Random House

SPANISH-ENGLISH
ENGLISH-SPANISH
Dictionary

Random House
SPANISH-ENGLISH
ENGLISH-SPANISH
Dictionary

Margaret H. Raventós, M.A.
Special Lecturer in Spanish at the
University of Manchester

Revised and Updated by
David L. Gold
Doctor in Romance Philology
University of Barcelona

Random House
NEW YORK

Hardcover edition of this dictionary published by Random House, Inc. in 1995. This dictionary was originally published by David McKay Company, Inc., under the title *Modern Spanish-English English-Spanish Dictionary*, in different form.

Library of Congress Cataloging-in-Publication Data
Raventós Margaret H. (Margaret Hamilton)
    Random House Spanish-English English-Spanish dictionary /
    Margaret H. Raventós ; revised and updated by David L. Gold.
       p.   cm.
    Originally published: 1995
    ISBN 0-679-78002-5 (paperback)
    1. Spanish language—Dictionaries—English. 2. English language—
Dictionaries—Spanish. I. Gold, David L. II. Title.
[PC4640.R32 1997]
463'.21—dc21   97-244
                                              CIP

Typeset and printed in the United States of America

Visit the Random House Web site at http://www.randomhouse.com/

ISBN: 0-679-78002-5 (paperback)
First Paperback Edition
0 9 8 7 6 5 4 3 2 1

New York Toronto London Sydney Auckland

Contents

Preface

Selection of Vocabulary

The aim of this dictionary is to cover as much current vocabulary as possible, as well as certain items found in standard works of Modern Spanish and English literature.

This dictionary includes items often omitted in other bilingual dictionaries—road and street signs, for example—though few things could be as frustrating (and, sometimes, as dangerous) as seeing such signs but not knowing what they mean (in this dictionary, all kinds of public notices are enclosed by the symbols « » in Spanish and by double quotation marks in English). Also, many vocabulary items consisting of more than one word have been treated here (see for instance do in the English-Spanish section).

For lack of space, however, not every current or useful item could be included and a selection of material was thus necessary.

Spanish Spelling and Alphabetization

On January 1, 1959, the Spanish language academies changed certain spelling rules and on April 27, 1994, they eliminated ch and ll as separate letters of the alphabet. Thus, whereas words like chico and chocolate were formerly alphabetized under their own letter (ch, which came between c and d) and words like llamar and llegar were formerly alphabetized under their own letter (ll, which came between l and m), words containing ch or ll, in whatever part of the word they may appear, are now alphabetized as they would be in English (chico therefore now appears under c and llegar under l).

Field Labels

Only essential field labels are given in this dictionary. For example, the label *medicine* or *pathology* is unnecessary at flebitis 'phlebitis' (in the Spanish-English section) because both the Spanish and the English words refer only to the pathological condition so called in those languages.

In contrast to that entry, we do need a label at foca 'seal' (in the Spanish-English section) because English seal has several meanings and only the zoological one is intended here. Anglophones looking up foca thus need the label *zoology* (hispanophones need no label because they know that foca is the name of an animal, hence they will correctly assume that seal is intended only in its zoological sense).

Spatial Labels for Spanish

Little of what has been written on how Spanish differs from place to place is reliable. For example, the Spanish-English section of one dictionary offers alborotos *Central America* 'popcorn', cabritos *Chile* 'popcorn', and palomitas 'popcorn', but the English-Spanish section of the very same dictionary has popcorn 'alborotos' *the River Plate region and Peru*, 'cabritas', and 'palomitas de maíz'.

In the absence of trustworthy sources, spatial labels are best dispensed with, though a few are given in this dictionary when a less than universal usage is found in a certain country.

Spatial characterizations in this dictionary should be interpreted in a minimal way. For instance, *Mexican* means that the usage so labeled is found in Mexico but it says nothing about whether that usage is present or absent elsewhere (something which only further research could determine).

Subentries

If a main entry head is repeated in a subentry in exactly the same form, it is abbreviated to its first letter (for instance, at fin in the Spanish-English section we find a f. de, which stands for a fin de). If the main entry head appears in any other form, the full form is given in the subentry (thus, at fin, the subentry head a fines de is spelled without abbreviation).

Irregular Spanish Verbs and the Direction "See . . ."

If a Spanish verb is irregular, it has been treated in one of two ways: either its principal parts are shown (see for example the end of the entry for caber) or you are referred to an analogous irregular verb for guidance (see for example the end of the entry for comparecer, where you are directed to conocer). Thus, since the irregular form conozco, is shown at conocer (it being irregular in the sense that it has a z), you may infer that comparecer has the irregular form comparezco.

One of the consequences of the changes in Spanish spelling of January 1, 1959, is that a new kind of orthographically irregular verb has come into existence (for example ahijar, ahincar, ahitar, ahuchar, ahumar, ahusar, cohibir, desahuciar, prohibir, prohijar, rehilar, rehusar, sahumar, sobrehilar, and trashumar).

If "See . . . " is all you find at an entry, you are being directed to a synonym. Thus, "descompasarse See descomedirse" means that the translations of descomedirse are those of descompasarse too.

Spanish Equivalents of 'you'

Today's Spanish, when taken as a whole, has at least six equivalents of 'you': tú, vos, usted (abbreviated to Vd.), su merced (all of which are used in addressing one person), ustedes (abbreviated to Vds.), vosotros, vosotras, and sus mercedes (all used in addressing more than one person).

When you occurs in this dictionary, usually only one of those words has been chosen to translate it, though three are never used here: su merced, sus mercedes, because they are now limited to only a small area of the Spanish-speaking world (the Cundinamarca Savanna, in Colombia) and even there they are now obsolescent, and vos, because the verb forms corresponding to this pronoun often vary from country to country.

Usually, the selection of one pronoun or another in this dictionary has been arbitrary, in which case any of the others could just as easily have been chosen. For example, for How are you? the translation '¿Cómo está Vd.?' is offered, yet any of the other pronouns could appear instead (with, in certain cases, a different verb form, for instance '¿Cómo están Vds.?').

In certain cases, however, not all pronouns (whether actually used or just implicit) would be appropriate. For example, among the translations of please . . . are imperative forms of servirse . . . . Because servirse in this sense is a formal usage (found mostly in impersonal writing like application blanks), it is not found in any familiar form of the imperative. The dictionary therefore gives ¡sírvase . . . ! (where the understood subject is usted, a formal pronoun). It could also have given ¡sírvanse . . . ! (where the understood subject is ustedes, likewise a formal pronoun), but not any form in which the subject were an informal pronoun.

Masculine and Feminine, Male and Female

As women engage in more and more activities once the domain of men, a growing number of Spanish nouns formerly used only in the masculine gender are being used in the feminine too. This dictionary thus labels nauta, paracaidista, púgil, pugilista, recluta, reservista, and seminarista, for example, as both masculine and feminine (the gender to be chosen depending on the gender of the person in question). For the user's convenience, the gender of Spanish nouns is indicated not only in the Spanish-English section but also in the English-Spanish one.

Many sample Spanish phrases and sentences in this dictionary can refer to people of either gender. For example, under wish in the English-Spanish section the sample sentence I wished him a Merry Christmas is translated 'Le deseé unas Pascuas muy felices' and 'Le felicité las Pascuas'. Since they both also mean 'I wished her a Merry Christmas', the sentence could as easily have contained her rather than him. It should therefore not be inferred that every phrase or sentence referring to a male cannot refer to a female (or vice versa). In this dictionary, male and female references have been chosen randomly, hopefully in about equal number.

In other cases, a slight change is needed to turn a male reference into a female one or vice versa. For instance, He was within an ace of being killed (under within, prep., in the English-Spanish section) is rendered by 'Por poco le matan'. Changing he to she and le to la will yield a correct equivalence referring to a female. Since it would have taken up too much space to indicate those alternate equivalences, they are not given here, but with just an elementary knowledge of both languages, users of this dictionary will be able to make the necessary changes and thus have at their disposal many more sample phrases and sentences than it supplies.

A dictionary of any living language can always be improved, all the more so a dictionary of two living languages. Additions, corrections, and other suggestions will be received with thanks. They should be addressed to:

Reference & Information Publishing
Random House, Inc.
201 East 50th St.
New York, NY 10022-7703
U.S.A.

To Sol Steinmetz, editorial director of Random House Reference, and to his staff go my thanks for their help in seeing this dictionary into print.

D.L.G.
January
1995

The Basics of Standard Spanish Pronunciation

Whereas the fit between English spelling and pronunciation has for centuries been less than ideal (think, for example, of the various pronunciations of -ough, as in **although, bough, cough,** and **slough**), the fit between today's Spanish spelling and pronunciation is quite good, thanks to the regulatory efforts of the Spanish academies.

Because of that good fit, Spanish-speakers learn to read and spell faster than English-speakers, there is no such thing as a Spanish spelling bee, and Spanish spelling is a good basis for teaching the rudiments of Spanish pronunciation. The following instructions thus take spelling as their starting point. Pronunciation is described in two ways: with phonetic symbols (enclosed in slashes or brackets) and by way of approximate comparisons with English. A wavy line separates variants (like **esnob ~ snob**). A stress mark (') means that the syllable following it is stressed (as in [re'lo]). An asterisk indicates a nonexistent form (like English *llion). A right-facing "arrow"(>), or "greater than" sign, means 'became in Spanish' (as in English **rum** and French **rhum** > **ron ~ romo**).

As may be expected of a language that has been used for many centuries, over a vast area, and by diverse people, Spanish is now pronounced in various ways. Of the many current pronunciations, two are offered as most suitable for speakers of Spanish as a second language. The two standards are identical to a large extent, differing chiefly with respect to the pronunciation of c before e; c before i; z in any position; and, optionally, ll in any position.

To the extent that the two standards differ, features belonging to just one of them are labeled either *Standard 1* or *Standard 2* below. Features labeled *Standard 1* are accepted as standard in Spain but not in the Western Hemisphere. Features labeled *Standard 2* are accepted as standard in the Western Hemisphere but not in Spain. If you speak Spanish mostly with Spaniards or mostly with people in or from the Western Hemisphere, your choice of standard will thus be straightforward. If you speak with people from both areas, you can either try to master both standards or, if you want to follow just one of them no matter to whom you speak, pick Standard 2.

In the Western Hemisphere, features labeled *Standard 1* are often either erroneously admired as being "the correct pronunciation of the language" or, quite the opposite, disdained as highfalutin (which are precisely the same reactions to British English frequently heard in English-speaking areas outside Europe). Neither standard, however, is intrinsically better than the other.

If possible, review the material given here with a speaker of Standard Spanish and hear how the sample words, phrases, and sentences are pronounced.

a is pronounced /a/, which is similar to the second vowel of the English interjection **aha!** and the vowel of the English interjection **ah,** although much shorter in duration.

See also "Diphthongs and Triphthongs" below.

b has three pronunciations. At the beginning of an utterance, after [m] (whether represented by **m** or by **n**), or after [n] (whether represented by **n** or by **m**), the letter b is pronounced [b], which is similar to the pronunciation of the first consonant of English **beach, broth, pebble,** etc. For example, in the sentence **Bulgaria envió a ambos embajadores en un barco japonés,** each of the four instances of b (and the one instance of v) is so pronounced.

Before /č/, /f/, /t/, /k/, /s/, /x/, or /θ/ in the same word (see ch [under c], f, t, c, g, and c respectively for interpreting those symbols), b is pronounced [p] (see p for interpreting that symbol), as in **subtítulo, absceso, subjefe,** and, in Standard 1, **subcentral.** That rule also holds before [p] in the same word (with the further result that [p] + [p] is reduced to [p]; hence the first two syllables of **subproducto,** for example, are [supro]) and for [p] before /s/ in the same word (with the further result that [ps] may be reduced to [s.] In certain words, nonpronunciation of b became so widespread that the only spelling now used is without that letter, for instance **ofuscar** and its derivatives (contrast English **obfuscate, obfuscation,** etc.).

At the end of a word, more than one pronunciation of b may be heard. For example, **club** may be [klub], [kluβ], or [klu]. Its plural (**clubs**) may be [klups], [klus], and possibly [kluβs] (unless the plural **clubes** is used, whose universal pronunciation is [kluβes] (see the next paragraph for interpreting [β] and e for interpreting [ɛ)]. All of the foregoing holds for compounds of **club**, like **aeroclub**. In **esnob** ~ snob, the final **b** is pronounced [b].

In all other positions (for example, **habas, hablar**, and **habré**), **b** is pronounced [β] a sound absent in English, which is made by bringing the lips close together without letting them touch each other (as if you were blowing dust away or blowing out a match or candle), expelling air through the mouth, and vibrating the vocal cords. This sound is thus similar to /v/ (as in English **very** and **vowel**), except that the latter is made by making the lower lip touch the upper teeth. English-speakers should not mistake Spanish [β] for English /v/.

It follows from the foregoing that if the position of **b** in the utterance changes, its pronunciation may change. Contrast, for example, these three utterances: (1) **Bulgaria mandó embajadores a ambos países**, (2) **En Bulgaria viven unos cuantos rusos**, and (3) **Iremos a Bulgaria**. In (1), the **b** of **Bulgaria** is pronounced [b] because it comes at the beginning of an utterance; in (2) the same **b** is also pronounced [b] because it comes after [m] (see the instructions for **n** on its pronunciation as [m]); but in (3) the same **b** is pronounced [β] because none of the conditions for pronouncing it [b] is met.

Similarly, when the word **baba** is pronounced in isolation, the first **b** is rendered [b] and the second one [β], but in the phrase **la baba**, the first **b** is no longer at the beginning of an utterance (nor is it preceded by the sounds [m] or [n]), hence the phrase is pronounced [laβaβa].

Or, if the **b** of **club** is pronounced, it will be [β] before a vowel. So too the final letter of **esnob**, which is always pronounced.

See also **v** and, on **tranvía**, "Miscellaneous" below.

c has several pronunciations. If it is followed by **e** or **i**, the letter **c** is pronounced /θ/ in Standard 1 and [s] in Standard 2. The pronunciation of /θ/ in Spanish is similar to that of **th** in English **thatch, think**, etc., but made with somewhat more protrusion of the tongue. The sound [s] is similar to the pronunciation of **s** in English **say, simple**, etc., though in northern Spain [s] is often produced with the tip of the tongue higher in the mouth than in other varieties of Spanish, the result being that this sound has a hushing quality there (similar to Modern Greek /s/), which English-speakers should not mistake for /š/, which is the pronunciation of **sh** in English **shall, should**, etc.

Although Standard 1 has /θ/ for **c** before **e**

or **i**, people who use that pronunciation will not be put off if they hear you pronounce the **c** as [s], because the latter is widespread (though not standard) in Spain. In the Western Hemisphere, **c** before **e** or **i** is always pronounced [s] and never /θ/. Speakers of Western Hemispheric Spanish will react to /θ/ either as "the correct pronunciation" ("though we don't use it") or as a highfalutin pronunciation (unless it comes from people who are to the manner born, i.e., many Spaniards). Thus, whereas it is desirable though not obligatory that you use Standard 1 in Spain, you would be well advised to use only Standard 2 in the Western Hemisphere, where /θ/ is bound to elicit a sharp reaction of one kind or another (as sharp as British **drawing pin, lorry**, or **trunk call** instead of **thumbtack, truck, long-distance call** would probably elicit in the United States).

Most speakers pronounce the combination **ch**, wherever it is found, as /č/, which is similar to the pronunciation of **ch** in English **child, church**, etc. Speakers who know Catalan or, at least, are aware of the Catalan pronunciation of **ch**, may pronounce this letter combination as /k/ in Catalan-origin proper nouns used in Spanish, like the family names **Escrich** and **Roch** (see the next paragraph on Spanish /k/). The letter combination **tch** (as in **catch**) is pronounced /č/ (in general, that sound at the end of a word is extremely rare, being limited to Catalan-origin proper nouns ending in -ch but not pronounced in Catalan fashion and to recent borrowings from English like **catch** and **punch**).

If **c** ends a syllable that is not the last syllable in the word and the next syllable begins with any consonant except /t/ (for instance **accionista, facsímil**, and **técnico**), you have an alternative: **c** may be pronounced either /k/ or /g/. Spanish /k/ is similar to the pronunciation of **c** in English **escape, scandal**, etc., but different from that of **c** in English **cape, coop**, etc. To achieve a good rendition of Spanish /k/, hold your open palm in front of your mouth and pronounce first **cape** and **coop**, then **escape** and **scandal**. When pronouncing the first two words, you felt a noticeable puff of air on your palm, but in the last two words you felt almost no puff at all. A noticeable puff of air accompanying a speech sound is called *aspiration;* sounds pronounced with aspiration are *aspirated;* and those pronounced without it are *unaspirated.* Spanish /k/ (like Spanish /p/ and /t/) is always unaspirated, wherever it occurs. Thus, you should have no trouble with Spanish **escapar** and **escándalo** because /k/ occurs after [s] and as an English speaker you will automatically pronounce it as unaspirated (just as you would the **c** of the English cognates of those words: **escape** and **scandal**). It is in other positions that you have to be careful not to aspirate: claro, crear, tocología, etc. (contrast them with their English cognates, all of which have an aspirated /k/: clear, create, tocology). See g for interpreting [g]. Note that if c is followed by c, the next letter is always e or i (as in accionista and confección). In such cases, you have an alternative with respect to the first c (either /k/ or [g] is correct) and the second c is pronounced according to either of the instructions given above for c before e or i.

If c ends a syllable that is not the last syllable in the word and the next syllable begins with /t/, it is pronounced /k/ in most words (like actor and actriz) and in at least one you may pronounce it /k/ or not pronounce it at all (coctel and its plurals: coctels ~ cocteles). In the place name Vitoria the absence of /k/ has been universal for so long that is that is now its only spelling (in contrast to the female given name Victoria and the common noun victoria).

If c or k ends the last syllable of the word, that letter is pronounced /k/ at least in cinc ~ zinc, clac, copec, frac, Nueva York, and tic-tac, whereas in biftec, bistec, and coñac many speakers do not pronounce it (likewise in the plural of the last word, coñacs).

In all other cases (as in aclarar, acoplar, acreditar, capaz, chucruta, claro, and creer), c is pronounced /k/.

See also k, ll (under l), q, s, and z.

d has several pronunciations. At the beginning of an utterance, after [n], or after /l/, this letter is pronounced [d], which is similar to the pronunciation of d in English dear, dust, etc., with this difference: in the production of Spanish [d], the tongue touches the lower edge of the upper front incisors.

When between two vowels, when preceded by a vowel and followed by r, or when at the end of a word and not preceded by r (as in pedir, Pedro, and libertad), the letter d is pronounced [ð], which is similar to the pronunciation of th in English that, there, etc., but less interdental than English [ð] (in the production of the Spanish sound, the tip of the tongue gently touches the lower edge of the upper incisors).

If d is at the end of a word and it is preceded by r (as in lord, milord), it is silent. In the plurals, no matter how they are spelled, d is never present, hence never pronounced: lores, milores.

It follows from the foregoing that if the position of d in the utterance changes, its pronunciation may change. Contrast, for example, these three utterances: (1) Dinamarca mandó embajadores a doce países, (2) En Dinamarca viven unos cuantos americanos, and (3) Iremos a Dinamarca. In (1), the d of Dinamarca is pronounced [d] because it comes at the beginning of an utterance; in (2) the same d is also pronounced [d] because it comes after [n]; but in (3) the same d is pronounced [ð] because none of the conditions for pronouncing it [d] is met. Similarly, when the word dedo is pronounced in isolation, the first d is rendered [d] (and the second one [ð]), but in the phrase mi dedo, the first d is no longer at the beginning of an utterance (nor is it preceded by [n] or /l/); hence the phrase is pronounced [miðeðo].

e has two pronunciations. The instruction given in some books that e is pronounced [e] when stressed and [ɛ] when unstressed does not hold true for today's Spanish and may never have been an accurate description of its pronunciation in any variety of the language.

Here are better guidelines for e (except when it is part of a diphthong or triphthong):

If e is found in a syllable ending in a consonant (see "Syllabification" below), it is pronounced [ɛ], which is similar to the pronunciation of è in French or to the vowel of bet, let, met, etc., as pronounced in Standard English, that is, with considerable lowering of the jaw. For example, embaldosar, fresco, hablen, and mestizo.

If e ends a syllable and the next one begins with r, rr, or t, it is pronounced [ɛ]. For instance, pero, caballete (the first e), cerrar, and jinete.

Otherwise, e is pronounced [e], which is similar to the pronunciation of é in French, that is, the jaw is lowered only minimally (the closest English comes to having a sound like [e] is probably the vowel of ache, rake, stake, etc.). For example, caballete (the second e), hablé, mesa, and poeta. Caballete thus has both renditions of e, though the plural of that word, caballetes, has only [ɛ], because here the last syllable ends in a consonant.

Many Spanish verbs show variation between -ar and -ear, like bazucar ~ bazuquear, chapurrar ~ chapurrear (e is optional in Yugoeslavia ~ Yugoslavia and in yugoeslavo ~ yugoslavo). See also "Diphthongs and Triphthongs" below.

f is pronounced /f/, which is similar to the pronunciation of f in English fate, feet, etc. For example, afectar, fecha, golf, golfo, ¡uf!. See also h.

g has several pronunciations. At the beginning of an utterance and when followed by a, o, u, or a consonant letter except n (as in gato, goma, gusto, glaciar, or grave), g is pronounced [g], which is similar to the pronunciation of g in English get, go, gumption, etc.

At the beginning of a word and when followed by n, the letter g is silent (as in gnomo). That pronunciation is in fact so widespread and reputable that a g-less spelling is now acceptable and is in fact preferred in this dictionary (see "Miscellaneous" below).

When g is preceded by n and is followed in the next syllable of the same word by a, o, u, ü, or a consonant letter (as in angosto, ángulo, ungüento, englobar, and engrasar), it is pronounced [g].

When g occurs at the end of a syllable and is preceded by n, it is silent, as in bumerang. In older borrowings from other languages, that g was systematically or sometimes omitted, as in sterling > esterlina, pudding > pudín.

Before e or i (as in gemir and gigante), except if it comes at the end of a word, the letter g is pronounced /x/, which is absent in most varieties of current English. This sound is similar to the pronunciation of ch in German Bach, that of ch in Israeli Hebrew zecher, and that of ch in Scots English loch, Lochaber, etc. Press the back of the tongue against the soft palate, expel air (as if coughing), and do not vibrate the vocal chords.

If g ends a syllable that is not the last syllable of the word (as in dogma and the first syllable of zigzag), this letter is pronounced [g]. In such cases, the next syllable always begins with a consonant.

Otherwise, g is pronounced [ɣ], a sound absent in English, which is made by bringing the back of the tongue close to the soft palate (without letting them touch), expelling air through the mouth, and vibrating the vocal chords. Examples are hago and hígado.

It follows from the foregoing that if the position of g in the utterance changes, its pronunciation may change. Contrast, for example, these three utterances: (1) Grecia mandó embajadores, (2) En Grecia viven unos cuantos italianos, and (3) Iremos a Grecia. In (1), the g of Grecia is pronounced [g] because it comes at the beginning of an utterance; in (2) the same g is also pronounced [g] because it comes after [n]; but in (3) the same g is pronounced [ɣ] because none of the conditions for pronouncing it [g] is met.

h is silent. In older Spanish, this letter was pronounced /h/ (a sound similar to the first consonant of here, how, and huddle in Standard English), which has remained in a few words in the guise of /x/ (see g for interpreting that symbol). In such cases, h has been replaced by j (cante jondo and joder, from older cante hondo and hoder respectively).

In at least four words, both spellings remain standard: halar ~ jalar, halón ~ jalón, holgorio ~ jolgorio, ¡hopo! and ¡jopo! (in the first variant of each pair, the h is not now pronounced). To at least some Spanish ears, the variants with /x/ are more emphatic or affective than those without it.

Since h is now silent, its presence or absence does not affect pronunciation. Thus, Ghana and Lesotho, for example, are pronounced exactly as if spelled without that letter. In some words, h is optional and the tendency to omit it can only be encouraged: armonizar ~ harmonizar, baraúnda ~ barahúnda, Rodesia ~ Rhodesia.

Many words that in older Spanish had f now have h. In a few instances, variants with both f and h remain in today's Spanish. They may be either full synonyms of each other or less than full synonyms (like faz and haz, forma and horma).

See also g and w.

i has two pronunciations. When representing a full vowel, it is pronounced [i], which is similar to the vowel of English beet, feet, sheen, etc., but shorter (for instance, dicho, isla, and cursi). When bearing a dieresis, this letter is likewise pronounced [i], as in pïada (were the dieresis absent, ia here would represent a diphthong).

When i represents part of a diphthong or a triphthong (see "Diphthongs and Triphthongs" below), it is pronounced [y], which is similar to the pronunciation of y in English year, yes, or yolk. Thus, miel and tiesto are pronounced [myɛl] and [tyɛsto].

See also y.

j is almost always pronounced /x/ (see g for interpreting that symbol). A notable exception is reloj, which many speakers pronounce [re'lo]. That pronunciation of reloj is so widespread that reló is an alternate spelling of the singular form, but only in informal writing. In the plural, everyone pronounces /x/ and therefore writes the j: relojes.

See x.

k, which is now found only in recent borrowings from other languages, is pronounced /k/ (see c for interpreting that symbol). The letter combination ck (as in crack, flashback, shock, snack, stock) is pronounced /k/.

l when not doubled is pronounced /l/, which is formed by putting the tip of the tongue against the sockets of the upper incisors, the remainder of the tongue lying flat. Spanish /l/ thus does not have the hollow sound of English /l/, in whose formation the back of the tongue rises toward the palate.

The letter combination ll (which always begins a syllable) has two pronunciations in Standard Spanish: /λ/ (which is similar to the pronunciation of lli in English million or that of li in vermilion) and [y], which is similar to the pronunciation of y in English year, yes, or yolk. Since English words like million and vermilion actually have [ly] rather than /λ/, that is, [l] ends one syllable of those English words and [y] begins the next one (whereas Spanish ll, except at the end of a word, always begins a syllable), English-speakers should be careful not to misinterpret /λ/ as [ly]. To achieve a good rendition of Spanish /λ/, pronounce million as if it did not contain mi-, that is, as if it were *llion. Good practice words are those beginning with ll (like llamar, llegar, and llorar) since here you are forced to pronounce /λ/ at the beginning of a syllable. See also ñ and "Syllabification" below.

In Spain, although /λ/ is still prestigious, it has been going out of use for decades as more and more people switch to [y] (in the unvarnished pronunciation of Madrid, for example, /λ/ has disappeared entirely). Spaniards now using /λ/ natively are mostly from northern Spain or, if not from that part of the country, they first learned [y] and later intentionally replaced that sound by the more prestigious /λ/. You may thus use either pronunciation in speaking to Spaniards, but /λ/ has a cachet in Spain that [y] lacks. Standard 1 therefore has /λ/.

In the Western Hemisphere, ll is pronounced /λ/, [y], /ž/, or /š/, according to area or speaker (/ž/ is similar to the pronunciation of z in English azure and of zs in the name Zsa Zsa; /š/ is similar to the pronunciation of sh in English shall, should, etc.). You may want to pick the sound your interlocutors use or, if you want to choose a SINGLE pronunciation that most speakers of Western Hemispheric Spanish will find acceptable (whatever they themselves use), take /λ/ or [y] (though /λ/ might sound a tad highfalutin to certain Spanish-speakers in the Western Hemisphere who do not use it themselves).

If you want to pick a SINGLE pronunciation of ll acceptable both in Spain and in the Western Hemisphere, take /λ/. However, if you do, you should also choose Standard 1 for the pronunciation of c before e or i and of z when speaking to Spaniards, since it seems that no speakers of the language in Spain who pronounce ll as /λ/ follow Standard 2 for those other two letters. With regard to the Western Hemisphere, since Standard 2 for those other two letters co-occurs there with all of the pronunciations of ll (/λ/, [y], /ž/, /š/), you have four choices, the only selection not recommended for this part of the

Spanish-speaking world being Standard 1 for c before e or i and for z in all positions (whatever pronunciation of ll you may choose).

l is optional in belfo ~ befo.

m: Traditionally, Spanish does not have [m] at the end of a word when it is pronounced in isolation. Consequently, in many words borrowed from other languages ending in that sound, it was replaced by [n] (see the next section for interpreting that symbol) and the word was respelled accordingly (for example, harén, ínterin, Jerusalén, macadán, querubín, ron, serafín). However, a few words (all learned borrowings from Latin and recent borrowings from other languages) end in m (for example, álbum, factótum, ídem, médium, memorándum, ultimátum, and vademécum) and that letter also appears in the Spanish names of many places outside Spanish-speaking areas, like Bírmingham, Búckingham, Siam, and Vietnam. Both [m] and [n] are heard in such words, depending on people's ability to pronounce [m] at the end of a word (as more and more Spanish-speakers study other languages, they find it easier to produce that sound in that position) and their interest in maintaining the supposedly "correct" (i.e., non-Spanish) pronunciation of that letter. The unaffected pronunciation is [n] (and mm in súmmum is always pronounced as if it were a single m), but if in another form of the word the m is followed by a vowel, it is pronounced according to rule, i.e., [m] (as in siamés).

In all other positions, m is pronounced [m], which is similar to the pronunciation of m in English make, might, etc. For example, amar, almirante, ambos, mayor.

n has several pronunciations. If immediately followed by a labial consonant (represented by b, f, m, p, or v) whether in the same word or in the next one, it is pronounced [m] (as in the words anfitrión, inmediato, anverso or the sentences insiste en bucear, insiste en pelear, and en muchos casos hay más). Since [m] + [m] is reduced to a single [m], en muchos casos actually has just one [m].

It follows from the foregoing that the word tampoco and the phrase tan poco are pronounced identically, as are the word ciempiés and the phrase cien pies (each of those words is in fact derived from the corresponding phrase); Edimburgo and Nuremberg also show the replacement of [n] by [m] before a labial.

However, [n] + [m] (as in insomne) is not reduced.

Before /k/ or [g] (as in aunque and angosto), n is pronounced [ŋ], which is similar to the final consonant of long, sing, and song as pronounced in Standard English.

In all other positions (as in **Anatolia, andan** and **nombrar**), n is pronounced [n], which is similar to the pronunciation of n in English **hand, near,** etc.

Instances of [n] + [n] are reduced to a single [n], as in the words **ennegrecer, ennoblecer, perenne, sinnúmero** or a phrase like **sin número** (the word **connoto** and the phrase **con Otto** are thus pronounced identically), though an effect of the double [n] remains: the preceding e is pronounced [ɛ], not [e], that is, as if the first syllable ended in the first [n].

Instances of [m] + [n], however, are not reduced (as in **amnesia** and **amnistiar**).

Spanish-speakers who know Catalan or, at least, are aware of the pronunciation of ny in that language at the end of a word, pronounce it [n] in Catalan-origin proper nouns used in Spanish (like the family names **Capmany, Castany,** and **Fortuny**). Others pronounce it [ni].

See also m, "Stress," and, on **tranvía,** "Miscellaneous" below.

ñ is pronounced /ɲ/ which is similar to the pronunciation of ny in English **canyon** or ni in English **onion**. Since English words like those two actually have [ny] rather than /ɲ/ (that is, [n] ends one syllable and [y] begins the next one), English-speakers should be careful not to misinterpret /ɲ/ as [ny]. To achieve a good rendition of Spanish /ɲ/ (which always begins a syllable), pronounce **canyon** as if it did not contain ca-, that is, as if it were *nyon, or **onion** as if it were *nion. Good practice words are those beginning with ñ (like **ñiquiñaque** and **ñoño**) since here you are forced to pronounce /ɲ/ at the beginning of a syllable.

See also ll (under l).

o has two pronunciations, neither of which can easily be described with reference to English. In a syllable ending in a consonant (see "Syllabification" below), this letter is pronounced somewhat like the o of English **port** or **short** (for instance **pondré** and **sondear**). Otherwise (that is, when o ends the syllable), it is pronounced somewhat like the o of English **coke** or **tote** (for instance, **codo** and **lodo**). The words **costo** and **zonzo** thus contain an example of each kind of o. The two kinds of /o/ are similar to the closed and open /o/ of Italian.

See also "Diphthongs and Triphthongs" below.

p, where it is pronounced, stands for [p], which is similar to the pronunciation of p in English **space, spear, spook,** etc., but different from that of p in English **pike, peak, poke,** etc. To achieve a good rendition of Spanish [p], hold your open palm in front of your mouth and pronounce first **pike, peak, poke,** then **space, spear, spook.** When pronouncing the first three words, you felt a noticeable puff of air on your palm, but in the last three words you felt almost no puff at all. A noticeable puff of air accompanying a speech sound is called *aspiration;* sounds pronounced with aspiration are *aspirated;* and those pronounced without it are *unaspirated.* Spanish [p] (like Spanish /k/ and /t/) is always unaspirated, wherever it occurs. Thus, you should have no trouble with Spanish **espacio, especial, especie,** etc. because here [p] occurs after [s] and as an English-speaker you will automatically pronounce it as unaspirated (just as you would the English cognates of those words: **space, special,** and **species**). It is in other positions that you have to be careful not to aspirate: **particular, poeta, puerta,** etc. (contrast them with their English cognates, all of which have an aspirated [p]: **particular, poet, port**).

Spanish ps at the beginning of a word is pronounced [s]. Some pretentious Spanish-speakers may tell you that the "correct" pronunciation is [ps], but that would be as artificial as pronouncing English **psyche, psychology,** etc., in that way. In fact, non-pronunciation of p in the combination ps at the beginning of a word is so entrenched in Spanish that the preferred spelling is now s (this dictionary thus gives only **sicología, sicólogo,** etc. and not the older spellings **psicología, psicólogo,** etc.). See "Miscellaneous" below.

Before /t/, some speakers pronounce p as [p] and some do not pronounce it at all. Thus, some write **excerpta, septiembre,** etc., and some **excerta, setiembre,** etc. Although both are correct, the spelling with p is preferred in this dictionary (except in the first word, for which both forms are given). Whether or not one pronounces the p of **óptimo,** it seems that standard spelling requires that the word always be spelled with that letter.

At the end of a word, you may have an alternative: in **galop,** for example, the p may be pronounced [p] or be silent. The number of instances in which p is silent or may be silent is small.

q is always followed by ue or ui. The sequence que is pronounced either [kɛ] or [ke] and qui is pronounced [ki] (for example, **quince**) or [ky] (for instance, **quien**) (see "Diphthongs and Triphthongs" below).

To represent the sound sequences [kwe], [kwɛ], and [kwi], Spanish has cue, cue, and cui respectively (as in **cueva, cuestión,** and **cuidar**).

Because q is always followed by u, if Spanish-speakers borrow words containing just q from other languages, that letter is changed to **k**. Thus, the Spanish names of Iraq and Qatar, for example, are **Irak** and **Katar.**

r has two pronunciations. At the beginning of a word or when it comes after **l, n,** or **s** (for example, **reir, alrededor, enrojecer,** and **Israel**), this letter has the same pronunciation as **rr** (see below).

If b ends one syllable and r begins the next one in the same word (see "Syllabification" below), r is pronounced exactly like **rr** (for example **subrayar** if syllabified **sub-ra-yar**). If **b + r** belong to the same syllable (for instance **bramar** and **lubricar**), r is pronounced with one flip of the upper front part of the tongue against the sockets of the upper incisors (for instance **subrayar** if syllabified **su-bra-yar**). See "Syllabification" below on the alternative now permitted in words beginning with the prefix **sub-**.

In all other positions, r is also pronounced with one flip of the upper front part of the tongue against the sockets of the upper incisors (for instance, **leer, para, pera, pero, tercero,** and **treinta**).

rr is pronounced with a trill (several flips) of the upper front part of the tongue against the sockets of the upper incisors (for instance, **parra, perra, perro,** and **sierra**). Thus, **para** and **parra** are different words, with different pronunciations and different meanings. The same applies to **caro** and **carro, pera** and **perra, pero** and **perro, torero** and **torrero,** and other pairs of words.

s has several pronunciations. When it represents the plural ending of nouns recently borrowed from other languages, it is silent in certain words, like **cabarets, carnets, complots, conforts, superávits, tíckets, trusts, vermuts.**

Before the letters b, v, d, g (but only when this letter is not followed by e or i), l, m, n, or r (whether any of those eight letters appear in the same word as s or they appear in the next word), you have an alternative (in both standards) if s is not the last letter of the word: it may be pronounced [z] (a sound similar to the pronunciation of z in English zebra, zoo, etc.) or [s] (see c for interpreting that symbol): **esbelto, esdrújulo, esgrimir, isla, esmalte, Israel, los baúles, los varones, los dedos, los guantes, los lagos, los maestros, los nervios, los ratones,** etc. If s is the last letter, only [s] is found (for instance, in the family name **Pons**).

If s is followed by r (whether in the same word or in the next one), besides the two pronunciations suggested above [s] or [z]), a third possibility is not to pronounce the s at all and, as a compensation, trill the r more. The word **Israel** (and its derivatives) thus has three pronunciations: [isrraɛl], [izrraɛl], and [irrraɛl].

Otherwise, s is pronounced [s] (as in **ese, especial, hablas, hasta, insistir, seco**).

If s is followed by h, the foregoing paragraph applies, except in the case of Spanish words recently borrowed from other languages or words modeled on such recently borrowed words, in which **sh** constitutes a unit, to be pronounced /š/ (a sound similar to the pronunciation of sh in English shall, sheet, should, etc.). Thus, in **deshacer,** an old Spanish word not recently borrowed from another language, the instructions about s apply and the h is silent (hence the first two syllables of that word are [desa]), whereas in **riksha** and **yídish,** sh is pronounced /š/.

Spanish spelling does not distinguish the two kinds of **sh,** which you can, however, partly distinguish in this way: **sh** at the beginning or at the end of a word is of recent non-Spanish origin. If **sh** appears in the middle of a word, you have to know its origin to determine how that letter combination should be pronounced, though this rule of thumb will almost always hold: a word beginning **desh-** is likely not to be a recent borrowing from another language; rather, it probably consists of the centuries-old Spanish negating prefix **des-** and a word beginning with **h-**. Furthermore, the recent borrowings are often easily identified because of their unusual spelling (for example, it is clear that **riksha** is new).

Traditionally, no Spanish words began with s followed by a consonant, as a result of which Spanish-speakers either dropped s when borrowing non-Spanish words so beginning or, more frequently, added e to them: Dutch **sloeren** > **eslora,** Dutch **skiff,** English **skiff,** French **esquif,** French **skiff,** Italian **schifo,** and/or Portuguese **esquife** > **esquife,** English **sterling** > **esterlina,** Italian **strambotto** > **estrambote,** Latin **scientia** > **ciencia,** etc.

S is optional in **quizá** ~ **quizás.**

See also b, c, t, z, and "Syllabification" below.

t, except before l in the same word, is pronounced [t], which is similar to the pronunciation of t in English stake, steer, stoop, etc., but different from that of t in English take, teak, took, etc. To achieve a good rendition of Spanish /t/, hold your open palm in front of your mouth and pronounce first take, teak, took, then stake, steer, stoop. When pronouncing the first three words, you felt a noticeable puff of air on your palm, but in the last three words you felt almost no puff at all. A noticeable puff of air is called *aspiration;* sounds pronounced with aspiration are *aspirated;* and those pronounced without it are *unaspirated*. Spanish /t/ (like Spanish /k/ and /p/) is always unaspirated, wherever it occurs. Thus, you should have no trouble producing an unaspirated /t/ in Spanish estado, estimar, estúpido, etc. because here /t/ occurs after [s] and as an English-speaker you will automatically pronounce it as unaspirated (just as you would the English cognates of those words: state, esteem, and stupid). It is in other positions that you have to be careful not to aspirate: tocar, tabla, Túnez, etc. (contrast them with their English cognates, all of which have an aspirated /t/: touch, table, Tunisia). Furthermore, Spanish /t/ is made by touching the tip of the tongue against the upper incisors (in contrast to English /t/, in whose production the tongue touches the gums).

In three positions, t may not be pronounced as described above. First, before l or m in the same word (as in atleta, aritmético, and ritmo) you have an alternative: t may be pronounced as described or it may be pronounced [ð] (see d for interpreting that symbol).

Second, the t of the prefix post- is not pronounced if it is followed by any pronounced consonant letter except r, so much so that alternate spellings without t are also found and they are in fact the preferable ones, for instance, posguerra and posmeridiano. (but also postergar, etc.).

Third, t at the end of a word may be silent. Probably many, most, or all Spanish-speakers pronounce it in cenit, déficit, fagot, mamut, superávit, and el Tíbet ~ el Tibet, whereas in other words final t is silent, for instance cabaret, carnet, complot, tícket, trust, and vermut, which are pronounced as if written *cabaré, *carné, *compló, *tique, *trus, and *vermú (the plurals are pronounced identically to their singulars. In still other words you have an alternative: confort is pronounced either [kom'for] or [kom'fort] (the plural conforts has both variants too).

u has several pronunciations. In the combinations gue, gui, que, and qui, the letter u is silent. For example, guedeja [ɡeðexa] ~ [ɣeðexa], quedar [keðar], and quien [kyɛn] (see q and e on the pronunciation of those letters).

When u represents part of a diphthong or a triphthong (see "Diphthongs and Triphthongs" below), it is pronounced [w], which is similar to the first sound of English win and won. Thus, puesto and seudónimo, for example, are pronounced [pwɛsto] and [sewðonimo].

If a u bears a dieresis, it is pronounced [w]. Thus, lingüista is pronounced [lingwista].

In all other cases, u is pronounced [u], which is similar to the vowel of English coot or toot, although in the production of the Spanish sound the lips are more rounded and the vowel is of shorter duration than in the production of the English one. For example, ducha, hubo, u, Unamuno, and uno.

v has two pronunciations. At the beginning of an utterance or after n (which in this position is pronounced [m]), the letter v is pronounced [b], which is similar to the first consonant of English beach, broth, pebble, etc. In all other positions, this letter is pronounced [β] (see b for interpreting that symbol). For example, in the sentence ¿Verdad que en el anverso de la medalla se ve un pavo real?, the first and fifth words have [b] and the tenth and twelfth have [β].

Therefore, the instructions for pronouncing b and those for pronouncing v are identical (depending on the position of those letters in the utterance), as a consequence of which pairs of words like baca and vaca or hube and uve are homophones in today's Spanish and, as a further consequence of which, if you hear [b] or [β], you cannot tell whether it is to be represented by b or by v unless you know how to spell the word.

If people try to tell you that b is pronounced in one way and v in another in today's Spanish, tell them that is a figment of their imagination. Spelling differences (like baca vs. vaca) are misleading them into thinking they hear a difference (or believing there should be a difference) when none in fact exists. The fact that native speakers of the language less skilled in spelling often write b when v is required or vice versa is proof enough that no difference in pronunciation is made.

w, which is found only in borrowings from Germanic languages and French, has several pronunciations. In several words, it is pronounced as if it were b or v and in such cases alternate spellings with v are found too: wagneriano ~ vagneriano, Westfalia ~ Vestfalia. The forms with v are preferable.

In at least a few words, w is pronounced [w] (a sound similar to the first sound of English win and won) and for one of them an alternate spelling with u exists: Malawi, Taiwán, Zimbabwe.

In whisky, the letter combination wh is pronounced [w] by those who want to show off their knowledge of English and [gw] or [ɣw] by those who speak normally (the choice of [gw] or [ɣw] depends on the position of the word in the utterance; see the instructions for g).

Whereas **Trans World Airlines** is shortened to the initialism **TWA** in English, in Spanish it is shortened to the acronym **la TWA**, which is pronounced /la'tua/.

x has several pronunciations. For a time, the recommended pronunciation was [ks]. Later, [gz] in certain positions was allowed as an alternate pronunciation. Today, those instructions, especially the one calling for [ks] wherever **x** occurs, would probably result in a pronunciation no native speaker uses and which would sound artificial. The following suggestions are more realistic for our times.

If **x** occurs before a consonant (as in **experiencia, extremidad** and **mixto**), pronounce it [s]. That pronunciation is probably most frequent in words beginning with the prefix **ex-** followed by a consonant, for example **excelente**, widely pronounced [esθelɛnte] or [eselɛnte]. In the latter pronunciation, [s] + [s] becomes a single [s], though an effect of the double [s] remains: the preceding **e** is pronounced [ɛ], not [e], that is, as if the first syllable ended in a consonant, i.e., as if it ended in the first [s].

If **x** occurs between vowels, you have an alternative in certain words (**examen** and **exiguo**, for example, may be pronounced with [ks], [gz], or [s]) but not in others (for instance, all Spanish-speakers, it seems, now pronounce **sexo** with [ks]).

At the end of a word, the pronunciation of **x** is in flux. In **ántrax, Benelux, dux, fénix, látex,** and **tórax,** [ks] seems to be most frequent if not universal today, whereas in **clímax** and **flux,** [s] may now be more frequent.

At least some exceptions to those pronunciations are heard in words of Native American origin: for example, in **México** and **mexicano,** the **x** is now always pronounced [x] (those are the spellings official and universal in Mexico; elsewhere, **Méjico, mejicano** are used); in **Xochimilco** (a Mexican place name), the **x** is always pronounced [s].

Further exceptions are certain given and family names, which are found in two variants: one preserving a now archaic spelling with **x** (like **Xavier** and **Ximénez**) and the other spelled in modern fashion with **j** (**Javier** and **Jiménez**). Here, **x** is pronounced /x/, that is, just like **j.**

y has several pronunciations. In the word **y,** it is pronounced [i] (see **i** for interpreting that symbol).

When it represents the first or last segment of a diphthong or triphthong (see "Diphthongs and Triphthongs" below), as in **ya, yegua, yunque, ley, rey, soy,** and **Paraguay,** the letter **y** is pronounced [y] (see **ll** [under **l**] for interpreting that symbol).

In certain varieties of Spanish, [y] is pronounced with more occlusion, so that it has come to be close to [ž] if not actually that sound (see **ll** [under **l**] for interpreting the latter symbol); and in still other varieties it is pronounced with so much occlusion that it has come to be close to [ǰ] if not actually that (ǰ] is similar to the first consonant of English **Jacob, Jerusalem, Jew,** etc.). Both Standard 1 and Standard 2 have [y] rather than [ž] or [ǰ], except in the emphatic pronunciation of **yo** (as in ¡**yo, y yo sólo, soy el dueño aquí!**), for which [ǰo] is a widespread rendition acceptable in both standards.

Certain family names have two spelling variants, an archaic one with **y** and one spelled in modern fashion with **i** (like **Yglesias ~ Iglesias**). Here, **y** is pronounced /i/, that is, just like **i.**

See also **n** with regard to **ny.**

z has several pronunciations. In Standard 1, you have an alternative:

(1) In all positions, pronounce it [θ] (see **c** for interpreting that symbol). Or,

(2) Before the letters **b, v, d, g, l, m, n,** or **r** (whether in the same word or in the next one), pronounce it [ð] (see **d** for interpreting that symbol) and in all other positions pronounce it [θ] (see **c** for interpreting that symbol).

In Standard 2, you have an alternative:

(3) In all positions, pronounce it [s] (see **s** for interpreting that symbol). Or,

(4) Before the letters **b, v, d, g, l, m, n,** or **r** (whether in the same word or in the next one), pronounce it [z] and in all other positions pronounce it [s] (see **s** for interpreting that symbol).

That is to say, if you pronounce **c** before **e** or **i** as [θ], you must follow instruction (1) or (2) above. If you pronounce **c** before **e** or **i** as [s], you must follow instruction (3) or (4) above.

Furthermore, if you choose to pronounce **s** as [s] before **b, v, d, g, l, m, n,** or **r,** you must pronounce **z** before any of those eight letters as [θ] (= Standard 1) or as [s] (= Standard 2); if you choose to pronounce **s** as [z], you must pronounce **z** before any of those eight letters as [ð] (= Standard 1) or [z] (= Standard 2).

Thus, in the sentence **César el hazmerreír de toda la isla,** for example, you have these choices for the **c** of the first word, the **z** of the third word, and the **s** of the seventh word:

c [θ] + z [θ] + s [s] (= Standard 1)
c [θ] + z [ð] + s [z] (= Standard 1)
c [s] + z [s] + s [s] (= Standard 2)
c [s] + z [z] + s [z] (= Standard 2)

The same restrictions apply to any individual word. Thus, civilización, for example, must be pronounced either [θiβiliθaθyon] (= Standard 1) or [siβilisasyon] (= Standard 2).

Diphthongs and Triphthongs

Spanish has fifteen diphthongs and eight triphthongs.

Eight of the diphthongs begin with a semivowel:

ia [ya] is spelled ya at the beginning of a word, e.g., desahuciar, yámbico.
ua [wa] (e.g., guardar).
ie [ye] or [yɛ] is spelled ye at the beginning of a word, e.g., agüero, bien, higiene, siete, yema. The rules for choosing [e] or [ɛ] (see e) apply to [ye] and [yɛ] too.
ue [we] or [wɛ] is spelled üe after g that is not pronounced [x], e.g., huelga, hueste, huevo, vergüenza. The rules for choosing [e] or [ɛ] (see e) apply to [we] or [wɛ] too.
io and yo [yo], e.g., soslayar, yo. The spelling io at the beginning of a word is an imitation of Greek.
uo [wo] (e.g., arduo).
iu [yu] is spelled yu at the beginning of a word, e.g., triunfo, yugo.
ui [wi] (spelled uy in muy), e.g., cuidar, muy. For uy representing [uy], see uy in the next section.

Take care to pronounce diphthongs beginning with a semivowel as diphthongs and not as two syllables. Thus, whereas English barrio has three syllables, Spanish barrio has two (ba-rrio), pronounced [barryo].

Seven of the diphthongs end in a semivowel:

ai [ay] is spelled ay at the end of most words; rarely, ay is found in the middle of a word (e.g., aimará ~ aymará, hay, Raimundo, Seychelles). If ay occurs before a vowel in the same word, it represents not a diphthong but /a/ + /y/ and each of those sounds belongs to a different syllable (thus, aya and haya for example are syllabified a-ya and ha-ya).
au [aw] (e.g., caudillo).
ei is almost always pronounced [ey] and is almost always spelled ey at the end of a word, e.g., reina, rey. A pronunciation exception is reir, which is pronounced as if spelled *reír. If ey occurs before a vowel in the same word, it represents not a diphthong but /e/ + /y/ and each of those sounds belongs to a different syllable (thus, reyes and leyenda for instance are syllabified re-yes and le-yen-da).
eu [ew] (e.g., seudónimo).
oi is almost always pronounced [oy] and is

spelled oy at the end of a word (e.g., hoy) and in certain family names in other positions too (like Goytisolo). A pronunciation exception is oir, which is pronounced as if spelled *oír. If oy occurs before a vowel in the same word, it represents not a diphthong but /o/ + /y/ and each of those sounds belongs to a different syllable (thus, Goya is syllabified Go-ya).
uy, which always occurs at the end of a word, is almost always pronounced [uy] (as in ¡huy!, Jujuy). The exception is muy, whose pronunciation is given in the previous section. If uy occurs before a vowel in the same word, it represents not a diphthong but /u/ + /y/ and each of those sounds belongs to a different syllable (thus, cuyo and tuyas are syllabified cu-yo and tu-yas).

The triphthongs are:

iai [yay] (e.g., despreciáis).
iau [yaw] (e.g., miau).
iei [yey] (e.g., despreciéis).
uai [way] (spelled uay at the end of a word), e.g., evaluáis, Uruguay.
uau [waw] (e.g., guau).
uei [wey] (spelled uey at the end of a word), e.g., evaluéis, buey.

Syllabification

Spanish is a consonant-vowel language, that is, syllables preferably end in a vowel (though many exceptions are found). Therefore, a single consonant and the vowel following it usually form a syllable or, expressed otherwise, a single consonant between two vowels usually goes with the following vowel (thus, ba-jo, a-dhe-sión). Since ch, ll, ñ, and rr represent a single consonant, the syllabification is, for example, mu-cha-cho, ha-llar, ni-ño, ba-rrio, and haz-me-rreír.

The consonant clusters bl, cl, dl, fl, gl, pl, tl, br, cr, dr, fr, gr, pr, and tr form a syllable with the following vowel, for instance, ha-blar, a-cla-rar, a-flo-jar, a-glo-me-rar, a-pla-zar, a-tle-ta, a-bra-zar, a-cre-di-tar, a-drede, a-fran-ce-sar, a-gre-gar, and a-pren-der.

When representing /š/, sh is not divided, whereas if a consonant letter + h is found in the middle of a word and the h is silent, the h begins a new syllable: al-ha-ra-ca, clor-hi-dra-to, des-hi-dra-tar, in-hu-ma-ción.

All other clusters of two consonants between vowels (including diphthongs and triphthongs) are usually divided, so that the first consonant belongs to the preceding syllable and the second consonant to the following syllable, for example, a-cos-tar-se, ac-tuar, cuer-do, en-car-gar, es-la-vo, fras-co, Is-ra-el, llan-ta, per-di-ción, sol-da-dura, and der-vi-che. Subject to that rule are also instances of double c or n, as in per-fec-ción and en-ne-gre-cer.

If a cluster of three or more consonants stands between vowels, the last two consonants are usually bl, cl, dl, fl, gl, pl, tl, br, cr, dr, fr, gr, pr, or tr and they go with the following syllable, for instance, tem-blar, ten-dré, ex-plo-tar, tem-prano.

If a cluster of three or more consonants stands between vowels and if the second consonant is s, the s goes with the preceding syllable, for example ins-tan-te and pers-pec-ti-va.

If one vowel follows another and they do not constitute a diphthong (see above), they belong to separate syllables, for instance, ma-es-tro, cre-o, le-er, to-a-lla. Accordingly, if i or u (which represent respectively [y] or [w] in diphthongs and triphthongs) represents a vowel, it belongs in a separate syllable and that fact is indicated by a stress mark. Thus, ahínco (three syllables: a-hín-co), búho (two syllables: bú-ho), desahúcio (four syllables: de-sa-hú-cio), traído (three syllables: tra-í-do), prohíbo (three syllables: pro-hí-bo), Raúl (two syllables: Ra-úl), haría (three syllables: ha-rí-a), haríais (three syllables: ha-rí-ais), etc.

If y is preceded and followed by a vowel, it forms a diphthong with the following one and therefore belongs in the following syllable, for instance, ca-yo, tu-yo, cre-yó. In fact, all diphthongs and triphthongs (see the list above) form syllables of their own. In contrast, identical contiguous vowels (as in creer) and vowels that do not form diphthongs or triphthongs (as in leal), as well as diphthongs or triphthongs dissolved by the stress mark (see the examples from ahínco to haríais in the previous paragraph), form separate syllables (thus, cre-er, le-al, etc.).

It is permissible but not obligatory to set aside the foregoing rules in the case of prefixes, which one may consider as forming syllables of their own (whether or not such would be the case if the rules were followed) or which one may subject to the rules. For example, ab-ro-ga-ción or a-bro . . . , des-a-bro-char or de-sa . . . , ex-a-cer-ba-ción or e-xa . . . , sub-li-mar or su-bli . . . (in each pair, the first variant reflects treatment of the prefix as a syllable in its own right, no matter what the rules would require, and the second variant shows syllabification when the rules are suspended). The same applies to solid compounds: nos-o-tros or no-so-tros, vos-o-tras or vo-so-tras, etc.

The foregoing paragraph not withstanding, the rules must be followed with respect to a succession of three consonant letters, the second of which is s, in which case s belongs with the preceding, not the following letter

(thus, as already noted, ins-tante, pers-pect-ti-va, not in-st . . . , per-sp . . .) and with respect to prefixes if the first letter immediately following them is h (thus, des-ha-cer and des-hi-dra-tar, not de-sha . . . or de-shi . . .).

Stress

Most Spanish words have only one primary stress, which can be determined from the spelling according to these rules:

(1) If a word is spelled with a stress mark, stress the syllable in which it is found (like águila, bíceps, fórceps, hablarán, Martí-nez), the only exception being ó, which is not stressed (this is the form taken by the conjunction o when it appears between two Arabic numerals, the purpose of the mark being solely to prevent misinterpretation of the conjunction as the Arabic numeral for zero; thus, 6 ó 7, for instance, means '6 or 7').

(2) If a word contains no stress mark:
  [2.A] Stress the last syllable if the word ends in:
    [2.A.i] a vowel letter + y (like convoy, Uruguay, virrey),
    [2.A.ii] a consonant letter other than n or s (like consentir, David, lateral),
    [2.A.iii] n not preceded by a vowel letter (like Isern),
    [2.A.iv] s not preceded by a vowel letter (like Fontanals, Casals).
  [2.B] Stress the next-to-last syllable if the word ends in:
    [2.B.i] a vowel letter other than y (like casi, habla, hable, hablo, fatuo, patria, sitio),
    [2.B.ii] a vowel letter + n (like consienten, hablan),
    [2.B.iii] a vowel letter + s (like consientes, hablas).

Catalan-origin names like Capmany, Castany, Fortuny are stressed on the vowel immediately preceding -y (thus, stress [man], [tan], [tun]).

The triplets árbitro, arbitro, arbitró; público, publico, publicó; término, termino, terminó; tráfago, trafago, trafagó; and válido, valido, validó illustrate several possibilities.

Miscellaneous

It is noted above that [m] + [m], [n] + [n], [p] + [p], and [s] + [s] are respectively reduced to one [m], [p], and [s]. Since the number of instances of [s] + [s] is not the same in all varieties of Spanish, the number of reductions to [s] varies accordingly. For example, **absceso** is pronounced [apseso] only where **c** before **e** (or **i**) is pronounced [s] (otherwise it is rendered [apθeso]); see also **excelente** in the remarks on **x**.

Reduction of identical contiguous sounds (whether vowels or consonants) is widespread in Spanish, whether within a word or between two words. Thus, [a] + [a] is reduced to [a] both in the word **portaaviones** and in a phrase like **a ambos**; or, [ɛ] + [e] is reduced to [e] in the word **sobreexcitar** and in a phrase like **este efecto** (in this regard, [e] and [ɛ] are considered "identical"; the same holds true for the two kinds of /o/; hence reduction is found in a sentence like **escojo ocho opciones**). The spellings **guardagujas, guardalmacén, remplazar, sobrentender**, etc., are in fact used too and they are preferable. In many cases, only spellings reflecting a reduction are now found, for example, **aprensión, prensil,** and **represible** (contrast those forms with their English cognates: **apprehension, prehensile,** and **reprehensible**).

In certain cases, however, two contiguous sounds are pronounced separately (by some speakers) or reduced to a single, slightly longer than usual one (by other speakers), for example in **creer** and its derivatives having **ee**. When to reduce to a single vowel and when not to reduce or to reduce to a single, slightly longer vowel must be learned individually for each word.

Other simplifications preferred in this dictionary are, at the beginning of a word, **g** instead of **gn**, **m** instead of **mn**, and **s** instead of **ps** (see, for example, **nomo, nemotecnia,** and **seudónimo**), as well as spellings like **oscuro** and **sustituir**.

Two sounds may influence each other. **Tranvía**, for example, is pronounced [trambia] because the sound represented by **v** causes the **n** to be pronounced [m] and the sound represented by **n** causes the **v** to be pronounced [b].

In both standards, vowels are relatively short, though in stressed syllables and when a vowel results from a reduction of two identical vowels, they are slightly longer than usual (thus, sentences **vi a ambos** and **vi ambos**, for instance, differ slightly in the length of /a/). You need not make an effort to lengthen a vowel in a stressed syllable because that will in most cases come naturally as a result of the stress on the vowel in that syllable. In Buenos Aires Spanish, as a consequence of Italian influence, stressed syllables are noticeably longer than unstressed ones. That feature is not recommended.

English, especially British English, is a stress-timed language (it has rhythm in which stressed syllables tend to occur at regular intervals of time, regardless of the number of intervening unstressed syllables) whereas Spanish is a syllable-timed language (with rhythm in which syllables are approximately equal in duration and thus tend to follow one another at regular intervals). Consequently, speakers of English, especially British English, tend to reduce unstressed syllables (as in the British pronunciation of **momentary, pattern,** and **secretary**), whereas Spanish-speakers tend to pronounce each syllable distinctly and do not often slur over any of them. Spanish-speakers thus often react to English-accented Spanish as one in which *se comen las vocales* 'the vowels are swallowed up' and speakers of English (especially of British English) tend to react to Spanish-accented English as "overly precise" (to get an idea of the difference between stress- and syllable-timed languages, contrast American and British pronunciations of **momentary** and **secretary:** Americans pronounce each syllable of those words with more or less the same degree of distinctiveness, whereas Britishers pronounce only the first syllable distinctly and slur over the others; thus, American English is more syllable-timed and British English more stress-timed). To pronounce Spanish correctly, English-speakers should therefore give each vowel its full value.

Formerly, in the Spanish-speaking world, the pronunciation and spelling of words borrowed from other languages were routinely changed so that they conformed to Spanish norms. Thus for example, bowline > bolina, coolie > culí, goal > gol, kerosene > kerosén, ketch > queche, Quaker > cuáquero, shilling > chelín, sweater > suéter, trolley bus > trolebús, volt > voltio, yacht > yate; English and/or French bureau > buró, English jacket and/or French jaquette > chaqué and chaqueta; English packet boat and/or French paquebot > paquebote; English pudding and/or French pudding > pudín; English and/or French restaurant > restaurante ~ restorán; English role and/or French rôle > rol; English toupée and/or French toupet > tupé; French bivouac > vivac (which was later completely hispanized to vivaque), boudin > budín, boulevard > bulevar, bourgeois > burgués, corset > corsé, meeting > mitin, nécessaire > neceser, purée > puré, terreplain > terraplén, vaudou > vodú; German Schomberg > chambergo; and, from various languages, zar 'tsar'. Or, non-Spanish /š/ usually became /č/ (not only in chambergo but also in bolchevique, chal, champán ~ champaña, champú, coqueluche,

derviche, and **fetiche**) or /s/ (as in **Visnú**).

Now, however, the trend is to retain non-Spanish spellings, though not necessarily non-Spanish pronunciations, with the result that the good fit between Spanish spelling and pronunciation is in certain words absent.

After the death of Francisco Franco (1975), the non-Spanish languages of Spain, long discouraged or suppressed in various ways up to that time, gained or regained their legitimate rights, although an unfortunate consequence thereof has been the use of non-Spanish spellings in certain Spanish words referring to elements of the cultures of which those languages are the vehicle. Thus, not uncommon in today's Spanish are Cata-lan spellings like "Catalunya" and "Convergencia i Unió" and Basque spellings like "batzoki," "txistu," and "txistulari." The Spanish language academies recognize only **Cataluña, Convergencia y Unión, bachoqui, chistu**, and **chistulari**.

All of which is to say that from the spelling of a recent Spanish borrowing from another language you may not be able to infer its pronunciation fully. But, on the whole, the number of Spanish words in which the fit between spelling and pronunciation is less than optimal or whose pronunciation is in some way unusual is still small.

D.L.G.

Spanish Irregular Verbs

Infinitive	Present	Future	Preterit	Past Part.
andar	ando	andaré	anduve	andado
caber	quepo	cabré	cupe	cabido
caer	caigo	caeré	caí	caído
conducir	conduzco	conduciré	conduje	conducido
dar	doy	daré	di	dado
decir	digo	diré	dije	dicho
estar	estoy	estaré	estuve	estado
haber	he	habré	hube	habido
hacer	hago	haré	hice	hecho
ir	voy	iré	fui	ido
jugar	juego	jugaré	jugué	jugado
morir	muero	moriré	morí	muerto
oir	oigo	oiré	oí	oído
poder	puedo	podré	pude	podido
poner	pongo	pondré	puse	puesto
querer	quiero	querré	quise	querido
saber	sé	sabré	supe	sabido
salir	salgo	saldré	salí	salido
ser	soy	seré	fui	sido
tener	tengo	tendré	tuve	tenido
traer	traigo	traeré	traje	traído
valer	valgo	valdré	valí	valido
venir	vengo	vendré	vine	venido
ver	veo	veré	vi	visto

Los sonidos del inglés americano

Vocales y diptongos

a se pronuncia más cerrado que la *a* de *paro* (por ejemplo: **act, at, bat, hat, marry**); también se encuentra este sonido en palabras deletreadas con: -ah- (d*ah*lia), -ai- (pl*ai*d), -al- (h*al*f), -au- (l*au*gh), -ua- (g*ua*rantee).

a se pronuncia más cerrado que la *e* de *hablé* y como si fuera seguido de *i* (por ejemplo: **age, gate, rate**); también se encuentra este sonido en palabras deletreadas con: -ai- (r*ai*n, *ai*r), -aigh- (str*aigh*t), -au- (g*au*ge), -ay- (s*ay*), -ea- (st*ea*k), -ei- (v*ei*l, w*ei*gh), -ey- (ob*ey*).

a equivale aproximadamente a la *a* de *sentado* y *bajo* (por ejemplo: **ah, father, part**); también se encuentra este sonido en palabras deletreadas con: -al- (c*al*m), -e(r)- (s*er*geant), -ea(r)- (h*ear*t), -ua- (g*ua*rd).

a equivale aproximadamente a la *e* de las palabras francesas *de* y *le* (por ejemplo: *al*one, *a*bout); también se encuentra este sonido en palabras deletreadas con: -e- (syst*e*m), -i- (eas*i*ly), -o- (gall*o*p), -u- (circ*u*s), -y- (mart*y*r).

e equivale aproximadamente a la *e* de *templo* y *perro* (por ejemplo: **edge, set, merry**); también se encuentra este sonido en palabras deletreadas con: a- (*a*ny, m*a*ny), -ai- (s*ai*d), -ay- (s*ay*s), -ea- (l*ea*ther), -ei- (h*ei*fer), -eo- (j*eo*pardy), -ie- (fr*ie*nd).

e equivale aproximadamente a la *i* de *Chile* (por ejemplo: **be, equal, secret**); también se encuentra este sonido en palabras deletreadas con: ea- (*ea*ch, t*ea*), -ee- (f*ee*, k*ee*p), -ei- (rec*ei*ve), -eo- (p*eo*ple), -ey- (k*ey*), -ie- (f*ie*ld), -y (c*i*ty).

i se pronuncia menos cerrado que la *i* de *Chile* (por ejemplo: **if, big, fit, mirror**); también se encuentra este sonido en palabras deletreadas con: e- (*E*ngland), -ee- (b*ee*n), -ei- (counterf*ei*t), -ia- (carr*ia*ge), -ie- (s*ie*ve), -o- (w*o*men), (b)u(s)- (b*u*siness), -y- (s*y*mpathetic).

i equivale aproximadamente a la *ai* de *aire*, *baile* (por ejemplo: **bite, ice, pirate**); también se encuentra este sonido en palabras deletreadas con: ais- (*ai*sle), -ei- (h*ei*ght, st*ei*n), eye (*eye*), -ie (p*ie*), -igh (h*igh*), is- (*i*sland), -uy (b*uy*), -y (cycle, sky), -ye (l*ye*).

o se pronuncia más cerrado que la *o* de *supo* (por ejemplo: **hope, go, oh, over**); también se encuentra este sonido en palabras deletreadas con: -au- (m*au*ve), -aux (f*aux* pas), -eau (b*eau*), -ew (s*ew*), -oa- (r*oa*d), -oe (t*oe*), -oo- (br*oo*ch), -ot (dep*ot*), -ou- (s*ou*l), -ow (fl*ow*), -owe- (*owe*).

o se pronuncia más cerrado que la *o* de *corre* (por ejemplo: **alcohol, order, raw**); también se encuentra este sonido en palabras deletreadas con: -a- (t*a*ll), -al- (w*al*k),-au- (*au*thor, v*au*lt), -augh- (c*augh*t), -oa- (br*oa*d), -oo- (fl*oo*r), -ough- (s*ough*t).

oi equivale aproximadamente a la *oy* de *doy* (por ejemplo: **oil, joint, voice**); también se encuentra este sonido en palabras deletreadas con: -awy- (l*awy*er), -oy- (b*oy*).

oo se pronuncia menos cerrado que la *u* de *insulto* (por ejemplo: **book, foot**); también se encuentra el sonido en palabras deletreadas con: -o- (w*o*lf), -ou- (t*ou*r), -u- (p*u*ll).

oo se pronuncia más largo que la *u* de *susto* (por ejemplo: **too, ooze, fool**); también se encuentra este sonido en palabras deletreadas con: -eu- (man*eu*ver), -ew (gr*ew*), -o (wh*o*), -o . . . e (m*o*ve), -oe (can*oe*), -ou- (tr*ou*pe), -u . . . e (r*u*le), -ue (fl*ue*), -ui- (s*ui*t).

ou equivale aproximadamente a la *au* de *aurora* (por ejemplo: **loud, out**); también se encuentra este sonido en palabras deletreadas con -ow (br*ow*, c*ow*, pl*ow*).

u equivale aproximadamente a la *iu* de *ciudad* (por ejemplo: **cue, use, utility**); también se encuentra este sonido en palabras deletreadas con: -eau- (b*eau*ty), -eu- (f*eu*d), -ew (f*ew*), hu- (*hu*man), hu . . . e (*hu*ge), -iew (v*iew*), you (*you*), yu . . e (*yu*le).

u es sonido intermedio entre la *o* de *borro* y la *a* de *barro*, algo parecido a la prounuciación de la *eu* francesa de *peur*; (por ejemplo: **up, sun, mud**); también se encuentra este sonido en palabras deletreadas con: o- (*o*ther), -o- (s*o*n), -oe- (d*oe*s), o . . . e (l*o*ve), -oo- (bl*oo*d), -ou (tr*ou*ble).

Consonantes

b equivale aproximadamente a la *b* de *burro* y *hombre* (por ejemplo: **bed, amber,**

rub); también se encuentra en palabras deletreadas con -bb- (ho*bb*y) y -be (lo*be*).

ch equivale aproximadamente a la *ch* española (por ejemplo: **chief, beach**); también se encuentra en palabras deletreadas con: -tch- (ca*tch*, bu*tch*er), -te- (righ*te*ous), -ti- (ques*ti*on), -tu- (na*tu*ral).

d equivale aproximadamente a la *d* de *onda* (por ejemplo: **do, odor, red**); también se encuentra en palabras deletreadas con -dd- (la*dd*er) y -de (fa*de*).

f equivale aproximadamente a la *f* española (por ejemplo: **feed, safe**); también se encuentra en palabras deletreadas con -ff- (mu*ff*in) y -fe (li*fe*).

g equivale aproximadamente a la *g* de *globo* (por ejemplo: **give, fog**); también se encuentra en palabras deletreadas con -gg (e*gg*), gh- (*gh*ost), y -gue (pla*gue*).

h se pronuncia más aspirado pero menos áspero que la *j* española en *jabón* (por ejemplo: **hit, hope**); también se encuentra en palabras deletreadas con wh- (*wh*ere, *wh*ich, *wh*o).

j equivale aproximadamente a la *y* de *yo* en su pronunciación enfática (p.ej. . . . *yo, y yo sólo soy el dueño aquí!*) o como la *y* de *cónyuge* en ciertas modalidades del español (por ejemplo: **just, joke**); también se encuentra en palabras deletreadas con: -dg- (ju*dg*e), -di- (sol*di*er), -ge (sa*ge*), -gg- (exa*gg*erate), gi- (*gi*n).

k (por ejemplo: **keep, make, token**); tras consonante equivale aproximadamente a la *k* española; en otras posiciones se pronuncia como los anglohablantes con fuerte acento inglés pronuncian la *k* española, o sea con aspiración; también se encuentra en palabras deletreadas con: -c- (*c*ar), -cc- (a*cc*ount), ch- (*ch*aracter), -ck (ba*ck*).

l se pronuncia aproximadamente como la *l* de *lago* (por ejemplo: **leap, sail**); también se encuentra en palabras deletreadas con -le (mi*le*) y -ll (ca*ll*), y puede formar sílaba (p.ej. **bottle** y **middle**).

m equivale aproximadamente a la *m* española (por ejemplo: **more, drum, him, summer**).

n equivale aproximadamente a la *n* de *bueno* (por ejemplo: **now, sunny**); también se encuentra en palabras deletreadas con gn- (*gn*at) y kn- (*kn*ife), y puede formar sílaba (p.ej. **button** y **mitten**).

ng (por ejemplo: **sing, Washington**) equivale aproximadamente a la *n* de *blanco*.

p (por ejemplo: **pool, spool, supper, stop**) tras consonante equivale aproximadamente a la *p* española; en otras posiciones se pronuncia como los anglohablantes con fuerte acento inglés pronuncian la *p* española, o sea con aspiración.

r se pronuncia como los anglohablantes con fuerte acento inglés pronuncian la *r* de *pero*, o sea que se eleva la punta de la lengua hacia el paladar (sin tocarlo) y doblada para atrás (por ejemplo: **red, hurry, near**); también se encuentra en palabras deletreadas con -re (pu*re*), rh- (*rh*ythm), y wr- (*wr*ong).

s equivale aproximadamente a la *s* de *salir*, pero algo más tensa y larga (por ejemplo: **see, kiss**); también se encuentra en palabras deletreadas con: ce- (*ce*nter, ra*ce*r), ci- (*ci*ty, a*ci*d), -ce (mi*ce*), ps- (*ps*yche), sc- (*sc*ene).

sh equivale aproximadamente a la *ch* de las palabras francesas *changer* and *chapeau* (por ejemplo: **ship, wash**); también se encuentra en palabras deletreadas con: -ce- (o*ce*an), -ch- (ma*ch*ine), -ci- (spe*ci*al), s(u)- (*s*(u)gar), -sci- (con*sci*ence), -si- (man*si*on), -ss- (ti*ss*ue, mi*ss*ion), -ti- (cap*ti*on).

t (por ejemplo: **team, ten, steam, bit**); tras consonante equivale aproximadamente a la *t* española; en otras posiciones se pronuncia como los anglohablantes con fuerte acento inglés pronuncian la *t* de *también* o de *tomar*, o sea con aspiración; también se encuentra en palabras deletreadas con: -bt (dou*bt*), -cht (ya*cht*), -ed (talk*ed*), -ght (bou*ght*), -te (bi*te*), th- (*th*yme), -tt- (bo*tt*om), tw- (*tw*o).

th (por ejemplo: **thin, ether, path**) equivale aproximadamente a la *z* española en el norte de España.

th (por ejemplo: **that, the, either, smooth**) equivale aproximadamente a la *d* de *adoptar*.

v (por ejemplo: **voice, river, live**) equivale aproximadamente a la *b* de *haba* pero labiodental en vez de bilabial.

w (por ejemplo: **west, witch, away**) equivale aproximadamente a la *u* de *puesto*.

y (por ejemplo: **yes, beyond**) equivale aproximadamente a la *i* de *bien*; también se encuentra en palabras deletreadas con -i- (on*i*on, un*i*on, -j- (halleluj*ah*), and -ll- (torti*ll*a).

z (por ejemplo: **zoo, lazy, zone**) equivale aproximadamente a la *s* de *isla* y *mismo* en ciertas modalidades del español, pero con más sonoridad; también se encuentra en algunas palabras deletreadas con: -s (ha*s*), -se (ri*se*), x- (*x*ylophone), y -zz- (bu*zz*ard, fu*zz*); o con el sonido /zh/ en **azure, brazier,** que equivale aproximadamente a la *ll* del español de la gente mayor de la ciudad de Buenos Aires (o sea, como la *j* de la palabra francesa *bonjour*). El sonido /sh/ también se encuentra en ciertas palabras deletreadas con -ge (gara*ge,* mira*ge*), -si- (vi*si*on), y su- (plea*su*re).

Las formas del verbo inglés

1. Se forma la 3ª persona singular del tiempo presente exactamente al igual que el plural de los sustantivos, añadiendo **-es** o **-s** a la forma sencilla según las mismas reglas, así:

(1)	teach	pass	wish	fix	buzz		
	teaches	passes	wishes	fixes	buzzes		
(2)	place	change	judge	please	freeze		
	places	changes	judges	pleases	freezes		
(3a)	find	sell	clean	hear	love	buy	know
	finds	sells	cleans	hears	loves	buys	knows
(3b)	think	like	laugh	stop	hope	meet	want
	thinks	likes	laughs	stops	hopes	meets	wants
(4)	cry	try	dry	carry	deny		
	cries	tries	dries	carries	denies		

Cinco verbos muy comunes tienen 3ª persona singular irregular:

(5)	go	do	say	have	be
	goes	does	says	has	is

2. Se forman el tiempo pasado y el participio de modo igual, añadiendo a la forma sencilla la terminación **-ed** o **-d** según las reglas que siguen:

(1) Si la forma sencilla termina en **-d** o **-t,** se le pone **-ed** como sílaba aparte:

end	fold	need	load	want	feast	wait	light
ended	folded	needed	loaded	wanted	feasted	waited	lighted

(2) Si la forma sencilla termina en cualquier otra consonante, se añade también **-ed** pero sin hacer sílaba aparte:

(2a)	bang	sail	seem	harm	earn	weigh
	banged	sailed	seemed	harmed	earned	weighed
(2b)	lunch	work	look	laugh	help	pass
	lunched	worked	looked	laughed	helped	passed

(3) Si la forma sencilla termina en **-e,** se le pone sólo **-d:**

(3a)	hate	taste	waste	guide	fade	trade
	hated	tasted	wasted	guided	faded	traded
(3b)	free	judge	rule	name	dine	scare
	freed	judged	ruled	named	dined	scared
(3c)	place	force	knife	like	hope	base
	placed	forced	knifed	liked	hoped	based

(4) Una **-y** final que sigue a cualquier consonante se cambia en **-ie** al añadir la **-d** del pasado/participio:

cry	try	dry	carry	deny
cried	tried	dried	carried	denied

3. Varios verbos muy comunes forman el tiempo pasado y el participio de manera irregular. Pertenecen a tres grupos.

(1) Los que tienen una sola forma irregular para tiempo pasado y participio, como los siguientes:

bend	bleed	bring	build	buy	catch	creep	deal
bent	bled	brought	built	bought	caught	crept	dealt
dig	feed	feel	fight	find	flee	get	hang
dug	fed	felt	fought	found	fled	got	hung
have	hear	hold	keep	lead	leave	lend	lose
had	heard	held	kept	led	left	lent	lost
make	mean	meet	say	seek	sell	send	shine
made	meant	met	said	sought	sold	sent	shone
shoot	sit	sleep	spend	stand	strike	sweep	teach
shot	sat	slept	spent	stood	struck	swept	taught

(2) Los que tienen una forma irregular para el tiempo pasado y otra forma irregular para el participio, como los siguientes:

be	beat	become	begin	bite
was	beat	became	began	bit
been	beaten	become	begun	bitten
blow	break	choose	come	do
blew	broke	chose	came	did
blown	broken	chosen	come	done
draw	drink	drive	eat	fall
drew	drank	drove	ate	fell
drawn	drunk	driven	eaten	fallen
fly	forget	freeze	give	go
flew	forgot	froze	gave	went
flown	forgotten	frozen	given	gone
grow	hide	know	ride	ring
grew	hid	knew	rode	rang
grown	hidden	known	ridden	rung
rise	run	see	shake	shrink
rose	ran	saw	shook	shrank
risen	run	seen	shaken	shrunk
sing	sink	speak	steal	swear
sang	sank	spoke	stole	swore
sung	sunk	spoken	stolen	sworn
swim	tear	throw	wear	write
swam	tore	threw	wore	wrote
swum	torn	thrown	worn	written

(3) Los que no varían del todo, la forma sencilla funcionando también como pasado/participio; entre éstos son de mayor frecuencia:

bet	burst	cast	cost	cut
hit	hurt	let	put	quit

read	set	shed	shut	slit
spit	split	spread	thrust	wet

El plural del sustantivo inglés

A la forma singular se añade la terminación **-es** o **-s** de acuerdo con las reglas siguientes.

(1) Si el singular termina en **-ch, -s, -sh, -x** o **-z**, se le pone **-es** como sílaba aparte:

match	glass	dish	box	buzz
matches	glasses	dishes	boxes	buzzes

(2) Si el singular termina en **-ce, -ge, -se** o **-ze,** se le pone una **-s** que con la vocal precedente forma sílaba aparte:

face	page	house	size
faces	pages	houses	sizes

(3) Una **-y** final que sigue a cualquier consonante se cambia en **-ie** a ponérsele la **-s** del plural:

sky	city	lady	ferry	penny
skies	cities	ladies	ferries	pennies

(4) Los siguientes sustantivos comunes tienen plural irregular:

Man	woman	child	foot	mouse	goose
men	women	children	feet	mice	geese
wife	knife	life	half	leaf	deer
wives	knives	lives	halves	leaves	deer

List of Abbreviations Used in this Dictionary

a adjective
abb abbreviation
acc accusative
adv adverb
aer aeronautics
agr agriculture
anat anatomy
ant antiquated
arch architecture
archeol archeology
art. article
art art
ast astronomy
astrol astrology
aut automobiles
aux auxiliary
biol biology
bot botany
cards card games
carp carpentry
chem chemistry
com commerce
comp comparative
condit conditional
conjunc conjunction
cul culinary
dance dancing
dat dative
dim diminutive
ecc ecclesiastical
elec electricity
eng engineering
ent entomology
euphem euphemism
f feminine
fig figurative
fig inf used figuratively in
    informal speech or writing
fut future
gen generally; genitive

geog geography
geol geology
geom geometry
gram grammar
gym gymnastics
her heraldry
hist history
icht ichthyology
imperf imperfect
impers impersonal
ind indicative
indef art. indefinite article
inf informal
infin infinitive
insep inseparable
interj interjection,
    exclamation
interr interrogative
iron ironical
irr irregular
law law
ling linguistics
lit literature
m masculine
mas masonry
math mathematics
mech mechanics
med medical
met metallurgy
mf masculine or feminine
mil military
min mineralogy
mus music
myth mythology
n noun
naut nautical
nav naval
neut neuter
opt optics
orn ornithology

part participle
pers personal; person
pharm pharmacy
phil philosophy
phon phonetics
phot photography
phys physics
physiol physiology
pl plural
poet poetic
pol political
pol econ political economy
poss possessive
prep preposition
pres present
print printing
pron pronoun
psy psychology
rad radio
rw railway
s substantive, noun
sew sewing
sing singular
spirit spiritualism
sport sports
subjunc subjunctive
sup superlative
surg surgery
surv surveying
tan tanning
theat theater
theol theology
univ university
v aux auxiliary verb
vi intransitive verb
vr reflexive verb
vt transitive verb
WH Western Hemispheric
    Spanish
zool zoology

SPANISH-ENGLISH
Dictionary

A

a *f,* name of the letter A

a *prep* to; at; on; by; in, into; up to; according to; if, etc. 1. Denotes the direct complement of verb before objects representing specified persons or animals, personified nouns, pronouns referring to specific persons (**alguien, entrambos, cualquiera,** etc.), demonstrative or relative pronouns, collective nouns representing persons (**el público, la muchedumbre,** etc.), names of countries, cities, rivers, etc., except where these invariably take the def. art., e.g. **Dejé a Varsovia,** I left Warsaw, *but* **Dejé el Perú,** I left Peru. 2. Introduces indirect obj. when this is a noun governed by a verb implying motion, or an emphatic pers. pron., e.g. **Nos conviene a ti y a mí,** It suits both you and me. It is also used before indirect obj. to avoid ambiguity when there is both an indirect and direct obj. 3. Denotes the complement of verb when this is an infin., e.g. **Enseñó a pintar a María,** He taught Mary to paint. 4. Indicates direction or destination, e.g. **Vamos a Edimburgo,** We are going to Edinburgh. 5. Signifies location, or point of time when action takes place, e.g. **Vinieron a las doce.** They came at twelve o'clock. 6. Describes position of persons or things, e.g. **Se sentaron a la puerta,** They sat down at the door. **La casa queda a la derecha,** The house is on the right. 7. Denotes interval of time or place between one thing and another, e.g. **de tres a cinco de la tarde,** from three to five in the afternoon, **de calle a calle,** from street to street. 8. Expresses manner of action, e.g. **a la francesa,** in the French way, **bordado a mano,** embroidered by hand. 9. Indicates rate or price, e.g. **a cuatro pesetas la libra,** at four pesetas the lb. 10. Indicates difference or comparison, e.g. **Va mucho de querer a hacer,** There's a difference between wishing and doing. 11. Sometimes is synonymous with **hasta, según, hacia** and governs almost all parts of speech. Has many idiomatic uses. 12. Before infin. sometimes has conditional sense, e.g. **A haber sabido las noticias no lo hubiéramos hecho,** If we had heard the news we would not have done it. 13. With nouns and adjectives forms adverbial phrases, e.g. **poco a poco,** little by little, **a veces,** sometimes, **a ciegas,** blindly, etc. **A + el** becomes **al,** e.g. **al rey,** to the king. **Al + infin.** means when or on, e.g. **al marcharme yo,** when I left (on my leaving)

abacería *f,* grocery shop

abacero (-ra) *n* grocer

ábaco *m, arch* abacus; counting frame

abad *m,* abbot

abadesa *f,* abbess

abadía *f,* abbacy; abbey

abajamiento *m,* lowering; letting down

abajar *vt* to lower

abajo *adv* under; underneath; below; down. Used immediately after noun in adverbial phrases, e.g. **cuesta a.,** downhill, downstairs. *interj* Down with! e.g., **¡A. el rey!** Down with the king! **venirse a.,** to fall down; *fig* collapse

abalanzamiento *m,* balancing; rushing upon; dashing

abalanzar *vt* to balance; impel violently; *vr* throw oneself upon; attack, rush upon; (*with prep a*) rush into, risk. **Se abalanzó hacia ellos,** He rushed toward them

abalorio *m,* glass bead; bead work

abanderado *m,* standardbearer; (Argentina) valedictorian

abanderar *vt* to register (a ship)

abanderizar *vt* to organize in groups; *vr* band together

abandonado *a* deserted; forlorn; helpless; indolent, careless; slovenly

abandonamiento *m,* desertion; forlornness; helplessness; carelessness; slovenliness

abandonar *vt* to forsake, desert; neglect; leave; give up; renounce; *vr* neglect oneself; grow discouraged; (*with prep a*) give oneself over to

abandono *m,* abandonment; defencelessness; forlornness; dilapidation; renunciation; neglect; slovenliness; debauchery

abanicar *vt* to fan

abanico *m,* fan; anything fan-shaped; *inf* sword; railway signal; *naut* derrick. **en a.,** fan-shaped

abaniqueo *m,* fanning; swinging, oscillation; gesticulation

abaratar *vt* to cheapen, make less expensive; *vr* fall in price

abarca *f,* leather sandal, worn chiefly in the Basque provinces

abarcador(-ra) *n* one who clasps or embraces; monopolist

abarcadura *f,* **abarcamiento** *m,* inclusion; scope

abarcar *vt* to clasp, encircle; include, comprise; undertake, attempt; monopolize

abarquillar *vt* to shape into a roll; roll; curl

abarracar(se) *vi* and *vr mil* to go into barracks

abarrancadero *m,* rough road; ravine, precipice; *fig* difficult situation

abarrancar *vt* to ditch; make a ravine; *vr* fall into a pit; stick (in the mud, etc.); get into difficulties; *naut* run aground

abastar see **abastecer**

abastecedor (-ra) *a* provisioning, supplying. *n* provider; purveyor, supplier; caterer

abastecer *vt irr* to supply, provide; purvey. See **conocer**

abastecimiento *m,* providing; supply, provision; catering; supplies

abasto *m,* provisions, food; *com* supply. *adv* plentifully, abundantly

abatanar *vt* to full (cloth)

abate *m,* abbé

abatido *a* dejected, depressed; spiritless; discouraged; crushed, humbled; *com* depreciated

abatimiento *m,* dejection, depression; humiliation; discouragement; falling; lowering; (*aer naut*) drift

abatir *vt* to knock down; overthrow; demolish; lower, take down; droop; humiliate; discourage; *naut* dismantle; *vi* (*naut aer*) drift; *vr* be despondent, despair; humble oneself; swoop down (of birds). **a. el vuelo,** to fly down

ABC *m,* ABCs (e.g. **el ABC de la física,** the ABCs of physics)

abdicación *f,* abdication

abdicar *vt* to abdicate; revoke; cancel; give up (rights, opinions)

abdomen *m,* abdomen

abdominal *a* abdominal

abecé *m,* ABCs

abecedario *m,* ABC, alphabet; reading book, primer

abedul *m,* birch tree; birch wood

abeja *f,* bee. **a. maestra,** queen bee. **a. obrera,** worker

abejar *m,* beehive

abejero (-ra) *n* beekeeper

abejón *m,* drone; hornet

abejorro *m,* bumblebee

abellacar *vt* to make a rogue of; *vr* become a rogue

aberración *f,* deviation; error, lapse; (*ast phys biol*) aberration

abertura *f,* opening; aperture, gap, hole; fissure, cleft; mountain pass; naturalness, frankness

abeto *m,* yew-leaved fir

abetunado *a* bituminous

abiertamente *adv* openly; frankly.

abierto *a* free, unobstructed; open, not enclosed; open,

2

full-blown (flowers); frank, sincere. *adv* openly
abigarrado *a* variegated; varied; speckled
abigarrar *vt* to variegate; vary; speckle; fleck; spot; dapple
abigotado *a* having a thick moustache
abintestato *a law* intestate
abiselar *vt* to bevel
abismal *a* abysmal
abismar *vt* to plunge into an abyss; depress, sadden; *vr* despair; be plunged in thought, be abstracted; be amazed
abismo *m*, chasm, abyss, gulf; hell
abjuración *f*, abjuration
abjurar *vt* to forswear, retract
ablactar *vt* to wean
ablandamiento *m*, softening; placating
ablandante *a* softening; placatory
ablandar *vt* to soften; appease, placate; loosen; relax; *vi* and *vr* be softened; be appeased; grow less stormy; (elements) decrease in force
ablandecer *vt irr* to soften. See **conocer**
ablución *f*, ablution
abnegación *f*, abnegation, self-sacrifice
abnegado *a* self-sacrificing
abnegarse *vr irr* to deprive oneself, sacrifice oneself. See **cegar**
abobado *a* bewildered; foolish-looking, silly
abobar *vt* to daze, bewilder; make stupid
abocado *a* full-flavoured, pleasant (of wine)
abocar *vt* to seize with the mouth; bring nearer; transfer (contents of one jug to another); *vr* meet, assemble; *vi* *naut* enter (a channel, port, etc.). **abocarse (con . . .),** to contact (. . .), get in touch (with . . .)
abocetado *a art* unfinished; sketchy
abochornado *a* flushed (of the face); ashamed; embarrassed
abochornar *vt* to overheat, make flushed; shame; embarrass; *vr* (plants) dry up
abofetear *vt* to slap, hit; buffet
abogacía *f*, legal profession; practice of law; advocacy
abogado (-da) *n* lawyer
abogar *vi* to defend at law; intercede for; advocate, champion
abolengo *m*, lineage, descent, family; inheritance
abolición *f*, abolition
abolir *vt* to abolish; cancel; annul
abolladura *f*, bruise; dent; embossment
abollar *vt* to bruise; dent
abollonar *vt* to emboss, do raised work on; *vr* (vines) sprout
abombado *a* convex; domed
abombar *vt* to make convex; *inf* deafen, bewilder; *vr* begin to putrefy; get intoxicated
abominable *a* abominable
abominación *f*, abomination; loathing, detestation
abominar *vt* to abominate, loathe, detest
abonable *a* subscribable; payable
abonado (-da) *a* trustworthy, reliable; ready, prepared, inclined. *n* subscriber; season ticket holder (for concerts, etc.)
abonanzar *vi impers* to clear up, be fine (weather)
abonar *vt* to guarantee; go surety for; improve, better; manure; ratify, confirm; pay; *com* place to the credit of; *vr* subscribe, become a subscriber; take out (season tickets, etc.)
abonaré *m*, *com* due bill; promissory note, I.O.U.
abono *m*, subscription; voucher; guarantee; manure. **a. verde,** leaf mold. **en a. de,** in payment of; in support of
aboquillado *a* tipped (of cigarettes)
abordaje *m*, *naut* boarding of a ship
abordar *vt naut* to board a ship; *naut* collide, run into; accost, tackle; undertake; *vi naut* put into port
aborigen *a* aboriginal
aborígenes *m pl*, aborigines
aborrachado *a* bright red; highly colored; flushed

aborrascarse *vr* to grow stormy
aborrecedor (-ra) *a* hateful. *n* hater, loather
aborrecer *vt irr* to hate, loathe; desert offspring (animals, birds). See **conocer**
aborrecible *a* hateful, detestable
aborrecimiento *m*, hate, detestation; dislike
abortar *vt* to abort; foil (a plot); *vi med* miscarry; fail, go awry
abortivo *a* abortive
aborto *m*, abortion; miscarriage; monster; failure
abotagarse *vr* to swell up, become bloated
abotonador *m*, button-hook
abotonar *vt* to button; *vi* bud, sprout
abozalar *vt* to muzzle
abra *f*, cove, small bay; narrow gorge; fissure, cleft
abrasador *a* burning, flaming
abrasamiento *m*, burning; ardour, heat
abrasar *vt* to burn; dry up, parch (plants); squander, waste; shame; *vi* burn; *vr* be very hot, glow; burn with passion
abrasión *f*, abrasion
abrasivo *a* and *m*, abrasive
abrazadera *f*, clasp; clamp
abrazamiento *m*, embracing
abrazar *vt* to embrace, clasp in one's arms; follow, adopt; engage in; seize, take advantage of; comprise, include; surround; take in hand; clamp; clasp. **abrazarse a,** to clutch, hang on to
abrazo *m*, embrace
abrelatas *m*, can opener
abrevadero *m*, watering place (for cattle)
abrevar *vt* to water cattle; irrigate, water
abreviación *f*, abbreviation, shortening; summary; hastening
abreviador *m*, abridger, condenser
abreviar *vt* to abbreviate, shorten; hasten, accelerate; condense, abridge. **a. tiempo,** to save time. **Y para a. . . . ,** And, to cut a long story short . . .
abreviatura *f*, abbreviation, contraction; shorthand
abridor *m*, opener; ear-ring (for keeping holes in ears open). **a. de guantes,** glove-stretcher. **a. de láminas,** engraving needle. **a. de latas,** can opener
abridura *f*, (act of) opening (e.g. of a trunk)
abrigada *f*, **abrigadero** *m*, sheltered place
abrigar *vt* to shelter, protect (against the cold, etc.); defend, help; hold (opinions); nurse (a hope, etc.); cover; *vr* take shelter; wrap oneself up
abrigo *m*, shelter; defence; protection; help; sheltered place; wrap, coat; *naut* haven
abril *m*, April; youth; *pl poet* years
abrillantar *vt* to cut in facets like a diamond; polish, burnish; cause to shine; *fig* improve, add lustre to
abrir *vt* to open; reveal; unlock; slide the bolt of; extend, spread out; cleave; engrave; clear (the way, etc.); begin; head, lead; separate; dig; inaugurate. *vi* unfold (flowers); expand; **en un abrir y cerrar de ojos,** in the twinkling of an eye, in the wink of an eye; *vr* open; expand; (*with con*) confide in. **a. el camino (a . . .),** to pave the way (for . . .). **abrirse camino,** to make one's way; **abrirse paso a codazos,** to elbow one's way out, (or through)
abrochador *m*, button-hook
abrochamiento *m*, buttoning; fastening
abrochar *vt* to button; fasten, clasp; hook up (a dress, etc.); buckle
abrogación *f*, repeal, annulment
abrogar *vt* to repeal, annul
abrojo *m*, thistle; *bot* caltrops; thorn, prickle; *pl* submerged rocks in sea
abroncar *vt inf* to bore, annoy
abrumador *a* burdensome, crushing, oppressive; troublesome, tiresome; exhausting
abrumar *vt* to weigh down; overwhelm, oppress; weary, exhaust; *vr* grow misty
abrupto *a* steep; rough, broken (ground); rugged
absceso *m*, abscess

absentismo *m*, absenteeism
ábside *mf*, *arch* apse. *m*, *ast* apsis
absolución *f*, (*ecc* and *law*) absolution; remission, pardon
absoluta *f*, *mil* discharge
absolutismo *m*, absolutism
absolutista *mf* absolutist
absoluto *a* absolute; categorical; *inf* despotic. **en a.**, absolutely
absolver *vt irr* to absolve; acquit (of a charge). *law* **a. de la instancia,** to dismiss the case. See **mover**
absorbente *a* and *m*, absorbent
absorber *vt* to absorb; consume, use up; attract, hold (the attention, etc.); imbibe
absorción *f*, absorption
absortar *vt* to amaze, dumbfound
absorto *a* amazed, astounded; abstracted, lost in thought
abstemio *a* abstemious
abstención *f*, abstention
abstenerse *vr irr* to refrain; abstain. See **tener**
abstinencia *f*, abstinence; fasting
abstinente *a* abstemious; temperate
abstracción *f*, abstraction; preoccupation; absent-mindedness
abstracto *a* abstract. **en a.**, in the abstract
abstraer *vt irr* to abstract; consider separately; *vi* (*with de*) do without, exclude; *vr* be preoccupied; let one's thoughts wander. See **traer**
abstraído *a* retired, recluse; preoccupied; absent-minded
abstruso *a* abstruse
absurdidad *f*, absurdity; folly, nonsense
absurdo *a* ridiculous, absurd. *m*, piece of folly, nonsense
abuchear *vt vi* to boo, hoot, jeer
abuela *f*, grandmother; old woman, dame
abuelo *m*, grandfather; ancestor *gen pl*; old man; *pl* grandparents
abulia *f*, lack of will-power, abulia
abúlico *a* abulic, lacking will-power
abultado *a* bulky, large; voluminous; exaggerated
abultamiento *m*, bulkiness; enlargement, increase; mound; exaggeration
abultar *vt* to enlarge, increase; exaggerate; model in rough (sculpture); *vi* be bulky; be large
abundancia *f*, abundance, plenty
abundante *a* abundant, plentiful; abounding (in)
abundar *vi* to be plentiful, abound
abundoso *a* See **abundante**
aburrido *a* boring, tedious, dull; tired, weary
aburrimiento *m*, boredom, dullness; wearisomeness, tediousness
aburrir *vt* to bore; *inf* spend (time, money); (birds) desert the nest; *vr* grow bored; be weary
abusar *vi* to abuse; exceed one's rights, go too far; (*with de*) take advantage of
abusivo *a* abusive
abuso *m*, abuse. **a. de confianza,** abuse of trust
abyección *f*, degradation, misery; abjectness, servility
abyecto *a* abject, wretched; servile
acá *adv* hither, here; at this time, now. **a. y acullá,** hither and thither. **desde ayer a.,** from yesterday until now
acabable *a* terminable, finishable; achievable
acabado *a* complete; perfect; expert, consummate; old, worn out; ill, infirm. *m*, finish
acabamiento *m*, finishing, completion; end; death, decease
acabar *vt* to end, terminate; finish; complete, perfect; kill; (*with con*) destroy, finish off; suppress; squander; *vi* end; die; be destroyed; (*with de + infin*) to have just (e.g. **Acaba de salir,** He has just gone out); *vr* end, be exhausted, run out of (e.g. **Se le acabó el dinero,** His money ran out); fade, grow weak; be destroyed. **Se les acabaron las dudas,** Their doubts were cleared up. **a.**

de desconcertar, to nonplus completely; **a. de decidirse,** to come to a decision; **a. de saber,** to finally learn
acacia *f*, *bot* acacia
academia *f*, academy
academicismo *m*, academicism, academism
académico (-ca) *a* academic. *n* academician. **a. de la lengua,** member of the Royal Spanish Academy
acaecer *vi irr* to happen, occur. See **conocer**
acaecimiento *m*, happening, occurrence, event
acalambrarse (muscle) to contract with cramps. **Estar acalambrado,** to have cramps
acalenturarse *vr* to grow feverish
acallar *vt* to quieten, hush; soothe, appease
acalorado *a* hot; fervent; *fig* heated
acaloramiento *m*, excitement, agitation, vehemence; ardour
acalorar *vt* to warm; aid, encourage; excite, stimulate; stir, move (to enthusiasm); inflame, rouse; tire (by exercise); *vr* grow hot; become agitated or excited; become heated (arguments)
acamar *vt* to lay flat (plants by the wind); *vr* be flattened (plants); lie down (animals); go rotten (fruit)
acampar *vi* and *vt* to encamp
acanalar *vt* to groove; striate, flute; corrugate; furrow, channel
acantilado *a* steep, precipitous; shelving (ocean-bed). *m*, cliff
acanto *m*, (*arch bot*) acanthus
acantonamiento *m*, billeting; cantonment
acantonar *vt* to billet or quarter troops
acaparador (-ra) *n* monopolist
acaparar *vt com* to monopolize, corner; seize, take possession of
acápite *m*, *WH* new paragraph
acaracolado *a* spiral, winding, twisting
acardenalar *vt* to bruise; *vr* be bruised; be covered with livid marks
acarear *vt* to face; face up to, meet with courage
acariciador (-ra) *a* caressing, loving. *n* fondler
acariciar *vt* to caress; brush, touch lightly; cherish, treat affectionately; toy with (a suggestion)
acarreador (-ra) *n* carrier, carter
acarreamiento, acarreo *m*, cartage, carting; transport, carriage; occasioning
acarrear *vt* to cart, transport; occasion, bring (gen. evil). **La guerra acarreó la carestía,** The war brought scarcity
acartonado *a* shriveled; shrunken; of cardboard; *fig* forced (dialogue)
acaso *m*, chance. *adv* by chance; perhaps, perchance. **por si a.,** in case (e.g. **Por si a. venga,** In case he comes)
acatable *a* venerable, worthy
acatadamente *adv* with respect, humbly
acatamiento *m*, respect; reverence; observance
acatar *vt* to treat with respect, honor, revere; observe
acatarrarse *vr* to catch a cold
acaudalado *a* wealthy, well-to-do
acaudalar *vt* to make money; hoard up wealth; acquire (learning, etc.)
acaudillar *vt mil* to command, lead; head (a party, etc.)
acceder *vi* (*with prep a*) to concede, grant; accede to, agree to
accesibilidad *f*, accessibility; approachableness
accesible *a* accessible; approachable
accesión *f*, agreement, acquiescence; accession; accessory; feverish attack
acceso *m*, access; paroxysm, outburst; *med* attack
accesorio *a* accessory
accesorios *m pl*, accessories; *theat* properties
accidentado *a* rough, uneven; stormy, troubled (life, etc.)
accidental *a* accidental; *m*, *mus* accidental
accidentar *vt* to cause (someone) an accident; *vr* be the victim of an accident; be seized by a fit

accidente *m*, chance; accident, mishap; illness, indisposition; *med* fit; *gram* accidence; *mus* accidental. **a. del trabajo,** accident at work. **por a.,** by chance, accidentally

acción *f*, action; battle; skirmish; *mech* drive; *com* share; gesture; lawsuit; *lit* action (of play, etc.); *art* posture, pose. **a. de gracias,** thanksgiving; *com* **a. liberada,** paid-up share. **a. privilegiada,** preference share

accionar *vi* to gesture, gesticulate

accionista *mf com* shareholder

acechar *vt* to spy upon, watch; lie in ambush for

acecho *m*, spying upon, watch; waylaying, ambush. **al a.,** in ambush; on the watch

acechona *f*, waylaying; ambush

acecinar *vt* to salt and dry (meat); *vr* (persons) wither, dry up

acedar *vt* to make bitter, sour; embitter, displease; *vr* turn sour; wither (plants)

acefalía *f*, acephalia, headlessness

acéfalo *a* acephalous

aceitar *vt* to oil, lubricate; rub with oil

aceite *m*, olive oil; oil. **a. de hígado de bacalao,** cod-liver oil. **a. de linaza,** linseed oil. **a. de ricino,** castor-oil. **a. de trementina,** oil of turpentine

aceitera *f*, woman who sells oil; oil can; oil bottle; *pl* cruet

aceitero *m*, oil seller. *a* oil

aceitoso *a* oily

aceituna *f*, *bot* olive

aceitunado *a* olive-colored

aceitunero (-ra) *n* olive picker; olive seller. *m*, warehouse for storing olives

aceituno *m*, olive tree

aceleración *f*, speed, haste; acceleration

aceleradamente *adv* hastily, swiftly

acelerador *a* accelerating. *m*, hastener; *aut* accelerator

acelerar *vt* to hasten, speed up; accelerate

acémila *f*, beast of burden, mule

acendrado *a* pure, unblemished, spotless

acendrar *vt* to refine (metals); purify, make spotless

acento *m*, accent; tone, inflection; *poet* voice, words. **a. agudo,** acute accent. **a. circunflejo,** circumflex accent. **a. grave,** grave accent. **a. ortográfico,** graphic accent, written accent. **a. tónico,** tonic accent

acentuación *f*, accentuation, stress; emphasis

acentuar *vt* to accent; stress, emphasize; *vr* become evident, become marked, be noticeable

aceña *f*, water-mill; irrigation water-wheel; chain-well

acepción *f*, meaning, significance, acceptation. **a. de personas,** partiality, preference

acepilladura *f*, sweeping, brushing; planing; wood-shaving

acepillar *vt* to sweep, brush; plane; *inf* brush up, polish up

aceptabilidad *f*, acceptability

aceptable *a* acceptable

aceptación *f*, acceptance; popularity; approval

aceptador (-ra) *a* accepting. *n* acceptor

aceptar *vt* to accept; approve; accept a challenge; *com* honor

acequia *f*, ditch, trench; irrigation channel

acequiero *m*, keeper of irrigation ditches

acera *f*, sidewalk, pavement. **a. del sol,** sunny side of the street

acerado *a* steel; steel-like; strong, tough; mordant, incisive

acerar *vt* to steel; treat (liquids) with steel; harden, make obdurate

acerbidad *f*, bitterness, acerbity, sourness; harshness, cruelty

acerbo *a* sour, tart, bitter; cruel, harsh

acerca de *adv* about, concerning

acercamiento *m*, approach

acercar *vt* to bring nearer; *vr* be near at hand, draw near; *(with prep a)* approach

acerico *m*, small cushion; pincushion

acero *m*, steel; blade, sword; *pl* bravery, spirit; *inf* good appetite. **a. inoxidable,** stainless steel

acérrimo *a sup* extremely strong, mighty; most harsh; most resolute, unflinching; very strong (taste, smell)

acerrojar *vt* to lock, padlock; bolt

acertado *a* well-aimed; fitting, suitable; wise; successful

acertar *vt irr* to hit the mark; find, come across; succeed (in), achieve; guess, find out; **No acertaba a explicármelo,** I couldn't quite understand it. **a. por chambra,** to make a lucky guess. *vi* be successful; thrive (of plants); *(with prep a + infin)* happen, occur, come to pass. *Pres. Ind.* **acierto, aciertas, acierta, aciertan.** *Pres. Subjunc.* **acierte, aciertes, acierte, acierten**

acertijo *m*, riddle

acervo *m*, pile, heap; *fig* storehouse, wealth (e.g. of words)

acetato *m*, acetate

acético *a* acetic

acetileno *m*, acetylene

achacar *vt* to attribute, impute, assign. **achacable a,** imputable to

achacoso *a* ailing, ill, sickly

achantarse *vr inf* to hide from danger; put up with, bear

achaparrado *a* stocky

achaque *m*, ailment, illness (permanent); *inf* period, menstruation; pregnancy; matter, affair; pretext; failing, bad habit. **En a. de . . . ,** Re . . . , concerning . . .

achatamiento *m*, flattening

achatar *vt* to flatten, make flat

achicado *a* childish

achicar *vt* to make smaller, diminish; drain, bail out; depreciate, belittle

achicarse *inf* to sing small

achicharrar *vt cul* to overcook; overheat; annoy, importune

achicoria *f*, chicory

achique *m*, bailing, draining

achispado *a inf* tipsy

achubascarse *vr* to become overcast, grow stormy

achuchar *vt inf* to squeeze, hug; jostle, push against

achuchón *m*, *inf* shove, push; hug, squeeze

achulado *a inf* brazen, tough

aciago *a* unhappy, ill-omened; fateful

acíbar *m*, aloe tree; bitter aloes; sorrow, bitterness

acibarar *vt* to add bitter aloes to; embitter, sadden

acicalado *a* polished; neat; well-groomed. *m*, polishing, burnishing (of weapons)

acicalador (-ra) *a* polishing. *n* polisher. *m*, burnisher (machine)

acicalar *vt* to burnish (weapons); adorn, deck; *vr* dress oneself with care

acicate *m*, Moorish spur; incitement, stimulus

acicatear *vt* to induce, spur on. **a. la curiosidad,** arouse curiosity

acidez *f*, acidity, bitterness

acidia *f*, indolence; sluggishness

ácido *a* acid; sour; harsh. *m*, acid. **a. fénico,** carbolic acid. **a. graso,** fatty acid

acidular *vt chem* to acidulate

acídulo *a chem* acidulous

acierto *m*, good hit, bull's-eye; success; achievement; cleverness; dexterity, skill; wisdom, sense; tact

acimut *m*, *ast* azimuth

aclamación *f*, acclamation; shout of acclamation. **por a.,** unanimously

aclamador (-ra) *a* acclaiming. *n* applauder, acclaimer

aclamar *vt* to acclaim; applaud

aclaración *f*, explanation; elucidation

aclarado *m*, rinse; rinsing

aclarador, aclaratorio *a* explanatory

aclarar *vt* to clarify, purify; clear; rinse (clothes); explain; thin; *vi* clear; (sky) clear up; dawn

aclimatación *f*, acclimatization

aclimatar *vt* to acclimatize

acné *m*, acne

acobardar *vt* to intimidate, frighten

acocear *vt* to kick; *inf* insult, humiliate

acocharse *vr* to squat, crouch

acodalar *vt* to prop

acodiciar *vt* to yearn for, covet, desire

acogedizo *a* gathered haphazardly

acogedor (-ra) *a* welcoming, friendly; inviting (e.g. a chair or room); *n* protector

acoger *vt* to receive, welcome, admit; protect, harbour; *vr* take refuge; (*with prep a*) make use of, resort to; **acogerse a sagrado,** seek sanctuary

acogida *f*, reception, welcome; protection, shelter; meeting place; confluence (of waters). **tener buena a.,** to be well received

acogollar *vt* to protect, cover (plants); *vi* sprout, shoot

acogotar *vt* to fell by a blow on the neck; *inf* knock out

acolada *f*, accolade

acolitar *vi* to serve as an altar boy, serve as an altar girl

acólito *m*, acolyte

acometedor (-ra) *a* capable, enterprising; aggressive. *n* aggressor, attacker

acometer *vt* to attack furiously; undertake; take in hand; overcome (of sleep, etc.)

acometida *f*, **acometimiento** *m*, assault, onrush; undertaking

acometividad *f*, aggressiveness

acomodable *a* easily arranged

acomodación *f*, adjustment; adaptation; accommodation

acomodadizo *a* accommodating, easy-going

acomodado *a* suitable; convenient; wealthy, well-off; comfort-loving; moderate, low (of price)

acomodador (-ra) *n* theater attendant, usher

acomodamiento *m*, agreement, transaction; accommodation

acomodar *vt* to arrange, adjust, accommodate; adapt; appoint; place; reconcile; employ, take on; equip, provide; lodge; *vi* suit, be convenient; *vr* compromise, agree

acomodaticio *a* accommodating

acomodo *m*, post, employment; arrangement; settlement

acompañamiento *m*, accompaniment; following, retinue; *mus* accompaniment; *theat* crowd, chorus

acompañanta *f*, chaperon; maid, servant

acompañante *m*, *mus* accompanist

acompañar *vt* to accompany; follow, escort; enclose (a letter, etc.); *mus* accompany

acompasado *a* rhythmic; deliberate, slow

acondicionado *a* conditioned; (*with bien or mal*) in good or bad condition; of good or bad quality; good- or ill-natured. **reflejo acondicionado** *med* conditioned reflex

acondicionar *vt* to prepare; mend, repair; *vr* condition oneself

acongojar *vt* to sadden, grieve; oppress

aconsejable *a* advisable

aconsejar *vt* to advise; *vr* (*with con*) consult, ask advice of

aconsonantar *vt* and *vi* to rhyme

acontecedero *a* possible

acontecer *vi* *irr* *impers* to happen. See **conocer**

acontecimiento *m*, event, occurrence

acopiar *vt* to collect, amass, gather

acopio *m*, collection, store; accumulation, gathering

acopladura *f*, **acoplamiento** *m*, (*carp mech*) joint; coupling; yoking; mating (of animals)

acoplar *vt* to join, couple; yoke; mate (animals); reconcile (opinions); *vr* *inf* fall in love

acoquinar *vt* *inf* to intimidate, terrify

acorazado *a* (*nav mil*) armoured, iron-clad. *m*, iron-clad, battleship

acorazar *vt* (*nav mil*) to armour

acorcharse *vr* to dry up, shrivel; go numb (limbs)

acordadamente *adv* by common consent, unanimously; deliberately, after due thought

acordar *vt* *irr* to decide unanimously; resolve; remind;

tune; harmonize (colors); *vi* agree; *vr* remember; come to an agreement. **Si mal no me acuerdo,** If memory serves me right. *Pres. Ind.* **acuerdo, acuerdas, acuerda, acuerdan.** *Pres. Subjunc.* **acuerde, acuerdes, acuerde, acuerden**

acorde *a* agreed; in harmony; in agreement. *m*, *mus* chord; harmony

acordeón *m*, accordion; (slang) crib sheet

acordonar *vt* to lace; cordon off, surround; mill (coins)

acornear *vt* to butt, toss (bulls)

acorralamiento *m*, corralling, penning

acorralado *a* at bay, intimidated

acorralar *vt* to corral, pen; confine; corner, silence (in argument); frighten; harass

acorrer *vt* to aid, assist; *vi* run, hasten; *vr* take refuge

acortamiento *m*, shortening

acortar *vt* to shorten; *vr* be speechless, be shy. **a. las velas,** to take in sail

acosador (-ra) *a* persecuting. *n* persecutor

acosamiento *m*, persecution

acosar *vt* to persecute relentlessly; annoy, harass

acostado *a* in bed; stretched out; *her* couchant

acostar *vt* *irr* to lay down, stretch out; put to bed; *vi* lean, tilt; *vr* lie down; go to bed; *naut* come alongside. See **contar**

acostumbrado *a* accustomed, usual

acostumbrar *vt* to habituate, accustom; *vi* be in the habit of (e.g. **Acostumbramos ir a la playa en el verano,** We generally go to the seashore in summer); *vr* (*with prep a*) become used to

acotación *f*, noting; marginal note; stage direction; ordnance survey number

acotar *vt* to annotate; mark out boundaries; fix, establish; accept; *inf* choose; testify; fill in elevation figures (on a map); *vr* seek refuge

acotillo *m*, sledgehammer

acre *a* bitter, sour; harsh; biting, mordant. *m*, acre (land measure)

acrecencia *f*, **acrecentamiento** *m*, increase; addition

acrecentar *vt* *irr* to increase; augment; promote, prefer. See **acertar**

acrecer *vt* *irr* to increase; augment. See **conocer**

acreción *f*, accretion

acreditado *a* accredited, well-reputed; respected

acreditar *vt* to prove; verify, accredit; recommend; sanction, authorize; vouch for, guarantee; *com* credit

acreedor (-ra) *n* creditor; claimant. *a* deserving. **a. hipotecario,** mortgagee

acreencia *f*, debt; *com* claim

acribillar *vt* to riddle with holes; wound repeatedly; pelt; torment; *inf* pester, harass

acriminación *f*, accusation

acriminador (-ra) *a* incriminating. *n* accuser

acriminar *vt* to accuse, charge

acrimonia *f*, acrimony

acrisolar *vt* to refine, purify (metals); perfect; clarify, elucidate

acrobacia *f*, acrobatics

acróbata *mf* acrobat

acrobático *a* acrobatic

acromatópsico *a* color-blind

acrópolis *f*, acropolis

acróstico *a* and *m*, acrostic

acta *f*, minutes, record; certificate of election (as deputy to Cortes, etc.); *pl* deeds (of a martyr). **a. matrimonial,** marriage register

actitud *f*, attitude

activar *vt* to stimulate, make active; accelerate, hasten

actividad *f*, activity; movement, bustle. **en a.,** in action; at work

activo *a* active. *m*, *com* assets

acto *m*, act, deed, action; act, law; act (of a play); public ceremony; *pl* minutes (of a meeting), proceedings (of a conference). **a. continuo** *or* **a. seguido,** immediately afterwards. **a. vandálico,** act of vandalism. **los Actos de los Apóstoles,** Acts of the Apostles. **en a.,** in the

act (of doing). **en el a.**, in the act; immediately
actor *m*, actor; *law* plaintiff
actriz *f*, actress
actuación *f*, operation, functioning; action; *pl* legal functions, judicial acts
actual *a* present; contemporary
actualidad *f*, present, present time; topic of interest. **actualidades**, current events. **en la a.**, at the present time
actuar *vt* to operate, set in motion; *vi* act; exercise legal functions
actuario (de seguros) *m*, actuary
acuarela *f*, water-color painting
acuarelista *mf* water-colorist
acuario *m*, aquarium; Aquarius
acuartelamiento *m*, billeting (of troops); billet, quarters
acuartelar *vt* to billet
acuático, acuátil *a* aquatic
acuatinta *f*, aquatint
acuchillado *a* taught by experience, schooled
acuchillar *vt* to hack, cut about; stab, put to the sword; slash (sleeves, etc.); *vr* fight with swords, daggers
acucia *f*, fervor, zeal; yearning, longing
acuciar *vt* to incite; goad; stimulate; encourage
acuciosidad *f*, eagerness, fervor, zeal
acucioso *a* eager, fervent, keen, zealous
acuclillarse *vr* to squat, crouch
acudir *vi* to go, repair (to); come; go or come to the aid of; attend, be present; **No me acude ningún ejemplo a la memoria,** No example comes to mind; resort (to), seek protection; reply, respond
acueducto *m*, aqueduct
acuerdo *m*, motion, resolution; decision; harmony, agreement; opinion, belief; remembrance; report; meeting (of members of a tribunal); *art* harmony (of colors). **de a.**, in agreement, in conformity; unanimously. **estar de a. (con),** to agree (with). **estar de acuerdo en** (+ inf.), to agree to (+ inf.) **ponerse de a.**, to come to an understanding
acuitar *vt* to distress, trouble; grieve
acullá *adv* afar, yonder, in the distance
acumulación *f*, accumulation, collection
acumulador (-ra) *a* accumulative. *m*, accumulator, storage battery. *n* collector, accumulator
acumulamiento *m*, accumulation (act)
acumular *vt* to accumulate, amass, collect; accuse, charge with
acuñación *f*, minting, coining; wedging
acuñador (-ra) *n* coiner, stamper; wedge. *m*, coining machine
acuñar *vt* to mint, stamp, coin; wedge
acuosidad *f*, wateriness
acuoso *a* aqueous, watery
acurrucarse *vr* to huddle; curl up; crouch
acusación *f*, accusation; *law* charge; *law* prosecution
acusado (-da) *a* accused; prominent; well-defined; *n* accused; *law* defendant
acusador (-ra) *a* accusing. *n* accuser; *law* prosecutor
acusar *vt* to accuse; blame; denounce; *com* acknowledge receipt; *law* prosecute; *law* charge. **acusarle a uno las cuarenta,** *inf* to give someone a piece of one's mind
acusatorio *a* accusatory
acusón (-ona) *n* *inf* telltale, sneak, informer
acústica *f*, acoustics
acústico *a* acoustic
adagio *m*, adage; *mus* adagio
adalid *m*, chieftain; head, leader
adamado *a* effeminate; refined; genteel
adamantino *a* adamantine
adaptabilidad *f*, adaptability
adaptación *f*, adaptation
adaptar *vt* to adapt, make suitable; *vr* adapt oneself
adarme *m*, tittle, jot. **por adarmes,** in bits and pieces, in drabs and driblets
adecentar *vt* to make decent; tidy up; *vr* tidy oneself

adecuación *f*, adequacy; suitability
adecuado *a* adequate; suitable
adecuar *vt* to proportion, fit; *fig* tailor
adefesio *m*, *inf* folly, absurdity (gen. *pl*); extravagant attire; guy, sight
adelantado *a* precocious; forward, pert; fast (clocks); early (of fruit); excellent; capable, proficient. *m*, *ant* provincial governor *or* chief justice *or* captain-general (Spanish history). **por a.**, in advance
adelantamiento *m*, promotion, furtherance; progress, advancement; betterment, improvement; *ant* office of **adelantado;** anticipation
adelantar *vt* to advance, move on; hasten; forestall; overtake; put on (the hands of clocks); improve, better; beat, excel; place in front; *vi* progress, advance; be fast (clocks); grow, develop; *vr* come forward
adelante *adv* on, forward; further on; straight ahead. **¡A.!** Onward!; Come in! **de hoy en a.**, henceforth, from today
adelanto *m*, anticipation; progress; *com* payment in advance. **el a. de la hora,** moving the clock forward
adelfa *f*, *bot* rose-bay, oleander
adelgazamiento *m*, loss of weight; slenderness; thinness
adelgazar *vt* to make slender or thin; *fig* split hairs; whittle, taper; *vi* grow slender or thin
ademán *m*, posture, attitude; gesture; *pl* behaviour, manners
además *adv* besides, in addition; moreover. **a. de,** as well as
adentellar *vt* to bite, sink the teeth into
adentro *adv* inside, within
adentros *m pl*, private thoughts (e.g. **Pensé para mis adentros,** I thought to myself). *Interj* **¡Adentro!** Come in!; Go in!
adepto *a* affiliated; adept, proficient
aderezamiento *m*, dressing; seasoning; embellishment
aderezar *vt* to deck, embellish; cook; *cul* season; *cul* dress; prepare; repair, mend; guide, direct; dress (cloth)
aderezo *m*, dressing, adornment; beautifying; finery, ornament; preparation; seasoning; set of jewels; horse's trappings; gum starch (for dressing cloth); equipment
adeudar *vt* to owe; be dutiable (goods); *com* debit; *vi* become related (by marriage); *vr* run into debt
adeudo *m*, debt; customs duty; *com* debit
adherencia *f*, adherence; adhesion
adherente *a* adhesive; connected, attached. *mf* adherent, follower; *m pl*. **adherentes,** accessories, requisites
adherirse *vr* *irr* to adhere, stick; follow; believe (in). See **herir**
adhesión *f*, adhesion; adherence
adhesivo *a* adhesive
adición *f*, addition
adicional *a* additional, extra
adicionar *vt* to add up; add to
adicto (-ta) *a* addicted, fond; joint. *n* addict; follower, disciple
adiestrador (-ra) *n* trainer, coach; guide, teacher
adiestrar *vt* to train, coach; guide, teach; lead; *vr* practise, perfect oneself
adietar *vt* *med* to put on a diet
adinerado *a* wealthy, well-off, rich
adiós *interj* Good-bye!; Hello, God be with you! (used as greeting). *m*, farewell
adiposo *a* adipose
aditamento *m*, addition
adive *m*, jackal
adivinación *f*, divination; guess
adivinador (-ra) *a* prophesying, divining. *n* soothsayer
adivinanza *f*, divination; riddle; puzzle. **adivinanzas,** guessing games. **no estar para jugar a las a.,** to be in no mood for guessing games
adivinar *vt* to prophesy, foretell; divine, guess; solve, guess (riddles, etc.)

adivino (-na) *n* soothsayer, prophet
adjetivo *a* adjectival. *m*, adjective
adjudicación *f*, adjudication, award
adjudicador (-ra) *n* adjudicator
adjudicar *vt* to adjudge; award; *vr* appropriate
adjudicatario (-ia) *n* recipient (of a prize, etc.); grantee
adjuntar *vt* to enclose (with a letter, etc.)
adjunto *a* attached; enclosed, accompanying; assistant, deputy; adjectival. *m*, addition, supplement
administración *f*, administration; direction, control; administratorship
administrador (-ra) *a* administrative. *n* administrator. **a. de correos**, postmaster
administrar *vt* to control, manage; provide, supply; administer. **administrarse el tiempo**, to budget one's time
administrativo *a* administrative, executive
admirable *a* admirable
admirablemente *adv* admirably, excellently
admiración *f*, amazement; admiration; wonder; exclamation mark
admirador (-ra) *a* admiring. *n* admirer
admirar *vt* to admire; surprise, amaze (e.g. **Me admira su acción**, His action surprises me); to see (e.g. **Desde la colina se pueden admirar varios edificios de la ciudad**, From the hill several buildings in the city can be seen); *vr* (*with de*) be surprised at or by
admirativo *a* admiring; admirable, excellent
admisibilidad *f*, allowability, permissibility
admisible *a* admissible; permissible
admisión *f*, admission; acceptance; allowance
admitir *vt* to admit; receive, accept; tolerate, brook; allow, permit
admonición *f*, admonition, warning; reprimand
adobar *vt* to prepare; *cul* garnish; pickle (meat); cook; dress (hides)
adobo *m*, repairing; dressing (for cloth, leather); *cul* savory sauce; pickling sauce; make-up, cosmetic
adocenado *a* ordinary; narrow-minded
adoctrinar *vt* to instruct
adolecer *vi irr* to fall ill; (*with de*) suffer from (diseases, defects); *vr* be sorry for, regret. See **conocer**
adolescencia *f*, adolescence
adolescente *a* and *mf* adolescent
adonde *adv* (*interr* **a dónde**) where to, whither (e.g. **¿A dónde fuiste?** Where did you go to?)
adondequiera *adv* wherever
adopción *f*, adoption
adoptador (-ra) *a* adopting. *n* adopter
adoptar *vt* to adopt (children); make one's own, embrace (opinions); take (decisions)
adoptivo *a* adoptive
adoquín *m*, cobble-stone; *fig* blockhead
adoquinado *m*, cobbling, paving. *m*, cobbled pavement
adoquinar *vt* to pave with cobble-stones
adorable *a* adorable
adoración *f*, worship, adoration. **A. de los Reyes**, Adoration of the Magi; Epiphany
adorador (-ra) *a* adoring. *n* adorer
adorar *vt* to adore; worship; (*with en*) dote on; *vi* pray
adormecedor *a* soporific, drowsy
adormecer *vt irr* to make drowsy; soothe, lull; hush to sleep; *vr* go to sleep; (limbs) fall asleep; (*with en*) persist in. See **conocer**
adormecimiento *m*, sleepiness; lulling asleep; numbness
adormitarse *vr* to doze, take a nap, snooze
adornamiento *m*, adornment, decoration
adornar *vt* to deck, beautify; decorate; trim, embellish; adorn (of virtues, etc.)
adorno *m*, decoration, adornment; ornament; trimming. **de a.**, ornamental; flowering (shrubs)
adquiridor (-ra) *a* acquiring. *n* acquirer
adquirir *vt irr* to acquire, get; achieve, obtain. *Pres. Ind.* **adquiero, adquieres, adquiere, adquieren.** *Pres. Subjunc.* **adquiera, adquieras, adquiera, adquieran**

adquisición *f*, acquirement; acquisition. **poder de a.**, purchasing power
adquisidor (-ra) *a* acquiring. *n* acquirer, obtainer
adquisitivo *a* acquisitive
adquisividad *f*, acquisitiveness
adrazo *m*, salt-water still
adrede *adv* on purpose, intentionally
adrenalina *f*, adrenaline
adriático *a* Adriatic
adscribir *vt* to ascribe, attribute; appoint (to a post, etc.)
adscripción *f*, ascription, attribution; appointment
aduana *f*, customs house, customs. **pasar por la a.**, to go through customs
aduanero *a* customs. *m*, customs officer
aducir *vt irr* to adduce, allege, cite; add. See **conducir**
adueñarse (-de) *vr* to appropriate, take possession (of)
adulación *f*, adulation, flattery
adulador (-ra) *a* fawning. *n* flatterer
adular *vt* to flatter, fawn upon, adulate
adulteración *f*, adulteration; falsification
adulterador (-ra) *a* adulterant. *n* adulterator; falsifier; coiner
adulterar *vi* to commit adultery; *vt* adulterate; falsify
adulterino *a* adulterous; false
adulterio *m*, adultery
adúltero (-ra) *a* adulterous; corrupt. *n* adulterer
adulto (-ta) *a* and *n* adult
adunar *vt* to join, unite; unify, combine
adusto *a* extremely hot (of climate); grave, austere; standoffish, reserved
advenedizo *a* foreign, alien; strange, unknown; upstart; newly rich
advenimiento *m*, advent, arrival; ascension (to the throne)
advenir *vi irr* to come, arrive; happen, befall. See **venir**
adventicio *a* casual, accidental; *bot* adventitious
adverbio *m*, adverb
adversario (-ia) *n* adversary, rival; opponent
adversidad *f*, adversity, misfortune, sorrow
adverso *a* unfavorable, contrary, adverse; opposite
advertencia *f*, warning; introduction, preface; remark
advertido *a* capable, clever; experienced; expert
advertir *vt irr* to observe, notice; warn; advise; feel, be conscious of; point out, indicate; inform; discover. See **sentir**
Adviento *m*, *ecc* Advent
adyacente *a* adjacent, near-by, neighboring
aedo *m*, *poet* poet
aeración *f*, aeration
aéreo *a* aerial; airborne; airy; air; aeronautic; unsubstantial, fantastic. **correo a.**, airmail. **línea aérea** airline
aerobismo *m*, aerobics
aerodinámica *f*, aerodynamics
aeronauta *mf* aeronaut, balloonist
aeronáutica *f*, aeronautics
aeronáutico *a* aeronautic
aeropuerto *m*, airport
aeróstato *m*, dirigible
afabilidad *f*, affability, geniality, friendliness
afable *a* affable, genial, pleasant
afamado *a* famous, well-known
afamar *vt* to make famous
afán *m*, effort; manual labor; desire, anxiety **a. de mando**, thirst for power
afanar *vt* to press, urge on; filch; *vr* toil, labor; (*with por*) work hard to, try to
afanoso *a* hard, laborious; hard-working, painstaking; eager, anxious
afasia *f*, *med* aphasia
afear *vt* to make ugly; distort, deform; blame; criticize
afección *f*, fondness, affection; complaint, ailment, trouble
afectación *f*, affectation
afectado *a* affected

afectar *vt* to feign, assume; affect; move, touch; *law* encumber

afectivo *a* affective

afecto *a* fond, affectionate; *law* encumbered; (*with prep a*) addicted to. *m*, emotion, sentiment; affection

afectuosidad *f*, affectionateness

afectuoso *a* affectionate, fond

afeitada *f*, shave, shaving

afeitar *vt* to shave; make up (one's face); adorn, beautify

afeite *m*, cosmetic; make-up (for the complexion)

afelpado *a* velvet-like, plushy

afeminación *f*, effeminacy; weakness, languor

afeminado *a* effeminate

afeminar *vt* to make effeminate; weaken; *vr* grow effeminate

aferradamente *adv* tenaciously, persistently, obstinately

aferramiento *m*, seizing, clutching; *naut* furling; *naut* grappling; mooring, anchoring; obstinacy

aferrar *vt* to seize, clutch; *naut* take in, furl; *naut* grapple; *vi naut* anchor; *vr* (*with con, en, a*) persist in, insist on

afestonado *a* festooned

Afganistán Afghanistan

afgano (-na) *a* and *n* Afghan

afianzamiento *m*, fastening, fixing; propping; grasping; guarantee, security

afianzar *vt* to fasten, fix; prop; consolidate (e.g. one's power); guarantee, be security for; grasp

afición *f*, propensity, inclination; fondness. **tomar a. (a),** to take a liking to

aficionado (-da) *a* amateur. *n* amateur, fan, enthusiast. **ser a a.,** to be fond of, have a liking for

aficionar *vt* to inspire liking or affection; *vr* (*with prep a*) take a liking to, grow fond of; become an enthusiast of

afijo *m*, *gram* affix

afiladera *f*, whetstone, grindstone

afilado *a* sharp, keen (of edges)

afilador *m*, grinder (of scissors, etc.); razor strop

afilalápices *m*, pencil sharpener

afilar *vt* to sharpen; grind, whet; taper; *vr* grow thin; taper

afiliación *f*, affiliation

afiliar *vt* (*with prep a*) to affiliate with; *vr* (*with prep a*) become affiliated with; join, become a member of

afiligranado *a* filigree; delicate, fine; slender

afilón *m*, steel, knife sharpener; razor-strop

afín *a* nearby, contiguous; similar, related. *mf* relative by marriage

afinador *m*, tuning key; tuner (of pianos, etc.)

afinar *vt* to finish, perfect; *fig* polish, refine; tune (musical instruments); refine (metals); *vi* sing in tune; *vr* grow refined

afinidad *f*, affinity, analogy; relationship (by marriage); *chem* affinity

afirmación *f*, affirmation, statement

afirmadamente *adv* firmly

afirmar *vt* to make firm; fix, fasten; affirm; *vr* steady oneself; hold on to

afirmativa *f*, affirmative

afirmativo *a* affirmative

aflicción *f*, affliction, grief

aflictivo *a* sorrowful, grievous

afligidamente *adv* sorrowfully

afligir *vt* to sadden; afflict, trouble; *vr* lament, mourn

aflojamiento *m*, slackening; loosening; diminution

aflojar *vt* to slacken; loosen; *vi* relax, weaken; abate, diminish. **a. el paso,** to slow down

afluencia *f*, crowd, concourse; eloquence, fluency

afluente *a* fluent, eloquent. *m*, tributary (river)

afluir *vi irr* to crowd, swarm; flow (into). See **huir**

afonía *f*, *med* aphonia, loss of voice; hoarseness

afónico *a* hoarse

aforismo *m*, aphorism

aforrador (-ra) *n* one who lines jackets, etc.

aforrar *vt* to line (clothes, etc.); *vr* wrap oneself up; *inf* gormandize

afortunadamente *adv* luckily, fortunately

afortunado *a* lucky, fortunate; happy; stormy

afortunar *vt* to bring luck to, make happy

afrancesado (-da) *a* Francophile; Frenchified. *n* Francophile

afrancesamiento *m*, adoption of the French way of life; servile imitation of everything French

afrancesar *vt* to make French, gallicize; Frenchify; *vr* become a Francophile

afrenta *f*, insult, affront; disgrace

afrentar *vt* to insult; *vr* be ashamed

afrentoso *a* insulting, outrageous; disgraceful

África Africa

africanismo *m*, Africanism

africano -na *a* and *n* African

afrodisíaco *a* and *m*, aphrodisiac

afrontar *vt* to place opposite; confront; face (danger, etc.)

afuera *adv* outside, out.

afueras *f pl*, suburbs, outskirts

agachada *f*, crouch, duck; jerk

agachar *vt inf* bend, bow; *vr inf* crouch down; lie low, hide

agalla *f*, oak-apple; tonsil (gen. *pl*); *zool* gill; *inf* gall, cheek

ágape *m*, agape; banquet, feast

Agar Hagar

agárico *m*, *bot* agaric

agarrada *f*, *inf* brawl, scuffle

agarradero *m*, handle; heft; *inf* influence, pull

agarrado *a inf* tight-fisted, mean

agarrar *vt* to grip, grasp; seize, take; *inf* nab (jobs); *vr* grip, hold on

agarro *m*, hold; grip, grasp

agarrotar *vt* to garrotte; tighten (ropes, etc.); press, squeeze; *vr* (limbs) go numb

agasajar *vt* to indulge, spoil, pet; receive kindly; entertain; caress

agasajo *m*, indulgence, kindness; affability, geniality; entertainment; gift, offering

ágata *f*, *min* agate

agauchado *a* gaucho-like

agazapar *vt inf* to nab, catch; *vr inf* squat, crouch

agencia *f*, influence, agency

agenciar *vt* to negotiate, arrange; procure, manage

agenda *f*, notebook; agenda

agente *m*, agent. **a. de bolsa** *or* **a. de cambio,** bill broker. **a. de negocios,** business agent. **a. de policía,** police officer. **a. fiscal,** revenue officer

agerasia *f*, sickness-free old age

agestado *a* used generally with advs. **bien** *or* **mal,** well or ill-featured

agigantado *a* enormous, gigantic; outstanding, extraordinary

ágil *a* agile, nimble; easy to use (e.g. **un libro ágil,** a book easy to use)

agilidad *f*, agility, nimbleness

agilizar *vt* to make agile, limber; refresh one's knowledge of (e.g. **Quiero agilizar mi español,** I want to refresh my knowledge of Spanish); to enable; *vr* limber up

agitación *f*, shaking; agitation, excitement

agitador (-ra) *a* stirring; agitating. *n* agitator. *m*, stirrer, stirring rod

agitar *vt* to stir; shake; agitate, excite **a. una cuestión,** raise a question; discuss a question

aglomeración *f*, agglomeration

aglomerado *m*, briquette

aglomerar *vt* to agglomerate, amass

aglutinación *f*, agglutination

aglutinar(se) *vt* and *vr* to stick, agglutinate

agnosticismo *m*, agnosticism

agnóstico (-ca) *a* and *n* agnostic

agobiar *vt* to bow, bend down; *fig* weigh down, oppress; *vr* bend (beneath a weight)

agobio *m*, bowing, bending down; oppression, burden, weight

agolparse *vr* to rush, crowd, swarm

agonía *f*, agony, anguish

agónico *a* dying; agonizing

agonizante *a* dying

agonizar *vt* to attend a dying person; *inf* pester, annoy; *vi* be dying (gen. **estar agonizando**)

agorar *vt* to prophesy, foretell

agorero (-ra) *a* prophetic; ill-boding. *n* seer, augur

agostarse *vt* and *vr* to dry up, shrivel

agosto *m*, August; harvest. *inf* **hacer su a.**, to make hay while the sun shines

agotable *a* exhaustible

agotado *a* exhausted; out of print (of books)

agotador *a* exhausting; exhaustive

agotamiento *m*, exhaustion

agotar *vt* to drain off (water); empty (a glass); exhaust; run through (money); study thoroughly, examine closely (a subject)

agraciado *a* graceful; pretty

agraciar *vt* to lend grace to; make pretty; favor

agradable *a* agreeable, pleasant

agradar *vi* to be pleasing, like, please (e.g. **Me agrada su sinceridad,** I like his sincerity)

agradecer *vt irr* to be grateful for; thank for; *fig* repay, requite. See **conocer**

agradecido *a* grateful; thankful

agradecimiento *m*, gratitude; thankfulness

agrado *m*, pleasure; desire, liking; amiability, affability

agrandar *vt* to enlarge

agrario *a* agrarian

agravación *f*, **agravamiento** *m*, aggravation, worsening

agravador *a* aggravating; worsening; increasing

agravar *vt* to aggravate, increase; oppress (taxes, responsibilities); make worse; exaggerate; *vr* grow worse

agraviador -ra *a* offensive. *n* offender

agraviar *vt* to offend; wrong; *vr* take offence, be insulted

agravio *m*, offence, insult; wrong, injury

agraz *m*, unripened grape; verjuice; *fig* bitterness

agredir *vt* to attack

agregación *f*, association, aggregation; total, collection, aggregate

agregado *m*, aggregate; assistant; attaché

agregar *vt* to add; collect, amass; appoint (to a post). **agregarse a . . . ,** to join . . . (e.g. an association)

agresión *f*, aggression

agresivo *a* aggressive

agresor (-ra) *a* and *n* aggressor

agreste *a* rural, rustic; wild; uncouth, rude

agriar *vt* to make bitter or sour; exasperate, provoke

agrícola *a* agricultural; *mf* agriculturalist, farmer

agricultura *f*, agriculture

agridulce *a* bitter-sweet

agrietarse *vr* to crack, split

agrimensor *m*, surveyor

agrimensura *f*, surveying

agrio *a* bitter, sour; rough, uneven (ground); brittle; sharp (of color contrast); unsociable; disagreeable

agrisetado *a* flowered (of materials)

agronomía *f*, agronomy

agrónomo *a* agronomic. *m*, agronomist

agrupación *f*, congregation, assembly; group; crowd; crowding, grouping

agrupar *vt* to assemble, group; *vr* crowd, cluster

agrura *f*, bitterness; sourness; asperity

agua *f*, water; rain; slope of a roof; *pl* shot or watered effect on silks, etc.; medicinal waters; waves; water (of precious stones). **a. abajo,** down-stream. **a. arriba,** upstream. **a. bendita,** holy water. **a. cruda,** hard water. **a. de colonia,** eau de Cologne. **a. dulce,** fresh water. **a. fresca,** cold water. **a. nieve,** sleet. **a. oxigenada,** hydrogen peroxide. *fig inf* **estar con el a. al cuello,** to be in low water. *fig inf* **estar entre dos aguas,** to be between two fires. *naut* **hacer a.,** to leak.

Todo eso es ya a. pasada, That's all water under the bridge

aguacero *m*, heavy rainfall, shower

aguada *f*, water supply on board ship; flood (in mines); watering station; *art* water color

aguadero *m*, (animals') watering place

aguado *a* watery; abstemious; watered

aguador (-ra) *n* water carrier, water seller; drawer (of water)

aguafiestas *mf fig inf* wet blanket

aguafuerte *f*, etching

aguaje *m*, tide, waves; sea current; water supply (on board ship); wake (of a ship)

aguamanil *m*, washstand; pitcher, ewer

aguamanos *m*, water for washing hands; pitcher

aguamarina *f*, aquamarine

aguamiel *f*, honey and water, hydromel

aguantable *a* tolerable, bearable

aguantar *vt* to bear, tolerate, endure; restrain, resist, oppose; *vr* bear in silence, keep quiet

aguante *m*, patience, endurance; resistance

aguar *vt* to water down (wine, etc.); spoil (fun, etc.); *vr* be filled with water; be flooded; become watery or thin

aguardar *vt* to await; expect; allow time to (debtors)

aguardentería *f*, liquor shop

aguardentoso *a* spirituous, containing **aguardiente;** hoarse, husky (of the voice)

aguardiente *m*, liquor. **a. de caña,** rum

aguardo *m*, ambush (for a hunter)

aguarrás *m*, oil of turpentine

aguatinta *f*, aquatint

aguatocha *f*, pump (for water, etc.)

aguaturma *f*, Jerusalem artichoke

agudeza *f*, sharpness; keenness; distinctness; alertness; cleverness; witty sally, repartee; wit; swiftness

agudo *a* sharp; alert, clever; (*geom med*) acute; fine, keen; rapid; high-pitched; strong (of scents, etc.)

agüero *m*, omen, sign; prophecy, prediction

aguerrido *a* veteran, war-hardened

aguerrir *vt defective* to harden to war; toughen

aguijada *f*, goad, spur

aguijar *vt* to prick (with a goad); urge on, encourage (animals); incite, instigate; spur on; *vi* walk swiftly

aguijón *m*, goad; sting; thorn, prickle; spur; incitement, stimulus. **tener aguijones,** to be on pins and needles

aguijonazo *m*, prick (with a goad)

águila *f*, eagle; master mind. **a. caudal** or **a. real,** royal eagle. **á. o sol,** heads or tails (Mexico)

aguileña *f*, *bot* columbine

aguileño *a* aquiline

aguilón *m*, arch gable; boom (of a crane)

aguinaldo *m*, Christmas present; New Year's gift

aguja *f*, needle; hand, pointer; hatpin; engraver's burin; switch; *rw* point; *rw* rail; obelisk; spire; bodkin; knitting needle; crochet hook; (compass) needle. *pl bot* plumelet. **a. capotera, a. de zurcir,** darning needle. **a. de marear** *naut*, binnacle; mariner's compass. **a. de media,** knitting needle. **a. espartera,** packing needle

agujerear *vt* to perforate, make holes in

agujero *m*, hole, aperture; needle maker or seller; needle case

agujeta *f*, lace (for shoes, etc.); *pl* muscular pains, aches; tip, gratuity

agusanarse *vr* to become worm-infested

aguzadura *f*, sharpening, grinding, whetting

aguzar *vt* to sharpen; grind, whet; stimulate, encourage; urge on, incite

ahechadura *f*, chaff (of grain)

ahembrado *a* effeminate

aherrojar *vt* to put (a prisoner) in irons; oppress

aherrumbrar *vt* to give the color or taste of iron to; *vr* taste or look like iron; go rusty

ahí *adv* there; over there. **de a.,** thus, so. **por a.,** somewhere about, near at hand.

ahidalgado *a* gentlemanly; noble, generous

ahijado (-da) *n* godchild; protégé

ahijar *vt* to adopt (children); mother (animals); attribute, impute; *vi* bring forth offspring; *bot* sprout. See **prohibir**

ahincado *a* earnest, eager

ahincar *vt* to urge, press; *vr* hurry, hasten. See **prohibir**

ahínco *m*, earnestness, eagerness

ahitar *vt* to stuff with food; bore, disgust. See **prohibir**

ahíto *a* full of food; *fig* fed up. *m*, indigestion

ahogado (-da) *a* drowned; suffocated; stuffy, unventilated; stifling. *n* drowned person; victim of suffocation

ahogamiento *m*, drowning; suffocation

ahogar *vt* to drown; suffocate; put out (the fire); stifle (yawns, etc.); suppress, extinguish; tire; overwater (plants); *vr naut* sink, founder; drown; suffocate

ahogo *m*, anxiety, grief; difficulty in breathing, oppression; asthma; embarrassment; suffocation; straitened circumstances

ahondamiento *m*, in-depth treatment (e.g. **el a. de un problema,** in-depth treatment of a problem)

ahondar *vt* to deepen; excavate, dig; go into thoroughly; go deep into, penetrate; *vr* (earth) subside

ahora *adv* now; very soon; just now, a short time ago. *conjunc* whether; now. **a. bien,** well now, given that. **a. mismo,** immediately, at once. **por a.,** for the present

ahorcado (-da) *n* hanged man

ahorcar *vt* to execute by hanging, hang. *inf* **a. los hábitos,** to leave the priesthood, cease to be an ecclesiastic

ahormar *vt* to adjust, shape; break in (new shoes); make (a person) see reason

ahorquillar *vt* to prop up (trees) with forks; *vr* grow forked

ahorrar *vt* to free (slaves); save, economize; avoid, eschew; *vr* avoid; remove clothing

ahorro *m*, economy, thrift; *pl* savings

ahuchar *vt* to hoard; expel, drive away. See **desahuciar**

ahuciar *vt* take possession of (a house)

ahuecar *vt* to hollow out; loosen; shake out; puff out, inflate; put on a solemn voice; hoe, dig; *inf vr* puff oneself out; put on airs

ahumada *f*, smoke signal

ahumado *a* smoked; smoky

ahumar *vt* to smoke (herrings, etc.); fill with smoke; *vi* smoke, burn; *vr* be full of smoke; taste smoked; *inf* get drunk. See **desahuciar**

ahusado *a* spindle-shaped

ahuyentar *vt* to frighten off; drive away; dismiss, banish (anxiety, etc.); *vr* flee

airadamente *adv* wrathfully, angrily

airado *a* angry

airar *vt* to annoy, anger; *vr* grow annoyed

aire *m*, air; atmosphere (sometimes *pl*); breeze, wind; bearing, appearance; vanity; (horse's) gait; futility, frivolity; grace, charm; gracefulness; *mus* air; *mus* tempo. **a. popular,** popular tune. **al a. libre,** in the open air, outdoors. *inf* **beber los aires (por),** to yearn (for)

aireación *f*, airing; ventilation

airear *vt* to air; ventilate; aerate; *vr* take the air; catch a chill

airosidad *f*, gracefulness; jauntiness

airoso *a* airy, open; windy, breezy, fresh; graceful; handsome; jaunty; victorious, successful

aislacionamismo *m*, *pol* isolationism

aislacionista *mf pol* isolationist

aislado *a* isolated; remote; individual; single; *elec* insulated

aislador *m*, *phys* insulator

aislamiento *m*, isolation; *phys* insulation

aislante *a* isolating; insulating

aislar *vt* to isolate; *elec* insulate; *vr* become a recluse; become isolated

¡ajá! *interj inf* Aha! Good!

ajaquecarse *vr* to have a headache

ajar *vt* to crease, crumple, spoil; humiliate; *vr* fade, wither (flowers)

ajear *vi* (partridge) to squawk (when cornered)

ajedrecista *mf* chess player

ajedrez *m*, chess

ajenjo *m*, *bot* wormwood; absinthe

ajeno *a* alien; belonging to another; various, diverse; free, exempt; unsuitable; irrelevant

ajetrear *vt* to tire out, exhaust; *vr* be overtired

ajetreo *m*, exhaustion, fatigue

ajo *m*, garlic; *inf* make up, paint; disreputable affair, shady business; curse, oath. *inf* **revolver el a.,** to stir up trouble

ajorca *f*, bracelet; slave bangle

ajornalar *vt* to hire by the day

ajuar *m*, trousseau; household equipment

ajustado (-ra) *a* exact; tight-fitting; trim

ajustador (-ra) *a* adjusting. *n* adjuster. *m*, tight-fitting jacket

ajustamiento *m*, adjustment; agreement

ajustar *vt* to adjust; fit; arrange; make an agreement about; reconcile; settle (accounts); engage, employ; retain (a barrister); regulate; tune up (a motor); *vi* fit; *vr* adapt oneself. *inf* **a. cuentas viejas,** to settle old accounts

ajuste *m*, fitting; adjustment; agreement; arrangement; *print* make-up. reconciliation; settlement; regulation; engagement, appointment

ajusticiado (-da) *n* executed person

ajusticiar *vt* to put to death

al (contraction of *a* + *el*). I. *prep a* + *m. def. art.*, to the, e.g. **Han ido al mar,** They have gone to the sea. 2. *prep a* + *el* used as *dem. pron* to that, to the one, e.g. **Mi sombrero se parece mucho al que tiene Vd.,** My hat is very similar to the one you have. *al* + *infin.* means when, as, at the same time as, e.g. **Al llamar a la puerta la vi en el jardín,** As I was knocking at the door, I saw her in the garden

ala *f*, *zool* wing; row, line; brim (of a hat); eaves; (*arch aer mil bot*) wing; blade (of propeller); fin (of fish); *fig* courage. **a. del corazón,** *anat* auricle. **arrastrar el a.,** to woo, flirt with. *fig* **cortar** (*or* **quebrar**) **las alas (a),** to clip a person's wings

Alá *m*, Allah

alabador (-ra) *n* praiser, extoller

alabanza *f*, praise; eulogy

alabar *vt* to praise; *vr* brag, boast

alabarda *f*, halberd

alabardero *m*, halberdier; *theat* claque, clapper

alabastrino *a* alabastrine, alabaster

alabastro *m*, alabaster

alacena *f*, cupboard; recess; closet; safe (for food)

alacrán *m*, scorpion

alacridad *f*, alacrity, eagerness

alado *a* winged; feathered; *fig* soaring

alambicado *a* sparing, frugal; subtle; euphuistic

alambicar *vt* to distil; examine carefully, scrutinise; make over-subtle or euphuistic (of style)

alambique *m*, still

alambrada *f*, *mil* wire-entanglement

alambrado *m*, wire-netting; *mil* wire-entanglement; wire cover

alambrar *vt* to wire (fence)

alambre *m*, wire; sheep bells. **a. espinoso,** barbed wire

alambrera *f*, wire fence; wire-netting; wire cover

alambrista *mf* tight-rope walker; (Mexico) wetback

alameda *f*, poplar wood or grove; avenue of poplars

álamo *m*, poplar. **a. temblón,** aspen tree

alano *m*, mastiff

alarde *m*, *mil* parade; display, ostentation. **hacer a. de,** to brag about

alargamiento *m*, lengthening; stretching

alargar *vt* to lengthen; prolong; pass, hand (things); pay out (ropes, etc.); increase; *vr* go away, depart; be wordy, spread oneself; lengthen

alarido *m*, yell, shout; shriek, scream; howl; yelp; cry (of a seagull)

alarma *f*, alarm. **a. aérea,** air-raid warning

alarmante *a* alarming

alarmar *vt* to give the alarm; frighten; *vr* be alarmed

alarmista *mf* alarmist

alazán *a* sorrel-colored. *m*, sorrel horse

alazo *m*, flap or stroke of the wings

alba *f*, dawn; *ecc* alb, vestment. **al a.,** at dawn

albacea *mf* executor, executrix; testator

albanés (-esa) *a* and *n* Albanian. *m*, Albanian language

albañil *m*, mason, bricklayer

albañilería *f*, masonry; bricklaying

albarda *f*, pack-saddle

albardilla *f*, small saddle; pad; small pillow; *arch* coping

albaricoque *m*, apricot

albaricoquero *m*, apricot tree

albarrada *f*, stone wall; mud fence

albatros *m*, albatross

albear *vi* to become white, whiten

albedrío *m*, free will; fancy, caprice

albéitar *m*, veterinary surgeon; farrier

alberca *f*, reservoir, tank; vat; artificial lake

albergar *vt* to shelter; nourish, harbor; *vi* and *vr* take refuge or shelter; lodge

albergue *m*, shelter, refuge; den, lair; hospitality; lodging; asylum

albo *a* pure white

albóndiga *f*, forced meat ball, rissole

albor *m*, whiteness; dawnlight, dawn. **a. de la vida,** life's dawning, childhood

alborada *f*, dawn; reveille; *mil* dawn attack; *mus* aubade

alborear *vi* to grow light, dawn

albornoz *m*, burnouse

alborotado *a* impulsive; turbulent; noisy; excitable

alborotar *vt* to disturb; *vi* make a noise; be gay; *vr* riot; grow rough (sea)

alboroto *m*, noise; confusion; tumult; riot; rejoicing, gaiety; *pl* popcorn

alborozar *vt* to overjoy, gladden; *vr* rejoice, be glad

alborozo *m*, gladness, rejoicing, joy

albricias *f pl*, reward for bringer of good tidings. *interj* **¡A.!** Joy! Congratulations!

álbum *m*, album

albúmina *f*, albumin

albur *m*, *icht* dace; chance, risk. **al a. de,** at the risk of

alcachofa *f*, artichoke

alcahueta *f*, procuress, go-between

alcahuete *m*, procurer, go-between, pimp, pander; *fig inf* protector, screen; *inf* scandalmonger

alcahuetear *vt* to procure, act as a go-between for; *vi* be a pimp or a procuress

alcaide *m*, governor of a fortress *ant*; governor of a prison

alcalde *m*, mayor; magistrate. *inf* **tener el padre a.,** to have a friend at court

alcaldesa *f*, mayoress

alcaldía *f*, office or authority of an alcalde

álcali *m*, *chem* alkali

alcalino *a* alkaline

alcaloide *m*, *chem* alkaloid

alcance *m*, reaching, attainment; range (of firearms, etc.); scope; arm's length or reach; pursuit; stop press *or* extra edition (newspapers); *com* deficit; importance; *pl* talent; capacity. **al a. de la voz,** within call. **hombre de cortos alcances,** a limited, dull man. **poner al a. de,** to make available to; make intelligible to

alcancía *f*, money-box; coin bank, piggy bank

alcanfor *m*, camphor

alcanforado *a* camphorated

alcantarilla *f*, little bridge; sewer; culvert; bed for electric cable

alcantarillado *m*, sewage system; main sewer

alcanzable *a* obtainable; attainable

alcanzadizo *a* attainable, easily reached

alcanzar *vt* to overtake; reach; range (of guns, etc.); attain, achieve; understand; *fig* equal (in attainments); live at the same time as, be contemporaneous with; be

capable of, be able; *vi* reach; share, participate in; be enough

alcaparra *f*, *bot* caper; caper bush

alcaucil *m*, (in most places) wild artichoke; (in some places) cultivated artichoke

alcazaba *f*, fortress (within a walled town or city), casbah

alcázar *m*, fortress; royal residence, castle; *naut* quarter-deck

alción *m*, *orn* kingfisher

alcista *mf* speculator (on Stock Exchange)

alcoba *f*, bedroom; alcove, recess; Moorish flute

alcohol *m*, alcohol; galena; eye black (cosmetic); spirits of wine. **a. desnaturalizado,** industrial alcohol, methylated spirit. **a. metílico,** wood alcohol

alcohólico *a* alcoholic

alcoholismo *m*, alcoholism

alcor *m*, hill; slope

Alcorán *m*, Koran

alcornoque *m*, cork tree; dunderhead, dolt

alcorza *f*, *cul* icing, sugar-paste

alcorzar *vt cul* to ice, cover with sugar; decorate, adorn

alcurnia *f*, lineage, family, descent

alcuza *f*, oil-bottle; oil-can; cruet

aldaba *f*, door knocker; bolt, latch; *pl* protectors, influential helpers. *inf* **tener buenas aldabas,** to have plenty of pull

aldabada *f*, rap with the knocker; sudden shock

aldabeo *m*, knocking

aldea *f*, village

aldeano (-na) *a* village; country, ignorant. *n* villager; countryman, peasant

aldehído *m*, *chem* aldehyde

aleación *f*, alloy

alear *vi* to flutter, beat the wings; flap one's arms; recuperate, grow well; *vt* alloy

aleatorio *a* accidental, fortuitous

aleccionamiento *m*, teaching, training, coaching

aleccionar *vt* to teach, train, coach

aledaño *a* adjoining; border. *m*, boundary, border

alegación *f*, allegation, statement

alegar *vt* to allege, state; cite; *vi law* bring forward, adduce

alegato *m*, *law* speech (for the prosecution or defence)

alegoría *f*, allegory

alegórico *a* allegorical

alegorizar *vt* to interpret allegorically, treat as an allegory

alegrar *vt* to make happy, gladden, rejoice; adorn, beautify; stir (fires); *vr* be glad, rejoice; *inf* be merry (tipsy)

alegre *a* joyful, glad; cheerful, gay; bright (colors, etc.); pretty, attractive; *inf* risqué; *inf* flirtatious, light

alegría *f*, joy, gladness; cheerfulness, gaiety; *pl* public rejoicings

alegrón *m*, sudden unexpected joy; *inf* flash of light. *a inf* flirtatious

alejamiento *m*, placing at a distance, removal; withdrawal

Alejandría Alexandria

alejar *vt* to place at a distance, remove; withdraw; ward off (dangers, etc.); *vr* depart, go away; withdraw. **alejarse de,** to abandon (a belief, custom, superstition, etc.)

alelar *vt* to make silly or stupid

aleluya *mf*, alleluia. *m*, Eastertide. *f*, small Easter cake; *inf* daub, poor painting; *inf* doggerel; joy, rejoicing

alemán (-ana) *a* and *n* German. *m*, German language.

Alemania Germany

alentada *f*, deep breath

alentado *a* valiant, spirited; proud

alentador *a* encouraging, inspiring, stimulating

alentar *vi irr* to breathe; *vt* encourage, inspire; *vr* be encouraged. See **sentar**

alerce *m*, larch tree and wood

alergia *f*, allergy

alergólogo *m*, allergist

alero *m*, projecting roof; splashboard (of carriages); eaves; gable end

alerón *m*, *aer* aileron

alerta *adv* watchfully. *interj* Take care! Look out! **estar ojo a.,** to be on the watch

alerto *a* watchful, alert

aleta *f*, *dim* small wing; fin

aletargado *a* lethargic; comatose

aletargamiento *m*, lethargy

aletargar *vt* to cause lethargy; *vr* become lethargic

aletazo *m*, flapping, beating (of wings); *inf* theft

aletear *vi* to flap the wings, flutter; move the arms up and down; become convalescent

aleteo *m*, fluttering, flapping of wings; beating, palpitation (of heart)

aleve *a* See **alevoso**

alevosía *f*, *law* malice; treachery

alevoso *a law* malicious; treacherous

alfabético *a* alphabetical

alfabetización *f*, literacy work

alfabetizador *m*, literacy worker

alfabeto *m*, alphabet. **a. manual,** sign language

alfalfa *f*, *bot* lucerne

alfar *m*, potter's workshop; pottery, earthenware

alfarería *f*, pottery shop; potter's workshop; potter's craft

alfarero *m*, potter

alfeñique *m*, *cul* icing, sugarpaste; *inf* affectation

alférez *m*, *mil* ensign; second lieutenant; lieutenant. *nav* **a. de fragata,** sub-lieutenant. *nav* **a. de navío,** lieutenant

alfil *m*, bishop (in chess)

alfiler *m*, pin; brooch with a pin; tiepin; *pl* pin-money, dress-allowance; *fig inf* **no estar uno con sus alfileres,** to have a slate loose. *inf* **vestido de veinticinco alfileres,** dressed to the nines

alfiletero *m*, needle-case

alfombra *f*, carpet; rug

alfombrado *m*, carpeting

alfombrar *vt* to carpet

alfombrilla eléctrica *f*, electric pad or blanket

alfombrista *m*, carpet merchant; layer of carpets

alforja *f*, saddle-bag; *mil* knapsack

alforza *f*, *sew* tuck; *inf* scar

alforzar *vt sew* to tuck

alga *f*, alga, seaweed

algalia *f*, civet

algarabía *f*, Arabic; *inf* gibberish; din of voices, uproar

algarada *f*, troop of horse; uproar, hubbub; outcry

algarroba *f*, *bot* carob bean

algazara *f*, Moorish war cry; rejoicing, merriment; noise, clamor

álgebra *f*, algebra; art of bone setting

algebraico *a* algebraic

algebrista *mf* bonesetter; algebraist

álgido *a* icy cold

algo *indef pron* some, something (e.g. **Se ve que hay a. que le molesta,** You can see that something is irritating him). *adv* somewhat, a bit. **en a.,** in some way

algodón *m*, cotton plant; cotton flower; cotton fabric; candy floss (UK), cotton candy (USA). **a. en rama,** cotton-wool. **a. hidró-filo,** absorbent cotton wool. **a. pólvora,** nitrocellulose

algodonal *m*, cotton plantation

algodonero (-ra) *a* cotton. *n* cotton merchant

alguacil *m*, policeman, constable; *ant* city governor; short-legged spider

alguien *indef pron* someone, somebody, e.g. **Dime si viene a.,** Tell me if anyone comes

algún *abb* of **alguno** bef. *m sing* noun, e.g. **a. libro**

alguno *a* (*abb* **algún** bef. *m, sing*) some, any. *indef pron* someone, somebody; *pl* some, some people. **alguno que otro,** a few

alhaja *f*, jewel; ornament; treasure, precious object; *inf* gem, excellent person (also ironic, e.g. **Es una a.,** He's a fine fellow)

alhajar *vt* to adorn with jewels, bejewel; furnish, equip

alharaca *f*, vehemence, demonstration, fuss (gen. *pl*)

alheña *f*, *bot* privet; henna

alhóndiga *f*, corn exchange; public granary

aliado (-da) *a* allied. *n* ally

alianza *f*, alliance; pact, agreement; relationship (by marriage); sum total, whole (of factors, etc.); wedding-ring

aliarse *vr* to join together, become allies; be associated

alicaído *a* drooping; *inf* weak, exhausted; discouraged, downhearted; come down in the world

alicates *m pl*, pincers, pliers

aliciente *m*, attraction, inducement

alícuota *f*, *a* aliquot; proportional. **partes alícuotas,** aliquot parts

alienación *f*, alienation

alienado *a* insane, mad

alienar *vt* See **enajenar**

alienista *mf med* alienist

aliento *m*, breathing; breath; courage, spirit; encouragement. **el posterior a.,** one's last breath. **cobrar a.,** to regain one's breath; take heart. **de un a.,** in one breath; without stopping

alifafe *m*, *inf* ailment; tumor on horse's hock

aligación *f*, binding together, alligation

aligeramiento *m*, lightening, reduction in weight

aligerar *vt* to lighten, make less heavy; quicken, hasten; ease, alleviate; moderate; shorten, abbreviate

alígero *a poet* winged; fleet, swift

alimaña *f*, destructive animal

alimentación *f*, nourishment; feeding

alimentar *vt* to feed; nourish; encourage, foment; assist, aid; keep, support

alimenticio *a* nourishing; feeding

alimento *m*, food, nourishment; stimulus, encouragement; *pl* alimony; allowance

alindar *vt* to mark the boundary of; beautify, adorn; *vi* border, be contiguous

alineación *f*, alignment

alinear *vt* to align, range in line; dress (troops); *vr* fall into line

aliñar *vt* to decorate, adorn; *cul* season; prepare; set (bones)

aliño *m*, decoration, ornament; preparation; condiment, seasoning; setting (bones)

aliquebrado *a* broken-winged; *inf* down in the mouth

alisador (-ra) *a* smoothing; polishing. *n* polisher

alisar *vt* to smooth; polish; sleek; plane; comb lightly

alisios *m pl*, trade winds

aliso *m*, alder tree and wood

alistador *m*, enroller

alistamiento *m*, enlistment; conscription; enrolment

alistar *vt* to enrol, list; enlist; conscript; prepare, get ready; *vr* enrol; *mil* enlist; get ready

aliviar *vt* to lighten; alleviate, mitigate; relieve; ease; quicken (one's step); hasten, speed up; steal

alivio *m*, lightening; relief; alleviation; ease

aljaba *f*, quiver (for arrows)

aljibe *m*, tank, cistern; watership or tanker

aljófar *m*, small irregular shaped pearl; dew-drop, rain-drop, tear drop

aljofifa *f*, floorcloth

allá *adv* there; to that place. **más a.,** farther on, beyond. Used in conjunction with phrases of time, indicates remoteness, e.g. **a. en tiempos de los Reyes Católicos,** long ago in the time of the Catholic Monarchs. **a. por 1900,** way back in 1900

allanamiento *m*, leveling, flattening; condescension, affability; (police) raid, (police) search acceptance of a judicial finding

allanar *vt* to level, flatten; overcome (difficulties); soothe; break into (a house, etc.); give entrance to the police; *vr* collapse (buildings, etc.); abide by, adapt oneself (to); condescend, be affable. **a. el camino (a . . .),** to pave the way (for . . .)

allegado (-da) *a* near, allied; related. *n* follower, ally

allegar *vt* to gather, collect; draw nearer; *agr* reap; add; *vi* arrive

allende *adv* beyond; besides. **de a. el mar,** from beyond the sea

allí *adv* there; to that place, thereto; thereupon, then. **por a.,** through there; that way

alma *f,* soul; living person; essence, core; vivacity, animation; energy, vitality; spirit, ghost; core (of a rope). **a. de cántaro,** fool, ninny. **a. de Dios,** simple soul, kind person. **a. en pena,** soul in purgatory. **¡A. mía!** My darling! **con todo el a.,** with all my heart. **Lo siento en el a.,** I feel it deeply

almacén *m,* warehouse; store, shop

almacenaje *m,* cost of storage

almacenar *vt* to store; put in store; hoard

almacenero *m,* warehouseman, storekeeper

almacenista *mf* owner of a store; assistant, salesman (saleswoman)

almáciga *f,* mastic; tree plantation or nursery

almagre *m, min* red ocher; stain, mark

almanaque *m,* calendar, almanac

almeja *f, icht* clam

almenara *f,* beacon fire

almendra *f,* almond; kernel; crystal drop (of chandeliers, etc.); cocoon; bean (of cocoa tree, etc.). **a. garapiñada,** sugar almond

almendro *m,* almond tree

almendruco *m,* green almond

almete *m,* casque, helmet; helmeted soldier

almiar *m,* haystack, hayrick

almíbar *m,* sugar syrup; nectar

almibarado *a* syrupy; *inf* sugary

almibarar *vt* to coat with sugar; preserve (fruit) in syrup; flatter with sweet words

almidón *m,* starch

almidonado *a* starched; *fig inf* stiff, unbending; prim, starchy

almidonar *vt* to starch

alminar *m,* minaret (of mosque)

almiranta *f,* admiral's wife; flagship

almirantazgo *m,* Admiralty; admiralship; Admiralty Court

almirante *m,* admiral

almizcle *m,* musk

almizcleño *a* musk (of scents)

almizclero *a* musky. *m, zool* musk-deer

almocafre *m, agr* hoe; trowel, dibble

almohada *f,* pillow; pillowcase; cushion. *inf* **aconsejarse** *or* **consultar con la a.,** to think over (a matter) carefully, sleep on it

almohadilla *f, dim* small cushion; lace or sewing cushion; pin cushion

almohadillado *a* cushioned; padded

almoneda *f,* auction; furniture sale

almonedear *vt* to auction; sell off (furniture)

almorranas *f pl,* hemorrhoids

almorzar *vi irr* to lunch; breakfast. See **forzar**

almuecín, almuédano *m,* muezzin

almuerzo *m,* luncheon; breakfast (not so usual)

alocado *a* feather-brained, reckless; crazy, wild

alocución *f,* allocution, address, harangue

áloe *m, bot* aloe

alojado (-da) *m,* billeted soldier. *n* lodger

alojamiento *m,* lodging; dwelling; *mil* billeting; *naut* steerage; camp, encampment

alojar *vt* to lodge; billet; quarter (troops); insert, introduce; *vi* and *vr* lodge; live, dwell

alondra *f, orn* lark

alopatía *f, med* allopathy

alpaca *f,* alpaca (animal and fabric); nickel silver

alpargata *f,* sandal with hemp sole

alpargatero (-ra) *n* manufacturer or seller of alpargatas

Alpes, los the Alps

alpestre *a* Alpine; rock (of plants); mountainous, lofty

alpinismo *m,* mountaineering

alpinista *mf* mountaineer, climber

alpino *a* Alpine

alpiste *m,* bird seed

alpro *f,* (Alianza para el Progreso)

alquería *f,* farmstead

alquiladizo *a* rentable, hirable

alquilador (-ra) *n* hirer

alquilamiento *m,* See **alquiler**

alquilar *vt* to rent; hire out; hire; *vr* hire oneself out, serve on a wage basis

alquiler *m,* hiring out; renting; rental; hire; wages. **de a.,** for hire, on hire

alquimia *f,* alchemy

alquímico *a* alchemic

alquimista *mf* alchemist

alquitrán *m,* tar, pitch. **a. mineral,** coal tar

alquitranado *a* tarred. *m, naut* tarpaulin

alrededor *adv* around, round about. **a. de,** around; approximately, about (e.g. **a. de cinco dólares,** about $5)

alrededores *m pl,* environs, surrounding country

Alsacia Alsace

alsaciano (-na) *a* and *n* Alsatian

alta *f,* certificate of discharge from hospital

altanería *f,* hawking; haughtiness, disdain; superciliousness

altanero *a* soaring, high-flying (of birds); supercilious; haughty, disdainful

altar *m,* altar. **a. mayor,** high altar

altavoz *m,* loudspeaker; megaphone

altearse *vr* to rise, grow steep (of land)

alterabilidad *f,* alterability, changeability

alteración *f,* alteration, change; debasement (of coinage); agitation

alterar *vt* to change, alter; debase (coinage); disturb, agitate; *vr* grow angry; become excited

altercación, *f.* **altercado** *m,* altercation, quarrel

altercar(se) and *vr* to quarrel, dispute, altercate

alternación *f,* alternation

alternado *a* alternated

alternador *a* alternating. *m, elec* alternator

alternante *a* alternating

alternar *vt* to alternate; make one's debut as a **matador;** *vi* alternate; (*with con*) have dealings with, know

alternativa *f,* alternative, option; service performed by turns; alternation

alternativo *a* alternative

alterno *a* alternative; *bot* alternate

alteza *f,* altitude, height; sublimity, perfection; **(A.)** Highness (title)

altibajo *m,* embossed velvet; *pl inf* rough ground; *inf* vicissitudes of fortune

altillo *m,* hillock, eminence; garret, attic

altímetro *m, aer* altimeter

altiplanicie *f,* plateau; highland

altisonante *a* sonorous; sublime; high-flown, pompous

altitud *f,* altitude, height

altivez *f,* arrogance, haughtiness

altivo *a* arrogant, haughty

alto *a* high; tall; difficult, arduous; sublime; deep; most serious (of crimes, etc.); dear (of price); small, early (hours). *m,* height; eminence, hill; story, floor; *mil* halt; red light (traffic light). *adv* up, above, on high; loudly. *interj* **¡A.!** *mil* Halt! *mil* **A. Mando,** High Command. **las altas horas de la noche,** the small (or early) hours. **en alta voz,** in a loud voice. **en alto,** on high; up above. **hacer alto,** to halt, stop

altoparlante *m, rad* loudspeaker

altozano *m,* mound, hillock; viewpoint, open space

altruismo *m,* altruism

altruista *a* altruistic. *mf* altruist

altura *f,* height; altitude; *geom* altitude or height; top, peak; sublimity; tallness

alucinación *f,* **alucinamiento,** *m,* hallucination

alucinado *m*, person suffering from hallucinations
alucinador *a* hallucinatory, deceptive
alucinar *vt* to dazzle, fascinate; deceive
alud *m*, avalanche
aludir *vi* to allude (to); refer (to), cite
alumbrado *m*, lighting; *pl* illuminati
alumbramiento *m*, lighting, supply of light; childbirth
alumbrar *vt* to light, illuminate; give sight to the blind; instruct, teach; inflict (blows); hoe vine roots; *vi* give birth to a child; *vr inf* grow tipsy
alumbre *m*, alum
aluminio *m*, aluminum
alumno (-na) *n* ward, adopted child; pupil. **a. externo**, day pupil. **a. interno**, boarder
alunizar *vi* to land on the moon
alunizaje *m*, landing on the moon, moon-landing
alusión *f*, allusion
alusivo *a* allusive, suggestive; hinting
aluvial *a* alluvial
aluvión *m*, alluvium. **de a.**, alluvial
alza *f*, rise (of temperature, etc.); increase (in price); front sight (of guns)
alzacuello *m*, high collar, clerical collar; neck stock
alzada *f*, horse's stature; mountain pasture; *law* appeal
alzado *a* fraudulent (of bankruptcy); fixed (of price). *m*, theft; *arch* front elevation
alzamiento *m*, raising, lifting; higher bid (at auction); rising, rebellion; fraudulent bankruptcy
alzaprima *f*, lever; wedge; bridge (of string instruments)
alzar *vt* to raise; lift up; elevate (the Host); steal, remove; hide; gather in the harvest; build, construct; *naut* heave; *vr* rise (of temperature, mercury, price, etc.); make a fraudulent bankruptcy; *law* appeal; (*with con*) run off with, steal. *naut* **a. la vela**, to set sail
ama *f*, mistress of the house; owner; housekeeper; wet nurse. **a. de casa**, housemaker, housewife. **a. de leche**, foster-mother. **a. de llaves** *or* **a. de gobierno**, housekeeper. **a. seca**, children's nurse
amabilidad *f*, lovableness; kindness; niceness, goodness, helpfulness
amable *a* lovable; kind; nice, good, helpful
amador (-ra) *a* loving. *n* lover, admirer
amadrigar *vt* to welcome, receive well; *vr* go into a burrow or lair; go into seclusion
amaestrar *vt* to train, instruct; tame; break in (horses)
amagar *vt and vi* to threaten; *vt* show signs of (diseases, etc.); *vr inf* hide
amago (**contra . . .**), threat (to . . .), menace (to . . .)
amainar *vt naut* to take in the sails; *vi* drop (of the wind); *vi and vt* relax (efforts, etc.)
amaine *m*, dropping, abatement (of the wind)
amalgama *f*, *chem* amalgam
amalgamación *f*, amalgamation
amalgamar *vt* to amalgamate; *vr* be amalgamated
amamantamiento *m*, suckling, nursling
amamantar *vt* to suckle
amancebado *m*, concubine
amancillar *vt* to discredit, dishonor; tarnish; stain
amanecer *vi irr* to dawn; arrive *or* be somewhere *or* be doing, at dawn (e.g. **Amanecimos en el barco**, Dawn came while we were on the ship. **Amanecimos escribiendo la carta**, The day broke as we were writing the letter); appear at daybreak; begin to appear. *m*, dawn, daybreak. See **conocer**
amanerado *a* mannered; affected
amaneramiento *m*, manneredness; mannerism
amanerarse *vr* to acquire mannerisms or tricks of style; become affected
amansador (-ra) *a* soothing, calming. *n* appeaser
amansamiento *m*, taming; appeasement; soothing; breaking in (horses)
amansar *vt* to tame; appease, moderate; soothe, pacify; break in (horses)
amante *a* loving. *mf* lover
amanuense *mf* amanuensis, secretary, clerk

amanzanar to lay out the streets of
amañar *vt* to execute with skill; *vr* grow skilful
amaño *m*, skill, dexterity; *pl* schemes, intrigues; tools, equipment
amapola *f*, poppy
amar *vt* to love
amaranto *m*, *bot* amaranth
amarar *vi* to alight on the water (of hydroplanes)
amargar *vi* to taste or be bitter; *vt* make bitter; embitter
amargo *a* bitter; embittered; grievous, sad. *m*, bitterness; *pl* bitters
amargor *m*, **amargura**, *f*, bitter taste, bitterness; trouble, affliction, pain
amaricado *a inf* effeminate
amarilis *f*, *bot* amaryllis; *poet* shepherdess
amarillear *vi* to look yellow; turn yellow; tend to yellow
amarillento *a* yellowish, turning yellow
amarilleo *m*, yellowing
amarillez *f*, yellowness
amarillo *a* and *m*, yellow
amarra *f*, *naut* cable, thick rope
amarradero *m*, *naut* mooring berth; mooring-post; hitchingpost or ring
amarraje *m*, *naut* mooring charge
amarrar *vt* to tie up, lash; moor
amarre *m*, mooring; hitching
amartelar *vt* to make jealous; court, woo, make love to; *vr* be jealous; fall madly in love
amartillar *vt* to hammer, knock; cock (firearms)
amasadera *f*, kneading-trough
amasador (-ra) *a* kneading. *n* kneader
amasar *vt* to knead; massage; scheme, plot
amasia *f*, concubine
amasiato *m*, concubinage
amasijo *m*, *cul* dough; kneading; portion of plaster or mortar; *inf* hotchpotch, mixture; scheme, plot
amatista *f*, amethyst
amatorio *a* amatory
amazacotado *a* heavy, dense; *fig* stodgy (of writings, etc.)
amazona *f*, Amazon; independent woman; woman rider; woman's riding habit
ambages *m pl*, maze, intricate paths; circumlocutions
ámbar *m*, amber. **a. gris**, ambergris
ambarino *a* amber
Amberes Antwerp
ambición *f*, ambition
ambicionar *vt* to long for; desire eagerly; be ambitious to
ambicioso *a* ambitious; eager, desirous
ambidextro *a* ambidextrous
ambiente *a* ambient, surrounding. *m*, air, atmosphere; environment
ambigú *m*, cold buffet; buffet (in theaters, etc.)
ambigüedad *f*, ambiguity
ambiguo *a* ambiguous
ámbito *m*, precincts; boundary, limit; compass, scope
amblar *vi* to pace (of a horse)
ambos, *a m pl*, **ambas** *a f pl*, both, e.g. **ambas casas**, both houses
ambulancia *f*, ambulance. **a. de correos**, railway post office. **a. fija**, field-hospital
ambulante *a* walking; traveling, wandering
amedrentador *a* frightening; terrible; intimidating
amedrentar *vt* to frighten, scare; intimidate
ameliorar *vt* to better, improve
amelonado *a* melon-shaped; *inf* madly in love
amén *m*, amen, so be it. **a. de**, besides, in addition to. *inf* **en un decir a.**, in a trice
amenaza *f*, threat
amenazador, **amenazante** *a* menacing, threatening
amenazar *vt* to threaten; *vt* and *vi* presage, be pending
amenguamiento *m*, lessening, diminution; discredit; loss of prestige

amenguar *vt* to lessen, decrease; dishonor, discredit
amenidad *f*, amenity; agreeableness
amenizar *vt* to make pleasant or attractive
ameno *a* pleasant; entertaining; agreeable, delightful
América America
América del Norte North America
América del Sur South America
americana *f*, (man's) jacket
americanismo *m*, usage typical of Western-Hemisphere Spanish
americano *a* American
ameritar *vt* WH to deserve, merit
ametrallador *m*, machine-gunner
ametralladora *f*, machine-gun
amianto *m*, *min* amianthus, asbestos
amiba *f*, *zool* ameba
amicísimo *a sup*. **amigo,** most friendly
amiga *f*, woman friend; mistress, lover; dame, schoolmistress; dame school
amigabilidad *f*, friendliness, amicability
amigable *a* friendly, amicable; harmonious; suitable
amígdala *f*, tonsil
amigdalitis *f*, tonsillitis
amigo (-ga) *a* friendly; fond, addicted. *n* friend. *m*, lover. *inf* **ser muy a. de,** to be very friendly with; be very keen on or fond of
amilanado *a* cowed, spiritless
amilanar *vt* to terrify, intimidate; *vr* grow discouraged
aminorar *vt* to diminish, lessen
amir *m*, emir, Arab prince or chief
amistad *f*, friendship; liaison; favor; *pl* acquaintances, friends
amistar *vt* to introduce, make known to each other; bring about a reconciliation between or with
amistoso *a* friendly
amnesia *f*, amnesia
amnistía *f*, amnesty
amnistiar *vt* to concede an amnesty, pardon
amo *m*, head of the house; master; owner; overlord; overseer. **a. de huéspedes,** keeper of a boarding house. **Nuestro A.** Our Lord. *inf* **ser el a. del cotarro,** to rule the roost
amodorramiento *m*, stupor, deep sleep
amodorrarse *vr* to fall into a stupor; fall into a heavy sleep
amoladera *f*, whetstone
amolador *m*, scissors grinder; knife grinder; sharpener
amoladura *f*, grinding, whetting, sharpening
amolar *vt irr* to grind, sharpen; *inf* pester, annoy. See **colar**
amoldar *vt* to mold; adjust; *vr* adapt oneself
amonedación *f*, coinage, minting
amonedar *vt* to coin, mint
amonestación *f*, warning; advice. **correr las amonestaciones,** to publish banns of marriage
amonestador (-ra) *a* warning, admonitory. *n* admonisher
amonestar *vt* to warn; advise; rebuke; *ecc* publish bans of marriage
amoníaco *m*, ammonia
amontillado *m*, kind of pale, dry sherry
amontonamiento *m*, accumulation; gathering, collection; piling up, heaping
amontonar *vt* to pile up, heap; gather; collect; accumulate; *vr inf* fly into a rage
amor *m*, love; beloved; willingness, pleasure; *pl* love affairs; caresses. **a. propio,** self-esteem; vanity. *inf* **con mil amores,** with great pleasure. **por a. de,** for love of; for the sake of
amoral *a* amoral
amoralidad *f*, amorality
amoratado *a* livid, bluish
amorcillo *m*, *dim*. little love; unimportant love affair; Cupid
amordazamiento *m*, muzzling; gagging
amordazar *vt* to muzzle; gag; prevent speaking

amorfo *a* amorphous
amorío *m*, *inf* wooing, love making; *pl* love affairs
amoroso *a* loving; gentle; mild, balmy
amorrar *vi inf* to hang one's head; sulk, be sullen
amortajar *vt* to wrap in a shroud; enshroud
amortiguador *m*, *mech* shock absorber. *aut* **a. de los muelles,** shock-absorber
amortiguamiento *m*, softening, deadening; mitigation, lessening
amortiguar *vt* to soften, deaden; absorb (shocks); moderate, mitigate; soften (colors)
amortización *f*, amortization
amortizar *vt* to amortize; recover, redeem; suppress, abolish (posts)
amoscarse *vr inf* to be piqued or annoyed; become agitated
amostazar *vt inf* to annoy; *vi* become peeved
amotinador (-ra) *a* mutinous, rebellious. *n* rebel, mutineer; rioter
amotinar *vt* to incite to rebellion; unbalance, unhinge (mind); *vr* rebel; riot; *fig* be unhinged
amovible *a* movable, removable; removable (of officials, etc.)
amovilidad *f*, movability, removability; liability to discharge or dismissal
amparador (-ra) *a* protective; sheltering. *n* protector, defender, helper; shelterer
amparar *vt* to protect, favor, help; shelter; *vr* take refuge, take shelter; defend oneself
amparo *m*, shelter, refuge; protection, favor, help; defense
amper *m*, *elec* ampere
amperímetro *m*, *elec* ammeter
amperio *m*, *elec* ampere
ampliable *a* amplifiable
ampliación *f*, enlargement, increase, extension; *phot* enlargement
ampliador (-ra) *a* enlarging. *n* enlarger
ampliadora *f*, *phot* enlarger
ampliar *vt* to extend, enlarge, increase; *phot* enlarge
amplificación *f*, extension, amplification; *phot* enlargement
amplificar *vt* to enlarge; extend; increase; amplify, expatiate upon
amplio *a* wide; extensive; roomy, ample; prolix
amplitud *f*, extension; width; spaciousness, amplitude
ampolla *f*, blister; ampoule; bubble; *elec* bulb
ampulosidad *f*, pomposity, redundancy (of style)
ampuloso *a* pompous, high-flown (style)
amputación *f*, amputation
amputar *vt* to amputate
amuchachado *a* boyish
amueblar *vt* to furnish; provide with furniture
amuleto *m*, amulet, charm
amurallar *vt* to surround with a wall, wall
amusgar *vt* and *vi* to flatten the ears (animals); *vt* screw up the eyes (to see better)
ana *f*, ell (measure)
anabaptismo *m*, Anabaptism
anabaptista *mf* Anabaptist
anacardo *m*, cashew (nut)
anacoreta *mf* anchorite, hermit
anacreóntico *a* Anacreontic
anacrónico *a* anachronous
anacronismo *m*, anachronism
añade *mf* duck
anadear *vi* to waddle (like a duck)
anadeo *m*, waddle
anadino (-na) *n* duckling
anadón *m*, drake
anáfora *f*, anaphora
anafrodisíaco *a* anaphrodisiac
anagrama *m*, anagram
analectas *f*, *pl* analects
anales *m*, *pl* annals
analfabetismo *m*, illiteracy

analfabeto (-ta) *a* and *n* illiterate
analgesia *f*, analgesia
analgésico *a* and *m*, *med* analgesic
análisis *m*, analysis; *gram* parsing
analista *mf* analyst
analizar *vt* to analyse
analogía *f*, analogy
analógico, análogo *a* analogous
ananás *m*, pineapple
anaquel *m*, shelf, ledge
anaranjado *a* and *m*, orange (color)
anarquía *f*, anarchy
anárquico *a* anarchical
anarquismo *m*, anarchism
anarquista *mf* anarchist
anatema *mf*, anathema
anatematizar *vt* to anathematize, denounce
anatomía *f*, anatomy
anatómico *a* anatomical
anatomista *mf* anatomist
anca *f*, croup, hindquarters of a horse
ancianidad *f*, old age; seniority; oldness
anciano (-na) *a* old; ancient. *n* old person
ancla *f*, anchor. **a. de la esperanza,** sheet anchor. **echar anclas,** to anchor
ancladero, anclaje *m*, anchorage
anclar *vi* to anchor
áncora *f*, anchor; refuge, haven
ancho *a* wide, broad. *m*, width, breadth. *inf* **a mis (tus, sus,** etc.) **anchas** *or* **anchos,** at my (your, his, etc.) ease, with complete freedom
anchoa *f*, anchovy
anchura *f*, width, breadth; ease, freedom; extent
anchuroso *a* very wide; extensive; spacious
andada *f*, wandering, roving; hard bread roll; pasture; *pl* trail, tracks. *fig inf* **volver a las andadas,** to return to one's old tricks
andaderas *f pl*, go-cart (for learning to walk)
andadoba *f*, lansquenet (card game)
andador *a* walking; swift walking; wandering. *m*, walker; garden path; *pl* leading-strings, reins
andadura *f*, walk, gait; pace, step
Andalucía Andalusia
andaluz (-za) *a* and *n* Andalusian
andaluzada *f*, *inf* exaggeration, tall story
andamio *m*, scaffolding; stand, platform
andanada *f*, *naut* broadside; cheapest priced seat in a bullring; *inf* dressing-down, scolding
andante *a* walking, strolling; errant (of knights). *a* and *m*, *mus* andante
andanza *f*, happening, occurrence; *pl* doings, deeds. **buena a.,** good fortune
andar *vi irr* to walk; move; work, operate, run (machines, etc.); progress, get along (negotiations, etc.); be, feel; elapse (of time); be occupied; behave; (*with prep a*) administer (blows, etc.); (*with en*) upset, turn over (papers, etc.); ride in or on (cars, bicycles, etc.); be engaged in; (*with con*) use, handle; *vt* traverse. *m*, gait, walk. **a. por los cuarenta,** to be in one's forties. **a. con paños tibios,** not to be firm. **a. con pies de plomo,** to be extremely cautious. **a. tras,** to follow, go after; persecute; desire ardently (things). *fig inf* **andarse a la flor del berro,** to sow one's wild oats. *fig inf* **andarse por las ramas,** to beat about the bush. **¡Anda!** Get along with you!; Hurry up!; You don't say so! **¡Andando!** Let's get going!, Let's get a move on it! *Preterite* **anduve,** etc. *Imperf subjunc* **anduviese,** etc.
andariego *a* swift walking; wandering, vagrant
andarín (-ina) *n* good walker; professional walker
andas *f pl*, kind of stretcher; bier
andén *m*, railway platform
andero *m*, bearer (of a bier)
andino *a* Andean
andorrano (-na) *a* and *n* Andorran
andrajo *m*, rag, wisp of cloth, tatter
andrajoso *a* ragged, tattered

andurriales *m pl*, byways, unfrequented paths; remote places
anécdota *f*, anecdote
anecdótico *a* anecdotal
anegación *f*, drowning; flooding, inundation
anegar *vt* to drown; inundate; shipwreck; *vr* drown; be flooded
anejo *a* attached, annexed. *m*, annexed borough
anemia *f*, anemia
anémico *a* anemic
anémona, anémone *f*, anemone. **anémona de mar,** sea-anemone
anestesia *f*, anesthesia
anestesiador (-ra) *n* anesthetist
anestesiar *vt* to anesthetize
anestésico *a* and *m*, anesthetic
aneurisma *mf med* aneurism
anexar *vt* to annex
anexión *f*, annexation
anexo *a* attached, joined. *m*, annex
anfibio *a* amphibious. *m*, amphibian
anfiteatro *m*, amphitheater; operating theater; dissecting room; morgue; *theat* dress-circle
anfitrión *m*, *inf* host, one who entertains guests
ánfora *f*, amphora
angarillas *f pl*, hand barrow; table cruet; yoke and panniers
ángel *m*, angel. **á. de la guarda,** guardian angel. **estar con los ángeles,** to be in Heaven (euphem. for 'to be dead')
angelical, angélico *a* angelic; divine, excellent
angina *f*, *med* angina, tonsillitis. **a. de pecho,** angina pectoris
anglicanismo *m*, Anglicanism
anglicano (-na) *a* and *n* Anglican
anglicismo *m*, anglicism
anglo (-la) *a* and *n* Angle. *a* Anglo-
angloamericano (-na) *a* and *n* Anglo-American
anglófilo (-la) *n* Anglophile
anglosajón (-ona) *a* and *n* Anglo-Saxon. *m*, Anglo-Saxon language
angostar *vi* and *vt* to narrow; tighten
angosto *a* narrow; tight
angostura *f*, narrowness; tightness; narrow pass; strait; *fig* tight corner, fix
anguila *f*, *icht* eel; *pl naut* slipway, slips
angula *f*, *icht* elver (young eel)
angular *a* angular
ángulo *m*, angle. **á. inferior izquierdo,** lower lefthand corner. **á. inferior derecho,** lower righthand corner. **á. superior izquierdo,** upper lefthand corner. **á. superior derecho,** upper righthand corner. **á. recto,** right angle
anguloso *a* angulate; angular, gaunt; cornered
angustia *f*, anguish, grief
angustiante *a* distressing
angustiar *vt* to grieve; afflict; *vr* be full of anguish
anhelación *f*, panting, hard breathing; yearning, longing
anhelar *vi* to pant, breathe with difficulty; *vi* and *vt* long for, yearn for, desire
anhélito *m*, pant, hard breathing
anhelo (de) *m*, longing (for), desire (for), yearning (for)
anheloso *a* difficult, labored (of breathing); anxious, longing
anidar *vi* to nest (birds); swell; *vt* shelter, protect; *vr* nest; dwell; nestle
anilla *f*, curtain ring; *pl* gymnastic rings
anillo *m*, finger ring; small ring; coil (of serpents and ropes). *inf* **venir como a. al dedo,** to fit like a glove; come just at the right moment
ánima *f*, soul, spirit; soul in purgatory; bore (of firearms); *pl* prayer bell for the souls of the departed
animación *f*, liveliness, gaiety; animation, vivacity; bustle, movement

animal *m*, animal; *inf* dolt, brute. *a* animal; *inf* brutish, doltish

animalada *f*, *inf* stupidity, foolishness

animalidad *f*, animalism

animar *vt* to animate; encourage, incite; invigorate, enliven; make gay, cheer up; make attractive, adorn; *vr* take heart; make up one's mind; cheer up; grow gay

animismo *m*, animism

ánimo *m*, soul, spirit; courage; endurance, fortitude; will, intention; mind. **con ánimo de + inf.**, with the intention of + *ger.* **¡Á.!** Courage!

animosidad *f*, hatred, animosity, dislike

animoso *a* spirited, lively; valiant

aniñado *a* childlike, childish

aniquilable *a* destructible

aniquilación *f*, destruction, annihilation; suppression; decay

aniquilador (-ra) *a* destructive, annihilating. *n* destroyer

aniquilamiento *m*, See **aniquilación**

aniquilar *vt* to annihilate, destroy completely; *vr* waste away, decay

anís *m*, aniseed, anise; anisette (liqueur)

anisar *vt* to flavor with aniseed

anisete *m*, anisette

aniversario *a* annual. *m*, anniversary

Anjeo Anjou

ano *m*, anus

anoche *adv* last night; the previous night

anochecer *vi irr* to grow night; become dark; be in a place *or* be doing something at nightfall (e.g. **Anochecimos en Lérida,** We were in Lerida at nightfall). *vr poet* be obscured or darkened. *m*, nightfall, dusk. See **conocer**

anochecida *f*, dusk, late twilight

anodino *a med* anodyne; ineffective, useless; inoffensive. *m*, anodyne

anomalía *f*, anomaly, inconstancy, irregularity; *ast* anomaly

anómalo *a* anomalous, abnormal, unusual

anonadación, *f.* anonadamiento *m*, destruction, annihilation; despair, melancholy; suppression

anonadar *vt* to destroy, annihilate; suppress; *fig* overwhelm, depress; humble

anónimo *a* anonymous. *m*, anonymity; anonymous letter; unsigned literary work

anormal *a* abnormal; irregular, unusual. *mf* abnormal person

anormalidad *f*, abnormality; irregularity, inconsistency

anotación *f*, annotation

anotador (-ra) *n* annotator

anotar *vt* to annotate; note down

anquilostoma *m*, *med* hookworm

ánsar *m*, goose; drake

ansarino *a* goose. *m*, gosling

anseático *a* Hanseatic

ansia (de) *f*, anxiety, trouble; grief; longing (for), yearning (for); greed

ansiar *vt* to long for, yearn for; covet, desire

ansiedad *f*, anxiety, anguish, worry

ansión *f*, intense desire

ansioso *a* anxious; grievous, painful; eager, desirous; greedy

anta *f*, *zool* elk; obelisk

antagónico *a* antagonistic

antagonismo *m*, antagonism

antagonista *mf* antagonist, adversary

antaño *adv* last year, yesteryear; long ago

antártico *a* antarctic

ante *m*, *zool* elk; suede; buffalo

ante *prep* in the presence of, before; regarding, in the face of (e.g. **a. deber tan alto,** in the face of so noble a duty)

anteado *a* beige, buff-colored, fawn

anteanoche *adv* the night before last

anteayer *adv* the day before yesterday

antebrazo *m*, forearm

antecámara *f*, antechamber

antecedente *m*, antecedent. **antecedentes** *m pl* background (of a case, situation, etc.)

antecedentemente *adv* previously

anteceder *vt* to precede

antecesor (-ra) *a* previous. *n* predecessor. *m*, forebear, ancestor

antecoger *vt* to carry in front, lead before; pick too soon

antecomedor *m*, breakfast nook, breakfast room

antedata *f*, antedate

antedatar *vt* to antedate

antedicho *a* aforementioned, aforesaid

antediluviano *a* antediluvian

antelación *f*, advance, anticipation

antemano, de *adv* in advance, beforehand

antemeridiano *a* antemeridian, forenoon

antena *f*, antenna; *rad* aerial

antenacido *a* born prematurely

antenombre *m*, title (placed before name)

anteojera *f*, horse's blinker; eyeglass case

anteojo *m*, spy-glass, small telescope; *pl* horse's blinkers; eyeglasses, glasses; spectacles; goggles

antepagar *vt* to pay in advance

antepalco *m*, vestibule of a box in a theater

antepasado *a* previous, past. *m*, ancestor (gen. *pl*)

antepecho *m*, parapet; windowsill; railing, balustrade; front (of a theater box, etc.); *naut* bulwark

antepenúltimo *a* antepenultimate, second from the last

anteponer *vt irr* to place before; prefer, favor. See **poner**

anteproyecto *m*, first sketch, preliminary work or plan

antepuerta *f*, door-curtain, portiere; *mil* anteport

anterior *a* previous, former; anterior; aforementioned, preceding

anteriormente *adv* beforehand, previously

antes *adv* before; rather, on the contrary; previously. **a. bien,** rather, sooner. **a. con a.** *or* **cuanto a.,** as soon as possible

antesala *f*, antechamber

antevíspera *f*, two days previously

antiaéreo *a* antiaircraft. *m pl.* **(cañones) antiaéreos,** A.A. guns

anticiclón *m*, anticyclone

anticipación *f*, anticipation; advance

anticipada *f*, foul thrust (in fencing, etc.)

anticipadamente *adv* in advance; prematurely

anticipado *a* in advance; premature

anticipador *a* anticipatory

anticipar *vt* to anticipate; foresee; forestall; advance (money); lend; *vr* happen before time; (*with prep a*) act in advance of, anticipate; get ahead of oneself

anticipo *m*, anticipation, advance; advance payment; sum of money lent

anticlerical *a* anticlerical

anticlímax *m*, anticlimax

anticonstitucional *a* unconstitutional

Anticristo *m*, Antichrist

anticuado *a* antiquated, ancient

anticuario *m*, antiquarian, antique dealer

antídoto *m*, antidote

antiesclavista *a* antislavery. *mf* antislavist

antiespasmódico *a* and *m*, *med* antispasmodic

antiestético *a* unesthetic

antietimológico *a* non-etymological, unetymological

antifaz *m*, mask; face-covering

antiflogístico *a* and *m*, *med* antiphlogistic

antigramatical *a* ungrammatical

antigualla *f*, antique; ancient custom; anything out-of-date

antiguamente *adv* in time past, formerly

antiguamiento *m*, seniority

antigüedad *f*, antiquity; ancients; length of service (in an employment); *pl* antiquities

antiguo *a* ancient, very old; antique; senior (in an employment); former. *m*, senior member (of a community, etc.). *m pl*, ancients. **A. Testamento,** Old Testament. **de a.,** from ancient times. **en lo antiguo,** in ancient times; in former times, in days of yore

antillano (-na) *a* and *n* of or from the Antilles

Antillas, las the Antilles

antílope *m*, antelope

antimacasar *m*, antimacassar

antimilitarismo *m*, antimilitarism

antimilitarista *a* antimilitaristic

antimonárquico *a* antimonarchical

antimonio *m*, *met* antimony

antipalúdico *a* antimalarial

antipapa *m*, antipope

antipara *f*, screen, shield

antiparras *f pl*, *inf* spectacles, eyeglasses, glasses

antipatía *f*, antipathy

antipático *a* disagreeable; unattractive

antipatriótico *a* unpatriotic

antípoda *a* and *m*, or *f*, antipode

antiquísimo *a sup*, **antiguo,** most ancient

antirrepublicano *a* antirepublican

antisemita *a* anti-Semitic. *mf* anti-Semite

antisemitismo *m*, anti-Semitism

antiséptico *a* and *m*, antiseptic

antisifilítico *a med* anti-syphilitic

antisocial *a* antisocial

antítesis *f*, antithesis

antitético *a* antithetic, contrasted

antófago *a* anthophagous, flower-eating

antojadizo *a* capricious, fanciful, whimsical

antojarse *vr* to have a fancy for, want (e.g. **Se me antoja marcharme al campo,** I have a yen to go to the country); suspect, imagine

antojo *m*, caprice, fancy, whim; desire, will; *pl* birthmark

antología *f*, anthology

antólogo *m*, anthologist

antonomasia *f*, antonomasia. **por a.,** by analogy, by transference

antorcha *f*, torch, flambeau

antracita *f*, anthracite

ántrax *m*, *med* anthrax

antro *m*, cave, cavern; *anat* antrum

antropofagia *f*, cannibalism, anthropophagy

antropófago (-ga) *a* cannibalistic. *n* cannibal

antropología *f*, anthropology

antropológico *a* anthropological

antropólogo *m*, anthropologist

antropometría *f*, anthropometry

antropomorfo *a* anthropomorphous

antroposofía *f*, anthroposophy

antruejo *m*, three days of carnival before Lent

anual *a* yearly, annual

anualidad *f*, annuity

anuario *m*, directory, yearbook, handbook

anubarrado *a* covered with clouds, cloudy

anublado *a* lowering, overcast; clouded

anublar *vt* to cloud; darken, obscure; blight (plants); *vr* cloud over; become blighted or mildewed

anudar *vt* to knot; tie, fasten; join; continue; **a. amistad de,** to strike up a friendship with. **a. la corbata,** to put on one's tie, tie one's tie; *vr* grow stunted

anulable *a* annulable, voidable

anulación *f*, annulment, abrogation

anular *a* annular, ring-shaped. *vt* to annul; *math* cancel out

anuloso *a* annulate, formed of rings

anunciación *f*, *ecc* Annunciation; announcement

anunciador (-ra), *n* **anunciante** *mf* announcer; advertiser

anunciar *vt* to announce; publish, proclaim; advertise; foretell, presage. **Anuncian lluvia,** The forecast calls for rain

anuncio *m*, announcement; publication, proclamation;

advertisement; presage, omen. **a. luminoso,** sky-sign

anverso *m*, obverse, face

anzuelo *m*, fish-hook; *cul* fritter; *inf* attraction, inducement

añadido *m*, hair-switch; make-weight

añadidura *f*, addition; make-weight, extra

añadir *vt* to add; increase

añagaza *f*, decoy bird; enticement, lure

añejo *a* very old

añicos *m pl*, fragments, small pieces. **hacer a.,** to break into fragments

añil *m*, indigo; indigo blue

año *m*, year; *pl* birthday. **a. bisiesto,** leap-year. **a. económico,** fiscal year. **A. Nuevo,** New Year. **tener (siete) años,** to be (seven) years old. **los Años Bobos,** the period from 1874 to 1898 in Spain

añoranza *f*, homesickness, loneliness; nostalgia

añorar *vi* to be homesick or lonely

añoso *a* very old, full of years

añublo *m*, mildew

aojamiento *m*, evil eye, wicked spell

aojar *vt* to bewitch, place under a spell; spoil, frustrate

aojo *m*, evil eye; magic spell

aorta *f*, *anat* aorta

aovillarse *vr* to roll oneself into a ball; curl up

apabullante *a* crushing, flattening

apacentadero *m*, grazing land, pasture

apacentamiento *m*, pasturage; grazing

apacentar *vt irr* to put out to grass; teach, instruct; satisfy (one's desires); *vr* graze (cattle). See **acertar**

apacibilidad *f*, agreeableness; mildness; peaceableness

apacible *a* agreeable; mild; peaceable; calm, peaceful

apaciguamiento *m*, appeasement, soothing, pacification

apaciguar *vt* to appease, pacify; calm

apadrinar *vt* to act as godfather to; be best man to (at a wedding); act as a second for (in a duel); sponsor; favor

apagable *a* extinguishable

apagado *a* timid, nervous; pale (of colors); dull, lusterless

apagador (-ra) *a* quenching. *n* extinguisher. *m*, candle-snuffer; damper (of a piano)

apagaincendios *m*, ship's fire-extinguisher

apagamiento *m*, quenching, extinguishment

apagar *vt* to extinguish, put out; *fig* quench, moderate; slake (lime); *art* tone down (colors); shut off (engines)

apagarrisas *mf* crapehanger, killjoy, wet blanket

apagavelas *m*, candle-snuffer

apalabrar *vt* to make an appointment with; discuss, consider

apaleamiento *m*, beating, thrashing

apalear *vt* to beat, thrash; knock down with a stick

apandillarse *vr* to form a gang or group

apañar *vt* to take away, remove; seize; steal; dress, get ready; *inf* wrap up; patch, repair; *vr inf* grow skilful

apaño *m*, dexterity, skill; craft, guile

aparador *m*, shop window; sideboard; workshop; *ecc* credence (table)

aparato *m*, apparatus; equipment, utensils; pomp, ostentation; symptoms; sign, circumstance, token. **a. digestivo,** digestive system; digestive tract. **a. fonador,** speech apparatus

aparatoso *a* showy, ostentatious. **incendio. a.,** conflagration, large fire

aparcería *f*, partnership (in a farm)

aparear *vt* to match, make equal; pair; mate (animals); *vr* form up in pairs

aparecer(se) *vi* and *vr irr* to appear; seem; be. See **conocer**

aparecido *m*, apparition, specter

aparejador (-ra), *m*, overseer, foreman; *naut* rigger

aparejar *vt* to prepare, make ready; saddle (horses); prime, size; rig (a ship)

aparejo *m*, preparation, arrangement; harness, trappings; *naut* rigging; *naut* gear; priming, sizing; *mech* tackle; *pl* equipment

aparentar vt to pretend, simulate

aparente a seeming, apparent; obvious, visible; suitable, proper

aparición f, appearance, arrival; apparition, phantom

apariencia f, appearance, looks, probability, likelihood; outward semblance; pl theat scenery

apartadamente adv apart, in private; secretly

apartadero m, passing place for cars; railway siding; grass verge. **a. ferroviario,** railway marshaling yard

apartado a distant, far off; secluded; different. m, post-office box; secluded room; smelting house; sorting of cattle; selection of bulls for a bullfight

apartamiento m, separation; withdrawal, retiral; seclusion; apartment, flat; law withdrawal of an action

apartar vt to separate; remove (e.g. an obstacle), take away; rw shunt; dissuade; sort; vr obtain a divorce; law withdraw an action. **apartarse de la tradición,** to depart from tradition

aparte adv aside, on one side; separately; theat aside; besides; beyond. m, theat aside; paragraph; space between words. **¡Aparte!** Move to one side!

apartidario a non-partisan

apasionado (-da) a impassioned; fervent, devoted; passionate; enthusiastic. n admirer, lover; enthusiast

apasionamiento m, passion

apasionar vt to arouse to passion; pain; vr (with por) grow passionately fond of; become enthusiastic for

apatía f, apathy

apático a apathetic

apeadero m, mounting-block; halt, stopping place; wayside railway station; pied-à-terre, occasional dwelling

apear vt to dismount; hobble (horse); survey, map out; fell a tree; fig overcome (difficulties); inf dissuade; prop; remove, bring down; scotch (a wheel); vr dismount; alight, step off

apechugar vi to push with the breast; inf put up with reluctantly

apedazar vt to tear; break; mend, repair

apedrear vt to stone; stone to death; vi impers hail; vr be damaged by hail (crops)

apegarse vr to grow fond (of), become attached (to)

apego m, fondness, inclination; affection, attachment

apelación f, law appeal; inf doctor's consultation

apelante a and mf law appellant

apelar vi law to appeal; (with prep a) have recourse to; vi be of the same color (horses)

apellidar vt to name, call; acclaim; call to arms; vr be named

apellido m, surname; nickname; call to arms; clamor; name

apenar vt to grieve, afflict; cause sorrow

apenas adv scarcely; immediately, as soon as; with trouble or difficulty

apéndice m, appendix, supplement; anat appendix

apendicitis f, appendicitis

Apeninos, los the Apennines

apeo m, survey; scaffolding; prop, support

apercibimiento m, preparation; provision; warning; law summons

apercibir vt to prepare, furnish; warn; law summon

apergaminado a parchment; parchment-like

apergaminarse vr inf to shrivel, dry up (with old age, etc.)

aperitivo a aperitive. m, aperient; aperitive, appetiser

apertura f, opening; inauguration; reading (of a will)

apesadumbrar vt to sadden, afflict, grieve

apestar vt to infect with the plague; catch the plague; fig corrupt; inf pester, annoy; vi stink

apestoso a stinking, putrid

apetecer vt irr to want, desire; attract. See **conocer**

apetecible a attractive, desirable

apetencia f, appetite; desire

apetito m, appetite

apetitoso a appetising; tasty, savory; attractive

apiadarse vr (with de) to have compassion on, be sorry for

ápice m, apex; peak, summit, top; orthographic accent; iota, tittle; crux (of a problem)

apicultor (-ra) n apiarist, beekeeper

apicultura f, apiculture, beekeeping

apilar vt to pile, heap

apiñado a crowded, serried

apiñamiento m, crowding; congestion

apiñar vt to group together, crowd; vr crowd

apio m, celery

apisonadora f, steam-roller; roller

apisonar vt to roll, stamp, flatten, ram down; tamp, pack down (e.g. tobacco in a pipe)

apizarrado a slate-colored

aplacable a appeasable, placable

aplacamiento m, appeasement

aplacar vt to appease, calm; moderate, mitigate

aplacible a agreeable, pleasant

aplanar vt to flatten, level; roll (pastry); inf dumbfound, overwhelm; vr collapse (buildings); lose heart

aplastar vt to flatten, squash, crush; inf squash flat, floor

aplaudir vt to applaud, clap; praise, commend, approve

aplauso m, applause; clapping, plaudit; approbation, commendation

aplazamiento m, postponement; appointment, summons

aplazar vt to summon, arrange a meeting; postpone; adjourn

aplicabilidad f, applicability

aplicable a applicable

aplicación f, application; diligence, assiduity; appliqué, ornamentation

aplicado a diligent, hardworking; appliqué

aplicar vt to apply; impute; intend, destine (for processions); law adjudge; vr engage in; apply oneself. **a. el oído,** to listen intently. **a. sanciones,** pol to impose sanctions

aplomado a self-possessed, dignified; leaden, lead-colored

aplomar vt and vi to plumb, test with a plumb-line; vr collapse, fall down

aplomo m, self-possession, dignity; sang-froid

apocado a spiritless, timid; base, mean

Apocalipsis m, Apocalypse

apocalíptico a apocalyptic

apocamiento m, timidity, pusillanimity; depression, discouragement; shyness; baseness, meanness

apocar vt to diminish, reduce; humiliate, scorn

apócrifo a fictitious, false; apocryphal. **Apócrifos,** Apocrypha

apodar vt to nickname

apoderado a authorized. m, attorney; deputy; proxy

apoderar vt to authorize; grant powers of attorney to; vr (with de) seize, take possession of

apodo m, nickname

apogeo m, ast apogee; fig zenith, peak (of fame, etc.)

apolillar vt to eat clothes (moths); vr be moth-eaten

apolíneo a Apollo-like

apologético a apologetic

apologista mf apologist

apólogo m, apologue, moral fable

apoltronarse vr to grow idle

apoplejía f, apoplexy

apoplético (-ca) a and n apoplectic

aporrear vt to beat, cudgel; vr work hard, slog away

aportación f, contribution; occasionment

aportar vt to cause, occasion; contribute; vi naut reach port; **El buque aportó a Nueva York,** The ship reached New York, The ship sailed into New York harbor; arrive at an unexpected place

aposentador m, usher; mil billeting officer

aposentar vt to lodge, give hospitality to; vr lodge, settle down

aposento m, room; suite, apartments; lodging, accommodation; theat box

aposición *f, gram* apposition

apósito *m,* poultice, external application; (medical) dressing

apostadero *m, naut* naval station; placing or stationing (of soldiers)

apostar *vt irr* to bet; station (soldiers); *vi* compete, rival. See **contar**

apostasía *f,* apostasy

apóstata *mf* apostate

apostilla *f,* marginal note, gloss

apóstol *m,* apostle

apostólico *a* apostolic

apóstrofe *m,* or *f,* apostrophe, hortatory exclamation

apóstrofo *m, gram* apostrophe

apostura *f,* neatness, spruceness

apotegma *m,* apothegm, maxim

apoteosis *f,* apotheosis

apoyar *vt* (*with* **en**) to lean against; rest upon; *vt* uphold, favor; confirm, bear out; droop the head (horses); second (a motion); *vi* (*with* **en**) rest on; lean against; *vr* (*with* **en**) rest on; lean against; **apoyarse de codos,** to lean on one's elbows; be upheld by; *fig* be founded on; *fig* depend on, lean on

apoyo *m,* support, prop; windowsill, sill; assistance; backing, support

apreciable *a* appreciable; estimable; important

apreciación *f,* appreciation; valuation, estimate

apreciador (**-ra**) *a* appreciatory. *n* appreciator

apreciar *vt* to estimate (values); appreciate; like, esteem, have a regard for

apreciativo *a* appreciative

aprecio *m,* valuation; appreciation, regard

aprehender *vt* to apprehend, catch; seize (contraband); understand, grasp

aprehensión *f,* seizure, apprehension

apremiador, apremiante *a* urgent, pressing

apremiar *vt* to hurry; urge, press; force, oblige; burden, oppress (with taxes)

apremio *m,* insistence, pressure; compulsion; demand note

aprendedor (**-ra**) *n* learner

aprender *vt* to learn. **a. de memoria,** to learn by heart

aprendiz (**-za**) *n* apprentice

aprendizaje *m,* apprenticeship. **hacer el a.,** to serve an apprenticeship

aprensión *f,* capture; fear, apprehension; suspicion, fancy; prejudice, scruple

aprensivo *a* apprehensive, nervous, fearful

apresar *vt* to nab, catch; capture (a ship); imprison; fetter

aprestar *vt* to prepare, arrange; dress (fabrics)

apresto *m,* preparation, arrangement; dressing (for cloth)

apresurar *vt* to quicken; *vr* hasten, be quick

apretado *a* difficult, dangerous; tight; crabbed (of handwriting); clustered (e.g. **casas apretadas alrededor de la sinagoga,** houses clustered around the synagogue). *inf* mean, close-fisted. *m,* small close handwriting

apretadura *f,* tightening, compression

apretar *vt irr* to tighten; compress; urge on, press; harass, vex; trouble, worry; speed up; squeeze; press (bells, gun triggers, etc.); *vi* increase, grow worse (storms, heat, etc.); pinch, hurt (shoes). **a. los pasos,** to quicken one's pace. *inf* **a. a correr,** to take to one's heels. **¡Aprieta!** *inf* Nonsense! It can't be! See **acertar**

apretón *m,* squeeze, grip, pressure; *inf* sprint, spurt; *inf* fix, pickle. **a. de manos,** handshake

apretujamiento *m,* squeezing together

apretujar *vt inf* to squeeze, hug

aprieto *m,* crowd, crush; urgency; *inf* jam, trouble, fix

aprisa *adv* quickly, in a hurry

aprisco *m,* cattle-shed; sheepfold

aprisionar *vt* to imprison; bind, fetter; tie

aprobación *f,* approbation, approval, commendation; ratification (of a bill); pass (in an examination)

aprobado *m,* pass certificate (in examinations)

aprobar *vt irr* to approve; pass (in an examination). See **contar**

apropiación *f,* appropriation; application; adaptation

apropiado *a* appropriate, suitable, proper

apropiar *vt* to appropriate; adapt, fit; *vr* appropriate, take possession

aprovechable *a* usable, available

aprovechado *a* advantageous; assiduous, conscientious; capable; thrifty

aprovechador *a* self-seeking

aprovechamiento *m,* utilization, employment; exploitation; profitable use

aprovechar *vi* to be advantageous or useful; be beneficial; make progress (in studies, etc.); *vt* use; profit by; *vr* take advantage of, make use of. **¡Que aproveche!** May it do you good! (said to anyone eating)

aprovisionar *vt* to provision, supply

aproximación *f,* approximation; consolation prize (in a lottery)

aproximadamente *adv* approximately; nearly, almost

aproximar *vt* to bring or draw nearer; *vr* approach; be almost, be approximately; draw closer

aptitud *f,* aptitude, ability; fitness; propensity

apto *a* suitable, fitting; competent. **no apta para menores,** not suitable for children (of films, etc.)

apuesta *f,* bet, wager; competition

apuestas benéficas de fútbol football pools

apuesto *a* elegant; handsome, well set-up

apuntación *f,* noting down; note; *mus* notation

apuntador (**-ra**) *n* note-taker; observer. *m, theat* prompter; *theat* stage-manager

apuntalar *vt* to prop, prop up, underpin, bolster

apuntamiento *m,* summary; *law* indictment, minute

apuntar *vt* to aim (a gun, etc.); point to, indicate; note down; mark; sketch; sharpen; bet (at cards); fasten temporarily; *inf* mend; *theat* prompt; suggest, hint (e.g. **La fecha está apuntada en vanos manuscritos,** The date is hinted at in various manuscripts); *vi* begin to appear. *inf* **a. y no dar,** to promise and do nothing

apunte *m,* abstract; note; annotation; sketch; *theat* prompt or prompter *or* prompt book *or* cue; stake in a card game

apuñalado *a* dagger-shaped

apuñalar *vt* to stab, attack with a dagger

apurado *a* poor, needy; dangerous; difficult; accurate, exact; hurried

apurar *vt* to purify; drain; exhaust; finish, conclude; examine closely, scrutinize (e.g. **apurar una materia,** to exhaust a subject, examine a subject thoroughly); irritate, make impatient; urge on, hasten; *vr* be anxious, fret

apuro *m,* difficulty, fix; poverty, want; anxiety, worry. **pasar apuros,** to have a hard time

aquejar *vt* to afflict; weary, beset, harass; *vr* complain; hurry

aquel, *a m* **aquella,** *a f* **aquellos,** *a m pl* **aquellas** *a f pl,* that, those; that or those over there (farther off than **ese**)

aquel *m,* charm, attraction, it

aquél, aquélla, aquéllos, aquéllas *dem pron m, f,* sing. and pl., that, the one, those, those ones; the former. e.g. **La casa que ve usted a lo lejos aquélla es la vivienda de mi tío,** The house that you see in the distance, that is my uncle's dwelling. **Éste no me gusta pero aquél sí,** I do not like the latter, but I like the former

aquelarre *m,* witches' sabbath

aquello *dem pron neut* that; the fact; the matter, the affair, the former (remark, idea, etc.). e.g. **Todo a. por fin acabó,** All that came to an end at last. **a. de,** the fact that

aquende *adv* on this side (rarely used)

aquí *adv* here. **de a.,** hence the fact that. **¡He a.!** Behold!

aquiescencia *f,* consent, acquiescence

aquietar *vt* to calm, soothe

aquilatar *vt* to assay; scrutinize; examine, weigh up (persons)

aquistar *vt* to attain, acquire

ara *f*, altar; **en aras de,** in honor of; for the sake of

árabe *a* Arab, Arabic. *mf* Arab. *m*, Arabic (language)

arabesco *a* Arabic. *m*, *art* arabesque

Arabia Saudita Saudi Arabia

arábigo *a* Arabic. *m*, Arabic (language)

arácnido *m*, *zool* arachnid

arado *m*, plow

arador *a* plowing. *m*, plowman. **a. de la sarna,** *ent* scabies mite

aragonés (-esa) *a* and *n* Aragonese

arahuaco *a* and *n* Arawak, Arawakian

arancel *m*, tariff, duty, tax

arancelar to charge tuition for (e.g. **a. la universidad,** charge tuition for college studies)

arancelario *a* tariff, tax; customs

arándano *m*, *bot* bilberry

arandela *f*, candle-dripper; *mech* washer; wall candelabrum

araña *f*, spider; chandelier

arañacielos *m*, skyscraper

arañar *vt* to scratch; *inf* scrape together, hoard

arañazo *m*, scratch

arar *vt* to plough. **a. en el mar,** to labor in vain

arbitrador (-ra) *n* arbitrator

arbitraje *m*, arbitration; arbitrament; *d*ecision

arbitrar *vt* to judge freely; *law* arbitrate, mediate; devise; invent; marshal (money, resources, etc.); draft (a law) *vr* make shift, contrive

arbitrariedad *f*, arbitrariness

arbitrario *a* arbitral, mediatory; arbitrary, capricious

arbitrio *m*, free will; arbitration; means, way; discretion; arbitrament, judgment; *pl* rates, municipal taxes

árbitro (-ra) *a* arbitrary. *n* arbiter. *m*, *s*port umpire; referee

árbol *m*, tree; *mech* shaft; *naut* mast; axis of a winding stair. **a. de amor** *or* **a. de Judas,** Judas tree. **a. de la ciencia (del bien y del mal),** Tree of Knowledge (of good and evil). **a. de levas,** *mech* camshaft. **a. del pan,** breadfruit tree. *naut* **a. mayor,** mainmast. **a. motor** *mech*, drivingshaft

arbolado *a* tree-covered, wooded. *m*, copse, woodland

arboladura *f*, *naut* masts and spars

arbolar *vt* to hoist (flags); *naut* fit with masts; place upright; *vr* rear, prance (horses)

arboleda *f*, copse, grove, spinney

arbotante *m*, flying buttress

arbusto *m*, shrub, woody plant

arca *f*, chest; money-box, coffer; ark; *pl* (treasury) vaults. **a. caudal,** strong box. **a. de agua,** watertower. **a. de la alianza,** *or* **a. del testamento,** Ark of the Covenant (Bible). **a. de Noé,** Noah's Ark; lumber box

arcabucero *m*, arquebusier; maker of arquebuses

arcabuz *m*, arquebus

arcada *f*, arcade; series of arches; *pl* sickness, nausea

árcade *a* and *mf* Arcadian

arcaico *a* archaic

arcaísmo *m*, archaism

arcángel *m*, archangel

arcano *a* secret. *m*, mystery, arcanum

arce *m*, *bot* maple tree

archifeliz *a* extremely happy, in bliss

archimandrita *m*, archimandrite

archimillonario (-ia) *a* and *n* multimillionaire

archipiélago *m*, archipelago

Archipiélago de Colón *m*, Galapagos Islands

archivar *vt* to place in an archive; file (papers)

archivero *m*, archivist, keeper of the archives; librarian; registrar; (Mexico) file cabinet, filing cabinet

archivista *mf* archivist; file clerk, filing clerk

archivo *m*, archives

arcilla *f*, clay

arcilloso *a* clayey, like or full of clay

arcipreste *m*, archpriest

arco *m*, *geom* arc; *mil* bow; bow (of a stringed instrument); hoop (of casks, etc.); *arch* arch. **a. del cielo** *or* **a. de San Martín** *or* **a. iris,** rainbow. **a. voltaico,** electric arc. *mus* **para a.,** for strings

arder *vi* to burn; shine, gleam; *fig* burn (with passion, etc.); *vt* to set alight, burn

ardid *a* crafty. *m*, trick, stratagem

ardiente *a* burning; ardent, passionate; vehement; enthusiastic; flame-colored; fiery-red

ardilla *f*, squirrel

ardite *m*, ancient Spanish coin of little value; *fig* farthing, fig, straw. **no valer un a.,** to be not worth a straw

ardor *m*, great heat; zeal, earnestness; passion, ardor; courage

ardoroso *a* ardorous

arduo *a* arduous

área *f*, area; small plot of ground; common threshing floor; arc (surface measure)

arena *f*, sand; arena; grit, gravel. **a. movediza,** quicksand

arenal *m*, quicksand; sand pit; sandy place

arenero (-ra) *n* sand merchant. *m*, sand-box (carried by railway engines)

arenga *f*, harangue, discourse

arenilla *f*, sand (for drying writing)

arenisca *f*, sandstone

arenisco *a* sandy

arenque *m*, herring

arete *m*, earring

argamasa *f*, mortar

argayo *m*, landslide; (Asturias) **a. de nieve,** avalanche

Árgel *m*, Algiers

Argelia Algeria

argelino (-na) *a* and *n* Algerian

argentado *a* silvered; silvery

argénteo *a* silver; silvery

argentífero *a* silver-yielding

argentino (-na) *a* silvery. *a* and *n* Argentinian. *m*, Argentinian gold coin

argento *m*, silver. **a. vivo,** mercury

argolla *f*, thick metal ring (for hitching, etc.); croquet (game); stocks, pillory; hoop, iron arch

argonauta *m*, *myth* Argonaut; *zool* paper nautilus, argonaut

argucia *f*, sophism, quibble; subtlety

argüir *vt irr* to deduce, imply; prove; reveal, manifest; accuse; *vi* argue, debate; dispute, oppose. See **huir**

argumentador (-ra) *a* argumentative. *n* arguer

argumentar *vi* to argue; dispute; oppose

argumento *m*, contention, case; theme (of a book, etc.); argument, discussion

aridez *f*, aridity, dryness; drought; sterility, barrenness; dullness, lack of interest

árido *a* dry, arid; sterile, barren; uninteresting, dull

ariete *m*, *mil* battering ram

ario (-ia) *a* and *n* Aryan

arisco *a* unsociable, surly; wild, shy (animals)

arista *f*, *bot* arista, awn, beard; pebble; edge, side

aristocracia *f*, aristocracy

aristócrata *mf* aristocrat

aristocrático *a* aristocratic

aristotélico *a* Aristotelian

aristotelismo *m*, Aristotelianism

aritmética *f*, arithmetic

aritmético (-ca) *a* arithmetical. *n* arithmetician

arlequín *m*, harlequin; *inf* fool, buffoon; Neapolitan ice-cream

arlequinada *f*, harlequinade; buffoonery

arma *f*, weapon; *mil* arm, branch; bull's horn; *pl* troops, army; means, way; arms, coat of arms. **a. arrojadiza,** missile. **a. blanca,** steel weapon. **a. de fuego,** firearm. **¡Armas al hombro!** Shoulder Arms! **armas portátiles,** small arms. *inf* **de armas tomar,** belligerent; resolute. **pasar por las armas,** *mil* to shoot. **presentar las armas,** *mil* to present arms. **ser a. de dos filos,** *fig* to cut both ways

armada *f,* navy, armada; fleet, squadron

armadía *f,* raft, pontoon

armador (-ra) *n* supplier, outfitter. *m,* shipowner; pirate, privateer; jacket; assembler, fitter

armadura *f,* armature, armor; frame, framework; skeleton (of a building); skeleton (of vertebrates); *phys* armature; plate armor (of persons)

armamento *m, mil* armament; arms, military equipment

armar *vt* to arm; *mech* mount; man (guns); put together, assemble; roll (a cigaret); reinforce (concrete); *inf* arrange, prepare; *inf* occasion (quarrels); *inf* outfit; *naut* equip; commission (a ship); *vr* prepare oneself, arm oneself. **a. caballero,** to knight. **a. los remos,** to ship the oars. *inf* **armarla,** to cause a row or quarrel

armario *m,* cupboard; wardrobe. **a. de luna,** wardrobe with a mirror

armatoste *m,* unwieldy piece of furniture; *fig inf* dead weight, clumsy person; snare

armazón *f,* frame, framework; ship's hulk. *m, anat* skeleton

armenio (-ia) *a* and *n* Armenian. *m,* Armenian language

armería *f,* armory; heraldry; gunsmith's craft or shop

armero *m,* gunsmith, armorer; stand for weapons. **a. mayor,** Royal Armorer

armiño *m,* ermine

armisticio *m,* armistice

armón de artillería *m,* gun-carriage

armonía *f,* harmony; friendship, concord; *mus* harmony

armónica (de boca) *f,* mouth-organ

armónico *a* harmonious. *a* and *m, mus* harmonic

armonio *m,* harmonium

armonioso *a* harmonious

armonización *f, mus* harmonization

armonizar *vt* to bring into harmony; *mus* harmonize

arnés *m,* armor; harness; *pl* horse trappings; *inf* equipment, tools

aro *m,* hoop; rim (of wheel, etc.); napkin-ring; croquet hoop; *bot* wild arum; child's hoop. **a. de empaquetadura,** *mech* gasket

aroma *m,* aroma, fragrance; balsam; sweet-smelling herb

aromático *a* aromatic

arpa *f,* harp. **a. eolia,** Eolian harp

arpar *vt* to scratch, claw; tear, rend

arpegio *m, mus* arpeggio

arpía *f,* harpy

arpicordio *m,* harpsichord

arpista *mf* harpist, harp player

arpón *m,* harpoon

arponear *vt* to harpoon

arponero *m,* harpooner; harpoon maker

arquear *vt* to arch; bend; beat (wool); gauge (ship's capacity); *vi* retch

arqueo *m,* arching; bending, curving; *naut* tonnage; gauging (of ship's capacity); *com* examination of deposits and contents of safe

arqueología *f,* archeology

arqueológico *a* archeological

arqueólogo *m,* archeologist

arquero *m, com* cashier; treasurer; *mil* archer

arquitecto *m,* architect. **a. de jardines,** landscape gardener

arquitectónico *a* architectural

arquitectura *f,* architecture

arquitrabe *m,* architrave

arrabal *m,* suburb, district; *pl* outskirts

arracada *f,* pendant-earring

arracimarse *vr* to cluster; group

arraigadamente *adv* deeply, firmly

arraigado *a* deep-rooted; firm; convinced

arraigar *vi* to take root; *vi* and *vr fig* become established, take hold; *vr* settle; take up residence

arraigo *m,* rooting; settlement, establishment; landed property

arrancaclavos *m,* nail-puller

arrancadero *m,* sport starting-point

arrancar *vt* to uproot; pull out; wrench; tear off; extirpate; obtain by threats; clear one's throat; *vt* and *vi naut* put on speed; *vi* start (a race); *inf* leave, quit; derive, originate **¡Arrancan!** And they're off! (races)

arranque *m,* uprooting; extirpation; wrenching, pulling, seizing; stimulus (of passion); sudden impulse; *mech* start; *mech* starter. **a. automático,** self-starter

arras *f pl,* dowry; coins given by bridegroom to his bride; earnest money, token

arrasamiento *m,* demolition, destruction; leveling

arrasar *vt* to demolish, destroy; level; fill to the brim; *vi* and *vr* clear up (sky). **ojos arrasados de lágrimas,** eyes brimming with tears

arrastrado *a inf* poverty-stricken, wretched; *inf* knavish; unhappy, unfortunate

arrastrar *vt* to drag; trail; convince; haul; *vi* trail along or touch the ground; trump (at cards); *vr* crawl, creep; shuffle along; humble oneself

arrastre *m,* dragging, trailing; haulage; trumping (at cards)

¡arre! *interj* Gee up! Get along!

arrear *vt* to spur on, whip up (horses, etc.). *interj inf* **¡Arrea!** Hurry up! Get on!

arrebañar *vt* to pick clean, clear; eat or drink up

arrebatado *a* precipitate, headlong; rash; flushed, red

arrebatador *a* overwhelming; violent; bewitching, captivating; delightful

arrebatamiento *m,* abduction; seizure; fury; ecstasy

arrebatar *vt* to abduct, carry off; seize, grab; attract, charm; grip (the attention); *vr* be overcome with rage

arrebatiña *f,* grab; scuffle, scrimmage

arrebato *m,* fit (gen. of anger); ecstasy, rapture

arrebol *m,* red flush in the sky; rouge; *pl* red clouds

arrebozar *vt* to muffle; envelop

arrebujarse *vr* to huddle; wrap oneself up

arrechucho *m, inf* fit of rage; sudden slight ailment

arreciar *vi* to increase in intensity; *vr* grow strong

arrecife *m,* reef (in the sea); stone-paved road

arredrar *vt* to separate, remove; force back, repel; terrify

arregazar(se) *vt* and *vr* to tuck up one's skirts

arreglado *a* regular; regulated; ordered; methodical

arreglar *vt* to regulate; arrange; adjust, put right; tidy; make up (the face); *vr* (*with prep a*) conform to; (*with con*) reach an agreement with. **Me voy a a.,** I am going to make myself presentable. *inf* **arreglárselas,** to shift for oneself

arreglo *m,* arrangement; rule; regulation; method, order; agreement; adjustment; compromise

arrellanarse *vr* to settle comfortably in one's chair; be happy in one's work

arremangar *vt* to roll up (sleeves, trousers, etc.); *vr inf* make a decision

arremango *m,* rolling or tucking up (of sleeve, etc.)

arremetedor (-ra) *n* attacker, assailant

arremeter *vt* to attack, assail; *vi* launch oneself (at); *fig* spoil the view, shock the eye

arremetida *f,* attack, assault

arremolinarse *vr* to crowd, cluster, group

arrendador (-ra) *n* landlord; renter; hirer; tenant

arrendamiento *m,* letting, renting; hiring; rental; agreement, lease

arrendar *vt irr* to let, lease; hire; rent (as a tenant); train (horses); tie up (horses); restrain; mimic, imitate. See **recomendar**

arrendatario (-ia) *a* rent, lease. *n* tenant; lessee; hirer. **a. de contribuciones,** tax farmer

arreo *m,* ornament; apparel; *pl* horse trappings; appurtenances, equipment

¡Arrepa! But look!, Hold on!, Hold your horses!, Not so fast!

arrepentimiento *m*, repentance

arrepentirse *vr irr* to repent. See **sentir**

arrestado *a* courageous, audacious, bold

arrestar *vt* to arrest, detain; *vr* be bold, dare

arresto *m*, arrest; detention; imprisonment; audacity, boldness

arriada *f*, lowering (of a boat); taking in (of sail)

arriar *vt naut* to strike (colors); take in (sail); pay out (ropes, etc.); lower (boats); flood, inundate

arriate *m*, garden border; avenue, walk; trellis (for plants)

arriba *adv* up, above; overhead; upstairs; earlier, before; upwards (with prices). *interj* ¡A.! Up with!; Long live! **de a. abajo,** from head to foot, from one end to the other; completely, wholly

arribada *f, naut* arrival. **de a.,** emergency (port)

arribar *vi naut* to arrive; put into an emergency port; reach, arrive at; *inf* convalesce; attain; *naut* drift

arribista *mf* social climber

arribo *m*, arrival

arriero *m*, farrier; muleteer

arriesgado *a* dangerous, risky; rash, daring

arriesgar *vt* to risk; *vr* run into danger; dare, risk

arrimar *vt* to bring or draw near; abandon (professions, etc.); lay aside, discard; *inf* administer (blows); *naut* stow (cargo); *vr* (*with prep a*) lean against, rest on; join, go with; seek the protection of. **Cada cual se arrima a su cada cual,** Birds of a feather flock together

arrimo *m*, bringing or placing near; leaning or resting against; abandonment, giving up; protection; staff, support

arrinconado *a* remote, secluded; forgotten, neglected

arrinconar *vt* to discard, lay aside; corner, besiege; set aside, dismiss; forsake; *vr* go into retirement, withdraw

arriscado *a* craggy, rugged; bold, resolute; sprightly, handsome

arro, arro, arro purrrr (echoic of a cat's purr)

arroba *f*, weight of 25 lb.; variable liquid measure

arrobamiento *m*, ecstasy; rapture; trance

arrobar *vt* to charm, entrance; *vr* be enraptured; be in ecstasy

arrodillar *vt* to cause to kneel down; *vi* and *vr* kneel down

arrogancia *f*, arrogance; courage; majesty, pride

arrogante *a* arrogant, haughty; courageous; proud, majestic

arrogar *vt* to adopt (as a son); *vr* usurp, appropriate

arrojadizo *a* easily cast or hurled; projectile

arrojado *a* bold, determined; rash

arrojar *vt* to throw, hurl, cast; shed (light, etc.; e.g. **La cuenta arroja un total de cien dólares,** The bill shows a total of a hundred dollars); *com* show (a balance, etc.); put out (sprouts); dismiss, send away; *vr* cast oneself; (*with prep a*) hurl oneself against or upon; undertake, venture upon. **a. de sí (a),** to get rid of, dismiss

arrojo *m*, daring, intrepidity; boldness

arrollar *vt* to roll; make into a roll, roll up; defeat (the enemy); silence, confound; rock to sleep; bear along, carry off

arromar *vt* to blunt; flatten

arropamiento *m*, wrapping up, covering, muffling

arropar *vt* to wrap up, cover

arrostrar *vt* to confront, defy, face up to; *vr* fight hand to hand. **a. las consecuencias,** *fig* to face the music

arroyada *f*, gorge, gully; course, channel; flood

arroyo *m*, stream, brook; street gutter; road, street; *fig* flood, plenty

arroz *m*, rice

arrozal *m*, rice field

arruga *f*, wrinkle; fold, pleat; crease

arrugamiento *m*, wrinkling; fold, pleating; crumpling, creasing; corrugation

arrugar *vt* to wrinkle; pleat; corrugate; crumple, crease. **a. el ceño,** to knit one's brow, scowl

arruinamiento *m*, ruin, decay, decline

arruinar *vt* to ruin; destroy, damage severely

arrullar *vt* to bill and coo (doves); lull to sleep; *inf* whisper sweet words to, make love to

arrullo *m*, cooing of doves; lullaby

arrumaco *m, inf* embrace, caress (gen. *pl*); ornament in bad taste

arrumaje *m, naut* stowage; clouds on the horizon

arrurruz *m*, arrowroot

arsenal *m*, dockyard; arsenal; *fig* store (of information, etc.)

arsénico *m*, arsenic

arte *mf*, art; skill; ability, talent; guile, craftiness. **las bellas artes,** fine arts. *inf* **no tener a. ni parte en,** to have nothing to do with, have no part in

artefacto *m*, machine, mechanism, apparatus; device, appliance. **a. atómico,** atomic bomb

arteria *f, med* artery; main line (of communication)

artería *f*, craftiness, guile

arterial *a* arterial

artesa *f*, wooden trough; kneading bowl

artesano (-na) *n* artisan; mechanic

artesiano *a* artesian

artesón *m*, bucket, pail; *arch* curved ceiling-panel; paneled ceiling

artesonado *a arch* paneled (ceiling). *m*, paneled ceiling

ártico *a* Arctic

articulación *f*, joint, articulation; jointing; enunciation, pronunciation

articular *vt* to joint, articulate; enunciate, pronounce clearly

articulista *mf* article writer

artículo *m*, finger knuckle; heading; article; *anat* joint; *gram* article; *pl* goods, things. **a. de fondo,** leading article (in a newspaper). **a. de primera necesidad,** prime necessity, essential

artífice *mf* craftsman, artificer; author, creator; forger

artificial *a* artificial

artificio *m*, skill, art; appliance, contraption, mechanism; trick, cunning device; guile, craftiness

artificioso *a* skilful; artificial; crafty, cunning

artillería *f*, artillery. **a. de costa,** coastal guns. **a. ligera, a. montada, a. rodada** *or* **a. volante,** field artillery

artillero *m*, gunner

artimaña *f*, trick, ruse, stratagem

artista *mf* artist; performer

artístico *a* artistic

artrítico *a med* arthritic

artritis *f, med* arthritis

arveja *f, bot* vetch

arzobispado *m*, archbishopric

arzobispo *m*, archbishop

as, *m*, Roman copper coin; ace (*aer* cards, etc.)

asa *f*, handle; pretext, excuse

asado *m, cul* roast

asador *m, cul* roasting-spit; roaster

asadura *f, cul* chitterlings; offal

asalariar *vt* to fix a salary for

asaltador (-ra) *a* attacking. *n* assailant, attacker

asaltar *vt* to storm, besiege; assault, attack; occur to (ideas); come on suddenly (illness)

asalto *m*, storming, besieging; assault, attack; bout (in fencing, boxing, wrestling); round (in a fight)

asamblea *f*, congregation, assembly; meeting; legislative assembly; *mil* assembly (bugle call)

asambleísta *mf* member of an assembly

asar *vt cul* to roast; grill; *vr* be burning-hot; *fig* burn (with enthusiasm)

asaz *adv* sufficiently, enough; very; in abundance. *a* sufficient; many

asbesto *m*, asbestos

ascalonia *f, bot* shallot

ascendencia *f*, lineage, ancestry, origin

ascendente *a* ascending

ascender *vi irr* to ascend, climb; be promoted; (*with prep a*) amount to (bills, etc.); *vt* promote. See **entender**

ascendiente *mf* ancestor, forbear. *m*, influence, ascendancy

ascensión *f,* ascension; promotion; *ast* exaltation
ascenso *m,* ascent; promotion, preferment
ascensor *m,* lift, elevator
ascensorista *mf* elevator operator
asceta *mf* ascetic
ascético *a* ascetic
ascetismo *m,* asceticism
asco *m,* nausea; repugnance, loathing; revolting thing. *inf* **Me da a.,** It sickens me
ascua *f,* live coal, ember. **estar como una a. de oro,** to be as bright as a new pin. **estar en ascuas,** *fig* to be on pins
aseado *a* clean, tidy
asear *vt* to tidy, make neat; clean up; decorate, adorn
asechanza *f,* ambush; trick, snare, stratagem
asechar *vt* to ambush, waylay; *fig* lay snares for
asediador (-ra) *n* besieger
asediar *vt* to besiege; pester, importune
asedio *m,* siege; importunity
asegurado (-da) *a* insured. *n* insured person
asegurador (-ra) *n* insuring. *n* insurer
asegurar *vt* to fasten, make secure; pinion, grip; reassure, soothe; assert, state; *com* insure; guarantee; ensure, secure; *vr com* insure oneself; *(with de)* make sure of
asemejar *vt* to imitate, copy; make similar to; *vr (with prep a)* be like, be similar to
asenderear *vt* to make a pathway through; persecute, harass
asenso *m,* assent. **dar a.,** to believe, give credence (to)
asentaderas *f pl, inf* buttocks, seat
asentado *a* prudent, circumspect; permanent, stable
asentamiento *m,* seating; settlement, residence; prudence, judgment
asentar *vt irr* to seat; place; fasten, fix; found; plant (flags); pitch (a tent); establish, make firm; smooth; hone (razors); estimate, budget, arrange, set forth; note down; affirm, believe; *com* enter (in an account); *vi* fit (clothes); *vr* seat oneself; alight (birds); settle (liquids); *arch* settle, subside; to be located (e.g. **El edificio se asienta en una esquina,** The building is located on a corner). **a. la mano en,** to strike hard. See **acertar**
asentimiento *m,* assent; consent, approval
asentir *vi irr* to assent, agree; *(with en)* consent to. See **sentir**
aseñorado *a* refined, gentlemanly; ladylike; presumptuous
aseo *m,* cleanliness, neatness
asepsia *f,* asepsis
asequible *a* attainable; obtainable
aserción *f,* assertion
aserradero *m,* sawmill; saw-pit
aserrador (-ra) *n* sawyer
aserrar *vt irr* to saw. See **acertar**
aserrín *m,* sawdust
asertivo *a* assertive
aserto *m,* assertion
asesinar *vt* to assassinate, murder
asesinato *m,* assassination, murder
asesino *mf* assassin, murderer; murderess
asesor (-ra) *n* assessor
asesorar *vt* to give advice; *vr* take legal advice; seek advice
asestar *vt* to aim (firearms); fire; deal (a blow)
aseveración *f,* assertion, statement
aseveradamente *adv* affirmatively
aseverar *vt* to affirm, assert
asfaltado *m,* asphalting; asphalt pavement
asfaltar *vt* to asphalt
asfalto *m,* asphalt
asfixia *f, med* asphyxia
asfixiante *a* asphyxiating
asfixiar *vt* to asphyxiate
asfódelo *m, bot* asphodel
así *adv* thus, so, in this way; like this (e.g. **en días a.,** on

days like this); even if; so that, therefore. **a. a.,** middling, so-so. **a. como a.,** as well as; as soon as. **a. las cosas,** that being the case, **a. que,** as soon as, immediately; consequently, thus
Asia Menor Asia Minor
asiático (-ca) *a* and *n* Asiatic
asidero *m,* hold, grasp; handle, haft; pretext, excuse
asido a wedded to (e.g. a belief)
asiduidad *f,* assiduity
asiduo *a* assiduous
asiento *m,* seat; place, position; site; base (of a vase, etc.); lees, sediment; indigestion; *arch* subsidence, settling; treaty, pact; contract; note, reminder; *com* entry; permanence, stability; prudence; bit (of a bridle); *pl* buttocks, seat. **estar de a.,** to be established (in a place)
asignación *f,* assignation; appropriation (of money); salary; portion, share
asignar *vt* to assign; apportion; destine, intend; appoint
asignatura *f,* subject (of study in schools, etc.)
asilar *vt* to give shelter to; receive; put into an institution
asilo *m,* shelter, refuge; sanctuary, asylum; *fig* protection, defence; home, institution
asimetría *f,* asymmetry
asimétrico *a* asymmetrical
asimiento *m,* hold, grasp; attachment, affection
asimilable *a* assimilable
asimilación *f,* assimilation
asimilar *vt* to compare, liken; *(bot zool gram)* assimilate; *vi* resemble, be like; *fig* assimilate, digest (ideas)
asimismo *adv* similarly, likewise
asir *vt irr* to grasp, take hold of; seize; *vi* take root (plants); *vr (with de)* lay hold of; take advantage of; make an excuse to. *Pres. Ind.* **asgo, ases,** etc. *Pres. Subjunc.* **asga,** etc.
asirio (-ia) *a* and *n* Assyrian. *m,* Assyrian language
asistencia *f,* presence, attendance; minimal attendance required (e.g. **Los alumnos tienen que completar una a.,** Pupils must attend a certain number of classes) assistance, help; service, attendance; medical treatment; remuneration; *pl* allowance. **a. pública,** Public Assistance. **a. social,** social work
asistenta *f,* daily maid; waiting-maid
asistente *m,* assistant; *mil* orderly
asistir *vt* to accompany; assist, help; attend, treat; *(with de)* act as; *vi (with prep a)* be present at, attend; follow suit (in cards)
asma *f,* asthma
asmático (-ca) *a* asthmatic. *n* asthma sufferer
asnal *a* asinine; brutish, stupid
asno *m,* ass
asociación *f,* association; company, partnership; society, fellowship
asociado (-da) *n* associate; member; partner
asociar *vt* to associate; *vr* associate oneself; join together; form a partnership
asolación, f. asolamiento *m,* destruction, ruin
asolar *vt irr* to destroy, devastate, lay flat; *vr* wither; settle (liquids). See **contar**
asoldar *vt irr* to employ, engage, hire. See **contar**
asolear *vt* to expose to the sun; *vr* sun oneself; become sunburnt
asomada *f,* brief appearance; vantage point
asomar *vt* to show, allow to appear, put forth; *vi* begin to show; *vr* show oneself, appear; *inf* be flushed (with wine); *(with prep a, por)* look out of. **asomarse a la ventana,** to show oneself at, or look out of, the window
asombrar *vt* to shade, shadow; darken (a color); terrify; amaze
asombro *m,* fright, terror; amazement; wonder, marvel
asombroso *a* amazing; marvellous, wonderful
asonancia *f,* assonance; congruity, harmony
asonante *a* and *m,* assonant
asordar *vt* to deafen

aspa *f,* cross; sail of a windmill

aspaviento *m,* exaggerated display of emotion; gesture (of horror, etc.); **hacer aspavientos,** to make a fuss

aspecto *m,* look, appearance; aspect, outlook

aspereza *f,* roughness, harshness; ruggedness, rockiness; severity, asperity

áspero *a* rough, harsh; uneven, rocky; jarring, grating; hard, severe

aspersión *f, ecc* aspersion; sprinkling

áspid *m,* asp, viper

aspiración *f,* breath; breathing; aspiration, desire; *mus* pause

aspirador (de polvo) *m,* vacuum cleaner

aspirante *m,* aspirant, novice; office-seeker; applicant

aspirar *vt* to breathe in, inhale; *gram* aspirate; *(with prep a)* aspire to, desire

aspirina *f,* aspirin

asquear *vi* and *vt* to hate, loathe

asquerosidad *f,* filthiness, loathsomeness; vileness, hatefulness

asqueroso *a* nauseating; loathsome, revolting; vile, hateful

asta *f,* lance, spear, pike; horn (of bull); antler; flagstaff; shaft. **a media a.,** at half-mast

asterisco *m,* asterisk

astigmático *a* astigmatic

astigmatismo *m,* astigmatism

astil *m,* handle, pole, shaft; bar of a balance; beam feather

astilla *f,* splinter

astillar *vt* to splinter, chip

astillero *m,* shipyard; rack for lances and pikes

astilloso *a* splintery, fragile

astracán *m,* astrakhan

astringente *a* astringent

astringir *vt* to tighten up; compress; constrain

astro *m,* heavenly body

astrolatría *f,* astrolatry, star worship

astrología *f,* astrology

astrológico *a* astrological

astrólogo (-ga) *n* astrologist

astronauta *m,* astronaut

astronomía *f,* astronomy

astronómico *a* astronomical

astrónomo *m,* astronomer

astucia *f,* astuteness, guile, craftiness

asturiano (-na) *a* and *n* Asturian

astuto *a* guileful, crafty, astute

Asuero Ahasuerus

asueto *m,* day's holiday

asumir *vt* to assume; adopt, appropriate

asunción *f,* assumption

asunto *m,* matter, theme, subject; business, affair

asustadizo *a* timid, nervous, easily frightened

asustar *vt* to frighten; **que asusta,** terribly (e.g. **Es de una ñoñería que asusta,** It's a terribly timid thing to do) *vr* be frightened

atablar *vt* to roll, flatten (earth)

atacado *a inf* hesitant; mean, stingy

atacador (-ra) *a* attacking. *n* aggressor, attacker

atacar *vt* to attack; fasten, button; fit (clothes); ram (guns); *fig* press hard, corner (persons). **a. a los nervios,** to jar on the nerves

atadero *m,* rope, tie, cord; hook, ring, etc. (for hitching); hindrance, impediment; hitching or fastening point

atado *m,* bundle, roll

atadura *f,* tying, stringing, fastening, tie; knot; connection

atajar *vi* to take a short cut; *vt* intercept, cut off; screen off, divide; impede, stop; interrupt (people); **atajarle la palabra a uno,** to cut somebody off, interrupt *vr* be overcome (by fear, shame, etc.)

atajo *m,* short cut, quick way; cutting, abbreviation; division. *inf* **echar por el a.,** to go to the root of (a matter)

atalaya *f,* look out, watch tower; observation point. *m,* lookout

atalayar *vt* to scan, watch; spy upon

atalón *m,* atoll, coral island

atañadero: en lo atañadero a with regard to, with respect to

atañer *vi impers* to concern, affect; belong, pertain

ataque *m, (mil med)* attack; quarrel, fight

atar *vt* to tie; fasten; lace; stop, paralyse; *vr* get in a fix; confine oneself. **a. cabos,** to put two and two together

atardecer *vi irr impers* to grow dusk. See **conocer**

atardecer *m,* dusk, evening

atarear *vt* to set to work, assign work to; *vr* work hard

atarugar *vt* to wedge; stop up; plug; block; *inf* silence, shut up; stuff, cram; *vr fig inf* lose one's head

atasajar *vt* to cut up, jerk (beef, etc.)

atascadero *m,* deep rut, boggy place; impediment, obstacle

atascar *vt* to plug; block up; stop (a leak); hinder, obstruct; *vr* stick in the mud; be held up or delayed; *inf* get stuck in a speech

atasco *m,* obstruction, block

ataúd *m,* coffin

Ataulfo Ataulf

ataviar *vt* to deck, apparel, adorn

atavío *m,* get-up, dress, apparel; *pl* ornaments

atavismo *m,* atavism

ate *m,* (Mexico) kind of Turkish delight

ateísmo *m,* atheism

atelaje *m,* team, yoke (of horses); trappings, harness; *inf* trousseau

atemperación *f,* moderation, mitigation; tempering

atemperar *vt* to moderate, mitigate; adapt, adjust; temper, cool. **atemperarse a la realidad,** to adjust to reality

Atenas Athens

atenazar *vt* to grip, grasp; torture

atención *f,* attention; solicitude, kindness; courtesy, civility; *pl* business affairs. *interj* **¡A.!** Take care! Look out!; *mil* Attention! **en a. (a),** taking into consideration. **estar en a.,** (patient) to be under treatment

atender *vt irr* to await, expect; take care of, look after; *vi (with prep a)* attend to, listen to; *vi* remember. See **entender**

ateneo *m,* atheneum. *a* Athenian

atenerse *vr irr (with prep a)* to abide by; resort to, rely on. See **tener**

ateniense *a* and *mf* Athenian

atentado *a* prudent, sensible; secret, silent. *m,* infringement, violation; attempt (on a person's life); crime

atentar *vt irr* to do illegally; attempt a crime; *vr* proceed cautiously; restrain oneself. See **acertar**

atento *a* attentive; courteous, civil. *adv* taking into consideration. **su atenta (atta),** *com* your favor

atenuación *f,* attenuation, diminution

atenuante *a* attenuating; extenuating (of circumstances)

atenuar *vt* to attenuate, diminish; extenuate

ateo (-ea) *a* atheistic. *n* atheist

aterciopelado *a* velvety

aterirse *vr defective* to grow stiff with cold

aterrador *a* terrifying, dreadful

aterraje *m, (aer, naut)* landing

aterramiento *m,* horror, terror; terrorization; *naut* landing; ruin, demolition

aterrar *vt irr* to demolish; discourage; cover with earth; *vi* land; *vr naut* draw near to land. See **acertar**

aterrizaje *m, aer* landing. **a. forzoso,** forced landing. **campo de a.,** landing field

aterrizar *vi aer* to land, touch down

aterrorizar *vt* to terrify; terrorize

atesorar *vt* to hoard, treasure up

atestación *f,* attestation, affidavit

atestar *vt irr* to stuff, cram; insert; *inf* stuff with food; crowd, fill with people. See **acertar**

atestar *vt* to attest, testify

atestiguación *f,* deposition, testimony
atestiguar *vt* to testify, attest
atetar *vt* to suckle; *vi* suck
atezado *a* bronzed, sunburnt; black
ático *a* Attic; *m,* penthouse
atiesar *vt* to stiffen
atildar *vt* to place a tilde over; blame, criticize; decorate, ornament
atimia *f,* loss of status
atinado *a* pertinent, relevant
atinar *vi* to find by touch; discover by chance; guess; hit the mark
atinente a . . . concerning . . .
atisbadura *f,* watching, spying, prying
atisbar *vt* to spy upon, watch
atisbo *m,* prying, watching; suspicion, hint
atisbón *a* penetrating (mind, vision)
atizador *m,* poker (for the fire)
atizar *vt* to poke (the fire); dowse, snuff; trim (lamps); excite, rouse; *inf* slap, wallop
atlántico *a* Atlantic. *m,* Atlantic Ocean
Atlántida Atlantis
atleta *m,* athlete
atlético *a* athletic
atletismo *m,* athletics
atmósfera *f,* atmosphere
atmosférico *a* atmospheric
atolladero *m,* rut; mud; bog
atolón *m,* atoll, coral island
atolondrado *a* scatter-brained, flighty
atolondramiento *m,* rashness, recklessness; bewilderment
atolondrar *vt* to bewilder, confuse
atómico *a* atomic
atomización *f,* atomization
átomo *m,* atom; speck, particle
atónito *a* amazed, astounded
atontar *vt* to confuse, daze; make stupid; stun
atormentador (-ra) *a* torturing. *n* tormentor; torturer
atormentar *vt* to torment; torture; grieve, harass
atorrante *a* and *mf* (Argentina) good-for-nothing
atracadero *m,* jetty, landingstage
atracar *vt inf* to stuff with food; *naut* tie up, moor; hold up, rob; *vi naut* moor, stop; *vr inf* guzzle, gorge
atracción *f,* attraction
atraco (a) *m,* hold up (of), ambush (of)
atracón *m, inf* gorge, fill; surfeit. **darse atracones de,** to gorge oneself on
atractivo *a* attractive. *m,* attraction, charm
atractriz *a* attracting; *f,* force of attraction; (fig.) lure
atraer *vt irr* to attract; charm, enchant. See **traer**
atragantarse *vr* to choke; *inf* be at a loss, dry up (in conversation)
atraíble *a* attractable, able to be attracted
atrancar *vt* to bar the door; obstruct, block; hinder; *vi inf* stride; skip (in reading)
atrapar *vt inf* grab, seize, catch; net, obtain; deceive
atrás *adv* behind, back; past; previously. **¡A.!** Back!
años a., years ago
atrasado *a* slow (of clocks); backward; old-fashioned; hard-up, poor. **a. mental,** retarded person
atrasar *vt* to delay, retard; fix a later date than the true one; put back (clocks). *vi* be slow (clocks); *vr* be late; be left behind
atraso *m,* delay; backwardness, dullness; slowness (clocks); lateness; *pl* arrears. **El reloj lleva cinco minutos de a.,** The watch is five minutes slow
atravesado *a* slightly squint-eyed; mongrel, crossbreed; half-caste; ill-intentioned
atravesar *vt irr* to lay across, put athwart; cross, traverse; pierce; obstruct; *naut* lie to; *vr* be among, mingle (with); interrupt; interfere, take part; quarrel; occur, arise. See **confesar**
atrayente *a* attractive
atreverse *vr* to dare, risk, venture; be overbold or insolvent

atrevido *a* bold, audacious; hazardous, dangerous; brazen, impudent
atribuible *a* attributable
atribución *f,* attribution; perquisite, attribute
atribuir *vt irr* to impute, attribute; assign, turn over to; *vr* take upon oneself, assume. See **huir**
atributo *m,* attribute, quality
atril *m,* lectern, reading desk; music stand
atrincherar *vt* to protect with entrenchments; *vr* entrench oneself
atrio *m,* atrium; hall, vestibule; *arch* parvis
atrocidad *f,* atrocity, cruelty; *inf* terrific amount; enormity, crime
atrofia *f,* atrophy
atrofiarse *vr* to atrophy
atronado *a* harebrained, foolish
atronar *vt irr* to deafen, stun with noise; confuse, daze. See **tronar**
atropelladamente *adv* in disorder, helter-skelter
atropellado *a* rash, foolhardy
atropellar *vt* to trample upon; thrust out of the way; knock down; disregard, violate (feelings); insult, abuse; transgress; do hastily; *vr* act rashly
atropello *m,* trampling; road accident; knocking over; upsetting; violation; outrage
atroz *a* atrocious, savage; monstrous, outrageous; *inf* terrific, enormous
atufar *vt* to irritate, vex; *vr* grow irritated; turn sour (wine, etc.)
atún *m,* tunny fish
aturdido *a* reckless, scatterbrained, silly; thoughtless; stunned
aturdimiento *m,* daze; confusion, bewilderment
aturdir *vt* to daze; confuse, bewilder; amaze; stun
atusar *vt* to trim (hair, beard); *agr* prune; smooth down (hair); *vr* dress over-carefully
audacia *f,* audacity
audaz *a* audacious, daring
audibilidad *f,* audibility
audición *f,* audition
audiencia *f,* audience, hearing; *law* audience; audience chamber
audífono *m,* hearing aid
audioteca *f,* audio library
auditivo *a* auditory
auditor *m,* magistrate, judge
auditorio *a* auditory. *m,* audience
auge *m, fig* zenith, height; *ast* apogee
augusto *a* august, awesome
aula *f,* lecture or class room; *poet* palace
aullador *a* howling
aullar *vi* to howl; bay
aullido *m,* howl; baying
aumentar(se) *vt vi vr* to increase, augment
aumentativo *a gram* augmentative
aumento *m,* increase; progress; enlargement. **ir en a.,** to increase; advance, progress; prosper
aun *adv* even. **A. los que viven lejos han de oíros,** Even those who live far must hear you. **a. así** *or* a. siendo así, even so. **a. ayer,** only yesterday. **a. cuando,** even if. **más a.,** even more. **ni a. si,** not even if.
aún *adv* still, yet. **A. no te creen** *or* No te creen a., They still don't believe you ¿A. se lo darás? *or* ¿Se lo darás a.? Will you still give it to her?
aunque *conjunc* although, even if, even though. It takes the Indicative referring to statement of fact and Subjunctive referring to a hypothesis, e.g. **A. vino, no lo hizo,** Although he came, he did not do it. **A. él cantase yo no iría allí,** Even though he sang (were to sing), I should not go there
aura *f,* zephyr, gentle breeze; popularity, approbation; aura. **a. epiléptica,** *med* epileptic aura
áureo *a* gold, gilt; golden
auricular *a* auricular. *m,* little finger; receiver, ear-piece (of a telephone); earphone (radio)

aurífero *a* gold-yielding, auriferous

auriga *m,* charioteer

aurora *f,* dawn; genesis, beginnings. **a. boreal,** aurora borealis, Northern Lights

auscultación *f, med* auscultation

auscultar *vt med* to auscultate

ausencia *f,* absence. **en ausencia de,** in the absence of

ausentar *vt* to send away; *vr* absent oneself

ausente *a* absent. *mf* absent person

auspicio *m,* augury, prediction; favor, patronage; *pl* auspices

austeridad *f,* austerity; mortification of the flesh

austero *a* austere, ascetic; severe, harsh; honest, upright

austral *a* southerly, austral

australiano (-na) *a* and *n* Australian

austríaco (-ca) *a* and *n* Austrian

Austrias, los the Hapsburgs (ruling house of Spain, 1516–1700)

austrófilo *a* and *n* Austrophile

autenticación *f,* authentication

autenticar *vt* to authenticate, attest; prove genuine

autenticidad *f,* authenticity

auténtico *a* authentic

auto *m, law* sentence, decision; *theat* one-act allegory (gen. religious); *pl* proceedings. **a. de fe,** auto-da-fé. **a. de reconocimiento,** search-warrant. **a. sacramental,** one-act religious drama on theme of mystery of the Eucharist. **hacer a. de fe de,** to burn

autobiografía *f,* autobiography

autobús *m,* motor bus, bus

autocitarse *vr* to quote from one's own works

autoclave *m,* pressure cooker

autocracia *f,* autocracy

autócrata *mf* autocrat

autocrático *a* autocratic

autocrueldad *f,* self-inflicted pain

autodescubrimiento *m,* self-discovery

autodidacto *a* autodidactic; self-educated, self-taught

autódromo *m,* speedway

autógeno *a* autogenous, self-generating

autogiro *m, aer* autogyro

autografía *f,* autography

autográfico *a* autographic, in lithographic reproduction

autógrafo *a* autographical. *m,* autograph

autoinducción *f,* self-induction

autómata *m,* automaton

automático *a* automatic. *m, sew* press stud

automatismo *m,* automatism

automejoramiento *m,* self-improvement

automóvil *m,* automobile, motor car. *a* automatic

automovilismo *m,* motoring

automovilista *mf* motorist

autonombrarse *vr* to call oneself, go by the name of

autonomía *f,* autonomy

autónomo *a* autonomous

autopista *f,* motor road

autopsia *f, med* autopsy, post-mortem

autor (-ra) *n* agent, originator; author; inventor; *law* perpetrator

autoridad *f,* authority; pomp, show

autoritario *a* authoritarian; authoritative

autorización *f,* authorization

autorizado *a* approved, authorized, responsible

autorizar *vt* to authorize; *law* attest, testify; cite, prove by reference; approve; exalt

autorretratarse *vr* to have one's portrait painted, sit for one's portrait

autorretrato *m,* self-portrait

autostopista *mf* hitchhiker (Spain)

autosugestión *f,* autosuggestion

auxiliador (-ra) *a* assistant; helpful. *n* helper, assistant

auxiliar *vt* to help, aid; attend (the dying). *m, univ* lecturer. *a* assisting

auxiliaría *f, univ* lectureship

auxilio *m,* help, aid, assistance

aval *m, com* endorsement; voucher

avalar *vt* to enhance. **avalado por la tradición,** hallowed by tradition

avalentado *a* boastful, bragging

avalorar *vt* to value, estimate; put spirit into, encourage

avance *m,* advance; advance payment; balance sheet; attack

avanzada *f, mil* advance guard

avanzado *a* advanced, progressive

avanzar *vt* to advance; promote; *vi* advance; attack; grow late (time)

avanzo *m,* balance sheet; price estimate

avaricia *f,* greed, avarice

avaricioso, avariento *a* avaricious, greedy

avaro (-ra) *a* miserly; greedy. *n* miser

avasallador *a* dominating; *fig* overwhelming; enslaving

avasallar *vt* to subdue, dominate; *vr* become a vassal; surrender, yield

ave *f,* bird. **a. de paso,** migratory bird; *fig* bird of passage. **a. de rapiña,** bird of prey. **a. fría,** *orn* plover. **ave cantora,** songbird

avecinarse *vr* to be approaching (e.g. **el año que avecina,** the coming year)

avellana *f,* hazel nut

avellanarse *vr* to shrivel

avellano *m, bot* hazel

avemaría *f,* Hail Mary (prayer); Angelus; rosary bead. *inf* **en un a.,** in a trice

avena *f,* oats; *poet* oaten pipe. **a. loca,** wild oats

avenal *m,* oatfield

avenar *vt* to drain (land); drain off (liquids)

avenencia *f,* agreement, arrangement; transaction; conformity, harmony

avenida *f,* flood, spate; avenue; abundance; way, approach (to a place)

avenido *a* (*with bien or mal*) well *or* ill-suited

avenidor (-ra) *n* arbitrator, mediator

avenir *vt irr* to reconcile; *vi* happen (used in infinitive and third singular and plural); *vr* be reconciled; agree; compromise, give way; harmonize (things) (*with con*) get on with, agree with. See **venir**

aventador *m, agr* winnower; pitchfork

aventajado *a* outstanding, talented; advantageous. *m, mil* private who enjoys extra pay

aventajar *vt* to improve, better; promote, prefer; excel; *vr* (*with prep a*) surpass, excel. **Te aventajo en diez años,** I'm ten years older than you

aventamiento *m,* winnowing

aventar *vt irr* to fan; air, ventilate; winnow; *inf* drive away, expel; *vr* be inflated; *inf* flee; smell (bad meat). See **sentar**

aventura *f,* adventure; chance, luck; risk, danger

aventurar *vt* to risk, hazard

aventurero (-ra) *a* adventurous; unscrupulous; intriguing; undisciplined (of troops). *n* adventurer

avergonzar *vt irr* to shame; make shy, abash; *vr* be ashamed; be shy or sheepish. *Pres. Ind.* **avergüenzo, avergüenzas, avergüenza, avergüenzan.** *Pres. Subjunc.* **avergüence, avergüences, avergüence, avergüencen**

avería *f,* aviary; damage (to merchandise); loss, harm; *elec* fault; breakdown. **a. gruesa,** general average (marine insurance)

averiarse *vr* to be damaged; deteriorate; break down

averiguable *a* examinable, investigable; discoverable

averiguación *f,* inquiry, investigation; discovery

averiguar *vt* to investigate, inquire into; discover, ascertain. **¡averígüelo Vargas!** Beats me!, Search me!

averío *m,* flock of birds

Averno *m, poet* Avernus, Hades

aversión *f,* aversion, repugnance

avestruz *m,* ostrich

avetado *a* veined, mottled, streaked

avezar *vt* to accustom; *vr* grow accustomed (to)

aviación *f,* aviation

aviador *m,* aviator
aviar *vt* to outfit, equip; prepare, make ready; *inf* speed up; caulk (ship). *fig inf* **estar aviado,** to be in a mess
avidez *f,* avidity, greed; longing, desire
ávido *a* avid, greedy
avieso *a* twisted, crooked; ill-natured; sinister
avillanado *a* countrified; gross, vulgar; boorish
avinagrado *a inf* crabbed, sour, testy
avío *m,* preparation, provision; picnic lunch; money advanced (to miners or laborers); *pl inf* equipment, tools. **avíos de pesca,** fishing tackle
avión *m,* airplane; *orn* martin or swift. **a. de bombardeo,** bomber. **a. de caza,** fighter plane. **a. de combate nocturno,** night fighter. **a. de hostigamiento,** interceptor. **a. de reacción,** jet airplane. **a. de transporte,** *aer* transport. **a. en picado,** dive-bomber. **a. taxi,** air taxi. **por a.,** by airmail «**Avión**» "Airmail"
avioneta *f,* light airplane, small airplane
avisado *a* shrewd, sensible. **mal a.,** ill-advised, imprudent
avisar *vt* to inform, acquaint; warn; advise
aviso *m,* notice, announcement; warning; advice; care, caution; attention; shrewdness, prudence. **estar sobre a.,** to be on call; be on the alert
avispa *f,* wasp
avispado *a inf* smart, clever, quick; wide-awake
avispar *vt* to goad, prick; *inf* rouse, incite; *vr* be uneasy, fret
avispero *m,* wasp's nest; swarm of wasps; *fig inf* hornet's nest
avispón *m,* hornet
avistamiento *m,* sighting, spotting (e.g. of a ship)
avistar *vt* to descry, sight, spot; *vr* **avistarse con,** to interview
avituallar *vt* to victual, supply with food
avivar *vt* to enliven; stimulate, encourage; stir (fire); trim (wicks); brighten (colors); inflame; vivify, invigorate; *vi* revive, recover
avizor *m,* watcher, spy. *a* watchful, vigilant
avizorar *vt* to watch, spy upon
avutarda *f,* bustard
axila *f, bot* axil; *anat* axilla, armpit
axioma *m,* axiom
axiomático *a* axiomatic
¡ay! *interj* Alas! Woe is me! *m,* complaint, sigh
aya *f,* governess
ayer *adv* yesterday; a short while ago; in the past. *m,* past
ayo *m,* tutor
ayuda *f,* help, assistance; enema; clyster; watch dog. *m,* **a. de cámara,** valet
ayudador (-ra) *a* helping, assisting. *n* helper
ayudante *m,* assistant; teaching assistant; *mil* adjutant. **a. a cátedra,** *univ* assistant lecturer. **a. de plaza,** post adjutant
ayudar *vt* to assist; help, aid; *vr* make an effort; avail oneself of another's help
ayunador (-ra) *a* fasting. *n* faster; abstainer
ayunar *vi* to fast
ayuno *m,* fast. *a* fasting; ignorant, unaware. **en a.** *or* **en ayunas,** before breakfast, fasting; *inf* ignorant, unaware

ayuntamiento *m,* meeting, assembly; municipal government; town hall; sexual union
azabache *m, min* jet
azada *f, agr* spade; hoe
azadón *m, agr* hoe
azafata *f,* queen's waiting-maid *ant;* flight attendant
azafate *m,* flat basket; small tray
azafrán *m, bot* saffron; crocus
azafranado *a* saffron-colored
azahar *m,* flower of orange, lemon or sweet lime tree
azar *m,* chance, hazard; unexpected misfortune; losing card or throw of dice
azararse *vr* to go wrong, fail (negotiations, etc.); grow nervous; become confused; blush
azaroso *a* unlucky, ill-omened; hazardous
ázimo *a* unleavened (bread)
ázoe *m,* nitrogen
azogar *vt* to silver (mirrors, etc.); slake lime; *vr* suffer from mercury poisoning; *inf* grow uneasy, be agitated
azogue *m, min* mercury, quick-silver; market-place
azolve *m,* silt
azoramiento *m,* alarm, terror; confusion, stupefaction; incitement
azorar *vt* to alarm, terrify; confuse, stun, dumbfound; excite, stimulate; encourage
azotacalles *mf inf* idler, street loafer
azotaina *f, inf* whipping, spanking
azotamiento *m,* flogging, beating, whipping
azotar *vt* to whip, beat, flog; acourge, ravage; knock against or strike repeatedly
azotazo *m,* spank
azote *m,* whip; scourge; lash, blow with a whip; spank, slap; misfortune, disaster. *inf* **azotes y galeras,** monotonous diet
azotea *f,* flat terrace roof
azteca *a* and *mf* Aztec
azozador party whip, whip
azúcar *m,* sugar. **a. blanco** *or* **a. de flor,** white sugar. **a. de pilón,** loaf sugar. **a. moreno,** brown sugar. **a. quebrado,** brown sugar. **a. y canela,** sorrel gray (of horses)
azucarado *a* sugary; sugared, sugar-coated; *inf* honeyed, flattering
azucarar *vt* to coat with sugar; sweeten; *inf* soften, mitigate; *vr* crystallize; go sugary (jam)
azucarera *f,* sugar-basin
azucarero *a* sugar-producing (e.g. province)
azucarillo *m, cul* bar made of white of egg and sugar for sweetening water
azucena *f,* white lily. **a. de agua,** water-lily
azuela *f,* adze
azufrar *vt* to sulphurate
azufre *m,* sulphur
azufroso *a* sulphurous
azul *a* and *m,* blue. **a. celeste,** sky blue, azure. **a. de mar** *or* **a. marino,** navy blue. **a. de ultramar,** ultramarine. **a. turquí,** indigo
azulado *a* bluish, blue
azulear *vi* to look bluish, have a blue tint
azulejo *m,* ornamental glazed tile
azumbre *f,* liquid measure (just over 2 liters)
azuzar *vt* to set on (dogs); irritate, provoke; incite, urge

B

baba *f,* saliva; secretion (of snails, etc.); viscous fluid (of plants). *inf* **caérsele (a uno) la b.,** to ooze satisfaction; be dumbfounded
babador, babero *m,* bib, feeder
babear *vi* to dribble, slaver; *fig inf* slobber over, be sloppy
babel *m,* babel
babélico *a* Babelian, Babel-like confused; unintelligible
Babia, estar en to be daydreaming

babieca *mf inf* stupid person. **Babieca** *f,* the Cid's horse
Babilonia Babylon
babilónico *a* Babylonian
bable *m,* Asturian (language)
babor *m, naut* larboard, port
babosa *f,* slug; young onion
baboso *a* slavering; *fig inf* "sloppy"; *inf* incompetent, useless
babucha *f,* heelless slipper, babouche

babuino *m, zool* baboon

baca *f,* luggage carrier (on roof of bus, etc.)

bacalao *m,* codfish

bacanales *f pl,* Bacchanalia

bacante *f,* Bacchante

bacará *m,* baccarat (card game)

baceta *f,* pool (in card games)

bache *m,* rut (in road); pothole

bacheo *m,* repairing of streets

bachiller *mf* high-school graduate *m, inf* babbler. *f.* **bachillera,** *inf* blue-stocking; garrulous woman

bachillerarse *vr* to graduate as a bachelor

bachillerato *m,* baccalaureate, bachelor's degree

bacía *f,* bowl; barber's circular shaving-dish; barber's trade sign

bacilar *a* bacillary

bacilo *m,* bacillus

bacterial, bacteriano *a* bacterial

bactericida *m,* bactericide

bacteriología *f,* bacteriology

bacteriológico *a* bacteriological

bacteriólogo *m,* bacteriologist

báculo *m,* staff; walking-stick; *fig* support. **b. episcopal,** bishop's crozier

badajo *m,* clapper (of a bell); chatterbox, gossip

badana *f,* cured sheepskin, chamois leather, wash-leather; sweat band; *inf* **zurrar (a uno) la b.,** to take the hide off; insult

badén *m,* channel made by rain, furrow; conduit

badil *m,* fire-shovel

badulaque *m, inf* good-for-nothing

bagaje *m, mil* baggage; beast of burden, transport animal; luggage

bagatela *f,* trifle, oddment, bagatelle

bagazo *m,* oilcake, bagasse

bagual *a WH* untamed, wild; doltish, dull. *m,* untamed horse, wild horse

bahía *f,* bay, harbor

bailable *a* dance (of music). *m, theat* dance number

bailador (-ra) *n* dancer

bailar *vi* to dance; spin round. **b. al son que le toca,** to adapt oneself to circumstances

bailarín *a* dancing. *m,* professional dancer. **b. de cuerda, bailarín de la cuerda floja,** tightrope dancer

bailarina *f,* ballerina

baile *m,* dance; ball; ballet. **b. de máscaras, b. de trajes,** fancy-dress ball. **b. de San Vito,** St. Vitus' dance. **b. ruso,** ballet

bailotear *vi* to jig about; dance

baja *f,* drop, diminution; fall (in price, etc.); *mil* casualty; discharge. *inf* **darse de b.,** to leave an employment

bajada *f,* descent, fall; slope, incline; hollow, depression. **b. de aguas,** roof gutter

bajalato *m,* pashalik

bajamar *f,* low tide

bajamente *adv* basely, abjectly

bajar *vi* to descend; go down; get off; drop; fall, decrease; *vt* lower, take down, bring down; let down; dismount, alight; bend, droop; drop; reduce (price); dip lower (voices); humiliate, humble; **b. a tierra,** to step ashore; **b. la cabeza ante,** to submit to (e.g. a judgment) *vr* alight, dismount; humble oneself

bajel *m, naut* galley, ship

bajeza *f,* base action; meanness; *fig* humble estate, lowliness. **b. de ánimo,** timorousness

bajío *m, naut* shallows, shoal; depression, hollow

bajista *mf* speculator, bear (Stock Exchange)

bajo *a* low; short, not tall; downcast; under; subordinate; pale (of colors); humble (origin); base; coarse, vulgar; cheap (price); low (sounds). *m,* depth; shoal, sand bank; *mus* bass; *pl* petticoats, skirts; horses' hoofs. *adv* beneath, below. *prep* under, beneath. **b. juramento,** upon oath. **bajo relieve,** bas relief. **en voz baja,** in a low voice. **planta baja,** ground floor. **por lo b.,** in a whisper; in secret, on the sly

bajolatino *a* Low Latin

bajón *m, mus* bassoon; bassoon player; *fig inf* downfall

bajonista *mf* bassoon player

bala *f,* bullet, ball; bale. **b. fría,** spent bullet. **b. luminosa,** tracer bullet. **b. perdida,** stray bullet. *inf* **como una b.,** like a shot

balada *f,* ballad, song

baladí *a* worthless, insignificant

baladro *m,* yell, outcry, shout

baladrón *a* braggart

baladronada *f,* bravado, bragging

balagar *m,* straw rick

bálago *m,* straw; soap-ball; straw rick

balance *m,* balance; swinging, oscillation; rolling, rocking (of a ship, etc.); doubt, insecurity, *com* balance; *com* balance sheet

balancear *vi* to swing; oscillate; vacillate, hesitate; *vt* balance; *vr* balance oneself; rock or swing oneself

balanceo *m,* balancing; rocking; swinging; rolling (of a ship, etc.)

balancín *m,* swing-bar; whipple-tree; balance beam; tight-rope dancer's pole; minting-mill; yoke (for carrying pails); *pl naut* lifts

balandra *f, naut* sloop, cutter

balanza *f,* balance; scale; judgment; comparison. **b. de comercio,** balance of trade. **en balanzas,** in doubt or danger, in the balance

balar *vi* to bleat (sheep)

balasto *m, rw* ballast

balaustrada *f,* balustrade

balaustre *m,* baluster

balazo *m,* shot; bullet wound

balbucear *m,* stammering; babbling; lisping; **balbuceos** *fig* beginnings, early stages (e.g. **los b. de la literatura yídica,** the beginnings of Yiddish literature)

balbuciente *a* stammering; babbling; lisping

balbucir *vi irr defective* to stammer; lisp; babble; read hesitantly. See **lucir**

Balcanes, los the Balkans

balcánico *a* Balkan

balcón *m,* balcony

baldaquín *m,* canopy, baldachin

baldar *vt* to cripple; impede, obstruct

balde *m,* bucket

balde (en) *adv* in vain. **de b.,** gratis, free of charge

baldear *vt naut* to wash the decks

baldío *a* untilled; fallow; useless, worthless; vagrant

baldón *m,* insult; dishonor

baldonar *vt* to insult

baldosa *f,* paving stone; tile

baldrufa *f,* top, spinning top

balduque *m,* red tape

Baleares, las Islas the Balearic Islands

baleárico *a* Balearic

balido *m,* bleat, bleating

balística *f,* ballistics

baliza *f, naut* buoy, beacon

balizamiento *m,* marking with beacons, marking with buoys; traffic signs and signals

ballena *f,* whale; whalebone

ballenero *a* whaling. *m,* whaler

ballesta *f,* crossbow; spring (of carriages)

ballestería *f,* archery; crossbowmen

ballestero *m,* archer; crossbowman; crossbow maker

balneario *a* pertaining to public baths; bathing; holiday; spa. *m,* watering place, spa

balompié *m,* football (game)

balón *m,* large ball; football; *chem* balloon; bundle; bale. **b. de ensayo,** *fig* feeler

baloncesto *m, sport* basket ball

balota *f,* ballot

balotaje *m,* balloting; run-off election

balotar *vi* to ballot

balsa *f,* pond; raft

balsadera *f,* ferry

balsámico *a* balmy

bálsamo *m,* balm

balsero *m*, ferryman; rafter (person fleeing a country by raft, rowboat, etc.)

balso *m*, *naut* sling

báltico *a* Baltic. **el Mar Báltico** the Baltic Sea

baluarte *m*, bulwark; bastion; protection, defence

bambalina *f*, fly (theatrical scenery)

bamboleante *a* swaying, swinging; *fig* tottering (e.g. empire)

bambolearse *vr* to sway; swing; totter; be shaky; stagger

bamboleo *m*, rocking; swinging; tottering; staggering; reeling

bambolla *f*, *inf* ostentation, swank

bambú *m*, bamboo

banal *a* banal, commonplace

banana *f*, banana

banasta *f*, big basket

banastero (-ra) *n* basket maker or dealer

banasto *m*, big round basket

banca *f*, bench; card game; stall; *com* banking

bancada *f*, rowing seat

bancal *m*, oblong garden plot; terrace

bancario *a* banking, bank

bancarrota *f*, bankruptcy. **hacer b.**, to go bankrupt

banco *m*, form, bench; rowing seat; settle; seat; *carp* bench; *com* bank; *naut* bar, shoal; school (of fish). **b. azul**, government benches in Spanish Parliament. **b. de arena**, sand-bank. **b. de descuento**, discount bank. **b. de emisión, banco emisor**, bank of issue. **b. de hielo**, iceberg. **b. de nivel**, benchmark

banda *f*, wide ribbon; sash; ribbon, insignia; strip; border; party, group; gang; flock (of birds); zone, belt; side (of ship); *mus* band; cushion (billiards); *her* bar, bend. **b. elástica**, rubber band. *naut* **dar a la b.**, to lie along

bandada *f*, flock (of birds)

bandeja *f*, tray, salver

bandera *f*, banner, flag; colors, standard. **b. de popa**, ensign. **jurar la b.**, (*mil nav*) to take the oath of allegiance

banderilla *f*, banderilla (bullfighting)

banderillear *vt* to put banderillas on bulls

banderillero *m*, man who puts banderillas on bulls

banderín *m*, *dim* small flag; recruiting post

banderizo *a* factious; vehement, excitable

banderola *f*, banderole, pennon; bannerole

bandido (-da) *a* and *n* outlaw, fugitive. *m*, bandit; highwayman; rogue, desperado

bando *m*, proclamation, order; faction, group, party

bandola *f*, *mus* pandora, pandore

bandolerismo *m*, brigandage

bandolero *m*, robber, footpad, brigand

bandolín *m*, mandolin

bandurria *f*, *mus* mandolin

banjo *m*, banjo

banquero *m*, banker

banqueta *f*, three-legged stool; seat; footstool

banquete *m*, banquet, feast

banquetear *vt* and *vi* to banquet

banqueteo *m*, banqueting, feasting

bañado *m*, chamber pot; *WH* marshy land, marsh; **bañados** *pl* marsh

bañador (-ra) *a* bathing. *n* bather. *m*, bathing dress; bath, vat

bañar *vt* to bathe; coat, cover; dip; lave, wash; *fig* bathe (of sunlight, etc.). *vr* take a bath; bathe

bañera *f*, bath attendant; bathtub

bañista *mf* bather; one who takes spa waters

baño *m*, bathing; bath; bathroom; bathtub; bagnio; Turkish prison; covering, coat; *pl* mineral baths, spa. **b. de mar**, sea bath. **b. de María**, double saucepan. **b. de sol**, sunbath. **casa de baños**, public baths. **cuarto de b.**, bathroom

bao *m*, *naut* beam

baptisterio *m*, baptistery; *ecc* font

baquelita *f*, bakelite

baqueta *f*, ramrod; *pl* drumsticks; *mil* gauntlet

bar *m*, bar; café

barahúnda *f*, See **baraúnda**

baraja *f*, pack (of cards); game of cards

barajar *vt* to shuffle (cards); jumble, mix; *vi* quarrel

baranda *f*, handrail, banister; cushion (of billiard table)

barandilla *f*, *dim* railing

baratija *f*, (gen. *pl*) trifle, oddment

baratillo *m*, second-hand article, frippery; second-hand shop or stall; bargain counter

barato *a* cheap; easy. *m*, bargain sale. *adv* cheaply

baratura *f*, cheapness

baraúnda *f*, uproar, confusion

barba *f*, chin; beard; whiskers; fin; barb (of a feather); *m*, actor who plays old men. *f pl*, fibers of plants. **b. bien poblada**, a thick beard. **barbas de ballena,** whalebone. *fig inf* **echar a las barbas**, to throw in a person's face. **en la barba, en las barbas**, to ones face (e.g. **Me lo dijeron en las barbas.** They told me so to my face). **hacer la b.**, to shave; *inf* annoy

barbacoa *f*, *WH* barbecue; trellis (for climbing plants)

barbado *a* bearded. *m*, shoot; sucker; transplanted plant

barbárico *a* barbarian; barbaric

barbaridad *f*, barbarity; blunder; atrocity; outrage; *inf* huge amount. **¡Qué b.!** How awful! You don't say so!

barbarie *f*, barbarism; barbarity, cruelty

barbarismo *m*, barbarism; cruelty; barbarians

bárbaro (-ra) *a* and *n* barbarian. *a* fierce; headstrong; uncivilized. **como un b.**, like crazy (e.g. **estudiar como un b.**, to study like crazy)

barbechar *vt* to plow; leave fallow

barbecho *m*, *agr* fallow; first plowing

barbería *f*, barber shop

barbero *m*, barber

barbihecho *a* fresh-shaved

barbilampiño *a* smooth-faced, beardless, clean-shaven

barbilindo *a* dandified, dappy; *m*, dandy

barbilla *f*, point of the chin; chin. **acariciar la b. (de),** to chuck under the chin

barbiquejo *m*, *naut* bobstay; hat-guard

barbudo *a* heavily bearded

barbulla *f*, *inf* babble, chatter, murmur of voices

barca *f*, small boat, bark; barge. **b. de pasaje,** ferryboat. **b. plantaminas** minelayer

barcada *f*, boat-load; ferry crossing

barcaza *f*, *naut* lighter; barge. **b. de desembarco,** landingcraft

barcelonés (-esa) *a* and *n* of or from Barcelona

barcino *a* ruddy (of animals); fawn and white; *inf* turncoat (of politicians)

barco *m*, boat; ship; hollow, rut. **b. barredero**, trawler. **b. siembraminas**, minelayer

barda *f*, horse armor; thatch; *carp* shingle; (Mexico) cement fence, cement wall

bardal *m*, thatched wall; mud wall

bardar *vt* to thatch

bardo *m*, poet, bard

bario *m*, barium

barítono *m*, baritone

barloventear *vi naut* to tack; ply to windward; *inf* wander about

barlovento *m*, *naut* windward

barnacla *m*, barnacle

barniz *m*, varnish; glaze; smattering, veneer

barnizar *vt* to varnish; glaze

barométrico *a* barometric

barómetro *m*, barometer

barón *m*, baron

baronesa *f*, baroness

baronía *f*, barony

barquero *m*, boatman; bargee; *ent* water-boatman

barquillero *m*, seller of wafers; waffle-iron

barquillo *m*, wafer, cornet

barquín *m*, furnace bellows

barra *f*, bar; ingot; railing (in courtroom); sandbank; fault (in cloth); lever, crossbar; (in cricket) bail; *mus* bar. **b. de jabón de afeitar,** shaving-stick. **a barras derechas,** without deceit

barrabasada f, inf wilfulness, escapade

barraca f, cabin, hut; stall; sideshow. **b. de tiro,** shooting gallery

barracón m, side-show; stall

barragana f, concubine, mistress

barranca, f, **barranco** m, furrow, channel, rut; gorge; difficulty, fix

barrancoso a rutty, uneven

barredor (-ra) n sweeper

barredura f, sweeping; pl sweepings; rubbish

barrena f, borer, gimlet, drill, auger. aer **b. de cola,** tailspin

barrenar vt to drill, bore; blast (in quarries)

barrendero (-ra) n sweeper, scavenger

barrenero m, driller; blaster

barreno m, blast hole; bore, drill; vanity

barreño m, earthenware bowl (for dish washing, etc.)

barrer vt to sweep; fig clear, make a clean sweep

barrera f, barrier; barricade; fig obstacle. **b. de golpe,** automatic gate (at level crossings, etc.). **b. de minas,** minefield

barriada f, district; quarter (of a city)

barrica f, cask; barrel

barricada f, barricade

barriga f, inf belly

barrigón, barrigudo a pot-bellied

barril m, barrel; cask; water-butt

barrilero m, cooper

barrilete m, dim keg; clamp; naut mouse

barrio m, district, quarter; suburb. **barrios bajos,** slums, back streets. **el otro b.,** the other world, Eternity

barrizal m, muddy place; claypit

barro m, mud; clay; earthenware drinking vessel; inf money

barroco a baroque

barroso a muddy; pimpled; mud-colored

barrote m, thick iron bar; stave, bond

barruntar vt to conjecture; suspect

barrunto m, conjecture; indication, sign

bártulos m pl, household goods; fig means, wherewithal

barullo m, inf confusion, disorder; mob

basa f, base; arch pedestal; foundation, basis

basalto m, basalt

basar vt to base, place on a base; fig found, base; vr (with en) rely upon, base oneself on

basca f, (gen. pl) nausea; retching; wave of anger

báscula f, weighing-machine, platform-scale; weighbridge

base f, base; (chem geom mil) base; basis; arch pedestal; mus root. **sin b.,** baseless

básico a basic

Basilea Basel, Basle

basílica f, palace; church, basilica

basilisco m, basilisk; antique cannon

basquear vi to retch; feel squeamish

bastante a sufficient, enough. adv sufficiently; enough; fairly; a good deal; somewhat. **Hace b. calor,** It is quite hot. **Tengo b.,** I have enough. **Tenemos b. tiempo,** We have sufficient time

bastar vi to suffice. **¡Basta!** Enough! No more! Stop! **¡Basta de . . . !** Enough of . . . ! **Basta decir que . . . ,** Suffice it to say that . . .

bastardía f, bastardy, illegitimacy; baseness, meanness

bastardilla f, print italics

bastardo (-da) a bastard; spurious. n bastard

bastear vt sew to baste

bastidor m, embroidery frame; art stretcher (for canvas); theat wing; mech underframe; chassis, carriage; frame (of a window). fig **entre bastidores,** behind the scenes

bastilla f, sew hem; bastille

bastimentar vt to provision; supply

bastimento m, supplies; provisioning

bastión m, bastion

basto m, pack-saddle; ace of clubs; clubs (cards). a rude; tough; fig unpolished, rough

bastón m, cane, walking-stick; rod (of office); truncheon. **b. de junquillo,** Malacca cane. **empuñar el b.,** to take control, take over. **meter el b.,** to mediate

bastonear vt to cane; stir with a stick

basura f, rubbish, refuse; dung; sweepings

basurero m, dustman; dunghill, rubbish dump; kitchen middens; dust-bin

bata f, dressing-gown; smoking-jacket; old-fashioned dress; overall, smock

batacazo m, bump, noise of a fall; pol dark horse

batahola f, inf hurly-burly, hubbub

batalla f, battle; fig struggle, conflict; tournament; art battle-piece. **b. campal,** pitched battle

batallador a fighting, warlike

batallar vi to battle, fight; dispute, argue; hesitate

batallón m, battalion

batanero m, fuller

batata f, sweet potato

batayola f, naut rail

batea f, wooden tray; punt

batería f, (mil elec naut) battery. **b. de cocina,** kitchen utensils. **b. de pilas secas,** dry battery. **b. de teatro,** stage lights. **b. eléctrica,** electric battery

baticola f, crupper

batida f, game drive; attack; met beating

batido a beaten (of metals); shot (of silk); trodden, worn (roads, etc.). m, cul batter; hunting party

batidor m, beater; scout; outrider; hair comb; cul whisk. **b. de oro** (or de plata), gold (or silver) beater

batiente m, jamb (of door, etc.); damper (piano); leaf (of door); place where sea beats against cliffs, etc.

batihoja m, gold beater; metal worker

batimiento m, beating

batín m, smoking-jacket; man's dressing-gown

batintín m, Chinese gong

batir vt to beat, slap; demolish; dismantle, take down (stall, etc.); hammer, flatten; batter; fig beat (of sun, etc.); stir; pound; churn; comb (hair); vanquish, defeat; coin; reconnoiter, beat; throw down or drop; vr fight; swoop (birds of prey). **b. palmas,** to clap, applaud

batista f, cambric, batiste

baturrillo m, hotchpotch (gen. food); inf farrago, medley

batuta f, baton, conductor's wand. **llevar la b.,** inf boss the show, call the music, be in charge, to rule the roost

baúl m, trunk; inf belly. **b. escaparate** or **b. mundo,** wardrobe trunk

bauprés m, naut bowsprit

bausán (-ana) n guy, strawman; puppet; fool, idiot; lazybones

bautismo m, baptism

bautista m, baptizer, baptist. **San Juan B.,** St. John the Baptist

bautisterio m, baptistery

bautizar vt to baptize, christen; inf nickname; inf water (wine); accidentally shower with water

bautizo m, baptism; christening party

bávaro(-ra) a and n Bavarian

baya f, berry

bayadera f, Indian dancing girl

bayeta f, baize; flannel

bayo (-ya) a bay (of horses)

Bayona Bayonne

bayoneta f, bayonet. **b. calada,** fixed bayonet

bayonetazo m, bayonet thrust

baza f, tricks taken (playing cards). fig inf **meter b.,** to stick one's oar in

bazar m, bazaar; shop, store; department store

bazo m, anat spleen. a yellow-brown

bazucar, bazuquear vt to shake or stir (liquids)

bazuqueo m, shaking or stirring of liquids

be *f,* letter B. *m,* baa
beata *f,* devout woman; *inf* pious hypocrite, prude; Sister of Mercy; over-religious woman
beatería *f,* sanctimoniousness; bigotry
beatificación *f,* beatification
beatificar *vt* to make happy; sanctify; beatify
beatífico *a* beatific
beatitud *f,* blessedness, beatitude; happiness
beato (-ta) *a* happy; blessed, beatified; devout; prudish. *n* devout person; over-pious person
bebé *m,* baby
bebedero *a* drinkable. *m,* drinking trough or place
bebedizo *a* drinkable. *m,* draught of medicine; love-potion; poisonous drink
bebedor (-ra) *a* drinkable. *n* drinker; toper
beber *vt* to drink; absorb; *vi* toast, drink to the health (of); tipple. *m,* drinking; drink
bebida *f,* drink; beverage; alcoholic liquor
beca *f,* academic scarf or sash; scholarship, exhibition
becado, becario *m,* exhibitioner, scholarship holder
becerra *f,* calf; *bot* snapdragon
becerro *m,* bullock; bull calf; calf-skin. **b. marino,** *zool* seal
Beda el Venerable the Venerable Bede
bedel *m,* beadle; servitor, university porter
beduino (-na) *a* and *n* Bedouin. *m,* savage, bloodthirsty man
befar *vt* to mock, ridicule
befo *a* thick-lipped; knock-kneed. *m,* animal's lip
begonia *f, bot* begonia
bejín *m, bot* puff-ball; spoilt child
bejuco *m,* rattan
beldad *f,* beauty; belle
beldar *vt agr* to winnow
Belén Bethlehem
belén *m,* nativity, manager; *inf* bedlam; *inf* gossip
belfo *a* thick-lipped
belga *a* and *mf* Belgian
Bélgica Belgium
bélgico *a* Belgian
Belgrado Belgrade
Belice Belize
belicista *adj* war, militaristic; *mf* warmonger
bélico *a* warlike, military
belicosidad *f,* bellicosity
belicoso *a* bellicose, aggressive; warlike
beligerancia *f,* belligerency
beligerante *a* and *mf* belligerent
belitre *a inf* knavish, cunning
bellaco (-ca) *a* artful, cunning. *n* knave
belladona *f,* belladonna
bellaquería *f,* roguery, knavery, cunning
bellasombra *f,* umbra tree
belleza *f,* beauty, loveliness, fairness
bello *a* beautiful
bellota *f,* acorn; carnation bud; ornamental button, knob
bellote *m,* round-headed nail
bemol *a* and *m, mus* flat. *inf* **tener bemoles,** to be thorny, be difficult
bencina *f,* benzine; petrol
bendecir *vt irr* to praise, extol; bless; dedicate, consecrate. See **decir**
bendición *f,* benediction; blessing; consecration; *pl* marriage ceremony. **b. de la mesa,** grace before meals
bendito *a* holy, blessed; fortunate; simple. **ser un b.,** to be a simpleton; be a good soul. **¡Benditos los ojos que te ven!** It's so nice to see you!
benedictino (-na) *a* and *n* Benedictine. *m,* Benedictine liqueur
beneficencia *f,* beneficence; charitable institutions
beneficiación *f,* benefaction
beneficiado (-da) *n* beneficiary. *m,* incumbent of a benefice
beneficiador (-ra) *n* benefactor
beneficiar *vt* to benefit; improve; cultivate (land); ex-

ploit (mine); purchase (directorship, etc.); sell at a loss (bonds, etc.)
beneficiario (-ia) *n* beneficiary
beneficiencia *f,* beneficence, charity
beneficio *m,* benefit; profit; cultivation (land, etc.); working (mine); *ecc* benefice; *theat* benefit
beneficioso *a* beneficial; useful
benéfico *a* beneficent; kind, helpful; charitable
benemérito *a* benemeritus, worthy, meritorious
beneplácito *m,* approbation; consent
benevolencia *f,* benevolence, goodwill
benévolo *a* benevolent, kind
Bengala Bengal
bengalí *a* and *mf* Bengali
benignidad *f,* kindness; mildness (of the weather, etc.)
benigno *a* kind; benign; mild; balmy
beodo (-da) *a* drunk, intoxicated. *n* drunkard
Berbería Barbary
bereber *a* and *mf* Berber
berenjena *f,* eggplant
bergante *m,* rascal, rogue
bergantín *m, naut* brig, brigantine
berilo *m,* beryl
Berlín Berlin
berlinés (-esa) *a* and *n* of or from Berlin
bermejear *vi* to be or look reddish
bermejo *a* reddish; red; redgold; carroty (of hair)
bermellón *m,* vermilion
Berna Berne
bernardina *f,* lie; boast; gibberish
bernardo (-da) *a* and *n ecc* Bernardine (Order of St. Bernard)
berquelio *m,* berkelium
berrear *vi* to low, bellow; yell, squall; shriek; *vr* reveal, confess
berrido *m,* lowing, bellowing; *inf* yell
berrinche *m, inf* tantrum, fit, fit of sulks
berro *m,* watercress
berroqueña *f,* granite
berza *f,* cabbage
besamanos *m,* ceremony of kissing royal hand, levee; kissing fingers (in salute)
besar *vt* to kiss; *inf* brush against, touch (of things); *vr* kiss one another; *inf* bang into, knock against one another
beso *m,* kiss; knock, collision
bestia *f,* quadruped (especially horses or mules); beast. *mf inf* nasty piece of work. **b. de carga,** beast of burden. **como una b.,** like a dog (e.g. **Trabajo como una b.** I work like a dog)
bestial *a* bestial; brutal; beastly
bestialidad *f,* brutality; bestiality; beastliness
bestialismo *m,* bestiality (sexual orientation)
besuquear *vt inf* to cover with kisses; *vr inf* spoon, make love
besuqueo *m, inf* kissing and spooning
bético *a* Andalusian
betún *m,* bitumen; shoe blacking; kind of cement. **b. de Judea** *or* **b. judaico,** asphalt
bey *m,* bey
bezo *m,* blubber lip; proud flesh (of a wound)
bezudo *a* thick-lipped
biberón *m,* feeding bottle
Biblia *f,* Bible
bíblico *a* biblical
bibliófilo *m,* bibliophile
bibliografía *f,* bibliography
bibliográfico *a* bibliographical
biblioteca *f,* library; book series. **b. por subscripción,** circulating library
bibliotecario (-ia) *n* librarian
bibliotecnia, bibliotecología, biblioteconomía *f,* library science
bicarbonato *m,* bicarbonate
bíceps *m,* biceps
bicho *m,* any small animal or reptile; quadruped; fight-

ing bull; scarecrow, sight. **b. viviente,** *inf* living soul. **mal b.,** rogue

bicicleta *f,* bicycle, bike. **ir** (*or* **andar** *or* **montar**) **en b.,** to bicycle, bike, go by bicycle, go by bike

bicoca *f, inf* trifle, bagatelle

bicolor *a* bicolored

bidé *m,* bidet

biela *f,* axle-tree; connecting-rod; big-end

bielda *f,* pitchfork; *agr* winnowing

bien *m,* ideal goodness, perfection; benefit, advantage; welfare; *pl* property, wealth. *adv* well; willingly; happily; perfectly; easily; enough, sufficient; all right! very well! **b. que,** although. **b. de equipo,** capital good. **bienes muebles,** movables, goods and chattels. **bienes raíces,** real estate. **el B. y el Mal,** Good and Evil. **¡Está b.!** All right! **no b.,** scarcely, as soon as. **si b.,** although, even if. **¿Y b.?** And so what? Well, then; What next?

bienal *a* biennial

bienamado *a* dearly beloved

bienandante *a* prosperous; happy

bienandanza *f,* happiness, welfare; prosperity

bienaventurado *a* blessed, holy; happy; *inf* over-simple, innocent, foolish

bienaventuranza *f,* blessedness

bienestar *m,* wellbeing; ease; comfort

bienhablado *a* well-spoken; civil, polite

bienhadado *a* fortunate, happy

bienhechor (-ra) *a* kind, helpful. *n* benefactor

bienintencionado *a* well-meaning

bienio *m,* biennium, space of two years, period of two years

bienquisto *a* respected; generally esteemed

bienvenida *f,* safe or happy arrival; welcome. **dar la b.,** to welcome

bienvivir *vi* to live comfortably; live decently or uprightly

bies *m,* bias, cross; slant

biftec *m,* beefsteak

bifurcación *f,* bifurcation; fork, branch, junction

bifurcarse *vr* to fork, branch

bigamia *f,* bigamy

bígamo (-ma) *a* bigamous. *n* bigamist

bigornia *f,* anvil

bigote *m,* moustache; *pl* whiskers

bigotudo *a* moustached, whiskered

bikini *m,* bikini

bilateral *a* bilateral

bilbaíno *a* pertaining to or native of Bilbao

bilingüe *a* bilingual

bilioso *a* bilious

bilis *f,* bile

billar *m,* billiards; billiard table

billete *m,* note, short letter; ticket; banknote. **b. circular,** excursion ticket. **b. de abono,** season ticket. **b. de andén,** platform ticket. **b. de banco,** banknote. **b. de favor,** free ticket. **b. de ida y vuelta,** round trip ticket. **b. entero,** full fare. **b. kilométrico,** tourist ticket. **b. sencillo,** one-way. **medio b.,** half-fare

billón *m,* billion

bimestral *a* bimonthly

bimestre *a* bimonthly. *m,* two months' duration; money paid or received at two-monthly intervals

bimotor *a* two-motor. *m,* twin-engined aircraft

binario *a* binary

binóculo *m,* opera glasses

binomio *a* and *m,* binomial

biofísica *f,* biophysics

biografía *f,* biography

biográfico *a* biographical

biógrafo (-fa) *n* biographer; (Chile) movie theater (e.g. **¡Vamos al biógrafo!** Let's go to the movies!)

biología *f,* biology

biológico *a* biological

biólogo *m,* biologist

biombo *m,* screen

bioquímica *f,* biochemistry

bioquímico *m,* biochemist

bipartido *a* bipartite

bípedo *a* and *m,* biped

biplano *m,* biplane

biplaza *a* two-seater

birla *f,* skittle

birlar *vt* to bowl from where the bowl stopped; *inf* knock down; snatch away; *inf* rob

birlocha *f,* child's kite

birlocho *m,* barouche

Birmania Burma

birmano (-na) *a* and *n* Burmese

birreta *f,* biretta

birrete *m,* biretta; university cap; cap

bis *adv* twice; repeat; encore. *a* duplicate; **B** (in addresses, e.g., **Calle de Alcalá 18bis,** 18b Alcalá St.)

bisabuela *f,* great-grandmother

bisabuelo *m,* great-grandfather

bisagra *f,* hinge; shoemaker's polisher

bisbís *m,* game of chance

bisbisar *vt inf* to mutter; whisper

bisbiseo *m, inf* muttering; murmuring; whispering

bisecar *vt* to bisect

bisección *f, geom* bisection

bisectriz *f,* bisector

bisel *m,* bevel, chamfer

bisiesto *a* leap and *m,* leap (year)

bisílabo *a* two-syllabled

bismuto *m,* bismuth

bisnieto (-ta) *n* great-grandchild

bisonte *m,* bison

bisoño (-ña) *a* inexperienced, raw. *n* recruit; *inf* greenhorn

bistec *m,* beef steak

bisturí *m,* surgical knife

bisunto *a* grubby, greasy

bisutería *f,* imitation jewelry

bituminoso *a* bituminous

bivalvo *a* bivalve

Bizancio Byzantium

bizantinismo *m,* Byzantinism

bizantino *a* Byzantine

bizarría *f,* handsomeness; dash; verve; gallantry, courage; magnificence; liberality; whim, caprice

bizarro *a* handsome; dashing; gallant, courageous; liberal; splendid, magnificent

bizcaitarrismo *m,* doctrine of Basque autonomy; Basque autonomy movement

bizco *a* squint-eyed, cross-eyed

bizcocho *m,* biscuit; spongecake; bisque

bizma *f,* poultice. **poner bizmas,** to poultice

biznieto *n* See **bisnieto**

blanca *f,* old Spanish coin; *inf* penny; *mus* minim. **sin b.,** penniless

blanco *a* white; fair-skinned; blank, vacant; *inf* cowardly. *m,* target; blank left in writing; white person; interval. **b. de España,** whiting. **b. de la uña,** half-moon of the nail. **dar en el b.,** to hit the mark. **en b.,** blank, unused; *inf* in vain; uncomprehendingly; (of nights) sleepless

blancor, *m.* **blancura** *f,* whiteness; fairness (of skin)

blandear *vt* to moderate, soothe; brandish; *vi fig* give way, yield

blandir *vt* to brandish, wield, flourish

blando *a* soft; mild (weather); delicate; kind; peaceable; delicate, effeminate; *inf* cowardly

blandón *m,* wax taper

blandura *f,* softness; poultice; blandishment, compliment; mildness (of weather); gentleness, affability; luxury

blanquear *vt* to bleach; whitewash; whiten; *vi* appear white; show white

blanquecino *a* whitish

blanqueo *m,* whitening; whitewashing; bleaching

blanquizal *m,* pipe-clay

blasfemador (-ra) *a* blaspheming. *n* blasphemer
blasfemar *vi* to blaspheme; curse, swear
blasfemia *f,* blasphemy; insult
blasfemo (-ma) *n* blasphemer. *a* blasphemous
blasón *m,* heraldry; escutcheon; glory, honor. **una familia con antiguos blasones,** a family of ancient lineage
blasonar *vt* to blazon; *vi* boast, brag, blazon abroad
bledo *m,* blade, leaf. **no importar un b.,** not to matter a straw
blenda *f, min* blende
blindado *a nav* armored, ironclad
blindaje *m, nav* armor-plating; *mil* blindage
blindar *vt* to plate with armor, to case with steel
blocao *m, mil* blockhouse
blonda *f,* blonde (of lace)
blondo *a* fair, blond, flaxen-haired
bloque *m,* block, slab
bloquear *vt* to blockade; besiege
bloqueo *m,* blockade; siege; blocking; freezing (of assets). **violar el b.,** to run the blockade
blusa *f,* blouse
boa *f,* boa, large snake. *m,* boa (fur)
boato *m,* outward show, ostentation
bobería *f,* foolishness, stupidity
bóbilis, bóbilis (de) *adv inf* free of charge; without effort
bobina *f,* bobbin, spool, reel; *elec* coil; spool (of fishing rod)
bobo (-ba) *a* stupid, idiotic; simple, innocent. *n* fool. *m,* clown, jester
boca *f,* mouth; pincers (of crustaceans); entrance or exit; mouth (of a river), gulf, inlet; orifice, opening; muzzle (of guns); cutting edge (of tools); taste (of wine, etc.). **b. abajo,** face down, prone. **b. arriba,** on one's back, face up, supine. **b. del estómago,** pit of the stomach. **b. rasgada,** large mouth. **a b.,** verbally. **a b. de jarro,** point-blank. **a pedir de b.,** just as one would wish. **de b.,** by word of mouth. *inf* **sin decir esta b. es mía,** without a word, in silence
bocacalle *f,* entrance (to a street); street junction
Bocacio Boccaccio
bocadillo *m,* narrow ribbon; sandwich
bocado *m,* mouthful. **b. de reyes,** delicacy, exquisite dish (of food); snack; bite; (horse's) bit; bridle; *pl* preserved fruit cut up
bocamanga *f,* wrist (of sleeve)
bocanada *f,* mouthful (of liquid); cloud (of smoke). **b. de aire,** gust of wind
boceto *m,* sketch; outline; rough-cast model
bocha *f, sport* bowl; *pl* bowls
bochorno *m,* sultry weather; heat, stuffiness; blush, hot flush; shame
bochornoso *a* sultry; shameful
bocina *f,* trumpet; megaphone; foghorn; hooter; *aut* horn; horn (of gramophone); *ast* Ursa Minor
bocio *m, med* goiter
bocoy *m,* hogshead; large cask
boda *f,* wedding, marriage. **bodas de oro,** fiftieth (golden) anniversary. **bodas de plata,** silver wedding anniversary
bodega *f,* wine-cellar; storeroom; stockroom; granary; *WH* grocery store; *naut* hold (of ship)
bodegón *m,* eating-house; tavern; *art* still-life; genre picture
bóer *a* and *mf* Boer
bofes *m pl,* lungs, lights. *inf* **echar los b.,** to work oneself to death
bofetada *f,* **bofetón** *m,* blow, slap; box on the ear
boga *f,* rowing; fashion, vogue; *mech* bogie. *mf* oarsman, rower. **estar en b.,** to be fashionable
bogador (-ra) *n* rower, oarsman
bogar *vi* to row
bogavante *m,* lobster
bogotano (-na) *a* and *n* of or from Bogotá
bohemio (-ia) *a* and *n* gipsy; bohemian; Bohemian. *m,* archer's short cloak

boicotear *vt* to boycott
boicot, boicoteo *m,* boycott
boina *f,* Basque cap; beret
boj *m,* box tree; boxwood, box oak; shoemaker's tool
bola *f,* globe; ball; *sport* bowl; *arch* balloon; *inf* trick, lie; (Cuba) rumor. **b. de nieves,** snowball. *inf* **dejar rodar la b.,** to let things slide
bolardo *m,* bollard
bolchevique *a* and *mf* bolshevist
bolchevismo *m,* Bolshevism
bolchevista *mf* bolshevist
bolea *f,* (tennis) volley; throw
bolera *f,* bowling alley
bolero *m,* bolero; dancer; *inf* top hat
boleta *f,* admission ticket; billet ticket; warrant; voucher; summons; ticket, traffic ticket
boletín *m,* bulletin; admission ticket; pay warrant; *com* price list; learned periodical. **b. de noticias,** news bulletin. **b. meteorológico,** weather report
boliche *m,* jack (in bowls); cup-and-ball toy; small oven (for charcoal); dragnet. **juego de b.,** bowls
bólido *m, ast* bolide, meteor
bolillo *m,* bobbin (lace making)
bolina *f, naut* bowline; *naut* sounder; *inf* uproar, tumult
bolita *f,* pellet
boliviano(-na) *a* and *n* Bolivian. *m,* silver coin
bollo *m,* bread roll; bun; bulge, bruise (in metal); *med* lump
bollón *m,* round-headed or brass-headed nail; *bot* bud (especially vines)
bolo *m,* skittle, ninepin; pillow (for lace making); Cuban coin; *med* large pill; *fig inf* blockhead; *pl* skittles (game of)
boloñés (-esa) *a* and *n* Bolognese
bolsa *f,* purse; bag; footmuff; fold, pucker; pouch; exchange, stock exchange, capital, money; prize money; *med* sac; *min* pocket. **b. de estudio,** scholarship grant. **b. de trabajo,** labor exchange. **b. de valores,** stock exchange. **bajar** (*or* **subir**) **la b.,** to fall (or rise) (of stock exchange quotations). **jugar a la b.,** to speculate on the stock exchange
bolsillo *m,* pocket; purse; money
bolsista *mf* stock-broker; speculator (on the stock exchange)
bomba *f, mech* pump; pumping engine; bomb; *mil* shell; lamp globe; *inf* improvised verses; *inf* drinking bout. **¡B.!** Listen! Here goes! **b. de incendios,** fire-engine. **b. marina,** waterspout. **b. de mecha atrasada,** time bomb. **b. volante,** flying-bomb. **a prueba de b.,** bombproof. **arrojar bombas,** to bomb. *inf* **caer como una b.,** to be a bombshell
bombachos *a* baggy, loose-fitting; *m pl,* plus fours
bombardear *vt* to bombard; bomb; shell
bombardeo *m,* bombardment, bombing; shelling
bombardero *m,* gunner, bombardier; *aer* bomber. **b. pesado,** *aer* heavy bomber. **Servicio de b.,** Bomber Command
bombástico *a* bombastic, high sounding
bombazo *m,* bombshell; bomb crater; noise of an exploding bomb
bombear *vt* to pump; bombard, shell; praise
bombero *m,* worker of a pressure pump; fireman; mortar, howitzer
bombilla *f, naut* lantern; (*elec phys*) bulb; small pump; straw for drinking maté *WH*
bombillo *m,* w.c. siphon; handpump
bombo *m,* big drum or player of it; *naut* barge, ferry; ballot box; exaggerated praise
bombón *m,* bonbon, sweet
bombonera *f,* box for toffee, etc.
Bona Bonn
bonachón *a inf* genial, good-natured
bonaerense *a* and *mf* of or from the Province of Buenos Aires
Bonaira Bonaire
bonancible *a* calm (of weather, sea)

bonanza *f,* fair weather; prosperity

bondad *f,* goodness; kindness, helpfulness. **Tenga la b. de . . . ,** Be good enough to . . . , Please . . .

bondadoso *a* good, kind

bonete *m,* academic cap; *zool* reticulum (ruminants); *ecc* biretta. **gran b.,** important person. *inf* **a tente b.,** insistently

bonetero (-ra) *n* seller or maker of caps and birettas

bonificación *f,* bonus; allowance, discount

bonísimo, *a sup* **bueno** extremely good

bonito *a* pretty; graceful; (ironical) fine. *m, icht* striped tunny

bono *m,* voucher; *com* bond, certificate. **b. postal,** postal money order. **bono del gobierno,** government bond

boñiga *f,* cow-dung, animal manure

boqueada *f,* gasp, opening of the mouth. **dar las boqueadas, estar en las últimas boqueadas,** to be at the last gasp

boquear *vi* to gasp; be dying; *inf* be at last gasp (of things); *vt* say, utter

boquera *f,* sluice (in irrigation canal)

boquerón *m,* large opening; *icht* anchovy (fish); whitebait

boquete *m,* narrow entrance, aperture; gap, breach; hole

boquiabierto *a* open-mouthed; amazed

boquiancho *a* wide-mouthed

boquiasombrado *a* gaping

boquilla *f, dim* small mouth; mouthpiece (of wind instruments, etc.); cigar- or cigarette-holder; gas-burner; nozzle; tip (of cigarettes)

boquirroto *a inf* loquacious, indiscreet

borbollar *vi* to bubble, foam, froth

borbollón, borbotón *m,* gushing, bubbling, welling up. **a borbollones,** in a torrent; hastily, impetuously

borbónico *a* Bourbon

borbotar *vi* to gush out, well up

borceguí *m,* buskin, boot

borda *f,* hut, cabin; *naut* gunwale

bordado *m,* embroidery

bordador (-ra) *n* embroiderer

bordar *vt* to embroider; *fig* perform perfectly

borde *m,* edge; fringe; verge; rim; mount (of a picture); brim (of a hat); side (of ship); *a* wild (of plants); illegitimate. **estar lleno hasta los bordes,** to be full to the brim

bordear *vt* to border, trim with a bordear; line (a street, e.g. **Diez mil personas bordearon las calles durante el desfile,** Ten thousand people lined the streets during the parade)

bordelés (-esa) *a* and *n* of or from Bordeaux

bordillo *m,* curbstone, curb.

bordo *m,* side (of ships); border, edge. **a b.,** on board

bordón *m,* pilgrim's staff; monotonous repetition; refrain; *mus* bass string; *fig* guide, stay

borgoña *m,* Burgundy wine

borgoñón (-ona) *a* and *n* Burgundian

bórico *a* boric

borla *f,* tassel; puff (for powder). *fig* **tomar la b.,** to take one's doctorate, graduate

borne *m,* tip (of lance); *elec* terminal

bornear *vt* to bend, twist; *arch* hoist into position; *vr* warp (wood)

borra *f,* yearling ewe; thickest wool; wad-stuffing; lees, sediment; fluff, dust; *inf* trash. **b. de algodón,** cotton-waste

borrachera *f,* drunkenness; orgy, carousal; *inf* blunder

borrachín (-ina) *n* tippler, toper

borrachito *a* high (on liquor), tipsy

borracho (de) *a* drunk (on), intoxicated (with); *inf* blind (with rage, etc.). *n* tippler, drunkard

borrador *m,* rough draft. **en borrador,** in the works (e.g. **Tiene dos ensayos en borrador,** She has two essays in the works). **estar en borrador,** to be in the works

borradura *f,* erasure

borrajear *vt* to scribble

borrar *vt* to erase; cross out; blot out; *fig* obliterate

borrasca *f,* storm, tempest; peril, danger; *inf* orgy

borrascosidad *f,* storminess

borrascoso *a* stormy; disordered, turbulent

borrego (-ga) *n* lamb; *inf* nincompoop, simpleton; *m pl,* fleecy clouds; white horses (waves)

borrico (-ca) *n* donkey; fool. *m, carp* sawing-horse

borrón *m,* blot; rough draft; defect; *fig* stigma

borroso *a* blurred, indistinct; full of dregs, muddy

boscaje *m,* grove, group of trees, thicket

Bósforo, el the Bosporus

bosque *m,* wood, forest

bosquejar *vt art* to sketch; sketch out, draft; model in rough (sculpture); outline

bosquejo *m,* outline, sketch; rough plan or idea; unfinished work. **en bosquejo,** grosso modo

bostar *m,* ox barn

bostezar *vi* to yawn

bostezo *m,* yawning; yawn

bota *f,* small wineskin; barrel, butt; boot. **b. de montar,** riding boot. **botas de campaña,** top-boots. **botas de vadear,** waders

botada, botadura *f,* launching (of a ship)

botador *m,* thrower; boating-pole; *carp* nail-puller

botafuego *m, mil* linstock; *inf* quick-tempered, irascible person

botalón *m, naut* boom. **b. de foque,** jib-boom

botánica *f,* botany

botánico (-ca) *a* botanical. *n* botanist

botar *vt* to fling; launch (boat); *naut* shift the helm; *vi* jump; bounce, rebound; rear, prance (horses)

botarate *m, inf* madcap, devil-may-care

botarel, botarete *m, arch* abutment, buttress, flying buttress

botarga *f,* motley; harlequin

bote *m,* thrust (with lance, etc.); rearing (of horse); rebound; *aer* bump; open boat; small bottle, jar. **b. salvavidas,** lifeboat. *inf* **de b. en b.,** chockfull

botella *f,* bottle; bottleful; flask

botica *f,* chemist's shop; medicines, remedies; physic; store, shop; medicine chest

boticario *m,* apothecary, chemist

botija *f,* earthen jug; *slang* chunky person

botijo *m,* earthenware jar with spout and handle

botillería *f,* ice-cream bar

botín *m,* gaiter; buskin; booty

botiquín *m,* first-aid kit; medicine chest

botón *m,* bud; button; knob, handle; switch (electric); press button (bell); *bot* center; button (on a foil); *mech* stud

botonero (-ra) *n* button maker or seller

bóveda *f, arch* vault, arch; crypt; cavern. **b. celeste,** sky

bovino *a* bovine

boxeador *m,* boxer

boxear *vi sport* to box

boxeo *m, sport* boxing

boya *f, naut* buoy; float

boyante *a* floating; light, buoyant; prosperous

boyar *vi naut* to float

boyera *f,* ox-stall

boyero *m,* cowherd

boza *f,* painter (of a boat)

bozal *m,* muzzle; nosebag; harness bells. *mf inf* greenhorn; *a* wild, untamed (horses)

bozo *m,* down which precedes beard; muzzle; headstall; lips, snout

bracero *m,* one who offers his arm (to a lady); day laborer; strong man. **de b.,** arm-in-arm

bracete *m,* small arm. **de b.,** arm-in-arm

bracmán *m,* Brahmin

braga *f,* (gen. *pl*) breeches; knickerbockers; hoist or pulley rope

bragazas *m, inf* weak-willed, fellow, soft specimen

braguero *m, med* truss

bragueta *f,* fly (of breeches)

brahmanismo *m,* Brahmanism

bramante *a* roaring. *m*, twine, pack-thread

bramar *vi* to roar; rage; *fig* howl (of the wind, etc.)

bramido *m*, bellowing; roaring; yell of rage; *fig* howling (wind, sea, etc.)

brancada *f*, drag net

branquia *f*, (gen. *pl*) *icht* gill

branquial *a* branchiate

braquicefalia *f*, brachycephaly

braquiotomía *f*, *surg* brachiotomy, amputation of the arms

brasa *f*, live coal. **estar como en brasas**, to be like a cat on hot bricks

brasero *m*, brazier

Brasil Brazil

brasileño (-ña) *a* and *n* Brazilian

bravata *f*, bravado; threat

braveza *f*, ferocity, savageness; valor; violence, fury (of elements)

bravío *a* savage, untamed; wild (plants); uncultured

bravo *a* valiant; surly, rude; independent, strong-minded, good, excellent; savage (animals); stormy (sea); rough, rugged; violent, angry; *inf* sumptuous, magnificent.

bravura *f*, ferocity (animals); courage (persons); boastful threat

braza *f*, *naut* fathom; stroke (in swimming)

brazado *m*, armful

brazal *m*, armlet, brassard

brazalete *m*, bracelet; brassard

brazo *m*, arm; upper arm; front paw; *mech* arm; branch (of chandelier, etc.); bough; arm (of chair); power, courage; *pl* protectors; workmen, hands. **b. de mar,** firth, arm of the sea. **a b. partido,** in unarmed fight, man to man. **con los brazos abiertos,** welcomingly; willingly, gladly. **dar los brazos (a),** to embrace. *inf* **hecho un b. de mar,** dressed up to the nines

brea *f*, pitch, tar; sacking, canvas

brebaje *m*, beverage; unpleasant drink; *naut* draught (of beer, grog, etc.)

brecha *f*, *mil* breach; opening; *fig* impression (on mind). **morir en la b.,** to fight to the last ditch; die in harness

brécol *m*, *bot* broccoli

brega *f*, fight; quarrel; disappointment, trick. **andar a la b.,** to work hard. **dar b.,** to play a trick

bregar *vi* to fight; work hard; *fig* struggle; **bregarse con,** to tackle (a problem)

Brema Bremen

breña *f*, rough ground, bramble patch

breñal *m*, scrub, brushwood

breñoso *a* rugged, rocky

Bretaña Brittany

brete *m*, fetters, shackles; *fig* fix, squeeze, tight spot, tight squeeze (e.g. **Estoy en un brete.** I'm in a tight spot)

bretón (-ona) *a* and *n* Breton. *m*, Breton (language)

breva *f*, early fig; early acorn; *fig* advantage, "plum"; *inf* peach (girl); *inf* windfall, piece of luck; Havana cigar

breve *a* brief; concise. *m*, papal brief. *f*, *mus* breve. **en b.,** shortly, concisely; in a short while, soon

brevedad *f*, brevity

breviario *m*, breviary

brezal *m*, heath, moor

brezo *m*, *bot* heath

bribón (-ona) *n* rogue, ruffian. *a* knavish, dishonest; lazy

bribonada *f*, knavery, mischievous trick

bribonear *vi* to idle; play tricks, be a rogue

bribonería *f*, rascality, vagrant life

brida *f*, bridle

brigada *f*, *mil* brigade; *naut* division of fleet; beasts of burden. **brigada millonaria,** (Castroist Cuba) team of thirty sugarcane cutters who cut a million or more arrobas in one harvest

brigadier *m*, brigadier-general

brillante *a* sparkling, brilliant; *fig* outstanding. *m*, diamond

brillantez *f*, brightness, luster; fame; *fig* brilliance

brillantina *f*, brilliantine

brillar *vi* to shine, sparkle, gleam, glisten; *fig* be brilliant or outstanding

brillo *m*, brilliancy, brightness, shine; fame, glory; distinction, brilliance, splendour

brincar *vi* to spring, leap, skip, frisk; *fig inf* skip, omit; *inf* grow angry; *vt* jump a child up and down

brinco *m*, leap, spring; skip, frolicking

brindar *vi* to invite, provoke (of things); (*with prep a or por*) drink the health of, toast; *vt* and *vi* give, present; offer; *vr* offer one's services

brindis *m*, toast (drink)

brío *m*, vigor; spirit, courage; gusto, verve

brioso *a* vigorous, enterprising; spirited, courageous; dashing, lively

briqueta *f*, briquette

brisa *f*, breeze; grape pressings

británico *a* British

brizna *f*, shred, paring; blade (grass); filament, fiber; string (of bean-pod, etc.); splinter, chip

broca *f*, reel; tack (shoemaker's); *mech* drill, bit

brocado *m*, brocade. *a* brocade or embroidered like brocade

brocal *m*, puteal (of a well); mouthpiece (of wineskin); metal ring (of sword-sheath)

brocamantón *m*, large jeweled brooch

brocatel *m*, imitation brocade

brocha *f*, brush. **b. de afeitar,** shaving brush. **de b. gorda,** crudely painted. **pintor de b. gorda,** decorator

brochada *f*, stroke (of the brush)

brochado *a* brocaded, embossed

brochadura *f*, fastening, set of hooks and eyes

broche *m*, clasp, fastening; brooch; hooks and eyes

brochón *m*, whitewash brush

broma *f*, merriment; joke, jest; ship-worm. **b. literaria,** literary hoax

bromear(se) *vi* and *vr* to joke, make fun

bromista *a* joking, jesting; mischievous. *mf* genial person; prankster, tease

bromo *m*, bromine

bromuro *m*, bromide

bronca *f*, *inf* shindy

bronce *m*, bronze; brass; *poet* gun, bell, trumpet; bronze statue; sunburn

bronceado *a* bronzed; sunburnt. *m*, sunburn

broncear *vt* to bronze; sunburn

bronco *a* rough, coarse; brittle; (of metals); harsh (voice, musical instruments); rigid, stiff; surly

bronconeumonía *f*, bronchopneumonia

bronquial *a* bronchial

bronquio *m*, (gen. *pl*) bronchi

bronquitis *f*, bronchitis

broquel *m*, shield; *fig* protection

broquelero *m*, shield maker; quarrelsome man

broqueta *f*, skewer

brotadura *f*, budding

brotar *vi* to germinate, sprout; gush forth (water); issue forth, burst out; *fig* appear (of rash); *fig* begin to appear; *vt* to bring forth; produce (of earth)

brote *m*, bud, sprout; *fig* germ, genesis; iota, jot, atom

broza *f*, garden rubbish; debris; thicket

bruces (a or de) *adv* face downwards. **caer de b.,** to fall flat. Also with other verbs: *dar, echarse,* etc.

bruja *f*, witch; owl; *inf* hag

Brujas Bruges

brujear *vi* to practise witchcraft

brujería *f*, witchcraft

brujo *m*, magician, wizard

brújula *f*, magnetic needle; compass; mariner's compass. **b. de bolsillo,** pocket compass. **b. giroscópica,** gyrocompass

bruma *f*, haze; sea-mist

brumoso *a* misty, hazy

bruno *a* dark brown

bruñido *m*, polishing; burnish

bruñidor (-ra) *a* polishing. *n* burnisher. *m*, polisher (instrument)

bruñir *vt* to polish, burnish; *inf* apply make up

brusco *a* brusque, rude; blunt; sudden, unexpected; sharp (of bends)

Bruselas Brussels

bruselense *a* and *mf* of or from Brussels

brusquedad *f*, brusquerie, rudeness; bluntness; suddenness, unexpectedness; sharpness (of a bend)

brutal *a* brutal

brutalidad *f*, brutality; *fig* brutishness; viciousness

bruto *a* stupid, unreasonable; vicious; unpolished, rough. *m*, animal (gen. quadruped). **en b.**, in the rough; *com* in bulk. **diamante en b.**, an uncut diamond

bruza *f*, strong brush; scrubbing brush

Bs. As. abbrev. of Buenos Aires

bu *m*, *inf* bogey man

buba *f*, pustule; *pl* buboes

bubónico *a* bubonic

bucal *a* buccal

bucanero *m*, buccaneer

Bucarest Bucharest

búcaro *m*, arsenican clay; jar made of arsenican clay

buceador *m*, diver

bucear *vi* to work as a diver; swim under water; *fig* investigate

bucéfalo *m*, bucephalus; *inf* fool, blockhead

buceo *m*, diving; dive; *fig* investigation

buche *m*, craw or crop; mouthful; wrinkle, pleat; *inf* stomach, belly. *fig inf* inmost heart

bucle *m*, ringlet, curl

bucólico *a* bucolic

búdico *a* Buddhist

budismo *m*, Buddhism

budista *a* and *mf* Buddhist

budín *m*, pudding

buen *a abb* of **bueno**, good. Used before *m*, singular nouns and infinitives used as nouns, e.g. **un b. libro,** a good book. **el b. cantar,** good singing

buenamente *adv* easily; comfortably, conveniently; willingly

buenaventura *f*, good luck; fortune told from hand

bueno (see buen) *a* good; kind; useful; convenient; pleasant; healthy; large (drink, etc.); simple, innocent; suitable; sufficient; opportune. **¡B.!** Good!; Enough!; All right! **a buenas,** willingly. **de buenas a primeras,** at first sight, from the beginning. **hacer bueno,** to prove, justify (a claim)

buey *m*, ox. **b. suelto,** *inf* freelance; bachelor

búfalo (-la) *n* buffalo

bufanda *f*, scarf

bufar *vi* to bellow; snort; *inf* snort with rage

bufete *m*, desk, writing table; lawyer's office or practice; sideboard

bufido *m*, snort; bellow

bufo *a* comic. *m*, clown, buffoon

bufón *m*, buffoon, clown; jester. *a* comical, clownish

bufonada *f*, buffoonery, clowning; raillery, taunt

bufonear(se) *vr* and *vi* to joke, jest, parody

bufonería. See **bufonada**

buhardilla *f*, garret; skylight

búho *m*, owl; *inf* hermit, unsociable person

buhonería *f*, pedling, hawking; pedler's wares

buhonero *m*, pedler

buido *a* sharp-pointed; sharp

buitre *m*, vulture

bujía *f*, candle; candlestick; *elec* candle-power; *aut* sparking plug

bula *f*, (Papal) bull

bulbo *m*, *bot* bulb. **b. dentario,** pulp (of teeth)

bulboso *a* bulbous

bulevar *m*, boulevard, promenade

búlgaro (-ra) *a* and *n* Bulgarian

bulla *f*, noise; bustle; confusion; fuss. *inf* **meter a b.,** to throw into great confusion

bullente *adj* boiling, bubbling; frothey (beer); swarming, teeming. **b. de sol,** drenched in sunlight, sundrenched

bullebulle *mf* busybody; madcap

bullicio *m*, noise, bustle; rioting; uproar

bullicioso *a* noisy, merry, boisterous; rebellious; lively, restless

bullir *vi* to boil; foam, bubble; *fig* seethe; *fig* swarm (insects); bustle; *vt* move, stir; *vr* stir, give signs of life

bulto *m*, bulk, mass, size; form of person, etc., seen indistinctly; swelling; bust, statue; bundle, package, piece of luggage; pillowcase. *fig inf* **poner de b.,** to put clearly, emphasize. **ser de b.,** to be obvious

bumerang *m*, boomerang

buñolería *f*, bun or waffle shop

buñuelo *m*, bun; waffle, fritter; *fig* botch

buque *m*, ship, vessel; capacity of ship; ship's hull. **b. barreminas,** minesweeper. **b. de guerra,** battleship, man-of-war. **b. de vapor,** steamer. **b. de vela,** sailing ship. **b. escuela,** trainingship. **b. mercante,** merchant vessel. **b. submarino,** submarine. **b. transbordador,** train-ferry

burbuja *f*, bubble

burbujear *vi* to bubble

burdel *m*, brothel; *inf* untidy, noisy place. *a* lascivious

burdo *a* coarse, tough

burgalés (-esa) *a* and *n* of or from Burgos

burgo *m*, borough, burgh

burgomaestre *m*, burgomaster

burgués (-esa) *a* and *n* bourgeois

burguesía *f*, bourgeoisie

buriel *a* dark red

buril *m*, burin, engraver's tool

burla *f*, mockery; joke, jest; trick. **b. burlando,** without effort; negligently. **de burlas,** in fun. **entre burlas y veras,** half-jokingly

burlador *a* mocking. *m*, libertine, rake; deceiver

burlar *vt* to play a trick on; deceive; disappoint; *vr* and *vi* (*with de*) make fun of, laugh at, ridicule

burlesco *a* jocular, comic, burlesque

burlón (-ona) *a* joking; mocking, scoffing. *n* joker; scoffer

buró *m*, bureau, writing-desk

burocracia *f*, bureaucracy

burócrata *mf* bureaucrat

burocrático *a* bureaucratic

burocratismo *m*, bureaucracy, red tape

burra *f*, she-ass; foolish, unteachable woman; painstaking, patient woman

burrajo *m*, dry stable dung used as fuel

burro *m*, ass, donkey; sawing-horse; card game

bursátil *a com* relating to the stock exchange; financial

busca *f*, search; hunting party; research; pursuit

buscado *adj* deliberate, intentional (negligence, etc.)

buscador (-ra) *n* searcher; investigator. *m*, finder (of a camera, etc.)

buscapié *m*, hint or suggestion; *fig* feeler

buscapiés *m*, squib, cracker

buscar *vt* to search, look for; pursue. **ir a b.,** to go to look for, go and get; bring, fetch

buscarruidos *mf inf* quarrel maker

buscavidas *mf inf* busybody; *inf* go-getter

buscón (-ona) *n* searcher; pickpocket, thief, swindler, rogue

buscona *f*, prostitute

busilis *m*, *inf* knotty problem, snag; **ahí está el b.,** there's the rub; core, main point

búsqueda (de) *f*, search (for)

busto *m*, *art* bust, head and shoulders

butaca *f*, armchair; *theat* orchestra stall; seat (in movies, etc.)

butifarra *f*, sausage made principally in Catalonia and the Balearic Islands; *inf* badly fitting stocking

buz *m*, respectful kiss

buzo *m*, diver

buzón *m*, mailbox; letter-box; canal, channel; sluice

C

C. abbrev. of ciudadano
¡ca! interj Fancy! Oh no!
cabal a just, exact; perfect; complete; faultless. interj Exactly! **por sus cabales,** according to plan; perfectly
cábala f, cabala; divination; inf intrigue. **hacer cábalas,** to venture a guess
cabalgada f, cavalcade; foray, raid
cabalgador (-ra) n rider, horseman
cabalgadura f, riding horse; beast of burden
cabalgar vi to ride a horse; ride in procession
cabalgata f, cavalcade; troop of horse
cabalístico a cabalistic; mysterious
caballa f, mackerel
caballada f, pack of horses; stud (of horses)
caballeresco a gentlemanly; knightly; chivalrous
caballerete m, dim inf foppish young man, dandy
caballería f, riding animal; cavalry; knightly deed or quest; any of Spanish Military Orders; knight-errantry; knighthood; chivalry; share of the spoils of war; horsemanship. **c. andante,** knight-errantry. **c. ligera,** mil light horse. **c. mayor,** horses, mares, mules. **c. menor,** asses, donkeys
caballeriza f, stable; stud of horses; staff of a stable
caballerizo m, head stable-groom. **c. mayor del rey,** Master of the King's Horse
caballero m, gentleman; cavalier; knight. **c. andante,** knight-errant. inf **c. de industria,** adventurer, sharper. **el C. de la Mancha,** the Knight of La Mancha. **el C. Sin Miedo y Sin Tacha,** the Seigneur de Bayart. **c. del hábito,** knight of one of the Spanish Military Orders. **c. novel,** untried knight. **armar c.,** to dub a knight
caballerosidad f, gentlemanliness; nobility; generosity; chivalry
caballeroso a gentlemanly; noble; generous; chivalrous
caballete m, ridge (of a roof); mil wooden horse; brake (for flax and hemp); agr furrow; easel; sawing-frame; trestle; bridge (of the nose)
caballito m, dim little horse; pl merry-go-round; automatic horse gambling game; circus equestrian act. **c. del diablo,** dragonfly
caballo m, horse; (chess) knight; (Spanish cards) queen; sawing-frame; pl cavalry. **c. balancín,** rocking horse. **c. de batalla,** war-horse; fig hobby-horse; forte; crux. **c. de cartón,** hobby-horse; rocking horse. **c. de carrera,** racehorse. **c. de tiro,** draft-horse. **c. de vapor,** horsepower. **c. marino,** sea-horse. **a c.,** on horseback. **A c. regalado no le mires el diente,** Never look a gift horse in the mouth. **caer bien a c.,** to have a good seat (on a horse). **ser un c. loco en una cacharrería,** to be like a bull in a china shop
cabaña f, hut, cabin, cottage; flock (of sheep); drove (of mules); art pastoral scene; balk (billiards)
cabaret m, cabaret, nightclub
cabaretero m, nightclub owner
cabecear vi to nod; shake the head in disapproval; move the head from side to side; toss the head (horses); (aer naut) pitch; sway (of a carriage); lean; vt refoot (socks); head (wine)
cabeceo m, nod, shake (of head); (naut aer) pitching; lurching (of a carriage, etc.); bight (of river)
cabecera f, top, upper portion, head; seat of honor; bedhead; river source; capital (country or county); illustrated chapter heading; pillow; inscription, heading
cabecilla dim f, small head. mf inf hothead. m, rebel leader
cabellera f, head of long hair; hair-switch; tail (of comet)

cabello m, hair; head of hair; silk (of maize). fig inf **asirse de un c.,** to clutch at a straw
cabelludo a hairy; bot fibrous
caber vi irr to be room for, contain; fit into, go into (e.g. **No cabemos todos en este coche,** There isn't room for all of us in this car); happen, befall, have (e.g. **No les cupo tal suerte,** They did not have such luck—Such luck did not befall them); be possible (e.g. **Todo cabe en Dios,** All things are possible with God). **No cabe más,** There's no room for anything else; fig That's the limit. fig **no c. en sí,** to be beyond oneself (with joy, pride, etc.). **No cabe duda de que,** There's no doubt that. Pres. Ind. **quepo, cabes,** etc. Fut. **cabré,** etc. Conditional **cabría,** etc. Preterite **cupe, cupiste,** etc. Pres. Subjunc. **quepa, quepas,** etc. Imperf. Subjunc. **cupiese,** etc.
cabestrar vt to halter
cabestrillo m, sling; thin chain (for ornament). **en c.,** in a sling (e.g. **Tenía el brazo en c.,** His arm was in a sling)
cabestro m, halter; sling; leading ox
cabeza f, head; top, upper end; nail-head; brain; mind; judgment; self-control; edge (of book); peak, summit; source, origin; individual, person; head of cattle; capital city. m, leader, chief, head. mech **c. de biela,** big-end. inf **c. de chorlito,** scatterbrain (person). **c. de hierro,** blockhead. mil **c. de puente,** bridgehead. **c. de partido,** principal town of a region. **c. de turco,** scapegoat. **irse la c. (a alguien),** to feel giddy. fig inf **meter a uno en la c.,** to put into someone's head. inf **quebrarse la c.,** to rack one's brains. inf **quitar a uno de la c. (una cosa),** to dissuade; get an idea out of someone's head
cabezada f, blow with or on the head; nod; headshake; headstall; naut pitching. **dar cabezadas,** to nod, go to sleep
cabezal m, small head pillow; surg pad; bolster; narrow mattress; mech head
cabezo m, summit (of mountain); hill; naut reef
cabezón m, tax-register; collar-band; head-opening (of a garment)
cabezudo a large-headed; inf obstinate; inf heady (of wine). m, carnival grotesque
cabida f, space, capacity; extent, area
cabildear vi to canvass votes, lobby
cabildo m, ecc chapter; municipal council; meeting, or meeting place of council. **c. abierto,** town meeting
cabina f, cabin. **c. telefónica** phone booth
cabizbajo a crestfallen; pensive, melancholy
cable m, cable; string (of bridge); cable's length; **c. aéreo,** overhead cable. **c. alimentador,** feed line. m, eléctrico, electric cable
cabo m, end, extremity; stump, stub; handle, shaft, haft; leader; geog cape; end, conclusion; naut rope; ply (of wool, etc.); mil corporal; pl accessories (clothes); horse's tail and mane. **c. de maestranza,** foreman. **c. de mar,** naval quartermaster. **c. furriel,** mil quartermaster. **al c.,** in the end. **llevar a c.,** to finish
Cabo de Buena Esperanza Cape of Good Hope
Cabo de Hornos Cape Horn
cabotaje m, naut coasting trade
cabra f, nanny-goat; goat. **c. montesa,** wild goat
cabrahigo m, wild fig; wild fig tree
cabrerizo (-za) a goatish. m, goatherd
cabrero (-ra) m, goatherd
cabrestante m, naut capstan
cabria f, winch, hoist
cabrilla f, carp saw-horse; pl ast Pleiades; burn marks on legs from sitting too near fire; white crests (of waves)

cabrillear *vi* to foam, froth (the sea)

cabrío *a* goatish. *m*, herd of goats. **macho c.**, male goat, he-goat

cabriola *f*, fouetté (in dancing); spin in the air (acrobats); curvet (horses); caper

cabriolar *vi* to curvet; caper, skip

cabriolé *m*, cabriolet; short cape with or without sleeves

cabritilla *f*, dressed kid; lambskin, etc.

cabrito *m*, *zool* kid; *pl* toasted maize, popcorn

cabrón *m*, billy goat, buck, he-goat; *inf* complaisant husband, cuckhold; *Chile* owner or operator of a brothel

cabrona *f*, *Chile* bawd, madam

cabruno *a* goatish

cabujón *m*, *min* uncut gem; unpolished ruby; *pl* vignettes

cacahual *m*, cacao plantation

cacahuete *m*, *bot* peanut, monkey nut

cacao *m*, *bot* cacao tree; cacaonut

cacarear *vi* to crow, cackle; *vt inf* boast

cacareo *m*, crowing, cackling; *inf* boast

cacatúa *f*, cockatoo

cacera *f*, irrigation channel

cacería *f*, hunting party; hunting bag; booty; *art* hunting scene

cacerola *f*, stew-pot, casserole

cachalote *m*, sperm whale

cachano *m*, Old Nick

cachar *vt* to break in fragments; split (wood)

cacharrería *f*, crockery store

cacharro *m*, coarse earthenware vessel; *inf* decrepit, worthless object

cachazudo *a* phlegmatic, slow

cachear *vt* to search (a person) for weapons

Cachemira Kashmir

cachemira *f*, cashmere

cacheo *m*, search (of persons) for weapons

cachete *m*, blow on the head or face with one's fist; cheek (especially fat one)

cachetero *m*, dagger

cachetina *f*, hand-to-hand fight

cachiporra *f*, club, bludgeon

cachivache *m*, *inf* (gen. *pl*) trash; pots, pans, utensils

cacho *m*, small slice (gen. of bread or fruit)

cachón *m*, breaker, wave; small waterfall

cachorro (-rra) *n* puppy; cub. *m*, small pistol

cachuela *f*, Extremaduran pork stew

cacillo *m*, ladle; basting spoon

cacique *m*, Indian chief, cacique; *inf* political "boss"

caciquismo *m*, political "bossism"

caco *m*, pickpocket, thief; *inf* poltroon

cacofonía *f*, cacophony

cacografía *f*, cacography

cacto *m*, cactus

cacumen *m*, *inf* brains, acumen

cada *a* every, each. **c. cual,** each. **c. que,** whenever; every time that. **c. y cuando que,** whenever

cadalso *m*, scaffold; platform, stand

cadáver *m*, corpse

cadavérico *a* cadaverous, ghastly

cadena *f*, chain; link, tie; *fig* bond; *fig* sequence (of events); *law* imprisonment; *arch* buttress; grand chain (dancing); **c. de montañas,** range of mountains. **c. perpetua,** life imprisonment

cadencia *f*, cadence; rhythm; *mus* measure, time; *mus* cadenza

cadencioso *a* rhythmic

cadente *a* falling, declining; decaying, dying; rhythmic

cadera *f*, hip; flank

caderillas *f pl*, bustle, panniers

cadete *m*, *mil* cadet

cadi *mf* caddy

Cádiz Cadiz

caducar *vi* to become senile; become invalid, be annulled; expire, lapse; *fig* be worn out

caduceo *m*, Mercury's wand

caducidad *f*, decrepitude; lapse, expiry

caduco *a* senile; decrepit; perishable; lapsed; obsolete

caduquez *f*, senility

caedizo *a* ready to fall; timid, cowardly, weak

caer *vi irr* to fall, drop; drop out or off; suit, fit, become; fail; fade (colors); *fig* drop (voice); (*with sobre*) attack, fall upon; (*with en*) fall in or on to; decay, collapse; understand; (*with preps. a, hacia*) *fig* look on to, face; (*with por, en*) *fig* fall on, occur on; *vr aer* crash; fly off (buttons, etc.). **c. de cabeza,** to fall head foremost. **c. en conflicto (con),** to come into conflict (with) **c. en las manos de uno,** to come into somebody's possession (come to be owned by somebody). **c. en gracia,** to make a good impression, arouse affection. **caerse de suyo,** to be self-evident. **c. por tierra,** (plan, etc.) to fall through. **Cayó enfermo,** He was taken ill. **cayendo y levantado,** dying *Pres. Ind.* **caigo, caes,** etc. *Pres. Part.* **cayendo.** *Preterite* **cayó cayeron.** *Pres. Subjunc.* **caiga,** etc.

café *m*, coffee (tree, berry, drink); café, coffeehouse. **c. con leche,** café au lait

cafeína *f*, caffeine

cafetal *m*, coffee plantation

cafetera *f*, coffeepot; *Peru* cab, taxi

cafeto *m*, coffee tree

cafiche *m*, *Argentina, Chile* pimp

caficultor *m*, coffee-grower

caficultura *f*, coffee-growing

cafúa *f*, *Argentina* clink, slammer

cagadas *f pl*, droppings, dung

cagar(se) *vi vt vr* to evacuate (bowels); *vt inf* spoil, make a botch of

cagarruta *f*, dung of sheep, deer, rabbits, etc.

caída *f*, falling; fall; ruin; failure; close (of day); *fig* falling off; hanging (curtains, etc.); diminution; incline; *pl* coarse wool; *inf* repartee. **a la c. de la tarde,** at the end of the afternoon. **a la c. del sol,** at sunset

caído (-da) *a* debilitated, languid; lapsed; (of a shoulder) sloping. **los caídos,** the fallen, the dead (in war, etc.)

caimán *m*, alligator; *inf* shark, astute person

caja *f*, box; safe, cash box; coffin; (of a vehicle) body; *mus* drum; case (of piano, watch, etc.); cavity; well (of a stair); *com* cash; cash-desk; cashier's office; *bot* sheath. **c. de ahorros,** savings bank. **c. de caudales,** strong-box. *print* **c. de imprenta,** type case. **c. de música,** musical box. **c. de reclutamiento,** recruiting office. **c. de velocidades,** gearbox. **c. registradora,** cash register. **c. torácica,** rib cage, thoracic cage

cajero (-ra) *m*, boxmaker; *n com* cashier; pedler **c. automático,** automatic teller, automatic teller machine, bank machine, money machine

cajetilla *f*, packet (cigarettes, etc.)

cajista *mf print* compositor

cajón *m*, chest, locker, case; drawer. **c. de municiones,** ammunition-box

cajonera *f*, *ecc* chest of drawers in sacristy; *agr* frame

cal *f*, lime. **c. muerta,** slaked lime. **c. viva,** quicklime. *fig inf* **de c. y canto,** tough, strong

cala *f*, sample slice (of fruit); *naut* hold; *surg* probe; cove, small bay; *bot* iris

calabacera *f*, *bot* pumpkin or gourd plant

calabacín *m*, kind of vegetable marrow; *inf* dolt

calabaza *f*, *bot* pumpkin (plant and fruit); gourd; *inf* dolt. **dar calabazas,** to refuse (suitor); flunk (an examinee). *inf* **llevar calabazas,** to get the sack; be jilted

calabobos *m*, *inf* drizzle

calabocero *m*, jailer

calabozo *m*, dungeon; prison cell; pruning knife

calabrés (-esa) *a* and *n* Calabrian

calada *f*, soaking, wetting through; flight of bird of prey; swoop. **dar una c.,** *fig inf* to dress down

calado *a* soaked, wet through. *m*, *sew* open-work; fretwork; *naut* draught of a ship; water level; *pl* lace. **c. hasta los huesos,** soaked to the skin; madly in love

calador *m*, one who does open or fretwork; caulking iron; borer; *surg* probe

calafate *m*, caulker

calafatear *vt naut* to caulk

calamar *m*, *zool* squid, calamary

calambre *m*, cramp. **c. del escribiente,** writer's cramp

calamidad *f*, misfortune, calamity

calamina *f*, *min* calamine

calamitoso *a* calamitous; unfortunate, unhappy

cálamo *m*, ancient flute; stalk (of grass); *poet* pen

calamocano *a* maudlin, tipsy

calandria *f*, *orn* calender, lark; *mech* calender; treadmill. *mf inf* malingerer

calaña *f*, sample; model; pattern; kind, quality; temperament; cheap fan

calar *vt* to permeate, soak through; pierce; do openwork (in cloth, paper, metal); cut a sample slice from fruit; pull (hat, etc.) well down on head; put down (an eyeshade or visor); fix (bayonets, etc.); *inf* understand (persons); *inf* guess, realize; *naut* let down; *vi naut* draw (water); *vr* be drenched, wet through; swoop (birds of prey); *inf* sneak in. *a* calcareous

calar *m*, limestone deposit or region

calavera *f*, skull. *m*, dare-devil, madcap; roué

calaverada *f*, *inf* dare-devilment, foolishness; escapade

calcañar *m*, heel (of foot)

calcar *vt* to trace (drawing); press with foot; copy servilely, imitate

calcáreo *a* calcareous

calce *m*, rim of a wheel; wedge; tyre

calcés *m*, *naut* masthead

calceta *f*, stocking; fetter. *inf* **hacer c.,** to knit

calcetería *f*, hosiery shop; hosiery trade

calcetero (-ra) *n* hosier; hose maker or darner

calcetín *m*, sock

calcificación *f*, *med* calcification

calcinación *f*, calcination

calcinar *vt* to calcine

calcio *m*, calcium

calco *m*, tracing (drawing)

calcografía *f*, chalcography

calcografiar *vt* to transfer; make chalcographies of

calcomanía *f*, transfer

calculación *f*, calculation

calculadamente *adv* calculatedly

calculado *a* calculated

calculador *a* calculating. *m*, calculating machine, comptometer

calcular *vt* to calculate

cálculo *m*, calculation; *math* estimate; investigation; conjecture; (math med) calculus. **c. hepático,** *med* gallstone

Calcuta Calcutta

calda *f*, heating; *pl* hot mineral baths

Caldea Chaldea

caldear *vt* to heat

caldeo (-ea) *a* and *n* Chaldean

caldeo *m*, heating

caldera *f*, cauldron; cauldron full; *WH* teapot; *eng* boiler. **c. de vapor,** steam-boiler

calderería *f*, coppersmith's trade and shop

calderero *m*, boiler maker; coppersmith; tinker

calderilla *f*, holy water stoup; any copper coin

caldero *m*, small cauldron; casserole; kettle

calderón *m*, large cauldron; *mus* rest; *mus* trill; pause

caldo *m*, broth; salad dressing; *pl agr* oil, wine, vegetable juices

calefacción *f*, heating. **c. central,** central heating

calendario *m*, calendar. **c. deportivo,** fixture card. **c. gregoriano,** Gregorian calendar

calendas *f pl*, calends. **en las c. griegas,** at the Greek calends

caléndula *f*, marigold

calentador *a* heating, warming. *m*, heater; warming-pan

calentamiento *m*, heating, warming

calentar *vt irr* to heat, warm; rev-up (an engine); hasten; *inf* spank; *vr* warm oneself; be in heat (animals); grow excited. See **acertar**

calentura *f*, fever

calenturiento *a* feverish

calera *f*, lime-kiln; fishing smack

calesa *f*, calash, calèche, chaise (two-wheeled carriage)

caleta *f*, cove, creek

caletre *m*, *inf* discernment, head, sense

calibrar *vt* to calibrate; gauge

calibre *m*, *mech* gauge; bore, caliber; diameter (tubes, pipes, etc.)

calidad *f*, quality; role; character, temperament; condition, requisite; importance, gravity; personal particulars; nobility; *pl* qualities of the mind. **c. originaria,** rank and birth. **c. de oficio,** justification for action. **en c. de,** in the capacity of

cálido *a* warm, hot; warming, heating; vehement, ardent; *art* warm

calidoscópico *a* kaleidoscopic

calidoscopio *m*, kaleidoscope

calientalibros *m*, bookworm (person)

calientapiés *m*, footwarmer

calientaplatos *m*, hot plate, plate-warmer

caliente *a* warm, hot; excited; *art* warm

calientito *a* piping hot

califa *m*, caliph

califal *a* caliphal

califato *m*, caliphate

calificable *a* classifiable; qualifiable

calificación *f*, classification; qualification; judgment; mark, place (examinations)

calificar *vt* to class; authorize; judge (qualities); *fig* ennoble; *vr* prove noble descent

calificativo *a gram* qualifying. *m*, epithet

californio (-ia) *a* and *n* Californian

caliginoso *a* murky, dark

caligrafía *f*, calligraphy

calígrafo *m*, calligraphist

calinoso *a* hazy

caliqueño *m*, cheroot

calistenia *f*, callisthenics

cáliz *m*, chalice; *poet* cup; *bot* calyx

caliza *f*, limestone

calizo *a* calcareous

callado *a* silent; reserved; secret

callar(se) *vi* and *vr* to say nothing, keep silent; stop speaking; stop making any sound (persons, animals, things); *vt* conceal, keep secret; omit, leave out; *inf interj* **¡Calle!** You don't say so! **Quien calla otorga,** Silence gives consent

calle *f*, street. *inf* **abrir c.,** to clear the way. *inf* **dejar en la c.,** to leave destitute. *inf* **echar a la c.,** put out of the house, to throw out of the house; make known, publish. **ponerse en la c.,** to go out

calleja, callejuela *f*, small street, alley, side street

callejear *vi* to walk the streets, wander about the streets, loaf around the streets

callejero *a* fond of gadding. *m*, street directory

callejón *m*, alley, lane. **c. sin salida,** cul-de-sac; *fig* impasse

callicida *m*, corn cure

callista *mf* chiropodist

callo *m*, corn, callosity; *med* callus; *pl* tripe

calloso *a* callous, horny

calma *f*, calm, airlessness; serenity, composure; quiet, tranquillity, peace. **c. chicha,** dead calm. **en c.,** at peace; tranquil; calm (of the sea)

calmante *a* calming, soothing. *med a* and *m*, sedative, tranquilizer

calmar *vt* to soothe, calm; moderate, mitigate; pacify; quench (thirst); *vi* grow calm; moderate; be becalmed

calmoso *a* calm, tranquil; *inf* sluggish, lazy; imperturbable

calor *m*, heat; ardor, vehemence; cordiality; *fig* heat (of battle); excitement

caloría *f, phys* calorie
calórico *a phys* caloric, thermic
calorífero *a* heat-giving. *m,* heater, radiator
calorífico *a* calorific
calumnia *f,* calumny; *law* slander
calumniador (-ra) *a* slandering. *n* calumniator, slanderer
calumniar *vt* to calumniate; *law* slander
calumnioso *a* calumnious, slanderous
caluroso *a* hot, warm; cordial, friendly; enthusiastic; ardent, impassioned; excited
calva *f,* bald patch on head; worn place (cloth, etc.); bare spot, clearing (trees, etc.)
Calvario *m,* Calvary; *inf* series of disasters; *inf* debts
calvero *m,* clearing (in a wood); chalk or marl pit
calvicie *f,* baldness
calvinismo *m,* Calvinism
calvinista *mf* Calvinist. *a* Calvinistic
calvo *a* bald; bare, barren (land); worn (cloth, etc.)
calza *f,* breeches (gen. *pl*); wedge; *inf* stocking. *inf* **tomar calzas,** to beat it
calzada *f,* roadway. **c. romana,** Roman road
calzado *m,* footwear, shoes
calzador *m,* shoehorn
calzadura *f,* wedging (of a wheel); act of putting on shoes; felloe of a wheel
calzar *vt* to put on shoes; wear (spurs, gloves, etc.); wedge, block (wheel); scotch (a wheel). *fig inf* **c. el coturno,** don the buskin; write in the sublime style; write a tragedy, write tragedies. **calzarse a una persona,** to have a person in one's pocket
calzón *m,* breeches (gen. *pl*). *fig inf* **ponerse los calzones,** to wear the breeches (of a woman)
calzonazos *m, inf* weak-willed, easily led fellow
calzoncillos *m pl,* drawers, pants
cama *f,* bed; bedstead; bedhanging; lair, form; floor (of a cart); check (of bridle) (gen. *pl*). **c. de campaña,** camp bed. **c. de matrimonio,** double bed. **c. de monja,** single bed. **c. de operaciones,** operating table. **c. turca,** settee-bed. **guardar c.,** to stay in bed
camada *f,* brood, litter; *inf* gang
camafeo *m,* cameo
camaleón *m,* chameleon; *inf* changeable person
cámara *f,* chamber; hall; house (of deputies); granary; *naut* state room; chamber (firearms, mines); *phys* camera; human excrement; *aut* inner tube. **c. acorazada,** strong-room. **c. alta,** Upper House, **c. baja** *or* **c. de los comunes,** lower house, house of commons. **c. de comercio,** chamber of commerce. **c. oscura,** (optics) dark room
camarada *mf* pal, companion, comrade
camaradería *f,* comradeship, companionship
camarera *f,* waiting-maid; waitress; chambermaid; stewardess
camarero *m,* waiter; papal chamberlain; chamberlain; steward; valet. **c. mayor,** lord chamberlain
camarilla *f,* palace or other clique, coterie; *inf* backscratch
camarín *m, theat* dressing-room; closet; boudoir; cage (of a lift); niche
camarón *m,* prawn, shrimp; tip, reward
camarote *m,* cabin; berth
cambalachear *vt inf* to barter
cámbaro *m,* sea-crab
cambiable *a* exchangeable; changeable
cambiante *a* exchanging; changing. *m,* sheen, luster (gen. *pl*); money changer
cambiar *vt* to exchange; convert. *vt* and *vi* change, alter; *vi* and *vr* to veer (wind). **c. de aguas,** *poet* to move (change one's residence). **c. de aire,** get a change of scenery. **c. de frente,** to face about; *fig* change front
cambio *m,* exchange; change; *com* rate of exchange; money change; *com* premium on bills of exchange. **a c. de, en c. de,** in exchange for; instead of. **en c.,** instead, on the other hand. **c. de velocidad,** *aut* gear-changing. **letra de c.,** bill of exchange. **libre c.,** free trade

cambista *mf* money changer. *m,* banker
Camboya Cambodia
Cambrige Cambridge
camelar *vt inf* to woo; seduce
camelia *f,* camelia. **c. japonesa,** japonica
camelo *m, inf* eyewash
camellero *m,* camel keeper or driver
camello *m,* camel. **c. pardal,** giraffe
camellón *m,* furrow; drinking trough; *Mexico* island, traffic island, median strip
Camerún Cameroons
camilla *f,* couch; small round skirted table with brazier underneath; stretcher, litter
camillero *m, mil* stretcher-bearer
caminador *a* in the habit of walking a great deal
caminante *mf* walker, traveler
caminar *vi* to travel; walk; *fig* move on, go (inanimate things). *fig* **c. derecho,** to walk uprightly
caminata *f,* long, tiring walk; excursion
caminejo *m,* worn path
camino *m,* road; route; journey; way, means; **c. de hierro,** railway. **c. de mesa,** table-runner. **c. de sirga,** towpath. **c. real,** highway, main road. **de c.,** on the way, in passing. **ponerse en c.,** to set out
camión *m,* truck. **c. de volteo, c. volquete** dump truck; *Mexico* bus
camioneta *f,* light truck, pick-up truck; *WH* station wagon
camisa *f,* shirt, stiff shirt; thin skin (of fruit); sloughed skin of snakes; coat (of whitewash, etc.); *mech* jacket; mantle (gas). **c. de fuerza,** straitjacket. **dejar sin c.,** *inf* to leave penniless
camisería *f,* shirt shop or factory
camisero (-ra) *n* shirt maker or seller
camiseta *f,* vest, T-shirt. **c. de fútbol,** soccer player's jersey
camisola *f,* stiff shirt; ruffled shirt
camisón *m,* large wide shirt; night shirt
camomila *f,* chamomile
camorra *f, inf* brawl, shindy. **armar c.,** to start a row
campal *a* field, country
campamento *m,* camping; *mil* encampment; camp; jamboree
campana *f,* bell; anything bell-shaped; church, parish. **c. de chimenea,** mantelpiece. **c. de hogar,** hood, shutter (of a fireplace)
campanada *f,* peal of a bell; scandal
campanario *m,* belfry, bell tower
campanear *vi* to ring bells frequently
campaneo *m,* bell-ringing; chime
campanero *m,* bell-founder; bell ringer
campanil *m,* small belfry, campanile
campanilla *f,* hand-bell; bubble; any bell-shaped flower
campanillazo *m,* loud peal of a bell
campante *a* outstanding; *inf* proud, satisfied
campanudo *a* bell-shaped; sonorous (of words); pompous (of speech)
campaña *f,* level country; campaign. *naut* voyage, cruise. **correr la c.,** to reconnoiter. **la C. del Desierto,** the War against the Gauchos (in Argentina)
campar *vi* to camp. *inf* **c. por sus respetos,** to stand on one's own feet
campeador *a* mighty in battle
campear *vi* to go out to graze; grow green (crops); excel; *mil* be engaged in a campaign, reconnoiter
campechano *a inf* hearty; frank; cheerful; generous
campeche *m, bot* logwood
campeón *m,* champion; advocate, defender
campeonato *m,* championship
campesinado *m,* peasantry
campesino (-na) *a* rural, rustic. *n* country dweller
campestre *a* rural
campiña *f,* expanse of cultivated land; countryside, landscape
campo *m,* country (as opposed to urban areas); field; *fig*

sphere, province; (*phys her mil*) field; *art* ground; *mil* camp, army; plain ground (of silks, etc.). «**C. Abierto»,** "Miscellaneous" (e.g. as the title of a section in a book catalog). **c. de aterrizaje,** *aer* landing-field. **c. de batalla,** battlefield. **c. de concentración,** concentration camp. **c. de experimentación,** testing ground. **c. de golf,** golf course. **c. de prisioneros** *mil* prison camp. **c. de tiro,** rifle-range. **c. santo,** graveyard. **c. visual,** field of vision. **a c. abierto,** in the open air. **a c. travieso,** cross-country

camuflaje *m,* camouflage
camuflar *vt* to camouflage
can *m,* dog; trigger; *arch* modillion; *ast* Dog Star
cana *f,* gray hair
Canadá Canada
canadiense *a* and *mf* Canadian
canal *m,* canal. *mf, geol* subterranean waterway; channel; *anat* canal, duct; defile, narrow valley; gutter; drinking trough; animal carcass. **abrir en c.,** to open up, split open
Canal de la Mancha English Channel
canalera *f,* roof gutter
canaleta *f,* (wooden) trough; gutter (on roof)
canalete *m,* paddle
canalización *f,* canalization; *elec* main, mains; piping; tubing
canalizar *vt* to make canals or channels; regulate waters of rivers, etc.; canalize
canalón *m,* gutter, spout; shovel hat; pantile
canalla *f, inf* mob, rabble. *m, inf* scoundrel
canallesco *a* scoundrelly, knavish; despicable
canana *f,* cartridge belt
canapé *m,* sofa
Canarias, las Islas the Canary Islands
canario (-ia) *m,* canary. *a* and *n* pertaining to or native of the Canary Islands.
canasta *f,* hamper, basket; card game
canastilla *f,* small basket; layette
canastillo *m,* basket-work tray
cáncamo *m,* ring-bolt
cancamusa *f, inf* trick, deception
cancel *m,* draftscreen; *ecc* screen
cancela *f,* wrought-iron door
cancelación *f,* cancellation; expunging
cancelar *vt* to cancel; expunge, annul; abolish, blot out; pay off, clear (a mortgage)
cancelaría *f,* papal chancery
cancelario *m,* chancellor (universities)
cáncer *m,* cancer
cancerar *vt* to consume; weaken; mortify; *vr* suffer from cancer; become cancerous
cancerbero *m, myth* Cerberus; *fig* unbribable guard
canceroso *a* cancerous
cancha *f, sport* fronton; (tennis) court; cockpit; yard; hippodrome; widest part of a river; road; toasted maize
canciller *m,* chancellor; foreign minister; assistant vice-consul
cancillería *f,* chancellorship; chancellery; foreign ministry
canción *f,* song; lyric poem; musical accompaniment; old name for any poetical composition. **volver a la misma c.,** *fig* to be always harping on the same theme
cancionero *m,* collection of songs and verses; songbook
cancionista *mf* singer; song writer
candado *m,* padlock; earring
candeal *a* white (of bread)
candela *f,* candle; horse-chestnut flower; candlestick; *inf* fire. **en c.,** *naut* vertical (of masts, etc.)
candelabro *m,* candelabrum
candelaria *f,* Candlemas
candelero *m,* candlestick; lamp; candle maker or seller; *naut* stanchion
candente *a* candescent, red-hot
candidatear *vi* to run (for office)
candidato (-ta) *n* candidate
candidatura *f,* candidature

candidez *f,* simplicity, ingenuousness; candidness
cándido *a* white; simple, ingenuous; candid, frank
candil *m,* oil lamp; Greek lamp; tips of stag's horns; *inf* cock of a hat
candileja *f,* oil reservoir of lamp; *pl* footlights, floats
candor *m,* extreme whiteness; sincerity, candor; simplicity, innocence
candoroso *a* candid, open; simple, honest
canela *f, bot* cinnamon; *fig* anything exquisitely perfect
canelo *m,* cinnamon tree. *a* cinnamon-colored
cangilón *m,* pitcher, jar; bucket (for water); dredging bucket
cangreja *f, naut* gaffsail. **c. de mesana,** *naut* jigger
cangrejo *m,* crab. **c. de mar,** sea-crab. **c. ermitaño,** hermit crab
canguro *m,* kangaroo
caníbal *a* and *mf* cannibal
canibalismo *m,* cannibalism
canica *f,* marble (for playing with)
canícula *f,* dog days; *ast* Dog star
caniculares *m pl* dog days
canijo *a inf* delicate, sickly; anemic, stunted
canilla *f,* long bone of leg or arm; any principal bones in bird's wing; tap, faucet; spool, reel; fault (in cloth)
canino *a* canine
canje *m,* (diplomacy, *mil., com.*) exchange, substitution. **c. de prisioneros,** exchange of prisoners
canjear *vt* to exchange
cano *a* white-haired, hoary; ancient; *poet* white
canoa *f,* canoe; launch. **c. automóvil,** motor launch
canoero (-ra) *n* canoeist
canódromo *m,* dog-race track
canon *m,* rule; (*ecc print*) canon; catalog; part of the Mass; *mus* canon, catch; tax. *pl* canon law
canonesa *f,* canoness
canónico *a* canonic, canonical
canónigo *m,* canon; prebendary
canonización *f,* canonization
canonizar *vt* to canonize; extol, exalt; approve, acclaim
canonjía *f,* canonry, canonship; *inf* sinecure
canoso *a* white-haired, hoary
cansado (-da) *a* tired; weary; exhausted; decadent; tiresome; *inf* fed up. *n* bore, tedious person
cansancio *m,* fatigue, weariness
cansar *vt* to tire, weary; *agr* exhaust soil; bore; badger; annoy; *vr* be tired; grow weary
cansino *a* worn-out (of horses, etc.)
cantable *a* singable; *mus* cantabile
cántabrico (-ca) *a* and *n* Cantabrian
cantante *a* singing. *mf* professional singer
cantar *vi* to sing; twitter, chirp; extol; *inf* squeak, creak; *fig* call (cards); *inf* squeal, confess. *m,* song. **C. de los Cantares,** Song of Songs. **cantarlas claras,** to call a spade a spade
cántara *f,* pitcher, jug
cantárida *f,* Spanish fly
cántaro *m,* pitcher, jug; jugful; varying wine measure; ballot box; tax on spirits and oil
cantata *f,* cantata
cantatriz *f,* singer, prima donna
cante *m,* song; singing
cantera *f, min* quarry; capacity, talent
cantería *f,* stone-cutting; quarrying; building made of hewn stone
cantero *m,* stone-cutter; quarryman
cántico *m, ecc* canticle; *poet* poem
cantidad *f,* quantity; large part; portion; sum of money; quantity (prosody). **c. llovida,** rainfall
cantiga *or* **cántiga** *f,* old poetic form designed to be sung
cantil *m,* cliff; steep rock
cantimplora *f,* water cooler; canteen (of water); siphon
cantina *f,* wine cellar; canteen; refreshment room
cantinero *m,* sutler; owner of a canteen
canto *m,* singing; song; canto; epic or other poem; end, rim, edge; non-cutting edge (knives, swords); pebble,

stone; angle (of a building). *mus* **c. llano**, plain-song. **al c. del gallo**, at cockcrow. **de c.**, on edge

cantón *m*, province, region; corner (of a street); cantonment; *her* canton, quartering

cantonera *f*, corner-piece (books, furniture, etc., as ornament); angle-iron; bracket, small shelf

cantor (-ra) *a* singing. *n* singer; song-bird

Cantórbery Canterbury

canturía *f*, singing exercise; vocal music; monotonous song; droning; *mus* execution, technique

canturreo, *m*, **canturria** *f*, humming; droning

canturriar *vi inf* to hum, sing under one's breath

caña *f*, stalk; reed; bone of arm or leg; leg (of a trouser, stocking, boot, etc.); marrow; *bot* cane; tumbler, glass; wine measure; gallery (of mine); *pl* mock joust on horseback using **cañas** as spears. **c. de azúcar**, sugar-cane. **c. de pescar**, fishing rod. **c. del timón**, tiller *naut*

cañada *f*, glen, gulch, gully, hollow, ravine, vale, cattle path; *WH* brook, cattle track

cañal *m*, cane-break; weir (for fish)

cañamazo *m*, hempen canvas; embroidery canvas; embroidered canvas

cañamelar *m*, sugar-cane plantation

cáñamo *m*, hemp

cañamón *m*, hemp-seed

cañar *m*, canebrake; growth of reeds; fishgarth made of reeds

cañavalera *f*, canefield

cañaveral *m*, cane-brake; *WH* bamboo field

cañazo *m*, blow with a cane

cañería *f*, conduit; pipe; piping

cañero *m*, pipe layer

caño *m*, pipe, tube, sewer; organ pipe; jet (of water); mine gallery

cañón *m*, pipe, cylindrical tube; flue; quill (of birds); cannon; soft down; *arch* shaft (of column); stack (of a chimney). **c. antiaéreo**, A.A. gun. **c. antianque**, anti-tank gun. **c. de escalera**, well of a staircase; *slang* terrific-looking, absolutely gorgeous (e.g. mujer cañón)

cañonazo *m*, cannon shot; roar of a cannon

cañonear *vt* to bombard

cañoneo *m*, cannonade; bombardment

cañonera *f*, embrasure (for cannon)

cañonería *f*, *mil* group of cannon; *mus* set of organ pipes

cañonero *m*, gunboat

cañuto *m*, *bot* internode; small pipe or tube; *inf* talebearer

caoba *f*, *bot* mahogany

caos *m*, chaos; confusion

caótico *a* chaotic

capa *f*, cloak; cape; *ecc* cope; coating; layer; cover; coat (animals); *fig* cloak, disguise; *geol* stratum. **la c. del cielo**, the canopy of heaven. *fig inf* **echar la c. al toro**, to throw one's cap over the windmill. *naut* **estarse** (*or* **ponerse**) **a la c.**, to lie to

capacete *m*, helmet

capacidad *f*, capacity; extension, space; mental capacity, talent; opportunity, means; *law* capacity. **c. de compra**, buying power, purchasing power. **c. de producción**, output

capacitación *f*, qualification, (act of) qualifying; (act of) training

capacitar *vt* to capacitate, qualify, enable

capadura *f*, castration

capar *vt* to castrate, geld; *inf* diminish, reduce

caparazón *m*, caparison, horse blanket; waterproof cover; hood (of carriages); nosebag; shell (insects, crustaceans)

capataz *m*, foreman; steward; overseer

capaz *a* capacious; large, spacious; capable, competent; *law* able

capcioso *a* deceitful, artful; captious, carping

capear *vt* to steal a cape; play the bull with a cape (bullfighting); *inf* put off with excuses, deceive; *naut* lie to

capelo *m*, cardinal's hat; cardinalate

capellán *m*, chaplain; any ecclesiastic

capellanía *f*, chaplaincy

capeo *m*, playing the bull with a cape (bullfighting)

caperuza *f*, hood, pointed cap; *arch* coping-stone

capigorrón *a inf* loafing. *m*, loafer, idler

capilar *a* capillary

capilaridad *f*, capillarity

capilla *f*, cowl, hood; chapel; *ecc* chapter; *ecc* choir. **c. ardiente**, chapelle ardente. **estar en c.**, to await execution (criminals); *inf* be in suspense, await anxiously

capillero *m*, sexton; churchwarden

capillo *m*, baby's bonnet; cocoon of silkworm; flowerbud

capirotazo *m*, box on the ear; fillip

capirote *m*, academic hood and cap; hood (falconry); tall pointed cap. **ser tonto de c.**, *inf* to be a complete fool

capitación *f*, poll-tax, capitation

capital *a* relating to the head; capital (sins, etc.); main, principal. *m*, capital, patrimony; *com* capital stock. *f*, capital (city). **c. pagado**, paid-in capital stock

capitalismo *m*, capitalism

capitalista *a* capitalistic. *mf* capitalist

capitalización *f*, capitalization

capitalizar *vt* to capitalize

capitán *m*, captain, skipper; chief, leader; ringleader. *aer* **c. de aviación**, group captain. **c. de fragata**, *nav* commander. **c. de puerto**, harbor master. **c. general de ejército**, field-marshal

capitana *f*, admiral's ship; *inf* captain's wife

capitanear *vt* to captain, command; *fig* guide, lead

capitanía *f*, captaincy; captainship

capitel *m*, *arch* capital

capitolio *m*, dignified building; *arch* acropolis; Capitol

capitulación *f*, agreement, pact; capitulation; *pl* marriage articles

capitular *a* capitulary, belonging to a Chapter. *m*, capitular, member of a Chapter. *vi* to make an agreement; capitulate; sing prayers; arrange order

capítulo *m*, *ecc* Chapter; meeting of town council, etc.; chapter (of book); item (in a budget); determination, decision

capó *m*, *aut* hood

capón *a* castrated; gelded. *m*, capon; bundle of firewood or vines

caponera *f*, coop for fattening capons; *inf* gaol; *inf* place where one lives well free of charge

capota *f*, *bot* head of teasel; bonnet; hood (of vehicles)

capote *m*, short, brightly colored cape (used by bullfighters); cape coat; (cards) slam; *inf* scowl

capricho *m*, caprice, fancy; strong desire

caprichoso *a* capricious; whimsical

caprichudo *a* headstrong; capricious

Capricornio *m*, Capricorn

cápsula *f*, cartridge-case; bottlecap; (*bot med chem zool*) capsule

captar *vt* gain, attract (goodwill, attention, etc.); *mech* collect; monitor (foreign broadcasts)

captor *m*, capturer

captura *f*, *law* capture; seizing, arrest

capturar *vt* to capture; arrest, apprehend

capucha *f*, hood; cowl; *print* circumflex accent

capuchina *f*, Capuchin nun; *bot* nasturtium; table-lamp with an extinguisher

capuchino (-na) *a* and *n* Capuchin

capucho *m*, cowl

capullo *m*, cocoon; flower bud; acorn cup; *anat* prepuce

caqui *m*, khaki; khaki color

cara *f*, face; likeness, aspect; façade; front; surface; side (of metal, etc.); mien. **c. a c.**, face to face; frankly; openly. *inf* **c. de juez**, severe face. *inf* **c. de pascua**, smiling face. *inf* **c. de vinagre**, sour face. **c. o cruz**, heads or tails. **de c.**, opposite. **hacer a dos caras**, to be deceitful, be two-faced. **hacer c. (a)**, to stand up to

caraba *f*, *slang* 25-centimo coin

cárabe m, amber

carabina f, carbine; rifle

carabinazo m, report of a carbine

carabinero m, carabineer; customs' guard, revenue guard; customs officer, customs official

caracol m, snail; snail's shell; cure; *zool* cochlea; winding stair. **c. marino,** periwinkle. **¡Caracoles!** Fancy!

caracola f, conch shell used as a horn

caracolear vi to prance from side to side (horses)

carácter m, sign, mark; character, writing (gen. *pl*); style of writing; brand (animals); nature, temperament; character, individuality, strong-mindedness, energy, firmness; condition, state, capacity. **comedia de c.,** psychological play. **en su c. de,** as in one's capacity as. **caracteres de imprenta,** printing types

característica f, quality, characteristic; *math* characteristic; actress who plays the part of an old woman

característico a characteristic, distinctive. m, actor who plays roles of old men

caracterización f, characterization; *theat* make-up

caracterizar vt to characterize; confer an office, honor, dignity, on; *theat* create a character; vr *theat* to make up, dress as, a character

caraísmo m, Karaism

caraíta a and mf Karaite

¡caramba! interj gosh!; blast!

carámbano m, icicle

carambola f, cannon (billiards); inf double effect; inf trick, deception

caramelo m, caramel; toffee

caramillo m, flageolet; small flute, pipe; gossip, intrigue

carantamaula f, inf hideous mask; ugly person

carapacho m, carapace, shell

carátula f, mask; fig dramatic art, the theater

caravana f, caravan, group of traders, pilgrims, etc. (especially in East); inf crowd of excursionists, picnickers, etc.

¡caray! interj blast!; gosh!

carbólico a carbolic

carbón m, coal; charcoal; black chalk, crayon. **c. bituminoso,** soft coal. **c. de coque,** coke. **c. de leña,** charcoal. **c. mineral,** coal, anthracite. **mina de c.,** coal-mine

carboncillo m, charcoal crayon

carbonear vt to turn into charcoal; *naut* coal

carboneo m, coaling

carbonera f, coal-cellar, coal-house, etc.; coal-scuttle; woman who sells charcoal or coal; charcoal burner

carbonería f, coal or charcoal merchant's office

carbonero a relating to coal or charcoal. m, collier; charcoal maker; coal merchant; *naut* coal-ship

carbónico a *chem* carbonic

carbonífero a carboniferous

carbonizar vt to carbonize

carbono m, *chem* carbon

carbonoso a carbonaceous; coaly

carbunco m, *med* carbuncle

carbúnculo m, carbuncle, ruby

carburador m, carburetor

carcaj m, quiver (for arrows)

carcajada f, burst of laughter, guffaw. **reírse a carcajadas,** to roar with laughter

carcajearse vi to guffaw

carcamal m, inf dotard

cárcel f, prison, jail

carcelario a prison, jail

carcelero (-ra) a jail. n jailer

cárcola f, treadle (of a loom)

carcoma f, wood-worm; dry rot; fig gnawing care; spendthrift

carcomer vt to gnaw wood (worms); fig undermine (health, etc.); vr be worm-eaten

carda f, card, carding; teasel head; card brush; inf reprimand

cardador (-ra) n carder, comber

cardadura f, carding; carding frame

cardar vt to card, tease; brush up (felt, etc.)

cardenal m, cardinal; cardinal bird; bruise

cardenalato m, cardinalate, cardinalship

cardenillo m, verdigris; *art* verditer

cárdeno a livid

cardíaco a *med* cardiac

cardinal a principal; cardinal (point); *gram* cardinal (number)

cardiógrafo m, *med* cardiograph

cardiograma m, *med* cardiogram

cardizal m, waste land covered with thistles and weeds

cardo m, *bot* thistle

carear vt to confront; compare; vi turn towards, face; vr meet; come together

carecer vi irr to be short; lack, need (e.g. **Carece de las condiciones necesarias,** It lacks the necessary conditions). See **conocer**

carena f, *naut* bottom; careening

carenar vt to careen

carencia f, shortage, lack

carestía f, shortage, scarcity; famine; dearness, high price

careta f, mask; beekeeper's veil; fencing mask. fig **quitar la c. (a),** to unmask

carey m, *zool* shell turtle; tortoise-shell

carga f, loading; *elec* charging, charge; load; burden, weight; cargo; explosive charge; fig imposition; tax; duty, obligation. *naut* **c. de profundidad,** depth charge

cargadero m, place where goods are loaded or unloaded

cargado a loaded; heavy, sultry; strong (tea, coffee). **c. de cadenas,** (prisoner, etc.) in chains. **c. de espaldas,** round-shouldered

cargador m, loader; porter; dockhand; pitchfork; rammer; *mech* stoker; *elec* charger

cargamento m, *naut* cargo, freight, shipload

cargar vt to load; charge (guns, etc.); stoke; overburden; tax, impose; blame for, charge with; inf annoy, bore; *Argentina* inf to kid, tease; *com* charge, book; *mil* attack; (football) tackle; vi tip, slope; (with con) carry away; be loaded with (fruit); assume responsibility; (with sobre) importune, urge; lean against; vr turn (head, etc.); lower, grow darker (sky); (with de) be abundant (in or with); load oneself with

cargazón f, cargo; loading; heaviness; darkness (of the sky)

cargo m, loading; load, weight; post, office; duty, obligation; management, charge; care; *com* debit; accusation. **com el c. y la data,** debit and credit. **hacerse c. de,** to take charge of; understand; consider carefully. **ser en c. (a),** to be debtor (to)

cariancho a inf broadfaced

cariacontecido a crestfallen, disappointed; glum

cariarse vr to become carious

cariátide f, *arch* caryatid

caribe a Caribbean. mf cannibal, savage

caricatura f, caricature

caricaturesco a caricaturish

caricaturista mf caricaturist

caricaturizar vt to caricature

caricia f, caress

caridad f, charity; charitableness; alms

caries f, caries

carilargo a inf long-faced

carilla f, dim small face; mask; page (of a book)

carilleno a inf plump-faced, round-faced

carillón m, peal (of bells)

cariño m, affection; love; caress affectionately (gen. *pl*); fondness, inclination. **con c.,** affectionately

cariñoso a affectionate; loving; kind

carirredondo a inf roundfaced

carismático a charismatic

caritativo a charitable

cariz m, appearance of the sky; look, face; aspect; inf outlook (for a business deal, etc.)

carlista *a* and *mf* Carlist

carmelita *a* and *mf* Carmelite

carmen *m*, country house and garden (Granada); song; poem

carmesí *a* crimson. *m*, crimson color; cramoisy

carmín *m*, red, carmine color; red wild rose-tree and flower

carnada *f*, bait

carnaje *m*, salted meat

carnal *a* carnal; lascivious; materialistic, worldly; related by blood

carnalidad *f*, carnality

carnaval *m*, carnival. **martes de c.,** Shrove Tuesday

carnavalesco *a* carnival

carne *f*, flesh; meat; pulpy part of fruit; carnality. **c. concentrada,** meat extract. **c. congelada,** frozen meat. **c. de gallina** *fig* gooseflesh. **c. de membrillo,** quince cheese or conserve. **c. y hueso,** *fig* flesh and blood. *inf* **cobrar carnes,** to put on weight. **poner toda la c. en el asador,** *inf* to put all one's eggs in one basket

carnerada *f*, flock of sheep

carnerero (-ra) *n* shepherd

carnero *m*, sheep; mutton; mortuary; charnel-house; family burial vault. **c. marino,** *zool* seal

carnestolendas *f pl* three days of carnival before Ash Wednesday

carnet *m*, notebook, diary; identity card; membership card, pass. **c. de chófer,** driving license

carnicería *f*, butcher's shop; carnage, slaughter

carnicero *a* carnivorous; inhuman, cruel. *m*, butcher

carnívoro *a* carnivorous. *m*, carnivore

carnosidad *f*, proud flesh; local fat; fatness

carnoso *a* meaty; fleshy; full of marrow; *bot* pulpy, juicy

caro *a* beloved; expensive; dear. *adv* expensively; dear

carolingio (-ia) *a* and *n* Carolingian

carótida *f*, carotid artery

carpa *f*, *icht* carp. **c. dorada,** goldfish

carpanta *f*, *inf* violent hunger

Cárpatos, los Montes the Carpathian Mountains

carpeta *f*, table or chest cover, doily; writing case; portfolio; docket, letter file

carpetazo, dar *vt* to shelve (a project, etc.)

carpintear *vi* to carpenter

carpintería *f*, carpenter's shop; carpentry

carpinteril *a* carpentering

carpintero *m*, carpenter, joiner; *theat* scene-shifter. **c. de carretas,** wheelwright. **c. de ribera,** shipwright

carraca *f*, rattle; ratchet-drill

Carrapempe *m*, Old Nick

carrascal *m*, field of pinoaks

carraspear *vi* to clear one's throat, cough

carraspera *f*, *inf* hoarseness

carraspique *m*, *bot* candytuft

carrera *f*, run; race; racing; racecourse; *ast* course; high road; route; *mas* layer, course; line, row; *fig* ladder (in stockings, etc.); course; duration (of life); career, profession; conduct; girder. **c. de fondo,** long-distance race. **c. de relevos, c. de equipos,** relay race. **a c. abierta, a c. tendida,** at full speed

carrerista *mf* racing enthusiast; professional racer

carreta *f*, long, narrow two-wheeled cart; wagon; tumbril

carretada *f*, cart-load; *inf* great deal, mass

carretaje *m*, cartage, transport

carrete *m*, spool, reel, bobbin; fishing reel; *elec* coil; *phot* film spool

carretear *vt* to cart; drive a cart

carretela *f*, calash

carretera *f*, high road

carretería *f*, number of carts; carting trade; cartwright's yard

carretero *m*, cartwright; carter, driver

carretilla *f*, wheelbarrow; hand cart; railway truck; squib. **de c.,** *inf* mechanically, without thought; (*with saber, repetir,* etc.) by rote

carretón *m*, truck, trolley; hand cart

carril *m*, wheel mark; furrow, rut; cart road, narrow road; rail (railways, etc.)

carrillera *f*, jaw (of some animals); chin strap; *pl* bonnet strings, etc.

carrillo *m*, cheek; jowl

carriola *f*, truckle bed; curricle

carro *m*, cart; cartload; car, chariot; carriage (of a typewriter, etc.); chassis; *ast* Plow, Great Bear. **mil c. blindado,** armored car. **mil c. de asalto,** tank. **c. de mudanzas,** moving van. **c. de regar,** watercart

carrocería *f*, place where carriages are made, sold, repaired; *aut* coachwork, body shop

carrocha *f*, eggs (of insects)

carrochar *vi* to lay eggs (insects)

carromato *m*, road wagon; covered wagon

carroña *f*, putrid flesh, carrion

carroza *f*, elegant coach; state coach; carriage; float (for tableaux, etc.); *naut* awning

carruaje *m*, carriage; any vehicle

carta *f*, letter; charter; royal order; playing card; chart, map. **c. certificada,** registered letter. **c. de amparo,** safe-conduct. **c. de crédito,** *com* letter of credit. **c. de marear,** sea chart. **c. de naturaleza,** naturalization papers. **c. de pésame,** letter of condolence. **c. de venta,** *com* bill of sale. **c. ejecutoria de hidalguía,** letters patent of nobility. **carta-poder,** letter of proxy, proxy. **cartas rusas,** (game of) consequences. **poner las cartas boca arriba,** *fig* to lay one's cards on the table

cartabón *m*, set-square; shoemaker's slide; quadrant

cartaginés (-esa) *a* and *n* Carthaginian

Cartago Carthage

cartapacio *m*, note-book; schoolbag, satchel; file, batch of papers

cartear *vi cards* to play low; *vr* to correspond by letter

cartel *m*, placard, poster; cartel; pasquinade, lampoon. **fijar carteles,** to placard

cartela *f*, tablet (for writing); slip (of paper, etc.); *arch* console, bracket

cartelera *f*, billboard

cartelero *m*, billpaster, billsticker

carteo *m*, correspondence (by letter)

cartera *f*, pocketbook; wallet; dispatch-case; portfolio; notebook; pocket flap; office of a cabinet minister; *com* shares

cartería *f*, sorting room (in a post-office)

carterista *mf* pickpocket

cartero *m*, mail carrier, postman

cartesiano (-na) *a* and *n* Cartesian

Cartesio Descartes

carteta *f*, lansquenet (card game)

cartilaginoso *a* cartilaginous

cartílago *m*, cartilage

cartilla *f*, first reading book; primer; certificate of ordination; note-book; liturgical calendar. **c. de racionamiento,** ration book

cartografía *f*, cartography

cartógrafo *m*, map maker

cartón *m*, pasteboard, cardboard; *arch* bracket; *art* cartoon, design

cartuchera *f*, cartridge-pouch; cartridge-belt

cartucho *m*, cartridge; paper cone

cartuja *f*, Carthusian Order or monastery

cartujano *a* Carthusian

cartujo *m*, Carthusian monk; *inf* taciturn, reserved man

cartulina *f*, Bristol board, oaktag, pasteboard, card

carúncula *f*, caruncle, comb of cock, etc.

casa *f*, house; home; household; residence, dwelling; family house; *com* firm. **c. consistorial,** town hall. **c. cuna,** crèche. **c. de campo,** country-house. **c. de empeño,** pawnshop. **c. de huéspedes,** boarding house, lodging-house. **c. de los sustos,** haunted house (at amusement park). **c. de moneda,** mint. **c. de socorro,** First Aid Post. **c. de vecindad,** tenement. **c. mala,** house of ill repute. **c. solar** *or* **c. solariega,** family seat. **en c.**, at home (also sport usage). **poner c.**, to set up house

casaca *f*, dress coat. **volver la c.**, to become a turncoat, change one's allegiance

casación *f, law* cassation

casadero *a* marriageable

casadoro *m, Costa Rica* bus

casamata *f, mil* casemate

casamiento *m*, marriage; wedding

casar *vt* to marry (of a priest); *law* repeal; *inf* marry off; join; match, harmonize; *vi* and *vr* (*with con*) to get married

casar *m*, group of houses

casca *f*, grape skin; tan (bark); shell, peel, rind

cascabel *m*, small bell (for harness, etc.). **serpiente de c.**, rattlesnake. *inf* **ser un c.**, to be feather-brained

cascabeleo *m*, jingling of bells

cascabillo *m*, husk (of cereals)

cascada *f*, cascade; waterfall

cascadura *f*, cracking, crack

cascajo *m*, gravel, shingle; *inf* broken, old things, junk; nuts

cascanueces *m*, nutcrackers

cascar *vt* to crack, split, break; *inf* beat; *fig inf* break down (of health); *vi inf* talk, chatter

cáscara *f*, shell; peel, rind; bark. *med* **c. sagrada**, cascara

cascarón *m*, eggshell; *arch* vault

cascarrabias *mf inf* spitfire

casco *m*, cranium; broken fragment of china, glass, etc.; crown of hat; helmet; tree of saddle; bottle; tank, pipe; barrel; *naut* hull; hoof; quarter (of fruit); *pl inf* head. **c. colonial**, sun-helmet. **c. respiratorio**, smoke-helmet

cascote *m*, rubble, ruins

caseoso *a* cheesy

caserío *m*, group of houses; country house

casero *a* home made; home bred; familiar; informa; *inf* domesticated, home-loving; domestic. *m*, landlord; caretaker; tenant

caserón *m*, large tumbledown house, mansion, hall

caseta *f*, hut; cottage; booth, stall. **c. de baños**, bathing van

casi *adv* almost, nearly. **c. c.**, very nearly

casilla *f*, hut; cabin; lodge; ticket office; pigeon-hole. *aer* **c. del piloto**, cockpit

casillero *m*, file cabinet, filing cabinet; locker (as in a locker room); set of pigeonholes; *sports* scoreboard; *rw* crossing guard

casino *m*, casino; club

caso *m*, happening, event; chance, hazard; occasion, opportunity; case, matter; (*med gram*) case. **en el c. de**, in a position to (e.g. **No estamos en el c. de pagar tanto dinero.** We are in no position to pay so much money). **en tal c.**, in such a case. **en todo c.**, in any case. **no hacer c. de**, to take no notice of. **venir al c.**, to be opportune

caspa *f*, dandruff; scab

caspio *a* Caspian

¡cáspita! *interj* Amazing! Wonderful!

casquete *m*, helmet; skullcap; half wig

casquijo *m*, gravel

casquillo *m*, tip, cap, ferrule; socket; arrow-head; metal cartridge-case

casquivano *a inf* giddy, feather-brained

casta *f*, race; caste; breed (animals); kind, species, quality. **de buena c.**, pedigree (e.g. **perros de buena c.**, pedigree dogs)

castaña *f, bot* chestnut; knot, bun (of hair)

castañar *m*, chestnut plantation or grove

castañetear *vi* to play the castanets; snap one's fingers; chatter (of teeth); knock together (of knees)

castaño *a* chestnut-colored. *m*, chestnut tree; chestnut wood. **c. de Indias**, horse-chestnut tree

castañuela *f*, castanet. **tocar las castañuelas**, to play the castanets

castellán *m*, castellan

castellano (**-na**) *n* Castilian; Spaniard. *m*, Spanish (language); castellan. *a* Castilian; Spanish

casticismo *m*, purity (of language); Spanish spirit; traditionalism

castidad *f*, chastity

castigador *a* punishing. *m*, punisher; *inf* lady-killer

castigadora *f, inf* man-hunter

castigar *vt* to punish; chastise; chasten, advise; pain, grieve; correct, edit; decrease (expenses); *com* allow a discount

castigo *m*, punishment; emendation, correction

Castilla Castile

castillo *m*, castle; howdah. **c. de naipes**, house of cards. **c. de proa**, *naut* forecastle. **c. fuerte**, fortified castle. *inf* **hacer castillos en el aire**, to build castles in the air or in Spain

castizo *a* pure-blooded; prolific; pure (of language); typically Spanish; traditional

casto *a* chaste; pure, unsullied

castor *m, zool* beaver (animal and fur); soft, woollen cloth

castración *f*, castration, gelding

castrado *a* castrated. *m, inf* eunuch

castrador *m*, castrator, gelder

castrapo *m*, mixed Spanish and Galician spoken in Galicia, Spain

castrar *vt* to castrate, geld; prune; remove honeycomb from hives; weaken

castrense *a* military

castrista *v* and *mf* Castroite

casual *a* accidental, casual

casualidad *f*, chance, coincidence. **por c.**, by chance. **ser mucha c. que . . .**, to be too much of a coincidence that . . .

casucha *f, inf* tumbledown hut

casuista *a* casuistic. *mf* casuist

casuística *f*, casuistry

casulla *f*, chasuble

cata *f*, tasting; taste, sample

catabolismo *m*, catabolism

cataclismo *m*, cataclysm

catacumbas *f pl*, catacombs

catador *m*, taster, sampler

catadura *f*, tasting; look, countenance (gen. qualified)

catafalco *m*, catafalque

catalán (**-ana**) *a* and *n* Catalan, Catalonian. *m*, Catalan (language)

catalejo *m*, telescope

cataléptico *a* cataleptic

catálisis *f, chem* catalysis

catalítico *a* catalytic

catalogar *vt* to catalogue, list

catálogo *m*, catalogue, list

Cataluña Catalonia

cataplasma *f*, cataplasm

catapulta *f*, catapult

catar *vt* to taste, sample; see, examine; inspect; regard

catarata *f*, cataract, waterfall; *med* cataract (of the eyes)

catarral *a* catarrhal

catarro *m*, catarrh; common cold

catástrofe *f, lit* tragic climax; catastrophe

catastrófico *a* catastrophic

catavino *m*, taster (cup)

catavinos *m*, professional wine taster; *inf* tippler, tavern haunter

cate *m, slang* flunk (failure in a course at school)

catecismo *m*, catechism

catecúmeno (**-na**) *n* catechumen

cátedra *f*, university chair; chair in a Spanish **instituto**; professorship; university lecture room; subject taught by professor; reading desk, lectern; *ecc* throne; *ecc* see. **c. del espíritu santo**, pulpit. **c. de San Pedro**, Holy See

catedral *f*, and a cathedral

catedrático (**-ca**) *n* professor

categoría *f, phil* category; class, rank

categórico *a* categorical, downright

cateo *m, WH* sampling; prospecting; house search (by the police)

catequismo *m,* catechism; question and answer method of teaching

catequista *mf* catechist

catequizar *vt* to catechize; persuade, induce

caterva *f,* crowd, throng; jumble, collection

catéter *m, surg* probe; catheter

catódico *a elec* cathodic

cátodo *m,* cathode

catolicidad *f,* catholicity; catholic world

catolicismo *m,* Catholicism

católico (-ca) *a* universal, catholic; infallible. *a* and *n* Catholic (by religion)

catorce *a* fourteen; fourteenth. *m,* number fourteen; fourteenth (of days of month)

catorzavo *a* fourteenth

catre *m,* camp-bed; truckle-bed; cot

caucáseo (-ea) *a* and *n* Caucasian

Cáucaso, el the Caucasus

cauce *m,* river or stream bed; ditch, irrigation canal

cauchal *m,* rubber plantation

cauchera *f,* rubber tree

cauchero *m,* rubber planter

caucho *m,* caoutchouc, rubber

caución *f,* caution, precaution; surety; security

caucional *a* See **libertad**

caudal *m,* wealth, capital; flow, volume (of water); plenty, abundance (e.g. **un c. de conocimientos,** a wealth of knowledge)

caudaloso *a* carrying much water; wealthy; abundant

caudillo *m,* head, leader; chief tain. **el C.,** (title of Francisco Franco)

causa *f,* cause; reason, motive; lawsuit; *law* trial. **c. final,** *phil* final cause. **c. pública,** public welfare. **ser c. bastante para . . . ,** to be reason enough to . . .

causador (-ra) *a* motivating. *n* occasioner, originator

causalidad *f,* causality

causante *a* causative, causing. *m, law* principal; *Mexico* taxpayer

causar *vt* to cause; occasion

causticidad *f,* causticity; mordacity

cáustico *a* burning, caustic; scathing; mordant; *surg* caustic

cautela *f,* caution; astuteness, cunning

cauteloso *a* cautious; cunning

cauterio *m,* cautery

cauterización *f,* cauterization

cauterizar *vt* to cauterize

cautivar *vt* to capture; captivate, charm; attract; *vi* become a prisoner

cautiverio *m,* captivity

cautivo (-va) *a* and *n* captive

cauto *a* cautious; prudent; sly

cava *f,* digging (especially vines); wine cellar in royal palaces

cavador (-ra) *n* digger, hoer

cavadura *f,* digging, hoeing; sinking (wells)

cavar *vt* to dig, hoe; sink (wells); *vi* hollow; *fig* go deeply into a thing

caverna *f,* cavern, cave; *med* cavity (generally in the lung)

cavernícola *a* cave. **hombre c.,** cave-man

cavernoso *a* cavernous; caverned; *fig* hollow (cough, etc.); deaf

cavidad *f,* cavity; sinus; cell

cavilación *f,* caviling

cavilar *vt* to cavil; criticize

caviloso *a* captious

cayado *m,* crook; bishop's crozier

caz *m,* channel, canal; head-race; flume

caza *f,* hunting; hunt, chase; game. *m, aer* fighter. **aer c. lanzacohetes,** rocket-launching aircraft. **c. nocturno,** night fighter. *naut* **dar c.,** to pursue

cazaautógrafos *m,* autograph hunter

cazabombardero *m, aer* fighter bomber

cazadero *m,* hunting ground

cazador *a* hunting. *m, mil* chasseur; huntsman

cazadora *f,* huntress; jacket; forage cap

cazadotes *m,* dowry hunter

cazafortunas *mf* fortune hunter

cazar *vt* to hunt, chase; *fig inf* run to earth; *fig inf* catch out; *inf* overcome by flattery

cazasubmarino *m,* submarine chaser

cazatorpedero *m, naut* torpedo-boat destroyer

cazo *m,* ladle; dipper

cazolada *f,* panful

cazoleta *f,* small pan; bowl (of pipe, etc.); sword guard; boss of a shield; pan (of a firelock)

cazuela *f,* earthenware cooking dish; stew-pot; part of theater formerly reserved for women; *theat* gallery

cazumbrón *m,* cooper

cazurro *a inf* unsociable; surly, boorish

c.c.p. abbrev. of **con copia para**

ce *f,* name of the letter C. *interj* Look! Chist! **ce por be,** in detail

cebada *f,* barley (plant and grain). **c. perlada,** pearl barley

cebadal *m,* barley field

cebadera *f,* nose-bag; barley bin

cebadero *m,* barley dealer

cebado *a* on the prowl; having tasted human flesh (animal)

cebar *vt* to feed or fatten (animals); fuel, feed (furnace, etc.); prime, charge (fire-arms, etc.); start up (machines); bait (fish hook); stimulate (passion, etc.); *vi* stick in, penetrate (nails, screws, etc.); *vr* put one's mind to; grow angry. **cebarse en vanas esperanzas,** to nurture vain hopes

cebo *m,* fodder; detonator; encouragement, food; bait

cebolla *f,* onion; onion bulb; any bulbous stem; oil bulb (of lamp). **c. escalonia,** shallot

cebollana *f,* chive

cebollero (-ra) *n* onion seller

cebolleta *f,* leek; young onion

cebollino *m,* onion seed; onion bed; chive

cebra *f,* zebra

ceca *f,* mint (for coining money); name of mosque in Cordova. **de C. en Meca,** from pillar to post, hither and thither

cecear *vi* to lisp

ceceo *m,* lisping

ceceoso *a* lisping

cecial *m,* dried fish

cecina *f,* dried salt meat

cedazo *m,* sieve, strainer

ceder *vt* to cede, give up; transfer; *vi* give in, yield; diminish, decrease (fever, storm, etc.); fail, end; happen, turn out; sag, give, stretch. **No c. la fama a,** to be no less famous than

cedro *m,* cedar tree; cedar wood. **c. dulce,** red cedar

cédula *f,* document, certificate, card. *ecc* **c. de comunión,** Communion card. **c. personal,** identity card. **c. real,** royal letters patent

céfiro *m,* west wind; *poet* zephyr

cegajoso *a* blear-eyed

cegar *vi irr* to become blind; *vt* to put out the eyes; *fig* blind; wall up, close up, stop up; infatuate. *Pres. Ind.* **ciego, ciegas, ciega, ciegan.** *Pres. Subjunc.* **ciegue, ciegues, ciegue, cieguen**

cegato *a inf* short-sighted

ceguedad, ceguera *f,* blindness; delusion; ignorance

Ceilán Ceylon

ceja *f,* eyebrow; cloud cap; mountain peak; *mus* bridge (of stringed instruments). *fig* **quemarse las cejas,** to burn the midnight oil

cejar *vi* to go backwards; give way, hesitate

cejijunto *a* having eyebrows that almost meet, beetle-browed

cejo *m,* river mist

cejudo *a* having long thick eyebrows

celada *f*, helmet; ambush; fraud, trick

celador (-ra) *a* watchful, zealous. *n* supervisor; caretaker; guard (at a museum, etc.)

celaje *m*, sky with scudding clouds (gen. *pl*); skylight, window; promising sign, presage

celar *vt* to be zealous in discharge of duties; spy upon; watch; oversee, superintend; conceal; engrave

celda *f*, cell

celdilla *f*, cell (bees, wasps, etc.); (*zool bot*) cell; *bot* capsule

celebérrimo, *a sup* **célebre** most celebrated

celebración *f*, celebration; applause

celebrador (-ra) *n* celebrator; applauder

celebrante *a* celebrating. *m*, *ecc* celebrant

celebrar *vt* to celebrate; applaud; praise; venerate; hold, conduct; **c. que** + *subj*, to be happy that, be glad that. *vt* and *vi ecc* officiate; *vr* take place

célebre *a* famous

celebridad *f*, fame, celebrity; magnificence, show, pomp

celeridad *f*, celerity

celeste *a* celestial, heavenly

celestial *a* celestial, heavenly; perfect, delightful; *inf* foolish (ironical)

celestina *f*, procuress (allusion to *Tragicomedia de Calixto y Melibea*)

celestinaje *m*, pandering, procuring

celibato *m*, celibacy; *inf* bachelor

célibe *a* celibate, unmarried. *mf* unmarried person

celo *m*, enthusiasm, ardor; religious zeal; devotion; jealousy; heat, rut; *pl* jealousy, suspicion. **dar celos (a),** to make jealous

celosía *f*, lattice; Venetian blind

celoso *a* zealous; jealous; suspicious

celta *a* Celtic. *mf* Celt

célula *f*, cell

celular *a* cellular

celuloide *f*, celluloid

celulosa *f*, cellulose

celuloso *a* cellular

cementación *f*, cementation

cementar *vt* to cement

cementerio *m*, cemetery

cemento *m*, cement

cena *f*, evening meal; supper; Last Supper

cenacho *m*, marketing bag

cenáculo *m*, cenacle

cenador *m*, diner out; arbor, pergola

cenagal *m*, quagmire; *fig* impasse

cenagoso *a* miry, muddy

cenar *vi* to dine, sup; *vt* eat for evening meal, sup off

cenceño *a* slim, thin

cencerrada *f*, noisy mock serenade given to widows or widowers on the first night of their new marriage

cencerrear *vi* to jingle; *inf* play out of tune; bang in the wind, rattle; squeak

cencerreo *m*, jingling; jangle; rattling; squeaking

cencerro *m*, cow-bell

cendal *m*, gauze; *ecc* stole; barbs of a feather

cenefa *f*, border; valance, flounce; edging

cenicero *m*, ash-pan; ash-pit; ash-tray

ceniciento *a* ash colored, ashen. **la Cenicienta,** Cinderella

cenit *m*, *ast* zenith; *fig* peak, summit

ceniza *f*, ash, cinders

cenotafio *m*, cenotaph

censo *m*, census; agreement for settlement of an annuity; annual ground rent; leasehold

censor *m*, censor; censorious person; *univ* proctor

censual *a* pertaining to census, annuity, rents

censualista *mf* annuitant

censura *f*, censorship; criticism; blame, reproach; scandal, gossip; *psy* censorship

censurable *a* reprehensible; censorable

censurar *vt* to judge; censure; criticize

centauro *m*, *myth* centaur

centavo *m*, hundredth part; cent

centella *f*, lightning; spark; flash; *fig* spark (of anger, affection, etc.)

centellador *a* flashing

centellear *vi* to flash; twinkle; sparkle

centelleo *m*, scintillation; sparkle; flash

centén *m*, Spanish gold coin once worth 100 reals and later 25 pesetas

centena *f*, hundred

centenal, centenar *m*, hundred; centenary; rye field. **a centenares,** by the hundred, in crowds

centenario (-ia) *a* centenary. *n* centenarian. *m*, centenary

centeno *m*, *bot* rye

centésimo *a* and *m*, hundredth

centígrado *a* centigrade

centigramo *m*, centigram

centilitro *m*, centiliter

centímetro *m*, centimeter. **c. cúbico,** cubic centimeter, milliliter

céntimo *a* hundredth. *m*, centime (coin)

centinela *mf mil* sentry, sentinel; person on watch. **estar de c.,** to be on sentry duty; be on guard

centolla *f*, marine crab

centón *m*, patchwork quilt

central *a* central; centric. *f*, head office; central depot; mother house. **c. de fuerza,** power-house. **c. telefónica,** telephone exchange

centralilla, centralita *f*, local exchange; private exchange

centralismo *m*, centralism

centralista *a* centralistic. *mf* centralist

centralización *f*, centralization

centralizador *a* centralizing

centralizar *vt* to centralize

centrar *vt* to center

céntrico *a* central, centric; centrally located; downtown

centrífugo *a* centrifugal

centrípeto *a* centripetal

centro *m*, center; headquarters, meeting place, club; center, hub; middle; core (of a rope); *fig* focus. *phys* **c. de gravedad,** center of gravity. **c. de mesa,** table center-piece. *anat* **centro nervioso,** nerve center

centroamericano (-na) *a* and *n* Central American

céntuplo *a* centuple

centuria *f*, century

centurión *m*, centurion

ceñidamente tightly (e.g. **un argumento c. organizado,** a tightly organized plot)

ceñido *a* thrifty; wasp-waisted, slender waisted; fitting (of garments)

ceñidor *m*, girdle, belt

ceñir *vt irr* to girdle; surround; shorten, abbreviate; *vr* be moderate (speech, expenditure, etc.); conform, confine oneself (to). **ceñirse a las reglas,** to abide by the rules. *Pres. Ind.* **ciño, ciñes, ciñen.** *Pres. Part.* **ciñendo.** *Preterite* **ciñó, ciñeron.** *Pres. Subjunc.* **ciña,** etc. *Imperf. Subjunc.* **ciñese,** etc.

ceño *m*, band, hoop; frown; *fig* dark outlook

ceñudo *a* frowning

cepillar *vt* to brush; plane; smooth

cepa *f*, stump; vine-stock; root (tails, antlers, etc.); *fig* origin, trunk (of a family); *biol* strain. **de la más pura c.,** of the best quality

cepillo *m*, brush; *carp* plane; poor-box, offertory-box. **c. para los dientes,** toothbrush. **c. para ropa,** clothes-brush. **c. para el suelo,** scrubbing-brush. **c. para las uñas,** nail-brush

cepo *m*, bough; wooden stocks; snare; trap; poor-box; collecting-box

cera *f*, beeswax; wax; wax candles, etc., used at a function. *inf* **ser como una c.,** to be like wax (in the hands of)

cerador *m*, floor waxer (person)

ceradora *f*, floor waxer (machine)

cerámica *f*, ceramics; ceramic art, pottery

cerámico *a* ceramic

cerbatana *f,* blow-pipe, popgun; pea-shooter; ear-trumpet

cerca *f,* fence, wall

cerca *adv* near. **c. de,** near to; almost, nearly (e.g. **c. de las once,** nearly eleven o'clock)

cercado *m,* enclosure, fenced in place; fence

cercanía *f,* nearness, proximity; (gen. *pl*) outskirts, surroundings

cercano *a* near, neighboring; impending, early

cercar *vt* to enclose; build a wall or fence round; to lay siege to; crowd round; *mil* surround

cercenamiento (a) *m,* curtailment (of)

cercenar *vt* to lop off the ends, clip; curtail, diminish; abridge; whittle

cerciorar *vt* to assure, confirm; *vr* make sure

cerco *m,* ring, hoop; fence; siege; small conversational circle; spin, circling; halo (sun, moon); frame; sash (of a window). **poner c. (a),** to lay siege to, blockade

cerda *f,* sow; bristle

Cerdeña Sardinia

cerdo *m,* pig, hog

cerdoso *a* bristly

cereal *a* and *m,* cereal

cerebelo *m, anat* cerebellum

cerebral *a* cerebral

cerebro *m,* cerebrum; brain; intelligence

cerebro-espinal *a* cerebrospinal

ceremonia *f,* ceremony; function, display; formality. **de c.,** ceremonial; formally. **por c.,** for politeness' sake

ceremonial *a* ceremonial. *m,* ceremony; rite; protocol (rules of behavior)

ceremonioso *a* ceremonious; formal, over-courteous

cerero *m,* wax-chandler

cereza *f,* cherry

cerezal *m,* cherry orchard

cerezo *m,* cherry tree; cherry wood

cerilla *f,* wax taper; match; ear wax

cerner *vt irr* to sieve; watch, observe; *fig* sift, clarify; *vi* bolt (of plants); drizzle; *vr* waddle; hover; threaten (of evil, etc.). *Pres. Ind.* **cierno, ciernes, cierne, ciernen.** *Pres. Subjunc.* **cierna, ciernas, cierna, ciernan**

cernícalo *m, orn* kestrel; *inf* lout

cernidillo *m,* drizzle; teetering walk

cernido *m,* sifting, sieving; sifted flour

cerniduras *f pl,* siftings

cero *m, math* zero; naught; (tennis) love. *fig inf* **ser un c.,** to be a mere cipher

cerote *m,* cobbler's wax. *inf* fear

cerquillo *m,* tonsure; welt (of a shoe)

cerquita *adv* very near, hard by

cerradero, m, cerradera *f,* bolt staple; catch of a lock; clasp or strings of a purse

cerradizo *a* closable, lockable

cerrado *a* closed; compact; incomprehensible, obscure; overcast, cloudy; *inf* taciturn; secretive. *m,* enclosure

cerradura *f,* fastening, lock; closing, locking

cerraja *f,* lock (of a door); bolt

cerrajería *f,* locksmith's craft; locksmith's workshop or shop

cerrajero *m,* locksmith

cerramiento *m,* closing, locking up; fence; enclosure, shooting preserve; partition wall

cerrar *vt irr* to close; lock, fasten, bolt; shut up; *mech* shut off, turn off; fold up; block or stop up; seal (letters, etc.); close down; terminate; obstruct; (*with con*) attack; *vi* close; close in (of night, etc.); *vr* heal up (wounds); close (flowers); *rad* close down; crowd together; *fig* stand firm. *inf* **cerrarse la espuela,** to take a nightcap, have a last drink. **c. la marcha,** to bring up the rear. **al c. la edición,** stop press. See **acertar**

cerrazón *f,* dark, overcast sky heralding a storm

cerril *a* rough, rocky; wild, untamed (cattle, horses); *inf* boorish

cerrillar *vt* to mill coins

cerro *m,* neck of an animal; spine, backbone; hill. *fig*

irse por los cerros de Úbeda, to go off the track, indulge in irrelevancies

cerrojo *m,* bolt (of a door, etc.); lock (of a door, gun, etc.)

certamen *m,* contest; competition; match

certero *a* well-aimed; sure, well-timed; knowledgeable, sure

certeza, certidumbre *f,* certitude, assurance

certificación *f,* certification; certificate; affidavit

certificado *a* certified; registered. *m,* registered letter; certificate

certificar *vt* to certify; register (letter, etc.)

certificatorio *a* certifying or serving to certify

certísimo *a* learned form of the superlative of **cierto** (see **certísimo**)

certitud *f,* certitude

cervantino *a* Cervantine

cervato *m,* fawn

cervecería *f,* brewery; ale-house

cervecero (-ra) *n* brewer; beer seller

cerveza *f,* beer, ale. **c. negra,** stout

cerviz *f,* cervix, nape (of neck). **doblar** (*or* **bajar**) **la c.,** to humble oneself

cesación *f,* cessation, stopping

cesante *a* dismissed; pensioned off. **declarar c. (a),** to dismiss (a person from a post). **estar c.,** to be out of a job

cesantía *f,* status of dismissed or retired official; retirement pension

cesar *vi* to cease, stop, end; leave an employment; desist; retire

cesáreo *a* Cesarean; imperial

cese *m,* stopping of payment for an employment

cesión *f,* cession; transfer; resignation; *law* release

cesionario (-ia) *n* cessionary, transferee

cesionista *mf* grantor, transferer

césped *m,* grass, sward; sod, lawn

cesta *f,* basket, hamper; *sport* racket; cradle (for a wine bottle)

cestada *f,* basketful

cestería *f,* basketmaking, basketweaving; basket factory; basket shop; basketwork

cestero (-ra) *n* basket maker or seller

cesto *m,* basket, hamper, skip

cesura *f,* cesura

cetáceo *a* and *m, zool* cetacean

cetorrino *m,* basking shark

cetrería *f,* falconry

cetrino *a* greenish-yellow; sallow; citrine; melancholy; reserved, aloof

cetro *m,* scepter; verge; reign

Cevenes, los the Cevennes

chabacanería *f,* bad taste; vulgarity

chabacano *a* vulgar, common; rude, uncouth

chacal *m, zool* jackal

cháchara *f, inf* empty chatter; verbiage

chacharear *vi* to chatter; gabble, cackle

chacharero *a inf* chattering; talkative

chacolotear *vi* to clatter, clink (loose horseshoe)

chacota *f,* merriment, mirth

chacotear *vi inf* to be merry, have fun

chacotón *a* of a boisterous humor

chafado *a* taken aback; disappointed

chafallar *vt inf* to mend carelessly; botch

chafandín *m,* vain fool

chafar *vt* to flatten; crumple, crease (clothes); *inf* heckle

chafarrinar *vt* to stain, mark, blot

chaflán *m,* bevel edge, chamfer

chagrén *m,* shagreen leather

chal *m,* shawl

chalán *m,* horse-dealer

chalana *f, naut* wherry, lighter

chalanear *vt* to bargain; indulge in sharp practice

chalar *vt* to drive mad; enamour

chaleco *m,* waistcoat; cardigan

chalina *f,* flowing scarf, artist's bow

Chalo pet form of the male given name *Carlos* 'Charles', hence = English *Chuck; Bud, Mac* (in direct address to a male whose name one does not know)

chalote *m*, shallot

chalupa *f*, shallop; launch; canoe; long boat, ship's boat

chamar *vt inf* to palm off, barter

chamarasca *f*, brushwood, tinder

chamarilero (-ra) *n* secondhand dealer

chamarreta *f*, sheepskin jacket; *Mexico* jacket

chambelán *m*, court chamberlain

chambergo *a* pertaining to the Chambergo regiment. *m*, broad-brimmed hat

chambón *a inf* awkward, clumsy; lucky

chambonada *f*, *inf* blunder; fluke, chance

chambra *f*, dressing-jacket, peignoir, negligee

chamicera *f*, piece of scorched earth (woodland, etc.)

chamorro *a* close-cropped, shorn (hair)

champán *m*, champagne. **c. obrero,** *humorous* cider

champaña *m*, champagne

champar *vt inf* to cast in a person's face, remind

champú *m*, shampoo

chamuscar *vt* to scorch; singe

chamusquina *f*, scorching; singeing; *inf* brawl

chanada *f*, *inf* trick, mischievous act

chancearse *vr* to joke

chancero *a* joking, facetious

chanchollada *f*, dirty trick, foul play, trick

chanchullo *m*, *inf* fraud

canciller *m*, chancellor

chancillería *f*, chancery

chancla *f*, down at heel shoe; heelless slipper

chancleta *f*, heelless slipper, babouche. *mf inf* ninny

chancleteo *m*, clicking of heelless slippers

chanclo *m*, overshoe; Wellington

chanfaina *f*, *cul* savory fricassee

chanflón *a* tough, coarse; ungainly

chantaje *m*, blackmail

chantajista *mf* blackmailer

chantar *vt* to put on, clothe; *inf* tell plainly. *inf* **c. sus verdades,** to tell hometruths

chanza *f*, joke, jest

chanzoneta *f*, canzonetta; *inf* joke

chapa *f*, plate, sheet; veneer; clasp; *inf* prudence, common sense; rouge. **c. de hierro,** sheet-iron. **c. de identidad,** number plate

chapado a la antigua *a* old-fashioned

chapalear *vi* to dabble in water; splash; clatter (of a horseshoe)

chapaleo *m*, dabbling, paddling; splash; clattering, clink (of a horseshoe)

chapaleteo *m*, lapping of water; splashing (of rain)

chaparrear *vi* to pour with rain

chaparrón *m*, heavy shower of rain, downpour

chapear *vt* to veneer; *vi* clatter (loose horseshoe)

chapeo *m*, hat

chaperón *m*, hood

chapeta *f*, *dim* clasp; red flush or spot on cheek

chapetón (-ona) *n WH* recently arrived European, especially Spaniard

chapín *m*, cork-soled leather overshoe (for women) *ant*

chapino *a* and *m*, *Mexico contemptuous* Guatemalan

chapitel *m*, *arch* capital; spire

chapodar *vt* to prune, lop off branches; cut down, reduce

chapotear *vt* to sponge, moisten, damp; *vi* paddle, splash; dabble or trail the hands (in water)

chapoteo *m*, moistening, sponging; paddling, splashing; dabbling

chapucear *vt* to botch, do badly; bungle

chapuceramente *adv* awkwardly. **hablar el japonés c.,** to speak broken Japanese

chapucería *f*, roughness, poor workmanship; botch

chapucero *a* rough, badly finished; bungling, clumsy, awkward

chapurrado *a* broken (e.g. **hablar un italiano c.,** to speak broken Italian)

chapurrar, chapurrear *vt* to speak badly (a language); jabber; *inf* mix (drinks)

chapuz *m*, ducking, submerging; plunge; unimportant job; clumsiness

chapuzar *vt* to duck, submerge; plunge

chaqué *m*, morning coat; morning suit

chaqueta *f*, jacket; *mech* casing

chaquete *m*, backgammon

chaquetilla *f*, short jacket; coatee; blazer

chaquetón *m*, short coat. **c. de piloto,** *aer* pea-jacket

charabán *m*, charabanc

charada *f*, charade

charanguero *a* rough, badly finished; clumsy. *m*, Andalusian boat

charca *f*, pond, pool; reservoir

charco *m*, puddle; *inf* sea

charla *f*, *inf* chatter; conversation; talk, informal lecture

charlar *vi inf* to prattle, chatter; chat, converse; give a talk (on)

charlatán (-ana) *a* loquacious, garrulous; indiscreet; fraudulent, false. *n* charlatan; chatterer

charlatanería *f*, loquacity, garrulity; quackery

charlatanismo *m*, charlatanism, quackery

charnela *f*, hinge; hinged joint

charol *m*, japan, varnish; patent leather

charolar *vt* to japan, varnish

charolista *m*, varnisher

charpa *f*, pistol-belt; sling

charrán (-ana) *n* rogue, trickster

charranada *f*, roguery, knavery

charrería *f*, tawdriness; gaudiness

charretera *f*, *mil* epaulet; garter

charro *a* churlish, coarse; flashy, tawdry

chasca *f*, brushwood, firewood

chascar *vi* to creak, crack; clack (the tongue); swallow

chascarrillo *m*, *inf* amusing anecdote, good story

chasco *m*, trick, practical joke; disappointment. **llevarse un c.,** to meet with a disappointment

chasis *m*, *aut* chassis; *phot* plate-holder; *mech* underframe

chasquear *vt* to play a trick on; wag (one's tongue); crack (a whip, one's knuckles); break a promise, disappoint; *vi* creak, crack; meet with a disappointment

chasquido *m*, crack (of whip); creaking (of wood); click (of the tongue)

chatarra *f*, scrap iron; junk

chato *a* flat-nosed; flat

chauvinismo *m*, chauvinism

chaval *a inf* young. *m*, lad

chaveta *f*, *mech* bolt, pin, peg, cotter, key

che *f*, name of the letter *ch*

checo (-ca) *a* and *n* Czech. Czech (language)

checoslovaco (-ca) *a* Czechoslovakian. *n* Czechoslovak

Checoslovaquia Czechoslovakia

Chejov Chekov

chelín *m*, shilling

Chengis-Jan Genghis Khan

chepa *f*, *inf* hunch (back); hump

cheque *m*, check. **c. cruzado,** crossed check

chica *f*, girl; *inf* dear

chicana *f*, chicanery

chicano (-na) *a* and *n* Chicano, American of Mexican ancestry

chícharo *m*, pea

chicharrón *m*, *cul* crackling; burnt meat; *inf* sunburnt person

chichón *m*, bruise, bump

chichonera *f*, child's protective hat (something like a straw crash-helmet)

chicle *m*, chewing gum

chiclero *m*, chicle-gatherer

chico (-ca) *a* little, small; young. *m*, little boy; youth; *inf* old boy, dear. **Es un buen c.,** He's a good fellow

chicoleo *m*, *inf* compliment

chicote *mf* sturdy child. *m*, *inf* cigar

chifla *f*, whistling, whistle; tanner's paring knife

chiflado *a inf* cracked, daft; crack-brained

chifladura *f,* whistling; *inf* whim, mania, hobby

chiflar *vi* to whistle; *vt* to make fun of, hiss; pare or scrape leather; *inf* swill, tipple; *vr inf* have a slate loose; be slightly mad; *inf* lose one's head over, adore

chifle *m,* whistle, whistling; decoy call (birds)

chile *m, bot* red pepper, chilli

chileno (-na) *a* and *n* Chilean

chillador *a* screaming, shrieking

chillar *vi* to scream, shriek; creak; squeak; jabber (monkeys, etc.); *art* be strident (of colors)

chillería *f,* shrieking, screaming

chillido *m,* scream, shriek; squeak (of mice, etc.); jabber (of monkeys, etc.)

chillón *a inf* screaming, yelling; strident, piercing; crude, loud (colors)

chimenea *f,* chimney; funnel; fireplace; kitchen range

chimpancé *m,* chimpanzee

china *f,* pebble; porcelain, china; Chinese silk

chinche *f,* bedbug; thumbtack, drawing-pin. *mf inf* bore

chinchona *f,* quinine

chinchorrería *f, inf* impertinence, tediousness; gossip

chinela *f,* mule, slipper; overshoe, patten *ant*

chinero *m,* china cupboard

chinesco *a* Chinese. **a la chinesca,** in Chinese fashion

chino (-na) *a* and *n* Chinese. *m,* Chinese (language)

Chipre Cyprus

chipriota *a* and *mf* Cypriot

chiquero *m,* pigsty; stable for bulls

chiquillada *f,* childishness, puerility

chiquillería *f, inf* crowd of children

chiquillo (-lla) *n* small boy

chiquito (-ta) *a dim* **chico,** tiny, very small. *n* little one, small boy

chirimía *f,* flageolet. *m,* flageolet player

chiripa *f,* (billiards) fluke; *inf* happy coincidence, stroke of luck; lucky guess

chirivía *f, bot* parsnip; *orn* wagtail

chirlar *vi inf* to gabble, talk loudly

chirlo *m,* knife wound, sabre cut; knife scar

chirona *f, inf* jail

chirriador *a* sizzling, crackling; creaking, squeaking

chirriar *vi* to sizzle, crackle; creak, squeak; squawk; *inf* croak, sing out of tune

chirrido *m,* squawk; croaking; noise of grasshoppers; squeaking; creaking, creak

¡chis! *interj* Shh! Silence!

chisme *m,* gossip, tale; *inf* small household utensil, trifle

chismear *vt* to tell tales, gossip

chismero (-ra), chismoso (-sa) *a* gossiping, talebearing. *n* gossip, tale bearer

chispa *f,* spark; ember; *elec* spark; tiny diamond; small particle; wit; quickwittedness; *inf* drunkenness. **c. del encendido,** ignition spark

chispazo *m,* flying out of a spark, sparking; damage done by spark; *inf* gossip, rumor

chispeante *a* sparking; sparkling; *fig* scintillating (with wit etc.)

chispear *vi* to throw out sparks, spark; sparkle, gleam; *fig* scintillate; drizzle gently

chisporrotear *vi inf* to sputter; fizz

chisporroteo *m, inf* sputtering; fizz

chisposo *a* sputtering, throwing out sparks

chistar *vi* to speak, break silence (gen. used negatively)

chiste *m,* witticism, bon mot; amusing incident; joke

chistera *f,* creel (for fish); *inf* top-hat, tile

chistoso *a* joking; amusing, funny

chiticallando *adv* quietly, stealthily; *inf* on the quiet, in secret

¡chito! ¡chitón! *interj* Hush! Sh!

chiva *f, Panama* bus

chivo *n zool* kid. **c. expiatorio,** scapegoat

chocante *a* colliding; provoking; shocking; surprising

chocar *vi* to collide; strike (against); run into; fight, clash; *vt* clink (glasses); provoke, annoy; surprise, shock. **¡Choca cinco!** Clasp five!, Gimme five!, Put it

there!, Give some skin! (invitation to shake hands)

chocarrería *f,* coarse joke

chochear *vi* to be senile; *fig inf* dote (on)

chocho *a* senile; *fig inf* doting

choco *m,* small hump, hunchback

chocolate *m,* chocolate; drinking chocolate. **c. a la española,** thick chocolate. **c. a la francesa,** French drinking chocolate

chocolatería *f,* chocolate factory or shop

chocolatero (-ra) *a* fond of chocolate. *n* chocolate maker or seller

chófer *m,* chauffeur; driver

chopera *f,* grove or plantation of black poplar trees

chopo *m, bot* black poplar; *inf* gun

choque *m,* collision; shock; jar; *med* concussion; fight; clink (of glasses); clash; *mil* skirmish

choricera *f,* sausage-making machine

choricero (-ra) *a* sausage maker

chorizo *m,* kind of pork sausage; counterweight

chorrear *vi* to spout, jet; drip; *fig inf* trickle, arrive slowly

chorreo *m,* drip, dripping; spouting, gushing

chorrera *f,* spout; drip; jabot, lace front

chorro *m,* jet; stream (of water, etc.); *fig* shower. **a chorros,** in a stream; in abundance, plentifully

chova *f,* rook; carrion crow; jackdaw

choza *f,* hut, cabin; cottage

chubasco *m,* squall, downpour; storm; transitory misfortune

chuchería *f,* gewgaw, trinket; savory titbit; snaring, trapping

chucruta *f,* sauerkraut

chueca *f,* round head of a bone; small ball; game like shinty; *inf* practical joke

chufa *f, bot* chufa; *inf* joke, trick

chufería *f,* place where drink made of **chufas** is sold

chufla *f,* flippant remark

chufleta *f, inf* joke; taunt

chulada *f,* mean trick, base action; drollery

chulería *f,* drollness; attractive personality

chuleta *f, cul* cutlet, chop; mutton-chop; *inf* slap

chulo *a* droll, amusing; attractive. *m,* slaughterhouse worker; bullfighter's assistant; pimp; rogue

chumbera *f,* prickly pear; Indian fig

chunga *f, inf* banter, teasing

chupada *f,* sucking; suck; suction

chupado de cara, c. de mofletes *a* lantern-jawed

chupador *a* sucking. *m,* baby's comforter or dummy

chupar *vt* to suck; absorb (of plants); *fig inf* drain, rob; *vr* grow thin. **chuparse los dedos,** *inf* to lick one's lips; be delighted

chupatintas *m, inf* scrivener, clerk (scornful)

churdón *m,* raspberry cane; raspberry; raspberry vinegar

churrería *f,* place where **churros** are made or sold

churrero (-ra) *n* maker or seller of **churros**

churrigueresco *a* Churrigueresque

churro *a* coarse (of wool). *m, cul* a kind of fritter eaten with chocolate, coffee, etc.

churumbela *f, mus* pipe; reed for drinking mate *WH*

chusco *a* droll, witty, amusing

chusma *f,* galley hands, crew; rabble, mob

chutar *vt sport* to shoot (a goal)

chuzo *m, mil* pike

chuzón *a* wily, suspicious, cunning

cianuro *m,* cyanide

ciar *vi* to go backwards; *naut* row backwards; *fig* make no headway (negotiations)

ciática *f,* sciatica

ciático *a* sciatic

ciborio *m,* ciborium

cicatería *f,* niggardliness, avarice

cicatero *a* avaricious, niggardly, mean

cicatriz *f,* cicatrice; *fig* scar, mark, impression

cicatrización *f,* cicatrization

cicatrizar *vt* to cicatrize, heal; *vr* scar over

ciclamino *m,* cyclamen
cíclico *a* cyclic, cyclical
ciclismo *m,* bicycling
ciclista *mf* cyclist
ciclo *m,* cycle (of time). **c. artúrico, c. de Artús,** Arthurian Cycle. **c. de conferencias,** series of lectures
ciclón *m,* cyclone
ciclópeo *a* cyclopean
ciclostilo *m,* cyclostyle
cicuta *f,* hemlock
cid *m,* great warrior, chief. **el Cid,** national hero of Spanish wars against the Moors
cidra *f,* citron
cidro *m,* citron tree
ciego *a* blind; dazed, blinded; choked up. *m,* blind man; *anat* cæcum. **a ciegas,** blindly; heedlessly
cielo *m,* sky, firmament; atmosphere; climate; paradise; Providence; bliss, glory; roof, canopy; *inf* darling. **a c. abierto,** in the open air. **parecer un c.,** to be heavenly
ciempiés *m,* centipede
cien *a* abb. **ciento,** hundred. Used always before substantives (e.g. **c. hombres,** 100 men)
ciénaga *f,* swamp; morass
ciencia *f,* science; knowledge; erudition, ability. **ciencias naturales,** natural science. **a c. cierta,** for certain, without doubt (gen. with *saber*)
cienmilésimo *a* hundred-thousandth
cieno *m,* slime, mud; silt
científico *a* scientific. *m,* scientist
ciento (cf. **cien**) *a* hundred; hundredth. *m,* hundred. **por c.,** per cent.
cierne, en in flower; *fig* in the early stages, in embryo
cierre *m,* closing, shutting; closing time of shops, etc.; fastening; fastener; clasp (of a necklace, handbag, etc.). **c. cremallera,** zip fastener. **c. metálico,** doorshutter
ciertamente *adv* certainly; undoubtedly; indeed
ciertísimo *a* everyday form of the superlative of **cierto** (see **certísimo**)
cierto *a* certain, sure; true; particular (e.g. **c. hombre,** a certain man (note no *def. art.*)). **un c. sabor,** a special flavor. **una cosa cierta,** something certain. **no, por c.,** no, certainly not. **por c.,** truly, indeed
cierva *f,* hind
ciervo *m,* stag. **c. volante,** stagbeetle
cierzo *m,* northerly wind
cifra *f,* number; figure; sum total; cipher, code; monogram; abbreviation
cifrar *vt* to write in cipher; summarize, abridge; (*with en*) be dependent on; depend on
cigarra *f, ent* cicada, harvest fly
cigarral *m,* (Toledo) countryhouse and garden or orchard
cigarrera *f,* woman who makes or sells cigars; cigar-cabinet; cigar-case
cigarrillo *m,* cigarette
cigarro *m,* cigar
cigüeña *f, orn* stork; *mech* crank
ciliar *a* ciliary
cilicio *m,* hairshirt
cilindrar *vt* to roll; calendar; bore
cilindrero *m,* organ grinder
cilíndrico *a* cylindrical
cilindro *m,* cylinder; roller
cima *f,* summit; top of trees; apex; *arch* coping; head (thistle, etc.); *fig* aim, goal, end
cimbalero (-ra) *n* cymbalist
címbalo *m,* cymbal
cimborrio *m, arch* cupola; cimborium
cimbrar, cimbrear *vt* to bend; brandish; *vr* sway (in walking)
cimbreño *a* graceful, lithe, willowy
cimbreo *m,* swaying, bending
cimentar *vt irr* to lay foundations; refine (gold, metals, etc.); found; *fig* ground (in virtue, etc.). See **acertar**
cimera *f,* crest of helmet
cimiento *m,* foundation (of a building); bottom; groundwork; origin, base. **abrir los cimientos,** to lay the foundations
cimitarra *f,* scimitar
cinabrio *m,* cinnabar; vermilion
cinc *m,* zinc
cincel *m,* chisel; burin, engraver
cincelador (-ra) *n* engraver; chiseler
cincelar *vt* to chisel; carve; engrave
cincha *f,* girth of a saddle
cinchar *vt* to tighten the saddle girths
cincho *m,* belt, girdle; iron hoop
cinco *a* and *m,* five; fifth. **a las c.,** at five o'clock
cincuenta *a* and *m,* fifty; fiftieth
cincuentavo *a* fiftieth
cincuentenario *m,* fiftieth anniversary
cincuentón (-ona) *a* and *n* fifty years old (person)
cine, cinema *m,* cinema, movies. **c. sonoro,** sound film
cinemática *f, phys* kinematics
cinematografía *f,* cinematography
cinematografiar *vt* to film
cinematográfico *a* cinematographic
cinematógrafo *m,* cinematograph; cinema
cínico *a* cynical; impudent; untidy. *m,* cynic
cinismo *m,* cynicism
cinta *f,* ribbon; tape; strip; film (cinematograph). **c. métrica,** tape-measure
cintillo *m,* hatband; small ring set with gems
cinto *m,* belt, girdle. **c. de pistolas,** pistol-belt
cinteca *f,* tape library
cintura *f,* waist; belt, girdle
cinturón *m,* large waist; belt girdle; sword-belt; that which encircles or surrounds. **c. de seguridad,** seat belt
ciprés *m, bot* cypress tree or wood
cipresal *m,* cypress grove
cipresino *a* cypress; cypresslike
circasiano (-na) *a* and *n* Circassian
circo *m,* circus; amphitheater
circón *m,* zircon
circuir *vt. irr* to surround, encircle. See **huir**
circuito *m,* periphery; contour; (*elec phys*) circuit. **corto c.,** short circuit
circulación *f,* circulation; traffic. **c. de la sangre,** circulation of the blood. **calle de gran c.,** busy street
circular *a* circular. *f,* circular. *vt* to pass round; *vi* circle; circulate; move in a circle; move about; run, travel (traffic)
circulatorio *a* circulatory
círculo *m,* circle; circumference; circuit; casino, social club
circuncidar *vt* to circumcise; modify, reduce
circuncisión *f,* circumcision
circunciso *a* circumcised
circundar *vt* to surround
circunferencia *f,* circumference
circunflejo *a* circumflex. **acento c.,** circumflex accent
circunlocución *f,* circumlocution
circunnavegación *f,* circumnavigation
circunnavegar *vt* to circumnavigate
circunscribir *vt* to circumscribe. *Past Part.* **circunscrito**
circunscripción *f,* circumscription
circunspección *f,* circumspection; seriousness, dignity
circunspecto *a* circumspect; serious, dignified
circunstancia *f,* circumstance; incident, detail; condition. **c. agravante,** aggravating circumstance. **c. atenuante,** extenuating circumstance. **bajo las circunstancias,** in the circumstances. **de circunstancias,** occasional (e.g. **poesías de circunstancias,** occasional verse). **estar al nivel de las circunstancias,** to rise to the occasion
circunstanciado *a* circumstantiated, detailed
circunstancial *a* circumstantial; occasional (e.g. **poesías circunstanciales,** occasional verse)
circunstante *a* surrounding; present. *mf* person present, bystander
circunvecino *a* adjacent, neighboring
circunvolución *f,* circumvolution

cirial *m,* processional candlestick

cirio *m,* wax candle

cirro *m, med* scirrhus; *bot* tendril; *zool* cirrus

cirrosis *f,* cirrhosis

cirroso *a med* scirrhous; (*zool bot*) cirrose

ciruela *f,* plum; prune. **c. claudia, c. veidal,** greengage. **c. damascena,** damson

ciruelo *m,* plum tree

cirugía *f,* surgery

cirujano *m,* surgeon

cisco *m,* coal dust, slack coal; *inf* hubbub, quarrel

cisma *m,* or *f,* schism; disagreement, discord. **el C. de Occidente,** the Western Schism

cismático *a* schismatic; discordant, inharmonious

cisne *m,* swan

cisterciense *a* Cistercian

cisterna *f,* water-tank, cistern

cístico *a* cystic

cistitis *f,* cystitis

cita *f,* appointment; quotation, citation

citable *a* quotable

citación *f,* quotation; *law* summons

citar *vt* to make an appointment; cite, quote; *law* summon. **c. en comparecencia,** to summon to appear in court

cítara *f, mus* zither

citatorio *m,* summons

citerior *a* hither, nearer

citrato *m, chem* citrate

cítrico *a* citric

ciudad *f,* city; municipal body. **la c. señorial,** the Aristocratic City (Ponce, Puerto Rico)

ciudadanía *f,* citizenship

ciudadano (-na) *a* city; civic, born in or belonging to a city. *n* citizen; burgess; bourgeois. **c. de honor,** freeman (of a city)

ciudadela *f,* citadel

cívico *a* civic; patriotic

civicultura *f,* raising of civets

civil *a* civil; civilian; polite

civilidad *f,* politeness, civility

civilización *f,* civilization

civilizador *a* civilizing

civilizar *vt* to civilize; educate; *vr* grow civilized; be educated

civismo *m,* civism; patriotism; civics

cizalla *f,* shears, shearing machine; metal filings

cizaña *f, bot* darnel, tare; vice, evil; dissension, discord (gen. with *meter* and *sembrar*)

clac *m,* opera-hat; tricorne

clamar *vi* to cry out; *fig* demand (of inanimate things); vociferate; speak solemnly

clamor *m,* outcry, shouting; shriek, complaint; knell, tolling of bells

clamorear *vt* to implore, clamor (for); *vi* toll (of bells)

clamoroso *a* noisy, clamorous

clandestino *a* clandestine, secret

clangor *m, poet* blare, bray (of trumpet)

claqué *m,* tap-dance

clara *f,* white of egg; bald patch (in fur); *inf* fair interval on a rainy day

claraboya *f,* skylight; *arch* clerestory

claramente *adv* clearly, evidently

clarear *vt* to clear; give light to; *vi* to dawn; grow light; *vr* be transparent; *inf* reveal secrets unwittingly

clarete *m,* claret (wine); claret color. *a* claret; claret-colored

claridad *f,* clearness; transparency; lightness, brightness; distinctness; clarity; good reputation, renown; plain truth, home truth (gen. *pl*)

clarificación *f,* clarification; purifying, refining

clarificar *vt* to illuminate; clarify, purify; refine (sugar, etc.)

clarín *m,* bugle; clarion; organ stop; bugler

clarinete *m,* clarinet; clarinet player

clarión *m,* white chalk, crayon

clarividencia *f,* perspicuity, clear-sightedness

clarividente *a* perspicacious, clear-sighted

claro *a* clear; light, bright; distinct; pure, clean; transparent, translucent; light (of colors); easily understood; evident, obvious; frank; cloudless; shrewd, quick-thinking; famous. *m,* skylight; space between words; break in a speech; space in procession, etc.; *art* (gen. *pl*) high lights. *interj* **¡C.!** or **¡C. está!** Of course! **a las claras,** openly, frankly

claroscuro *m,* chiaroscuro; monochrome

clase *f,* class, group; kind, sort, quality; class (school, university); lecture room; lecture, lesson; order, family. **c. dirigente,** ruling class. **c. media,** middle class. **c. social,** social class

clasicismo *m,* classicism

clasicista *a* and *mf* classicist

clásico *a* classic; notable; classical. *m,* classic

clasificación *f,* classification

clasificador (-ra) *n* classifier. **c. de billetes,** ticket-punch

clasificar *vt* to classify, arrange. **c. correspondencia,** to file letters

claudicación *f,* limping; negligence; hesitancy, weakness; backing down

claudicar *vi* to limp; be negligent; hesitate, give way

claustral *a* cloistral

claustro *m,* cloister; council, faculty, senate (of university); monastic rule

claustrofobia *f,* claustrophobia

cláusula *f,* clause. **c. de negación implícita,** contrary-to-fact clause. **c. principal,** main clause. **c. subordinada,** dependent clause, subordinate clause. **c. sustantiva,** noun clause

clausura *f,* sanctum of convent; claustration; solemn ending ceremony of tribunal, etc. **la vida de c.,** monastic or conventual life

clava *f,* club, truncheon; *naut* scupper

clavadizo *a* nail-studded (doors, etc.)

clavar *vt* to nail; fasten with nails; pierce, prick; set gems (jeweler); spike (cannon, gum); *fig* fix (eyes, attention, etc.); *inf* cheat

clave *m,* clavichord. *f,* code, key; *mus* clef; *arch* keystone; plug (telephones); **c. (de),** key to. *mus* **c. de sol,** treble clef

clavel *m, bot* carnation plant and flower

clavelito *m, bot* pink plant and flower

clavero (-ra) *n* keeper of the keys. *m,* clove tree

clavetear *vt* to stud with nails; *fig* round off (business affairs)

clavicordio *m,* clavichord

clavícula *f,* clavicle

clavija *f,* peg, pin; plug; peg of stringed instrument; axle-pin

clavo *m,* nail, spike, peg; corn (on foot); anguish. **c. de especia,** clove. **c. de herradura,** hob-nail

claymore *f,* claymore

clemátide *f, bot* clematis

clemencia *f,* mildness; clemency; mercy

clemente *a* mild; clement; merciful

cleptomanía *f,* kleptomania

cleptómano (-na) *a* and *n* kleptomaniac

clerecía *f,* clergy

clerical *a* belonging to the clergy; clerical

clericalismo *m,* clericalism

clerigalla *f,* (*contemptuous*) dog-collar men

clérigo *m,* cleric, clergyman; clerk (in Middle Ages)

clero *m,* clergy

cliente *mf* client, customer; protégé, ward

clientela *f,* patronage, protection; clientele

clima *m,* climate, clime

climatérico *a* climacteric

climático *a* climatic

climatología *f,* climatology

clímax *m,* climax

clínica *f,* clinic, nursing home; department of medicine or surgery

clínico *a* clinical
clíper *m*, (*aer* and *naut*) clipper
clisar *vt print* to cast from a mold, stereotype
clisé *m*, *print* stereotype plate
cloaca *f*, sewer, drain; *zool* cloaca
cloquear *vi* to go broody (hen); cluck
cloqueo *m*, cluck, clucking
cloquera *f*, broodiness (hens)
clorato *m*, chlorate
clorhidrato *m*, hydrochloride
clorhídrico *a* hydrochloric
cloro *m*, chlorine
clorofila *f*, chlorophyll
cloroformizar *vt* to chloroform
cloroformo *m*, chloroform
clorosis *f*, chlorosis
cloruro *m*, chloride
club *m*, club
clueca *f*, broody hen
clueco *a* broody (hens); *inf* doddering
C.N.T. initialism of Confederación Nacional de Trabajo
coacción *f*, coercion
coactivo *a* coercive
coadjutor *m*, co-worker, assistant
coadunar *vt* to join or mingle together
coadyuvar *vt* to assist
coagulación *f*, coagulation
coagular *vt* to coagulate; clot; curdle
coágulo *m*, clot; coagulation; congealed blood
coalición *f*, coalition
coartada *f*, alibi. **probar la c.**, to prove an alibi
coartar *vt* to limit, restrict
coautor (-ra) *n* co-author
cobalto *m*, cobalt
cobarde *a* cowardly; irresolute. *m*, coward
cobardía *f*, cowardice
cobayo *m*, guinea-pig
cobertera *f*, lid, cover
cobertizo *m*, overhanging roof; shack, shed, hut. **c. de aeroplanos,** *aer* hangar
cobertura *f*, covering; coverlet; wrapping
cobija *f*, imbrex tile; cover
cobijar *vt* to cover; shelter
cobra *f*, *zool* cobra; rope or thong for yoking oxen; retrieval (of game)
cobradero *a* that which can be collected, recoverable
cobrador *m*, collector, receiver. *a* collecting. **c. de tranvía,** tram conductor
cobranza *f*, receiving, collecting; collection of fruit or money
cobrar *vt* to collect (what is owed); charge; earn; regain, recover; feel, experience (emotions); wind, pull in (ropes, etc.); gain, acquire; retrieve (game); *vr* recuperate. **c. ánimo,** to take courage. **c. cariño (a),** to grow fond of. **c. fuerzas,** to gather strength. **c. importancia,** to gain importance. **¿Cuánto cobra Vd.?** How much do you charge? How much do you earn?
cobre *m*, *min* copper; copper kitchen utensils; *pl mus* brass
cobrizo *a* containing copper; copper-colored
cocacolonizar *vt* (United States) to gain economic control of . . . and introduce into its pop culture
cocacolonización *f*, economic domination by the United States and introduction of its pop culture
cocaína *f*, cocaine
cocción *f*, coction
coceador *a* inclined to kick; kicking (animals)
coceadura *f*, kicking
cocear *vi* to kick; *inf* kick against, oppose
cocedero *a* easily cooked
cocer *vt. irr* to boil; cook; bake (bricks, etc.); digest; *surg* suppurate; *vi* boil (of a liquid); ferment; *vr* suffer pain or inconvenience over a long period. *Pres. Ind.* **cuezo, cueces, cuece, cuecen.** *Pres. Subjunc.* **cueza, cuezas, cueza, cuezan**
coche *m*, carriage, car. **c. camas,** sleeping car. **c. -cam-**

ioneta, station wagon. **c. cerrado,** *aut* sedan. **c. de muchos caballos,** high-powered car. **c. de plaza,** hackney-carriage. **c. fúnebre,** hearse. **c. -línea,** inter-city bus. *f, Ecuador* puddle
cochera *f*, coach house; tramway depot
cochero *m*, coachman; driver. *a* easily cooked
¡cochi! (call to pigs)
cochina *f*, sow
cochinería *f*, *inf* filthiness; mean trick
cochinilla *f*, wood louse; cochineal insect; cochineal
cochinillo, *m*, sucking-pig. **c. de Indias,** guinea-pig
cochino *m*, pig; *inf* filthy person. *a* filthy
cocido *a* boiled, cooked, baked. *m*, dish of stewed meat, pork, chicken, with peas, etc.
cociente *m*, quotient
cocimiento *m*, cooking; decoction
cocina *f*, kitchen; pottage; broth; cookery. **c. de campaña,** field-kitchen. **c. económica,** cooking range
cocinar *vt* to cook; *vi inf* meddle, interfere
cocinería *f*, *naut* galley
cocinero (-ra) *n* cook, chef
cocinilla *f*, spirit-stove
coco *m*, *bot* coconut tree and fruit; coconut shell; grub, maggot; bogeyman; hobgoblin; *inf* grimace. *inf* **ser un c.,** to be hideously ugly
cocacolismo *n inf* economic dependence on the United States and adoption of its pop culture
cocodrilo *m*, crocodile
cócora *mf inf* bore, nosy Parker
cocotal *m*, grove of coconut palms
cocotero *m*, coconut palm
coctel *m*, cocktail
cocuyo *m*, firefly
codal *a* cubital. *m*, shoot of a vine; prop, strut; frame of a hand-saw
codazo *m*, blow or nudge of the elbow. **dar codazos,** to elbow, shoulder out of the way
codear *vi* to jostle; elbow, nudge; *vr* be on terms of equality with
codeína *f*, codeine
codelincuente *mf* partner in crime, accomplice
codera *f*, elbow rash; elbow-piece or patch
codeso *m*, laburnum
códice *m*, codex
codicia *f*, covetousness; greed
codiciar *vt* to covet
codicilo *m*, codicil
codicioso (-sa) *a* covetous; *inf* hardworking. *n* covetous person
codificación *f*, codification
codificar *vt* to codify, compile
código *m*, code of laws. **c. civil,** civil laws. **c. de la circulación, c. de la vía pública,** highway code, traffic code. *naut* **c. de señales,** signal code. **c. penal,** criminal laws. **c. postal,** zip code
codillo *m*, knee (of quadrupeds); shaft (of branch); bend (pipe, tube); stirrup
codo *m*, elbow; angle, bend (pipe, tube); cubit. *inf* **hablar por los codos,** to chatter
codorniz *f*, *orn* quail
coeducación *f*, co-education
coeficiente *m*, coefficient
coercer *vt* to restrain, coerce
coerción *f*, *law* coercion
coercitivo *a* coercive
coetáneo (-ea) *a* contemporaneous. *n* contemporary
coevo *a* coeval
coexistencia *f*, co-existence
coexistir *vi* to co-exist
cofia *f*, hairnet; coif
cofín *m*, basket
cofradía *f*, confraternity, brotherhood or sisterhood **c. de gastronomía,** eating club (US), dining society (UK)
cofre *m*, trunk, chest (for clothes); coffer
cogedor *m*, collector, gatherer; dustpan; coal-shovel
coger *vt* to seize, hold; catch; take, collect, gather; have

room for; take up or occupy space; find; catch in the act; attack, surprise; reach; **c. un berrinche,** have a fit, have a tantrum. *vi* have room, fit

cogida *f,* gathering, picking; *inf* fruit harvest; toss (bull-fighting)

cogido *m,* pleat, fold; crease. **estar c. de tiempo** to be pressed for time.

cogitabundo *a* very pensive

cognación *f,* cognation; kinship

cognoscitivo *a* cognitive

cogollo *m,* heart (of lettuce, etc.); shoot; topmost branches of pine tree

cogote *m,* nape (of neck)

cogulla *f,* monk's habit

cohabitación *f,* cohabitation

cohabitar *vt* to cohabit

cohechador (**-ra**) *a* bribing. *n* briber

cohechar *vt* to bribe, corrupt, suborn

cohecho *m,* bribing; bribe

coheredero (**-ra**) *n* co-heir

coherencia *f,* coherence, connection

coherente *a* coherent

cohesión *f,* cohesion

cohesivo *a* cohesive

cohete *m,* rocket

cohetero *m,* firework manufacturer

cohibir *vt* to restrain; repress. See **Prohibir.**

cohombrillo *m, dim* gherkin

cohombro *m,* cucumber

cohonestar *vt fig* to gloss over, cover up; make appear decent (actions, etc.)

cohorte *f,* cohort

coincidencia *f,* coincidence

coincidir *vt* to coincide; (two or more people) be in the same place at the same time. **c. con que . . .** to agree that . . .

coito *m,* coitus

cojear *vi* to limp; wobble, be unsteady (of furniture); *fig inf* go wrong or astray; *inf* suffer from (vice, bad habit)

cojera *f,* lameness, limp

cojijoso *a* peevish

cojín *m,* cushion; pad; pillow (for lace-making)

cojinete *m,* small cushion; *mech* bearing. **c. de bolas,** ball-bearing

cojo *a* lame; unsteady, wobbly (of furniture, etc.)

col *f,* cabbage. **c. de Bruselas,** Brussels sprouts

cola *f,* tail; train (of gown); shank (of a button); queue; tailpiece (of a violin, etc.); appendage; glue. **c. de milano,** *carp* dovetail. **c. de pescado,** isinglass. **formar c.,** to line up, queue up

colaboración *f,* collaboration. **en c.,** joint (e.g. **obra en colaboración,** joint work)

colaboracionista *mf* collaborationist

colaborador (**-ra**) *n* collaborator

colaborar *vt* to collaborate

colación *f,* conferment of a degree; collation (of texts); light repast; cold supper; area of a parish

colada *f,* wash; bleaching; mountain path; *met* casting; *inf* trusty sword (allusion to name of one of the Cid's swords)

coladero *m,* colander, sieve, strainer; narrow path

colador *m,* colander

coladura *f,* straining, filtration; *inf* untruth; *inf* howler, mistake

colapso *m, med* prostration, collapse

colar *vt irr* to filter, strain; bleach; *met* cast; *vi* go through a narrow place; *inf* drink wine; *vr* thread one's way; *inf* enter by stealth, steal in; *inf* tell untruths. *Pres. Ind.* **cuelo, cuelas, cuela, cuelan.** *Pres. Subjunc.* **cuele, cueles, cuele, cuelen**

colateral *a* collateral

colcha *f,* bedspread, counterpane, quilt

colchadura *f,* quilting

colchero *m,* quilt maker

colchón *m,* mattress. **c. de muelles,** spring-mattress. **c. de viento,** air-bed

colchonero *m,* mattress maker or seller

colchoneta *f,* pad, thin mattress

coleada *f,* wag of the tail

colear *vi* to wag the tail

colección *f,* collection

coleccionador (**-ra**) *n* collector

coleccionar *vt* to collect

coleccionista *mf* collector

colecta *f,* assessment; collection (of donations); *ecc* collect; voluntary offering

colectivero *m,* bus driver

colectividad *f,* collectivity; body of people

colectivismo *m,* collectivism

colectivista *a* collectivist

colectivo *a* collective; *Argentina* (local) bus

colector *m,* gatherer; collector; tax-collector; water-pipe; water-conduit; *elec* commutator, collector

colega *m,* colleague

colegiado *a* collegiate

colegial (**-la**) *a* college, collegiate. *n* student; pupil; *fig inf* novice.

colegiarse *vr* to meet as an association (professional, etc.)

colegiata *f,* college church

colegiatura *f,* scholarship, fellowship (money granted a student); tuition (fee paid by a student), tuition fee, tuition fees

colegio *m,* college; school; academy; association (professional); council, convocation; college or school buildings. **c. de abogados,** bar association. **c. de cardenales,** College of Cardinals. **c. electoral,** polling-booth. **c. militar,** military academy

colegir *vt irr* to collect; gather; deduce, infer. See **elegir**

cólera *f,* bile, anger. *m,* cholera. **montar en c.,** to fly into a rage

colérico *a* angry; choleric; suffering from cholera

colesterina *f, chem* cholesterol

coleta *f,* pigtail; queue; *inf* postscript

coletazo *m,* blow with one's tail, lash with one's tail; lash of a dying fish; *fig* last hurrah

coleto *m,* leather jerkin; *inf* body of a man

colgadero *a* able to be hung up. *m,* coat-hanger, hook

colgadizo *a* hanging. *m,* overhanging roof

colgadura *f,* hangings, drapery, tapestries. **c. de cama,** bedhangings

colgajo *m,* tatter; bunch (of grapes, etc.); *surg* skin lap

colgar *vt irr* to hang up; decorate with hangings; *inf* hang, kill; *vi* hang, be suspended; *fig* be dependent. See **contar**

colibrí *m,* hummingbird

cólico *m,* colic

colicuar *vt* to dissolve

coliflor *f,* cauliflower

coligarse *vr* to confederate, unite

colilla *f,* stub (of a cigar or cigarette)

colina *f,* hill; cabbage seed; *chem* choline

colindante *a* adjacent, contiguous

coliseo *m,* coliseum; theater

colisión *f,* collision; abrasion, bruise; *fig* clash (of ideas)

colitis *f,* colitis

collado *m,* hill, hillock

collar *m,* necklace; chain of office or honor; collar (dogs, etc.)

collera *f,* **collerón,** *m,* horse collar

colmado *a* abundant. *m,* provision shop

colmar *vt* to fill to overflowing; bestow generously, heap upon

colmena *f,* beehive

colmenero (**-ra**) *n* beekeeper

colmillo *m,* canine tooth; tusk; fang

colmilludo *a* having large canine teeth; tusked; fanged; sagacious

colmo *m,* overflow; highest point; completion, limit, end. **ser el c.,** *inf* to be the last straw. **el c. de los colmos,** the absolute limit

colocación *f,* placing, putting; situation, place; employment; *sport* placing; order, arrangement; *ling* collocation

colocar *vt* to place, put, arrange; place in employment. **c. bajo banderas,** to draft (into the armed forces). *vr* place oneself

colofón *m, print* colophon

colofonia *f,* solid resin (for bows of stringed instruments, etc.)

coloide *a* and *m,* colloid

colombiano (**-na**) *a* and *n* Colombian

colombina *f,* columbine

colombofilia *f,* pigeon fancying

colonia *f,* colony; plantation

colonial *a* colonial

colonización *f,* colonization

colonizador (**-ra**) *a* colonizing. *n* colonizer

colonizar *vt* to colonize; settle

colono *m,* settler, colonist; farmer

coloquio *m,* colloquy, conversation, talk; colloquium

color *m,* color; dye; paint; rouge; coloring; pretext, excuse; character, individuality; *pl* natural colors. **c. estable, c. sólido,** fast color. **mudar de c.,** to change color. **de c.,** colored. **so c.,** under the pretext. **ver las cosas c. de rosa,** to see things through rose-colored glasses

coloración *f,* coloration, painting

colorado *a* colored. *WH* red, reddish; *inf* blue, obscene; specious

colorante *a* coloring. *m,* dyestuff; coloring (substance)

colorar *vt* to color; dye

colorear *vt* to color; pretext; *fig* whitewash, excuse; *vi* show color; be reddish; grow red, ripe (tomatoes, cherries, etc.)

colorero *m,* dyer

colorete *m,* rouge

colorido *m,* coloring, color

colorín *m,* goldfinch; bright color

colorista *a* and *mf* colorist

colosal *a* colossal, enormous; extraordinary, excellent

coloso *m,* colossus; *fig* outstanding person or thing, giant; **el C. del Norte, el Gran C. del Norte,** (contemptuous epithet for the United States of America)

columbino *a* pertaining to a dove; dovelike; candid, innocent; purply-red

columbrar *vt* to discern in the distance, glimpse; conjecture, guess

columna *f, mil arch print* column; *fig* protection, shelter; *naut* stanchion. **c. cerrada,** *mil* etc. mass formation. **c. de los suspiros,** agony column (in a newspaper)

columnata *f,* colonnade

columpiar *vt* to swing; dangle (one's feet); *vr inf* sway in walking; swing

columpio *m,* swing

colusión *f,* collusion

colusorio *a* collusive

coma *f, gram* comma. *m, med* coma

comadre *f,* midwife; *inf* procuress, go-between; *inf* pal, gossip

comadrear *vi inf* to gossip

comadreja *f, zool* weasel

comadrón *m,* accoucheur

comadrona *f,* midwife

comandancia *f, mil* command; commandant's H.Q.

comandante *m,* commandant; commander; major; squadron-leader. *a mil* commanding. **c. en jefe,** commanding officer

comandar *vt mil* to command

comandita *f, com* sleeping partnership; private company

comando *m, mil* commando

comarca *f,* district, region

comatoso *a* comatose

comba *f,* bend, warping; jump rope, skipping-rope; camber (of road)

combadura *f,* curvature; warping; camber (of a road)

combar *vt* to bend; twist; warp; camber

combate *m,* fight, combat; mental strife; contradiction, opposition. **c. judicial,** trial by combat. **dejar fuera de c.,** (*a*) (boxing) to knock out

combatiente *m,* combatant, soldier

combatir *vi* to fight; *vt* attack; struggle against (winds, water, etc.); contradict, oppose; *fig* disturb, trouble (emotions)

combinación *f,* combination; list of words beginning with same letter; project; concurrence; underskirt, petticoat. **estar en c. (con),** to be in cahoots (with), connive (with)

combinar *vt* to combine; (*mil nav*) join forces; arrange, plan; *chem* combine; **combinar para + inf.** (two or more people) to make arrangements to + inf.

combustible *a* combustible. *m,* fuel

combustión *f,* combustion. **c. activa,** rapid combustion. **c. espontánea,** spontaneous combustion

comedero *a* edible. *m,* feeding-trough; dining-room

comedia *f,* comedy; play; theater; comic incident; *fig* play-acting, theatricalism. **c. alta,** art theater. **c. de costumbres,** comedy of manners. **c. de enredo,** play with very involved plot. *inf* **hacer la c.,** to play-act, pretend

comediante *m,* actor; *inf* dissembler.

comedianta *f,* actress

comedido *a* courteous; prudent; moderate

comedimiento *m,* courtesy; moderation; prudence

comedir *vt irr* to prepare, premeditate; *vr* restrain oneself, be moderate; offer one's services. See **pedir**

comedor *a* voracious. *m,* dining-room

comendador *m,* knight commander

comendatorio *a* commendatory (of letters)

Comenio Comenius

comensal *mf* table companion

comentador (**-ra**) *n* commentator

comentar *vt* explain (document); *inf* comment

comentario (**a**) *m,* commentary (on)

comentarista *mf* commentator

comento *m,* comment; commentary

comenzante *mf* beginner, novice. *a* initial

comenzar *vt vi irr* to begin, commence. See **empezar**

comer *m,* eating; food. *vi* to eat; feed; dine. *vt* eat; *inf* enjoy an income; waste (patrimony); consume, exhaust; fade (of colors); *vr* be troubled, uneasy, remorseful. **ser de buen c.,** to have a good appetite; taste good. **tener que c.,** to be obliged to eat; have to eat; have enough to eat

comerciable *a* marketable; sociable, pleasant (of persons)

comercial *a* commercial

comerciante *a* trading. *mf* merchant, trader

comerciar *vt* to trade; have dealings (with)

comercio *m,* trade, commerce; intercourse, traffic; illicit sexual intercourse; shop, store; tradesmen; commercial quarter of town

comestible *a* edible, eatable. *m,* (gen. *pl*) provisions

cometa *m, ast* comet. *f,* kite (toy). **c. celular,** box-kite

cometedor (**-ra**) *n* perpetrator

cometer *vt* to entrust, hand over to; commit (crime, sins, etc.); *com* order

cometido *m,* charge, commission; moral obligation; function

comezón *f,* itching, irritation; hankering, longing

comicidad *f,* comic element; comic spirit

cómico *a* comic; funny, comical. *m,* actor; comedian. **c. de la legua,** strolling player

comida *f,* food; meal; dinner; eating. **c. de gala,** state banquet. **c. de prueba,** *med* test meal

comienzo *m,* beginning, origin

comilón (**-ona**) *a inf* gluttonous. *n* glutton

comillas *f pl, gram* inverted commas

comino *m, bot* cumin. **no valer un c.,** to be not worth a jot

comisar *vt* to confiscate, sequestrate

comisaría *f,* commissaryship; commissariat. **c. de policía,** police station

comisario *m*, deputy, agent; commissary, head of police; commissioner. **alto c.,** high commissioner. **c. propietario,** stockholders' representative
comisión *f*, perpetration, committal; commission; committee; *com* commission
comisionado (-da) *a* commissioned. *m*, commissary
comisionar *vt* to commission
comisionista *mf com* commission agent
comiso *m, law* confiscation, sequestration; contraband
comité *m*, committee
comitiva *f*, retinue, following
como *adv* like, as; in the same way; thus, accordingly; in the capacity of; so that; since. *conjunc* if (*followed by subjunc.*); because. **c. no,** unless. **¿Cómo?** How? In what way? Why? Pardon? What did you say? *interj* **¡Cómo!** What! You don't say! **¡Cómo no!** Why not! Of course! Surely! **¿Cómo que . . . ?** What do you mean that . . . ?
cómo *m*, the wherefore. **no saber el porqué ni el c.,** not to know the why or wherefore
cómoda *f*, chest of drawers
comodidad *f*, comfort; convenience; advantage; utility, interest
comodín *m*, (in cards) joker
cómodo *a* comfortable; convenient; opportune
comodón *a inf* comfort-loving; easy-going; egoistical
comodoro *m, naut* commodore
comoquiera que *adv* by any means that, anyway; whereas, given that
compacidad *f*, compactness
compacto *a* compact, dense; close (type)
compadecer *vt irr* to pity; *vr* (*with* **de**) sympathize with; pity; harmonize, agree with. See **conocer**
compadre *m, inf* pal
compaginación *f*, joining, fixing; *print* making-up
compaginar *vt* to fit together; join, put in order; harmonize, square (e.g. **compaginé una cuenta con la otra,** I squared one account with the other); *print* make up
compañero (-ra) *n* companion, comrade; fellow-member; partner (games); *fig* pair, fellow, mate (things). **c. de armas,** brother-in-arms, companion-at-arms. **c. de cabina,** boothmate. **c. de exilio,** companion in exile, fellow exile. **c. de generación,** contemporary, person of the same generation. **c. de viaje,** traveling companion; *pol* fellow traveler (communist sympathizer)
compañía *f*, company; society, association; theatrical company; (*com mil*) company. **C. de Jesús,** Order of Jesus. **c. de la zarza,** guild of guards and woodcutters for autos de fe. **c. de navegación,** shipping company. **c. por acciones,** joint stock company
comparable *a* comparable
comparación *f*, comparison
comparar *vt* to compare; collate
comparativo *a* comparative
comparecencia *f*, (gen. *law*) appearance
comparecer *vi irr law* to appear (before tribunal, etc.); present oneself. See **conocer**
comparendo *m, law* summons
comparsa *f*, retinue; *theat* chorus; troop of carnival revelers dressed alike. *mf theat* supernumerary actor
comparte *mf law* partner; accomplice
compartimiento *m*, share, division; railway carriage. *naut* **c. estanco,** compartment
compartir *vt* to share out, divide; participate
compás *m*, compasses; callipers; size; compass, time; range of voice; (*naut min*) compass; *mus* time, rhythm, bar, marking time. **c. de mar,** mariner's compass. **c. de puntas,** dividers, callipers. **fuera de c.,** *mus* out of time; out of joint (of the times). *mus* **llevar el c.,** to beat time
compasar *vt* to measure with compasses; arrange or apportion accurately; *mus* put into bars
compasillo *m, mus* ⁴⁄ measure
compasivo *a* compassionate; tender-hearted
compatibilidad *f*, compatibility

compatible *a* compatible
compatriota *mf* compatriot
compeler *vt* to compel, force
compendiar *vt* to abridge, summarize
compendio *m*, compendium. **en c.,** briefly
compendioso *a* summary, condensed; compendious
compenetración *f*, co-penetration; intermingling
compenetrado (de) *a* thoroughly convinced (of)
compenetrarse *vr* to co-penetrate; intermingle
compensación *f*, compensating; compensation
compensar *vt* to equalize, counterbalance; compensate
compensatorio *a* compensatory; equalizing
competencia *f*, competition, contest; rivalry; competence; aptitude; *law* jurisdiction
competente *a* adequate, opportune; rightful, correct; apt, suitable; learned, competent
competer *vi irr* to belong to; devolve on; concern. See **pedir**
competición *f*, competition
competidor (-ra) *n* competitor
competir *vi irr* to compete, contest; be equal (to), vie (with). See **pedir**
compilación *f*, compilation
compilador (-ra) *n* compiler. *a* compiling
compilar *vt* to compile
compinche *mf inf* pal, chum
complacencia *f*, satisfaction, pleasure
complacer *vt irr* to oblige, humor; *vr* (*with* **en**) be pleased or satisfied with; delight in, like to. See **nacer**
complaciente *a* pleasing; obliging, helpful
complejidad *f*, complexity
complejo *a* complex; intricate. *m*, complex. **c. de inferioridad,** inferiority complex
complementario *a* complementary
complemento *m*, complement (all meanings)
completar *vt* to complete; perfect
completo *a* full; finished; perfect
complexión *f*, physical constitution
complexo *a* complex; intricate
complicación *f*, complication
complicar *vt* to complicate; muddle, confuse; *vr* be complicated; be muddled or confused
cómplice *mf* accomplice
complicidad *f*, complicity
complot *m, inf* conspiracy, plot, intrigue
complutense *a* native of, or belonging to, Alcalá de Henares
componedor (-ra) *n* repairer; arbitrator; bone-setter; *mus* composer; writer, author, compiler; *print* compositor
componenda *f*, mending, repair; *inf* settlement; compromise, arbitration; *inf* shady business
componente *a* and *m*, component
componer *vt irr* to construct, form; *mech* resolve; compose, create; *print* compose; prepare, concoct, mend, repair; settle (differences); remedy; trim; correct, adjust; *lit mus* compose; add up to, amount to; *vi* write (verses); *mus* compose; *vr* dress oneself up. **c. el semblante,** to compose one's features; deal craftily. **componérselas,** to fix matters, use one's wits. See **poner**
componible *a* reparable, mendable; able to be arranged or adjusted
comportamiento *m*, conduct; deportment
comportar *vt* to tolerate; *vr* behave, comport oneself
composición *f*, composition; repair; arrangement, compromise; *print* composition; *gram* compound; *chem* constitution; *mech* resolution
compositor (-ra) *n mus* composer; *print* compositor
Compostela Compostella
compostura *f*, composition, structure; repair; neatness (of person); adulteration; arrangement, agreement; discretion, modesty
compota *f*, fruit preserve, compote; thick sauce
compotera *f*, jam or preserve dish
compra *f*, buying; marketing, shopping; purchase.

estar de compras, *euphem* to be in the family way. **ir de compras,** to go shopping

comprable *a* purchasable

comprador (-ra) *a* purchasing. *n* purchaser; buyer; shopper

comprar *vt* to buy; bribe

comprender *vt* to encircle, surround; include, comprise, contain; understand

comprensible *a* comprehensible

comprensión *f*, comprehension, understanding

comprensivo *a* understanding; comprehensive

compresa *f*, *med* compress, swab; pack (for the face, etc.)

compresión *f*, compression; squeeze

compresivo *a* compressive

compresor *m*, compressor; *aut aer* supercharger

comprimido *m*, tablet, pill

comprimir *vt* to compress; squeeze; restrain; *vr* restrain oneself

comprobación *f*, verification; checking; proof

comprobante *a* verifying; confirmatory

comprobar *vt irr* to verify, check; confirm, prove. See **probar**

comprobatorio *a* confirmatory; verifying; testing

comprometedor *a inf* compromising; jeopardizing

comprometer *vt* to submit to arbitration; compromise; imperil, jeopardize; *vr* pledge oneself; *inf* compromise oneself

comprometido *a* awkward, embarrassing; (e.g. literature of a writer) committed, engagé

compromiso *m*, compromise, agreement, arbitration, commitment, obligation; appointment, engagement; jeopardy; difficulty

compuerta *f*, half-door, wicket, hatch; floodgate, sluice. **c. flotante,** floating dam

compuesto *a* and *past part* made-up, built-up; composite; circumspect; *bot gram* compound. *m*, composite; preparation, compound

compulsar *vt* to collate; *law* make a transcript of

compulsivo *a* compelling

compunción *f*, compunction

compungir *vt* to cause remorse or pity; *vr* repent; sympathize with, pity

computable *a* computable

computación *f*, **cómputo** *m*, calculation, computation

computador (-ra) *n* computer

computar *vt* to compute

computista *mf* computer

cómputo *m*, computation; estimate

comulgar *vt* to administer Holy Communion; *vi* receive Holy Communion

comulgatorio *m*, communion rail, altar rail

común *a* general, customary, ordinary; public, communal; universal, common; vulgar, low. *m*, community, population; water-closet. **en c.,** in common; generally. **por lo c.,** generally. **sentido c.,** common sense

comunal *a* communal; common. *m*, commonalty

comunero *a* popular, affable, democratic. *m*, joint owner; commoner; *hist* commune

comunicable *a* communicable; communicative, sociable

comunicación *f*, communication; (telephone) call, message; letter (to the press); *mil* communiqué; *pl* lines of communication, transport

comunicado *m*, official communication, communiqué; letter (to the press)

comunicante *a* communicating

comunicar *vt* to communicate; transmit; impart; share; *vr* **comunicarse con,** (door) to open onto (e.g. **Esta puerta se comunica con el jardín.** This door opens onto the garden); communicate, converse, correspond with each other

comunicativo *a* communicative; talkative, not reserved

comunidad *f*, the common people; community; generality, majority; *pl hist* Commune

comunión *f*, communion; intercourse, fellowship; *ecc* Communion

comunismo *m*, communism

comunista *a* and *mf* communist

comunistófilo, comunistoide *a* fellow-traveling; *n* fellow traveler

comúnmente *adv* commonly, generally; frequently

con *prep* with; by means of; in the company of; towards, to; although (followed by *infin.,* but generally translated by an inflected verb, e.g. **C. ser almirante, no le gusta el mar,** Although he is an admiral, he doesn't like the sea); by (followed by *infin.* and generally translated by a gerund, e.g. **c. hacer todo esto,** by doing all this). **c. bien,** safe and sound, safely (e.g. **Llegamos con bien.** We arrived safely.) **c. cuentagotas,** sparingly; stingily. **c. que,** so, then. **c. tal que,** provided that, on condition that. **c. todo,** nevertheless. **¿Con . . . ?** Is this . . . ? (on the telephone, e.g. **¿Con el Sr. Piñangos?** Is this Mr. Piñangos?)

conato *m*, effort, endeavor; tendency; *law* attempted crime

concatenación *f*, concatenation

concavidad *f*, concavity; hollow

cóncavo *a* concave. *m*, concavity; hollow

concebible *a* conceivable

concebimiento *m*. See **concepción**

concebir *vi irr* to become pregnant; conceive, imagine; understand; *vt* conceive, acquire (affection, etc.). See **pedir**

concedente *a* conceding

conceder *vt* to confer, grant; concede; agree to

concejal *m*, councillor; alderman

concejil *a* pertaining to a municipal council; public

concejo *m*, town council; town hall; council meeting

concentración *f*, concentration

concentrado *a* concentrated; (of persons) reserved

concentrar *vt* to concentrate

concéntrico *a* concentric

concepción *f*, conception; idea, concept; *ecc* Immaculate Conception

conceptismo *m*, *lit* Concetism (cf. *Euphuism*)

conceptista *a* and *mf* concettist

concepto *m*, idea, concept; epigram; opinion. **en mi c.,** in my opinion; judgment. **por c. de,** in payment of

conceptualismo *m*, conceptualism

conceptuar *vt* to judge, take to be; believe; imagine

conceptuoso *a* witty, ingenious

concernencia *f*, respect, relation

concerniente *a* concerning

concernir *vi irr defective* to concern. See **discernir**

concertadamente *adv* methodically, orderly; by arrangement, or agreement

concertar *vt irr* to arrange, settle, adjust; bargain; conclude (business deal); harmonize; compare, correlate; tune instruments; *vi* reach an agreement. See **acertar**

concertina *f*, concertina

concertista *mf mus* performer, soloist; *mus* manager. **c. de piano,** concert pianist

concesión *f*, conceding, grant; concession; lease

concesionario *m*, *law* concessionaire, leaseholder

conciencia *f*, consciousness; conscience; conscientiousness. **c. doble,** dual personality. **ancho de c.,** broadminded. **a c.,** conscientiously

concienzudo *a* of a delicate conscience, scrupulous; conscientious

concierto *m*, methodical arrangement; agreement; *mus* concert; *mus* concerto. **de c.,** by common consent

conciliable *a* reconcilable compatible

conciliábulo *m*, conclave, private meeting; secret meeting

conciliación *f*, conciliation; similarity, affinity; protection, favor

conciliador *a* conciliatory

conciliar *m,* councilor. *vt* to conciliate; *fig* reconcile (opposing theories, etc.). **c. el sueño,** to induce sleep, woo sleep. *vr* win liking (or sometimes dislike)

concilio *m,* council; *ecc* assembly; conciliary decree; findings of council

concinidad *f,* concinnity

concino *a* concinnous

concisión *f,* conciseness, brevity

conciso *a* concise

concitar *vt* to stir up, foment

conciudadano (-na) *n* fellow citizen; fellow countryman

cónclave *m,* conclave; meeting

concluir *vt irr* to conclude, finish; come to a conclusion, decide; infer, deduce; convince by reasoning; *law* close legal proceedings; *vr* expire, terminate. **c. con,** to put an end to. See **huir**

conclusión *f,* finish, end; decision; close, denouement; theory, proposition (gen. *pl*); deduction, inference; *law* close. **en c.,** in conclusion

conclusivo *a* final; conclusive

concluyente *a* concluding; convincing; conclusive

concomer *vi inf* to give a shrug, shrug one's shoulders; fidget with an itch. **c. de placer,** to itch with pleasure

concomitancia *f,* concomitance

concomitante *a* and *m,* concomitant

concordable *a* conformable

concordador (-ra) *a* peacemaking. *n* peacemaker

concordancia *f,* harmony, agreement; (*mus gram*) concord; *pl* concordance

concordar *vt irr* to bring to agreement; *vi* agree. See **acordar**

concordato *m,* concordat

concorde *a* agreeing; harmonious

concordia *f,* concord, agreement, harmony; written agreement

concreción *f,* concretion

concretar *vt* to combine, bring together; make concise; resume; *vr fig* confine oneself (to a subject) to hammer out, work out (an agreement)

concreto *a* concrete, real, not abstract. **en c.,** in definite terms; finally, to sum up

concubina *f,* concubine, mistress

concubinato *m,* concubinage

conculcación *f,* trampling, treading; violation

conculcador *m,* violator

conculcar *vt* to trample under foot, tread on; break, violate

concupiscencia *f,* concupiscence, lust; greed

concupiscente *a* concupiscent, lustful; greedy

concurrencia *f,* assembly; coincidence; attendance; help, influence

concurrido *a* crowded; busy; frequented

concurrir *vi* to coincide; contribute; meet together; agree, be of same opinion; compete (in an examination, etc.)

concurso *m,* crowd, concourse; conjunction, coincidence; help; competition; (tennis) tournament; competitive examination; invitation to offer tenders. **c. de acreedores,** creditors' meeting. **c. interno,** competitive examination for a position open to staff members only

concusión *f,* concussion; shock; extortion

concha *f,* shell; turtle-shell; prompter's box; cove, creek; anything shell-shaped. *fig* **meterse en su c.,** to retire into one's shell. *inf* **tener más conchas que un galápago,** to be very cunning

conchado *a* scaly, having a shell

condado *m,* earldom; county

condal *a* of an earl, earl's; of a count, count's; of Barcelona

conde *m,* earl; king of the gypsies

condecir (con) *vi* to agree (with)

condecoración *f,* conferment of an honor, decoration; medal

condecorar *vt* to confer a decoration or medal

condena *f,* law sentence; punishment; penalty

condenable *a* culpable, guilty; worthy of damnation

condenado (-da) *a* damned; wicked, harmful. *n law* convicted criminal

condenador *a* condemning; incriminating; blaming

condenar *vt law* to pronounce sentence (on), convict; condemn; disapprove; wall or block or close up. **c. a galeras,** to condemn to the gallies. *vr* blame oneself; be eternally damned

condenatorio *a* condemnatory; incriminating

condensación *f,* condensation

condensador *a* condensing. *m,* (*elec mech chem*) condenser

condensante *a* condensing

condensar *vt* to condense; thicken; abridge

condesa *f,* countess

condescendencia *f,* affability, graciousness

condescender *vi irr* to be obliging, helpful, agreeable. See **entender**

condescendiente *a* affable, gracious

condestable *m, hist* constable, commander-in-chief

condición *f,* condition; quality; temperament, character; (social) position; rank, family; nobility, circumstance; stipulation, condition, requirement. **estar en condiciones de,** to be in a position to. **no estar en condiciones de,** to be in no condition to

condicional *a* conditional

condicionar *vi* to come to an agreement, arrange; *vt* impose conditions

condigno *a* condign

condimentación *f, cul* seasoning

condimentar *vt* to flavor, season (food)

condimento *m,* condiment, flavoring

condiscípulo *m,* schoolfellow

condolencia *f,* compassion; condolence

condolerse *vr* (*with de*) to sympathize with, be sorry for. See **doler**

condonar *vt* to condone

conducción *f.* **conducencia,** *f,* transport, conveyance, carriage; guiding; direction, management; *phys* conduction; *mech* control-gear. *aut* **c. a izquierda,** left-hand drive

conducente *a* conducting, conducive

conducir *vt irr* to transport, convey, carry; *phys* conduct; guide, lead; manage, direct; *aut* drive; conduce; *vi* be suitable; *vr* behave, conduct oneself. *Pres. Ind.* **conduzco, conduces,** etc. *Preterite* **conduje, condujiste,** etc. *Pres. Subjunc.* **conduzca, conduzcas,** etc. *Imperf. Subjunc.* **condujese,** etc.

conducta *f,* transport, conveyance; management, conduct, direction; behavior

conductibilidad *f, phys* conductivity

conductivo *a* conductive

conducto *m,* pipe, conduit, drain, duct; *fig* channel, means; *anat* tube

conductor (-ra) *n* guide; leader; driver (vehicles); *m, phys* conductor. **c. de caballos,** teamster. **c. de entrada,** *rad* lead-in. **c. del calor,** heat-conductor. **c. eléctrico,** electric wire or cable

conectar *vt elec* to connect, switch on; couple; attach, join

conectivo *a* connective; (*elec mech*) connecting

conejera *f,* rabbit-warren; *inf* low dive or haunt

conejillo de Indias *m,* guineapig

conejo *m,* rabbit

conejuno *a* rabbit, rabbit-like

conejuna *f,* rabbit fur, coney

conexión *f,* connection; *elec* switching on, connection; joint; joining; *pl* friends, connections; *elec* wiring

conexo *a* connected

confabulación *f,* confabulation, conspiracy

confabular *vi* to confer; *vr* scheme, plot

confalón *m,* standard, banner

confección *f,* making; confection; making-up; concoction, remedy; ready-made garment

confeccionador (-ra) *n* maker (of clothes, etc.)

confeccionar *vt* to make; prepare; make up (pharmaceuticals)

confederación *f*, alliance, pact; confederacy, federation

confederarse *vr* to confederate, be allied

conferencia *f*, conference, meeting; lecture; (telephone) long-distance call (US), trunk call (UK)

conferenciante *mf* lecturer

conferenciar *vi* to confer

conferir *vt irr* to grant, concede; consider, discuss; compare, correlate. See **herir**

confesable *a* acknowledgeable, avowable

confesar *vt irr* to avow, declare; acknowledge, admit; *ecc* hear confession; *vr ecc* confess. *Pres. Ind.* **confieso, confiesas, confiesa, confiesan.** *Pres. Subjunc.* **confiese, confieses, confiese, confiesen**

confesión *f*, confession

confesional *a* confessional

confesionario, confesonario, confesorio *m*, *ecc* confessional

confeso *a* confessed; converted (of Jews). *m*, *ecc* lay brother

confesor *m*, confessor

confeti *m*, confetti

confianza *f*, confidence, trust; assurance, courage; over-confidence, conceit; intimacy; familiarity. **de c.,** reliable (e.g. **persona de c.,** reliable person); informal (e.g. **reunión de c.,** informal meeting). **en c.,** in confidence, confidentially

confianzudo *a inf* overconfident

confiar *vi* (*with en*) to trust in, hope; *vt* (*with prep a* or *en*) entrust, commit to the care of; confide in

confidencia *f*, trust; confidence; confidential information

confidencial *a* confidential

confidente (-ta) *a* trustworthy, true. *m*, seat for two. *n* confidant(e); spy

configuración *f*, configuration, form, lie

configurar *vt* to shape

confín *m*, boundary, frontier; limit. *a* boundary

confinado *a* banished. *m*, *law* prisoner

confinar *vi* (*with con*) to be bounded by, contiguous to; *vt* banish; place in confinement

confirmación *f*, corroboration; *ecc* confirmation

confirmar *vt* to corroborate; uphold; *ecc* confirm

confirmatorio *a* confirmatory

confiscación *f*, confiscation

confiscar *vt* to confiscate

confitar *vt* to candy, crystallize or preserve (fruit, etc.); *fig* sweeten

confite *m*, bonbon, sugared almond, etc.

confitería *f*, confectionery

confitero (-ra) *n* confectioner

confitura *f*, preserve, jam

conflagración *f*, conflagration, blaze; uprising, rebellion

conflicto *m*, strife, struggle; spiritual conflict; *fig* difficult situation

confluencia *f*, confluence; crowd

confluir *vi irr* to meet, flow together (rivers); run together (roads); crowd. See **huir**

conformación *f*, conformation; make-up, structure (e.g. of an organization)

conformar *vt* to fit, adjust; *vr* agree, be of the same opinion; submit, comply; to make up (e.g. **los grupos sociales que conforman este país,** the social groups who make up this country)

conforme *a* similar, alike; consistent; in agreement; long-suffering, resigned. *adv* according (to), in proportion (to)

conformidad *f*, conformity; similarity; resignation; agreement, harmony; proportion, symmetry. **de c.,** by common consent. **en c.,** according to

confort *m*, comfort

confortante *a* comforting; consoling; strengthening (of beverages)

confortar *vt* to comfort, reassure; encourage; console

confortativo *a* comforting; comfortable; strengthening, warming (of beverages); encouraging, cheering

confrontación *f*, confrontment; comparison (of texts, etc.)

confrontar *vt* to bring face to face; compare, correlate; *vi* face; (*with con*) be contiguous to, border on

confucianismo *m*, Confucianism

confundible *a* mistakable, liable to be confused

confundimiento *m*, confounding; mistaking; confusion

confundir *vt* to mix, confuse; jumble together; mistake; *fig* confound (in argument); humble; bewilder, perplex; *vr* be mixed together; mistake, confuse; be ashamed; be bewildered

confusión *f*, confusion; perplexity; shame; jumble

confuso *a* mixed, upset; jumbled; obscure; indistinct; blurred; bewildered

confutación *f*, confutation

confutar *vt* to confute

conga *f*, conga (dance; drum)

congelación *f*, freezing; congealment. **punto de c.,** freezing point

congelar *vt* to congeal; freeze

congeniar *vi* to be congenial

congénito *a* congenital

congestión *f*, *med* congestion

congestionar *vt* to congest; *vr med* be overcharged (with blood)

conglomeración *f*, conglomeration

conglomerar *vt* to conglomerate

congoja *f*, anguish, anxiety, grief

congraciarse (*con*), *vr* to ingratiate oneself (with), get into the good graces (of)

congratulación *f*, congratulation

congratular *vt* to congratulate; *vr* congratulate oneself

congratulatorio *a* congratulatory

congregación *f*, gathering, meeting, congregation; brotherhood, guild

congregar(se) *vt* and *vr* to meet, assemble

congresista *mf* member of a congress

congreso *m*, congress; conference, meeting; sexual intercourse

congrio *m*, conger eel

congruencia *f*, suitability, convenience; *math* congruence

congruente *a* convenient, opportune; *math* congruent

cónico *a* conical, tapering *math* conic

conífera *f*, conifer

conífero *a* coniferous

conjetura *f*, conjecture

conjetural *a* conjectural

conjeturar *vt* to conjecture surmise

conjugación *f*, conjugation

conjugar *vt* to conjugate

conjunción *f*, connection, union association; (*ast gram*) conjunction

conjuntivitis *f*, conjunctivitis

conjunto *a* united, associated adjoining; mingled, mixed (with) bound, affiliated. *m*, whole; combo, ensemble (of musicians). **c. habitacional,** housing complex, housing project

conjura, conjuración *f*, conspiracy, plot

conjurador (-ra) *n* conspirator, plotter; exorcist

conjurar *vi* to conspire, plot *vt* swear, take an oath; exorcise; implore, beg; ward off (danger)

conjuro *m*, plot, conspiracy, spell, incantation; entreaty

conllevar *vt* to share (troubles) bear, put up with; endure

conmemoración *f*, commemoration

conmemorar *vt* to commemorate

conmemorativo *a* commemorative

conmensurable *a* commensurable

conmigo *pers. pron* 1st pers. sing. *mf* with myself, with me

conminar *vt* to threaten

conminatorio *a* threatening

conmiseración f, commiseration, compassion, pity

conmoción f, disturbance (mind or body); upheaval, commotion. **c. eléctrica,** electric shock

conmovedor a moving, pitiful; stirring, thrilling

conmover vt irr to perturb, stir; move to pity. **c. los cimientos de,** to shake the foundations of; vr be emotionally moved. See **mover**

conmutable a commutable

conmutación f, commutation

conmutador m, elec commutator; change-over switch

conmutar vt to commute; elec switch, convert

conmutatriz f, elec converter

connato a contemporary

connatural a innate, inborn

connaturalizar vt to connaturalize

connaturalizarse (con) vr to become accustomed (to), become acclimated (to)

connivencia f, connivance

connotación f, connotation

connotar vt to connote

cono m, (geom bot) cone. **el C. Sur,** the Southern Cone

conocedor (-ra) n one who knows; connoisseur; expert

conocer vt irr to know; understand; observe, perceive; be acquainted (with); conjecture; confess, acknowledge; know carnally; vr know oneself; know one another. **conocerle a uno la voz,** to recognize somebody's voice (e.g. **Le conozco la voz.** I recognize her by her voice.) **conocerle a uno en su manera de andar,** to recognize somebody by his gait, recognize somebody by his walk. Pres. Ind. **conozco, conoces,** etc. Pres. Subjunc. **conozca,** etc.

conocido (-da) a illustrious, distinguished. n acquaintance

conocimiento m, knowledge; understanding; intelligence; acquaintance (not friend); consciousness; com bill of lading; pl knowledge, learning

conque conjunc so, so that (e.g. ¿**C.** Juan se va? So John's going away?)

conquista f, conquest

conquistador (-ra) a conquering. n conqueror

conquistar vt to conquer; fig captivate, win

consabido a aforesaid, beforementioned

consagración f, consecration; dedication

consagrar vt to consecrate; dedicate, devote; deify; vr (with prep a) dedicate oneself to, engage in

consanguíneo a consanguineous

consanguinidad f, consanguinity

consciente a conscious; aware; sane. m, psy conscious

conscripción f, conscription

conscripto m, conscript

consecución f, obtainment; attainment

consecuencia f, consequence, outcome; logical consequence, conclusion; importance; consistence (of people)

consecuente a consequent, resultant; consistent. **c. consigo mismo,** self-consistent m, consequence; math consequent

consecutivo a consecutive, successive

conseguir vt irr to obtain, achieve. See **seguir**

conseja f, story, fairy-tale; old wives' tale

consejero (-ra) n adviser; member of council. m. **c. de estado,** counselor of state

consejo m, advice; council, commission, board; council chamber or building. **c. de administración,** board of directors. **c. de guerra,** council of war. **c. del reino,** council of the realm. **c. privado,** privy council

consenso m, consensus of opinion, unanimity

consentido a complaisant (of husband); spoilt, over-indulged

consentimiento m, consent; assent

consentir vt irr to permit, allow; believe; tolerate, put up with; over-indulge, spoil; vr crack, give way (furniture, etc.). **c. en,** to consent to; to agree to. See **sentir**

conserje m, concierge, porter; warden or keeper (of castle, etc.)

conserjería f, conciergerie, porter's lodge; warden's dwelling (in castles, etc.)

conserva f, jam; preserve; pickles; naut convoy. **en c.,** preserved, tinned

conservación f, upkeep; preservation, maintenance; cul preserving; conservation. **c. refrigerada,** cold-storage

conservador (-ra) a keeping, preserving. a and n preserver; pol conservative; traditionalist. m, curator

conservadurismo m, conservatism

conservar vt to keep, maintain, preserve; keep up (custom, etc.); guard; cul preserve. **c. en buen estado,** to keep in repair

conservatorio m, conservatoire; academy. **c. de música,** academy of music, conservatoire

considerable a considerable; worthy of consideration, powerful; numerous; large; important

consideración f, consideration, attention; reflection, thought; civility; importance. **en c. de,** considering

considerado a considerate; prudent; distinguished; important

considerar vt to consider, reflect upon; treat with consideration (persons); judge, estimate, feel (e.g. **Considero que . . .** I feel that . . .)

consigna f, mil watchword; left luggage office

consignador (-ra) n com consigner, sender

consignar vt to assign, lay aside; deposit; com consign; entrust, commit; put in writing; law deposit in trust; book (a suspect)

consignatario m, law trustee; mortgagee; com consignee. **c. de buques,** shipping agent

consigo pers. pron 3rd sing. and pl. mf with himself, herself, oneself, yourself, yourselves, themselves

consiguiente a consequent, resulting. m, consequence. **por c.,** in consequence

consistencia f, solidity; consistence, density; consistency, congruity, relevance

consistente a of a certain consistency; solid

consistir vi (with en) to consist in; be comprised of; be the result of

consistorio m, consistory; municipal council (in some Spanish towns); town hall

consola f, console table; piertable; mech bracket

cónsola f, radio cabinet

consolable a consolable

consolación f, consolation

consolador (-ra) n comforter, consoler

consolar vt irr to comfort, console. **consolarse de + inf.,** to console oneself for + pp. See **contar**

consolidación f, consolidation; stiffening

consolidar vt to consolidate; strengthen; combine, unite; vr law unite

consomé m, consommé

consonancia f, harmony; agreement

consonante a consonant, consistent. m, rhyme. f, gram consonant

consonantismo m, consonantism, consonant system

consorcio m, partnership; trust; intimacy, common life

consorte mf consort; companion, associate, partner; spouse

conspicuo a outstanding, distinguished; conspicuous

conspiración f, conspiracy

conspirador (-ra) n conspirator

conspirar vi to conspire; plot, scheme; tend, combine

constancia f, constancy, steadfastness; stability, steadiness; transcript (of grades). **c. de estudios,** transcript (of grades)

constante a constant; durable; mech steady, non-oscillating. m, constant

Constantinopla Constantinople

Constanza Constance (female given name and lake)

constar vi to be evident, be clear; (with de) be composed of, consist of, comprise

constelación f, ast constellation; climate

consternación f, dismay, alarm

consternarse *vr* to be dismayed or alarmed
constipado *m, med* cold; chill
constiparse *vr* to catch a cold or chill
constitución *f,* constitution; composition; make-up (e.g. **la c. del suelo,** the make-up of the soil)
constitucional *a* constitutional
constituir *vt irr* to constitute, form; found, establish; (*with en*) appoint, nominate; *fig* place in (a difficult situation, etc.); *vr* (*with en* or *por*) be appointed or authorized; be under (an obligation). See **huir**
constituyente, constitutivo *a* and *m,* constituent
constreñir *vt irr* to constrain, oblige; constrict; constipate. See **ceñir**
constricción *f,* constriction; contraction, shrinkage
construcción *f,* construction; art or process of construction; fabric, structure; *gram* construction; building, erection. **c. de caminos,** road making. **c. naval,** shipbuilding
constructor (-ra) *a* building, constructive. *n* builder; constructor
construir *vt irr* to construct; build, make; *gram* construct. See **huir**
consuelo *m,* consolation; comfort, solace; joy, delight
cónsul *m,* consul
consulado *m,* consulate. **c. general,** consulate general
consulta *f,* deliberation, consideration; advice; reference; conference, consultation
consultar *vt* to discuss, consider; seek advice, consult. **consultarlo con la almohada,** *fig* to sleep on it, think it over, mull it over
consultor (-ra) *a* consultative, advisory; consulting. *n* consultant; adviser. **c. externo,** outside consultant
consultorio *m, med* consulting rooms; surgery; technical information bureau
consumación *f,* consummation; completion, attainment; extinction, end
consumado *a* consummate; *inf* thorough, perfect
consumar *vt* to consummate; complete, accomplish, perfect
consumido *a inf* emaciated, wasted away; timid, spiritless
consumidor (-ra) *a* consuming. *n* consumer, user
consumir *vt* to destroy; consume, use; waste away, wear away; *ecc* take communion; *inf* grieve; *vr* be destroyed; *inf* be consumed with grief
consumo *m,* consumption; demand. **c. de combustible,** fuel consumption
contabilidad *f,* bookkeeping; accounts; accounting
contable *m,* bookkeeper
contacto *m,* contact (also *elec mil*). **en c.,** in common (e.g. **Los dos libros tienen mucho en c.** The two books have much in common.)
contado *a* few; infrequent; rare. **al c.,** *com* cash down. **por de c.,** presumably; of course, naturally
contador *a* counting. *m,* accountant; *law* auditor; counter (in banks); *elec* meter, counter; *naut* purser. **c. oficial,** *Argentina* certified public accountant. **c. público titulado,** certified public accountant
contaduría *f,* accountancy; counting house; accountant's office; auditorship; *theat* box-office; *naut* purser's office
contagiar *vt* to infect; corrupt, pervert; *vr* (*with con, de* or *por*) be infected by or through
contagio *m,* infection; contagious disease; *fig* contagion, perversion, corruption
contagioso *a* infectious; *fig* catching, contagious
contaminación *f,* contamination, pollution
contaminar *vt* to pollute, contaminate; infect; *fig* corrupt
contante *a* ready (of money)
contar *vt irr* to count; recount, tell; place to account; include, count among; *vi* calculate, compute. **contarle a uno las cuarenta,** *inf* to give someone a piece of one's mind. **c. con,** to rely upon; reckon upon. *Pres. Ind.* **cuento, cuentas, cuenta, cuentan.** *Pres. Subjunc.* **cuente, cuentes, cuente, cuenten**

contemplación *f,* meditation, contemplation; consideration
contemplar *vt* to consider, reflect upon; look at, contemplate; indulge, please
contemplativo *a ecc* contemplative; reflective, thoughtful; kind, indulgent
contemporáneo (de) *a* contemporaneous (to *or* with) *n* contemporary
contemporizar *vi* to temporize, gain time
contencioso *a* contentious, argumentative; *law* litigious
contender *vi irr* to contain; restrain, hold back; comprise; *vr* control oneself. See **entender**
contendiente *mf* contestant
contener *vt irr* to contain; include; comprise; hold back; restrain; check, repress; hold down, subdue; suppress, put down; *vr* contain oneself; keep one's temper; keep quiet; refrain. See **tener**
contenido *m,* contents. *a* contained; *fig* restrained; reserved (of persons)
contentamiento *m,* contentment
contentar *vt* to satisfy, please; *com* endorse; *vr* be pleased or satisfied
contento *a* happy; content; satisfied; pleased. *m,* pleasure; contentment. **no caber de c.,** to be overjoyed
contestación *f,* reply, answer; discussion, argument, dispute
contestar *vt* to reply, answer; confirm, attest; *vi* accord, harmonize
contexto *m,* context
contextura *f,* structure; context; physique, frame
contienda *f,* struggle, fight; quarrel, dispute; discussion
contigo *pers. pron* 2nd sing. *mf* with thee, with you
contigüidad *f,* proximity, nearness
contiguo *a* adjacent, near
continencia *f,* moderation, self-restraint; continence; chastity; containing
continental *a* continental. *m,* express messenger service; *Puerto Rico* person from the mainland United States
continente *a* continent. *m,* container; demeanor, bearing; *geog* continent; mainland
contingencia *f,* contingency; risk, danger
contingente *a* incidental; fortuitous; dependent; *m, mil* taskforce, contingent
continuación *f,* continuation; prolongation; sequel (of a story, etc.)
continuador (-ra) *n* continuer
continuar *vt* to continue; *vi* continue; last, remain, go on; *vr* be prolonged
continuidad *f,* continuity
continuo *a* continuous, steady, uninterrupted; persevering, tenacious; persistent, lasting, unremitting. *m,* a united whole. **de c.,** continuously
contonearse *vr* to swing the hips (in walking); strut
contorno *m,* contour, outline; (gen. *pl*) environs, surrounding district
contorsión *f,* contortion
contorsionista *mf* contortionist
contra *prep* against, counter, athwart; opposed to, hostile to; in front of, opposite; towards. *m,* opposite view or opinion. *f, inf* difficulty, trouble. **c. la corriente,** upstream. **el pro y el c.,** the pros and cons. **en c.,** in opposition, against
contraalmirante *m,* rear admiral
contraataque *m,* counterattack
contraaviso *m,* countermand
contrabajo *m,* doublebass; player of this instrument; deep bass voice
contrabalancear *vt* to counterbalance; *fig* compensate
contrabandista *a* smuggling. *mf* smuggler
contrabando *m,* contraband; smuggling
contracción *f,* contraction; shrinkage; abridgment; abbreviation
contracubierta *f,* book jacket, jacket
contradanza *f,* square dance

contradecir *vt irr* to contradict; *vr* contradict oneself. See **decir**

contradicción *f,* contradiction

contradictorio *a* contradictory

contraer *vt irr* to shrink, reduce in size, shorten; abridge; contract (matrimony, obligations); *fig* acquire (diseases, habits); *vr* shorten, contract, shrink. See **traer**

contrafuerte *m,* buttress, counterfort, abutment; *geog* spur

contrahacer *vt irr* to forge, counterfeit; mimic; imitate. See **hacer**

contrahecho *a* deformed

contralor *m,* comptroller

contraloría *f,* comptrollership, office of comptroller (position); comptroller's office (place)

contralto *m,* contralto (voice)

contraluz *f,* counterlight

contramaestre *m, naut* boatswain; overseer, superintendent, foreman

contramarcha *f,* retrogression; *mil* countermarch

contramedida *f,* counter-measure

contraorden *f,* countermand

contrapedalear *vi* to backpedal

contrapelo *a adv* the wrong way of the hair, against the grain; *inf* reluctantly, distastefully

contrapeso *m,* counterpoise, counterweight; balancing-pole (acrobats); *fig* counterbalance; makeweight

contraponer *vt irr* to compare; place opposite; oppose. See **poner**

contraproducente *a* counteractive, counterproductive, unproductive, self-deceiving; self-defeating

contrapuesto *a* opposing, divergent

contrapunto *m,* counterpoint

contrariar *vt* to counter, oppose; impede; vex, annoy

contrariedad *f,* contrariety, opposition; obstacle; vexation, trouble

contrario (-ia) *a* opposite; hostile, opposed; harmful; adverse, contrary. *n* adversary; opponent. *m,* obstacle. *f.* **contraria,** contrary, opposite. **al contrario,** on the contrary. **llevar la contraria (a),** to oppose; contradict

contrarreforma *f,* counter-Reformation

contrasentido *m,* wrong sense, opposite sense (of words); contradiction of initial premise; self-contradiction; nonsense

contraseña *f,* countersign; *mil* password

contrastar *vt* to contrast; oppose, resist; check (weights and measures); assay; *mech* calibrate, gauge; *vi* contrast

contraste *m,* contrast; opposition, difference; weights and measures inspector; dispute, clash. **en c. a,** in contrast to

contrata *f,* **contrato,** *m,* contract. **contrato de arrendamiento,** lease

contratación *f,* hiring; *com* transaction; commerce, trade

contratapa *f,* back cover (of a periodical, etc.)

contratar *vt* to contract, enter into an agreement; make a bargain (with), deal (with); hire, contract

contratiempo *m,* mishap, accident

contratista *mf* contractor

contratorpedero *m,* torpedoboat destroyer

contravención *f,* contravention; violation. **en c. a,** in violation of

contraveneno *m, med* antidote; remedy, precaution

contravenir *vt irr* to infringe, contravene. See **venir**

contraventana *f,* shutter (for windows)

contravidriera *f,* storm window

contrayente *a* contracting. *mf* contracting party (used of matrimony)

contribución *f,* contribution; tax. **c. sobre la propiedad,** property tax

contribuir *vt irr* to pay (taxes); contribute. See **huir**

contribuyente *a* contributing; contributory. *mf* contributor; taxpayer

contrición *f,* contrition

contrincante *m,* competitor, candidate (public examinations); rival, opponent

contrito *a* contrite

control *m,* control; checking. **c. de precios,** price control

controlar *vt* to control

controversia *f,* controversy

controvertir *vi* and *vt irr* to dispute, argue against, deny. See **sentir**

contumacia *f,* obstinacy; *law* contumacy

contumaz *a* stubborn; impenitent; *law* contumacious; *med* obstinate, resistant (to cure)

contumelia *f,* contumely

conturbar *vt* to perturb, make anxious, disturb; *vr* be perturbed

contuso *a* contused, bruised

convalecencia *f,* convalescence; convalescent home

convalecer *vi irr* to convalesce, get better; *fig* recover, regain (influence, etc.). See **conocer**

convaleciente *a* and *mf* convalescent

convalidar *vt* to ratify, confirm

convecino *a* nearby; neighboring

convencedor *a* convincing

convencer *vt* to convince; prove beyond doubt, demonstrate to (persons); be convincing (e.g. **No convence,** It's not convincing; He's not convincing.) *vr* be convinced

convencimiento *m,* conviction, belief, assurance

convención *f,* pact, formal agreement; harmony, conformity; convention

convencional *a* conventional (all meanings)

convencionalismo *m,* conventionality

convenido *a* agreed

conveniencia *f,* conformity, harmony, adjustment; experience, suitability, convenience; advantage; agreement, pact; post as domestic; ease, comfort; *pl* income; social conventions

conveniente *a* convenient, opportune; suitable, fitting; profitable; useful; decorous. **tener por c. + inf,** to think it fitting to + *inf,* find it appropriate to + *inf*

convenio *m,* pact, treaty; *com* agreement, contract

convenir *vi irr* to agree; assemble, congregate; belong; be suitable; *vr* agree; suit oneself. **No me conviene salir esta tarde,** It does not suit me to go out this afternoon. **Me convendría pasar un mes allí,** It would be a good idea (or a wise thing) for me to spend a month there. See **venir**

convento *m,* convent; monastery; religious community

conventual *a* conventual; monastic. *m, ecc* conventual

convergencia *f,* convergence

convergir *vi* to converge; *fig* coincide (views, etc.)

conversación *f,* conversation; intercourse, company; *law* criminal conversation

conversar *vi* to converse; chat; live with others; know socially

conversión *f,* conversion; change, transformation; *com* conversion; *mil* wheel; wheeling

converso (-sa) *n* convert

convertible *a* convertible

convertir *vt irr* to change, transform; convert; reform; *vr* be transformed; be converted; be reformed. See **sentir**

convexidad *f,* convexity

convexo *a* convex

convicción *f,* conviction; certitude; *law* conviction

convicto (-ta) *a* and *n law* convict

convidado (-da) *n* guest

convidar *vt* to invite (persons); encourage, provoke; entice, attract; *vr* invite oneself; offer one's services

convincente *a* convincing

convite *m,* invitation; banquet; party

convivencia *f,* coexistence, common life, life together. **c. pacífica,** peaceful coexistence

convivial *a* convivial

convivir *vi* to live together, live under the same roof

convocación f, convocation
convocar vt to convene, convoke
convoy m, convoy; escort; following; cruet-stand
convoyar vt to convoy, escort
convulsión f, convulsion
convulsivo a convulsive
conyugal a conjugal
cónyuge mf husband or (and) wife (used gen. in pl)
coñac m, brandy
cooperación f, cooperation
cooperador (-ra) a cooperative. n cooperator, collaborator
cooperar vt to cooperate
cooperativa f, cooperative society
cooperativo a cooperative
coordenada f, coordinate
coordinación f, coordination
coordinar vt to coordinate, classify
copa f, wineglass, goblet; glassful; top branches (of trees); crown (of hat); cards heart; gill (liquid measure); inf drink, glass; pl cards hearts (in Spanish pack, goblets)
copartícipe mf co-partner, partaker, participant
copec m, kopeck
Copenhague Copenhagen
copernicano a Copernican
copero m, cupbearer; sideboard; cocktail cabinet
copete m, lock, tress (hair); tuft, crest; forelock (horses); head, top (ice-cream, drinks); inf **de alto c.**, aristocratic; socially prominent
copia f, abundance, plenty; copy, reproduction; transcript; imitation
copiador (-ra) a copying. n copier; transcriber. m, copybook
copiar vt to copy
copioso a abundant, plentiful
copla f, couplet; popular four-line poem; couple, pair; pl inf verses
coplero (-ra) n balladmonger; poetaster
copo m, cop (of a spindle); snowflake
copón m, large goblet; ecc ciborium, chalice
coprófago a coprophagous
copropietario (-ia) n coproprietor, coowner
cóptico a Coptic. m, Coptic (language)
copto (-ta) n Copt
cópula f, connection; coupling; joining; copulation
copularse vr to copulate
coque m, coke
coqueluche f, whooping cough
coqueta f, coquette, flirt
coquetear vi to flirt
coqueteo m, coquetry; flirtation
coquetería f, coquetry
coquetón a coquettish
coracero m, cuirassier
coraje m, courage, valor; anger
coral m, coral. f, coral snake. m, bot coral tree; pl coral beads
coral a choral
coralina f, coral (polyp).
coraza f, cuirass; shell (of tortoise); armor-plate, armor (ships, etc.)
corazón m, heart; courage, spirit; love, tenderness; goodwill, benevolence; core (of a fruit); fig pith. **de c.**, sincerely. **tener el c. en la mano,** to wear one's heart on one's sleeve
corazonada f, feeling, instinct; presentiment, apprehension
corbata f, necktie; scarf; ribbon (insignia)
corbatería f, necktie shop
corbatero m, necktie maker; necktie dealer; tie rack
corbeta f, corvette
Córcega Corsica
corcel m, charger or battle horse
corchea f, mus quaver
corchete m, sew hook and eye; hook

corcho m, bot cork, cork bark; stopper, cork; cork mat; bee hive
corcova f, hump, abnormal protuberance
corcovado (-da) a hunchbacked, crooked. n hunchback
corcovear vi to curvet, caper
cordaje m, naut cordage, tackling, rope
cordel m, cord; naut line. **a c.,** in a straight line
cordelería f, rope making; ropeyard; cordage
cordelero (-ra) n rope maker
cordera f, ewe lamb; sweet, gentle woman
cordero m, lamb; dressed lambskin; peaceable, mild man; Jesus (gen. **Divino C.**)
cordial a warming, invigorating; affectionate, loving, friendly. m, med cordial
cordialidad f, cordiality, friendliness
cordillera f, mountain range
Córdoba Cordova
cordobán m, cured goatskin; Cordovan leather, Spanish leather
cordobés (-esa) a and n Cordovan
cordón m, cord; cordon; ecc rope girdle; arch stringcourse
cordoncillo m, rib (in cloth); ridge, milling (of coins); sew piping
cordura f, good sense, prudence
Corea Korea
corego, corega m, choragus
coreografía f, choreography; art of dancing
coreográfico a choreographic
coreógrafo m, choreographer
corintio (-ia) a and n Corinthian
Corinto Corinth
corista m, ecc chorister. mf theat member of the chorus
cornada f, horn thrust or wound (bulls, etc.)
cornalina f, min cornelian
cornamenta f, horns (bulls, deer, etc.)
córnea f, cornea
corneja f, carrion or black crow
córneo a horny, corneous
corneta f, mus bugle; mus cornet; swineherd's horn; mil pennon. m, bugler; mil cornet. **c. de monte,** hunting horn
cornetín m, dim **corneta,** mus cornet; cornet player
cornezuelo m, dim little horn; med ergot; bot variety of olive
cornisa f, cornice
cornucopia f, cornucopia, horn of plenty; sconce; mirror
cornudo a horned. m, cuckold. **el C.,** the Devil
coro m, choir; chorus; arch choir. **hacer c. (a),** to listen to, support. **saber de c.,** to know by heart
corolario m, corollary
corona f, garland, wreath; halo; (ast arch) corona; crown (of tooth); crown (of head); tonsure; crown (coin); royal power; kingdom; triumph; reward; summit, height, peak; circlet (for candles)
coronación f, coronation; coping stone
coronamiento m, coronation; coping stone; fig crowning touch; naut taffrail
coronar vt to crown; crown (in draughts); complete, round off; vr be crowned; crown oneself; be tipped or capped
coronel m, colonel
coronela f, inf colonel's wife
coronelía f, colonelcy
coronilla f, dim small crown; crown of head; fig inf **estar hasta la c.,** to be fed up
coroza f, dunce's cap
corpiño m, bodice
corporación f, corporation, body, association
corporal a and m, ecc corporal
corporativo a corporate, corporative
corpóreo a corporeal
corporizar vt to embody
corpulento a corpulent, stout
Corpus m, Corpus Christi

corpúsculo m, corpuscle

corral m, yard; pen, enclosure, corral; old-time theater. **c. de madera,** timber yard. *inf* **hacer corrales,** to play truant

correa f, leather strap or thong; flexibility; *mech* belt, band

corrección f, correction; correctness; punishment; emendation. **c. de pruebas,** proofreading, proofing, reading proof

correcional a correctional. m, reformatory

correctivo a and m, corrective

correcto a correct; well-bred; unexceptionable, irreproachable; regular (of features)

corredera f, link (engines); *mech* slide; *naut* log; racecourse; *inf* procuress

corredizo a easy to untie; running (of knots); sliding

corredor (-ra) n runner. m, com broker; corridor; *inf* meddler; *inf* procurer, pimp. a running. **c. de bolsa,** stockbroker

corregible a corrigible

corregidor m, Spanish magistrate; *ant* mayor

corregidora f, wife of corregidor; mayoress

corregir vt irr to correct; scold, punish; moderate, counteract; *mech* adjust; vr mend one's ways. **c. pruebas,** to read proof. *Pres. Ind.* **corrijo, corriges, corrige, corrigen.** *Pres. Part.* **corrigiendo.** *Pres. Subjunc.* **corrija, corrijas,** etc. *Imperf. Subjunc.* **corrigiese,** etc.

correlación f, correlation

correligionario (-ia) n coreligionist; fellow-supporter or believer

correo m, courier; mail; post-office; letters. **c. aéreo,** air-mail. **c. certificado,** registered mail. **a vuelta de c.,** by return of mail. **tren c.,** mail train

correr vi to run; race; sail, steam; flow; blow; flood; extend, stretch; pass (of time); fall due (salary, etc.); be current or general; (*with con*) be in charge of or responsible for; vt run (a horse); fasten, slide (bolts, etc.); draw (curtains); undergo, suffer; sell, auction; *inf* steal; *fig* embarrass; spread (a rumor, etc.); catch, make (bus, train, etc.); vr slide, glide, slip; run (of colors); *inf* spread oneself, talk too much. **c. cañas,** to participate in a mock joust using reeds as spears

correría f, raid, foray; excursion, trip

correspondencia f, relationship, connection; intercourse, communication; correspondence, letters; equivalence, exact translation

corresponder vi to requite, repay; be grateful; belong to, concern; devolve upon, fall to; suit, harmonize (with); fit; vr correspond by letters; like or love each other

correspondiente a suitable; proportionate; corresponding. *mf* correspondent

corresponsal *mf* correspondent (especially professional); *com* agent

corretear vi to wander about the streets; gad

correveidile *mf inf* tale-bearer, gossip

corrida f, race, run; *aer* taxying; bull fight (abb. for **c. de toros**)

corrido a extra, over (of weight); embarrassed; experienced

corriente a current, present; well-known; usual, customary; fluent (style); ordinary, average; easy. f, flow, stream; *fig* course (of events, etc.); *elec* current. adv quite, exactly. *elec* **c. alterna,** alternating current. **c. continua,** direct current. **c. de aire,** draught. **estar al c.,** to be informed (of something)

Corriente del Golfo Gulf Stream

corrillo m, knot, group, huddle (of people)

corro m, circle, group; ring (for children's games)

corroboración f, corroboration, confirmation

corroborar vt to fortify; corroborate, support

corroborativo a corroborative

corroer vt irr to corrode, waste away; *fig* gnaw. See **roer**

corromper vt to rot; mar; spoil, ruin; seduce; corrupt (texts); bribe; *fig* contaminate, corrupt; vi stink; vr putrefy, not; be spoilt; *fig* be corrupted

corrosión f, corrosion

corrosivo a corrosive

corrugación f, corrugation, wrinkling

corrupción f, rot, putrefaction; corruption, depravity; decay; stink; bribery; falsification (of texts); corruption (of language, etc.)

corrupto a corrupt

corruptor (-ra) n corrupter

corsario m, pirate; privateer

corsé m, corset

corsetería f, corset shop or manufactory

corso (-sa) a and n Corsican

corta f, felling, cutting

cortacircuitos m, *elec* circuit breaker, cut-out; disconnecting switch

cortado a fitting, proportioned; disjointed (style); confused, shamefaced

cortador m, cutter; cutter-out (dresses, etc.); butcher

cortadura f, cut, wound; cutting (from periodicals); defile; *pl* clippings, cuttings

cortafrío m, cold chisel; *carp* hammer-head chisel

cortalápices m, pencil sharpener

cortante a cutting; sharp; piercing (of wind, etc.); trenchant

cortapapel m, paper-knife

cortapisa f, condition, stipulation

cortaplumas m, penknife

cortapuros m, cigar cutter

cortar vt to cut; cut out (dresses, etc.); switch off, turn off (water, electricity, etc.); cleave, divide; cut (cards); pierce (wind, etc.); interrupt, impede; omit, cut; *fig* interrupt (conversation); decide, determine; vr be confused or shamefaced; curdle, turn sour (e.g. **Se cortó la leche,** The milk turned sour); split, fray; chap

cortavidrios m, diamond, glasscutter

cortaviento m, windscreen

corte f, court (royal); retinue; yard; *pl* Spanish parliament. m, cutting, cut; blade, cutting edge; cutting out, dressmaking; length, material required for garment, shoes, etc.; cut, fit; style; book edge; *arch* section; means, expedient; counting of money (in a till). **c. de caja,** counting of money (in a till). **c. trasversal,** side view

cortedad f, shortness, brevity; smallness; stupidity; dullness; timidity, shyness. **c. de fuerzas,** lack of strength

cortejar vt to accompany, escort; woo, court

cortejo m, courtship, wooing; suite, accompaniment; gift, present; homage, attention; *inf* lover, beau

cortés a polite, attentive, courteous, civil

cortesana f, courtesan

cortesano a court; courtly. m, courtier

cortesía f, politeness, courtesy; attentiveness; civility; gift, present; favor. **c. internacional,** courtesy of nations. **c. de boca mucho vale y poco cuesta.** Courtesy is worth much and costs little

corteza f, bot bark; *anat* cortex; skin, peel, crust; aspect, appearance; roughness. **c. terrestre,** Earth's crust, crust of the Earth. **de c.,** superficial (e.g. explanation)

cortijo m, farmhouse and land

cortina f, curtain; *fig* veil; *inf* heel taps; *mil* curtain, screen. **c. de fuego de artillería,** anti-aircraft barrage. **c. de globos de intercepción,** balloon barrage. **c. de humo,** smoke screen. **c. metálica,** metal shutter

cortinaje m, curtains, hangings

corto a short, brief; timid, bashful; concise; defective; stupid, dull; tongue-tied, inarticulate. **c. circuito,** *elec* short-circuit. **c. de alcances,** dull-witted. **c. de vista,** short-sighted

coruscar vi to glitter, shine

corvadura f, bend; curvature

corvea f, corvée

corveta f, curvet, prancing

corvetear vi to curvet

corzo m, roe-deer, fallow-deer

cosa f, thing. **c. rara,** strange to relate; an extraordinary

thing. **como si tal c.**, as though nothing had happened. *inf* **poquita c.**, a person of no account
cosaco (-ca) *a* and *n* Cossack
coscorrón *m*, blow on the head, cuff
cosecha *f*, harvest; harvest time; reaping, gathering, lifting; yield, produce; crop, shower (of honors, etc.). **c. de vino**, vintage
cosechar *vi* and *vt* to harvest, reap
coseno *m*, cosine
coser *vt* to sew, stitch; join, unite; press together (lips, etc.). **c. a puñaladas**, to stab repeatedly
Cosme Cosmo
cosmético *a* and *m*, cosmetic
cósmico *a* cosmic
cosmografía *f*, cosmography
cosmógrafo *m*, cosmographer
cosmonave *f*, spaceship
cosmopolita *a* and *mf* cosmopolitan
cosmopolitismo *m*, cosmopolitanism
cosmos *m*, cosmos
cospel *m*, blank (from which to stamp coins); to ken; subway to ken
cosquillas *f pl*, tickling. **hacer c. (a)**, to tickle
cosquillear *vt* to tickle
cosquilleo *m*, tickle, tickling
cosquilloso *a* ticklish; hypersensitive, touchy
costa *f*, cost; expense; coast; *pl law* costs. **a c. de**, by dint of; at the cost of. **a toda c.**, at all costs
Costa del Oro, la the Gold Coast
Costa de Marfil Ivory Coast
costado *m*, *anat* side; *mil* flank; side; *pl* line of descent, genealogy. *naut* **dar el c.**, to be broadside on
costal *m*, sack, bag
costanero *a* sloping; coast, coastal
costar *vi irr* to cost; cause. See **contar**
costarriqueño (-ña) *a* and *n* Costa Rican
coste *m*, cost, price
costear *vt* to pay for, defray the expense of; *naut* coast; *vr* pay (for itself)
costilla *f*, (*anat aer naut arch*) rib; *fig inf* better half, wife; *pl inf* back, behind
costillaje, costillar *m*, *anat* ribs; *naut* ship's frame
costoso *a* expensive, costly; valuable; dear, costly, difficult
costra *f*, crust; scab; rind (of cheese)
costumbre *f*, habit; custom
costumbrista *mf* writer on everyday life and customs. *a* (of literary work) dealing with life and customs
costura *f*, sewing; seam; needlework; *carp* joint; riveting
costurera *f*, seamstress
costurero *m*, work-box, sewing bag
cota *f*, *surv* elevation, height; coat (of mail); quota. **c. de malla,** chain-mail
cotangente *f*, cotangent
cotejar *vt* to compare; collate
cotejo *m*, comparison; collation
cótel *m*, cocktail, drink
cotelera *f*, cocktail shaker
cotí *m*, ticking (cloth)
cotidiano *a* daily
cotillón *m*, cotillion
cotizable *a* valued at; (of prices, shares) quoted
cotización *f*, *com* quotation; *com* rate. **boletín de c.,** price list (of shares, etc.)
cotizar *vt com* to quote (prices, rates)
coto *m*, enclosed ground; boundary stone; preserve, covert; hand's breadth; end, stop, limit. **c. de caza**, game preserve
cotorra *f*, small green parrot; magpie; *inf* chatterbox
cotufa *f*, earthnut; titbit; *inf* **pedir cotufas en el golfo,** to ask for the moon
coturno *m*, buskin
coyote *m*, coyote, prairie wolf; *Mexico* fixer (anyone who can pull strings to cut red tape or achieve something illegally); smuggler (of goods or people)
coyuntura *f*, *anat* joint; juncture, occasion

coz *f*, kick, recoil (of gun); butt (of a rifle); *inf* slap in the face, unprovoked rudeness. **dar coces,** to kick
craneal *a* cranial
cráneo *m*, cranium, skull
crápula *f*, drunkenness; depravity, immorality, debauchery
craquear *vt* to crack (petroleum)
crasitud *f*, greasiness; fatness; crassness
craso *a* fat, greasy; thick; unpardonable, crass (often with *ignorancia*). *m*, fatness; ignorance
creación *f*, creation; universe, world; foundation, establishment; appointment (dignitaries)
creador (-ra) *n* creator, originator. *m*, God. *a* creative
crear *vt* to create; found, institute, establish; make, appoint
crecer *vi irr* to grow; grow up; increase in size; grow longer; wax (moon); come in (of the tide); increase in value (money); *vr* become more sure of oneself; swell with pride; grow in authority. See **nacer**
creces *f pl*, increase, interest. **con c.,** fully, amply. **pagar con c.,** *fig* to pay with interest
crecida *f*, swollen river or stream; food; rising (of the tide)
crecido *a* grown up; considerable; abundant, plentiful; large; full; serious, important
crecidos *m pl*, widening stitches (knitting)
creciente *a* growing; rising (of the tide); crescent (moon). *m*, *her* crescent. *f*, rising of the tide; crescent moon
crecimiento *m*, growing; growth, development; increase (in value, money); waxing (of moon)
credencial *a* accrediting
credenciales *f pl*, credentials
credibilidad *f*, credibility
crédito *m*, belief, credence; assent, acquiescence; reputation, name; favor, popularity, acceptance; *com* credit; *com* letter of credit. **créditos activos,** assets. **créditos pasivos,** liabilities. **a c.,** on credit
credo *m*, creed. *inf* **en un c.,** in a jiffy
credulidad *f*, credulity
crédulo *a* credulous
creencia *f*, belief; religion, sect, faith
creer *vt irr* to believe; think, consider, opine; think likely or probable. **¡Ya lo creo!** I should just think so! Rather! **creerse la divina garza,** *Mexico* to think one is God's gift to the world. **creerse descender del sobaco de Jesucristo,** to think one's God's gift to the world. *Pres. Part.* **creyendo.** *Preterite* **creyó, creyeron.** *Imperf. Subjunc.* **creyese,** etc.
creíble *a* credible
crema *f*, cream (off milk); custard mold, cream, shape; face cream; cold cream; elect, flower (of society, etc.)
cremación *f*, cremation; burning, incineration
cremallera *f*, *mech* rack, ratch; zip fastener. **colgar la c.,** to give a house-warming
crematístico *a* economic, financial
crematorio *m*, crematorium. *a* burning; cremating
cremor *m*, *chem* cream of tartar
cremoso *a* creamy
crencha *f*, parting (of the hair); each side of parting
creosota *f*, creosote
crepitación *f*, crackling, sputtering; hissing; roar (of a fire); *med* crepitation
crepitar *vi* to crackle; sputter; hiss; roar (of a fire); *med* crepitate
crepuscular *a* twilight
crepúsculo *m*, twilight, half light
cresa *f*, maggot; cheese-mite; fly's egg
Creso Croesus
crespo *a* curly, frizzy (hair); rough (of animal's fur); curled (leaves); artificial, involved (style)
crespón *m*, crape
cresta *f*, comb (of cock, etc.); tuft, topknot (birds); plume; summit, top (of mountains); crest (of a wave); *her* crest
crestado *a* crested

Creta Crete

creta *f*, chalk

cretense *a* Cretan

cretinismo *m*, cretinism

cretino (-na) *a* and *n* cretin

creyente *a* believing; religious. *mf* believer

cría *f*, rearing; bringing up; nursing; suckling; breeding; brood; litter

criada *f*, servant, maid

criadero *m*, *min* vein, deposit; tree nursery, plantation; breeding farm or place. *a* prolific

criado *m*, servant. *a* bred, brought up (used with *bien* or *mal*, well *or* badly brought up)

criador (-ra) *n* breeder, keeper, raiser. *a* creating; rearing; creative; fertile, rich

crianza *f*, feeding, suckling; lactation; manners. **buena** (or **mala**) **c.**, good (or bad) breeding or upbringing

criar *vt* to create; procreate; rear, educate, bring up; feed, nurse, suckle; raise (birds, animals); inspire, give rise to. **Me crié raquítico,** I grew up delicate

criatura *f*, being, creature; man, human being; infant; small child; fetus; *fig* puppet, tool

criba *f*, sieve, cribble

cribar *vt* to sieve; riddle (earth, etc.)

crimen *m*, crime. **c. pasional,** crime of passion

criminal *a* and *m*, criminal

criminalidad *f*, guilt; crime ratio; delinquency

criminalista *mf* criminal lawyer; criminologist

criminología *f*, criminology

crin *f*, horsehair; (gen. *pl*) mane

crinolina *f*, crinoline

crío *m*, *inf* kid, brat

criollo (-lla) *a* and *n* creole. *a* indigenous, native

cripta *f*, crypt

criptografía *f*, cryptography

criquet *m*, *sport* cricket

crisálida *f*, chrysalis

crisantemo *m*, chrysanthemum

crisis *f*, crisis. **c. de desarrollo,** growing pains. **c. de vivienda,** housing shortage

crisma *m*, or *f*, chrism

crisol *m*, crucible; melting pot

crispado *a* stiffened

crispar *vt* to cause to contract or twitch; *vr* twitch. *inf* **Se me crispan los nervios,** My nerves are all on edge

cristal *m*, crystal; glass; windowpane; mirror; water. **c. tallado,** cut glass

cristalería *f*, glassware; glass manufacture; glass panes; glass and china shop

cristalino *a* crystalline. *m*, lens (of the eye)

cristalización *f*, crystallization

cristalizar *vi* to crystallize; *fig* take shape; *vt* cause to crystallize

cristalografía *f*, crystallography

cristiandad *f*, Christendom

cristianismo *m*, Christianity; Christendom

cristianizar *vt* to convert to Christianity, christianize

cristiano (-na) *a* and *n* Christian. *a inf* watered (of wine). *m*, *inf* Spanish (contrasted with other languages); *inf* soul, person

cristino (-na) *a* and *n* supporting, or follower of, Queen Regent Maria Cristina during Carlist wars

cristo *m*, Christ; crucifix. *inf* **donde C. dio las tres voces,** in the middle of nowhere

cristus *m*, Christ-cross; alphabet. **no saber el c.,** to be extremely ignorant

criterio *m*, criterion, standard; judgment, discernment; opinion. **a c. de,** in the opinion of. **según mi c.,** in my opinion

crítica (a) *f*, criticism (of)

criticar *vt* to criticize; censure, find fault with, blame

crítico *a* critical; censorious; dangerous, difficult; *med* critical. *m*, critic; fault-finder

criticón (-ona) *a* censorious, hyper-critical. *n* fault-finder

croar *vi* (frog) to croak

Croacia Croatia

croata *a* and *mf* Croatian

croché *m*, crochet work

crol *m*, crawl (swimming)

cromado *a* chromium-plated

cromático *a* chromatic

cromato *m*, chromate

crómico *a* chromic

cromo *m*, chrome; chromium; chromolithograph

crónica *f*, chronicle; diary of events

crónico *a* chronic; inveterate

cronista *mf* chronicler

cronología *f*, chronology

cronológico *a* chronological

cronómetro *m*, stop-watch

croqueta *f*, croquette

croquis *m*, sketch, outline, drawing. **c. de nivel,** (optical) foresight

crótalo *m*, rattlesnake; snapper (kind of castanet)

cruce *m*, crossing; point of intersection; crossroads

crucero *m*, *ecc* cross-bearer; crossroads; *arch* transept; *ast* Cross; *naut* cruiser

crucificar *vt* to crucify; *fig inf* torment, torture

crucifijo *m*, crucifix

crucifixión *f*, crucifixion

cruciforme *a* cruciform

crucigrama *m*, crossword puzzle

cruda *f*, *Mexico* hangover

crudelísimo *a sup* **cruel,** most cruel, exceedingly cruel

crudeza *f*, rawness, uncookedness; unripeness; rawness (silk, etc.); crudeness; harshness; *inf* boasting

crudo *a* uncooked, raw; green, unripe; indigestible; raw, natural, unbleached; harsh, cruel; cold, raw; *inf* boastful. **crudos de petróleo,** *m pl* crude oil

crueldad *f*, cruelty; harshness

cruento *a* bloody

crujía *f*, passage, corridor; *naut* midship gangway

crujidero *a* crackling; creaking; crispy; clattering; rustling; chattering

crujido *m*, creak, crack, crackling, rustle

crujir *vi* to creak, crackle, rustle

crup *m*, croup

crupié *m*, croupier

crustáceo *a* and *m*, crustacean

crux *f*, cross; tails (of coin); withers (of animals); insignia, decoration; affliction, trouble; *ast* Southern Cross; *print* dagger, obelisk, obelus. **c. doble,** diesis, double dagger. **c. de mayo,** May cross. **c. gamada,** swastika. *inf* **¡C. y raya!** An end to this! **en c.,** in the shape of a cross. *inf* **hacerse cruces,** to be left speechless, be dumbfounded

cruzada *f*, crusade; crossroads; campaign

cruzado *a* cross; double-breasted (of coats). *m*, crusader; member of military order

cruzamiento *m*, crossing; intersection

cruzar *vt* to cross; intersect; interbreed; bestow a cross upon; *naut* cruise; *vr* take part in a crusade; cross one another; coincide; *geom* intersect

cu *f*, name of the letter Q

cuacuac *m*, quack (of a duck)

cuaderna *f*, *naut* ship's frame, timber; double fours (backgammon)

cuaderno *m*, notebook, jotter, account book; *inf* card pack. *naut* **c. de bitácora,** logbook

cuadra *f*, stable; ward, dormitory; hall, large room; quarter of a mile

cuadrado *a* square; perfect, exact. *m*, square; (*carp mil math*) square; window-frame; clock (of a stocking)

cuadragenario *a* forty years old

cuadragésima *f*, Quadragesima

cuadragésimo *a* fortieth

cuadrángulo *m*, quadrangle

cuadrante *m*, quadrant; dial, face

cuadrar *vt* (*math carp*) to square; make square; *vi* correspond, tally; fit, be appropriate. *vr mil* stand at attention; *fig inf* dig one's heels in

cuadrática *f*, quadratic equation

cuadrático *a* quadratic

cuadratura *f*, squareness; (*math ast*) quadrature

cuadrienio *m*, space of four years

cuadriga *f*, quadriga

cuadrilátero *m*, quadrilateral; boxing ring. *a* quadrilateral

cuadrilongo *a* and *m*, oblong

cuadrilla *f*, gang; company, band, group; police patrol; quadrille (dance); matadors and their assistants (at a bull fight). **c. carrillana,** track gang

cuadrimotor *a aer* four-engined

cuadrivio *m*, quadrivium

cuadro *m*, square; picture-frame; frame (of bicycle); flowerbed; *theat* tableau, scene; spectacle, sight; board (of instruments); description (in novel, etc.); *mil* command, officers; square (of troops). **c. de distribución,** *elec* main switchboard. **c. enrejado,** play pen. **cuadro de costumbres,** word-picture of everyday life and customs. **cuadro vivo,** tableau vivant. **a cuadros,** checked, in squares

cuadrúpedo (-da) *a* and *n* quadruped

cuadruple *a* quadruple

cuadruplicar *vt* to quadruple

cuajada *f*, curd (of milk)

cuajar *m*, maw (of a ruminant)

cuajar *vt* to coagulate; curdle; *vi inf* achieve, get away with; *vr* be coagulated or curdled; *inf* be packed or chock full; get stuck (e.g. a piece of food in one's throat)

cuajarón *m*, clot (of blood, etc.)

cuajo *m*, rennet; coagulation; curdling; *anat* abomasum

cual *rel. pron* sing. *mf* and *neut. pl* **cuales,** which; who; such as (e.g. **Le detuvieron sucesos cuales suelen ocurrir,** He was detained by events such as usually happen). **a c. mas,** vying (with) (e.g. **Los dos canónigos a c. más grueso,** The two canons each fatter (vying in fatness) than the other). **c.** is used with *def. art* **el (la, lo, los, las) cual(es),** who; which, when the antecedent is a noun (e.g. **Juan saltó en el barco, el c. zarpó en seguida,** John jumped into the boat which sailed at once). **por lo c.,** for which reason. *adv* like (gen. literary or poet.). **¿cuál?** *interr. pron* (no article) which? what? e.g. **Aquí tienes dos cuadros, ¿cuál de ellos te gusta?** Here are two pictures, which one do you like? Also expresses an implicit question, e.g. **No sé cuál te guste,** I don't know which you will like. **¡cuál!** *adv interj* how! **c. . . . c.** *indef pron* some . . . some

cualesquier *a pl* of **cualquier**

cualesquiera *a pl* of **cualquiera**

cualidad *f*, quality; characteristic; talent

cualitativo *a* qualitative

cualquier *abb* of **cualquiera,** any; *pl* **cualesquier.** Only used as abb. *before* noun

cualquiera *a mf* any, e.g. **una canción c.,** any song. *pron* anybody, each, anyone whatsoever, whoever (e.g. **¡C. diría que no te gusta!** Anyone would say you don't like it!) *inf* **un c.,** a nobody

cuán *adv* how (e.g. **¡C. bello es!** How beautiful it is). Used only before *a* or *adv.* Abb. of **cuánto**

cuando *adv* when; if. *interr* **¿cuándo?** *conjunc* although; since; sometimes; *prep* during (e.g. **c. la guerra,** during the war) **c. más,** at most, at best. **c. menos,** at the least. **c. no,** if not (e.g. **Es agnóstica cuando no atea,** She's an agnostic, if not an atheist) **de c. en c.,** from time to time

cuandoquiera *adv* whenever

cuanta, teoría de la *f*, quantum theory

cuantía *f*, quantity, amount; importance, rank, distinction

cuantiar *vt* to value, estimate; tax

cuantidad *f*, quantity

cuantioso *a* large, considerable; numerous; plentiful, abundant

cuantitativo *a* quantitative

cuanto *a* as much as, all the; *pl* as many as, all the (e.g. **Te daré cuantas muñecas veas allí,** I'll give you all the dolls you see there). *a. correlative* the . . . the, as . . . as (e.g. **C. más tanto, mejor,** The more the better). **cuánto,** *a* and *pron interr* and *interj* how much; *pl* how many (e.g. **¡Cuánto tiempo sin verla!** How long without seeing her!) *pron neut* **cuanto,** as much as, all that (e.g. **Te daré c. quieras,** I shall give you all that you wish). *adv* **cuanto,** as soon as. **c. antes,** as soon as possible. **c. a** *or* **en c. a,** concerning. *adv* and *conjunc* **c. más,** all the more (e.g. **Se lo diré c. más que tenía esa intención,** I shall tell him all the more because I meant to do so). *adv* **en c.,** as soon as, immediately (e.g. **Lo haré en c. venga,** I shall do it immediately he comes). **en c. a,** with regard to. **por c.,** inasmuch, for this reason. *adv interr* **¿Cuánto?** How much? How long? *adv interj* How! How much! (e.g. **¡Cuánto me gustaría ir!** How much I should like to go!)

cuaquerismo *m*, Quakerism

cuáquero (-ra) *n* Quaker

cuarenta *a* and *m*, forty; fortieth

cuarentena *f*, fortieth; period of forty days, months or years; Lent; quarantine

cuarentón (-ona) *n* person forty years old

cuaresma *f*, Lent

cuaresmal *a* Lenten

cuarta *f*, quarter, fourth; hand's breadth; *mus* fourth; *ast* quadrant

cuartana *f*, quartan (fever)

cuarteadura *f*, crack

cuartear *vt* to quarter, divide into quarters; cut or divide into pieces

cuartel *m*, barracks; *naut* hatch; quarter, fourth; *her* quarter; district, ward; flowerbed; *inf* house, accommodation; *mil* quarter, mercy; *mil* billet, station. **mil c. general,** general headquarters

cuartelada *f*, *naut* quarter; military rebellion, military uprising, mutiny

cuartelar *vt her* to quarter

cuartelazo *m*, military rebellion, military uprising, mutiny

cuarterón (-ona) *n* quadroon

cuarteta *f*, quatrain

cuarteto *m*, *mus* quartet; *poet* quatrain

cuartilla *f*, sheet of paper; liquid measure; quarter of an arroba; pastern (horses)

cuarto *m*, room; quarter, fourth; point (of compass); watch (on battleships); *ast* quarter, phase; portion, quarter; joint (of meat); *pl* quarters (of animals); *inf* penny, farthing. *a* quarter, fourth. **c. creciente,** first phase (of moon). **c. de hora,** quarter of an hour. **en c.,** *print* in quarto. *inf* **no tener un c.,** to be broke

cuarzo *m*, quartz

cuasi *adv* almost, nearly, quasi

cuasidelito *m*, *law* technical offence

cuasimodo *m*, *ecc* Low Sunday, Quasimodo

cuaterna *f*, quaternion

cuatrillón *m*, quadrillion

cuatrimestre *a* of four months' duration. *m*, space of four months

cuatrimotor *m*, *aer* four-engine airplane

cuatrisílabo *a* quadrisyllabic

cuatro *a* four; fourth. *m*, figure four; fourth (of days of months); playing-card with four spots; *mus* quartet. **el c. de mayo,** the fourth of May. **Son las c.,** It is four o'clock

cuatrocientos *a* four hundred; four hundredth

cuba *f*, barrel, cask; tub, vat; *inf* pot-bellied person; *inf* drunkard, toper

cubano (-na) *a* and *n* Cuban

cubería *f*, cooperage

cubeta *f*, *dim* keg, small cask; bucket, pail; *phot* developing dish

cubicar *vt math* to cube; *geom* measure the volume of

cúbico *a* cubic

cubículo *m*, cubicle

cubierta f, cover; envelope; casing; deck (of ship); tire cover; book-jacket; pretext, excuse. **c. de escotilla,** naut companion-hatch. **c. de paseo,** promenade deck

cubierto m, cover, place at table; course (of a meal); table d'hôte, complete meal; roof. **un c. de doscientas pesetas,** a two hundred peseta meal

cubil m, lair, den (of animals)

cubilete m, cul mold; dice box; conjurer's cup

cubismo m, cubism

cubista mf cubist. a cubistic

cubo m, bucket, pail; mech socket; math cube; hub (of a wheel); mill-pond

cubrecama m, bedspread

cubrecorsé m, camisole

cubrimiento m, covering

cubrir vt to cover; mil defend; spread over, extend over; conceal, hide; com cover; dissemble; arch roof; vr cover one's head; pay, meet (debts, etc.); cover or protect oneself (by insurance, etc.). Past Part. **cubierto**

cucaña f, greasy pole; inf snip, cinch, bargain

cucaracha f, cockroach

cuchara f, spoon; ladle; naut boat scoop; scoop, dipper. fig **meter c.,** to stick one's oar in

cucharada f, spoonful; ladleful

cuchicheador (-ra) n whisperer

cuchichear vi to whisper

cuchicheo m, whisper; whispering; murmur

cuchillada f, knife thrust or wound; pl (in sleeves, etc.) slashes; fight, blows

cuchillería f, cutlery; cutler's shop

cuchillero m, cutler

cuchillo m, knife; sew gore, gusset (gen. pl); authority, power; anything triangular in shape. **pasar a c.,** to put to the sword

cuclillas, en adv in a squatting position

cuclillo m, orn cuckoo; inf cuckold

cuco a inf pretty, cute; crafty, smart

cucú m, cry of the cuckoo

Cucufo m, the Devil

cuculla f, cowl, hood

cucurucho m, paper cornet

cuello m, anat neck; neck (of bottle, etc.); sew neck; collar; necklet (of fur, etc.)

cuenca f, socket (of eye); geog catchment-basin; gorge, deep valley. **c. de un río,** river-basin

cuenta f, count, counting; calculation; account; bead; charge, responsibility; reckoning; explanation, reason; com bill. **c. a cero, c. a la inversa, c. atrás,** countdown. **c. corriente,** current account. **cuentas alegres, cuentas galanas,** inf idle dreams, illusions. **c. pendiente,** outstanding account. inf **caer en la c.,** to tumble to, realize. **llevar la c.,** to reckon, keep account. **sin c.,** countless. **tener en c.,** to bear in mind

cuentacorrentista mf one who has a bank account

cuentagotas m, dropper, dropping tube

cuentakilómetros m, speedometer

cuentapasos m, pedometer

cuentista mf storyteller; inf gossip

cuento m, story, tale; narrative; calculation; inf gossip, fairytale; math million. **c. de viejas,** old wives' tale. fig inf **dejarse de cuentos,** to go straight to the point. inf **Va de c.,** It is told, they say

cuerda f, rope; cord; string; geom chord; mus string; catgut; chain (of clock); mus chord; vocal range. **dar c. (a),** to wind up (a watch); lead on, make talk. **de cuerdas cruzadas,** overstrung (of a piano)

cuerdo a sane; prudent; levelheaded

cuerno m, anat horn; feeler, antenna; mus horn; horn (of the moon). **c. de abundancia,** horn of plenty. inf **poner en los cuernos de la luna,** to praise to the skies

cuero m, hide, pelt; leather. **c. charolado,** patent leather. **en cueros,** stark naked

cuerpo m, anat body or trunk; flesh (as opposed to spirit); bodice; volume, book; main portion; collection; size, volume; physical appearance; corpse; group, as-

sembly; corporation, association; geom solid; chem element; thickness, density; mil corps. **c. de bomberos,** fire brigade. **c. de guardia,** guardhouse. **c. de la vida,** staff of life; inf **dar con el c. en tierra,** to fall flat. **de c. entero,** art full-length (portrait). **en c.,** without a coat, lightly clad. **un c. a c.,** a clinch (in wrestling)

cuervo m, raven; crow

cuesco m, stone, seed, pip

cuesta f, slope, incline, gradient. **c. abajo (arriba),** down (up) hill. **a cuestas,** on one's back; having the responsibility of

cuestión f, problem, question; quarrel, disagreement; affair, matter; torture

cuestionable a doubtful, questionable

cuestionar vt to discuss, debate

cuestionario m, questionnaire

cueva f, cave, cavern; basement, cellar. fig **c. de ladrones,** den of thieves

cuévano m, hamper, basket

cuidado m, carefulness, pains; attention; charge, care, responsibility; anxiety, fear. interj ¡C.! Careful! Look out! **Me tiene sin c. su opinión,** I am not interested in his (your) opinion. inf **estar al c. de,** to be under the direction of. **estar de c.,** to be dangerously ill

cuidadoso (de) a careful (about or with); anxious (about); concerned (with); watchful; conscientious

cuidar vt to care for; tend; take care of, look after; mind, be careful of; vr look after oneself

cuita f, misfortune, anxiety, trouble

cuitado a unfortunate, worried; timid, bashful, humble

culata f, anat haunch; butt (of fire-arms); back, rear; aut sump

culatazo m, recoil (of fire-arms)

culebra f, snake; inf trick, joke; inf sudden uproar. **hacer c.,** to stagger along

culebrear vi to wriggle; grovel; meander, wind

culebreo m, wriggling; meandering, winding

culí m, coolie

culinario a culinary

culminación f, culmination, peak; ast zenith

culminante a culminating; fig outstanding

culminar vi to culminate (in)

culo m, buttocks, seat; rump; anus; base, bottom. **c. de lámpara,** arch pendant; print tail-piece

culpa f, fault; blame. **echar la c. (a),** to blame. **por c. de,** through the fault of. **tener la c.,** to be to blame

culpabilidad f, guilt

culpable a culpable

culpado (-da) n culprit

culpar vt to blame, accuse; criticize, censure

culteranismo, cultismo m, involved literary style (cf. Euphuism)

cultígeno m, cultigen

cultismo m, cultism (Gongorism); learned form, learnedism, learned word

cultivable a cultivable

cultivación f, cultivation; culture

cultivador (-ra) n cultivator; planter

cultivar vt to cultivate; develop; exercise, practise (professions); culture (bacteriology)

cultivo m, cultivation; farming; culture (bacteriological)

culto a cultivated; educated; cultured; elegant, artificial (style). m, worship; cult; religion, creed; homage

cultura f, cultivation; culture. **de c. universitaria,** college-educated

cultural a cultural

cumbre f, peak, crest, summit; fig zenith, acme

cumpleaños m, birthday

cumplidamente adv fully, completely

cumplido a complete; thorough; long; plentiful; courteous, punctilious; fulfilled. m, courtesy, attention; formality. **gastar cumplidos,** to stand on ceremony; be formal

cumplimentar vt to congratulate; perform, carry out

cumplimentero a over-complimentary; inf gushing

cumplimiento *m,* fulfilment, performance; courtesy, formality; completion; complement

cumplir *vt* to perform, carry into effect; reach (of age); keep (promises). **c. su palabra,** to keep one's word; *vi* perform a duty; expire, fall due; serve the required term of military service; be necessary, behove; *vr* be fulfilled, come true. **por c.,** as a matter of form

cumulativo *a* cumulative

cúmulo *m,* heap, pile; great many, host, mass, myriad; (cloud) cumulus, thunderhead

cuna *f,* cradle; foundling hospital; birthplace; origin, genesis; *pl* cat's cradle (game)

cundir *vi* to extend, spread (gen. liquids); be diffused (news); expand, grow

cuneiforme *a* wedge-shaped, cuneiform

cunero (-ra) *n* foundling, orphan

cuña *f,* wedge; *mech* quoin. *mil* **practicar una c.,** to make a wedge

cuñada *f,* sister-in-law

cuñado *m,* brother-in-law

cuño *m,* die, stamp; *fig* impression; mark on silver, hallmark. **de viejo c.,** old-guard (e.g. socialites)

cuota *f,* quota; share; subscription; fee

cupé *m,* coupé

Cupido *m,* Cupid; philanderer

cuplé *m,* couplet; song

cupo *m,* quota; share; tax rate; *mil* contingent

cupón *m,* coupon

cúpula *f, arch* dome, cupola; *bot* cup

cuquería *f,* craftiness, smartness; cuteness, prettiness

cura *m,* parish priest; *inf* Roman Catholic priest. *f,* cure (e.g. **La enfermedad tiene c.,** The illness can be cured); healing; remedy. **c. de almas,** cure of souls. **primera c.,** first aid. *inf* **c. de misa y olla,** ignorant priest

curable *a* curable

curación *f,* cure, remedy; healing

curador (-ra) *n* curer, salter. *m,* (*Scots law*) curator. *a* curing; healing

curaduría *f, law* guardianship

curanderismo *m,* quackery, charlatanism; quack medicine

curandero (-ra) *n* quack doctor; charlatan

curar *vi* to heal, cure; (*with de*) take care of; care about, mind; *vt* cure, salt; treat medically (bandage, give medicines, etc.); cure (leather); bleach (cloth); season (timber); *fig* remedy (an evil)

curasao *m,* curaçao (drink)

curativo *a* curative

curato *m, ecc* parish, cure

Curazao Curaçao

cúrcuma *f,* turmeric

curdo, (-da) *a* Kurdish. *n* Kurd

cureña *f,* gun-carriage

curia *f, law* bar; tribunal; *ecc* curia; care, attention

curiana *f,* cockroach

curiche *m,* swamp

curiosamente *adv* curiously; carefully, attentively; neatly

curiosear *vi* to pry; be curious (about); meddle, be a busybody

curiosidad *f,* curiosity; inquisitiveness, meddlesomeness; neatness; carefulness, conscientiousness; curio

curioso *a* curious; inquisitive; interesting, odd; neat, clean; conscientious, careful

Curita *f, trademark* Band-Aid

cursado *a* experienced, versed

cursante *m,* student

cursar *vt* to frequent, visit; do repeatedly; study, attend classes, take courses (e.g. **¿En qué escuela cursan?** At what school are you studying?); expedite (public admin.)

cursi *a inf* vulgar, in bad taste; loud, crude

cursilería *f, inf* vulgarity, bad taste

cursillo *m,* minicourse, short course; short series of lectures

cursiva *f,* italics. **en c.,** in italics, italicized

cursivo *a* cursive

curso *m,* course, direction; duration, passage (time); progress; route; course of study; academic year; succession, series; *com* tender

curtido *m,* tanning; leather; tanned leather (gen. *pl*)

curtidor *m,* tanner

curtiduría *f,* tannery

curtimiento *m,* tanning; effect of weather on the complexion; toughening-up; hardening

curtir *vt* to tan; *fig* bronze (complexions); make hardy, harden up; *vr* be weatherbeaten; be hardy. *inf* **estar curtido en,** to be experienced in; be expert at

curul *a* curule *m,* seat (in parliament)

curva *f,* curve; bend. *surv* **c. de nivel,** contour line

curvatura, curvidad *f,* curvature

curvilíneo *a* curvilinear

curvo *a* curved; bent. *m,* curve

cúspide *f,* peak, summit; (*geom arch*) cusp

custodia *f,* custody; guardianship, care; *ecc* monstrance; custodian, keeper; guardian; guard

custodiar *vt* to watch, guard; look after, care for; *naut* convoy

custodio *a* guardian; guarding; custodial. *m,* custodian; guard. **angel c.,** guardian angel

cutáneo *a* cutaneous, skin

cúter *m, naut* cutter

cutícula *f,* cuticle

cutis *m,* complexion; skin (sometimes *f*)

cuyo (cuya, cuyos, cuyas) *rel pron poss* whose, of which (e.g. **el viejo cuya barba era más blanca que la nieve,** the old man whose beard was whiter than snow). *interr* **¿Cúyo?** Whose? (e.g. **¿Cúyos son estos lápices?** Whose pencils are these?) (gen. **de quién** or **de quiénes** is used rather than **cúyo**). *m,* beau, lover

D

dable *a* practicable, possible

daca Give me!

dactilografía *f,* typewriting

dactilógrafo (-fa) *n* typist

dactilología *f,* dactylology

dádiva *f,* gift, present

dadivosidad *f,* generosity

dadivoso *a* generous, liberal

dado *m,* die; *arch* dado. *conjunc* **d. que,** given that, supposing that. **cargar los dados,** to load the dice

dador (-ra) *n* giver, donor. *m, com* bearer; *com* drawer (of a bill of exchange)

daga *f,* dagger

daguerrotipo *m,* daguerreotype

daifa *f,* concubine

dalia *f, bot* dahlia

dallar *vt* to scythe (grass)

dalle *m,* scythe

dálmata *a* and *mf* Dalmatian

dalmática *f,* dalmatic, loose tunic or vestment

dalmático (-ca) *a* and *n* Dalmatian

daltoniano *a* color-blind

daltonismo *m,* color-blindness

dama *f,* lady; noblewoman; lady-in-waiting; lady-love; mistress, concubine; queen (chess); king (checkers); *theat* **d. primera,** leading lady

damajuana *f,* demijohn

damas *f pl,* checkers (game)

damasceno (-na) *a* and *n* Damascene

Damasco Damascus
damasco *m*, damask
damasquino *a* damascened (swords, etc.)
damería *f*, prudery, affectation
damisela *f*, damsel; *inf* woman of the town
damnificar *vt* to injure
dandi *m*, dandy
dandismo *m*, dandyism
danés (-esa) *a* Danish. *n* Dane. *m*, Danish (language)
danta *f*, *zool* tapir
dantesco *a* Dantesque
danubiano *a* Danubian
Danubio, el the Danube
danza *f*, dance; set (of dancers); *fig inf* dirty business. **d. de arcos,** dance of the arches. **d. de cintas,** maypole dance. **d. de monos,** amusing spectacle
danzador (-ra) *n* dancer; *a* dancing
danzante (-ta) *n* dancer; *fig inf* live wire; *inf* busybody
danzar *vt* and *vi* to dance; *vi* jump up and down, rattle; *inf* interfere, meddle
danzarín (-ina) *n* good dancer; *inf* meddler; *inf* playboy
danzón *m*, Cuban dance
dañable *a* harmful; worthy of condemnation
dañado *a* evil, perverse; damned; spoiled, damaged
dañador (-ra) *a* harmful. *n* injurer, offender
dañar *vt* to hurt, harm; damage, spoil; *vr* spoil, deteriorate
dañino *a* destructive (often of animals); hurtful, harmful. **animales dañinos,** vermin, pests
daño *m*, hurt; damage; loss. *law* **daños y perjuicios,** damages. **hacerse d.,** to hurt oneself
dañoso *a* hurtful, harmful
dar *vt irr* to give; wish, express (congratulations, etc.); hand over; concede, grant; inspire; produce, yield; cause, create; sacrifice; propose, put forward; take (a walk); believe, consider; deliver (blows, etc.); administer (medicine); provide with; apply, coat with; occasion; perform (plays); propose (a toast); give forth, emit; set (norms), render (thanks, etc.); hold (banquets, etc.); proffer, hold out; *vi* to strike (clocks); (*with prep a*) overlook, look on to (e.g. **Su ventana da a la calle,** His window looks on to the street); (*with con*) find, meet (things, persons); (*with de*) fall on, fall down (e.g. **Dio de cabeza,** He fell head first. **Dio de espaldas,** He fell on his back); (*with en*) fall into, incur; insist on or persist in (doing something); acquire the habit of (e.g. **Dieron en no venir a vernos,** They took to not coming to see us); solve, guess (riddles, etc.); strike, wound, hurt (e.g. **La bala le dio en el brazo,** The bullet struck him in the arm); (*with por*) decide on (e.g. **Di por no hacerlo,** I decided not to do it). *vr* to yield, give in; (*with prep a*) engage in, devote oneself to; (*with por*) think or consider oneself (e.g. **Me di por muerto,** I gave myself up for dead). **d. alas a,** to propagate, spread (a belief). **darse a la vela,** to set sail. **darse la mano,** to shake hands. **darse por buenos,** to make up a quarrel, be friends. **darse prisa,** to hurry up, make haste. **darse uno a conocer,** to make oneself known. **darse uno por entendido,** to show that one understands; be grateful. **No se me da un bledo,** I don't care a straw. **d. abajo,** to fall down. **d. bien por mal,** to return good for evil. **d. a conocer,** to make known. **d. a entender,** to suggest, hint. **d. a luz,** to give birth; publish, issue. **d. cuenta de,** to give an account of. **d. de baja,** *mil* to muster out, discharge. **d. de comer,** to feed. **d. de sí,** to stretch, expand; produce, yield; give of itself (oneself, himself, themselves) (either in good or bad sense). **d. diente con diente,** to chatter (of teeth), shiver. **d. el pésame,** to tender condolences. **d. en cara,** *fig inf* to throw in one's face. **d. en el clavo,** *fig* to hit the mark. **d. en qué pensar,** to make suspicious, cause to think. **d. fe,** to certify, attest. **d. fiado,** to give on credit. **d. fianza,** to give security. **d. fin a,** to finish. **d. licencia,** to permit, allow. **d. los buenos días,** to wish good day or good morning. **d. mal,** to have bad luck at cards. **d. parte de,** to announce; issue a communiqué about (e.g. **Dieron parte de la pérdida del buque,** They announced the loss of the ship). **d. prestado,** to lend. **d. qué decir,** to cause a scandal. **d. qué hacer,** to cause trouble. **d. razón de,** to give an account of. **d. sobre uno,** to assault a person. **d. un abrazo,** to embrace. **d. voces,** to shriek; call out. *inf* **Donde las dan las toman,** It's only tit-for-tat. *inf* **No me da la real gana,** I darn well don't want to. *Pres. Ind.* **doy, das,** etc. *Preterite* **di, diste,** etc. *Pres. Subjunc.* **dé,** etc. *Imperf. Subjunc.* **diese,** etc.
Dardanelos, los the Dardanelles
dardo *m*, (*mil sport*) dart; *icht* dace; lampoon
dares y tomares *m*, *pl* give and take; *inf* back-chat. Generally used with *andar*, *haber* or *tener*
dársena *f*, *naut* dock
darviniano *a* Darwinian
darvinismo *m*, Darwinism
darvinista *mf* Darwinian
data *f*, date (calendar); *com* credit
datar *vt* to date; *vi* (*with de*) date from; *vr com* credit
dátil *m*, *bot* date
datilado *a* date-like or date-colored
datilera *f*, *bot* date-palm
dativo *m*, *gram* dative
dato *m*, datum; basis, fact
davídico *a* Davidic
de *f*, name of letter D. *prep* of (possessive) (e.g. **Este cuadro es de Vd.,** This picture is yours); from (place and time) (e.g. **Vengo de Madrid,** I come from Madrid. **de vez en cuando,** from time to time); with, of, from, as the result of (e.g. **Lloraban de miedo,** They were crying with fright. **Murió de un ataque del corazón,** He died from a heart attack); for, to (e.g. **Es hora de marchar,** It is time to leave); with (of characteristics) (e.g. **el señor de los lentes,** the gentleman with the eyeglasses. **el cuarto de la alfombra azul,** the room with the blue carpet); when, as (e.g. **De niños nos gustaban los juguetes,** When we were children we liked toys); by (e.g. **Es un ensayo del mismo autor,** It is an essay by the same author. **Fue amado de todos,** He was loved by all. **Es hidalgo de nacimiento,** He is a gentleman by birth). Indicates the material of which a thing is made (e.g. **La mesa es de mármol,** The table is marble). Indicates contents of a thing (e.g. **un vaso de leche,** a glass of milk). Shows manner in which an action is performed (e.g. **Lo hizo de prisa,** He did it hurriedly). Shows the use to which an article is put (e.g. **una mesa de escribir,** a writing-table. **una máquina de coser,** a sewing-machine. **un caballo de batalla,** a war-horse). Sometimes used for emphasis (e.g. **El tonto de tu secretario,** That fool of a secretary of yours). Used by Spanish married women before husband's family name (e.g. **Señora Martínez de Cabra,** Mrs. Cabra (née Martínez)). Used after many adverbs (generally of time or place) to form prepositional phrases (e.g. **detrás de,** behind. **enfrente de,** opposite to; in front of. **de acá para allá,** here and there. **de allí a poco,** shortly afterward. **de allí a pocos días,** a few days later. **de bamba,** by chance. **de cabo a rabo,** from cover to cover. **además de,** besides, etc.). Used at beginning of various adverbial phrases (e.g. **de noche,** by night. **de día,** by day. **de antemano,** previously, **la persona de mi derecha** the person at my right, etc.). Used partitively before nouns, pronouns, adjectives (e.g. **Estas historias tienen algo de verdad,** These stories have some truth in them. **¿Qué hay de nuevo?** What's the news?) Forms many compound words (e.g. **deponer, denegar,** etc.). With **"uno"** means "at" (e.g. **Lo cogió de un salto,** He caught it at one bound). **de a** is used before expressions of price, weight, etc. (e.g. **un libro de a cinco pesetas,** a five-peseta book)
dea *f*, *poet* goddess
deán *m*, dean
debajo *adv* underneath; below

debate *m*, discussion, debate; dispute
debatible *a* debatable
debatir *vt* to discuss, debate, argue
debe *m*, *com* debtor
debelación *f*, conquest
debelador (-ra) *a* conquering. *n* conqueror
debelar *vt* to conquer, overthrow
deber *vt* to owe (e.g. **Le debo mil pesetas,** I owe him one thousand pesetas). Used as auxiliary verb followed by infinitive, ought to, be obliged to (e.g. **Debía haberlo hecho,** I ought to have done it. **Deberá hacerlo,** He will have to do it); be destined to (e.g. **La princesa que más tarde debió ser reina,** The princess who later was destined to be queen); be essential, must (e.g. **La cuestión debe ser resuelta,** The question must be settled); (*with de* + *infin.*) be probable (indicates supposition) (e.g. **Debe de tener cincuenta años,** He is probably about fifty. **Debía de sufrir del corazón,** He probably suffered from heart trouble); (preceded by a negative *with de* + *infin.*) be impossible (e.g. **No debe de ser verdad,** It can't be true)
deber *m*, duty, obligation; debt. **hacer su d.,** to do one's duty
debidamente *adv* justly, rightly; duly
debido *a* correct, due. **d. a,** owing to, because of
débil *a* weak; *fig* spineless; frail
debilidad *f*, weakness; feebleness
debilitación *f*, debilitation
debilitante *a* weakening
debilitar *vt* to weaken; *vr* become weak
débito *m*, debit, debt; duty
debutar *vi* to appear for the first time, make one's début
década *f*, decade
decadencia *f*, decadence, decline
decadente *a* decadent, decaying
decaer *vi irr* to fail (persons); decay, decline. See **caer**
decagramo *m*, decagram
decaimiento *m*, decadence; *med* prostration
decalaje *m*, *aer* stagger
decalitro *m*, decaliter
decálogo *m*, decalogue, the Ten Commandments
decámetro *m*, decameter
decampar *vi* *mil* to decamp
decanato *m*, deanery; *univ* dean's rooms
decano *m*, senior member; *univ* dean
decantación *f*, decantation
decantar *vt* to decant (wines); praise
decapitación *f*, decapitation
decapitar *vt* to decapitate, behead
decena *f*, ten; *mus* tenth
decenal *a* decennial
decenario *m*, decade
decencia *f*, propriety, decency; decorum, modesty
decenio *m*, decade
deceno *a* tenth
decentar *vt irr* to begin, cut (loaves, etc.); *fig* undermine (health, etc.); *vr* suffer from bedsores. See **acertar**
decente *a* decent, honest; respectable; suitable; tidy
decepción *f*, disillusionment, disappointment
dechado *m*, model, ideal; *sew* sampler; exemplar, ideal
decible *a* expressible
decidero *a* that which can be safely said
decidido *a* decided; resolute, determined
decidir *vt* to resolve, decide; *vr* make up one's mind
decidor (-ra) *a* talkative, fluent, eloquent. *n* good talker
decigramo *m*, decigram
décima *f*, tenth; tithe; ten-line stanza of eight-syllable verse
decimal *a* decimal; pertaining to tithes. **sistema d.,** metric system
decímetro *m*, decimeter
décimo *a* tenth. *m*, tenth part; tenth of a lottery ticket
decimoctavo *a* eighteenth
decimocuarto *a* fourteenth
decimonono *a* nineteenth
decimoquinto *a* fifteenth

decimoséptimo *a* and *m*, seventeenth
decimosexto *a* sixteenth
decimotercio *a* thirteenth
decir *vt irr* to say; name; indicate, show; tell. **d. bien,** to go with, suit; speak the truth; be eloquent. **d. entre** (*or* **para**) **sí,** to say to oneself. *inf* **d. nones,** to refuse. **¡Diga!** Hello! (telephone). *inf* **el que dirán,** public opinion (what will people say!). **Es d.,** That is to say. **Se dice,** It is said, people say. *Pres. Ind.* **digo, dices,** etc. *Pres. Part.* **diciendo.** *Past Part.* **dicho.** *Fut.* **diré,** etc. *Condit.* **diría,** etc. *Preterite* **dije,** etc. *Pres. Subjunc.* **diga,** etc. *Imperf. Subjunc.* **dijese,** etc.
decir *m*, saying, saw; maxim, witticism (often *pl.*)
decisión *f*, decision, resolution; *law* judgment; firmness, strength (of character)
decisivo *a* decisive
declamación *f*, declamation, oration; *theat* delivery; recitation
declamador (-ra) *a* declamatory. *n* reciter; orator
declamar *vi* to make a speech, declaim; recite
declamatorio *a* declamatory, rhetorical
declaración *f*, declaration; exposition, explanation; confession; statement; *law* deposition. **d. jurada,** affidavit, sworn statement
declaradamente *adv* avowedly
declarante *a* declaring. *mf law* deponent
declarar *vt* to declare; make clear, explain; *law* find; *vi law* give evidence; *vr* avow, confess (one's sentiments, etc.); show, reveal itself
declarativo, declaratorio *a* explanatory, declaratory
declinación *f*, fall, descent; decadence, decay; *ast* declination; *gram* declension. *inf* **no saber las declinaciones,** not to know one's ABC, be very ignorant
declinante *a* declining; sloping
declinar *vi* to slope; diminish, fall; decline, deteriorate; *fig* near the end; *vt gram* decline
declive, m. declividad *f*, slope, incline; gradient
decocción *f*, decoction
decoloración *f*, decoloration; decolorization
decomisar *vt* to confiscate, seize
decoración *f*, decoration; ornament, embellishment; *theat* scenery
decorado *m*, *theat* scenery, décor
decorador *m*, decorator
decorar *vt* to adorn, ornament; *poet* decorate, honor
decorativo *a* decorative
decoro *m*, respect, reverence; prudence, circumspection; decorum, propriety; integrity, decency; *arch* decoration
decoroso *a* decorous, honorable, decent
decrecer *vi irr* to decrease, grow less. See **conocer**
decreciente *a* decreasing
decrepitación *f*, *chem* decrepitation, crackling
decrepitar *vi chem* to decrepitate, crackle
decrépito *a* decrepit
decrepitud *f*, decrepitude
decretar *vt* to decree, decide; *law* give a judgment (in a suit)
decreto *m*, decree, order; judicial decree
decuplar, decuplicar *vt* to multiply by ten
décuplo *a* tenfold
decurso *m*, course, lapse (of time)
dedada *f*, thimbleful, finger; pinch
dedal *m*, thimble; finger-stall
dédalo *m*, labyrinth
dedeo *m*, *mus* touch
dedicación *f*, dedication (all meanings)
dedicar *vt* to dedicate; devote; consecrate; *vr* (*with prep a*) dedicate oneself to, engage in
dedicatoria *f*, dedication (of a book, etc.)
dedicatorio *a* dedicatory
dedil *m*, finger-stall
dedillo, saber al *fig* to have at one's fingertips, know perfectly
dedo *m*, finger; toe; finger's breadth. **d. anular,** third (ring) finger. **d. de en medio** *or* **del corazón,** middle

finger. **d. índice,** forefinger. **d. meñique,** little finger. **d. pulgar,** thumb or big toe. *fig inf* **a dos dedos de,** within an inch of. *fig inf* **chuparse los dedos,** to smack one's lips over. *inf* **estar unidos como los dedos de la mano,** to be as thick as thieves

deducción *f,* inference, deduction; derivation; (*mus math*) progression

deduciente *a* deductive

deducir *vt irr* to deduce, infer; deduct, subtract; *law* plead, allege in pleading. See **conducir**

deductivo *a* deductive

defecación *f,* purification; defecation

defecar *vt* to clarify, purify; defecate

defección *f,* defection

defectible *a* deficient; imperfect

defecto *m,* defect, fault; imperfection

defectuoso *a* imperfect, defective

defender *vt irr* to defend, protect; maintain, uphold; forbid; hinder; *vr* defend oneself. See **entender**

defendible *a* defensible

defensa *f,* defence; protection; (hockey) pad; *law* defense; *sport* back; *pl mil* defenses; *naut* fenders. **d. química,** chemical warfare. *mil* **defensas costeras,** coastal defenses

defensiva *f,* defensive

defensivo *a* defensive. *m,* safeguard

defensor (-ra) *n* defender. *m, law* counsel for the defense

deferencia *f,* deference

deferente *a* deferential

deferir *vi irr* to defer, yield; *vt* delegate. *Pres. Ind.* **defiero, defieres, defiere, defieren.** *Pres. Part.* **defiriendo.** *Preterite* **defirió, defirieron.** *Pres. Subjunc.* **defiera,** etc. *Imperf. Subjunc.* **defiriese,** etc.

deficiencia *f,* defect, deficiency

deficiente *a* faulty, deficient

déficit *m,* deficit

definible *a* definable

definición *f,* definition; decision

definido *a* definite

definir *vt* to define; decide

definitivo *a* definitive. **en definitiva,** definitely; in short

deflagración *f,* sudden blaze, deflagration

deflagrador *m, elec* deflagrator

deflagrar *vi* to go up in flames

deformación *f,* deformation; *rad* distortion

deformado *a* deformed; misshapen

deformador (-ra) *a* disfiguring, deforming. *n* disfigurer

deformar *vt* to deform; *vr* become deformed or misshapen

deformidad *f,* deformity; gross error; vice, lapse

defraudación *f,* defrauding; deceit

defraudador (-ra) *n* defrauder

defraudar *vt* to defraud; usurp; frustrate, disappoint; impede

defuera *adv* outwardly, externally

defunción *f,* decease, death

degeneración *f,* degeneration. **d. grasienta,** fatty degeneration

degenerado (-da) *a* and *n* degenerate

degenerar *vi* to degenerate

deglución *f,* swallowing, deglutition

deglutir *vi* and *vt* to swallow

degollación *f,* decollation, throat slitting

degolladero *m,* slaughterhouse; execution block

degollador *m,* executioner

degolladura *f,* slitting of the throat

degollar *vt irr* to behead; slit the throat; *fig* destroy; (*fig theat*) murder; *inf* annoy, bore. *Pres. Ind.* **degüello, degüellas, degüella, degüellan.** *Pres. Subjunc.* **degüelle, degüelles, degüelle, degüellen**

degollina *f, inf* massacre

degradación *f,* degradation; humiliation, debasement; *art* gradation, shading (colors, light)

degradante *a* degrading, humiliating

degradar *vt* to degrade; humiliate; *art* grade, blend; *vr* degrade oneself

degüello *m,* decollation; havoc, destruction; haft (of swords, etc.)

degustación *f,* act of tasting or sampling

dehesa *f,* pasture, meadow

deicida *mf* deicide (person)

deicidio *m,* deicide (act)

deidad *f,* divinity; deity, idol

deificación *f,* deification

deificar *vt* to deify; overpraise

deífico *a* deific, divine

deísmo *m,* Deism

deísta *mf* deist. *a* deistic

dejación *f,* relinquishment, abandonment

dejadez *f,* slovenliness; neglect; laziness; carelessness

dejado *a* lazy; neglectful; slovenly; discouraged, depressed

dejamiento *m,* relinquishment; negligence; lowness of spirits; indifference

dejar *vt* to leave; omit, forget, allow, permit (e.g. **Déjame salir,** Let me go out); yield, produce, entrust, leave in charge; believe, consider; intend, appoint; cease, stop; forsake, desert; renounce, relinquish; bequeath; give away; *vr* neglect oneself; engage (in); lay oneself open to, allow oneself; abandon oneself (to); fling oneself (into); *fig* be depressed or languid; (*with de + infin.*) cease to (e.g. **Se dejó de hacerlo,** He stopped doing it); *vi* (*with de + adjective*) be none the less, be rather (e.g. **No deja de ser sorprendente,** It isn't any the less surprising). **d. aparte,** to omit, leave out. **d. atrás,** to overtake; *fig* leave behind, beat. **d. caer,** to let fall. **dejarse caer,** to let oneself fall; *fig inf* to let fall, utter; appear suddenly. **dejarse vencer,** to give way, allow oneself to be persuaded

dejo *m,* relinquishment; end; accent (of persons); savor, after-taste; negligence; *fig* touch, flavor

del contraction of **de + el,** (*def. art. m.*) of the (e.g. **del perro,** of the dog)

delación *f,* accusation, denunciation

delantal *m,* apron

delante *adv* before, in front, in the presence (of)

delantera *f,* front, front portion; *theat* orchestra stall, front seat; front (of garment). **tomar la d.,** to take the lead; *inf* steal a march on

delantero *a* fore, front. *m,* postilion; *sport* forward. **d. centro,** *sport* centerforward

delatable *a* impeachable; blameworthy

delatar *vt* to inform against, accuse; impeach

delator (-ra) *a* denunciatory, accusing. *n* denouncer, informer

delectación *f,* delectation, pleasure

delegación *f,* delegation; proxy

delegado (-da) *n* delegate; proxy

delegar *vt* to delegate

deleitable *a* delightful

deleitar *vt* to delight, charm, please; *vr* delight (in)

deleite *m,* delight; pleasure

deleitoso *a* delightful, pleasant

deletéreo *a* deleterious; poisonous

deletrear *vi* to spell; *fig* decipher

deletreo *m,* spelling; *fig* decipherment

deleznable *a* fragile, brittle; slippery; brief, fugitive, transitory

délfico *a* Delphic

delfín *m,* (*icht ast*) dolphin; dauphin

delfina *f,* dauphiness

Delfos Delphi

delgadez *f,* thinness; slenderness; leanness

delgado *a* slim; thin; scanty; poor (of land); sharp, perspicacious

delgaducho *a* slenderish, somewhat thin

deliberación *f,* deliberation; consideration; discussion

deliberadamente *adv* deliberately

deliberante *a* deliberative, considering

deliberar *vi* to deliberate, consider; *vt* decide after reflection; discuss

delicadez *f*, weakness; delicacy; hypersensitiveness; amiability

delicadeza *f*, delicacy; fastidiousness; refinement, subtlety; sensitiveness; consideration, tact; scrupulosity

delicado *a* courteous; tactful; fastidious; weak, delicate; fragile, perishable; delicious, tasty; exquisite; difficult, embarrassing; refined, discriminating, sensitive; scrupulous; subtle; hypersensitive, suspicious. **d. de salud**, in poor health

delicia *f*, pleasure, delight; sensual pleasure

delicioso *a* delightful, agreeable, pleasant

delimitar *vt* to delimit

delincuencia *f*, delinquency

delincuente *a* and *mf* delinquent

delineación *f*, delineation; diagram, design, plan

delineador (**-ra**), *n* **delineante** *m*, draftsman, designer

delineamiento *m*, delineation

delinear *vt* to delineate; sketch; describe

delinquimiento *m*, delinquency; crime

delinquir *vi irr* to commit a crime. *Pres. Ind.* **delinco.** *Pres. Subjunc.* **delinca**

deliquio *m*, faint, swoon

delirante *a* delirious

delirar *vi* to be delirious; act or speak foolishly

delirio *m*, delirium; frenzy; foolishness, nonsense. **d. de grandezas**, illusions of grandeur

delito *m*, delict, offense against the law, crime

delta *f*, fourth letter of Greek alphabet. *m*, delta (of a river)

delusorio *a* deceptive

demacración *f*, emaciation

demacrado *a* emaciated

demacrarse *vr* to become emaciated

demagogia *f*, demagogy

demagógico *a* demagogic

demagogo (**-ga**) *n* demagogue

demanda *f*, petition, request; collecting (for charity); collecting box; want ad; question; search; undertaking; *com* order or demand; *law* claim

demandadero (**-ra**) *n* convent or prison messenger; errandboy

demandado (**-da**) *n law* defendant; *law* respondent

demandante *mf law* plaintiff

demandar *vt* to ask, request; desire, yearn for; question; *law* claim

demarcación *f*, demarcation, limit

demarcar *vt* to fix boundaries, demarcate

demás *a* other. *adv* besides. **lo d.**, the rest. **los (las) d.**, the others. **por d.**, useless; superfluous. **por lo d.**, otherwise; for the rest

demasía *f*, excess; daring; insolence; guilt, crime. **en d.**, excessively

demasiado *a* too; too many; too much. *adv* excessively

demencia *f*, madness, insanity

demencial *a* insane

dementar *vt* to render insane; *vr* become insane

demente *a* insane, mad. *mf* lunatic

demérito *m*, demerit, fault

demeritorio *a* undeserving, without merit

demisión *f*, submission, acquiescence

democracia *f*, democracy

demócrata *mf* democrat

democrático *a* democratic

democratizar *vt* to make democratic

demoledor (**-ra**) *a* demolition. *n* demolisher

demoler *vt irr* to demolish, destroy, dismantle. See **moler**

demolición *f*, demolition, destruction, dismantling

demoníaco *a* devilish; possessed by a demon

demonio *m*, devil; evil spirit. *interj* **¡Demonios!** Deuce take it! *inf* **tener el d. en el cuerpo,** to be always on the move, be very energetic

demontre *m*, *inf* devil

demora *f*, delay; *naut* bearing; *com* demurrage

demorar *vt* to delay; *vi* stay, remain, tarry; *naut* bear

demostrable *a* demonstrable

demostración *f*, demonstration; proof

demostrador (**-ra**) *a* demonstrating. *n* demonstrator

demostrar *vt irr* to demonstrate, explain; prove; teach. See **mostrar**

demostrativo *a* demonstrative. *gram* **pronombre d.**, demonstrative pronoun

demudación *f*, change; alteration

demudar *vt* to change, vary; alter, transform; *vr* change suddenly (color, facial expression, etc.); grow angry

denario *a* denary. *m*, denarius

denegación *f*, denial; refusal

denegar *vt irr* to deny, refuse. See **acertar**

dengoso *a* fastidious, finicky

dengue *m*, affectation, faddiness, fastidiousness

denigrable *a* odious

denigración *f*, slander, defamation (of character)

denigrante *a* slanderous

denigrar *vt* to slander; insult

denodado *a* valiant, daring

denominación *f*, denomination

denominador *a* denominating *m*, *math* denominator

denominar *vt* to name, designate

denostada *f*, insult

denostar *vt irr* to revile, insult. See **acordar**

denotar *vt* to denote, indicate

densidad *f*, density; closeness, denseness; *phys* specific gravity; obscurity

denso *a* compact, close; thick, dense; crowded; dark, confused

dentado *a* toothed; pronged; dentate

dentadura *f*, set of teeth (real or false). **d. de rumiante**, teeth like an ox. **d. postiza**, false teeth

dental *a* dental

dentar *vt irr* to provide with teeth, prongs, etc.; *vi* cut teeth. See **sentar**

dentellada *f*, gnashing or chattering of teeth; bite; toothmark

dentellar *vt* to chatter, grind, gnash (teeth)

dentellear *vt* to bite, sink the teeth into

dentera *f*, (**dar**) to set one's teeth on edge; *fig inf* make one's mouth water

dentición *f*, teething, dentition

dentífrico *m*, toothpaste

dentista *mf* dentist

dentro *adv* within, inside. **d. de poco**, soon, shortly. **por d.**, from the inside; on the inside

dentudo *a* having large teeth

denudación *f*, denudation; *geol* erosion

denudar *vt* to denude

denuedo *m*, courage, daring

denuesto *m*, insult

denuncia *f*, denunciation, accusation

denunciante *a* accusing. *mf law* denouncer

denunciar *vt* to give notice, inform; herald, presage; declare, proclaim; denounce; *law* accuse

denunciatorio *a* denunciatory

deparar *vt* to furnish, offer, present

departamental *a* departmental

departamento *m*, department; compartment (railway); branch, section. **d. de lactantes,** nursery (in a hospital)

departir *vi* to converse

depauperación *f*, impoverishment; *med* emaciation

depauperar *vt* to impoverish; *vr med* grow weak, become emaciated

dependencia *f*, dependence; subordination; dependency; *com* branch; firm, agency; business affair; kinship or affinity; *pl arch* offices; *com* staff; accessories

depender *vi* (*with de*) to be subordinate to; depend on; be dependent on, need

dependiente (**-ta**) *a* and *n* dependent, subordinate. *m*, employee; shop assistant

depilación *f*, depilation

depilar *vt* to depilate

depilatorio *m*, depilatory

deplorar *vt* to deplore, lament

deponente *a* deposing; affirming. *mf* deponent. *gram* **verbo d.**, deponent verb

deponer *vt irr* to lay aside; depose, oust; affirm, testify; remove, take from its place; *law* depose. See **poner**

deportación *f*, deportation

deportar *vt* to exile; deport

deporte *m*, sport; *pl* games. **d. de vela,** sailing; boating

deportismo *m*, sport

deportista *a* sporting. *mf* sportsman (sportswoman)

deportivo *a* sporting

deposición *f*, affirmation, statement; *law* deposition; degradation, removal (from office, etc.)

depositador (-ra) *a* depositing. *n* depositor

depositar *vt* to deposit; place in safety; entrust; lay aside, put away; *vr chem* settle

depositaría *f*, depository; trusteeship; accounts office

depositario (-ia) *a* pertaining to a depository. *n* depositary, trustee

depósito *m*, deposit; depository; *com* depot, warehouse; *chem* deposit, sediment; tank, reservoir; *mil* depot. **d. de bencina, d. de gasolina,** gas tank; service station. **d. de municiones,** munitions dump. *com* **en d.,** in bond. **Queda hecho el d. que marca la ley,** Copyright reserved

depravación *f*, depravity

depravar *vt* to deprave, corrupt; *vr* become depraved

deprecación *f*, supplication, petition; deprecation

deprecar *vt* to supplicate, petition; deprecate

depreciación *f*, depreciation, fall in value

depreciar *vt* to depreciate, reduce the value (of)

depredación *f*, depredation, robbery

depredar *vt* to pillage

depresión *f*, depression. **d. nerviosa,** nervous breakdown

depresivo *a* depressive; humiliating

deprimir *vt* to depress, compress, press down; depreciate, belittle; *vr* be compressed

depuración *f*, cleansing, purification; *pol* purge

depurar *vt* to cleanse, purify; *pol* purge

derecha *f*, right hand; *pol* (gen. *pl*) Right. *mil* ¡**D.!** Right Turn! **a la d.,** on the right

derechamente *adv* straight, directly; prudently, justly; openly, frankly

derechera *f*, direct road

derechista *mf pol* rightist

derecho *a* straight; upright; right (not left); just, reasonable; *sport* forehand. *adv* straightaway. *m*, right; law; just claim; privilege; justice, reason; exemption; right side (cloth, etc.); *pl* dues, taxes; fees. **d. a la vía,** right of way. **d. de apelación,** right to appeal. **d. de visita,** (international law) right of search. **derechos de aduana,** customhouse duties. **derechos de entrada,** import duties. **según d.,** according to law. **usar de su d.,** to exercise one's right

derechura *f*, directness, straightness; uprightness

deriva *f*, (*naut aer*) drift, leeway

derivación *f*, origin, derivation; inference, consequence; *gram* derivation

derivar *vi* to originate; *naut* drift; *vt* conduct, lead; *gram* derive; *elec* tap

derivativo *a* derivative

dermatitis *f*, dermatitis

dermatología *f*, dermatology

dermatólogo *m*, dermatologist

derogación *f*, repeal, annulment; deterioration

derogar *vt* to annul, repeal; destroy, suppress

derogatorio *a law* repealing

derrama *f*, apportionment of tax

derramado *a* extravagant, wasteful

derramamiento *m*, pouring out; spilling; scattering

derramar *vt* to pour out; spill; scatter; apportion (taxes); publish abroad, spread; *vr* be scattered; overflow

derrame *m*, spilling; leakage; overflow; scattering; slope

derredor *m*, circumference. **al** (*or* **en**) **d.,** round about

derrelicto *a* abandoned; derelict. *m, naut* derelict

derrengado *a* crooked; crippled

derretimiento *m*, melting; thaw; liquefaction; *inf* burning passion

derretir *vt irr* to melt, liquefy; waste, dissipate; *vr* be very much in love; *inf* be susceptible (to love); *inf* long, be impatient. See **pedir**

derribar *vt* to demolish; knock down; fell; throw down; *aer* shoot down; throw (in wrestling); *fig* overthrow; demolish, explode (a myth); control (emotions); *vr* fall down; prostrate oneself; throw oneself down. **d. el chapeo,** *humorous* to doff one's hat

derribo *m*, demolition; debris, rubble; throw (in wrestling)

derrocadero *m*, rocky precipice

derrocar *vt* to throw down from a rock; demolish (buildings); overthrow, oust

derrochador (-ra) *a* wasteful, extravagant. *n* spendthrift

derrochar *vt* to waste, squander

derroche *m*, squandering

derrota *f*, road; route, path; *naut* course; *mil* defeat

derrotar *vt* to squander; destroy, harm; *mil* defeat; *vr naut* drift, lose course

derrotero *m, naut* course; *naut* ship's itinerary; number of sea charts; means to an end, course of action

derrotismo *m*, defeatism

derrotista *mf* defeatist

derruir *vt irr* to demolish (a building). See **huir**

derrumbadero *m*, precipice; risk, danger

derrumbamiento *m*, landslide; collapse, downfall

derrumbar *vt* to precipitate; *vr* throw oneself down, collapse, tumble down (buildings, etc.)

derrumbe *m*, collapse; subsidence

derviche *m*, dervish

desabarrancar *vt* to pull out of a ditch or rut; extricate (from a difficulty)

desabillé *m*, deshabille

desabor *m*, insipidity

desabotonar *vt* to unbutton; *vi* open (flowers)

desabrido *a* insipid, poor-tasting; inclement (weather); disagreeable; unsociable; homely, plain (woman)

desabrigar *vt* to uncover; leave without shelter

desabrigo *m*, want of clothing or shelter; poverty, destitution

desabrimiento *m*, insipidity; harshness, disagreeableness; melancholy, depression

desabrir *vt* to give a bad taste (to food); annoy, trouble

desabrochar *vt* to unbutton, untie; open; *vr inf* confide, open up

desacatar *vt* to behave disrespectfully (towards); lack reverence

desacato *m*, irreverence; disrespect

desacertado *a* wrong, erroneous; imprudent

desacertar *vi irr* to be wrong; act imprudently. See **acertar**

desacierto *m*, mistake, miscalculation, blunder

desacomodado *a* lacking means of subsistence; poor; unemployed (servants); troublesome

desacomodar *vt* to incommode, make uncomfortable, inconvenience; dismiss, discharge

desaconsejado *a* ill-advised

desaconsejar *vt* to advise against, dissuade

desacoplar *vt* to disconnect

desacordar *vt irr mus* to put out of tune; *vr* (*with de*) forget. See **acordar**

desacorde *a* discordant, inharmonious; *mus* out of tune

desacostumbrado *a* unaccustomed; unusual

desacostumbrar *vt* to break of a habit

desacotar *vt* to remove (fences); refuse, deny; *vi* withdraw (from agreement, etc.)

desacreditar *vt* to discredit

desacuerdo *m*, disagreement, discord; mistake; forgetfulness; swoon, loss of consciousness

desadeudar *vt* to free from debt

desadornar *vt* to denude of ornaments

desadorno *m*, lack of ornaments; bareness

desafecto *a* disaffected; hostile. *m*, disaffection

desaferrar *vt irr* to untie, unfasten; *fig* wean from; *naut* weigh anchor. See **acertar**

desafiador (-ra) *a* challenging. *n* challenger. *m*, duelist

desafiar *vt* to challenge; compete with; oppose

desafinar *vi mus* to go out of tune; *fig inf* speak out of turn

desafío *m*, challenge; competition; duel

desaforado *a* lawless; outrageous; enormous

desaforar *vt* to infringe (laws, etc.); *vr* be disorderly

desaforrar *vt* to remove the lining of or from

desafortunado *a* unfortunate

desafuero *m*, act of injustice; outrage, excess

desagarrar *vt inf* to release, loosen; unhook

desagraciado *a* ugly, unsightly

desagraciar *vt* to disfigure, make ugly

desagradable *a* disagreeable; unpleasant

desagradar *vi* to be disagreeable, displease (e.g. Me desagrada su voz, I find his voice unpleasant)

desagradecer *vt irr* to be ungrateful (for). See **conocer**

desagradecido *a* ungrateful

desagradecimiento *m*, ingratitude

desagrado *m*, displeasure, dislike, dissatisfaction

desagraviar *vt* to make amends, apologize; indemnify

desagravio *m*, satisfaction, reparation; compensation

desagregar(se) *vt* and *vr* to separate

desaguadero *m*, drain, waste pipe

desaguar *vt* to drain off; dissipate; *vi* flow (into sea, etc.)

desagüe *m*, drainage; outlet, drain; catchment

desaguisado *a* outrageous, lawless. *m*, offense, insult

desahogado *a* brazen, insolent; clear, unencumbered; in comfortable circumstances

desahogar *vt* to ease, relieve; *vr* unburden oneself; recover (from illness, heat, etc.); get out of debt; speak one's mind

desahogo *m*, relief, alleviation; ease; comfort, convenience; freedom, frankness; unburdening (of one's mind). *inf* **vivir con d.,** to be comfortably off

desahuciar *vt* to banish all hope; give up, despair of the life of; put out (tenants). When the third syllable of this verb is stressed, it is spelled with **ú:** *Pres. Ind.* **desahúcio, desahúcias, desahúcia, desahúcian.** *Pres. Subj.* **desahúcie, desahúcies, desahúcie, desahúcien.** *Imp.* **desahúcia, desahúcie, desahúcien**

desahúcio *m*, ejection, dispossession (of tenants)

desahumar *vt* to clear of smoke

desairado *a* unattractive, graceless, ugly; unsuccessful, crestfallen; slighted

desairar *vt* to disdain, slight, disregard; underrate (things)

desaire *m*, gracelessness, ugliness; insult, slight

desalabanza *f*, disparagement; criticism

desalabar *vt* to censure, disparage

desalación *f*, desalinization

desalado *a* anxious, precipitate, hasty

desalar *vt* to remove the salt from; take off wings; *vr* walk or run at great speed; long for, yearn

desalentar *vt irr* to make breathing difficult (work, fatigue); discourage; *vr* be depressed or sad. See **sentar**

desaliento *m*, depression, discouragement, dismay

desalinear *vt* to throw out of the straight

desaliñado *a* slovenly; slipshod

desaliñar *vt* to disarrange, make untidy, crumple

desaliño *m*, untidiness, slovenliness; negligence, carelessness

desalmado *a* soulless, conscienceless; cruel

desalmamiento *m*, inhumanity, consciencelessness; cruelty

desalmidonar *vt* to remove starch from

desalojamiento *m*, dislodgement, ejection

desalojar *vt* to dislodge, remove, eject; *vi* move out, remove

desalquilado *a* untenanted, vacant

desalquilar *vt* to leave, or cause to leave, rented premises

desalterar *vt* to soothe, calm

desamar *vt* to cease to love; hate

desamarrar *vt* to untie; separate; *naut* unmoor

desamor *m*, indifference; lack of sentiment or affection; hatred

desamotinarse *vr* to cease from rebellion; submit

desamparar *vt* to abandon, forsake; leave (a place)

desamparo *m*, desertion; need

desamueblado *a* unfurnished

desamueblar *vt* to empty of furniture

desandar lo andado *vt irr* to retrace one's steps. See **andar**

desangrar *vt med* to bleed; drain (lake, etc.); impoverish, bleed; *vr* lose much blood

desanidar *vi* to leave the nest; *vt* eject, expel

desanimado *a* downhearted; (of places) dull, quiet

desanimar *vt* to discourage, depress

desanublar, vt desanublarse *vr* to clear up (weather)

desanudar *vt* to untie; disentangle

desaojar *vt* to cure of the evil eye

desapacibilidad *f*, disagreeableness, unpleasantness

desapacible *a* disagreeable; unpleasant; unsociable

desaparecer *vt irr* to cause to disappear; *vi* and *vr* disappear. See **conocer**

desaparecido *a* late (deceased); *mil* missing

desaparejar *vt* to unharness

desaparición *f*, disappearance

desapegar *vt* to unstick, undo; *vr* be indifferent, cast off a love or affection

desapego *m*, lack of affection or interest, coolness

desapercibido *a* unnoticed; unprovided, unprepared

desapercibimiento *m*, unpreparedness

desapestar *vt* to disinfect

desapiadado *a* merciless

desaplicación *f*, laziness, lack of application; carelessness, negligence

desaplicado *a* lazy; careless

desapoderado *a* precipitate, uncontrolled; furious, violent

desapoderar *vt* to dispossess, rob; remove from office

desapolillar *vt* to free from moths; *vr inf* take an airing

desaposentar *vt* to evict; drive away

desapreciar *vt* to scorn

desaprender *vt* to unlearn

desaprensivo *a* unscrupulous

desapretar(se) *vt* and *vr irr* to slacken. See **acertar**

desaprisionar *vt* to release from prison

desaprobación *f*, disapproval

desaprobar *vt irr* to disapprove; disagree with. See **probar**

desapropiamiento *m*, renunciation or transfer of property

desapropiarse *vr* to renounce or transfer (property)

desaprovechado *a* unprofitable; backward; unintelligent

desaprovechar *vt* to take no advantage of, waste; *vi fig* lose ground, lose what one has gained

desapuntar *vt* to unstitch; lose one's aim

desarbolar *vt naut* to unmast

desarenar *vt* to clear of sand

desarmar *vt* to disarm; dismantle, dismount; appease

desarme *m*, disarming; disarmament

desarraigar *vt* to pull up by root (plants); extirpate, suppress; eradicate (opinion, etc.); exile

desarraigo *m*, uprooting; extirpation; eradication; exile

desarrebujar *vt* to disentangle, uncover; explain

desarreglado *a* disarranged; untidy; intemperate, immoderate

desarreglar *vt* to disarrange

desarreglo *m*, disorder; disarrangement; irregularity

desarrendar *vt irr* to unbridle a horse; end a tenancy or lease. See **recomendar**

desarrollar *vt* to unroll; increase, develop, grow, unfold; explain (theory); *vr* develop, grow

desarrollo *m*, unrolling; development, growth; explanation

desarropar *vt* to uncover, remove the covers, etc. from

desarrugar *vt* to take out wrinkles or creases

desarticulación *f*, disarticulation

desarticular *vt* to disarticulate; *mech* disconnect

desaseado *a* dirty; unkempt, slovenly

desaseo *m*, dirtiness; slovenliness

desasimiento *m*, loosening; liberality; disinterestedness; indifference, coldness

desasir *vt irr* to loosen, undo. *vr* disengage oneself. See **asir**

desasnar *vt inf* to instruct, educate, polish

desasosegar *vt irr* to disturb, make anxious. See **cegar**

desasosiego *m*, uneasiness, disquiet

desastre *m*, disaster, calamity

desastroso *a* unfortunate, calamitous

desatacar *vt* to unfasten, undo, unbutton

desatadura *f*, untying

desatar *vt* to untie; melt, dissolve; elucidate, explain; *vr* loosen the tongue; lose self control; lose all reserve; unbosom oneself

desatascar *vt* to pull out of the mud; free from obstruction; extricate from difficulties

desataviar *vt* to strip of ornaments

desatavío *m*, carelessness in dress, slovenliness

desatención *f*, inattention, abstraction; incivility

desatender *vt irr* to pay no attention to; disregard, ignore. See **entender**

desatentado *a* imprudent, ill-advised; excessive, immoderate

desatento *a* inattentive, abstracted; discourteous

desatinado *a* foolish, imprudent, wild

desatinar *vt* to bewilder; *vi* behave foolishly; lose one's bearings

desatino *m*, folly, foolishness, imprudence, rashness; blunder, faux pas, mistake

desatracar *vi naut* to push off

desatrancar *vt* to unbar the door; remove obstacles

desaturdir *vt* to rouse (from torpor, etc.)

desautorizar *vt* to remove from authority; discredit

desavenencia *f*, disharmony, disagreement

desavenido *a* disagreeing, discordant

desavenir *vt irr* to upset. See **venir**

desaventajado *a* disadvantageous; unfavorable, inferior

desaviar *vt* to lead astray; deprive of a necessity; *vr* lose one's way

desayunador *m*, breakfast nook

desavisado *a* unaware, unprepared

desavisar *vt* to take back one's previous advice

desayunarse *vr* to have breakfast, eat breakfast

desayuno *m*, breakfast

desazón *f*, insipidity, lack of flavor; poorness (soil); anxiety, trouble; vexation

desazonar *vt* to make insipid; make anxious, worry; vex; *vr* feel out of sorts

desbancar *vt* to break the bank (gambling); supplant

desbandada *f*, dispersal, rout. **a la d.,** in confusion or disorder

desbandarse *vr* to disband, retreat in disorder; *mil* desert

desbaratado *a inf* corrupt, vicious

desbaratar *vt* to spoil, destroy; dissipate, waste; foil, thwart (a plot); *mil* rout; *vi* talk foolishly; *vr* go too far, behave badly

desbarbado *a* beardless

desbastar *vt carp* to plane, dress; polish, refine, civilize

desbocado *a* (of tools) blunt; runaway (of a horse); *inf* foul-tongued

desbocar *vt* to break the spout or neck (of jars, etc.); *vi* run (into) (of streets, etc.); *vr* bolt (horses); curse, swear

desboquillar *vt* to remove or break a stem or mouthpiece

desbordamiento *m*, overflowing, flood

desbordarse *vr* to overflow; lose self-control. **d. en alabanzas para,** to heap praise on

desbravar *vt* to break in (horses, etc.); *vi* grow less savage; lose force, decrease

desbrozar *vt* to free of rubbish, clear up

descabalgadura *f*, alighting (from horses, etc.)

descabalgar *vi* to alight (from horse); *vt* dismantle (gun)

descabellado *a* disheveled; ridiculous, foolish

descabellar *vt* to disarrange, ruffle (hair)

descabezado *a* headless; rash, impetuous

descabezar *vt* to behead; cut the top off (trees, etc.); *fig inf* break the back of (work); *vi* abut, join; *vr* (*with con* or *en*) rack one's brains about

descalabazarse *vr inf* to rack one's brains

descalabradura *f*, head wound or scar

descalabrar *vt* to wound in the head; wound; harm

descalabro *m*, misfortune, mishap

descalzar *vt* to remove the shoes and stockings; undermine; *vr* remove one's shoes and stockings; lose a shoe (horses)

descalzo *a* barefoot

descaminar *vt* to lead astray; pervert, corrupt

descamisado (**-da**) *a inf* shirtless; ragged, poor. *n inf* down and out, outcast; vagabond

descansadero *m*, resting place

descansado *a* rested, refreshed; tranquil

descansar *vi* to rest, repose oneself; have relief (from anxiety, etc.); sleep; *agr* lie fallow; sleep in death; (*with en*) trust, have confidence in; (*with sobre*) lean on or upon; *vt* (*with sobre*) rest (a thing) on another. **¡Que en paz descanse!** May he rest in peace!

descanso *m*, rest, repose; relief (from care); landing of stairs; *mech* bench, support; *mil* stand easy

descarado *a* impudent, brazen

descararse *vr* to behave impudently

descarbonizar *vt* to decarbonize

descarburación *f*, decarbonization

descarga *f*, unloading; *naut* discharge of cargo; *elec* discharge; *mil* volley. **d. cerrada,** dense volley, fusillade

descargadero *m*, wharf

descargador *m*, unloader, docker; *elec* discharger

descargar *vt* to unload; *mil* fire; unload (fire-arms); *elec* discharge; rain (blows) upon; *fig* free, exonerate; *vi* disembogue (of rivers); burst (clouds); *vr* relinquish (employment); shirk responsibility; *law* clear oneself

descargo *m*, unloading; *com* acquittance; *law* answer to an impeachment

descargue *m*, unloading

descarnado *a* fleshless; scraggy; spare, lean

descarnador *m*, dental scraper; tanner's scraper

descarnar *vt* to scrape off flesh; corrode; inspire indifference to earthly things

descaro *m*, impudence

descarriar *vt* to lead astray; *vr* be lost, be separated (from others); *fig* go astray

descarrilamiento *m*, derailment

descarrilar *vi* to run off the track, be derailed

descarrío *m*, losing one's way

descartar *vt* to put aside; *vr* discard (cards); shirk, make excuses

descarte *m*, discard (cards); excuse, pretext

descascarar *vt* to peel; shell; *vr* peel off

descendencia *f*, descendants, offspring; lineage, descent

descender *vi irr* to descend; flow (liquids); (*with de*) descend from, derive from; *vt* lower, let down. See **entender**

descendiente *mf* descendant, offspring. *a* descending

descendimiento *m*, descent

descenso *m*, descent; lowering, letting down; degradation

descentralización *f*, decentralization

descentralizar *vt* to decentralize

desceñir(se) *vt* and *vr irr* to ungird, remove a girdle, etc. See **ceñir**

descepar *vt* to tear up by the roots; *fig* extirpate

descercado *a* unfenced, open

descercar *vt* to pull down a wall or fence; *mil* raise a siege

descerrajar *vt* to remove the locks (of doors, etc.)

descifrable *a* decipherable

descifrador *m*, decipherer, decoder

descifrar *vt* to decipher; decode

descinchar *vt* to loosen or remove girths (of horse)

desclavar *vt* to remove nails; unnail, unfasten

descoagular *vt* to liquefy, dissolve, melt

descobijar *vt* to uncover; undress

descocado *a inf* brazen, saucy

descoco *m, inf* impudence

descogollar *vt* to prune a tree of shoots; remove hearts (of lettuces, etc.)

descolar *vt irr* to cut off or dock an animal's tail. See **colar**

descolgar *vt irr* to unhang; lower; *vr* lower oneself (by rope, etc.); come down, descend; *inf* come out (with), utter. See **volcar**

descoloramiento *m*, discoloration

descolorar *vt* to discolor; *vr* be discolored

descolorido *a* discolored; pale-colored; pallid

descollar *vi irr* to excel, be outstanding. See **degollar**

descomedido *a* excessive, disproportionate; rude

descomedimiento *m*, disrespect, lack of moderation, rudeness

descomedirse *vr irr* to be disrespectful or rude. See **pedir**

descompasarse *vr* See **descomedirse**

descomponer *vt irr* to disorder, disarrange; *chem* decompose; unsettle; *vr* go out of order; rot, putrefy; be ailing; lose one's temper. See **poner**

descomposición *f*, disorder, confusion; discomposure; *chem* decomposition; putrefaction

descompostura *f*, decomposition; slovenliness, dirtiness, untidiness; impudence, rudeness

descompuesto *a* rude, impudent

descomunal *a* enormous, extraordinary

desconcertar *vt irr* to disorder, disarrange; dislocate (bones); disconcert, embarrass; *vr* disagree; be impudent. See **acertar**

desconcharse *vr* to flake off, peel

desconcierto *m*, disorder, disarrangement; dislocation; embarrassment; disagreement; impudence

desconectar *vt* to disconnect; switch off

desconfianza *f*, lack of confidence

desconfiar *vi* to lack confidence

desconformidad *f*, See **disconformidad**

desconformismo *m*, non-conformism

desconocer *vt irr* to forget; be unaware of; deny, disown; pretend ignorance; not to understand (persons, etc.). See **conocer**

desconocido (**-da**) *a* unknown; ungrateful. *n* stranger; ingrate

desconocimiento *m*, unawareness; ignorance; ingratitude

desconsiderado *a* inconsiderate; discourteous; rash

desconsolación *f*, affliction, trouble

desconsolar *vt irr* to afflict, make disconsolate; *vr* grieve, despair. See **colar**

desconsuelo *m*, anguish, affliction, despair

descontar *vt irr com* to make a discount; ignore, discount; take for granted, leave aside. See **contar**

descontentadizo *a* discontented, difficult to please; fastidious, finicky

descontentar *vt* to displease; *vr* be dissatisfied

descontento *m*, discontent, dissatisfaction

descontextualizar *vt* to take out of context

descontrolarse *vr* to lose control, lose control of oneself

desconveniencia *f*, inconvenience, unsuitability, disagreement

desconvenir *vi irr* to disagree; be unsuitable, unsightly or odd (things). See **venir**

descorazonamiento *m*, depression, despair

descorazonar *vt* to tear out the heart; depress, discourage

descorchar *vt* to take the cork from cork tree; draw a cork (bottles); force, break into (safes)

descorrer *vt* to re-run (race, etc.); draw back (curtains, etc.); *vi* run, flow (liquids)

descorrimiento *m*, overflow (liquids)

descortés *a* impolite

descortesía *f*, impoliteness, discourtesy

descortezadura *f*, peeling (of bark)

descortezar *vt* to decorticate; remove crust (bread, etc.); polish, civilize

descoser *vt sew* to unpick; *vr* be unpicked; be indiscreet or tactless

descosido *a* tactless, talkative; *fig* disjointed; desultory; unsewn. *m, sew* rent, hole

descoyuntamiento *m*, dislocation (bones); irritation, bore; ache, pain

descoyuntar *vt* to dislocate (bones); bore, annoy; *vr* be dislocated

descrédito *m*, fall in value (things); discredit (persons)

descreer *vt irr* to disbelieve; depreciate, disparage (persons). See **creer**

descreído (**-da**) *a* unbelieving. *n* unbeliever; infidel

describir *vt* to describe; outline, sketch. *Past Part.* **descrito**

descripción *f*, description; *law* inventory

descriptible *a* describable

descriptivo *a* descriptive

descuajar *vt* to liquefy; *inf* discourage; *agr* pull up by the root

descuartizar *vt* to quarter; joint (meat); *inf* carve, cut into pieces, break up

descubierto *a* bareheaded; exposed. *m*, deficit. **al d.,** openly; in the open, without shelter. **girar en d.,** to overdraw (a bank account)

descubridero *m*, viewpoint, lookout

descubridor (**-ra**) *n* discoverer; inventor; explorer. *m, mil* scout

descubrimiento *m*, find; discovery; revelation; newly discovered territory

descubrir *vt* to reveal; show; discover; learn; unveil (memorials, etc.); *vr* remove one's hat; show oneself, reveal one's whereabouts. *Past Part.* **descubierto**

descuello *m*, extra height; *fig* pre-eminence; arrogance

descuento *m*, reduction; *com* rebate, discount

descuidado *a* negligent; careless; untidy; unprepared

descuidar *vt* to relieve (of responsibility, etc.); distract, occupy (attention, etc.); *vi* and *vr* be careless; *vr* (*with de* or *en*) neglect

descuido *m*, carelessness, negligence; oversight, mistake; incivility; forgetfulness; shameful act

desde *prep* since, from (time or space); after (e.g. **d. hoy,** from today). **d. la ventana,** from the window. **d. allá,** from the other world. **d. aquella época,** since that time

desdecir *vi irr* (*with de*) to degenerate, be less good than; be discordant, clash; be unworthy of; *vr* unsay one's words, retract. See **decir**

desdén *m*, indifference, coldness; disdain, scorn

desdentado *a* toothless; *zool* edentate

desdentar *vt* to remove teeth

desdeñar *vt* to scorn; *vr* (*with de*) dislike, be reluctant

desdeñoso *a* disdainful, scornful

desdevanar *vt* to unwind thread, etc.

desdibujado *a* badly drawn; blurred, confused

desdicha *f*, misfortune; extreme poverty, misery. **por d.,** unfortunately

desdichado *a* unfortunate; *inf* timid, weak-kneed

desdicharse *vr* to bewail one's fate

desdinerarse una fortuna *vr* to spend a fortune

desdoblar *vt* to unfold

desdorar *vt* to remove the gilt; *fig* tarnish, sully

desdoro *m*, discredit, dishonor

deseable *a* desirable

desear vt to desire; yearn or long for

desecar vt to dry; vr be desiccated

desechar vt to reject, refuse; scorn; cast out, expel; put away (thoughts, etc.); cast off (old clothes); turn (key); give up

desecho m, residue, rest, remains; cast-off; scorn

desembalar vt to unpack

desembanastar vt to take out of a basket; inf unsheath (sword); vr break loose (animals); inf get out, alight

desembarazar vt to clear of obstruction; disembarrass, free; vacate; vr fig rid oneself of obstacles

desembarazo m, freedom, insouciance, naturalness

desembarcadero m, landing-stage

desembarcar vt to unload; vi disembark; alight from vehicle

desembarco m, disembarkation, landing; staircase landing

desembargar vt to free of obstacles or impediments; law remove an embargo

desembargo m, law removal of an embargo

desembarque m, disembarkation, landing

desembarrancar vt and vi naut to refloat

desembaular vt to unpack from a trunk; disinter, empty; inf unbosom oneself

desembocadero m, exit, way out; mouth (rivers, etc.)

desembocadura f, mouth (rivers, etc.); street opening

desembocar vi (with en) to lead to, end in; flow into (rivers)

desembolsar vt to take out of a purse; pay, spend

desembolso m, disbursement; expenditure

desemboscarse vr to get out of the wood; extricate oneself from an ambush

desembozar vt to unmuffle

desembozo m, uncovering of the face

desembragar vt mech to disengage (the clutch, etc.)

desembravecer vt irr to tame, domesticate. See **conocer**

desembriagar(se) vt and vr to sober up (after a drinking bout)

desembrollar vt inf to disentangle, unravel

desemejanza f, unlikeness

desemejar vi to be unlike; vt disfigure, deform

desempacar vt to unpack

desempapelar vt to unwrap, remove the paper from; remove wallpaper

desempaquetar vt to unpack

desemparejar vt to split (a pair); make unequal

desemparentado a without relatives

desempedrar vt irr to take up the flags (of a pavement). See **acertar**

desempeñar vt to redeem (pledges); free from debt; fulfil (obligations, etc.); take out of pawn; hold, fill (an office); extricate (from difficulties, etc.); perform, carry out; theat act

desempeño m, redemption of a pledge; fulfilment (of an obligation, etc.); performance, accomplishment; theat acting of a part

desempolvar vt to free from dust, dust

desenamorar vt to kill the affection of; vr fall out of love

desencadenar vt to unchain, unfetter; fig unleash, let loose; vr fig break loose

desencajamiento m, disjointedness, dislocation; ricketiness, broken-down appearance

desencajar vt to disconnect, disjoint; dislocate; vr be out of joint; be contorted (of the face); be tired looking

desencaje m, See **desencajamiento**

desencallar vt naut to float a grounded ship

desencantar vt to disenchant

desencanto m, disenchantment; disillusionment

desencerrar vt irr to set at liberty; unlock; disclose, reveal. See **acertar**

desenchufar vt to disconnect, unplug (electric plugs, etc.)

desenclavijar vt to remove the pegs or pins; disconnect, disjoint

desencoger vt to unfold, spread out; vr grow bold

desencolerizar vt to placate; vr lose one's anger, grow calm

desenconar vt to reduce (inflammation); appease (anger, etc.); vr become calm

desencono m, reduction of inflammation; appeasement (of anger, etc.)

desencordelar vt to untie the ropes (of), unstring

desencorvar vt to straighten (curves, etc.)

desenfadado a expeditious; natural, at ease; gay; forward, bold; wide, spacious

desenfadar vt to appease, make anger disappear

desenfado m, freedom; ease; unconcern, frankness

desenfardar vt to unpack bales

desenfrailar vt to leave the cloister, become secularized; inf emancipate oneself

desenfrenar vt to unbridle (horses); vr give rein to one's passions, etc.; break loose (storms, etc.)

desenfreno m, license, lasciviousness; complete freedom from restraint

desengalanar vt to strip of ornaments

desenganchar vt to unhook; uncouple; unfasten; unharness

desengañador a undeceiving

desengañar vt to undeceive, disillusion

desengaño m, undeceiving, disabuse; disillusionment

desengarzar vt to loosen from its setting; unlink, unhook, unclasp

desengastar vt to remove from its setting (jewelry, etc.)

desengrasar vt to remove the grease from, clean; vi inf grow thin

desenlace m, loosening, untying; lit denouement, climax (of play, etc.)

desenlazar vt to untie, unloose; lit unravel (a plot)

desenlosar vt to remove flagstones

desenmarañar vt to disentangle; fig straighten out

desenmascarar vt to remove the mask from; fig unmask

desenmudecer vi irr to be freed of a speech impediment; break silence, speak. See **conocer**

desenojar vt to soothe, appease; vr distract oneself, amuse oneself

desenojo m, relenting, abatement of anger

desenredar vt to disentangle; fig set right; straighten out; vr extricate oneself, get out of a difficulty

desenredo m, disentanglement; lit climax

desentablar vt to tear up planks or boards; disorder, disrupt

desentenderse vr irr (with de) to pretend to be ignorant of; take no part in. See **entender**

desenterrador m, disinterrer, unearther

desenterramiento m, disinterment; fig unearthing, recollection

desenterrar vt irr to unbury, disinter; rummage out; fig unearth, bring up, recall. See **acertar**

desentoldar vt to take away an awning; fig strip of ornament

desentonar vt to humiliate; vi mus be out of tune; speak rudely; vr be inharmonious; raise the voice (anger, etc.), behave badly

desentono m, bad behavior, rudeness; mus discord; grating quality or harshness (of voice)

desentorpecer vt irr to restore feeling to (numbed limbs); free from torpor; vr become bright and intelligent. See **conocer**

desentramparse vr inf free oneself from debt

desentrañar vt to disembowel; fig unravel, penetrate; vr give away one's all

desentronizar vt to dethrone; dismiss from office

desentumecer vt irr to free from numbness (limbs); vr be restored to feeling (numb limbs). See **conocer**

desenvainar vt to unsheath; inf reveal, bring into the open

desenvoltura f, naturalness, ease, freedom; eloquence, facility (of speech); effrontery, audacity, shamelessness (especially in women)

desenvolver *vt irr* to unroll; unfold; *fig* unravel, explain; *fig* develop, work out (theories, etc.); *vr* unroll; unfold; lose one's timidity, blossom out; be over-bold; extricate oneself (from a difficulty). See **resolver**

desenvuelto *a* natural, easy; impudent, bold

deseo *m,* desire, will, wish

deseoso *a* desirous, wishful

desequilibrar(se) *vt and vr* to unbalance

desequilibrio *m,* lack of balance; confusion, disorder; mental instability

deserción *f, mil* desertion. **d. estudiantil,** school dropout

desertar *vt mil* to desert; *inf* quit

desertor *m, mil* deserter; *inf* quitter

deservicio *m,* disservice

desesperación *f,* desperation, despair; frenzy, violence

desesperado *a* desperate, hopeless; frenzied

desesperanza *f,* despair; hopelessness

desesperanzar *vt* to render hopeless; *vr* despair, lose hope

desesperar *vt* to make hopeless; *inf* annoy, make furious; *vr* lose hope, despair; be frenzied

desestañar *vt* to unsolder

desestimación *f,* disrespect, lack of esteem; rejection

desestimar *vt* to scorn; reject

desfachatado *a inf* impudent, brazen

desfachatez *f, inf* effrontery, cheek

desfalcador (-ra) *a* embezzling. *n* embezzler

desfalcar *vt* to remove a part of; embezzle

desfalco *m,* diminution, reduction; embezzlement

desfallecer *vt irr* to weaken; *vi* grow weak; faint, swoon. See **conocer**

desfallecimiento *m,* weakness, languor; depression, discouragement; faint, swoon

desfavorable *a* unfavorable; hostile, contrary

desfavorecer *vt irr* to withdraw one's favor, scorn; disfavor; oppose. See **conocer**

desfiguración *f,* deformation; disfigurement

desfigurar *vt* to deform, misshape; disfigure; *fig* disguise, mask; obscure, darken; distort, misrepresent; *vr* be disfigured (by rage, etc.)

desfijar *vt* to unfix, pull off, remove

desfiladero *m,* defile, gully

desfilar *vi* to walk in file; *inf* file out; *mil* file or march past

desfile *m, mil* march past; parade; walk past; procession

desflecarse (en) *vr* to disintegrate (into)

desfloración *f,* defloration

desflorar *vt* to tarnish, stain; deflower, violate; *fig* touch upon, deal lightly with

desfortalecer *vt irr mil* to dismantle a fortress. See **conocer**

desfruncir *vt* to unfold, shake out

desgaire *m,* untidiness, slovenliness; affectation of carelessness (in dress); scornful gesture. **al d.,** with an affectation of carelessness, negligently

desgajar *vt* to tear off a tree branch; break; *vr* break off; dissociate oneself (from)

desgalgar *vt* to throw headlong

desgana *f,* lack of appetite; lack of interest, indifference; reluctance

desganar *vt* to dissuade; *vr* lose one's appetite; become bored or indifferent, lose interest

desgarbado *a* slovenly, slatternly; gawky, graceless

desgarrado *a* dissolute, vicious; impudent, brazen

desgarrador *a* tearing; heart-rending

desgarrar *vt* to tear; *vr* leave, tear oneself away

desgarro *m,* tearing; rent, breach; boastfulness, impudence; effrontery

desgastar *vt* to corrode, wear away; spoil, corrupt; *vr* lose one's vigor, grow weak; wear away

desgaste *m,* attrition; wearing down or away; corrosion; wear and tear

desgobernado *a* uncontrolled (of persons)

desgobernar *vt irr* to upset or rise against the government; dislocate (bones); *naut* neglect the tiller; *vr* affect

exaggerated movements in dancing. See **recomendar**

desgobierno *m,* misgovernment; mismanagement; maladministration; disorder, tumult

desgomar *vt* to ungum (fabrics)

desgorrarse *vr* to doff one's cap, doff one's hat

desgoznar *vt* to unhinge; *vr fig* lose one's self-control

desgracia *f,* misfortune, adversity; mishap, piece of bad luck; disgrace, disfavor; disagreeableness, brusqueness; ungraciousness. **por d.,** unhappily, unfortunately

desgraciado *a* unfortunate, unhappy; unlucky; dull, boring; disagreeable

desgraciar *vt* to displease; spoil the development (of), destroy; maim; *vr* fall out of friendship; be out of favor; turn out badly, fail; be destroyed or spoiled; be maimed

desgranar *vt agr* to thresh, flail; *vr* break (string of beads, etc.)

desgrasante *m,* grease remover

desgreñar *vt* to dishevel the hair; *vr inf* pull each other's hair, come to blows

desguarnecer *vt irr* to strip of trimming; *mil* demilitarize; *mil* disarm; dismantle; unharness. See **conocer**

desguazar *vt* to break up (ships)

deshabitado *a* uninhabited, empty

deshabitar *vt* to desert, quit, leave (a place)

deshabituar *vt* to disaccustom; *vr* lose the habit, become unaccustomed

deshacer *vt irr* to undo; destroy; *mil* rout, defeat; take to pieces; melt; pulp (paper); untie (knots, etc.); open (parcels); diminish, decrease; break in pieces, smash; *fig* obstruct, spoil; *vr* be wasted or spoiled; be full of anxiety; vanish; try or work very hard; injure oneself; be emaciated, grow extremely thin; (*with de*) part with. **d. agravios,** to right wrongs. See **hacer**

desharrapado *a* tattered, shabby

deshebillar *vt* to unbuckle

deshebrar *vt* to unravel; shred

deshecha *f,* pretense, evasion; courteous farewell; obligatory departure

deshechizar *vt* to disenchant

deshelar *vt irr* to thaw, melt. See **acertar**

desherbar *vt irr* to pull up weeds. See **acertar**

desheredación *f,* disinheritance

desheredar *vt* to disinherit; *vr fig* lower oneself

desherrar *vt irr* to unfetter, unchain; strike off horseshoes; *vr* lose a shoe (horses). See **acertar**

desherrumbrar *vt* to remove the rust from; clean off rust from

deshidratación *f,* dehydration

deshidratar *vt* to dehydrate

deshielo *m,* thaw

deshilado *a* in single file. *m, sew* drawn-thread work (gen. *pl*). **a la deshilada,** *mil* in file formation; secretly

deshiladura *f,* unraveling

deshilar *vt* to unravel; *sew* draw threads; *cul* shred, grate

deshilvanado *a fig* disjointed, disconnected

deshilvanar *vt sew* to remove the tacking threads

deshincar *vt* to pull out, remove, draw out

deshinchar *vt* to remove a swelling; deflate; lessen the anger of; *vr* decrease, subside (swellings); deflate; *inf* grow humble

deshojar *vt* to strip off leaves or petals

deshollejar *vt* to skin, peel (fruit); shell (peas, etc.)

deshollinador *m,* chimney-sweep; wall-brush; chemical chimney cleaner

deshollinar *vt* to sweep chimneys; clean down walls; *inf* examine closely

deshonestidad *f,* immodesty, shamelessness; indecency

deshonesto *a* shameless, immodest; dissolute, vicious; indecent

deshonor *m,* dishonor; disgrace, insult

deshonra *f,* dishonor

deshonrabuenos *mf inf* slanderer; degenerate

deshonrador (-ra) *a* dishonorable. *n* dishonorer

deshonrar *vt* to dishonor; insult; seduce (women)

deshonroso *a* dishonorable, insulting, indecent

deshora *f*, inconvenient time. **a d.**, *or* **a deshoras,** at an inconvenient time, unseasonably; extempore

deshuesar *vt* to bone, remove the bone (from meat); stone (fruit)

deshumedecer *vt irr* to dry; *vr* become dry. See **conocer**

desidia *f*, negligence; laziness

desidioso *a* negligent; lazy

desierto *a* deserted, uninhabited, solitary. *m*, desert; wilderness

designación *f*, designation; appointment

designar *vt* to plan, intend; designate; appoint

designio *m*, intention, idea

desigual *a* unequal; uneven (ground); rough; arduous, difficult; changeable

desigualar *vt* to make unequal; *vr* prosper

desigualdad *f*, inequality; unevenness, rockiness; *fig* changeability; variability

desilusión *f*, disillusionment; disappointment

desilusionar *vt* to disillusion; *vr* become disillusioned; be undeceived

desinclinar *vt* to dissuade

desinfección *f*, disinfection

desinfectante *a* and *m*, disinfectant

desinfectar *vt* to disinfect

desinflación *f*, deflation

desinflar *vt* to deflate

desinterés *m*, disinterestedness

desinteresado *a* disinterested; generous

desinteresarse *vr* to lose interest, grow indifferent

desistencia, *f*, **desistimiento** *m*, desistance, ceasing

desistir *vi* to desist; cease; *law* renounce

desjuntamiento *m*, separation; division

desjuntar(se) *vt* and *vr* to separate; divide

deslavado *a* brazen, impudent

deslavar *vt* to wash superficially; spoil by washing, take away the body of (cloth, etc.)

desleal *a* disloyal, treacherous

deslealtad *f*, disloyalty

desleír *vt irr* to dissolve; dilute. See **reír**

deslenguado *a* shameless, foulmouthed

deslenguar *vt* to remove the tongue; *vr inf* be insolent

desliar *vt* to untie, undo, unloose

desligadura *f*, untying, loosening

desligar *vt* to unfasten, unbind; *fig* solve, unravel; relieve of an obligation; *mus* play staccato; *vr* come unfastened, grow loose. **desligarse de,** to weasel out of, wiggle out of (a promise)

deslindador *m*, one who fixes boundaries or limits

deslindar *vt* to fix the boundaries (of); limit, circumscribe

deslinde *m*, demarcation, boundary

desliz *m*, slipping, slip, slide; skid; indiscretion, slip; peccadillo, trifling fault

deslizadero *m*, slippery place; chute

deslizadizo *a* slippery

deslizar *vt* to slip, slide; skid; *vr* commit an indiscretion; speak or act unwisely; escape, slip away; slip; skid

deslucido *a* fruitless, vain; stupid, clumsy, awkward; discolored; tarnished, dull; unsuccessful

deslucimiento *m*, clumsiness, gracelessness; failure, lack of success

deslucir *vt irr* to fade; discolor, stain; tarnish; spoil; sully the reputation of; *vr* do a thing badly, fail at. See **lucir**

deslumbrador *a* dazzling

deslumbramiento *m*, brilliant light, glare, dazzle; bewilderment, confusion

deslumbrar *vt* to dazzle; confuse, bewilder; *fig* daze (with magnificence)

deslustrar *vt* to dull, dim, tarnish; frost (glass); discredit, sully (reputation)

deslustre *m*, dullness, tarnish; frosting (of glass); disgrace, stigma

deslustroso *a* ugly, unsuitable, unbecoming

desmadejar *vt* to debilitate, enervate

desmán *m*, outrageous behavior; disaster, misfortune

desmandado *a* disobedient

desmandar *vt* to cancel, revoke (orders); withdraw (an offer). *vr* behave badly; stray

desmantelado *a* dismantled, dilapidated

desmantelamiento *m*, dismantling; dilapidation

desmantelar *vt* to dismantle; abandon, forsake

desmaña *f*, lack of dexterity, clumsiness, awkwardness

desmañado *a* clumsy, awkward, unhandy

desmayado *a* pale, faint (of colors); weak (of a voice)

desmayar *vt* to cause to faint; *vi* grow discouraged, lose heart; *vr* swoon, faint

desmayo *m*, depression, discouragement; faint, swoon

desmedido *a* disproportionate; excessive

desmedirse *vr* to misbehave, go too far

desmedrado *a* thin, emaciated; deteriorated, spoiled

desmedrar *vt* to spoil, ruin; *vi* deteriorate; decline

desmedro *m*, impairment; decline, deterioration. **en d. de,** to the detriment of

desmejora *f*, deterioration

desmejorar *vt* to spoil, impair, cause to deteriorate; *vr* deteriorate; *vi* and *vr* decline in health; lose one's beauty

desmelenar *vt* to ruffle or dishevel the hair

desmembración *f*, dismemberment

desmembrar *vt* to dismember; separate, divide

desmemoriarse *vr* to forget, lose one's memory

desmenguar *vt* to reduce, decrease; *fig* diminish

desmentida *f*, action of giving the lie to

desmentir *vt irr* to give the lie to; contradict, deny; lower oneself; behave unworthily; *vi* deviate (from right direction, etc.). See **sentir**

desmenuzar *vt* to crumble, break into small pieces; *fig* examine in detail; *vr* be broken up

desmeollar *vt* to remove the marrow of

desmerecedor *a* unworthy

desmerecer *vt irr* to become undeserving of; *vi* deteriorate; be inferior to. See **conocer**

desmesura *f*, insolence; disproportion; excess

desmesurado *a* disproportionate; excessive, enormous; insolent, uncivil

desmesurar *vt* to disarrange, disorder; *vr* be insolent

desmigajar(se) *vt* and *vr* to crumble

desmigar *vt cul* to make breadcrumbs

desmilitarizar *vt* to demilitarize

desmochar *vt* to lop off the top; pollard (trees)

desmonetización *f*, demonetization; conversion of coin into bullion

desmonetizar *vt* to convert money into bullion; demonetize; *vr* depreciate (shares, etc.)

desmontable *a* movable; sectional

desmontadura *f*, clearing; deforestation; leveling; demounting, dismounting

desmontar *vt* to clear wholly or partly of trees or shrubs; clear up (rubbish); level (ground); dismantle; dismount; uncock (firearms); *vi* and *vr* dismount (from horse, etc.)

desmonte *m*, clearing of trees and shrubs; clearing, cleared ground; timber remaining

desmoralización *f*, demoralization, corruption

desmoralizador *a* demoralizing

desmoralizar *vt* to demoralize, corrupt

desmoronamiento *m*, crumbling; decay, ruin

desmoronar *vt* to destroy, decay; crumble; *vr* crumble away, fall into ruin; decline, decay; wane, fade (power, etc.)

desmovilización *f*, demobilization

desmovilizar *vt* to demobilize

desnacificación *f*, denazification

desnatar *vt* to skim; *fig* take the cream or best

desnaturalización *f*, denaturalization

desnaturalizar *vt* to denaturalize; exile; deform, disfigure, pervert; *vr* give up one's country

desnivel *m*, unevenness; slope, drop

desnivelar(se) *vi* and *vr* to become uneven

desnudar *vt* to undress; *fig* despoil, strip, denude; *vr* undress oneself; deprive oneself

desnudez f, nudity; nakedness; bareness; plainness
desnudo a nude; ill-clad; bare, naked; clear, patent; fig destitute (of grace, etc.). m, art nude
desnutrición f, malnutrition
desobedecer vt irr to disobey. See **conocer**
desobediencia f, disobedience
desobediente a disobedient
desobligar vt to free from obligation; offend, hurt
desocupación f, lack of occupation; leisure
desocupado a idle; vacant, unoccupied
desocupar vt to empty; vacate; vr give up an employment or occupation
desodorante a and m, deodorant
desoír vt irr to pay no attention, pretend not to hear. See **oír**
desojar vt to break the eye of (needles, etc.); vr gaze intently
desolación f, destruction, desolation; affliction
desolador a desolate; grievous
desolar vt irr to lay waste, destroy; vr grieve, be disconsolate. See **contar**
desoldar vt to unsolder; vr become unsoldered
desolladero m, slaughterhouse
desollado a inf impertinent, barefaced. m, carcass
desolladura f, flaying, skinning; inf slander
desollar vt irr to flay, skin; harm, discredit. **d. vivo**, inf to extort an exorbitant price; slander. See **contar**
desopinado a discredited
desopinar vt to discredit, defame
desorden m, disorder, disarray; confusion; excess
desordenado a disordered; vicious; licentious
desordenar vt to disorder; confuse; vr go beyond the just limits; behave badly; be impertinent
desorganización f, disorganization
desorganizador a disorganizing
desorganizar vt to disorganize; disband
desorientación f, disorientation, loss of bearings; lack of method, confusion
desorientar vt to disorient; perplex, confuse; vr lose one's way; be disoriented
desovar vi to spawn
desove m, spawning; spawning season
desovillar vt to unwind; uncoil; uncurl; explain, clarify
despabiladeras f pl, snuffers
despabilado a alert, wide-awake; watchful, vigilant
despabiladura f, snuff of a candle, lamp, etc.
despabilar vt to snuff (a candle); trim (lamps); hasten, expedite; finish quickly; steal, rob; fig quicken (intelligence, etc.). inf kill; vr rouse oneself, wake up
despachador (-ra) n dispatcher, sender
despachar vt to expedite; dispatch, conclude; forward, send; attend to correspondence; sell; dismiss; inf serve in a shop; inf kill; vi hasten; carry letters to be signed (in offices, etc.); vr get rid of
despacho m, transaction, execution; study; office, room; department; booking-office; dispatch, shipment; expedient; commission, warrant; dispatch (diplomatic); telegram; telephone message. **d. particular**, private office
despachurrar vt inf to crush, squash; recount in a muddled fashion; fig squash flat, confound
despacio adv slowly; little by little; deliberately; leisurely. interj Careful! Gently now!
despacito adv inf very slowly
despalmador m, dockyard
despalmar vt naut to careen, caulk
despampanar vt agr to prune vines; inf amaze, stun, astound; vr inf relieve one's feelings; vr inf receive a serious injury (through falling)
desparpajar vt to spoil; vi inf chatter
desparpajo m, inf loquaciousness, pertness; disorder, muddle
desparramar vt to disperse, scatter; squander, waste (money, etc.); vr amuse oneself; be dissipated
despavorido a terrified, panicstricken

despechar vt to anger; make despair; inf wean; vr be angry; be in despair
despecho m, rancor, malice; despair. **a d. de**, in spite of
despechugar vt to cut off the breast (fowls); vr inf show the bosom
despectivo a contemptuous, depreciatory
despedazar vt to cut or break into pieces; fig break (heart, etc.)
despedida f, dismissal, discharge; seeing off (a visitor, etc.); farewell, good-by
despedir vt irr to throw out, emit, cast up; dismiss, discharge; see off (on a journey or after a visit); banish (from the mind); get rid of; vr say good-by; leave (employment). See **pedir**
despedregar vt to clear of stones
despegadamente adv uninterestedly, unconcernedly, indifferently
despegado a inf indifferent, unconcerned, cold
despegar vt to unstick; unglue; separate, detach; vr become estranged; come apart or unstuck; vi aer take off. **sin d. los labios**, without saying a word
despegue m, aer take-off
despeinar vt to disarrange the hair; undo the coiffure
despejado a lively, sprightly; logical, clear-cut; cloudless; spacious, unobstructed, clear
despejar vt to clear, free of obstacles; **d. el camino de**, to clear the way for; fig elucidate, solve; math find the value of; vr smarten up, grow gay; amuse oneself; clear up (weather, sky, etc.); improve (a patient)
despejo m, freeing of obstacles; smartness, gaiety; grace, elegance; perkiness; clear-sightedness, intelligence
despeluzar vt to disorder the hair; cause the hair to stand on end; horrify; vr stand on end (hair); be horrified or terrified
despeluznante a hair-raising, terrifying
despellejar vt to flay, skin; slander
despendedor (-ra) n spendthrift, waster
despender vt to spend; waste
despensa f, larder, pantry; store (of food); naut steward's room; stewardship
despensero (-ra) n steward; caterer; victualler; naut steward
despeñadero m, precipice, crag; dangerous undertaking, risk. a steep, precipitous
despeñar vt to precipitate, fling down from a height, hurl down; vr fling oneself headlong; throw oneself into (vices, etc.)
despeño m, precipitation; headlong fall; fig collapse, ruin
despepitar vt to remove seeds or pips; vr vociferate; act wildly; inf desire, long (for)
desperdiciador (-ra) a squandering, wasting. n squanderer
desperdiciar vt to squander; fig misspend, waste
desperdicio m, waste; remains, leftovers (gen. pl)
desperdigar vt to separate, sever; scatter
desperecerse vr irr to crave, yearn (for). See **conocer**
desperezarse vr to stretch oneself
desperfecto m, imperfection, flaw; slight deterioration
despernado a weary, footsore
despertador (-ra) a awakening. n awakener. m, alarm clock; incentive, stimulus
despertar vt irr to awaken; bring to mind, recall; incite, stimulate; vi waken; fig wake up, become more intelligent. See **acertar**
despiadado a cruel, merciless
despicar vt to satisfy, content; vr revenge oneself
despierto a wide-awake, clever
despilfarrado a ragged, shabby; wasteful; spendthrift
despilfarrar vt to squander, waste
despilfarro m, slovenliness; waste, extravagance; mismanagement, maladministration
despintar vt to paint out; wash off the paint; efface, blot out; disfigure, deform; vi be unlike or unworthy (of); vr fade (colors); forget

despiojar *vt* to remove lice, delouse; *inf* rescue from misery

despique *m*, vengeance, revenge

despistar *vt* to throw off the scent; mislead

desplacer *vt irr* to displease. *m*, disgust, displeasure, sorrow. See **placer**

desplantar(se) *vt* and *vr* to deviate from the vertical

desplazamiento *m*, *naut* displacement

desplegadura *f*, unfolding

desplegar *vt irr* to unfold; spread open; *fig* reveal, disclose, explain; evince, display; *mil* deploy troops; *vr* unfold, open (flowers, etc.); *mil* deploy. See **cegar**

despliegue *m*, unfolding; spreading out; evincing, demonstration; *mil* deployment

desplomar *vt* to put out of the straight, cause to lean (walls, buildings); *vr* lean, tilt (buildings); topple, fall down (walls, etc.); collapse (people); be ruined

desplome *m*, collapse

desplomo *m*, tilt, cant, deviation from vertical

desplumar *vt* to remove feathers, pluck; rob, despoil

despoblación *f*, depopulation. **d. forestal**, deforestation

despoblado *m*, wilderness; deserted place

despoblar *vt* to depopulate; despoil, rob; *vr* become depopulated

despojador (-ra) *a* robbing, despoiling. *n* despoiler

despojar *vt* to plunder, despoil; dispossess; *vr* (*with de*) remove (garments, etc.); relinquish, give up

despojo *m*, pillaging, spoliation; booty, plunder; butcher's offal; *pl* remains, leavings; debris, rubble; corpse

despolvorear *vt* to remove dust; *fig* shake off

desposado *a* recently married; fettered, handcuffed. **los desposados**, the newlyweds

desposar *vt* to perform the marriage ceremony; *vr* become betrothed; marry

desposeer *vt* to dispossess; *vr* renounce one's possessions. See **creer**

desposeimiento *m*, dispossession

desposorio *m*, betrothal, promise of marriage; (gen. *pl*) wedding, marriage

déspota *m*, despot, tyrant

despótico *a* tyrannical

despotismo *m*, despotism

despotricarse *vr* to rave (against), rail (against)

despreciable *a* worthless, contemptible

despreciar *vt* to scorn, despise; *vr* despise oneself

despreciativo *a* contemptuous, scornful

desprecio *m*, contempt, scorn

desprender *vt* to loosen, remove, unfix; give off (gases, etc.); *vr* work loose, give way; deduce, infer; give away, deprive oneself (of)

desprendido *a* disinterested; generous

desprendimiento *m*, loosening; removal, separation; emission; indifference, lack of interest; generosity; impartiality

despreocupación *f*, fair mindedness, impartiality; lack of interest

despreocupado *a* unprejudiced, broadminded; indifferent, uninterested

despreocuparse *vr* to shake off prejudice; (*with de*) pay no attention to; set aside

desprestigiar *vt* to discredit; *vr* lose prestige; lose caste

desprestigio *m*, loss of prestige, discredit

desprevenido *a* unprepared, improvident

desproporción *f*, disproportion

desproporcionado *a* disproportionate; out of proportion

despropósito *m*, nonsense, absurdity

desproveer *vt irr* to deprive of necessities. See **creer**

despueble *m*, depopulation

después *adv* afterwards, after, next (of time and place) (e.g. **Vendrá d. de Pascua,** He will come after Easter. **Zaragoza viene d. de Madrid,** Saragossa comes after Madrid)

despuntar *vt* to blunt the point; *naut* double, sail round; *vi* show green, sprout; appear (the dawn); grow clever; *fig* stand out, excel

desquiciamiento *m*, unhinging; disconnecting; *fig* upsetting, throwing out of gear; downfall, fall from favor

desquiciar *vt* to unhinge; disconnect; *fig* throw out of gear, upset; banish from favor; *vr* become unhinged; *fig* be disordered; upset

desquitar(se) *vt* and *vr* to retrieve a loss; take revenge, retaliate

desquite *m*, compensation; revenge

destacamento *m*, *mil* detachment

destacar *vt mil* to detach; *vr* excel; be prominent; be conspicuous; *art* stand out

destajador *m*, smith's hammer

destajar *vt* to cut (cards); set forth conditions, stipulate, contract

destajista *mf* pieceworker; jobber (worker)

destajo *m*, piecework; job. **a d.,** quickly and diligently. *inf* **hablar a d.,** to chatter, talk too much

destapar *vt* to remove the cover or lid; reveal, uncover; *vr* be uncovered; reveal oneself. **no destaparse,** to keep quiet, be mum

destartalado *a* tumble-down, rickety; poverty-stricken

destechado *a* roofless

destejar *vt* to remove tiles or slates; leave unprotected

destejer *vt* to unweave, unravel; *fig* undo, spoil

destello *m*, gleam, sparkle, brilliance; flash, beam, ray; *fig* gleam (of talent)

destemplado *a* out of tune; inharmonious; intemperate; *art* inharmonious; *inf* out of sorts, indisposed

destemplanza *f*, inclemency, rigor (weather); intemperance, excess, abuse; *inf* indisposition; lack of moderation (actions, speech)

destemplar *vt* to disturb, upset, alter; *mus* put out of tune; put to confusion; *vr* be unwell; *fig* go too far, behave badly; lose temper (metals)

destemple *m*, *mus* being out of tune; *med* indisposition; uncertainty (weather); lack of temper (metals); disturbance, disorder; intemperance, excess, confusion

desternillarse de risa to shake with laughter

desterrado (-da) *a* exiled. *n* exile

desterrar *vt irr* to banish; shake off the soil; *fig* discard, lay aside; extirpate (an error). See **recomendar**

destetar *vt* to wean

destete *m*, weaning

destiempo, a *adv* untimely, inopportunely

destierro *m*, banishment, exile; place of exile; remote place

destilación *f*, distillation

destilador (-ra) *n* distiller. *m*, still

destilar *vt* to distil; filter; *vi* to drip

destilatorio *a* distilling. *m*, distillery; still

destilería *f*, distillery

destinación *f*, destination

destinar *vt* to destine; appoint; assign

destino *m*, fate, destiny; post, appointment; destination. **con d. a,** going to, bound for

destitución *f*, destitution; discharge, dismissal

destituir *vt irr* (*with de*) to dismiss or discharge from (employment); deprive of. See **huir**

destorcer *vt irr* to untwist; straighten out; *vr naut* drift. See **torcer**

destornillado *a* reckless; *fig inf* with a screw loose

destornillador *m*, screwdriver

destornillamiento *m*, unscrewing

destornillar *vt* to unscrew; *vr* act rashly

destrenzar *vt* to unplait. **destrenzarse las cintas,** to unlace one's shoes

destreza *f*, dexterity; agility

destrón *m*, blind person's guide

destronamiento *m*, dethronement

destronar *vt* to dethrone, depose; oust

destroncamiento *m*, detruncation

destroncar *vt* to lop, detruncate (trees); dislocate, disjoint; mutilate; *fig* ruin, seriously harm; tire out; *vr* be exhausted or tired

destrozar *vt* to destroy; break in pieces, shatter; *mil* wipe out, annihilate; squander, dissipate

destrozo *m*, destruction, ruin; shattering; *mil* rout; dissipation, waste

destrozón *a* hard on wearing apparel, shoes, etc.

destrucción *f*, destruction; ruin, irreparable loss

destructible *a* destructible

destructivo *a* destructive

destructor (-ra) *a* destructive. *n* destroyer. *m, nav* destroyer

destruible *a* destructible

destruir *vt irr* to destroy, ruin, annihilate; frustrate, blast, disappoint; deprive of means of subsistence; squander, waste; *vr math* cancel. See **huir**

desuello *m*, flaying, skinning; forwardness, impertinence; extortion, fleecing. *fig inf* ¡Es un d.! It's highway robbery!

desunión *f*, disunion, separation; *fig* discord, disharmony

desunir *vt* to disunite, separate; *fig* cause discord or disharmony

desusarse *vr* to fall into disuse, become obsolete

desuso *m*, disuse

desvaído *a* gaunt, lanky; pale, faded, dull (of colors)

desvainar *vt* to shell (peas, beans)

desvalido *a* unprotected, helpless

desvalijar *vt* to rifle (a suitcase, etc.); swindle

desvalimiento *m*, defenselessness, lack of protection; lack of favor; desertion, abandonment

desvalorización *f*, devaluation

desván *m*, garret

desvanecer *vt irr* to cause to disappear; disintegrate; make vain; remove; *vr* evaporate; faint, swoon; grow vain or conceited. See **conocer**

desvanecimiento *m*, faintness, loss of consciousness; vanity, conceit

desvarar *vt* to slip, slide; *naut* refloat

desvariar *vi* to be delirious; rave, talk wildly

desvarío *m*, foolish action, absurdity; delirium; monstrosity; whim, caprice

desvedar *vt* to raise a ban or prohibition

desvelar *vt* to keep awake; *vr* be sleepless; (*with por*) take great care over

desvelo *m*, sleeplessness, vigil; care, attention, vigilance; anxiety. **con d.**, watchfully

desvencijar *vt* to loosen, disconnect, disjoint; *vr* work loose, become disjointed

desventaja *f*, disadvantage. **estar en d.**, to be at a disadvantage

desventajoso *a* disadvantageous

desventura *f*, misfortune

desventurado *a* unfortunate; timid, faint-hearted; miserly

desvergonzado *a* shameless, brazen, impudent

desvergonzarse *vr irr* to be brazen, be impudent. See **avergonzar**

desvergüenza *f*, insolence; shamelessness

desvestir(se) *vt* and *vr irr* to undress. See **pedir**

desviación *f*, deviation, deflection

desviadero *m*, diversion; *rw* siding

desviar *vt* to divert, deflect; dissuade

desvío *m*, deviation; indifference, coldness; repugnance

desvirgar *vt* to deflower

desvirtuar *vt* to decrease in strength or merit

desvivirse *vr* (*with por*) to adore, love dearly; yearn for, be dying to; do one's best to please, (e.g. **Juan se desvive por servirme,** John does his best to help me)

detallar *vt* to tell in detail; relate

detalle *m*, detailed account; detail, particular

detallismo *m*, meticulous attention to details

detective *mf* detective

detector *m*, detector; *rad* catwhisker

detención *f*, stop, halt; delay; prolixity; arrest, detention. **con d.**, carefully, meticulously

detener *vt irr* to detain, stop; arrest; retain, keep; *vr* go

slowly; tarry; halt, stop; (*with en*) pause over, stop at. See **tener**

detenido *a* timid, irresolute; miserable, mean

deterioración *f*, deterioration

deteriorar(se) *vt* and *vr* to deteriorate

determinación *f*, determination; daring; decision

determinado *a* resolute, determined

determinar *vt* to determine, limit; discern, distinguish; specify, appoint; decide, resolve; *law* define, judge; *vr* make up one's mind

determinativo *a* determining

determinismo *m*, determinism

determinista *mf* determinist. *a* deterministic

detersorio *a* and *m*, detergent

detestable *a* detestable

detestación *f*, detestation

detestar *vt* to abominate, detest

detonación *f*, detonation

detonador *m*, detonator

detonar *vi* to detonate

detracción *f*, detraction

detractor (-ra) *a* slandering *n* detractor, slanderer

detraer *vt irr* to detract, take away; separate; slander. See **traer**

detrás *adv* behind, after (place). **por d.**, in the rear; *fig* behind one's back

detrimento *m*, detriment; moral harm. **en d. de**, to the detriment of

deuda *f*, debt; fault, offence; sin. **d. exterior,** foreign debt. **estar en d. con,** to be indebted to. **Perdónanos nuestras deudas,** Forgive us our trespasses

deudo *m*, relative, kinsman; kinship, relationship

deudor (-ra) *a* indebted. *n* debtor. **d. hipotecario,** mortgagor

devanadera *f*, bobbin, reel, spool; winder (machine)

devanador (-ra) *n* winder (person). *m*, spool, bobbin

devanar *vt* to reel, wind. *inf* **devanarse los sesos,** to rack one's brains

devanear *vi* to rave, talk nonsense

devaneo *m*, delirium; foolishness, nonsense; dissipation; love affair

devastación *f*, devastation

devastar *vt* to devastate, lay waste; *fig* destroy, ruin

develador *m*, betrayer

devengar *vt* to have a right to, earn (salary, interest, etc.)

devoción *f*, piety; affection, love; pious custom; prayer

devocionario *m*, prayer book

devolución *f*, restitution, return; its devolution

devolutivo *a law* returnable

devolver *vt irr* to restore to original state; return, give back; repay. See **resolver**

devorador (-ra) *a* devouring. *n* devourer

devorar *vt* to devour; destroy, consume

devoto (-ta) *a* devout, pious; devoted, fond. *n* devotee. *m*, object of devotion

día *m*, day; daylight; *pl* name or saint's day; birthday (e.g. **Hoy son los días de María,** This is Mary's saint's day (or birthday)). **d. de Año Nuevo,** New Year's Day. **d. de asueto,** day off. **d. de ayuno** or **de vigilia,** fast day. **d. del cura,** *humorous* wedding day. **d. del juicio,** Day of Judgment. **d. de los difuntos,** All Souls' Day. **d. de recibo,** at home day. **d. de Reyes,** Epiphany (when Spanish children receive their Christmas presents). **d. de trabajo** or **d. laborable,** working day. **d. por medio,** every other day. **días caniculares,** dog days. **d. por d.,** day by day. **al d.,** up to date; per day. **al otro d.,** next day. **¡Buenos días!** Good morning! Good day! **de d.,** by day. **d. en d.,** from day to day. **de un d. a otro,** any time now, very soon. **el d. de mañana,** tomorrow, the near future. **un d. sí y otro no,** every other day. **vivir al d.,** to live up to one's income

diabético *a* diabetic

diablillo *m*, *dim* devilkin, imp; *inf* madcap

diablo *m*, devil; Satan; *fig* fiend. *inf* **d. cojuelo,** mischievous devil; *fig inf* imp. *inf* **Anda el d. suelto,** The Devil's abroad, there's trouble. *inf* **tener el d. en el cuerpo,** to be as clever as the Devil; be mischievous

diablura *f,* mischief, prank; devilry

diabólico *a* diabolical, devilish; *inf* fiendish, iniquitous

diaconisa *f,* deaconess

diácono *m,* deacon

diadema *f,* diadem; crown; tiara

diafanidad *f,* transparency

diáfano *a* transparent, diaphanous

diafragma *m, anat mech* diaphragm; sound-box (of a phonograph)

diagnosticar *vt med* to diagnose

diagnóstico *a* diagnostic. *m,* diagnosis. **d. precoz,** early diagnosis

diagonal *a* diagonal; oblique

diagrama *m,* diagram

diagramación *f,* layout (of a publication)

dialectal *a* dialect

dialéctica *f,* dialectic

dialéctico *a* dialectic. *m,* logician

dialecto *m,* dialect

dialogar *vi* to hold dialogue, converse; *vt* write dialogue

diálogo *m,* dialogue

diamante *m,* diamond; miner's lamp; glass-cutting diamond. **d. bruto,** rough diamond

diamantífero *a* diamond-bearing

diamantino *a* diamantine; *poet* adamant

diamantista *mf* diamond-cutter; diamond merchant

diametral *a* diametrical

diámetro *m,* diameter

diana *f, mil* reveille; bull's-eye (of a target); the moon

¡diantre! *interj inf* the deuce!   ♦

diapasón *m, mus* tuning fork; diapason; neck (of violins, etc.). **d. normal,** tuning fork. **d. vocal,** pitch-pipe

diapositiva *f, phot* diapositive; (lantern) slide

diario *a* daily. *m,* diary; daily paper; daily expenses. **d. de navegación,** ship's log. **d. de viaje,** travel diary, trip journal

diarista *mf* journalist, diarist

diarrea *f,* diarrhea

diatónico *a mus* diatonic

diatriba *f,* diatribe

diávolo *m,* diabolo (game)

dibujante *m,* sketcher; draftsman; designer

dibujar *vt art* to draw; describe, depict; *vr* appear, be revealed; be outlined, stand out

dibujo *m,* drawing; sketch, design, pattern; depiction, description. **d. a la pluma,** pen-and-ink drawing. **d. a pulso,** freehand drawing. **d. del natural,** drawing from life

dicción *f,* word; diction, language, style

diccionario *m,* dictionary

díceres *m pl WH* news

diciembre *m,* December

dictado *m,* title of honor; dictation; *pl* promptings (of heart, etc.). **escribir al d.,** to write to dictation

dictador *m,* dictator

dictadura *f,* dictatorship

dictáfono *m,* dictaphone

dictamen *m,* judgment, opinion

dictaminar *vi* to give judgment or opinion

dictar *vt* to dictate; suggest, inspire. **dictar fallo,** to hand down a decision, render judgment

dictatorial, dictatorio *a* dictatorial

dicterio *m,* taunt, insult

dicha *f,* happiness; good fortune. **por d.,** by chance; fortunately

dicharacho *m, inf* vulgar expression, slangy expression

dicho *m,* saying; phrase, expression; witty remark; *law* declaration; *inf* insult. *past part* **decir,** "said." **D. y hecho,** No sooner said than done. **Del d. al hecho hay muy gran trecho,** There's many a slip 'twixt the cup and the lip. **Lo d. d.,** The agreement stands

dichoso *a* happy; lucky; *inf* blessed, wretched, darn

didáctica *f,* didactics

didáctico *a* didactic

diecinueve *a* and *m,* nineteen

diecinuevavo *a* and *m,* nineteenth

dieciochavo *a* and *m,* eighteenth

dieciocheno *a* See **décimoctavo**

dieciocho *a* and *m,* eighteen

dieciséis *a* and *m,* sixteen

dieciseisavo *a* and *m,* sixteenth

dieciseiseno *a* See **décimosexto**

diecisiete *a* and *m,* seventeen

diecisieteavo *a* and *m,* seventeenth

diente *m,* tooth; tooth (of saw, etc.); tusk; cog (of wheel); prong (of fork); tongue (of a buckle). **d. de leche,** milk-tooth. **d. de león,** dandelion. **d. de perro,** *sew* feather-stitch. *inf* **dar d. con d.,** to chatter (teeth). *fig inf* **enseñar** (*or* **mostrar**) **los dientes,** to show one's teeth; threaten. *inf* **estar a d.,** to be famished. **hablar entre dientes,** to mutter; fume, grumble. *inf* **tener buen d.,** to have a good appetite. **traer a uno entre dientes,** to loathe someone; speak scandal of

Diepa Dieppe

diestra *f,* right hand; protection

diestro *a* right (hand); skilful, dextrous; shrewd; astute, cunning; favorable. happy. *m,* expert fencer; bullfighter; halter; bridle

dieta *f, med* diet; *inf* fast, abstinence; legislative assembly; travel allowance (gen. *pl*); day's journey of ten leagues; daily fee (gen. *pl*)

dietario *m,* household accounts' book

dietética *f,* dietetics

dietético *a* dietetic

dietista *mf* dietician

diez *a* ten; tenth. *m,* ten; decade of rosary

diezmar *vt* to tithe; decimate; punish every tenth person

diezmero (-ra) *n* tax-gatherer

diezmesino *a* ten months old

diezmilésimo *a* ten-thousandth

diezmo *m,* ten per cent tax; tithe

difamación *f,* defamation, libel

difamador (-ra) *a* libeling. *n* libeler

difamar *vt* to libel; denigrate

difamatorio *a* libelous, defamatory

diferencia *f,* unlikeness, dissimilarity; *math* difference; dissension, disagreement. **a d. de,** unlike; in contrast to

diferenciación *f,* differentiation. **d. del trabajo,** division of labor

diferencial *a* differential

diferenciar *vt* to differentiate; change the function (of); *vi* dissent, disagree; *vr* be different, differ; distinguish oneself

diferente *a* different, various

diferir *vt irr* to delay, retard; postpone; suspend, interrupt; *vi* be different. See **discernir**

difícil *a* difficult

dificultad *f,* difficulty; impediment, obstacle; objection

dificultar *vt* to raise difficulties; put obstacles in the way; *vi* think difficult (of achievements)

dificultoso *a* difficult; *inf* ugly (face, figure, etc.)

difidencia *f,* mistrust; lack of faith, doubt

difidente *a* mistrustful

difracción *f,* diffraction

difractar *vt* to diffract

difteria *f,* diphtheria

difundir *vt* to diffuse (fluids); spread, publish, divulge; *rad* broadcast

difunto (-ta) *a* and *n* deceased. *m,* corpse

difusión *f,* diffusion; prolixity; *rad* broadcasting

difusivo *a* diffusive

difuso *a* widespread, diffuse; prolix, wordy

digerible *a* digestible

digerir *vt irr* to digest; bear patiently; consider carefully; *chem* digest. See **sentir**

digestible *a* easily digested
digestivo *a* digestive
digesto *m*, law digest
digitación *f, mus* fingering
digital *a* digital. *f, bot* foxglove, digitalis
dígito *a* digital. *m, (ast math)* digit
dignación *f*, condescension
dignarse *vr* to deign, condescend
dignatario *m*, dignitary
dignidad *f*, dignity, stateliness; serenity, loftiness; high office or rank; high repute, honor; *ecc* dignitary
dignificar *vt* to dignify
digno *a* worthy, deserving; upright, honorable; fitting, suitable, appropriate
digresión *f*, digression
dije *m*, charm; trinket, any small piece of jewelry; *inf* person of excellent qualities, jewel
dilacerar *vt* to lacerate, tear flesh; *fig* discredit
dilación *f*, delay
dilapidación *f*, waste, dissipation, squandering
dilapidar *vt* to waste, squander
dilatación *f*, expansion; enlargement, widening; prolongation; *surg* dilatation; respite (in trouble)
dilatador *a* dilating. *m, surg* dilater
dilatar *vt* to dilate, enlarge; expand; delay, postpone; spread, publish abroad; prolong; *vr* expand; be prolix, spread oneself
dilatorio *a* procrastinating, dilatory
dilección *f*, affection, love
dilema *m*, dilemma
diletantismo *m*, dilettantism
diligencia *f*, care, conscientiousness, industry; haste, briskness; diligence (coach); *inf* business, occupation. **hacer sus diligencias,** to try one's best
diligenciar *vt* to set on foot, put into motion
diligente *a* diligent, conscientious, industrious; speedy, prompt
dilucidación *f*, elucidation, clarification
dilucidar *vt* to elucidate, clarify
dilución *f*, dilution
diluir *vt irr* to dilute. See **huir**
diluviano *a* diluvian
diluviar *vi* to teem with rain
diluvio *m*, flood, inundation; *inf* very heavy rain, deluge; overabundance
dimanación *f*, emanation, source
dimanar *vi (with de)* to rise in (rivers); proceed from, originate in
dimensión *f*, dimension; size, extent
dimes y diretes *m pl, inf* back-chat
diminutivo *a* diminutive; diminishing; *gram* diminutive
diminuto *a* defective, incomplete; minute, very small
dimisión *f*, resignation (of office, etc.)
dimisorias *f pl, ecc* letter dimissory. *inf* **dar d. a uno,** to give a person his marching orders, dismiss
dimitente *a* resigning; retiring. *mf* resigner (of a post)
dimitir *vt* to resign (office, post, etc.)
Dinamarca Denmark
dinamarqués (-esa) *a* Danish. *n* Dane
dinámica *f*, dynamics
dinámico *a* dynamic
dinamita *f*, dynamite
dinamo *f*, dynamo
dinasta *mf* dynast
dinastía *f*, dynasty
dinástico *a* dynastic
dineral *m*, large amount of money, fortune
dinero *m*, money; Peruvian coin; wealth, fortune; currency. **d. contante, d. junto,** ready cash, **Poderoso caballero es Don D.,** Money talks
dinosauro *m*, dinosaur
dintel *m*, lintel
diocesano *a* diocesan
diocesis *f*, diocese
Dios *m*, God; deity. **¡D. le guarde!** God keep you! **¡D.**

lo quiera! God grant it! **D. mediante,** God willing (D.V.). **¡D. mío!** Good gracious! **De menos nos hizo D.,** Nothing is impossible, Never say die. *inf* **haber** (*or* armarse) **la de D. es Cristo,** to be the deuce of a row. **¡No lo quiera D.!** God forbid! **¡Plegue a D.!** Please God! **¡Por D.!** For goodness sake! Heavens! **¡Válgame D.!** Bless me! **¡Vaya Vd. con D.!** Goodbye! Off with you! Depart! **¡Vive D.!** By God!
diosa *f*, goddess
diploma *m*, license, bull; diploma. **d. de suficiencia,** general diploma
diplomacia *f*, diplomacy; tactfulness; *inf* astuteness
diplomático *a* diplomatic; tactful; *inf* astute. *m*, diplomat. **cuerpo d.,** diplomatic corps
dipsomanía *f*, dipsomania
dipsómano (-na) *n* dipsomaniac
diptongo *m*, diphthong
diputación *f*, deputation; mission
diputado (-da) *n* deputy, delegate. **d. a Cortes,** member of the Spanish Parliament, congressman
diputar *vt* to appoint, depute; delegate; empower
dique *m*, dike; dam; dry dock; *fig* bulwark, check; **d. flotante,** floating dock
dirección *f*, direction; management, control, guidance; directorate; instruction; information; order, wish, command; editorial board; directorship, managership; (postal) address; managerial office. **d. cablegráfica,** cable address. **d. particular,** home address
directiva *f*, board, governing body
directivo *a* directive, control, ling, guiding, managing
directo *a* direct; straight
director (-ra) *a* directing, controlling. *n* director; manager; principal, head (schools, etc.); editor. **d. del ceremonial,** chief of protocol. **d. de escena,** stagemanager. **d. espiritual,** *ecc* father confessor. **d. gerente,** managing director
directorio *a* directory, advising. *m*, directory; directorate, board of directors
dirigible *m*, airship
dirigir *vt* to direct; regulate; govern; supervise; guide; *mus* conduct; address (an envelope, etc.); keep (a shop, etc.); edit; put (a question); point (a gun); cast (a glance); *vr* go; wend one's way. **d. la palabra (a),** to speak to, address. **d. la vista a,** to look towards, look in the direction of, turn towards, turn in the direction of
dirigirse a, to go towards; make one's way to
dirimir *vt* to annul, make void; break, dissolve; settle (disputes, etc.)
discernidor (-ra) *n* discerner. *a* discerning
discernimiento *m*, discernment; judgment; discrimination
discernir *vt irr* to discern, distinguish. *Pres. Ind.* **discierno, disciernes, discierne, disciernen.** *Pres. Subjunc.* **discierna, disciernas, discierna, disciernan**
disciplina *f*, discipline; system, philosophy, education; submission, obedience; subject (arts or science); *pl* scourge
disciplinante *a* disciplinary. *m*, scourge
disciplinar *vt* to train; educate; scourge, beat; discipline; *vr* scourge oneself
disciplinario *a* disciplinary
discipulado *m*, pupilship, studentship; discipleship, teaching; discipleship; body of pupils (of a school, etc.)
discípulo (-la) *n* pupil, student; disciple, follower
disco *m*, discus; disk; phonograph record; *ast* disk. **d. de señales,** railway signal. **d. giratorio,** turntable (of a phonograph)
discóbolo *m*, discus thrower
díscolo *a* willful, unmanageable
disconformidad *f*, disagreement; disconformity
discontinuo *a* intermittent, discontinuous
discordancia *f*, discord, disagreement
discordar *vi* to be discordant; disagree; *mus* be out of tune
discorde *a* discordant; *mus* dissonant
discordia *f*, discord, disagreement

discreción *f*, discretion; circumspection; prudence, good sense; shrewdness; pithy or clever saying. **a d.,** at discretion; at will; voluntarily. *mil* **darse** (*or* **entregarse**) **a d.,** to surrender unconditionally
discrecional *a* optional, voluntary
discrepancia *f*, discrepancy; disagreement
discrepar *vi* to be discrepant; differ; disagree
discreto *a* discreet; ingenious, witty
disculpa *f*, excuse
disculpabilidad *f*, pardonableness
disculpable *a* excusable
disculpar *vt* to excuse; forgive, pardon; *vr* apologize; excuse oneself
discurrir *vi* to wander, roam; flow, run (rivers, etc.); (*with en*) consider, think about; (*with sobre*) discourse on; *vt* invent; conjecture
discursivo *a* discursive; thoughtful, reflective
discurso *m*, reasoning power; oration, discourse; consideration, reflection; speech, conversation; dissertation. **d. aceptatorio,** acceptance speech
discusión *f*, discussion
discutible *a* debatable; disputable
discutir *vt* to discuss, debate, consider
disecar *vt anat* to dissect; stuff animals; mount plants
disección *f*, dissection
disector *m*, dissector, anatomist
diseminación *f*, dissemination
diseminar *vt* to disseminate; spread
disensión *f*, dissension
disentería *f*, dysentery
disentimiento *m*, dissent
disentir *vi irr* to dissent; disagree. See **sentir**
diseñador *m*, delineator, drawer
diseñar *vt* to outline, sketch
diseño *m*, outline, sketch; plan; description
disertación *f*, dissertation
disertar *vi* (*with sobre*) to discourse on, discuss, treat of
diserto *a* eloquent
disfavor *m*, disfavor, discourtesy, slight
disforme *a* deformed; ugly; enormous
disfraz *m*, disguise; mask; fancy dress; pretence
disfrazar *vt* to disguise; dissemble, misrepresent; *vr* disguise oneself; wear fancy dress
disfrutar *vt* to enjoy (health, comfort, friendship, etc.); reap the benefit of; *vi* take pleasure in, enjoy
disfrute *m*, enjoyment, use, benefit
disgregación *f*, separation, disjunction
disgregar *vt* to separate, disjoin
disgustado *a* annoyed; discontented, dissatisfied; melancholy, depressed
disgustar *vt* to displease, dissatisfy; annoy; *fig* depress; *vr* quarrel, fall out. **Me disgusta la idea de marcharme,** I don't like the idea of going away
disgusto *m*, displeasure, dissatisfaction; discontent; annoyance; affliction, sorrow, trouble; quarrel; boredom; repugnance
disidente *a* dissenting. *mf* dissenter, nonconformist
disidir *vi* to dissent
disímil *a* dissimilar, different, unlike
disimulación *f*, dissimulation, pretence
disimulado *a* feigned, pretended
disimular *vt* to dissemble; pretend, feign; put up with, tolerate; misrepresent, misinterpret
disimulo *m*, pretence, dissimulation; tolerance, patience
disipación *f*, dispersion; dissipation, frivolity; immorality
disipado *a* spendthrift; dissipated, frivolous
disipar *vt* to disperse; squander; *vr* evaporate; vanish, fade, disappear
dislate *m*, absurdity, nonsense
dislocación *f*, dislocation
dislocar *vt* to dislocate; *vr* dislocate; sprain
disminución *f*, diminution. **ir (una cosa) en d.,** to diminish, decrease; taper, grow to a point
disminuido físico *m*, physically impaired person, physically handicapped person

disminuir *vt and vi irr* to diminish, decrease. See **huir**
disociación *f*, dissociation. **d. nuclear,** nuclear fission
disociar *vt* to dissociate, separate; *chem* dissociate
disoluble *a* dissoluble
disolución *f*, dissolution; immorality, laxity; disintegration; loosening, relaxation
disolutivo *a* dissolvent, solvent
disoluto *a* dissolute, vicious
disolvente *m*, dissolvent, solvent
disolver *vt irr* to loosen, undo; *chem* dissolve; separate, disintegrate; annul. See **resolver**
disonancia *f*, dissonance; disagreement; *mus* dissonant
disonante *a* dissonant; discordant, inharmonious
disonar *vi irr* to be inharmonious; disagree. See **sonar**
dísono *a* dissonant
dispar *a* unequal; unlike, different
disparadero *m*, trigger of a firearm
disparador *m*, shooter, firer; trigger (of firearms); ratchet (of watch)
disparar *vt* to shoot, fire; throw or discharge with violence; *vr* run precipitately; rush (towards); bolt (horses); race (of a machine); explode, go off; *inf* go too far, misbehave
disparatado *a* foolish; absurd, unreasonable
disparatar *vi* to act or speak foolishly
disparate *m*, foolishness, nonsense
disparidad *f*, disparity, dissimilarity
disparo *m*, shooting; explosion; racing (of an engine); discharge; foolishness
dispendio *m*, squandering, extravagance
dispendioso *a* costly, expensive
dispensa *f*, dispensation; privilege
dispensable *a* dispensable; excusable
dispensación *f*, dispensation; exemption
dispensar *vt* to grant, concede, distribute; exempt; excuse, forgive
dispensario *m*, dispensary
dispepsia *f*, dyspepsia
dispéptico (**-ca**) *a* and *n* dyspeptic
dispersar *vt* to disperse, scatter, separate; *mil* rout
dispersión *f*, dispersion
disperso *a* dispersed, scattered; *mil* separated from regiment
displicencia *f*, disagreeableness, coldness; hesitation, lack of enthusiasm
displicente *a* unpleasant, disagreeable; difficult, peevish
disponer *vt irr* to arrange, dispose; direct, order; decide; prepare, get ready; *vi* (*with de*) dispose of, make free with; possess; have at one's disposal; *vr* prepare oneself to die; make one's will; get ready. See **poner**
disponible *a* disposable; available
disposición *f*, arrangement; order, instruction; decision; preparation; aptitude, talent; disposal; condition of health; temperament; grace of bearing; promptitude, competence; measure, step, preliminary; *arch* plan; proviso, stipulation; symmetry. **A la d. de Vd,** I (we, he, it, etc.) am at your disposal. **hallarse en d. de hacer una cosa,** to be ready to do something. **última d.,** last will and testament
dispositivo *a* directory, advisory
dispuesto *a* ready, prepared; handsome, gallant; clever, wide-awake. **bien d.,** well-disposed; well, healthy. **mal d.,** ill-disposed; disinclined; out of sorts, indisposed
disputa *f*, dispute. **sin d.,** undoubtedly
disputar *vt* to argue, debate; dispute, question; *fig* fight for
disquisición *f*, disquisition
distancia *f*, distance; interval of time; difference, dissimilarity; unfriendliness, coolness
distanciar *vt* to separate, place farther apart
distante *a* separated; distant; far off
distar *vi* to be distant (time and place); be different, unlike
distender(se) *vt and vr med* to distend, swell

distinción *f,* distinction, differentiation; difference, individuality; privilege, honor; clarity, order; distinction (of bearing or mind). **a d. de,** unlike, different from

distinguible *a* distinguishable

distinguido *a* distinguished, illustrious

distinguir *vt* to distinguish, discern; differentiate; characterize; esteem, honor, respect; discriminate; see with difficulty; make out; *vr* be different; excel, distinguish oneself

distintivo *a* distinguishing; distinctive. *m,* distinguishing mark

distinto *a* different; distinct; clear

distracción *f,* distraction; abstraction, heedlessness, absentmindedness; pleasure, amusement; licentiousness

distraer *vt irr* to lead astray; distract (attention); influence for bad; amuse. *vr* be absentminded; amuse oneself. See **traer**

distraído *a* abstracted, absentminded; inattentive; licentious

distribución *f,* distribution; (gen. *pl*) share

distribuidor (-ra) *a* distributing. *n* distributor

distribuir *vt irr* to distribute; share out, divide. See **huir**

distributivo *a* distributive

distrito *m,* district

disturbio *m,* disturbance

disuadir *vt* to dissuade

disuasión *f,* dissuasion

disuasivo *a* dissuasive

disyunción *f,* disjunction

ditirambo *m,* dithyramb; excessive praise

diurético *a* diuretic

diurno *a* diurnal

diva *f,* prima donna; woman singer

divagación *f,* wandering, roaming; digression

divagar *vi* to wander, roam; digress

diván *m,* divan (Turkish supreme council); divan, sofa; collection of Arabic, Persian or Turkish poems

divergencia *f,* divergence; disagreement

divergente *a* divergent; conflicting, dissentient

divergir *vi* to diverge; dissent

diversidad *f,* diversity, unlikeness, difference; variety

diversificar *vt* to differentiate; vary

diversión *f,* pastime, amusement; *mil* diversion

diverso *a* diverse, unlike; *pl* various, many

divertido *a* amusing, funny, entertaining

divertir *vt irr* to lead astray, turn aside; entertain; *mil* create a diversion. *vr* amuse oneself. See **sentir**

dividendo *m,* dividend. *com* **d. activo,** dividend

dividir *vt* to divide; distribute; stir up discord; *vr* (*with de*) part company with, leave

divieso *m, med* boil

divinamente *adv* divinely; excellently, admirably, perfectly

divinidad *f,* divinity, Godhead; person or thing of great beauty

divinizar *vt* to deify; sanctify; extol

divino *a* divine; excellent, admirable, superb

divisa *f,* badge, emblem; *her* motto

divisar *vt* to glimpse, descry

divisibilidad *f,* divisibility

divisible *a* divisible

división *f,* division, partition; discord; (*math mil*) division; hyphen; apportionment; district, ward

divisor (-ra) *a* dividing, separating. *m, math* divisor. *n* divider, separator

divisoria *f,* dividing line

divisorio *a* dividing

divorciar *vt* to divorce; separate; *vr* be divorced, be separated

divorcio *m,* divorce

divulgación *f,* spreading, publication, propagation

divulgar(se) *vt* and *vr* to spread abroad, publish

do *m, mus* doh, C. *poet* where

dobladillo *m, sew* hem; turn-up (of a trouser)

doblado *a* stocky, thickset, sturdy; rocky, rough, uneven; dissembling. *m,* garret

dobladura *f,* fold, crease; crease mark

doblamiento *m,* doubling; folding

doblar *vt* to double, multiply by two; fold, double; bend; persuade, induce; *naut* double, sail round; turn, walk round; *vi ecc* ring the passing bell; *theat* double a role; *vr* fold, double; bend; bow; stoop; allow oneself to be persuaded

doble *a* double, twofold; duplicate; insincere, false; thick (cloth); *bot* double (flowers); hardy, robust. *m,* fold, crease; *ecc* passing-bell; Spanish dance step. *adv* double, twice. *ecc* **rito d.,** full rites

doblegar *vt* to fold; bend; brandish; dissuade in favor of another proposition; *vr* submit, give way, acquiesce

doblete *a* of medium thickness. *m,* imitation jewel

doblez *m,* fold, crease; fold mark. *mf,* double dealing, treachery

doblilla *f,* twenty-real coin

doblón *m,* doubloon

doce *a* twelve. *m,* twelve; twelfth (of the month). **las d.,** twelve o'clock

docena *f,* dozen. **la d. del fraile,** baker's dozen

docente *a* teaching

dócil *a* docile; obedient; flexible, easily worked (metals, etc.)

docilidad *f,* docility; obedience; flexibility

docto *a* learned, erudite

doctor (-ra) *n* doctor; physician; teacher. *f, inf* bluestocking

doctorado *m,* doctorate

doctorarse *vr* to get one's doctorate

doctrina *f,* doctrine; instruction, teaching; theory, conception; *ecc* sermon

doctrinar *vt* to teach, instruct

documentación *f,* documentation; collection of documents, papers

documental *a* documental. *m,* documentary film

documentar *vt* to document

Dodecaneso, el the Dodecanese

dogal *m,* halter; noose; slipknot. *fig* **estar con el d. a la garganta,** to be in a fix

dogma *m,* dogma

dogmático *a* dogmatic

dogmatizar *vt* to teach heretical doctrines; dogmatize

dólar *m,* dollar

dolencia *f,* ailment; pain; ache

doler *vi irr* to be in pain; be reluctant; *vr* be sorry, regretful; grieve; sympathize, be compassionate; complain. *Pres. Ind.* **duelo, dueles, duele, duelen.** *Pres. Subjunc.* **duela, duelas, duela, duelan**

doliente *a* suffering; ill; afflicted, sad. *mf* sufferer, ill person. *m,* chief mourner

dolo *m,* fraud; deception; deceit; *law* premeditation

dolor *m,* pain, ache; mental suffering. **d. sordo,** dull pain

dolorido *a* painful; afflicted, sad

doloroso *a* sad, regrettable; mournful, sorrowful; pitiful; painful

doloso *a* deceitful, fraudulent

domable *a* tamable; controllable

domador (-ra) *n* subduer, controller; wild animal tamer; horsebreaker

domadura *f,* taming, breaking in; controlling (emotions)

domar *vt* to tame, break in; control, repress (emotions)

domesticable *a* tamable; domesticable

domesticar *vt* to tame; domesticate; *vr* grow tame; become domesticated

domesticidad *f,* domesticity

doméstico (-ca) *a* domestic, domesticated; tame. *n* domestic worker

domiciliar *vt* to domicile; *vr* become domiciled, settle down

domiciliario *a* domiciliary

domicilio *m,* domicile; house

dominación *f,* domination; power, authority; command (of a military position, etc.); *mil* high ground; *pl* dominions, angels

dominador *a* dominating; overbearing

dominante *a* dominating; overbearing, domineering; dominant. *f, mus* dominant

dominar *vt* to dominate; repress, subdue; *fig* master (branch of knowledge); *vi* stand out; *vr* control oneself

dómine *m, inf* teacher; pedant, know-all

domingo *m,* Sunday. **d. de Cuasimodo,** Low Sunday. **d. de Pentecostés,** Whitsuntide Sunday. **d. de Ramos,** Palm Sunday. **d. de Resurrección,** Easter Sunday

dominguero *a inf* Sunday; special, excursion (trains)

dominicano (-na) *a* and *n* Dominican; native of Santo Domingo

dominio *m,* authority, power; rule, sovereignty; dominion (country); domain

dominó *m,* domino; game of dominoes

don *m,* gift; quality, characteristic; talent. **d. de gentes,** the human touch; charm

don *m,* title of respect equivalent to English Mr. or Esquire. Used only before given name and *not* before a family name, e.g. **don Juan Martínez,** *or* **don Juan**

donación *f,* donation, gift, grant

donador (-ra) *a* donating. *n* donor

donaire *m,* discretion, wit; witticism; gracefulness, elegance

donar *vt* to bestow, give; transfer; grant

donatario *m,* recipient, grantee

donativo *m,* gift, present, donation

doncel *m,* squire, youth not yet armed; knight; male virgin; king's page

doncella *f,* virgin, maid; maidservant; lady's maid

doncellez *f,* virginity; maidenhood

donde *adv* where, wherein. Sometimes used as relative pronoun "in which" (e.g. **La casa d. estaba,** The house in which I was). *interrog* **¿dónde? ¿A dónde va Vd.?** Where are you going to? **¿De dónde viene Vd.?** Where do you come from? **¿Por dónde se va a Madrid?** Which is the way to Madrid?

dondequiera *adv* wherever, anywhere, everywhere

donoso *a* witty; graceful

donostiarra *a* and *mf* of or from San Sebastian (N. Spain)

donosura *f,* wit; grace; dash, verve

doña *f,* feminine equivalent of **don** (e.g. **D. Catalina Palacios)**

dorado *a* golden, gilded; fortunate, happy. *m,* gilding

dorador *m,* gilder

doradura *f,* gilding

dorar *vt* to gild; make golden; *fig* gild the pill; *cul* toast lightly; *vr* become golden

dórico *a* Doric

dormidero *a* soporiferous, narcotic

dormilón (-ona) *a inf* sleepy. *n* sleepyhead

dormir *vi irr* to sleep; spend the night; *fig* grow calm; sleep (tops); (*with sobre*) sleep on, consider; *vt* put to sleep; *vr* go to sleep; go slow over, neglect; be dormant; go numb (limbs). **d. como un lirón,** to sleep like a top. *inf* **d. la mona,** to sleep oneself sober. **entre duerme y vela,** half-awake. *Pres. Ind.* **duermo, duermes, duerme, duermen.** *Pres. Part.* **durmiendo.** *Preterite* **durmió, durmieron.** *Pres. Subjunc.* **duerma, duermas, duerma, duerman**

dormitar *vi* to doze

dormitivo *a* and *m,* sedative

dormitorio *m,* dormitory; bedroom

dorsal *a* dorsal

dorso *m,* back; dorsum

dos *a* two. *m,* two; second (of the month). **las d.,** two o'clock. **d. a d.,** two against two. **de d. en d.,** two by two. *inf* **en un d. por tres,** in a twinkling

doscientos *a* and *m,* two hundred; two hundredth

dosel *m,* canopy; dais

dosis *f,* dose; quantity

dotación *f,* endowment; *naut* crew; staff, workers; equipment

dotar *vt* to give as dowry; endow, found; *fig* endow (with talents, etc.); equip; apportion (salary)

dote *mf,* dowry. *f,* (gen. *pl*) gifts, talents. **dotes de mando,** capacity for leadership

dracma *f,* drachma; dram

draga *f,* dredger

dragado *m,* dredging

dragaminas *m, nav* minesweeper

dragar *vt* to dredge

dragón *m,* dragon; *bot* snapdragon; *mil* dragoon; *zool* dragon, giant lizard; *ast* Draco

dragona *f,* female dragon; *mil* shoulder-strap

drama *m,* play; drama. **d. lírico,** opera

dramática *f,* dramatic art

dramático *a* dramatic; vivid, unexpected, moving

dramaturgo *m,* dramatist, playwright

drenaje *m,* drainage (of land and wounds)

Dresde Dresden

dril *m,* drill, cotton cloth

droga *f,* drug; falsehood, deception; nuisance

droguería *f,* chemist's shop; drug trade

droguero (-ra) *n* chemist, druggist

dromedario *m, zool* dromedary

druida *m,* Druid

dualidad *f,* duality

ducado *m,* dukedom; duchy; ducat

ducentésimo *a* two hundredth

ducha *f,* shower-bath; douche; stripe in cloth; furrow

ducho *a* experienced, skilful

dúctil *a* ductile (metals); adaptable, docile, flexible

ductilidad *f,* ductility; adaptability

duda *f,* doubt, hesitation; problem. **sin d.,** doubtless

dudable *a* doubtful

dudar *vi* to be in doubt; *vt* doubt, disbelieve

dudoso *a* doubtful; uncertain, not probable

duela *f,* hoop, stave

duelista *mf* dueler; duelist

duelo *m,* sorrow, grief; mourning; mourners; duel; (gen. *pl*) troubles, trials. **duelos y quebrantos,** *cul* fried offal. **sin d.,** in abundance

duende *m,* imp, elf, sprite, ghost

dueña *f,* owner, proprietress, mistress; duenna; married lady *ant*

dueño *m,* owner, proprietor; master (of servants). **d. de sí mismo,** self-controlled

Duero, el the Douro

duetista *mf* duetist

dula *f,* common pasture ground or herds

dulce *a* sweet; fresh, pure; fresh, not salty; fragrant; melodious; pleasant, agreeable; tender, gentle; soft (metals). *m,* sweetmeat, bonbon. **d. de almíbar,** preserved fruit.

dulcedumbre *f,* sweetness; softness

dulcémele *m,* dulcimer

dulcera *f,* preserve dish, fruit dish

dulcería *f,* See **confitería**

dulcificar *vt* to make sweet; alleviate, sweeten

dulcinea *f, inf* sweetheart; ideal

dulzaina *f, mus* flageolet

dulzura *f,* sweetness; gentleness; pleasure; meekness; agreeableness

duna *f,* (gen. *pl*) sand dune

Dunas, las the Downs

Dunquerque Dunkirk

dúo *m, mus* duet

duodécimo *a* twelfth

duodeno *a* twelfth. *m, anat* duodenum

duplicación *f,* duplication

duplicado *m,* duplicate

duplicar *vt* to duplicate; double

duplicidad *f,* duplicity, falseness

duplo *a* double

duque *m,* duke

duquesa *f,* duchess

duración *f,* duration; durability

duradero *a* lasting; durable
durante *adv* during
durar *vi* to continue; endure, last
dureza *f,* hardness; *med* callosity; severity, harshness
durmiente *a* sleeping. *mf* sleeper; *m, arch* dormant
duro *a* hard; firm, unyielding; vigorous, robust; severe, inclement; exacting, cruel; *mus* metallic, harsh; *art* crude, too sharply defined; miserly, avaricious; obstinate; self-opinionated; unbearable, intolerable; merciless, hard; harsh (style). *m,* Spanish coin worth five pesetas
dux *m,* doge

E

e *f,* letter E. *conjunc* used instead of *y* (and) before words beginning with *i* or *hi,* provided this last is not followed by a diphthong (e.g. **e invierno, e hijos,** *but* **y hierro**)
¡ea! *interj* Well!; Come on!; Let's see! (often used with **pues**)
ebanista *mf* cabinetmaker
ebanistería *f,* cabinetmaker's shop; cabinetmaking or work
ébano *m,* ebony
ebonita *f,* ebonite, vulcanite
ebrio *a* intoxicated, inebriated
ebullición *f,* boiling, ebullition
ebúrneo *a* eburnine, ivory-like
echada *f,* throw, cast; pitch; fling; length of a man
echador (-ra) *n* thrower. *m, inf* chucker-out
echadura *f,* sitting on eggs to hatch them; (gen. *pl*) gleanings
echamiento *m,* throw, fling; throwing, casting; expulsion; rejection
echar *vt* to throw, fling; eject, drive away; cast out, expel; put forth, sprout; emit, give forth; cut (teeth); dismiss, discharge; couple (animals); pour (liquids); place, apply; put into, fill; turn (keys, locks); impute; attribute; impose (penalty, taxes, etc.); play (game); try one's luck; distribute; publish, make known; perform (plays); (*with por*) go in direction of; (*with prep a* + *infin.*) begin to (**e. a andar,** to begin to walk); *vr* throw oneself down, lie down; sit on eggs (birds); abate, calm (wind); apply oneself, concentrate on; rush (towards), fling oneself (upon). **e. abajo,** to overthrow; demolish. **e. aceite al fuego,** to add fuel to the flames. **e. a perder,** to spoil, deteriorate. *naut* **e. a pique,** to sink. **e. a vuelo,** to ring (bells). **e. carnes,** to put on weight, grow fat. **e. cuentas,** to reckon up. **e. de menos,** to miss; mourn absence of. **e. de ver,** to notice. *fig* **e. en cara,** to throw in one's face, reproach. **echarla de majo,** to play the gallant. **e. las cartas al correo,** to post the letters. **e. las cartas,** to tell fortunes. **e. el pie atrás,** *fig* to climb down; *fig* back out. **e. raíces,** to take root; **e. las bases de, e. los cimientos de,** to lay the foundation of, lay the foundation for. *fig* become established. **e. rayos por la boca,** to fly into a rage. **e. suertes,** to draw lots. **echarlo todo a rodar,** to spoil everything. **e. una mano,** to lend a hand
echazón *f,* throw, cast; jetsam
eclecticismo *m,* eclecticism
ecléctico (-ca) *a* and *n* eclectic
eclesiástico *a* ecclesiastical. *m,* ecclesiastic, clergyman; Ecclesiasticus
eclipsar *vt ast* to eclipse; surpass, outvie; *vr ast* be in eclipse; disappear
eclipse *m, ast* eclipse; retirement, withdrawal
écloga *f,* eclogue
eco *m,* echo; verse-echo; muffled sound; slavish imitation or imitator
economato *m,* trusteeship; cooperative store
econometría *f,* econometrics
economía *f,* economy, thrift; structure, organization; poverty, shortage; saving (of time, labor, etc.); *pl* savings. **e. dirigida,** planned economy. **e. doméstica,** domestic economy. **e. política,** political economy
económico *a* economic; thrifty; avaricious; cheap
economista *mf* economist
economizar *vt* to economize; save
ecónomo *m,* trustee, guardian

ecuación *f,* (*math* and *ast*) equation. **e. personal,** personal equation
ecuador *m,* equator
ecuánime *a* calm, unruffled; impartial
ecuanimidad *f,* calmness, serenity; impartiality
ecuatorial *a* equatorial
ecuatoriano (-na) *a* and *n* Ecuadorian
ecuestre *a* equestrian
ecuménico *a* ecumenical
eczema *m,* eczema
edad *f,* age; epoch; period. **e. de piedra,** Stone Age. **e. media,** Middle Ages. **de cierta e.,** middle-aged. **ser mayor de e.,** to have attained one's majority. **ser menor de e.,** to be a minor
edecán *m,* aide-de-camp
edema *m,* edema
Edén *m,* Eden; *fig* paradise
edición *f,* edition. **e. diamante,** miniature edition. **e. príncipe,** first edition
edicto *m,* edict, decree; public notice
edificación *f,* building, construction; edification
edificador (-ra) *a* uplifting, edifying; building. *n* builder
edificante *a* building, constructing; edifying
edificar *vt* to build, construct; edify
edificio *m,* building, structure, fabric
Edimburgo Edinburgh
editar *vt* (of a publisher) to publish; edit
editor (-ra) *n* publisher; editor
editorial *a* publishing; editorial. *m,* editorial, leading article
edredón *m,* down of an eiderduck; eiderdown, quilt
eduardiano (-na) *a* and *n* Edwardian
educable *a* educable
educación *f,* upbringing; education; good breeding, good manners
educado *a* educated. **ser mal e.,** to be badly brought up; be ill-mannered
educador (-ra) *a* educating. *n* educator
educando (-da) *n* pupil
educar *vt* to educate; bring up, train, teach, develop
educativo *a* educational, educative
educción *f,* eduction; inference, deduction
educir *vt irr* to educe; infer, deduce. See **conducir**
efe *f,* name of letter F
efectismo *m,* sensationalism; striving after effect
efectista *a* (*art lit*) striking, sensational
efectivo *a* effective; real. *m,* cash. **hacer e.,** to put into effect
efecto *m,* effect, result; purpose, intent; impression; *pl* assets; goods, chattels. **efectos de escritorio,** stationery. **efectos públicos,** public securities. **en e.,** in fact, actually. **llevar a e.,** to put into effect; make effective
efectuación *f,* accomplishment, execution
efectuar *vt* to accomplish, effect; make (a payment); *vr* be effected; happen, take place
eferente *a* efferent
efervescencia *f,* effervescence; excitement, enthusiasm
efervescente *a* effervescent
Éfeso Ephesus
eficacia *f,* efficacy; effectiveness
eficaz *a* efficacious; effective
eficiencia *f,* efficiency
eficiente *a* efficient, effective

efigie *f*, effigy; image, representation, symbol
efímero *a* ephemeral; brief
eflorescencia *f*, *chem* efflorescence
efluvio *m*, effluvium; exhalation
efugio *m*, subterfuge, evasion
efusión *f*, effusion; *fig* spate (of words, etc.)
efusivo *a* effusive, expansive
Egeo, Mar Aegean Sea
égida *f*, shield; egis, protection
egipcíaco (-ca), egipcio (-ia) *a* and *n* Egyptian
Egipto Egypt
egiptólogo (-ga) *n* Egyptologist
égloga *f*, eclogue
egoísmo *m*, egoism
egoísta *a* egoistic. *mf* egoist
egolatría *f*, self-love
egotismo *m*, egotism
egotista *a* egotistical. *mf* egotist
egregio *a* distinguished, celebrated
egresado *m*, graduate (of a certain school)
eje *m*, axis; axle-tree; shaft; pivot, fundamental idea. **e. trasero,** rear-axle
ejecución *f*, accomplishment, performance; execution, technique; death penalty
ejecutable *a* feasible, practicable
ejecutante *mf mus* executant, performer
ejecutar *vt* to discharge, perform; put to death; (*art mus*) execute; serve (a warrant, etc.); *law* seize (property)
ejecutivo *a* executive; urgent
ejecutor *m*, executor
ejecutoria *f*, letters patent of nobility; *law* judgment, sentence
ejecutoría *f*, executorship
ejemplar *a* exemplary. *m*, copy, specimen; precedent; example; warning
ejemplificar *vi* to exemplify
ejemplo *m*, example, precedent; illustration, instance; specimen. **dar e.,** to set an example. **por e.,** for example
ejercer *vt* to practise (a profession); perform, fulfil; exercise, use
ejercicio *m*, exercise; practice; performance; exertion, effort; *mil* exercises (gen. *pl*). **ejercicios espirituales,** spiritual exercises. **ejercicios físicos,** physical training
ejercitar *vt* to exercise; train, teach; *vr* exercise; practice
ejército *m*, army
el *def art. m, sing* the
él *pers pron sing m*, he; it (*f*. **ella.** *neut* **ello**) (e.g. **Lo hizo él,** He did it). Also used with prep. (e.g. **Lo hicimos por él,** We did it for him)
elaboración *f*, elaboration, working out
elaborado *a* elaborate
elaborar *vt* to elaborate; produce, work out
elasticidad *f*, elasticity; adaptability
elástico *a* elastic; adaptable. *m*, elastic tape; elastic material
ele *f*, name of letter L
elección *f*, choice; election; selection; discrimination
electivo *a* elective
electo *m*, elect, candidate elect
elector (-ra) *n* elector, voter. *m*, German prince *ant*
electorado *m*, electorate
electoral *a* electoral
electricidad *f*, electricity
electricista *mf* electrician
eléctrico *a* electric; electrical
electrificación *f*, electrification
electrificar *vt* to electrify
electrizar *vt* to electrify; startle; *vr* be electrified
electrocución *f*, electrocution
electrocutar *vt* to electrocute
electrodinámica *f*, electrodynamics
electrodo *m*, electrode
electroimán *m*, electromagnet
electrólisis *f*, electrolysis
electrólito *m*, electrolyte

electrolizar *vt* to electrolyze
electromagnético *a* electromagnetic
electromotriz *a* electromotive. **fuerza e.,** electromotive force
electrón *m*, electron
electroquímica *f*, electrochemistry
electroscopio *m*, electroscope
electrotecnia *f*, electrical engineering
electroterapia *f*, *med* electrotherapy
elefante (-ta) *n* elephant
elefantíasis *f*, elephantiasis
elefantino *a* elephantine
elegancia *f*, elegance, grace; fashionableness; *lit* beauty of style
elegante *a* elegant; graceful, lovely; fashionable, stylish
elegíaco *a* elegiac
elegía *f*, elegy
elegibilidad *f*, eligibility
elegible *a* eligible
elegir *vt irr* to select, prefer; elect. *Pres. Ind.* **elijo, eliges, elige, eligen.** *Pres. Part.* **eligiendo.** *Preterite* **eligió, eligieron.** *Pres. Subj.* **elija,** etc.
elemental *a* elemental; fundamental; elementary
elemento *m*, element; component, constituent; *elec* element; *pl* rudiments. *mil* **elementos de choque,** shock troops
elevación *f*, lifting, raising; height, high ground; elevation; altitude; *fig* eminence; elevation, advancement; ecstasy; raising (of the voice)
elevado *a* sublime, lofty
elevar *vt* to raise, lift; *fig* exalt; *vr* be in ecstasy, be transported. **elevarse de categoría,** to rise in status
elfo *m*, elf
elidir *vt* (phonetics) to elide
eliminación *f*, elimination
eliminador *a* eliminatory. *m*, eliminator
eliminar *vt* to eliminate
elipse *f*, ellipse
elipsis *f*, ellipsis
elíptico *a* elliptic
elíseo *m*, Elysium. *a* Elysian. **campos elíseos,** Elysian fields
elocución *f*, elocution; style of speech
elocuencia *f*, eloquence
elocuente *a* eloquent
elogiador (-ra) *a* eulogistic. *n* eulogist
elogiar *vt* to eulogize, praise
elogio *m*, eulogy, praise. **«Elogio de la Locura»,** "In Praise of Folly"
elucidación *f*, elucidation, explanation
elucidar *vt* to elucidate, clarify
eludible *a* escapable, avoidable
eludir *vt* to elude, avoid
ella *pers. pron 3rd sing. f* she; it. See **él**
elle *f*, name of letter LL
ello *pers. pron 3rd sing. neut* that, the fact, it. **Ello es que ...,** The fact is that ... **No tengo tiempo para ello,** I have no time for that
ellos, ellas *pers. pron 3rd pl. m* and *f*, they. See **él**
emaciación *f*, emaciation
emanación *f*, emanation; effluvium
emanar *vi* to emanate (from), originate (in)
emancipación *f*, emancipation; enfranchisement
emancipador (-ra) *a* emancipatory. *n* emancipator
emancipar *vt* to emancipate, free; enfranchise; *vr* emancipate oneself; become independent; free oneself
emascular *vt* to emasculate
embadurnar *vt* to smear, smudge, daub
embajada *f*, embassy; ambassadorship; embassy building; *inf* message
embajador *m*, ambassador; emissary
embajadora *f*, wife of ambassador; woman ambassador
embalador *m*, packer
embalaje *m*, packing; bale; wrapper; packing charge
embalar *vt* to pack
embaldosado *m*, tiled pavement or floor

embaldosar *vt* to tile, pave with tiles
embalsamador *a* embalming. *m*, embalmer
embalsamar *vt* to embalm; perfume
embalse *m*, dam; damming, impounding (of water)
embanastar *vt* to place in a basket; crowd, squeeze
embarazada *a f*, pregnant
embarazar *vt* to impede, hinder, embarrass; *vr* be hindered or embarrassed; be pregnant
embarazo *m*, difficulty, impediment; pregnancy; timidity, embarrassment
embarazoso *a* embarrassing; inconvenient; difficult, troublesome
embarcación *f*, ship, vessel; embarkation
embarcadero *m*, wharf, dock; quay; pier; jetty
embarcador *m*, shipper
embarcar *vt* to embark, ship; board (boat, train, etc.); *vr* embark; board
embarco *m*, embarking, embarkation
embargar *vt* to obstruct, impede; *law* seize; suspend, paralyse
embargo *m*, *law* seizure; embargo. **sin e.**, nevertheless, however
embarque *m*, loading, embarkation (goods)
embarrancar *vi naut* to run aground; *vr naut* be stuck on a reef or in the mud
embarrilar *vt* to barrel
embarullar *vt inf* to mix up, muddle; do hastily and badly
embasamiento *m*, *arch* foundation
embastar *vt sew* to baste; tack
embaste *m*, *sew* basting; tacking stitch
embate *m*, beating of the waves; sudden attack; unexpected misfortune
embaucamiento *m*, trick, deception
embaucar *vt* to deceive, hoodwink
embaular *vt* to pack in a trunk; *inf* stuff with food
embazar *vt* to dye brown; hinder; amaze; *vr* be amazed; be tired or bored; be satiated
embebecer *vt irr* to entertain, amuse; engross, fascinate; *vr* be dumbfounded. See **conocer**
embebecimiento *m*, astonishment; absorption, engrossment
embeber *vt* to absorb; contain; shrink, contract; saturate; insert, introduce; incorporate; *vi* shrink; *vr* be amazed; master or absorb (a subject). **embebido en sus pensamientos**, absorbed in thought
embelecar *vt* to dupe, deceive, trick
embeleco *m*, deception, fraud
embelesar *vt* to astonish; fascinate, enchant; *vr* be astonished or fascinated
embeleso *m*, astonishment; fascination; charm
embellecer *vt irr* to embellish; *vr* beautify oneself. See **conocer**
embellecimiento *m*, beautifying, embellishment
emberizo *m*, *orn* yellow-hammer
embermejecer *vt irr* to dye red; shame, make blush; *vi* turn red or reddish; *vr* blush. See **conocer**
embestida *f*, assault, attack, onrush; *inf* importunity
embestir *vt irr* to rush upon, assault; *inf* importune, be a nuisance to; *vi fig inf* clash, be inharmonious. See **pedir**
emblema *m*, emblem; symbol; badge
emblemático *a* emblematic; symbolical
embobamiento *m*, stupefaction, amazement
embobar *vt* to entertain, fascinate; *vr* be dumbfounded
embobecer *vt irr* to make stupid. See **conocer**
embobecimiento *m*, stupefaction
embocadero *m*, narrow entrance, bottleneck; mouth of a channel
embocadura *f*, entrance by a narrow passage; *mus* mouthpiece; flavor (of wine); estuary, mouth of a river; *theat* proscenium
embocar *vt* to put in the mouth; go through a narrow passage; deceive; *inf* devour, wolf; initiate a business deal
embolia *f*, embolism

émbolo *m*, *mech* piston, plunger
embolsar *vt* to place money in a purse; collect (a debt, etc.)
emborrachar *vt* to intoxicate; daze, stupefy; *vr* become intoxicated; run (of dyes)
emborrascarse *vr* to be furious; become stormy (weather); *fig* go downhill (business concern)
emborronar *vt* to blot; scribble, write hastily
emboscada *f*, ambuscade, ambush; intrigue, spying
emboscar *vt mil* to set an ambush; *vr* lie in ambush
embosquecer *vi irr* to become wooded. See **conocer**
embotar *vt* to blunt (cutting edge); *vi fig* weaken; *vr* become blunt
embotellado *m*, bottling; *fig* bottleneck
embotellador (-ra) *n* bottler. *f*, **embotelladora**, bottling outfit
embotellar *vt* to bottle; bottle up, prevent from escaping
embotijar *vt* to put into jars; *vr inf* be enraged
embozar *vt fig* to cloak, dissemble; muffle; *vr* muffle oneself up
embozo *m*, anything used to cover or muffle the face; pretense, pretext; facings (gen. *pl*); yashmak
embragar *vt* to sling, lift; *mech* let in the clutch
embrague *m*, hoisting, slinging; *mech* clutch
embravecer *vt irr* to infuriate; *vr* be enraged; be boisterous (sea). See **conocer**
embravecimiento *m*, fury, rage
embrazadura *f*, grasping, clasping; handle, clasp
embreadura *f*, tarring
embrear *vt* to tar, paint with pitch
embriagador *a* intoxicating
embriagar *vt* to intoxicate; enrapture; *vr* become inebriated
embriaguez *f*, intoxication, inebriation; rapture
embriología *f*, embryology
embrión *m*, embryo; germ, rough idea
embrionario *a* embryonic
embrocación *f*, *med* embrocation
embrollar *vt* to entangle; embroil
embrollo *m*, tangle; falsehood; difficult situation
embromar *vt* to tease, chaff; trick, deceive; waste the time of; annoy; harm
embrujar *vt* to bewitch
embrutecer *vt irr* to make brutish or stupid; *vr* become brutish. See **conocer**
embudo *m*, *chem* funnel
embuste *m*, lie, fraud; *pl* trinkets
embustero (-ra) *a* deceitful, knavish. *n* liar, cheat, trickster
embutido *m*, inlaid work; *cul* sausage
embutir *vt* to inlay; stuff full, cram; *vt* and *vr inf* stuff with food
eme *f*, name of letter M
emergencia *f*, emergence; accident, emergency
emergente *a* emergent
emerger *vi* to emerge; have its source (rivers, etc.)
emérito *a* emeritus
emético *a* and *m*, emetic
emigración *f*, emigration; migration; number of emigrants
emigrado *m*, emigrant, emigré
emigrante *a* and *mf* emigrant
emigrar *vi* to emigrate; migrate
emigratorio *a* emigration
eminencia *f*, highland; importance, prominence; outstanding personality, genius; title given to cardinals
eminente *a* high, elevated; prominent, illustrious
emirato *m*, emirate
emisario (-ia) *n* emissary
emisión *f*, emission; *rad* broadcast; *com* issue (bonds, etc.); floating (of a loan)
emisor *m*, *elec* transmitter
emisora *f*, *rad* broadcasting station
emitir *vt* to emit; *rad* broadcast; *com* issue (bonds, paper money, etc.); utter, give voice to

emoción *f*, emotion

emocional *a* emotional; emotive

emocionante *a* moving, causing emotion; thrilling

emocionar *vt* to cause emotion, move; *vr* be stirred by emotion; be thrilled

emoliente *a* and *m*, emollient

emolumento *m*, emolument (gen. *pl*)

emotivo *a* emotive

empachado *a* awkward, clumsy

empachar *vt* to hinder, impede; disguise, dissemble; *vr* overeat, stuff; be bashful

empacho *m*, bashfulness, timidity; embarrassment, impediment; indigestion, satiety

empadronamiento *m*, census

empadronar *vt* to take the census

empalagar *vt* to cloy (of food); tire, annoy

empalagoso *a* sickly, oversweet; cloying; *fig* sugary, honeyed

empalar *vt* to impale

empalizada *f*, stockade, fencing

empalmar *vt* to dovetail; splice (ropes); clamp; *fig* combine (plans, actions, etc.); *vi* join (railroad lines); couple (railroad trains); *vr* palm (as in conjuring)

empalme *m*, connection; splicing; *fig* combination (of plans, etc.); railroad junction; continuation; palming, secreting

empanada *f*, savory turnover or pie; secret negotiations, intrigue

empanar *vt* to bread; *cul* cover with breadcrumbs; *agr* sow grain

empantanar *vt* to turn into marsh; embog; delay, embarrass

empañar *vt* to swaddle; tarnish, dim; blur; *fig* sully (fame, etc.)

empapar *vt* to saturate; absorb; impregnate; *vr* be saturated; absorb; *fig* be imbued

empapelado *m*, paperhanging; wallpaper

empapelador *m*, paperhanger

empapelar *vt* to wrap in paper; paper (a room, etc.)

empaque *m*, packing; paneling; *inf* mien, air; pomposity

empaquetador (-ra) *n* packer

empaquetar *vt* to pack; make up parcels or packages; overcrowd

emparedado (-da) *a* cloistered, reclusive. *n* recluse. *m*, *cul* sandwich

emparedar *vt* to shut up, immure; *vr* become a recluse

emparejar *vt* to pair, match; equalize, make level; *vi* come abreast (of); be equal

emparentar *vi irr* to become related by marriage. See **acertar**

emparrado *m*, vine arbor; vine prop; pergola

empastadura *f*, filling (of teeth)

empastar *vt* to cover with glue or paste; bind in boards (books); fill (teeth). **empastado en tela,** clothbound

empaste *m*, pasting, gluing; filling (teeth)

empatar *vt* to equal, tie with

empate *m*, tie, draw; dead heat

empecatado *a* willful; evil-minded, wicked; incorrigible, impenitent; extremely unlucky

empecer *vt irr* to harm, damage; *vi* hinder. See **conocer**

empedernido *a* stony-hearted, cruel

empedrado *a* dappled (horses); *fig* flecked (with clouds). *m*, paving; pavement

empedrador *m*, stone paver

empedrar *vt irr* to pave with stones. See **acertar**

empegadura *f*, coat of pitch

empegar *vt* to coat with pitch; mark with pitch (sheep)

empeine *m*, groin; instep

empellar *vt* to push, jostle

empellón *m*, hard push. *inf* **a empellones,** by pushing and shoving

empenachado *a* plumed

empeñado *a* violent, heated (of disputes)

empeñar *vt* to pledge, leave as surety; pawn; oblige, compel; appoint as mediator; *vr* bind oneself, be under

an obligation; (*with en*) insist on; persist in; *vr* intercede; mediate; *mil* begin (a battle). **empeñado en,** determined to, intent on

empeño *m*, pledge, surety; obligation, engagement; fervent desire; purpose, intention; determination, resolve; guarantor; *inf* influence, favor

empeoramiento *m*, worsening; deterioration

empeorar *vt* to make worse; *vi* and *vr* deteriorate, grow worse

empequeñecer *vt irr* to diminish, lessen; make smaller; belittle. See **conocer**

emperador *m*, emperor

emperatriz *f*, empress

emperezar *vt* to obstruct, hinder; *vr* be lazy

empernar *vt* to peg, bolt

empero *conjunc* but; nevertheless

empezar *vt irr* to begin, commence; initiate; *vi* begin. *Pres. Ind.* **empiezo, empiezas, empieza, empiezan.** *Preterite* **empecé, empezaste,** etc. *Pres. Subjunc.* **empiece, empieces, empiece, empecemos, empecéis, empiecen**

empicotar *vt* to pillory

empinado *a* steep; lofty; arrogant; exalted

empinar *vt* to raise; tip, tilt (drinking vessels); *vr* stand on tiptoe; rear, prance; tower, rise; *aer* zoom, climb steeply. *inf* **e. el codo,** to lift the elbow, tipple

empingorotado *a* important, prominent; *inf* stuck-up

empíreo *a* empyreal; heavenly, divine. *m*, empyrean

empírico (-ca) *a* empiric. *n* quack, charlatan

empirismo *m*, empiricism

empizarrado *m*, slate roof

empizarrar *vt* to roof with slate

emplastar *vt med* to apply plasters; make up; paint; *inf* hinder, obstruct; *vr* be smeared

emplasto *m*, *med* plaster; poultice; *inf* put-up job, fraud

emplazamiento *m*, placing, location; site; *law* summons; *naut* berth

emplazar *vt* to convene, arrange a meeting; *law* summon

empleado (-da) *n* employee; clerk. **e. público,** civil servant

emplear *vt* to employ; lay out, invest (money); use; *vr* be employed or occupied

empleo *m*, employment; investment, laying out (of money); occupation; post, office

emplomar *vt* to lead, solder or cover with lead; affix lead seals on or to; weight (a stick, etc.)

emplumar *vt* to feather; decorate with feathers; tar and feather

emplumecer *vi irr* to fledge, grow feathers. See **conocer**

empobrecer *vt irr* to impoverish; *vi* and *vr* become poor; decay. See **conocer**

empobrecimiento *m*, impoverishment

empollar *vt* to hatch; *vi* produce a brood (of bees); *inf* brood on, consider; *inf* grind, cram, swot (of students)

empollón (-ona) *n inf* plodder, grind, swot

empolvar *vt* to cover with dust; powder

emponzoñamiento *m*, poisoning

emponzoñar *vt* to poison; pervert, corrupt

emporio *m*, emporium

empotrar *vt* to embed, implant; fix down

emprendedor *a* capable, efficient, enterprising

emprender *vt* to undertake; (*with prep a or con*) *inf* accost, tackle, buttonhole

empresa *f*, undertaking, task; motto, device; intention; design; management, firm; enterprise, deal

empresarial *a* entrepreneurial

empresario *m*, contractor; theatrical manager

empréstito *m*, loan

empujar *vt* to push; *fig* exert pressure, influence

empuje *m*, push; *arch* pressure; energy; power, influence

empujón *m*, violent thrust or push. *inf* **a empujones,** by pushing and shoving; intermittently

empuñadura *f*, hilt (of a sword); *inf* preamble

empuñar *vt* to grasp; grip; clutch

emu *m*, emu

emulación *f*, emulation, competition, rivalry

emulador *a* emulative

emular *vt* to emulate, rival, compete with

émulo (-la) *a* emulative, rival. *n* competitor, rival

emulsión *f*, emulsion

emulsivo *a* emulsive

en *prep* in; into; on, upon; at; by. **en Madrid,** in Madrid. **en junio,** in June. **Se echó en un sillón,** He threw himself into an armchair. **Se transformó en mariposa,** It turned into a butterfly. **Hay un libro en la mesa,** There is a book on the table. **María está en casa,** Mary is at home. **en un precio muy alto,** at a very high price. **El número de candidatos ha disminuido en un treinta por ciento,** The number of candidates has decreased by thirty percent. **En** appears in a number of adverbial phrases, e.g. **en particular,** in particular, **en secreto,** in secret, **en seguida,** immediately. When it is used with a gerund, it means after, as soon as, when, e.g. **En llegando a la puerta llamó,** When he arrived at the door, he knocked. **En todas partes se cuecen habas,** That happens everywhere; It happens in the best of families

enagua *f*, slip, crinoline, petticoat

enajenación *f*, transference, alienation (property); abstraction, absent-mindedness. **e. mental,** lunacy

enajenar *vt* to transfer (property)

enaltecer *vt irr* to elevate, raise; exalt. See **conocer**

enamoradizo *a* susceptible, easily enamoured; fickle

enamorado *a* in love, lovesick; easily enamoured

enamorar *vt* to arouse love in; court, make love to; *vr* fall in love; (with *de*) become fond of (things)

enano (-na) *a* small, dwarf. *n* dwarf

enarbolar *vt* to hoist (flags); *vr* prance (horses); become angry

enardecer *vt irr* to kindle, stimulate (passion, quarrel, etc.); *vr* be afire (with passion); *med* be inflamed. See **conocer**

encabestrar *vt* to halter; lead, dominate

encabezamiento *m*, census taking; tax register; tax assessment; heading, inscription, running head

encabezar *vt* to take the census of; put on the tax register; open a subscription list; put a heading or title to; lead, head; *vr* compound, settle by agreement (taxes, etc.)

encabritarse *vr* to rear, prance (horses)

encadenamiento *m*, fettering, chaining; connection, link, relation

encadenar *vt* to chain, fetter; *fig* link up, connect; *fig* paralyze. **encadenar el interés de,** to capture the interest of

encajar *vt* to insert, fit one thing inside another; force in; fit tightly; *inf* be opportune, fit in (often with *bien*); *vr* squeeze or crowd in; *inf* butt in, interfere

encaje *m*, fitting, insertion; socket, groove; joining; lace; inlay, mosaic

encajera *f*, lace maker or seller

encaladura *f*, whitewashing

encalar *vt* to whitewash

encalmado *a* calm; *com* dull

encalmarse *vr* to become calm (wind, weather)

encalvecer *vi irr* to grow bald. See **conocer**

encalladero *m*, *naut* sandbank, reef, shoal

encallar *vi naut* to run aground; *fig* be held up (negotiations, etc.)

encamado *a* bedridden, confined to one's bed; *m*, person confined to his bed

encamarse *vr* to go to bed (gen. illness); be laid flat (grain, etc.); crouch

encaminadura *f*, **encaminamiento** *m*, directing, forwarding, routing

encaminar *vt* to guide; direct; regulate; manage; promote, advance; *vr* (*with prep a*) make for, go in the direction of

encandecer *vt irr* to make incandescent. See **conocer**

encandilar *vt* to dazzle; mislead; *inf* poke (the fire); *vr* be bloodshot (eyes)

encanecer *vi irr* to grow gray- or white-haired; grow mold; grow old. See **conocer**

encanijar *vt* to make weak, sickly (gen. of babies); *vr* be delicate or ailing

encantado *a inf* daydreaming, abstracted; haunted; rambling (of houses)

encantador *a* captivating, bewitching, delightful. *m*, sorcerer, magician. **e. de serpientes,** snake charmer

encantamiento *m*, enchantment, spell, charm

encantar *vt* to enchant, weave a spell; delight, captivate, charm

encañada *f*, gorge, ravine

encañado *m*, trellis; pipeline

encañar *vt* to run water through a pipe; stake plants; wind thread on a spool

encañonar *vt* to run into pipes; pleat, fold

encapotarse *vr* to muffle oneself in a cloak; scowl; be overcast; lower (sky)

encapricharse *vr* to take a fancy (to); insist on having one's own way, be stubborn

encapuchar *vt* to cover or hide with a hood

encaramar *vt* to raise, lift; climb; praise, extol. **e. al poder,** to put in power (e.g. a dictator). **encaramarse por,** to climb up

encarar *vt* to place face to face; aim (at); *vt* and *vr* face; come face to face

encarcelación *f*, incarceration

encarcelar *vt* to imprison, jail; *carp* clamp

encarecer *vt irr* to raise the price; overpraise, exaggerate; recommend strongly; *vi* and *vr* increase in price. See **conocer**

encarecimiento *m*, increase (in price); enhancement; exaggeration. **con e.,** insistently, earnestly

encargado *m*, person in charge; manager; agent, representative. **e. de negocios,** chargé d'affaires

encargar *vt* to enjoin; commission; recommend; advise; *com* order

encargo *m*, charge, commission; order; office, employ; responsibility

encariñarse (*con*), *vi* to become fond (of)

encarnación *f*, incarnation

encarnadino *a* incarnadine

encarnado *a* incarnate; flesh-colored; red

encarnar *vi* to incarnate; pierce the flesh; *fig* leave a strong impression; *vt* symbolize, personify; *vr* mingle, blend

encarnizado *a* bloodshot (eyes); flesh-colored; bloody, cruel (gen. of battles)

encarnizamiento *m*, cruelty, fury

encarnizar *vt* to infuriate; *vr* devour flesh (animals); persecute, ill-treat

encaro *m*, stare, gaze; aim

encarrilar *vt* to set on the track or rails (vehicles); *fig* put right, set on the right track

encartamiento *m*, proscription; charter

encartar *vt* to proscribe, outlaw; place on the tax register; *law* summon, cite

encartonar *vt* to cover with cardboard; bind in boards (books)

encasar *vt surg* to set (a bone)

encasillado *m*, set of pigeonholes

encasillar *vt* to pigeonhole; file, classify

encasquetar(se) *vt* and *vr* to pull a hat well down on the head; *vr* get a fixed idea

encastillar *vt* to fortify with castles; *vr* retire to a castle; be headstrong, obstinate

encauzamiento *m*, channeling; *fig* direction

encauzar *vt* to channel; *fig* direct, guide

encefalitis *f*, encephalitis. **e. letárgica,** encephalitis lethargica, sleeping sickness. **enceguedor** *a* blinding, dazzling

encéfalo *m*, *anat* brain

encenagarse *vr* to wallow in mire; muddy oneself; take to vice

encendedor *a* lighting. *m*, lighter. **e. de bolsillo,** pocket lighter

encender *vt irr* to light; switch on; set fire to, kindle; arouse (emotions); inflame, incite; *vr* blush. See **entender**

encendido *a* high-colored; inflamed; ardent. *m, aut* ignition

encerado *a* wax-colored. *m*, oilskin; sticking plaster; blackboard; tarpaulin

enceramiento *m*, waxing

encerar *vt* to wax, varnish with wax; stain with wax; inspissate (lime)

encerotar *vt* to wax (thread)

encerrar *vt irr* to shut up, imprison; include, contain; *vr* go into seclusion. See **acertar**

encerrona *f, inf* voluntary retreat; *fig inf* tight corner

encespedar *vt* to cover with sod

enchufar *vt* to connect tubes; *fig* combine (jobs, etc.); *elec* plug, connect

enchufe *m*, joint, fitting together (of tubes); *elec* wall socket, plug; part-time post; *inf* cushy job. **e. de reducción,** *elec* adapter

encía *f*, gum (of the mouth)

encíclica *f*, encyclical

enciclopedia *f*, encyclopedia

enciclopédico *a* encyclopedic

encierro *m*, act of closing or shutting up; prison; retreat, confinement

encima *adv* over; above; at the top; besides; (*with de*) on, on top of. **por e. de esto,** over and above this, besides this

encina *f, bot* evergreen or holm oak

encinar *m*, grove of evergreen or holm oaks

encinta *a f*, pregnant

encintar *vt* to decorate with ribbons

enclavar *vt* to nail; pierce; embed; *inf* deceive

enclenque *a* ailing, weak; puny, anemic

enclocar *vi irr* to begin to brood (hens). See **contar**

encobar *vi* to hatch eggs

encoger *vt* to shrink, contract, recoil; discourage; *vi* shrink (wood, cloth, etc.); *vr* shrink from, recoil; be discouraged; be timid or bashful

encogimiento *m*, shrinkage; contraction; depression, discouragement; timidity; bashfulness

encoladura *f*. **encolamiento** *m*, gluing; sizing

encolerizar *vt* to anger; *vr* be angry

encomendar *vt irr* to charge with, entrust; recommend, commend; *vr* (*with prep a*) put one's trust in; send greetings to. See **acertar**

encomiar *vt* to eulogize, praise

encomiástico *a* encomiastic

encomienda *f*, commission, charge; knight commandership; insignia of knight commander; land formerly granted in America to *conquistadores*; recommendation, commendation; protection, defense; *pl* greetings, compliments, messages

encomio *m*, eulogy; strong recommendation

enconar *vt* to irritate, exasperate; *vr med* be inflamed; be exasperated; (*with en*) burden one's conscience with

encono *m*, rancor, resentment, ill will

encontrado *a* facing, opposite, in front; hostile, inimical, opposed (to)

encontrar *vt irr* to meet; find; *vi* meet; encounter unexpectedly; (*with con*) run into, collide with; *vr* be antagonistic; find; feel, be; differ, disagree (opinions); (*with con*) meet, come across. **e. eco,** to strike a responsive chord. **encontrarse con el cura de su pueblo,** to find someone who knows all about, meet someone who knows all about. **¿Cómo se encuentra Vd?** How are you? *Pres. Ind.* **encuentro,** etc. *Pres. Subjunc.* **encuentre,** etc.

encontrón *m*, collision, violent impact

encopetado *a* conceited, proud; of noble descent; prominent, important

encorajar *vt* to encourage, inspire, hearten; *vr* be angry

encordelar *vt* to cord, rope

encorsetar *vt* to correct

encorvadura *f*, bending, curving

encorvar *vt* to bend, curve; *vr* have a leaning toward, favor

encostrar *vt* to cover with a crust; *vr* form a crust

encrespador *m*, curling irons

encrespar *vt* to curl (hair); enrage; *vr* be curly (hair); stand on end (hair, feathers, from fright); be angry; grow rough (sea); become complicated, entangled

encrestado *a* crested; haughty, arrogant

encrestarse *vr* to stiffen the comb or crest (birds)

encrucijada *f*, crossroad, intersection; ambush

encrudecer *vt irr* to make raw-looking; annoy; *vr* be annoyed. See **conocer**

encuadernación *f*, bookbinding; binding (of a book); bookbinder's workshop. **e. en tela,** cloth binding

encuadernador (-ra) *n* bookbinder

encuadernar *vt* to bind (a book)

encuadrar *vt* to frame; fit one thing into another, insert; limit; *mil* enlist

encubar *vt* to put into casks (wine, etc.)

encubiertamente *adv* secretly; deceitfully

encubierto *a* concealed; secret

encubridor (-ra) *a* concealing, hiding. *n* hider; harborer; accomplice; receiver (of stolen goods); *law* accessory after the fact

encubrimiento *m*, hiding, concealment; *law* accessory before (after) the fact; receiving (of stolen goods)

encubrir *vt* to conceal; receive (stolen goods); *law* prosecute as an accessory. *Past. Part.* **encubierto**

encuentro *m*, collision; meeting, encounter; opposition, hostility; *mil* fight, skirmish; *arch* angle. **ir al e. de,** to go in search of. **salir al e. (de),** to go to meet; resist

encuesta *f*, investigation, examination

encumbrado *a* elevated, high

encumbramiento *m*, act of elevating; height; aggrandizement, advancement

encumbrar *vt* to raise, elevate; exalt, promote; ascend, climb to the top; *vr* be proud; be lofty, tower

encurtido *m*, pickle

encurtir *vt* to pickle

ende *adv ant* there. **por e.,** therefore

endeble *a* weak, frail

endeblez *f*, weakness

endémico *a med* endemic

endemoniado *a* devil-possessed; *inf* fiendish, malevolent

endemoniar *vt* to possess with a devil; *inf* enrage

endentar *vt irr mech* to cut the cogs (of a wheel); engage, interlock (gears, wheels, etc.). See **regimentar**

endentecer *vi irr* to cut teeth. See **conocer**

enderezamiento *m*, straightening; directing, guiding; putting right, correction

enderezar *vt* to straighten; direct, guide; put right, correct; *vi* take the right road; *vr* straighten oneself; prepare to

endeudarse *vr* to contract debts; to be under an obligation

endiablado *a* ugly, monstrous; *inf* fiendish

endiosar *vt* to deify; *vr* be puffed up with pride; be abstracted or lost in ecstasy

endocrino *a* endocrine

endocrinología *f*, endocrinology

endomingarse *vr* to put on one's Sunday best

endosante *m*, endorser

endosar *vt com* to endorse; transfer, pass on

endoso *m, com* endorsement

endrino *m*, sloe tree. *a* blue-black, sloe-colored

endulzar *vt* to sweeten; soften, mitigate

endurecer *vt irr* to harden; toughen, inure; make severe or cruel; *vr* grow hard; become hardened or robust; be harsh or cruel. **endurecerse al trabajo,** to become hardened to work. See **conocer**

endurecimiento *m*, hardness; obstinacy, tenacity

ene *f*, name of letter N

enemiga *f*, hostility, enmity

enemigo (-ga) *a* hostile. *n* enemy; antagonist. *m*, devil

enemistad *f*, enmity, hostility

enemistar *vt* to make enemies of; *vr (with con)* become an enemy of; cease to be friendly with

energía *f*, energy, vigor

enérgico *a* energetic, vigorous

energúmeno (-na) *n* energumen

enero *m*, January

enervación *f*, enervation

enervar *vt* to enervate, weaken; *fig* take the force out of (reasons, etc.)

enfadar *vt* to make angry; *vr* become angry

enfado *m*, anger; annoyance; trouble, toil

enfadoso *a* vexatious; troublesome, wearisome

enfaldada *f*, skirtful

enfaldar *vt* to tuck up the skirts; lop off lower branches (of trees)

enfangarse *vr* to cover oneself with mud; *inf* dirty one's hands, sully one's reputation; wallow in vice

enfardar *vt* to pack; make bales or bundles

énfasis *m*, or *f*, emphasis

enfático *a* emphatic

enfermar *vi* to fall ill; *vt* cause illness; *fig* weaken. **Enfermó del corazón,** He fell ill with heart trouble.

enfermedad *f*, illness; *fig* malady, distemper. **e. del sueño,** sleeping sickness

enfermera *f*, nurse

enfermería *f*, infirmary; hospital; first-aid station

enfermero *m*, nurse

enfermizo *a* ailing, delicate; unhealthy, unwholesome

enfermo (-ma) *a* ill; *fig* corrupt, diseased; delicate, sickly. *n* patient. **e. venéreo,** person with a venereal disease

enfilar *vt* to place in line; string; *mil* enfilade

enflaquecer *vt irr* to make thin; weaken, enervate; *vi* grow thin; lose heart. See **conocer**

enflaquecimiento *m*, loss of flesh; discouragement

enfocar *vt* to focus; envisage

enfoque *m*, focus

enfoscado *a* ill-humored; immersed in business matters

enfrascar *vt* to bottle; *vr (with en)* plunge into, entangle oneself in (undergrowth, etc.); become engrossed or absorbed in

enfrenar *vt* to bridle; curb (a horse); restrain, repress; check

enfrente *adv* in front, opposite, facing; in opposition

enfriadero *m*, cooling place, cold cellar, root cellar

enfriamiento *m*, cooling

enfriar *vt* to cool; *fig* chill, make indifferent; *vr* grow cold; *fig* grow stormy (weather)

enfurecer *vt irr* to enrage. See **conocer**

enfurecimiento *m*, fury

enfurruñarse *vr inf* to fume, be angry; be disgruntled

engalanar *vt* to decorate, embellish. **engalanado como nunca,** dressed to the nines, dressed to kill

enganchar *vt* to hook; couple, connect; hitch, harness, yoke; *inf* seduce, hook; *mil* bribe into army; *vr* be hooked or caught on a hook; *mil* enlist

enganche *m*, hooking; coupling (of railroad trains, etc.); connection; yoke, harness; hook; *inf* enticement; *mil* enlistment

engañadizo *a* easily deceived, simple

engañador (-ra) *a* deceiving; deceptive. *n* deceiver, impostor

engañar *vt* to deceive; defraud, cheat; beguile, while away; hoax, humbug; *vr* be mistaken; deceive oneself. **e. como a un chino,** *inf* to pull the wool over a person's eyes. **Las apariencias engañan,** Appearances are deceptive

engañifa *f*, *inf* swindle, fraud

engaño *m*, deceit; deception, illusion; fraud; falsehood

engañoso *a* deceitful, false; fraudulent; deceptive, misleading

engarabatar *vt inf* to hook; *vr* become hooked, curved, crooked

engarce *m*, hooking; coupling; setting (of jewels)

engarzar *vt* to link, couple, enchain; hook; curl; set (jewels)

engastar *vt* to set (jewels)

engaste *m*, setting (of jewels)

engatusar *vt inf* to wheedle, coax, flatter

engendrador (-ra) *a* engendering; original. *n* begetter

engendrar *vt* to procreate; engender, produce, cause

engendro *m*, fetus; abnormal embryo; literary monstrosity

englobar *vt* to include, comprise, embrace

engolfarse *vr* to sail out to sea; *(with en)* *fig* be absorbed in

engomar *vt* to gum

engordar *vt* to fatten; *vi* grow fat; *inf* prosper, grow rich

engorde *m*, fattening (of stock)

engorro *m*, impediment, obstacle, difficulty

engorroso *a* difficult, troublesome

engranaje *m*, *mech* gearing, gear; *fig* connection, link

engrandecer *vt irr* to enlarge; augment; eulogize; promote, exalt. See **conocer**

engrandecimiento *m*, enlargement; increase; exaggeration, eulogization; advancement, promotion

engrasado *m*, oiling; greasing

engrasador *m*, greaser, lubricator; oiler

engrasar *vt* to grease; lubricate, oil; manure; stain with grease

engreimiento *m*, conceit, vanity

engreír *vt irr* to make conceited; *vr* become vain or conceited. See **reír**

engrescar(se) *vt* and *vr* to start a quarrel

engrosar *vt irr* to fatten, thicken; *fig* increase, swell; manure; *vi* put on weight, grow fat. See **contar**

engrudar *vt* to paste, glue

engrudo *m*, paste, glue

enguantarse *vr* to put on one's gloves

enguijarrado *a* pebbled. *m*, pebbled path

engullir *vt* to gobble, swallow

enhebrar *vt* to thread (needles); string

enhestar *vt irr* to erect; set upright; *vr* rise; rear up; straighten oneself up. See **acertar**

enhiesto *a* upright, erect

enhorabuena *f*, congratulation. *adv* well and good. **dar la e.,** to congratulate

enhoramala *adv* in an evil hour. *inf* **¡Vete e.!** Go to the devil!

enhorquetado *a* in the saddle

enhuerar *vt* to addle; *vi* become addled

enigma *m*, enigma

enigmático *a* enigmatical

enjabonar *vt* to soap; *inf* soap down, flatter

enjaezar *vt* to harness (a horse)

enjalbegar *vt* to whitewash

enjambrar *vt* to hive bees; *vi* multiply, increase

enjambre *m*, swarm (of bees); crowd

enjaretado *m*, latticework

enjaular *vt* to cage; *inf* jail

enjoyar *vt* to adorn with jewels; beautify; set with precious stones

enjuagadura *f*, rinsing (the mouth); rinse water; mouthwash

enjuagar *vt* to rinse; *vr* rinse the mouth

enjuague *m*, rinse; rinsing; mouthwash; tooth mug; scheme, plan

enjugar *vt* to dry; cancel, write off; wipe, mop (perspiration, tears, etc.); *vr* grow lean

enjuiciar *vt* to submit a matter to arbitration; *law* prosecute; *law* render judgment; *law* adjudicate (a case)

enjundia *f*, animal fat or grease; *fig* substance, meat; strength, vigor; constitution, temperament

enjuto *a* dry; lean. *m pl*, brushwood; *cul* canapés, savories

enlace *m*, connection; link; tie; *chem* bond; alliance, relationship; marriage

enladrillado *m*, brick floor or pavement

enlardar *vt cul* to baste

enlazar *vt* to tie, bind; join, link; lasso; *vr* marry; be allied, related. **e. con,** to connect with (of trains); link up with

enlentecerse *vr* to decelerate, go slow, slow down

enlodar *vt* to muddy; *fig* smirch, sully

enloquecer *vt irr* to drive insane; *vi* go mad. See **conocer**

enlosado *m*, tile floor

enlosar *vt* to pave with flags

enlucir *vt irr* to plaster (walls); polish (metals). See **lucir**

enlutar *vt* to put in mourning, drape with crepe; darken, obscure; sadden; *vr* go into mourning; become dark

enmaderar *vt* to panel in wood, board up

enmarañar *vt* to tangle, disorder (hair, etc.); complicate, confuse; *vr* be tangled; be sprinkled with clouds

enmaridar *vi* to become a wife

enmarillecerse *vr irr* to grow yellow. See **conocer**

enmascarar *vt* to mask; disguise, dissemble; *vr* be masked

enmasillar *vt* to putty

enmendar *vt irr* to correct, improve; reform; compensate, indemnify; *law* repeal; *vr* be improved or corrected; mend one's ways. See **acertar**

enmienda *f*, correction; reform; indemnity; compensation; amendment; *pl agr* fertilizers

enmohecer *vt irr* to rust; *vr* become moldy. See **conocer**

enmudecer *vt irr* to silence; *vi* become dumb; be silent. See **conocer**

enmugrecer *vt irr* to cover with grime; *vr* be grimy, dirty. See **conocer**

ennegrecer *vt irr* to dye black; make black; *vr* become black; become dark or cloudy. See **conocer**

ennoblecer *vt irr* to ennoble; enrich, embellish; adorn, befit. See **conocer**

ennoblecimiento *m*, ennoblement; enrichment

enojadizo *a* irritable, peevish

enojar *vt* to anger; annoy, irritate; *vr* be angry; rage, be rough (wind, sea)

enojo *m*, anger; resentment; vexations, troubles, trials (gen. *pl*). **con gran e. de,** much to the annoyance of

enojoso *a* annoying; troublesome, tiresome

enorgullecer *vt irr* to make proud; *vr* be proud. See **conocer**

enorme *a* enormous, huge; monstrous, heinous

enormidad *f*, hugeness; enormity; wickedness

enramada *f*, bower; thick foliage

enramar *vt* to intertwine branches; embower; *vi* branch (trees)

enrarecer *vt irr* to rarefy; *vr* become rarefied; grow rare. See **conocer**

enrarecimiento *m*, rarefaction

enredadera *f*, convolvulus. *a f*, climbing, twining (plant)

enredador (-ra) *a* mischievous, willful; intriguing, scheming; *inf* gossiping, meddlesome. *n* intriguer; *inf* meddler

enredar *vt* to catch in a net; put down nets or snares; entangle; sow discord; compromise, involve (in difficulties); *vi* be mischievous; *vr* be entangled; be involved (in difficulties)

enredo *m*, tangle; mischief, prank; intrigue, malicious falsehood; difficult situation; plot

enredoso *a* tangled; fraught with difficulties

enrejado *m*, railing, paling; trellis or latticework; *sew* openwork

enrejar *vt* to fence with a railing; cover with grating

enriquecer *vt irr* to enrich; exalt, aggrandize; *vi* grow rich; prosper, flourish. See **conocer**

enriscado *a* craggy, rocky

enriscar *vt* to raise; *vr* hide among crags

enristrar *vt* to couch (a lance); string (onions, etc.);

fig surmount (difficulties); go straight to (a place)

enrojecer *vt irr* to redden; make blush; *vr* grow red; blush. See **conocer**

enroscar *vt* to twist, twine; *vr* turn (screw); twist; coil

ensaimada *f*, Spanish pastry cake

ensalada *f*, salad; hodgepodge

ensaladera *f*, salad bowl

ensalmar *vt surg* to set (bones); cure by spells

ensalmo *m*, spell, charm. **por e.,** as if by magic, rapidly

ensalzar *vt* to exalt, promote; praise

ensamblador *m*, joiner, assembler

ensambladura *f*, assemblage, joinery; joining; dovetailing

ensamblar *vt* to assemble; join, dovetail, mortise

ensanchador *m*, glove stretcher

ensanchar *vt* to widen, enlarge, extend; *sew* let out, stretch; *vr* put on airs

ensanche *m*, dilatation, widening; stretch; extension; *sew* turnings, letting out; (city) extension

ensangrentar *vt irr* to stain with blood; *vr* be bloodstained; be overhasty. See **regimentar**

ensañar *vt* to irritate, infuriate; *vr* be merciless (with vanquished)

ensartar *vt* to string (beads); thread (needles); spit, pierce; tell a string (of falsehoods)

ensayador *m*, metal assayer

ensayar *vt* to try out; *chem* test; *theat* rehearse; assay

ensaye *m*, assaying (of metals)

ensayista *mf* essayist

ensayo *m*, test, trial; *lit* essay; assay; experiment; rehearsal. **e. general,** dress rehearsal

ensenada *f*, cove, inlet

enseña *f*, ensign, standard

enseñanza *f*, teaching; education; example, experience. **e. primaria,** elementary education. **e. secundaria,** secondary education. **e. superior,** higher education

enseñar *vt* to teach, instruct; train; point out; exhibit, show; *vr* become accustomed. **e. la oreja,** *fig* to show the cloven hoof

enseñorearse *vr* to take possession (of)

enseres *m pl*, household goods; utensils; equipment

ensilladero *m*, paddock

ensillar *vt* to saddle

ensimismarse *vr* to be lost in thought

ensoberbecer *vt irr* to make haughty; *vr* become arrogant; grow rough (sea). See **conocer**

ensordecedor *a* deafening

ensordecer *vt irr* to deafen; *vi* become deaf; keep silent, refuse to reply. See **conocer**

ensuciar *vt* to soil, dirty; *fig* sully; *vr* be dirty; *inf* accept bribes

ensueño *m*, dream; illusion, fancy

entablado *m*, stage, dais; wooden floor; planking

entablar *vt* to plank, floor with boards; board up; *surg* splint; undertake, initiate (negotiations, etc.); begin (conversations, etc.); *vr* settle (winds). **e. acción judicial,** to take legal action

entalegar *vt* to put into sacks or bags; hoard (money)

entalladura *f*, carving; sculpture; *carp* mortise, notch

entallar *vt* to carve; sculpture; engrave; notch, groove; tap (trees); fit (well or ill) at the waist

entallecer *vi irr* to sprout (plants). See **conocer**

entapizar *vt* to hang with tapestry; upholster; *fig* cover, carpet

entarimado *m*, wooden floor; dais

ente *m*, entity, being; *inf* object, individual

enteco *a* sickly, ailing, delicate

entendederas *f pl*, *inf* understanding

entendedor (-ra) *a* understanding, comprehending. *n* one who understands. **A buen e. pocas palabras,** A word to the wise is sufficient

entender *vt irr* to comprehend, understand; know; deduce, infer; intend; believe; (*with de*) be familiar with or knowledgeable about; (*with en*) have as a profession or trade; be engaged in; have authority in; *vr* understand oneself; have a reason (for behavior); understand each other; have an amatory understanding; be meant, signify; (*with con*) have an understanding with. **a mi e.,** in my opinion, as I see it. *Pres. Ind.* **entiendo, entiendes, entiende, entienden.** *Pres. Subjunc.* **entienda, entiendas, entienda, entiendan**

entendido *a* learned, knowledgeable

entendimiento *m*, understanding; mind, reason, intelligence

enteramente *adv* completely, entirely, wholly

enterar *vt* to inform, advise

entereza *f*, entirety; completeness; impartiality, integrity; fortitude, constancy; strictness, rigour

enternecer *vt irr* to soften, make tender; move to pity; *vr* be touched by compassion. See **conocer**

enternecimiento *m*, compassion, pity; tenderness

entero *a* entire; whole; robust, healthy; upright, just; constant, loyal; virgin; pure; *inf* strong, tough (cloth); *math* integral

enterrador *m*, gravedigger

enterrar *vt irr* to inter; outlive; bury, forget. See **acertar**

entibiar *vt* to make lukewarm; *fig* cool, temper

entidad *f*, entity; value, importance

entierro *m*, interment, burial; grave; funeral; buried treasure

entoldar *vt* to cover with an awning; hang with tapestry, etc., drape; cover (sky, clouds)

entomología *f*, entomology

entomológico *a* entomological

entomólogo *m*, entomologist

entonación *f*, intonation; modulation (voice); conceit

entonado *m*, haughty, conceited

entonar *vt* to modulate (voice); intone; blow (organ bellows); lead (song); *med* tone up; *art* harmonize; *vr* become conceited; *com* improve, harden (stock, etc.)

entonces *adv* then, at that time; in that case, that being so

entonelar *vt* to put in barrels or casks

entontecer *vt irr* to make stupid or foolish; *vr* become stupid. See **conocer**

entornar *vt* to leave ajar; half-close; upset, turn upside down

entorpecer *vt irr* to numb, make torpid; confuse, daze; obstruct, delay; *vr* go numb; be confused. See **conocer**

entorpecimiento *m*, numbness, torpidity; stupidity, dullness; delay, obstruction

entrada *f*, entrance; door, gate; admission; *cul* entree; admission ticket; *theat* house; takings, gate; *mil* entry; beginnings (of month, etc.); intimacy; right of entry. **entradas y salidas,** comings and goings; collusion; *com* ingoing and outgoing

entrampar *vt* to trap (animals); swindle; *fig inf* entangle (business affairs); *inf* load with debts; *vr* be bogged down; *inf* be in debt

entrante *a* incoming, entrant; next, coming (month)

entraña *f*, entrail; *pl* heart; *fig* center, core; humaneness; temperament. *inf* **no tener entrañas,** to be heartless, be without feeling

entrañable *a* intimate; dearly loved

entrar *vi* (*with en*) to enter, go into, come in; flow into; *fig* have access to; join, become a member; *fig* be taken by (fever, panic, etc.); *mil* enter; be an ingredient of; (*with por, en*) penetrate, pierce; (*with de*) embrace (professions, etc.); (*with prep a + infin*) begin to; (*with en + noun*) begin to be (e.g. **e. en calor,** begin to be hot) or begin to take part in (e.g. **e. en lucha,** begin to fight); *vt* introduce, make enter; *mil* (*with en*) occupy; *vr* (*with en*) squeeze in. **e. en apetito,** to work up an appetite, get an appetite. *inf* **no e. ni salir en,** to take no part in. *inf* **No me entra,** I don't understand it

entre *prep* between; among; to. **e. joyas,** among jewels. **E. las dos se escribió la carta,** Between them, they wrote the letter. **Dije e. mí,** I said to myself. **los días de e. semana,** weekdays. **e. tanto,** in the meanwhile.

entreabrir *vt* to leave ajar; half-open. *Past Part.* **entreabierto**

entreacto *m*, interval, entr'acte; small cigar

entrecano *a* going gray, grayish (hair)

entrecejo *m*, space between the eyebrows; frown

entrecoger *vt* to intercept, catch; constrain, compel

entrecortado *a* intermittent (sounds); faltering, broken (voice)

entrecubiertas *f pl*, *naut* between decks

entredicho *m*, prohibition; *ecc* interdiction

entredós *m*, *sew* insertion

entrefino *a* middling, fairly fine

entrega *f*, handing over; delivery; *lit* part, serial; installment. **por entregas,** as a serial, serial (of stories)

entregar *vt* to hand over; deliver; surrender; *vr* give oneself up; surrender; submit; (*with prep a*) engage in, be absorbed in; (*with prep a or en*) give oneself over to (vice, etc.)

entreguista *mf* defeatist

entrelazar *vt* to interlace, intertwine; interweave

entrelistado *a* striped

entrelucir *vi irr* to show through, be glimpsed. See **lucir**

entremedias *adv* in between, halfway; in the meantime

entremés *m*, hors d'oeuvres (gen. *pl*); interlude, one-act farce

entremesista *mf* author of, or actor in, one-act farces

entremeter *vt* to place between or among; *vr* intrude; meddle, pry

entremetido (-da) *a* meddlesome. *n* busybody, meddler

entremetimiento *m*, meddlesomeness

entremezclar *vt* to intermingle

entrenador (-ra) *n* trainer; *sport* coach

entrenamiento *m*, training, exercise

entrenar(se) *vt* and *vr* to train; exercise; *sport* coach

entreoír *vt* to overhear; hear imperfectly

entrepaño *m*, *arch* panel; pier (between windows, etc.)

entrepiernas *f pl*, crotch

entrepuente *m*, *naut* between decks; steerage quarters

entresacar *vt* to choose or pick out; thin out (plants); thin (hair)

entresuelo *m*, mezzanine, entresol; ground floor

entresueño *m*, daydream

entretalladura *f*, bas-relief

entretallar *vt* to carve in bas-relief; engrave; *sew* do openwork; intercept; *vr* connect, dovetail

entretejer *vt* to interweave; interlace; *lit* insert

entretela *f*, *sew* interlining

entretener *vt irr* to keep waiting; make more bearable; amuse, entertain; delay, postpone; maintain, upkeep; *vr* amuse oneself. See **tener**

entretenido *a* amusing, entertaining

entretenimiento *m*, amusement; pastime, diversion; upkeep, maintenance

entretiempo *m*, between seasons, spring or autumn

entreventana *f*, space between windows

entreverado *a* variegated; streaky (of bacon)

entreverar *vt* to intermingle

entrevía *f*, railroad gauge

entrevista *f*, meeting, interview

entristecer *vt irr* to sadden; *vr* grieve. See **conocer**

entristecimiento *m*, sadness

entrometer *vt* See **entremeter**

entronar *vt* See **entronizar**

entroncar *vt* to prove descent; *vi* be related, or become related (by marriage)

entronerar *vt* to pocket (in billiards)

entronización *f*, enthronement

entronizar *vt* to enthrone; exalt

entronque *m*, blood relationship, cognation; junction

entumecer *vt irr* to numb; *vr* go numb; swell, rise (sea, etc.). See **conocer**

enturbiar *vt* to make turbid or cloudy; confuse, disorder; *vr* become turbid; be in disorder

entusiasmar *vt* to inspire enthusiasm; *vr* be enthusiastic

entusiasmo *m*, enthusiasm
entusiasta *a* enthusiastic. *mf* enthusiast
enumeración *f*, enumeration
enumerar *vt* to enumerate
enunciación *f*, statement, declaration, enunciation
enunciar *vt* to state clearly, enunciate
envainar *vt* to sheathe
envalentonamiento *m*, boldness; braggadocio, bravado
envalentonar *vt* to make bold (gen. in a bad sense); *vr* strut, brag; take courage
envanecer *vt irr* to make vain or conceited; *vr* be vain; be conceited
envanecimiento *m*, conceit, vanity
envasador (-ra) *n* packer. *m*, funnel
envasar *vt* to bottle; barrel; sack (grain, etc.); pack in any container; pierce (with sword)
envase *m*, bottling; filling; container; packing
envejecer *vt irr* to make old, wear out; *vi* grow old. See **conocer**
envenenador (-ra) *n* poisoner
envenenamiento *m*, poisoning
envenenar *vt* to poison; corrupt, pervert; put a malicious interpretation on; embitter; *vr* take poison
envergadura *f*, wingspan
envés *m*, wrong side of anything; *inf* back. **al e.**, wrong side out
enviado *m*, messenger; envoy. **e. extraordinario,** special envoy
enviar *vt* to send, dispatch
enviciar *vt* to corrupt, make vicious; *vr* (*with con, en*) take to (drink, etc.)
envidia *f*, envy; emulation; desire (to possess)
envidiable *a* enviable
envidiar *vt* to envy, grudge; emulate
envidioso *a* envious
envilecer *vt irr* to debase; *vr* degrade oneself. See **conocer**
envío *m*, *com* remittance; consignment
envite *m*, stake (at cards); offer; push, shove
enviudar *vi* to become a widow or widower
envoltorio *m*, bundle
envoltura *f*, swaddling clothes; covering; wrapping
envolver *vt irr* to enfold; envelop; wrap up, parcel; *fig* contain, enshrine; swaddle, swathe; roll into a ball; confound (in argument); *mil* outflank; implicate (person). See **mover**
enyesado *m*, plastering; stucco
enyesar *vt* to plaster; *surg* apply a plaster bandage
enzarzar *vt* to fill or cover with brambles; *vr* be caught on brambles; set one person against another; get in difficulties; quarrel
eñe *f*, name of letter Ñ
eón *m*, eon
eperlano *m*, smelt
épica *f*, epic
épico *a* epic
epicúreo (-ea) *a* epicurean; sensual, voluptuous. *n* epicure
epidemia *f*, epidemic
epidémico *a* epidemic
epifanía *f*, Epiphany, Twelfth Night
epiglotis *f*, epiglottis
epígrafe *m*, epigraph, inscription; title, motto
epigrafía *f*, epigraphy
epigrama *m*, inscription; epigram
epigramático (-ca) *a* epigrammatic. *n* epigrammatist
epilepsia *f*, epilepsy
epiléptico (-ca) *a* and *n* epileptic
epilogar *vt* to summarize, recapitulate
epílogo *m*, recapitulation; summary, digest; epilogue
episcopado *m*, episcopate; bishopric
episódico *a* episodic
episodio *m*, episode; digression
epístola *f*, epistle
epistolar *a* epistolary

epitafio *m*, epitaph
epíteto *m*, epithet
epítome *m*, epitome; summary, abstract
época *f*, epoch, period; space of time. **é. de celo,** mating season. **é. de lluvias,** rainy season. **é. de secas,** dry season. **en aquella é.,** at that time
épodo *m*, *poet* epode
epopeya *f*, epic poem; *fig* epic
equidad *f*, fairness; reasonableness; equity
equidistancia *f*, equidistance
equidistante *a* equidistant
equilibrar *vt* to balance; *fig* maintain in equilibrium, counterbalance
equilibrio *m*, equilibrium; equanimity; *fig* balance
equilibrista *mf* equilibrist, tightrope walker
equino *a* equine. *m*, *arch* echinus; sea urchin
equinoccio *m*, equinox
equipaje *m*, luggage, baggage; *naut* crew
equipar *vt* to equip, furnish
equipo *m*, outfitting, furnishing; equipment; team; trousseau
equis *f*, name of letter X
equitación *f*, horsemanship, riding
equitativo *a* equitable, just, fair
equivalencia *f*, equivalence, equality
equivalente *a* equivalent
equivaler *vi irr* to be equivalent; *geom* be equal. See **valer**
equivocación *f*, error, mistake
equivocadamente *adv* mistakenly, by mistake
equivocar *vt* to mistake; *vr* be mistaken or make a mistake. **equivocarse de medio a medio,** to be off by a long shot
equívoco *a* equivocal, ambiguous. *m*, equivocation
era *f*, era; threshing floor; vegetable or flower bed
erario *m*, public treasury, exchequer
erección *f*, raising; erection, elevation; foundation, institution
eremita *mf* hermit
ergio *m*, erg
erguir *vt irr* to raise; straighten; lift up; *vr* straighten up; tower; grow proud. *Pres. Ind.* **irgo** (or **yergo**), **irgues, irguen.** *Pres. Part.* **irguiendo.** *Preterite* **irguió, irguieron.** *Pres. Subjunc.* **irga** or **yerga**, etc.
erial *m*, uncultivated land
erigir *vt* to found, establish; promote, exalt. **erigirse contra,** to rise up against
erisipela *f*, erysipelas
erizado *a* standing on end (of hair); prickly, covered with bristles or quills. **e. de espinas,** bristling with thorns; covered with bristles or quills
erizar *vt* to set on end (hair); beset with difficulties; *vr* stand on end, bristle (hair, quills, etc.)
erizo *m*, hedgehog; husk (of some fruits); *inf* touch-me-not, unsociable person; *mech* sprocket wheel. **e. de mar,** sea urchin
ermita *f*, hermitage
ermitaño *m*, hermit
erosión *f*, erosion
erótico *a* erotic
errabundo *a* wandering, errant, vagrant
erradamente *adv* erroneously
erradicable *a* eradicable
erradicación *f*, eradication
erradicar *vt* to eradicate
errante *a* wandering; erring; errant
errar *vi irr* to err, fail; rove, roam; wander (attention, etc.); *vr* be mistaken. *aut* **e. el encendido,** to misfire. *Pres. Ind.* **yerro, yerras, yerra, yerran.** *Pres. Subjunc.* **yerre, yerres, yerre, yerren**
errata *f*, misprint
errático *a* wandering, vagrant; *med* erratic
erre *f*, name of letter R
erróneo *a* erroneous, mistaken
error *m*, error. **error de más,** an overestimate. **error de menos,** an underestimate

eructar *vi* to eructate, belch
eructo *m*, eructation, belching
erudición *f*, erudition
erudito *a* learned, erudite. *m*, scholar. **e. a la violeta,** pseudo-learned
erupción *f*, *med* rash; eruption
eruptivo *a* eruptive
es *irr 3rd pers. sing Pres. Ind.* of ser, is
esa *f*, *dem a* that. **ésa,** *f*, *dem. pron* that one; the former; the town in which you are (e.g. **Iré a é. mañana,** I shall come to your town tomorrow). Used generally in letters. See **ése**
esbeltez *f*, slenderness
esbelto *a* tall and slim and graceful, willowy
esbozar *vt* to sketch, outline
esbozo *m*, sketch; outline, rough plan, first draft
escabechar *vt* to pickle; dye (the hair, etc.); *inf* kill in anger; *inf* fail (an examination)
escabeche *m*, *cul* pickle; hair dye
escabechina *f*, *inf* heavy failure (in an examination)
escabel *m*, footstool; small backless chair; *fig* stepping-stone
escabioso *a* scabby, scabious
escabro *m*, scab, mange
escabroso *a* rough; rocky; uneven; rude, unpolished, uncivil; risqué, improper
escabullirse *vr irr* to escape; run away; slip out unnoticed. See **mullir**
escafandra *f*, diving suit, diving outfit
escala *f*, ladder; (*mus math*) scale; dial (of machines); proportion, ratio; stage, stopping place; measuring rule; *naut* port of call. **e. de toldilla,** companion ladder. *mus* **e. mayor,** major scale. **e. menor,** minor scale. *naut* **hacer e. en un puerto,** to call at a port
escalada *f*, escalade
escalafón *m*, salary scale; roll, list
escalamiento *m*, scaling, climbing; storming
escalar *vt* to scale; climb, ascend; storm, assail, enter or leave violently
escaldadura *f*, scalding; scald
escaldar *vt* to scald; make red-hot; *vr* scald or burn oneself. **Gato escaldado del agua fría huye,** Once bitten, twice shy
escalera *f*, staircase; stair. **e. abajo,** below stairs. **e. de caracol,** spiral staircase. **e. de mano,** ladder. **e. de tijera,** stepladder. **e. móvil,** escalator
escalfar *vt* to poach (eggs); burn (bread)
escalinata *f*, outside staircase or flight of steps, perron
escalofrío *m*, (gen. *pl*) shiver, shudder
escalón *m*, step, stair; rung (of a ladder); *fig* stepping-stone; grade, rank. **en escalones,** in steps
escalpar *vt* to scalp
escalpelo *m*, scalpel
escama *f*, *zool* scale; anything scale-shaped; flake; suspicion, resentment
escamar *vt* to scale (fish); make suspicious. *vr inf* be suspicious or disillusioned
escamondar *vt agr* to prune
escamoso *a* scaly
escamotear *vt* to make disappear; palm (in conjuring); steal
escamoteo *m*, disappearance; stealing
escampada *f*, *inf* clear interval on a rainy day
escampar *vi* to cease raining; clear up (of the weather, sky); stop (work, etc.)
escamujar *vt agr* to cut out superfluous wood (of trees, etc.)
escanciar *vt* to pour out wine; *vi* drink wine
escandalizar *vt* to shock, scandalize; disturb with noise; *vr* be vexed or irritated
escándalo *m*, scandal; commotion, uproar; bad example; viciousness; astonishment
escandaloso *a* disgraceful, scandalous; turbulent
escandallo *m*, *naut* deep-sea lead; random test
Escandinavia Scandinavia
escandinavo (-va) *a* and *n* Scandinavian

escandir *vt* to scan (verse)
escansión *f*, scansion
escantillón *m*, template, pattern; rule
escaño *m*, bench with a back
escapada *f*, escape; escapade
escapar *vt* to spur on (a horse); *vi* escape; flee; avoid, evade; *vr* escape; leak (gas, etc.). **Se me escapó su nombre,** His name escaped me. **e. por un pelo,** to have a narrow escape
escaparate *m*, showcase, cabinet; shop window
escapatoria *f*, escape, flight; *inf* way out, loophole
escape *m*, flight; evasion; escape (gas, etc.); *aut* exhaust. **a e.,** at full speed
escápula *f*, scapula
escaque *m*, square (chessboard or checkerboard); *pl* chess
escaqueado *a* checked, worked in squares
escara *f*, scar
escarabajo *m*, beetle, scarab; *fig inf* dwarf; *pl inf* scrawl
escaramuza *f*, skirmish
escaramuzar *vi* to skirmish
escarapela *f*, cockade, rosette; brawl
escarbadientes *m*, toothpick
escarbar *vt* to scratch, scrabble (fowls); rootle, dig; rake out (the fire); inquire into
escarcha *f*, hoarfrost
escarchar *vt cul* to frost, ice; spread with frosting; *vi* freeze lightly
escarda *f*, weeding; *fig* weeding out
escardador (-ra) *n* weeder
escardar *vt* to weed; *fig* separate good from bad
escarificación *f*, scarification
escarlata *f*, scarlet; scarlet cloth
escarlatina *f*, scarlet fever
escarmentar *vt irr* to reprehend or punish severely; *vi* learn from experience, be warned. See **acertar**
escarmiento *m*, disillusionment, experience; warning; punishment, fine
escarnecedor (-ra) *a* mocking. *n* mocker
escarnecer *vt irr* to mock. See **conocer**
escarnio *m*, gibe, jeer
escarola *f*, endive; frilled ruff
escarpa *f*, steep slope, declivity; escarpment
escarpado *a* steep, precipitous
escarpín *m*, pump, slipper
escasear *vt* to dole out, give grudgingly; save, husband; *vi* be scarce or short; grow less
escasez *f*, meanness, frugality; want; shortage, scarcity
escaso *a* scarce; short; bare; parsimonious
escatimar *vt* to cut down, curtail
escatimoso *a* malicious, guileful
escayola *f*, plaster of Paris
escena *f*, *theat* stage; scene; scenery; theater, drama; spectacle, sight; episode, incident. **director de e.,** producer. **poner en e.,** *theat* to produce
escenario *m*, *theat* stage; scenario
escénico *a* scenic
escenografía *f*, scenography
escenógrafo (-fa) *n* scenographer, scene painter
escepticismo *m*, scepticism
escéptico (-ca) *a* sceptical. *n* sceptic
escindir *vt* to split
escisión *f*, cleavage, split; splitting; schism; disagreement
esclarecer *vt irr* to illuminate; ennoble, make illustrious; *fig* enlighten; elucidate; *vi* dawn. See **conocer**
esclarecido *a* distinguished, illustrious
esclavina *f*, short cape
esclavitud *f*, slavery; fraternity
esclavizar *vt* to enslave
esclavo (-va) *n* slave; member of a brotherhood. *a* enslaved. *f*, slave bracelet; ID bracelet
esclerosis *f*, sclerosis
esclerótica *f*, sclerotic
esclusa *f*, lock; sluice gate; weir
esclusero *m*, lock keeper

escoba *f*, broom, brush; *bot* yellow broom

escobada *f*, sweep, stroke (of a broom)

escobar *vt* to sweep with a broom

escobazo *m*, brush with a broom

escobero *m*, brush maker or seller

escobilla *f*, brush

escobina *f*, metal filing; woodshaving

escocer *vi irr* to smart; *fig* sear; *vr* hurt, smart; be chafed. See **mover**

escocés (-esa) *a* Scots, Scottish. *n* Scot

Escocia Scotland

escoda *f*, claw hammer

escofina *f*, rasp, file

escoger *vt* to choose, select

escogido *a* choice, select

escolar *a* school; pupil. *m*, pupil

escolasticismo *m*, scholasticism

escolástico *a* scholastic

escollera *f*, breakwater, sea wall, jetty

escollo *m*, reef; danger, risk; difficulty, obstacle

escolopendra *f*, centipede; hart's-tongue fern

escolta *f*, escort, guard

escoltar *vt* to escort; guard, conduct

escombrar *vt* to remove obstacles, free of rubbish; *fig* clean up

escombro *m*, debris, rubble, rubbish; mackerel

esconder *vt* to hide, conceal; *fig* contain, embrace; *vr* hide

escondidas, a *adv* secretly

escondite, escondrijo *m*, hiding place. **jugar al escondite,** to play hide-and-seek

escopeta *f*, shotgun. **e. de aire comprimido,** air gun, popgun. **e. de pistón,** repercussion gun. **e. de viento,** air gun

escopetazo *m*, gunshot; gunshot wound; *fig* bombshell

escopetear *vt* to shoot repeatedly

escopetero *m*, musketeer; gunsmith; man with a gun

escoplear *vt carp* to notch; chisel; gouge

escoplo *m*, chisel

escorbuto *m*, scurvy

escoria *f*, dross, slag; scoria, volcanic ash; *fig* dregs

escorial *m*, slag heap

escorpión *m*, scorpion; Scorpio

escorzo *m*, *art* foreshortening

escotado *a* low-cut (of dresses)

escotadura *a* low neck (of a dress); piece cut out of something; *theat* large trapdoor; recess

escotar *vt* to cut low in the neck (of dresses); pay one's share (of expenses)

escote *m*, low neck (of a dress); shortness (of sleeves); share (of expenses); lace yoke

escotilla *f*, *naut* hatch

escozor *m*, smart, pricking pain; irritation, prickle; heartache

escriba *m*, (*Jewish hist.*) scribe

escribanía *f*, secretaryship; notaryship; bureau, office; writing case; inkstand

escribano *m*, notary public; secretary

escribiente *mf* clerk

escribir *vt* to write; *vr* enlist; enroll; correspond by writing. Past Part. **escrito**

escrito *m*, writing, manuscript; literary or scientific work; *law* writ. **por e.,** in writing

escritor (-ra) *n* writer, author

escritorio *m*, escritoire; office

escritura *f*, writing; handwriting; *law* deed; literary work. **Sagrada E.,** Holy Scripture

escrófula *f*, scrofula

escrofuloso *a* scrofulous

escroto *m*, scrotum

escrúpulo *m*, scruple, qualm; conscientiousness; scruple (pharmacy)

escrupulosidad *f*, conscientiousness, scrupulousness

escrupuloso *a* scrupulous; exact, accurate

escrutador (-ra) *n* scrutinizer. *a* examining, inspecting

escrutar *vt* to scrutinize, examine; count (votes)

escrutinio *m*, scrutiny, examination; count (votes)

escuadra *f*, carpenter's square; architect's square; *nav* fleet; *aer* squadron; *mil* squad. **e. de agrimensor,** *surv* cross-staff

escuadrar *vt* (*carp* and *mas*) to square

escuadrilla *f*, squadron (airplanes, small ships)

escuadrón *m*, squadron

escualidez *f*, squalor, sordidness

escuálido *a* filthy, squalid; sordid; thin

escucha *f*, listening; peephole; *mil* sentinel

escuchar *vt* to listen; attend to, heed; *vr* like the sound of one's own voice

escudar *vt* to shield, protect

escudero *m*, squire, page; gentleman; shield maker

escudete *m*, escutcheon; shield; gusset; white water lily

escudilla *f*, bowl

escudo *m*, shield; escudo; escutcheon; protection, defense; ward (of a keyhole)

escudriñador (-ra) *a* searching; curious, prying. *n* scrutinizer; pryer

escudriñar *vt* to scrutinize; scan; investigate; pry into

escuela *f*, school; school building; style; (*lit* and *art*) school. **e. de artes y oficios,** industrial school. **e. industrial,** technical school. **e. normal,** normal school

escueto *a* dry, bare, unadorned; simple, exact; unencumbered

esculpir *vt* to sculpture; engrave

escultor (-ra) *n* sculptor

escultórico *a* sculptural

escultura *f*, sculpture; carving; modeling

escupidera *f*, spittoon

escupir *vi* to expectorate; *vt fig* spit out; cast away, throw out

escurreplatos *m*, dishrack, draining rack

escurrido *a* narrow-hipped; skintight (of skirts)

escurridor *m*, colander, sieve; dishrack; drainingboard

escurriduras *f pl*, lees, dregs

escurrir *vt* to drain to the dregs; wring, press out, drain; *vi* trickle, drip; slip, slide; *vr* slip away, edge away; escape, slip out; skid

esdrújulo *a gram* of words where the accent falls on the antepenultimate syllable

ese *f*, name of letter S; S-shaped link (in a chain). *inf* **andar haciendo eses,** to reel about drunkenly

ese *m*, *dem a* (*f*, **esa.** *pl* **esos, esas**) that; those. **ése,** *m*, *dem pron* (*f*, **ésa.** *neut* **eso.** *pl* **ésos, ésas**) that one; the former (e.g. **Me gusta éste, pero ése no me gusta,** I like this one, but I do not like that one

esencia *f*, essence, nature, character; extract; *chem* essence

esencial *a* essential

esfera *f*, *geom* sphere, globe, ball; sky; rank; face, dial; province, scope

esférico *a* spherical

esfinge *f*, sphinx

esforzado *a* valiant, courageous; spirited

esforzador *a* encouraging

esforzar *vt irr* to encourage; invigorate; *vr* make an effort. See **contar**

esfuerzo *m*, effort; courage; spirit; vigor; exertion; strain; *mech* stress. **sin e.,** effortless

esfumar *vt art* shade; *art* stump; dim; *vr* disappear

esfumino *m*, *art* stump

esgrima *f*, (art of) fencing

esgrimidor *m*, fencer, swordsman

esgrimir *vt* to fence; fend off

esguazar *vt* to ford (a river)

esguince *m*, dodging, twist; expression or gesture of repugnance; *med* sprain

eslabón *m*, link (in a chain); steel for producing fire. **e. perdido,** *fig* missing link

eslabonar *vt* to link; connect, unite

eslavo (-va) *a* Slavic. *n* Slav

eslora *f*, *naut* length (of a ship)

eslovaco (-ca) *a* Slovakian. *n* Slovak

esloveno (-na) *a* and *n* Slovene

esmaltador (-ra) *n* enameler

esmaltar *vt* to enamel; decorate, adorn

esmalte *m*, enamel; enamelwork; smalt; brilliance

esmerado *a* careful, painstaking

esmeralda *f*, emerald

esmerar *vt* to polish; *vr (with en)* take great pains with (or to)

esmeril *m*, emery

esmerilar *vt* to polish with emery

esmero *m*, great care, conscientiousness

esmoladera *f*, grindstone

esnob *a* snobbish. *mf* snob

eso *neut dem pron* that; the fact that; that idea, affair, etc.; about (of time) (e.g. **Vendrá a e. de las nueve,** He will come about nine o'clock). **Eso** refers to an abstraction, never to one definite object. **No me gusta e.,** I don't like that kind of thing. **e. es,** that's it. **por e.,** therefore, for that reason

esófago *m*, esophagus

esotérico *a* esoteric

espaciar *vt* to space; *print* lead; *vr* spread oneself, enlarge (upon)

espacio *m*, space; capacity; interval, duration; slowness; *print* lead

espaciosidad *f*, spaciousness; capacity

espada *f*, sword; matador; swordsman; (cards) spade. **entre la e. y la pared,** *fig* between a rock and a hard place; between undesirable alternatives.

espadachín *m*, good swordsman; bully, quarrelsome fellow

espadaña *f*, open belfry; gladiolus

espadería *f*, sword cutler's workshop or shop

espadero *m*, sword cutler

espadín *m*, small dress sword

espahi *m*, spahi

espalda *f*, *anat* back (often *pl*); *pl* rear, back portion; *mil* rear guard. **de espaldas,** with one's (its, his, etc.) back turned; on one's (its, etc.) back

espaldar *m*, backpiece of a cuirass; back (of chair); garden trellis, espalier

espaldarazo *m*, accolade

espaldera *f*, espalier, trellis

espantadizo *a* easily frightened

espantapájaros *m*, scarecrow

espantar *vt* to frighten, terrify; chase off; *vr* be amazed; be scared

espanto *m*, terror, panic; dismay; amazement; threat

espantoso *a* horrible, terrifying, awesome; amazing

España Spain

español (-la) *a* Spanish. *n* Spaniard. *m*, Spanish (language). **a la española,** in Spanish fashion

españolía *f*, Spanish colony, Spanish community (outside Spain)

españolismo *m*, love of things Spanish; Hispanism

españolizar *vt* to hispanize; *vr* adopt Spanish customs

esparadrapo *m*, court plaster

esparavel *m*, casting net

esparcimiento *m*, scattering; naturalness, frankness; geniality

esparcir *vt* to scatter, sprinkle, disperse; spread, publish abroad; entertain; *vr* be scattered; amuse oneself

espárrago *m*, asparagus

esparraguera *f*, asparagus plant; asparagus bed; asparagus dish

Esparta Sparta

espartano (-na) *a* and *n* Spartan

espartería *f*, esparto industry, esparto shop

esparto *m*, esparto grass

espasmo *m*, spasm

espasmódico *a* spasmodic

espátula *f*, spatula; palette knife

especia *f*, spice. **nuez de e.,** nutmeg

especial *a* special; particular

especialidad *f*, speciality; branch (of learning)

especialista *mf* specialist

especialización *f*, specialization

especializarse *vr* to specialize

especie *f*, class, kind; species; affair, matter, case; idea, image; news; pretext, appearance

especiería *f*, spice trade; spice shop

especiero (-ra) *n* spice merchant; spice rack

especificación *f*, specification. **e. normalizada,** standard specification

especificar *vt* to specify, particularize

específico *a* and *m*, specific patent medicine

espécimen *m*, specimen, sample

especioso *a* lovely, perfect; specious

espectacular *a* spectacular

espectáculo *m*, spectacle, sight; show, display

espectador (-ra) *n* spectator

espectral *a* spectral; faint, dim

espectro *m*, phantom, specter; *phys* spectrum

especulación *f*, conjecture; *com* speculation

especulador (-ra) *n* speculator

especular *vt* to examine, look at; *(with en)* reflect on, consider; *vi com* speculate

especulativo *a* speculative; thoughtful, meditative

espejería *f*, mirror shop or factory

espejero *m*, mirror manufacturer or seller

espejismo *m*, mirage; illusion

espejo *m*, mirror; *fig* model. **e. de cuerpo entero,** full-length mirror. **e. retrovisor,** rearview mirror

espejuelo *m*, small mirror; *min* selenite; *min* sheet of talc; *pl* lenses, eyeglasses

espeluznante *a* hair-raising

espeluznar *vt* to dishevel; untidy (hair, etc.); *vr* stand on end (hair)

espera *f*, waiting; expectation; *law* adjournment; caution, restraint; *law* respite

esperantista *mf* Esperantist

esperanto *m*, Esperanto

esperanza *f*, hope

esperanzar *vt* to inspire hope in

esperar *vt* to hope; expect; await; *(with en)* have faith in. **e. sentado,** *fig inf* to whistle for

esperma *f*, sperm, semen. **e. de ballena,** spermaceti

esperpento *m*, *inf* scarecrow, grotesque; folly, madness; fantastic dramatic composition

espesar *vt* to thicken; make closer; tighten (fabrics); *vr* thicken; grow denser or thicker

espeso *a* thick; dense; greasy, dirty

espesor *m*, thickness; density

espesura *f*, thickness; density; thicket; filth

espetar *vt* *cul* to spit, skewer; pierce; *inf* utter, give; *vr* be stiff or affected; *inf* push oneself in, intrude

espetera *f*, kitchen or pot rack

espetón *m*, *cul* spit; poker; large pin

espía *mf* spy. *f*, *naut* warp

espiar *vt* to spy upon, watch; *vi naut* warp

espiche *m*, sharp-pointed weapon or instrument; spit, spike

espiga *f*, *bot* spike, ear; sprig; *carp* peg; tang, shank (of sword); *carp* tenon, dowel; *naut* masthead; *her* garb

espigador (-ra) *n* gleaner

espigar *vt* to glean; *carp* tenon; *vi bot* begin to show the ear or spike; *vr bot* bolt; shoot up, grow (persons)

espigón *m*, sting; sharp point; breakwater; bearded spike (corn, etc.)

espigueo *m*, gleaning

espín *m*, porcupine

espina *f*, thorn; prickle; splinter; fish bone; *anat* spine; suspicion, doubt

espinaca *f*, spinach

espinal *a* spinal

espinar *m*, thorn brake; *fig* awkward position. *vt* to prick, wound, hurt

espinazo *m*, backbone

espineta *f*, spinet; virginals

espinilla *f*, shinbone; blackhead

espinoso *a* thorny; difficult, intricate

espión *m*, See **espía**

espionaje *m*, espionage; spying

espira *f,* *(geom arch)* helix; turn, twist (of winding stairs); whorl (of a shell)

espiración *f,* expiration; respiration

espiral *a* spiral. *f, geom* spiral; spiral watchspring

espirar *vt* to exhale, breathe out; inspire; encourage; *vi* breathe; breathe out; *poet* blow (wind)

espiritisimo *m,* spiritualism

espiritista *a* spiritualist. *mf* spiritualist

espiritoso *a* lively, active, spirited; spirituous

espíritu *m,* spirit; apparition, specter; soul; intelligence, mind; mood, temper, outlook; underlying principle, spirit; devil (gen. *pl*) vigor, ardor, vivacity; *chem* essence; *chem* spirits; turn of mind. **E. Santo,** Holy Ghost

espiritual *a* spiritual

espiritualidad *f,* spirituality

espiritualismo *m, phil* spiritualism

espiritualizar *vt* to spiritualize

espita *f,* spigot, tap; *inf* tippler

esplender *vi poet* to shine

esplendidez *f,* liberality, abundance; splendor, pomp

espléndido *a* magnificent; liberal; resplendent (gen. *pl*)

esplendor *m,* splendor, brilliance; distinction, nobility

esplendoroso *a* splendid, brilliant, radiant

espliego *m,* lavender

esplín *m,* spleen, melancholy

espolada *f,* prick with the spur

espolear *vt* to prick with the spur; encourage, stimulate

espoleta *f,* fuse (of explosives); breastbone (of fowls); wishbone. **e. de tiempo, e. graduada,** time fuse. **e. de seguridad,** safety fuse

espolón *m,* spur (of a bird or mountain range); *naut* ram; breakwater; buttress; *naut* fender

espolvorear *vt* to sprinkle with powder

espondeo *m,* (metrical foot) spondee

esponja *f,* sponge

esponjadura *f,* sponging

esponjar *vt* to make spongy; sponge; *vr* swell with pride; *inf* bloom with health

esponjera *f,* sponge holder

esponjosidad *f,* sponginess

esponjoso *a* spongy, porous

esponsales *m pl,* betrothal; marriage contract

espontaneidad *f,* spontaneity

espontáneo *a* spontaneous

espora *f,* spore

esporádico *a* sporadic

esportillo *m,* bass, frail

esposa *f,* wife; *pl* handcuffs

esposo *m,* husband; *pl* husband and wife

espuela *f,* spur; stimulus; *(orn bot)* spur. **e. de caballero,** larkspur

espulgar *vt* to delouse; examine carefully

espuma *f,* froth, foam; *cul* scum; *fig* the best of anything, flower; *fig inf* **crecer como la e.,** to flourish like weeds

espumadera *f,* skimming ladle

espumajear *vi* to foam at the mouth

espumajoso *a* frothy, foaming

espumar *vt* to skim (soup, etc.); *vi* foam; increase rapidly

espumoso *a* frothy, foaming

espurio *a* bastard; spurious

esputo *m,* sputum

esqueje *m, agr* cutting

esquela *f,* note; (printed) card

esqueleto *m,* skeleton; *inf* skinny person; framework

esquema *f,* diagram, layout sketch; scheme, plan. **e. de una máquina,** drawing of a machine

esquemático *a* schematic; diagrammatic

esquematizar *vt* to plan, outline

esquí *m,* ski, snowshoe

esquiador *m,* skier

esquiar *vi* to ski

esquife *m,* skiff

esquila *f,* cattle bell; small bell, hand bell; sheep shearing; *(icht bot)* squill

esquilador *a* shearing. *m,* sheep shearer

esquiladora *f,* shearing machine

esquilar *vt* to shear, clip (sheep, etc.)

esquileo *m,* shearing; shearing time or place

esquilmar *vt* to harvest; impoverish

esquilmo *m,* harvest

esquimal *a* and *mf* Eskimo

esquina *f,* corner

esquinado *a* having corners; *fig* difficult to approach (people)

esquirla *f,* splinter (of a bone); shrapnel

esquirol *m, inf* strikebreaker, blackleg

esquisto *m, min* slate; shale

esquivar *vt* to avoid; *vr* slip away, disappear; excuse oneself

esquivez *f,* unsociableness; unfriendliness, aloofness

esquivo *a* unsociable, elusive, aloof

esquizado *a* mottled (of marble)

estabilidad *f,* stability; fastness (of colors)

estabilizar *vt* to stabilize

estable *a* stable; fast (of colors)

establecer *vt irr* to establish, found, institute; decree; *vr* take up residence; open (a business firm). See **conocer**

establecimiento *m,* law, statute; foundation, institution; establishment

establero *m,* stablegroom

establo *m,* stable

estaca *f,* stake, pole; *agr* cutting; cudgel

estacada *f,* fence; *mil* palisade; place fixed for a duel

estacar *vt* to stake; fence; tie to a stake; *vr fig* be as still as a post

estación *f,* position, situation; season; station (railroad, etc.); depot; time, period; stop, halt; building, headquarters; *bot* habitat; *(surv geom ecc)* station

estacional *a* seasonal; *ast* stationary

estacionamiento *m,* stationariness; *aut* parking

estacionar *vt* to station, place; *aut* park (a car); *vr* remain stationary; place oneself

estacionario *a* motionless; *ast* stationary. *m,* stationer

estada *f,* sojourn

estadía *f,* stay, sojourn; *art* sitting (of a model)

estadio *m,* racetrack; stadium; furlong

estadista *mf.* statistician; statesman, stateswoman

estadística *f,* statistics

estadístico *a* statistical

estadizo *a* stagnant

estado *m,* state; condition; rank, position; *pol* state; profession; status; *com* statement. **e. de guerra,** state of war; martial law. **e. mayor central,** *(nav mil)* general staff. **e. tapón,** *pol* buffer state. **tomar e.,** to marry; *ecc* profess; be ordained a priest

Estados Unidos de América United States of America

estadounidense *a* United States

estafa *f,* swindle

estafador (-ra) *n* swindler

estafar *vt* to swindle

estafeta *f,* courier, messenger; branch post office; diplomatic pouch

estafilococo *m,* staphylococcus

estagnación *f,* stagnation

estalactita *f,* stalactite

estalagmita *f,* stalagmite

estallar *vi* to explode; burst; *fig* break out

estallido *m,* explosion, report; crash, crack; *fig* outbreak; *aut* **e. de un neumático,** blowout (of a tire)

estambre *m,* woolen yarn, worsted; stamen

estameña *f,* serge

estampa *f,* illustration, picture; print; aspect; printing press; track, step; *met* boss, stud

estampación *f,* stamping; printing; imprinting. **e. en seco,** tooling (of a book)

estampado *a* printed (of textiles). *m,* textile printing; printed fabric

estampar *vt* to print, stamp; leave the print (of); bestow, imprint. **e. en relieve,** to emboss. **e. en seco,** to tool (a book)

estampería *f,* print or picture shop; trade in prints

estampero *m,* print dealer, picture dealer

estampido *m,* report, bang, detonation; crash

estampilla *f,* rubber stamp; seal

estampillar *vt* to stamp, imprint

estancación *f,* stagnation

estancado *a* stagnant; blocked, held up

estancar *vt* to check, stem; set up a monopoly; *fig* hold up (negotiations, etc.); *vr* be stagnant

estancia *f,* stay, residence; dwelling; lounge, living-room; stanza; *WH* farm

estanciero *m, WH* farmer

estanco *a naut* watertight. *m,* monopoly; shop selling government monopoly goods; archive

estandarte *m,* standard, flag. **e. real,** royal standard

estanque *m,* tank; pool; reservoir

estanquero (-ra) *n* seller of government monopoly goods (tobacco, matches, etc.)

estante *a* present; extant; permanent. *m,* shelf; bookcase; bin (for wine)

estantería *f,* shelving; shelves, bookcase

estantigua *f,* hobgoblin, specter; *fig inf* scarecrow

estañador *m,* tinsmith

estañar *vt* to tin; solder

estaño *m,* tin

estaquilla *f,* peg, cleat

estar *vi irr* to be. Indicates: 1. Position or place (e.g. **Está a la puerta,** He is at the door). 2. State (e.g. **Las flores están marchitas,** The flowers are faded). 3. Used to form the continuous or progressive tense (e.g. **Siempre está (estaba) escribiendo,** He is (was) always writing). 4. In contrast to verb *ser,* indicates impermanency (e.g. **Está enfermo,** He is ill). 5. **Estar** forms an apparent passive where no action is implied (e.g. **El cuadro está pintado al óleo,** The picture is painted in oils). 6. Used in some impersonal expressions (e.g. **¡Bien está!** All right! **¡Claro está!** Of course! etc.). **e. de,** to be in, or on, or acting as (e.g. **e. de prisa,** to be in a hurry. **e. de capitán,** to be acting as a captain). **e. para,** to be on the point of; to be nearly; to be in the mood for. **e. para llover,** to be on the point of raining. **e. por,** to remain to be done; have a mind to (e.g. **La historia está por escribir,** The story remains to be written). **e. bien,** to be well (healthy). *mech* **e. bajo presión,** to have the steam up. *pol* **e. en el poder,** to be in office. **e. en una cuenca,** *Dominican Republic* to be broke. **¿A cómo** (*or* **A cuántos**) **estamos?** What is the date? *Pres. Ind.* **estoy, estás, está, estamos, estáis, están.** *Preterite* **estuve,** etc. *Pres. Subjunc.* **esté, estés, esté, estén.** *Imperf. Subjunc.* **estuviese,** etc.

estarcir *vt* to stencil

estatal *a* state

estática *f, mech* statics

estático *a* static

estatua *f,* statue

estatuaria *f,* statuary

estatuir *vt irr* to establish, order. See **huir**

estatura *f,* stature, height (of persons)

estatuto *m,* statute, law

estay *m, naut* stay. **e. mayor,** *naut* mainstay

este *m,* east

este *m, dem a* this (*f,* **esta,** *pl* **estos, estas,** these). **éste,** *m, dem pron* this one; the latter. (*f,* **ésta,** *neut* **esto,** *pl* **éstos, éstas,** these ones; the latter) (e.g. **Aquel cuadro no es tan hermoso como éste,** That picture is not as beautiful as this one)

estela *f,* wake, track (of a ship)

estenografía *f,* shorthand

estenográfico *a* shorthand

estenógrafo (-fa) *n* stenographer

estenordeste *m,* east-northeast

estentóreo *a* stentorian

estepa *f,* steppe, arid plain

estera *f,* matting

esterar *vt* to cover with matting; *vi inf* muffle oneself up

estercoladura *f,* manuring

estercolar *vt* to manure

estercolero *m,* manure pile; driver of a dung cart

estereoscopio *m,* stereoscope

esterería *f,* matting factory, matting shop

esterero (-ra) *n* matting maker, matting seller

estéril *a* sterile, barren; unfruitful, unproductive

esterilidad *f,* sterility; barrenness, unfruitfulness

esterilización *f,* sterilization

esterilizador *a* sterilizing. *m,* sterilizer

esterilizar *vt* to make barren; *med* sterilize

esterilla *f,* mat, matting

esterlina *a f,* sterling. **libra e.,** pound sterling

esternón *m,* sternum

estero *m,* salt marsh

estertor *m,* stertorous breathing, rattle

estesudeste *m,* east-southeast

estética *f,* aesthetics. *a* aesthete

estético *a* aesthetic *m,* aesthete

estetoscopio *m,* stethoscope

esteva *f,* plow handle

estevado *a* bandy-legged

estiaje *m,* low water level (of rivers)

estibador *m,* stevedore, dock worker

estibar *vt naut* to stow

estiércol *m,* dung; manure

estigio *a* Stygian; (*fig poet*) infernal

estigma *m,* stigma

estigmatizar *vt* to brand; stigmatize; insult

estilar *vi* to be accustomed; *vt* draw up (document)

estilete *m,* stiletto, dagger; needle, hand, pointer; *med* stylet

estilista *mf* stylist

estilística *f,* stylism, stylistics

estilizar *vt* to stylize

estilo *m,* (*art arch lit*) style, writing instrument; gnomon, pointer; manner, way; *bot* style. **por el e.,** in some such way, like that

estilográfico *a* stylographic. **pluma estilográfica,** fountain pen

estima *f,* appreciation, esteem, consideration

estimable *a* estimable

estimación *f,* valuation, estimate; regard, esteem. **e. prudente,** conservative estimate

estimar *vt* to value, estimate; esteem, judge

estimulante *m, med* stimulant. *a* stimulating

estimular *vt* to stimulate, excite; goad on, encourage, incite

estímulo *m,* stimulus; incitement, encouragement

estío *m,* summer

estipendiar *vt* to pay a stipend to

estipendiario *m,* stipendiary

estipendio *m,* stipend, pay, remuneration

estipulación *f,* stipulation; *law* clause, condition

estipular *vt* to stipulate; arrange terms; *law* covenant

estirado *a* stretched out; tight, stiff; wire-drawn (metals); stiff, pompous; parsimonious

estirador *m,* wire drawer

estirar *vt* to stretch; iron roughly (clothes); *met* wire-draw; dole out (money); *fig* stretch, go beyond the permissible; *vr* stretch oneself

estirpe *f,* race, stock, lineage

estival *a* summer

esto *dem pron neut* this, this matter, this idea, etc. Always refers to abstractions, never to a definite object. **e. de,** the matter of. **e. es,** that's it; namely. **por e.,** for this reason. **a todo e.,** meanwhile

estocada *f,* sword thrust

Estocolmo Stockholm

estofa *f, sew* quilting; kind, quality

estofado *m,* stew. *a sew* quilted; stewed

estofar *vt sew* to quilt; make a stew

estoicismo *m,* stoicism

estoico (-ca) *n* stoic. *a* stoical

estolidez *f,* idiocy

estólido (-da) *a* idiotic. *a* idiot

estomacal *a* stomach

estómago *m,* stomach
estomático *a* pertaining to the mouth, oral
estomatitis *f,* stomatitis
estonio (-ia) *a* and *n* Estonian. *m,* Estonian (language)
estopa *f,* tow; oakum
estopilla *f,* batiste, lawn; calico, cotton cloth
estopín *m, mil* quick march
estoque *m,* rapier; narrow sword
estoquear *vt* to wound or kill with a rapier
estoqueo *m,* swordplay
estorbador (-ra) *a* obstructive. *n* obstructer
estorbar *vt* to obstruct, impede; hinder
estorbo *m,* obstruction; hindrance, nuisance
estornino *m,* starling
estornudar *vi* to sneeze
estornudo *m,* sneezing; sneeze
estrabismo *m, med* strabismus, squint, cast
estrada *f,* road, highway
estrado *m,* dais
estrafalario *a inf* slovenly, untidy; *inf* eccentric, odd
estragar *vt* to corrupt, spoil, vitiate; ruin, destroy
estrago *m,* devastation, destruction, ruin, havoc
estrambote *m,* refrain
estrambótico *a inf* eccentric
estrangul *m, mus* mouthpiece
estrangulación *f,* strangulation; *aut* throttling
estrangulador (-ra) *a* strangling. *n* strangler. *m, aut* throttle
estrangular *vt* to strangle
estraperlista *mf* black marketeer
estraperlo *m,* black market
Estrasburgo Strasbourg
estratagema *f,* stratagem, trick
estrategia *f,* strategy
estratégico *a* strategic
estratego *m,* strategist
estratificación *f,* stratification
estrato *m, geol* stratum
estratosfera *f,* stratosphere
estraza *f,* rag. **papel de e.,** brown paper
estrechar *vt* to make narrower, tighten; hold tightly, clasp; compel, oblige; *vr* tighten oneself up; reduce one's expenses; *fig* tighten the bonds (of friendship, etc.). **e. la mano,** to shake hands
estrechez *f,* narrowness; tightness; scantiness; poverty, want. **e. de miras,** narrowmindedness
estrecho *a* narrow; tight; intimate, close; austere, rigid; meanspirited. *m, geog* strait
estregadera *f,* shoe scraper; scourer
estregar *vt irr* to rub, scour, scrub, scrape, scratch. See **cegar**
estrella *f,* star; fortune, fate; anything star-shaped; *fig* star. **e. de la pantalla,** movie star. **e. de mar,** starfish. **e. de rabo,** comet. **e. fugaz,** shooting star. **tener e.,** to be born under a lucky star
estrellado *a* star-shaped; full of stars, starry; shattered, broken; fried (eggs)
estrellamar *f,* starfish
estrellar *vt inf* to shatter, break into fragments; fry (eggs); *vr* be starry or sprinkled with stars; be dashed against; fail in, come up against
estrellón *m,* large, artificial star (painted or otherwise); star-like firework
estremecer *vt irr* to cause to tremble; perturb; *vr* shudder, tremble. See **conocer**
estremecimiento *m,* shudder, trembling; agitation
estrenar *vt* to use or do for the first time; inaugurate; give the first performance of (plays, etc.); *vr* do for the first time; *com* make the first sale of the day
estreno *m,* commencement, inauguration; first appearance; *theat* first performance, opening night, premiere
estrenque *m,* strong esparto rope
estrenuo *a* strong, energetic, agile
estreñimiento *m,* constipation
estreñir *vt* to constipate
estrépito *m,* clamor, din, great noise; fuss, show

estrepitoso *a* noisy, clamorous
estreptococo *m,* streptococcus
estreptomicina *f,* streptomycin
estría *f,* arch fluting, stria
estribadero *m,* prop, support, strut
estribar *vi* (*with en*) to lean on, rest on, be supported by; *fig* be based on
estribillo *m,* refrain
estribo *m,* stirrup; footboard, step, running board (of vehicles); *arch* buttress or pier; *fig* stay, support; *anat* stapes; *mech carp* stirrup piece. **perder los estribos,** to lose patience, forget oneself
estribor *m,* starboard
estricnina *f,* strychnine
estricto *a* strict, exact; unbending, severe
estridente *a* strident, shrill
estridor *m,* strident or harsh sound; screech; creak
estro *m,* inspiration
estrofa *f,* strophe; verse, stanza
estropajo *m,* scourer, dishcloth; worthless person or thing
estropajoso *a inf* indistinct, stammering; dirty and ragged; tough (meat, etc.)
estropear *vt* to spoil, damage; ruin, undo, spoil (plans, effects, etc.); ill-treat, maim; *vr* hurt oneself, be maimed; spoil, deteriorate
estropicio *m, inf* crash (of china, etc.)
estructura *f,* fabric, structure; *fig* construction
estructural *a* structural
estruendo *m,* din, clatter; clamor, noise; ostentation
estruendoso *a* noisy
estrujar *vt* to squeeze, crush (fruit); hold tightly, press, squeeze, bruise; *fig* squeeze dry
estrujón *m,* squeeze, pressure; final pressing (grapes)
estuario *m,* estuary
estucado *m,* stucco
estucar *vt* to stucco
estuco *m,* stucco; plaster
estuche *m,* case; casket; box; cover; sheath
estudiante *mf* student
estudiantil *a inf* student
estudiantina *f,* strolling band of students playing and singing, generally in aid of charity
estudiantino *a inf* student
estudiantón *m, inf* grind
estudiar *vt* to study. **e. de,** study to be a (e.g. **e. de rabino,** study to be a rabbi); learn; *art* copy
estudio *m,* study; sketch; disquisition, dissertation; studio; diligence; *art* study; reading room, den
estudiosidad *f,* studiousness
estudioso *a* studious
estufa *f,* heating stove; hothouse; hot room (in bathhouses); drying chamber; *elec* heater
estufador *m,* stewpot or casserole
estufilla *f,* muff; small brazier
estufista *mf* stove maker or repairer, stove seller
estulto *a* foolish
estupefacción *f,* stupefaction
estupefacto *a* stupefied, stunned, amazed
estupendo *a* wonderful, marvelous
estupidez *f,* stupidity
estúpido *a* stupid
estupor *m, med* stupor; astonishment
estupro *m, law* rape
estuque *m,* stucco
estuquería *f,* stuccowork
esturión *m,* sturgeon
esvástica *f,* swastika
etapa *f, mil* field ration; *mil* halt, camp; stage, juncture. **a pequeñas etapas,** by easy stages (of a journey)
etcétera etcetera
éter *m,* ether; *poet* sky
etéreo *a* etheric; ethereal
eterizar *vt* to etherize
eternidad *f,* eternity
eternizar *vt* to drag out, prolong; eternize, perpetuate

eterno *a* eternal, everlasting; lasting, enduring
ética *f*, ethics
ético *a* ethical. *m*, moralist
etimología *f*, etymology
etimológico *a* etymological
etimologista *mf* etymologist
etimólogo *m*, etymologist
etiología *f*, etiology
etíope *a* and *mf* Ethiopian
Etiopía Ethiopia
etiqueta *f*, etiquette; label
etiquetero *a* ceremonious, stiff; prim
étnico *a* ethnic; heathen
etnografía *f*, ethnography
etnográfico *a* ethnographic
etnología *f*, ethnology
etnólogo *m*, ethnologist
etrusco (-ca) *a* and *n* Etruscan
eubolia *f*, discretion in speech
eucalipto *m*, eucalyptus
Eucaristía *f*, Eucharist
euclídeo *a* Euclidean
eufemismo *m*, euphemism
eufonía *f*, euphony
eufónico *a* euphonious
euforia *f*, resistance to disease; buoyancy, well-being
eufuismo *m*, euphuism
eugenesia *f*, eugenics
eugenésico *a* eugenic
eunuco *m*, eunuch
euritmia *f*, eurythmics
eurítmico *a* eurythmic
euro *m*, *poet* east wind
Europa Europe
europeizar *vt* to Europeanize
europeo (-ea) *a* and *n* European
éuscaro *a* Basque. *m*, Basque (language)
eutanasia *f*, euthanasia
evacuación *f*, evacuation
evacuar *vt* to vacate; evacuate, empty; finish, conclude (a business deal, etc.)
evadir *vt* to avoid, elude; *vr* escape; elope
evaluación *f*, valuation; estimation
evaluar *vt* to evaluate, estimate; gauge; value
evangélico *a* evangelical
evangelio *m*, Gospel; Christianity; *inf* indisputable truth
evangelista *m*, evangelist
evangelizar *vt* to evangelize
evaporación *f*, evaporation
evaporar(se) *vt* and *vr* to evaporate; disappear, vanish
evasión, evasiva *f*, subterfuge, evasion; flight, escape
evasivo *a* evasive
evento *m*, happening, event; contingency
eventual *a* possible, fortuitous; accidental (expenses); extra (emoluments)
eventualidad *f*, eventuality
evicción *f*, law eviction
evidencia *f*, proof, evidence. **ponerse en e.**, to put oneself forward
evidenciar *vt* to show, make obvious
evidente *a* obvious, evident
evitable *a* avoidable
evitación *f*, avoidance
evitar *vt* to avoid; shun, eschew
evocación *f*, evocation
evocador *a* evocative
evocar *vt* to evoke
evolución *f*, evolution; development; (*mil nav*) maneuver; change; *geom* involution
evolucionar *vi* to evolve; (*nav mil*) maneuver; change, alter
evolucionismo *m*, evolutionism
evolutivo *a* evolutional
ex *prefix* out of; from; formerly
exacción *f*, exaction; tax
exacerbación *f*, exacerbation

exacerbar *vt* to exasperate; exacerbate
exactitud *f*, exactitude; correctness; punctuality
exacto *a* exact; correct; punctual
exactor *m*, tax collector; tyrant, oppressor
exageración *f*, exaggeration
exagerador (-ra) *a* given to exaggerating. *n* exaggerater
exagerar *vt* to exaggerate
exaltación *f*, exaltation
exaltar *vt* to exalt, elevate; extol; *vr* grow excited or agitated
examen *m*, inquiry; investigation, research; examination; *geol* survey. **e. parcial,** quiz (at school)
examinador (-ra) *n* examiner
examinando (-da) *n* candidate, examinee
examinar *vt* to inquire into; investigate; inspect; examine; *vr* take an examination
exangüe *a* bloodless, pale; exhausted, weak; dead
exánime *a* lifeless; spiritless, weak
exasperación *f*, exasperation
exasperador, exasperante *a* exasperating
exasperar *vt* to exasperate; irritate, annoy
excarcelar *vt* to release from jail
excavación *f*, excavation
excavador (-ra) *n* excavator. *f*, *mech* excavator
excavar *vt* to hollow; excavate; *agr* hoe (roots of plants)
excedente *a* exceeding; excessive; surplus
exceder *vt* to exceed; *vr* forget oneself, go too far
excelencia *f*, excellence, superiority; Excellency (title)
excelente *a* excellent; first-rate
excelso *a* lofty, high; eminent, mighty; sublime
excentricidad *f*, eccentricity
excéntrico *a* unconventional; erratic; *geom* eccentric
excepción *f*, exception
excepcional *a* exceptional
exceptuar *vt* to except
excerpta, excerta *f*, excerpt, extract
excesivo *a* excessive
exceso *m*, excess; *com* surplus; *pl* crimes, excesses. **e. de peso** *or* **e. de equipaje,** excess baggage
excipiente *m*, excipient
excisión *f*, excision
excitabilidad *f*, excitability
excitable *a* excitable, high-strung
excitación *f*, excitation; excitement
excitador *a* exciting, stimulating. *m*, *phys* exciter
excitar *vt* to excite, stimulate, provoke; *elec* energize; *vr* become agitated or excited
exclamación *f*, exclamation, interjection
exclamar *vi* to exclaim
exclamatorio *a* exclamatory
excluir *vt irr* to exclude, keep out; reject, bar. See **huir**
exclusiva *f*, exclusion; special privilege, sole right
exclusive *adv* exclusively; excluded
exclusivismo *m*, exclusivism
exclusivista *a* exclusive. *mf* exclusivist
exclusivo *a* exclusive
excomulgado (-da) *a* and *n ecc* excommunicate; *inf* wicked (person)
excomulgar *vt* to excommunicate
excomunión *f*, excommunication
excoriar *vt* to flay, excoriate; *vr* graze oneself
excrecencia *f*, excrescence
excreción *f*, excretion
excremento *m*, excrement
excretar *vi* to excrete
excretorio *a* excretory
exculpación *f*, exoneration
exculpar(se) *vt* and *vr* to exonerate
excursión *f*, excursion, trip; *mil* incursion
excursionismo *m*, sightseeing; hiking
excursionista *mf* excursionist; hiker
excusa *f*, excuse
excusabaraja *f*, basket with a lid
excusado *a* excused; exempt; unnecessary, superfluous; reserved, private. *m*, lavatory, toilet

excusar *vt* to excuse; avoid, ward off, prevent; exempt; *vr* excuse oneself

execración *f,* execration

execrar *vt* to execrate; denounce; loathe

exención *f,* exemption

exentar *vt* to exempt

exento *a* exempt; free, liberated; open (of buildings, etc.)

exequias *f pl,* obsequies

exfoliar *vt* to strip off; *vr* flake off

exhalación *f,* exhalation; shooting star; lightning; emanation, effluvium

exhalar *vt* to exhale, give off; *fig* give vent to

exhausto *a* exhausted

exhibición *f,* exhibition

exhibicionismo *m,* exhibitionism

exhibicionista *mf* exhibitionist

exhibir *vt* to exhibit, show

exhortación *f,* exhortation

exhortar *vt* to exhort

exhumación *f,* exhumation

exhumar *vt* to exhume, disinter

exigencia *f,* exigency; demand

exigente *a* exigent

exigir *vt* to exact, collect; need, require; demand

exigüidad *f,* exiguousness

exiguo *a* exiguous, meager

eximio *a* most excellent; illustrious

eximir *vt* to exempt

existencia *f,* existence; *pl com* stock on hand

existir *vi* to exist, be; live

éxito *m,* success; result, conclusion

éxodo *m,* Exodus; exodus, emigration. **é. rural,** rural depopulation

exoneración *f,* exoneration

exonerar *vt* to exonerate; discharge (from employment)

exorbitancia *f,* exorbitance

exorbitante *a* exorbitant, excessive

exorcismo *m,* exorcism

exorcista *m,* exorcist

exorcizar *vt* to exorcize

exordio *m,* exordium, introduction

exornar *vt* to adorn; embellish (*lit* style)

exótico *a* exotic, rare

expandir *vt* to expand

expansibilidad *f, phys* expansibility

expansión *f,* expansion; recreation, hobby

expansivo *a* expansive; communicative, frank

expatriación *f,* expatriation

expatriarse *vr* to emigrate, leave one's country

expectación *f,* expectation; expectancy

expectante *a* expectant

expectativa *f,* expectancy; expectation

expectoración *f,* expectoration

expectorar *vt* to expectorate

expedición *f,* expedition; speed, promptness; *ecc* bull, dispensation; excursion; forwarding, dispatch

expediente *m, law* proceedings; file of documents; expedient, device, means; expedition, promptness; motive, reason; provision

expedir *vt irr* to expedite; forward, send, ship; issue, make out (checks, receipts, etc.); draw up (documents); dispatch, deal with. See **pedir**

expedito *a* expeditious, speedy

expeler *vt* to expel, discharge, emit

expendedor (-ra) *a* spending. *n* spender; agent; retailer; seller; *law* **e. de moneda falsa,** distributor of counterfeit money

expendeduría *f,* shop where government monopoly goods are sold (tobacco, stamps, etc.)

expender *vt* to spend (money); *com* retail; *com* sell on commission; *law* distribute counterfeit money

expensas *f pl,* costs, charges

experiencia *f,* experience; practice, experiment

experimentación *f,* experimenting

experimentar *vt* to test, try; experience; feel

experimento *m,* experiment

experto (-ta) *a* practiced, expert. *n* expert

expiación *f,* expiation

expiar *vt* to expiate, atone for; pay the penalty of; *fig* purify

expiatorio *a* expiatory

expiración *f,* expiration

expirar *vi* to die; *fig* expire; die down; exhale, expire

explanación *f,* leveling; explanation, elucidation

explanada *f,* esplanade; *mil* glacis

explanar *vt* to level; explain

explayar *vt* to extend, enlarge; *vr* spread oneself, enlarge (upon); enjoy an outing; confide (in)

explicación *f,* explanation; elucidation

explicar *vt* to explain; expound; interpret, elucidate; *vr* explain oneself

explicativo *a* explanatory

explícito *a* explicit, clear

exploración *f,* exploration

explorador *a* exploring. *m,* explorer; prospector; boy scout; *mil* scout

explorar *vt* to explore; investigate; *med* probe

exploratorio *a* exploratory

explosión *f,* explosion; outburst, outbreak. **hacer falsas explosiones,** *mech* to misfire

explosivo *a* and *m,* explosive. **e. violento,** high explosive

explotación *f,* development, exploitation

explotar *vt* to work (mines); *fig* exploit

expoliación *f,* spoliation

expoliar *vt* to despoil

exponente *a* and *mf* exponent. *m, math* index

exponer *vt irr* to show, expose; expound, interpret; risk, jeopardize; abandon (child). See **poner**

exportación *f,* exportation; export

exportador (-ra) *a* export. *n* exporter

exportar *vt* to export

exposición *f,* exposition, demonstration; petition; exhibition; *lit* exposition; *phot* exposure; orientation, position

expósito (-ra) *a* and *n* foundling

expositor (-ra) *a* and *n* exponent. *n* exhibitor

expremijo *m,* cheese vat

exprés *a* express. *m,* messenger or delivery service; express train; transport office

expresar *vt* to express (all meanings)

expresión *f,* statement, utterance; phrase, wording; expression; presentation; manifestation; gift, present; squeezing; pressing (of fruits, etc.)

expresivo *a* expressive; affectionate

expreso *a* express; clear, obvious. *m,* courier, messenger

exprimelimones *m,* **exprimidera,** *f,* lemon squeezer

exprimidor de la ropa *m,* wringer, mangle

exprimir *vt* to squeeze, press (fruit); press, hold tightly; express, utter

expropiación *f,* expropriation

expropiar *vt* to expropriate; commandeer

expugnar *vt mil* to take by storm

expulsar *vt* to expel, eject, dismiss

expulsión *f,* expulsion

expurgar *vt* to cleanse, purify; expurgate

expurgatorio *a* expurgatory. *m, ecc* index

exquisitez *f,* exquisiteness

exquisito *a* exquisite, choice; delicate, delicious

extasiarse *vr* to fall into ecstasy; marvel (at), delight (in)

éxtasis *m,* ecstasy; rapture

extático *a* ecstatic

extemporáneo *a* untimely; inopportune, inconvenient

extender *vt irr* to spread; reach, extend; elongate; enlarge, amplify; unfold, open out, stretch; draw up (documents); make out (checks, etc.); *vr* stretch out; lie down; spread, be generalized; extend; last (of time);

record; stretch, open out. **extenderse en,** to expatiate on. See **entender**

extensión *f,* extension; expanse; length; extent; duration; extension (logic)

extensivo *a* extensive, spacious; extensible

extenso *a* extensive, vast

extensor *a* extensor. *m,* chest expander

extenuación *f,* emaciation, weakness; extenuation

extenuar *vt* to exhaust, weaken; *vr* become weak

exterior *a* external; foreign (trade, etc.). *m,* outside, exterior; outward appearance

exterioridad *f,* outward appearance; outside, externality; *pl* ceremonies, forms; ostentation

exteriorizar *vt* to exteriorize, reveal

exterminador (-ra) *a* exterminating. *n* exterminator

exterminar *vt* to exterminate; devastate

exterminio *m,* extermination; devastation

externado *m,* day school

externarse *vr* to stand out

externo (-na) *a* external. *n* day

extinción *f,* extinction; extinguishment; abolition, cancellation

extinguir *vt* to extinguish; destroy

extintor *m,* fire extinguisher

extirpación *f,* extirpation

extirpador (-ra) *a* extirpating. *n* extirpator

extirpar *vt* to extirpate; *fig* eradicate

extorsión *f,* extortion

extorsionar *vt* to extort

extra *prefix* outside, without, beyond. *prep* besides. *a* extremely, most. *m, inf* extra

extracción *f,* extraction; drawing (lottery); origin, lineage; exportation

extractar *vt* to abstract, summarize

extracto *m,* abstract, summary; *chem* extract

extractor *a* extracting. *m,* extractor

extradición *f,* extradition

extraer *vt irr* to extract; draw out; export; *chem* extract. See **traer**

extranjero (-ra) *a* alien, foreign. *n* foreigner. *m,* abroad, foreign country

extrañar *vt* to exile; alienate, estrange; wonder at; miss, feel the loss of; *vr* be exiled; be estranged; be amazed (by); refuse (to do a thing)

extrañeza *f,* strangeness; estrangement; surprise

extraño *a* strange, unusual; foreign, extraneous

extraoficial *a* unofficial

extraordinario *a* extraordinary; special. *m, cul* extra course

extraterritorialidad *f,* exterritoriality

extravagancia *f,* eccentricity; queerness; folly

extravagante *a* eccentric; queer, strange; absurd

extravertido *m,* extrovert

extraviar *vt* to mislead; mislay; *vr* lose one's way; be lost (of things); *fig* go astray

extravío *m,* deviation, divergence; error; aberration, lapse

extremado *a* extreme

extremar *vt* to take to extremes; *vr* do one's best

extremaunción *f,* extreme unction

extremeño (-ña) *a* and *n* Extremaduran

extremidad *f,* end; extremity; remotest part; edge; limit; *pl* extremities

extremista *a* and *mf* extremist

extremo *a* last, ultimate; extreme; furthest; great, exceptional; utmost. *m,* end, extreme; highest degree; extreme care; *pl* excessive emotional display

extremoso *a* immoderate, exaggerated; very affectionate

extrínseco *a* extrinsic

exuberancia *f,* abundance; exuberance

exuberante *a* abundant, copious; exuberant

exudar *vi* and *vt* to exude

exultación *f,* exultation; rejoicing

exultante *a* exultant

exultar *vi* to exult

exvoto *m,* votive offering

eyaculación *f, med* ejaculation

eyacular *vt med* to ejaculate

F

fa *m, mus* fa, F

fabada *f,* dish of broad beans with pork, sausage or bacon

fábrica *f,* manufacture; making; factory, works; fabric, structure, building; creation; invention. **f. de papel,** paper mill. **marca de f.,** trademark

fabricación *f,* make; making; construction. **f. en serie,** mass production

fabricador (-ra) *a* creative, inventive. *n* fabricator; maker

fabricante *a* manufacturing. *m,* manufacturer; maker

fabricar *vt* to manufacture; make; construct, build; devise; invent, create

fabril *a* manufacturing

fabriquero *m,* manufacturer; churchwarden; charcoal burner

fábula *f,* rumor, gossip; fiction; fable; story, plot; mythology; myth; laughingstock; falsehood.

fabulista *mf* fabulist; mythologist

fabulosidad *f,* fabulousness

fabuloso *a* fabulous; fictitious; incredible, amazing

faca *f,* jackknife

facción *f,* rebellion; faction, party, band; feature (of the face) (gen. *pl*); military exploit; any routine military duty

faccionario *a* factional

faccioso (-sa) *a* factional; factious, seditious. *n* rebel

faceta *f,* facet (gems); aspect, view

facha *f, inf* countenance, look, face; guy, scarecrow. *naut* **ponerse en f.,** to lie to

fachada *f,* facade, front (of a building, ship, etc.); *inf*

build, presence (of a person); frontispiece (of a book)

fachenda *f, inf* boastfulness, vanity

facial *a* facial; intuitive

fácil *a* easy; probable; easily led; docile; of easy virtue (women). *adv* easy

facilidad *f,* easiness; facility, aptitude; ready compliance; opportunity

facilitación *f,* facilitation

facilitar *vt* to facilitate, expedite; provide, deliver

facineroso *a* criminal, delinquent. *m,* criminal; villain

facistol *m, ecc* lectern; chorister's stand

facsímile *m,* facsimile

factibilidad *f,* feasibility, practicability

factible *a* feasible, practicable

facticio *a* factitious, artificial

factor *m, com* factor, agent; *math* factor; element; consideration

factoría *f,* agency; factorage; factory; merchants' trading post, especially in a foreign country

factótum *m, inf* factotum, handyman; *inf* busybody; confidential agent or deputy

factura *f, com* invoice, bill, account; *art* execution; workmanship; making

facturar *vt com* to invoice; register (luggage on a railroad)

facultad *f,* faculty; mental or physical aptitude, capability; authority, right; science, art; *univ* faculty; license

facultar *vt* to authorize, permit

facultativo *a* belonging to a faculty; optional, permissive. *m,* physician

facundia *f,* eloquence

facundo *a* eloquent

faena *f*, manual labor; mental work; business affairs (gen. *pl*)

faetón *m*, phaeton

fagocito *m*, phagocyte

fagot *m*, bassoon

fagotista *mf* bassoon player

faisán (-ana) *orn* cock (hen) pheasant

faisanera *f*, pheasantry

faja *f*, belt; sash, scarf; corset, girdle; *geog* zone; newspaper wrapper; *arch* fascia; swathing band

fajar *vt* to swathe; swaddle (a child)

fajero *m*, swaddling band

fajín *m*, ceremonial ribbon or sash worn by generals, etc.

fajina *f*, stack; brushwood; (*fort.*) fascine

fajo *m*, bundle, sheaf; *pl* swaddling clothes

falacia *f*, fraud, deceit; deceitfulness; fallacy

falange *f*, *mil* phalanx; *anat* phalange; (*Spanish pol.*) Falange

falangista *a* and *mf* Falangist

falaz *a* deceitful; fallacious

falda *f*, skirt; lap, flap, panel (of a dress); slope (of a hill); the lap; loin (of beef, etc.); brim of a hat; *pl inf* petticoats, women. **f. escocesa**, kilt. **f.-pantalón**, divided skirt, culottes.

faldellín *m*, skirt; underskirt

faldero *a* lap (dog); fond of the company of women

faldillas *f pl*, coattails

faldistorio *m*, faldstool

faldón *m*, long, flowing skirt; shirttail; coattail

falibilidad *f*, fallibility

falible *a* fallible

falla *f*, deficiency, defect; failure; *geol* displacement; bonfire (Valencia); *min* slide

fallar *vt law* to pass sentence; *vi* be deficient

falleba *f*, shutter bolt

fallecer *vi irr* to die; fail. See **conocer**

fallecimiento *m*, death, decease

fallido *a* frustrated; bankrupt

fallo *m*, *law* verdict; judgment

falsario *a* falsifying, forging, counterfeiting; deceiving, lying. *m*, falsifier, forger, counterfeiter

falseamiento *m*, falsifying; forging

falsear *vt* to falsify; forge; counterfeit; penetrate; *vi* weaken; *mus* be out of tune (strings)

falsedad *f*, falseness; falsehood

falsete *m*, spigot; *mus* falsetto voice

falsificación *f*, falsification; forgery

falsificador *a* falsifying; forging. *m*, falsifier; forger

falsificar *vt* to forge, counterfeit; falsify

falso *a* false; forged, counterfeit; treacherous, untrue, deceitful; incorrect; sham; vicious (horses). **de f.,** falsely; deceitfully

falta *f*, lack, shortage; defect; mistake; *sport* fault; shortcoming; nonappearance, absence; deficiency in legal weight of coin; *law* offense. **f. de éxito,** failure. **hacer f.,** to be necessary. **sin f.,** without fail

faltar *vi* to be lacking; fail, die; fall short; be absent from an appointment; not to fulfill one's obligations. **f. a,** to be unfaithful to, break (e.g. **Faltó a su palabra,** He broke his promise). *inf* **¡No faltaba más!** I should think not!; That's the limit!

falto *a* lacking, wanting; defective; wretched, mean, timid. **f. de personal,** short-handed

faltriquera *f*, pocket; hip pocket

falúa *f*, *naut* tender; longboat

falucho *m*, felucca

fama *f*, rumor, report; reputation; fame

famélico *a* ravenous

familia *f*, family; household; kindred. **ser de f.,** to run in the family

familiar *a* family; familiar; well known; unceremonious; plain, simple; colloquial (language). *m*, *ecc* familiar; servant; intimate friend; familiar spirit

familiaridad *f*, familiarity

familiarizar *vt* to familiarize; *vr* become familiar; accustom oneself

familiarmente *adv* familiarly

famoso *a* famous; notorious; *inf* excellent, perfect; *inf* conspicuous

fámula *f*, *inf* female servant

fámulo *m*, servant of a college; *inf* servant

fanal *m*, lantern (of a lighthouse); *naut* poop lantern; lantern; lamp glass

fanático (-ca) *a* fanatical. *n* fanatic; *inf* fan, enthusiast

fanatismo *m*, fanaticism

fanatizar *vt* to make fanatical; turn into a fanatic

fandango *m*, lively Andalusian dance

fanega *f*, grain measure about the weight of 1.60 bushel; land measure (about $1\frac{1}{2}$ acres)

fanfarrón (-ona) *a inf* boastful, swaggering. *n* swashbuckler; boaster

fanfarronear *vi* to swagger; brag

fanfarronería *f*, bragging

fango *m*, mud, mire; degradation

fangoso *a* muddy, miry

fantasear *vi* to let one's fancy roam; boast

fantasía *f*, fancy, imagination; fantasy; caprice; fiction; *inf* presumption; *mus* fantasia

fantasma *m*, ghost, phantom; vision; image, impression; presumptuous person. *f, inf* scarecrow; apparition

fantasmagoría *f*, phantasmagoria

fantasmagórico *a* phantasmagoric

fantástico *a* fanciful, imaginary; fantastic, imaginative; presumptuous, conceited

fantoche *m*, puppet; *inf* yes-man, mediocrity

faquín *m*, porter, carrier

faquir *m*, fakir

faradio *m*, farad

faralá *m*, flounce, frill

farándula *f*, profession of low comedian; troupe of strolling players; cunning trick

farandulero *m*, actor, strolling player. *a inf* plausible

faraón *m*, pharaoh; faro (card game)

fardel *m*, bag, knapsack; bundle

fardo *m*, bundle, bale, package

farfulla *f, inf* mumbling; gibbering. *mf inf* mumbler

farfullar *vt inf* to mumble; gibber; *inf* act in haste

faringe *f*, pharynx

faríngeo *a* pharyngeal

faringitis *f*, pharyngitis

farisaico *a* pharisaical

fariseísmo *m*, cant, hypocrisy

fariseo *m*, Pharisee; hypocrite

farmacéutico *a* pharmaceutical. *m*, pharmacist

farmacia *f*, pharmacy

farmacología *f*, pharmacology

farmacológico *a* pharmacological

farmacólogo *m*, pharmacologist

faro *m*, lighthouse; beacon, guide; *aut* headlight

farol *m*, lantern, lamp; streetlamp; cresset

farola *f*, lamppost (generally with several branches); lantern

farolero *m*, lantern maker; lamplighter; lamp tender. *a inf* swaggering, braggart

fárrago *m*, hodgepodge

farsa *f*, old name for a play; farce; theatrical company; poor, badly constructed play; sham, trick, deception

farsante *m*, comedian; *ant* actor; *fig inf* humbug

fascinación *f*, evil eye; enchantment, fascination

fascinador (-ra) *a* bewitching; fascinating. *n* charmer

fascinante *a* fascinating

fascinar *vt* to bewitch; place under a spell; deceive, impose upon; attract, fascinate

fascismo *m*, fascism

fascista *a* and *mf* fascist

fase *f*, phase; aspect

fastidiar *vt* to disgust, bore; annoy; *vr* be bored

fastidio *m*, sickness, squeamishness; annoyance, boredom, dislike, repugnance

fastidioso *a* disgusting, sickening; annoying; boring, tiresome

fastuoso *a* ostentatious; pompous

fatal *a* fatal, mortal; predetermined, inevitable; ill-fated, unhappy, disastrous; evil

fatalidad *f,* fatality; inevitability; disaster, ill-fatedness

fatalismo *m,* fatalism

fatalista *a* fatalistic. *mf* fatalist

fatalmente *adv* inevitably, unavoidably; unhappily, unfortunately; extremely badly

fatídico *a* prophetic (gen. of evil)

fatiga *f,* fatigue; toil; difficult breathing; hardship, troubles (gen. *pl.*)

fatigar *vt* to tire; annoy; *vr* be tired

fatigoso *a* tired; tiring; tiresome, annoying

fatuidad *f,* fatuousness, inanity, foolishness; conceit; priggishness

fatuo *a* fatuous, foolish; conceited; priggish. *m,* self-satisfied fool. **fuego f.,** will-o'-the-wisp

fauces *f pl,* gullet

fauna *f,* fauna

fauno *m,* faun

fausto *m,* pomp, magnificence, ostentation. *a* fortunate, happy

fautor *m,* protector, helper; accomplice. **f. de guerra,** warmonger

favonio *m, poet* zephyr, westerly wind

favor *m,* aid, protection, support; favor, honor, service; love favor, sign of favor. **a f. de,** in favor of; on behalf of

favorable *a* kind, helpful; favorable

favorecedor (-ra) *a* favoring, helping. *n* helper; protector

favorecer *vt irr* to aid, protect, support; favor; do a service, grant a favor. See **conocer**

favoritismo *m,* favoritism

favorito (-ta) *a* and *n* favorite

fayenza *f,* faience

faz *f,* face; external surface of a thing, side; frontage

fe *f,* faith; confidence, trust, good opinion; belief; solemn promise; assertion; certificate, attestation; faithfulness. **f. de erratas,** *print* errata. **dar f.,** *law* to testify. **de buena f.,** in good faith. **en f.,** in proof

fealdad *f,* ugliness; base action

febo *m,* Phoebus; *poet* sun

febrero *m,* February

febril *a* feverish; ardent, violent; passionate

fecal *a* fecal

feculento *a* starchy; dreggy

fecundación *f,* fecundation

fecundar *vt* to fertilize; fecundate

fecundidad *f,* fecundity; fertility, fruitfulness

fecundizar *vt* to fertilize; make fruitful

fecundo *a* fertile, fecund, prolific; abundant

fecha *f,* date. **a la f.,** at present, now. **hasta la f.,** up to the present (day)

fechar *vt* to date, write the date

federación *f,* federation, league

federal *a* federal. *mf* federalist

federalismo *m,* federalism

federalista *a* federal, federalist. *mf* federalist

federativo *a* federative

fehaciente *a law* authentic, attested

feldespato *m,* feldspar

felicidad *f,* happiness; contentment, satisfaction; good fortune

felicitación *f,* congratulation

felicitar *vt* to congratulate; wish well; *vr* congratulate oneself

feligrés (-esa) *n* parishioner

feligresía *f,* parish

felino *a* and *m,* feline

feliz *a* happy; fortunate; skillful, felicitous (of phrases, etc.)

felón (-ona) *n* felon

felonía *f,* felony

felpa *f,* plush; *inf* drubbing, beating

felpilla *f,* chenille

felpudo *a* plush

femenino *a* feminine; female; *fig* weak

fementido *a* sly, false, treacherous, unfaithful

feminismo *m,* feminism

feminista *a* feminist. *mf* feminist

fémur *m,* femur, thigh bone

fenecer *vt irr* to conclude, finish; *vi* die; be ended. See **conocer**

fenecimiento *m,* end; death

fenicio (-ia) *a* and *n* Phoenician

fénico *a* phenic, carbolic

fénix *f,* phoenix

fenomenal *a* phenomenal; *inf* terrific

fenómeno *m,* phenomenon; *inf* something of great size

feo *a* ugly; alarming, horrid; evil. *m, inf* slight, insult

feraz *a* fruitful, fertile

féretro *m,* coffin; bier

feria *f,* fair, market; workday; holiday; rest

feriar *vt* to buy at a fair; bargain. *vi* cease work, take a holiday

fermentación *f,* fermentation

fermentar *vi* to ferment; be agitated; *vt* cause to ferment

fermento *m,* ferment; leaven; *chem* enzyme

ferocidad *f,* ferocity, cruelty

feroz *a* ferocious, cruel

férreo *a* ferrous; hard, tenacious. **línea férrea,** railroad

ferrería *f,* ironworks

ferretería *f,* ironworks; ironmonger's shop; ironware, hardware

férrico *a* ferric

ferrífero *a* iron-bearing

ferrocarril *m,* railroad, railway; railroad train. **f. de cremallera,** rack railroad. **f. funicular,** funicular railway

ferroso *a* ferrous

ferroviario *a* railroad, railway. *m,* railroad employee

fértil *a* fertile; fruitful, productive

fertilidad *f,* fertility

fertilización *f,* fertilization

fertilizar *vt* to fertilize, make fruitful

férula *f,* ferule; *surg* splint; *fig* yoke, rule

fervor *m,* intense heat; fervor, devotion; zeal

fervoroso *a* fervent, zealous, devoted

festejar *vt* to feast, entertain; woo; celebrate; *vr* amuse oneself

festejo *m,* feast, entertainment; courtship, wooing; *pl* public celebrations

festín *m,* private dinner or party; sumptuous banquet

festival *m,* musical festival; festival

festividad *f,* festivity; *ecc* celebration, solemnity; witticism

festivo *a* joking, witty; happy, gay; solemn, worthy of celebration. **día f.,** holiday

festón *m,* garland, wreath; festoon; border; scalloped edging

festonear *vt* to garland, festoon; border

fetal *a* fetal

fetiche *m,* fetish

fetichismo *m,* fetishism

fetidez *f,* fetidness, fetor, stink

fétido *a* stinking, fetid

feto *m,* fetus

feudal *a* feudal; despotic

feudalismo *m,* feudalism

feudo *m,* fief; fee. **f. franco,** freehold

fez *m,* fez

fiado, al *adv* on credit. **en f.,** on bail

fiador (-ra) *m,* guarantor; bail. *m,* fastener, loop (of a coat, clock, etc.); safety catch, bolt. **salir f.,** to be surety (for); post bail

fiambre *m,* cold meat, cold dish; *inf* stale, out-of-date news, etc.; *inf* corpse

fiambrera *f,* lunchbox, lunchpail

fianza *f,* guarantee, bail; surety; security. *law* **dar f.,** to guarantee; post bail

fiar *vt* to go surety for, post bail; sell on credit; trust; confide; *vr (with de)* confide in; trust

fibra *f,* fiber; filament; energy, strength; *min* vein; grain (of wood)

fibroso *a* fibrous; fibroid

ficción *f,* falsehood; invention; fiction, imaginative creation; pretense

ficha *f,* chip, counter; domino; index card, filing card. **f. antropométrica,** personal particulars card

fichar *vt* to record personal particulars on a filing card; file, index

fichero *m,* filing cabinet; card catalog

fichú *m,* fichu, scarf

ficticio *a* fictitious

fidedigno *a* trustworthy, bona fide

fideicomisario *m, law* fiduciary, trustee

fideicomiso *m, law* trust

fidelidad *f,* fidelity, honesty; loyalty; punctiliousness

fideos *m pl,* vermicelli. *m, inf* scraggy person

fiduciario *a law* fiduciary. *m, law* trustee

fiebre *f,* fever; great agitation, excitement. **f. de oro,** gold fever. **f. palúdica,** malarial fever. **f. puerperal,** puerperal fever. **f. tifoidea,** typhoid fever

fiel *a* faithful, loyal; true, exact. *m,* axis; pointer (of a scale or balance)

fieltro *m,* felt

fiera *f,* wild beast; cruel person

fiereza *f,* savageness, wildness; cruelty, fierceness; deformity

fiero *a* wild, savage; ugly; huge, enormous; horrible, alarming; haughty

fiesta *f,* merriment, gaiety; entertainment, feast; *inf* joke; festivity, celebration; public holiday; caress, cajolery (gen. *pl*); *pl* holidays. **f. fija** *ecc* immovable feast. *inf* **estar de f.,** to be making merry. **hacer f.,** to take a holiday. *inf* **Se acabó la f.,** It's all over and done with

figón *m,* eating house, diner

figulino *a* fictile, made of terra cotta

figura *f,* shape, form; face; *art* image, figure; *law* form; court card; *mus* note; *theat* character, role; *(geom gram dancing)* figure. **f. de nieve,** snowman. *naut* **f. de proa,** figurehead. *fig* **f. decorativa,** figurehead. *fig* **hacer f.,** to cut a figure

figurado *a* figurative; rhetorical

figurar *vt* to shape, mold; simulate, pretend; represent; *vi* be numbered among; cut a figure; *vr* imagine

figurativo *a* figurative; symbolical

figurilla *mf inf* ridiculous, dwarfish figure. *f, art* statuette

figurín *m,* fashion plate or model

fijación *f,* fixing; nailing; sticking, posting; attention, fixity; *chem* fixation; firmness, stability

fijador *m, (med phot)* fixative; setting lotion; *art* varnish. *a* fixing

fijamente *adv* firmly; attentively

fijar *vt* to fix; glue, stick; nail; make firm; settle, appoint (a date); fix, concentrate (attention, gaze); *(phot med)* fix; *vr* decide; notice (e.g. **No me había fijado,** I hadn't noticed). **f. anuncios,** to post bills

fijeza *f,* fixedness; firmness, stability; constancy, steadfastness

fijo *a* firm; fixed; stable; steadfast; permanent; exact. **de f.,** certainly, without doubt

fila *f,* line, row; *mil* rank; antipathy, hatred. **en f.,** in a line

filacteria *f,* phylactery

filamento *m,* filament

filantropía *f,* philanthropy

filantrópico *a* philanthropic

filántropo *m,* philanthropist

filarmónico *a* philharmonic

filatelia *f,* philately, stamp collecting

filatélico *a* philatelic

filatelista *mf* philatelist, stamp collector

filete *m, arch* filet; *cul* small spit; filet (of meat or fish); thread of a screw; *sew* hem

filiación *f,* filiation; affiliation, relationship; *mil* regimental register

filial *a* filial; affiliated

filibustero *m,* filibuster

filiforme *a* filamentous

filigrana *f,* filigree; watermark (of paper); *fig* delicate creation

filípica *f,* philippic

Filipinas, las the Philippines

filipino (-na) *a* and *n* Philippine

filisteo (-ea) *a* and *n* philistine

filme *m,* (cinema) film

filmar *vt* to film

filo *m,* cutting edge; dividing line

filología *f,* philology

filológico *a* philological

filólogo *m,* philologist

filomela *f, poet* nightingale

filón *m, min* vein, lode; *fig* gold mine

filosofar *vi* to philosophize

filosofía *f,* philosophy. **f. moral,** moral philosophy. **f. natural,** natural philosophy

filosófico *a* philosophic

filósofo *m,* philosopher. *a* philosophic

filoxera *f,* phylloxera

filtración *f,* filtration

filtrar *vt* to filter; *vi* filter through, percolate; *vr fig* disappear (of money, etc.)

filtro *m,* filter, strainer; love potion, philter

fin *m,* finish, end, conclusion; purpose, goal, aim; limit, extent. **a f. de,** in order to, so that. **a fines de,** toward the end of (with months, years, etc.) (e.g. **a fines de octubre,** toward the end of October). **en f.,** at last; in fine; well then! **por f.,** finally

finado (-da) *n* deceased, dead person

final *a* final. *m,* end, finish; *sport* final (gen. *pl*)

finalidad *f,* finality; purpose

finalista *mf sport* finalist

finalizar *vt* to conclude, finish; *vi* be finished; close (stock exchange)

finalmente *adv* finally

financiar *vt* to finance

financiero *a* financial. *m,* financier

finanzas *f pl,* finance

finar *vi* to die; *vr* desire, long for a thing

finca *f,* land, real estate; house property, country house, ranch

fineza *f,* fineness; excellence, goodness; kindness, expression of affection; good turn, friendly act; gift; beauty, delicacy

fingido *a* pretended; assumed; feigned; sham

fingimiento *m,* pretense; affectation, assumption

fingir *vt* to pretend, feign; imagine

finiquitar *vt* to close and pay up an account; *inf* end

finiquito *m,* closing of an account; final receipt, quittance; quietus

finito *a* finite

finlandés (-esa) *a* Finnish. *n* Finn. *m,* Finnish (language)

Finlandia Finland

fino *a* fine; excellent, good; slim, slender, thin; delicate, subtle; dainty (of people); cultured, polished; constant, loving; sagacious, shrewd; *min* refined

finta *f,* feint (in fencing); menace, threat

finura *f,* fineness; excellence; delicacy; courtesy

fiordo *m,* fjord

firma *f,* signature; act of signing; *com* firm name, firm

firmamento *m,* firmament

firmante *a* signing. *mf* signatory

firmar *vt* to sign

firme *a* firm; hard; steady, solid; constant, resolute, loyal. *m,* foundation, base. *mil* **¡Firmes!** Attention! **batir de f.,** to strike hard

112

firmeza *f*, stability, firmness; constancy, resoluteness, loyalty

fiscal *a* fiscal. *m*, attorney general; public prosecutor; meddler. **f. de quiebras**, official receiver

fiscalizar *vt* to prosecute; pry into; meddle with; censure, criticize

fisco *m*, national treasury, exchequer, revenue

fisgar *vt* to harpoon; pry; *vi* mock, make fun of

fisgón (-ona) *a* prying; mocking. *n* pryer; mocker; eavesdropper

fisgoneo *m*, prying; eavesdropping

física *f*, physics

físico *a* physical. *m*, physicist; physician; physique

fisiología *f*, physiology

fisiológico *a* physiological

fisiólogo *m*, physiologist

fisioterapia *f*, physiotherapy

fisonomía *f*, physiognomy

fístula *f*, pipe, conduit; *mus* pipe; *surg* fistula

fisura *f*, fissure

flaccidez *f*, flabbiness

fláccido *a* flaccid, soft, flabby

flaco *a* thin; weak, feeble; *fig* weak-minded; dispirited. *m*, failing, weakness. *inf* **hacer un f. servicio**, to do an ill turn. **estar f. de memoria**, to have a weak memory

flagelación *f*, flagellation

flagelante *m*, flagellant

flagelar *vt* to scourge; *fig* lash

flagelo *m*, whip, scourge

flagrante *a poet* refulgent; present; actual. **en f.**, in the very act, flagrante delicto

flagrar *vi poet* to blaze, be refulgent

flamante *a* resplendent; brand-new; fresh, spick-and-span

flamenco (-ca) *m*, *orn* flamingo. *a* and *n* Flemish. *a* Andalusian; gypsy; buxom, fresh

flan *m*, baked custard, creme caramel. **estar como un f.**, to shake like a leaf, be nervous

flanco *m*, side; *mil* flank

Flandes Flanders

flanquear *vt mil* to flank

flanqueo *m*, *mil* outflanking

flaquear *vi* to grow weak; weaken; totter (buildings, etc.); be disheartened, flag

flaqueza *f*, weakness; thinness; faintness, feebleness; frailty, fault; loss of zeal

flato *m*, flatulence, gas

flatulento *a* flatulent, gassy

flauta *f*, flute

flautín *m*, piccolo

flautista *mf* flutist

flebitis *f*, phlebitis

flebotomía *f*, phlebotomy, bloodletting

flecha *f*, arrow, dart

flechar *vt* to shoot an arrow or dart; wound or kill with arrows; *inf* inspire love; *vi* bend a bow to shoot

flechazo *m*, wound with an arrow; *inf* love at first sight

flechero *m*, archer; arrow maker

fleco *m*, fringe; fringe (of hair)

fleje *m*, iron hoop (for barrels, etc.)

flema *f*, phlegm; sluggishness

flemático *a* phlegmatic; sluggish

flemón *m*, gumboil; abscess

flequillo *m*, fringe (of hair)

fletamento *m*, chartering (a ship)

fletar *vt* to charter a ship; embark merchandise or people

flete *m*, freightage; cargo, freight

flexibilidad *f*, flexibility; suppleness, adaptability

flexible *a* pliant, supple; flexible, adaptable. *m*, *elec* flex

flexión *f*, flexion; bend, bending; deflection

flirtear *vi* to flirt

flirteo *m*, flirtation

flojedad *f*, flabbiness; weakness; feebleness; laziness, negligence

flojo *a* flabby; slack, loose; weak, feeble; lazy, slothful; poor (of a literary work, etc.)

floqueado *a* fringed

flor *f*, flower; best (of anything); bloom (on fruit); virginity; grain (of leather); compliment (gen. *pl*); menstruation (gen. *pl*). **f. de especia**, mace. **f. de la edad**, prime, youth. **f. del cuclillo**, mayflower. **f. del estudiante**, French marigold. **flores de mano**, artificial flowers. **flores de oblón**, hops. **a f. de**, on the surface of, level with. **andarse en flores**, *fig* to beat about the bush. **echar flores**, to pay compliments. **en f.**, in bloom

flora *f*, flora

floración *f*, flowering

floral *a* floral. **juegos florales**, poetry contest

florear *vt* to adorn with flowers; *vi* execute a flourish on the guitar

florecer *vi irr* to flower, bloom; flourish, prosper; *vr* grow mold (of cheese, etc.). See **conocer**

floreciente *a* flowering; prosperous

florecimiento *m*, flowering; prosperity

Florencia Florence

florentino (-na) *a* and *n* Florentine

floreo *m*, witty conversation; flourish (on the guitar or in fencing)

florero *m*, vase; flower pot; *art* flower piece

florescencia *f*, flowering; flowering season, florescence

floresta *f*, grove, wooded park, woodland; *fig* collector of beautiful things; anthology

florete *m*, fencing foil

floricultor (-ra) *n* floriculturist

floricultura *f*, floriculture

floridamente *adv* elegantly, with a flourish

florido *a* flowery; best, most select; florid, ornate

florilegio *m*, anthology, collection

florín *m*, florin

florista *mf* artificial-flower maker; florist; flower seller

florón *m*, large flower; *arch* fleuron; honorable deed

flósculo *m*, *bot* floret

flota *f*, fleet of merchant ships. **f. aérea**, air force

flotación *f*, floating. *naut* **línea de f.**, water line

flotador *a* floating. *m*, float

flotamiento *m*, floating

flotante *a* floating

flotar *vi* to float on water or in air

flote *m*, floating. **a f.**, afloat; independent, solvent

flotilla *f*, flotilla; fleet of small ships. **f. aérea**, air fleet

fluctuación *f*, fluctuation; hesitation, vacillation

fluctuante *a* fluctuating

fluctuar *vi* to fluctuate; be in danger (things); vacillate, hesitate; undulate; oscillate

fluidez *f*, fluidity

flúido *a* fluid; fluent. *m*, fluid; *elec* current

fluir *vi irr* to flow. See **huir**

flujo *m*, flow, flux; rising tide. **f. de sangre**, hemorrhage

fluorescencia *f*, fluorescence

fluorescente *a* fluorescent

fluvial *a* fluvial

flux *m*, flush (in cards)

foca *f*, *zool* seal

focal *a* focal

foco *m*, focus; center; origin; source; *theat* spotlight; core (of an abscess)

fofo *a* spongy, soft; flabby

fogata *f*, bonfire

fogón *m*, fire, cooking area, kitchen range, kitchen stove; furnace of a steamboiler; vent of a firearm

fogonazo *m*, powder flash

fogonero *m*, stoker

fogosidad *f*, enthusiasm; vehemence; ardor

fogoso *a* ardent; vehement; enthusiastic

folclórico *a* pertaining to folklore

folclorista *mf* folklorist

foliar *vt* to number the pages of a book

folículo *m*, follicle

folio *m*, leaf of a book or manuscript, folio. **en f.**, in folio

follaje *m*, foliage; leafy ornamentation; crude, unnecessary decoration; verbosity

folletín *m*, feuilleton, literary article; serial story; *inf* dime novel, potboiler

folletinista *mf* pamphleteer

folleto *m*, pamphlet, leaflet

follón *a* lazy; caddish; craven

fomentación *f*, *med* fomentation, poultice

fomentador *a* fomenting. *m*, fomenter

fomentar *vt* to warm, foment; incite, instigate; *med* apply poultices

fomento *m*, heat, shelter; fuel; protection, encouragement; *med* fomentation

fonda *f*, inn; restaurant

fondeadero *m*, anchorage, anchoring ground

fondear *vt naut* to sound; search a ship; examine carefully; *vi naut* anchor

fondillos *m pl*, seat (of the trousers)

fondista *mf* owner of an inn or restaurant

fondo *m*, bottom (of a well, etc.); bed (of the sea, etc.); depth; rear, portion at the back; ground (of fabrics); background; *com* capital; *com* stock; *fig* fund (of humor, etc.); character, nature; temperament; *fig* substance, core, essence; *naut* bottom; *pl com* resources, funds. **f. de amortización,** sinking fund. **f. doble** *or* **f. secreto,** false bottom. **f. muerto, f. perdido** *or* **f. vitalicio,** life annuity. *com* **fondos inactivos,** idle capital. **a fondo,** completely, thoroughly. **artículo de f.,** editorial, lead article. *sport* **carrera de f.,** long-distance race. *naut* **irse a f.,** to sink, founder

fonética *f*, phonetics

fonético *a* phonetic

fonetista *mf* phonetician

fonógrafo *m*, phonograph

fonología *f*, phonology

fonológico *a* phonological

fontanar *m*, spring, stream

fontanería *f*, pipe laying, plumbing

fontanero *m*, pipe layer; plumber

forajido (-da) *a* fugitive, outlawed. *n* robber, fugitive

forastero (-ra) *a* strange, foreign; alien, exotic. *n* stranger

forcejear *vi* to struggle; try, strive; oppose, contradict

forcejo *m*, struggle; endeavor; opposition, hostility

fórceps *m pl*, forceps

forense *a* forensic

forestal *a* forestal

forillo *m*, *theat* backdrop

forja *f*, forge

forjador *m*, smith, ironworker

forjar *vt* to forge; fabricate; create; counterfeit

forma *f*, shape, form; arrangement; method; style; manifestation, expression; formula, formulary; ceremonial; *print* form; manner; means, way; mold, matrix; style of handwriting. *law* **en debida f.,** in due form

formación *f*, formation; form, contour, shape; (*mil geol*) formation. **f. del censo,** census taking

formador *a* forming, shaping

formal *a* apparent, formal; serious, punctilious, steady; truthful, reliable; sedate; orderly, regular, methodical

formaldehído *m*, formaldehyde

formalidad *f*, orderliness, propriety; formality; requirement, requisite; ceremony; seriousness, sedateness; punctiliousness

formalismo *m*, formalism; bureaucracy, red tape

formalizar *vt* to put into final form; legalize; formulate; enunciate; *vr* take seriously (a joke)

formar *vt* to shape; form; educate, mold; *mil* form. **formarle causa a uno,** to bring charges against someone. *vr* develop, grow

formativo *a* formative

formato *m*, *print* format; *chem* formate

formidable *a* formidable, awe-inspiring; huge, enormous

fórmula *f*, formula; prescription; mode of expression. (*math chem*) **f. clásica,** standard formula

formular *vt* to formulate; prescribe

formulario *m*, *law* formulary; handbook

formulismo *m*, formulism; bureaucracy, red tape

fornicación *f*, fornication

fornicador (-ra) *a* and *n* fornicator

fornicar *vi* to fornicate

fornido *a* stalwart, muscular, strong

foro *m*, forum; law courts; law, bar, legal profession; *theat* back scenery; leasehold

forraje *m*, forage, fodder; foraging

forrajeador *m*, forager

forrajear *vt* to gather forage, go foraging

forrar *vt sew* to line; cover, encase, make a cover for

forro *m*, lining, inner covering; cover (of a book)

fortalecedor *a* fortifying

fortalecer *vt irr* to fortify. See **conocer**

fortaleza *f*, vigor; fortitude; fortress; natural defense. **aer f. volante,** flying fortress

fortificable *a* fortifiable

fortificación *f*, fortification

fortificador *a* fortifying

fortificar *vt* to fortify

fortísimo *a sup* **fuerte** extremely strong

fortuito *a* fortuitous, chance

fortuna *f*, fate, destiny; fortune, capital, estate; tempest. **por f.,** fortunately. **probar f.,** to try one's luck

forzado *a* forced, obliged. *m*, convict condemned to the galleys

forzador *m*, violator, seducer

forzar *vt irr* to force, break open; take by force; rape, ravish; oblige, compel. *Pres. Ind.* **fuerzo, fuerzas, fuerza, fuerzan.** *Preterite* **forcé, forzaste,** etc. *Pres. Subjunc.* **fuerce, fuerces, fuerce, forcemos, forcéis, fuercen**

forzoso *a* obligatory, unavoidable, necessary

forzudo *a* brawny, stalwart

fosa *f*, grave; socket (of a joint). **f. común,** potter's field.

fosar *vt* to undermine; dig a trench around

fosfato *m*, phosphate

fosforecer *vi* to phosphoresce. See **conocer**

fosforera *f*, matchbox

fosforero (-ra) *n* match seller

fosforescencia *f*, phosphorescence

fosforescente *a* phosphorescent

fósforo *m*, phosphorus; match; morning star

fósil *a* and *m*, fossil; *inf* antique

fosilizarse *vr* to become fossilized

foso *m*, hole, hollow, pit; trench; pit (in garages); *theat* room under the stage.

foto *f*, snapshot, photo

fotocopia *f*, photocopy

fotogénico *a* photogenic

fotograbado *m*, photogravure

fotografía *f*, photography; photograph

fotografiar *vt* to photograph

fotográfico *a* photographic

fotógrafo *m*, photographer

fotograma *m*, (cinema) shot

fotoquímica *f*, photochemistry

fotostato *m*, photostat

frac *m*, tail coat

fracasar *vi* to break, crumble, be shattered; collapse (of plans, etc.); fail; be disappointed

fracaso *m*, shattering; collapse (of plans, etc.); disaster; failure, disappointment, downfall

fracción *f*, division into parts; fraction. **f. impropia,** *math* improper fraction

fractura *f*, fracture. **f. conminuta,** compound fracture

fracturar *vt* to fracture

fragancia *f*, fragrance, perfume; renown, good name

fragante *a* fragrant; perfumed; flagrant

fragata *f*, frigate

frágil *a* fragile, brittle; perishable, frail; weak, sinful

fragilidad *f*, fragility; frailty, sinfulness

fragmentario *a* fragmentary
fragmento *m*, fragment
fragor *m*, noise, crash
fragosidad *f*, roughness, rockiness, unevenness
fragoso *a* craggy, rocky; rough; noisy, clamorous
fragua *f*, forge
fraguado *m*, forging; *mas* setting
fraguar *vt* to forge, work; plot, scheme; *vi* set (concrete, etc.)
fraile *m*, friar, monk. *inf* **f. de misa y olla,** ignorant friar
frailesco *a* *inf* pertaining to friars, friar-like
frambuesa *f*, raspberry
francachela *f*, *inf* binge
francés (-esa) *a* French. *n* Frenchman (-woman). *m*, French (language). **a la francesa,** in French fashion
francesilla *f*, *cul* French roll
Francia France
franciscano (-na) *a* and *n* Franciscan
francmasón (-ona) *n* Freemason
francmasonería *f*, freemasonry
franco *a* generous, liberal; exempt; sincere, genuine, frank; duty-free; Frank; Franco (in compound words). *m*, franc (coin). **f. de porte,** post-free; prepaid
Franco-Condado Franche-Comté
francotirador *m*, sharpshooter, franc tireur
franela *f*, flannel
frangir *vt* to divide, quarter
frangollar *vt* to scamp, skimp (work); botch, bungle
franja *f*, fringe; border, trimming; stripe. *rad* **f. undosa,** wave band
franjar *vt sew* to fringe, trim
franqueadora *f*, postage meter
franquear *vt* to exempt; make free, make a gift of; clear the way; stamp, prepay; free (slaves); *vr* fall in easily with others' plans; make confidences
franqueo *m*, exemption; bestowal, making free; postage, stamping; enfranchisement (of slaves)
franqueza *f*, exemption, freedom; generosity, liberality; sincerity, frankness
franquicia *f*, exemption from excise duties
franquista *mf* Franquist, supporter of Franco
frasco *m*, bottle, flask; powder flask or horn. **f. cuentagotas,** drop bottle
frase *f*, sentence; phrase; epigram; idiom, style. **f. hecha,** cliché
frasear *vt* to phrase
fraseología *f*, phraseology; wording
fratás *m*, plastering trowel
fraternal *a* brotherly
fraternidad *f*, fraternity, brotherhood
fraternizar *vi* to fraternize
fraterno *a* fraternal
fratricida *a* fratricidal. *mf* fratricide
fratricidio *m*, fratricide (act)
fraude *m*, fraud, deception
fraudulento *a* fraudulent
fray *m*, *abb* **fraile.** Always followed by a proper name (e.g. **F. Bartolomé,** Friar Bartholomew)
frazada *f*, blanket
frecuencia *f*, frequency. **f. radioeléctrica,** radiofrequency
frecuentación *f*, frequenting, visiting
frecuentador (-ra) *n* frequenter
frecuentar *vt* to frequent
frecuente *a* frequent
fregadero *m*, kitchen sink
fregado *m*, scrubbing; rubbing; scouring; washing; *inf* murky business
fregador *m*, kitchen sink; scrub brush; dishcloth. **f. mecánico de platos,** dishwasher
fregar *vt irr* to rub; scour; wash (dishes). See **cegar**
fregona *f*, kitchen maid
fregotear *vt inf* to clean or scour inefficiently
freiduría *f*, fried-fish shop
freír *vt irr cul* to fry. See **reír**

fréjol *m*, kidney bean
frenar *vt* to restrain, hold back; bridle, check; *mech* brake
frenesí *m*, madness, frenzy; vehemence, exaltation
frenético *a* mad, frenzied; vehement, exalted
freno *m*, bridle; *mech* brake; restraint, check. **f. de pedal,** foot brake. **f. neumático,** vacuum brake, pneumatic brake
frente *f*, brow, forehead; front portion; countenance; head; heading; beginning (of a letter, etc.). *m*, *mil* front. *mf* facade; front; obverse (of coins). *adv* in front, opposite. **f. a f.,** face to face. **con la f. levantada,** with head held high; proudly; insolently. **de f.,** abreast
freo *m*, strait, narrow channel
fresa *f*, strawberry plant and fruit (especially small or wild varieties); *mech* milling cutter, miller
fresadora *f*, milling machine
fresal *m*, strawberry bed
fresca *f*, cool air; fresh air; *inf* home truth
fresco *a* cool; fresh, new; recent; buxom, fresh-colored; calm, serene; *inf* impudent, cheeky, bold; thin (cloths). *m*, coolness; fresh air; *art* fresco. **al f.,** in the open air. **hacer f.,** to be cool or fresh
frescote *a inf* ruddy and corpulent
frescura *f*, coolness; freshness; pleasant verdure and fertility; *inf* cheek, nerve; piece of insolence; uncon-cern, indifference; calmness, serenity
fresero (-ra) *n* strawberry seller
fresneda *f*, ash grove
fresno *m*, *bot* ash
fresón *m*, strawberry (large, cultivated varieties)
fresquera *f*, meat locker; cool place
fresquista *mf* fresco painter
friable *a* brittle; friable, powdery
frialdad *f*, coldness, chilliness; *med* frigidity; indifference, lack of interest; foolishness; negligence
fríamente *adv* coldly; coolly, with indifference; dully, flatly
fricción *f*, friction
friccionar *vt* to rub; give a massage
friega *f*, friction, massage
frigidez *f*, See **frialdad**
frígido *a* frigid
frigio *a* and *n* Phrygian
frigorífico *a* refrigerative. *m*, refrigerator, cold-storage locker
frío *a* cold; *med* frigid; indifferent, uninterested; dull, uninteresting; inefficient. *m*, coldness, chill; cold
friolera *f*, bagatelle, trifle, mere nothing
friolero *a* sensitive to cold
frisa *f*, frieze cloth
frisar *vt* to frizz, curl (cloth); scrub, rub; *vi* approach, be nearly (e.g. **Frisa en los setenta años,** He's nearly seventy)
Frisia Friesland
friso *m*, frieze; dado; border
frisón (-ona) *a* and *n* Frisian
fritada *f*, *cul* fry, fried food
frito *a* fried
fritura *f*, frying; fried food
frivolidad *f*, frivolity
frivolité *m*, *sew* tatting
frívolo *a* frivolous, superficial; futile, unconvincing
fronda *f*, *bot* leaf; frond (of ferns); *pl* foliage
frondosidad *f*, luxuriance of foliage
frondoso *a* leafy
frontera *f*, frontier; facade
fronterizo *a* frontier; facing, opposite
frontero *a* facing, opposite. *m*, (*ant mil*) frontier commander
frontispicio *m*, frontispiece; facade; *fig inf* face, dial
frontón *m*, pelota court; jai alai court; *arch* pediment
frotamiento, frote *m*, rubbing, friction
frotar *vt* to rub
frotis *m*, *med* smear
fructífero *a* fruitful, fructiferous

fructuoso *a* fruitful, fertile; useful

frufrú *m,* rustle (of silk, etc.)

frugal *a* frugal; saving, economical

frugalidad *f,* frugality, abstemiousness, moderation

fruición *f,* enjoyment; fruition; satisfaction

fruir *vi irr* to enjoy what one has long desired. See **huir**

frunce *m, sew* shirring; gather; ruffling; tuck; pucker; wrinkle

fruncimiento *m,* wrinkling; puckering; *sew* shirring

fruncir *vt* to frown; purse (the lips); pucker; *sew* shirr, pleat, gather; reduce in size; conceal the truth; *vr* pretend to be prudish. **f. el ceño,** to knit one's brow, scowl

fruslería *f,* trifle, nothing

frustración *f,* frustration

frustrar *vt* to disappoint; frustrate, thwart

fruta *f,* fruit; *inf* consequence, result. **f. de hueso,** stone fruit. *cul* **f. de sartén,** fritter

frutal *a* fruit-bearing. *m,* fruit tree

frutar *vi* to bear fruit

frutería *f,* fruit

frutero (-ra) *a* fruit. *n* fruit seller. *m,* fruit dish; *art* painting of fruit; basket of imitation fruit

frútice *m,* bush, shrub

fruticultura *f,* fruit farming

fruto *m,* fruit; product, result; profit, proceeds; *agr* grain

fu spitting (of cats). *interj* expression of scorn. *inf* **ni f. ni fa,** neither one thing nor the other

fucilazo *m,* heat lightning

fucsia *f,* fuchsia

fuego *m,* fire; conflagration; firing (of firearms); beacon; hearth, home; rash; ardor; heat (of an argument, etc.); *interj* ¡F.! *mil* Fire! **fuegos artificiales,** fireworks. **a sangre y f.,** by fire and sword. *mil* **hacer f.,** to fire (a weapon). **pegar f.,** to set on fire

fuelle *m,* bellows; bag (of a bagpipe); *sew* pucker, wrinkle; hood (of a carriage, etc.); wind cloud; *inf* talebearer. **f. de pie,** foot pump

fuente *f,* stream, spring; fountain; meat dish; genesis, origin; source, headwaters; tap

fuera *adv* outside, out. *interj* get out! **f. de,** besides, in addition to. **f. de alcance,** out of reach. **f. de sí,** beside oneself (with rage, etc.). **de f.,** from the outside. **por f.,** on the outside, externally

fuero *m,* municipal charter; jurisdiction; compilation of laws; legal right or privilege; *pl inf* arrogance. **los fueros de León,** the laws of León

fuerte *a* strong, resistant; robust; spirited, vigorous; hard (of diamonds, etc.); rough, uneven; impregnable; terrible, tremendous; overweight (of coins); active; efficacious, effective; expert, knowledgeable; *gram* strong; intense; loud; tough. *m,* fort; talent, strong point; *mus* forte. *adv* strongly; excessively. **tener genio f.,** to be quick-tempered

fuerza *f,* strength; power, might; force, efficacy; fortress; *sew* stiffening; sinew power; violence; toughness, durability, solidity; potency; authority; courage; vigor; *pl fig inf* livewires, influential people. **a f. de,** by means of, by dint of. **a la f.,** forcibly. **en f. de,** because of, on account of. **por f. mayor,** by main force. **ser f.,** to be necessary

fuga *f,* flight, escape, running away; leak (gas, etc.); elopement; *mus* fugue; ardor, strength. **f. de cerebros,** brain drain

fugarse *vr* to run away; elope; escape

fugaz *a* fugitive; fleeting, brief

fugitivo (-va) *a* fugitive; runaway, escaping; transient. *n* fugitive

fulano (-na) *n* so-and-so, such a person **f., zutano, y mengano,** *inf* Tom, Dick, and Harry

fulcro *m,* fulcrum

fulgente, fúlgido *a* brilliant, shining

fulgor *m,* brilliance, brightness

fulgurar *vi* to shine, be resplendent, scintillate; flare

fulguroso *a* shining, sparkling

fúlica *f, orn* coot

fulminante *a med* fulminant; fulminating; thundering. *m,* percussion cap

fulminar *vt* to fulminate (all meanings)

fulminato *m, chem* fulminate

fulmíneo, fulminoso *a* fulminous, pertaining to lightning

fullería *f,* cheating at play; craftiness, low guile

fullero (-ra) *a* cheating; crafty, astute. *n* cheat, cardsharper

fumadero *m,* smoking room

fumador (-ra) *a* smoking. *n* smoker. «**No fumadores**», "Nonsmoking" (area)

fumar *vi* to smoke; *vr inf* dissipate, waste

fumarola *f,* fumarole

fumigación *f,* fumigation

fumigador (-ra) *n* fumigator

fumigar *vt* to fumigate

fumigatorio *a* fumigatory. *m,* perfume burner

fumista *m,* stove maker or seller

fumistería *f,* stove factory or store

funámbulo *n* tightrope walker, acrobat

función *f,* function; working, operation; *theat* performance; activity, duty; ceremony; celebration; *math* function; *mil* battle

funcional *a* functional

funcionamiento *m,* functioning

funcionar *vi* to function, work. «**No funciona**», "Out of order"

funcionario *m,* functionary, official; civil servant

funda *f,* case, cover, sheath; hold-all. **f. de almohada,** pillowcase

fundación *f,* foundation

fundadamente *adv* with reason, on good evidence

fundador (-ra) *n* founder, creator; originator

fundamental *a* fundamental

fundamento *m, mas* foundation; basis; basic principle, reason; origin, root

fundar *vt* to build, erect; base; found, institute; create, establish; *vr* (*with en*) found, base upon. **f. una compañía,** *com* to float a company

fundición *f,* foundry; smelting, founding, casting; cast iron; *print* font

fundido fotográfico *m,* composite photograph

fundidor *m,* founder, smelter.

fundir *vt* to melt; found, smelt; cast (metals); *vr* join together, unite; *elec* blow (fuses)

fúnebre *a* funeral; dismal, lugubrious, mournful

funeral *a* funeral

funerales *m pl,* funeral; *ecc* memorial masses

funerala, (a la) *adv mil* with reversed arms

funeraria *f,* funeral home, undertaker

funerario *a* funeral

funéreo *a* funereal, mournful

funesto *a* unlucky, unfortunate; mournful, melancholy, sad

fungoso *a* spongy, fungous

funicular *a* funicular

furgón *m,* wagon; van; guard's van, baggage car, luggage cart. **f. postal,** mail truck

furia *f, myth* fury; rage, wrath; fit of madness; raging, violence (of the elements); speed, haste

furibundo *a* frantic, furious; raging

fúrico *a* stark raving mad

furioso *a* furious, enraged; mad, insane; violent, terrible; enormous, excessive

furor *m,* fury, rage; poetic frenzy; violence; furor

furriel *m,* quartermaster

furtivo *a* furtive; covert, clandestine; pirate (editions)

fusa *f,* demisemiquaver

fusco *a* dark

fuselado *a* streamlined

fuselaje *m,* fuselage

fusible *a* fusible. *m, elec* fuse; fuse wire

fusil *m,* rifle

fusilamiento *m,* execution by shooting

fusilar *vt* to execute by shooting; *inf* plagiarize

fusilazo *m*, rifle shot

fusión *f*, melting, liquefying; fusion, blending; mixture, union; *com* merger, amalgamation

fusionar *vt* to blend, fuse, merge; *vr com* combine, form a merger

fusta *f*, brushwood; whip

fuste *m*, wood, timber; *poet* saddle; *fig* core, essence; importance, substance; shaft of a lance; *arch* shaft. **hombre de buen f.**, a man with a good (physical) constitution

fustigar *vt* to whip, lash; rebuke harshly

fútbol *m*, football; soccer

futbolista *mf* football player; soccer player

fútil *a* futile, ineffectual, worthless

futilidad *f*, futility, worthlessness

futura *f*, *law* reversion (of offices); *inf* fiancée

futurismo *m*, futurism

futurista *mf* futurist

futurístico *a* futuristic

futuro (-ra) *a* future. *m*, future. *n inf* betrothed

G

gabacho (-cha) *a* and *n* (*inf* scornful) Frenchman

gabán *m*, overcoat; cloak

gabardina *f*, gabardine; weatherproof coat

gabarra *f*, *naut* lighter, gabbard, barge

gabarro *m*, flaw (in cloth); knot (in stone); snag, drawback; slip, error (in accounts)

gabela *f*, duty, tax; imposition, burden

gabinete *m*, study, library; sitting room; den; *pol* cabinet; collection, museum, gallery; laboratory; boudoir; studio; display cabinet. **g. de lectura,** reading room

gablete *m*, *arch* gable

gacel, m. gacela *f*, gazelle

gaceta *f*, bulletin, review, record; newspaper; gazette (official Spanish government organ); *inf* newshound

gacetero (-ra) *n* newsdealer. *m*, news reporter

gacetilla *f*, news in brief, miscellany column, society news; gossip column; *inf* newshound

gacetillero *m*, paragrapher, penny-a-liner; reporter

gacha *f*, unglazed crock; *pl* pap; porridge

gaché *m*, (among the Romany) Andalusian; *inf* fellow

gacho *a* drooping, bent downward; slouch (hat); (of ears) lop

gachón *a inf* attractive, charming

gaditano (-na) *a* and *n* native of, or pertaining to, Cadiz

gaélico *a* and *m*, Gaelic

gafar *vt* to claw; seize with a hook, hook; mend with a bracket (pottery)

gafas *f pl*, spectacles; goggles; spectacle earhooks; grapplehooks

gafete *m*, hook and eye; clasp

gaita *f*, bagpipe; hand organ; kind of clarinet; *inf* neck. **g. gallega,** bagpipe

gaitería *f*, crude, gaudy garment or ornament

gaitero *a inf* overmerry; loud, crude. *m*, piper

gajes *m pl*, salary; emoluments; perquisites

gajo *m*, branch, bough (gen. cut); little cluster (of grapes); bunch (of fruit); quarter (of oranges, etc.); prong (of forks, etc.)

gala *f*, evening or full dress; grace, wit; flower, cream, best; gala; *pl* finery; trappings; wedding presents. **de g.,** full dress. **hacer g. de,** to glory in, boast of

galactita *f*, fuller's earth

galaico *a* See **gallego**

galán *m*, handsome, well-made man; lover, wooer, gallant; *theat* leading man or one of leading male roles

galancete *m*, handsome little man; *theat* male juvenile lead

galano *a* smart, well-dressed; agreeable, pleasing; beautiful; ornamented; *fig* elegant (speech, style, etc.)

galante *a* gallant, courtly, attentive; flirtatious (of women); licentious

galanteador *a* flirtatious. *m*, philanderer; wooer

galantear *vt* to court; flirt with; make love to; *fig* procure assiduously

galanteo *m*, courtship; flirtation; love-making; wooing

galantería *f*, courtesy; attention, compliment; elegance, grace; gallantry; generosity, liberality

galanura *f*, showiness, gorgeousness; elegance, grace; prettiness

galápago *m*, freshwater tortoise; cleat

galardón *m*, reward, recompense; prize

galardonar *vt* to reward, recompense

gálata *a* and *mf* Galatian

galbana *f*, laziness, inertia

galbanoso *a inf* slothful

galdrufa *f*, top, spinning top

galeote *m*, galley slave

galera *f*, van, wagon, cart; *naut* galley; prison for women; *print* galley. **echar a galeras,** to condemn to the galleys

galerada *f*, galley proof

galería *f*, gallery; corridor, passage; collection of paintings; *min* gallery, drift; *theat* gallery

galerna *f*, tempestuous northwest wind (gen. on Spanish north coast)

Gales Wales

galés (-esa) *a* Welsh. *n* Welshman. *m*, Welsh (language)

galga *f*, boulder, rolling stone; greyhound bitch

galgo *m*, greyhound. **g. ruso,** borzoi

Galia Gaul

gálibo *m*, *naut* mold; elegance

galicado *a* gallicized

galicismo *m*, gallicism

gálico *m*, syphilis. *a* gallic

Galilea Galilee

galileo (-ea) *a* and *n* Galilean

galimatías *m*, *inf* gibberish, nonsense

gallardear *vi* to behave with ease and grace

gallardete *m*, pennant; bunting

gallardía *f*, grace, dignity; spirit, dash; courage; liveliness

gallardo *a* handsome, upstanding; gallant; spirited; fine, noble; lively

gallear *vi inf* to put on airs; be a bully; shout, bawl (with anger, etc.); *fig inf* stand out

gallego (-ga) *a* and *n* Galician. *m*, Galician (language)

galleta *f*, biscuit; *inf* slap; anthracite, lump coal; small jar or vessel

gallina *f*, hen. *mf inf* coward. **g. ciega,** blindman's buff. **inf acostarse con las gallinas,** to go to bed early

gallinaza *f*, hen dung

gallinero (-ra) *n* poultry dealer. *m*, henhouse; brood of hens; *theat* gallery; babel, noisy place

gallito *m*, small cock; cock of the walk; bully

gallo *m*, *orn* cock; *inf* false note (in singing); *inf* boss, chief. **g. de viento,** weathercock. *inf* **alzar el g.,** to put on airs, boast. **Cada g. canta en su muladar,** Every man is boss in his own house. *inf* **Otro g. nos cantara,** Our lot (or fate) would have been very different

gallofero (-ra) *a* mendicant, vagabond. *n* beggar

galocha *f*, patten, clog; cap with earflaps

galón *m*, galloon, braid; *mil* stripe; gallon (measure)

galoneadura *f*, braiding, trimming

galonear *vt* to trim with braid

galop *m*, galop; gallopade

galopante *a* galloping (of consumption, etc.)

galopar *vi* to gallop; *mech* wobble

galope *m*, gallop. *a* or **de g.,** at the gallop; on the run; quickly. **andar a g. corto,** to canter

galopillo *m*, scullion

galopín *m*, ragamuffin, urchin; rogue, knave; *inf* clever rogue; *naut* cabin boy

galvanización f, galvanization

galvanizar vt elec to galvanize; electroplate; fig shock into life

gama f, mus scale; gamut, range; doe

gambito m, gambit (in chess)

gamella f, trough (for washing, feeding animals, etc.)

gamo m, buck (of the fallow deer)

gamuza f, chamois; chamois leather

gana f, appetite; wish, desire. **de buena g.**, willingly. **de mala g.**, reluctantly. **tener g.** (**de**), to wish, desire, want. **no tener g.**, to have no appetite, not be hungry. **No me da la g.**, I don't want (to), I won't

ganable a attainable; earnable

ganadería f, livestock; strain (of cattle); cattle raising; stock farm; cattle dealing

ganadero m, cattle raiser or dealer; herdsman

ganado m, livestock, herd; flock; hive (of bees); inf mob. **g. mayor**, cattle, mules, horses. **g. menor**, sheep, goats, etc. **g. moreno**, hogs, swine. **g. vacuno**, cattle

ganador (**-ra**) a winning. n winner

ganancia f, winning; gain, profit

ganancial, ganancioso a gainful, profitable; lucrative

ganapán m, laborer; porter; inf boor

ganar vt to gain; win; conquer; arrive at; earn; surpass, beat; achieve; acquire; vi prosper

ganchero m, lumberjack

ganchillo m, crochet hook; crochet. **hacer g.**, to crochet

gancho m, hook; stump (of a branch); shepherd's crook; crochet hook; inf trickster, pimp; inf scribble

ganchoso a hooked; bent; curved

gandujar vt sew to pleat, tuck, shirr

gandul (**-la**) a inf lazy. n lazybones, loafer

gandulería f, loafing, idleness

ganga f, min gangue, matrix; bargain, cinch

ganglio m, ganglion

gangoso a nasal; with a twang (of speech)

gangrena f, gangrene

gangrenarse vr to become gangrenous, mortify

gangrenoso a gangrenous

ganguear vi to speak nasally, or with a twang

ganoso a wishful, desirous, anxious

gansada f, inf impertinence, foolishness

ganso (**-sa**) n goose, gander; slow-moving person; yokel, bumpkin

Gante Ghent

ganzúa f, skeleton key; inf picklock, burglar; inf pumper, inquisitive person

gañán m, farm worker; day laborer; brawny fellow

gañido m, yowl, yelp, howl

gañir vi irr to yowl, yelp, howl (of dogs, etc.); crow, croak; inf talk hoarsely. See **mullir**

garabatear vi to hook, catch with hooks; scribble; fig inf beat around the bush

garabateo m, hooking; scribbling

garabato m, hook; agr weed clearer; scrawl, scribble; inf charm, sex appeal; pothook; boat hook; pl gestures, movements (with the hands)

garaje m, garage

garambaina f, tawdry finery gaudiness; pl inf grimaces of affectation; inf scribble, scrawl

garante mf guarantor; reference (person). a responsible, guaranteeing

garantía f, guarantee; security, pledge; law warranty

garantir vt to guarantee; warrant, vouch for

garapiñar vt to ice, freeze (drinks, syrups, etc.); cul candy, coat with sugar

garapiñera f, ice-cream freezer

garbanzo m, chickpea. **g. negro**, fig black sheep

garbillar vt agr to sift; min riddle

garbo m, jaunty air; grace, elegance; frankness; generosity, liberality

garboso a attractive; handsome, sprightly, gay; graceful; munificent

garduña f, weasel; marten

garduño (**-ña**) n inf sneak thief

garete (**ir** or **irse al**) naut to be adrift

garfa f, claw (of a bird or animal)

garfear vi to catch with a hook, hook

garfio m, grappling iron, hook, drag hook, cramp; gaff

gargajear vi to expectorate

gargajo m, phlegm

garganta f, throat; gullet; instep; defile; neck, shaft, narrowest part

gargantear vi to warble, trill

gárgara f, gargling (gen. pl). **hacer gárgaras,** to gargle

gargarismo m, gargling; gargle

gárgol a rotten (eggs). m, groove, mortise

gárgola f, arch gargoyle; linseed

garguero m, windpipe; esophagus

garita f, sentry box; porter's lodge; hut; cabin. **g. de señales,** (railroad) signal box

garitero m, gambling house keeper; gambler

garito m, gambling house; profits of a gambling house

garra f, paw with claws; talon; hand; mech clamp, claw. fig **caer en las garras de,** to fall into the clutches (of)

garrafa f, decanter, carafe; carboy

garrapata f, ent tick

garrapatear vi to scribble

garrapato m, scribble, scrawl

garrido a handsome; gallant; elegant; graceful

garroba f, carob bean

garrocha f, goad. **salto a la g.**, pole jumping

garrotazo m, blow with a truncheon or cudgel. **dar garrotazos de ciego,** to lay about one

garrote m, truncheon, club; med tourniquet; garrote. **dar g.** (**a**), to strangle

garrotillo m, croup

garrucha f, pulley; mech gin block

garrulidad f, garrulity, loquaciousness

gárrulo a twittering, chirping (birds); garrulous; murmuring, babbling (wind, water, etc.)

garza f, heron

garzo a blue (gen. of eyes)

gas m, gas; fumes. **g. asfixiante,** poison gas. **cámara de g.,** gasbag, gas chamber

gasa f, gauze. **tira de g.,** black mourning band

gascón (**-ona**) a and n Gascon

gasconada f, bravado, gasconade

gaseosa f, aerated water

gaseoso a gaseous

gasista mf gas fitter; gasman

gasolina f, gasoline, petrol

gasómetro m, gas meter; gasometer

gastado a worn; worn-out; exhausted

gastador (**-ra**) a extravagant, wasteful. n spendthrift. m, mil sapper; convict condemned to hard labor

gastar vt to spend (money); wear out; exhaust; ruin, destroy; display or have habitually; possess, use, wear; vr wear out; run down (of a battery)

gasto m, spending; expenditure; consumption (of gas, etc.); expense, cost, charge; wear (and tear). **g. suplementario,** extra charge

gástrico a gastric

gastritis f, gastritis

gastronomía f, gastronomy

gastronómico a gastronomic

gastrónomo (**-ma**) n gastronome

gata f, she-cat; wreath of mist; inf Madrilenian woman. **a gatas,** on all fours

gatada f, inf sly trick

gatear vi to climb like a cat; inf crawl on all fours; vt inf scratch (of a cat); steal, pinch

gatera f, cat hole (in a door, etc.)

gatillo m, dim small cat; dental forceps; trigger (of gun); inf juvenile petty thief

gato m, cat; tomcat; moneybag or its contents; mech jack; mousetrap; inf cat burglar, sneak thief; inf Madrilenian; carp clamp. **g. atigrado,** tiger cat. **g. de algalia,** civet cat. **g. de Angora,** Persian cat. **g. montés,** wildcat. **g. romano,** tabby cat. **dar g. por liebre,** to serve cat for hare, to deceive; misrepresent. inf **Hay g.**

encerrado, There's more to this than meets the eye

gatuno *a* feline

gaucho (-cha) *n* gaucho; cowboy, rider

gaveta *f,* drawer (of a desk)

gavia *f,* main topsail; *pl* topsails; crow's-nest

gavilán *m,* sparrow hawk; thistle flower

gavilla *f,* sheaf (of corn, etc.); gang, rabble

gaviota *f,* seagull

gavota *f,* gavotte

gayo *a* gay, happy; showy, attractive. **gaya ciencia,** minstrelsy, art of poetry

gazapera *f,* rabbit warren; *inf* thieves' den; *inf* brawl

gazapo *m,* young rabbit; *inf* cunning fellow; fib, lie; slip, blunder

gazmoñería *f,* prudery, priggish affectation

gazmoño *a* hypocritical, prudish, priggish

gaznápiro (-ra) *n* ninny, simpleton

gaznate *m,* windpipe

gazpacho *m,* cold soup containing bread, onions, vinegar, olive oil, garlic, etc.

ge *f,* name of the letter G

gehena *m,* gehenna, hell

géiser *m,* geyser

gelatina *f,* gelatin. **g. incendiaria,** napalm. **g. seca,** cooking gelatin

gelatinoso *a* gelatinous

gélido *a poet* icy; very cold

gema *f,* gem; *bot* bud

gemelo (-la) *a* and *n* twin. *m pl,* field or opera glasses, binoculars; cuff links; *ast* Gemini

gemido *m,* groan, lament, moan

gemidor *a* groaning, moaning; wailing (of the wind, etc.)

gemir *vi irr* to moan, groan, lament; *fig* wail, howl. See **pedir**

gene *m,* gene

genealogía *f,* genealogy

genealógico *a* genealogical

genealogista *mf* genealogist

generación *f,* generation, reproduction; species; generation

generador *a* generative. *m, mech* generator

general *a* general; universal; widespread; common, usual. *m, (mil ecc)* general. **g. de división,** *mil* major general. **en** *or* **por lo g.,** generally

generalato *m,* generalship

generalidad *f,* majority, bulk; generality

generalísimo *m,* generalissimo, commander in chief

generalización *f,* generalization

generalizar *vt* to generalize; *vr* become widespread or general

generar *vt* to generate

genérico *a* generic

género *m,* kind; class; way, mode; *com* goods; species; genus; *gram* gender; cloth, material. **g. chico,** short theatrical pieces (gen. one act). **g. humano,** humankind

generosidad *f,* hereditary nobility; generosity, magnanimity; liberality, munificence; courage

generoso *a* noble (by birth); magnanimous; generous (of wine); munificent; courageous; excellent

genésico *a* genetic

génesis *m,* Genesis. *f,* beginning, origin

genial *a* of genius; highly talented; brilliant; characteristic, individual; pleasant; cheerful

genialidad *f,* genius; talent; brilliance; eccentricity, oddity

genio *m,* nature, individuality, temperament; temper; character; talent; genius; genie, spirit. **corto de g.,** unintelligent. **mal g.,** bad temper

genital *a* genital. *m,* testicle (gen. *pl*)

genitivo *a* reproductive, generative. *m, gram* genitive

Génova Genoa

genovés (-esa) *a* and *n* Genoese

gente *f,* people, a crowd; nation; army; *inf* family; followers, adherents. **g. baja,** rabble. **g. de bien,** honest

folk; respectable people. **g. de paz,** friends (reply to sentinel's challenge). **g. fina,** nice, cultured people. **g. menuda,** children, small fry

gentecilla *f, dim inf* rabble; contemptible people

gentil *a* pagan, idolatrous; spirited, dashing, handsome; notable, extraordinary; graceful, charming

gentileza *f,* grace; elegance; beauty; verve, sprightliness; courtesy; show, ostentation

gentilhombre *m,* gentleman; handsome man; kind sir! **gentileshombres de cámara,** gentlemen-in-waiting

gentilicio *a* national; family

gentílico *a* pagan, idolatrous

gentilidad *f,* idolatry, paganism; heathendom

gentío *m,* crowd, throng

gentualla, gentuza *f,* canaille, rabble

genuflexión *f,* genuflection

genuino *a* pure; authentic, genuine

geodesia *f,* geodesy

geodésico *a* geodesic

geofísico *m,* geophysicist

geografía *f,* geography

geográfico *a* geographical

geógrafo *m,* geographer

geología *f,* geology

geológico *a* geological

geólogo *m,* geologist

geometría *f,* geometry. **g. del espacio,** solid geometry

geométrico *a* geometrical

geranio *m,* geranium

gerencia *f, com* managership; manager's office; management

gerente *m, com* manager

germanía *f,* thieves' slang; association of thieves; sixteenth-century political brotherhood

germánico *a* germanic

germanófilo (-la) *a* and *n* germanophile

germen *m,* germ, sprout; *bot* embryo; genesis, origin

germinación *f,* germination

germinar *vi* to germinate, sprout; develop, grow

germinativo *a* germinative

gerundio *m, gram* gerund; *inf* pompous ass; *inf* tubthumper

gesta *f,* heroic deed. **cantar de g.,** epic or heroic poem

gestación *f,* gestation

gestear *vi* to gesture, grimace

gesticulación *f,* gesticulation; grimace

gesticular *vi* to grimace, gesticulate. *a* gesticulatory

gestión *f,* negotiation; management, conduct; effort, exertion; measure

gestionar *vt* to negotiate; conduct; undertake; take steps to attain

gesto *m,* gesture; facial expression; grimace; face, visage

gestor (-ra) *n* manager; partner; promoter. *a* managing

Getsemaní Gethsemane

giba *f,* hump, hunchback; *inf* nuisance, inconvenience

gibón *m,* gibbon

giboso *a* hunchbacked

gibraltareño *a* Gibraltarian

gigante *a* gigantic. *m,* giant.

giganta *f,* giantess

gigantesco *a* giant, gigantic; *fig* outstanding

gigantez *f,* gigantic size

gigantón (-ona) *n* enormous giant; carnival grotesque

gimnasia *f,* gymnastics

gimnasio *m,* gymnasium; school, academy

gimnasta *mf* gymnast

gimnástico *a* gymnastic

gimotear *vi inf* to whine (often used scornfully)

gimoteo *m, inf* whining, whimpering

ginebra *f,* gin (drink); confusion; babble, din

ginebrés (-esa), ginebrino (-na) *a* and *n* Genevan

gineceo *m, (bot* and in ancient Greece) gynaecium

ginecología *f,* gynecology

ginecológico *a* gynecological

ginecólogo (-ga) *n* gynecologist

girado *m, com* drawee

girador *m, com* drawer
giralda *f,* weathercock in the shape of a person or animal; tower at Seville
girar *vi* to revolve; deal (with), concern; turn, branch (streets, etc.); *com* trade; *mech* turn on, revolve; *vt* and *vi com* draw, cash. **g. en descubierto,** *com* to overdraw
girasol *m,* sunflower
giratorio *a* revolving, gyrating; swiveling
giro *m,* revolution, turn; revolving; trend; course (of affairs); style, turn (of phrase); threat; knife gash; *com* draft, drawing; *com* line of business, speciality. **g. postal,** postal order
giroscopio *m,* gyroscope
gitanería *f,* cajolery, wheedling; gypsies; gypsy saying or action
gitanesco *a* gypsy, gypsy-like
gitano (-na) *a* gypsy; gypsy-like; seductive, attractive; sly. *n* gypsy
glaciar *m,* glacier
gladiador *m,* gladiator
gladiatorio *a* gladiatorial
glándula *f,* gland
glicerina *f,* glycerin, glycerol
globo *m, geom* sphere; globe, world; globe (*elec gas*); balloon. **g. aerostático,** air balloon. **g. terrestre,** world; geographical globe
globular *a* globular
glóbulo *m,* globule.
globuloso *a* globulous
gloria *f,* heavenly bliss; fame, glory; delight, pleasure; magnificence, splendor; *art* apotheosis, glory. *m, ecc* doxology
gloriar *vt* to praise; *vr* (*with de or en*) boast about; be proud of, rejoice in
glorieta *f,* bower, arbor; open space in a garden; street square
glorificación *f,* glorification
glorificador *a* glorifying
glorificar *vt* to exalt, raise up; glorify, extol; *vr* (*with de or en*) be proud of; glory in; boast of
glorioso *a* glorious; *ecc* blessed; boastful, bragging
glosa *f,* gloss; explanation, note
glosador (-ra) *n* glossator; commentator. *a* explanatory
glosar *vt lit* to gloss
glosario *m,* glossary
glosopeda *f,* foot-and-mouth disease
glotón (-ona) *a* greedy, gluttonous. *n* glutton
glotonería *f,* gluttony, greed
glucosa *f,* glucose
glúteo *a* gluteal
glutinoso *a* glutinous
gn- For words so beginning, see spellings without **g.**
gobernación *f,* government; governor's office or building; ministry of the interior, home office (abb. for **ministerio de G.**)
gobernador (-ra) *a* governing, *n* governor
gobernalle *m,* helm
gobernante *a* governing. *m, inf* self-appointed director or manager
gobernar *vt irr* to govern, rule; lead, conduct; manage; steer; control; *vi* govern; *naut* obey the tiller. See **recomendar**
gobierno *m,* government (all meanings); *naut* helm; control (of machines, business, etc.)
goce *m,* enjoyment; possession
godo (da) *a* Gothic; aristocratic, noble. *n* Goth; aristocrat
gol *m, sport* goal
gola *f,* throat; gullet; gorget; tucker, bib
goleta *f,* schooner
golf *m,* golf. **palo de g.,** golf club
golfear *vi* to loaf
golfería *f,* loafing; vagabondage; loafers
golfo (-fa) *m, geog* gulf; sea, ocean. *n* ragamuffin, urchin. *m, inf* loafer; lounge lizard, wastrel
Golfo Pérsico Persian Gulf

golilla *f,* ruff; *m, inf* magistrate
gollería *f,* dainty, tidbit; *inf* affectation, persnicketiness
gollete *m,* gullet; neck (of a bottle, etc.); *mech* nozzle
golondrina *f, orn* swallow. **g. de mar,** tern
golosina *f,* tidbit, delicacy; desire, caprice; pleasant useless thing
goloso *a* fond of sweet things; greedy, desirous; appetizing
golpe *m,* blow, knock; pull (at the oars); ring (of a bell); *mech* stroke; crowd; fall (of rain, etc.); mass, torrent; misfortune; shock, collision; spring lock; beating (of the heart); flap (of a pocket); *sew* passementerie; surprise; point, wit; bet. **g. de estado,** coup d'état. **g. de fortuna,** stroke of fortune. **g. de mano,** rising, insurrection. **g. en vago,** blow in the air; disappointment. **g. franco,** *sport* free kick. **de g.,** suddenly; quickly
golpeadura *f.* **golpeo** *m,* knocking, striking; beating, throbbing
golpear *vt* and *vi* to knock, strike; beat, throb
goma *f,* gum, rubber; India rubber; rubber band
gomería *f,* tire store
gomero *a* gum; rubber. *m, WH* rubber planter
gomorresina *f,* gum resin
gomoso *a* gummy; gum
gónada *f,* gonad
góndola *f,* gondola
gondolero *m,* gondolier
gongorino *a* gongoristic, euphuistic
gonorrea *f,* gonorrhea
gordo *a* fat, stout; greasy, oily; thick (thread, etc.). *m,* animal fat, suet. *inf* **ganar el g.,** to win first prize (in a lottery, etc.)
gordura *f,* grease, fat; stoutness, corpulence
gorgojo *m,* weevil; *fig* dwarf
gorgoritear *vi inf* to trill, quaver
gorgorito *m, inf* quaver, tremolo, trill (gen. *pl*)
gorgoteo *m,* gurgle
gorjear *vi* to trill, warble; twitter; *vr* crow (of a baby)
gorjeo *m,* trill, shake; warbling, twitter; crowing, lisping (of a child)
gorra *f,* cap; bonnet; *mil* busby; hunting cap. **vivir de g.,** *inf* to sponge
gorrión *m,* sparrow
gorrista *mf inf* parasite; sponger
gorro *m,* cap; bonnet
gorrón *m,* smooth, round pebble; *mech* pivot, gudgeon; sponger, waster. *a* parasitical
gota *f,* drop (of liquid); gout
gotear *vi* to drop, trickle, drip; leak; drizzle; give or receive in driblets
goteo *m,* trickling, dripping
gotera *f,* dripping; trickle; leak; leakage; valance
gótico *a* Gothic; noble, illustrious
gotoso (-sa) *a* gouty. *n* sufferer from gout
goyesco *a* Goyesque
gozar *vt* to enjoy, have; take pleasure (in), delight (in); know carnally; *vi* (*with de*) enjoy; have, possess
gozne *m,* hinge
gozo *m,* enjoyment, possession; gladness, joy; *pl* couplets in honor of the Virgin Mary or a saint. *inf* **¡Mi g. en el pozo!** I'm sunk! All is lost!
gozoso *a* glad, happy. *adv* gladly; with pleasure
grabado *m,* engraver's art; engraving; illustration, picture. **g. al agua fuerte,** etching. **g. al agua tinta,** aquatint
grabador (-ra) *n* engraver
grabadura *f,* act of engraving
grabar *vt* to engrave; *fig* leave a deep impression
gracejo *m,* humor, wit; cheerfulness
gracia *f,* grace; attraction, grace; favor; kindness; jest, witticism; pardon, mercy; pleasant manner; obligingness, willingness; *pl* thanks, thank you. **gracias a,** thanks to. **¡Gracias a Dios!** Thank God! Thank goodness! **las Gracias,** the Three Graces
grácil *a* slender; small
graciosidad *f,* beauty, perfection, grace

gracioso (-sa) *a* attractive, graceful, elegant; witty, humorous; free, gratis. *n theat* comic role; *m, theat* fool

grada *f*, step, stair; gradin, seat; stand, gallery; *agr* harrow; *naut* runway; *pl* perron, flight of stairs

gradación *f*, gradation; climax

gradería *f*, flight of steps

grado *m*, step, stair; degree (of relationship); university degree; grade, class (in schools); (*fig geom phys*) degree; will, desire. **de buen g.**, willingly. **en sumo g.**, in the highest degree

graduación *f*, graduation; *mil* rank; rating (of a ship's company). **g. de oficial**, *mil* commission

graduado *a* graded; *mil* brevet. *m*, graduate

gradual *a* gradual

graduar *vt* to classify; *mil* grade; confer a degree on; measure; test; *com* standardize; *mech* calibrate; *vr* graduate, receive a degree. **g. la vista**, to test the eyes. **graduarse de oficial**, *mil* to get one's commission

gráfica *f*, graph

gráfico *a* graphic; vivid

grafito *m*, graphite

grafología *f*, graphology

grajear *vi* to caw; gurgle, burble (of infants)

grajo *m*, *orn* rook

gramática *f*, grammar. *inf* **g. parda**, horse sense

gramático *a* grammatical. *m*, grammarian

gramo *m*, gram

gramófono *m*, phonograph

gran *a abb* See **grande.** Used before a singular noun. big; great; grand

grana *f*, grain, seed; seed time; cochineal; kermes; red

granada *f*, *mil* grenade, shell; pomegranate

granadero *m*, grenadier; *inf* very tall person

granadilla *f*, passionflower

granadina *f*, grenadine

granar *vi agr* to seed; run to seed

granate *m*, garnet; dark red

Gran Bretaña Great Britain

Gran Canaria Grand Canary

grande *a* big, large; great, illustrious; grand. *m*, great man; grandee. **en g.**, in a large size; as a whole; in style, lavishly

grandeza *f*, largeness; greatness, magnificence; grandeeship; vastness, magnitude

grandilocuencia *f*, grandiloquence

grandílocuo *a* grandiloquent

grandiosidad *f*, grandeur, greatness

grandioso *a* grandiose, magnificent

grandor *m*, size

granear *vt agr* to sow; grain (of leather)

granero *m*, granary; grain-producing country

granito *m*, *dim* small grain; granite; small pimple

granizar *vi* to hail, sleet; *vi and vt fig* shower down, deluge

granizo *m*, hail, sleet; hailstorm; *fig* shower, deluge

granja *f*, farm; farmhouse; dairy farm, dairy

granjear *vt* to trade, profit, earn; obtain, acquire; *vr* gain, win

granjería *f*, farming; agricultural profits; earnings, profits

granjero (-ra) *n* farmer

Gran Lago Salado, el the Great Salt Lake

grano *m*, *agr* grain; seed; bean (coffee, etc.); particle; markings, grain (of wood, etc.); pimple; grain (measure). *fig inf* **ir al g.**, to go to the root of the matter; come to the point

granuja *f*, grape pit. *m*, *inf* urchin, scamp; knave, rogue

granujiento *a* pimply

gránulo *m*, granule

granuloso *a* granulous

grapa *f*, cramp, dowel, clamp; block hook; *elec* cleat; staple

grasa *f*, fat; grease; oil; dripping, suet

grasiento *a* greasy; grubby, dirty

gratificación *f*, monetary reward; fee, remuneration; gratuity

gratificar *vt* to recompense; please, gratify

gratis *a* and *adv* gratis

gratitud *f*, gratitude

grato *a* pleasing, agreeable; free, gratuitous

gratuito *a* gratuitous, free; baseless, unfounded

grava *f*, gravel; stone chip, pebble; metal (of a road)

gravamen *m*, obligation; burden; tax

gravar *vt* to burden, weigh upon; tax

grave *a* heavy; important, momentous; grave; dignified, serious; sedate; tiresome; low-pitched, low; *gram* grave accent

gravedad *f*, *phys* gravity

gravitación *f*, *phys* gravitation; seriousness; sedateness; importance; enormity, gravity

gravitar *vi* to gravitate; lean or rest (upon)

gravoso *a* grievous, oppressive; onerous; costly

graznar *vi* to caw; cackle; quack; croak; sing stridently, screech

graznido *m*, caw; cackle; croaking; quack; screech

Grecia Greece

greco (-ca) *a* and *n* Greek

grecorromano *a* Greco-Roman

gregario *a* gregarious

gregoriano *a* Gregorian

gregüescos *m pl*, wide breeches (sixteenth and seventeenth centuries)

gremial *a* pertaining to a guild, union, or association. *m*, member of a guild, union, or association

gremio *m*, guild, corporation, union; society, association; (univ.) general council

greña *f*, tangled lock (of hair) (gen. *pl*); tangle, confused mass

gresca *f*, uproar, tumult; fight, row

grey *f*, flock, drove, herd; *ecc* flock, company; people, nation

grial *m*, grail

griego (-ga) *a* and *n* Greek. *m*, Greek (language); *inf* gibberish

grieta *f*, fissure; crevice; chink; split; flaw; vein (in stone, etc.); *mech* leak

grietado *a* fissured; cracked

grifo *m*, griffin; tap; cock

grillo *m*, cricket; *bot* shoot; *pl* fetters, irons, chains; *fig* shackles

grima *f*, revulsion, horror

gringo (-ga) *n inf* foreigner (scornful)

gripe *f*, influenza; grippe

gris *a* and *m*, gray

grisú *m*, firedamp

gritador (-ra) *a* shouting. *n* shouter

gritar *vi* to shout, yell, scream; howl down; hoot

gritería *f*, shouting, yelling, clamor

grito *m*, shout, yell, shriek, scream. *inf* **poner el g. en el cielo**, to cry to high heaven, complain

groenlandés (-esa) *a* Greenland. *n* Greenlander

Groenlandia Greenland

grog *m*, grog

grosella *f*, currant. **g. blanca**, gooseberry

grosería *f*, rudeness; roughness (of workmanship); ignorance; rusticity

grosero *a* coarse; rough; thick; unpolished, rude

grotesco *a* grotesque, absurd

grúa *f*, *mech* crane, hoist, derrick. **g. de pescante**, jib crane. **g. móvil**, traveling crane

gruesa *f*, twelve dozen, gross

grueso *a* stout, corpulent; large. *m*, bulk, body; major portion, majority; thick stroke (of a letter); thickness, density. **en g.**, in bulk

grulla *f*, *orn* crane

grumete *m*, ship's boy, cabin boy

grumo *m*, clot; heart (of vegetables); bunch, cluster; bud

gruñido *m*, grunt; growl

gruñidor *a* grunting; growling

gruñir *vi* to grunt; growl; grumble; squeak, creak (doors, etc.). *Pres. Part.* **gruñendo.** *Pres. Ind.* **gruño, gruñes,** etc.

grupa *f,* croup (of a horse); pillion (of a motorcycle)

grupera *f,* pillion (of a horse, etc.)

grupo *m,* knot, cluster; band, group; *art* group; *mech* set

gruta *f,* cavern, grotto

guacamayo *m,* macaw

guadamecí *m,* embossed decorated leather

guadaña *f,* scythe

guagua, *f Caribbean* bus

gualdo *a* yellow, golden

gualdrapa *f,* saddlecloth, trappings; *inf* tatter, rag

guante *m,* glove. **g. con puño,** gauntlet glove. **g. de boxeo,** boxing glove. **g. de cabritilla,** kid glove. **arrojar el g.,** to throw down the gauntlet; challenge, defy

guantelete *m,* gauntlet

guantería *f,* glove trade, shop, or factory

guantero (-ra) *n* glove maker or seller, glover

guapear *vi inf* to make the best of a bad job; *inf* pride oneself on being well dressed

guapeza *f,* prettiness; *inf* resolution, courage; *inf* smartness or showiness of dress; boastful act or behavior

guapo *a* pretty; handsome; *inf* daring, enterprising; *inf* smart, well-dressed, foppish; *inf* handsome. *m,* braggart, brawler; beau, lover; *inf* fine fellow, son of a gun

guarda *mf* keeper, guard. *f,* guarding, keeping, custodianship, preservation; guardianship; observance, fulfilment; flyleaf, end page (books); warder (of locks or keys); *mech* guard; guard (of a fan)

guardabarrera *mf* gatekeeper at a level crossing (railroad)

guardabarro *m,* mudguard

guardabosque *mf* gamekeeper

guardabrisa *m, aut* windshield; glass candle shield

guardacostas *m,* coast guard; *naut* revenue cutter

guardafrenos *m,* brakeman (railroad)

guardagujas *m,* pointsman (railroad)

guardainfante *m,* farthingale, crinoline

guardalmacén *mf* storekeeper

guardameta *mf* goalkeeper

guardamuebles *m,* furniture warehouse

guardapelo *m,* locket

guardapolvo *m,* dustcover; light overcoat; inner case of a pocket watch

guardar *vt* to keep; preserve, retain; maintain, observe; save, put aside, lay away; defend, protect; guard; *vr (with de)* avoid, guard against. **g. compás con,** to be in tune with. **guardarse mucho,** to think twice before. **g. silencio,** to keep silent. ¡**Guarda**! Take care! ¡**Guárdate del agua mansa**! Still waters run deep!

guardarropa *m,* cloakroom. *mf* cloakroom attendant; keeper of the wardrobe. *m,* wardrobe, clothes closet

guardarropía *f,* theatrical wardrobe

guardavía *m,* signalman (railroad)

guardería *f,* day nursery, day-care center

guardia *f,* guard, escort; protection; (*mil naut*) watch; regiment, body (of troops); guard (fencing). *m,* guardsman; policeman. **g. de asalto,** armed police. **g. de corps,** royal bodyguard. **g. civil,** civil guard. **g. marina,** midshipman. **g. municipal,** city police. *mil* **montar la g.,** to mount guard

guardián (-ana) *n* keeper; custodian; warden. *m,* watchman; jailer

guardilla *f,* attic, garret

guarecer *vt irr* to shelter, protect, aid; preserve, keep; cure; *vr* take shelter. See **conocer**

guarida *f,* lair, den; refuge, shelter; haunt, resort

guarismo *m, math* figure; number, numeral

guarnecer *vt irr* to decorate, adorn; *sew* trim, face, border; *mil* garrison; *mas* plaster. See **conocer**

guarnecido *m, mas* plastering

guarnición *f, sew* trimming, ornament, border, fringe; *mech* packing; *mil* garrison; setting (of jewels); guard (of a sword, etc.); *pl* harness; fittings

guarnir *vt naut* to reeve

guasa *f, inf* dullness, boringness; joke. **de g.,** jokingly

guasón *a inf* dull, tedious; humorous, jocose

guatemalteco (-ca) *a* and *n* Guatemalan

guau *m,* bowwow, bark of a dog

guayaba *f,* guava; guava jelly

Guayana Guiana

gubernamental *a* governmental

gubernativo *a* governmental; administrative

gubia *f, carp* chisel; gouge

guedeja *f,* long tress or lock of hair; forelock; lion's mane

Guernesey Guernsey

guerra *f,* war; struggle, fight; *fig* hostility. *inf* **dar g.,** to give trouble, annoy. **en g. con,** at war with. **la g. de Cuba,** the Spanish-American War

guerrear *vi* to make war, fight; oppose

guerrero (-ra) *a* war, martial; warrior; *inf* troublesome, annoying. *n* fighter. *m,* warrior, soldier

guerrillear *vi* to wage guerrilla warfare; fight as a guerrilla

guerrillero *m,* guerrilla fighter

guía *mf* guide, conductor; adviser, director. *f,* guide, aid; guidebook; *mech* guide, slide; directory; signpost. **g. de ferrocarriles,** train schedule, railroad timetable. **g. de teléfonos,** telephone directory

guiar *vt* to guide; lead, conduct; *mech* work, control; *aut* drive; pilot; teach, direct, govern

guija *f,* pebble

guijarro *m,* smooth, round pebble; boulder; cobblestone

guijarroso *a* pebbly, cobbled

guijo *m,* gravel; granite chips; pebble

guillotina *f,* guillotine; paper-cutting machine

guillotinar *vt* to guillotine, decapitate

guinda *f,* mazard cherry; *naut* height of masts

guinea *f,* guinea

guinga *f,* gingham

guiñada *f,* wink; blink; *naut* yaw

guiñapo *m,* rag, tatter; sloven, ragamuffin

guiñar *vt* to wink; blink; *naut* yaw; *vr* wink at each other

guiño *m,* wink

guión *m,* royal standard; banner; summary; leader of a dance; *gram* hyphen; subtitle (in films). **g. mayor,** *gram* dash

guipuzcoano (-na) *a* and *n* Guipuzcoan

guirigay *m, inf* gibberish; uproar, babble

guirnalda *f,* garland, wreath

guisa *f,* way, manner; will, desire. **a g. de,** in the manner or fashion of

guisado *m, cul* stew; cooked dish

guisante *m, agr* pea; pea plant. **g. de olor,** sweetpea

guisar *vt* to cook; stew; *cul* prepare, dress; adjust, arrange

guiso *m, cul* cooked dish

guitarra *f,* guitar

guitarrista *mf* guitar player

guito *a* vicious (horses, mules)

gula *f,* greed, gluttony

gusaniento *a* worm-eaten; maggoty

gusano *m,* worm; caterpillar; maggot; meek, downtrodden person. **g. de seda,** silkworm

gusanoso *a* wormy

gustar *vt* to taste, savor; try; *vi* be pleasing, give pleasure; like. **Me gusta el libro,** I like the book. **La película no me gustó,** I didn't like the film. **g. de,** to like, is used only when a person is the subject

gusto *m,* taste; flavor, savor; pleasure, delight; will, desire; discrimination, taste, style, fashion, manner; whim, caprice. **a g.,** to taste; according to taste. **con mucho g.,** with great pleasure. **dar g.,** to please. **de buen g.,** in good taste

gustoso *a* savory, palatable; willingly, with pleasure; pleasant, agreeable

gutagamba *f,* gamboge (yellow)

gutapercha *f,* guttapercha

gutural *a* guttural

H

haba *f*, broad bean; bean (coffee, cocoa, etc.). **h. de las Indias,** sweetpea. **Esas son habas contadas,** That's a certainty

Habana, la Havana

habanero (-ra), habano (-na) *a* and *n* Havanese, from Havana. *m*. **habano,** Havana cigar

habar *m*, bean field

haber *m*, estate, property (gen. *pl*); income; *com* credit balance. **h. monedado,** specie

haber *vt irr* to have; catch, lay hands on (e.g. **El reo fue habido,** The criminal was caught). *v aux* (e.g. **Hemos escrito la carta,** We have written the letter). *v impers* to happen, take place; be. *3rd pers. sing Pres. Ind.* **ha** is replaced by **hay,** meaning there is or there are (e.g. **No hay naranjas en las tiendas,** There are no oranges in the shops). In certain weather expressions, **hay** means it is (e.g. **Hay luna,** It is moonlight). Used of expressions of time, **haber** means to elapse and **ha** (*3rd pers. sing Pres. Ind.*) has adverbial force of 'ago' (e.g. **muchos días ha,** many days ago). **h. de,** to be necessary (less strong than **h. que**) (e.g. **Hemos de verle mañana,** We must see him tomorrow. **He de hacer el papel de Manolo,** I am to play the part of Manolo). **h. que,** to be unavoidable, be essential. With this construction the form **hay** is used (e.g. **Hay que darse prisa,** We (or one) must hurry. **No hay que enojarse,** There's no need to get annoyed). **no h., más que pedir,** to leave nothing to be desired. **no h. tal,** to be no such thing. *inf* **habérselas con,** to quarrel or fall out with. **Hubo una vez . . . ,** Once upon a time . . . **¡No hay de qué!,** Don't mention it!; Not at all!; You're welcome! **No hay para que . . . ,** There's no point in. . . . **poco tiempo ha,** a little while ago. **¿Qué hay?** What's the matter?; What's new? **¿Qué hay de nuevo?** What's new? *Pres. Ind.* **he, has, ha, hemos, habéis, han.** *Fut.* **habré,** etc. *Condit.* **habría,** etc. *Preterite* **hube, hubiste, hubo, hubimos, hubisteis, hubieron.** *Pres. Subjunc.* **haya,** etc. *Imperf. Subjunc.* **hubiese,** etc.

habichuela *f*, kidney bean

hábil *a* clever; skillful; able; lawful

habilidad *f*, ability; skill; accomplishment; craftsmanship, workmanship

habilidoso *a* accomplished; able; skillful

habilitación *f*, habilitation; paymastership; equipment; furnishing

habilitado *m*, paymaster

habilitar *vt* to qualify; equip; furnish; habilitate; enable; *com* capitalize

habitabilidad *f*, habitability

habitable *a* habitable

habitación *f*, habitation, dwelling; room in a house; residence; (*bot zool*) habitat; caretaking

habitante *m*, inhabitant

habitar *vt* to inhabit, reside in

hábito *m*, attire; *ecc* habit; use, custom; skill, facility; *pl* vestments; gown, robe. **tomar el h.,** to become a monk or nun

habitual *a* habitual, usual

habituar *vt* to accustom; *vr* accustom oneself; grow used (to)

habitud *f*, habit, custom; connection, relationship

habla *f*, speech; language; dialect; discourse. **al h.,** within speaking distance

hablado *a* spoken. **bien h.,** well-spoken; courteous. **mal h.,** ill-spoken; rude

hablador (-ra) *a* talkative; gossipy. *n* chatterbox; gossip

habladuría *f*, gossip; impertinent chatter

hablanchín *a inf* chattering, gossiping

hablar *vi* to speak; converse; express oneself; arrange; (*with de*) speak about; discuss; gossip about; criticize; (*with por*) intercede on behalf of; *vt* speak (a language);

say, speak; *vr* speak to one another. **no hablarse,** to not be on speaking terms. **h. a gritos,** to shout. **h. alto,** to speak loudly or in strong terms. **h. bien** (*or* **mal**), to be well- (or ill-) spoken; be polite (or rude). **h. claro,** to speak frankly. **h. consigo** *or* **h. entre sí,** to talk to oneself. *inf* **h. cristiano, h. en cristiano,** to speak clearly or intelligibly; speak frankly. **hablarlo todo,** to talk too much. **h. por h.,** to talk for talking's sake. *inf* **h. por los codos,** to chatter. **h. sin ton ni son,** to speak foolishly

hablilla *f*, rumor, tittletattle, gossip

hacecillo *m*, small sheaf; small bundle; *bot* fascicle; beam (of light)

hacedero *a* feasible, practicable

hacedor *m*, maker; steward, manager; Creator

hacendado (-da) *a* landed. *n* landowner; *WH* cattle rancher

hacendista *mf* political economist

hacendoso *a* diligent, hard-working

hacer *vt irr* to make; fashion, form, construct; do, perform; cause, effect; arrange, put right; contain; accustom, harden; pack (luggage); imagine, invent, create; improve, perfect; compel, oblige; deliver (speeches); compose; earn; *math* add up to; suppose, imagine (e.g. **Sus padres hacían a María en casa,** Her parents imagined that Mary was at home); put into practice, execute; play the part of or act like (e.g. **h. el gracioso,** to play the buffoon); shed, cast (e.g. **El roble hace sombra,** The oak casts a shadow); assemble, convoke (meetings, gatherings); give off, produce (e.g. **La chimenea hace humo,** The chimney is smoking); perform (plays); (*with el, la, lo, and some nouns*) pretend to be (e.g. **Se hizo el desconocido,** He pretended to be ignorant). (**h.** followed by infin. is sometimes translated by a past participle in English (e.g. **Lo hice h.,** I had it done.)) *vi* to matter, be important, signify (e.g. **Su llegada no hace nada al caso,** His arrival makes no difference to the case. **Se me hace muy poco . . . ,** It matters to me very little . . .); be fitting or suitable; concern, be pertinent; match, go with; agree, be in harmony; (*with de*) act as, discharge duties of temporarily (e.g. **h. de camarero,** to be a temporary waiter); (*with por*) try to, attempt to (e.g. **Haremos por decírselo,** We shall try to tell him). *vi impers* Used in expressions concerning: 1. the weather. 2. lapse of time. English uses the verb 'to be' in both cases, e.g.:

1. **hace buen** (*or* **mal**) **tiempo,** it is fine (or bad) weather. **hace mucho frío,** it is very cold. **hace sol,** it is sunny. **hace viento,** it is windy. **¿Qué tiempo hace?** What is the weather like?

2. **hace** + an expression of time is followed by **que** introducing a clause (e.g. **Hace dos horas que llegamos,** It is two hours since we arrived) or **hace** + an expression of time may be followed by **desde** + a noun (e.g. **Hace dos años desde aquel día,** It is two years since that day) When an action or state that has begun in the past is still continuing in the present, the Spanish verb is in the Pres. Ind., whereas the English verb is in the Perfect (e.g. **Hace un mes que la veo todos los días,** I have been seeing her every day for a month). This rule holds good with other tenses. English Pluperfect, Future Perfect, Conditional Perfect become in Spanish Imperfect, Future, Conditional, respectively. *naut* **h. agua,** to leak. **h. aguas,** to pass water, urinate. **h. alarde de,** to boast of. **h. América,** to strike it rich. **h. el amor a,** to make love to, court, woo. **h. autoridad,** to be authoritative. **h. a todo,** to have many uses; be adaptable. **h. bancarrota,** to go bankrupt. **h. un berrinche,** to make a fit, have a tantrum. **hacerse un berrinche,** to have a fit, have a tantrum. *fig inf* **h. buena,** to justify. **h. calceta,** to knit. **h. cara**

or **frente a,** to face; resist. **h. caso,** to take notice, mind (e.g. **¡No hagas caso!** Never mind!). **h. causas,** to bring charges, institute proceedings. **h. cuentas,** to reckon up. **h. daño,** to harm. *inf* **h. de las suyas,** to behave in his usual manner or play one of his usual tricks. **h. diligencias por,** to endeavor to. **h. fiesta,** to take a holiday. **h. fuerza,** to struggle. **h. fuerza a,** *fig* to do violence to (e.g. **Hizo fuerza a sus creencias,** He did violence to his beliefs). **h. h.,** to cause to be made (e.g. **He hecho hacer un vestido,** I have had a dress made). **h. juego,** to make a set, match (e.g. **El sombrero hace juego con el traje,** The hat goes with the dress). **h. la corte (a),** to court, woo. *fig inf* **h. la vista gorda,** to turn a blind eye. **h. la vida del claustro,** to lead a cloistered existence. **h. mal,** to do wrong; be harmful (food, etc.). **h. pedazos,** to break. **h. pinos** (or **pinitos**) to totter; toddle; stagger. *aer* **h. rizos,** to loop the loop. **h. saber,** to make known; notify. **h. seguir,** to forward (letters). **h. señas,** to make signs (wave, beckon, etc.). *inf* **h. una que sea sonada,** to cause a big scandal. **¡Hágame el favor!** Please! *Pres. Ind.* **hago, haces,** etc. *Fut.* **haré,** etc. *Condit.* **haría,** etc. *Imperat.* **haz, haga, hagamos, haced, hagan.** *Preterite* **hice, hiciste, hizo, hicimos, hicisteis, hicieron.** *Pres. Subjunc.* **haga,** etc. *Imperf. Subjunc.* **hiciese,** etc.

hacerse *vr irr* to become (e.g. **Se ha hecho muy importante,** It (or he) has become very important); grow up (e.g. **Miguel se ha hecho hombre,** Michael has grown up (become a man)); develop, mature; pass oneself off as, pretend to be; (*with prep a*) become accustomed to or used to (e.g. **Me haré a este clima,** I shall grow used to this climate); withdraw or retire to (of places); (*with de or con*) provide oneself with. **h. a la vela,** to set sail. **h. a (uno),** to seem (e.g. **Eso que me cuentas se me hace increíble,** What you tell me seems incredible). *inf* **h. chiquito,** to be modest. **h. tarde,** to grow late; *fig* be too late. See **hacer**

hacia *prep* toward, near, about. **h. adelante,** forward, onward

hacienda *f,* country estate, land; property; *pl* domestic tasks; cattle. **h. pública,** public funds. **ministerio de h.,** national treasury, exchequer

hacina *f, agr* stack; heap, pile

hacinamiento *m,* stacking, piling; accumulation

hacinar *vt agr* to stack sheaves; accumulate, amass; pile up, heap

hacha *f,* large candle; torch; ax. **h. pequeña,** hatchet

hachazo *m,* stroke of an ax

hache *f,* name of the letter H

hachero *m,* candlestick; woodcutter, axman

hacho *m,* torch; beacon

hada *f,* fairy

hado *m,* fate; destiny

hagiografía *f,* hagiography

hagiógrafo *m,* hagiographer

Haití Haiti

haitiano (-na) *a* and *n* Haitian

halagar *vt* to caress; flatter; coax; please, delight

halago *m,* flattery; coaxing; caress; source of pleasure, delight

halagüeño *a* flattering; pleasing; caressing; hopeful, promising

halar *vt naut* to haul, tow

halcón *m,* falcon

halconero *m,* hawker, hunter

hálito *m,* breath; vapor; *poet* breeze

hallado *a* and *Past Part.* found, met. **bien h.,** welcome; happy, contented. **mal h.,** unwelcome; uneasy, discontented

hallador (-ra) *n* finder

hallar *vt* to find; meet; observe; discover; find out; *vr* be present; be, find oneself

hallazgo *m,* finding; thing found; finder's reward

halo *m,* halo

halterofilia *f,* weightlifting

hamaca *f,* hammock

hamadríade *f,* hamadryad

hambre *f,* hunger; famine; desire, yearning. **tener h.,** to be hungry

hambriento *a* hungry; famished; *fig* starved (of affection, etc.)

Hamburgo Hamburg

hamo *m,* fishhook

hampa *f,* rogue's life; gang of rogues; underworld, slum

hangar *m,* hangar

hanseático *a* Hanseatic

haragán (-ana) *a* lazy, idle. *n* idler, lazybones

harapiento *a* ragged

harapo *m,* tatter, rag

haraposo *a* ragged

harén *m,* harem

harina *f,* flour; powder; farina. *inf* **ser h. de otro costal,** to be a horse of another color

harinero *a* relating to flour. *m,* flour merchant; flour bin

harinoso *a* floury, mealy; farinaceous

harmónica *f, (phys math)* harmonic

harmonizar *vt* to arrange (music)

harnero *m,* sieve

harón *a* slothful, slow; lazy, idle

harpillera *f,* sackcloth, sacking

hartar *vt* to satiate; tire, annoy; satisfy the appetite; shower (with blows, etc.)

hartazgo *m,* satiety

harto *a* satiated; tired (of), *adv* enough

hartura *f,* satiety; abundance

hasta *prep* until; as far as; down or up to. *conjunc* also, even. **h. la vista,** See you! Ciaio! Au revoir! **h. mañana,** until tomorrow

hastial *m,* gable, end wall; boor, lout

hastío *m,* loathing; distaste; nausea

hato *m,* personal clothing; herd of cattle; gang (of suspicious characters); crowd, mob; *inf* group, party. *inf* **liar el h.,** to pack up

Hawai Hawaii

hay there is; there are. See **haber**

haya *f,* beech tree; beechwood

Haya, La The Hague

hayal *m,* wood of beech trees, beech plantation

hayuco *m,* beech mast

haz *m,* bundle, sheaf; *mil* file; *pl* fasces. *f,* visage; surface, face. **h. de la tierra,** face of the earth. **h. de luz,** beam of light. *fig* **ser de dos haces,** to be two-faced

haz *2nd pers Imperat* **hacer**

hazaña *f,* exploit, prowess

hazañoso *a* heroic, dauntless, courageous

hazmerreír *m, inf* laughingstock

he *interj* and *adv* Hallo! Hist! Behold! **¡Heme aquí!** Here I am. **he aquí,** here is . . .

hebilla *f,* buckle

hebra *f,* thread; fiber; flesh; *min* vein, streak; filament (textiles); grain (of wood); *pl poet* hair. *inf* **pegar la h.,** to start a conversation

hebraísmo *m,* Hebraism

hebraísta *m,* Hebraist

hebreo (-ea) *a* Hebraic, Jewish. *n* Jew. *m,* Hebrew (language)

Hébridas, las the Hebrides

hecatombe *f,* hecatomb; slaughter, massacre

hechicería *f,* sorcery; spell, enchantment

hechicero *a* bewitching; magic; charming, attractive

hechizar *vt* to bewitch; charm, attract, delight

hechizo *m,* magic spell; fascination, charm; delight, pleasure

hecho *a* developed, mature; accustomed, used; perfected, finished; ready-made. **h. una furia,** like a fury, very angry. **bien h.,** well-made, well-proportioned; well or rightly done

hecho *m,* deed, action; fact; happening, event. **los Hechos de los Apóstoles,** the Acts of the Apostles

hechura *f,* making, make; creation; form; figure, statue; *lit* composition; build (of body); *fig* puppet, creature; *pl* price paid for work done. **de h. sastre,** *a* tailor-made

hectárea *f*, hectare

hectógrafo *m*, hectograph

hectogramo *m*, hectogram

hectolitro *m*, hectoliter

hectovatio *m*, hectowatt

heder *vi irr* to stink; be intolerable. See **entender**

hediondez *f*, stink, stench

hediondo *a* stinking; intolerable, pestilential; obscene

hedonismo *m*, hedonism

hedonista *mf* hedonist

hegeliano *a* Hegelian

hegemonía *f*, hegemony

helada *f*, frost. **h. blanca,** hoarfrost

heladera *f*, refrigerator

helado *a* frozen; ice-cold; astounded, disdainful. *m*, iced drink; sherbet, ice cream

helamiento *m*, icing; freezing

helar *vt irr* to freeze; ice, chill; astound; discourage; *vr* become iced; freeze; become ice-cold. *v impers* to freeze. See **acertar**

helecho *m*, fern

helénico *a* Hellenic

helenismo *m*, Hellenism

helenista *mf* Hellenist

helenizar *vt* to Hellenize

hélice *f*, spiral, helical line; screw, propeller; *geom* helix; *ast* Ursa Major

helicóptero *m*, *aer* helicopter

helio *m*, helium

heliógrafo *m*, heliograph

helioscopio *m*, helioscope

helióstato *m*, heliostat

helioterapia *f*, heliotherapy

heliotropismo *m*, heliotropism

heliotropo *m*, heliotrope; agate

helvecio (-ia) *a* and *n* Helvetian

hembra *f*, female; *inf* woman; nut of a screw; eye of a hook. *inf* **una real h.,** a fine figure of a woman

hemiciclo *m*, hemicycle; floor (of a legislative building)

hemisférico *a* hemispherical

hemisferio *m*, hemisphere

hemofilia *f*, hemophilia.

hemoglobina *f*, hemoglobin

hemorragia *f*, hemorrhage

hemorroides *f*, hemorrhoids

henchido *a* swollen

henchimiento *m*, swelling; inflation; filling

henchir *vt irr* to fill; stuff; swell. *Pres. Ind.* **hincho, hinches, hinche, hinchen.** *Pres. Part.* **hinchiendo.** *Pres. Subjunc.* **hincha,** etc. *Imperf. Subjunc.* **hinchiese,** etc. *Imperat.* **hinche, hincha, hinchamos, henchid, hinchan**

hendedura *f*, fissure; rift

hender *vt irr* to split, crack; *fig* cleave (air, water, etc.); make one's way through. See **entender**

hendidura *f*, split, fissure, crack, chink

henil *m*, hayloft

heno *m*, hay

hepático *a* hepatic

heráldica *f*, heraldry

heráldico *a* heraldic

heraldo *m*, herald; harbinger

herbaje *m*, herbage; pasture, grass; thick woolen cloth

herbario *m*, herbalist, botanist; herbarium. *a* herbal

herbívoro *a* herbivorous

herbolaria *f*, herbal

herborizar *vi* to botanize

hercúleo *a* herculean

heredad *f*, landed property; country estate

heredar *vt* to inherit; make a deed of gift to; inherit characteristics, etc.; take as heir

heredera *f*, heiress

heredero *m*, heir; inheritor. **h. aparente,** heir apparent. **presunto h.,** heir presumptive

hereditario *a* hereditary

hereje *mf* heretic

herejía *f*, heresy

herencia *f*, inheritance; heredity; heritage

heresiarca *mf* heresiarch

herético *a* heretical

herida *f*, wound; insult; anguish. **h. contusa,** contusion. **h. penetrante,** deep wound

herir *vt irr* to wound; strike, harm; *fig* pierce (of sun's rays); *fig* pluck (strings of a musical instrument); impress (the senses); affect (the emotions); offend (gen. of words). *Pres. Part.* **hiriendo.** *Pres. Ind.* **hiero, hieres, hiere, hieren.** *Preterite* **hirió, hirieron.** *Pres. Subjunc.* **hiera, hieras, hiera, hiramos, hiráis, hieran.** *Imperf. Subjunc.* **hiriese,** etc.

hermafrodita *a* and *mf* hermaphrodite

hermafroditismo *m*, hermaphroditism

hermana *f*, sister; twin, pair (of things). **h. de leche,** foster sister. **h. política,** sister-in-law

hermanar *vt* to join; mate; harmonize; *vt* and *vr* be the spiritual brother of, be compatible

hermanastra *f*, stepsister

hermanastro *m*, stepbrother

hermandad *f*, brotherhood; friendship, intimacy; relationship (of one thing to another); confraternity. **Santa H.,** Spanish rural police force instituted in the fifteenth century

hermano *m*, brother; pair, twin (of things); *ecc* brother. **h. de raza,** member of the same race. **h. político,** brother-in-law

hermético *a* hermetic

hermosear *vt* to embellish, beautify, adorn

hermoso *a* beautiful; shapely; handsome; fine, wonderful (weather, view, etc.)

hermosura *f*, beauty; pleasantness, attractiveness, perfection of form; belle

hernia *f*, hernia

héroe *m*, hero

heroicidad *f*, heroism

heroico *a* heroic

heroína *f*, heroine

heroismo *m*, heroism

herpes *m pl*, or *f pl*, herpes

herrada *f*, pail

herradero *m*, branding of livestock

herrador *m*, blacksmith

herradura *f*, horseshoe

herraje *m*, ironwork

herramienta *f*, tool; set of tools

herrar *vt irr* to shoe horses; brand (cattle); decorate with iron. See **acertar**

herrería *f*, forge; ironworks; blacksmith's shop; clamor, tumult, confusion

herrero *m*, smith

herrete *m*, ferrule, tag

herrumbre *f*, rust; taste of iron

herrumbroso *a* rusty

hervidero *m*, boiling, bubbling; *fig* ebullition; swarm, crowd

hervir *vi irr* to boil; foam and froth (sea); seethe (emotions); surge (crowds); (*with en*) abound in, swarm with. See **sentir**

hervor *m*, boiling; ebullition, vigor, zest; seething, agitation

hesitación *f*, hesitation, doubt, uncertainty

hesitar *vi* to hesitate, vacillate

heteo (-ea) *a* and *n* Hittite

heterodina *a f*, *rad* heterodyne

heterodoxia *f*, heterodoxy

heterodoxo *a* heterodox

heterogeneidad *f*, heterogeneity

heterogéneo *a* heterogeneous

hético *a* hectic, consumptive

hexagonal *a* hexagonal

hexágono *m*, hexagon

hexámetro *m*, hexameter

hez *f*, (gen. *pl* **heces**) lees, dregs

hiato m, hiatus
hibernal a wintry
hibernés a Hibernian
hibisco m, hibiscus
hibridación f, hybridization
hibridismo m, hybridism
híbrido a and m, hybrid
hidalgo (-ga) n noble, aristocrat. a noble; illustrious; generous
hidalguía f, nobility; generosity, nobility of spirit
hidra f, zool hydra; poisonous snake; ast Hydra
hidratar vt chem to hydrate
hidrato m, hydrate. **h. de carbono,** carbohydrate
hidráulica f, hydraulics
hidráulico a hydraulic
hidroavión m, flying boat
hidrocarburo m, hydrocarbon
hidrocéfalo a hydrocephalic
hidrodinámica f, hydrodynamics
hidroeléctrico a hydroelectric
hidrofobia f, hydrophobia; rabies
hidrógeno m, hydrogen
hidrografía f, hydrography
hidrología f, hydrology
hidropesía f, dropsy
hidrópico a dropsical
hidroplano m, seaplane
hidroquinona f, hydroquinone
hidroscopio m, hydroscope
hidrostática f, hydrostatics
hidroterapia f, hydrotherapy
hiedra f, ivy
hiel f, gall, bile, bitterness, affliction; pl troubles
hielo m, ice, frost; freezing, icing; stupefaction; indifference, coldness. inf **estar hecho un h.,** to be as cold as ice
hiena f, hyena
hierático a hieratical
hierba f, grass; small plant; herb. **h. cana,** groundsel. **mala h.,** weed
hierbabuena f, bot mint
hierofante m, hierophant
hierra f, branding time
hierro m, iron; brand with hot iron; iron or steel head of a lance, etc.; instrument or shape made of iron; weapon of war. pl fetters. **h. colado,** cast iron. **h. dulce,** wrought iron. **h. en planchas,** sheet iron. **h. viejo,** scrap iron
hígado m, liver; courage
higiene f, hygiene; cleanliness, neatness. **h. privada,** personal hygiene. **h. pública,** public health
higiénico a hygienic
higo m, fig. **h. chumbo,** prickly pear
higrómetro m, hygrometer
higuera f, fig tree
hija f, daughter; native of a place; offspring
hijastro (-ra) n stepchild
hijo m, son; child; native of a place; offspring; shoot, sprout; pl descendants. **h. de la cuna,** foundling. **h. de leche,** foster child. **h. natural,** natural child. **h. político,** son-in-law
hijuela f, little daughter; small mattress; small drain; side road; accessory, subordinate thing; piece of material for widening a garment; law part of an inheritance
hila f, row, line; gut; surg lint (gen. pl)
hilacha f, thread raveled from cloth; fiber, filament. **h. de vidrio,** spun glass
hilado m, spinning; thread, yarn
hilandería f, spinning; spinning mill; mill. **h. de algodón,** cotton mill
hilandero (-ra) n spinner
hilar vt to spin; reason, infer, discourse
hilaridad f, hilarity; quiet happiness
hilaza f, yarn
hilera f, line, file, row; fine yarn; mil file, rank; met wire drawer; mas course (of bricks)

hilo m, thread; linen; wire; mesh (spiders, silkworm's web, etc.); edge (of a blade); thin stream (of liquid); thread (of discourse)
hilván m, sew basting; tack
hilvanar vt sew to baste
himalayo a Himalayan
himen m, hymen
himeneo m, marriage, wedding
himnario m, hymnal
himno m, hymn
hin m, whinny, neigh
hincapié m, foothold. **hacer h.,** to insist, make a stand
hincar vt to thrust in; drive in, sink; vr kneel. **h. el diente,** to bite. **h. la uña,** to scratch. **hincarse de rodillas,** to kneel down
hinchado a puffed up, vain; pompous, high-flown, redundant (style)
hinchar vt to inflate; puff out (the chest); swell (of a river, etc.); exaggerate (events); vr swell; grow vain, be puffed up
hinchazón f, swelling; vanity, presumption; pomposity, euphuism (style)
hiniesta f, Spanish broom
hinojo m, bot fennel; knee. **de hinojos,** on bended knee
hipar vi to hiccup; pant (of dogs); be overanxious; be overtired; sob, cry
hipérbole f, hyperbole
hiperbólico a hyperbolical
hipercrítico m, hypercritic. a hypercritical
hipertrofiarse vr to hypertrophy
hípico a equine
hipnosis f, hypnosis
hipnótico a hypnotic. m, hypnotic drug
hipnotismo m, hypnotism
hipnotización f, hypnotization
hipnotizar vt to hypnotize
hipo m, hiccup; sob; longing, desire; dislike, disgust
hipocondría f, hypochondria
hipocondríaco (-ca) a hypochondriacal. n hypochondriac
hipocrático a Hippocratic
hipocresía f, hypocrisy
hipócrita a hypocritical. mf hypocrite
hipodérmico a hypodermic
hipódromo m, hippodrome, racetrack
hipopótamo m, hippopotamus
hipostático a hypostatic
hipoteca f, mortgage
hipotecable a mortgageable
hipotecar vt to mortgage
hipotecario a belonging to a mortgage
hipotenusa f, hypotenuse
hipótesis f, hypothesis
hipotético a hypothetical
hirsuto a hirsute, hairy
hirviente a boiling
hisca f, birdlime
hisopear vt ecc to sprinkle, asperse
hisopo m, bot hyssop; ecc hyssop, sprinkler
hispánico a Spanish
hispanismo m, Hispanism
hispanista mf Hispanist
hispanoamericano (-na) a and n Spanish-American, Hispano-American
histeria f, hysteria
histérico a hysterical; hysteric
histerismo m, med hysteria
histología f, histology
histólogo m, histologist
historia f, history; narrative, story; tale; inf gossip (gen. pl); art historical piece. **h. natural,** natural history. **h. sagrada,** biblical history. fig inf **dejarse de historias,** to stop beating around the bush
historiador (-ra) n historian
historiar vt to narrate, relate; record, chronicle
histórico a historical; historic

historieta *f,* short story; anecdote
historiografía *f,* historiography
historiógrafo *m,* historiographer
histriónico *a* histrionic
hitlerismo *m,* Hitlerism
hito *m,* milestone; boundary mark; *fig* mark, target. **de h. en h.,** from head to foot
hocico *m,* snout; *inf* face, mug; *inf* angry gesture; *naut* prow. **meter el h.,** to stick one's nose into other people's business
hogaño *adv inf* during this year; at the present time
hogar *m,* hearth, fireplace; home, house; family life; firebox (of a locomotive)
hoguera *f,* bonfire
hoja *f, bot* leaf; petal; sheet (metal, paper, etc.); page (of book); blade (sharp instruments); leaf (door, window); sword. **h. de servicios,** service or professional record. **h. de tocino,** side of bacon. **h. extraordinaria,** extra, special edition (of a newspaper). **h. volante,** handbill, supplement. **volver la h.,** to turn over (pages); change one's opinion; turn the conversation
hojalata *f,* tin plate
hojalatería *f,* tinware; tin shop
hojalatero *m,* tinsmith
hojaldre *m,* or *f,* puff pastry
hojarasca *f,* withered leaves; excessive foliage; rubbish, trash
hojear *vt* to turn the leaves of a book; skip, skim, read quickly; *vi* exfoliate
hojuela *f, dim* little leaf; *bot* leaflet; pancake
¡hola! *interj* Hallo! Goodness!
Holanda Holland
holandés (-esa) *a* and *n* Dutchman (-woman) *m,* Dutch (language)
holgado *a* leisured, free; loose, wide; comfortable; well-off, rich
holganza *f,* repose, leisure, ease; idleness; pleasure
holgar *vi irr* to rest; be idle; be glad; be unused or unnecessary (things). *vr* enjoy oneself, amuse oneself; be glad. See **contar**
holgazán (-ana) *a* idle. *n* idler
holgazanear *vi* to idle
holgazanería *f,* idleness, sloth
holgorio *m,* rejoicing, festivity, merriment
holgura *f,* enjoyment, merrymaking; width; comfort, ease; *mech* free play
hollar *vt irr* to trample under foot; humiliate. See **degollar**
hollejo *m,* peel, thin skin (of fruit); *agr* chaff
hollín *m,* soot
holocausto *m,* holocaust
hológrafo *m,* holograph
hombradía *f,* manliness; courage
hombre *m,* man; adult; omber (cards). *interj* **¡h.!** *inf* Old fellow! You don't say so! **¡h. al agua!** Man overboard! **h. de bien,** honest, honorable man. **h. de estado,** statesman. **h. de muchos oficios,** jack-of-all-trades. **h. de negocios,** businessman; man of affairs. **h. de pro,** worthy man; famous man. **ser muy h.,** to be a real man, be very manly
hombrera *f,* epaulette; shoulderpad
hombro *m,* shoulder. **echar al h.,** to shoulder; undertake, take the responsibility of. **encogerse de hombros,** to shrug one's shoulders; be indifferent or uninterested
hombruno *a inf* mannish (of a woman)
homenaje *m,* allegiance; homage; veneration, respect
homeópata *a* homeopathic. *mf* homeopath
homeopatía *f,* homeopathy
homérico *a* Homeric
homicida *a* murderous, homicidal. *mf* murderer (-ess)
homicidio *m,* homicide (act)
homilía *f,* homily
homogeneidad *f,* homogeneity
homogéneo *a* homogeneous
homólogo *a* homologous

homónimo *a* homonymous. *m,* homonym
homosexual *a* and *mf* homosexual
honda *f,* sling, catapult
hondear *vt naut* to sound, plumb; *naut* unload
hondo *a* deep; low; *fig* profound; deep, intense (emotion). *m,* depth
hondón *m,* depth, recess
hondonada *f,* hollow; glen; valley
hondura *f,* depth
hondureño (-ña) *a* and *n* Honduran
honestidad *f,* honorableness; virtue; respectability; modesty; courtesy
honesto *a* honorable, virtuous, modest; honest, just
hongo *m,* fungus; toadstool; bowler hat
honor *m,* honor; fame; reputation (women); modesty (women); praise; *pl* rank, position; honors
honorable *a* honorable
honorario *a* honorary. *m,* honorarium, fee
honorífico *a* honorary; honorable
honra *f,* self-respect, honor, personal dignity; reputation; chastity and modesty (women); *pl* obsequies
honradez *f,* honesty; honorableness, integrity; respectability
honrado *a* honest; honorable
honrar *vt* to respect; honor; *vr* to be honored
honroso *a* honor-giving, honorable
hora *f,* hour; opportune moment; *pl* book of hours. **horas hábiles,** working hours. **horas muertas,** wee hours; wasted time. **a última h.,** at the last minute. **dar la h.,** to strike the hour. **¿Qué h. es?** What time is it?
horaciano *a* Horatian
horadar *vt* to bore, pierce
horario *a* hourly. *m,* timetable; hour hand of a clock; watch
horca *f,* gibbet, gallows; *agr* pitchfork; fork; prop for trees
horcajadas (a) *adv* astride
horcajadura *f,* crotch
horchata *f,* drink made of chufas or crushed almonds
horda *f,* horde
horizontal *a* horizontal
horizonte *m,* horizon. **nuevos horizontes,** new opportunities
horma *f,* mold; cobbler's last; stone wall. *fig inf* **hallar la h. de su zapato,** to find what suits one; meet one's match
hormiga *f,* ant
hormigón *m,* concrete. **h. armado,** ferro-concrete
hormiguear *vi* to itch; crowd, swarm
hormiguero *m,* anthill; crowd, swarm
hormona *f,* hormone
hornero (-ra) *n* baker
horno *m,* oven; furnace; kiln; bakery. **h. alfarero,** firing oven (for pottery). **h. de cocina,** kitchen stove. **h. de cuba,** blast furnace. **h. de ladrillo,** brick kiln. **alto h.,** iron-smelting furnace
horóscopo *m,* horoscope
horquilla *f,* forked stick; hairpin; hatpin; *agr* fork; hook. **viraje en h.,** hairpin turn
horrendo *a* horrible, frightful
hórreo *m,* granary, barn
horribilidad *f,* horribleness
horribilísimo *a sup* most horrible, exceedingly horrible
horrible *a* horrible
horrífico *a* horrific
horripilante *a* hair-raising, horrifying
horrísono *a poet* horrid-sounding, terrifying
horror *m,* horror; horribleness; atrocity, enormity
horrorizar *vt* to horrify; *vr* be horrified, be terrified
horroroso *a* dreadful, horrible; horrid; *inf* hideous, most ugly
hortaliza *f,* green vegetable, garden produce
hortelano *m,* market gardener
hortensia *f,* hydrangea
horticultor (-ra) *n* horticulturalist

horticultura *f*, horticulture
horticultural *a* horticultural
hosanna *m*, hosanna
hosco *a* dark brown; unsociable, sullen; crabbed
hospedaje *m*, lodging; board, payment
hospedar *vt* to lodge, receive as a guest; *vr* and *vi* lodge, stay
hospedería *f*, hostelry, inn; lodging
hospedero (-ra) *n* innkeeper
hospicio *m*, hospice; almshouse, workhouse; lodging; orphanage
hospital *m*, hospital; hospice. **h. de sangre,** field hospital
hospitalario *a* hospitable
hospitalidad *f*, hospitality; hospitableness; hospital
hostelero (-ra) *n* innkeeper
hostería *f*, hostelry; inn
hostia *f*, *ecc* wafer, Host; sacrificial victim
hostigamiento *m*, harassment. **h. sexual,** sexual harassment
hostigar *vt* to chastise; harass; tease, annoy
hostil *a* hostile
hostilidad *f*, hostility
hostilizar *vt* to commit hostile acts against; antagonize
hotel *m*, hotel; villa
hotelero (-ra) *n* hotelkeeper
hoy *adv* today; at present. **h. día** *or* **h. en día,** today. **h. por h.,** day by day; at the present time. **de h. en adelante,** from today forward
hoya *f*, hole; grave; valley, glen; bed (of a river)
hoyo *m*, hole; pockmark; grave; hollow
hoyuelo *m*, *dim* little hole; dimple
hoz *f*, sickle; defile
hozar *vt* to root (pigs, etc.)
hucha *f*, large chest; strongbox; savings
hueco *a* empty; hollow; vain; hollow (sound); pompous (style); spongy, soft; inflated. *m*, hollow; interval of time or place; *inf* vacancy; gap in a wall, etc.
huelga *f*, strike; leisure; lying fallow; merrymaking. **h. de brazos caídos,** sit-down strike. **h. patronal,** lock-out strike
huelguista *mf* striker
huella *f*, footprint, track; footstep; tread (of stairs); *print* impression; vestige, trace. **h. digital,** fingerprint
huérfano (-na) *n* orphan. *a* unprotected, uncared for
huero *a* addled; empty, hollow
huerta *f*, kitchen garden; orchard; irrigation land
huerto *m*, orchard; kitchen garden
hueso *m*, bone; stone (of fruit); kernel, core; drudgery; cheap, useless thing of poor quality. *inf* **no dejar un h. sano,** to tear (a person) to pieces. **tener los huesos molidos,** to be tired out; be bruised
huésped (-da) *n* guest; host; innkeeper
hueste *f*, (gen. *pl*) army on the march, host; party, supporters
huesudo *a* bony
hueva *f*, fish roe
huevera *f*, egg seller; eggcup
huevo *m*, egg. **h. duro,** hard-boiled egg. **h. estrellado,** fried egg. **h. pasado por agua,** soft-boiled egg. **huevos revueltos,** scrambled eggs
hugonote (-ta) *a* and *n* Huguenot
huida *f*, flight, escape; bolting (of a horse); outlet
huir *vi irr* to flee; fly (of time); elope; run away, bolt; (with *de*) avoid. *Pres. Part.* **huyendo.** *Pres. Ind.* **huyo, huyes, huyen.** *Preterite* **huyó, huyeron.** *Pres. Subjunc.* **huya,** etc. *Imperf. Subjunc.* **huyese,** etc.

hule *m*, oilcloth; rubber
hulla *f*, coal mine, coal, soft coal
hullera *f*, colliery, coal mine
humanidad *f*, humanity; human nature; human weakness; compassion; affability; *inf* stoutness; *pl* study of humanities
humanismo *m*, humanism
humanista *mf* humanist. *a* humanistic
humanitario *a* humanitarian
humanizar *vt* to humanize
humano *a* human; understanding, sympathetic. *m*, human being
humareda *f*, cloud of smoke
humeante *a* smoking; smoky
humear *vi* to give forth smoke; give oneself airs
humedad *f*, humidity; dampness; moisture
humedecer *vt irr* to moisten, wet, damp; *vr* grow moist. See **conocer**
húmedo *a* humid; damp; wet
húmero *m*, humerus
humildad *f*, humility; lowliness; humbleness
humilde *a* meek; lowly; humble
humillación *f*, humiliation
humillante *a* humiliating; debasing; mortifying
humillar *vt* to humble; humiliate; *vr* humble oneself
humo *m*, smoke; vapor, fume; vanity, airs
humor *m*, *med* humor; temperament, disposition; mood. **de buen h.,** good-tempered. **de mal h.,** ill-tempered
humorada *f*, humorous saying, extravagance, witticism
humorismo *m*, humor, comic sense; humorousness
humorista *mf* humorist
humorístico *a* humorous
humoso *a* smoky, reeky
hundible *a* sinkable
hundido *a* sunken (of cheeks, etc.); hollow, deep-set (of eyes)
hundimiento *m*, sinking; collapse; subsidence (of earth)
hundir *vt* to sink; oppress; confound; destroy, ruin; *vr* collapse (building); sink; *fig inf* disappear
húngaro (-ra) *a* and *n* Hungarian. *m*, Hungarian (language)
Hungría Hungary
huno (-na) *n* Hun
huracán *m*, hurricane
hurañía *f*, shyness, unsociableness; diffidence; wildness (of animals, etc.)
huraño *a* shy, unsociable; diffident; wild (of animals, etc.)
hurgar *vt* to stir; poke, rake; touch; rouse, incite. *vr* pick one's nose
hurgón *m*, fire rake, poker; *inf* sword
hurgonada *f*, raking (of the fire, etc.)
hurí *f*, houri
hurón (-ona) *n* ferret. *a* shy, unsociable
¡hurra! *interj* Hurrah!
hurtadillas (a) *adv* by stealth, secretly
hurtar *vt* to steal; encroach (sea, river); plagiarize; *vr* hide oneself
hurto *m*, theft. **coger con el h. en las manos,** *fig* to catch red-handed
husmear *vt* to sniff out; *inf* pry; *vi* smell bad (of meat)
huso *m*, spindle; bobbin
¡huy! *interj* (denoting pain or surprise) Oh!

I

ibérico *a* Iberian
ibero (-ra) *a* and *n* Iberian
íbice *m*, ibex
icnografía *f*, ichnography

icnográfico *a* ichnographical
icono *m*, icon
iconoclasta *a* iconoclastic. *mf* iconoclast
iconografía *f*, iconography

ictericia *f,* jaundice
ictiología *f,* ichthyology
ictiólogo *m,* ichthyologist
ida *f,* setting out, departure, going; impetuous action; precipitancy; track, trail (of animals). **de i. y vuelta,** round trip (of tickets)
idea *f,* idea. *inf* **¡Qué ideas tienes!** What (odd) ideas you have!
ideación *f,* ideation
ideal *a* ideal; perfect. *m,* model; ideal
idealidad *f,* ideality
idealismo *m,* idealism
idealista *a* idealistic. *mf* idealist
idealización *f,* idealization
idealizar *vt* to idealize
idealmente *adv* ideally
idear *vt* to imagine; devise; plan; design; draft, draw up
ídem *adv* idem
idéntico *a* identical
identidad *f,* identity
identificable *a* identifiable
identificación *f,* identification
identificar *vt* to identify; recognize; *vr (with con)* identify oneself with
ideografía *f,* ideography
ideograma *m,* ideogram, ideograph
ideología *f,* ideology. **i. racista,** racial ideology
ideológico *a* ideological
ideólogo (-ga) *n* ideologist; dreamer, planner
idílico *a* idyllic
idilio *m,* idyll
idioma *m,* language, tongue
idiomático *a* idiomatic
idiosincrasia *f,* idiosyncrasy
idiosincrásico *a* idiosyncratic
idiota *a* idiot; idiotic. *mf* idiot
idiotez *f,* idiocy
idiotismo *m, gram* idiom; ignorance
idólatra *a* idolatrous; adoring. *mf* idolater, heathen
idolatrar *vt* to idolize; worship, love excessively
idolatría *f,* idolatry; adoration, idolization
ídolo *m,* idol
idoneidad *f,* fitness, suitability; competence; capacity
idóneo *a* suitable; competent, fit
idus *m pl,* ides
iglesia *f,* church. **i. colegial,** collegiate church. **cumplir con la i.,** to discharge one's religious duties. **llevar a una mujer a la i.,** to lead a woman to the altar
ígneo *a* igneous
ignición *f,* ignition
ignominia *f,* ignominy, disgrace
ignominioso *a* ignominious
ignorancia *f,* ignorance. **pretender i.,** to plead ignorance
ignorante *a* ignorant; unaware, uninformed. *mf* ignoramus
ignorar *vt* to be unaware of, not to know
ignoto *a* unknown, undiscovered
igual *a* equal; level; even, smooth; very similar; alike; uniform; proportionate; unchanging; constant; indifferent; same. *mf* equal. *m, math* equal sign. **al i.,** equally. **sin i.,** peerless, without equal. **Me es completamente i.,** It's all the same to me
iguala *f,* equalizing; leveling; agreement, arrangement; cash adjustment
igualación *f,* equalization; leveling; arrangement; agreement; matching; *math* equation
igualador *a* equalizing; leveling
igualar *vt* to equalize, make equal; match; pair; level, flatten; smooth; adjust; arrange, agree upon; weigh, consider; *math* equate; *vi* be equal
igualdad *f,* equality; uniformity, harmony; evenness; smoothness; identity, sameness. **i. de ánimo,** equability, equanimity
igualitario *a* equalizing; egalitarian
igualmente *adv* equally; the same, likewise

ijada *f,* side, flank; pain in the side
ijadear *vi* to pant
ijar *m,* See **ijada**
ilación *f,* connection, reference
ilegal *a* illegal
ilegalidad *f,* illegality
ilegible *a* illegible, unreadable
ilegitimidad *f,* illegitimacy
ilegítimo *a* illegitimate; false
íleon *m,* ilium
ileso *a* unharmed, unhurt
iletrado *a* unlettered, uncultured
Ilíada *f,* Iliad
iliberal *a* illiberal; narrow-minded
iliberalidad *f,* illiberality; narrow-mindedness
ilícito *a* illicit
ilicitud *f,* illicitness
ilimitado *a* unlimited, boundless
iliterato *a* illiterate, uncultured
ilógico *a* illogical
ilota *mf* helot
iluminación *f,* illumination; lighting. **i. intensiva,** floodlighting
iluminador (-ra) *a* lighting; illuminating. *n art* illuminator
iluminar *vt* to illuminate; light; *art* illuminate; enlighten
iluminativo *a* illuminating
ilusión *f,* illusion; illusoriness; hope; dream
ilusionarse *vr* to harbor illusions
ilusivo *a* deceptive, illusive
iluso *a* deceived, deluded; dreamy; visionary
ilusorio *a* illusory; deceptive; null
ilustración *f,* illustration, picture; enlightenment; explanation; illustrated newspaper or magazine; erudition, knowledge; example, illustration
ilustrado *a* erudite, learned; knowledgeable, well-informed
ilustrador (-ra) *a* illustrative. *n* illustrator
ilustrar *vt* to explain, illustrate; enlighten, instruct; illustrate (books); make illustrious; inspire with divine light
ilustrativo *a* illustrative
ilustre *a* illustrious, distinguished
ilustrísimo *a sup* most illustrious (title of bishops, etc.)
imagen *f,* image; effigy, statue; idea; metaphor, simile. **i. nítida,** sharp image
imaginable *a* imaginable
imaginación *f,* imagination
imaginar *vi* to imagine; *vt* suppose, conjecture; discover, invent; imagine. **¡Imagínese!** Just imagine!
imaginario *a* imaginary
imaginativa *f,* imagination; common sense
imaginativo *a* imaginative
imaginería *f,* imagery
imán *m,* magnet; attraction, charm; imam
imanación *f,* magnetization
imanar *vt* to magnetize
imbécil *a* imbecile; stupid, idiotic. *mf* imbecile
imbecilidad *f,* imbecility; folly, stupidity
imberbe *a* beardless. *inf* **joven i.,** stripling
imbibición *f,* imbibing, absorption
imborrable *a* ineffaceable
imbuir *vt irr* to imbue. See **huir**
imitable *a* imitable
imitación *f,* imitation; reproduction, copy
imitado *a* imitation; imitated
imitador (-ra) *a* imitation; imitative. *n* imitator
imitar *vt* to imitate; counterfeit
imitativo *a* imitative
impacción *f,* impact
impaciencia *f,* impatience
impacientar *vt* to make impatient, annoy; *vr* grow impatient
impaciente *a* impatient
impacto *m,* impact. **i. de lleno,** direct hit

impalpabilidad *f*, impalpability
impalpable *a* impalpable
impar *a* odd; unpaired; single, uneven. **número impar,** odd number
imparcial *a* impartial
imparcialidad *f*, impartiality
imparisilábico *a* imparisyllabic
impartible *a* indivisible
impasibilidad *f*, impassivity, indifference
impasible *a* impassive
impavidez *f*, dauntlessness; serenity in the face of danger
impávido *a* dauntless; calm, composed, imperturbable
impecabilidad *f*, impeccability, perfection
impecable *a* impeccable, perfect
impedido *a* disabled
impedimento *m*, obstacle; hindrance; *law* impediment
impedir *vt irr* to impede; obstruct; prevent; thwart; disable; delay; *poet* amaze. See **pedir**
impeler *vt* to push; incite; drive; urge
impender *vt* to spend money
impenetrabilidad *f*, impenetrability; imperviousness; obscurity, difficulty
impenetrable *a* impenetrable, dense; impervious; *fig* unfathomable; obscure
impenitencia *f*, impenitence
impenitente *a* impenitent
impensado *a* unexpected, unforeseen
imperante *a* ruling, dominant
imperar *vi* to rule; command
imperativo *a* commanding. *a* and *m, gram* imperative
imperatorio *a* imperial, imperatorial
imperceptible *a* imperceptible
imperdible *m*, safety pin
imperdonable *a* unpardonable, inexcusable
imperecedero *a* undying, eternal, everlasting
imperfección *f*, imperfection, inadequacy; fault, blemish; weakness
imperfecto *a* imperfect; inadequate; faulty. *a* and *m, gram* imperfect
imperial *a* imperial. *f*, upper deck of a bus or streetcar
imperialismo *m*, imperialism
imperialista *a* imperialistic. *mf* imperialist
impericia *f*, inexpertness; unskillfulness, unhandiness
imperio *m*, empire; rule, reign; command, sway; imperial dignity; arrogance, haughtiness. *fig inf* **valer un i.,** to be priceless
imperioso *a* imperious
imperito *a* inexpert; clumsy, unskilled
impermeabilidad *f*, watertightness; imperviousness; impermeability
impermeabilizar *vt* to waterproof
impermeable *a* watertight, impermeable; impervious. *m*, raincoat, mackintosh
impersonal *a* impersonal
impertérrito *a* unafraid, dauntless
impertinencia *f*, impertinence, insolence; peevishness; fancy, whim; overexactness, meticulousness; interference, intrusion
impertinente *a* impertinent; irrelevant; inopportune; officious, interfering
impertinentes *m pl*, lorgnettes
imperturbabilidad *f*, imperturbability
imperturbable *a* calm, imperturbable
impetrar *vt* to obtain by entreaty; implore
ímpetu *m*, impetus, momentum; speed, swiftness; violence
impetuosidad *f*, impetuosity
impetuoso *a* impetuous; precipitate
impiedad *f*, cruelty, harshness; irreligion
impío *a* impious, wicked; irreverent, irreligious
implacabilidad *f*, implacability, relentless
implacable *a* implacable
implantación *f*, inculcation, implantation
implantar *vt* to inculcate, implant (ideas, etc.)
implicación *f*, implication; contradiction (in terms); complicity

implicar *vt* to implicate; imply, infer; involve, entangle; *vi* imply contradiction (gen. with negatives)
implicatorio *a* contradictory; implicated (in crime)
implícito *a* implicit; implied
implorante *a* imploring
implorar *vt* to implore, entreat
implume *a* without feathers, unfeathered
impolítico *a* impolitic; unwise, inexpedient; tactless
impoluto *a* unpolluted, spotless, pure
imponderabilidad *f*, imponderability
imponderable *a* imponderable, immeasurable; most excellent
imponente *a* imposing; awe-inspiring
imponer *vt irr* to exact; impose; malign, accuse falsely; instruct, acquaint; *fig* impress (with respect, etc.); invest or deposit (money); *print* impose; give, bestow (a name). *vr* assert oneself. See **poner**
imponible *a* taxable; ratable
impopular *a* unpopular
impopularidad *f*, unpopularity
importable *a* importable
importación *f*, *com* importation; import
importador (-ra) *a* import, importing. *n* importer
importancia *f*, importance; magnitude
importante *a* important
importar *vi* to matter; be important; concern, interest; *vt* amount to; import; include, comprise. **¡No importa!** It doesn't matter! Never mind!
importe *m*, amount; value, cost. **i. bruto,** gross or total amount. **i. líquido** *or* **neto,** net amount
importunación *f*, importuning; importunity
importunadamente *adv* importunately
importunar *vt* to importune, pester
importunidad *(also **importunación**) f*, importunity
importuno *a* importunate, inopportune, ill-timed; persistent; tedious
imposibilidad *f*, impossibility
imposibilitado *a* disabled, crippled; incapable, unable
imposibilitar *vt* to disable; render unable; make impossible
imposible *a* impossible
imposición *f*, imposition; exaction; tax, duty, tribute; *print* makeup **i. de manos,** *ecc* laying on of hands
impostor (-ra) *n* impostor
impostura *f*, swindle, imposture; aspersion; slur, imputation
impotable *a* undrinkable
impotencia *f*, impotence
impotente *a* impotent; powerless
impracticabilidad *f*, impracticability; impassability (of roads, etc.)
impracticable *a* impracticable; impossible; impassable (roads, etc.)
imprecación *f*, imprecation; curse, malediction
imprecar *vt* to imprecate, curse
impregnación *f*, impregnation, permeation, saturation
impregnar *vt* impregnate; to permeate; *vr* become impregnated
impremeditado *a* unpremeditated
imprenta *f*, printing; printing house or office; print; letterpress
impreparación *f*, unpreparedness
imprescindible *a* indispensable, essential
impresión *f*, printing; impression; effect; influence; imprint, stamp; *print* impression; print. **impresión digital,** fingerprint
impresionable *a* impressionable, susceptible
impresionante *a* impressing; moving, affecting
impresionar *vt* to impress; affect; fix in the mind; *fig* move deeply, stir; *(rad* cinema) record
impresionismo *m*, impressionism
impresionista *mf* impressionist. *a* impressionistic
impreso *m*, (gen. *pl*) printed matter
impresor *m*, printer
imprevisión *f*, lack of foresight; improvidence
imprevisto *a* unforeseen, unexpected, sudden

imprevistos *m pl*, incidental expenses
imprimación *f*, priming (of paint, etc.)
imprimar *vt* to prime (of paint)
imprimir *vt* to print; stamp; impress upon (the mind)
improbabilidad *f*, improbability
improbable *a* improbable
improbo *a* vicious, corrupt, dishonest; hard, arduous
improductivo *a* unproductive; unprofitable, fruitless
impronta *f*, *art* cast, mold
impronunciable *a* unpronounceable; ineffable
improperio *m*, insult, affront
impropiedad *f*, inappropriateness; unsuitableness; impropriety
impropio *a* unsuitable; inappropriate; inadequate; improper
improporcionado *a* disproportionate, out of proportion
impróvido *a* improvident, heedless
improvisación *f*, improvisation
improvisador (-ra) *n* improviser
improvisamente *adv* unexpectedly, suddenly
improvisar *vt* to improvise
improviso, improvisto *a* unexpected, unforeseen. **al** (*or* **de**) **improviso,** unexpectedly
imprudencia *f*, imprudence, rashness, indiscretion
imprudente *a* imprudent, unwise, rash
impúbero *a* below the age of puberty
impudencia *f*, impudence, impertinence
impudente *a* brazen, impudent
impudicia *f*, immodesty, brazenness
impúdico *a* immodest, brazen
impuesto *m*, tax; duty. **i. de utilidades,** income tax. **i. sucesorio,** inheritance tax
impugnable *a* impugnable, refutable
impugnación *f*, refutation; contradiction
impugnar *vt* to refute, contradict; oppose; criticize
impulsar *vt* to impel; prompt; cause; drive, operate, propel
impulsión *f*, impulse; impetus; *mech* operation, driving; propulsion
impulsivo *a* impulsive; irreflexive, precipitate
impulso *m*, stimulus, incitement; impulse, desire; *mech* drive, impulse
impulsor (-ra) *a* driving, impelling. *n* driver, operator
impune *a* unpunished
impunemente *adv* with impunity
impunidad *f*, impunity
impureza *f*, impurity; lack of chastity; obscenity, indecency
impurificar *vt* to defile; make impure; adulterate
impuro *a* impure; adulterated; polluted; immoral, unchaste
imputable *a* imputable
imputación *f*, imputation
imputador (-ra) *n* imputer, attributer
imputar *vt* to impute; attribute
inacabable *a* endless, interminable, ceaseless; wearisome
inaccesibilidad *f*, inaccessibility
inaccesible *a* inaccessible; incomprehensible
inacción *f*, inaction
inaceptable *a* unacceptable
inactividad *f*, inactivity; quiescence; idleness
inactivo *a* inactive; idle; unemployed; *naut* laid-up
inadaptable *a* inadaptable
inadecuado *a* inadequate, insufficient
inadmisible *a* inadmissible
inadvertencia *f*, inadvertence; oversight, mistake, slip
inadvertido *a* unnoticed; inattentive; inadvertent, unintentional; negligent
inafectado *a* unaffected, natural
inagotable *a* inexhaustible, unfailing; abundant
inaguantable *a* unbearable, intolerable
inajenable *a* inalienable
inalámbrica *f*, radio station
inalienable *a* inalienable

inalterable *a* unalterable
inamovibilidad *f*, immovability
inamovible *a* immovable
inanición *f*, inanition
inanimado *a* inanimate
inapagable *a* inextinguishable
inapelable *a* unappealable; irremediable, inevitable
inapetencia *f*, lack of appetite
inaplazable *a* undeferable, unable to be postponed
inaplicable *a* inapplicable
inaplicación *f*, laziness, inattention, negligence
inaplicado *a* lazy; inattentive; careless
inapreciable *a* inappreciable; invaluable
inarmónico *a* unharmonious, discordant
inarticulado *a* inarticulate
inasequible *a* unattainable; out of reach
inaudible *a* inaudible
inaudito *a* unheard of, unprecedented; extraordinary, strange
inauguración *f*, inauguration; induction; inception, commencement
inaugural *a* inaugural
inaugurar *vt* to inaugurate; induct
inaveriguable *a* unascertainable
inca *mf* Inca
incaico *a* Incan
incalculable *a* incalculable; innumerable
incalificable *a* indescribable, unclassable; vile
incandescencia *f*, incandescence, white heat
incandescente *a* incandescent
incansable *a* indefatigable; unflagging; unwearying
incapacidad *f*, incapacity; incompetence
incapacitar *vt* to incapacitate; disable
incapaz *a* incapable, incompetent; inefficient
incasable *a* unmarriageable; antimarriage
incautarse *vt* to seize, take possession (of)
incauto *a* incautious; unwary
incendiar *vt* to set on fire, set alight
incendiario (-ia) *a* and *n* incendiary
incendiarismo *m*, incendiarism
incendio *m*, conflagration, fire; consuming passion
incensar *vt irr ecc* to cense, incense; flatter. See **acertar**
incensario *m*, incense burner, incensory
incentivo *m*, incentive; encouragement
incertidumbre *f*, uncertainty, incertitude
incesable, incesante *a* incessant, continuous
incesto *m*, incest
incestuoso *a* incestuous
incidencia *f*, incidence
incidental *a* incidental
incidente *a* incidental. *m*, incident, event, occurrence
incidir *vi* (*with en*) to incur, fall into (e.g. **Incidió en el pecado,** He fell into sin)
incienso *m*, incense; flattery
incierto *a* untrue, false; uncertain; unknown
incineración *f*, incineration
incinerador *m*, incinerator
incinerar *vt* incinerate, reduce to ashes
incipiente *a* incipient
incircunciso *a* uncircumcised
incisión *f*, incision
incisivo *a* sharp, keen; incisive, sarcastic, caustic
inciso *m*, clause; comma
incitación *f*, incitement; *fig* spur, stimulus
incitar *vt* to incite; stimulate, encourage
incivil *a* rude, discourteous, uncivil
incivilidad *f*, rudeness, incivility
inclasificable *a* unclassifiable
inclemencia *f*, harshness, severity; inclemency (of the weather). **a la i.,** at the mercy of the elements
inclemente *a* inclement
inclinación *f*, inclination; slope; slant; tendency, propensity; predilection, fondness; bow (in greeting); *geom* inclination
inclinar *vt* to incline, tilt, slant; bow; bend; influence; persuade; *vi* resemble; *vr* lean; stoop; tilt; tend, incline

(to), view favorably (e.g. **Me inclino a creerlo,** I am inclined to believe it)

ínclito *a* famous, celebrated

incluir *vt irr* to comprise, embrace, contain; include, take into account. See **huir**

inclusa *f,* foundling home

inclusión *f,* inclusion; relationship, intercourse, friendship

inclusive *adv* including

inclusivo *a* inclusive

incluso *adv* including, inclusive. *prep* even

incoar *vt* to begin (especially lawsuits)

incoativo *a* inceptive

incobrable *a* irrecoverable; irredeemable

incógnita *f, math* X; unknown quantity; secret motive; unknown lady

incógnito *a* unknown. *m,* incognito, assumed name, disguise

incoherencia *f,* incoherence

incoherente *a* incoherent, disconnected, illogical

íncola *mf* resident, dweller, inhabitant

incoloro *a* colorless, uncolored

incólume *a* unharmed, unscathed; untouched, undamaged

incombustibilidad *f,* incombustibility

incomodar *vt* to disturb, incommode, inconvenience; annoy; *vr* disturb oneself, put oneself out; grow angry. **¡No se incomode!** Please don't move!; Please don't be angry!

incomodidad *f,* discomfort; inconvenience; trouble, upset; annoyance

incómodo *a* uncomfortable; inconvenient; troublesome, tiresome. *m,* discomfort; inconvenience

incomparable *a* incomparable

incompartible *a* indivisible

incompasivo *a* unsympathetic, hard

incompatibilidad *f,* incompatibility

incompatible *a* incompatible

incompetencia *f,* incompetence

incompetente *a* incompetent

incomplejo, incomplexo *a* noncomplex, simple

incompleto *a* incomplete

incomponible *a* unrepairable, unmendable

incomprensibilidad *f,* incomprehensibility

incomprensible *a* incomprehensible

incomprensión *f,* incomprehension

incomunicado *a* in solitary confinement (of a prisoner)

incomunicar *vt* to sentence to solitary confinement; isolate, deprive of means of communication; *vr* become a recluse

inconcebible *a* inconceivable

inconciliable *a* irreconcilable

incondicional *a* unconditional

inconexión *f,* disconnectedness

inconexo *a* unconnected; incoherent

inconfeso *a* unconfessed

incongruencia *f,* incongruity

incongruente *a* incongruous, inappropriate

inconmensurabilidad *f,* incommensurability

inconmovible *a* immovable; unflinching, unshakable

inconmutable *a* unalterable, immutable, unchangeable

inconquistable *a* unconquerable; *fig* resolute, inflexible

inconsciencia *f,* unconsciousness; subconscious

inconsciente *a* unconscious, involuntary; subconscious

inconsecuencia *f,* inconsequence; inconsistency

inconsecuente *a* inconsequential; inconsistent

inconsideración *f,* thoughtlessness

inconsiderado *a* thoughtless; heedless, selfish

inconsiguiente *a* illogical, inconsistent

inconsistencia *f,* inconsistency

inconsistente *a* inconsistent

inconsolable *a* inconsolable

inconstancia *f,* inconstancy, infidelity

inconstante *a* inconstant, fickle

inconstitucional *a* unconstitutional

incontaminado *a* uncontaminated

incontestable *a* undeniable, unquestionable

incontinencia *f,* incontinence

incontinente *a* incontinent

incontrastable *a* insuperable, invincible; undeniable, unanswerable; *fig* unshakable, inconvincible

incontrovertible *a* undeniable, incontrovertible

inconvencible *a* inconvincible

inconveniencia *f,* discomfort; inconvenience; unsuitability

inconveniente *a* awkward, inconvenient; uncomfortable; inappropriate. *m,* inconvenience; obstacle, impediment; disadvantage

inconvertible *a* inconvertible

incorporación *f,* incorporation

incorporar *vt* to incorporate; cause to sit up, lift up; *vr* sit up, raise oneself; become a member, join (associations); be incorporated; blend, mix

incorporeidad *f,* incorporeity

incorpóreo *a* incorporeal; immaterial

incorrección *f,* incorrectness; indecorum, impropriety

incorrecto *a* incorrect; indecorous, unbecoming, improper

incorregible *a* incorrigible

incorrupción *f,* incorruption; purity; integrity; wholesomeness

incorrupto *a* incorrupt; pure; chaste

incredibilidad *f,* incredibility

incredulidad *f,* incredulity, scepticism

incrédulo (-la) *a* incredulous; atheistic. *n* atheist; unbeliever, sceptic

increíble *a* incredible; marvelous, extraordinary

incremento *m,* increment, increase

increpación *f,* scolding, harsh rebuke

increpar *vt* to scold, rebuke harshly

incriminante *a* incriminating

incriminar *vt* to incriminate, accuse; exaggerate (a charge, etc.)

incruento *a* bloodless, unstained with blood

incrustación *f,* incrustation; *art* inlay

incubación *f,* hatching; *med* incubation

incubadora *f,* incubator (for chickens)

incubar *vi* to sit on eggs (of hens); *vt* hatch; *med* incubate

inculcación *f,* inculcation, instillment

inculcar *vt* to press one thing against another; instill, inculcate; *vr* grow more fixed in one's views

inculpable *a* blameless, innocent

inculpar *vt* to blame; accuse

incultivable *a* uncultivatable; untillable

inculto *a* uncultivated, untilled; uncultured; uncivilized

incultura *f,* lack of cultivation; lack of culture

incumbencia *f,* obligation, moral responsibility, duty

incumbir *vi* to be incumbent on; concern

incumplimiento *m,* nonfulfilment

incurable *a* incurable; inveterate, hopeless

incuria *f,* negligence, carelessness

incurioso *a* incurious

incurrir *vi* (*with en*) to fall into (error, etc.); incur (dislike, etc.)

incursión *f,* incursion; inroad

indagación *f,* investigation, inquiry

indagador (-ra) *a* investigating, inquiring. *n* investigator

indagar *vt* to investigate, examine; inquire. **i. precios,** to inquire about prices

indebido *a* undue, immoderate improper; illegal, illicit

indecencia *f,* indecency; obscenity; impropriety

indecente *a* indecent; obscene; improper

indecible *a* unutterable, ineffable, unspeakable

indeciso *a* undecided; hesitant, irresolute; vague; noncommittal

indeclinable *a* obligatory; unavoidable; *gram* indeclinable, uninflected

indecoro *m*, impropriety, indecorum

indecoroso *a* indecorous, unbecoming; base, mean

indefectible *a* unfailing; perfect

indefectiblemente *adv* invariably

indefendible *a* indefensible

indefenso *a* unprotected, defenseless

indefinible *a* indefinable, vague; indescribable

indefinido *a* indefinite, vague; undefined; *gram* indefinite

indeleble *a* indelible

indeliberado *a* unpremeditated; unconsidered

indemne *a* unharmed, undamaged

indemnidad *f*, indemnity

indemnización *f*, compensation, indemnification; indemnity

indemnizar *vt* to indemnify, compensate

indemostrable *a* indemonstrable, incapable of demonstration

independencia *f*, independence

independiente *a* independent; self-contained

indescifrable *a* undecipherable; illegible

indestructible *a* indestructible

indeterminado *a* indeterminate; vague, doubtful, uncertain; hesitant, irresolute; *math* indeterminate

indiano (-na) *a* and *n* Indian; East Indian; West Indian. *m*, nouveau riche, one who returns rich from the Western Hemisphere

indicación *f*, indication; sign, evidence; intimation, hint

indicador *a* indicative. *m*, indicator. **i. del nivel de gasolina**, gas gauge

indicar *vt* to indicate; show; point out; simply, suggest; intimate

indicativo *a* indicative. *a* and *m*, *gram* indicative

índice *m*, index; indication, sign; library catalogue; catalogue room; hand (of a clock); pointer, needle (of instruments); gnomon (of a sundial); *math* index; forefinger. **I. expurgatorio**, the Index

indicio *m*, indication; sign; evidence. **indicios vehementes**, circumstantial evidence

índico *a* Indian

indiferencia *f*, indifference

indiferente *a* indifferent

indígena *a* native, indigenous. *mf* native

indigencia *f*, destitution, indigence; impecuniosity

indigente *a* destitute, indigent; impecunious

indigestión *f*, indigestion

indigesto *a* indigestible; *lit* muddled, confused; unsociable, brusque

indignación *f*, indignation, anger

indignado *a* indignant

indignar *vt* to anger, make indignant; *vr* grow angry

indignidad *f*, unworthiness; indignity; personal affront

indigno *a* unworthy; base, despicable

índigo *m*, indigo

indio (-ia) *a* Indian; blue. *n* Indian. *m*, indium

indirecta *f*, hint, covert suggestion, innuendo. *inf* **i. del padre Cobos**, strong hint

indirecto *a* indirect

indisciplina *f*, indiscipline

indisciplinado *a* undisciplined

indiscreción *f*, indiscretion

indiscreto *a* indiscreet

indiscutible *a* unquestionable, undeniable

indisoluble *a* indissoluble

indispensable *a* indispensable

indisponer *vt irr* to make unfit or incapable; indispose, make ill; (*with con or contra*) set against, make trouble with; *vr* be indisposed; (*with con or contra*) quarrel with. See **poner**

indisposición *f*, reluctance, disinclination; indisposition, brief illness

indisputable *a* indisputable

indistinguible *a* undistinguishable

indistinto *a* indistinct; indeterminate; vague

individual *a* individual; peculiar, characteristic. *m*, (tennis) single

individualidad *f*, individuality

individualismo *m*, individualism

individualista *a* individualistic. *mf* individualist

individuo (-ua) *a* individual; indivisible. *m*, individual; member, associate; *inf* self. *n inf* person

indivisibilidad *f*, indivisibility

indivisible *a* indivisible

indiviso *a* undivided

indócil *a* unmanageable; disobedient; brittle, unpliable (of metals)

indocilidad *f*, indocility; disobedience; brittleness (of metals)

indochino (-na) *a* and *n* Indochinese

indoeuropeo *a* Indo-European

indoísmo *m*, Hinduism

índole *f*, temperament, nature; kind, sort

indolencia *f*, idleness, indolence

indolente *a* nonpainful; indifferent, insensible; idle, indolent

indoloro *a* painless

indomable *a* untamable; invincible; indomitable; ungovernable, unmanageable

indomado *a* untamed

indómito *a* untamed; untamable; unmanageable, unruly; indomitable

indonesio (-ia) *a* and *n* Indonesian

indostanés *a* Hindustani

indostani *m*, Hindustani (language)

indubitable *a* unquestionable

inducción *f*, persuasion; *phys* induction

inducir *vt irr* to persuade, prevail upon; induce; infer, conclude. See **conducir**

inductivo, inductor *a* inductive

indudable *a* indubitable

indulgencia *f*, overkindness, tenderness; *ecc* indulgence

indulgente *a* indulgent, tender; tolerant

indultar *vt* to pardon; exempt

indulto *m*, amnesty; exemption; forgiveness; *ecc* indult

indumentaria *f*, clothing; outfit (of clothes)

industria *f*, assiduity, industriousness; pains, effort, ingenuity; industry. **i. pesada**, heavy industry. **i. cárnica**, meat industry. **i. extractivos**, mining industry

industrial *a* industrial. *m*, industrialist

industrialismo *m*, industrialism

industrialización *f*, industrialization

industriar *vt* to teach, train; *vr* find a way, manage, succeed in

industrioso *a* industrious; diligent, assiduous

inédito *a* unpublished; unedited

inefable *a* ineffable

ineficacia *f*, inefficiency; ineffectiveness

ineficaz *a* ineffective; inefficient

ineludible *a* unavoidable

ineptitud *f*, ineptitude

inepto *a* inept, incompetent; unfit, unsuitable

inequívoco *a* unequivocal

inercia *f*, inertia

inerme *a* defenseless, unprotected; (*bot zool*) unarmed

inerte *a* inert

inescrutable *a* inscrutable, unfathomable

inesperado *a* unexpected, sudden

inestabilidad *f*, instability

inestable *a* unstable

inestimable *a* inestimable

inevitable *a* inevitable

inexactitud *f*, inexactitude, inaccuracy; error, mistake

inexacto *a* inexact, inaccurate; erroneous

inexcusable *a* inexcusable, unforgivable; indispensable

inexhausto *a* inexhaustible

inexistente *a* nonexistent

inexorable *a* inexorable

inexperiencia *f*, inexperience

inexperto *a* inexperienced; inexpert

inexplicable *a* inexplicable
inexplorado *a* unexplored
inexplosible *a* inexplosive
inexpresivo *a* inexpressive; reticent
inexpugnable *a* impregnable; *fig* unshakable, firm; obstinate
inextinguible *a* inextinguishable; everlasting, perpetual
infalibilidad *f*, infallibility
infalible *a* infallible
infamación *f*, defamation
infamador (-ra) *a* slandering. *n* slanderer
infamar *vt* to defame, slander
infame *a* infamous, vile
infamia *f*, infamy; baseness, vileness
infancia *f*, infancy, babyhood; childhood
infanta *f*, female child under seven years; infanta, any Spanish royal princess; wife of a Spanish royal prince
infantado *m*, land belonging to an *infante* or *infanta*
infante *m*, male child under seven years; infante, any Spanish royal prince except an heir-apparent; infantryman. **i. de coro,** choir boy
infantería *f*, infantry
infanticida *a* infanticidal. *mf* infanticide (person)
infanticidio *m*, infanticide (act)
infantil *a* infantile, babyish; innocent, candid
infatigable *a* unwearying, indefatigable
infatuación *f*, infatuation
infatuar *vt* to infatuate; *vr* become infatuated
infausto *a* unlucky, unfortunate
infección *f*, infection
infeccioso *a* infectious
infectar *vt* to infect; corrupt, pervert; *vr* become infected; be corrupted
infecto *a* infected; corrupt, perverted; tainted
infecundidad *f*, sterility
infecundo *a* sterile, barren
infelice *a* *poet* unhappy, unfortunate
infelicidad *f*, unhappiness
infeliz *a* unhappy; unfortunate; *inf* simple, good-hearted
inferencia *f*, inference, connection
inferior *a* inferior; lower; second-rate; subordinate. *mf* inferior, subordinate
inferioridad *f*, inferiority
inferir *vt irr* to infer, deduce; involve, imply; occasion; inflict. See **sentir**
infernáculo *m*, hopscotch
infernal *a* infernal; devilish, fiendish; wicked, inhuman; *inf* confounded
infierno *a* *poet* infernal
infértil *a* infertile
infestación *f*, infestation
infestar *vt* to infest, swarm in; infect; injure, damage
infesto *a* *poet* harmful, dangerous
inficionar *vt* to infect; pervert, corrupt
infidelidad *f*, faithlessness, infidelity; disbelief in Christian religion; unbelievers, infidels
infidelísimo, *a* *sup* **infiel** most disloyal; most incorrect; most incredulous, faithless
infidencia *f*, disloyalty, faithlessness
infiel *a* unfaithful, disloyal; inaccurate, incorrect; infidel, unbelieving. *mf* infidel, nonbeliever
infierno *m*, hell; hades (gen. *pl*); *fig inf* inferno. **en el quinto i.,** very far off, at the end of the world. **en los quintos infiernos,** at the end of nowhere
infiltración *f*, infiltration; inculcation, implantation
infiltrar *vt* to infiltrate; imbue, inculcate
ínfimo *a* lowest; meanest, vilest, most base; cheapest, poorest (in quality)
infinidad *f*, infinity; infinitude; great number
infinitivo *a* and *m*, *gram* infinitive
infinito *a* infinite; endless; boundless; countless. *m*, *math* infinite. *adv* excessively, immensely
infinitud *f*, See **infinidad**
inflación *f*, inflation; distension; pride, vanity

inflacionismo *m*, inflationism
inflacionista *mf* inflationist
inflamabilidad *f*, inflammability
inflamable *a* inflammable
inflamación *f*, inflammation; *eng* ignition
inflamador *a* inflammatory
inflamar *vt* to set on fire; *fig* inflame, excite; *vr* take fire; *med* become inflamed; grow hot or excited
inflamatorio *a med* inflammatory
inflar *vt* to inflate; blow up, distend; throw out (one's chest); exaggerate; make haughty or vain; *vr* be swollen or inflated; be puffed up with pride
inflexibilidad *f*, inflexibility; rigidity; immovability, constancy
inflexible *a* inflexible
inflexión *f*, bending, flexion; diffraction (optics); inflection
infligir *vt* to impose, inflict (penalties)
influencia *f*, influence; power, authority; *elec* charge
influir *vt irr* to influence; affect; (*with en*) cooperate in, assist with. See **huir**
influjo *m*, influence; flux, inflow of the tide
influyente *a* influential
infolio *m*, folio
información *f*, information; legal inquiry; report; research, investigation
informador (-ra) *a* informing, acquainting. *n* informant
informal *a* informal, irregular; unreliable (of persons); unconventional
informalidad *f*, irregularity; unconventionality; unreliability
informante *mf* informant
informar *vt* to inform, acquaint with; *vi law* plead; *vr* (*with de, en, or sobre*) find out about, investigate
informática *f*, information sciences
informativo *a* informative
informe *a* formless, shapeless. *m*, report, statement; information; *law* plea; *pl* data, particulars; references
infortificable *a* unfortifiable
infortuna *f*, *astrol* evil influence
infortunado *a* unfortunate
infortunio *m*, misfortune; unhappiness, adversity; mischance, ill luck
infracción *f*, transgression, infringement
infracto *a* imperturbable
infractor(-ra) *a* infringing. *n* transgressor, infringer
infrangible *a* unbreakable
infranqueable *a* insuperable, unsurmountable
infrarrojo *a* infrared
infrascrito *a* undersigned; undermentioned
infrecuente *a* infrequent
infringir *vt* to infringe, transgress, break
infructífero *a* unfruitful; worthless, useless
infructuosidad *f*, unfruitfulness; worthlessness, uselessness
infructuoso *a* fruitless; useless, worthless
infumable *a* unsmokable (of tobacco)
infundado *a* unfounded, groundless
infundio *m*, *inf* nonsense, untruth
infundir *vt* to infuse, imbue with
infusión *f*, infusion
ingeniar *vt* to devise, concoct, plan; *vr* contrive, find a way, manage
ingeniería *f*, engineering
ingeniero *m*, engineer. **i. agrónomo,** agricultural engineer. **i. de caminos, canales y puertos,** civil engineer. **i. radiotelegrafista,** radio engineer. **cuerpo de ingenieros,** royal engineers
ingenio *m*, mind; inventive capacity; imaginative talent; man of genius; talent, cleverness; ingeniousness; machine; guillotine (bookbinding)
ingeniosidad *f*, ingeniousness; witticism, clever remark
ingenioso *a* talented, clever; ingenious
ingénito *a* unengendered, unconceived; innate, inborn

ingente *a* huge, enormous

ingenuidad *f*, ingenuousness, naiveté

ingenuo *a* ingenuous, naive, artless, unaffected

Inglaterra England

ingle *f*, groin

inglés (-esa) *a* English; British. *n* Englishman; Briton. *m*, English (language); *inf* creditor. **a la inglesa**, in English fashion. **marcharse a la inglesa**, *inf* to take French leave

inglesismo *m*, Anglicism

ingobernable *a* ungovernable, unruly

ingratitud *f*, ingratitude

ingrato *a* ungrateful; irksome, thankless; disagreeable

ingrávido *a* light weight

ingrediente *m*, ingredient

ingresar *vi* to return, come in (money); (*with en*) join, become a member of, enter

ingreso *m*, joining, entering, admission; *com* money received; opening, commencement; *pl* earnings, takings, revenue

ingurgitación *f*, *med* ingurgitation

ingurgitar *vt* to ingurgitate, swallow

inhábil *a* unskillful; unpracticed; incompetent, unfit; unsuitable, ill-chosen

inhabilidad *f*, unskillfulness; incompetence; unsuitability; inability

inhabilitación *f*, incapacitation; disqualification; disablement

inhabilitar *vt* to make ineligible; disqualify; incapacitate, make unfit; *vr* become ineligible; be incapacitated

inhabitable *a* uninhabitable

inhabitado *a* uninhabited, deserted

inhalación *f*, inhalation

inhalador *m*, *med* inhaler

inhalar *vt* to inhale

inhallable *a* nowhere to be found, unfindable

inhereditable *a* uninheritable

inherencia *f*, inherency

inherente *a* inherent, innate

inhestar *vt irr* to raise, lift up; erect. See **acertar**

inhibición *f*, inhibition

inhibir *vt law* to inhibit; *vr* inhibit or restrain oneself. See **prohibir**

inhibitorio *a law* inhibitory

inhonesto *a* indecent, obscene; immodest

inhospedable, inhospitalario *a* inhospitable; bleak, uninviting; exposed

inhospitalidad *f*, inhospitality

inhumación *f*, inhumation, burial

inhumadora *f*, crematory

inhumanidad *f*, inhumanity; brutality

inhumano *a* inhuman; brutal, barbarous

inhumar *vt* to bury, inter

iniciación *f*, initiation

iniciador (-ra) *a* initiating; *n* initiator

inicial *a* and *f*, initial

iniciar *vt* to initiate; admit, introduce; originate; *vr* be initiated; *ecc* take minor or first orders

iniciativa *f*, initiative

inicuo *a* iniquitous, most unjust, wicked

inimaginable *a* inconceivable

inimicísimo *a sup* **enemigo** most hostile

inimitable *a* inimitable

ininteligible *a* unintelligible

iniquidad *f*, iniquity, wickedness

injerir *vt irr* to insert, place within, introduce; interpolate; *vr* meddle. See **sentir**

injertar *vt agr* to graft

injerto *m*, *agr* graft; grafting; grafted plant, briar, or tree

injuria *f*, insult; slander; outrage; wrong, *f*, injustice; harm, damage

injuriador (-ra) *a* insulting. *n* offender, persecutor

injuriar *vt* to insult; slander; outrage; wrong, persecute; harm, damage

injurioso *a* insulting; slanderous; offensive, abusive; harmful

injusticia *f*, injustice; lack of justice; unjust action

injustificable *a* unjustifiable

injustificado *a* unjustified

injusto *a* unjust; unrighteous

inllevable *a* unbearable, intolerable

inmaculado *a* immaculate, pure

inmanejable *a* unmanageable; uncontrollable

inmanencia *f*, immanence

inmanente *a* immanent

inmarcesible, inmarchitable *a* unfading, imperishable

inmaterial *a* incorporeal; immaterial

inmaterialidad *f*, incorporeity; immateriality

inmaturo *a* immature; unripe

inmediación *f*, nearness, proximity; contact; *pl* outskirts, neighborhood, environs

inmediatamente *adv* near; immediately, at once

inmediato *a* adjoining, close, nearby; immediate, prompt

inmejorable *a* unsurpassable, unbeatable

inmemorable, inmemorial *a* immemorial

inmensidad *f*, vastness, huge extent; infinity; infinite space; immensity; huge number

inmenso *a* vast; infinite; immense; innumerable

inmensurable *a* immeasurable, incalculable

inmerecido *a* undeserved, unmerited

inmérito *a* wrongful, unjust

inmeritorio *a* unmeritorious, unpraiseworthy

inmersión *f*, immersion; dip

inmigración *f*, immigration

inmigrante *a* and *mf* immigrant

inmigrar *vi* to immigrate

inminencia *f*, imminence

inminente *a* imminent

inmiscuir *vt* to mix; *vr* meddle. May be conjugated regularly or like **huir**

inmisión *f*, inspiration

inmobiliario *a* concerning real estate

inmoble *a* immovable; motionless, immobile, stationary; *fig* unshakable, unflinching

inmoderación *f*, immoderateness, excess

inmoderado *a* immoderate; unrestrained, excessive

inmodestia *f*, immodesty

inmodesto *a* immodest

inmolación *f*, immolation

inmolador (-ra) *a* sacrificing. *n* immolator

inmolar *vt* to immolate; *fig* sacrifice, give up; *vr fig* sacrifice oneself

inmoral *a* immoral

inmoralidad *f*, immorality

inmortal *a* immortal

inmortalidad *f*, immortality

inmortalizar *vt* to immortalize

inmotivado *a* unfounded, without reason

inmoto *a* motionless, stationary

inmóvil *a* immovable, fixed; motionless; steadfast, constant

inmovilidad *f*, immovability; immobility; constancy, steadfastness

inmovilizar *vt* to immobilize

inmueble *m*, *law* immovable estate

inmundicia *f*, filth, nastiness; dirt; rubbish, refuse; obscenity, indecency

inmundo *a* dirty, filthy; obscene, indecent; unclean

inmune *a* exempt; *med* immune

inmunidad *f*, exemption; immunity

inmunizar *vt* to immunize

inmutabilidad *f*, immutability, changelessness; imperturbability

inmutable *a* immutable, unchangeable; imperturbable

inmutación *f*, change, alteration, difference

inmutar *vt* to change, alter, vary; *vr* change one's expression (through fear, etc.)

innato *a* innate; inherent; instinctive, inborn

innatural *a* unnatural

innavegable *a* unnavigable; unseaworthy (of ships)

innecesario *a* unnecessary
innegable *a* undeniable; indisputable, irrefutable
innoble *a* plebeian; ignoble
innocuo *a* harmless, innocuous
innovación *f*, innovation
innovador (-ra) *a* innovatory. *n* innovator
innovar *vt* to introduce innovations
innumerabilidad *f*, countless number, multitude
innumerable *a* innumerable, countless
innúmero *a* countless, innumerable
inobediencia *f*, disobedience
inobediente *a* disobedient
inobservable *a* unobservable
inobservancia *f*, inobservance
inobservante *a* unobservant
inocencia *f*, innocence; simplicity, candor; harmlessness
inocentada *f*, *inf* naïve remark or action; fool's trap; practical joke
inocente *a* innocent; candid, simple; harmless; easily deceived
inocentón *a* *inf* extremely credulous and easily taken in
inocuidad *f*, innocuousness
inoculación *f*, inoculation
inoculador *m*, inoculator
inocular *vt* to inoculate; pervert, corrupt; contaminate
inodoro *a* odorless. *m*, toilet, lavatory
inofensivo *a* inoffensive, harmless
inolvidable *a* unforgettable
inoperable *a* inoperable
inopia *f*, poverty; scarcity
inopinable *a* indisputable, unquestionable
inopinado *a* unexpected, sudden
inoportunidad *f*, inopportuneness, unseasonableness; unsuitability
inoportuno *a* inopportune, untimely
inordenado *a* inordinate, immoderate, excessive
inorgánico *a* inorganic
inoxidable *a* rustless
inquebrantable *a* unbreakable; final, irrevocable
inquietador (-ra) *a* disturbing. *n* disturber
inquietar *vt* to disturb; trouble, make anxious; worry; *vr* be disquieted, worry
inquieto *a* restless; unquiet; fidgety; disturbed, anxious, worried, uneasy
inquietud *f*, restlessness; uneasiness; worry; trouble, care, anxiety
inquilinato *m*, tenancy; rent; *law* lease; (rental) rates
inquilino (-na) *n* tenant; lessee
inquina *f*, dislike, grudge
inquinar *vt* to contaminate, corrupt, infect
inquiridor (-ra) *a* inquiring, examining. *n* investigator
inquirir *vt* *irr* to inquire; examine, look into. See **adquirir**
inquisición *f*, inquiry, investigation; *ecc* Inquisition
inquisidor (-ra) *a* inquiring, investigating. *n* investigator. *m*, *ecc* inquisitor; judge
inquisitorial *a* inquisitorial
insaciabilidad *f*, insatiability
insaciable *a* insatiable
insalivación *f*, insalivation
insalubre *a* unhealthy
insanable *a* incurable
insania *f*, insanity
insano *a* insane, mad
inscribir *vt* to inscribe; record; enter (a name on a list, etc.), register, enroll; engrave; *geom* inscribe. *Past Part.* **inscrito**
inscripción *f*, inscription; record, enrollment; registration; government bond
insecable *a* undryable, undrying
insecticida *a* insecticide
insectívoro *a* insectivorous
insecto *m*, insect
inseguridad *f*, insecurity
inseguro *a* insecure; unsafe; uncertain

insensatez *f*, folly, foolishness
insensato *a* foolish, stupid, mad
insensibilidad *f*, insensibility; imperception; callousness, hard-heartedness
insensibilizar *vt* to make insensible (to sensations)
insensible *a* insensible; imperceptive, insensitive; unconscious, senseless; imperceptible, inappreciable; callous
inseparabilidad *f*, inseparability
inseparable *a* inseparable
insepulto *a* unburied (of the dead)
inserción *f*, insertion; interpolation; grafting
insertar *vt* to insert; introduce; interpolate; *vr* (*bot zool*) become attached
inservible *a* useless; unfit; unsuitable
insidia *f*, insidiousness; snare, ambush
insidiador (-ra) *a* ensnaring. *n* schemer, ambusher
insidiar *vt* to waylay, ambush; set a trap for; scheme against
insidioso *a* insidious; treacherous; scheming, guileful
insigne *a* illustrious, famous; distinguished
insignia *f*, symbol; badge; token; banner, standard; *naut* pennant; *pl* insignia
insignificancia *f*, meaninglessness; unimportance, triviality; insignificance, insufficiency
insignificante *a* meaningless; unimportant; insignificant, small
insinuación *f*, insinuation; hint; implication; suggestion
insinuador *a* insinuating; suggestive, implicative
insinuar *vt* to insinuate; suggest, hint; *vr* ingratiate oneself; creep in
insinuativo *a* insinuative
insipidez *f*, tastelessness, insipidity; *fig* dullness
insípido *a* tasteless, insipid; dull, uninteresting, boring
insistencia *f*, insistence
insistente *a* insistent
insistir *vi* (*with en or sobre*) to lay stress upon, insist on; persist in
ínsito *a* inherent, innate
insociabilidad *f*, unsociability
insociable *a* unsociable
insolación *f*, insolation, exposure to the sun; sunstroke
insolar *vt* to expose to the sun's rays; *vr* contract sunstroke
insoldable *a* unsolderable, unable to be soldered
insolencia *f*, insolence; impudence, impertinence
insolentarse *vr* to grow insolent; be impudent
insolente *a* insolent; impudent, impertinent
insólito *a* unaccustomed; infrequent; unusual; unexpected
insolubilidad *f*, insolubility
insoluble *a* insoluble
insoluto *a* unpaid, outstanding
insolvencia *f*, insolvency
insolvente *a* insolvent
insomne *a* sleepless
insomnio *m*, insomnia
insondable *a* unfathomable, bottomless; inscrutable, secret
insoportable *a* intolerable, unbearable
insostenible *a* indefensible; arbitrary, baseless
inspección *f*, inspection; supervision; examination; inspectorship; inspector's office
inspeccionar *vt* to inspect; survey, examine. **i. una casa**, to view a house
inspector (-ra) *a* inspecting, examining. *n* supervisor. *m*, inspector; surveyor
inspiración *f*, inspiration; inhalation
inspirador (-ra) *a* inspiring. *n* inspirer
inspirar *vt* to breathe in, inhale; blow (of the wind); inspire; *vr* be inspired; (*with en*) find inspiration in, imitate
instabilidad *f*, instability; unsteadiness; shakiness; unreliability, inconstancy
instable *a* unstable

instalación *f*, plant, apparatus; erection, fitting; induction; installment, settling in

instalador (-ra) *n* fitter; one who installs (electricity, etc.)

instalar *vt* to appoint, induct; erect (a plant, etc.); install, put in; lay on; *elec* wire; *vr* install oneself, settle down

instancia *f*, instance; argument; suggestion; supplication; request; formal petition. **de primera i.**, in the first instance, firstly

instantánea *f*, *phot* snapshot

instantáneo *a* instantaneous

instante *a* urgent. *m*, second; instant, moment. **a cada i.**, every minute; frequently. **al i.**, at once, immediately. **por instantes**, continually; immediately

instar *vt* to press; persuade; insist upon; *vi* be urgent, press

instauración *f*, restoration; renewal; renovation

instaurador (-ra) *a* renovating, renewing. *n* restorer, renovator

instaurar *vt* to restore; repair; renovate, renew

instaurativo *a* restorative

instigación *f*, instigation, incitement

instigador (-ra) *n* instigator

instigar *vt* to instigate, incite; induce

instilación *f*, instillment, pouring drop by drop; inculcation, implantation

instilar *vt chem* instill; implant, inculcate

instintivo *a* instinctive

instinto *m*, instinct. **por i.**, by instinct, naturally

institución *f*, setting up, establishment; institution; teaching, instruction; *pl* institutes, digest

institucional *a* institutional

instituir *vt irr* to found, establish; institute; instruct, teach. See **huir**

instituto *m*, institute; secondary school. **i. de belleza**, beauty parlor, beauty salon

institutor *m*, founder, instituter; tutor

institutriz *f*, governess

instrucción *f*, teaching, instruction; knowledge, learning; education; *pl* orders; rules; instruction. **i. primaria**, primary education. **i. pública**, public education

instructivo *a* instructive

instructor (-ra) *a* instructive. *n* instructor

instruido *a* cultured, well-educated; knowledgeable

instruir *vt irr* to teach, instruct; train; inform, acquaint with; *law* formulate. See **huir**

instrumentación *f*, *mus* instrumentation

instrumental *a* instrumental

instrumentar *vt mus* to score

instrumentista *mf mus* instrumentalist; instrument maker

instrumento *m*, tool, implement; machine, apparatus; *mus* instrument; means, medium; legal document. **i. de cuerda**, string instrument. **i. de percusión**, percussion instrument. **i. de viento**, wind instrument

insuave *a* unpleasant (to the senses); rough

insubordinación *f*, insubordination, rebellion

insubordinado *a* insubordinate, unruly

insubordinar *vt* to rouse to rebellion; *vr* become insubordinate, rebel

insubsistencia *f*, instability

insubsistente *a* unstable; groundless, unfounded

insubstancial *a* insubstantial, unreal, illusory; pointless, worthless, superficial

insubstancialidad *f*, superficiality, worthlessness

insuficiencia *f*, insufficiency, shortage; incompetence, inefficiency

insuficiente *a* insufficient, scarce, inadequate

insufrible *a* insufferable, unbearable, intolerable

insular *a* insular

insulina *f*, insulin

insulsez *f*, insipidity, tastelessness; dullness; tediousness

insulso *a* insipid, tasteless; tedious; dull

insultador (-ra) *a* insulting. *n* insulter

insultante *a* insulting

insultar *vt* to insult; call names; *vr* take offense

insulto *m*, insult; sudden attack; sudden illness, fit

insumable *a* incalculable; excessive, exorbitant

insumergible *a* unsinkable

insumiso *a* rebellious

insuperable *a* insuperable

insurgente *a* insurgent, rebellious. *m*, rebel

insurrección *f*, insurrection

insurreccionar *vt* to incite to rebellion; *vr* rise in rebellion

insurrecto (-ta) *n* rebel

insustancial *a* See **insubstancial**

insustituible *a* indispensable

intacto *a* untouched; intact, uninjured; whole, entire; complete; pure

intachable *a* irreproachable; impeccable, perfect

intangibilidad *f*, intangibility

intangible *a* intangible

integración *f*, integration

integral *a* integral

integrar *vt* to integrate; *com* repay

integridad *f*, wholeness; completeness; integrity, probity, honesty; virginity

íntegro *a* integral, whole; upright, honest

integumento *m*, integument; pretense, simulation

intelectiva *f*, understanding

intelecto *m*, intellect

intelectual *a* intellectual

intelectualidad *f*, understanding, intellectuality; intelligentsia

intelectualismo *m*, intellectualism

inteligencia *f*, intelligence; intellect; mental alertness; mind; meaning, sense; experience, skill; understanding, secret agreement; information, knowledge; Intelligence, Secret Service

inteligente *a* intelligent; clever; skillful; capable, competent

inteligibilidad *f*, intelligibility

inteligible *a* intelligible; understandable; able to be heard

intemperancia *f*, intemperance, lack of moderation

intemperante *a* intemperate

intemperie *f*, stormy weather. **a la i.**, at the mercy of the elements; in the open air

intempestivo *a* inopportune, ill-timed

intención *f*, intention; determination, purpose; viciousness (of animals); caution. *inf* **con segunda i.**, with a double meaning, slyly

intencionado *a* intentioned, disposed

intencional *a* intentional, designed, premeditated

intendencia *f*, management; supervision; administration; *pol* intendancy. *mil* **cuerpo de i.**, quartermaster corps, army supply corps

intendente *m*, director; manager; *pol* intendant. **i. de ejército**, quartermaster general

intensar *vt* to intensify

intensidad *f*, intensity; ardor; vehemence

intensificar *vt* to intensify

intensivo *a* intensive

intenso *a* intense; ardent; fervent, vehement

intentar *vt* to intend, mean; propose; try, endeavor; initiate. **i. fortuna**, to try one's luck

intento *m*, intention, determination; purpose. **de i.**, on purpose; knowingly

intentona *f*, *inf* foolhardy attempt

interacción *f*, interaction; reciprocal effect; *chem* reaction

intercalación *f*, interpolation; insertion

intercalar *vt* to intercalate; interpolate, include, insert

intercambiable *a* interchangeable

intercambio *m*, interchange

interceder *vi* to intercede, plead for

interceptación *f*, interception

interceptar *vt* to intercept; interrupt; hinder

intercesión f, intercession
intercesor (-ra) a interceding. n intercessor
intercutáneo a intercutaneous
interdecir vt irr to forbid, prohibit. See **decir**
interdicción f, interdiction, prohibition
interdicto m, interdict
interés m, interest; yield, profit; advantage; com interest; inclination, fondness; attraction, fascination; pl money matters. **i. compuesto,** compound interest.
intereses creados, bonds of interest; vested interests
interesado a involved, concerned; biased; selfish
interesante a interesting
interesar(se) vi and vr to be interested; vt com invest; interest
interfecto (-ta) n law victim (of murder)
interferencia f, phys interference
interfoliar vt to interleave (of books)
ínterin m, interim. adv meanwhile, in the meantime
interinamente adv in the interim; provisionally
interinar vt to discharge (duties) provisionally, act temporarily as
interino a acting, provisional, temporary
interior a interior; inner; inside; indoor; inland; internal, domestic (policies, etc.); inward, spiritual. m, interior, inside; mind, soul; pl entrails
interjección f, gram interjection, exclamation
interlinear vt to write between the lines; print lead
interlocución f, dialogue, conversation
interlocutorio a law interlocutory
intérlope a interloping. mf interloper
interludio m, interlude
intermediario (-ia) a and n intermediary. m, com middleman
intermedio a intermediate. m, interim; theat interval. **por i. de,** through, by the mediation of
intermisión f, intermission, interval
intermitencia f, intermittence
intermitente a intermittent
intermitir vt to interrupt, suspend, discontinue
internación f, going inside; penetration; taking into
internacional a international
internacionalismo m, internationalism
internacionalista mf internationalist
internacionalización f, internationalization
internado m, boarding school
internamiento m, internment
internar vt to take or send inland; vi penetrate; vr (with en) go into the interior of (a country); get into the confidence of; study deeply (a subject)
interno (-na) a interior; internal; inner; inside; boarding (student). n boarding school student; med intern
internodio m, internode
internuncio m, ecc internuncio; interlocutor; representative
interoceánico a interoceanic
interpaginar vt to interleave (of books)
interpelación f, law interpellation; appeal
interpelar vt law to interpellate; appeal to, ask protection from
interpolación f, interpolation, insertion; interruption
interpolador (-ra) n interpolator; interrupter
interpolar vt to interpolate; interject
interponer vt irr to interpose, insert, intervene; designate as an arbitrator; vr intervene. See **poner**
interposición f, interposition; intervention; mediation, arbitration
interpresa f, mil surprise attack
interpretación f, interpretation; translation
interpretador (-ra) a interpretative. n interpreter
interpretar vt to interpret; translate; attribute; expound, explain. **i. mal,** to misconstrue; translate wrongly
interpretativo a interpretative
intérprete mf interpreter
interregno m, interregnum. **i. parlamentario,** parliamentary recess

interrogación f, interrogation, question; gram question mark
interrogador (-ra) n questioner
interrogante a interrogating. m, print question mark
interrogar vt to interrogate, question
interrogativo a interrogative
interrogatorio m, interrogatory
interrumpir vt to interrupt; hinder, obstruct; elec break contact
interrupción f, interruption; stoppage (of work); elec break
interruptor (-ra) a interrupting. n interrupter. m, elec switch, interruptor. **i. de dos direcciones,** elec two-way switch
intersecarse vr geom to intersect
intersección f, geom intersection
intersticio m, interstice, crack, crevice; interval, intervening space
intervalo m, interval
intervención f, intervention; mediation, intercession; auditing (of accounts)
intervenir vi irr to take part (in); intervene, interfere; arbitrate, mediate; happen, occur; vt com audit. See **venir**
interventor (-ra) a intervening. n one who intervenes. m, auditor; inspector
intervocálico a intervocalic
intestado (-da) a and n law intestate
intestinal a intestinal
intestino a intestinal. m, intestine
íntima, intimación f, intimation, notification
intimar vt to intimate; inform, notify; vr penetrate; vr and vi become intimate or friendly
intimidación f, intimidation, terrorization
intimidad f, intimacy
intimidar vt to intimidate, terrorize, cow
íntimo a intimate; deep-seated; inward; private, personal
intitular vt to give a title to, entitle, call; vr call oneself
intolerable a intolerable; unbearable
intolerancia f, narrow-mindedness, intolerance, bigotry
intolerante a narrow-minded, illiberal; med intolerant
intonso a long-haired, unshorn; boorish, ignorant
intoxicación f, poisoning
intoxicar vt to poison
intraducible a untranslatable
intramuros adv within the town walls, within the city
intranquilidad f, disquiet, restlessness; anxiety
intranquilizador a disquieting, perturbing
intranquilizar vt to disquiet, make uneasy, worry
intranquilo a uneasy, anxious
intransferible a untransferable, not transferable
intransigencia f, intolerance, intransigence
intransigente a intolerant, intransigent
intransitable a impassable; unsurmountable
intransitivo a intransitive
intratable a intractable; impassable; rough; unsociable, difficult
intrauterino a intrauterine
intravenoso a intravenous
intrepidez f, intrepidity, dauntlessness, gallantry
intrépido a intrepid, dauntless, gallant
intriga f, scheme, intrigue; entanglement; lit plot
intrigante mf intriguer, schemer
intrigar vi to intrigue, scheme, plot
intrincación f, intricacy
intrincado a intricate
intrincar vt to complicate; obscure, confuse
íntríngulis m, inf ulterior motive
intrínseco a intrinsic, inherent; essential
introducción f, introduction
introducir vt irr to introduce; insert; fit in; drive in; present, introduce; bring into use; cause, occasion; show in, bring in; vr interfere, meddle; enter. See **conducir**
introductor (-ra) n introducer

introito *m*, preamble, introduction; *ecc* introit; (*theat ant*) prologue

intromisión *f*, intromission; interference; *geol* intrusion

introspección *f*, introspection

introverso *a* introvert

intruso (-sa) *a* intruding, intrusive. *n* intruder

intuición *f*, intuition

intuir *vt irr* to know by intuition. See **huir**

intuitivo *a* intuitive

intuito *m*, glance, look, view

intumescencia *f*, intumescence

inulto *a poet* unavenged, unpunished

inundación *f*, flood; flooding; excess, superabundance

inundar *vt* to flood; swamp; *fig* inundate, overwhelm

inurbanidad *f*, discourtesy, impoliteness

inurbano *a* discourteous, uncivil, impolite

inusitado *a* unusual, unaccustomed; rare

inútil *a* useless

inutilidad *f*, uselessness

inutilizar *vt* to render useless; disable, incapacitate; spoil, damage

invadeable *a* impassable, unfordable

invadir *vt* to invade

invaginación *f*, invagination

invalidación *f*, invalidation

invalidar *vt* to invalidate

invalidez *f*, invalidity; disablement; infirmity

inválido (-da) *a* weak, infirm; invalid, null; disabled. *n* invalid; disabled soldier

invariabilidad *f*, invariability

invariable *a* invariable

invariación *f*, invariableness

invariante *m*, invariant

invasión *f*, invasion, encroachment, incursion

invasor (-ra) *a* invading; *med* attacking. *n* invader

invectiva *f*, invective

invencibilidad *f*, invincibility

invencible *a* invincible

invención *f*, invention, discovery; deception, fabrication, lie; creative imagination; finding (e.g. **i. de la Santa Cruz,** Invention of the Holy Cross)

invencionero (-ra) *n* inventor; schemer, deceiver

invendible *a* unsalable

inventar *vt* to invent; create; imagine; concoct, fabricate (lies, etc.)

inventariar *vt* to make an inventory of; *com* take stock of

inventario *m*, inventory; *com* stock taking

inventiva *f*, inventiveness, ingenuity; creativeness

inventivo *a* inventive

invento *m*, See **invención**

inventor (-ra) *n* inventor, discoverer; liar, storyteller

inverecundia *f*, impertinence, impudence

inverecundo *a* shameless, brazen

inverisímil *a* See **inverosímil**

invernáculo *m*, greenhouse; conservatory

invernada *f*, winter season; hibernation

invernadero *m*, winter quarters; greenhouse

invernal *a* wintry; winter

invernar *vi irr* to winter; hibernate; be wintertime. See **acertar**

invernizo *a* wintry, winter

inverosímil *a* unlikely, improbable

inverosimilitud *f*, improbability

inversamente *adv* inversely

inverso *a* inverse; inverted

invertebrado *a* and *m*, invertebrate

invertir *vt irr* to invert, transpose; reverse; *com* invest; spend (time). See **sentir**

investidura *f*, investiture

investigación *f*, investigation, examination; research; inquiry

investigador (-ra) *a* investigating. *n* investigator; researcher

investigar *vt* to investigate, examine; research on

investir *vt irr* to confer upon, decorate with; invest, appoint. See **pedir**

inveterado *a* inveterate

inviable *a* unfeasible

invicto *a* invincible; unconquered

invierno *m*, winter; rainy season

inviolabilidad *f*, inviolability. **i. parlamentaria,** parliamentary immunity

inviolable *a* inviolable; infallible

inviolado *a* inviolate

invisibilidad *f*, invisibility

invisible *a* invisible

invitación *f*, invitation

invitado (-da) *n* guest

invitar *vt* to invite; urge, request; allure, attract

invocación *f*, invocation

invocador (-ra) *n* invoker

invocar *vt* to invoke

involucro *m*, involucre

involuntariedad *f*, involuntariness

involuntario *a* involuntary

invulnerabilidad *f*, invulnerability

invulnerable *a* invulnerable

inyección *f*, injection

inyectado *a* bloodshot (of eyes)

inyectar *vt* to inject

ipecacuana *f*, ipecac

iperita *f*, mustard gas

ir *vi irr* to go; bet (e.g. **Van cinco pesetas que no lo hace,** I bet five pesetas he doesn't do it); be different, be changed (e.g. **¡Qué diferencia va entre esto y aquello!** What a difference there is between this and that!); suit, be becoming, fit (e.g. **El vestido no te va bien,** The dress doesn't suit you); extend; lead, go in the direction of (e.g. **Este camino va a Lérida,** This road leads to Lerida); get along, do, proceed, be (e.g. **¿Cómo te va estos días?** How are you getting along these days?); come (e.g. **Ahora voy,** I'm coming now); *math* carry (e.g. **siete y van cuatro,** seven, and four to carry); *math* leave (e.g. **De quince a seis van nueve,** Six from fifteen leaves nine). With a gerund, **ir** indicates the continuance of the action, or may mean to become or to grow (e.g. **Iremos andando hacia el mar,** We shall go on walking toward the sea, or **Entre tanto iba amaneciendo,** In the meanwhile it was growing light). With a past participle, **ir** means 'to be' (e.g. **Voy encantado de lo que he visto,** I am delighted with what I have seen). With *prep a + infin,* **ir** means to prepare (to do) or to intend (to do) or to be on the point of doing (e.g. **Van a cantar la canción que te gusta,** They are going (or preparing) to sing the song you like). With *prep a + noun,* **ir** indicates destination (e.g. **Voy al cine,** I'm going to the cinema. **¿A dónde vamos?** Where are we going to?). **ir** + *con* means to go in the company of, or to do a thing in a certain manner (e.g. **Hemos de ir con cuidado,** We must go carefully). **ir** + *en* means to concern, interest (e.g. **¿Qué le va a él en este asunto?** What has this affair to do with him?). **ir** + *por* means to follow the career of, become (e.g. **Juan va por abogado,** John is going to be a lawyer). It also means to go and bring, or to go for (e.g. **Iré por agua,** I shall go and bring (or for) water). *vr* to go away, leave, depart; die; leak (of liquids); evaporate; overbalance, slip (e.g. **Se le fueron los pies,** He slipped (and lost his balance)); be worn out, grow old, deteriorate; be incontinent; *fig inf* **írsele a uno una cosa,** not to notice or not to understand a thing. *naut* **irse a pique,** to founder, sink. **Se le fueron los ojos tras María,** He couldn't keep his eyes off Mary. **i. a caballo,** to ride, go on horseback. **i. adelante,** to go on ahead, lead; *fig inf* forge ahead, go ahead. **i. al cuartel,** to go into the army. **i. a una,** to cooperate in. **i. bien** *fig inf* to go on well; be well. **i. de brazo,** to walk arm in arm. **i. de compras,** to go shopping. **i. de juerga** *inf* to go on a binge. **i. de bicicleta** *or* **en coche,** to go by bicycle or to ride (in a car or carriage). **i. por,** to do things in order, take one thing at a time. *fig inf* **i. tirando,** to carry on, manage. **¿Cómo**

le va? How are things with you? How are you getting along? *inf* **no irle ni venirle a uno nada en un asunto,** to be not in the least concerned in (an affair). **¡Qué va!** Rubbish! Nothing of the sort! **¿Quién va?** *mil* Who goes there? **Vamos,** Let's go (also used as an exclamation: Good gracious! You don't say so! Well!) **Vamos a ver . . . ,** Let's see. . . . **¡Vaya!** What a . . . !; Come now! Never mind! **¡Vaya a paseo!** *or* **¡Vaya con su música a otra parte!** Take yourself off! Get out! **¡Vaya con Dios!** God keep you! Good-bye! *Pres. Ind.* **voy, vas, va, vamos, váis, van.** *Pres. Part.* **yendo.** *Preterite* **fui, fuiste, fue, fuimos, fuisteis, fueron.** *Imperf.* **iba,** etc. *Pres. Subjunc.* **vaya,** etc. *Imperf. Subjunc.* **fuese,** etc. *Imperat.* **vé**

ira *f,* wrath, anger; vengeance; raging, fury (of elements); *pl* cruelties, acts of vengeance

iracundia *f,* irascibility, irritability; anger

iracundo *a* irascible, irritable, choleric; angry; raging, tempestuous

Irak Iraq

iranio (-ia) *a* and *n* Iranian

irascibilidad *f,* irascibility; petulance

iridiscencia *f,* iridescence

iridiscente *a* iridescent

iris *m,* rainbow; *anat* iris (of the eye)

irisación *f,* irisation

irisar *vi* to be iridescent

irlandés (-esa) *a* and *n* Irishman (woman)

Irlanda Ireland

ironía *f,* irony

irónico *a* ironical

iroqués (-esa) *a* and *n* Iroquois

irracional *a* irrational; illogical, unreasonable; *math* irrational, absurd

irracionalidad *f,* irrationality, unreasonableness

irradiación *f,* radiation, irradiation

irradiar *vt* to radiate, irradiate

irrazonable *a* unreasonable

irreal *a* unreal

irrealidad *f,* unreality

irrealizable *a* unachievable, unattainable

irrebatible *a* irrefutable, evident

irreconciliable *a* irreconcilable, intransigent

irrecuperable *a* irretrievable

irredimible *a* irredeemable

irreemplazable *a* irreplaceable

irreflexión *f,* thoughtlessness; impetuosity

irreflexivo *a* thoughtless; rash, impetuous

irreformable *a* unreformable

irrefragable *a* indisputable, unquestionable

irrefrenable *a* unmanageable, uncontrollable

irrefutable *a* irrefutable

irregular *a* irregular; infrequent, rare

irregularidad *f,* irregularity; abnormality; *inf* moral lapse

irreligión *f,* irreligion

irreligiosidad *f,* impiety, godlessness

irreligioso *a* irreligious, impious

irremediable *a* irremediable

irremediablemente *adv* unavoidably; hopelessly

irremisible *a* unpardonable, inexcusable

irremunerado *a* unremunerated, gratuitous

irreparable *a* irreparable

irreprensible *a* blameless, unexceptionable

irreprochable *a* irreproachable

irresistible *a* irresistible; ravishing

irresolución *f,* vacillation, indecision

irresoluto *a* hesitant, irresolute

irrespetuoso *a* disrespectful

irresponsabilidad *f,* irresponsibility

irresponsable *a* irresponsible

irreverencia *f,* irreverence

irreverente *a* irreverent

irrevocabilidad *f,* irrevocability, finality

irrevocable *a* irrevocable

irrigación *f,* irrigation

irrigador *m,* spray, sprinkler; *med* syringe, spray

irrigar *vt* (*med agr*) to irrigate

irrisible *a* ridiculous, laughable, absurd

irrisión *f,* derision; laughingstock

irrisorio *a* ridiculous; derisive

irritabilidad *f,* irritability, petulance, irascibility

irritable *a* irritable

irritación *f, med* irritation; petulance, exasperation

irritador *a* irritating; exasperating. *m,* irritant

irritante *a* irritating; exasperating

irritar *vt* to exasperate, annoy; provoke, inflame; (*med law*) irritate

írrito *a law* null, void

irrogar *vt* to occasion (damage, harm)

irrompible *a* unbreakable

irrumpir *vi* to enter violently, break in

irrupción *f,* irruption, incursion, invasion

irruptor *a* invading, attacking

isabelino *a* Isabelline (pertaining to Spanish Queen Isabella II (reigned 1830–68)); bay (of horses)

isla *f,* island; block (of houses)

islámico *a* Islamic

islamismo *m,* Islam

islamita *a* and *mf* Muslim

islandés (-esa), islándico (-ca) *a* Icelandic. *n* Icelander. *m,* Icelandic (language)

Islandia Iceland

isleño (-ña) *a* island. *n* islander; native of the Canary Islands

isleta *f,* islet

islote *m,* barren islet

ismaelita *a* and *mf* Ishmaelite

isométrico *a* isometric

isomorfo *a* isomorphic

isotermo *a* isothermal

isótope, isótopo *m,* isotope

israelita *mf* Israelite. *a* Israeli

istmeño (-ña) *n* native of an isthmus

ístmico *a* isthmian

istmo *m,* isthmus

Istmo de Suez, el the Suez Canal

Ítaca Ithaca

Italia Italy

italianismo *m,* Italianism

italianizar *vt* to italianize

italiano (-na) *a* and *n* Italian. *m,* Italian (language)

itálico *a* italic

iteración *f,* iteration, repetition

iterar *vt* to repeat, reiterate

iterativo *a* iterative, repetitive

itinerario *a* and *m,* itinerary

izar *vt naut* to hoist

izote *m,* yucca

izquierda *f,* left, left-hand side; *pol* left. **¡I.!** *mil* Left face! **a la i.,** on the left

izquierdo *a* left, left-hand; left-handed; bent, twisted, crooked

J

jabalí *m,* wild boar

jabalina *f,* sow of wild boar; javelin

jabato *m,* young wild boar

jabón *m,* soap. **j. blando,** soft soap. **j. de olor** *or* **j. de tocador,** toilet soap. **j. de sastre,** French chalk, steatite

jabonadura *f,* soaping; *pl* soapsuds, lather

jabonar *vt* to soap; wash; *inf* dress down, scold

jaboncillo *m,* toilet soap; steatite

jabonera *f,* soapdish or box; soapwort

jabonería *f,* soap factory or shop

jabonoso *a* soapy
jaca *f,* pony; filly
jácara *f,* gay, roguish ballad; song and dance
jácena *f,* arch beam, girder
jacinto *m,* hyacinth; jacinth. **j. de ceilán,** zircon. **j. occidental,** topaz. **j. oriental,** ruby
jaco *m,* short coat of mail; hack, jade
jacobinismo *m,* Jacobinism
jacobino (-na) *n* Jacobin
jactancia *f,* bragging, boasting
jactancioso (-sa) *a* boastful. *n* braggart
jactarse *vr* to brag, boast
jaculatoria *f,* ejaculatory prayer
jaculatorio *a* ejaculatory
jade *m, min* jade
jadeante *a* panting
jadear *vi* to pant
jadeo *m,* pant; panting; hard breathing
jaez *m,* harness (gen. *pl*); kind, sort; *pl* trappings
jaguar *m,* jaguar
¡ja, ja, ja! *interj* Ha! ha! ha!
jalbegar *vt* to whitewash; make up the face
jalbegue *m,* whitewash
jalde *a* bright yellow
jalea *f,* jelly. **j. de membrillo,** quince jelly
jalear *vt* to encourage, urge on (by shouts, etc.)
jaleo *m,* act of encouraging dancers by clapping, shouting, etc.; Andalusian song and dance, *inf* uproar
jalón *m,* surveying rod
jamaicano (-na) *a* and *n* Jamaican
jamás *adv* never. **nunca j.,** never. **por siempre j.,** for always, forever
jamba *f,* jamb (of a door or window)
jamelgo *m,* sorry nag, miserable hack
jamón *m,* ham
jamona *f, inf* plumpish middle-aged woman
jansenismo *m,* Jansenism
jansenista *mf* and *a* Jansenist
Japón Japan
japonés (-esa) *a* and *n* Japanese. *m,* Japanese (language)
jaque *m,* check (in chess); braggart. **j. mate,** checkmate. **en j.,** at bay
jaquear *vt* to check (in chess); *mil* harass the enemy
jaqueca *f,* migraine, sick headache. *inf* **dar una j.,** to annoy
jarabe *m,* syrup. **j. tapatío,** Mexican hat dance
jarana *f,* roundhouse; *inf* revelry; fight, roughhouse; trick, deception
jarcia *f,* equipment; *naut* tackle, rigging (gen. *pl*); fishing tackle; *inf* heap, mixture, medley
jardín *m,* garden
jardinar *vt* to landscape
jardinera *f,* plant stand, jardiniere; open streetcar
jardinería *f,* gardening
jardinero (-ra) *n* gardener
jareta *f, sew* running hem; *naut* netting
jarra *f,* jar, jug. **en jarras,** arms akimbo
jarrero *m,* jug seller or manufacturer
jarrete *m,* calf (of the leg)
jarretera *f,* garter. **Orden de la J.,** Order of the Garter
jarro *m,* pitcher; jug; jar; vase
jarrón *m,* garden urn; vase
jaspe *m,* jasper
jaspeado *a* marbled, mottled; dappled; frosted (of glass)
jauja *f, fig* paradise, land of milk and honey
jaula *f,* cage; crate; miner's cage
jauría *f,* pack of hounds
javanés (-esa) *a* and *n* Javanese
jazmín *m,* jasmine. **j. amarillo,** yellow jasmine. **j. de la India,** gardenia
jefa *f,* forewoman; manager; leader, head
jefatura *f,* chieftainship; managership; leadership. **j. de policía,** police station or headquarters
jefe *m,* chief; head, leader; manager; *mil* commanding

officer. *mil* **j. de estado mayor,** chief of staff. **j. del tren,** railroad guard
jengibre *m,* ginger
jeque *m,* sheik
jerarca *m,* hierarch
jerarquía *f,* hierarchy
jerárquico *a* hierarchical
jeremiada *f,* lamentation
jerez *m,* sherry
jerga *f,* thick frieze cloth; jargon
jergón *m,* straw or hay mattress, pallet; misfit (garments); *inf* fat, lazy person
Jericó Jericho
jerigonza *f,* jargon; gibberish
jeringa *f,* syringe
jeringar *vt* to inject; syringe; *inf* annoy
jeringuilla *f,* small syringe; mock orange
jeroglífico *a* hieroglyphic. *m,* hieroglyph
jersey *m,* jersey, sweater
Jerusalén Jerusalem
jesuita *m,* Jesuit
jesuita, jesuítico *a* jesuitical
Jesús *m,* Jesus. *interj* Goodness!; Bless you! (said to someone after sneezing). **¡ay J.!** Alas! *inf* **en un decir J.,** in a trice
jeta *f,* hog's snout; blubber lip; *inf* face, mug
jibia *f,* cuttlefish
jícara *f,* small cup
jifa *f,* meat offal
jifia *f,* swordfish
jilguero *m,* goldfinch
jinete *m,* horseman, rider; horse soldier, cavalryman
jingoísmo *m,* jingoism
jip *m,* jeep
jipijapa *f,* very fine straw. **sombrero de j.,** panama hat
jira *f,* strip of cloth; picnic; tour
jirafa *f,* giraffe
jirón *m,* rag; piece of a dress, etc.; portion of a whole
jiujitsu *m,* jujitsu
jocosidad *f,* pleasantry, jocularity; joke
jocoso *a* waggish; jocose, joyous
jocundidad *f,* jocundity
jocundo *a* jocund
jofaina *f,* washbowl
jónico (-ca) *a* Ionic. *n* Ionian. *m,* (metrics) Ionic foot
Jordán Jordan (river)
Jordania Jordan (country)
jornada *f,* day's journey; journey, trip; *mil* expedition; duration of a working day; opportunity; span of life; act of a drama. **a grandes jornadas,** by forced marches, rapidly
jornal *m,* day's wages or labor
jornalear *vi* to work by the day
jornalero (-ra) *n* day laborer; wage earner
joroba *f,* hump; *inf* impertinence, nuisance
jorobado (-da) *a* humpbacked. *n* hunchback
jota *f,* name of letter J; popular Spanish dance; jot, tittle (always used negatively). **no saber j.,** to be completely ignorant
joven *a* young. *mf* young man or woman
jovenzuelo (-la) *n* youngster, boy
jovialidad *f,* joviality, cheerfulness
joya *f,* jewel; present; *arch* astragal; *fig* a jewel of a person
joyería *f,* jeweler's shop or workshop
joyero *m,* jeweler; jewel box
juanete *m,* bunion; prominent cheekbone; *naut* topgallant sail
juanetudo *a* having bunions; with prominent cheekbones
jubilación *f,* retirement; pensioning off; pension
jubilado *a* retired
jubilar *vt* to pension off; excuse from certain duties; *inf* put aside as useless (things); *vr* rejoice; retire or be pensioned off
jubileo *m,* jubilee

júbilo *m*, rejoicing, merriment. **j. de vivir,** joie de vivre
jubiloso *a* jubilant, happy
jubón *m*, doublet; bodice
judaico *a* Judaic
judaísmo *m*, Judaism
judas *m*, Judas; traitor
judería *f*, Jewry
judesmo *m*, Judezmo (Romance language of Jews)
judía *f*, Jew (female); Jewish quarter, Jewish neighborhood; haricot bean. **judías verdes,** string beans
judicatura *f*, judicature; judgeship; judiciary
judío (-ía) *a* Jewish. *n* Jew. **j. errante,** wandering Jew
juego *m*, play, sport; gambling; hand (of cards); set; suite; *mech* play, working. **j. de café,** coffee set. **j. de los cientos,** piquet. **j. de manos,** sleight of hand, conjuring. **j. de naipes,** game of cards. **j. limpio,** fair play. **j. sencillo,** single (at tennis). **j. sucio,** foul play. **juegos florales,** floral games, poetry contest. **juegos malabares,** juggling. **en j.,** in operation; at stake. **entrar en j.,** to come into play. **hacer j.,** to match. **hacer juegos malabares,** to juggle
juerga *f*, *inf* spree, binge. **ir de j.,** *inf* to go on a binge
jueves *m*, Thursday. **¡No es cosa del otro j.!** *inf* It's no great shakes! It's nothing to write home about!
juez *m*, judge. **j. arbitrador,** arbitrator; referee. **j. municipal,** magistrate
jugada *f*, play; playing; move, throw; *fig* bad turn
jugador (-ra) *a* gambling; playing. *n* gambler; player. **j. de manos,** conjurer
jugar *vi irr* to play; frolic; take part in a game; gamble; make a move (in a game); *mech* work; handle (a weapon); *com* intervene; *vt* play (a match); bet; handle (a weapon); risk. **j. el lance,** *fig* to play one's cards well. **j. limpio,** to play fair; *fig inf* be straightforward. **j. sucio,** to play foul. **jugarse el todo por el todo,** to stake everything. *Pres. Ind.* **juego, juegas, juega, juegan.** *Pres. Subjunc.* **juegue, juegues, juegue, jueguen**
jugarreta *f*, *inf* bad play; dirty trick
juglar *m*, entertainer; buffoon, juggler; minstrel
juglaresco *a* pertaining to minstrels
jugo *m*, sap; juice; *fig* essence. **j. de muñeca,** elbow grease
jugosidad *f*, juiciness, succulence; *fig* pithiness
jugoso *a* juicy, succulent; *fig* pithy
juguete *m*, toy; plaything; *fig* puppet
juguetear *vi* to frolic, gambol
jugueteo *m*, gamboling; play, dalliance
juguetería *f*, toy trade; toy shop
juguetón *a* playful
juicio *m*, judgment; wisdom, prudence; sanity, right mind; opinion; horoscope. **j. final,** Last Judgment. **j. sano,** right mind. **asentar el j.,** to settle down, become sensible. **estar fuera de j.,** to be insane. **pedir en j.,** to sue at law

juicioso *a* judicious; prudent
julio *m*, July; *elec* joule
jumento *m*, ass; beast of burden
juncal *a* reedy; rushy; *inf* slim, lissome
juncar *m*, reedy ground
junco *m*, *bot* rush, reed; *naut* junk
juncoso *a* reed-like; rushy; reedy
junio *m*, June
junquillo *m*, jonquil; *arch* reed molding
junta *f*, joint; assembly, council; committee; union, association; session, sitting; entirety, whole; board, management. **j. de comercio,** board of trade. **j. directiva,** managerial board
juntamente *adv* jointly; simultaneously
juntar *vt* to join, unite (*with prep a or con*); couple; assemble; amass; leave ajar (door); *vr* (*with con*) frequent company of; meet; join; copulate
junto *a* united, together. *adv* (*with prep a*) near; *adv* together, simultaneously. **en j.,** altogether, in all
juntura *f*, joining; joint; seam; juncture
jura *f*, solemn oath; swearing
jurado *m*, jury; jury
juramentar *vt* to swear in; *vr* take an oath
juramento *m*, oath; curse, imprecation. **j. falso,** perjury, **prestar j.,** to take an oath
jurar *vt* to swear an oath; swear allegiance; *vi* curse, be profane
jurídico *a* juridical, legal
jurisconsulto *m*, jurisconsult
jurisdicción *f*, *law* jurisdiction; boundary; authority
jurisprudencia *f*, jurisprudence
jurista *mf* jurist
justa *f*, joust; tournament; contest
justar *vi* to joust
justicia *f*, justice; equity, right; penalty, punishment; righteousness; court of justice; *inf* death penalty, execution. **administrar j.,** to dispense justice
justiciero *a* just
justificable *a* justifiable
justificación *f*, justification, impartiality, fairness; convincing proof
justificar *vt* to justify, vindicate; adjust, regulate; prove innocent; *vr* justify oneself; prove one's innocence
justillo *m*, jerkin
justipreciar *vt* to appraise, value
justiprecio *m*, appraisement, valuation
justo *a* just; righteous, virtuous; exact, accurate; tight-fitting, close. *adv* justly; exactly; tightly
Jutlandia Jutland
juvenil *a* young
juventud *f*, youthfulness, youth; younger generation
juzgado *m*, court of law; jurisdiction; judgeship
juzgar *vt* to judge, pass sentence on; decide, consider

K

ka *f*, name of the letter K
káiser *m*, kaiser
kan *m*, khan
kantiano *a* Kantian
Kenia Kenya
kermese *f*, kermis, festival
kerosén *m*, kerosene
kilo *prefix* meaning a thousand. *m*, *abb* kilogram

kilociclo *m*, *elec* kilocycle
kilogramo *m*, kilogram (2.17 lb.)
kilolitro *m*, kiloliter
kilometraje *m*, number of kilometers; mileage
kilométrico *a* kilometric. **billete k.,** tourist ticket
kilómetro *m*, kilometer (about $\frac{5}{8}$ mile)
kilovatio *m*, *elec* kilowatt
kiosco *m*, kiosk

L

la *def art. f, sing* the (e.g. **la mesa,** the table). **la** is replaced by el *m, sing* before feminine nouns beginning with stressed *a* or *ha* (e.g. **el hambre,** hunger). **la** is

sometimes used before names of famous women (e.g. **la Juana de Arco, la Melba** (Joan of Arc, Melba)) and is generally not translated. *pers pron acc f sing* her; it (e.g. **La veo venir,** I see her coming). *dem. pron* followed by *de,* or by *que* introducing relative clause, that of, that which, the one that, she who (e.g. **La casa está lejos de la en que escribo,** The house is far from the one in which I write). **la de** is used familiarly for Mrs. (e.g. **la de Jiménez,** Mrs. Jimenez). **la** means some, any, one, as substitution for noun already given (e.g. **Su hija lo haría si la tuviera,** Her daughter would do it if she had one)

lábaro *m,* labarum, standard

laberíntico *a* labyrinthine

laberinto *m,* labyrinth; *fig* tangle, complication; *anat* labyrinth of the ear

labia *f, inf* blarney, gab

labial *a* labial

labihendido *a* harelipped

labio *m,* lip; rim, edge. **l. leporino,** harelip. **cerrar los labios,** to close one's lips; keep silent

labor *f,* work, toil; sewing; needlework; husbandry, farming; silkworm egg; *min* working; trimming; plowing, harrowing

laborable *a* workable; cultivable, tillable. **día l.,** workday

laborar *vt* to work; till; plow; construct; *vi* scheme, plot, plan

laboratorio *m,* laboratory

laborear *vt* to work; till, cultivate; *naut* reeve

laboreo *m,* tilling, cultivation; working, development (of mines, etc.)

laboriosidad *f,* laboriousness, diligence

laborioso *a* industrious, diligent; laborious, tedious, hard

laborista *a* and *mf* belonging to the Labor Party

labra *f,* stonecutting; carving or working (metal, stone, or wood)

labrada *f,* fallow land ready for sowing

labradero *a* workable; cultivable, tillable

labrado *a* and *past part* worked; fashioned; carved; embroidered; figured, patterned. *m,* (gen. *pl*) cultivated ground

labrador *m,* laborer, worker; farmer; peasant

labradora *f,* peasant girl; farm girl

labradoresco, labradoril *a* rustic, peasant, farming

labrandera *f,* seamstress

labrantío *a* tillable, cultivable. *m,* farming

labranza *f,* tillage, cultivation; farm; farmland; farming; employment, work

labrar *vt* to work, do; carve; fashion, construct, make; *agr* cultivate, till; plow; embroider; sew; bring about, cause; *vi fig* impress deeply, leave a strong impression

labriego (-ga) *n* agricultural laborer; peasant

laca *f,* lac; lacquer, varnish; *art* lake (pigment)

lacayo *m,* groom; lackey, footman

lacear *vt sew* to trim with bows; tie, lace; snare, trap

laceración *f,* laceration

lacerado *a* unhappy, unfortunate; leprous

lacerar *vt* to lacerate, mangle, tear; distress, wound the feelings of

lacería *f,* poverty, misery; toil, drudgery; trouble, affliction

lacero *m,* cowboy, one who uses a lasso; poacher

lacio *a* drooping, limp; withered, faded; straight (hair)

lacónico *a* laconic; concise; Laconian

lacra *f,* aftereffect, trace (of illness); vice; fault

lacrar *vt* to impair the health; infect with an illness; injure, prejudice (the interests, etc.); seal with sealing wax

lacre *m,* sealing wax. *a* red

lacrimal *a* lachrymal

lacrimoso *a* tearful, lachrymose

lactancia *f,* lactation

lactar *vt* to suckle; feed with milk; *vi* take or drink milk

lácteo *a* lacteal; milky

lacustre *a* lacustrine, lake

ladear *vt* to incline; tilt; turn aside, twist; skirt, pass

close to; reach by a roundabout way, go indirectly to; *vr* tilt; be in favor of, incline to; be equal to

ladeo *m,* tilt; sloping; turning aside

ladera *f,* slope, incline; hillside

ladería *f,* terrace on a hillside

ladero *a* lateral

ladilla *f,* crab louse

ladino *a* eloquent; versatile linguistically; wily, crafty; *m,* Ladino (variety of Judezmo)

lado *m,* side; edge, margin; slope, declivity; faction, party; side, flank; face (of a coin); *fig* aspect, view; line of descent; means, way; favor, protection; *pl* helpers, protectors; advisers. **al l.,** near at hand. *inf* **dar de l.** **(a),** to cool off, fall out with. **dejar a un l. (una cosa),** to omit, pass over (a thing). **mirar de l.** *or* **de medio l.,** to look upon with disapproval; steal a look at

ladrador *a* barking

ladrar *vi* to bark; *inf* threaten without hurting

ladrido *m,* bark, barking; slander, gossip

ladrillado *m,* brick floor or pavement

ladrillar *vt* to floor or pave with bricks. *m,* brickyard; brickkiln

ladrillero (-ra) *n* brickmaker

ladrillo *m,* brick; tile

ladrón (-ona) *a* robbing, thieving. *n* thief, robber; burglar. *m.* **l. de corazones,** ladykiller

ladronera *f,* thieves' den; thieving, pilfering; strongbox

lagar *m,* wine or olive press

lagarta *f,* female lizard; *inf* she-serpent, cunning female

lagartera *f,* lizard hole

lagartija *f,* wall lizard, small lizard

lagarto *m,* lizard; *inf* sly, artful person, fox; *inf* insignia of Spanish Military Order of Santiago

lago *m,* lake

lagotear *vi inf* to wheedle, play up to

lagotería *f,* wheedling, coaxing, flattery

lágrima *f,* tear; drop (of liquid); exudation, ozzing (from trees)

lagrimal *a* lachrymal

lagrimear *vi* to shed tears

lagrimeo *m,* weeping, crying; watering of the eyes

lagrimoso *a* tearful; watery (of eyes); sad, tragic

laguna *f,* small lake, lagoon; lacuna; gap, hiatus

lagunoso *a* boggy, marshy

laical *a* lay, secular

laicismo *m,* secularism

laico *a* lay, secular

lama *f,* ooze, slime. *m,* lama, Buddhist priest

lamaísmo *m,* lamaism

lameculos *mf inf* toady

lamedura *f,* licking; lapping

lamentable *a* lamentable

lamentación *f,* lamentation; lament

lamentador (-ra) *a* lamenting, wailing. *n* wailer, mourner

lamentar *vt* to mourn, lament, bewail; *vr* bemoan, bewail

lamento *m,* lament

lamentoso *a* lamenting, afflicted; lamentable

lamer *vt* to lick; pass the tongue over; touch lightly; lap

lámina *f,* sheet (of metal); lamina; engraving; illustration, picture; engraving plate

laminación *f,* lamination, rolling (of metals)

laminado *a* laminate; rolled (metals). *m,* rolling (of metals)

laminador *m,* rolling mill (for metals)

laminar *a* laminate; laminated. *vt* to roll (metals); laminate; lick

lámpara *f,* lamp; radiance, light, luminous body; grease spot. **l. de los mineros** *or* **l. de seguridad,** safety lamp. **l. de soldar,** blowpipe. **l. termiónica,** *rad* thermionic valve. **atizar la l.,** to trim the lamp; *inf* refill drinking glasses

lamparería *f,* lamp factory; lamp shop

lamparero (-ra), *n* **lamparista** *mf* lamplighter; lamp maker or seller

lamparilla f, night-light; *bot* aspen; small lamp
lamparón m, scrofula, king's evil; tumor (disease of horses)
lampiño a beardless, clean-shaved; smooth-faced; *bot* nonhirsute
lampista mf See **lamparero**
lamprea f, lamprey
lana f, wool; fleece; woolen garments or cloth; woolen trade (gen. *pl*)
lanar a wool; wool-bearing. **ganado l.,** sheep
lance m, throw, cast; casting a fishing line; catch of fish; crisis, difficult moment; *lit* episode; quarrel; move (in a game). *fig* **l. apretado,** difficult position, tight corner. **l. de fortuna,** chance, fate. **l. de honor,** affair of honor; duel
lancear vt to wound with a lance; lance
lancero m, *mil* lancer; *pl* lancers (dance and music)
lanceta f, lancet
lancha f, *naut* launch; lighter; ship's boat; small boat; flagstone. **l. bombardera** or **l. cañonera,** gunboat. **l. de salvamento,** ship's lifeboat. **l. escampavía,** patrol boat
lancinar vt *med* to lance
landa f, lande
landó m, landau
lanero a woolen. m, wool merchant; wool warehouse
langosta f, locust; lobster. **l. migratoria,** locust
langostín m, crayfish
languidecer vi *irr* to languish, pine. See **conocer**
languidez f, lassitude, inertia; languor
lánguido a listless, weak, languid; halfhearted; languishing, languorous
lanolina f, lanolin
lanosidad f, woolliness; down (on leaves, etc.)
lanoso, lanudo a woolly
lanza f, lance, spear; lancer; nozzle (of a hosepipe). **correr lanzas,** to joust (in a tournament). **estar con la l. en ristre,** to have the lance in rest; be prepared or ready. *inf* **ser una l.,** to be very clever
lanzabombas m, (*aer nav*) bomb release
lanzada f, lance or spear thrust
lanzadera f, weaver's shuttle; sewing machine shuttle. *inf* **parecer una l.,** to be constantly on the go
lanzador (-ra) m. batsman. n thrower, caster, tosser
lanzallamas m, flamethrower
lanzamiento m, throwing; cast, throw; *law* dispossession; *naut* launching
lanzaminas m, minelayer
lanzar vt to throw, cast, hurl; *naut* launch; vomit; *law* dispossess; *agr* take root; vr hurl oneself, rush; take (to), embark (upon)
lanzatorpedos (tubo) m, torpedo tube
lañar vt to clamp; clean fish (for salting)
lapa f, barnacle, limpet
lapicero m, pencil holder, pencil case; mechanical pencil
lápida f, memorial tablet; gravestone
lapidación f, lapidation, stoning
lapidar vt to stone, lapidate; throw stones at
lapidario a lapidary
lapislázuli m, lapis lazuli
lápiz m, graphite; pencil; crayon. **l. para los labios,** lipstick
lapizar m, graphite mine. vt to pencil
lapón (-ona) a Lappish. n Laplander. m, Sami (language)
Laponia Lapland
lapso m, lapse, period, passage; slip, error, failure
laquear vt to lacquer, paint
lar m, home; *pl* lares
lardear vt *cul* to baste
lardo m, lard; animal fat
lardoso a greasy; fat; oily
larga f, longest billiard cue; delay (gen. *pl*). **a la l.,** in the long run
largamente adv fully, at length; generously; widely, extensively; comfortably

largar vt to slacken, loosen; *naut* unfurl; set at liberty; *fig inf* let fly (oaths, etc.); administer (blows, etc.); vr *inf* quit, leave (in a hurry or secretly); *naut* set sail
largo a long; generous, liberal; abundant, plentiful; protracted; prolonged; expeditious; *pl* many long (e.g. **por largos años,** for many long years). m, *mus* largo; length. *inf* **¡L. de aquí!** Get out! **a la larga,** in length; eventually, finally; slowly; with many digressions. **a lo l.,** lengthwise; along the length (of); in the distance, far off; along, the length (of). *fig* **ponerse de l.,** to make one's debut in society; come of age
largor m, **largura** f, length
largueza f, length; generosity, munificence
largura f, length
laringe f, larynx
laríngeo a laryngeal
laringitis f, laryngitis
larva f, larva; worm, grub; specter, phantom
las *def art. f pl,* of **la** the. *pers pron acc f pl,* of **la,** them
lascivia f, lasciviousness
lascivo a lascivious, lewd; wanton
lasitud f, lassitude, weariness, exhaustion
laso a weary, exhausted; weak; untwisted (of silk, etc.)
lástima f, compassion, pity; pitiful sight; lamentation. **dar l.,** to cause pity. **Es l.,** It's a pity. **tener l. (a** or **de) to be sorry for (persons)**
lastimador a harmful, injurious; painful
lastimar vt to hurt, harm, injure; pity; *fig* wound, distress; vr (*with de*) be sorry for or about; complain, lament
lastimero a pitiful; mournful; injurious, harmful
lastimoso a pitiful, heartbreaking; mournful
lastrar vt to ballast
lastre m, ballast; good sense, prudence
lata f, can, tin; tin plate; can of food. **en l.,** canned, tinned (of food). *inf* **Es una l.,** It's a bore, It's an awful nuisance
latamente adv extensively, at length; broadly
latente a latent
lateral a lateral
látex m, latex
latido m, yelp, bark; beat; throb; palpitation
latifundios m pl, latifundia (large agricultural estates)
latigazo m, lash; crack of a whip; sudden blow of fate; *inf* draft (of wine, etc.); harsh scolding; *naut* jerk or flapping (of sails)
látigo m, whip, lash; cinch, girth of a saddle
latín m, Latin. **bajo l.,** low Latin. *inf* **saber l.,** to know the score; be smart
latinajo m, *inf* bad Latin
latinidad f, Latinity
latinismo m, Latinism
latinista mf Latinist
latinizar vt to latinize; vi *inf* use Latin phrases
latino a Latin; lateen sail
latinoamericano (-na) a and n Latin-American
latir vi to yelp, howl; bark; throb, palpitate, beat
latitud f, latitude; area, extent; breadth
latitudinario a latitudinarian
lato a extensive; large; broad (of word meanings)
latón m, brass
latonería f, brassworks; brass shop
latoso a boring, troublesome, annoying
latrocinio m, larceny
latvio (-ia) a and n Latvian
laúd m, lute
laudable a praiseworthy, laudable
láudano m, laudanum
laudatorio a laudatory
laurear vt to crown with laurel; honor, reward
laurel m, bay tree. **l. cerezo,** laurel. **l. rosa,** rosebay, oleander
láureo a laurel
lauréola f, laurel wreath
lauro m, bay tree; glory, triumph
Lausana Lausanne

lava *f,* lava
lavable *a* washable
lavabo *m,* washstand; cloakroom, lavatory
lavada *f,* load of wash, load
lavadedos *m,* fingerbowl
lavadero *m,* washing place; laundry
lavado *m,* washing; cleaning; wash. **l. al seco,** dry cleaning
lavadura *f,* washing
lavamanos *m,* washstand; lavatory
lavamiento *m,* washing, cleansing, ablution
lavanda *f,* lavender
lavandera *f,* laundress; washerwoman
lavandería *f,* laundry
lavandero *m,* laundry; laundryman
lavaplatos *m,* dishwasher
lavar *vt* to wash; *fig* wipe out, purify; paint in watercolors. **l. al seco,** to dry-clean
lavativa *f,* enema; syringe, clyster; *inf* nuisance, bore
lavatorio *m,* washing, lavation; *ecc* lavabo; lavatory, washing place; *ecc* maundy
lavazas *f pl,* dirty soapy water
laxante *a* and *m,* laxative
laxar *vt* to loosen, relax; soften
laxitud *f,* laxity
laxo *a* lax; slack
laya *f, agr* spade; kind, sort, class
layar *vt agr* to fork
lazar *vt* to lasso
lazareto *m,* leper hospital; quarantine hospital
lazarillo *m,* boy who guides a blind person
lazarino *a* leprous
lázaro *m,* lazar, beggar
lazo *m,* bow; knot of ribbons; tie; ornamental tree; figure (in dancing); lasso; rope, bond; lace (of a shoe); *fig* trap, snare; bond, obligation; slipknot. **l. corredizo,** running knot. *fig inf* **armar l.,** to set a trap. *inf* **caer en el l.,** to fall into the trap, be deceived
le *pers pron dat m,* or *f, 3rd pers sing* to him, to her, to it, to you (e.g. **María le dio el perro,** Mary gave him (her, you) the dog). Clarity may require the addition of **a él, a ella, a usted** (e.g. **Le dio el perro a ella,** etc.). *pers pron acc m, 3rd pers sing* him (e.g. **Le mandé a casa,** I sent him home)
leal *a* loyal; faithful (animals)
lealtad *f,* loyalty; faithfulness; sincerity, truth
lebrel *m,* greyhound
lección *f,* reading; lesson; oral test; warning, example. **l. práctica,** object lesson. **dar l.,** to give a lesson. **tomar la l.,** to hear a lesson
leccionista *mf* private teacher, coach, tutor
lechas *f pl,* soft roe; milt
leche *f,* milk; milky fluid of some plants and seeds. *inf* **estar con la l. en los labios,** to be young and inexperienced
lechera *f,* milkmaid; milk can or jug
lechería *f,* dairy; dairy shop
lechero (-ra) *a* dairy, milk; milky; milch, milk-giving. *n* milk seller. **industria lechera,** dairy farming
lecho *m,* bed; couch; animal's bed, litter; riverbed; bottom of the sea; layer; *geol* stratum
lechón *m,* suckling pig; hog; *inf* slovenly man
lechoso *a* milky
lechuga *f,* lettuce; frill, flounce. *inf* **como una l.,** as fresh as a daisy
lechuguero (-ra) *n* lettuce seller
lechuguilla *f,* ruff; ruche
lechuguina *f, inf* affected, overdressed young woman
lechuguino *m,* lettuce plant; *inf* young blood, gallant; *inf* foppish young man
lechuza *f,* barn owl
lector (-ra) *n* reader; lecturer
lectura *f,* reading; lecture; culture, knowledge
ledo *a* happy, content
leer *vt irr* to read; explain, interpret; teach; take part in an oral test. See **creer**

lega *f, ecc* lay sister
legación *f, ecc* legateship; legation
legado *m,* legacy; legate
legajo *m,* bundle, docket; file
legal *a* legal; legitimate; upright, trustworthy
legalidad *f,* legality
legalización *f,* legalization
legalizar *vt* to legalize
legamente *adv* ignorantly, stupidly
légamo *m,* mud, slime
legamoso *a* slimy
legaña *f,* bleariness (of the eyes)
legañoso *a* bleary-eyed
legar *vt* to bequeath; send as a legate
legatario (-ia) *n* legatee, one to whom a legacy is bequeathed
legendario *a* legendary
legibilidad *f,* legibility
legible *a* legible
legión *f,* legion
legionario *a* and *m,* legionary
legislación *f,* legislation
legislador (-ra) *a* legislative. *n* legislator
legislar *vi* to legislate
legislativo *a* legislative
legislatura *f,* legislature
legista *mf* jurist; student of law
legítima *f,* portion of a married man's estate that cannot be willed away from his wife and children
legitimación *f,* legitimation
legitimar *vt* to legitimize
legitimidad *f,* legitimacy
legítimo *a* legitimate; real, true
lego *a* lay, secular. *m,* layman
legua *f,* league (approximately 5.573 meters). **a la l., de cien leguas, desde media l.,** from afar
legumbre *f,* pulse; vegetable
leguminoso *a* leguminous
leído *a* well-read
leila *f,* nocturnal Moorish merrymaking or dance
lejanía *f,* distance
lejano *a* distant, remote, far off
lejía *f,* lye; bleaching solution; *inf* dressing-down, scolding
lejos *adv* far off, far, distant. *m,* perspective, view from afar; *art* background. **a lo l.,** far off, in the distance. **de** or **desde l.,** from afar, from a distance
lelo *a* stupid; fatuous, inane
lema *m,* chapter heading; argument, summary; motto; theme, subject
lémur *m,* lemur
lencería *f,* linen goods; linen merchant's shop; linen closet
lencero *m,* linen merchant
lene *a* smooth, soft; kind, sweet, gentle; lightweight
lengua *f, anat* tongue; mother tongue, language; clapper of a bell; information. *mf* spokes. **l. de escorpión** or **mala l.,** scandalmonger, backbiter. **l. de fuego,** *ecc* tongue of fire, flame. **l. del agua,** waterline, shoreline. **l. de oc,** langue d'oc. **l. de oil,** langue d'oil. **l. de tierra,** neck of land, promontory. **l. viva,** modern language. *inf* **andar en lenguas,** to be on every lip, be famous. *inf* **hacerse lenguas de,** to praise to the skies. *inf* **irse (a uno) la l.,** to be indiscreet, talk too much. **poner l.** or **lenguas en,** to gossip about. *inf* **tener mucha l.,** to be very talkative. **tomar l.** or **lenguas,** to find out about, inform oneself on
lenguado *m, icht* sole
lenguaje *m,* language; style; speech, idiom. **l. vulgar,** common speech
lengüeta *f, dim* little tongue; *mus* tongue (of wind instruments); barb (of an arrow); needle (of a balance)
lenidad *f,* lenience, indulgence, mercy
Leningrado Leningrad
lenitivo *a* lenitive; soothing. *m, med* lenitive; *fig* balm (of sorrow, etc.)

lente *m*, lens; *pl* eyeglasses. **l. de aumento,** magnifying glass

lenteja *f*, lentil; lentil plant

lentejuela *f*, sequin

lentitud *f*, lentitude; slowness, deliberation

lento *a* slow, deliberate; sluggish, heavy; *med* glutinous, adhesive

leña *f*, firewood; *inf* beating, birching. *fig* **echar l. al fuego,** to add fuel to the flame. *fig* **llevar l. al monte,** to carry coals to Newcastle

leñador (-ra) *n* woodcutter; firewood dealer

leñera *f*, woodpile; woodshed

leño *m*, wooden log; wood, timber; *poet* ship; *inf* blockhead

leñoso *a* woody, ligneous

león *m*, lion. *ast* Leo; valiant man. **l. marino,** sea lion

leona *f*, lioness

leonera *f*, lion cage; lion's den; *inf* gambling den; *inf* lumber room

leonero (-ra) *n* lionkeeper; *inf* keeper of a gambling house

leonés (-esa) *a* and *n* Leonese

leonino *a* leonine

leopardo *m*, leopard

lepra *f*, leprosy

leproso *a* leprous

lerdo *a* slow, lumbering (gen. horses); stupid, slow-witted, dull

les *pers pron dat 3rd pers pl mf*, to them (e.g. **Les dimos las flores,** We gave them flowers. **Les hablé del asunto,** I spoke to them about the matter)

lesbio (-ia) *a* and *n* lesbian

lesión *f*, lesion, wound; *fig* injury

lesionar *vt* to wound; *fig* injure

lesna *f*, awl

leso *a* wounded, hurt; offensive, injurious; *fig* unbalanced, perturbed (of the mind). **crimen de lesa majestad,** crime of lèse-majesté

letal *a* lethal; deadly

letanía *f*, *ecc* litany

letargia *f*, *med* lethargy

letárgico *a* lethargic

letargo *m*, lethargy; indifference, apathy

Letonia Latvia

letra *f*, letter (of alphabet); *print* type; penmanship, hand; *fig* letter, literal meaning; words (of a song); inscription; *com* bill, draft; cunning, shrewdness; *pl* learning, knowledge. **l. abierta,** *com* open credit. **l. de cambio,** *com* bill of exchange. **l. gótica,** Gothic characters. **l. itálica,** italics. **l. mayúscula,** capital letter. **l. paladial,** palatal. **facultad de letras,** faculty of arts. **La l. con sangre entra,** Learning is acquired with pain. **primeras letras,** early education, first letters

letrado *a* learned, educated; *inf* presumptuous; pedantic. *m*, lawyer

letrero *m*, label; inscription; poster, bill; sign, indicator. **l. luminoso,** illuminated sign

letrilla *f*, short poem, often set to music

letrina *f*, latrine

leucocito *m*, leucocyte

leva *f*, *naut* weighing anchor; *mil* levy, forced enrolment; tappet; *mech* lever; *mech* cam; *inf* **irse a l. y a monte,** to flee, beat it, quit

levadizo *a* able to be raised or lowered (bridges). **puente l.,** drawbridge

levadura *f*, leaven, yeast; rising (of bread)

levantada *f*, act of rising from bed

levantamiento *m*, raising, lifting; rebellion, revolt; ennoblement, elevation; settlement of accounts

levantar *vt* to raise, lift; pick up; build, construct; cancel, remove; encourage, rouse; recruit, enlist; cut (cards); leave, abandon; survey; disturb (game); produce, raise (a swelling); found, institute; increase (prices); raise (the voice); *fig* ennoble, elevate; cause, occasion; libel, accuse falsely; *vr* rise; get up; stand up;

stand out, be prominent; rebel; leave one's bed after an illness. **l. bandera,** to rebel. **l. el campo,** to break camp. **levantarse del izquierdo,** *inf* to get out of bed on the wrong side

levante *m*, east; Levant; east wind

levantino (-na) *a* and *n* Levantine

levar *vt naut* to weigh anchor; *vr* set sail

leve *a* light (in weight); unimportant, trifling

levedad *f*, lightness (in weight); unimportance, levity, flippancy

leviatán *m*, leviathan

levita *m*, Levite; deacon. *f*, frock coat

levitación *f*, levitation

levítico *a* Levitical. *m*, Leviticus

levitón *m*, frock coat

léxico *m*, lexicon

lexicografía *f*, lexicography

lexicógrafo *m*, lexicographer

lexicólogo *m*, lexicologist

ley *f*, law; precept; regulation, rule; doctrine; loyalty, faithfulness; affection, love; legal standard (weights, measures, quality); ratio of gold or silver in coins, jewelry; statute, ordinance; *pl* the Law. **l. de préstamo y arriendo,** Lend-Lease Act. **ley suntuaria,** sumptuary law. *inf* **a la l.,** with care and decorum. **a l. de caballero,** on the word of a gentleman. **de buena l.,** *a* excellent; *adv* genuinely; in good faith. **de mala l.,** *a* disreputable, base; *adv* in bad faith

leyenda *f*, legend; inscription; story, tale

leyente *a* reading. *mf* reader

lezna *f*, awl

lía *f*, plaited esparto rope; *pl* lees, dregs

liar *vt* to fasten or tie up; wrap up, parcel; roll (a cigarette); *inf* entangle, embroil; *vr* take a lover, enter on a liaison. *inf* **liarlas,** to quit, sneak off; *inf* kick the bucket, die

libación *f*, libation

Líbano, el Lebanon

libar *vt* to suck; perform a libation; sip, taste; sacrifice

libelista *mf* libeler

libelo *m*, libel; *law* petition

libélula *f*, dragonfly

liberación *f*, liberation, freeing; receipt, quittance; *law* reconveyance (of mortgages)

liberador (-ra) *a* liberating, freeing. *n* liberator

liberal *a* generous, openhanded; liberal, tolerant; learned (of professions). *a* and *mf pol* liberal

liberalidad *f*, generosity, magnanimity

liberalismo *m*, liberalism

liberalizar *vt* to liberalize, make liberal

liberar *vt* to liberate

libérrimo *a sup* extremely free, most free

libertad *f*, liberty, freedom; independence; privilege, right (gen. *pl*); exemption; licentiousness; forwardness, familiarity; naturalness, ease of manner; facility, capacity; immunity. **l. caucional,** freedom on bail, release on bail. **l. de cultos,** freedom of worship; religious toleration. **l. vigilada,** *law* probation. **poner en l.,** to set at liberty; (*with de*) *fig* free from

libertador (-ra) *a* liberating, freeing. *n* liberator, deliverer

libertar *vt* to liberate, free; save, deliver; exempt

libertario (-ia) *a* anarchistic. *n* anarchist

libertinaje *m*, libertinage, licentiousness

libertino (-na) *a* debauched, licentious. *m*, libertine. *n* child of a freed slave

liberto (-ta) *n* freed slave, freedman

Libia Libya

libídine *f*, lust

libidinoso *a* libidinous, lustful

libio *a* and *n* Libyan

libra *f*, pound (measure, coinage); *ast* Libra. **l. esterlina,** pound sterling. **l. medicinal,** pound troy

libración *f*, oscillation; *ast* libration

librador (-ra) *a* freeing, liberating. *n* deliverer, liberator. *m*, *com* drawer (of bill of exchange, etc.)

libramiento *m*, liberation, deliverance; *com* delivery; order of payment

libranza *f*, *com* draft

librar *vt* to liberate, free; protect (from misfortune); *com* draw (a draft); *com* deliver; place confidence in; issue, enact; *vi* bring forth children; *vr (with de)* escape from; get rid of

libre *a* free; at liberty, disengaged; unhampered, untrammeled; independent; bold, brazen; dissolute, vicious; exempt; vacant, unoccupied; unmarried; clear, free; mutinous, rebellious; isolated, remote; innocent; unharmed. **l. cambio**, free trade

librea *f*, livery

librecambio *m*, free trade

librecambista *a* free trade. *mf* free trader

librepensador (-ra) *a* freethinking. *n* freethinker

librepensamiento *m*, free thought

librería *f*, bookshop; book trade, bookselling; bookcase

librero *m*, bookseller. **l. anticuario**, antiquarian bookseller; rare-book dealer

libreta *f*, *cul* 1-lb. loaf; notebook; passbook, bankbook

libretista *mf* librettist

libreto *m*, libretto

librillo *m*, *dim* small book; book of cigarette papers; tub, pail; *zool* omasum

libro *m*, book; *mus* libretto; *zool* omasum. **l. copiador**, *com* letter book. **l. de actas**, minute book. **l. de caja**, *com* cash book. **l. de cheques**, checkbook. **l. de facturas**, *com* invoice book. **l. de reclamaciones**, complaint book. **l. de texto**, textbook. **l. diario**, *com* daybook. **l. mayor**, ledger. **l. talonario**, receipt book. *fig inf* **hacer l. nuevo**, to turn over a new leaf; introduce innovations

licencia *f*, permission, license; licentiousness; boldness, insolence; *univ* bachelor's degree, licentiate. **l. absoluta**, *mil* discharge

licenciado (-da) *a* pedantic; free, exempt; licensed. *n* *univ* bachelor; licentiate. *m*, discharged soldier

licenciar *vt* to allow, permit; license; dismiss, discharge; confer degree of bachelor or licentiate; *mil* discharge; *vr* become licentious; receive bachelor's degree or licentiate

licenciatura *f*, degree of licentiate or bachelor; graduation as such; licentiate course of study

licencioso *a* licentious, dissolute

liceo *m*, lyceum

licitación *f*, bidding (at auction)

licitador *m*, bidder (at auction)

licitar *vt* to bid for (at auction)

lícito *a* permissible, lawful

licor *m*, liquor, alcoholic drink; liquid

licorera *f*, liqueur set; decanter

licoroso *a* aromatic, generous (of wines)

licuadora *f*, blender

licuar *vt* to liquefy

licuefacción *f*, liquefaction

lid *f*, combat, fight; dispute, controversy. **en buena l.**, in fair fight; by fair means

líder *m*, leader; chief

lidia *f*, fighting; bullfight

lidiador (-ra) *n* combatant, fighter

lidiar *vi* to fight; *fig* struggle; *(with contra or con)* oppose, fight against; *vt* fight (a bull). **¡Cuánto tienen que l. con . . . !** *fig* What a struggle they have with . . . !

liebre *f*, hare

liendre *f*, nit

lienza *f*, narrow strip (of cloth)

lienzo *m*, linen; cotton; cambric; hemp cloth; *art* canvas

liga *f*, garter; bandage; birdlime; mixture, blend; *met* alloy; alliance, coalition; league (football, etc.)

ligación *f*, tying; binding; union

ligado *m*, *mus* legato; *mus* tie

ligadura *f*, bond, tie; binding, fastening; *fig* shackle, link; *(surg mus)* ligature; *naut* lashing

ligamento *m*, tie, bond; mixture; *anat* ligament

ligar *vt* to tie, bind; *met* alloy; join, connect; render im-

potent by sorcery; *mus* slur (notes); *vr* ally, join together; *fig* bind oneself. **l. cabos**, to put two and two together

ligazón *f*, fastening; union; bond

ligereza *f*, lightness (of weight); swiftness, nimbleness; fickleness; tactless remark, indiscretion

ligero *a* light (in weight); swift, nimble; light (sleep); unimportant, insignificant; easily digested (food); thin (fabrics, etc.); fickle, changeable. **l. de cascos**, frivolous, gay. **a la ligera**, lightly; quickly; without fuss. **de l.**, impetuously, thoughtlessly; easily, with ease

lignito *m*, lignite

lija *f*, dogfish; sandpaper

lijar *vt* to sandpaper

lila *f*, lilac bush and flower; lilac color. *a inf* foolish, vain

liliputiense *a* and *mf* Lilliputian

lima *f*, sweet lime, citron fruit; lime tree; file (tool); filing, polishing

limadura *f*, filing; polishing; *pl* filings

limar *vt* to file, smooth with a file; *fig* touch up, polish

limazo *m*, slime, viscosity (especially of snails, etc.)

limbo *m*, limbo; edge, hem; *(ast bot)* limb; limb (of a quadrant, etc.). *inf* **estar en el l.**, to be bewildered or abstracted

limen *m*, *poet* threshold; *psy* limen

limeño (-ña) *a* and *n* native of or belonging to Lima (Peru)

limero (-ra) *n* seller of sweet limes. *m*, sweet lime tree (citron)

limitación *f*, limitation; limit, extent, bound; district, area

limitado *a* dull-witted, limited

limitáneo *a* bordering

limitar *vt* to limit; curb, restrict; bound

límite *m*, limit, extent; boundary, border; end, confine

limítrofe *a* bordering, contiguous

limo *m*, mud, mire, slime

limón *m*, lemon; lemon tree

limonada *f*, lemonade. **l. seca**, lemonade powder

limonar *m*, lemon grove

limonero (-ra) *n* lemon seller. *m*, lemon tree

limosna *f*, alms

limosnear *vi* to beg, ask alms

limosnero *a* charitable, generous. *m*, almoner

limoso *a* slimy, muddy

limpiabarros *m*, shoe scraper

limpiabotas *m*, bootblack (person)

limpiachimeneas *m*, chimney-sweep

limpiador (-ra) *a* cleaning. *n* cleaner

limpiadura *f*, cleaning; *pl* rubbish

limpiamente *adv* cleanly; dexterously, neatly; sincerely, candidly; generously, charitably

limpiametales *m*, metal polish

limpiaparabrisas *m*, windshield wiper

limpiapipas *m*, pipe cleaner

limpiar *vt* to clean; *fig* cleanse, clear; empty, free (from); *agr* thin out; *inf* steal, pinch; *inf* win (gambling); *vr* clean oneself

limpiauñas *m*, orange stick (for fingernails)

limpidez *f*, *poet* limpidity

límpido *a* *poet* limpid

limpieza *f*, cleanliness; cleaning; chastity; purity; altruism; uprightness, integrity; neatness, tidiness; dexterity, skill, precision; fair play

limpio *a* clean; pure, unalloyed, unmixed; neat, tidy; pure-blooded; unharmed, free. **en l.**, in substance; as a fair copy; clearly; *com* net

linaje *m*, lineage, family; offspring; kind; sort, quality

linajudo (-da) *a* highborn. *n* noble, aristocrat; one who alleges his noble descent

linar *m*, field of flax

linaza *f*, linseed

lince *m*, lynx; fox; crafty person

linchamiento *m*, lynching

linchar *vt* to lynch

lindar *vi* to run together, be contiguous

linde *mf* limit, extent; boundary

lindero *a* bordering, contiguous. *m,* boundary. *inf* **con linderos y arrabales,** with many digressions

lindeza *f,* beauty, loveliness; witticism; *pl* (*inf ironical*) insults

lindo *a* lovely, beautiful; perfect, exquisite. *m, inf* fop (gen. **lindo don Diego**)

línea *f,* line; kind, class; ancestry, lineage; limit, extent; *mil* file; equator. **l. aérea,** airline. *naut* **l. de flotación,** waterline. **l. de toque,** touchline (in soccer). **l. recta,** direct line (of descent)

lineal *a* lineal

lineamento *m,* lineament

linear *a* linear. *vt* to line, mark with lines; *art* sketch

linfa *f, med* lymph; vaccine; *poet* water

linfático *a* lymphatic

lingote *m,* ingot; bar (of iron). **l. de fundición,** pig iron

lingüista *mf* linguist

lingüística *f,* linguistics

lingüístico *a* linguistic

linimento *m,* liniment

lino *m, bot* flax; linen; *poet* ship's sail, canvas

linóleo *m,* linoleum

linotipia *f,* linotype

linterna *f,* lantern; lighthouse; lamp. **l. sorda,** dark lantern

lío *m,* bundle; *inf* muddle, imbroglio; *inf* liaison, amour. *inf* **armar un l.,** to make a muddle, cause trouble. *inf* **hacerse un l.,** to get in a fix; get in a muddle

liquen *m,* lichen

liquidable *a* liquefiable

liquidación *f,* liquefaction; *com* clearance, sale; *com* settlement

liquidar *vt* to liquefy; *com* settle; *com* liquidate; finish; *vr* liquefy

liquidez *f,* liquidness

líquido *a* liquid; *com* net. *m,* liquid; *com* net profit

lira *f, mus* lyre; *ast* Lyra; lira (coin)

lírica *f,* lyrical verse, lyric

lírico *a* lyrical

lirio *m,* lily. **l. cárdeno,** yellow flag (iris). **l. de los valles,** lily of the valley

lirismo *m,* lyricism

lirón *m, zool* dormouse; *inf* sleepyhead

Lisboa Lisbon

lisbonense *a* and *mf* **lisbonés (-esa)** *a* and *n* Lisboan

lisiado *a* lame, crippled

lisiar *vt* to cripple, lame; *vr* be disabled; be lame

liso *a* smooth; sleek; unadorned, plain; unicolored

lisonja *f,* flattery, adulation

lisonjear *vt* to flatter; fawn upon; *fig* delight (the ear). **lisonjearse de . . . ,** to flatter oneself on . . .

lisonjero (-ra) *a* flattering; sweet, pleasant (sounds). *n* flatterer

lista *f,* strip of cloth; streak; rib; stripe; catalog, list. **l. de correos,** general delivery, poste restante. **l. de platos,** bill of fare. **pasar l.,** to call the roll; check the list

listado *a* streaked; striped; ribbed

listo *a* clever; expeditious, diligent; ready, prepared

listón *m,* ribbon; strip (of wood)

lisura *f,* smoothness; sleekness; flatness; sincerity

litera *f,* litter; *naut* berth

literal *a* literal

literario *a* literary

literatear *vi* to write on literary subjects

literato (-ta) *a* literary. *n* writer, litterateur

literatura *f,* literature

litigación *f,* litigation

litigante *mf* litigant

litigar *vt* to litigate; *vi* dispute, argue

litigio *m,* lawsuit; dispute, argument

litigioso *a* litigious; quarrelsome, disputatious

litisexpensas *f pl, law* costs of a suit; legal expenses

litografía *f,* lithography

litografiar *vt* to lithograph

litográfico *a* lithographic

litoral *a* and *m,* littoral

litro *m,* liter

Lituania Lithuania

lituano (-na) *a* and *n* Lithuanian. *m,* Lithuanian (language)

liturgia *f,* liturgy

litúrgico *a* liturgical

liviandad *f,* lightness (of weight); fickleness; unimportance; frivolity; lewdness; act of folly, indiscretion

liviano *a* light weight; fickle; unimportant, trifling, frivolous; lascivious

lividez *f,* lividness

lívido *a* livid

liza *f,* list (at a tournament); arena

llaga *f,* ulcer; sore; grief, affliction; *fig* thorn in the flesh

llagar *vt* to ulcerate; make or produce sores; *fig* wound; *vr* be covered with sores

llama *f,* flame; ardor, vehemence; marsh; *zool* llama

llamada *f,* call; *mil* call-to-arms, call. **l. molestosa,** annoyance call, nuisance call

llamado *a* called; so-called

llamador (-ra) *n* caller. *m,* door knocker; doorbell

llamamiento *m,* calling; call; divine summons, inspiration; invocation, appeal; summons, convocation

llamar *vt* to call; invoke, call upon; summon, convoke; name; attract; *vi* knock (at a door); ring (a bell); *vr* be named, be called; *naut* veer (wind). **Se llama Pedro,** His name is Peter

llamarada *f,* flame, flash; blaze, flare (of anger, etc.)

llamativo *a* striking, showy; provocative

llamear *vi* to throw out flames, blaze

llana *f,* mason's trowel; plain; surface of a page

llanada *f,* plain

llanamente *adv* frankly, plainly; naturally, simply; candidly, sincerely

llanero (-ra) *n* plain dweller

llaneza *f,* naturalness; candor; familiarity; simplicity (of style)

llano *a* flat, level; smooth, even; shallow (of receptacles); unaffected, homely, natural; plain (of dresses); manifest, evident; easy; straightforward, candid; informal; simple (of style). *m,* plain; level stretch of ground

llanta *f, aut* tire; rim, felloe. **l. de rueda,** wheel, rim

llanto *m,* weeping, flood of tears

llanura *f,* smoothness, evenness, levelness; plain

llar *m,* hearth

llave (de) *f,* key (to); spigot (of), faucet (of), tap (of); spanner, wrench; *elec* switch; clock winder; *mus* key, clef; *arch* keystone; *print* brace; *mech* wrench; lock (of a gun); tuning key; piston (of musical instruments); lock (in wrestling); *fig* key (of a problem or a study). **l. de transmisión,** sender (telegraphy). **l. inglesa,** monkey-wrench, spanner. **l. maestra,** master key, skeleton key. **echar la l.,** to lock. **torcer la l.,** to turn the key

llavero (-ra) *n* keeper of the keys. *m,* key ring. **l. de cárcel,** turnkey

llavín *m,* yale key, latchkey

llegada *f,* arrival, advent

llegar *vi* to arrive; last, endure; reach; achieve a purpose; be sufficient, suffice; amount (to); make; *vt* bring near, draw near; gather; *vr* come near, approach; adhere. **l. a ser,** to become. **l. a un punto muerto,** to reach a deadlock. **l. hasta . . . ,** to stretch as far as . . .

llena *f,* spate, overflow

llenar *vt* to fill; occupy (a post); satisfy, please; fulfill; satiate; pervade; fill up (a form); *vi* be full (of the moon); *vr inf* stuff, overeat; *fig inf* be fed-up

lleno *a* full; replete; abundant; complete. *m,* full moon; *theat* full house; *inf* glut, abundance; perfection. **de l., de l. en l.,** entirely, completely

llenura *f,* abundance, plenty

lleva, llevada *f,* carrying, bearing

llevadero *a* tolerable, bearable

llevar *vt* to carry, transport; charge (a price); yield, produce; carry off, take away; endure, bear; persuade;

guide, take; direct; wear (clothes); carry (a handbag, etc.); introduce, present; gain, achieve; manage (a horse); pass, spend (of time); (*with past part*) have (e.g. **Llevo escrita la carta,** I have written the letter); *math* carry; (*with prep. a*) surpass, excel. **l. a cabo,** to accomplish. **l. a cuestas,** to carry on one's back; support. **l. la correspondencia,** to look after the correspondence. **l. la delantera,** to take the lead. **l. luto,** to be in mourning. **llevarse bien,** to get on well, agree

llorar *vi* to weep, cry; drip; water (eyes); *vt* lament, mourn; bewail one's troubles

lloriquear *vi* to whine, snivel

lloriqueo *m*, whining, sniveling

lloro *m*, weeping, crying; flood of tears

llorón *a* weeping; sniveling, whining. *m*, long plume. **niño llorón,** crybaby

lloroso *a* tearful; grievous, sad; sorrowful

llovedizo *a* leaky; rainy

llover *vi impers irr* to rain; come in abundance (of troubles, etc.); *vr* leak (roofs, etc.). **l. a cántaros,** to rain in torrents, rain cats and dogs. **l. sobre mojado,** to add insult to injury. **como llovido,** unexpectedly. See **mover**

llovido *m*, stowaway

llovizna *f*, drizzle, fine rain

lloviznar *vi* to drizzle

lluvia *f*, rain; rainwater; *fig* shower; rose (of watering can)

lluvioso *a* rainy, showery

lo *def art. neut* the thing, part, fact, what, that which. Used before adjectives, past participles, sometimes before nouns and adverbs (e.g. **Lo barato es caro,** Cheap things are dear (in the long run).) **Lo mío es mío, pero lo tuyo es de ambos,** What's mine is mine, but what is yours belongs to both of us. **Juan siente mucho lo ocurrido,** John is very sorry for what has happened. **a lo lejos,** in the distance). **lo . . . que,** how (e.g. **No sabes lo bueno que es,** You don't know how good he is). *pers pron acc m*, or *neut* him, it; that, it (e.g. **Lo harán mañana,** They will do it tomorrow). Means some, any, one, as substitute for noun already mentioned (e.g. **Carecemos de azúcar; no lo hay,** We are short of sugar; there isn't any). **Lo cortés no quita lo valiente,** One can be courteous and still insistent

loa *f*, praise, eulogy; *theat* prologue; short dramatic piece; *ant*; dramatic eulogy

loable *a* praiseworthy

loador (-ra) *a* eulogizing. *n* eulogist

loar *vt* to praise; commend

lobero *a* wolf; wolfish

lobezno *m*, wolf cub

lobo (-ba) *n* wolf. *m*, (*bot anat*) lobe; *inf* drinking fit. **l. marino,** *zool* seal. *inf* **pillar un l.,** to get drunk

lóbrego *a* murky, dark; dismal; mournful, lugubrious

lobreguez *f*, obscurity, gloom, darkness

lóbulo *m*, lobe

lobuno *a* wolf, wolfish

locación *f*, *law* lease; agreement, contract

local *a* local. *m*, premises; place, spot, scene.

localidad *f*, location; locality; place, spot; seat (in theaters, etc.)

localización *f*, localization, placing; place

localizar *vt* to localize

locamente *adv* insanely, madly; extraordinarily, extremely

loción *f*, lotion

loco (-ca) *a* insane, mad; rash, foolish, crazy; excessive, enormous; amazing; extraordinary; infatuated. *n* lunatic; rash person. *fig inf* **Es un l. de atar,** He's completely crazy!

locomoción *f*, locomotion

locomotor *a* locomotive

locomotora *f*, locomotive

locomóvil *a* and *f*, locomotive

locuacidad *f*, loquacity

locuaz *a* loquacious

locución *f*, style of speech; phrase, idiom; *gram* locution

locuelo (-la) *n* madcap

locura *f*, insanity, lunacy; madness, fury; folly, foolishness

locutor (-ra) *n* (radio) announcer; commentator

locutorio *m*, locutory; phone booth

lodazal, lodazar *m*, muddy place; quagmire

lodo *m*, mud

lodoso *a* muddy

logarítmico *a* logarithmic

logaritmo *m*, logarithm

logia *f*, (Freemason's) lodge

lógica *f*, logic. *inf* **l. parda,** common sense

lógico (-ca) *a* logical. *n* logician

logística *f*, logistics

lograr *vt* to achieve, attain, obtain; enjoy; (*with infin*) succeed in; *vr* succeed in, achieve; reach perfection

logrear *vi* to borrow or lend at interest

logrero (-ra) *n* moneylender; monopolist, profiteer

logro *m*, achievement, attainment; profit, gain; usury, money-lending

loma *f*, knoll, hill

lombarda *f*, red cabbage

Lombardía Lombardy

lombardo (-da) *a* of or from Lombardy. *n* native of Lombardy (Italy). *m*, mortgage bank

lombriz *f*, earthworm, common worm. **l. intestinal,** intestinal worm. **l. solitaria,** tapeworm

lomo *m*, loin, back of a book; ridge between furrows; *pl* ribs; loins

lona *f*, canvas, sailcloth

londinense *a* London. *mf* Londoner

Londres London

longanimidad *f*, longanimity, fortitude

longaniza *f*, *cul* pork sausage

longevidad *f*, longevity

longevo *a* long-lived

longísimo *a sup* **luengo** exceedingly long

longitud *f*, length; longitude. **l. de onda,** *rad* wavelength

lonja *f*, slice, rasher; *com* exchange; market; grocery store; woolen warehouse

lonjista *mf* provision merchant, grocer

lontananza *f*, distance (also *art*). **en l.,** in the distance, far off

loor *m*, praise

loquear *vi* to play the fool; romp

lord *m*, lord; *pl* **lores,** lords

loro *m*, *orn* parrot

los *def art. m pl*, the (e.g. **l. sombreros,** the hats). *pers. pron acc 3rd pers m pl*, them. **Tus cigarrillos no están sobre la mesa; los tengo en mi bolsillo,** Your cigarettes are not on the table; I have them in my pocket. Means some, any, ones, as substitution for noun already stated (e.g. **Los cigarros están en la caja si los hay,** The cigars are in the box, if there are any). Used demonstratively followed by *de* or *que* introducing relative clause, those of; those which, those who; the ones that (who) (e.g. **Estaba leyendo algunos libros de los que tienes en tu cuarto,** I was reading some books from among those which you have in your room)

losa *f*, flagstone; slab; tombstone

lote *m*, lot, portion, share

lotería *f*, lottery; lotto (game); lottery office

lotero (-ra) *n* seller of lottery tickets

loto *m*, lotus; lotus flower or fruit

loza *f*, porcelain, china

lozanía *f*, luxuriance (of vegetation); vigor, lustiness; arrogance

lozano *a* luxuriant, exuberant; vigorous, lusty; arrogant

lubricación *f*, lubrication

lubricador *m*, lubricator

lubricante *a* lubricant

lubricar *vt* to lubricate

lúbrico *a* slippery, smooth; lascivious, lustful

lucera *f*, skylight

Lucerna Lucerne

lucerna *f*, large chandelier; skylight

lucero *m*, evening star; any bright star; white star (on a horse's head); brilliance, radiance; *pl poet* eyes, orbs. **l. del alba,** morning star

lucha *f*, fight; struggle; wrestling match; argument, disagreement. **l. grecorromana,** wrestling. **l. igualada,** close fight. **l. libre,** catch-as-catch-can

luchador (-ra) *n* fighter; struggler

luchar *vi* to fight hand to hand; wrestle; fight; struggle; argue

lucidez *f*, brilliance, shine; lucidity, clarity

lucido *a* splendid, brilliant; sumptuous; fine, elegant

lúcido *a poet* brilliant; lucid; clear

luciente *a* bright, shining

luciérnaga *f*, glowworm

lucimiento *m*, brilliance, luster; success, triumph; elegance; display, ostentation

lucir *vi irr* to shine, scintillate; excel, outshine; be successful; *vt* illuminate; display, show off; show; *vr* dress elegantly; be successful; excel, be brilliant. *Pres. Ind.* **luzco, luces,** etc. *Pres. Subjunc.* **luzca,** etc.

lucrativo *a* lucrative

lucro *m*, gain, profit

lucroso *a* profitable

luctuoso *a* lugubrious, mournful

lucubración *f*, lucubration

ludibrio *m*, mockery, ridicule

luego *adv* immediately; afterward, later; then; soon, presently. *conjunc* therefore. **l. que,** as soon as. **desde l.,** immediately, at once; of course, naturally; in the first place. **hasta l.,** au revoir, good-by for the present

luengo *a* long

lugar *m*, place; spot; village, town, city; region, locality; office, post; passage, text; opportunity, occasion; cause, motive; place on a list; room, space; seat. **l. común,** commonplace. **en l. de,** instead of. **en primer l.,** firstly, in the first place. **hacer l.,** to make room, make way. *law* **No ha l.,** The petition is refused. **tener l.,** to take place; have the time or opportunity (to)

lugarejo *m*, hamlet

lugareño (-ña) *a* peasant, regional. *n* villager, peasant

lugarteniente *m*, lieutenant; substitute, deputy

lúgubre *a* lugubrious, dismal, mournful

luis *m*, louis (French coin)

lujo *m*, luxury; abundance, profusion. **artículos de l.,** luxury goods

lujoso *a* luxurious; abundant, profuse

lujuria *f*, lasciviousness; excess, intemperance

lujuriante *a* luxuriant, abundant, profuse

lujurioso *a* lascivious, voluptuous

lumbago *m*, lumbago

lumbre *f*, fire; light; splendor, lustre; transom window, opening, skylight; *pl* tinderbox

lumbrera *f*, luminary; skylight; dormer window; eminent authority

luminar *m*, luminary (also *fig*)

luminaria *f*, illumination; fairy lamp, small light; lamp burning before the Sacrament in Catholic churches

luminosidad *f*, luminosity

luminoso *a* luminous; bright

luna *f*, moon; mirror; satellite; sheet of plate glass. **l. creciente,** new or rising moon. **l. de miel,** honeymoon. **l. llena,** full moon. **l. menguante,** waning moon. **media l.,** crescent moon

lunado *a* half-moon, crescent

lunar *m*, beauty spot; *fig* stain, blot (on reputation, etc.); blemish, slight imperfection. *a* lunar

lunático (-ca) *a* and *n* lunatic

lunes *m*, Monday

luneta *f*, lens (of eyeglasses), *theat* orchestra stall; (*arch mil*) lunette

lupa *f*, magnifying glass

lupanar *m*, brothel

lupino *a* wolf-like, lupine. *m, bot* lupine

lúpulo *m, bot* hop

lusitano (-na) *a* and *n* Lusitanian

lustrador *m*, polisher. **l. de piso,** floor polisher

lustrar *vt* to lustrate, purify; polish, burnish; roam, journey

lustre *m*, polish, sheen, gloss; glory, luster

lustro *m*, lustrum, period of five years; chandelier

lustroso *a* shining, glossy; brilliant; glorious, noble

luteranismo *m*, Lutheranism

luterano (-na) *a* and *n* Lutheran

luto *m*, mourning; grief, affliction; *pl* mourning draperies. **estar de l.,** to be in mourning

luxación *f, surg* luxation, dislocation

Luxemburgo Luxembourg

luz *f*, light; glow; brightness, brilliance; information, news; *fig* luminary; day, daylight; *pl* culture, learning; windows. **luces de estacionamiento,** parking lights. **a buena l.,** in a good light; in a favorable light; after due consideration. **a primera l.,** at dawn. **dar a l.,** to publish (a book); bring forth (children); reveal. **entre dos luces,** in the dawn light; in the twilight; *inf* tipsy. **media l.,** half-light, twilight

M

maca *f*, bruise or blemish on fruit; defect, flaw; *inf* fraud, swindle

macabro *a* macabre

macadán *m*, macadam

macagua *f, orn* macaw

macanudo *a* (*inf WH*) extraordinary; enormous; robust; fine, excellent

macareno (-na) *n* inhabitant of the Macarena district of Seville. *m, inf* braggart

macarrones *m pl*, macaroni; *naut* stanchions

macarrónico *a* macaronic, recondite, stylized

macarse *vr* to go bad, rot (fruit)

macedón (-ona), macedonio (-ia) *a* and *n* Macedonian

maceración *f*, maceration; steeping, soaking; mortification of the flesh

macerar *vt* to macerate; steep, soak; mortify

macero *m*, mace bearer

maceta *f, dim* small mace; handle, haft (of tools); stone-cutter's hammer; flowerpot

macetero *m*, flowerpot stand

machaca *f*, pestle; pulverizer. *mf inf* bore, tedious person

machacador (-ra) *a* crushing, pounding. *n* beater, crusher, pounder

machacar *vt* to crush, pound; *vi* importune; harp on a subject

machacón *a* tiresome, prolix

machado *m*, hatchet, ax

machetero *m*, one who cuts sugarcane with a machete

machihembrar *vt carp* to dovetail

machina *f*, derrick, crane; pile driver

macho *m*, male; male animal (he-goat, stallion, etc.); male plant; hook (of hook and eye); screw; *met* core; tap (tool); *inf* dunderhead, fool; *arch* buttress. *a* male; stupid, ignorant; vigorous, strong. **m. cabrío,** he-goat

machucadura *f*, **machucamiento** *m*, pounding, crushing; bruising

machucar *vt* to crush, pound; bruise

machucho *a* prudent, sensible; adult, mature

macicez *f*, solidity; massiveness; thickness

macilento *a* thin, lean, emaciated

macillo *m, dim* small mace; hammer (of a piano)
macis *f, cul* mace
macizar *vt* to block up, fill up
macizo *a* massive; compact, solid; *fig* well-founded, unassailable; thick; strong. *m,* solidity, compactness; bulk, volume; flowerbed; solid tire
macrocosmo *m,* macrocosm
mácula *f,* stain, spot; *fig* blot, blemish; *inf* trick, deception; *ast* macula
macuquero *m,* unauthorized worker of abandoned mines
madeja *f,* skein, hank; lock of hair; *inf* dummy, useless person
madera *f,* wood; timber; *inf* kind, sort; *mus* wind instruments. **m. contrachapada,** plywood. **m. de construcción,** timber. **maderas de sierra,** lumber wood. *inf* **ser de mala m.,** to be a ne'er-do-well
maderada *f,* lumber wood
maderaje *m,* woodwork, timber work
maderero *m,* timber merchant; lumberjack; carpenter
maderia *f,* timber yard
madero *m,* wooden beam; log, piece of lumber; ship, vessel; *inf* blockhead or insensible person
madrastra *f,* stepmother; anything unpleasant
madraza *f, inf* overindulgent mother
madre *f,* mother; matron; cause, genesis; *inf* dame, mother; riverbed; dam; womb; main sewer; chief irrigation channel. **m. de familia,** mother; housewife. **m. de leche,** wet nurse. **m. política,** mother-in-law; stepmother. *inf* **sacar de m. (a),** to provoke, irritate (a person)
madreperla *f,* mother-of-pearl
madrépora *f,* white coral, madrepore
madreselva *f,* honeysuckle
madrigado *a* twice-married (women); *inf* experienced, wide-awake
madrigal *m,* madrigal
madriguera *f,* rabbit warren; burrow, den, hole, lair; haunt of thieves, etc.
madrileño (-ña) *a* and *n* Madrilenian
madrina *f,* godmother; matron of honor or bridesmaid; sponsor; patroness; prop; stanchion
madroncillo *m,* strawberry
madroño *m,* strawberry tree; tuft, spot; tassel
madrugada *f,* dawn, daybreak; early rising. **de m.,** at dawn
madrugador (-ra) *a* early rising. *n* early riser
madrugar *vi* to get up early; gain time; anticipate, be beforehand
maduración *f,* ripening; mellowing; preparation; ripeness; maturity
madurador *a* ripening; maturing
maduramente *adv* maturely; sensibly
madurar *vt* to ripen; mature; think out; *vi* ripen; grow mature, learn wisdom
madurez *f,* ripeness; maturity; mellowness; wisdom
maduro *a* ripe; mature; mellow; adult; wise
maestra *f,* schoolmistress; teacher, instructor; queen bee; guide, model
maestral *a* referring to the grand master of one of the Spanish military orders; teaching, pedagogic. *m,* mistral (wind); cell of a queen bee
maestrear *vt* to direct, control, manage; prune vines; *vi inf* bully, domineer
maestría *f,* mastery, skill; *univ* master's degree
maestril *m,* queen cell (of bees)
maestro *a* masterly; excellent; chief, main; midship. *m,* master, expert; teacher; instructor; master craftsman; *univ* master; *mus* composer; *naut* mainmast. **m. de armas,** fencing master. **m. de capilla,** *ecc* choirmaster. **m. de obras,** building contractor; master builder. **El ejercicio hace m.,** Practice makes perfect
Magallanes, Estrecho de Straits of Magellan
magdalena *f,* madeleine (cake); magdalen, penitent. *inf* **estar hecha una M.,** to be inconsolable
magia *f,* magic

mágica *f,* magic; enchantress, sorceress
mágico *a* magic; marvelous, wonderful. *m,* magician; enchanter, wizard
magín *m, inf* imagination; head, mind
magisterio *m,* teaching profession; teaching diploma; teaching post; pedantry, pompousness. **ejercer su m. en,** to be employed as a teacher in
magistrado *m,* magistrate; magistracy
magistral *a* magistral; authoritative, magisterial; pedantic, pompous
magistratura *f,* magistracy
magnanimidad *f,* magnanimity; generosity, liberality
magnánimo *a* magnanimous, generous, noble
magnate *m,* magnate
magnesia *f,* magnesia
magnesio *m,* magnesium
magnético *a* magnetic
magnetismo *m,* magnetism
magnetizar *vt* to magnetize; mesmerize
magneto *m,* magneto
magnificar *vt* to magnify, enlarge; praise, extol
magnificencia *f,* magnificence, pomp, splendor
magnífico *a* magnificent; splendid, wonderful, fine; excellent
magnitud *f,* magnitude; quantity; importance
magno *a* great; famous. **Alejandro M.,** Alexander the Great
magnolia *f,* magnolia
mago *m,* magician; *pl* magi
magra *f,* rasher (of bacon, ham)
magrez, magrura *f,* leanness; scragginess
magro *a* lean; scraggy. *m, inf* lean pork
magulladura *f,* **magullamiento** *m,* bruising; bruise, contusion
magullar *vt* to bruise
mahometano (-na) *a* and *n* Muslim
mahometismo *m,* Islam
mahonesa *f,* mayonnaise
maíz *m,* corn
maizal *m,* cornfield
maja *f,* belle
majada *f,* sheepfold; dung
majadería *f,* impertinence, insolence
majadero *a* persistent, tedious. *m,* bobbin (for lace making); pestle. *n* fool, bore
majador *m,* pestle
majar *vt* to pound, crush; *inf* importune, annoy
majestad *f,* majesty (title); dignity; stateliness
majestuosidad *f,* majesty; dignity
majestuoso *a* majestic; stately; dignified
majo *a* arrogant, aggressive; gaudily attired, smart; dashing, handsome; attractive, pretty; elegant, well-dressed. *m,* beau, gallant, man about town
majuelo *m,* new vine; species of white hawthorn
mal *a abb* **malo.** Used only before *m sing* nouns (e.g. **un m. cuarto de hora,** a bad quarter of an hour). *m,* evil; damage; harm; misfortune; illness; disease; trouble (e.g. **El m. es,** The trouble is). **m. de altura,** air sickness. **m. de ojo,** evil eye. **m. de piedra,** lithiasis, stone. **m. francés,** syphilis. **el m. menor,** the lesser of two evils. *interj* **¡M. haya!** A curse upon! **echar a m.,** to scorn (things); waste, squander. **llevar a m. (una cosa),** to take (a thing) badly, complain. **No hay m. que por bien no venga,** It's an ill wind that blows no one any good, Every cloud has a silver lining. **parar en m.,** to come to a bad end
mal *adv* badly; unfavorably; wrongly; wickedly; with difficulty; scarcely, barely. **m. que bien,** willingly or unwillingly; rightly or wrongly. **de m. en peor,** from bad to worse
mala *f,* mail, post. **m. real,** royal mail
malabarista *mf* juggler
malaconsejado *a* ill-advised; imprudent
malacostumbrado *a* badly trained, spoiled; having bad habits
malagueña *f,* popular song of lament

malagueño *a* of or from Málaga

malandante *a* evildoing; unfortunate, miserable; poor

malandanza *f,* evildoing; misfortune, misery; poverty

malandrín *a* wicked, ill-disposed. *m,* scoundrel, miscreant

malaquita *f,* malachite

malaria *f,* malaria

malaventura *f,* misfortune, adversity, bad luck

malaventurado *a* unfortunate, unlucky

malayo (-ya) *a* Malay. *n* Malayan

malbaratador (-ra) *a* wasteful, spendthrift. *n* squanderer, spendthrift

malbaratar *vt* to squander, waste; sell at a loss

malcasado *a* adulterous, unfaithful

malcasar(se) *vt* and *vr* to marry badly

malcomido *a* underfed

malcontento (-ta) *a* dissatisfied, discontented; rebellious. *n* malcontent, rebel

malcriado *a* badly brought up; ill-bred; spoiled, peevish

maldad *f,* badness; depravity, wickedness

maldecidor (-ra) *a* slanderous. *n* scandalmonger, slanderer

maldecir *vt irr* to curse; *vt* and *vi* slander, backbite. See **decir**

maldiciente *a* defamatory, slanderous; cursing, reviling. *m,* slanderer; curser

maldición *f,* malediction; curse, imprecation

maldispuesto *a* indisposed, ill; reluctant

maldita *f, inf* tongue. *inf* **soltar la m.,** to say too much, go too far

maldito *a* accursed; wicked; damned; poor (of quality); *inf* not a . . .

maleabilidad *f,* malleability, flexibility

maleable *a* malleable, flexible

maleante *a* rascally, villainous. *mf* evildoer

malecón *m,* breakwater

maledicencia *f,* slander, abuse, backbiting; cursing

maleficencia *f,* wrongdoing

maleficio *m,* (magic) curse; spell; charm

maléfico *a* malefic, harmful. *m,* sorcerer

malestar *m,* indisposition, slight illness; discomfort

maleta *f,* suitcase, valise, grip; *m, inf* clumsy matador; duffer (at games, etc.). **hacer la m.,** to pack a suitcase; *inf* prepare for a journey, get ready to leave

maletero *m,* seller or maker of traveling bags; porter

maletín *m,* small suitcase or valise

malevolencia *f,* malevolence, hatred, malice

malévolo *a* malevolent, malicious

maleza *f,* weeds; undergrowth; thicket

malgastador (-ra) *a* thriftless, wasteful. *n* squanderer

malgastar *vt* to waste (time); squander, throw away (money)

malhablado *a* foul-tongued, indecent

malhadado *a* ill-fated, unhappy

malhecho *a* deformed, twisted (persons). *m,* evil deed, wrongdoing

malhechor (-ra) *n* malefactor; evildoer

malhumorado *a* ill-humored, bad-tempered

malicia *f,* wickedness, evil; malice, maliciousness; acuteness, subtlety, shrewdness; craftiness, guile; *inf* suspicion

maliciar *vt* to suspect; spoil, damage; hurt, harm

malicioso *a* malicious; vindictive; wicked; shrewd, clever; *inf* suspicious; artful

malignidad *f,* malignancy, spite, ill will

maligno *a* malignant, spiteful; wicked; *med* malignant

malintencionado *a* ill-intentioned, badly disposed

malla *f,* mesh (of a net); coat of mail; *pl theat* tights. **m. de alambre,** wire netting. **cota de m.,** coat of mail

Mallorca Majorca

mallorquín (-ina) *a* and *n* Majorcan. *m,* Majorcan (variety of Catalan or Spanish)

malmandado *a* disobedient; reluctant, unwilling

malmaridada *f,* adultress, faithless wife

malo *a* bad; wicked; evil; injurious; harmful; illicit; licentious; ill; difficult; troublesome, annoying; *inf* mischievous; knavish; rotten, decaying. *interj* **¡M.!** That's bad!; You shouldn't have done that!; That's a bad sign! **de malas,** unluckily, unhappily. **el M.,** the Evil One, the Devil. **estar m.,** to be ill. **Lo m. es,** The trouble is, The worst of it is. **por malas o por buenas,** willynilly, willingly or unwillingly. **ser m.,** to be wicked; be evil; behave badly (children)

malograr *vt* to lose (time); waste, throw away (opportunities); *vr* fall through, fail; wither, fade; die early, come to an untimely end

malogro *m,* loss, waste (time, opportunity); frustration; decline, fading; untimely death

malparar *vt* to ill-treat; damage. **quedar malparado,** to get the worst of

malparir *vt med* to miscarry

malparto *m,* miscarriage; abortion

malquerencia *f,* ill will, aversion, dislike

malquistar *vt* to stir up trouble; make unpopular; estrange; *vr* make oneself disliked

malquisto *a* unpopular, disliked

malsano *a* unhealthy

malta *m,* malt

maltés (-esa) *a* and *n* Maltese

maltraer *vt irr* to ill-treat; insult. See **traer**

maltratamiento *m,* abuse, ill usage; damage, deterioration

maltratar *vt* to ill-treat; abuse, insult; misuse, spoil, damage

maltrato *m,* maltreatment; misuse

maltrecho *a* ill-treated, bruised; abused, insulted; damaged

maltusianismo *m,* Malthusianism

maltusiano *a* Malthusian

Malucas, las the Moluccas

malucho *a inf* off-color, below par, not well

malva *f,* mallow. **m. real, m. rosa,** or **m. loca,** hollyhock. **ser como una m.,** *fig inf* to be a clinging vine

malvado *a* evil, malevolent, fiendish. *n* villain, fiend

malvasía *f, bot* malvasia; malmsey (wine)

malvavisco *m, bot* marshmallow

malvender *vt* to sell at a loss

malversación *f,* malversation, maladministration; misappropriation (of funds)

malversador (-ra) *n* bad or corrupt administrator

malversar *vt* to misappropriate (funds)

mama *f, inf* mamma, mommy; breast; udder

mamá *f,* mamma

mamar *vt* to suck (the breast); *inf* wolf, swallow; learn from an early age; enjoy, obtain unfairly; *vr* get drunk

mamario *a* mammary

mamarracho *m, inf* scarecrow, dummy; anything grotesque looking

mameluco *m,* mameluke; *inf* ninny, fool

mamífero *a* mammalian. *m,* mammal

mamotreto *m,* notebook, memorandum; *inf* large book or bulky file of papers

mampara *f,* folding screen; screen; partition

mamparo *m,* bulkhead

mampostería *f,* masonry, stonemasonry

mampostero *m,* stonemason

mamut *m,* mammoth

maná *m,* manna

manada *f,* handful; herd, flock; group, drove, crowd

manadero *m,* herdsman, drover; spring, stream

manantial *m,* fountain, source, spring; head (of a river)

manar *vi* to flow, stream; be plentiful

manatí *m,* sea cow, manatee

mancar *vt* to injure, maim; *vi* grow calm (elements)

manceba *f,* concubine; girl

mancebía *f,* brothel; youth, young days

mancebo *m,* youth, stripling; bachelor; shop assistant

mancha *f,* spot, smear, stain; blotch; plot of ground; patch of vegetation; stigma, disgrace

manchar *vt* to stain; smear; spot; speckle; disgrace; tarnish

manchego (-ga) *a* and *n* of or from La Mancha (Spain)

manchuriano (-na) *a* and *n* Manchurian

mancilla *f*, stain; slur

mancillar *vt* to stain; *fig* smirch

manco (-ca) *a* maimed, disabled; one-handed; one-armed; armless; handless; incomplete, faulty. *n* disabled person

mancomunidad *f*, association, society; community, union; commonwealth; regional legislative assembly

manda *f*, offer, suggestion, proposition; legacy

mandadero (-ra) *n* convent or prison messenger; errand boy (girl)

mandado *m*, order, command; errand

mandamiento *m*, order, command; *ecc* commandment; *law* writ; *pl inf* one's five fingers

mandar *vt* to order, command; bequeath, will; send; control, drive; promise, offer; order (e.g. **Mandó hacerse un traje,** He ordered a suit to be made); *vr* walk unaided (convalescents, etc.); lead into one another (rooms, etc.); **¿Quién manda aquí?** Who is in charge here?

mandarín *m*, mandarin; *inf* bureaucrat

mandarina *f*, mandarin (classical Chinese); mandarin orange

mandatario *m*, mandatary

mandato *m*, mandate; command; *ecc* maundy. *pol* mandate. **cuarto m.,** fourth term (of President, Governor, etc.)

mandíbula *f*, jaw; jawbone, mandible

mandil *m*, long leather apron; apron; Freemason's apron; close-meshed fishing net

mandilón *m*, *inf* coward, nincompoop

mandioca *f*, manioc, cassava; tapioca

mando *m*, authority, power; (*mil nav*) command; *eng* regulation; controls (of a machine, etc.). **m. a distancia,** remote control. *aer* **m. de dos pilotos,** dual-controlled. **mandos gemelos,** dual control. **al m. de,** under the command of; under the direction of

mandolín *m*. **mandolina** *f*, mandolin

mandón *a* domineering, bossy

mandrágora *f*, mandrake

mandril *m*, *mech* mandrel, chuck; *zool* mandrill

manear *vt* to hobble (a cow, etc.); manage, control

manecilla *f*, *dim* little hand; hand of a clock; *print* fist

manejable *a* manageable, controllable

manejar *vt* to handle; use, wield; control; manage, direct; ride (horses); *vr* manage to move around (after an accident, illness)

manejo *m*, handling; use, wielding; control; management, direction; horsemanship; intrigue

maneota *f*, hobble, shackle

manera *f*, manner, way, means; behavior, style (gen. *pl*); class (of people); *art* style, manner. **a la m. de,** like, in the style of. **de esa m.,** in that way; according to that, in that case. **de m. que,** so that. **en gran m.,** to a great extent. **sobre m.,** exceedingly

manga *f*, sleeve; bag; grip; handle; pipe (of a hose); strainer; waterspout; body of troops; beam, breadth of a ship; *pl* profits. **m. de viento,** whirlwind. **echar de m. a,** to make use of a person. *inf* **estar de m.,** to be in league. **tener m. ancha,** to be broad-minded. *fig inf* **traer (una cosa) en la m.,** to have (something) up one's sleeve

mangana *f*, lasso

manganeso *m*, manganese

manganilla *f*, sleight of hand; hoax, trick

mangle *m*, mangrove tree

mango *m*, handle, haft, stock; mango. **m. de cuchillo,** knife handle

mangonear *vi inf* to loaf, roam about; interfere, meddle

mangonero *a inf* meddlesome

mangosta *f*, mongoose

mangote *m*, *inf* long, wide sleeve; black oversleeve

manguera *f*, hose; sleeve, tube; airshaft; waterspout

manguero *m*, fireman; hoseman

manguito *m*, muff; black oversleeve; wristlet, cuff; *mech* bush, sleeve

manía *f*, mania, obsession; whim, fancy

maníaco (-ca) *a* maniacal; capricious, extravagant. *n* maniac

maniatar *vt* to handcuff; hobble (a cow, etc.)

maniático (-ca) *a* maniacal; capricious; faddy, fussy. *n* crank

manicomio *m*, insane asylum, mental hospital

manicura *f*, manicure

manicuro (-ra) *n* manicurist

manida *f*, lair, den; dwelling, habitation

manifestación *f*, declaration, statement; exhibition; demonstration; *ecc* exposition (of the Blessed Sacrament)

manifestante *mf* demonstrator

manifestar *vt irr* to declare, make known, state; exhibit, show; *ecc* to expose (the Blessed Sacrament). See **acertar**

manifiesto *a* obvious, evident. *m*, manifesto; *naut* manifest; *ecc* exposition of the Blessed Sacrament. **poner de m.,** to show; make public; reveal

manigua *f*, thicket, jungle (in Cuba)

manija *f*, handle, stock, haft; hand lever; clamp; tether (for horses, etc.)

manileño (ña) *a* and *n* Manilan

manilla *f*, bracelet; handcuff, manacle

maniobra *f*, operation, process; *mil* maneuver; intrigue; tackle, gear; handling, management; *naut* working of a ship; *pl* shunting (trains)

maniobrar *vi mil* to maneuver; *naut* handle, work (ships)

manipulación *f*, handling; manipulation; control, management

manipulador *a* manipulative. *m*, sending key (telegraphy)

manipular *vt* to handle; manipulate; manage, direct

manípulo *m*, maniple

maniqueo (-ea) *a* Manichean *n* Manichee

maniquete *m*, black lace mitten

maniquí *m*, mannequin; dummy; *inf* puppet, weak person

manirroto (-ta) *a* wasteful, extravagant. *n* spendthrift

manivela *f*, *mech* crank, lever

manjar *m*, dish, food; pastime, recreation, pleasure. **m. blanco,** blancmange

mano *f*, hand; coat, coating; quire (of paper); front paw (animals); elephant's trunk; side, hand; hand (of a clock); game (of cards, etc.); lead (at cards); way, means; ability; power; protection, favor; compassion; aid, help; scolding; *mus* scale; pestle; workers. *inf* editing, correction of a literary work (gen. by a person more skilled than the author). **m. de mortero,** pestle. **m. de obra,** (manual) labor. **manos muertas,** *law* mortmain. **m. sobre m.,** with folded hands; lazily, indolently. **a la m.,** at hand, nearby; within one's grasp. **a manos llenas,** in abundance, abundantly. **bajo m.,** in an underhand manner, secretly. **buenas manos,** cleverness, ability; dexterity. **de primera m.,** firsthand, new. **estar dejado de la m. de Dios,** to be very unlucky; be very foolish. **poner la m. en,** to ill-treat; slap, buffet. **Si a m. viene . . . ,** If by chance . . . **tender la m.,** to put out one's hand, shake hands. **traer entre manos,** to have on hand, be engaged in

manojo *m*, bunch, handful. **a manojos,** in handfuls; plentifully, in abundance

manolo (-la) *n* inhabitant of low quarters of Madrid noted for pride, gaiety, quarrelsomeness, and wit

manopla *f*, gauntlet

manoseado *a* hackneyed

manosear *vt* to handle; paw, touch repeatedly; finger

manoseo *m*, handling; fingering; *inf* pawing, feeling

manotada *f*, slap, cuff

manotear *vt* to slap, cuff; *vi* gesticulate, gesture with the hands

manoteo *m*, gesticulation with the hands

manquedad *f*, disablement of hand or arm; lack of one of these; defect; incompleteness

mansalva (a) *adv* without danger

mansedumbre *f*, meekness; kindness; gentleness

mansión *f*, stay, visit; dwelling, abode; mansion

manso *a* soft, gentle; meek, mild; tame; peaceable, amiable; calm

manta *f*, blanket; horse blanket; traveling rug; *inf* hiding, thrashing. **m. de viaje,** traveling rug. *inf* **a m. de Dios,** in abundance. **dar una m.,** to toss in a blanket. *fig inf* **tirar de la m.,** to let the cat out of the bag

manteamiento *m*, tossing in a blanket

mantear *vt* to toss in a blanket

manteca *f*, lard; cooking fat; grease; *Argentina* butter. **como m.,** as mild as milk, as soft as butter

mantecada *f*, buttered toast

mantecado *m*, French ice cream

mantecoso *a* greasy

mantel *m*, tablecloth; altar cloth

mantelería *f*, table linen

mantelete *m*, (*ecc mil*) mantlet

mantener *vt irr* to maintain; keep, feed; support; continue, persevere with; uphold, affirm; keep up; *vr* support oneself; remain in a place; (*with en*) continue to uphold (views, etc.), persevere in. **mantenerse firme,** *fig* to stand one's ground. See **tener**

mantenimiento *m*, maintenance; support; sustenance, nourishment; affirmation; upkeep; livelihood

manteo *m*, tossing in a blanket; long cloak

mantequera *f*, churn; dairymaid; butter dish

mantequero *m*, dairyman; butter dish

mantequilla *f*, butter

mantero *m*, blanket seller or maker

mantilla *f*, mantilla; saddlecloth. *pl* baby's long clothes. **estar en mantillas,** to be in swaddling clothes; *fig* be in early infancy

manto *m*, cloak, cover, disguise; *zool* mantle; *min* layer

mantón *m*, shawl. **m. de Manila,** Manila shawl

mantuano (-na) *a* and *n* Mantuan

manuable *a* easy to handle or use, handy

manual *a* manual; handy, easy to use; docile, peaceable. *m*, manual, textbook; *ecc* book of ritual; notebook

manubrio *m*, handle, crank

manuela *f*, open carriage (Madrid)

manufactura *f*, manufacture; manufactured article; factory

manufacturar *vt* to manufacture

manufacturero *a* manufacturing

manumisión *f*, freeing (of slaves), manumission

manumitir *vt law* to free, enfranchise (slaves)

manuscrito *a* and *m*, manuscript

manutención *f*, maintenance; upkeep; protection

manzana *f*, apple; block (of houses); city square; Adam's apple

manzanal *m*, apple orchard; apple tree

manzanar *m*, apple orchard

manzanilla *f*, white sherry wine; *bot* chamomile; chamomile tea; knob, ball (on furniture); pad (on an animal's foot)

manzano *m*, apple tree

maña *f*, skill, dexterity; craftiness, guile; vice, bad habit (gen. *pl*). **darse m. para,** to contrive to

mañana *f*, morning; tomorrow. *m*, future, tomorrow. *adv* tomorrow; in time to come; soon. **¡M.!** Tomorrow! Another day! Not now! (generally to beggars). **de m.,** early in the morning. **muy de m.,** very early in the morning. **pasado m.,** the day after tomorrow

mañanica *f*, early morning

mañear *vt* to arrange cleverly; *vi* behave shrewdly

mañero *a* shrewd, clever; easily worked; handy

mañoso *a* clever, skillful; crafty; vicious, with bad habits

mañuela *f*, low guile

mapa *m*, map; card. **m. en relieve,** relief map. **m. del estado mayor,** ordnance map. *inf* **no estar en el m.,** to be off the map; be most unusual (of things)

mapache *m*, raccoon

mapamundi *m*, map of the world

maqueta *f*. (*art arch*) model

maquiavélico *a* Machiavellian

maquiavelismo *m*, Machiavellism

maquillaje *m*, makeup, cosmetics; making up (of the face)

maquillar (se) *vt* and *vr* to make up (the face, etc.)

máquina *f*, machine, mechanism; engine; apparatus; plan, scheme; machine, puppet; *inf* mansion, palace; plenty; locomotive; fantasy, product of the imagination. **m. de vapor,** steam engine. **m. de arrastre,** traction engine; tractor. **m. de coser,** sewing machine. **m. de escribir,** typewriter. **m. fotográfica,** camera. **m. de impresionar,** movie camera. **m. de imprimir,** printing machine. **m. herramienta,** machine tool. **m. neumática,** air pump

maquinación *f*, intrigue, machination

maquinador (-ra) *n* intriguer, schemer

maquinal *a* mechanical

maquinar *vt* to intrigue, scheme, plot

maquinaria *f*, machinery; applied mechanics; mechanism

maquinista *mf* driver, enginer; mechanic; machinist; locomotive driver

mar *mf* sea; great many, abundance. **m. bonanza** *or* **m. en calma,** calm sea. **m. de fondo** *or* **m. de leva,** swell. **alta m.,** high seas. **a mares,** plentifully. **arar en el m.,** to labor in vain. *naut* **hacerse a la m.,** to put out to sea. **la m. de historias,** a great number of stories

Mar Caspio Caspian Sea

maraña *f*, undergrowth; tangle; *fig* difficult position; intrigue; silk waste

marasmo *m*, *med* marasmus, atrophy; inactivity, paralysis

maravedí *m*, maravedi (old Spanish coin of fluctuating value)

maravilla *f*, marvel, wonder; admiration; amazement; marigold. **a m.,** wonderfully. **a las mil maravillas,** to perfection, excellently. **por m.,** by chance; occasionally

maravillar *vt* to amaze, cause admiration; *vr* (*with de*) marvel at, admire; be amazed by

maravilloso *a* marvelous, wonderful

marbete *m*, label, tag; edge, border

marca *f*, mark, sign; brand; frontier zone, border country; standard, norm (of size); make, brand; measuring rule; *sport* record. **m. de fábrica,** brand, trademark. **m. de ley,** hallmark. **m. registrada,** registered name. **de m.,** excellent, of excellent quality

marcado *a* marked; pronounced; strong (of accents)

marcador *a* marking. *m*, marker; scoreboard; bookmark

marcar *vt* to mark; brand; embroider initials on linen; tell the time (watches); show the amount (cash register, etc.); dial (telephone); *sport* score (a goal); notice, observe; set aside, earmark; *vr naut* check the course. **m. el compás** to beat time

marcha *f*, departure; running, working; *mil* march; speed (of trains, ships, etc.); *mus* march; progress, course (of events). **m. atrás,** backing, reversing. **m. de ensayo,** trial run. **m. forzada,** *mil* forced march. **a largas marchas,** with all speed. **a toda m.,** at top speed; full speed ahead; by forced marches; *mil* **batir la m.,** to strike up a march. **en m.,** underway; working; in operation

marchamero *m*, customs official who checks and marks goods

marchamo *m*, customs mark on checked goods

marchar *vi* to run; work; function; go; leave, depart; progress, proceed; *mil* march; go (clocks); *vr* leave, go away

marchitable *a* perishable, fragile

marchitamiento *m*, withering

marchitar *vt* to wither, fade; blight, spoil; weaken; *vr* wither; be blighted

marchitez *f*, witheredness; fadedness

marchito *a* withered; faded; blighted, frustrated

marcial *a* martial; courageous, militant
marcialidad *f,* war-like spirit, militancy
marciano *a* Martian
marco *m,* mark (German coin); boundary mark; frame (of a picture, etc.). **m. de ventana,** window frame
Mar de las Indias Indian Ocean
Mar del Norte North Sea
marea *f,* tide; strand, water's edge; light breeze; drizzle; dew; street dirt. **m. creciente,** flood tide. **m. menguante,** ebb tide. **m. muerta,** neap tide
mareaje *m,* seamanship; ship's course
marear *vt* to navigate; sell; sell publicly; *inf* annoy; *vr* be seasick; feel faint; feel giddy; be damaged at sea (goods)
marejada *f,* surge, swell; high sea; tidal wave; commotion, uproar
mareo *m,* seasickness; nausea, dizziness; *inf* irritation, tediousness
mareta *f,* movement of the waves; sound, noise (of a crowd)
marfil *m,* ivory
marfileño *a* ivory; ivory-like
marfuz *a* spurned, rejected; deceitful
marga *f,* loam, marl
margarina *f,* margarine
margarita *f,* pearl; marguerite, oxeye daisy; daisy; periwinkle
margen *mf* edge, fringe, border, verge; margin (of a book); opportunity; marginal note. **dar m. para,** to provide an opportunity for; give rise to
marginal *a* marginal
margoso *a* loamy, marly
marica *f,* magpie. *m,* (*offensive*) homosexual; milksop
maricón *m,* (*offensive*) homosexual
maridable *a* marital, matrimonial
maridaje *m,* conjugal union and harmony; intimate relationship (between things)
maridar *vi* to get married; mate, live as husband and wife; *vt* unite, link, join together
marido *m,* husband
marihuana *f,* marijuana
marimacho *m, inf* mannish woman
marina *f,* coast, seashore; *art* seascape; seamanship; navy, fleet. **m. de guerra,** navy. **m. mercante,** merchant navy
marinera *f,* sailor's blouse
marinería *f,* profession of a sailor; seamanship; crew of a ship; sailors (as a class)
marinero *m,* sailor, seaman. **m. de agua dulce,** freshwater sailor (a novice). **m. práctico,** able seaman. **a la marinera,** in a seaman-like fashion
marinesco *a* seamanly
marino *a* marine, sea; seafaring; shipping. *m,* sailor, mariner
marioneta *f,* marionette, puppet
mariposa *f,* butterfly; night-light
mariposear *vi* to flutter, flit, fly about; flirt, be fickle; follow about, dance attendance on
mariquita *f, ent* ladybird; parakeet.
marisabidilla *f, inf* blue-stocking, know-it-all
mariscal *m, mil* marshal; field marshal; blacksmith
marisco *m,* shellfish
marisma *f,* bog, morass, swamp
marital *a* marital
marítimo *a* maritime, sea
marjal *m,* marshland, fen
marmita *f,* stewpot; copper, boiler
marmitón *m,* kitchen boy, scullion
mármol *m,* marble; work executed in marble
marmolería *f,* marble works; work executed in marble
marmolista *mf* marble cutter; dealer in marble
marmóreo *a* marble; *poet* marmoreal
marmota *f, zool* marmot; sleepyhead, dormouse
Mar Muerto Dead Sea
maroma *f,* rope, hawser
marqués *m,* marquis
marquesa *f,* marchioness

marquesina *f,* marquee
marquetería *f,* marquetry
marrana *f,* sow; *inf* slattern, slut
marrano *m,* pig, hog; Marrano
marras (de) *adv* long ago, in the dim past
marrasquino *m,* maraschino liqueur
marro *m,* tick, tag (game)
Mar Rojo Red Sea
marrón *a* maroon; brown. *m,* brown color; maroon color; quoit
marroquí *a* and *mf* Moroccan. *m,* Morocco leather
marroquín (-ina), marrueco (-ca) *a* and *n* Moroccan
Marruecos Morocco
marrullería *f,* flattery, cajolery
marrullero (-ra) *a* wheedling, flattering. *n* wheedler, cajoler
Marsella Marseilles
marsellés (-esa) *a* and *n* of or from Marseilles. *f.* **la Marsellesa,** the Marseillaise
marsopa *f,* porpoise
marta *f,* sable; marten
Marte *m,* Mars
martes *m,* Tuesday. **m. de carnaval,** mardi gras
martillar *vt* to hammer; oppress
martillazo *m,* hammer blow
martilleo *m,* hammering; noise of the hammer; clink, clatter
martillo *m,* hammer; oppressor, tyrant; auction rooms. **a m.,** by hammering. **de m.,** wrought (of metals)
martín pescador *m,* kingfisher
martinete *m,* hammer (of a pianoforte); pile driver; drop hammer. **m. de báscula,** tilt hammer
Martinica Martinique
mártir *mf* martyr
martirio *m,* martyrdom
martirizar *vt* to martyr; torture, torment, martyrize; tease, annoy
martirologio *m,* martyrology
marxismo *m,* Marxism
marxista *a* and *mf* Marxist
marzo *m,* March
mas *conjunc* but; yet
más *adv comp* more; in addition, besides; rather, preferably. *math* plus. **el (la,** etc.**) más,** *adv sup* the most, etc. **m. bien,** more; rather; preferably. **m. que,** only; but; more than; although, even if. **a lo m.,** at the most; at the worst. **a m.,** besides, in addition. **de m.,** superfluous, unnecessary, unwanted. **no ... m. que,** only. **por m. que,** however; even if. **sin m. ni m.,** without further ado. **M. vale un mal arreglo que un buen pleito,** A bad peace is better than a good war
masa *f,* mass; dough; whole, aggregate; majority (of people); mortar. **en la m. de la sangre,** *fig* in the blood, in a person's nature
masada *f,* farmhouse and stock
masadero *m,* farmer; farm laborer
masaje *m,* massage
masajista *mf* masseur; masseuse
mascadura *f,* chewing
mascar *vt* to chew; masticate; *inf* mumble, mutter
máscara *f,* mask; fancy dress; pretext, excuse. *mf* masquerader, reveler; *pl* masquerade. **m. para gases,** gas mask
mascarada *f,* masquerade; company of revelers
mascarero (-ra) *n* theatrical costumer, fancy-dress dealer
mascarilla *f,* death mask
mascarón *m,* large mask; *arch* gargoyle. **m. de proa,** *naut* figurehead
mascota *f,* mascot
masculinidad *f,* masculinity
masculino *a* masculine; male; manly, vigorous
mascullar *vt inf* to chew; mutter, mumble
masera *f,* kneading bowl; cloth for covering dough
masilla *f,* mastic, putty
masón (-ona) *n* Freemason

masonería *f,* freemasonry
masónico *a* masonic
masoquismo *m,* masochism
mastelero *m, naut* topmast
masticación *f,* mastication
masticar *vt* to masticate, eat; *inf* chew upon, consider
masticatorio *a* masticatory
mástil *m, naut* mast; upright, stanchion; pole (of a tent); stem, trunk; neck (of a guitar, etc.)
mastín *m,* mastiff
mastodonte *m,* mastodon
mastoides *a* mastoid
mastuerzo *m,* watercress; fool, blockhead
masturbación *f,* masturbation
masturbarse *vr* to masturbate
mata *f,* plant, shrub; stalk, sprig; grove, copse. **m. de pelo,** mat of hair
matacandelas *m,* candle snuffer
matachín *m,* mummer; butcher; *inf* swashbuckler
matadero *m,* slaughterhouse, abattoir
matadura *f,* sore (on animals)
matafuego *m,* fire extinguisher; fireman
matalotaje *m,* ship's supplies, stores; *inf* hodgepodge
matamoros *a* swashbuckling, swaggering
matamoscas *m,* fly swatter
matanza *f,* killing, massacre, slaughter; butchery (animals); *inf* persistence, determination
matar *vt* to kill; quench (thirst); put out (fire, light); slake (lime); tarnish (metal); bevel (corners, etc.); pester, importune; suppress; compel; *art* tone down; *vr* kill oneself; be disappointed, grieve; overwork. **estar a m.,** to be at daggers drawn. **matarse por,** to try hard to; work hard for
matasanos *m, inf* quack (doctor); bad doctor
matasellos *m,* cancellation, postmark
mate *a* matte, unpolished, dull. *m,* checkmate (chess); maté, Paraguayan tea; gourd; vessel made from gourd, coconut, etc.
maté *m,* maté, Paraguayan tea
matemáticas *f pl,* mathematics. **m. prácticas,** applied mathematics. **m. teóricas,** pure mathematics
matemático *a* mathematical; exact. *m,* mathematician
materia *f,* matter; theme, subject matter; subject (of study); matter, stuff, substance; pus, matter; question, subject; reason, occasion. **m. colorante,** dye. **materias plásticas,** plastics. **materias primas,** raw materials. **en m. de,** concerning; in the matter of
material *a* material; dull, stupid, limited. *m,* material; ingredient; plant, factory; equipment. **m. móvil ferroviario,** rolling stock (railroads)
materialidad *f,* materiality; external appearance (of things)
materialismo *m,* materialism
materialista *a* materialistic. *mf* materialist
materializar *vt* to materialize; *vr* materialize; grow materialistic, grow less spiritual
maternidad *f,* maternity, motherhood
materno *a* maternal
matiz *m,* combination of colors; tone, hue; shade (of meaning, etc.)
matizar *vt* to combine, harmonize (colors); tint, shade; tinge (words, etc.)
matojo *m,* shrub, bush
matorral *m,* thicket, bush, undergrowth
matraca *f,* rattle; *inf* scolding, dressing-down; insistence, importunity
matraquear *vi* to make a noise with a rattle; *inf* scold
matriarcado *m,* matriarchy
matricida *mf* matricide (person)
matricidio *m,* matricide (crime)
matrícula *f,* list, register; matriculation; registration number (of a car, etc.). **m. de buques,** maritime register. **m. de mar,** mariner's register; maritime register
matriculación *f,* matriculation; registration
matricular *vt* to matriculate; enrol; *naut* register; *vr* matriculate; enroll, register

matrimonial *a* matrimonial
matrimonio *m,* marriage, matrimony; married couple. **m. a yuras,** secret marriage. **m. de la mano izquierda** *or* **m. morganático,** morganatic marriage. **contraer m.,** to get married
matritense *a* and *mf* Madrilenian
matriz *f,* uterus, womb; matrix, mold; *min* matrix; nut; female screw
matrona *f,* married woman; matron; midwife; female customs officer
matusalén *m,* Methuselah, very old man
matute *m,* smuggling; contraband; gambling den
matutero (-ra) *n* smuggler, contrabandist
matutino *a* matutinal, morning
maula *f,* trash; remnant; deception, fraud, trick. *mf inf* good-for-nothing; lazybones. *inf* **ser buena m.,** to be a trickster or a fraud
maulería *f,* remnant stall; trickery
maullar *vi* to meow, mew (cats)
maullido *m,* meow, cry of the cat
Mauricio, Isla de Mauritius
mauritano (-na) *a* and *n* Mauritian
mausoleo *m,* mausoleum
maxilar *a* maxillary. *m,* jaw
máxima *f,* maxim, rule, precept, principle
máxime *adv* principally, chiefly
máximo *a sup* **grande** greatest, maximum, top. *m,* maximum
maya *f,* common daisy; May queen
mayal *m,* flail
mayo *m,* May; maypole; bouquet, wreath of flowers; *pl* festivities on eve of May Day
mayólica *f,* majolica
mayonesa *f,* mayonnaise
mayor *a comp* **grande** bigger; greater; elder; main, principal; older; high (mass, etc.); *mus* major. *mf* major (of full age). *a sup* **grande. el, la, lo mayor, los (las) mayores,** the biggest, greatest; eldest; chief, principal. **por m.,** in short, briefly; *com* wholesale
mayor *m,* head, director; chief clerk; *mil* major; *pl* ancestors
mayoral *m,* head shepherd; coachman, driver; foreman, overseer, supervisor, steward
mayorazgo *m, law* entail; entailed estate; heir (to an entail); eldest son; right of primogeniture
mayordoma *f,* steward's wife; housekeeper; stewardess
mayordomo *m,* steward, superintendent; butler; major-domo, royal chief steward
mayoría *f,* majority
mayormente *adv* chiefly; especially
mayúscula *f,* capital letter, upper-case letter
mayúsculo *a* large; capital (letters). **letra mayúscula,** capital letter, upper-case letter
maza *f,* mallet; club; bludgeon; mace; bass drum stick; pile driver; bone, stick, etc., tied to dog's tail in carnival; *inf* pedant, bore; important person, authority. **m. de polo,** polo mallet
mazacote *m,* concrete; roughhewn work of art; *inf* stodgy overcooked dish; bore, tedious person
mazamorra *f,* dish made of cornmeal; biscuit crumbs; broken fragments, remains
mazapán *m,* marzipan
mazmorra *f,* dungeon
mazo *m,* mallet; bundle, bunch; importunate person; clapper (of a bell)
mazonería *f,* stonemasonry
mazonero *m,* stonemason
mazorca *f,* spindleful; spike, ear (of corn); cocoa berry; camarilla, group
mazurca *f,* mazurka
me *pers pron acc or dat 1st sing mf* me; to me
meandro *m,* meandering, twisting, winding; wandering
meato *m,* meatus
Meca, la Mecca

mecánica *f,* mechanics; mechanism, machinery; *inf* worthless thing; mean action

mecánico *a* mechanical; power-operated; base, ill-bred. *m,* engineer; mechanic

mecanismo *m,* mechanism; works, machinery

mecanizar *vt* to mechanize

mecanografía *f,* typewriting

mecanografiar *vt* to typewrite, type

mecanográfico *a* typewriting, typing; typewritten, typed

mecanografista *mf* **mecanógrafo (-fa)** *n* typist

mecedor *a* rocking, swaying. *m,* swing

mecedora *f,* rocking chair

mecenas *m,* Maecenas, patron

mecer *vt* to stir, mix; shake; rock; swing

mecha *f,* wick; bit, drill; fuse (of explosives); match (for cannon, etc.); fat bacon (for basting); lock of hair; skein, twist

mechar *vt cul* to baste, lard

mechero *m,* gas burner; pocket lighter; socket of a candlestick

mechón *m,* tuft, skein, bundle; lock of hair; wisp

medalla *f,* medal; medallion; plaque, round panel; *inf* piece of eight (coin)

medallón *m,* large medal; medallion; locket

médano *m,* sand dune

media *f,* stocking

mediación *f,* mediation, arbitration; intercession

mediado *a* half-full. **a mediados (del mes,** etc.**),** toward the middle (of the month, etc.)

mediador (-ra) *n* mediator, arbitrator; intercessor

medianamente *adv* moderately; passably, fairly well

medianero (-ra) *a* middle; intervening, intermediate; mediatory. *n* mediator. *m,* owner of a semidetached house or of one in a row

medianía *f,* average; medium, mediocrity; moderate wealth or means

mediano *a* medium, average; moderate; *inf* middling, passable, fair

medianoche *f,* midnight

mediante *a* mediatory. *adv* by means of, by, through

mediar *vi* to reach the middle; get halfway; elapse half a given time; intercede, mediate; arbitrate; be in between or in the middle; intervene, take part

medicación *f,* medication

medicamento *m,* medicament, medicine, remedy

medicar *vt* to medicate

medicastro *m,* unskilled physician; quack, charlatan

medicina *f,* medicine; medicament

medicinar *vt* to attend; treat (patients)

medición *f,* measuring; measurements; survey (land); scansion

médico (-ca) *a* medical. *n* doctor of medicine. **m. de cabecera,** family doctor. **m. general,** general practitioner

medida *f,* measurement; measuring stick; measure, precaution (gen. with *tomar, adoptar,* etc.); gauge; judgment, wisdom; meter; standard. **a m. que,** while, at the same time as. **tomar las medidas (a),** *fig* to take a person's measure, sum him up. **tomar sus medidas,** to take his (their) measurements; take the necessary measures. **un traje hecho a m.,** a suit made to measure

medieval *a* medieval

medio *a* half; middle; intermediate; halfway. *m,* half; middle; *art* medium; spiritualist medium; proceeding, measure, precaution; environment, medium; middle way, mean; *sport* halfback. **m. galope,** canter. **m. tiempo,** *sport* halftime. **a medias,** by halves; half, partly. **de por m.,** by halves; in between; in the way. **estar de por m.,** to be in the way; take part in. *inf* **quitar de en m.,** to get rid of. *inf* **quitarse de en m.,** to go away, remove oneself

mediocre *a* mediocre

mediocridad *f,* mediocrity; insignificance

mediodía *m,* noon, meridian; south

medioeval *a* medieval

mediopelo *m,* lower middle class

mediquillo *m, inf* quack; medicine man (in the Philippines)

medir *vt irr* to measure; (metrics) scan; survey (land); compare; *vr* measure one's words; act with restraint. See **pedir**

meditabundo *a* pensive, meditative, thoughtful

meditación *f,* meditation; consideration, reflection

meditador *a* meditative, thoughtful

meditar *vt* to meditate, consider, muse

meditativo *a* meditative

mediterráneo *a* mediterranean; inland, landlocked

médium *m, spirit* medium

medra *f,* progress; improvement, betterment; growth; prosperity

medrar *vi* to flourish, grow; become prosperous or improve one's position

medro *m,* improvement, progress. See **medra**

medroso *a* timid, frightened; frightful, horrible

médula *f,* marrow; *bot* pith; *fig* essence, core

medusa *f,* jellyfish

mefistofélico *a* Mephistophelian

mefítico *a* noxious, mephitic, poisonous

megáfono *m,* megaphone

megalómano (-na) *n* megalomaniac

mejicano (-na) *a* and *n* Mexican

Méjico Mexico

mejilla *f, anat* cheek

mejillón *m,* sea mussel

mejor *a comp* **bueno** better. *adv* better; rather; sooner; preferably. *a sup* **bueno. el, la, lo mejor; los, las mejores,** the best; most preferable. **m. que m.,** better and better. *inf* **a lo m.,** probably, in all probability. **tanto m.,** so much the better

mejora *f,* improvement; bettering; progress; higher bid (at auctions)

mejorable *a* improvable

mejoramiento *m,* betterment, improvement

mejorar *vt* to improve; better; outbid; *vi* grow better (in health); improve (weather); make progress; rally (of markets). **Mejorando lo presente,** Present company excepted

mejoría *f,* improvement, progress; betterment; superiority; advantage, profit

mejunje *m, inf* brew, potion, cure-all, stuff

melado *a* honey-colored. *m,* cane syrup

melancolía *f,* melancholia; sadness, depression, melancholy

melancólico *a* melancholy, sad; depressing

melaza *f,* molasses

melena *f,* long side whiskers; loose, flowing hair (in women); overlong hair (in men); lion's mane. *inf* **andar a la m.,** to start a fight or quarrel. *inf* **traer a la m.,** to drag by the hair, force

melifluidad *f,* mellifluence, sweetness

melifluo *a* mellifluous, sweet-voiced; honeyed

melindre *m,* honey fritter; affectation, scruple, fastidiousness; narrow ribbon

melindroso *a* overfastidious, affected, prudish

mella *f,* nick, notch; dent; gap; harm, damage (to reputation, etc.). **hacer m.,** *fig* to make an impression (on the mind); *mil* breach, drive a wedge

mellar *vt* to nick, notch; dent; damage

mellizo (-za) *a* and *n* twin

melocotón *m,* peach; peach tree

melocotonero *m,* peach tree

melodía *f,* melody, tune; melodiousness

melódico *a* melodic, melodious

melodioso *a* melodious, tuneful, sweet-sounding

melodrama *m,* melodrama

melodramático *a* melodramatic

melón *m,* melon

melosidad *f,* sweetness

meloso *a* honeyed; sweet; gentle; mellifluous

membrana *f,* membrane

membrete *m,* note, memorandum; note or card of invitation; superscription, heading; address (of person)

membrillo *m,* quince tree; quince; quince jelly

membrudo *a* brawny, strong, muscular

memo *a* silly, stupid

memorable *a* memorable

memorándum *m,* notebook, jotter; memorandum

memorar(se) *vt* and *vr* to remember, recall

memoria *f,* memory; remembrance, recollection; monument; memorial; report; essay, article; codicil; memorandum; record, chronicle; *pl* regards, compliments, greetings; memoirs; memoranda. **inf m. de grillo,** poor memory. **de m.,** by heart. **flaco de m.,** forgetful. **hacer m.,** to remember

memorial *m,* notebook; memorial, petition

memorialista *mf* secretary, amanuensis

memorioso *a* mindful, unforgetful

mena *f, min* ore

menaje *m,* household or school equipment or furniture

mención *f,* mention. **m. honorífica,** honorable mention. **hacer m. de,** to mention

mencionar *vt* to mention

mendacidad *f,* mendacity, untruthfulness

mendaz *a* mendacious, untruthful

mendelismo *m,* Mendelism

mendicante *a* begging; *ecc* mendicant. *mf* beggar

mendicidad *f,* mendicancy, begging

mendigar *vt* to beg for alms; entreat, supplicate

mendigo (-ga) *n* beggar

mendoso *a* mendacious, untruthful; mistaken

mendrugo *m,* crust of bread

menear *vt* to sway, move; wag; shake; manage, control, direct; *vr inf* get a move on; sway, move; wriggle

meneo *m,* swaying movement; wagging; shaking; wriggling; management, direction; *aer* bump; *inf* spanking

menester *m,* lack, shortage; necessity; occupation, employment; *pl* physical necessities; *inf* tools, implements, equipment. **haber m.,** to need, require. **ser m.,** to be necessary or requisite

menesteroso *a* indigent, poverty-stricken, needy

menestra *f,* vegetable soup; dried vegetable (gen. *pl*)

menestral (-la) *n* artisan; worker; mechanic

mengano (-na) *n* so-and-so (used instead of the name of the person)

mengua *f,* decrease; lack, shortage; waning (of the moon, etc.); dishonor, disgrace; poverty

menguado (-da) *a* timid, cowardly; silly, stupid; mean, avaricious. *n* coward; fool; skinflint. *m,* narrowing stitch when knitting socks

menguante *a* ebb; waning; decreasing. *f,* ebb tide; decadence, decline. **m. de la luna,** waning of the moon

menguar *vi* to decrease; decline, decay; wane; ebb; narrow (socks); *vt* diminish; disgrace, discredit

menina *f,* child attendant (on Spanish royalty)

menino *m,* Spanish royal page; little dandy

menjurje *m,* See **mejunje**

menopausia *f,* menopause

menor *a comp* less, smaller; younger, minor; *mus* minor. *m,* minor. *f,* (logic) minor. *a sup* **el, la, lo m.; los, las menores,** the least; smallest; youngest. **m. de edad,** minor (in age). **por m.,** at retail; in detail

Menorca Minorca

menoría *f,* subordination, dependence; inferiority; minority (underage); childhood, youth

menos *adv* less; minus; least; except. **m. de** *or* **m. que,** less than. **al m., por lo m.,** at least. **a m. que,** unless. **De m. nos hizo Dios,** Never say die, Nothing is impossible. **poco más o m.,** more or less, about

menoscabar *vt* to lessen, diminish, decrease; deteriorate, damage; disgrace, discredit

menoscabo *m,* decrease, diminishment; harm, damage, loss

menospreciable *a* despicable, contemptible

menospreciador (-ra) *a* scornful. *n* scorner, despiser

menospreciar *vt* to despise, scorn; underestimate, have a poor opinion of

menospreciativo *a* scornful, slighting, derisive

menosprecio *m,* scorn, derision; underestimation

mensaje *m,* message; official communication

mensajería *f,* carrier service; steamship line

mensajero (-ra) *n* messenger; errand boy

menstruación *f,* menstruation

menstruar *vi* to menstruate

mensual *a* monthly

mensualidad *f,* monthly salary, monthly payment

mensurable *a* measurable

mensurar *vt* to measure

menta *f,* menthe, mint; peppermint

mentado *a* celebrated, distinguished, famous

mental *a* mental

mentalidad *f,* mentality

mentalmente *adv* mentally

mentar *vt irr* to mention. See **sentar**

mente *f,* mind; intelligence, understanding; will, intention

mentecatería *f,* folly, stupidity

mentecato (-ta) *a* foolish, silly; feeble-minded, simple. *n* fool, idiot

mentir *vi irr* to lie, be untruthful; deceive, mislead; falsify; *poet* belie; disagree, be incompatible; *vt* break a promise, disappoint. **m. como un bellaco,** to lie like a trooper See **sentir**

mentira *f,* lie, falsehood; error (in writing); *inf* white spot (on a fingernail); cracking (of fingerjoints). **m. oficiosa,** white lie. **Parece m.,** It seems incredible

mentiroso *a* lying, false; full of errors (literary works); deceptive

mentís *m,* giving the lie (literally, you lie); proof, demonstration (of error)

mentol *m,* menthol

mentón *m,* chin

mentonera *f,* chin rest

menú *m,* menu

menudamente *adv* minutely; in detail, circumstantially

menudear *vt* to do frequently; do repeatedly; *vi* happen frequently; describe in detail; *com* sell by retail

menudencia *f,* minuteness, smallness; exactness, care, accuracy; trifle, worthless object; small matter; *pl* offal; pork sausages

menudeo *m,* repetition; description in detail; *com* retail. **al m.,** at retail

menudillos *m pl,* giblets; offal

menudo *a* minute, tiny; despicable; thin; small; vulgar; meticulous, exact; small (money). *m,* small coal; *m pl,* offal, entrails; small change (money). **a m.,** often, frequently. **por m.,** in detail, carefully; *com* in small lots

meñique *a inf* very small. *m,* little finger (in full, **dedo m.)**

meollo *m,* brain; *anat* marrow; *fig* essence, core, substance; understanding; *inf* **no tener m. (una cosa),** to be worthless, unsubstantial (things)

mequetrefe *m, inf* coxcomb, whippersnapper

meramente *adv* solely, simply, merely

mercachifle *m,* peddler; small merchant

mercadear *vi* to trade, traffic

mercadeo *m,* marketing (study of markets)

mercader *m,* dealer, merchant, trader. **m. de grueso,** wholesaler

mercadería *f,* See **mercancía**

mercado *m,* market; marketplace

mercancía *f,* goods, merchandise; commerce, trade, traffic

mercante *a* trading; commercial. *m,* merchant, dealer, trader

mercantil *a* mercantile, commercial

mercantilismo *m,* mercantilism

merced *f,* salary, remuneration; favor, benefit, kindness; will, desire, pleasure; mercy, grace; courtesy title given to untitled person (e.g. **vuestra m.,** your honor. Has now become **usted** and is universally used). **m. a,**

thanks to. **estar uno a m. de,** to live at someone else's expense, be dependent on

mercenario (-ia) *n ecc* member of the Order of la Merced. *m, mil* mercenary; day laborer. *a* mercenary

mercería *f,* haberdashery, mercery

mercerizar *vt* to mercerize

mercero *m,* haberdasher, mercer

mercurio *m,* mercury, quicksilver; *ast* Mercury

merecedor *a* deserving, worthy

merecer *vt irr* to deserve, be worthy of; attain, achieve; be worth; *vi* deserve, be deserving. **m. bien de,** to deserve well of; have a claim on the gratitude of. See **conocer**

merecido *m,* due reward

merecimiento *m,* desert; merit

merendar *vi irr* to have lunch; pry into another's affairs; *vt* have (a certain food) for lunch. *inf* **merendarse (una cosa),** to obtain (a thing), have it in one's pocket. See **recomendar**

merendero *m,* lunchroom; tearoom

merengue *m, cul* meringue

meretriz *f,* prostitute

meridiana *f,* daybed, chaise longue; siesta

meridiano *a* meridian. *m,* meridian. **a la meridiana,** at noon

meridional *a* meridional, southern

merienda *f,* tea, snack; lunch; *inf* hunchback. *inf* **juntar meriendas,** to join forces, combine interests

merino *a* merino. *m,* merino wool; shepherd of merino sheep

meritísimo *a sup* most worthy, most deserving

mérito *m,* merit; desert; worth, excellence. **de m.,** excellent, notable. **hacer m. de,** to mention

meritorio *a* meritorious. *m,* unpaid worker, learner

merluza *f,* hake; *inf* drinking bout. *inf* **pescar una m.,** to get drunk

merma *f,* decrease, drop; loss, waste, reduction; leakage

mermar *vi* to diminish, waste away, decrease; evaporate; leak; *vt* filch, pilfer; reduce, decrease

mermelada *f,* conserve, preserve; jam; marmalade

mero *a* mere; simple; plain

merodeador *a* marauding. *m,* marauder, raider

merodear *vi* to maraud, raid

merodeo *m,* raiding, marauding

mes *m,* month; menses, menstruation

mesa *f,* table; board, directorate; meseta, tableland; staircase landing; flat (of a sword, etc.); game of billiards. **m. de batalla,** post office sorting table. **m. de caballete,** trestle table. **m. de noche,** bedside table. **m. de tijeras,** folding table. **m. giratoria,** turntable. **alzar** (*or* **levantar**) **la m.,** to clear the table. **cubrir** (*or* **poner**) **la m.,** to set the table

mesada *f,* monthly wages, monthly payment

mesadura *f,* tearing of the hair or beard

mesarse *vr* to tear one's hair or beard

mesenterio *m,* mesentery

meseta *f,* staircase landing; plateau, tableland

mesiánico *a* Messianic

Mesías *m,* Messiah

mesilla *f,* small table; laughing admonition; landing (of a stair)

mesmerismo *m,* mesmerism

mesnada *f,* association, company, society

mesocracia *f,* mesocracy; middle class, bourgeoisie

mesón *m,* inn, tavern

mesonero (-ra) *n* innkeeper

mesta *f,* ancient order of sheep farmers; *pl* confluence, meeting (of rivers)

mester *m,* craft, occupation. **m. de clerecía,** learned poetic meter of the Spanish Middle Ages. **m. de juglaría,** popular poetry and troubadour songs

mestizo *a* half-breed; hybrid; cross-breed

mesura *f,* sedateness; dignity; courtesy; moderation

mesurado *a* sedate; dignified; moderate, restrained, temperate

meta *f,* goalpost *fig* aim, end; goal; goalkeeper

metabolismo *m,* metabolism

metafísica *f,* metaphysics

metafísico *a* metaphysical. *m,* metaphysician

metáfora *f,* metaphor

metafórico *a* metaphorical

metal *m,* metal; brass; timbre of the voice; state, condition; quality, substance; *her* gold or silver; *mus* brass (instruments)

metalario *m,* metalworker

metálico *a* metallic. *m,* metalworker; coin, specie; bullion

metalistería *f,* metalwork

metalizar *vt* to metallize, make metallic; *vr* become metallized; grow greedy for money

metalurgia *f,* metallurgy

metalúrgico *a* metallurgical. *m,* metallurgist

metamorfosis *f,* metamorphosis

metano *m,* methane

metatarso *m,* metatarsus

metátesis *f,* metathesis

metedor (-ra) *n* placer, inserter; smuggler, contrabandist

metempsicosis *f,* metempsychosis

metemuertos *inf* meddler, Nosy Parker

meteórico *a* meteoric

meteorito *m,* meteorite

meteoro *m,* meteor

meteorología *f,* meteorology

meteorológico *a* meteorological

meteorologista *mf* meteorologist; weather forecaster

meter *vt* to place; put; introduce, insert; stake (gambling); smuggle; cause, occasion; place close together; persuade to take part in; *sew* take in fullness; deceive, humbug; cram in, pack tightly; *naut* take in sail; *vr* interfere, butt in; meddle (with); take up, follow (occupations); be overfamiliar; disembogue, empty itself (rivers, etc.); attack with the sword; (*with prep a*) follow (occupations); become, turn (e.g. **meterse a predicar,** to turn preacher; (*with con*) pick a quarrel with. **meterse en precisiones,** to go into details. *inf* **meterse en todo,** to be very meddlesome

metesillas y sacamuertos *m,* scene shifter, stagehand

meticulosidad *f,* meticulosity; timorousness

meticuloso *a* meticulous, fussy; timid, nervous

metido *a* tight; crowded; crabbed (of handwriting). *m, sew* material for letting out (seams). **m. en años,** quite old (person)

metílico *a* methylic

metimiento *m,* insertion, introduction; influence, sway

metódico *a* methodical

metodismo *m,* Methodism

metodista *a* methodistic. *mf* Methodist

método *m,* method

metodología *f,* methodology

metralla *f, mil* grapeshot, shrapnel

métrica *f,* metrics

métrico *a* metric; metrical

metro *m,* (verse) meter; meter (measurement); subway, underground railway

metrónomo *m,* metronome

metrópoli *f,* metropolis, capital; see of a metropolitan bishop; mother country

metropolitano *a* metropolitan. *m,* metropolitan bishop

México Mexico

mezcla *f,* mixture; blend, combination; mixed cloth, tweed; mortar

mezclar *vt* to mix, blend, combine; *vr* mix, mingle; take part; interfere, meddle; intermarry

mezcolanza *f, inf* hodgepodge

mezquindad *f,* poverty; indigence; miserliness; paltriness; meanness, poorness

mezquino *a* needy, impoverished; miserly, stingy; small, diminutive; unhappy; mean, paltry

mezquita *f,* mosque

mi *poss pron* my. *m, mus* mi, E

mí *pers pron acc gen dat 1st pers sing* me. Used only after prepositions (e.g. **Lo hicieron por mí,** They did it for me)

miaja *f,* See **migaja**

miasma *m,* miasma

miasmático *a* miasmatic, malarious

miau *m,* meow

mica *f, min* mica; coquette, flirt

micción *f,* micturition

micho (-cha) *n inf* puss, pussycat

micología *f,* mycology

micra *f,* micron, thousandth part of a millimeter

microbiano *a* microbial, microbic

microbio *m,* microbe

microbiología *f,* microbiology

microbrigada *f,* team of volunteer workers (Castroist Cuba)

microcéfalo *a* microcephalous

microcosmo *m,* microcosm

micrófono *m,* microphone

microonda *f,* microwave

microscópico *a* microscopic

microscopio *m,* microscope

miedo *m,* fear, apprehension, terror. **m. al público,** stagefright. **tener m.,** to be afraid

miedoso *a inf* fearful, nervous

miel *f,* honey. **m. de caña,** sugarcane syrup. *inf* **quedarse a media m.,** to see one's pleasure snatched away. *inf* **ser de mieles,** to be most pleasant or agreeable

mielitis *f,* myelitis

miembro *m, anat* limb; penis; member, associate; part, portion, section; *math* member

miente *f,* thought, imagination, mind. **parar** *or* **poner mientes en,** to consider, think about. **venírsele a las mientes,** to occur to one's mind

mientras *adv* while. **m. más . . .,** the more . . . . **m. que,** while (e.g. **m. que esperaba en el jardín,** while he was waiting in the garden). **m. tanto,** in the meanwhile

miércoles *m,* Wednesday. **m. de ceniza,** Ash Wednesday

mierda *f,* (*vulgar*) shit; *inf* filth

mies *f,* cereal plant, grain; harvest time; *pl* grain fields

miga *f,* breadcrumb; crumb; *inf* essence, core; substance; bit, scrap; *pl* fried breadcrumbs. *inf* **hacer buenas** (*or* **malas**) **migas,** to get on well (*or* badly) together

migaja *f,* breadcrumb; bit, scrap; trifle, mere nothing; *pl* crumbs (from the table); remains, remnants

migajón *m,* crumb (of a loaf); *fig inf* essence, substance, core

migración *f,* migration; emigration

migraña *f,* migraine

migratorio *a* migratory

mijo *m,* millet; maize

mil *a* thousand; thousandth; many, large number. *m,* thousand; thousandth. *inf* **Son las m. y quinientas,** It's extremely late (of the hour)

miladi *f,* my lady

milagrero *a inf* miraculous

milagro *m,* miracle; marvel, wonder. **¡M.!** Amazing! Just fancy!

milagroso *a* miraculous; marvelous, wonderful

milanés (-esa) *a* and *n* Milanese

milano *m, orn* kite

mildeu *m,* mildew

milenario *a* millenary; millennial. *m,* millenary; millennium

milésimo *a* thousandth

milicia *f,* militia; military; art of war; military profession

miliciano *a* military. *m,* militiaman

miligramo *m,* milligram

mililitro *m,* milliliter

milímetro *m,* millimeter

militante *a* militant

militar *a* military. *m,* soldier. *vi* to fight in the army; struggle (for a cause); *fig* militate (e.g. **Las circunstancias militan en favor de** (*or* **contra**) **sus ideas,** Circumstances militate against his ideas)

militarismo *m,* militarism

militarista *a* militaristic. *mf* militarist

militarizar *vt* to militarize; make war-like

milla *f,* mile

millar *m,* thousand; vast number (gen. *pl*)

millón *m,* million

millonario (-ia) *a* and *n* millionaire

millonésimo *a* millionth

milmillonésimo *a* billionth

milord *m,* my lord. *pl* **milores,** my lords

mimar *vt* to spoil, overindulge; caress, fondle

mimbre *mf* osier; willow tree. *m,* wicker

mimbrear *vi* to sway, bend

mimbrera *f,* osier; osier bed; willow

mímica *f,* mimicry; mime

mímico *a* mimic

mimo *m,* mimic, buffoon; mime; caress, expression of affection, tenderness; overindulgence

mimoso *a* affectionate, demonstrative

mina *f,* mine; excavation, mining; underground passage; lead (in a pencil); (*mil nav*) mine; *fig* gold mine. *mil* **m. terrestre,** landmine

minador *m,* excavator; *nav* minelayer; *mil* sapper

minar *vt* to excavate, mine; *fig* undermine; (*mil nav*) mine; work hard for

minarete *m,* minaret

mineraje *m,* exploitation of a mine, mining; mineral products

mineral *a* and *m,* mineral

mineralogía *f,* mineralogy

mineralógico *a* mineralogical

mineralogista *mf* mineralogist

minería *f,* mining, mineworking; mineworkers

minero *a* mining. *m,* miner, mineworker; source, origin

miniar *vt art* to illuminate

miniatura *f,* miniature

miniaturista *mf* miniaturist

mínima *f, mus* minim; very small thing or portion

mínimo *a sup* **pequeño** smallest; minimum; meticulous, precise. *m,* minimum; (meteorological) trough

ministerial *a* ministerial

ministerio *m,* office, post; *pol* cabinet; ministry; government office; government department.

ministrar *vt* and *vi* to fill; administer (an office); *vt* minister to; give, provide

ministro *m,* instrument, agency; minister of state, cabinet minister; clergyman, minister; minister plenipotentiary; policeman. **m. de estado,** secretary of state. **m. de gobernación,** secretary of the interior. **m. de hacienda,** treasurer. **m. de relaciones extranjeras,** foreign secretary. **primer m.** prime minister

minoración *f,* reduction, decrease

minorar *vt* to diminish, decrease

minoría *f,* minority, smaller number; minority (of age)

minoridad *f,* minority (of age)

minucia *f,* smallness; morsel, mite; *pl* details, trifles, minutiae

minuciosidad *f,* meticulousness, minuteness, precision

minucioso *a* meticulous, precise, minute

minué *m,* minuet

minúsculo *a* minute, very small

minuta *f,* memorandum, minute; note; list, catalogue

minutario *m,* minute book

minutero *m,* minute hand (of a clock)

minuto *a* minute, very small. *m,* minute

mío *m.* **mía,** *f,* (*m pl.* **míos,** *f pl.* **mías**) *poss pron* mine (e.g. **Las flores son mías,** The flowers are mine). **Mi** is used before nouns, *not* **mío.** Also used with article (e.g. **Este sombrero no es el mío,** This hat is not mine (my one)). **de mío,** by myself, without help. *inf* **¡Esta es la mía!** This is my chance!

miope *a* myopic. *mf* myopic person

miopía *f,* shortsightedness

miosota *f,* myosotis, forget-me-not

mira *f,* sight (optical instruments, guns); intention, design; *mil* watchtower; care, precaution. **andar, estar** *or* **quedar a la m.,** to be vigilant, be on the lookout

mirada *f,* look; gaze. **lanzar miradas de carnero degollado (a),** to cast sheep's eyes at

miradero *m,* object of attention, cynosure; observation post, lookout

mirador (-ra) *n* spectator. *m,* *arch* oriel; enclosed balcony; observatory

miramiento *m,* observation, gazing; scruple, consideration; precaution, care; thoughtfulness

mirar *vt* to look at, gaze at; observe, behold; watch; consider, look after; value, appreciate; concern; believe, think; *(with prep a)* overlook, look on to; face; *(with por)* care for, protect; look after, consider. **m. contra el gobierno,** *inf* to be squint-eyed. **m. de hito en hito,** to look over, stare at. **mirarse en (una cosa),** to consider (a matter) carefully

miríada *f,* myriad, huge number

mirilla *f,* peephole

miriñaque *m,* trinket, ornament; crinoline

mirlarse *vr* *inf* to give oneself airs

mirlo *m,* blackbird; *inf* pompous air

mirón *a* inquisitive, curious

mirra *f,* myrrh

mirto *m,* myrtle

misa *f,* (*ecc mus*) mass. **m. de difuntos,** requiem mass. **m. del gallo,** midnight mass. **m. mayor,** high mass. **m. rezada,** low mass. **como en m.,** in profound silence. **oír m.,** to attend mass

misal *m,* missal

misantropía *f,* misanthropy

misantrópico *a* misanthropic

misántropo *m,* misanthrope

miscelánea *f,* medley, assortment, miscellany

misceláneo *a* assorted, miscellaneous, mixed

miscible *a* mixable

miserable *a* miserable, unhappy; timid, pusillanimous; miserly, mean; despicable

miseria *f,* misery; poverty, destitution; avarice, miserliness; *inf* poor thing, trifle

misericordia *f,* mercy, compassion

misericordioso *a* merciful, compassionate

mísero *a* *inf* fond of churchgoing

misérrimo *a* *sup* most miserable

misión *f,* mission; vocation; commission, duty, errand

misionar *vi* to missionize, act as a missionary; *ecc* conduct a mission

misionero *m,* missioner; missionary

Misisipi, el the Mississippi

misiva *f,* missive

mismo *a* same; similar; self (e.g. **ellos mismos,** they themselves); very, same (e.g. **Ahora m. voy,** I'm going this very minute). **Me da lo m.,** It makes no difference to me. **por lo m.,** for that selfsame reason

misógamo (-ma) *n* misogamist

misógino *m,* misogynist

misterio *m,* mystery

misterioso *a* mysterious

mística *f,* **misticismo** *m,* mysticism

místico *a* mystic

mistificación *f,* mystification; mystery; deception

mistificar *vt* to mystify; deceive

Misuri, el the Missouri

mitad *f,* half; middle, center. *fig inf* **cara a m.,** better half. *inf* **mentir por la m. de la barba,** to lie barefacedly

mítico *a* mythical

mitigación *f,* mitigation

mitigador (-ra) *a* mitigatory. *n* mitigator

mitigar *vt* to mitigate, moderate, alleviate; appease

mitin *m,* mass meeting

mito *m,* myth

mitología *f,* mythology

mitológico *a* mythological

mitologista, mitólogo *m,* mythologist

mitón *m,* mitten

mitra *f,* miter; bishopric; archbishopric

mitrado *a* mitred

mixto *a* mixed, blended; hybrid; composite; mongrel. *m,* mixed train (carrying freight and passengers); sulphur match

mixtura *f,* mixture, blend; compound; mixture (medicine)

¡miz, miz! puss, puss!

moabita *mf* Moabite

mobiliario *a* movable (goods). *m,* furniture

moblaje *m,* household goods and furniture

mocasín *m,* moccasin

mocedad *f,* youth, adolescence; mischief, prank. *fig inf* **correr sus mocedades,** to sow one's wild oats

mochila *f,* knapsack; nosebag; military rations for a march

mocho *a* blunted, topless, lopped; *inf* shorn, cropped. *m,* butt, butt end

mochuelo *m,* owl; *inf* difficult job

moción *f,* motion, movement; impulse, tendency; divine inspiration; motion (of a debate)

moco *m,* mucus; candle drips; snuff of a candle. *inf* **caérsele el m.,** to be very simple, be easily deceived

mocoso (-sa) *a* running of the nose, sniffling; unimportant, insignificant. *n* coxcomb, stripling

moda *f,* fashion. **estar** *or* **ser de m.,** to be fashionable, be in fashion. **la última m.,** the latest fashion

modales *m pl,* manners, behavior

modalidad *f,* form, nature; *mus* modality

modelado *m,* *art* modeling

modelar *vt* *art* to model; *vr* model oneself (on), copy

modelo *m,* example, pattern; model. *mf* *art* life model

moderación *f,* moderation; restraint, temperance, equability

moderado *a* moderate; restrained, temperate

moderador (-ra) *a* moderating. *n* moderator

moderantismo *m,* moderate opinion; moderate political party

moderar *vt* to moderate; temper, restrain; *vr* regain one's self-control; behave with moderation

modernidad *f,* modernity

modernismo *m,* modernism

modernista *a* modernistic; modern. *mf* modernist

modernización *f,* modernization

modernizar *vt* to modernize

moderno *a* modern. *m,* modern. **a la moderna,** in modern fashion

modestia *f,* modesty

modesto *a* modest

módico *a* moderate (of prices, etc.)

modificable *a* modifiable

modificación *f,* modification

modificador, modificante *a* modifying, moderating

modificar *vt* to modify; moderate

modismo *m,* idiom, idiomatic expression

modista *mf* dressmaker; couturier; milliner

modo *m,* mode, method, style; manner, way; moderation, restraint; civility, politeness (often *pl*); *mus* mode; *gram* mood. **m. de ser,** nature, temperament. **de m. que,** so that. **de ningún m.,** not at all, by no means. **de todos modos,** in any case

modorra *f,* deep sleep, stupor

modorro *a* drowsy, heavy

modoso *a* demure; well-behaved

modulación *f,* modulation

modulador (-ra) *a* modulative. *n* modulator, *m,* *mus* modulator

modular *vt* and *vi* to modulate

mofa *f,* mockery, ridicule, jeering

mofador (-ra) *a* jeering. *n* scoffer, mocker

mofarse *vr* (*with de*) to make fun of, jeer at

mofeta *f,* noxious gas; damp (gas); *zool* skunk

moflete *m,* *inf* plump cheek

mofletudo *a* plump-cheeked

mogol (-la) *a* and *n* Mongolian.
mogote *m*, hill; pyre, stack
mohicano *a* and *n* Mohican
mohín *m*, grimace
mohína *f*, grudge, rancor; sullenness; sulkiness
mohíno *a* depressed, gloomy; sulky; black or black-nosed (of animals)
moho *m*, mold, fungoid growth; moldiness; moss. *inf* **no criar m.**, to be always on the move
mohoso *a* mossy; moldy
mojada *f*, wetting; *inf* stab; sop of bread
mojador (-ra) *n* wetter. *m*, stamp moistener
mojar *vt* to wet; moisten; *inf* stab, wound with a dagger; *vi* take part in; meddle, interfere; *vr* get wet
mojicón *m*, kind of spongecake; *inf* slap in the face
mojiganga *f*, masquerade, mummer's show; farce; funny sight, figure of fun
mojigatería *f*, hypocrisy; sanctimoniousness; prudery
mojigato (-ta) *a* hypocritical; sanctimonious; prudish. *n* hypocrite; bigot; prude
mojón *m*, boundary marker; milestone; heap. **m. kilométrico**, milestone
molar *a* molar
moldavo (-va) *a* and *n* Moldavian
molde *m*, mold, matrix; *fig* model, pattern. **de m.**, printed; suitably, conveniently; perfectly. **letra de m.**, printed letters, print
moldeador (-ra) *n* molder
moldear *vt* to mold, cast
moldura *f*, molding
moldurar *vt carp* to mold
molécula *f*, molecule
molecular *a* molecular
moler *vt irr* to grind, crush; tire, exhaust; ill-treat; pester, annoy. **m. a palos**, to beat black and blue. *Pres. Ind.* **muelo, mueles, muele, muelen.** *Pres. Subjunc.* **muela, muelas, muela, muelan**
molestia *f*, inconvenience, trouble; annoyance; discomfort, pain; bore, nuisance. **Es una m.**, It's a nuisance
molesto *a* inconvenient, troublesome; annoying; painful; uncomfortable; boring, tedious
moletón *m*, flannelet
molicie *f*, softness, smoothness; effeminacy, weakness
molienda *f*, milling; grinding; mill; portion ground at one time; *inf* exhaustion, fatigue; *inf* nuisance
molificar *vt* to mollify, appease
molimiento *m*, milling; grinding; exhaustion, fatigue
molinera *f*, (woman) miller; miller's wife
molinero *a* mill. *m*, miller
molinillo *m*, hand mill, small grinder; mincing machine; beater. **m. de café**, coffee mill
molino *m*, mill; harum-scarum, rowdy; bore, tedious person; *inf* mouth. **m. de rueda de escalones**, treadmill. **m. de viento**, windmill
molleja *f*, gizzard
mollera *f*, crown of the head; brains, sense. *inf* **ser duro de m.**, to be obstinate; be stupid
molusco *m*, mollusk
momentaneidad *f*, momentariness
momentáneo *a* momentary, brief; instantaneous, immediate
momento *m*, moment, minute; importance; *mech* moment. **al m.**, immediately. **a cada m.**, all the time; frequently. **por momentos,** continually; intermittently
momería *f*, mummery
momero (-ra) *n* mummer
momia *f*, mummy
momificación *f*, mummification
momificar *vt* to mummify; *vr* become mummified
mona *f*, female monkey; *inf* imitator; drinking bout; drunk. *inf* **Aunque la m. se vista de seda, m. se queda,** Breeding will tell. *inf* **ser la última m.**, to be of no account, be unimportant
monacal *a* monkish, monastic
monacillo *m*, *ecc* acolyte

monada *f*, mischievous prank; affected gesture or grimace; small, pretty thing; childish cleverness; flattery; rash act; *pl* monkey shines
monaguillo *m*, *ecc* acolyte
monarca *mf* monarch
monarquía *f*, monarchy
monárquico (-ca) *a* monarchic. *n* monarchist
monarquismo *m*, monarchism
monasterio *m*, monastery; convent
monástico *a* monastic
monda *f*, skinning, peeling; *agr* pruning; cleansing
mondadientes *m*, toothpick
mondar *vt* to skin, peel; *agr* prune; cut the hair; cleanse; free of rubbish; *inf* deprive of possessions; *vr* pick one's teeth
mondo *a* simple, plain; bare; unadulterated, pure
moneda *f*, coin, piece of money; coinage; *inf* wealth; cash. **m. corriente**, currency. **m. metálica**, specie. **pagar en buena m.**, to give entire satisfaction. **pagar en la misma m.**, to pay back in the same coin, return like for like. *inf* **ser m. corriente**, to be usual or very frequent
monedero *m*, coiner, minter; handbag; purse
monería *f*, mischievous trick; unimportant trifle; pretty thing; childish cleverness, pretty ways
monetario *a* monetary. *m*, collection of coins and medals
monetización *f*, monetization
monigote *m*, *inf* boor; grotesque, puppet
monitor *m*, monitor
monitorio *a* monitory
monja *f*, nun; *pl* sparks
monje *m*, monk
monjil *a* nun-like. *m*, nun's habit
mono *a inf* pretty, attractive; amusing, funny. *m*, monkey; person given to grimacing; rash youth; coverall. *inf* **estar de monos**, to be on bad terms
monocromo *a* monochrome; monochromatic
monóculo *m*, monocle
monogamia *f*, monogamy
monógamo *a* monogamous. *n* monogamist
monografía *f*, monograph
monograma *m*, monogram
monolítico *a* monolithic
monolito *m*, monolith
monólogo *m*, monologue
monomanía *f*, monomania
monomaníaco (-ca) *n* monomaniac
monopatín *m*, scooter
monoplano *m*, monoplane
monopolio *m*, monopoly
monopolista *mf* monopolist
monopolizar *vt* to monopolize
monosilábico *a* monosyllabic
monosílabo *m*, monosyllable
monoteísmo *m*, monotheism
monoteísta *mf* monotheist
monotipia *f*, monotype
monotonía *f*, monotony; monotone
monótono *a* monotonous
monroísmo *m*, Monroe doctrine
monseñor *m*, monsignor
monserga *f*, *inf* rigmarole; jargon
monstruo *m*, monster; freak, monstrosity; cruel person; hideous person or thing
monstruosidad *f*, monstrousness, monstrosity
monstruoso *a* monstrous, abnormal; enormous; extraordinary; atrocious, outrageous
monta *f*, mounting a horse; total; *mil* mounting signal; breeding station (horses)
montacargas *m*, hoist, lift; freight elevator
montador *m*, mounter; mounting block
montadura *f*, mounting; mount, setting (of jewels)
montaje *m*, assembling, setting up (machines); presentation (of a book); (cinema) montage
montano *a* hilly, mountainous

montante *m*, upright, stanchion; tent pole

montaña *f*, mountain; mountainous country. **montañas rusas,** roller coaster (at an amusement park)

montañés (-esa) *a* mountain. *n* mountain dweller; native of Santander

montañoso *a* mountainous; hilly

montar *vi* to ascend, climb up, get on top; mount (a horse); ride (a horse); be important; *vt* get on top of; ride (a horse); total, amount to; set up (apparatus, machinery); *naut* sail around, double; set, mount (gems); cock (firearms); fine for trespassing; wind (a clock); command (a ship); *naut* carry, be fitted with (guns, etc.). **m. a horcajadas en,** to mount astride; straddle. **montarse en cólera,** to fly into a rage

montaraz *a* mountain-dwelling; wild, savage; rude, uncivilized, uncouth. *m*, gamekeeper, forester

montazgo *m*, toll payable for cattle moving from one province to another

monte *m*, mount, hill; woodland; obstacle, impediment. **m. de piedad,** pawnshop. **m. pío,** savings fund

montenegrino (-na) *a* and *n* Montenegrin

montera *f*, cap; glass roof

montería *f*, hunt, chase; art of hunting

montero (-ra) *n* hunter, huntsman

montés *a* wild, savage, untamed

montevideano (-na) *a* and *n* Montevidean

montículo *m*, mound, hill

montón *m*, heap, pile; *inf* abundance, lot. *inf* **a, de *or* en m.,** all jumbled up together. **a montones,** in abundance

montuoso *a* mountainous

montura *f*, riding animal, mount; horse trappings; setting up, mounting (artillery, etc.)

monumental *a* monumental

monumento *m*, monument; document, record; tomb

monzón *mf*, monsoon

moña *f*, doll; dressmaker's model; bow for the hair; bullfighter's black bow; baby's bonnet; *inf* drinking bout

moño *m*, bun, chignon; topknot (birds); bunch of ribbons; *pl* tawdry trimmings

moqueta *f*, moquette

moquete *m*, slap in the face

moquillo *m*, distemper (of animals)

mora *f*, blackberry; mulberry; bramble; Moorish girl, Moorish woman

morada *f*, dwelling, abode; sojourn, stay

morado *a* purple

morador (-ra) *n* dweller; sojourner

moral *a* moral, ethical. *f*, morality, ethics; morale. *m*, blackberry bush

moraleja *f*, moral, lesson

moralidad *f*, morality

moralista *mf* moralist

moralización *f*, moralization

moralizador (-ra) *a* moralizing. *n* moralizer

moralizar *vt* to reform, correct; *vi* moralize

moratoria *f*, moratorium

moravo (-va) *a* and *n* Moravian

morbidez *f*, *art* morbidezza; softness

mórbido *a* morbid, diseased; *art* delicate (of flesh tones); soft

morbo *m*, illness. **m. gálico,** syphilis

morboso *a* ill; morbid, unhealthy

morcilla *f*, *cul* black pudding; (*inf theat*) gag

morcillero (-ra) *n* seller of black puddings; (*inf theat*) actor who gags

mordacidad *f*, corrosiveness; mordacity, sarcasm; *cul* piquancy

mordaz *a* corrosive; sarcastic, caustic, mordant; *cul* piquant

mordaza *f*, gag

mordedor *a* biting; scandalmongering

mordedura *f*, bite, biting

morder *vt irr* to bite; nibble, nip; seize, grasp; corrode; eat away; slander; etch. *Pres. Ind.* **muerdo, muerdes,**

muerde, muerden. *Pres. Subjunc.* **muerda, muerdas, muerda, muerdan**

mordiente *m*, fixative (for dyeing); mordant. *a* mordant (of acid)

mordiscar *vt* to nibble, bite gently; bite

mordisco *m*, nibble; nibbling; bite; biting; piece bitten off

morena *f*, moraine

moreno (-na) *a* dark brown; swarthy complexioned; dark (of people). *n inf* negro, mulatto

morera *f*, mulberry bush

morería *f*, Moorish quarter

morfina *f*, morphine

morfinómano (-na) *n* morphine addict

morfología *f*, morphology

morfológico *a* morphological

morganático *a* morganatic

moribundo (-da) *a* moribund, dying. *n* dying person

morillo *m*, andiron, fire-dog

morir *vi irr* to die; fade, wither; decline, decay; disappear; yearn (for); long (to); go out (lights, fire); *vr* die; go numb (limbs); (*with por*) adore, be mad about. *inf* **m. vestido,** to die a violent death. **¡Muera!** Down with! *Past Part.* **muerto.** For other tenses see **dormir**

morisco (-ca) *a* Moorish. *n* Morisco, Moor converted to Christianity

morisma *f*, Mohammedanism; multitude of Moors

mormón (-ona) *n* Mormon

mormónico *a* Mormon

mormonismo *m*, Mormonism

moro (-ra) *a* Moorish. *n* Moor; Mohammedan. *inf* **haber moros y cristianos,** to be the deuce of a row. *inf* **Hay moros en la costa,** The coast is not clear; There's trouble in the offing

morosidad *f*, slowness, delay; sluggishness, sloth

moroso *a* slow, dilatory; sluggish, lazy

morra *f*, crown of the head

morral *m*, nose-bag; knapsack; game-bag; *inf* lout

morriña *f*, cattle plague, murrain; *inf* depression, blues; homesickness

morrión *m*, morion (helmet)

morro *m*, anything round; hummock, hillock; round pebble; headland, cliff

morsa *f*, walrus

mortaja *f*, shroud, winding sheet

mortal *a* mortal; fatal, deadly; on the point of death; great, tremendous; certain, sure. *mf* mortal

mortalidad *f*, humanity, human race; mortality, death-rate

mortandad *f*, mortality, number of deaths

mortecino *a* dead from natural causes (animals); weak; fading; dull, dead (of eyes); flickering; on the point of death or extinction

mortero *m*, mortar (for building); *mil* mortar; pounding mortar

mortífero *a* deadly, mortal

mortificación *f*, *med* gangrene; humiliation, wounding; mortification (of the flesh)

mortificar *vt med* to mortify; humiliate, wound, hurt; mortify (the flesh); *vr* become gangrenous

mortuorio *a* mortuary. *m*, funeral, obsequies

mosaico *a* and *m*, mosaic

mosca *f*, fly; *inf* nuisance; bore, pest; cash; *pl* sparks. *inf* **m. muerta,** underhanded person. *inf* **papar moscas,** to gape, be dumbfounded. *inf* **soltar la m.,** to give or spend money unwillingly

moscardón *m*, gadfly

moscatel *a* muscatel. *m*, muscatel (grapes and wine); *inf* pest, tedious person

moscovita *a* and *mf* Muscovite

Moscú Moscow

mosquear *vt* to drive off flies; reply crossly; whip; *vr* be exasperated; brush aside obstacles

mosquero *m*, flypaper

mosquete *m*, musket

mosquetería *f*, musketry; (*ant theat*) male members of the audience who stood at the back of the pit

mosquetero *m*, musketeer; (Spanish theater of the sixteenth and seventeenth centuries) male member of the audience who stood at the back of the pit

mosquitero *m*, mosquito net

mosquito *m*, mosquito; midge, gnat; *inf* tippler, drunkard

mostacera *f*, mustard pot

mostacho *m*, mustache, whiskers; *inf* smudge on the face

mostaza *f*, mustard plant or seed; *cul* mustard

mostela *f*, sheaf (of corn, etc.)

mosto *m*, must, unfermented wine

mostrador (-ra) *n* one who shows, exhibitor. *m*, shop counter; face of a watch

mostrar *vt irr* to show; indicate, point out; demonstrate, prove; manifest, reveal; *vr* show oneself, be (e.g. **Se mostró bondadoso,** He showed himself to be kind). *Pres. Ind.* **muestro, muestras, muestra, muestran.** *Pres. Subjunc.* **muestre, muestres, muestre, muestren**

mostrenco *a inf* stray, vagrant, homeless; *inf* dull, ignorant; *inf* fat, heavy

mota *f*, fault in cloth; mote, defect, fault; mound, hill; thread of cotton, speck of dust, etc.; fleck (of the sun, etc.); spot

mote *m*, maxim, saying; motto, device; catchword, slogan; nickname

motear *vt* to speckle, dot, variegate, spot

motejar *vt* to nickname, call names, dub

motete *m*, motet

motín *m*, mutiny; riot

motivar *vt* to motivate, cause; explain one's reasons

motivo *a* motive. *m*, cause, motive; *mus* motif. **con m. de,** on account of, because of. **de m. propio,** of one's own free will

motocicleta *f*, motorcycle

motociclista *mf* motorcyclist

motor (-ra) *a* motive, driving. *m*, motor, engine. *n* (person) mover, motive force. **m. de combustión interna,** internal combustion engine. **m. de retroacción,** jet engine

motorista *mf* motorist, driver

movedizo *a* movable; insecure, unsteady; shaky; changeable, vacillating

mover *vt irr* to move; operate, drive; sway; wag; persuade, induce; excite; move (to pity, etc.) (*with prep a*) cause; *vi* sprout (plants); *vr* move. *Pres. Ind.* **muevo, mueves, mueve, mueven.** *Pres. Subjunc.* **mueva, muevas, mueva, muevan**

movible *a* movable; insecure, shaky. *m*, motive, cause, incentive

movilidad *f*, mobility; changeableness, inconstancy

movilización *f*, mobilization

movilizar *vt* to mobilize

movimiento *m*, movement; perturbation, excitement; *mus* movement; *lit* fire, spirit; *mech* motion, movement. **mil m. envolvente,** encircling movement

moza *f*, maid; girl; waitress. **m. de partido,** party girl, prostitute. **buena m.,** fine, upstanding young woman

mozalbete *m*, lad, stripling, boy

mozárabe *a* Mozarabic. *mf* Mozarab

mozo *a* young, unmarried. *m*, boy, youth; bachelor; waiter; porter. **m. de cordel** *or* **m. de esquina,** street porter, message boy. **m. de estación,** railroad porter. **buen m.,** fine, upstanding young man

muaré *m*, moiré silk

muceta *f*, *univ* hood, short cape (of a graduate's gown)

muchacha *f*, girl, lass; female servant

muchachada *f*, childish prank

muchachez *f*, boyhood; girlhood

muchachil *a* boyish; girlish

muchacho *m*, boy, youth; male servant

muchedumbre *f*, abundance, plenty; crowd, multitude; mass, mob

muchísimo *a sup* very much. *adv* very great deal, very much

mucho *a* much; plenty of; very; long (time); *pl* many, numerous. *adv* a great deal; much; very much; yes, certainly; frequently, often; very (e.g. **Me alegro m.,** I am very glad); to a great extent; long (time). **con m.,** by far, easily. **ni con m.,** nor anything like it, very far from it. **ni m. menos,** and much less. **por m. que,** however much

mucílago *m*, mucilage, gum

mucosidad *f*, mucosity

mucosa *f*, mucous membrane

mucoso *a* mucous

muda *f*, change, transformation; change of clothes; molting season; molt, sloughing of skin (snakes, etc.); change of voice (in boys)

mudable *a* changeable, inconstant

mudanza *f*, change; furniture removal; step, figure (in dancing); changeability, inconstancy

mudar *vt* to change; alter, transform; exchange; remove; dismiss (from employment); molt; slough the skin (snakes, etc.); change the voice (boys); *vr* alter one's behavior; change one's clothes; change one's residence; change one's expression; *inf* go away, depart

mudéjar *m*, *arch* style containing Moorish and Christian elements. *mf* Moor who remained in Spain under Christian rule

mudez *f*, dumbness; silence, muteness

mudo *a* dumb; silent, mute, quiet

mueblaje *m*, household goods and furniture

mueble *m*, piece of furniture; furnishing

mueblería *f*, furniture store or factory

mueblista *mf* furniture maker; furniture dealer

mueca *f*, grimace

muela *f*, grindstone; molar (tooth); millstone; flat-topped hill. **m. del juicio,** wisdom tooth. **dolor de muelas,** toothache

muellaje *m*, wharfage, dock dues

muelle *a* soft, smooth; voluptuous, sensuous; luxurious. *m*, spring (of a watch, etc.); wharf, quay; freight platform (railroad). **m. real,** mainspring (of a watch). **m. del volante,** hairspring.

muérdago *m*, mistletoe

muermo *m*, glanders

muerte *f*, death; destruction, annihilation; end, decline. *inf* **una m. chiquita,** a nervous shudder. **a m.,** to the death, with no quarter. **de m.,** implacably, inexorably (of hatred); very seriously (of being ill). **dar m. (a),** to kill. **estar a la m.,** to be on the point of death. **a cada m. de un obispo,** once in a blue moon

muerto (-ta) *a* dead; slaked (lime); *mech* neutral; faded, dull (colors); languid, indifferent. **m.** is used in familiar speech as *past part* **matar** (e.g. **Le ha muerto,** He has killed him). *n* corpse. *inf* **desenterrar los muertos,** to speak ill of the dead. *inf* **echarle a uno el m.,** to pass the buck. *inf* **estar m. por,** to be dying, yearning for. **ser el m.,** to be dummy (at cards)

muesca *f*, notch, mortise, groove

muestra *f*, shop sign; sample, specimen; pattern, model; demeanor; watch or clock face; sign, indication; poster, placard; *mil* muster roll. **hacer m.,** to show

muestrario *m*, sample book, collection of samples

mufla *f*, muffler (of a furnace)

mugido *m*, mooing or lowing (of cattle)

mugir *vi* to low or moo (cattle); bellow, shout; rage (elements)

mugre *f*, grease, grime, dirt

mugriento *a* grimy, greasy

muguete *m*, lily of the valley

mujer *f*, woman; wife. **m. de la vida airada** *or* **m. del partido** *or* **m. pública,** prostitute. **m. de la luna,** man in the moon. **m. de su casa,** good housewife. **tomar m.,** to take a wife

mujeriego *a* womanly, feminine; (of men) dissolute, given to philandering. **cabalgar a mujeriegas,** to ride sidesaddle

mujeril *a* womanly, feminine

mula *f,* female mule; mule (heelless slipper). *inf* **Se me fue la m.,** My tongue ran away with me

muladar *m,* refuse heap, junkpile, dunghill

mular *a* mule; mulish

mulatero *m,* mule hirer; muleteer

mulato (-ta) *a* and *n* mulatto

muleta *f,* crutch; bullfighter's red flag; support, prop

mullir *vt irr* to make soft, shake out (wool, down, etc.); *fig* prepare the way; *agr* hoe the roots (of vines, etc.). *Pres. Part.* **mullendo.** *Preterite* **mulló, mulleron.** *Imperf. Subjunc.* **mullese,** etc.

mulo *m,* mule

multa *f,* fine

multar *vt* to impose a fine on

multicolor *a* multicolored

multiforme *a* multiform

multilátero *a* multilateral

multimillonario (-ia) *a* and *n* multimillionaire

multiplicación *f,* multiplication

multiplicador (-ra) *n* multiplier. *m, math* multiplier

multiplicando *m,* multiplicand

multiplicar((se) *vt* and *vr* to multiply; reproduce

multiplicidad *f,* multiplicity

múltiplo *a* and *m,* multiple

multisecular *a* age-old, many centuries old

multitud *f,* multitude, great number; crowd; rabble, masses, mob

mundanal, mundano *a* worldly, mundane

mundanalidad *f,* worldliness

mundial *a* world, worldwide

mundo *m,* world, universe; human race; earth; human society; world (of letters, science, etc.); secular life; *ecc* vanities of the flesh; geographical globe. **echar al m.,** to give birth to; produce, bring forth. **el Nuevo M.,** the New World, America. *inf* **medio m.,** half the earth, a great crowd. *inf* **ponerse el m. por montera,** to treat the world as one's oyster. **ser hombre del m.,** to be a man of the world. *inf* **tener m.** *or* **mucho m.,** to be very experienced, know the world. **todo el m.,** everyone. **venir al m.,** to be born. **ver m.,** to travel, see the world

mundología *f,* worldliness, experience of the world

munición *f, mil* munition; small shot. *mil* **m. de boca,** fodder and food supplies

municionar *vt* to munition, furnish with munitions

municionero (-ra) *n* purveyor, supplier

municipal *a* municipal. *m,* policeman

municipalidad *f,* municipality

municipio *m,* municipality, town council

munificencia *f,* munificence, generosity

munífico *a* munificent, generous

muñeca *f, anat* wrist; doll; puppet; dressmaker's dummy; polishing pad; mannequin; boundary marker; *inf* flighty young woman

muñeco *m,* boy doll; puppet; *inf* playboy

muñir *vt irr* to summon, convoke; arrange, dispose. See **mullir**

muñón *m, surg* stump of an amputated limb; *mech* gudgeon

mural *a* mural

muralla *f,* town wall; rampart, fortification

murar *vt* to surround with a wall, wall in

murciano (-na) *a* and *n* Murcian

murciélago *m, zool* bat

murga *f,* band of street musicians

murmullo *m,* whisper; whispering; rustling; purling, lapping, splashing; mumbling, muttering

murmuración *f,* slander, backbiting, gossip

murmurador (-ra) *a* gossiping, slanderous. *n* gossip, backbiter

murmurar *vi* to rustle (leaves, etc.); purl, lap, splash (water); whisper; mumble, mutter; *vi* and *vt inf* slander, backbite

murmurio *m,* rustling; lapping (of water); whispering; murmur; *inf* slander

muro *m,* wall; defensive wall, rampart

musa *f,* muse

musaraña *f, zool* shrew; any small animal; *inf* ridiculous effigy, guy. *inf* **mirar a las musarañas,** to be absent-minded

muscular *a* muscular

musculatura *f,* musculature

músculo *m,* muscle; strength, brawn

musculoso *a* muscular; strong, brawny

muselina *f,* muslin

museo *m,* museum. **m. de pintura,** art gallery, picture gallery

musgo *m,* moss

musgoso *a* mossy, moss-grown

música *f,* music; melody, harmony; musical performance; musical composition; group of musicians; sheet music. *inf* **m. celestial,** vain words, moonshine. *inf* **m. ratonera,** badly played music. *inf* **¡Vaya con su m. a otra parte!** Get out! Go to hell!

musical *a* musical

músico (-ca) *a* music. *n* musician. **m. ambulante,** strolling musician. **m. mayor,** bandleader

musitar *vi* to mutter, mumble

muslo *m,* thigh

mustio *a* sad, disheartened, depressed; faded, withered

musulmán (-ana) *a* and *n* Muslim

mutabilidad *f,* mutability, changeability

mutación *f,* change, mutation; sudden change in the weather; *theat* change of scene

mutilación *f,* mutilation; damage; defacement

mutilar *vt* to mutilate; spoil, deface, damage; cut short; reduce

mutis *m, theat* exit. **hacer m.** *theat* to exit; keep quiet, say nothing

mutismo *m,* mutism, dumbness; silence, speechlessness

mutualidad *f,* reciprocity, mutuality, interdependence; principle of mutual aid; mutual aid society

mutualismo *m,* mutualism, organized mutual aid

mutualista *mf* member of a mutual aid society

mutuante *mf com* lender

mutuo *a* reciprocal, mutual, interdependent

muy *adv* very; very much; much. Used to form absolute superlative (e.g. **m. rápidamente,** very quickly). Can modify adjectives, nouns used adjectivally, adverbs, participles (e.g. **María es m. mujer,** Mary is very much a woman (very womanly)). **m. temprano,** very early. **M. señor mío,** Dear Sir (in letters)

N

naba *f,* swede, turnip

nabar *m,* turnip field

nabo *m,* turnip; turnip root; any root stem; *naut* mast; stock (of a horse's tail)

nácar *m,* mother-of-pearl

nacarado, nacáreo *a* nacreous, mother-of-pearl

nacer *vi irr* to be born; rise (rivers, etc.); sprout; grow (plumage, fur, leaves, etc.); descend (lineage); appear (stars, etc.); originate; *fig* issue forth; appear suddenly;

(with prep a or *para)* be destined for, have a natural leaning toward. **n. con pajitas de oro en la cuna,** to be born with a silver spoon in one's mouth. *vr* grow; sprout; *sew* split at the seams. *Pres. Ind.* **nazco, naces,** etc. *Pres. Subjunc.* **nazca,** etc.

nacido *a* and *past part* born; suitable, fit. *m,* (gen. *pl*) the living and the dead. **bien n.,** noble, well-born; well-bred. **mal n.,** base-born; ill-bred

naciente *a* growing; nascent. *m,* east

nacimiento *m*, birth; source (of rivers, etc.); birthplace; origin; lineage; *ast* rising; nativity crib, manger. **de n.,** from birth; by birth; born

nación *f*, nation; country; *inf* birth

nacional *a* national; native. *mf* citizen, national

nacionalidad *f*, nationality

nacionalismo *m*, nationalism

nacionalista *a* and *mf* nationalist

nacionalización *f*, naturalization; nationalization; acclimatization

nacionalizar *vt* to naturalize; nationalize

nacionalsindicalismo *m*, national syndicalism

nacionalsocialismo *m*, national socialism, nazism

nada *f*, void, nothingness. *pron indef* nothing. *adv* by no means. **casi n.,** very little, practically nothing. **¡De n.!** Not at all! Don't mention it! You're welcome! **No vale para n.,** He (it, she) is of no use

nadaderas *f pl*, water wings (for swimming)

nadador (-ra) *n* swimmer. *a* swimming

nadar *vi* to swim; float; have an abundance (of); *inf* be too large (of garments, etc.). **n. y guardar la ropa,** *fig* to sit on the fence

nadería *f*, trifle

nadie *pron indef* no one. *m, fig* a nobody

nadir *m*, nadir

nado *a* by swimming; afloat

nafta *f*, naphtha

naftalina *f*, naphthalene

naipe *m*, playing card; pack of cards

naire *m*, elephant keeper or trainer

nalga *f*, (gen. *pl*) buttock(s)

nana *f*, *inf* grandma; lullaby

nao *f*, ship

napoleónico *a* Napoleonic

Nápoles Naples

napolitano (-na) *a* and *n* Neapolitan

naranja *f*, orange. **n. dulce,** blood orange. **n. mandarina,** tangerine. *inf* **media n.,** better half

naranjada *f*, orangeade

naranjal *m*, orange grove

naranjero (-ra) *n* orange seller

naranjo *m*, orange tree; *inf* lout, blockhead

narciso *m*, narcissus; dandy, fop. **n. trompón,** daffodil

narcótico *a* and *m*, narcotic

narcotizar *vt* to narcotize

narcotraficante *mf* drug dealer

nardo *m*, tuberose, spikenard, nard

narguile *m*, hookah, hubble-bubble, narghile

narigudo *a* large-nosed; nose-shaped

nariz *f*, nose; nostril; snout; nozzle; sense of smell; bouquet (of wine). **n. perfilada,** well-shaped nose. **n. respingona,** snub nose. *inf* **meter las narices,** to meddle, interfere

narración *f*, narration, account

narrador (-ra) *a* narrative. *n* narrator

narrar *vt* to narrate, tell, relate

narrativa *f*, narrative; account; narrative skill

narrativo, narratorio *a* narrative

nata *f*, cream; *fig* the flower, elite; *pl* whipped cream with sugar

natación *f*, swimming. **n. a la marinera,** trudgen stroke

natal *a* natal; native. *m*, birth; birthday

natalicio *a* natal. *a* and *m*, birthday

natalidad *f*, birth rate

natatorio *a* swimming. *m*, swimming pool

natillas *f pl*, custard

natividad *f*, nativity; birth; Christmas

nativo *a* indigenous; native; innate

nato *a* born; inherent; ex officio

natura *f*, nature; *mus* major scale

natural *a* natural; native; indigenous; spontaneous; sincere, candid; physical; usual, ordinary; *mus* natural; unadulterated, pure; *her* proper. *mf* native, citizen. *m*, temperament; disposition; instinct (of animals); natu-

ral inclination. **al n.,** naturally, without art. **del n.,** *art* from life

naturaleza *f*, nature; character; disposition; instinct; temperament; nationality, origin; naturalization; kind, class; constitution, physique. **n. humana,** humankind. **n. muerta,** *art* still life

naturalidad *f*, naturalness; nationality

naturalista *mf* naturalist

naturalización *f*, naturalization; acclimatization

naturalizar *vt* to naturalize; acclimatize; *vr* become naturalized; become acclimatized

naturalmente *adv* naturally; of course

naturismo *m*, nature cure

naufragar *vi* to be shipwrecked; fail, be unsuccessful

naufragio *m*, shipwreck; disaster, loss

náufrago (-ga) *n* shipwrecked person. *m*, shark

náusea *f*, nausea (*pl* more usual); repugnance

nauseabundo, nauseoso *a* nauseous; nauseating, repugnant

nauta *mf* mariner

náutica *f*, navigation; yachting; seamanship

náutico *a* nautical

navaja *f*, razor; clasp knife; boar tusk; sting; *inf* slanderous tongue. **n. de afeitar,** (shaving) razor

navajada *f*, slash with a razor

navajero *m*, razor case

naval *a* naval

Navarra Navarre

navarro (-ra) *a* and *n* Navarrese

nave *f*, ship; *arch* nave. **n. aérea,** airship. *arch* **n. lateral,** aisle. **n. principal,** *arch* nave

navegable *a* navigable

navegación *f*, navigation; sea voyage

navegante *a* voyaging; navigating. *m*, navigator

navegar *vi* to navigate; sail; fly

navidad *f*, nativity; Christmas; *pl* Christmastime

naviero *a* shipping. *m*, ship owner

navío *m*, warship; ship. **n. de transporte,** transport. **n. de tres puentes,** three-decker

náyade *f*, naiad, water nymph

nazareno (-na) *a* and *n* Nazarene; Christian

Nazaret Nazareth

nazismo *m*, nazism

neblina *f*, fog; mist

nebulosidad *f*, nebulousness; cloudiness

nebuloso *a* foggy; misty; cloudy; somber, melancholy; confused, nebulous

necedad *f*, silliness

necesario *a* necessary; unavoidable

neceser *m*, dressing case. *sew* **n. de costura,** workbox

necesidad *f*, necessity; poverty, want; shortage, need; emergency. **de n.,** necessarily

necesitado (-da) *a* needy, poor. *n* poor person

necesitar *vt* to necessitate; compel, oblige; *vi* be necessary, need

necio *a* stupid; senseless; unreasonable

necrología *f*, necrology, obituary

necromancía *f*, necromancy

neerlandés *a* Dutch

nefando *a* iniquitous

nefario *a* nefarious

nefasto *a* disastrous, ill-omened

nefrítico *a* nephritic

nefritis *f*, nephritis

negable *a* deniable

negación *f*, negation; privation; negative; nay; *gram* negative particle; *law* traverse

negado *a* inept, unfitted; stupid

negar *vt irr* to deny; refuse; prohibit; disclaim; dissemble; disown; *law* traverse; *vr* refuse, avoid; decline (to receive visitors). See **acertar**

negativa *f*, denial; refusal; *phot* negative

negativo *a* negative

negligencia *f*, negligence; omission; carelessness; forgetfulness

negligente *a* negligent; careless; neglectful

negociable *a* negotiable

negociación *f*, negotiation; business affair, deal

negociado *m*, department, section (of a ministry, etc.); business

negociante *m*, businessman. *a* negotiating; trading

negociar *vi* to trade, traffic; negotiate

negocio *m*, occupation; trade; business; employment; transaction; *pl* business affairs. **hombre de negocios,** businessman

negra *f*, black girl, black woman; *inf* honey, *WH* sweetheart

negrecer *vi irr* to become black. See **conocer**

negrero (-ra) *n* slave trader

negro *a* black; dark; melancholy; disastrous; *her* sable. *m*, black; black (color). **n. de humo,** lampblack

negrura *f*, blackness

negruzco *a* blackish

nemotécnica *f*, mnemonics

nene (-na) *n inf* baby; darling

nenúfar *m*, white water lily

neo *m*, neon

neocelandés (-esa) *a* New Zealand. *n* New Zealander

neófito (-ta) *n* neophyte

neoguineano *a* New Guinean

neolítico *a* neolithic

neologismo *m*, neologism

neoyorquino (-na) *a* New York. *n* New Yorker

nepotismo *m*, nepotism

Neptuno *m*, *ast* Neptune; *poet* sea

nereida *f*, nereid, sea nymph

nervio *m*, nerve; sinew; *bot* vein; vigor; *mus* string. **n. ciático,** sciatic nerve

nervioso *a* nervous; overwrought, agitated; vigorous; neural; sinewy; jerky (of style, etc.)

nervosidad *f*, nervousness; nervosity; flexibility (metals); jerkiness (of style, etc.); force, efficacy

nervudo *a* strong-nerved, vigorous

nesga *f*, sew gore

neto *a* neat; clean; pure; *com* net. *m*, *arch* dado

neumático *a* pneumatic. *m*, rubber tire

neumococo *m*, pneumococcus

neurálgico *a* neuralgic

neurastenia *f*, neurasthenia

neurasténico (-ca) *a* and *n* neurasthenic

neurología *f*, neurology

neurólogo *m*, neurologist

neurópata *mf* neuropath

neurosis *f*, neurosis. **n. de guerra,** war neurosis; shell shock

neurótico (-ca) *a* and *n* neurotic

neutral *a* neutral; indifferent

neutralidad *f*, neutrality; impartiality, indifference

neutralizar *vt* to neutralize; counteract, mitigate

neutro *a* neuter; *chem* neutral; *mech* neuter; sexless

nevada *f*, snowfall

nevar *vi irr impers* to snow. *Pres. Ind.* **nieva.** *Pres. Subjunc.* **nieve**

nevera *f*, refrigerator; icehouse

nevero *m*, ice-cream man; iceman

nevisca *f*, light snowfall

nevoso *a* snowy

nexo *m*, nexus; connection, union

ni *conjunc* neither, nor. **ni bien ni mal,** neither good nor bad. **ni siquiera,** not even. **¡Ni crea!, ¡Ni creas!** Nonsense!

niara *f*, haystack, rick

nicaragüeño (-ña) *a* and *n* Nicaraguan

nicho *m*, niche; recess (in a wall)

nicotina *f*, nicotine

nidada *f*, nest full of eggs; brood, clutch

nidal *m*, nest; nest egg; haunt; cause, foundation

nido *m*, nest; den; hole; dwelling; haunt. **n. de ametralladoras,** *mil* pillbox

niebla *f*, fog; mist; cloud; mildew; haze

nieto (-ta) *n* grandchild; descendant

nieve *f*, snow; whiteness. **deportes de n.,** winter sports

nigromancia *f*, necromancy

nigromante *m*, necromancer

nihilismo *m*, nihilism

nihilista *mf* nihilist

Nilo, el the Nile

nimbo *m*, halo, nimbus

nimiedad *f*, prolixity; *inf* fussiness; fastidiousness, delicacy

nimio *a* prolix; *inf* fussy; fastidious; *inf* parsimonious

ninfa *f*, nymph; *ent* chrysalis

ningún *a abb* of **ninguno.** Used before *m*, *sing* nouns only. **De n. modo,** In no way! Certainly not!

niña *f*, girl. **n. del ojo,** pupil (of the eye). **n. de los ojos,** apple of one's eye, darling

niñada *f*, childishness, foolish act

niñera *f*, nursemaid

niñería *f*, childish act; trifle; childishness, folly

niñez *f*, childhood; beginning, early days; *fig* cradle

Nínive Nineveh

niño (-ña) *a* childish; young; inexperienced; imprudent. *n* child; young or inexperienced person. **n. de la doctrina,** charity child. **n. terrible,** enfant terrible. **desde n.,** from childhood

nipón (-ona) *a* and *n* Japanese

níquel *m*, *chem* nickel

niquelar *vt* to chrome-plate

nirvana *m*, nirvana

níspero *m*, medlar tree; medlar

níspola *f*, medlar

nitidez *f*, brightness, neatness, cleanliness

nítido *a* bright, neat, clean (often *poet.*)

nitrato *m*, nitrate

nítrico *a* nitric

nitrógeno *m*, nitrogen

nivel *m*, level; levelness. **n. de albañil,** plummet. **n. de burbuja,** spirit level. **a n.,** on the level. **estar al n. de las circunstancias,** to rise to the occasion; save the day

nivelación *f*, leveling

nivelador (-ra) *a* leveling. *n* leveler

nivelar *vt* to level; *fig* make equal

níveo *a* snowy; snow-white

Niza Nice

no *adv* no; not. **no bien,** no sooner. **no sea que,** unless. **no tal,** no such thing

noble *a* noble, illustrious; generous; outstanding, excellent; aristocratic. *mf* nobleman (-woman)

nobleza *f*, nobility

noche *f*, night; darkness; confusion, obscurity. *inf* **n. toledana,** restless night. **¡Buenas noches!** Good night! **de n.,** by night. **esta n.,** tonight

nochebuena *f*, Christmas Eve

nochebueno *m*, yule log; Christmas cake

nocherniego *a* night, nocturnal

noción *f*, notion, idea; *pl* elementary knowledge

nocividad *f*, noxiousness

nocivo *a* noxious

nocturno *a* nocturnal; melancholy. *m*, *mus* nocturne

nodriza *f*, wet nurse

nogal *m*, walnut tree; walnut wood

nómada *a* nomadic

nomadismo *m*, nomadism

nombradía *f*, renown

nombramiento *m*, naming; appointment; nomination

nombrar *vt* to name; nominate; appoint; mention (in dispatches, etc.)

nombre *m*, name; title; reputation; proxy; *gram* noun; *mil* password. **n. de pila,** Christian name. **por n.,** called; by name. **Su n. anda puesto en el cuerno de la Luna,** He (she) is praised to the skies

nomenclatura *f*, nomenclature

nómina *f*, list, register; payroll; amulet

nominación *f*, nomination, appointment

nominador (-ra) *a* nominating. *n* nominator

nominal *a* nominal

nominalismo *m*, nominalism

nominalista *a* nominalistic. *mf* nominalist

nomo *m*, gnome

nóstico (-ca) *a* and *n* gnostic

non *a* odd (of numbers)

nonada *f*, nothing, practically nothing

nonagenario (-ia) *a* and *n* nonagenarian

nonagésimo *a* ninetieth

nones *m*, *pl* certainly not, definitely not, nope

nopal *m*, nopal, prickly pear tree

noque *m*, tanner's vat

noquear *vt* (*boxing*) to knock out, K.O.

norabuena *f*, congratulation

nordeste *m*, northeast

nórdico (-ca) *a* and *n* Nordic

noria *f*, water well; chain pump; *inf* hard, monotonous work

norma *f*, square (used by builders, etc.); *fig* norm, standard, model

normal *a* normal, usual; standard, average. *f*, normal school, teacher's college (also **escuela n.**)

normalidad *f*, normality

normalista *mf* student at a teacher's college

normalización *f*, normalization; standardization

normalizar *vt* to make normal; standardize

Normandía Normandy

normando (-da) *a* Norman. *n* Northman; Norman

nornordeste *m*, northnortheast

nornorueste *m*, northnorthwest

noroeste *m*, northwest

norte *m*, north pole; north; north wind; polestar; *fig* guide

norteamericano (-na) *a* and *n* North American; (*U.S.A.*) American

norteño *a* northerly, northern

Noruega Norway

noruego (-ga) *a* and *n* Norwegian. *m*, Norwegian (language)

nos *pers pron pl mf acc* and *dat* (direct and indirect object) of **nosotros**, us; to us (e.g. **Nos lo dio,** He gave it to us)

nosotros, nosotras *pers pron pl mf* we; us. Also used with preposition (e.g. **Lo hicieron por nosotros,** They did it for us)

nostalgia *f*, nostalgia

nostálgico *a* nostalgic; melancholy; homesick

nota *f*, mark, sign; annotation, comment; *mus* note; memorandum; *com* bill, account; criticism, imputation; mark (in exams); repute, renown; note (diplomatic)

notabilidad *f*, notability

notable *a* notable, remarkable; outstanding, prominent; with distinction (examination mark). *m pl*, notabilities

notación *f*, (*mus math*) notation; annotation

notar *vt* to mark, indicate; observe, notice; note down; annotate; dictate, read out; criticize, reproach; discredit

notaría *f*, profession of a notary; notary's office

notarial *a* notarial

notario *m*, notary public

noticia *f*, rudiment, elementary knowledge; information; news (gen. *pl*); *pl* knowledge. **atrasado de noticias,** *fig* behind the times

noticiar *vt* to inform, give notice

noticiario *m*, news bulletin, newsreel.

noticiero *m*, newspaper

noticioso *a* informed; learned; newsy

notificación *f*, *law* notification. **n. de reclutamiento,** draft notice

notificar *vt* to notify officially; inform; warn

noto *a* known. *m*, south wind

notoriedad *f*, notoriety, publicity; flagrancy; fame, renown

notorio *a* well-known; notorious, obvious; flagrant

novatada *f*, *inf* ragging (of a freshman); blunder

novato (-ta) *a* new, inexperienced. *n* novice, beginner

novecientos *a* and *m*, nine hundred

novedad *f*, newness, novelty; change, alteration; latest

news; surprise; *pl* novelties. **sin n.,** no change; all well (or as usual); safely, without incident

novel *a* new; inexperienced

novela *f*, novel; tale; falsehood. **n. caballista,** western, cowboy story. **n. por entregas,** serial (story)

novelero (-ra) *a* fond of novelty and change; fond of novels; fickle. *n* newshound, gossip

novelesco *a* novelistic; imaginary

novelista *mf* novelist

novelística *f*, art of novel writing

novena *f*, *ecc* novena, religious services spread over nine days

noveno *a* and *m*, ninth

noventa *a* and *m*, ninety; ninetieth

novia *f*, bride; fiancée

noviazgo *m*, engagement, betrothal

noviciado *m*, novitiate; training, apprenticeship

novicio (-ia) *n* *ecc* novice; beginner, apprentice; unassuming person

noviembre *m*, November

novillada *f*, herd of young bulls; bullock baiting

novillo *m*, bullock. **hacer novillos,** to play truant

novilunio *m*, new moon

novio *m*, bridegroom; fiancé; novice, beginner

novísimo *a sup* **nuevo** newest; latest, most recent

nubada *f*, cloudburst, rainstorm; abundance, plenty

nubarrón *m*, dense, lowering cloud, storm cloud

nube *f*, cloud; *fig* screen, impediment. **n. de verano,** summer cloud; passing annoyance

nublado *a* cloudy; overcast. *m*, storm cloud; menace, threat; multitude, crowd

nublarse *vr* to cloud over

nubloso *a* cloudy; unfortunate, unhappy

nuca *f*, nape

núcleo *m*, kernel; stone, pip (of fruit); nucleus; *fig* core, essence

nudillo *m*, knuckle; *mas* plug

nudo *m*, knot; (*bot med*) node; joint; *naut* knot; *fig* bond, tie; *fig* crux, knotty point. **n. al revés,** granny knot. **n. de comunicaciones,** communication center. **n. de marino,** reef knot. **n. de tejedor,** sheet bend (knot). **n. en la garganta,** *fig* lump in the throat (from emotion)

nudoso *a* knotted, knotty; gnarled

nuera *f*, daughter-in-law

nuestro, nuestra *poss pron 1st pers pl mf* our; ours. **los nuestros,** our friends, supporters, party, profession, etc.

nueva *f*, news

Nueva Caledonia New Caledonia

Nueva Escocia Nova Scotia

Nueva Gales del Sur New South Wales

Nueva Guinea New Guinea

nuevamente *adv* again

Nueva Orleans New Orleans

Nueva York New York

Nueva Zelanda, Zelandia New Zealand

nueve *a* nine; ninth. *m*, number nine; ninth (of the month) (e.g. **el nueve de marzo,** March 9th). **a las nueve,** at nine o'clock

nuevo *a* new; fresh; newly arrived; inexperienced; unused, scarcely worn. **de n.,** again. **¿Qué hay de n.?** What's the news? What's new?

nuez *f*, walnut; *anat* Adam's apple. **n. moscada,** nutmeg

nulidad *f*, nullity; incompetence, ineptitude; worthlessness

nulo *a* null, void; incapable; worthless

numen *m*, divinity; inspiration

numeración *f*, calculation; numbering

numerador *m*, numerator

numerar *vt* to number; enumerate; calculate

numerario *a* numerary. *m*, cash

numérico *a* numerical

número *m*, number; figure; numeral; size (of gloves, etc.); quantity; issue, copy; rhythm; *gram* number;

item (of a program); *pl ecc* Numbers. **n. del distrito postal,** ZIP code. **n. quebrado,** *math* fraction. **sin n.,** numberless
numeroso *a* numerous; harmonious
numismática *f*, numismatics
nunca *adv* never. **n. jamás,** nevermore. **N. digas «De esta agua no beberé!»** Never say "Never!"
nuncio *m*, messenger; papal nuncio; *fig* harbinger
nupcial *a* nuptial

nupcialidad *f*, marriage rate
nupcias *f pl*, nuptials, marriage
nutria *f*, otter, nutria
nutrición *f*, nourishment; nutrition
nutrido *a* abundant; numerous
nutrimento *m*, nutriment; nourishment; nutrition; *fig* food, encouragement
nutrir *vt* to nourish; encourage; *fig* fill
nutritivo *a* nourishing, nutritive

Ñ

ñaques *m pl*, odds and ends, rubbish
ñiquiñaque *m*, *inf* good-for-nothing, wastrel; *inf* trash

ñoñería *f*, *inf* drivel; folly, stupidity
ñoño (-ña) *a inf* sentimental; foolish, idiotic. *n* fool.

O

o *f*, letter O. *conjunc* or, either. **o** becomes **u** before words beginning with **o** or **ho** (e.g. **gloria u honor**)
oasis *m*, oasis; *fig* refuge, haven
obcecación *f*, blindness; obstinacy; obsession
obcecar *vt* to blind; obsess; *fig* dazzle; darken
obduración *f*, obstinacy, stubbornness, obduracy
obedecer *vt irr* to obey; *fig* respond; bend, yield (metals, etc.); *vi* result (from), arise (from). See **conocer**
obedecimiento *m*, **obediencia** *f*, obedience
obediente *a* obedient; docile
obelisco *m*, obelisk
obertura *f*, *mus* overture
obesidad *f*, obesity
obeso *a* obese
óbice *m*, obstacle, impediment
obispado *m*, bishopric
obispalía *f*, bishop's palace; bishopric
obispo *m*, bishop. **o. sufragáneo,** suffragan bishop
óbito *m*, death, demise
obituario *m*, obituary; obituary column
objeción *f*, objection
objetar *vt* to object to, oppose
objetivar *vt* to view objectively
objetividad *f*, objectivity
objetivo *a* objective. *m*, *opt* eyepiece; object finder; aim, goal
objeto *m*, object; subject, theme; purpose; aim, goal. **sin o.,** without object; aimlessly
oblea *f*, seal, wafer
oblicuidad *f*, obliqueness
oblicuo *a* slanting, oblique
obligación *f*, obligation; *com* bond; *com* debenture; *pl* responsibilities; *com* liabilities
obligacionista *mf com* bond holder, debenture holder
obligado *m*, contractor (to a borough, etc.); *mus* obbligato
obligar *vt* to compel, oblige, constrain; lay under an obligation; *law* mortgage; *vr* bind oneself, promise
obligatorio *a* obligatory
oblongo *a* oblong
oboe *m*, oboe; oboe player, oboist
óbolo *m*, obol, ancient Greek coin
obra *f*, work; anything made; literary, artistic, scientific production; structure, construction; repair, alteration (to buildings, etc.); means, influence, power; labor, or time spent; action, behavior. **o. de caridad,** charitable act. **o. maestra,** masterpiece. **obras públicas,** public works. **poner por o.,** to put into effect; to set to work on. **o. de,** about, approximately
obrar *vt* to work; make, do; execute, perform; affect; construct, build; *vi* be, exist (things); act, behave. **o. mal,** to behave badly, do wrong
obrero (-ra) *a* working. *n* worker; *pl* workers
obscenidad *f*, obscenity
obsceno *a* obscene

obsequiar *vt* to entertain, be attentive (to); give presents (to); court, make love to. **Me obsequia con un reloj,** He is presenting me with a watch
obsequio *m*, attention; gift; deference. **en o. de,** as a tribute to
obsequioso *a* obliging, courteous, attentive
observable *a* observable
observación *f*, observation; remark
observador (-ra) *a* observing. *n* observer
observancia *f*, observance; respect, reverence
observar *vt* to notice; inspect, examine; fulfill; remark; watch, spy upon; *ast* observe
observatorio *m*, observatory
obsesión *f*, obsession
obsesionar *vt* to obsess
obseso *a* obsessed
obsidiana *f*, obsidian
obsolecer *vi* to obsolesce, become obsolete
obsoleto *a* obsolete
obstáculo *m*, impediment; obstacle
obstante, no *adv* in spite of; nevertheless
obstar *vi* to impede, hinder
obstetra *mf* obstetrician
obstetricia *f*, obstetrics
obstinación *f*, obstinacy
obstinado *a* obstinate, stubborn
obstinarse *vr* (*with en*) to persist in, insist on, be stubborn about
obstinaz *a* obstinate
obstrucción *f*, obstruction
obstruccionismo *m*, obstructionism
obstruccionista *mf* obstructionist
obstruir *vt irr* to obstruct; block; hinder; *vr* become choked or stopped up (pipes, etc.). See **huir**
obtención *f*, obtainment; attainment, realization
obtener *vt irr* to obtain; attain; maintain, preserve. See **tener**
obturador *m*, stopper; shutter (of a camera)
obturar *vt* to stopper, plug; block, obstruct
obtuso *a* blunt, dull; (*geom* and *fig*) obtuse
obús *m*, howitzer; *mil* shell
obviar *vt* to obviate
obvio *a* obvious, evident, apparent
oca *f*, goose
ocasión *f*, occasion; opportunity; motive, cause; danger; risk; *inf* **asir la o. por la melena,** to take time by the forelock. **de o.,** second-hand
ocasional *a* chance, fortuitous; occasional
ocasionar *vt* to cause, occasion; excite, provoke; risk, endanger
ocaso *m*, sunset; west; dusk; decadence, decline
occidental *a* Western
occidente *m*, West, Occident
occipital *a anat* occipital
occiso *a* murdered; killed

oceánico *a* oceanic

océano *m*, ocean; immensity, abundance

oceanografía *f*, oceanography

ocelote *m*, ocelot

ochava *f*, eighth; *ecc* octave

ochavo *m*, *ant* small Spanish copper coin

ochenta *a* and *m*, eighty; eightieth

ochentón (-ona) *n* octogenarian

ocho *a* eight; eighth. *m*, figure eight; playing card with eight pips; eight; eighth day (of the month). **las o.,** eight o'clock

ochocientos *a* and *m*, eight hundred; eight-hundredth

ocio *m*, leisure, idleness; *pl* pastimes; leisure time

ociosidad *f*, idleness, laziness; leisure

ocioso (-sa) *a* idle; useless, worthless; unprofitable, fruitless. *n* idle fellow

ocre *m*, ocher

octágono *a*, octagon

octava *f*, octave

octaviano *a* Octavian

octavo *a* eighth. *m*, eighth. **en o.,** in octavo

octeto *m*, octet

octogenario (-ia) *a* and *n* octogenarian

octogésimo *a* eightieth

octubre *m*, October

óctuple *a* octuple, eightfold

ocular *a* ocular. *m*, eyepiece

oculista *mf* oculist

ocultación *f*, hiding, concealment

ocultamente *adv* secretly

ocultar *vt* to hide, conceal; disguise; keep secret

ocultismo *m*, occultism

oculto *a* hidden; secret; occult. **en o.,** secretly, quietly

ocupación *f*, occupancy; occupation, pursuit; employment, office, trade

ocupado *a* occupied; busy

ocupante *m*, occupant

ocupar *vt* to take possession of; obtain or hold (job); occupy, fill; inhabit; employ; hinder, embarrass; hold the attention (of); *vr* (*with en*) be engaged in, be occupied with; (*with con*) concentrate on (a business affair, etc.)

ocurrencia *f*, occurrence, incident; bright idea; witty remark

ocurrir *vi* to anticipate; happen, take place; occur, strike (ideas)

oda *f*, ode

odalisca *f*, odalisk

odiar *vt* to hate

odio *m*, hatred; malevolence

odioso *a* hateful, odious

odisea *f*, odyssey

odontología *f*, odontology

odontólogo *m*, odontologist

odorífero *a* odoriferous, fragrant

odre *m*, goatskin, wineskin; *inf* wine bibber

oesnorueste *m*, westnorthwest

oessudueste *m*, westsouthwest

oeste *m*, west

ofender *vt* to ill-treat, hurt; offend, insult; anger, annoy; *vr* be offended

ofendido *a* offended; resentful

ofensa *f*, injury, harm; offense, crime

ofensiva *f*, *mil* offensive. **tomar la o.,** to take the offensive

ofensivo *a* offensive

ofensor (-ra) *n* offender

oferta *f*, offer; gift; proposal; *com* tender. **o. y demanda,** supply and demand

ofertorio *m*, *ecc* offertory

oficial *a* official. *m*, official; officer; clerk; executioner; worker

oficiala *f*, trained female worker

oficialidad *f*, officialdom; officers

oficiar *vt ecc* to celebrate or serve (mass); communicate officially, inform; *inf* (*with de*) act as

oficina *f*, workshop; office; pharmaceutical laboratory; *pl* cellars, basement (of a house)

oficinesco *a* bureaucratic, red-tape

oficinista *mf* clerk, office employee, office worker

oficio *m*, occupation, employment; office, function, capacity; craft; operation; trade, business; official communication; office, bureau; *ecc* office. **Santo O.,** Holy Office. *fig* **buenos oficios,** good offices

oficiosidad *f*, diligence, conscientiousness; helpfulness, friendliness; officiousness

oficioso *a* conscientious; helpful, useful; officious; meddlesome; unofficial, informal

ofrecer *vt irr* to offer; present; exhibit; consecrate, dedicate; *vr* occur, suggest itself; volunteer. **¿Qué se le ofrece?** What do you require? What would you like? See **conocer**

ofrecimiento *m*, offer, offering

ofrenda *f*, *ecc* offering; gift, present

oftalmología *f*, ophthalmology

oftalmólogo *m*, oculist, ophthalmologist

ofuscación *f*. **ofuscamiento** *m*, obfuscation, dazzle; dimness of sight; mental confusion, bewilderment

ofuscar *vt* to dazzle, daze; dim, obfuscate; confuse, bewilder

ogro *m*, ogre

ohmio *m*, ohm

oídas, de *adv* by hearsay

oído *m*, sense of hearing; ear. **de o.,** by ear. **decir al o.,** to whisper in a person's ear. *mus* **duro de o.,** hard of hearing; having a bad ear (for music). **estar sordo de un o.,** to be deaf in one ear

oidor *m*, hearer; judge, *ant* magistrate

oir *vt irr* to hear; give ear to, listen; understand. *Pres. Part.* **oyendo.** *Pres. Ind.* **oigo, oyes, oye, oyen.** *Preterite* **oyó, oyeron.** *Pres. Subjunc.* **oiga,** etc. *Imperf. Subjunc.* **oyese,** etc.

oíslo *mf inf* better half

ojal *m*, buttonhole; slit, hole

¡ojalá! *interj* If only that were so! God grant!

ojeada *f*, glance

ojear *vt* to look at, stare at; bewitch; scare, startle

ojera *f*, dark shadow (under the eye); eye bath

ojeriza *f*, ill-will, spite

ojeroso *a* having dark shadows under the eyes, wan, haggard

ojete *m*, eyelet

ojinegro *a* black-eyed

ojiva *f*, ogive

ojo *m*, eye; hole; slit; socket; keyhole; eye (of a needle); span (of a bridge); core (of a corn); attention, care; mesh; spring, stream; well (of a staircase); *pl* darling. **¡Ojo!** Take care! **o. avizor,** sharp watch; lynx eye. **Ojos que no ven, corazón que no siente,** Out of sight, out of mind. **o. saltón,** prominent, bulging eye. **o. vivo,** bright eye. **a o. de buen cubero,** at a guess. **a ojos vistas,** visibly; patently

ola *f*, billow; wave (atmospheric)

ole *m*, Andalusian dance

¡olé! *interj* Bravo!

oleada *f*, big wave, breaker; swell (of the sea); *fig* surge (of a crowd)

oleaginoso *a* oleaginous

oleaje *m*, swell, surge, billowing

olear *vt* to administer extreme unction

óleo *m*, oil; *ecc* holy oil (gen. *pl*). **al ó.,** in oils

oleoducto *m*, oil pipeline

oler *vt irr* to smell; guess, discover; pry, smell out; *vi* smell; (*with prep a*) smell of; smack of, be reminiscent of. *Pres. Ind.* **huelo, hueles, huele, huelen.** *Pres. Subjunc.* **huela, huelas, huela, huelan**

olfatear *vt* to sniff, snuff, smell; *inf* pry into

olfativo, olfatorio *a* olfactory

olfato *m*, sense of smell; shrewdness

olfatorio *a* olfactory

oliente (mal) *a* evil-smelling

oligarquía *f*, oligarchy

oligárquico *a* oligarchic
olímpico *a* Olympic; Olympian
oliva *f,* olive tree; olive; barn owl; peace
olivar *m,* olive grove
olivo *m,* olive tree
olmeda *f,* **olmedo** *m,* elm grove
olmo *m,* elm tree
olor *m,* odor, scent, smell; hope, promise; suspicion, hint; reputation. **o. de santidad,** odor of sanctity
oloroso *a* fragrant, perfumed
olvidadizo *a* forgetful
olvidar(se) *vt* and *vr* to forget; neglect, desert. **Se me olvidó el libro,** I forgot the book. **Me olvidé de lo pasado,** I forgot the past
olvido *m,* forgetfulness; indifference, neglect; oblivion
olla *f,* stew pot; Spanish stew; whirlpool. **o. podrida,** rich Spanish stew containing bacon, fowl, meat, vegetables, ham, etc. **las ollas de Egipto,** the fleshpots of Egypt
ombligo *m,* navel; *fig* core, center
ominoso *a* ominous
omisión *f,* omission; carelessness, negligence; neglect
omiso *a* omitted; remiss; careless. **hacer caso o. de,** to set aside, ignore
omitir *vt* to omit
ómnibus *m,* bus
omnímodo *a* all-embracing
omnipotencia *f,* omnipotence
omnipotente *a* omnipotent, all-powerful
omnisciencia *f,* omniscience
omniscio *a* omniscient
omnívoro *a* omnivorous
omoplato *m,* scapula, shoulder blade
once *a* eleven; eleventh. *m,* eleven; eleventh (of the month). **las o.,** eleven o'clock
onceno *a* eleventh
onda *f,* wave; *fig* flicker (of flames); *sew* scallop; *phys* wave; ripple; *pl* waves (in hair). **rad o. corta,** short wave. **o. etérea,** ether wave. **o. sonora,** sound wave
ondeado *a* undulating; wavy; scalloped
ondeante *a* waving; flowing
ondear *vi* to wave; ripple; undulate; roll (of the sea); float, flutter, stream; *sew* scallop; *vr* swing, sway
ondeo *m,* waving; undulation
ondina *f,* undine, water sprite
ondulación *f,* undulation; wave; wriggling; twisting. **o. permanente,** permanent wave, perm
ondulado *a* wavy; undulating; scalloped
ondular *vi* to writhe, squirm, wriggle; twist; coil; *vt* wave (in hair)
oneroso *a* onerous, heavy; troublesome
ónice *m,* onyx
onomástico *a* onomastic. **día o.,** saint's day
onomatopeya *f,* onomatopoeia
onza *f,* ounce. **por onzas,** by ounces; sparingly
onzavo *a* and *m,* eleventh
opacidad *f,* opacity; obscurity; gloom
opaco *a* opaque; dark; gloomy, sad
opalescente *a* opalescent
opalino *a* opaline
ópalo *m,* opal
opción *f,* option; choice, selection; *law* option
ópera *f,* opera
operación *f, surg* operation; execution, performance; *com* transaction
operar *vt surg* to operate; *vi* act, have an effect; operate, control; *com* transact
operario (-ia) *n* worker, hand; operator; mechanic
opereta *f,* operetta, light opera
opinar *vi* to have or form an opinion, think; judge, consider
opinión *f,* opinion, view; reputation
opio *m,* opium. **fumadero de o.,** opium den
opíparo *a* magnificent, sumptuous (banquets, etc.)
oponer *vt irr* to oppose; resist, withstand; protest against; *vr* oppose; be contrary or hostile (to); face, be

opposite; object (to), set oneself against; compete (in public exams.). See **poner**
oporto *m,* port (wine)
oportunidad *f,* opportunity, occasion
oportunismo *m,* opportunism
oportunista *a* and *mf* opportunist
oportuno *a* opportune, timely
oposición *f,* opposition; resistance; antagonism; public competitive exam for a post; (*ast pol*) opposition
opositor (-ra) *n* opponent; competitor
opresión *f,* oppression; hardship; pressure. **o. de pecho,** difficulty in breathing
opresor (-ra) *a* oppressive. *n* oppressor
oprimir *vt* to oppress; treat harshly; press, crush; choke
oprobio *m,* opprobrium
optar *vt* to take possession of; (*with por*) choose
óptica *f, phys* optics; peepshow
óptico *a* optic, optical. *m,* optician
optimismo *m,* optimism
optimista *mf* optimist. *a* optimistic
óptimo *a sup* **bueno** best, optimal, optimum
opugnar *vt* to resist violently; *mil* assault, attack; impugn, challenge
opulencia *f,* opulence, riches; excess, superabundance
opulento *a* opulent, rich
opúsculo *m,* monograph, opuscule
oquedad *f,* hollow, cavity; superficiality, banality
ora *adv* now
oración *f,* oration, speech; prayer; *gram* sentence
oráculo *m,* oracle
orador (-ra) *n* orator; speech maker. *m,* preacher
oral *a* oral; verbal; buccal
orangután *m,* orangutan
orar *vi* to harangue, make an oration; pray; *vt* request, beg
orate *mf* lunatic
oratoria *f,* oratory, eloquence
oratorio *a* oratorical. *m,* oratory, chapel; *mus* oratorio
orbe *m,* sphere; orb; world
órbita *f, ast* orbit; *fig* sphere; *anat* orbit, eye socket
Órcades, las the Orkneys
ordalía *f,* (medieval hist.) ordeal
orden *mf* order, mode of arrangement; succession, sequence; group; system; orderliness, neatness; coherence, plan; *ecc* order, brotherhood; (*zool bot*) group, class; *arch* order; *math* degree. *f,* precept, command; *com* order; *pl ecc* ordination. (*mil naut*) **o. de batalla,** battle array. **o. de caballería,** order of knighthood. **o. del día,** order of the day. *ecc* **dar órdenes,** to ordain. **en o.,** in order; with regard (to). **por su o.,** in its turn; successively
ordenación *f,* order, orderly arrangement; disposition; ordinance, precept; *ecc* ordination
ordenador *m Spain* computer
ordenamiento *m,* ordaining; ordinance; edict
ordenancista *mf mil* martinet; disciplinarian
ordenanza *f,* order, method; command, instruction; ordinance, regulation (gen. *pl*). *m, mil* orderly
ordenar *vt* to put in order, arrange; command, give instructions to; decree; direct, regulate; *ecc* ordain; *vr* (*with de*) *ecc* be ordained as
ordeñadero *m,* milk pail
ordeñar *vt* to milk
ordinal *a* ordinal. *m,* ordinal number
ordinariez *f,* rudeness, uncouthness; vulgarity
ordinario *a* ordinary, usual; vulgar, coarse, uncultured; rude; commonplace, average, mediocre. *m, ecc* ordinary; carrier; courier. **de o.,** usually, ordinarily
orear *vt* to ventilate; *vr* dry; air; take the air
orégano *m,* wild marjoram
oreja *f,* external ear; lug; tab, flap; tongue (of a shoe). *inf* **con las orejas caídas,** down in the mouth, depressed
orejera *f,* earflap; mold board (of a plow)
orejudo *a* large- or long-eared
oreo *m,* zephyr; ventilation; airing
orfanato *m,* orphanage, orphan asylum

orfandad *f,* orphanhood; defenselessness, lack of protection

orfebre *mf* gold- or silversmith

orfebrería *f,* gold- or silverwork

orfeón *m,* choral society

organdí *m,* organdy

orgánico *a* organic; harmonious; *fig* organized

organillero(-ra) *n* organ grinder

organillo *m,* barrel organ

organismo *m,* organism; organization, association

organista *mf* organist

organización *f,* organization; order, arrangement

organizador (-ra) *a* organizing. *n* organizer

organizar *vt* to organize; regulate; constitute

órgano *m, mus* organ; (*anat bot*) organ; means, agency. **o. de manubrio,** barrel organ

orgasmo *m,* orgasm

orgía *f,* orgy

orgullo *m,* pride; arrogance

orgulloso *a* proud; haughty

orientación *f,* orientation; exposure, prospect; bearings

oriental *a* Oriental, Eastern. *mf* Oriental

orientalismo *m,* Orientalism

orientalista *mf* Orientalist

orientar *vt* to orientate; *vr* find one's bearings; familiarize oneself (with)

oriente *m,* Orient, the East; luster (of pearls); youth, childhood; origin, source

orificio *m,* orifice; hole

oriflama *f,* oriflamme; standard, flag

origen *m,* origin, source, root; stock, extraction; reason, genesis. **dar o. a,** to give rise to. **país de o.,** native land

original *a* original; earliest, primitive; new, first-hand; novel, fresh; inventive, creative; eccentric; quaint. *m,* original manuscript; original; sitter (for portraits); eccentric

originalidad *f,* originality

originar *vt* to cause, originate; invent; *vr* spring from, originate (in)

originario *a* original, primary; primitive; native (of)

orilla *f,* limit, edge; hem, border; selvage; shore, margin; bank (of a river, etc.); sidewalk; brink, edge. **a la o.,** on the brink; nearly

orillar *vt* to settle, arrange, conclude; *vi* reach the shore or bank; *sew* leave a hem; *sew* border; leave a selvage on cloth

orillo *m,* selvage (of cloth)

orín *m,* rust; *pl* urine

orinal *m,* chamber pot, urinal

orinar *vi* to urinate

oriundo *a* native (of); derived (from)

orla *f,* border, fringe; selvage (of cloth, garments); ornamental border (on diplomas, etc.)

orlar *vt* to border; edge, trim

ornamentación *f,* ornamentation

ornamental *a* ornamental

ornamentar *vt* to ornament; embellish

ornamento *m,* ornament; decoration; gift, virtue, talent; *pl ecc* vestments

ornar *vt* to ornament, adorn, embellish

ornato *m,* decoration, ornament

ornitología *f,* ornithology

ornitológico *a* ornithological

ornitólogo *m,* ornithologist

oro *m,* gold; gold coins or jewelery; *fig* riches; *pl* diamonds (cards). **o. batido,** gold leaf. **o. en polvo,** gold dust. *fig* **como un o.,** shining with cleanliness. **el as de oros,** the ace of diamonds

orondo *a* hollow; *inf* pompous; *inf* swollen, spongy

oropel *m,* brass foil; showy, cheap thing; trinket; tinsel

oropéndola *f,* oriole

orquesta *f,* orchestra

orquestación *f,* orchestration

orquestal *a* orchestral

orquestar *vt* to orchestrate

orquídea *f,* orchid

ortega *f, orn* grouse

ortiga *f, bot* nettle

orto *m,* rising (of sun, stars)

ortodoxia *f,* orthodoxy

ortodoxo *a* orthodox

ortografía *f,* orthography

ortográfico *a* orthographical

ortopedia *f,* orthopedics

ortopédico (-ca) *a* orthopedic. *n* orthopedist

ortopedista *mf* orthopedist

oruga *f,* caterpillar

orzuelo *m, med* sty; trap (for wild animals)

os *pers pron* 2nd *pl mf dat* and *acc* of **vos** and **vosotros** you, to you

osa *f,* she-bear; *ast* **O. mayor,** Big Bear; **O. menor,** Little Bear

osadía *f,* boldness, audacity

osado *a* daring, bold

osamenta *f,* skeleton; bones (of a skeleton)

osar *vi* to dare; risk, venture

osario *m,* charnel house, ossuary

oscilación *f,* oscillation

oscilante *a* oscillating

oscilar *vi* to oscillate, sway; hesitate, vacillate

ósculo *m,* kiss, osculation

oscurantismo *m,* obscurantism

oscurantista *a* and *mf* obscurantist

oscurecer *vt irr* to darken; *fig* tarnish, dim, sully; confuse, bewilder; express obscurely; *art* shade; *vn* grow dark; *vr* cloud over (sky); *inf* disappear (things, gen. by theft). See **conocer**

oscuridad *f,* darkness; gloom, blackness; humbleness; obscurity, abstruseness

oscuro *a* dark; humble, unknown; abstruse, involved; obscure; uncertain, dangerous. **a oscuras,** in the dark; ignorant

óseo *a* osseous

osera *f,* bear's den

osezno *m,* bear cub

osificación *f,* ossification

osificarse *vr* to ossify

ósmosis *f,* ósmosis

oso *m,* bear. **o. blanco,** polar bear

Ostende Ostend

ostensible *a* ostensible; obvious

ostensión *f,* show, display, manifestation

ostensivo *a* ostensive

ostentación *f,* manifestation; ostentation

ostentar *vt* to exhibit, show; boast, show off

ostentoso *a* magnificent, showy, ostentatious

osteología *f,* osteology

osteópata *mf* osteopath

osteopatía *f,* osteopathy

ostra *f,* oyster. **vivero de ostras,** oyster bed

ostracismo *m,* ostracism

otear *vt* to observe; look on at

otero *m,* hill, height, eminence

otología *f,* otology

otólogo *m,* otologist

otomana *f,* ottoman, couch

otomano *a* Ottoman

otoñal *a* autumnal, autumn, fall

otoño *m,* autumn, fall

otorgamiento *m,* granting; consent, approval; license, award

otorgar *vt* to grant; concede, approve; *law* grant, stipulate, execute

otro (-ra) *a* other, another. *n* another one

otrosí *adv* besides, moreover

ovación *f,* ovation, triumph; applause

ovacionar *vt* to applaud

oval *a* oval

óvalo *m,* oval

ovario *m,* ovary

oveja *f,* ewe

ovejuno *a* relating to ewes or sheep, sheep-like

ovillar *vi* to wind thread into a ball; *vr* curl up; huddle

ovillo *m*, ball, bobbin (of thread); tangled heap (of things)

ovíparo *a* oviparous

OVNI *m*, UFO

ovulación *f*, ovulation

óvulo *m*, ovule

oxidación *f*, oxidation

oxidar *vt* oxidize; *vr* become oxidized

óxido *m*, oxide. **ó. de carbono,** carbon monoxide. **ó. de cinc,** zinc oxide

oxígeno *m*, oxygen

oyente *mf* hearer; *pl* audience

ozono *m*, ozone

P

pabellón *m*, pavilion; colors, flag; bell tent. **p. británico,** Union Jack. **p. de reposo,** rest home. **en p.,** stacked (of arms)

pábulo *m*, food; *fig* pabulum

pacedero *a agr* grazing, meadow

pacer *vi irr agr* to graze; *vt* nibble away; eat away. See **nacer**

paciencia *f*, patience

paciente *a* patient; long-suffering; complacent. *mf med* patient

pacienzudo *a* extremely patient or long-suffering

pacificación *f*, pacification; serenity, peace of mind

pacificador (-ra) *a* peace making; pacifying. *n* peace maker

pacificar *vt* to pacify; *vi* make peace; *vr* grow quiet, become calm (sea, etc.)

pacífico *a* pacific, meek, mild; peace-loving, peaceful. **el Océano P.,** the Pacific Ocean

pacifismo *m*, pacifism

pacifista *a* and *mf* pacifist

pacotilla *f*, goods. *inf* **hacer su p.,** to make one's packet or fortune. **ser de p.,** to be poor stuff; be jerry-built (of houses)

pactar *vt* to stipulate, arrange; contract

pacto *m*, agreement, contract; pact

padecer *vi irr* to suffer; feel keenly; experience, undergo; tolerate. **p. desnudez,** to go unclothed. **p. hambre,** to go hungry. See **conocer**

padecimiento *m*, suffering

padrastro *m*, stepfather; cruel father; *fig* impediment, obstacle; hangnail

padrazo *m*, *inf* indulgent father

padre *m*, father; stallion; head (of the family, etc.); *ecc* father; genesis, source; author, creator; *pl* parents; ancestors. **p. adoptivo,** foster father. **p. de familia,** paterfamilias. **P. Eterno,** Eternal Father. **p. nuestro,** Lord's Prayer. **P. Santo,** Holy Father, the Pope

padrear *vi* to take after one's father; *zool* reproduce, breed

padrino *m*, godfather; sponsor; second (in duels, etc.); patron; best man

padrón *m*, census; pattern, model; memorial stone

paella *f*, *cul* savory rice dish of shellfish, chicken, and meat

paga *f*, payment; amends, restitution; pay; payment of fine; reciprocity (in love, etc.)

pagadero *a* payable. *m*, date and place when payment is due

pagador (-ra) *n* payer. *m*, teller; wages clerk; paymaster

pagaduría *f*, pay office

paganismo *m*, paganism; heathenism

pagano (-na) *a* and *n* pagan; heathen

pagar *vt* to pay; make restitution, expiate; return, requite (love, etc.); *vr* (*with de*) become fond of; be proud of. **p. adelantado,** to prepay. **com p. al contado,** to pay cash. **p. la casa,** to pay the rent (for one's residence)

pagaré *m*, *com* promissory note, I.O.U.

página *f*, page (of a book); episode, occurrence

paginación *f*, pagination

paginar *vt* to paginate

pago *m*, payment; recompense, reward; region of vineyards, olive groves, etc.

pagoda *f*, pagoda, temple; idol

paguro *m*, hermit crab

pailebote *m*, schooner

país *m*, country, nation; region; *art* landscape. **del p.,** typical of the country of origin (gen. of food)

paisaje *m*, countryside; landscape, scenery

paisajista, paisista *mf* landscape painter

paisano (-na) *n* compatriot; peasant; civilian

Países Bajos, los the Low Countries, the Netherlands

paja *f*, straw; chaff; trash; *fig* padding. **ver la p. en el ojo del vecino y no la viga en el nuestro,** to see the mote in our neighbor's eye and not the beam in our own

pajar *m*, barn

pájara *f*, hen (bird); kite (toy); *inf* jay; prostitute. **p. pinta,** game of forfeits

pajarear *vt* to snare birds; loaf, idle about

pajarera *f*, aviary

pajarero *m*, bird catcher or seller. *a inf* frivolous, giddy; *inf* gaudy (colors)

pajarita *f*, bow tie

pájaro *m*, bird. **p. bobo,** penguin. **p. carpintero,** woodpecker. *fig inf* **p. gordo,** big gun. **p. mosca,** hummingbird

pajarota *f*, *inf* canard, false report

paje *m*, page; *naut* cabin boy

pajera *f*, hayloft

pajizo *a* made of straw; covered or thatched with straw; strawcolored

pala *f*, paddle; blade (of an oar); shovel; spade; baker's peel (long-handled shovel); cutting edge of a spade, hoe, etc.; *sport* racket; vamp, upper (of a shoe); pelota or jai alai racket; tanner's knife; *inf* guile, cunning; cleverness, dexterity. **p. de hélice,** propeller blade. **p. para pescado,** fish server. *inf* **corta p.,** ignoramus; blockhead

palabra *f*, word; power of speech; eloquence; offer, promise; *pl* magic formula, spell. **p. de clave,** code word. **p. de matrimonio,** promise of marriage. **p. de rey,** inviolable promise. **palabras cruzadas,** crossword puzzle. **bajo p. de,** under promise of. **cuatro palabras,** a few words; short conversation. **de p.,** verbally, by word of mouth. **dirigir la p. a,** to address, speak to. **faltar a su p.,** to break one's promise. **llevar la p.,** to be spokesperson. **medias palabras,** halfwords; hint, insinuation. **su p. empeñada,** one's solemn word. **tener la p.,** to have the right to speak (in meetings, etc.) (e.g. **El señor Martínez tiene la p.,** Mr. Martínez has the floor)

palabrería *f*, verbosity, wordiness

palabrota *f*, *inf* coarse language; long word

palaciego (-ga) *a* pertaining to palaces; *fig* courtesan. *n* courtier

palacio *m*, palace; mansion

palada *f*, shovelful, spadeful; oar stroke

paladar *m*, *anat* palate; taste; discernment, sensibility

paladear *vt* to taste with pleasure, savor; enjoy, relish

paladín *m*, paladin

paladino *a* public, clear, open

palafrén *m*, palfrey

palafrenero *m*, groom; stablehand

palanca *f*, *mech* lever; handle; bar; (high) diving board. **p. de arranque,** starting gear. **p. de cambio de velocidad,** gear-changing lever. **p. de mando,** control stick

palangana *f*, washbasin
palanganero *m*, washstand
palanqueta *f*, *dim* small lever; jimmy
palastro *m*, sheet iron or steel
palatinado *m*, Palatinate
palatino *a* palatine
palatizar *vt* to palatilize
palazón *f*, woodwork
palco *m*, *theat* box; stand, raised platform, enclosure. **p. de platea**, orchestra
palenque *m*, enclosure; stand; platform; palisade
paleografía *f*, paleography
paleógrafo *m*, paleographer
paleolítico *a* paleolithic
paleología *f*, paleology
paleontología *f*, paleontology
Palestina Palestine
palestra *f*, tilt yard
paleta *f*, *dim* little shovel; trowel; *art* palette; fireplace shovel; mason's trowel; *anat* shoulder blade; blade (of a propeller, ventilator, etc.); *chem* spatula
paliación *f*, palliation; excuse
paliar *vt* to dissemble, excuse; palliate, mitigate
paliativo *a* palliative; extenuating
palidecer *vi irr* to turn pale. See **conocer**
palidez *f*, pallor, paleness
pálido *a* pale, pallid
paliducho *a* somewhat pale, palish; sallow
palillo *m*, *dim* small stick; toothpick; bobbin (for lacemaking); drumstick; *fig* chatter; *pl* castanets
palimpsesto *m*, palimpsest
palinodia *f*, *lit* palinode. **cantar la p.**, to eat one's words, recant
palio *m*, Greek mantle; cape; *ecc* pallium; canopy, awning
palique *m*, *inf* chat. **estar de p.**, to be having a chat
paliquear *vi* to chat
paliza *f*, caning, beating
palizada *f*, paling, fence; palisade, stockade. **p. de tablas**, hoarding
palma *f*, palm tree; palm leaf; date palm; palm (of the hand); hand; triumph. **llevarse la p.**, to bear away the palm; take the cake
palmada *f*, slap; *pl* hand-clapping
palmado *a* web (of feet); palmy
palmar *a* palmaceous; palmar; clear, obvious. *m*, palm grove
palmatoria *f*, ferule, ruler; candlestick
palmear *vi* to clap hands
palmera *f*, palm tree
palmeta *f*, ferrule, ruler
palmetazo *m*, slap on the hand with a ruler; *fig* slap in the face
Palmira Palmyra
palmo *m*, span; hand's breadth. **p. a p.**, inch by inch, piecemeal
palmotear *vt* to applaud; clap
palo *m*, stick; rod; pole; timber, wood; wooden log; *naut* mast; blow with a stick; execution by hanging; suit (of playing cards); fruit stalk; *her* pale. **p. de Campeche**, logwood. **p. de hule**, rubber tree. **p. de rosa**, tulipwood. *naut* **p. mayor**, mainmast. *naut* **a p. seco**, under bare poles. **de tal p., tal astilla**, a chip off the old block; like father like son. **estar del mismo p.**, to be of the same mind, agree
paloma *f*, dove; pigeon; gentle person; *pl naut* white horses. **p. buchona**, pouter pigeon. **p. mensajera**, carrier pigeon. **p. torcaz**, wood pigeon
palomar *m*, dovecote; pigeon loft
palomero (-ra) *n* pigeon fancier; pigeon dealer
palomino *m*, young pigeon
palomo *m*, male pigeon; wood pigeon
palotes *m pl*, drumsticks; pothooks (in writing)
palpabilidad *f*, palpability
palpable *a* palpable, tangible
palpación *f*, *med* palpation

palpar *vt* to palpate, examine by touch; grope, walk by touch; *fig* see clearly
palpitación *f*, beating (of a heart); *med* palpitation; convulsive movement
palpitante *a* palpitating; quivering; beating; (of a question) burning
palpitar *vi* to beat (heart); throb, palpitate; shudder, move convulsively; *fig* manifest itself (passions, etc.)
palpo *m*, palp, feeler
palúdico *a* marshy, swampy; malarial
paludismo *m*, malaria; paludism
palurdo (-da) *a inf* gross, rude, boorish. *n* boor
palustre *m*, mason's trowel. *a* marshy, swampy
pamela *f*, wide-brimmed straw sailor (woman's hat)
pamema *f*, *inf* unimportant trifle; *inf* caress
pampa *f*, pampa, treeless plain
pámpano *m*, young vine shoot; vine leaf
pamplina *f*, *inf* nonsense, rubbish
pan *m*, bread; loaf; *cul* piecrust; *fig* food; wheat; gold leaf; *pl* cereals. **p. ázimo**, unleavened bread. **p. de oro**, gold leaf. **llamar al p. p. y al vino vino**, to call a spade a spade. **venderse como p. bendito**, to sell like hot cakes
pana *f*, velveteen, velours
panacea *f*, panacea; cure-all
panadería *f*, bakery trade or shop; bakery
panadero (-ra) *n* baker. *m pl*, Spanish dance
panadizo *m*, *med* whitlow; *inf* ailing person, crock
panal *m*, honeycomb; wasp's nest
Panamá Panama
panameño (-ña) *a* and *n* Panamanian
panamericanismo *m*, pan-Americanism
panarra *m*, *inf* simpleton
páncreas *m*, pancreas
pancreático *a* pancreatic
panda *f*, gallery of a cloister. *mf zool* panda
pandémico *a* pandemic
pandemónium *m*, pandemonium
pandereta *f*, tambourine
pandero *m*, tambourine; *inf* windbag
pandilla *f*, league, group; gang (of burglars, etc.); party, crowd, band
pane *f*, breakdown
panecillo *m*, *dim* roll (of bread)
panegírico *a* and *m*, panegyric
panegirista *mf* panegyrist; eulogizer
panel *m*, panel
panetela *f*, panada
pánfilo (-la) *a* sluggish, phlegmatic, slow-moving. *n* sluggard
panfleto *m*, pamphlet
paniaguado *m*, servant; favorite, protégé
pánico *a* and *m*, panic
panoja *f*, *bot* panicle; *bot* ear, beard, awn
panoli *a inf* doltish, stupid
panoplia *f*, panoply; collection of arms
panorama *m*, panorama; view
panorámico *a* panoramic
pantalón *m*, pant, trouser (gen. *pl*); knickers. **p. de corte**, striped trousers. **pantalones bombachos**, plus fours
pantalla *f*, lampshade; face screen; movie screen; shade, reflector
pantano *m*, marsh, swamp; impediment; artificial pool
pantanoso *a* marshy, swampy; *fig* awkward, full of pitfalls
panteísmo *m*, pantheism
panteísta *a* pantheistic. *mf* pantheist
panteón *m*, pantheon
pantera *f*, panther
pantomima *f*, pantomime; mime
pantoque *m*, *naut* bilge
pantorrilla *f*, calf (of the leg)
pantuflo *m*, house slipper
panza *f*, paunch, stomach; belly (of jugs, etc.). *inf* **un cielo de p. de burra**, a dark gray sky

panzudo *a* paunchy

pañal *m*, diaper; shirttail; *pl* long clothes, swaddling clothes; infancy

pañería *f*, drapery stores; drapery

pañero (-ra) *n* draper

paño *m*, woolen material; cloth, fabric; drapery, hanging; tapestry; linen, bandage; tarnish or other mark; *naut* canvas; *sew* breadth, width (of cloth); panel (in a dress); floor cloth, duster; livid mark on the face; *pl* garments. **p. de lágrimas**, consoler, sympathizer. **p. mortuorio**, pall (on a coffin). **paños menores**, underwear. **p. verde**, gambling table. **al p.**, *theat* from the wings, from without. *inf* **poner el p. al púlpito**, to hold forth, spread oneself

pañoleta *f*, kerchief, triangular scarf; fichu

pañuelo *m*, kerchief; handkerchief

papa *m*, pope; *inf* papa, daddy. *f*, *inf* potato; stupid rumor; nonsense; *pl* pap; *cul* sop; food

papá *m*, *inf* papa, daddy

papada *f*, double chin; dewlap

papado *m*, papacy

papagayo *m*, parrot

papamoscas *m*, *orn* flycatcher; *inf* simpleton

papanatas *m*, *inf* simpleton

papar *vt* to sip, take soft food; *inf* eat; neglect, be careless about

paparrucha *f*, *inf* stupid rumor; nonsense

papel *m*, paper; document; manuscript; *theat* role, part; pamphlet; sheet of paper; paper, monograph, essay; guise, role; *theat* character. **p. carbón, p. carbónico**, carbon paper. **p. celofán**, cellophane. **p. cuadriculado**, graph paper, cartridge paper. **p. de calcar**, carbon paper; tracing paper. **p. de escribir**, writing paper. **p. de estaño**, tinfoil. **p. de estraza**, brown paper. **p. de fumar**, cigarette paper. **p. de lija**, emery- or sandpaper. **p. de paja de arroz**, rice paper. **p. de seda**, tissue paper. **p. de tornasol**, litmus paper. **p. del estado**, government bonds. **p. higiénico**, toilet paper. **p. moneda**, paper money. **p. pintado**, wallpaper. **p. secante**, blotting paper. **p. sellado**, official stamped paper. **hacer buen (mal) p.**, to do well (badly). **hacer el p. (de)**, *theat* to act the part (of); feign, pretend

papelear *vi* to turn over papers, search among them; *inf* cut a dash

papeleo *m*, bureacracy, red tape

papelera *f*, mass of papers; desk (for keeping papers)

papelería *f*, heap of papers; stationer's shop; stationery

papelero (-ra) *a* paper, stationery. *n* paper maker; stationer

papeleta *f*, slip or scrap of paper

papelista *mf* paper maker; stationer; paperhanger

papelucho *m*, old or dirty piece of paper; trash, worthless writing; *inf* rag (newspaper)

papera *f*, mumps

papilla *f*, pap; guile, wiliness

papillote *m*, curl-paper

papiro *m*, papyrus

papista *a* and *mf* papist

papo *m*, dewlap; gizzard (of a bird); goiter. **p. de cardo**, thistledown

paquebote *m*, *naut* packet; mail boat; liner

paquete *m*, packet; parcel, package

paquidermo *m*, pachyderm

par *a* equal; alike; corresponding. *m*, pair, couple; team (of oxen, mules); peer (title); rafter (of a roof); *mech* torque, couple; *elec* cell. *f*, par. **a la p.**, jointly; simultaneously; *com* at par. **a pares**, two by two. **de p. en p.**, wide-open (doors, etc.). **sin p.**, peerless, excellent

para *prep* in order to; for; to; for the sake of (e.g. **Lo hice p. ella**, I did it for her sake); enough to (gen. with *bastante*, etc.); in the direction of, toward; about to, on the point of (e.g. **Está p. salir**, He is on the point of going out). Expresses:

1. *Purpose* (e.g. **La educan p. bailarina**, They are bringing her up to be a dancer. **Lo dije p. ver lo que harías**, I said it to (in order to) see what you would do)

2. *Destination* (e.g. **Salió p. Londres**, He left for London)

3. *Use* (e.g. **seda p. medias**, silk for stockings. **un vaso p. flores**, a vase for flowers)

4. *An appointed time* (e.g. **Lo pagaré p. Navidad**, I will pay it at Christmas)

p. con, toward (a person) (e.g. **Ha obrado muy bien p. con mi hermano**, He has behaved very well toward my brother)

p. coneretar, to be exact, to wit

p. que, in order to, so that (e.g. **Lo puse en la mesa p. que lo vieses**, I put it on the table so that you would see it)

¿P. qué? Why? For what reason?

p. siempre, forever. **decir p. sí**, to say to oneself. **sin qué ni p. qué**, without rhyme or reason

parábola *f*, parable; *geom* parabola

parabrisas *m*, windshield

paracaídas *m*, parachute

paracaidista *mf* parachutist

paráclito *m*, Paraclete

parachoques *m*, *aut* bumper; buffer (railroad)

parada *f*, stopping, halting; stop; stoppage, suspension; halt; *mil* review; interval, pause; cattle stall; dam; gambling stakes; parry (in fencing); relay (of horses). **p. de coches**, taxi rank. **p. de tranvía**, streetcar stop. **p. discrecional**, request stop (buses, etc.)

paradero *m*, railroad station; stopping place; end, conclusion; whereabouts

paradisíaco *a* paradisaical

parado *a* still; indolent, lazy; unoccupied, leisured; silent, reserved; timid; unemployed

paradoja *f*, paradox

paradójico *a* a paradoxical

parador *m*, inn, tavern, hostelry

parafina *f*, paraffin

parafinar *vt* to paraffin

parafrasear *vt* to paraphrase

paráfrasis *f*, paraphrase

paraguas *m*, umbrella

paraguayo (-ya) *a* and *n* Paraguayan

paragüería *f*, umbrella shop

paragüero (-ra) *n* umbrella maker, umbrella seller. *m*, umbrella stand

paraíso *m*, paradise; garden of Eden; heaven; (*inf theat*) gallery, gods

paraje *m*, place, locality, spot; state, condition

paralela *f*, *mil* parallel; *pl* parallel bars (for gymnastic exercises)

paralelismo *m*, parallelism

paralelo *a* parallel; analogous; similar. *m*, parallel, similarity; *geog* parallel

paralelogramo *m*, parallelogram

parálisis *f*, paralysis

paralítico (-ca) *a* and *n* paralytic

paralización *f*, paralysis; cessation; *com* dullness, quietness

paralizar *vt* to paralyze; stop

paramento *m*, ornament; trappings (of a horse); face (of a wall); facing (of a building). **paramentos sacerdotales**, liturgical vestments or ornaments

páramo *m*, paramo, treeless plain; desert, wilderness

parangón *m*, comparison; similarity

parangonar *vt* to compare

paraninfo *m*, *arch* paranymph, university hall; best man (weddings); messenger of good

paranoico *a*, paranoiac

parapetarse *vr* to shelter behind a parapet; take refuge behind

parapeto *m*, parapet

parapoco *mf* *inf* ninny, numskull

parar *vi* to stop, halt; end, finish; lodge; come into the hands of; *vt* stop; detain; prepare; bet, stake; point (hunting dogs); parry (fencing); *vr* halt; be interrupted

p. mientes en, to notice; consider. **sin p.,** immediately, at once; without stopping

pararrayos *m*, lightning conductor

parasitario, parasítico *a* parasitic

parásito *m*, parasite; *fig* sponger; *pl rad* interference. *a* parasitic

parasitología *f*, parasitology

parasol *m*, sunshade; *bot* umbel

paratifoidea *f*, paratyphoid

parca *f*, Fate; *poet* death. **las Parcas,** the Three Fates

parcela *f*, plot, parcel (of land); atom, particle

parche *m*, *med* plaster; *aut* patch; drum; drumhead, parchment of drum; patch, mend

parcial *a* partial, incomplete; biased, prejudiced; factional, party; participatory

parcialidad *f*, partiality, bias, prejudice; party, faction, group; intimacy, friendship

parco *a* scarce, scanty; temperate, moderate; frugal

¡pardiez! *interj inf* By gad!

pardo *a* brown; gray, drab, dun-colored; cloudy, dark; husky (voices). *m*, leopard

pardusco *a* grayish; fawn-colored

parear *vt* to pair, match; put in pairs; compare

parecer *vi irr* to appear; look, seem; turn up (be found). *impers* believe, think (e.g. **me parece,** it seems to me, I think, my opinion is); *vr* look alike, resemble one another. See **conocer**

parecer *m*, opinion, belief; appearance, looks

parecido *a* (*with bien or mal*) good- or bad-looking. *m*, resemblance

pared *f*, wall; partition wall; side, face. **p. maestra,** main wall. **p. medianera,** party wall. **Las paredes oyen,** The walls have ears. *inf* **pegado a la p.,** confused, taken aback

pareja *f*, pair; dance partner; couple. **p. desparejada,** mismatched pair. **parejas mixtas,** mixed doubles (in tennis). **correr parejas** *or* **correr a las parejas,** to be equal; go together, happen simultaneously; be on a par

parejo *a* equal; similar; smooth, flat; even, regular

parentela *f*, relatives, kindred; parentage

parentesco *m*, kinship; relationship; affinity; *inf* connection, link

paréntesis *m*, parenthesis; digression. **entre p.,** incidentally

paresa *f*, peeress

paria *mf* pariah; outcast

parida *a f*, newly delivered of a child

paridad *f*, parity; analogy, similarity

pariente (-ta) *n* relative, relation; *inf* husband (wife)

parihuela *f*, wheelbarrow; stretcher

parir *vt* to give birth to; *fig* bring forth; reveal, publish; *vi* lay eggs

París Paris

parisiense *a* and *mf* Parisian

parla *f*, speech; loquaciousness, eloquence; verbiage

parlamentar *vi* to converse; discuss (contracts, etc.); *mil* parley

parlamentario *a* parliamentarian. *m*, member of parliament

parlamentarismo *m*, parliamentarianism

parlamento *m*, legislative assembly; parliament; discourse, speech; *theat* long speech; *mil* parley

parlanchín *a inf* talkative, chattering, loquacious

parlar *vt* and *vi* to speak freely or easily; chatter; reveal, speak indiscreetly; babble (of streams, etc.)

parlero *a* talkative; gossiping, indiscreet; talking (birds); *fig* expressive (eyes, etc.); prattling, babbling (brook, etc.)

parlotear *vi inf* to chatter, gossip

parloteo *m*, chattering, gossip

parmesano (-na) *a* and *n* Parmesan

parnaso *m*, Parnassus; anthology of verse

paro *m*, *inf* work stoppage; lockout; *orn* tit. **p. forzoso,** unemployment

parodia *f*, parody

parodiar *vt* to parody

parodista *mf* parodist

parótida *f*, parotid gland; parotitis, mumps

parotiditis *f*, parotitis, mumps

paroxismo *m*, *med* paroxysm; frenzy, ecstasy, fit

parpadear *vi* to blink

parpadeo *m*, blinking

párpado *m*, eyelid

parque *m*, park; depot, park; paddock, pen. **p. de atracciones,** pleasure ground. **p. de** (*or* **para**) **automóviles,** car park, parking lot

parquedad *f*, scarcity; moderation, temperance; parsimony, frugality

parra *f*, vine. **hoja de p.,** *fig* fig leaf

párrafo *m*, paragraph; *gram* paragraph sign. **p. aparte,** new paragraph. **echar un p.,** to chat, gossip

parranda *f*, *inf* binge; strolling band of musicians. **ir de p.,** to go on a binge

parricida *mf* parricide (person)

parricidio *m*, parricide (act)

parrilla *f*, *cul* griller, broiler; grill, gridiron; *eng* grate. *cul* **a la p.,** grilled

párroco *m*, parish priest; parson

parroquia *f*, parish church; parish; clergy of a parish; clientele, customers

parroquial *a* parochial

parroquiano (-na) *a* parochial. *n* parishioner; client, customer

parsi *m*, Parsee; Parseeism

parsimonia *f*, frugality, thrift; prudence, moderation

parsimonioso *a* parsimonious

parte *f*, part; share; place; portion; side, faction; *law* party; *theat* part, role. *m*, communication, message; telegraph or telephone message; (*mil nav*) communiqué. *f pl*, parts, talents. **p. actora,** *law* prosecution. **p. de la oración,** part of speech. **partes litigantes,** *law* contending parties. **dar p.,** to notify; (*mil naut*) report; give a share (in a transaction). **de algún tiempo a esta p.,** for some time past. **de p. de,** in the name of, from. **en p.,** partly. **por todas partes,** on all sides, everywhere. **ser p. a** *or* **ser p. para que,** to contribute to. **tener de su p. (a),** to count on the favor of. **la quinta p.,** one-fifth, etc.

partear *vt* to assist in childbirth

partera *f*, midwife

partero *m*, accoucheur

partición *f*, partition, distribution; (*aer naut*) accommodation

participación *f*, participation; notice, warning; announcement (of an engagement, etc.); *com* share

participante *a* and *mf* participant

participar *vi* to participate, take part (in), share; *vt* inform; announce (an engagement, etc.)

partícipe *a* sharing. *mf* participant

participio *m*, participle

partícula *f*, particle, grain; *gram* particle

particular *a* private; peculiar; special, particular; unusual; individual. *m*, private individual. *m*, matter, subject. **en p.,** especially; privately

particularidad *f*, individuality; speciality; rareness, unusualness; detail, circumstance; intimacy, friendship

particularizar *vt* to detail, particularize; single out, choose; *vr* (*with en*) be characterized by

partida *f*, departure; entry, record (of birth, etc.); certificate (of marriage, etc.); *com* item; *com* lot, allowance; *mil* guerrilla; armed band; expedition, excursion; game (of cards, etc.); rubber (at bridge, etc.); *inf* conduct, behavior; place, locality; death. *com* **p. doble,** double entry. **Las siete Partidas,** code of Spanish laws compiled by Alfonso X (1252–84)

partidarismo *m*, partisanship

partidario (-ia) *a* partisan. *n* adherent, disciple. *m*, partisan, guerrilla

partido *m*, party, group, faction; profit; *sport* match; team; agreement, pact. **p. conservador,** *pol* conservative party. **p. obrero** *or* **p. laborista,** *pol* labor party.

buen p., *fig* good match, catch. **sacar p. de,** to take advantage of, make the most of. **tomar p.,** to enlist; join, become a supporter (of)

partidor *m,* divider, apportioner; cleaver, chopper; hewer

partir *vt* to divide; split; crack, break; separate; *math* divide; *vi* go, depart; start (from). **p. como el rayo,** be off like a flash. *vr* disagree, become divided; leave, depart

partitura *f, mus* score

parto *m,* parturition, birth; newborn child; *fig* creation, offspring; important event

parturienta *a f,* parturient

parva *f,* light breakfast; threshed or unthreshed grain; heap, mass

parvedad *f,* smallness; scarcity; light breakfast (taken on fast days)

parvo *a* little, small

párvulo (-la) *n* child. *a* small; innocent, simple; lowly, humble

pasa *f,* raisin; *naut* channel; passage, flight (of birds). **p. de Corinto,** currant

pasacalle *m, mus* lively march

pasada *f,* passing, passage; money sufficient to live on; passage, corridor. **dar p.,** to let pass, put up with. *inf* **mala p.,** bad turn, dirty trick

pasadera *f,* steppingstone

pasadero *a* passable, traversable; fair (health); tolerable, passable. *m,* steppingstone

pasadizo *m,* narrow corridor or passage; alley, narrow street; *naut* alleyway

pasado *m,* past; *pl* ancestors. **Lo p., p.,** What's past is past. **p. de moda,** out of fashion, unfashionable

pasador *m,* bolt, fastener; *mech* pin, coupler; pin (of brooches, etc.); colander; *naut* marlin spike; shirt stud

pasajaretas *m,* bodkin

pasaje *m,* passing; passage; fare; passage money; *naut* complement of passengers; channel, strait; (*mus lit*) passage; *mus* modulation, transition (of voice); voyage; passage; covered way; road

pasajero (-ra) *a* crowded public (thoroughfare); transitory, fugitive; passing; temporary. *n* passenger

pasamanería *f,* passementerie work, industry or shop

pasamano *m,* passementerie; banister, handrail; *naut* gangway

pasante *a her* passant. *m,* student teacher; articled clerk; apprentice; student. **p. de pluma,** law clerk

pasaporte *m,* passport; license, permission. **dar el p. (a),** *inf* to give the sack (to)

pasar *vt* to pass; carry, transport; cross over; send; go beyond, overstep; run through; pierce; upset; overtake; transfer; suffer, undergo; sieve; study; dry (grapes, etc.); smuggle; surpass; omit; swallow (food); approve; dissemble; transform; spend (time); *vi* pass; be transferred; have enough to live on; cease; last; die; pass away; pass (at cards); be transformed; be current (money); be salable (goods); (*with prep a + infin*) begin to; (*with por*) pass as; have a reputation as; visit; (*with sin*) do without. *impers* happen, occur. *vr* end; go over to another party; forget; go stale or bad; *fig* go too far, overstep the mark; permeate. **p. contrato,** to draw up a contract; sign a contract. **p. la voz,** to pass the word along. **p. por alto (de),** to omit, overlook. **p. de largo,** to go by without stopping. **pasarse de listo,** to be too clever. **¡No pases cuidado!** Don't worry!

pasarela *f,* gangplank

pasatiempo *m,* pastime, hobby, amusement

pasavante *m, naut* safe conduct; navicert

pascua *f,* Passover; Easter; Christmas; Twelfth Night; Pentecost; *pl* twelve days of Christmas. **P. florida,** Easter Sunday. **dar las pascuas,** to wish a merry Christmas. **¡Felices pascuas!** Merry Christmas!

pascual *a* paschal

pase *m,* pass (with the hands and in football, etc.); safe conduct; free pass; thrust (in fencing)

paseante *mf* stroller, promenader, passerby

pasear *vt* to take a walk; parade up and down, display; *vi* take a walk; go for a drive; go for a ride (on horseback, etc.); stroll up and down; *vr* touch upon lightly, pass over; loaf, be idle; drift; float

paseo *m,* walk, stroll; drive; outing, expedition; promenade; boulevard. **p. a caballo,** ride on horseback

pasiega *f,* wet nurse

pasillo *m,* gallery; corridor; lobby; railway carriage; *sew* basting stitch

pasión *f,* suffering; passivity; passion; desire; *ecc* passion. **con p.,** passionately

pasional *a* passionate; of passion

pasionaria *f,* passionflower

pasiva *f, gram* passive

pasividad *f,* passivity

pasivo *a* passive; inactive; *com* sleeping (partner); *gram* passive. *m, com* liabilities

pasmar *vt* to freeze to death (plants); dumbfound, amaze, stun; chill; *vr* be stunned or amazed

pasmo *m,* amazement, astonishment; wonder, marvel; *med* tetanus, lockjaw

pasmoso *a* astounding, amazing; wonderful

paso *a* dried (of fruit)

paso *m,* step; pace; passage, passing; way; footstep; progress, advancement; passage (in a book); *sew* tacking stitch; occurrence, event; *theat* short play; gait, walk; strait, channel; migratory flight (birds); *mech* pitch; event or scene from the Passion; armed combat; death; *pl* measures, steps. *adv* softly, in a low voice; gently. **p. a nivel,** level crossing. **p. a p.,** step by step. **p. doble,** quick march; Spanish dance. **p. volante,** (gymnastics) giant stride. **a cada p.,** at every step; often. **al p.,** without stopping; on the way, in passing. **ceder el p.,** to allow to pass. **de p.,** in passing; incidentally. **llevar el p.,** to keep in step. **marcar el p.,** to mark time. **salir al p. (a),** to waylay, confront; oppose. **seguir los pasos (a),** to follow; spy upon

pasquín *m,* **pasquinada** *f,* pasquinade, lampoon

pasta *f, cul* dough; paste; pastry; piecrust; batter; *cul* noodle paste; paper pulp; board (bookbinding). **ser de buena p.,** to be good-natured

pastar *vt* to take to pasture; *vi* graze, pasture

pastel *m,* cake; *art* pastel; pie; *inf* plot, secret understanding; cheating (at cards); *print* pie; *inf* fat, stocky person

pastelear *vi inf* to indulge in shady business (especially in politics)

pastelería *f,* cake bakery; cake shop; confectioner's art; confectionery

pastelero (-ra) *n* confectioner, pastry cook; *fig inf* spineless person, jellyfish

pastelillo *m, cul* turnover

pastelista *mf* pastelist

pastelón *m,* meat or game pie

pasteurización *f,* pasteurization

pasteurizar *vt* to pasteurize

pastilla *f,* tablet, cake; lozenge; pastille, drop; tread (of a tire)

pasto *m,* grazing land, pasture; fodder; *fig* fuel, food; spiritual food. **a p.,** in plenty, abundantly. **de p.,** of daily use

pastor (-ra) *n* shepherd. *m, ecc* pastor

pastoral *a* rustic, country; *ecc* pastoral, *f,* pastoral poem; *ecc* pastoral letter

pastorear *vt* to graze, put to grass; *ecc* have charge of souls

pastorela *f,* pastoral

pastoreo *m,* pasturage, grazing

pastoría *f,* pastorate

pastoril *a* shepherd, pastoral

pastoso *a* doughy; mealy; pasty; mellow

pata *f,* paw and leg (animals); foot (of table, etc.); duck; *inf* leg. **p. de gallo,** blunder; crow's-foot, wrinkle. **meter la p.,** to interfere, put one's foot in it. *inf* **tener mala p.,** to be unlucky

patada *f,* kick, stamp; *inf* step, pace

patagón (-ona) *a* and *n* Patagonian
patalear *vi* to stamp (with the feet)
pataleo *m*, kicking; stamping
pataleta *f*, *inf* convulsion; feigned hysterics
patán *m*, *inf* yokel; boor, churl
patanería *f*, *inf* boorishness, churlishness
patarata *f*, trash, useless thing; extravagant courtesy
patata *f*, potato
patatal, patatar *m*, potato patch
patatús *m*, *inf* petty worry; mishap; *med* stroke, fit
patear *vt inf* to stamp; *fig* walk on, treat badly; *vi inf* stamp the feet; be furiously angry; (*golf*) putt
patena *f*, engraved medal worn by country women; *ecc* paten
patentar *vt* to issue a patent; take out a patent, patent
patente *a* obvious, patent; *f*, patent; warrant, commission; letters patent. **p. de invención,** patent. **p. de sanidad,** clean bill of health
patentizar *vt* to make evident
paternidad *f*, paternity
paterno *a* paternal
patético *a* pitiable; pathetic, moving
patiabierto *a inf* knock-kneed
patibulario *a* heartrending, harrowing
patíbulo *m*, scaffold
paticojo *a inf* lame; wobbly; unsteady
patilla *f*, side whisker (gen. *pl*); *pl* old Nick, the Devil
patín *m*, skate; runner (of a sled); (*aer* and of vehicles) skid; *mech* shoe. **p. del diablo,** scooter. **p. de ruedas,** roller skate
patinador (-ra) *n* skater
patinaje *m*, skating; skidding (of planes and vehicles)
patinar *vi* to skate; slip, lose one's footing; skid (vehicles and planes)
patinazo *m*, skid (of a vehicle)
patinete *m*, child's scooter
patio *m*, courtyard; *theat* pit
patitieso *a inf* paralyzed in the hands or feet; openmouthed, amazed; stiff, unbending, proud
patituerto *a* crooked-legged; pigeon-toed; *inf* lopsided
patizambo *a* knock-kneed
pato *m*, duck; *inf* **pagar el p.,** to be a scapegoat
patógeno *a* pathogenic
patojo *a* waddling
patología *f*, pathology
patológico *a* pathological
patólogo *m*, pathologist
patoso *a fig* heavy, pedestrian, tedious
patraña *f*, nonsense, rubbish, fairy tale
patria *f*, motherland, native country; native place. **p. chica,** native region
patriarca *m*, patriarch
patriarcado *m*, patriarchy
patriarcal *a* patriarchal
patricio (-ia) *a* and *n* patrician
patrimonio *m*, patrimony
patriota *mf* patriot
patriótico *a* patriotic
patriotismo *m*, patriotism
patrocinar *vt* to protect, defend; favor, sponsor; patronize
patrocinio *m*, protection, defense; sponsorship; patronage
patrón (-ona) *n* patron, sponsor; patron saint; landlord; employer. *m*, coxswain; *naut* master, skipper; pattern, model; standard. **p. de oro,** gold standard
patronato *m*, patronage, protection; employers' association; charitable foundation. **p. de turismo,** tourist bureau
patronímico *a* and *m*, patronymic
patrono (-na) *n* protector; sponsor; patron; patron saint; employer
patrulla *f*, *mil* patrol; group, band
patrullar *vi mil* patrol; march about
patudo *a inf* large-footed

paulatinamente *adv* slowly, by degrees
pauperismo *m*, destitution, pauperism
paupérrimo *a sup* **pobre** exceedingly poor
pausa *f*, pause, interruption; delay; *mus* rest; *mus* pause. **a pausas,** intermittently
pausado *a* deliberate, slow. *adv* slowly, deliberately
pausar *vi* to pause
pauta *f*, standard, norm, design; *fig* guide, model
pavada *f*, flock of turkeys
pavana *f*, pavane, stately dance
pavero (-ra) *a* vain; strutting. *n* turkey keeper or vendor. *m*, broad-brimmed Andalusian hat
pavimentación *f*, paving, flagging
pavimento *m*, pavement
pavo (-va) *a orn* turkey. **p. real,** peacock. *inf* **pelar la pava,** to serenade, court
pavón *m*, *orn* peacock; peacock butterfly; preservative paint (for steel, etc.); gunmetal
pavonear *vi* to strut, peacock (also *vr*); *inf* hoodwink, dazzle
pavor *m*, terror, panic
pavoroso *a* fearful, awesome, dreadful
payasada *f*, clowning, practical joke; clown's patter
payaso *m*, clown
paz *f*, peace; harmony, concord; peaceableness. **¡P. sea en esta casa!** Peace be upon this house! (salutation). **estar en p.,** to be at peace; be quits, be even. **poner** (*or* **meter**) **p.,** to make peace (between dissentients). **venir de p.,** to come with peaceful intentions
pazguato (-ta) *n* simpleton, booby
pazpuerca *f*, slattern
pe *f*, name of the letter P. *inf* **de pe a pa,** from A to Z, from beginning to end
peaje *m*, toll (on bridges, roads, etc.)
peatón *m*, pedestrian; walker; country postman
pebete *m*, joss stick; fuse; *inf* stench
peca *f*, mole, freckle
pecado *m*, sin; fault; excess; defect; *inf* the Devil. **p. capital,** mortal sin
pecador *a* sinful. *m*, sinner. **¡P. de mí!** Poor me!
pecadora *f*, sinner; *inf* prostitute
pecaminoso *a* sinful
pecar *vi* to sin; trespass, transgress; (*with de*) be too . . . (e.g. **El libro peca de largo,** The book is too long)
peceño *a* pitch-black (horses, etc.); tasting of pitch
pecera *f*, goldfish bowl; aquarium
pechera *f*, shirt front; chest protector; bib, tucker; shirt frill; *inf* bosom
pecho *m*, *anat* chest; breast; bosom; mind, conscience; courage, endurance; *mus* quality (of voice); incline, slope. **p. arriba,** uphill. **abrir su p.** (*a* or con), to unbosom oneself to. **dar el p.** (a), to suckle. **de pechos,** leaning on. **echar el p. al agua,** *fig* to embark courageously upon. **tomar a pechos** (una cosa), to take (a thing) very seriously; take to heart
pechuga *f*, breast (of a bird); *inf* breast, bosom; slope, incline
pecio *m*, flotsam
pécora *f*, sheep, head of sheep; wily woman, serpent
pecoso *a* freckled; spotted (with warts)
pecuario *a agr* stock; cattle
peculiar *a* peculiar, individual
peculiaridad *f*, peculiarity
peculio *m*, private money or property
pecunia *f*, *inf* cash
pecuniario *a* pecuniary
pedagogía *f*, education, pedagogy
pedagógico *a* educational, pedagogic
pedagogo *m*, schoolmaster; educationalist; *fig* mentor
pedal *m*, *mech* treadle, lever, *mus* pedal; *mus* sustained harmony. *aut* **p. de embrague,** clutch pedal
pedalear *vi* to pedal
pedante *a* pedantic. *mf* pedant
pedantería *f*, pedantry
pedazo *m*, bit, piece; lump; fragment, portion. *inf* **p. del alma, p. del corazón, p. de las entrañas,** loved one,

dear one. **a pedazos** or **en pedazos,** in pieces, in bits.

hacer pedazos, to break into fragments

pedernal m, flint; anything very hard

pedestal m, pedestal; base; stand; fig foundation

pedestre a pedestrian; dull, uninspired

pediatra mf pediatrician

pedicuro m, chiropodist

pedido m, com order; request, petition

pedigüeño a importunate, insistent

pedimento m, petition, demand; law claim; law motion

pedir vt irr to ask, request; com order; demand; necessitate; desire; ask in marriage. **p. en juicio,** law to bring an action against. inf **pedírselo (a uno) el cuerpo,** to desire (something) ardently. **a p. de boca,** according to one's wish. Pres. Part. **pidiendo.** Pres. Ind. **pido, pides, pide, piden.** Preterite **pidió, pidieron.** Pres. Subjunc. **pida,** etc. Imperf. Subjunc. **pidiese,** etc.

pedo m, fart

pedómetro m, pedometer

pedrada f, casting a stone; blow with a stone; innuendo

pedrea f, stone throwing; fight with stones; shower of hailstones

pedregal m, stony ground

pedregoso a stony

pedrera f, stone quarry

pedrería f, precious stones

pedrisco m, hailstone; shower of stones; pile of stones

pedrusco m, inf rough, unpolished stone

pega f, sticking; cementing; joining; pitch; varnish; inf joke; beating; orn magpie

pegadizo a sticky, gummy, adhesive; detachable, removable; fig clinging, importunate (of people)

pegado m, sticking plaster; patch

pegajoso a sticky, gluey; viscid; contagious, catching; inf oily, unctuous; fig inf cadging, sponging

pegar vt to stick; cement; join, fasten; press (against); infect with (diseases); hit, strike; give (a shout, jump, etc.); patch; vi spread, catch (fire, etc.); fig make an impression, have influence; be opportune; vr cul stick, burn; meddle; become enthusiastic about; take root in the mind. **p. un tiro (a),** to shoot

Pegaso m, Pegasus

pegote m, sticking plaster; fig inf sponger; inf patch

peinado m, hairdressing or style; headdress. a inf effeminate, overelegant (men); overcareful (style). **un p. al agua,** a finger wave

peinador (-ra) m, peignoir, dressing gown. n hairdresser

peinadura f, brushing or combing of hair; pl hair combings

peinar vt to comb, dress the hair; card (wool); cut away (rock)

peine m, comb; mech hackle, reed; instep; inf crafty person

peinería f, comb factory or shop

peinero m, comb manufacturer or seller

peineta f, high comb (for mantillas, etc.)

peladilla f, sugared almond; smooth, small pebble

pelado a plucked; bare, unadorned; needy, poor; hairless; skinned; peeled; without shell; treeless

peladura f, peeling; shelling; skinning; plucking (feathers)

pelafustán m, inf good-for-nothing, scamp

pelagatos m, inf miserable wretch

pelágico a pelagian, oceanic

pelagra f, pellagra

pelaje m, fur, wool

pelamesa f, brawl, fight; lock, tuft (of hair)

pelapatatas m, potato peeler

pelar vt to tear out or cut the hair; pluck; skin; peel; shell; rob, fleece; vr lose one's hair

peldaño m, step, stair, tread, rung

pelea f, battle; quarrel, dispute; fight (among animals); effort, exertion; fig struggle

peleador a fighting; quarrelsome, aggressive

pelear vi to fight; quarrel; struggle, strive. **p. como**

perro y gato, to fight like cat and mouse. vr come to blows; fall out, become enemies

pelechar vi to get a new coat (of animals); grow new feathers (of birds); inf prosper, flourish; grow well

pelele m, effigy; inf nincompoop

peletería f, furrier; fur shop

peletero m, furrier; skinner

peliagudo a long-haired (animals); inf complicated, difficult; wily, downy

pelícano m, pelican

pelicorto a short-haired

película f, film. **p. fotográfica,** roll of film. **p. sonora,** sound film

peligrar vi to be in danger

peligro m, danger, peril. **correr p.** or **estar en p.,** to be in danger

peligroso a dangerous, perilous, risky

pelilargo a long-haired

pelirrojo a red-haired

pelleja f, hide, skin (of animals); sheepskin

pellejo m, hide; pelt; skin; wineskin; inf drunkard; peel, skin (of fruit)

pelliza f, fur or fur-trimmed coat

pellizcar vt to pinch, tweak, nip; pilfer

pellizco m, pinch, nip, tweak; pilfering, pinching; bit, pinch

pelmazo m, squashed mass; inf idler, sluggard; inf bore

pelo m, hair; down (on birds and fruit); fiber, filament; hair trigger (firearms); hairspring (watches); kiss (in billiards); nap (of cloth), grain (of wood); flaw (in gems); raw silk. **p. de camello,** camel's hair. **a p.,** in the nude; without a hat; opportunely. **en p.,** bareback (of horses). **hacerse el p.,** to do one's hair; have one's hair cut. inf **no tener p. de tonto,** to be smart, clever. inf **no tener pelos en la lengua,** to be outspoken. inf **tomar el p. (a),** to pull a person's leg. **venir a p.,** to be apposite; come opportunely

pelón a hairless; fig inf broke, fleeced

pelonería f, inf poverty, misery

peloponense a and mf Peloponnesian

pelota f, ball; ball game. **p. base,** baseball. **p. vasca,** pelota. **en p.,** stark naked

pelotari m, professional pelota player

pelotazo m, knock or blow with a ball

pelotear vt to audit accounts; vi play ball; throw, cast; quarrel; argue

pelotera f, inf brawl

pelotón m, big ball; lump of hair; crowd, multitude; mil platoon. **p. de ejecución,** firing squad

peltre m, pewter

peluca f, wig; periwig; inf scolding

peludo a hairy. m, long-haired rug

peluquería f, hairdressing establishment; hairdressing trade

peluquero (-ra) n hairdresser; barber

peluquín m, small wig

pelusa f, down, soft hair; fluff, nap

pena f, punishment, penalty; grief; pain, suffering; difficulty, trouble; mourning veil; hardship; embarrassment; tail feather. **p. capital** or **p. de la vida,** capital punishment. **a duras penas,** with great difficulty. **so p. de,** under penalty of. **valer** (or **merecer**) **la p.,** to be worth while

penable a punishable

penacho m, topknot, crest (of birds); plume, panache; inf pride, arrogance

penado (-da) a difficult, laborious; painful, troubled, afflicted. n convict

penal a penal; punitive

penalidad f, trouble, labor, difficulty; law penalty

penar vt to penalize; punish; vi suffer; undergo purgatorial pains; vr suffer anguish. **p. por,** to long for

penca f, bot fleshy leaf; lash, strap, cat-o'-nine-tails

penco m, inf wretched nag

pendejo m, pubic hair; inf coward; jerk

pendencia f, fight; quarrel

pendenciar *vi* to fight; quarrel

pendenciero *a* quarrelsome, aggressive

pender *vi* to hang; depend; be pending

pendiente *a* pending; hanging; *com* outstanding. *m*, earring; pendant. *f*, slope, incline; gradient

péndola *f*, feather, plume; quill pen; pendulum (of a clock)

pendolista *mf* calligrapher

pendón *m*, pennon, banner; *bot* shoot; *inf* lanky, slatternly woman; *pl* reins

péndulo *a* pendulous, hanging. *m*, pendulum

pene *m*, penis

penetrabilidad *f*, penetrability

penetración *f*, penetration; understanding, perspicuity; sagacity, shrewdness

penetrador *a* penetrating, perspicacious; sagacious, acute

penetrante *a* penetrating; deep; piercing (of sounds); acute, shrewd

penetrar *vt* to penetrate; permeate; master, comprehend; *(with en)* enter

penetrativo *a* piercing

penicilina *f*, penicillin

península *f*, peninsula. **la P.** the Iberian Peninsula

Península Ibérica, la the Iberian Peninsula

penique *m*, penny

penitencia *f*, penitence, repentance; penance

penitencial *a* penitential

penitenciaría *f*, penitentiary

penitenciario *a* penitentiary

penitente *a* penitent, repentant. *mf* penitent

penoso *a* laborious, difficult; grievous; painful; troublesome; *inf* foppish

pensado *a* premeditated, deliberate. **de p.,** intentionally. **mal p.,** malicious, evil-minded

pensador *a* thinking; pensive. *m*, thinker

pensamiento *m*, mind; thought; idea; suspicion, doubt; heartsease pansy; maxim; intention, project

pensar *vt irr* to think; purpose, intend; *(with en, sobre)* reflect upon; think about; *vt* feed (animals). **p. entre sí, p. para consigo** *or* **p. para sí,** to think to oneself. See **acertar**

pensativo *a* reflective, pensive

pensil *a* hanging. *m*, hanging garden; delightful garden

pensión *f*, pension, allowance; boarding house, private hotel; scholarship grant; cost of board; trouble, drudgery

pensionado (-da) *a* pensioned; retired. *n* scholarship holder. *m*, boarding school

pensionar *vt* to pension, grant a pension to; charge a pension on

pensionista *mf* pensioner; boarder

pentágono *m*, pentagon. *a* pentagonal

pentagrama *or* **pentágrama** *m*, *mus* pentagram, stave

pentámetro *m*, pentameter

Pentateuco *m*, Pentateuch

Pentecostés *m*, Pentecost, Whitsuntide

penúltimo *a* next to the last, penultimate

penuria *f*, scarcity; want, penury

peña *f*, crag, rock; boulder; group of friends; club. **ser una p.,** to be stony-hearted

peñasco *m*, craggy peak

peñascoso *a* craggy, rocky

peñón *m*, rock; cliff; peak

peón *m*, pedestrian; laborer; *South America* farmhand; top (toy); piece (chess, checkers); *mech* axle; infantryman. **p. caminero,** road mender. **p. de ajedrez,** pawn (in chess)

peonada *f*, day's manual labor; gang of laborers

peonía *f*, peony

peonza *f*, top; teetotum

peor *a comp* **malo** worse. *adv comp* **mal,** worse. *a sup* **el (la, lo) peor; los (las) peores,** the worst. **p. que p.,** worse and worse. **tanto p.,** so much the worse

pepino *m*, cucumber plant; cucumber; *fig* pin, straw

pepita *f*, *min* nugget; pip, seed (of fruit)

peplo *m*, Greek tunic, peplum

péptico *a* peptic

pequeñez *f*, littleness, smallness; pettiness; childhood; infancy; trifle, insignificant thing; meanness, baseness

pequeño *a* little, small; petty; very young; short, brief; humble, lowly

pera *f*, pear; goatee; *fig* plum, sinecure

peral *m*, pear tree; pearwood

perca *f*, *icht* perch

percal *m*, percale, calico

percalina *f*, percaline, binding cloth

percance *m*, perquisite, attribute (gen. *pl*); disaster, mischance

percebe *m*, (gen. *pl*) goose barnacle

percentaje *m*, percentage

percepción *f*, perception; idea, conception

perceptible *a* perceptible

perceptivo *a* perceptive

perceptor (-ra) *a* perceptive. *n* observer

percha *f*, stake, pole; coat hanger; perch (for birds); rack (for hay); hall stand, coat and hat stand, coatrack

perchero *m*, hall stand; clothes rack; row of perches (for fowl, etc.)

percibir *vt* to collect, draw, receive; perceive; understand, grasp

percibo *m*, perceiving; collecting, drawing, receiving

percolador *m*, percolator (coffee)

percusión *f*, percussion; shock, vibration

percusor *m*, hammer (of a firearm)

percutir *vt* to percuss, strike

perdedor (-ra) *a* losing. *n* loser

perder *vt* to lose; throw away, squander; spoil, destroy; *vi* fade (of colors); *vr* lose one's way, be lost; be confused or perplexed; be shipwrecked; take to vice, become dissolute; be spoiled or destroyed; disappear; love madly. **p. la chaveta (por),** to go out of one's head (for), be wild (about). **p. la ocasión,** to let the chance slip. **p. los estribos,** to lose patience. **p. terreno,** to lose ground. **perderse de vista,** to be lost to sight. **echarse a p.,** to spoil, be damaged. See **entender**

perdición *f*, loss; perdition, ruin; damnation; depravity, viciousness

pérdida *f*, loss; waste. **p. cuantiosa,** heavy losses

perdidamente *adv* ardently, desperately; uselessly

perdigón *m*, young partridge; decoy partridge; hailstone, pellet, shot

perdigonada *f*, volley of hailstone; hailstone wound

perdiguero (-ra) *n* game dealer; setter, retriever

perdiz *f*, partridge. **p. blanca,** ptarmigan

perdón *m*, pardon, forgiveness; remission. **con p.,** with your permission; excuse me

perdonable *a* pardonable, excusable

perdonar *vt* to pardon, forgive; remit, excuse; exempt; waste, lose; give up (a privilege)

perdonavidas *m*, *inf* bully, braggart

perdulario *a* careless, negligent; slovenly; vicious, depraved

perdurable *a* perpetual, everlasting; enduring, lasting

perdurar *vi* to last, endure

perecedero *a* brief, fugitive, transient; perishable. *m*, *inf* poverty, want

perecer *vi irr* to end, finish; perish, die; suffer (damage, grief, etc.); be destitute; *vr* (*with por*) long for, crave; desire ardently. See **conocer**

peregrinación *f*, journey, peregrination; pilgrimage

peregrinamente *adv* rarely, not often; beautifully, perfectly

peregrinar *vi* to journey, travel; make a pilgrimage

peregrino (-na) *a* and *n* pilgrim. *a* migratory (birds); rare, unusual; extraordinary, strange; beautiful, perfect

perejil *m*, parsley; *inf* ornament or apparel (gen. *pl*); *pl* honors, titles

perengano (-na) *n* so-and-so, such a one

perenne *a* incessant, constant; *bot* perennial

perennidad *f*, perpetuity
perentoriedad *f*, peremptoriness; urgency
perentorio *a* peremptory; conclusive, decisive; urgent, pressing
pereza *f*, laziness; languor, inertia; slowness, deliberateness
perezoso *a* lazy; languid; slothful; slow, deliberate. *m*, *zool* sloth
perfección *f*, perfection; perfecting, perfect thing, virtue, grace
perfeccionamiento *m*, perfecting; progress, improvement
perfeccionar *vt* to perfect; complete
perfectamente *adv* perfectly; quite, entirely
perfecto *a* perfect; excellent, very good; complete; whole; *gram* perfect
perfidia *f*, perfidy, treachery
pérfido *a* perfidious, treacherous
perfil *m*, ornament, decoration; outline, contour; profile; section (of metal); fine stroke (of letters); *pl* finishing touches; politeness, attention, courtesy. **de p.**, in profile; sideways
perfilado *a* long, elongated (of faces, etc.)
perfilar *vt* to draw in profile; outline; *vr* place oneself sideways, show one's profile; *inf* dress up, titivate
perforación *f*, perforation, boring; hole
perforador *a* perforating, boring. *m*, *mech* drill
perforar *vt* to perforate, pierce; bore, drill, make a hole in
perfumador (-ra) *a* perfuming. *n* perfumer. *m*, perfume burner
perfumar *vt* to perfume; *vi* give off perfume
perfume *m*, perfume; scent, fragrance
perfumería *f*, scent factory; perfumery; perfume shop
perfumista *mf* perfumer
perfunctorio *a* perfunctory
pergamino *m*, parchment, vellum; document; diploma; *pl* aristocratic descent
pericardio *m*, pericardium
pericia *f*, expertness; skilled workmanship
pericial *a* expert, skillful
perico *m*, parakeet
periferia *f*, periphery
periférico *a* peripheral
perifollos *m pl*, *inf* frills, flounces, finery
perifrástico *a* periphrastic
perilla *f*, pear-shaped ornament; goatee; imperial. **p. de la oreja**, lobe of the ear. **venir de p.**, to be most opportune
perillán *m*, *inf* rascal, rogue
perímetro *m*, perimeter; precincts
perínclito *a* distinguished, illustrious; heroic
perineo *m*, perineum
perinola *f*, top, teetotum
periodicidad *f*, periodicity
periódico *a* periodic. *m*, newspaper; periodical publication
periodicucho *m*, rag (bad newspaper)
periodismo *m*, journalism
periodista *mf* journalist
periodístico *a* journalistic
período *m*, period; *phys* cycle; menstruation period; *gram* clause; age, era
periostio *m*, periosteum
peripatético *a* peripatetic
peripecia *f*, sudden change of fortune, vicissitude
peripuesto *a* *inf* overelegant, spruce, too well-dressed; smart
periquete *m*, *inf* jiffy, trice
periquito *m*, parakeet; budgerigar
periscopio *m*, periscope
perito (-ta) *a* expert; skillful, experienced. *n* expert
peritoneo *m*, peritoneum
perjudicador (-ra) *a* injurious, prejudicial. *n* injurer
perjudicar *vt* to harm, damage, injure; prejudice
perjudicial *a* injurious, noxious, harmful; prejudicial

perjuicio *m*, injury, damage; harm; *law* prejudice
perjurador (-ra) *n* perjurer
perjurar *vi* to perjure oneself, commit perjury; swear, curse
perjurio *m*, perjury
perjuro (-ra) *a* perjured, forsworn. *n* perjurer
perla *f*, pearl; *arch* bead; *fig* treasure, jewel, dear. **de perlas**, excellent; exactly right
perlero *a* pearl
perlesía *f*, paralysis; palsy
perlino *a* pearly, pearl-colored
permanecer *vi irr* to stay, remain. **p. en posición de firme**, to stand at attention. See **conocer**
permanencia *f*, stay, sojourn; permanence
permanente *a* permanent; lasting, enduring
permanganato *m*, permanganate
permeabilidad *f*, permeability
permisible *a* permissible, allowable
permisivo *a* permissive
permiso *m*, permission, leave; permit; (*mil* etc.) pass. **¡Con p.!** Excuse me!; Allow me!
permitir *vt* to permit, allow
permuta *f*, exchange
permutación *f*, permutation, interchange
permutar *vt* to exchange
pernear *vi* to kick; *inf* bustle; fret, be impatient
pernetas, en *adv* barelegged
perniciosidad *f*, perniciousness
pernicioso *a* pernicious
pernil *m*, *anat* hock; ham; leg of pork; leg (of trousers)
pernio *m*, hinge (of doors, windows)
perniquebrar *vt irr* to break the legs of. See **quebrar**
perno *m*, bolt, pin, spike
pernoctar *vi* to spend the night (away from home)
pero *conjunc* but. *m*, *inf* defect; difficulty, snag
perogrullada *f*, *inf* truism
perol *m*, *cul* pan
peroné *m*, fibula
peroración *f*, peroration
perorar *vi* to make a speech; *inf* speak pompously; ask insistently
peróxido *m*, peroxide
perpendicular *a* perpendicular. *f*, perpendicular
perpetración *f*, perpetration
perpetrar *vt* to perpetrate
perpetua *f*, *bot* immortelle, everlasting
perpetuación *f*, perpetuation
perpetuar *vt* to perpetuate; *vr* last, endure
perpetuidad *f*, perpetuity
perpetuo *a* everlasting; lifelong
perplejidad *f*, perplexity, bewilderment, doubt
perplejo *a* perplexed, bewildered, doubtful
perquirir *vt irr* to search carefully. See **adquirir**
perra *f*, bitch; *inf* sot, drunkard; tantrums. **p. chica**, five-cent coin. **p. gorda**, ten-cent coin
perrada *f*, pack of dogs; *inf* dirty trick
perrengue *m*, *inf* short-tempered person
perrera *f*, dog kennel; useless toil; *inf* tantrums
perrería *f*, pack of dogs; *inf* dirty trick; fit of anger
perrero *m*, dog fancier; kennel worker
perro *m*, dog. **p. caliente** hot dog. **p. danés**, Great Dane. **p. de aguas**, poodle; spaniel. **p. de casta**, thoroughbred dog. **p. de lanas** poodle. **p. de muestra**, pointer. **p. de presa**, bulldog. **p. de San Bernardo**, St. Bernard (dog). **p. de Terranova**, Newfoundland (dog). **p. del hortelano**, dog in the manger. **p. dogo** bulldog. **p. esquimal** husky. **p. faldero**, lap dog. **p. lobo**, wolfhound. **p. pachón**, dachshund. **p. pastor alemán** *or* **p. policía**, German shepherd. **p. pequinés**, Pekingese. **p. perdiguero**, retriever. **p. pomerano**, spitz, Pomeranian (dog). **p. sabueso español**, spaniel. **p. zorrero**, foxhound. *inf* **A p. viejo no hay tus tus**, You can't fool an old dog. **vivir como perros y gatos**, to live like cat and dog
perruno *a* dog, dog-like
persa *a* and *mf* Persian. *m*, Persian (language)

persecución *f*, pursuit; persecution; annoyance, importuning

perseguidor (-ra) *a* pursuing; tormenting. *n* pursuer; tormentor, persecutor

perseguimiento *m*, pursuit

perseguir *vi irr* to pursue; persecute, torment; importune. See **seguir**

perseverancia *f*, perseverance

perseverante *a* persevering; constant

perseverar *vi* to persevere; last, endure

persiana *f*, Venetian blind; flowered silk material

pérsico *a* Persian. *m*, peach tree; peach

persignar *vt* to sign; make the sign of the cross over; *vr* cross oneself

persistencia *f*, persistence

persistente *a* persistent

persistir *vi* to persist

persona *f*, person; personage; character (in a play, etc.); (*gram ecc*) person. **de p. a p.**, in private, face to face

personaje *m*, important person, personage; character (in a play, etc.)

personal *a* personal. *m*, staff, personnel

personalidad *f*, personality

personalismo *m*, personality; personal question

personalizar *vt* to become personal, be offensive

personalmente *adv* personally

personarse *vr* to present oneself, call, appear

personificación *f*, personification

personificar *vt* to personify

perspectiva *f*, perspective; view; outlook; aspect, appearance. **p. aérea**, bird's-eye view

perspicacia *f*, perspicacity, shrewdness

perspicaz *a* perspicacious, clear-sighted

perspicuidad *f*, perspicuity

perspicuo *a* lucid, clear

persuadir *vt* to persuade

persuasible *a* persuadable

persuasión *f*, persuasion; belief, conviction, opinion

persuasiva *f*, persuasiveness

persuasivo *a* persuasive

pertenecer *vi irr* to belong; relate, concern. See **conocer**

perteneciente *a* belonging (to), pertaining (to)

pertenencia *f*, ownership, proprietorship; property, accessory

pértiga *f*, long rod; pole. **salto de p.**, pole vaulting

pertinacia *f*, pertinacity, doggedness

pertinaz *a* pertinacious, stubborn, dogged

pertinencia *f*, relevance, appropriateness

pertinente *a* relevant, apposite; appropriate

pertrechar *vt* to supply, equip; prepare, make ready

pertrechos *m pl*, *mil* armaments, stores; equipment, appliances

perturbación *f*, disturbance; agitation

perturbador (-ra) *a* disturbing. *n* disturber; heckler

perturbar *vt* to disturb; agitate

Perú Peru

peruano (-na) *a* and *n* Peruvian

perversidad *f*, wickedness, depravity

perversión *f*, perversion; wickedness, evil

perversivo *a* perversive

perverso *a* wicked, iniquitous, depraved

pervertir *vt irr* to pervert, corrupt; distort. See **sentir**

pesa *f*, weight; clock weight; gymnast's weight. **pesas y medidas,** weights and measures

pesacartas *m*, letter scale, letter balance

pesada *f*, weighing

pesadez *f*, heaviness; obesity; tediousness, tiresomeness; slowness; fatigue

pesadilla *f*, nightmare

pesado *a* heavy; obese; deep (of sleep); oppressive (of weather); slow; unwieldy; tedious; impertinent; dull, boring; offensive

pesadumbre *f*, heaviness; grief, sorrow; trouble, anxiety

pésame *m*, expression of condolence. **dar el p.,** to present one's condolences

pesantez *f*, weight, heaviness; seriousness, gravity

pesar *m*, grief, sorrow; remorse. **a p. de**, in spite of

pesar *vi* to weigh; be heavy; be important; grieve, cause regret (e.g. **Me pesa mucho,** I am very sorry); influence, affect; *vt* weigh; consider. **Mal que me (te,** etc.) **pese . . . ,** Much as I regret . . .

pesario *m*, pessary

pesaroso *a* regretful, remorseful; sorrowful

pesca *f*, fishery; angling, fishing; catch of fish. **p. a la rastra,** trawling. **p. deportiva** sport fishing. **p. mayor,** deep-sea fishing

pescadería *f*, fishery; fish store; fish market

pescadilla *f*, *icht* whiting

pescado *m*, fish (out of the water); salt cod

pescador (-ra) *n* fisherman; angler

pescante *m*, driving seat; coach box; jib (of a crane)

pescar *vt* to fish; *inf* catch in the act; acquire. **p. a la rastra,** to trawl

pescozón *m*, slap on the neck or head

pescuezo *m*, neck; throat; haughtiness, arrogance. **torcer el p.,** to wring the neck (of chickens, etc.)

pesebre *m*, manger, stable; feeding trough

pésimamente *adv* extremely badly

pesimismo *m*, pessimism

pesimista *a* pessimistic. *mf* pessimist

pésimo *a sup* **malo** extremely bad

peso *m*, weighing; weight; heaviness; gravity; importance; influence; load; peso (coin); scale, balance. **p. bruto,** gross weight. **p. de joyería,** troy weight. **p. específico,** *phys* specific gravity. **p. pluma,** (*boxing*) featherweight

pespunte *m*, backstitch

pesquera *f*, fishing ground, fishery

pesquería *f*, fishing, angling; fisherman's trade; fishing ground, fishery

pesquero *a* fishing (of boats, etc.)

pesquisa *f*, investigation, examination; search

pesquisar *vt* to investigate, look into; search

pestaña *f*, eyelash; *sew* edging, fringe; ear, lug; *naut* fluke

pestañear *vi* to wink; blink; flutter the eyelashes

pestañeo *m*, winking; blinking

peste *f*, plague, pestilence; nauseous smell; epidemic; pest; vice; *pl* oaths, curses. **p. bubónica,** bubonic plague. **p. roja** syphilis. **p. de las abejas,** foul brood. **echar pestes,** to swear; fume

pestífero *a* noxious

pestilencia *f*, plague, pestilence

pestilente *a* pestilential

pestillo *m*, latch; lock bolt. **p. de golpe,** safety latch

petaca *f*, cigarette or cigar case; tobacco pouch

pétalo *m*, petal

petardista *mf* swindler, impostor

petardo *m*, detonator; torpedo; firecracker; fraud

petición *f*, petition, request

peticionario (-ia) *n* petitioner. *a* petitionary

petimetra *f*, stylish and affected young woman

petimetre *m*, fop

petirrojo *m*, robin

petitorio *a* petitionary. *m*, *inf* importunity

peto *m*, breastplate; front (of a shirt); bib

pétreo *a* petrous

petrificación *f*, petrifaction

petrificar *vt* to petrify; *vr* become petrified

petrografía *f*, petrology

petróleo *m*, petroleum; oil, mineral oil. **p. bruto,** crude oil. **p. de lámpara,** kerosene

petrolero (-ra) *a* oil, petroleum. *n* petroleum seller; incendiarist. *m*, oil tanker

petrolífero *a* oil-bearing

petroso *a* stony, rocky

petulancia *f*, insolence; vanity

petulante *a* insolent; vain

pez *m*, fish; *pl* Pisces. *f*, *chem* pitch. **p. sierra,** swordfish

pezón *m, bot* stalk; nipple; axle pivot; point (of land, etc.)

pezonera *f,* linchpin

pezuña *f,* cloven hoof (of cows, pigs, etc.)

piada *f,* chirping, twittering

piadoso *a* compassionate; kind, pitiful; pious, religious

piafar *vi* to stamp, paw the ground (horses)

piamontés (-esa) *a* and *n* Piedmontese

pianista *mf* piano maker; piano dealer; pianist

piano *m,* pianoforte. **p. de cola,** grand piano. **p. de media cola,** baby grand. **p. vertical,** upright piano

piante *a* chirping, twittering

piar *vi* to chirp, twitter

piara *f,* herd of swine; pack (of horses, etc.)

pica *f, mil* pike; bullfighter's goad; pike soldier; stone-cutter's hammer. **a p. seca,** in vain. **pasar por las picas,** to suffer hardship. **poner una p. en Flandes,** to triumph over great difficulties

picacho *m,* peak, summit

picada *f,* prick; bite; peck; *aer* dive

picadero *m,* riding school; paddock (of a racetrack)

picado *a sew* pinked. *m, cul* hash

picador *m,* horse trainer; meat chopper; horseman armed with a goad (bullfights)

picadura *f,* puncture; prick; sting; *sew* pinking; peck (of birds); cut tobacco; black tobacco; beginning of caries in teeth

picajoso *a* hypersensitive, touchy, peevish

picamaderos *m,* woodpecker

picante *a* piquant; mordant; hot, highly seasoned. *m,* mordancy; pungency

picapleitos *m, inf* shady lawyer, pettifogger

picaporte *m,* latch, door catch; door knocker

picar *vt* to prick; sting; peck; bite; chop fine; mince; nibble (of fishing); irritate (the skin); *sew* pink; burn (the tongue); eat (grapes); goad; spur; stipple (walls); stimulate, encourage; split, cleave; *mil* harass; vex; *mus* play staccato; *vi* burn (of the sun); smart (of cuts, etc.); eat sparingly; *aut* knock; (*with en*) knock at (doors, etc.); *vr* be moth-eaten; go rotten (fruit, etc.); grow choppy (of the sea); be piqued; boast

pícaramente *adv* knavishly, cunningly

picardear *vi* to play the rogue; behave mischievously

picardía *f,* knavery, roguery; mischievousness; practical joke; wantonness

picaresco *a* roguish, picaresque, knavish

pícaro (-ra) *a* knavish; base, vile; astute; mischievous. *n* rogue

picatoste *m,* kind of fritter

picaza *f,* magpie

picazo *m,* blow with a pike or anything pointed; peck, tap with a beak (of birds); sting

picazón *f,* itch, irritation; annoyance

pícea *f, bot* spruce

píceo *a* piscine, fish-like

pichel *m,* tankard

pichón (-ona) *m,* male pigeon. *n inf* darling

pico *m,* beak (of birds); peak; woodpecker; odd amount (e.g. **treinta y p.,** thirty-odd); sharp point; spout (of a jug, etc.); *inf* mouth; blarney, gab. **p. de cigüeña,** crane's-bill. **p. de oro,** silver-tongued orator

picor *m,* burning sensation in the mouth; smarting; itching, irritation

picoso *a* pitted, marked by smallpox

picota *f,* pillory; peak; spire

picotazo *m,* peck; dab; sting, bite

picoteado *a* peaked, having points

picotear *vt* to peck (of a bird); *vi* to toss the head (of horses); *inf* chatter senselessly; *vr inf* slang each other

picotero *a inf* chattering, talkative; indiscreet

pictografía *f,* picture writing

pictórico *a* pictorial

picudo *a* pointed, peaked; having a spout; *inf* chattering

pie *m,* foot; stand, support; stem (of a glass, etc.); standard (of a lamp); *bot* trunk, stem; sapling; lees, sediment; *theat* cue; foot (measure); custom; (metrics) foot; motive, cause; pretext; (metrics) meter. **p. de cabra,** crowbar. **p. de imprenta,** printer's mark, printer's imprint. **p. de piña,** clubfoot. **p. de rey,** caliper. **p. palmado,** webfoot. **al p. de la letra,** punctiliously. *inf* **andar con pies de plomo,** to walk warily. **a p.,** on foot. **a p. firme,** without budging; steadfastly. *inf* **buscar tres pies al gato,** to look for something that isn't there; twist a person's words. **de a p.,** on foot. **en p. de guerra,** on a wartime footing. *inf* **poner pies en polvorosa,** to quit

piedad *f,* piety; pity, compassion; *art* pietà

piedra *f,* stone; tablet; *med* gravel. **p. de amolar,** whetstone, grindstone. **p. angular,** cornerstone (also *fig*). **p. caliza,** limestone. **p. clave,** keystone. **p. de construcción,** building stone; child's block. **p. de toque,** touchstone, test. **p. filosofal,** philosopher's stone. **p. fundamental,** foundation stone. **p. miliaria,** milestone. **p. mortuoria,** tombstone. *fig inf* **no dejar p. sin remover,** to leave no stone unturned. **no dejar p. sobre p.,** to demolish, destroy completely

piel *f,* skin; fur; hide; leather; peel (of some fruits); rind (of bacon). **p. de gallina,** *fig* goose flesh. **p. de rata,** horse blanket. **p. de Rusia,** Russian leather.

piélago *m,* high seas; sea, ocean; glut, superabundance

pienso *m, agr* fodder

pierna *f, anat* leg; *mech* shank; leg of a compass. *inf* **a p. suelta,** at one's ease. **en piernas,** barelegged

pietismo *m,* pietism

pietista *a* pietistic. *mf* pietist

pieza *f,* portion; piece; component part; room; *theat* play; roll (of cloth); piece (in chess, etc.); coin; piece (of music). **p. de recambio** *or* **p. de repuesto,** spare part. **p. de recibo,** reception room. *inf* **quedarse en una p.,** to be struck dumb

pífano *m,* fife; fife player, fifer

pigmentación *f,* pigmentation

pigmentario *a* pigmentary

pigmento *m,* pigment

pigmeo (-ea) *a* and *n* pygmy

pignoración *f,* hypothecation; pawning; mortgage

pignorar *vt* to hypothecate; pawn; mortgage

pigre *a* lazy; negligent, careless

pigricia *f,* laziness; negligence

pijama *m,* pajamas

pila *f,* trough, basin; heap, pile; *elec* battery; *ecc* parish; pier, pile; *phys* cell. **p. atómica,** atomic pile. **p. bautismal,** *ecc* font

pilar *m,* fountain basin; milestone; pillar

pilastra *f,* pier, pile; pilaster

píldora *f, med* pill; *inf* disagreeable news

pillador (-ra) *a* pillaging, plundering. *n* plunderer

pillaje *m,* pillaging, looting; robbery, theft

pillar *vt* to pillage; steal, rob; seize, snatch; *inf* surprise, find out (in a lie, etc.). **pillarse el dedo,** to get one's finger caught (in a door, etc.)

pillastre *m, inf* rogue, ragamuffin

pillear *vi inf* to lead a rogue's life

pillería *f, inf* gang of rogues; *inf* rogue's trick

pillo *m,* rogue, knave

pilón *m,* fountain basin; pestle; loaf sugar; pylon

pilongo *a* thin, lean

píloro *m,* pylorus

pilotaje *m,* pilotage; piling, pilework. **examen de p.,** flying test

pilotar *vt* to pilot

pilote *m, eng* pile

pilotear *vt* to pilot

piloto *m,* pilot; mate (in merchant ships). **p. de pruebas,** test pilot

pimentero *m,* pepper plant; pepper shaker

pimentón *m,* red pepper, cayenne

pimienta *f,* pepper. **p. húngara,** paprika. *inf* **ser como una p.,** to be sharp as a needle

pimiento *m,* pimento; capsicum; red pepper; pepper plant. **p. de cornetilla,** chili pepper

pimpollo *m*, sapling; sprout, shoot; rosebud

pina *f*, conical stone; felloe (of a wheel)

pinacoteca *f*, art gallery, picture gallery

pináculo *m*, pinnacle, summit; climax, culmination; *arch* finial

pinar *m*, pinewood

pincarrasco *m*, pin oak

pincel *m*, paintbrush; artist, painter; painting technique. **p. para las cejas,** eyebrow pencil

pincelada *f*, brushstroke. **dar la última p.,** to add the finishing touch

pincelero (-ra) *n* seller or maker of paintbrushes; brush box

pinchadura *f*, prick, puncture, piercing; sting; nipping, biting

pinchar *vt* to prick; puncture; pierce; sting; nip, bite. **no p. ni cortar,** to be ineffective (of persons)

pinchazo *m*, prick; puncture; sting; incitement

pinche *m*, scullion

pineda *f*, pinewood

pingajo *m*, *inf* tatter, rag

pingajoso *a inf* tattered, ragged

pingo *m*, *inf* tatter, rag; *pl inf* cheap clothes

pingüe *a* fat, greasy; fertile, rich

pingüino *m*, penguin

pino *a* steep. *m*, *bot* pine, deal; *poet* ship. **p. de tea,** pitch pine. **p. silvestre,** red fir

pinocha *f*, pine needle

pinta *f*, spot; marking; mark; fleck; look, appearance; pint (measure); drop, drip; spot ball (in billiards)

pintamonas *mf inf* dauber

pintar *vt* to paint; describe, picture; exaggerate; *vi* show, manifest itself; *vr* make up (one's face). *inf* **pintarse solo para,** to be very good at, excel at

pintiparado *a* most similar, very alike; fitting, apposite

pintiparar *vt inf* to compare

pintor (-ra) *n* painter, artist. **p. callejero,** sidewalk artist, pavement artist. **p. de brocha gorda,** house painter

pintoresco *a* picturesque, quaint, pretty

pintoresquismo *m*, picturesqueness

pintorrear *vt inf* to daub, paint badly

pintura *f*, painting; paint, pigment; picture, painting; description. **p. a la aguada,** watercolor painting. **p. al fresco,** fresco. **p. al látex,** latex paint. **p. al óleo,** oil painting. **p. al pastel,** pastel drawing

pinturería *f*, paint store

pinturero *a inf* affected, conceited; dandified, overdressed

pinza *f*, clamp. **p. de la ropa,** clothes peg

pinzas *f pl*, pincers; pliers; tweezers; forceps. **p. hemostáticas,** arterial forceps

pinzón *m*, chaffinch

piña *f*, pineapple; cluster, knot (of people, etc.); pinecone

piñón *m*, pine nut; *mech* pinion, chain wheel

pío *a* pious; compassionate; good; piebald. *m*, chirping, cheep; *inf* longing

piojo *m*, louse

piojoso *a* lousy; avaricious, stingy

pionero *m*, pioneer

piorrea *f*, pyorrhea

pipa *f*, barrel, cask; tobacco pipe; pip (of fruits)

pipar *vi* to smoke a pipe

pipeta *f*, pipette

pipiar *vi* to chirp, twitter

pique *m*, pique, resentment. **a p. de,** on the verge of, about to. **echar a p.,** *naut* to sink; destroy. **irse a p.,** to sink, founder

piquero *m*, pike soldier

piqueta *f*, pick, mattock; mason's hammer

piquete *m*, puncture, small wound; *mil* picket; pole, stake; small hole (in garments); picket (in strikes)

pira *f*, funeral pyre; bonfire

piragua *f*, piragua, canoe

pirámide *f*, pyramid

pirarse *vr inf* to slip away

pirata *a* piratical *mf* pirate; savage, cruel person

piratear *vi* to play the pirate

piratería *f*, piracy; plunder, robbery

pirático *a* piratical

pirenaico, pirineo *a* Pyrenean

pirético *a* pyretic

piriforme *a* pear-shaped

Pirineos, los the Pyrenees

piromancia *f*, pyromancy

piropear *vt inf* to pay compliments to

piropo *m*, carbuncle; *inf* compliment. **echar piropos,** to pay compliments

pirotecnia *f*, pyrotechnics

pirotécnico *a* pyrotechnical. *m*, pyrotechnist

pirrarse *vr inf* to desire ardently

pírrico *a* Pyrrhic

pirueta *f*, pirouette, twirl

pisada *f*, treading, stepping; footprint, footstep; stepping on a person's foot. **seguir las pisadas de alguien,** *fig* to follow in someone's footsteps, imitate someone

pisano (-na) *a* and *n* Pisan

pisapapeles *m*, paperweight

pisar *vt* to tread upon; trample upon; crush; *mus* press (strings); trespass upon

pisaverde *m*, *inf* fop, dandy

piscicultura *f*, pisciculture, fish farming

piscina *f*, fishpond; swimming pool; *ecc* piscina

piscolabis *m*, *inf* snack, light meal

piso *m*, treading, trampling; story, floor; flooring; apartment. **p. bajo,** ground floor

pisón *m*, rammer, ram

pisotear *vt* to trample; crush under foot; tread on; step on; humiliate, treat inconsiderately

pisoteo *m*, trampling under foot; treading

pista *f*, track, trail (of animals); circus ring; racetrack, racecourse. **p. de patinar,** skating rink. **p. de vuelo,** *aer* landing field. *inf* **seguir la p. a,** to spy upon

pistacho *m*, pistachio

pistar *va* to pestle, pound

pistero *m*, feeding cup

pistilo *m*, pistil

pistola *f*, pistol. **p. ametralladora,** machine gun.

pistolera *f*, holster; pistol case

pistolero *m*, gangster

pistoletazo *m*, pistol shot; pistol wound

pistón *m*, *mus* piston; *mil* percussion cap; *mech* piston

pitada *f*, blast on a whistle; whistling; impertinence

pitagórico (-ca) *a* and *n* Pythagorean

pitanza *f*, alms, charity; *inf* daily food; pittance, scanty remuneration

pitar *vi* to play the whistle; *vt* pay (debts); smoke; give alms to

pitido *m*, blast on a whistle; whistling (of birds)

pitillera *f*, cigarette case; female cigarette maker

pito *m*, whistle; *mus* fife. *inf* **Cuando pitos flautas, cuando flautas pitos,** It's always the unexpected that happens. *inf* **no valer un p.,** to be not worth a straw

pitoflero (-ra) *n* mediocre performer (gen. on a wind instrument); *inf* talebearer, gossip

pitón *m*, *zool* python; nascent horn (of goats, etc.); spout; protuberance; *bot* sprout

pitonisa *f*, *myth* pythoness; witch, enchantress

pitorrearse *vr* to ridicule, mock

pituitario *a* pituitary

pituso *a* small and amusing (of children)

pivote *m*, pivot, swivel, gudgeon

piyama *m*, pajamas

pizarra *f*, slate; blackboard

pizarral *m*. **pizarrería** *f*, slate quarry

pizarrero *m*, slater

pizarrín *m*, slate pencil

pizca *f*, *inf* atom, speck, crumb; jot, whit. **¡Ni p.!** Not a scrap!

pizpireta *a f, inf* coquettish; smart; dressed up

placa *f,* plate, disk; *art* plaque; *phot* plate; star (insignia). **p. recordatorio,** commemorative plaque

placabilidad *f,* placability, appeasability

pláceme *m,* congratulation

placentero *a* agreeable, pleasant

placer *vt irr* to please, give pleasure to, gratify. *m, naut* reef, sandbank; pleasure; wish, desire; permission, consent; entertainment, diversion. **a p.,** at one's convenience; at leisure. *Pres. Ind.* **plazco, places,** etc. *Preterite* **plugo, pluguieron.** *Pres. Subjunc.* **plazca,** etc. *Imperf. Subjunc.* **pluguiese,** etc.

placibilidad *f,* agreeableness, pleasantness

placible *a* agreeable, pleasant

placidez *f,* placidity, calmness, serenity

plácido *a* placid, calm, serene

placiente *a* pleasing, attractive

plácito *m,* decision, judgment, opinion

plafón *m,* ceiling light; *arch* panel

plaga *f,* plague; disaster, calamity; epidemic; glut; pest; grief

plagar *vt (with de)* to infect with; *vr (with de)* be covered with; be overrun by; be infested with

plagiar *vt* to plagiarize, copy; kidnap, hold for ransom

plagiario (-ia) *n* plagiarist

plagio *m,* plagiary; kidnapping

plan *m,* plan; scheme; plane. **p. quinquenal,** five-year plan

plana *f,* sheet, page; mason's trowel; plain. **p. mayor,** *(mil nav)* staff

planadora *f,* steamroller

plancha *f,* sheet, slab, plate; flatiron; horizontal suspension (in gymnastics); *naut* gangway, gangplank; *inf* howler

planchado *m,* ironing; ironing to be done or already finished

planchador (-ra) *n* ironer

planchar *vt* to iron, press with an iron

planchear *vt* to plate (with metal)

planeador *m, aer* glider

planear *vt* to plan out; make plans for; *vi aer* glide

planeo *m, aer* glide

planeta *m,* planet

planetario *a* planetary. *m,* planetarium

planicie *f,* levelness, evenness; plain

plano *a* flat, level; plane. *m, geom* plane; plan, map; *aer* aileron, wing

planta *f, bot* plant; sole (of the foot); plantation; layout, plan; position of the feet (in dancing, fencing); scheme, project. **p. baja,** ground floor. **p. vivaz,** perennial plant. *inf* **buena p.,** good appearance

plantación *f,* planting; plantation, nursery

plantador (-ra) *n* planter. *m, agr* dibble. *f.* **plantadora,** mechanical planter

plantar *vt* to plant; erect; place; found, set up; pose (a problem); raise (a question, etc.); *inf* leave in the lurch; *vr* take up one's position; jib (of horses); oppose

planteamiento *m,* execution; putting into practice; planning; statement (of problems)

plantel *m,* nursery garden; training school, nursery

plantilla *f,* young plant; insole (of shoes); *mech* template, jig

plantío *m,* plantation, afforestation; planting. *a* planted or ready for planting (ground)

plantón *m,* plant or sapling ready for transplanting; *bot* cutting; doorkeeper, porter. **dar un p. (a),** to keep (a person) waiting a long time

plañidera *f,* paid mourner

plañidero *a* mournful, piteous, anguished

plañido *m,* lament, weeping, wailing

plañir *vi and vt irr* to lament, wail, weep. See **tañer**

plasma *m,* plasma

plasmar *vt* to mold, throw (pottery)

plástica *f,* art of clay modeling; plastic

plasticidad *f,* plasticity

plástico *a* plastic; flexible, malleable, soft

plata *f,* silver; silver (coins); money; white. **p. labrada,** silverware

plataforma *f,* platform; running board (of a train); *rw* turntable

plátano *m,* banana tree, banana; plantain; plane tree

platea *f, theat* pit. **butaca de p.,** pit stall

plateado *a* silvered; silver-plated; silvery

plateador *m,* plater

platear *vt* to electroplate, silver

platería *f,* silversmith's art or trade; silversmith's shop or workshop

platero *m,* silversmith; jeweler

plática *f,* conversation; exhortation, sermon; address, discourse

platicar *vt* and *vi* to converse (about)

platija *f,* plaice

platillo *m,* saucer; kitty (in card games); pan (of a scale); *pl* cymbals

platinado *m,* plating

platino *m,* platinum

platívolo *m,* flying saucer

plato *m,* plate; dish; *cul* course, dish; pan (of a scale). **p. sopero,** soup plate. **p. trinchero,** meat dish. *inf* **comer en un mismo p.,** to be on intimate terms. **nada entre dos platos,** much ado about nothing

platónico *a* Platonic

platonismo *m,* Platonism

plausibilidad *f,* plausibility

plausible *a* plausible, reasonable

playa *f,* beach, seashore, strand

plaza *f,* square (in a town, etc.); marketplace; fortified town; space; duration; employment, post.; *com* market. **p. de armas,** garrison town; military camp. **p. de toros,** bullring. **p. fuerte,** strong place, fortress. **sentar p.,** to enlist in the army

plazo *m,* term, duration; expiration of term, date of payment; installment. **a plazos,** *com* by installments, on the installment system

plazoleta *f,* small square (in gardens, etc.)

pleamar *f, naut* high water

plebe *f,* common people; rabble, mob

plebeyo (-ya) *a* plebeian. *n* commoner, plebeian

plebiscito *m,* plebiscite

plectro *m,* plectrum

plegable *a* foldable

plegadera *f,* folder; folding knife; paper folder

plegadizo *a* folding; collapsible; jointed

plegado *m,* pleating; folding

plegador *a* folding. *m,* folding machine

plegadura *f,* folding, doubling; fold, pleat

plegar *vt irr* to fold; pleat; *sew* gather; *vr* submit, give in. See **acertar**

plegaria *f,* fervent prayer

pleitear *vt* to go to court about; indulge in litigation

pleitista *a* quarrelsome, litigious

pleito *m,* action, lawsuit; dispute, quarrel; litigation. **p. de familia,** family squabble. **ver el p.,** *law* to try a case

plenamente *adv* fully, entirely

plenario *a* full, complete; *law* plenary

plenilunio *m,* full moon

plenipotencia *f,* full powers (diplomatic, etc.)

plenipotenciario *a and m,* plenipotentiary

plenitud *f,* fullness, completeness; plenitude, abundance

pleno *a* full. *m,* general meeting

pleonasmo *m, gram* pleonasm

pleonástico *a* pleonastic

pleuresía *f,* pleurisy

plexo *m,* plexus

pléyades *f pl,* Pleiades

pliego *m,* sheet (of paper); letter, packet of papers

pliegue *m,* fold, pleat; *sew* gather

plinto *m, arch* plinth (of a column); baseboard

plisar *vt* to pleat; fold

plomada *f,* plummet; sounding lead; plumb, lead

plomería *f,* plumbing; plumbing business; lead roofing

plomero *m*, plumber

plomizo *a* lead-like; lead-colored, gray

plomo *m*, lead (metal); plummet; bullet; *inf* bore, tedious person

pluma *f*, feather; pen; plumage; quill; penmanship; writer; writing profession. **p. estilográfica**, fountain pen. **a vuela p.**, as the pen writes, written in a hurry

plumado *a* feathered

plumaje *m*, plumage, feathers; plume

plúmbeo *a* plumbeous, leaden

plúmeo *a* feathered, plumed

plumero *m*, feather duster; plume, feather; plumage

plumón *m*, down; feather bed

plumoso *a* feathered

plural *a* and *m*, plural

pluralidad *f*, plurality; multitude, number

pluralizar *vt* to pluralize

plurilingüe *a* multilingual

pluscuamperfecto *m*, pluperfect

plusmarquista *mf sport* recordholder

plutocracia *f*, plutocracy

plutócrata *mf* plutocrat

plutocrático *a* plutocratic

plutónico *a geol* Plutonic

pluviómetro *m*, rain gauge

poblacho *m*, miserable town or village

población *f*, peopling; population; town

poblado *m*, inhabited place; town; village

poblador (-ra) *a* populating. *n* colonist, settler

poblar *vt irr* to colonize; people, populate; breed fast; stock, supply; *vr* put forth leaves (of trees). See **contar**

pobre *a* poor; indigent, needy; mediocre; unfortunate; humble, meek. *mf* beggar, pauper, needy person. *inf* **ser p. de solemnidad**, to be down and out

pobrero *m*, *ecc* distributor of alms

pobretería *f*, poverty; needy people

pobretón *a* extremely needy

pobreza *f*, poverty, need; shortage; timidity; *min* baseness; poorness (of soil, etc.)

pocero *m*, well digger

pocilga *f*, pigsty; *inf* filthy place

poción *f*, potion, drink; mixture, dose

poco *a* little, scanty; *pl* few. *m*, small amount, a little. *adv* little; shortly, in a little while. **p. a p.**, by degrees, little by little; slowly. **p. más o menos**, more or less, approximately. **por p.**, almost, nearly (always used with the present tense, e.g. **Por p. me caigo**, I almost fell). **tener en p. (a)**, to have a poor opinion of; undervalue

poda *f*, *agr* pruning; pruning season

podadera *f*, pruning knife

podar *vt agr* to prune, trim

poder *m*, power; authority; jurisdiction; *law* power of attorney; strength; ability; proxy; efficacy; possession; *pl* authority; power of attorney. **los poderes constituidos**, the established authorities; the powers that be. **p. de adquisición**, purchasing power. **casarse por poderes**, to be married by proxy

poder *vt irr* to be able to (e.g. **Podemos comprar estas naranjas**, We can (are able to) buy these oranges). **Dice que la calamidad podía haberse evitado**, He says that the disaster could have been averted). *inf* also expresses possibility (e.g. **Pueden haber ido a la ciudad**, They may have gone to the city. **¡Qué distinta pudo haber sido su vida!** How different his life might have been!). *impers* be possible. **a más no p.**, of necessity, without being able to help it; to the utmost. **no p. con**, to be unable to control or manage. **no p. hacer más**, to have no alternative, have to; be unable to do more. **no p. menos de**, to be obliged to, have no alternative but. **no p. contener su emoción**, to be overcome with emotion. **no p. ver a**, to hate (persons). *impers* **Puede que venga esta tarde**, He may come (perhaps he will come) this afternoon. *Pres. Part.* **pudiendo**. *Pres. Ind.* **puedo, puedes, puede, pueden**. *Fut.* **podré**, etc. *Condit.* **podría**, etc. *Preterite*

pude, pudiste, etc. *Pres. Subjunc.* **pueda, puedas, pueda, puedan**. *Imperf. Subjunc.* **pudiese**, etc.

poderío *m*, power, authority; sway, rule; dominion; wealth

poderoso *a* powerful; opulent; effective, efficacious; mighty, magnificent

podredumbre *f*, decay; pus; *fig* canker, anguish

podredura, podrición *f*, putrefaction; decay

podrido *a* rotten; putrid; corrupt; decayed

podrir *vt* See **pudrir**

poema *m*, poem. **p. sinfónico**, tone poem

poesía *f*, poetry, verse; lyric, poem

poeta *m*, poet

poetastro *m*, poetaster

poética *f*, poetics

poético *a* poetical

poetisa *f*, poetess

poetizar *vi* to write verses; *vt* poeticize

polaco (-ca) *a* Polish. *n* Pole. *m*, Polish (language)

polainas *f pl*, leggings, puttees, gaiters

polar *a* polar

polaridad *f*, polarity; polarization

polarización *f*, polarization

polarizar *vt* to polarize

polca *f*, polka

polea *f*, pulley; *naut* block

polémica *f*, polemic, controversy, dispute

polémico *a* polemical

polemista *mf* disputant, controversialist

polen *m*, pollen

poliandria *f*, polyandry

polichinela *m*, Punchinello

policía *f*, police; government, polity, administration; civility, courtesy; cleanliness, tidiness. *m*, policeman. **p. urbana**, city police

policíaco *a* police; detective

policromo *a* polychrome

poliedro *m*, polyhedron

polifacético *a* many-sided

polifonía *f*, polyphony

polifónico *a* polyphonic

poligamia *f*, polygamy

polígamo (-ma) *a* polygamous. *n* polygamist

poligloto (-ta) *n* polyglot. *f*, polyglot Bible

polígono *a* polygonal. *m*, polygon

polilla *f*, moth; moth grub; destroyer, ravager

polimorfismo *m*, *chem* polymorphism

polimorfo *a* polymorphous

Polinesia Polynesia

polinesio (-ia) *a* and *n* Polynesian

polinización *f*, pollination

poliomielitis *f*, poliomyelitis, polio

pólipo *m*, *zool* polyp; octopus; *med* polyp

polisílabo *a* polysyllabic. *m*, polysyllable

polista *mf* polo player

politécnico *a* polytechnic

politeísmo *m*, polytheism

politeísta *a* polytheistic. *mf* polytheist

política *f*, politics; civility, courtesy; diplomacy; tact; policy

politicastro *m*, corrupt politician

político *a* political; civil, courteous; in-law, by marriage (relationships). *m*, politician

politiquear *vi inf* to dabble in politics, talk politics

politizarse *vr* to enter the political arena

póliza *f*, com policy; com draft; share certificate; revenue stamp; admission ticket; lampoon. **p. a prima fija**, fixed-premium policy. **p. de seguros**, insurance policy. **p. dotal**, endowment policy

polizón *m*, loafer, tramp; stowaway; bustle (of a dress)

polla *f*, pullet; *inf* flapper, young woman

pollada *f*, brood, hatch (especially of chickens)

pollastro (-ra) *n* pullet.

pollera *f*, female poultry breeder or seller; chicken coop; go-cart

pollería *f*, poultry market or shop

pollero *n* poultry breeder; poulterer. *m*, hen coop
pollino (-na) *n* young ass; donkey
pollo *m*, chicken; *inf* youth, stripling; *fig inf* downy bird. *inf* **p. pera,** young blood, lad. **sacar pollos,** to hatch chickens
polo *m*, pole (all meanings); *fig* support; popular Andalusian song; *sport* polo. **de p. a p.,** from pole to pole
polonés (-esa) *a* Polish. *n* Pole
polonesa *f*, polonaise; short coat
Polonia Poland
poltrón *a* lazy, idle
poltronería *f*, idleness, laziness
polución *f*, *med* ejaculation
poluto *a* filthy, unclean
Pólux *m*, Pollux
polvareda *f*, dust cloud; storm, agitation
polvera *f*, powder bowl; powder puff; powder compact
polvo *m*, dust; powder; pinch (of snuff, etc.); *pl* face or dusting powder. **Se hizo como por polvos de la madre celestina,** It was done as if by magic. *inf* **limpio de p. y paja,** gratis, for nothing; net (of profit)
pólvora *f*, gunpowder; bad temper. **p. de algodón,** guncotton.
polvorear *vt* to powder, dust with powder
polvoriento *a* dusty; powdery, covered with powder
polvorín *m*, very fine powder; powder magazine; powder flask
polvoroso *a* dusty; covered with powder
pomada *f*, pomade; salve, ointment
pomar *m*, orchard (especially an apple orchard)
pómez *f*, pumice stone **(piedra p.)**
pomo *m*, *bot* pome; pomander; nosegay; pommel, hilt (of a sword); handle; rose (of watering can)
pomología *f*, pomology, art of fruit growing
pompa *f*, pomp, splendor; ceremonial procession; air bubble; peacock's outspread tail; *naut* pump; billowing of clothes in the wind
Pompeya Pompeii
pompeyano *a* Pompeian
pomposidad *f*, pomposity
pomposo *a* stately, ostentatious, magnificent; inflated, pompous; florid, bombastic
pómulo *m*, cheekbone
ponche *m*, punch, toddy
ponchera *f*, punch bowl
poncho *a* lazy, negligent. *m*, military cloak; poncho, cape
ponderación *f*, weighing; reflection, consideration; exaggeration
ponderador *a* reflective, deliberate; exaggerated
ponderar *vt* to weigh; consider, ponder; exaggerate; overpraise
ponderosidad *f*, heaviness; ponderousness, dullness
ponderoso *a* heavy; ponderous; circumspect
ponedero *a* egg-laying (of hens). *m*, nest
ponencia *f*, clause, section; office of referee or arbitrator; report, referendum
poner *vt irr* to place, put; arrange; set (the table); bet, stake; appoint (to an office); call, name; lay (eggs); set down (in writing); calculate, count; suppose; leave to a person's judgment; risk; contribute; prepare; need, take; cause, inspire (emotions); make, cause; adapt; add; cause to become (angry, etc.); insult; praise; (*with prep a* + *infin*) begin to. **p. a contribución,** to lay under contribution, turn to account, utilize. **ponerle el cascabel al gato** *or* **el collar al gato,** to bell the cat. **p. los cuernos (a),** to cuckold. **p. al corriente,** to bring up to date, inform. **p. a prueba,** to test. **p. casa,** to set up house. *inf* **p. colorado a,** to make blush. **p. coto a,** to put a stop to, check. **p. en comparación,** to compare. **p. conato en,** to put a great deal of effort into. **p. en cotejo,** to collate. **p. en limpio,** to make a fair copy (of). **p. en marcha,** to start, set in motion. **p. en práctica,** to put into effect. **p. por caso,** to take as an example (e.g. **Pongamos por caso . . .** For example, . . .). **p. por encima (de),** to prefer. *vr* to place

oneself; become; put on (garments, etc.); dirty or stain oneself; set (of the sun, stars); oppose; deck oneself, dress oneself up; arrive; (*with prep a* + *infin*) begin to. **ponerse al corriente,** to bring oneself up to date. **ponerse bien,** to improve; get better (in health). **ponerse colorado,** to blush, flush. **p. una base racional a la fe,** to give faith a rational foundation. **p. los cimientos de,** lay the foundation of, lay the foundations for. **p. una conferencia,** to make a long-distance call. *Pres. Ind.* **pongo, pones,** etc. *Fut.* **pondré,** etc. *Condit.* **pondría,** etc. *Imperat.* **pon.** *Past Part.* **puesto.** *Preterite* **puse, pusiste,** etc. *Pres. Subjunc.* **ponga,** etc. *Imperf. Subjunc.* **pusiese,** etc.
ponientada *f*, steady west wind
poniente *m*, west; west wind
pontazgo *m*, bridge toll
pontear *vt* to bridge; make bridges
pontificado *m*, pontificate, papacy
pontífice *m*, pontifex; pope, pontiff; archbishop; bishop
pontificial *a* and *m*, pontifical
pontificio *a* pontifical
pontón *m*, *mil* pontoon; hulk used as a prison, hospital, store, etc.; wooden bridge
pontonero *m*, pontoneer, military engineer
ponzoña *f*, poison, venom
ponzoñoso *a* poisonous, venomous; noxious; harmful
popa *f*, *naut* stern, poop. **en p.,** abaft, astern, aft
popelina *f*, poplin
populachería *f*, cheap popularity with the rabble
populachero *a* mob, vulgar
populacho *m*, mob, rabble
popular *a* popular
popularidad *f*, popularity
popularizar *vt* to popularize; *vr* grow popular
popularmente *adv* popularly
populoso *a* populous, crowded
popurrí *m*, *cul* stew; potpourri; miscellany
poquedad *f*, paucity, scarcity; timidity, cowardice; trifle, mere nothing
poquísimo *a sup* **poco** very little
poquito *m*, very little
por *prep* for; by; through, along; during; because, as (e.g. **Lo desecharon p. viejo,** They threw it away because it was old); however (e.g. **p. bonito que sea,** however pretty it is); during; in order to (e.g. **Lo hice p. no ofenderla,** I did it in order not to offend her); toward, in favor of, for; for the sake of; on account of, by reason of (e.g. **No pudo venir p. estar enfermo,** He could not come on account of his illness); via, by (e.g. **p. correo aéreo,** by airmail); as for (e.g. **P. mí, lo rechazo,** As for me, I refuse it. **p. mi cuenta,** to my way of thinking; on my own); in exchange for (e.g. **Me vendió dos libros p. seis dólares,** He sold me two books for six dollars); in the name of; as a substitute for, instead of (e.g. **Hace mi trabajo p. mí,** He is doing my work for me); per. **Por** has several uses: 1. Introduces the agent after a passive (e.g. **La novela fue escrita p. él,** The novel was written by him). 2. Expresses movement through, along or about (e.g. **Andaban p. la calle,** They were walking along (or down) the street). 3. Denotes time at or during which an action occurs (e.g. **Ocurrió p. entonces un acontecimiento de importancia,** About that time an important event occurred). 4. Expresses rate or proportion (e.g. **seis por ciento,** six percent). 5. With certain verbs, means 'to be' and expresses vague futurity (e.g. **El libro queda p. escribir,** The book remains to be written). **p. cortesía,** by courtesy, out of politeness. **p. cortesía de,** by courtesy of. **p. escrito,** in writing. **p. fas or p. nefas,** by fair means or foul; at any cost. **p. mucho que,** however great, however much; in spite of, notwithstanding. **¿P. qué?** Why? **p. si acaso,** in case, if by chance. **estar p.,** to be about to; be inclined to. **P. un clavo se pierde la herradura,** For want of a nail, the shoe was lost.
porcelana *f*, porcelain, china; chinaware

porcentaje *m*, percentage
porche *m*, porch, portico
porcino *a* porcine. *m*, young pig; bruise
porción *f*, portion; *com* share; *inf* crowd; allowance, pittance
porcionista *mf* shareholder; sharer; boarding school student
porcuno *a* porcine, hoggish
pordiosear *vi* to ask alms, beg
pordioseo *m*, asking alms, begging
pordiosero (-ra) *a* begging. *n* beggar
porfía *f*, obstinacy; importunity; tenacity. **a p.,** in competition
porfiadamente *adv* obstinately
porfiado *a* obstinate, obdurate, persistent
porfiar *vi* to be obstinate, insist; persist
pórfido *m*, porphyry
pormenor *m*, particular, detail (gen. *pl*); secondary matter
pormenorizar *vt* to describe in detail
pornografía *f*, pornography
pornográfico *a* pornographic, obscene
poro *m*, pore
porosidad *f*, porosity, permeability
poroso *a* porous, leaky
porque *conjunc* because, for; in order that
porqué *m*, reason, wherefore, why; *inf* money. **el cómo y el p.,** the why and the wherefore
porquería *f*, *inf* filth, nastiness; dirty trick; rudeness, gross act; trifle, thing of no account
porquerizo, porquero *m*, swineherd
porra *f*, club, bludgeon; last player (in children's games); *inf* vanity, boastfulness; bore, tedious person
porrada *f*, blow with a club; buffet, knock, fall; *inf* folly; glut, abundance
porrazo *m*, blow with a club; buffet, knock, fall
porrear *vi* *inf* to insist, harp on
porrería *f*, *inf* folly; obduracy, persistence
porreta *f*, green leaves of leeks, onions, and cereals. *inf* **en p.,** stark-naked
porrino *m*, seed of a leek; young leek plant
porrón *m*, winebottle with a spout; earthenware jug
portaaviones *m*, aircraft carrier
portacartas *m*, mailbag
portachuelo *m*, defile, narrow mountain pass
portada *f*, front, facade; frontispiece, title page; portal, doorway
portado (bien *or* **mal)** *a* well- or ill-dressed or behaved
portador (-ra) *n* carrier. *m*, *com* bearer; *mech* carrier
portaestandarte *m*, standard-bearer
portafolio *m*, portfolio
portafusil *m*, rifle sling
portal *m*, entrance, porch; portico; city gate
portalámpara *f*, lamp holder; *elec* socket
portalibros *m*, bookstrap
portalón *m*, gangway
portamanteo *m*, traveling bag
portamonedas *m*, pocketbook; handbag, purse
portanuevas *mf* bringer of news, newsmonger
portaobjetos *m*, stage (of a microscope)
portaplumas *m*, pen holder
portar *vt* to retrieve (of dogs); carry (arms); *vr* behave (well or badly); bear oneself, act; be well, or ill (in health)
portátil *a* portable
portatostadas *m*, toast rack
portavoz *m*, megaphone; spokesman, mouthpiece
portazgo *m*, toll; tollbooth
portazguero *m*, toll collector
portazo *m*, bang of the door; slamming the door in a person's face
porte *m*, transport; *com* carriage; postage; freight, transport cost; porterage; behavior, conduct; bearing, looks; capacity, volume; size, dimension; nobility (of descent); *naut* tonnage. **p. pagado,** charges prepaid
porteador *m*, carrier; porter; carter

portear *vt* to carry, transport; *vr* migrate (of birds)
portento *m*, marvel, prodigy, portent
portentoso *a* marvelous, portentous
porteo *m*, porterage, cartage
portería *f*, porter's lodge; porter's employment; *sport* goal
portero (-ra) *n* doorman, doorkeeper; porter; concierge; janitor; *sport* goalkeeper. **p. eléctrico,** door buzzer
portezuela *f*, *dim* small door; carriage door; pocket flap
pórtico *m*, portico, piazza; porch; vestibule, hall
portillo *m*, breach, opening; defile, narrow pass; *fig* loophole
portón *m*, hall door, inner door
portorriqueño (-ña) *a* and *n* Puerto Rican
portuario *a* dock, port
portugués (-esa) *a* and *n* Portuguese. *m*, Portuguese (language)
portuguesada *f*, exaggeration
porvenir *m*, future time
¡pórvida! *interj* By the saints! By the Almighty!
pos *prefix* after; behind. Also *adv* **en p.,** with the same meanings
posa *f*, tolling bell; *pl* buttocks
posada *f*, dwelling; inn, tavern; lodging; hospitality
posaderas *f pl*, buttocks
posadero (-ra) *n* innkeeper; boardinghouse keeper
posar *vi* to lodge, live; rest; alight, perch; *vt* set down (a burden); *vr* settle (liquids); (*with en or sobre*) perch upon
posdata *f*, P.S., postscript
pose *f*, *phot* time exposure; *inf* pose
poseedor (-ra) *n* possessor, holder
poseer *vt irr* to own, possess; know (a language, etc.); *vr* restrain oneself. **estar poseído por,** to be possessed by (passion, etc.); be thoroughly convinced of. See **creer**
posesión *f*, ownership, occupancy; possession; property, territory (often *pl*)
posesionarse *vr* to take possession; lay hold (of)
posesivo *a* possessive
poseso *a* possessed of an evil spirit
posesor (-ra) *n* owner, possessor
posfecha *f*, postdate
posguerra *f*, postwar period
posibilidad *f*, possibility; probability; opportunity, means, chance; *pl* property, wealth
posibilitar *vt* to make possible, facilitate
posible *a* possible. *m pl*, property, personal wealth. **hacer lo p.** *or* **hacer todo lo p.,** to do everything possible; do one's best
posición *f*, placing; position; situation; status
positivamente *adv* positively, definitely
positivismo *m*, positivism
positivista *a* positivistic. *mf* positivist
positivo *a* positive; certain, definite; (*math elec*) plus; true, real
pósito *m*, public granary; cooperative association
posma *f*, *inf* sluggishness, sloth
posmeridiano *a* and *m*, postmeridian
poso *m*, sediment; lees, dregs; repose, quietness
posponer *vt irr* (*with prep* a) to place after; make subordinate to; value less than. See **poner**
posta *f*, post horse; stage, post; stake (cards)
postal *a* postal. *f*, postcard, postal card
poste *m*, post, stake
postema *f*, tumor, abscess; bore, tedious person
postergación *f*, delay; delaying; relegation; disregard of seniority (in promotion)
postergar *vt* to delay; disregard a senior claim to promotion
posteridad *f*, descendants; posterity
posterior *a* back, rear; hind; subsequent
posterioridad *f*, posteriority
posteriormente *adv* later, subsequently
postigo *m*, secret door; grating, hatch; postern; shutter (of a window)

postillón *m*, postilion

postizo *a* false, artificial, not natural. *m*, switch of false hair

postor *m*, bidder (at an auction)

postración *f*, prostration; exhaustion; depression, distress

postrar *vt* to cast down, demolish; prostrate, exhaust; *vr* kneel down; be prostrated or exhausted

postre *a* last (in order). *m*, *cul* dessert. **a la p.,** at last, finally

postrero *a* last (in order); rearmost, hindmost

postrimeramente *adv* lastly, finally

postrimería *f*, *ecc* last period of life

postulación *f*, entreaty, request

postulado *m*, assumption; supposition; working hypothesis; *geom* postulate

postulante (-ta) *n* *ecc* postulant, applicant, candidate

postular *vt* to postulate

póstumo *a* posthumous

postura *f*, posture, bearing; laying (of an egg); bid (at an auction); position; agreement, pact; bet, stake; planting; transplanted tree. **p. de vida,** way of life

potable *a* drinkable. **agua p.,** drinking water

potación *f*, potation, drink

potaje *m*, stew, potage; dried vegetables; mixed drink; hotchpotch

potasa *f*, potash

potasio *m*, potassium

pote *m*, pot; jar; flowerpot; *cul* cauldron; *cul* stew

potencia *f*, power; potency; *mech* performance, capacity; strength, force; *math* power; rule, dominion

potencial *a* potential

potentado *m*, potentate

potente *a* potent; powerful; *inf* enormous

potestad *f*, authority, power; podesta, Italian magistrate; potentate; *math* power; *pl* angelic powers

potestativo *a* *law* facultative

potingue *m*, *inf* brew; mixture; lotion; medicine; filthy place, pigsty

potra *f*, filly

potrada *f*, herd of colts

potrear *vt* *inf* to tease, annoy

potro *m*, colt, foal; rack (for torture); vaulting horse. **p. mesteño,** mustang

poyo *m*, stone seat

pozal *m*, pail, bucket

pozo *m*, well; shaft (in a mine). *aut* **p. colector,** crankcase

práctica *f*, practice; custom, habit; method; exercise

practicabilidad *f*, feasibility

practicable *a* feasible, practicable

prácticamente *adv* practically, in practice

practicante *m*, medical practitioner; medical student; *med* intern; first-aid practitioner

practicar *vt* to execute, perform; practice; make

práctico *a* practical; experienced, expert; workable. *m*, *naut* pilot

pradeño *a* meadow, prairie

pradera *f*, meadow, field; lawn

pradería *f*, meadowland, prairie

prado *m*, meadow; grassland; field; lawn; walk (in cities)

Praga Prague

pragmatismo *m*, pragmatism

pragmatista *a* pragmatic. *mf* pragmatist

pravedad *f*, wickedness, immorality, depravity

pravo *a* wicked, immoral, depraved

pre *m*, *mil* daily pay. *prep insep* pre-

preámbulo *m*, preamble, preface; importunate digression

prebenda *f*, *ecc* prebend, benefice; *inf* sinecure

preboste *m*, provost

precario *a* precarious, uncertain, insecure

precaución *f*, precaution, safeguard

precaucionarse *vr* to take precautions, safeguard oneself

precautelar *vt* to forewarn; take precautions

precaver *vt* to prevent, avoid; *vr* (*with de or contra*) guard against

precavido *a* cautious, forewarned

precedencia *f*, priority, precedence; superiority; preference, precedence

precedente *a* preceding. *m*, antecedent; precedent

preceder *vt* to precede; have precedence over, be superior to

preceptivo *a* preceptive; didactic

precepto *m*, precept; order, injunction; rule, commandment. **de p.,** obligatory

preceptor (-ra) *n* teacher, instructor, tutor, preceptor

preces *f pl*, *ecc* prayers; entreaties

preciado *a* excellent, esteemed, precious; boastful

preciar *vt* to esteem, value; valuate, price; *vr* boast

precintar *vt* to seal; rope, string, tie up

precinto *m*, sealing; roping, tying up; strap

precio *m*, price, cost; recompense, reward; premium; rate; reputation, importance; esteem. **p. de tasa,** controlled price

preciosidad *f*, preciousness; exquisiteness, fineness; richness; wittiness; *inf* loveliness, beauty; thing of beauty

precioso *a* precious; exquisite, fine, rare; rich; witty; *inf* lovely, delicious, attractive

precipicio *m*, precipice; heavy fall; ruin, disaster

precipitación *f*, precipitancy, haste; rashness; *chem* precipitation

precipitadamente *adv* precipitately, in haste; rashly, foolishly

precipitado *a* precipitate; rash, thoughtless. *m*, *chem* precipitate

precipitar *vt* to precipitate, hurl headlong; hasten; *chem* precipitate; *vr* hurl oneself headlong; hasten, rush

precipitoso *a* precipitous; rash, heedless

precisamente *adv* exactly, precisely, just; necessarily. **Y p. en aquel instante llegó,** And just at that moment he arrived

precisar *vt* to fix, arrange; set forth, draw up; state; compel, force, oblige

precisión *f*, accuracy, precision; necessity, conciseness, clarity; compulsion, obligation

preciso *a* necessary, unavoidable; concise, clear; precise, exact

precitado *a* aforementioned

preclaro *a* illustrious, distinguished, celebrated

precocidad *f*, precocity

precognición *f*, foreknowledge

preconcebido *a* preconceived

preconcepto *m*, preconceived idea, preconceived notion

preconizar *vt* to eulogize, praise publicly

preconocer *vt irr* to know beforehand; foresee. See **conocer**

precoz *a* precocious

precursor (-ra) *a* precursory; preceding, previous. *n* precursor

predecesor (-ra) *n* predecessor

predecir *vt irr* to foretell, prophesy. See **decir**

predestinación *f*, predestination

predestinado (-da) *a* predestined; foreordained. *n* one of the predestined

predestinar *vt* to predestine, foreordain

predeterminación *f*, predetermination

predeterminar *vt* to predetermine

prédica *f*, *inf* (contemptuous) sermon

predicación *f*, preaching; homily, sermon

predicadera *f*, pulpit; *pl inf* talent for preaching

predicado *m*, (*gram phil*) predicate

predicador (-ra) *a* preaching. *n* preacher

predicamento *m*, predicament; reputation

predicar *vt* to publish; manifest; preach; *vi* overpraise; *inf* lecture, scold. **p. en el desierto,** to preach to the wind

predicción *f*, prediction, prophecy

predilección *f*, predilection, preference, partiality
predilecto *a* favorite, preferred
predisponer *vt irr* to predispose. See **poner**
predisposición *f*, predisposition; tendency, prejudice
predominación *f*, predominance
predominante *a* predominant; prevailing
predominar *vi* and *vt* to predominate; prevail; tower above; overlook
predominio *m*, predominance, ascendancy, preponderance
preeminencia *f*, preeminence
preeminente *a* preeminent
preexistencia *f*, preexistence
preexistente *a* preexistent
preexistir *vi* to preexist, exist before
prefacio *m*, introduction, preface, prologue; *ecc* preface
prefecto *m*, prefect
prefectura *f*, prefecture
preferencia *f*, preference; superiority. **de p.,** preferred, favorite; preferably
preferente *a* preferable; preferential; preferred (of stock)
preferible *a* preferable
preferir *vt irr* to prefer; excel, exceed. *Pres. Part.* **prefiriendo.** *Pres. Ind.* **prefiero, prefieres, prefiere, prefieren.** *Preterite* **prefirió, prefirieron.** *Pres. Subjunc.* **prefiera, prefieras, prefiera, prefieran.** *Imperf. Subjunc.* **prefiriese,** etc.
prefijar *vt* to prefix
prefijo *m*, prefix
prefinir *vt* to fix a time limit for
prefulgente *a* brilliant, shining, resplendent
pregón *m*, public proclamation; marriage banns
pregonar *vt* to proclaim publicly; cry one's wares; publish abroad; eulogize, praise; proscribe, outlaw. **p. a los cuatro vientos,** *inf* to shout from the rooftops
pregonería *f*, office of the town crier
pregonero *m*, town crier
preguerra *f*, prewar period
pregunta *f*, question; *com* inquiry; questionnaire, interrogation. *inf* **andar** (*or* **estar**) **a la cuarta p.,** to be very hard up, be on the rocks. **hacer una p.,** to ask a question
preguntador (-ra) *a* questioning; inquisitive. *n* questioner; inquisitive person
preguntar *vt* to question, ask; (*with por*) inquire for; *vr* ask oneself, wonder
prehistoria *f*, prehistory
prehistórico *a* prehistoric
prejuicio *m*, prejudice
prejuzgar *vt* to prejudge, judge hastily
prelacía *f*, prelacy
prelación *f*, preference
prelado *m*, prelate
preliminar *a* preliminary, prefatory. *m*, preliminary
preludiar *vi* and *vt mus* to play a prelude (to); *vt* prepare, initiate
preludio *m*, introduction, prologue; *mus* prelude; *mus* overture
prematuro *a* premature, untimely; unseasonable; immature, unripe
premeditación *f*, premeditation
premeditar *vt* to premeditate, plan in advance
premiador (-ra) *a* rewarding. *n* rewarder
premiar *vt* to reward, requite
premio *m*, prize; reward; premium; *com* interest. **p. en metálico,** cash prize. *inf* **p. gordo,** first prize (in a lottery)
premioso *a* tight; troublesome, annoying; stern, strict; slow-moving; burdensome, hard; labored (of speech or style)
premisa *f*, premise; sign, indication
premonitorio *a* premonitory
premura *f*, urgency, haste
prenda *f*, pledge; token, sign; jewel; article of clothing; talent, gift; loved one; *pl* game of forfeits

prendador (-ra) *n* pledger
prendamiento *m*, pawning
prendar *vt* to pawn; charm, delight; *vr* (*with de*) take a liking to
prender *vt* to seize; arrest; capture, catch. *vi* take root (plants); catch fire; be infectious
prendería *f*, second-hand shop
prendero (-ra) *n* second-hand dealer
prendimiento *m*, seizure, capture; arrest
prenombre *m*, given name, praenomen
prensa *f*, press; printing press; newspapers, the press. **dar a la p.,** to publish
prensado *m*, **prensadura** *f*, pressing; flattening; squeezing
prensar *vt* to press; squeeze
prensil *a* prehensile
preñado *a* pregnant; bulging, sagging (walls, etc.); swollen. *m*, pregnancy
preñez *f*, pregnancy; suspense
preocupación *f*, anxiety, preoccupation; prejudice
preocupadamente *adv* preoccupiedly, absentmindedly; with prejudice
preocupar *vt* to preoccupy; make anxious; bias, prejudice; *vr* be anxious; be prejudiced
preordinar *vt ecc* to predestine
preparación *f*, preparation; treatment; compound, specific
preparado *a* ready, prepared. *m*, preparation, patent food, etc.
preparar *vt* to prepare; *vr* prepare oneself; qualify
preparativo *a* preparatory. *m*, preparation
preparatorio *a* preparatory
preponderancia *f*, preponderance
preponderante *a* preponderant; dominant
preponderar *vi* to preponderate; dominate; outweigh
preponer *vt irr* to put before. See **poner**
preposición *f*, preposition
prepósito *m*, chairman, head, president; *ecc* provost
prepucio *m*, prepuce
prerrafaelista *a* and *mf* Pre-Raphaelite
prerrogativa *f*, prerogative
presa *f*, hold, grasp; seizure, capture; booty; dam; lock (on rivers, canals); weir; ditch, trench; embankment; slice, bit. **hacer p.,** to seize; take advantage of (circumstances)
presagiar *vt* to prophesy, presage, bode
presagio *m*, presage, sign; presentiment, foreboding
présbita *a* long-sighted, farsighted
presbiterado *m*, priesthood; holy orders
presbiteriano (-na) *a* and *n* Presbyterian
presbítero *m*, priest
presciencia *f*, prescience, foresight
presciente *a* prescient, farsighted
prescindible *a* nonessential, able to be dispensed with
prescindir *vi* (*with de*) to pass over, omit; do without. **Prescindiendo de esto . . . ,** Leaving this aside. . . .
prescribir *vt* to prescribe, order
prescripción *f*, prescription
presea *f*, jewel, object of value
presencia *f*, presence, attendance; appearance, looks; ostentation. **p. de ánimo,** presence of mind
presenciar *vt* to be present at; witness, behold
presentación *f*, presentation; introduction
presentar *vt* to show; present, make a gift of; introduce (persons); *vr* occur; present oneself; offer one's services
presente *a* present. *m*, gift; present time. *law* **Por estas presentes . . . ,** By these presents . . . . **tener p.,** to remember
presentimiento *m*, presentiment, apprehension
presentir *vt irr* to have a presentiment of. See **sentir**
preservación *f*, preservation, protection, saving
preservar *vt* to preserve, protect, save
preservativo *a* preservative. *m*, preservative, safeguard, protection
presidencia *f*, presidency; chairmanship; presidential seat or residence

presidencial *a* presidential

presidenta *f,* female president; president's wife; chairwoman

presidente *m,* president; chairman; head, director; presiding judge

presidiar *vt* to garrison

presidiario *m,* convict

presidio *m,* garrison; garrison town; fortress; penitentiary; imprisonment; *law* hard labor; assistance, protection

presidir *vt* to preside over; act as chairperson for; influence, determine

presilla *f,* loop, shank, noose; press stud

presión *f,* pressure

preso (-sa) *n* prisoner, captive; convict

prestación *f,* lending, loan. **p. vecinal,** corvée

prestador (-ra) *a* lending, loan. *n* lender

prestamente *adv* expeditiously, promptly

prestamista *mf* moneylender; pawnbroker

préstamo *m,* loan; lending. **casa de préstamos,** pawnshop

prestar *vt* to lend; assist; pay (attention); give; *vi* be useful; give, expand; *vr* be suitable; lend itself; offer oneself. **tomar prestado,** to borrow

prestatario (-ia) *n* money borrower, debtor

preste *m,* celebrant of high mass. **el p. Juan,** title of Prester John

presteza *f,* speed; promptness, dispatch

prestidigitación *f,* prestidigitation

prestidigitador (-ra) *n* juggler, conjurer

prestigio *m,* magic spell, sorcery; trick, illusion (of conjurers, etc.); influence, prestige

prestigioso *a* illusory; influential

presto *a* quick, speedy; prompt, ready. *m,* pressure cooker. *adv* immediately; soon; quickly. **de p.,** speedily

presumido *a* conceited, vain; presumptuous

presumir *vt* to suppose, presume; *vi* be conceited

presunción *f,* supposition, presumption; vanity, presumptuousness

presuntivo *a* presumptive

presuntuosidad *f,* presumptuousness

presuntuoso *a* presumptuous, vain

presuponer *vt irr* to presuppose, assume; budget, estimate. See **poner**

presuposición *f,* presupposition

presupuesto *m,* motive, reason; supposition, assumption; estimate; *com* tender; national budget

presuroso *a* swift, speedy

pretencioso *a* pretentious, vain

pretender *vt* to seek, solicit; claim; apply for; attempt, try; woo, court

pretendiente (-ta) *n* pretender; candidate; petitioner; suitor

pretensión *f,* pretension; claim; *pl* ambitions

pretérito *a* past. *m,* preterite

pretextar *vt* to allege as a pretext or excuse

pretexto *m,* pretext, excuse

prevalecer *vi irr* to prevail; be dominant; take root (plants). See **conocer**

prevaleciente *a* prevailing; prevalent

prevaricación *f,* prevarication

prevaricador (-ra) *n* prevaricator

prevaricar *vi* to prevaricate

prevención *f,* prevention; precaution; prejudice; police station; *mil* guard room; foresight, prevision; preparation. **de p.,** as a precaution

prevenido *a* prepared; cautious, forewarned

prevenir *vt irr* to prepare; prevent, avoid; warn; prejudice; occur, happen; *fig* overcome (obstacles); *vr* be ready; be forewarned. See **venir**

preventivo *a* preventive

prever *vt irr* to foresee, forecast, anticipate. See **ver**

previamente *adv* previously, in advance

previo *a* previous, advance

previsión *f,* forecast; foresight, prevision, prescience. **p. social,** social insurance

previsor *a* farsighted, provident

prieto *a* almost black, blackish; tight; mean, avaricious

prima *f, ecc* prime; *com* premium; female cousin

primacía *f,* supremacy, preeminence; primacy; primateship

primada *f, inf* act of sponging on, taking advantage of

primado *m,* primate; primateship

primario *a* primary. *m,* professor who gives the first lecture of the day

primavera *f,* springtime; primrose; figured silk material; beautifully colored thing; youth; prime

primaveral *a* spring, spring-like

primeramente *adv* first; in the first place

primerizo (-za) *n* novice; beginner; apprentice; firstborn

primero *a* first; former; excellent, first-rate. *adv* first; in the first place. **primera enseñanza,** primary education. **primera materia,** raw material. **primer plano,** *art* foreground. **primera cura,** first aid. **de buenas a primeras,** all at once, suddenly

primicia *f,* first fruits; offering of first fruits; *pl* first effects

primitivo *a* original, early; primitive

primo (-ma) *a* first; excellent, fine. *n* cousin; *inf* simpleton; *inf* pigeon, dupe. **p. carnal,** first cousin. *inf* **hacer el p.,** to be a dupe. *inf* **ser prima hermana de,** to be the twin of (of things)

primogénito (-ta) *a* and *n* firstborn

primogenitura *f,* primogeniture

primor *m,* exquisite care; beauty, loveliness; thing of beauty

primoroso *a* beautiful; exquisitely done; dexterous, skillful

princesa *f,* princess

principado *m,* principality; princedom; superiority, preeminence

principal *a* chief, principal; illustrious; fundamental, first. *m,* head, principal (of a firm); *com* capital, principal; first floor

principalmente *adv* principally, chiefly

príncipe *m,* leader; prince. **p. de Asturias,** prince of Asturias. **p. de la sangre,** prince of the blood royal

principesco *a* princely

principiante (-ta) *n* beginner, novice; apprentice

principiar *vt* to begin, commence

principio *m,* beginning; principle; genesis, origin; rudiment; axiom; constituent. **al p.,** at first. **a principios,** at the beginning (of the month, year, etc.). **en p.,** in principle

pringar *vt cul* to soak in fat; stain with grease; *inf* wound; take part in a business deal; slander; *vr inf* appropriate, misuse (funds, etc.)

pringoso *a* greasy

pringue *mf,* animal fat, lard; grease spot

prior *m,* prior; parish priest

priora *f,* prioress

prioridad *f,* priority

prisa *f,* haste, speed; skirmish, foray. **a toda p.,** with all speed. **correr p.,** to be urgent. **dar p.,** to hasten, speed up. **darse (or estar de) p.,** to hurry

prisión *f,* prison, jail; seizure; captivity, imprisonment; *fig* bond; obstacle, shackle; *pl* fetters

prisionero (-ra) *n* prisoner; *fig* victim (of passion, etc.)

prisma *m,* prism

prismáticos *m pl,* field glasses

pristino *a* pristine

privación *f,* privation; lack, shortage; deprivation; degradation

privada *f,* toilet, privy, water closet

privadamente *adv* privately; individually, separately

privado *a* private; individual, personal. *m,* favorite; confidant

privanza *f,* court favor, intimacy of princes

privar *vt* to deprive; dismiss (from office); interdict, forbid; *vi* prevail, be in favor; *vr* swoon; deprive oneself

privilegiar *vt* to privilege; bestow a favor on

privilegio *m*, privilege; prerogative; concession; copyright; patent

pro *mf* advantage, benefit. **el p. y el contra,** the pros and cons. **en p.,** in favor

proa *f*, prow, bow

probabilidad *f*, probability

probable *a* probable; likely; provable

probación *f*, proof, test; novitiate, probation

probado *a* tried, tested, proved

probar *vt irr* to prove; test; taste; try on (clothes); *vi* suit; (*with prep a + infin*) try to. **p. fortuna,** to try one's luck. *Pres. Ind.* **pruebo, pruebas, prueba, prueban.** *Pres. Subjunc.* **pruebe, pruebes, prueben**

probatorio *a* probationary

probidad *f*, probity, trustworthiness, honesty

problema *m*, problem

problemático *a* problematical, uncertain

probo *a* honest, trustworthy

procacidad *f*, insolence, pertness

procaz *a* insolent, pert, brazen

procedencia *f*, origin, source; parentage, descent; port of sailing or call

procedente *a* arriving or coming from

proceder *vi* to proceed; behave; originate, arise; continue, go on; act. *law* **p. contra,** to proceed against (a person)

procedimiento *m*, proceeding, advancement; procedure; legal practice; process

proceloso *a* tempestuous

prócer *a* exalted, eminent; lofty. *m*, exalted personage

procesado (-da) *n* defendant

procesamiento *m*, suing, suit; indictment

procesar *vt law* to proceed against, sue

procesión *f*, proceeding, emanating; procession; *inf* train, string. **andar** (*or* **ir**) **por dentro la p.,** to feel keenly without betraying one's emotion

proceso *m*, process; progress, advancement; lapse of time; lawsuit

proclama *f*, proclamation; announcement; publication of marriage banns

proclamación *f*, proclamation; acclaim, applause

proclamar *vt* to proclaim; acclaim; publish abroad; reveal, show

proclividad *f*, proclivity, tendency

procomún *m*, social or public welfare

procreación *f*, procreation

procreador (-ra) *a* procreative. *n* procreator

procrear *vt* to procreate, beget, engender

procuración *f*, procurement; assiduity, care; *law* power of attorney; *law* attorneyship

procurador (-ra) *m*, proxy; *law* attorney; proctor. *n* procurer

procurar *vt* to try, attempt; procure, get; exercise the profession of a lawyer

prodigalidad *f*, prodigality, lavishness; waste, extravagance

prodigar *vt* to waste, squander; lavish, bestow freely; *vr* make oneself cheap

prodigio *m*, marvel, wonder; prodigy; monster; miracle

prodigiosidad *f*, prodigiousness

prodigioso *a* wonderful; prodigious; monstrous; miraculous

pródigo (-ga) *a* wasteful, extravagant; lavish, generous. *n* spendthrift, wastrel, prodigal

producción *f*, production; output, yield; generation (of heat, etc.); crop

producir *vt irr* to produce; generate; yield, give; cause, occasion; publish; *vr* explain oneself; arise, appear, be produced. **p. efecto,** to have effect; take effect. See **conducir**

productividad *f*, productivity

productivo *a* productive; fertile; profitable

producto *m*, produce; product; profit; yield, gain; *math* product. *chem* **p. derivado,** by-product

productor (-ra) *a* productive. *n* producer

proemio *m*, prologue, preface, introduction

proeza *f*, prowess, gallantry; skill

profanación *f*, profanation

profanador (-ra) *n* profaner, transgressor

profanar *vt* to profane

profanidad *f*, profanity

profano *a* profane; dissolute; pleasure-loving, worldly; immodest; lay, ignorant

profecía *f*, prophecy; *ecc* Book of the Prophets; opinion, view

proferir *vt irr* to utter, pronounce. See **herir**

profesar *vt* to exercise, practice (professions); *ecc* profess; believe in; teach

profesión *f*, profession; trade, occupation; avowal, admission

profesional *a* professional

profesionalismo *m*, professionalism

profeso (-sa) *a ecc* professed. *n* professed monk

profesor (-ra) *n* teacher; professor

profesorado *m*, teaching staff; teaching profession; professorship; professorate

profeta *m*, prophet; seer

profético *a* prophetic

profetisa *f*, prophetess

profetizar *vt* to prophesy; imagine, suppose

proficiente *a* proficient

profiláctico *a and m*, prophylactic

prófugo (-ga) *a and n* fugitive from justice. *m, mil* one who evades military service

profundamente *adv* profoundly; acutely, deeply

profundidad *f*, depth; profundity, obscurity; *geom* depth; concavity; intensity (of feeling); vastness (of knowledge, etc.)

profundizar *vt* to deepen; hollow out; *fig* go into deeply, fathom

profundo *a* deep; low; *fig* intense, acute; abstruse, profound; *fig* vast, extensive; high. *m*, depth, profundity; *poet* ocean, the deep; *poet* hell

profuso *a* profuse, abundant; extravagant, wasteful

progenie *f*, descendants

prognosis *f*, prognosis; forecast

programa *m*, program; edict, public notice; plan, scheme; *univ* calendar; syllabus; timetable

progresar *vt and vi* to make progress; progress, advance

progresión *f*, progression; advancement, progress

progresista *a pol* progressive. *mf* progressive

progresivo *a* progressive; advancing

progreso *m*, progress, advancement; growth; improvement, development

prohibente *a* prohibitory, prohibitive

prohibición *f*, forbidding, prohibition

prohibicionista *mf* prohibitionist. *a* prohibitionist

prohibir *vt* to forbid, prohibit. «**Prohibido el paso,**» "No thoroughfare"

prohibitivo, prohibitorio *a* prohibitive

prohijador (-ra) *n* adopter (of a child)

prohijamiento *m*, child adoption; fathering (of a bill, etc.)

prohijar *vt* to adopt (children, ideas); *fig* father

prohombre *m*, master of a guild; respected, well-liked man

prójimo *m*, fellow man, brother, neighbor.

prole *f*, progeny, young offspring

proletariado *m*, proletariat

proletario *a* poor; common, vulgar. *m*, plebeian; pauper; proletarian

prolífico *a* prolific; abundant, fertile

prolijidad *f*, verbosity, prolixity; nicety, scruple; importunity, tediousness

prolijo *a* verbose, prolix; fussy, fastidious; tedious, importunate

prologar *vt* to prologue; provide with a preface

prólogo *m*, preface; prologue; introduction

prolongación *f*, lengthening; prolongation, protraction; extension

prolongado *a* prolonged; oblong, long

prolongar *vt* to lengthen; *geom* produce; prolong, spin out

promediar *vt* to distribute or divide into two equal portions; average; *vi* arbitrate; place oneself between two people; reach half-time

promedio *m*, average; middle, center

promesa *f*, promise; augury, favorable sign

prometedor (-ra) *a* promising. *n* promiser

prometer *vt* to promise; attest, certify; *vi* promise well, look hopeful; *vr* devote oneself to service of God; anticipate confidently, expect; become engaged (marriage). *inf* **prometérselas muy felices,** to have high hopes

prometido (-da) *n* betrothed. *m*, promise

prometimiento *m*, promise; promising

prominencia *f*, prominence, protuberance; eminence, hill

prominente *a* prominent, protuberant; eminent, elevated

promiscuar *vi* to eat meat and fish on fast days

promiscuidad *f*, promiscuity; ambiguity

promiscuo *a* indiscriminate, haphazard, promiscuous; ambiguous

promisión *f*, promise

promisorio *a* promissory

promoción *f*, promotion; batch, class, year (of recruits, students, etc.)

promontorio *m*, headland; promontory; cumbersome object

promotor (-ra) *a* promotive. *n* promoter; supporter

promover *vt irr* to promote, further, advance; promote (a person). **p. un proceso (a),** to bring a suit (against). See **mover**

promulgación *f*, promulgation

promulgar *vt* to publish officially, proclaim; promulgate. *law* **p. sentencia,** to pass judgment

pronombre *m*, pronoun

pronosticación *f*, prognostication; presage

pronosticar *vt* to prognosticate, forecast; presage

pronóstico *m*, omen, prediction; almanac; prognosis; sign, indication. **p. del tiempo,** weather forecast

prontitud *f*, quickness, promptness; quick-wittedness; *fig* sharpness, liveliness; celerity, dispatch

pronto *a* quick, speedy; prompt; ready, prepared. *m, inf* sudden decision. *adv* immediately; with all speed; soon. **de p.,** suddenly; without thinking. **por lo p.,** temporarily, provisionally

prontuario *m*, compendium, handbook; summary

pronunciación *f*, pronunciation

pronunciamiento *m*, military uprising; political manifesto; *law* pronouncement of sentence

pronunciar *vt* to pronounce, articulate; decide, determine; *law* pronounce judgment; give or make (a speech)

propagación *f*, propagation; dissemination; transmission

propagador *a* propagative. *m*, propagator

propaganda *f*, propaganda organization; propaganda

propagandista *mf* propagandist

propagar *vt* to reproduce; propagate, disseminate; *vr* reproduce, multiply; propagate, spread

propalar *vt* to disseminate, spread abroad

propasarse *vr* to go too far, forget oneself; overstep one's authority

propender *vi* to be inclined, have a leaning toward

propensión *f*, propensity, inclination; tendency

propenso *a* inclined, disposed; liable

propiamente *adv* properly, suitably

propiciación *f*, propitiation

propiciador (-ra) *a* propitiatory. *n* propitiator

propiciar *vt* to propitiate, appease

propiciatorio *a* propitiatory

propicio *a* propitious, auspicious; kind, favorable

propiedad *f*, estate, property; ownership; landed property; attribute, quality, property; *art* resemblance, naturalness

propietario (-ia) *a* proprietary. *n* proprietor, owner

propina *f*, gratuity, tip. *inf* **de p.,** in addition, extra

propinar *vt* to treat to a drink; administer (medicine); *inf* give (slaps, etc.)

propincuidad *f*, propinquity, proximity

propincuo *a* near, contiguous, adjacent

propio *a* own, one's own; typical, characteristic; individual, peculiar; suitable, apt; natural, real; same. *m*, messenger; *pl* public lands

proponente *a* proposing. *m*, proposer; *com* tenderer

proponer *vt irr* to propose, suggest; make a proposition; propose (for a post, office, etc.); *math* state; *vr* intend, purpose. **proponerse para un empleo,** to apply for a post. See **poner**

proporción *f*, proportion; chance, opportunity; size; *math* proportion

proporcionado *a* fit, suitable; proportionate; symmetrical

proporcional *a* proportional

proporcionar *vt* to allot, proportion; supply, provide, give; adapt

proposición *f*, proposition; motion (in a debate)

propósito *m*, proposal; intention, aim; subject, question, matter. **a p.,** suitable, apropos; by the way, incidentally. **de p.,** with the intention, proposing. **fuera de p.,** irrelevant

propuesta *f*, proposal, tender

propugnar *vt* to defend, protect

propulsar *vt* to repulse, throw back; propel, drive

propulsión *f*, repulse; propulsion

propulsor *a* driving, propelling. *m*, propeller

prorrata *f*, quota, share, apportionment. **a p.,** in proportion

prorratear *vt* to apportion, distribute proportionately, prorate

prorrogación *f*, prorogation, adjournment; extension (of time); renewal (of a lease, etc.)

prorrogar *vt* to extend, prolong; defer, suspend, prorogue; renew (leases, etc.)

prorrumpir *vt* (*with en*) to burst out; utter, give vent to, burst into

prosa *f*, prose; prosaism, prosaic style; *inf* dull verbosity; monotony, tediousness

prosaico *a* prosaic; prosy; monotonous, tedious; matter-of-fact

prosapia *f*, family, lineage, descent

proscenio *m*, proscenium

proscribir *vt* to proscribe, outlaw; forbid, prohibit. *Past Part.* **proscrito**

proscripción *f*, proscription

proscrito (-ta) *n* outlaw, exile

prosecución *f*, prosecution, performance; pursuit

proseguir *vt irr* to continue, proceed with. See **pedir**

proselitismo *m*, proselytism

prosélito *m*, convert, proselyte

prosificar *vt* to turn verse into prose

prosista *mf* prose writer

prosodia *f*, prosody

prospecto *m*, prospectus

prosperar *vt* to prosper; protect; *vi* flourish, prosper

prosperidad *f*, prosperity; wealth; success

próspero *a* favorable, propitious, fortunate; prosperous

próstata *f*, prostate

prostitución *f*, prostitution

prostituir *vt irr* to prostitute; *vr* become a prostitute; sell oneself, debase oneself. See **huir**

prostituta *f*, prostitute

protagonista *mf* hero or heroine, principal character; leading figure, protagonist

protección *f*, protection, defense; favor, aid

proteccionismo *m*, protectionism

proteccionista *mf* protectionist

protector *a* protective. *m*, protector; guard

protectorado *m*, protectorate

protectriz *f*, protectress

proteger *vt* to protect, defend; favor, assist

protegido (-da) *n* protégé

proteico *a* protean

proteína *f*, protein

protervia *f*, depravity, perversity

protervo *a* depraved, perverse

protesta, protestación *f*, protest; protestation, declaration

protestante *a* and *mf* Protestant

protestantismo *m*, Protestantism

protestar *vt* to declare, attest; *(with contra)* protest against; *(with de)* affirm vigorously

protesto *m*, *com* protest; objection

protocolizar *vt* to protocol, draw up

protocolo *m*, protocol

protoplasma *m*, protoplasm

prototipo *m*, model, prototype

protuberancia *f*, protuberance, projection, swelling

provecto *a* ancient, venerable; mature, experienced

provecho *m*, gain, benefit; profit; advantage; progress, proficiency. **¡Buen p.!** Enjoy your food! Enjoy your meal! **ser de p.**, to be advantageous or useful

provechoso *a* beneficial; profitable; advantageous; useful

proveedor (-ra) *n* provider; purveyor, supplier

proveer *vt irr* to provide; furnish; supply; confer (an honor or office); transact, arrange. **p. de,** to furnish or supply with; fit with. See **creer**

provenir *vi irr (with de)* to originate in, proceed from. See **venir**

Provenza Provence

provenzal *a* and *mf* Provençal. *m*, Provençal (language)

proverbio *m*, proverb; omen; *pl* Book of Proverbs

providencia *f*, precaution, foresight; provision, furnishing; measure, preparation. **la Divina P.,** Providence

providencial *a* providential

próvido *a* provident, thrifty, careful; kind, favorable

provincia *f*, province; *fig* sphere

provincial *a* provincial. *m*, *ecc* provincial

provincialismo *m*, provincialism

provinciano (-na) *a* provincial. *n* provincial, rustic, countryman; native of Biscay

provisión *f*, stock, store; provision; supply; food supply (gen. *pl*); catering; means, way

provisional *a* temporary, provisional

provisor *m*, purveyor, supplier; *ecc* vicar general

provocación *f*, provocation

provocador (-ra) *a* provocative. *n* provoker; instigator

provocar *vt* to provoke; incite; irritate; help, assist; *inf* vomit

provocativo *a* provocative

próximamente *adv* proximately; soon; approximately

proximidad *f*, nearness, proximity (in time or space)

próximo *a* near, neighboring; next; not distant (of time)

proyección *f*, projection (all meanings)

proyectante *a* projecting, jutting

proyectar *vt* to throw, cast; plan, contrive; design; project; *vr* jut out; be cast (a shadow, etc.)

proyectil *m*, projectile

proyectista *mf* planner

proyecto *a* placed in perspective. *m*, project, plan, scheme; planning; intention, idea

proyector (-ra) *n* designer, planner. *m*, searchlight; spotlight; projector

prudencia *f*, prudence, sagacity, caution; moderation

prudencial *a* prudent, discreet; safe

prudente *a* prudent, cautious; provident

prueba *f*, proof; test; testing; trial; fitting (of garments); sample; taste; *law* evidence; *(phot print)* proof. *law* **p. de indicios** or **p. indiciaria,** circumstantial evidence. *phot* **p. negativa,** negative. *com* **a p.,** on approval; on trial; up to standard, perfect. **a p. de,** proof against (water, etc.). **poner a p.,** to put to the test, try out

prurito *m*, pruritus; desire, longing

Prusia Prussia

ps- For words so beginning (e.g. *psicología, psiquiatría*), see spellings without **p**

púa *f*, prong; tooth (of a comb); quill (of a porcupine); *agr* graft; plectrum (for playing the mandolin, etc.); anxiety, grief; pine needle; *inf* crafty person

púber *a* pubescent

pubertad *f*, puberty

púbico *a* pubic

publicación *f*, publication; announcement, proclamation; revelation; publishing of marriage banns

publicador (-ra) *a* publishing. *n* publisher; announcer

publicar *vt* to publish; reveal; announce, proclaim; publish (marriage banns)

publicidad *f*, publicity; advertising, propaganda

publicista *mf* publicist; publicity agent

público *a* well-known, universal; common, general; public. *m*, public; audience; gathering, attendance. **dar al p.** or **sacar al p.,** to publish

pucherazo *m*, *inf* electoral fraud, vote-fixing

puchero *m*, *cul* kind of stew; stew pot; *inf* daily food; puckering of the face preceding tears

pudendo *a* shameful, monstrous, obscene

pudicia *f*, modesty; bashfulness; chastity

púdico *a* modest; bashful; chaste

pudiente *a* rich, wealthy; powerful

pudín *m*, pudding

pudor *m*, modesty; bashfulness, shyness

pudoroso *a* modest; shy

pudrición *f*, putrefaction

pudrir *vt* to rot, putrefy; irritate, worry, provoke; *vi* rot in the grave; *vr* rot; be consumed with anxiety

puebla *f*, town; population; gardener's seed setting

pueblo *m*, town; village, hamlet; people, population, inhabitants; common people; working classes; nation

puente *mf* bridge; *mus* bridge (of stringed instruments); *naut* bridge; *carp* crossbeam, transom. **p. colgante,** suspension bridge. **p. levadizo,** drawbridge. **hacer p. de plata (a),** to remove obstacles for, make plain sailing

puerca *f*, sow; *inf* slattern; harridan, termagant

puerco *m*, pig; wild boar. *a* filthy; rough, rude; low, mean. **p. espín** or **p. espino,** porcupine. **p. marino,** dolphin. **p. montés** or **p. salvaje,** wild boar

puericultura *f*, child care

pueril *a* childish, puerile; foolish, silly; trivial

puerilidad *f*, puerility; foolishness; triviality

puerro *m*, leek

puerta *f*, door; gate; goal (football, soccer, hockey); means, way. **p. batiente,** swinging door. **p. caediza,** trapdoor. **p. corrediza,** sliding door. **p. de servicio,** tradesman's entrance. **p. falsa** or **p. secreta,** secret door; side door. **p. trasera,** back door. **a p. cerrada,** in camera; in secret. *inf* **dar con la p. en las narices (de),** to slam the door in a person's face; offend, insult. **llamar a la p.,** to knock at the door; be on the verge of happening. **tomar la p.,** to depart, go away

puerto *m*, harbor; port; defile, narrow pass; refuge, haven. **p. fluvial,** river port. **p. franco,** free port. **tomar p.,** to put into port; take refuge

pues *conjunc* then; since; as; for, because; well. *adv* yes, certainly. *conjunc* **p. que,** since, as

puesta *f*, *ast* setting, sinking; stake (in gambling). **p. al día,** aggiornamento, updating; modernization. **p. de largo,** coming of age; coming-out party. **p. del sol,** sunset

puesto *m*, post, job; booth, stall; beat, pitch; place, position; state, condition; *mil* encampment, barracks; office, position. **p. de los testigos,** witness box. **p. de mando,** command, position of authority.

puesto *a* (with **bien** or **mal**) well- or badly dressed. *conjunc* **p. que,** since, as; although

púgil *mf* pugilist, boxer

pugilato *m*, boxing; boxing match

pugilista *mf* boxer

pugna *f*, fight, struggle; rivalry, conflict

pugnante *a* hostile, conflicting, rival

pugnar *vi* to fight; quarrel; *(with con, contra)* struggle against, oppose; *(with por, para)* strive to

pugnaz *a* pugnacious

puja *f,* outbidding (at an auction); higher bid; push, thrust

pujador (-ra) *n* bidder or outbidder (at an auction)

pujante *a* strong, powerful, vigorous

pujanza *f,* strength, vigor

pujar *vt* to push on; bid or outbid (at an auction); *vi* stutter; hesitate, falter; *inf* show signs of weeping

pujo *m,* irresistible impulse; desire; will; purpose, intention

pulchinela *m,* Punchinello

pulcritud *f,* beauty, loveliness, delicacy; fastidiousness, subtlety

pulcro *a* beautiful, lovely; delicate, fine; fastidious, subtle

pulga *f,* flea; small top (toy). **el juego de la p.,** tiddlywinks. *inf* **tener malas pulgas,** to be irritable

pulgada *f,* inch

pulgar *m,* thumb

pulgón *m,* aphid, greenfly

pulgoso *a* full of fleas

pulidez *f,* elegance, fineness; polish, smoothness; neatness

pulido *a* elegant, fine; polished, smooth; neat

pulidor *m,* polisher (machine)

pulimentar *vt* to polish, burnish

pulir *vt* to polish, burnish; give the finishing touch to; beautify, decorate; *fig* polish up, civilize; *vr* beautify oneself; become polished and polite

pulmón *m,* lung

pulmonar *a* pulmonary

pulmonía *f,* pneumonia

pulpa *f,* fleshy part of fruit; *anat* pulp; wood pulp

pulpejo *m, anat* fleshy part, fat portion (of thumbs, etc.)

pulpería *f, WH* grocery, grocery store, general store

púlpito *m,* pulpit

pulpo *m,* octopus. *inf* **poner como un p.,** to beat to a pulp

pulposo *a* pulpy, pulpous

pulquérrimo *a sup* **pulcro** most lovely, most exquisite

pulsación *f,* pulsation; throb, beat

pulsar *vt* to touch, feel; take the pulse of; *fig* explore (a possibility); *vi* beat (the heart, etc.)

pulsera *f,* bracelet; wrist bandage. **p. de pedida,** betrothal bracelet

pulso *m,* pulse; steadiness of hand; tact, diplomacy, circumspection. **a p.,** freehand (drawing). **tomar a p. (una cosa),** to try a thing's weight. **tomar el p. (a),** to take a person's pulse

pulular *vi* to pullulate, sprout; abound, be plentiful; swarm, teem; multiply (of insects)

pulverización *f,* pulverization; atomization

pulverizador *m,* atomizer, sprayer; scent spray

pulverizar *vt* to pulverize, grind, make into powder; atomize; spray

pulla *f,* lewd remark; strong hint; witty comment

¡pum! *interj* Bang! Thump!

pundonor *m,* (**punto de honor**) point of honor, sense of honor

pundonoroso *a* careful of one's honor; honorable, punctilious

pungir *vt* to prick, pierce; revive an old sorrow; *fig* wound, sting (passions)

punible *a* punishable

púnico *a* Punic

punitivo *a* punitive, punitory

punta *f,* sharp end, point; butt (of a cigarette); end, point, tip; cape, headland; trace, touch, suspicion; nib (of a pen); pointing (pointer dogs); *her* point; *pl* point lace. **p. de París,** wire nail. **p. seca,** drypoint, engraving needle. **sacar p.,** to sharpen; *inf* twist (a remark)

puntación *f,* dotting, placing dots over (letters)

puntada *f, sew* stitch; innuendo, hint

puntal *m, naut* draft, depth; stanchion, prop, brace, pile; *fig* basis, foundation

puntapié *m,* kick

punteado *m,* plucking the strings of a guitar, etc.; sewing

puntear *vt* to make dots; *mus* pluck the strings of; play the guitar; sew; *art* stipple; *vi naut* tack

puntera *f,* mend in the toe of a stocking; toe cap; new piece on the toe of shoe; *inf* kick

puntería *f,* aiming (of a firearm); aim, sight (of a firearm); marksmanship

puntero *a* of a good aim, having a straight eye. *m,* pointer, wand; stonecutter's chisel

puntiagudo *a* pointed, sharp-pointed

puntilla *f,* narrow lace edging; headless nail, wire nail; brad, tack. **de puntillas,** on tiptoe

puntillismo *m,* pointillisme

puntilloso *a* punctilious; overfastidious, fussy

punto *m.;* dot; point; pen nib; gun sight; *sew* stitch; dropped stitch, hole; weaving stitch, mesh; *gram* full stop, period; hole (in belts for adjustment); place, spot; point, mark; subject matter; *mech* cog; degree, extent; taxi stand; instant; infinitesimal amount; opportunity, chance; vacation, recess; aim, goal; point of honor. **p. de congelación,** freezing point. **p. de ebullición,** boiling point. **p. de fuga,** vanishing point. **p. de fusión,** melting point. **p. de partida,** starting point. **p. de vista,** point of view. **p. final,** *gram* period, full stop. **p. interrogante,** question mark. **p. menos,** a little less. **p. y coma,** semicolon. **p. cardinal,** cardinal point. **p. suspensivo,** *gram* ellipsis point, suspension point, leader, dot. **a p.,** in readiness; immediately. **en p.,** sharp, prompt (e.g. **a las seis en p.,** at six o'clock sharp)

puntoso *a* many-pointed

puntuación *f,* punctuation; *sport* score

puntual *a* punctual; punctilious; certain, indubitable; suitable, convenient

puntualidad *f,* punctuality; punctiliousness; certainty; exactitude, accuracy

puntualizar *vt* to describe in detail; give the finishing touch to; perfect; impress on the mind

puntualmente *adv* punctually; carefully, diligently; exactly

puntuar *vt* to punctuate

punzada *f,* prick, sting; puncture, piercing; sudden pain, twinge, stitch; *fig* anguish, pain

punzar *vt* to pierce, puncture; prick; punch, perforate; *vi* revive, make itself felt (pain or sorrow)

punzón *m,* awl; punch; die; engraver's burin

puñado *m,* handful; a few, some, a small quantity. **a puñados,** in handfuls; liberally, lavishly

puñal *m,* dagger

puñalada *f,* dagger thrust; stab, wound; *fig* unexpected blow (of fate). **p. por la espalda,** stab in the back

puñalero *m,* dagger maker or seller

puñetazo *m,* blow with the fist

puño *m,* fist; handful; cuff (of a sleeve); wristband; handle, head, haft; hilt (of a sword); *pl inf* guts, courage. **p. de amura,** *naut* tack. **p. de un manillar,** handlebar grip. *inf* **meter en un p.,** to overawe. *inf* **ser como un p.,** to be tightfisted; be small (in stature)

pupila *f,* female child ward; *anat* pupil; *inf* cleverness, talent

pupilaje *m,* pupilage, minority; boarding house, guesthouse; boarding school; price of board residence; dependence, bondage

pupilo (-la) *n* ward, minor; boarder; boarding school student

pupitre *m,* desk, school desk

puramente *adv* purely; simply, solely; *law* unconditionally, without reservation

puré *m,* purée, thick soup

pureza *f,* purity; perfection, excellence; chastity; disinterestedness, genuineness; clearness

purga *f,* laxative, purge; waste product
purgación *f,* purging; menstruation; gonorrhea
purgante *a* purgative. *m,* purge, cathartic
purgar *vt* to cleanse, purify; expiate, atone for; (*med law*) purge; suffer purgatorial pains; clarify, refine; *vr* rid oneself, purge oneself
purgativo *a* purgative
purgatorio *m,* purgatory. *a* purgatorial
puridad *f,* purity; secrecy, privacy. **en p.,** openly, without dissembling; secretly, in private
purificación *f,* purification; cleansing
purificador (-ra) *a* purifying; cleansing. *n* purifier; cleanser
purificar *vt* to purify; cleanse; *vr* be purified
purificatorio *a* purificatory
Purísima (la) *f,* the Most Blessed Virgin
purista *mf* purist
puritanismo *m,* Puritanism
puritano (-na) *a* puritanical. *n* Puritan
puro *a* pure; undiluted; unalloyed; unmixed; disinter-

ested, honest; virgin; absolute, sheer; mere, simple. *m,* cigar. **de p.,** by sheer . . . , by dint of
púrpura *f,* purple; *poet* blood; purpura; *her* purpure; purple (cloth); dignity of an emperor, cardinal, consul
purpurear *vi* to look like purple; be tinged with purple
purpúreo, purpurino *a* purple
purulencia *f,* purulence
purulento *a* purulent
pus *m,* pus, matter
pusilánime *a* pusillanimous, timid, cowardly
pusilanimidad *f,* pusillanimity, timidity, cowardice
pústula *f,* pustule
puta *f,* whore
putativo *a* putative
puto *m,* male prostitute
putrefacción *f,* putrefaction; rottenness, putrescence
putrefacto *a* rotten, decayed
pútrido *a* putrid, rotten
puya *f,* goad
puyazo *m,* prick with a goad

Q

que *pron. rel* all genders sing. and pl. who; which; that; whom; when (e.g. **Un poema en que habla de su juventud,** A poem in which he speaks of his youth. **El libro que tengo aquí,** The book (that) I have here. **No es oro todo lo que reluce,** All that glitters is not gold. **Un día que nos vimos,** One day when we met. *interr* **¿qué?** what? *interj* what a ———! what! how! (e.g. **¿Qué hay?** What's the matter? **¡Qué día más hermoso!** What a lovely day! **¿qué de . . . ?** how many? **¿qué tal?** how? *inf* **¿Qué tal estás hoy?** How are you today? **¿qué tanto?** how much?) **¿a qué?** why? for what reason? (e.g. **¿A qué negarlo?** Why deny it?). *conjunc* that (e.g. **Me dijo que vendría,** He said (that) he would come). Means 'so that,' 'that,' 'for,' in commands (e.g. **Mandó que le trajesen el libro,** He ordered that they bring him the book (He ordered them to bring him the book)). Note that the translation of **que** is often omitted in English.

In compound tenses where the participle is placed first, **que** means 'when' (e.g. **llegado que hube,** when I had arrived). In comparisons, **que** means 'than' (e.g. **más joven que yo,** younger than I).

With subjunctives and expressing commands or wishes, **que** means 'let' (e.g. **¡Que venga!** Let him come!) Preceding a subjunctive, **que** is generally translated by 'to' (e.g. **Quiero, que venga** *or* **que llueva,** I want him to come *or* I want it to rain). Also means 'may' (e.g. **¡Que lo pase bien!** May you enjoy yourself! (I hope you . . .)). **es (era) que,** the fact is (was) that . . . **que . . . que,** whether . . . or . . .
quebrada *f,* mountain gorge; *com* bankruptcy
quebradizo *a* brittle, fragile; ailing, infirm; delicate, frail
quebrado (-da) *m, math* fraction; *n com* bankrupt. *a* rough, uneven (ground); *med* ruptured; bankrupt; ailing, broken-down
quebradura *f,* snap, breaking; gap, crevice; hernia
quebraja *f,* split, crack; flaw (in wood, metal, etc.)
quebrantahuesos *m,* sea eagle, osprey; *inf* bore, tedious person
quebrantamiento *m,* crushing; splitting, cleaving; fracture, rupture; profanation, desecration; burglary; violation, breaking, infringement; fatigue; *law* annulment; exhaustion
quebrantanueces *m,* nutcrackers
quebrantaolas *m,* breakwater
quebrantar *vt* to break, shatter; crush, pound; transgress, infringe; break out, force; tone down, soften; moderate, lessen; bore, exhaust; move to pity; *inf* break in (horses); profane; overcome (difficulties); as-

suage, placate; *law* revoke (wills); *vr* be shaken or bruised, suffer from aftereffects
quebranto *m,* breaking, shattering; crushing, pounding; infringement; breaking out (from prison); weakness, exhaustion; compassion, pity; loss, damage; pain, suffering
quebrar *vt irr* to break, shatter; crush; impede, hinder; make pale (color, gen. of complexion); mitigate, moderate; bend, twist; overcome (difficulties); *vi* break off (a friendship); weaken, give way; go bankrupt; *vr med* suffer from hernia; be interrupted (of mountain ranges). **quebrarse los ojos,** to strain one's eyes. *Pres. Ind.* **quiebro, quiebras, quiebra, quiebran.** *Pres. Subjunc.* **quiebre, quiebres, quiebre, quiebren**
queche *m,* ketch
queda *f,* curfew; curfew bell
quedada *f,* stay, sojourn
quedar *vi* to stay, sojourn; remain; be left over; (*with por* + *infin.*) remain to be (e.g. **Queda por escribir,** It remains to be written); (*with por*) be won by or be knocked down to; be, remain in a place; end, cease; (*with en*) reach an agreement (e.g. **Quedamos en no ir,** We have decided not to go). **q. en esta alternativa . . . ,** to face this alternative: . . . . *vr* remain; abate (wind); grow calm (sea); (*with con*) keep, retain possession of. **q. bien o mal,** to behave well or badly, come off well or badly (in business affairs, etc.). **quedarse muerto,** to be astounded
quedo *a* still, motionless; quiet, tranquil. *adv* in a low voice; quietly, noiselessly. **de q.,** slowly, gradually. *interj* **¡Q.!** Quiet!
quehacer *m,* odd job; task; business (gen. *pl*)
queja *f,* lamentation, grief; complaint, grudge; quarrel
quejarse *vr* to lament; complain, grumble; *law* lodge an accusation (against)
quejido *m,* complaint, moan
quejoso *a* querulous, complaining
quejumbre *f,* complaint, whine; querulousness
quejumbroso *a* complaining, grumbling
quema *f,* burn; burning; fire, conflagration
quemadero *a* burnable. *m,* stake (for burning people)
quemado *m,* burned patch of forest; *inf* anything burned or burning
quemador (-ra) *m,* jet, burner. *n* incendiary
quemadura *f,* burn; scald; burning
quemajoso *a* smarting, burning, pricking
quemar *vt* to burn; dry up, parch; scorch; tan, bronze; scald; throw away, sell at a loss; *vi* burn, be excessively hot; *vr* be very hot; be dried up with the heat; burn with (passions); *inf* be near the attainment of a desired

end. **quemarse las cejas,** to burn the midnight oil, study too hard

quemazón *f,* burning; conflagration; intense heat; *inf* smarting; *inf* hurtful remark; *inf* vexation, soreness

querella *f,* complaint; quarrel, fight

querellarse *vr* to complain; lament, bemoan; *law* lodge an accusation; *law* contest a will

querelloso *a* complaining, grumbling, querulous

querencia *f,* love, affection; homing instinct; lair; natural inclination or desire

querer *vt irr* to desire, wish; want, will; attempt, endeavor; *(with a)* love. *impers* be on the point of. **q. decir,** to mean. **¿Qué quiere decir esto?** What does this mean? **sin q.,** unintentionally. See **entender**

querer *m,* affection, love

querido (-da) *n* lover; beloved; darling. *a* dear

querub, querube *poet* **querubín** *m,* cherub

querúbico *a* cherubic

quesera *f,* dairymaid; dairy; cheese vat; cheese board; cheese dish

quesería *f,* dairy; cheese shop; season for making cheese

queso *m,* cheese. **q. de bola,** Dutch cheese. **q. rallado,** grated cheese

quetzal *m,* quetzal

quevedos *m pl,* glasses, eyeglasses; pince-nez

¡quia! *interj inf* You don't say so!

quianti *m,* chianti

quicial *m,* doorjamb

quicio *m,* threshold; hinge; *mech* bushing. **fuera de q.,** out of order; unhinged. **sacar de q.,** to displace (things); annoy, irritate; drive crazy

quiebra *f,* breach, crack; rut, fissure; loss; bankruptcy

quiebro *m,* twisting of the body, dodging; *mus* trill

quien *rel pron mf pl* **quienes.** *interr* **quién, quiénes** who; whom; he (she, etc.) who, anyone who, whoever; which; whichever (e.g. **mis padres a quienes respeto,** my parents whom I respect. **Quien te quiere te hará llorar,** Whoever (he, those, who) love(s) you will make you weep. **¿Quién está a la puerta?** Who is at the door? **¿De quién es?** Whose is it? To whom does it belong?). *indef pron* one (*pl* some)

quienquiera *indef pron mf pl* **quienesquiera,** whosoever, whichever, whomsoever

quietación *f,* quieting, soothing

quietador (-ra) *a* tranquilizing, soothing. *n* soother

quietismo *m,* quietism

quietista *mf* quietist. *a* quietistic

quieto *a* quiet, still; peaceful, tranquil; virtuous, respectable

quietud *f,* stillness, repose; peacefulness; rest, quietness

quif *m,* hashish, marijuana

quijada *f,* jawbone, jaw; *mech* jaw

quijo *m,* ore (gold or silver)

quijotada *f,* quixotic action, quixotism

quijote *m,* cuisse; thigh guard; quixotic person

quijotesco *a* quixotic

quijotería *f,* **quijotismo** *m,* quixotism

quilate *m,* carat; degree of excellence (gen. *pl*). *inf* **por quilates,** in small bits, parsimoniously

quilla *f,* naut keel; breastbone (of birds)

quillotrar *vt inf* to encourage, incite; woo, make love to; consider; *vr inf* fall in love; dress up; whine, complain

quillotro *m, inf* incentive; indication, sign; love affair; puzzle, knotty point; compliment; dressing up

quimera *f,* chimera; fancy, vision; quarrel, dispute

quimérico *a* chimerical, fanciful

quimerista *mf* dreamer, visionary; quarreler, disputant

química *f,* chemistry

químico *a* chemical. *m,* chemist. **productos químicos,** chemicals

quimono *m,* kimono

quina *f,* cinchona; quinine; *pl* Arms of Portugal. *inf* **tragar q.,** to suffer in patience, put up with

quinario *a* quinary

quincalla *f,* cheap jewelery; fancy goods

quincallería *f,* cheap jewelery shop; hardware factory or industry; cheap jewelry; fancy goods

quince *a* and *m,* fifteen; fifteenth

quinceañero *f,* sweet sixteen party, sweet sixteen (in Spanish-speaking areas, held at age fifteen)

quincena *f,* fortnight, two weeks; bimonthly pay; *mus* fifteenth

quincenal *a* fortnightly; lasting a fortnight, lasting two weeks

quinceno *a* fifteenth

quincuagenario *a* quinquagenarian

quincuagésimo *a* fiftieth

quindécimo *a* fifteenth

quinientos *a* five hundred; five-hundredth. *m,* five hundred

quinina *f,* quinine

quinqué *m,* oil lamp, student's lamp, table lamp; perspicuity, talent

quinquenio *m,* period of five years, lustrum

quinta *f,* country house; *mus* fifth; conscripting men into army by drawing lots; *mil* draft

quintaesencia *f,* quintessence

quintal *m,* hundredweight

quintar *vt* to draw one out of every five; draw lots for conscription into the army; *vi* reach the fifth (day, etc., gen. of the moon)

quintería *f,* farm

quintero *m,* farmer; farmworker

quinteto *m,* quintet

quintilla *f,* five-line stanza of eight syllables

Quintín, San. armarse (*or* **haber**) **la de San Q.** to quarrel, make trouble; be a row

quinto *a* fifth. *m,* one-fifth; *mil* conscript; duty of twenty percent; *law* fifth part of an estate. **quinta columna,** fifth column. **quinta esencia,** quintessence

quintuplicar *vt* to quintuplicate

quíntuplo *a* fivefold, quintuple

quinzavo *a* and *m,* fifteenth

quiñón *m,* share of land owned jointly, share of the profits

quiosco *m,* kiosk, stand; pavilion, pagoda. **q. de música,** bandstand

quiquiriquí *m,* cock-a-doodle-doo; *fig inf* cock of the walk

quiromancia *f,* chiromancy, palmistry

quiromántico (-ca) *n* chiromancer, palmist

quirúrgico *a* surgical

quirurgo *m,* surgeon

quisicosa *f, inf* riddle, puzzle, enigma

quisquilla *f,* trifle, quibble, scruple; prawn, shrimp

quisquilloso *a* quibbling, overscrupulous, fastidious; hypersensitive; irascible, touchy

quistarse *vr* to make oneself well-liked or loved

quiste *m, med* cyst

quita *f, law* discharge (of part of a debt)

quitaesmalte *m,* nail polish remover (for fingernails)

quitamanchas *mf,* dry cleaner, clothes cleaner

quitamotas *mf inf* flatterer, adulator

quitanieve *m,* snowplow

quitanza *f,* quittance; quietus

quitapesares *m, inf* consolation, solace, comfort

quitar *vt* to remove; take off or away; clear (the table); rob, steal; prevent, impede; parry (in fencing); separate; redeem (pledges); forbid; annul, repeal (laws, etc.); free from (obligations); *vr* shed, take off, remove; get rid of; leave, quit. **quitarse de encima (a),** to get rid of someone or something. **q. el polvo,** to dust. **de quita y pon,** detachable, removable; adjustable

quitasol *m,* parasol, sunshade

quitasueño *m, inf* sleep banisher, anxiety

quite *m,* hindering, impeding; obstruction; parry (in fencing). **estar al q.,** to be ready to protect someone

quizá, quizás *adv* perhaps. **q. y sin q.,** without doubt, certainly

R

rabadán *m,* head shepherd or herdsman
rabadilla *f,* rump, croup
rábano *m,* radish. **r. picante,** horseradish
rabel *m, mus* rebec; *inf* backside, seat
rabera *f,* tail-end; chaff, siftings
rabí *m,* rabbi
rabia *f,* rabies, hydrophobia; anger, fury. *inf* **tener r. (a),** to hate
rabiar *vi* to suffer from hydrophobia; groan with pain; be furious; *(with por)* yearn for, desire. **a r.,** excessively
rabicorto *a* short-tailed
rabieta *f, inf* tantrum
rabilargo *a* long-tailed
rabínico *a* rabbinical
rabinismo *m,* rabbinism
rabino *m,* rabbi. **gran r.,** chief rabbi
rabioso *a* rabid; furious, angry; vehement. **perro r.,** mad dog
rabo *m,* tail; *bot* stalk; *inf* train (of a dress); shank (of a button). **r. del ojo,** corner of the eye. *fig inf* **ir r. entre piernas,** to have one's tail between one's legs
rabón *a* tailless, docked; bobtailed
rabudo *a* big-tailed
racimo *m,* bunch (of grapes or other fruits); cluster; raceme
racimoso *a* racemose
raciocinación *f,* ratiocination
raciocinar *vi* to reason
raciocinio *m,* reasoning; ratiocination; discourse, speech
ración *f,* ration; portion (in a restaurant); meal allowance; *ecc* prebendary. *inf* **r. de hambre,** starvation diet; pittance, starvation wages
racional *a* reasonable, logical; rational
racionalidad *f,* reasonableness; rationality
racionalismo *m,* rationalism
racionalista *a* and *mf* rationalist. *a* rationalistic
racionalización *f,* rationalization
racionamiento *m,* rationing. *f.* **cartilla de r.,** ration book
racionar *vt* to ration
rada *f,* bay, cove; *naut* road, roadstead
radar *m,* radar
radiación *f,* radiation; *rad* broadcasting
radiactividad *f,* radioactivity
radiactivo *a* radioactive
radiador *m,* radiator (for heating); *aut* radiator
radial *a* radial
radiante *a phys* radiating; brilliant, shining; *fig* beaming (with satisfaction)
radiar *vi phys* to radiate; *vt* broadcast (by radio)
radical *a* radical; fundamental; *pol* radical. *m, gram* root; *(math chem)* radical. *mf pol* radical
radicalismo *m,* radicalism
radicar(se) *vi* and *vr* to take root. **r. una solicitud,** file an application, submit an application. *vi* be (in a place)
radio *m, (geom anat)* radius; radium. *f,* radio
radioaficionado (-da) *n* radio amateur; *inf* ham, wireless fan or enthusiast
radioaudición *f,* radio broadcast
radiocomunicación *f,* radio transmission
radiodifundir *vt rad* to broadcast
radiodifusión, radioemisión *f, rad* broadcast; broadcasting
radioemisora *f,* radio station
radioescucha *mf* radio listener
radiofotografía *f,* radiophotography; x-ray photograph. **tomar una r. de,** to x-ray
radiofrecuencia *f,* radiofrequency
radiografía *f,* radiography
radiografiar *vt* to x-ray, radiograph

radiografista *mf* radiographer
radiograma *m,* radiogram, cable
radiolocación *f,* radiolocation
radiología *f,* radiology
radiólogo *mf* radiologist
radiometría *f,* radiometry
radiómetro *m,* radiometer
radiorreceptor *m,* receiver, wireless set
radioscopia *f,* radioscopy
radioyente *mf* radio listener
radiotelefonía *f,* radiotelephony
radiotelegrafía *f,* radiotelegraphy
radiotelegrafiar *vt* to radiotelegraph
radiotelegráfico *a* radiotelegraphic, wireless
radiotelegrafista *mf* wireless operator
radiotelegrama *m,* radiogram, radiotelegram
radioterapia *f,* radiotherapy, radiotherapeutics
radiotransmisor *m,* (radio) transmitter
raedera *f,* scraper
raedor *a* scraping; abrasive
raedura *f,* scraping; rubbing; fraying
raer *vt irr* to scrape; abrade; fray; *fig* extirpate. See **caer**
ráfaga *f,* gust or blast of wind; light cloud; flash (of light)
rafe *m,* eaves
rafia *f,* raffia
raído *a* frayed, threadbare; brazen, barefaced
raíz *f,* root. **r. amarga,** horseradish. **r. cuadrada (cúbica),** square (cubed) root. **r. pivotante,** tap root. **a r.,** close to the root, closely. **a r. de,** as a result of; after. **de r.,** from the root, entirely. **echar raíces,** to take root
raja *f,* split, crack; chip, splinter (of wood); slice (of fruit, etc.)
rajá *m,* rajah
rajadura *f,* splitting; crack, split, crevice; *geol* break
rajar *vt* to crack, split; slice; *vi inf* boast; chatter; *vr* crack, split; *inf* take back one's words
ralea *f,* kind, quality; *(inf* scornful) race, lineage
ralear *vi* to grow thin (cloth, etc.); behave true to type (gen. in a bad sense)
rallador *m, cul* grater
rallar *vt cul* to grate; *inf* bother, annoy
rallo *m, cul* grater; rasp
ralo *a* sparse, thin
rama *f,* bough, branch; *fig* branch (of family). *fig inf* **andarse por las ramas,** to beat around the bush. **en r.,** *com* raw; unbound (of books)
ramaje *m,* thickness of branches, denseness of foliage
ramal *m,* strand (of rope); halter; branch line (of a railroad); fork (of a road, etc.); ramification, division
ramalazo *m,* blow with a rope; mark left by this; bruise
rambla *f,* bed, channel, course; avenue, boulevard (in Catalonia)
ramera *f,* whore
ramificación *f,* ramification; *anat* bifurcation
ramificarse *vr* to branch, fork; *fig* spread
ramillete *m,* bouquet; table centerpiece; *bot* cluster
ramo *m, bot* branch; twig, spray; bouquet, bunch; wreath; *fig* branch (of learning, etc.); *com* line (of business); *fig* touch, slight attack. **Domingo de Ramos,** Palm Sunday
ramoso *a* branchy, thick with branches
rampa *f,* gradient, incline; *mil* ramp; launching site
ramplón *a* stout, heavy (of shoes); coarse; vulgar; bombastic
rana *f,* frog. **r. de San Antonio,** tree frog
ranchero *m, mil* cook; small farmer; *WH* rancher
rancho *m,* mess, rations; settlement, camp; hut, cabin; *inf* group, huddle; *WH* ranch; *naut* gang. **hacer r.,** *inf* to make room
rancidez *f,* rancidness; staleness; rankness; antiquity

198

ranciedad *f*, rancidness; antiquity, oldness; mustiness
rancio *a* rancid, rank; mellow (of wine); ancient; traditional; musty
rango *m*, grade, class; range; (*mil nav* and *social*) rank; file, line
ranúnculo *m*, buttercup
ranura *f*, groove; rabbet; slot, notch
rapacidad *f*, rapacity, avidity, greed
rapador *a* scraping. *m*, *inf* barber
rapapolvo *m*, *inf* severe scolding, dressing-down
rapar(se) *vt* and *vr* to shave; *vt* crop, cut close (hair); *inf* steal, pinch
rapaz *a* rapacious. *m*, young boy. **ave r.**, bird of prey
rapaza *f*, young girl
rape *m*, *inf* hasty shave or haircut. **al r.**, close-cropped
rapé *m*, snuff
rapidez *f*, speed, swiftness, rapidity
rápido *a* quick, swift; express (trains). *m*, torrent, rapid; express train
rapiña *f*, robbery, plundering, sacking
rapiñar *vt inf* to steal, pinch
raposa *f*, vixen, fox; *inf* wily person
raposo *m*, (male) fox
raposear *vi* to behave like a fox
rapsodia *f*, rhapsody
raptar *vt* to abduct; rob
rapto *m*, abduction; rape; snatching, seizing; ecstasy, trance; *med* loss of consciousness
raptor *m*, kidnapper, abductor
raquero *a* pirate. *m*, wrecker; pickpocket, dock rat
raqueta *f*, racket (tennis, badminton, squash rackets); croupier's rake. **r. de nieve,** snowshoe
raquianestesia *f*, spinal anesthesia
raquídeo *a* spinal
raquítico *a med* rachitic; small, minute; weak, feeble; rickety
raquitismo *m*, rickets
rarefacción *f*, rarefaction
rarefacer(se) *vt* and *vr* to rarefy. See **satisfacer**
rareza *f*, rareness, unusualness; eccentricity, whim; oddity, curio
raridad *f*, rarity; thinness; scarcity
raro *a* rare, unusual, uncommon; notable, outstanding; odd, eccentric, queer; rarefied (gases, etc.). **rara vez,** seldom. **lo r. de,** the strange thing about (e.g. **Lo r. del caso es . . . ,** the strange thing about the case is . . .)
ras *m*, level. **a r.,** flush (with), nearly touching
rasa *f*, worn place in cloth; clearing, glade
rasar *vt* to level with a strickle; graze, brush, touch lightly; *vr* grow clear (of the sky, etc.)
rascacielos *m*, skyscraper
rascador *m*, scraper; ornamental hairpin
rascadura *f*, scraping; scratching
rascar *vt* to scratch; claw; scrape; twang (a guitar, etc.). *inf* **¡Que se rasque!** Let him put up with it! Let him lump it!
rascatripas *m*, *inf* caterwauler, squeaker (of violinists, etc.)
rascón *a* sour, tart
rasgadura *f*, tearing; tear, rip, rent
rasgar(se) *vt* and *vr* to tear, rip; *vt* strum the guitar
rasgo *m*, flourish (of the pen); felicitous expression; characteristic, quality; *pl* features (of the face)
rasgón *m*, rip, tear
rasguear *vt* to strum, twang (the guitar); *vi* write with a flourish
rasgueo *m*, flourish (on a guitar); scratch (of a pen)
rasguñar *vt* to scratch, scrape; claw; *art* sketch
rasguño *m*, scratch; *art* sketch, outline
raso *a* flat; free of obstacles; glossy; clear (sky, etc.); plain; undistinguished; backless (chairs). *m*, satin. **al r.,** in the open air
raspa *f*, *bot* beard (of cereals); fishbone; bunch of grapes; *bot* husk; *carp* scraper
raspador *m*, eraser; scraper, rasp
raspadura *f*, scraping; erasing; shavings, filings

raspar *vt* to scrape; erase; rob, steal; burn, bite (wine, etc.)
rastra *f*, trace, sign; sled; string of onions, etc.; anything dragging; *agr* harrow; *agr* rake. **a la r.**, dragging; reluctantly. **pescar a la r.**, to trawl
rastreador *m*, *naut* minesweeper. *a* dragging
rastrear *vt* to trace, trail; drag, trawl; surmise, conjecture, investigate; *vi agr* rake; fly low
rastreo *m*, dragging (of lakes, etc.)
rastrero *a* dragging, trailing; low-flying; servile, abject; *bot* creeping. *m*, slaughterhouse employee
rastrillador (-ra) *n* raker; hackler
rastrilladora *f*, mechanical harrow
rastrillaje *m*, raking
rastrillar *vt* to rake; dress, comb (flax)
rastrillo *m*, *agr* rake; hackle; portcullis; *agr* rack
rastro *m*, *agr* rake; track, trail; wholesale meat market; slaughterhouse; trace, vestige; second-hand market (in Madrid)
rastrojo *m*, stubble; stubble field
rasura *f*, shaving
rasurar(se) *vt* and *vr* to shave
rata *f*, rat. *m*, *inf* pickpocket. **r. almizclera,** muskrat. *inf* **más pobre que las ratas,** poorer than a church mouse
rataplán *m*, rub-a-dub-dub, beating of a drum
ratear *vt* to rebate pro rata; apportion; thieve on a small scale, filch; *vi* crawl, creep
ratería *f*, filching, petty theft, picking pockets; meanness, parsimony
ratero (-ra) *n* pilferer, petty thief, pickpocket
ratificación *f*, ratification
ratificador (-ra) *n* ratifier
ratificar *vt* to ratify
ratificatorio *a* ratifying, confirmatory
rato *m*, short interval of time, while. **buen (mal) r.,** pleasant (unpleasant) time. **r. perdido,** leisure moment. **a ratos,** sometimes, occasionally. **de r. en r.,** from time to time. **pasar el r.,** *inf* to while away the time
ratón (-ona) *n* mouse
ratonera *f*, mousetrap; mousehole; mouse nest. *fig* **caer en la r.,** to fall into a trap
ratonero, ratonesco, ratonil *a* mousy
rauco *a* poet hoarse
raudal *m*, torrent, cascade; *fig* flood, abundance
raudo *a* swift, rapid
ravioles *m pl*, ravioli
raya *f*, stripe, streak; limit, end; part (of the hair); boundary; *gram* dash; score (some games). *m*, *icht* ray. **pasar de r.,** to go too far; misbehave
rayadillo *m*, striped cotton
rayano *a* neighboring; border; almost identical, very similar
rayar *vt* to draw lines; streak; stripe; cross out; underline; rifle (a gun); *vi* verge (on), border (on); appear (of dawn, daylight); excel; be similar. **Raya en los catorce años,** He is about fourteen
rayo *m*, *phys* beam, ray; thunderbolt; flash of lightning; spoke; quick-witted person; capable, energetic person; sudden pain; disaster, catastrophe. **r. de sol,** sunbeam. **r. católico,** cathode ray. **r. x,** x-ray. *fig* **echar rayos,** to breathe forth fury
rayón *m*, rayon
raza *f*, race; breed; lineage, family; kind, class; crack, crevice. **de r.,** purebred
razón *f*, reason; reasoning; word, expression; speech, argument; motive, cause; order, method; justice, equity; right, authority; explanation; *math* ratio, proportion. **r. de estado,** raison d'état, reasons of state. *com* **r. social,** firm, trade name. **a r. de,** at a rate of. **dar la r. (a),** to agree with. **estar puesto en r.,** to stand to reason. **tener r.,** to be in the right
razonable *a* reasonable; moderate
razonador (-ra) *n* reasoner
razonamiento *m*, reasoning

razonar *vi* to reason; speak; *vt* attest, confirm
razzia *f,* foray; pillaging, sacking; police raid
re *m, mus* re, D
reabsorción *f,* reabsorption
reacción *f,* reaction. **r. de Bayardo,** quick reaction of someone always ready to help those in distress
reaccionar *vi* to react
reaccionario (-ia) *a* and *n* reactionary
reaccionarismo *m,* reactionism
reacio *a* recalcitrant
reactivo *m,* reagent. *a* reactive; reacting
readmisión *f,* readmission
readmitir *vt* to readmit
reajustar *vt* to readjust
real *a* actual, real; kingly; royal; royalist; *fig* regal; *inf* fine, handsome. *m,* silver coin, real; *m pl,* encampment, camp. **alzar el r.,** *mil* to strike camp. **asentar el r.,** *mil* to encamp. **r. decreto,** royal decree. **sitio r.,** royal residence. **un r., sobre otro,** *inf* cash in full
realce *m,* raised or embossed work; renown, glory; *art* high light
realeza *f,* royalty, royal majesty
realidad *f,* reality; sincerity; truth. **en r.,** in fact, actually
realismo *m,* realism; regalism; royalism
realista *a* realistic; royalist. *mf* realist; royalist; regalist
realizable *a* realizable; practicable
realización *f,* realization; performance, execution
realizar *vt* to perform, execute, carry out; *com* realize. **r. beneficio,** to make a profit
realmente *adv* really, truly; actually
realzar *vt* to heighten, raise; emboss; exalt; enhance; *art* intensify (colors, etc.)
reanimar *vt* to reanimate; revive, restore, resuscitate; encourage
reanudación *f,* resumption, renewal
reanudar *vt* to resume, continue
reaparecer *vi irr* to reappear. See **conocer**
reaparición *f,* reappearance
rearmamento *m,* rearmament
rearmar *vi* to rearm
reasegurador *m,* underwriter
reasegurar *vt* to reinsure, underwrite
reaseguro *m,* reinsurance, underwriting
reasumir *vt* to reassume; resume
reasunción *f,* reassumption; resumption
reata *f,* string of horses or mules. **de r.,** in single file; *inf* blindly, unquestioningly; *inf* at once
rebaja *f,* diminution; *com* discount, rebate; remission
rebajar *vt* to lower; curtail, lessen; remit; *com* reduce in price; *mech* file; *elec* step down; humble, humiliate; *vr* cringe, humble oneself
rebajo *m,* reduction (in price, etc.); rabbet
rebanada *f,* slice, piece (of bread, etc.)
rebanar *vt* to cut into slices; split
rebaño *m,* flock, drove, herd; *ecc* flock
rebasar *vt* to exceed, go beyond; *mil* bypass
rebate *m,* altercation, dispute, quarrel
rebatiña *f,* grab; scrimmage. **andar a la r.,** to scuffle
rebatir *vt* to repulse, repel; fight again; fight hard; oppose, resist; *com* deduct; refuse, reject
rebato *m,* alarm, tocsin; *mil* surprise attack; panic, dismay
rebeca *f,* cardigan, jersey
rebeco *m, zool* chamois
rebelarse *vr* to mutiny, rebel; oppose, resist
rebelde *a* mutinous, rebellious; wilful, disobedient; stubborn. *mf* rebel
rebeldía *f,* rebelliousness; willfulness; stubbornness; *law* nonappearance
rebelión *f,* insurrection, revolt
rebién *adv* very well, extremely well
rebisabuelo (-la) *n.* See **tatarabuelo**
reblandecer *vt irr* to soften; *vr* become soft. See **conocer**
reblandecimiento *m,* softening; *med* flabbiness

reborde *m,* rim, edge; *mech* flange. **r. de acera,** curb
rebordear *vt* to flange
rebosar *vi* to overflow, run over; *fig* abound in; express one's feelings
rebotar *vi* to rebound; clinch (nails, etc.); refuse; *vr* change color; *inf* be vexed
rebote *m,* rebounding; rebound
rebotica *f,* back room of a pharmacy; back of a shop
rebozar *vt* to muffle up; coat with batter
rebozo *m,* muffling up, hiding the face; head shawl; pretense, excuse. *fig* **sin r.,** openly
rebramo *m,* barking of deer, stags, etc.
rebueno *a inf* extremely good, fine
rebullicio *m,* uproar, clamor
rebullir *vi* to stir, show signs of movement; *fig* swarm, seethe
rebusca *f,* close search; gleaning; remains
rebuscado *a* affected, unnatural (of style)
rebuscar *vt* to search for; glean
rebuznar *vi* to bray
rebuzno *m,* braying
recadero (-ra) *n* messenger, errand boy
recado *m,* message; greeting, note; gift, present; daily marketing; outfit, implements; precaution, safeguard
recaer *vi irr* to fall again; *med* relapse; lapse, backslide; devolve, fall upon. See **caer**
recaída *f,* falling again; *med* relapse; lapse
recalar *vt* to impregnate; *naut* call at (a port), come within sight of land
recalcada *f,* pressing down, squeezing; emphasis; *naut* list
recalcar *vt* to press down; squeeze; pack tight; stress, emphasize; *vi naut* list; *vr inf* say over and over, savor one's words
recalcitrante *a* obdurate, recalcitrant
recalentador *m, mech* superheater
recalentar *vt irr* to overheat; superheat; reheat. See **sentar**
recamado *m,* raised embroidery
recámara *f,* dressing room; explosives chamber; breech of a gun; *inf* caution
recambio *m,* spare, spare part; *com* re-exchange
recantación *f,* retraction, recantation
recapacitar *vi* to search one's memory; think over
recapitulación *f,* summary, résumé
recapitular *vt* to recapitulate, summarize
recargar *vt* to recharge; load again; reaccuse; overcharge; overdress or overdecorate; *vr med* become more feverish. **r. acumuladores,** to recharge batteries
recargo *m,* charge; new load; *law* new accusation; overcharge, extra cost; *med* temperature increase
recatado *a* prudent, discreet, circumspect; modest, shy
recatar *vt* to hide, conceal; *vr* be prudent or cautious
recato *m,* caution, prudence; modesty, shyness, reserve
recauchutar *vt* to retread (tires)
recaudación *f,* collecting; collection (of taxes, etc.); tax collector's office
recaudador *m,* tax collector
recaudar *vt* to collect, recover (taxes, debts, etc.); deposit, place in custody
recaudo *m,* collecting; collection (of taxes, etc.); precaution, safeguard; *law* surety
recelar *vt* to suspect, fear, mistrust; *vr (with de)* be afraid or suspicious of
recelo *m,* suspicion, mistrust, doubt, fear
receloso *a* suspicious, distrustful, doubtful
recepción *f,* receiving, reception; admission, acceptance; reception, party; *law* cross-examination
receptáculo *m,* receptacle, container; *fig* refuge; *bot* receptacle
receptador (-ra) *n* receiver (of stolen goods); accomplice
receptivo *a* receptive
receptor (-ra) *a* receiving. *n* recipient. *m, elec* receiver; wireless set. **r. de galena,** crystal set. **r. telefónico,** telephone receiver

receta *f, med* prescription; *cul* recipe

recetar *vt med* to prescribe; *inf* demand

rechapear *vt* to replate

rechazar *vt* to repulse; resist; refuse; oppose, deny (the truth of); contradict

rechazo *m*, recoil; rebound; refusal

rechinamiento, rechino *m*, squeaking, creaking; gnashing (of teeth)

rechinar *vi* to squeak, creak; gnash (teeth); chatter (teeth); do with a bad grace

rechoncho *a* squat, stocky

reciamente *adv* hard; strongly, firmly, vigorously

recibí *m, com* receipt

recibidor (-ra) *a* receiving. *n* recipient. *m*, reception room

recibimiento *m*, reception; welcome, greeting; reception room, waiting room; hall, vestibule

recibir *vt* to obtain, receive; support, bear; suffer, experience (attack, injury); approve; accept, receive; entertain; stand up to (attack); *vr (with de)* graduate as, take office as

recibo *m*, reception; *com* receipt; reception room, waiting room; hall, vestibule. *com* **acusar r.**, to acknowledge receipt

recidiva *f, med* relapse

recién *adv* recently, newly. Shortened form of **reciente** before a past participle (e.g. **r. llegado,** newly arrived)

reciente *a* recent; new; fresh

recinto *m*, precincts; neighborhood; premises, place

recio *a* strong; robust; bulky, thick; rough, uncouth; grievous, hard; severe (weather); impetuous, precipitate

recipiente *a* receiving. *m*, receptacle, container, vessel

reciprocar *vt* to reciprocate

reciprocidad *f*, reciprocity; reciprocation

recíproco *a* reciprocal

recitación *f*, recitation

recitado *m*, recitative

recitador (-ra) *n* elocutionist, reciter

recitar *vt* to recite, declaim

reclamación *f*, reclamation; objection, opposition; *com* claim

reclamar *vi* to oppose, object to; *poet* resound; *vt* call repeatedly; *com* claim; decoy (birds)

reclamo *m*, decoy bird; enticement, allurement; *law* reclamation; advertisement. **objeto de r.,** advertising sample. **venta de r.,** bargain sale

reclinación *f*, reclining; leaning

reclinatorio *m*, couch; prie-dieu

recluir *vt irr* to immure, shut up; detain, arrest. See **huir**

reclusión *f*, confinement, seclusion; prison

recluso (-sa) *n* recluse

recluta *f*, recruiting. *mf mil* recruit

reclutador *m*, recruiting office

reclutamiento *m*, recruiting

reclutar *vt* to enlist recruits, recruit

recobrar *vt* to recover, regain; *vr* recuperate; regain consciousness

recobro *m*, recovery; *mech* pick-up

recocer *vt irr* to reboil; recook; overboil; overcook; anneal (metals); *vr fig* to be tormented (by emotion), be all burned up. See **cocer**

recodo *m*, bend, turn, loop

recogedor *a* sheltering. *m, agr* gleaner

recoger *vt* to gather, pick; pick up; retake; collect (letters from a mailbox, etc.); amass; shrink, narrow; keep; hoard; shelter; reap, pick; *vr* withdraw, retire; go home; go to bed; retrench, economize; give oneself to meditation

recogida *f*, collection (of letters from a mailbox); withdrawal; retirement; harvest

recogido *a* recluse; cloistered, confined

recogimiento *m*, gathering, picking; collection, accumulation; seclusion; shelter; women's reformatory

recolección *f*, summary, résumé; harvest; collection (of taxes, etc.); *ecc* convent of a reformed order; mystic ecstasy

recoleto *a ecc* reformed (of religious orders); recluse

recomendable *a* commendable, recommendable

recomendación *f*, recommendation (all meanings)

recomendar *vt irr* to recommend (all meanings); entrust, commend. *Pres. Ind.* **recomiendo, recomiendas, recomienda, recomiendan.** *Pres. Subjunc.* **recomiende, recomiendes, recomiende, recomienden**

recompensa *f*, compensation; recompense, reward

recompensar *vt* to compensate; requite; reward, recompense

recomposición *f*, recomposition

recomprar *vt* to repurchase

reconcentrar *vt* to concentrate; dissemble; *vr* withdraw into oneself, meditate

reconciliable *a* reconcilable

reconciliación *f*, reconciliation

reconciliador (-ra) *a* reconciliatory. *n* reconciler

reconciliar *vt* to reconcile; *ecc* reconsecrate; *ecc* hear a short confession; *vr* become reconciled; *ecc* make an additional confession

recondicionar *vt* to rebuild, overhaul, recondition

recóndito *a* recondite

reconocer *vt irr* to examine, inspect; recognize; admit, acknowledge; own, confess; search; *pol* recognize; *mil* reconnoiter; *(with por)* adopt as (a son, etc.); recognize as; *vr* be seen, show; acknowledge, confess; know oneself. **Bien se reconoce que no está aquí,** It's easy to see he's not here. See **conocer**

reconocido *a* grateful

reconocimiento *m*, examination, inspection; recognition; acknowledgement, admission; search; *mil* reconnoitering; adoption; gratitude

reconquista *f*, reconquest

reconquistar *vt* to reconquer; *fig* recover, win back

reconstitución *f*, reconstitution

reconstituir *vt irr* to reconstitute. See **huir**

reconstituyente *m, med* tonic

reconstrucción *f*, reconstruction

reconstruir *vt irr* to reconstruct, rebuild; recreate. See **huir**

reconvención *f*, rebuke, reproof; recrimination; *law* countercharge

reconversión *f*, reconversion

recopilación *f*, summary, compendium; collection (of writings); digest (of laws)

recopilador *m*, compiler

recopilar *vt* to compile, collect

recordar *vt irr* to cause to remember, remind; remember; *vi* remember; awake. See **acordar**

recordatorio *m*, reminder. *a* commemorative (e.g. a plaque)

recorrer *vt* to travel over; pass through; wander around; examine, inspect; read hastily; overhaul, renovate

recorrido *m*, journey, run; *mech* stroke; overhaul. **r. de despegue,** *aer* take-off run

recortado *a bot* jagged, incised. *m*, paper cutout

recortar *vt* to clip, trim, pare; cut out; *art* outline; *vr* stand out (against), be outlined (against)

recorte *m*, clipping, paring; cutting; cutout; *art* outline; *pl* snippets, clippings. **r. de periódico,** newspaper cutting, newspaper clipping

recostar *vt irr (with en or contra)* to lean, rest against; *vr (with en or contra)* lean against, rest on; lean back; recline. See **contar**

recreación *f*, recreation, hobby

recrear *vt* to entertain, amuse; *vr* amuse oneself; delight (in), enjoy

recreo *m*, recreation, hobby; playtime, recess (in schools); place of amusement. **salón de r.,** recreation room

recriminación *f*, recrimination

recriminador *a* recriminatory

recriminar *vt* to recriminate

recrudecer(se) *vi* and *vr irr* to recur, return. See **conocer**

recrudescencia *f*, recrudescence, recurrence

rectángulo *m*, rectangle. *a* rectangular

rectificable *a* rectifiable

rectificación *f*, rectification; *mech* grinding

rectificador *m*, rectifier

rectificar *vt* to rectify; *mech* grind; *vr* mend one's ways; *mil* **r. el frente**, to straighten the line

rectilíneo *a* rectilinear

rectitud *f*, straightness; rectitude, integrity; exactness; righteousness

recto *a* straight; upright; erect; literal (meaning); just, fair; single-breasted (of coats); *m*, right angle; rectum

rector (-ra) *n* director; principal, headmaster. *m, ecc* rector

rectorado *m*, principalship, headmaster- (mistress-) ship, directorship; *ecc* rectorship

rectoría *f*, rectorate, rectorship

recua *f*, drove of beasts of burden; *inf* string or line (of things)

recubrir *vt* to re-cover; coat; plate. *Past Part.* **recubierto**

recuento *m*, calculation; recount; inventory

recuerdo *m*, memory, remembrance; memento; *pl* greetings, regards

reculada *f*, drawing back; recoil

recular *vi* to recoil, draw back; *inf* go back on, give up

recuperable *a* recoverable, recuperable

recuperación *f*, recovery, recuperation; *chem* recovery

recurrente *a* recurrent

recurrir *vi* to recur; (*with prep a*) have recourse to; appeal to

recurso *m*, recourse, resort; choice, option; reversion; petition; *law* appeal; *pl* means of livelihood; *fig* way out, last hope

recusar *vt* to refuse; challenge the authority (of)

red *f*, net; network; hairnet; railing, grating; *fig* snare; system (of communications, etc.); *fig* combination (of events, etc.); *elec* mains. **r. de arrastre**, trawl net. *fig inf* **caer en la r.**, to fall into the trap

redacción *f*, phrasing; editorial office; editing; editorial board

redactar *vt* to write, phrase; draw up; edit

redactor (-ra) *a* editorial. *n* editor

redada *f*, cast (of a fishing net); haul, catch

redecilla *f*, *dim* small net; netting; hairnet

redención *f*, redemption; ransom; deliverance, salvation; redeeming, paying off (a mortgage, etc.)

redentor (-ra) *a* redeeming, redemptive. *n* redeemer

redificar *vt* to rebuild

redifusión *f*, *rad* relay

redil *m*, sheepfold

redimible *a* redeemable

redimir *vt* to ransom; redeem, buy back; pay off (a mortgage, etc.); deliver, free; *ecc* redeem

reditar *vt* to reprint, reissue

rédito *m*, *com* income, revenue, interest, profit

redoblamiento *m*, redoubling; bending back (of nails, etc.); rolling (of a drum)

redoblar *vt* to redouble; repeat; bend back (nails, etc.); *vi* roll (a drum)

redoble *m*, doubling, redoubling; repetition; roll (of a drum)

redoma *f*, flask, vial

redomado *a* astute, crafty, sly; complete, perfect

redonda *f*, district; pasture ground; *naut* square sail; *mus* semibreve. **a la r.**, around

redondear *vt* to make round; round; free (from debt, etc.); *vr* acquire a fortune; clear oneself (of debts, etc.)

redondel *m*, traffic circle, rotary, roundabout

redondez *f*, roundness

redondo *a* round; circular; unequivocal, plain. *m*, round, circle; *inf* cash

reducción *f*, reduction; *mil* defeat, conquest; decrease; *com* rebate; (*math chem*) reduction

reducible *a* reducible

reducir *vt irr* to reduce; decrease, cut down; break up; *art* scale down; *elec* step down; subdue; (*chem math surg*) reduce; exchange; divide into small fragments; persuade; *vr* be obliged to, have to; live moderately. See **conducir**

reducto *m*, *mil* redoubt (of fortifications)

redundancia *f*, redundance

redundante *a* redundant

redundar *vi* to overflow; be excessive or superfluous; (*with en*) redound to

reduplicación *f*, reduplication

reduplicar *vt* to reduplicate

ree For words so beginning (e.g. *reeditar, reexportar*), see spellings with one **e**

refacción *f*, refection, light meal; compensation, reparation

refajo *m*, skirt, underskirt

refección *f*, refection, light meal

refectorio *m*, refectory

referencia *f*, report, account; allusion; regard, relation; *com* reference (gen. *pl*); consideration

referente *a* concerning, related (to)

referir *vt irr* to narrate; describe; direct, guide; relate, refer, concern; *vr* allude (to); refer (to); concern. See **sentir**

refinación *f*, refining

refinado *a* refined; polished, cultured; crafty

refinador *m*, refiner

refinamiento *m*, refinement, subtlety, care

refinar *vt* to refine, purify; polish, perfect

refinería *f*, refinery

reflector *a* reflecting. *m*, reflector; searchlight; shade (for lamps, etc.)

reflejar *vi phys* to reflect; *vt* consider; show, mirror; *vr fig* be reflected, be seen

reflejo *m*, reflection; image; glare. *a* reflex; considered, judicious

reflexión *f*, *phys* reflection; consideration, thought

reflexionar *vt* (*with en or sobre*) to consider, reflect upon

reflexivo *a phys* reflective; thoughtful

reflorecer *vi irr* to flower again; return to favor (ideas, etc.). See **conocer**

reflujo *m*, reflux, refluence; ebb tide

refocilar *vt* to warm up, brace up; give pleasure to; *vr* enjoy oneself

reforma *f*, reform; improvement; reformation; *hist* Reformation

reformación *f*, reform, improvement

reformador (-ra) *a* reformatory, reforming. *n* reformer

reformar *vt* to remake; reshape; repair, mend, restore; improve, correct; *ecc* reform; reorganize; *vr* mend one's ways, improve; control oneself

reformatorio *m*, reformatory. *a* reforming, reformatory

reformista *mf* reformist, reformer. *a* reformatory

reforzador *m*, *phot* reinforcing bath; *elec* booster

reforzamiento *m*, stiffening, reinforcing

reforzar *vt irr* to reinforce, strengthen, stiffen; encourage, inspirit. See **forzar**

refractar *vt* to refract

refractario *a* stubborn; (*phys chem*) refractory; unmanageable, unruly; fireproof

refrán *m*, proverb

refranero *m*, collection of proverbs

refregamiento *m*, rubbing; scrubbing, scouring

refregar *vt irr* to rub; scrub, scour; *fig inf* rub in, insist on. See **cegar**

refrenamiento *m*, curbing; control, restraint

refrenar *vt* to curb, check (horses); control, restrain

refrendar *vt* to countersign, endorse, legalize

refrescante *a* refreshing, cooling

refrescar *vt* to cool, chill; repeat; *fig* brush up, revise; *vi* be rested or refreshed; grow cooler; take the air; freshen (wind); take a cool drink; *vr* grow cooler; take the air; take a cool drink

refresco *m*, refreshment; cool drink
refriega *f*, affray, scuffle, rough-and-tumble
refrigeración *f*, refrigeration
refrigerador *m*, refrigerator
refrigerante *a* refrigerative; chilling; cooling. *m*, cooling chamber, cooler
refrigerar *vt* to chill; cool; freeze, refrigerate; refresh
refrigerio *m*, coolness; consolation; refreshment, food
refringente *a phys* refringent
refuerzo *m*, reinforcement, strengthening; aid, help
refugiado (-da) *a* and *n* refugee
refugiar *vt* to protect, shelter; *vr* take refuge
refugio *m*, refuge, shelter, protection; traffic island. **r. antiaéreo,** air raid shelter. **r. para peatones,** traffic island
refulgencia *f*, resplendence, splendor, brilliance
refulgente *a* resplendent, refulgent, dazzling
refulgir *vi* to shine, be dazzling
refundición *f*, recasting (of metals); adaptation; rehash, refurbishing
refundir *vt* to recast (metals); include, comprise; adapt; rehash, refurbish; *vi fig* promote, contribute to
refunfuñador *a* grumbling, fuming
refunfuñar *vi* to grumble, growl, fume
refunfuño *m*, grumble, fuming; snort
refutable *a* refutable
refutación *f*, refutation
refutar *vt* to refute
regadera *f*, watering can; irrigation canal; sprinkler
regadío *m*, irrigated land; irrigation, watering. *a* irrigated
regajal, regajo *m*, pool, puddle; stream, brook
regalado *a* delicate, highly bred; luxurious, delightful
regalar *vt* to make a gift of, give; caress, fondle; indulge, cherish; entertain, regale; *vr* live in luxury
regalía *f*, royal privilege; right, exemption; perquisite, emolument
regalismo *m*, regalism
regalista *a* and *mf* regalist
regaliz *m*, **regaliza** *f*, licorice
regalo *m*, gift, present; satisfaction, pleasure; entertainment, regalement; luxury, comfort
regalón *a inf* pampered
regañadientes, a *adv* unwillingly, grumblingly
regañar *vi* to snarl (dogs); crack (skin of fruits); grumble, mutter; *inf* quarrel; *vt inf* scold
regaño *m*, angry look or gesture; *inf* scolding
regañón (-ona) *a inf* grumbling, complaining; scolding. *n inf* grumbler
regar *vt irr* to water, sprinkle with water; flow through, irrigate; spray; *fig* shower (with), strew. See **cegar**
regata *f*, regatta; small irrigation channel (for gardens, etc.)
regate *m*, twist of the body, sidestep; dribbling; (in soccer); *inf* dodging, evasion
regatear *vt* to haggle over, beat down (prices); resell, retail; dribble (a ball); *fig inf* dodge, avoid; *vi* bargain, haggle; *naut* take part in a regatta, race
regateo *m*, haggling, bargaining
regatero (-ra) *a* retail. *n* retailer
regatón (-ona) *m*, ferrule, tip. *a* haggling, bargaining. *n* haggler; retailer
regatonear *vt* to resell at retail
regazo *m*, lap, knees; *fig* heart, bosom
regencia *f*, regency
regeneración *f*, regeneration
regenerador (-ra) *n* regenerator. *a* regenerative, reforming
regenerar *vt* to regenerate, reform
regenta *f*, wife of the president of a court of session
regentar *vt* to fill temporarily (offices); rule, govern; manage, run (businesses)
regente *a* ruling. *mf* regent. *m*, president of a court of session; manager
regicida *mf* regicide (person)
regicidio *m*, regicide (act)

regidor *a* ruling, governing. *m*, magistrate, alderman
régimen *m*, administration, management; regime; (*med gram*) regimen; *mech* rating
regimentación *f*, regimentation
regimentar *vt irr* to form into regiments; regiment. *Pres. Ind.* **regimento, regimientas, regimienta, regimientan.** *Pres. Subjunc.* **regimiente, regimientes, regimiente, regimienten**
regimiento *m*, *mil* regiment; administration, rule
regio *a* royal; magnificent, regal
región *f*, region, country; area, tract, space. **r. industrial,** industrial area
regionalismo *m*, regionalism
regionalista *mf* regionalist. *a* regional
regir *vt irr* to govern, rule; administer, conduct; *gram* govern; *vi* be in force (laws, etc.); work, function; *naut* obey the helm. See **pedir**
registrador *a* recording. *m*, registrar, keeper of records; recorder. **caja (registradora),** (cash) register
registrar *vt* to examine, inspect; search; copy, record; mark the place (in a book); observe, note; (of thermometers, etc.) record, show; look on to (houses, etc.); *vr* register (hotels, etc.)
registro *m*, search; registration, entry; record; recording; reading (of a thermometer, etc.); *mech* damper; registry; register (book); *mus* range, compass (voice); *mus* register (organ); (*mech print*) register; bookmark. **r. civil,** register of births, marriages, and deaths
regla *f*, ruler, measuring stick; rule, principle, guide; precept; system, policy; *med* period; moderation; method, order. **r. de cálculo,** slide rule. **r. T,** T-square. **en r.,** in due form. **por r.,** general, generally, as a rule
reglamentación *f*, regulation; rules and regulations
reglamentar *vt* to regulate
reglamento *m*, bylaw; regulation, ordinance
reglar *vt* to rule (lines); regulate; govern; control; *vr* restrain oneself, mend one's ways
regocijado *a* merry, joyful, happy
regocijar *vt* to cheer, delight; *vr* enjoy oneself, rejoice
regocijo *m*, happiness, joy; cheer, merriment
regordete *a inf* chubby
regresar *vi* to return
regresión *f*, return; retrogression; regression
regreso *m*, return
reguera *f*, irrigation channel, ditch
reguero *m*, trickle
regulación *f*, regulation; *mech* control, timing
regulador *m*, *mech* governor, regulator. *a* regulating, controlling
regular *vt* to adjust, regulate; *mech* govern. *a* methodical, ordered; moderate; average, medium; (*ecc mil geom gram*) regular; so-so, not bad; probable. **por lo r.,** generally
regularidad *f*, regularity
regularización *f*, regularization; regulation
regularizar *vt* to regularize; regulate
regurgitar *vi* to regurgitate
rehabilitación *f*, rehabilitation
rehabilitar *vt* to rehabilitate; *vr* rehabilitate oneself
rehacer *vt irr* to remake; repair, mend; *vr* recover one's strength; control one's emotions; *mil* rally. See **hacer**
rehén *m*, hostage (gen. *pl*); *mil* pledge, security
rehenchir *vt irr* to restuff; refill, recharge. See **henchir**
reherir *vt irr* to repulse. See **herir**
rehilar *vt* to spin too much or twist the yarn; *vi* totter, stagger; whizz (arrows, etc.)
rehuir *vt irr* to withdraw; avoid; reject. See **huir**
rehusar *vt* to refuse, reject. See **desahuciar**
reimponer *vt irr* to reimpose. See **poner**
reimportación *f*, reimportation
reimpresión *f*, reprint
reimprimir *vt* to reprint
reina *f*, queen; queen (in chess); queen bee; peerless beauty, belle
reinado *m*, reign; heyday, fashion
reinante *a* reigning; prevalent

reinar *vi* to reign; influence; endure, prevail

reincidencia *f*, relapse (into crime, etc.), recidivism

reincidente *mf* backslider

reincidir *vi* to relapse (into crime, etc.)

reincorporar *vt* to reincorporate; *vr* join again, become a member again

reingresar *vi* to reenter

reingreso *m*, reentry

reino *m*, kingdom

reinstalación *f*, reinstatement

reinstalar *vt* to reinstate; *vr* be reinstalled

reintegración *f*, reintegration

reintegrar *vt* to reintegrate; *vr* be reinstated, recuperate, recover

reir *vi irr* to laugh; sneer, jeer; *fig* smile (nature); *vt* laugh at; *vr inf* (*with de*) scorn. **reírse a carcajadas,** to shout with laughter. *Pres. Part.* **riendo.** *Pres. Ind.* **río, ríes, ríe, ríen.** *Preterite* **rió, rieron.** *Pres. Subjunc.* **ría,** etc. *Imperf. Subjunc.* **riese,** etc.

reiteración *f*, reiteration, repetition

reiteradamente *adv* repeatedly, reiteratively

reiterar *vt* to reiterate, repeat

reiterativo *a* reiterative

reivindicación *f*, *law* recovery

reivindicar *vt law* to recover

reja *f*, colter, plowshare; plowing, tilling; grating, grille

rejado *m*, railing, grating

rejilla *f*, grating; grille, lattice; luggage rack (in a train); cane (for chairs, seats, etc.); wire mesh; small brazier; *elec* grid; *mech* grate

rejuntar *vt* to point (a wall)

rejuvenecer *vt irr* to rejuvenate; *fig* revive; bring up to date; *vi* and *vr* be rejuvenated, grow young again, rejuvenesce. See **conocer**

rejuvenecimiento *m*, rejuvenation

relación *f*, relation; connection (of ideas); report, statement; narrative, account; *math* ratio; *law* brief; intercourse, association, dealings (gen. *pl*); list; analogy, relation. **tener relaciones con,** to have dealings with; be engaged or betrothed to; woo, court

relacionar *vt* to recount, narrate, report; connect, relate; *vr* be connected

relajación *f*, relaxation; recreation; laxity, dissoluteness

relajar *vt* to relax; recreate, amuse; make less rigorous; *law* remit; *vr* become relaxed; be dissolute, lax, or vicious

relamer *vt* to lick again; *vr* lick one's lips; *fig* overpaint, make up too much; ooze satisfaction, brag

relamido *a* overdressed; affected

relámpago *m*, lightning; flash, gleam; streak of lightning (of quick persons or things); flash of wit, witticism

relampaguear *vi* to lighten (of lightning); flash, gleam

relapso *a* relapsed, lapsed (into error, vice)

relatar *vt* to relate, narrate, report

relatividad *f*, relativeness; *phys* relativity

relativo *a* relevant, pertinent; relative, comparative; *gram* relative

relato *m*, narration, account, report

relator (**-ra**) *a* narrating. *n* narrator. *m*, *law* reporter

relavar *vt* to rewash, wash again

relección *f*, reelection

releer *vt irr* to reread; revise. See **creer**

relegación *f*, relegation

relegar *vt* to banish; relegate, set aside

relegir *vt irr* to reelect. See **elegir**

relente *m*, night dew, dampness; *inf* cheek, impudence

relevación *f*, *art* relief; release; remission, exemption

relevar *vt art* to work in relief; emboss; relieve, free; dismiss; excuse, pardon; aid, succor; *fig* aggrandize; *mil* relieve; *vi* carve in relief

relevo *m*, relay; *mil* relief

relicario *m*, reliquary

relieve *m*, *art* relief; *pl* leftovers, remains (of food). **alto r.,** high relief. **bajo r.,** low relief

religar *vt* to retie, fasten again; fasten more securely; solder

religión *f*, religion; creed, faith, philosophy; devotion, religious practice. **r. reformada,** Protestantism. **entrar en r.,** *ecc* to profess

religionario *m*, Protestant

religiosidad *f*, religiosity; religiousness; conscientiousness, punctiliousness

religioso (**-sa**) *a* religious; punctilious, conscientious; moderate. *n* religious

relinchar *vi* to whinny, neigh

relincho *m*, neigh, whinny

reliquia *f*, residue (gen. *pl*); *ecc* relic; vestige, remnant, memento; permanent disability or ailment

rellanar *vt* to make level again; *vr* stretch oneself at full length

rellano *m*, landing (of a staircase); level stretch (of ground)

rellenar *vt* to refill, replenish; fill up; *mas* plug, point; *cul* stuff; *inf* cram with food (gen. *vr*)

relleno *m*, *cul* stuffing; replenishing; filling; *fig* padding (of speeches, etc.)

reloj *m*, clock; watch. **r. de arena,** hourglass. **r. de bolsillo,** watch. **r. de la muerte,** deathwatch beetle. **r. de péndulo,** grandfather clock. **r. de pulsera,** wristwatch. **r. de repetición,** repeater. **r. de sol** or **r. solar,** sundial

relojera *f*, clock stand; watch case

relojería *f*, watch or clock making; jeweler, watch maker's shop

relojero (**-ra**) *n* watch maker, watch repairer

reluciente *a* shining, sparkling; shiny

relucir *vi irr* to glitter, sparkle, gleam; *fig* shine, excel. See **lucir**

reluctante *a* unruly, refractory, disobedient

relumbrante *a* resplendent, dazzling

relumbrar *vi* to be resplendent, shine, glitter

remachar *vt* to rivet; *fig* clinch

remache *m*, riveting; rivet

remanente *m*, remains, residue

remanso *m*, backwater; stagnant water; sloth, dilatoriness

remar *vi* to row, paddle, scull; toil, strive

rematadamente *adv* completely, entirely, absolutely

rematado *a* beyond hope, extremely ill; utterly lost; *law* convicted

rematar *vt* to end, finish; finish off, kill; knock down at auction; *sew* finish; *vi* end; *vr* be ruined or spoiled

remate *m*, end, conclusion; extremity; *arch* coping; *arch* terminal; highest bid; auction. **de r.,** utterly hopeless

rembarcar *vt* to reembark, reship

rembarque *m*, reembarkation, reshipment

rembolsable *a* repayable

rembolsar *vt* to recover (money); refund, return (money)

rembolso *m*, repayment. **contra r.,** cash on delivery, C.O.D.

remedar *vt* to copy, imitate; mimic

remediador (**-ra**) *a* remedying. *n* benefactor, helper

remediar *vt* to remedy; aid, help; save from danger; prevent (trouble)

remedio *m*, remedy; emendation, correction; help; refuge, protection; *med* remedy. **No hay más r.,** There's nothing else to do, It's only way open. **no tener más r.,** to be unable to help (doing something), be obliged to

remedo *m*, imitation; poor copy

remembranza *f*, remembrance, memory

rememorar *vt* to remember, recall to mind

remendar *vt irr* to mend, patch; darn; repair; correct. See **recomendar**

remendón (**-ona**) *n* cobbler; mender of old clothes

remero (**-ra**) *n* oarsman, rower; sculler

remesa *f*, remittance; consignment, shipment

remesar(se) *vt* and *vr* to pluck out (hair); *vt com* remit; consign

remiendo *m*, *sew* patch; mend, darn; emendation; *inf* insignia of one of the Spanish military orders. **a remiendos,** *inf* piecemeal

remilgarse *vr* to preen oneself, be overdressed

remilgo *m,* affectation; mannerism; prudery, squeamishness

reminiscencia *f,* reminiscence; memory, recollection

remirado *a* wary, cautious, prudent, circumspect

remirar *vt* to revise, go over again; *vr* take great care over; behold with pleasure

remisión *f,* sending; remission; pardon, forgiveness; foregoing, relinquishment; abatement, diminution; *lit* reference, allusion

remiso *a* timid, spiritless; languid, slow

remitente *mf* sender. *a* sending

remitir *vt* to remit, send; pardon, forgive; defer, postpone; abate, diminish; relinquish, forgo; *lit* refer; *vr* remit, submit, consult; refer (to), cite

remo *m,* oar, scull, paddle; arm or leg (of men or animals, gen. *pl*); wing (gen. *pl*); hard, continuous toil; galleys. **al r.,** by dint of rowing; *inf* struggling with hardships

remojar *vt* to soak, steep; celebrate by drinking

remojo *m,* soaking, steeping

remolacha *f,* beet

remolcador *m, naut* tow, tug. *a naut* towing

remolcar *vt* (*naut aut*) to tow; *fig* press into service, use

remolinar *vi* to spin, whirl, eddy; *vr* throng, swarm

remolino *m,* whirlwind; eddy, swirl; whirlpool; crowd, throng, swarm; disturbance, riot

remolonear *vi inf* to loiter, lag; avoid work; be lax or dilatory

remolque *m,* towage, towing; towline; barge; *aut* trailer. **a r.,** on tow

remonta *f,* resoling (of shoes); leather gusset (of riding breeches); *mil* remount

remontar *vt* to scare off (game); *mil* supply with fresh horses; resole (shoes); *fig* rise to great heights (of oratory, etc.); *vr* soar (of birds); (*with prep a*) date from, go back to; originate in

remoquete *m,* blow with the fist; witticism; *inf* flirtation, courtship

rémora *f, icht* remora; delay, hindrance

remorder *vt irr* to bite again or repeatedly; *fig* gnaw, nag, cause uneasiness or remorse; *vr* show one's feelings. See **morder**

remordimiento *m,* remorse

remotamente *adv* distantly, remotely; unlikely; vaguely, confusedly

remoto *a* distant, remote; unlikely, improbable

remover *vt irr* to remove, move; stir; turn over; dismiss, discharge. See **mover**

remozar *vt* to cause to appear young; freshen up, bring up to date; *vr* look young

remplazar *vt* to replace; exchange, substitute; succeed, take the place of

remplazo *m,* replacement; exchange, substitute; successor; *mil* replacement

remuda *f,* replacement, exchange

remudar *vt* to replace

remuneración *f,* remuneration; reward

remunerador (-ra) *a* remunerative, recompensing. *n* remunerator

remunerar *vt* to recompense, reward

remusgar *vi* to suspect, imagine

renacentista *a* renaissance

renacer *vi irr* to be reborn. See **nacer**

renacimiento *m,* rebirth; Renaissance

renacuajo *m,* tadpole; *mech* frog; *inf* twerp

renano *a* Rhenish

rencarcelar *vt* to reimprison

rencarnación *f,* reincarnation

rencarnar(se) *vi* and *vr* to be reincarnated

rencilla *f,* grudge, grievance, resentment

rencilloso *a* peevish, easily offended, touchy

rencor *m,* rancor, spite, old grudge. **guardar r.,** to bear malice

rencoroso *a* rancorous, malicious, spiteful

rencuadernar *vt* to rebind (books)

rencuentro *m,* collision; *mil* encounter, clash

rendición *f,* surrender; yield, profit

rendido *a* submissive, obsequious

rendija *f,* crevice, cleft, crack, fissure

rendimiento *m,* weariness, fatigue; submissiveness, obsequiousness; yield, profit; *mech* efficiency

rendir *vt irr mil* to cause to surrender; defeat; overcome, conquer; give back, return; yield, provide; tire, exhaust; vomit; pay, render; *vr* be exhausted, be worn out; surrender. *mil* **r. el puesto,** to retire from or give up a post. See **pedir**

renegado (-da) *n* renegade, apostate; turncoat; *inf* malignant person. *a* renegade

renegador (-ra) *n* blasphemer; foul-mouthed person

renegar *vt irr* to deny, disown; loathe, hate; *vi* (*with de*) apostatize; blaspheme; *inf* curse. See **cegar**

renganchar(se) *vt* and *vr mil* to reenlist

renganche *m, mil* reenlistment

renglón *m, print* line; *pl* writing, composition

reniego *m,* blasphemy; *inf* foul language, cursing

renitencia *f,* repugnance

reno *m,* reindeer

renombrado *a* illustrious, famous

renombre *m,* surname; renown, reputation, fame

renovable *a* renewable, replaceable

renovación *f,* replacement; renewal; renovation; transformation, reform

renovador (-ra) *n* reformer; renovator. *a* renovating; reforming

renovar *vt irr* to renew; renovate; replace; exchange; reiterate, repeat. See **contar**

renta *f,* yield, profit; income; revenue; government securities; rent; tax

rentar *vt* to yield, produce an income

rentero (-ra) *n* tenant farmer. *m,* one who farms out land

rentista *mf* financier; bondholder; person who lives on a private income, rentier

rentístico *a* revenue, financial

renuente *a* refractory, willful

renuevo *m, bot* shoot; renewal

renuncia, renunciación *f,* renunciation; resignation; abandonment, relinquishment

renunciar *vt* to renounce; refuse; scorn; abandon, relinquish; resign; revoke (at cards). **r. a,** to give up

renuncio *m,* revoke (cards); *inf* falsehood

reñidamente *adv* strongly, stubbornly, fiercely

reñir *vi irr* to quarrel, dispute; fight; be on bad terms, fall out; *vt* scold; fight (battles, etc.). See **ceñir**

reo *mf* criminal; offender, guilty party; *law* defendant

reojo *m,* (**mirar de**) to look out of the corner of the eye; *fig* look askance

reorganizador (-ra) *a* reorganizing. *n* reorganizer

reorganizar *vt* to reorganize

reóstato *m,* rheostat

repantigarse *vr* to stretch out one's legs, make oneself comfortable

reparable *a* remediable, reparable; worthy of note

reparación *f,* repair, mending; reparation, satisfaction; indemnity, compensation

reparada *f,* shying (of horses)

reparador *a* repairing, mending; faultfinding; restoring; satisfying, compensating

reparar *vt* to repair; restore; consider; correct, remedy; atone for, expiate; indemnify; hold up, detain; protect, guard; (*with en*) notice; *vi* halt, be detained; *vr* control oneself

reparo *m,* repair; restoration; remedy; note, reflection; warning; doubt, scruple; guard, protection; parry (at fencing)

repartición *f,* distribution

repartidero *a* distributable

repartidor (-ra) *a* distributing. *n* distributor; tax assessor

repartimiento *m*, distribution, allotment; assessment

repartir *vt* to distribute; share out; allot; deal (cards); assess; *com* deliver

reparto *m*, distribution; assessment; delivery (of letters, etc.); *theat* cast; deal (at cards)

repasar *vt* to pass by again; peruse, reexamine; brush up, revise; skim, glance over; mend, repair (garments); edit, revise; hone

repaso *m*, second passage through; reexamination, perusal; revision, editing; brushing up, revision; repair, mending; *inf* dressing-down, scolding

repatriación *f*, repatriation

repatriado (-da) *n* repatriate

repatriar *vt* to repatriate; *vi* and *vr* return to one's own country

repecho *m*, steep slope. **a r.,** uphill

repelar *vt* to pull by the hair; put through its paces (of a horse); clip, cut; remove, diminish

repeler *vt* to repel, throw back; reject, refute

repelo *m*, anything against the grain; *inf* skirmish; reluctance, repugnance

repente *m*, *inf* sudden or unexpected movement. **de r.,** suddenly

repentino *a* sudden, unexpected

repentizar *vi* *mus* to sight-read

repercusión *f*, repercussion; vibration

repercutir *vi* to recoil, rebound; *vr* reverberate; reecho; *fig* have repercussions; *vt med* repel

repertorio *m*, repertory

repesar *vt* to reweigh, weigh again

repetición *f*, repetition; *art* replica, copy; repeater (in clocks); recital

repetidamente *adv* repeatedly

repetidor *a* repeating

repetir *vt irr* to repeat, do over again; reiterate; *art* copy, make a replica of; recite. See **pedir**

repicar *vt* to chop, mince; peal (of bells); prick again; *vr* pride oneself (on), boast

repique *m*, chopping, mincing; peal, pealing (of bells); disagreement, grievance

repisa *f*, *arch* bracket; ledge; shelf. **r. de chimenea,** mantelpiece

replantar *vt* to replant; transplant

repleción *f*, repletion, satiety

replegar *vt irr* to refold, fold many times; *vr mil* retreat in good order. See **cegar**

repleto *a* replete

réplica *f*, reply, answer; replica

replicar *vi* to contradict, dispute; answer, reply. **¡No me repliques!** *inf* Don't answer back!

repliegue *m*, double fold, crease; doubling, folding; *mil* withdrawal

repoblación *f*, repeopling, repopulation

repoblar *vt* to repeople, repopulate

repollo *m*, white cabbage; heart (of lettuce, etc.)

reponer *vt irr* to replace; reinstate; restore; reply; *vr* recover, regain (possessions); grow well again; grow calm. See **poner**

reportación *f*, serenity, moderation

reportaje *m*, journalistic report

reportar *vt* to restrain, moderate; achieve, obtain; carry; bring; *vr* control oneself

reporte *m*, report, news; rumor

reporterismo *m*, newspaper reporting

reportero (-ra) *a* news, report. *n* reporter

reposado *a* quiet, peaceful, tranquil

reposar *vi* to rest, repose oneself; sleep, doze; lie in the grave; settle (liquids); rest (on)

reposición *f*, replacement; restoration; renewal; recovery (of health); *theat* revival

repositorio *m*, repository

reposo *m*, rest, repose; peace, tranquility; sleep

repostería *f*, confectioner's shop; pantry; butler's pantry

repostero *m*, confectioner, pastry cook

repregunta *f*, cross-examination

repreguntar *vt* to cross-examine

reprender *vt* to scold, reprimand, rebuke

reprensible *a* reprehensible, censurable

reprensión *f*, scolding, reprimand, rebuke

represa *f*, damming, holding back (water); dam, lock; restraining, controlling

represalia *f*, reprisal (gen. *pl*); retaliation

represar *vt* to dam, harness (water); *naut* retake, recapture; *fig* restrain, control

representación *f*, representation; *theat* performance; authority; dignity; *com* agency; portrait, image; depiction, expression; petition

representador *a* representative

representante *a* representative. *mf* representative; actor; performer

representar *vt* to represent; *theat* perform; depict, express; describe, portray; *vr* imagine, picture to oneself

representativo *a* representative

represión *f*, repression; recapture

represivo *a* repressive

reprimenda *f*, rebuke, reprimand

reprimir *vt* to repress, restrain, control; *vr* restrain oneself

reprobación *f*, censure; reprobation

reprobar *vt irr* to reprove; censure; fail (in an exam). See **probar**

réprobo (-ba) *n* reprobate

reprochar *vt* to reproach

reproche *m*, reproaching; rebuke, reproach

reproducción *f*, reproduction. **r. a gran escala,** large-scale model

reproducir *vt irr* to reproduce. See **conducir**

reproductor (-ra) *a* reproductive. *n* breeding animal

reps *m*, rep (fabric)

reptil *a* reptilian; crawling. *m*, reptile

república *f*, republic; state, commonwealth. **la r. de las letras,** the republic of letters

República Dominicana Dominican Republic

República Malgache Republic of Madagascar

republicanismo *m*, republicanism

republicano (-na) *a* and *n* republican

repudiación *f*, repudiation

repudiar *vt* to cast off (a wife); repudiate, renounce

repuesto *a* retired, hidden. *m*, stock, provision; serving table; pantry; stake (at cards, etc.). **de r.,** spare, extra

repugnancia *f*, inconsistency, contradiction; aversion, dislike; reluctance; repugnance

repugnante *a* repugnant, loathsome

repugnar *vt* to contradict, be inconsistent with; hate, be averse to (e.g. **La idea me repugna,** I hate the idea)

repujado *m*, repoussé work

repujar *vt* to work in repoussé

repulir *vt* to repolish, reburnish; *vt* and *vr* make up too much, overdress

repulsa *f*, snub, rebuff; rejection; repulse

repulsar *vt* to decline, reject; repulse; deny, refuse; rebuff

repulsión *f*, repulsion; rebuff; aversion, dislike

repulsivo *a* repellent

repunta *f*, headland, cape; *fig* first sign; *inf* disgust; caprice; fight

reputación *f*, reputation

reputar *vt* to believe, consider (e.g. **Le reputo por honrado,** I believe him to be an honorable man); appreciate, esteem

requebrar *vt irr* to break into smaller pieces; make love to, woo; compliment, flatter. See **quebrar**

requemado *a* sunburned; brown

requemar *vt* to burn again; overcook; dry up, parch (of plants, etc.); burn (the mouth) (of spicy foods, etc.); *vr fig* suffer inwardly

requerimiento *m*, requirement, demand; *law* summons

requerir *vt irr* to inform, notify; examine; need, necessitate; require; summon; woo; persuade. See **sentir**

requesón *m*, cream cheese; curd

requetebién *adv inf* exceedingly well

requiebro *m,* compliment, expression of love; wooing, flirtation

requisa *f,* inspection, visitation; *mil* requisitioning

requisar *vt mil* to requisition

requisito *m,* requisite

res *f,* animal, beast; head of cattle

resabiar *vt* to make vicious, cause bad habits; *vr* contract bad habits or vices; be discontented; relish

resabio *m,* disagreeable aftertaste; bad habit, vice

resaca *f,* surf, undertow, surge; *com* redraft

resalado *a inf* very witty; most attractive

resaltar *vi* to rebound; project, jut out; grow loose, fall out; *fig* stand out, be prominent

resalto *m,* rebound; projection

resarcir *vt* to compensate, indemnify

resbaladizo *a* slippery; difficult, delicate (of a situation)

resbalar *vi* to slip; slide; skid; err, fall into sin

resbalón *m,* slip; slide; skid; temptation, error

rescatador (-ra) *n* ransomer; rescuer

rescatar *vt* to ransom; redeem, buy back; barter; free, rescue; *fig* redeem (time, etc.)

rescate *m,* ransom; redemption; barter; amount of ransom

rescindir *vt* to annul, repeal, rescind

rescisión *f,* annulment, abrogation

rescoldo *m,* ember, cinder; scruple, qualm, doubt

resentimiento *m,* deterioration, impairment; animosity, resentment

resentirse *vr irr* to deteriorate, be impaired; be hurt or offended. See **sentir**

reseña *f, mil* review; short description; review (of a book)

reseñar *vt mil* to review; describe briefly, outline

reserva *f,* store, stock; exception, qualification; reticence; restraint, moderation; (*ecc law*) reservation; (*mil naut*) reserve. **sin r.,** frankly, without reserve

reservación *f,* reservation; scruple

reservado *a* reserved, reticent; prudent, moderate; kept, reserved. *m,* reserved compartment; private apartment, private garden, etc.

reservar *vt* to keep, hold; postpone; reserve (rooms, etc.); exempt; keep secret; withhold (information); *ecc* reserve; *vr* await a better opportunity; be cautious

reservista *a* (*mil nav*) reserved. *mf* reservist

resfriado *m, med* cold, chill

resfriar *vt* to chill; *fig* cool, moderate; *vi* grow cold; *vr* catch a cold; *fig* cool off (of love, etc.)

resguardar *vt* to protect; shelter; *vr* take refuge; (*with de*) guard against; (*with con*) shelter by

resguardo *m,* protection, guard; *com* guarantee, security; *com* voucher; preservation; vigilance (to prevent smuggling, etc.); contraband guards

residencia *f,* stay, residence; home, domicile; *ecc* residence

residencial *a* residential; resident, residentiary

residente *a* resident. *mf* inhabitant. *m,* resident, minister resident (diplomatic)

residir *vi* to live, inhabit; reside officially; be found, be, exist

residuo *m,* residuum, remainder; *math* remainder; *chem* residue

resignación *f,* resignation; fortitude, submission

resignar *vt* to resign, relinquish; *vr* submit, resign oneself

resina *f,* resin

resinoso *a* resinous

resistencia *f,* resistance, opposition; endurance; (*phys mech psy*) resistance

resistente *a* resistant; tough; hardy (of plants)

resistir *vi* to resist, oppose; reject; *vt* endure, bear; resist; *vr* fight, resist

resma *f,* ream (of paper)

resolución *f,* decision; boldness, daring; determination; resolution; decree

resoluto *a* resolute, bold; brief, concise; able, expert

resolver *vt irr* to determine, decide; summarize; solve; dissolve; analyze; (*phys med*) resolve; *vr* decide, determine; be reduced to, become; *med* resolve. *Pres. Ind.* re-**suelvo, resuelves, resuelve, resuelven.** *Past Part.* **resuelto.** *Pres. Subjunc.* **resuelva, resuelvas, resuelva, resuelvan**

resollar *vi irr* to breathe; pant. See **degollar**

resonancia *f,* resonance, sonority, ring; fame, reputation

resonante *a* resonant; resounding

resonar *vi irr* to resound, echo. See **tronar**

resoplido, resoplo *m,* heavy breathing, pant, snort

resorber *vt* to reabsorb

resorción *f,* reabsorption

resorte *m, mech* spring; elasticity; *fig* means, instrument

respaldo *m,* back (of chairs, etc.); reverse side (of a piece of paper)

respectivo *a* respective

respecto *m,* relation, regard, reference. **con r. a,** *or* **r. a,** with regard to, with respect to, concerning

respetabilidad *f,* respectability; worthiness

respetable *a* worthy of respect; respectable; *fig* considerable, large

respetar *vt* to respect, revere

respeto *m,* respect, honor; consideration, reason. **de r.,** spare, extra; special, ceremonial

respetuoso *a* venerable, worthy of honor; respectful, courteous

respingar *vi* to flinch, wince, kick; *inf* be uneven, rise (hem of garments); *inf* do (a thing) grumblingly

respingo *m,* wincing; jerk, shake; *inf* gesture of reluctance or dislike

respirable *a* breathable

respiración *f,* breathing, respiration; ventilation

respiradero *m,* ventilator; air hole, vent; rest, breathing space

respirador *a* breathing; respiratory. *m,* respirator

respirar *vi* to breathe; exhale, give off; take courage; have a breathing space, rest; *inf* speak. **sin r.,** continuously, without stopping for breath

respiratorio *a* respiratory

respiro *m,* breathing; breathing space, respite

resplandecer *vi irr* to glitter, gleam; shine, excel. See **conocer**

resplandeciente *a* glittering, resplendent, shining

resplandor *m,* radiance, brilliance; glitter, gleam; majesty, splendor

responder *vt* to reply; satisfy, answer; *vi* reecho; requite, return; produce, provide; *fig* answer, have the desired effect; *com* (*with de*) answer for, guarantee; *com* correspond

respondón *a inf* pert, impudent, cheeky, given to answering back

responsabilidad *f,* responsibility

responsable *a* responsible

responso *m, ecc* response, responsory

respuesta *f,* answer, reply; response; refutation; repartee

resquebradura *f,* fissure, crevice, crack

resquebrajarse *vr* to crack, split

resquemar *vt* to bite, sting (of hot dishes)

resquicio *m,* crack, chink, slit; opportunity

resta *f, math* subtraction; *math* remainder

restablecer *vt irr* to reestablish; restore; *vr* recover one's health; reestablish oneself. See **conocer**

restablecimiento *m,* reestablishment; restoration

restañar *vt* to re-tin; staunch

restar *vt math* to subtract; deduct; return (a ball); *vi* remain. **No me resta más que decir adiós,** It only remains for me to say good-by

restauración *f,* restoration; renovation

restaurador (-ra) *a* restorative. *n* restorer

restaurante *m,* restaurant

restaurantero *m,* restaurant operator; restaurant owner; restaurateur

restaurar *vt* to recover, recuperate; renovate, repair; restore

restaurativo *a* and *m*, restorative
restinga *f*, sandbank, bar
restitución *f*, restitution
restituible *a* returnable, replaceable
restituir *vt irr* to return, give back; restore; reestablish; *vr* return to one's place of departure. See **huir**
restorán *m*, restaurant
resto *m*, rest, balance; *math* remainder; *pl* remains
restricción *f*, limitation, restriction
restrictivo *a* restrictive; restraining
restringir *vt* to limit, restrict; contract
resucitar *vt* to raise from the dead; *fig inf* revive; *vi* resuscitate
resuelto *a* audacious, daring; resolute, capable
resuello *m*, breathing; panting, hard breathing
resulta *f*, consequence, result; decision, resolution; vacant post. **de resultas de,** as the result of; in consequence of
resultado *m*, result, consequence, outcome
resultante *a* resulting. *f*, *mech* resultant
resultar *vi* to result, follow; turn out, happen; result (in); *inf* turn out well. **El vestido no me resulta,** The dress isn't a success on me
resumen *m*, summary. **en r.,** in short
resumir *vt* to summarize, abridge; sum up, recapitulate; *vr* be contained, be included
resurgimiento *m*, resurgence, revival
resurgir *vi* to reappear, rise again, revive; resuscitate
resurrección *f*, resurrection
resurtir *vi* to rebound
retablo *m*, *arch* altarpiece, retable; frieze; series of pictures
retaguardia *f*, rear guard. **a r.,** in the rear. **picar la r.,** to harass the rear guard
retajar *vt* to cut in the round; circumcise
retal *m*, clipping, filing, shaving; remnant
retama *f*, *bot* broom. **r. común** *or* **r. de olor,** Spanish broom. **r. de escobas,** common broom
retar *vt* to challenge; *inf* reproach, accuse
retardación *f*, retardment
retardar *vt* to retard, delay
retardo *m*, delay, retardment
retazo *m*, remnant, cutting; excerpt, fragment
retemblar *vi* to quiver, tremble constantly
retén *m*, stock, reserve, provision; *mil* reserve
retención *f*, retention
retener *vt irr* to keep, retain; recollect, remember; keep back; *law* detain; deduct. See **tener**
retenidamente *adv* retentively
retentiva *f*, retentiveness, memory
retentivo *a* retentive
reticencia *f*, reticence
reticente *a* reticent
retículo *m*, reticulum, network; *phys* reticle
retina *f*, retina
retintín *m*, ringing; tinkling; *inf* sarcastic tone
retiñir *vi* to tinkle, clink; jingle
retirada *f*, withdrawal; retirement; seclusion, refuge; *mil* retreat
retirado *a* remote, secluded; *mil* retired
retirar *vt* to withdraw; remove; repel, throw back; hide, put aside; *vr* withdraw; retire; *mil* retreat
retiro *m*, withdrawal; removal; seclusion, privacy; *mil* retreat; retirement; *ecc* retreat. **dar el r. (a),** to place on the retired list
reto *m*, challenge; threat
retocar *vt* to touch again or repeatedly; *phot* retouch; restore (pictures); *fig* put the finishing touch to
retoñar *vi* to sprout, shoot; *fig* revive, resuscitate
retoño *m*, sprout, shoot
retoque *m*, frequent touching; finishing touch; touch, slight attack
retorcer *vt irr* to twist; contort; confound with one's own argument; misconstrue, distort; *vr* contort; writhe. See **torcer**
retórica *f*, rhetoric; *pl inf* quibbling

retórico (-ca) *a* rhetorical. *n* rhetorician
retornar *vt* to return, give back; turn, twist; turn back; *vi* and *vr* return, go back
retorno *m*, return, going back; recompense, repayment; exchange; return journey
retorsión *f*, twisting, writhing; *fig* misconstruction
retorta *f*, *chem* retort
retortijón *m*, twisting, curling. **r. de tripas,** stomachache
retozar *vi* to skip, frisk, frolic, gambol; romp; *fig* be aroused (passions)
retozón *a* frolicsome
retracción *f*, drawing back, retraction
retractación *f*, retractation, recantation
retractar *vt* to retract, recant, withdraw
retráctil *a* retractile
retraer *vt irr* to bring back again; dissuade; buy back, redeem; *vr* take refuge; retire; withdraw; go into seclusion. See **traer**
retraído *a* fugitive, refugee; retired, solitary; timid, nervous, unsociable
retraimiento *m*, withdrawal; seclusion, privacy; refuge, asylum, sanctuary; timidity, unsociability
retrasar *vt* to postpone, delay; turn back (the clock); *vi* be slow (of clocks); *vr* be behind time, be late; be backward (persons)
retraso *m*, lateness; delay, dilatoriness; loss of time (clocks); setting back (of the clock) (e.g. **El reloj lleva cinco minutos de r.,** The clock is five minutes slow)
retratar *vt* to paint or draw the portrait of; portray, describe; photograph; copy, imitate
retratista *mf* portrait painter; photographer; portrayer
retrato *m*, portrait; portrayal; *fig* image, likeness
retrechería *f*, *inf* craftiness, evasiveness
retreta *f*, *mil* retreat; tattoo
retrete *m*, toilet, water closet
retribución *f*, recompense, reward
retribuir *vt irr* to recompense, reward. See **huir**
retroactivo *a* retroactive
retroceder *vi* to withdraw, move back, draw back; recede
retroceso *m*, retrocedence, withdrawal; *med* retrogression
retrogradación *f*, retrogression
retrógrado *a* retrogressive, retrograde; *pol* reactionary
retronar *vi irr* to bang, thunder, resound with noise. See **tronar**
retrospección *f*, retrospection
retrospectivo *a* retrospective
retrotraer *vt irr* to antedate. See **traer**
retruécano *m*, antithesis; play on words, pun
retumbante *a* resounding; pompous, high-flown
retumbar *vi* to resound, echo, reverberate; roll (of thunder); roar (of a cannon)
retumbo *m*, reverberation, echo; rumble; roll (of thunder); roar (of a cannon, etc.)
reuma *m*, rheumatism
reumático *a* rheumatic
reumatismo *m*, rheumatism
reunión *f*, reunion, union; meeting; assembly, gathering
reunir *vt* to reunite; unite; join; gather, assemble; *vr* meet, assemble; unite
revacunación *f*, revaccination
revacunar *vt* to revaccinate
revalidación *f*, ratification, confirmation
revalidar *vt* to ratify, confirm; *vr* pass a final examination
revejido *a* prematurely old
revelación *f*, revelation; *phot* developing
revelador *a* revealing. *m*, *phot* developer
revelar *vt* to reveal; *phot* develop
revendedor (-ra) *a* reselling, retail. *n* retailer
revender *vt* to resell; retail (goods)
reventa *f*, resale; retail
reventar *vi irr* to burst, explode; break in foam (waves);

burst forth; *fig* burst (with impatience, etc.); *inf* explode (with anger, etc.); *vt* break, crush; *fig* wear out, exhaust; *inf* irritate, vex; *vr* burst; *fig* be exhausted. See **sentar**

reventón *a* bursting. *m*, explosion, bursting; steep hill; hole, fix, difficulty; uphill work, heavy toil

rever *vt irr* to look at again, revise; *law* retry. See **ver**

reverberación *f*, reflection (of light); reverberation, resounding

reverberar *vi* to reflect; resound, reverberate

reverbero *m*, reverberation; reflector

reverdecer *vi irr* to grow green again; revive, acquire new vigor. See **conocer**

reverencia *f*, respect, veneration; bow; curtsy; *ecc* reverence (title)

reverencial *a* reverential, respectful

reverenciar *vt* to revere; honor; respect

reverendo *a* reverend; venerable; *inf* overprudent

reversibilidad *f*, reversibility

reversión *f*, reversion

reverso *m*, wrong side, back; reverse side (of coins)

reverter *vi irr* to overflow. See **entender**

revertir *vi law* to revert

revés *m*, wrong side, back, reverse; cuff, slap; backhand (in ballgames); check, setback, reverse; disaster, misfortune. **al r.,** on the contrary; wrong side out. **de r.,** from left to right, counterclockwise

revesado *a* complicated, difficult; willful

revestimiento *m, mas* lining, coating

revestir *vt irr* to dress; *mas* coat, line; *fig* cover, clothe; *vr* be dressed or dress oneself; *fig* be captivated (by an idea); become haughty or full of oneself; rise to the occasion, develop qualities necessary. See **pedir**

reviejo *a* very old. *m*, dead branch (of trees)

revisar *vt* to revise; examine

revisión *f*, revision; reexamination; *law* retrial

revisor *a* revising, examining. *m*, reviser; ticket inspector

revista *f*, reexamination, revision; review, periodical; *theat* revue; reinspection; review (of a book, etc.); *law* new trial; *mil* review. **pasar r.,** to inspect; review

revistero (-ra) *n* reviewer, writer of reviews

revivificación *f*, revivification

revivificar *vt* to revivify, revive

revivir *vi* to resuscitate; revive

revocación *f*, revocation, cancellation, annulment

revocar *vt* to revoke, annul; dissuade; repel, throw back; wash (walls); *law* discharge

revolcadero *m*, bathing place (of animals)

revolcar *vt irr* to knock down, trample underfoot; lay flat (in an argument); *vr* wallow; dig one's heels in, be obstinate. See **volcar**

revolotear *vi* to flutter, fly around; twirl; *vt* hurl, toss

revoltillo *m*, jumble, hodgepodge; confusion, tangle

revoltoso *a* rebellious; mischievous, willful; intricate

revolución *f*, turn, revolution; rebellion, uprising; revolution

revolucionar *vt* to revolutionize

revolucionario (-ia) *a* and *n* revolutionary

revolver *vt irr* to turn over; turn upside down; wrap up; revolve; stir; reflect upon, consider; upset, cause disharmony; search through, disorder (papers, etc.); *vr* move from side to side; change (in the weather). See **resolver**

revólver *m*, revolver

revoque *m, mas* washing, whitewash; plastering

revuelco *m*, wallowing

revuelo *m*, second flight (of birds); irregular course of flight; disturbance, upset

revuelta *f*, second turn or revolution; revolt, rebellion; quarrel, fight; turning point; change of direction, turn; change (of opinions, posts, etc.)

revueltamente *adv* in confusion, higgledy-piggledy

revulsión *f*, revulsion

reexaminación *f*, reexamination

reexaminar *vt* to reexamine

rexpedir *vt* to forward, send on

reexportación *f*, reexport

reexportar *vt com* to reexport

rey *m*, king (in cards, chess); queen bee; *inf* swineherd; *fig* king, chief. **her r. de armas,** king-of-arms. **reyes magos,** magi. **día de Reyes,** Twelfth Night. **servir al r.,** to fight for the king

reyerta *f*, quarrel, row, rumpus

reyezuelo *m*, kinglet, petty king; golden-crested wren

rezagar *vt* to leave behind; postpone, delay; *vr* lag behind, straggle

rezar *vt* to pray, say prayers; say mass; *inf* state, say; *vi* pray; *inf* fume, grumble. **El edicto reza así,** The edict runs like this, The edict reads like this

rezo *m*, prayer; devotions

rezongar *vi* to grouse, grumble

rezumar(se) *vr* and *vi* to percolate, ooze through; *inf* leak out, be known

ría *f*, estuary, river mouth, firth

riachuelo *m*, rivulet, stream

riada *f*, flood. *aer* **r. de acero,** rain of flak

ribaldería *f*, ribaldry

ribaldo *a* ribald. *m*, knave

ribazo *m*, slope, incline

ribera *f*, bank, margin, shore, strand

ribereño (-ña) *a* and *n* riparian

ribero *m*, embankment, wall

ribete *m*, binding, border, trimming; stripe; increase, addition; dramatic touch, exaggeration; *pl* indications, signs

ribetear *vt sew* to bind, trim, edge

ricacho (-cha) *n inf* newly rich person, nouveau riche

ricahembra *f*, lady; daughter or wife of a Spanish noble *ant*

ricamente *adv* richly, opulently; beautifully, splendidly; luxuriously

ricino *m*, castor oil plant

rico *a* wealthy, rich; abundant; magnificent, splendid; delicious. **r. como Creso,** rich as Croesus

ricohombre *m*, nobleman *ant*

ricura *f*, *inf* richness, wealth

ridiculez *f*, absurd action or remark; ridiculousness; affectation; folly

ridiculizar *vt* to ridicule, poke fun at

ridículo *a* ridiculous, absurd; grotesque; preposterous, outrageous. *m*, reticule

riego *m*, watering, spraying; irrigation

riel *m*, ingot; rail (of a train or streetcar)

rielar *vi* to glimmer, glisten; glitter; shimmer

rienda *f*, rein (gen. *pl*); restraint; *pl* administration, government. **a r. suelta,** swiftly; without restraint

riesgo *m*, risk, danger

rifa *f*, raffle; quarrel, disagreement

rifar *vt* to raffle; *vi* quarrel, fall out

rifle *m*, rifle

rigidez *f*, stiffness; rigidity; harshness

rígido *a* stiff; rigid; inflexible; severe, harsh

rigodón *m*, rigadoon

rigor *m*, severity, sternness; rigor; hardness; inflexibility; *med* rigor. **en r.,** strictly speaking. **ser de r.,** to be essential, be indispensable

rigorista *mf* martinet

riguroso *a* rigorous; harsh, cruel; austere, rigid; strict, exact, scrupulous

rijoso *a* quarrelsome; lascivious

riksha *m*, rickshaw

rima *f*, rhyme, rime; heap; *pl* lyrics

rimador (-ra) *a* rhyming, rimer. *n* rhymer, rimer

rimar *vi* to compose verses; *vi* and *vt* rhyme, rime

rimbombo *m*, reverberation (of a sound)

rimero *m*, heap, pile

Rin, el the Rhine

rincón *m*, corner, angle; retreat, hiding place; *inf* home, nest, nook

rinconada *f*, corner, angle

rinconera *f*, corner cupboard; corner table

ringlera *f*, file, line, row

ringlero *m*, guiding line for writing

ringorrangos *m pl, inf* exaggerated flourishes in writing; *inf* unnecessary frills or ornaments

rinoceronte *m*, rhinoceros

riñón *m*, kidney; *fig* center, heart; *pl anat* back

río *m*, river; *fig* stream, flood

rioja *m*, red wine from Rioja

ripio *m*, remains, rest; debris, rubbish; *lit* padding; verbiage, prolixity. **no perder r.**, to lose no occasion or opportunity

riqueza *f*, riches, wealth; abundance; richness, magnificence

risa *f*, laugh; laughter; cause of amusement, joke

risco *m*, crag

riscoso *a* craggy

risible *a* laughable

risoles *m pl*, rissoles

risotada *f*, loud laugh

ristra *f*, string (of onions, etc.); file, line, row

risueño *a* smiling; cheerful; pleasant, agreeable; favorable, hopeful

rítmico *a* rhythmic

ritmo *m*, rhythm

rito *m*, rite

ritualismo *m*, ritualism

ritualista *mf* ritualist

rivalidad *f*, rivalry, competition; hostility

rivalizar *vi* to compete, rival

rizado *m*, curling; pleating, crimping; rippling, ruffling

rizar *vt* to curl (hair); ripple, ruffle (of water); pleat, crimp; *vr* be naturally wavy (of hair)

rizo *m*, curl, ringlet; cut velvet. *aer* **hacer el r.**, to loop the loop; *naut* to take in reefs

rizoso *a* naturally curly or wavy (hair)

ro, ro m, hushaby!

roano *a* roan (of horses)

robador (-ra) *a* robbing. *n* robber, thief. *m*, abductor

robar *vt* to rob; abduct; wash away, eat away (rivers, sea); remove honey from the hive; draw (in cards, dominoes); *fig* capture (love, etc.)

roblar *vt* to reinforce, strengthen; clinch

roble *m*, oak tree; oak; *fig* bulwark, tower of strength

robledo *m*, oak grove

roblón *m*, rivet

robo *m*, theft, robbery; booty

robustecer *vt irr* to strengthen. See **conocer**

robustez *f*, strength, robustness

robusto *a* vigorous, robust, hearty, strong

roca *f*, rock; *fig* tower of strength

roce *m*, rubbing, brushing, touching, friction; social intercourse

rociada *f*, dewing; sprinkling; dew-wet grass given as medicine to horses and mules; *fig* shower; general slander; harsh rebuke

rociar *vi* to fall as dew; drizzle; *vt* sprinkle, spray; *fig* shower (with)

rocín *m*, sorry nag; hack; *inf* ignoramus, boor

rocinante *m*, poor nag (alluding to Don Quixote's horse)

rocío *m*, dew; dewdrop; drizzle, light shower; *fig* sprinkling, spray

rocoso *a* rocky

rodaballo *m*, turbot; *inf* crafty man

rodada *f*, wheel mark or track

rodado *a* dappled (of horses)

rodaje *m*, wheeling; shooting (of a film)

rodante *a* rolling

rodar *vi* to roll; revolve, turn; run on wheels; wander, roam; be moved about; be plentiful, abound; happen successively; *(with por)* fall down, roll down

Rodas Rhodes

rodear *vi* to walk around; go by a roundabout way; *fig* beat around the bush; *vt* encircle, surround; besiege; *WH* round up (cattle)

rodela *f*, round shield; buckler

rodeno *a* red (of rocks, earth, etc.)

rodeo *m*, encirclement; indirect and longer way; trick to evade pursuit; *WH* rodeo, roundup; stockyard, cattle enclosure; *fig* beating around the bush; evasive reply

rodera *f*, rail, track, line; cart rut or track

Rodesia Rhodesia

rodilla *f*, knee; floor cloth. **de rodillas**, on one's knees. **ponerse de rodillas**, *or* **hincar las rodillas**, to kneel down

rodillazo *m*, push with the knee

rodillera *f*, kneecap, kneepad; mend at the knee of garments; bagginess of trouser knees

rodillo *m*, roller; traction engine; *print* inking roller; garden roller. **r. de pastas**, *cul* rolling pin

rododendro *m*, rhododendron

rodrigón *m*, stake, prop (for plants); *inf* old retainer who serves as a ladies' escort

roedor *a* gnawing; *fig* nagging; biting. *a* and *m*, rodent

roedura *f*, biting, gnawing; corrosion

roer *vt irr* to gnaw, nibble, eat; corrode, wear away; trouble, afflict. *Pres. Ind.* **roigo, roes**, etc. *Preterite* **royó, royeron.** *Imperf. Subjunc.* **royese**, etc.

rogación *f*, request, supplication, entreaty; *ecc* rogation

rogador (-ra) *a* requesting; beseeching. *n* suppliant

rogar *vt irr* to request; beseech, beg. See **contar**

rogativo *a* supplicatory, petitioning

roído *a* gnawed, eaten; *inf* miserable, stingy

rojal *a* red (of soil, etc.). *m*, red earth

rojear *vi* to appear red; be reddish

rojete *m*, rouge

rojez *f*, redness

rojizo *a* reddish

rojo *a* red; fair; red-gold (of hair); *pol* radical, red

rol *m*, roll, list

roldana *f*, pulley wheel

rollizo *a* round; plump, sturdy. *m*, log

rollo *m*, roll; *cul* rolling pin; log; town cross or pillar; anything rolled (paper, etc.); twist (of tobacco)

Roma Rome

romance *a* and *m*, romance (language). *m*, Spanish; ballad; romance of chivalry; *pl fig* fairy tales, excuses. **en buen r.**, *fig* in plain words

romancear *vt* to translate from Latin into the spoken language; translate into Spanish; paraphrase the Spanish to assist translation

romancero (-ra) *n* balladeer. *m*, collection of ballads

romancista *mf* romancist

románico *a arch* Romanesque

romanista *mf* expert in Roman law or Romance languages and literature

romanizar *vt* to romanize; *vr* become romanized

romano (-na) *a* and *n* Roman. **a la romana**, in the Roman way. **cabello a la romana**, *inf* bobbed hair

romanticismo *m*, romanticism

romántico (-ca) *a* romantic; emotional; fanciful. *n* romantic; romanticist

rombo *m*, rhombus

romería *f*, pilgrimage; excursion, picnic (made on a saint's day)

romero (-ra) *m*, rosemary. *n* pilgrim

romo *a* blunt, dull, unsharpened; flat (of noses)

rompecabezas *m*, bludgeon; knuckleduster; *inf* teaser, puzzle, riddle; jigsaw puzzle

rompeimágenes *mf* iconoclast

rompeolas *m*, jetty, breakwater

romper *vt* to break; shatter, break into fragments; spoil, ruin; break up, plow; *fig* cut, divide (of water, etc.); *fig* end, break; interrupt; infringe, break; *vi* break; break (of waves); sprout, flower; (*with prep a*) begin to. **Rompió a hablar**, He broke into speech. *Past Part.* **roto**

rompiente *a* breaking. *m*, reef, shoal

rompimiento *m*, break, rupture; crack, split; breakage; infringement; plowing up; *fig* dividing (water, etc.); spoiling, ruining; opening (of buds, etc.)

ron *m*, rum

roncar *vi* to snore; *fig* roar, howl (of the sea, wind, etc.); *inf* brag

roncear *vi* to be dilatory or unwilling; *inf* flatter, cajole; *naut* lag behind, sail slowly

roncero *a* dilatory, slow; grumbling, complaining; cajoling, flattering

roncha *f*, wheal; bruise, bump; *inf* money lost through trickery; thin, round slice

ronco *a* hoarse, husky

ronda *f*, round, beat, patrol; serenading party; *inf* round (of drinks)

rondador *m*, watchman; roundsman; serenader; night wanderer

rondalla *f*, tale, fairy tale

rondar *vi* to patrol, police; walk the streets by night; serenade; *vt* haunt; hover about; *inf* overcome (of sleep, etc.)

rondó *m*, rondo

ronquear *vi* to be hoarse

ronquera *f*, hoarseness

ronquido *m*, snore; hoarse sound

ronronear *vi* to purr (of cats)

ronzal *m*, halter

ronzar *vt* to munch, crack with the teeth

roña *f*, mange (in sheep); grime, filth; mold; moral corruption; *inf* stinginess; *inf* trick, deception

roñería *f*, *inf* meanness, stinginess

roñoso *a* scabby; filthy; rusty; *inf* mean, stingy

ropa *f*, fabric, material, stuff; clothes, wearing apparel; garment, outfit; robe (of office). **r. blanca,** underclothes; (domestic) linen. **r. hecha,** ready-made clothing. **r. talar,** long gown; cassock

ropaje *m*, clothes, garments; vestments; drapery; *fig* form, outline

ropavejería *f*, old-clothes shop

ropavejero (-ra) *n* old-clothes dealer

ropería *f*, clothier's shop or trade; wardrobe; cloakroom

ropero (-ra) *n* clothier; keeper of the wardrobe. *m*, wardrobe; charitable organization

ropilla *f*, doublet

ropón *m*, a loose-fitting gown generally worn over clothes

roque *m*, rook (in chess)

roqueño *a* rocky; hard as rock

roquete *m*, *ecc* rochet; barb of a lance

rorro *m*, *inf* infant, baby

rosa *f*, rose; anything rose-shaped; artificial rose; red spot on the body; *arch* rose window; *pl* rosettes. *m*, rose color. **r. de los vientos,** mariner's compass. **r. laurel,** oleander

rosado *a* rose-colored; rose; rosé (wines)

rosal *m*, rose tree. **r. de tallo,** standard rose tree

rosaleda, rosalera *f*, rose garden

rosario *m*, rosary; *fig* string; chain pump; *inf* backbone

rosbif *m*, roast beef

rosca *f*, screw and nut; *cul* twist (of bread or cake); spiral

roscado *a* twisted, spiral

rosear *vi* to turn to rose, become rose-colored

Rosellón Rousillon

róseo *a* rose-colored

roseta *f*, *dim* small rose; rosette; rose of a watering can; rosette copper; *pl* toasted maize. **r. de fiebre,** rush of fever

rosetón *m*, large rosette; *arch* rose window

rosicler *m*, rose-pink (first flush of dawn)

rosillo *a* light red; roan (of horses)

rosmaro *m*, manatee, sea cow

roso *a* bald, worn; red

rosquilla *f*, ring-shaped cake

rosquillero (-ra) *n* seller of rosquillas

rostrituerto *a* *inf* wry-faced (from sadness or anger)

rostro *m*, human face; bird's beak; face, visage. **conocer de r.,** to know by sight. **dar en r.,** *fig* to throw in one's face

rota *f*, *mil* defeat; *ecc* Rota; *bot* rattan

rotación *f*, rotation. **r. de cultivos,** rotation of crops

rotativa *f*, rotary printing press

rotativo *a* rotary

rotatorio *a* rotary

roto *a* shabby, ragged; vicious, debauched

rotograbado *m*, rotogravure

rotonda *f*, rotunda

rótula *f*, rotula, patella

rotular *vt* to label; give a title or heading to

rótulo *m*, title; poster, placard; label

rotundamente *adv* tersely, roundly, plainly

rotundidad *f*, rotundity; roundness; finality (of words, etc.)

rotundo *a* round; rotund; sonorous; final, plain (of words, etc.)

rotura *f*, breaking, shattering; plowing up; breakage; rupture

roturar *vt* *agr* to break up, plow up

roya *f*, rust, mildew; tobacco

roza *f*, *agr* clearing (of weeds, etc.); ground ready for sowing. **de r. abierta,** open cast (of mining)

rozadura *f*, rubbing, friction; abrasion, chafing

rozagante *a* long and elaborate (dresses); upstanding; handsome; strapping, fine

rozamiento *m*, grazing, brushing, rubbing; discord, disharmony, disagreement; *mech* friction

rozar *vt* *agr* to clear of weeds; crop, nibble; scrape; brush against, touch; *vi* brush, rub, touch; *vr* have dealings with, know; stammer; be like, resemble

rúa *f*, village street; highway

ruar *vi* to walk or ride through the streets; parade through the streets flirting with the ladies

rubéola *f*, rubella

rubí *m*, ruby; jewel (of a watch)

rubia *f*, *bot* madder; blonde (girl, woman)

rubicundez *f*, rubicundity, ruddiness, redness

rubicundo *a* red-gold; ruddy-complexioned; reddish

rubio *a* red-gold, gold; fair, blond

rublo *m*, ruble

rubor *m*, blush, flush; bashfulness

ruborizarse *vr* to blush; be shamefaced

ruboroso *a* shamefaced; blushing

rúbrica *f*, rubric; personal mark, flourish added to one's signature

rubricar *vt* to sign and seal; sign with an X or other symbol; sign with a flourish

rubro *a* red

rucio *a* fawn, light-gray (of animals); *inf* going gray, gray-haired

rudamente *adv* rudely, abruptly, churlishly; roughly

rudeza *f*, roughness; rudeness, uncouthness; stupidity

rudimentario *a* rudimentary

rudimento *m*, embryo; *pl* rudiments

rudo *a* rough; unfinished; uncouth, boorish, rude; stupid

rueca *f*, distaff (in spinning); spinning wheel; curve, twist

rueda *f*, wheel; group, circle; spread of a peacock's tail; roller, castor; round piece or slice; turn, chance; succession (of events); wheel (used for torture). **r. libre,** freewheeling. *inf* **hacer la r. (a),** to flatter, make a fuss of

ruedero *m*, wheelwright

ruedo *m*, turning, rotation; circumference; lined hem of a cassock; circuit

ruego *m*, request, entreaty

rufián *m*, ruffian; pimp

rufianesco *a* ruffianly

rufo *a* fair; red-haired; curly-haired

rugido *m*, roaring, roar; creaking; gnashing; rumbling

rugir *vi* to roar; squeak, creak; gnash (the teeth)

ruibarbo *m*, rhubarb

ruido *m*, noise, din; disturbance; rumor. **hacer** (*or* **meter**) **r.,** to cause a sensation. *inf* **ser más el r. que las nueces,** to be much ado about nothing

ruidoso *a* noisy; notable

ruin *a* base, vile; despicable; mean; puny

ruina *f*, ruin, downfall; financial ruin; fall, decline; *pl* ruins

ruinar *vt* to ruin

ruindad *f*, baseness; meanness; pettiness, unworthiness; mean trick, despicable action

ruinoso *a* half-ruined; ruinous; useless, worthless

ruiseñor *m*, nightingale

ruleta *f*, roulette

rumano (-na) *a* and *n* Romanian. *m*, Romanian (language)

rumbo *m*, *naut* course, way, route; direction; *inf* swank. **con r. a**, headed for, in the direction of. **hacer r. a**, to sail for; make for

rumboso *a inf* pompous, dignified; open-handed, generous

rumia *f*, rumination; cud

rumiante *a* and *mf zool* ruminant. *a inf* reflective, meditative

rumiar *vt zool* to ruminate; *inf* reflect upon, chew on; *inf* fume, rage

rumor *m*, noise; rumor; murmur, babble; dull sound

runa *f*, rune

rúnico *a* runic

runrunearse *v impers* to be rumored

rupia *f*, rupee

ruptura *f*, *fig* rupture; *surg* hernia

rural *a* rustic, rural

ruralmente *adv* rurally

Rusia Russia

rusificar *vt* to russianize

ruso (-sa) *a* and *n* Russian. *m*, Russian (language)

rusticación *f*, rustication

rusticar *vi* to rusticate

rusticidad *f*, rusticity; boorishness, coarseness

rústico *a* rustic, country; boorish, uncouth. *m*, country-man; yokel; peasant. **en rústica**, in paper covers (of books)

ruta *f*, route; *fig* way. **r. de evitación**, bypass, detour

ruteno (-na) *a* and *n* Ruthenian. *m*, Ruthenian (language)

rutilante *a poet* sparkling, glowing

rutilar *vi poet* to gleam, sparkle

rutina *f*, routine

rutinario *a* routine

rutinero (-ra) *a* routinistic. *n* routinist

S

sábado *m*, Saturday; Jewish sabbath. **s. de gloria**, Easter Saturday

sábalo *m*, *icht* shad

sabana *f*, savannah

sábana *f*, bed sheet; altar cloth. *inf* **pegársele (a uno) las sábanas**, to be tied to the bed, get up late

sabandija *f*, any unpleasant insect or reptile; *fig* vermin

sabanero (-ra) *n* savannah dweller. *a* savannah

sabanilla *f*, small piece of linen (kerchief, towel, etc.); altar cloth

sabañón *m*, chilblain

sabatario *a* sabbatarian

sabático *a* sabbatical

sabatino *a* Saturday, Sabbath

sabedor *a* aware; knowledgeable, knowing

sabelotodo *mf inf* know-it-all

saber *m*, learning; wisdom

saber *vt irr* to know; be able to, know how; *vi* know; be shrewd, be well aware of; (*with prep a*) taste of; be like or similar to. **s. al dedillo**, *fig* to have at one's fingertips. **a s.**, viz., namely. *inf* **no s. cuántas son cinco**, not to know how many beans make five. **no s. dónde meterse**, to be overcome by shame; have the jitters. **No sé cuántos**, I don't know how many. **No sé quién**, I don't know who (which person). **No sé qué**, I don't know what. **un no sé qué**, a certain something; a touch (of). **¡Quién sabe!** Who knows!; Time will tell. *Pres. Ind.* **sé, sabes**, etc. *Fut.* **sabré**, etc. *Condit.* **sabría**, etc. *Preterite* **supe**, etc. *Pres. Subjunc.* **sepa**, etc. *Imperf. Subjunc.* **supiese**, etc.

sabiamente *adv* wisely, prudently

sabidillo (-lla) *a* and *n inf* know-it-all

sabiduría *f*, prudence; wisdom; erudition, learning; knowledge, awareness. **Libro de la S. de Salomón**, Book of Wisdom

sabiendas, a *adv* knowingly, consciously

sabihondo (-da) *a n inf* know-it-all

sabino (-na) *a* and *n* Sabine. *a* roan (of horses)

sabio (-ia) *a* wise; learned, erudite; prudent, sagacious; knowing (of animals); performing (of animals). *n* wise person; scholar, erudite person

sablazo *m*, saber thrust or wound; *inf* sponging, taking advantage of. **dar un s. (a)**, *inf* to sponge on; touch for money

sable *m*, saber; *her* sable; *inf* talent for sponging on people. *a her* sable

sablear *vi inf* to touch for invitations, loans, etc.; cadge

sablista *mf inf* sponger, cadger

saboneta *f*, hunting case watch, hunter

sabor *m*, taste, flavor; impression, effect. **a s.**, to taste; at pleasure

saboreamiento *m*, savoring; relishing, enjoyment

saborear *vt* to flavor, season; relish, savor; appreciate, enjoy; *vr* relish, savor; enjoy

saboreo *m*, tasting; savoring; relishing

sabotaje *m*, sabotage

saboteador *m*, saboteur

Saboya Savoy

saboyano (-na) *a* and *n* Savoyard

sabroso *a* tasty, savory, well-seasoned; delightful, delicious; *inf* piquant, racy

sabueso *m*, cocker spaniel. **s. de artois**, hound

sabuloso *a* sandy

saburra *f*, fur (on the tongue)

saca *f*, drawing out, removing; export, transport, shipping; removal, extraction; legal copy (of a document). **estar de s.**, to be on sale; *inf* be marriageable (of women)

sacabocados *m*, punch (tool); *inf* cinch, easy matter

sacabotas *m*, bootjack

sacabrocas *m*, tack puller

sacabuche *m*, *mus* sackbut; sackbut player; *inf* insignificant little man; *naut* hand pump

sacacorchos *m*, corkscrew

sacacuartos *m*, *inf* catchpenny

sacada *f*, territory cut off from a province

sacadineros *m*, *inf* catchpenny

sacamanchas *mf*. See **quitamanchas**

sacamantas *m*, *inf* tax collector

sacamiento *m*, removing, taking out

sacamuelas *mf* dentist; charlatan, quack; *inf* windbag

sacapotras *m*, *inf* unskilled surgeon

sacar *vt* to draw out; extract; pull out; take out; remove; dispossess, turn out; free from; relieve; examine, investigate; extort (the truth); extract (sugar, etc.); win (prizes, games); copy; discover, find out; elect by ballot; obtain, achieve; exclude; show, exhibit; quote, mention; produce, invent; manufacture; note down; put forth; unsheath (swords); bowl (in cricket); serve (in tennis). **s. a bailar**, to invite to dance. **s. a luz**, to publish, print; reveal, bring out. **s. a paseo**, to take for a walk. **s. de pila**, to be a godfather or godmother to. **s. en claro** *or* **s. en limpio**, to copy; conclude, infer, gather. **sacarse en conclusión que . . .** , the conclusion is that . . .

sacarificar *vt* to saccharify

sacarina *f,* saccharine
sacasillas *m, inf theat* stagehand
sacerdocio *m,* priesthood
sacerdotal *a* priestly
sacerdote *m,* priest
sacerdotisa *f,* priestess. **sumo s.,** high priestess
saciable *a* satiable
sachar *vt* to weed
sacho *m,* weeder
saciar *vt* to satisfy; satiate; *vr* be satiated
saciedad *f,* satiety, surfeit
saco *m,* handbag; sack, bag; sackful; sack coat; *biol* sac; *mil* sack, plundering. **s. de noche,** dressing case, weekend case. *inf* **no echar en s. roto,** not to forget, to remember
sacramentalmente *adv* sacramentally; in confession
sacramentar *vt* to consecrate; administer the Blessed Sacrament; hide, conceal
sacramentario (-ia) *n* sacramentalist; sacramentarian
sacramento *m,* sacrament; *ecc* Host; *ecc* mystery. **s. del altar,** Eucharist. **con todos los sacramentos,** with all the sacraments; done in order, complete with all formalities. **recibir los sacramentos,** to receive the last sacraments
sacratísimo *a* most sacred
sacrificadero *m,* place of sacrifice
sacrificador (-ra) *a* sacrificing. *n* sacrificer
sacrificar *vt* to sacrifice; slaughter; *vr* consecrate oneself to God; sacrifice oneself; devote or dedicate oneself (to)
sacrificio *m,* sacrifice; offering, dedication; surrendering, forgoing; compliance, submission. **s. del altar,** sacrifice of the mass
sacrilegio *m,* sacrilege
sacrílego *a* sacrilegious
sacristán *m,* sacristan; sexton; hoop (for dresses). *inf* **s. de amén,** yes-man. *inf* **ser gran s.,** to be very crafty
sacristana *f,* wife of a sacristan or sexton; nun in charge of a convent sacristy
sacristanía *f,* office of a sacristan or sexton
sacristía *f,* sacristy; vestry; office of a sacristan or sexton
sacro *a* sacred; *anat* sacral
sacrosanto *a* sacrosanct
sacudida *f,* shake, shaking; jerk, jar, jolt; twitch, pull; *aer* bump
sacudido *a* unsociable; difficult, wayward; determined, bold
sacudidor (-ra) *a* shaking; jerking. *n* shaker. *m,* carpet beater; duster
sacudidura *f,* shaking (especially to remove dust); jerking
sacudimiento *m,* shake, shaking; jerk; twitch, pull; jolt
sacudir *vt* to shake; flap, wave; jerk, twitch; beat, bang; shake off; *vr* shake off, avoid
sadismo *m,* sadism
sadista *mf* sadist
sadístico *a* sadistic
saduceo (-ea) *a* Sadducean. *n* Sadducee
saeta *f,* arrow, dart; clock hand, watch hand; magnetic needle; short sung expression of religious ecstasy; *ast* Sagitta
saetada *f,* **saetazo** *m,* arrow wound
saetera *f,* loophole; small window
saetero *a* arrow, arrow-like. *m,* archer, bowman
sáfico *a* Sapphic
saga *f,* saga
sagacidad *f,* sagacity
sagaz *a* sagacious, shrewd; farseeing; quick on the scent (dogs)
sagital *a* arrow-shaped
sagitario *m,* archer; *ast* Sagittarius
sagrado *a* sacred; holy; sacrosanct, venerable; accursed, detestable. *m,* sanctuary, refuge; haven
sagrario *m,* sanctuary; sacrarium
sagú *m,* sago
Sáhara, el the Sahara
sahornarse *vr* to chafe, grow sore

sahorno *m,* chafing, abrasion
sahumado *a* improved, rendered more excellent; perfumed; fumigated
sahumador *m,* perfumer; fumigating vessel
sahumar *vt* to perfume; fumigate. See **desahuciar**
sahumerio *m,* perfuming; fumigation; fume, smoke
saín *m,* fat, grease; sardine oil (for lamps); grease spot (on clothes)
sainar *vt* to fatten up (animals)
sainete *m, cul* sauce; *theat* one-act parody or burlesque; farce; delicacy, tidbit; delicate taste (of food)
sainetero *m,* writer of sainetes
sainetesco *a* pertaining to sainetes; burlesque, satirical
sajar *vt surg* to scarify
Sajonia Saxony
sajón (-ona) *a* and *n* Saxon
sal *f,* salt; wit; grace, gracefulness. **s. de cocina,** common kitchen salt. **s. de la Higuera,** Epsom salts. **s. gema,** rock salt. **s. marina,** sea salt. **sales inglesas,** smelling salts. *inf* **estar hecho de s.,** to be full of wit. *inf* **hacerse s. y agua,** to melt away, disappear (of riches, etc.)
sala *f,* drawing room; large room, hall; *law* courtroom; *law* bench; **s. de apelación,** court of appeal. **s. de hospital,** hospital ward. **s. de justicia,** court of justice. **s. de lectura,** reading room. *law* **guardar s.,** to respect the court
salacidad *f,* lewdness, salaciousness
saladar *m,* salt marsh
saladero *m,* salting or curing place; *WH* meat packing factory
saladillo *m,* salt pork
salado *a* salty, briny; brackish; witty; attractive, amusing
salador (-ra) *a* salting, curing. *n* salter, curer. *m,* curing place
saladura *f,* salting, curing
salamandra *f,* salamander; fire sprite
salar *vt* to salt; season with salt; oversalt; cure, pickle (meat, etc.)
salario *m,* salary
salaz *a* lewd, lecherous
salazón *f,* salting, curing; salt meat or fish trade
salazonero *a* salting, curing
salchicha *f,* sausage
salchichería *f,* sausage shop
salchichero (-ra) *n* sausage maker, sausage seller
salchichón *m, cul* salami, kind of sausage
saldar *vt com* to settle, pay in full; sell out cheap; balance
saldista *mf* remnant buyer
saldo *m, com* balance; closing of an account; bargain sale. **s. acreedor,** credit balance. **s. deudor,** debit balance. **s. líquido,** net balance
salero *m,* saltshaker, saltcellar; salt storage warehouse; *inf* wit
saleta *f, dim* small hall; royal antechamber; court of appeal
salida *f,* going out; leaving; departure; sailing; exit, way out; projection, protrusion; *fig* escape, way out; outcome, result; witty remark; *mil* sally; *com* outlay, expense; *com* opening, sale, salability; environs, outskirts. **s. de dólares,** dollar drain. **s. de tono,** *inf* an impertinent remark. **dar s.,** *com* to enter on the credit side
salidero *a* fond of going out; *m,* exit, way out
salidizo *m, arch* projection. *a* projecting
saliente *a* outgoing; salient, projecting. *m,* east; projection; salient. **s. continental,** continental shelf
salina *f,* salt mine; saltworks
salinero *m,* salt merchant; salter; salt worker
salino *a* saline. *m, med* saline
salir *vi irr* to go out; depart, leave; succeed in getting out; escape; appear (of the sun, etc.); sprout, show green; fade, come out (of stains); project, stand out; grow, develop; turn out, result; happen, take place; cost; sail; end (of seasons, time); lead off, start (some games); be published (books); do (well or badly), suc-

ceed or fail; appear, show oneself; be drawn, win (lottery tickets); balance, come out right (accounts); be elected; become; give up (posts); lead to (of streets, etc.); *naut* overtake; (*with prep a*) guarantee, be surety for; resemble, be like; (*with con*) utter, come out with; commit, do inopportunely; succeed in, achieve (e.g. **Salió con la suya,** He got his own way); (*with de*) originate in; break away from (traditions, conventions); get rid of; (*with por*) stand up for, protect; go surety for, guarantee. *vr* leak; boil over; overflow; (*with con*) achieve, get; (*with de*) *fig* break away from. *theat* **s. a la escena,** to enter, come on to the stage. **s. de,** to recover from (an illness). **no acabar de s. de,** to not be completely recovered from. **s. del apuro,** to get out of trouble. **s. de estampía,** to stampede (of animals). **s. pitando,** *inf* to get out in a hurry. **Esta idea no salió de Juan,** This wasn't John's idea. **salga lo que saliere,** *inf* come what may. . . . *Pres. Ind.* **salgo, sales,** etc. *Fut.* **saldré,** etc. *Condit.* **saldría,** etc. *Pres. Subjunc.* **salga,** etc.

salitral *a* nitrous. *m,* saltpeter bed

salitre *m,* saltpeter

salitrería *f,* saltpeter works

salitrero *n* saltpeter worker or dealer

saliva *f,* saliva. *inf* **tragar s.,** to put up with; be unable to speak through emotion

salivación *f,* salivation

salival *a* salivary

salivar *vi* to salivate; spit

salmantino (-na) *a* and *n* Salamanca

salmear *vi* to intone psalms

salmista *mf* psalmist; psalmodist, psalm chanter

salmo *m,* psalm

salmodia *f,* psalmody; *inf* drone; psalter

salmodiar *vi* to chant psalms; *vt* drone

salmón *m,* salmon

salmonado *a* salmon-like

salmonera *f,* salmon net

salmonete *m,* red mullet

salmuera *f,* brine

salobre *a* salt, salty; brackish

salobridad *f,* saltiness

salomar *vi naut* to sing chanteys

salón *m,* drawing room; large room or hall; reception room; salon, reception, social gathering. **s. de muestras,** showroom

saloncillo *m, dim* small room; *theat* greenroom; rest room

salpicadura *f,* sprinkling, spattering, splashing

salpicar *vt* to sprinkle, scatter; bespatter, splash

salpicón *m, cul* kind of salmagundi; *inf* hodgepodge; spattering

salpimentar *vt irr* to season with pepper and salt; sprinkle; *fig* leaven, enliven (a speech, etc.). See **regimentar**

salpresar *vt* to preserve in salt, salt

salpullido *m,* rash, skin eruption

salsa *f,* sauce; gravy. **s. mahonesa** or **s. mayonesa,** mayonnaise sauce. **s. mayordoma,** sauce maître d'hôtel

salsera *f,* sauce boat, gravy boat

saltabanco *m,* mountebank; street entertainer, juggler

saltabarrancos *mf inf* madcap, harum-scarum

saltable *a* jumpable

saltadero *m,* jumping ground; fountain, jet

saltador (-ra) *a* jumping. *n* jumper; acrobat. *m,* jump rope, skip rope

saltamontes *m,* grasshopper

saltaojos *m,* peony

saltaparedes *mf inf* madcap, romp

saltar *vi* to jump, leap, spring; prance; frisk, gambol; rebound; blow up; burst, break asunder; pop (of corks); fly off, come off (buttons, etc.); gush out, shoot up (liquids); break apart, be shattered; be obvious, stand out; come to mind, suggest itself; show anger; *fig* let slip, come out with (remarks); *vt* leap or jump over; poke

out (eyes); cover (the female); omit, pass over; blow up, explode. **s. a la cuerda,** to jump rope, play with a skip rope. **s. a la vista,** to be obvious, leap to the eye. **s. diciendo,** *inf* to come out with, say

saltarín (-ina) *a* dancing. *n* dancer

saltatriz *f,* ballet dancer, female acrobat

saltatumbas *m, (inf* contemptuous) cleric who makes his living off funerals

salteador *m,* highwayman

salteamiento *m,* highway robbery, holdup; assault, attack

saltear *vt* to hold up and rob; assault, attack; jump from one thing to another, do intermittently; forestall; surprise, amaze

salterio *m,* psaltery

saltimbanco, saltimbanqui *m, inf.* See **saltabanco**

salto *m,* jump, leap, bound; leapfrog (game); precipice, ravine; waterfall; assault; important promotion; omission (of words). **s. de agua,** waterfall. **s. de cama,** peignoir, bathrobe. **s. de campana,** overturning. *inf* **s. de mal año,** sudden improvement in circumstances. **s. de mata,** flight, escape. **s. mortal,** leap of death; somersault. **s. de pie,** spillway. **dar un s.,** to leap. **en un s.,** at one jump; swiftly

saltón *a* jumping, leaping; prominent (teeth, eyes). *m,* grasshopper

salubérrimo *a sup* **salubre** most healthy

salubre *a* salubrious, healthful

salubridad *f,* healthfulness

salud *f,* health; salvation; welfare, well-being; *ecc* state of grace; *pl* civilities, greetings. **¡S. y pesetas!** Here's to your good health and prosperity! (on drinking). **gastar s.,** to enjoy good health. *inf* **vender** (*or* **verter) s.,** to look full of health

saludable *a* healthy, wholesome

saludador (-ra) *a* greeting, saluting. *n* greeter. *m,* charlatan, quack

saludar *vt* to greet, salute; hail (as king, etc.); send greetings to; bow; *mil* fire a salute

saludo *m,* greeting, salutation; bow; (*mil nav*) salute

salutación *f,* greeting, salutation; Ave Maria

salutífero *a* salubrious

salva *f,* salutation, greeting; (*mil nav*) salvo, volley; salute (of guns); salver; ordeal (to establish innocence); solemn assurance, oath; sampling, tasting (of food, drink). **s. de veintiún cañonazos,** twenty-one–gun salute

salvación *f,* liberation, deliverance; salvation

salvado *m,* bran

salvador (-ra) *a* saving, redeeming. *n* deliverer. *m,* redeemer

salvadoreño (-ña) *a* and *n* Salvadorean

salvaguardia *m,* guard, watch. *f,* safeguard; protection, defense; safe conduct, passport

salvajada *f,* savagery, brutal action

salvaje *a* wild (plants, animals); rough, uncultivated; uncultured, uncivilized. *mf* savage

salvajismo *m,* savagery

salvamano, a *adv* safely

salvamente *adv* safely, securely

salvamento *m,* salvation; deliverance, security, safety; place of safety; salvage

salvante *adv inf* except, save

salvar *vt* to save; *ecc* redeem; avoid (difficulty, danger); exclude, except; leap, jump; pass over, clear; *law* prove innocent; *naut* salve. **s. la diferencia,** to bridge the gap. *vi* taste, sample (food, drink); *vr* be saved from danger; *ecc* be redeemed

salvavidas *m,* life belt; safety belt; life preserver; traffic island

¡salve! *interj poet* hail!; Hail Mary, Salve Regina

salvedad *f,* qualification, reservation

salvia *f, bot* sage

salvilla *f,* salver

salvo *a* safe, unharmed; excepting, omitting. *adv* except. **a s.,** safely, without harm. **a su s.,** to his (her, their) satisfaction; at his (her, etc.) pleasure. **dejar a s.,** to exclude, leave aside. **en s.,** in safety

salvoconducto *m,* safe conduct, pass

sallar *vt* to weed

samarita *a* and *mf* **samaritano (-na)** *a* and *n* Samaritan

sambenito *m,* penitent's gown (Inquisition); disgrace, dishonor

Samotracia Samothrace

samotracio (-ia) *a* and *n* Samothracian

samoyedo (-da) *n* Samoyed

san *a abb* of **santo.** Used before masculine singular names of saints except **Santos Tomás** (*or* **Tomé**)**, Domingo, Toribio**

sanable *a* curable

sanador (-ra) *a* healing, curing. *n* healer

sanalotodo *m, inf* cure-all, universal remedy

sanar *vt* to cure, heal; *vi* recover, get well; heal

sanatorio *m,* sanatorium; convalescent home

sanción *f,* authorization, consent; sanction; penalty

sancionable *a* sanctionable

sancionar *vt* to authorize, approve; sanction

sancochar *vt cul* to parboil, half-cook

sanchopancesco *a* like or pertaining to Sancho Panza

sandalia *f,* sandal

sándalo *m,* sandalwood

sandez *f,* foolishness, stupidity; folly

sandía *f,* watermelon

sandio *a* foolish, inane

sandunga *f, inf* attractiveness, winsomeness, grace

sandunguero *a inf* attractive, appealing, winsome

saneado *a* unencumbered, nontaxable, free

saneamiento *m,* guarantee, security; indemnity; stabilization (of currency); drainage

sanear *vt com* to guarantee, secure; indemnify; stabilize (currency); drain (land, etc.)

Sanedrín *m,* Sanhedrin

sangradera *f,* lancet; channel, sluice, drain

sangrador *m,* phlebotomist; outlet, drainage

sangradura *f,* inner bend of the arm; *surg* bleeding; draining off

sangrar *vt surg* to bleed; drain off; *inf* extort money, bleed; *print* indent; draw off resin (from pines, etc.); *vi* bleed; *vr* bleed; have oneself bled; run (of colors)

sangre *f,* blood; lineage, family. **s. fría,** sang-froid. **a s. fría,** in cold blood, premeditated. **a s. y fuego,** by fire and sword, without quarter. *inf* **bullir la s.,** to have youthful blood in one's veins. **llevar en la s.,** *fig* to be in the blood. **subírsele la s. a la cabeza,** to grow excited. *fig inf* **tener s. de horchata,** to have milk and water in one's veins

sangría *f, surg* bloodletting; resin cut (on pines, etc.)

sangriento *a* bloody, bloodstained; bloodthirsty, cruel; mortal (insults, etc.); *poet* blood-colored

sangüesa *f,* raspberry

sanguijuela *f,* leech; *fig inf* sponger

sanguina *f,* red crayon drawing, sanguine

sanguinaria *f,* bloodstone

sanguinario *a* vengeful, bloody, cruel

sanguíneo *a* blood; sanguineous; sanguine, fresh-complexioned; blood-colored

sanguinolento *a.* See **sangriento**

sanidad *f,* safety, security; healthiness; health department. **s. interior,** Public Health. **S. militar,** army medical corps

sanitario *a* sanitary, hygienic. *m, mil* medical officer

sano *a* healthy; safe, secure; healthful, wholesome; unhurt, unharmed; upright, honest; sincere; *inf* entire, undamaged; sane. **s. y salvo,** safe and sound. *inf* **cortar por lo s.,** to cut one's losses

sánscrito *a* and *m,* Sanscrit

santa *f,* female saint

santabárbara *f, nav* magazine

santamente *adv* in a saintly manner; simply

santero (-ra) *a* given to image worship. *n* accomplice (of a burglar); caretaker (of a hermitage); beggar

¡Santiago! *interj* St. James! (Spanish war cry). *m,* attack, assault

santiamén *m, inf* trice, twinkling

santidad *f,* sanctity; saintliness; godliness. **Su S.,** His Holiness

santificación *f,* sanctification

santificador (-ra) *a* sanctifying. *n* sanctifier

santificar *vt* to sanctify, make holy; consecrate; dedicate; keep (feast days)

santiguada *f,* crossing oneself; rough treatment, harsh reproof

santiguar *vt* to make the sign of the cross over; *inf* beat, rain blows on; *vr* cross oneself; *inf* be dumbfounded

santísimo *a sup* most saintly, most holy

santo *a* holy; saintly; saint (see **san**); consecrated; inviolate, sacred; *inf* simple, sincere, ingenuous. *m,* saint; image of a saint; saint's day, name day (of a person); *mil* password. **Santa Hermandad,** Holy Brotherhood (former name of the Spanish rural police force). **S. Oficio,** Holy Office, Inquisition. **S. y bueno,** Well and good, All right! *inf* **alzarse con él y la limosna,** to take the lot, make off with everything. **llegar y besar el s.,** to do in a trice. *inf* **No es s. de mi devoción,** I'm not very keen on him. *inf* **todo el s. día,** the whole blessed day

santón *m,* dervish, santon. *inf* hypocrite, sham saint

santoral *m,* book of saints; calendar of saints; choir book

santuario *m,* sanctuary

santurrón (-ona) *a* sanctimonious; hypocritical; prudish. *n* hypocrite

santurronería *f,* sanctimoniousness

saña *f,* fury, blind rage; lust for revenge, cruelty

sañoso, sañudo *a* furious, blind with rage; cruel

sapidez *f,* flavor, sapidity

sápido *a* tasty, savory

sapiencia *f,* wisdom; knowledge; erudition

sapino *m,* fir (tree)

sapo *m,* toad

saque *m, sport* serve, service; service or bowling line; *sport* server; *sport* bowler; bowling (in cricket)

saqueador (-ra) *a* looting, pillaging. *n* pillager, plunderer

saquear *vt* to pillage, plunder, sack

saqueo *m,* plundering, pillage, sacking

saquila *f,* small sackful (especially of grain)

sarampión *m,* measles

sarao *m,* soirée, evening party

sarasa *m, (inf* and contemptuous) pansy, faggot

sarcasmo *m,* sarcasm

sarcástico *a* sarcastic

sarcia *f,* load, cargo

sarcófago *m,* sarcophagus

sarda *f,* mackerel

sardana *f,* traditional Catalonian dance

sardina *f,* sardine. **s. arenque,** herring. **como sardinas en banasta,** *fig* packed like sardines

sardinal *m,* sardine net

sardinero (-ra) *a* sardine. *n* sardine seller or dealer. *m,* famous district of Santander

sardineta *f,* sprat; small sardine; *mil* chevron

sardo (-da) *a* and *n* Sardinian

sardónico *a* sardonic

sarga *f,* (silk) serge; willow

sargenta *f,* sergeant's wife; *inf* mannish, overbearing woman

sargentear *vt* to be in charge as a sergeant; command, captain; *inf* boss

sargento *m,* sergeant

sarmentoso *a* vine-like; twining

sarmiento *m,* vine shoot

sarna *f,* scabies; itch. **s. perruna,** mange. **más viejo que la s.,** *inf* older than the plague

sarnoso *a* itchy; mangy

sarraceno (-na) *a* Saracen. *n* Saracen; Moor

sarracina *f,* scuffle

sarrillo *m,* death rattle, rale; arum lily
sarro *m,* furry encrustation, scale; film; tartar (on teeth)
sarta *f,* string, link (of pearls, etc.); file, line
sartén *f,* frying pan. **tener la s. por el mango,** *inf* to be top dog
sastra *f,* female tailor; tailor's wife
sastre *m,* tailor. **ser buen s.,** *inf* to be an expert (in)
sastrería *f,* tailoring; tailor's shop
Satanás *m,* Satan; devil
satánico *a* satanic
satélite *m,* satellite; follower, admirer, sycophant
satén *m,* sateen
satinar *vt* to calender; glaze; satin (paper)
sátira *f,* satire
satírico *a* satiric
satirizar *vi* to write satires; *vt* satirize
sátiro *m,* satyr; *theat* indecent play
satisfacción *f,* settlement, payment; atonement, expiation; satisfaction; gratification; amends; complacency, conceit; contentment; apology. **tomar s.,** to avenge oneself
satisfacer *vt irr* to pay, settle; atone for, expiate; gratify; quench; fulfill, observe; compensate, indemnify; discharge, meet; convince, persuade; allay, relieve; reward; explain; answer, satisfy; *vr* avenge oneself; satisfy oneself. *Pres. Ind.* **satisfago, satisfaces,** etc. *Fut.* **satisfaré,** etc. *Condit.* **satisfaría,** etc. *Preterite* **satisfice,** etc. *Past Part.* **satisfecho.** *Pres. Subjunc.* **satisfaga,** etc. *Imperf. Subjunc.* **satisficiese,** etc.
satisfactorio *a* satisfactory
satisfecho *a* self-satisfied, complacent; happy, contented
sátrapa *m,* satrap; *inf* cunning fellow
saturación *f,* saturation
saturar *vt* to satiate, fill; saturate
saturnino *a* saturnine, melancholy, morose
saturnismo *m,* saturnism, lead poisoning
Saturno *m,* Saturn
sauce *m,* willow. **s. llorón,** weeping willow
saúco *m,* elder tree
saurio *a* and *m,* saurian
savia *f,* sap; energy, zest
sáxeo *a* stone, stony
saxófono *or* **saxofón** *m,* saxophone
saya *f,* skirt; long tunic
sayal *m,* thick woolen material
sayo *m,* loose smock; *inf* any garment. **cortar un s. (a),** *inf* to gossip behind a person's back
sayón *m,* executioner; *inf* hideous-looking man
sazón *f,* ripeness, maturity; season; perfection, excellence; opportunity; taste, flavor; seasoning. **a la s.,** at that time, then. **en s.,** in season; opportunely
sazonador (-ra) *a* seasoning. *n* seasoner
sazonar *vt cul* to season; mature; *vr* mature, ripen
se *object pron reflexive 3rd sing* and *pl mf* 1. Used as accusative (direct object) himself, herself, yourself, themselves, yourselves (e.g. **Juan se ha cortado,** John has cut himself). 2. Used as dative or indirect object to himself, at himself, herself, themselves, etc. (e.g. **María se mira al espejo,** Mary looks at herself in the mirror). Reciprocity is also expressed by reflexive (e.g. **No se hablan,** They do not speak to one another). When a direct object pron. (accusative) and an indirect object pron., both in the 3rd pers. (sing. or pl.), are used together, the indirect object pron. becomes **se** (instead of **le** or **les**) (e.g. **Se lo doy,** I give it to him). Many Spanish reflexive verbs have English equivalents that are not reflexive (e.g. **desayunarse,** to breakfast, **arrepentirse,** to repent, **quejarse,** to complain). Some intransitive (neuter) verbs have a modified meaning when used reflexively (e.g. **marcharse,** to go away, **dormirse,** to fall asleep). The passive may be formed by using **se** + 3rd pers. sing. of verb (e.g. **se dice,** it is said, people say). A number of impersonal phrases are also formed in this way (e.g. **«Se alquila,»** "To Let," **«Se vende,»** "For Sale"). The imperative is used in the

same way (e.g. **Véase la página dos,** See page two)
sebáceo *a* sebaceous
sebo *m,* tallow; candle grease; fat, grease
seboso *a* tallowy; fat, greasy
seca *f,* drought; *naut* unsubmerged sandbank
secadero *m,* drying place, drying room
secadora *f,* dryer, drying machine, clothesdryer. **s. de cabello,** hairdryer
secafirmas *m,* blotting pad
secamente *adv* tersely, brusquely, curtly; dryly
secamiento *m,* drying
secano *m,* nonirrigated land; *naut* unsubmerged sandbank; anything very dry
secante *a* drying. *a* and *f, geom* secant. **papel s.,** blotting paper
secar *vt* to dry; desiccate; annoy, bore; *vr* dry; dry up (of streams, etc.); wilt, fade (of plants); become parched; grow thin, become emaciated; be very thirsty; become hard-hearted
sección *f,* act of cutting; section, part, portion; *geom mil* section. **s. cónica,** conic section. **s. de amenidades,** entertainment section (of a newspaper). **s. de reserva,** *mil* reserve list
seccionar *vt* to divide into sections, section
seccionario *a* sectional
secesión *f,* secession
secesionista *a* and *mf* secessionist
seco *a* dry; dried up, parched; faded, wilted; dead (plants); dried (fruits); thin, emaciated; unadorned; barren, arid; brusque, curt; severe, strict; indifferent, unenthusiastic; sharp (sounds); dry (wines). **a secas,** only; solely; simply, just. **en s.,** on dry land; curtly. *inf* **dejar s. (a),** to dumbfound, petrify
secreción *f,* segregation, separation; *med* secretion
secreta *f, law* secret trial or investigation; *ecc* secret(s); toilet, water closet
secretar *vt med* to secrete
secretaría *f,* secretaryship; secretary's office, secretariat
secretario (-ia) *n* secretary; amanuensis, clerk. *m,* actuary; registrar. **s. de asuntos exteriores** *or* **s. de asuntos extranjeros,** foreign secretary. **s. particular,** private secretary
secretear *vi inf* to whisper, have secrets
secreteo *m, inf* whispering, exchanging of secrets
secreto *m,* secret; secrecy, silence; confidential information; mystery; secret drawer. *a* secret; private, confidential. **en s.,** in secret, confidentially. **s. a voces,** open secret
secta *f,* sect
sectario (-ia) *a* and *n* sectarian. *n* fanatical believer
sectarismo *m,* sectarianism
sector *m,* sector
secuaz *mf* follower, disciple
secuela *f,* sequel, result
secuencia *f, ecc* sequence; (cinema) sequence
secuestrador (-ra) *a* sequestrating. *n* sequestrator
secuestrar *vt* to sequester; kidnap
secuestro *m,* sequestration; kidnapping; *surg* sequestrum
secular *a* secular, lay; centennial; age-old, ancient; *ecc* secular
secularización *f,* secularization
secularizar *vt* to secularize; *vr* become secularized
secundar *vt* to second, aid
secundario *a* secondary; accessory, subordinate; *geol* mesozoic
sed *f,* thirst; desire, yearning, appetite. **apagar (or matar) la s.,** to quench one's thirst. **tener s.,** to be thirsty
seda *f,* silk; bristle (boar, etc.). **s. cordelada,** twist silk. **s. ocal,** floss silk. **s. vegetal** *or* **s. artificial,** artificial silk. *inf* **como una s.,** as smooth as silk; sweet-tempered; achieved without any trouble
sedación *f,* calming, soothing
sedal *m,* fish line
sedar *vt* to soothe, calm

sedativo *a* and *m, med* sedative

sede *f, ecc* see; bishop's throne; *fig* seat (of government, etc.); Holy See (also **Santa S.**)

sedentario *a* sedentary

sedeño *a* silky; silken, made of silk

sedería *f,* silk goods; silks; silk shop

sedero (-ra) *a* silk. *n* silk weaver or worker; silk merchant

sedición *f,* sedition

sedicioso *a* seditious

sediento *a* thirsty; parched, dry (land); eager (for), desirous (of)

sedimentación *f,* sedimentation

sedimentar *vt* to leave a sediment; *vr* settle, form a sediment

sedimento *m,* sediment; dregs, lees; scale (on boilers)

sedoso *a* silky, silk-like

seducción *f,* seduction; temptation, blandishment, wile; charm, allurement

seducir *vt irr* to seduce; tempt, lead astray; charm, attract; corrupt, bribe. See **conducir**

seductivo *a* tempting; seductive, charming

seductor (-ra) *a* tempting; charming. *n* seducer; charming person

sefardí *mf* Iberian Jew or Jewess; *pl* Sephardim. *a* Sephardic

segadera *f,* sickle

segadero *a* reapable, able to be reaped

segador *m,* reaper, harvester

segadora *f,* mowing machine, harvester; woman harvester

segar *vt irr* to scythe, cut down; reap, harvest; mow. See **cegar**

seglar *a* secular, lay. *mf* layman

segmento *m,* segment; *geom* segment. **s. de émbolo,** piston ring

segoviano (-na) *a* and *n* Segovian

segregación *f,* segregation

segregar *vt* to segregate, separate; *med* secrete

seguida *f,* continuation, prolongation. **de s.,** continuously; immediately. **en s.,** at once, immediately

seguidamente *adv* continuously; immediately

seguidilla *f,* popular Spanish tune and dance and verse sung to them; *inf* diarrhea

seguido *a* continuous, successive; direct, straight

seguidor (-ra) *a* following. *n* follower, disciple

seguimiento *m,* following, pursuit; continuation, resumption

seguir *vt irr* to follow; go after, pursue; prosecute, execute; continue, go on; accompany, go with; exercise (a profession); subscribe to, believe in; agree with; persecute; pester, annoy; imitate; *law* institute (a suit); handle, manage; *vr* result, follow as a consequence; follow in order, happen by turn; originate. *Pres. Part.* **siguiendo.** *Pres. Ind.* **sigo, sigues, sigue, siguen.** *Pres. Subjunc.* **siga,** etc. *Imperf. Subjunc.* **siguiese**

según *adv* according to; as. **s. parece,** as it seems. **s. y como,** as, according to

segunda *f, mus* second

segundar *vt* to repeat, do again; *vi* be second, follow the first

segundero *a agr* of the second flowering or fruiting. *m,* second hand (of a watch)

segundo *a* second. *m,* second in command, deputy head; *ast geom* second. **segunda intención,** double meaning. **segunda velocidad,** *aut* second gear. **de segunda mano,** second-hand. **sin s.,** without peer or equal

segundogénito (-ta) *a* and *n* secondborn

segundón *m,* second son; any son but the eldest

segurador *m,* surety, security (person)

seguramente *adv* securely, safely; surely, of course, naturally

seguridad *f,* security; safety; certainty; trustworthiness; *com* surety. **con toda s.,** with complete safety, surely, absolutely. **de s.,** *a* safety

seguro *a* secure; safe; certain, sure; firm, fixed; reliable, trustworthy; unfailing. *m,* certainty; haven, place of safety; *com* insurance; permit; *mech* ratchet. **s. contra incendio, accidentes, robo,** fire, accident, burglary insurance. **s. sobre la vida,** life insurance. **de s.,** surely, certainly. **en s.,** in safety

seis *a* six; sixth. *m,* six; sixth (of the month); playing card or domino with six spots. **Son las s.,** It is six o'-clock

seiscientos *a* six hundred; six-hundredth. *m,* six hundred

selección *f,* selection, choice. **s. natural,** natural selection

seleccionar *vt* to select, choose

selectivo *a* selective

selecto *a* choice, select, excellent

sellador (-ra) *a* sealing, stamping. *n* sealer, stamper

selladura *f,* sealing, stamping

sellar *vt* to seal; stamp; end, conclude; close

sello *m,* seal; stamp. **s. fiscal,** stamp duty. **s. postal,** postage stamp

selva *f,* forest, wood; jungle

Selva Negra, la the Black Forest

selvático *a* sylvan, wood, forest; wild

selvoso *a* wooded, sylvan

semafórico *a* semaphoric

semáforo *m,* semaphore, traffic light.

semana *f,* week; week's salary. **S. Mayor** or **S. Santa,** Holy Week. **entre s.,** during the week, on weekdays; weekdays

semanal *a* weekly; of a week's duration

semanario *a* weekly. *m,* weekly periodical

semanero *a* employed by the week

semántica *f,* semantics

semántico *a* semantic

semblante *m,* facial expression, countenance; face; appearance, look, aspect. **componer el s.,** to pull oneself together, straighten one's face. **mudar de s.,** to change color, change one's expression; alter (of circumstances)

semblanza *f,* biographical sketch. **s. literaria,** short literary biography

sembradera *f,* sowing machine

sembradío *a agr* ready for sowing

sembrado *m,* sown land

sembrador (-ra) *a* sowing. *n* sower

sembradura *f, agr* sowing

sembrar *vt irr agr* to sow; scatter, sprinkle; spread, disseminate. See **sentar**

semeja *f,* resemblance, similarity; indication, sign (gen. *pl*)

semejante *a* like, similar; such a; *math* similar. *m,* similarity, imitation. *mf* fellow man

semejanza *f,* similarity, likeness. **a s. de,** in the likeness of; like

semejar(se) *vi* and *vr* to resemble

semen *m,* semen; *bot* seed

semental *a agr* seed; breeding (of male animals). *m,* stallion

sementar *vt agr* to sow

sementera *f, agr* sowing; sown land; seedbed; seedtime; *fig* hotbed, nursery, genesis

sementero *m,* seed bag; seed bed

semestral *a* biannual, half-yearly; lasting six months

semestre *a* biannual. *m,* half-year, period of six months; six months' salary; semester

semicircular *a* semicircular

semicírculo *m,* semicircle

semidifunto *a* half-dead

semidiós *m,* demigod

semidiosa *f,* demigoddess

semidormido *a* half-asleep

semiesférico *a* hemispherical

semilla *f, bot* seed; *fig* germ, genesis

semillero *m,* seedbed; nursery; *fig* hotbed, origin

semilunio *m, ast* half-moon

seminario *m*, seedbed; nursery; genesis, origin; seminary; tutorial. **s. conciliar,** theological seminary

seminarista *mf* seminarist

semiótica *f*, *med* symptomatology; semiotics

semita *mf* Semite. *a* Semitic

semítico *a* Semitic

semitismo *m*, Semitism

semitono *m*, *mus* semitone

semitransparente *a* semitransparent

semivivo *a* half-alive

sémola *f*, semolina

sempiterna *f*, everlasting flower; thick woolen material

sempiterno *a* eternal

sen *m*, senna

Sena, el the Seine

sena *f*, *bot* senna; six-spotted die

senado *m*, senate; senate house; any grave assembly

senador *m*, senator

senaduría *f*, senatorship

senario *a* senary

senatorio *a* senatorial

sencillez *f*, simplicity; naturalness; easiness; ingenuousness, candor

sencillo *a* simple; unmixed; natural; thin, light (fabric); easy; ingenuous, candid; unadorned, plain; single; sincere

senda *f*, path, footpath; way; means

senderear *vt* to conduct along a path; make a pathway; *vi* attain by tortuous means

sendero *m*, footpath, path

sendos, sendas *a m*, and *f pl*, one each (e.g. **Les dio sendos lápices,** He gave them each a pencil)

senectud *f*, old age

senegalés (-esa) *a* and *n* Senegalese

senescal *m*, seneschal

senil *a* senile

senilidad *f*, senility

seno *m*, hollow; hole; concavity; bosom, breast; chest; uterus, womb; any internal cavity of the body; bay, cove; lap (of a woman); interior (of anything), heart; gulf; *math* sine; *anat* sinus

sensación *f*, sensation

sensacional *a* sensational

sensacionalista *a* sensationalist

sensatez *f*, prudence, good sense

sensato *a* prudent, wise

sensibilidad *f*, sensibility

sensibilizar *vt phot* to sensitize

sensible *a* sensible, sensitive; tender, feeling; perceptible; noticeable, definite; sensitive; sad, regrettable

sensiblemente *adv* appreciably; perceptibly; painfully, sadly

sensiblería *f*, sentimentality, sentimentalism

sensiblero *a* oversentimental

sensitiva *f*, sensitive plant, mimosa

sensitivo *a* sensuous; sensitive, sensible

sensorio *a* sensory. *m*, sensorium

sensual *a* sensual; sensitive, sensible; carnal, voluptuous

sensualidad *f*, sensuality; sensualism

sensualismo *m*, sensualism; *phil* sensationalism

sensualista *mf phil* sensationalist; sensualist

sentadero *m*, resting place, improvised seat

sentado *a* prudent, circumspect

sentar *vt irr* to seat; *vi* inf suit, agree with (e.g. **No me sienta este clima** (este plato), This climate (dish) doesn't suit me); fit, become; *inf* please, satisfy, be agreeable to; *vr* sit down; *inf* leave a mark on the skin. *Pres. Ind.* **siento, sientas, sienta, sientan.** *Pres. Subjunc.* **siente, sientes, siente, sienten**

sentencia *f*, opinion, belief; maxim; *law* verdict, sentence; decision, judgment. *law* **fulminar** (or **pronunciar**) **la s.,** to pass sentence

sentenciador *a law* sentencing

sentenciar *vt law* to sentence; *inf* destine, intend

sentencioso *a* sententious

sentidamente *adv* feelingly; sadly, regretfully

sentido *m*, sense (hearing, seeing, touch, smell, taste); understanding, sense; meaning, interpretation, signification; perception, discrimination; judgment; direction, way. *a* and *past part* felt; expressive; hypersensitive, touchy. **s. común,** common sense. **costar un s.,** *fig inf* to cost a fortune. **perder el s.,** to lose consciousness

sentimental *a* emotional; sentimental; romantic

sentimentalismo *m*, emotional quality; sentimentalism

sentimiento *m*, feeling, sentiment; sensation, impression; grief, sorrow. **Le acompaño a usted en su s.,** I sympathize with you in your sorrow (bereavement)

sentina *f*, well (of a ship); *naut* bilge; cesspool; sink of iniquity

sentir *vt irr* to feel, experience; hear; appreciate; grieve, regret; believe, consider; envisage, foresee; *vr* complain; suffer; think or consider oneself; crack; feel, be; go rotten, decay (gen. with *estar + past part.*). *m*, view, opinion; feeling. **sin s.,** without feeling; without noticing. *Pres. Part.* **sintiendo.** *Pres. Ind.* **siento, sientes, siente, sienten.** *Preterite* **sintió, sintieron.** *Pres. Subjunc.* **sienta, sientas, sienta, sintamos, sintáis, sientan.** *Imperf. Subjunc.* **sintiese,** etc.

seña *f*, sign, mark; gesture; *mil* password; signal; *pl* address, domicile. **s. mortal,** definite or unmistakable sign. **dar señas,** to show signs, manifest. **hablar por señas,** to converse by signs

señal *f*, mark, sign; boundary stone; landmark; scar; signal; trace, vestige; indication, symptom, token; symbol, sign; image, representation; prodigy, marvel; deposit, advance payment. **s. de aterrizaje,** *aer* landing signal. **s. de niebla,** fog signal. **señales horarias,** *rad* time signal. **en s.,** as a sign, in proof of. **s. luminosa de la circulación,** traffic light, traffic robot

señaladamente *adv* especially, particularly, notably

señalado *a* famous, celebrated; important, notable

señalador *m*, *Argentina* bookmark

señalamiento *m*, marking; pointing out; appointment, designation

señalar *vt* to mark; indicate, point out; fix, arrange; wound; signal; stamp; appoint (to office); *vr* excel

señero *a* solitary, isolated

señor *a inf* gentlemanly. *m*, owner, master; mister, esquire; **(S.)** the Lord; lord, sire. **s. de horca y cuchillo,** feudal lord, lord of life and death

señora *f*, lady; owner, mistress; madam; wife. **s. de compañía,** chaperon; lady companion. **Nuestra S.,** Our Lady

señorear *vt* to control, run, manage; master; domineer; appropriate, seize; dominate, overlook; restrain (emotions); *vr* behave with dignity

señoría *f*, lordship (title and person); lordship, jurisdiction; area, territory; control, restraint

señoría *f*, dignity, sedateness; self-control

señorial *a* manorial; noble, dignified, lordly

señoril *a* lordly, noble, aristocratic

señorío *m*, lordship; jurisdiction, dominion

señorita *f*, young lady; miss; *inf* mistress of the house

señorito *m*, young gentleman; *inf* master of the house; master (address); *inf* young man about town

señuelo *m*, decoy; bait; allurement, attraction. **caer en el s.,** *fig inf* to fall into the trap

sepancuantos *m*, *inf* scolding, rebuke; spanking

separación *f*, separation

separado *a* separate

separador (-ra) *a* separating. *n* separator. *m*, filter. **s. de aceite,** oil filter

separar *vt* to separate; divide; dismiss (from a post); lay aside; *vr* retire, resign; separate

separatismo *m*, separatism

separatista *a* and *mf* separatist

septeno *a*. See **séptimo**

septentrión *m*, *ast* Great Bear; north

septentrional *a* north; northern
septeto *m*, septet
septicemia *f*, septicemia
séptico *a* septic
septiembre *m*, September
septillo *m*, *mus* septuplet
séptima *f*, *mus* seventh
séptimo *a* and *m*, seventh
septuagenario (-ia) *a* and *n* septuagenarian
septuagésimo *a* seventieth; septuagesimal. *m*, seventieth
séptuplo *a* sevenfold
sepulcral *a* sepulchral
sepulcro *m*, sepulcher
sepultador (-ra) *a* burying. *n* gravedigger; burier
sepultar *vt* to inter, bury; hide, cover up
sepultura *f*, interment; grave; tomb
sepulturero *m*, gravedigger
sequedad *f*, dryness, barrenness; acerbity, sharpness
sequía *f*, drought
séquito *m*, following, suite, retinue; general approval, popularity
ser *m*, essence, nature; being; existence, life. **El S. Supremo,** The Supreme Being, God
ser *vi irr* to be (e.g. **El sombrero es azul,** The hat is blue). **Ser** may agree with either subject or complement, though when latter is *pl* the verb tends to be so too (e.g. **Son las once, (horas),** It is eleven o'clock. **Cien libras son poco dinero,** A hundred pounds is a small amount). If verbal complement is pers. pron., **ser** agrees with it both in number and person (e.g. **Son ellos,** It is they. **Soy yo,** It is I). In impers. phrases the pron. is not expressed (e.g. **Es difícil,** It is difficult. **Es sorprendente,** It is surprising). **ser** means to exist (e.g. **Pienso luego soy,** I think, therefore I am). **ser** (also **ser de** with nouns or obj. prons.) means to belong to, be the property of (e.g. **Este gato es mío,** This cat is mine. **El libro es de Juan,** The book belongs to John). Signifies to happen, occur (e.g. **¿Cómo fue eso?** How did that happen?). Means to be suitable or fitting (e.g. **Este vestido no es para una señora mayor,** This dress is not suitable for an elderly lady). Expresses price, to be worth (e.g. **¿A cuánto es la libra?** How much is it a pound?; How much is the pound (sterling) worth?). Means to be a member of, belong to (e.g. **Es de la Academia Española,** He is a member of the Spanish Academy). Means to be of use, be useful for (e.g. **Esta casa no es para una familia numerosa,** This house is no use for a large family). **Ser** expresses nationality (e.g. **Son francesas,** They are French. **Somos de Londres,** We are from London). *Auxiliary verb* used to form passive tense (e.g. **Esta historia ha sido leída por muchos,** This story has been read by many. **Fueron mandados al Japón,** They were sent to Japan. **s. de ver,** to be worth seeing. **s. para poco,** to be of little use, amount to little. **s. testigo de,** to witness. **¡Cómo es eso!** How can that be! Surely not! **¡Cómo ha de s.!** How should it be!; One must resign oneself. **Érase una vez** *or* **que érase,** Once upon a time. **es a saber,** viz., that is to say. **un sí es no es,** a touch of, a suspicion of). *Pres. Part.* **siendo.** *Pres. Ind.* **soy, eres, es, somos, sois, son.** *Fut.* **seré,** etc. *Condit.* **sería,** etc. *Preterite* **fui, fuiste, fue, fuimos, fuisteis, fueron.** *Imperf.* **era,** etc. *Past Part.* **sido.** *Pres. Subjunc.* **sea,** etc. *Imperf. Subjunc.* **fuese,** etc. *Imperat.* **sé**
sera *f*, large frail
seráfico *a* seraphic
serafín *m*, seraphim
serbal *m*, service tree
serena *f*, serenade; *inf* dew
serenar *vt* to calm; soothe; clear; *vr* grow calm; clear up (weather); clear (liquids); be soothed or pacified
serenata *f*, serenade
serenidad *f*, serenity, composure, tranquility; Serene Highness (title)

sereno *a* cloudless, fair; composed, serene. *m*, dew; night watchman
sericultor *m*, silk cultivator, sericulturist
sericultura *f*, silk culture
serie *f*, series, sequence, succession; *math* progression; (*biol elec*) series; break (in billiards)
seriedad *f*, seriousness, earnestness; gravity; austerity; sternness; importance; sincerity; solemnity
serigrafía *f*, silkscreen printing
serio *a* serious, earnest; grave; austere; stern; important; sincere, genuine; solemn. **en s.,** seriously
sermón *m*, sermon; scolding. **dar un s.,** to give a sermon; scold
sermonar *vi* to preach
sermonear *vi* to preach sermons; *vt* scold
sermoneo *m*, *inf* scolding
seroja *f*, withered leaves; brushwood
serpear *vi* to wind, twist; wriggle, squirm; coil
serpenteado *a* winding
serpentear *vi* to wind, twist, meander; stagger along; wriggle; coil; *aer* yaw
serpenteo *m*, winding, twisting; wriggling; coiling; *aer* yaw
serpentín *m*, *chem* worm; coil (in industry); *min* serpentine
serpentina *f*, *min* serpentine; paper streamer
serpentino *a* serpentine; *poet* winding, sinuous
serpiente *f*, snake, serpent; Satan, the Devil; *ast* Serpent. **s. de anteojos,** cobra. **s. de cascabel,** rattlesnake
serpollo *m*, *bot* shoot, new branch; sprout; sucker
serrado *a* serrate
serrallo *m*, harem, seraglio; brothel
serrana, serranilla *f*, pastoral poem
serranía *f*, mountainous territory
serrano (-na) *a* mountain, highland. *n* highlander, mountain dweller
serrucho *m*, handsaw. **s. de calar,** fretsaw
Servia Serbia
servible *a* serviceable; useful
servicial *a* useful, serviceable; obliging, obsequious
servicio *m*, service; domestic service; cult, devotion; care, attendance; military service; set, service; department, section; present of money; cover (cutlery, etc., at table); domestic staff, servants. **s. informativo,** news service. **s. nocturno permanente,** all-night service. **hacer un flaco s. (a),** *inf* to do someone an ill turn. **prestar servicios,** to render service, serve
servidor (-ra) *n* servant, domestic; name by which one refers to oneself (e.g. **Un s. lo hará con mucho gusto,** I (your servant) will do it with much pleasure). *m*, wooer, lover; bowler (in cricket). **los servidores de una ametralladora,** the crew (of a gun). **Quedo de Vd. atento y seguro s.,** I remain your obedient servant (in letters), Yours faithfully
servidumbre *f*, serfdom; servitude; servants, domestic staff; obligation, duty; enslavement (by passions); right of way; use, service
servil *a* servile; humble
servilismo *m*, servility; abjectness; absolutism (Spanish history)
servilleta *f*, table napkin. **s. higiénica,** sanitary napkin
servilletero *m*, napkin ring
servio (-ia) *a* and *n* Serbian
servir *vi irr* to be employed (by), be in the service (of); serve (as), perform the duties (of); be of use; wait (on), be subject to. *mil* serve in the armed forces; wait at table; be suitable or favorable; *sport* serve; perform a service; follow the lead (cards); (*with de*) act as, be a deputy for; be a substitute for; *vt* serve; worship; do a favor to; woo, court; serve (food, drink); *vr* be pleased or willing, deign; help oneself to (food); (*with de*) make use of. **no s. para nada,** to be good for nothing, be useless. **No sirves para tales cosas,** You are no good at this sort of thing. **Para s. a Vd,** At your service. **¡Sírvase de . . . !** (followed by infin.), Please! **s. de,** to

serve as (e.g. **s. de base a,** to serve as a basis for). See **pedir**
sésamo *m,* sesame
sesenta *a* and *m,* sixty; sixtieth
sesentavo *a* and *m,* sixtieth
sesentón (-ona) *n inf* person of sixty
sesga *f, sew* gore
sesgadamente *adv* on the slant; askew; obliquely
sesgado *a* oblique, slanting
sesgar *vt sew* to cut on the bias; slant, slope; place askew, twist to one side
sesgo *a* slanting, oblique; serious-faced. *m,* slope, slant, obliquity; compromise, middle way. **al s.,** on the slant
sesión *f,* session, meeting; conference, consultation; *law* sitting; term. **abrir la s.,** to open the meeting. **levantar la s.,** to adjourn the meeting
seso *m,* brain; prudence; *pl* brains. **perder el s.,** to go mad; *fig* lose one's head
sestear *vi* to take an afternoon nap; rest; settle
sesudez *f,* prudence, shrewdness
sesudo *a* sensible, prudent
seta *f,* mushroom. **s. venenosa,** poisonous toadstool
setal *m,* mushroom bed, patch, or field
setecientos *a* and *m,* seven hundred; seven-hundredth
setenta *a* and *m,* seventy; seventieth
setentavo *a* and *m,* seventieth
setentón (-ona) *n* septuagenarian
seter *m,* setter (dog)
setiembre *m.* See **septiembre**
seto *m,* fence; hedge
seudo *a* pseudo
seudónimo *m,* pseudonym
severamente *adv* severely, harshly
severidad *f,* severity; harshness; strictness, rigor; austerity, seriousness
severo *a* severe; harsh; strict, rigid, scrupulous, exact; austere, serious
sevillanas *f pl,* Sevillian dance and its music
sevillano (-na) *a* and *n* of or from Seville, Sevillian
sexagenario (-ia) *n* sexagenarian
sexagésimo *a* sixtieth
sexo *m,* sex; (sexual) organ
sexología *f,* sexology
sexólogo (-ga) *n* sexologist
sexta *f, ecc* sext; *mus* sixth
sextante *m, math* sextant
sexteto *m,* sextet
sexto *a* sixth
sextuplicación *f,* multiplication by six
sextuplicar *vt* to multiply by six, sextuple
séxtuplo *a* sixfold
sexualidad *f,* sexuality
si *m, mus* B, seventh note of the scale. *conjunc* if; whether; even if, although. In conditional clause, **si,** meaning if, is followed by indicative tense unless statement be contrary to fact (e.g. **Si pierdes el tren, volverás a casa,** If you miss your train you will return home, *but* **Si hubieran venido habríamos ido al campo,** If they had come (but they didn't) we would have gone to the country). **Si** is used at the beginning of a clause to make expressions of doubt, desire, or affirmation more emphatic (e.g. **¡Si lo sabrá él, con toda su experiencia!** Of course he knows it, with all his experience. **¿Si será falsa la noticia?** Can the news be false?) **Si** also means whether (e.g. **Me preguntaron si era médico o militar,** They asked me whether I was a doctor or a soldier). Sometimes means even if, although (e.g. **Si viniesen no lo harían,** Even if they came they would not do it. **como si,** as if. **por si acaso,** in case, in the event of. **si bien,** although.
sí *pers pron reflexive 3rd pers m,* and *f, sing* and *pl* himself, herself, itself, themselves. Always used with prep. (e.g. **para sí,** for himself, herself, etc. **de por sí,** separately, on its own. **decir para sí,** to say to oneself)
sí *adv* yes. **sí** *or* **sí que** is frequently used to emphasize a verb generally in contrast to a previous negative (e.g.

Ellos no lo harán, pero yo sí, They won't do it but I will). Often translated by 'did' (e.g. **No lo vi todo, pero lo que sí vi,** I didn't see it all, but what I did see . . .). *m,* assent; yes; consent. **dar el sí,** to say yes; agree; accept an offer of marriage
siamés (-esa) *a* and *n* Siamese. *m,* Thai (language)
sibarita *a* sybaritic. *mf* sybarite
sibarítico *a* sybaritic; sensual
sibaritismo *m,* sybaritism
siberiano (-na) *a* and *n* Siberian
sibila *f,* sibyl
sibilante *a* sibilant
sibilino *a* sibylline
sicario *m,* paid assassin
Sicilia Sicily
siciliano (-na) *a* and *n* Sicilian
sicoanálisis *m,* psychoanalysis
sicoanalista *mf* psychoanalyst
sicoanalizar *vt* to psychoanalyze
sicofanta, sicofante *m,* sycophant
sicología *f,* psychology
sicológico *a* psychological
sicólogo (-ga) *n* psychologist
sicomoro *m,* sycamore
sicopático *a* psychopathic
sicosis *f, med* psychosis
sicoterapia *f,* psychotherapy
SIDA *m,* AIDS
sideral, sidéreo *a* sidereal
sidra *f,* cider
siega *f,* reaping, harvesting; harvest time; harvest, crop
siembra *f, agr* sowing; seedtime; sown field
siempre *adv* always. **s. que,** provided that; whenever. **para s.,** forever. **por s. jamás,** for always, for ever and ever
siempreviva *f, bot* everlasting flower. **s. mayor,** houseleek
sien *f, anat* temple
sierpe *f,* serpent, snake; anything that wriggles; kite (toy); *bot* sucker; hideous person
sierra *f, carp* saw; ridge of mountains; sawfish; slope; hillside. **s. de cerrojero,** hacksaw. **s. de cinta,** handsaw
siervo (-va) *n* slave; servant; serf
siesta *f,* noonday heat; afternoon nap
siete *a* seven; seventh. *m,* seven; seventh (days of the month); playing card with seven spots; number seven. **las s.,** seven o'clock. *inf* **más que s.,** more than somewhat, extremely
sietemesino (-na) *n* seven-month-old child; *fig inf* young cock
sífilis *f,* syphilis
sifilítico (-ca) *a* and *n* syphilitic
sifón *m,* siphon; siphon bottle; soda water; *mech* trap
sigilar *vt* to seal; hide, conceal
sigilo *m,* seal; secrecy, concealment; silence, reserve
sigiloso *a* secret, silent
sigla *f,* acronym
siglo *m,* century; long time, age; social intercourse, society, world. **s. de oro,** golden age. **en** *or* **por los siglos de los siglos,** for ever and ever
signar *vt* to sign; make the sign of the cross over; *vr* cross oneself
signatario (-ia) *a* and *n* signatory
signatura *f, print* signature; mark, sign; *mus* signature
significación *f,* **significado** *m,* meaning; importance, significance
significante *a* significant
significar *vt* to signify, indicate; mean; publish, make known; *vi* represent, mean; be worth
significativo *a* significant
signo *m,* sign, indication, token; sign, character; *math* symbol; sign of the zodiac; *mus* sign; *med* symptom; *ecc* gesture of benediction; destiny, fate
siguemepollo *m, inf* streamer

siguiente *a* following; next, subsequent. **el día s.,** the next day

sílaba *f*, syllable

silabario *m*, speller, spelling book

silabear *vi* and *vt* to pronounce by syllables, syllabize

silabeo *m*, pronouncing syllable by syllable, syllabication

silábico *a* syllabic

sílabo *m*, syllabus, list

silba *f*, hissing (as a sign of disapproval)

silbador (-ra) *a* whistling; hissing. *n* whistler; one who hisses

silbar *vi* to whistle; whizz, rush through the air; *vi* and *vt theat* hiss

silbato *m*, whistle; air hole

silbido, silbo *m*, whistle, whistling; hiss, hissing

silenciador *m*, (*aut* firearms) silencer

silenciar *vt* to silence; keep secret

silenciario *a* vowed to perpetual silence

silencio *m*, silence; noiselessness, quietness; omission, disregard; *mus* rest. **en s.,** in silence; quietly; uncomplainingly. **pasar en s. (una cosa),** to pass over (something) in silence, omit. **s. de muerte,** deathly silence

silencioso *a* silent; noiseless; tranquil, quiet. *m*, (*aut* firearms) silencer

silesio (-ia) *a* and *n* Silesian

sílfide *f*, **silfo** *m*, sylph

silicato *m*, *chem* silicate

sílice *f*, *chem* silica

silla *f*, chair; riding saddle; *mech* rest, saddle; *ecc* see. **s. de manos,** sedan chair. **s. de montar,** riding saddle. **s. de posta,** post chaise. **s. de ruedas,** wheelchair. **s. de tijera,** deck chair; campstool. **s. giratoria,** swivel chair. **s. poltrona,** easy chair. *inf* **pegársele la s.,** to overstay one's welcome

sillar *m*, ashlar, quarry stone; horseback

sillería *f*, set of chairs; pew, choir stalls; chair factory; shop where chairs are sold; chair making; *mas* ashlar masonry

sillero (-ra) *n* chair maker or seller; saddler

silleta *f*, bedpan; fireman's lift

silletero *m*, runner, sedan chair carrier

sillín *m*, light riding saddle; seat, saddle (of bicycles, etc.)

sillón *m*, armchair; sidesaddle. **s.-cama,** reclining chair. **s. de mimbres,** cane chair

silo *m*, *agr* silo; dark cavern, dark cave

silogismo *m*, syllogism

silogístico *a* syllogistic

silueta *f*, silhouette; figure

silúrico *a* silurian

siluro *m*, catfish; *nav* self-propelling torpedo

silva *f*, literary miscellany; metrical form

silvestre *a bot* wild; sylvan; uncultivated; savage

silvicultor *m*, forester

silvicultura *f*, forestry

sima *f*, abyss, chasm

simbiosis *f*, symbiosis

simbólico *a* symbolical

simbolismo *m*, symbolism

simbolista *mf* symbolist

simbolización *f*, symbolization

simbolizar *vt* to symbolize, represent

símbolo *m*, symbol. **s. de la fe,** *ecc* Creed

simetría *f*, symmetry

simétrico *a* symmetric; symmetrical

simetrizar *vt* to make symmetrical

símico *a* simian

simiente *f*, seed; semen; germ, genesis, origin

simiesco *a* apish, ape-like

símil *a* similar. *m*, comparison; simile

similar *a* similar

similitud *f*, similarity

simio (-ia) *n* ape

simón *m*, horse cab; cabdriver

simonía *f*, simony

simpatía *f*, liking, understanding, affection; fellow feeling; sympathy

simpático *a* friendly, nice, decent, congenial; sympathetic. **gran s.,** *anat* sympathetic

simpatizar *vi* to get on well, be congenial

simple *a* simple; single, not double; insipid; easy; plain, unadorned; stupid, silly; pure, unmixed; easily deceived, simple; naïve, ingenuous; mere; mild, meek. *mf* simpleton; fool

simpleza *f*, foolishness, stupidity; simplicity

simplicidad *f*, simplicity; candour, ingenuousness

simplicísimo *a sup* most simple, exceedingly simple

simplificable *a* simplifiable

simplificación *f*, simplification, simplifying

simplificador *a* simplifying

simplificar *vt* to simplify

simplista *mf* herbalist

simulación *f*, pretense, simulation

simulacro *m*, image, simulacrum; vision, fancy; *mil* mock battle

simuladamente *adv* pretendedly

simulador (-ra) *a* feigned. *n* dissembler

simular *vt* to feign, pretend

simultanear *vt* to perform simultaneously

simultaneidad *f*, simultaneousness

simultáneo *a* simultaneous

simún *m*, sandstorm

sin *prep* without (e.g. **Lo hizo s. hablar,** He did it without speaking). **s. embargo,** nevertheless. **s. fin,** endless. **s. hilos,** radio, wireless

sinagoga *f*, synagogue

sinapismo *m*, *med* mustard plaster; *inf* pest, bore

sincerarse *vr* to justify oneself; vindicate one's actions

sinceridad *f*, sincerity

sincero *a* sincere

síncopa *f*, *mus* syncopation; *gram* syncope

sincopar *vt* to syncopate; abbreviate

síncope *m*, syncope

sincrónico *a* synchronous

sincronismo *m*, synchronism

sincronizar *vt* to synchronize; *rad* tune in

sindéresis *f*, discretion, good sense

sindicación *f*, syndication

sindicado *m*, syndicate

sindical *a* syndical

sindicalismo *m*, syndicalism, trade unionism

sindicalista *mf* syndicalist, trade unionist. *a* syndicalistic, trade unionist

sindicar *vt* to accuse, charge; censure; syndicate

sindicato *m*, syndicate; trade union. **s. gremial,** trade union. **S. Internacional de Trabajadoras de la Aguja,** International Ladies' Garment Workers' Union

sindicatura *f*, (official) receivership

síndico *m*, *com* receiver, trustee

síndrome *m*, syndrome

sinecura *f*, sinecure

sinergia *f*, synergy

sinfín *m*, countless number

sinfonía *f*, symphony

sinfónico *a* symphonic

sinfonista *mf* composer of symphonies, player in a symphony orchestra

sinfonola *f*, jukebox

Singapur Singapore

singladura *f*, *naut* day's sailing; nautical twenty-four hours (beginning at midday)

singlar *vi naut* to sail a given course

singular *a* singular, single; individual; extraordinary, remarkable. *a* and *m*, *gram* singular

singularidad *f*, individuality, peculiarity; strangeness, remarkableness; oddness, eccentricity

singularizar *vt* to particularize, single out; *gram* make singular, singularize; *vr* distinguish oneself, stand out; be distinguished (by)

sinhueso *f*, *inf* tongue (organ of speech)

sínico *a* Chinese

siniestra *f,* left, lefthand
siniestro *a* left (side); vicious, perverse; sinister; unlucky. *m,* viciousness, depravity (gen. *pl*); shipwreck, sinking; disaster, catastrophe; *com* damage, loss
sinnúmero *m,* countless number
sino *m,* fate, destiny. *conjunc* but; except (e.g. **No lo hicieron ellos s. yo,** They didn't do it, I did. **no . . . s.,** not . . . , but); only (e.g. **No sólo lo dijo él s. ella,** Not only he said it, but she did too)
sínodo *m, (ecc ast)* synod; council
sinología *f,* sinology
sinólogo *m,* sinologist
sinonimia *f,* synonymy
sinónimo *a* synonymous. *m,* synonym
sinopsis *f,* synopsis
sinóptico *a* synoptic
sinrazón *f,* injustice, wrong
sinsabor *m,* unpleasantness, trouble; grief, anxiety
sintáctico *a* syntactic
sintaxis *f,* syntax
síntesis *f,* synthesis
sintético *a* synthetic
sintetizar *vt* to synthesize
sintoísmo *m,* Shintoism
síntoma *m,* symptom
sintomático *a* symptomatic
sintomatología *f,* symptomatology
sintonización *f, rad* tuning in
sintonizador *m, rad* tuner
sintonizar *vt rad* to tune in
sinuosidad *f,* sinuosity
sinuoso *a* sinuous, winding
sinvergüenza *mf* rascal, knave, rogue
Sión Zion
sionismo *m,* Zionism
sionista *a* and *mf* Zionist
siquiatra *m,* psychiatrist
siquiatría *f,* psychiatry
síquico *a* psychic
siquiera *conjunc* although, even if. **s. . . . s.,** whether . . . or. *adv* at least; even (e.g. **Hay que pedir mucho para tener s. la mitad,** One must ask a great deal to get even half). **ni s.,** not even (e.g. **No había nadie, ni s. un perro,** There was no one, not even a dog)
Siracusa Syracuse
siracusano (-na) *a* and *n* Syracusan
sirena *f,* mermaid, siren; siren; foghorn
sirga *f,* towline
sirgar *vt naut* to track, tow
Siria Syria
siríaco (-ca) *a* and *n* Syriac
sirio (-ia) *a* and *n* Syrian. *m,* Sirius
siroco *m,* sirocco
sirte *f,* sandbank, submerged rock
sirvienta *f,* female servant
sirviente *a* serving. *m,* servant
sisa *f,* pilfering; *sew* dart. **s. dorada,** gold lacquer
sisador (-ra) *n* filcher, pilferer
sisar *vt* to pilfer, filch, steal; *sew* take in, make darts in
sisear *vi* and *vt* to hiss (disapproval); sizzle
sísmico *a* seismic
sismógrafo *m,* seismograph
sismología *f,* seismology
sismológico *a* seismological
sismómetro *m,* seismometer
sistema *m,* system. **s. ferroviario,** railroad system. **s. métrico,** metric system
sistemático *a* systematic
sistematización *f,* systematization
sistematizar *vt* to systematize
sístole *f,* systole
sitiador *a* besieging. *m,* besieger
sitial *m,* ceremonial chair
sitiar *vt mil* to lay siege to; surround, besiege
sitio *m,* place, spot; room, space; site; locality; *mil* siege, blockade. **No hay s.,** There's no room

sito *past part* situated, located
situación *f,* situation; position; circumstances; condition, state; location
situado *past part* situated, placed. *m,* income, interest
situar *vt* to situate, locate, place; assign funds; *vr* place oneself
smoking *m,* tuxedo, tux, dinner jacket
snobismo *m,* snobbery
so *prep* under (used only with **color, pena, pretexto, capa**) (e.g. **so color de,** under the pretext of). *interj* **¡So!** Whoa! (to horses)
soba *f,* rubbing; kneading; massaging; drubbing, beating; handling, touching
sobacal *a* underarm, axillary
sobaco *m,* armpit; *bot* axil
sobajar *vt* to squeeze, press
sobaquera *f, sew* armhole; dress shield
sobar *vt* to rub; knead; massage; beat, thrash; handle, touch, paw (persons); soften
soberanear *vi* to tyrannize, domineer
soberanía *f,* sovereignty; dominance, sway, rule; dignity, majesty
soberano (-na) *a* sovereign; superb; regal, majestic. *n* ruler, lord. *m,* sovereign (coin)
soberbia *f,* arrogance, haughtiness; conceit, presumption; ostentation, pomp; rage, anger
soberbio *a* haughty, arrogant; conceited; superb, magnificent; lofty, soaring; spirited (of horses)
sobón *a inf* overdemonstrative, mushy; *inf* lazy
sobordo *m, naut* manifest, freight list
sobornación *f,* bribing; bribery
sobornador (-ra) *a* bribing. *n* briber
sobornar *vt* to bribe
soborno *m,* bribing; bribe; inducement
sobra *f,* excess, surplus; insult, outrage; *pl* leftovers (from a meal); remains, residue; rubbish, trash. **de s.,** in abundance; in excess, surplus; unnecessary, superfluous; too well
sobradamente *adv* abundantly; in excess
sobrado *a* excessive; brazen, bold; wealthy, rich. *m,* garret
sobrante *a* surplus, leftover, remaining. *m,* remainder, surplus, excess
sobrar *vt* to exceed; have too much of (e.g. **Me sobran mantas,** I have too many blankets); *vi* be superfluous; remain, be left. *inf* **Aquí sobro yo,** I am in the way here, My presence is superfluous
sobrasada *f,* spicy sausage
sobre *prep* upon, on; above, over; concerning, about; apart from, besides; about (e.g. **s. las nueve,** at about nine o'clock) (indicates approximation); toward; after. *m,* envelope; address, superscription. **s. cero,** above freezing (Fahrenheit); above zero (Centigrade). **s. el nivel del mar,** above sea level. **s. manera,** excessively, extremely. **s. todo,** especially
sobreabundancia *f,* superabundance, excess
sobreabundante *a* superabundant
sobreabundar *vi* to be superabundant
sobreagudo *a* and *m, mus* treble (pitch)
sobrealiento *m,* heavy, painful breathing
sobrealimentación *f,* overfeeding; *aut* supercharge
sobrealimentar *vt aut* to supercharge
sobreasar *vt* to roast or cook again
sobrecama *f,* bedspread, quilt
sobrecarga *f,* overload; rope, etc., for securing bales and packs; additional trouble or anxiety
sobrecargar *vt* to overload; weigh down; *sew* oversew, fell
sobrecargo *m, naut* purser; flight attendant
sobrecarta *f,* envelope (for a letter)
sobreceja *f,* brow, lower forehead; frown
sobrecejo *m,* frown
sobrecielo *m,* canopy
sobrecoger *vt* to take by surprise; *vr* be frightened or apprehensive
sobrecogimiento *m,* fright, apprehension

sobrecomida *f*, dessert

sobrecoser *vt sew* to oversew, whip

sobrecrecer *vi irr* to grow too much. See **conocer**

sobrecubierta *f*, second lid or cover; dust jacket (of a book); *naut* upper deck

sobrecuello *m*, overcollar; loose collar

sobredicho *a* aforementioned, aforesaid

sobredorar *vt* to gild (metals); make excuses for

sobreedificar *vt* to build upon or above

sobreexcitar *vt* to overexcite

sobrefaz *f*, surface, exterior

sobreganar *vt* to make an excess profit

sobreguarda *m*, head guard; extra or second guard

sobreherido *a* lightly wounded

sobrehilar *vt* to oversew or overcast. See **prohibir**

sobrehumano *a* superhuman

sobrellenar *vt* to fill full

sobrellevar *vt* to help in the carrying of a burden; endure, bear; make excuses for, overlook; help

sobremesa *f*, tablecloth; after-dinner conversation. **de s.**, *fig* at the dinner table

sobrenadar *vi* to float

sobrenatural *a* supernatural; extraordinary, singular

sobrenombre *m*, additional surname; nickname

sobrentender *vt irr* to take for granted, understand as a matter of course; *vr* go without saying. See **entender**

sobrepaga *f*, overpayment; extra pay

sobreparto *m*, time after parturition; afterbirth

sobrepasar *vt* to exceed; outdo, excel

sobrepelliz *f*, surplice

sobreponer *vt irr* to place over; overlap; *vr* rise above (circumstances); dominate (persons). See **poner**

sobreprecio *m*, extra charge, rise in price

sobreproducción *f*, overproduction

sobrepuerta *f*, curtain pelmet; door curtain

sobrepujar *vt* to excel, surpass, outdo

sobrequilla *f*, keelson

sobrerrealista *a* and *mf* surrealist

sobrerrealismo *m*, surrealism

sobresaliente *a* overhanging; projecting; distinctive, outstanding; excellent, remarkable. *m*, "excellent" (mark in examinations). *mf theat* understudy

sobresalir *vi irr* to overhang, project; stand out; be conspicuous or noticeable; excel; distinguish oneself. See **salir**

sobresaltar *vt* to assail, rush upon; startle, frighten suddenly; *vi art* stand out, be striking; *vr* be startled or frightened

sobresalto *m*, sudden attack; unexpected shock; agitation; sudden fear. **de s.**, unexpectedly

sobresanar *vi* to heal superficially but not deeply; conceal, dissemble

sobrescribir *vt* to label; address, superscribe. *Past Part.* **sobrescrito**

sobrescrito *m*, address, superscription

sobresello *m*, second seal

sobrestante *m*, overseer; supervisor; foreman; inspector

sobresueldo *m*, additional salary, bonus

sobresuelo *m*, second flooring

sobretarde *f*, early evening, late afternoon

sobretodo *m*, overcoat

sobrevenida *f*, sudden arrival

sobrevenir *vi irr* occur, take place; supervene. See **venir**

sobrevidriera *f*, storm window; wire-mesh window guard

sobrevienta *f*, gust of wind; fury, violence; shock, surprise. **a s.**, suddenly

sobreviviente *a* surviving. *mf* survivor

sobrevivir *vi* to survive

sobriedad *f*, sobriety, moderation

sobrina *f*, niece

sobrino *m*, nephew

sobrio *a* sober, moderate, temperate

socaliña *f*, cunning, craft

socaliñero (-ra) *a* cunning. *n* trickster

socalzar *vt mas* to underpin

socapa *f*, blind, pretext. **a s.**, secretly; cautiously

socarra *f*, scorching, singeing; craftiness

socarrón *a* cunning, deceitful; malicious, sly (of humor, etc.)

socarronería *f*, cunning, craftiness; slyness (of humor, etc.); knavish action

socava *f*, undermining; *agr* hoeing round tree roots

socavar *vt* to undermine

sociabilidad *f*, sociability

sociable *a* sociable; social

social *a* social

socialdemócrata *a* and *mf* social democrat

socialismo *m*, socialism

socialista *mf* socialist. *a* socialistic

socialización *f*, socialization

socializar *vt* to socialize

sociedad *f*, society; association; *com* partnership; *com* company. *com* **s. anónima,** incorporated company, limited company. **S. de las Naciones,** League of Nations. **s. de socorros mutuos,** mutual aid society. **s. en comandita,** private company

socio (-ia) *n* associate, partner; member. **s. comanditario,** *com* silent partner

sociología *f*, sociology

sociológico *a* sociological

sociólogo (-ga) *n* sociologist

socolor *m*, pretext. *adv* (also **so c.**) under pretext

socollada *f*, *naut* flapping (of sails); pitching (of a ship)

socorredor (-ra) *a* aiding, succoring. *n* helper

socorrer *vt* to aid, succor, assist; pay on account

socorrido *a* helpful, generous, prompt to assist; well-equipped, well-furnished; well-supplied

socorro *m*, aid, help, assistance; payment on account; *mil* relief (provisions or arms)

socrático *a* socratic

sodio *m*, sodium

sodomía *f*, sodomy

sodomita *mf* sodomite. *a* sodomitic

soez *a* base, vile; vulgar

sofá *m*, sofa, couch

sofaldar *vt* to tuck up the skirts; disclose, reveal

sofisma *m*, sophism, fallacy

sofista *a* sophistic. *mf* sophist, quibbler

sofistería *f*, sophistry

sofístico *a* sophistic, fallacious

soflama *f*, thin flame; glow; flush, blush; specious promise, deception

soflamar *vt* to shame, make blush; promise with intent to deceive, swindle; *vr cul* burn

sofocación *f*, suffocation, smothering; shame; anger

sofocador, sofocante *a* suffocating; stifling

sofocar *vt* to suffocate, smother; extinguish; dominate, oppress; pester, importune; shame, make blush, make angry; agitate; *vr* be ashamed; be angry

sofocleo *a* Sophoclean

sofoco *m*, mortification, chagrin; shame; anger; suffocation, smothering; hot flush

sofreír *vt irr* to fry lightly. See **reír**

sofrenada *f*, sudden check, pulling up short (of horses); harsh scolding; moral restraint

sofrenar *vt* to pull up, check suddenly (horses); scold harshly; restrain, repress (emotions)

soga *f*, rope; land measure (varies in length). *m*, *inf* rogue, knave

soguería *f*, rope making; rope walk; rope shop; ropes

soguero *m*, rope maker or seller

soja *f*, soybean

sojuzgador (-ra) *a* conquering, oppressive. *n* conqueror, oppressor

sojuzgar *vt* to conquer, oppress, subdue

sol *m*, sun; sunlight; day; Peruvian coin; *mus* G, fifth note of the scale, sol. **de s. a s.,** from sunrise to sunset. **hacer s.,** to be sunny. **morir uno sin s. sin luz y sin moscas,** *inf* to die abandoned by all. **no dejar a s. ni a**

sombra, *inf* to follow everywhere; pester constantly.
tomar el s., to bask in the sun
solado *m,* paving; tile floor
solador *m,* tiler
solamente *adv* only; exclusively; merely, solely. **s. que,** only that; nothing but
solana *f,* sunny corner; Solarium
solanera *f,* sunburn; sunny spot
solapa *f,* lapel; excuse, pretext. **de s.,** *inf* secretly
solapado *a* cunning, sly
solapar *vt sew* to provide with lapels; *sew* cause to overlap; dissemble; *vi sew* overlap
solapo *m,* lapel; *inf* slap, buffet. **a s.,** *inf* secretly, slyly
solar *vt irr* to pave; sole (shoes). *m,* family seat, manor house; building site; lineage, family. *a* solar. See **colar**
solariego *a* memorial; of an old and noble family
solas, a *adv* alone, in private
solaz *m,* consolation; pleasure; relief, relaxation. **a s.,** enjoyably, pleasantly
solazar *vt* to solace, comfort; amuse, entertain; rest; *vr* be comforted; find pleasure (in)
soldada *f,* salary, wages, emoluments; *(nav mil)* pay
soldadesca *f,* soldiering, military profession; troops. **a la s.,** in a soldier-like way
soldadesco *a* military, soldier
soldado *m,* soldier; defender, partisan. **s. raso,** *mil* private
soldador *m,* solderer, welder; soldering iron
soldadura *f,* welding, soldering; correction, emendation
soldar *vt irr* to weld; mend by welding; correct, put right; *mil* wipe out, liquidate. See **contar**
solecismo *m,* solecism
soledad *f,* solitude; loneliness; homesickness; *pl* melancholy Andalusian song and dance (also *f pl.* **soleares**)
solemne *a* solemn; magnificent; formal; serious, grave, important; pompous; *inf* downright, complete
solemnidad *f,* solemnity; magnificence; formality; gravity, seriousness; solemn ceremony; religious ceremony; legal formality
solemnización *f,* solemnization
solemnizar *vt* to solemnize, celebrate; extol
soler *vi irr defective* to be in the habit, be used; happen frequently (e.g. **Solía hacerlo los lunes,** I generally did it on Mondays. **Suele llover mucho aquí,** It rains a great deal here). See **moler**
solercia *f,* shrewdness, ability, astuteness
solevantado *a* agitated; restless
solevantar *vt* to raise, push up; incite to rebellion. **s. con gatos,** *mech* to jack up
solfa *f, mus* sol-fa
solfear *vt mus* to sing in sol-fa; *inf* spank, buffet; *inf* scold
solfeo *m, mus* sol-fa; *inf* spanking, drubbing
solicitación *f,* request; application; solicitation; wooing; search (for a post); attraction, inducement
solicitador (-ra) *a* soliciting. *n* solicitor. *m,* agent; applicant
solicitante *mf* applicant, candidate
solicitar *vt* to solicit; request; apply for; make love to, court; seek (posts, etc.); try to, attempt to; manage (business affairs); *phys* attract; appeal to
solícito *a* solicitous; conscientious; careful
solicitud *f,* diligence, conscientiousness; solicitude; request; application; appeal, entreaty; petition; *com* demand. **a s.,** on request
solidaridad *f,* solidarity
solidario *a law* jointly responsible or liable
solideo *m, ecc* small skullcap
solidez *f,* solidity; *fig* force, weight (of arguments, etc.)
solidificación *f,* solidification
solidificar(se) *vt* and *vr* to solidify
sólido *a* compact, solid; thick; fast or lasting (of colors); indisputable, convincing. *m,* (geom phys) solid; solidus (ancient coin)
soliloquiar *vi inf* to soliloquize, talk to oneself
soliloquio *m,* soliloquy

solio *m,* throne
solista *mf* soloist
solitario (-ia) *a* abandoned, deserted; solitary; secluded; solitude-loving. *n* recluse. *m,* solitaire diamond; hermit; solitaire (card game). **hacer solitarios,** to play solitaire (card game)
sólito *a* accustomed, wonted; customary, habitual
soliviantar *vt* to rouse, incite, excite
soliviar *vt* to help to lift up; *vr* half get up, raise oneself
sollastre *m,* scullion; brazen rogue
sollozante *a* sobbing
sollozar *vi* to sob
sollozo *m,* sob
solo *a* sole, only; alone; lonely; deserted, forsaken. *m,* solo performance; (cards) solo; solitaire (card game). **a solas,** alone; without help, unaided
sólo *or* **solo** *adv* only; merely, solely; exclusively
solomillo *m,* sirloin; filet (of meat)
solsticio *m,* solstice. **s. hiemal,** winter solstice. **s. vernal,** summer solstice
soltar *vt irr* to loosen; let go; disengage; untie; release; let drop; let out (a laugh, etc.); solve; *inf* utter; turn on (taps); set free; *vr* work loose; grow skillful; *(with prep. a + infin.)* begin to do (something). See **contar**
soltera *f,* spinster
soltería *f,* bachelorhood; spinsterhood
soltero *a* unmarried, single. *m,* bachelor
solterón *m,* confirmed bachelor
solterona *f,* confirmed old maid
soltura *f,* loosening; untying; freedom from restraint; ease, independence; impudence; immorality, viciousness; facility of speech; *law* release
solubilidad *f,* solubility
soluble *a* soluble, dissolvable; solvable
solución *f,* dissolution, loosening; *(math chem)* solution; answer, solution; payment, satisfaction; *lit* climax; conclusion, end (of negotiations)
solucionar *vt* to solve, find a solution for
solvencia *f, com* solvency
solventar *vt* to pay or settle accounts; solve (problems, difficulties)
solvente *a com* solvent
somático *a* somatic, corporeal
somatología *f,* somatology
sombra *f,* shadow; shade; darkness, dimness; specter; phantom; defense, refuge, protection; resemblance, likeness; defect; *inf* luck; gaiety, charm; trace, vestige; *art* shading, shadow. **sombras chinescas,** shadow show. **a la s.,** in the shade; *inf* in jail. **hacer s.,** to shade; *fig* stand in the light, be an obstacle; protect. **ni por s.,** by no means; without warning. **no tener s. de,** to have not a trace of .... **tener buena s.,** *inf* to be witty or amusing and agreeable. **tener mala s.,** *inf* to bring bad luck, exert an evil influence upon; be dull and disagreeable
sombrear *vt* to shadow, shade; *art* shade; *vi* begin to show (of mustaches, beards)
sombrera *f,* milliner; hatbox
sombrerería *f,* hat shop or trade; hat factory
sombrerero *m,* hatter; hat manufacturer
sombrerete *m, mech* bonnet, cap; cowl
sombrero *m,* hat; *mech* cap, cowl; sounding board; head (of mushrooms, toadstools). **s. calañés,** Andalusian hat. **s. chambergo,** broad-brimmed plumed hat. **s. de canal** *or* **teja,** shovel hat (worn by clergymen). **s. de copa,** top hat. **s. de jipijapa,** Panama hat. **s. de tres picos,** three-cornered hat, cocked hat. **s. flexible,** soft felt hat. **s. hongo,** bowler (hat)
sombría *f,* shady spot
sombrilla *f,* sunshade
sombrío *a* dark; shadowy; overcast; *art* shaded; gloomy, melancholy
someramente *adv* superficially; briefly, summarily
somero *a* superficial, shallow; summary, rudimentary, brief
someter *vt* to put down, defeat; submit, place before;

subject. **s. a votación,** to put to a vote. *vr* yield, surrender; (*with prep a*) undergo

sometimiento *m,* defeat; submission (to arbitration, etc.); subjection

somnambulismo *m,* somnambulism, sleepwalking

somnámbulo (-la) *a* somnambulistic. *n* somnambulist

somnífero *a* soporiferous

somnílocuo *a* somniloquous, sleeptalking

somnolencia *f,* somnolence

son *m,* sound; rumor; reason, motive; means, way; guise, manner. **al s. de,** to the sound of; to the music of. **en s. de,** in the manner of, as, like, under pretext of

sonadera *f,* nose blowing

sonado *a* famous; much admired or talked of. **hacer una que sea sonada,** *inf* to cause a great scandal; do something noteworthy

sonaja *f,* metal jingles on a tambourine; baby's rattle

sonajero *m,* baby's rattle

sonar *vi irr* to sound; be quoted, be mentioned; ring; *inf* be familiar, remember (e.g. **No me suena el nombre,** I don't remember the name); (*with prep a*) be reminiscent of; *vt* sound; ring; play on; clink; *vr* be rumored, be reported; blow one's nose. *Pres. Ind.* **sueno, suenas, suena, suenan.** *Pres. Subjunc.* **suene, suenes, suene, suenen**

sonata *f,* sonata

sonda *f, naut* taking of soundings, heaving the lead; sound, plummet, lead; dragrope; probe, sound

sondar *vt naut* to take soundings; probe; *inf* sound, try to find out; bore, drill

sondeable *a* fathomable

sondeo *m, naut* sounding; *min* drilling; probing

sonetear, sonetizar *vi* to write sonnets

sonetista *mf* sonneteer

soneto *m,* sonnet

sonido *m,* sound; literal meaning; rumor, report

sonochar *vi* to keep watch in the early hours of the night

sonoridad *f,* sonorousness

sonoro *a* sounding; resonant, loud; sonorous

sonreír, sonreírse *vi* and *vr irr* to smile; *vi* look pleasant (landscape, etc.); look favorable (of circumstances). **sonreír tras la barba,** to laugh to oneself. See **reír**

sonriente *a* smiling

sonrisa *f,* smile

sonrojar *vt* to cause to blush; *vr* blush

sonrosado *a* rosy, rose-colored, pink

sonrosar *vt* to make rose-colored; *vr* blush, flush

sonroseo *m,* blush, flush

sonsaca *f,* removal by stealth; pilfering; enticement; *fig* pumping (of a person for information)

sonsacar *vt* to remove by stealth; steal, pilfer; entice away; *fig* pump (a person for information), draw out

sonsonete *m,* rhythmic tapping or drumming; monotonous sound (gen. unpleasant); sarcastic tone of voice

soñador (-ra) *a* dreamy, sleepy. *n* dreamer

soñar *vt* to dream; imagine, conjure up; (*with con*) dream of; (*with prep a*) dream (of persons)

soñoliento *a* sleepy, drowsy; soothing; slow, leisurely

¡Soo! *interj* Whoa! (command to horses, etc.)

sopa *f,* sop, piece of bread; soup. **s. boba,** beggar's portion; life of ease at others' expense. **andar a la s.,** to beg one's way. **hecho una s.,** *inf* wet through

sopapo *m,* chuck under the chin; *inf* slap; valve

sopera *f,* soup tureen

sopero *m,* soup plate, soup bowl. *a* fond of soup

sopesar *vt* to try the weight of

sopetón *m,* blow, cuff. **de s.,** suddenly

soplada *f,* puff of wind

soplado *a inf* overelegant; haughty, stiff. *m,* fissure, chasm

soplador (-ra) *a* instigatory. *m,* blower, fan. *n* instigator; blower

soplar *vi* to blow; *vt* blow; blow away; inflate, blow up; filch, steal; instigate, inspire; accuse; fan; prompt, help

out; *vr inf* eat and drink too much; *inf* be puffed up, grow haughty. *interj* **¡Sopla!** *inf* You don't say so!

soplete *m,* blowpipe

soplo *m,* blow; blowing; instant, trice; *inf* hint, tip; *inf* accusation; *inf* tale-bearer; puff, breath (of wind)

soplón (-ona) *a inf* tale-bearing, backbiting. *n* talebearer. *m, aut* scavenger

soponcio *m, inf* fainting fit

sopor *m,* stupor; deep sleep

soporífero *a* soporiferous

soportable *a* bearable

soportador (-ra) *a* supporting. *n* supporter

soportal *m,* portico

soportar *vt* to bear; carry, support; put up with, tolerate

soporte *m,* rest, support; *mech* bearing; *mech* bracket, support

sopuntar *vt* to underline in dots

sor *f, ecc* sister (used of nuns)

sorbedor (-ra) *a* supping, sipping. *n* sipper

sorber *vt* to suck; imbibe; swallow; *fig* absorb eagerly (ideas); sip

sorbete *m,* sherbet, iced drink; French ice cream

sorbo *m,* sucking; imbibition; swallow; sip; mouthful, gulp

sordamente *adv* secretly, quietly

sordera *f,* deafness

sordidez *f,* sordidness

sórdido *a* dirty, squalid; mean, niggardly; sordid

sordina *f, mus* sordine, mute; *mus* damper. **a la s.,** on the quiet, in secret

sordo *a* deaf; silent, quiet; dull, muted (of sounds); insensible, inanimate; obdurate, uncompliant. **a la sorda o a lo s. o a sordas,** in silence, quietly

sordomudez *f,* deaf-muteness, deaf-mutism

sordomudo (-da) *a* and *m* deaf-mute

sorna *f,* slowness, sluggishness; craftiness, guile, knavery; malice

sorprendente *a* surprising, amazing

sorprender *vt* to surprise, amaze

sorpresa *f,* surprise; amazement; shock

sortear *vt* to raffle; draw lots for; avoid artfully (difficulties, etc.); fight (bulls)

sorteo *m,* raffle; casting lots

sortero (-ra) *n* sorcerer; holder of a draw ticket

sortija *f,* ring (for a finger); ring (for a curtain, etc.); curl

sortilegio *m,* sorcery, magic

sortílego (-ga) *a* magic. *n* sorcerer, fortuneteller

sosa *f,* sodium carbonate, soda ash. **s. cáustica,** sodium-hydroxide, caustic soda, soda

sosegado *a* tranquil, peaceful, calm

sosegador (-ra) *a* soothing, calming. *n* appeaser, soother

sosegar *vt irr* to soothe, quiet; reassure; appease, moderate; *vi* grow still; rest, sleep; *vr* grow quiet; calm down, be appeased; grow still. See **cegar**

sosería *f,* insipidness; lack of wit, dullness; stupidity

sosia *m,* double, exact likeness (of persons)

sosiego *m,* calm; peace, tranquility

soslayar *vt* to slant, place in an oblique position; *fig* go around (a difficulty)

soslayo *a* slanting. **al s.,** obliquely, on the slant; askance

soso *a* saltless, insipid; dull, uninteresting; heavy (of people)

sospecha *f,* suspicion

sospechar *vt* and *vi* to suspect

sospechoso *a* suspicious. *m,* suspect

sostén *m,* support; *mech* stand, support; brassiere, bra, bustier; steadiness (of a ship)

sostenedor (-ra) *a* supporting. *n* supporter

sostener *vt irr* to support; defend, uphold; bear, tolerate; help, aid; maintain, support. **s. una conversación,** to carry on a conversation. See **tener**

sostenido *a mus* sostenuto, sustained. *a* and *m, mus* sharp

sostenimiento *m,* support; defense; toleration; endurance; maintenance, sustenance

sota *f*, jack, knave (in cards); *inf* baggage, hussy. *m*, foreman, supervisor. *prep* deputy, substitute (e.g. **sotamontero**, deputy huntsman)

sotabanco *m*, attic, garret

sotana *f*, gown, cassock, robe

sótano *m*, basement, cellar

sotavento *m*, leeward. **a s.**, on the lee

sotechado *m*, hut, shed

soterrar *vt irr* to bury in the ground; hide, conceal. See **acertar**

sotileza *f*, fine cord for fishing (in Santander province)

soto *m*, thicket, grove, copse

soviético *a* soviet

sovietismo *m*, sovietism

sovietizar *vt* to sovietize

sovoz, a *adv* in a low voice

su, sus *poss pron* 3rd pers *mf sing* and *pl* his, her, its, one's, your, their

suasorio *a* suasive, persuasive

suave *a* soft, smooth; sweet; pleasant, harmonious, quiet; slow, gentle; meek; delicate, subtle

suavidad *f*, softness, smoothness; sweetness; pleasantness; quietness; gentleness; meekness; delicacy

suavizador *a* softening, smoothing; soothing, quietening. *m*, razor strop

suavizar *vt* to soften; smooth; strop (a razor); moderate, temper; *mech* steady; quieten; ease

subalpino *a* subalpine

subalternar *vt* to put down, subdue

subalterno *a* subordinate. *m*, subordinate; *mil* subaltern

subarrendar *vt irr* to sublet. See **recomendar**

subarrendatario (-ia) *n* sublessee

subarriendo *m*, sublease, sublet

subasta *f*, auction sale. **sacar a pública s.**, to sell by auction

subastar *vt* to auction

subcentral *f*, substation

subclase *f*, subclass

subcolector *m*, assistant collector

subcomisión *f*, subcommittee

subconsciencia *f*, subconscious

subcutáneo *a* subcutaneous

subdelegar *vt* to subdelegate

subdirector (-ra) *n* deputy, assistant director

súbdito (-ta) *a* dependent, subject. *n* subject (of a state)

subdividir *vt* to subdivide

subdominante *f*, *mus* subdominant

subgénero *m*, subgenus

subgobernador *m*, deputy governor, lieutenant governor

subibaja *f*, seesaw, teetertotter

subida *f*, ascension, ascent; upgrade; rise; carrying up; raising (of a theater curtain)

subidero *m*, uphill road; mounting block; way up (to a higher level)

subido *a* strong (of scents); deep (of colors); expensive, high-priced; best, finest

subidor *m*, porter, carrier; elevator

subintendente *m*, deputy or assistant intendant

subir *vi* to ascend, climb, go up; mount; rise; *com* amount (to), reach; prosper, advance, be promoted; grow more acute (of illnesses); intensify; *mus* raise the pitch (of an instrument or voice); *vt* ascend, mount; pick up, take up; raise up; place higher; build up, make taller; straighten up, place in a vertical position; increase, raise (in price or value); *vr* ascend, climb. **s. a caballo,** to mount a horse. **subirse a la cabeza,** *inf* to go to one's head (of alcohol, etc.)

subitáneo *a* sudden

súbito *a* unexpected, unforeseen; sudden; precipitate, impulsive. *adv* suddenly (also **de s.**)

subjefe *m*, deputy chief, second in command

subjetividad *f*, subjectivity

subjetivismo *m*, subjectivism

subjetivo *a* subjective

subjuntivo *a* and *m*, subjunctive

sublevación *f*, **sublevamiento** *m*, rebellion, mutiny, uprising

sublevar *vt* to rouse to rebellion; excite (indignation, etc.); *vr* rebel

sublimación *f*, sublimation

sublimado *m*, *chem* sublimate

sublimar *vt* to exalt, raise up; *chem* sublimate

sublime *a* sublime

sublimidad *f*, sublimity, majesty, nobility

submarino *a* submarine. *m*, submarine. **s. de bolsillo** or **s. enano,** midget submarine

suboficial *m*, *mil* subaltern; *nav* petty officer

subordinación *f*, dependence, subordination

subordinado (-da) *a* and *n* subordinate

subordinar *vt* to subordinate

subpolar *a* subpolar

subprefecto *m*, subprefect

subproducto *m*, by-product

subrayar *vt* to underline; emphasize

subrepción *f*, underhand dealing; *law* subreption

subrepticio *a* surreptitious; clandestine

subrogación *f*, surrogation

subrogar *vt law* to surrogate, elect as a substitute

subs—For words so beginning not found here, see **sus**-

subsanar *vt* to make excuses for; remedy, put right; indemnify

subscriptor (-ra) *n* subscriber

subsección *f*, subsection

subsecretaría *f*, assistant secretaryship; assistant secretary's office

subsecretario (-ia) *n* assistant secretary

subsecuente *a* subsequent

subsidiario *a* subsidized; subsidiary

subsidio *m*, subsidy

subsiguiente *a* subsequent; next

subsistencia *f*, permanence; stability; subsistence, maintenance; livelihood

subsistir *vi* to last, endure; subsist, live; make a livelihood

subsuelo *m*, subsoil, substratum

subteniente *m*, *mil* second lieutenant

subterfugio *m*, subterfuge, trick

subterráneo *a* underground, subterranean. *m*, subterranean place

subtítulo *m*, subtitle; caption

subtropical *a* subtropical

suburbano (-na) *a* suburban. *n* suburbanite

suburbio *m*, suburb

subvención *f*, subsidy, subvention, grant

subvencionar *vt* to subsidize

subvenir *vt irr* to help, succor; subsidize. See **venir**

subversivo *a* subversive

subvertir *vt irr* to subvert, overturn, ruin. See **sentir**

subyugación *f*, subjugation

subyugador (-ra) *a* subjugating. *n* conqueror

subyugar *vt* to subjugate, overcome

succión *f*, suction

sucedáneo *m*, *med* succedaneum

suceder *vi* to follow, come after; inherit, succeed. *impers* happen, occur

sucedido *m*, *inf* event, occurrence

sucesión *f*, succession; series; offspring, descendants; *law* estate

sucesivo *a* successive. **en lo s.**, in future

suceso *m*, happening, occurrence; course (of time); outcome, result

sucesor (-ra) *a* succeeding. *n* successor

suciedad *f*, dirt; filth, nastiness; obscenity

sucinto *a* succinct, brief, concise

sucio *a* dirty, unclean; stained; easily soiled; *fig* sullied, spotted; obscene; dirty (of colors); *fig* tainted, infected. **jugar s.**, *sport* to play in an unsporting manner

suco *m*, juice

sucoso *a* juicy

suculencia *f*, succulence; juiciness

suculento *a* succulent; juicy
sucumbir *vi* to yield, give in; die, succumb; lose a lawsuit
sucursal *a* branch. *f, com* branch (of a firm)
sud *m,* south (gen. **sur**). Used in combinations like **sudamericano**
sudadero *m,* horse blanket; sudatorium, sweating bath
sudafricano (-na) *a* and *n* South African
sudamericano (-na) *a* and *n* South American
Sudán, el the Sudan
sudante *a* sweating, perspiring
sudar *vi* and *vt* to perspire, sweat; ooze; *vi inf* toil; *vt* bathe in sweat; *inf* give reluctantly. **s. frío,** to break out in a cold sweat. **s. la gota gorda,** *fig inf* to be in a stew
sudario *m,* shroud
sudeste *m,* southeast; southeast wind
sudexpreso *m,* southern express
sudoeste *m,* southwest; southwest wind
sudor *m,* sweat, perspiration; toil; juice, moisture, sap, gum
sudoroso *a* sweaty
sudsudeste *m,* southsoutheast
sudsudoeste *m,* southsouthwest
Suecia Sweden
sueco (-ca) *a* Swedish. *n* Swede. *m,* Swedish (language)
suegra *f,* mother-in-law
suegro *m,* father-in-law
suela *f,* sole (of a shoe); *icht* sole; tanned leather; base. **no llegarle a uno a la s. del zapato,** *inf* to be not fit to hold a candle to.
sueldo *m,* salary, wages; *ant* Spanish coin. **a s.,** for a salary, salaried
suelo *m,* ground, earth; soil; bottom, base; sediment, dregs; site, plot; floor; flooring; story; land, territory; hoof (of horses); earth, world; *pl* chaff of grain. **s. natal,** native land; **besar el s.,** *inf* to fall flat. **dar consigo en el s.,** to fall down. **dar en el s. con,** to throw down; damage, spoil. *inf* **estar (una cosa) por los suelos,** to be dirt cheap
suelta *f,* loosening, unfastening; hobble (for horses); relay of oxen. **dar s. a,** to let loose, allow to go out for a time
suelto *a* swift; competent, efficient; odd, separate; licentious; flowing, easy (style); loose, unbound. *m,* single copy (of a newspaper); loose change; newspaper paragraph
sueño *m,* dream; sleep; drowsiness, desire for sleep; vision, fancy. **s. pesado,** deep sleep. **conciliar el s.,** to court sleep. **echar un s.,** *inf* to take a nap. **en sueños,** in a dream; while asleep. **entre sueños,** between sleeping and waking. **¡Ni por sueño!** *inf* Certainly not! I wouldn't dream of it!
suero *m,* serum. **s. de la leche,** whey
suerte *f,* chance, luck; good luck; destiny, fate; condition, state; kind, species, sort; way, manner; bullfighter's maneuver; parcel of land. **de s. que,** so that; as a result. **echar suertes,** to draw lots. **tener buena s.,** to be lucky
sueste *m,* southeast; sou'wester (cap)
suéter *m,* sweater
suevo (-va) *a* and *n* Swabian
suficiencia *f,* sufficiency; talent, aptitude; pedantry. **a s.,** enough
suficiente *a* sufficient, enough; suitable
sufijo *m,* suffix
sufismo *m,* Sufism
sufragar *vt* to assist, aid; favor; pay, defray
sufragio *m,* aid, assistance; *ecc* suffragium, pious offering; vote; suffrage
sufragista *f,* suffragette
sufrible *a* bearable, endurable
sufrido *a* long-suffering, resigned; complaisant (of husbands); dirt-resistant (colors)
sufrimiento *m,* suffering, pain; affliction; tolerance
sufrir *vt* to suffer, undergo, experience; bear, endure;

tolerate, put up with; allow, permit; resist, oppose; expiate; *vi* suffer
sugerir *vt irr* to suggest. See **sentir**
sugestión *f,* suggestion
sugestionable *a* easily influenced, open to suggestion
sugestionador *a* suggestive
sugestionar *vt* to suggest hypnotically; dominate, influence
sugestivo *a* suggestive, stimulating
suicida *a* suicidal, fatal. *mf* suicide (person)
suicidarse *vr* to commit suicide
suicidio *m,* suicide (act)
Suiza Switzerland
suiza *f,* row, rumpus, scrap
suizo (-za) *a* and *n* Swiss
sujeción *f,* subjection, domination; fastening, fixture; obedience, conformity
sujetador *m,* clamp; clip
sujetar *vt* to fasten, fix; hold down; grasp, clutch; subdue; *vr (with prep a)* conform to, obey. **s. con alfileres,** to pin up. **s. con tornillos,** to screw down
sujeto *a* liable, subject. *m,* topic, subject; person, individual; *gram phil* subject
sulfatar *vt* to sulphate
sulfato *m,* sulphate
sulfurar *vt* to sulphurate; *vr* grow irritated, become angry
sulfúrico *a* sulphuric
sulfuro *m,* sulphide
sulfuroso *a* sulphurous
sultán *m,* sultan
sultana *f,* sultana
sultanía *f,* sultanate
suma *f,* total; amount, sum; *math* addition; summary, digest; computation. **en s.,** in brief, in short, finally
sumador (-ra) *n* summarizer; computator, adder
sumamente *adv* extremely, most
sumar *vt* to sum up, summarize; *math* add up
sumaria *f,* written indictment
sumariamente *adv* concisely, in brief; *law* summarily
sumario *a* brief, concise, abridged; *law* summary. *m,* summary, résumé, digest
sumergible *a* sinkable; submergible. *m,* submarine
sumergir *vt* to dip, immerse; sink, submerge; *fig* overwhelm (with grief, etc.); *vr* sink; dive; be submerged
sumersión *f,* immersion, dive, submersion
sumidero *m,* cesspool; drain; sink; pit, gully
suministración *f.* See **suministro**
suministrador (-ra) *n* purveyor
suministrar *vt* to purvey, supply, provide
suministro *m,* purveyance; provision; supply
sumir *vt* to sink; submerge; *ecc* consummate; *fig* overwhelm (with grief, etc.); *vr* fall in, become sunken (of cheeks, etc.); sink; be submerged
sumisión *f,* submission, obedience; *com* estimate, tender
sumiso *a* submissive, docile
sumista *mf* quick reckoner, computator. *m,* condenser, summarizer, abridger
sumo *a* supreme; high; tremendous, extraordinary. **a lo s.,** at the most; even if, although. **en s. grado,** in the highest degree
suntuosidad *f,* magnificence, luxury
suntuoso *a* magnificent, luxurious, sumptuous
supeditación *f,* subjection
supeditar *vt* to oppress; overcome, conquer; subordinate
superabundancia *f,* superabundance, excess; glut
superabundante *a* superabundant, excessive
superádito *a* superadded
superar *vt* to overcome, conquer; surpass; do better than
superávit *m, com* balance, surplus
superchería *f,* trickery, guile
superchero *a* guileful, wily

superconsciencia *f*, higher consciousness
supereminencia *f*, supereminence, greatest eminence
supereminente *a* supereminent
superentender *vt irr* to supervise, superintend. See **entender**
supererogación *f*, supererogation
superestructura *f*, superstructure
superficial *a* surface, shallow; superficial, rudimentary; futile
superficialidad *f*, superficiality; futility; shallowness
superficie *f*, area; surface; outside, exterior. **s. de rodadura**, tire tread
superfino *a* superfine
superfluidad *f*, superfluity
superfluo *a* superfluous, redundant
superfortaleza volante *f*, *aer* superfortress
superhombre *m*, superman
superintendencia *f*, supervision; superintendentship; higher administration
superintendente *mf* superintendent; supervisor
superior *a* higher, upper; excellent, fine; superior; higher (education, etc.). *m*, head, director; superior
superiora *f*, mother superior
superioridad *f*, superiority
superlativo *a* and *m*, superlative
superno *a* supreme
supernumerario (-ia) *a* and *n* supernumerary
superposición *f*, superposition
superproducción *f*, overproduction; superproduction
superrealismo *m*, surrealism
superrealista *a* surrealist
superstición *f*, superstition
supersticioso *a* superstitious
supervención *f*, *law* supervention
supervivencia *f*, survival
superviviente *a* surviving. *mf* survivor
supino *a* supine; foolish, stupid. *m*, *gram* supine
suplantación *f*, supplanting
suplantador (-ra) *a* supplanting. *n* supplanter
suplantar *vt* to forge, alter (documents); supplant
suplefaltas *mf* scapegoat
suplementario *a* supplementary, additional
suplemento *m*, supplement; supply, supplying; newspaper supplement; *geom* supplement
suplente *m*, substitute, proxy; *fig* makeweight
súplica *f*, supplication, prayer; request
suplicación *f*, entreaty, supplication; *law* petition
suplicante *a* supplicatory; *law* petitioning. *mf* supplicator; *law* petitioner
suplicar *vt* to beg, supplicate; request; *law* appeal
suplicio *m*, torment, torture; execution; place of torture or execution; affliction, anguish. **último s.**, capital punishment
suplir *vt* to supply, furnish; substitute, take the place of; overlook, forgive
suponer *vt irr* to suppose, take for granted; simulate; comprise, include; *vi* carry weight, wield authority. See **poner**
suposición *f*, supposition; conjecture, assumption; distinction, talent, importance; falsity, falsehood
supositorio *m*, suppository
suprasensible *a* supersensible
supremacía *f*, supremacy
supremo *a* supreme; matchless, incomparable; last
supresión *f*, suppression; destruction, eradication; omission
suprimir *vt* to suppress; destroy, eradicate; omit, leave out. **s. una calle al tráfico**, to close a street to traffic, ban traffic from a street
supuesto *a* supposed; so-called; reputed. *m*, supposition, hypothesis. **por s.**, presumably; doubtless
supuración *f*, suppuration
supurar *vi* to suppurate
suputar *vt* to calculate, compute
sur *m*, south; south wind

surcador *m*, plowman
surcar *vt* to plow furrows; furrow, line; cut, cleave (water, etc.)
surco *m*, furrow; wrinkle, line; groove, channel; rut
surgidero *m*, *naut* road, roadstead
surgir *vi* to spout, gush, spurt; *naut* anchor; appear, show itself; come forth, turn up
surrealismo *m*, surrealism
surrealista *a* and *mf* surrealist
surtida *f*, hidden exit; false door; *naut* slipway
surtidero *m*, outlet, drain; jet, fountain
surtido *a* mixed, assorted. *m*, variety, assortment; stock, range. **de s.**, in everyday use
surtidor (-ra) *n* purveyor, supplier. *m*, fountain, jet. **s. de gasolina**, gasoline pump, gas pump
surtimiento *m*, assortment; stock
surtir *vt* to provide, supply, furnish; *vi* spurt, gush
surto *a* calm, reposeful; *naut* anchored
¡sus! *interj* Come on! Hurry up!
susceptibilidad *f*, susceptibility
susceptible *a* susceptible, open to; touchy, oversensitive
suscitar *vt* to cause, originate; provoke, incite; *vr* arise, take place
suscribir *vt* to sign; agree to; *vr* subscribe, contribute; take out a subscription (to a periodical, etc.). *Past Part.* **suscrito**
suscripción *f*, subscription; agreement, accession
susodicho *a* aforesaid
suspender *vt* to suspend, hang up; postpone, defer, stop; amaze, dumbfound; suspend (from employment); fail (an exam); adjourn (meetings); *vr* rear (of horses)
suspensión *f*, suspension; postponement, stoppage, deferment; amazement; failure (in an exam); adjournment (of a meeting); springs (of a car). *com* **s. de pagos**, suspension of payments. **con mala s.**, badly sprung (of a car)
suspensivo *a* suspensive
suspensivos *m*, *pl* suspension points, ellipsis points
suspenso *a* amazed, bewildered. *m*, failure slip (in an exam). **en s.**, in suspense
suspicacia *f*, suspiciousness; mistrust, uneasiness
suspicaz *a* suspicious, mistrustful
suspirado *a* eagerly desired, longed for
suspirar *vt* and *vi* to sigh. **s. por**, to long for
suspiro *m*, sigh; breath; glass whistle; *mus* brief pause, pause sign. **último s.**, *inf* last kick, end
suspirón *a* given to sighing
sustancia *f*, substance, juice, extract, essence; *fig* core, pith; *fig* meat; wealth, estate; worth, importance; nutritive part; *inf* common sense. *anat* **s. gris**, gray matter. **en s.**, in short
sustanciación *f*, substantiation
sustancial *a* substantial, real; important, essential; nutritive; solid
sustanciar *vt* to substantiate; summarize, extract, abridge
sustancioso *a* substantial; nutritive
sustantivo *a* and *m*, *gram* substantive, noun
sustentable *a* arguable, defensible
sustentación *f*, maintenance; defense
sustentar *vt* to sustain, keep; support, bear; nourish, feed; uphold, advocate. **s. un ciclo de conferencias**, to give a series of lectures
sustento *m*, maintenance, preservation; nourishment, sustenance; support
sustitución *f*, substitution
sustituible *a* substitutive, replaceable
sustituir *vt irr* to substitute. See **huir**
sustitutivo *a* substitutive
sustituto (-ta) *n* substitute
susto *m*, fright, shock; apprehension. **dar un s. (a)**, to scare
sustracción *f*, subtraction
sustraendo *m*, *math* subtrahend

sustraer *vt irr* to remove, separate; rob, steal; *math* subtract; *vr* depart, remove oneself; avoid. See **traer**

sustrato *m*, substratum

susurrador (-ra) *a* whispering; murmuring; rustling. *n* whisperer

susurrante *a* whispering; murmuring; rustling

susurrar *vi* to whisper; murmur; rustle; babble, purl, prattle (of water); *vi* and *vr* be whispered abroad

susurro *m*, whispering, whisper; murmur; rustle; lapping

sutil *a* fine, thin; penetrating, subtle, keen

sutileza, sutilidad *f*, fineness, thinness; subtlety, penetration. **sutileza de manos,** dexterity; light-fingeredness; sleight of hand

sutilizaciones *f, pl* casuistry, hairsplitting, quibbling

sutilizar *vt* to make thin, refine; *fig* finish, perfect; *fig* split hairs, make subtle distinctions

sutura *f*, suture

suyo, suya *m,* and *f, pl* **suyos, suyas,** *poss pron* and *a 3rd pers* his; hers; its; yours; theirs; of his, of hers, etc. (e.g. **Este libro es suyo,** This book is his (hers, yours, theirs). **Este libro es uno de los suyos,** This book is one of his (hers, etc.). **(suyo** is often used with def. art. **el, la,** etc.) **los suyos,** his (hers, yours, etc.) family, following, adherents, etc. **de suyo,** of its very nature, of itself; spontaneously. **salirse con la suya,** to get one's own way. *inf* **ver la suyo,** to see one's opportunity

T

tabacal *m*, tobacco plantation

tabacalero (-ra) *a* tobacco. *n* tobacco merchant; tobacco planter

tabaco *m*, tobacco plant, tobacco leaf; tobacco; cigar. **t. de pipa,** pipe tobacco. **t. flojo,** mild tobacco. **t. rubio,** Virginia tobacco

tabalear(se) *vt* and *vr* to rock, sway, swing; *vi* drum with the fingers

tabaleo *m*, swaying, rocking; drumming with the fingers

tabanco *m*, market stall

tábano *m, ent* horsefly

tabanque *m*, potter's wheel

tabaque *m*, small osier basket (for fruit, sewing, etc.); large tack

tabaquera *f*, tobacco jar, tobacco tin; bowl of pipe tobacco; tobacco pouch; snuffbox

tabaquería *f*, tobacconist's shop

tabaquero (-ra) *n* worker in a tobacco factory; tobacconist

tabaquismo *m*, nicotinism, nicotine poisoning

tabaquista *mf* tobacco expert; heavy smoker

tabardillo *m*, fever. **t. de tripas,** typhoid. **t. pintado,** typhus

tabardo *m*, tabard

taberna *f*, public house, tavern

tabernáculo *m*, tabernacle

tabernario *a* public house, tavern; low, vulgar

tabernera *f*, publican's wife; barmaid

tabernero *m*, publican; barman, drawer

tabicar *vt* to wall or board up; hide, cover up

tabique *m*, partition wall, inside wall; thin wall

tabla *f*, plank of wood, board; *met* plate; slab; flat side, face (of wood); *sew* box pleat; table (of contents, etc.); *art* panel; vegetable garden; butcher's slab; butcher's stall; *pl* tablets (for writing); (*math* etc.) tables; stalemate (chess, checkers); draw (in an election); *theat* boards, stage. **t. de armonía,** sounding board (of musical instruments). **t. de lavar,** washboard. **t. de materias,** table of contents. **t. de multiplicación,** multiplication table. **t. rasa,** clean sheet (of paper, etc.); complete ignorance. **T. Redonda,** Round Table (of King Arthur). **escapar** or **salvarse en una t.,** to have a narrow escape, escape in the nick of time

tablacho *m*, sluice gate. **echar el t.,** *inf* to interrupt the flow of someone's remarks

tablado *m*, flooring; platform; *theat* stage; scaffold, gibbet. **sacar al t.,** to produce, put on the stage; to make known, publish

tablazón *f*, planks, boards; flooring; *naut* deck planks or sheathing

tablear *vt* to saw into planks; *sew* make box pleats in; hammer iron into sheets

tablero *m*, board (of wood); paneling, boarding; slab; shop counter; board (checkers, chess). **t. de instrumentos,** dashboard; instrument panel

tableta *f*, tablet; pastille, lozenge

tablilla *f*, small board; tablet; bulletin board, notice board

tablón *m*, thick plank; wooden beam; *inf* drinking bout

tabú *m*, taboo

tabuco *m*, miserable little room; hovel

taburete *m*, stool; tabouret

tacañería *f*, miserliness, niggardliness; craftiness

tacaño *a* miserly, niggardly; crafty

tacha *f*, imperfection, defect; spot, stain; fault; large tack. **poner t.,** to criticize, object to

tachable *a* censurable, blameworthy

tachar *vt* to criticize, blame; cross out, erase; charge, accuse

tacho de basura *m, Argentina* garbage can

tachón *m*, round-headed ornamental nail; *sew* gold or silver studs, trimming; crossing out, erasure

tachonar *vt* to stud with round-headed nails; *sew* trim with gold or silver studs or trimming

tachoso *a* imperfect, defective, faulty; spotted, stained

tachuela *f, carp* tack

tácito *a* silent, unexpressed; tacit, implied

taciturnidad *f*, taciturnity; reserve; melancholy

taciturno *a* taciturn; reserved; dismal, gloomy, melancholy

taco *m*, stopper, plug; billiard cue; rammer; wad, wadding (in a gun); pop gun; taco (food); tear-off calendar; *inf* snack; obscenity, oath. **t. de papel,** writing tablet

tacón *m*, heel (of a shoe)

taconear *vi* to stamp with one's heels; walk heavily on one's heels; walk arrogantly

taconeo *m*, drumming or stamping of one's heels (gen. in dancing)

táctica *f*, method, technique; *mil* tactics; policy, way, means

táctico *a* tactical. *m, mil* tactician

táctil *a* tactile

tacto *m*, sense of touch; touch, feel; touching; skill; tact

tafetán *m*, taffeta; *pl* flags, standards. **t. de heridas** or **t. inglés,** court plaster

tafilete *m*, morocco leather

tahalí *m*, sword shoulder belt

tahona *f*, horse mill; bakery; baker's shop

tahonero (-ra) *n* miller; baker

tahúr *m*, gambler; cardsharper

tahurería *f*, gambling den; gambling; cheating at cards

Tailandia Thailand

taimado *a* knavish, crafty; obstinate, headstrong

taimería *f*, cunning, craftiness

taita *m*, daddy

taja *f*, cut, cutting; slice; washboard

tajada *f*, slice; strip, portion; steak, filet; *inf* cough; drinking bout; hoarseness

tajadera *f*, cheese knife; chisel; *pl* sluice gate

tajado *a* steep, sheer (of cliffs, etc.)

tajadura *f*, cutting, dividing, dissection

tajamar *m*, cutwater; breakwater; raft

tajar *vt* to cut, chop; sharpen, trim (quill pens)

tajea *f,* culvert; aqueduct; drain; watercourse

Tajo, el the Tagus

tajo *m,* cut, incision; task; cutting (in a mountain, etc.); cut, thrust (of sword); executioner's block; chopping board; washboard; steep cliff, precipice

tajón *m,* butcher block; chopping board

tal *a pl* **tales,** such; said (e.g. **el t. Don Juan,** the said Don Juan). **tal** is always used before nouns and (except when meaning 'the said') without def. art. **un t.,** a certain (e.g. **un t. hombre,** a certain man). *pron* some, some people; someone; such a thing. *adv* so, thus. **t. para cual,** two of a kind, a well-matched pair; tit for tat. **con t. que,** *conjunc* on condition that, provided that. **No hay t.,** There is no such thing. *inf* **¿Qué t.?** How are you? What's the news? What's new?

tala *f,* felling or cutting down (of trees); cropping of grass (ruminants)

talabarte *m,* sword belt

talabartería *f,* saddlery

talabartero *m,* saddler

talador (-ra) *a* felling, cutting; destructive. *n* feller, cutter; destroyer

taladrar *vt* to drill, bore, gouge holes; pierce, perforate; punch (a ticket); assail or hurt the ear (sounds); *fig* go into deeply (a subject)

taladro *m,* drill, gimlet, gouge; drill hole, bore; puncher (for tickets, etc.)

tálamo *m,* marriage bed; (*bot anat*) thalamus

talán *m,* peal, tolling (of a bell)

talanquera *f,* barricade; parapet, fence, wall; refuge, asylum; safety, security

talante *m,* mode of execution, technique; personal appearance, mien; disposition, temperament; wish, desire; aspect, appearance. **de buen (mal) t.,** willingly (unwillingly)

talar *a* full-length, long (of gowns, robes, etc.)

talar *vt* to fell, chop down (trees); ravage, lay waste; prune (gen. olive trees)

talco *m, min* talc; sequin, tinsel

talcualillo *a inf* not too bad, fairly good; slightly better (of health)

taled *m,* prayer shawl, tales, tallit

talega *f,* sack, bag; sackful; money bag; *pl inf* cash wealth

talego *m,* narrow sack; *inf* dumpy person

talento *m,* talent (Greek coin); talent, gift, quality; intelligence, understanding; cleverness

talentoso *a* talented

tálero *m,* thaler (old German coin)

talión *m,* **(ley de)** law of retaliation

talismán *m,* talisman

talla *f,* carving (especially wood); cutting (of gems); reward for apprehension of a criminal; ransom; stature, height, size; height measuring rod

tallado *a* **bien** (or **mal**), well (or badly) carved; well (or badly) proportioned, of a good (or bad) figure

tallado *m,* carving

tallador *m,* metal engraver; die sinker

tallar *vt art* to carve; engrave; cut (gems); value, estimate; measure height (of persons)

tallarín *m,* (gen. *pl*) *cul* noodle

talle *m,* figure, physique; waist; fit (of clothes); appearance, aspect. *inf* **largo de t.,** long-waisted; long drawn out, overlong. **tener buen t.,** to have a good figure

tallecer *vi irr bot* to sprout, shoot. See **conocer**

taller *m,* workshop; factory; mill; workroom, atelier; industrial school; school of arts and crafts; studio

tallista *mf* engraver; wood carver; sculptor

tallo *m, bot* stalk; stem; slice of preserved fruit; cabbage. **t. rastrero,** *bot* runner

talludo *a* long-stalked; lanky, overgrown; no longer young, aging (of women); habit-ridden

talmúdico *a* Talmudic

talón *m,* heel; heel (of a shoe); *com* counterfoil; luggage receipt; *com* sight draft; coupon; heel (of a violin bow). *inf* **apretar los talones,** to take to one's heels. *inf* **pi-**

sarle (a uno) los talones, to follow on a person's heels; rival successfully

talonada *f,* dig in with the spurs

talonario *m,* stub book

tamaño *a comp* so big; so small (e.g. **La conocí tamaña,** I knew her when she was so high) (indicating her size with a gesture)); so great, so large (e.g. **tamaña empresa,** so great an undertaking). *m,* size

tamarindo *m,* tamarind

tambaleante *a* tottering, rickety; staggering

tambalear(se) *vi* and *vr* to totter, sway, shake; reel, stagger

tambaleo *m,* swaying; tottering; rocking; shaking; staggering, reeling

tambarillo *m,* chest with an arched lid

también *adv* also, too; in addition, as well

tambor *m, mus* drum; drummer; embroidery frame; *mech* drum, cylinder; roaster (for coffee, chestnuts, etc.). **t. mayor,** drum major. **a t.** (*or* **con t.**) **batiente,** with drums beating; triumphantly, with colors flying

tamborear *vi* to totter, sway; stagger, reel

tamboreo *m,* tottering, swaying; staggering, reeling

tamboril *m,* tabor

tamborilada *f, inf* slap on the back or face; *inf* fall on the bottom

tamborilear *vi* to play the tabor; *vt* eulogize, extol

tamborilero *m,* tabor player

tamborín *m,* tabor

Támesis, el the Thames

tamiz *m,* sieve

tamizar *vt* to sieve

tamo *m,* fluff; chaff

tampoco *adv* neither, not . . . either, nor . . . either; no more (e.g. **No lo ha hecho María t.,** Mary hasn't done it either)

tampón *m,* stamp moistener; *surg* tampon

tan *adv abb* **tanto** so, as. Used before adjectives and adverbs, excepting **más, mejor, menos, peor,** which need **tanto. t. . . . como,** as . . . as. **t. siquiera,** even (see **siquiera**). **t. sólo,** only, solely (e.g. **No vengo t. sólo para saludarte,** I do not come merely to greet you). **qué . . . t.,** what a . . . (e.g. **¡Qué día t. hermoso!** What a lovely day!)

tanda *f,* turn; opportunity; task; shift, relay; game (of billiards); bad habit; collection, batch, group; round (of a game); (*dance*) set

tándem *m,* tandem

tandeo *m,* allowance of irrigation water, turn for using water

Tangañica Tanganyika

tangente *a* and *f, geom* tangent

Tánger Tangier

tangerino (-na) *a* and *n* of or from Tangier, Tangerine

tanque *m, mil* tank; cistern, tank, reservoir; ladle, dipper

tanteador *m, sport* scorer, marker; scoreboard

tantear *vt* to measure, compare; consider fully; test, try out; *fig* probe, sound (persons); estimate roughly; *art* sketch, block in; *vt* and *vi sport* keep the score of

tanteo *m,* measurement, comparison; test; rough estimate; *sport* score

tanto *a* so much; as much; very great; as great; *pl* **tantos,** so many; as many (e.g. **Tienen tantas flores como nosotros,** They have as many flowers as we). In comparisons **tanto** is used before **más, mejor, menos, peor,** but generally **tan** is used before adjectives and adverbs (e.g. **¡Tanto peor!** So much the worse!). *pron dem* that (e.g. **por lo t.,** therefore, on that account). *m,* so much, a certain amount; copy of a document; man, piece (in games); point (score in games); *com* rate (e.g. **el t. por ciento,** the percentage, the rate); *pl* approximation, odd (e.g. **Llegaron cien hombres y tantos,** A hundred-odd men arrived). *adv* so much; as much; so, in such a way. **t. . . . como,** the same as, as much as. **t. . . . cuanto,** as much as. **t. más,** the more. **t. menos,** the less (e.g. **Cuanto más (menos) dinero tiene t. más (menos) quiere,** The more (less) money he has, the more (less) he wants. **t. más (menos)** . . . **cuanto que,** all the more (less) . . . because. **algún t.,** a certain amount, somewhat. **al t. de (una cosa),** aware of, acquainted with (a thing). **en t.** or **entre t.,** meanwhile. **las tantas,** *inf* late hour, wee hours. **No es para t.,** *inf* It's not as bad as that, there's no need to make such a fuss; he (she, it) isn't equal to it. **otro t.,** the same, as much; as much more. **un t.,** a bit, somewhat

tañedor (-ra) *n mus* player

tañer *vt irr mus* to play; *vi* sway, swing. **t. la occisa,** to sound the death (in hunting). *Pres. Part.* **tañendo.** *Preterite* **tañó, tañeron.** *Imperf. Subjunc.* **tañese,** etc.

tañido *m,* tune, sound, note; toll, peal; ring

taoísmo *m,* Taoism

taoísta *mf* Taoist

tapa *f,* lid; cover; cover (of books)

tapaboca *m,* blow on the mouth; *f,* scarf, muffler; *inf* remark that silences someone

tapada *f,* veiled woman, one whose face is hidden

tapadera *f,* loose lid, top, cover

tapadero *m,* stopper

tapador (-ra) *a* covering. *n* coverer. *m,* stopper; lid; cover

tapagujeros *m, inf* unskilled mason or bricklayer; *fig inf* stopgap (person)

tapar *vt* to cover; cover with a lid; muffle up, veil; hide, keep secret; close up, stop up

taparrabo *m,* loincloth; swimming trunks

tapete *m,* rug; tablecover. *inf* **t. verde,** gaming table. *fig* **estar sobre el t.,** to be on the carpet, be under consideration

tapia *f,* adobe; mud wall; fence. *inf* **más sordo que una t.,** as deaf as a post

tapiar *vt* to wall up; put a fence around, fence in

tapicería *f,* set of tapestries; tapestry work; art of tapestry making; upholstery; tapestry storehouse or shop

tapicero *m,* tapestry weaver or maker; upholsterer; carpet layer; furnisher

tapioca *f,* tapioca

tapiz *m,* tapestry; carpet

tapizar *vt* to cover with tapestry; cover, clothe; upholster; carpet; hang with tapestry; furnish with hangings or drapes

tapón *m,* stopper; cork (of a bottle); plug; *surg* tampon

taponar *vt* to stopper, cork; plug; *surg* tampon; *mil* seal off

taponazo *m,* pop (of a cork)

tapujarse *vr* to wrap oneself up, muffle oneself

tapujo *m,* scarf, muffler, face covering; disguise; *inf* pretense, subterfuge

taquera *f,* rack (for billiard cues)

taquería *f,* taco stand

taquigrafía *f,* shorthand

taquigrafiar *vt* to write in shorthand

taquigráfico *a* shorthand

taquígrafo (-fa) *n* shorthand writer, stenographer

taquilla *f,* booking office; box office; grille, window (in banks, etc.); rolltop desk, cupboard for papers; *theat* takings, cash

taquillero (-ra) *n* booking office clerk

tara *f,* tally stick; *com* tare

taracea *f,* inlaid work, marquetry

taracear *vt* to inlay

tarambana *mf inf* madcap

tarantela *f,* tarantella

tarántula *f,* tarantula

tararear *vt* to hum a tune

tararreo *m,* humming, singing under one's breath

tarasca *f,* figure of a dragon (carried in Corpus Christi processions); *inf* hag, trollop

tarascada *f,* bite, nip; *inf* insolent reply

tarascar *vt* to bite; wound with the teeth

tardanza *f,* delay, tardiness; slowness

tardar *vi* to delay; be tardy, arrive late; take a long time. **a más t.,** at the latest

tarde *f,* afternoon. *adv* late. ¡**Buenas tardes!** Good afternoon! **de t. en t.,** from time to time, sometimes. **hacerse t.,** to grow late. **Más vale t. que nunca,** Better late than never

tardecer *vi impers irr* to grow dusk. See **conocer**

tardecica, tardecita *f,* dusk, late afternoon

tardíamente *adv* late; too late

tardío *a* late; backward; behind; slow, deliberate

tardo *a* slow, slothful, tardy; late; dilatory; stupid, slow-witted; badly spoken, inarticulate

tarea *f,* task, work

tarifa *f,* price list; tariff

tarifar *vt* to put a tariff on

tarima *f,* stand, raised platform

tarín barín *adv inf* more or less, about

tarja *f,* large shield; ancient coin; tally stick. *inf* **beber sobre t.,** to drink on credit

tarjar *vt* to reckon by tally

tarjeta *f,* buckler, small shield; *arch* tablet bearing an inscription; title (of maps and charts); visiting card; invitation (card). **t. de visita,** visiting card. **t. postal,** postcard, postal card

tarquín *m,* mud, mire

tárraga *f,* old Spanish dance

tarro *m,* jar, pot

tarso *m, anat* tarsus, ankle; *zool* hock; *orn* shank

tarta *f,* cake pan; cake; tart

tártago *m,* spurge; *inf* misfortune, disappointment

tartajear *vi* to stammer; stutter

tartajeo *m,* stammering; stutter

tartajoso (-sa) *a* stammering; stuttering. *n* stutterer

tartalear *vi inf* to stagger, totter; be speechless, be dumbfounded

tartamudear *vi* to stammer, stutter

tartamudeo *m.* **tartamudez** *f,* stammering; stuttering

tartamudo (-da) *n* stammerer

tartán *m,* tartan

tartana *f, naut* tartan; covered two-wheeled carriage

tartáreo *a poet* infernal, hellish

Tartaria Tartary

tártaro (-ra) *m,* cream of tartar; tartar (on teeth); *poet* hell, hades.. *a* and *n* Tartar

tartufo *m,* hypocrite

tarugo *m,* thick wooden peg; stopper; wooden block

tasa *f,* assessment, valuation; valuation certificate; fixed price; standard rate; measure, rule

tasación *f,* valuation; assessment

tasador *m,* public assessor; valuer

tasajo *m,* salt meat; piece of meat

tasar *vt* to value; price; fix remuneration; tax; regulate; rate; dole out sparingly

tasca *f,* gambling den; tavern

tascar *vt* to dress (hemp, etc.); graze, crop the grass

tasquera *f, inf* quarrel, row, rumpus

tasquil *m,* wood splinter, chip

tata *m, inf WH* daddy

tatarabuela *f,* great-great-grandmother

tatarabuelo *m,* great-great-grandfather

tataradeudo (-da) *n* very old relative; ancestor

tataranieta *f,* great-great-granddaughter

tataranieto *m,* great-great-grandson

tatas, andar a *vt* to walk on all fours

¡**tate!** *interj* Stop!; Be careful!; Go slowly!; Now I understand!, Of course!

tatuaje *m,* tattooing

tatuar *vt* to tattoo

taumaturgia *f,* thaumaturgy, wonder-working

taumaturgo *m,* thaumaturge, magician

taurino *a* taurine; pertaining to bullfights

Tauro *m,* Taurus

tauromaquia *f,* bullfighting, tauromachy

tautología *f,* tautology

taxi *m,* taxi

taxidermia *f,* taxidermy

taxidermista *mf* taxidermist

taxista *m,* taxi driver

taxonomía *f*, taxonomy
taz a taz *adv* in exchange, without payment; even
taza *f*, cup; cupful; basin (of a fountain)
tazar(se) *vt* and *vr* to fray (of cloth)
tazmía *f*, tithe contribution; share of tithes; tithe register
tazón *m*, large cup; bowl
te *f*, name of the letter T. *mf* dat. and acc. of *pers pron 2nd pers sing* thee; you; to thee, to you. Never used with a preposition
té *m*, tea
tea *f*, torch; firebrand
teatral *a* theatrical
teatralidad *f*, theatricality
teatro *m*, theater; stage; dramatic works; dramatic art; drama, plays. **t. de variedades,** music hall. **t. por horas,** theater where short, one-act plays are staged hourly
tebano (-na), tebeo (-ea) *a* and *n* Theban
Tebas Thebes
teca *f*, teak
techado *m*, ceiling; roof
techador *m*, roofer
techar *vt* to roof
techo *m*, roof; ceiling; dwelling, habitation
techumbre *f*, ceiling; roof
tecla *f*, key (of keyed instruments); typewriter, linotype, or calculating machine key; *fig* difficult or delicate point. *inf* **dar en la t.,** to hit on the right way of doing a thing
teclado *m*, keyboard
tecleado *m*, *mus* fingering
teclear *vi* to finger the keyboard; run one's fingers over the keyboard; *inf* drum or tap with the fingers; *vt* tap (the keys, etc.); *inf* try out various schemes
tecleo *m*, fingering the keys; *inf* drumming with the fingers; scheme, means
técnica *f*, technique
tecnicismo *m*, technical jargon; technicality, technical term
técnico *a* technical. *m*, technician
tecnicolor *m*, technicolor
tecnología *f*, technology
tecnológico *a* technological
tecnólogo *m*, technologist
tedero *m*, torch seller; torch holder
tedio *m*, tedium, boredom, ennui
tedioso *a* tedious, boring
tegumento *m*, integument, tegument
teísmo *m*, theism
teísta *a* theistic. *mf* theist
teja *f*, tile, slate. *inf* **de tejas abajo,** in the normal way; in the world of men. **de tejas arriba,** in a supernatural way; in heaven
tejadillo *m*, roof (of a vehicle)
tejado *m*, roof
tejar *m*, tile works. *vt* to roof with tiles
tejavana *f*, penthouse, open shed
tejedor (-ra) *a* weaving; *inf* scheming. *n* weaver; *inf* schemer
tejedura *f*, weaving; fabric; texture
tejeduría *f*, art of weaving; weaving shed or mill
tejemaneje *m*, *inf* cleverness, knack
tejer *vt* to weave; plait; spin a cocoon; arrange, regulate; concoct, hatch (schemes); wind in and out (in dancing)
tejero *m*, tile manufacturer
tejido *m*, texture, weaving; textile; *anat* tissue; fabric, material
tejo *m*, quoit, discus; metal disk; yew tree
tejón *m*, *zool* badger
tela *f*, fabric, material, cloth; membrane; film (on liquids); spiderweb, cobweb; inner skin (of fruit, vegetables); film over the eye; matter, subject; scheme, plot. **t. metálica,** wire gauze. **en t. de juicio,** under consideration, in doubt. **llegarle a uno a las telas del corazón,** to hurt deeply, cut to the quick

telar *m*, loom, weaving machine; *theat* gridiron
telaraña *f*, cobweb; mere trifle, bagatelle. *inf* **mirar las telarañas,** to be absent-minded
telarañoso *a* cobwebby
telecomunicación *f*, telecommunication
telefonear *vt* to telephone, call
telefonía *f*, telephony. **t. sin hilos,** wireless telephony, broadcasting
telefónico *a* telephonic
telefonista *mf* telephone operator
teléfono *m*, telephone. **t. automático,** dial telephone. **llamar por t.** (a), to telephone, call, ring up
telefundir *vt* to telecast
telegrafía *f*, telegraphy. **t. sin hilos,** wireless telegraphy
telegrafiar *vt* to telegraph
telegráfico *a* telegraphic
telegrafista *mf* telegraph operator
telégrafo *m*, telegraph. **t. sin hilos,** wireless telegraph. *inf* **hacer telégrafos,** to talk by signs
telegrama *m*, telegram
telemetría *f*, telemetry
telémetro *m*, telemeter, rangefinder
teleología *f*, teleology
telepatía *f*, telepathy
telepático *a* telepathic
telescópico *a* telescopic
telescopio *m*, telescope
telespectador *m*, TV viewer, member of the television audience
teletipo *m*, teleprinter
televisión *f*, television
telilla *f*, film (on liquids); thin fabric
telón *m*, *theat* curtain; drop scene. **t. contra incendios, t. de seguridad,** *theat* safety curtain. **t. de boca,** drop curtain. **t. de foro,** drop scene
tema *m*, theme, subject; *mus* motif, theme; thesis, argument. *f*, obstinacy; obsession, mania; hostility, grudge, rancor
temático *a* thematic; pigheaded, obstinate
temblador (-ra) *a* trembling, shaking. *n* Quaker
temblante *a* shaking; quivering. *m*, bracelet
temblar *vi irr* to tremble, shake; wave, quiver; shiver with fear. See **acertar**
temblequear, tembletear *vi inf* tremble; shake with fear
temblón *a inf* trembling, shaking. *m*, *inf* aspen
temblor *m*, shake, trembling, shiver. **t. de tierra,** earthquake
tembloroso, tembloso *a* trembling, shaking, shivering, quivering
temedero *a* fearsome, dread
temedor (-ra) *a* fearful. *n* fearer, dreader
temer *vt* to fear, dread; suspect, imagine; *vi* be afraid
temerario *a* reckless, impetuous; thoughtless, hasty
temeridad *f*, recklessness, impetuosity, temerity; thoughtlessness; act of folly; rash judgment
temerón *a inf* swaggering, bombastic
temeroso *a* frightening, dread; fearful, timid; afraid, suspicious
temible *a* dread, awesome
temor *m*, fear
temoso *a* obstinate, headstrong
témpano *m*, tabor; drumhead; block, flat piece; side of bacon. **t. de hielo,** iceberg, ice floe
temperación *f*, tempering
temperamento *m*, temperament, nature; compromise, agreement
temperar *vt* to temper
temperatura *f*, temperature
temperie *f*, weather conditions
tempestad *f*, storm
tempestividad *f*, opportuneness, seasonableness
tempestivo *a* opportune, seasonable
tempestuoso *a* stormy
templa *f*, tempera; *pl anat* temples

templado *a* moderate; temperate (of regions); luke-warm; *mus* in tune; restrained (of style); *inf* brave, long-suffering. **estar bien** (*or* **mal**) **templado,** *inf* to be well (*or* badly) tuned (of musical instruments); be in a good (*or* bad) temper; be good- (*or* ill-) natured

templario (-ra) *n* tuner. *m*, tuning key

templadura *f*, tuning; tempering

templanza *f*, moderation; sobriety; mildness of climate

templar *vt* to tune; met temper; moderate; warm; allay, appease; anneal; *art* harmonize, blend; *naut* trim the sails; *vr* control oneself, be moderate; *vi* grow warm

templario *m*, Knight Templar

temple *m*, weather conditions; temperature; temper (of metals, etc.); nature, disposition; bravery; mean, average; *mus* tuning. **al t.,** in tempera

templete *m*, *dim* shrine; niche (for statues); kiosk, pavilion

templo *m*, temple

temporada *f*, space of time, season, while. **de t.,** seasonal; temporary. **estar de t.,** to be out of town, on holiday

temporal *a* temporal; temporary; secular, lay; transient, fugitive. *m*, storm, tempest; rainy period; seasonal laborer

temporalidad *f*, secular character; temporality secular possession (gen. *pl*)

temporáneo, temporario *a* temporary, impermanent, fleeting

témporas *f pl*, Ember days

temporejar *vt naut* to lie to in a storm

temporero *a* temporary (of work)

temporizar *vi* to while away the time; temporize

tempranal *a* early fruiting

tempranero *a* early

temprano *a* early. *adv* in the early hours; prematurely, too soon

temulento *a* intoxicated, drunken

ten con ten *m*, *inf* tact, diplomacy

tenacear *vi* to insist, be obstinate

tenacidad *f*, adhesiveness; resistance, toughness; obstinacy, tenacity

tenacillas *f pl*, *dim* small tongs; candle snuffers; sugar tongs; curling irons; tweezers

tenaz *a* adhesive; hard, resistant, unyielding; tenacious, obstinate

tenaza *f*, claw (of a lobster, etc.); *pl* tongs; pincers; pliers; dental forceps

tenazada *f*, seizing with tongs; strong bite, snap; rattle of tongs

tenazón (**a** or **de**) *adv* without taking aim, wildly; unexpectedly

tenca *f*, tench

tención *f*, retention, holding; grip

tendal *m*, awning; sheet for catching olives

tendedero *m*, drying ground

tendedura *f*, laying out; stretching

tendencia *f*, tendency

tendencioso *a* tendentious, biased

tender *vt irr* to hang out; unfold, spread out; extend, hold out; *mas* plaster; *vi* tend, incline; *vr* lie down at full length; place one's cards on the table; gallop hard (of horses). See **entender**

tendero (-ra) *n* shopkeeper; retailer. *m*, tent maker

tendido *m*, row of seats in a bullfight arena; clothes hung out to dry; clear sky; *mas* plaster

tendón *m*, tendon

tenducha *f*, *inf* wretched little shop

tenebrosidad *f*, gloom, darkness, obscurity

tenebroso *a* dark, gloomy

tenedero *m*, *naut* anchoring ground, anchorage

tenedor *m*, table fork; possessor, retainer; *com* holder; payee. **t. de libros,** bookkeeper

teneduría *f*, employment of a bookkeeper. **t. de libros,** bookkeeping

tenencia *f*, possession; tenancy, occupation; lieutenancy

tener *vt irr* to have; hold; grasp; possess; own; uphold, maintain; contain; include; hold fast, grip; stop; keep (promises); lodge, accommodate; (*with en*) value, estimate (e.g. **Le tengo en poco,** I have a poor opinion of him); (*with para*) be of the opinion that (e.g. **tengo para mí,** my opinion is); (*with por*) believe, consider; *vi* be wealthy; *vr* steady oneself; hold on to; lean (on); rest (on); defend oneself; uphold; rely on; (*with por*) consider oneself as. **tener** is used to express: 1. *Age* (e.g. **¿Cuántos años tiene Vd?** How old are you?). 2. *Possession* (e.g. **Tenemos muchos sombreros,** We have a great many hats). 3. *Measurements* (e.g. **El cuarto tiene dieciocho metros de largo,** The room is eighteen meters long). Translated by 'be' when describing some physical and mental states (e.g. **Tenemos miedo,** We are afraid. **Tengo sueño,** I am sleepy. **Tienen frío (calor),** They are cold (hot)). Used as *auxiliary verb* replacing **haber** in compound tenses of transitive verbs (e.g. **Tengo escritas las cartas,** I have written the letters). **t. a bien,** to think fit, please, judge convenient. **t. algo en cuenta a uno,** to hold something against someone. **t. a menos de hacer (una cosa),** to scorn to do (a thing). **t. cruda,** to have a hangover. **t. curiosidad por,** to be curious about. **t. curiosidad por que** + *subj* to be interested that. **t. en aprecio,** to appreciate, esteem, value. **t. en cuenta,** to bear in mind. **t. en menos (a),** to despise (a person). **t. gana,** to want, wish; feel disposed; have an appetite. **t. lugar,** to take place, occur. **t. muchas partes cruzadas,** to be well-traveled. **t. mucho colegio** to be well-educated. **t. muy en cuenta,** to certainly bear in mind. **t. poco colegio,** to have had little education. **t. presente,** to remember. **t. que,** to have to (e.g. **tengo que hacerlo,** I must do it). **t. que ver (con),** to have something to do (with), be related to. **no tenerlas todas consigo,** *inf* to have the jitters. *Pres. Ind.* **tengo, tienes, tiene, tenemos, tenéis, tienen.** *Preterite* **tuve,** etc. *Fut.* **tendré,** etc. *Condit.* **tendría,** etc. *Pres. Subjunc.* **tenga,** etc. *Imperf. Subjunc.* **tuviese,** etc.

tenguerengue, en *adv inf* rickety, insecure

tenia *f*, tapeworm; *arch* fillet, narrow molding

teniente *a* owning; holding; unripe (of fruit); *inf* slightly deaf; stingy, mean. *m*, deputy, substitute; *mil* first lieutenant, lieutenant. **t. coronel,** lieutenant colonel. **t. de navío,** naval lieutenant. **t. general,** *mil* lieutenant general. **t. general de aviación,** air marshal

tenis *m*, tennis

tenor *m*, import, contents (of a letter, etc.); constitution, composition; *mus* tenor

tenorio *m*, rake, Don Juan, philanderer

tensar *vt* to tighten; tense

tensión *f*, tautness; tension; strain, stress; *elec* tension

tenso *a* taut; tight; tense

tentación *f*, temptation; attraction, inducement

tentáculo *m*, tentacle; feeler

tentadero *m*, yard for trying out young bulls for bullfighting

tentador (-ra) *a* tempting; attractive. *n* tempter. *m*, the Devil

tentalear *vt* to examine by touch

tentar *vt irr* to touch, feel; examine by touch; incite, encourage; try, endeavor; test; tempt; *surg* probe. See **sentar**

tentativa *f*, endeavor, attempt; preliminary exam (at some univs.)

tentativo *a* tentative, experimental

tentemozo *m*, support, prop; tumbler (toy)

tentempié *m*, *inf* snack, bite

tenue *a* thin; slender, delicate; trivial, worthless, insignificant; pale; faint

tenuidad *f*, slenderness; delicacy; triviality, insignificance; paleness; faintness

teñidura *f*, dyeing, staining

teñir *vt irr* to dye; *art* darken; color, tinge; *vr* be dyed; be tinged or colored. See **ceñir**

teocracia *f,* theocracy
teocrático *a* theocratic
teodolito *m,* theodolite
teologal *a* theological
teología *f,* theology, divinity
teológico *a* theological
teologizar *vi* to theologize
teólogo *a* theological. *m,* theologian, divine; student of theology
teorema *m,* theorem
teoría *f,* theory
teórica *f,* theory
teórico *a* theoretical, speculative. *m,* theorist
teorizar *vt* to consider theoretically, theorize about
teoso *a* resinous, gummy
teosofía *f,* theosophy
teosófico *a* theosophical
teósofo *m,* theosophist
tepe *m,* sod, cut turf
terapeuta *mf* therapeutist
terapéutica *f,* therapeutics
terapéutico *a* therapeutic
terapia *f,* therapy
teratología *f,* teratology
tercena *f,* warehouse for storing government monopoly goods (tobacco, etc.)
tercenista *mf* person in charge of a tercena
tercer *a abb* of **tercero** third. Used before *m, sing* nouns
tercera *f,* procuress; *mus* third
tercería *f,* arbitration, mediation; temporary occupation of a fortress, etc.
tercero (-ra) *a* third; mediatory. *n* third; mediator. *m,* pimp; *ecc* tertiary; tithes collector; third person. **¡A la tercera va la vencida!** Third time lucky!
terceto *m,* tercet, triplet
tercia *f,* one-third; *ecc* tierce, third hour; storehouse for tithes. **tercias reales,** royal share of ecclesiastical tithes
terciana *f,* tertian fever
terciar *vt* to slant; sling sideways; divide into three; equalize weight (on beasts of burden); plow or dig for the third time; *agr* prune; *vr* be opportune, come at the right time. *vi* mediate, arbitrate; make up a number (for cards, etc.); reach the third day (of the moon); take part, participate
terciario *a* third, tertiary; *geol* tertiary. *m, ecc* tertiary
tercio *a* a third. *m,* one-third; *mil* infantry regiment; *ant,* body of foreign volunteers; fishermen's association; *pl* brawny limbs of a man. **hacer t.,** to take part in; make up the number of. **hacer buen (or mal) t. a alguien,** to do someone a good (or bad) turn
terciopelo *m,* velvet; velveteen
terco *a* pigheaded, obstinate; hard, tough
tergiversación *f,* tergiversation, vacillation
tergiversar *vt* to tergiversate, shuffle, vacillate
termal *a* thermal
termas *fpl,* thermal springs, hot mineral baths; thermal
térmico *a* a thermic
terminable *a* terminable
terminación *f,* conclusion, termination; end, finish; ending of a word; *gram* termination
terminador (-ra) *a* concluding. *n* finisher
terminal *a* terminal; final. *m, elec* terminal. **t. de carga,** cargo terminal
terminante *a* conclusive, definite; categorical
terminar *vt* to end, conclude; complete; *vr* and *vi* end
término *m,* limit, end; term, expression; boundary marker; district, suburb; space, period; state, condition; boundary; aim; appearance, demeanor, behavior (gen. *pl*); completion; *mus* tone; (*math law logic*) term. **t. medio,** *math* average; medium; compromise, middle way. **correr el t.,** to lapse (of time). **en primer t.,** *art* in the foreground. **medios términos,** evasions, excuses. **primer t.,** (cinema) closeup
terminología *f,* terminology
termita *f,* thermite. *m,* termite

termodinámica *f,* thermodynamics
termoeléctrico *a* thermoelectric
termómetro *m,* thermometer
Termópilas Thermopylae
termos *m,* thermos, vacuum bottle
termoscopio *m,* thermoscope
termóstato *m,* thermostat
termostático *a* thermostatic
terna *f,* triad, trio; set of dice
ternario *a* ternal, ternary
terne *a inf* bullying, braggartly; persistent, obstinate; robust. *mf* bully
ternera *f,* female calf; veal
ternero *m,* male calf
terneza *f,* tenderness, kindness; softness; softheartedness; endearment, caress, compliment (gen. *pl*)
ternilla *f,* cartilage, gristle
ternísimo *a sup* **tierno** most tender
terno *m,* triad; suit of clothes, three-piece suit; oath, curse
ternura *f,* softness; softheartedness; tenderness, kindness, sweetness
terquedad, terquería, terqueza *f,* obstinacy, obduracy
terracota *f,* terra cotta
terrado *m,* flat roof
Terranova Newfoundland
terraplén *m,* embankment; *mil* terreplein
terraplenar *vt* to fill up with earth; fill in (a hollow); make into an embankment; terrace
terrateniente *mf* landowner
terraza *f,* terrace; flat roof; flower border (of a garden)
terrazgo *m,* tillable land; rent for farming land
terregoso *a* lumpy, full of clods (of soil)
terremoto *m,* earthquake
terrenal *a* terrestrial
terreno *a* terrestrial. *m,* ground, land; *fig* sphere; region; soil; plot of land. **ganar t.,** *fig* to win ground, make progress. **medir el t.,** *fig* to feel one's way
térreo *a* earthy
terrero *a* earthly; low-flying, almost touching the ground; humble. *m,* flat roof; pile or mound of earth; deposit of earth, alluvium; target; mineral refuse
terrestre *a* terrestrial, earthly
terrezuela *f,* poor soil
terribilidad *f,* terribleness, horribleness; rudeness
terribilísimo *a sup* most terrible
terrible *a* terrible, horrible; rude, unsociable, ill-humored; enormous, huge
terrífico *a* terrible, frightful
territorial *a* territorial
territorialidad *f,* territoriality
territorio *m,* territory; jurisdiction. **t. bajo mandato,** mandated territory
terrizo *a* earthen
terrón *m,* clod (of earth); lump; *pl* lands, landed property. **t. de azúcar,** lump of sugar
terrorismo *m,* terrorism
terrorista *mf* terrorist
terrosidad *f,* earthiness
terroso *a* earthy; earthen
terruño *m,* plot of ground; native earth; country; soil
terso *a* smooth, shiny, glossy; *lit* elegant, polished (style)
tersura *f,* smoothness, glossiness; elegance (of style)
tertulia *f,* regular social meeting (gen. in cafés); conversational group; party; part of Spanish cafés set apart for players of chess, etc. **hacer t.,** to meet for conversation
tertuliano (-na) *n* **tertuliante,** *mf* **tertulio (-ia),** *n* member of a tertulia
terzuelo *m,* third, third part
Tesalia Thessaly
tesar *vt naut* to make taut; *vi* step backward, back (oxen)
tesela *f,* tessera, square used in mosaic work
teselado *a* tessellated
tesina *f,* master's essay, thesis

tesis *f*, thesis

teso *a* tight, taut, tense. *m*, hilltop; bulge, lump

tesón *m*, persistence, obstinacy, tenacity

tesonería *f*, stubbornness, obstinacy

tesorería *f*, treasury; treasuryship

tesorero (-ra) *n* treasurer

tesoro *m*, treasure; public treasury; hoard; *fig* gem, excellent person; thesaurus. **t. de duende,** fairy gold

tespíades *f pl*, the muses

testa *f*, head; face, front; *inf* sense, acumen. **t. coronada,** crowned head

testación *f*, erasure, crossing out

testado *a* testate

testador (-ra) *n* testator

testaferro *m*, *fig* figurehead, proxy

testamentar *vt* to bequeath

testamentaria *f*, execution of a will; *law* estate; executors' meeting

testamentario *a* testamental, testamentary

testamento *m*, *law* will; testament. **Antiguo T.,** Old Testament. **ordenar** (*or* **otorgar**) **su t.,** to make one's will

testar *vi* to make a will; *vt* erase, cross out

testarada *f*, a blow with the head; pigheadedness, stubbornness

testarrón *a inf* pigheaded

testarudez *f*, obstinacy, obduracy

testarudo *a* stubborn, obstinate

testera *f*, front, face; front seat (in a vehicle); upper half of an animal's face; tester, canopy

testículo *m*, testicle

testificación *f*, testification

testificar *vt* to testify; affirm, assert; attest, prove

testigo *mf* witness. *m*, proof, evidence. *law* **t. de cargo,** witness for the prosecution. *law* **t. de descargo,** witness for the defense. **t. de vista,** eyewitness. *law* **hacer testigos,** to bring forward witnesses

testimonial *a* confirmatory, proven

testimoniar *vt* to attest, confirm, bear witness to

testimoniero (-ra) *a* slanderous; hypocritical. *n* slanderer, hypocrite

testimonio *m*, testimony, proof; slander; affidavit

testuz *m*, front of the head (of some animals); nape (of animals)

teta *f*, mammary gland, breast; teat, dug, udder. **dar la t. (a),** to suckle

tétano, tétanos *m*, tetanus

tetera *f*, teapot; teakettle

tetilla *f*, *dim* rudimentary teat or nipple; nipple (of a nursing bottle)

tétrico *a* gloomy; somber

tetuaní *a* and *mf* of or from Tetuan

teutón (-ona) *n* Teuton. *a* Teutonic

teutónico *a* Teutonic

textil *a* and *m*, textile

texto *m*, text; quotation, citation; textbook

textorio *a* textile

textual *a* textual

textualista *mf* textualist

textura *f*, texture; weaving; structure (of a novel, etc.); animal structure

tez *f*, complexion, skin

ti *pers pron 2nd sing mf dat acc abl* thee, you. Always used with prep. (e.g. **por ti,** by thee (you))

tía *f*, aunt; *inf* wife, mother, dame; *inf* coarse creature. **t. abuela,** grandaunt, great-aunt. *inf* **quedarse para t.,** to be left an old maid

tiara *f*, ancient Persian headdress; papal tiara; coronet; dignity and power of the papacy

tiberino *a* Tiberine

tibetano (-na) *a* and *n* Tibetan. *m*, Tibetan (language)

tibia *f*, flute; tibia

tibieza *f*, tepidity; indifference, lack of enthusiasm

tibio *a* tepid, warm; indifferent, unenthusiastic

tiburón *m*, shark

ticket *m*, ticket; pass, membership card

tictac *m*, ticktock (of a clock)

tiempo *m*, time; season; epoch, period; chance, opportunity; leisure, free time; weather; *mus* tempo; *gram* tense; *naut* storm. **t. ha,** many years ago, long ago. **t. medio** *or* **medio t.,** *sport* halftime. **abrir el t.,** to clear up (of the weather). **ajustar los tiempos,** to fix the date (chronology). **a largo t.,** after a long time. **andando el t.,** in the course of time. **a su t.,** in due course, at the proper time. **a t.,** in time, at the right time. **a un t.,** simultaneously, at the same time. **cargarse el t.,** to cloud over (of the sky). **con t.,** in advance, with time; in time. **correr el t.,** to pass, move on (of time). **de t. en t.,** from time to time. **engañar** (*or* **entretener**) **el t.,** to kill time, while away the hours. *inf* **en t., de Maricastaña** *or* **del rey Perico,** long, long ago. **fuera de t.,** unseasonably, inopportunely; out of season. **ganar t.,** to gain time; *inf* hurry. **hacer t.,** to wait, cool one's heels; *fig* mark time. **perder el t.,** to waste time; misspend or lose time. **sentarse el t.,** to clear up (of the weather). **tomarse t. (para),** to postpone, take time for (or to)

tienda *f*, tent; *naut* awning, canopy; shop, store. **t. de antigüedades,** antique shop. **t. de campaña,** bell tent, pavilion. **t. oxígena,** oxygen tent

tienta *f*, astuteness; cleverness; *surg* probe; trying out young bulls for the bullring. **a tientas,** by touch, gropingly

tientaparedes *mf* one who gropes one's way

tiento *m*, touching, feeling; touch, feel; blind person's cane; tightrope walker's pole; manual control, steady hand; caution, care, tact; *mus* preliminary flourish; *inf* slap buffet; tentacle. **a t.,** by touch; unsurely, gropingly

tierno *a* soft; tender; kind; sweet; delicate; softhearted; fresh, recent; affectionate

tierra *f*, world, planet; earth; soil; ground; cultivated ground, land; homeland, native land; region; district, territory. **t. adentro,** inland. **t. de batán,** fuller's earth. **t. de Promisión,** Promised Land. **t. de Siena,** sienna. **besar la t.,** *inf* to fall down. **dar en t. con,** to throw down; demolish. **echar en t.,** *naut* to put ashore, land. **echar por t.,** *fig* to overthrow, destroy. **echar t. a,** *fig* to bury, forget. *inf* **la t. de María Santísima,** Andalusia. **por t.,** overland. **saltar en t.,** to land, disembark. **venir** (*or* **venirse**) **a t.,** to fall down, topple over

Tierra Santa Holy Land

tieso *a* hard, rigid, stiff; healthy, robust; taut; spirited; courageous; obstinate; stiff-necked; distant, formal. *adv* firmly, strongly

tiesto *m*, flowerpot; broken piece of earthenware

tiesura *f*, hardness, rigidity, stiffness; physical fitness; courageousness; obstinacy; formality, stiffness

tifoidea *f*, typhoid

tifón *m*, typhoon

tifus *m*, typhus. **t. exantemático,** trench fever

tigre *m*, tiger; ferocious person

tigresa *f*, tigress

tigridia *f*, tiger lily

tijera *f*, scissors (gen. *pl*); any scissor-shaped instrument; shears; drainage channel; carpenter's horse; scandalmonger, gossip

tijereta *f*, vine tendril; earwig

tijeretada *f*, cut or snip with scissors

tijeretear *vt* to cut with scissors; *inf* interfere arbitrarily

tijereteo *m*, scissor cut; click of the scissors

tila *f*, lime tree or flower; linden tree or flower; infusion made of lime flowers

tildar *vt* to cross out, erase; stigmatize; place a tilde over a letter

tilde *mf*, bad reputation; tilde; *f*, jot, iota

tilín *m*, tinkle, peal (of a bell)

tillar *vt* to lay wood floors

tilo *m*, lime tree

timador (-ra) *n inf* swindler, sharper, cheat

timar *vt* to swindle, cheat, deceive; *vr inf* exchange looks or winks

timba *f, inf* casino, gambling den; game of chance

timbal *m,* kettledrum

timbalero *m,* kettledrum player

timbrador *m,* stamper; stamping machine; rubber stamp

timbrar *vt* to stamp; place the crest over a coat of arms

timbre *m,* postage stamp; heraldic crest; excise stamp; bell, push-button; *mus* timbre; noble deed; personal merit

timidez *f,* timidity, nervousness

tímido *a* timid, nervous

timo *m, inf* swindling, trick; thymus

timón *m, naut* helm; rudder; management, direction; stick of a rocket. **t. de dirección,** *aer* tailfin

timonear *vi naut* to steer

timonel, timonero *m,* helmsman, coxswain

timorato *a* godfearing; timid, vacillating

tímpano *m, anat* eardrum, tympanum; *mus* kettledrum; *arch* tympanum; *print* tympan

tina *f,* vat; flour bin; large earthenware jar; wooden tub; bath

tinada *f,* woodpile; cow shed

tinaja *f,* large earthenware jar; jarful

tinajero *m,* seller of earthenware jars

tinelo *m,* servants' hall

tinerfeño (-ña) *a* and *n* of or from Tenerife

tinglado *m,* overhanging roof; open shed; penthouse; intrigue

tiniebla *f,* gloom, darkness (gen. *pl*); *pl* profound ignorance; confusion of mind; *ecc* tenebrae

tino *m,* skilled sense of touch; good eye, accurate aim; judgment, shrewdness; vat. **sacar de t. (a),** to bewilder, confuse; irritate, exasperate. **sin t.,** without limit, excessively

tinta *f,* color, tint; ink; staining, dyeing; dye, stain; *pl* shades, colors; *art* mixed colors ready for painting. **t. china,** India ink. **t. simpática,** invisible ink. **recargar las tintas,** *fig* to overpaint, lay the colors on too thick. *inf* **saber de buena t. (una cosa),** to learn (a thing) from a reliable source

tintar *vt* to dye; color, tinge, stain

tinte *m,* dyeing, staining; color; dye; stain; dye house; pretext, disguise

tintero *m,* inkwell. *inf* **dejar** (*or* **quedársele a uno) en el t.,** to forget, omit (to say, write)

tintín *m,* ring, peal; clink; chink

tintinar *vi* to ring, tinkle; clink; jingle

tintineo *m,* ringing, tinkling; clinking; jingle

tintirintín *m,* bray of a trumpet

tinto *a* red (of wine). *m,* red wine; dark red

tintorería *f,* dyeing industry; dyeing and dry-cleaning shop

tintorero (-ra) *n* dyer; dry cleaner

tintura *f,* dyeing, staining; color, tint; dye; stain; tincture; smattering, slight knowledge

tinturar *vt* to dye; color, tinge, stain; give a superficial notion of

tiña *f,* ringworm; *inf* meanness, stinginess

tiñoso *a* mangy; afflicted with ringworm; *inf* mean, stingy

tiñuela *f,* shipworm

tío *m,* uncle; gaffer; fellow, chap; fool; stepfather; father-in-law. **t. abuelo,** granduncle, great-uncle

tiovivo *m,* merry-go-round

tipiadora *f,* typewriter

típico *a* typical

tiple *m,* soprano or treble voice. *mf* soprano

tipo *m,* model, pattern; type; print, type; species, group (of animals, etc.); *inf* guy, chap

tipografía *f,* typography

tipográfico *a* typographical

tipógrafo *m,* typographer

típula *f,* daddy-longlegs

tiquismiquis *m pl,* ridiculous scruples; affected courtesies. *a inf* faddy, fussy

tira *f,* strip, band, ribbon; stripe, rib. **t. cómica,** comic strip

tirabotas *m,* buttonhook

tirabuzón *m,* corkscrew; ringlet, curl; hair curler

tirada *f,* throwing; drawing, pulling; cast, throw; distance, space; *print* edition, issue; circulation (of a newspaper, etc.); stroke (in golf); lapse, interval (of time). **t. aparte,** reprint (of an article, etc.)

tiradero *m,* shooting butt

tirado *a inf* dirt-cheap. *m,* wire drawing

tirador (-ra) *n* thrower, caster; drawer, puller; marksman. *m,* handle, knob; *mech* trigger; bell rope, bell pull; *print* pressman. **t. de bota,** boot tag. **t. de gomas,** catapult. **t. de oro,** gold wire drawer

tiralíneas *m,* ruling pen

tiramiento *m,* pulling; stretching

tiramira *f,* long, narrow mountain range; long line of persons or things; distance

tiranía *f,* tyranny, despotism

tiranicida *mf* tyrannicide (person)

tiranicidio *m,* tyrannicide (act)

tiránico *a* tyrannical

tiranización *f,* tyranny, tyrannization

tiranizar *vt* to tyrannize over

tirano (-na) *a* tyrannous, tyrannical; *fig* overwhelming, dominating. *n* tyrant

tirante *a* taut; tense, strained. *m,* trace (of a harness); shoulderstrap; suspender (gen. *pl*); *arch* tie

tirantez *f,* tautness; tension, strain; straight distance between two points. **estado de t.,** *pol* strained relations

tiranuelo *m,* petty tyrant

tirar *vt* to throw, cast; fling, aim, toss; throw down, overthrow; pull; draw; discharge, shoot; stretch, pull out; rule, draw (lines); squander, waste; *print* print; *vi* attract; pull; (*with prep a*) turn to, turn in the direction of; incline, tend to; incline toward, have a tinge of (colors); try, aspire to; (*with de*) wield, unsheath, draw out (firearms, arms); *vr* cast oneself, precipitate oneself; throw oneself on. *inf* **ir tirando,** to carry on, get along somehow

tirilla *f,* sew shirt neckband

tiritaña *f,* thin silk material; *inf* mere nothing, trifle

tiritar *vi* to shiver with cold

tiritón *m,* shiver, shudder

Tiro Tyre

tiro *m,* throwing; throw, cast; toss, fling; try (in football); shooting; piece of artillery; report, shot (of a gun); discharge (firearms); shooting range or gallery; team (of horses); range (of firearms, etc.); hoisting cable; flight (of stairs); min shaft; *inf* trick; robbery, theft; innuendo, insinuation; grave harm or injury; *pl* sword belt. **t. de pichón,** pigeon shooting. **t. par,** four-in-hand. **a t.,** within firing range; within reach. **de tiros largos,** *inf* in full regalia

tirocinio *m,* apprenticeship

tiroideo *a* thyroid

tiroides *f,* thyroid gland

Tirol, el the Tyrol

tirón *m,* novice, beginner; pull, tug, heave. **de un t.,** with one tug; at one stroke, at one blow

tiroriro *m, inf* sound of a wind instrument; *pl inf* wind instruments

tirotearse *vr mil* to exchange fire; indulge in repartee

tiroteo *m,* shooting, exchange of shots; crackle (of rifle fire)

Tirreno, el Mar the Tyrrhenian Sea

tirria *f, inf* hostility, grudge, dislike

tirulato *a* dumbfounded, stupefied

tisana *f,* tisane

tísico (-ca) *a* tuberculous. *n* sufferer from tuberculosis, consumptive

tisis *f,* tuberculosis

tisú *m,* silver or gold tissue

titánico *a* titanesque; colossal, huge

títere *m,* puppet; *fig inf* dummy, grotesque; *inf* fool; obsession, fixed idea; *pl inf* circus; Punch and Judy show. *inf* **echar los títeres a rodar,** to upset the whole show; quarrel, fall out with. *inf* **no dejar t. con**

cabeza, to destroy entirely, smash up completely; leave no one

titerero (-ra), titiritero (-ra), n titerista mf puppet showman; acrobat; juggler

tití m, marmoset

titilación f, quiver, tremor; twinkling, winking, gleam

titilador, titilante a quivering, trembling; twinkling

titilar vi to quiver, tremble; twinkle

titiritaina f, inf muffled strains of musical instruments; merrymaking, uproar

titiritar vi to tremble, shiver, shudder

titiritero (-ra) n puppet master; acrobat

titubear vi to totter, sway, rock; stutter, stammer; toddle; hesitate, vacillate

titubeo m, tottering, swaying; stuttering; hesitation

titulado m, titled person; one who holds an academic title

titular a titular. vt to entitle, call; vi obtain a title (of nobility); vr style oneself, call oneself

título m, title; heading; inscription; pretext, excuse; diploma, certificate; claim, right; noble title and its owner; section, clause; (univ.) degree; com stock certificate, bond; com title; caption; qualification, right, merit; basis of a claim or privilege; pl com securities, stocks. t. de la columna, print running title. títulos de propiedad, title deeds. t. del reino, title of nobility. a t., under pretext

tiza f, chalk; whiting; calcined stag's antler

tiznar vt to make sooty; dirty, stain, begrime; fig sully, tarnish

tizne m, (sometimes f) soot; charcoal; stain (on one's honor, etc.); agr blight

tizón m, firebrand; agr blight; fig stain (on one's honor, etc.)

tizona f, inf sword (by allusion to name of that of the Cid)

tizonear vi to poke or rake the fire

toalla f, towel. t. continua, roller towel. t. rusa, Turkish towel

toallero m, towel rail

tobillera f, inf girl, flapper

tobillo m, ankle

tobogán m, toboggan; chute (in apartment buildings or amusement parks)

toca f, headdress; toque; wimple; coif

tocable a touchable

tocado a fig touched, half-crazy. m, headdress; coiffure, hairdressing

tocador (-ra) n mus player. m, dressing table; kerchief; boudoir; cloakroom; dressing room; dressing case

tocamiento m, touching, feeling; touch; fig inspiration

tocante a touching. t. a, concerning, with regard to

tocar vt to touch, feel; mus play; knock, rap; summon; ring, peal; brush against; discover by experience; persuade, inspire; mention, touch upon; naut touch bottom; art retouch, touch up. vi belong; stop (at), touch at; be one's turn; concern, interest; be one's lot; adjoin, be near to; be opportune; be allied or closely related to; find the scent (of dogs). t. en un puerto, naut to touch at a port. Ahora me toca a mí, Now it's my turn. Es un problema que me toca de cerca, It is a problem that touches me very nearly. a toca teja, inf in ready cash

tocayo (-ya) n namesake

tochedad f, boorishness, loutishness

tocho a boorish, loutish, countrified. m, iron bar

tocinería f, pork butcher's shop

tocinero m, pork butcher

tocino m, bacon; salt pork

tocología f, tokology, obstetrics

tocón m, stump (of a tree or an amputated limb)

todavía adv still; even; nevertheless; yet. No han venido t., They have not come yet. Queda mucho que hacer t., There is still much to be done.

todo a all; whole, entire; every, each. m, whole, entirety; whole word (in charades); all; pl all; everyone.

adv wholly, entirely. t. lo posible, everything possible; all one can, one's best. t. lo que, all that which. ante t., in the first place; especially, particularly. así y t., nevertheless. a t. esto, in the meanwhile. con t. or con t. esto or con t. y esto, nevertheless, in spite of this. del t., wholly, completely. jugar el t. por el t., to risk everything on the outcome. sobre t., especially. y t., in addition, as well. Todos somos hijos de Adán y Eva, sino que nos diferencia la lana y la seda, We are all equal, but some of us are more equal than others

todopoderoso a all-powerful, almighty. m, the Almighty, God

toga f, toga; robe, gown

toisón m, fleece. t. de oro, Golden Fleece

Tokio Tokyo

toldadura f, awning; canopy; hanging, curtain

toldillo m, covered litter or sedan chair; WH mosquito net

toldo m, awning; canopy; pomp, show

tole m, outcry, uproar, tumult

toledano (-na) a and n Toledan

tolerable a bearable, tolerable

tolerancia f, tolerance, forbearance; permission

tolerante a tolerant, broad-minded

tolerantismo m, religious toleration

tolerar vt to put up with, bear, tolerate; overlook, allow, forgive

tolla f, marsh, bog

tollina f, inf spanking, whipping

tolmo m, tor

tolondro a stupid, heedless, reckless. m, bump, bruise

tolonés (-esa) a and n of or from Toulon

Tolosa Toulouse

tolva f, chute (for grain, etc.)

toma f, taking; receiving; conquest, capture; dose (of medicine)

tomada f, taking; take; capture

tomadero m, handle, haft

tomadura f, taking; receiving; dose (of medicine). inf t. de pelo, leg-pull, joke

tomar vt to take; pick up; conquer; eat; drink; adopt; employ; contract (habits); engage (employees); rent; understand; steal; remove; buy; suffer; fig overcome (by laughter, sleep, etc.); choose; possess physically; vi (with por) go in the direction of; vr grow rusty; go moldy; (with con) quarrel with. t. a chacota, to take as a joke. t. a pechos, to take to heart. t. el fresco, to take the air. tomarla con, to contradict, oppose; bear a grudge. t. la delantera, to take the lead; excel, beat. t. las de Villadiego, inf to quit, show one's heels. t. por su cuenta, to undertake, take charge of; take upon oneself. t. su desquite con, to get even with. Más vale una toma que dos te daré, A little help is worth a lot of promises. ¡Toma! inf Fancy! You don't say!; Of course! There's nothing new about that!

tomatal m, tomato bed, tomato patch

tomate m, tomato; tomato plant; inf hole, potato (in stockings, etc.)

tomatera f, tomato plant

tomatero (-ra) n tomato seller

tómbola f, raffle (gen. for charity); jumble sale

tomillo m, thyme

tomo m, volume, book; importance, worth

ton m, abb tono. sin t. ni son, inf without rhyme or reason

tonada f, words of a song and its tune

tonadilla f, dim short song; comic song; theat musical interlude ant

tonadillero (-ra) n composer or singer of tonadillas

tonal a tonal

tonalidad f, tonality

tonar vi poet to thunder or lightning

tonel m, barrel; cask; butt

tonelada f, ton

tonelería f, cooperage; collection or stock of casks and barrels

tonelero *m*, cooper

tonga, tongada *f*, layer, stratum; *inf* task

tónica *f*, *mus* keynote

tónico *a* tonic. *m*, *med* tonic; pick-me-up

tonificador, tonificante *a* strengthening, invigorating tonic

tonillo *m*, *dim* monotonous singsong voice; regional accent

tonina *f*, tuna; dolphin

tono *m*, inflection, modulation; (*mus med art*) tone; pitch, resonance, energy, strength; style; manner, behavior; *mus* key; mode of speech. **bajar el t.**, *fig inf* to change one's tune. **inf darse t.**, to put on side, give oneself airs. **de buen (mal) t.**, in good (bad) taste

tonsila *f*, tonsil

tonsilitis *f*, tonsillitis

tonsura *f*, shearing; hair cutting; *ecc* tonsure

tonsurar *vt* to shear, clip; cut the hair off; *ecc* tonsure

tontaina *mf inf* ninny, fool

tontear *vi* to behave foolishly; play the fool

tontería *f*, foolishness, stupidity; piece of folly; trifle, bagatelle

tontiloco *a inf* crazy, daft

tontillo *m*, dress bustle; hoop (for dresses)

tontivano *a* vain, conceited

tonto (-ta) *a* silly, stupid, simple; foolish, absurd. *n* fool, idiot. *m*, short coat, stroller. **t. de capirote,** *inf* an utter fool. **a tontas y a locas,** without rhyme or reason, topsy-turvy. **volver t. (a),** *fig inf* to drive crazy

topacio *m*, topaz

topar *vt* (*with con*) to run into, collide with, hit; meet unexpectedly; come across, find; *vi* butt (of horned animals); take a bet (in cards); consist in (of obstacles); meet with (difficulties); *inf* be successful

tope *m*, projection, part that juts out; obstacle, impediment; collision, bump; crux, difficult point; quarrel, fight; *mech* stop; *naut* masthead; *rw* buffer. **hasta el t.,** completely full, full to the brim

topera *f*, molehill

topetada *f*, butt (of horned animals); *inf* knock, bang

topetar *vt* and *vi* to butt (of horned animals); *vt* meet, run into

topetón *m*, butt; collision, impact, bump; blow on the head

tópico *a* topical. *m*, topic, theme

topo *m*, *zool* mole; *inf* clumsy or shortsighted person; dolt, ninny

topografía *f*, topography

topográfico *a* topographical

topógrafo *m*, topographer

toque *m*, touch, touching; pealing, ringing (of bells); crux, essence; test, proof; touchstone; *met* assay; warning; *inf* tap (on the shoulder, etc.); *art* touch. **t. de luz,** *art* light (in a picture). **t. de obscuro,** *art* shade (in a picture). **t. de queda,** curfew. **t. de tambor,** beating of a drum. **dar un t. a,** *inf* to put to the test; pump (for information)

toquero (-ra) *n* manufacturer of headdresses

toquetear *vt* to keep touching, handle repeatedly

toquilla *f*, hatband, hat trimming; kerchief; small shawl

torácico *a* thoracic

toral *a* principal, chief, main

tórax *m*, thorax

torbellino *m*, whirlwind; spate of things; *inf* madcap

torcedero *a* twisted, crooked

torcedor *a* twisting. *m*, twister; cause of continual anxiety

torcedura *f*, twisting; sprain, wrench

torcer *vt irr* to twist; bend; turn, bear (of roads, etc.); slant, slope, incline; misconstrue, pervert; dissuade; wrench, sprain (muscles); corrupt (justice). **t. el gesto,** to make a wry face. *vr* turn sour (of wine, milk); *fig* go astray; turn out badly (of negotiations). *Pres. Ind.* **tuerzo, tuerces,** etc. *Pres. Subjunc.* **tuerza, tuerzas, tuerza, tuerzan**

torcida *f*, wick (of lamps, etc.)

torcido *a* bent, crooked, sloping, inclined; curved; dishonest, tortuous. *m*, silk twist

torcijón *m*, stomachache

torcimiento *m*, twisting; twist, turn; circumlocution; digression

tordo *a* piebald, black-and-white. *m*, *orn* thrush. **t. de campanario** or **t. de Castilla,** starling

toreador *m*, bullfighter

torear *vi* and *vt* to fight bulls; *vt* ridicule; exasperate, provoke; *inf* string along, deceive

toreo *m*, bullfighting

torera *f*, bullfighter's jacket

torero *a inf* bullfighting. *m*, bullfighter

torete *m*, *dim* small bull; *inf* problem, difficult question; engrossing topic of conversation

toril *m*, pen for fighting bulls

torio *m*, thorium

tormenta *f*, storm; misfortune, calamity; indignation, agitation

tormento *m*, torment; torture; pain; anxiety, anguish. **dar t. (a),** to torture; inflict pain (on)

tormentoso *a* stormy, tempestuous; *naut* pitching, rolling

torna *f*, return; restitution; backwater

tornaboda *f*, day after a wedding; rejoicings of this day

tornada *f*, return home; return visit, revisit; *poet* envoy

tornadizo (-za) *a inf* changeable. *n* turncoat

tornamiento *m*, return; change, transformation

tornar *vt* to return, give back; change, transform; *vi* return, go back; continue

tornasol *m*, sunflower; sheen, changing light; *chem* litmus

tornasolado *a* shot (of silk, etc.)

tornasolar *vt* to look iridescent; change the color of, cause to appear variegated

tornátil *a* turned (in a lathe); inconstant, changeable; *poet* spinning, revolving

tornatrás *mf* half-caste

tornaviaje *m*, return journey

tornavoz *m*, soundboard, sounding board

torneador *m*, turner; jouster, fighter in a tournament

tornear *vt sport* to put a spin on (balls); turn in a lathe; *vi* turn around, spin; fight in a tournament; turn over in the mind

torneo *m*, tournament

tornería *f*, turnery

tornero *m*, turner; lathe maker; convent messenger

tornillero *m*, (*inf mil*) deserter

tornillo *m*, screw; (*inf mil*) desertion

torniquete *m*, turnstile; tourniquet. **dar t. (a),** to pervert, misinterpret (meanings)

torniscón *m*, *inf* slap, buffet, blow; pinch

torno *m*, lathe; turntable (of a convent, etc.); turn, rotation; windlass; dumbwaiter; axletree; spinning wheel; bend, loop (in a river). **en t.,** round about, around; in exchange

toro *m*, bull; Taurus; *pl* bullfight. *inf* **t. corrido,** tough nut to crack, wise guy. *inf* **Ciertos son los toros,** So it's true (gen. of bad news)

toronja *f*, grapefruit

toroso *a* strong, vigorous, robust

torpe *a* heavy, slow, encumbered; torpid; clumsy, unskilled; stupid, dull-witted; obscene, indecent; base, infamous; ugly

torpedeamiento *m*, torpedoing, sinking

torpedear *vt* to torpedo

torpedeo *m*, torpedoing

torpedero *m*, torpedo boat

torpedo *m*, *icht* torpedo fish, electric ray; torpedo; sports car. **t. automóvil,** self-propelling torpedo

torpeza *f*, slowness, heaviness; torpidity; stupidity; lack of skill, clumsiness; indecency; ugliness; baseness, infamy

tórpido *a* torpid

torrar *vt* to toast, brown

torre *f*, tower; belfry, steeple; turret; rook (in chess);

naut gun turret; stack, pile (of chairs, etc.); country house with a garden. **t. del tráfico,** traffic light. **t. de viento,** castle in the air, castle in Spain

torrefacción *f,* toasting (of coffee, etc.)

torrencial *a* torrential

torrente *m,* torrent; *fig* spate, rush; crowd

torreón *m,* large fortified tower

torrero *m,* lighthouse keeper; gardener

torreznero (-ra) *n inf* lazybones, idler

torrezno *m,* rasher of bacon

tórrido *a* torrid

torsión *f,* twisting, torsion

torta *f,* cake; pastry, tart; *inf* slap. **t. de reyes,** traditional Twelfth Night cake

tortada *f,* meat pie, game pie

tortedad *f,* twistedness, crookedness

tortera *f,* cake pan; baking dish; whorl (of a spindle)

tortícolis *m,* crick (in the neck)

tortilla *f,* omelet. **t. a la española,** potato omelet. **hacer t.,** to smash to atoms. **Se volvió la t.,** *inf* The tables are turned

tórtola *f,* turtledove

tórtolo *m,* male turtledove; *inf* devoted lover

tortuga *f,* turtle; tortoise. **a paso de t.,** at a snail's pace

tortuosidad *f,* tortuousness; winding; indirectness; deceitfulness

tortuoso *a* tortuous; winding; disingenuous, deceitful

tortura *f,* twistedness; torture, torment; anguish, grief. **una t. china,** excruciating torture

torturador *a* torturing, tormenting

torturar *vt* to torture

torva *f,* squall of rain or snow

torzal *m,* sewing silk; twist, plait

tos *f,* cough. **t. ferina,** whooping cough

Toscana Tuscany

tosco *a* rough, unpolished; coarse; boorish, uncouth

toser *vi* to cough

tósigo *m,* poison, venom; anguish; affliction

tosigoso *a* poisoned, venomous

tosquedad *f,* roughness, lack of polish; coarseness; boorishness, uncouthness

tostada *f, cul* toast

tostadera *f,* toasting fork

tostado *a* golden brown, tanned. *m,* roasting (of coffee, etc.)

tostador (-ra) *n* toaster (of peanuts, etc.). *m,* toaster (utensil); coffee or peanut roaster

tostadura *f,* toasting; roasting (of coffee, etc.)

tostón *m,* buttered toast; anything overtoasted; roast pig; *inf* nuisance, bore

total *a* total, entire, whole; general. *m,* total. *adv* in short; so, therefore

totalidad *f,* whole; aggregate, entirety

totalitario *a* totalitarian

tótem *m,* totem

totemismo *m,* totemism

toxicidad *f,* toxicity

tóxico *a* toxic. *m,* toxic substance

toxicología *f,* toxicology

toxicológico *a* toxicological

toxicólogo *m,* toxicologist

toxina *f,* toxin

tozo *a* dwarfish, small

tozudez *f,* obstinacy

tozudo *a* obstinate, obdurate

tozuelo *m,* scruff, fat nape (of animals)

traba *f,* setting (of a saw's teeth); tether (for horses); difficulty, obstacle; fastening; bond, tie; shackle; *law* distraint

trabacuenta *f,* mistake in accounts; argument, difference of opinion

trabajado *a* and *past part* wrought; fashioned; labored, exhausted, weary

trabajador (-ra) *a* working; conscientious. *n* worker

trabajar *vi* to work; function; stand the strain, resist (of machines, etc.); exert oneself, strive; toil, labor; oper-

ate, work; produce, yield (the earth fruits, etc.); *vt* work; till, cultivate; exercise (a horse); worry, annoy, weary; operate, drive; *vr* make every effort, work hard

trabajo *m,* work; toil, labor; operation, working; difficulty, obstacle; literary work; hardship, trouble; process; *pl* poverty; hardship. **t. a destajo,** piecework. **t. al ralenti,** go-slow tactics. **trabajos forzados** (*or* **forzosos**), *law* hard labor. **pasar trabajos,** to undergo hardships

trabajosamente *adv* painstakingly

trabajoso *a* difficult, hard; ailing, delicate; needy; afflicted

trabalenguas *m, inf* tongue twister, jawbreaker

trabamiento *m,* joining, fastening; uniting; initiation, commencement; shackling; hobbling (of horses)

trabar *vt* to join, unite, fasten; grasp, seize; set the teeth (of a saw); thicken; begin, initiate; hobble (of horses); reconcile, bring together, harmonize; shackle; *law* distrain; *vr* speak with an impediment; stutter, hesitate. **t. amistad,** to make friends. **t. conversación,** to get into conversation. **Se me trabó la lengua,** I began to stutter

trabazón *f,* join, union, fastening; connection; thickness, consistency

trabilla *f,* vest strap; dropped stitch (in knitting)

trabuca *f,* squib, Chinese firecracker, riprap

trabucar *vt* to turn upside down, upset; confuse, bewilder; mix up, confuse (news, etc.); pronounce or write incorrectly

trabucazo *m,* shot or report of a blunderbuss; *inf* calamity, unexpected misfortune

trabuco *m, mil* catapult; blunderbuss

trabuquete *m,* catapult

tracamundana *f, inf* barter, exchange of trash; hubbub, uproar

tracción *f,* pulling; traction

Tracia Thrace

tracoma *f,* trachoma

tracto *m,* tract, area, expanse; lapse of time

tractor *m,* tractor. **t. de orugas,** caterpillar tractor

tractorista *mf* driver of a tractor, tractor driver

tradición *f,* tradition

tradicional *a* traditional

tradicionalismo *m,* traditionalism

tradicionalista *a* traditionalistic. *mf* traditionalist

traducción *f,* translation; interpretation, explanation

traducible *a* translatable

traducir *vt irr* to translate; interpret, explain; express. See **conducir**

traductor (-ra) *n* translator; interpreter

traedizo *a* portable, movable

traer *vt irr* to bring; attract; cause, occasion; wear, have on; quote, cite (as proof); compel, force; persuade; conduct, lead (persons); be engaged in; *vr* dress (well *or* badly). **t. consigo,** to bring with it; have or carry or bring with one. **t. entre manos,** to have on hand. *Pres. Ind.* **traigo, traes,** etc. *Pres. Part.* **trayendo.** *Preterite* **traje, trajiste,** etc. *Pres. Subjunc.* **traiga,** etc. *Imperf. Subjunc.* **trajese,** etc.

trafagador *m,* dealer, trafficker, merchant

tráfago *m,* traffic, trade; toil, drudgery

trafalmejas *a inf* rowdy, crazy, *mf inf* rowdy

traficante *mf* dealer, merchant, trader

traficar *vi* to trade; travel

tráfico *m,* traffic; trade, commerce

tragaderas *f pl,* throat, gullet. *inf* **tener buenas t.,** to be very credulous; be tolerant (of evil)

tragadero *m,* throat, gullet; sink, drain; hole, plug

tragador (-ra) *n* glutton, guzzler

tragahombres *mf inf* braggart, bully

trágala *m,* (**trágala tú, servilón**), title of Spanish Liberal song aimed at Absolutists; *inf* take that!

tragaleguas *mf inf* fast walker

tragaluz *m,* skylight; fan light

tragantón (-ona) *a inf* guzzling, greedy. *n* glutton

tragantona *f, inf* spread, large meal; swallowing with difficulty; *fig* hard pill to swallow

tragaperras *m, inf* vending machine, catchpenny

tragar *vt* to swallow; eat ravenously, devour; engulf, swallow up; believe, take in; tolerate, put up with; dissemble; consume, absorb

tragedia *f,* tragedy

trágico (-ca) *a* tragic. *n* tragedian; writer of tragedies

tragicomedia *f,* tragicomedy

tragicómico *a* tragicomic

trago *m,* swallow, gulp, draft; *fig inf* bitter pill. **a tragos,** *inf* little by little, slowly

tragón (-ona) *a inf* greedy, gluttonous. *n* glutton

tragonear *vt inf* to devour, eat avidly

traición *f,* treason, treachery. **a t.,** treacherously

traicionar *vt* to betray

traicionero (-ra) *a* treacherous. *n* traitor

traída *f,* conduction. **t. de aguas,** water supply

traidor (-ra) *a* treacherous. *n* traitor

traílla *f,* lead, leash (for animals)

traje *m,* dress, apparel; outfit, costume; suit. **t. de americana,** lounge suit. **t. de ceremonia** *or* **t. de etiqueta,** full-dress uniform; evening dress (men). **t. de luces,** bullfighter's gala outfit. **t. de montar,** riding habit. **t. de noche,** evening dress (women). **t. paisano,** civilian dress; lounge suit

trajín *m,* carriage, transport; busyness, moving around; bustle; clatter

trajinar *vt* to carry, transport; *vi* be busy, go about one's business

tralla *f,* rope, cord; lash (of a whip); whip

trama *f,* woof, texture (of cloth); twisted silk; intrigue, scheme; *lit* plot; olive flower

tramar *vt* to weave; prepare, hatch (plots); *fig* prepare the way for; *vi* flower (of trees, especially olive)

tramitación *f,* transaction, conduct; procedure, method

tramitar *vt* to transact, conduct, settle

trámite *m,* transit; negotiation, phase of a business deal; requirement, condition

tramo *m,* plot of ground; flight of stairs, staircase; stretch, expanse, reach, tract

tramontana *f,* north wind; arrogance, haughtiness

tramontano *a* ultramontane, from beyond the mountains

tramontar *vi* to cross the mountains; sink behind the mountains (of the sun); *vr* run away, escape

tramoya *f, theat* stage machinery; trick, deception, hoax

tramoyista *mf* stage carpenter; stagehand; scene-shifter; trickster, impostor, swindler

trampa *f,* trap, snare; trapdoor; flap of a shop counter; trouser fly; trick, swindle; overdue debt. *fig inf* **caer en la t.,** to fall into the trap. *inf* **coger en la t.,** to catch in a trap; catch in the act

trampal *m,* bog, marsh

trampantojo *m, inf* optical illusion, swindle

trampeador *a inf* swindling. *n* trickster, swindler

trampear *vi inf* to obtain money on false pretenses; struggle on (against illness, etc.); keep oneself alive, make shift; *vt* defraud, swindle

trampolín *m,* springboard; diving board; *fig* jumping-off place

tramposo (-sa) *n* debtor; cardsharper; swindler

tranca *f,* thick stick, cudgel; bar (of a window, etc.)

trancada *f,* stride

trancar *vt* to bar the door; *vi inf* oppose, resist

trancazo *m,* blow with a stick; influenza, flu

trance *m,* crisis, difficult juncture; danger, peril. **t. de armas,** armed combat. **a todo t.,** at all costs, without hesitation

tranco *m,* stride; threshold. *inf* **en dos trancos,** in a trice

tranquera *f,* stockade, palisade

tranquilar *vt com* to check off

tranquilidad *f,* tranquility, peace, quietness; composure, serenity

tranquilizador *a* tranquilizing, soothing

tranquilizar *vt* to calm, quiet; soothe

tranquilo *a* tranquil, quiet, peaceful; serene, composed

transacción *f,* compromise, arrangement; transaction, negotiation, deal

transalpino *a* transalpine

transandino *a* transandean

transatlántico *a* transatlantic. *m,* (transatlantic) liner

transbordar *vt* to transship; transfer, remove goods from one vehicle to another

transbordo *m,* transshipment, transshipping; transfer, removal

transcendencia *f* See **trascendencia**

transcendental *a.* See **trascendental**

transcribir *vt* to transcribe; copy. *Past Part.* **transcrito**

transcripción *f,* transcription; copy, transcript

transcurrir *vi* to elapse, pass (time)

transcurso *m,* passage, lapse, course (of time)

transepto *m,* transept

transeúnte *a* transient, temporary. *mf* passerby; visitor, sojourner

transferencia *f,* transfer (from one place to another); *law* conveyance, transference. **t. bancaria,** bank draft

transferidor (-ra) *a* transferring. *n* transferrer; *law* transferor

transferir *vt irr* to transfer, move from one place to another; *law* convey (property, etc.); postpone. See **sentir**

transfiguración *f,* transfiguration

transfigurar *vt* to transfigure

transfijo *a* transfixed

transfixión *f,* transfixion

transformable *a* transformable

transformación *f,* transformation

transformador *a* transformative. *m, elec* transformer

transformar *vt* to transform; reform (persons); *vr* be transformed; reform, mend one's ways

transfregar *vt irr* to rub, scrub. See **cegar**

transfretar *vt naut* to cross the sea; *vi* spread

tránsfuga *mf* **tránsfugo** *m,* fugitive; political turncoat

transfundir *vt* to transfuse, pour from one vessel to another; imbue, transmit

transfusor *a* transfusive

transgredir *vt* to transgress, infringe

transgresión *f,* infringement, violation, transgression

transgresor (-ra) *a* infringing. *n* transgressor, violator

transiberiano *a* trans-Siberian

transición *f,* transition, change

transido *a* exhausted, worn-out, spent; niggardly, mean

transigencia *f,* tolerance, forbearance, indulgence

transigente *a* tolerant, forbearing

transigir *vi* to be tolerant; be broad-minded. *vt* put up with, tolerate

transitable *a* passable, traversable

transitar *vi* to cross, pass through; travel

transitivo *a* transitive

tránsito *m,* passage, crossing; transit; stopping place; transition, change; gallery of a cloister; *ecc* holy death. **de t.,** temporarily; in transit (of goods). **hacer tránsitos,** to break one's journey, stop

transitorio *a* transitory, fugitive, fleeting

translimitación *f,* trespass; bad behavior; armed intervention in a neighboring state

translimitar *vt* to overstep the boundaries (of a state, etc.); overstep the limits (of decency, etc.)

translucidez *f,* translucence, semitransparency

translúcido *a* translucent, semitransparent

transmarino *a* transmarine

transmigración *f,* transmigration

transmigrar *vi* to migrate; transmigrate (of the soul)

transmisión *f,* transmission. **t. del pensamiento,** thought transference

transmisor *a* transmitting. *m, elec* transmitter, sender

transmitir *vt* to transmit; *mech* drive

transmutable *a* transmutable

transmutación *f*, transmutation, transformation, change

transmutar *vt* to transmute, transform, change

transmutativo *a* transmutative

transoceánico *a* transoceanic

transpacífico *a* transpacific

transparencia *f*, transparency; obviousness

transparentarse *vr* to be transparent; show through; *fig* reveal, give away (secrets)

transparente *a* transparent; translucent; evident, obvious. *m*, windowshade, blind

transpiración *f*, transpiration; perspiration

transpirar *vi* to perspire; transpire

transpirenaico *a* trans-Pyrenean

transponer *vt irr* to move, transfer; transplant; transpose; *vr* hide behind; sink behind the horizon (of the sun, stars); be half-asleep. See **poner**

transportable *a* transportable

transportación *f*. See **transporte**

transportador (-ra) *a* transport. *n* transporter. *m, geom* protractor

transportamiento *m*. See **transporte**

transportar *vt* to transport; *mus* transpose; carry; *vr fig* be carried away by (anger, rapture)

transporte *m*, transport, carriage; cartage; *naut* transport; strong emotion, transport, ecstasy

transposición *f*, transposition

transpositivo *a* transpositive

transubstanciación *f*, transubstantiation

transubstanciar *vt* to transubstantiate, transmute

transversal, transverso *a* transverse

tranvía *m*, street railway; streetcar. **t. de sangre,** horse-drawn streetcar.

tranviario *a* streetcar. *m*, streetcar employee

trapacear *vi* to cheat, swindle

trapacete *m, com* daybook

trapacista *mf* trickster, swindler, knave

trapajoso *a* ragged, shabby, tattered

trápala *f*, noise, confusion, hubbub; noise of horse's hoofs, gallop; *inf* trick, swindle; prattling, babbling. *mf inf* babbler, prattler; trickster

trapalear *vi* to walk noisily, tramp; *inf* chatter, babble

trapatiesta *f, inf* brawl, row, quarrel

trapaza *f*, hoax, swindle

trapecio *m*, trapeze; *geom* trapezium, trapezoid

trapería *f*, old-clothes shop; old clothes, rags, trash, frippery

trapero (-ra) *n* old-clothes seller; rag merchant; rag-picker

trapezoide *m*, trapezium, trapezoid

trapichear *vi inf* to make shift, endeavor

trapiento *a* ragged, shabby

trapillo *m, inf* poverty-stricken lover; nest egg, savings. *inf* **de t.,** in a state of undress, in négligé

trapío *m, inf* spirit of a fighting bull; verve, dash, independent air (of women)

trapisonda *f, inf* uproar, brawl; hubbub, bustle; snare, fix

trapisondear *vi inf* to be given to brawling; scheme, intrigue

trapisondista *mf* brawler; schemer, trickster

trapo *m*, rag; *naut* canvas; bullfighter's cape; *pl* garments, bits and pieces. *inf* **poner como un t. (a),** to dress down, scold. *inf* **soltar el t.,** to burst out crying or laughing

trapujo *m, inf* trick; subterfuge

traque *m*, report, bang (of a rocket, etc.); fuse (of a firework)

tráquea *f*, trachea

traqueotomía *f*, tracheotomy

traquetear *vi* to crack, bang, go off with a report; rattle; jolt (of trains, etc.). *vt* shake, stir; *inf* paw, handle too much

traqueteo *m*, banging (of fireworks); creaking; rattling; jolting (of trains, etc.)

traquido *m*, report (of a gun); crack (of a whip); creak

tras *prep* after; behind; following, in pursuit of; trans- (in compounds). *m, inf* buttock; sound of a blow, bang, bump. **t. t. t.,** knocking (at a door); banging

trasalcoba *f*, dressing room

trasbarrás *m*, bang, bump, noise

trascendencia *f*, transcendence, excellence; consequence, result

trascendental *a* transcendental; important, far-reaching

trascender *vi irr* to spread to, influence; become known, leak out; exhale a scent; *vt* investigate, discover. See **entender**

trascocina *f*, back kitchen

trascolar *vt irr* to filter, strain; cross over, traverse. See **colar**

trascordarse *vr irr* to mix up, make a muddle of, forget. See **acordar**

trasechar *vt* to ambush, waylay

trasegar *vt irr* to upset, turn upside down; transfer, move from one place to another; empty, pour out, upset (liquids). See **cegar**

traseñalar *vt* to re-mark, mark again

trasera *f*, rear, back, rear portion

trasero *a* rear, back. *m*, hindquarters, rump; buttocks, seat; *pl inf* ancestors

trasgo *m*, imp, sprite, puck

trashumante *a* nomadic (of flocks)

trashumar *vi* to go from winter to summer pasture (or vice versa) (of flocks)

trasiego *m*, emptying, pouring out, upsetting (of liquids); decanting (of wines)

traslación *f*, removal, transfer; alteration (of the date for a meeting); metaphor

trasladable *a* removable, movable, transferable

trasladar *vt* to remove, transfer; move from one place to another; alter (the date of a meeting); translate; copy, transcribe; *vr* remove (from a place)

traslado *m*, removal; transfer; transcription

traslapar *vt* to cover, overlap

traslapo *m*, overlap, overlapping

traslucirse *vr irr* to be transparent or translucent; shine through; come out (of secrets); infer, gather. See **lucir**

traslumbramiento *m*, dazzle, glare, brilliance

traslumbrar *vt* to dazzle; *vr* flicker, glimmer; fade quickly, disappear

trasluz *m*, reflected light. **al t.,** against the light

trasmañana *adv* the day after tomorrow

trasmañanar *vt* to put off from day to day

trasminar *vt* to undermine, excavate; *vi* percolate, ooze; penetrate, spread

trasnochada *f*, previous night, last night; night's vigil; sleepless night; *mil* night attack

trasnochado *a* stale, old; weary; hackneyed; drawn, pinched

trasnochador (-ra) *n* one who watches by night or stays up all night; *inf* night owl, reveler

trasnochar *vi* to stay up all night; watch through the night; spend the night; *vt* sleep on, leave for the following day

trasnoche, trasnocho *m, inf* night out; night vigil

trasoir *vt irr* to hear incorrectly, misunderstand. See **oir**

trasojado *a* haggard, tired-eyed

trasoñar *vt irr* to imagine, mistake a dream for reality. See **contar**

traspalar *vt* to fork (grain); shovel; transfer, move

trasparencia *f*. See **transparencia**

traspasar *vt* to transfer, move; cross; *law* convey, make over to; pierce; transgress, flout; exceed one's authority; *fig* go too far; reexamine, go over again; give intolerable pain (of illness, grief). **se traspasa,** to be disposed of (houses, etc.)

traspaso *m*, transport, transfer; *law* conveyance; property transferred; price agreed upon

traspié *m*, slip, catching of the foot, stumble; heel of the foot. **dar traspiés,** *inf* to blunder

trasplantación f, **trasplante** m, transplantation; emigration

trasplantar vt agr to transplant; vr emigrate

trasplante m, planting out

traspuesta f, transposition; back quarters; rear (of a house); back yard

traspunte m, theat prompter

traspuntín m, aut folding seat

trasquilar vt to cut the hair unevenly; shear (sheep); inf cut down, diminish

trasquilón m, cropping (of hair); shearing; inf money stolen by pilfering

trastada f, inf dirty trick, mean act

traste m, fret (of stringed instruments); tasting cup. **dar al t. con,** to spoil, upset, damage. inf **sin trastes,** topsy-turvy, without method

trastear vt to play well (on the mandolin, etc.); inf manage tactfully; vi move around, change (furniture, etc.); discuss excitedly

trastejar vt to repair the roof; renew slates; overhaul

trastienda f, back of a shop; room behind a shop; inf wariness, caution

trasto m, piece of furniture; (household) utensil; lumber, useless furniture; theat wing or set piece; inf useless person, ne'er-do-well; oddment, thing; pl implements, equipment

trastornable a easily overturned or upset; easily agitated

trastornar vt to turn upside down; perturb, disturb; fig overpower (of scents, etc.); disorder, upset; dissuade; make mad; derange the mind

trastorno m, upset; perturbation, anxiety; disorder; mental derangement; confusion (of the senses)

trastrabillar vi to stumble, slip; totter, sway; hesitate; stutter, be tongue-tied

trastrás m, inf last but one (in games)

trastrocamiento m, alteration, change; disarrangement

trastrocar vt irr to alter, change, disarrange; change the order of. See **contar**

trasudar vt to perspire

trasudor m, light perspiration

trasuntar vt to copy, transcribe; summarize

trasunto m, copy, transcript; imitation

trasver vt irr to see through or between, glimpse; see incorrectly. See **ver**

trasverter vt irr to overflow. See **entender**

trata f, slave trade. **t. de blancas,** white slave traffic

tratable a easily accessible, sociable, unpretentious

tratadista mf writer of a treatise; expert, writer on special subjects

tratado m, pact, agreement; treaty; treatise

tratador (-ra) n arbitrator

tratamiento m, treatment; courtesy title; address, style; med treatment; process

tratante m, merchant, dealer

tratar vt to handle, use; conduct, manage; have dealings with, meet, know (e.g. **Yo no le trato,** I don't know him); behave well or badly toward; care for, treat; discuss, deal with (e.g. **¿De qué trata el libro?** What is the book about?); propose, suggest; chem treat; (with de) address as, call; vi have amorous relations; (with de) try to, endeavor to; (with en) trade in; vr look after oneself, treat oneself; conduct oneself

trato m, use, handling; management; conduct, behavior; manner, demeanor; appellation, title; commerce, traffic; dealings, intercourse; treatment; agreement, arrangement. **t. colectivo,** collective bargaining

traumático a traumatic

traumatismo m, traumatism

través m, slant, slope; mishap; (mil arch) traverse. **a t.** or **al t.,** across; through. **de t.,** athwart; through

travesaño m, crossbar; bolster; rung (of a ladder); carp traverse

travesear vi to run about, romp, be mischievous; lead a vicious life; speak wittily; move ceaselessly (of water, etc.)

travesía f, crossing; traverse; crossroad; side road or street; distance, space; sea crossing; crosswise position; stretch of road within a town

travestido a disguised, dressed up

travesura f, romping, frolic; mischief; prank; quick-wittedness

traviesa f, sleeping car, sleeper (railroad); arch rafter; distance between two points

travieso a transverse, crosswise; mischievous, willful; debauched; clever, subtle; ever-moving (of streams, etc.)

trayecto m, run, distance, journey; stretch, expanse, tract; fare stage

trayectoria f, trajectory; journey

traza f, plan, design, draft; scheme, project; idea, proposal; aspect, appearance; means, manner. **Hombre pobre todo es trazas,** A poor man is full of schemes (for bettering himself)

trazado m, designing, drawing; design, draft, model, plan; course, direction (of a canal, etc.)

trazador (-ra) n draftsman, designer; planner, schemer

trazar vt to plan, draft, design; make a drawing of; trace; describe; map out, arrange

trazo m, line, stroke; outline, contour, form, line; art fold in drapery; stroke of the pen

trebejar vi to frolic, skip, play

trebejo m, chessman, chess piece; utensil, article (gen. pl); plaything

trébol m, clover

trece a and m, thirteen, thirteenth. m, thirteenth (day of the month)

trecemesino a thirteen months old

trecho m, distance, space; interval (of time). **a trechos,** at intervals. **de t. en t.,** from time to time

trefe a pliable, flexible; light; spurious (of coins)

tregua f, truce, respite, rest. **dar treguas,** to afford relief, give a respite; give time

treinta a and m, thirty; thirtieth. m, thirtieth (day of the month)

treintañal a thirty years old

treintavo a thirtieth

treintena f, thirtieth (part)

tremebundo a fearsome, dread

tremedal m, bog; quagmire

tremendo a fearful, formidable; awesome; inf tremendous, enormous

trementina f, turpentine

tremesino a three months old

tremolar vt and vi to wave, fly (of banners); fig make a show of

tremolina f, noise of the wind; inf hubbub, confusion

trémulo a trembling, tremulous

tren m, supply, provision; outfit; equipment; pomp, show; railroad train; following, train. **t. ascendente,** up train (from coast to interior). inf **t. botijo,** excursion train. **t. con coches corridos,** corridor train. **t. correo,** mail train. **t. descendente,** down train (from interior to coast). **t. mixto,** train carrying passengers and freight. **t. ómnibus,** accommodation train, slow, stopping train. **t. rápido,** express

trencilla f, braid, trimming

trencillar vt to trim with braid, braid

treno m, threnody

Trento Trento

trenza f, plait, braid; plait of hair; bread twist. **en t.,** in plaits, plaited (of hair)

trenzadera f, linen tape

trenzar vt to plait, braid; vi curvet, prance

trepa f, perforation, boring, piercing; climbing; creeping; inf half-somersault; grain, surface (of wood); craftiness, slyness; deception, fraud; beating, drubbing

trepador a climbing; crawling; bot creeping, climbing. m, climbing place

trepanación f, trepanning

trepanar *vt* to trepan

trepante *a* creeping; *bot* twining, climbing

trepar *vi* to climb, ascend; *bot* climb or creep; bore, perforate

trepatrepa *m*, jungle gym, monkey bars

trepidación *f*, trepidation, dread; vibration; jarring; shaking

trepidar *vi* to shiver, shudder; vibrate; shake; jar

trépido *a* shuddering, shivering; vibrating

tres *a* three; third. *m*, figure three; third (day of the month); three (of playing cards); trio. *inf* **como t. y dos son cinco**, as sure as two and two make four

trescientos *a* and *m*, three hundred; three-hundredth

tresillo *m*, omber (card game); *mus* triplet

tresnal *m*, *agr* stook, cock, sheaf

treta *f*, scheme; trick, hoax; feint (in fencing)

trezavo *a* thirteenth

tría *f*, selection, choice; worn place (in cloth)

triangulación *f*, triangulation

triángulo *a* triangular. *m*, (*geom mus*) triangle. **t. acutángulo**, acute triangle. **t. obtusángulo**, obtuse triangle. **t. rectángulo**, right-angled triangle

triar *vt* to select, pick out; *vi* fly in and out of the hive (of bees); *vr* grow threadbare, become worn

tribu *f*, tribe; species, family

tribulación *f*, tribulation, suffering

tribuna *f*, tribune; platform, rostrum, pulpit; spectators' gallery; stand. **t. de la prensa**, press gallery. **t. del jurado**, jury box. **t. del órgano**, organ loft

tribunado *m*, tribunate

tribunal *m*, law court; *law* bench; judgment seat; tribunal; board of examiners. **t. de menores**, children's court, juvenile court. *naut* **t. de presas**, prize court. **t. de primera instancia**, *law* petty sessions. **t. militar**, court-martial

tribuno *m*, tribune; political speaker

tributar *vt* to pay taxes; offer, render (thanks, homage, etc.)

tributario (-ia) *a* tributary; tax-paying, contributive. *n* taxpayer. *m*, tributary (of a river)

tributo *m*, contribution; tax; tribute, homage; census

tricenal *a* of thirty years' duration; occurring every thirty years

tricentésimo *a* three-hundredth

triciclo *m*, tricycle

tricolor *a* three-colored

tricorne *a* *poet* three-cornered, three-horned

tricornio *a* three-cornered. *m*, three-cornered hat

tricotomía *f*, trichotomy, division into three

tricromía *f*, three-color process

tridente *a* tridentate, three-pronged. *m*, trident

tridentino *a* Tridentine

trienal *a* triennial

trienio *m*, space of three years

trifásico *a* three-phase

trifolio *m*, trefoil

trigal *m*, wheat field

trigésimo *a* thirtieth

trigo *m*, wheat plant; ear of wheat; wheat field (gen. *pl*); wealth, money. **t. sarraceno**, buckwheat. **t. tremés** *or* **t. trechel** *or* **t. tremesino** *or* **t. de marzo**, summer wheat

trigonometría *f*, trigonometry

trigueño *a* brunette, dark

triguero *a* wheat; wheat-growing. *m*, grain sieve; grain merchant

trilátero *a* three-sided, trilateral

trilingüe *a* trilingual

trilla *f*, red mullet; *agr* harrow; threshing; threshing season

trillado *a* frequented, trodden, worn (of paths); hackneyed

trilladora *f*, threshing machine

trillar *vt* to thresh; *inf* frequent; ill-treat

trillo *m*, threshing machine; harrow

trillón *m*, trillion

trilogía *f*, trilogy

trimestral *a* quarterly; terminal (in schools, etc.)

trimestre *a* quarterly; terminal. *m*, quarter, three months; term (in schools, etc.); quarterly payment; quarterly rent

trinado *m*, *mus* trill; twittering, shrilling (of birds)

trinar *vi* *mus* to trill; twitter, shrill; *inf* get in a temper, be furious

trincapiñones *m*, *inf* scatterbrained youth

trincar *vt* to fasten securely; tie tightly; pinion; *naut* lash, make fast; cut up, chop; *inf* tipple; *vi naut* sail close to the wind

trincha *f*, vest strap

trinchante *m*, table carver; carving fork; stonecutter's hammer

trinchar *vt* to carve (at table); *inf* decide, dispose

trinchera *f*, *mil* trench; cutting (for roads, etc.); trench coat

trinchero *m*, platter, trencher; serving table, side table

trineo *m*, sledge, sleigh

trinidad *f*, trinity

trinitaria *f*, *bot* heartsease

trinitario (-ia) *a* and *n* *ecc* Trinitarian

trino *a* triune; ternary. *m*, *mus* trill

trinomio *m*, trinomial

trinquete *m*, *naut* mainmast; mainsail; *sport* rackets; *mech* ratchet

trinquis *m*, *inf* draft, drink

trío *m*, trio

tripa *f*, entrail, gut; *inf* belly; inside (of some fruits). **hacer de tripas corazón**, *inf* to take heart, buck up. **revolver las tripas (a)**, *fig inf* to make one sick

tripartición *f*, tripartition

tripartir *vt* to divide into three

tripartito *a* tripartite

tripicallos *m pl*, *cul* tripe

triple *a* triple; three-ply (of yarn)

triplicación *f*, trebling

triplicar *vt* to treble

trípode *m*, (sometimes *f*) three-legged stool or table; tripod; trivet

Trípoli Tripoli

tríptico *m*, triptych

triptongo *m*, triphthong

tripulación *f*, crew (ships and aircraft)

tripulante *m*, crew member

tripular *vt* to provide with a crew, man; equip, furnish; serve in, work as the crew of

trique *m*, crack, creak. *inf* **a cada t.**, at every moment

triquiñuela *f*, *inf* evasion, subterfuge

triquitraque *m*, tap, rap; crack; firework

tris *m*, crack, noise of glass, etc., cracking; *inf* instant, trice. **estar en un t. (de)**, to be on the verge (of), within an inch (of)

trisar *vt* to crack, break, splinter (of glass); *vi* chirp, twitter (especially of swallows)

trisca *f*, cracking, crushing, crackling (of nuts, etc.); noise, tumult

triscar *vi* to make a noise with the feet; gambol, frolic; creak, crack; *vt* blend, mingle; set the teeth of a saw

trisecar *vt* to trisect

trisección *f*, trisection

trisemanal *a* three times weekly; every three weeks

trisílabo *a* trisyllabic

trismo *m*, lockjaw, trismus

triste *a* unhappy, sorrowful; melancholy, gloomy; sad; piteous, unfortunate; useless, worthless

tristeza, tristura *f*, unhappiness; melancholy, gloom; sadness; piteousness

tritón *m*, merman

triturar *vt* to crumble, crush; chew; masticate; ill-treat, bruise; refute, contradict

triunfada *f*, trumping (at cards)

triunfador (-ra) *a* triumphant. *n* victor

triunfal *a* triumphal

triunfante *a* triumphant

triunfar *vi* to triumph; be victorious, win; trump (at cards); spend ostentatiously

triunfo *m*, triumph; victory; trump card; success; booty, spoils of war; conquest

triunvirato *m*, triumvirate

trivial *a* well-known, hackneyed; frequented, trodden; commonplace, mediocre; trivial, unimportant

trivialidad *f*, banality, triteness; mediocrity; triviality

trivio *m*, road junction

triza *f*, fragment, bit; *naut* rope. **hacer trizas**, to smash to bits

trizar *vt* to smash up, destroy

trocable *a* exchangeable

trocada, a la *adv* contrariwise; in exchange

trocador (-ra) *n* exchanger

trocar *vt irr* to exchange; vomit; distort, misconstrue, mistake; *vr* change, alter one's behavior; change places with another; be transferred. See **contar**

trocha *f*, short cut; trail, path, track

trochemoche, a *adv inf* without rhyme or reason, pell-mell

trocear *vt* to divide into pieces

trofeo *m*, trophy; victory; military booty

troglodita *a* and *mf* troglodyte. *m*, *fig* savage, barbarian. *mf* glutton

troglodítico *a* troglodytic

troj *f*, granary

trojero *m*, granary keeper

trola *f*, *inf* lie, nonsense, hoax

trole *m*, trolley

trolebús *m*, trolley car

trolero *a inf* deceiving, lying

tromba *f*, waterspout

trombón *m*, trombone; trombone player. **¡Trombones y platillos!** Great Scot!

trombosis *f*, thrombosis

trompa *f*, elephant's trunk; *mus* horn; proboscis (of insects); waterspout; humming top. **t. de Falopio**, fallopian tube

trompada *f*, *inf* bang, bump; blow, buffet, slap; collision

trompazo *m*, heavy blow, knock, bang

trompear *vi* to play with a top; *vt* knock about

trompero *m*, top maker. *a* deceiving, swindling

trompeta *f*, trumpet; bugle. *m*, trumpeter; bugler; *inf* ninny. **t. de amor**, sunflower

trompetada *f*, *inf* stupid remark, piece of nonsense

trompetazo *m*, bray of a trumpet; bugle blast; *inf* stupid remark

trompetear *vi inf* to play the trumpet or bugle

trompeteo *m*, trumpeting, trumpet call; sound of the bugle

trompetería *f*, collection of trumpets; metal organ pipes

trompetero *m*, trumpet or bugle maker or player

trompetilla *f*, *dim* little trumpet; ear trumpet

trompicar *vt* to make stumble, trip. *vi* stumble, trip up

trompicón *m*, stumble

trompo *m*, humming or spinning top; *inf* dolt, idiot

tronada *f*, thunderstorm

tronado *a* worn-out; threadbare, old; poor, poverty-stricken; down at the heels

tronar *v impers irr* to thunder; *vi* growl, roar (of guns); *inf* go bankrupt, be ruined; *inf* protest against, attack; (*with con*) quarrel with. *Pres. Ind.* **trueno, truenas, truena, truenan.** *Pres. Subjunc.* **truene, truenes, truene, truenen**

troncal *a* trunk; main, principal

tronchar *vt* to break off, lop off (branches)

troncho *m*, *bot* stem, stalk, branch

tronco *m*, *anat bot* trunk; main body or line (of communications); trunk line; common origin, stock; *inf* blockhead, dolt; callous person. *fig* **estar hecho un t.**, to lie like a log; sleep like a log

tronera *f*, *naut* porthole; embrasure; slit window; pocket of a billiards table. *mf inf* madcap, harum-scarum

tronido *m*, roll of thunder

trono *m*, throne; *ecc* tabernacle; shrine; kingly might; *pl* thrones, hierarchy of angels

tronzador *m*, two-handled saw

tronzar *vt* to smash, break into bits; *sew* pleat; exhaust, overtire

tropa *f*, crowd (of people); troops, military; *mil* call to arms; *pl* army. **t. de línea**, regiment of the line. **tropas de asalto**, storm troopers. **tropas de refresco**, fresh troops. **en t.**, in a crowd; in groups

tropel *m*, rush, surge (of crowds, etc.); bustle, confusion; crowd, multitude; heap, jumble (of things). **en t.**, in a rush; in a crowd

tropelía *f*, rush, dash; violence; outrage

tropezar *vi irr* to stumble, slip; (*with con*) meet unexpectedly or accidentally come up against, be faced with (difficulties); quarrel with or oppose; fall into (bad habits). See **empezar**

tropezón *m*, stumbling, slipping; stumbling block, obstacle. **a tropezones**, *inf* stumblingly; by fits and starts

tropical *a* tropical

trópicos *m pl*, tropics

tropiezo *m*, stumble; stumbling block, obstacle; hitch; impediment; slip, peccadillo, fault; difficulty, embarrassment; fight, skirmish; quarrel

tropismo *m*, tropism

tropo *m*, trope, figure of speech

troquel *m*, die, mold

trotaconventos *f*, *inf* go-between, procuress

trotamundos *m*, *inf* globetrotter

trotar *vi* to trot; *inf* hurry, get a move on

trote *m*, trot; toil, drudgery. **t. corto**, jog-trot. **al t.**, with all speed

trotón (-ona) *a* trotting. *m*, horse. *f*, chaperone

trova *f*, verse; song, lay, ballad; love song

trovador (-ra) *m*, troubadour, minstrel. *n* poet

trovadoresco *a* pertaining to minstrels, troubadour

trovar *vi* to compose verses; write ballads; misconstrue, misinterpret

Troya Troy

troyano (-na) *a* and *n* Trojan

trozo *m*, part, fragment; piece, portion; *lit* selection. **t. de abordaje**, *nav* landing party

trucha *f*, trout. **t. asalmonada**, salmon trout

truchuela *f*, small trout; salt cod

truco *m*, trick, deception

truculencia *f*, harshness, cruelty, truculence

truculento *a* fierce, harsh, truculent

trueco *m*, exchange. **a t. de**, in exchange for; on condition that

trueno *m*, thunder; report, noise (of firearms); *inf* rake, scapegrace

trueque *m*, exchange. **a.** (*or* **en**) **t.**, in exchange

trufa *f*, *bot* truffle; nonsense, idle talk

trufar *vt cul* to stuff with truffles; *vi inf* lie, tell fibs

truhán (-ana) *a* knavish, roguish, comic. *n* knave, rogue; clown, buffoon

truhanear *vi* to be a trickster, behave like a knave; play the clown

truhanería *f*, knavery, act of a rogue; clowning, buffoonery; collection of rogues

truhanesco *a* knavish, scoundrelly; clownish

trujal *m*, oil or grape press; oil mill; vat for soap making

trujar *vt* to partition off

trulla *f*, uproar, tumult; crowd, throng

truncar *vt* to shorten, truncate; decapitate, mutilate; omit, cut out (words, etc.); curtail, abridge; mutilate, deform (texts, etc.)

truque *m*, card game; kind of hopscotch

trust *m*, *com* trust

tú *pers pron 2nd sing mf* thou, you. **tratar de t.** (**a**), to address familiarly; be on intimate terms with

tu *poss pron mf* thy, your. Used only before nouns

tuberculina *f*, tuberculin

tubérculo *m*, (*zool med*) tubercle; *bot* tubercle, tuber

tuberculoso *a* tubercular, tuberculous

tubería *f,* piping, tubing; pipe system; pipe factory
tuberosa *f,* tuberose
tuberoso *a* tuberous
tubo *m,* pipe, tube; lamp chimney; flue; *anat* duct, canal. **t. acústico,** speaking tube. **t. de ensayo,** test tube. **t. de escape,** exhaust pipe. **t. lanzatorpedos,** torpedo tube. **t. termiónico,** *rad* thermionic valve
tubular *a* tubular
tucán *m,* toucan
tudesco *a* German
tueco *m,* stump (of a tree); wormhole (in wood)
tuerca *f,* nut (of a screw)
tuerto *a* one-eyed. *m, law* tort; *pl* afterpains. **a t.,** unjustly
tueste *m,* toasting
tuétano *m,* marrow. *inf* **hasta los tuétanos,** to the depths of one's being
tufillas *mf inf* easily irritated person
tufo *m,* strong smell, poisonous vapor; *inf* stink; side, airs, conceit (often *pl*); lock of hair over the ears
tugurio *m,* shepherd's hut; miserable little room; *inf* haunt, low dive
tul *m,* tulle
tulipa *f,* small tulip; lampshade
tulipán *m,* tulip
tullido *a* partially paralyzed; maimed, crippled
tullir *vt irr* to maim, cripple; paralyze; *vr* become paralyzed; be crippled. See **mullir**
tumba *f,* tomb; tumble, overbalancing; somersault; Catherine wheel
tumbar *vt* to knock down; kill, drop; *inf* overpower, overcome (of odors, wine). *vi* fall down; *naut* run aground; *vr inf* lie down, stretch oneself out
tumbo *m,* tumble, overbalancing; undulation (of ground); rise and fall of sea waves; imminent danger; book containing deeds and privileges of monasteries and churches
tumbón *a inf* crafty, sly; idle, lazy. *m,* trunk with an arched lid
tumefacción *f,* swelling
tumefacto, túmido *a* swollen
tumor *m,* tumor
túmulo *m,* tumulus; catafalque; mound of earth
tumulto *m,* riot, uprising; tumult, commotion, disturbance
tumultuario, tumultuoso *a* noisy, tumultuous, confused
tuna *f,* prickly pear tree or fruit; vagrant life; strolling student musicians (playing to raise money for charity)
tunante *a* rascally, roguish. *mf* rascal, scoundrel
tunantuelo (-la) *n inf* imp, little rascal
tunda *f,* shearing of cloth; *inf* sound beating, hiding
tundear *vt* to beat, drub, buffet
tundidora *f,* woman who shears cloth; cloth-shearing machine; lawn mower
tundir *vt* to shear (cloth); mow (grass); *inf* beat, wallop
tunecino (-na) *a* and *n* Tunisian
túnel *m,* tunnel

Túnez Tunis, Tunisia
tungsteno *m,* tungsten
túnica *f,* tunic, chiton; tunicle; robe
Tunicia Tunisia
tuno (-na) *a* knavish, rascally. *n* rascal, scoundrel
tupé *m,* forelock (of a horse); toupee; *inf* cheek, nerve
tupido *a* thick, dense; obtuse, dull, stupid
tupir *vt* to thicken, make dense; press tightly; *vr* stuff oneself with food or drink
turba *f,* crowd, multitude; peat
turbación *f,* disturbance; upset; perturbation; bewilderment, confusion; embarrassment
turbador (-ra) *a* disturbing, upsetting. *n* disturber, upsetter
turbamulta *f, inf* mob, rabble
turbante *a* upsetting, perturbing. *m,* turban
turbar *vt* to disturb, upset; make turbid, muddy; bewilder, confuse; embarrass
turbera *f,* peat bog
turbiedad *f,* muddiness (of liquids); obscurity
turbina *f,* turbine
turbio *a* turbid, muddy; troublous; turbulent, disturbed; obscure, confused (style); indistinct, blurred, *m pl,* lees, sediment (of oil)
turbión *m,* brief storm, squall; *fig* shower, rush
turbulencia *f,* turbidity, muddiness; turbulence, commotion; disturbance, confusion
turbulento *a* muddy, turbid; turbulent, disturbed; confused
turca *f, inf* drinking bout
turco (-ca) *a* Turkish. *n* Turk. *m,* Turkish (language)
turgencia *f,* swelling, turgidity
turgente *a med* turgescent; *poet* turgid, prominent, swollen
Turingia Thuringia
turismo *m,* touring, tourist industry. **coche de t.,** touring car
turista *mf* tourist
turno *m,* turn. **por t.,** in turn
turquesa *f,* turquoise
turquesco *a* Turkish
Turquía Turkey
turrón *m,* kind of nougat; almond paste; *inf* soft job, sinecure; civil service job
turulato *a inf* dumbfounded, speechless, inarticulate
¡tus! *interj* word for calling dogs. **sin decir t. ni mus,** *inf* without saying anything
tutear *vt* to address as tú (instead of the formal usted); treat familiarly
tutela *f,* guardianship; tutelage; protection, defense
tuteo *m,* the use in speaking to a person of the familiar tú instead of the formal usted
tutor (-ra) *n* guardian. *m,* stake (for plants); protector, defender
tutoría *f.* See **tutela**
tuyo, tuya, tuyos, tuyas *poss pron 2nd sing* and *pl mf* thine, yours. Used sometimes with def. art. (e.g. **Este sombrero es el tuyo,** This hat is yours)

U

u *f,* letter U. *conjunc* Used instead of **o** or before words beginning with **o** or **ho** (e.g. **fragante u oloroso**)
ubérrimo *a sup* most fruitful; very abundant
ubicación *f,* situation, position, location
ubicar *vt* to place, situate; *vi* and *vr* be situated
ubicuidad *f,* ubiquity
ubicuo *a* omnipresent; ubiquitous
ubre *f,* udder
Ucrania Ukraine
ucranio (-ia) *a* and *n* Ukrainian
ucelele *m,* ukulele
¡uf! *interj* ugh!
ufanarse *vr* to pride oneself, put on airs

ufanía *f,* pride, conceit
ufano *a* conceited, vain; satisfied, pleased; expeditious, masterly
ujier *m,* usher
úlcera *f,* ulcer
ulceración *f,* ulceration
ulcerar(se) *vt* and *vr* to ulcerate
ulceroso *a* ulcerous
ulterior *a* farther, ulterior; subsequent
ulteriormente *adv* subsequently, later
ultimación *f,* ending, finishing
ultimar *vt* to end, conclude
ultimátum *m,* ultimatum

último *a* last; farthermost; ultimate; top; final, definitive; most valuable, best; latter; recent. «**Última Hora.**» "Stop Press." **a última hora,** *fig* at the eleventh hour. **en estos últimos años,** in recent years. **a últimos de mes,** towards the end of the month. **el ú. piso,** the top floor. **por ú.,** finally. *inf* **estar en las últimas,** to be at the end, be finishing

ultra, *adv* besides; (with words like *mar*) beyond; (as prefix) excessively

ultrajar *vt* to insult; scorn, despise

ultraje *m,* insult, outrage

ultrajoso *a* offensive, insulting, abusive

ultramar *m,* overseas, abroad

ultramarino *a* oversea; ultramarine. *m,* foreign produce (gen. *pl*)

ultramontano *a* ultramontane

ultrarrojo *a* infrared

ultratumba *adv* beyond the grave

ultravioleta *a* ultraviolet

úlula *f,* screech owl

ululación *f,* screech, howl; hoot of an owl

ulular *vi* to howl, shriek, screech; hoot (of an owl)

ululato *m,* ululation

umbilical *a* umbilical

umbral *m,* threshold; *fig* starting point; *arch* lintel. **atravesar (or pisar) los umbrales,** to cross the threshold

umbría *f,* shady place

umbrío *a* shady, dark

umbroso *a* shady

un *abb* of **uno, a,** one. Used before *m, sing f,* **una,** *indef art.* a, an; a; one

unánime *a* unanimous

unanimidad *f,* unanimity. **por u.,** unanimously

unción *f,* anointing; *ecc* Extreme Unction; unction, fervor

uncir *vt* to yoke

undécimo *a* eleventh

undísono *a poet* sounding, sonorous (waves, etc.)

undoso *a* wavy, rippling

undulación *f,* undulation; *phys* wave

undular *vi* to undulate; wriggle; float, wave (flags, etc.)

undulatorio *a* undulatory

ungimiento *m,* anointment

ungir *vt* to anoint

ungüento *m,* ointment; lotion; *fig* balm, unguent

unicelular *a* unicellular

único *a* unique; sole, solitary, only. **Lo ú. que se puede hacer es . . .,** The only thing one can do is . . .

unicolor *a* of one color

unicornio *m,* unicorn

unidad *f,* unity; unit; (*math mil*) unit. **u. de bagaje,** piece of baggage. (of drama) **u. de lugar,** unity of place. **u. de tiempo,** unity of time

unidamente *adv* jointly; harmoniously

unificación *f,* unification

unificar(se) *vt* and *vr* to unify, unite

uniformación *f,* standardization

uniformar *vt* to make uniform, standardize; put into uniform; *vr* become uniform

uniforme *a* uniform; same, similar. *m,* uniform

uniformidad *f,* uniformity

unigénito *a* only-begotten. *m,* Christ

unilateral *a* one-sided, unilateral

unión *f,* union; correspondence, conformity; agreement; marriage; alliance, federation; composition; mixture; combination; proximity, nearness; (mystic) union

unionista *mf pol* unionist

Unión Soviética Soviet Union

unir *vt* to unite, join; mix, combine; bind, fasten; connect, couple; bring together; marry; *fig* harmonize, conciliate; *vr* join together, unite; be combined; marry; (*with prep* a *or* con) be near to; associate with

unísono *a* unisonant. **al u.,** in unison; unanimously

unitario (-ia) *a* and *n* Unitarian

universal *a* universal; well-informed; widespread

universalidad *f,* universality

universalizar *vt* to make universal, generalize

universidad *f,* university; universality; universe

universitario *a* a university

universo *a* universal. *m,* universe

uno (*f,* **una**) *a* a, one; single, only; same; *pl* some; about, nearly. *m,* one (number). **Tiene unos doce años,** He is about twelve. **unas pocas manzanas,** a few apples. *pron* someone; one thing, same thing; *pl* some people. **No sabe uno qué creer,** One doesn't know what to believe. **Unos dicen que no, otros que sí,** Some (people) say no, others yes. **Juan no tiene libros y le voy a dar uno,** John has no books and I am going to give him one. **Todo es uno,** It's all the same. **u. a u.,** one by one. **u. que otro,** a few. **u. y otro,** both. **unos cuantos,** a few, some. **Es la una,** It is one o'clock

untar *vt* to anoint; grease, oil; *inf* bribe; *vr* smear oneself with grease or similar thing; *fig inf* line one's pockets. **u. el carro,** *fig* to grease the wheels

unto *m,* grease; animal fat; *fig* balm

untuoso *a* fat, greasy

uña *f,* nail (of fingers or toes); hoof, trotter, claw; stinging tail of scorpion; thorn; stump of tree branch; *naut* fluke; *fig inf* light fingers (gen. *pl*). **afilarse las uñas,** to sharpen one's claws, prepare for trouble. **comerse las uñas,** to bite one's nails. **caer en las uñas de,** to fall into the clutches of. **hincar la u. (en),** to stick the claws into; to defraud, overcharge. **ser u. y carne,** to be devoted friends

uñarada *f,* scratch with nails

uñero *m,* ingrowing nail, ingrown nail

¡upa! *interj* Up you get! Up you go! Upsy daisy! (gen. to children)

Urales, los the Urals

uranio *m,* uranium

urbanidad *f,* civility, good manners, urbanity

urbanismo *m,* town planning; housing scheme

urbanización *f,* urbanization

urbanizar *vt* to civilize, polish; urbanize

urbano *a* urban, city; urbane

urbe *f,* city, metropolis

urbícola *mf* city dweller

urdemalas *mf,* schemer, intriguer

urdidera *f,* warping-frame

urdimbre *f,* warp; scheming, plotting

urdir *vt* to warp; weave; scheme, intrigue

uréter *m,* ureter

uretra *f,* urethra

urgencia *f,* urgency; necessity; compulsion

urgente *a* urgent

urgir *vi* to be urgent; be valid, be in force (laws)

úrico *a* uric

urinario *a* urinary. *m,* urinal

urna *f,* urn; ballot box; glass case

urraca *f,* magpie

uruguayo (-ya) *a* and *n* Uruguayan

usado *a* worn out; accustomed, efficient. *com* **al u.,** in the usual form. **ropa usada,** second-hand clothing, worn clothing

usanza *f,* custom, usage

usar *vt* to use; wear, make use of; follow (trade, occupation); *vi* be accustomed

uso *m,* use; custom; fashion; habit; wear and tear. **al u.,** according to custom. **al u. de,** in the manner of

usted *mf* you. *pl* **ustedes.** Often abbreviated to **Vd, V, Vds, VV** or **Ud, Uds**

usual *a* usual; general, customary; sociable

usufructo *m, law* usufruct; life-interest; profit

usura *f,* usury; profiteering. **pagar con u.,** to pay back a thousandfold

usurario *a* usurious

usurear *vi* to lend or borrow with usury; profiteer, make excess profits

usurero (-ra) *n* usurer; profiteer

usurpación *f,* usurpation
usurpador (-ra) *a* usurping. *n* usurper
usurpar *vt* to usurp
utensilio *m,* utensil; tool, implement (gen. *pl*)
uterino *a* uterine
útero *m,* uterus
útil *a* useful; profitable; *law* lawful (of days, etc.). *m,* usefulness, profit; *pl* **útiles,** utensils, tools
utilidad *f,* utility; usefulness; profit
utilitario *a* utilitarian
utilitarismo *m,* utilitarianism
utilizable *a* utilizable
utilización *f,* utilization
utilizar *vt* to utilize
utillaje *m,* machinery
utópico *a* Utopian
uva *f,* grape. **u. espina,** kind of gooseberry. **u. moscatel,** muscatel grape. *inf* **hecho una u.,** dead-drunk
uvero (-ra) *a* pertaining or relating to grapes, grape. *n* grape seller
uxoricidio *m,* uxoricide (act)
uxorio *a* uxorious

V

v *f,* letter V. **v doble** *or* **doble v,** letter W. **V** *or* **Vd, VV,** *abbs* **vuestra(s) merced(es),** *mf sing* and *pl* you
vaca *f,* cow. **v. de San Antón,** *ent* ladybug
vacación *f,* vacation, holiday (gen. *pl*); vacancy; act of vacating (employment). **vacaciones retribuídas,** paid vacation
vacada *f,* herd of cows
vacancia *f,* vacancy
vacante *a* vacant. *f,* vacancy
vacar *vi* to be vacant; take a holiday; retire temporarily; (*with prep a*) dedicate oneself to, engage in
vaciadero *m,* rubbish dump; sewer, drain
vaciado *m,* plaster cast; *arch* excavation
vaciamiento *m,* emptying; molding, casting; depletion
vaciar *vt* to empty; drain, drink; mold, cast; *arch* excavate; hone; copy; *vi* flow (into) (rivers); *vr inf* blurt out
vaciedad *f,* emptiness; foolishness, inanity
vacilación *f,* swaying; tottering; staggering; hesitation, perplexity
vacilante *a* swaying; tottering; staggering; hesitating, vacillating
vacilar *vi* to sway; totter; stagger; flicker; hesitate
vacío *a* empty, void; fruitless, vain; unoccupied, vacant, deserted; imperfect; hollow, empty; conceited, immature. *m,* hollow; *anat* flank; vacancy; shortage; *phys* vacuum. **v. de aire,** airpocket. **de v.,** unloaded (carts, etc.). **en v.,** in vacuo. *inf* **hacer el v. (a),** to send to Coventry
vacuidad *f,* emptiness; vacuity
vacuna *f,* cowpox; vaccine. **v. antivariolosa,** smallpox vaccine
vacunación *f,* vaccination
vacunar *vt* to vaccinate; inoculate
vacuno *a* bovine
vacuo *a* empty; vacant. *m,* void; vacuum
vadeable *a* fordable (rivers, etc.); *fig* surmountable
vadear *vt* to ford, wade; *fig* overcome (obstacles); *fig* sound, find out the nature (of); *vr* behave
vademécum *m,* vade mecum; school satchel
vado *m,* ford; expedient, help
vagabundear *vi* to wander, roam, loiter
vagabundeo *m,* vagabondage
vagabundo (-da) *a* roving, wandering; vagrant. *n* tramp, vagabond
vagamundear *vi.* See **vagabundear**
vagancia *f,* vagrancy
vagar *m,* leisure; interval, pause. *vi* be idle or at leisure; wander, roam
vagido *m,* cry, wail (infants)
vagneriano *a* Wagnerian
vago (-ga) *a* vagrant, idle; vague; *art* indefinite, blurred. *n* idler. *m,* tramp; loafer. **en v.,** unsuccessfully, vainly
vagón *m,* wagon; (railway) coach. **v. comedor,** dining car
vagoneta *f,* open truck (railways, mines, etc.)
vaguear *vi* to roam, wander; loaf
vaguedad *f,* vagueness; vague remark
vaharada *f,* whiff, exhalation
vahído *m,* vertigo
vaho *m,* vapor, fume

vaina *f,* scabbard; *bot* sheath, pod; case (scissors, etc.)
vainilla *f, bot* vanilla; *sew* drawn-thread work
vaivén *m,* swing, sway, seesaw; instability, fluctuation
vajilla *f,* china; dinner service
val *m, abb* **valle**
Valdepeñas *m,* red wine from Valdepeñas
vale *m, com* bond, I.O.U., promissory note; voucher; valediction
valedero *a* valid, binding
valedor (-ra) *n* protector, sponsor
valencia *f,* valency
valenciano (-na) *a* and *n* Valencian
valentía *f,* bravery; heroic deed; boast; (*art lit*) dash, imagination, fire; superhuman effort
valentón *a* boastful, blustering
valer *vt irr* to protect; defend; produce (income, etc.); cost; *vi* be worth; deserve; have power or authority; be of importance or worth; be a protection; be current (money); be valid; *vr* (*with de*) make use of. *m,* value, worth. **v. la pena,** to be worthwhile. **v. tanto como cualquiera,** to be as good as the next guy, be as good as the next fellow. **¡Válgame Dios!** Heavens! Bless me! **Más vale así,** It's better thus. **Vale más ser cola de león que cabeza de ratón.** Better a big frog in a small puddle than a small frog in a big puddle. *Pres. Ind.* **valgo, vales,** etc. *Fut.* **valdré,** etc. *Condit.* **valdría,** etc. *Pres. Subjunc.* **valga,** etc.
valeriana *f,* valerian
valeroso *a* active, energetic; courageous; powerful
valetudinario *a* valetudinarian
valía *f,* value, price; influence, worth; faction, party. **a las valías,** at the highest price
validación *f,* validation; force, soundness
validar *vt* to make strong; validate
validez *f,* validity
valido *a* favorite, esteemed. *m,* court favorite; prime minister
válido *a* firm, sound, valid; strong, robust
valiente *a* strong, robust; courageous; active; excellent; excessive, enormous (gen. *iron*); boastful
valija *f,* valise, suitcase, grip; mail bag; mail
valimiento *m,* value; favor; protection, influence
valioso *a* valuable; powerful; wealthy
valisoletano (-na) *a* and *n* of or from Valladolid
valla *f,* barricade, paling; stockade; *fig* obstacle. **v. publicitaria,** billboard
vallado *m,* stockade; enclosure
valle *m,* valley; vale; river-basin
valón *a* Walloon
valona *f,* Vandyke collar
valor *m,* worth, value; price; courage; validity; power; yield, income; insolence; *pl com* securities
valoración *f,* valuation; appraisement
valorar *vt* to value; appraise
valorización *f,* valuation
valquiria *f,* Valkyrie
vals *m,* waltz
valsar *vi* to waltz
valuación *f.* See **valoración**
valuar *vt* to value; appraise; assess

valva *f, zool* valve
válvula *f, mech* valve. *aut* **v. de cámara (del neumático),** tire-valve. **v. de seguridad,** safety-valve
vampiro *m,* vampire; *fig* bloodsucker
vanagloria *f,* vaingloriousness, conceit
vanagloriarse *vr* to be conceited
vanaglorioso (-sa) *a* conceited. *n* boaster
vanamente *adv* vainly; without foundation; superstitiously; arrogantly
vandálico *a* Vandal
vandalismo *m,* vandalism; destructiveness
vándalo (-la) *a* and *n* Vandal
vanguardia *f,* vanguard; *pl* outerworks. **a v.,** in the forefront
vanidad *f,* vanity; ostentation; empty words; illusion. *inf* **ajar la v. de,** to take (a person) down a peg
vanidoso (-sa) *a* vain; ostentatious. *n* conceited person
vano *a* vain; hollow, empty; useless, ineffectual; unsubstantial, illusory. *m,* span (bridge). **v. único,** single span. **en v.,** uselessly, in vain
vapor *m,* steam, vapor; fainting fit; steamboat; *pl* hysterics. **v. de ruedas, v. de paleta,** paddle steamer. **v. volandero,** tramp steamer. **al v.,** full steam ahead; *inf* with all speed
vaporable *a* vaporizable
vaporación *f,* evaporation
vaporización *f,* vaporization
vaporizador *m,* vaporizer; spray, sprayer
vaporizar *vt* to vaporize; spray
vaporoso *a* vaporous; ethereal; gauzy
vapulación *f,* **vapulamiento** *m,* whipping
vapular *vt* to whip
vapuleo *m,* whipping, spanking
vaquería *f,* herd of cattle; dairy; dairy farm
vaquero (-ra) *n* cowboy; **vaqueros,** *m, pl* jeans
vaquilla *f,* heifer
vara *f,* staff; rod; wand (of authority); vara (nearly one yard); shaft (of cart). **v. de aforar,** water gauge
varada *f, naut* running aground
varadero *m,* shipyard
varar *vi naut* to run aground; *fig* be held up (negotiations, etc.); *vt naut* put in dry dock
varear *vt* to knock down (fruit from tree); beat (with a rod); measure with a rod; sell by the rod; *vr* grow thin
variabilidad *f,* variableness
variable *a* variable; changeable, inconsistent
variación *f,* variation
variado *a* varied; variegated
variante *a* varying. *f,* variant; discrepancy
variar *vt* to vary; change; *vi* change; be different
varice *f,* varix
varicela *f,* chicken pox
varicoso *a* varicose
variedad *f,* variety; change; inconstancy, instability; alteration; variation; *biol* variety
varilla *f, dim* rod; rib (fan, umbrella). **v. de virtudes,** conjurer's wand. *mech* **v. percusora,** tappet rod
vario *a* different, diverse; inconstant, changeable; variegated; *pl* some, a few
variopinto *a* motley
varón *m,* male; man
varonil *a* male; manly
Varsovia Warsaw
varsoviano (-na) *a* and *n* of or from Warsaw
vasallaje *m,* vassalage; dependence; tribute money
vasallo (-lla) *n* vassal. *a* vassal; dependent
vasco (-ca), vascongado (-da) *a* and *n* Basque
vascuence *m,* Basque (language); *inf* gibberish
vaselina *f,* vaseline
vasija *f,* vessel, receptacle, jar
vaso *m,* receptacle; glass, tankard, mug; glassful; (*naut anat bot*) vessel; garden-urn; vase
vástago *m,* stem, shoot; offspring, descendant; piston rod
vastedad *f,* extensiveness, largeness, vastness

vasto *a* vast, extensive
vate *m,* bard; seer
vaticano *a* and *m,* Vatican
vaticinar *vt* to prophesy, foretell
vaticinio *m,* prediction
vatímetro *m,* water meter
vatio *m,* watt. **v. hora,** watt hour
ve *f,* name of the letter V. **v. doble** *or* **doble v.,** name of the letter W
vecinal *a* neighboring
vecindad *f,* neighborhood. **buena v.,** good neighborliness. **hacer mala v.,** to be a nuisance to one's neighbors
vecindario *m,* neighborhood; population of a district
vecino (-na) *a* neighboring; near; similar. *n* neighbor; citizen; inhabitant
vector *m,* carrier (of disease)
veda *f,* close season; prohibition
vedamiento *m,* prohibition
vedar *vt* to forbid; prevent
vedija *f,* tangled lock of hair; piece of matted wool; curl (of smoke)
veedor (-ra) *a* prying. *n* busy-body. *m,* inspector; overseer
vega *f,* fertile lowland plain; meadow
vegada *f.* See **vez**
vegetable *a* and *m,* vegetable
vegetación *f,* vegetation
vegetal *a* vegetal; plant. *m,* vegetable, plant
vegetar *vi* to flourish, grow (plants); *fig* vegetate
vegetarianismo *m,* vegetarianism
vegetariano (-na) *a* and *n* vegetarian
vegetativo *a* vegetative
vehemencia *f,* vehemence
vehemente *a* vehement; vivid
vehículo *m,* vehicle; means, instrument
veinte *a* and *m,* twenty; twentieth
veintena *f,* a score
veinticinco *a* and *m,* twenty-five; twenty-fifth
veinticuatro *a* and *m,* twenty-four; twenty-fourth
veintidós *a* and *m,* twenty-two; twenty-second
veintinueve *a* and *m,* twenty-nine; twenty-ninth
veintiocho *a* and *m,* twenty-eight; twenty-eighth
veintiséis *a* and *m,* twenty-six; twenty-sixth
veintisiete *a* and *m,* twenty-seven; twenty-seventh
veintitrés *a* and *m,* twenty-three; twenty-third
veintiuno *a* and *m,* twenty-one; twenty-first. Abbreviates to **veintiún** before a noun (even if one or more adjectives intervene)
vejación *f,* ill-treatment, persecution
vejamen *m,* irritation, provocation; taunt; lampoon
vejar *vt* to ill-treat, persecute; plague
vejatorio *a* vexing, annoying
vejete *m, inf* silly old man
vejez *f,* oldness; old age; platitude. **vejeces,** *pl* ailments of old age. *inf* **a la v., viruelas,** the older the madder
vejiga *f,* bladder; blister. **v. natatoria,** float (of a fish)
vela *f,* vigil; watch; pilgrimage; sentinel, watchman; candle; *naut* sail; awning; night work, overtime. **v. de cangreja,** boom sail. **v. de mesana,** mizzen sail. **v. de trinquete,** foresail. **v. latina,** lateen sail. **a toda v.,** with all speed. **alzar velas,** to hoist sail. **en v.,** wakeful, without sleep. *inf* **estar entre dos velas,** to be tipsy
velación *f,* vigil; watch; marriage ceremony of veiling (gen. *pl*)
velada *f,* vigil; watch; evening party
velado *a* veiled; dim; (of voice) thick, indistinct
velador (-ra) *a* watchful; vigilant. *m,* candlestick; small round table. *n* watcher, guard
velar *vi* to watch, be wakeful; work overtime or at night; *ecc* watch; *fig* (with *por*) watch over, defend; *vt* veil; conceal; *phot* blur; (with *prep a*) wake (corpse); sit with (patient at night)
veleidad *f,* velleity; fickleness
veleidoso *a* inconstant, changeable

velero (-ra) *m*, sailing ship; sailmaker. *n* candlemaker
veleta *f*, weathercock; float, quill (fishing). *mf* changeable person
vello *m*, down, soft hair
vellocino *m*, wool; fleece
vellón *m*, fleece; copper and silver alloy formerly used in sense of 'sterling'; *ant* copper coin
vellosidad *f*, downiness, hairiness
velloso *a* downy, hairy
velludo *a* hairy, downy. *m*, plush, velvet
velo *m*, veil; curtain; *ecc* humeral veil; excuse, pretext; *zool* velum. **v. del paladar,** soft palate. **correr el v.,** to disclose a secret. **tomar el v.,** to take the veil, become a nun
velocidad *f*, speed; *mech* velocity. *aer* **v. ascensional,** rate of climb. *mech* **v. del choque,** speed of impact. **en gran v.,** by passenger train. **en pequeña v.,** by goods train
velocípedo *m*, velocipede
velódromo *m*, velodrome
velón *m*, oil lamp
veloz *a* swift; quick-thinking or acting
vena *f*, (*bot anat*) vein; streak, veining (in wood or stone); *min* seam; underground spring; inspiration. **estar de v.,** to be in the mood; be inspired
venablo *m*, javelin
venado *m*, venison; deer
venal *a* venous; saleable; venal
venalidad *f*, saleableness; venality
vencedor (-ra) *a* conquering. *n* conqueror
vencer *vt* to conquer; defeat; overcome, rise above; outdo, excel; restrain, control (emotions); convince, persuade; *vi* succeed, triumph; *com* fall due, mature; *com* expire; *vr* control oneself; twist, incline
vencible *a* conquerable; superable
vencimiento *m*, defeat; conquest, victory; bend, twist (of things); *com* expiration; *com* maturity (of a bill)
venda *f*, bandage; fillet. **tener una v. en los ojos,** to be blind (to the truth)
vendaje *m*, bandage
vendar *vt* to bandage; *fig* blind (generally passions)
vendaval *m*, strong wind
vendedor (-ra) *a* selling. *n* seller
vender *vt* to sell; betray; *vr* sell oneself; be sold; risk all (for someone); *fig* give away (secret); (*with por*) sell under false pretences. **v. al contado,** to sell for cash. **v. al por mayor,** to sell wholesale. **v. al por menor,** to sell retail. **venderse caro,** to be unsociable
vendí *m*, *com* certificate of sale
vendible *a* purchasable; saleable
vendimia *f*, vintage; profit, fruits
vendimiador (-ra) *n* vintager
vendimiar *vt* to harvest the grapes; take advantage of; *inf* kill
Venecia Venice
veneciano (-na) *a* and *n* Venetian
veneno *m*, poison; venom; danger (to health or soul); evil passion
venenosidad *f*, poisonousness
venenoso *a* poisonous, venomous
venera *f*, scallop-shell (pilgrim's badge); badge, decoration
veneración *f*, respect, veneration
venerador (-ra) *a* venerating. *n* venerator, respector
venerar *vt* to venerate; worship
venéreo *a* venereal
venero *m*, spring of water; horary line on sundial; origin, genesis; *min* bed
venezolano (-na) *a* and *n* Venezuelan
vengador (-ra) *a* avenging. *n* avenger
venganza *f*, revenge
vengar *vt* to avenge; *vr* avenge oneself
vengativo *a* vindictive
venia *f*, pardon, forgiveness; permission; inclination of head (in greeting); *law* license issued to minors to manage their own estate

venial *a* venial
venialidad *f*, veniality
venida *f*, arrival, coming; return; attack (fencing); precipitancy
venidero *a* future
venideros *m pl*, successors; posterity
venir *vi* to come; arrive; turn up (at cards); fit, suit; consent, agree; *agr* grow; follow, come after, succeed; result, originate; occur (to the mind); feel, experience; (*with prep* a + *infin.*) happen finally, come to pass; (*with en*) decide, resolve; *vr* ferment. **v. a menos,** to deteriorate, decline; come upon evil days. **v. a pelo,** to come opportunely, be just right. **v. a ser,** to become. **venirse abajo,** to fall, collapse. **¿A qué viene este viaje?** What is the purpose of this journey? **el mes que viene,** next month. **El vestido te viene muy ancho,** The dress is too wide for you. **Me vino la idea de marcharme,** It occurred to me to leave. **en lo por venir,** in the future. *Pres. Ind.* **vengo, vienes, viene, venimos, venís, vienen.** *Pres. Part.* **viniendo.** *Fut.* **vendré,** etc. *Condit.* **vendría,** etc. *Preterite* **vine, viniste, vino, vinimos, vinisteis, vinieron.** *Pres. Subjunc.* **venga,** etc. *Imperf. Subjunc.* **viniese,** etc.
venoso *a* veined; venous
venta *f*, selling; sale; inn; *inf* wilderness; *pl com* turnover. **v. pública,** auction. **a la v.,** on sale. **la V. de la Mesilla,** the Gadsden Purchase
ventada *f*, gust of wind
ventaja *f*, advantage; profit
ventajoso *a* advantageous
ventana *f*, window. **v. de guillotina,** sash window. **v. saladiza,** bay window. **echar algo por la v.,** to waste a thing
ventanal *m*, large window
ventanilla *f*, small window (as in railway compartments); grill (ticket office, bank, etc.); nostril
ventarrón *m*, high wind
ventear *v impers* to blow (of the wind); *vt* sniff air (animals); air, dry; investigate; *vr* be spoiled by air (tobacco, etc.)
ventero (-ra) *n* innkeeper
ventilación *f*, ventilation; ventilator; current of air
ventilador *m*, ventilating fan; ventilator
ventilar *vt* to ventilate; shake, winnow; air; discuss
ventisca *f*, snowstorm
ventiscar, ventisquear *v impers* to snow with a high wind
ventisquero *m*, glacier; snowfield, snowdrift; snowstorm
ventolera *f*, gust of wind; *inf* boastfulness; whim, caprice
ventor (-ra) *n* pointer (dog)
ventosa *f*, vent (pipes, etc.); *zool* sucker; *surg* cupping glass
ventosidad *f*, flatulence
ventoso *a* windy; flatulent
ventrículo *m*, ventricle
ventrílocuo (-ua) *a* ventriloquial. *n* ventriloquist
ventriloquia *f*, ventriloquism
ventrudo *a* big-bellied
ventura *f*, happiness; chance, hazard; risk, danger. **a la v.,** at a venture. **buena v.,** good luck. **por v.,** perhaps; by chance; fortunately
venturoso *a* fortunate
Venus *m*, Venus. *f*, beautiful woman, beauty
ver *vt irr* to see; witness, behold; visit; inspect, examine; consider; observe; know, understand; (*with de* + *infin.*) try to; *vr* be seen; show oneself, appear; experience, find oneself; exchange visits; meet. **v. mundo,** to travel. **V. y creer,** Seeing is believing. **A mi v.,** In my opinion. **¡A v.!** Let's see!; Wait and see! **no tener nada que v. con,** to have no connection with, nothing to do with. **Veremos,** Time will tell. **Verse en la casa,** to be a stay-at-home. **Ya se ve,** Of course, Naturally. *Pres. Ind.* **veo, ves,** etc. *Imperf.* **veía,** etc. *Past Part.* **visto.** *Pres. Subjunc.* **vea,** etc. *Imperf. Subjunc.* **viese,** etc.

vera *f*, edge; border; shore. **a la v.**, on the edge, on the verge

veracidad *f*, truthfulness, veracity

veranadero *m*, summer pasture

veraneante *mf* summer resident, summer vacationist, holiday-maker

veranear *vi* to spend the summer

veraneo *m*, summer vacation, summer holidays, summering

veraniego *a* summer; light, unimportant

verano *m*, summer; dry season *WH*

veras *f pl*, reality, truth; fervor, earnestness. **de v.**, really; in earnest

veraz *a* truthful, veracious

verbal *a* verbal; oral

verbena *f*, *bot* verbena, vervain; fair held on eve of a saint's day

verbigracia *adv* for instance. *m*, example

verbo *m*, word; vow; *gram* verb. **v. activo** *or* **v. transitivo,** active or transitive verb. **v. auxiliar,** auxiliary verb. **v. intransitivo** *or* **v. neutro,** intransitive or neuter verb. **v. reflexivo** *or* **v. recíproco,** reflexive verb

verbosidad *f*, verbosity

verboso *a* verbose, prolix

verdad *f*, truth, veracity; reality. **a la v.**, indeed; without doubt. **en v.**, in truth; indeed. **cantar cuatro verdades a alguien,** to tell someone a few home truths. **la pura v.**, the plain truth

verdadero *a* true; real; sincere; truthful

verdal *a* green. **ciruela v.**, greengage

verde *a* green; unripe; fresh (vegetables); youthful; immature, undeveloped; obscene, dissolute. *m*, green (color); verdure, foliage

verdear *vi* to look green; be greenish; grow green

verdecer *vi irr* to grow green, be verdant. See **conocer**

verdegay *a* and *m*, bright green

verdemar *a* and *m*, sea-green

verdín *m*, verdure; mold; verdigris

verdinegro *a* dark green

verdor *m*, verdure; greenness; strength; youth (also *pl*)

verdoso *a* greenish

verdugo *m*, hangman, executioner; wale, mark; shoot of tree; switch; whip; *fig* scourge; tyrant

verdulera *f*, greengrocer; market woman; *inf* harridan

verdulería *f*, greengrocer's shop

verdulero *m*, greengrocer

verdura *f*, verdure; green garden produce, vegetables (gen. *pl*); *art* foliage; obscenity

verecundo *a* bashful

vereda *f*, footpath; sheep track

veredicto *m*, *law* verdict; judgment, considered opinion

verga *f*, steel bow of crossbow; *naut* yard; *inf* penis

vergajo *m*, rod (for punishment)

vergel *m*, orchard

vergonzoso (-sa) *a* shameful; bashful, shamefaced. *n* shy person

vergüenza *f*, shame; self-respect; bashfulness, timidity; shameful act; public punishment

vericueto *m*, narrow, stony path

verídico *a* veracious; true, exact

verificación *f*, verification, checking; *law* **v. de un testamento,** probate

verificador (-ra) *a* verifying, checking. *n* inspector, checker

verificar *vt* to prove; verify; *vr* take place, happen; check; come true. *elec* **v. las conexiones,** to check the connections

verisímil *a* credible, probable

verisimilitud *f*, credibility

verismo *m*, realism; truthfulness

verja *f*, grating, grill; railing

vermífugo *a* and *m*, vermifuge

verminoso *a* verminous

vermut *m*, vermouth

vernáculo *a* native, vernacular

vernal *a* vernal

veronés (-esa) *a* and *n* Veronese

verónica *f*, *bot* speedwell; veronica (bullfighting)

verosímil *a* credible, probable

verosimilitud *f*, verisimilitude, probability

verraco *m*, boar

verruga *f*, *med* wart; *inf* bore; defect

versar *vi* to revolve; (*with sobre*) concern, deal with (book, etc.); *vr* become versed (in)

versátil *a* *zool* versatile; changeable; fickle

versatilidad *f*, *zool* versatility; changeableness; fickleness

versículo *m*, versicle; verse (of the Bible)

versificación *f*, versification

versificador (-ra) *n* versifier

versificar *vi* to write verses; *vt* put into verse, versify

versión *f*, translation; version; account

verso *m*, poetry, verse; stanza; line (of a poem). **v. suelto,** blank verse

vertebrado *a* and *m*, *zool* vertebrate

vertedor *m*, drain, sewer; chute

verter *vt irr* to pour, spill; empty; translate; *vi* flow. See **entender**

vertical *a* and *f*, vertical

verticalidad *f*, verticality

vértice *m*, vertex

vertiente *a* emptying. *mf*, slope, incline; watershed

vertiginoso *a* giddy; vertiginous

vértigo *m*, giddiness, faintness

vesícula *f*, blister; (*anat bot*) vesicle

vespertino *a* evening

vestíbulo *m*, hall, vestibule foyer

vestido *m*, dress; clothes

vestidura *f*, garment; *pl* vestments

vestigio *m*, footprint; trace, mark; remains; *fig* vestige

vestir *vt irr* to clothe, dress; adorn; embellish (ideas); *fig* disguise (truth); simulate, pretend; *vi* be dressed; *vr* dress oneself; *fig* be covered. See **pedir**

vestuario *m*, clothing, dress; *theat* wardrobe or dressing room; *ecc* vestry; *mil* uniform

Vesubio Vesuvius

veta *f*, vein; stripe, rib (fabric)

veterano (-na) *a* and *n* veteran

veterinaria *f*, veterinary science

veterinario *a* veterinary. *m*, veterinary surgeon

veto *m*, veto; prohibition

vetustez *f*, antiquity, oldness

vetusto *a* ancient, very old

vez *f*, time, occasion; turn; *pl* proxy, deputy, substitute. **a la v.**, simultaneously. **alguna v.**, sometime. **a su v.**, in its (her, his, their) turn. **a veces,** sometimes. **de una v.**, at the one time. **de v. en cuando,** from time to time. **en v. de,** instead of. **hacer las veces de,** to be a substitute for. **otra v.**, again. **Su cuarto es dos veces más grande que éste,** His room is twice as large as this one

vía *f*, way; road; railway track or gauge; *anat* tract; (mystic) way; route; conduct; *pl* procedure. **v. ancha,** broad gauge (railway). **v. angosta,** narrow gauge. **v. de agua,** *naut* leak. *law* **v. ejecutiva,** seizure, attachment. **v. férrea,** railway. **v. láctea,** Milky Way. **v. muerta,** railway siding. **v. principal,** main line. **v. pública,** public thoroughfare. **v. romana,** Roman road. **v. secundaria,** *rw* side line. **por v. aérea,** by air, by airplane

viabilidad *f*, viability

viable *a* viable; practicable; workable; passable

viaducto *m*, viaduct

viajante *mf* traveling salesman, commercial traveler

viajar *vi* to travel, journey, voyage

viaje *m*, journey; voyage; water-supply; travel journal; *naut* **v. de ensayo,** trial trip. **v. redondo,** circular tour. **¡Buen v.!** Have a good trip! Bon voyage!

viajero (-ra) *a* traveling. *n* traveler; passenger

vianda *f*, viand, victual (gen. *pl*); meal

viático *m*, *ecc* viaticum; provisions for a journey

víbora *f,* viper

viborezno *m,* young viper

vibración *f,* vibration; jar, jolt; thrill

vibrante *a* shaking; vibrant; thrilling

vibrar *vt* to shake, oscillate; *vi* vibrate; jar, jolt; quiver, thrill

vibratorio *a* vibratory, vibrative

vicaría *f,* vicarage; vestry

vicario *a* vicarious. *m,* vicar; curate; deputy

vicealmirante *m,* vice-admiral

vicecanciller *m,* vice-chancellor

vicecónsul *m,* vice-consul

viceconsulado *m,* vice-consulate

vicepresidente (-ta) *n* vice president

vicesecretario (-ia) *n* assistant secretary

viciar *vt* to corrupt; adulterate; forge; annul; interpret maliciously, misconstrue; *vr* become vicious

vicio *m,* vice; defect; error, fraud; bad habit; excess, exaggerated desire; viciousness (animals); overgrowth (plants); peevishness (children). **tener el v. de,** to have the bad habit of. **el v. del juego,** fondness for gambling

vicioso *a* vicious; vigorous, overgrown; abundant; *inf* spoilt (children)

vicisitud *f,* vicissitude

víctima *f,* victim

¡víctor! *interj* Victor!; Long live!; Hurrah!

victoria *f,* victory, triumph; victoria

victoriano (-na) *a* and *n* Victorian

victorioso *a* victorious

vid *f,* vine

vida *f,* life; livelihood; human being; biography; vivacity. **v. airada,** dissolute life. **la v. allende la muerte,** life after death. **de por v.,** for life. **darse buena v.,** to live comfortably; enjoy one's life. **dar mala v.,** to illtreat. **en la v.,** in life; never. **ganarse la v.,** to make one's living

vidente *m,* clairvoyant; seer

videograbación *f,* videotape

vidriar *vt* to glaze (earthenware)

vidriera *f,* glass window (gen. stained or colored)

vidriero *m,* glazier. *a* made of glass

vidrio *m,* glass; anything made of glass; fragile thing; touchy person. **v. inastillable,** safety-glass. **v. jaspeado,** frosted glass. **v. pintado** *or* **v. de color,** stainedglass. **v. plano,** plate glass. **v. soplado,** blown glass

vidrioso *a* brittle; slippery; fragile; hypersensitive; *fig* glazed (eyes)

vieja *f,* old woman

viejo *a* old; ancient; former; old-fashioned; worn out. *m,* old man

Viena Vienna

vienés (-esa) *a* and *n* Viennese

viento *m,* wind; scent (of game, etc.); guy (rope); upheaval; vanity. **v. en popa,** *naut* following wind; without a hitch, prosperously. **vientos alisios,** tradewinds. **v. terral,** land wind. **a los cuatro vientos,** in all directions. **contra v. y marea,** *fig* against all obstacles. **correr malos vientos,** to be unfavorable (of circumstances). **refrescar el v.,** to stiffen (of the breeze)

vientre *m,* stomach; belly; vitals; *law* venter

viernes *m,* Friday. **V. Santo,** Good Friday

viga *f,* beam, rafter; girder; joist; mill beam. **v. maestra,** main beam or girder

vigente *a* valid; in force (laws, customs)

vigésimo *a* twentieth

vigía *f,* watch tower; (gen. *m*) look-out, watch

vigilancia *f,* watchfulness, vigilance; watch patrol

vigilante *a* watchful. *m,* watcher; watchman. **v. escolar,** truant officer

vigilar *vi* to watch over; supervise

vigilia *f,* vigil; wakefulness; night study; *ecc* vigil, eve; wake; *mil* watch. **día de v.,** fast-day

vigor *m,* strength; activity; vigor, efficiency; validity

vigorizar *vt* to invigorate; exhilarate; encourage

vigorosidad *f,* vigorousness

vigoroso *a* strong, vigorous

vihuela *f,* lute

vil *a* vile, infamous; base; despicable; untrustworthy

vileza *f,* baseness; vileness, infamy

vilipendiar *vt* to revile

vilipendio *m,* vilification; contempt

villa *f,* villa; country house; town

villancico *m,* carol

villanesco *a* peasant; rustic, country

villanía *f,* humbleness of birth; vileness; villainy

villano (-na) *n* peasant. *a* rustic, country; boorish; base

vilo, en *adv* hanging in the air; *fig* in suspense

vilorta *f,* hoop; *mech* washer

vinagre *m,* vinegar

vinagrera *f,* vinegar bottle; table cruet

vinagreta *f,* vinegar sauce

vinagroso *a* vinegary; *inf* bad-tempered, acid

vinatero (-ra) *n* wine merchant. *a* wine

vincapervinca *f, bot* periwinkle

vinculación *f, law* entail

vincular *vt law* to entail; *fig* base; *vr* perpetuate. *a law* entail

vínculo *m,* tie, bond; *law* entail

vindicación *f,* vindication; justification; excuse

vindicador (-ra) *n* vindicator. *a* vindicative

vindicar *vt* to avenge; vindicate; justify; excuse

vindicativo *a* avenging; vindicatory

vinícola *a* wine-growing; wine

vinicultor (-ra) *n* wine grower, viniculturalist

vinicultura *f,* wine-growing, viniculture

vinificación *f,* vinification

vinillo *m,* thin, weak wine

vino *m,* wine; fermented fruit juice. **v. de Oporto,** port wine. **v. generoso,** well-matured wine. **v. tinto,** red wine

vinosidad *f,* vinosity

vinoso *a* vinous; fond of wine

viña *f,* vineyard

viñador *m,* vineyard-keeper; vine-cultivator

viñedo *m,* vineyard

viñeta *f,* vignette

viola *f, mus* viola; *bot* viola, pansy. *mf* viola player

violación *f,* violation; infringement

violado *a* violet

violador (-ra) *n* violator. *m,* seducer

violar *vt* to violate; infringe; rape; spoil, harm

violencia *f,* violence; outrage; rape

violentar *vt* to force; falsify, misinterpret; force an entrance; *vr* force oneself

violento *a* violent; repugnant; impetuous, hasty-tempered; unnatural, false; unreasonable

violeta *f, bot* violet. *m,* violet color. **v. de febrero,** snowdrop

violín *m,* violin

violinista *mf* violinist

violón *m,* double-bass, bass viol; double-bass player

violoncelista *mf* cellist

violoncelo *m,* cello

viperino *a* viperine; venomous, evil

vira *f,* welt (of a shoe); dart

viraje *m, aut* change of direction; bend, turn

virar *vt naut* to put about; *phot* tone; *vi naut* tack; *aut* change direction. **v. de bordo,** *naut* to lay off

virgen *mf* virgin. *f, ast* Virgo

virgiliano *a* Virgilian

virginal *a* virginal; pure, unspotted

virginidad *f,* virginity

virgulilla *f,* comma; cedilla; accent; apostrophe; fine line

viril *a* manly, virile. *m,* clear glass screen

virilidad *f,* virility

virote *m,* arrow; shaft; *inf* young blood

virreina *f,* vicereine

virreinato *m,* viceroyship

virrey *m,* viceroy

virtual *a* virtual; implicit

virtualidad *f*, virtuality
virtualmente *adv* virtually; tacitly
virtud *f*, virtue; power; strength, courage; efficacy. **en v. de,** in virtue of
virtuosidad *f*, virtuosity
virtuoso *a* virtuous; powerful, efficacious. *m*, virtuoso, artist
viruela *f*, smallpox (gen. *pl*)
virulencia *f*, virulence
virulento *a* virulent
virus *m*, virus
viruta *f*, wood-shaving
vis cómica *f*, the comic spirit
visaje *m*, grimace
visar *vt* to visa; endorse
viscosidad *f*, viscosity
viscoso *a* viscous, sticky
visera *f*, visor; eye-shade; peak (of a cap)
visibilidad *f*, visibility
visigodo (-da) *a* Visigothic. *n* Visigoth
visigótico *a* Visigothic
visillo *m*, window-blind
visión *f*, seeing, sight; queer sight; vision; hallucination; *inf* scarecrow, sight
visionario (-ia) *a* and *n* visionary
visir *m*, vizier. **gran v.,** grand vizier
visita *f*, visit; visitor; inspection. **v. de cumplido,** formal call. **v. de sanidad,** health inspection. **hacer una v.,** to pay a call
visitación *f*, visitation; visit
visitador (-ra) *n* regular visitor. *m*, inspector. *a* visiting; inspecting
visitar *vt* to visit; inspect; *med* attend; *ecc* examine. **v. los monumentos,** to see the sights, go sightseeing
visiteo *m*, receiving or paying of visits
vislumbrar *vt* to glimpse; surmise, conjecture
vislumbre *f*, glimmer, glimpse; surmise, glimmering (gen. *pl*); semblance, appearance
viso *m*, view point, elevation; glare; shimmer, gleam; colored slip under transparent dress; semblance. **de v.,** prominent (persons)
visón *m*, mink
víspera *f*, eve; *ecc* day before festival; prelude, preliminary. *pl ecc* vespers. **en vísperas de,** on the eve of
vista *f*, vision, sight; view; eyes; eyesight; meeting, interview; *law* hearing (of a case); apparition; picture of a view; clear idea; connection (of things); proposition, intention; glance; *pl* window, door, skylight, opening for light. **v. corta,** short sight. **v. de lince,** sharp eyes. **a primera v.,** at first sight. **a v. de,** in sight of; in the presence of. **conocer de v.,** to know by sight. **dar una v.,** to take a look. **doble v.,** second sight; clairvoyance. **en v. de,** in view of, considering. **estar a la v.,** to be evident. *inf* **hacer la v. gorda,** to turn a blind eye. **¡Hasta la v.!** Good-bye! **perder de v. (a),** to lose sight of
vistazo *m*, glance. **echar un v.,** to cast a glance
visto *past part irr* **ver.** *law* whereas. **bien v.,** approved. **mal v.,** disapproved. **V. Bueno (V⁰ B⁰)** Approved, Passed. **v. que,** since, inasmuch as
vistoso *a* showy, gaudy; beautiful
visual *a* visual
vital *a* vital; essential
vitalicio *a* lifelong. *m*, life-insurance
vitalidad *f*, vitality
vitalizar *vt* to vitalize
vitamina *f*, vitamin
vitando *a* odious; bad; vital
vitela *f*, vellum
vitícola *a* viticultural. *mf* viticulturist
viticultura *f*, viticulture
¡vítor! *interj* Victor!; Hurrah!; Long live!
vitorear *vt* to cheer; applaud, acclaim
vítreo *a* glassy, vitreous
vitrificar(se) *vt* and *vr* to vitrify
vitrina *f*, show-case; display cabinet

vitriólico *a* vitriolic
vitriolo *m*, vitriol
vitualla *f*, (gen. *pl*) victuals, provisions
vituperable *a* blameworthy, vituperable
vituperador (-ra) *a* vituperative. *n* vituperator
vituperar *vt* to censure, blame, vituperate
vituperio *m*, vituperation
viuda *f*, widow
viudedad *f*, widow's pension
viudez *f*, widowhood, widowerhood
viudita *f*, young widow
viudo *m*, widower
¡viva! *interj* Long live!; Hurrah!
vivacidad *f*, vivacity, gaiety; ardor, warmth; brightness
vivamente *adv* quickly, lively
vivandera *f*, vivandiere
vivandero *m*, sutler
vivaque *m*, bivouac
vivaquear *vi* to bivouac
vivar *m*, warren; aquarium; breeding ground; well (of a fishing boat)
vivaracho *a inf* sprightly, cheery, lively
vivaz *a* vigorous; quick-witted; sprightly; *bot* perennial; vivid, bright
víveres *m pl*, provisions; *mil* stores
vivero *m*, *bot* nursery; vivarium; small marsh
viveza *f*, quickness, briskness; vehemence; perspicuity; witticism; resemblance; brightness (eyes, colors); thoughtless word or act
vividero *a* habitable
vívido *a poet* vivid
vividor (-ra) *a* frugal, thrifty; dissolute. *n* liver; long-liver; libertine, rake
vivienda *f*, dwelling
viviente *a* living
vivificación *f*, vivification
vivificante *a* vivifying
vivificar *vt* to vivify; comfort
vivir *vi* to be alive, live; last, endure; *(with en)* inhabit. *m*, life. **¿Quién vive?** *mil* Who goes there? **v. a costillas ajenas,** to live at someone else's expense, live off someone else
vivisección *f*, vivisection
vivo *a* alive; intense, strong; bright; *mil* active; subtle, ingenious; precipitate; *fig* lasting, enduring; diligent; hasty; persuasive, expressive. *m*, edge. **al v., a lo v.,** to the life; vividly
vizcaíno (-na) *a* and *n* Biscayan
Vizcaya, el Golfo de the Bay of Biscay
vizcondado *m*, viscounty
vizconde *m*, viscount
vizcondesa *f*, viscountess
vocablo *m*, word
vocabulario *m*, vocabulary
vocación *f*, vocation; trade, profession
vocal *a* vocal; oral. *f*, *gram* vowel. *mf* voting member
vocalismo *m*, vocalism, vowel system
vocalización *f*, vocalization
vocalizar *vi* to vocalize
vocear *vi* to cry out, shout; *vt* proclaim; call for; acclaim
vocerío *m*, shouting; clamor, outcry
vociferación *f*, vociferation, outcry
vociferar *vt* to boast (of); *vi* shout, vociferate
vocinglería *f*, clamor; babble, chatter
vocinglero *a* vociferous; prattling, babbling
vodca *m*, vodka
volada *f*, short flight. *mech* **v. de grúa,** jib
voladura *f*, explosion; blasting
volandas (en), volandillas (en) *adv* in the air, as though flying; *inf* in a trice
volante *a* flying; wandering, restless. *m*, frill, flounce; screen; fan (of a windmill); *mech* flywheel; *mech* balance wheel (watches); coiner's stamp mill; shuttle-cock. *aut* **v. de dirección,** steering-wheel
volantón (-ona) *n* fledgeling
volar *vi irr* to fly (birds, insects, aviation); float in the

air; hurry; disappear suddenly; burst, explode; jut out (buttresses, etc.); cleave (air) (arrows, etc.); *fig* spread (rumors); *vt* explode; blast; anger. See **contar**

volatería *f,* fowling; fowls; poultry; flock of birds; *fig* crowd (of ideas)

volátil *a* volatile; inconstant

volatilizar *vt* to volatilize

volatinero (-ra) *n* tight-rope walker, acrobat

volcán *m,* volcano; violent passion. **v. extinto,** extinct volcano

volcánico *a* volcanic

volcar *vt irr* to overturn, capsize; make dizzy; cause a change (of opinion); annoy; *vi* overturn. *Pres. Ind.* **vuelco, vuelcas, vuelca, vuelcan.** *Preterite* **volqué,** **volcaste,** etc. *Pres. Subjunc.* **vuelque, vuelques,** **vuelque, vuelquen**

volear *vt* to strike in the air, volley; *agr* sow broadcast

voleo *m,* volley (tennis, etc.); high kick; straight punch

volframio *m,* wolfram, tungsten

volición *f,* volition

volquete *m,* tip-cart

voltaico *a* voltaic

voltaje *m,* voltage

voltario *a* versatile; capricious, headstrong

volteador (-ra) *n* acrobat

voltear *vt* to whirl, turn; overturn; change place (of); *arch* construct an arch or vault; *vi* revolve; tumble, twirl (acrobats)

volteo *m,* turning, revolution; whirl; overturning; twirling; *elec* voltage

voltereta *f,* somersault

volteriano *a* Voltairian

voltímetro *m,* voltmeter

voltio *m,* volt

volubilidad *f,* inconstancy, fickleness

voluble *a* easily turned; inconstant, changeable; *bot* twining

volumen *m,* bulk, size; volume, book

volumétrico *a* volumetric

voluminoso *a* voluminous, bulky

voluntad *f,* will, volition; wish; decree; free will; intention; affection; free choice; consent. **a v.,** at will; by choice. **de buena v.,** of good will; willingly, with pleasure. **de su propia v.,** of one's own free will. **mala v.,** hostility, ill-will

voluntario (-ia) *a* voluntary; strong-willed. *n* volunteer

voluntarioso *a* self-willed

voluptuosidad *f,* voluptuousness

voluptuoso *a* voluptuous

volver *vt irr* to turn; turn over; return; pay back; direct, aim; translate; restore; change, alter; close (doors, etc.); vomit; reflect, reverberate; *vi* come back; continue (speech, etc.); bend, turn (roads); (*with prep a +* *infin.*) do something again (e.g. **v. a leer,** to read over again); (*with por + noun*) protect; *vr* become; go sour; turn. **v. a las filas,** *mil* to reduce to the ranks. **v. en sí,** to regain consciousness. **v. la cabeza,** to turn one's head. **volverse atrás,** *fig* to back out. **volverse loco,** to go mad. See **resolver**

vomitar *vt* to vomit; *fig* vomit forth; *fig* spit out (curses, etc.); *inf* burst into confidences

vomitivo *a* and *m,* emetic

vómito *m,* vomit

voracidad *f,* voracity

vorágine *f,* vortex, whirlpool

voraz *a* voracious

vórtice *m,* whirlpool; *fig* vortex

vos *pers pron 2nd pers sing* and *pl* you.

vosotros, vosotras *pers pron 2nd pers pl mf* you

votación *f,* voting

votador (-ra) *n* voter; swearer

votar *vi* and *vt* to vote; make a vow; curse, swear. **v.** **una proposición de confianza,** to pass a vote of confidence

votivo *a* votive

voto *m,* vote; vow; voter; prayer; curse; desire; opinion. **v. de calidad,** casting vote. **v. de confianza,** vote of confidence

voz *f,* voice; sound, noise; cry, shout (gen. *pl*); word; expression; *mus* singer or voice; *gram* mood; vote; rumor; instruction, order. **v. común,** general opinion. **a voces,** in a shout, loudly. **llevar la v. cantante,** *inf* to have the chief say

vuelco *m,* overturning

vuelo *m,* flight; wing; *sew* skirt-fullness; ruffle, frill; *arch* buttress. **v. a ciegas,** *aer* blind flying. **v. de distancia,** long-distance flight. **v. de patrulla,** patrol or reconnaissance flight. **v. de reconocimento,** reconnaissance flight. **v. nocturno,** *aer* night flying. **v. sin** **parar,** non-stop flight. **al v.,** on the wing; in passing; quickly. **alzar** (*or* **levantar**) **el v.,** to take flight

vuelta *f,* revolution, turn; bend, curve; return; restitution; recompense; repetition; wrong side; beating; *sew* facing, cuff; change (money); conning (lessons, etc.); stroll, walk; change; vault, ceiling; *sport* round; *mech* **vueltas por minuto,** revolutions per minute. **a v. de** **correo,** by return mail, by return of post. **a la v.,** on returning; overleaf. **dar la v.,** to turn round, make a détour. **dar una v.,** to take a stroll. **dar vueltas,** to revolve; search (for); consider. **media v.,** half turn

vuestro, vuestra, vuestros, vuestras *poss pron 2nd pl* *mf* your, yours

vulcanita *f,* vulcanite.

vulcanización *f,* vulcanization

vulcanizar *vt* to vulcanize

vulgar *a* popular; general, common; vernacular; mediocre

vulgaridad *f,* vulgarity

vulgarismo *m,* vulgarism

vulgarización *f,* vulgarization; popularization

vulgarizar *vt* to vulgarize; popularize; translate into the vernacular; *vr* grow vulgar

vulgata *f,* Vulgate

vulgo *m,* mob

vulnerabilidad *f,* vulnerability

vulnerable *a* vulnerable

vulpeja *f,* vixen

vulpino *a* vulpine; crafty

W

wagneriano *a* Wagnerian

wáter *m,* toilet, water-closet

whisky *m,* whiskey

X

xenofobia *f,* xenophobia, hatred of foreigners

xilófago *a* xylophagous, wood-boring. *m,* wood-borer

xilófono *m,* xylophone

xilografía *f,* xylography

Y

y *conjunc* and. See **e**

ya *adv* already; formerly; soon; now; finally; immediately; well, yes, quite. Used of past, present and future time, and in various idiomatic ways. **Ha venido ya,** He has already come. **¡Ya caerá!** His time will come!, He will get his comeuppance! **Ya vendrá,** He will come soon. **¡Ya voy!** Coming! **¡Ya lo creo!** Of course!; I should think so! **¡Ya!** Quite!; I understand. **ya no,** no longer. **ya que,** since

yacente *a* recumbent, reclining (statues, etc.)

yacer *vi irr* to be lying at full length; lie (in the grave); be situated, be; lie (with), sleep (with); graze by night. *Pres. Ind.* **yazgo** *or* **yazco, yaces,** etc. *Pres. Subjunc.* **yazga** *or* **yazca,** etc.

yaciente *a* recumbent

yacija *f,* bed; couch; tomb

yacimiento *m, geol* bed, deposit

yacio *m,* india-rubber tree

yak *m,* yak

yámbico *a* and *m,* (metrics) iambic

yanqui *a* and *mf contemptuous and offensive* North American (gen. U.S.A.)

yarda *f,* yard (English measure)

yate *m, naut* yacht

ye *f,* name of the letter Y

yegua *f,* mare

yelmo *m,* helmet

yema *f,* bud; yolk (of egg); sweetmeat; *fig* best of anything. **y. del dedo,** finger-tip

yermo *a* uninhabited, deserted; uncultivated. *m,* wilderness, desert

yerno *m,* son-in-law

yerro *m,* error; mistake; fault

yerto *a* stiff, rigid

yesca *f,* tinder; fuel, stimulus

yeso *m,* gypsum, calcium sulphate; plaster; plaster cast

yídish *n* and *a* Yiddish

yo *pers pron 1st sing mf* I. **el yo,** the ego

yodo *m,* iodine

yuca *f,* yucca

yucateco (-ca) *a* and *n* from or pertaining to Yucatan

yugo *m,* yoke; nuptial tie; oppression; *naut* transom; *fig* **sacudir el y.,** to throw off the yoke

Yugo(e)slavia Yugoslavia

yugo(e)slavo (-va) *a* and *n* Yugoslav

yugular *a anat* jugular. *m,* jugular vein

Yukón, el the Yukon

yunque *m,* anvil; patient, undaunted person; hard worker; *anat* incus

yunta *f,* yoke (of oxen, etc.)

yute *m,* jute fiber or fabric

yuxtaponer *vt irr* to juxtapose. See **poner**

yuxtaposición *f,* juxtaposition

Z

zabarcera *f,* vegetable seller

zaborda *f,* zabordamiento *m, naut* grounding, stranding

zabordar *vi naut* to run aground, strand

zacatín *m,* street or square where clothes are sold

zafar *vt* to embellish, garnish, adorn; *naut* lighten (a ship); *vr* escape, hide oneself; (*with de*) excuse oneself, avoid; get rid of

zafarrancho *m, naut* clearing the decks; *inf* damage; *inf* scuffle

zafiedad *f,* rudeness, ignorance, boorishness

zafio *a* rude, unlettered, boorish

zafiro *m,* sapphire

zafra *f,* olive oil container; sugar crop or factory; *min* waste

zaga *f,* rear. *m,* last player. **en z.,** behind. *inf* **no quedarse en z.,** not to be left behind; be not inferior

zagal *m,* youth; strong, handsome lad; young shepherd; full skirt

zagala *f,* maiden, girl; young shepherdess

zagual *m,* paddle

zaguán *m,* entrance hall; vestibule

zaguero *a* loitering, straggling. *m, sport* back

zahareño *a* untamable, wild (birds); unsociable, disdainful

zaherimiento *m,* upbraiding; nagging

zaherir *vt irr* to upbraid, reprehend; nag. See **herir**

zahína *f, bot* sorghum

zahón *m,* leather apron (worn by cowboys)

zahorí *m,* soothsayer; waterfinder; sagacious person

zahúrda *f,* pigsty

zaino *a* treacherous; vicious (horses); chestnut (horses); black (cows)

zalagarda *f,* ambush; skirmish; snare, trap; *inf* trick, ruse; *inf* mock battle

zalamería *f,* adulation, flattery

zalamero (-ra) *a* wheedling, flattering. *n* flatterer

zalea *f,* sheepskin

zalear *vt* to shake; frighten away (dogs)

zalema *f,* salaam

zamacuco *m, inf* oaf, dolt; *inf* drinking bout

zamarra *f,* sheepskin jacket

zamarrear *vt* to worry, shake (prey); *fig inf* beat up; *inf* floor, confound

zambo *a* knock-kneed

zambomba *f,* rustic drum

zambra *f,* Moorish festival; *inf* merrymaking; Moorish boat

zambuco *m, inf* concealment (especially of cards)

zambullida *f,* plunge, submersion; thrust (in fencing)

zambullir *vt* to plunge in water, submerge; *vr* dive; hide oneself, cover oneself

zampar *vt* to conceal (one thing in another); eat greedily; (*with en*) arrive suddenly

zampatortas *mf inf* glutton

zampoña *f,* rustic flute; *inf* unimportant work

zanahoria *f,* carrot

zanca *f,* long leg (birds); *inf* long thin leg; *arch* stringboard (of stairs)

zancada *f,* swift stride

zancadilla *f,* trip (wrestling); *inf* trick, deceit. **echar la z. (a),** to trip up

zancajear *vi* to stride about

zancajo *m,* heel-bone; torn heel (stocking, shoe); *inf* ill-shaped person. *inf* **no llegarle al z.,** to be immensely inferior to someone

zancajoso *a* flatfooted; slovenly

zanco *m,* stilt. *fig inf* **andar** (*or* **estar**) **en zancos,** to have gone up in the world

zancudo *a* long-legged

zangandungo (-ga) *n inf* loafer

zanganear *vi inf* to loaf

zángano *m,* drone; *inf* idler, parasite

zangolotear *vt inf* to shake violently; *vi* fuss about, bustle; *vr* rattle (windows, etc.)

zangoloteo *m,* shaking; rattling

zanguango *m, inf* lazybones

zanja *f*, trench, ditch; drain; furrow
zanjar *vt* to excavate; *fig* remove (obstacles)
Zanzíbar Zanzibar
zapa *f*, shovel, spade; *mil* sap; sandpaper
zapador *m*, *mil* sapper
zapapico *m*, pick-ax; mattock
zapaquilda *f*, *inf* she-cat
zapar *vi mil* to sap
zaparrastrar *vi inf* to trail along the floor (dresses)
zapata *f*, half-boot; piece of leather used to stop creaking of a hinge; *arch* lintel; (*naut mech*) shoe
zapatazo *m*, blow with a shoe; fall, thud; stamping (horses); flap (of sail)
zapateado *m*, dance in which rhythmic drumming of heels plays important part
zapatear *vt* to hit with a shoe; stamp feet; drum heels (in dancing); *inf* ill-treat; thump ground (rabbits); *vi* stamp (horses); *naut* flap (sails); *vr fig* stand one's ground
zapateo *m*, stamping; rhythmic drumming of heels
zapatera *f*, cobbler's wife; woman who makes or sells shoes
zapatería *f*, shoemaking; shoe shop
zapatero *m*, shoemaker; shoe seller. **z. remendón**, cobbler
zapateta *f*, caper, leap
zapatilla *f*, slipper; trotter, hoof
zapato *m*, shoe
¡zape! *interj inf* shoo! Used for frightening away cats; exclamation of surprise or warning
zapear *vt* to scare away cats; *inf* frighten off
zaque *m*, leather bottle, wineskin; *inf* drunkard, sot
zaquizamí *m*, garret; dirty little house or room
zar *m*, tsar
zarabanda *f*, saraband; *inf* racket, row
zaragata *f*, *inf* fight, brawl
Zaragoza Saragossa
zaragozano (-na) *a* and *n* Saragossan
zaragüelles *m*, *pl* wide pleated breeches
zaranda *f*, sieve, strainer, colander
zarandajas *f*, *pl inf* odds and ends
zarandar *vt* to sieve (grapes, grain); strain; *inf* pick out the best; *vr inf* move quickly
zarandillo *m*, small sieve, strainer; *inf* a live wire, energetic person; Spanish dance
zaraza *f*, chintz
zarcillo *m*, earring; *bot* tendril; *agr* trowel
zarco *a* light blue (generally eyes or water)
zarina *f*, tsarina
zarpa *f*, *naut* weighing anchor; paw
zarpada *f*, blow with a paw
zarpar *vt* and *vi naut* to weigh anchor, sail
zarza *f*, *bot* bramble, blackberry bush
zarzal *m*, bramble patch
zarzamora *f*, blackberry
zarzaparrilla *f*, sarsaparilla
zarzo *m*, hurdle; wattle
zarzoso *a* brambly
zarzuela *f*, comic opera; musical comedy
zarzuelista *mf* writer or composer of comic operas
¡zas! *m*, sound of a bang or blow
zascandil *m*, *inf* busybody
zatara *f*, raft
zeda *f*, name of the letter Z
zedilla *f*, cedilla
zenit *m*. See **cenit**

zepelín *m*, Zeppelin
zeta *f*. See **zeda**
zigzag *m*, zigzag
zigzaguear *vi* to zigzag
zinc *m*, zinc
zipizape *m*, *inf* row, quarrel
zoca *f*, square
zócalo *m*, arch socle
zoclo *m*, clog, sabot
zoco *m*, square; market; clog, sabot
zodiaco *m*, zodiac
zona *f*, girdle, band; strip (of land); zone; *med* shingles. **z. de depresión**, air pocket. **z. templada**, temperate zone. **z. tórrida**, torrid zone
zonal *a* zonal
zoología *f*, zoology
zoológico *a* zoological
zoólogo *m*, zoologist
zopenco *a inf* oafish
zopo *a* maimed, deformed (hands, feet)
zoquete *m*, *carp* block; dowel; hunk of bread; *inf* short, ugly man; *inf* dunderhead
zorcico *m*, Basque song and dance
zorra *f*, vixen; fox; *inf* cunning person; *inf* prostitute; *inf* drinking bout; truck, dray
zorrera *f*, foxhole
zorrería *f*, foxiness; *inf* cunning
zorro *m*, fox; fox-skin; *inf* knave
zóster *f*, *med* shingles
zote *a* dull, ignorant
zozobra *f*, *naut* foundering, capsizing; anxiety
zozobrar *vi naut* to founder, sink; *naut* plunge, shiver; be anxious, vacillate
zueco *m*, sabot, clog
zulú *a* and *mf* Zulu
Zululandia Zululand
zumaque *m*, *bot* sumach tree; *inf* wine
zumba *f*, cow bell; jest
zumbar *vi* to buzz, hum; ring (of the ears); whizz; twang (of a guitar, etc.); *fig inf* be on the brink
zumbido *m*, buzzing, humming; ringing (in the ears); whizz; twanging (of a guitar, etc.); *inf* slap, blow
zumbón *a* waggish, jocose
zumo *m*, sap; juice; profit, advantage
zumoso *a* succulent, juicy
zupia *f*, wine lees; cloudy wine; *fig* dregs
zurcido *m*, sew darn; mend
zurcidor (-ra) *n* darner, mender. **z. de voluntades**, *humorous* pimp
zurcidura *f*, darning; mending; darn
zurcir *vt* to darn; mend, repair; join; *fig* concoct, weave
zurdo *a* left-handed
zurra *f*, *tan* currying; *inf* spanking; *inf* quarrel
zurrador *m*, *tan* currier, dresser
zurrapa *f*, (gen. *pl*) sediment, lees, dregs
zurrar *vt* to curry (leather); *inf* spank; *inf* dress down, scold
zurriagazo *m*, lash with a whip; *fig* blow of fate
zurriago *m*, whip
zurribanda *f*, *inf* whipping; fight, quarrel
zurriburri *m*, *inf* ragamuffin; mob; uproar
zurrido *m*, *inf* blow; dull noise
zurrir *vi* to have a confused sound, hum, rattle
zurrón *m*, shepherd's pouch; leather bag; *bot* husk
zutano (-na) *n inf* so-and-so, such a one
Zuyderzee, el the Zuider Zee

ENGLISH-SPANISH
Dictionary

A

a *n* (letter) a, *f; mus* la, *m.* **symphony in A major,** sinfonía en la mayor, *f.* **A1,** de primera clase; de primera calidad, excelente
a, an *indef art.* (one) un, *m;* una, *f;* (with weights, quantities) el, *m;* la, *f;* (with weeks, months, years, etc.) por, al, *m;* a la, *f.* The indef. art. is omitted in Spanish before nouns expressing nationality, profession, rank, and generally before a noun in apposition. It is omitted also before certain words such as **mil, ciento, otro, semejante, medio,** etc. Not translated in book titles, e.g., **A History of Spain,** Historia de España. *prep* a. In phrases such as **to go hunting,** ir a cazar. As prefix, see **abed, ashore,** etc. **Madrid, a Spanish city,** Madrid, ciudad de España. **three times a month,** tres veces al mes. **ten dollars an hour,** diez dólares por hora. **thirty miles an hour,** treinta millas por hora. **a certain Mrs. Brown,** una tal Sra. Brown. **a thousand soldiers,** mil soldados. **half an hour later,** media hora después
aback *adv naut* en facha; *fig* sorprendido, desconcertado. **to take a.,** desconcertar, coger desprevenido (a)
abacus *n* ábaco, *m*
abaft *adv naut* hacia la popa, en popa; atrás
abandon *vt* abandonar; dejar; desertar, desamparar; renunciar; entregar. *n* entusiasmo, fervor, *m;* naturalidad, *f.* **to a. oneself to,** (despair, vice, etc.) entregarse a
abandoned *a* entregado a los vicios, vicioso
abandonment *n* abandono, *m;* renunciación, *f;* deserción, *f*
abase *vt* humillar; degradar; abatir
abasement *n* humillación, degradación, *f;* abatimiento, *m*
abash *vt* avergonzar; confundir, desconcertar
abashed *a* avergonzado, confuso, consternado
abate *vt* disminuir, reducir; (a price) rebajar; (suppress) suprimir, abolir; (remit) condonar, remitir; (annul) anular; (moderate) moderar; (of pride, etc.) humillar; (of pain) aliviar. *vi* disminuir; moderarse; (of the wind and *fig*) amainar; cesar; apaciguarse, calmarse
abatement *n* disminución, *f;* reducción, *f;* mitigación, *f;* (of price) rebaja, *f;* supresión, *f;* remisión, *f;* (annulment) anulación, *f;* (of pride) humillación, *f;* (of the wind and of enthusiasm, etc.) amaine, *m;* (of pain, etc.) alivio, *m*
abattoir *n* matadero, *m*
abbey *n* abadía, *f*
abbreviate *vt* abreviar; condensar, resumir
abbreviation *n* abreviación, *f;* resumen, *m,* condensación, *f;* (of a word) abreviatura, *f*
abdicate *vt* renunciar; (a throne) abdicar
abdication *n* renuncia, *f;* abdicación, *f*
abdomen *n* abdomen, *m*
abdominal *a* abdominal
abduct *vt* raptar, secuestrar
abduction *n* rapto, *m;* (anat phil) abducción, *f*
abductor *n anat* abductor, *m;* raptor, *m*
aberration *n* aberración (also *ast phys biol*), *f*
abet *vt* ayudar, apoyar, favorecer; incitar, alentar; (in bad sense) ser cómplice de
abetment *n* ayuda, *f,* apoyo, *m;* instigación, *f*
abettor *n* instigador (-ra); cómplice, *mf*
abeyance *n* suspensión, *f;* expectativa, esperanza, *f.* **in a.,** en suspenso; vacante; latente
abhor *vt* detestar, odiar, aborrecer; repugnar
abhorrence *n* detestación, *f,* odio, aborrecimiento, *m;* repugnancia, *f*
abhorrent *a* detestable, odioso, aborrecible; repugnante
abide *vi* morar, quedar. *vt* aguardar; *inf* aguantar, sufrir.
to a. by, atenerse a, cumplir; sostener

abiding *a* permanente, constante, perenne
ability *n* habilidad, facultad, *f,* poder, *m;* talento, *m,* capacidad, *f.* **to the best of my a.,** lo mejor que yo pueda
abject *a* abyecto, miserable; despreciable, vil; servil
abjure *vt* abjurar; renunciar; retractar
ablaze *adv* en llamas, ardiendo. *a* brillante; (with, of anger, etc.) dominado por
able *a* capaz (de); (clever) hábil; competente; en estado (de); *law* apto legalmente, capaz; bueno, excelente. **to be a. to,** poder; ser capaz de; (know how) saber. **a.-bodied,** fuerte, fornido. **a.-bodied seaman,** marinero práctico, *m*
abloom *adv* en flor
ablution *n* ablución, *f*
ably *adv* hábilmente; competentemente
abnegation *n* abnegación, *f*
abnormal *a* anormal; irregular
abnormality *n* anormalidad, *f;* irregularidad, *f*
abnormally *adv* anormalmente; demasiado
aboard *adv* a bordo. *prep* a bordo de. **to go a.,** embarcarse, ir a bordo. **All a.!** ¡Viajeros a bordo!; (a train) ¡Viajeros al tren!
abode *n* morada, habitación, *f;* residencia, *f;* (stay) estancia, *f*
abolish *vt* abolir, suprimir, anular
abolition *n* abolición, supresión, *f;* anulación, *f*
abolitionism *n* abolicionismo, *m*
abolitionist *n* abolicionista, *mf*
abominable *a* abominable, aborrecible; repugnante, execrable; *inf* horrible
abominably *adv* abominablemente
abominate *vt* abominar, aborrecer, detestar
abomination *n* abominación, *f;* aborrecimiento, *m;* horror, *m*
aboriginal *a* aborigen; primitivo
aborigines *n pl* aborígenes, *m pl*
abort *vi* abortar, malparir; *fig* malograrse
abortion *n* aborto, *m; fig* fracaso, malogro, *m*
abortive *a* abortivo
abound *vi* abundar (en)
about *adv* (around) alrededor; (round about) a la redonda, en torno; (all over) por todas partes; (up and down) acá y acullá; por aquí, por ahí; en alguna parte; por aquí; (in circumference) en circunferencia; (almost) casi, aproximadamente; (by turns) por turnos, en rotación. *prep* alrededor de; en torno; por; (near to) cerca de; (on one's person) sobre; (on the subject of) sobre; (concerning) acerca de; (over) por, a causa de; en; (of) de; (with time by the clock) a eso de, sobre; (towards) hacia; (engaged in) ocupado en; (on the point of) a punto de. **a. here,** por aquí. **a. nothing,** por nada. **a. supper time,** hacia la hora de cenar. **a. three o'clock,** a eso de las tres. **A. turn!** ¡Media vuelta! (a la izquierda or a la derecha). **He wandered a. the streets,** Vagaba por las calles. **somewhere a.,** en alguna parte. **to be a. to,** estar para, estar a punto de. **to bring a.,** ocasionar. **to come a.,** suceder. **to know a.,** saber de. **to set a.,** empezar, iniciar; (a person) acometer. **What are you thinking a.?** ¿En qué piensas?
above *adv* arriba; en lo alto; encima; (superior) superior; (earlier) antes; (higher up on a page, etc.) más arriba; (in heaven) en el cielo. *prep* encima de; por encima de; sobre; (beyond) fuera de; fuera del alcance de; (superior to) superior a; (more than) más de; (too proud to) demasiado orgulloso para; (too good to) demasiado bueno para; (in addition to) además de, en adición a; (with degrees of temperature) sobre. *a* anterior; (with past participles) antes. **from a.,** desde arriba. **a. all,** sobre todo. **over and a.,** además de. **a. board,** *adv* abiertamente, con las cartas boca arriba. *a*

franco y abierto. **a. mentioned,** supradicho, susodicho, antes citado

abrasion *n* abrasión, *f;* rozadura, *f; geol* denudación, *f*

abrasive *a* abrasivo. *n* substancia abrasiva, *f,* abrasivo, *m*

abreast *adv* de frente, al lado uno de otro; *naut* por el través. **to keep a. of the times,** mantenerse al dia. **to ride six a.,** cabalgar a seis de frente. **a. with,** al nivel de, a la altura de

abridge *vt* abreviar; resumir, condensar, compendiar; disminuir; reducir

abridgment *n* abreviación, *f;* resumen, *m,* sinopsis, *f;* disminución, *f;* reducción, *f*

abroad *adv* (out) fuera, afuera; (gone out) salido; ausente; (everywhere) en todas partes; (in foreign lands) en el extranjero. **to go a.,** salir de casa, echarse a la calle; ir al extranjero; (of rumors, etc.) propagarse, rumorearse

abrogation *n* abrogación, anulación, *f*

abrupt *a* (precipitous) escarpado, precipitado, abrupto; (unexpected) repentino, inesperado; (of persons) brusco, descortés; (of style) seco

abruptly *adv* bruscamente; repentinamente

abruptness *n* precipitación, *f;* brusquedad, *f*

abscess *n* absceso, *m*

abscond *vi* evadirse; huir, escaparse; (with money) desfalcar

absence *n* ausencia, *f;* alejamiento, *m;* (of mind) abstracción, *f,* ensimismamiento, *m;* (lack) falta, *f.* **leave of a.,** permiso para ausentarse, *m; mil* licencia, *f,* permiso, *m*

absent *a* ausente; alejado (de); (in mind) abstraído, ensimismado, distraído. *vt* ausentarse; alejarse. **the a.,** los ausentes. **a.-mindedness,** ensimismamiento, *m,* abstracción, *f*

absentee *n* ausente, *mf*

absenteeism *n* absentismo, *m*

absently *adv* distraídamente

absinthe *n* ajenjo, *m*

absolute *a* absoluto; perfecto; puro; (unconditional) incondicional; (downright) categórico; completo; (true) verdadero; (unlimited) ilimitado. **the a.,** lo absoluto

absolutely *adv* absolutamente; enteramente, completamente; realmente, categóricamente

absolution *n* (*ecc law*) absolución, *f*

absolutism *n* absolutismo, despotismo, *m*

absolutist *n* absolutista, *mf*

absolve *vt* absolver; (free) exentar, eximir; librar; exculpar

absorb *vt* absorber; (drink) beber; (use) gastar; (of shocks) amortiguar; (*fig* digest) asimilar; (engross) ocupar (el pensamiento, etc.). **to be absorbed in,** *fig* enfrascarse en, engolfarse en, estar entregado a

absorbent *a* and *n* absorbente, *m.* **a. cotton,** algodón hidrófilo, *m*

absorbing *a* absorbente; *fig* sumamente interesante

absorption *n* absorción, *f;* (*fig* digestion) asimilación, *f;* (engrossment) enfrascamiento, *m,* preocupación, abstracción, *f*

abstain *vi* abstenerse (de); evitar

abstemious *a* abstemio, abstinente; sobrio; moderado

abstention *n* abstención, *f;* abstinencia, *f;* privación, *f*

abstinence *n* abstinencia, *f.* **day of a.,** día de ayuno, *m*

abstinent *a* abstinente; sobrio

abstract *a* abstracto. *n* extracto, resumen, *m;* abstracción, *f. vt* abstraer; separar; extraer; (précis) resumir; (steal) substraer. **in the a.,** en abstracto

abstracted *a* distraído, desatento, absorto, ensimismado

abstraction *n* abstracción, *f;* (of mind) preocupación, desatención, *f;* (stealing) substracción, *f*

abstruse *a* abstruso, ininteligible; obscuro; recóndito

absurd *a* absurdo, grotesco; ridículo, disparatado; cómico

absurdity *n* absurdidad, ridiculez, *f;* disparate, *m,* tontería, *f*

abundance *n* abundancia, copia, *f;* muchedumbre (de), multitud (de), *f;* riqueza, *f;* prosperidad, *f*

abundant *a* abundante, copioso; rico. **to be a. in,** abundar en

abundantly *adv* en abundancia, abundantemente

abuse *n* abuso, *m;* (bad language) insulto, *m,* injuria, *f. vt* (ill-use) maltratar; (misuse) abusar (de); (revile) insultar, injuriar; (deceive) engañar

abuser *n* abusador (-ra); injuriador (-ra); (defamer) denigrante, *mf*

abusive *a* abusivo; (scurrilous) insultante, injurioso, ofensivo

abusively *adv* insolentemente, ofensivamente

abut (on) *vi* lindar con; terminar en; estar adosado a

abysmal *a* abismal

abyss *n* abismo, *m,* sima, *f;* (hell) infierno, *m*

acacia *n* acacia, *f*

academic *a* académico

academician *n* académico, miembro de la Academia, *m*

academy *n* academia, *f;* conservatorio, *m;* (school) colegio, *m;* (of riding, etc.) escuela, *f.* **A. of Music,** Conservatorio de Música, *m*

accede *vi* (to a throne) ascender (al trono); tomar posesión (de); (join) hacerse miembro (de); aceptar; (agree) acceder (a), consentir (en), convenir (en)

accelerate *vt* acelerar; apresurar; (shorten) abreviar

acceleration *n* aceleración, *f*

accelerator *n* (of a vehicle) acelerador, *m*

accent *n* acento (all meanings), *m. vt* acentuar

accentuate *vt* acentuar; dar énfasis a

accept *vt* aceptar; (believe) creer; recibir; admitir; (welcome) acoger

acceptability *n* aceptabilidad, *f;* mérito, *m*

acceptable *a* aceptable; admisible; agradable; (welcome) bien acogido

acceptably *adv* aceptablemente; agradablemente

acceptance *n* aceptación, *f.* **a. speech** discurso aceptatorio; (approval) aprobación, *f;* (welcome) buena acogida, *f; com* aceptación, *f*

access *n* acceso, *m;* entrada, *f;* (way) camino, *m; med* ataque, *m;* (fit) transporte, *m;* (advance) avance, *m.* **easy of a.,** accesible; fácil de encontrar

accessibility *n* accesibilidad, *f*

accessible *a* accesible; asequible

accession *n* (to the throne, etc.) advenimiento, *m;* aumento, *m;* (acquisition) adición, *f;* adquisición, *f; law* accesión, *f*

accessory *a* accesorio; secundario; suplementario, adicional. *n* accesorio, *m; law* cómplice, *mf.* **a. before the fact,** instigador (-ra). **a. after the fact,** encubridor (-ra)

accident *n* accidente, *m;* (chance) casualidad, *f;* (mishap) contratiempo, *m.* **by a.,** por casualidad, accidentalmente. **a. insurance,** seguro contra accidentes, *m*

accidental *a* accidental, casual, fortuito. *n mus* accidente, *m*

accidentally *adv* accidentalmente; por casualidad; sin querer

acclaim *vt* aclamar; proclamar; vitorear, aplaudir

acclamation *n* aclamación, *f;* aplauso, vítor, *m*

acclimatization *n* aclimatación, *f*

acclimatize *vt* aclimatar

accolade *n* acolada, *f,* espaldarazo, *m*

accommodate *vt* acomodar; ajustar; adaptar; (reconcile) reconciliar; (provide) proveer, proporcionar; (oblige) complacer; (fit) poner, instalar; (lodge) hospedar; (lend) prestar; (hold) tener espacio para, contener; (give a seat to) dar un sitio a. **to a. oneself to,** adaptarse a

accommodating *a* acomodadizo; (obliging) servicial

accommodation *n* acomodación, *f;* ajuste, *m;* adaptación, *f;* (arrangement) arreglo, *m;* (reconciliation) reconciliación, *f;* (lodging) alojamiento, *m;* (aer naut) partición, *f;* (space, room or seat) sitio, *m;* (loan) préstamo, *m.* **We found the accommodations good in**

this hotel, Estuvimos muy bien en este hotel. **a. ladder,** escalera real, *f*

accompaniment *n* acompañamiento, *m*

accompanist *n* acompañante (-ta)

accompany *vt* acompañar

accompanying *a* anexo *n* acompañamiento, *m*

accomplice *n* cómplice, comparte, *mf*

accomplish *vt* llevar a cabo, efectuar; terminar; (fulfil) cumplir; perfeccionar; (achieve) conseguir, lograr

accomplished *a* consumado; perfecto; culto; (talented) talentoso

accomplishment *n* efectuación, *f*; realización, *f*, logro, *m*; (fulfilment) cumplimiento, *m*; (gift) prenda, *f*, talento, *m*; *pl* **accomplishments,** partes, dotes, *f pl*; conocimientos, *m pl*

accord *n* acuerdo, *m*; unión, *f*; consentimiento, *m*; concierto, *m*, concordia, *f*; voluntad, *f*. *vt* otorgar, conceder. *vi* estar de acuerdo (con); armonizar (con). **of one's own a.,** espontáneamente. **with one a.,** unánimemente

accordance *n* acuerdo, *m*, conformidad, *f*; arreglo, *m*. **in a. with,** de acuerdo con, según, con arreglo a

according *adv* según, conforme. **a. as,** conforme a, a medida que. **a. to,** según

accordingly *adv* en consecuencia, por consiguiente; pues

accordion *n* acordeón, *m*. **to a.-pleat,** *vt* plisar

accost *vt* abordar, acercarse a; dirigirse a, hablar

account *vt* (judge) considerar, creer, juzgar, tener por. *vi* (for) explicar; (understand) comprender; (be responsible) responder de, dar razón de; justificar

account *n* (bill) cuenta, *f*; factura, *f*; (narrative) narración, relación, *f*; (description) descripción, *f*; historia, *f*; versión, *f*; (list) enumeración, *f*; (reason) motivo, *m*, causa, *f*; (importance) importancia, *f*; (weight) peso, *m*; (news) noticias, *f pl*; (advantage) provecho, *m*, ventaja, *f*. **by all accounts,** según lo que se oye, según voz pública. **current a.,** cuenta corriente, *f*. **outstanding a.,** cuenta pendiente, *f*. **on a.,** a cuenta. **on a. of,** a causa de, por motivo de. **on no a.,** de ninguna manera. **on that a.,** por lo tanto. **to be of no a.,** ser insignificante; ser de poca importancia; *inf* ser la última mona. **to give an a.,** contar, hacer una relación (de). **to give an a. of oneself,** explicarse. **to keep a.,** llevar la cuenta. **to settle accounts,** ajustar cuentas. **to take into a.,** considerar. **to turn to a.,** sacar provecho de. **a. book,** libro de cuentas, *m*

accountability *n* responsabilidad, *f*

accountable *a* responsable

accountancy *n* contabilidad, *f*

accountant *n* contador, *m*. **chartered a.,** contador autorizado, *m*. **accountant's office,** contaduría, *f*

accouterment *n* atavío, *m*; equipo, *m*

accredit *vt* acreditar

accretion *n* acrecentamiento, aumento, *m*; *law* accesión, *f*

accrue *vi* resultar (de), proceder (de); originarse (en); aumentar

accumulate *vt* acumular; amontonar, atesorar. *vi* acumularse; aumentarse, crecer

accumulation *n* acumulación, *f*; amontonamiento, *m*

accumulative *a* acumulador; adquisitivo, ahorrador

accumulator *n elec* acumulador, *m*

accuracy *n* exactitud, corrección

accurate *a* exacto, correcto, fiel; (of persons) exacto, minucioso; (of apparatus) de precisión

accurately *adv* con exactitud, correctamente; con precisión

accursed *a* maldito.

accusation *n* acusación, *f*. **to lodge an a.,** querellarse ante el juez

accusatory *a* acusatorio

accuse *vt* acusar

accused *n law* acusado (-da)

accuser *n* acusador (-ra)

accustom *vt* acostumbrar (a), habituar (a)

accustomed *a* acostumbrado, usual; general; característico

ace *n* as, *m*; *fig* pelo, *m*. **to be within an ace of,** estar a dos dedos de

acerbity *n* acerbidad, *f*; *fig* aspereza, *f*; severidad, *f*; sequedad, *f*

acetate *n* acetato, *m*

acetic *a* acético

acetylene *n* acetileno, *m*. **a. lamp,** lámpara de acetileno, *f*

ache *n* dolor, *m*; pena, *f*. *vi* doler. **My head aches,** Me duele la cabeza, Tengo dolor de cabeza

achievable *a* alcanzable, asequible; factible

achieve *vt* conseguir, lograr; (reach) alcanzar; (obtain) obtener, ganar

achievement *n* logro, *m*, realización, *f*; obtención, *f*; (deed) hazaña, *f*; (work) obra, *f*; (success) éxito, *m*; (discovery) descubrimiento, *m*; (victory) victoria, *f*

aching *n* dolor, *m*; pena, angustia, *f*. *a* doliente; afligido

achromatic *a* acromático

achromic *a* acrómico

acid *a* and *n* ácido, *m*. **fatty a.,** ácido graso, *m*

acidify *vt* acidificar

acidity *n* acidez, *f*

acidosis *n med* acidismo, *m*

acidulous *a* acídulo

acknowledge *vt* reconocer; confesar; (reply to) contestar a; (appreciate) agradecer. **to a. receipt,** *com* acusar recibo

acknowledgment *n* reconocimiento, *m*; confesión, *f*; (appreciation) agradecimiento, *m*; (reward) recompensa, *f*; (of a letter) acuse de recibo, *m*

acme *n* cumbre, *f*; *fig* auge, apogeo, *m*

acne *n* acné, *m*

acolyte *n* acólito, monacillo (male) *m*, acólita, monacilla *f*, (female)

acorn *n* bellota, *f*. **a. cup,** capullo de bellota, *m*. **a.-shaped,** en forma de bellota, abellotado

acoustic *a* acústico

acoustics *n pl* acústica, *f*

acquaint *vt* dar a conocer, comunicar, informar (de), dar parte (de); familiarizar (con). **to be acquainted with,** conocer; saber. **to make oneself acquainted with,** familiarizarse con; entablar amistad con

acquaintance *n* conocimiento, *m*; (person) conocido (-da); *pl* **acquaintances,** amistades, *f pl*. **to make their a.,** conocer (a), llegar a conocer (a)

acquiesce *vi* asentir (en), consentir (a)

acquiescence *n* acquiescencia, *f*, consentimiento, *m*

acquiescent *a* conforme; resignado

acquire *vt* adquirir, obtener; (diseases, habits) contraer; ganar; (learn) aprender

Acquired Immune Deficiency Syndrome *n* el síndrome de Inmunodeficiencia Adquirida, *m*

acquirement *n* adquisición, *f*; (learning) conocimiento, *m*; (talent) talento, *m*

acquirer *n* adquisidor (-ra)

acquisition *n* adquisición, *f*

acquisitive *a* adquisitivo

acquit *vt* (of a debt) pagar; exonerar; *law* absolver; (a duty) cumplir. **to a. oneself well (badly),** portarse bien (mal); salir bien (mal)

acquittal *n* (of a debt) pago, *m*; *law* absolución, *f*; (of a duty) cumplimiento, *m*

acquittance *n* descargo, *m*; quitanza, *f*

acre *n* (measure) acre, *m*; *pl* **acres,** terrenos, campos, *m pl*

acreage *n* acres, *m pl*

acrid *a* acre

acrimonious *a* acrimonioso, áspero; mordaz, sarcástico

acrimony *n* acrimonia, acritud, *f*; sarcasmo, *m*

acrobat *n* acróbata, *mf*

acrobatic *a* acrobático

acrobatics *n pl* acrobacia, *f*

acronym *n* sigla, *f*

acropolis *n* acrópolis, *f*

across adv a través, de través, transversalmente; (on the other side) al otro lado; de una parte a otra; (of the arms, etc.) cruzados, m pl. prep a través de; al otro lado de; (upon) sobre; por. **He went a. the road,** Cruzó la calle. **to run a.,** correr por; tropezar con; dar con. **a. country,** a campo travieso. **a. the way,** en frente
acrostic n (poema) acróstico, m, a acróstico
act n acción, obra, f, hecho, m; acto, m; law ley, f; theat acto, m. **in the act,** en el acto. **in the act (of doing),** en acto de (hacer algo). **in the very act,** en flagrante. **the Acts of the Apostles,** los Actos de los Apóstoles. **act of God,** fuerza mayor, f. **act of indemnity,** bill de indemnidad, m
act vt (a play) representar, hacer; (a part) desempeñar, hacer (un papel); (pretend) simular, fingir. vi obrar, actuar; (behave) portarse, conducirse; (function) funcionar; producir su efecto; (feign) fingir; (as a profession) ser actor. **to act as,** hacer de; cumplir las funciones de. **to act as a second,** (in a duel) apadrinar. **to act for,** representar; ser el representante de. **to act upon,** obrar sobre; afectar; influir en
acting n (of a play) representación (de una comedia), f; (of an actor) interpretación (de un papel), f; (as a hobby) el hacer comedia; (dramatic art) arte dramática, f. a interino, suplente; comanditario. **He is a. captain,** Está de capitán. **a. partner,** socio (-ia) comanditario (-ia)
action n acción, f; función, f; operación, f; (movement) movimiento, m; (effect) efecto, m; influencia, f; law proceso, m; mil batalla, acción, f; lit acción, f. **in a.,** en actividad; en operación; mil en el campo de batalla. **man of a.,** hombre de acción, m. **to be killed in a.,** morir en el campo de batalla. **to bring an a. against,** pedir en juicio, entablar un pleito contra. **to put into a.,** hacer funcionar; introducir. **to take a.,** tomar medidas (para). **to take a. against,** prevenirse contra; law proceder contra
actionable a procesable, punible
active a activo; ágil; diligente; mil vivo; enérgico; gram activo. **to make a.,** activar, estimular
activity n actividad, f
actor n actor, m; (in comedy) comediante, m
actress n actriz, f; (in comedy) comedianta, f
actual a actual, existente; real, verdadero
actuality n realidad, f
actually adv en efecto, realmente, en realidad
actuary n actuario de seguros, m
actuate vt mover, animar, excitar
acumen n cacumen, m, agudeza, sagacidad, f
acute a agudo; (shrewd) perspicaz; (of a situation) crítico. **a. accent,** acento agudo, m. **a.-angled,** acutángulo
acutely adv agudamente; (deeply) profundamente
acuteness n agudeza, f; (shrewdness) perspicacia, penetración, f
ad n anuncio, m. See **advertisement**
adage n refrán, proverbio, decir, m
adagio n adagio, m
Adam n Adán, m. **Adam's apple,** nuez de la garganta, f
adamant a firme, duro, inexorable
adamantine a adamantino
adapt vt adaptar; ajustar, acomodar; aplicar; (a play, etc.) refundir, arreglar; mus arreglar
adaptability n adaptabilidad, f
adaptable a adaptable
adaptation n adaptación, f; (of a play, etc.) refundición, f; (mus etc.) arreglo, m
adapter n (of a play, etc.) refundidor (-ra); elec enchufe de reducción, m
add vt añadir; juntar; (up) sumar. **add insult to injury,** al mojado echarle agua, añadir a una ofensa otra mayor. **to add to,** añadir a; (increase) aumentar, acrecentar. **to add up,** sumar. **to add up to,** subir a; (mean) querer decir.
adder n víbora, serpiente, f

addict n adicto (-ta). **to a. oneself to,** dedicarse a, entregarse a
addicted a aficionado (a), amigo (de), dado (a); adicto (a)
addiction n afición, propensión, f; adicción, f
addition n añadidura, f; math adición, suma, f. **in a. (to),** además (de), también
additional a adicional
addled a huero, podrido; fig confuso
address n (on a letter) sobrescrito, m; (of a person) dirección, f, señas, f pl; (speech) discurso, m; (petition) memorial, m, petición, f; (dedication) dedicatoria, f; (invocation) invocación, f; (deportment) presencia, f; (tact) diplomacia, habilidad, f; pl **addresses,** corte, f. vt (a ball) golpear; (a letter) dirigir, poner el sobrescrito a; (words, prayers) dirigir (a); hablar, hacer un discurso. **to a. oneself to a task,** dedicarse a (or entregarse a or emprender) una tarea. **to deliver an a.,** pronunciar un discurso. **to pay one's addresses to,** cortejar, hacer la corte (a), galantear
addressee n destinatario (-ia)
adduce vt aducir, alegar; aportar
Aden Adén m
adenoids n pl amígdalas, f pl
adept a adepto, versado, consumado. n adepto, m
adequacy n adecuación, f; suficiencia, f; competencia, f
adequate a adecuado; proporcionado; suficiente; competente; a la altura (de)
adequately adv adecuadamente
adhere vi adherirse; pegarse; ser fiel (a); persistir (en)
adherence n fig adhesión, f
adherent n partidario (-ia)
adhesion n adherencia, f; (to a party, etc.) adhesión, f
adhesive a adhesivo; (sticky) pegajoso. **a. tape,** esparadrapo, m; elec cinta aisladora adherente, f
adipose a adiposo
adjacent a próximo, contiguo, adyacente, vecino
adjective n adjetivo, m
adjoin vt estar contiguo a, lindar con; juntar. vi colindar
adjoining a vecino, de al lado, adyacente; cercano
adjourn vt aplazar, diferir; (a meeting, etc.) suspender; levantar. vi retirarse. **The debate was adjourned,** Se suspendió el debate. **to a. a meeting,** levantar la sesión
adjournment n aplazamiento, m; (of a meeting) suspensión (de la sesión), f
adjudicate vt adjudicar; law declarar; juzgar. vi ejercer las funciones del juez; fallar, dictar sentencia
adjudication n adjudicación, f; law fallo, m, sentencia, f; (of bankruptcy) declaración (de quiebra), f; concesión, f, otorgamiento, m
adjudicator n adjudicador (-ra)
adjunct n atributo, m; accesorio, m; adjunto, m; gram adjunto, m
adjure vt conjurar; rogar encarecidamente
adjust vt ajustar; regular; arreglar; (correct) corregir; adaptar
adjustable a ajustable; regulable; desmontable; quita y pon
adjustment n ajuste, m; regulación, f; arreglo, m; (correction) corrección, f; adaptación, f; com prorrateo, m
adjutant n mil ayudante, m
administer vt administrar; (laws) aplicar; (blows, etc.) dar; (an office) ejercer; (govern) regir, gobernar; (provide) suministrar; (an oath) tomar; (justice) hacer; (the sacraments) administrar; (with to) contribuir a. **to a. an oath,** tomar juramento (a)
administration n administración, f; (government) gobierno, m; dirección, f; (of laws) aplicación, f; distribución, f
administrative a administrativo; gubernativo
administrator n administrador, m
administratrix n administradora, f
admirable a admirable
admirably adv admirablemente
admiral n almirante, m. **A. of the Fleet,** almirante supremo, m. **admiral's ship,** capitana, f

admiration n admiración, f
admire vt sentir admiración por; (love) amar; (like) gustar; (respect) respetar
admirer n admirador (-ra); (amateur) aficionado (-da), apasionado (-da); (partisan) satélite, m; (lover) enamorado, amante, m
admiring a admirativo, de admiración
admissible a admisible; aceptable; lícito, permitido
admission n admisión, f; recepción, f; entrada, f; confesión, f, reconocimiento, m. **No a.!** Entrada prohibida. **right of a.,** derecho de entrada, m. **A. free,** Entrada libre. **a. ticket,** entrada, f
admit vt admitir; recibir; dejar entrar; hacer entrar, introducir; (hold) contener; (concede) conceder; (acknowledge) reconocer, confesar. **to a. of,** permitir; sufrir
admittance n admisión, f; entrada, f. **No a.!** Prohibida la entrada
admittedly adv según opinión general; sin duda
admonish vt (advise) aconsejar; amonestar, advertir; (reprimand) reprender
admonition n amonestación, f; advertencia, f; admonición, f
admonitory a amonestador
ad nauseam adv hasta la saciedad
ado n (noise) ruido, m; (trouble) trabajo, m, dificultad, f; (fuss) barahúnda, f. **much ado about nothing,** mucho ruido y pocas nueces, nada entre dos platos. **without more ado,** sin más ni más
adolescence n adolescencia, f
adolescent a and n adolescente, mf
adopt vt adoptar
adopted a adoptivo
adoption n adopción, f; (choice) elección, f
adoptive a adoptivo
adorable a adorable
adoration n adoración, f. **A. of the Magi,** Adoración de los Reyes, f
adore vt adorar
adorer n adorador (-ra); amante, m
adoringly adv con adoración
adorn vt adornar, embellecer; (fig of persons) adornar con su presencia
adornment n adorno, m; ornamento, m; embellecimiento, m
adrenalin n adrenalina, f
Adriatic, the el (Mar) Adriático, m
adrift a and adv a merced de las olas; a la ventura. **to turn a.,** inf poner de patitas en la calle
adroit a hábil
adulate vt adular
adulation n adulación, f
adulatory a adulador
adult a and n adulto (-ta)
adult education n educación de los adultos, f
adulterate vt adulterar; falsificar; contaminar. a adulterado; falsificado; impuro
adulteration n adulteración, f; falsificación, f; impureza, f; contaminación, f
adulterer n adúltero, m
adulteress n adúltera, f
adulterous a adúltero
adultery n adulterio, m. **to commit a.,** cometer adulterio, adulterar
advance n avance, m; (progress) progreso, adelantamiento, m; (improvement) mejora, f; (of shares) alza, f; (of price) subida, f; (loan) préstamo, m; (in rank) ascenso, m; pl **advances,** (overtures) avances, m pl; (proposals) propuestas, f pl; (of love) requerimientos amorosos, m pl. **in a.,** de antemano, con anticipación, con tiempo, previamente; (of money) por adelantado. **a. guard,** mil avanzada, f. **a. payment,** anticipo, m, paga por adelantado, f
advance vt avanzar; (suggest) sugerir, proponer; (encourage) fomentar; (a person) ascender; (improve) mejorar; (of events, dates) adelantar; (of prices, stocks)

hacer subir; (money) anticipar; (of steps) tomar. vi avanzar; (progress) progresar; (in rank, studies, etc.) adelantar; (of prices) subir
advanced a avanzado; (developed) desarrollado; (mentally, of children) precoz; (course) superior. **a. research,** investigaciones superiores. **a. standing,** equivalencias, f pl. **a. views,** ideas avanzadas, f pl
advancement n adelantamiento, m; progreso, m; (encouragement) fomento, m; (in employment) promoción, f; prosperidad, f
advancing a que avanza; (of years) que pasan
advantage n ventaja, f; superioridad, f; (benefit) provecho, beneficio, m; interés, m; ocasión favorable, oportunidad, f; (tennis) ventaja, f. **to have the a. of,** tener la ventaja de. **to show to a.,** embellecer, realzar; aumentar la belleza (etc.) de. **to take a. of,** sacar ventaja de, aprovecharse de; (deceive) engañar. **to take a. of the slightest pretext,** asirse de un cabello
advantageous a ventajoso, provechoso. **to be a.,** ser de provecho
advent n advenimiento, m, llegada, f; ecc Adviento, m
adventitious a adventicio (all uses)
adventure n aventura, f; riesgo, m; (chance) casualidad, f; com especulación, f, vt aventurar, arriesgar. vi arriesgarse, osar
adventurer n aventurero, m; (one living by his wits) caballero de industria, m; (in commerce) especulador, m
adventuresome a de aventura
adventuress n aventurera, f
adventurous a aventurero; osado, audaz; (dangerous) peligroso, arriesgado
adverb n adverbio, m
adversary n adversario (-ia)
adverse a adverso; hostil (a); malo; desfavorable; (opposite) opuesto
adversity n adversidad, f
advertise vt anunciar. vi poner un anuncio; (oneself) llamar la atención
advertisement n anuncio, m; (poster) cartel, m; (to attract attention) reclamo, m. **to put an a. in the paper,** poner un anuncio en el periódico. **a. hoarding,** cartelera, f
advertiser n anunciante, mf
advertising n anuncios, m pl; publicidad, propaganda, f; medios publicitarios, m pl
advice n consejo, m; (warning) advertencia, amonestación, f; (news) noticia, f, aviso, m; com comunicación, f; (belief) parecer, m, opinión, f. **piece of a.,** consejo, m. **to follow the a. of,** seguir los consejos de. **to give a.,** dar consejos
advisability n conveniencia, f; prudencia, f
advisable a conveniente, aconsejable; prudente
advise vt aconsejar; (inform) avisar, informar
advised a avisado; premeditado. **ill-a.,** mal aconsejado; imprudente. **well-a.,** bien aconsejado; prudente
adviser n consejero (-ra)
advisory a asesor, consultivo, consultativo
advocacy n defensa, f; apología, f; abogacía, intercesión, f
advocate n law abogado (-da); defensor (-ra); (champion) campeón, m. vt abogar, defender; sostener, apoyar; recomendar
adze n azuela, f
Aegean, the el (Mar) Egeo, m
aegis n égida, f; protección, f
aerated a aerado; (of lemonade, etc.) gaseoso. **a. waters,** aguas gaseosas, f pl
aeration n aeración, f
aerial a aéreo, de aire; etéreo; fantástico. n (radio) antena, f. **indoor a.,** antena interior, f
aerobics n aerobismo m
aerodynamics n aerodinámica, f
aeronaut n aeronauta, mf
aeronautical a aeronáutico
aeronautics n aeronáutica, f
afar adv a lo lejos, en la distancia. **from a.,** desde lejos

affability *n* afabilidad, condescendencia, urbanidad, *f*

affable *a* afable, condescendiente

affably *adv* afablemente

affair *n* asunto, *m*, cosa, *f*; cuestión, *f*; (business) negocio, *m*; (*fam* applied to a machine, carriage, etc.) artefacto, *m*; (of the heart) amorío, *m*. **a. of honour,** lance de honor, *m*

affect *vt* afectar; influir; *med* atacar; (move) impresionar, conmover; enternecer; (harm) perjudicar; (frequent) frecuentar; (like) gustar de; (love) amar; (wear) vestir; (use) gastar, usar; (feign) aparentar; (boast) hacer alarde de

affectation *n* afectación, *f*

affected *a* afectado; influido; *med* atacado; (moved) conmovido, impresionado; enternecido; (inclined) dispuesto, inclinado; (artificial) artificioso; amanerado, afectado; (of style) rebuscado, artificial

affecting *a* conmovedor, emocionante

affection *n* afecto, cariño, *m*; amor, *m*; apego, *m*; simpatía, *f*; (emotion) emoción, *f*, sentimiento, *m*; *med* afección, enfermedad, *f*

affectionate *a* afectuoso, cariñoso; mimoso; (tender) tierno; expresivo

affectionately *adv* afectuosamente. **Yours a.,** tu cariñoso . . . , tu . . . , que te quiere

affective *a* afectivo

affidavit *n* declaración jurada, declaración jurídica *f*, atestiguación, *f*

affiliate *vt* afiliar; adoptar; *law* imputar; *law* legitimar

affiliation *n* afiliación, *f*; adopción, *f*; legitimación de un hijo, *f*

affinity *n* afinidad, *f*

affirm *vt* afirmar, aseverar, declarar; confirmar. *vi law* declarar ante un juez

affirmation *n* afirmación, aserción, *f*; confirmación, *f*; *law* declaración, deposición, *f*

affirmative *a* afirmativo. *n* afirmativa, *f*

affix *vt* fijar; pegar; añadir; (seal, one's signature) poner. *n gram* afijo, *m*

afflict *vt* afligir, atormentar, aquejar

affliction *n* aflicción, *f*; tribulación, pesadumbre, *f*; calamidad, *f*; miseria, *f*; (ailment) achaque, *m*

affluence *n* afluencia, *f*; abundancia, *f*; riqueza, *f*; opulencia, *f*

affluent *a* abundante; rico; opulento

afflux *n* afluencia, *f*; *med* aflujo, *m*

afford *vt* dar, proporcionar; producir; ofrecer; (bear) soportar; poder con; (financially) tener medios para; permitirse el lujo de; (be able) poder. **I could not a. to pay so much,** No puedo (podía) pagar tanto

afforest *vt* convertir en bosque

afforestation *n* conversión en bosque, *f*; plantación de un bosque, *f*

affray *n* riña, refriega, *f*

affront *n* afrenta, *f*, insulto, agravio, *m*. *vt* insultar, ultrajar, afrentar; (offend) ofender

Afghan *a* and *n* afgano (-na)

Afghanistan Afganistán, *m*

afield *adv* en el campo; lejos. **to go far a.,** ir muy lejos

afire *adv* en fuego, en llamas; *fig* ardiendo

aflame *adv* en llamas; *fig* encendido

afloat *adv* a flote; *naut* a bordo; (solvent) solvente; en circulación; (floating) flotante; (swamped) inundado; (in full swing) en marcha, en movimiento

afoot *adv* a pie; en marcha, en movimiento; en preparación. **to set a.,** iniciar, poner en marcha

aforementioned *a* antedicho, ya mencionado

aforesaid *a* consabido, dicho; susodicho

afraid *a* espantado; temeroso, miedoso. **I'm a. that . . . ,** Me temo que. . . . **to be a.,** tener miedo. **to make a.,** dar miedo (a)

afresh *adv* de nuevo, otra vez

African *a* and *n* africano (-na)

aft *adv* en popa; a popa. **fore and aft,** de proa a popa

after *prep* (of place) detrás de; (of time) después de; (behind) en pos de; (following) tras; (in spite of) a pesar de; (in consequence of) después de, a consecuencia de; (in accordance with) según; (in the style of) al estilo de, en imitación de. *adv* (later) después, más tarde; (subsequently) después (que); (when) cuando. *a* futuro, venidero. **day a. day,** día tras día. **on the day a.,** al día siguiente. **soon a.,** poco después. **to look a.,** cuidar de. **to go a.,** ir a buscar; seguir. **the day a. tomorrow,** pasado mañana. **What are you a.?** ¿Qué buscas? **a. all,** después de todo. **a. the manner of,** a la moda de, según la moda de; al estilo de. **a.-dinner conversation,** conversación de sobremesa, *f*. **a. glow,** resplandor crepuscular, reflejo del sol poniente en el cielo, *m*. **a. life,** vida futura, *f*. **a. pains,** dolores de sobreparto, *m pl*. **a. taste,** dejo, resabio, *m*

afterbirth *n* placenta, *f*

aftermath *n* consecuencias, *f pl*, resultado, *m*

afternoon *n* tarde, *f*. **Good a.!** ¡Buenas tardes! **a. nap,** siesta, *f*. **a. tea,** el té de las cinco

afterthought *n* reflexión tardía, *f*; segunda intención, *f*. **to have an a.,** pensar en segundo lugar

afterwards *adv* después; más tarde

again *adv* (once more) otra vez, de neuvo; por segunda vez, dos veces; (on the other hand) por otra parte; (moreover) además; (likewise) también; (returned) de vuelta. Sometimes translated by prefix **re** in verbs. **as much a.,** otro tanto. **never a.,** nunca más. **not a.,** no más. **now and a.,** de vez en cuando. **to do a.,** volver a hacer, hacer de nuevo. **a. and a.,** repetidas veces

against *prep* (facing) enfrente de; contra; (in preparation for) para; (contrary to) contrario a; (opposed to) opuesto a; (near) cerca de. **to be a.,** oponer; estar enfrente de. **a. the grain,** a contrapelo

agate *n* ágata, *f*; heliotropo, *m*

age *n* edad, *f*; (generation) generación, *f*; (epoch) siglo, período, *m*; época, *f*; (old age) vejez, *f*; (majority) mayoría de edad, *f*, vi envejecer. **at any age,** a cualquier edad. **the golden age,** la edad de oro; (in literature, etc.) el siglo de oro. **from age to age,** por los siglos de los siglos. **to be of age,** ser mayor de edad. **to be under age,** ser menor de edad. **to come of age,** llegar a la mayoría de edad. **She is six years of age,** Ella tiene seis años. **age-old,** secular

aged *a* de la edad de; (old) anciano, viejo. **a girl a. four,** una niña de cuatro años

ageless *a* siempre joven; eterno

agency *n* órgano, *m*, fuerza, *f*; acción, *f*; influencia, *f*; intervención, *f*; mediación, *f*; *com* agencia, *f*. **through the a. of,** por la mediación (or influencia) de

agenda *n* agenda, *f*

agent *n* agente, *m*; *com* representante, *mf*; *law* apoderado (-da). **business a.,** agente de negocios, *m*

agglomerate *vt* and *vi* aglomerar(se)

agglomeration *n* aglomeración, *f*

agglutinate *vt* and *vi* aglutinar(se)

aggrandize *vt* engrandecer

aggrandizement *n* engrandecimiento, *m*

aggravate *vt* agravar, hacer peor; intensificar; (annoy) irritar, exasperar

aggravating *a* agravante, agravador; (tiresome) molesto; (annoying) irritante. **a. circumstance,** circunstancia agravante, *f*

aggravation *n* agravación, *f*, intensificación, *f*; (annoyance) irritación, *f*

aggregate *a* total. *n* agregado, conjunto, *m*. **in the a.,** en conjunto

aggression *n* agresión, *f*

aggressive *a* agresivo

aggressiveness *n* carácter agresivo, *m*, belicosidad, *f*

aggressor *n* and *n* agresor (-ra)

aggrieved *a* afligido; ofendido; lastimero

aghast *a* horrorizado, espantado; (amazed) estupefacto

agile *a* ágil; ligero; vivo

agility *n* agilidad, *f*; ligereza, *f*

agitate *vt* agitar; excitar; inquietar, perturbar; discutir. **to a. for,** luchar por; excitar la opinión pública en favor de

agitating *a* agitador
agitation *n* agitación, *f*; perturbación, *f*; discusión, *f*
agitator *n* agitador (-ra); (apparatus) agitador, *m*
aglow *a* and *adv* brillante, fulgente; encendido
agnostic *a* and *n* agnóstico (-ca)
agnosticism *n* agnosticismo, *m*
ago *adv* hace. **a short while ago,** hace poco. **How long ago?** ¿Cuánto tiempo hace? **long ago,** hace mucho. **many years ago,** hace muchos años. **I last saw him ten years ago,** La última vez que le vi fue hace diez años
agog *a* agitado; ansioso; excitado; impaciente; curioso. *adv* con agitación; con ansia; con curiosidad
agonize *vt* atormentar. *vi* sufrir intensamente; retorcerse de dolor
agonizing *a* (of pain) intenso, atormentador
agonizingly *adv* dolorosamente
agony *n* agonía, *f*; angustia, *f*; paroxismo, *m*. **a. column,** columna de los suspiros, *f*
agrarian *a* agrario
agree *vi* estar de acuerdo. **Do you a. or disagree?** ¿Coincides o discrepas?; convenir (en); acordar; ponerse de acuerdo, entenderse; (suit) sentar bien, probar; (consent) consentir (en); *gram* concordar, (get on well) llevarse bien; (correspond) estar conforme (con). **to a. to,** convenir en, consentir en. **to a. with,** estar de acuerdo con, apoyar; dar la razón a; (suit) sentar bien; *gram* concordar
agreeable *a* agradable; afable, amable; (pleasant) ameno, grato; conforme; dispuesto a (hacer algo); conveniente
agreeableness *n* (of persons) afabilidad, amabilidad, *f*; amenidad, *f*; deleite, *m*; conformidad, *f*
agreeably *adv* agradablemente; de acuerdo (con), conforme (a)
agreed *a* convenido, acordado; (approved) aprobado. *interj* ¡convenido! ¡de acuerdo!
agreement *n* acuerdo, *m*; pacto, *m*; acomodamiento, concierto, *m*; contrato, *m*; com convenio, *m*; conformidad, *f*; consentimiento, *m*; *gram* concordancia, *f*. **in a.,** conforme. **in a. with,** de acuerdo con; según. **to reach an a.,** ponerse de acuerdo
agricultural *a* agrícola. **a. engineer,** ingeniero agrónomo, *m*. **a. laborer,** labriego, *m*. **a. show,** exposición agrícola, *f*
agriculturalist *n* agrícola, *mf*
agriculture *n* agricultura, *f*
agronomist *n* agrónomo, *m*
agronomy *n* agronomía, *f*
aground *adv* *naut* varado, encallado. **running a.,** varada, *f*. **to run a.,** varar
ague *n* fiebre intermitente, *f*; *fig* escalofrío, *m*
ah! *interj* ¡ah! ¡ay!
aha! *interj* ¡ajá!
ahead *adv* delante; enfrente; al frente (de); a la cabeza (de); adelante; hacia delante; *naut* por la proa. **Go a.!** ¡Adelante! **It is straight a.,** Está directamente enfrente. **to go straight a.,** ir hacia delante; seguir (haciendo algo)
ahoy! *interj* ¡ah del barco!
aid *n* ayuda, *f*; socorro, auxilio, *m*; subsidio, *m*, *vt* ayudar; socorrer, auxiliar. **in aid of,** pro, en beneficio de. **first aid,** primera cura, *f*. **first aid post,** puesto de socorro, *m*. **to come or go to the aid of,** acudir en defensa de
aide-de-camp *n* edecán, *m*
AIDS *n* el SIDA, *m*
ail *vt* afligir, doler; pasar. *vi* estar indispuesto (or enfermo). **What ails you?** *inf* ¿Qué te pasa?
ailing *a* enfermizo, enclenque, achacoso
ailment *n* enfermedad, *f*, achaque, *m*
aim *n* (of firearms) puntería, *f*; (mark) blanco, *m*; *fig* objeto, fin, *m*; *fig* intención, *f*, propósito, *m*, *vt* (a gun) apuntar; dirigir; (throw) lanzar; (a blow) asestar. *vi* apuntar (a); (a remark at) decir por; aspirar (a); intentar, proponerse. **Is your remark aimed at me?** ¿Lo

dices por mí? **to aim high,** apuntar alto; *inf* picar alto. **to miss one's aim,** errar el tiro. **to take aim,** apuntar. **with the aim of,** con objeto de, a fin de
aimless *a* **aimlessly,** *adv* sin objeto, a la ventura
air *n* aire, *m*, (all meanings). **by air,** en avión; (of mail) por avión; (of goods) por vía aérea. **in the air,** al aire; al aire libre; (as though flying) en volandas. **in the open air,** al aire libre, al fresco, a la intemperie. **to be on the air,** *rad* hablar por radio. **to give oneself airs,** darse tono, tener humos. **to take the air,** tomar el fresco; despegar. **air balloon,** globo aerostático, *m*; (toy) globo, *m*. **air-base,** base aérea, *f*. **air-bed,** colchón de viento, *m*. **air-borne (to become),** levantar el vuelo, despegar. **air-brake,** *mech* freno neumático, *m*. **air-chamber,** cámara de aire, *f*. **air chief marshal,** general del ejército del aire, *m*. **air-cock,** válvula de escape de aire, *f*. **air commodore,** general de brigada de aviación, *m*. **air conditioning,** purificación de aire, *f*. **air-cooled,** enfriado por aire. **air crash,** accidente de aviación, *m*. **air current,** corriente de aire, *f*. **air-cushion,** almohadilla neumática, *f*. **air-field,** campo de aviación, *m*. **air fleet,** flotilla aérea, *f*. **air force,** fuerza aérea, flota aérea, *f*. **air-gun,** escopeta de viento, *f*. **air-hole,** respiradero, *m*. **air-hostess,** azafata, *f*. **air-lift,** puente aéreo, *m*. **air-liner,** avión de pasajeros, *m*. **airline** linea aérea, aerolínea, *f*. **airmail,** correo aéreo, *m*. **by airmail,** por avión. **air-pocket,** bolsa (or vacío, *m*) de aire, *f*. **air pollution** contaminación atmosférica, *f*. **air pump,** bomba neumática, *f*. **air-raid** bombardeo aéreo, *m*. **air-raid shelter,** refugio antiaéreo, *m*. **air-raid warning,** alarma aérea, *f*. **air-route,** vía aérea, *f*. **air-screw,** hélice de avión, *f*. **air-shaft,** respiradero de mina, *m*. **air shuttle,** puente aéreo, *m*. **air squadron,** escuadrilla aérea, *f*. **air stream,** chorro de aire, *m*. **air taxi,** avión taxi, *m*. **air-tight,** herméticamente cerrado. **air valve,** válvula de aire, *f*. **air vice-marshal,** general de división de aviación, *m*, *vt* airear, orear; secar al aire; ventilar; *fig* sacar a lucir, emitir; *fig* ostentar
aircraft *n* aparato, avión, *m*. **a. barrage,** cortina de fuego de artillería, *f*. **a.-carrier,** porta-aviones, *m*. **factory,** fábrica de aeroplanos, *f*
airily *adv* ligeramente, sin preocuparse; alegremente
airiness *n* airosidad, *f*; ventilación, *f*; situación airosa, *f*; (lightness) ligereza, *f*; alegría, *f*; frivolidad, *f*
airing *n* aireación, *f*; ventilación, *f*; secamiento, *m*; (walk) vuelta, *f*, paseo, *m*. **to take an a.,** dar una vuelta
airless *a* sin aire; falto de ventilación; sofocante
airman *n* aviador, *m*
airplane *n* aeroplano, avión, *m*. **jet-propelled a.,** aeroplano de reacción, *m*. **model a.,** aeroplano en miniatura, *m*
airport *n* aeropuerto, *m*
airship *n* aeronave, nave aérea, *f*
airsick *a* mareado en el aire, mareado
airway *n* vía aérea, *f*
airwoman *n* aviadora, *f*
airy *a* aéreo; (breezy) airoso; ligero; vaporoso; alegre; (vain) vano; (flippant) frívolo
aisle *n* nave lateral, ala, *f*
ajar *a* entreabierto, entornado. **to leave a.,** dejar entreabierto, entornar
akimbo *adv* en jarras. **with arms a.,** con los brazos en jarras
akin *a* consanguíneo, emparentado; análogo, relacionado; semejante
alabaster *n* alabastro, *m*, *a* alabastrino
alacrity *n* alacridad, *f*
alarm *n* alarma, *f*, toque de alarma, *m*; (tocsin) rebato, *m*; sobresalto, *m*, alarma, *f*, *vt* alarmar; *mil* dar la señal de alarma (a); asustar. **to give the a.,** dar la alarma. **a. bell,** timbre de alarma, *m*. **a. clock,** despertador, *m*. **a. signal,** señal de alarma, *f*
alarming *a* alarmante

alarmingly *adv* de un modo alarmante; espantosamente
alarmist *n* alarmista, *mf*
alas! *interj* ¡ay!
alb *n* alba, *f*
Albanian *a* and *n* albanés (-esa); (language) albanés, *m*
albatross *n* albatros, *m*
albeit *conjunc* aunque, si bien; sin embargo
albinism *n* albinismo, *m*
albino *a* albino
album *n* álbum, *m*
albumin *n* albúmina, *f*
alchemist *n* alquimista, *m*
alchemy *n* alquimia, *f*
alcohol *n* alcohol, *m*. **industrial a.**, alcohol desnaturalizado, *m*. **wood a.**, alcohol metílico, alcohol de madera, *m*
alcoholic *a* alcohólico
alcoholism *n* alcoholismo, *m*
alcoholize *vt* alcoholizar
alcove *n* alcoba, *f*; nicho, *m*
alder *n* (tree and wood) aliso, *m*
alderman *n* concejal, *m*
ale *n* cerveza, *f*. **ale-house**, cervecería, *f*
alert *a* alerto; vigilante; despierto; vivo. *n* sirena, *f*. **to be on the a.**, estar sobre aviso; estar vigilante
alertly *adv* alertamente
alertness *n* vigilancia, *f*; viveza, *f*; prontitud, *f*
Alexandria Alejandría, *f*
alga *n* alga, *f*
algebra *n* álgebra, *f*
algebraic *a* algebraico
Algeria Argelia, *f*
Algerian *a* and *n* argelino (-na)
Algiers Argel, *m*
alias *adv* alias, por otro nombre. *n* nombre falso, seudónimo, *m*
alibi *n* *law* coartada, *f*. **to prove an a.**, probar la coartada
alien *a* ajeno; (foreign) extranjero; extraño; contrario. *n* extranjero (-ra). **a. to**, ajeno a; repugnante a. **Aliens Department**, Sección de Extranjeros, *f*
alienable *a* enajenable
alienate *vt* alejar, hacer indiferente; (property) enajenar, traspasar
alienation *n* desvío, *m*; enajenación, *f*; traspaso, *m*; enajenación mental, *f*
alight *vi* apearse (de), bajar (de); desmontar (de); (of birds, etc.) posarse (sobre)
alight *a* encendido, iluminado; en llamas
align *vt* alinear
alignment *n* alineación, *f*
alike *a* semejante; igual. *adv* del mismo modo; igualmente
alimentary *a* nutritivo; alimenticio. **a. canal**, tubo digestivo, *m*
alimentation *n* alimentación, *f*
alimony *n* *law* alimentos, *m pl*, pensión alimenticia, *f*
alive *a* viviente; vivo; del mundo; (busy) animado, concurrido; (aware) sensible; (alert) lleno de vida, enérgico, despierto. **He is still a.**, Aún vive. **He is the best man a.**, Es el mejor hombre que existe, Es el mejor hombre del mundo. **half-a.**, semivivo. **while a.**, en vida. **a. to**, consciente de, sensible de. **a. with**, plagado de, lleno de
alkali *n* álcali, *m*
alkaline *a* alcalino
alkaloid *n* alcaloide, *m*
all *a* todo, *m*; toda, *f*; todos, *m pl*; todas, *f pl*; (in games) iguales. *adv* enteramente, completamente; del todo; absolutamente. **after all**, después de todo; sin embargo. **at all**, nada; de ninguna manera; en absoluto. **fifteen all**, (tennis) quince iguales. **for good and all**, para siempre. **if that's all**, si no es más que eso. **in all**, en conjunto. **It is all one to me**, Me da igual. **not at all**, de ningún modo, nada de eso; nada; (never) jamás;

(as a polite formula) No hay de qué. **once for all**, una vez por todas; por última vez. **That is all**, Eso es todo. **all along**, (of time) siempre, todo el tiempo; (of place) a lo largo de, de un extremo a otro de. **all but**, (almost) casi, por poco; (except) todo menos. **all joking aside**, fuera de burla. **all of them**, todos ellos, *m pl*; todas ellas, *f pl*. **All right!** ¡Bien! ¡Está bien! ¡Entendido! **all that**, todo eso; (as much as) cuanto. **all that which**, todo lo que. **all those who**, todos los que, *m pl*; todas las que, *f pl*. **all the more**, cuanto más. **all the same**, sin embargo, a pesar de todo. **all the worse**, tanto peor
all *n* todo, *m*; todos, *m pl*; todas, *f pl*; (everyone, all men) todo el mundo. **to lose one's all**, perder todo lo que se tiene. **All is lost**, Todo se ha perdido. **all told**, en conjunto
all (in compounds) **all-absorbing**, que todo lo absorbe; sumamente interesante. **all-bountiful**, de suma bondad. **all-conquering**, invicto. **all-consuming**, que todo lo consume; irresistible; ardiente. **all-enduring**, resignado a todo. **All Fools' Day**, Día de los Inocentes, *m*, (December 28). **all-fours**, a cuatro patas; a gatas. **to go on all fours**, andar a gatas. **All hail!** ¡Salud! ¡Bienvenido! **all-important**, sumamente importante. **all-in insurance**, seguro contra todo riesgo, *m*. **all-in wrestling**, lucha libre, *f*. **all-loving**, de un amor infinito. **all-merciful**, de una compasión infinita, sumamente misericordioso. **all-powerful**, omnipotente, todo poderoso. **all-round**, completo, cabal; universal. **an all-round athlete**, un atleta completo. **All Souls' Day**, Día de las Ánimas, Día de los difuntos, *m*. **all-wise**, omniscio
Allah *n* Alá, *m*
allay *vt* calmar; (relieve) aliviar; apaciguar
allaying *n* alivio, *m*; apaciguamiento, *m*
allegation *n* alegación, *f*
allege *vt* afirmar, declarar; alegar
allegiance *n* lealtad, *f*; fidelidad, *f*; obediencia, *f*
allegorical *a* alegórico
allegory *n* alegoría, *f*
alleluia *n* aleluya, *mf*
allergic *a* alérgico
allergist *n* alergólogo, *m*
allergy *n* alergia, *f*
alleviate *vt* aliviar
alleviation *n* alivio, *m*; mitigación, *f*
alley *n* callejuela, *f*, callejón, *m*; avenida, *f*; (skittle a.) pista de bolos, *f*. **a.-way**, *naut* pasadizo, *m*
alliance *n* alianza, *f*; parentesco, *m*
allied *a* aliado; allegado
alligator *n* caimán, *m*. **a. pear**, avocado, *m*
alliteration *n* aliteración, *f*
allocate *vt* asignar, destinar; distribuir, repartir
allocation *n* asignación, *f*; distribución, *f*, repartimiento, *m*
allot *vt* repartir; asignar; destinar
allotment *n* repartimiento, *m*, distribución, *f*; porción, *f*; lote, *m*; parcela de tierra, huerta, *f*
allow *vt* permitir; autorizar; dejar; tolerar, sufrir; (provide) dar; conceder, otorgar; (acknowledge) admitir; confesar; (discount) descontar; (a pension) hacer; deducir. **to a. for**, tener en cuenta; ser indulgente con; deducir; dejar (espacio, etc.) para
allowable *a* admisible, permisible; lícito, legítimo
allowance *n* ración, *f*; (discount) descuento, *m*; pensión, *f*; concesión, *f*; excusa, *f*; (subsidy) subsidio, *m*; (bonus) abono, *m*; (monthly) mesada, *f*. **to make a. for**, tener presente; hacer excusas para, ser indulgente con
alloy *n* aleación, *f*; liga, *f*; mezcla, *f*. *vt* alear, ligar; mezclar
allspice *n* guindilla de Indias, *f*
all-star game *n* juego de estrellas, *m*
allude *vi* aludir (a), referirse (a)
allure *vt* convidar, provocar; atraer; seducir, fascinar
allurement *n* (snare) añagaza, *f*; atracción, *f*; tentación, *f*, seducción, *f*

alluring *a* atractivo, seductor, tentador; (promising) halagüeño

allusion *n* alusión, referencia, *f*; insinuación, *f*

allusive *a* alusivo

ally *n* aliado (-da), allegado (-da); asociado (-da); (state) aliado, *m*. *vt* unir. **to become allies,** aliarse

almanac *n* almanaque, *m*

almighty *a* omnipotente

almond *n* almendra, *f*; (tree) almendro, *m*. **bitter a.,** almendra amarga, *f*. **green a.,** almendruco, *m*. **milk of almonds,** horchata de almendras, *f*; (for the hands) loción de almendras, *f*. **sugar a.,** almendra garapiñada, *f*. **a.-eyed,** con, or de, ojos rasgados. **a. paste,** pasta de almendras, *f*. **a.-shaped,** en forma de almendra, almendrado

almost *adv* casi; por poco

alms *n* limosna, *f*. **to ask a.,** pedir limosna, mendigar. **to give a.,** dar limosna. **a.-box,** cepillo de limosna, *m*

almsgiving *n* caridad, *f*

aloe *n* áloe, *m*; *pl* **aloes,** *med* acíbar, *m*

aloft *adv* arriba, en alto

alone *a* solo; solitario. *adv* a solas, sin compañía; solamente; únicamente. **to leave a.,** dejar solo; dejar en paz

along *adv* adelante; a lo largo; todo el tiempo. *prep* a lo largo de; por; al lado (de); en compañía (de). **Come a.!** ¡Ven! **all a.,** todo el tiempo, desde el principio; a lo largo de. **a. with,** junto con; en compañía de

alongside *adv* al lado, *naut* al costado. *prep* junto a, al lado de; *naut* al costado de. **to bring a.,** *naut* abarloar. **to come a.,** *naut* acostarse

aloof *adv* a distancia; lejos. *a* altanero, esquivo; reservado. **to keep a.,** mantenerse alejado

aloofness *n* alejamiento, *m*; esquivez, *f*; reserva, *f*

aloud *adv* en alta voz, alto

alpaca *n* alpaca, *f*

alphabet *n* alfabeto, *m*; abecedario, *m*

alphabetical *a* alfabético

Alpine *a* alpestre, alpino

Alps, the los Alpes, *m*

already *adv* ya; previamente

Alsace Alsacia, *f*

Alsatian *a* and *n* alsaciano (-na†). **A. dog,** perro policía, perro pastor alemán, perro lobo, *m*

also *adv* también, igualmente, además

altar *n* altar, *m*. **high a.,** altar mayor, *m*. **to lead a woman to the a.,** llevar a una mujer a la iglesia. **a.-cloth,** mantel del altar, *m*. **a.-piece,** retablo, *m*. **a.-rail,** mesa del altar, *f*

altar boy *n* acólito, monaguillo, *m*

altar girl *n* acólita, monaguilla, *f*

altar server *n* acólito, monaguillo, *m* (male), acólita, monaguilla, *f* (female)

alter *vt* cambiar; alterar; modificar; corregir; transformar; (clothes) arreglar. *vi* cambiar

alterable *a* alterable

alteration *n* cambio, *m*, alteración, *f*; modificación, *f*; corrección, *f*; innovación, *f*; (to buildings, etc.) reforma, *f*; renovación, *f*; arreglo, *m*

altercation *n* altercación, *f*

alternate *a* alternativo; (bot and of rhymes) alterno. *vt* and *vi* alternar

alternately *adv* alternativamente; por turno

alternating *a* alternador. **a. current,** *elec* corriente alterna, *f*

alternation *n* alternación, *f*; (of time) transcurso, *m*; turno, *m*

alternative *n* alternativa, *f*, *a* alternativo, alterno. **to have no a. but,** no poder menos de

alternatively *adv* alternativamente

alternator *n* *elec* alternador, *m*

although *conjunc* aunque, bien que; si bien; no obstante, a pesar de

altimeter *n* *aer* altímetro, *m*

altitude *n* altitud, elevación, *f*; altura, *f*

alto *n* (voice) contralto, *m*; (singer) contralto, *mf*; viola, *f*

altogether *adv* completamente; del todo; en conjunto

alto-relievo *n* alto relieve, *m*

altruism *n* altruísmo, *m*

altruist *n* altruista, *mf*

aluminum *n* aluminio, *m*

aluminum foil *n* hoja de aluminio, *f*

always *adv* siempre

amalgam *n* amalgama, *f*; mezcla, *f*

amalgamate *vt* amalgamar; combinar, unir. *vi* amalgamarse; combinarse, unirse

amalgamation *n* amalgamación, *f*; combinación, *f*; mezcla, *f*

amanuensis *n* amanuense, *mf*; secretario (-ia)

amass *vt* acumular, amontonar

amateur *a* and *n* aficionado (-da), (sports) no profesional. **a. theatricals,** función de aficionados, *f*

amateurish *a* no profesional; de aficionado; superficial; (clumsy) torpe

amatory *a* amatorio

amaze *vt* asombrar, sorprender; pasmar; confundir

amazed *a* asombrado; sorprendido; admirado; asustado

amazement *n* asombro, pasmo, *m*; sorpresa, *f*; (wonderment) admiración, *f*; estupor, *m*

amazing *a* asombroso, pasmoso; sorprendente

amazingly *adv* asombrosamente

Amazon *n* amazona, *f*

Amazon River, the el (Río de las) Amazonas, *m*

ambassador *n* embajador, *m*

ambassadress *n* embajadora, *f*

amber *n* ámbar, *m*, *a* ambarino

ambergris *n* ámbar gris, *m*

ambidextrous *a* ambidextro

ambiguity *n* ambigüedad, *f*

ambiguous *a* ambiguo, equivoco

ambition *n* ambición, *f*

ambitious *a* ambicioso. **to be a. to,** ambicionar

amble *n* (of a horse) paso de andadura, *m*; paso lento, *m*. *vi* (of a horse) andar a paso de andadura; andar lentamente

ambulance *n* ambulancia, *f*. **a. corps,** cuerpo de sanidad, *m*. **a. man,** sanitario, *m*

ambulatory *n* paseo, *m*; claustro, *m*, *a* ambulante

ambush *n* acecho, *m*, aschanza, *f*; *mil* emboscada, *f*. *vt* acechar, asechar; *mil* emboscar; sorprender. **to be in a.,** emboscarse, estar en acecho

ameba *n* amiba, *f*

amelioration *n* mejora, *f*

amen *n* amén, *m*

amenable *a* sujeto (a); responsable; dócil; fácil de convencer, dispuesto a ser razonable; dispuesto a escuchar. **to make a. to reason,** hacer razonable

amend *vt* enmendar; modificar. *vi* reformarse

amendment *n* enmienda, *f*; modificación, *f*

amends *n* *pl* reparación, *f*; satisfacción, *f*; compensación, *f*. **to make a.,** dar satisfacción

amenity *n* amenidad, *f*

America América, *f*

American *n* americano (-na); (U.S.A.) norteamericano (-na). *a* americano, de América; norteamericano, de los Estados Unidos. **Central A.,** *a* and *n* centroamericano (-na). **A. bar,** bar americano, *m*

Americanism *n* americanismo, *m*

Americanize *vt* americanizar

amethyst *n* amatista, *f*

amiability *n* amabilidad, afabilidad, cordialidad, *f*

amiable *a* amable, afable, cordial

amiably *adv* amablemente, con afabilidad

amianthus *n* amianto, *m*

amicable *a* amigable, amistoso

amicably *adv* amigablemente

amice *n* amito, *m*

amid, amidst *prep* en medio de; entre; rodeado por

amidships *adv* en el centro del buque, en medio del navío

amiss *adv* mal; de más; (ill) indispuesto, enfermo; (inopportunely) inoportunamente. *a* malo. **It would**

not come a., No vendría mal. **to take a.,** llevar a mal

ammeter *n elec* amperímetro, *m*

ammonia *n* amoníaco, *m*

ammoniacal *a* amoniacal

ammunition *n* munición, *f*. **a. box,** cajón de municiones, *m*

amnesia *n* amnesia, *f*

amnesty *n* amnistía, *f*. **to concede an a. to,** amnistiar

amok (to run a.) atacar a ciegas

among *prep* en medio de; entre; con

amoral *a* amoral

amorality *n* amoralidad, *f*

amorous *a* amoroso; (tender) tierno

amorousness *n* erotismo, *m*; galantería, *f*

amorphous *a* amorfo

amortization *n* amorcización, *f*

amortize *vt* amortizar

amount *n* importe, *m*, suma, *f*; cantidad, *f*, *vi* (to) subir a, ascender a, llegar a; valer; reducirse a. **gross a.,** importe bruto, *m*. **net a.,** importe líquido, importe neto, *m*. **It amounts to the same thing, then,** Es igual entonces, Viene a ser lo mismo pues. **What he says amounts to this,** Lo que dice se reduce a esto

amperage *n* amperaje, *m*

ampere *n* amper, amperio, *m*

amphibian *n* anfibio, *m*

amphibious *a* anfibio

amphitheater *n* anfiteatro, *m*

amphora *n* ánfora, *f*

ample *a* amplio; abundante; extenso, vasto; (sufficient) bastante, suficiente

amplification *n* amplificación, *f*

amplifier *n* amplificador, *m*

amplify *vt* amplificar; aumentar, ampliar

amplitude *n* amplitud, *f*; abundancia, *f*; extensión, *f*

amply *adv* ampliamente; abundantemente; suficientemente

amputate *vt* amputar

amputation *n* amputación, *f*

amulet *n* amuleto, *m*

amuse *vt* divertir, entretener, distraer. **to a. oneself,** divertirse; pasarlo bien

amusement *n* diversión, *f*, entretenimiento, *m*; (hobby) pasatiempo, *m*. **a. park,** parque de atracciones, *m*

amusing *a* divertido, entretenido; (of people) salado

amusingly *adv* de un modo divertido, entretenidamente

an. See **a**

Anabaptism *n* anabaptismo, *m*

Anabaptist *n* anabaptista, *mf*

anachronism *n* anacronismo, *m*

anachronistic *a* anacrónico

anagram *n* anagrama, *m*

analects *n pl* analectas, *f pl*

analgesia *n* analgesia, *f*

analgesic *a* and *n* analgésico, *m*.

analogous *a* análogo

analogy *n* analogía, *f*

analyse *vt* analizar

analysis *n* análisis, *m*

analyst *n* analista, *mf*

analytical *a* analítico

anaphora *n* anáfora, *f*

anaphrodisiac *a* anafrodisíaco

anarchic *a* anárquico

anarchism *n* anarquismo, *m*

anarchist *n* anarquista, *mf*

anarchy *n* anarquía, *f*

anastigmatic *a* anastigmático

anathema *n* anatema, *mf*

anathematize *vt* anatematizar

anatomic *a* anatómico

anatomically *adv* anatómicamente; físicamente

anatomist *n* anatomista, *mf*

anatomy *n* anatomía, *f*

ancestor *n* antepasado, abuelo, *m*

ancestral *a* de sus antepasados; de familia; hereditario. **a. home,** casa solariega, *f*

ancestry *n* antepasados, *m pl*; linaje, abolengo, *m*; estirpe, *f*; nacimiento, *m*; origen, *m*

anchor *n* ancla, *f*. *fig* áncora, *f*. *vt* sujetar con el ancla. *vi* anclar, echar anclas, fondear. **at a.,** al ancla. **drag a.,** ancla flotante, ancla de arrastre, *f*. **sheet a.,** ancla de la esperanza, *f*; *fig* ancla de salvación, *f*. **to drop a.,** anclar. **to ride at a.,** estar al ancla. **to weigh a.,** levar el ancla

anchorage *n* anclaje, *m*; ancladero, fondeadero, *m*; derechos de anclaje, *m pl*

anchorite *n* anacoreta, *mf*

anchovy *n* anchoa, *f*, boquerón, *m*

ancient *a* anciano; antiguo. *n pl* **ancients,** los antiguos. **from a. times,** de antiguo. **most a.,** antiquísimo

and *conjunc* y; (before stressed i or hi) e; (after some verbs and before infin.) de, a; que; (with) con; (often not translated before infins.). **Better and better,** Mejor que mejor. **I shall try and do it,** Trataré de hacerlo. **to come and see,** venir a ver. **We shall try and speak to him,** Procuraremos hablar con él

Andalusia Andalucía, *f*

Andalusian *a* andaluz. *n* andaluz (-za). **A. hat,** sombrero calañés, *m*

Andean *a* andino

Andes, the los Andes, *f*

andiron *n* morillo, *m*

Andorran *a* and *n* andorrano (-na)

androgynous *a* andrógino

anecdotal *a* anecdótico

anecdote *n* anécdota, *f*

anemia *n* anemia, *f*

anemic *a* anémico

anemometer *n* anemómetro, *m*

anemone *n* anémona, anémone, *f*

aneroid *a* aneroide. *n* barómetro aneroide, *m*

anesthesia *n* anestesia, *f*

anesthetic *a* and *n* anestésico, *m*.

anesthetist *n* anestesiador (-ra)

anesthetize *vt* anestesiar

aneurism *n* aneurisma, *mf*

angel *n* ángel, *m*

angelic *a* angélico

angelica *n* angélica, *f*

angelus *n* ángelus, *m*

anger *n* cólera, ira, *f*, enojo, *m*, *vt* enojar, encolerizar; hacer rabiar

angina *n* angina, *f*. **a. pectoris,** angina de pecho, *f*

angle *n* ángulo, *m*; rincón, *m*; esquina, *f*; (of a roof) caballette, *m*; *fig* punto de vista, *m*, *vi* pescar con caña. **at an a.,** a un lado. **a.-iron,** hierro angular, *m*. **to a. for,** pescar; *fig* procurar obtener

Angle *a* and *n* anglo (-la)

angler *n* pescador (-ra) de caña

Anglican *a* and *n* anglicano (-na)

Anglicanism *n* anglicanismo, *m*

Anglicism *n* anglicismo, inglesismo, *m*

Anglicize *vt* inglesar

angling *n* pesca con caña, *f*

Anglo- (in compounds) anglo-. **A.-American,** *a* and *n* angloamericano (-na). **A.-Indian,** *a* and *n* angloindio (-ia). **A.-Saxon,** *a* and *n* anglosajón (-ona); (language) anglosajón, *m*

anglomania *n* anglomanía, *f*

anglophile *n* anglófilo (-la)

anglophobia *n* anglofobia, *f*

angora *n* angora, *f*. **a. cat,** gato de angora, *m*. **a. rabbit,** conejo de angora, *m*

angrily *adv* airadamente

angry *a* (of persons) enfadado, enojado, airado; (of waves, etc.) furioso; *med* inflamado; (red) rojo; (scowling) cenudo; (dark) obscuro. **to be a.,** estar enojado. **to grow a.,** enojarse, enfadarse; (of waves) encresparse; (of the sky) obscurecerse. **to make a.,** enojar

anguish *n* agonía, *f*; dolor, *m*; angustia, *f*. *vt* angustiar
angular *a* angular; (of features, etc.) anguloso
angularity *n* angulosidad, *f*
anhydrous *a* anhidro
aniline *n* anilina, *f*
animal *a* and *n* animal *m*. **a. fat,** grasa animal, *f*. **a. kingdom,** reino animal, *m*. **a. spirits,** *phil* espíritus animales, *m pl*; brío, *m*, energía, *f*
animalism *n* animalidad, *f*; sensualidad, *f*
animate *vt* animar; inspirar. *a* animado; viviente
animated *a* animado; vivo, lleno de vida
animation *n* animación, *f*; vivacidad, *f*; calor, fuego, *m*
animism *n* animismo, *m*
animosity *n* animosidad, hostilidad, *f*
aniseed *n* anís, *m*
anisette *n* (liqueur) anisete, *m*
ankle *n* tobillo, *m*. **a. bone,** hueso del tobillo, *m*. **a. sock,** calcetín corto, *m*
anklet *n* brazalete para el tobillo, *m*; (support) tobillera, *f*
annals *n pl* anales, *m pl*
anneal *vt* (metals) recocer; (glass) templar; (with oil) atemperar
annex *vt* unir, juntar; anexar. *n* anexo, *m*
annexation *n* anexión, *f*
annihilate *vt* aniquilar
annihilation *n* aniquilación,
anniversary *a* and *n* aniversario, *m*.
annotate *vt* anotar, acotar, comentar, hacer anotaciones a
annotation *n* anotación, *f*; nota, *f*
annotator *n* anotador (-ra), comentador (-ra)
announce *vt* proclamar; declarar; publicar; anunciar
announcement *n* proclama, *f*; declaración, *f*; publicación, *f*; anuncio, *m*; (of a betrothal) participación, *f*
announcer *n* anunciador (-ra); (radio or TV) locutor (-ra)
annoy *vt* exasperar, irritar, disgustar; molestar, incomodar
annoyance *n* disgusto, *m*, exasperación, *f*; molestia, *f*, fastidio, *m*
annoying *a* enojoso, molesto, fastidioso
annual *a* anual. *n* anuario, *m*; calendario, *m*; planta anual, *f*
annually *adv* anualmente, cada año
annuitant *n* censualista, *mf*
annuity *n* anualidad, pensión vitalicia, *f*
annul *vt* anular
annulment *n* anulación, *f*
annunciation *n* anunciación, *f*. **the A.,** la Anunciación
anodyne *a* and *n* anodino, *m*
anoint *vt* untar; (before death) olear; (a king, etc.) ungir
anointing *n* unción, *f*
anomalous *a* anómalo
anomaly *n* anomalía, *f*
anonymity *n* anónimo, *m*
anonymous *a* anónimo. **a. letter,** anónimo, *m*
anonymously *adv* anónimamente
another *a* otro; (different) distinto. *n* otro, *m*; otra, *f*. **For one thing . . . and for a.,** En primer lugar . . . y además (y por otra cosa). **one after a.,** uno después de otro. **They love one a.,** Ellos se aman. **They sent it from one to a.,** Lo mandaron de uno a otro
answer *n* contestación, respuesta, *f*; (refutation) refutación, *f*; (pert reply) réplica, *f*; (solution) solución, *f*; *math* resultado, *m*; *law* contestación a la demanda, *f*
answer *vt* responder, contestar; (a letter, etc.) contestar a; (refute) refutar; (reply pertly) replicar; (write) escribir; (return) devolver; (suit) servir; (a bell, etc.) acudir a; (the door) abrir. *vi* contestar; (succeed) tener éxito; dar resultado. **to a. by return,** contestar a vuelta de correo, **to a. back,** replicar. **to a. for,** ser responsable por; ser responsable de; (speak for) hablar por; (guarantee) garantizar, responder de
answerable *a* responsable; refutable; (adequate) adecuado. **to make a. for,** hacer responsable de

answering machine *n* contestador telefónico, contestador, *m*
ant *n* hormiga, *f*. **ant-eater,** oso hormiguero, *m*. **ant-hill,** hormiguero, *m*
antagonism *n* antagonismo, *m*, hostilidad, oposición, *f*
antagonist *n* antagonista, *mf*
antagonistic *a* antagónico, hostil
antagonize *vt* contender; hacer hostil (a)
antarctic *a* antártico. *n* polo antártico, *m*
antecedent *a* and *n* antecedente, *m*.
antechamber *n* antecámara, antesala, *f*
antedate *vt* antedatar; anticipar
antediluvian *a* antediluviano
antelope *n* antílope, *m*
antenna *n* antena, *f*
anterior *a* anterior
anthem *n* antífona, *f*
anthologist *n* antólogo, *m*
anthology *n* antología, floresta, *f*
anthracite *n* antracita, *f*, carbón mineral, *m*
anthrax *n* ántrax, *m*
anthropological *a* antropológico
anthropologist *n* antropólogo, *m*
anthropology *n* antropología, *f*
anti-aircraft *a* antiaéreo. **A.A. gun,** cañon antiaéreo, *m*
antibody *n* anticuerpo, *m*
antic *n* travesura, *f*
Antichrist *n* Anticristo, *m*
anticipate *vt* (foresee) prever; anticipar; adelantarse a; (hope) esperar; (frustrate) frustrar; (enjoy) disfrutar con anticipación de
anticipation *n* anticipación, *f*; adelantamiento, *m*; esperanza, expectación, *f*. **in a. of,** en espera de
anticipatory *a* anticipador
anticlerical *a* anticlerical
anticlericalism *n* anticlericalismo, *m*
anticlimax *n* anticlímax, *m*
antidote *n* antídoto, contraveneno, *m*
antifreeze *n* anticongelante, *m*
Antilles, the las Antillas, *f*
antimony *n* antimonio, *m*
antipathetic *a* antipático
antipathy *n* antipatía, *f*
antipode *n pl* antípodas, *mf pl*
antiquarian *a* anticuario
antiquary *n* anticuario, *m*
antiquated *a* anticuado
antique *a* antiguo. *n* antigüedad, antigualla, *f*. **a. dealer,** anticuario, *m*. **a. shop,** tienda de antigüedades, *f*
antiquity *n* antigüedad, *f*; ancianidad, *f*
antireligious *a* antirreligioso
antirepublican *a* antirrepublicano
anti-Semitic *a* antisemita
anti-Semitism *n* antisemitismo, *m*
antiseptic *a* and *n* antiséptico, *m*
antisocial *a* antisocial
antithesis *n* antítesis, *f*
antithetic *a* antitético
antitoxin *n* antitoxina, *f*
antler *n* asta, *f*
antonym *n* contrario, *m*
antrum *n* antro, *m*
Antwerp Amberes, *m*
anus *n* ano, *m*
anvil *n* yunque, *m*, bigornia, *f*
anxiety *n* inquietud, intranquilidad, *f*; preocupación, *f*; ansiedad, *f*; curiosidad, *f*; impaciencia, *f*; (wish) deseo, afán, *m*
anxious *a* inquieto, intranquilo; preocupado; ansioso; impaciente; deseoso. **to be a.,** estar inquieto; apurarse. **to be a. to,** ansiar, tener deseos de. **to make a.,** preocupar, inquietar, intranquilizar
anxiously *adv* con inquietud; ansiosamente; impacientemente

any *a* cualquiera; (before the noun only) cualquier; (some) algún, *m*; alguna, *f*; (every) todo; (expressing condition or with interrogatives or negatives, following the noun) alguno, *m*; alguna, *f*, (is often not translated in a partitive sense, e.g. **Have you any butter?** ¿Tienes mantequilla?) *pron* algo; (with the relevant noun) algún, etc.; lo, *m*, and *neut*; la, *f*; los, *m pl*; las, *f pl*. **He hasn't any pity,** No tiene piedad alguna. **at any rate,** de todos modos; por lo menos. **If there is any,** Si lo (la, etc.) hay. **in any case,** venga lo que venga. **not any,** ninguno, *m*; ninguna, *f*. **Whether any of them . . . ,** Si alguno de ellos . . . **any further,** más lejos. **any longer,** más largo; (of time) más tiempo. **any more,** nada más; nunca más

anybody *n* and *pron* (someone) alguien; cualquiera, *mf*; (everyone) todo el mundo; (with a negative) nadie; (of importance) persona de importancia, *f*. **hardly a.,** casi nadie

anyhow *adv* de cualquier modo; (with a negative) de ningún modo; de cualquier manera; (at least) por lo menos, en todo caso; (carelessly) sin cuidado

anyone *n*. See **anybody**

anything *n* algo, *m*, alguna cosa, *f*; (negative) nada; cualquier cosa, *f*; todo (lo que). **a. but,** todo menos

anyway *adv* de todos modos, con todo; venga lo que venga; (anyhow) de cualquier modo

anywhere *adv* en todas partes, dondequiera; en cualquier parte; (after a negative) en (or a) ninguna parte

A.O.B. (any other business) asuntos varios (on an agenda)

aorta *n* aorta, *f*

apart *adv* aparte; a un lado; separadamente; separado (de); apartado (de). **a. from,** aparte de, dejando a un lado. **to keep a.,** mantener aislado; distinguir (entre). **to take a.,** desarmar. **wide a.,** muy distante

apartment *n* cuarto, *m*, habitación, *f*; (flat) piso, *m*

apathetic *a* apático; indiferente

apathy *n* apatía, *f*; indiferencia, *f*

ape *n* simio, *m*

Apennines, the los Apeninos, *m*

aperitive *a* and *n* aperitivo, *m*.

aperture *n* abertura, *f*; agujero, *m*; orificio, *m*

apex *n* ápice, *m*

aphasia *n* afasia, *f*

aphorism *n* aforismo, *m*

aphrodisiac *a* and *n* afrodisíaco, *m*

apiary *n* colmenar, *m*

apiece *adv* cada uno; por persona

apish *a* simiesco, de simio; (affected) afectado; (foolish) tonto

aplomb *n* confianza en sí, *f*, aplomo, *m*

apocalypse *n* Apocalipsis, *m*

apocalyptic *a* apocalíptico

apocopate *vt* apocopar

Apocrypha *n* libros apócrifos, *m pl*

apocryphal *a* apócrifo

apogee *n* apogeo, *m*

apologetic *a* apologético

apologist *n* apologista, *mf*

apologize *vi* presentar sus excusas; disculparse, excusarse; (regret) sentir

apology *n* excusa, disculpa, *f*; defensa, apología, *f*; (makeshift) substituto, *m*

apoplectic *a* and *n* apoplético (-ca)

apoplexy *n* apoplegía, *f*

apostasy *n* apostasía, *f*

apostate *n* apóstata, *mf*, renegado (-da)

apostatize *vi* apostatar, renegar

apostle *n* apóstol, *m*. **Apostles' Creed,** el Credo de los Apóstoles

apostolic *a* apostólico

apostrophe *n* apóstrofe, *mf*; (punctuation mark) apóstrofo, *m*

apothecary *n* apotecario, *m*

Apothecaries weight peso de boticario, *m*

apothegm *n* apotegma, *m*

apotheosis *n* apoteosis, *f*

appal *vt* horrorizar, espantar, aterrar

appalling *a* espantoso, horrible

apparatus *n* aparato, *m*; máquina, *f*; instrumentos, *m pl*

apparel *n* ropa, *f*; vestiduras, *f pl*; ornamento, *m*. *vt* vestir

apparent *a* aparente; visible; evidente, manifiesto; (of heirs) presunto. **to become a.,** manifestarse

apparently *adv* al parecer, aparentemente

apparition *n* aparición, *f*, fantasma, espectro, *m*

appeal *n* súplica, *f*; llamamiento, *m*; (charm) atracción, *f*, encanto, *m*; *law* apelación, alzada, *f*. *vi* (to) suplicar (a); hacer llamamiento (a); poner por testigo (a); recurrir a; llamar la atención de; interesar (a); (attract) atraer, encantar; *law* apelar. **It doesn't a. to him,** No le atrae, No le gusta. **to allow an a.,** revocar una sentencia apelada. **without a.,** inapelable

appealing *a* suplicante; atrayente

appealingly *adv* de un modo suplicante

appear *vi* (of persons and things) aparecer; (seem) parecer; (before a judge) comparecer, presentarse (ante el juez); (of books) publicarse; (of lawyers) representar; (of the dawn) rayar; (of the sun, etc.) salir; (show itself) manifestarse. **to cause to a.,** hacer presentarse; (show) hacer ver; (prove) demostrar, probar

appearance *n* aparición, *f*; (show, semblance or look, aspect) apariencia, *f*; presencia, *f*; aspecto, *m*; (in court of law) comparecencia, *f*; (of a book) publicación, *f*; (arrival) llegada, *f*; (view) perspectiva, *f*; (ghost) aparición, *f*, fantasma, *m*. **first a.,** (of an actor, etc.) debut, *m*; (of a play) estreno, *m*. **to all appearances,** según las apariencias. **to make one's first a.,** aparecer por primera vez; *theat* debutar. **Appearances are deceptive,** Las apariencias engañan

appease *vt* apaciguar, aplacar, pacificar; satisfacer

appeasement *n* apaciguamiento, aplacamiento, *m*, pacificación, *f*; satisfacción, *f*

appellant *a* and *n* *law* apelante, *mf*

appellation *n* nombre, *m*; título, *m*

append *vt* añadir; (a seal) poner; (enclose) incluir, anexar

appendage *n* accesorio, *m*; (bot zool) apéndice, *m*

appendicitis *n* apendicitis, *f*

appendix *n* apéndice, *m*

appertain *vi* pertenecer (a)

appetite *n* apetito, *m*; *fig* hambre, *f*; deseo, *m*. **to have a bad a.,** no tener apetito, estar desganado. **to have a good a.,** tener buen apetito. **to whet the a.,** abrir el apetito

appetizer *n* aperitivo, *m*

appetizing *a* apetitoso

applaud *vt* and *vi* aplaudir; aclamar, ovacionar; celebrar

applause *n* aplauso, *m*; ovación, *f*; aprobación, alabanza, *f*

apple *n* manzana, *f*. **the a. of one's eye,** la niña de los ojos. **a. orchard,** manzanar, *m*. **a. sauce,** compota de manzanas, *f*. **a. tart,** pastel de manzanas, *m*. **a. tree,** manzano, *m*

appliance *n* aparato, *m*; instrumento, *m*; utensilio, *m*; máquina, *f*

applicability *n* aplicabilidad, *f*

applicable *a* aplicable

applicant *n* candidato, *m*; aspirante, *m*; solicitante, *mf*

application *n* aplicación, *f*; solicitud, *f*, petición, *f*; empleo, *m*. **on a.,** a solicitar

appliqué *a* aplicado. *n* aplicación, *f*

apply *vt* aplicar; (use) emplear; (place) poner; (give) dar; (the brakes) frenar; *vi* ser aplicable; ser a propósito; dirigirse (a); acudir (a); (for a post) proponerse para. **a. for,** solicitar, pedir; (a post) proponerse para. **a. for admission (to . . .),** solicitar el ingreso en (. . .). **a. oneself to,** ponerse a; dedicarse a, consagrarse a

appoint *vt* (prescribe) prescribir, ordenar; señalar; asignar; (furnish) amueblar; equipar; (create) crear, establecer; (to a post) nombrar, designar; (manage) gobernar; organizar. **at the appointed hour,** a la hora señalada. **well-appointed,** bien amueblado; bien equipado

appointive *a* por nombramiento

appointment *n* (assignation) cita, *f;* (to a post) nombramiento, *m;* (post, office) cargo, *m;* creación, *f.* **By Royal A.,** Proveedor de la Real Casa. **to make an a. with,** citar

apportion *vt* dividir; distribuir; prorratear; (taxes) derramar

apportionment *n* repartimiento, *m,* distribución, *f;* división, *f;* prorrateo, *m*

apposite *a* a propósito, pertinente, oportuno; justo

appositeness *n* pertinencia, oportunidad, *f*

appraisal *n* valoración, valuación, *f;* estimación, *f*

appraise *vt* valorar, tasar; estimar

appreciable *a* apreciable, perceptible

appreciably *adv* sensiblemente

appreciate *vt* (understand) darse cuenta de, comprender; estimar; apreciar; (distinguish) distinguir. *vi* encarecer, aumentar en valor; (of shares) subir, estar en alza

appreciation *n* (understanding) comprensión, *f;* apreciación, *f;* (recognition, etc.) aprecio, reconocimiento, *m;* (in value) aumento (en valor), *m;* subida de precio, *f*

appreciative *a* apreciativo

appreciatively *adv* con aprecio

appreciator *n* apreciador (-ra)

apprehend *vt* aprehender, prender; comprender, aprehender; (fear) temer

apprehension *n* aprehensión, comprensión, *f;* (fear) aprensión, *f;* (seizure) aprehensión, presa, *f*

apprehensive *a* aprehensivo; (fearful) aprensivo

apprehensiveness *n* aprehensión, *f;* (fear) aprensión, *f,* temor, *m*

apprentice *n* aprendiz (-za). **to bind a.,** poner de aprendiz

apprenticeship *n* aprendizaje, *m.* **to serve an a.,** hacer el aprendizaje

apprise *vt* dar parte (de), informar (de)

approach *vt* acercarse a; aproximarse a; (pull, etc. nearer) acercar, aproximar; (resemble) parecerse a, ser semejante a; (speak to) hablar con; entablar negociaciones con. *vi* acercarse, aproximarse. *n* acercamiento, *m;* (arrival) llegada, *f;* aproximación, *f;* (of night, etc.) avance, *m;* (entrance) entrada, *f;* avenida, *f;* vía, *f;* (step) paso, *m;* (to a subject) punto de vista (sobre), concepto (de), *m;* (introduction) introducción, *f; pl* **approaches,** (environs) alrededores, *m pl,* inmediaciones, *f pl;* (seas) mares, *m pl;* (overtures) avances, *m pl*

approachable *a* accesible

approaching *a* venidero, próximo, cercano

approbation *n* asentimiento, *m;* aprobación, *f*

appropriate *a* apropiado; conveniente; *vt* adueñarse de, tomar posesión de, apropiar

appropriately *adv* propiamente; convenientemente; justamente

appropriateness *n* conveniencia, *f;* justicia, *f*

appropriation *n* apropiación, *f;* aplicación, *f;* empleo, *m*

approval *n* aprobación, *f;* consentimiento, *m.* **on a.,** a prueba

approve *vt* aprobar; confirmar; (sanction) autorizar, sancionar; ratificar; estar contento (de); (oneself) demostrarse. *vi* aprobar

approved *a* aprobado; bien visto; (on documents) Visto Bueno (V° B°)

approximate *a* aproximado. *vt* acercar. *vi* aproximarse (a)

approximately *adv* aproximadamente, poco más o menos

approximation *n* aproximación, *f*

appurtenance *n* accesorio, *m,* pertenencia, *f*

apricot *n* albaricoque, *m.* **a. tree,** albaricoquero, *m*

April *n* abril, *m, a* abrileño. **A. Fool's Day,** el 1° de abril; (in Spain) el Día de los Inocentes (December 28)

apron *n* delantal, *m;* (of artisans and freemasons) mandil, *m.* **to be tied to a mother's a.-strings,** estar cosido a las faldas de su madre. **a.-stage,** proscenio, *m.* **a.-string,** cinta del delantal, *f*

apse *n* ábside, *mf*

apt *a* apto, listo; propenso (a), inclinado (a); expuesto (a); (suitable) apropiado, oportuno

aptitude *n* aptitud, disposición, facilidad, *f*

aptly *adv* apropiadamente; justamente, bien

aquamarine *n* aguamarina, *f*

aquarelle *n* acuarela, *f*

aquarellist *n* acuarelista, *mf*

aquarium *n* acuario, *m*

Aquarius *n* Acuario, *m*

aquatic *a* acuático

aquatint *n* acuatinta, *f*

aqueduct *n* acueducto, *m*

aqueous *a* ácueo, acuoso

aquiline *a* aguileño

Arab *a* árabe. *n* árabe, *mf*

arabesque *n* arabesco, *m*

Arabian *a* árabe, arábigo. **The A. Nights,** Las Mil y Una Noches

Arabic *a* arábigo. *n* (language) arábigo, árabe, *m*

Arabist *n* arabista, *mf*

arable *a* cultivable, labrantío

Aragonese *a* and *n* aragonés (-esa)

arbiter *n* árbitro (-ra), arbitrador (-ra)

arbitrariness *n* arbitrariedad, *f*

arbitrary *a* arbitrario

arbitrate *vi* arbitrar, juzgar como árbitro; someter al arbitraje

arbitration *n* arbitraje, *m*

arbitrator. See **arbiter**

arbour *n* glorieta, *f,* emparrado, *m*

arc *n* arco, *m.* **arc-light,** lámpara de arco, *f*

arcade *n* arcada, *f;* galería, *f;* pasaje, *m*

arch *n* arco, *m;* (vault) bóveda, *f. vt* abovedar; arquear; encorvar

arch *a* (roguish) socarrón; (coy) coquetón

arch- *prefix* archi-

archaic *a* arcaico

archaism *n* arcaísmo, *m*

archangel *n* arcángel, *m*

archbishop *n* arzobispo, *m*

archenemy *n* mayor enemigo (-ga); Demonio, *m*

archeological *a* arqueológico

archeologist *n* arqueólogo, *m*

archeology *n* arqueología, *f*

archer *n* flechero, saltero, *m; mil* arquero, *m*

archery *n* ballestería, *f*

archery range *n* campo de tiro con arco, *m*

archfiend *n* demonio, *m*

arching *n* arqueo, *m*

archipelago *n* archipiélago, *m*

architect *n* arquitecto, *m*

architectural *a* arquitectónico

architecturally *adv* arquitectónicamente; desde el punto de vista arquitectónico

architecture *n* arquitectura, *f*

archive *n* archivo, *m*

archivist *n* archivero, *m*

archness *n* coquetería, *f;* malicia, *f*

archway *n* arcada, *f,* pasaje abovedado, *m;* arco, *m*

arctic *a* ártico; muy frío. **A. Circle,** Círculo ártico, *m*

ardent *a* ardiente; apasionado, vehemente; fogoso

ardently *adv* ardientemente; con vehemencia, apasionadamente

ardor *n* ardor, *m*

arduous *a* arduo, difícil

arduousness *n* dificultad, arduidad, *f*

are *pl* of present indicative of **be.** See **be. There are,** Hay

area *n* área, *f;* superficie, *f;* (extent) extensión, *f;* espacio, *m;* región, *f;* (of a house) patio, *m;* (of a concert hall, etc.) sala, *f*

area code *n* característica, *f*, (Chile), código territorial (Spain), prefijo (Spain), código interurbano, código (Argentina), *m*

arena *n* arena, *f*

argent *n poet* blancura, *f*; *her* argén, *m*

Argentinian *a* and *n* argentino (-na)

argonaut *n* (*zool* and *myth*) argonauta, *m*

argot *n* jerga, *f*; (thieves') germanía, *f*

arguable *a* discutible

argue *vt* discutir; persuadir; (prove) demostrar. *vi* argüir, discutir; sostener. **to a. against,** hablar en contra de, oponer

arguing *n* razonamiento, *m*; argumentación, *f*; discusión, *f*

argument *n* argumento, *m*

argumentative *a* argumentador; contencioso

arid *a* árido, seco

aridity *n* aridez, *f*

Aries *n* Aries, *m*

arise *vi* levantarse; (appear) surgir, aparecer; ofrecerse, presentarse; (of sound) hacerse oír; provenir (de); proceder (de); (result) hacerse sentir; (rebel) sublevarse

aristocracy *n* aristocracia, *f*

aristocrat *n* aristócrata, *mf*

aristocratic *a* aristocrático

Aristotelian *a* aristotélico

Aristotelianism *n* aristotelismo, *m*

arithmetic *n* aritmética, *f*

arithmetical *a* aritmético

ark *n* arca, *f*. **Noah's ark,** arca de Noé, *f*. **Ark of the Covenant,** arca de la alianza, *f*

arm *n* (*anat geog mech* and *fig*) brazo, *m*; (lever) palanca, *f*; (of a tree) rama, *f*, brazo, *m*; (sleeve) manga, *f*; *naut* cabo de una verga, *m*; (weapon) arma, *f*; (of army, navy, etc.) ramo, *m pl.* **arms,** *her* armas, *f pl*, escudo, *m*. **in arms,** en brazos; armado; en oposición. **To arms!** ¡A las armas! **to keep at arm's length,** guardar las distancias; tratar fríamente. **to lay down arms,** rendir las armas. **to present arms,** presentar las armas. **to receive with open arms,** recibir con los brazos abiertos. **to take up arms,** alzarse en armas, empuñar las armas. **under arms,** sobre las armas. **with folded arms,** con los brazos cruzados. **arm in arm,** del bracete, de bracero. **arm of the sea,** brazo de mar, *m*. **arm-rest,** brazo, *m*

arm *vt* armar; proveer (de); (*fig* fortify) fortificar. *vi* armarse

armada *n* armada, *f*

armament *n* armamento, *m*

armchair *n* sillón, *m*, silla poltrona, *f*

armed *a* armado

Armenian *a* and *n* armenio (-ia); (language) armenio, *m*

armful *n* brazado, *m*

armhole *n* sobaquera, *f*

arming *n* armamento, *m*

armistice *n* armisticio, *m*

armless *a* sin brazos

armor *n* armadura, *f*; (for ships, etc.) blindaje, *m*. *vt* blindar, acorazar. **(to) a.-plate,** *vt* blindar. *n* coraza, plancha blindada, *f*

armored *a* blindado, acorazado. **a. car,** carro blindado, *m*. **a. cruiser,** crucero acorazado, *m*

armory *n* armería, *f*

army *n* ejército, *m*; multitud, muchedumbre, *f*. **to be in the a.,** ser del ejército. **to go into the a.,** alistarse. **a. corps,** cuerpo del ejército, *m*. **a. estimates,** presupuesto del ejército, *m*. **a. list,** escalafón del ejército, *m*. **A. Medical Corps,** Sanidad Militar, *f*. **A. Supply Corps,** Cuerpo de Intendencia, *m*

aroma *n* aroma, *m*

aromatic *a* aromático

around *prep* alrededor de; por todas partes; cerca de; (with words like corner) a la vuelta de. *adv* alrededor; a la redonda, en torno; por todas partes; de un lado para otro

arouse *vt* despertar; excitar. **a. (someone's) suspicions,** despertar las sospechas (de fulano)

arpeggio *n* arpegio, *m*

arraign *vt* acusar; *law* procesar

arraignment *n* acusación, *f*; *law* procesamiento, *m*

arrange *vt* arreglar; acomodar; poner en orden, clasificar; (place) colocar; (order) ordenar, disponer; (contrive) agenciar; organizar; preparar; *mus* adaptar; (of differences) concertar, ajustar. *vi* convenir, concertarse; arreglar; hacer preparativos

arrangement *n* arreglo, *m*; clasificación, *f*; disposición, *f*; (agreement) acuerdo, *m*; *mus* adaptación, *f*; *pl* **arrangements,** preparativos, *m pl*

array *n* (of troops) orden de batalla, *mf*; formación, *f*; colección, *f*; (dress) atavío, *m*, *vt* poner en orden de batalla; formar (las tropas, etc.); ataviar, adornar

arrears *n pl* atrasos, *m pl*. **in a.,** atrasado

arrest *vt* detener, impedir; (the attention) atraer; (capture) arrestar, prender; (judgment) suspender. *n* (stop) interrupción, parada, *f*; (hindrance) estorbo, *m*; (detention) arresto, *m*, detención, *f*; (of a judgment) suspensión, *f*. **under a.,** bajo arresto

arresting *a* que llama la atención, notable, muy interesante; asombroso, chocador

arrival *n* llegada, venida, *f*, advenimiento, *m*; *naut* arribada, *f*; entrada, *f*; el, *m*, (la, *f*), que llega. **on a.,** al llegar, a la llegada. **the new arrivals,** los recién llegados

arrive *vi* llegar; aparecer; (happen) suceder; *naut* arribar; entrar. **to a. at,** (a place or conclusion) llegar a

arrogance *n* arrogancia altivez, soberbia, *f*

arrogant *a* altivo, arrogante, soberbio

arrogate *vt* arrogar

arrow *n* saeta, flecha, *f*. **a.-head,** punta de flecha, *f*. **a.-shaped,** en forma de flecha, sagital. **a. wound,** flechazo, saetazo, *m*

arsenal *n* arsenal, *m*

arsenic *n* arsénico, *m*

arson *n* incendio premeditado, *m*

art *n* arte, *mf*; (cleverness) habilidad, *f*; (cunning) artificio, *m*. **Faculty of Arts,** Facultad de Letras, *f*. **fine arts,** bellas artes, *f pl*. **art exhibition,** exposición de pinturas, *f*. **art gallery,** museo de pinturas, *m*. **art school,** colegio de arte, *m*

arterial *a* arterial; (of roads) de primera clase. **a. forceps,** pinzas hemostáticas, *f pl*

artery *n* arteria, *f*

artesian *a* artesiano

artful *a* hábil, ingenioso; (crafty) astuto

artfully *adv* ingeniosamente; con astucia

artfulness *n* habilidad, ingeniosidad, *f*; astucia, maña, *f*

arthritic *a* artrítico

arthritis *n* artritis, *f*

artichoke *n* alcachofa, *f*. **Jerusalem a.,** aguaturma, *f*

article *n* artículo, *m*; (object) objeto, *m*, cosa, *f*; *pl* **articles,** escritura, *f*; contrato, *m*; estatutos, *m pl*. *vt* escriturar; contratar. **leading a.,** artículo de fondo, *m*. **articles of apprenticeship,** contrato de aprendizaje, *m*. **articles of association,** estatutos de asociación, *m pl*. **articles of war,** código militar, *m*

articulate *vt* articular; pronunciar, articular. *vi* estar unido por articulación; articular. *a* articulado; claro; expresivo

articulation *n* articulación, *f*, (all meanings)

artifice *n* artificio, *m*; arte, *m*, or *f*, habilidad, *f*

artificer *n* artífice, *mf*

artificial *a* artificial; falso, fingido; afectado. **a. flowers,** flores de mano, *f pl*. **a. silk,** seda artificial, seda vegetal, *f*

artificiality *n* artificialidad, *f*; falsedad, *f*; afectación, *f*

artificially *adv* artificialmente; con afectación

artillery *n* artillería, *f*. **field a.,** artillería volante (or ligera or montada), *f*. **a. practice,** ejercicio de cañón, *m*

artilleryman *n* artillero, *m*

artisan *n* artesano (-na)

artist *n* artista, *mf*; (painter) pintor (-ra)

artiste *n* artista, *mf*
artistic *a* artístico
artistically *adv* artísticamente
artistry *n* habilidad artística, *f*, arte, *mf*
artless *a* natural; sencillo, cándido, inocente
artlessly *adv* con naturalidad; con inocencia
artlessness *n* naturalidad, *f*; sencillez, candidez, inocencia, *f*
art museum *n* museo de arte, *m*
Aryan *a* ario
as *adv conjunc rel pron* como; así como; (followed by infin.) de; (in comparisons) tan . . . como; (while) mientras; a medida que; (when) cuando, al (followed by infin.); (since) puesto que, visto que; (because) porque; (although) aunque; por; (according to) según; en; (in order that) para (que). **as a rule,** por regla general. **Once as he was walking,** Una vez mientras andaba. **as . . . as,** tan . . . como. **as far as,** hasta; en cuanto a. **as from,** desde. **as good as,** tan bueno como. **as if,** como si. **as it were,** por decirlo así, en cierto modo. **as many,** otros tantos (e.g. **six embassies in as many countries,** seis embajadas en otros tantos países). **as many as,** tanto . . . como; todos los que. **as soon as,** en cuanto, luego que, así que. **as soon as possible,** cuanto antes. **as sure as can be,** sin duda alguna. **as to,** en cuanto a. **as usual,** como de costumbre. **as well,** también. **as well as,** (besides) además de; tan bien como. **as yet,** todavía.
asbestos *n* asbesto, amianto, *m*
ascend *vt* and *vi* subir; (on, in) subir a; ascender; (rise) elevarse; (a river) remontar. **to a. the stairs,** subir las escaleras. **to a. the pulpit,** subir al púlpito. **to a. the throne,** subir al trono
ascendancy *n* ascendiente, influjo, *m*
ascendant *n* elevación, *f. a* ascendente; predominante. **to be in the a.,** *fig* ir en aumento; predominar
ascending *a* ascendente
ascension *n* subida, ascensión, *f*; (of the throne) advenimiento (al trono), *m.* **The A.,** La Ascensión
ascent *n* subida, *f*, ascenso, *m*; elevación, *f*; (slope) cuesta, pendiente, *f*
ascertain *vt* averiguar, descubrir
ascertainable *a* averiguable, descubrible
ascertainment *n* averiguación, *f*
ascetic *a* ascético. *n* asceta, *mf*
asceticism *n* ascetismo, *m*
ascribable *a* imputable, atribuible
ascribe *vt* atribuir, adscribir, imputar
ascription *n* atribución, adscripción, *f*
asepsis *n* asepsia, *f*
aseptic *a* aséptico
asexual *a* asexual
ash *n* ceniza, *f*; cenizas, *f pl*; (tree and wood) fresno, *m*; *pl* **ashes,** cenizas, *f pl*; restos mortales, *m pl.* **mountain ash,** serbal, *m.* **ash-bin,** basurero, *m.* **ash-coloured,** ceniciento. **ash grove,** fresneda, *f.* **ashtray,** cenicero, *m.* **Ash Wednesday,** miércoles de ceniza, *m*
ashamed *a* avergonzado. **to be a. of,** avergonzarse de. **to be a. of oneself,** avergonzarse, tener vergüenza de sí mismo
ashen *a* ceniciento; (of ash wood) de fresno; pálido como un muerto
ashlar *n* sillar, *m*
ashore *adv* a tierra; en tierra. **to go** or **put a.,** desembarcar
Asia Minor Asia Menor, *f*
Asiatic *a* and *n* asiático (-ca)
aside *adv* a un lado; aparte. *n theat* aparte, *m.* **to set a.,** poner a un lado; (omit) dejar aparte; descontar; abandonar; (a judgment) anular. **to take a.,** llevar aparte
asinine *a* asnal
ask *vt* (a question; enquire) preguntar; (request; demand) pedir; (beg) rogar; (invite) invitar. **to ask a question,** hacer una pregunta. **to ask about,** preguntar acerca de. **to ask after,** preguntar por. **to ask down,** invitar a bajar; invitar a visitar (a alguíen). **to**

ask for, pedir; preguntar por. **ask for the moon,** pedir cotofas en el golfo. **to ask in,** invitar (a alguien) a entrar
askance *adv* al (or de) soslayo, de reojo; con recelo
askew *adv* oblicuamente; al lado; a un lado; sesgadamente
aslant *prep* a través de
asleep *a* and *adv* dormido. **to be a.,** estar dormido. **to fall a.,** dormirse
asparagus *n* espárrago, *m.* **a. bed,** esparraguera, *f*
aspect *n* aspecto, *m*; vista, *f*; apariencia, *f*, semblante, *m.* **to have a southern a.,** dar (mirar) al sur
asperity *n* aspereza, *f*
aspersion *n ecc* aspersión, *f*; calumnia, *f*; insinuación, *f*
asphalt *n* asfalto, *m*, *vt* asfaltar
asphyxia *n* asfixia, *f*
asphyxiate *vt* asfixiar
asphyxiating *a* asfixiante
aspirant *n* aspirante, candidato, *m*
aspirate *vt* aspirar. *n* letra aspirada, *f*
aspiration *n* aspiración, ambición, *f*; deseo, anhelo, *m*; *gram* aspiración, *f*
aspire *vi* aspirar (a), pretender, ambicionar; alzarse
aspirin *n* aspirina, *f*
ass *n* asno, *m*
assail *vt* atacar, acometer, arremeter
assailable *a* atacable
assailant *n* asaltador (-ra)
assassin *n* asesino, *mf*
assassinate *vt* asesinar
assassination *n* asesinato, *m*
assault *n* asalto, *m*; acometida, embestida, *f*; *fig* ataque, *m. vt* asaltar; acometer, embestir; atacar. **to take by a.,** tomar por asalto
assay *n* ensayo, *m*, *vt* ensayar, aquilatar
assayer *n* ensayador, *m*
assaying *n* ensaye, *m*
assemblage *n* reunión, *f*; (of a machine) montaje, *m*; (of people) muchedumbre, *f*, concurso, *m*; (of things) colección, *f*, grupo, *m*
assemble *vt* (persons) reunir, convocar; (things and persons) juntar; (a machine, etc.) armar, ensamblar. *vi* reunirse, congregarse; acudir
assembly *n* asamblea, *f*; reunión, *f*; *ecc* concilio, *m.* **a. line,** cadena de montaje, línea de montaje, *f.* **a. room,** sala de reuniones, *f*; sala de baile, *f*
assent *n* asentimiento, consentimiento, *m*; aprobación, *f*; (parliamentary, *law*) sanción, *f. vi* asentir (a), consentir (en); aprobar
assert *vt* mantener, defender; declarar, afirmar; hacer valer, reclamar. **to a. oneself,** imponerse, hacerse sentir; hacer valer sus derechos
assertion *n* aserción, afirmación, *f*; defensa, *f*; reclamación, *f*
assertive *a* afirmativo; dogmático
assess *vt* tasar, valorar; fijar, señalar; repartir (contribuciones, etc.)
assessment *n* tasación, *f*; fijación, *f*; repartimiento, *m*
assessor *n law* asesor (-ra); (of taxes) repartidor (-ra); (valuer) tasador, *m.* **public a.,** tasador, *m*
asset *n* ventaja, *f*; adquisición, *f*; cualidad, *f*; *pl* **assets,** fondos, *m pl*; *com* activo, *m*, créditos activos, *m pl*
assiduity *n* asiduidad, *f*
assiduous *a* asiduo
assiduously *adv* asiduamente, con asiduidad
assign *vt law* ceder; señalar, asignar; (appoint) destinar; fijar; atribuir, imputar. *n* cesionario (-ia)
assignation *n* asignación, *f*; cita, *f*; *law* cesión, *f*
assignment *n law* cesión, *f*; escritura de cesión, *f*; atribución, *f*; parte, porción, *f*
assimilable *a* asimilable
assimilate *vt* asimilar; incorporarse. *vi* mezclarse
assimilation *n* asimilación, *f*; incorporación, *f*
assimilative *a* asimilativo
assist *vt* ayudar; auxiliar, socorrer; (uphold) apoyar; (further) promover, fomentar. *vi* (be present) asistir (a)

assistance *n* ayuda, *f*; auxilio, socorro, *m*; apoyo, *m*; (furtherance) fomento, *m*. **public a.**, asistencia pública, *f*

assistant *n* ayudante, *m*; *ecc* asistente, *m*; (in a shop) dependiente (-ta); colaborador (-ra); (university) auxiliar, *m*; sub-. **a. secretary,** subsecretario (-ia). **a. secretaryship,** subsecretaría, *f*

associate *n* asociado (-da); miembro, *m*; socio (-ia); compañero (-ra), amigo (-ga); colega, *m*; colaborador (-ra); (confederate) cómplice, *mf a* asociado; auxiliar. *vt* asociar; unir, juntar. **to a. oneself with,** asociarse con; asociarse a. **to a. with,** frecuentar la compañía de, ir con

association *n* asociación, *f*; unión, *f*; sociedad, *f*; compañía, corporación, *f*; (connection) relación, *f*. **a. football,** fútbol, *m*

assonance *n* asonancia, *f*

assort *vt* clasificar; mezclar

assorted *a* surtido, mezclado. **They are a well-a. pair,** Son una pareja bien avenida

assortment *n* clasificación, *f*, arreglo, *m*; surtido, *m*, mezcla, *f*

assuage *vt* mitigar; suavizar; calmar; aliviar

assume *vt* asumir; tomar; apropiarse; (wear) revestir; (suppose) suponer; poner por caso

assumed *a* fingido, falso; supuesto

assumption *n* asunción, *f*; apropiación, arrogación, *f*; suposición, *f*. **Feast of the A.,** Fiesta de la Asunción, *f*

assurance *n* garantía, *f*; promesa, *f*; confianza, seguridad, *f*; (in a good sense) aplomo, *m*, naturalidad, *f*; (in a bad sense) presunción frescura, *f*, descaro, *m*; *com* seguro, *m*

assure *vt* asegurar

assured *a* aseguardo; seguro

assuredly *adv* seguramente

asterisk *n* asterisco, *m*

astern *adv* a popa; de popa; en popa; atrás

asthma *n* asma, *f*

asthmatic *a* asmático

astigmatic *a* astigmático

astigmatism *n* astigmatismo, *m*

astir *adv* en movimiento; (out of bed) levantado; excitado

astonish *vt* sorprender, asombrar

astonished *a* atónito, estupefacto

astonishing *a* sorprendente, asombroso

astonishment *n* asombro, *m*, sorpresa, estupefacción, *f*

astound *vt* aturdir, pasmar. **to be astounded,** *inf* quedarse muerto

astounding *a* asombroso

astray *adv* desviado, extraviado; por el mal camino. **to go a.,** errar el camino, perderse; *fig* descarriarse

astride *adv* a horcajadas. *prep* a horcajadas sobre; a ambos lados de

astringent *a* astringente

astrologer *n* astrólogo (-ga)

astrological *a* astrológico

astrology *n* astrología, *f*

astronaut *n* astronauta, *mf*

astronomer *n* astrónomo, *m*

astronomical *a* astronómico

astronomy *n* astronomía, *f*

astrophysics *n* astrofísica, *f*

astute *a* astuto, sagaz; (with knave, etc.) redomado, pícaro

astuteness *n* astucia, sagacidad, *f*

asunder *adv* en dos; separadamente; lejos uno de otro

asylum *n* asilo, *m*; (for the insane) manicomio, *m*

asymmetrical *a* asimétrico

asymmetry *n* asimetría, *f*

at *prep* a; en casa de; en; de; con; por; (before) delante de. Sometimes forms part of verb, e.g. **to aim at,** apuntar. **to look at,** mirar. May be translated by using pres. part., e.g. **They were at play,** Estaban jugando. **at a bound,** de un salto. **at peace,** en paz. **at the doctor's,** en casa del médico. **at the crack of dawn,** al

rayar el alba, al romper el alba. **at the head,** a la cabeza. **John is at Brighton,** Juan está en Brighton. **at first,** al principio. **at last,** por fin. **at no time,** jamás. **at once,** en seguida. **at most,** a lo más. **at all events,** en todo caso. **What is he getting at?** ¿Qué quiere saber? **at home,** en casa. **at-home day,** día de recibo, *m*

atavism *n* atavismo, *m*

atavistic *a* atávico

atheism *n* ateísmo, *m*

atheist *n* ateo (-ea)

atheistic *a* ateo

Atheneum *n* ateneo, *m*

Athenian *a* and *n* ateniense *mf*

Athens Atenas, *f*

athlete *n* atleta, *m*

athletic *a* atlético

athletics *n* atletismo, *m*

athwart *adv* de través. *prep* al través de; contra

Atlantic *a* and *n* atlántico *m*. **A. Charter,** Carta del Atlántico, *f*. **A. liner,** transatlántico, *m*

Atlantis Atlántida, *f*

atlas *n* atlas, *m*

atmosphere *n* aire, *m*; atmósfera, *f*; *fig* ambiente, *m*

atmospheric *a* atmosférico

atmospherics *n pl* perturbaciones eléctricas atmosféricas, *f pl*

atoll *n* atolón, *m*

atom *n* átomo, *m*. **splitting of the a.,** escisión del átomo, *f*

atomic *a* atómico. **a. bomb,** bomba atómica, *f*. **a. pile,** pila atómica, *f*. **a. theory,** teoría atómica, *f*

atomize *vt* pulverizar

atomizer *n* pulverizador, *m*

atone *vi* (for) expiar

atonement *n* expiación, *f*

atonic *a* átono, atónico

atrocious *a* atroz; horrible

atrocity *n* atrocidad, *f*

atrophy *n* atrofia, *f*, *vi* atrofiarse

attach *vt* (*law* of goods) embargar; (*law* of persons) arrestar; (fix) fijar; (tie) atar; (join) juntar; (stick) pegar; (connect) conectar; (hook) enganchar; (with a brooch, etc.) prender; (blame, etc.) imputar; (importance, etc.) dar, conceder; (assign) asignar; (attract) atraer; (enclose) adjuntar, incluir. *vi* pertenecer (a), ser indivisible (de). **to a. oneself to,** pegarse a; adherirse a, asociarse con; acompañar; hacerse inseparable de

attaché *n* agregado, *m*. **a. case,** maletín, *m*

attachment *n* (*law* of goods) embargo, *m*; (*law* of persons) arresto, *m*; unión, *f*; conexión, *f*; (hooking) enganche, *m*; (with a brooch, etc.) prendimiento, *m*; (tying) atadura, *f*; (fixing) fijación, *f*; (affection) apego, cariño, *m*; (friendship) amistad, *f*

attack *n* ataque, *m*; *mil* ofensiva, *f*; (access) acceso, *m*. *vt* atacar

attacker *n* atacador (-ra), asaltador (-ra)

attain *vt* alcanzar, conseguir, lograr. *vi* llegar a; alcanzar

attainable *a* asequible, realizable; accesible

attainment *n* consecución, obtención, *f*; logro, *m*; *pl* **attainments,** prendas, dotes, *f pl*

attempt *vt* (try) procurar, tratar de, intentar; ensayar; querer; *law* hacer una tentativa (de), atentar. *n* tentativa, prueba, *f*; esfuerzo, ensayo, *m*; (criminal) atentado, *m*, tentativa, *f*

attend *vi* prestar atención (a); escuchar; (look after) cuidar (de); (serve) servir; (accompany) acompañar; (await) esperar. *vt* (be present) asistir (a); (of a doctor) visitar; (accompany) acompañar; (bring) acarrear, traer; (follow) seguir. **to be attended with,** traer consigo, acarrear

attendance *n* asistencia, presencia, *f*; (those present) público, *m*, concurrencia, *f*; servicio, *m*; (train) acompañamiento, *m*; *med* asistencia, *f*, tratamiento médico, *m*. **to be in a.,** acompañar (a)

attendant *a* que acompaña; que sigue; concomitante. *n* criado (-da); (keeper) guardián (-ana); (nurse) enfermero (-ra); (in a cloakroom) guardarropa, *f*; (in a theater) acomodador (-ra); (on a train) mozo, *m*; (waiter) camarero, *m*; (at baths) bañero (-ra)

attention *n* atención, *f*; cuidado, *m*. **A.!** ¡Atención!; *mil* ¡Firmes! **to pay a.**, prestar atención. **to stand to a.**, cuadrarse, permanecer en posición de firmes

attentive *a* atento; solícito; cortés, obsequioso

attentively *adv* con atención, atentamente; solícitamente

attentiveness *n* cuidado, *m*; cortesía, *f*

attenuate *vt* atenuar

attenuating *a* atenuante. **a. circumstance,** circunstancia atenuante, *f*

attenuation *n* atenuación, *f*

attest *vt* atestar. *vi* atestiguar, deponer, dar fe

attestation *n* atestación, deposición, *f*; (certificate) certificado, *m*, fe, *f*

attic *n* buhardilla, guardilla, *f*, desván, sotabanco, *m*

Attic *a* ático

attire *n* atavío, *m*; (dress) traje, *m*; (finery) galas, *f pl*, *vt* ataviar, vestir; engalanar

attitude *n* actitud, *f*; postura, *f*; posición, *f*

attorney *n* (solicitor) abogado (-da); (agent) apoderado (-da); (public) procurador, *m*. **power of a.**, poderes, *m pl* procuración, *f*. **A.-general,** fiscal, *m*

attract *vt* atraer; (charm) seducir, cautivar, apetecer; (invite) convidar; (goodwill, etc.) captar

attraction *n* atracción, *f*; atractivo, aliciente, encanto, *m*

attractive *a* atrayente; atractivo, seductivo; apetecible; encantador

attractively *adv* atractivamente

attributable *a* imputable, atribuible

attribute *vt* atribuir (a), achacar (a), imputar (a). *n* atributo, *m*

attribution *n* atribución, imputación, *f*; atributo, *m*

attrition *n* atrición, *f*

auburn *a* castaño, rojizo

auction *n* subasta, almoneda, *f*; venta pública, pública subasta, *f*, *vt* subastar. **to put up to a.**, sacar a pública subasta

auctioneer *n* subastador (-ra)

audacious *a* atrevido, audaz, osado, temerario; (shameless) descarado, impudente

audaciously *adv* osadamente; descaradamente

audacity *n* audacia, osadía, temeridad, *f*, atrevimiento, *m*; (shamelessness) descaro, *m*, desvergüenza, *f*

audibility *n* audibilidad, perceptibilidad, *f*

audible *a* audible, oíble

audibly *adv* en forma audible, perceptiblemente, en alta voz

audience *n* (interview and *law*) audiencia, *f*; oyentes, *m pl*, auditorio, público, *m*. **to give a.**, dar audiencia. **a. chamber,** sala de recepción, *f*

audiofrequency *n* audiofrecuencia, *f*

audit *vt* intervenir, examinar (cuentas). *n* intervención, *f*, ajuste (de cuentas), *m*

audition *n* audición, *f*

auditor *n* (hearer) oyente, *mf*; interventor, contador, *m*

auditorium *n* sala de espectáculos, *f*

auditory *a* auditivo, auditorio

Augean *a* de Augeas; muy sucio

auger *n* taladro, *m*

aught *n* algo. **For a. I know,** Por lo que yo sepa

augment *vt* aumentar, acrecentar. *vi* aumentarse, acrecentarse

augmentation *n* aumento, acrecentamiento, *m*; añadidura, *f*

augmentative *a* aumentativo

augur *n* agorero (-ra). *vt and vi* presagiar, anunciar; pronosticar, agorar

augury *n* predicción, *f*; agüero, presagio, pronóstico, *m*

August *n* agosto, *m*

august *a* augusto

Augustan *a* (of Roman emperor) augustal. **A. Age,** siglo de Augusto, *m*

Augustinian *a* and *n ecc* agustino (-na)

aunt *n* tía, *f*. **great-a.,** tía abuela, *f*. **A. Sally,** el pim, pam, pum

aura *n* exhalación, *f*; influencia psíquica, *f*; *med* aura, *f*

aural *a* auricular. **a. surgeon,** otólogo, *m*

auricle *n* (of the heart) aurícula, ala del corazón, *f*; oreja, *f*, pabellón de la oreja, *m*

aurora *n* aurora, *f*. **a. borealis,** aurora boreal, *f*

auspice *n* auspicio, *m*

auspicious *a* propicio, favorable, feliz

auspiciously *adv* prósperamente, felizmente

auspiciousness *n* buenos auspicios, *m pl*; felicidad, *f*

austere *a* severo, austero, adusto; ascético; (of style) desnudo

austerity *n* austeridad, severidad, *f*; ascetismo, *m*; (of style) desnudez, *f*

Australian *a* and *n* australiano (-na)

Austrian *a* and *n* austríaco (-ca)

authentic *a* auténtico

authenticate *vt* autenticar

authentication *n* autenticación, *f*

authenticity *n* autenticidad, *f*

author *n* autor, *m*

authoress *n* autora, *f*

author index *n* índice de autores, *m*

authoritarian *a* autoritario

authoritative *a* autoritario

authority *n* autoridad, *f*; poder, *m*. **to have on the best a.**, tener de muy buena fuente

authorization *n* autorización, *f*

authorize *vt* autorizar

authorship *n* profesión de autor, *f*; paternidad (literaria), *f*; origen, *m*

autobiographical *a* autobiográfico

autobiography *n* autobiografía, *f*

autocracy *n* autocracia, *f*

autocrat *n* autócrata, *mf*

autocratic *a* autocrático

autograph *n* autógrafo, *m*

autography *n* autografía, *f*

automatic *a* automático. **a. gate,** (at level crossings, etc.) barrera de golpe, *f*. **a. machine,** máquina automática, *f*; *inf* tragaperras, *m*. **a. pencil,** lapicero, *m*

automatically *adv* automáticamente

automatism *n* automatismo, *m*

automaton *n* autómata, *m*

automobile *n* automóvil, *m*

autonomous *a* autónomo

autonomy *n* autonomía, *f*

autopsy *n* autopsia, *f*

autosuggestion *n* autosugestión, *f*

autumn *n* otoño, *m*

autumnal *a* otoñal, de otoño

auxiliary *a* auxiliar. *n* auxiliador, *m*

avail *vi* servir; valer; importar. *vt* aprovechar. **to a. oneself of,** valerse de, aprovecharse de. **to no a.,** en balde

availability *n* utilidad, *f*; disponibilidad, *f*; provecho, *m*; (validity) validez, *f*

available *a* útil; disponible; aprovechable; válido

avalanche *n* alud, lurte, *m*

avarice *n* avaricia, *f*

avaricious *a* avaro, avaricioso

ave *interj* ¡ave! *n* avemaría, *f*; despedida, *f*

avenge *vt* vengar; vindicar. **to a. oneself for,** vengarse de

avenger *n* vengador (-ra)

avenging *a* vengador

avenue *n* avenida, *f*

aver *vt* afirmar, asegurar

average *n* promedio, término medio, *m*; (marine insurance) avería, *f*, *a* de promedio; típico; corriente; normal. *vt* hallar el término medio (de); proporcionar; ser por término medio. **general a.,** (marine insurance) avería gruesa, *f*. **on the a.,** por término medio

averse *a* opuesto (a); desinclinado (a); enemigo (de); repugnante. **to be a. to,** no gustar de; oponerse a; estar desinclinado a; ser enemigo de; repugnar
aversion *n* aversión, *f;* repugnancia, *f*
avert *vt* apartar; (avoid) evitar
aviary *n* avería, pajarera, *f*
aviation *n* aviación, *f*
aviator *n* aviador (-ra)
avid *a* ávido
avidity *n* avidez, *f*
avidly *adv* ávidamente, con avidez
avocation *n* pasatiempo, *m,* distracción, *f;* ocupación, *f;* profesión, *f*
avoid *vt* evitar; (pursuit) evadir, eludir; guardarse (de), rehuir; *law* anular
avoidable *a* evitable, eludible
avoidance *n* evitación, *f*
avow *vt* confesar; declarar
avowal *n* confesión, admisión, *f*
avowedly *adv* por confesión propia
avuncular *a* avuncular
await *vt* aguardar, esperar
awake *vt* despertar. *vi* despertarse. *a* despierto; vigilante; consciente (de); atento (a)
awakening *n* despertamiento, *m*
award *n* sentencia, decisión, *f;* adjudicación, *f;* (prize) premio, *m. vt* adjudicar; otorgar, conceder. **She was awarded a professorship in Greek,** Ganó unas oposiciones para una cátedra de griego
aware *a* consciente, sabedor. **to be well a. of,** saber muy bien. **to make a. of,** hacer saber
awash *adv* a flor de agua
away *adv* a distancia, a lo lejos, lejos; (absent) ausente; (out) fuera; (unceasingly) sin parar, continuamente; (wholly) completamente; (visibly) a ojos vistas. In verbs of motion **a.** is rendered by the reflexive, e.g. **to go a.,** marcharse. Sometimes not translated, e.g. **to take a.,** quitar. *interj* ¡fuera de aquí! ¡márchese Vd.!; ¡vámonos! ¡adelante! **nine miles a.,** a nueve millas de

distancia. **a. in the distance,** allá a lo lejos. **She sang a.,** Ella seguía cantando
awe *n* temor reverente, *m;* horror, *m;* respeto, *m;* reverencia, *f, vt* intimidar, aterrar; infundir respeto (a). **to stand in awe of,** tener respeto (a), reverenciar
awesome *a* pavoroso, temible, aterrador; terrible; (august) augusto; (imposing) imponente
awestruck *a* espantado, aterrado
awful *a* terrible, pavoroso; horrible; temible; atroz; *inf* enorme. **How a.!** *inf* ¡Qué barbaridad!
awfully *adv* terriblemente; horriblemente; *inf* muy
awfulness *n* lo terrible; lo horrible; atrocidad, *f;* (of a crime, etc.) enormidad, *f*
awkward *a* difícil; peligroso; delicado; embarazoso; (of time, etc.) inconveniente, inoportuno; (of things) incómodo; (clumsy) torpe, desmañado; desagradable; (ungraceful) sin gracia. **the a. age,** la edad difícil
awkwardly *adv* torpemente; incómodamente; mal; con dificultad; sin gracia. **He is a. placed,** Se encuentra en una situación difícil
awkwardness *n* dificultad, *f;* peligro, *m;* delicadeza, *f;* inconveniencia, inoportunidad, *f;* (clumsiness) torpeza, desmaña, *f;* (ungracefulness) falta de gracia, *f*
awl *n* lezna, *f,* punzón, *m*
awning *n* toldo, palio, *m; naut* toldilla, *f*
awry *adv* a un lado; oblicuamente; *fig* mal. *a* torcido; *fig* descarriado
ax *n* hacha, *f*
axiom *n* axioma, *m*
axiomatic *a* axiomático
axis *n* eje, *m; zool* axis, *m.* **A. power,** nación del Eje
axle *n* eje, *m;* peón, árbol (de una rueda), *m.* **back a.,** eje trasero, *m.* **differential a.,** eje diferencial, *m.* **front a.,** eje delantero, *m*
ay *interj* sí. *n* voto afirmativo, *m*
aye *adv* siempre. **for aye,** por (or para) siempre
azalea *n* azalea, *f*
Aztec *a* and *n* azteca, *mf*
azure *n* azul celeste, *m*

B

b *n* (letter) be, *f; mus* si, *m*
baa *n* balido, be, *m, vi* balar, dar balidos
babble *n* (chatter) charla, *f;* (of a child) gorjeo, *m;* (confused sound) vocinglería, barbulla, *f,* rumor, *m;* (of water) murmullo, susurro, *m. vi* charlar; (of children) gorjearse; (incoherently) balbucir; (water) murmurar, susurrar; (a secret) descubrir
babbler *n* charlatán (-ana)
babbling *n* garrulería, locuacidad, *f;* (incoherent speech) balbuceo, *m.* (of water) murmullo, *m. a* gárrulo, locuaz; balbuciente; murmurante
babel *n* babel, *m*
baboon *n* babuino, *m*
baby *n* bebé, crío, *m;* niño (-ña) de pecho; *fig* gran bebé, *m;* niño mimado, *m, a* infantil. **b. blue,** azul claro, *m.* **b. doll,** muñeca bebé, *f.* **b. grand piano,** piano de media cola, *m*
baby carriage *n* coche de niños, *m*
baby-faced *a* con mejillas mofletudas
babyhood *n* infancia, niñez, *f*
babyish *a* infantil, aniñado, pueril
Babylon babilonia, *f*
babysitter *n* cuidaniños, *mf*
baccalaureate *n* bachillerato, *m*
baccarat *n* bacará, *m*
bachelor *n* soltero, célibe, *m;* (of a university) licenciado, bachiller, *m;* (as a title) caballero, *m.* **confirmed b.,** soltaron, *m.* **degree of b.,** licenciatura, *f.* **to receive the degree of b.,** licenciarse, bachillerarse
bachelorhood *n* soltería, *f,* celibato, *m*
bacillus *n* bacilo, *m*
back *n anat* espalda, *f;* (of an animal) lomo, espinazo, *m;*

(reins, loins) riñones, *m pl;* (of chairs, sofas) respaldo, *m;* (of a book) lomo, *m;* (back, bottom) fondo, *m;* parte posterior, parte de atrás, *f;* (of a hand, brush and many other things) dorso, *m;* (of a coin) reverso, *m;* el otro lado de alguna cosa; (in football, hockey) defensa, *m; theat* foro, *m;* (of fire-arms) culata, *f;* (of a knife) canto, *m;* (upper portion) parte superior, *f. a* posterior, trasero; de atrás; (remote) alejado, apartado; inferior; (overdue) past; out of date) atrasado; (earlier) anterior; *anat* dorsal. **at the b.,** detrás; en el fondo; en la última fila. **at the b. of one's mind,** por sus adentros, en el fondo del pensamiento. **behind one's b.,** a espaldas de uno, en ausencia de uno. **half-b.,** medio, *m.* **on one's b.,** boca arriba; a cuestas. **to see the b. of,** *inf* ver por última vez, desembarazarse de. **to turn one's b. on,** volver la espalda (a). **with one's b. to the engine,** de espaldas a la máquina. **b. to b.,** espalda con espalda
back *vt* empujar hacia atrás; (a vehicle) dar marcha atrás; hacer retroceder; (line) reforzar; (support) apoyar; (sign) endosar; (bind) forrar; (bet on) apostar a; (a sail) fachear. *vi* retroceder; dar marchar atrás; (of the wind) girar; (with on to) dar sobre, dominar; (with down) abandonar (una pretensión, etc.). **to b. out,** salir, marcharse; volverse atrás; (retract) desdecirse
back *adv* detrás; atrás; otra vez, de nuevo; (returned) de vuelta; a alguna distancia; (at home) en casa. *interj* ¡atrás! **A few weeks b.,** Hace unas semanas, Unas semanas atrás. **It stands b. from the road,** Está a alguna distancia del camino. **to go b. to,** (of families, etc.) remontar a. **to come b.,** regresar. **to come b. again,** regresar de nuevo, regresar por segunda vez
back axle *n* eje trasero, *m*

backbite vt cortar (a uno) un sayo, desollarle (a uno) vivo, murmurar de

backbiter n mala lengua, f, murmurador (-ra)

backbiting n murmuración, detracción, maledicencia, f, a murmurador, detractor

backbone n espinazo, m, columna vertebral, f. **to the b.,** hasta la médula

backchat n dimes y diretes, m pl; insolencia, f. **to indulge in b.-c.,** andar en dimes y diretes

back door n puerta trasera, puerta de servicio, f

backed a (lined) forrado, m (in compounds; of persons) de espalda; (of chairs) de respaldo

backer n (better) apostador, m; protector (-ra, -triz)

backfire n contrafuego m, falsa explosión, f

backgammon n chaquete, m

back garden n jardín de atrás, m

background n fondo, m; art último término, m. **in the b.,** en el fondo; art en último término; fig en las sombras; alejado, a distancia

backhand n sport revés, m

backhanded a de revés, dado con el revés de la mano; fig ambiguo, equívoco

backing n forro, m; (lining) refuerzo, m; (of a vehicle) marcha atrás, f; retroceso, m; (betting) el apostar (a); (wagers) apuestas, f pl; (fig support) apoyo, m, ayuda, f; garantía, f

backlog n com rezago de pedidos, m

back number n (of a periodical) número atrasado, m

back pedal vi contrapedalear

back premises n parte trasera (de una casa, etc.), f

backroom n cuarto interior, m, habitación trasera, f. **b. boy,** investigador ocupado en trabajos secretos para el gobierno, m

back seat n asiento trasero, m; fondo, m. **to take a b.-s.,** permanecer en el fondo, ceder el paso

back shop n trastienda, f

backside n trasero, m, posaderas, nalgas, f pl

backslide vi recaer, reincidir

backslider n (in religion or politics) apóstata, mf; reincidente, mf

backsliding n apostasía, f; reincidencia, f

backstage n foro, fondo del escenario, m, adv hacia el foro; detrás de bastidores

backstaircase n escalera de servicio, f; escalera secreta, f

backstairs n escalera de servicio, f; fig vías secretas, f pl, a de cocina; fig secreto

backstitch n sew pespunte, m, vt and vi pespuntar

back street n calle secundaria, callejuela, f; pl **back streets,** barrios bajos, m pl

backstroke n reculada, f; sport revés, m

back tooth n muela, f

back view n vista de detrás, f

backward a hacia atrás; vuelto hacia atrás; (in development) atrasado, poco avanzado; lento; negligente; (shy) modesto; (late) tardío; atrasado; retrógrado; (dull) torpe; retrospectivo. adv hacia atrás; al revés; (of falling) de espaldas; (of time) al pasado. **to go b. and forward,** ir y venir. **b. and forward,** de acá para allá

backwardness n atraso, m; lentitud, f; negligencia, f; modestia, f; (lateness) tardanza, f; atraso, m; (dullness) torpeza, f; falta de progreso, f

backwards adv. See **backward**

backwash n agua de rechazo, f

backwater n remanso, f

back wheel n rueda trasera, f, vi contrapedalear

backwoods n monte, m, selva, f

back yard n corral, m

bacon n tocino, m

bacteria n bacteria, f

bacterial a bacterial, bacteriano

bactericide n bactericida, m

bacteriological a bacteriológico

bacteriologist n bacteriólogo, m

bacteriology n bacteriología, f

bad a malo; (wicked) perverso; (ill) enfermo, malo (with estar); (naughty; undutiful) malo (with ser); (of coins) falso; (of debts) incobrable; (rotten) podrido; (harmful) nocivo; (dangerous) peligroso; (of pains, a cold) fuerte; intenso; (of a shot) errado; (mistaken) equivocado; (unfortunate) desgraciado. n el mal, lo malo; (persons) los malos. **from bad to worse,** de mal en peor. **It's too bad!** ¡Esto es demasiado! **to go bad,** (fruit) macarse; (food) estropearse. **bad habit,** mala costumbre, f, vicio, m. **to have the bad habit of,** tener el vicio de. **bad temper,** malhumor, mal genio, m. **bad tempered,** malhumorado. **bad turn,** flaco servicio, m, mala pasada, f

badge n insignia, f; (decoration) condecoración, f; símbolo, emblema, m; (mark) marca, f

badger n tejón, m, vt cansar, molestar

Bad Lands (of Nebraska and South Dakota) Tierras malas f pl; (of Argentina) la Travesía, f

badly adv mal. **extremely b.,** pésimamente. **to want something b.,** necesitar algo con urgencia. **b. done,** mal hecho. **b. disposed,** malintencionado

badminton n el juego del volante, m

badness n maldad, f; mala calidad, f; lo malo

bad-smelling a maloliente

baffle vt desconcertar; (bewilder) tener perplejo (a); contrariar, frustrar; (obstruct) impedir; (avoid) evitar. **to b. description,** no haber palabras para describir

baffling a desconcertante; difícil; confuso; perturbador; (of people) enigmático

bag n saco, m; talega, f; (hand) bolsa, f; saco (de mano), m; (for tools) capacho, m; (for sewing) costurero, m; (of bagpipes) fuelle, m; (saddle) alforja, f; (briefcase) cartera, f; (suitcase) maleta, f; (under the eye) ojera, f; (game shot) caza, f. vt entalegar; coger, cazar; matar; tomar. vi (of garments) arrugarse. **to clear out bag and baggage,** liar el petate. **a bag of bones,** (person) un manojo de huesos. **bag wig,** peluquín, m

bagatelle n bagatela, friolera, f; (game) billar romano, m

bagful n saco, m; bolsa, f

baggage n equipaje, m; mil bagaje, m; (madcap) pícara, f; (jade) mujerzuela, f. **b. master,** (railway) factor, m. **b. car,** furgón de equipajes, m

baggage rack n (of automobile) portaequipajes, m

baggy a (creased, of trousers) con rodilleras, arrugado; (wide) bombacho

bagpipe n gaita, f

bagpiper n gaitero, m

bah interj ¡bah!

Bahamas, the las Islas Bahamas, las Islas Lucayas, f

bail n law fianza, caución, f; (person) fiador (-ra); (cricket) travesaño, m, barra, f. vt law poner en libertad bajo fianza; salir fiador (por); (a boat) achicar. **on b.,** en fiado. **to go b.,** dar fianza, fiar.

bailiff n law agente ejecutivo, m; alguacil, m; mayordomo, m; capataz, m

bait n cebo, m; anzuelo, m; (fodder) pienso, m, vt cebar; (feed) dar pienso (a); azuzar; atormentar; (attract) atraer

baiting n cebadura, f; combate, m; tormenta, f

baize n bayeta, f. **green b.,** tapete verde, m

bake vt cocer; hacer (pan, etc.). **I like to bake cakes,** Me gusta hacer pasteles; fig endurecer. vi cocerse

bakelite n bakelita, f

baker n panadero, hornero, m. **a baker's dozen,** la docena del fraile

bakery n panadería, f

baking n cocimiento, m, cocción, f; (batch) hornada, f; el pan (pan, etc.) a inf abrasador. **b.-dish,** tortera, f. **b.-powder,** levadura química, f

balance n balanza, f; equilibrio, m; com balance, saldo, m; (in a bank) saldo (a favor del cuentacorrentista), m; math resto, m; ast Libra, f; (pendulum) péndola, f; (counterweight) contrapeso, m. **credit b.,** saldo acreedor, m. **debit b.,** saldo deudor, m. **net b.,** saldo líquido, m. **to lose one's b.,** perder el equilibrio. **to strike a b.,**

hacer balance. **b. of power,** equilibrio político, *m.* **b. of trade,** balanza de comercio, *f.* **b.-sheet,** balance, avanzo, *m.* **b. wheel,** (of watches) volante, *m*
balance *vt* balancear, abalanzar; contrapesar; (accounts) saldar; equilibrar; comparar; considerar, examinar. *vi* balancearse; ser de igual peso; equilibrarse; (accounts) saldarse
balance of trade *n* balanza comercial, *f*
balancing *n* balanceo, *m; com* balance, *m.* **b.-pole,** balancín, *m*
balconied *a* con balcones, que tiene balcones
balcony *n* balcón, *m;* galería, *f; theat* anfiteatro, *m*
bald *a* calvo; (of style) seco, pobre; *fig* desnudo, árido, pelado; sin adorno; (simple) sencillo. **to grow b.,** ponerse calvo, encalvecer
balderdash *n* galimatías, *m,* jerigonza, *f;* disparate, *m*
baldly *adv* secamente; sencillamente
baldness *n* calvicie, *f;* (of style) sequedad, pobreza, *f;* (bareness) desnudez, aridez, *f*
bale *n* (bundle) fardo, *m;* (of cotton, paper, etc.) bala, *f*
Balearic *a* baleárico
Balearic Islands, the las Islas Baleares, *f*
baleful *a* malicioso, siniestro, maligno
balefully *adv* malignamente
balk *n* obstáculo, *m;* (beam) viga, *f;* (billiards) cabaña, *f. vt* frustrar; impedir. *vi* resistirse, rehusar
Balkan *a* balcánico
Balkans, the los Balcanes, *m*
ball *n* globo, *m,* esfera, *f;* (plaything) pelota, *f;* (as in billiards, cricket, croquet) bola, *f;* (in football, basket-ball) balón, *m;* (shot) bala, *f;* (of wool, etc.) ovillo, *m;* (of the eye) globo (del ojo), *m;* (of the thumb) yema (del pulgar), *f;* (of the foot) planta (del pie), *f;* (dance) baile, *m. vi* apelotonarse. **red b.,** (in billiards) mingo, *m.* **to play b.,** jugar a la pelota. **to roll oneself into a b.,** aovillarse, hacerse un ovillo. **b.-and-socket joint,** articulación esférica, *f.* **b.-bearing,** cojinete de bolas, *m*
ballad *n* romance, *m;* (song) balada, *f*
balladmonger *n* coplero (-ra)
ballast *n* (*naut* and *fig*) lastre, *m; rw* balasto, *m. vt* lastrar; llenar de balasto
ballerina *n* bailarina, *f*
ballet *n* baile ruso, ballet, *m;* baile, *m.* **b. master,** director de ballet, *m*
ballistics *n* balística, *f*
balloon *n* globo aerostático, *m; chem* balón, *m;* (toy) globo, *m; arch* bola, *f.* **captive b.,** globo cautivo, *m.* **b. barrage,** cortina de globos de intercepción, *f.* **b.-tyre,** neumático balón, *m*
balloonist *n* aeronauta, *mf*
ballot *n* votación, *f;* papeleta para votar, cédula de votación, *f. vi* votar, balotar. **b. box,** urna electoral, *f*
ballpoint pen *n* pluma esférica, *f,* birome, *m* (Argentina), punto-bola, *m* (Bolivia), esfero, *m* (Colombia)
ballroom *n* salón de baile, *m;* salón de fiestas, *m*
ballroom dancing *n* baile de salón, *m*
balm *n* bálsamo, *m; fig* ungüento, *m*
balminess *n* fragancia, *f;* aroma, *m;* (gentleness) suavidad, *f*
balmy *a* balsámico; fragante; aromático; (soft) suave; (soothing) calmante
balsam *n* bálsamo, *m*
Baltic *a* báltico
Baltic, the el (Mar) Báltico, *m*
baluster *n* balaustre, *m*
balustrade *n* balaustrada, barandilla, *f,* antepecho, *m*
bamboo *n* bambú, *m*
bamboozle *vt* engatusar, embaucar
bamboozler *n* embaucador (-ra)
bamboozling *n* embaucamiento, engaño, *m*
ban *n* interdicción, *f;* prohibición, *f;* bando, *m. vt* prohibir; proscribir
banal *a* banal, vulgar, trivial
banality *n* banalidad, vulgaridad, trivialidad, *f*
banana *n* (tree and fruit) plátano, *m;* (fruit) banana, *f.* **b. plantation,** platanar, *m*

band *n* lista, tira, *f;* zona, *f;* (black mourning) tira de gasa, *f;* (sash) faja, *f;* (ribbon) banda; cinta, *f;* (bandage) venda, *f; mech* correa, *f; arch* listón, *m; mus* banda, *f;* (group) pandilla, *f,* grupo, *m. vt* congregar, reunir. *vi* reunirse, asociarse. **b.-saw,** sierra de cinta, *f*
bandage *n* vendaje, *f,* vendaje, *m, vt* vendar, poner un vendaje en (limbs, etc. or persons)
bandaging *n* vendaje, *m*
banderol *n* banderola, *f*
bandit *n* bandido, bandolero, *m*
bandmaster *n* músico mayor, *m;* director de orquesta, *m*
bandsman *n* músico, *m*
bandstand *n* quiosco de música, *m*
bandy *vt* cambiar, trocar; pasar de uno a otro
bandy-legged *a* estevado zanquituerto
bane *n* (poison) veneno, *m;* perdición, ruina, *f;* (nuisance) plaga, *f*
baneful *a* pernicioso, funesto; dañino; maligno
banefully *adv* funestamente; malignamente
bang *n* golpe, golpazo, *m;* (of an explosive, fire-arm) estallido, *m,* detonación, *f;* (of a firework) traque, *m;* (of a door) portazo, *m;* (with the fist) puñetazo, *m;* (noise) ruido, *m;* (fringe) flequillo, *m. vt* golpear; (beat) sacudir; (throw) lanzar, arrojar con violencia; (a door, etc.) cerrar de golpe, cerrar con violencia. *vi* golpear; estallar; (thunder) retronar; (in the wind) cencerrear. *interj* ¡pum! ¡zas!
banging *n* golpeadura, *f;* sacudidura, *f;* detonación, *f;* ruido, *m*
bangle *n* (slave b.) esclava, *f;* pulsera, *f;* brazalete, *m;* (for ankles) ajorca, *f*
banish *vt* desterrar; apartar; (from the mind) despedir, ahuyentar; (suppress) suprimir
banishment *n* destierro, *m;* expulsión, *f;* relegación, *f;* (suppression) supresión, *f*
banister *n* baranda, *f,* pasamano, *m*
banjo *n* banjo, *m*
banjoist *n* tocador (-ra) de banjo
bank *n* (of rivers, etc.) ribera, orilla, *f,* margen, *m;* (of clouds) banda, capa, *f;* (of sand, fog, snow) banco, *m;* (embankment) terraplén, *m; com* banco, *m;* (gaming) banca, *f;* (for foreign exchange) casa de cambio, *f.* **b. account,** cuenta corriente, *f.* **b. book,** libreta de banco, *f.* **b. clerk,** empleado del banco, *m.* **b. holiday,** fiesta oficial, *f.* **b.-note,** billete de banco, *m.* **b. stock,** acciones de un banco, *f pl*
bank *vt* estancar, represar; amontonar; poner (dinero) en un banco, depositar en un banco. *vi* tener cuenta corriente en un banco; (gaming) tener la banca; ser banquero; *aer* inclinarse al virar
banker *n* banquero, *m,* (also at cards); (money-changer) cambista, *mf*
banking *n* banca, *f; aer* vuelo inclinado, *m, a com* bancario. **b. house,** casa de banca, *f*
bankrupt *a* insolvente, quebrado. *n* quebrado (-da). **to go b.,** declararse en quiebra, hacer bancarrota
bankruptcy *n* bancarrota, quiebra, *f; fig* pobreza, decadencia, *f.* **fraudulent b.,** quiebra fraudulenta, *f.* **b. court,** tribunal de quiebras, *m*
banner *n* bandera, *f*
banns *n pl* amonestaciones, *f pl.* **to forbid the b.,** impedir las amonestaciones. **to publish the b.,** decir las amonestaciones
banquet *n* banquete, *m, vt* and *vi* banquetear
banqueting *a* de banquetes. **b. hall,** sala de banquetes, *f*
bantam *n* gallina enana, *f.* **b. weight,** (*sport*) *a* de peso gallo. *n* peso gallo, *m*
banter *vt* and *vi* tomar el pelo (a). *n* chistes, *m pl,* burlas, *f pl*
baptism *n* bautismo, *m; fig* bautizo, *m*
baptist *n* bautista, *m.* **St. John the B.,** San Juan Bautista
baptistry *n* baptisterio, bautisterio, *m*
baptize *vt* bautizar

baptizing n bautizo, m

bar n barra, f; (of chocolate, soap) pastilla, f; her banda, f; (on a window) reja, f; (of a door) tranca, f, barrote, m; (bar lever) palanca, f; (of a balance) astil, m; mus barra, f; (in the sea, etc.) banco, alfaque, m; (barrier) barrera, f; (barrister's profession) foro, m, curia, f; fig tribunal, m; (in a court) barra, f; fig impedimento, m; (of light) rayo, m; (stripe) raya, f; (for refreshments) bar, m; mostrador del bar, m. vt atrancar, abarrotar; impedir, obstruir; prohibir; exceptuar, excluir; (streak) rayar. **the b.,** el cuerpo de abogados. **to be called to the b.,** ser recibido como abogado en los tribunales. **b.-tender,** camarero del bar, m

bar association n colegio de abogados, m

barb n púa, f; (of an arrow, fish-hook, etc.) lengüeta, f; (of a lance) roquete, m; (of fish) barbilla, f; (of a feather) barba, f; (horse) caballo berberisco, m. vt proveer de púas; armar de lengüetas

Barbados Isla de Barbados, f

barbarian a bárbaro, barbárico. n bárbaro (-ra)

barbaric a barbárico, salvaje

barbarism n barbarismo, salvajismo, m; crueldad, f; (of style) barbarismo, m

barbarity n barbaridad, ferocidad, f

barbarous a feroz, cruel, salvaje; inculto

barbarously adv bárbaramente, cruelmente

barbarousness n barbaridad, f; crueldad, ferocidad, f

Barbary Berbería, f

barbecue n barbacoa, f

barbed wire n alambre de púas, alambre espinoso, m

barber n barbero, m. **barber shop,** barbería, f

Barcelona (of or from) a and n barcelonés (-esa)

bard n bardo, vate, m

bare a desnudo; descubierto; vacío; (mere) mero, solo; (worn) raído; pelado, raso; (unadorned) sencillo; (unsheathed) desnudo; (arid) árido; (curt) seco; (unprotected) desabrigado; pobre. vt desnudar; descubrir; revelar. **He bared his head,** Se descubrió. **to lay b.,** dejar al desnudo; revelar

bareback a que monta en pelo. adv en pelo

barefaced a descarado, desvergonzado, cínico

barefoot a descalzo

bareheaded a sin sombrero, descubierto

barelegged a en pernetas, en piernas

barely adv apenas; escasamente; meramente, solamente

bareness n desnudez, f; desadorno, m; (aridity) aridez, f; pobreza, f

bargain n contrato, m; pacto, acuerdo, m; (purchase) ganga, f. vi negociar; (haggle) regatear; (expect) esperar. **into the b.,** de añadidura, también. **It is a b.,** Es una ganga; Trato hecho. **to get the best of the b.,** salir ganando. **to strike a b.,** cerrar un trato. **b. counter,** sección de saldos, f. **b. sale,** venta de saldos, f

bargainer n negociador (-ra); regatón (-ona)

bargaining n negociación, gestión, f; (haggling) regateo, m

barge n (for freight) barcaza, gabarra, m; falúa, f; lancha, f. vi (into) tropezar con; dar empujones

baritone n chem bario, m

barium n chem bario, m

bark n (of a tree) corteza, f; (quinine) quina, f; (boat, poet) barca, f; naut buque de tres palos, m; (of a dog) ladrido, m; (of a fox) aullido, m; (of a gun) ruido, m. vi (of a dog) ladrar; (of a fox) aullar; (of a gun) tronar

barking n ladrido, m; (of stags) rebramo, m; (of foxes) aullidos, m pl; (of guns) trueno, m

barley n cebada, f, a de cebada. **pearl b.,** cebada perlada, f. **b.-bin,** cebadera, f. **b. dealer,** cebadero, m. **b. field,** cebadal, m. **b.-water,** hordiate, m

barm n (froth on beer) giste, m; (leaven) levadura, f

barmaid n moza de bar, camarera, f

barn n pajar, granero, hórreo, m. **b.-owl,** lechuza, f

barnacle n lapa, f, barnacla, m

barometer n barómetro, m

barometric a barométrico

baron n barón, m

baroness n baronesa, f

Baron Munchausen el Baron de la Castaña

baroque a barroco. **the b.,** lo barroco

barrack n mil cuartel, m, caserna, f, vt acuartelar

barrage n presa de contención, f; mil cortina de fuego, f; (barrier) barrera, f; (of questions) lluvia, f. **b. balloon,** globo de intercepción, m

barrel n barril, m; tonel, m, cuba, f; (of a gun) cañón, m; mech cilindro, m; (of an animal) cuerpo, m. vt embarrilar, entonelar. **b.-organ,** organillo, órgano de manubrio, m

barrelled a embarrilado; (of guns, generally in compounds) de . . . cañones. **double-b. gun,** escopeta de dos cañones, f

barren a estéril; (of ground) árido; (fruitless) infructuoso

barrenness n esterilidad, f; aridez, sequedad, f; (fruitlessness) inutilidad, f

barrens n yermo, m sing, yerma, f sing

barricade n barricada, f; barrera, f, vt cerrar con barricadas; obstruir

barricading n el cerrar con barricadas; la defensa con barricadas (de)

barrier n barrera, f; impedimento, m; (for customs duties) portazgo, m

barring prep salvo, excepto, con la excepción de, menos

barrister n abogado (-da)

barrow n carretón, m; carretilla, f; (tumulus) túmulo, m

barter n cambio, trueque, m; tráfico, m, vt and vi cambiar, trocar; traficar

barterer n traficante, mf

basal a básico, fundamental

basalt n basalto, m

base a bajo, vil, ruin; soez; indigno; impuro; (of metals) de mala ley. n base, f; fundamento, m; pie, m; arch pedestal, m; (mil chem geom) base, f; (of a vase) asiento, m, vt basar; fundar. **b. action,** bajeza, f. **b. line,** sport línea de base, f. **b. metal,** metal común, m

baseball n pelota base, f

baseless a sin base; sin fundamento; insostenible

basely adv bajamente, vilmente

baseness n bajeza, vileza, ruindad, f

basement n sótano, m

bashful a vergonzoso, ruboroso; tímido, corto; (unsociable) huraño, esquivo

bashfully adv vergonzosamente; tímidamente

bashfulness n vergüenza, f, rubor, m; encogimiento, m, timidez, cortedad, f; (unsociableness) huraña, esquivez, f

basic a básico; fundamental

basic commodity n artículo básico, producto primario, m

basil (sweet) n bot albahaca, f

basilica n basílica, f

basilisk n basilisco, m

basin n vasija, f; (for washing) jofaina, f; (barber's) bacía, f; (of a fountain) taza, f; anat bacinete, m; (of a harbor) concha, f; (of a river) cuenca, f; (in the earth) hoya, f; (dock) dársena, f

basis n base, f; fundamento, m; elemento principal, m

bask vi calentarse; (in the sun) tomar el sol

basket n cesta, f; canasta, f; (frail) espuerta, f. **flat b.,** azafate, m. **large b.,** banasta, f. **b. with a lid,** excusabaraja, f. **b. ball,** baloncesto, m. **b. maker** or **dealer,** banastero, cestero, m. **b. work** or **shop** or **factory,** cestería, f. **b. work chair,** sillón de mimbres, m

basketful n cesta, cestada, f

Basle Basilea, f

Basque a and n vasco (-ca), vascongado (-da). n (language) vascuence, m

Basque Provinces, the las Provincias Vascongadas

bas-relief n bajo relieve, m

bass n mus bajo, m; (for tying) esparto, m, a mus bajo. **double b.,** contrabajo, m. **figured b.,** bajo cifrado, m.

b. clef, clave de fa, *f.* **b. string,** bordón, *m.* **b. voice,** voz baja, *f*

bassinet *n* cochecito de niño, *m*

bassoon *n mus* bajón, fagot, *m*

bassoonist *n* bajonista, fagotista, *mf*

bastard *n* bastardo (-da), hijo (-ja) natural. *a* bastardo, ilegítimo; espurio

baste *vt sew* bastear, hilvanar, embastar; *cul* enlardar, lardear

basting *n sew* embaste, *m; cul* lardeamiento, *m.* **b. spoon,** cacillo, *m.* **b. stitch,** pasillo, *m*

bastion *n* bastión, baluarte, *m.* **to fortify with bastions,** abastionar

bastioned *a* abastionado, con bastiones

bat *n zool* murciélago, *m;* (in cricket) paleta, *f;* (in table tennis) pala, *f. vi* (cricket) golpear con la paleta. See **without**

batch *n* (of loaves, etc.) hornada, *f;* lote, *m;* (of recruits) promoción, *f*

bath *n* baño, *m;* (room) cuarto de baño, *m;* (vat) bañador, *m;* (for swimming) piscina cubierta, *f;* (in the open air) piscina al aire libre, *f; phot* baño, *m,* solución, *f. vt* bañar, lavar. **hot mineral baths,** termas, *f pl.* **Order of the B.,** Orden del Baño, *f.* **public baths,** casa de baños, *f.* **reinforcing b.,** *phot* reforzador, *m.* **to take a b.,** bañarse, tomar un baño. **b.-chair,** cochecillo de inválido, *m.* **b.-robe,** bata de baño, *f,* albornoz, *m.* **b. room,** cuarto de baño, *m.* **b. towel,** toalla del baño, *f.* **b. tub,** bañera, *f,* baño, *m*

bathe *vt* bañar, lavar; (of light, etc.) bañar, envolver. *vi* bañarse. *n* baño, *m.* **to go for a b.,** ir a bañarse

bather *n* bañista, *mf;* bañador (-ra)

bathing *a* de baño; balneario, *n* baño, *m.* **b. cap,** gorro de baño, *m.* **b. dress,** traje de baño, *m.* **b. gown,** albornoz, *m,* bata de baño, *f.* **b. machine,** caseta de baños, *f.* **b.-pool,** piscina, *f.* **b.-resort,** estación balnearia, *f.* **b.-shoes,** calzado de baño, *m*

bathos *n* paso de lo sublime a lo ridículo, *m;* anticlímax, *m*

batiste *n;* batista, *f*

baton *n* bastón de mando, *m; mus* batuta, *f;* (policeman's) porra, *f*

battalion *n* batallón, *m*

batten *vi* engordar (de); medrar, prosperar. **to b. down,** cerrar las escotillas

batter *n cul* batido, *m;* pasta, *f; sport* lanzador, *m. vt* apalear, golpear; (demolish) derribar, demoler; (with artillery) cañonear; batir. **to coat with b.,** rebozar. **to b. down,** derribar

battering ram *n* ariete, *m*

battery *n* (*mil nav*) batería, *f; elec* pila, batería, *f; law* agresión, *f.* **dry b.,** batería de pilas, *f.* **storage b.,** acumulador, *m.* **b. cell,** pila de batería eléctrica, *f*

battle *n* batalla, *f;* pelea, *f,* combate, *m;* (struggle) lucha, *f. vi* batallar, pelear; luchar. **b.-array,** orden de batalla, *f.* **b.-axe,** hacha de combate, *f.* **b.-cruiser,** acorazado, *m.* **b.-field,** campo de batalla, *m.* **b.-front,** frente de combate, *m.* **b.-piece,** *art* batalla, *f.* **b.-ship,** buque de guerra, *m*

battledore (and shuttlecock) *n* raqueta (y volante), *f*

battlement *n* almenaje, *m;* muralla almenada, *f*

bauble *n* (trifle) chuchería, fruslería, *f;* (fool's) cetro de bufón, *m*

bauxite *n* bauxita, *f*

Bavaria Baviera, *f*

Bavarian *a* and *n* bávaro (-ra)

bawdy *a* obsceno, indecente, escabroso

bawl *vi* chillar, vocear

bawling *n* vocerío, *m,* chillidos, *m pl*

bay *n geog* bahía, *f;* (small) abra, *f; bot* laurel, *m;* (horse) bayo, *m;* (howl) aullido, *m; arch* abertura, *f; rw* andén, *m. a* (of horses) bayo, isabelino. *vi* aullar. **at bay,** en jaque, acorralado. **sick-bay,** enfermería, *f.* **to keep at bay,** tener a distancia; tener alejado; entretener. **bay rum,** ron de malagueta, *m.* **bay window,** ventana salediza, *f*

baying *n* aullido, *m*

bayonet *n* bayoneta, *f, vt* herir o matar con bayoneta. **fixed b.,** bayoneta calada, *f.* **b. charge,** carga de bayoneta, *f.* **b. thrust,** bayonetazo, *m*

Bayonne Bayona, *f*

bazaar *n* bazar, *m*

be *vi* ser; (of position, place, state, temporariness) estar; (exist) existir; (in impersonal expressions) haber; (of expressions concerning the weather and time) hacer; (remain) quedar; (leave alone) dejar; (do) hacer; (of one's health) estar; (of feeling cold, hot, afraid, etc. and of years of one's age) tener; (live) vivir; (belong) ser (de), pertenecer (a); (matter, concern) importar (a); (happen) ocurrir, suceder; (find oneself) hallarse, encontrarse, estar; (arrive) llegar (a); (cost) costar; (be worth) valer; (celebrate, hold) celebrarse, tener lugar; (forming continuous tense with present participle active or passive) estar; (with past participle forming passive) ser (this construction is often replaced by reflexive form when no ambiguity is entailed); (with infinitive expressing duty, intention) haber de; (must) tener que. **He is a soldier (doctor, etc.),** Es soldado (médico, etc.). **He is on guard,** Está de guardia. **They were at the door (in the house, etc.),** Estaban a la puerta (en la casa, etc.). **I am writing a letter,** Estoy escribiendo una carta (but this form is often replaced by a simple tense, e.g. escribo . . .). **It remains to be written,** Queda por escribir. **What is to be done?** ¿Qué hay que hacer? **Woe is me!** ¡Ay de mí! **to be hot (cold),** (of things) estar caliente (frío); (of weather) hacer calor (frío); (of persons) tener calor (frío). **How is John? He is well,** ¿Cómo está Juan? Está bien de salud. **It is daylight,** Es de día. **It is cloudy,** Está nublado. **She is 10,** Tiene diez años. **They are afraid,** Tienen miedo. **I am to go there tomorrow,** He de ir allí mañana. **What is to be will be,** Lo que tiene que ser será. **If John were to come we could go into the country,** Si viniera Juan podríamos ir al campo. **Be that as it may,** Sea como sea. **It is seven years since we saw him,** Hace siete años que no le vemos. **We have been here for three years,** Hace tres años que estamos aquí, Llevamos tres años aquí. **There is or there are,** Hay. **There will be many people,** Habrá mucha gente. **There were many people,** Había mucha gente. **There are many people,** Hay mucha gente. **It is three miles to the next village,** Estamos a tres millas del pueblo próximo. **So be it!** Así sea. **Your pen is not to be seen,** Tu pluma no se ve. **It is to be hoped that . . . ,** Se espera que . . . ; ¡Ojalá que . . . ! **The door is open,** La puerta está abierta. **The door was opened by Mary,** La puerta fue abierta por María. **He was accused of being a fascist,** Lo acusaron de fascista. **to be about to,** estar por; (of a more imminent action) estar para, estar a punto de. **to be in,** estar dentro; estar en casa. **to be off,** marcharse, irse. **Be off!** ¡Márchate! ¡Vete!; ¡Fuera! **to be out,** estar fuera; haber salido; no estar en casa; (of a light, etc.) estar apagado. **to be up,** estar levantado. **to be up to,** proyectar, traer entre manos; urdir, maquinar

beach *n* playa, *f;* costa, *f. vt* (a boat) encallar en la costa. **b. shoes,** playeras, *f pl.* **b. suit,** vestido de playa, *m*

beach club *n* club de playa, *m*

beacon *n* (lighthouse) faro, *m;* (buoy) baliza, *f,* fanal, *m;* (watch-tower) atalaya, *f; fig* guía, *f. vt* iluminar. **b. fire,** almenara, *f*

bead *n* cuenta, *f;* (of glass) abalorio, *m;* (drop) gota, *f; arch* perla, *f;* (bubble) burbuja, *f;* (foam) espuma, *f; pl* **beads,** rosario, *m, vt* adornar con abalorios. **to tell one's beads,** rezar el rosario. **b. work,** abalorio, *m*

beading *n* abalorio, *m; arch* friso, listón, *m*

beadle *n* bedel, *m*

beadleship *n* bedelía, *f*

beagle *n* perro sabueso, *m*

beak *n* pico, *m;* punta, *f; naut* espolón, *m.* **to tap with the b.,** picotear

beaked *a* que tiene pico; (in compounds) de . . . pico

beaker *n* copa, *f; chem* vaso de precipitado, *m*

beam *n arch* madero, *m*, viga, *f;* (width of a ship) manga, *f;* (of a balance) palanca, *f;* (of a plough) cama, *f;* (of light) rayo, destello, *m; phys* rayo, *m;* (smile) sonrisa brillante, *f; pl* **beams,** (of a building) envigado, *m;* (of a ship) baos, *m pl.* **main b.,** *arch* viga maestra, *f.* **on her b.-ends,** de costado; *fig* arruinado; en la miseria. **b. feather,** astil, *m.* **b. of light,** rayo de luz, haz de luz, *m*

beam *vt* lanzar, emitir; difundir. *vi* brillar, fulgurar, destellar; estar radiante, estar rebosando de alegría

beaming *a* brillante; radiante

bean *n* haba, *f;* judía, alubia, *f;* (of coffee) grano, *m.* **broad b.,** haba, *f.* **French, haricot, kidney b.,** judía, *f.* **string b.,** judía verde, *f.* **b. field,** habar, *m*

bear *n zool* oso, *m;* (she-bear) osa, *f;* (Stock Exchange) bajista, *mf.* **Great B.,** *ast* Osa Mayor, *f,* Septentrión, *m.* **Little B.,** *ast* Osa Menor, *f.* **polar b.,** oso blanco, *m.* **b.-cub,** osezno, *m.* **bear's den,** osera, *f.* **b.-garden,** patio de osos, *m; inf* merienda de negros, *f.* **b.-hunting,** caza de osos, *f.* **b.-like,** osuno. **b.-pit,** recinto de los osos, *m*

bear *vt* and *vi* (carry) llevar; (show) ostentar; (company, etc.) hacer; (profess) profesar; (of spite, etc. and of relation) guardar; (have) tener; (fruit) dar; (give birth to) parir; (support) sostener; (endure) aguantar; (suffer) padecer, sufrir; (tolerate) tolerar, sufrir; (a strain, an operation, etc.) resistir; (lean on) apoyarse en; (experience) experimentar; (produce) producir, dar; (enjoy) disfrutar de; (use) usar; (impel) empujar; (occupy, hold) ocupar; (go) dirigirse. **It was suddenly borne in on them that . . . ,** De pronto vieron claro que . . . **I cannot b. any more,** No puedo más. **We cannot b. him,** No le aguantamos, No le sufrimos. **His language won't b. repeating,** Su lenguaje no puede repetirse. **to bring to b.,** ejercer (presión, etc.). **to b. a grudge,** guardar rencor (a), tener ojeriza (a). **to b. arms,** llevar armas; servir en el ejército o la milicia. **to b. company,** hacer compañía (a), acompañar (a). **to b. in mind,** tener en cuenta, tener presente; acordarse de. **to b. oneself,** conducirse, portarse. **to b. to the right,** ir hacia la derecha. **to b. witness,** atestiguar. **to b. false witness,** levantar falso testimonio. **to b. away,** llevarse; ganar. **to b. down,** hundir; derribar; bajar. **to b. down on,** avanzar rápidamente hacia; correr hacia; *naut* arribar sobre; (attack) caer sobre. **to b. in,** llevar adentro. **to b. off,** llevarse; ganar; *naut* apartarse de la costa. **to b. on, upon,** apoyarse en; (refer to) referirse a. **to b. out,** llevar fuera; confirmar; apoyar; justificar. **to b. up,** llevar arriba; llevar a la cumbre (de); sostener; (recover) cobrar ánimo; (against) resistir; hacer frente a. **to b. with,** soportar; sufrir; aguantar; llevar con paciencia; ser indulgente con

bearable *a* soportable; aguantable; tolerable

beard *n* barba, *f;* (of cereals) raspa, arista, *f, vt* desafiar. **thick b.,** barba bien poblada, *f*

bearded *a* con barba, barbudo

beardless *a* barbilampiño, desbarbado, imberbe, lampiño

bearer *n* llevador (-ra), portador (-ra); (of a bier) andero, *m; com* dador, portador, *m.* **good b.,** *agr* árbol fructífero, *m.* **to b.,** *com* al portador

bearing *n* porte, *m;* postura, *f;* presencia, *f;* conducta, *f;* aspecto, *m;* relación, *f;* (meaning) significación, *f; naut* demora, orientación, *f; mech* cojinete, soporte, *m;* (endurance) tolerancia, *f; pl* (of a building) (way) camino, *m; her* escudo de armas, *m.* **to get one's bearings,** orientarse; encontrar el camino. **to lose one's bearings,** desorientarse; perderse. **to have a b. on,** tener relación con; tener que ver con; influir en

bearish *a* osuno; rudo, áspero

bearskin *n* piel de oso, *f;* birretina, *f*

beast *n* animal, bruto, *m;* cuadrúpedo, *m;* (cattle) res, *f;* bestia, *f.* **wild b.,** fiera, *f.* **b. of burden,** acémila, bestia de carga, *f.* **b. of prey,** animal de rapiña, *m*

beastliness *n* bestialidad, brutalidad, *f;* obscenidad, *f*

beastly *a* bestial, brutal; obsceno; *inf* horrible

beat *n* latido, *m,* pulsación, *f;* golpe, *m;* (of a drum) toque (de tambor), *m;* (of a clock) tictac, *m;* sonido repetido, *m;* vibración, *f*

beat *vt* and *vi* batir; golpear; (thrash) pegar, dar una paliza (a); (to remove dust, etc.) sacudir; (shake) agitar; (the wings) aletear; (hunting) batir; (excel) exceder, superar; ganar; (defeat) vencer; (of the rain, etc.) azotar; (a drum) tocar; (of the sun) batir, dar (en); (throb) latir, palpitar, pulsar. **to b. about the bush,** andarse por las ramas. **to stop beating about the bush,** dejarse de historias. **to b. a retreat,** *mil* emprender la retirada; huir. **to b. black and blue,** moler a palos. **to b. hollow,** vencer completamente; ganar fácilmente; aventajar con mucho. **to b. it,** *inf* escaparse corriendo. **to b. time,** *mus* llevar el compás; triunfar sobre la vejez. **to b. to it,** *inf* tomar la delantera. **to b. against,** golpear contra; chocar contra. **to b. back,** rechazar; (sobs, etc.) ahogar; reprimir. **to b. down,** (prices) regatear; (of the sun) caer de plomo, caer de plano; reducir; suprimir; destruir. **to b. off,** rechazar; echar a un lado. **to b. out,** hacer salir; (metals) batir; (a tune) llevar el compás (de). **to b. up,** *cul* batir; (a mattress) mullir; asaltar; maltratar

beaten *a* (of paths) trillado; (conquered) vencido; (of metals) batido; (dejected) deprimido; (trite) trivial, vulgar

beater *n* batidor, *m;* (for carpets) sacudidor (de alfombras), *m; cul* batidor, *m*

beatific *a* beatífico

beatification *n* beatificación, *f*

beatify *vt* beatificar

beating *n* batimiento, *m;* vencimiento, *f;* (thrashing) paliza, *f;* (of the heart, etc.) palpitación, *f,* latido, *m;* (of metals) batida, *f;* (of a drum) rataplán, toque de tambor, *m;* (of waves) embate, *m;* (of wings) aleteo, aletazo, *m*

beatitude *n* beatitud, *f*

beau *n* galán, *m;* (fop) petimetre, *m*

beautiful *a* bello, lindo, hermoso; magnífico; excelente; exquisito; elegante; encantador, delicioso

beautifully *adv* bellamente; (richly) ricamente; admirablemente; magníficamente; elegantemente

beautify *vt* embellecer; hermosear; adornar. **to b. oneself,** arreglarse, ponerse elegante

beautifying *n* embellecimiento, *m;* adorno, *m*

beauty *n* belleza, hermosura, lindeza, *f;* magnificencia, *f;* excelencia, *f;* elegancia, *f;* encanto, *m;* (belle) beldad, Venus, *f.* **to lose one's b.,** desmejorarse, perder su hermosura. **b. contest,** concurso de belleza, *m.* **b. parlor,** salón de belleza, instituto de belleza, *m.* **b. sleep,** el primer sueño de la noche. **b. spot,** lunar, *m;* lunar postizo, *m;* (place) sitio hermoso, *m.* **b. treatment,** masaje facial, *m*

beaver *n* castor, *m;* (hat) sombrero de copa, *m;* (of helmet) babera, *f*

because *conjunc* porque. **b. of,** debido a, a causa de

beckon *vt* and *vi* hacer señas (a); llamar por señas, llamar con la mano

become *vi* volverse; llegar a ser, venir a ser; convertirse en; ponerse; hacerse; (befit) convenir; (suit) ir bien (a), favorecer. **He became red,** Se enrojeció. **The hat becomes you,** El sombrero te va bien. **He became king,** Llegó a ser rey. **What has b. of her?** ¿Qué es de ella? (Where is she?) ¿Qué se ha hecho de ella? **b. binding,** adquirir carácter de compromiso

becoming *a* propio; correcto; decoroso; (suitable) conveniente; (of dress) que favorece, que va bien. **This dress is to you,** Este vestido te favorece

becomingly *adv* decorosamente

bed *n* cama, *f,* lecho, *m;* (of sea) fondo, *m;* (of river) cauce, *m; geol* yacimiento, *m;* (in a garden) cuadro, macizo (de jardín), *m;* (of a machine) asiento, *m;* (of a building) cimiento, *m; fig* fundamento, *m,* base, *f, vt* (plants) plantar; (fix) fijar, poner. **double bed,** cama de matrimonio, *f.* **single bed,** cama de monja, *f.* **in**

bed, en cama. **to be gone to bed,** haber ido a la cama. **to be in bed,** estar acostado. **to get into bed,** meterse en cama. **to get out of bed,** levantarse de la cama. **to go to bed,** acostarse, ir a la cama. **to make the beds,** hacer las camas. **to put to bed,** acostar. **to stay in bed,** quedarse en cama, guardar cama. **bed-bug,** chinche, *f.* **bed-clothes,** ropa de cama, *f.* **bed-cover,** cubrecama, colcha, *f.* **bed-head,** cabecera, *f.* **bed-pan,** silleta, *f.* **bed-sore,** úlcera de decúbito, *f*

bedaub, bedazzle. See **daub, dazzle**

bedchamber *n* dormitorio, *m*, alcoba, *f*

bedded *a* con . . . cama(s). **a double-b. room,** un cuarto con dos camas; un cuarto con cama de matrimonio

bedding *n* ropa de cama, *f*; cama para el ganado, *f*

bedeck *vt* embellecer, adornar, engalanar

bedfellow *n* compañero de almohada, compañero de cama

bedlam *n* belén, manicomio, *m*; *fig* babel, *m*

Bedouin *a* and *n* beduino (-na)

bedraggled *a* mojado y sucio

bedridden *a* postrado en cama, inválido

bedrock *n* lecho de roca, *m*; *fig* principios fundamentales, fundamentos, *m pl*

bedroom *n* cuarto de dormir, dormitorio, *m*, habitación, *f*

bedside *n* lado de cama, *m*; cabecera, *f.* **b. manner,** mano izquierda, diplomacia, *f.* **b.-table,** mesa de noche, *f*

bedspread *n* colcha, cubrecama, sobrecama, *f*

bedstead *n* cama, *f*

bedtime *n* hora de acostarse, *f*

bee *n* abeja, *f*; (meeting) reunión, *f*, *a* abejuno. **queen bee,** rey, *m*, abeja maestra, *f.* **to have a bee in one's bonnet,** tener una manía (or idea fija). **to make a bee-line for,** ir directamente a. **bee-eater,** *orn* abejaruco, *m.* **bee hive,** colmena, *f*; abejar, *m.* **bee-keeper,** apicultor (-ra), colmenero (-ra), abejero (-ra). **bee's wax,** cera de abeja, *f*

beech *n* haya, *f.* **plantation of b. trees,** hayal, *m.* **b.-nut,** hayuco, *m*

beef *n* carne de vaca, *f*; (flesh) carne, *f*; (strength) fuerza, *f.* **roast b.,** rosbif, *m.* **b.-tea,** caldo, *m*

beefsteak *n* biftec, bistec, *m*

beer *n* cerveza, *f.* **b. barrel,** barril de cerveza, *m.* **b.-house,** cervecería, *f.* **b. mug,** jarro para la cerveza, *m*

beery *a* de cerveza; (tipsy) achispado

beet *n* remolacha, *f.* **b. sugar,** azúcar de remolacha, *m*

beetle *n* escarabajo, *m.* **b.-browed,** cejijunto

beetroot *n* remolacha, *f*

befall *vi* acontecer, suceder, ocurrir. *vt* ocurrir (a), acontecer (a)

befeathered *a* plumado; adornado con plumas

befit *vt* convenir (a), ser digno de

befitting *a* conveniente, apropiado; digno; oportuno

before *adv* delante; al frente; (of time), antes, anteriormente; (of order) antes; (already) ya. *prep* delante de; en frente de; (of time, order) ante; (in the presence of) ante, en presencia de; (rather than) antes de. **b. going,** antes de marcharse. **B. I did it,** Antes de que lo hiciera; Antes de hacerlo. **as never b.,** como nunca. **b. long,** en breve, dentro de poco. **b.-mentioned,** antes citado. **b. the mast,** al pie del mástil, e.g. **two years b. the mast,** dos años al pie del mástil.

beforehand *adv* previamente, de antemano

befoul *vt* ensuciar; *fig* manchar, difamar

befriend *vt* proteger, ayudar, favorecer, amparar

beg *vt* pedir, implorar, suplicar. *vi* mendigar, pordiosear; vivir de limosna. **I beg to propose,** Me permito proponer; Tengo el gusto de proponer; (the health of) Brindo a la salud de. **I beg your pardon!** ¡Vd. dispense! (when passing in front of anyone, etc.) Con permiso; (in conversation for repetition of a word) ¿Cómo? **to beg the question,** dar por sentado lo mismo que se trata de probar. **His conduct begs de-**

scription, No hay palabras para su comportamiento

beget *vt* procrear, engendrar; causar; suscitar

begetter *n* procreador (-ra); creador (-ra)

begetting *n* procreación, *f*; origen, *m*, causa, *f*

beggar *n* mendigo (-ga), pordiosero (-ra). **beggars can't be choosers,** a falta de pan, se conforma con tortillas (Mexico); *vt* empobrecer; arruinar. **to b. description,** no haber palabras para describir

beggarliness *n* mendicidad, *f*; pobreza, *f*

beggarly *a* miserable, pobre

beggary *n* miseria, pobreza, *f*

begging *a* mendicante, pordiosero. *n* mendicidad, *f*, pordioseo, *m.* **to go b.,** andar mendigando. **b. letter,** carta pidiendo dinero, *f*

begin *vt* and *vi* empezar; comenzar; iniciar; (a conversation) entablar; (open) abrir; inaugurar; tener su principio; nacer. **to b. to,** empezar a; (start on) ponerse a; (with laughing, etc.) romper a. **to b. with,** empezar por; para empezar, en primer lugar

beginner *n* principiante (-ta); (novice) novato (-ta); iniciador (-ra); autor (-ra)

beginning *n* principio, comienzo, *m*; origen, *m.* **at the b.,** al principio; (of the month) a principios (de). **from the b. to the end,** desde el principio hasta el fin, *inf* de pe a pa. **in the b.,** al principio. **to make a b.,** comenzar, empezar

begone *interj* ¡fuera! ¡márchate! ¡vete!

begonia *n* begonia, *f*

begrudge *vt* envidiar

beguile *vt* engañar; defraudar; (time) entretener; (charm) encantar, embelesar

beguilement *n* engaño, *m*; (of time) entretenimiento, *m*; (charm) encanto, *m*

beguilingly *adv* encantadoramente

behalf *n* (preceded by on or upon) por; (from) de parte (de); a favor (de); en defensa (de)

behave *vi* (oneself) conducirse, portarse; (act) obrar, proceder. **to b. badly,** portarse mal; obrar mal. **B.!** ¡Pórtate bien!

behavior *n* conducta, *f*; comportamiento, *m*; proceder, *m*; (manner) modales, *m pl*; *biol* reacción, *f*

behaviorism *n psy* behaviorismo, *m*

behead *vt* decapitar, descabezar

beheading *n* decapitación, *f*

behest *n* mandato, mando, *m*

behind *adv* detrás; por detrás; atrás; hacia atrás; en pos; (of time and order) después; (late and in arrears) con retraso; (old-fashioned) atrasado. *prep* detrás de; por detrás de; inferior a; menos avanzado que. *n inf* trasero, *m.* **from b.,** por detrás. **to be b. time,** retrasarse; llegar tarde. **b. the back of,** a espaldas de. **b. the scenes,** entre bastidores. **b. the times,** *fig* atrasado de noticias; pasado de moda. **the ideology b. the French Revolution,** la ideología que informó la Revolución Francesa.

behindhand *a* (out of date) atrasado; (late) tardío; *adv* con retraso

behold *vt* ver, mirar, contemplar; presenciar. *interj* ¡he aquí! ¡mira!

beholden *a* obligado, agradecido

beholder *n* espectador (-ra). **the beholders,** los que lo presenciaban

beholding *n* contemplación, vista, *f*

behove *vt* incumbir, tocar, corresponder

beige *n* beige, color arena, *m*

being *n* existencia, *f*; operación, *f*; ser, *m*; (spirit) alma, *f*, espíritu, *m*; esencia, *f.* **human b.,** ser humano, *m*, alma viviente, *f.* **for the time b.,** por ahora, por el momento

bejewel *vt* enjoyar, adornar con joyas

belabor *vt* apalear, golpear

belated *a* tardío

belay *vt* amarrar

belch *n* eructo, *m*; detonación, *f*; (of a volcano) erupción, *f. vi* eructar. *vt* vomitar; (curses, etc.) escupir; despedir, arrojar

belching *n* eructación, *f;* (of smoke, etc.) vómito, *m*, emisión, *f*

beleaguer *vt* sitiar

belfry *n* campanario, *m*

Belgian *a* and *n* belga, *mf*

Belgium Bélgica, *f*

Belgrade Belgrado, *m*

belie *vt* desmentir, contradecir; defraudar

belief *n* creencia, *f;* fe, *f;* opinión, *f,* parecer, *m;* (trust) confianza, *f.* **in the b.** **that,** creyendo que, en la creencia de que

believable *a* creíble

believe *vt* and *vi* creer; opinar, ser de la opinión, parecer (a uno); confiar, tener confianza. **I b. not,** Creo que no, Me parece que no. **I b. so,** Creo que sí, Me parece que sí. **to make (a person) b.,** hacer (a uno) creer. **to b. in,** creer en; confiar en, tener confianza en

believer *n* persona que cree, *f;* creyente, *mf*

belittle *vt* achicar; conceder poca importancia a

bell *n* campana, *f;* (hand-bell) campanilla, *f;* (small, round) cascabel, *m;* (on cows, etc.) esquila, *f;* (electric, push, or bicycle) timbre, *m;* (jester's) cascabeles, *m pl;* (cry of stag) bramido, *m.* *vt* poner un cascabel (a). *vi* (stags) bramar, roncar. **To bear away the b.,** *fig* llevarse la palma. **to ring the b.,** tocar el timbre; agitar la campanilla. **to ring the bells,** tocar las campanas. **to b. the cat,** ponerle el cascabel al gato, ponerle el collar al gato. **b.-boy,** botones, mozo de hotel, *m.* **b.-clapper,** badajo, *m.* **b.-flower,** campanilla, *f.* **b.-founder,** campanero, *m.* **b.-mouthed,** abocinado. **b.-pull,** tirador de campanilla, *m.* **b.-ringer,** campanero, *m.* **b.-shaped,** campanudo. **b.-tent,** pabellón, *m.* **b. tower,** campanario, *m*

belladonna *n* belladona, *f*

belle *n* beldad, *f*

belles-lettres *n pl* bellas letras, *f pl*

bellicose *a* belicoso, agresivo

bellicosity *n* belicosidad, *f*

belligerency *n* beligerancia, *f*

belligerent *a* beligerante; belicoso, guerrero. *n* beligerante, *mf*

bellow *n* (shout) grito, *m;* rugido, bramido, *m;* (of guns) trueno, *m.* *vi* gritar, vociferar; rugir, bramar; tronar

bellowing *n.* See **bellow**

bellows *n* fuelle, *m*

belly *n* vientre, *m,* barriga, *f;* (of a jug, etc.) panza, *f;* estómago, *m;* (womb) seno, *m.* *vt* hinchar. *vi* hincharse

belong *vi* pertenecer (a); tocar (a), incumbir (a); (to a place) ser de; residir en

belongings *n pl* efectos, *m pl;* posesiones, *f pl;* (luggage) equipaje, *m*

beloved *a* muy amado, muy querido. *n* querido (-da)

below *adv* abajo; (under) debajo; (further on) más abajo; (in hell) en el infierno; (in this world) en este mundo, aquí abajo. *prep* bajo; (underneath) debajo de; (after) después de; (unworthy of) indigno de; inferior a. **The valley lay b. us,** El valle se extendía a nuestros pies. **b. zero,** bajo cero

belt *n* cinturón, *m;* (of a horse) cincha, *f;* (corset) faja, *f; geog* zona, *f;* (of a machine) correa (de transmisión), *f*

beltway *n* anillo periférico, *m*

belvedere *n* mirador, *m*

bemoan *vt* deplorar, lamentar

bemoaning *n* lamentación, *f*

bemuse *vt* confundir, desconcertar

bench *n* banco, *m;* (with a back) escaño, *m;* mesa de trabajo, *f;* (carpenter's, shoemaker's, in a boat, in parliament) banco, *m;* (judges) tribunal, *m*

bend *n* corvadura, curva, vuelta, *f;* (in a river, street) recodo, *m;* (on a road) codo viraje, *m;* (of the knee) corva, *f;* (in a pipe) codo, *m; naut* nudo, *m; her* banda, *f.* **sheet b.,** (knot) nudo de tejedor, *m*

bend *vt* encorvar; doblegar; torcer; (the head) bajar; (the body) inclinar; (steps) dirigir, encaminar; (the mind) aplicarse, dedicarse. *vi* encorvarse; doblegarse; torcerse; (arch) arquear; inclinarse. **to b. the knee,**

arrodillarse. **on bended knee,** de rodillas. **to b. back,** *vt* redoblar. *vi* redoblarse; inclinarse hacia atrás. **to b. down,** agacharse; inclinarse. **to b. forward,** inclinarse hacia delante. **to b. over,** inclinarse encima de

bendable *a* que puede doblarse; plegadizo; flexible

bending *n* doblamiento, *m;* flexión, *f;* inclinación, *f. a* doblado; inclinado

beneath *adv* abajo; debajo; (at one's feet) a los pies de uno. *prep* bajo; debajo de; al pie de; (unworthy, inferior) indigno. **He married b. him,** Se casó fuera de su clase

Benedictine *a* benedictino. *n* benedictino, *m;* (liqueur) benedictino, *m*

benediction *n* bendición, *f;* gracia divina, merced, *f*

benefaction *n* beneficiación, *f;* buena obra, *f;* beneficio, favor, *m*

benefactor *n* bienhechor, *m;* protector, *m;* patrono, *m;* fundador, *m*

benefactress *n* bienhechora, *f;* protectora, *f;* patrona, *f;* fundadora, *f*

benefice *n* beneficio eclesiástico, *m,* prebenda, *f*

beneficence *n* beneficiencia, caridad, *f,* buenas obras, *f pl*

beneficent *a* benéfico, caritativo

beneficial *a* beneficioso; provechoso, útil

beneficiary *n* beneficiado (-da), beneficiario (-ia)

benefit *n* beneficio, bien, *m;* provecho, *m,* utilidad, *f;* (favor) favor, *m; theat* beneficio, *m;* (help) ayuda, *f,* servicio, *m.* *vt* beneficiar; aprovechar; (improve) mejorar. *vi* (with by) sacar provecho de; ganar. **for the b. of,** para; en pro de, a favor de. **b. society,** sociedad benéfica, *f*

benevolence *n* benevolencia, bondad, *f;* liberalidad, *f;* caridad, *f;* favor, *m*

benevolent *a* benévolo; bondadoso; caritativo. **b. society,** sociedad de beneficencia, *f*

benevolently *adv* benignamente, con benevolencia

Bengal Bengala, *f*

benighted *a* sorprendido por la noche; *fig* ignorante

benign, benignant *a* benigno

bent *n* talento, *m;* inclinación, afición, *f, a* torcido, encorvado; resuelto

benumb. See **numb**

benzine *n* bencina, *f*

bequeath *vt* legar, dejar (en el testamento); transmitir

bequest *n* legado, *m*

Berber *a* and *n* bereber, *mf*

bereave *vt* privar (de), quitar; arrebatar; afligir. **the bereaved parents,** los padres afligidos

bereavement *n* privación, *f;* (by death) pérdida, *f;* aflicción, *f*

bereft *a* privado (de); desamparado; indefenso. **utterly b.,** completamente solo

beret *n* boina, *f*

Berlin *a* and *n* (of or from) berlinés (-esa). *n* (carriage) berlina, *f*

Bermudas, the, *m* las Islas Bermudas

Bernard *n* Bernardo, *m.* **St. B. dog,** perro de San Bernardo, *m*

Berne Berna, *f*

berry *n* baya, *f;* (of coffee, etc.) fruto, *m, vi* dar bayas; coger bayas

berth *n* (bed) litera, *f;* (cabin) camarote, *m;* (anchorage) anclaje, fondeadero, *m;* (job) empleo, *m, vt* (a ship) fondear. **to give a wide b. to,** *naut* ponerse a resguardo de; apartarse mucho de; evitar

beseech *vt* suplicar, rogar, implorar; (ask for) pedir con ahinco

beseeching *a* suplicante, implorante. *n* súplica, *f;* ruego, *m*

beseechingly *adv* suplicantemente

beset *vt* atacar, acosar; aquejar, acosar, perseguir. **beset by personal misfortune,** acosado por las desgracias personales; (block) obstruir; (surround) rodear, cercar

besetting *a* usual, frecuente; obsesionante

beside, besides *prep* al lado de; cerca de; (compared

with) en comparación de, comparado con; (in addition) además de; aparte de; excepto. *adv* además, también. **to be beside oneself,** estar fuera de sí

besiege *vt* sitiar; (assail) asaltar, asediar; (surround) rodear; importunar

besieged *n* sitiado (-da)

besieger *n* sitiador, *m*

besieging *a* sitiador. *n* sitio, asalto, *m*; asedio, *m*, importunación, *f*

besmear *vt* embadurnar, ensuciar

besotted *a* estúpido; embrutecido; atontado

bespangled *a* adornado con lentejuelas; brillante (con); (studded) salpicado (de)

bespatter *vt* manchar; derramar; salpicar

bespeak *vt* reservar; (goods) encargar; (signify) demostrar, indicar, significar; *poet* hablar

besprinkle *vt* rociar

best *a sup* of **good** and **well,** mejor; el (la) mejor, *m, f.,* los (las) mejores, *m pl, f pl. adv* mejor; el mejor; (most) más. **as b. I can,** como mejor pueda. **at the b.,** cuando más, en el mejor caso. **He did it for the b.,** Lo hizo con la mejor intención. **the b.,** lo mejor. **to be at one's b.,** brillar; lucirse. **to do one's b.,** hacer todo lo posible. **to get the b. of,** llevar la mejor parte de; triunfar de (or sobre). **to make the b. of,** sacar el mayor provecho de. **The next b. thing to do is . . . ,** Lo mejor que queda ahora por hacer es . . . **b. man,** padrino de boda, *m.* **to be b. man to,** apadrinar, ser padrino de. **b. seller,** libro que se vende más, libro favorito, *m*

bestial *a* bestial

bestiality *n* bestialidad, *f*

bestir (oneself) *vr* menearse, moverse; preocuparse; (hurry) darse prisa

bestow *vt* (place) poner; (with upon) conferir, conceder, otorgar; (a present) regalar

bestowal *n* puesta, *f*; otorgamiento, *m*, concesión, *f*; (of a present) regalo, *m*, dádiva, *f*

bestride *vt* montar a horcajadas en; poner una pierna en cada lado de; cruzar de un tranco

bestseller *n* campeón de venta, éxito editorial, triunfo de librería, *m*

bet *n* apuesta, postura, *f, vi* apostar; (gamble) jugar. **What do you bet?** ¿Qué apuesta Vd.?

betake (oneself) *vr* acudir (a); darse (a); marcharse

bethink (oneself) *vr* pensar, reflexionar; (remember) recordar, hacer memoria; ocurrirse

Bethlehem Belén, *m*

betimes *adv* pronto; de buena hora, temprano; con tiempo

betoken *vt* presagiar, prometer; indicar

betray *vt* traicionar; revelar, descubrir; (a woman) seducir; (show) dejar ver

betrayal *n* traición, *f*; (of confidence) abuso (de confianza), *m*; (of a woman) seducción, *f*

betrayer *n* traidor (-ra)

betroth *vt* desposar(se) con, prometer(se). **to be betrothed to,** estar desposado con

betrothal *n* desposorio, *m*, esponsales, *m pl*; (duration) noviazgo, *m*

betrothed *n* desposado (-da), futuro (-ra)

better *a comp* of **good,** mejor; superior. *adv* mejor; más. *vt* mejorar; exceder. *n* apostador (-ra). **He has bettered himself,** Ha mejorado su situación. **It is b. to . . . ,** Es mejor . . . , Vale más . . . (followed by infin.). **little b.,** poco mejor; algo mejor; poco más. **much b.,** mucho mejor. **our betters,** nuestros superiores. **so much the b.,** tanto mejor. **the b. to,** para mejor. **to be b.,** ser mejor; (of health) estar mejor. **to get b.,** mejorar. **to get the b. of,** triunfar sobre, vencer. **b. half,** *inf* media naranja, *f.* **b. off,** mejor situado, más acomodado

betterment *n* mejora, *f*, mejoramiento, *m*; adelantamiento, avance, *m*

betting *n* apuesta, *f*

bettor *n* apostador (-ra)

between *prep* entre; en medio de; de. **the break b. Mr.**

X and Mrs. Y, el rompimiento del Sr. X y la Sra. Y. *adv* en medio; entre los dos. **far b.,** a grandes intervalos. **b. now and then,** desde ahora hasta entonces. **b. one thing and another,** entre una cosa y otra. **b. ourselves,** entre nosotros

bevel *n* bisel, *m*, *vt* abiselar

beverage *n* brebaje, *m*, bebida, *f*

bevy *n* grupo, *m*; (of birds) bandada, *f*; (of roes) manada, *f*

bewail *vt* lamentar, llorar

bewailing *n* lamentación, *f*

beware *vi* guardarse (de); cuidar (de); desconfiar (de). *interj* ¡cuidado! ¡atención! **B. of imitations!** ¡Desconfiad de las imitaciones!

bewilder *vt* aturdir, abobar; dejar perplejo (a); confundir

bewildered *a* aturdido, abobado; perplejo; confuso

bewildering *a* incomprensible; complicado

bewilderment *n* aturdimiento, *m*; perplejidad, *f*; confusión, *f*

bewitch *vt* hechizar; fascinar, encantar

bewitching *a* encantador, hechicero, fascinante. *n* embrujamiento, encantamiento, *m*

bewitchingly *adv* de un modo encantador

bewitchment *n.* See **bewitching**

beyond *prep* más allá de; más lejos que; (behind) tras, detrás de; (of time) después de; *fig* fuera del alcance de; (without) fuera de; (above) encima de; (not including) aparte. *adv* más allá; más lejos; detrás. **b. doubt,** fuera de duda. **b. question,** indiscutible. **b. the sea,** allende el mar. **That is b. me,** Eso es demasiado para mí; Eso no está en mi mano; Eso está fuera de mi alcance. **the back of b.,** donde Cristo dio las tres voces, las quimbambas. **the B.,** la otra vida

Bhután Bután, *m*

bias *n* sesgo, bies, través, *m*; *fig* prejuicio, *m*; parcialidad, *f*, *vt* influir; predisponer. **to cut on the b.,** cortar al sesgo

biassed *a* parcial; tendencioso

bib *n* babero, *m*; pechera, *f*, *vi* beber mucho, empinar el codo

Bible *n* Biblia, *f*

biblical *a* bíblico. **b. history,** historia sagrada, *f*

bibliographer *n* bibliógrafo (-fa)

bibliographical *a* bibliográfico

bibliography *n* bibliografía, *f*

bibliophile *n* bibliófilo, *m*

bibulous *a* bebedor, borrachín

bicarbonate *n* bicarbonato, *m*

bicentenary *n* segundo centenario, *m*

biceps *n* bíceps, *m*

bichloride *n* bicloruro, *m*

bicker *vi* disputar, altercar; (of stream, etc.) murmurar, susurrar; (of flame) bailar, centellear

bickering *n* altercado, argumento, *m*

bicycle *n* bicicleta, *f*, *vi* andar en bicicleta, ir de bicicleta

bicycling *n* ciclismo, *m*

bicyclist *n* biciclista, *mf*

bid *n* (at auction) postura, *f*; (bridge) puja, *f*; oferta, *f*, *vt* mandar, ordenar, invitar a; (at an auction) pujar, licitar. **to make a bid for,** (attempt) hacer un esfuerzo para; procurar. **to bid fair,** prometer; dar indicios de; dar esperanzas de. **to bid goodbye to,** decir adiós (a), despedirse de. **to bid welcome,** dar la bienvenida (a)

biddable *a* obediente, dócil; manso

bidder *n* postor, *m*, pujador (-ra). **the highest b.,** el mejor postor

bidding *n* (order) orden, *f*; instrucción, *f*; invitación, *f*; (at an auction) postura, licitación, *f*. **to do a person's b.,** hacer lo que se le manda

bide *vt* aguardar, esperar. **to b. by,** (fulfil) cumplir con

bidet *n* bidé, *m*

biennial *a* bianual, bienal

bier *n* andas, *f pl*; féretro, ataúd, *m*

bifocal *a* bifocal

bifurcate *vt* and *vi* bifurcar(se)

bifurcation *n* bifurcación, *f*

big *a* grande; grueso; (grown up) mayor; (tall) alto; voluminoso; (vast) extenso, vasto; (full) lleno (de); (with young) preñada; importante. **to talk big**, echarla de importante. **big-boned**, huesudo. **big-end**, *aut* biela, *f.* **big game**, caza mayor, *f.* **big gun**, *inf* pájaro gordo, *m*

bigamist *n* bígamo (-ma)

bigamous *a* bígamo

bigamy *n* bigamia, *f*

bight *n* (in a rope) vuelta (de un cabo), *f*; (bay) ensenada, *f*

bigness *n* grandor, *m*; gran tamaño, *m*; altura, *f*; (tallness of a person) gran talle, *m*; (vastness) extensión, *f*; importancia, *f*

bigot *n* fanático (-ca)

bigoted *a* fanático, intolerante

bigotry *n* fanatismo, *m*, intolerancia, *f*

bikini *n* bikini, *m*

bilateral *a* bilateral

bilberry *n* arándano, *m*

bile *n* bilis, hiel, *f*; mal humor, *m*, cólera, *f*

bilge *n* *naut* pantoque, *m*, sentina, *f.* **b. water**, agua de pantoque, *f*

bilingual *a* bilingüe

bilious *a* bilioso

bill *n* (parliamentary) proyecto de ley, *m*; *law* escrito, *m*; *com* cuenta, *f*; (poster) cartel, *m*; (program) programa, *m*; (cast) repertorio, *m*; (bank note) billete de banco, *m*; (of a bird) pico, *m*; (for pruning) podadera, *f.* **due b.**, *com* abonaré, *m.* **Post no bills!** Se prohíbe fijar carteles. **b. of exchange**, letra de cambio, *f.* **b. of fare**, lista de platos, *f*; *fig* programa, *m.* **b. of health**, patente de sanidad, *f.* **b. of lading**, conocimiento de embarque, *m.* **b. of rights**, declaración de derechos, *f.* **b. of sale**, contrato de venta, *m*, carta de venta, *f.* **b.-broker**, agente de bolsa, agente de cambio, *m.* **b.-poster**, fijador de carteles, cartelero, *m*

bill *vt* anunciar; publicar; poner en el programa; fijar carteles en. **to b. and coo**, (doves) arrullar; *inf* besuquearse

billboard, *n* tablero publicitario, *m*

billed *a* (in compounds) de pico

billet *n* alojamiento, *m*; (of wood) pedazo (de leña), *m*; (job) empleo, destino, *m*, *vt* alojar (en or con)

billeting *n* alojamiento, *m.* **b. officer**, *mil* aposentador, *m*; oficial encargado de encontrar alojamiento, *m*

billiards *n pl* billar, *m.* **billiard ball**, bola de billar, *f.* **billiard cue**, taco, *m.* **billiard cushion**, baranda de la mesa de billar, *f.* **billiard marker**, marcador, *m.* **billiard match**, partida de billar, *f.* **billiard player**, jugador (-ra) de billar. **billiard room**, sala de billar, *m.* **billiard table**, mesa de billar, *f*

billing *n* facturación, *f*

billion *n* billón, *m*; (U.S.A. and France) mil millones, *m pl*

billionth *a* billonésimo; (U.S.A. and France) milmillonésimo

bill of particulars *n* relación detallada, *f*

billow *n* oleada, *f*; *poet* ola, *f*; *fig* onda, *f.* *vi* hincharse, encresparse; ondular

billowy *a* ondulante, ondeante

bimonthly *a* bimestral

bin *n* hucha, *f*, arcón, *m*; recipiente, *m*; depósito, *m*; cajón, *m*; (for wine) estante, *m*

binary *a* binario

bind *vt* atar; unir, ligar; amarrar; (in sheaves) agavillar; (bandage) vendar; sujetar; fijar; aprisionar; (a book) encuadernar; *sew* ribetear; (oblige) obligar; comprometer; (constipate) estreñir; contratar (como aprendiz). **I feel bound to**, Me siento obligado a. **to b. over**, obligar a comparecer ante el juez

binder *n* encuadernador (-ra); *agr* agavilladora, *f*

binding *a* válido, valedero; obligatorio; **become b.**, adquirir carácter de compromiso; *med* constrictivo. *n* atadura, ligación, *f*; (of books) encuadernación, *f*; *sew* ribete, *m*

binge *n* parranda, juerga, *f.* **to go on the b.**, ir de parranda, ir de picos pardos, ir de juerga

binnacle *n* *naut* bitácora, *f*

binocular *a* binocular. *n pl* **binoculars**, binóculos, gemelos, *m pl*

binomial *a* and *n* binomio *m*.

biochemist *n* bioquímico, *m*

biochemistry *n* bioquímica, *f*

biographer *n* biógrafo (-fa)

biographical *a* biográfico

biography *n* biografía, vida, *f*

biological *a* biológico

biologist *n* biólogo, *m*

biology *n* biología, *f*

bipartite *a* bipartido

biped *n* bípedo, *m*, *a* bípedo, bípede

birch *n* *bot* abedul, *m*; (rod) vara, *f. a* de abedul. *vt* pegar con una vara, dar una paliza (a)

bird *n* pájaro, *m*; ave, *f.* **Birds of a feather flock together**, Cada cual se arrima a su cada cual. **hen b.**, pájara, *f.* **b.-call**, voz del pájaro, *f*, canto del ave, *m.* **b. catcher or vendor**, pajarero, *m.* **bird's-eye view**, vista de pájaro, perspectiva aérea, *f.* **b.-fancier**, aficionado (-da) a las aves; criador (-ra) de pájaros. **b.-like**, como un pájaro; de pájaro. **b.-lime**, liga, *f.* **to go b.-nesting**, ir a coger nidos de pájaros. **b. of paradise**, ave del paraíso, *f.* **b. of passage**, ave de paso, *f.* **b. of prey**, ave rapaz, *f.* **b.-seed**, alpiste, *m*

birth *n* nacimiento, *m*; (act of) parto, *m*, origen, *m*; (childhood) infancia, *f*; (family) linaje, *m*, familia, *f*; *fig* creación, *f.* **b.**, de nacimiento. **to give b. to**, dar a luz, echar al mundo, parir. **b. certificate**, partida de nacimiento, certificación de nacimiento, *f.* **b. control**, anticoncepcionismo, *m*, regulación de la fecundidad, *f.* **b.-mark**, antojos, *m pl.* **b.-place**, lugar de nacimiento, *m.* **b.-rate**, natalidad, *f*

birthday *n* cumpleaños, *m*

birthright *n* derecho de nacimiento, *m*; herencia, *f*

Biscayan *a* and *n* vizcaíno (-na)

Biscay, the Bay of el Golfo de Vizcaya, *m*

biscuit *n* galleta, *f*; bizcocho, *m.* **b. box or maker**, galletero, *m.* **b.-like**, abizcochado

bisect *vt* dividir en dos partes iguales; *geom* bisecar

bisexual *a* bisexual

bishop *n* obispo, *m*; (in chess) alfil, *m.* **bishop's crozier**, báculo episcopal, cayado, *m*

bismuth *n* bismuto, *m*

bison *n* bisonte, *m*

bisque *n* porcelana blanca, *f*, bizcocho, *m*

bistoury *n* bisturí, *m*

bit *n* pedazo, *m*; (of grass, etc.) brizna, *f*; (moment) instante, *m*; (quantity) cantidad, *f*; (of a drill) mecha, *f*; (part) parte, *f*; (passage) trozo, *m*; (horse's) bocado, *m*; *inf* miga, *f.* **a bit**, un tanto, algo, un poco. **in bits**, en pedazos. **Not a bit!** ¡Nada!; ¡Ni pizca!; ¡Claro que no! **bit by bit**, poco a poco, gradualmente. **to give someone a bit of one's mind**, contarle cuatro verdades. **to take the bit between one's teeth**, desbocarse; *fig* rebelarse. **Wait a bit!** ¡Espera un momento!

bitch *n* (female dog) perra, *f*; (fox) zorra, *f*; (wolf) loba, *f*

bite *n* mordedura, *f*; mordisco, *m*; (mouthful, snack) bocado, *m*; (of fish and insects) picada, *f*; (hold) asimiento, *m*; (sting, pain) picadura, *f*; (pungency) resquemor, *m*; (offer) oferta, *f*; (*fig* mordancy) mordacidad, acritud, *f. vt* and *vi* morder; (gnaw) roer; (of fish, insects) picar; (of hot dishes) resquemar; (of acids) corroer; (deceive) engañar, defraudar; (of wheels, etc.) agarrar; (hurt, wound) herir. **to b. one's tongue**, morderse la lengua. **to b. the dust**, caer al suelo

biting *a* (stinging) picante; (mordant) mordaz, acre; (of winds, etc.) penetrante; satírico. *n* mordedura, *f*, roedura, *f*

bitter *a* amargo; (sour) agrio, ácido; (of winds) penetrante; (of cold) intenso; cruel. **to the b. end**, hasta la muerte; hasta el último extremo. **b.-sweet,** agridulce

bitterly *adv* amargamente; intensamente; cruelmente

bitterness *n* amargura, *f*; (sourness) acidez, *f*; (of cold) intensidad, *f*; crueldad, *f*

bitters *n pl* (drink) bíter, *m*, angostura, *f*

bitumen *n* betún, *m*

bituminous *a* bituminoso, abetunado

bivalve *n* bivalvo, *m*

bivouac *n mil* vivaque, *m*, *vi* vivaquear

bizarre *a* raro, extravagante; grotesco

black *a* negro; obscuro; (sad) triste, melancólico; funesto; (wicked) malo, perverso; (sullen) malhumorado. *n* (color) negro, *m*; (mourning) luto, *m*; (negro) negro, *m*; (negress) negra, *f*; (stain) mancha, *f*; (dirt) tizne, *m*. *vt* ennegrecer; tiznar. **in b. and white,** por escrito. **to look on the b. side,** verlo todo negro. **b. art,** nigromancia, *f*. **b.-currant,** grosella negra, *f*. **b.-eyed,** ojinegro, con ojos negros. **b.-haired,** pelinegro, de pelo negro. **b.-lead,** plombagina, *f*. **b.-list,** lista negra, *f*. **b.-market,** estraperlo, mercado negro, *m*. **b.-marketeer,** estraperlista, *mf* **b.-out,** oscurecimiento, apagamiento, *m*. **b.-pudding,** morcilla, *f*. **b. sheep,** oveja negra, *f*; *fig* oveja descarriada, *f*; (of a family) garbanzo negro, *m*. **b.-water fever,** melanuria, *f*

blackberry *n* mora, zarzamora, *f*; (bush) zarza, *f*, moral, *m*

blackbird *n* mirlo, *m*

blackboard *n* encerado, *m*, pizarra, *f*

blacken *vt* ennegrecer; tiznar; *fig* manchar, desacreditar. *vi* ennegrecerse

black eye *n* ojo como un tomate, ojo morado, *m*

Black Forest, the la Selva Negra, *f*

blackguard *n* tipo de cuidado, perdido, *m*

blackhead *n* espinilla, *f*

blacking *n* betún, *m*

blackish *a* negruzco

blackmail *n* chantaje, *m*, *vt* hacer víctima de un chantaje; arrancar dinero por chantaje (a)

blackmailer *n* chantajista, *mf*

blackness *n* negrura, *f*; obscuridad, *f*; (wickedness) maldad, perversidad, *f*

Black Sea, the el Mar Negro, *m*

blacksmith *n* herrero, *m*. **blacksmith's forge,** herrería, *f*

bladder *n anat* vejiga, *f*; ampolla, *f*; (of sea-plants) vesícula, *f*; (of fish) vejiga natatoria, *f*

blade *n* (leaf) hoja, *f*; (of grass, etc.) brizna, *f*; (of sharp instruments) hoja, *f*; (of oar) pala, *f*; (of propeller) paleta, ala, *f*

bladed *a* de . . . hojas. **a two-b. knife,** un cuchillo de dos hojas

blame *n* culpa, *f*; responsabilidad, *f*; censura, *f*. *vt* culpar, echar la culpa (a); tachar, censurar, criticar; acusar. **You are to b. for this,** Vd. tiene la culpa de esto

blameless *a* inculpable; inocente; intachable; elegante

blamelessness *n* inculpabilidad, inocencia, *f*; elegancia, *f*

blameworthy *a* culpable, digno de censura, vituperable

blanch *vt cul* mondar; hacer palidecer. *vi* palidecer, perder el color

blanching *n* palidecimiento, *m*; *cul* mondadura, *f*

blancmange *n* manjar blanco, *m*

bland *a* afable, cortés; dulce, agradable

blandish *vt* adular, halagar, acariciar

blandishment *n* adulación, *f*, halago, *m*, caricia, *f*

blandness *n* afabilidad, urbanidad, *f*; dulzura, *f*

blank *a* en blanco; (empty) vacío; desocupado; pálido; (confused) confuso, desconcertado; (expressionless) sin expresión; (of verse) suelto; sin adorno. *n* blanco, hueco, *m*; papel en blanco, *m*; laguna, *f*. **b. cartridge,** cartucho para salvas, cartucho de fogueo, *m*. **b. verse,** verso suelto, *m*

blanket *n* manta, frazada, *f*; (of a horse) sudadero *m*; *fig* capa, *f*. *vt* cubrir con una manta. **to toss in a b.,** man-

tear. **wet b.,** aguafiestas, *mf*. **b. maker or seller,** mantero, *m*. **b. vote,** voto colectivo, *m*

blanketing *n* manteamiento, *m*

blankly *adv* con indiferencia; sin comprender; (flatly) categóricamente

blankness *n* confusión, *f*, desconcierto, *m*; (emptiness) vaciedad, *f*; indiferencia, *f*; incomprensión, *f*

blare *n* sonido de la trompeta o del clarín, *poet* clangor, *m*; (of a car horn) ruido, *m*. *vi* sonar

blarney *n* labia, *f*. *vt* lisonjear

blaspheme *vi* blasfemar. *vt* renegar de, maldecir

blasphemer *n* blasfemador (-ra), blasfemo (-ma)

blasphemous *a* blasfemo, blasfematorio

blasphemy *n* blasfemia, *f*

blast *n* (of wind) ráfaga (de viento), *f*; (of a trumpet, etc.) trompetazo, son, *m*; (of a whistle) pitido, *m*; (draft) soplo, *m*; explosión, *f*; *fig* influencia maligna, *f*. *vt* (rock) barrenar, hacer saltar; (wither) marchitar, secar; *fig* destruir; (curse) maldecir. **in full b.,** en plena marcha. **b.-furnace,** alto horno, horno de cuba, *m*. **b. hole,** barreno, *m*

blaster *n* barrenero, *m*

blasting *n* (of rock) voladura, *f*; (withering) marchitamiento, *m*; *fig* destrucción, ruina, *f*; (cursing) maldiciones, *f pl*. **a.** destructor; *fig* funesto. **b. charge,** carga explosiva, *f*

blatant *a* ruidoso; agresivo; llamativo; (boastful) fanfarrón

blaze *n* llama, *f*; fuego, *m*; conflagración, *f*; luz brillante, *f*; (of anger, etc.) acceso, *m*. *vi* llamear, encenderse en llamas; brillar, resplandecer. **a b. of colour,** una masa de color. **Go to blazes!** ¡Vete al infierno!

blazon *n her* blasón, *m*; *fig* proclamación, *f*, *vt* blasonar; adornar; proclamar

bleach *n* lejía, *f*. *vt* blanquear; descolorar. *vi* ponerse blanco; descolorarse

bleaching *n* blanqueo, *m*. **b. powder,** hipoclorito de cal, *m*

bleak *a* yermo, desierto; frío; expuesto; (sad) triste; severo

bleakness *n* situación expuesta, *f*; desnudez, *f*; frío, *m*; (sadness) tristeza, *f*; severidad, *f*

bleary-eyed *a* legañoso, cegajoso

bleat *n* balido, *m*, *vt* and *vi* balar, dar balidos

bleating *a* balador, que bala. *n* balido, *m*

bleed *vi* sangrar, echar sangre; sufrir. *vt* sangrar; arrancar dinero a

bleeding *n* hemorragia, *f*; sangría, *f*

blemish *n* imperfección, *f*, defecto, *m*; (on fruit) maca, *f*; (stain) mancha, *f*, deshonra, *f*

blend *n* mezcla, mixtura, *f*; combinación, *f*; fusión, *f*. *vt* mezclar; combinar. *vi* mezclarse; combinarse

blende *n min* blenda, *f*

blending *n* mezcla, *f*; fusión, *f*

bless *vt* bendecir; consagrar; (praise) alabar, glorificar; hacer feliz (a). **B. me!** ¡Válgame Dios!

blessed *a* bendito; *ecc* beato, bienaventurado; (dear) querido; feliz; *inf* maldito

blessedness *n* felicidad, *f*; bienaventuranza, *f*

blessing *n* bendición, *f*; (grace) bendición de la mesa, *f*; (mercy) merced, gracia, *f*; favor, *m*; (good) bien, *m*. **He gave them his b.,** Les echó su bendición

Bless you! (to someone who has sneezed) ¡Jesús!

blight *n agr* tizne, tizón, *m*; (of cereals) añublo, *m*; (mould) roña, *f*; (greenfly) pulgón, *m*; *fig* influencia maligna, *f*; (frustration) desengaño, *m*; (spoil-sport) aguafiestas, *mf* *vt* atizonar; anublar; (wither) marchitar, secar; *fig* frustrar, destruir; malograr

blighter *n* bribón, *m*

blind *a* ciego; (secret) secreto; (of a door, etc.) falso; (closed) cerrado, sin salida; (unaware) ignorante; sin apreciación (de). **to be b.,** ser ciego; *fig* tener una venda en los ojos. **to be b. in one eye,** ser tuerto. **to turn a b. eye,** hacer la vista gorda. **b. alley,** callejón sin salida, *m*. **b. as a bat,** más ciego que un topo. **b. flying,** *aer* vuelo a ciegas, *m*. **b. man,** ciego, hombre ciego, *m*. **b. obedience,** obediencia ciega, *f*. **b. side,** (of persons) lado débil, *m*. **b. woman,** ciega, mujer ciega, *f*

blind *vt* cegar; poner una venda en los ojos (de); (dazzle) deslumbrar; hacer cerrar los ojos a; hacer ignorar

blind *n* persiana, *f*; (Venetian) celosía, *f*; (deception) pretexto, *m*; velo, *m*

blindfold *vt* vendar los ojos (a); *fig* poner una venda en los ojos (de). *a and adv* con los ojos vendados; a ciegas; con los ojos cerrados

blindly *adv* ciegamente; a ciegas; ignorantemente

blindman's buff *n* gallina ciega, *f*

blindness *n* ceguedad, *f*; ofuscación, *f*; ignorancia, *f*

blink *n* parpadeo, *m*, guiñada, *f*; (of light) destello, *m*; reflejo, *m*; *vi* parpadear, pestañear; (of lights) destellar

blinkers *n pl* anteojeras, *f pl*

bliss *n* felicidad, *f*; deleite, placer, *m*; *ecc* gloria, *f*

blissful *a* feliz

blissfully *adv* felizmente

blissfulness *n*. See **bliss**

blister *n med* vesícula, *f*; ampolla, *f*; (bubble) burbuja, *f*. *vt* ampollar; *fig* herir

blithe *a* alegre

blithely *adv* alegremente

blitheness *n* alegría, *f*

blitzkrieg *n* blitzkrieg, *m*, guerra relámpago, *f*

blizzard *n* ventisca, nevasca, *f*

bloated *a* abotagado, hinchado; orgulloso; indecente

bloater *n* arenque ahumado, *m*

blob *n* masa, *f*; mancha, *f*; gota, *f*

block *n* bloque, *m*; (log) leño, *m*; *naut* polea, *f*; (for beheading and of a butcher) tajo, *m*; (for mounting) apeadero, *m*; (of shares, etc.) lote, *m*; (of houses) manzana, *f*; (jam) atasco, *m*; (obstruction) obstrucción, *f*; (for hats) forma, *f*. **A chip off the old b.,** De tal palo tal astilla. **b. and tackle,** *naut* polea con aparejo. **b.-hook,** grapa, *f*. **b.-house,** *mil* blocao, *m*

block *vt* bloquear; cerrar (el paso); (stop up) atarugar, atascar; (a wheel) calzar; (a bill, etc.) obstruir; (hats) poner en forma. **to b. the way,** cerrar el paso.

blockade *n* bloqueo, *m*, *vt* bloquear. **to run the b.,** violar el bloqueo

blockhead *n* leño, zoquete, imbécil, *m*

blond(e) *a* (of hair) rubio; (of complexion) de tez blanca. *n* hombre rubio, *m*; (woman) rubia, mujer rubia, *f*. **peroxide b.,** rubia oxigenada, *f*. **b. lace,** blondina, *f*

blood *n* sangre, *f*; (relationship) parentesco, *m*; (family) linaje, *m*, prosapia, *f*; (life) vida, *f*; (sap) savia, *f*; jugo, *m*; (horse) caballo de pura raza, *m*; (dandy) galán, *m*. *vt* sangrar. **bad b.,** mala sangre, *f*; odio, *m*; mala leche, *f*. **blue b.,** sangre azul, *f*. **in cold b.,** a sangre fría, *f*. **My b. is up,** Se me enciende la sangre. **My b. runs cold,** Se me hiela la sangre. **to be in the b.,** llevar en la sangre. **b.-bank,** banco de sangre, *m*. **b.-bath,** matanza, *f*. **b.-colored,** de color de sangre, sanguíneo. **b.-feud,** venganza de sangre, *f*. **b.-guilt,** culpabilidad de homicidio, *m*. **b.-heat,** calor de sangre, *m*. **b.-letting,** sangría, *f*. **b. orange,** naranja dulce, *f*. **b.-plasma,** plasma sanguíneo, *m*. **b.-poisoning,** septicemia, *f*; infección, *f*. **b.-pressure,** presión sanguínea, *f*. **b. purity,** limpieza de sangre, *f*. **b.-red,** rojo como la sangre. **b.-relation,** pariente (-ta) consanguíneo(a). **b.-relationship,** consanguinidad, *f*. **b.-stain,** mancha de sangre, *f*. **b.-stained,** ensangrentado, manchado de sangre. **b.-stone,** sanguinaria, *f*. **b.-sucker,** sanguijuela, *f*; *fig* vampiro, *m*; (usurer) avaro (-ra). **b.-vessel,** vaso sanguíneo, *m*

blooded *a* de sangre . . . ; de casta . . .

bloodhound *n* sabueso, *m*

bloodily *adv* sangrientamente; cruentamente; con ferocidad, cruelmente

bloodiness *n* estado sangriento, *m*; crueldad, ferocidad, *f*

bloodless *a* exangüe; pálido; incruento; anémico; indiferente

bloodshed *n* efusión de sangre, *f*; matanza, carnicería, *f*

bloodshot *a* (of the eye) inyectado

bloodthirstiness *n* sed de sangre, *f*

bloodthirsty *a* sanguinario, carnicero

bloody *a* sangriento; (of battles) encarnizado; (cruel) sanguinario, cruel

bloom *n* flor, *f*; florecimiento, *m*; (on fruit) flor, *f*; (prime) lozanía, *f*; (on the cheeks) color sano, *m*. *vi* florecer. **in b.,** en flor

blooming *a* florido; en flor; fresco; lozano; brillante

blossom *n* flor, *f*. *vi* florecer. **to b. out into,** hacerse, llegar a ser; (wear) lucir; (buy) comprarse

blossomed *a* con flores, de flores

blossoming *n* floración, *f*

blot *n* borrón, *m*; mancha, *f*. *vt* manchar; (erase) tachar; (dry) secar. **to b. out,** borrar; destruir; secar con papel secante

blotch *n* (on the skin, or stain) mancha, *f*

blotter *n com* libro borrador, *m*; teleta, *f*

blotting paper *n* papel secante, *m*

blouse *n* blusa, *f*

blow *n* golpe, *m*; bofetada, *f*; (with the fist) puñetazo, *m*; (with the elbow) codazo, *m*; (with a club) porrazo, *m*; (with a whip) latigazo, *m*; (blossoming) floración, *f*; (disaster) desastre, *m*, tragedia, *f*. **to come to blows,** venirse a las manos. **at a b.,** con un solo golpe; de una vez. **We are going for a b.,** Vamos a tomar el fresco. **b. below the belt,** golpe bajo, *m*. **b. in the air,** golpe en vago, *m*. **b. of fate,** latigazo de la fortuna, *m*

blow *vi* (of wind) soplar (el viento), hacer viento, correr aire; (pant) jadear, echar resoplidos; (of fuses) fundirse. *vt* (wind instruments) tocar; soplar; (inflate) inflar; (swell) hinchar. **to b. a kiss,** tirar un beso. **to b. one's nose,** sonarse las narices. **to b. away,** dispar; ahuyentar; llevar (el viento). **to b. down,** echar por tierra, derribar (el viento). **to b. in,** llevar adentro, hacer entrar (el viento); (windows, etc.) quebrar (el viento). **to b. off,** quitar (el viento). **to b. open,** abrir (el viento). **to b. out,** hacer salir (el viento); llevar afuera (el viento); (a light) matar de un soplo, apagar soplando. **to b. over,** pasar por (el viento); soplar por; disiparse; olvidarse. **to b. up,** (inflate) inflar; (the fire) avivar (el fuego); (explode) volar; (swell) hinchar

blowing *n* soplo, *m*; violencia, *f*; (blossoming) florecimiento, *m*. **b. up,** voleo, *m*; explosión, *f*

blow-up *n* (photograph) fotografía ampliada, *f*

blowzy *a* desaliñado

blubber *vi* gimotear; berrear. *n* (of the whale) grasa de ballena, *f*. **b.-lip,** bezo, *m*. **b.-lipped,** bezudo

bludgeon *n* cachiporra, porpa, *f*; garrote, *m*; estaca, *f*. *vt* golpear con una porra, dar garrotazos (a)

blue *a* azul; (with bruises) amoratado; (sad) deprimido, melancólico; (obscene) verde; (dark) sombrío; (traditionalist) conservador. *n* azul, *m*; (sky) cielo, *m*; (for clothes) añil de lavandera, *m*; *pl* **blues,** melancolía, depresión, *f*; (homesickness) morriña, *f*. *vt* (laundry) añilar. **to look b.,** parecer deprimido; (of prospects, etc.) ser poco halagüeño. **b. black,** azul negro, *m*; (of hair) azabache, *m*. **b.-bottle,** *ent* moscón, *m*. **b.-eyed,** con ojos azules. **b. gum,** eucalipto, *m*. **B. Peter,** bandera de salida, *f*. **b. print,** fotocopia, *f*; plan, *m*

bluebell *n* campanilla, *f*

blueness *n* color azul, *m*

bluestocking *n* marisabidilla, doctora, *f*

bluff *a* (of cliffs, etc.) escarpado; (of persons) franco, campechano, brusco

bluffness *n* franqueza, brusquedad, *f*

bluish *a* azulado

bluishness *n* color azulado, *m*

blunder *n* desacierto, desatino, *m*; equivocación, *f*; (in a translation, etc.) falta, *f*. *vi* tropezar (con); desacertar; equivocarse; *inf* meter la pata. *vt* manejar mal; estropear

blunderer *n* desatinado (-da)

blundering *a* desacertado; equivocado; imprudente *n*. See **blunder**

blunt *a* romo, embotado; obtuso; (abrupt) brusco; franco; descortés; (plain) claro. *vt* enromar, embotar; (the point) despuntar; *fig* hacer indiferente; (pain) mitigar

bluntly *adv* sin filo; sin punta; bruscamente, francamente; claramente

bluntness *n* embotamiento, *m*; *fig* brusquedad, franqueza, *f*; claridad, *f*

blur *n* borrón, *m*; mancha, *f*; imagen indistinta, *f*. *vt* borrar; manchar; *phot* velar

blurred *a* borroso; indistinto; turbio

blurt (out) *vt* proferir bruscamente; revelar sin querer

blush *n* rubor, *m*; rojo, *m*. *vi* enrojecerse, ruborizarse, ponerse colorado; avergonzarse (por)

blushing *a* ruboroso; rojo

bluster *vi* (of the wind) soplar con furia; (of waves) encresparse, embravecerse; (of persons) bravear, fanfarronear. *n* furia, violencia, *f*; tumulto, *m*; fanfarronería, *f*

blustering *a* (of wind) violento, fuerte; (of waves) tumultuoso; (of people) fanfarrón, valentón

boar *n* verraco, *m*; (wild) jabalí, *m*

board *n* tabla, *f*; (for notices) tablón, *m*; (b. residence) pensión, *f*; (table) mesa, *f*; (food) comida, *f*; (for chess, checkers) tablero, *m*; (sign) letrero, *m*; (of instruments) cuadro, *m*; (bookbinding) cartón, *m*; *naut* bordo, *m*; (committee) junta, dirección, *f*; tribunal, *m*; *pl* boards *theat* tablas, *f pl*. **above b.,** abiertamente, sin disimulo. **free on b.,** (f.o.b.) franco a bordo. **in boards,** (of books) encartonado. **managerial b.,** junta directiva, *f*. **on b.,** a bordo. **on the boards,** *theat* en las tablas. **to go on b.,** ir a bordo. **b. and lodging,** pensión completa, casa y comida, *f*. **b. of directors,** consejo de administración, *m*. **b. of examiners,** tribunal de exámenes, *m*. **b. of trade,** junta de comercio, *f*; ministerio de comercio, *m*

board *vt carp* entablar, enmaderar; embarcar en; (*nav* a ship) abordar; (lodge) alojar, tomar a pensión

boarder *n* huésped (-da); (at school) pensionista, *mf* alumno (-na) interno (-na)

boarding *n* entablado, *m*; (planking) tablazón, *f*; (of a ship) abordaje, *m*; (of a train) subida (al tren), *f*. **b.-house,** casa de huéspedes, pensión, *f*. **b.-school,** pensionado, *m*

boarding gate *n* puerta de embarque, *f*

boast *n* jactancia, *f*; ostentación, *f*; (honor) gloria, *f*. *vi* jactarse, vanagloriarse; alabarse; ostentar. **to b. about,** jactarse de; hacer gala de; gloriarse en

boaster *n* vanaglorioso (-sa), jactancioso (-sa)

boastful *a* vanaglorioso, jactancioso; ostentador

boastfully *adv* con jactancia; con ostentación

boastfulness *n* vanagloria, jactancia, *f*; fanfarronería, *f*; ostentación, *f*

boasting *n* alardeo, *m*; fanfarronería, *f*

boat *n* barco, *m*; bote, *m*; (in a fun fair) columpio, *m*, lancha, *f*; (for sauce or gravy) salsera, *f*. *vi* ir en barco; (row) remar; navegar. **to b. down,** bajar en barco. **to b. up,** subir en barco. **b. building,** construcción de barcos, *f*. **b. club,** club náutico, *m*. **b. crew,** tripulación de un barco, *f*. **b.-hook,** bichero, garabato, *m*. **b.-house,** cobertizo de las lanchas, *m*. **b.-load,** barcada, *f*. **b.-race,** regata, *f*. **b.-scoop,** achicador, *m*. **b.-shaped,** en forma de barco. **b.-train,** tren que enlaza con un vapor, *m*

boating *n* pasear en bote, *m*; manejo de un bote, *m*; (rowing) remo, *m*. **b.-pole,** botador, *m*

boatman *n* barquero, *m*

boatswain *n* contramaestre, *m*. **boatswain's mate,** segundo contramaestre, *m*

bob *n* (curtsey) reverencia, *f*; (woman's hair) pelo a la romana, *m*; (of bells) toque (de campana), *m*. *vi* saltar; moverse. *vt* cortar corto. **long bob,** (hair) melena, *f*. **to bob up,** ponerse de pie; surgir. **to bob up and down,** subir y bajar; bailar. **bob-tail,** rabo corto, *m*. **bobtailed,** rabón

Bob (pet form of *Robert*) Beto (Mexico)

bobbin *n* carrete, huso, *m*; (of wool, etc.) ovillo, *m*; (of looms, sewing machines) bobina, *f*; (in lace-making) bolillo, palillo, *m*

bobsleigh *n* trineo doble, *m*

bode *vt* presagiar, prometer. **to b. ill,** prometer mal. **to b. well,** prometer bien

bodice *n* corpiño, *m*

bodied *a* (in compounds) de cuerpo-

bodiless *a* incorpóreo

bodily *a* del cuerpo; físico; corpóreo; real; material; (of fear) de su persona. *adv* corporalmente; en persona, personalmente; en conjunto, enteramente; en una pieza

boding *a* ominoso, amenazador. *n* presagio, *m*; agüero, *m*

body *n anat* cuerpo, *m*; (trunk) tronco, *m*; (corpse) cadáver, *m*; (of a vehicle) caja, *f*; (of a motor-car) carrocería, *f*; (of a ship) casco, *m*; (of a church) nave, *f*; (centre) centro, *m*; (of a book, persons, consistency and *ast*) cuerpo, *m*; (person) persona, *f*; corporación, *f*; grupo, *m*; (of an army) grueso (de ejercito), *m*; organismo, *m*. **in a b.,** en masa, juntos (juntas); en corporación. **to have enough to keep b. and soul together,** tener de que vivir. **b.-snatcher,** junta cadáveres *mf* ladrón de cadáveres, *m*. **b.-snatching,** robo de cadáveres, *m*

bodyguard *n* guardia de corps, *f*; guardia, *f*; (escort) escolta, *f*

body language *n* el lenguaje del cuerpo, *m*

bog *n* pantano, marjal, *m*, marisma, *f*

bogey *n* duende, *m*; (to frighten children) coco, *m*; (nightmare) pesadilla, *f*

boggy *a* pantanoso, fangoso

bogus *a* postizo, falso

Bohemian *a* and *n* bohemio (-ia)

boil *vi* bullir, hervir; (cook) cocer. *vt* hervir; cocer. *n* ebullición, *f*; *med* divieso, *m*. **to b. away,** consumirse hirviendo; *chem* evaporar a seco. **to b. over,** rebosar

boiler *n cul* marmita, olla, *f*; (of a furnace) caldera, *f*. **double-b.,** baño de María, *m*. **steam-b.,** caldera de vapor, *f*. **b.-maker,** calderero, *m*. **b. room,** cámara de la caldera, *f*. **b.-suit,** mono, *m*

boiling *n* ebullición, *f*, hervor, *m*; (cooking) cocción, *f*, *a* hirviente. **b. point,** punto de ebullición, *m*

boisterous *a* (of persons) exuberante, impetuoso; (stormy) tempestuoso, borrascoso; violento

boisterously *adv* impetuosamente, ruidosamente; tempestuosamente; con violencia

boisterousness *n* exuberancia, impetuosidad, *f*; violencia, *f*; tempestuosidad, borrascosidad, *f*

bold *a* intrépido, audaz; (determined) resuelto; (forward) atrevido; (showy) llamativo; (clear) claro. **b.-faced,** descarado, desvergonzado. **b.-faced type,** letra negra, *f*

boldly *adv* intrépidamente; descaradamente; resueltamente; claramente

boldness *n* intrepidez, valentía, *f*; resolución, *f*; (forwardness) osadia, *f*, descaro, atrevimiento, *m*; claridad, *f*

Bolivian *a* and *n* boliviano (-na)

Bolognese *a* and *n* boloñés (-esa)

Bolshevik *a* and *n* bolchevique, *mf*

Bolshevism *n* bolchevismo, *m*

Bolshevist *n* bolchevista, *mf*

bolster *n* travesaño, *m*. *vt* apuntalar; *fig* apoyar

bolt *n* pasador, cerrojo, *m*; (pin) perno, *m*; (knocker) aldaba, *f*; (roll) rollo, *m*; (flight) huida, *f*; (of a crossbow) flecha, *f*; (from the blue) rayo, *m*. *adv* (upright) recto como una flecha; enhiesto; rígido. **b. and nut,** perno y tuerca, *m*

bolt *vt* echar el cerrojo (a); empernar; (*fam* eat) zampar. *vi* huir; (horses) desbocarse, disparase; (plants) cerner. **to b. down,** cerrar con cerrojo. **to b. in,** entrar corriendo, entrar de repente. **to b. off,** marcharse corriendo. **to b. out,** *vi* salir de golpe. *vt* cerrar fuera

bolus *n* bolo, *m*

bomb *n* bomba, *f*, *vt* bombardear. **to be a b.-shell,** *fig*

caer como una bomba. **b.-carrier,** portabombas, *m*. **b. crater,** bombazo, *m*. **b.-release,** *(aer nav)* lanzabombas, *m*. **b.-sight,** mira de avión de bombardeo, *f*
bombard *vt* bombardear, bombear; *fig* llover (preguntas, etc.) sobre
bombardier *n* bombardero, *m*
bombardment *n* bombardeo, *m*
bombast *n* ampulosidad, pomposidad, *f*
bombastic *a* bombástico, altisonante, pomposo
bomber *n* avión de bombardeo, bombardero, *m*. **dive b.,** bombardero en picado, *m*. **heavy b.,** bombardero pesado, *m*. **light b.,** bombardero ligero, *m*. **b. command,** servicio de bombardero, *m*
bombproof *a* a prueba de bomba
bonafide *a* fidedigno
bonbon *n* bombón, confite, dulce, *m*. **b. box,** bombonera, *f*
bond *n* lazo, vínculo, *m*; *chem* enlace, *m*; (financial) obligación, *f*; (security) fianza, *f*; (Customs) depósito, *m*; *pl* **bonds,** cadenas, *f pl, a* esclavo. **in b.,** en depósito. **bonds of interest,** intereses creados, *m pl*. **b.-holder,** obligacionista, *mf*
bondage *n* esclavitud, *f*; servidumbre, *f*; cautiverio, *m*; prisión, *f*
bone *n* hueso, *m*; (of fish) espina (de pez), *f*; (whale b.) ballena, *f*; *pl* **bones,** cuerpo, *m*, *vt* deshuesar; poner ballenas (a or en). **to be all skin and bones,** estar en los huesos. **to have a b. to pick with,** tener que arreglar las cuentas con. **b.-ash,** cendra, *f*
boned *a* (in compounds) de huesos; deshuesado, sin hueso
boner *n* gazapo, *m*, patochada, plancha, *f*
bonfire *n* fogata, hoguera, *f*
Bonn Bona, *f*
bonnet *n* capota, *f*; (of babies) gorra, *f*; (of men) boina, *f*; (of chimney and of machines) sombrerete, *m*
bonny *a* sano; hermoso; (fat) gordo
bonus *n* paga extraordinaria, bonificación, *f*; sobresueldo, *m*; (of food, etc.) ración extraordinaria, *f*
bon vivant *n* alegre, vividor, *m*
bon voyage *interj* ¡buen viaje! ¡feliz viaje!
bony *a* huesudo; (of fish-bones) lleno de espinas; óseo
booby *n* pazguato, bobo, *m*. **b.-prize,** último premio, *m*. **b.-trap,** trampa, *f*; mil mina, *f*
book *n* libro, *m*; volumen, tomo, *m*; (of an opera) libreto, *m*, *vt* anotar en un libro; apuntar; (seats) tomar (localidades); (tickets) sacar (billetes); (of the issuing clerk) dar; (reserve) reservar; inscribir; consignar (a suspect); (engage) contratar; (invite) comprometer. **to turn the pages of a b.,** hojear un libro. **b.-ends,** sostén para libros, sujetalibros, *m*. **b.-keeper,** tenedor de libros, *m*. **b.-keeping,** teneduría de libros, *f*. **b.-maker,** apostador de profesión, *m*. **b. of reference,** libro de consulta, *m*. **b.-plate,** exlibris, *m*. **b.-post,** tarifa de impresos, *f*. **b.-shop,** librería, *f*. **b.-trade,** venta de libros, *f*; comercio de libros, *m*
bookbinder *n* encuadernador (-ra) de libros
bookbinding *n* encuadernación de libros, *f*
bookcase *n* armario de libros, *m*
booking *n* (of rooms, etc.) reservación, *f*; (of tickets) toma, *f*; *com* asiento, *m*; (engagement) contratación, *f*. **b.-clerk,** vendedor (-ra) de billetes. **b.-office,** despacho de billetes, *m*; taquilla, *f*
bookish *a* aficionado a los libros; docto, erudito
bookishness *n* afición a los libros, *f*; erudición, *f*
bookmark *n* marcador, *m*
bookseller *n* librero, *m*
bookselling *n* venta de libros, *f*; comercio de libros, *m*
bookshelf *n* estante para libros, *m*
bookstall *n* puesto de libros, *m*
bookstrap *n* portalibros, *m*
bookworm *n* polilla que roe los libros, *f*; *fig* ratón de biblioteca, *m*
boom *n naut* botavara, *f*; (of a crane) aguilón, *m*; (noise) ruido, *m*; (of the sea) bramido, *m*; (thunder) trueno, *m*; (in a port) cadena de puerto, *f*; *com* actividad, *f*; *(fig*

peak) auge, *m*, *vi* sonar; bramar; tronar; *com* subir; ser famoso. **b. sail,** vela de cangreja, *f*
boomerang *n* bumerang, *m*
boon *n* favor, *m*, merced, *f*; bien, *m*, ventaja, *f*; don, *m*; privilegio, *m*, *a* (of friends) íntimo
boor *n* monigote, patán, palurdo, *m*
boorish *a* rudo, zafio, rústico, cerril
boorishness *n* zafiedad, patanería, tosquedad, *f*
boost *vt elec* aumentar la fuerza de; *inf* empujar; subir; (advertise) dar bombo (a)
boot *n* bota, *f*; (of a car) compartimiento para equipaje, *m*. **button-boots,** botas de botones, *f pl*. **riding-boots,** botas de montar, *f pl*. **to b.,** además, de añadidura. **b.-maker,** zapatero, *m*. **b.-tag,** tirador de bota, *m*. **b.-tree,** horma de bota, *f*
bootblack *n* limpiabotas, *m*
booted *a* con botas, calzado con botas; (in compounds) de botas . . .
bootee *n* botín, *m*
booth *n* puesto, *m*, barraca, *f*
bootlace *n* cordón para zapatos, *m*
bootlegger *n* contrabandista de alcohol, *m*
boots *n* mozo de hotel, botones, *m*
booty *n* botín, *m*; tesoro, *m*
booze *vi* emborracharse. *n* alcohol, *m*; borrachera, *f*
boozer *n* borracho (-cha)
boracic *a* bórico. *n* ácido bórico, *m*
borax *n* bórax, *m*
Bordeaux *a* and *n* (of or from) bordelés (-esa). *n* (wine) vino de Burdeos, *m*
bordello *n* burdel, *m*
border *n* borde, *m*; (of a lake, etc.) orilla, *f*; (edge) margen, *m*; (of a diploma, etc.) orla, *f*; *sew* ribete, *m*, orla, *f*; (fringe) franja, *f*; (garden) arriate, *m*; (territory) frontera, *f*; límite, confín, *m*. *vt sew* orlar, ribetear; ornar (de); (of land) lindar con. **to b. on,** (of land) tocar, lindar con; (approach) rayar en. **b. country,** región fronteriza, *f*
borderer *n* habitante de una zona fronteriza, *m*; escocés (-esa) de la frontera con Inglaterra
borderland *n* zona fronteriza, *f*; lindes, *m pl*
borderline *n* frontera, *f*; límite, *m*; margen, *m*, *a* fronterizo; lindero; (uncertain) dudoso, incierto
bore *n* taladro, barreno, *m*; perforación, *f*; (hole) agujero, *m*; (of guns) calibre, *m*; (wave) oleada, *f*; (nuisance) fastidio, *m*; (dullness) aburrimiento, tedio, *m*; (person) pelmazo, *m*, machaca, *mf vt* taladrar, barrenar, horadar; perforar; hacer un agujero (en); (exhaust) aburrir; fastidiar. **It's a b.,** Es una lata. **to be bored,** aburrirse, fastidiarse
boredom *n* aburrimiento, *m*; tedio, hastío, *m*
boric *a* bórico
boring *a* aburrido, pesado, tedioso; molesto, fastidioso. *n* taladro, *m*; horadación, *f*; sondeo, *m*; perforación, *f*
born *a* nacido; (by birth) de nacimiento; (b. to be) destinado a; natural (de). **He was b. in 1870.** Nació en 1870. **to be b.,** nacer, venir al mundo. **to be b. again,** renacer, volver a nacer. **well-b.,** bien nacido. **b. with a silver spoon in one's mouth,** Nacido de pie, Nacido un domingo
-borne trasmitido por . . . (e.g. **anthropod-b.,** trasmitido por los antrópodos)
borough *n* burgo, *m*; villa, *f*; ciudad, *f*. **b. surveyor,** arquitecto municipal, *m*
borrow *vt* pedir prestado; apropiarse, adoptar; copiar; (arithmetic) restar; (a book from a library) tomar prestado. **May I b. your pencil?** ¿Quieres prestarme tu lápiz?
borrower *n* el (la) que pide o toma prestado
borrowing *n* el pedir prestado, acto de pedir prestado, *m*
bosh *n* patrañas, tonterías, *f pl*; palabrería, *f*
Bosnian *a* bosnio
bosom *n* pecho, *m*; (heart) corazón, *m*; (of the earth, etc.) seno, *m*. **b. friend,** amigo (-ga) del alma, amigo (-ga) íntimo (-ma)

Bosphorus, the el Bósforo, *m*
boss *n* (of a shield) corcova saliente, *f;* tachón, *m; arch* pinjante, *m. inf* amo, *m;* jefe, *m. vt* mandar; dominar.
  political b., cacique, *m*
bossism *n* caudillaje, *m*
bossy *a* mandón, autoritario
botanical *a* botánico. **b. garden,** jardín botánico, *m*
botanist *n* botánico (-ca)
botany *n* botánica, *f*
botch *n* (clumsy work) chapucería, *f;* remiendo, *m. vt* chapucear, chafallar; (patch) remendar
both *a* and *pron* ambos, *m pl;* ambas, *f pl;* los dos, *m pl;* las dos, *f pl, adv* tan(to) . . . como; (and) y; a la vez, al mismo tiempo. **It appealed both to the young and the old,** Gustó tanto a los jóvenes como a los viejos. **b. of you,** ustedes dos, vosotros dos, vosotras dos. **b. pretty and useful,** bonito y útil a la vez
bother *n* molestia, *f;* fastidio, *m;* (worry) preocupación, *f;* dificultad, *f;* (fuss) alboroto, *m. vt* molestar, fastidiar; preocupar. *vi* preocuparse
bottle *n* botella, *f;* (smaller) frasco, *m;* (babies) biberón, *m;* (for water) cantimplora, *f, vt* embotellar, envasar, enfrascar. **to b. up,** (liquids, capital, armies, navies) embotellar; (feelings) refrenar. **to bring up on the b.,** criar con biberón. **b.-green,** verde botella, *m.* **b.-neck,** (in an industry) embotellado, *m;* (in traffic) atascadero, *m.* **b.-washer,** fregaplatos, *mf;* (machine) máquina para limpiar botellas, *f*
bottle cap *n* corchalata, *f*
bottled *a* en botella; (of fruit, vegetables) conservado
bottleful *n* botella, *f*
bottler *n* embotellador (-ra)
bottling *n* embotellado, *m;* envase, *m.* **b. outfit,** embotelladora, *f;* (for fruit, etc.) aparato para conservar frutas o legumbres, *m*
bottom *n* base, *f;* (deepest part) fondo, *m;* (last place) último lugar, *m;* fundamento, *m;* (of a chair) asiento, *m;* (of a page, table, mountain, etc.) pie, *m;* (posterior) culo, *m;* (of a river) lecho, *m;* (of the sea) fondo, *m;* (of a ship) casco, *m;* (of a skirt) orilla, *f;* (truth) realidad, verdad, *f;* (basis) origen, *m,* causa, *f.* **at b.,** en realidad. **at the b.,** en el fondo. **false b.,** fondo doble, fondo secreto, *m.* **to be at the b. of,** ocupar el último lugar en; ser el causante de. **to get to the b. of,** descubrir la verdad de; profundizar en, analizar. **to sink to the b.,** (of ships) irse a pique
bottomed *a* (in compounds) de fondo . . .
bottomless *a* sin fondo; (of chairs, etc.) sin asiento; (unfathomable) insondable
boudoir *n* tocador, gabinete de señora, *m*
bough *n* rama, *f,* brazo (de un árbol) *m*
boulder *n* roca, peña, *f;* canto rodado, *m;* bloque de roca, *m*
boulevard *n* bulevar, *m*
Boulogne Boloña, *f*
bounce *n* bote, rebote, *m;* salto, *m;* (boasting) fanfarronería, *f, vi* rebotar; saltar, brincar. *vt* hacer botar o saltar
bouncing *a* (healthy) sano, robusto; vigoroso, fuerte
bound *n* límite, *m;* (jump) salto, brinco, *m, vt* limitar, confinar. *vi* saltar, brincar; (bounce) botar. **within bounds,** dentro del límite. **b. for,** con destino a; (of ships) con rumbo a
boundary *n* límite, lindero, término, *m;* frontera, *f;* raya, *f.* **b. stone,** mojón, *m*
bounden *a* obligatorio, forzoso; indispensable
boundless *a* sin límites, infinito; inmenso
bounteous, bountiful *a* dadivoso, generoso; bondadoso
bountifulness *n* munificencia, dadivosidad, generosidad, *f*
bounty *n* generosidad, munificencia, *f;* don, *m;* (subsidy) subvención, *f*
bouquet *n* ramo, ramillete (de flores), *m;* perfume, *m;* (of wine) nariz, *f*
Bourbon *a* borbónico. *n* Borbón (-ona)

bourgeois *a* and *n* burgués (-esa)
bourgeoisie *n* burguesía, mesocracia, *f*
bout *n* turno, *m;* (in fencing, boxing, wrestling) asalto, *m;* (of illness, coughing) ataque, *m;* (fight) lucha, *f,* combate, *m;* (of drinking) borrachera, *f*
bovine *a* bovino, vacuno
bow *n* (weapon) arco, *m;* (of a saddle) arzón (de silla), *m; mus* arco, *m;* (knot) lazo, *m;* (greeting) saludo, *m;* reverencia, inclinación, *f;* (of a boat) proa, *f.* **to tie a bow,** hacer un lazo. **bow and arrows,** arco y flechas, *m.* **bow-legged,** patizambo. **bow window,** ventana saliente, *f*
bow *vi* inclinarse; hacer una reverencia, saludar; (remove the hat) descubrirse; *fig* inclinarse (ante); (submit) someterse (a), reconocer; agobiarse; *mus* manejar el arco. *vt* (usher in) introducir en, conducir a; doblar; inclinar. **to bow down (to),** humillarse ante; obedecer; (worship) reverenciar, adorar. **to bow out,** despedir con una inclinación del cuerpo
bowel *n* intestino, *m; pl* **bowels,** *fig* seno, *m,* entrañas, *f pl*
bower *n* (arbor) enramada, *f;* glorieta, *f;* (boudoir) tocador de señora, *m*
bowing *n mus* arqueada, *f;* saludo, *m, a* (of acquaintance) superficial
bowl *n* receptáculo, *m;* (of a fountain) taza, *f;* (of a pipe) cazoleta, *f;* (barber's) bacía, *f;* (for washing) jofaina, *f;* (for punch) ponchera, *f;* (goblet) copa, *f;* (for soup) escudilla, *f;* (for fruit) frutero, *m;* (of a spoon) paleta, *f;* (ball) boliche, *m. vt* tirar; (in cricket) sacar; (a hoop) jugar con; (in ninepins) tumbar con una bola. **to b. along,** recorrer; ir en coche o carruaje (por). **to b. over,** *fig* dejar consternado (a), desconcertar
bowler *n* (in cricket) servidor, *m;* (hat) sombrero hongo, *m;* (skittle player) jugador de bolos, *m*
bowling *n* (in cricket) saque, *m;* (skittles) juego de bolos, *m;* juego de boliche, *m.* **b. alley,** bolera, pista de bolos, *f,* salón de boliche, *m.* **b.-green,** bolera en césped, *f*
bowls *n* juego de boliche, *m*
bowsprit *n* bauprés, *m*
bowstring *n* cuerda de arco, *f*
bow tie *n* pajarita, *f*
bow-wow *n* guau, *m*
box *n* caja, *f;* (case) estuche, *m;* (luggage) baúl, *m,* maleta, *f;* (for a hat) sombrerera, *f; bot* boj, *m; theat* palco, *m;* (for a sentry, signalman, etc.) garita, casilla, *f;* (on a carriage) pescante, *m;* (blow) cachete, *m,* bofetada, *f;* (for a horse) vagón, *m.* **post office box,** apartado de correos, *m.* **box-kite,** cometa celular, *f.* **box-maker,** cajero, *m.* **box office,** taquilla, *f.* **box-pleat,** *sew* tabla, *f*
box *vt* encajonar, meter en una caja. *vi* boxear. **to box the ears of,** calentar las orejas de. **to box up,** encerrar
boxer *n sport* boxeador, pugilista, *m*
boxing *n* encajonamiento, *m;* envase, *m; sport* boxeo, pugilato, *m.* **B. Day,** Día de San Esteban, *m,* (A Spanish child receives its Christmas presents on the Día de Reyes (Twelfth Night).) **b.-gloves,** guantes de boxeo, *m pl.* **b.-ring,** cuadrilátero de boxeo, *m*
box-office success *n* éxito de taquilla, *m*
boy *n* muchacho, niño, rapaz, *m;* (older) chico, joven, *m.* **new boy,** nuevo alumno, *m.* **old boy,** (of a school) antiguo alumno, *m;* (fam address) chico. **small boy,** chiquillo, pequeño, crío, *m.* **b. doll,** muñeco, *m.* **boy scout,** muchacho explorador, *m*
boycott *vt* boicotear. *n* boicot, *m*
boyhood *n* muchachez, mocedad, *f;* (childhood) niñez, *f*
boyish *a* muchachil; pueril; de niñez
brace *n* (prop) puntal, barrote, *m;* abrazadera, *f; carp* berbiquí, *m;* viento, tirante, *m;* freno (for the teeth), *m;* (pair) par, *m; pl* **braces,** tirantes, *m pl. vt* apuntalar; asegurar; *carp* ensamblar; *naut* bracear; (trousers) tirar; *fig* fortalecer, refrescar
bracelet *n* pulsera, *f,* brazalete, *m,* ajorca, *f*

bracing *a* (of air, etc.) fortificante, tónico; estimulador

bracken *n* helecho, *m*

bracket *n* consola, *f*; *arch* repisa, *f*; soporte, *m*; (on furniture, etc.) cantonera, *f*; *print* paréntesis angular, *m*; (for a light) brazo (de alumbrado), *m*. *vt print* poner entre paréntesis; juntar. **in brackets**, entre paréntesis. **They were bracketed equal,** Fueron juzgados iguales

brackish *a* salobre

brag *vi* jactarse, fanfarronear. *n* jactancia, *f*. **to b. about,** hacer alarde de

braggart *a* baladrón, jactancioso. *n* jactancioso, fanfarrón, *m*

bragging *n* jactancia, *f*

Brahmin *n* brahmán, *m*

Brahminism *n* brahmanismo, *m*

braid *n* trencilla, *f*, cordoncillo, *m*; (for trimming) galón, *m*; (plait) trenza, *f*. *vt* (hair) trenzar; (trim) galonear; acordonar, trencillar

brain *n* cerebro, *m*; entendimiento, *m*, inteligencia, *f*; talento, *m*; (common sense) sentido común, *m*; *pl* **brains,** sesos, *m pl*, (animal and human); cacumen, *m*. *vt* romper la crisma (a). **to blow one's brains out,** levantarse la tapa de los sesos. **to rack one's brains,** devanarse los sesos. **Brains Trust,** masa cefálica, *f*; consorcio de inteligencias, *m*. **b.-box,** cráneo, *m*. **b.-fever,** fiebre cerebral, *f*. **b.-storm,** crisis nerviosa, *f*. **b.-wave,** idea luminosa, *f*. **b.-work,** trabajo intelectual, *m*

brainchild *n* engendro, *m*

brain drain *n* fuga de cerebros, *f*

brained *a* de cabeza, de cerebro

brainless *a* sin seso; tonto

brainy *a* sesudo, inteligente, talentudo

braise *vt cul* asar

brake *n* (of vehicles and *fig*) freno, *m*; (flax and hemp) caballete, *m*; (carriage) break, *m*; (thicket) matorral, *m*. *vt* (vehicles) frenar; (hemp, etc.) rastrillar. **foot-b.,** freno de pedal, *m*. **hand-b.,** freno de mano, *m*. **to b. hard,** frenar de repente. **to release the b.,** quitar el freno

bramble *n* zarza, *f*. **b. patch,** breña, *f*, zarzal, *m*

brambly *a* zarzoso

bran *n* salvado, *m*

branch *n* (of a tree, a family) rama, *f*; (of flowers, of learning) ramo, *m*; (of a river) tributario, afluente, *m*; (of roads, railways) ramal, *m*; (of a firm) sucursal, dependencia, *f*. *a* sucursal, dependiente; (of roads, railways) secundario. *vi* echar ramas; bifurcarse, dividirse; ramificarse. **to b. off,** bifurcarse, ramificarse. **to b. out,** extenderse; emprender cosas nuevas

branched *a* con ramas; *bot* ramoso; (of candlesticks) de . . . brazos

branchiness *n* ramaje, *m*, frondosidad, *f*

branching *n* ramificación, *f*; división, *f*. **b. off,** bifurcación, *f*

brand *n* tizón, *m*; (torch) tea, *f*; (on cattle, etc.) hierro, *m*; (trademark) marca de fábrica, *f*; marca, *f*; (stigma) estigma, *m*. *vt* marcar con el hierro, herrar; marcar; estigmatizar, tildar. **b.-new,** flamante

branding *n* (of livestock) herradero, *m*; (of slaves, criminals) estigmatización, *f*; difamación, *f*. **b.-iron,** hierro de marcar, *m*

brandish *vt* blandir

brandy *n* coñac, *m*

brass *n* latón, *m*; *mus* metal, *m*; (tablet) placa conmemorativa, *f*; *inf* dinero, *m*. **the b.,** *mus* el metal. **b. band,** banda de instrumentos de viento, *f*. **b.-neck,** *inf* cara dura, *f*. **b. works** or **shop,** latonería, *f*

brassiere *n* sostén, *m*

brat *n* crío, *m*

bravado *n* bravata, *f*

brave *a* valiente, animoso, intrépido; espléndido, magnífico; bizarro. *n* valiente, *m*. *vt* desafiar, provocar; arrostrar

bravely *adv* valientemente; espléndidamente; bizarramente

bravery *n* valentía, *f*, valor, *m*, intrepidez, *f*, coraje, *m*; esplendidez, suntuosidad, *f*; bizarría, *f*

bravo *n* bandido, *m*; asesino pagado, *m*, *interj* ¡bravo! ¡ole!

bravura *n* bravura, *f*

brawl *n* camorra, reyerta, pelotera, *f*. *vi* alborotar; (of streams) murmurar. **to start a b.,** armar camorra

brawler *n* camorrista, *mf*

brawling *n* alboroto, *m*, vocinglería, *f*; (of streams) murmullo, *m*

brawn *n* *cul* embutido, *m*; músculo, *m*; (strength) fuerza, *f*

brawny *a* membrudo, musculoso, forzudo

bray *n* rebuzno, *m*; (of trumpets) clangor, *m*, *vi* rebuznar; sonar

brazen *a* de latón; (of voice) bronca; desvergonzado, descarado

brazier *n* (fire) brasero, *m*; latonero, *m*

Brazil el Brasil, *m*

Brazilian *a* and *n* brasileño (-ña)

Brazil nut *n* nuez del Brasil, *f*

breach *n* violación, contravención, *f*; (gap) abertura, *f*; *mil* brecha, *f*. *vt mil* hacer brecha (en); (in a line of defence) hacer mella (en). **b. of confidence,** abuso de confianza, *m*. **b. of promise,** incumplimiento de la palabra de casamiento, *m*. **b. of the peace,** alteración del orden público, *m*; quebrantamiento de la paz, *m*

bread *n* pan, *m*. **to earn one's b. and butter,** ganarse el pan. **brown b.,** pan moreno, *m*. **unleavened b.,** pan ázimo, *m*. **b. and butter,** pan con mantequilla, *m*; *fig* sustento diario, *m*. **b.-basket,** cesta de pan, *f*; *inf* estómago, *m*. **b.-bin,** caja del pan, *f*. **b.-crumb,** miga, *f*; migaja, *f*. **b.-knife,** cuchillo para cortar el pan, *m*. **b. poultice,** cataplasma de miga de pan, *f*. **b.-winner,** ganador (-ra) del pan, trabajador (-ra)

breadfruit tree *n* árbol del pan, *m*

breadth *n* anchura, *f*; latitud, *f*; liberalidad, *f*; *sew* ancho de una tela, *m*

breadthways *adv* a lo ancho

break *n* rotura, *f*; (opening) abertura, *f*; *geol* rajadura, *f*; (fissure) grieta, *f*; solución de continuidad, *f*; interrupción, *f*; (billiards) serie, *f*; (change) cambio, *m*; (in a boy's voice) muda (de la voz), *f*; (blank) vacío, *m*; (in the market) baja, *f*; intervalo, *m*; descanso, *m*; pausa, *f*; (truce) tregua, *f*; (clearing) clara, *f*; *mus* quiebra (de la voz), *f*; (carriage) break, *m*; (*fam* folly) disparate, *m*. **with a b. in one's voice,** con voz entrecortada. **b. of day,** aurora, alba, *f*. **at the b. of day,** al despuntar el alba

break *vt* romper; quebrar; quebrantar; fracturar; (breach) abrir brecha en; (in two) partir, dividir; (into pieces) hacer pedazos, despedazar; (into small pieces) desmenuzar; (into crumbs) desmigajar; (destroy) destrozar; (a blow) parar; (a law) infringir, violar; (the bank in gambling) quebrar; (a journey, etc.) interrumpir; (of a habit) desacostumbrar, hacer perder el vicio de; (a promise) no cumplir, faltar a; (a record) superar; (plow ground) roturar; (spoil) estropear; arruinar; *com* ir a la quiebra; (an official) degradar; (an animal) domar, amansar; (*fig* crush) subyugar; (betray) traicionar; (*fig* of silence, a spell, a lance, peace, the ranks) romper; (cushion) amortiguar; (lessen) mitigar; (disclose) revelar; *elec* interrumpir. **to b. one's promise,** faltar a su palabra. **to b. the ice,** *fig* romper el hielo. **to b. asunder,** romper en dos (partes); dividir. **to b. down,** derribar; echar abajo; destruir; (suppress) suprimir; subyugar; abolir; disolver. **to b. in,** (animals) domar, amaestrar; (persons) disciplinar; (new shoes) ahormar, romper. **to b. in two,** partir; dividir en dos; (split) hender. **to b. off,** separar, quitar; (a branch) desgajar; *fig* romper; interrumpir; cesar. **to b. open,** forzar, abrir a la fuerza. **to b. up,** hacer pedazos; (scatter) poner en fuga, dispersar; hacer levantar la sesión; (the ground) roturar; (parliament) disolver; (a ship) desguazar, deshacer (un buque)

break *vi* romperse; quebrarse; (of beads)

desgranarse; (burst) reventar, estallar; (of abscesses) abrirse; (of a boy's voice) mudar; (*fig* and of clouds, etc.) romperse; desaparecer; (of the dawn) despuntar (el alba), amanecer; (sprout) brotar; (of a ball) torcerse; (of fine weather) terminar; (change) cambiar; (of a storm) estallar. **to b. loose,** desasirse; *fig* desencadenarse. **to b. away,** escaparse, fugarse; (from a habit) romper con, independizarse de (another country); disiparse. **to b. down,** (of machinery, cars) averiarse; (fail) frustrarse, malograrse; (weep) deshacerse en lágrimas; (lose one's grip) perder la confianza en sí; (in health) sufrir una crisis de salud. **The car broke down,** El auto tuvo una avería. **to b. in,** (of burglars) forzar la entrada; irrumpir (en), penetrar (en); exclamar. **to b. in on,** sorprender; entrar de sopetón; invadir; interrumpir; caer sobre; molestar. **to b. into,** (force) forzar; (utter) romper a, prorrumpir en; empezar (a); pasar de repente a; (of time, etc.) ocupar; hacer perder. **to b. off,** (of speech) interrumpirse; cesar; (detach) desprenderse, separarse; (of branches) desgajarse. **to b. out,** huir, escaparse; *fig* estallar; aparecer; declararse; (of fire) tomar fuego; derramarse; (of an eruption) salir. **to b. over,** derramarse por; bañar. **to b. through,** abrirse paso (por); abrirse salida (por); atravesar; *fig* penetrar; (of the sun, etc.) romper (por). **to b. up,** (depart) separarse; (of meetings) levantarse la sesión; dispersarse; (smash) hacerse pedazos; disolverse; (of a school) cerrarse, empezar las vacaciones; (melt) fundir; desbandarse; (of a camp) levantar (el campo); (grow old) hacerse viejo; (be ill) estar agotado. **to b. with,** romper con; cesar; reñir con

breakable *a* quebradizo, frágil

breakage *n* rompimiento, quebrantamiento, *m*; cosa rota, *f*; fractura, *f*

breakdown *n* accidente, *m*; (of a machine) avería, *f*; *aut* pane, *f*; (failure) fracaso, *m*, falta de éxito, *f*; deterioración, *f*; (in health) crisis de salud, *f*. **b. gang,** pelotón de reparaciones, *m*

breaker *n* oleada, *f*

breakfast *n* desayuno, *m*. *vi* desayunar(se), tomar el desayuno. **to have a good b.,** desayunar bien. **b.-cup,** tazón, *m*. **b.-time,** hora del desayuno, *f*

breaking *n* rompimiento, *m*; quebrantamiento, *m*; fractura, *f*; ruptura, *f*; (in two) división, *f*; (into pieces) despedazamiento, *m*; (into small pieces) desmenuzamiento, *m*; (destruction) destrozo, *m*; (of a blow) parada, *f*; (of a law, etc.) violación, *f*; (of one's word) no cumplimiento, *m*; (of a journey, of sleep, etc.) interrupción, *f*; (escape) escape, *m*, huida, *f*; (of an animal) domadura, *f*; (of a boy's voice) muda (de la voz), *f*; (of news) revelación, *f*. **b. down,** demolición, *f*; (of negotiations) suspensión, *f*. **b. in,** irrupción, *f*; (of an animal) domadura, *f*; (training) entrenamiento, *m*. **b. open,** forzamiento, *m*; quebranto, *m*. **b. out,** huida, *f*, escape, *m*; *fig* estallido, *m*; aparición, *f*; declaración, *f*; (scattering) derramamiento, *m*; (of a rash) erupción, *f*. **b. up,** dispersión, *f*; disolución, *f*; fin, *m*; ruina, *f*; (of a school) cierre, *m*; (change in weather) cambio, *m*; (of a meeting) levantamiento (de una sesión), *m*; (of the earth) roturación, *f*

breakneck *a* rápido, veloz, precipitado

breakwater *n* malecón, rompeolas, *m*

bream *n icht* sargo, *m*, besugo, *m*. **sea-b.,** *m*

breast *n* pecho, *m*; (of birds) pechuga, *f*; (of female animals) teta, mama, *f*; (heart) corazón, *m*, *vt* (the waves) cortar (las olas); luchar con; *fig* arrostrar, hacer frente a. **b.-bone,** esternón, *m*. **b. high,** alto hasta el pecho. **b.-pin,** alfiler de pecho, *m*. **b.-pocket,** bolsillo de pecho, *m*. **b.-stroke,** estilo pecho, *m*

breast cancer *n* el cáncer del seno, *m*

breasted *a* de pecho . . .; de pechuga . . .; de tetas . . . **a double-b. jacket,** una chaqueta cruzada. **a single-b. jacket,** una chaqueta

breastwork *n mil* parapeto, *m*

breath *n* aliento, *m*; suspiro, *m*; (phonetics) aspiración, *f*; (breeze) soplo (de aire), *m*; (of scandal, etc.) mur-

murio, *m*; (fragrance) perfume, *m*, fragancia, *f*; (life) vida, *f*. **in a b.,** de un aliento. **in the same b.,** sin respirar. **out of b.,** sin aliento. **under one's b.,** por lo bajo, entre dientes. **to draw b.,** tomar aliento. **to get one's b. back,** cobrar aliento. **to hold one's b.,** contener el aliento. **to take one's b. away,** *fig* dejar consternado (a)

breathable *a* respirable

breathe *vi* respirar; vivir; (of air, etc.) soplar; (take air) tomar el fresco; (rest) tomar aliento. *vt* respirar; exhalar; dar aire (a); (whisper) murmurar; (convey) expresar, revelar; (infuse) infundir. **to b. forth fury,** echar rayos. **to b. hard,** jadear. **to b. one's last,** exhalar el último suspiro. **to b. in,** inspirar

breathing *n* respiración, *f*; (of the air, etc.) soplo, *m*; (phonetics) aspiración, *f*. *a* que respira; viviente. **hard** or **heavy b.,** jadeo, resuello, resoplido, *m*. **b.-space,** *fig* respiro, *m*

breathless *a* jadeante, sin aliento; (dead) muerto; (sultry) sin un soplo de aire; intenso, profundo; (of haste) precipitado

breathlessly *adv* anhelosamente; con expectación

breathlessness *n* falta de aliento, *f*; respiración difícil, *f*; (death) muerte, *f*; (of weather) falta de aire, *f*

bred *a* criado. **ill (well) b.,** mal (bien) criado. **pure-b.,** de raza

breech *n anat* trasero, *m*; (of fire-arms) recámara, *f*

breeches *n* calzones, *m pl*; pantalones, *m pl*. **riding-b.,** pantalones de montar, *m pl*. **to wear the b.,** *fig* ponerse los calzones

breed *n* casta, raza, *f*; tipo, *m*; clase, *f*, *vt* procrear; engendrar, crear; (bring up) educar; criar. *vi* reproducirse; sacar cría; multiplicarse. **to b. in-and-in,** procrear sin mezclar razas

breeder *n* criador (-ra); animal reproductor, *m*

breeding *n* reproducción, *f*; cría, *f*; (upbringing) crianza, *f*; educación, *f*; instrucción, *f*; producción, *f*; creación, *f*, *a* de cría; (of male animals) semental, prolífico. **bad b.,** mala crianza, *f*. **good b.,** buena crianza, *f*. **cross b.,** cruzamiento de razas, *m*. **B. will out,** Aunque la mona se vista de seda, mona se queda. **b. farm,** criadero, *m*

breeze *n* brisa, *f*, vientecillo, soplo de aire, *m*; (argument) altercación, *f*, argumento, *m*; (of coke) cisco de coque, *m*. **fresh b.,** brisa fresca, *f*. **light b.,** brisa floja, *f*. **strong b.,** viento fuerte, viento muy fresco, *m*

breezy *a* con brisa, fresco; expuesto a la brisa; oreado; (of manner) animado, jovial

Bremen Brema, *f*

brethren *n pl* hermanos, *m pl*

Breton *a* and *n* bretón (-ona). *n* (language) bretón, *m*

brevet *n mil* graduación honoraria, *f*; nombramiento honorario, *m*. *vt mil* graduar

breviary *n* breviario, *m*

brevity *n* brevedad, *f*; concisión, *f*

brew *n* mezcla, *f*; brebaje, *m*. *vt* hacer (cerveza, té, etc.); preparar, mezclar; *fig* urdir, tramar. *vi* prepararse; urdirse; (storm) gestarse.

brewer *n* cervecero (-ra)

brewery *n* cervecería, fábrica de cerveza, *f*

brewing *n* elaboración de cerveza, *f*

briar *n* (wild rose) rosal silvestre, *m*; (heather) brezo, *m*. **b. pipe,** pipa de brezo, *f*

bribable *a* sobornable

bribe *n* soborno, cohecho, *m*. *vt* sobornar, cohechar. **to take bribes,** dejarse sobornar

briber *n* cohechador (-ra)

bribery *n* soborno, *m*

brick *n* ladrillo, *m*; (for children) piedra de construcción, *f*; bloque, *m*; *inf* buen chico, *m*, joya, *f*, a de ladrillo. *vt* enladrillar. **b.-floor,** ladrillado, *m*; **b.-kiln,** horno de ladrillo, *m*. **b.-maker,** ladrillero, *m*. **b.-yard,** ladrillar, *m*

bricklayer *n* albañil, *m*

bricklaying *n* albañilería, *f*

brickwork *n* masonería, *f*

bridal *a* nupcial; de la boda; de la novia. **b. bed,** tálamo, *m.* **b. cake,** torta de la boda, *f.* **b. shop,** tienda para novias, *f.* **b. shower,** despedida de soltera, despedida de soltería, *f.* **b. song,** epitalamio, *m.* **b. veil,** velo de la novia, velo nupcial, *m.* **b. wreath,** corona de azahar, *f*

bride *n* novia, desposada, *f*; (after marriage) recién casada, *f*

bridegroom *n* novio, *m*; (after marriage) recién casado, *m*

bridesmaid *n* madrina de boda, *f*; niña encargada de sostener la cola de la novia, *f*

bridge *n* (engineering, *mus naut*) puente, *m*; lomo (de la nariz), *m*; (game) bridge, *m*, *vt* construir un puente (sobre), pontear; (obstacles) salvar; evitar; (fill in) ocupar, llenar. **auction b.,** bridge por subasta, *m*. **contract b.,** bridge por contrato, *m*. **suspension-b.,** puente colgante, *f*. **b. toll,** pontazgo, *m*

bridgehead *n* cabeza de puente, *f*

bridle *n* brida, *f*; freno, *m*. *vt* embridar, enfrenar; *fig* reprimir. *vi* (of horses) levantar la cabeza; (of persons) erguirse; hacer un gesto despreciativo. **snaffle b.,** bridón, *m*. **b. path,** camino de herradura, *m*

brief *a* breve, corto; conciso; lacónico, seco; rápido; fugaz, pasajero. *n* (papal) breve, *m*; *law* relación, *f*; escrito, *m*. *vt* (a barrister) instruir. **to hold a b. for,** defender, abogar por. **b.-case,** portapapeles, *m*; cartera (grande), *f*

briefly *adv* brevemente; en pocas palabras; sucintamente; (tersely) secamente

brier *n* rosal silvestre, *m*; zarza, *f*

brigade *n mil* brigada, *f*; cuerpo, *m*; asociación, *f*

brigadier *n* brigadier, *m*

brigand *n* bandolero, bandido, *m*

brigandage *n* bandolerismo, *m*

bright *a* brillante, reluciente; vivo; cristalino; subido; claro; optimista; alegre; inteligente; (quick-witted) agudo; ilustre; (smiling) risueño; (of future, etc.) halagüeño. **to be as b. as a new pin,** estar como una ascua de oro. **b. blue,** azul subido, *m*. **b.-eyed,** con ojos vivos, con ojos chispeantes, ojialegre

Bright's disease *n* enfermedad de Bright, glomerulonefritis, *f*

brighten *vt* hacer brillar; (polish) pulir; (make happy) alegrar; (improve) mejorar. *vi* (of the weather) aclarar, despejarse (el cielo); sentirse más feliz; mejorar

brightly *adv* brillantemente; alegremente

brightness *n* brillo, *m*; claridad, *f*; esplendor, *m*; (of colors) brillantez, *f*; vivacidad, *f*; inteligencia, *f*; agudeza de ingenio, *f*

brilliance *n* fulgor, brillo, *m*, refulgencia, *f*; esplendor, *m*; lustre, *m*; talento, *m*; brillantez, gloria, *f*

brilliant *a* brillante. *n* (gem) brillante, *m*. **to be b.,** (in conversation, etc.) (be clever) ser brillante

brilliantine *n* brillantina, *f*

brim *n* (of a glass, etc.) borde, *m*; (of a hat) ala, *f*; margen, *m*, orilla, *f*. **to be full to the b.,** estar lleno hasta los bordes; *fig* rebosar. **eyes brimming with tears,** ojos arrasados de lágrimas

brimful *a* hasta el borde (or los bordes); *fig* rebosante

brimless *a* (of hats) sin ala

brimmed *a* (of hats) con ala

brimstone *n* azufre, *m*

brindled *a* atigrado, abigarrado

brine *n* salmuera, *f*; mar, *m*; *poet* lágrimas, *f pl*

bring *vt* traer; llevar; (take a person or drive a vehicle) conducir; *fig* acarrear, traer; causar, ocasionar; producir; crear; (induce) persuadir; hacer (ver, etc.); (be worth) valer; (sell for) vender por; *law* entablar (un pleito, etc.); (before a judge) hacer comparecer (ante); (present) presentar; (attract) atraer; (place) poner. **to b. home,** llevar a casa; *fig* hacer ver, hacer sentir; demostrar; (a crime) probar contra. **to b. near,** acercar. **to b. about,** efectuar, poner por obra; causar, ocasionar; (achieve) lograr, conseguir. **to b. again,** traer otra vez, llevar de nuevo. **to b. away,** llevarse. **to b. back,** devolver; traer; (of memories) recor-

dar. **to b. down,** llevar abajo, bajar; (of persons) hacer bajar; (humble) humillar; hacer caer; (of prices) hacer bajar; arruinar; destruir. **to b. down the house,** *theat* hacer venirse el teatro abajo. **to b. forth,** (give birth to) dar a luz; producir; causar; sacar a luz. **to b. forward,** hacer adelantarse; empujar hacia adelante; *fig* avanzar; (allege) alegar; *com* llevar a nueva cuenta; presentar, producir. **brought forward,** *com* suma y sigue. **to b. in,** (things) llevar adentro; (persons) hacer entrar; introducir; aparecer con, presentarse con; (meals) servir; producir; declarar; (a verdict) dictar (sentencia de), fallar. **to b. into being,** poner en práctica; dar origen (a). **to b. off,** (a ship) poner a flote; (rescue) salvar, rescatar; (carry out) efectuar, poner en práctica; (achieve) conseguir, lograr. **B. me the glass off the table,** Tráeme el vaso que hay en la mesa. **to b. on,** causar, inducir; acarrear; iniciar. **He brought a book on to the stage,** Entró en escena llevando un libro (or con un libro). **to b. out,** sacar; poner afuera; (a person) hacer salir; publicar; (a play) poner en escena; sacar a luz; (an idea, jewels, etc.) sacar a lucir; revelar; demostrar; hacer aparecer; (a girl in society) poner de largo (a). **to b. over,** llevar al otro lado; hacer venir; traer; conducir; hacer cruzar; (convert) convertir. **to b. round,** traer; llevar; (from a swoon) sacar de un desmayo; curar; persuadir; conciliar. **to b. through,** hacer atravesar; llevar a través de; ayudar a salir (de un apuro); (an illness) curar de. **to b. to,** traer a; llevar a; (from a swoon) hacer volver en sí; *naut* ponerse a la capa. **He cannot b. himself to,** No puede persuadirse a. **to b. together,** reunir; (things) juntar; amontonar; reconciliar; poner en paz. **to b. under,** someter; sojuzgar; incluir. **to b. up,** llevar arriba, subir; (a person) hacer subir; hacer avanzar; (a price) hacer subir; ir (a); andar; (breed) criar; (educate) educar, criar; (in a discussion) hacer notar; vomitar. **to b. up the rear,** ir al fin (de); *mil* ir a la retaguardia. **well** (or **badly) brought up,** bien (o mal) educado. **to b. upon oneself,** buscarse, incurrir (en). **to b. up-to-date,** poner al día; refrescar; rejuvenecer

bringing *n* acción de llevar o traer, *f*; conducción, *f*; transporte, *m*. **b. forth,** producción, *f*. **b. in,** introducción, *f*. **b. out,** producción, *f*; publicación, *f*; (of a girl in society) puesta de largo, *f*. **b. under,** reducción, *f*; subyugación, *f*. **b. up,** educación, crianza, *f*

brink *n* borde, margen, *m*; (of water) orilla, *f*; *fig* margen, *m*. **on the b.,** al margen; a la orilla. **to be on the b. of,** (doing something) estar para, estar a punto de

briny *a* salado

briquette *n* briqueta, *f*, aglomerado de carbón, *m*

brisk *a* activo; vivo; animado; rápido, acelerado; enérgico

brisket *n* falda, *f*

briskly *adv* vivamente; enérgicamente; aprisa

briskness *n* actividad, *f*; viveza, *f*; animación, *f*; rapidez, *f*; energía, *f*

bristle *n* cerda, seda, *f*, *vi* erizarse

bristling *n* sardina noruega, .

bristly *a* erizado, cerdoso; espinoso; hirsuto

Bristol board *n* cartulina, *f*

British *a* británico. **the B.,** el pueblo británico; los ingleses

British Commonwealth, the la Mancomunidad Británica, *f*

Briton *n* inglés (-esa). **ancient B.,** britano (-na)

Brittany Bretaña, *f*

brittle *a* frágil, quebradizo, deleznable, friable

brittleness *n* fragilidad, friabilidad, *f*

broach *n cul* espetón, asador, *m*. *vt* espitar (un barril); abrir; *fig* introducir

broad *a* ancho; grande; (extensive) vasto, extenso; **a b. confession,** una confesión amplia; (full) pleno; (of accents) marcado; (of words) lato; (clear) claro; (of the mind) liberal, tolerante; (of humor, etc.) grosero; (general) general, comprensivo. **in b. daylight,** en pleno día. **b.-brimmed,** de ala ancha. **b.-faced,** cariancho.

b.-minded, tolerante, liberal, ancho de conciencia, abierto al mundo. **b.-mindedness,** tolerancia, liberalidad, *f.* **to be b.-minded,** ser tolerante, tener manga ancha. **b.-shouldered,** ancho de espaldas

broadcast *n agr* siembra al vuelo; *f; rad* radiodifusión, radiotransmisión, emisión, *f, a* radiado. *adv* por todas partes; extensamente. *vt agr* sembrar a vuelo; *rad* radiodifundir, radiar, transmitir por radio; (news, etc.) diseminar

broadcaster *n* (lecturer) conferenciante, *mf; radiodifusor (-ra); (announcer) locutor (-ra)

broadcasting *n* radiación, radiodifución, *f; radio, f.* **b.-station,** estación de radio, emisora, *f.* **b.-studio,** estudio de emisión, *m*

broaden *vt* ampliar, ensanchar. *vi* ampliarse, ensancharse

broad-leaved *a* frondoso

broadly *adv* anchamente; con marcado acento dialectal; de una manera general

broadness *n* anchura, *f;* extensión, vastedad, *f;* tolerancia, *f;* liberalidad, *f;* grosería, *f;* (of accent) acento marcado, *m*

broadside *n* (of a ship) costado, *m;* (of guns) andanada, *f; fig* batería, *f; print* cara de un pliego, *f.* **to be b. on,** dar al costado

brocade *a* and *n* brocado *m.. vt* decorar con brocado. **imitation b.,** brocatel, *m*

brocaded *a* decorado con brocado; de brocado

broccoli *n* bróculi, brécol, *m*

brochure *n* folleto, *m*

brogue *n* acento, *m;* acento irlandés, *m;* (shoe) zapato grueso, *m*

broil *vt* emparrillar, asar. *vi* asarse

broke *a* quebrado

broken *a* roto; quebrado; (spiritless) abatido, desalentado; (infirm) agotado, debilitado; (ruined) arruinado; (of ground) desigual, escabroso; (of a language) chapucero; (spoilt) estropeado; imperfecto; incompleto; (loose) suelto; (of a horse, etc.) domado; (of the weather) variable; (of sleep) interrumpido; (of the heart, of shoes, etc.) roto; (of the voice, sobs, sighs) entrecortado; (of the voice through old age, etc.) cascada; (incoherent) incoherente. **b.-down,** (tired) rendido, agotado; arruinado; (not working) estropeado. **b.-hearted,** roto el corazón, angustiado. **b.-winged,** aliquebrado. **I speak broken Spanish,** Hablo el español chapuceramente

brokenly *adv* (of the voice) con voz entrecortada; a ratos; interrumpidamente

brokenness *n* interrupción, *f;* (of the ground) desigualdad, *f;* (of speech) imperfección, *f*

broker *n* corredor, *m;* (stock) corredor de bolsa, *m*

brokerage *n* corretaje, *m*

bromide *n* bromuro, *m*

bromine *n* bromo, *m*

bronchi *n pl* bronquios, *m pl*

bronchitis *n* bronquitis, *f*

broncopneumonia *n* bronconeumonía, *f*

Brontosaurus *n* brontosauro, *m*

bronze *n* bronce, *m;* objeto de bronce, *m, a* de bronce. *vt* broncear. **B. Age,** Edad de Bronce, *f*

brooch *n* broche, *m;* alfiler de pecho, *m*

brood *n* (of birds) nidada, *f;* (of chickens) pollada, *f;* (other animals) cría, *f;* prole, *f, vi* empollar. **to b. over,** meditar sobre, rumiar; (of mountains, etc.) dominar

broody *a* (of hens) clueca, *f*

brook *n* arroyo, riachuelo, *m, vt* tolerar, sufrir, permitir

broom *n* escoba, *f; bot* retama, *f;* hiniesta, *f.* **common b.,** retama de escobas, *f.* **Spanish b.,** retama común, retama de olor, hiniesta, *f.* **b.-handle,** palo de escoba, *m*

broomstick *n* palo de escoba, *m*

broth *n* caldo, *m*

brothel *n* burdel, lupanar, *m,* casa de trato, *f*

brother *n* hermano, *m;* (colleague) colega, *m; inf* compañero, *m.* **foster-b.,** hermano de leche, *m.* **half-b.,**

medio hermano, *m.* **step-b.,** hermanastro, *m.* **b.-in-law,** hermano político, cuñado, *m.* **b.-officer,** compañero de promoción, *m*

brotherhood *n* fraternidad, *f; ecc* cofradía, *f;* hermandad, *f*

brotherliness *n* fraternidad, *f*

brotherly *a* fraterno

brow *n* frente, *f;* ceja, *f;* (of a hill) cresta, cumbre, *f;* (edge) borde, *m.* **to knit one's b.,** fruncir el ceño

browbeat *vt* intimidar, amenazar

browbeating *n* intimidación, *f*

brown *a* castaño; (gallicism often used of shoes, etc.) marrón; pardo; (of complexion, eyes, hair) moreno; (dark brown) bruno; (blackish) negruzco; (toasted) tostado; (burnt) quemado. *n* color moreno, *m;* color pardo, *m;* castaño, *m;* (from the sun) bronce, *m. vt* (toast) tostar; (a person) volver moreno, broncear; (meat) asar. *vi* tostarse; volverse moreno, broncearse; asarse. **b. bear,** oso pardo, *m.* **b. owl,** autillo, *m.* **b. paper,** papel de estraza, *m.* **b. study,** ensimismamiento, *m,* meditación, *f.* **b. sugar,** azúcar moreno (or quebrado), *m*

brownie *n* duende benévolo, *m*

brownish *a* morenucho; que tira a castaño o a bruno; parduzco; trigueño

brownness *n* color moreno, *m*

browse *vi* pacer; (through a publication) hojear (un libro)

browsing *n* apacentamiento, *m;* hojeo (de un libro), *m;* lectura, *f,* estudio, *m*

Bruges Brujas, *f*

bruise *n* cardenal, *m;* abolladura, *f;* (in metal) bollo, *m;* (on fruit) maca, *f. vt* acardenalar, magullar; abollar; (fruit) macar

bruising *n* magullamiento, *m;* (of metal) abolladura, *f;* (crushing) machacadura, *f;* (boxing) boxeo, pugilato, *m*

brunette *n* trigueña, morena, *f*

brunt *n* peso, *m;* golpe, *m;* choque, *m;* esfuerzo, *m.* **to bear the b.,** soportar el peso; sufrir el choque, *inf* pagar el pato

brush *n* cepillo, *m;* (broom) escoba, *f;* (for whitewashing, etc.) brocha, *f;* (for painting) pincel, *m;* (of a fox) cola (de zorro), *f;* (undergrowth) breñal, matorral, *m;* (fight) escaramuza, *f;* (argument) altercación, *f.* **scrubbing-b.,** cepillo para fregar, *m.* **shoe-b.,** cepillo para limpiar los zapatos, *m.* **stroke of the b.,** brochada, *f;* pincelada, *f.* **whitewash-b.,** brochón, *m.* **b. maker or seller,** escobero (-ra); pincelero (-ra)

brush *vt* cepillar; (sweep) barrer; frotar; (touch) rozar; (touch lightly) acariciar. **to b. against,** rozar, tocar. **to b. aside,** echar a un lado; *fig* no hacer caso de; ignorar. **to b. off,** sacudir(se); quitar(se); (sweep) barrer. **to b. up,** cepillar; (wool) cardar; (tidy) asear; (a subject) refrescar; repasar

brushing *n* acepilladura, *f;* (sweeping) barredura, *f;* (touching) roce, rozamiento, *m;* (of hair) peinadura, *f*

brushwood *n* enjutos, *m pl,* chamarasca, *f;* matorral, *m*

brusque *a* brusco, seco

brusquely *adv* secamente

brusqueness *n* brusquedad, *f*

Brussels *a* bruselense; de Bruselas. **B. lace,** encaje de Bruselas, *m*

Brussels sprouts *n pl* bretones, *m pl*

brutal *a* bestial, brutal; salvaje, inhumano

brutality *n* brutalidad, bestialidad, *f;* barbaridad, ferocidad, *f*

brutalize *vt* embrutecer

brutally *adv* brutalmente

brute *n* bruto, animal, *m;* salvaje, bárbaro, *m.* **b. force,** la fuerza bruta

brutish *a* bruto; sensual, bestial; grosero; salvaje; estúpido; ignorante. **to become b.,** embrutecerse

bubble *n* burbuja, *f;* borbollón, *m, vi* burbujear; borbollar, bullir, hervir

bubbling *n* burbujeo, *m;* hervidero, *m;* (of brooks) murmullo, *m, a* burbujeante; hirviente; (of brooks) parlero; (of wine) espumoso, efervescente

bubonic *a* bubónico. **b. plague,** peste bubónica, *f*

buccaneer *n* corsario, *m*; aventurero, *m*

Bucharest Bucarest, *m*

buck *n zool* gamo, *m*; (male) macho, *m*; (fop) galán, petimetre, *m, vi* (of a horse) caracolear; fanfarronear. **to pass the b.,** *inf* echarle a uno el muerto. **b.-rabbit,** conejo, *m.* **to b. up,** hacer de tripas corazón

bucket *n* cubo, balde, *m*, cubeta, *f*

buckle *n* hebilla, *f. vt* enhebillar, abrochar con hebilla. *vi* doblarse. **to b. to,** ponerse a hacer algo con ahinco

buckled *a* con hebillas

buckler *n* broquel, *m*, rodela, tarjeta, *f*

buckram *n* bocací, *m*

buckshot *n* perdigón, *m*

buckskin *n* ante, *m*

buckwheat *n* alforfón, trigo sarraceno, *m*

bucolic *a* bucólico, pastoril

bud *n* brote, *m*; botón, capullo, *m*; (of vines) bollón, *m*; (of vegetables) gema, *f. vi* brotar, germinar. *vt* injertar de escudete

Buddhism *n* budismo, *m*

Buddhist *n* budista, *mf*

budding *n* brotadura, *f*; (of roses, etc) injerto de escudete, *m*; *fig* germen, *m*

budge *vi* moverse, menearse. *vt* mover

budgerigar *n* periquito, *m*

budget *n* presupuesto, *m*; (of news, etc.) colección, *f. vi* presuponer

Buenos Aires (of or from) *a* and *n* bonaerense, *mf*

buff *n* color de ante, *m*; piel de ante, *f.* **b.-colored,** anteado

buffalo *n* búfalo, *f*

buffer *n* (railway) parachoques, *m*; (of cars) amortiguador, *m.* **b. state,** estado tapón, *m*

buffet *n* bofetón, *m*; bofetada, *f*; bar, *m. vt* abofetear; golpear; luchar con las olas

buffoon *n* bufón, *m*

buffoonery *n* bufonería, *f*

bug *n* chinche, *f*

bugbear *n* pesadilla, *f*

bugle *n* corneta, trompeta, *f*; (bead) abalorio, *m.* **b. blast,** trompetazo, *m*

bugler *n* trompetero, *m*

build *vt* edificar; (engines, ships, organs, etc.) construir; (a nest and *fig*) hacer; (have built) hacer, edificar; crear; formar; fundar. *n* estructura, *f*; (of the body) hechura, *f*; talle, *m.* **to b. castles in Spain,** hacer castillos en el aire. **built-up area,** zona urbana, *f.* **to b. up,** construir, levantar; (block) tapar; (business, reputation) establecer, crear. **to b. upon,** *fig* contar con, confiar en; esperar de

builder *n* constructor, *m*; maestro de obras, *m*; (laborer) albañil, *m*; creador (-ra), fundador (-ra); arquitecto, *m*

building *n* edificación, *f*; construcción, *f*; edificio, *m*; fundación, *f*; creación, *f.* **b. contractor,** maestro de obras, *m.* **b. material,** material de construcción, *m.* **b. site,** solar, terreno, *m.* **b. timber,** madera de construcción, *f*

built-in *a* empotrado. **b. closet,** armario empotrado, *m*

bulb *n bot* bulbo, *m*; (elec phys) bombilla, *f*; (of an oil lamp) cebolla, *f*

bulbous *a* bulboso

Bulgarian *a* and *n* búlgaro (-ra)

bulge *n* bulto, *m*; hinchazón, *f*; protuberancia, *f*; *mil* bolsa (en el frente), *f. vi* hincharse; estar lleno (de)

bulging *a* lleno (de); con bultos; hinchado (de)

bulk *n* volumen, tamaño, *m*; (larger part) grueso, *m*; mayor parte, *f*; (of people) mayoría, *f*; (of a ship) capacidad, *f.* **in b.,** *com* en bruto, en grueso. **to b. large,** tener mucha importancia

bulkhead *n naut* mamparo, *m*

bulkiness *n* abultamiento, *m*; volumen, tamaño, *m*

bulky *a* voluminoso, grande, grueso

bull *n* toro, *m*; *ast* Tauro, *m*; (of some animals) macho,

m; (Stock Exchange) alcista, *mf*; (of the Pope) bula (del Papa), *f.* **a b. in a china shop,** un caballo loco en una cacharrería. **to fight bulls,** torear. **b.-calf,** ternero, *m.* **bull's eye,** blanco, *m*; acierto, *m.* **b. fight,** corrida de toros, *f.* **b. fighter's gala uniform,** traje de luces, *m.* **b.-ring,** plaza de toros, *f*

bulldog *n* perro dogo, perro de presa, *m*

bulldozer *n* (excavator) tozodora, *f*

bullet *n* bala, *f.* **spent b.,** bala fría, *f.* **stray b.,** bala perdida, *f.* **b.-proof,** a prueba de bala, blindado

bulletin *n* boletín, *m*

bulletin board *n* tablero de anuncios, tablero de avisos, tablón, *m*

bulletproof vest *n* chaleco blindado, *m*

bullfighter *n* torero, *m* (on foot), toreador, *m* (on horseback)

bullfinch *n* pinzón real, *m*

bullion *n com* metálico, *m*; oro (or plata) en barras, *m, f.*

bullock *n* becerro, *m*; buey, *m*

bullpen *n* toril, *m* (bullfighting); calentador, *m* (baseball)

bully *n* valentón, perdonavidas, gallito, *m*; rufián, *m. vt* intimidar; tratar mal. **b. beef,** vaca en lata, *f*

bulrush *n* anea, *f*

bulwark *n* baluarte, *m*; *naut* antepecho, *m*

bumblebee *n* abejorro, *m*

bump *n* golpe, *m*; ruido, *m*; choque, *m*; (bruise) chichón, *m*, roncha, *f*; *aer* sacudida, *f*, meneo, *m. vi* (into, against) tropezar con; (along) saltar en. *vt* chocar (contra)

bumper *n* copa llena hasta los bordes, *f*, vaso lleno, *m*; (of a car) parachoques, *m.* **a b. harvest,** una cosecha abundante

bumpkin *n* patán, villano, *m*

bumptious *a* fatuo, presuntuoso, presumido

bumptiousness *n* fatuidad, presunción, *f*

bumpy *a* (of surface) desigual, escabroso; (of a vehicle) incómodo, con mala suspensión

bun *n* buñuelo, bollo, *m*; (hair) moño, *m*

bunch *n* (of fruit) racimo, *m*; manojo, *m*; (of flowers) ramo, *m*; (tuft) penacho, *m*; (gang) pandilla, *f, vi* arracimarse; agruparse

bundle *n* atado, lío, *m*; (of papers) legajo, *m* (of sticks) haz, *m*; (sheaf) fajo, *m*; (package) paquete, *m*; fardo, hatillo, *m*; (roll) rollo, *m. vt* atar, liar; envolver; empaquetar; (stuff) meter, introducir. **to b. in,** meter dentro (de). **to b. out,** despachar sin ceremonia, poner de patitas en la calle

bung *n* tapón, tarugo, *m, vt* atarugar

bungalow *n* casa de un solo piso, *f*

bungle *vt* estropear; hacer mal. *n* equivocación, *f*, yerro, *m*; cosa (obra) mal hecha, *f*

bungling *a* chapucero, torpe

bunion *n* juanete (del pie), *m*

bunk *n* litera, *f*, *vi inf* poner pies en polvorosa, pirarse

bunker *n naut* pañol, *m*; (for coal) carbonera, *f*; (golf) hoya de arena, *f*

bunkum *n* patrañas, *f pl*

bunting *n* gallardete, *m*

buoy *n* boya, *f*, *vt* boyar; abalizar; *fig* sostener. **light b.,** boya luminosa, *f*

buoyancy *n* flotación, *f*; *fig* optimismo, *m*, alegría, *f*

buoyant *a* boyante; ligero

burden *n* carga, *f*, peso, *m*; (of a ship) tonelaje, *m*, capacidad, *f*; (of a song) estribillo, *m*; (gist) esencia, *f. vt* cargar. **to be a b. on,** pesar sobre

burdensome *a* pesado, oneroso, gravoso; abrumador

burdensomeness *n* pesadez, *f*; agobio, *m*

bureau *n* buró, secreter, *m*; escritorio, *m*; (office) dirección, oficina, *f*; departamento, *m*

bureaucracy *n* burocracia, *f*

bureaucrat *n* burócrata, *mf*; *inf* mandarín, *m*

bureaucratic *a* burocrático

burgher *n* ciudadano (-na), vecino (-na)

burglar *n* ladrón de casas, escalador, *m.* **cat b.,** gato, *m.*

b. alarm, alarma contra ladrones, *f.* **b. insurance,** seguro contra robo, *m*

burglary *n* robo nocturno de una casa, *m*

burgle *vi* robar una casa de noche. *vt* robar

burgomaster *n* burgomaestre, *m*

Burgundian *a* and *n* borgoñón (-ona)

burgundy *n* vino de Borgoña, borgoña, *m*

burial *n* entierro, *m*. **b.-ground,** campo santo, cementerio, *m*. **b. service,** misa de difuntos, *f.* **b. society,** sociedad de entierros, *f*

burlap *n* arpillera, *f*

burlesque *a* burlesco. *n* parodia. *f. vt* parodiar

burliness *n* corpulencia, *f*

burly *a* corpulento, fornido

Burma Birmania, *f*

Burmese *a* and *n* birmano (-na)

burn *vt* quemar; calcinar; (bricks) cocer; cauterizar; (the tongue) picar; (dry up) secar; (the skin by sun or wind) tostar. *vi* quemar; arder; *fig* abrasarse (en). **b. at the stake,** *vt* quemar en la hoguera. **to b. to ashes,** reducir a cenizas. **to b. away,** consumir(se). **to b. oneself,** quemarse. **to b. up,** quemar del todo, consumir. **to b. with,** *fig* abrasarse en

burn *n* quemadura, *f*; (stream) arroyo, *m*

burnable *a* combustible

burner *n* quemador (-ra); mechero, *m*

burning *n* quema, *f*; incendio, *m*; fuego, *m*; (inflammation) inflamación, *f*; (pain) quemazón, *f*; abrasamiento, *m. a* en llamas; ardiente; intenso; (notorious) notorio, escandaloso; abrasador; palpitante. **b. question,** cuestión palpitante, *f*

burnish *n* bruñido, *m*; lustre, brillo, *m*, *vt* bruñir; pulir, pulimentar, dar brillo a; (weapons) acicalar. *vi* tomar lustre

burnisher *n* bruñidor, acicalador, *m*

burnishing *n* bruñido, *m*; pulimento, *m*; (of weapons) acicalado, *m*

burnouse *n* albornoz, *m*

burr *n bot* cáliz de flor con espinas, *m*; *mech* rebaba, *f*; sonido fuerte de la erre, *m*

burrow *n* madriguera, *f*, vivar, *m*; (for rabbits) conejera, *f. vt* amadrigar; minar

bursar *n* tesorero, *m*; becario, *m*

bursary *n* tesorería, *f*; beca, *f*

burst *n* estallido, *m*, explosión, *f*; (in a pipe) avería, *f*, (fit) acceso, *m*; transporte, *m*; (effort) esfuerzo, *m*; (expanse) extensión, *f*, panorama, *m*. **b. of applause,** salva de aplausos, *f*

burst *vi* estallar; reventar; quebrarse; romperse; (overflow) desbordar; (of seams) nacerse; derramarse (por); (into laughter) romper a; (into tears) deshacerse en. *vt* quebrar; romper; hacer estallar. **to b. upon the view,** aparecer de pronto. **to b. into,** irrumpir en; (exclamations, etc.) prorrumpir en. **to b. into tears,** romper a llorar, deshacerse en lágrimas. **to b. open,** abrir con violencia; forzar

bursting *n* estallido, *m*; quebrantamiento, *m*; (overflowing) desbordamiento, *m*

bury *vt* enterrar, sepultar; sumergir; (hide) esconder, ocultar; (forget) echar tierra a

bus *n* autobús, ómnibus, *Mexico* camión, *Caribbean* guagua, *m*. **double-decker bus,** ómnibus de dos pisos, *m*. **to travel by bus,** ir en autobús. **bus station,** estación de autobuses, *f*

busby *n* birretina, gorra de húsar, *f*

bush *n* arbusto, matojo, *m*; (undergrowth) maleza, *f*; tierra virgen, *f*; *mech* manguito, *m*

bushel *n* medida de áridos, *f*, (In England 8 gallons or 36.37 liters)

bushiness *n* espesura, *f*; densidad, *f*

bushy *a* lleno de arbustos; denso; espeso; grueso; (eyebrows, etc.) poblado

busily *adv* diligentemente, solícitamente; afanosamente, laboriosamente. **He was b. occupied in . . . ,** Estaba muy ocupado en . . .

business *n* ocupación, *f*; quehaceres, *m pl*; (matter) asunto, *m*, cosa, *f*; empleo, oficio, *m*; *com* negocio(s), *m*, *pl*.; casa comercial, *f*; (trade) comercio, *m*; (clients, connection) clientela, *f*; (right) derecho, *m*; *theat* juego escénico, *m*, pantomima, *f*. **He had no b. to do that,** No tenía derecho a hacer eso. **Mind your own b.!** ¡No te metas donde no te llaman! **on b.,** por negocios. **to be in b. for oneself,** tener negocios por su propia cuenta. **to mean b.,** hacer algo en serio; estar resuelto. **to send about his b.,** mandar a paseo (a). **to set up in b.,** establecer un negocio. **b. affairs,** negocios, *m pl.* **b. agent,** agente de negocios, *m*. **b. hours,** horas de trabajo, *f pl.* **b.-like,** formal, práctico, sistemático. **b. man,** hombre de negocios, negociante, *m*

business administration *n* administración de empresas, *f*

bust *n art* busto, bulto, *m*; pecho, *m*. **b. bodice,** sostén, *m*

bustard *n* avutarda, *f*

bustle *n* actividad, animación, *f*; confusión, *f*; (of a dress) polizón, tontillo, *m*. *vi* menearse, darse prisa. *vt* dar prisa (a)

bustling *a* activo; ocupado, atareado; animado; bullicioso, ruidoso

busy *a* ocupado; atareado; activo, diligente; (of places) animado, bullicioso; (of streets) de gran circulación; (officious) entremetido. **to b. oneself,** ocuparse (en, con); dedicarse (a), entregarse (a); (interfere) entremeterse (con). **to be b.,** estar ocupado; estar atareado, tener mucho que hacer. **b.-body,** bullebulle, *mf,* entremetido (-da), chismoso (-sa)

busyness *n* ocupación, *f*; laboriosidad, *f*; actividad, *f*

but *conjunc prep adv* pero; sino; (only) solamente; (except) menos; excepto; (almost) casi; que no; si no; (that) que; (nevertheless) sin embargo, empero, no obstante; (without) sin, sin que; (of time recently passed) no más que, tan recientemente. *n* pero, *m*. **He cannot choose but go,** No puede hacer otra cosa que marcharse. **to do nothing but . . . ,** hacer únicamente . . . , no hacer más que . . . **but for,** a no ser por. **but yesterday,** solamente ayer. **but then (or but yet),** pero

butcher *n* carnicero, *m*. *vt* matar reses; hacer una carnicería en. **butcher's boy,** mozo del carnicero, *m*. **butcher's shop,** carnicería, *f*

butchery *n* carnicería, *f*; matanza, *f*

butler *n* mayordomo, *m*. **butler's pantry,** despensa, repostería, *f*

butt *n* (cask) tonel, *m*, pipa, *f*; (for water) barril, *m*; (of a cigarette, etc.) colilla, *f*; (of fire-arms) culata, *f*; (handle) mango, cabo, *m*; (billiards) mocho, *m*; (earthwork) terrero, *m*; (fig object) objeto (de), *m*; (of bulls, etc.) topetada, *f*; *pl* **butts,** campo de tiro, *m*; (target) blanco, *m. vt* (toss) topar, acornear; (meet) tropezar (con). **to b. in,** *inf* entrometerse, meter baza; encajarse

butter *n* mantequilla, *f*, *vt* untar con mantequilla. **b.-dish,** mantequera, *f.* **b.-fingers,** torpe, *m.* **b.-knife,** cuchillo para mantequilla, *m.* **b.-milk,** suero de mantequilla, *m.* **b.-print,** molde para mantequilla, *m.* **b.-sauce,** mantequilla fundida, *f*

buttercup *n* ranúnculo, botón de oro, *m*

butterfly *n* mariposa, *f*

butterscotch *n* dulce de azúcar y mantequilla, *m*

buttery *n* despensa, *f*

buttocks *n pl* nalgas, posaderas, *f pl*

button *n* botón, *m*; *pl* **buttons,** botones, paje, *m*. *vt* abotonar, abrochar. *vi* abotonarse, abrocharse. **to press the b.,** apretar el botón. **b.-hook,** abotonador, *m*

buttonhole *n* ojal, *m*; flor que se lleva en el ojal, *f*. *vt sew* hacer ojales; (embroidery) hacer el festón; *inf* importunar

buttoning *n* abrochamiento, *m*

buttress *n* estribo, macho, contrafuerte, *m*; *fig* apoyo, sostén, *m*. *vt* afianzar, estribar; *fig* apoyar, sostener. **flying-b.,** arbotante, *m*

buxom *a* (of a woman) fresca, guapetona, frescachona

buxomness *n* frescura, *f*
buy *vt* comprar; obtener; (achieve) lograr; (bribe) sobornar. **to buy on credit,** comprar al fiado. **to buy back,** comprar de nuevo; redimir; (ransom) rescatar. **to buy for,** (a price) comprar por; (purpose or destination) comprar para. **to buy in,** (at an auction) comprar por cuenta del dueño. **to buy off,** librarse de uno con dinero. **to buy out,** (of a business) comprar la parte de un socio. **to buy up,** comprar todo, acaparar
buyable *a* comprable, que se puede comprar
buyer *n* comprador (-ra)
buying *n* compra, *f*. **b. back,** rescate, *m*. **b. up,** acaparamiento, *m*
buying power *n* capacidad de compra, *f*, valor adquisitivo, *m*
buzz *n* zumbido, *m*; (whisper) susurro, murmullo, *m*; (of a bell) sonido (del timbre), *m*, *vi* zumbar; susurrar
buzzer *n* zumbador, *m*; sirena, *f*; (bell) timbre, *m*
buzzing *a* zumbador, que zumba, *n*. See **buzz**
by *prep* por; de; en; a; con; (of place) cerca de, al lado de; (according to) según, de acuerdo con; (in front of, past) delante (de); (at the latest) antes de, al más tardar; (expressing agency) por; (by means of) mediante; (through, along) por; (upon) sobre; (for) para; (under) bajo. **He will be here by Wednesday,** Estará aquí para el miércoles; (not later than) Estará aquí antes del miércoles (or el miércoles al más tardar). **How did he come by it?** ¿Cómo llegó a su poder? **He will come by train,** Vendrá en tren. **I know her by sight,** La conozco de vista. **There are three children by the first marriage,** Hay tres niños del primer matrimonio. **He goes by the name of Pérez,** Se le conoce por (or bajo) el nombre de Pérez. **six feet by eight,** seis pies por ocho. **They called her by her name,** La llamaron por su nombre. **two by two,** dos por dos. **The picture was painted by Cézanne,** El cuadro fue pintado por Cézanne. **drop by drop,** gota a gota. **by a great deal,** con mucho. **by all means,** naturalmente; de todos modos; cueste lo que cueste. **by chance,** por ventura. **by day (night),** de día (noche). **by daylight,** a la luz del día. **by doing it,** con hacerlo. **by myself,** solo; sin ayuda. **"By Appointment"** «Cita Previa». **by chance or by mischance,** por ventura o por desdicha. **an hour away by car,** a una hora de automóvil. **music by Brahms,** música de Brahms. **pull by the hair,** tirar por el pelo. **take by the hand,** llevar de la mano.
by *adv* (near) cerca; (before) delante; al lado; a un lado; aparte; (of time) pasado. **to put by,** (keep) guardar; (throw away) desechar; (accumulate) acumular; (put out of the way) arrinconar. **to pass by,** pasar; pasar delante (de). **by and by,** luego, pronto; más tarde. **by now,** ya, antes de ahora. **by the way,** entre paréntesis, a propósito; de paso; al lado del camino. **by-election,** elección parcial, *f*. **by-law,** reglamento, *m*. **by-pass,** ruta de evitación, *f*, desvío, *m*; (*mech elec*) derivación, *f*. *vi* desviarse de; *mil* rebasar. **by-product,** derivado, *m*; *chem* producto derivado, *m*; *fig* consecuencia, *f*; resultado, *m*
bye *n* (in cricket) meta, *f*. **by the bye,** a propósito, entre paréntesis
bygone *a* pasado. **Let bygones be bygones,** Lo pasado pasado
byplay *n* pantomima, *f*, gestos, *m pl*; *theat* juego escénico, *m*, escena muda, *f*
bystander *n* espectador (-ra); *pl* **bystanders,** los circunstantes
bystreet *n* callejuela, *f*; calle pobre, *f*
byway *n* camino desviado, *m*; *fig* senda indirecta, *f*; *pl* **byways,** andurriales, *m pl*
byword *n* proverbio, *m*; objeto de burla o escándalo, *m*
Byzantine *a* bizantino
Byzantine Empire, the el Imperio Bizantino, *m*
Byzantium Bizancio, *m*

C

c *n* (letter) c, *f*; *mus* do, *m*
cab *n* (horse-drawn) simón, *m*; (taxi) coche de alquiler, *m*; (of a locomotive) cabina del conductor, *f*. **cab-rank,** punto de coches, *m*
cabala *n* cábala, *f*
cabaret *n* cabaret, *m*; taberna, *f*
cabbage *n* col, berza, *f*. **red c.,** lombarda, *f*. **c. butterfly,** mariposa de col, *f*
cabin *n* cabaña, choza, *f*; *naut* camarote, *m*; (railway) garita, *f*; *aer* cabina, *f*. **c. boy,** grumete, galopín, mozo de cámara, *m*. **c. trunk,** baúl mundo, *m*
cabinet *n* (piece of furniture) vitrina, *f*; colección, exposición, *f*; *pol* gabinete, *m*; (of a radio) cónsola, *f*. **c.-maker,** ebanista, *m*. **c.-making,** ebanistería, *f*. **c. meeting,** consejo de ministros, *m*. **c. minister,** ministro, *m*
cable *n* amarra, maroma, *f*; cable, *m*; cable(grama), *m*, *vt* cablegrafiar. **electric c.,** cable eléctrico, *m*. **overhead c.,** cable aéreo, *m*
cabman *n* cochero de punto, simón, *m*
caboose *n* *naut* cocina, *f*
cache *n* escondite, escondrijo, *m*
cackle *vi* (of a hen) cacarear; (of a goose) graznar; (of humans) chacharear. *n* cacareo, *m*; graznido, *m*; cháchara, *f*
cacophony *n* cacofonía, *f*
cactus *n* cacto, *m*
cad *n* sinvergüenza, *m*; tipo de cuidado, *m*
cadaverous *a* cadavérico
caddish *a* mal educado, grosero
caddy *n* (for tea) cajita para té, *f*; (golf) cadi, *mf*
cadence *n* cadencia, *f*
cadet *n* hermano menor, *m*; *mil* cadete, *m*
cadge *vi* sablear. *vt* dar un sablazo (a)
cadger *n* sablista, *mf*; mendigo, *m*; (loafer) golfo, *m*
Cadiz Cádiz, *m*
cadmium *n* cadmio, *m*
café *n* café, *m*
cafeteria *n* bar automático, *m*
caffeine *n* cafeína, *f*
cage *n* (animal's, bird's) jaula, *f*; (of a lift) camarín, *m*; (for transporting miners) jaula, *f*. *vt* enjaular; encerrar
Cain, to raise armar la de Dios es Cristo
cairn *n* montón de piedras, *m*
Cairo el Cairo, *m*
cajole *vt* lisonjear; engatusar, embromar; instar
cajolery *n* zalamerías, *f pl*; marrullería, *f*, engatusamiento, *m*
cake *n* cul pastel, *m*, torta, *f*; (of chocolate, etc.) pastilla, *f*. *vt* and *vi* cuajar; formar costra; (with mud) enlodar. **to sell like hot cakes,** venderse como pan bendito. **to take the c.,** llevarse la palma. **c. of soap,** pastilla de jabón, *f*. **c.-shop,** pastelería, *f*
calamine *n* calamina, *f*
calamitous *a* calamitoso, desastroso
calamity *n* calamidad, *f*; desastre, *m*
calash *n* (carriage) calesa, carretela, *f*; (hood) capota, *f*
calcium *n* calcio, *m*
calculate *vt* calcular; adaptar. **to c. on,** contar con
calculated *a* premeditado. **to be c. to,** conducir a; ser a propósito para
calculatedly *adv* calculadamente
calculating *n* cálculo, *m*, *a* calculador; (of persons) interesado; (shrewd) perspicaz; atento. **c. machine,** máquina de calcular, *f*, calculador, *m*
calculation *n* cálculo, *m*; calculación, *f*
calculus *n* cálculo, *m*
Calcutta Calcutta, *f*

calendar *n* calendario, *m*; almanaque, *m*; (university, etc.) programa, *m*

calender *n* calandria, *f*, *vt* calandrar, cilindrar

calf *n* becerro (-rra), ternero (-ra); (young of other animals) hijuelo, *m*; (of the leg) pantorrilla, *f*; (leather) cuero de becerro, *m*; piel, *f*. **calf's-foot,** pie de ternera, *m*. **c. love,** amor de muchachos, *m*

calibrate *vt* calibrar

calibre *n* calibre, *m*

calico *n* indiana, *f*; percal, *m*. **c.-printer,** fabricante de estampados, *m*

Californian *a* californio. *n* californio (-ia)

caliph *n* califa, *m*

calk. See **caulk**

call *n* llamada, *f*; (shout) grito, *m*; (of a bird) canto, *m*; (signal) señal, *f*; (visit) visita, *f*; (by a ship) escala, *f*; mil toque, *m*; (need) necesidad, *f*; (of religion, etc.) vocación, *f*; invitación, *f*; (demand) demanda, *f*; exigencia, *f*. **They came at my c.,** Acudieron a mi llamada. **c. to arms,** llamada, llamada a filas, *f*. **port of c.,** puerto de escala, *m*. **telephone c.,** llamada telefónica, *f*. **to pay a c.,** hacer una visita. **within c.,** al alcance de la voz. **c.-box,** cabina del teléfono, *f*. **c.-boy,** ayudante del traspunte, *m*

call *vi* llamar; gritar, dar voces; (visit) visitar, hacer una visita (a); venir; (stop) parar; (of a ship) hacer escala. *vt* llamar; (a meeting, etc.) convocar; (awaken) despertar, llamar; (say) decir; (appoint) nombrar; (at cards) declarar. **She is called Dorothy,** Se llama Dorotea. **Madrid calling!** ¡Aquí Radio Madrid! **Will you c. me at eight o'clock, please?** Haga el favor de despertarme (llamarme) a las ocho. **to c. at a port,** hacer escala en un puerto. **to c. a halt,** hacer alto. **to c. a strike,** declarar una huelga. **to c. names,** vituperar, injuriar. **to c. to account,** pedir cuentas (a). **to c. to arms,** llamar al arma; alarmar. **to c. to mind,** acordarse (de), recordar. **to c. to witness,** hacer testigo (de). **to c. back,** *vt* llamar; hacer volver; (unsay) desdecir. *vi* (return) volver; venir a buscar; ir a buscar. **I called back for the parcel,** Volví a buscar el paquete. **to c. for,** pedir a gritos; llamar; (demand) pedir; exigir; (collect a person) pasar a buscar; (parcels, etc.) ir (or venir) a recoger. **He called for help,** Pidió socorro a gritos. **to c. forth,** producir; provocar; inspirar; revelar; (bring together) reunir. **to c. in,** hacer entrar; invitar; (a specialist, etc.) llamar; (worn coin) retirar de la circulación; recoger. **to c. in question,** poner en duda. **to c. off,** (dogs, etc.) llamar; (a strike) cancelar; parar; terminar; (a person) disuadir (de); (postpone) aplazar; suspender; (refrain) desistir (de). **to c. on,** (visit) hacer una visita (a), ir a ver, visitar; (of a doctor) visitar; (a person to do something) recurrir (a); (for a speech) invitar (a hablar); (invoke) invocar. **I shall now c. on Mr. Martínez,** Doy la palabra al señor Martínez. **to c. out,** *vt* hacer salir; provocar; inspirar; (challenge) desafiar, retar. *vi* gritar. **c. the roll,** pasar lista. **to c. over,** (names) pasar lista (de). **to c. up,** hacer subir; (to the army) llamar a filas (a); (telephone) llamar por teléfono (a); (memories) evocar. **to c. upon.** See **to c. on**

caller *n* visita, *f*

calligraphist *n* calígrafo, *m*

calligraphy *n* caligrafía, *f*

calling *n* llamamiento, *m*; (occupation) profesión, *f*; empleo, *m*; vocación, *f*; (of a meeting) convocación, *f*

callipers *n pl* compás de puntas, pie de rey, *m*

callisthenics *n pl* calistenia, *f*

callosity *n* callosidad, *f*

callous *a* (of skin) calloso; *fig* insensible, duro, inhumano

callously *adv* sin piedad

callousness *n* falta de piedad, inhumanidad, dureza, *f*

callow *a* (of birds) implume; (inexperienced) bisoño, inexperto, novato

callus *n* callo, *m*

calm *n* calma, *f*; paz, tranquilidad, *f*; sosiego, *m*; sereni-

dad, *f*. *a* (of the sea) en calma; tranquilo; sereno; sosegado. *vt* calmar; tranquilizar; apaciguar. *vi* calmarse; tranquilizarse; sosegarse. **dead c.,** calma chicha, *f*

calming *a* calmante

calmly *adv* tranquilamente, sosegadamente; con calma

calmness *n* calma, tranquilidad, *f*; ecuanimidad, serenidad, *f*

caloric *a* calórico

calorie *n* caloría, *f*

calumniation *n* calumnia, *f*

calumniator *n* calumniador (-ra)

calumny *n* calumnia, *f*

calvary *n* calvario, *m*

calve *vi* (of a cow, etc.) parir

Calvinism *n* calvinismo, *m*

Calvinist *n* calvinista, *mf*

Calvinistic *a* calvinista

calyx *n* cáliz, *m*

cam *n mech* leva, *f*. **camshaft,** árbol de levas, *m*

camaraderie *n* compañerismo, *m*

camber *n* comba(dura), *f*

cambric *n* batista, *f*

camel *n* camello (-lla). **c.-driver,** camellero, *m*. **camel's hair,** pelo de camello, *m*

camellia *n* camelia, *f*

cameo *n* camafeo, *m*

camera *n phot* máquina fotográfica, *f*. **folding c.,** máquina fotográfica plegable, *f*. **in c.,** a puerta cerrada. **c. obscura,** cámara obscura, *f*

Cameroons, the el Camerón, los Camerones, *m*

camouflage *n* camuflaje, *m*, *vt* camuflar

camp *n* campamento, *m*; campo, *m*; *fig* vida de cuartel, *f*; (for school children, etc.) colonia, *f*; (party) partido, *m*. *vi* acampar; vivir en tiendas de campaña. **to break c.,** levantar el campo. **c.-bed,** cama de campaña, *f*. **c.-stool,** silla de campaña, *f*

campaign *n* campaña, *f*. *vi* hacer una campaña

campaigner *n* veterano, *m*; propagandista, *mf*

campaigning *n* campañas, *f pl*

camphor *n* alcanfor, *m*

camphorated *a* alcanforado

campus *n* recinto, *m* (Puerto Rico), ciudad universitaria, *f*

can *v auxil* poder; (know how to) saber. **You can go to the village when you like,** Puedes ir al pueblo cuando quieras. **I cannot allow that,** No puedo permitir eso. **What can they mean?** ¿Qué quieren decir? **If only things could have been different!** ¡Si solamente las cosas hubiesen sido distintas! **Can you come to dinner on Saturday?** ¿Puede Vd. venir a cenar el sábado? **I can come later if you like,** Puedo (or Podría) venir más tarde si Vd. quiere. **Mary can** (knows how to) **play the piano,** María sabe tocar el piano **You can't eat your cake and have it too.** No hay rosa sin espinas

can *n* lata, *f*; (for carrying sandwiches, etc.) fiambrera, *f*. *vt* conservar en latas. **canopener,** abrelatas, *f*

Canada el Canadá, *m*

Canadian *a* canadiense. *n* canadiense, *mf*

canaille *n* gentualla, gentuza, *f*

canal *n* canal, *m*

canalization *n* canalización, *f*

canalize *vt* canalizar

canary *n* canario (-ia); color de canario, *m*; vino de Canarias, *m*. **roller c.,** canario de raza flauta, *m*. **c.-seed,** alpiste, *m*

Canary Islands, the las Islas Canarias, *m*

cancel *vt* cancelar; revocar; borrar; anular. **to c. out,** *math* anular

cancellation *n* cancelación, *f*; revocación, *f*; anulación, *f*

cancer *n med* cáncer, *m*; *ast* Cáncer, *m*

cancerous *a* canceroso. **to become c.,** cancerarse

candelabrum *n* candelabro, *m*

candescent *a* candente

candid *a* franco; sincero. **If I am to be c.,** Si he de decir la verdad, Si he de ser franco
candidate *n* candidato (-ta); aspirante, *m*
candidature *n* candidatura, *f*
candidly *adv* francamente; sinceramente
candidness *n* franqueza, *f*; sinceridad, *f*
candied *a* (of peel, etc.) almibarado, garapiñado
candle *n* vela, candela, *f*. **wax c.,** cirio, *m*. **You cannot hold a c. to him,** No llegas a la suela de su zapato, Ni llegas a sus pies, Ni le llegas a los pies. **The game is not worth the c.,** La cosa no vale la pena. **to burn the c. at both ends,** consumir la vida. **c.-grease,** sebo, *m*. **c.-light,** luz de las velas, *f*; luz artificial, *f*. **c.-maker,** candelero, *m*. **c.-power,** *elec* potencia luminosa, bujía, *f*. **c.-snuffer,** apagavelas, matacandelas, *m*
Candlemas *n* candelaria, *f*
candlestick *n* candelero, *m*, palmatoria, *f*; (processional) cirial, *m*
candor *n* franqueza, *f*; sinceridad, *f*; candor, *m*
candy *n* caramelo, bombón, *m*, *vt* garapiñar, almibarar
candytuft *n* carraspique, *m*
cane *n bot* caña, *f*; (for chair seats, etc.) rejilla, *f*; (walking stick) bastón, *m*; (for punishment) vara, *f*. *vt* apalear, pegar. **sugar-c.,** caña de azúcar, *f*. **c.-break,** cañaveral, *m*. **c. chair,** sillón de mimbres, *m*. **c.-sugar,** azúcar de caña, *m*. **c.-syrup,** miel de caña, *f*
canine *a* canino. *n* (tooth) diente canino, *m*
caning *n* paliza, *f*
canister *n* bote, *m*, cajita, *f*
canker *n* úlcera, *f*; (in trees) cancro, *m*; *fig* cáncer, *m*, *vt* roer; *fig* corromper
canned *a* en lata
cannibal *n* caníbal, *mf* antropófago (-ga). *a* caníbal, antropófago
cannibalism *n* canibalismo, *m*, antropofagía, *f*
canning *n* conservación en latas, *f*. **c. factory,** fábrica de conservas alimenticias, *f*
cannon *n* (fire-arm) cañón, *m*; (billiards) carambola, *f*, *vi* carambolear. **to c. into,** chocar con. **c.-ball,** bala de cañón, *f*. **c.-shot,** cañonazo, *m*
cannonade *n* cañoneo, *m*
canny *a* cuerdo, sagaz
canoe *n* canoa, *f*; piragua, *f*, *vi* ir en canoa
canoeist *n* canoero (-ra)
canon *n* (*ecc mus print*) canón, *m*; (dignitary) canónigo, *m*; (criterion) criterio, *m*. **c. law,** derecho canónico, *m*
canonical *a* canónico
canonization *n* canonización, *f*
canonize *vt* canonizar
canopy *n* dosel, toldo, *m*; palio, *m*; *fig* capa, bóveda, *f*. **the c. of heaven,** la capa (or bóveda) del cielo
cant *vt* inclinar; ladear. *vi* inclinarse; (be a hypocrite) camandulear. *n* (slope) inclinación, *f*, sesgo, desplomo, *m*; (hypocrisy) gazmoñería, *f*
Cantabrian *a* cántabrico
cantankerous *a* irritable, intratable, malhumorado
cantankerousness *n* mal humor, *m*, irritabilidad, *f*
cantata *n* cantata, *f*
canteen *n* cantina, *f*; (water bottle) cantimplora, *f*. **c. of cutlery,** juego de cubiertos, *m*
canter *n* medio galope, *m*, *vi* andar a galope corto
Canterbury Cantórbery, Cantuaria, *f*
canticle *n* cántico, *m*
canting *a* hipócrita
canto *n* canto, *m*
canton *n* (province and *her*) cantón, *m*, *vt* (of soldiers) acantonar
cantonment *n* acantonamiento, cantón, *m*
cantor *n ecc* chantre, *m*
canvas *n* lona, *f*; *art* lienzo, *m*; *naut* vela, *f*, paño, *m*. **under c.,** en tiendas de campaña; (of ships) a toda vela
canvass *vt* (votes, etc.) solicitar
canvasser *n* solicitador (-ra) (de votos, etc.)
canvassing *n* solicitación (de votos, etc.), *f*
canyon *n* cañón, *m*
canzonet *n* chanzoneta, *f*

cap *n* gorra, *f*; (with a peak) montera, *f*; (type of military headgear with brim at front) quépis, *m*; (cardinal's) birrete, *m*; *univ* bonete, *m*; (pointed) caperuza, *f*; (woman's old-fashioned) cofia, *f*; (jester's) gorro de bufón, *m*; (on a bottle) cápsula, tapa, *f*. *vt univ* conferir el grado (a). **cap and bells,** gorro de bufón, *m*. **cap and gown,** birrete y muceta, toga y birrete, toga y bonete. **to throw one's cap over the windmill,** echar la capa al toro. **to cap it all,** ser el colmo
capability *n* capacidad, *f*; aptitud, *f*
capable *a* capaz; competente; (of improvement) susceptible; (full of initiative) emprendedor
capably *adv* competentemente
capacious *a* espacioso; grande; extenso
capaciousness *n* capacidad, *f*; amplitud, *f*
capacitate *vt* capacitar
capacity *n* capacidad, *f*; calidad, *f*; aptitud, *f*. **in one's c. as,** en calidad de. **seating c.,** número de asientos, *m*; (in aircraft) número de plazas, *m*
caparison *n* caparazón, *m*
cape *n* (cloak) capa, *f*; (short) capotillo, *m*, capeta, *f*; (fur) cuello, *m*; *geog* cabo, promontorio, *m*. **c. coat,** capote, *m*
Cape Horn Cabo de Hornos, *m*
caper *vi* (gambol) brincar, saltar; cabriolar, corcovear; (play) juguetear. *n* travesura, *f*; zapateta, *f*; cabriola, *f*; (whim) capricho, *m*; *bot* alcaparra, *f*. **to c. about,** dar saltos, brincar; juguetear
capillarity *n* capilaridad, *f*
capillary *a* capilar. *n* vaso capilar, *m*
capital *a* capital; mortal; de muerte; de vida; principal; (of letters) mayúscula; (very good) excelente. *n* (city) capital, *f*; (letter) (letra) mayúscula, *f*; *com* capital, *m*; *arch* capitel, chapitel, *m*. **floating c.,** capital fluctuante, *m*. **idle c.,** fondos inactivos, *m pl*. **c. punishment,** pena de muerte, pena capital, pena de la vida, *f*. **C.!** ¡Estupendo! ¡Excelente! **to make c. out of,** aprovecharse de, sacar ventaja de
capitalism *n* capitalismo, *m*
capitalist *n* capitalista, *mf*
capitalistic *a* capitalista
capitalization *n* capitalización, *f*
capitalize *vt* capitalizar
capitally *adv* estupendamente
capitation *n* capitación, *f*
Capitol *n* Capitolio, *m*
capitulate *vi* capitular
capitulation *n* capitulación, *f*
capon *n* capón, *m*
caprice *n* capricho, *m*
capricious *a* caprichoso
capriciousness *n* carácter inconstante, *m*; lo caprichoso
Capricorn *n* Capricornio, *m*
capsize *vt naut* hacer zozobrar; volcar. *vi naut* zozobrar; volcarse
capsizing *n naut* zozobra, *f*; vuelco, *m*
capsule *n* (*bot med chem zool*) cápsula, *f*
captain *n* (*mil nav aer* and *sport*) capitán, *m*, *vt* capitanear. **to c. a team,** ser el capitán de un equipo. **group c.,** *aer* capitán de aviación, *m*
captaincy *n* capitanía, *f*
caption *n* (arrest) arresto, *m*; (heading) encabezamiento, título, pie, *m*; (cinema) subtítulo, *m*
captious *a* capcioso, caviloso
captivate *vt* cautivar, seducir
captivating *a* encantador, seductor
captive *a* cautivo, *n* cautivo (-va), prisionero (-ra), preso (-sa). **c. balloon,** globo cautivo, globo de observación, *m*
captivity *n* cautiverio, *m*
captor *n* el, *m*, (*f*, la) que hace prisionero (-ra)
capture *n* captura, *f*; presa, toma, *f*; *law* captura, *f*. *vt* prender, capturar; tomar
Capuchin *a* capuchino. *n* capuchino, *m*. **C. nun,** capuchina, *f*
car *n* (chariot) carro, *m*; (tram) tranvía, *m*; (motor) au-

tomóvil, coche, *m*; (on a train) coche vagón, *m*. **sleeping car,** coche camas, *m*. **car park,** parque de automóviles, *m*

carabineer *n* carabinero, *m*

carafe *n* garrafa, *f*

caramel *n* caramelo, *m*; azúcar quemado, *m*

carapace *n* carapacho, *m*

carat *n* quilate, *m*

caravan *n* caravana, *f*; coche de gitanos, *m*; coche habitación, *m*

caraway *n* alcaravea, *f*

carbarn *n* encierro, *m* (Mexico), cochera, cochera de tranvías, *f*, cobertizo, cobertizo para tranvías, *m*

carbide *n* carburo, *m*

carbine *n* carabina, *f*

carbohydrate *n* hidrato de carbono, *m*

carbolic *a* carbólico. **c. acid,** ácido fénico, *m*

carbon *n* carbono, *m*. **c. copy,** copia en papel carbón, *f*. **c. dioxide,** anhídrido carbónico, *m*. **c. monoxide,** óxide de carbono, *m*. **c. paper,** papel carbón, papel de calcar, *m*

carbonate *n* carbonato, *m*

carbonated *a* (beverage) carbónico (formal), con gas (informal)

carbonic *a* carbónico

carbonization *n* carbonización, *f*

carbonize *vt* carbonizar

carboy *n* damajuana, garrafa, *f*

carbuncle *n med* carbunco, *m*; (stone) carbúnculo, *m*

carburetor *n* carburador, *m*

carcass *n* (animal) res muerta, *f*; (corpse) cadáver, *m*; (body) cuerpo, *m*; (of a ship) casco, *m*

carcinoma *n* carcinoma, *m*

card *n* (playing) naipe, *m*; (pasteboard) cartulina, *f*; (visiting, postal, etc.) tarjeta, *f*; (index) ficha, *f*; (for wool, etc.) carda, *f*. *vt* (wool, etc.) cardar. **I still have a c. up my sleeve,** Me queda todavía un recurso. **to lay one's cards on the table,** poner las cartas boca arriba. **to play one's cards well,** *fig* jugar el lance. **admission c.,** billete de entrada, *m*. **post c.,** tarjeta postal, *f*. **visiting c.,** tarjeta de visita, *f*. **c.-case,** tarjetero, *m*. **c.-index,** fichero, *m*. *vt* poner en el fichero. **c.-sharper,** fullero, *m*. **c.-table,** mesa de juego, *f*. **c. trick,** juego de manos con cartas, *m*

cardboard *n* cartón, *m*, a de cartón

cardiac *a* cardíaco

cardigan *n* rebeca, chaqueta de punto, *f*

cardinal *a* cardinal. *n* cardenal, *m*. **c. number,** número cardinal, *m*. **c. points,** puntos cardinales, *m pl*

cardinalate *n* cardenalato, *m*

carding *n* (of wool, etc.) cardadura, *f*. **c. machine,** carda mecánica, *f*

cardiogram *n* cardiograma, *m*

cardiograph *n* cardiógrafo, *m*

care *n* cuidado, *m*; atención, *f*; inquietud, ansia, *f*; (charge) cargo, *m*. *vi* preocuparse; tener interés; (suffer) sufrir. **I don't c.,** Me es igual; No me importa. **I don't c. a straw,** No se me da un bledo. **They don't c. for eggs,** No les gustan los huevos. **We don't c. what his opinion is,** Su opinión nos tiene sin cuidado (or no nos importa). **to c. for,** cuidar, mirar por; (love) querer (a); (like) gustar. **Take c.!** ¡Cuidado! ¡Ojo! **Take c. not to spoil it!** ¡Ten cuidado que no lo estropees! **Would you c. to . . . ?** ¿Le gustaría . . . ? ¿Tendría inconveniente en . . . ? **c. of,** (on a letter, etc.) en casa de. **c.-free,** *a* libre de cuidados

careen *vt* carenar. *vi* dar a la banda

careening *n* carena, *f*

career *n* carrera, *f*; curso, *m*. *vi* correr a carrera tendida; galopar

careful *a* cuidadoso (de); atento (a); prudente. **Be c.!** ¡Cuidado! **to be c.,** tener cuidado

carefully *adv* con cuidado. **drive c.,** manejar con cuidado; cuidadosamente; prudentemente; atentamente

carefulness *n* cuidado, *m*; atención, *f*; prudencia, *f*

careless *a* sin cuidado; indiferente (a); insensible (a); negligente; (of mistakes, etc.) de (or por) negligencia

carelessly *adv* indiferentemente; negligentemente; descuidadamente

carelessness *n* indiferencia, *f*; negligencia, *f*; descuido, *m*; omisión, *f*

caress *n* caricia, *f*, *vt* acariciar

caressing *a* acariciador

caretaker *n* (of museums, etc.) guardián (-ana); (of flats, etc.) portero (-ra)

careworn *a* devorado de inquietud, ansioso

cargo *n* cargamento, *m*, carga, *f*. **c.-boat,** barco de carga, *m*

Caribbean *a* caribe

Caribbean Sea, the el Mar Caribe, *m*

caricature *n* caricatura, *f*, *vt* caricaturizar

caricaturist *n* caricaturista, *mf*

caries *n* caries, *f*

carious *a* cariado. **to become c.,** cariarse

Carmelite *a* carmelita. *n* carmelita, *mf*

carmine *n* carmín, *m*, a de carmín

carnage *n* carnicería, *f*

carnal *a* carnal; sensual

carnality *n* carnalidad, *f*

carnally *adv* carnalmente

carnation *n* clavel, *m*

carnival *n* carnaval, *m*, a de carnaval, carnavalesco

carnivore *n* carnívoro, *m*

carnivorous *a* carnívoro

carol *n* villancico, *m*; canto, *m*. *vi* cantar alegremente; (of birds) trinar, gorjear

Carolingian *a* carolingio

carotid *n* carótida, *f*

carousal *n* borrachera, *f*; holgorio, *m*, jarana, *f*

carouse *vi* emborracharse. *n* borrachera, orgía, *f*

carp *n* carpa, *f*, *vi* criticar, censurar

Carpathian Mountains, the los Montes Carpotes, *m*

carpel *n* carpelo, *m*

carpenter *n* carpintero, *m*, *vi* carpintear. **carpenter's bench,** banco de carpintero, *m*. **carpenter's shop,** carpintería, *f*

carpentry *n* carpintería, *f*

carpet *n* alfombra, *f*; *fig* tapete, *m*. *vt* cubrir de una alfombra, alfombrar; entapizar. **to be on the c.,** estar sobre el tapete. **c.-beater,** sacudidor de alfombras, *m*. **c. merchant,** alfombrista, *m*. **c. slippers,** zapatillas de fieltro, *f pl*. **c.-sweeper,** aspirador de polvo, *m*

carpeting *n* alfombrado, *m*

carping *a* capcioso, criticón

carriage *n* (carrying) transporte, porte, *m*; (deportment) porte, continente, *m*, presencia, *f*; (vehicle) carruaje, *m*; carroza, *f*; coche, *m*; (railway) departamento, *m*; (chassis) chasis, bastidor, *m*; (of a typewriter, etc.) carro, *m*. **hackney c.,** coche de plaza, *m*. **c. and pair,** carroza de dos caballos, *f*. **c. door,** portezuela, *f*. **c.-forward,** porte debido. **c.-free,** franco de porte. **c.-paid,** porte pagado

carrier *n* el, *m*, (*f*, la) que lleva; portador (-ra); *com* mensajero, *m*; (on a car, bicycle) portaequipajes, *m*; (of a disease) vector, *m*; (aircraft) porta-aviones, *m*. **c.-pigeon,** paloma mensajera, *f*

carrion *n* carroña, *f*. **c.-crow,** chova, *f*

carrot *n* zanahoria, *f*

carry *vt* llevar; transportar; traer; conducir; (*mil* of arms) portar; (have with one) tener consigo; (an enemy position) tomar, ganar; (a motion) aprobar; (oneself) portarse; (one's point, etc.) ganar; (in the mind) retener; (conviction) convencer; (involve) implicar; (influence) influir; (send) despachar, enviar; (contain) incluir, comprender. *vi* (of the voice, etc.) alcanzar, llegar. **The noise of the guns carried a long way,** El ruido de los cañones se oía desde muy lejos. **to fetch and c.,** traer y llevar. **to c. all before one,** vencer todos los obstáculos. **to c. into effect,** poner en efecto. **to c. one's audience with one,** captar (or cautivar) su auditorio. **to c. oneself well,** tener buena presencia. **to c. on**

one's back, llevar a cuestas. **to c. the day,** quedar victorioso, quedar señor del campo. **to c. weight,** *fig* ser de peso. **to c. along,** llevar; (drag) arrastrar; conducir; acarrear. **to c. away,** llevar; llevarse, llevar consigo; (kidnap) robar, secuestrar; (of emotions) dominar; (by enthusiasm) entusiasmar; (inspire) inspirar. **to c. forward,** llevar a cabo; avanzar; fomentar; (bookkeeping) pasar a cuenta nueva. **to c. off,** (things) llevarse; (persons) llevar consigo (a); (abduct or steal) robar; (kill) matar; (a prize) ganar. **to c. (a thing) off well,** llevar la mejor parte, salir vencedor. **to c. on,** *vt* (a discussion, etc.) seguir, continuar. **c. on a conversation,** llevar una conversación; mantener; (a business, etc.) tener; dirigir. *vi* ir tirando; seguir trabajando. **to c. out,** realizar, llevar a cabo; hacer, ejecutar, efectuar; (a promise) cumplir. **to c. through,** llevar a cabo
carrying *n* transporte, *m*; (of a motion) adopción, *f*
cart *n* carro, *m*. *vt* acarrear; llevar. **c.-horse,** caballo de tiro, *m*. **c.-load,** carretada, *f*, carro, *m*. **c.-wheel,** rueda de carro, *f*; (somersault) voltereta, *f*
cartage *n* carretaje, transporte, porte, *m*
carte blanche *n* carta blanca, *f*
cartel *n* cartel, *m*
carter *n* carretero, *m*
Cartesian *a* cartesiano. *n* cartesiano (-na)
Carthage Cartago, *m*
Carthaginian *a* cartaginés. *n* cartaginés (-esa)
Carthusian *a* cartujano. **C. monk,** cartujo, *m*
cartilage *n* cartílago, *m*
cartilaginous *a* cartilaginoso
cartographer *n* cartógrafo, *m*
cartography *n* cartografía, *f*
cartomancy *n* cartomancia, *f*
carton *n* caja de cartón, *f*
cartoon *n* (design for tapestry, etc.) cartón, *m*; caricatura, *f*
cartoonist *n* caricaturista, *mf*
cartridge *n* cartucho, *m*. **blank c.,** cartucho sin bala, *m*. **c.-belt,** cartuchera, canana, *f*. **c.-case,** cápsula de proyectil, *f*
carve *vt* tallar, labrar; grabar; cortar; (meat, etc.) trinchar; (a career, etc.) hacer, forjarse
carver *n* tallador, *m*; (at table) trinchador, *m*; (implement) trinchante, *m*
carving *n* talla, *f*; (design) tallado, *m*. **c.-knife,** trinchante, *m*
cascade *n* cascada, catarata, *f*, salto de agua, *m*; *fig* chorro, *m*. *vi* chorrear
case *n* caso, *m*; *law* proceso, *m*, causa, *f*; *gram* caso, *m*; *med* caso, *m*; enfermo (-ma); (box) caja, *f*; (for scissors, etc.) vaina, *f*; (for a cushion, etc.) funda, *f*; (for jewels, manicure implements, etc.) estuche, *m*; (of a piano, watch and *print*) caja, *f*; (for documents) carpeta, *f*; (glass) vitrina, *f*; (for a book) sobrecubierta, *f*; (dressing) neceser, *m*. *vt* cubrir; forrar; resguardar. **packing-c.,** caja de embalaje, *f*. **c. of goods,** caja de mercancías, *f*; bulto, *m*. **in any c.,** en todo caso; venga lo que venga. **in c.,** por si acaso. **in c. of emergency,** en caso de urgencia. **in such a c.,** en tal caso. **in the c. of,** en caso de; respecto a. **lower c.,** *print* caja baja, *f*. **upper c.,** *print* caja alta, *f*. **c.-hardened,** (of iron) templado; *fig* endurecido, indiferente
case closed! ¡asunto concluido!
casement window *n* ventana, *f*
cash *n* efectivo, metálico, *m*; dinero contante, *m*; *inf* dinero, *m*; *com* caja, *f*. *vt* cobrar; pagar, hacer efectivo. **hard or ready c.,** dinero contante, *m*. **to pay c.,** pagar al contado. **c. on delivery,** (C.O.D.) contra reembolso. **c. on hand,** efectivo en caja, *m*. **c.-book,** libro de caja, *m*. **c.-box,** caja, *f*. **c.-desk,** caja, *f*. **c. down,** pago al contado, *m*. **c. prize,** premio en metálico, *m*. **c.-register,** caja registradora, *f*
cashew *n* anacardo, *m*
cashier *n* cajero (-ra). *vt* degradar. **cashier's desk,** caja, *f*
cash machine *n* cajero automático, *m*

cashmere *n* cachemira, *f*
casino *n* casino, *m*
cask *n* pipa, barrica, *f*, tonel, *m*; cuba, *f*
casket *n* cajita, arquilla, *f*, cofrecito, *m*
Caspian *a* caspio
Caspian Sea, the el (Mar) Caspio, *m*
casserole *n* cacerola, *f*
cassock *n* sotana, *f*
cast *vt* arrojar, tirar; (in fishing, the anchor, dice, darts, lots, a net, glances, blame, etc.) echar; (skin) mudar; (lose) perder; (a shadow, etc.) proyectar; (a vote) dar; (mold) vaciar; (accounts) echar, calcular; (a horoscope) hacer; (the parts in a play) repartir; (an actor for a part) dar el papel de; (metals) colar, fundir. **the shadow c. by the wall,** la sombra proyectada por el muro. **to c. anchor,** echar anclas, anclar. **to c. in one's lot with,** compartir la suerte de. **to c. something in a person's teeth,** echar en cara (a). **to c. lots,** echar suertes. **to c. about,** meditar, considerar; imaginar; (devise) inventar. **to c. aside,** desechar; poner a un lado; abandonar. **to c. away,** tirar lejos; desechar; (money) derrochar, malgastar. **to be c. away,** *naut* naufragar. **to c. down,** (overthrow) derribar, destruir; (eyes) bajar; (depress) desanimar, deprimir; (humiliate) humillar. **to be c. down,** estar deprimido. **c. iron,** *n* hierro colado, hierro fundido, *m*. **c.-iron,** *a* de hierro colado; *fig* inflexible. **to c. off,** quitarse; desechar; (a wife) repudiar; (desert) abandonar; (free oneself) librarse (de). **c.-off,** *n* desecho, *m*. **c.-off clothing,** ropa de desecho, *f*. **to c. out,** echar fuera; hacer salir; excluir. **to c. up,** echar; vomitar; (a sum) sumar; (something at a person) reprochar
cast *n* (of dice, fishing-line) echada, *f*; (of a net) redada, *f*; (worm) molde, *m*; (of a play) reparto, *m*; (of mind) inclinación, *f*; (in the eye) defecto en la mirada, *m*; (of colour) matiz, tinte, *m*. **c. of features,** facciones, *f pl*; fisonomía, *f*. **plaster c.,** vaciado, *m*
castanets *n pl* castañuelas, *f pl*
castaway *n* náufrago (-ga); *fig* perdido (-da)
caste *n* casta, *f*; clase social, *f*. **to lose c.,** desprestigiarse
castigate *vt* castigar
Castile Castilla, *f*
Castilian *a* castellano. *n* castellano (-na); (language) castellano, *m*
casting *n* lanzamiento, *m*; (of metals) fundición, colada, *f*; obra de fundición, *f*. **c.-net,** esparavel, *m*. **c.-vote,** voto de calidad, *m*
castle *n* castillo, *m*; (in chess) torre, *f*, roque, *m*. **to build castles in Spain,** hacer castillos en el aire
castor *n* *zool* castor, *m*; (for sugar) azucarero, *m*; (cruet) convoy, *m*; (on chairs, etc.) ruedecilla, roldana, *f*. **c.-oil,** aceite de ricino, *m*. **c.-sugar,** azúcar en polvo, *m*
castrate *vt* castrar, capar
castration *n* castración, capadura, *f*
casual *a* fortuito, accidental; ligero, superficial; *inf* despreocupado. **c. worker,** jornalero, *m*
casually *adv* por casualidad; de paso; negligentemente
casualness *n* *inf* negligencia, despreocupación, *f*
casualty *n* víctima, *f*; herido, *m*; *mil* baja, *f*; *pl* **casualties,** heridos, *m pl*; muertos, *m pl*. **c.-list,** lista de víctimas, *f*; *mil* lista de bajas, *f*
casuist *n* casuista, *mf*
casuistry *n* casuística, *f*
cat *n* gato (-ta). **She is an old cat,** Ella es una vieja chismosa. **to be like a cat on hot bricks,** estar como en brasas. **to let the cat out of the bag,** tirar de la manta. **to lead a cat-and-dog life,** vivir como perros y gatos. **cat's-cradle,** (game) cunas, *f pl*. **cat's paw,** (person) hombre de paja, *m*; *naut* bocanada de viento, *f*. **cat o' nine tails,** gato de siete colas, *m*, penca, *f*
catwhisker, *rad* detector, *m*
cataclysm *n* cataclismo, *m*
catacombs *n pl* catacumbas, *f pl*
catafalque *n* catafalco, *m*
Catalan *a* catalán (-ana). *n* catalán; (language) catalán, *m*

catalepsy *n* catalepsia, *f*
catalogue *n* catálogo, *m*, *vt* catalogar
Catalonia Cataluña, *f*
catalysis *n* catálisis, *f*
cat-and-mouse *n* el juego de ratón, *m*
catapult *n* *mil* catapulta, *f*; *aer* catapulta (para lanzar aviones), *f*; (toy) tirador de gomas, *m*. *vt* tirar con una catapulta (or con un tirador de gomas); (throw) lanzar
cataract *n* catarata, cascada, *f*, salto de agua, *m*; (of the eye) catarata, *f*
catarrh *n* catarro, *m*; constipado, resfriado, *m*
catastrophe *n* catástrofe, *f*, desastre, *m*; (in drama) desenlace, *m*
catastrophic *a* catastrófico
catcall *n* silbido, *m*
catch *vt* coger; agarrar, asir; (capture) prender, haber; (a disease) contraer; (habit) tomar; (on a hook, etc.) enganchar; (surprise) sorprender; (understand) comprender; (hear) oír; (with blows, etc.) dar. *vi* (of a lock) encajarse; (become entangled) engancharse; (of a fire) encenderse. **to c. a glimpse of,** ver por un instante (a); alcanzar a ver, entrever. **to c. at,** asir; agarrarse (a); echar mano de; procurar asir; alargar la mano hacia; (an idea, etc.) adoptar con entusiasmo. **to c. on,** (be popular) tener éxito; (understand) comprender. **to c. out,** coger en el acto; coger en un error; *sport* coger. **to c. up,** coger; interrumpir. **to c. up with,** (a person) alcanzar; (news) ponerse al corriente de
catch *n* presa, *f*; (of fish) redada, pesca, *f*; (of a window, etc.) cerradura, *f*; (latch) pestillo, *m*; (trick) trampa, *f*; *mus* canon, *m*. **a good c.,** (matrimonial) un buen partido. **to have a c. in one's voice,** hablar con voz entrecortada. **c.-as-c.-can,** lucha libre, *f*
catching *a* contagioso
catchment *n* desagüe, *m*
catchword *n* reclamo, *m*; (theater cue) pie, apunte, *m*; (slogan) mote, *m*
catchy *a* atractivo. **It's a c. tune,** Es una canción que se pega
catechism *n* catequismo, *m*
categorical *a* categórico
category *n* categoría, *f*
cater *vi* proveer, abastecer. **to c. for all tastes,** atender a todos los gustos
caterer *n* despensero (-ra)
catering *n* provisión, *f*
caterpillar *n* oruga, *f*. **c. tractor,** tractor de orugas, *m*
caterwaul *vi* (of a cat) maullar
caterwauler *n* (violinist, etc.) rascatripas, *m*
caterwauling *n* maullidos, *m pl*; música ratonera, *f*
catfish *n* siluro, *m*
catgut *n* *surg* catgut, *m*; *mus* cuerda, *f*
catharsis *n* *med* purga, *f*; *fig* catarsis, *f*
cathedral *n* catedral, *f*
Catherine wheel *n* *arch* rosa, *f*; (fireworks) rueda de Santa Catalina, *f*; (somersault) tumba, *f*
catheter *n* catéter, *m*
cathode *n* cátodo, *m*. **c. rays,** rayos catódicos, *m pl*. **c. ray tube,** tubo de rayos catódicos, *m*
cathodic *a* catódico
catholic *a* católico
Catholicism *n* catolicismo, *m*
catkin *n* amento, *m*. **male c.,** amento macho, *m*
catlike *a* de gato; gatuno
cattle *n* ganado vacuno, *m*; ganado, *m*; animales, *m pl*. **c.-dealer,** ganadero, *m*. **c.-lifter,** hurtador de ganado, *m*. **c.-pen,** corral, *m*. **c.-raiser,** criador de ganado, *m*. **c.-raising,** ganadería, *f*. **c.-ranch,** hacienda de ganado, estancia, *f*. **c.-show,** exposición de ganado, *f*. **c.-truck,** vagón de ferrocarril para ganado, *m*
cattle rustler *n* abigeo, cuatrero, ladrón de ganado, *m*
cattle rustling *n* abigeato, *m*
catty *a* gatuno; malicioso, chismoso
Caucasian *a* and *n* caucáseo (-ea)
Caucasus, the el Cáucaso
cauldron *n* caldera, *f*

cauliflower *n* coliflor, *f*
caulk *vt* calafatear
caulker *n* calafate, *m*
caulking *n* calafateado, *m*. **c. iron,** calador, *m*
causality *n* causalidad, *f*
causative *a* causante
cause *n* causa, *f*; (reason) motivo, *m*, razón, *f*; (lawsuit) proceso, *m*. *vt* causar; ocasionar, suscitar; (oblige) hacer, obligar (a). **final c.,** *phil* causa final, *f*. **to have good c. for,** tener buen motivo para
causeway *n* dique, *m*; acera, *f*
caustic *a* cáustico; *fig* mordaz. **c. soda,** sosa cáustica, *f*
caustically *adv* mordazmente, con sarcasmo
causticity *n* causticidad, *f*
cauterization *n* cauterización, *f*
cauterize *vt* cauterizar
cautery *n* cauterio, *m*
caution *n* prudencia, cautela, *f*; (warning) amonestación, *f*; aviso, *m*. *vt* amonestar. **to proceed with c.,** ir con prudencia; ir despacio
"Caution" (road sign) «Precaución»
cautionary *a* (of tales) de escarmiento
cautious *a* cauteloso, cauto; prudente, circunspecto
cautiously *adv* cautamente; prudentemente. **to go c.,** *inf* ir con pies de plomo
cavalcade *n* cabalgata, *f*
cavalier *n* jinete, *m*; caballero, *m*; galán, *m*, *a* arrogante, altanero
cavalry *n* caballería, *f*. **c.-man,** jinete, soldado de a caballo, *m*
cave *n* cueva, caverna, *f*. **to c. in,** hundirse; desplomarse; *fig* rendirse. **c.-man,** hombre cavernícola, *m*
cavern *n* caverna, *f*
cavernous *a* cavernoso
caviar *n* caviar, *m*
cavil *vi* cavilar
cavity *n* cavidad, *f*; hoyo, *m*; hueco, *m*; (in a lung) caverna, *f*
cavy *n* cobayo (-ya), conejillo (-lla) de las Indias
caw *n* graznido, *m*, *vi* graznar, grajear
cawing *n* graznidos, *m pl*
cayenne *n* pimentón, *m*
cease *vi* cesar (de), dejar de; parar. *vt* cesar de; parar de; (payments, etc.) suspender; discontinuar. **C. fire!** ¡Cesar fuego!
ceaseless *a* incesante, continuo, sin cesar
ceaselessly *adv* sin cesar, incesantemente
ceasing *n* cesación, *f*. **without c.,** sin cesar
cedar *n* (tree and wood) cedro, *m*. **red c.,** cedro dulce, *m*
cede *vt* ceder, traspasar; (admit) conceder
cedilla *n* zedilla, *f*
ceiling *n* techo, *m*; *aer* altura máxima, *f*. **c. price,** máximo precio, *m*
celebrant *n* *ecc* celebrante, *m*
celebrate *vt* celebrar; solemnizar. **Their marriage was celebrated in the autumn,** Su casamiento se solemnizó en el otoño
celebrated *a* célebre, famoso
celebration *n* celebración, *f*; festividad, *f*
celebrity *n* celebridad, *f*
celerity *n* celeridad, *f*
celery *n* apio, *m*
celestial *a* celestial
celibacy *n* celibato, *m*
celibate *a* célibe. *n* célibe, *mf*
cell *n* celda, *f*; (*bot biol*) célula, *f*; (bees, wasps) celdilla, *f*; *elec* elemento, *m*
cellar *n* sótano, *m*; (wine) bodega, *f*
cellist *n* violoncelista, *mf*
cello *n* violoncelo, *m*
cellophane *n* (papel) celofán, *m*
cellular *a* celular, celuloso
cellule *n* célula, *f*
celluloid *n* celuloide, *f*

cellulose *n* celulosa, *f*
Celt *n* celta, *mf*
Celtiberian *a* celtibérico
Celtic *a* celta
cement *n* cemento, *m*, *vt* cementar
cemetery *n* cementerio, *m*
cenotaph *n* cenotafio, *m*
cense *vt* incensar
censer *n* incensario, *m*
censor *n* censor, *m*, *vt* censurar. **banned by the c.**, prohibido por la censura
censorious *a* severo; crítico
censoriousness *n* severidad, propensión a censurar, *f*
censorship *n* censura, *f*
censure *vt* censurar, culpar, criticar
census *n* censo, *m*. **to take the c.**, formar el censo, levantar el censo, tomar el censo, empadronar
census-taking *n* la formación del censo, la formación de los censos, *f*, el levantamiento del censo, el levantamientos de los censos, *m*
cent *n* (coin) centavo, *m*. **per c.**, por ciento. **not to have a c., not to have a c. to one's name**, no tener donde caer muerto
centaur *n* centauro, *m*
centenarian *a* and *n* centenario (-ia)
centenary *n* centenario, *m*, *a* centenario
center *n* centro, *m*; medio, *m*. *a* central; centro. *vt* centrar; concentrar (en). **nervous centers**, centros nerviosos, *m pl*. **c.-forward**, *sport* delantero centro, *m*. **c.-half**, *sport* medio centro, *m*. **c. of gravity**, centro de gravedad, *m*. **c.-piece**, centro, *m*
centerfold *n* páginas centrales, *f pl*
centigrade *a* centígrado
centigrame *n* centigramo, *m*
centilitre *n* centilitro, *m*
centime *n* céntimo, *m*
centimeter *n* centímetro, *m*. **cubic c.**, centímetro cúbico, *m*
centipede *n* ciempiés, *m*
central *a* central; céntrico. **The house is very c.**, La casa es muy céntrica. **C. American**, *a* and *n* centroamericano (-na). **c. depot**, central, *f*. **c. heating**, calefacción central, *f*
centralism *n* centralismo, *m*
centralist *n* centralista, *mf*
centralization *n* centralización, *f*
centralize *vt* centralizar
centrally *adv* centralmente; céntricamente
centric *a* céntrico; central
centrifugal *a* centrífugo
centripetal *a* centrípeto
centumvir *n* centunviro, *m*
centuple *a* céntuplo
centuplicate *vt* centuplicar
centurion *n* centurión, *m*
century *n* siglo, *m*, centuria, *f*
ceramic *a* cerámico
ceramics *n* cerámica, *f*
Cerberus *n* Cancerbero, *m*
cereal *a* cereal. *n* cereal, *m*
cerebellum *n* cerebelo, *m*
cerebral *a* cerebral
cerebrospinal *a* cerebroespinal
cerebrum *n* cerebro, *m*
ceremonial *a* ceremonial; de ceremonia. *n* ceremonial, *m*
ceremonially *adv* ceremonialmente; con ceremonia
ceremonious *a* ceremonioso
ceremoniously *adv* ceremoniosamente
ceremoniousness *n* ceremonia, formalidad, *f*
ceremony *n* ceremonia, *f*. **to stand on c.**, gastar cumplidos. **without c.**, sin cumplidos
cerise *a* de color cereza
certain *a* (sure) seguro; cierto; (unerring) certero. **a c. man**, cierto hombre. **I am c. that . . .**, Estoy seguro de que . . . **to know for c.**, saber con toda seguridad,

saber a ciencia cierta. **to make c. of**, asegurarse de
certainly *adv* seguramente; ciertamente; (as a reply) sin duda; naturalmente. **c. not**, no, por cierto; claro que no
certainty *n* certidumbre, *f*; seguridad, *f*; convicción, *f*. **of a c.**, seguramente
certificate *n* certificado, *m*; fe, *f*; partida, *f*; *com* bono, título, *m*; diploma, *m*. *vt* certificar. **birth c.**, partida de nacimiento, *f*. **death c.**, partida de defunción, *f*. **marriage c.**, partida de casamiento, *f*
certificated *a* (of teachers, etc.) con título
certify *vt* certificar; atestiguar; declarar
certitude *n* certeza, certidumbre, *f*
Cerulean *a* cerúleo
Cervantine *a* cervantino
cervix *n* *anat* cerviz, *f*
Cesarean *a* cesáreo
cessation *n* cesación, *f*
cession *n* cesión, *f*
cessionary *n* cesionario (-ia)
cesspool *n* sumidero, *m*
cetacean *a* cetáceo. *n* cetáceo, *m*
Ceylon Ceilán, *m*
cf. cfr.
chafe *vt* (rub) frotar; (make sore) escocer, rozar. *vi* raerse, desgastarse; escocerse; *fig* impacientarse; *fig* irritarse, enojarse
chaff *n* (of grain) ahechadura, *f*; (in a general sense and *fig*) paja, *f*; tomadura de pelo, burla, *f*. *vt* (a person) tomar el pelo (a), burlarse de
chaffinch *n* pinzón, *m*
chafing *n* frotación, *f*; (soreness) excoriación, *f*; *fig* impaciencia, *f*. **c.-dish**, escalfador, *m*
chagrin *n* mortificación, decepción, *f*, disgusto, *m*, *vt* mortificar
chain *n* cadena, *f*, *vt* encadenar. **c. of mountains**, cadena de montañas, cordillera, *f*. **c.-gang**, cadena de presidiarios, *f*. **c.-mail**, cota de malla, *f*. **c.-stitch**, cadeneta, *f*. **c.-stores**, empresa con sucursales, *f*. **in chains**, cargado de cadenas (e.g., **prisoners in chains**, prisioneros cargados de cadenas)
chair *n* silla, *f*; *univ* cátedra, *f*; (of a meeting) presidencia, *f*. *vt* llevar en hombros (a). **C.!** ¡Orden! **easy-c.**, (silla) poltrona, *f*. **to be in the c.**, ocupar la presidencia; presidir. **to take a c.**, sentarse, tomar asiento. **to take the c.**, presidir. **swivel-c.**, silla giratoria, *f*. **wheel-c.**, silla de ruedas, *f*. **c.-back**, respaldo de una silla, *m*
chairman *n* presidente (-ta). **to act as c.**, presidir
chairmanship *n* presidencia, *f*
chaise longue *n* meridiana, tumbona, *f*
Chaldea Caldea, *f*
Chaldean *a* caldeo
chalet *n* chalet, *m*
chalice *n* cáliz, *m*
chalk *n* creta, *f*; (for writing, etc.) tiza, *f*, yeso, *m*. *vt* marcar con tiza; dibujar con tiza. **to c. up**, apuntar. **not by a long c.**, no con mucho
chalky *a* cretáceo; cubierto de yeso; (of the complexion) pálido
challenge *n* provocación, *f*; (of a sentry) quién vive, *m*; (to a duel, etc.) desafío, reto, *m*; *law* recusación, *f*; concurso, *m*. *vt* (of a sentry) dar el quién vive (a); desafiar; provocar; *law* recusar
challenger *n* desafiador (-ra)
challenging *a* desafiador, provocador
chamber *n* cuarto, *m*; sala, *f*; (bed-) dormitorio, *m*, alcoba, *f*; cámara, *f*; *mech* cilindro, *m*; (in a gun) cámara, *f*. **c. concert**, concierto de música de cámara, *m*. **c.-maid**, camarera, *f*. **c. music**, música de cámara, *f*. **c. of commerce**, cámara de comercio, *f*. **c.-pot**, orinal, *m*
chamberlain *n* camarero, *m*. **court c.**, chambelán, *m*. **Lord C.**, camarero mayor, *m*
chameleon *n* camaleón, *m*
chamfer *n* chaflán, bisel, *m*

chamois *n* gamuza, *f;* rebeco, *m.* **c. leather,** piel de gamuza, *f*
chamomile *n* camomila, manzanilla, *f*
champ *vt* mascar; morder. *vi fig* impacientarse
champagne *n* (vino de) champaña, *m*
champion *n* campeón, *m;* defensor (-ra)
championship *n* campeonato, *m;* (of a cause) defensa, *f*
chance *n* casualidad, *f;* suerte, fortuna, *f;* posibilidad, *f;* probabilidad, *f;* esperanza, *f;* (opportunity) ocasión, oportunidad, *f. a* fortuito; accidental. *vi impers* suceder, acontecer. *vt* arriesgar; probar. **by c.,** por casualidad; por ventura. **if by c.,** si acaso. **If it chances that . . . ,** Si sucede que; Si a mano viene que . . . **The chances are that . . . ,** Las probabilidades son que . . . **There is no c.,** No hay posibilidad; No hay esperanza. **to let the c. slip,** perder la ocasión. **to take a c.,** aventurarse, arriesgarse. **to c. to do,** hacer algo por casualidad. **to c. upon,** encontrar por casualidad.
chancel *n* antealtar, entrecoro, *m*
chancellery *n* cancillería, *f*
chancellor *n* canciller, *m; univ* cancelario, *m.* **C. of the Exchequer,** Ministro de Hacienda, *m*
chancellorship *n* cancillería, *f*
chancery *n* chancillería, *f;* (papal) cancelaría, *f*
chandelier *n* araña de luces, *f*
chandler *n* velero, *m*
change *vt* cambiar; transformar; modificar; (clothes) mudarse (de); (one thing for another) trocar; sustituir (por). *vi* cambiar; (clothes) mudarse. **All c.!** ¡Cambio de tren! **to c. a check,** cambiar un cheque. **to c. color,** cambiar de color; (of persons) mudar de color. **to c. countenance,** demudarse. **to c. front,** *fig* cambiar de frente. **to c. hands,** (of shops, etc.) cambiar de dueño. **to c. one's clothes,** cambiar de ropa, mudarse de ropa. **to c. one's mind,** cambiar de opinión. **to c. one's tune,** cambiar de tono. **to c. the subject,** cambiar de conversación. **to c. trains,** cambiar de trenes
change *n* cambio, *m;* transformación, *f;* modificación, *f;* variedad, *f;* (of clothes, feathers) muda, *f;* (*theat* of scene) mutación, *f;* (money) cambio, *m;* (small coins) suelto, *m;* (stock) bolsa, *f;* lonja, *f;* vicisitud, *f;* (of bells) toque (de campanas), *m.* **for a c.,** para cambiar, como un cambio; para variar. **small c.,** suelto, *m,* moneda suelta, *f.* **c. for the better,** cambio para mejor, *m.* **c. for the worse,** cambio para peor, *m.* **c. of clothes,** cambio de ropa, *m;* **c. of front,** *fig* cambio de frente, *m.* **c. of heart,** cambio de sentimientos, *m;* conversión, *f.* **c. of life,** menopausia, *f.* **c.-over,** cambio, *m*
changeability *n* mutabilidad, *f;* inconstancia, volubilidad, *f*
changeable *a* voluble; variable; cambiable
changeless *a* immutable; constante
changeling *n* niño (-ña) cambiado (-da) por otro
changing *a* cambiante. **c.-room,** vestuario, *m*
channel *n* (of a river, etc.) cauce, *m;* canal, *m;* (irrigation) acequia, *f;* (strait) estrecho, *m; fig* conducto, *m;* (furrow) surco, *m,* estría, *f;* (of information, etc.) medio, *m. vt* acanalar; (furrow) surcar; (conduct) encauzar
chant *n* canto llano, *m;* salmo, *m. vt* salmodiar; cantar; recitar
chantey *n* saloma, *f*
chaos *n* caos, *m*
chaotic *a* caótico, desordenado
chaotically *adv* en desorden
chap *vt* agrietar. *vi* agrietarse. *n inf* chico, *m*
chapbook *n* librito de cordel, *m*
chapel *n* capilla, *f;* templo disidente, *m*
chaperon *n* dama de compañía, señora de compañía, dueña, *f, vt* acompañar
chaplain *n* capellán, *m*
chaplaincy *n* capellanía, *f*
chaplet *n* guirnalda, *f;* rosario, *m;* (necklace) collar, *m*
chapter *n* (in a book) capítulo, *m; ecc* cabildo, capítulo,

m. **a c. of accidents,** una serie de desgracias. **c. house,** sala capitular, *f*
char *vt* (a house, etc.) fregar, hacer la limpieza de; (of fire) carbonizar. *n inf* fregona, asistenta, *f*
character *n* carácter, *m;* (of a play) personaje, *m;* (role) papel, *m;* (eccentric) tipo, *m.* **Gothic characters,** caracteres góticos, *m pl.* **in c.,** característico; apropiado. **in the c. of,** en el papel de. **out of c.,** nada característico; no apropiado. **principal c.,** protagonista, *mf.* **c. actor,** actor de carácter, *m.* **c. actress,** actriz de carácter
characteristic *a* característico, típico. *n* característica, peculiaridad, *f,* rasgo, *m*
characterization *n* caracterización, *f*
characterize *vt* caracterizar
characterless *a* sin carácter; insípido, soso
charade *n* charada, *f*
charcoal *n* carbón de leña, *m;* (for blacking the face, etc.) tizne, *m; art* carboncillo, *m.* **c. burner,** carbonera, *f.* **c. crayon,** carboncillo, *m.* **c. drawing,** dibujo al carbón, *m*
charge *vt* cargar; (enjoin) encargar; (accuse) acusar (de); (with price) cobrar; (with a mission, etc.) encomendar, confiar; *mil* acometer, atacar. *vi mil* atacar; (a price) cobrar, pedir. **How much do you c.?** ¿Cuánto cobra Vd.? **to c. with a crime,** acusar de un crimen
charge *n* (load) carga, *f;* (price) precio, *m;* gasto, *m;* (on an estate, etc.) derechos, *m pl;* (task) encargo, *m;* (office or responsibility) cargo, *m;* (guardianship) tutela, *f;* (care) cuidado, *m;* exhortación, *f; law* acusación, *f; mil* ataque, *m.* **He is in c. of . . . ,** Está encargado de . . . ; Es responsable de . . . **The diamonds are in the c. of . . . ,** Los diamantes están a cargo de. **depth c.,** carga de profundidad, *f.* **extra c.,** gasto suplementario, *m;* (on a train) suplemento, *m.* **free of c.,** gratis. **c. for admittance,** entrada, *f.* **to bring a c. against,** acusar de. **to give (someone) in c.,** entregar (una persona) a la policía. **to take c. of,** encargarse de
chargé d'affaires *n* encargado de negocios, *m*
charger *n* caballo de guerra, corcel, *m*
chariness *n* cautela, *f*
chariot *n* carro, *m*
charioteer *n* auriga, *m*
charitable *a* caritativo; benéfico
charitableness *n* caridad, *f*
charity *n* caridad, *f;* beneficencia, *f;* (alms) limosna, *f.* **c. child,** niño (-ña) de la doctrina
charlatan *n* charlatán (-ana); (quack) curandero, *m*
charlatanism *n* charlatanismo, *m;* curanderismo, *m*
charm *n* hechizo, *m;* ensalmo, *m;* (amulet) amuleto, *m;* (trinket) dije, *m;* (general sense) encanto, atractivo, *m. vt* encantar, hechizar, fascinar
charming *a* encantador; atractivo, seductor, fascinador
charm school *n* academia de buenos modales, *f*
chart *n naut* carta de marear, *f;* (graph) gráfica, *f. vt* poner en una carta
charter *n* carta, *f;* (of a city, etc.) fuero, *m;* cédula, *f. vt* (a ship) fletar; (hire) alquilar. **royal c.,** cédula real, *f*
Chartism *n* el cartismo, *m*
chartist *n* cartista, *mf*
charwoman *n* fregona, asistenta; mujer de hacer faenas, *f*
chary *a* cauteloso; desinclinado; frugal
chase *n* caza, *f;* seguimiento, *m. vt* cazar; dar caza (a); perseguir; (drive off) ahuyentar; *fig* disipar, hacer desaparecer; (engrave) cincelar. **to c. to,** dar caza (a). **to go on a wild goose c.,** buscar pan de trastrigo
chasm *n* sima, *f,* precipicio, *m; fig* abismo, *m*
chassis *n* chasis, *m*
chaste *a* casto
chasten *vt* castigar; corregir; humillar, mortificar
chastened *a* sumiso, dócil
chastise *vt* castigar
chastisement *n* castigo, *m*
chastity *n* castidad, *f*
chat *vi* charlar, conversar. *n* conversación, charla, *f.*

They are having a c., Están charlando, Están de palique

chattels *n pl* bienes muebles, efectos, *m pl*

chatter *vi* charlar; hablar por los codos, chacharear; (of water) murmurar; (of birds) piar; (of monkeys, etc.) chillar; (of teeth) rechinar; (of a person's teeth) dar diente con diente. *n* charla, *f*; cháchara, parla, *f*; (of water) murmureo, *m*; (of birds) gorjeo, *m*; (of monkeys, etc.) chillidos, *m pl*

chatterbox *n* badajo, *m*, cotorra, *f*

chatterer *n* hablador (-ra)

chattering *n* charla, cháchara, *f*; (of teeth) rechinamiento, *m*, *a* gárrulo, chacharero, locuaz

chauffeur *n* chófer, *m*

chauvinism *n* chauvinismo, *m*

cheap *a* barato; (of works of art) cursi. *adv* barato. **dirt c.,** baratísimo. **to be dirt c.,** estar por los suelos. **to hold** (something) **c.,** tener en poco, estimar en poco

cheapen *vt* disminuir el valor de; reducir el precio de

cheaply *adv* barato; a bajo precio

cheapness *n* baratura, *f*; precio módico, *m*; mal gusto, *m*, vulgaridad, *f*

cheat *n* engaño, fraude, *m*, estafa, *f*; (person) fullero (-ra), trampista, *mf* embustero (-ra). *vt* engañar; defraudar; (at cards) hacer trampas. **He cheated me out of my property,** Me defraudó de mi propiedad

cheating *n* engaño, *m*; fraude, *m*; (at cards) fullerías, *f pl*

check *n* (chess) jaque, *m*; revés, *m*; impedimento, *m*; contratiempo, *m*; (of a bridle) cama, *f*; (control) freno, *m*; control, *m*; (checking) verificación, *f*; (ticket) papeleta, *f*; (counterfoil) talón, *m*; (square) cuadro, *m*; (bill) cuenta, *f*; (bank) cheque, *m*. *vt* (chess) jaquear; (hamper) refrenar; detener; contrarrestar; (test) verificar. *vi* detenerse. **to c. off,** marcar. **to c. oneself,** detenerse; contenerse. **to c. up,** comprobar. **crossed c.,** cheque cruzado, *m*. **c. book,** libro de cheques, *m*

checked *a* (cloth) a cuadros

checker *vt* escaquear; (variegate) motear, salpicar; diversificar. **a checkered career,** una vida accidentada

checking *n* represión, *f*; control, *m*; verificación, *f*; comprobación, *f*

checkmate *n* mate, jaque, mate, *m*. *vt* dar mate (a); (plans, etc.) frustrar

checks and balances *n pl* frenos y contrapesos, *m pl*

cheek *n* mejilla, *f*; *inf* descaro, *m*; insolencia, *f*. **They have plenty of c.,** Tienen mucha cara dura. **c. by jowl,** cara a cara; al lado de. **c.-bone,** pómulo, *m*

cheekiness *n* cara dura, insolencia, *f*

cheeky *a* insolente, descarado; (pert) respondón

cheep *n* pío, *m*, *vi* piar

cheer *n* alegría, *f*, regocijo, *m*; vítor, *m*; aplauso, *m*. *vt* animar; alegrar, regocijar; vitorear, aplaudir. **to be of good c.,** estar alegre; ser feliz. **C. up!** ¡Ánimo! **to c. up,** animarse, cobrar ánimo

cheerful *a* alegre; jovial; de buen humor. **It is a c. room,** Es un cuarto alegre

cheerfully *adv* alegremente; (willingly) con mucho gusto, de buena gana

cheerfulness *n* alegría, *f*; jovialidad, *f*; buen humor, *m*

cheering *n* vítores, *m pl*, aclamaciones, *f pl*, *a* animador

cheerleader *n* porro, *m*

cheerless *a* triste; sin alegría; (dank) obscuro, lóbrego

cheese *n* queso, *m*. **cream c.,** queso de nata, *m*. **grated c.,** queso rallado, *m*. **c.-dish,** quesera, *f*. **c.-mite,** cresa, *f*. **c.-paring,** *n* corteza de queso, *f*. *a inf* tacaño. **c.-vat,** quesera, *f*

cheesy *a* caseoso

chemical *a* químico. **c. warfare,** defensa química, *f*

chemicals *n pl* productos químicos, *m pl*

chemise *n* camisa (de mujer), *f*

chemist *n* químico, *m*. **chemist's shop,** farmacia, *f*; droguería, *f*

chemistry *n* química, *f*

chenille *n* felpilla, *f*

cherish *vt* amar, querer; (a hope, etc.) abrigar, acariciar

cherry *n* (fruit) cereza, *f*; (tree and wood) cerezo, *m*. **c. brandy,** aguardiente de cerezas, *m*. **c. orchard,** cerezal, *m*

cherub *n* querub(e), querubín, *m*

cherubic *a* querúbico

chess *n* ajedrez, *m*. **c.-board,** tablero de ajedrez, *m*

chessman *n* pieza de ajedrez, *f*

chest *n* arca, *f*, cofre, *m*; cajón, *m*; *anat* pecho, *m*. **to throw out one's c.,** inflar el pecho. **c.-expander,** extensor, *m*. **c. of drawers,** cómoda, *f*

chested *a* (in compounds) de pecho . . .

chestnut *n* (tree) castaño, *m*; (fruit) castaña, *f*; (color) castaño, color castaño, *m*; (horse) caballo castaño, *m*; (joke) chiste del tiempo de Maricastaña, *m*, *a* castaño. **horse-c. tree,** castaño de Indias, *m*

chevron *n* *her* cabrío, *m*; (*mil* etc.) sardineta, *f*

chew *vt* mascar, mascullar; (ponder) masticar

chewing *n* masticación, *f*. **c.-gum,** chicle, *m*

chianti *n* (wine) quianti, *m*

chiaroscuro *n* claroscuro, *m*

chic *n* chic, *m*, elegancia, *f*

chicanery *n* sofistería, *f*

chicken *n* pollo, *m*. **c.-hearted,** medroso, cobarde, timorato. **c.-pox,** varicela, *f*

chickenwire *n* alambrillo, *m*

chickpea *n* garbanzo, *m*

chickweed *n* pamplina, *f*

chicory *n* achicoria, *f*

chide *vt* reprender, reñir

chidingly *adv* en tono de represión

chief *n* jefe, *m*, *a* principal; primero; en jefe; mayor. **c.-of-staff,** jefe de estado mayor, *m*

chiefly *adv* principalmente; sobre todo

chieftain *n* caudillo, *m*; (of a clan) cabeza, jefe, *m*

chiffon *n* chifón, *m*, gasa, *f*

chiffonier *n* cómoda, *f*

chignon *n* moño, *m*

chilblain *n* sabañón, *m*

child *n* niño (-ña); hijo (-ja). **from a c.,** desde niño, desde la niñez. **with c.,** encinta, embarazada. **How many children have you?** ¿Cuántos hijos tiene Vd.? **child's play,** juegos infantiles, *m pl*; *fig* niñerías, *f pl*. **c. welfare,** puericultura, *f*

childbirth *n* parto, *m*

childhood *n* niñez, infancia, *f*. **from his c.,** desde su niñez, desde niño

childish *a* de niño; aniñado; pueril; fútil. **to grow c.,** chochear

childishly *adv* como un niño

childishness *n* puerilidad, *f*; futilidad, *f*

child labor *n* trabajo de menores, trabajo infantil, *m*

childless *a* sin hijos; sin niños

childlike *a* de niño, aniñado; pueril

children. See **child**

Chilean *a* and *n* chileno (-na)

chili *n* chile, pimento de cornetilla, *m*

chill *n* frío, *m* (of fear, etc.) estremecimiento, *m*; (illness) resfriado, *m*; (unfriendliness) frialdad, frigidez, *f*, *a* frío; (unfriendly) frígido. *vt* enfriar; helar; (with fear, etc.) dar escalofríos (de); (discourage) desalentar. *vi* tener frío; tener escalofríos. **to take the c. off,** templar, calentar un poco

chilliness *n* frío, *m*; (unfriendliness) frialdad, frigidez, *f*

chilly *a* frío; (sensitive to cold) friolero; (of politeness, etc.) glacial, frígido

chime *n* juego de campanas, *m*; repique, campaneo, *m*; armonía, *f*. *vi* (of bells) repicar; *fig* armonizar. **to c. the hour,** dar la hora

chimera *n* quimera, *f*

chimerical *a* quimérico

chimney *n* chimenea, *f*; (of a lamp) tubo (de lámpara), *m*. **c.-corner,** rincón de chimenea, *m*. **c.-pot,** sombrerete de chimenea, *m*. **c.-stack,** chimenea, *f*. **c.-sweep,** limpiador de chimeneas, deshollinador, *m*

chimpanzee *n* chimpancé, *m*

chin *n* barbilla, barba, *f*, mentón, *m*. **c.-rest,** mentonera,

f. **c.-strap,** barboquejo, *m*; venda para la barbilla, *f*
china *n* china, porcelana, *f*; loza, *f. a* de porcelana; de loza. **c. cabinet,** chinero, *m*
chinchilla *n* (animal and fur) chinchilla, *f*
Chinese *a* and *n* chino (-na); (language) chino, *m*. **C. lantern,** farolillo de papel, *m*. **C. white,** óxido blanco de cinc, *m*
chink *n* resquicio, *m*, grieta, hendidura, *f*; (clink) retintín, tintineo, *m. vi* tintinar
chintz *n* zaraza, *f*
chip *n* astilla, *f*; (counter) ficha, *f. vt* picar; cincelar. **a c. off the old block,** de tal palo tal astilla. **c. potatoes,** patatas fritas, *f pl*
chiromancy *n* quiromancia, *f*
chiropodist *n* pedicuro, *m*, callista, *mf*
chiropody *n* pedicura, *f*
chiropractor *n* quiropráctico, *m*
chirp *vi* piar, gorjear, *m*
chirping *n* píada, *f, a* gárrulo, piante
chisel *n* escoplo, cincel, *m*, *vt* cincelar. **cold c.,** cortafrío, *m*
chitchat *n* charla, *f*
chitterlings *n* asadura, *f*
chivalrous *a* caballeroso
chivalry *n* caballería, *f*; caballerosidad, *f*. **novel of c.,** novela de caballería, *f*
chive *n bot* cebollana, *f*, cebollino, *m*
chloral *n* cloral, *m*
chlorate *n* clorato, *m*
chloride *n* cloruro, *m*
chlorine *n* cloro, *m*
chloroform *n* cloroformo, *m*, *vt* cloroformizar
chlorophyll *n* clorófila, *f*
chock-full *a* lleno de bote en bote
chocolate *n* chocolate, *m*, *a* de chocolate. **thick drinking-c.,** chocolate a la española, *m*. **thin drinking-c.,** chocolate a la francesa. *m*. **c. shop,** chocolatería, *f*
choice *n* selección, *f*; preferencia, *f*; elección, *f*; opción, *f*; alternativa, *f*; lo más escogido. *a* escogido, selecto; excelente. **for c.,** con preferencia
choir *n* coro, *m*. **c.-boy,** niño del coro, *m*. **c.-master,** maestro de capilla, *m*
choke *vi* ahogarse; atragantarse; obstruirse. *vt* ahogar; estrangular. **to c. with laughter,** ahogarse de risa. **to c. back,** (words) tragar. **to c. off,** (a person) disuadir (de); quitarse de encima(a). **to c. up,** obstruir, cerrar, obturar; (hide) cubrir, tapar
choking *a* asfixiante, sofocante. *n* ahogamiento, sofocación, *f*
cholera *n* cólera, *m*
choleric *a* colérico
cholesterol *n* colesterina, *f*
choline *n* colina, *f*
choose *vt* escoger; elegir; optar por; (wish) querer, gustar. **They will do it when they c.,** Lo harán cuando les parezca bien. **If you c.,** Si Vd. quiere; Si Vd. gusta. **He was chosen as Mayor,** Fue elegido alcalde. **There is nothing to c. between them,** No hay diferencia entre ellos; Tanto vale el uno como el otro. **You cannot c. but love her,** No puedes menos de quererla
choosing *n* selección, *f*; (for an office, etc.) elección, *f*
chop *vt* cortar; (mince) picar; (split) hender, partir. *n* (meat) chuleta, *f*; (jaw) quijada, *f*. **to c. down,** (trees) talar. **to c. off,** separar; cortar; tajar. **to c. up,** cortar en pedazos
chopper *n* hacha, *f*
choppy *a* picado, agitado
chopstick *n* palillo chino, *m*
choragus *n* corega, corego, *m*
choral *a* coral
chord *n* cuerda, *f*; *mus* acorde, *m*; **the right c.,** *fig* la cuerda sensible
choreographer *n* coreógrafo, *m*
choreographic *a* coreográfico
choreography *n* coreografía, *f*
chorister *n* corista, *m*

chorus *n* coro, *m*; (in revues) comparsa, *f*, acompañamiento, *m*; (of a song) refrán, *m*. **to sing in c.,** cantar a coro. **c. girl,** corista, *f*
chosen *a* escogido; elegido. **the c.,** los elegidos
chrestomathy *n* crestomatía, *f*
Christ *n* Cristo, Jesucristo, *m*
christen *vt* bautizar
Christendom *n* cristianismo, *m*, cristiandad, *f*
christening *n* bautizo, *m*, *a* bautismal, de bautizo
christian *a* cristiano. *n* cristiano (-na). **c. name,** nombre de pila, *m*
christianity *n* cristianismo, *m*
Christmas *n* Navidad, *f*. **A Merry C.!** ¡Felices Pascuas (de Navidad)! **Father C.,** Padre Noel, *m*; (Sp. equivalent) Los Reyes Magos. **C. box,** regalo de Navidad, *m*. **C. card,** felicitación de Navidad, *f*. **C. carol,** villancico de Navidad, *m*. **C. Day,** día de Navidad, *m*. **C. Eve,** Nochebuena, *f*. **C.-tide,** Navidades, *f pl*. **C. tree,** árbol de Navidad, *m*
Christopher Columbus Cristóbal Colón, *m*
chromate *n* cromato, *m*
chromatic *a* cromático
chrome *n* cromo, *m*. **c. yellow,** amarillo de cromo, *m*
chromic *a* crómico
chromium *n* cromo, *m*. **c.-plated,** cromado
chromosome *n* cromosoma, *m*
chronic *a* crónico; inveterado
chronicle *n* crónica, *f*, *vt* narrar
chronicler *n* cronista, *mf*
chronological *a* cronológico. **in c. order,** por orden cronológico
chronology *n* cronología, *f*
chronometer *n* cronómetro, *m*
chrysalis *n* crisálida, *f*
chrysanthemum *n* crisantemo, *m*
chubbiness *n* gordura, *f*
chubby *a* regordete, gordito. **c.-cheeked,** mofletudo
chuck *vt* (throw) lanzar, arrojar; (discontinue) abandonar, dejar. *n* (in a lathe) mandril, *m*. **to c. under the chin,** acariciar la barbilla (a). **to c. away,** derrochar; malgastar, perder. **to c. out,** echar, poner en la calle
chuckle *vi* reír entre dientes. *n* risa ahogada, *f*; risita, *f*
chum *n* compinche, camarada, *mf*. **to c. up with,** ser camarada de
chunk *n* pedazo, trozo, *m*
church *n* iglesia, *f*; (Protestant) templo, *m*, *vt* (a woman) purificar. **poor as a c. mouse,** más pobre que las ratas. **the C. of England,** la iglesia anglicana. **to go to c.,** ir a misa; ir al templo. **c. music,** música sagrada, *f*
churchyard *n* cementerio, *m*
churl *n* patán, *m*
churlish *a* grosero, cazurro; (mean) tacaño, ruin
churn *n* mantequera, *f*. *vt* (cream) batir; *fig* azotar, agitar
chute *n* (for grain, etc.) manga de tolva, *f*; vertedor, *m*; (in flats and fun fairs) tobogán, deslizadero, *m*
ciborium *n* (chalice) copón, *m*; (tabernacle) sagrario, *m*; *arch* ciborio, *m*
cicada *n* cigarra, *f*
cicatrice *n* cicatriz, *f*
cicatrization *n* cicatrización, *f*
cicatrize *vt* cicatrizar. *vi* cicatrizarse
cider *n* sidra, *f*
cigar *n* cigarro, *m*. **c.-box,** cigarrera, *f*. **c.-case,** petaca, cigarrera, *f*. **c.-cutter,** corta-puros, *m*
cigarette *n* cigarrillo, pitillo, *m*. **c.-butt,** colilla, *f*. **c.-case,** pitillera, *f*. **c.-holder,** boquilla, *f*. **c.-lighter,** encendedor de cigarrillos, *m*. **c.-paper,** papel de fumar, *m*
cinch *n* (of a saddle) cincha, *f*; *inf* ganga, *f*; *inf* seguridad, *f*. **c.-strap,** látigo, *m*
cinchona *n* quina, cinchona, *f*
cinder *n* ceniza, *f*; carbonilla, *f*. **red-hot c.,** rescoldo, *m*. **c.-track,** pista de ceniza, *f*
cinema, cinematograph *n* cine, cinematógrafo, *m*
cinematographic *a* cinematográfico

cinematography *n* cinematografía, *f*
cinemogul *n* magnate del cine, *mf*
cinnamon *n* (spice) canela, *f*; (tree) canelo, *m*; color de canela, *m*
cipher *n* math cero, *m*; *fig* nulidad, *f*; (code) cifra, *f*; monograma, *m*. **to be a mere c.,** ser un cero
Circassian *a* circasiano. *n* circasiano (-na)
circle *n* círculo, *m*; (revolution) vuelta, *f*; (group) grupo; *m*; (club, etc.) centro, *m*; (cycle) ciclo, *m*. *vt* dar vueltas alrededor de; rodear; ceñir; (on an application, examination, etc.) encerrar en un círculo. *vi* dar vueltas; (aircraft) volar en círculo; (of a hawk, etc.) cernerse. **dress-c.,** *theat* anfiteatro, *m*. **the family c.,** el círculo de la familia. **to come full c.,** dar la vuelta. **upper c.,** *theat* segundo piso, *m*. **vicious c.,** círculo vicioso, *m*
circlet *n* (of flowers, etc.) corona, *f*; (ring) anillo, *m*
circuit *n* circuito, *m*; (tour) gira, *f*; (revolution) vuelta, *f*; (radius) radio, *m*. **short c.,** corto circuito, *m*. **c.-breaker,** corta-circuitos, *m*
circuit court of appeals *n* tribunal colegial de circuito, *m*
circuitous *a* indirecto; tortuoso
circuitously *adv* indirectamente
circular *a* circular; redondo. *n* carta circular, *f*; circular, *f*. **c. tour,** viaje redondo, *m*
circularize *vt* enviar circulares (a)
circulate *vi* circular. *vt* hacer circular; poner en circulación; (news, etc.) divulgar, diseminar
circulating library *n* biblioteca por subscripción, *f*
circulation *n* circulación, *f*; (of a newspaper, etc.) tirada, circulación, *f*. **c. of the blood,** circulación de la sangre, *f*
circulatory *a* circulatorio
circumcise *vt* circuncidar
circumcised *a* circunciso
circumcision *n* circuncisión, *f*
circumference *n* circunferencia, *f*
circumflex *a* circunflejo. **c. accent,** acento circunflejo, *m*, (informal) capucha, *f*
circumlocution *n* circumlocución, *f*
circumnavigate *vt* circunnavegar
circumnavigation *n* circunnavegación, *f*
circumscribe *vt* circunscribir; *fig* limitar
circumscribed *a* circunscripto; *fig* limitado
circumscription *n* circunscripción, *f*; *fig* limitación, restricción, *f*
circumspect *a* circunspecto; discreto, correcto; prudente
circumspection *n* circunspección, *f*; prudencia, *f*
circumspectly *adv* con circunspección; prudentemente
circumstance *n* circunstancia, *f*; detalle, *m*. **aggravating c.,** circunstancia agravante, *f*. **attenuating c.,** circunstancia atenuante, *f*. **in the circumstances,** en las circunstancias. **in easy circumstances,** en buena posición, acomodado. **Do you know what his circumstances are?** ¿Sabes cuál es su situación económica? **under the circumstances,** bajo las circunstancias
circumstantial *a* circunstancial; detallado. **c. evidence,** prueba de indicios, *f*
circumvent *vt* frustrar; impedir
circumvention *n* frustración, *f*
circumvolution *n* circunvolución, *f*
circus *n* circo, *m*; plaza redonda, *f*; (traffic) redondel, *m*
cirrhosis *n* cirrosis, *f*
cirrus *n* (all meanings) cirro, *m*
cistern *n* tanque, *m*; cisterna, *f*, aljibe, *m*
citadel *n* ciudadela, *f*
citation *n law* citación, *f*; cita, *f*
citation dictionary *n* diccionario de autoridades, *m*
cite *vt* citar
citizen *n* ciudadano (-na); vecino (-na); natural, *mf*. **fellow c.,** conciudadano, *m*; compatriota, *mf*
citizenship *n* ciudadanía, *f*
citrate *n* citrato, *m*
citric *a* cítrico

citrine *a* cetrino
citron *n* (fruit) cidra, *f*; (tree) cidro, *m*
city *n* ciudad, *f*, *a* municipal
city-state *n* ciudad-estado, *f*, (plural: ciudades-estado)
civet *n* algalia, *f*
civic *a* cívico; municipal
civics *n* civismo, *m*
civil *a* civil; doméstico; (polite) cortés, atento; (obliging) servicial. **C. Aeronautics Board,** Dirección general de aeronáutica civil, *f*. **c. defense,** defensa pasiva, *f*. **c. engineer,** ingeniero de caminos, canales y puertos, *m*. **C. Service,** cuerpo de empleados del Estado, *m*
civilian *a* civil. *n* ciudadano (-na). **c. dress,** traje paisano, *m*
civility *n* civilidad, cortesía, *f*
civilization *n* civilización, *f*
civilize *vt* civilizar
civilized *a* civilizado
civilizing *a* civilizador
civilly *adv* civilmente, cortésmente
clack *n* golpeo, ruido sordo, *m*
clad *a* vestido
claim *vt* reclamar; pretender exigir; *law* demandar; (assert) afirmar. *n law* pedir en juicio. *n* reclamación, *f*; pretensión, *f*; *law* demanda, *f*; (in a gold-field, etc.) concesión, *f*; (right) derecho, *m*. **to lay c. to,** pretender a; exigir. **to put in a c. for,** reclamar
claimant *n law* demandante, *mf*; pretendiente (-ta); *com* acreedor (-ra)
clairvoyance *n* doble vista, *f*
clairvoyant *n* vidente, *m*
clam *n* almeja, chirla, *f*
clamber *vi* trepar, encaramarse. *n* subida difícil, *f*
clamminess *n* viscosidad, humedad, *f*
clammy *a* viscoso; húmedo, mojado
clamor *n* clamor, estruendo, *m*; gritería, vocería, *f*. *vi* gritar, vociferar. **to c. against,** protestar contra. **to c. for,** pedir a voces
clamorous *a* clamoroso, ruidoso, estrepitoso
clamp *n* grapa, *f*; abrazadera, *f*; *carp* tornillo, *m*; (pile) montón, *m*. *vt* empalmar; sujetar, lañar
clan *n* clan, *m*; familia, *f*; partido, grupo, *m*
clandestine *a* clandestino, furtivo
clandestinely *adv* en secreto, clandestinamente
clang *vi* sonar; (of a gate, etc.) rechinar. *vt* hacer sonar. *n* sonido metálico, *m*; estruendo, *m*
clank *vi* dar un ruido metálico; crujir. *vt* hacer sonar; (glasses) hacer chocar. *n* ruido metálico, *m*; el crujir
clannish *a* exclusivista
clansman *n* miembro de un clan, *m*
clap *vt* (hands) batir; (spurs, etc.) poner rápidamente; (one's hat on) encasquetarse (el sombrero); (shut) cerrar apresuradamente. *vi* aplaudir. *n* (of the hands) palmada, *f*; (of thunder) trueno, *m*; (noise) ruido, *m*. **to c. eyes on,** echar la vista encima de. **to c. someone on the back,** dar una palmada en la espalda (a). **to c. the hands,** batir las palmas
clapper *n* (of a bell) badajo, *m*
clapping *n* aplausos, *m pl*
claque *n* claque, *f*
claret *n* clarete, *m*
clarification *n* clarificación, *f*; elucidación, *f*
clarify *vt* clarificar; elucidar, aclarar
clarinet *n* clarinete, *m*
clarinettist *n* clarinete, *m*
clarion *n* clarín, *m*
clarity *n* claridad, *f*; lucidez, *f*
clash *vi* chocar; encontrarse; (of events) coincidir; (of opinions, etc.) oponerse, estar en desacuerdo; (of colors) desentonar, chocar. *n* estruendo, fragor, *m*; choque, *m*; *mil* encuentro, *m*; (of opinions, etc.) desacuerdo, *m*; disputa, *f*
clasp *vt* (a brooch, etc.) abrochar, enganchar; (embrace) abrazar; (of plants, etc.) ceñir. *n* (brooch) broche, *m*; (of a belt) hebilla, *f*; (of a necklace, handbag, book) cierre, *m*; (for the hair) pasador, *m*. **to c. someone in**

one's arms, tomar en los brazos (a), abrazar. **c.-knife,** navaja, *f*

class *n* clase, *f;* (kind) especie, *f;* (of exhibits, etc.) categoría, *f. vt* clasificar. **in a c. by itself,** único en su línea. **the lower classes,** las clases bajas. **the middle classes,** la clase media. **the upper classes,** la clase alta. **c.-mate,** condiscípulo (-la). **c.-room,** sala de clase, *f,* salón de clase, *f.* **c. war,** lucha de clases, *f*

classic *a* clásico, *m*

classical *a* clásico

classicism *n* clasicismo, *m*

classicist *a* and *n* clasicista, *mf*

classifiable *a* clasificable

classification *n* clasificación, *f*

classified *a* (secreto) reservado, secreto; (advertisement) por palabras

classified advertisement *n* anuncio por palabras, *m*

classify *vt* clasificar

clatter *vi* hacer ruido; (knock) golpear; (of loose horseshoes) chacolotear. *vt* hacer ruido con; chocar (una cosa contra otra). *n* ruido, *m;* (hammering) martilleo, *m;* (of horseshoes) chacoloteo, *m;* (of a crowd) estruendo, *m,* bulla, *f.* **John clattered along the street,** Los pasos de Juan resonaban por la calle

clause *n gram* cláusula, *f; law* condición, estipulación, cláusula, *f*

claustrophobia *n* claustrofobia, *f*

clavichord *n* clavicordio, *m*

clavicle *n* clavícula, *f*

claw *n* garra, *f;* (of a lobster, etc.) tenaza, *f;* (hook) garfio, gancho, *m. vt* arañar, clavar las uñas en; (tear) desgarrar. **c.-hammer,** martillo de orejas, *m*

clay *n* arcilla, *f;* barro, *m;* (pipe) pipa de barro, *f.* **c.-pit,** barrizal, *m*

clayey *a* arcilloso

clean *a* limpio; puro, casto. *adv* limpio; completamente; exactamente. **to make a c. sweep (of),** no dejar títere con cabeza. **to make a c. breast of,** confesar sin tormento, no quedarse con nada en el pecho. **to show a c. pair of heels,** tomar las de Villadiego. **c. bill of health,** patente de sanidad, *m.* **c.-cut,** bien definido; claro. **c.-limbed,** bien proporcionado, gallardo. **c.-shaven,** lampiño; sin barba, bien afeitado

clean *vt* limpiar; (streets) barrer; (a floor) fregar; (dryclean) lavar al seco. **to c. one's hands (teeth),** limpiarse las manos (los dientes). **to c. up,** limpiar; (tidy) asear; poner en orden

cleaner *n* limpiador (-ra); (charwoman) fregona, *f;* (stain remover) sacamanchas, *m;* (drycleaner, person) tintorero (-ra)

cleaning *n* limpieza, *f, a* de limpiar. **dry-c.,** lavado al seco, *m.* **c. rag,** trapo de limpiar, *m*

cleanliness *n* limpieza, *f;* aseo, *m*

cleanness *n* limpieza, *f;* aseo, *m;* pureza, *f*

cleanse *vt* limpiar; lavar; purgar; purificar

cleansing *n* limpieza, *f;* lavamiento, *m;* purgación, *f;* purificación, *f*

clear *a* claro; (of the sky) sereno, despejado; transparente; (free (from)) libre (de); (open) abierto; (of profit, etc.) neto; (of thoughts, etc.) lúcido; (apparent) evidente; explícito; (of images) distinto; absoluto; (whole) entero, completo. **c. majority,** mayoría absoluta, *f.* **c. profit,** beneficio neto, *m.* **c.-cut,** bien definido. **c.-headed,** perspicaz; inteligente. **c.-sighted,** clarividente

clear *vt* aclarar; despejar; limpiar; librar (de); quitar; (one's throat) carraspear; (*com* stock) liquidar; (of a charge) absolver; (one's character) vindicar; (avoid, miss) evitar; (jump) salvar, saltar; (a court, etc.) desocupar; (a debt) satisfacer; (an account) saldar; (a mortgage) cancelar; (win) ganar; hacer un beneficio de; (through customs) despachar en la aduana. *vi* (of sky, etc.) serenarse; escampar; (of wine, etc.) aclararse; despacharse en la aduana. **to c. the table,** levantar la mesa, levantar los manteles. **to c. the way,** abrir calle; *fig* abrir paso. **to c. away,** *vt* quitar; disipar. *vi* disiparse.

to c. off, *vt* (finish) terminar; (debts) pagar; (discharge) despedir. *vi* (of rain) despejarse, escampar; marcharse. **to c. out,** *vt* limpiar; (a drain, etc.) desatascar; vaciar; echar. *vi* marcharse, escabullirse. **C. out!** ¡Fuera! **c. the decks,** hacer zafarrancho. **c. the decks for action,** hacer zafarrancho. **to c. up,** *vt* poner en orden; (a mystery, etc.) aclarar, resolver, *vi* (of weather) serenarse, escampar, despejarse

clearance *n* (of trees, etc.) desmonte, *m;* eliminación, *f;* expulsión, *f; mech* espacio muerto, *m;* despacho de aduana, *m.* **to make a c. of,** deshacerse de. **c. sale,** liquidación, venta de saldos, *f*

clearing *n* (in a wood) claro, *m;* desmonte, *m;* (*com* of goods) liquidación, *f;* (of one's character) vindicación, *f.* **c.-house,** casa de compensación, *f*

clearly *adv* claramente

clearness *n* claridad, *f*

cleavage *n* (of weather) benignidad, *f;* (of character, etc.) clemencia, *f*

cleave *vt* partir; abrir; (air, water, etc.) surcar, hender. *vi* partirse; (stick) pegarse, adherirse

cleaver *n* partidor, *m;* hacha, *f*

clef *n* clave, *f.* **treble c.,** clave de sol, *f*

cleft *n* hendedura, fisura, rendija, abertura, *f.* **c.-palate,** paladar hendido, *m*

clematis *n* clemátide, *f*

clemency *n* (of weather) benignidad, *f;* (of character, etc.) clemencia, *f*

clement *a* (of weather) benigno; (of character, etc.) clemente, benévolo

clench *vt* agarrar; (teeth, etc.) apretar; (a bargain) cerrar, concluir

clergy *n* clero, *m,* clérigos, *m pl*

clergyman *n* clérigo, *m*

cleric *n* eclesiástico, *m*

clerical *a* clerical; de oficina. **c. error,** error de oficina, *m.* **c. work,** trabajo de oficina, *m*

clericalism *n* clericalismo, *m*

clerk *n* (clergyman) clérigo, *m;* (in an office) oficinista, escribiente, *m;* oficial, *m;* secretario, *m*

clerkship *n* puesto de oficinista, *m;* escribanía, *f;* secretaría, *f*

clever *a* listo, inteligente; ingenioso; hábil; (dexterous) diestro

cleverly *adv* hábilmente; diestramente, con destreza

cleverness *n* talento, *m;* inteligencia, *f;* habilidad, *f;* (dexterity) destreza, *f*

cliché *n* frase hecha, frase de cajón, *f*

click *vi* (of the tongue) dar un chasquido; (of a bolt, etc.) cerrarse a golpe; hacer tictac. *vt* (one's tongue) chascar; (a bolt, etc.) cerrar a golpe. *n* golpe seco, *m;* tictac, *m;* (of the tongue) chasquido, *m.* **to c. one's heels together,** hacer chocar los talones

client *n* cliente, *mf;* (customer) parroquiano (-na)

clientele *n* clientela, *f*

cliff *n* acantilado, *m,* roca, escarpa, *f*

cliff dweller *n* hombre de la roca, hombre de las rocas, *m,* mujer de la roca, mujer de las rocas, *f*

climate *n* clima, *m*

climatic *a* climático

climatology *n* climatología, *f*

climax *n* culminación, *f;* (rhetoric) clímax, *m;* gradación, *f;* punto más alto, apogeo, cenit, *m;* (of a play, etc.) desenlace, *m*

climb *vt* and *vi* trepar; escalar; montar; subir; ascender. **rate of c.,** *aer* velocidad ascensional, *f.* **to c. down,** bajar; *fig* echar el pie atrás. **to c. over,** (obstacles) salvar. **to c. up,** encaramarse por; subir por; montar

climber *n* alpinista, *mf;* (plant) trepadera, enredadera, *f;* (social) arribista, *mf*

clime *n* clima, *m*

clinch *vt* (nails, etc.) remachar, rebotar; (a bargain, etc.) cerrar; (an argument, etc.) remachar. *n* (wrestling) cuerpo a cuerpo, *m*

cling *vi* pegarse (a); agarrarse (a); (of scents) pegarse; (follow) seguir. **They clung together for an instant,** Quedaron abrazados un instante

clinging *a* tenaz; (of plants, etc.) trepador; (of persons) manso, dócil. **to be a c. vine,** *inf* ser una malva

clinic *n* clínica, *f*

clinical *a* clínico. **c. thermometer,** termómetro clínico, *m*

clink *vi* retiñir; (of glasses) chocarse. *vt* hacer sonar; (glasses) chocar. *n* retintín, *m;* (of a hammer) martilleo, *m;* sonido metálico, *m;* (of glasses) choque, *m*

clip *vt* (grasp) agarrar; (sheep, etc.) esquilar; (trim) recortar, cercenar; (prune) podar; (a ticket) taladrar. *n* pinza, *f;* (paper-clip) sujetapapeles, *m; mech* grapa, escarpia, *f;* (for ornament) sujetador, *m.* **to c. a person's wings,** *fig* cortar (or quebrar) las alas (a)

clipper *n* (person) esquilador (-ra); (*naut* and *aer*) clíper, *m;* *pl* **clippers,** tenazas de cortar, *f pl;* (for pruning) podaderas, *f pl;* (punch) taladro, *m*

clipping *n* (of sheep, etc.) esquileo, *m;* (of a newspaper, etc.) recorte, *m*

clique *n* camarilla, *f*

cliquish *a* exclusivista

cloak *n* capa, *f;* manto, *m; fig* velo, *m. vt* encapotar; embozar; (conceal) ocultar, encubrir. **c. and sword play,** comedia de capa y espada, *f.* **c.-room,** guardarropa, *m;* (ladies') tocador, *m;* (on a station) consigna, *f*

clock *n* reloj, *m;* (of a stocking) cuadrado, *m.* **It is six o'clock,** Son las seis. **c.-face,** esfera de reloj, *f.* **c.-maker,** relojero, *m.* **c.-making,** relojería, *f.* **c.-work,** aparato de relojería, *m.* **to go like c.-work,** ir como un reloj. **c.-work train,** tren de cuerda, *m*

clockwise *a* and *adv* en el sentido de las agujas del reloj; de derecha a izquierda

clod *n* (of earth) terrón, *m;* (corpse) tierra, *f;* (person) zoquete, *m.* **c.-hopper,** patán, *m*

clog *n* (shoe) zueco, zoclo, *m;* (obstacle) estorbo, obstáculo, *m. vt* embarazar; estorbar, impedir; (block) obturar, cerrar; *fig* paralizar

cloister *n* claustro, *m;* convento, *m. vt* enclaustrar

cloistered *a* enclaustrado; retirado, aislado

cloistered nun *n* monja de claustro, *f*

close *a* estrecho; (of a prisoner) incomunicado; (reticent) reservado; (niggardly) tacaño, avaro; (scarce) escaso; (of friends) íntimo; (equal) igual; (lacking space) apretado; (dense) denso; (thick) tupido, compacto; (of a copy, etc.) fiel, exacto; (thorough) concienzudo; (careful) cuidadoso; (attentive) atento; (to the roots) a raíz; (of shaving) bueno; (of weather) pesado, sofocante; (of rooms) mal ventilado. **at c. quarters,** de cerca. **It is c. to eight o'clock,** Son casi las ocho. **to press c.,** perseguir de cerca; fatigar. **c. at hand, c. by,** cerca; al lado; a mano. **c.-cropped,** (of hair) al rape. **c. fight,** lucha igualada, *f.* **c.-fisted,** tacaño, apretado. **c.-fitting,** ajustado, ceñido al cuerpo; pequeño. **c. season,** veda, *f.* **c.-up,** *n* (cinema) primer plano, *m*

close *n* (end) fin, *m,* conclusión, *f;* (of day) caída, *f; mus* cadencia, *f;* (enclosure) cercado, *m;* (square) plazoleta, *f;* (alley) callejón, *m;* (of a cathedral) patio, *m.* **at the c. of day,** a la caída de la tarde. **to bring to a c.,** terminar; llevar a cabo. **to draw to a c.,** tocar a su fin; estar terminando

close *vt* cerrar; (end) concluir, terminar; poner fin a. *vi* cerrar(se); (of a wound) cicatrizarse, cerrarse; (end) terminar(se), acabar, concluir. **to c. the ranks,** cerrar filas. **to c. about,** (surround) rodear, cercar; (envelop) envolver. **to c. down,** *vt* cerrar. *vi* cerrar; *rad* cerrarse. **to c. in,** (surround) cercar; (of night) cerrar; caer; (envelop) envolver; (of length of days) acortarse. **to c. in on,** cercar. **to c. round,** envolver; (of water) tragar. **to c. up,** *vt* cerrar; cerrar completamente; obstruir. *vi* (of persons) acercarse; (of a wound) cicatrizarse; cerrar

closed *a* cerrado. **"Road C.,"** Paso Cerrado. **to have a c. mind,** ser cerrado de mollera; sufrir de estrechez de miras

closely *adv* estrechamente; de cerca; (carefully) cuidadosamente; (exactly) exactamente; (attentively) con atención, atentamente

closeness *n* estrechez, *f;* densidad, *f;* (nearness) proximidad, *f;* (of a copy, etc.) fidelidad, exactitud, *f;* (stuffiness), falta de aire, *f;* (of friendship) intimidad, *f;* (stinginess) tacañería, *f;* (reserve) reserva.

closet *n* camarín, *m;* (cupboard) alacena, *f;* (water) excusado, *m*

closing *n* cerramiento, *m;* (of an account) saldo, *m.* **c. time,** cierre, *m,* hora de cerrar, *f*

closure *n* conclusión, *f; pol* clausura, *f*

clot *n* coágulo, grumo, *m. vt* coagular. *vi* coagularse, cuajarse

cloth *n* tela, *f;* paño, *m;* (table) mantel, *m;* (clergy) clero, *m.* **She cleaned the books with a c.,** Ella limpió los libros con un paño. **in c.,** (of books) en tela

clothe *vt* vestir; cubrir; (with authority, etc.) revestir. **to c. oneself,** vestirse

clothes *n pl* vestidos, *m pl,* ropa, *f.* **a suit of c.,** un traje. **old c. shop,** ropavejería, *f.* **c.-basket,** cesta de la colada, *f.* **c.-brush,** cepillo para ropa, *m.* **c.-hanger,** percha, *f.* **c.-horse,** enjugador, *m.* **c.-line,** cuerda de la ropa, *f.* **c.-peg,** pinza de la ropa, *f.* **c.-prop,** palo para sostener la cuerda de la colada, *m*

clothier *n* ropero, *m.* **clothier's shop,** ropería, *f*

clothing *n* vestidos, *m pl,* ropa, *f.* **article of c.,** prenda de vestir, *f*

clotted *a* grumoso

cloud *n* nube, *f. vt* anublar, oscurecer; empañar; (blot out) borrar. *vi* anublarse. **to be under a c.,** estar bajo sospecha. **summer c.,** nube de verano, *f.* **storm-c.,** nubarrón, *m.* **c.-burst,** nubada, *f,* chaparrón, *m.* **c.-capped,** coronado de nubes

cloudiness *n* nebulosidad, *f;* obscuridad, *f;* (of liquids) turbiedad, *f*

cloudless *a* sin nubes, despejado; sereno, claro

cloudy *a* nublado, nubloso; obscuro; (of liquids) turbio

clove *n* clavo de especia, *m;* (of garlic) diente de ajo, *m.* **c.-tree,** clavero, *m*

cloven *a* hendido. **to show the c. hoof,** enseñar la oreja. **c. hoof,** pezuña, *f*

clover *n* trébol, *m.* **to be in c.,** nadar en la abundancia

clown *n* patán, *m;* bufón, tonto, *m;* (in a circus) payaso, *m. vi* hacer el tonto, hacer el payaso

clowning *n* payasada, *f*

clownish *a* grosero; palurdo, zafio; bufón

cloy *vt* empalagar

cloying *a* empalagoso

club *n* porra, cachiporra, clava, *f;* (gymnastic) maza, *f;* (hockey) bastón de hockey, *m;* (golf) palo de golf, *m;* (in cards) basto, *m;* (social) club, *m. vt* golpear. **to c. together,** asociarse, unirse. **We clubbed together to buy him a present,** Entre todos le compramos un regalo. **c.-house,** club, *m*

clubfoot *n* pie calcáneo, pie contrahecho, pie de piña, pie equino, pie talo, pie zambo, *m*

clubman *n* miembro de un club, *m*

cluck *vi* cloquear. *n* cloqueo, *m*

clucking *n* cloqueo, *m*

clue *n* indicio, *m;* (to a problem) clave, *f;* (of a crossword) indicación, *f;* idea, *f*

clump *n* bloque, pedazo, *m;* (of trees) grupo, *m;* (of feet) ruido, *m*

clumsily *adv* torpemente; pesadamente

clumsiness *n* torpeza, *f;* falta de maña, *f;* pesadez, *f*

clumsy *a* torpe; desmañado; chapucero, sin arte; (lumbering) pesado; (in shape) disforme

cluster *n* (of currants, etc.) racimo, *m;* (of flowers) ramillete, *m;* grupo, *m. vi* arracimarse; agruparse. **They clustered round him,** Se agrupaban a su alrededor

clutch *vt* agarrar; sujetar, apretar. *n mech* embrague, *m;* (of eggs) nidada, *f; fig* garras, *f pl.* **to fall into the clutches of,** caer en las garras de. **to make a c. at,** procurar agarrar. **to throw in the c.,** *mech* embragar. **to throw out the c.,** *mech* desembragar. **c. pedal,** pedal de embrague, *m*

clutter *n* desorden, *m,* confusión, *f, vt* desordenar

coach *n* carroza, *f;* charabán, *m; rw* vagón, coche, *m;*

(hackney) coche de alquiler, *m; sport* entrenador, *m;* (tutor) profesor particular, *m. vt sport* entrenar; (teach) preparar, dar lecciones particulares (a). **through c.,** coche directo, *m.* **c.-box,** pescante, *m.* **c.-house,** cochera, *f*

coaching *n sport* entrenamiento, *m;* lecciones particulares, *f pl*

coachman *n* cochero, *m*

coagulate *vi* coagularse. *vt* coagular, cuajar

coagulation *n* coagulación, *f*

coal *n* carbón, *m;* pedazo de carbón, *m;* (burning) brasa, *f. vi* carbonear, hacer carbón. *vt* proveer de carbón; carbonear. **to carry coals to Newcastle,** llevar leña al monte, elevar aqua al mar. **to haul a person over the coals,** reprender a alguien. **c.-barge,** (barco) carbonero, *m.* **c.-black,** negro como el azabache. **c.-cellar, house,** carbonera, *f.* **c.-dust,** cisco, *m.* **c.-field,** yacimiento de carbón, *m.* **c.-gas,** gas de hulla, *m.* **c.-heaver,** cargador de carbón, *m.* **c.-merchant,** carbonero, *m.* **c.-mine,** mina de carbón, *f.* **c.-miner,** minero de carbón, *m.* **c.-scuttle,** carbonera, *f.* **c.-tar,** alquitrán mineral, *m*

coalesce *vi* fundirse; unirse; incorporarse

coalescence *n* fusión, *f;* unión, *f;* incorporación, *f*

coalition *n* coalición, *f*

coarse *a* (in texture) basto; burdo; tosco; (gross) grosero; vulgar. **c.-grained,** de fibra gruesa; (of persons) vulgar, poco fino

coarsen *vt* (of persons) embrutecer. *vi* embrutecerse; (of the skin) curtirse

coarseness *n* basteza, *f;* tosquedad, *f;* (of persons) grosería, indelicadeza, *f;* vulgaridad, *f*

coast *n* costa, *f;* litoral, *m. vi* costear; deslizarse en un tobogán; dejar muerto el motor. **The c. is not clear,** Hay moros en la costa. **c.-guard,** guardacostas, *m.* **c.-line,** litoral, *m*

coastal *a* costanero, costero. **c. defences,** defensas costeras, *f pl*

coaster *n naut* barco costanero, barco de cabotaje, *m*

coasting *n naut* cabotaje, *m*

coat *n* abrigo, *m;* gabán, *m;* chaqueta, *f;* (animal's) capa, *f;* (of paint) mano, *f. vt* recubrir; (with paint, etc.) dar una mano de. **fur c.,** abrigo de pieles, *m.* **sports c.,** Americana sport, *f.* **c. of arms,** escudo de armas, *m.* **c. of mail,** cota de malla, *f.* **c.-hanger,** percha, *f*

coating *n* (of paint, etc.) capa, mano, *f*

co-author *n* coautor, *m*

coax *vt* instar; halagar; persuadir (a)

coaxing *n* ruegos, *m pl;* mimos, *m pl,* caricias, *f pl;* persuasión, *f. a* mimoso, zalamero; persuasivo

cob *n* (horse) jaca, *f;* (lump) pedazo, *m;* (swan) cisne macho, *m*

cobalt *n* cobalto, *m.* **c. blue,** azul cobalto, *m*

cobble *n* (stone) guijarro, *m, vt* (with stones) empedrar con guijarros; (shoes) remendar

cobbler *n* zapatero remendón, *m.* **cobbler's last,** horma, *f.* **cobbler's wax,** cerote, *m*

cobblestone *n* guijarro, *m,* piedra, *f*

cobelligerent *n* cobeligerante, *mf*

cobra *n* cobra, serpiente de anteojos, *f*

cobweb *n* telaraña, *f*

cobwebby *a* cubierto de telarañas; transparente; de gasa

cocaine *n* cocaína, *f*

coccyx *n* cóccix, *m, inf* rabadilla, *f*

cochlea *n* caracol (del oído), *m*

cock *n* gallo, *m;* (male) macho, *m;* (tap) grifo, *m,* espita, *f;* (of a gun) martillo, *m;* (weather-vane) veleta, *f;* (of hay) montón, *m. vt* (a gun) amartillar; (a hat) ladear; (raise) erguir, enderezar. **a cocked hat,** un sombrero de tres picos. **at half c.,** (of a gun) desamartillada *f.* **He cocked his head,** Erguió la cabeza. **The dog cocked its ears,** El perro aguzó las orejas. **to c. one's eye at,** lanzar una mirada (a). **c.-a-doodle-doo,** quiquiriquí, *m.* **c.-a-hoop,** triunfante, jubiloso; arrogante. **c.-crow,** canto del gallo, *m.* **c.-fight,** riña de gallos, *f.*

c.-of-the-walk, gallito, *m.* **c.-sure,** pagado de sí mismo; completamente convencido

cockerel *n* gallo joven, gallito, *m*

cocker spaniel *n* cóquer, *m*

cockle *n* (bivalve) bucarda, *f. vi* arrugarse; (warp) torcerse; doblarse. **c.-shell,** (pilgrims') concha, *f;* (boat) cascarón de nuez, *m*

Cockney *a* londinense, de Londres. *n* londinense, *mf*

cockpit *n* gallería, *f; aer* casilla del piloto, *f; fig* arena, *f*

cockroach *n* cucaracha, *f*

cockscomb *n* cresta de gallo, *f*

cocktail *vt* (drink) cótel, coctel, *m.* **to shake a c.,** mezclar un coctel. **c. party,** coctel *m.* **c. shaker,** cotelera, *f*

cocky *a* fatuo, presuntuoso

cocoa *n* cacao, *m*

coconut *n* coco, *m; inf* cabeza, *f.* **c. milk,** agua de coco, *f.* **c. shy,** pim, pam, pum, *m.* **c. tree,** cocotero, *m*

cocoon *n* capullo, *m*

cod *n* bacalao, *m.* **cod-liver oil,** aceite de hígado de bacalao, *m*

coddle *vt* criar con mimo, mimar, consentir

code *n* código, *m;* clave, *f;* (secret) cifra, *f. vt* poner en cifra. **signal c.,** *naut* código de señales, *m.* **c. word,** palabra de clave, *f*

codeine *n* codeína, *f*

codex *n* códice, *m*

codicil *n* codicilio, *m*

codification *n* codificación, *f*

codify *vt* codificar

coeducation *n* coeducación, *f*

coefficient *n* coeficiente, *m*

coequality *n* coigualdad, *f*

coerce *vt* forzar, obligar; constreñir

coercion *n* coerción, coacción, *f*

coercive *a* coercitivo, coactivo

coeval *a* coevo

coexist *vi* coexistir

coexistence *n* coexistencia, *f*

coffee *n* café, *m.* **black c.,** café solo, *m.* **white c.,** café con leche, *m.* **c.-bean,** grano de café, *m.* **c.-cup,** taza para café, *f.* **c.-house,** café, *m.* **c.-mill,** molinillo de café, *m.* **c.-plantation,** cafetal, *m.* **c.-pot,** cafetera, *f.* **c.-set,** juego de café, *m.* **c.-tree,** cafeto, *m*

coffer *n* cofre, *m;* arca, caja, *f*

coffin *n* ataúd, féretro, *m;* caja, *f*

cog *n mech* diente (de rueda), *m*

cogency *n* fuerza, *f*

cogent *a* convincente, fuerte; urgente

cogitate *vi* pensar, considerar, meditar

cogitation *n* reflexión, meditación, consideración, *f*

cognac *n* coñac, *m*

cognate *a* (of stock) consanguíneo; afín; análogo; semejante

cognition *n* cognición, *f*

cognitive *a* cognoscitivo

cognizance *n* conocimiento, *m;* jurisdicción, *f*

cogwheel *n* rueda dentada, *f*

cohabit *vi* cohabitar

cohabitation *n* cohabitación, *f*

coheir *n* coheredero, *m*

coheiress *n* coheredera, *f*

cohere *vi* pegarse, adherirse; unirse

coherent *a* coherente; consecuente

cohesion *n* cohesión, *f;* coherencia, *f*

cohort *n* cohorte, *f*

coif *n* cofia, *f;* toca, *f*

coiffure *n* peinado, *m;* tocado, *m*

coil *vt* arrollar; (*naut* of ropes) adujar. *vi* arrollarse; enroscarse; serpentear. *n* rollo, *m;* (of a serpent and ropes) anillo, *m;* (of hair) trenza, *f; elec* carrete, *m.* **coil of smoke,** nube de humo, *f.* **to c. up,** hacerse un ovillo

coiling *n* arrollamiento, *m;* serpenteo, *m*

coin *n* moneda, *f; inf* dinero, *m. vt* acuñar; (a new word) inventar. **to pay back in the same c.,** pagar en la misma moneda

coinage *n* acuñación, *f*; moneda, *f*; sistema monetario, *m*; invención, *f*; (new word) neologismo, *m*

coincide *vi* coincidir (con); estar conforme, estar de acuerdo

coincidence *n* coincidencia, *f*; (chance) casualidad, *f*

coiner *n* acuñador de moneda, *m*; monedero falso, *m*; (of phrases, etc.) inventor, *m*

coitus *n* coito, *m*

coke *n* (carbón de) coque, *m*

colander *n* colador, *m*

cold a frío. *n* frío, *m*; *med* catarro, constipado, *m*. **I am c.,** Tengo frío. **It is c.,** Está frío; (weather) Hace frío. **to catch a c.,** acatarrarse, resfriarse. **to grow c.,** enfriarse; (of the weather) empezar a hacer frío. **in c. blood,** a sangre fría. **c.-blooded,** (fishes, etc.) de sangre fría; (chilly, of persons) friolero; (pitiless) insensible, sin piedad; (of actions) a sangre fría, premeditado. **c.-chisel,** cortafrío, *m*. **c. cream,** crema (para el cutis), *f*. **c.-hearted,** seco, insensible. **c.-shoulder,** *n* frialdad, *f*. *vt* tratar con frialdad (a). **c.-storage,** conservación refrigerada, *f*

coldly *adv* fríamente

coldness *n* frío, *m*; (of one's reception, etc.) frialdad, *f*; (of heart) inhumanidad, *f*

coleopterous *a* coleóptero

colic *n* cólico, *m*

coliseum *n* coliseo, *m*

colitis *n* colitis, *f*

collaborate *vi* colaborar (con)

collaboration *n* colaboración, *f*

collaborationist *n* colaboracionista, *mf*

collaborator *n* colaborador (-ra); (quisling) colaboracionista, *mf*

collapse *n* derrumbamiento, *m*; desplome, *m*; *med* colapso, *m*; (of buildings and *fig*) hundimiento, *m*; (of plans) frustración, *f*; (failure) fracaso, *m*. *vi* derrumbarse; (of buildings, etc.) hundirse, venirse abajo; (of persons, fall) desplomarse; *med* sufrir colapso; (of plans, etc.) frustrarse, venirse abajo. **George came to us after the c. of France,** Jorge vino a quedarse con nosotros después del hundimiento de Francia

collapsible *a* plegable

collar *n* (of a garment and of fur) cuello, *m*; (of a dog, etc., and necklace) collar, *m*. *vt* (seize) agarrar. **detachable c.,** cuello suelto, *m*. **high c.,** alzacuello, *m*. **c.-bone,** clavícula, *f*

collate *vt* cotejar; (to a benefice) colacionar

collateral *a* colateral

collation *n* colación, *f*

colleague *n* colega, *m*; compañero (-ra)

collect *vt* (assemble) reunir; (catch) coger; acumular; (call for) pasar a buscar, ir (or venir) a buscar; (pick up) recoger; (taxes, etc.) recaudar; coleccionar; (one's strength, etc. and debts, etc.) cobrar; (letters) recoger. *vi* reunirse, congregarse; acumularse. *n ecc* colecta, *f*. **to c. oneself,** reponerse

collected *a* (of persons) seguro de sí.

collection *n* reunión, *f*; (of data, etc.) acumulación, *f*; (of pictures, stamps, etc.) colección, *f*; (of a debt, etc.) cobranza, *f*; (of taxes, etc.) recaudación, *f*; (from a mail box) recogida, *f*; (of laws, etc.) compilación, *f*; *ecc* ofertorio, *m*; (of donations) colecta, *f*

collection agency *n* agencia de cobros de cuentas, *f*

collective *a* colectivo. **c. bargaining,** regateo colectivo, trato colectivo, *m*

collectivism *n* colectivismo, *m*

collector *n* (of pictures, etc.) coleccionador (-ra), coleccionista, *mf*; cobrador, *m*; *elec* colector, *m*

college *n* colegio, *m*; escuela, *f*; universidad, *f*. **C. of Cardinals,** Colegio de Cardenales, *m*

collegiate *a* colegial, colegiado. **c. church,** iglesia colegial, *f*

collide *vi* chocar (contra), topar (con); estar en conflicto (con). **c. head-on,** chocar frontalmente

collie *n* perro de pastor escocés, *m*

collier *n* minero de carbón, *m*; (barco) carbonero, *m*

collision *n* choque, *m*, colisión, *f*; (of interests, etc.) antagonismo, conflicto, *m*. **to come into c. with,** chocar con

Cologne Colonia, *f*

colloid *a* coloide. *n* coloide, *m*

colloquial *a* familiar

colloquialism *n* expresión familiar, *f*

colloquially *adv* en lenguaje familiar; familiarmente

colloquy *n* coloquio, *m*

collusion *n* colusión, *f*. **to be in c.,** *law* coludir; conspirar, estar de manga

Colombia Colombia, *f*

Colombian *a* colombiano. *n* colombiano (-na)

colon *n anat* colon, *m*; (punctuation) dos puntos, *m pl*

colonel *n* coronel, *m*

colonial *a* colonial. *n* habitante de las colonias, *m*. **C. Office,** Ministerio de Asuntos Coloniales, *m*

colonist *n* colono, *m*; colonizador (-ra)

colonization *n* colonización, *f*

colonize *vt* colonizar. *vi* establecerse en una colonia

colonizer *n* colonizador (-ra)

colonizing *n* colonización, *f*, *a* colonizador

colonnade *n* columnata, *f*

colony *n* colonia, *f*

color *n* color, *m*; colorido, *m*; tinta, *f*; materia colorante, *f*; *pl* **colors,** insignia, *f*; bandera, *f*, estandarte, *m*; *naut* pabellón, *m*. *vt* colorear; pintar; iluminar; (influence) influir, afectar. *vi* colorarse; ruborizarse; encenderse. **fast c.,** color estable, color sólido, *m*. **regimental colors,** bandera del regimiento, *f*. **with colors flying,** con tambor batiente, a banderas desplegadas. **to be off c.,** estar maluco, estar indispuesto. **to change c.,** (of persons) mudar de color, mudar de semblante. **to give c. to,** (a story, etc.) hacer verosímil. **to lay the colors on too thick,** recargar las tintas. **to pass with flying colors,** salir triunfante. **under c. of,** so color de, a pretexto de. **c.-blind,** daltoniano. **c.-blindness,** daltonismo, *m*

Colorado beetle *n* escarabajo de la patata, *m*

colored *a* colorado; de color

colorimeter *n* colorímetro, *m*

coloring *n* (substance) colorante, *m*; (act of) coloración, *f*; *art* colorido, *m*; (of complexion) colores, *m pl*

colorist *n* colorista, *mf*

colorless *a* sin color, incoloro; *fig* insípido

colossal *a* colosal, gigantesco; enorme; *inf* estupendo

colossus *n* coloso, *m*

colt *n* potro, *m*; (boy) muchacho alegre, *m*

colter *n* reja, reja del arado, *f*

colt's-foot *n bot* fárfara, *f*

columbine *n bot* aguileña, *f*; (in pantomime) Colombina, *f*

column *n* columna, *f*. **Fifth c.,** quinta columna, *f*

columned *a* con columnas

columnist *n* periodista, *m*

coma *n* coma, *m*

comatose *a* comatoso

comb *n* peine, *m*; (for flax) carda, *f*; (curry) almohaza, *f*; (of cock) cresta, carúncula, *f*; (of a wave) cima, cresta, *f*; (honey) panal, *m*, *vt* (hair) peinar; (flax) rastrillar, cardar. **c. and brush,** cepillo y peine, *m*. **high c.,** peineta, *f*. **to c. one's hair,** peinarse

combat *vt* luchar contra, combatir, resistir. *vi* combatir, pelear. *n* combate, *m*; lucha, batalla, *f*. **in single c.,** cuerpo a cuerpo

combatant *n* combatiente, *m*, *a* combatiente

combative *a* belicoso, pugnaz

combination *n* combinación, *f*; mezcla, *f*; unión, *f*; asociación, *f*; *pl* **combinations.** camisa pantalón, *f*. **c. lock,** cerradura de combinación, *f*

combine *vt* combinar; reunir, juntar; *chem* combinar. *vi* combinarse; asociarse (con); *com* fusionarse. *n* asociación, *f*; *com* monopolio, *m*

combings *n pl* peinaduras, *f pl*

combustible *a* combustible. *n* combustible, *m*

combustion *n* combustión, *f*. **rapid c.,** combustión

rápida, *f.* **spontaneous c.**, combustión espontánea, *f*
come *vi* venir; llegar; avanzar; acercarse; (happen) suceder, acontecer; (result) resultar; (find oneself) encontrarse, hallarse; (become) llegar a ser; (begin to) ponerse (a), empezar (a). **Coming!** ¡Voy! ¡Allá voy! **C., c.!** ¡Vamos! ¡No es para tanto! ¡Ánimo! **I am ready whatever comes,** Estoy preparado venga lo que venga. **He comes of a good family,** Es (Viene) de buena familia. **I came to know him well,** Llegué a conocerle bien. **I don't know what came over me,** No sé lo que me pasó. **When I came to consider it,** Cuando me puse a considerarlo. **The bill comes to six thousand pesetas,** La cuenta sale a seis mil pesetas. **He comes up before the judge tomorrow,** Ha de comparecer ante el juez mañana. **What you say comes to this,** Lo que dice Vd. se reduce a esto. **What is the world coming to?** ¿A dónde va parar el mundo? **It does not c. within my scope,** No está dentro de mi alcance. **to c. apart,** deshacerse; romperse; dividirse. **to c. home to,** *fig* impresionar mucho, tocar en lo más íntimo; hacer comprender (a). **to c. into bloom,** empezar a tener flores, florecer. **to c. into one's head,** venir a las mientes. **to c. into the world,** venir al mundo. **to c. near,** acercarse; aproximarse, estar próximo. **to c. next,** venir después; suceder luego. **to c. to an end,** terminar, acabarse. **to c. to blows,** venir a las manos. **to c. to grief,** salir mal parado; (of schemes, etc.) malograrse. **to c. to hand,** venir a mano; (of letters) llegar a las manos (de). **to c. to life,** despertar; animarse; resucitarse. **to c. to nothing,** frustrarse; no quedar en nada. **to c. to pass,** suceder; realizarse. **to c. to terms,** ponerse de acuerdo. **to c. true,** cumplirse, verificarse. **to c. about,** suceder, acontecer, tener lugar; (of the wind) girar. **to c. across,** dar con, encontrar por casualidad; tropezar con. **to c. after,** (a situation) solicitar; (follow) seguir (a); venir más tarde (que); (succeed) suceder. **to c. again,** volver. **to c. along,** caminar (por); andar (por); (arrive) llegar. **C. along!** ¡Ven! ¡Vamos! ¡Andamos! **to c. at,** alcanzar; (attack) embestir, atacar; (gain) obtener, adquirir. **to c. away,** irse, marcharse; (break) deshacerse. **to c. back,** volver. **c.-back,** *n inf* respuesta, *f*; contraataque, *m*. **to c. before,** llegar antes; preceder (a). **to c. between,** interponerse (entre), intervenir. **to c. by,** pasar por, pasar junto a; (acquire) obtener, adquirir; (achieve) conseguir. **to c. down,** bajar, descender; (in the world) venir a menos; (be demolished) demolerse; (collapse) derrumbarse, hundirse; (of prices) bajar; (of traditions, etc.) llegar e.g. **This work has c. down to us in two fifteenth-century manuscripts** Esta obra nos ha llegado en dos manuscritos del siglo quince; (fall) caer. **c.-down,** *n* caída, *f*; frustración, *f*; desengaño, *m*; desprestigio, *m*; pérdida de posición, *f.* **to c. down on a person,** cantar la cartilla (a). **to c. forward,** avanzar, adelantarse; (offer) ofrecerse; presentarse. **to c. in,** entrar; (of money) ingresar; (of trains, etc.) llegar; (of the tide) crecer; (of the new year) empezar; (of fashion) ponerse de moda; (be useful) servir (para). **C. in!** ¡Adelante! ¡Pase Vd.! **to c. into,** (a scheme) asociarse con; (property) heredar; (the mind) presentarse a la imaginación, ocurrirse (a). **to c. off,** (happen) tener lugar; realizarse, efectuarse; (be successful) tener éxito; (break off) separarse (de); romperse. **to c. off well,** tener éxito; (of persons) salir bien. **c. off the press,** salir de prensas. **to c. on,** avanzar; (of actors) salir a la escena; (progress) hacer progresos; (develop) desarrollarse; (of pain, etc.) acometer (a); (arrive) llegar; (of a lawsuit) verse. **C. on!** ¡Vamos! ¡En marcha! **to c. out,** salir; (of stars) nacer; (of buds, etc.) brotar; (of the moon, etc.) asomarse; (of stains) borrarse, salir; (of a book) ver la luz, publicarse; (of secrets) divulgarse, saberse; (of a girl in society) ponerse de largo; (on strike) declararse en huelga; (of fashions, etc.) aparecer. **to c. out with,** (a remark) soltar; (oaths, etc.) prorrumpir (en); (disclose) revelar, hacer público. **to c. round,** (to see someone) venir a ver (a);

(coax) engatusar; (after a faint, etc.) volver en sí; (after illness) reponerse; (to another's point of view) aceptar, compartir. **to c. through,** pasar por; (trials, etc.) subir; salir de; (of liquids) salirse. **to c. to,** volver en sí. **to c. together,** reunirse, juntarse; venir juntos; unirse. **to c. under,** venir (or estar) bajo la jurisdicción de; (the influence of) estar dominado por; (figure among) figurar entre, estar comprendido en. **to c. up,** subir; (of sun, moon) salir; (of plants) brotar; (of problems, etc.) surgir; (in conversation) discutirse; (before a court) comparecer. **to c. up to,** (equal) igualar, ser igual (a); rivalizar con; (in height) llegar hasta. **He came up to them in the street,** Les abordó (or se les acercó) en la calle. **We have c. up against many difficulties,** Hemos tropezado con muchas dificultades. **This novel does not c. up to his last,** Esta última novela no es tan buena como la anterior. **The party did not c. up to their expectations,** La reunión no fue tan divertida como esperaban. **to c. up with,** (a person) alcanzar (a). **to c. upon,** encontrar, hallar; tropezar con; encontrar por casualidad. **to c. upon evil days,** venir a menos

comedian *n* actor cómico, comediante, *m*
comedy *n* comedia, *f.* **c. of manners,** comedia de costumbres, *f*
comeliness *n* hermosura, *f*
comely *a* hermoso
comer *n* el, *m*, (*f*, la) que viene. **all comers,** todo el mundo. **first c.,** primer (-ra) venido (-da)
comet *n* cometa, *m*
comfort *vt* consolar, confortar; (encourage) animar; (reassure) alegrar. *n* consuelo, *m*; satisfacción, *f*; comodidad, *f*; bienestar, *m*. **He lives in great c.,** Vive con mucha comodidad. **c.-loving,** comodón
comfortable *a* cómodo; (with income) suficiente; (consoling) consolador. **to make oneself c.,** ponerse cómodo
comfortably *adv* cómodamente; suficientemente; fácilmente; con facilidad; (well) bien. **He is c. off,** Está bien de dinero
comforter *n* consolador (-ra); (baby's) chupador, *m*; (scarf) bufanda, *f*
comforting *a* consolador
comfortless *a* incómodo, sin comodidad; desconsolador; (of persons) inconsolable, desconsolado
comic *a* cómico; bufo; satírico. *n* cómico, *m*; *pl* **comics,** (printed) historietas cómicas, *f pl.* **c. opera,** ópera cómica, *f.* **c. paper,** periódico satírico, *m*
comical *a* cómico; divertido, gracioso
coming *a* (with year, etc.) próximo, que viene; (promising) de porvenir; (approaching) que se acerca. *n* venida, *f*; llegada, *f*; advenimiento, *m*. **c.-out party,** puesta de largo, *f.* **comings and goings,** entradas y salidas, *f pl*
comma *n* coma, *f.* **inverted commas,** comillas, *f pl*
command *vt* mandar, ordenar; (silence, respect, etc.) imponer; (an army, fleet, etc.) comandar; capitanear; (one's emotions) dominar; (have at one's disposal) disponer de; (a military position, view) dominar; (sympathy, etc.) despertar, merecer; (of price) venderse por. *vi* mandar. *n* orden, *f*; (*mil nav*) mando, *m*; (of an army, etc.) comandancia, *f*; (of one's emotions, etc.) dominio, *m*; (of a military position, etc.) dominación, *f*; disposición, *f.* **By Royal C.,** Por Real Orden; (of shops, etc.) Proveedor de la Real Casa. **The house commands lovely views of the mountains,** La casa tiene hermosas vistas de las montañas. **word of c.,** orden, *f.* **Yours to c.,** A la disposición de Vd.
commandant *n* comandante, *m*
commandeer *vt* (conscript) reclutar; *mil* requisar; expropiar
commander *n mil* comandante, *m*; *nav* capitán de fragata, *m*; (of order of Knighthood) comendador, *m.* **c.-in-chief,** generalísimo, *m.* **C. of the Faithful,** Comendador de los creyentes, *m*
commanding *a mil* comandante; imponente; (of man-

ner) imperioso; dominante. **c. officer,** comandante en jefe, *m*

commandment *n* precepto, mandamiento, *m*. **the Ten Commandments,** los diez mandamientos

commando *n mil* comando, *m*

commemorate *vt* conmemorar

commemoration *n* conmemoración, *f*

commemorative *a* conmemorativo

commence *vt* comenzar, empezar, principiar. *vi* comenzar. **He commenced to eat,** Empezó a comer

commencement *n* principio, comienzo, *m*

commend *vt* (entrust) encomendar; recomendar; alabar

commendable *a* loable; recomendable

commendation *n* aprobación, alabanza, *f*, aplauso, *m*

commendatory *a* (of letters) comendatorio

commensurable *a* conmensurable

commensurate *a* proporcionado (a); conforme (a)

comment *n* observación, *f*; (on a work) comento, *m*; explicación, nota, *f*. *vi* hacer una observación (sobre); (a work) comentar, anotar. **to c. unfavorably on,** criticar

commentary *n* comentario, *m*; (on a person, etc.) comentos, *m pl,* observaciones, *f pl*

commentator *n* comentador (-ra); (of a work) comentarista, *mf*

commerce *n* comercio, *m*; negocios, *m pl*; (social) trato, *m*

commercial *a* comercial; mercantil. **c. traveler,** viajante, *mf*

commercialism *n* mercantilismo, *m*

commercialize *vt* hacer objeto de comercio

commercially *adv* comercialmente

commingle *vt* mezclar. *vi* mezclarse

commiserate *vi* compadecerse (de), apiadarse (de)

commiseration *n* conmiseración, compasión, *f*

commissariat *n* comisaría, *f*; *inf* despensa, *f*

commissary *n* comisario, *m*

commission *n* comisión, *f*; *mil* graduación de oficial, *f*. *vt* comisionar; (a ship) poner en servicio activo, armar; (appoint) nombrar. **in c.,** en servicio, activo. **out of c.,** (of ships) inutilizado; inservible. **c. agent,** comisionista, *mf* **to gain one's c.,** *mil* graduarse de oficial. **to put out of c.,** retirar del servicio; poner fuera de combate; estropear

commissionaire *n* portero, *m*

commissioned *a* comisionado. **c. officer,** oficial, *m*

commissioner *n* comisario, *m*. **High C.,** alto comisario, *m*. **c. for oaths,** notario, *m*. **c. of police,** jefe de policía, *m*

commit *vt* entregar (a); (a crime) cometer; (to prison) encarcelar; (for trial) remitir. **to c. oneself,** comprometerse. **to c. to memory,** aprender de memoria. **to c. to writing,** poner por escrito

commitment *n* (financial, etc.) obligación, responsabilidad, *f*; compromiso, *m*

committal *n* (of an offence) comisión, *f*; (placing, entrusting) entrega, *f*; (to prison) encarcelamiento, *m*; (legal procedure) auto de prisión, *m*

committee *n* comité, *m*; comisión, junta, *f*; consejo, *m*. **They decided in c.,** Tomaron la resolución en comité. **c. of management,** consejo de administración, *m*

commodious *a* espacioso, grande

commodiousness *n* espaciosidad, *f*

commodity *n* artículo, *m*, mercancía, *f*

commodore *n nav* jefe de escuadra, *m*; comodoro, *m*

common *a* común; general, corriente; universal; vulgar; (disparaging) cursi; (elementary) elemental. *n* pastos comunes, *m pl*. **He is not a c. man,** No es un hombre cualquiera; No es un hombre vulgar. **in c.,** en común. **the c. man,** el hombre medio. **the c. people,** el pueblo. **c. sense,** sentido común, *m*. **c. soldier,** soldado raso, *m*. **c. speech,** lenguaje vulgar, *m*. **c. usage,** uso corriente, *m*

commoner *n* plebeyo (-ya)

commonly *adv* comúnmente, por lo general

commonness *n* frecuencia, *f*; vulgaridad, *f*

commonplace *n* lugar común, *m*; trivialidad, *f*. *a* trivial

commons *n* el pueblo; (House of) Cámara de los Comunes, *f*; (food) provisiones, *f pl.* **to be on short c.,** comer mal, estar mal alimentado

Commonwealth *n* estado, *m*; república, *f*; comunidad (de naciones), *f*; mancomunidad, *f*. **the Commonwealth of Puerto Rico,** el Estado Libre Asociado de Puerto Rico, *m*

commotion *n* confusión, *f*; conmoción, perturbación, *f*; tumulto, *m*

communal *a* comunal

commune *n* comuna, *f*; comunión, *f*, *vi* conversar (con). **to c. with oneself,** hablar consigo

communicable *a* comunicable

communicant *n ecc* comulgante, *mf*; (of information) informante, *mf*

communicate *vt* comunicar; (diseases) transmitir. *vi* comunicarse (con); *ecc* comulgar

communication *n* comunicación, *f*. **lines of c.,** comunicaciones, *f pl.* **to get into c. with,** ponerse en comunicación con. **c.-cord,** (in a railway carriage) timbre de alarma, *m*

communicative *a* comunicativo; expansivo

communicativeness *n* carácter expansivo, *m*; locuacidad, *f*

communion *n* comunión, *f*. **Holy c.,** comunión, *f*. **to take c.,** comulgar. **c. card,** cédula de comunión, *f*. **c. cup,** cáliz, *m*. **c. table,** sagrada mesa, *f*; altar, *m*

communiqué *n* comunicación, parte, *f*. **to issue a c.,** dar parte

communism *n* comunismo, *m*

communist *n* comunista, *mf a* comunista

community *n* comunidad, *f*. **the c.,** la nación; el público. **c. center,** centro social, *m*

commutation *n* conmutación, *f*; reducción, *f*

commute *vt* conmutar; reducir

compact *n* (pact) acuerdo, pacto, *m*; (powder) polvorera, *f. a* compacto; firme; sólido; apretado, cerrado; (of persons) bien hecho; (of style) conciso, sucinto

compactness *n* compacidad, *f*; (of style) concisión, *f*

companion *n* compañero (-ra); camarada, *mf*; (of an Order) caballero, *m*, (or dama, *f*). *vt* acompañar. **lady c.,** señora de compañía, *f*. **c.-hatch,** cubierta de escotilla, *f*. **c.-ladder,** escala de toldilla, *f*

companionable *a* sociable, amistoso

companionably *adv* sociablemente, amistosamente

companionship *n* compañía, *f*; compañerismo, *m*

company *n* (*com mil* etc.) compañía, *f*; (ship's) tripulación, *f*. **I will keep you c.,** Te haré compañía. **to part c. with,** separarse de. **Present c. excepted!** ¡Mejorando lo presente! **They are not very good c.,** No son muy divertidos

company store *n* tienda de raya, *f* (Mexico)

comparable *a* comparable

comparably *adv* comparablemente

comparative *a* comparativo; relativo

comparatively *adv* comparativamente; relativamente

compare *vt* comparar. *vi* compararse; poder compararse. **beyond c.,** sin comparación; sin igual. **to c. favorably with,** no perder por comparación con. **to c. notes,** cambiar impresiones

comparison *n* comparación, *f*. **in c. with,** comparado con

compartment *n* compartimiento, *m*; *rw* departamento, *m*

compass *n* circuito, *m*; límites, *m pl*; alcance, *m*; (of a voice) gama, *f*; *naut* brújula, *f*; *pl* **compasses,** compás, *m*. *vt* (achieve) conseguir; (plan) idear, **mariner's c.,** compás de mar. *m*, rosa de los vientos, *f*. **pocket c.,** brújula de bolsillo, *f*. **to c. about,** cercar, rodear

compassion *n* compasión, *f*. **to have c. on,** apiadarse de, compadecerse de

compassionate *a* compasivo, piadoso. **c. leave,** permiso, *m*

compassionately *adv* compasivamente, con piedad

compatibility *n* compatibilidad, *f*
compatible *a* compatible, conciliable
compatriot *n* compatriota, *mf*
compel *vt* obligar (a), forzar (a); exigir; imponer. **His attitude compels respect,** Su actitud impone el respeto
compelling *a* compulsivo
compendious *a* compendioso, sucinto
compendium *n* compendio, *m*; resumen, *m*
compensate *vt* compensar; (reward) recompensar; (for loss, etc.) indemnizar. **to c. for,** compensar; indemnizar contra
compensation *n* compensación, *f*; (reward) recompensa, *f*; (for loss, etc.) indemnización, *f*
compensatory *a* compensatorio
compete *vi* competir (con); rivalizar; ser rivales; (in a competition) concurrir
competence *n* aptitud, *f*; capacidad, *f*; competencia, *f*
competent *a* competente; capaz
competently *adv* competentemente
competition *n* competencia, competición, rivalidad, *f*; emulación, *f*; (contest, etc.) concurso, *m*. **spirit of c.,** espíritu de competencia, *m*
competitive *a* competidor; de competición. **c. examination,** oposición, *f*
competitor *n* competidor (-ra)
compilation *n* compilación, *f*
compile *vt* compilar
compiler *n* compilador (-ra)
complacence *n* complacencia, satisfacción, *f*; contento de sí mismo, *m*
complacent *a* satisfecho; pagado de sí mismo
complacently *adv* con satisfacción
complain *vi* quejarse; lamentarse; *law* querellarse. **He complains about everything,** Se queja de todo
complainant *n* *law* demandante, *mf*
complaint *n* queja, *f*; lamento, *m*; *law* demanda, *f*; (illness) enfermedad, *f*. **to lodge a c. (against),** quejarse (de)
complaisance *n* afabilidad, cortesía, *f*
complaisant *a* complaciente, cortés, afable; (of husbands) consentido, sufrido
complement *n* complemento, *m*; total, número completo, *m*. *vt* completar
complementary *a* complementario
complete *a* entero; completo; perfecto; acabado. *vt* completar; acabar; (happiness, etc.) coronar, poner el último toque (a); (years) cumplir; (forms) llenar
completely *adv* completamente, enteramente
completeness *n* entereza, *f*; totalidad, *f*
completion *n* terminación, *f*, fin, *m*
complex *a* complejo. *n* complejo, *m*. **inferiority c.,** complejo de inferioridad, *m*
complexion *n* tez, *f*, cutis, *m*; *fig* carácter, *m*
complexity *n* complejidad, *f*
compliance *n* condescendencia, *f*; (subservience) sumisión, *f*; obediencia, *f*. **in c. with,** de acuerdo con, en conformidad con
compliant *a* condescendiente; sumiso, dócil; obediente
complicate *vt* complicar
complicated *a* complejo; complicado; enredado
complication *n* complicación, *f*
complicity *n* complicidad, *f*. **c. in a crime,** complicidad en un crimen
compliment *n* cumplido, *m*, cortesía, *f*; requiebro, *inf* piropo, *m*; favor, *m*; honor, *m*; (greeting) saludo, *m*; (congratulation) felicitación, *f*. *vt* cumplimentar; requebrar; (flatter) adular, lisonjear; (congratulate) felicitar. **They did him the c. of reading his book,** Le hicieron el honor de leer su libro. **to pay compliments,** hacer cumplidos; *inf* echar piropos
complimentary *a* lisonjero; galante. **c. ticket,** billete gratuito, *m*
comply *vi* (with) cumplir, obedecer; conformarse (con); consentir
component *a* componente. *n* componente, *m*

comport *vt* (oneself), comportarse
comportment *n* comportamiento, *m*, conducta, *f*
compose *vt* (all meanings) componer. **to c. oneself,** serenarse, calmarse. **to c. one's features,** componer el semblante
composed *a* sereno, tranquilo, sosegado
composer *n* compositor (-ra)
composite *a* compuesto; mixto. *n* compuesto, *m*; *bot* planta compuesta, *f*
composition *n* (all meanings) composición, *f*
compositor *n* *print* cajista, *mf*
composure *n* tranquilo, serenidad, calma, *f*; sangre fría, *f*, aplomo, *m*
compote *n* compota, *f*
compound *vt* mezclar, componer; concertar. *a* compuesto. *n* compuesto, *m*; mixtura, *f*. **c. interest,** interés compuesto, *m*
comprehend *vt* comprender
comprehensible *a* comprensible
comprehensibly *adv* comprensiblemente
comprehension *n* comprensión, *f*
comprehensive *a* comprensivo
comprehensiveness *n* alcance, *m*, extensión, *f*
compress *vt* comprimir; condensar; reducir, abreviar. *n* compresa, *f*
compression *n* compresión, *f*
compressor *n* compresor, *m*
comprise *vt* comprender, abarcar, incluir
compromise *n* compromiso, *m*, transacción, *f*; componenda, *f*. *vt* (settle) componer, arreglar; (jeopardize) arriesgar; comprometer. *vi* transigir. **to c. oneself,** comprometerse
compromising *a* comprometedor
comptometer *n* calculador, *m*
compulsion *n* compulsión, fuerza, *f*. **under c.,** a la fuerza
compulsory *a* obligatorio. **c. measures,** medidas obligatorias, *f pl.* **c. powers,** poderes absolutos, *m pl*
compunction *n* compunción, *f*, remordimiento, *m*; escrúpulo, *m*. **without c.,** sin escrúpulo
computable *a* calculable
computation *n* computación, *f*, cómputo, *m*
compute *vt* computar, calcular
computer *m* computador, *m* (Western Hemisphere), ordenador, *m* (Spain)
computer center *n* centro calculador, centro de computación, *m*
comrade *n* camarada, *mf* compañero (-ra)
comradeship *n* compañerismo, *m*
con *vt* estudiar; leer con atención; *naut* gobernar (el buque)
concatenation *n* concatenación, *f*
concave *a* cóncavo
conceal *vt* esconder, ocultar; (the truth, etc.) encubrir, callar; disimular
concealed *a* oculto; escondido; disimulado. **c. lighting,** iluminación indirecta, *f*. **c. turning,** (on a road) viraje oculto, *m*
concealment *n* ocultación, *f*; encubrimiento, *m*; (place of) escondite, *m*; secreto, *m*
concede *vt* conceder
conceit *n* presunción, vanidad, fatuidad, *f*, envanecimiento, *m*. **to have a good c. of oneself,** estar pagado de sí mismo
conceited *a* presumido, fatuo, vanidoso
conceivable *a* concebible, imaginable
conceivably *adv* posiblemente
conceive *vt* concebir; (affection, etc.) tomar; (an idea, etc.) formar; (plan) formular, idear. *vi* concebir; (understand) comprender; (suppose) imaginar, suponer
concentrate *vt* concentrar. *vi* concentrarse; (on, upon) dedicarse (a), entregarse (a); prestar atención (a), concentrar atención (a)
concentrated *a* concentrado
concentration *n* concentración, *f*. **c. camp,** campo de concentración, *m*

concentric *a* concéntrico

concept *n* concepto, *m*

conception *n* concepción, *f;* conocimiento, *m;* idea, *f,* concepto, *m.* **to have not the remotest c. of,** no tener la menor idea de

conceptualism *n* conceptualismo, *m*

concern *vt* tocar, tener que vercon, importar, concernir; interesar; referirse (a); tratar (de); (trouble) preocupar, inquietar; (take part in) ocuparse (de or con). *n* asunto, *m,* cosa, *f;* (share) interés, *m;* (anxiety) inquietud, *f;* solicitud, *f;* (business) casa comercial, firma, *f.* **as concerns . . . ,** en cuanto a . . . , respecto a . . . **It concerns the date of the next meeting,** Es cuestión de la fecha de la próxima reunión. **It is no c. of yours,** No tiene nada que ver contigo. **The book is concerned with the adventures of two boys,** El libro trata de las aventuras de dos muchachos

concerned *a* ocupado (en); afectado (en); (in a crime) implicado (en); (troubled) preocupado; inquieto, agitado

concerning *prep* tocante a, con respecto a, referente a, sobre

concert *n* acuerdo, concierto, *m,* armonía, *f; mus* concierto, *m, vt* concertar, acordar. **in c. with,** de acuerdo con. **c. hall,** sala de conciertos, *f*

concerted *a* concertado

concertina *n* concertina, *f*

concerto *n* concierto, *m*

concession *n* concesión, *f;* privilegio, *m*

concessionaire *n* concesionario, *m*

concierge *n* conserje, *m*

conciliate *vt* conciliar

conciliation *n* conciliación, *f*

conciliatory *a* conciliador

concise *a* conciso, breve, sucinto

concisely *adv* concisamente

concision *n* concisión, *f*

conclave *n* conciliábulo, *m;* (of cardinals) conclave, *m*

conclude *vt* concluir. *vi* concluirse

conclusion *n* conclusión, *f.* **in c.,** en conclusión, para terminar. **to come to the c. that . . . ,** concluir que . . .

conclusive *a* conclusivo, concluyente, decisivo

conclusively *adv* concluyentemente

conclusiveness *n* carácter decisivo, *m,* lo concluyente

concoct *vt* confeccionar; inventar

concoction *n* confección, *f;* mezcla, *f;* invención, *f;* (of a plot) maquinación, *f*

concomitant *a* concomitante. *n* concomitante, *m*

concord *n* concordia, buena inteligencia, armonía, *f;* (mus gram) concordancia, *f;* (of sounds) armonía, *f*

concordance *n* concordia, armonía, *f;* (book) concordancias, *f pl*

concordat *n* concordato, *m*

concourse *n* concurrencia, muchedumbre, *f*

concrete *a* concreto; de hormigón. *n* hormigón, *m. vt* concretar; cubrir de hormigón. **reinforced c.,** hormigón armado, *m*

concretion *n* concreción, *f*

concubine *n* concubina, manceba, *f*

concur *vi* coincidir, concurrir; estar de acuerdo, convenir (en)

concurrence *n* (agreement) acuerdo, consentimiento, *m,* aprobación, *f*

concurrent *a* concurrente; unánime; coincidente

concurrently *adv* concurrentemente

concussion *n* concusión, *f; med* concusión cerebral, *f*

condemn *vt* condenar; censurar, culpar; (forfeit) confiscar. **condemned cell,** celda de los condenados a muerte, *f*

condemnation *n* condenación, *f;* censura, *f*

condensation *n* condensación, *f*

condense *vt* condensar. *vi* condensarse

condenser *n* (elec mech chem) condensador, *m*

condescend *vi* dignarse; (in a bad sense) consentir (en); (with affability) condescender

condescending *a* condescendiente

condescendingly *adv* con condescendencia

condescension *n* condescendencia, *f;* afabilidad, *f*

condign *a* condigno

condiment *n* condimento, *m*

condition *n* condición, *f;* estado, *m; pl* **conditions,** condiciones, *f pl;* circunstancias, *f pl.* **on c. that,** con tal que; siempre que, dado que. **to be in no c. to,** no estar en condiciones de. **to change one's c.,** cambiar de estado. **to keep oneself in c.,** mantenerse en buena forma

conditional *a* condicional. **to be c. on,** depender de

conditionally *adv* condicionalmente

conditioned *a* acondicionado. **c. reflex,** reflejo acondicionado, *m*

condole *vi* condolerse (de); (on a bereavement) dar el pésame

condolence *n* condolencia, *f.* **to present one's condolences,** dar el pésame

condom *n* condón, *m*

condone *vt* condonar, perdonar

conduce *vi* contribuir, conducir

conducive *a* que contribuye, conducente; favorable

conduct *n* conducta, *f. vt* conducir; guiar; *mus* dirigir; (oneself) portarse, conducirse; *phys* conducir. *vi mus* dirigir (una orquesta, etc.); *phys* ser conductor. **conducted tour,** excursión acompañada, *f;* viaje acompañado, *m*

conduction *n* conducción, *f*

conductive *a* conductivo

conductivity *n* conductibilidad, *f*

conductor *n* (guide) guía, *mf;* (of an orchestra) director, *m;* (on a tram, etc.) cobrador, *m; phys* conductor, *m*

conduit *n* conducto, *m;* cañería, *f;* canal, *m*

cone *n* (bot geom etc.) cono, *m*

confabulation *n* confabulación, *f*

confection *n* confección, *f, vt* confeccionar

confectioner *n* confitero (-ra); pastelero (-ra)

confectionery *n* confitería, pastelería, repostería, *f*

confederate *a* confederado; aliado. *n* confederado, *m;* (in crime) cómplice, *mf. vt* confederar. *vi* confederarse; aliarse

confederation *n* confederación, *f*

confer *vt* conceder, conferir; (an honor, etc.) otorgar, investir (con). *vi* consultar (con); deliberar, considerar

conference *n* conferencia, consulta, *f;* conversación, *f*

conferment *n* otorgamiento, *m;* concesión, *f*

confess *vt* confesar, reconocer; *inf* admitir; (of a priest) confesar; (of a penitent) confesarse. *vi* hacer una confesión; (one's sins) confesarse. **I c. that I was surprised,** No puedo negar que me sorprendió

confessed *a* confesado, declarado

confession *n* confesión, *f;* reconocimiento, *m;* declaración, *f;* religión, *f;* (creed) credo, *m.* **to go to c.,** confesarse. **to hear a c.,** confesar (a)

confessional *n* confesionario, *m*

confessor *n* confesor, *m*

confetti *n pl* confeti, papel picado *m,* serpentina, *f*

confidant *n* confidente, *m*

confidante *n* confidenta, *f*

confide *vi* confiar (a or en). *vt* confiar

confidence *n* confianza, *f;* seguridad, *f;* (revelation) confidencia, *f.* **in c.,** en confianza. **over-c.,** presunción, *f.* **to have c. in,** tener confianza en. **c. man,** caballero de industria, estafador, *m.* **c. trick,** timo, *m*

confident *a* confiado; seguro; (conceited) presumido

confidential *a* confidencial; de confianza. **c. clerk,** empleado (-da) de confianza. **c. letter,** carta confidencial, *f*

confidentially *adv* en confianza, confidencialmente

confidently *adv* confiadamente

confiding *a* confiado

confidingly *adv* con confianza

configuration *n* configuración, *f*

confine *vt* limitar; (imprison) encerrar. **confined space,** espacio limitado, *m.* **to be confined,** (of a woman) estar de parto, parir. **to be confined to one's**

room, no poder dejar su cuarto. **to c. oneself to,** limitarse a

confinement *n* encierro, *m,* prisión, *f;* reclusión, *f;* (of a woman) parto, *m.* **to suffer solitary c.,** estar incomunicado

confines *n pl* límites, *m pl;* confines, *m pl;* fronteras, *f pl*

confirm *vt* confirmar; corroborar; *ecc* confirmar

confirmation *n* confirmación, *f;* (of a treaty) ratificación, *f; ecc* confirmación, *f*

confirmatory *a* confirmatorio

confirmed *a* inveterado

confiscate *vt* confiscar

confiscation *n* confiscación, *f*

conflagration *n* conflagración, *f,* incendio, *m*

conflict *n* conflicto, *m;* lucha, *f. vi* estar opuesto (a), estar en contradicción (con)

conflicting *a* opuesto; incompatible; (of evidence) contradictorio

confluence *n* confluencia, *f*

conform *vt* ajustar, conformar. *vi* ajustarse (a), amoldarse (a); conformarse (a); adaptarse (a)

conformation *n* conformación, *f*

conformity *n* conformidad, *f.* **in c. with,** en conformidad con, con arreglo a

confound *vt* confundir. **C. it!** ¡Demonio!

confounded *a* perplejo; *inf* maldito

confraternity *n* cofradía, hermandad, *f*

confront *vt* hacer frente (a), afrontar; salir al paso; confrontar

Confucianism *n* el confucianismo, *m*

confuse *vt* turbar, aturdir; confundir (con); (the issue) obscurecer; (disconcert) desconcertar, dejar confuso (a); dejar perplejo (a). **You have confused one thing with another,** Has confundido una cosa con otra. **My mind was confused,** Mis ideas eran confusas; Tenía la cabeza trastornada

confused *a* confuso

confusing *a* turbador; desconcertante. **It is all very c.,** Todo ello es muy difícil de comprender

confusion *n* confusión, *f.* **covered with c.,** confuso, avergonzado. **to be in c.,** estar confuso; estar en desorden

confute *vt* (a person) confundir; (by evidence) refutar, confutar

congeal *vt* congelar; (blood) coagular. *vi* congelarse, helarse; coagularse

congealment *n* congelación, *f;* (of blood) coagulación, *f*

congenial *a* (of persons) simpático; propicio, favorable; agradable

congenital *a* congénito

congest *vt* atestar; amontonar; *med* congestionar

congested *a med* congestionado; (of places) atestado de gente; (of mayor densidad de población. **c. area,** área de mayor densidad de población; concurrido. **c. area,** área de mayor densidad de población

congestion *n med* congestión, *f;* densidad del tráfico, *f;* mayor densidad de población, *f*

conglomerate *a* conglomerado. *n* conglomerado, *m*

conglomeration *n* conglomeración, *f*

congratulate *vt* felicitar, dar la enhorabuena (a); congratular

congratulation *n* felicitación, enhorabuena, *f;* congratulación, *f*

congratulatory *a* de felicitación, congratulatorio

congregate *vi* congregarse, reunirse, juntarse

congregation *n* congregación, *f;* asamblea, reunión, *f;* (in a church) fieles, *m pl;* (parishioners) feligreses, *m pl*

congress *n* congreso, *m.* **C.-man,** miembro del Congreso, *m*

conical *a* cónico

conifer *n* conífera, *f*

coniferous *a* conífero

conjectural *a* conjetural

conjecture *n* conjetura, *f,* *vt* conjeturar

conjoint *a* asociado, conjunto

conjointly *adv* juntamente, en común

conjugal *a* conyugal

conjugate *vt* conjugar. *vi* conjugarse

conjugation *n* conjugación, *f*

conjunction *n* conjunción, *f.* **in c. with,** de acuerdo con

conjunctive *a* conjuntivo. *n* conjunción, *f*

conjunctivitis *n* conjuntivitis, *f*

conjure *vt* (implore) rogar, suplicar. *vi* (juggle) hacer juegos de manos. **a name to c. with,** un nombre todopoderoso. **to c. up,** (spirits) conjurar; *fig* evocar

conjurer, conjuror *n* (magician) nigromante, *m;* prestidigitador, *m.* **conjuror's wand,** varilla de virtudes, *f*

conjuring *n* prestidigitación, *f,* juegos de manos, *m pl.* **c. trick,** juego de manos, *m.* **c. up,** evocación, *f*

connect *vt* juntar, unir; (relate) relacionar; asociar; (elec and *mech)* conectar. *vi* juntarse, unirse; relacionarse; asociarse; (of events) encadenarse; (of trains) enlazar. **This train connects with the Madrid express,** Este tren enlaza con el expreso de Madrid. **They are connected with the Borgia family,** Están emparentados con los Borgia, Son parientes de los Borgia

connected *a* conexo; (coherent) coherente; relacionado; asociado; (in a crime) implicado; (by marriage, etc.) emparentado

connectedly *adv* coherentemente

connecting *a* que une; (mech and elec) conectivo; (of doors, etc.) comunicante. **c.-link,** *mech* varilla de conexión, *f; fig* lazo, *m.* **c.-rod,** biela, *f*

connection, connexion *n* conexión, *f;* unión, *f;* (of ideas) relación, *f;* (junction) empalme, *m;* (of trains, boats) enlace, *m;* (intimacy) intimidad, *f;* (relative) pariente, *m;* (of a firm, etc.) clientela, *f; elec* conexión, *f.* **in c. with,** con referencia a; en asociación con. **in this c.,** respecto a esto

conning tower *n* torre de mando, *f*

connivance *n* consentimiento, *m;* complicidad, *f*

connive (at) *vi* hacer la vista gorda, ser cómplice (en)

connotation *n* connotación, *f*

connote *vt* connotar

connubial *a* conyugal

conquer *vt* conquistar; vencer. *vi* triunfar

conquering *a* conquistador, vencedor; triunfante, victorioso

conqueror *n* conquistador, *m;* vencedor, *m*

conquest *n* conquista, *f.* **to make a c. of,** conquistar

consanguineous *a* consanguíneo

consanguinity *n* consanguinidad, *f*

conscience *n* conciencia, *f.* **in all c.,** en verdad. **with a clear c.,** con la conciencia limpia. **c.-stricken,** lleno de remordimientos

conscienceless *a* desalmado, falto de conciencia

conscientious *a* concienzudo; diligente. **c. objector,** objetor de conciencia, *m*

conscientiously *adv* concienzudamente

conscientiousness *n* conciencia, diligencia, *f;* rectitud, *f*

conscious *a* consciente. *n psy* consciente, *m.* **to become c.,** (after unconsciousness) volver en sí. **to become c. of,** darse cuenta de

consciously *adv* conscientemente, a sabiendas

consciousness *n* conciencia, *f;* conocimiento, sentido, *m.* **to lose c.,** perder el conocimiento, perder el sentido. **to recover c.,** recobrar el sentido, volver en sí

conscript *n* conscripto, *m, a* conscripto. *vt* reclutar

conscription *n* conscripción, *f*

consecrate *vt* consagrar; bendecir

consecration *n* consagración, *f;* dedicación, *f*

consecutive *a* consecutivo

consecutively *adv* consecutivamente

consensus *n* consenso, *m,* unanimidad, *f.* **c. of opinion,** opinión general, *f*

consent *vi* consentir. *n* consentimiento, *m;* permiso, *m,* aquiescencia, *f.* **by common c.,** de común acuerdo

consequence *n* consecuencia, *f;* resultado, *m;* importancia, *f*, **in c.**, por consiguiente. **in c. of**, de resultas de. **of no c.**, sin importancia

consequences *n* (game) cartas rusas, *f pl*

consequent *a* consecuente, consiguiente

consequential *a* consecuente; (of persons) fatuo, engreído

consequently *adv* por consiguiente, en consecuencia

conservation *n* conservación, *f*. **c. of energy,** conservación de energía, *f*

conservatism *n* conservadurismo, *m*

conservative *a* preservativo; conservador. *n* conservador (-ra). **c. party,** partido conservador, *m*

conservatoire *n* conservatorio de música, *m*

conservatory *n* invernáculo, invernadero, *m*

conserve *vt* conservar

consider *vt* considerar, pensar meditar; tomar en cuenta; examinar; (deem) juzgar; (believe) creer, estar convencido de (que); (of persons) considerar. **all things considered,** considerando todos los puntos, después de considerarlo todo

considerable *a* considerable

considerably *adv* considerablemente

considerate *a* considerado, solícito

considerately *adv* con consideración, solícitamente

consideration *n* consideración, *f*; reflexión, deliberación, *f*; remuneración, *f*. **out of c. for,** en consideración de; por consideración a. **to take into c.,** tomar en cuenta, tomar en consideración

considered *a* considerado

considering *prep* en consideración de, considerando, en vista de

consign *vt* consignar; *fig* enviar. **to c. to oblivion,** sepultar en el olvido

consignee *n* consignatorio, *m*

consignment *n* consignación, *f*; envío, *m*

consignor *n* consignador, *m*

consist *vi* consistir (en); ser compatible (con). **to c. of,** componerse de, consistir de

consistence, consistency *n* consistencia, *f*; compatibilidad, *f*; lógica, *f*; (of persons) consecuencia, *f*

consistent *a* compatible; lógico; (of persons) consecuente

consistently *adv* conformemente (a); consecuentemente

consolation *n* consuelo, *m*, consolación *f*

console *vt* consolar; confortar. *n arch* cartela, *f*. **c. table,** consola, *f*

consolidate *vt* consolidar. *vi* consolidarse

consolidation *n* consolidación, *f*

consoling *a* consolador; confortador

consols *n pl* (títulos) consolidados, *m pl*

consonance *n* consonancia, *f*

consonant *a* consonante

consort *n* consorte, *mf*. **to c. with,** frecuentar la compañía de; ir con; acompañar (a). **prince c.,** príncipe consorte, *m*

conspicuous *a* conspicuo; prominente; notable. **to be c.,** destacarse; llamar la atención. **to make oneself c.,** ponerse en evidencia, llamar la atención

conspicuously *adv* visiblemente; muy en evidencia

conspiracy *n* conspiración, *f*; complot, *m*

conspirator *n* conspirador (-ra)

conspire *vi* conspirar

constable *n* agente de policía, *m*; (historical) condestable, *m*. **chief c.,** jefe de policía, *m*

constabulary *n* policía, *f*

constancy *n* constancia, *f*

constant *a* constante; incesante. *n* constante, *m*

Constantinople Constantinopla, *f*

constantly *adv* constantemente

constellation *n* constelación, *f*

consternation *n* consternación, *f*; espanto, terror, *m*

constipate *vt* estreñir

constipation *n* estreñimiento, *m*, constipación de vientre, *f*

constituency *n* distrito electoral, *m*

constituent *a* constituyente. *n* constituyente, *m*; componente, *m*; elector (-ra)

constitute *vt* constituir; nombrar; autorizar

constitution *n* constitución, *f*

constitutional *a* constitucional

constitutionally *adv* constitucionalmente

constrain *vt* obligar, forzar. **I felt constrained to help them,** Me sentí obligado a ayudarles

constrained *a* (of smiles, etc.) forzado; (of silences) violento; (of persons) avergonzado

constraint *n* fuerza, compulsión, *f*; (of atmosphere) tensión, *f*; (reserve) reserva, *f*; vergüenza, *f*

constrict *vt* apretar, estrechar

constriction *n* constricción, *f*

construct *vt* edificar; construir

construction *n* construcción, *f*; interpretación, *f*. **to put a wrong c. on,** interpretar mal

constructional *a* construccional

constructive *a* constructor

constructor *n* constructor, *m*

construe *vt* construir; (translate) traducir; *fig* interpretar

consul *n* cónsul, *m*

consular *a* consular

consular fees *n pl* derechos consulares, *m pl*

consulate *n* consulado, *m*. **c. general,** consulado general, *m*

consult *vt* consultar. *vi* consultar (con), aconsejarse (con)

consultant *n* (*med* and other uses) especialista, *m*

consultation *n* consulta, *f*

consultative *a* consultativo

consulting *a* consultor. **c. hours,** horas de consulta, *f pl*. **c. rooms,** consultorio, *m*

consume *vt* consumir; (eat) comerse, tragarse. *vi* consumirse. **to be consumed by envy,** estar consumido por la envidia. **to be consumed by thirst,** estar muerto de sed

consumer *n* consumidor (-ra)

consummate *a* consumido, perfecto. *vt* consumar

consummation *n* consumación, *f*

consumption *n* consumo, *m*; gasto, *m*; *med* tuberculosis, *f*. **fuel c.,** consumo de combustible, *m*

consumptive *a* destructivo; *med* tísico, hético. *n* tísico (-ca)

contact *n* contacto, *m*, *vt* ponerse en contacto con. **to be in c. with,** estar en contacto con

contagion *n* contagio, *m*

contagious *a* contagioso

contain *vt* contener; incluir; *geom* encerrar; (arithmetic) ser divisible por; (oneself) dominarse. **I could not c. myself,** No pude dominarme

container *n* recipiente, *m*; envase, *m*; (box) caja, *f*

contaminate *vt* contaminar; corromper

contamination *n* contaminación, *f*

contemplate *vt* contemplar; meditar, considerar; (plan) tener intención de, pensar, proponerse

contemplation *n* contemplación, *f*; meditación, *f*; expectación, esperanza, *f*; (plan) proyecto, *m*. **to have something in c.,** proyectar algo

contemplative *a* contemplativo

contemplatively *adv* contemplativamente; atentamente

contemporaneous *a* contemporáneo

contemporary *a* contemporáneo; (of persons) coetáneo; (of events, etc.) actual. *n* contemporáneo (-ea)

contempt *n* desprecio, menosprecio, *m*; desdén, *m*. **c. of court,** falta de respeto a la sala, *f*

contempt of court *n* rebeldía a la corte, *f*

contempt of law *n* rebeldía a la ley, *f*

contemptible *a* menospreciable, despreciable; vil

contemptibly *adv* vilmente

contemptuous *a* desdeñoso; despectivo; de desprecio. **to be c. of,** desdeñar; menospreciar, tener en poco (a)

contemptuously *adv* con desprecio, desdeñosamente

contend *vi* contender; (affirm) sostener, mantener. **He contended that . . .** , Sostuvo que . . . ; **contending party,** *law* parte litigante, *f*

content *n* contenido, *m*; capacidad, *f*; (emotion) contento, *m*; satisfacción, *f. a* contento; satisfecho (de). *vt* contentar; satisfacer. **to one's heart's c.**, a pedir de boca; a gusto de uno; cuanto quisiera

contented *a* satisfecho, contento

contentedly *adv* con satisfacción, contentamente

contention *n* disputa, controversia, discusión, *f*; argumento, *m*, opinión, *f*

contentious *a* contencioso

contentment *n* contentamiento, *m*; contento, *m*

contest *vt* disputar; (a suit) defender; (a match, an election, etc.) disputar. *n* disputa, *f*; combate, *m*, lucha, *f*; (competition) concurso, *m*

contestant *n* contendiente, *mf*

context *n* contexto, *m*

contiguity *n* contigüidad, *f*

contiguous *a* contiguo, lindero, adyacente

continence *n* continencia, *f*

continent *a* continente. *n* continente, *m*

continental *a* continental

continental shelf *n* plataforma continental, *f*

contingency *n* contingencia, *f*

contingent *a* contingente. *n mil* contingente, *m*. **to be c. on,** (of events) depender de

continual *a* continuo

continually *adv* continuamente

continuance *n* continuación, *f*

continuation *n* continuación, *f*; prolongación, *f*

continue *vi* continuar; seguir; prolongarse; durar. *vt* continuar; seguir; proseguir; perpetuar; (in an office) retener. **to be continued,** se continuará, continuará, seguirá

continuer *n* continuador (-ra)

continuity *n* continuidad, *f*

continuous *a* continuo. **c. performance,** sesión continua, *f*

continuously *adv* de continuo, continuamente

contort *vt* retorcer

contortion *n* contorsión, *f*

contortionist *n* contorsionista, *m*

contour *n* contorno, *m*; curva de nivel, *f*. **c. map,** mapa con curvas de nivel, *m*

contraband *n* contrabando, *m*

contrabandist *n* contrabandista, *mf*

contrabass *n* contrabajo, *m*

contraception *n* anticoncepción, *f*

contraceptive *n* anticonceptivo, *m*

contract *n* pacto, *m*; (*com* and *law*) contrato, *m*; (betrothal) esponsales, *m pl*; (marriage) capitulaciones, *f pl*; (cards) "Bridge," *m. vt* contraer; (acquire) adquirir, contraer; (a marriage, etc.) contraer; (be betrothed to) desposarse con; (by formal contract) contratar; pactar. *vi* (shrink) contraerse, encogerse; comprometerse por contrato. **breach of c.,** no cumplimiento de contrato, *m.* **c. party,** (of matrimony) contrayente, *mf*

contractile *a* contráctil

contraction *n* contracción, *f* (act or process); forma contracta, *f* (like *isn't* or *can't*)

contractor *n* contratista, *mf*

contradict *vt* contradecir; desmentir

contradiction *n* contradicción, *f*; negación, *f*

contradictory *a* contradictorio; opuesto (a), contrario (a)

contralto *n* (voice) contralto, *m*; (woman) contralto, *f*

contraption *n inf* artefacto, *m*

contrapuntal *a mus* de contrapunto

contrariness *n inf* testarudez, terquedad, *f*

contrariwise *adv* al contrario; al revés

contrary *a* contrario; opuesto (a); desfavorable, poco propicio; (of persons) difícil, terco. *n* contraria, *f*; (logic) contrario, *m*, *adv* en contra, contrariamente. **on the c.,** al contrario. **to be c.,** (of persons) llevar la contraria

contrast *n* contraste, *m. vt* contrastar (con). *vi* contrastar (con), hacer contraste (con)

contravene *vt* contravenir; atacar, oponerse (a)

contravention *n* contravención, *f*

contribute *vt* contribuir; (an article) escribir

contribution *n* contribución, *f*; (to a review, etc.) artículo, *m*

contributor *n* contribuyente, *mf*; (to a journal) colaborador (-ra)

contributory *a* contribuyente

contrite *a* penitente, arrepentido, contrito

contritely *adv* contritamente

contrition *n* contrición, penitencia, *f*, arrepentimiento, *m*

contrivance *n* invención, *f*; (scheme) treta, idea, estratagema, *f*; (machine) aparato, mecanismo, artefacto, *m*

contrive *vt* inventar; idear, proyectar. *vi* (succeed in) lograr, conseguir; (manage) arreglárselas

control *n* autoridad, *f*; dominio, *m*; gobierno, *m*; dirección, *f*; regulación, *f*; (restraint) freno, *m*; (*biol* and *spirit*) control, *m*; (of a vehicle) conducción, *f*; manejo, *m*, manipulación, *f*; *pl* **controls,** *mech* mando, *m. vt* dirigir, regir; regular; usar, manejar, manipular; controlar; (dominate) dominar; (curb) refrenar, reprimir; (command) mandar. **He lost c. of the car,** Perdió el mando (or control) del automóvil. **out of c.,** fuera de mando, fuera de control. **remote c.,** mando a distancia, *m.* **to c. oneself,** dominarse, contenerse. **to lose c. of oneself,** no lograr dominarse, perder el control. **c. stick,** *aer* palanca de mando, *f.* **c. tower,** *aer* torre de mando, *f*

controller *n* interventor, *m*; (device) regulador, *m*

controlling *n* See **control.** *a* regulador

controversial *a* debatible, discutible

controversy *n* controversia, *f*; argumento, *m*; altercación, disputa, *f*

contumacious *a* contumaz

contumacy *n* contumacia, *f*

contumely *n* contumelia, *f*

contusion *n* herida contusa, *f*

conundrum *n* acertijo, rompecabezas, *m*; problema, *m*

convalesce *vi* convalecer, estar convaleciente

convalescence *n* convalecencia, *f*

convalescent *a* convaleciente. *n* convaleciente, *mf*. **c. home,** casa de convalecencia, *f*

convene *vt* (a meeting) convocar; (person) citar. *vi* reunirse

convenience *n* conveniencia, *f*; (comfort) comodidad, *f*; utilidad, *f*; (advantage) ventaja, *f*; (public) retretes, *m pl*. **at one's c.,** cuando le sea conveniente a uno. **to make a c. of,** abusar de. **with all modern conveniences,** con todo el confort moderno

convenient *a* conveniente; apropiado; cómodo. **I shall make it c. to see him at 6 p.m.,** Arreglaré mis asuntos para verle a las seis

conveniently *adv* cómodamente; oportunamente; sin inconveniente

convent *n* convento, *m*

convention *n* convención, *f*

conventional *a* convencional

conventual *a* conventual. *n* conventual, *m*

converge *vi* convergir

convergence *n* convergencia, *f*

convergent *a* convergente

conversance *n* familiaridad, *f*, conocimiento, *m*

conversant *a* familiar, versado, conocedor. **c. with,** versado en

conversation *n* conversación, *f.* **to engage in c. with,** entablar conversación con

conversational *a* de conversación; (talkative) locuaz

conversationally *adv* en tono familiar; familiarmente; en conversación

converse *vi* conversar. **to c. by signs,** hablar por señas

conversely *adv* recíprocamente

conversion *n* conversión, *f*

convert *vt* convertir; transformar. *n* converso (-sa). **to become a c.,** convertirse

convertible *a* convertible; transformable

convex *a* convexo

convey *vt* transportar; conducir, llevar; (a meaning, etc.) comunicar, dar a entender; expresar; *law* traspasar

conveyance *n* transporte, *m*; conducción, *f*; medio de transporte, *m*; vehículo, *m*; carruaje, *m*; (of property) traspaso, *m*; (document) escritura de traspaso, *f*. **public c.,** coche de alquiler, *m*; ómnibus, *m*

convict *n* convicto, *m*; presidiario, *m*. *vt law* condenar; culpar. **c. settlement,** colonia penal, *f*

conviction *n* (of a prisoner) condenación, *f*; (belief) convencimiento, *m*, convicción, *f*

convince *vt* convencer

convincing *a* convincente

convivial *a* convivial

conviviality *n* jovialidad, *f*

convocation *n* convocación, *f*

convoke *vt* convocar

convolution *n* circunvolución, *f*; espira, *f*

convoy *vt* convoyar, escoltar. *n* convoy, *m*. **to sail in a c.,** navegar en convoy

convulse *vt* agitar; sacudir; estremecer. **to be convulsed with laughter,** desternillarse de risa, morirse de risa

convulsion *n* convulsión, *f*; conmoción, *f*

convulsive *a* convulsivo

coo *vi* arrullar; (of infants) gorjearse. *n* arrullo, *m*

cooing *n* arrullo, *m*

cook *n* cocinero (-ra). *vt* guisar, cocer, cocinar; (falsify) falsear

cooker *n* cocina, *f*. **gas c.,** cocina de gas, *f*

cookery *n* cocina, *f*. **c.-book,** libro de cocina, *m*

cooking *n* arte de guisar, *m*, or *f*; cocina, *f*; (of accounts, etc.) falsificación, *f*. **c. range,** cocina económica, *f*. **c.-stove,** cocina, *f*. **c. utensils,** batería de cocina, *f*

cool *a* fresco; bastante frío; (not ardent and of receptions, etc.) frío; (calm) sereno, imperturbable. *n* fresco, *m*. *vi* enfriarse; (of love, etc.) resfriarse; (of the weather) refrescar; (of persons) refrescarse. *vt* refrescar; enfriar. **to grow cooler,** (of weather) refrescarse; (of persons) tener menos calor. **It is c.,** Hace fresco. **to be as c. as a cucumber,** tener sangre fría. **c. drink,** bebida fría, *f*. **c.-headed,** sereno, imperturbable

coolie *n* culí, *m*

cooling *n* enfriamiento, *m*, *a* refrescante

coolly *adv* frescamente; fríamente, con frialdad; imperturbablemente; (impudently) descaradamente

coolness *n* frescura, *f*; (of a welcome, etc.) frialdad, *f*; (sangfroid) sangre fría, serenidad, *f*; aplomo, *m*

coop *n* gallinero, *m*; caponera, *f*, *vt* enjaular; encerrar. **to keep** (someone) **cooped up,** tener encerrado (a)

cooper *n* tonelero, barrilero, *m*, *vt* hacer barriles

cooperate *vi* cooperar; colaborar

cooperation *n* cooperación, *f*

cooperative *a* cooperativo. **c. society,** cooperativa, *f*

coopt *vt* elegir por votación

coordinate *vt* coordinar. *n math* coordenada, *f*. *a* coordenado

coordination *n* coordinación, *f*

coot *n* fúlica, *f*

cop *n* (police officer) chapa (Ecuador), polizonte, *mf*

copartner *n* copartícipe, *mf*; socio (-ia)

cope *n ecc* capa, *f*; (of heaven) dosel, *m*, bóveda, *f*. **to c. with,** contender con; (a difficulty) hacer cara a, arrostrar

copeck *n* copec, *m*

Copenhagen Copenhague, *m*

Copernican *a* copernicano

copier *n* copiador (-ra)

coping *n arch* albardilla, *f*. **c.-stone,** teja cumbrera, *f*; *fig* coronamiento, *m*

copious *a* copioso, abundante

copiously *adv* en abundancia

copiousness *n* abundancia, *f*

copper *n* cobre, *m*; (coin) calderilla, *f*; (vessel) caldera, *f*. *a* de cobre. **c.-colored,** cobrizo. **c.-smith,** calderero, *m*. **c.-sulphate,** sulfato de cobre, *m*

copperplate *n* lámina de cobre, *f*; grabado en cobre, *m*

coppery *a* cobrizo

coppice *n* soto, bosquecillo, *m*. **c. with standards,** monte medio, *m*

coproprietor *n* copropietario, *m*

copse *n* arboleda, *f*, bosquecillo, *m*

Coptic *a* cóptico, copto. *n* (language) copto, cóptico, *m*

copulate *vi* copularse

copulation *n* cópula, *f*

copy *n* copia, *f*; (of a book) ejemplar, *m*; (of a paper) número, *m*; manuscrito, *m*; (subject-matter) material, *m*. *vt* copiar; imitar; tomar como modelo (a). **rough c.,** borrador, *m*. **c.-book,** cuaderno de escritura, *m*

copy editor *n* redactor de textos, *m*

copying *n* imitación, *f*; transcripción, *f*. **c. ink,** tinta de copiar, *f*

copyist *n* copiador (-ra); (plagiarist) copiante, *mf*

copyright *n* derechos de autor, *m pl*; propiedad literaria, *f*. *a* protegido por los derechos de autor. *vt* registrar como propiedad literaria. **C. reserved,** Derechos reservados, Queda hecho el depósito que marca la ley

copywriter *n* escritor de anuncios, *m*

coquet *vi* coquetear; *fig* jugar (con)

coquetry *n* coquetería, *f*

coquette *n* coqueta, *f*

coquettish *a* coquetón; atractivo

coral *n* coral, *m*; (polyp) coralina, *f*. *a* de coral, coralino. **white c.,** madrépora, *f*. **c. beads,** corales, *m pl*. **c.-island,** atalón, *m*. **c.-reef,** escollo de coral, *m*. **c. snake,** coral, *f*

corbel *n arch* ménsula, *f*

cord *n* cuerda, *f*; cordel, *m*; cordón, *m*. *vt* encordelar. **spinal c.,** médula espinal, *f*. **umbilical c.,** cordón umbilical, *m*

cordial *a* cordial; sincero, fervoroso. *n* cordial, *m*

cordiality *n* cordialidad, *f*

cordon *n* cordón, *m*; cinto, *m*. **to c. off,** acordonar

Cordova Córdoba, *f*

cordovan *a* cordobés. *n* (leather) cordobán, *m*

corduroy *n* pana de cordoncillo, *f*

core *n* (of a fruit) corazón, *m*; (of a rope) alma, *f*, centro, *m*; (of an abscess) foco, *m*; (of a corn) ojo, *m*; *fig* núcleo, *m*; esencia, *f*; lo esencial

coreligionist *n* correligionario (-ia)

corespondent *n* cómplice en un caso de divorcio, *mf*

Corinth Corinto, *m*

Corinthian *a* corintio. *n* corintio (-ia)

cork *n* corcho, *m*; (of a bottle) tapón, *m*, *a* de corcho. *vt* tapar con corcho, taponar; (wine) encorchar; (the face) tiznar con corcho quemado. **pop of a c.,** taponazo, *m*. **to draw a c.,** descorchar. **c.-jacket,** chaleco salvavidas, *m*. **c. tree,** alcornoque, *m*

corkscrew *n* sacacorchos, *m*

cormorant *n* cormorán, *m*

corn *n* grano, cereal, *m*; (wheat) trigo, *m*; (maize) maíz, *m*; (single seed) grano, *m*; (on the foot, etc.) callo, *m*. **Indian c.,** maíz, *m*. **c. cure,** callicida, *m*. **c.-exchange,** bolsa de granos, *f*. **c.-field,** campo de trigo, *m*. **c.-flower,** aciano, *m*

cornea *n* córnea, *f*

corner *n* ángulo, *m*; (of a street or building) esquina, *f*; (of a room) rincón, *m*; *aut* viraje, *m*; *com* monopolio, *m*; (of the eye) rabo, *m*; (Assoc. football) "corner," *m*. *vt* arrinconar; acorralar; *com* acaparar. **the four corners of the earth,** las cinco partes del mundo. **a tight c.,** un lance apretado, un apuro. **to drive into a c.,** *fig* poner entre la espada y la pared. **to look out of the c. of the eye,** mirar de reojo. **to turn the c.,** doblar la esquina; *fig* pasar la crisis. **c.-cupboard,** rinconera, *f*. **c. seat,** asiento del rincón, *m*. **c.-stone,** piedra angular, *f*.

cornered *a* (of a person) acorralado, en aprieto; (of

hats) de . . . picos. **three-c. hat,** sombrero de tres picos, *m*

cornet *n* (musical instrument) corneta, *f*; mil corneta, *m*; (paper) cucurucho, *m*. **c.** **player,** cornetín, *m*

cornflour *n* harina de maíz, *f*

cornice *n* cornisa, *f*

Cornish *a* de Cornualles

cornucopia *n* cornucopia, *f*

corollary *n* corolario, *m*

corona *n* (*ast arch*) corona, *f*

coronation *n* coronación, *f*

coroner *n* juez de guardia, *mf*, médico forense, *m*

coronet *n* (of a peer, etc.) corona, *f*; tiara, *f*; guirnalda, *f*

corporal *a* corporal, *n* mil cabo, *m*; (altar-cloth) corporal, *m*. **c. punishment,** castigo corporal, *m*

corporate *a* corporativo

corporation *n* corporación, *f*; concejo, cabildo municipal, *m*; (*com* U.S.A.) sociedad anónima, *f*

corporeal *a* corpóreo

corps *n* cuerpo, *m*

corpse *n* cadáver, *m*

corpulence *n* gordura, obesidad, *f*

corpulent *a* corpulento, grueso, gordo

corpus *n* cuerpo, *m*. **C. Christi,** Corpus, *m*. **c. delicti,** cuerpo del delito, *m*

corpuscle *n* corpúsculo, *m*

correct *a* correcto; exacto, justo. *vt* corregir; rectificar; amonestar, reprender

correction *n* corrección, *f*; rectificación, *f*

corrective *a* correctivo. *n* correctivo, *m*

correctness *n* corrección, *f*; exactitud, *f*; justicia, *f*

correlate *vt* poner en correlación. *vi* tener correlación

correlation *n* correlación, *f*

correspond *vi* corresponder (a); (by letter) escribirse, corresponderse

correspondence *n* correspondencia, *f*; *com* correo, *m*. **c. course,** curso por correspondencia, *m*

correspondent *n* correspondiente, *mf*; (*com* and journalist) corresponsal, *mf*. **special c.,** corresponsal extraordinario, *m*

corresponding *a* correspondiente. **c. member,** miembro correspondiente, *m*

corridor *n* corredor, pasillo, *m*; (railway) pasillo, *m*; *pol* corredor, *m*. **c. train,** tren con coches corridos, *m*

corroborate *vt* corroborar, confirmar

corroboration *n* corroboración, confirmación, *f*

corroborative *a* corroborativo, confirmatorio

corrode *vt* corroer, morder; *fig* roer

corrosion *n* corrosión, *f*

corrosive *a* corrosivo; mordaz

corrugate *vt* arrugar. *vi* arrugarse

corrugated *a* arrugado; ondulado. **c. iron,** chapa canaleta, *f*

corrugation *n* corrugación, *f*, arrugamiento, *m*

corrupt *a* corrompido; vicioso, desmoralizado. *vt* corromper. *vi* corromperse

corrupter *n* corruptor (-ra)

corruption *n* corrupción, *f*

corsage *n* corpiño, *m*

corset *n* corsé, *m*, *vt* encorsetar. **c. shop,** corsetería, *f*

Corsica Córcega, *f*

Corsican *a* corso. *n* corso (-sa)

cortege *n* séquito, acompañamiento, *m*; desfile, *m*

cortex *n bot anat* corteza, *f*

cortisone *n* (drug) cortisona, *f*

Corunna La Coruña, *f*

coruscation *n* brillo, *m*

corvette *n* corbeta, *f*

cosignatory *n* cosignatario (-ia)

cosine *n* coseno, *m*

cosiness *n* comodidad, *f*

cosmetic *a* cosmético. *n* afeite, cosmético, *m*

cosmic *a* cósmico

cosmographer *n* cosmógrafo, *m*

cosmography *n* cosmografía, *f*

cosmopolitan *a* cosmopolita. *n* cosmopolita, *mf*

cosmopolitanism *n* cosmopolitismo, *m*

cosmos *n* cosmos, universo, *m*

Cossack *a* cosaco. *n* cosaco (-ca)

cosset *vt* mimar, consentir

cost *vi* costar. *n* costa, *f*, coste, precio, *m*; *fig* costa, *f*; *pl* **costs,** *law* costas, *f pl*. **at all costs,** cueste lo que cueste, a toda costa. **to my c.,** a mi costa. **c. of living,** coste de la vida, *m*. **to c. a fortune,** costar un sentido

Costa-Rican *a* costarriqueño. *n* costarriqueño (-ña)

coster *n* vendedor (-ra) ambulante

costliness *n* alto precio, *m*; suntuosidad, *f*

costly *a* costoso; suntuoso, magnífico

costume *n* traje, *m*; (fancy-dress) disfraz, *m*; (tailored) traje sastre, *m*; "Costume," (among credits in films and plays) «Vestuario»

costumier *n* modista, *mf*; sastre, *m*

cot *n* (hut) choza, cabaña, *f*; (child's) camita, *f*

coterie *n* círculo, grupo, *m*; (clique) camarilla, *f*

cotillion *n* cotillón, *m*

cottage *n* cabaña, choza, *f*; casita, *f*, hotelito, *m*; torre, villa, *f*

cotter *n* chaveta, llave, *f*

cotton *n* algodón, *m*, *a* de algodón. **I don't c. to the idea at all,** No me gusta nada la idea; La idea no me seduce. **sewing-c.,** hilo de coser, *m*. **c. goods,** géneros de algodón, *m pl*. **c. mill,** hilandería de algodón, algodonería, *f*. **c. plantation,** algodonal, *m*. **c.-seed oil,** aceite de semilla de algodón, *m*. **c.-spinner,** hilandero (-ra) de algodón. **c.-wool,** algodón en rama, *m*. **c.-yarn,** hilo de algodón, *m*

cottony *a* algodonoso

couch *n* sofá, canapé, *m*; (bed) lecho, *m*; (lair) cama, *f*. *vt* (lay down) acostar, echar; (a lance) enristrar; (express) expresar, redactar. *vi* acostarse; (crouch) agacharse; estar en acecho

cough *vi* toser. *n* tos, *f*. **to c. up,** escupir, expectorar. **c.-drop,** pastilla para la tos, *f*

coughing *n* tos, *f*

could. See **can**

council *n* consejo, *m*; junta, *f*; *ecc* concilio, *m*. **Privy C.,** consejo privado, *m*. **C. of the Realm,** Concejo del Reino, *m*. **to hold c.,** celebrar un consejo; aconsejarse (con); consultarse. **town c.,** ayuntamiento, *m*. **c. chamber,** sala consistorial, *f*; sala de actos, *f*. **c. houses,** casas baratas, *f pl*. **c. of war,** consejo de guerra, *m*

councilor *n* concejal, *m*; miembro de la junta, *m*

counsel *n* consultación, *f*; deliberación, *f*; consejo, *m*; *law* abogado, *m*. *vt* aconsejar. **a c. of perfection,** un ideal imposible. **to keep one's own c.,** no decir nada, callarse, guardar silencio. **to take c. with,** consultar (a), aconsejarse con

counselor *n* consejero, *m*. **c. of state,** consejero de estado, *m*

count *vt* contar; calcular; (consider) creer, considerar. *vi* contar. *n* cuenta, *f*; (of votes) escrutinio, *m*; *law* capítulo, *m*. **John simply doesn't c.,** Juan no cuenta para nada. **Erudition alone counts for very little,** La mera erudición sirve para muy poco. **to keep c. of,** tener cuenta de. **to lose c. of,** perder cuenta de. **to c. on,** contar con; (doing something) esperar. **to c. up,** contar

count *n* (title) conde, *m*

countenance *n* semblante, *m*; expresión de la cara, *f*; aspecto, *m*; (favor) apoyo, *m*, ayuda, *f*. *vt* autorizar, aprobar; apoyar, ayudar. **to put (a person) out of c.,** desconcertar (a)

counter *n* (in a bank) contador, *m*; (in a shop) mostrador, *m*; (in games) ficha, *f*, *adv* contra, al contrario; al revés. *a* opuesto (a), contrario (a). *vt* parar; contestar. **to run c. to my inclinations,** oponerse a mis deseos. **to c. with the left,** (boxing) contestar con la izquierda. **c.-attack,** contraataque, *m*. **c.-attraction,** atracción contraria, *f*. **c.-offensive,** contraofensiva, *f*.

c.-reformation, contrarreforma, *f.* **c.-revolution,** contrarevolución, *f*

counteract *vt* neutralizar; frustrar

counterbalance *n* contrapeso, *m, vt* contrabalancear; compensar, igualar

counterblast *n* denunciación, *f*; respuesta, *f*

countercharge *n* recriminación, *f. vt* recriminar; *law* reconvenir

counterfeit *a* falso, espurio; fingido. *n* falsificación, *f*; imitación, *f*; moneda falsa, *f*; (person) impostor (-ra). *vt* imitar; (pretend) fingir; (coins, handwriting, etc.) falsificar

counterfeiter *n* falsario (-ia)

counterfoil *n* talón, *m*

countermand *vt* contramandar; (an order) revocar, cancelar. *n* contraorden, *f*; revocación, *f*

countermarch *n* contramarcha, *f*

countermeasure *n* contramedida, *f*

counterpane *n* sobrecama, colcha, *f*

counterpart *n* contraparte, *f*; (of a document) duplicado, *m*

counterplot *n* contratreta, *f*

counterpoint *n mus* contrapunto, *m*

counterpoise *n* contrapeso, *m*; equilibrio, *m, vt* contrabalancear, contrapesar

countersign *n* contraseña, *f, vt* refrendar

countess *n* condesa, *f*

counting *n* cuenta, *f*; numeración, *f*; (of votes) escrutinio, *m.* **c.-house,** contaduría, *f*

countless *a* innumerable. **a c. number,** un sinfín, un sinnúmero

countrified *a* rústico, campesino

country *n* país, *m*; (fatherland) patria, *f*; región, campiña, tierra, *f*; (as opposed to town) campo, *m. a* del campo; campesino, campestre, rústico. **He lives in the c.,** Vive en el campo. **c. club,** club campestre, *m.* **c. cousin,** provinciano (-na). **c.-dance,** baile campestre, *m.* **c. gentleman,** hacendado, *m.* **c. girl,** campesina, *f*; aldeana, *f.* **c.-house,** finca, *f*; casa de campo, *f.* **c. life,** vida del campo, *f.* **c.-seat,** finca, *f*

countryman *n* campesino, *m*; hombre del campo, *m*; compatriota, *m*

countryside *n* campo, *m*; campiña, *f*

countrywoman *n* campesina, *f*; compatriota, *f*

county *n* condado, *m*; provincia, *f.* **c. council,** diputación provincial, *f.* **c. town,** cabeza de partido, *f*; ciudad provincial, *f*

county seat *n* cabecera municipal, cabeza de partido, *f*

coup *n* golpe, *m.* **c. d'état,** golpe de estado, *m*

coupe *n* cupé, *m*

couple *n* par, *m*; (in a dance, etc.) pareja, *f. vt* enganchar, acoplar; (in marriage) casar; (animals) aparear; (ideas) asociar; (names) juntar. **the young (married) c.,** el matrimonio joven

couplet *n* copla, *f*

coupling *n* enganche, acoplamiento, *m*; (of railway carriages) enganche, *m*; (of ideas) asociación, *f*

coupon *n* talón, *m*; cupón, *m*

courage *n* valor, *m.* **C.!** ¡Ánimo! **to muster up c.,** cobrar ánimo

courageous *a* valiente

courageously *adv* valientemente

courier *n* correo, *m*, estafeta, *f*; (guide) guía, *m*; (newspaper) estafeta, *f*

course *n* curso, *m*; (of time) transcurso, *m*; (of events) marcha, *f*; (of a river, etc.) cauce, *m*; (of stars) carrera, *f*, curso, *m*; (of a ship) derrota, *f*, rumbo, *m*; (way) camino, *m*, ruta, *f*; (of conduct) línea de conducta, *f*; actitud, *f*; (of study) curso, *m*; (of a meal) plato, *m*; (of an illness) desarrollo, *m*; *med* tratamiento, *m.* **He took it as a matter of c.,** Lo tomó sin darle importancia. **in due c.,** a su tiempo debido. **in the c. of time,** andando el tiempo, en el transcurso de los años. **of c.,** claro está; naturalmente. **Are you coming tomorrow? Of c.!** ¿Vienes mañana? ¡Ya lo creo! **the best c. to take,** lo mejor que se puede hacer, el mejor plantamiento, *m*

course *vt* cazar, perseguir; *poet* correr por, cruzar. *vi* (of blood, etc.) correr; cazar

court *n* (yard) patio, *m*; (tennis) campo de tenis, *m*; (fives, racquets) cancha, *f*; (royal) corte, *f*; (of justice) tribunal, *m*; (following) séquito, acompañamiento, *m. vt* hacer la corte (a); cortejar, pretender; solicitar; (sleep) conciliar. **to pay c. to,** (a woman) galantear, pretender; (a person) hacer la rueda (a). **to respect the c.,** *law* guardar sala. **c. of appeal,** sala de apelación, *f.* **c. of justice,** sala de justicia, *f*; tribunal de justicia, *m.* **supreme c.,** tribunal supremo, *m.* **c.-card,** figura, *f.* **c.-dress,** traje de corte, *m.* **c. house,** palacio de justicia, *m.* **c. jester,** bufón, *m.* **c.-martial,** tribunal militar, *m.* **c.-plaster,** tafetán inglés, tafetán de heridas, *m.* **c.-room,** sala de justicia, *f*

courteous *a* cortés

courteousness *n* cortesía, *f*

courtesan *n* cortesana, *f*

courtesy *n* cortesía, *f*; favor, *m*, merced, *f*; permiso, *m*

courtier *n* cortesano, palaciego, *m*

courtliness *n* cortesía, urbanidad, *f*; dignidad, *f*; elegancia, *f*

courtly *a* cortés, galante; digno; elegante

courtship *n* noviazgo, *m*; galanteo, *m*

courtyard *n* patio, *m*

cousin *n* primo (-ma). **first c.,** primo (-ma) carnal. **second c.,** primo (-ma) segundo (-da)

cove *n* cala, abra, ensenada, *f*

covenant *n* contrato, *m*; estipulación, *f*; pacto, *m*; alianza, *f. vt* prometer; estipular

Coventry, to send to, hacer el vacío (a)

cover *vt* cubrir; abrigar; (dissemble) disimular; (a distance) recorrer; (comprise) comprender, abarcar; (with confusion, etc.) llenar (de); (with a revolver, etc.) amenazar (con); (an overdraft, etc.) garantizar; (of stallions) cubrir; (of a hen and eggs) empollar; (a story, journalism) investigar. *n* cubierta, *f*; (for a chair, umbrella, etc.) funda, *f*; (of a saucepan, jar, etc.) tapa, *f*; (dish-cover) tapadera, *f*; (of a book) cubierta, tapa, *f*; (of a letter) sobre, *m*; (shelter) abrigo, *m*; protección, *f*; (undergrowth) maleza, *f*; *fig* velo, manto, *m*; (pretence) pretexto, *m*; *com* garantía, *f*; (of tire) cubierta de neumático, *f.* **to c. oneself with glory,** cubrirse de gloria. **to c. up,** cubrir completamente; (with clothes) arropar; (wrap up) envolver. **to c. with a revolver,** amenazar con un revólver. **to read a book from c. to c.,** leer un libro del principio al fin. **to take c.,** refugiarse, tomar abrigo. **under c.,** bajo tejado; al abrigo

cover charge *n* consumo mínimo, precio del cubierto, *m*

covering *n* cubrimiento, *m*; cubierta, *f*; envoltura, *f*; capa, *f*, abrigo, *m.* **c. letter,** carta adjunta, *f*

coverlet *n* colcha, sobrecama, *f*

covert *n* guarida, *f. a* oculto; furtivo

covertly *adv* secretamente, furtivamente

covet *vt* codiciar; ambicionar, suspirar por

covetous *a* codicioso; ávido; ambicioso

covetously *adv* codiciosamente; ávidamente

covetousness *n* codicia, avaricia, *f*; avidez, *f*; ambición, *f*

cow *vt* intimidar, acobardar

cow *n* vaca, *f*; (of other animals) hembra, *f.* **c.-bell,** cencerro, *m*, zumba, *f.* **c.-catcher,** *aut* salvavidas, *m.* **c.-hide,** cuero, cuero de vaca, zurriago, *m*; penca, *f.* **c.-house,** establo, *m*, boyera, *f.* **c.-pox,** vacuna, *f*

coward *n* cobarde, *m*, *a* cobarde

cowardice *n* cobardía, *f*

cowardly *a* cobarde

cowboy *n* vaquero, *m*; gaucho, "cowboy," *m*

cower *vi* no saber dónde meterse; temblar, acobardarse

cowherd *n* vaquero, boyero, *m*

cowl *n* capucha, *f*; (of a chimney) sombrerete, *m*

cowlike *a* de vaca; bovino

coworker *n* colaborador (-ra)

cowshed *n* establo, *m*

cowslip *n* prímula, *f*

cox *n* timonel, *m*

coxcomb *n* (of a jester) gorra de bufón, *f*; mequetrefe, *m*

coxswain *n* patrón, *m*; (of a rowboat) timonel, *m*

coy *a* modoso, tímido; coquetón

coyly *adv* tímidamente; con coquetería

coyness *n* timidez, modestia, *f*; coquetería, *f*

cozy *a* cómodo; agradable; caliente. **You ate very c. here,** Estás muy bien aquí

crab *n* (sea) cangrejo de mar, cámbaro, *m*; (river) cangrejo, *m*; *ast* Cáncer, *m*. *vt* (thwart) frustrar. **hermit c.,** cangrejo ermitaño, *m*. **c.-apple,** manzana silvestre, *f*. **c.-louse,** ladilla, *f*

crabbed *a* áspero, hosco, desabrido, arisco; (of handwriting) apretado, metido

crack *vt* hender; quebrantar, romper; (nuts) cascar; (a whip and fingers) chasquear; (a bottle of wine) abrir. *vi* (of earth, skin, etc.) agrietarse; romperse, quebrarse; (of the voice) romper; (of the male voice) mudar. *n* hendedura, rendija, *f*; quebraja, *f*; (of a whip) chasquido, *m*; (of a rifle) estallido, *m*; (blow) golpe, garrotazo, *m*, *a* excelente, de primera categoría; estupendo. **to c. a joke,** decir un chiste. **to c. up,** *vt* dar bombo (a), alabar. *vi* (in health) quebrantarse; (airplane) cuartearse, estrellarse. **c.-brained,** chiflado; estúpido, loco

cracked *a* grietado; (of a bell, etc.) hendido; (of the voice) cascada; (of a person) chiflado

cracker *n* (firework) petardo, *m*; buscapiés, *m*

crackle *vi* (of burning wood, etc.) crepitar; (rustle) crujir; (of rifle fire) tirotear. *n* crepitación, *f*; crujido, *m*; (of rifle fire) tiroteo, *m*

crackling *n*. See **crackle;** *cul* chicharrón, *m*

Cracow Cracovia, *f*

cradle *n* cuna, *f*; *fig* niñez, infancia, *f*; (for a limb) arco de protección, *m*; (for winebottle) cesta, *f*. *vt* mecer. **c.-song,** canción de cuna, *f*

craft *n* (guile) astucia, *f*; (skill) habilidad, *f*; arte, *mf*; (occupation) oficio manual, *m*; profesión, *f*; (guild) gremio, *m*; (boat) barco, *m*, embarcación, *f*

craftily *adv* astutamente

craftiness *n* astucia, *f*

craftsman *n* artífice, *m*; arte sano, *m*; artista, *m*

craftsmanship *n* arte, *m*, or *f*; habilidad, *f*; artificio, *m*

crafty *a* astuto, taimado

crag *n* peña, *f*, risco, despeñadero, *m*

cragginess *n* escabrosidad, aspereza, fragosidad, *f*

craggy *a* escabroso, escarpado, peñascoso, riscoso

cram *vt* henchir; atestar; (one's mouth) llenar (de); (poultry) cebar; (a pupil) preparar para un examen; (a subject) empollar. *vi* (with food) atracarse. **The room was crammed with people,** La sala estaba atestada de gente

cramp *n* *med* calambre, *m*; (numbness) entumecimiento, *m*; (rivet) grapa, *f*. *vt* dar calambre (a); (numb) entumecer; (fasten) lañar; (*fig* hamper) estorbar. **to c. someone's style,** cortar los vuelos (a). **writer's c.,** calambre del escribiente, *m*

cramped *a* (of space) apretado, estrecho; (of writing) menuda

cranberry *n* arándano, *m*

crane *n* *orn* grulla, *f*; (machine) grúa, *f*. **jib c.,** grúa de pescante, *f*. **travelling c.,** grúa móvil, *f*. **to c. one's neck,** estirar el cuello. **crane's bill,** pico de cigüeña, *m*

cranium *n* cráneo, *m*

crank *n* (handle) manivela, *f*; (person) maniático (-ca). *vt* poner en marcha (un motor) con la manivela

crankiness *n* (crossness) irritabilidad, *f*, mal humor, *m*; (eccentricity) excentricidad, *f*

cranky *a* (cross) irritable, malhumorado; (eccentric) chiflado, maniático, excéntrico

cranny *n* hendedura, grieta, *f*

crape *n* crespón, *m*

crash *vi* caer estrepitosamente; romperse; estallarse; (of aircraft, cars) estrellarse; *fig* hundirse, arruinarse. *n* estrépito, estruendo, *m*; estallido, *m*; (of aircraft) ac-

cidente de aviación, *m*; (car) accidente, *m*, (or choque, *m*) de automóviles; (financial) ruina, *f*; *fig* hundimiento, *m*. **to c. into,** estrellarse contra, chocar con. **c. helmet,** casco, *m*. **c.-landing,** aterrizaje violento, *m*

crass *a* craso

crassness *n* estupidez, *f*

crate *n* (box) caja de embalaje, *f*; (basket) canasto, *m*, banasta, *f*

crater *n* cráter, *m*

cravat *n* corbata, *f*

crave *vt* suplicar, implorar. **to c. for,** perecer por, suspirar por, anhelar

craven *a* cobarde, pusilánime. *n* poltrón, cobarde, *m*

craving *n* deseo vehemente, *m*, sed, *f*

crawfish *n* cangrejo de río, *m*; cigala, *f*

crawl *vi* arrastrarse; andar a gatas; andar a paso de tortuga; (abase oneself) humillarse; (be full of) abundar (en). *n* paso de tortuga, *m*; (swimming) arrastre *m*

crayfish *n* cangrejo de río, *m*; cigala, *f*

crayon *n* carbón, *m*; pastel, *m*; (pencil) lápiz de color, *m*. *vt* dibujar con pastel, etc. **c. drawing,** dibujo al carbón, *m*

craze *vt* enloquecer, volver loco (a). *n* manía, *f*, capricho, entusiasmo, *m*; (fashion) moda, *f*

crazily *adv* locamente

craziness *n* locura, *f*

crazy *a* loco; chiflado; (of structure) dilapidado. **He is c. about music,** Está loco por la música. **to be completely c.,** (of persons) ser un loco de atar; ser completamente loco. **to drive c.,** volver loco (a)

creak *vi* (of shoes, chairs, etc.) crujir; (of gates, etc.) rechinar, chirriar. *n* crujido, *m*; chirrido, *m*

creaking *n*. See **creak**

creaky *a* crujiente, que cruje; chirriador

cream *n* crema, *f*; nata, *f*; *fig* flor, nata, *f*. *a* de nata. **whipped c.,** nata batida, *f*. **c. cake,** pastel de nata, *m*. **c.-cheese,** queso de nata, *m*. **c.-colored,** de color crema. **c.-jug,** jarro para crema, *m*. **c. of tartar,** cremor, tártaro, *m*

creamery *n* lechería, *f*

creamy *a* cremoso

crease *n* (wrinkle) arruga, *f*; (fold) pliegue, *m*; (in trousers) raya, *f*; (in cricket) línea de la meta, *f*. *vt* (wrinkle) arrugar; (fold) plegar; (trousers) poner la raya en. *vi* arrugarse

create *vt* crear; (appoint) nombrar; (produce) suscitar, producir

creation *n* creación, *f*; establecimiento, *m*; (appointment) nombramiento, *m*

creative *a* creador; de la creación

creativeness *n* facultad creativa, inventiva, *f*

creator *n* creador (-ra)

creature *n* criatura, *f*; animal, *m*. **c. comforts,** bienestar material, *m*

creche *n* casa cuna, *f*

credence *n* crédito, *m*, fe, creencia, *f*; *ecc* credencia, *f*. **to give c. to,** dar crédito (a), creer

credentials *n pl* credenciales, *f pl*

credibility *n* credibilidad, verosimilitud, *f*

credible *a* creíble, verosímil; (of persons) digno de confianza

credibly *adv* creíblemente

credit *n* crédito, *m*; reputación, *f*; honor, *m*; (*com* and banking) crédito, *m*; (in bookkeeping) data, *f*. *vt* dar fe (a), dar crédito (a); (*com* atribuir; (bookkeeping) acreditar. **It does them c.,** Les hace honor. **on c.,** a crédito, al fiado. **open c.,** *com* letra abierta, *f*. **to give on c.,** dar a crédito. **c. balance,** haber, *m*

creditable *a* loable, honroso, digno de alabanza

creditably *adv* honrosamente

creditor *n* acreedor (-ra); (bookkeeping) haber, *m*

credulity *n* credulidad, *f*

credulous *a* crédulo

credulously *adv* con credulidad, crédulamente

creed *n* credo, *m*

creek *n* caleta, abra, *f*

creel n (for fish) cesta de pescador, f
creep vi arrastrarse; (of plants and birds) trepar; (of infants) andar a gatas; (totter) hacer pinitos; (slip) deslizarse; (cringe) lisonjear, rebajarse; (of one's flesh) sentir hormigueo. **to c. about on tiptoe,** andar de puntillas. **to c. into a person's favor,** insinuarse en el favor de. **to c. in,** entrar sin ser notado (en); deslizarse en. **to c. on,** (of time) avanzar lentamente; (of old age, etc.) acercarse insensiblemente. **to c. out,** salir sin hacer ruido; escurrirse. **to c. up,** trepar por; subir a gatas
creeper n bot enredadera, f; orn trepador, m; zool reptil, m
creeping a bot trepante; zool trepador; (servile) rastrero
cremate vt incinerar
cremation n cremación, f
crematorium n crematorio, m; horno de incineración, m, inhumadora, f
creole a criollo. n criollo (-lla)
creolize vt acriollar
crescent n media luna, f; her creciente, m; calle en forma de semicírculo, f. a en forma de media luna; poet creciente
cress n bot berro, m
crest n (of a cock, etc.) cresta, f; (plume) penacho, m; (of a helmet) cimera, f; (of a hill) cumbre, cima, f; (of a wave) cresta, f. **family c.,** blasón, escudo, m
crestfallen a cabizbajo, cariacontecido
cretan a cretense. n cretense, mf
Crete Creta, f
cretin n cretino (-na)
cretinism n cretinismo, m
crevasse n grieta en un ventisquero, f
crevice n intersticio, m, rendija, grieta, f
crew n (of ships, boats, aircraft) tripulación, f; (of a gun) servidores de una ametralladora, m pl; (gang) pandilla, cuadrilla, f
crib n pesebre, m; (child's) camita de niño, f; (plagiary) plagio, m. vt (plagiarize) plagiar; (steal) hurtar
crick n (in the neck) tortícolis, m
cricket n ent grillo, m; (game) cricquet, m. **c. ball,** pelota de cricquet, f. **c. bat,** paleta de cricquet, f. **c. ground,** campo de cricquet, m. **c. match,** partido de cricquet, m
cricketer n jugador de cricquet, m
crier n (town) pregonero, m
crime n crimen, m; ofensa, f, delito, m
Crimea, the la Crimea, f
Crimean War, the la guerra de Crimea, la guerra de Oriente, f
criminal a criminal. n criminal, m; reo, mf **C. Investigation Department,** (nearest equivalent) policía secreta, f. **c. laws,** código penal, m
criminally adv criminalmente
criminologist n criminalista, m
criminology n criminología, f
crimp vt (hair) rizar
crimson n carmesí, m. a de carmesí. vt teñir de carmesí. vi enrojecerse
cringe vi temblar; asustarse, acobardarse; inclinarse (ante)
cringing a servil, humilde; adulador
crinkle vi arrugarse; rizarse. vt arrugar. n arruga, f
crinoline n crinolina, f, miriñaque, guardainfante, m
cripple n tullido (-da); cojo (-ja). vt lisiar, tullir, estropear; fig paralizar
crisis n crisis, f
crisp a (of hair and of leaves) crespo; (fresh) fresco; (stiff) tieso; (of style) nervioso, vigoroso; (of manner) decidido; (of repartee) chispeante; (of tone) incisivo
crisscross vt (a body of water or land) surcar
criterion n criterio, m
critic n crítico, m; censor, m
critical a crítico
criticism n crítica, f
criticize vt criticar; censurar

critique n crítica, f
croak vi (of frogs) croar; (of ravens) graznar; (of persons) lamentarse, gruñir
croaking n canto de la rana, m; graznido, m
Croat a croata. n croata, mf
Croatia Crocia, f
crochet n ganchillo, m, vi hacer ganchillo. vt hacer (algo) de ganchillo. **c. hook,** aguja de gancho, f, ganchillo, m. **c. work,** croché, ganchillo, m
crockery n loza, f, cacharros, m pl. **c. store,** cacharrería, f
crocodile n cocodrilo, m. **c. tears,** lágrimas de cocodrilo, f pl
crocus n azafrán, m
croft n campillo, m; (farm) heredad, f
crofter n colono, m
crone n bruja, f
crony n compinche, mf
crook n curva, f; (staff) cayado, m; (swindler) caballero de industria, estafador, m, vt doblar, encorvar
crooked a curvo; encorvado; torcido; ladeado; (deformed) contrahecho; (of paths, etc.) tortuoso; (dishonest) torcido, tortuoso
crookedly adv torcidamente; de través
crookedness n encorvadura, f; tortuosidad, f; sinuosidad, f
croon vt and vi canturrear; cantar
crooner n cantante, mf
crop n (of birds) buche, m; (whip) látigo, m, fusta, f; (handle) mango, m; (harvest) cosecha, f; (of the hair) cortadura, f. vt cortar; (nibble) rozar; (hair) rapar. **Eton c.,** pelo a la garçonne, m. **to c. up,** aparecer, surgir
crop rotation n la rotación de cultivos, f
croquet n juego de la argolla, juego de croquet, m
croquette n cul croqueta, f
crosier n báculo, cayado del obispo, m
cross n cruz, f; biol cruzamiento, m; (sew bias) bies, m. **in the shape of a c.,** en cruz. **the Red C.,** la Cruz Roja. **c.-bearer,** ecc crucero, m
cross vt cruzar; atravesar; pasar por; (a check and animals) cruzar; (thwart) contrariar. **It did not c. my mind,** No se me ocurrió. **Our letters must have crossed,** Nuestras cartas deben haberse cruzado. **to c. oneself,** ecc persignarse. **to c. out,** tachar, rayar. **to c. over,** vt atravesar, cruzar. vi ir al otro lado
cross a transversal; cruzado; oblicuo; (contrary) opuesto (a); (bad-tempered) malhumorado. **c.-breed,** a mestizo, atravesado. **c.-country,** a a campo travieso. **c.-examination,** law repregunta, f, contrainterrogatorio, m. **c.-examine,** vt law repreguntar; interrogar. **c.-eyed,** bizco. **c.-fire,** mil fuego cruzado, m sing fuegos cruzados, m pl; fig tiroteo, m. **c.-grained,** (of wood) vetisesgado; (of persons) áspero, intratable, desabrido. **c.-legged,** con las piernas cruzadas. **c.-purpose,** despropósito, m. **at c.-purposes,** a despropósito. **c.-question,** vt law repreguntar; interrogar. **c. reference,** contrarreferencia, f. **c. section,** sección transversal, f. **c.-stitch,** punto cruzado, m. **c.-word puzzle,** crucigrama, m
crossbar n travesaño, m
crossbeam n viga transversal, f
crossbench a atravesado
crossbred a cruzado, mestizo; híbrido
crossbreed n mestizo (-za); híbrido, m
crossing n cruzamiento, m; (of the sea) travesía, f; (intersection) cruce, m; paso, m. **level c.,** paso a nivel, m. **pedestrian c.,** paso para peatones, m. **c.-sweeper,** barrendero, m
crossly adv con mal humor, con displicencia, irritablemente
crossness n irritabilidad, f, mal humor, m
crossroad n travesía, f; cruce, m; pl **crossroads,** cruce, cruce de caminos, m sing encrucijada, f sing
crosswise adv en cruz; a través
crotch n (of a tree) bifurcación, f; anat horcajadura, f; (of breeches) entrepiernas, f pl

crotchet *n mus* semínima, *f*; (fad) capricho, *m*; extravagancia, excentricidad, *f*
crotchety *a* caprichoso; raro, excéntrico; difícil
crouch *vi* acurrucarse, agacharse, acuclillarse
croup *n* (disease) crup, garrotillo, *m*; (of a horse) grupa, anca, *f*
croupier *n* coime, crupié, *m*
crow *n orn* cuervo, *m*; *orn* grajo, *m*; (of a cock) canto del gallo, cacareo, *m*; (of an infant) gorjeo, *m*. *vi* (of a cock) cantar, cacarear; (of an infant) gorjearse. **as the c. flies,** en línea recta. **to c. over,** gallear, cantar victoria. **crow's-foot,** pata de gallo, *f*. **crow's-nest,** *naut* gavias, *f pl*
crowbar *n* alzaprima, palanca, *f*
crowd *n* multitud, muchedumbre, *f*; concurso, *m*; vulgo, *m*; (majority) mayoría, *f*; *theat* acompañamiento, *m*. *vi* reunirse, congregarse; agolparse, remolinarse, apiñarse. *vt* (fill) llenar; atestar. **in a c.,** en tropel. **So many ideas crowded in on me,** Se me ocurrieron tantas ideas a la vez. **to follow the c.,** seguir la multitud; *fig* ir con la mayoría. **to c. in,** entrar en tropel. **to c. round,** cercar, agruparse alrededor de. **to c. together,** apiñarse. **to c. up,** subir en masa, subir en tropel
crowded *a* lleno; atestado, apiñado; (weighed down) agobiado; (of hours, etc.) lleno
crowing *n* cacareo, canto del gallo, *m*; (of an infant) gorjeos, *m pl*; (boasting) jactancia, *f*
crown *n* corona, *f*; (of the head) coronilla, corona, *f*; (of a hat) copa, *f*; *arch* coronamiento, *m*. *vt* coronar. **c. prince,** príncipe heredero, *m*
crowning *n* coronamiento, *m*; *arch* remate, *m*, *a* final; supremo
crozier *n.* See **crosier**
crucial *a* decisivo, crítico; difícil
crucible *n* crisol, *m*
crucifix *n* crucifijo, *m*
crucifixion *n* crucifixión, *f*
cruciform *a* cruciforme
crucify *vt* crucificar
crude *a* crudo; (of colors) chillón, llamativo; (uncivilized) cerril, inculto; (vulgar) cursi; (of truth, etc.) desnudo
crudity *n* crudeza, *f*
cruel *a* cruel
cruelty *n* crueldad, *f*
cruet *n* ánfora, vinagrera, *f*; (stand) angarillas, *f pl*, convoy, *m*
cruise *vi* cruzar, navegar; (of cars) correr. *n* viaje por mar, *m*
cruiser *n* crucero, *m*
crumb *n* miga, *f*; (spongy part of bread) migaja, *f*. *vt* (bread) desmigajar; desmenuzar. **c. brush,** recogemigas, *m*
crumble *vt* desmigajar, desmenuzar. *vi* desmoronarse, desmigajarse; *fig* hundirse, derrumbarse; *fig* desaparecer
crumbling *n* (of buildings, etc.) desmoronamiento, *m*; *fig* destrucción, *f*
crumple *vt* arrugar, ajar. *vi* arrugarse. **to c. up,** *vt* (crush) estrujar; (persons) dejar aplastado. *vi* (collapse) hundirse, derrumbarse; (of persons) desplomarse; (despair) desalentarse
crunch *vt* mascar; hacer crujir. *vi* crujir
crupper *n* baticola, *f*
crusade *n* cruzada, *f*
crusader *n* cruzado, *m*
crush *vt* aplastar; (to powder) moler, triturar; (grapes, etc.) exprimir; (crease) arrugar; (opposition, etc.) vencer; (annihilate) aniquilar, destruir; (abash) humillar, confundir; (hope, etc.) matar; (of sorrow, etc.) agobiar. **We all crushed into his diningroom,** Fuimos en tropel a su comedor. **to c. up,** machacar, moler; (paper, etc.) estrujar
crushing *a* (of defeats and replies) aplastante; (of sorrow, etc.) abrumador

crust *n* (of bread, pie) corteza, *f*; (scab) costra, *f*; (of the earth, snow) capa, *f*. *vt* encostrar. *vi* encostrarse. **c. of bread,** mendrugo de pan, *m*
crustacean *a* crustáceo. *n* crustáceo, *m*
crustily *adv* irritablemente, malhumoradamente
crustiness *n* mal humor, *m*, aspereza, *f*
crusty *a* costroso; (of persons) malhumorado, irritable; áspero
crutch *n* muleta, *f*; (fork) horquilla, *f*; (crotch) horcajadura, *f*
crux *n* problema, *m*; (knotty point) nudo, *m*
cry *vi* (weep) llorar; (shout) gritar; (exclaim) exclamar. *vt* (one's wares) pregonar. *n* grito, *m*. **to cry for help,** pedir socorro a voces. **to cry to high heaven,** poner el grito en el cielo. **to cry one's eyes out,** llorar a mares. **to cry down,** desacreditar. **to cry off,** desdecirse; volverse atrás. **to cry out,** *vt* gritar. *vi* dar gritos; gritar; *fig* clamar. **cry-baby,** niño (-ña) llorón (-ona)
crying *a* urgente; notorio. *n* gritos, *m pl*; (weeping) llanto, *m*, lamentaciones, *f pl*; (tears) lágrimas, *f pl*
crypt *n* cripta, *f*
cryptic *a* secreto, oculto
cryptography *n* criptografía, *f*
crystal *n* cristal, *m*. **c. set,** *rad* receptor de galena, *m*
crystal ball *n* bola de cristal, esfera de cristal, *f*
crystalline *a* cristalino
crystallization *n* cristalización, *f*
crystallize *vt* and *vi* cristalizar
crystallography *n* cristalografía, *f*
cub *n* cachorro (-rra)
Cuban *a* cubano. *n* cubano (-na)
cubbyhole *n* refugio, *m*; garita, *f*; cuarto pequeño, *m*; chiribitil, *m*
cube *n* cubo, *m*; (of sugar) terrón, *m*. *vt* cubicar. **c. root,** raíz cúbica, *f*
cubic *a* cúbico
cubicle *n* cubículo, *m*
cubism *n* cubismo, *m*
cubist *n* cubista, *mf*
cubit *n* codo, *m*
cuckold *n* cornudo, *m*
cuckoo *n* cuclillo, *m*; (cry) cucú, *m*. **c.-clock,** reloj de cuclillo, *m*
cucumber *n* cohombro *m*
cud *n* rumia, *f*. **to chew the cud,** rumiar
cuddle *vt* abrazar. *n* abrazo, *m*. **to c. up together,** estar abrazados
cudgel *n* porra, estaca, tranca, *f*, *vt* aporrear, apalear. **to c. one's brains,** devanarse los sesos. **to take up the cudgels for,** salir en defensa de
cue *n theat* pie, *m*; (lead) táctica, *f*; (hint) indicación, *f*; (of hair) coleta, *f*; (billiard) taco (de billar), *m*. **to take one's cue from,** tomar como modelo (a); seguir el ejemplo de
cuff *vt* abofetear. *n* (blow) bofetón, *m*; (of sleeve) puño, *m*, bocamanga, valenciana, *f*. **c.-links,** gemelos, *m pl*
cuisine *n* cocina, *f*
cul-de-sac *n* callejón sin salida, *m*
culinary *a* culinario
cullender *n* colador, *m*
culminate *vi* culminar (en), terminar (en). **culminating point,** punto culminante, *m*
culmination *n* culminación, *f*; *fig* apogeo, punto culminante, *m*
culpability *n* culpabilidad, *f*
culpable *a* culpable
culpably *adv* culpablemente
culprit *n* culpado (-da)
cult *n* culto, *m*
cultivable *a* cultivable, labradero
cultivate *vt* cultivar
cultivated *a* cultivado; (of persons) culto, fino
cultivation *n* cultivación, *f*; (of the land) cultivo, *m*; (of persons, etc.) cultura, *f*
cultivator *n* cultivador (-ra); (machine) cultivador, *m*
cultural *a* cultural

culture *n* cultura, *f;* (bacteriology) cultivo, *m,* *vt* (bacteriology) cultivar
cultured *a* culto
culvert *n* alcantarilla, *f*
cumbersome *a* pesado; incómodo
cumulative *a* cumulativo
cumulus *n* cúmulo, *m*
cuneiform *a* cuneiforme
cunning *a* astuto, taimado. *n* (skill) habilidad, *f;* astucia, *f*
cup *n* taza, *f;* (*ecc* and *bot*) cáliz, *m;* *sport* copa, *f;* (hollow) hoyo, *m,* hondonada, *f.* **c.-final,** *sport* final de la copa, *m.* **c.-tie,** *sport* partido eliminatorio, *m*
cup-and-ball *n* boliche, *m*
cupboard *n* armario, *m;* (in the wall) alacena, *f.* **c. love,** amor interesado, *m*
cupful *n* taza, *f*
cupidity *n* avaricia, codicia, *f*
cup of sorrow *n* ramito de amargura, *m*
cupola *n* cúpula, *f*
cur *n* perro mestizo, *m;* canalla, *m*
curable *a* curable
curableness *n* curabilidad, *f*
curative *a* curativo, terapéutico
curator *n* (of a museum) director, *m;* (Scots law) curador, *m*
curb *n* (of a bridle) barbada, *f; fig* freno, *m;* (stone) bordillo, *m,* guarnición, *f. vt* (a horse) enfrenar; *fig* refrenar, reprimir; (limit) limitar
curd *n* requesón, *m;* cuajada, *f*
curdle *vt* coagularse; (of blood) helarse. *vt* coagular; (blood) helar
cure *n* cura, *f; ecc* curato, *m. vt* curar; (salt) salar; *fig* remediar. **to take a c.,** tomar una cura. **c.-all,** panacea, *f.* **c. of souls,** cura de almas, *f*
curer *n* (of fish, etc.) salador, *m;* (of evils, etc.) remediador, *m*
curfew *n* toque de queda, *m*
curia *n ecc* curia, *f*
curing *n* curación, *f;* (salting) saladura, *f*
curio *n* curiosidad, antigüedad, *f*
curiosity *n* curiosidad, *f*
curious *a* (all meanings) curioso
curiously *adv* curiosamente
curl *n* (of hair) rizo, bucle, *m;* (of smoke) penacho, *m. vt* rizar. *vi* rizarse; *sport* jugar al curling. **in c.,** rizado. **to c. one's lip,** hacer una mueca de desdén. **to c. up,** *vt* arrollar; *fig* dejar fuera de combate (a). *vi* hacerse un ovillo, enroscarse; (of leaves) abarquillarse; *fig* desplomarse; desanimarse. **c.-paper,** papillote, *m*
curlew *n orn* zarapito, *m*
curling *n* (game) curling, *m, a* rizado. **c.-tongs,** encrespador, *m*
curly *a* rizado, crespo
curmudgeon *n* erizo, misántropo, cara de viernes, *m*
currant *n* (dry) pasa de Corinto, *f;* (fresh) grosella, *f.* **black c.,** grosella negra, *f;* (bush) grosellero negro, *m.* **c.-bush,** grosellero, *m*
currency *n* uso corriente, *m;* moneda corriente, *f,* dinero, *m;* dinero en circulación, *m;* valor corriente, *m;* estimación, *f*
current *a* corriente; presente, de actualidad; (of money) en circulación. *n* (of water, etc., *fig elec*) corriente, *f.* **alternating c.,** *elec* corriente alterna, *f.* **direct c.,** *elec* corriente continua, *f.* **the c. number of a magazine,** el último número de una revista. **c. events,** actualidades, *f pl*
currently *adv* corrientemente, generalmente
curricle *n* carriola, *f*
curriculum *n* plan de estudios, *m;* curso, *m*
curriculum vitae *n* hoja de vida, *f*
curry *vt* (leather) zurrar; (a horse) almohazar; *cul* condimentar con cari. **to c. favor with,** insinuarse en el favor de. **c.-comb,** almohaza, *f*
curse *n* maldición, *f;* blasfemia, *f;* (ruin) azote, castigo, *m. vt* maldecir; (afflict) castigar. *vi* blasfemar, echar pestes
cursed *a* maldito; abominable, odioso

cursing *n* maldición, *f;* blasfemias, *f pl*
cursive *a* cursivo
cursorily *adv* rápidamente; de prisa; superficialmente
cursory *a* rápido; apresurado; superficial
curt *a* seco, brusco; corto
curtail *vt* abreviar; reducir; disminuir
curtailment *n* abreviación, *f;* reducción, *f;* disminución, *f*
curtain *n* cortina, *f; theat* telón, *m. vt* poner cortinas (a) **drop c.,** telón de boca, *m.* **iron c.,** *pol* telón de acero, *m.* **to c. off,** separar por cortinas. **c.-lecture,** reprimenda conyugal, *f.* **c.-raiser,** entremés, *m.* **c.-ring,** anilla, *f*
curtly *adv* secamente, bruscamente
curtness *n* brusquedad, sequedad, *f*
curtsey *n* reverencia, cortesía, *f, vi* hacer una reverencia
curvature *n* curvatura, *f*
curve *n* curva, *f; mech* codo, *m;* (*aut* of a road) viraje, *m. vt* encorvar, torcer. *vi* encorvarse, torcerse; (of a road) hacer un viraje.
curved *a* curvo
curvet *n* corveta, cabriola, *f, vi* corvetear, corcovear, cabriolar
curvilinear *a* curvilíneo
cushion *n* almohada, *f;* cojín, *m;* (billiards) banda, *f;* (of fingers, etc.) pulpejo, *m. vt* proveer de almohadas; (a shock) amortiguar; suavizar
custard *n* flan, *m,* natillas, *f pl*
custodian *n* custodio, *m;* guardián, *m;* (of a museum, etc.) director, *m*
custody *n* custodia, *f;* guarda, *f;* prisión, *f.* **in safe c.,** en lugar seguro. **to take** (a person) **into c.,** arrestar
custom *n* costumbre, *f;* uso, *m; com* parroquia, clientela, *f;* (sales) ventas, *f pl; pl* **Customs,** aduana, *f.* **to go through the Customs,** pasar por la aduana. **Customs duty,** derechos de aduana, *m pl.* **Customs officer,** aduanero, *m.* **c.-house,** aduana, *f*
customarily *adv* habitualmente, por lo general
customary *a* acostumbrado, usual, habitual
customer *n* cliente, *mf* parroquiano (-na). **He is a queer c.,** Es un tipo raro
customs barrier *n* barrera aduanera, barrera arancelaria, *f*
cut *vt* cortar; (diamonds) tallar; (hay, etc.) segar; (carve) labrar, tallar; (engrave) grabar; (a lecture, etc.) no asistir a; (cards) destajar, cortar; (*fig* wound) herir; (reduce) reducir; abreviar; (teeth) echar; (of lines) cruzar. *vi* cortar; cortar bien; (*fam* go) marcharse a prisa y corriendo. **I must get my hair cut,** He de hacerme cortar el pelo. **That cuts both ways,** Es una arma de dos filos. **His opinion cuts no ice,** Su opinión no cuenta. **Mary cut him dead,** María hizo como si no le reconociera. **to cut a caper,** dar saltos; hacer cabriolas. **to cut a person short,** echar el tablacho (a). **to cut and run,** poner los pies en polvorosa. **to cut for deal,** (cards) cortar para ver quién da las cartas. **to cut short,** (a career) terminar. **to cut to the quick,** herir en lo más vivo. **to cut across,** cortar al través; (fields, etc.) atravesar; tomar por un atajo. **to cut away,** *vt* quitar. *vi inf* poner pies en polvorosa. **to cut down,** derribar; (by the sword) acuchillar; (by death, etc.) segar, malograr; (expenses, etc.) reducir; (abbreviate) cortar, abreviar. **to cut off,** cortar, separar; amputar; (on a telephone) cortar la comunicación; (gas, water, etc.) cortar; (supply of food, etc.) interrumpir; (of death) llevarse. **to cut off with a shilling,** desheredar (a). **to cut out,** (dresses, etc.) cortar; (oust) suplantar. **He is not cut out for medicine,** No tiene la disposición para la medicina. **to cut up,** trinchar, cortar en pequeños trozos; (afflict) entristecer, afligir. **to cut up rough,** *inf* ponerse furioso
cut *a* cortado. **well-cut features,** facciones regulares, *f pl.* **cut and dried opinion,** opinión hecha, idea fija, *f;* ideas cerradas, *f pl.* **cut glass,** cristal tallado, *m*
cut *n* corte, *m;* (with a whip) latigazo, *m;* (with a sword) cuchillada, *f;* (with a sharp instrument) tajo, *m;* cor-

tadura, *f;* (in prices, etc.) reducción, *f;* (engraving) grabado, *m;* clisé, *m;* (of cards) corte, *m.* **short cut,** atajo, *m.* **the cut of a coat,** el corte de un abrigo. **to give** (someone) **the cut direct,** pasar cerca de (una persona) sin saludarle. **cut-out,** *n* (paper) recortado, *m; elec* cortacircuitos, *m.* **cut-throat,** *n* asesino, *m*
cutaneous *a* cutáneo
cute *a* cuco, listo; mono
cuteness *n* cuquería, inteligencia, *f;* monería, *f*
cuticle *n* cutícula, *f*
cutler *n* cuchillero, *m*
cutlery *n* cuchillería, *f*
cutlet *n* chuleta, *f*
cutter *n* cortador, *m; naut* cúter, *m;* escampavía, *f*
cutting *n* corte, *m;* (of diamonds) talla, *f;* (in a mountain, etc.) tajo, *m; agr* plantón, *m;* (of cloth) retazo, *m;* (newspaper) recorte, *m. a* cortante; (of remarks) mordaz. **newspaper c.,** recorte de periódico. **c. down,** (of trees) tala, *f;* reducción, *f*
cuttingly *adv* mordazmente, con malicia.
cuttlefish *n* jibia, *f*
cyanide *n* cianuro, *m*
cycle *n* ciclo, *m;* período, *m;* (bicycle) bicicleta, *f. vi* ir en bicicleta
cyclic *a* cíclico

cycling *n* ciclismo, *m*
cyclist *n* ciclista, *mf*
cyclone *n* ciclón, *m*
Cyclopean *a* ciclópeo
Cyclopean task *n* obra ciclópea, *f*
cygnet *n* pollo del cisne, *m*
cylinder *n* cilindro, *m; mech* tambor, *m.* **c. head,** culata, *f*
cylindrical *a* cilíndrico
cymbal *n* címbalo, platillo, *m*
cymbalist *n* cimbalero (-ra)
cynic *n* cínico, *m*
cynical *a* cínico
cynicism *n* cinismo, *m*
cynosure *n ast* Osa Menor, *f;* blanco, *m*
cypress *n* (tree and wood) ciprés, *m.* **c. grove,** cipresal, *m*
Cypriot *a* chipriota. *n* chipriota, *mf*
Cyprus Isla de Chipre, *f*
cyst *n* quiste, *m*
cystic *a* cístico
Czech *a* checo. *n* checo (-ca); (language) checo, *m*
Czechoslovak *n* checoslovaco (-ca)
Czechoslovakia Checoslovaquia, *f*
Czechoslovakian *a* checoslovaco

D

d *n* (letter) de, *f; mus* re, *m*
dab *vt* golpear suavemente, tocar; (sponge) esponjar; (moisten) mojar. *n* golpecito, golpe blando, *m;* (small piece) pedazo pequeño, *m;* (blob) borrón, *m;* (peck) picotazo, *m; inf* experto (-ta). **to dab at one's eyes,** secarse los ojos
dabble *vt* mojar (en). *vi* chapotear; (engage in) entretenerse en; (meddle in) meterse en; (speculate in) especular en. **to d. in politics,** meterse en política
dabbler *n* aficionado (-da)
dace *n* dardo, albur, *m*
dachshund *n* perro pachón, *m*
daddy *n* papaíto, *m.* **d.-longlegs,** típula, *f*
dado *n arch* dado, neto, *m;* friso, *m*
daffodil *n* narciso trompón, *m*
daft *a* bobo, tonto, chiflado; loco
dagger *n* daga, *f,* puñal, *m; print* cruz, *f.* **to be at daggers drawn,** estar a matar. **to look daggers (at),** lanzar miradas de odio (hacia), mirar echando chispas. **d. thrust,** puñalada, *f*
daguerreotype *n* daguerrotipo, *m*
dahlia *n* dalia, *f*
daily *a* diario, de todos los días; cotidiano. *adv* diariamente, cada día, todos los días; cotidianamente. *n* (paper) diario, *m.* **d. bread,** pan cotidiano, pan de cada día, *m.* **d. help,** (person) asistenta, *f.* **d. pay,** jornal, *m;* mil pre, *m*
daintily *adv* delicadamente; elegantemente; con primor
daintiness *n* delicadeza, *f;* elegancia, *f;* (beauty) primor, *m*
dainty *a* delicado; elegante; primoroso, exquisito; (fastidious) melindroso, difícil. *n* bocado exquisito, *m,* golosina, *f*
dairy *n* lechería, *f.* **d. cattle,** vacas lecheras, *f pl.* **d.-farm,** granja, *f.* **d.-farmer,** granjero (-ra). **d.-farming,** industria lechera, *f*
dairymaid *n* lechera, *f*
dairyman *n* lechero, *m*
dais *n* estrado, *m*
daisy *n* margarita, *f*
dale *n* valle, *m*
dalliance *n* (delay) tardanza, *f;* (play) jugueteo, *m;* diversiones, *f pl;* (caresses) caricias, *f pl,* abrazos, *m pl*
dally *vi* tardar, perder el tiempo; entretenerse, divertirse; (make love) holgar (con); (with an idea) entretenerse con, jugar con

Dalmatian *a* dalmático, dálmata. *n* dálmata, *mf.* **D. dog,** perro dálmata, *m*
dalmatic *n* dalmática, *f*
daltonism *n* daltonismo, *m*
dam *n* (of animals) madre, *f;* (of a river, etc.) presa, *f,* embalse, *m;* (mole) dique, *m;* pared de retención, *f. vt* represar, embalsar; cerrar; (restrain) contener, reprimir
damage *n* daño, perjuicio, *m;* mal, *m;* avería, *f;* pérdida, *f; (fam* price) precio, *m; pl* **damages,** *law* daños y perjuicios, *m pl. vt* dañar, perjudicar; estropear; deteriorar; (reputation, etc.) comprometer
damageable *a* que puede ser dañado; frágil
damaging *a* perjudicial; comprometedor
damascene *vt* damasquinar
Damascus Damasio, *m*
damask *n* (cloth) damasco, *m;* (steel) acero damasquino, *m. a* de damasco; damasquino. *vt* (metals) damasquinar; (cloth) adamascar. **d.-like,** adamascado. **d. rose,** rosa de Damasco, *f*
dame *n* dama, señora, *f; inf* madre, *f;* (schoolmistress) amiga, *f.* **to attend a d. school,** ir a la amiga
damming *n* embalse, *m,* represa, *f;* retención, *f;* represión, *f*
damn *vt* condenar al infierno; maldecir; vituperar. **D. it!** ¡Maldito sea!
damnable *a* detestable, infame; *inf* horrible
damnably *adv* abominablemente; *inf* horriblemente
damnation *n* condenación, perdición, *f;* maldición, *f;* vituperación, *f*
damned *a* condenado; maldito; detestable, odioso
damning *a* que condena; irresistible
damp *n* humedad, *f;* (mist) niebla, *f;* exhalación, *f;* (gas) mofeta, *f; fig* tristeza, depresión, *f. vt* humedecer, mojar; apagar, amortiguar; (depress) deprimir, entristecer; (stifle) ahogar; (lessen) moderar; (trouble) turbar. **d.-proof,** impermeable
damper *n* (of a chimney) registro de humos, *m;* (of a piano) batiente, *m;* (for stamps) mojador, *m;* (gloom) depresión, tristeza, *f;* (restraint) freno, *m*
dampish *a* algo húmedo
dampness *n* humedad, *f*
damsel *n* chica, muchacha, *f;* damisela, *f*
damson *n* ciruela damascena, *f.* **d. tree,** ciruelo damasceno, *m*
dance *n* danza, *f;* baile, *m. vi* bailar, danzar; saltar, brin-

car. *vt* bailar; hacer saltar. **to d. attendance on,** servir humildemente; hacer la rueda (a). **to lead someone a d.,** hacer bailar. **d. band,** orquestina, *f;* orquesta de jazz, *f.* **d. floor,** pista de baile, *f.* **d. hall,** salón de baile, *m.* **d. music,** música bailable, *f.* **d.-number,** (in a theater) bailable, *m.* **d. of death,** danza de la muerte, *f*

dancer *n* bailarín (-ina); danzador (-ra), bailador (-ra); *pl* **dancers,** (partners) parejas de baile, *f pl*

dancing *n* baile, *m,* danza, *f.* **d.-girl,** bailarina, *f;* (Indian) bayadera, *f.* **d.-master,** maestro de baile, *m.* **d. school,** academia de baile, *f.* **d. slipper,** zapatilla de baile, *f*

dandelion *n* diente de león, *m*

dandle *vt* mecer, hacer saltar sobre las rodillas, hacer bailar

dandruff *n* caspa, *f*

dandy *n* dandi, petimetre, barbilindo, *m*

Dane *n* danés (-esa). **Great D.,** perro danés, *m*

danger *n* peligro, *m;* riesgo, *m.* **out of d.,** fuera de peligro. **to be in d.,** correr peligro, peligrar, estar en peligro

dangerous *a* peligroso; arriesgado; nocivo

dangerously *adv* peligrosamente

dangerousness *n* peligro, *m*

dangle *vi* colgar, pender. *vt* dejar colgar; oscilar; (show) mostrar

Danish *a* danés, de Dinamarca. *n* (language) danés, *m*

dank *a* húmedo

dankness *n* humedad, *f*

Danube, the el (Río) Danubio, *m*

dapper *a* apuesto, aseado; activo, vivaz

dapple *vt* motear, salpicar, manchar. **d.-grey,** *a* rucio

dappled *a* (of horses) rodado, empedrado

Dardanelles, the los Dardanelos, *m*

dare *vi* atreverse, osar. *vt* arriesgar; desafiar, provocar; hacer frente a, arrostrar. *n* reto, *m.* **I d. say!** ¡Ya lo creo! ¡No lo dudo! **I d. say that . . . ,** No me sorprendería que . . . ; Supongo que . . . **d.-devil,** calavera, *m;* atrevido (-da), valeroso (-sa)

daring *a* intrépido, audaz; atrevido; (dangerous) arriesgado, peligroso. *n* audacia, osadía, *f,* atrevimiento, *m;* peligro, *m*

daringly *adv* atrevidamente

dark *a* oscuro; (of complexion, etc.) moreno; negro; lóbrego; (of colours) oscuro; misterioso; enigmático; secreto, escondido; (sad) funesto, triste; (evil) malo, malévolo; (ignorant) ignorante, supersticioso. *n* oscuridad, *f;* (shade) sombra, *f;* ignorancia, *f.* **after d.,** *n* nocturno. *adv* después del anochecer. **in the d.,** a oscuras; de noche; *fig* **be in the d.,** quedarse en la luna. **to become d.,** oscurecerse; (cloud over) anublarse; (become night) anochecer. **to keep d.,** *vt* tener secreto. *vi* esconderse. **d. ages,** los siglos de la ignorancia y de la superstición. **d.-eyed,** de ojos negros, ojinegro. **d. horse,** caballo desconocido, *m; pol* batacazo, *m.* **d. lantern,** linterna sorda, *f.* **d. room,** cuarto oscuro, *m; phot* laboratorio fotográfico, *m;* (optics) cámara oscura, *f*

darken *vt* obscurecer; sombrear; (of color) hacer más oscuro; (sadden) entristecer. *vi* obscurecerse; (of the sky) anublarse; (of the face with emotion) inmutarse.

darkening *n* oscurecimiento, *m*

darkly *adv* oscuramente; misteriosamente; con malevolencia; secretamente; (archaic) indistintamente

darkness *n* oscuridad, *f,* tinieblas, *f pl;* sombra, *f;* (of color) oscuro, *m;* (of the complexion) color moreno, *m;* (of eyes, hair) negrura, *f;* (night) noche, *f;* (ignorance) ignorancia, *f;* (privacy) secreto, *m.* **Prince of d.,** el príncipe de las tinieblas

darling *a* querido, amado; (greatest) mayor. *n* querido (-da); (favorite) el predilecto, la predilecta, el favorito, la favorita. **My d.!** ¡Amor mío! ¡Vida mía! ¡Pichoncito mío!

darn *vt* zurcir, remendar. *n* zurcido, remiendo, *m*

darner *n* zurcidor (-ra); (implement) huevo de zurcir, *m*

darning *n* zurcidura, *f;* zurcido, recosido, *m.* **d.-needle,** aguja de zurcir, *f.* **d. wool,** lana de zurcir, *f*

dart *n* dardo, *m;* movimiento rápido, *m;* avance rápido, *m; sew* sisa, *f. vi* lanzarse, abalanzarse (sobre); volar; correr, avanzar rápidamente. *vt* lanzar, arrojar; dirigir. **to make darts in,** *sew* sisar

Darwinian *a* darwiniano. *n* darwinista, *mf*

Darwinism *n* darwinismo, *m*

dash *n* (spirit) fogosidad, *f,* brío, *m;* energía, *f;* (impact) choque, golpe, *m;* (mixture) mezcla, *f;* (of a liquid) gota, *f;* (of the pen) rasgo, *m;* (attack) ataque, *m;* avance rápido, *m;* (a little) algo, un poco (de); *gram* raya, *f;* (show) ostentación, *f.* **He made a d. for the door,** Se precipitó a la puerta, Corrió hacia la puerta. **to cut a d.,** hacer gran papel. **d.-board,** tablero de instrumentos, *m*

dash *vt* arrojar con violencia; (break) quebrar, estrellar; (sprinkle) rociar (con), salpicar (con); (mix) mezclar; (knock) golpear; (disappoint) frustrar, destruir; (confound) confundir; (depress) desanimar. *vi* (rush) precipitarse; quebrarse, estrellarse; chocar (contra); (of waves) romperse. **to d. to pieces,** hacer añicos, estrellar. **to d. along,** avanzar rápidamente; correr. **to d. away,** *vi* marcharse apresuradamente. *vt* apartar bruscamente. **to d. down,** *vi* bajar aprisa. *vt* derribar; (overturn) volcar; (throw) tirar. **to d. off,** *vi* marcharse rápidamente. *vt* hacer apresuradamente; (a letter, etc.) escribir de prisa; (sketch) bosquejar rápidamente. **to d. out,** *vi* salir precipitadamente; lanzarse a la calle. *vt* (erase) borrar; hacer saltar. **to d. through,** atravesar rápidamente; hacer de prisa. **to d. up,** llegar a prisa; (sprout) saltar

dashing *a* valiente; (spirited) fogoso, gallardo; majo, brillante. *n* choque, *m;* (breaking) quebrantamiento, *m;* (of the waves) embate, *m*

dastardly *a* cobarde

data *n pl* datos, *m pl*

data processing *n* elaboración electrónica de datos, *f,* recuento de datos, *m*

date *n* fecha, *f;* (period) época, *f;* (term) plazo, *m;* (duration) duración, *f;* (appointment) cita, *f; bot* dátil, *m. vt* fechar, datar; poner fecha a; asignar. *vi* datar (de), remontar (a). **out of d.,** anticuado; pasado de moda; (of persons) atrasado de noticias. **to be up to d.,** ser nuevo; ser de última moda; (of persons) estar al día. **to bring up to d.,** renovar; (of persons) poner al corriente. **to fix the d.,** señalar el día; (chronologically) ajustar los tiempos. **to d.,** hasta la fecha. **under d. (of),** con fecha (de). **up to d.,** hasta hoy, hasta ahora. **What is the d.?** ¿Qué fecha es? ¿A cómo estamos hoy? ¿A cuántos estamos hoy? **d. palm,** datilera, *f*

date of expiry *n* fecha de caducidad, *f*

daub *vt* barrar, embadurnar; manchar, ensuciar; untar; (paint) pintorrear. *n* embadurnamiento, *m;* (picture) aleluya, *f*

dauber *n* chafalmejas, pintamonas, *mf* pintor (-ra) de brocha gorda

daughter *n* hija, *f.* **adopted d.,** hija adoptiva, *f.* **little d.,** hijuela, *f.* **d.-in-law,** nuera, *f*

daughterly *a* de hija

daunt *vt* intimidar, acobardar; dar miedo (a), espantar; (dishearten) desanimar

dauntless *a* impávido, intrépido

dauphin *n* delfín, *m*

dawdle *vi* perder el tiempo; haraganear, gandulear

dawdler *n* gandul (-la)

dawdling *a* perezoso, lento

dawn *n* alba, madrugada, primera luz, *f; fig* aurora, *f. vi* amanecer, alborear, romper el día; (appear) mostrarse, asomar. **at d.,** a primera luz, al amanecer, de madrugada, al alba. **It had not dawned on me,** No me había ocurrido

day *n* día, *m;* luz del día, *f;* (day's work) jornada, *f;* (battle) batalla, *f;* (victory) victoria, *f; pl* **days,** (time) tiempos, *m pl,* época, *f;* (life) vida, *f;* (years) años, *m pl, a* diario. **all day long,** durante todo el día. **any day,**

cualquier día. **by day,** de día. **by the day,** al día. **every day,** todos los días, cada día. **every other day,** un día sí y otro no, cada dos días. **from this day forward,** desde hoy en adelante. **from day to day,** de día en día. **Good day!** ¡Buenos días! **in these days,** en estos días. **in olden days,** en la antigüedad; *inf* en tiempos de Maricastaña. **in the days of,** en los tiempos de; durante los años de; durante la vida de. **next day,** el día siguiente. **(on) the next day,** al día siguiente, al otro día. **one of these days,** un día de éstos. **some fine day,** el mejor día, de un día a otro. **the day after tomorrow,** pasado mañana. **the day before yesterday,** anteayer. **the day before,** la víspera. **to win the day,** ganar el día, salir victorioso. **day after day,** cada día, día tras día. **day by day,** día por día. **day in, day out,** sin cesar, día tras día. **daybook,** *com* libro diario, *m.* **day's holiday,** día de asueto, *m;* día libre, *m.* **day laborer,** jornalero, *m.* **day nursery,** guardería de niños, *f.* **day-pupil,** alumno (-na) externo (-na). **day-school,** externado, *m.* **day shift,** turno de día, *m.* **day-star,** lucero del alba, *m.* **day ticket,** billete de excursión, *m*

daybreak *n* alba, *f,* amanecer, *m.* **at d.,** al romper el día, al amanecer

daydream *n* ensueño, *m;* ilusión, *f;* fantasía, visión, *f. vi lit* soñar despierto, dejar volar sus pensamientos; *fig* hacerse ilusiones

daydreamer *n* soñador (-ra); visionario (-ia)

daylight *n* luz del día, *f,* día, *m;* (contrasted with artificial light) luz natural, *f.* **in broad d.,** a plena calle, a plena luz, en plena luz del día. **It's d. robbery!** ¡Es un desuello! **d.-saving,** hora de verano, *f*

daytime *n* día, *m.* **in the d.,** durante el día

daze *vt* aturdir, confundir; (dazzle) deslumbrar. *n* aturdimiento, *m,* confusión, *f;* perplejidad, *f*

dazzle *vt* (camouflage) disfrazar; deslumbrar, ofuscar. *n* deslumbramiento, *m;* brillo, *m,* refulgencia, *f*

dazzling *a* deslumbrador; brillante

deacon *n* diácono, *m*

deaconess *n* diaconisa, *f*

dead *a* and *past part* muerto; inanimado; (withered) marchito; (deep) profundo; (unconscious) inerte; inmóvil; insensible; (numb) entumecido; (complete) absoluto, completo; (sure) certero, excelente; (useless) inútil; (of color and human character) apagado; sin espíritu; inactivo; (of eyes) mortecino; (of sound) sordo, opaco; (of villages, etc.) desierto, despoblado; (quiet) silencioso; (empty) vacío; (monotonous) monótono; (of fire) apagado; (with weight, language) muerto; *elec* interrumpido; *law* muerto civilmente. *adv* completamente, enteramente; del todo; directamente; exactamente; profundamente. **the d.,** los muertos. **in the d. of night,** en las altas horas de la noche. **to be d.,** estar muerto; haber muerto. **to be d. against,** estar completamente opuesto a. **to drop d.,** caer muerto; morir de repente. **to go d. slow,** ir muy lentamente. **to rise from the d.,** resucitar. **to sham d.,** hacer la mortecina, fingirse muerto. **to speak ill of the d.,** hablar mal de los muertos; *inf* desenterrar los muertos. **d. ball,** pelota fuera de juego, *f.* **d.-beat,** muerto de cansancio. **d. body,** cadáver, cuerpo muerto, *m.* **d. calm,** calma profunda, *f; naut* calma chicha, *f.* **d. certainty,** seguridad completa, *f.* **d.-drunk,** hecho una uva. **d. end,** callejón sin salida, *m.* **d. heat,** empate, *m.* **d. language,** lengua muerta, *f.* **d.-letter,** letra muerta, *f;* carta devuelta por no reclamada, *f.* **d.-lock,** punto muerto, *m.* **to reach a d.-lock,** llegar a un punto muerto. **d. march,** marcha fúnebre, *f.* **d. season,** temporada de calma, *f.* **d. set,** empeñado (en). **d. shot,** (person) tirador (-ra) certero (-ra) (shot) tiro certero, *m.* **d. silence,** silencio profundo, *m.* **d. stop,** parada en seco, *f.* **d. tired,** rendido, *m.* **d. weight,** peso muerto, *m.* **d. wood,** leña seca, *f;* material inútil, *m*

deaden *vt* amortiguar; (of pain) calmar; (remove) quitar; (of colours) apagar

deadening *n* amortiguamiento, *m*

deadliness *n* carácter mortal, *m;* implacabilidad, *f*

deadly *a* mortal; implacable; *inf* insoportable. *adv* mortalmente. **He was d. pale,** Estaba pálido como un muerto. **the seven d. sins,** los siete pecados mortales. **d. nightshade,** belladona, *f*

deadness *n* falta de vida, *f;* inercia, *f;* marchitez, *f;* (numbness) entumecimiento, *m;* desanimación, *f;* parálisis, *f*

Dead Sea, the el mar Muerto, *m*

Dead Sea Scrolls, the los rollos del mar Muerto, *m pl*

deaf *a* sordo. **d. people,** los sordos. **to be d.,** ser sordo; padecer sordera. **to be as d. as a post,** ser más sordo que una tapia. **to become d.,** ensordecer, volverse sordo. **to fall on d. ears,** caer en saco roto. **to turn a d. ear,** hacerse el sordo. **d. aid,** audífono, *m.* **d.-and-dumb,** sordomudo. **d.-and-dumb alphabet,** alfabeto manual, abecedario manual, *m.* **d.-mute,** sordomudo (-da). **d.-mutism,** sordomudez, *f*

deafen *vt* asordar, ensordecer

deafening *a* ensordecedor

deafly *adv* sordamente

deafness *n* sordera, *f*

deal *n* (transaction) negocio, trato, *m;* (at cards) reparto, *m;* (wood) pino, *m;* (plank) tablón de pino, *m.* **a d., a great d.,** mucho. **a very great d.,** muchísimo. **to conclude a d.,** cerrar un trato

deal *vt* repartir; (a blow) asestar, dar; (cards) dar; (justice) dispensar. **to be as d. a blow at,** asestar un golpe; *fig* herir (en); *fig* destruir de un golpe. **to d. in,** comerciar en, traficar en; ocuparse en; meterse en. **to d. out,** dispensar. **to d. with,** (buy from) comprar de; tener relaciones con, tratar; entenderse con; portarse con; (of affairs) ocuparse en, arreglar, dirigir; (contend) luchar con; (discuss) discutir, tratar de; (of books) versar sobre

dealer *n* traficante, *mf* mercader, *m;* (at cards) el que da las cartas

dealing *n* conducta, *f;* proceder, *m;* trato, *m;* tráfico, *m; pl* **dealings,** relaciones, *f pl;* transacciones, *f pl*

dean *n ecc* deán, *m; univ* decano, *m*

dear *a* (beloved) querido, amado; (charming) encantador, simpático; (in letters) estimado, querido; (favorite) predilecto; (expensive) caro. *n* querido (-da); persona querida, *f,* bien amado (-da). *adv* caro. **Oh d.!** ¡Dios mío! ¡Ay!

dearly *adv* tiernamente, entrañablemente; caro

dearness *n* cariño, afecto, *m,* ternura, *f;* (of price) precio alto, *m*

dearth *n* carestía, *f;* (of news, etc.) escasez, *f*

death *n* muerte, *f;* (*law* and announcements) fallecimiento, *m,* defunción, *f.* **to be at death's door,** estar a la muerte. **to put to d.,** ajusticiar. **to the d.,** a muerte. **untimely d.,** muerte repentina, *f;* malogro, *m.* **death's head,** calavera, *f.* **d. certificate,** partida de defunción, *f.* **d.-duties,** derechos de herencia, *m pl.* **d.-like,** cadavérico. **d.-mask,** mascarilla, *f.* **d. penalty,** pena de muerte, *f.* **d.-rate,** mortalidad, *f.* **d.-rattle,** sarrillo, *m.* **d.-trap,** lugar peligroso, *m; fig* trampa, *f.* **d.-warrant,** sentencia de muerte, *f.* **d.-watch beetle,** reloj de la muerte, *m*

deathbed *n* lecho mortuorio, lecho de muerte, *m.* **on one's d.,** en su lecho de muerte

deathblow *n* golpe mortal, *m*

deathless *a* inmortal, eterno

deathly *a* mortal

death toll *n* (of a bell) doble, toque de difuntos, *m;* (casualties) número de muertos, saldo de muertos, *m*

debacle *n fig* ruina, *f*

debar *vt* excluir, privar

debase *vt* degradar, humillar, envilecer; (the coinage) alterar (la moneda)

debasement *n* degradación, humillación, *f,* envilecimiento, *m;* (of the coinage) alteración (de la moneda), *f*

debasing *a* degradante, humillante

debatable *a* discutible

debate *n* debate, *m*; discusión, *f*; disputa, *f*. *vt* and *vi* debatir; discutir; disputar; considerar

debater *n* discutidor (-ra); orador (-ra).

debating *n* discusión, *f*; argumentación, *f*

debauch *vt* corromper, pervertir; (a woman) seducir, violar. *n* libertinaje, *m*; borrachera, *f*

debauched *a* vicioso, licencioso

debauchee *n* libertino, vicioso, *m*

debauchery *n* libertinaje, mal vivir, *m*, viciosidad, licencia, *f*

debenture *n* obligación, *f*. **d. holder,** obligacionista, *mf*

debilitate *vt* debilitar

debilitating *a* debilitante

debilitation *n* debilitación, *f*

debility *n* debilidad, *f*

debit *n* débito, cargo, *m*; saldo deudor, *m*; "debe" de una cuenta, *m*. *vt* adeudar. **d. and credit,** el cargo y la data. **d. balance,** saldo deudor, *m*

debonair *a* gallardo, gentil, donairoso; alegre

debonairly *adv* gallardamente; alegremente

débris *n* escombros, desechos, *m pl*; ruinas, *f pl*; *geol* despojos, *m pl*

debt *n* deuda, *f*. **a bad d.,** una deuda incobrable. **to be in the d. of,** ser en cargo a; deber dinero a; *fig* sentirse bajo una obligación. **to get into d.,** adeudarse, contraer deudas

debtor *n* deudor (-ra); *com* debe, *m*

debunk *vt* demoler

debut *n* (of a debutante) puesta de largo, *f*; (of a play, etc.) estreno, *m*. **to make one's d.,** ponerse de largo, presentarse en sociedad

debutante *n* debutante, *f*

decade *n* década, *f*, decenio, *m*; (of the rosary) decena, *f*

decadence *n* decadencia, *f*

decadent *a* decadente

decagramme *n* decagramo, *m*

decaliter *n* decalitro, *m*

decalogue *n* decálogo, *m*

decametre *n* decámetro, *m*

decamp *vi mil* decampar; escaparse, fugarse

decant *vt* decantar

decanter *n* garrafa, *f*

decapitate *vt* decapitar, descabezar

decapitation *n* decapitación, *f*

decarbonization *n* descarburación, *f*

decarbonize *vt* descarbonizar

decay *vi* (rot) pudrirse; degenerar; marchitarse; (of teeth) cariarse; (crumble) desmoronarse, caer en ruinas; decaer, declinar; (come down in the world) venir a menos, arruinarse. *n* pudrición, putrefacción, *f*; (of teeth) caries, *f*; (withering) marchitez, *f*; degeneración, *f*; desmoronamiento, *m*; ruina, *f*; (oldness) vejez, *f*; decadencia, declinación, *f*; (fall) caída, *f*

decease *n* fallecimiento, *m*, defunción, *f*, *vi* fallecer

deceased *n* finado (-da), difunto (-ta). *a* difunto

deceit *n* engaño, fraude, *m*; duplicidad, *f*

deceitful *a* engañoso, falso; embustero, mentiroso; ilusorio

deceitfully *adv* engañosamente

deceitfulness *n* falsedad, duplicidad, *f*

deceivable *a* fácil a engañar, engañadizo

deceive *vt* engañar; (disappoint) decepcionar, desilusionar; frustrar. **If my memory does not d. me,** Si la memoria no me engaña, Si mal no me acuerdo

deceiver *n* engañador (-ra); seductor, *m*

deceiving *a* engañador

December *n* diciembre, *m*

decency *n* decoro, *m*, decencia, *f*; pudor, *m*, modestia, *f*; conveniencias, *f pl*; *inf* bondad, *f*; (manners) cortesía, *f*, buenos modales, *m pl*

decennial *a* decenal

decent *a* decente; decoroso, honesto; púdico; (likable) simpático; (of things) bastante bueno; (honorable) honrado

decently *adv* decentemente

decentralization *n* descentralización, *f*

decentralize *vt* descentralizar

deception *n* engaño, *m*; ilusión, *f*

deceptive *a* engañoso, mentiroso, ilusorio

deceptively *adv* engañosamente

decide *vt* decidir; *law* determinar. *vi* decidir, resolver; acordar, quedar en; juzgar; *law* dictar sentencia, fallar

decided *a* decidido; (downright) categórico, inequívoco; resuelto; positivo; definitivo

decidedly *adv* decididamente; categóricamente; definitivamente

deciduous *a bot* caedizo

decigram *n* decigramo, *m*

decimal *a* decimal. **d. fraction,** fracción decimal, *f*. **d. point,** punto decimal, *m*. **d. system,** sistema métrico, *m*

decimate *vt* diezmar

decimation *n* gran mortandad, *f*; matanza, *f*

decimeter *n* decímetro, *m*

decipher *vt* descifrar; deletrear

decipherable *a* descifrable

decipherer *n* descifrador, *m*

decipherment *n* el descifrar; deletreo, *m*

decision *n* decisión, determinación, *f*; *law* sentencia, *f*, fallo, *m*; (agreement) acuerdo, *m*; (of character) firmeza, resolución, *f*

decisive *a* decisivo; terminante, conclusivo; crítico

decisively *adv* decisivamente

decisiveness *n* carácter decisivo, *m*; firmeza, resolución, *f*; decisión, *f*

deck *n* cubierta, *f*; (of cards) baraja (de naipes), *f*. *vt* adornar, ataviar; decorar. **between decks,** entrecubiertas, *f pl*. **lower d.,** cubierta, *f*. **promenade d.,** cubierta de paseo, *f*. **upper d.,** cubierta superior, *f*. **d.-cabin,** camarote de cubierta, *m*. **d.-chair,** silla de cubierta, silla de tijera, silla extensible, *f*. **d.-hand,** marinero, estibador, *m*

decked *a* ornado, ataviado; engalanado; *naut* de . . . puentes

declaim *vt* recitar. *vi* perorar, declamar

declamation *n* declamación, *f*

declamatory *a* declamatorio

declaration *n* declaración, *f*; manifiesto, *m*; proclamación, *f*

declaratory *a* declaratorio, declarativo

declare *vt* declarar; proclamar; afirmar; manifestar; confesar. *vi* declarar; *law* deponer, testificar. **to d. war (on)** declarar la guerra (a)

declaredly *adv* declaradamente, explícitamente, abiertamente

declension *n* declinación, *f*

declination *n* declinación, *f*

decline *n* declinación, decadencia, *f*; disminución, *f*; debilitación, *f*; (of the day) caída, *f*; (of stocks, shares) depresión, *f*; (illness) consunción, *f*; (*fig* setting) ocaso, *m*, *vi* declinar; inclinarse; decaer; disminuir; debilitarse; (refuse) negarse (a). *vt* (refuse) rechazar, rehusar; *gram* declinar; (avoid) evitar

declining *a* declinante. **in one's d. years,** en sus últimos años

declivity *n* cuesta, pendiente, *f*, declive, *m*

declutch *vi* desembragar

decoction *n* decocción, *f*

decode *vt* descifrar

decoder *n* descifrador, *m*

décolletee *a* escotado

decolouration *n* decoloración, *f*

decompose *vt* descomponer. *vi* descomponerse

decomposition *n* descomposición, *f*

decompressor *n* decompresor, *m*

decontaminate *vt* descontaminar

decontamination *n* descontaminación, *f*

decontrol *vt* suprimir las restricciones sobre

decorate *vt* adornar (con), embellecer; (by painting, etc.) decorar, pintar; (honor) investir (con), condecorar

decoration *n* decoración, *f; theat* decorado, *m;* (honor) condecoración, *f;* ornamento, *m*

decorative *a* decorativo

decorator *n* decorador, *m;* (interior) adornista, *m*

decorous *a* decoroso, decente; correcto

decorum *n* decoro, *m;* corrección, *f*

decoy *n* señuelo, *m;* añagaza, *f;* (trap) lazo, *m,* trampa, *f; fig* añagaza, *f. vt* (birds) reclamar, atraer con señuelo; *fig* tentar (con), seducir (con). **d. bird,** pájaro de reclamo, *m*

decrease *n* disminución, *f;* baja, *f;* reducción, *f;* (of the moon, waters) mengua, *f, vi* decrecer, disminuir; bajar; menguar. *vt* disminuir; reducir

decreasingly *adv* de menos en menos

decree *n* decreto, *m;* edicto, *m. vi* and *vt* decretar, mandar

decrepit *a* decrépito

decry *vt* desacreditar, rebajar

dedicate *vt* dedicar; consagrar; destinar; aplicar; (a book, etc.) dedicar. **to d. oneself to,** dedicarse a, consagrarse a, entregarse a

dedication *n* dedicación, *f;* consagración, *f;* (of a book, etc.) dedicatoria, *f*

dedicatory *a* dedicatorio

deduce *vt* derivar; deducir, inferir

deduct *vt* deducir; descontar

deduction *n* deducción, *f;* descuento, *m*

deductive *a* deductivo

deed *n* acción, *f;* hecho, acto, *m;* hazaña, *f;* (reality) realidad, *f; law* escritura, *f; law* contrato, *m.* **d. of gift,** escritura de donación, *f*

deem *vt* juzgar, creer, estimar

deep *a* profundo; (wide) ancho; (low) bajo; (thick) espeso; (of colours) subido; (of sounds) grave, profundo; (immersed (in)) absorto (en); (of the mind) penetrante; (secret) secreto; (intense) intenso, hondo; (cunning) astuto, artero; (dark) oscuro; (of mourning) riguroso. *n poet* piélago, mar, *m;* profundidad, *f;* abismo, *m, adv* profundamente; a una gran profundidad. **to be in d. waters,** *fig* estar con el agua al cuello. **to be three feet d.,** tener tres pies de profundidad. **to be d. in,** estar absorto en; (of debt) estar cargado de. **three d.,** tres de fondo. **d. into the night,** hasta las altas horas de la noche. **d.-felt,** hondamente sentido. **d. mourning,** luto riguroso, *m.* **d.-rooted,** arraigado. **d.-sea fishing,** pesca mayor, *f.* **d.-sea lead,** escandallo, *m.* **d.-seated,** íntimo, profundo; arraigado. **d.-set,** hundido

deepen *vt* profundizar, ahondar; (broaden) ensanchar; (intensify) intensificar; (increase) aumentar; (of colors) aumentar el tono de, intensificar. *vi* hacerse más profundo, hacerse más hondo; intensificarse; aumentarse; (of sound) hacerse más grave

deeply *adv* profundamente; intensamente; fuertemente

deepness *n* (cunning) astucia, *f;* see **depth**

deer *n* ciervo (-va), venado, *m, a* cervuno. **d.-hound,** galgo de cazar venados, *m.* **d.-skin,** piel de venado, *f.* **d.-stalking,** caza del ciervo, *f*

deface *vt* desfigurar, mutilar; estropear; (erase) borrar

defacement *n* desfiguración, mutilación, *f;* afeamiento, *m;* borradura, *f*

defamation *n* difamación, denigración, *f*

defamatory *a* difamatorio, denigrante

defame *vt* difamar, denigrar, calumniar

default *n* omisión, *f,* descuido, *m;* falta, *f;* ausencia, *f; law* rebeldía, *f. vi* dejar de cumplir; faltar; no pagar. *vt law* condenar en rebeldía. **in d. of,** en la ausencia de

defaulter *n* el, *m,* (*f,* la) que no cumple sus obligaciones; delincuente, *mf;* desfalcador (-ra) *law* rebelde, *mf*

defeat *vt* vencer, derrotar; frustrar; (reject) rechazar; (elude) evitar; *fig* vencer, triunfar sobre. *n* derrota, *f;* vencimiento, *m;* frustración, *f;* rechazamiento, *m.* **to d. one's own ends,** defraudar sus intenciones

defeatism *n* derrotismo, *m*

defeatist *n* derrotista, *mf*

defecate *vt* defecar

defecation *n* defecación, *f*

defect *n* defecto, *m;* imperfección, *f;* falta, *f*

defection *n* defección, *f;* deserción, *f;* (from a religion) apostasía, *f*

defective *a* defectuoso; *gram* defectivo; falto; imperfecto; (mentally) anormal. *n* persona anormal, *f,* anormal, *m*

defectiveness *n* imperfección, *f;* deficiencia, *f;* defecto, *m*

defend *vt* defender; proteger; preservar; sostener; (a thesis) sustentar

defendant *n law* acusado (-da), procesado (-da), demandado (-da)

defender *n* defensor (-ra); (of a thesis) sustentante, *mf*

defense *n* defensa, *f;* justificación, *f; pl* **defenses,** defensas, *f pl;* obras de fortificación, *f pl.* **for the d.,** (of witnesses) de descargo; (of counsel) para la defensa. **in d. of,** en defensa de. **in one's own d.,** en su propia defensa. **d. in depth,** *mil* defensa en fondo, *f*

defenseless *a* indefenso, sin defensa

defenselessness *n* incapacidad de defenderse, *f;* debilidad, *f,* desvalimiento, *m*

defensible *a* defendible; justificable

defensive *a* defensivo. *n* defensiva, *f.* **to be on the d.,** estar a la defensiva

defensively *adv* defensivamente

defer *vt* (postpone) diferir, aplazar; suspender. *vi* (yield) deferir, ceder; (delay) tardar, aguardar. **deferred payment,** pago a plazos, *m*

deference *n* deferencia, *f,* respeto, *m;* consideración, *f*

deferential *a* deferente, respetuoso

deferment *n* aplazamiento, *m;* suspensión, *f*

defiance *n* desafío, *m;* provocación, *f;* oposición, *f;* insolencia, *f.* **in d. of,** en contra de

defiant *a* provocativo; insolente

defiantly *adv* de un aire provocativo; insolentemente

deficiency *n* falta, deficiencia, *f;* imperfección, *f;* defecto, *m;* omisión, *f;* (scarcity) carestía, *f;* (in accounts) déficit, *m*

deficient *a* deficiente; falto, incompleto; imperfecto; pobre; defectuoso; (not clever at) débil (en); (mentally) anormal. **to be d. in,** carecer de; ser pobre en

deficit *n* déficit, *m;* descubierto, *m*

defile *n* desfiladero, *m. vt* contaminar; profanar; manchar; deshonrar. *vi mil* desfilar

defilement *n* contaminación, *f;* corrupción, *f;* profanación, *f*

definable *a* definible

define *vt* definir; (throw into relief) destacar; fijar; *law* determinar

definite *a* definido; positivo; categórico; exacto; concreto. **d. article,** artículo definido, *m*

definitely *adv* positivamente; claramente. **definitely not!** ¡definitivamente no!

definiteness *n* carácter definido, *m;* exactitud, *f;* lo categórico

definition *n* definición, *f*

definitive *a* definitivo

deflate *vt* desinflar. *vi* desinflarse, deshincharse

deflation *n* desinflación, *f*

deflect *vt* desviar; apartar. *vi* desviarse; apartarse

deflection *n* desviación, *f;* apartamiento, *m*

defloration *n* desfloración, *f*

deflower *vt* desflorar

deforestation *n* desforestación, desmontadura, despoblación forestal, *f*

deform *vt* deformar, desfigurar; afear

deformation *n* deformación, *f*

deformed *a* deformado; contrahecho

deformity *n* deformidad, *f*

defraud *vt* defraudar

defrauder *n* defraudador (-ra)

defrauding *n* defraudación, *f*

defray *vt* sufragar, costear, pagar

defrayal *n* pago, *m*

defrost *vt* deshelar

deft *a* diestro; hábil

deftly *adv* con destreza; hábilmente

deftness *n* destreza, *f*; habilidad, *f*

defunct *a* and *n* difunto (-ta)

defy *vt* desafiar; (face) arrostrar; (violate) contravenir

degeneracy *n* degeneración, *f*; depravación, degradación, *f*

degenerate *a* and *n* degenerado (-da). *vi* degenerar

degeneration *n* degeneración, *f*

degradation *n* degradación, *f*; abyección, *f*

degrade *vt* degradar; envilecer, deshonrar

degrading *a* degradante

degree *n* grado, *m*; punto, *m*; clase social, *f*. **by degrees,** poco a poco, gradualmente, **five degrees below zero,** cinco grados bajo cero. **in the highest d.,** en sumo grado, en grado superlativo. **to a certain d.,** hasta cierto punto. **to receive a d.,** graduarse

degree-granting institution *n* plantel habilitado para expedir títulos, *m*

dehydrate *vt* deshidratar

dehydration *n* deshidratación, *f*

de-ice *vt* deshelar

deicide *n* (act) deicidio, *m*; (person) deicida, *mf*

deification *n* deificación, *f*

deify *vt* deificar, endiosar

deign *vi* dignarse. *vt* conceder

deism *n* deísmo, *m*

deist *n* deísta, *mf*

deity *n* deidad, divinidad, *f*; dios, *m*

dejected *a* abatido, desanimado, deprimido

dejectedly *adv* tristemente, abatidamente

dejection *n* abatimiento, desaliento, *m*, melancolía, *f*

delay *n* retraso, *m*, dilación, tardanza, demora, *f*. *vt* retrasar, demorar; (a person) entretener; (postpone) aplazar; (obstruct) impedir. *vi* tardar; entretenerse. **without more d.,** sin más tardar

delectable *a* deleitoso, delicioso

delectably *adv* deliciosamente

delectation *n* delectación, *f*, deleite, *m*

delegacy *n* delegación, *f*

delegate *n* delegado (-da). *vt* delegar, diputar

delegation *n* delegación, *f*

delete *vt* suprimir, borrar

deleterious *a* deletéreo

deletion *n* supresión, borradura, *f*

deliberate *a* premeditado, intencionado; (slow) pausado, lento. *vi* and *vt* deliberar, discurrir, considerar

deliberately *adv* (intentionally) con premeditación, a sabiendas; (slowly) pausadamente, lentamente

deliberation *n* reflexión, deliberación, consideración, *f*; (slowness) lentitud, pausa, *f*

deliberative *a* deliberativo, de liberante

delicacy *n* delicadeza, *f*; fragilidad, *f*; suavidad, *f*; sensibilidad, *f*; escrupulosidad, *f*; (of health) debilidad, delicadez, *f*; (difficulty) dificultad, *f*; (food) manjar exquisito, *m*, golosina, *f*

delicate *a* delicado; fino; frágil; suave; exquisito; delicado (de salud); (of situations) difícil

delicatessen *n* (store) fiambrería, *f*

delicious *a* delicioso

deliciously *adv* deliciosamente

deliciousness *n* deleite, *m*, lo delicioso; excelencia, *f*; delicias, *f pl*

delict *n* delito, *m*

delictive *a* delictivo

delight *n* deleite, regocijo, *m*; encanto, *m*, delicia, *f*; placer, gozo, *m*. *vt* deleitar, encantar; halagar. *vi* deleitarse, complacerse. **to be delighted with,** estar encantado con. **to d. in,** deleitarse en, complacerse en; tomar placer en

delightful *a* delicioso, precioso, encantador

delightfully *adv* deliciosamente

delimit *vt* delimitar

delimitation *n* delimitación, *f*

delineate *vt* delinear, diseñar; *fig* pintar, describir

delineation *n* delineación, *f*; retrato, *m*; *fig* descripción, *f*

delineator *n* diseñador, *m*

delinquency *n* delincuencia, *f*; criminalidad, *f*; culpa, *f*; delito, *m*

delinquent *a* delincuente. *n* delincuente, *mf*

deliquescence *n* delicuescencia, *f*

deliquescent *a* delicuescente

delirious *a* delirante; desvariado; *inf* loco. **to be d.,** delirar, desvariar

delirium *n* delirio, desvarío, *m*. **d. tremens,** delírium tremens, *m*

deliver *vt* librar (de); salvar (de); (distribute) repartir; (hand over) entregar; (recite) recitar, decir; (a speech) pronunciar; comunicar; (send) despachar, expedir; (a blow) asestar; (give) dar; (bring) traer; (battle, a lecture) dar; (a woman, of a doctor) asistir en el parto (a); (a child) traer al mundo; (a judgment) pronunciar. **to be delivered (of a child),** dar a luz. **to d. oneself up,** entregarse. **delivered free,** porte pagado.

deliverance *n* libramiento, rescate, *m*; redención, salvación, *f*; (of a judgment) pronuncia, *f*

deliverer *n* libertador (-ra); salvador (-ra); (distributor) repartidor (-ra); entregador (-ra)

delivery *n* (distribution) reparto, *m*, distribución, *f*; entrega, *f*; *law* cesión, *f*; (of a judgment) pronuncia, *f*; (of a speech) pronunciación, *f*; (manner of speaking) declamación, *f*; dicción, *f*; (of a child) parto, *m*. **on d.,** al entregarse. **The letter came by the first d.,** La carta llegó en el primer reparto. **d. man,** mozo de reparto, *m*. **d. note,** nota de entrega, *f*. **d. van,** camión de reparto, *m*

delivery truck *n* camioneta de reparto, furgoneta, *f*, sedán de reparto, *m*

dell *n* hondonada, *f*; pequeño valle, *m*

delouse *vt* despiojar, espulgar

Delphi Delfos, *m*

delta *n* (Greek letter) delta, *f*; (of a river) delta, *m*

delude *vt* engañar; ilusionar. **to d. oneself,** engañarse

deluded *a* iluso, engañado, ciego

deluge *n* diluvio, *m*. *vt* diluviar; inundar (con)

delusion *n* engaño, *m*, ceguedad, *f*; error, *m*; ilusión, *f*

delve *vt* and *vi* cavar; *fig* ahondar (en), penetrar (en), investigar

demagogic *a* demagógico

demagogue *n* demagogo (-ga)

demagogy *n* demagogia, *f*

demand *n* exigencia, *f*; *com* demanda, *f*; petición, *f*; *pol* econ consumo, *m*. *vt* exigir; requerir; pedir; (claim) reclamar. **in d.,** en demanda. **on d.,** al solicitarse. **to be in d.,** ser popular. **d. note,** apremio, *m*

demanding *a* exigente

demarcate *vt* demarcar

demarcation *n* demarcación, *f*

demean (oneself) *vr* degradarse, rebajarse

demeanor *n* conducta, *f*; continente, porte, aire, *m*; (manners) modales, *m pl*

demented *a* demente, loco

demerit *n* demérito, *m*

demi *prefix* semi; casi. **d.-tasse,** taza cafetera, jícara, *f*

demigod *n* semidios, *m*

demigoddess *n* semidiosa, *f*

demijohn *n* damajuana, *f*

demilitarize *vt* desmilitarizar

demise *n* *law* traslación de dominio, *f*; sucesión de la corona, *f*; (death) óbito, fallecimiento, *m*

demisemiquaver *n* fusa, *f*

demobilization *n* desmovilización, *f*

demobilize *vt* desmovilizar

democracy *n* democracia, *f*

democrat *n* demócrata, *mf*

democratic *a* democrático. **to make d.,** democratizar

demolish *vt* demoler, derribar; *fig* destruir; (eat) engullir, devorar

demolisher *n* demoledor, *m*; *fig* destructor (-ra)

demolition *n* demolición, *f*; derribo, *m*, *a* demoledor; de demolición. **d. squad,** pelotón de demolición, *m*

demon *n* demonio, diablo, *m*

demonetization *n* desmonetización, *f*

demonetize *vt* desmonetizar

demoniacal *a* demoníaco

demonology *n* demonología, *f*

demonstrable *a* demonstrable

demonstrably *adv* demostrablemente

demonstrate *vt* demostrar; mostrar, probar. *vi* hacer una demostración

demonstration *n* demostración, *f*; manifestación, *f*

demonstrative *a* demostrativo; (of persons) expresivo, mimoso. **d. pronoun,** pronombre demostrativo, *m*

demonstrator *n* demostrador (-ra)

demoralization *n* desmoralización, *f*

demoralize *vt* desmoralizar

demoralizing *a* desmoralizador

demur *vi* dudar, vacilar; objetar, protestar; poner dificultades. *n* objeción, protesta, *f*

demure *a* serio, modoso recatado; púdico; de una coquetería disimulada

demurely *adv* modestamente; con recato; con coquetería disimulada

demureness *n* seriedad, *f*, recato, *m*; modestia fingida, coquetería disimulada, *f*

demy *n* papel marquilla, *m*; becario de Magdalen College, Oxford, *m*

den *n* madriguera, guardia, *f*; (of thieves) cueva, *f*; (in a zoo) cercado, recinto, *m*; (study) gabinete, *m*; (squalid room) cuartucho, *m*

denaturalization *n* desnaturalización, *f*

denaturalize *vt* desnaturalizar

denial *n* negación, *f*; rechazo, *m*; contradicción, *f*; negativa, *f*

denizen *n* habitante, *m*; ciudadano (-na)

Denmark Dinamarca, *f*

denominate *vt* denominar, nombrar

denomination *n* denominación, *f*; secta, *f*; clase, *f*

denominational *a* sectario

denominator *n* math denominador, *m*

denote *vt* denotar, indicar; significar

dénouement *n* desenlace, desenredo, *m*; solución, *f*

denounce *vt* denunciar; delatar, acusar

denouncer *n* denunciante, *mf* delator (-ra)

dense *a* denso; espeso, compacto; tupido; impenetrable; *inf* estúpido

densely *adv* densamente; espesamente. **d. populated,** con gran densidad de población

density *n* densidad, *f*; espesor, *m*; consistencia, *f*; *inf* estupidez, *f*

dent *n* mella, *f*; (in metal) abolladura, *f*, *vt* mellar; abollar

dental *a* dental. *n* letra dental, *f*. **d. forceps,** gatillo, *m*. **d. mechanic,** mecánico dentista, *m*. **d. surgeon,** odontólogo, *m*

dental floss *n* seda dental, *f*

dentifrice *n* dentífrico, *m*

dentist *n* dentista, *mf*; odontólogo, *m*

dentistry *n* odontología, *f*

dentition *n* dentición, *f*

denture *n* dentadura, *f*

denudation *n* denudación, *f*

denude *vt* denudar, despojar, privar (de)

denunciation *n* denuncia, *f*; acusación, delación, *f*

denunciatory *a* denunciatorio

Denver boot *n* cepo, *m*

deny *vt* negar; desmentir; rehusar; rechazar; renegar (de); (give up) renunciar, sacrificar. **to d. oneself,** privarse (de); sacrificar; negarse

deodorant *a* and *n* desodorante, *m*

deodorize *vt* desinfectar, destruir el olor de

depart *vi* marcharse, irse, partir; (of trains, etc., and meaning go out) salir; (deviate) desviarse (de), apartarse (de); (go away) alejarse; (leave) dejar; (disappear) desaparecer; (alter) cambiar; (die) morir

departed *a* (past) pasado; desaparecido; (dead) difunto, muerto. *n* difunto (-ta)

department *n* departamento, *m*; sección, *f*; (of learning) ramo, *m*; (in France) distrito administrativo, *m*. **d. store,** grandes tiendas, *f pl*, (Argentina), grandes almacenes, *m pl*

departmental *a* departamental

departure *n* partida, ida, *f*; (going out, and of trains, etc.) salida, *f*; (deviation) desviación, el apartarse. **d. from the rules,** el apartarse de las reglas), *f*; (disappearance) desaparición, *f*; (change) cambio, *m*; (giving up) renuncia, *f*; (death) muerte, *f*. **to take one's d.,** marcharse

depend *vi* depender. **to d. on,** depender de; (rest on) apoyarse en; (count on) contar con; (trust) fiarse de; tener confianza en, estar seguro de. **That depends!** ¡Eso depende!

dependable *a* digno de confianza; seguro

dependence, dependency *n* dependencia, *f*; subordinación, *f*; (trust) confianza, *f*

dependent *a* dependiente; subordinado; condicional. *n* dependiente, *m*. **to be d. on,** depender de

depict *vt* representar; pintar; dibujar; *fig* describir, retratar

depiction *n* representación, *f*; pintura, *f*; dibujo, *m*; *fig* descripción, *f*

depilate *vt* depilar

depilation *n* depilación, *f*

depilatory *a* and *n* depilatorio *m*.

deplete *vt* agotar; disipar

depletion *n* agotamiento, *m*

deplorable *a* lamentable, deplorable

deplorably *adv* lamentablemente

deplore *vt* deplorar, lamentar

deploy *vt* desplegar. *vi* desplegarse. *n* despliegue, *m*

deployment *n* despliegue, *m*

deponent *n* law declarante, deponente, *mf* *a* deponente. **d. verb,** verbo deponente, *m*

depopulate *vt* despoblar

depopulation *n* despoblación, *f*

deport *vt* deportar

deportation *n* deportación, *f*

deportment *n* comportamiento, *m*; porte, aire, *m*; conducta, *f*

depose *vt* destronar; (give evidence) testificar, declarar

deposit *n* depósito, *m*; *geol* yacimiento, filón, *m*; sedimento, *m*. *vt* depositar. **to leave a d.,** dejar un depósito. **d. account,** cuenta corriente, *f*

deposition *n* deposición, *f*; law testimonio, *m*, declaración, *f*; (from the Cross) descendimiento, *m*, (de la Cruz)

depositor *n* depositador (-ra)

depository *n* depositaría, *f*, almacén, *m*; (of knowledge, etc.) pozo, *m*

depot *n* almacén, *m*; (military headquarters) depósito, *m*; (for army vehicles, etc.) parque, *m*; (for buses, etc.) estación, *f*

depravation *n* depravación, *f*

depraved *a* depravado, perverso, vicioso

depravity *n* corrupción, maldad, perversión, *f*

deprecate *vt* desaprobar, criticar; lamentar, deplorar

deprecatingly *adv* con desaprobación, críticamente

deprecation *n* deprecación, *f*; desaprobación, crítica, *f*

deprecatory *a* deprecativo; de desaprobación, de crítica

depreciate *vt* depreciar, rebajar; *fig* tener en poco, menospreciar. *vi* depreciarse, deteriorarse; bajar de precio

depreciatingly *adv* con desprecio

depreciation *n* (in value) amortización, depreciación, *f*; *fig* desprecio, *m*

depreciatory *a* *fig* despectivo, despreciativo

depredation *n* depredación, *f*

depress *vt* deprimir; (weaken) debilitar; (humble) humillar; (dispirit) abatir, entristecer; (trade) desanimar, paralizar

depressed *a* deprimido, desalentado, melancólico, triste; (of an area) necesitado

depressing *a* melancólico, triste; pesimista

depressingly *adv* con tristeza; con pesimismo

depression *n* depresión, *f*; (hollow) hoyo, *m*; (sadness) desaliento, abatimiento, *m*, melancolía, *f*; (in prices) baja, *f*; (in trade) desanimación, parálisis, *f*; *ast* depresión, *f*

deprivation *n* privación, *f*; pérdida, *f*

deprive *vt* privar (de), despojar (de); defraudar (de); *ecc* destituir (de)

depth *n* profundidad, *f*; (thickness) espesor, *m*; fondo, *m*; (of night, winter, the country) medio, *m*; (of sound) gravedad, *f*; (of colour, feeling) intensidad, *f*; (abstruseness) dificultad, *f*; (sagacity) sagacidad, *f*; *pl* **depths**, profundidades, *f pl*; abismo, *m*; lo más hondo; lo más íntimo, *m*. **to be 4 feet in d.,** tener cuatro pies de profundidad. **to the depths of one's being,** hasta lo más íntimo de su ser; hasta los tuétanos. **d. charge,** carga de profundidad, *f*

deputation *n* deputación, delegación, *f*

deputize (for) *vi* desempeñar las funciones de, substituir

deputy *n* (substitute) lugarteniente, *m*; (agent) representante, *m*; apoderado, *m*; (parliamentary) diputado, *m*; (in compounds) sub, vice. **d.-governor,** subgobernador, *m*. **d.-head,** subjefe, *m*; (of a school) subdirector (-ra)

derail *vt* (hacer) descarrilar

derailment *n* descarrilamiento, *m*

derange *vt* desordenar; desorganizar; turbar; (mentally) trastornar, hacer perder el juicio (a)

derangement *n* desorden, *m*; turbación, *f*; (mental) trastorno, *m*, locura, *f*

derby *n* carrera del Derby, *f*; (hat) sombrero hongo, *m*

deregulate *vt* desregular

deregulation *n* desregulación, *f*

derelict *a* abandonado, derrelicto. *n* derrelicto, *m*

dereliction *n* abandono, *m*; omisión, negligencia, *f*; descuido, *m*

deride *vt* burlarse de, mofarse de; ridiculizar

derision *n* irrisión, *f*, menosprecio, *m*

derisive *a* irrisorio; irónico

derisively *adv* irrisoriamente; con ironía, irónicamente

derivation *n* derivación, *f*

derivative *a* derivativo. *n* derivado, *m*

derive *vt* derivar; obtener; extraer; *fig* sacar, hallar. *vi* (from) derivar de; proceder de; remontar a

dermatitis *n* dermatitis, *f*

dermatologist *n* dermatólogo, *m*

dermatology *n* dermatología, *f*

derogatory *a* despectivo, despreciativo; deshonroso

derrick *n* grúa, machina, *f*; abanico, *m*

descant *n mus* discante, *m*. *vi mus* discantar; discurrir (sobre), disertar (sobre)

descend *vi* descender, bajar; (be inherited) pasar a; (fall) caer; (of the sun) ponerse. *vt* bajar. **to d. from,** descender de. **to d. to,** (lower oneself) rebajarse; (consider) venir a, considerar. **to d. upon,** caer sobre; (arrive unexpectedly) llegar inesperadamente, invadir

descendant *n* descendiente, *mf*; *pl* **descendants,** descendencia, *f*

descent *n* descenso, *m*; bajada, *f*; (slope) pendiente, cuesta, *f*; (attack) invasión, *f*, ataque, *m*; (lineage) descendencia, alcurnia, procedencia, *f*; (inheritance) herencia, *f*; transmisión, *f*. **D. from the Cross,** Descendimiento de la Cruz, *m*

describable *a* descriptible

describe *vt* describir; pintar

description *n* descripción, *f*

descriptive *a* descriptivo

descry *vt* divisar, descubrir; *poet* ver

Desdemona Desdémona, *f*

desecrate *vt* profanar

desecration *n* profanación, *f*

desert *vt* abandonar; dejar; (mil etc.) desertar. *vi* desertar. *a* solitario; inhabitado; desierto; *fig* árido. *n* desierto, *m*; soledad, *f*; (merit) mérito, *m*. **to receive one's deserts,** llevar su merecido

deserted *a* abandonado; desierto; solitario; inhabitado, despoblado

deserter *n* desertor, *m*

desertion *n* abandono, *m*, deserción, *f*; (mil etc.) deserción, *f*

deserve *vt* and *vi* merecer

deservedly *adv* merecidamente

deserving *a* merecedor; meritorio. **to be d. of,** merecer

desiccate *vi* desecar. *vi* desecarse

design *n* proyecto, *m*; plan, *m*; intención, *f*, propósito, *m*; objeto, *m*; modelo, *m*; (pattern) diseño, dibujo, *m*; arte del dibujo, *m*. *vt* idear; proyectar; (destine) destinar, dedicar; diseñar, dibujar, delinear; planear. **by d.,** expresamente, intencionalmente

designate *vt* señalar; designar; (appoint) nombrar. *a* electo

designation *n* designación, *f*; nombramiento, *m*

designedly *adv* de propósito

designer *n* inventor (-ra), autor (-ra); delineador (-ra); dibujante, *mf*; (of public works, etc.) proyectista, *mf*

designing *a* intrigante, astuto

desirability *n* lo deseable; conveniencia, *f*; ventaja, *f*

desirable *a* deseable; conveniente; ventajoso; agradable; apetecible

desire *vt* desear; querer; ansiar, ambicionar; (request) rogar, pedir; (order) mandar. *n* deseo, *m*; ansia, aspiración, *f*; ambición, *f*; impulso, *m*; (will) voluntad, *f*. **to d. ardently,** perecerse por; suspirar por

desirous *a* deseoso (de); ambicioso (de); ansioso (de); impaciente (a); curioso (de)

desist *vi* desistir; dejar (de)

desk *n* pupitre, *m*; escritorio, buró, *m*; mesa de trabajo, *f*; (cashier's) caja, *f*; (teacher's, lecturer's; pulpit) cátedra, *f*

desolate *a* solitario; desierto; deshabitado; abandonado; arruinado; árido; (afflicted) desolado, angustiado. *vt* desolar; despoblar

desolation *n* desolación, *f*; aflicción, angustia, *f*, desconsuelo, *m*

despair *n* desesperación, *f*, *vi* perder toda esperanza. **His life is despaired of,** Se ha perdido la esperanza de salvarle (la vida). **to be in d.,** estar desesperado

despairing *a* desesperado

despairingly *adv* sin esperanza

desperate *a* desesperado; sin esperanza; irremediable; furioso; violento; (dangerous) arriesgado, peligroso; terrible

desperately *adv* desesperadamente; furiosamente; terriblemente

desperation *n* desesperación, *f*; furia, violencia, *f*

despicable *a* vil, despreciable; insignificante

despise *vt* despreciar; desdeñar

despiser *n* menospreciador (-ra)

despite *prep* a pesar de

despoil *vt* despojar, desnudar

despoiler *n* despojador (-ra)

despoliation *n* despojo, *m*

despondency *n* abatimiento, desaliento, *m*, desesperación, *f*

despondent *a* abatido, desanimado, deprimido

despondently *adv* con desaliento

despot *n* déspota, *m*

despotic *a* despótico

despotism *n* despotismo, *m*

dessert *n* postre, *m*, *a* de postre. **d. plate,** plato para postre, *m*. **d.-spoon,** cuchara de postre, *f*

destination *n* destinación, *f*

destine *vt* destinar; dedicar; predestinar

destiny *n* destino, *m*

destitute *a* indigente, menesteroso; desnudo (de); privado (de); desprovisto (de), falto (de); desamparado

destitution *n* destitución, indigencia, miseria, *f*; privación, falta, *f*; desamparo, *m*

destroy *vt* destruir; demoler; deshacer; (kill) matar; exterminar; (finish) acabar con

destroyer *n* destructor (-ra); *nav* destructor, cazatorpedero, *m*

destructible *a* destructible, destruible

destruction *n* destrucción, *f*; demolición, *f*; ruina, *f*; pérdida, *f*; muerte, *f*; exterminio, *m*; perdición, *f*

destructive *a* destructivo, destructor; (of animals) dañino. **d. animal,** animal dañino, *m*, alimaña, *f*

destructiveness *n* destructividad, *f*; instinto destructor, *m*

desultory *a* inconexo; sin método, descosido; irregular

detach *vt* separar, desprender; (unstick) despegar; *mil* destacar

detachable *a* separable, de quita y pon

detached *a* suelto, separado; (*fig* with outlook, etc.) imparcial; indiferente, despegado.

detachment *n* separación, *f*; *mil* destacamento, *m*; (*fig* of mind) imparcialidad, *f*; independencia (de espíritu, etc.), *f*; indiferencia, *f*

detail *n* detalle, *m*; pormenor, *m*, particularidad, *f*; circunstancia, *f*; *mil* destacamento, *m*. *vt* detallar; particularizar, referir con pormenores; *mil* destacar. **in d.,** detalladamente; al por menor; *inf* ce por be. **to go into details,** entrar en detalles

detain *vt* detener; (arrest) arrestar, prender; (withhold) retener; (prevent) impedir

detect *vt* descubrir; averiguar; (discern) discernir, percibir; *elec* detectar

detectable *a* perceptible

detection *n* descubrimiento, *m*; averiguación, *f*; percepción, *f*

detective *n* detective, *m*, *a* de detectives, policíaco. **d. novel,** novela policíaca, *f*

detector *n* descubridor, *m*; *elec* detector, *m*; *mech* indicador, *m*

detention *n* detención, *f*; (arrest) arresto, *m*; (confinement) encierro, *m*

deter *vt* desanimar, desalentar; acobardar; (dissuade) disuadir; (prevent) impedir

detergent *a* detersorio. *n* detersorio, *m*

deteriorate *vt* deteriorar. *vi* deteriorarse; empeorar

deterioration *n* deterioración, *f*; empeoramiento, *m*

determinable *a* determinable

determination *n* determinación, *f*; definición, *f*; resolución, decisión, *f*; *law* fallo, *m*; *med* congestión, *f*

determine *vt* determinar; definir; decidir, resolver; concluir; (fix) señalar; *law* sentenciar. *vi* resolverse; decidirse; (insist (on)) empeñarse en, insistir en

determined *a* determinado; resuelto, decidido; (of price) fijo

determining *a* determinante

determinism *n* determinismo, *m*

deterministic *a* determinista

deterrent *a* disuasivo. *n* freno, *m*. **to act as a d.,** servir como un freno

deterrent capability *n* poder de disuasión, *m*

detest *vt* detestar, abominar, aborrecer

detestable *a* detestable, aborrecible, abominable

detestation *n* detestación, abominación, *f*, aborrecimiento, *m*

dethrone *vt* destronar

detonate *vt* hacer detonar. *vi* detonar, estallar

detonation *n* detonación, *f*

detonator *n* detonador, *m*; señal detonante, *f*

detour *n* rodeo, *m*; desvío, *m*, desviación, *f*

detract *vt* quitar; (diminish) disminuir; (slander) detraer, denigrar

detraction *n* detracción, denigración, *f*

detractor *n* detractor (-ra); infamador (-ra)

detriment *n* detrimento, *m*; perjuicio, *m*; daño, *m*

detrimental *a* perjudicial

deuce *n* (dice, cards) dos, *m*; (tennis) "dos," *m*. **The d.!** ¡Diantre! **to be the d. of a row,** haber moros y cristianos. **D. take it!** ¡Demonios!

Deuteronomy *n* Deuteronomio, *m*

devaluation *n* desvalorización, *f*

devalue *vt* rebajar el valor de

devastate *vt* devastar, asolar

devastation *n* devastación, *f*

develop *vt* desarrollar; (make progress) avanzar, fomentar; perfeccionar; *phot* revelar. *vi* desarrollarse; crecer; avanzar, progresar; evolucionar

developer *n* *phot* revelador, *m*

development *n* desarrollo, *m*; evolución, *f*; progreso, avance, *m*; (encouragement) fomento, *m*; (event) acontecimiento, suceso, *m*; (product) producto, *m*; (working) explotación, *f*; *phot* revelación, *f*

deviate *vi* desviarse (de); (disagree) disentir (de)

deviation *n* desviación, *f*

device *n* (contrivance) aparato, artefacto, mecanismo, *m*; (invention) invento, *m*; (trick) expediente, artificio, *m*; (scheme) proyecto, *m*; (design) dibujo, emblema, *m*; (motto) divisa, leyenda, *f*; *pl* **devices,** placeres, caprichos, *m pl*

devil *n* diablo, Satanás, *m*; demonio, *m*; (printer's) aprendiz de impresor, *m*. **Go to the d.!** ¡Vete enhoramala! **He is a poor d.,** Es un pobre diablo. **little d.,** diablillo, *m*. **The devil's abroad,** Anda el diablo suelto. **The d. take it!** ¡Lléveselo el diablo! **to play the d. with,** arruinar por completo. **What the d.!** ¡Qué diablos! **d.-possessed,** endemoniado

devilish *a* diabólico, demoníaco; infernal

devilry *n* diablura, *f*; magia, *f*; demonología, *f*; (wickedness) maldad, *f*; crueldad, *f*

devious *a* desviado; tortuoso

deviousness *n* tortuosidad, *f*

devise *vt* idear, inventar; fabricar; *law* legar

deviser *n* inventor (-ra)

devitalize *vt* restar vitalidad, privar de vitalidad

devoid *a* desprovisto (de), privado (de); libre (de), exento (de)

devolve *vt* traspasar, transmitir. *vi* (on, upon) incumbir (a), corresponder (a), tocar (a)

devote *vt* dedicar; consagrar. **to d. oneself to,** darse a, dedicarse a; consagrarse a

devoted *a* fervoroso, apasionado; (faithful) fiel, leal

devotedly *adv* con devoción

devotee *n* devoto (-ta), admirador (-ra); aficionado (-da)

devotion *n* devoción, *f*; dedicación, *f*; (zeal) celo, *m*; afición, *f*; (loyalty) lealtad, *f*; *pl* **devotions,** rezos, *m pl*, oraciones, *f pl*

devotional *a* devoto, religioso, de devoción. **devotional literature,** literatura de devoción, *f*

devour *vt* devorar; consumir

devourer *n* devorador (-ra)

devouring *a* devorador; absorbente

devout *a* devoto, piadoso, practicante (e.g., **a d. Catholic,** un católico practicante)

devoutly *adv* piadosamente

devoutness *n* piedad, devoción, *f*

dew *n* rocío, sereno, relente, *m*; *fig* rocío, *m*, *vt* rociar; humedecer; (refresh) refrescar. **d.-drop,** aljófar, *m*, gota de rocío, *f*

dewlap *n* papada, *f*, papo, *m*

dewy *a* rociado, lleno de rocío; húmedo; (of eyes) lustroso

dexterity *n* destreza, *f*

dextrine *n* dextrina, *f*

dextrose *n* dextrosa, glucosa, *f*

dextrous *a* diestro; hábil, listo

diabetes *n* diabetes, *f*

diabetic *a* diabético

diabolical *a* diabólico

diadem *n* diadema, *f*

diagnose *vt* diagnosticar

diagnosis *n* diagnóstico, *m*, diagnosis, *f*

diagnostician *n* diagnóstico, *m*

diagonal *n* diagonal, *f*

diagram *n* diagrama, *m*; esquema, *f*; gráfico, *m*

diagrammatic *a* esquemático

dial *n* (sundial) reloj de sol, *m*; (of clocks, gas-meter) esfera, *f*; (of machines) indicador, *m*; (of a wireless set) cuadrante graduado, *m*; (of a telephone) marcador, disco, *m*. *vt* (a telephone number) marcar. **d. telephone,** teléfono automático, *m*

dialect *n* dialecto, *m*, habla, *f*, *a* dialectal

dialectic *a* dialéctico

dialectics *n* dialéctica, *f*

dialogue *n* diálogo, *m*. **to hold a d.,** dialogar

dialysis *n* diálisis, *f*

diameter *n* diámetro, *m*

diametrical *a* diametral

diamond *n* diamante, *m*; brillante, *m*; (tool) cortavidrios, *m*; (cards) oros (de baraja), *m pl*. **rough d.,** diamante bruto, *m*. **d.-bearing,** diamantífero. **d. cutter,** diamantista, *mf* **d. cutting,** talla de diamantes, *f*. **d. edition,** edición diamante, *f*. **d.-like,** adiamantado. **d. wedding,** bodas de diamante, *f pl*

diapason *n* diapasón, *m*

diaper *n* lienzo adamascado, *m*; (baby's) pañal, *m*; (woman's) servilleta higiénica, *f*

diaphanous *a* diáfano, transparente

diaphragm *n* diafragma, *m*

diarist *n* diarista, *mf*

diarrhea *n* diarrea, *f*

diary *n* diario, *m*

diastase *n* diastasa, *f*

diastole *n* diástole, *f*

diatribe *n* diatriba, denunciación violenta, *f*

dibble *n* plantador, *m*, *vt* and *vi* plantar con plantador

dice *n pl* dados, *m pl*. **to load the d.,** cargar los dados

dicky *n* (front) pechera postiza, *f*; (seat) trasera, *f*; (apron) delantal, *m*. **d. seat,** *inf* ahí te pudras, *m*

dictaphone *n* dictáfono, *m*

dictate *vt* dictar; mandar. *n* (order) dictamen, *m*; *fig* dictado, *m*

dictation *n* dictado, *m*. **to write from d.,** escribir al dictado

dictator *n* dictador, *m*

dictatorial *a* dictatorial, dictatorio, imperioso

dictatorship *n* dictadura, *f*

diction *n* dicción, *f*

dictionary *n* diccionario, *m*

dictum *n* dictamen, *m*; (saying) sentencia, *f*; *law* fallo, *m*

didactic *a* didáctico

die *vi* morir; fallecer, finar; (wither) marchitarse; (disappear) desvanecerse, desaparecer; (of light) palidecer; extinguirse; (end) cesar; (desire) ansiar, perecerse (por). **Never say die!** ¡Mientras hay vida, hay esperanza! **to die early,** morir temprano; malograrse. **to die a violent death,** tener una muerte violenta, *inf* morir vestido. **to die from natural causes,** morir por causas naturales; *inf* morir en la cama. **to die hard,** luchar contra la muerte; tardar en morir; tardar en desaparecer. **to die of a broken heart,** morir con el corazón destrozado, morir de pena. **to die away,** desaparecer gradualmente; extinguirse poco a poco; dejar de oírse poco a poco; cesar; pasar. **to die down,** extinguirse gradualmente; palidecer; dejar de oírse; desaparecer; (of the wind) amainar; perder su fuerza. **to die out,** desaparecer; olvidarse; dejar de existir; pasarse de moda

die *n* dado, *m*; *fig* suerte, *f*; (stamp) cuño, troquel, *m*; *arch* cubo, *m*. **The die is cast,** La suerte está echada. **die-sinker,** grabador en hueco, *m*

diehard *n* valiente, *m*; tradicionalista empedernido, *m*; partidario (-ia) entusiasta

Dieppe Diepa, *f*

dieresis *n* diéresis, crema, *f*

diesel *a* Diesel. **d. engine,** motor Diesel, *m*

diet *n* dieta, *f*, régimen dietario, *m*; (assembly) dieta, *f*. *vi* estar a dieta, hacer régimen

dietetic *a* dietético

dietetics *n* dietética, *f*

dietician *n* dietista, *mf*

differ *vi* diferenciarse; (contradict) contradecir; (disagree) no estar de acuerdo; disentir

difference *n* diferencia, *f*; disparidad, *f*; contraste, *m*; (of opinion) disensión, *f*; controversia, disputa, *f*. **to make no d.,** no hacer diferencia alguna; no afectar; dar lo mismo, no importar

different *a* distinto; diferente; vario, diverso

differential *a* diferencial. **d. calculus,** cálculo diferencial, *m*

differentiate *vt* diferenciar, distinguir. *vi* diferenciarse; distinguirse

differentiation *n* diferenciación, *f*

differently *adv* diferentemente

difficult *a* difícil. **to make d.,** dificultar

difficulty *n* dificultad, *f*. **d. in breathing,** opresión de pecho, *f*

diffidence *n* modestia, timidez, *f*; huraña, *f*; falta de confianza en sí mismo, *f*

diffident *a* modesto, tímido; huraño; sin confianza en sí mismo

diffidently *adv* tímidamente; vergonzosamente

diffract *vt* difractar

diffraction *n* difracción, *f*

diffractive *a* difrangente

diffuse *vt* difundir. *a* difuso; (long-winded) prolijo

diffuseness *n* difusión, *f*; prolijidad, *f*

diffusion *n* difusión, *f*; esparcimiento, *m*; diseminación, *f*

diffusive *a* difusivo

dig *vt* and *vi* cavar; excavar; (of animals) escarbar; (mine) zapar, minar; (into a subject) ahondar (en); (with the spurs) aguijonear, dar con las espuelas; (poke) clavar. **to dig in,** enterrarse; *mil* abrir trincheras; *inf* arreglarse las cosas. **to dig out,** excavar; sacar cavando, sacar con azadón; extraer. **to dig up,** desenterrar; descubrir

digest *vt* clasificar; codificar; (food, also *chem*. and *fig*. tolerate and think over) digerir; (of knowledge and territory) asimilar. *vi* digerir. *n* compendio, resumen, *m*; *law* digesto, *m*; recopilación, *f*. **This food is easy to d.,** Este alimento es fácil de digerir; Este alimento es muy ligero

digestibility *n* digestibilidad, *f*

digestible *a* digerible, digestible

digestion *n* digestión, *f*; (of ideas) asimilación, *f*; *chem* digestión, *f*

digestive *a* digestivo

digger *n* cavador (-ra)

digging *n* cavadura, *f*; excavación, *f*; *pl* **diggings,** minas, *f pl*; excavaciones, *f pl*; *inf* alojamiento, *m*, posada, *f*

digit *n* dígito, *m*

digital *a* digital, dígito

digitalin *n* digitalina, *f*

digitalis *n* digital, *f*

dignified *a* serio, grave; majestuoso; (worthy) digno; solemne; altivo; noble

dignify *vt* dignificar, honrar; exaltar; dar dignidad (a); ennoblecer

dignitary *n* dignatario, *m*; dignidad, *f*

dignity *n* dignidad, *f*; (rank) rango, *m*; (post) cargo, puesto, *m*; (honor) honra, *f*; (stateliness) majestad, *f*; mesura, seriedad, *f*; (haughtiness) altivez, *f*; (nobility) nobleza, *f*. **to stand on one's d.,** darse importancia

digress *vi* divagar

digression *n* digresión, divagación, *f*

dike *n* dique, *m*; (ditch) acequia, *f*; canal, *m*; (embankment) zanja, *f*, *vt* represar

dilapidated *a* arruinado, destartalado; (of fortune) dilapidado; (of persons, families) venido a menos; (shabby) raído

dilapidation *n* deterioración, *f*; ruina, *f*, estado ruinoso, *m*

dilatation *n* dilatación, *f*; ensanche, *m*

dilate *vt* dilatar; ensanchar. *vi* dilatarse. **to d. upon,** extenderse sobre, dilatarse en

dilator *n* dilatador, *m*

dilatoriness *n* tardanza, *f*; (slowness) lentitud, *f*

dilatory *a* dilatorio; (slow) lento

dilemma *n* dilema, *m*

dilettante *n* diletante, *m*; aficionado (-da)

dilettantism *n* diletantismo, *m*

diligence *n* diligencia, *f*; asiduidad, *f*; (care) cuidado, *m*; (coach) diligencia, *f*

diligent *a* diligente, asiduo, aplicado, industrioso; (painstaking) concienzudo

dilute *vt* diluir; *fig* adulterar. *a* diluido

dilution *n* dilución, *f*; *fig* adulteración, *f*

diluvian *a* diluviano

dim *a* (of light) apagado, débil, tenue; (of sight) turbio; (dark) sombrío, oscuro; (blurred, etc.) empañado; indistinto, confuso. *vt* obscurecer; empañar; (dazzle) ofuscar; (eclipse) eclipsar; reducir la intensidad (de una luz); (of memories) borrar. **dim intelligence,** de brumoso seso

dimension *n* dimensión, *f*; (size) tamaño, *m*; (scope) extensión, *f*, alcance, *m*

dimensional *a* dimensional

diminish *vt* disminuir; reducir; debilitar, atenuar. *vi* disminuir; reducirse; debilitarse, atenuarse

diminishing *a* menguante

diminution *n* disminución, *f*; reducción, *f*; atenuación, *f*

diminutive *a* diminutivo. *n* diminutivo, *m*

diminutiveness *n* pequeñez, *f*

dimly *adv* obscuramente; vagamente; indistintamente. **dimly lit,** apenas alumbrado

dimness *n* oscuridad, *f*; deslustre, *m*; (of light) tenuidad (de la luz), *f*; confusión, *f*

dimple *n* hoyuelo, *m*

dimpled *a* con hoyuelos, que tiene hoyuelos

din *n* estrépito, estruendo, ruido, *m*; algarabía, barahúnda, *f*, *vt* ensordecer

dine *vi* (in the evening) cenar; (at midday) comer. *vt* convidar a cenar o a comer. **to d. out,** cenar o comer fuera

diner *n* (on a train) coche comedor, coche restaurante, *m*; cenador, *m*; comedor, *m*

ding-dong *n* tintín, *m*

dinghy *n* lancha, *f*; canoa, *f*, bote, *m*. **rubber d.,** canoa de goma, *f*

dinginess *n* deslustre, *m*; suciedad, *f*; oscuridad, *f*; (of a person) desaseo, *m*

dingy *a* deslucido, empañado; sucio; oscuro; (of persons) desaseado

dining car *n* coche comedor, vagón restaurante, *m*

dining room *n* comedor, *m*; refectorio, *m*

dining table *n* mesa del comedor, *f*

dinner *n* (in the evening) cena, *f*; (at midday) comida, *f*. **over the d. table,** de sobremesa. **d.-jacket,** smoking, *m*. **d. party,** cena, *f*. **d. plate,** plato, *m*. **d. roll,** panecillo, *m*. **d. service,** vajilla, *f*

dinosaur *n* dinosauro, *m*

dint (by d. of) a fuerza de, a costa de

diocesan *a* diocesano

diocese *n* diócesis, *f*

Dionysus Thrax Dionisio el Tracio, *m*

dioxide *n* dióxido, *m*

dip *n* inmersión, *f*; baño, *m*; (in the ground) declive, *m*; (in the road) columpio, *m*, depresión, *f*; (slope) pendiente, *f*; (candle) vela de sebo, *f*; (of the horizon) depresión (del horizonte), *f*; (of the needle) inclinación (de la aguja), *f*. *vt* sumergir; bañar; (put) poner. *vi* inclinarse hacia abajo. **to dip into a book,** hojear un libro. **to dip the colors,** saludar con la bandera. **to dip the headlights,** bajar los faros

diphtheria *n* difteria, *f*

diphthong *n* diptongo, *m*

diploma *n* diploma, *m*

diplomacy *n* diplomacia, *f*; tacto, *m*

diploma mill *n* fábrica de títulos académicos, *f*

diplomat *n* diplomático, *m*

diplomatic *a* diplomático. **d. bag,** valija diplomática, *f*. **d. corps,** cuerpo diplomático, *m*

diplomatically *adv* diplomáticamente

dipper *n* (ladle) cazo, *m*; *ast* Osa Mayor, *f*

dipsomania *n* dipsomanía, *f*

dipsomaniac *n* dipsómano (-na)

diptych *n* diptica, *f*

dire *a* espantoso, horrible; cruel; funesto

direct *a* directo; claro, inequívoco; (of descent) recto; (of electric current) continuo; exacto. *adv* directamente. *vt* dirigir; (command) ordenar, encargar; dar instrucciones. **d. action,** acción directa, *f*. **d. current,** corriente continua, *f*. **d. line,** línea directa, *f*; (of descent) línea recta, *f*. **d. object,** acusativo, *m*. **d. speech,** oración directa, *f*

direct dialing *n* discado directo, *m*

direction *n* dirección, *f*; rumbo, *m*; instrucción, *f*; (on a letter) sobrescrito, *m*; señas, *f pl*. **in the d. of,** en la dirección de; hacia; *naut* con rumbo a. **in all directions,** por todas partes; a las cuatro vientos. **to go in the d. of,** ir en la dirección de; tomar por. **Directions for use,** Direcciones para el uso. **d. indicator, d. signal,** (on car) indicador de dirección, *m*

directive *a* directivo, director

directly *adv* directamente; inmediatamente, en seguida

directness *n* derechura, *f*

director *n* director (-triz, -ora), **managing d.,** director gerente, *m*

directorate *n* directorio, *m*, junta directiva, *f*; cargo de director, *m*

directory *n* directorio, *m*, guía, *f*. **telephone d.,** guía de teléfonos, *f*

dirge *n* endecha, *f*, lamento, *m*; canto fúnebre, *m*

dirigible *n* dirigible, *m*

dirt *n* mugre, suciedad, *f*; (mud) lodo, *m*; (earth) tierra, *f*; (dust) polvo, *m*; *fig* inmundicia, *f*. **d.-cheap,** sumamente barato. **to be d. cheap,** (of goods) estar por los suelos. **d.-track,** pista de ceniza, *f*. **d.-track racing,** carreras en pista de ceniza, *f pl*

dirtiness *n* suciedad, *f*; (untidiness) desaseo, *m*; sordidez, *f*; (meanness) bajeza, *f*

dirty *a* sucio; (untidy) desaseado; (muddy) enlodado; (dusty) polvoriento; (of weather) borrascoso; (sordid) sórdido; (base, mean) vil; (indecent) indecente, verde, obsceno. *vt* ensuciar. **d. trick,** mala pasada, *f*

disability *n* incapacidad, *f*; impotencia, *f*; desventaja, *f*

disable *vt* (cripple) estropear, tullir; hacer incapaz (de), incapacitar; imposibilitar; (destroy) destruir; *law* incapacitar legalmente

disabled *a* inválido; impedido, lisiado; (in the hand) manco; incapacitado; (of ships, etc.) fuera de servicio, estropeado. **d. soldier,** inválido, *m*

disablement *n* (physical) invalidez, *f*; inhabilitación, *f*; *law* impedimento, *m*

disabuse *vt* desengañar, sacar de un error

disadvantage *n* desventaja, *f*. **to be under the d. of,** sufrir la desventaja de

disadvantaged *a* (financially) de escasos recursos

disadvantageous *a* desventajoso

disaffected *a* desafecto

disaffection *n* desafecto, descontento, *m*

disagree *vi* no estar de acuerdo; diferir; (quarrel) reñir; (not share the opinion of) no estar de la opinión (de); (of food, etc.) sentar mal; no probar. **The meat disagreed with me,** La carne me sentó mal

disagreeable *a* desagradable; repugnante; (of persons) antipático, displicente

disagreeableness *n* lo desagradable; (of persons) displicencia, *f*

disagreeably *adv* desagradablemente; con displicencia

disagreement *n* desacuerdo, *m*; diferencia, *f*; desavenencia, *f*; discordia, *f*; (quarrel) riña, disputa, *f*; discrepancia, *f*

disallow *vt* negar; rechazar

disappear *vi* desaparecer. **to cause to d.,** hacer desaparecer

disappearance *n* desaparición, *f*

disappoint *vt* desilusionar; frustrar; (hopes) defraudar; (deprive) privar de; (annoy) contrariar; (break a promise) faltar (a la palabra)

disappointedly *adv* con desilusión, con desengaño

disappointing *a* desengañador; pobre; triste; poco halagüeño

disappointment *n* desengaño, *m*, decepción, *f*; frustración, *f*; desilusión, *f*; (vexation) contrariedad, *f*; contratiempo, *m*. **to suffer a d.**, sufrir un desengaño; *inf* llevarse un chasco

disapproval *n* desaprobación, *f*

disapprove *vt* desaprobar

disapproving *a* de desaprobación, severo

disapprovingly *adv* con desaprobación

disarm *vt* desarmar. *vi* desarmarse; deponer las armas

disarmament *n* desarme, *m*

disarrange *vt* desarreglar; descomponer, desajustar; (hair) despeinar

disarrangement *n* desarreglo, *m*; desajuste, *m*; desorden, *m*

disarray *n* desorden, desarreglo, *m*; confusión, *f*. *vt* desordenar, desarreglar

disarticulate *vt* desarticular

disarticulation *n* desarticulación, *f*

disaster *n* desastre, *m*; catástrofe, *m*; infortunio, *m*

disastrous *a* desastroso; funesto, trágico

disastrously *adv* desastrosamente

disastrousness *n* carácter desastroso, *m*

disavow *vt* repudiar; retractar

disavowal *n* repudiación, *f*

disband *vt* licenciar. *vi* desbandarse, dispersarse

disbelief *n* incredulidad, *f*; desconfianza, *f*

disbelieve *vt* and *vi* descreer, no creer; desconfiar (de)

disburse *vt* desembolsar, pagar

disbursement *n* desembolso, *m*

disc *n* disco, *m*

discard *vt* desechar, arrinconar; despedir; (at cards) descartar. *n* (at cards) descarte, *m*

discern *vt* discernir, distinguir, percibir

discerner *n* discernidor (-ra)

discernible *a* distinguible, perceptible

discerning *a* perspicaz, discernidor

discernment *n* discernimiento, *m*

discharge *vt* descargar; (a gun) disparar, tirar; (an arrow) lanzar; *elec* descargar; emitir; (dismiss) destituir, despedir; arrojar; *mil* licenciar; (exempt) dispensar (de); (exonerate) absolver, exonerar; (free) dar libertad (a); (from hospital) dar de baja (a); *law* revocar; (perform) cumplir, ejecutar; (pay) pagar, saldar; (of an abscess, etc.) supurar.

discharge *n* (of firearms) disparo, tiro, *m*; (of artillery) descarga, *f*; (of goods, cargo) descargue, *m*; *elec* descarga, *f*; (from a wound, etc.) pus, *m*, supuración, *f*; (from the intestine) flujo, *m*; (of a debt) pago, m.; *com* descargo, *m*; (receipt) carta de pago, quitanza, *f*; *mil* licencia absoluta, *f*; (dismissal) despedida, destitución, *f*; (exoneration) exoneración, *f*; (freeing) liberación, *f*; (from hospital) baja, *f*; (performance) cumplimiento, *m*; ejecución, *f*

disciple *n* discípulo (-la)

disciplinarian *n* disciplinario (-ia)

disciplinary *a* disciplinario

discipline *n* disciplina, *f*, *vt* disciplinar

disclaim *vt* renunciar (a); (repudiate) rechazar, repudiar

disclaimer *n* *law* renunciación, *f*; repudiación, *f*

disclose *vt* descubrir, revelar

disclosure *n* descubrimiento, *m*, revelación, *f*

discolor *vt* descolorar. *vi* descolorarse

discoloration *n* descoloramiento, *m*

discomfit *vt* desconcertar

discomfiture *n* desconcierto, *m*

discomfort *n* falta de comodidades, *f*; incomodidad, *f*; malestar, *m*; molestia, *f*; inquietud, *f*; dolor, *m*

discomposure *n* confusión, agitación, inquietud, *f*

disconcert *vt* desconcertar, turbar; (of plans, etc.) frustrar

disconnect *vt* separar; (of railway engines, etc.) desacoplar; desconectar; (of electric plugs) desenchufar

disconnected *a* inconexo; incoherente, deshilvanado

disconnectedness *n* inconexión, *f*; incoherencia, *f*

disconsolate *a* desconsolado, triste

disconsolately *adv* desconsoladamente, tristemente

disconsolateness *n* desconsuelo, *m*

discontent *n* descontento, disgusto, *m*, *vt* descontentar, desagradar

discontented *a* descontentadizo, descontento, disgustado

discontinuance *n* descontinuación, cesación, *f*; interrupción, *f*

discontinue *vt* descontinuar; cesar; interrumpir; (of payments, etc.) suspender. *vi* cesar

discontinuous *a* descontinuo; interrumpido; intermitente

discord *n* discordia, *f*; *mus* disonancia, *f*, desentono, *m*

discordant *a* discorde, poco armonioso; incongruo; *mus* disonante, desentonado. **to be d.,** discordar; ser incongruo; *mus* disonar

discount *n* descuento, *m*; rebaja, *f*. *vt* descontar; rebajar; balancear; (disconsider) desechar. **at a d.,** al descuento; bajo la par; fácil de obtener; superfluo; *fig* en disfavor, en descrédito. **rate of d.,** tipo de descuento, *m*. **d. for cash,** descuento por venta al contado, *m*

discourage *vt* desalentar, desanimar; oponerse a; disuadir; frustrar

discouragement *n* desaliento, *m*; desaprobación, oposición, *f*; disuasión, *f*; (obstacle) estorbo, *m*

discouraging *a* poco animador, que ofrece pocas esperanzas; (with prospect, etc.) nada halagüeño

discourse *n* discurso, *m*; plática, *f*; (treatise) disertación, *f*. *vi* (converse) platicar, conversar; (with on, upon) disertar sobre, discurrir sobre; tratar de

discourteous *a* descortés, desconsiderado

discourtesy *n* descortesía, *f*

discover *vt* descubrir; (see) ver; (realize) darse cuenta de; (show) manifestar; revelar

discoverable *a* que se puede descubrir; averiguable; distinguible, perceptible

discoverer *n* descubridor (-ra); revelador (-ra)

discovery *n* descubrimiento, *m*; revelación, *f*

discredit *n* descrédito, *m*; des honra, *f*; duda, *f*. *vt* dudar (de), no creer (en); desacreditar; deshonrar

discreditable *a* deshonroso, ignominioso, vergonzoso

discreet *a* discreto; prudente, circunspecto

discreetly *adv* discretamente; prudentemente

discrepancy *n* discrepancia, diferencia, *f*; contradicción, *f*

discrepant *a* discrepante; contradictorio, inconsistente

discretion *n* discreción, *f*; prudencia, circunspección, *f*; juicio, *m*; voluntad, *f*. **at d.,** a discreción. **at one's own d.,** a voluntad (de uno). **years of d.,** edad de discreción, *f*

discriminate *vi* distinguir (entre); hacer una distinción (en favor de or en perjuicio de). *vt* distinguir

discriminating *a* discerniente, que sabe distinguir, juicioso; culto; diferencial

discrimination *n* discernimiento, *m*; gusto, *m*; distinción, *f*; discriminación, *f*

discursive *a* discursivo; digresivo

discus *n* disco, *m*. **d. thrower,** discóbolo, *m*

discuss *vt* discutir; hablar de; debatir; (deal with) tratar; (fam a dish) probar; (a bottle of wine) vaciar

discussion *n* discusión, *f*, debate, *m*

disdain *n* desdén, *m*; altivez, *f*. *vt* desdeñar, desairar, despreciar. **to d. to,** desdeñarse de

disdainful *a* desdeñoso; altivo

disdainfully *adv* desdeñosamente

disease *n* enfermedad, *f*; *fig* mal, *m*. **infectious d.,** enfermedad contagiosa, *f*

diseased *a* enfermo; (of fruit, etc.) malo

disembark *vt* and *vi* desembarcar

disembarkation *n* desembarque, *m*; *mil* desembarco (de tropas), *m*

disembodied *a* incorpóreo

disembowel *vt* desentrañar, destripar

disenchant *vt* desencantar; deschechizar; desilusionar

disenchantment *n* desencanto, *m*; desilusión, *f*

disengage *vt* desasir; soltar; (gears) desembragar; (uncouple) desacoplar; (free) librar

disengaged *a* (free) libre

disentangle *vt* (undo) desatar, desanudar; separar; (of threads, etc., and *fig*) desenredar, desenmarañar. *vi* desenredarse

disentanglement *n* desatadura, *f*; separación, *f*; desenredo, *m*

disestablish *vt* separar (la Iglesia del Estado)

disestablishment *n* separación (de la Iglesia del Estado), *f*

disfavor *n* disfavor, *m*; (disapproval) desaprobación, *f*. *vt* desaprobar

disfigure *vt* desfigurar, afear; deformar; (mar) estropear

disfigurement *n* desfiguración, *f*; deformidad, *f*; defecto, *m*

disfranchise *vt* privar de los derechos civiles (a)

disfranchisement *n* privación de los derechos civiles, privación del derecho de votar, *f*

disgorge *vt* and *vi* vomitar; (of a river) desembocar (en); hacer restitución (de lo robado)

disgrace *n* vergüenza, ignominia, *f*; deshonra, *f*; (insult) afrenta, *f*; (scandal) escándalo, *m*; disfavor, *m*. *vt* deshonrar; despedir con ignominia. **in d.,** fuera de favor; desacreditado; (of children and animals) castigado

disgraceful *a* deshonroso; ignominioso; escandaloso

disgracefully *adv* escandalosamente

disgracefulness *n* ignominia, vergüenza, *f*; deshonra, *f*

disgruntled *a* refunfuñador, enfurruñado, malhumorado

disguise *n* disfraz, *m*; (mask) máscara, *f*. *vt* disfrazar; cubrir, tapar; (*fig* conceal) ocultar. **in d.,** disfrazado

disgust *n* repugnancia, aversión, *f*; aborrecimiento, *m*; asco, *m*. *vt* repugnar, inspirar aversión; disgustar; dar asco (a)

disgusted *a* asqueado; disgustado; furioso; (bored) aburrido

disgusting *a* repugnante; odioso, horrible; asqueroso

dish *n* (for meat, vegetables, fruit, etc.) fuente, *f*; (food) plato, *m*; *pl* **dishes,** platos, *m pl*, vajilla, *f*. *vt* servir; *inf* frustrar. **cooked d.,** guiso, *m*. **special d. for today,** plato del día, *m*. **to wash the dishes,** fregar los platos. **d.-cloth,** (for washing) fregador, *m*; (for drying) paño de los platos, *m*. **d.-cover,** cubre-platos, *m*. **d.-rack,** escurre-platos, *m*. **d.-washer,** lavaplatos, lavavajillas, *m*. **d.-water,** agua de lavar los platos, *f*

disharmony *n* falta de armonía, *f*; (disagreement) discordia, desavenencia, *f*; incongruencia, *f*; *mus* disonancia, *f*

dishearten *vt* desalentar, desanimar; desesperar; disuadir (a)

disheveled *a* despeinado, desgreñado; (untidy) desaseado

dishonest *a* falto de honradez, tramposo; fraudulento; falso, desleal

dishonestly *adv* de mala fe, sin honradez; fraudulentamente; deslealmente

dishonesty *n* falta de honradez, falta de integridad, *f*; fraude, *m*; falsedad, deslealtad, *f*

dishonor *n* deshonra, *f*, *vt* deshonrar; *com* no pagar, o no aceptar, un giro

dishonorable *a* deshonroso

dishonorer *n* deshonrador (-ra); profanador (-ra)

disillusion *vt* desengañar, desilusionar

disillusionment *n* desilusión, *f*, desengaño, desencanto, *m*

disinclination *n* aversión, *f*

disincline *vt* desinclinar

disinfect *vt* desinfectar

disinfectant *a* and *n* desinfectante *m*.

disinfection *n* desinfección, *f*

disingenuous *a* tortuoso, doble, falso, insincero

disinherit *vt* desheredar

disinheritance *n* desheredación, *f*

disintegrate *vt* despedazar, disgregar. *vi* disgregarse; desmoronarse

disintegration *n* disgregración, *f*; disolución, *f*; desmoronamiento, *m*

disinter *vt* desenterrar

disinterested *a* desinteresado

disinterestedness *n* desinterés, *m*

disinterment *n* desenterramiento, *m*

disjointed *a* dislocado; desarticulado; incoherente, inconexo; (of a speech, etc.) descosido

disjointedness *n* descoyuntamiento, desencajamiento, *m*; incoherencia, *f*

disk *n* disco, *m*

dislike *n* aversión, *f*; antipatía, *f*; (hostility) animosidad, *f*. *vt* desagradar, no gustar; repugnar. **I d. the house,** No me gusta la casa. **I d. them,** No me gustan

dislocate *vt* dislocar, descoyuntar; *fig* interrumpir

dislocation *n* dislocación, *f*, descoyuntamiento, *m*; *fig* interrupción, *f*

dislodge *vt* desalojar

dislodgement *n* desalojamiento, *m*

disloyal *a* desleal, infiel, falso

disloyalty *n* deslealtad, infidelidad, falsedad, *f*

dismal *a* lóbrego, sombrío; lúgubre; funesto; triste

dismantle *vt* (a ship or fort) desmantelar; (a machine) desmontar; (a house, etc.) desamueblar

dismantling *n* desmantelamiento, *m*

dismay *n* desmayo, desaliento, *m*; consternación, *f*; espanto, terror, *m*. *vt* desanimar; consternar; espantar, horrorizar

dismember *vt* desmembrar

dismemberment *n* desmembración, *f*

dismiss *vt* (from a job) despedir (de); (from an official position) destituir (de); (bid good-bye to) despedirse de; (after military parade) dar la orden de romper filas; (thoughts) apartar de sí; ahuyentar; (discard) desechar, descartar; (omit) pasar por alto de; (disregard) rechazar; (a parliament, etc.) disolver; (a law case) absolver de la instancia. **to d. in a few words,** tratar someramente; hablar brevemente de

dismissal *n* despedida, *f*; (from an official post) destitución, *f*; apartamiento, *m*; (discard) descarte, *m*; (of a parliament, etc.) disolución, *f*

dismount *vi* apearse, desmontar, echar pie a tierra; bajar. *vt* desmontar; (dismantle) desarmar

disobedience *n* desobediencia, *f*

disobedient *a* desobediente

disobey *vt* and *vi* desobedecer

disobliging *a* poco servicial

disobligingly *adv* descortésmente

disorder *n* desorden, *m*; confusión, *f*; (unrest) perturbación del orden público, *f*, motín, *m*; (disease) enfermedad, *f*; (mental) enajenación mental, *f*; trastorno, *m*. *vt* desordenar, desarreglar; (of health) perjudicar; (the mind) trastornar. **in d.,** en desorden, desarreglado; (helter-skelter) atropelladamente

disordered *a* en desorden; irregular, desordenado; (of the mind and bodily organs) trastornado; (ill) enfermo; (confused) confuso

disorganization *n* desorganización, *f*

disorganize *vt* desorganizar

disorganizing *a* desorganizador

disorientate *vt* desorientar

disorientation *n* desorientación, *f*

disown *vt* repudiar; negar; renegar de

disparage *vt* menospreciar; desacreditar; denigrar; (spoil) perjudicar; (scorn) despreciar

disparagement *n* menosprecio, *m*; denigración, *f*; desprecio, *m*

disparagingly *adv* con desprecio

disparity *n* disparidad, *f*

dispassionate *a* desapasionado, sereno; imparcial; moderado

dispassionately *adv* con imparcialidad; serenamente; con moderación

dispatch *n* despacho, *m*; *com* envío, *m*; (message) mensaje, *m*; (communiqué) parte, *f*; (cable) telegrama, *m*; (promptness) prontitud, presteza, *f*; (execution) ejecución, muerte, *f*. *vt* despachar; enviar, remitir; (*fam* kill) despachar. **d.-case,** cartera, *f*. **d.-rider,** mensajero motociclista, *m*

dispel *vt* disipar

dispensable *a* dispensable

dispensary *n* dispensario, *m*

dispensation *n* dispensación, *f*; (of the Pope, etc.) dispensa, *f*; (decree) ley, *f*, decreto, *m*; (of justice) administración, *f*

dispense *vt* dispensar; (of justice) administrar. **to d. with,** pasar sin, prescindir de

dispenser *n* dispensador (-ra); administrador (-ra)

dispersal *n* dispersión, *f*; disipación, *f*; esparcimiento, *m*

disperse *vt* dispersar; disipar; esparcir. *vi* dispersarse disiparse

dispirited *a* abatido, desanimado, deprimido; lánguido

dispiritedly *adv* desanimadamente, con desaliento; lánguidamente

displace *vt* desalojar; cambiar de situación; (of liquids) desplazar; (oust) quitar el puesto (a), destituir

displacement *n* desalojamiento, *m*; cambio de situación, *m*; (of liquid) desplazamiento, *m*; (from a post) destitución, *f*

display *n* exhibición, *f*; ostentación, *f*; presentación, *f*; (development) desarrollo, *m*; manifestación, *f*; (naval or military) maniobras, *f pl*; espectáculo, *m*; (pomp) pompa, *f*; fausto, *m*. *vt* exhibir; mostrar, manifestar; ostentar; (unfold) desplegar, extender; (develop) desarrollar. **d. cabinet,** vitrina, *f*

displease *vt* desagradar; ofender; enojar

displeasing *a* desagradable

displeasure *n* desagrado, *m*; disgusto, *m*; disfavor, *m*; indignación, *f*; enojo, *m*; (grief) angustia, *f*

disport *vi* (oneself), divertirse, entretenerse, recrearse; retozar, jugar

disposal *n* disposición, *f*; (transfer) cesión, enajenación, *f*; (sale) venta, *f*; (gift) donación, *f*. **I am at your d.,** Estoy a la disposición de Vd. **the d. of the troops,** la disposición de las tropas

dispose *vt* disponer; inclinar. *vi* disponer. **to d. of,** disponer de; (finish) terminar, concluir; (get rid of) deshacerse de; (give away) regalar; (sell) vender; (transfer) ceder; (of houses, etc.) traspasar; (kill) matar; (send) enviar; (use) servirse de; (refute) refutar. **"To be disposed of,"** (a business, etc.) «Se traspasa»

disposed *a* (in compounds) intencionado, dispuesto. **well-d.,** bien intencionado

disposition *n* disposición, *f*; (temperament) naturaleza, índole, *f*, temperamento, carácter, *m*; (humor) humor, *m*

dispossess *vt* desposeer (de); privar (de); desahuciar

dispossession *n* desposeimiento, *m*; desahúcio, *m*

disproportion *n* desproporción, *f*

disproportionate *a* desproporcionado

disproportionately *adv* desproporcionadamente

disprovable *a* refutable

disprove *vt* refutar

disputable *a* disputable; discutible

disputant *n* disputador (-ra)

dispute *n* disputa, controversia, *f*; altercación, *f*; discusión, *f*; debate, *m*. *vt* and *vi* disputar. **beyond d.,** *a* incontestable. *adv* incontestablemente; fuera de duda

disqualification *n* incapacidad, *f*; inhabilitación, *f*; impedimento, *m*; *sport* descalificación, *f*

disqualify *vt* incapacitar; inhabilitar; *sport* descalificar

disquiet *n* desasosiego, *m*; intranquilidad, inquietud, agitación, *f*. *vt* desasosegar, intranquilizar, perturbar, agitar

disquieting *a* intranquilizador, perturbador

disquisition *n* disquisición, *f*

disregard *n* indiferencia, *f*; omisión, *f*; descuido, *m*; (scorn) desdén, *m*. *vt* no hacer caso de, desatender; omitir; desconocer; descuidar; despreciar

disregardful *a* indiferente; negligente; desatento; desdeñoso

disrepair *n* deterioro, mal estado, *m*

disreputable *a* de mala fama; (shameful) vergonzoso, vil; (compromising) comprometedor; de mal aspecto, horrible; ruin

disreputably *adv* ruinmente; vergonzosamente

disrepute *n* disfavor, *m*; mala fama, *f*; deshonra, *f*; descrédito, *m*. **to come into d.,** caer en disfavor; perder su reputación

disrespect *n* falta de respeto, *f*; irreverencia, *f*

disrespectful *a* irrespetuoso, irreverente

disrobe *vt* desnudar. *vi* desnudarse

disrupt *vt* quebrar; desorganizar; interrumpir; separar

disruption *n* quebrantamiento, *m*; desorganización, *f*; interrupción, *f*; separación, *f*

dissatisfaction *n* descontento, desagrado, disgusto, *m*

dissatisfied *a* descontentado, malcontento, no satisfecho

dissect *vt* disecar; *fig* analizar

dissecting table *n* mesa de disección, *f*

dissection *n* disección, *f*; análisis, *m*

dissector *n* disector, *m*; *fig* analizador (-ra)

dissemble *vt* and *vi* disimular, fingir

dissembler *n* hipócrita, *mf*; disimulador (-ra)

disseminate *vt* diseminar; propagar, sembrar

dissemination *n* diseminación, *f*; propagación, *f*

dissension *n* disensión, *f*; disidencia, *f*

dissent *n* disentimiento, *m*, *vi* disentir, disidir

dissenter *n* disidente, *mf*

dissentient *a* disidente, divergente. **without one d. voice,** unánimemente

dissertation *n* disertación, *f*

disservice *n* deservicio, *m*

dissimilar *a* disímil, desemejante, diferente

dissimilarity *n* desemejanza, diferencia, disparidad, *f*

dissimulation *n* disimulación, *f*, disimulo, *m*

dissipate *vt* disipar; dispersar; (waste) derrochar, desperdiciar. *vi* disiparse; dispersarse; (vanish) desvanecerse; (of persons) ser disoluto

dissipated *a* (of persons) disipado, disoluto, vicioso

dissipation *n* disipación, *f*; (waste) derroche, *m*; libertinaje, *m*

dissociate *vt* disociar

dissociation *n* disociación, *f*

dissoluble *a* disoluble

dissolute *a* disoluto, vicioso, licencioso

dissoluteness *n* disolución, inmoralidad, *f*

dissolution *n* disolución, *f*; separación, *f*; muerte, *f*

dissolvable *a* soluble

dissolve *vt* disolver; derretir; (of parliament) prorrogar; (a marriage, etc.) anular; *fig* disipar. *vi* disolverse; derretirse; (vanish) desvanecerse; disiparse, evaporarse. **to d. into tears,** deshacerse en lágrimas

dissolvent *a* disolutivo. *n* disolvente, *m*

dissonance *n* disonancia, *f*; *fig* discordia, falta de armonía, *f*

dissonant *a* disonante, *f*, a disonante

dissuade *vt* disuadir (de), apartar (de)

dissuasion *n* disuasión, *f*

distaff *n* rueca, *f*

distance *n* distancia, *f*; lontananza, *f*; lejanía, *f*; trecho, *m*; (of time) intervalo, *m*; (difference) diferencia, *f*. **at a d.,** a alguna distancia; (from afar) desde lejos. **from a d.,** desde (or de) lejos. **in the d.,** a lo lejos, en lontananza. **to keep at a d.,** mantener lejos; guardar las distancias (con). **to keep one's d.,** mantenerse a distancia; no intimarse, guardar las distancias. **What is the d. from London to Madrid?** ¿Qué distancia hay desde Londres a Madrid?

distant *a* distante; lejano; remoto; (of manner) frío, reservado; (slight) ligero; (of references, etc.) indirecto.

He is a d. relation, Es un pariente lejano. **They are always rather d. with her,** La tratan siempre con bastante frialdad

distantly *adv* a distancia; a lo lejos; desde lejos; remotamente; (of manner) con frialdad; (slightly) ligeramente

distaste *n* aversión, repugnancia, *f*; disgusto, hastío, *m*

distasteful *a* desagradable

distemper *n* enfermedad, *f*; (in animals) moquillo, *m*; *fig* mal, *m*; (for walls) pintura al temple, *f*. *vt* desordenar, perturbar; (walls) pintar al temple

distend *vt* ensanchar; dilatar; inflar, henchir; *med* distender. *vi* ensancharse, etc.

distension *n* dilatación, *f*; inflación, *f*; henchimíento, *m*; *med* distensión, *f*

distil *vt* destilar; extraer. *vi* destilar; exudar

distillation *n* destilación, *f*; extracción, *f*; exudación, *f*

distiller *n* destilador (-ra)

distillery *n* destilería, *f*, destilatorio, *m*

distinct *a* distinto; diferente; claro; notable, evidente

distinction *n* distinción, *f*

distinctive *a* distintivo; característico

distinctive feature *n* *ling* rasgo pertinente, *m*

distinctly *adv* claramente; distintamente

distinctness *n* claridad, *f*; distinción, *f*; carácter distintivo, *m*

distinguish *vt* distinguir; discernir; caracterizar; (honor) honrar. *vi* distinguir, diferenciar

distinguishable *a* distinguible; perceptible, discernible

distinguished *a* distinguido; eminente; famoso, ilustre, egregio

distinguishing *a* distintivo

distort *vt* (twist) torcer; deformar; falsear; pervertir

distorting mirror *n* (at fairs) espejo de la risa, *m*; espejo deformador, *m*

distortion *n* deformación, *f*; torcimiento, *m*; contorsión, *f*; perversión, *f*; *rad* deformación, *f*

distract *vt* distraer; interrumpir; perturbar; (turn aside) desviar, apartar; (madden) enloquecer, volver loco (a)

distracted *a* aturdido; demente, loco

distractedly *adv* locamente; perdidamente

distraction *n* distracción, *f*; (amusement) diversion, *f*, pasatiempo, *m*; (bewilderment) confusión, *f*, aturdimiento, *m*; (madness) locura, *f*; frenesí, *m*. **to drive to d.,** trastornar, sacar de quicio.

distrain *vi* embargar

distraint *n* embargo, *m*

distraught *a* aturdido; desesperado; enloquecido

distress *n* dolor, *m*, aflicción, *f*; pena, *f*; miseria, penuria, *f*; (exhaustion) fatiga, *f*, cansancio, *m*; (pain) dolor, *m*; (misfortune) desdicha, *f*; apuro, *m*; (danger) peligro, *m*; *law* embargo, *m*. *vt* afligir, dar pena (a), llenar de angustia; cansar, fatigar; (pain) doler

distressed *a* afligido; necesitado, pobre

distressing *a* congojoso, doloroso, penoso

distributable *a* repartible

distribute *vt* (of justice, etc.) administrar; distribuir; repartir

distribution *n* (of justice) administración, *f*; distribución, *f*; reparto, *m*

distributive *a* distributivo

distributor *n* distribuidor (-ra); repartidor (-ra). **d. of false money,** expendedor (-ra) de moneda falsa

district *n* distrito, *m*; comarca, *f*; (of a town) barrio, *m*; (judicial) partido judicial, *m*; jurisdicción, *f*; región, zona, *f*

distrust *n* desconfianza, *f*; recelo, *m*, sospecha, *f*. *vt* desconfiar de, sospechar

distrustful *a* desconfiado, receloso, suspicaz

distrustfully *adv* desconfiadamente, con recelo

disturb *vt* perturbar; interrumpir; incomodar; (make anxious) inquietar; (alter) cambiar; (disarrange) desordenar, desarreglar. **to d. the peace,** perturbar el orden público

disturbance *n* perturbación, *f*; disturbio, *m*, conmoción, *f*; incomodidad, *f*; agitación, *f*; confusión, *f*; tumulto, *m*; desorden, *m*; *rad* parásitos, *m pl*

disturber *n* perturbador (-ra)

disturbing *a* perturbador; inquietador; conmovedor, impresionante, emocionante

disunion *n* desunión, *f*; discordia, *f*

disunite *vt* desunir; separar, dividir. *vi* separarse

disuse *n* desuso, *m*. *vt* desusar; desacostumbrar. **to fall into d.,** caer en desuso

ditch *n* zanja, *f*; (for defense, etc.) foso, *m*; (irrigation) acequia, *f*. *vt* zanjar; abarrancar. **to die in the last d.,** morir en la brecha

ditto *adv* ídem; también

ditty *n* canción, cantinela, *f*

diuretic *a* diurético

divan *n* diván, *m*

dive *n* buceo, *m*; *aer* picada, *f*, *vi* bucear; sumergirse (en); *aer* volar en picado; penetrar (en); (into a book) enfrascarse en. **to d. out,** salir precipitadamente. **to d.-bomb,** bombardear en picado. **d.-bomber,** avión en picado, *m*. **d.-bombing,** bombardeo en picado, *m*

diver *n* buceador, *m*; buzo, *m*; (bird) somorgujo, *m*

diverge *vi* divergir

divergence *n* divergencia, *f*

divergent *a* divergente

diverse *a* diverso, vario

diversify *vt* diversificar

diversion *n* diversión, *f*; entretenimiento, *m*, recreación, *f*; pasatiempo, *m*; placer, *m*; *mil* diversión, *f*

diversity *n* diversidad, variedad, *f*

divert *vt* desviar; (amuse) divertir, entretener

diverting *a* divertido, entretenido

divide *vt* dividir; partir; separar; (cut) cortar; (share) repartir, distribuir; (hair) hacer la raya (del pelo); (of voting) provocar una votación. *vi* dividirse; separarse; (of roads, etc.) bifurcarse; (of voting) votar. **divided skirt,** *n* falda pantalón, *f*

dividend *n* dividendo, *m*. **d. warrant,** cupón de dividendo, *m*

dividers *n pl* compás de puntas, *m*

dividing *a* divisorio, divisor

divination *n* adivinación, *f*

divine *a* divino; sublime; *inf* estupendo. *n* teólogo, *m*. *vt* (foretell) vaticinar, pronosticar; presentir; (guess) adivinar

diving *n* buceo, *m*; *aer* picado, *m*. **d.-bell,** campana de bucear, *f*. **d.-board,** (low) trampolín, *m*; (high) palanca, *f*. **d.-suit,** escafandra, *f*

divining rod *n* vara divinatoria, *f*

divinity *n* divinidad, *f*; teología, *f*

divisibility *n* divisibilidad, *f*

divisible *a* divisible

division *n* división, *f*; separación, *f*; (distribution) repartimiento, *m*; (mil math) división, *f*; sección, *f*; grupo, *m*; (voting) votación, *f*; (discord) discordia, desunión, *f*. **without a d.,** por unanimidad, sin división

divisor *n* math divisor, *m*

divorce *n* divorcio, *m*. *vt* divorciarse de; *fig* divorciar, separar. **to file a petition of d.,** poner una petición de divorcio

divorcee *n* (wife) divorciada, *f*; (husband) divorciado, *m*

divulge *vt* divulgar, revelar

dizzily *adv* vertiginosamente

dizziness *n* vértigo, *m*; mareo, *m*; (bewilderment) aturdimiento, *m*, confusión, *f*

dizzy *a* vertiginoso; mareado; confuso, perplejo, aturdido

do *vt* hacer; ejecutar; (one's duty, etc.) cumplir con; concluir; (cause) causar; (homage) rendir; (commit) cometer; (arrange) arreglar; (cook) cocer, guisar; (roast) asar; (fam cheat) engañar; (suit) convenir; (suffice) bastar; (act) hacer el papel (de); (fam treat) tratar (bien o mal); (learn) aprender; (exhaust) agotar; (walk) andar; (travel, journey) recorrer; (translate) traducir; (prepare) preparar. *vi* hacer; (behave) conducirse; (of health) estar (bien o mal); (act) obrar; (get on) ir; (be suitable, suit) convenir; (suffice) bastar; (of plants) florecer; (cook) cocerse; (last) durar. **Don't!** ¡No lo hagas! ¡Quieto! ¡Calla! **How do you do?** ¿Cómo está Vd.? ¡Buenos días! **Have done!** ¡Acaba de una vez! **It will do you good,** Te conviene; Te hará bien; **It will do you no harm,** No te perjudicará; No te hará daño. **I could do with one,** Me gustaría (tener) uno; (of drinks) Me bebería uno con mucho gusto. **That will do,** Eso basta; Se puede servirse de eso; Está bien así; (leave it alone) ¡Déjate de eso! (be quiet!) ¡No digas más! ¡Cállate! **That won't do,** Eso no es bastante; Eso no sirve; Eso no se hace así; Eso no se hace. **That will never do,** Eso no servirá; Eso no puede ser. **This will do,** (when buying an article) Me quedaré con éste; Me serviré de esto; Esto basta; Esto será suficiente; (is all right) Está bien así. **Thy will be done!** ¡Hágase tu voluntad! **to be doing,** estar haciendo; estar ocupado en (or con) hacer; (of food) estar cocinando. **to be done for,** estar perdido; estar muerto. **to do better,** hacer mejor (que); (mend one's ways) enmendarse, corregirse; (improve) mejorar, hacer progresos; (in health) encontrarse mejor. **to do nothing,** no hacer nada. **to do reverence,** rendir homenaje; inclinarse. **to do to death,** matar; asesinar; ejecutar. **to do violence to,** *fig* hacer fuerza a. **to do well,** hacer bien; obrar bien; (be successful) tener éxito; hacer buena impresión; (prosperous) tener una buena posición. **to do wonders,** hacer maravillas. **to have done with,** renunciar (a); dejar de usar; dejar de hacer, cesar; concluir, terminar; no tener más que ver con; (forsake) abandonar; (a person) romper con. **to have nothing to do,** no tener nada que hacer. **to have nothing to do with,** no tener nada que ver con; (of people) no tratar; (end a friendship) romper su amistad con, dejar de ver. **well done,** bien hecho; (of food) bien guisado; (of meat) bien asado. **What is to be done?** ¿Qué hay que hacer? ¿Qué se puede hacer? **What is to do?** ¿Qué pasa? ¿Qué hay? **When he had done speaking,** Cuando hubo terminado de hablar. **to do again,** hacer de nuevo, volver a hacer, rehacer; repetir. **He will not do it again,** No lo hará más. **to do away with,** quitar, eliminar; suprimir; hacer desaparecer; poner fin a; hacer cesar; destruir; matar. **to do by,** tratar (a), portarse con. **to do for,** arruinar; matar; (suffice) bastar para; ser a propósito para, servir para; (look after) cuidar; (as a housekeeper) dirigir la casa para. **to do out,** (a room) limpiar. **to do out of,** quitar; privar de; (steal) robar. **to do up,** (tie) atar; (fold) enrollar, plegar; envolver; (parcel) empaquetar; (arrange) arreglar; decorar; poner en orden; poner como nuevo; (iron) planchar; (launder) lavar y planchar; (tire) fatigar. **to do with,** (of people) tratar; (of things) tener que ver con; (put up with) poder con; poder sufrir. **to do without,** prescindir de; pasarse sin **do** as an auxiliary verb is not translated in Spanish, e.g. **I do believe,** creo. **Do not do that,** no hagas eso. **I did not know,** no sabía When it is used for emphasis, **do** is translated by **sí, ciertamente, claro** and similar words, e.g.: **She did not know, but he did,** Ella no lo sabía pero él sí **You do paint well,** Pintas muy bien por cierto **Do come this time,** No dejes de venir esta vez **docile** *a* dócil

docility *n* docilidad, *f*

dock *n* dique, *m,* dársena, *f;* (wharf) muelle, *m;* (in a law court) banquillo de los acusados, *m; bot* romaza, *f. vt* (a tail) descolar; cortar, cercenar; reducir; (money) descontar; (a ship) poner en dique. *vi* entrar en dársena, entrar en dique, entrar en muelle. **dry-d.,** dique seco, *m.* **floating-d.,** dique flotante, *m.* **d.-dues,** muellaje, *m.* **d. rat,** (thief) raquero, *m*

docker *n* estibador, descargador del muelle, *m*

docket *n* (bundle) legajo, *m;* extracto, *m;* minuta, *f;* (label) etiqueta, *f,* marbete, *m*

dockyard *n* arsenal, astillero, *m*

doctor *n* doctor (-ra); (medical practitioner) médico

(-ca), asistir; (repair) reparar, componer; adulterar; mezclar drogas con; falsificar. *vi* ejercer la medicina. **family d.,** médico de cabecera, *m.* **to graduate as a d.,** doctorarse. **d. of divinity, laws, medicine,** doctor (-ra) en teología, en derecho, en medicina, *m*

doctoral *a* doctoral

doctorate *n* doctorado, *m*

doctrinaire *a* and *n* doctrinario (-ia)

doctrinal *a* doctrinal

doctrine *n* doctrina, *f*

document *n* documento, *m. vt* documentar; probar con documentos. **d.-case,** carpeta, *f*

documentary *a* documental; escrito, auténtico. **d. film,** película documental, *f*

documentation *n* documentación, *f*

Dodecanese, the el Dodecaneso, *m*

dodge *n* esguince, regate, *m;* evasiva, *f;* (trick) estratagema, *m,* maniobra, *f;* artefacto, *m. vt* esquivar, evadir

doe *n* gama, *f.* **doe rabbit,** coneja, *f*

doer *n* hacedor (-ra); autor (-ra)

doeskin *n* ante, *m,* piel de gama, *f*

doff *vt* quitar; (of hats, etc.) quitarse; desnudarse de

dog *n* perro, *m;* (male) macho, *m;* (andiron) morillo, *m; ast* Can Mayor (or Menor), Sirio, *m. vt* perseguir; seguir los pasos de; espiar. **You can't deceive an old dog,** A perro viejo no hay tus tus. **to go to the dogs,** ir a las carreras de galgos; *fig* ir cuesta abajo. **mongrel dog,** perro mestizo, *m.* **thoroughbred dog,** perro de raza pura, *m.* **dog-collar,** collar de perro, *m; ecc* alzacuello, *m.* **dog-days,** días caniculares, *m pl,* canícula, *f.* **dog-eared** (of books) con las puntas de las hojas dobladas. **dog-fight,** lucha de perros, *f;* combate aéreo, *m.* **dog-fish,** lija, *f,* cazón, *m.* **dog in the manger,** el perro del hortelano. **dog-kennel,** perrera, *f.* **dog-latin,** bajo latín, *m.* **dog license,** matrícula de perros, *f.* **dog-racing,** carrera de galgos, *f.* **dog-rose,** escaramujo, *m.* **dog show,** exposición canina, *f.* **dog-tooth,** *arch* diente de perro, *m.* **dog-vane,** *naut* cataviento, *m*

doge *n* dux, *m*

dogged *a* persistente, tenaz, pertinaz, obstinado

doggedly *adv* tenazmente

doggedness *n* pertinacia, tenacidad, terquedad, persistencia, *f*

doggerel *n* malos versos, *m pl;* aleluyas, coplas de ciego, *f pl, a* malo, irregular

dogma *n* dogma, *m*

dogmatic *a* dogmático

dogmatize *vt* and *vi* dogmatizar; mostrarse dogmático

doh *n mus* do, *m*

doily *n* carpeta, *f,* pañito de adorno, *m*

doings *n pl* acciones, *f pl;* (deeds) hechos, *m pl;* (behavior) conducta, *f;* (happenings) acontecimientos, *m pl;* (works) obras, *f pl;* (things) cosas, *f pl*

doldrums *n pl* calmas ecuatoriales, *f pl*

dole *n* limosna, *f;* porción, *f.* **to d. out,** repartir; distribuir en porciones pequeñas; racionar; dar contra la voluntad de uno.

doleful *a* triste, lúgubre, melancólico; doloroso

dolefulness *n* tristeza, melancolía, *f;* dolor, *m*

doll *n* muñeca, *f*

dollar *n* dólar, *m*

dolly *n* muñeca, *f;* (for clothes) moza, *f.* **d.-tub,** cubo para la colada, *m*

dolman *n* dormán, *m*

dolphin *n* delfín, *m*

dolt *n* cabeza de alcornoque, *mf,* zamacuco, *m*

domain *n* territorio, *m;* heredad, posesión, propiedad, *f;* (empire) dominio, *m*

dome *n* cúpula, *f;* bóveda, *f;* (palace) palacio, *m*

domestic *a* doméstico; familiar; (home-loving) casero; (of animals) doméstico; (national) interior, nacional. *n* doméstico, sirviente, *m;* criada, *f.* **d. economy,** economía doméstica, *f*

domesticate *vt* domesticar

domesticated *a* (of animals) domesticado; (of persons) casero

domestication *n* domesticación, *f*

domesticity *n* domesticidad, *f*

domicile *n* domicilio, *m*, *vt* domiciliar

domiciliary *a* domiciliario

dominant *a* dominante; imperante. *n mus* dominante, *f*. **to be d.**, prevalecer

dominate *vt* and *vi* dominar

domination *n* dominación, *f*

domineer *vi* dominar, tiranizar. **to d. over,** mandar en

domineering *a* dominante, mandón, tiránico

Dominican *a* dominicano. *n* dominicano, *m*

Dominican Republic, the la República Dominicana, *f*

dominion *n* dominio, *m*; autoridad, soberanía, *f*; imperio, *m*; *pl* **dominions,** *ecc* dominaciones, *f pl*

Dominions, the los Dominios, *m*

domino *n* dominó, *m*. **to go d.**, nacer domino

don *n* (Spanish and Italian title) don, *m*; señor, *m*. *vt* ponerse, vestirse

donation *n* donación, dádiva, *f*; contribución, *f*

done *a* and *past part* hecho; (of food) cocido; (roasted) asado; (tired) rendido; (*fam* deceived) engañado. **Well d.!** ¡Bien hecho! **d. for,** arruinado; muerto; perdido; vencido; (spoilt) estropeado

donkey *n* borrico (-ca), burro (-rra). **d.-engine,** máquina auxiliar, *f*

donor *n* donador (-ra); dador (-ra)

doodle *v* borrajear, garabatear, hacer garabatos

doom *n* condena, *f*; (fate) suerte, *f*; (judgment) destino, *m*; ruina, *f*; juicio, *m*. *vt* sentenciar; condenar

doomsday *n* día del juicio final, *m*

door *n* puerta, *f*; entrada, *f*. **front d.,** puerta de entrada, *f*. **next d.,** la casa vecina; la puerta de al lado, la puerta vecina. **next d. neighbor,** vecino (-na) de al lado. **out of doors,** al aire libre; en la calle. **to knock at the d.,** llamar a la puerta. **to slam the d. in a person's face,** dar con la puerta en las narices de alguien. **d.-bell,** timbre (non-electric, campanilla, *f*) de llamada, *m*. **d.-jamb,** quicial, *m*. **d. keeper,** portero, *m*. **d.-knob,** tirador, *m*. **d.-knocker,** manija, *f*; picaporte, *m*, aldaba, *f*. **d.-plate,** placa, *f*. **d.-shutter,** cierre metálico, *m*. **d.-step,** peldaño de la puerta, *m*; umbral, *m*. **d.-way,** portal, *m*

dope *n* drogas, *f pl*, narcóticos, *m pl*; (news) información, *f*. **d. fiend,** morfinómano (-na)

dope-pusher *n* narcotraficante, *mf*

Doric *a* dórico

dormant *a* durmiente; latente; secreto; inactivo. **to go d.,** dormirse

dormer window *n* lumbrera, *f*

dormitory *n* dormitorio, *m*

dormouse *n* lirón, *m*

dorsal *a* dorsal

dorsum *n* dorso, *m*

dory *n* (fish) dorado, *m*

dose, dosage *n*; dosis, *f*

dossier *n* documentación, *f*

dot *n* punto, *m*; *mus* puntillo, *m*; *pl* **dots,** *gram* puntos suspensivos, *m pl*. *vt* poner punto (a una letra); (scatter) salpicar. **on the dot,** (of time) en punto. **to dot one's i's,** poner los puntos sobre las íes

dotage *n* senectud, chochera, *f*

dotard *n* viejo chocho, *m*; vieja chocha, *f*; *inf* carcamal, *m*

dote *vi* chochear. **to d. on,** adorar en, idolatrar

doting *a* chocho

double *a* and *adv* doble; dos veces; (in a pair) en par; en dos; doblemente; (deceitful) doble, de dos caras, falso; ambiguo. *n* doble, *m*; duplicado, *m*; *theat* contrafigura, *f*; *pl* **doubles,** (tennis) dobles, *m pl*, juego doble, *m*. *vt* doblar; duplicar; (fold) doblegar; (the fist) cerrar (el puño); (*theat* and *naut*) doblar. *vi* doblarse; (dodge) volverse atrás, hacer un rodeo, dar una vuelta; esquivarse. **to d. up,** *vt* envolver; arrollar; (a person) doblar. *vi* doblegarse; arrollarse; (collapse) desplomarse.

at the d., corriendo. **He was doubled up with pain,** El dolor le hacía retorcerse. **mixed doubles,** parejas mixtas, *f pl*; dobles mixtos, *m pl*. **double two,** (telephone) dos dos. **with a d. meaning,** con segunda intención. **d.-barrelled,** de dos cañones. **d.-bass,** contrabajo, *m*. **d. bed,** cama de matrimonio, *f*. **d.-bedded,** con cama de matrimonio; con dos camas. **d.-breasted,** cruzado. **d.-chin,** papada, *f*. **d.-dealing,** duplicidad, *f*. **d.-edged,** de doble filo. **d.-entry,** *com* partida doble, *f*. **d.-faced,** de dos caras. **d.-jointed,** con articulaciones dobles

double-spaced *a* a doble espacio, a dos espacios

doublet *n* (garment) jubón, justillo, *m*; pareja, *f*, par, *m*

doubling *n* doblamiento, *m*; doblez, plegadura, *f*; duplicación, *f*; (dodging) evasiva, *f*, esguince, *m*

doubloon *n* doblón, *m*

doubly *adv* doblemente; con duplicidad

doubt *n* duda, *f*; incertidumbre, *f*; sospecha, *f*. *vt* and *vi* dudar; sospechar; titubear, hesitar; temer. **beyond all d.,** fuera de duda. **no d.,** sin duda. **There is no d. that,** No hay duda de que, No cabe duda de que. **When in d. . . . ,** En caso de duda . . .

doubter *n* incrédulo (-la)

doubtful *a* dudoso; incierto; perplejo; ambiguo; (of places) sospechoso

doubtfully *adv* dudosamente; inciertamente; irresolutamente; ambiguamente

doubtfulness *n* duda, incertidumbre, *f*; ambigüedad, *f*

doubtless *adv* sin duda, por supuesto; probablemente

douche *n* ducha, *f*, *vt* duchar

dough *n* pasta, masa, *f*; (money) lana, *f*

dour *a* huraño, adusto, austero

dourly *adv* severamente

douse *vt* zambullir; (a sail) recoger; *inf* apagar

dove *n* paloma, *f*. **d.-cote,** palomar, *m*

Dover Dóver, *m*

dovetail *n carp* cola de milano, *f*, *vt carp* machihembrar, empalmar; *fig* encajar

dowager *n* viuda, *f*; matrona, *f*. **d. countess,** condesa viuda, *f*

dowager empress *n* emperatriz viuda, *f*

dowdiness *n* desaliño, desaseo, *m*; falta de elegancia, *f*

dowdy *a* desaliñado, desaseado; poco elegante. *n* mujer poco elegante, *f*

dowel *n* espiga, clavija, *f*, zoquete, *m*, *vt* enclavijar

down *n* (of a bird) plumón, *m*; (on a peach, etc.) pelusilla, *f*; (hair) vello, *m*; (before the beard) bozo, *m*; (of a thistle, etc.) vilano, *m*. **ups and downs,** vicisitudes, *f pl*

down *a* pendiente; (of trains, etc.) descendente. *adv* abajo; hacia abajo; (lowered) bajado; (of the eyes) bajos; (on the ground) en tierra, por tierra; (stretched out) tendido a lo largo; (depressed) triste, abatido; (ill) enfermo; (fallen) caído; (of the wind) cesado; (closed) cerrado; (exhausted) agotado; *com* al contado; (of temperature) más bajo. *prep* abajo de; abajo; en la dirección de; (along) a lo largo de; por. **"Down"** (on elevators) «Para bajar». *interj* ¡Abajo!; ¡A tierra! **He went d. the hill,** Bajaba la colina. **He is d. now,** Ha bajado ahora; Está abajo ahora; Está derribado ahora. **The sun has gone d.,** Se ha puesto el sol. **His stock has gone d.,** *fig inf* Ha caído en disfavor. **Prices have come d.,** Los precios han bajado. **Their numbers have gone d.,** Sus números han disminuido. **to be d. and out,** estar completamente arruinado, ser pobre de solemnidad. **to boil d.,** reducir hirviendo. **to come d. in the world,** venir a menos. **while I was going d. the river,** mientras iba río abajo, mientras bajaba al río. **d. below,** allá abajo; abajo; en el piso de abajo. **D. on your knees!** ¡De rodillas! **d. to,** hasta. **d. spout,** tubo de bajada, *m*. **D. with!** ¡Abajo! ¡Muera! **d.-stream,** agua abajo. **d. train,** tren descendente, *m*

down *vt* derribar; vencer. **to d. tools,** declararse en huelga

downcast *a* bajo; cabizbajo, deprimido, abatido

downfall n caída, f; derrumbamiento, m; (failure) fracaso, m; (fig ruin) decadencia, ruina, f
downhearted a descorazonado, alicaído, desalentado
downhill adv cuesta abajo, hacia abajo. a en declive, inclinado. **to go d.**, ir cuesta abajo
downiness n vellosidad, f
downpour n chubasco (Mexico), aguacero, chaparrón, m
downright a franco, sincero; categórico, terminante; absoluto. adv muy; completamente
downstairs adv escalera abajo; al piso de abajo; en el piso bajo; abajo. a del piso de abajo. n planta baja, f; piso de abajo, m. **to go d.**, bajar la escalera; ir al piso de abajo
downtrodden a oprimido, esclavizado
downward a descendente; inclinado. adv hacia abajo
downy a velloso; (fam of persons) con más conchas que un galápago
dowry n dote, mf. **to give as a d.**, dotar
dowse vt. See **douse**
doze vi dormitar. n sueño ligero, m
dozen n docena, f
drab a pardo, parduzco, grisáceo; (fig gris, monótono. n (slut) pazpuerca, f; (prostitute) ramera, f
drachma n dracma, f
draft n (detachment) destacamento, m; com giro, m, letra de cambio, f; (for the army, navy) conscripción, leva, f; (outline) bosquejo, m; proyecto, m; borrador, m. vt (detach) destacar; (recruit) reclutar; (outline) bosquejar, delinear; (draw up) redactar; proyectar
draft card n cartilla (Mexico), libreta de enrolamiento (Argentina), m
draft dodger n emboscado, prófugo, m
drafting n (mil nav) reclutamiento, m; (of a bill, etc.) redacción, f; (wording) términos, m pl
draftsman n dibujante, m; delineante, m; redactor, m
drag n (for dredging) draga, f; (harrow) rastrillo, m; (break) freno, m; (obstacle) estorbo, m; aer sonda, f. vt arrastrar; (fishing nets) rastrear; (harrow) rastrillar. vi (of the anchor) garrar; arrastrarse por el suelo; (of time) pasar lentamente; ir más despacio (que); (of interest) decaer, disminuir. **d.-hook,** garfio, m. **d.-net,** brancada, f
dragging n arrastre, m; (of lakes, etc.) rastreo, m, a rastrero; cansado
draggled a mojado y sucio
dragon n dragón, m. **d.-fly,** libélula, f, caballito del diablo, m
dragoon n mil dragón, m, vt someter a una disciplina rigurosa; obligar a la fuerza (a)
drain n desaguadero, m; (sewer) cloaca, alcantarilla, f; sumidero, m; agr acequia, f. vt desaguar; sanear; (lakes, etc.) desangrar; secar; (bail) achicar; (empty and drink) vaciar; (swallow) tragar; (fig of sorrow, etc.) apurar; (despoil) despojar; (deprive) privar (de); (impoverish) empobrecer; (exhaust) agotar. vi desaguarse; vaciarse; (with off) escurrirse. **to be well drained,** tener buen drenaje. **to d. the sump,** vaciar la culata. **to d. away,** vaciar. **d.-pipe,** tubo de desagüe, m
drainage n (of land) drenaje, m; desagüe, m; (of wounds) drenaje, m; (sewage) aguas del alcantarillado, f pl. **main d.,** drenaje municipal, m
draining a de desagüe; de drenaje. **d.-board,** escurridor, m
drake n ánade macho, m
dram n dracma, f; (of liquor) trago, m
drama n drama, m
dramatic a dramático
dramatically adv dramáticamente
dramatis personae n pl personajes, m pl
dramatist n dramaturgo, m
dramatization n versión escénica, f; descripción dramática, f; (of emotions) dramatización, f
dramatize vt dramatizar
drape vt colgar, cubrir; vestir
draper n pañero (-ra)

drapery n colgaduras, f pl; ropaje, m, ropas, f pl; pañería, f
drastic a drástico; enérgico, fuerte; **a drastic measure,** una medida avanzada, f
draught n (act of drawing) tiro, m; (of liquid) trago, m; (glass) vaso, m; (of a ship) calado, m; (of air) corriente de aire, f; (party) destacamento, m; n pl **draughts,** (game) damas, f pl. vt see **draft. on d.,** (of beer, etc.) por vaso. **d. horse,** caballo de tiro, m. **d. screen,** cancel, m
draughtboard n tablero de damas, m
draughtsman n dibujante, m; delineante, m; redactor, m; (piece in game) peón, m
draughtsmanship n arte del dibujo lineal, mf; redacción (de un proyecto de ley), f
draughty a que tiene corriente de aire; expuesto a los vientos. **This room is d.,** Hay corriente de aire en esta habitación
draw vt tirar; arrastrar; traer; (pluck) arrancar; (attract) atraer; (extract) extraer; sacar; hacer salir; (unsheath) desenvainar; (a bow-string) tender; (cards, dominoes) tomar, robar; (threads) deshilar; (disembowel) destripar; (a check, etc.) girar, librar; (of a ship) calar; (of lines) hacer (rayas); (curtains) correr; (to draw curtains back) descorrer; (salary, money) cobrar, percibir; (obtain) obtener; (persuade) persuadir, inducir; (inhale) respirar; (a sigh) dar; (win) ganar; (a conclusion) deducir, inferir; (a distinction) hacer formular; sport empatar; (a number, etc.) sortear; (suck) chupar; (tighten) estirar; (lengthen) alargar; (comfort, etc.) tomar; (inspiration) inspirarse en; (obtain money) procurarse (recursos); (withdraw funds) retirar; (write) escribir; (draw) dibujar; (trace) trazar; (provoke) provocar. **to be drawn,** (of tickets in a lottery and cards) salir. **to d. lots,** echar suertes. **to d. water,** sacar agua. **to d. along,** arrastrar; conducir. **to d. aside,** tomar a un lado, tomar aparte; quitar de en medio, poner a un lado; (curtains) descorrer. **to d. away,** (remove) quitar; (a person) llevarse (a); apartar. **to d. back,** hacer recular; hacer retirarse; hacer volverse atrás; (curtains) descorrer. **to d. down,** hacer bajar; tirar a lo largo de (or por); bajar; (attract) atraer. **to d. forth,** hacer salir; hacer avanzar; tirar hacia adelante; conducir; (develop) desarrollar; sacar; hacer aparecer; (comment, etc.) suscitar. **to d. in,** tirar hacia adentro; sacar; acercar; atraer. **to d. off,** sacar; retirar; quitar; (water from pipes, etc.) vaciar; print tirar; (turn aside) desviar. **to d. on,** (of apparel) ponerse; (boots) calzarse; (occasion) ocasionar. **to d. out,** sacar fuera; hacer salir; tirar (de); (extract) extraer; (trace) trazar; (a person) hacer hablar. **to d. over,** poner encima de; arrastrar por; hacer acercarse a, tirar hacia; atraer; persuadir. **d. prestige (from),** cobrar prestigio (de). **to d. round,** poner alrededor de. **to d. together,** reunir; acercar. **to d. up,** tirar hacia arriba; subir; sacar; extraer; (raise) levantar, alzar; (bring) traer; (bring near) acercar; (order) ordenar; mil formar; (a document) redactar; formular. **to d. oneself up,** erguirse
draw vi tirar; (shrink) encogerse; (wrinkle) arrugarse; (of chimneys, etc.) tirar; (a picture) dibujar; sport empatar; (move) moverse; avanzar, adelantarse; (of a ship) calar; (a sword) desnudar (la espada); (lots) echar suertes; (attract people) atraer gente; com girar. **to d. aside,** ponerse a un lado; retirarse. **to d. back,** retroceder, recular; retirarse; vacilar. **to d. in,** retirarse; (of days) hacerse corto; (of dusk) caer. **to d. off,** alejarse; apartarse, retirarse. **to d. on,** (approach) acercarse; avanzar; com girar contra; inspirarse en. **to d. out,** hacerse largo; (of a vehicle) ponerse en marcha, empezar a andar. **to d. round,** ponerse alrededor; reunirse alrededor de. **to d. together,** reunirse. **to d. up,** parar.
draw n tirada, f; (of lotteries) sorteo, m; sport empate, m; atracción, f; (fig feeler) tanteo, m. **to be a big d.,** ser una gran atracción
drawback n desventaja, f, inconveniente, m

drawbridge *n* puente levadizo, *m*

drawee *n com* girado, *m*

drawer *n* tirador (-ra); (of water) aguador (-ra); extractor (-ra); (in a public-house) mozo de taberna, *m*; (designer) diseñador, *m*; (sketcher) dibujante, *mf*; *com* girador, *m*; (receptacle) cajón, *m*; *pl* **drawers,** (men's) calzoncillos, *m pl*; (women's) pantalones, *m pl*

drawing *n* (pulling) tiro, *m*; atracción, *f*; (extraction) extracción, *f*; saca, *f*; (in raffles, etc. and of lots) sorteo, *m*; (of money) percibo, *m*; *com* giro, *m*; (sketch) dibujo, *m*; (plan) esquema, *f.* **free-hand d.,** dibujo a pulso, *m.* **d. from life,** dibujo del natural, *m.* **d.-board,** tablero de dibujo, *m.* **d.-paper,** papel para dibujar, *m.* **d.-pin,** chinche, *f.* **d.-room,** salón, *m*

drawl *vi* hablar arrastrando las palabras

drawn *past part* See **draw.** *a* (tired) ojeroso, con ojeras, con un aspecto de cansancio; (with pain) desencajado. **long d. out,** demasiado largo. **d. sword,** espada desnuda, *f.* **d.-thread work,** deshilados, *m pl*

dray *n* carro, *m.* **d.-horse,** caballo de tiro, *m*

dread *n* pavor, temor, terror, espanto, *m*; trepidación, *f*, miedo, *m.* *a* temible, espantoso, terrible; augusto. *vt* temer. *vi* tener miedo, temer. **in d. of,** con miedo de, con terror de

dreader *n* el, *m*, (*f*, la) que teme, temedor (-ra)

dreadful *a* terrible, pavoroso, espantoso, horroroso; formidable; augusto

dreadfully *adv* terriblemente, horriblemente

dreadfulness *n* horror, *m*

dreadnought *n* acorazado de línea, *m*

dream *n* sueño, *m*; ilusión, *f*; ensueño, *m*; fantasía, *f. vt* and *vi* soñar; imaginar. **He dreamed away the hours,** Pasaba las horas soñando. **I wouldn't d. of it!** ¡Ni por sueño! **in a d.,** en sueños; (waking) como en sueños; mecánicamente. **Sweet dreams!** ¡Duerme bien! **to d. of,** soñar con

dreamer *n* soñador (-ra); visionario (-ia)

dreamily *adv* como en sueños; soñolientamente; vagamente

dreaming *n* sueños, *m pl*

dreamland *n* reino de los sueños, *m*

dreamy *a* soñador; soñoliento; fantástico; (empty) vacío

dreariness *n* tristeza, *f*; melancolía, *f*; lobreguez, *f*

dreary *a* triste; melancólico; lóbrego

dredge *vt* dragar; (with sugar, etc.) espolvorear

dredger *n* draga, *f*; (for sugar) azucarera, *f*; (for flour) harinero, *m*

dredging *n* dragado, *m*; (sprinkling) salpicadura, *f.* **d. bucket,** cangilón, *m*

dregs *n pl* heces, *f pl*, posos, *m pl.* **to drain to the d.,** vaciar hasta las heces

drench *vt* mojar, calar. **He is drenched to the skin,** Está calado hasta los huesos

Dresden *n* Dresde, *f.* **D. china,** loza de Dresde, *f*

dress *vt* (with clothes) vestir; (arrange) arreglar; (the hair) peinar(se); (a wound) curar; (hides) adobar; (cloth) aprestar; (flax) rastrillar; (stone) labrar; (wood) desbastar; (prune) podar; (a garden) cultivar; (manure) abonar; *cul* aderezar; preparar; (season) condimentar; (a table) poner; (adorn) ataviar, adornar; revestir; (a dead body) amortajar. *vi* vestirse; ataviarse; (of troops) alinearse. **all dressed up and nowhere to go,** compuesta y sin novio. **dressed up to the nines,** vestido de veinticinco alfileres. **Left (Right) d.!** ¡A la izquierda (A la derecha) alinearse! **to d. down,** (scold) poner como un trapo (a), dar una calada (a). **to d. up,** *vt* ataviar; (disguise) disfrazar. *vi* ponerse muy elegante; disfrazarse

dress *n* (in general) el vestir; (clothes) ropa, *f*; (frock) vestido, traje, *m*; (uniform) uniforme, *m*; (*fig* covering) hábitos, *m pl*; (appearance) aspecto, *m*; forma, *f.* **full d.,** (uniform) uniforme de gala, *m*; (civilian, man's) traje de etiqueta, *m*; (woman's) traje de gala, *m.* **morning d.,** (man's) traje de paisano, *m*; (woman's) vestido de todos los días, *m*; (man's formal dress) chaqué, *m.*

ready-made d., traje hecho, *m.* **d. allowance,** alfileres, *m pl.* **d.-circle,** anfiteatro, *m.* **d.-coat,** frac, *m.* **d. protector,** sobaquera, *f.* **d. rehearsal,** ensayo general, *m.* **d. shirt,** camisa de pechera dura, *f.* **d. suit,** (with white tie) traje de frac, *m*; (with black tie) smoking, *m.* **d. sword,** espada de gala, *f.* **d. tie,** corbata de smoking (or de frac), *f*

dresser *n* el que adereza; (of wounds) practicante (de hospital), *m*; (valet) ayuda de cámara, *m*; (maid) doncella, *f*; (of skins) adobador de pieles, *m*; (furniture) aparador, *m*; (in the kitchen) armario de la cocina, *m*

dressing *n* el vestir(se); aderezamiento, *m*; (for cloth) apresto, *m*; (of leather) adobo, *m*; (of wood) desbaste, *m*; (of stone) labrado, *m*; (manuring) estercoladura, *f*; (sauce) salsa, *f*; (seasoning) condimentación, *f*; (of a wound) cura, *f*; (bandage) apósito, *m*, vendaje, *m.* **d.-case,** neceser, saco de noche, *m.* **d.-down,** *inf* rapapolvo, *m.* **d.-gown,** (woman's) salto de cama, quimono, *m*; (man's) batín, *m.* **d.-jacket,** chambra, *f*, peinador, *m.* **d.-room,** *theat* camarín, *m*; (in a house) trasalcoba, vestídor, *m.* **d.-station,** puesto de socorro, *m.* **d.-table,** tocador, *m*, mesa de tocador, *f*

dressmaker *n* modista, *mf*

dressmaking *n* confección de vestidos, *f*; arte de la modista, *mf*

dribble *vi* gotear; (slaver) babear. *vt* (in football) regatear. *n* (in football) regate, *m*

dried *a* seco; (of fruit) paso. **d. up,** (withered) marchito; (of people) enjuto. **d. fish,** cecial, *m.* **d. meat,** cecina, *f*

drift *n* (in a ship or airplane's course) deriva, *f*; (of a current) velocidad, *f*; (tendency) tendencia, *f*; (meaning) significación, *f*; (heap) montón, *m*; (aim) objeto, propósito, fin, *m*; *min* galería, *f*; (of dust, etc.) nube, *f*; (shower) lluvia, *f*; (impulsion) impulso, *m*; violencia, *f.* *vi* flotar, ir arrastrado por la corriente; amontonarse; *naut* derivar; *aer* abatir. *vt* llevar; amontonar. **drifts of sand,** arena movediza, *f.* **to d. into,** (war, etc.) entrar sin querer en; (habits) dar en la flor de; (a room, etc.) deslizarse en. **d.-wood,** madera de deriva, *f*

drill *n* (instrument) taladro, perforador, *m*, barrena, *f*; ejercicio, *m*, educación física, *f*; *mil* instrucción militar, *f*; (cloth) dril, *m*; *agr* sembradora mecánica, *f*; (for seeds) hilera, *f*; (discipline) disciplina, *f*; (teaching) instrucción, *f. vt* taladrar, barrenar; enseñar el ejercicio (a); enseñar la instrucción; disciplinar; (seed) sembrar en hileras. *vi* hacer el ejercicio; hacer la instrucción militar. **d. ground,** (in a barracks) patio de un cuartel, *m*; (in a school) patio de recreo, *m.* **d.-sergeant,** sargento instructor, *m*

drilling *n* (boring) perforación, *f*, barrenamiento, *m*; (of seeds) sembradura en hileras, *f*; ejercicios, *m pl*; (maneuvers) maniobras, *f pl*

drink *n* bebida, *f*; (glass of wine, etc.) copita, *f*; (of water, etc.) vaso, *m. vt* beber; tomar; (empty) vaciar. *vi* beber. **to d. the health of,** beber a la salud de, brindar por. **to give someone a d.,** dar a beber. **Would you like a d.?** ¿Quieres tomar algo? **to d. in,** absorber. **to d. off, up,** beber de un trago

drinkable *a* potable, bebedero

drinker *n* bebedor (-ra)

drinking *n* acción de beber, *m*; el beber, *m*; (alcoholism) bebida, *f. a* que bebe; aficionado a la bebida; (of things) para beber; (drinkable) potable; (tavern) de taberna. **d.-fountain,** fuente pública para beber agua, *f.* **d. place,** bebedero, *m*; bar, *m.* **d.-song,** canción de taberna, *f.* **d.-trough,** abrevadero, *m.* **d.-water,** agua potable, *f*

drip *vi* and *vt* chorrear, gotear; caer gota a gota; escurrir; destilar; chorrear. *n* goteo, *m*; gota, *f*; *arch* goterón, *m*

dripping *n* goteo, *m*; chorreo, *m*; (fat) grasa, *f*, *a* que gotea; mojado; que chorrea. **d.-pan,** grasera, *f*

drive *vt* empujar; arrojar; conducir; (grouse, etc.) batir; (a ball) golpear; (a nail, etc.) clavar; (oblige) compeler, forzar a; (a horse, plough, etc.) manejar; (*mech* work) mover; (cause to work, of machines) hacer funcionar;

(a tunnel, etc.) abrir, construir; (a bargain, etc.) hacer; (cause) impulsar, hacer; (mad, etc.) volver. *vi* lanzarse; (of rain) azotar; (a vehicle) conducir; (in a vehicle) ir en (coche, etc.). **to let d. at,** (aim) asestar. **to d. a wedge,** hacer mella. **to d. home an argument,** convencer; hacer convincente. **What is he driving at?** ¿Qué se propone?; ¿Qué quiere?; ¿Qué quiere decir con sus indirectas? ¿A dónde quiere llegar con esto? **to d. along,** ir en coche o carruaje por; pasearse en coche o carruaje; conducir un auto, etc., por. **to d. away,** *vt* echar; (chase) cazar; (flies, etc.) sacudirse, espantar; (care, etc.) ahuyentar; (of persons) apartar, alejar. *vi* (depart) marcharse (en coche, etc.). **to d. back,** *vt* rechazar; (a ball) devolver. *vi* volver (en auto, etc.); (arrive) llegar. **to d. down,** hacer bajar; arrojar hacia abajo; (in a vehicle) bajar (por). **to d. in, into,** *vt* hacer entrar; (of teeth, etc.) hincar; (nails) clavar; *fig* introducir. *vt* entrar (en coche, carruaje); llegar (en coche, etc.). **to d. off,** See **away. to d. off the stage,** hacer dejar la escena, silbar. **to d. on,** *vt* empujar; hacer avanzar; (attack) atacar. *vi* seguir su marcha; seguir avanzando; emprender la marcha. **to d. out,** *vt* expulsar; hacer salir; (chase) cazar. *vi* salir (en coche, etc.). **to d. up,** *vi* illegar (en coche, etc.); parar. **to d. up to,** avanzar hasta, llegar hasta; conducir (el coche, etc.) hasta

drive *n* paseo (en coche, etc.), *m*; (avenue) avenida, *f*; (distance) trayecto, *m*; (journey) viaje, *m*; *mech* acción, *f*; conducción, *f*; *m*; *mil* ataque, *m*; (of a person) energía, *f*; campaña vigorosa, *f*; impulso, *m*. **left (right) hand d.,** conducción a la izquierda (derecha). **to take a d.,** dar un paseo (en auto, etc.). **to take for a d.,** llevar a paseo en (auto, etc.)

drive-in *n* autocine, autocinema, *m*

drivel *n* vaciedades, patrañas, *f pl,* disparates, *m pl, vi* decir disparates, chochear

driver *n* conductor (-ra); chófer, *m*; (of an engine) maquinista, *m*; (of a cart) carretero, *m*; (of a coach, carriage) cochero, *m*; (of cattle, etc.) ganadero, *m*; (golf) conductor, *m*

"Driveway" «Vado Permante», «Paso de Carruajes»

driving *n* conducción, *f*; modo de conducir, *m*; paseo (en coche, etc.), *m*; impulsión, *f. a* de conducir; de chófer; para choferes; motor; propulsor; impulsor; de transmisión; *fig* impulsor; (violent) violento, impetuoso. **to go d.,** ir de paseo (en auto o carruaje). **d. license,** carnet de chófer, *m.* **d. mirror,** espejo retrovisor, *m.* **d. seat,** asiento del conductor, *m*; (of an old-fashioned coach, etc.) pescante, *m.* **d.-shaft,** *mech* árbol motor, *m.* **d. test,** examen para choferes, *m.* **d.-wheel,** volante, *m*; rueda motriz, *f.* **d.-whip,** látigo, *m*

drizzle *n* llovizna, *f, vi* lloviznar

droll *a* chusco, gracioso. *n* bufón, *m*

dromedary *n* dromedario, *m*

drone *n* abejón, *m; fig* zángano, *m*; (hum) zumbido, *m*; (of a song, voice) salmodia, *f, vt* and *vi* (hum) zumbar; (of a song, voice) salmodiar; (idle) zanganear

droning *a* zumbador; confuso

droop *vi* inclinarse; colgar; caer; (wither) marchitarse; (fade) consumirse; (pine) desanimarse. *vt* bajar; dejar caer. *n* caída, *f*; inclinación, *f*

drooping *a* caído; debilitado; lánguido; (of ears) gacho; (depressed) alicaído, deprimido

drop *n* gota, *f*; (tear) lágrima, *f*; (for the ear) pendiente, *m*; (sweet) pastilla, *f*; (of a chandelier) almendra, *f*; (fall) caída, *f*; (in price, etc.) baja, *f*; (slope) pendiente, cuesta, *f.* **by drops,** a gotas. **d. bottle,** frasco cuentagotas, *m.* **d.-curtain,** telón de boca, *m.* **d.-hammer,** martinete, *m.* **d.-head coupé,** cupé descapotable, *m.* **d.-scene,** telón de foro, *m*

drop *vt* verter a gotas; destilar; (sprinkle) salpicar, rociar; dejar caer; soltar; (lower) bajar; (of clothes, etc.) desprenderse de, quitar; (lose) perder; (a letter in a mailbox) echar; (leave) dejar; (give up) renunciar (a); desistir (de); abandonar; (kill) tumbar; (a hint) soltar;

(a curtsey) hacer. *vi* gotear, caer en gotas, destilar; (descend) bajar, descender; caer muerto; caer desmayado; (sleep) dormirse; (fall) caer; (of the wind) amainar; (of prices, temperature) bajar. **to let the matter d.,** poner fin a una cuestión. **to d. a line,** poner unas líneas. **to d. anchor,** anclar. **to d. behind,** quedarse atrás. **to d. down,** caer (a tierra). **to d. in,** entrar al pasar. **d. in on somebody,** pasarse por casa de fulano, pasarse por el despacho de (etc.). **to d. off,** separarse (de); disminuir; (sleep) quedar dormido; (die) morir de repente. **to d. out,** separarse; (from a race, etc.) retirarse (de); quedarse atrás; desaparecer; ausentarse, apartarse; (decrease) disminuir; decaer. **He has dropped out of my life,** Le he perdido de vista. **to d. through,** hacer por; frustrarse; no dar resultado

dropping *n* gotera, *f*; gotas, *f pl*; (fall) caída, *f*; *pl* **droppings** (of a candle) moco, *m*; (dung) cagadas, *f pl*. **Constant d. wears away the stone,** La gotera cava la piedra

dropsy *n* hidropesía, *f*

dross *n* escoria, *f*; (rubbish) basura, *f*

drought *n* aridez, *f*; (thirst) sed, *f*; (dry season) sequía, *f*

drove *n* manada, *f*, hato, *m*; (of sheep) rebaño, *m*; (crowd) muchedumbre, *f*

drown *vi* ahogarse. *vt* ahogar; sumergir; inundar; (*fig* of cries, sorrow, etc.) ahogar

drowning *n* ahogamiento, *m*; sumersión, *f*; inundación, *f. a* que se ahoga

drowse *vi* adormecerse

drowsily *adv* soñolientamente

drowsiness *n* somnolencia, *f*; sueño, *m*; (laziness) indolencia, pereza, *f*

drowsy *a* soñoliento; adormecedor, soporífero; (heavy) amodorrado. **to grow d.,** adormecerse. **to make d.,** adormecer

drubbing *n* tunda, zurra, felpa, *f*

drudgery *n* trabajo arduo, *m*, faena monótona, *f*

drug *n* droga, *f*; medicamento, *m*; narcótico, *m. vt* mezclar con drogas; administrar drogas (a); narcotizar. *vi* tomar drogas. **d. trade,** comercio de drogas, *m.* **d. traffic,** contrabando de drogas, narcotráfico *m*

drug addict *n* toxicómano, *m*

drug addiction *n* toxicomanía, *f*

druggist *n* droguero (-ra)

druid *n* druida, *m*

drum *n* tambor, *m*; (of the ear) tímpano (del oído), *m*; (cylinder) cilindro, *m*; (box) caja, *f*; *arch* cuerpo de columna, *m.* **bass d.,** bombo, *m.* **with drums beating,** con tambor batiente. **d.-head,** parche (del tambor), *m.* **d.-head service,** misa de campaña, *f.* **d.-major,** tambor mayor, *m*

drum *vt* and *vi* tocar el tambor; (with the fingers) tabalear, teclear; (with the heels) zapatear; (into a person's head) machacar. **to d. out,** *mil* expulsar a tambor batiente

drummer *n* tambor, *m*

drumming *n* ruido del tambor, *m*; (of the heels) taconeo, *m*; (of the fingers) tabaleo, tecleo, *m*

drumstick *n* palillo (de tambor), *m*

drunk *a* borracho, ebrio. *n* borracho, *m.* **to be d.,** estar borracho. **to get d.,** emborracharse; *inf* pillar un lobo. **to make d.,** emborrachar

drunkard *n* borracho (-cha)

drunken *a* borracho, ebrio

drunkenness *n* embriaguez, borrachera, ebriedad, *f*

dry *vi* secarse. *vt* secar; desaguar; (wipe) enjugar. **to dry one's tears,** enjugarse las lágrimas; *fig* secarse las lágrimas. **to dry up,** secarse; (of persons) acecinarse; (with old age) apergaminarse; (of ideas, etc.) agotarse; (be quiet) callarse

dry *a* seco; árido; estéril; (thirsty) sediento; (of wine) seco (U.S.A.) prohibicionista; (squeezed) exprimido; (of toast) sin mantequilla; (*fig* chilly) aburrido; (sarcastic) sarcástico; (of humour) agudo. **on dry land,** en seco. **dry battery,** pila seca, *f.* **to dry-clean,** lavar al seco. **dry-cleaner,** tintorero (-ra). **dry-cleaning,** lavado al seco, *m.* **dry-cleaning shop,** tintorería, *f.* **dry goods,** lencería, *f.* **dry land,** tierra firme, *f.* **dry measure,** medida para áridos, *f.* **dry-nurse,** ama seca, *f.* **dry-point,** punta seca, *f.* **dry-rot,** carcoma, *f.* **dry-shod,** con los pies secos

drying *n* secamiento, *m;* desecación, *f, a* secante; seco; para secar. **d. ground,** tendedero, *m.* **d. machine,** secadora, *f;* (for the hair) secadora de cabello, *f.* **d. room,** secadero, *m*

dryly *adv* secamente

dryness *n* sequedad, *f;* aridez, *f;* (of humour) agudeza, *f*

dual *a* doble; *gram* dual. **d. control,** mandos gemelos, *m pl.* **d. personality,** conciencia doble, *f*

dualism *n* dualismo, *m*

duality *n* dualidad, *f*

dub *vt* (a knight) armar caballero; (call) apellidar; (nickname) motejar, apodar

dubbing *n* (of films) doblaje, *m*

dubious *a* dudoso, incierto; indeciso; problemático; ambiguo

dubiously *adv* dudosamente

dubiousness *n* carácter dudoso, *m;* incertidumbre, *f;* ambigüedad, *f*

Dublin Dublín, *f*

Dubliner *n* dublinés (-esa)

ducat *n* ducado, *m*

duchess *n* duquesa, *f*

duchy *n* ducado, *m*

duck *n* pato (-ta), ánade, *mf; sport* cero, *m;* (darling) vida mía, querida, *f;* (jerk) agachada, *f;* (under the water) chapuz, *m;* (material) dril, *m; mil* auto anfibio, *m; pl* **ducks,** pantalones de dril, *m pl. vi* agacharse; (under water) chapuzarse. *vt* zabullir, sumergir; bajar, inclinar

ducking *n* chapuz, *m.* **d.-stool,** silla de chapuzar, *f*

duckling *n* anadino (-na)

duct *n* conducto, canal, *m; bot* tubo, *m*

ductile *a* dúctil

ductility *n* ductilidad, *f*

ductless *a* sin tubos

due *a* debido; (payable) pagadero; (fallen due) vencido; (fitting) propio; (expected) esperado. *n* impuesto, *m;* derecho, *m.* **in due form,** en regla. **in its due time,** a su tiempo debido. **to fall due,** vencerse. **due bill,** *com* abonaré, *m.* **due west,** poniente derecho, *m*

duel *n* duelo, lance de honor, *m; fig* lucha, *f.* **to fight a d.,** batirse en duelo

dueling *n* el (batirse en) duelo

duelist *n* duelista, *m*

duenna *n* dueña, *f*

duet *n* dúo, *m*

duettist *n* duetista, *mf*

duffer *n* estúpido (-da); ganso, *m;* (at games, etc.) maleta, *m*

dug *n* teta, *f*

dugout *n* trinchera, *f*

duke *n* duque, *m*

dukedom *n* ducado, *m*

dulcet *a* dulce

dulcimer *n* dulcémele, *m*

dull *a* (stupid) lerdo, estúpido, obtuso; (boring, tedious) aburrido; (of pain, sounds) sordo; (of colors and eyes) apagado; (of light, beams, etc.) sombrío; (not polished) mate; (pale) pálido; (insipid) insípido, insulso; (of people) soso, poco interesante; (dreary, sad) triste; (gray) gris; (of mirrors, etc.) empañado; (of weather) anublado; (of hearing) duro; (slow) lento; lánguido; insensible; (blunt) romo; *com* encalmado, inactivo. **to find life d.,** encontrar la vida aburrida. **d. of hearing,** duro de oído, algo sordo. **d. pain,** dolor sordo, *m.* **d. season,** temporada de calma, *f.* **d.-eyed,** con ojos apagados. **d.-witted,** lerdo

dull *vt* (make stupid) entontecer; (lessen) mitigar; (weaken) debilitar; (pain) calmar, aliviar; (sadden) entristecer; (blunt) embotar; (spoil) estropear; (a mirror,

etc.) empañar; (a polished surface) hacer mate, deslustrar; (of enthusiasm, etc.) enfriar; (tire) fatigar; (obstruct) impedir

dullness *n* (stupidity) estupidez, *f;* (boredom) aburrimiento, *m;* (heaviness) pesadez, *f;* (drowsiness) somnolencia, *f;* (insipidity) insipidez, insulsez, *f;* (of literary style) prosaísmo, *m;* (of persons) sosería, *f;* (of a surface) deslustre, *m;* (laziness) pereza, languidez, *f;* (slowness) lentitud, *f;* (tiredness) cansancio, *m;* (sadness) tristeza, *f;* (bluntness) embotamiento, *m;* (of hearing) dureza, *f; com* desanimación, *f*

dully *adv* (stupidly) estúpidamente; sin comprender; (insipidly) insípidamente; (not brightly) sin brillo; (slowly) lentamente; (sadly) tristemente; (tiredly) con cansancio; (of sound) sordamente

duly *adv* debidamente; puntualmente

dumb *a* mudo; callado; silencioso; *inf* tonto, estúpido. **to become d.,** enmudecer. **to strike d.,** dejar sin habla. **d.-bell,** barra con pesas, *f.* **d. show,** pantomima, *f.* **d. waiter,** bufete, *m*

dumbfound *vt* dejar sin habla; confundir; pasmar

dumbness *n* mudez, *f,* mutismo, *m;* silencio, *m*

dummy *n* (tailor's, etc.) maniquí, *m;* (puppet) títere, *m;* cabeza para pelucas, *f;* (figurehead) hombre de paja, testaferro, *m;* (baby's) chupador, *m;* (at cards) el muerto. *a* fingido. **to be d.,** (at cards) ser el muerto

dump *n* depósito, *m;* vaciadero, *m.* *vt* depositar; (goods on a market) inundar (con)

dumping *n* depósito, *m;* vaciamiento, *m;* (of goods on a market) inundación, *f.* **"D. prohibited,"** «Se prohibe arrojar la basura»

dumps *n* murria, *f*

dun *vt* apremiar, importunar

dun-colored *a* pardo

dunce *n* asno, bobo, zoquete, *m.* **dunce's cap,** coroza, *f*

dunderhead *n* cabeza de alcornoque, zoquete, *m*

dune *n* duna, *f*

dung *n* estiércol, *m;* (of rabbits, mice, deer, sheep, goats) cagarruta, *f;* (of cows) boñiga, *f;* (of hens) gallinaza, *f.* **d.-cart,** carro de basura, *m*

dungarees *n* mono, *m,* pantalones-vaquero, *m pl*

dungeon *n* mazmorra, *f,* calabozo, *m*

dunghill *n* muladar, *m*

Dunkirk Dunquerque, *m*

duodenum *n* duodeno, *m*

dupe *n* víctima, *f;* tonto (-ta). *vt* embelecar, engañar. **to be a d.,** *inf* hacer el primo

duplicate *a* duplicado, doble. *n* duplicado, *m;* copia, *f, vt* duplicar

duplication *n* duplicación, *f*

duplicator *n* copiador, *m*

duplicity *n* duplicidad, *f*

durability *n* duración, *f.* **This is a cloth of great d.,** Este es un paño que dura mucho, Este es un paño muy duradero

durable *a* duradero

duration *n* duración, *f*

duress *n* compulsión, *f;* (prison) prisión, *f*

during *prep* durante

dusk *n* atardecer, anochecer, *m;* (twilight) crepúsculo, *m;* (darkness) oscuridad, *f.* **at d.,** al atardecer, a la caída de la tarde

dusky *a* (swarthy) moreno; (black) negro; (dim, dark) oscuro; (of colors) sucio

dust *n* polvo, *m;* (cloud of dust) polvareda, *f;* (ashes) cenizas, *f pl;* (of coal) cisco, *m;* (sweepings) barreduras, *f pl;* (of grain) tamo, *m. vt* desempolvar, quitar (or sacudir) el polvo de; (cover with dust) polvorear; (scatter) salpicar; (sweep) barrer; (clean) limpiar. **d.-bin,** basurero, *m.* **d.-cart,** carro de la basura, *m.* **d. cloud,** polvareda, *f.* **d. jacket,** (books) sobrecubierta, *f.* **d.-pan,** recogedor de basura, *m.* **d.-sheet,** guardapolvo, *m.* **d. storm,** vendaval de polvo, *m*

duster *n* el, *m,* que quita el polvo; paño (para quitar el polvo), *m;* (of feathers) plumero, *m*

dustiness *n* empolvoramiento, *m*; estado polvoriento, *m*

dusting *n* limpieza, *f*; (sweeping) barredura, *f*; (powder) polvos antisépticos, *m pl*

dustman *n* basurero, *m*

dusty *a* polvoriento, polvoroso, empolvado; del color del polvo; (of colours) sucio. **It is very d.,** Hay mucho polvo. **to get d.,** llenarse (or cubrirse) de polvo

Dutch *a* holandés. **the D.,** los holandeses. **double D.,** griego, galimatías, *m*. **D. cheese,** queso de bola, *m*. **D. courage,** coraje falso, *m*. **D. woman,** holandesa, *f*

Dutchman *n* holandés, *m*

dutiable *a* sujeto a derechos de aduana

dutiful *a* que cumple con sus deberes; obediente, sumiso; respetuoso; excelente, muy bueno

dutifully *adv* obedientemente; respetuosamente

dutifulness *n* obediencia, docilidad, *f*; respeto, *m*

duty *n* deber, *m*; obligación, *f*; (greetings) respetos, *m pl*; (charge, burden) carga, *f*; (tax) derecho, impuesto, *m*; *mil* servicio, *m*; (guard) guardia, *f*. **off d.,** libre. **on d.,** de servicio. **to be on sentry d.,** estar de guardia. **to do d. as,** servir como. **to do one's d.,** hacer (or cumplir con) su deber. **to pay d. on,** pagar derechos de aduana sobre. **d.-free,** franco de derechos

dwarf *a* enano. *n* enano (-na). *vt* impedir el crecimiento de; empequeñecer

dwarfish *a* enano

dwell *vi* vivir, habitar; (with on, upon) (think about) meditar sobre, pensar en; (deal with) tratar de; hablar largamente de; (insist on) insister en; apoyarse en, hacer hincapié en; (pause over) detenerse en

dweller *n* habitante, *mf*; (more poetic) morador (-ra)

dwelling *n* vivienda, *f*; (abode) morada, habitación, *f*; residencia, *f*; casa, *f*; (domicile) domicilio, *m*. **d.-house,** casa, *f*

dwindle *vi* disminuirse; consumirse; (decay) decaer; (degenerate) degenerar. **to d. to,** reducirse a

dwindling *n* disminución, *f*

dye *vt* teñir, colorar. *vi* teñirse. *n* tinte, *m*; (colour) color, *m*. **fast dye,** tinte estable, *m*. **dye-house,** tintorería, *f*. **dye-stuff,** materia colorante, *f*. **dye-works,** tintorería, *f*

dyed-in-the-wool *a* de pies a cabeza

dyeing *n* teñidura, tintura, *f*; (as a trade) tintorería, *f*. **d. and dry-cleaning shop,** tintorería, *f*

dyer *n* tintorero (-ra)

dyestuff *n* materia colorante, materia de tinte, materia tintórea, *f*

dying *a* moribundo, agonizante; de la muerte; (of light) mortecino; (last) último; supremo; (languishing) lánguido; (deathbed) hecho en su lecho mortuorio. **to be d.,** estar agonizando; (of light) fenecer. **to be d. for,** estar muerto por

dynamic *a* dinámico

dynamics *n* dinámica, *f*

dynamite *n* dinamita, *f*

dynamo *n* dinamo, *f*

dynastic *a* dinástico

dynasty *n* dinastía, *f*

dysentery *n* disentería, *f*

dyspepsia *n* dispepsia, *f*

dyspeptic *a* dispéptico. *n* dispéptico (-ca)

E

e *n* (letter) e, *f*; *mus* mi, *m*

each *a* cada (invariable), todo. *pron* cada uno, *m*; cada una, *f*. **e. of them,** cada uno de ellos. **They help e. other,** Se ayudan mutuamente, Se ayudan entre sí. **to love e. other,** amarse

eager *a* impaciente; ansioso, deseoso; ambicioso

eagerly *adv* con impaciencia; con ansia; ambiciosamente

eagerness *n* impaciencia, *f*; ansia, *f*, deseo, *m*; (promptness) alacridad, *f*; (zeal) fervor, *m*

eagle *n* águila, *f*. **royal e.,** águila caudal, águila real, *f*. **e.-eyed,** con ojos de lince, de ojo avizor. **have the eyes of an e.,** tener ojos de lince, tener vista de lince

ear *n* (outer ear) oreja, *f*; (inner ear and sense of hearing) oído, *m*; *bot* espiga, panoja, *f*. **to begin to show the ear,** (grain) espigar. **to be all ears,** ser todo oídos. **to give ear,** dar oído. **to have a good ear,** tener buen oído. **to play by ear,** tocar de oído. **to turn a deaf ear,** hacerse el sordo. **ear-ache,** dolor de oídos, *m*. **ear-drum,** tímpano (del oído), *m*. **ear-flap,** orejera, *f*. **ear-phone, ear-piece,** auricular, *m*. **ear-piercing,** penetrante, agudo. **ear-shot,** alcance del oído, *m*. **to be within ear-shot,** estar al alcance del oído. **ear-trumpet,** trompetilla, *f*. **ear wax,** cerilla, *f*

eared *a* con orejas; de orejas; *bot* con espigas

earl *n* conde, *m*

earldom *n* condado, *m*

earlier, earliest *a comp* and *sup* más temprano; más primitivo; más antiguo; (first, of time) primero. *adv* más temprano; más pronto; antes

earliness *n* lo temprano; antigüedad, *f*, lo primitivo; (precocity) precocidad, *f*. **The e. of his arrival,** Su llegada de buena hora

early *a* temprano; primitivo; (of fruit, etc.) temprano, adelantado; (movement) primero (e.g. **early Romanticism,** el primer romanticismo); (person) de la primera época (e.g. **the early Cervantes,** Cervantes de la primera época); (work) un primer (e.g. **an early work of Unamuno's,** una primera obra de Unamuno's); (advanced) avanzado; (precocious) precoz; (first, of time)

primero; (in the morning) matutino; (near) próximo; cercano; (premature) prematuro; (of child's age) tierno; joven. **in the e. hours,** en las primeras horas; en las altas horas (de la noche). **e. age,** edad temprana, tierna edad, *f*. **e.-fruiting,** *agr* tempranal. **e. riser,** madrugador (-ra). **e.-rising,** *a* madrugador. **e. years,** primeros años, años de la niñez, *m pl*

early *adv* temprano; al principio (de); en los primeros días (de); desde los primeros días (de); (in the month, year) a principios (de); (in time) a tiempo; (in the day) de buena hora; (soon) pronto; (among the first) entre los primeros (de). **as e. as possible,** lo más temprano posible; lo más pronto posible. **to be e.,** llegar antes de tiempo; llegar de buena hora. **to get up e.,** madrugar. **to go to bed e.,** acostarse temprano. **too e.,** demasiado temprano. **e. in the morning,** de madrugada

earmark *vt* marcar; *fig* destinar, reservar

earn *vt* ganar; obtener, adquirir; (deserve) merecer

earnable *a* ganable

earnest *a* serio; fervoroso; diligente; sincero. **to be in e. about something,** tomarlo en serio; ser sincero (en). **e. money,** arras, *f pl*

earnestly *adv* seriamente; fervorosamente; con diligencia; sinceramente, de buena fe

earnestness *n* seriedad, *f*; fervor, celo, *m*; diligencia, *f*; sinceridad, buena fe, *f*

earnings *n pl com* ingresos, *m pl*; (salary) salario, *m*; estipendio, *m*; (of a workman) jornal, *m*

earring *n* pendiente, arete, *m*

earth *n* tierra, *f*; (of a badger, etc.) madriguera, *f*; *rad* tierra, *f*. *vt* cubrir con tierra; *rad* conectar con tierra. **clod of e.,** terrón, *m*. **half the e.,** *inf* medio mundo, *m*. **on e.,** en este mundo, sobre la tierra

earthen *a* terrizo, terroso; (of mud) de barro

earthenware *n* alfar, *m*, *a* de loza, de barro

earthiness *n* terrosidad, *f*

earthly *a* terrestre, terrenal; de la tierra; (fleshly) carnal; (worldly) mundano; material. **There is not an e. chance,** No hay la más mínima posibilidad

earthquake *n* terremoto, temblor de tierra, *m*
earth tremor movimiento sísmico, *m*
earthwork *n* terraplén, *m*
earthworm *n* gusano de tierra, *m*
earthy *a* térreo, terroso
earwig *n* tijereta, *f*
ease *n* bienestar, *m*; tranquilidad, *f*; descanso, *m*; (leisure) ocio, *m*; (comfortableness) comodidad, *f*; (freedom from embarrassment) naturalidad, *f*, desembarazo, desenfado, *m*; (from pain) alivio, *m*; (simplicity) facilidad, *f*. *vt* (widen) ensanchar; aflojar; (pain) aliviar; (lighten) aligerar; (moderate) moderar; (soften) suavizar; (free) librar; (one's mind) tranquilizar. **in my moments of e.,** en mis ocios, en mis momentos de ocio. **Stand at e.!** *mil* ¡En su lugar descansen! **to be at e.,** estar a sus anchas; encontrarse bien; comportarse con toda naturalidad. **with e.,** fácilmente. **to e. off,** *vt* (*naut* cables, sails) arriar. *vi* sentirse menos, cesar
easel *n* caballete (de pintor) *m*
easily *adv* fácilmente. **The engine runs e.,** El motor marcha bien
easiness *n* facilidad, *f*; sencillez, *f*; (of manner) desembarazo, *m*, naturalidad, *f*
east *n* este, *m*; oriente, *m*, (of countries) Oriente, *m*; Levante, *m*. *a* del este; del oriente; (of countries) de Oriente, oriental; levantino. **e. North e.,** estenordeste, *m*. **e. South e.,** estesudeste, *m*. **e. wind,** viento del este, *m*
Easter *n* Pascua de Resurrección, *f*. **E. egg,** huevo de Pascua, *m*. **E. Saturday,** sábado de gloria, *m*. **E. Sunday,** domingo de Pascua, *m*
easterly *a* del este; al este. *adv* hacia el este
eastern *a* del este; de Oriente; oriental. *n* oriental, *mf*
easternmost *a* situado más al este
East Indies Indias Orientales, *f pl*
eastward *adv* hacia el este, hacia oriente
easy *a* fácil; sencillo; (comfortable) cómodo; (free from pain) aliviado; *com* flojo; (well-off) acomodado, holgado; (calm) tranquilo; tolerante; natural; afable, condescendiente; (of virtue, women) fácil. *adv* con calma; despacio. **I must make myself e. about,** he de tranquilizarme sobre. **Stand e.!** ¡En su lugar descansen! **to take it e.,** tomarlo con calma. **e.-chair,** (silla) poltrona, *f*. **easy come, easy go,** lo que por agua, agua (Mexico and Colombia), los dineros del sacristán cantando vienen y cantando se van (Spain). **e.-going,** acomodadizo; indolente; (morally) de manga ancha; (casual) descuidado
eat *vt* comer; (meals, soup, refreshments) tomar; (with a good, bad appetite) hacer; consumir; (corrode) corroer; desgastar. *vi* comer; (*fam* of food) ser de buen (or mal) comer. **to eat one's breakfast (lunch),** tomar el desayuno, desayunar (almorzar). **to eat one's words,** retractarse. **to eat away,** comer; consumir; corroer. **to eat into,** (of chemicals) morder; (a fortune) consumir; gastar. **eat out of s.b.'s hand,** comer de la mano de fulano, comer en la mano de fulano. **to eat up,** devorar (also *fig*)
eatable *a* comestible, comedero. *n pl* **eatables,** comestibles, *m pl*
eater *n* el, *m*, (*f*, la) que come
eating *n* el comer; comida, *f*. **e. and drinking,** el comer y beber. **e.-house,** casa de comidas, *f*
eau de cologne *n* agua de Colonia, *f*
eaves *n* rafe, alero, *m*. **under the e.,** debajo del alero
eavesdrop *vi* escuchar a las puertas; fisgonear, espiar
eavesdropper *n* fisgón (-ona)
eavesdropping *n* fisgoneo, *m*
ebb *n* (of the tide) reflujo, *m*; menguante, *f*; *fig* declinación, *f*; *fig* decadencia, *f*; (of life) vejez, *f*. *vi* (of tide) menguar; declinar; decaer. **to ebb and flow,** fluir y refluir. **to ebb away from,** dejar; dejar aislado. **ebb-tide,** marea menguante, *f*
ebonite *n* ebonita, *f*
ebony *n* ébano, *m*

ebullience *n* efervescencia, exuberancia, *f*
ebullient *a* efervescente, exuberante
ebullition *n* (boiling) ebullición, *f*, hervor, *m*; *fig* efervescencia, *f*, estallido, *m*
eccentric *a* *geom* excéntrico; raro, original; extravagante, excéntrico. *n* persona excéntrica, *f*, original, *m*
eccentrically *adv* excéntricamente
eccentricity *n* *geom* excentricidad, *f*; rareza, extravagancia, excentricidad, *f*
Ecclesiastes *n* Eclesiastés, *m*
ecclesiastic *a* eclesiástico. *n* eclesiástico, clérigo, *m*
ecclesiastically *adv* eclesiásticamente
echo *n* eco, *m*; reverberación, resonancia, *f*. *vt* repercutir; *fig* repetir. *vi* resonar, retumbar, reverberar
echoing *a* retumbante. *n* eco, *m*
eclectic *a* and *n* ecléctico (-ca)
eclecticism *n* eclecticismo, *m*
eclipse *n* *ast* eclipse, *m*, *vt* eclipsar, hacer eclipse a. **to be in e.,** estar en eclipse
ecliptic *n* *ast* eclíptica, *f*, *a* elíptico
eclog *n* égloga, *f*
economic *a* económico
economical *a* económico
economics *n* economía política, *f*
economist *n* economista, *mf*
economize *vt* economizar, ahorrar. *vi* hacer economías
economy *n* economía, *f*. **domestic e.,** economía doméstica, *f*. **political e.,** economía política, *f*
ecstasy *n* éxtasis, arrebato, *m*; transporte, *m*. **to be in e.,** estar en éxtasis
ecstatic *a* extático
Ecuador el Ecuador
Ecuadorian *a* and *n* ecuatoriano (-na)
ecumenical *a* ecuménico
eczema *n* eczema, *f*
eddy *n* remolino, *m*, *vi* remolinar; *fig* remolinear
edelweiss *n* inmortal de las nieves, *f*
edema *n* *med* edema, *m*
Eden *n* Edén, *m*
edge *n* (of sharp instruments) filo, *m*; (of a skate) cuchilla, *f*; margen, *mf*; (shore) orilla, *f*; (of two surfaces) arista, *f*; (of books) borde, *m*; (of a coin) canto, *m*; (of a chair, a precipice, a forest, a curb, etc.) borde, *m*; (extreme) extremidad, *f*. **on e.,** de canto; *fig* ansioso. **to be on e.,** *fig* tener los nervios en punta. **to set on e.,** poner de canto; (of teeth) dar dentera
edge *vt* (sharpen) afilar; *sew* ribetear; orlar; poner un borde (a); (cut) cortar. **to e. away,** escurrirse. **to e. into,** insinuarse. *vi* deslizarse en. **to e. out,** salir poco a poco
edged *a* afilado, cortante; (in compounds) de . . . filos; (bordered) bordeado; (of books) de bordes . . .
edgeways *adv* de lado; de canto. **He couldn't get a word in e.,** No pudo meter baza en la conversación
edging *n* borde, *m*; ribete, *m*
edibility *n* el ser comestible
edible *a* comestible
edict *n* edicto, *m*
edification *n* edificación, *f*
edifice *n* edificio, *m*
edify *vt* edificar
edifying *a* edificante, edificador, de edificación
Edinburgh Edinburgo, *m*
Edipus complex *n* complejo de Edipo, *m*
edit *vt* editar; (a newspaper, journal) ser director de; (prepare for press) redactar; (correct) corregir
editing *n* trabajo editorial, *m*; redacción, *f*; dirección, *f*; corrección, *f*
edition *n* edición, *f*; *print* tirada, *f*. **first e.,** edición príncipe, *f*. **miniature e.,** edición diamante, *f*
editor *n* (of a book) editor, *m*; (of a newspaper, journal) director, *m*
editorial *a* de redacción; editorial. *n* editorial, artículo de fondo, *m*. **e. staff,** redacción, *f*

editorial board consejo de redacción, *m*
editorship *n* dirección (de un periódico, de una revista), *f*
editress *n* (of a paper, journal) directora, *f*; editora, *f*
educability *n* educabilidad, *f*
educable *a* educable
educate *vt* educar; formar; (accustom) acostumbrar
educated *a* culto
education *n* educación, *f*; enseñanza, *f*; pedagogía, *f*. **chair of e.**, cátedra de pedagogía, *f*. **early e.**, primeras letras, *f pl*. **higher e.**, enseñanza superior, *f*
educational *a* educativo; pedagógico; instructivo
educationalist *n* pedagogo, *m*
educative *a* educativo
educator *n* educador (-ra)
educe *vt* educir; deducir; *chem* extraer
eduction *n* educción, *f*
Edwardian *a* and *n* eduardiano (-na)
eel *n* anguila, *f*. **electric eel**, gimnoto, *m*. **eel-basket**, nasa para anguilas, *f*
eerily *adv* fantásticamente; de modo sobrenatural
eeriness *n* ambiente de misterio, *m*; efecto misterioso, *m*
eerie *a* misterioso, fantástico; sobrenatural; lúgubre
efface *vt* borrar, destruir; quitar. **to e. oneself**, retirarse; permanecer en el fondo
effacement *n* borradura, *f*
effect *n* efecto, *m*; impresión, *f*; (result) resultado, *m*, consecuencia, *f*, (meaning) substancia, *f*, significado, *m*; *pl* **effects**, efectos, bienes, *m pl*. *vt* efectuar; producir. **in e.**, en efecto, efectivamente. **of no e.**, inútil. **striving after e.**, efectismo, *m*. **to feel the effects of**, sentir los efectos de; padecer las consecuencias de. **to put into e.**, poner en práctica; hacer efectivo. **to take e.**, producir efecto; ponerse en vigor
effective *a* eficaz; (striking) de mucho efecto, poderoso, vistoso. **to make e.**, llevar a efecto
effectively *adv* eficazmente; (strikingly) con gran efecto; efectivamente, en efecto
effectiveness *n* eficacia, *f*; efecto, *m*
effectuate *vt* efectuar
effeminacy *n* afeminación, *f*
effeminate *a* afeminado, adamado. **to make e.**, afeminar
efferent *a* eferente
effervesce *vi* estar efervescente, hervir
effervescence *n* efervescencia, *f*
effervescent *a* efervescente
effete *a* gastado; estéril; decadente
effeteness *n* decadencia, *f*; esterilidad, *f*
efficacious *a* eficaz
efficacy *n* eficacia, *f*
efficiency *n* eficiencia, *f*; buen estado, *m*; habilidad, *f*; *mech* rendimiento, *m*
efficient *a* (e.g. medicine) eficaz; eficiente; (person) competente, capaz
efficiently *adv* eficientemente; eficazmente; competentemente
effigy *n* efigie, imagen, *f*
efflorescence *n chem* eflorescencia, *f*; *bot* florescencia, *f*
effluvium *n* efluvio, *m*
effort *n* esfuerzo, *m*. **to make an e.**, hacer un esfuerzo. **make every effort to**, hacer lo posible por + *inf*; empeñar sus máximos esfuerzos en el sentido de + *inf*
effortless *a* sin esfuerzo
effrontery *n* descaro, *m*, insolencia, *f*
effulgence *n* esplendor, fulgor, *m*
effulgent *a* fulgente, resplandeciente
effusion *n* efusión, *f*
effusive *a* efusivo; expansivo
egg *n* huevo, *m*. **to egg on**, incitar (a). **boiled egg**, huevo cocido, *m*. **fried egg**, huevo frito, *m*. **hard egg**, huevo duro, *m*. **poached egg**, huevo escalfado, *m*. **scrambled egg**, huevos revueltos, *m pl*. **soft egg**, huevo pasado por agua, *m*. **to lay eggs**, poner huevos. **to put all one's eggs in one basket**, *fig* poner toda la carne en el asador. **egg-cup**, huevera, *f*. **egg dealer**,

vendedor (-ra) de huevos. **egg flip**, huevo batido con ron, *m*. **eggplant**, berenjena, *f*. **egg-shaped**, aovado. **egg-shell**, cascarón, *m*, cáscara de huevo, *f*. **egg-shell china**, loza muy fina, *f*. **egg-spoon**, cucharita para comer huevos, *f*. **egg-whisk**, batidor de huevos, *m*
ego *n* yo
egoism *n* egoísmo, *m*
egoist *n* egoísta, *mf*
egoistic *a* egoísta
egoistically *adv* egoístamente
egotism *n* egotismo, *m*, egolatría, *f*
egotist *n* egotista, *mf*
egotistic *a* egotista
egregious *a* notorio
egress *n* salida, *f*
Egypt Egipto, *m*
Egyptian *a* egipcio. *n* egipcio (-ia); cigarrillo egipcio, *m*
Egyptologist *n* egiptólogo (-ga)
Egyptology *n* egiptología, *f*
eh? *interj* ¿eh? ¿qué?
eider *n orn* pato de flojel, *m*
eiderdown *n* edredón, *m*
eight *a* and *n* ocho *m*. **He is e. years old**, Tiene ocho años. **It is e. o'clock**, Son las ocho. **e.-day clock**, reloj con cuerda para ocho días, *m*. **e. hundred**, *a* and *n* ochocientos *m*.. **e.-syllabled**, octosilábico
eighteen *a* and *n* diez y ocho, *m*.
eighteenth *a* décimoctavo; (of the month) (el) diez y ocho, dieciocho; (of monarchs) diez y ocho. *n* décimoctava parte, *f*. **Louis the E.**, Luis diez y ocho
eightfold *a* óctuple
eighth *a* octavo, *m*; (of the month) (el) ocho; (of monarchs) octavo. *n* octavo, *m*
eighthly *adv* en octavo lugar
eightieth *a* octogésimo
eighty *a* and *n* ochenta, *m*.
either *a* and *pron* uno y otro, cualquiera de los dos; ambos (-as). *conjunc* o (becomes **u** before words beginning with **o** or **ho**). *adv* tampoco. **I do not like e.**, No me gusta ni el uno ni el otro (ni la una ni la otra). **e. ... or, o ... o**
ejaculate *vt* exclamar, lanzar; *med* eyacular
ejaculation *n* exclamación, *f*; *med* eyaculación, *f*
ejaculatory *a* jaculatorio
eject *vt* echar, expulsar; *law* desahuciar; (emit) despedir, emitir
ejection *n* echamiento, *m*, expulsión, *f*; *law* desahúcio, *m*; (emission) emisión, *f*
eke (out) *vt* aumentar, añadir a
elaborate *a* elaborado; primoroso; elegante; complicado; (detailed) detallado; (of meals) de muchos platos; (of courtesy, etc.) estudiado. *vt* elaborar; amplificar
elaborately *adv* primorosamente; elegantemente; complicadamente; con muchos detalles
elaborateness *n* primor, *m*; elegancia, *f*; complicación, *f*; (care) cuidado, *m*; minuciosidad, *f*
elaboration *n* elaboración, *f*
elapse *vi* transcurrir, andar, pasar
elastic *a* elástico. *n* elástico, *m*. **e. band**, anillo de goma, *m*; cinta de goma, *f*. **e. girdle**, faja elástica, *f*
elasticity *n* elasticidad, *f*
elate *vt* alegrar; animar
elatedly *adv* alegremente; triunfalmente
elation *n* alegría, *f*, júbilo, *m*; triunfo, *m*
elbow *n* codo, *m*; ángulo, *m*; (of a chair) brazo, *m*. *vt* codear, dar codazos (a). **at one's e.**, a la mano. **nudge with the e.**, codazo, *m*. **to be out at e.**, enseñar los codos, tener los codos raídos; ser harapiento. **to e. one's way**, abrirse paso a codazos. **e.-chair**, silla de brazos, *f*. **e.-grease**, jugo de muñeca, *m*. **e.-piece** or **patch**, codera, *f*. **e. room**, libertad de movimiento, *f*
elder *a comp* mayor. *n* persona mayor, *f*; señor mayor, *m*; (among Jews and in early Christian Church) anciano, *m*; *bot* saúco, *m*
elderly *a* mayor

eldest *a sup* old (el, la, etc.) mayor. **e. daughter,** hija mayor, *f.* **e. son,** hijo mayor, *m*
elect *vt* elegir. *a* elegido; predestinado. *n* electo, *m*; elegido, *m*
election *n theol* predestinación, *f*; elección, *f*. **by-e.,** elección parcial, *f*
electioneer *vi* solicitar votos; distribuir propaganda electoral
electioneering *n* solicitación de votos, *f*; propaganda electoral, *f*
elective *a* electivo. *n* (subject at school) materia optativa, *f*
elector *n* elector (-ra); (prince) elector, *m*
electoral *a* electoral. **e. register,** lista electoral, *f*
electoral college colegio de compromisarios, *m*
electorate *n* electorado, *m*
electric, electrical *a* eléctrico; *fig* vivo, instantáneo. **e. arc,** arco voltaico, *m*. **e. engineer,** ingeniero electricista, *m*. **electric fan,** (Spain) ventilador, (Western Hemisphere) ventilador eléctrico, *m*. **e. fire,** estufa eléctrica, *f*. **e. immersion heater,** calentador de agua eléctrico, *m*. **e. light,** luz eléctrica, *f*. **e. pad,** alfombrilla eléctrica, *f*. **e. shock,** conmoción eléctrica, *f*. **e. washing-machine,** lavadora eléctrica, *f*. **e. wire** or **cable,** conductor eléctrico, *m*
electrically *adv* por electricidad
electrician *n* electricista, *mf*
electricity *n* electricidad, *f*
electrification *n* electrificación, *f*
electrify *vt* electrificar; *fig* electrizar
electro *prefix* (in compounds) electro. **e.-chemistry,** electroquímica, *f*. **e.-dynamics,** electrodinámica, *f*. **e.-magnet,** electroimán, *m*. **e.-magnetic,** electromagnético. **e.-plate,** *vt* galvanizar, platear. *n* artículo galvanizado, *m*. **e.-therapy,** electroterapia, *f*
electrocute *vt* electrocutar
electrocution *n* electrocución, *f*
electrode *n* electrodo, *m*
electrolysis *n* electrólisis, *f*
electrolyte *n* electrólito, *m*
electrolyze *vt* electrolizar
electrometer *n* electrómetro, *m*
electromotive *a* electromotriz. **e. force,** fuerza electromotriz, *f*
electron *n* electrón, *m*
electroscope *n* electroscopio, *m*
elegance *n* elegancia, *f*
elegant *a* elegante; bello
elegantly *adv* elegantemente, con elegancia
elegiac *a* elegíaco
elegy *n* elegía, *f*
element *n* elemento, *m*; factor, *m*; ingrediente, *m*; *elec* par, elemento, *m*; *chem, phys* cuerpo simple, *m*; *pl* **elements,** rudimentos, *m pl*, nociones, *f pl*; (weather) intemperie, *f*; (Eucharist) el pan y el vino. **to be in one's e.,** estar en su elemento
elemental *a* elemental; rudimentario, lo elemental
elementariness *n* el carácter, elemental
elementary *a* elemental; rudimentario; primario. **e. education,** enseñanza primaria, *f*
elephant *n* elefante (-ta). **e. keeper** or **trainer,** naire, *m*
elephantiasis *n* elefantíasis, *f*
elephantine *a* elefantino
elevate *vt* (the Host) alzar; elevar; (the eyes, the voice) levantar; (honor) enaltecer
elevated *a* noble, elevado, sublime; edificante; (drunk) achispado
elevation *n* elevación, *f*; enaltecimiento, *m*; (of style, thought) nobleza, sublimidad, *f*; (hill) eminencia, altura, *f*
elevator *n* (lift) ascensor, *m*; (for grain, etc.) montacargas, *m*
elevator shaft caja, *f*, hueco pozo, *m*
eleven *a* once. *n* once, *m*. **It is e. o'clock,** Son las once
eleventh *a* onceno, undécimo; (of month) (el) once; (of

monarchs) once. *n* onzavo, *m*; undécima parte, *f*. **at the e. hour,** *fig* a última hora. **Louis the E.,** Luis once (XI)
elf *n* elfo, duende, *m*; (child) trasgo, *m*; (dwarf) enano, *m*
elfin *a* de duendes; de hada
elicit *vt* sacar; hacer contestar; hacer confesar; descubrir
elicitation *n* descubrimiento, *m*
elide *vt* elidir
eligibility *n* elegibilidad, *f*
eligible *a* elegible; deseable
eliminate *vt* eliminar; quitar
elimination *n* eliminación, *f*
eliminatory *a* eliminador
elision *n* elisión, *f*
elite *n* nata, flor, *f*
elixir *n* elixir, *m*
Elizabethan *a* de la época de la Reina Isabel I de Inglaterra
elk *n* ante, *m*
ell *n* (measure) ana, *f*
ellipse *n geom* elipse, *f*; óvalo, *m*
ellipsis *n gram* elipsis, *f*
elliptic *a geom, gram* elíptico
elm *n* olmo, *m*. **e. grove,** olmeda, *f*
elocution *n* elocución, *f*; (art of elocution) declamación, *f*
elocutionist *n* recitador (-ra), declamador (-ra)
elongate *vt* alargar; extender. *vi* alargarse; extenderse. *a* alargado; (of face) perfilado
elongation *n* alargamiento, *m*; prolongación, *f*; extensión, *f*
elope *vi* evadirse, huir; fugarse (con un amante)
elopement *n* fuga, *f*
eloquence *n* elocuencia, *f*
eloquent *a* elocuente
eloquently *adv* elocuentemente
else *adv* (besides) más; (instead) otra cosa, más; (otherwise) si no, de otro modo. **anyone e.,** (cualquier) otra persona; alguien más. **Anything e.?** ¿Algo más? **everyone e.,** todos los demás. **everything e.,** todo lo demás. **nobody e.,** ningún otro, nadie más. **nothing e.,** nada más. **or e.,** o bien, de otro modo; si no. **someone e.,** otra persona, otro. **somewhere e.,** en otra parte. **There's nothing e. to do,** No hay nada más que hacer; No hay más remedio
elsewhere *adv* a, or en, otra parte
elucidate *vt* elucidar, aclarar
elucidation *n* elucidación, aclaración, *f*
elucidatory *a* aclaratorio
elude *vt* eludir, evitar
elusive *a* (of persons) esquivo; fugaz; difícil de comprender
elusiveness *n* esquivez, *f*; fugacidad, *f*
Elysian *a* elíseo. **E. Fields,** campos elíseos, *m pl*
Elysium *n* elíseo, *m*
emaciate *vt* extenuar, demacrar, enflaquecer
emaciated *a* extenuado, demacrado. **to become e.,** demacrarse
emaciation *n* demacración, emaciación, *f*; *med* depauperación, *f*
emanate *vi* emanar (de), proceder (de)
emanation *n* emanación, *f*; exhalación, *f*
emancipate *vt* emancipar
emancipated *a* emancipado
emancipation *n* emancipación, *f*
emancipator *n* emancipador (-ra), libertador (-ra)
emancipatory *a* emancipador
emasculate *a* afeminado. *vt* emascular; *fig* afeminar; mutilar
emasculation *n* emasculación, *f*
embalm *vt* embalsamar; *fig* conservar el recuerdo de; perfumar
embalmer *n* embalsamador, *m*
embalmment *n* embalsamamiento, *m*

embankment *n* declive, *m*; ribera, *f*; terraplén, *m*; dique, *m*; (quay) muelle, *m*

embargo *n* embargo, *m*, *vt* embargar. **to put an e. on,** embargar. **to remove an e.,** sacar de embargo

embark *vi* embarcarse; lanzarse (a). *vt* embarcar

embarkation *n* (of persons) embarcación, *f*; (of goods) embarque, *m*

embarrass *vt* impedir; (financially) apurar; (perplex) tener perplejo; (worry) preocupar; (confuse) desconcertar, turbar; (annoy) molestar

embarrassed *a* turbado

embarrassing *a* embarazoso; desconcertante; molesto

embarrassingly *adv* de un modo desconcertante; demasiado

embarrassment *n* impedimento, *m*; (financial) apuro, *m*; (obligation) compromiso, *m*; (perplexity) perplejidad, *f*; (worry) preocupación, *f*; (confusion) turbación, *f*

embassy *n* embajada, *f*

embattled *a* en orden de batalla; *her* almenado

embed *vt* empotrar, enclavar; fijar

embellish *vt* embellecer; adornar

embellishment *n* embellecimiento, *m*; adorno, *m*

ember *n* rescoldo, *m*. **E. days,** témporas, *f pl*

embezzle *vt* desfalcar

embezzlement *n* desfalco, *m*

embezzler *n* desfalcador (-ra)

embitter *vt fig* amargar; envenenar

embittering *a* amargo

embitterment *n* amargura, *f*

emblazon *vt* blasonar; *fig* ensalzar

emblem *n* emblema, *m*

emblematic *a* emblemático

embodiment *n* incarnación, *f*; expresión, *f*; personificación, *f*; símbolo, *m*; síntesis, *f*

embody *vt* encarnar; expresar; personificar; incorporar; contener; formular; sintetizar. **to be embodied in,** quedar plasmado en

embolden *vt* animar, dar valor (a)

embolism *n med* embolia, *f*

emboss *vt* repujar, abollonar; estampar en relieve

embossment *n* abolladura, *f*; relieve, *m*

embrace *n* abrazo, *m*. *vt* abrazar, dar un abrazo (a); (fig. seize) aprovechar; (accept) aceptar; adoptar; (engage in) dedicarse a; (comprise) incluir, abarcar; (comprehend) comprender. **They embraced,** Se abrazaron

embroider *vt* bordar; embellecer; (a tale, etc.) exagerar; *vi* hacer bordado

embroiderer *n* bordador (-ra)

embroidery *n* bordado, *m*; labor, *f*. **e.-frame,** bastidor, *m*. **e. silk,** hilo de bordar, *m*

embroil *vt* enredar, embrollar; desordenar

embryo *n* embrión, *m*; *fig* germen, *m*. *a* embrionario

embryology *n* embriología, *f*

embryonic *a* embrionario

emend *vt* enmendar; corregir

emendation *n* enmienda, *f*; corrección, *f*

emerald *n* esmeralda, *f*, *a* de color de esmeralda. **e. green,** verde esmeralda, *m*

emerge *vi* emerger; surgir; *fig* salir; aparecer

emergence *n* emergencia, *f*; salida, *f*; aparición, *f*

emergency *n* urgencia, *f*; necesidad, *f*; emergencia, *f*; aprieto, *m*. **e. exit,** salida de urgencia, *f*. **e. port,** *naut* puerto de arribada, *m*

emergent *a* emergente; que sale; naciente

emery *n* esmeril, *m*. **to polish with e.,** esmerilar. **e.-paper,** papel de lija, *m*

emetic *a* and *n* emético, vomitivo, *m*.

emigrant *a* emigrante. *n* emigrante, *mf* emigrado, *m*

emigrate *vi* emigrar; *inf* trasladarse

emigration *n* emigración, *f*. **e. officer,** oficial de emigración, *m*

eminence *n* (hill) elevación, prominencia, *f*; eminencia (also as title), *f*; distinción, *f*

eminent *a* distinguido, eminente; famoso, ilustre; notable; conspicuo

eminently *adv* eminentemente

emir *n* amir, *m*

emissary *n* emisario (-ia); embajador (-ra); agente, *m*

emission *n* emisión, *f*

emit *vt* despedir; exhalar; emitir

emollient *a* emoliente, lenitivo. *n* emoliente, *m*

emolument *n* emolumento, *m*

emotion *n* emoción, *f*. **to cause e.,** emocionar

emotional *a* emocional, sentimental; emocionante

emotionalism *n* sentimentalismo, *m*

emotionalize *vt* considerar bajo un punto de vista sentimental

emotionally *adv* con emoción, sentimentalmente

emotionless *a* sin emoción

emotive *a* emotivo

emperor *n* emperador, *m*

emphasis (on) *n* énfasis (en), *mf*; insistencia especial (en), especial atención (a), *f*; accentuación, *f*

emphasize *vt* subrayar, dar énfasis a, poner de relieve, hacer resaltar, dar importancia a; acentuar; insistir en, hacer hincapié (en)

emphatic *a* enfático

emphatically *adv* con énfasis

empire *n* imperio, *m*

empiric *a* empírico

empiricism *n* empirismo, *m*

employ *n* empleo, *m*; servicio, *m*. *vt* emplear; ocupar; tomar; servirse de, usar. **How do you e. yourself?** ¿Cómo te ocupas? ¿Cómo pasas el tiempo?

employable *a* empleable; utilizable

employee *n* empleado (-da)

employer *n* el, *m*, (*f*, la) que emplea; dueño (-ña), amo (-a); patrón (-ona)

employment *n* empleo, *m*; uso, *m*; ocupación, *f*; aprovechamiento, *m*; (post) puesto, cargo, *m*; (situation) colocación, *f*. **e. exchange,** bolsa de trabajo, *f*

emporium *n* emporio, *m*; (store) almacén, *m*

empower *vt* autorizar; permitir; ayudar (a); dar el poder (para)

empress *n* emperatriz, *f*

emptiness *n* vaciedad, *f*; futilidad, *f*; vacuidad, *f*; (verbosity) palabrería, *f*

empty *a* vacío; (of a house, etc.) deshabitado, desocupado; (deserted) desierto; (vain) vano, inútil; frívolo; (hungry) hambriento. *n* envase vacío, *m*. *vt* vaciar; descargar. *vi* vaciarse; (river, etc.) desembocar; venir a morir en. **e.-handed,** con las manos vacías. **e.-headed,** casquivano

emptying *n* vaciamiento, *m*; abandono, *m*; *pl* **emptyings,** heces de la cerveza, *f pl*

emu *n* emu, *m*

emulate *vt* emular

emulation *n* emulación, *f*

emulative *a* emulador

emulsify *vt* emulsionar

emulsion *n* emulsión, *f*

emulsive *a* emulsivo

enable *vt* (to) hacer capaz (de); ayudar (a); autorizar (para); permitir (de)

enact *vt law* promulgar; decretar; (a part) hacer, desempeñar (un papel); (a play) representar; (happen) ocurrir, tener lugar

enaction *n law* promulgación, *f*

enamel *n* esmalte, *m*. *vt* esmaltar

enameler *n* esmaltador (-ra)

enameling *n* esmaltadura, *f*

enamor *vt* enamorar. **to be enamored of,** estar enamorado de; estar aficionado a

encamp *vt* and *vi* acampar

encampment *n* campamento, *m*

encase *vt* encajar; encerrar; (line) forrar

encasement *n* encaje, *m*; encierro, *m*

encephalitis *n* encefalitis, *f*. **e. lethargica,** encefalitis letárgica, *f*

enchant *vt* encantar, hechizar; fascinar, embelesar; deleitar

enchanter *n* encantador, *m*

enchanting *a* encantador, fascinador

enchantment *n* encantamiento, *m*; fascinación, *f*, encanto, deleite, *m*

enchantress *n* bruja, *f*; *fig* mujer seductora, *f*

encircle *vt* cercar; rodear; dar la vuelta (a)

enclose *vt* cercar; meter dentro de; encerrar; (with a letter, etc.) incluir, adjuntar

enclosed *a* (of letters) adjunto

enclosure *n* cercamiento, *m*; cercado, *m*; recinto, *m*; (wall) tapia, cerca, *f*; (with a letter) contenido adjunto, *m*

encomium *n* encomio, *m*

encompass *vt* cercar, rodear

encore *n* repetición, *f*, *interj* ¡bis!

encounter *n* encuentro, *m*; combate, *m*; conflicto, *m*; lucha, *f*. *vt* encontrar; atacar; tropezar con

encourage *vt* animar; alentar; estimular; incitar; ayudar; (approve) aprobar; (foster) fomentar

encouragement *n* ánimos, *m pl*; estímulo, incentivo, *m*; ayuda, *f*; (approval) aprobación, *f*; (promotion) fomento, *m*

encourager *n* instigador (-ra); ayudador (-ra); aprobador (-ra); fomentador (-ra)

encouraging *a* alentador; estimulante; fomentador; (favorable) halagüeño, favorable

encouragingly *adv* de un modo alentador; con aprobación

encroach *vi* usurpar; abusar (de); invadir; robar; (of sea, river) hurtar

encroaching *a* usurpador; invadiente

encroachment *n* usurpación, *f*; abuso, *m*; invasión, *f*

encrust *vt* encostrar; incrustar

encumber *vt* impedir, estorbar; llenar; (burden) cargar; (mortgage) hipotecar; (overwhelm) agobiar

encumbrance *n* impedimento, estorbo, *m*; gravamen, *m*; carga, *f*; (mortgage) hipoteca, *f*

encyclical *n* encíclica, *f*

encyclopedia *n* enciclopedia, *f*

encyclopedic *a* enciclopédico

encyclopedist *n* enciclopedista, *m*

end *n* fin, *m*; extremidad, *f*; extremo, *m*; conclusión, *f*; (point) punta, *f*; cabo, *m*; (district) barrio, *m*; cabeza, *f*; (death) muerte, *f*; (aim) objeto, intento, *m*; (purpose) propósito, *m*; (issue) resultado, *m*; (bit) fragmento, pedazo, *m*; (of a word) terminación, *f*. *vi* terminar; acabar; concluir; cesar; (in) terminar en; resultar en; (with) terminar con. *vt* terminar; acabar, dar fin a. **at an end**, terminado. **at the end**, al cabo (de); al extremo (de). **end of quotation**, fin de cita, final de la cita, *m*. **from end to end**, de un extremo a otro; de un cabo a otro. **in the end**, por fin, finalmente. **on end**, de pie, de cabeza, derecho; de punta; (of hair) erizado. **no end of**, un sinnúmero de. **to make both ends meet**, pasar con lo que se tiene. **to make an end of**, acabar con. **to put an end to**, poner fin a. **to the end that**, a fin de que, para que; con objeto de. **toward the end of**, (months, years, etc.) a fines de; a últimos de; hacia el fin de. **two hours on end**, dos horas seguidas. **end-paper**, guarda, *f*

endanger *vt* arriesgar, poner en peligro

endear *vt* hacer querer

endearing *a* que inspira cariño; atrayente; cariñoso

endearment *n* cariño, amor, *m*; caricia, terneza, *f*; palabra de cariño, *f*

endeavor *vi* procurar, intentar, hacer un esfuerzo. *n* esfuerzo, *m*, tentativa, *f*

endemic *a med* endémico

ending *n* fin, *m*; conclusión, *f*; *gram* terminación, *f*; cesación, *f*; (climax) desenlace, *m*

endive *n bot* escarola, *f*

endless *a* eterno; inacabable; infinito; sin fin; interminable; incesante

endlessly *adv* sin fin; incesantemente; sin parar

endlessness *n* eternidad, *f*; infinidad, *f*; continuidad, *f*

endocrine *a* endocrino. *n* secreción interna, *f*

endocrinology *n* endocrinología, *f*

end-of-season *a* por final de temporada (e.g., **end-of-season reductions**, rebajos por final de temporada, *m pl*. **end-of-season sale**, liquidación por final de temporada, *f*)

endogenous *a* endógeno

endorse *vt com* endosar; garantizar; (uphold) apoyar; confirmar

endorsee *n* endosatario (-ia)

endorsement *n com* endoso, *m*; aval, *m*, garantía, *f*; corroboración, confirmación, *f*

endorser *n com* endosante, *m*

endow *vt* dotar; fundar; crear

endowment *n* dotación, *f*; fundación, *f*; creación, *f*; (mental) inteligencia, *f*; cualidad, *f*; don, *m*. **e. policy**, póliza dotal, *f*

endurable *a* sufrible, soportable; tolerable

endurance *n* aguante, *m*; resistencia, *f*; sufrimiento, *m*; tolerancia, *f*; paciencia, *f*; (lastingness) duración, continuación, *f*. **beyond e.**, intolerable, inaguantable. **e. test**, prueba de resistencia, *f*

endure *vt* soportar; tolerar; aguantar; sufrir; resistir. *vi* sufrir; (last) durar, continuar

enduring *a* permanente, perdurable; continuo; constante

enduringness *n* (lastingness) permanencia, *f*; paciencia, *f*; aguante, *m*

enema *n* lavativa, enema, *f*

enemy *n* enemigo (-ga); adversario (-ia); (in war) enemigo, *m*. *a* del enemigo, enemigo. **to be one's own e.**, ser enemigo de sí mismo. **to become an e. of**, enemistarse con; hacerse enemigo de, volverse hostil a

energetic *a* enérgico

energy *n* energía, fuerza, *f*, vigor, *m*

enervate *vt* enervar; debilitar. *a* enervado

enervation *n* enervación, *f*; debilitación, *f*

enfeeble *vt* debilitar

enfeeblement *n* debilitación, *f*, desfallecimiento, *m*

enfold *vt* envolver; abrazar

enforce *vt* (a law) poner en vigor; (impose) imponer a la fuerza; hacer cumplir; conseguir por fuerza; (demonstrate) demostrar

enforcement *n* (of a law) ejecución (de una ley), *f*; imposición a la fuerza, *f*; observación forzosa, *f*

enfranchise *vt* emancipar; conceder derechos civiles (a)

enfranchisement *n* emancipación, *f*; concesión de derechos civiles, *f*

engage *vt* empeñar; contratar; tomar en alquiler; tomar a su servicio; (seats, etc.) reservar; (occupy) ocupar; (attention) atraer; (in) aplicarse a, dedicarse a; *mil* combatir con, librar batalla con; atacar; (of wheels) endentar con. *vi* obligarse; dedicarse (a); tomar parte (en); (bet) apostar; *mil* librar batalla; (fight) venir a las manos. **to be engaged in**, traer entre manos, ocuparse en. **to become engaged**, prometerse. **Number engaged!** (telephone) ¡Están comunicando!

engaged *a* ocupado; (betrothed) prometido; reservado

engagement *n* obligación, *f*; compromiso, *m*; (date) cita, *f*; (betrothal) palabra de casamiento, *f*; (battle) combate, *m*, batalla, *f*. **I have an e. at two o'clock.** Tengo una cita a las dos

engagement gift regalo de esponsales, *m*

engaging *a* simpático, atractivo

engagingly *adv* de un modo encantador

engender *vt fig* engendrar; excitar

engine *n* máquina, *f*; motor, *m*; (locomotive) locomotora, *f*; (pump) bomba, *f*. **to sit with one's back to the e.**, estar sentado de espaldas a la máquina (or locomotora). **e. builder**, constructor de máquinas, *m*. **e. driver**, maquinista, *mf*. **e. room**, cuarto de máquinas, *m*. **e. works**, taller de maquinaria, *m*

engineer *n* ingeniero, *m*; mecánico, *m*. *vt fig* gestionar; arreglar. **civil e.**, ingeniero de caminos, canales y puertos, *m*. **Royal Engineers**, Cuerpo de Ingenieros, *m*

engineering *n* ingeniería, *f*; *fig* manejo, *m*. *a* de ingeniería

England Inglaterra, *f*

English *a* inglés. *n* (language) inglés, *m*. **in E. fashion,** a la inglesa. **to speak E.,** hablar inglés. **to speak plain E.,** hablar sin rodeos; hablar en cristiano. **E. Church,** iglesia anglicana, *f*. **E.-teacher,** maestro (-ra) de inglés. **English-translator,** traductor al inglés, *m*

English Channel, the el Canal de la Mancha

Englishman *n* inglés, *m*

Englishwoman *n* inglesa, *f*

engrain *vt* inculcar

engrave *vt* grabar; esculpir, cincelar; *fig* grabar

engraver *n* grabador (-ra); (tool) cincel, *m*

engraving *n* grabadura, *f*; (picture) grabado, *m*. **e. needle,** punta seca, *f*

engross *vt* (a document) poner en limpio; redactar; (absorb) absorber

engrossing *a* absorbente

engulf *vt* hundir, sumir, sumergir

enhance *vt* realzar; intensificar; aumentar; mejorar

enhancement *n* realce, *m*; intensificación, *f*; aumento, *m*; mejoría, *f*

enigma *n* enigma, *m*

enigmatic *a* enigmático

enjoin *vt* imponer; ordenar, mandar; encargar

enjoy *vt* disfrutar; gustar de; gozar de; poseer, tener. **to e. oneself,** recrearse, regocijarse; (amuse oneself) divertirse; entretenerse; pasarlo bien. **Did you e. yourself?** ¿Lo pasaste bien?

enjoyable *a* agradable, divertido, entretenido

enjoyableness *n* lo agradable; lo divertido

enjoyably *adv* de un modo muy agradable

enjoyer *n* el, *m*, (*f*, la) que disfruta; poseedor (-ra); (amateur) aficionado (-da)

enjoyment *n* posesión, *f*; goce, disfruto, *m*; (pleasure) placer, *m*; aprovechamiento, *m*; utilización, *f*; (satisfaction) satisfacción, *f*

enlarge *vt* agrandar; aumentar; ensanchar; extender; *phot* ampliar; dilatar; (the mind, etc.) ensanchar. *vi* agrandarse; ensancharse; aumentarse; extenderse. **an enlarged heart,** dilatación del corazón, *f*. **to e. upon,** tratar detalladamente, explayarse en

enlargement *n* engrandecimiento, *m*; ensanchamiento, *m*; *phot* ampliación, *f*; *med* dilatación, *f*; aumento, *m*; amplificación, *f*; (of a town, etc.) ensanche, *m*

enlarger *n* *phot* ampliadora, *f*

enlighten *vt* iluminar; aclarar; informar

enlightened *a* culto; ilustrado; inteligente

enlightening *a* instructivo

enlightenment *n* ilustración, *f*; cultura, civilización, *f*

enlist *vt* *mil* reclutar; alistar; obtener, conseguir. *vi* *mil* sentar plaza, sentar plaza de soldado; engancharse; alistarse

enlistment *n* *mil* enganche, *m*; reclutamiento, *m*; alistamiento, *m*

enliven *vt* animar; avivar; alegrar

enmity *n* enemistad, enemiga, hostilidad, *f*

ennoble *vt* ennoblecer; ilustrar

ennui *n* tedio, *m*; aburrimiento, *m*

enormity *n* enormidad, *f*; gravedad, *f*; atrocidad, *f*

enormous *a* enorme, colosal

enormously *adv* enormemente

enormousness *n* enormidad, *f*

enough *a* bastante, suficiente. *n* lo bastante, lo suficiente. *adv* bastante; suficientemente. *interj* ¡bastante! ¡basta! **to be e.,** ser suficiente; bastar. **two are enough,** con dos tenemos bastante, con dos tengo bastante

enquire. See **inquire**

enrage *vt* enfurecer, hacer furioso; *inf* hacer rabiar

enraged *a* furioso

enrapture *vt* entusiasmar, extasiar; (intoxicate) embriagar; (charm) encantar, deleitar

enrich *vt* enriquecer; (adorn) adornar, embellecer; (the land) fertilizar

enrichment *n* enriquecimiento, *m*; embellecimiento, *m*; (of the land) abono, *m*

enroll *vt* alistar; matricular; inscribir; (perpetuate) inmortalizar

enrollment *n* alistamiento, *m*; inscripción, *f*

ensconce *vt* acomodar, colocar; ocultar

ensemble *n* conjunto, *m*

enshrine *vt* poner en sagrario; guardar con cuidado; *fig* guardar como una reliquia

enshroud *vt* amortajar; envolver; esconder

ensign *n* (badge) insignia, *f*; (flag) enseña, bandera, *f*; pabellón, *m*; bandera de popa, *f*; *mil* alférez, *m*; (U.S.A. navy) subteniente, *m*

enslave *vt* esclavizar; *fig* dominar

enslavement *n* esclavitud, *f*

ensue *vt* conseguir. *vi* resultar; suceder, sobrevenir

ensuing *a* (next) próximo; (resulting) resultante

ensure *vt* asegurar; estar seguro de que; garantizar

entail *vt* traer consigo, acarrear; *law* vincular; *n* *law* vinculación, *f*; herencia, *f*

entangle *vt* enredar; coger; *fig* embrollar

entanglement *n* enredo, *m*; complicación, *f*; intriga, *f*; (*mil* of wire) alambrada, *f*

entangling *a* enmarañador (e.g., **entangling alliances,** alianzas enmarañadoras, *f pl*)

enter *vt* entrar en; penetrar; (of thoughts) ocurrirse; (join) ingresar en; entrar en; (become a member of) hacerse miembro de; (enroll) alistarse; (a university) matricularse; (inscribe) inscribir, poner en la lista; (note) anotar, apuntar; (a protest) hacer constar; (make) hacer; formular. *vi* entrar; *theat* salir (a la escena); penetrar; *com* anotarse. **to e. for,** *vt* inscribir. *vi* inscribirse, tomar parte en. **to e. into,** entrar en; formar parte de; (conversation) entablar (conversación); (negotiations) iniciar; considerar; (another's emotion) acompañar en; (an agreement, etc.) hacer; (sign) firmar; (bind oneself) obligarse a, comprometerse a; tomar parte en; (undertake) emprender; empezar; adoptar. **to e. up,** anotar; poner en la lista; registrar. **to e. upon,** comenzar, emprender; tomar posesión de; encargarse de, asumir; inaugurar, dar principio a

enteric *a* entérico

enteritis *n* enteritis, *f*

enterprise *n* empresa, *f*; aventura, *f*; (spirit) iniciativa, *f*, empuje, *m*

enterprising *a* emprendedor, acometedor; de mucha iniciativa

entertain *vt* (an idea, etc.) acariciar, abrigar; considerar; (as a guest) agasajar, obsequiar; recibir en casa; (amuse) divertir, entretener. *vi* ser hospitalario; tener invitados en casa; dar fiestas

entertaining *a* entretenido, divertido

entertainingly *adv* entretenidamente; (witty) graciosamente

entertainment *n* convite, *m*; fiesta, *f*; reunión, *f*; banquete, *m*; (hospitality) hospitalidad, *f*; (amusement) diversión, *f*, entretenimiento, *m*; espectáculo, *m*; función, *f*; concierto, *m*

enthrall *vt* seducir, atraer, encantar; absorber, captar la atención

enthralling *a* absorbente; atrayente, halagüeño

enthrallment *n* absorción, *f*; atracción, *f*

enthrone *vt* entronizar

enthronement *n* entronización, *f*

enthusiasm *n* entusiasmo, *m*

enthusiast *n* entusiasta, *mf*

enthusiastic *a* entusiasta. **to make e.,** entusiasmar. **to be e.,** entusiasmarse

enthusiastically *adv* con entusiasmo

entice *vt* tentar, inducir; atraer, seducir

enticement *n* tentación, *f*; atractivo, *m*

enticing *a* seducente, atrayente; halagüeño

entire *a* entero; completo; intacto; absoluto; perfecto; íntegro; total

entirely *adv* enteramente; completamente; integralmente; totalmente

entirety *n* totalidad, *f*; integridad, *f*; todo, *m*
entitle *vt* (designate) intitular; dar derecho (a); autorizar. **to be entitled to,** tener derecho a
entity *n* entidad, *f*; ente, ser, *m*
entombment *n* sepultura, *f*, entierro, *m*
entomological *a* entomológico
entomologist *n* entomólogo, *m*
entomology *n* entomología, *f*
entourage *n* séquito, *m*; (environment) medio' ambiente, *m*
entr'acte *n* entreacto, *m*
entrails *n* entrañas, tripas, *f pl*, intestinos, *m pl*
entrain *vi* tomar el tren, subir al tren
entrance *n* entrada, *f*; *theat* salida (a la escena), *f*; (into a profession, etc.) ingreso, *m*; (beginning) principio, *m*; (door) puerta, *f*; (porch) portal, *m*; (of a cave) boca, *f*. **e. fee,** cuota de entrada, *f*. **e. hall,** zaguán, *m*. **e. money,** entrada, *f*
entrance *vt fig* encantar, fascinar; ecstasiar
entrancing *a* encantador
entreat *vt* suplicar, implorar, rogar
entreating *a* suplicante, implorante
entreatingly *adv* de un modo suplicante; insistentemente
entreaty *n* súplica, instancia, *f*, ruego, *m*
entree *n* entrada, *f*
entrench *vt* atrincherar
entrenchment *n* atrincheramiento, *m*; *mil* parapeto, *m*; (encroachment) invasión, *f*
entresol *n* entresuelo, *m*
entrust *vt* confiar a (or en), encomendar a; encargar
entry *n* entrada, *f*; (passage) callejuela, *f*; (note) inscripción, apuntación, *f*; *com* partida, *f*; (registration) registro, *m*. **double e.,** *com* partida doble, *f*. **single e.,** *com* partida simple, *f*
entwine *vt* entrelazar, entretejer
enumerate *vt* enumerar
enumeration *n* enumeración, *f*
enumerative *a* enumerativo
enunciate *vt* enunciar; articular
enunciation *n* enunciación, *f*; articulación, *f*
envelop *vt* envolver, cubrir
envelope *n* sobre, *m*
envelopment *n* envolvimiento, *m*; cubierta, *f*
enviable *a* envidiable
envious *a* envidioso. **an e. look,** una mirada de envidia
enviously *adv* con envidia
environment *n* medio ambiente, *m*
environs *n* inmediaciones, *f pl*, alrededores, *m pl*
envisage *vt* hacer frente a; contemplar; imaginar
envoy *n* enviado, *m*; mensajero (-ra)
envy *n* envidia, *f*, *vt* envidiar
enzyme *n* fermento, *m*, enzima, *f*
eon *n* eón, *m*
epaulette *n* hombrera, *f*
ephemeral *a* efímero; *fig* fugaz, pasajero
Ephesus Efiso, *m*
Ephraim Efraín, *m*
Ephraimite *n* and *adj* efraíta, *mf*
epic *a* épico. *n* epopeya, *f*
epicenter *n* epicentro, *m*
epicure *n* epicúreo (-ea)
epicurean *a* epicúreo
Epicureanism *n* epicureísmo, *m*
epidemic *n* epidemia, *f*; plaga, *f*, *a* epidémico
epidermis *n* epidermis, *f*
epiglottis *n* epiglotis, *f*
epigram *n* epigrama, *m*
epigrammatic *a* epigramático
epigraph *n* epígrafe, *m*
epigraphy *n* epigrafía, *f*
epilepsy *n* epilepsia, alferecía, *f*
epileptic *a* and *n* epiléptico (-ca). **e. fit,** ataque epiléptico, *m*. **e. aura,** aura epiléptica, *f*
epilog *n* epílogo, *m*
epiphany *n* epifanía, *f*

Epirus Epiro, *m*
episcopacy *n* episcopado, *m*
episcopal *a* episcopal
episcopalianism *n* episcopalismo, *m*
episode *n* suceso, incidente, *m*; *lit* episodio, *m*
episodic *a* episódico
epistle *n* epístola, *f*
epistolary *a* epistolar
epitaph *n* epitafio, *m*
epithet *n* epíteto, *m*
epitome *n* epítome, *m*
epitomize *vt* resumir, abreviar
epoch *n* época, edad, *f*
epode *n* épodo, *m*
Epsom salts *n* sal de la Higuera, *f*
equability *n* igualdad (de ánimo), ecuanimidad, *f*; uniformidad, *f*
equable *a* igual, ecuánime; uniforme
equably *adv* con ecuanimidad; igualmente; uniformemente
equal *a* igual; uniforme; imparcial; equitativo, justo. *n* igual, *mf*. *vt* ser igual a; equivaler a; igualar; *sport* empatar. **to be e. to,** (of persons) ser capaz de; servir para; atreverse a; (circumstances) estar al nivel de; sentirse con fuerzas para. **without e.,** sin igual; (of beauty, etc.) sin par. **e. sign,** *math* igual, *m*
equality *n* igualdad, *f*; uniformidad, *f*
equalization *n* igualación, *f*
equalize *vt* igualar
equalizing *a* igualador; compensador
equally *adv* igualmente; imparcialmente
equanimity *n* ecuanimidad, *f*
equation *n* ecuación, *f*
equator *n* ecuador, *m*
equatorial *a* ecuatorial
equerry *n* caballerizo del rey, *m*
equestrian *a* ecuestre
equiangular *a* equiángulo
equidistance *n* equidistancia, *f*
equidistant *a* equidistante
equilateral *a* equilátero
equilibrist *n* equilibrista, *mf*
equilibrium *n* equilibrio, *m*
equine *a* equino; hípico; de caballo
equinoctial *a* equinoccial. **e. gale,** tempestad equinoccial, *f*
equinox *n* equinoccio, *m*
equip *vt* proveer; pertrechar; equipar
equipage *n* (train) séquito, tren, *m*; (carriage) carruaje, *m*
equipment *n* habilitación, *f*; equipo, *m*; pertrechos, *m pl*; material, *m*; aparatos, *m pl*; armamento, *m*
equitable *a* equitativo, justo
equitableness *n* equidad, justicia, *f*
equitably *adv* equitativamente, con justicia
equity *n* equidad, *f*; imparcialidad, justicia, *f*
equivalence *n* equivalencia, *f*
equivalent *a* and *n* equivalente, *m*. **to be e. to,** equivaler a
equivocal *a* equívoco, ambiguo
equivocally *adv* equivocadamente
equivocate *vi* usar frases equívocas, emplear equívocos, tergiversar
equivocation *n* equívoco, *m*
era *n* época, era, *f*
eradiation *n* irradiación, *f*
eradicable *a* erradicable
eradicate *vt* erradicar; destruir, extirpar; suprimir
eradication *n* erradicación, *f*; destrucción, *f*; supresión, *f*
erasable *a* borrable
erase *vt* borrar; tachar
eraser *n* goma de borrar, *f*. **ink e.,** goma para tinta, *f*
erasure *n* borradura, *f*; tachón, *m*
ere *conjunc* antes de (que), antes de. *prep* antes de
erect *a* (upright) derecho; erguido; vertical; (uplifted)

levantado; (standing) de pie; (firm) firme, resuelto; (alert) vigilante. *vt* (build) edificar, construir; instalar; (raise) alzar; convertir

erectile *a* eréctil

erection *n* erección, *f*; construcción, edificación, *f*; (building) edificio, *m*; (structure) estructura, *f*; instalación, *f*; (assembling) montaje, *m*

erectly *adv* derecho

erectness *n* derechura, *f*

erg *n phys* ergio, *m*

ermine *n* armiño, *m*, *a* de armiño

erode *vt* corroer; comer; *geol* denudar

erosion *n* erosión, *f*

Erostrato Eróstrato

erotic *a* erótico

err *vi* desviarse; errar; desacertar; pecar

errand *n* mensaje, recado, *m*; encargo, *m*; misión, *f*. **e.-boy,** mandadero, mensajero, motril, mozo, recadero, *m*

errant *a* errante; (of knights) andante

erratic *a* (of conduct) excéntrico, irresponsable; (of thoughts, etc.) errante; *med* errático

erratum *n* errata, *f*

erring *a* extraviado; pecaminoso

erroneous *a* erróneo; falso; injusto

erroneously *adv* erróneamente; falsamente; injustamente

erroneousness *n* falsedad, *f*

error *n* error, *m*; equivocación, *f*, desacierto, *m*; (sin) pecado, *m*. **in e.,** por equivocación

erudite *a* erudito; sabio

erudition *n* erudición, *f*

erupt *vi* entrar en erupción, estar en erupción; *fig* salir con fuerza

eruption *n* erupción, *f*

erysipelas *n* erisipela, *f*

escalade *n* escalada, *f*, *vt* escalar

escalator *n* escalera automática, escalera eléctrica, escalera mecánica, escalera móvil, escalera rodante, *f*

escapable *a* evitable, eludible

escapade *n* escapada, *f*; aventura, *f*

escape *n* huida, fuga, *f*; evasión, evitación, *f*; (leak) escape, *m*; *fig* salida, *f*. *vt* eludir, evitar; (of cries, groans, etc.) dar, salir de. *vi* huir, fugarse, escapar; (slip away) escurrirse; librarse; salvarse; (leak) escaparse. **His name escapes me,** Se me escapa (or se me olvida) su nombre. **to e. notice,** pasar inadvertido. **to have a narrow e.,** salvarse en una tabla. **to e. from,** escaparse de; librarse de; huir de

escape clause *n* cláusula de salvaguardia, *f*

escaping *a* fugitivo

escarpment *n* escarpa, *f*

eschew *vt* evitar

eschewal *n* evitación, *f*

escort *n mil* escolta, *f*; (of ships) convoy, *m*; acompañamiento, *m*; acompañante, *m*. *vt mil* escoltar; (of ships) convoyar; acompañar

escritoire *n* escritorio, *m*

escudo *n* escudo, *m*

escutcheon *n* escudo, blasón, *m*

Eskimo *a* and *n* esquimal *mf*

esoteric *a* esotérico

esparto *n* esparto, *m*

especial *a* especial; particular

especially *adv* especialmente; ante todo; en particular

Esperantist *n* esperantista, *mf*

Esperanto *n* esperanto, *m*

espionage *n* espionaje, *m*

esplanade *n mil* explanada, *f*; bulevar, paseo, *m*

espousal *n* desposorio, *m*; *fig* adhesión (a una causa), *f*

espouse *vt* desposar; (a cause) abrazar; defender

espy *vt* divisar, ver, observar

esquire *n* escudero, *m*; (landowner) hacendado, *m*; (as a title) don (before given name)

essay *n* tentativa, *f*; *lit* ensayo, *m*, *vt* probar; procurar;

(on an examination) tema, *m*. **essay question,** tema, *m*

essayist *n* ensayista, *mf*

essence *n* esencia, *f*

essential *a* esencial; indispensable, imprescindible; intrínseco. *n* artículo de primera necesidad, *m*; elemento necesario, *m*

essentially *adv* esencialmente

establish *vt* establecer; fundar; crear; erigir; (constitute) constituir; (order) disponer; (prove) demostrar, probar; (take root, settle) arraigarse

established *a* establecido; arraigado; (proved) demostrado; bien conocido; (author) consagrado; (of churches) oficial

establishment *n* establecimiento, *m*; fundación, *f*; creación, *f*; institución, *f*; (building) erección, *f*; arraigo, *m*; (house) casa, *f*; (church) iglesia oficial, *f*; demostración, *f*; reconocimiento, *m*

estate *n* estado, *m*; clase, *f*; condición, *f*; (land) propiedad, finca, *f*; fortuna, *f*; (inheritance) heredad, *f*, patrimonio, *m*; *law* bienes, *m pl*. **personal e.,** bienes muebles, *m pl*; fortuna personal, *f*. **third e.,** estado llano, *m*. **e. agent,** agente de fincas, *m*; agente de casas, *m*

esteem *n* estima, *f*, aprecio, *m*; consideración, *f*, *vt* estimar, apreciar; creer, juzgar

ester *n chem* éster, *m*

esthete *n* estético, *m*

esthetic *a* estético

esthetically *adv* estéticamente

esthetics *n* estética, *f*

estimable *a* apreciable, estimable

estimableness *n* estimabilidad, *f*

estimate *n* estimación, tasa, *f*; cálculos, *m pl*; apreciación, *f*; opinión, *f*; *pl* **estimates,** presupuesto, *m*. *vt* (value) avalorar, tasar; calcular, computar; considerar. *vi* hacer un presupuesto

estimation *n* opinión, *f*; cálculo, cómputo, *m*; (esteem) aprecio, *m*, estima, *f*

Estonian *a* and *n* estonio (-ia); (language) estonio, *m*

estrange *vt* enajenar; ofender

estrangement *n* enajenación, alienación, *f*

estuary *n* estuario, *m*, ría, *f*

etcetera etcétera. (Used as noun, *f*)

etch *vt* grabar al agua fuerte

etcher *n* grabador (-ra) al agua fuerte

etching *n* aguafuerte, *f*; grabado al agua fuerte, *m*. **e. needle,** punta seca, aguja de grabador, *f*

eternal *a* eterno; incesante. *n* (E.) el Eterno

eternally *adv* eternamente

eternity *n* eternidad, *f*

eternize *vt* eternizar

ether *n* éter, *m*

ethereal *a* etéreo; vaporoso, aéreo

etheric *a* etéreo

etherize *vt* eterizar

ethical *a* ético, moral; *n* droga de ordenanza, *f*

ethics *n* ética, *f*; (filosofía) moral, *f*

Ethiopia Etiopia, *f*

ethnic *a* étnico

ethnographic *a* etnográfico

ethnography *n* etnografía, *f*

ethnologist *n* etnólogo, *m*

ethnology *n* etnología, *f*

ethyl *n chem* etilo, *m*

ethylene *n chem* etileno, *m*

etiquette *n* etiqueta, *f*

Eton coat *n* chaquetilla, *f*

Eton collar *n* cuello de colegial, *m*

Eton crop *n* pelo a la garçonne, *m*

Etna, Mount el Etna

Etruscan *a* and *n* etrusco (-ca)

etymological *a* etimológico

etymologist *n* etimólogo, *m*, etimologista, *mf*

etymology *n* etimología, *f*

eucalyptus *n* eucalipto, *m*

Eucharist n Eucaristía, f
eucharistic a eucarístico
Euclidean a euclídeo
eugenic a eugenésico
eugenics n eugenesia, f
eulogist n elogiador (-ra), loador (-ra)
eulogistic a elogiador
eulogize vt elogiar, alabar, encomiar
eulogy n elogio, encomio, m; alabanza, f; panegírico, m
eunuch n eunuco, m
euphemism n eufemismo, m
euphonious a eufónico
euphony n eufonía, f
euphuistic a alambicado, gongorino
Eurasian a and n eurasio (-ia)
eurhythmic a eurítmico
eurhythmics n euritmia, f
European a and n europeo (-ea)
europeanize vt europeanizar
euthanasia n eutanasia, f
evacuate vt evacuar
evacuation n evacuación, f
evade vt evadir, eludir; evitar, esquivar; rehuir
evaluate vt evaluar, estimar; calcular
evaluation n evaluación, estimación, f
evanescent a transitorio, fugaz, pasajero
evangelical a evangélico
evangelicalism n evangelismo, m
evangelist n evangelista, m
evangelize vt evangelizar
evaporate vi evaporarse; desvanecerse. vt evaporar
evaporation n evaporación, f; desvanecimiento, m
evaporative a evaporatorio
evasion n (escape) fuga, f; evasión, f; evasiva, f, efugio, m
evasive a evasivo, ambiguo
evasively adv evasivamente
evasiveness n carácter evasivo, m
eve n víspera, f; ecc vigilia, f. **on the eve of,** la víspera de; fig en vísperas de
even a (flat) llano; (smooth) liso; igual; (level with) al mismo nivel (de); uniforme; (of numbers) par; (approximate, of sums) redondo; rítmico; invariable, constante; (of temper) apacible; (just) imparcial; (monotonous) monótono, igual; (paid) pagado; (com of date) mismo. **to get e. with,** pagar en la misma moneda, vengarse de
even adv siquiera; aun; hasta; (also) también. **not e.,** ni siquiera. **e. as,** así como, del mismo modo que. **e. if,** aun cuando, si bien. **e. now,** aun ahora; ahora mismo. **e. so,** aun así; (nevertheless) sin embargo. **e. though,** aunque; suponiendo que
even vt igualar; (level) allanar, nivelar; (accounts) desquitar; compensar; hacer uniforme
evening n tarde, f, atardecer, m; noche, f; fig fin, m, a vespertino, de la tarde. **Good e.!** ¡Buenas tardes! ¡Buenas noches! **in the e.,** al atardecer. **tomorrow e.,** mañana por la tarde. **yesterday e.,** ayer por la tarde. **e. class,** clase nocturna, f. **e. dress,** (women) traje de noche, m; (men) traje de etiqueta, m. **e. meal,** cena, f. **e. paper,** periódico (or diario) de la noche, m. **evening primrose,** hierba del asno, onagra, f. **e. star,** estrella vespertina, estrella de la tarde, f; (Venus) lucero de la tarde, m
evenly adv igualmente; (on a level) a nivel; uniformemente; imparcialmente; (of speech) con suavidad
evenness n igualdad, f; (smoothness) lisura, f; uniformidad, f; imparcialidad, f; (of temper) ecuanimidad, serenidad, f
evensong n vísperas, f pl
event n incidente, suceso, acontecimiento, m; (result) consecuencia, f; resultado, m; caso, m; (athletics) prueba, f; (race) carrera, f. **at all events,** de todas maneras. **in such an e.,** en tal caso. **in the e. of,** en el caso de

eventful a lleno de acontecimientos; accidentado; memorable
eventual a eventual; final, último
eventuality n eventualidad, f
eventually adv a la larga, al fin
ever adv siempre; (at any time) jamás; alguna vez; nunca; (even) siquiera; (very) muy; (in any way) en modo alguno. **As fast as e. he can,** Lo más aprisa que pueda. **Be it e. so big,** Por grande que sea. **Did you e.!** ¡Habráse visto! ¡Qué cosa! **for e.,** para siempre. **for e. and e.,** para siempre jamás; (mostly ecclesiastical) por los siglos de los siglos; eternamente. **He is e. so nice,** Es muy simpático. **Hardly e.,** casi nunca. **I don't think I have e. been there,** No creo que haya estado nunca allí. **if e.,** si alguna vez; (rarely) raramente. **nor . . . e.,** ni nunca. **not . . . e.,** nunca. **e. after,** desde entonces; (afterward) después. **e. and anon,** de vez en cuando. **e. so little,** siquiera un poco; muy poco
evergreen a siempre verde. n planta vivaz, f. **e. oak,** encina, f
everlasting a eterno, perpetuo; (of colors) estable; incesante. **e. flower,** perpetua, f
evermore adv eternamente
every a todo; cada (invariable); todos los, m pl; todas las, f pl. **e. day,** todos los días, cada día. **e. now and then,** de cuando en cuando. **e. other day,** cada dos días
everybody n todo el mundo, m; todos, m pl; todas, f pl; cada uno, m; cada una, f
everyday a diario, cotidiano; corriente, de cada día, usual
everything n todo, m; (e. that, which) todo lo (que). **e. possible,** todo lo posible
everywhere adv por todas partes
evict vt desahuciar; expulsar
eviction n evicción, f, desahúcio, m; expulsión, f
evidence n law testimonio, m, deposición, f; indicios, m pl; evidencia, f; prueba, f; hecho, m, vt patentizar, probar. **to give e.,** dar testimonio, deponer
evident a evidente, patente, manifiesto; claro. **to be e.,** ser patente, estar a la vista
evidently adv evidentemente; claramente
evil a malo; malvado, perverso; de maldad; (unfortunate) aciago; de infortunio; (of spirits) diabólico, malo. n mal, m; maldad, perversidad, f; (misfortune) desgracia, f. **the E. One,** el Malo. e.-doer, malhechor (-ra). **e. eye,** mal de ojo, aojo, m. **e.-minded,** mal pensado; malintencionado. **e.-speaking,** maledicencia, calumnia, f. **e. spirit,** demonio, espíritu malo, m
evince vt evidenciar; mostrar
eviscerate vt destripar, desentrañar
evocation n evocación, f
evocative a evocador
evoke vt evocar
evolution n evolución, f; desarrollo, m; (nav, mil) maniobra, f; math extracción de una raíz, f; (revolution) revolución, vuelta, f
evolutionism n evolucionismo, m
evolutive a evolutivo
evolve vi evolucionar; desarrollarse. vt producir por evolución; desarrollar; pensar
ewe n oveja, f. **ewe lamb,** cordera, f
ewer n aguamanil, m
exacerbate vt exacerbar; agravar, empeorar
exacerbation n exacerbación, f; agravación, f
exact a exacto; fiel; metódico; estricto. vt exigir
exacting a exigente; severo, estricto; (hard) agotador, arduo
exaction n exigencia, f; extorsión, exacción, f
exactly adv exactamente; precisamente
exactness n exactitud, f
exaggerate vt exagerar; acentuar. vi exagerar
exaggerated a exagerado
exaggeration n exageración, f
exaggerator n exagerador (-ra)
exalt vt exaltar; enaltecer, elevar; (praise) glorificar, magnificar; (intensify) realzar; intensificar

exaltation *n* exaltación, elevación, *f;* alegría, *f,* júbilo, *m;* (ecstasy) éxtasis, arrobamiento, *m;* (of the Cross) exaltación, *f*
exalted *a* exaltado, eminente
exaltedness *n* exaltación, *f*
examination *n* examen, *m;* inspección, *f;* investigación, *f; law* interrogatorio, *m;* prueba, *f.* **to sit an e.,** examinarse. **written e.,** prueba escrita, *f*
examine *vt* examinar; inspeccionar; investigar; *law* interrogar; (search) reconocer; (by touch) tentar; observar; analizar. **to e. into,** examinar; considerar detenidamente; ahondar en
examinee *n* examinando (-da)
examiner *n* examinador (-ra); inspector (-ra)
examinership *n* cargo de examinador, *m*
examining *a* que examina; de examen; *law* interrogante
example *n* ejemplo, *m;* ilustración, *f;* (parallel) ejemplar, *m;* (warning) escarmiento, *m.* **for e.,** por ejemplo. **to set an e.,** dar ejemplo, dar el ejemplo.
exasperate *vt* exasperar, irritar; (increase) aumentar; (worsen) agravar
exasperating *a* exasperante, irritante, provocador
exasperation *n* exasperación, irritación, *f;* (worsening) agravación, *f;* enojo, *m*
excavate *vt* excavar; (hollow) vaciar
excavation *n* excavación, *f; arch* vaciado, *m*
excavator *n* excavador (-ra); (machine) excavadora, *f*
exceed *vt* exceder; (excel) superar, aventajar; (one's hopes, etc.) sobrepujar. *vi* excederse. **e. all expectations,** exceder a toda ponderación. **to e. one's rights,** abusar de sus derechos, ir demasiado lejos
exceedingly *adv* sumamente, extremadamente; sobre manera
excel *vt* aventajar, superar; vencer. *vi* sobresalir; distinguirse, señalarse; ser superior
excellence *n* excelencia, *f;* superioridad, *f;* perfección, *f;* mérito, *m;* buena calidad, *f*
excellency *n* (title) Excelencia, *f.* **Your E.,** Su Excelencia
excellent *a* excelente; superior; perfecto; magnífico; (in examinations) sobresaliente
excellently *adv* excelentemente; perfectamente; magníficamente
except *vt* exceptuar; omitir
except, excepting *prep* excepto, con excepción de; exceptuando; menos; salvo; fuera de. *conjunc* a menos que. **except for,** si no fuese por; con excepción de; fuera de
exception *n* excepción, *f;* objeción, protesta, *f.* **to make an e.,** hacer una excepción. **to take e. to,** protestar contra; tachar, criticar; desaprobar
exceptional *a* excepcional
excerpt *n* excerpta, *f,* extracto, *m, vt* extraer
excess *n* exceso, *m;* superabundancia, *f;* demasía, *f; com* superávit, *m.* **in e.,** en exceso, de sobra. **in e. of,** en exceso de; arriba de. **to e.,** excesivamente, demasiado. **e. fare,** suplemento, *m.* **e. luggage,** exceso de equipaje, *m;* (overweight) exceso de peso, *m*
excessive *a* excesivo; superabundante; inmoderado, desmesurado; exagerado
excessively *adv* excesivamente; exageradamente
excessiveness *n* exceso, *m;* superabundancia, *f;* exageración, *f*
exchange *n* cambio, trueque, *m;* (of prisoners) canje, *m;* (financial) cambio, *m;* (building) bolsa, lonja, *f;* (telephone) oficina central de teléfonos, *f. vt* cambiar (for, por); trocar; (replace) reemplazar; (prisoners) canjear; (of blows) darse; (pass from, into) pasar de . . . a. *vi* hacer un cambio. **in e. for,** en cambio de, a trueque de; por. **to e. greetings,** saludarse; cambiar saludos. **They exchanged looks,** Se miraron. **What is the rate of e.?** ¿Cuál es el tipo de cambio? **e. of prisoners,** canje de prisioneros, *m*
exchangeable *a* cambiable; trocable
exchequer *n* (public finance) Hacienda pública, *f;* teso-

rería, *f;* (funds) fondos, *m pl.* **Chancellor of the E.,** Ministro de Hacienda, *m*
excise *n* contribución indirecta, *f;* (customs and e.) Aduana, *f. vt* (cut) cortar, extirpar; imponer una contribución indirecta. **e. duty,** derecho de aduana, *m*
excise tax arbitrios, *m pl*
excision *n* excisión, *f;* extirpación, *f*
excitability *n* excitabilidad, *f*
excitable *a* excitable
excitation *n* excitación, *f*
excite *vt* emocionar; conmover; agitar; excitar; suscitar; provocar; incitar, instigar; (attention, interest) despertar; estimular. **to become excited,** emocionarse; exaltarse; (annoyed) acalorarse; (upset) agitarse
excitedly *adv* con emoción; acaloradamente; agitadamente
excitement *n* conmoción, *f;* agitación, *f;* (annoyance) acaloramiento, *m;* emoción, *f;* estímulo, *m;* instigación, *f,* fomento, *m;* (amusement) placer, *m*
exciting *a* emocionante; conmovedor; agitador; muy interesante
exclaim *vt* and *vi* exclamar. **to e. against,** clamar contra
exclamation *n* exclamación, *f.* **e. mark,** punto de exclamación, *m*
exclamatory *a* exclamatorio
exclude *vt* excluir; exceptuar; evitar; (refuse) rechazar
exclusion *n* exclusión, *f;* exceptuación, *f;* eliminación, *f*
exclusive *a* exclusivo; (snobbish) exclusivista. **e. of,** no incluido; aparte de
exclusively *adv* exclusivamente; únicamente
exclusiveness *n* carácter exclusivo, *m*
exclusivism *n* exclusivismo, *m*
exclusivist *n* exclusivista, *mf*
excommunicate *vt* excomulgar. *a* excomulgado
excommunication *n* excomunión, *f*
excrement *n* excremento, *m*
excrescence *n* excrecencia, *f*
excrescent *a* que forma excrecencia; superfluo
excrete *vt* excretar
excretion *n* excreción, *f*
excretory *a* excretorio
excruciating *a* atormentador, angustioso; (of pain) agudísimo
excursion *n* excursión, *f;* expedición, *f;* (digression) digresión, *f.* **e. ticket,** billete de excursión, *m.* **e. train,** tren de excursionistas, *m*
excursionist *n* excursionista, *mf;* turista, *mf*
excusable *a* disculpable, excusable
excusably *adv* excusablemente
excuse *n* excusa, *f;* disculpa, *f;* pretexto, *m;* justificación, defensa, *f.* **to give as an e.,** pretextar
excuse *vt* disculpar, excusar; dispensar (de); librar (de); (forgive) perdonar; (defend) justificar, defender; (minimize) paiar; (oneself) disculparse. **E. me!** ¡Con permiso!; ¡Perdone Vd.!; ¡Dispense Vd.!
execrable *a* execrable, abominable
execrate *vt* execrar, abominar. *vi* maldecir
execration *n* execración, abominación, *f;* maldición, *f*
execute *vt* (perform) ejecutar, poner en efecto, realizar; *(art, mus)* ejecutar; (part in a play) hacer, desempeñar; (fulfil) cumplir; *law* otorgar (un documento); (kill) ajusticiar
execution *n* efectuación, realización, *f;* *(art, mus)* ejecución, *f;* (of part in a play) desempeño (de un papel), *m;* (fulfilment) cumplimiento, *m; law* otorgamiento (de un documento), *m;* (killing) suplicio, *m,* ejecución de la pena de muerte, *f;* *(law seizure)* ejecución, *f*
executioner *n* verdugo, *m*
executive *a* ejecutivo; administrativo. *n* poder ejecutivo, *m*
executor *n* administrador testamentario, *m*
executorship *n* ejecutoría, *f*
executrix *n* administradora testamentaria, *f*
exegesis *n* exégesis, *f*
exegetical *a* exegético

exemplary *a* ejemplar
exemplification *n* ejemplificación, ilustración, demostración, *f*
exemplify *vt* ejemplificar; ilustrar, demostrar
exempt *vt* exentar, eximir; librar; dispensar, excusar. *a* exento; libre; excusado; inmune
exemption *n* exención, *f*; libertad, *f*; inmunidad, *f*
exercise *n* ejercicio, *m*; uso, *m*; (essay) ensayo, *m*; *pl* **exercises,** (on land or sea) maniobras, *f pl*. *vt* ejercer; usar, emplear; (train) ejercitar, entrenar; adiestrar; pasear, dar un paseo; (worry) preocupar. *vi* hacer ejercicio; ejercitarse; adiestrarse. **spiritual exercises,** ejercicios espirituales, *m pl*. **to take e. in the open air,** tomar ejercicio al aire libre. **to write an e.,** escribir un ejercicio. **e. book,** cuaderno de ejercicios, *m*
exert *vt* hacer uso de, emplear, ejercer, poner en juego; (deploy) desplegar. **to e. oneself,** hacer un esfuerzo (para); esforzarse (de); trabajar mucho; tratar (de); apurarse, tomarse mucha molestia; preocuparse
exertion *n* esfuerzo, *m*; uso, *m*; (exercise) ejercicio, *m*; (good offices) diligencias, gestiones, *f pl*; buenos oficios, *m pl*
exhalation *n* exhalación, *f*; efluvio, *m*; vapor, *m*; humo, *m*
exhale *vt* exhalar; emitir, despedir. *vi* evaporarse; disiparse
exhaust *vt* agotar; (empty) vaciar; (end) acabar; apurar; consumir; (tire) rendir, cansar mucho; (weaken) debilitar; (a subject) tratar detalladamente. *n mech* escape, *m*; emisión de vapor, *f*; vapor de escape, *m*. **e. pipe,** tubo de escape, *m*
exhaustible *a* agotable
exhausting *a* cansado, agotador
exhaustion *n* agotamiento, *m*; rendimiento, cansancio, *m*; lasitud, *f*; postración, *f*
exhaustive *a* completo; minucioso
exhaustively *adv* detenidamente; detalladamente; minuciosamente
exhaustiveness *n* lo completo; minuciosidad, *f*
exhibit *vt* exhibir; manifestar, ostentar; revelar, descubrir; presentar. *vi* exhibir, ser expositor. *n* objeto exhibido, *m*; *law* prueba, *f*
exhibition *n* exposición, *f*; (performance) función, *f*; espectáculo, *m*; exhibición, *f*; (showing) manifestación, *f*; (grant) bolsa de estudio, beca, *f*
exhibitionism *n* exhibicionismo, *m*
exhibitionist *n* exhibicionista, *mf*
exhibitor *n* expositor (-ra)
exhilarate *vt* alegrar, alborozar
exhilarating *a* alegre; estimulador; vigorizador, tonificante
exhilaration *n* alegría, *f*, alborozo, regocijo, *m*
exhort *vt* and *vi* exhortar
exhortation *n* exhortación, *f*
exhumation *n* exhumación, *f*
exhume *vt* exhumar
exigence *n* exigencia, *f*; urgencia, *f*; (need) necesidad, *f*
exigent *a* exigente; urgente
exiguous *a* exiguo
exiguousness *n* exigüidad, *f*
exile *n* destierro, *m*; (person) desterrado (-da). *vt* desterrar
exist *vi* existir
existence *n* existencia, *f*; (being) ser, *m*; (life) vida, *f*. **to bring into e.,** causar; producir
existentialism *n* existencialismo, *m*
existing *a* existente
exit *n* salida, *f*; partida, *f*; (death) muerte, *f*; *theat* mutis, *m*. *vi theat* hacer mutis. **to make one's e.,** salir; marcharse; irse; morir; *theat* hacer mutis
exodus *n* éxodo, *m*; salida, *f*; emigración, *f*; (Old Testament) Éxodo, *m*
exonerate *vt* exonerar
exoneration *n* exoneración, *f*
exorbitance *n* exorbitancia, *f*
exorbitant *a* exorbitante

exorcism *n* exorcismo, *m*
exorcist *n* exorcista, *m*
exorcize *vt* exorcizar, conjurar
exotic *a* exótico. *n* planta exótica, *f*; *fig* flor de estufa, *f*
expand *vt* extender; abrir; (wings, etc.) desplegar; (the chest, etc.) expandir; dilatar; (amplify) ampliar; (an edition) ampliar, aumentar; (develop) desarrollar; *fig* ensanchar; (increase) aumentar. *vi* dilatarse; hincharse; abrirse; extenderse; *fig* ensancharse; (increase) aumentarse
expanse *n* extensión, *f*
expansibility *n phys* expansibilidad, *f*; dilatabilidad, *f*
expansible *a phys* expansible; dilatable
expansion *n* expansión, *f*; extensión, *f*; dilatación, *f*; (amplification) ampliación, *f*; (development) desarrollo, *m*; *fig* ensanchamiento, *m*; (increase) aumento, *m*
expansionism *n* expansionismo, *m*
expansive *a* expansivo; (of persons) efusivo, expresivo, comunicativo, afable
expansiveness *n* expansibilidad, *f*; (of persons) afabilidad, *f*
expatiate (upon) *vi* extenderse en
expatiation *n* discurso, *m*; digresión, *f*
expatriation *n* expatriación, *f*
expect *vt* esperar; (await) aguardar; (suppose) suponer; (demand) exigir; (count on) contar con. *vi* creer
expectance *n* expectación, *f*; esperanza, *f*
expectant *a* expectante; (hopeful) esperanzudo; (pregnant) embarazada
expectantly *adv* con expectación
expectation *n* expectación, *f*; (hope) esperanza, expectativa, *f*; probabilidad, *f*
expectorate *vt* expectorar. *vi* escupir
expectoration *n* expectoración, *f*
expedience *n* conveniencia, *f*; oportunidad, *f*; aptitud, *f*; (self-interest) egoísmo, *m*
expedient *a* conveniente; oportuno; apto; prudente; político. *n* expediente, recurso, medio, *m*
expedite *vt* acelerar; facilitar; (send off) despachar
expedition *n* expedición, *f*; (haste) celeridad, diligencia, *f*
expeditionary *a* expedicionario. **e. force,** fuerza expedicionaria, *f*
expeditious *a* expedito, pronto
expeditiously *adv* expeditamente, prontamente
expeditiousness *n* prontitud, *f*
expel *vt* expeler, expulsar; echar, arrojar; despedir
expend *vt* gastar, expender; (time) perder
expenditure *n* gasto, desembolso, *m*; (of time) pérdida, *f*
expense *n* gasto, *m*; pérdida, *f*; costa, *f*; *pl* **expenses,** expensas, *f pl*, gastos, *m pl*. **at the e. of,** a costa de. **to be put to great e.,** tener que gastar mucho. **to pay one's expenses,** pagar sus gastos
expensive *a* costoso; caro
expensively *adv* costosamente
expensiveness *n* lo costoso; costa, *f*
experience *n* experiencia, *f*. *vt* experimentar; sentir; sufrir. **by e.,** por experiencia
experienced *a* experimentado; experto; hábil; (lived) vivido
experiment *n* experimento, *m*; prueba, *f*; ensayo, *m*, tentativa, *f*, *vi* experimentar; hacer una prueba
experimental *a* experimental; tentativo
experimentally *adv* experimentalmente; por experiencia
expert *a* experto; perito; hábil; (finished) acabado. *n* experto, *m*, especialista, *mf*
expertly *adv* expertamente; hábilmente
expertness *n* pericia, *f*; maestría, *f*; habilidad, *f*; (knowledge) conocimiento, *m*
expiable *a* que se puede expiar
expiate *vt* expiar; reparar
expiation *n* expiación, *f*
expiatory *a* expiatorio
expiration *n* (breathing out) espiración, *f*; (ending) ex-

piración, *f;* terminación, *f; com* vencimiento, *m;* (death) muerte, *f*

expiration date fecha de caducidad, *f*

expire *vi* (exhale) espirar; (die) morir, dar el último suspiro; (of fire, light) extinguirse; (end) expirar; terminar; *com* vencer

expiry *n* terminación, *f;* expiración, *f; com* vencimiento, *m*

explain *vt* explicar; aclarar; demostrar; exponer; (justify) justificar, defender. *vi* explicarse. **to e. away,** explicar; justificar

explainable *a* explicable

explanation *n* explicación, *f;* aclaración, *f*

explanatory *a* explicativo; aclaratorio

expletive *a* expletivo. *n* interjección, *f*

explicable *a* explicable

explicit *a* explícito

explode *vi* estallar; detonar; reventar. *vt* hacer estallar; (a mine) hacer saltar; (a belief, etc.) hacer abandonar; desechar

exploit *n* hazaña, proeza, *f;* aventura, *f. vt* explotar

exploitation *n* explotación, *f*

exploiter *n* explotador (-ra)

exploration *n* exploración, *f*

exploratory *a* exploratorio

explore *vt* explorar; examinar; averiguar; investigar; (*med surg*) explorar

explorer *n* explorador (-ra)

explosion *n* explosión, *f;* estallido, *m,* detonación, *f*

explosive *a* and *n* explosivo, *m.* **high e.,** explosivo violento, *m.* **explosives chamber,** recámara, *f*

explosiveness *n* propiedad explosiva, *f;* lo explosivo; violencia, *f*

exponent *a* and *n* exponente, *mf*

export *n* exportación, *f, vt* exportar. **e. licence,** permiso de exportación, *m.* **e. trade,** comercio de exportación, *m*

exportation *n* exportación, *f*

exporter *n* exportador (-ra)

expose *vt* exponer; arriesgar; (exhibit) exhibir, (unmask) desenmascarar; descubrir; revelar; *phot* exponer; (ridicule) ridiculizar

exposed *a* descubierto; no abrigado; expuesto, peligroso

exposition *n* explicación, interpretación, *f;* declaración, *f;* (exhibition) exposición, *f*

expostulate *vi* protestar, **to e. with,** reprochar; reconvenir

expostulation *n* protesta, *f;* reconvención, *f*

exposure *n* exposición, *f;* (aspect) orientación, *f;* (scandal) revelación, *f,* escándalo, *m;* peligro, *m;* exposición al frío or al calor, *f*

expound *vt* exponer, explicar; comentar

expounder *n* intérprete, *mf;* comentador (-ra)

express *a* (clear) categórico, explícito, claro; expreso; (exact) exacto; (quick) rápido. *n* (messenger, post) expreso, *m;* (train) (tren) expreso, (tren) rápido, *m;* (goods) exprés, *m. vt* expresar; (a letter, etc.) mandar por expreso

expressible *a* decible

expression *n* expresión, *f*

expressionless *a* sin expresión

expressive *a* expresivo; que expresa

expropriate *vt* expropiar

expropriation *n* expropiación, *f*

expulsion *n* expulsión, *f*

expunge *vt* borrar; testar; omitir

expunging *n* borradura, *f;* testación, *f;* omisión, *f*

expurgate *vt* expurgar

expurgation *n* expurgación, *f*

expurgator *n* expurgador, *m*

expurgatory *a* expurgatorio

exquisite *a* exquisito, precioso, primoroso; excelente; (acute) agudo, intenso; (keen) vivo. *n* elegante, petimetre, *m*

exquisitely *adv* primorosamente, pulcramente; a la perfección

exquisiteness *n* primor. *m;* pulcritud, perfección, *f;* excelencia, *f;* (of pain) intensidad, *f;* (keenness) viveza, *f*

ex-serviceman *n* excombatiente, antiguo soldado, *m*

extant *a* estante; existente; viviente

extempore *a* improvisado

extemporize *vt* and *vi* improvisar

extend *vt* extender; (hold out) tender, alargar; (lengthen) prolongar; (a period of time) prorrogar, diferir; (make larger) ensanchar; (increase) aumentar; dilatar; ampliar; (offer) ofrecer; *vi* extenderse; dilatarse; continuar; (give) dar de sí, estirarse; (last) prolongarse, durar; (become known) propagarse

extensible *a* extensible

extension *n* extensión, *f;* expansión, *f;* (increase) aumento, *m;* prolongación, *f;* ampliación, *f; com* prórroga, *f;* (telephone number) extensión, *f,* interno, *m*

extension cord *n* cordón de extensión, *m;* ladrón *m,* (Mexico; slang)

extensive *a* extenso, ancho, vasto; grande, considerable; (comprehensive) comprensivo

extensively *adv* extensamente; generalmente

extensiveness *n* extensión, *f;* amplitud, *f*

extensor *n anat* extensor, *m*

extent *n* extensión, *f;* (degree) punto, *m;* (limit) límite, *m.* **to a great e.,** en gran parte; considerablemente. **to some e.,** hasta cierto punto. **to the full e.,** en toda su extensión; completamente. **to what e.?** ¿hasta qué punto?

extenuate *vt* atenuar, desminuir, mitigar, paliar

extenuating *a* atenuante

extenuation *n* atenuación, mitigación, *f*

exterior *a* exterior, externo; de fuera; (foreign) extranjero. *n* exterior, *m;* aspecto, *m;* forma, *f*

exterminate *vt* exterminar

extermination *n* exterminio, *m*

exterminator *n* exterminador (-ra)

exterminatory *a* exterminador

external *a* externo, exterior; (foreign) extranjero. *n pl* **externals,** apariencias, *f pl;* aspecto exterior, *m;* comportamiento, *m*

externally *adv* exteriormente

exterritorial *a* extraterritorial

exterritoriality *n* extraterritorialidad, *f*

extinct *a* extinto; (of light, fire) extinguido; suprimido

extinction *n* extinción, *f*

extinguish *vt* extinguir; apagar; *fig* eclipsar

extinguishable *a* apagable

extinguisher *n* apagador (-ra); (for fires) extintor, *m;* (snuffer) matacandelas, *m*

extinguishment *n* apagamiento, *m;* extinción, *f;* abolición, *f;* (destruction) aniquilamiento, *m*

extirpate *vt* extirpar

extirpation *n* extirpación, *f*

extol *vt* elogiar, encomiar, alabar; cantar

extoller *n* alabador (-ra)

extort *vt* arrancar, sacar por fuerza; exigir por amenazas

extortion *n* extorsión, *f;* exacción, *f*

extortionate *a* injusto; opresivo; (of price) exorbitante, excesivo

extra *a* and *adv* adicional; extraordinario; suplementario; (spare) de repuesto. *prefix* (in compounds) extra. *n* extra, *m;* suplemento, *m;* (of a paper) hoja extraordinaria, *f;* (actor) supernumerario (-ia). **e. charge,** gasto suplementario, *m;* (on the railway, etc.) suplemento, *m.* **e.-mural,** *a* de extramuros.

extract *vt* sacar; (chem math) extraer; extractar; (obtain) obtener. *n chem* extracto, *m;* (excerpt) cita, *f*

extraction *n* saca, *f;* (chem) extracción, *f;* obtención, *f*

extradite *vt* entregar por extradición

extradition *n* extradición, *f*

extraneous *a* extraño; (irrelevant) ajeno (a)

extraordinarily *adv* extraordinariamente, singularmente

extraordinariness *n* lo extraordinario; singularidad, *f;* (queerness) rareza, *f*

extraordinary *a* extraordinario; singular; (queer) raro, excéntrico; (incredible) increíble

extravagance *n* (in spending) prodigalidad, *f*, derroche, *m*; (of dress, speech) extravagancia, *f*; (foolishness) disparate, *m*; (luxury) lujo, *m*

extravagant *a* extravagante; (queer) extraño, raro; (wasteful) pródigo; (of persons) gastador, manirroto; (of price) exorbitante; excesivo

extravagantly *adv* extravagantemente; de un modo extraño; pródigamente; profusamente; excesivamente

extreme *a* extremo. *n* extremo, *m*. **in e.**, extremamente, en extremo, en sumo grado. **to carry to extremes,** llevar a extremos; **E. Unction,** Extremaunción, *f*

extremely *adv* sumamente; *inf* muy

extremism *n* extremismo, *m*

extremist *a* and *n* extremista, *mf*

extremity *n* extremidad, *f*; (point) punta, *f*; necesidad, *f*; *pl* **extremities,** *anat* extremidades, *f pl*; (measures) medidas extremas, *f pl*

extricate *vt* desenredar; librar; sacar

extrication *n* liberación, *f*

extrinsic *a* extrínseco

extrovert *n* *psy* extravertido, *m*

exuberance *n* exuberancia, *f*

exuberant *a* exuberante

exudation *n* exudación, *f*

exude *vt* exudar; rezumar; sudar. *vi* exudar; rezumarse

exult *vi* exultar; alegrarse

exultant *a* exultante, triunfante

exultantly *adv* con exultación; triunfalmente

exultation *n* exultación, *f*; triunfo, *m*

eye *n* ojo, *m*; (sight) vista, *f*; (look) mirada, *f*; atención, *f*; (opinion) opinión, *f*, juicio, *m*; (of a needle, of cheese) ojo, *m*; (of a hook) corcheta, *f*; *bot* yema, *f*; (of a potato) grillo, *m*. *vt* ojear; fijar los ojos en; examinar, mirar detenidamente. **bright eyes,** ojos vivos, *m pl*. **prominent eyes,** ojos saltones, *m pl*. **He couldn't keep his eyes off Mary,** Se le fueron los ojos tras María. **as far as the eye can reach,** hasta donde alcanza la vista. **before one's eyes,** a la vista de uno, ante los ojos de uno. **in my (etc.) eyes,** *fig* según creo yo, en mi opinión. **in the twinkling of an eye,** en un abrir y cerrar de ojos. **with an eye to,** pensando en. **with my own eyes,** con mis propios ojos. **with the naked eye,** con la simple vista. **to keep an eye on,** vigilar. **to make eyes at,** guiñar el ojo; mirar con ojos de enamorado. **to have one's eyes opened,** *fig* caérsele la venda. **eye-bath,** ojera, *f*. **eye-opener,** revelación, sorpresa, *f*. **eye-pencil,** pincel para las cejas, *m*. **eye-piece,** objetivo, ocular, *m*. **eye-shade,** visera, *f*. **eye-tooth,** colmillo, *m*. **eye-witness,** testigo ocular, *mf*; testigo de vista, testigo presencial, *m*

eyeball *n* globo ocular, *m*

eyebrow *n* ceja, *f*

eye care atención de la vista, *f*

eyed *a* que tiene ojos; (in compounds) de ojos . . ., con ojos . . .; con los ojos; (of a needle) con el ojo . . . **She is a blue-eyed child,** Es una niña de ojos azules

eyeglass *n* lente, *m*

eyelash *n* pestaña, *f*

eyeless *a* sin ojos

eyelet *n* ojete, *m*

eyelid *n* párpado, *m*

eyesight *n* vista, *f*

eyewash *n* colirio, *m*; *inf* camelo, *m*. **That's all e.!** ¡Eso es un camelo!

eyrie *n* nido (of any bird of prey), nido de águila (eagle's) *m*

F

f *n* (letter) efe, *f*; *mus* fa, *m*. **f sharp,** fa sostenido, *m*

fa *n* *mus* fa, *m*

fable *n* fábula, leyenda, historia, *f*, apólogo, cuento, *m*; (untruth) invención, mentira, *f*

fabled *a* celebrado, famoso

fabric *n* obra, fábrica, *f*; estructura, construcción, *f*; (making) manufactura, *f*; (cloth) tejido, paño, *m*; textura, *f*

fabricate *vt* fabricar, construir; (invent) fingir, inventar

fabrication *n* fabricación, manufactura, *f*; construcción, *f*; (lie) invención, ficción, *f*

fabulist *n* fabulista, *mf*

fabulous *a* fabuloso

fabulousness *n* fabulosidad, *f*

façade *n* fachada, frente, *f*

face *n* superficie, *f*; (of persons) cara, *f*, rostro, *m*; (look) semblante, aire, *m*; (of coins) anverso, *m*; (grimace) mueca, *f*, gesto, *m*; (dial) esfera, *f*; (of gems) faceta, *f*; (of a wall) paramento, *m*; (front) fachada, frente, *f*; (effrontery) cara dura, *f*, descaro, *m*. **in the f. of,** ante; en presencia de. *mil* **Left f.!** ¡Izquierda! **on the f. of it,** juzgando por las apariencias. **to bring f. to f.,** confrontar (con). **to laugh in a person's f.,** reírse a la cara (de). **to make a f.,** hacer muecas. **to my f.,** en mi cara, en mis barbas. **to put a good f. on,** *fig* poner (or hacer) buena cara a. **to set one's f. against,** oponerse resueltamente a. **to straighten one's f.,** componer el semblante. **to throw in one's f.,** *fig* dar en rostro, dar en cara. **to wash one's f.,** lavarse la cara. **f. card,** figura (de la baraja), *f*. **f.-cloth,** paño para lavar la cara, *m*. **f. downward,** boca abajo. **f. lift,** operación estética facial, *f*. **f. of the waters,** faz de las aguas, *f*. **f. powder,** polvos de arroz, *m pl*. **f. to f.,** cara a cara, de persona a persona; frente a frente. **f. value,** significado literal, *m*; *com* valor nominal, *m*

face *vt* mirar hacia; confrontar; hacer cara (a); (of buildings, etc.) mirar a, caer a (or hacia); *fig* arrostrar, enfrentarse con; *sew* guarnecer, aforrar. *vi* estar orientado a. **to f. the facts,** enfrentarse con la realidad. **to f. the music,** *fig* arrostrar las consecuencias. **to f. about,** volver la espalda; *mil* dar una vuelta, cambiar de frente. **to f. up to,** *fig* hacer cara a

faced *a* con cara . . ., de cara . . .; *sew* forrado (de). **to be two-f.,** *fig* ser de dos haces

facer *n* puñetazo en la cara, *m*; *fig* dificultad insuperable, *f*, problema muy grande, *m*

facet *n* faceta, *f*

facetious *a* chancero, chistoso, jocoso

facetiousness *n* jocosidad, festividad, *f*

facial *a* facial. **f. expression,** expresión de la cara, *f*, semblante, *m*

facile *a* (frivolous) ligero (e.g., a deduction or inference)

facilitate *vt* facilitar

facilitation *n* facilitación, *f*

facility *n* facilidad, *f*; habilidad, destreza, *f*

facing *sew* vuelta, *f*; (of a building) paramento, *m*; (of lumber) chapa *f*; encaramiento, *m*

facsimile *n* facsímile, *m*

fact *n* (event) hecho, suceso, *m*; (datum) dato, *m*; realidad, verdad, *f*. **as a matter of f.,** en realidad. **in f.,** en efecto, en realidad. **I know as a f.,** Tengo por cierto. **The f. is . . . ,** La verdad es (que) . . . **the f. that,** el hecho de que

fact-finding informador (e.g. **send s.b. on a fact-finding mission,** enviar a fulano en misión informadora)

faction *n* facción, *f*, partido, bando, *m*; (tumult) alboroto, *m*

factional *a* partidario

factious *a* faccioso, sedicioso

factiousness *n* espíritu de facción, *m*; rebeldía, *f*

factitious *a* falso; artificial

factor *n* (fact) factor, elemento, *m*; consideración, *f*; *math* factor, *m*; *com* agente, factor, *m*

factory *n* fábrica, manufactura, *f*; taller, *m*. **F. Act,** ley de trabajadores industriales, *f*. **f. hand,** operario (-ia)

factotum *n* factótum, *m*

factual *a* basado en hechos, objetivo

faculty *n* facultad, *f*; (talent) habilidad, *f*, talento, *m*; (university division) facultad, *f*; (teachers as a group) claustro de profesores, claustro, profesorado, *m*; (authorization) privilegio, *m*, autoridad, *f*

fad *n* capricho, *m*, chifladura, *f*, dengue, *m*

faddiness *n* manías, *f pl*, excentricidad, *f*

faddist *n* chiflado (-da)

faddy *a* caprichoso, dengoso, difícil, excéntrico

fade *vi* (of plants) marchitarse, secarse; (of color) palidecer, descolorarse; (vanish) disiparse, desaparecer; (of persons) desmejorarse; (of stains) salir. *vt* descolorar. **to f. away,** desvanecer; (of persons) consumirse. **f.-out,** *n* (cinema) desaparecimiento gradual, *m*

faded *a* (of plants) seco, marchito, mustio; (of colors) descolorado, pálido; (of people) desmejorado

fadeless *a* de colores resistentes; eterno, no olvidado; siempre joven

fading *a* que palidece; (of flowers) medio marchito; (of light) mortecino, pálido; decadente. *n* desaparecimiento, *m*, marchitez, *f*; decadencia, *f*

fag *n inf* pitillo, *m*. **f.-end,** fin, *m*; restos, *m pl*, sobras, *f pl*; (of a cigarette) colilla, *f*; (*offensive*) maricón. *vi* trabajar mucho. *vt* fatigar mucho; hacer trabajar.

faggot *n* haz (or gavilla) de leña, *f*

faience *n* fayenza, *f*

fail *vi* faltar; fracasar, malograrse; no tener éxito, salir mal; (of strength) decaer, acabarse; (be short of) carecer (de); *com* hacer bancarrota, suspender pagos. *vt* abandonar; (disappoint) decepcionar, engañar; (in exams) suspender. **Do not f. to see her,** No dejes de verla. **He failed to do his duty,** Faltó a su deber

fail *n* without **f.,** sin falta

failing *n* falta, *f*; (shortcoming) vicio, flaco, *m*, debilidad, *f*; malogro, fracaso, *m*; decadencia, *f*

failure *n* fracaso, *m*; falta de éxito, *f*; (in exams) suspensión, *f*; (of power) no funcionamiento, *m*; omisión, *f*, descuido, *m*; *com* quiebra, bancarrota, *f*; (decay) decadencia, *f*. **on f. of,** al fracasar; bajo pena de

fain *a* deseoso, muy contento. **He was f. to . . .,** Se sintió obligado a . . . ; Quería

faint *a* débil; (dim) indistinto, vago, borroso; (of colors) pálido, desmayado; (weak) lánguido, desfallecido; (slight) superficial, rudimentario. *vi* perder el sentido, desmayarse. *n* desmayo, *m*. **to be f. with hunger,** estar muerto de hambre. **to cause to f.,** hacer desmayar. **f.-hearted,** pusilánime, medroso. **f.-heartedness,** pusilanimidad, *f*

faintly *adv* débilmente; en voz débil; indistintamente

faintness *n* languidez, debilidad, *f*; (swoon) desmayo, *m*; lo indistinto; lo borroso.

fair *n* feria, *f*; (sale) mercado, *m*; (exhibition) exposición, *f*

fair *a* (beautiful) hermoso, lindo, bello; (of hair) rubio; (of skin) blanco; (clear, fresh) limpio, claro; (good) bueno; (favorable) favorable, propicio, próspero; (of weather) despejado, sereno; (just) imparcial; (straightforward) honrado, recto, justo; (passable) regular, mediano; (of writing) legible; (proper) conveniente. *adv* honradamente; (politely) cortésmente; exactamente. **by f. means,** por medios honrados. **It's not f.!** ¡No hay derecho! **to become f.,** (of weather) serenarse. **to give a f. trial,** juzgar imparcialmente; law procesar imparcialmente. **to make a f. copy,** poner en limpio. **f.-haired,** de pelo rubio, rubio. **f. one,** una beldad, *f*. **f. play,** *sport* juego limpio, *m*; proceder leal, *m*. **f.-skinned,** de tez blanca, rubio. **f.-weather,** buen tiempo, *m*, bonanza, *f*. **f.-weather friends,** amigos de los días prósperos, *m pl*

fairing *n Brit* regalo de feria, *m*. **to give fairings,** feriar

fairly *adv* (justly) con imparcialidad; (moderately) bastante; totalmente, enteramente. **f. good,** bastante bueno; regular

fairness *n* belleza, hermosura, *f*; (of skin) blancura, *f*; (justness) imparcialidad, *f*; (reasonableness) justicia, equidad, *f*; (of hair) color rubio, oro, *m*

fairway *n naut* canalizo, paso, *m*; (golf) terreno sin obstáculos, *m*

fairy *n* hada, *f*, duende, *m*, a de hada, de duendes; *fig* delicado. **f.-gold,** tesoro de duendes, *m*; **f.-light,** lucecillo, *m*; luminaria, *f*. **f.-like,** aduendado, como una hada. **f.-ring,** círculo mágico, *m*. **f.-tale,** cuento de hadas, *m*; patraña, *f*, cuento de viejas, *m*

fairyland *n* país de las hadas, *m*

faith *n* fe, *f*; confianza, *f*; (doctrine) creencia, religión, filosofía, *f*; (honor) palabra, *f*. **in good f.,** de buena fe. **to break f.,** faltar a la palabra dada. **f.-healing,** curanderismo, *m*

faithful *a* fiel, leal; (accurate) exacto; (trustworthy) veraz. **the f.,** los creyentes

faithfully *adv* fielmente, lealmente; (accurately) con exactitud. **Yours f.,** Queda de Vd. su att. s.s.

faithfulness *n* fidelidad, lealtad, *f*; (accuracy) exactitud, *f*

faithless *a* infiel, desleal, pérfido

faithlessness *n* infidelidad, deslealtad, traición, *f*

fake *vt* imitar, falsificar. *n* imitación, falsificación, *f*. **to f. up,** inventar

Falangist *a* and *n* falangista *mf*

falcon *n* halcón, *m*. **f. gentle,** *orn* neblí, *m*

falconer *n* halconero, *m*

falconry *n* cetrería, *f*

fall *n* caída, *f*; (of temperature, mercury) baja, *f*; (of water) salto de agua, *m*, catarata, cascada, *f*; (in value) depreciación, *f*; (in price and Stock Exchange) baja, *f*; (descent) bajada, *f*; (autumn) otoño, *m*; (declivity) declinación, *f*, declive, desnivel, *m*; (ruin) ruina, *f*; destrucción, *f*; (of night, etc.) caída (de la noche), *f*; (of snow) nevada, *f*; (of rain) golpe, *m*; (*theat* of curtain) caída, bajada, *f*; (surrender) capitulación, rendición, *f*; (of earth) desprendimiento de tierras, *m*; (of the tide) reflujo, *m*

fall *vi* caer; (of mercury, temperature) bajar; (collapse) desplomarse, hundirse, derrumbarse; (die) caer muerto; (descend) descender; (*theat* of the curtain) bajar, caer; (of a river into the sea, etc.) desembocar, desaguar; (of hair, draperies) caer; (decrease) disminuir; (of spirits) ponerse triste, sentirse deprimido; (sin) caer; (come upon) sobrevenir; (of dusk, etc.) caer, llegar; (strike, touch) tocar; (as a share) tocar en suerte; (as a duty, responsibility) tocar, corresponder; (of seasons) caer en; (of words from the lips) caer de (los labios); (say) decir, pronunciar palabras; (of exclamations) escaparse; (become) venir a ser; (happen) suceder; (be) ser. **fallen upon evil days,** venido a menos. **His face fell,** Puso una cara de desengaño. **Christmas falls on a Thursday this year,** Navidad cae en jueves este año. **to let f.,** dejar caer. **to f. a-** (followed by verb) empezar a. **He fell a-crying,** Empezó a llorar. **to f. again,** volver a caer, recaer. **to f. among,** caer entre. **to f. astern,** quedarse atrás. **to f. away,** (leave) abandonar, dejar; (grow thin) enflaquecer; marchitarse; (crumble) desmoronarse. **to f. back,** retroceder, volver hacia atrás. **to f. back upon,** recurrir a; *mil* replegarse hacia. **to f. backward,** caer de espaldas, caer hacia atrás. **to f. behind,** quedarse atrás. **to f. down,** venirse a tierra; venirse abajo, dar consigo en el suelo, caer. **to f. due,** vencer. **to f. flat,** caer de bruces; (be unsuccessful) no tener éxito. **to f. in,** caer en; (collapse) desplomarse; *mil* alinearse; (expire) vencer. **to f. into,** caer en. **to f. in with,** tropezar con; reunirse con, juntarse con; (agree) convenir en; **to f. off,** caer de; (of leaves, etc.) desprenderse de, separarse de; (abandon) abandonar; (diminish) disminuir. **to f. on,** caer de (e.g. **to f. on one's back,** caer de espaldas);

(of seasons) caer en; (attack) echarse encima de, atacar. **to f. out,** (of a window, etc.) caer por; (happen) acontecer, suceder; (quarrel) pelearse, reñir; *mil* romper filas. **to f. out with,** reñir con. **to f. over,** volcar, caer; (stumble) tropezar con. **to f. short,** faltar; carecer, ser deficiente; (fail) malograrse, no llegar a sus expectaciones; (of shooting) errar el tiro. **to f. through,** caer por; (fail) malograrse, fracasar. **to f. to,** empezar a, ponerse a; (be incumbent on) tocar a, corresponder a; (attack) atacar. **to f. under,** caer debajo; caer bajo; sucumbir, perecer; (incur) incurrir en, merecer. **to f. upon,** (attack) caer sobre, acometer; acaecer, tener lugar; (be incumbent) tocar a

fallacious *a* falaz, engañoso, ilusorio

fallaciousness *n* falacia, *f*; engaño, *m*

fallacy *n* error, *m*, ilusión, *f*

fallen *a* caído; arruinado; degradado. **f. angel,** ángel caído, *m*. **f. woman,** perdida, mujer caída, *f*

fallibility *n* falibilidad, *f*

fallible *a* falible

falling *a* que cae, cayente. *n* caída, *f*; (of mercury, temperature) baja, *f*; (crumbling) desmoronamiento, *m*; (collapse) hundimiento, derrumbamiento, *m*; (of tide) reflujo, *m*; (of waterlevel) bajada, *f*; (in value) depreciación, *f*; (of prices and Stock Exchange) baja, *f*; (diminishment) disminución, *f*; (in level of earth) declinación, *f*; (com expiry) vencimiento, *m*; (theat of curtain) bajada, caída, *f*. **f. away,** (crumbling) desmoronamiento, *m*; desprendimiento de tierras, *m*; (desertion) deserción, *f*, abandono, *m*. **f. back,** retirada, *f*, retroceso, *m*. **f. down,** caída, *f*; derrumbamiento, *m*. **f. due,** vencimiento, *m*. **f. in,** hundimiento, *m*; (crumbling) desmoronamiento, *m*. **f. off,** caída de, *f*; (disappearance) desaparición, *f*; (diminution) disminución, *f*; (deterioration) deterioración, *f*. **f. out,** caída por, *f*; disensión, *f*. **f. short,** falta, *f*; carácter inferior, *m*; frustración, *f*. **f. star,** estrella fugaz, *f*

fallout caída radiactiva, llovizna radiactiva, precipitación radiactiva, *f*

fallow *a* (of color) leonado; *agr* barbechado; descuidado. *n* barbecho, *m*. *vt* barbechar. **to leave f.,** dejar en barbecho. **f. deer,** corzo (-za)

false *a* incorrecto, erróneo, equivocado; falso; (unfounded) infundado; (disloyal) infiel, traidor, desleal; (not real) postizo; artificial; de imitación; *mus* desafinado; (pretended) fingido; engañoso, mentiroso. **to play a person f.,** traicionar (a). **f. bottom,** fondo doble, *m*; **f. claim,** pretensión infundada, *f*. **f. door,** surtida, *f*. **f.-hearted,** pérfido, desleal. **f. teeth,** dientes postizos, *m pl*, dentadura postiza, *f*

falsehood *n* mentira, *f*

falseness *n* falsedad, *f*; (disloyalty) duplicidad, perfidia, traición, *f*

falsetto *n* falsete, *m*, voz de cabeza, *f*

falsification *n* falsificación, *f*; (of texts) corrupción, *f*

falsifier *n* falsificador (-ra)

falsify *vt* falsear, falsificar; (disappoint) defraudar, frustrar, contrariar

falter *vi* (physically) titubear; (of speech) balbucir, tartamudear; (of action) vacilar. **to f. out,** balbucir; hablar con voz entrecortada; decir con vacilación

faltering *a* titubeante; (of speech) entrecortado; vacilante. *n* temblor, *m*; vacilación, *f*

falteringly *adv* (of speech) balbuciente, en una voz temblorosa; con dificultad, vacilantemente

fame *n* fama, *f*; reputación, *f*; (renown) celebridad, *f*, renombre, *m*. **of ill f.,** de mala fama

famed *a* reputado; renombrado, célebre, famoso

familiar *a* íntimo, familiar; afable, amistoso; (ill-bred) insolente, demasiado familiar; (usual) corriente, usual, común; conocido. *n* amigo (-ga) íntimo (-ma); *ecc* familiar, *m*; demonio familiar, *m*. **to be f. with,** (a subject) estar versado en, conocer muy bien; (a person) tratar con familiaridad. **to become f. with,** acostumbrarse a; familiarizarse con; (a person) hacerse íntimo de

familiarity *n* intimidad, familiaridad, confianza, *f*; (friendliness) afabilidad, *f*; (over-familiarity) insolencia, demasiada familiaridad, *f*; (with a subject) conocimiento (de), *m*, experiencia (de), *f*

familiarize *vt* familiarizar, acostumbrar, habituar. *vr* familiarizarse

familiarly *adv* familiarmente; amistosamente

family *n* familia, *f*; (lineage) linaje, abolengo, *m*; (bot zool) familia, *f*; (of languages) grupo, *m*. *a* de familia; familiar; casero. **f. doctor,** médico de cabecera, *m*. **f. life,** vida de familia, *f*; hogar, *m*. **f. man,** padre de familia, *m*. **f. name,** apellido, *m*. **f. seat,** casa solar, *f*. **f. tree,** árbol genealógico, *m*

family quarrel disputa de familia, *f*

famine *n* hambre, *f*; carestía, escasez, *f*

famish *vt* matar de hambre. *vi* morirse de hambre

famished *a* hambriento

famous *a* famoso, célebre, renombrado; insigne, distinguido; *inf* excelente

famously *adv inf* muy bien, excelentemente

fan *n* abanico, *m*; *agr* aventador, *m*; *mech* ventilador, *m*; (on a windmill) volante, *m*; (amateur) aficionado (-da); (admirer) admirador (-ra); *arch* abanico, *m*. *vt* abanicar; *agr* aventar; ventilar. **fan oneself,** hacerse viento. **tap with a f.,** abanicazo, golpecito con el abanico, *m*. **f.-belt,** *mech* correa de transmisión del ventilador, *f*. **f.-light,** tragaluz, *m*. **f. maker** or **seller,** abaniquero (-ra). **f.-shaped,** en abanico, abanicado, en forma de abanico

fanatic *a* and *n* fanático (-ca)

fanaticism *n* fanatismo, *m*

fanaticize *vt* fanatizar

fancied *a* imaginario

fancier *n* aficionado (-da); (of animals) criador (-ra)

fanciful *a* romántico, caprichoso; fantástico

fancifulness *n* extravagancia, *f*; romanticismo, *m*

fancy *n* fantasía, imaginación, *f*; (idea) idea, *f*, ensueño, *m*; (caprice) capricho, antojo, *m*; (liking) afecto, cariño, *m*; gusto, *m*, afición, *f*; (wish) deseo, *m*; (fantasy) quimera, *f*, *a* imaginario; elegante, ornado; *com* de capricho, de fantasía; fantástico, extravagante. *vt* imaginar, figurarse; (like) gustar de; aficionarse a; antojarse. **I have a f. for . . . ,** Se me antoja. . . . **Just f.!** ¡Toma! ¡Quia! ¡Parece mentira! **to take a f. to,** (things) tomar afición a; (people) tomar cariño (a). **f.-dress,** disfraz, *m*. **f.-dress ball,** baile de trajes, *m*

fancy goods *n pl* artículos suntuarios *m pl*

fane *n* templo, *m*

fanfare *n* tocata de trompetas, *f*

fang *n* colmillo, *m*; raíz de un diente, *f*

fanged *a* que tiene colmillos; (of teeth) acolmillado

fangless *a* sin colmillos

fanner *n* abanicador (-ra); *agr* aventador, *m*

fanning *n* abaniqueo, *m*; *agr* avienta, *f*

fantastic *a* fantástico; extravagante

fantastically *adv* fantásticamente; extravagantemente

fantasy *n* imaginación, *f*; fantasía, quimera, visión, *f*; creación imaginativa, *f*

far *adv* lejos; a lo lejos; (much, greatly) mucho, en alto grado; (very) muy; (mostly) en gran parte. *a* lejano, distante; (farther) ulterior. **as far as,** tan lejos como; (up to, until) hasta; en cuanto, por lo que, según que. (e.g. **As far as we know,** Por lo que nosotros sepamos. **As far as we are concerned,** En cuanto a nosotros toca). **by far,** con mucho. **from far and near,** de todas partes. **from far off,** desde lejos. **He read far into the night,** Leyó hasta las altas horas de la noche. **how far?** ¿a qué distancia?; (to what extent) ¿hasta qué punto? ¿hasta dónde? **How far is it to . . . ?** ¿Qué distancia hay a . . . ? **in so far as,** en tanto que. **on the far side,** al lado opuesto; al otro extremo. **so far,** tan lejos; (till now) hasta ahora. **to go far,** ir lejos. **far away,** *a* distante, remoto, lejano; *fig* abstraído. *adv* muy lejos. **far beyond,** mucho más allá. **far-fetched,** increíble, improbable. **far-off,** *a* distante. *adv* a lo lejos, en lontananza. **far-reaching,** de gran alcance. **far-**

sighted, sagaz, presciente, previsor. **far-sightedness,** sagacidad, previsión, *f*

farce *n* farsa, *f*. *vt cul* embutir, rellenar

farcical *a* burlesco, cómico, sainetesco; absurdo, grotesco, ridiculo

fare *n* (price) pasaje, precio del billete, *m*; (traveler) viajero (-ra), pasajero (-ra); (food) comida, *f*. *vi* pasarlo (e.g. **to f. well,** pasarlo bien). **bill of f.,** menú, *m*. **full f.,** billete entero, *m*. **f. stage,** trayecto, *m*

farewell *n* despedida, *f*, adiós, *m*. *a* de despedida. *interj* ¡adiós! ¡quede Vd. con Dios! **to bid f. to,** despedirse de

farewell address *n* discurso de despedida *m*

farflung de gran alcance, extenso, vasto; (empire) dilatado

farina *n* harina (de cereales), *f*; *chem* fécula, *f*, almidón, *m*; *bot* polen, *m*

farm *n* granja, hacienda, quintería, finca, chacra, *f*, cortijo, *m*. *vt* cultivar, labrar (la tierra); (taxes) arrendar. *vi* ser granjero. **to f. out,** (taxes) dar en arriendo. **f. girl,** labradora, *f*. **f. house,** alquería, casa de labranza, granja, *f*. **f. laborer,** labriego, peón, *m*. **f. yard,** corral de una granja, *m*

farmer *n* granjero, hacendado, quintero, *m*, agrícola, *mf*; (small) colono, labrador, *m*; (of taxes) arrendatario, *m*

farmhand gañán, mozo, mozo de granja, peón *m*

farming *n* labranza, *f*, cultivo, *m*; agricultura, labor agrícola, *f*; (of taxes) arriendo, *m*. *a* de labranza, labradoril; agrícola

faro *n* (card game) faraón, *m*

farouche *a* huraño, esquivo

farrago *n* fárrago, *m*, mezcla, *f*

farrier *n* herrador, *m*

farther *adv* más lejos; (beyond) más adelante; (besides) además. *a* ulterior; más distante. **at the f. end,** al otro extremo; en el fondo. **f. on,** más adelante; más allá

farthest *adv* más lejos. *a* más lejano, más distante; extremo

farthing *n* cuarto, *m*; *fig* ardite, maravedí, *m*. **He hasn't a brass f.,** No tiene dos maravedís

fasces *n pl* fasces, *f pl*

fascicle *n bot* hacecillo, *m*

fascinate *vt* fascinar; encantar, hechizar, seducir

fascinating *a* fascinador; encantador, seduciente

fascination *n* fascinación, *f*; encanto, hechizo, *m*

Fascism *n* fascismo, *m*

Fascist *a* and *n* fascista *mf*

fashion *n* (form) forma, hechura, *f*; (way) modo, *m*; (custom) costumbre, *f*, uso, *m*; (vogue) moda, *f*; (high life) alta sociedad, *f*; (tone) buen tono, *m*. *vt* hacer, labrar; inventar. **in Spanish f.,** a la española, al uso de España. **the latest f.,** la última moda. **to be in f.,** estar de moda. **to go out of f.,** dejar de ser de moda, perder la popularidad. **f. book,** revista de modas, *f*. **f. plate,** figurín, *m*

fashionable *a* de moda; elegante; de buen tono. **to be f.,** estar en boga, ser de moda. **f. world,** mundo elegante, mundo de sociedad, *m*

fashionableness *n* buen tono, *m*; elegancia, *f*

fashionably *adv* a la moda, elegantemente

fashion show desfile de modas, *m*, exhibición de modas, *f*

fast *a* (firm) firme; (secure) seguro; (strong) fuerte; (fixed) fijo; (closed) cerrado; (of boats) amarrado; (tight) apretado; (of colors) estable; (of trains) rápido; (of sleep) profundo; (of friends) leal, seguro; (quick) rápido, veloz; (of a watch) adelantado; (dissipated) disoluto. *adv* firmemente, seguramente; (quickly) rápidamente; (of sleep) profundamente; (tightly) estrechamente, apretadamente; (of rain) (llover) a cántaros; (ceaselessly) continuamente; (often) frecuentemente; (entirely) completamente. **to be f.,** (clocks) adelantar. **to make f.,** *naut* amarrar, trincar. **f. asleep,** profundamente dormido. **f. color,** color estable, color sólido, *m*

fast *n* ayuno, *m*, *vi* ayunar. **to break one's f.,** romper

el ayuno. **f.-day,** día de ayuno, día de vigilia, *m*

fasten *vt* (tie) atar; (fix) fijar; sujetar; (stick) pegar; (a door) cerrar; (bolt) echar el cerrojo; *naut* trincar; (together) juntar, unir; (with buttons, hooks, etc.) abrochar; (on, upon) fijar en; *fig* imputar (a). *vi* fijarse; pegarse; (upon) agarrarse a, asir. **to f. one's eyes on,** fijar los ojos en. **to f. up,** cerrar; atar; (nail) clavar

fastener *n* (bolt) pasador, *m*; (for bags, jewelery, etc.) cierre, *m*; (buckle) hebilla, *f*; (of a coat, etc.) tiador, *m*; (of a book, file) sujetador, *m*; (lock) cerrojo, *m*. **paper-f.,** sujetador de papeles, *m*. **patent-f.,** botón automático, *m*

fastening *n* atadura, *f*; sujeción, *f*, afianzamiento, *m*; (together) union, *f*; (of a garment) brochadura, *f*; (of a handbag) cierre, *m*

fastidious *a* dengoso, melindroso, desdeñoso; (sensitive) sensitivo, delicado; (critical) discerniente, crítico

fastidiously *adv* melindrosamente

fastidiousness *n* dengues, melindres, *m pl*, nimiedad, *f*, desdén, *m*; sensibilidad, delicadeza, *f*; sentido crítico, *m*

fasting *n* ayuno, *m*. *a* and *part* de ayuno; en ayunas

fastness *n* firmeza, solidez, *f*; (stronghold) fortaleza, *f*; (retreat) refugio, *m*; (speed) velocidad, rapidez, *f*; (dissipation) disipación, *f*, libertinaje, *m*

fat *a* (stout) gordo, grueso; mantecoso, graso, seboso; (greasy) grasiento; (rich) fértil, pingüe; (productive) lucrativo. *n* (stoutness) gordura, *f*; (for cooking) manteca, *f*; (lard) lardo, *m*; (of animal or meat) grasa, *f*; sebo, saín, *m*; *fig* riqueza, *f*; *fig* fertilidad, *f*. **to grow fat,** engordar, ponerse grueso

fatal *a* fatal, mortal; funesto

fatalism *n* fatalismo, *m*

fatalist *n* fatalista, *mf*

fatalistic *a* fatalista

fatality *n* fatalidad, *f*; infortunio, *m*, calamidad, *f*; muerte, *f*

fatally *adv* mortalmente, fatalmente; inevitablemente

fate *n* destino, sino, hado, *m*, providencia, *f*; fortuna, suerte, *f*; destrucción, ruina, *f*; muerte, *f*. **the Three Fates,** las Parcas

fated *a* fatal, destinado; predestinado

fateful *a* decisivo, fatal; aciago, ominoso

father *n* padre, *m*. *vt* prohijar, adoptar; (on or upon) atribuir (a), imputar (a). **Eternal F.,** Padre Eterno, *m*. **Holy F.,** Padre Santo, *m*. **indulgent f.,** padre indulgente, padrazo, *m*. **Like f. like son,** De tal palo tal astilla. **f. confessor,** *ecc* director espiritual, *m*. **f.-in-law,** suegro, *m*

fatherhood *n* paternidad, *f*

fatherland *n* patria, madre patria, *f*

fatherless *a* sin padre, huérfano de padre

fatherliness *n* amor paternal, *m*; sentimiento paternal, *m*

fatherly *a* paternal, de padre

fathom *n naut* braza, *f*. *vt* sondear; *fig* profundizar, tantear; (a mystery) desentrañar

fathomless *a* insondable; *fig* incomprensible, impenetrable

fatigue *n* fatiga, *f*, cansancio, *m*; *mil* faena, *f*; *mech* pérdida de resistencia, *f*. *vt* fatigar, cansar. **to be fatigued,** estar cansado, cansarse, fatigarse. **f. party,** *mil* pelotón de castigo, *m*

fatiguing *a* fatigoso

fatness *n* (stoutness) gordura, carnosidad, *f*; grasa, *f*, gordo, *m*; (richness) fertilidad, *f*; lo lucrativo

fatten *vt* engordar; (animals) cebar, sainar; (land) abonar, fertilizar. *vi* ponerse grueso, echar carnes

fatty *a* untoso, grasiento; *chem* graso. **f. acid,** ácido graso, *m*. **f. degeneration,** degeneración grasienta, *f*

fatuity *n* fatuidad, necedad, *f*

fatuous *a* fatuo, necio, lelo

fault *n* defecto, mal, imperfección, *f*; (blame) culpa, *f*; (mistake) falta, *f*, error, *m*; (in cloth) canilla, barra, *f*; *geol* falla, quiebra, *f*; *elec* avería, *f*; *sport* falta, *f*, *vi sport* cometer una falta. **to a f.,** excesivamente. **to be at f.,**

(to blame) tener la culpa; (mistaken) estar equivocado; (puzzled) estar perplejo; (of dogs) perder el rastro. **to find f.,** tachar, culpar, criticar. **Whose f. is it?** ¿Quién tiene la culpa?

faultfinder *n* criticón (-ona)

faultiness *n* defectuosidad, imperfección, *f*

faultless *a* sin faltas; perfecto, sin tacha; impecable

faulty *a* defectuoso, imperfecto

faun *n* fauno, *m*

fauna *n* fauna, *f*

favor *n* favor, *m*; (protection) amistad, protección, *f*, amparo, *m*; (permission) permiso, *m*, licencia, *f*; (kindness) merced, gracia, *f*; (gift) obsequio, *m*; (favoritism) favoritismo, *m*, preferencia, *f*; (benefit) beneficio, *m*; (badge) colores, *m pl*; *com* grata, atenta, *f*. *vt* favorecer, apoyar; mirar con favor, mostrar parcialidad (hacia); (suit) favorecer; (be advantageous) ser propicio (a); (contribute to) contribuir a, ayudar; (resemble) parecerse (a). **Circumstances f. the idea,** Las circunstancias son propicias a la idea, Las circunstancias militan en pro de la idea. **I f. the teaching of modern languages,** Soy partidario de la enseñanza de lenguas vivas. **in f. of,** a favor de, en pro de. **in the f. of,** en el favor de. **out of f.,** fuera de favor; (not fashionable) fuera de moda. **to count on the f. of,** tener de su parte (a), contar con el apoyo de. **to do a f.,** hacer un favor. **to enjoy the f. of,** gozar del favor de. **to fall out of f.,** caer en desgracia; (go out of fashion) pasar de moda. **to grow in f.,** aumentar en favor

favorable *a* favorable; propicio, próspero

favorableness *n* lo favorable; lo propicio; benignidad, benevolencia, *f*

favorably *adv* favorablemente

favored *a* favorecido; predilecto; (in compounds) parecido, encarado

favoring *a* favorecedor, propicio

favorite *a* favorito; predilecto, preferido. *n* favorito (-ta). **court f.,** valido, privado, *m*; (mistress) querida (de un rey), *f*; (lover) amante (de una reina), *m*. **to be a f.,** ser favorito

favoritism *n* favoritismo, *m*

fawn *n zool* cervato, *m*; (color) color de cervato, color de ante, *m*. *a* de color de cervato, anteado, pardo; (of animals) rucio, pardo. *vt and vi* parir la cierva. *vi* acariciar; (on, upon) adular, lisonjear

fawning *n* adulación, *f*, *a* adulador, lisonjero

fear *n* miedo, temor, *m*; (apprehension) ansiedad, aprensión, *f*, recelo, *m*; (respect) veneración, *f*. *vt* temer; recelar; (respect) reverenciar. *vi* tener miedo; estar receloso, estar con cuidado. **for f. of,** por miedo de. **for f. that,** por temor de que, por miedo de que. **from f.,** por miedo. **There is no f. of . . .,** No hay miedo de (que) . . .

fearer *n* temedor (-ra), el (la) que teme

fearful *a* miedoso, aprensivo, receloso; (cowardly) tímido, pusilánime; (terrible) horrible, espantoso, pavoroso; *inf* tremendo, enorme

fearfully *adv* con miedo; tímidamente; (terribly) horriblemente; *inf* enormemente

fearfulness *n* temor, miedo, *m*; (horribleness) lo horrible

fearless *a* sin miedo, intrépido, audaz

fearlessness *n* intrepidez, valentía, *f*

fearsome *a* temible, horrible, espantoso

feasibility *n* practicabilidad, posibilidad, *f*

feasible *a* factible, hacedero, practicable, ejecutable

feast *n ecc* fiesta, *f*; banquete, *m*; *fig* abundancia, *f*, *vi* regalarse. *vt* festejar, agasajar; (delight) recrear, deleitar. **immovable f.,** *ecc* fiesta fija, *f*. **movable f.,** fiesta movible, *f*. **f. day,** día de fiesta, festividad *f*

feasting *n* banquetes, *m pl*; fiestas, *f pl*

feat *n* hazaña, proeza, *f*, hecho, *m*

feather *n* pluma, *f*; (of the tail) pena, *f*; *pl* **feathers,** plumaje, *m*; plumas, *f pl*. *vt* emplumar; adornar con plumas; (rowing) poner casi horizontal la pala del remo. **to f. one's nest,** *inf* hacer su agosto. **f.-bed,** plu-

món, colchón de plumas, *m*. **f.-brained,** casquivano, alocado, aturdido. **f.-duster,** plumero, *m*. **f.-stitch,** *sew* diente de perro, *m*. **f. weight,** (boxing) peso pluma, *m*

feathered *a* plumado, plumoso; adornado con plumas; (winged) alado

feathery *a* plumoso; como plumas

feature *n* rasgo, *m*, característica, *f*; (cinema) número de programa, *m*; *pl* **features** (of the face) facciones, *f pl*. *vt* dar importancia (a); (cinema) presentar. **f. film,** documentaria, *f*

febrile *a* febril

February *n* febrero, *m*

fecal *a* fecal

feces *n* heces, *f pl*; excremento, *m*

fecund *a* fecundo, fértil

fecundate *vt* fecundar

fecundity *n* fecundidad, fertilidad, *f*

federal *a* federal, federalista

federalism *n* federalismo, *m*

federalist *n* federalista, federal, *mf*

federate *vt* confederar. *vi* confederarse. *a* confederado

federation *n* confederación, federación, *f*; liga, unión, asociación, *f*

federative *a* federativo

fee *n* (feudal law) feudo, *m*; (homage) homenaje, *m*; (duty) derecho, *m*; (professional) honorario, estipendio, *m*; (to a servant) gratificación, *f*; (entrance, university, etc.) cuota, *f*; (payment) paga, *f*

feeble *a* débil; lánguido; enfermizo; (of light, etc.) tenue; *fig* flojo. **to grow f.,** debilitarse; disminuir. **f.-minded,** anormal

feebleness *n* debilidad, *f*; *fig* flojedad, *f*

feebly *adv* débilmente; lánguidamente

feed *n* alimento, *m*; (meal) comida, *f*; (of animals) pienso, forraje, *m*; *mech* alimentación, *f*. *vt* alimentar; dar de comer (a); (animals) cebar; *mech* alimentar; mantener; *fig* nutrir. *vi* comer, alimentarse; (graze) pastar. **to be fed up,** *inf* estar hasta la coronilla, estar harto. **to f. on,** alimentarse de; *fig* nutrirse de. **f. pipe,** tubo de alimentación, *m*

feedback *n* retrocomunicación, *f*

feeder *n* el, *m*, (*f*, la) que da de comer a; (eater) comedor (-ra); (of a river) tributario, afluente, *m*; (bib) babero, *m*; *mech* alimentador, *m*; (cup for invalids) pistero, *m*

feeding *n* alimentación, *f*, *a* alimenticio, de alimentación. **f.-bottle,** biberón, *m*. **f.-cup,** pistero, *m*. **f.-trough,** pesebre, *m*

feel *n* (touch) tacto, *m*; (feeling) sensación, *f*; (instinct) instinto, *m*, percepción innata, *f*

feel *vt* (touch) tocar, tentar, palpar; (experience) sentir; experimentar; (understand) comprender; (believe) creer; (be conscious of) estar consciente de; (the pulse) tomar; examinar. *vi* sentir, ser sensible; sentirse, encontrarse; (to touch) ser . . . al tacto, estar. **How do you f.?** ¿Cómo se siente Vd.? **I f. cold,** Tengo frío. **I f. for you,** Lo siento en el alma; Estoy muy consciente de ello. **I f. strongly that . . .,** Estoy convencido de que . . . **I f. that it is a difficult question,** Me parece una cuestión difícil. **It feels like rain,** Creo que va a llover. **to f. at home,** sentirse a sus anchas, sentirse como en su casa. **to f. hungry (thirsty),** tener hambre (sed). **to f. one's way,** andar a tientas; *fig* medir el terreno. **to f. soft,** ser blando al tacto. **to make itself felt,** hacerse sentir. **Your hands f. cold,** Tus manos están frías

feeler *n* (of insects) palpo, *m*, antena, *f*; tentáculo, *m*; *fig* tentativa, *f*, balón de ensayo, *m*

feeling *n* (touch) tacto, *m*; (sensation) sensación, *f*; (sentiment) sentimiento, *m*; emoción, *f*; (premonition) corazonada, intuición, premonición, *f*; (tenderness) ternura, *f*; (perception) sensibilidad, percepción, *f*; (passion) pasión, *f*; (belief) opinión, *f*, sentir, *m*. *a* sensible; tierno; (compassionate) compasivo; apasionado; (moving) conmovedor

feelingly *adv* con emoción; (strongly) enérgicamente,

vivamente; (understandingly) comprensivamente

feign *vt* fingir; (invent) inventar, imaginar; simular; (allege) pretextar; (dissemble) disimular. *vi* disimular

feint *n* artificio, engaño, *m*; (in fencing) treta, finta, *f*. *vi* hacer finta

feldspar *n min* feldespato, *m*

felicitate *vt* felicitar, congratular, dar el parabién (a)

felicitation *n* felicitación, *f*, parabién, *m*

felicitous *a* feliz, dichoso, afortunado; (of phrases, etc.) feliz, acertado; oportuno

felicity *n* felicidad, dicha, *f*

feline *a* felino, gatuno, de gato. *n* felino, *m*

fell *n* (skin) piel, *f*; (upland) altura, cuesta de montaña, *f*. *a* cruel, feroz; (unhappy) aciago, funesto. *vt* talar, cortar; (knock down) derribar; *sew* sobrecoser

feller *n* talador, leñador, *m*

felling *n* corta, tala, *f*

fellow *n* compañero (-ra); (equal) igual, *mf*; (in crime) cómplice, *mf*; (man) hombre, *m*; (boy, youth) chico, *m*; (colleague) colega, *m*; (of a society) miembro, *m*; (of a pair of objects) pareja, *f*; *inf* tipo, chico, *m*. **He's a good f.,** Es un buen chico. **How are you, old f.?** ¡Hombre! ¿Cómo estás? **f.-citizen,** conciudadano (-na). **f.-countryman,** compatriota, *m*; paisano (-na). **f.-creature,** semejante, *mf* **f.-feeling,** simpatía, comprensión mutua, *f*. **f.-member,** compañero (-ra); colega, *m*. **f.-passenger,** compañero (-ra) de viaje. **f.-prisoner,** compañero (-ra) de prisión. **f.-student,** condiscípulo (-la). **f.-worker,** compañero (-ra) de trabajo; (collaborator) colaborador (-ra); (colleague) colega, *m*

fellowship *n* coparticipación, *f*; (companionship) compañerismo, *m*; (brotherhood) comunidad, confraternidad, *f*; (society) asociación, *f*; (grant) beca, *f*; (of a university) colegiatura, *f*

felon *n* reo, criminal, *mf*; felón (-ona); malvado (-da); (swelling) panadizo, *m*

felonious *a* criminal; pérfido, traidor

felony *n* felonía, *f*

felt *n* fieltro, *m*. **a f. hat,** un sombrero de fieltro

female *n* hembra, *f*, *a* femenino. (**f.** is often rendered in Sp. by the feminine ending of the noun, e.g. **a f. cat,** una gata; **a f. friend,** una amiga.) **This is a f. animal,** Este animal es una hembra. **f. screw,** hembra de tornillo, tuerca, *f*

feminine *a* femenino; mujeril, afeminado. **in the f. gender,** en el género femenino

feminism *n* feminismo, *m*

feminist *n* feminista, *mf*

feministic *a* feminista

femur *n anat* fémur, *m*

fen *n* marjal, pantano, *m*

fence *n* cerca, *f*; (of stakes) estacada, palizada, *f*; (hedge) seto, *m*; (fencing) esgrima, *f*; *mech* guía, *f*; *inf* comprador (-ra) de efectos robados. *vi* esgrimir; *fig* defenderse; *inf* recibir efectos robados. *vt* cercar; estacar; *fig* defender; proteger. **to sit on the f.,** *fig* estar a ver venir

fencer *n* esgrimidor, *m*

fencing *n* esgrima, *f*; palizada, empalizada, *f*. **f. mask,** careta, *f*. **f. master,** maestro de esgrima, maestro de armas, *m*. **f. match,** asalto de esgrima, *m*

fencesitter *n* bailarín de la cuerda flaja, *m*

fend (off) *vt* parar; defenderse de, guardarse de. *vi* (for) mantener, cuidar de. **to f. for oneself,** ganarse la vida; defenderse

fender *n* (round hearth) guardafuegos, *m*; *naut* espolón, *m*, defensas, *f pl*; *aut* parachoques, *m*

fennel *n bot* hinojo, *m*

ferment *n* fermento, *m*; fermentación, *f*; *fig* agitación, conmoción, efervescencia *f*. *vt* hacer fermentar; *fig* agitar, excitar. *vi* fermentar, estar en fermentación; *fig* hervirse, agitarse, excitarse

fermentation *n* fermentación, *f*

fern *n* helecho, *m*

ferny *a* cubierto de helechos

ferocious *a* feroz, bravo, salvaje

ferocity *n* ferocidad, braveza, fiereza, *f*

ferreous *a* férreo

ferret *n zool* hurón (-ona); **to f. out,** cazar con hurones; (discover) husmear, descubrir

Ferris wheel *n* estrella giratoria, gran rueda, novia, rueda de feria, *f*

ferroconcrete *n* hormigón armado, *m*

ferrous *a* ferroso

ferruginous *a* ferruginoso; aherrumbrado, rojizo

ferrule *n* herrete, regatón, *m*, contera, *f*; garrucha de tornillos, *f*

ferry *n* barca de transporte, *f*; barca de pasaje, *f*, transbordador, *m*. *vt* transportar de una a otra orilla, llevar en barca. *vi* cruzar un río en barca. **ferry across** *vt* transbordar. **F.-Command,** servicio de entrega y transporte de aeroplanos, *m*

ferryman *n* barquero, *m*

fertile *a* fértil, fecundo; (rich) pingüe; *fig* prolífico, abundante

Fertile Crescent, the el Creciente Fértil *m*

fertility *n* fertilidad, fecundidad, *f*

fertilization *n biol* fecundación, *f*; *agr* fertilización, *f*, abono, *m*

fertilize *vt biol* fecundar; *agr* fertilizar, abonar

fertilizer *n* abono, *m*

ferule *n* palmatoria, palmeta, férula, *f*

fervent *a* ardiente; fervoroso, intenso; (enthusiastic) entusiasta, apasionado

fervently *adv* con fervor, con vehemencia

fervor *n* ardor, fervor, *m*, pasión, *f*; (enthusiasm) entusiasmo, celo, *m*; vehemencia, *f*

festal *a* de fiesta; alegre, festivo, regocijado

fester *vi* ulcerarse, enconarse; *fig* inflamarse, amargarse. *vt* ulcerar

festival *a* de fiesta. *n* festividad, *f*; *ecc* fiesta, *f*; (musical, etc.) festival, *m*

festive *a* de fiesta; festivo, alegre

festivity *n* festividad, fiesta, *f*; (merriment) alegría, *f*, júbilo, *m*

festoon *n* festón, *m*, guirnalda, *f*. *vt* festonear

festschrift *n* libro de homenaje, libro jubilar, *m*

fetal *a* fetal

fetch *vt* traer; ir a buscar; ir por; llevar; (conduct) conducir; (of tears) hacer derramar lágrimas, hacer saltársele las lágrimas; (blood) hacer correr la sangre; (produce, draw) sacar; (a blow, a sigh) dar; (acquire) conseguir; (charm) fascinar; (of price) venderse por. **to go and f.,** ir a buscar. **to f. and carry,** *vt* (news) divulgar, publicar. *vi* estar ocupado en oficios humildes, trajinar. **to f. away,** llevarse; ir a buscar; venir a buscar. **to f. back,** devolver; (of persons) traer (a casa, etc.); traer otra vez. **to f. down,** bajar, llevar abajo; hacer bajar. **to f. in,** hacer entrar; (place inside) poner adentro; (persons and things) llevar adentro. **to f. out,** hacer salir; (bring out things) sacar; (put out) poner afuera; (an idea, etc.) sacar a relucir. **to f. up,** (a parcel, etc.) subir; (a person) hacer subir; llevar arriba

fete *n* fiesta, *f*

fetid *a* fétido, hediondo

fetidness *n* fetidez, *f*, hedor, *m*

fetish *n* fetiche, *m*

fetishism *n* fetichismo, *m*

fetter *n* grillete, *m*; *pl* **fetters,** grillos, *m pl*, cadenas, *f pl*; prisión, cárcel, *f*. *vt* encadenar, atar

fettle *n* condición, *f*, estado, *m*

fetus *n* feto, *m*

feud *n* enemistad, riña, *f*; (feudal law) feudo, *m*

feudal *a* feudal. **f. lord,** señor feudal, señor de horca y cuchillo, *m*

feudalism *n* feudalismo, *m*

feudatory *a* and *n* feudatario (-ia)

fever *n* fiebre, *f*; calentura, *f*; (enthusiasm) pasión, afición, *f*. **to be in a f.,** tener fiebre; (agitated) estar muy agitado. **to be in a f. to,** estar muy impaciente de. **puerperal f.,** fiebre puerperal, *f*. **tertian f.,** fiebre terciana, *f*. **yellow f.,** fiebre amarilla, *f*

feverish *a* febril; *fig* ardiente, febril, vehemente. **to grow f.**, empezar a tener fiebre, acalenturarse

feverishness *n* calentura, *f*; (impatience) impaciencia, *f*

few *a* and *n* pocos, *m pl*; pocas, *f pl*; algunos, *m pl*; algunas, *f pl*; (few in number) número pequeño (de), *m*. **a good f.**, bastantes, *mf pl*. **not a f.**, no pocos, *m pl*, (pocas, *f pl*). **the f.**, la minoría, *f*. **f. and far between,** raramente, en raras ocasiones; pocos y contados **fewer** *a comp* menos. **The f. the better,** Cuantos menos mejor

fewest *a sup* (el) menos, *m*; el menor número (de), *m*; (el) menos posible de, *m*

fewness *n* corto número, *m*

fez *n* fez, *m*

fiancé(e) *n* novio (-ia); desposado (-da), prometido (-da)

fiasco *n* fiasco, mal éxito, fracaso, malogro, *m*

fiat *n* fiat, mandato, *m*, orden, *f*

fib *n* mentirilla, *f*, *vt* decir mentirillas, mentir

fibber *n* embustero (-ra), mentiroso (-sa)

fiber *n* fibra, *f*; filamento, *m*, hebra, *f*; (of grass, etc.) brizna, *f*; *fig* naturaleza, *f*

fibroid *a* fibroso. *n* fibroma, *m*

fibrous *a* fibroso

fibula *n* *anat* peroné, *m*

fichu *n* pañoleta, *f*, fichú, *m*

fickle *a* inconstante; mudable; (of persons) liviano, ligero, voluble

fickleness *n* inconstancia, *f*; mudanza, *f*; liviandad, ligereza, veleidad, volubilidad, *f*

fiction *n* ficción, *f*; invención, *f*; literatura narrativa, *f*; novelas, *f pl*. **legal f.,** ficción legal, ficción de derecho, *f*

fictitious *a* ficticio; imaginario; fingido

fictitiousness *n* carácter ficticio, *m*; falsedad, *f*

fiddle *n* violín, *m*. *vt* tocar . . . en el violín. *vi* tocar el violín; (fidget) jugar; perder el tiempo. **to play second f.,** tocar el segundo violín, *fig* ser plato de segunda mesa

fiddler *n* violinista, *mf*

fiddling *a* insignificante, trivial, frívolo

fidelity *n* fidelidad, *f*

fidget *vi* estar nervioso, estar inquieto; impacientarse; trajinar; (with) jugar con. *vt* molestar; impacientar

fidgetiness *n* inquietud, nerviosidad, *f*

fidgety *a* inquieto, nervioso. **to be f.,** tener hormiguillo

fiduciary *a* fiduciario. *n* fideicomisario (-ia)

fief *n* feudo, *m*

field *n* campo, *m*; (meadow) prado, *m*, pradera, *f*; (sown field) sembrado, *m*; (phys, her) campo, *m*; (of ice) banco, *m*; *min* yacimiento, *m*; (background) fondo, *m*; (campaign) campaña, *f*; (battle) batalla, lucha, *f*; (space) espacio, *m*; (of knowledge, etc.) especialidad, esfera, *f*; (hunting) caza, *f*; *sport* campo, *m*; (competitors) todos los competidores en una carrera, etc.; (horses in a race) el campo. *a* campal, pradeño; de campo; de los campos. *vt* *sport* parar y devolver la pelota. **in the f.,** *mil* en el campo de batalla, en campaña. **magnetic f.,** campo magnético, *m*. **to take the f.,** entrar en campaña. **f.-artillery,** artillería ligera, artillería montada, *f*. **f.-day,** (holiday) día de asueto, *m*; (day out) día en el campo, *m*; *mil* día de maniobras, *m*. **f.-glasses,** anteojos, gemelos, *m pl*. **f.-hospital,** hospital de sangre, *m*; ambulancia fija, *f*. **f.-kitchen,** cocina de campaña, *f*. **f.-marshal,** capitán general de ejército, *m*. **f.-mouse,** ratón silvestre, *m*. **f. of battle,** campo de batalla, *m*. **f. of vision,** campo visual, *m*. **f.-telegraph,** telégrafo de campaña, *m*

fielder *n* (baseball) jardinero (-ra)

field work prácticas de campo, *f pl*

fiend *n* diablo, demonio, *m*; malvado (-da); (addict) adicto (-ta). **morphia f.,** morfinómano (-na)

fiendish *a* diabólico, infernal; malvado, cruel, malévolo

fiendishness *n* perversidad, crueldad, *f*

fierce *a* salvaje, feroz, cruel; (of the elements) violento, furioso; (intense) intenso, vehemente

fiercely *adv* ferozmente; violentamente, con furia; intensamente, con vehemencia

fierceness *n* ferocidad, fiereza, *f*; violencia, furia, *f*; intensidad, vehemencia, *f*

fieriness *n* ardor, *m*; (flames) las llamas, *f pl*; (redness) rojez, *f*; (irritability) ferocidad, irritabilidad, *f*; (vehemence) pasión, vehemencia, *f*; (of horses) fogosidad, *f*

fiery *a* ardiente; (red) rojo; (irritable) feroz, colérico, irritable; (vehement) apasionado, vehemente; (of horses) fogoso

fife *n* *mus* pífano, pito, *m*

fifteen *a* and *n* quince *m*.; (of age) quince años, *m pl*

fifteenth *a* and *n* décimoquinto *m*.; (part) quinzavo, *m*, décimoquinta parte, *f*; (of the month) (el) quince, *m*; (of monarchs) quince; *mus* quincena, *f*

fifth *a* quinto; (of monarchs) quinto; (of the month) (el) cinco. *n* quinto, *m*; (part) quinto, *m*, quinta parte, *f*; *mus* quinta, *f*, **Charles V,** Carlos quinto. **f. column,** quinta columna, *f*

fifthly *adv* en quinto lugar

fiftieth *a* quincuagésimo; (part) quincuagésima parte, *f*, cincuentavo, *m*

fifty *a* and *n* cincuenta *m*.; (of age) cincuenta años, *m pl*

fiftyfold *a* and *adv* cincuenta veces

fig *n* higo, *m*; (tree) higuera, *f*; *fig* bledo, ardite, *m*. **green fig,** higo, *m*, breva, *f*. **I don't care a fig,** No se me da un higo. **to be not worth a fig,** no valer un ardite. **fig-leaf,** hoja de higuera, *f*; *fig* hoja de parra, *f*

fight *n* lucha, pelea, *f*, combate, *m*; batalla, *f*; (struggle) lucha, *f*; (quarrel) riña, pelea, *f*; (conflict) conflicto, *m*; (valor) coraje, brío, *m*. **hand-to-hand** *f*, cachetina, *f*. **in fair f.,** en buena lid. **to have a f.,** tener una pelea. **to show f.,** mostrarse agresivo

fight *vt* luchar contra, batirse con; (a battle) dar (batalla); (oppose) oponer; (defend) defender, pelear por; hacer batirse. *vi* luchar, batirse, pelear; (with words) disputar; (struggle) luchar; (make war) hacer la guerra; (in a tournament) tornear. **to f. one's way,** abrirse paso con las armas. **to f. against,** luchar contra. **to f. off,** librarse de; sacudirse. **to f. with,** luchar con; pelear con; reñir con

fighter *n* luchador (-ra); combatiente, *m*; guerrero, *m*; duelista, *m*; (boxer) boxeador, *m*; *aer* (avión de) caza, *m*. **night f.,** *aer* (avión de) caza nocturno, *m*. **f.-bomber,** *aer* caza bombardero, *m*. **F. Command,** *aer* servicio de aviones de caza, *m*

fighting *n* lucha, *f*, combate, *m*; el pelear; (boxing) boxeo, *m*, *a* combatiente; (bellicose) agresivo, belicoso. **f.-man,** combatiente, guerrero, *m*

figment *n* ficción, invención, *f*

figurative *a* figurado, metafórico; figurativo; simbólico

figuratively *adv* en sentido figurativo; metafóricamente

figure *n* figura, *f*; forma, *f*; (statue) estatua, figura, *f*; (of a person) silueta, *f*; talle, *m*; (number) cifra, *f*, número, *m*; (quantity) cantidad, *f*; (price) precio, *m*; *geom*, *gram*, *dance* (skating) figura, *f*; (appearance) presencia, *f*, aire, *m*; (picture) imagen, *m*; (on fabric) diseño, *m*; *mus* cifra, *f*; *pl* **figures,** aritmética, *f*, matemáticas, *f pl*. *vt* figurar; (imagine) figurarse, imaginar; *mus* cifrar. *vi* figurar, hacer un papel; (calculate) calcular, hacer cuentas. **to f. out,** calcular; (a problem, etc.) resolver. **a fine f. of a woman,** *inf* una real hembra, *f*, maniquí, *m*. **to be good at figures,** estar fuerte en matemáticas. **to cut a f.,** *fig* hacer figura. **to have a good f.,** tener buen talle. **f. of speech,** figura retórica, figura de dicción, *f*; (manner of speaking) metáfora *f*. **f. dance,** baile de figuras, *m*, contradanza, *f*. **f.-head,** *naut* mascarón, *m*, (or figura, *f*) de proa; *fig* figura decorativa, *f*

figured *a* estampado, con diseños, labrado

figurine *n* figurilla, *f*

filament *n* filamento, *m*; hebra, *f*

filamentous *a* filamentoso, fibroso

filbert *n* avellana, *f*; (tree) avellano, *m*

filch *vt* sisar, ratear

filching *n* sisa, *f*

file *n* (line) fila, hilera, sarta, línea, *f; mil* fila, *f;* (tool) lima, *f;* (rasp) escofina, *f;* (list) lista, *f,* catálogo, *m;* (for documents) carpeta, *f,* cartapacio, *m;* (bundle of papers) legajo, *m;* (for bills, letters, etc.) clasificador, *m;* archivo, *m;* (in an archives) expediente *m.* **in a f.,** en fila; en cola

file *vt* hacer marchar en fila; (smooth) limar; (literary work) pulir; (classify) clasificar; (note particulars) fichar; (keep) guardar; (a petition, etc.) presentar, registrar. *vi* marchar en fila. **to f. in,** entrar en fila. **to f. off,** desfilar. **to file a brief,** presentar un escrito. **to f. letters,** clasificar correspondencia. **to f. past,** *mil* desfilar

filial *a* filial

filiation *n* filiación, *f*

filibuster *n* filibustero, pirata, *m*

filigree *n* filigrana, *f, a* afiligranado

filing *n* (with a tool) limadura, *f;* clasificación, *f;* (of a petition, etc.) presentación, *f,* registro, *m; pl* **filings,** limaduras, *f pl,* retales, *m pl.* **f.-cabinet,** fichero, *m.* **f.-card,** ficha, *f*

fill *vt* llenar; (stuff) rellenar; (appoint to a post) proveer; (occupy a post) desempeñar; (imbue) henchir; (saturate) saturar; (occupy) ocupar; (a tooth) empastar; (fulfil) cumplir; (charge, fuel) cargar; (with food) hartar. *vi* llenarse. **fill an order,** servir un pedido. **fill a prescription,** surtir una receta. **to f. the chair,** ocupar la presidencia; (university) ocupar la cátedra. **to f. the place of,** ocupar el lugar de; substituir; suplir. **It will be difficult to find someone to f. his place,** Será difícil de encontrar uno que haga lo que hizo él. **to f. to the brim,** llenar hasta los bordes. **to f. in, f. out,** (a form) llenar (or completar) (una hoja); (insert) insertar, añadir; (a hollow) terraplenar. **to f. out,** or hinchar. *vi* hincharse; echar carnes; (of the face) redondearse. **to f. up,** colmar, llenar hasta los bordes; (an office) proveer; (block) macizar; (a form) completar, llenar

fillet *n* venda, cinta, *f;* (of meat or fish) filete, *m;* (of meat) solomillo, *m; arch* filete, *m. vt* atar con una venda o cinta; *cul* cortar en filetes

filling *n* envase, *m;* (swelling) henchimiento, *m;* (of a tooth) empastadura, *f;* (in or up, of forms, etc.) llenar, *m.* **f. station,** depósito de gasolina, *m*

fillip *n* capirotazo, *m;* (stimulus) estímulo, *m;* (trifle) bagatela, *f. vt and vi* dar un capirotazo (a); *vt* estimular, incitar

filly *n* jaca, potra, *f*

film *n* (on liquids) tela, *f;* membrana, *f;* (coating) capa ligera, *f;* (on eyes) tela, *f;* (cinema) película, cinta, *f; phot* película, *f; fig* velo, *m;* nube, *f, vi* cubrirse de un velo, etc. *vt* cubrir de un velo, etc.; filmar, fotografiar para el cine. **roll f.,** película fotográfica, *f.* **silent f.,** película muda, *f.* **talking f.,** película sonora, *f.* **to shoot a f.,** hacer una película. **to take part in a f.,** actuar, *or* tomar parte, en una película. **f. pack,** película en paquetes *f.* **f. star,** estrella de la pantalla (or del cine), *f*

film industry industria fílmica, *f*

filminess *n* transparencia, diafanidad, *f*

filmy *a* transparente, diáfano

filter *n* filtro, *m. vt* filtrar. *vi* infiltrarse; (*fig* of news) trascender, divulgarse. **f.-bed,** filtro, *m.* **f.-paper,** papel filtro, *m*

filth *n* inmundicia, suciedad, *f; fig* corrupción, *f; fig* obscenidad, *f*

filthiness *n* suciedad, *f;* escualidez, *f; fig* asquerosidad, *f; fig* obscenidad, *f*

filthy *a* inmundo, sucio; escuálido; *fig* asqueroso; *fig* obsceno

filtrate *n* filtrado, *m, vt* filtrar

filtration *n* filtración, *f*

fin *n* (of fish) aleta, ala, *f;* (of whale) barba, *f; aer* aleta, *f*

final *a* último, final; (conclusive) conclusivo, decisivo, terminante. *n sport* finales, *m pl; univ* último examen, *m.* **f. blow,** *fig* golpe decisivo, *m.* **f. cause,** *phil* causa final, *f*

finale *n* final, *m*

finalist *n sport* finalista, *mf*

finality *n* finalidad, *f;* (decision) determinación, resolución, decisión, *f*

finally *adv* por fin, finalmente, por último, a la postre; (irrevocably) irrevocablemente

finance *n* hacienda pública, *f,* asuntos económicos, *m pl;* finanzas, *f pl. vt* financiar

financial *a* financiero, monetario. **f. year,** año económico, *m*

financially *adv* del punto de vista financiero

financier *n* financiero, *m*

find *vt* encontrar, hallar; (discover) descubrir, dar con; (invent) inventar, crear; (supply) facilitar, proporcionar; (provide) proveer; (instruct) instruir; *law* declarar. *vi law* fallar, dar sentencia. *n* hallazgo, *m;* descubrimiento, *m.* **I found him out a long time ago,** *fig* Hace tiempo que me di cuenta de cómo era él. **I found it possible to go out,** Me fue posible salir. **The judge found them guilty,** El juez les declaró culpables. **to f. a verdict,** *law* dar sentencia, fallar. **to f. one's way,** encontrar el camino. **to f. oneself,** hallarse, verse, encontrarse. **to f. out,** averiguar, descubrir. **to f. out about,** informarse sobre (or de)

finder *n* hallador (-ra); (inventor) inventor (-ra), descubridor (-ra); (telescope, camera) buscador, *m*

finding *n* hallazgo, *m;* (discovery) descubrimiento, *m; law* fallo, *m,* sentencia, *f*

fine *n* multa, *f;* (end) fin, *m.* **in f.,** en fin, en resumen

fine *vt* multar, cargar una multa de

fine *a* (thin) delgado; (sharp) agudo; (delicate) fino, delicado; (minute) menudo; (refined) refinado, puro; (healthy) saludable; (of weather) bueno; magnífico; (beautiful) hermoso, lindo; excelente; (perfect) perfecto; (good) bueno; elegante; (showy) ostentoso, vistoso; (handsome) guapo; (subtle) sutil; (acute) agudo; (noble) noble; (eminent, accomplished) distinguido, eminente; (polished) pulido; (affected) afectado; (clear) claro; (transparent) transparente, diáfano. *adv* muy bien. **a f. upstanding young man,** un buen mozo. **a f. upstanding young woman,** una real moza. **He's a f. fellow,** (ironically) Es una buena pieza. **That is all very f. but . . . ,** Todo eso está muy bien pero. . . . **to become f.,** (weather) mejorar

finely *adv* finamente; menudamente; elegantemente; (ironically) lindamente

fineness *n* (thinness) delgadez, *f;* (excellence) excelencia, *f;* delicadeza, *f;* (softness) suavidad, *f;* elegancia, *f;* (subtlety) sutileza, *f;* (acuteness) agudeza, *f;* (perfection) perfección, *f;* (nobility) nobleza, *f;* (beauty) hermosura, *f*

finery *n* galas, *f pl,* atavíos magníficos, *m pl;* adornos, *m pl;* primor, *m,* belleza, *f*

finesse *n* sutileza, diplomacia, *f;* estratagema, artificio, *m;* (cunning) astucia, *f, vi* valerse de estratagemas y artificios

finger *n* dedo, *m;* (of a clock, etc.) manecilla, *f;* (measurement) dedada, *f; fig* mano, *f. vt* manosear, tocar; (soil) ensuciar con los dedos; (steal) sisar; (*mus* a keyed instrument) teclear, (a stringed instrument) tocar. **first f.,** dedo índice, *m.* **fourth f.,** dedo anular, *m.* **little f.,** dedo meñique, *m.* **second f.,** dedo de en medio, dedo del corazón, *m.* **to burn one's fingers,** quemarse los dedos; *fig* cogerse los dedos. **to have at one's f.-tips,** *fig* saber al dedillo. **f.-board,** (of piano) teclado, *m;* (of stringed instruments) diapasón, *m.* **f.-bowl,** lavadedos, lavafrutas, *m.* **finger's breadth,** dedo, *m.* **f.-mark,** huella digital, *f.* **f.-nail,** uña del dedo, *f.* **f.-print,** impresión digital, *f.* **f.-stall,** dedil, *m.* **f.-tip,** punta del dedo, yema del dedo, *f.* **f.-wave,** peinado al agua, *m*

fingered *a* (in compounds) con dedos, que tiene los dedos . . .

fingering *n* (touching) manoseo, *m; mus* digitación, *f;* (*mus* the keys) tecleo, *m;* (wool) estambre, *m*

finial *n* pináculo, *m*

finicky *a* (of persons) dengoso, remilgado; (of things) nimio

finish *n* fin, *m*, conclusión, terminación, *f*; (final touch) última mano, *f*; perfección, *f*; (of an article) acabado, *m*; *sport* llegada, (*horse race*) meta, *f*. *vt* terminar, acabar, concluir; llevar a cabo, poner fin a; (perfect) perfeccionar; (put finishing touch to) dar la última mano a; (kill) matar; (exhaust) agotar, rendir; (overcome) vencer. *vi* acabar; concluirse. **to f. off,** acabar, terminar; (kill) matar, acabar con; (destroy) destruir. **to f. up,** acabar; (eat) comer; (drink) beber

finishable *a* acabable

finished *a* acabado, terminado, completo; perfecto; (careful) cuidadoso

finished goods *n pl* bienes terminados, *m pl*

finisher *n* terminador (-ra), acabador (-ra); pulidor (-ra); (final blow) golpe de gracia, *m*

finishing *a* concluyente. *n* terminación, *f*, fin, *m*; perfección, *f*; (last touch) última mano, *f*. **to put the f. touch,** dar la última pincelada

finite *a* finito

Finland Finlandia, *f*

Finn *n* finlandés (-esa)

Finnish *a* finlandés. *n* (language) finlandés, *m*

fir *n* abeto, sapino, pino, *m*. **red fir,** pino silvestre, *m*. **fir-cone,** piña de abeto, *f*. **fir grove,** abetal *m*

fire *n* fuego, *m*; (conflagration) incendio, *m*; (on the hearth) lumbre, *f*, fuego, *m*; *fig* ardor, *m*, pasión, *f*; (shooting) fuego, tiro, *m*. **by f. and sword,** a sangre y fuego. **by the f.,** cerca del fuego; (in a house) al lado de la chimenea. **long-range f.,** *mil* fuego de largo alcance, *m*. **short-range f.,** *mil* fuego de corto alcance, *m*. **on f.,** en fuego, ardiendo, en llamas; *fig* impaciente; *fig* lleno de pasión. **to be between two fires,** *fig* estar entre dos aguas. **to make a f.,** encender un fuego. **to miss f.,** no dar en el blanco, errar el tiro. **to open f.,** *mil* hacer una descarga. **to set on f.,** prender fuego a, incendiar. **to take f.,** encenderse. **under f.,** bajo fuego. **f.-alarm,** alarma de incendios, *f*. **f.-arm,** arma de fuego, *f*. **f.-box,** hogar, *m*. **f.-brand,** tea, *f*. **f.-brigade,** cuerpo de bomberos, *m*. **f.-damp,** aire detonante, grisú, *m*, mofeta, *f*. **f.-dog,** morillo, *m*. **f.-drill,** (firefighters') instrucción de bomberos, *f*, (others') simulacro de incendio, *m*. **f.-engine,** autobomba, bomba, de incendios, *f*. **f.-escape,** escalera de incendios, *f*. **f.-extinguisher,** apagador de incendio, extintor, matafuego, *m*. **f.-guard,** vigilante de incendios, *m*; alambrera, *f*. **f.-hose,** manguera de incendios, *f*. **f.-insurance,** seguro contra incendios, *m*. **f.-irons,** badil *m*. y tenazas *f pl*. **f.-lighter,** encendedor, *m*. **f.-screen,** pantalla, *f*. **f.-ship,** brulote, *m*. **f.-shovel,** badil, *m*, paleta, *f*. **f.-spotter,** vigilante de incendios, *m*. **f.-sprite,** salamandra, *f*. **f.-watching,** servicio de vigilancia de incendios, *m*

fire *vt* incendiar, prender (or pegar) fuego a; quemar; (bricks) cocer; (fire-arms) disparar; (cauterize) cauterizar; (*fig* stimulate) estimular, excitar; (inspire) inspirar; (*inf* of questions) disparar; (*inf* sack) despedir. *vi* encenderse; (shoot) hacer fuego, disparar (un tiro); (*inf* away) disparar; (up) enojarse. **to f. a salute,** disparar un saludo. *mil* **F.!** ¡Fuego!

fire department *n* parque de bomberos, servicis de bomberos, servicio de incendios, parque de bombas (Puerto Rico), *m*

firefly *n* cocuyo, *m*

fireman *n* bombero, *m*; (of an engine, etc.) fogonero, *m*. **fireman's lift,** silleta, *f*

fireplace *n* chimenea francesa, chimenea, *f*; (hearth) hogar, *m*

fireproof *a* a prueba de incendios; incombustible

firer *n* disparador, *m*

firewood *n* leña, *f*. **f. dealer,** leñador (-ra), vendedor (-ra) de leña

firework *n* fuego artificial, *m*

firing *n* (of fire-arms) disparo, *m*; (burning) incendio, *m*, quema, *f*; (of bricks, etc.) cocimiento, *m*; (of pottery)

cocción, *f*; (cauterization) cauterización, *f*; (fuel) combustible, *m*; (*inf* sacking) despedida, *f*. **within f. range,** a tiro. **f.-line,** línea de fuego, *f*. **f.-oven,** (pottery) horno alfarero, *m*. **f.-squad,** pelotón de ejecución, *m*

firm *a* firme; (strong) fuerte; (secure) seguro; sólido; (resolute) inflexible, resoluto; severo; (steady) constante; (persistent) tenaz. *n com* casa (de comercio), empresa, *f*; razón social, *f*

firmament *n* firmamento, *m*

firmly *adv* firmemente; inflexiblemente; constantemente

firmness *n* firmeza, *f*; solidez, *f*; inflexibilidad, resolución, *f*; severidad, *f*; constancia, *f*; tenacidad, *f*

first *a* primero (primer before *m sing* nouns); (of monarchs) primero; (of dates) (el) primero. *n* primero, *m*; (beginning) principio, *m*. *adv* primero, en primer lugar; (before, of time) antes; (for the first time) por primera vez; (at the beginning) al principio; (ahead) adelante. **at f.,** al principio. **from the very f.,** desde el primer momento. **to appear for the f. time,** aparecer (or presentarse) por primera vez; *theat* debutar. **to go f.,** ir delante de todos, ir a la cabeza; ir adelante. **f. and foremost,** en primer lugar; ante todo. **f.-aid,** primera cura, *f*. **f.-aid post,** casa de socorro, *f*. **f.-aider,** practicante, *m*. **f.-born,** *a* and *n* primogénito (-ta). **f.-class,** *a* de primera clase; *fig* excelente. **f.-cousin,** primo (-ma) carnal, primo (-ma) hermano (-na). **f. edition,** edición príncipe, *f*. **f. floor,** primer piso, *m*. **f. fruits,** frutos primerizos, *m pl*; *fig* primicias, *f pl*. **f.-hand,** *a* original, de primera mano. **f. letters,** primeras letras, *f pl*. **f. night,** *theat* estreno, *m*. **f. of all,** primero, ante todo. **f.-rate,** *a* de primera clase

firstly *adv* en primer lugar, primero

firth *n* ría, *f*

fiscal *a* and *n* fiscal *m*.. **f. year,** año económico, *m*

fish *n* pez, *m*; (out of the water) pescado, *m*; *inf* tipo, indivíduo, *m*. *vt* pescar; (out) sacar. *vi* pescar; *fig* buscar. **fried f.,** pescado frito, *m*. **He is a queer f.,** Es un tipo muy raro. **to be neither f. nor fowl,** no ser ni carne ni pescado. **to feel like a f. out of water,** sentirse fuera de su ambiente. **to f. in troubled waters,** A río revuelto ganancia de pescadores. **f.-eating,** *a* ictiófago. **f.-fork,** tenedor de pescado, *m*. **f.-glue,** cola de pescado, *f*. **f.-hook,** anzuelo, *m*. **f.-knife,** cuchillo de pescado, *m*. **f.-like,** de pez; como un pez; parecido a un pez. **f. roe,** hueva, *f*. **f.-server,** pala para pescado, *f*

fishbone *n* espina de pescado, raspa de pescado, *f*

fisherman *n* pescador, *m*

fishery *n* pesquería, *f*

fishing *n* pesca, *f*, a de pescar. **to go f.,** ir de pesca. **f.-boat,** bote de pesca, *m*. **f.-floats,** levas, *f pl*. **f.-line,** sedal, *m*. **f.-net,** red de pesca, *f*. **f.-reel,** carretel, carrete, *m*. **f.-rod,** caña de pesca, *f*. **f.-tackle,** aparejo de pesca, *m*. **f.-village,** pueblo de pescadores, *m*

fishmeal harina de pescado, *f*

fishmonger *n* pescadero (-ra).

fishmonger's shop pescadería, *f*

fishpond *n* vivero, *m*, piscina, *f*

fishwife *n* pescadora, *f*

fishy *a* de pescado; (of eyes, etc.) de pez, como un pez; (in smell) que huele a pescado; *inf* sospechoso; (of stories) inverosímil

fissure *n* grieta, hendidura, rendija, *f*; (*anat, geol*) fisura, *f*

fissured *a* hendido

fist *n* puño, *m*; *print* manecilla, *f*; (handwriting) letra, *f*. **with clenched fists,** a puño cerrado

fisticuff *n* puñetazo, *m*; *pl* **fisticuffs,** agarrada, riña, *f*

fit *n* espasmo, paroxismo, *m*; ataque, *m*; (impulse) acceso, arranque, *m*; (whim) capricho, *m*; (of a garment) corte, *m*; (adjustment) ajuste, encaje, *m*. **by fits and starts,** a tropezones, espasmódicamente

fit *a* a propósito (para), bueno (para); (opportune) oportuno; (proper) conveniente; apto; (decent) decente; (worthy) digno; (ready) preparado, listo; (adequate) adecuado; (capable) capaz, en estado (de);

(appropriate) apropiado; (just) justo. **It is not in a fit state to be used,** No está en condiciones para usarse. **to be not fit for,** no servir para; (through ill-health) no tener bastante salud para. **to think fit,** creer (or juzgar) conveniente. **fit for use,** usable. **fit to eat,** comestible

fit vt ajustar, acomodar, encajar; adaptar (a); (furnish) proveer (de), surtir (con); (of tailor, dressmaker) entallar, probar; (of shoemaker) calzar; (of garments, shoes) ir (bien o mal); (prepare) preparar; (go with) ser apropiado (a); (adapt itself to) adaptarse a. vi ajustarse, acomodarse, encajarse; adaptarse; (clothes) ir (bien o mal). **to fit in,** vt encajar; incluir. vi encajarse; caber; adaptarse. **to fit out,** equipar; proveer (de); preparar. **to fit up,** montar, instalar; proveer (de). **to fit with,** proveer de

fitful a intermitente; espasmódico; caprichoso

fitfully adv por intervalos, a ratos; caprichosamente

fitly adv adecuadamente; justamente; apropiadamente

fitment n equipo, m; instalación, f; (of bookcase, etc.) sección, f; (furniture) pieza, f, mueble, m

fitness n conveniencia, f; aptitud, capacidad, f; oportunidad, f; salud, f; (good health) vigor, m

fitted a (of clothes) ajustado

fitter n ajustador, m; (mechanic) armador, mecánico, m; (tailoring) cortador, m; (dressmaking) probador (-ra)

fitting n encaje, ajuste, m; adaptación, f; (of a garment) prueba, f; (size) medida, f; (installation) instalación, f; **pl. fittings,** guarniciones, fpl; instalaciones, fpl; accesorios, m pl. a conveniente, justo; apropiado; adecuado; (worthy) digno; (of coats, etc.) ajustado. **f. room,** cuarto de pruebas, m. **f. in,** encaje, m. **f. out,** equipo, m. **f. up,** arreglo, m; (of machines) montaje, m; (of a house) mueblaje, m

five a and n cinco m.; (of the clock) las cinco, f pl; (of age) cinco años, m pl. **to be f.,** tener cinco años. **f. feet deep,** de cinco pies de profundidad. **f. feet high,** cinco pies de altura. **f.-finger exercises,** ejercicios de piano, m pl. **F.-Year Plan,** Plan Quinquenal, m

fivefold a quíntuplo

fix n aprieto, apuro, m; callejón sin salida, m. vt fijar; sujetar, afianzar; (bayonets) calar; (with nails) clavar; (phot, chem, med) fijar; (decide) establecer; (a date) señalar; (eyes, attention) clavar; (on the mind) grabar, estampar; (one's hopes) poner; (base) basar, fundar; (inf put right) arreglar, componer. vi fijarse; establecerse; determinarse. **to get in a fix,** hacerse un lío. **to fix a price,** fijar un precio. **to fix on, upon,** elegir, escoger; decidir, determinar. **to fix up,** arreglar; decidir; organizar; (differences) olvidar (sus disensiones)

fixation n obsesión, idea fija, f; (scientific) fijación, f

fixative n (med, phot) fijador, m; (dyeing) mordiente, m. a que fija

fixed a fijo; inmóvil; permanente; (of ideas) inflexible. **f. bayonet,** bayoneta calada, f. **f. price,** precio fijo, m. **f. star,** estrella fija, f

fixedly adv fijamente; resueltamente; firmemente

fixing n fijación, f; afianzamiento, m; arreglo, m; (of a date) señalamiento, m. **f. bath,** phot baño fijador, m

fixity n permanencia, f; inmovilidad, f; invariabilidad, f; firmeza, f

fixture n instalación, f; accesorio fijo, m; sport partido, m; inf permanencia, f. **f. card,** sport calendario deportivo, m

fizz n espuma, f; chisporroteo, m. inf champaña, m. vi (liquids) espumear; (sputter) chisporrotear

fizzle n (failure) fiasco, fracaso, m. vi chisporrotear; (out) apagarse; (fail) fracasar, no tener éxito

fjord n fiordo, m

flabbergast vt dejar con la boca abierta, dejar de una pieza

flabbiness, flaccidity n flaccidez, flojedad, f; med reblandecimiento, m; (of character) debilidad, flaqueza del ánimo, f

flabby, flaccid a fláccido, flojo; fig débil

flag n bandera, f; pabellón, estandarte, m; (small) banderola, f; (iris) (yellow) cala, f, (purple) lirio cárdeno, m; (stone) losa, f. **to dip the f.,** saludar con la bandera. **to hoist the f.,** izar la bandera. **to strike the f.,** bajar la bandera; (in defeat) rendir la bandera. **f. bearer,** portaestandarte, abanderado, m. **f.-day,** día de la banderita, m; (in U.S.A.) día de la bandera, m. **f.-officer,** almirante, m; vicealmirante, m; jefe de escuadra, m. **f. of truce,** bandera blanca, bandera de paz, f

flag vi flaquear, debilitarse; languidecer; (wither) marchitarse; decaer, disminuir. vt adornar con banderas; (signal) hacer señales con una bandera; (for a race, etc.) marcar con banderas; (with stones) enlosar, embaldosar.

flagellant n flagelante, m

flagellate vt flagelar

flagellation n flagelación, f

flageolet n mus caramillo, m, chirimía, f. **f. player,** chirimía, m

flagging n pavimentación, f; (floor) enlosado, m. a lánguido, flojo

flagon n frasco, m; botella, f

flagrancy n escándalo, m, notoriedad, f

flagrant a escandaloso, notorio

flagship n capitana, f

flagstaff n asta de bandera, f

flagstone n losa, lancha, f

flail n mayal, m

flair n instinto natural, m, comprensión innata, f; habilidad natural, f

flak n cortina (or barrera) antiaérea, f

flake n escama, f; laminilla, hojuela, f; (of snow) copo, m; (of fire) chispa, f. vt cubrir con escamas, etc.; exfoliar; (crumble) hacer migas de, desmigajar. vi escamarse; (off) exfoliarse; caer en copos

flaky a escamoso; en laminillas; (of pastry) hojaldrado. **f. pastry,** hojaldre, f

flamboyance n extravagancia, f, lit ampulosidad, f

flamboyant a arch flamígero; extravagante, llamativo, rimbombante; (of style) ampuloso. **f. gothic,** gótico florido, m

flame n llama, f; fig fuego, m. inf amorío, m, vi flamear, llamear; arder, abrasarse; (shine) brillar; (up, fig) inflamarse; acalorarse. **f.-colored,** de color de llama, anaranjado. **f.-thrower,** lanzallamas, m

flaming a llameante; abrasador; (of colors) llamativo, chillón; (of feelings) ardiente, fervoroso, apasionado

flamingo n orn flamenco, m

Flanders flandes, m

flange n mech reborde, m, vt rebordear

flank n (of animal) ijada, f; (human) costado, m; (of hill, etc.) lado, m, falda, f; mil flanco, m. a (mil nav) por el flanco. vt lindar con, estar contiguo a; (mil, nav) flanquear. vi estar al lado de; tocar a, lindar con.

flannel n franela, f, a de franela

flannelette n moletón, m

flap n golpe, m; (of a sail) zapatazo, m, sacudida, f; (of a pocket) cartera, tapa, f; (of skin) colgajo, m; (of a shoe, etc.) oreja, f; (of a shirt, etc.) falda, f; (of a hat) ala, f; (of trousers) bragueta, f; (rever) solapa, f; (of a counter) trampa, f; (of a table) hoja plegadiza, f; (of the wings) aletazo, m; (of w.c.) tapa, f. vt sacudir, golpear, batir; agitar; (the tail) menear. vi agitarse; (of wings) aletear; (of sails) zapatear, sacudirse; colgar. **f.-eared,** de orejas grandes y gachas

flapjack n cul torta de sartén, f; (for powder) polvorera, f

flapper n inf polla, tobillera, chica "topolino," f

flapping n batimiento, m; (waving) ondulación, f; (of sails) zapatazo, m; (of wings) aleteo, m

flare n fulgor, m, llama, f; hacha, f; aer cohete de señales, m; sew vuelo, m. vi relampaguear, fulgurar; brillar; (of a lamp) llamear; (up) encolerizarse; salirse de tino; (of epidemic) declararse; (war, etc.) desencadenarse

flash n relámpago, centelleo, m, ráfaga de luz, f; brillo,

m; (from a gun) fuego, fogonazo, *m*; (of wit, genius) rasgo, *m*; (of joy, etc.) acceso, *m*. *vi* relampaguear, fulgurar, centellear; brillar; cruzar rápidamente, pasar como un relámpago. *vt* hacer relampaguear; hacer brillar; (a look, etc.) dar; lanzar; (light) encender; (powder) quemar; transmitir señales por heliógrafo; *inf* sacar a relucir, enseñar. **shoulder-f.,** *mil* emblema, *m*. **to be gone like a f.,** desaparecer como un relámpago. **to f. out,** brillar, centellear. **f. of lightning,** relámpago, rayo, *m*. **f. of wit,** agudeza, *f*, rasgo de,ingenio, *m*

flashback *n* episodio intercalado, *m*, retrospección, *f*

flashily *adv* llamativamente, con mal gusto

flashing *n* centelleo, *m*, llamarada, *f*. *a* centellador, relampagueante; brillante; chispeante

flashlight *n* luz de magnesio, *f*; (torch) lamparilla eléctrica, *f*, rayo, *m* (Mexico); **f. photograph,** magnesio, *m*

flashy *a* llamativo, de mal gusto, charro; frívolo, superficial

flask *n* frasco, *m*, redoma, botella, *f*; (for powder) frasco, *m*; (vacuum) termos, *m*

flat *a* llano; (smooth) liso; (lying) tendido, tumbado; (flattened) aplastado; (destroyed) arrasado; (stretched out) extendido; (of nose, face) chato, romo; (of tire) desinflado; (uniform) uniforme; (depressed) desanimado; (uninteresting) monótono; (boring) aburrido; *com* paralizado; (downright) categórico; absoluto; (net) neto; *mus* bemol; (of boats) de fondo plano. *adv* See **flatly.** *n* planicie, *f*; (of a sword) hoja, *f*; (of the hand) palma, *f*; (land) llanura, *f*; (apartment) piso, *m*; *mus* bemol, *m*. **to fall f.,** caer de bruces; *fig* no tener éxito. **to make f.,** allanar. **to sing f.,** desafinar. **f. boat,** barco de fondo plano, *m*. **f.-footed,** de pies achatados; *fig* pedestre. **f.-iron,** plancha, *f*. **f. roof,** azotea, *f*

flatly *adv* de plano; a nivel; (plainly) llanamente, netamente; (dully) indiferentemente; (categorically) categóricamente

flatness *n* planicie, *f*; llanura, *f*; (smoothness) lisura, *f*; (evenness) igualdad, *f*; (uninterestingness) insulsez, insipidez, *f*; aburrimiento, *m*; (depression) desaliento, abatimiento, *m*

flatten *vt* aplanar, allanar; aplastar; (smooth) alisar; (even) igualar; (destroy) derribar, arrasar, destruir; (dismay) desconcertar; (out) extender. *vi* aplanarse, allanarse; aplastarse

flattening *n* achatamiento, *m*, allanamiento, *m*; aplastamiento, *m*; igualación, *f*

flatter *vt* adular, lisonjear, halagar; (of a dress, photograph, etc.) favorecer, (please the senses) regalar, deleitar; (oneself) felicitarse

flatterer *n* adulador (-ra), lisonjero (-ra)

flattering *a* adulador, lisonjero; (promising) halagüeño; favoreciente; deleitoso

flattery *n* adulación, *f*

flat tire llanta desinflada, *f*

flatulence *n* flatulencia, *f*

flatulent *a* flatulento

flaunt *vi* (flutter) ondear; pavonearse. *vt* desplegar; ostentar, sacar a relucir; enseñar

flaunting *n* ostentación, *f*; alarde, *m*. *a* ostentoso; magnífico; (fluttering) ondeante

flautist *n* flautista, *mf*

flavor *n* sabor, gusto, *m*; *cul* condimento, *m*; *fig* dejo, *m*. *vt cul* sazonar, condimentar; dar un gusto (de), hacer saborear (a); *fig* dar un dejo (de)

flavored *a* (in compounds) de sabor . . . ; sazonado; que tiene sabor de . . .

flavoring *n cul* condimento, *m*; *fig* sabor, dejo, *m*

flavorless *a* insípido, soso, sin sabor

flaw *n* desperfecto, *m*, imperfección, *f*; (crack) grieta, hendedura, *f*; (in wood, metals) quebraja, *f*; (in gems) pelo, *m*; (in fruit) maca, *f*; (in cloth) gabarro, *m*; *fig* defecto, error, *m*; (wind) ráfaga de viento, *f*

flawless *a* sin defecto; perfecto; impecable

flawlessness *n* perfección, *f*; impecabilidad, *f*

flax *n* lino, *m*. **to dress f.,** rastrillar lino. **f.-comb,** rastrillo, *m*. **f. field,** linar, *m*

flaxen *a* de lino; (fair) rubio, blondo. **f.-haired,** de pelo rubio

flay *vt* desollar; (criticize) despellejar

flaying *n* desuello, *m*, desolladura, *f*

flea *n* pulga, *f*. **f. bite,** picada de pulga, *f*

fleck *n* pinta, mancha, *f*, lunar, *m*; (of sun) mota, *f*; (speck) partícula, *f*; (freckle) peca, *f*. *vt* abigarrar; manchar; (dapple) salpicar, motear

fledged *a* emplumecido, plumado; alado; *fig* maduro

fledgeling *n* volantón, *m*; *fig* niño (-ña); *fig* novato (-ta)

flee *vi* huir, fugarse, escapar; (vanish) desaparecer; (avoid) evitar, huir de. *vt* abandonar

fleece *n* vellón, *m*; lana, *f*; toisón, *m*. *vt* esquilar; *fig inf* pelar. **Order of the Golden F.,** Orden del Toisón de Oro, *f*

fleecy *a* lanudo, lanar; (white) blanquecino; (of clouds) borreguero. **f. clouds,** borregos, *m pl*

fleet *n* (navy) armada, *f*; escuadra, flota, *f*; *fig* serie, *f*, *a* alado, rápido, veloz. **F. Air Arm,** Aviación Naval, *f*. **f.-footed,** ligero de pies

fleeting *a* fugaz, momentáneo, efímero, pasajero

Flemish *a* flamenco. *n* (language) flamenco, *m*

flesh *n* carne, *f*; (mankind) género humano, *m*, humanidad, *f*; (of fruit) pulpa, *f*. **a man of f. and blood,** un hombre de carne y hueso. **of one's own f. and blood,** de la misma sangre de uno. **to make one's f. creep,** dar carne de gallina (a). **f.-colored,** encarnado, de color de carne. **f.-eating,** carnívoro. **f. wound,** herida superficial, *f*

fleshiness *n* carnosidad, gordura, *f*

fleshpot *n* marmita, *f*; *fig* olla, *f*. **the fleshpots of Egypt,** las ollas de Egipto

fleshy *a* carnoso, grueso; (of fruit) pulposo; suculento

fleur-de-lis *n* flor de lis, *f*

flex *n elec* flexible, *m*. *vt* doblar. *vi* doblarse

flexibility *n* flexibilidad, *f*; (of style) plasticidad, *f*; docilidad, *f*

flexible *a* flexible; dúctil, maleable; (of style) plástico; (of voice) quebradizo; adaptable; dócil

flexion *n* flexión, *f*; *gram* inflexión, *f*; *gram* flexión, *f*

flexor *n anat* músculo flexor, *m*

flick *n* golpecito, toque, *m*; (of the finger) capirotazo, *m*; *inf* cine, *m*. *vt* dar un golpecito a; dar ligeramente con un látigo; sacudir. **f. one's wrist,** hacer girar la muñeca. **to f. over the pages of,** hojear

flicker *n* estremecimiento, temblor, *m*; fluctuación, *f*; (of bird) aleteo, *m*; (of flame) onda (de una llama), *f*; (of eyelashes) pestañeo, *m*; (of a smile) indicio, *f*. *vi* agitarse; (of flags) ondear; vacilar

flickering *a* tenue; vacilante

flier *n* volador (-ra); aviador (-ra); piloto, *m*; fugitivo (-va)

flight *n* vuelo, *m*; (of bird of prey) colada, *f*; (flock of birds) bandada, *f*; (migration) migración, *f*; (of time) transcurso, *m*; (of imagination, etc.) arranque, *m*; (volley) lluvia, *f*; (of airplanes) escuadrilla (de aviones), *f*; (of stairs) tramo, tiro, *m*; (staircase) escalera, *f*; (of locks on canal, etc.) ramal, *m*; (escape) huida, fuga, *f*. **long-distance f.,** *aer* vuelo de distancia, *m*. **non-stop f.,** *aer* vuelo sin parar, *m*. **reconnaissance f.,** *aer* vuelo de reconocimiento, vuelo de patrulla, *m*. **test f.,** *aer* vuelo de pruebas, *m*. **to put to f.,** ahuyentar, poner en fuga. **to take f.,** alzar el vuelo. **f.-lieutenant,** teniente aviador, *m*. **f.-sergeant,** sargento aviador, *m*

flight attendant *n* sobrecargo, *mf*

flightiness *n* frivolidad, veleidad, ligereza, *f*

flighty *a* frívolo, inconstante, veleidoso

flimsiness *n* falta de solidez, endeblez, *f*; fragilidad, *f*; (of arguments) futilidad, *f*

flimsy *a* endeble; frágil; fútil, insubstancial

flinch *vi* echarse atrás, retirarse (ante); vacilar, titubear. **without flinching,** sin vacilar; sin quejarse

fling *vt* arrojar, echar, tirar; lanzar; (scatter) derramar; (oneself) echarse; (oneself upon) echarse encima, *fig*

confiar en. *vi* lanzarse; marcharse precipitadamente; saltar. *n* tiro, *m*; (of dice, etc.) echada, *f*; (gibe) sarcasmo, *m*, burla, chufleta, *f*; (of horse) respingo, brinco, *m*; baile escocés, *m*. **in full f.,** en plena operación; en progreso. **to have one's f.,** darse un verde, correrla. **to f. away,** *vt* desechar; (waste) desperdiciar, malgastar, perder. *vi* marcharse enfadado; marcharse rápidamente. **to f. back,** (a ball) devolver; (the head) echar atrás. **to f. down,** tirar al suelo; arrojar; derribar. **to f. off,** *vt* rechazar; apartar; (a garment, etc.) quitar. *vi* marcharse sin más ni más. **to f. oneself down,** tumbarse, echarse; despeñarse (por). **to f. oneself headlong,** despeñarse. **to f. open,** abrir violentamente, abrir de repente. **to f. out,** *vt* echar a la fuerza; (a hand) alargar, extender. *vi* salir apresuradamente. **to f. over,** (upset) volcar; arrojar por; abandonar. **to f. up,** lanzar al aire; levantar, erguir; renunciar (a), abandonar; dejar

flint *n* pedernal, *m*; (for producing fire) piedra de encendedor, *f*

flinty *a* pedernalino; *fig* endurecido

flippancy *n* levedad, ligereza, *f*; frivolidad, *f*; impertinencia, *f*

flippant *a* poco serio, ligero; frívolo; impertinente

flipper *n* aleta, *f*

flirt *n* (man) coquetón, castigador, *m*; (woman) coqueta, castigadora, *f*. *vt* (shake) sacudir; (move) agitar; (wave) menear. *vi* flirtear, coquetear (toy with) jugar con; divertirse con

flirtation *n* flirteo, amorío, *m*

flirtatious *a* (of men) galanteador, castigador; (of women) coqueta

flit *vi* revolotear, mariposear; (move silently) deslizarse, pasar silenciosamente; (depart) irse, marcharse; mudarse por los aires. **to f. about,** ir y venir silenciosamente. **to f. past,** pasar como una sombra

flitch *n* (of bacon) hoja de tocino, *f*

float *n* masa flotante, *f*; (raft) balsa, *f*; *mech* flotador, *m*; (of fishing rod or net) corcho, *m*; (of fish) vejiga natatoria, *f*; (for swimming) nadadera, calabaza, *f*; (for tableaux) carroza, *f*; *pl* **floats,** *theat* candilejas, *f pl*. *vi* flotar; (flags, hair, etc.) ondear; (wander) vagar; *naut* boyar. *vt* poner a flote; hacer flotar; (a grounded ship) desencallar; (*com* a company) fundar; (a loan, etc.) emitir, poner en circulación; (launch a ship) botar; (flood) inundar

floating *n* flotación, *f*, flote, *m*; *com* fundación (de una compañía), *f*; (of a loan) emisión, *f*; (of a ship) botadura, *f*. *a* flotante; boyante; *com* en circulación, flotante; fluctuante, variable. **f. capital,** capital fluctuante, *m*. **f. debt,** deuda flotante, *f*. **f. dock,** dique flotante, *m*. **f. light,** buque faro, *m*. **f. population,** población flotante, *f*. **f. rib,** costilla flotante, *f*

flock *n* rebaño, *m*, manada, *f*; (of birds) bandada, *f*; *fig* grey, *f*; (crowd) multitud, muchedumbre, *f*; (parishioners) congregación, *f*; (of wool or cotton) vedija (de lana or de algodón), *f*; *pl* **flocks,** (for stuffing) borra, *f*. *vi* concurrirse, reunirse, congregarse; ir en tropel, acudir; (birds) volar en bandada. **f.-bed,** colchón de borra, *m*

floe *n* banco de hielo, *m*

flog *vt* azotar; castigar

flogging *n* azotaina, vapuleo, *m*

flood *n* inundación, *f*; (Bible) diluvio, *m*; (of the tide) flujo, *m*; *fig* torrente, *m*; (abundance) copia, abundancia, *f*; (fit) paroxismo, *m*. *vt* inundar; sumergir; (of tears) mojar. *vi* desbordar. **f. lighting,** iluminación intensiva, *f*

floodgate *n* compuerta (de esclusa), *f*

flooding *n* inundación, *f*; desbordamiento, *m*; *med* hemorragia uterina, *f*

floodtide *n* marea creciente, *f*

floor *n* suelo, piso, *m*; (wooden) entarimado, *m*; (story) piso, *m*; (of a cart) cama, *f*; *agr* era, *f*. *vt* entablar; echar al suelo, derribar; *fig* desconcertar, confundir. **on the f.,** en el suelo. **on the ground f.,** en el piso bajo. **to**

take the f., *fig* tener la palabra. **f.-polisher,** lustrador de piso, *m*

flooring *n* tablado, *m*, tablazón, *f*; piso, *m*

flop *n* golpe, *m*; ruido sordo, *m*; (splash) chapoteo, *m*; *inf* fiasco, *m*. *vi* dejarse caer

flora *n* flora, *f*

floral *a* floral. **f. games,** juegos florales, *m pl*

Florence Florencia, *f*

Florentine *a* and *n* florentino (-na)

florescence *n* florescencia, *f*

florid *a* florido; demasiado ornado, cursi, llamativo; (of complexion) rubicundo

floridness *n* floridez, *f*, estilo florido, *m*; demasiada ornamentación, vulgaridad, *f*, mal gusto, *m*; (of complexion) rubicundez, *f*

florin *n* florín, *m*

florist *n* florista, *mf*

floss *n* seda floja, filoseda, *f*; (of maize) penacho, *m*; (of a cocoon) cadarzo, *m*. **f. silk,** seda floja, *f*

flotilla *n* flotilla, *f*

flotsam *n* pecio, *m*

flounce *n* volante, *m*, *vi* saltar de impaciencia. **to f. out,** salir airadamente

flounder *n* (nearest equivalent) *icht* platija, *f*; tumbo, *m*. *vi* tropezar; revolcarse; andar dificultosamente

flour *n* harina, *f*, *vt* enharinar. **f.-bin,** tina, *f*, harinero, *m*. **f. merchant,** harinero, *m*

flourish *n* movimiento, *m*; gesto, saludo, *m*; (of a pen) plumada, *f*; (on the guitar, in fencing) floreo, *m*; preludio, *m*; (fanfare) tocata (de trompetas), *f*; (of a signature) rúbrica, *f*; (in rhetoric) floreo, *m*. *vi* (of plants) vegetar; (prosper) prosperar, medrar; florecer; (of the guitar, in fencing) florear; *mus* preludiar; (with a pen) hacer plumadas (or rasgos de pluma); (of a signature) firmar con rúbrica; (sound a fanfare) hacer una tocata (de trompetas). *vt* agitar en el aire, blandir

flourishing *a* (of plants) lozano, floreciente; (prosperous) próspero; (happy) feliz

flourmill *n* molino de harina, *m*, fábrica de harina, *f*, molina harinero, *m*

floury *a* harinoso

flout *vt* burlarse de; despreciar, no hacer caso de

flow *n* flujo, *m*; corriente, *f*; chorro, *m*; (of water) caudal, *m*; (output) producción total, cantidad, *f*; (of the tide) flujo (de la marea), *m*; (of words) facilidad, *f*. *vi* fluir, manar; correr; (of the tide) crecer (la marea); (pass) pasar, correr; (result) resultar (de), provenir (de); (of hair, drapery) caer, ondular; (abound) abundar (en). **to f. away,** escaparse, salir. **to f. back,** refluir. **to f. down,** descender, fluir hacia abajo; (of tears) correr por. **to f. from,** dimanar de; manar de; *fig* provenir de. **to f. in,** llegar en abundancia. **to f. into,** (rivers) desaguar en, desembocar en. **to f. over,** derramarse por. **to f. through,** fluir por; atravesar; (water) regar. **to f. together,** (rivers) confluir

flower *n* flor, *f*; (best) flor y nata, crema, *f*. *vi* florecer. **in f.,** en flor. **No flowers by request,** (for a funeral) No flores por deseo del finado. **f.-bud,** capullo, *m*. **f.-garden,** jardín, *m*. **f. girl,** florista, vendedora de flores, *f*. **f. market,** mercado de flores, *m*. **f.-piece,** florero, *m*. **f. pot,** tiesto, *m*, maceta, *f*. **f. show,** exposición de flores, *f*. **f. vase,** florero, *m*

flowerbed *n* cuadro, macizo, *m*

flower car coche portacoronas, *m*

flowered *a* (in compounds) con flores; con dibujos de flores

floweriness *n* abundancia de flores, *f*; (of style) floridez, *f*, estilo florido, *m*

flowering *n* florecimiento, *m*. *a* floreciente; con flores; (of shrubs) de adorno. **f. season,** época de la floración, *f*

flowery *a* florido

flowing *n* flujo, *m*; derrame, *m*. *a* fluente, corriente; (of tide) creciente; (waving) ondeante; suelto; (of style) flúido

flow of capital corriente de capital, *f*

fluctuate *vi* fluctuar, vacilar; variar

fluctuating *a* fluctuante, vacilante; variable; (hesitating) irresoluto, dudoso

fluctuation *n* fluctuación, *f;* cambio, *m,* variación, *f;* (hesitancy) indecisión, vacilación, *f*

flue *n* (of a chimney) cañón, *m;* (of a boiler) tubo, *m*

fluency *n* fluidez, *f*

fluent *a* flúido; fácil

fluently *adv* corrientemente, con facilidad, de corrido

fluff *n* borra, pelusa, *f;* tamo, *m*

fluffy *a* velloso; (feathered) plumoso; (woolly) lanudo; (of hair) encrespado

fluid *n* flúido, líquido, *m, a* flúido

fluidity *n* fluidez, *f*

fluke *n* (in billiards) chiripa, *f; naut* uña, *f; inf* carambola, chiripa, chambonada, *f.* **by a f.,** de carambola, por suerte. **f.-worm,** duela del hígado, *f*

flunkey *n* lacayo, *m; fig* adulador, *m*

fluorescence *n* fluorescencia, *f*

fluorescent *a* fluorescente

fluorine *n chem* flúor, *m*

fluorite *n* fluorita, *f*

flurry *n* (of wind) ráfaga, *f;* (squall) chubasco, *m;* agitación, *f;* conmoción, *f. vt* agitar

flush *n* rubor, *m;* (in the sky) arrebol, rojo, color de rosa, *m;* emoción, *f,* acceso, *m;* sensación, *f;* (at cards) flux, *m;* vigor, *m;* (flowering) floración, *f;* abundancia, *f;* (of youth, etc.) frescura, *f. a* (level) igual, parejo; abundante; (generous) pródigo, liberal; (rich) adinerado. *vi* ruborizarse, enrojecerse, ponerse colorado; (flood) inundarse, llenarse (de agua, etc.); (of sky) arrebolarse. *vt* inundar, limpiar con un chorro de agua, etc., lavar; (of blood) circular por; (redden) enrojecer; (make blush) hacer ruborizarse; (exhilarate) excitar, animar; (inflame) inflamar, encender; (make level) igualar, nivelar. **f. with,** a ras de

flushing *n* rojez, *f;* (cleansing) limpieza, lavadura, *f;* (flooding) inundación, *f*

fluster *n* agitación, confusión, *f,* aturdimiento, *m. vt* agitar, poner nervioso (a), aturdir; (oneself) preocuparse. *vi* agitarse; estar nervioso, estar perplejo; (with drink) estar entre dos vinos

flute *n* flauta, *f; arch* estría, *f;* (organ-stop) flautado, *m. vi* tocar la flauta, flautear; tener la voz flauteada. *vt* tocar (una pieza) en la flauta; (groove) encanutar, acanalar, estriar. **f. player,** flautista, *mf*

fluted *a* (grooved) acanalado

fluting *n mus* son de la flauta, *m;* (of birds) trinado, *m; arch* estría, *f; sew* rizado, *m*

flutter *n* (of wings) aleteo, *m;* (of leaves, etc.) murmurio, *m;* (of eyelashes) pestañeo, *m;* (of flags, etc.) ondeo, *m,* ondulación, *f;* (excitement) agitación, *f;* (stir) sensación, *f;* (gamble) jugada, *f. vi* (of birds) aletear; revolotear; (of butterflies) mariposear; (of flags) ondear; palpitar; (of persons) estar agitado. *vt* agitar; (the eyelashes) pestañear; (agitate) agitar, alarmar

fluttering *n* mariposeo, *m;* revoloteo, *m;* (of birds) aleteo, *m;* (of leaves, etc.) murmurio, *m;* (of flags, etc.) ondeo, *m,* ondulación, *f;* (of eyelashes) pestañeo, *m*

fluvial *a* fluvial

flux *n* flujo, *m*

fly *n* (insect) mosca, *f;* (on a fishhook) mosca artificial, *f;* (carriage) calesín, *m;* (of breeches) bragueta, *f; theat* bambalina, *f;* (of a tent) toldo, *m;* (flight) vuelo, *m;* (of a flag) vuelo, *m.* **fly-blown,** manchado por las moscas. **fly-by-night,** trasnochador (-ra). **fly-catcher,** *orn* papamoscas, *m;* matamoscas, *m.* **fly-fishing,** pesca con moscas artificiales, *f.* **fly-leaf,** guarda (de un libro), *f.* **fly-paper,** papel matamoscas, *m.* **fly-swatter,** matamoscas, *m.* **fly-wheel,** *mech* volante, *m*

fly *vi* volar; (flutter) ondear; (jump) saltar; (rush) lanzarse, precipitarse; (pass away) pasar volando, volar; (run off) marcharse a todo correr; (escape) huir, escapar; (seek refuge) refugiarse; (to the head, of intoxicants) subirse; (vanish) desaparecer. *vt* hacer volar; hacer ondear, enarbolar; (an airplane) pilotar, dirigir;

(flee from) huir de; evitar. **to let fly (at),** descargar, tirar; *fig* saltar la sinhueso. **to fly about,** volar en torno de; revolotear. **to fly at,** lanzarse sobre; acometer, asaltar. **to fly away,** emprender el vuelo. **to fly back,** volar hacia el punto de partida; (of doors, etc.) abrir, or cerrar, de repente. **to fly down,** volar abajo. **to fly in,** volar dentro de; volar adentro; (of airplanes) llegar (el avión). **to fly in pieces,** hacerse pedazos. **to fly into a rage,** montarse en cólera. **to fly low,** rastrear; *aer* volar a poca altura. **to fly off,** emprender el vuelo; (hasten) marcharse volando; (of buttons, etc.) saltar (de), separarse (de). **to fly open,** abrirse de repente. **to fly over,** volar por, volar por encima de. **to fly upwards,** volar hacia arriba; subir

flying *n* vuelo, *m. a* volante, volador; que vuela; de volar; volátil; (hasty) rápido; (flowing) ondeante, ondulante. **to shoot f.,** tirar al vuelo. **with f. colors,** con banderas desplegadas, triunfante. **f.-boat,** hidroavión, *m.* **f.-buttress,** botarel, arbotante, *m.* **f.-column,** *mil* cuerpo volante, *m.* **f.-fish,** (pez) volador, *m.* **f.-fortress,** *aer* fortaleza volante, *f.* **f.-officer,** oficial de aviación, *m.* **f.-sickness,** mal de altura, *m.* **f.-squad,** escuadra ligera, *f.* **f.-test,** *aer* examen de pilotaje, *m*

foal *n* potro (-ra). *vi* and *vt* parir una yegua

foam *n* espuma, *f. vi* espumar; (of horses, etc.) echar espumarajos. **to f. and froth,** (of the sea) hervir. **f. at the mouth,** echar espuma por la boca.

foam rubber *n* caucho esponjoso, *m,* espuma de caucho, *f,* espuma sintética, *f*

foamy *a* espumoso

fob *n* bolsillo del reloj, *m;* faltriquera pequeña, *f. vt* (off) engañar con

focal *a* focal

focus *n* foco, *m;* centro, *m. vt* enfocar; concentrar. *vi* convergir. **in f.,** en foco

fodder *n agr* pienso, forraje, *m. vt* dar forraje (a)

foe *n* enemigo, *m*

fog *n* neblina, niebla, *f; fig* confusión, *f; fig* perplejidad, *f. vt* obscurecer; *phot* velar; *fig* ofuscar. *vi* hacerse nebuloso; *phot* velarse. **fog-signal,** señal de niebla, *f*

fogbound *a* rodeado de niebla; detenido por la niebla

fogey *n* obscurantista, *m.* **He is an old f.,** Es un señor chapado a la antigua

fogginess *n* oscuridad, neblina, *f*

foggy *a* nebuloso; *phot* velado. **It is f.,** Hay niebla

foghorn *n* sirena, *f;* bocina, *f*

foible *n* flaco, *m,* debilidad, *f*

foil *n* (sword) florete, *m;* (coat) hoja, *f;* (of a mirror) azogado, *m. vt* frustrar. **f. a plot,** desbaratar un complot. **She makes a good f. for her sister's beauty,** Hace resaltar la belleza de su hermana

foiling *n* frustración, *f*

foist *vt* imponer; insertar, incluir; engañar (con)

fold *n* doblez, *f,* pliegue, *m,* arruga, *f; sew* cogido, *m;* (for sheep) redil, aprisco, *m; fig* iglesia, congregación de los fieles, *f;* (in compounds) vez, *f. vt* doblar, plegar, doblegar; (the arms) cruzar (los brazos); (embrace) abrazar; (wrap) envolver; (clasp) entrelazar; (sheep) meter en redil, encerrar. *vi* doblarse, plegarse; cerrarse

folder *n* doblador (-ra); plegadera, *f*

folding *n* plegadura, *f,* doblamiento, *m;* (of sheep) encerramiento, *m, a* plegadizo. **f.-door,** puerta plegadiza, *f.* **f.-machine,** plegador, *m.* **f.-seat,** *aut* traspuntín, *m.* **f.-table,** mesa de tijeras, *f;* mesa plegadiza, *f*

foliage *n* follaje, *m,* frondas, *f pl.* **thick f.,** frondosidad, *f*

folio *n* folio, *m;* (a volume) infolio, *m. a* de infolio. *vt* foliar

folk *n* (nation) pueblo, *m,* nación, *f;* gente, *f; pl* **folks,** *inf* familia, *f;* parientes, *m pl.* **f.-dance,** danza popular, *f*

folklore *n* folclore, *m,* tradiciones folclóricas, *f pl*

folklorist *n* folclorista, *mf*

folksong *n* canción popular, *f;* romance, *m;* copla, *f*

folktale *n* conseja, *f,* cuento popular, *m*

follicle *n* (anat, bot) folículo, *m*

follow *vt* seguir; (pursue) perseguir; (hunt) cazar; (adopt) adoptar; (understand) comprender; (notice) observar. *vi* ir, o venir, detrás; (of time) venir después; (gen. impers.) seguir, resultar; seguirse. **as follows,** como sigue. **I shall f. your advice,** Seguiré tus consejos. **to f. on the heels of,** *fig* pisar los talones (a). **to f. suit,** (at cards) asistir, jugar el mismo palo; *fig* imitar. **to f. up,** proseguir; continuar; (pursue) perseguir; (enhance) reforzar. **f.-me-lads,** *inf* siguemepollo, *m*

follower *n* seguidor (-ra); adherente, secuaz, *mf*; (imitator) imitador (-ra); (lover) novio, *m*; *pl* **followers,** acompañamiento, séquito, *m*

following *n* séquito, acompañamiento, *m*, comitiva, *f*; partidarios, *m pl*, adherentes, *mf pl. a* siguiente; próximo. **f. wind,** viento en popa, *m*

folly *n* locura, extravagancia, absurdidad, tontería, *f*, disparate, *m*

foment *vt* (poultice) fomentar; provocar, incitar, instigar; (assist) fomentar, proteger, promover

fomentation *n med* fomentación, *f*; provocación, instigación, *f*; fomento, *m*, protección, *f*

fomenter *n* fomentador (-ra), instigador (-ra)

fond *a* (credulous) vano, crédulo, vacío; (doting) demasiado indulgente; (loving) cariñoso, tierno, afectuoso; (addicted to) aficionado a, adicto a, amigo de. **to be f. of,** (things) tener afición a, estar aficionado de; (people) tener cariño (a). **to grow f. of,** (things) aficionarse a; (people) tomar cariño (a)

fondle *vt* mimar, acariciar; jugar (con.)

fondly *adv* (vainly) vanamente, sin razón; cariñosamente, tiernamente

fondness *n* cariño, afecto, *m*; (for things) afición, inclinación, *f*; gusto, *m*

font *n* pila bautismal, *f*; *poet* fuente, *f*; *print* fundición, *f*

food *n* alimento, *m*; comida, *f*, el comer; (of animals) pasto, *m*; *fig* pábulo, *m*; materia, *f*. **She gave him f.** Le dio de comer. **You have given me f. for thought,** Me has dado en qué pensar. **f.-card,** cartilla de racionamiento, **food, clothing, and shelter** comida, abrigo y vivienda, *f*. **F. Ministry,** Ministerio de Alimentación, *m*. **f. value,** valor nutritivo, *m*. **food poisoning,** intoxicación alimenticia, *f*

foodstuffs *n pl* comestibles, víveres, *m pl*

fool *n* tonto (-ta), mentecato (-ta), majadero (ra) necio (-ia); (jester) bufón, *m*; (butt of jest) hazmerreír, *m*; víctima, *f*; *cul* compota de frutas con crema, *f*, *vi* tontear, hacer tonterías. *vt* poner en ridículo (a); (deceive) engañar, embaucar; (with) jugar con. **to make a f. of oneself,** ponerse en ridículo. **to f. about,** *vi* perder el tiempo, vagabundear. **to f. away,** malgastar, malbaratar. **fool's bauble,** cetro de bufón, *m*. **fool's cap,** gorro de bufón, *m*

foolhardiness *n* temeridad, *f*

foolhardy *a* temerario, atrevido

fooling *n* payasada, bufonada, *f*; (deceiving) engaño, *m*, burla, *f*

foolish *a* imprudente; estúpido, tonto; ridículo, absurdo; imbécil

foolishly *adv* imprudentemente; tontamente; imbécilmente

foolishness *n* imprudencia, *f*; estupidez, tontería, *f*, disparate, *m*; ridiculez, *f* imbecilidad, *f*

foolproof *a* (of utensils, etc.) con garantía absoluta

foolscap *n* (nearest equivalent) papel de barba, *m*

fool's gold *n* pirita amarilla, *f*, sulfuro de hierro *m*

foot *n* pie, *m*; (of animals, furniture) pata, *f*; (of bed, sofa, grave, ladder, page, etc.) pie, *m*; (hoof) pezuña, *f*; (metric unit and measure) pie, *m*; *mil* infantería, *f*; (base) base, *f*; (step) paso, *m*. *a* mil de a pie; a pie. *vi* ir a pie; venir a pie; bailar. *vt* hollar; (account) pagar (una cuenta); (stockings) poner pie (a). **on f.,** a pie; (of soldiers) de a pie; (in progress) en marcha. **to go on f.,** ir a pie, andar. **to put one's best f. forward,** apretar el paso; *fig* hacer de su mejor. **to put one's f. down,** poner pies en pared, pararle fulano el alto. **to put one's f. in it,** meter la pata. **to rise to one's feet,**

ponerse de pie. **to set f. on,** pisar, hollar. **to set on f.,** poner en pie; *fig* poner en marcha. **to trample under f.,** pisotear. **f.-and-mouth disease,** glosopeda, *f*. **f.-brake,** freno de pedal, *m*. **f.-pump,** fuelle de pie, *m*. **f.-rule,** (nearest equivalent) doble decímetro, *m*. **f.-soldier,** soldado de a pie, infante, *m*

football *n* (game) fútbol, *m*; (ball) pelota de fútbol, *f*. **f. field,** campo de fútbol, *m*. **f. match,** partida de fútbol, *f*. **f. pools,** apuestas de fútbol, *f pl*; (in Spain) apuestas benéficas de fútbol, *f pl*

footballer *n* futbolista, *m*

footbath *n* baño de pies, *m*

footbridge *n* puente para peatones, *m*

footed *a* con pies; de pies . . . ; de patas . . .

footfall *n* pisada, *f*, paso, *m*

foothills *n pl* faldas de la montaña, *f pl*

foothold *n* hincapié, *m*; posición establecida, *f*

footing *n* hincapié, *m*; posición firme, *f*; condiciones, *f pl*; relaciones, *f pl*. **on a peacetime f.,** en pie de paz. **to be on an equal f.,** estar en pie de igualdad, estar en iguales condiciones. **to miss one's f.,** resbalar

footlights *n pl* canilejas, candilejas, *f pl*. **to get across the f.,** hacer contacto con el público

footman *n* lacayo, *m*

footnote *n* llamada a pie de página, nota a pie de página, *f*

footpath *n* senda, vereda, *f*, sendero, *m*

footprint *n* huella, pisada, *f*, vestigio, *m*

footsore *a* con los pies lastimados

footstep *n* paso, *m*; (trace) pisada, huella, *f*. **to follow in the footsteps of,** *fig* seguir las pisadas de

footstool *n* escabel, banquito, *m*

footwarmer *n* calientapiés, *m*

footwear *n* calzado, *m*

fop *n* petimetre, *m*

foppery *n* afectación en el vestir, *f*; vanidad, *f*

foppish *a* presumido, afectado; elegante

for *prep* (expressing exchange, price or penalty of, instead of, in support or favor of, on account of) por; (expressing destination, purpose, result) para; (during) durante, por; (for the sake of) para; (because of) a causa de; (in spite of) a pesar de; (as) como; (with) de; (in favor of) en favor de; (in election campaign) con (e.g., "Ecuadorians for Martínez!" ¡Ecuatorianos con Martínez!) (toward) hacia; (that) que, para que (with *subjunc*) a; (before) antes de; (searching for) en busca de; (bound for) con rumbo a; (regarding) en cuanto a; (until) hasta. **What's for dinner?** ¿Qué hay de comida? **center for . . .** centro de . . . (e.g., **Center for Applied Linguistics,** Centro de Lingüística Aplicada). **He is in business for himself,** Tiene negocios por su propia cuenta. **It is raining too hard for you to go there,** Llueve demasiado para que vayas allí. **It is not for him to decide,** No le toca a él decidirlo. **Were it not for . . . ,** Si no fuese por . . . **She has not been to see me for a week,** Hace una semana que no viene a verme. **It is impossible for them to go out,** Les es imposible salir. **but for all that,** pero con todo. **for ever,** por (or para) siempre. **for fear that,** por miedo de que. **for myself,** en cuanto a mí, personalmente. **for the present,** por ahora. **for what reason?** ¿para qué? ¿por cuál motivo? **for brevity's sake, for the sake of brevity,** por causa de la brevedad

for *conjunc* porque; visto que, pues, puesto que, en efecto, ya que

forage *n* forraje, *m*. *vt* and *vi* forrajear. **to f. for,** buscar. **f. cap,** gorra de cuartel, *f*

forager *n* forrajeador, *m*

foraging *n* forraje, *m*

forasmuch as *conjunc* puesto que, como que, ya que •

foray *n* correría, cabalgada, *f*; saqueo, *m*

forbear *vt* and *vi* dejar (de), guardarse (de); abstenerse de; evitar; reprimirse (de); rehusarse (de); (cease) cesar (de); (be patient) ser paciente; ser tolerante

forbearance *n* abstención, *f*; tolerancia, transigencia, *f*; indulgencia, *f*; paciencia, *f*

forbearing *a* tolerance, transigente; generoso, magnánimo; paciente

forbid *vt* prohibir, defender (de); impedir. **I f. you to do it,** Te prohibo hacerlo. **The game is forbidden,** El juego está prohibido. **They have forbidden me to . . . ,** Me han defendido de . . . **Heaven f.!** ¡Dios no lo quiera!

forbidden *a* prohibido; ilícito. **f. fruit,** fruto prohibido, *m*

forbidding *a* repugnante, horrible; antipático, desagradable; (dismal) lúgubre; (threatening) amenazador. *n* prohibición, *f*

force *n* fuerza, *f*; violencia, *f*; vigor, *m*; (efficacy) eficacia, *f*; (validity) validez, *f*; (power) poder, *m*; (motive) motivo, *m*, razón, *f*; (weight) peso, *m*, importancia, *f*; (police) policía, *f*; *pl* forces, *mil* fuerzas, tropas, *f pl.* **by main f.,** por fuerza mayor. **in f.,** vigente, en vigor. **to be in f.,** estar vigente

force *vt* forzar; (compel) obligar, constreñir, precisar; (ravish) violar; *cul* rellenar; (impose) imponer; (plants) forzar; (the pace) apresurar; (cause) hacer; (a lock, etc.) forzar. **to f. oneself into,** entrar a la fuerza en; (a garment) ponerse con dificultad; imponerse a la fuerza. **to f. oneself to,** esforzarse a. **to f. the pace,** forzar el paso. **to f. away,** ahuyentar. **to f. back,** hacer retroceder; rechazar; (a sigh, etc.) ahogar. **to f. down,** hacer bajar, obligar a bajar; (make swallow) hacer tragar; (of airplanes) hacer tomar tierra. **to f. in,** introducir a la fuerza; obligar a entrar. **to f. into,** meter a la fuerza; obligar a entrar (en). **to f. on, upon,** imponer. **to f. open,** abrir a la fuerza; (a lock) romper, forzar. **to f. out,** hacer salir; empujar hacia fuera; (words) pronunciar con dificultad. **to f. up,** obligar a subir; hacer subir; hacer vomitar

forced *a* forzado; forzoso; afectado. **f. landing,** *aer* aterrizaje forzoso, *m*. **f. march,** *mil* marcha forzada, *f*

forceful *a* See **forcible**

forcemeat *n* picadillo, *m*; relleno, *m*. **f. ball,** albóndiga, *f*

forceps *n pl* fórceps, *m pl*; pinzas, *f pl*. **arterial f.,** pinzas hemostáticas, *f pl*

forcible *a* fuerte; a la fuerza; violento; enérgico, vigoroso; poderoso; *lit* vívido, gráfico, vehemente. **f. feeding,** alimentación forzosa, *f*

forcibleness *n* fuerza, *f*; vigor, *m*, energía, *f*; vehemencia, *f*

forcibly *adv* a la fuerza

forcing *n* forzamiento, *m*; compulsión, *f*. **f. frame,** semillero, *m*, especie de invernadero, *f*

ford *n* esguazo, vado, *m*. *vt* esguazar, vadear

fordable *a* esguazable, vadeable

fore *a* delantero; *naut* de proa. *adv* delante; *naut* de proa. **f.-and-aft,** *naut* de popa a proa.

forearm *n* antebrazo, *m*. *vt* armar de antemano; preparar

forebear *n* antecesor, *m*, ascendiente, *mf*

forebode *vt* presagiar, augurar, anunciar; presentir

foreboding *n* presagio, augurio, *m*; presentimiento, *m*, corazonada, *f*

forecast *n* pronóstico, *m*; proyecto, plan, *m*, *vt* pronosticar; proyectar. **weather f.,** pronóstico del tiempo, *m*

forecastle *n naut* castillo de proa, *m*

foreclose *vt* excluir; impedir; vender por orden judicial; anticipar el resultado de; decidir de antemano

foreclosure *n* venta por orden judicial, *f*; juicio hipotecario, *m*

foredoom *vt* predestinar

forefather *n* antepasado, antecesor, *m*

forefinger *n* índice, dedo índice, *m*

forefoot *n* pata delantera, *f*

forefront *n* delantera, primera línea, *f*; frente, *m*; vanguardia, *f*. **in the f.,** en la vanguardia; en el frente

foregoing *a* precedente, anterior

foregone *a* decidido de antemano; previsto

foreground *n* primer plano, primer término, frente, *m*. **in the f.,** *art* en primer término

forehand *a* derecho. **f. stroke,** golpe derecho, *m*

forehead *n* frente, *f*

foreign *a* extranjero; extraño; exótico; exterior; (alien) ajeno. **f. affairs,** asuntos extranjeros, *m pl.* **f. body,** cuerpo extraño, *m*. **f. debt,** deuda exterior, *f*. **F. Legion,** tercio extranjero, *m*. **F. Office,** Ministerio de Relaciones Extranjeras, *m*. **f. parts,** extranjero, *m*. **f. policy,** política internacional, *f*. **F. Secretary,** Secretario de Asuntos Extranjeros, Secretario de Asuntos Exteriores, Ministro de Relaciones Extranjeras, *m*. **f. trade,** comercio con el extranjero, *m*

foreigner *n* extranjero (-ra)

foreignness *n* extranjerismo, *m*; (strangeness) extrañeza, *f*; lo exótico

foreknowledge *n* presciencia, precognición, *f*

foreland *n* promontorio, cabo, *m*

foreleg *n* pata delantera, *f*

forelock *n* guedeja, vedeja, *f*; (of a horse) copete, tupé, *m*. **to take time by the f.,** asir la ocasión por la melena

foreman *n* (of jury) presidente (del jurado), *m*; (of a farm) mayoral, *m*; (in a works) capataz, *m*

foremost *a* delantero; de primera fila; más importante. *adv* en primer lugar; en primera fila

forensic *a* forense, legal. **f. medicine,** medicina legal, *f*

foreordained *a* predestinado

forerunner *n* precursor (-ra), predecessor (-ra); (presage) anuncio, presagio, *m*

foresee *vt* prever, anticipar

foreseeing *a* presciente, sagaz

foreseer *n* previsor (-ra)

foreshadow *vt* anunciar, prefigurar; simbolizar; hacer sentir.

foreshorten *vt art* escorzar

foreshortening *n art* escorzo, *m*

foresight *n* presciencia, *f*; previsión, prudencia, *f*; (of gun) punto de mira, *f*; (optical) croquis de nivel, *m*

forest *n* bosque, *m*, selva, *f*. *vt* arbolar

forestall *vt* anticipar, saltear; prevenir; *com* acaparar

forestalling *n* anticipación, *f*

forestation *n* repoblación forestal, *f*

forester *n* silvicultor, guardamonte, ingeniero forestal, *m*; habitante de los bosques, *m*

forest fire incendio forestal, *m*

forestry *n* silvicultura, *f*

foresworn *a* perjuro

foretaste *n* muestra, *f*; presagio, *m*. *vt* gustar con anticipación

foretell *vt* predecir, profetizar; anunciar, presagiar

foreteller *n* profeta, *m*; presagio, *m*

foretelling *n* profecía, predicción, *f*

forethought *n* presciencia, previsión, *f*; prevención, *f*

forewarn *vt* prevenir

forewarning *n* presagio, *m*

forewoman *n* encargada, *f*; primera oficiala, *f*

foreword *n* prefacio, *m*, introducción, *f*

forfeit *n* pérdida, *f*; (fine) multa, *f*; (in games) prenda, *f*; (of rights, goods, etc.) confiscación, *f*. *a* confiscado. *vt* perder; perder el derecho o el título de

forfeiture *n* pérdida, *f*; confiscación, *f*; secuestro, *m*

forge *n* fragua, *f*; (smithy) herrería, *f*. *vt and vi* fraguar, forjar; (fabricate) inventar, fabricar; falsificar; (advance) avanzar lentamente. **to f. ahead,** abrirse camino; avanzar

forged *a* (of iron) forjado; (of checks, etc.) falso, falsificado

forger *n* falsificador (-ra), falsario (-ia); (creator) artífice, *mf*

forgery *n* falsificación, *f*

forget *vt* olvidar; descuidar. *vi* olvidarse. **to f. about,** olvidarse de, desacordarse de. **to f. oneself,** olvidarse de sí mismo; propasarse; (in anger) perder los estribos

forgetful *a* olvidadizo; descuidado, negligente

forgetfulness *n* olvido, *m*; descuido, *m*; falta de memoria, *f*

forget-me-not *n bot* miosota nomeolvides, *f*

forging n fraguado, m; falsificación, f

forgivable a perdonable, excusable

forgive vt perdonar, disculpar, condonar; (debts) remitir

forgiveness n perdón, m; condonación, f; (remission) remisión, f

forgiving a misericordioso, clemente, dispuesto a perdonar

forgo vt renunciar, sacrificar, privarse de; abandonar, ceder

forgoing n renunciación, f, sacrificio, m; cesión, f

"For Immediate Occupancy" «De Ocupación Inmediata»

fork n agr horca, horquilla, f; (table fork) tenedor, m; bifurcación, f; (of rivers) confluencia, f; (of branches) horcadura, f; (of legs) horcajadura, f; (for supporting trees, etc.) horca, f; mus diapasón normal, m. vt hacinar con horca. vi bifurcarse; ramificarse

forked a bifurcado, hendido, ahorquillado. **f. lightning,** relámpago, m. **f. tail,** cola hendida, f

forlorn a abandonado, desamparado, desesperado. **f. hope,** aventura desesperada, f

forlornness n desamparo, m, miseria, f; desolación, f, desconsuelo, m

form n forma, f; figura, f; (shadowy) bulto, m; (formality) formalidad, f; ceremonia, f; ecc rito, m; método, m; regla, f; (in a school) clase, f; (lair) cama, f; (seat) banco, m; (system) sistema, m; (ghost) espectro, m; aparición, f; (to fill up) documento, m; hoja, f; (state) condición, f; lit construcción, forma, f. **It is a matter of f.,** Es una pura formalidad. **in due f.,** en debida forma, en regla. **in the usual f.,** com al usado. **It is not good f.,** No es de buena educación

form vt formar; (a habit) contraer; (an idea) hacerse (una idea). vi formarse. **to f. fours,** mil formar a cuatro

formal a esencial; formal; ceremonioso, solemne; (of person) etiquetero, formalista. **f. call,** visita de cumplido, f

formaldehyde n formaldehído. m

formalism n formalismo, m

formality n formalidad, f; ceremonia, solemnidad, f

formally adv formalmente

format n formato, m

formation n formación, f; disposición, f, arreglo, m; organización, f; (mil, geol) formación, f

formative a formativo

forme n print forma, f, molde, m

former a primero; antiguo; anterior; pasado. **in f. times,** antes, antiguamente. **the f.,** ése, aquél, m; ésa, aquélla, f; aquéllos, m pl; aquéllas, f pl

former n formador (-ra); creador (-ra), autor (-ra)

formerly adv antiguamente, antes

formidable a formidable; terrible, espantoso

formless a informe

formlessness n falta de forma, f

formula n fórmula, f. **standard f.,** (math, chem) fórmula clásica, f

formulate vt formular

fornicate vi fornicar

fornication n fornicación, f

fornicator n fornicador (-ra)

forsake vt dejar, desertar; abandonar, desamparar; separarse de; (of birds, the nest) aborrecer; (one's faith) renegar de

forsaker n el, m, (la, f) que abandona; desertor, m; renegado (-da)

"For Sale" «Se Vende»

forsooth adv ciertamente, claro está

forswear vt abjurar; renunciar a. **to f. oneself,** perjurarse

forswearing n abjuración, f; renuncia, f; perjurio, m

fort n fortaleza, f, fuerte, m

forte n fuerte, m. a mus fuerte

forth adv (on) adelante, fuera; hacia adelante; (out) fuera; (in time) en adelante, en lo consecutivo; (show) a la vista. **and so f.,** y así en lo sucesivo; etcétera

forthcoming a próximo; futuro; en preparación

forthwith adv en seguida, sin tardanza

fortieth a cuadragésimo; cuarenta. n cuarentavo, m

fortifiable a fortificable

fortification n fortificación, f

fortify vt fortificar; fortalecer; confirmar; fig proveer (de)

fortitude n aguante, m, fortaleza, f, estoicismo, m

fortnight n quince días, m pl, dos semanas, f pl; quincena, f. **a f. ago,** hace quince días. **a f. tomorrow,** mañana en quince. **in a f.,** dentro de quince días; al cabo de quince días. **once a f.,** cada quince días

fortnightly a quincenal. adv cada dos semanas, dos veces al mes. n revista quincenal, f

fortress n fortaleza, plaza fuerte, f

fortuitous a fortuito, accidental

fortuitously adv accidentalmente

fortuity n casualidad, f; accidente, m

fortunate a dichoso, feliz; afortunado; próspero. **to be f.,** (of persons) tener suerte

fortunately adv afortunadamente, por dicha, felizmente

fortune n suerte, fortuna, f, destino, m; (money) caudal, m, fortuna, f; bienes, m pl; buena ventura, f. **good f.,** buena fortuna, dicha, f. **ill f.,** mala suerte, f. **to cost a f.,** costar un sentido. **to make one's f.,** enriquecerse; inf hacer su pacotilla. **to tell fortunes,** echar las cartas. **f. hunter,** buscador de dotes, cazador de dotes, cazador de fortunas, aventurero, m. **f.-teller,** adivinadora, f; echadora de cartas, f. **f.-telling,** buenaventura, f

forty a and n cuarenta, m. **He is turned f.,** Ha cumplido los cuarenta. **person of f.,** cuarentón (-ona). **She is f.,** Tiene cuarenta años

forum n foro, tribuna f, (e.g., **to serve as a forum for discussion,** servir de tribuna de discusión)

forward a avanzado; adelantado; (of position) delantero; (ready) preparado; (eager) pronto, listo, impaciente; activo, emprendedor; (of persons, fruit, etc.) precoz; (pert) insolente, desenvuelto, atrevido. adv adelante; hacia adelante; (of time) en adelante; (farther on) más allá; hacia el frente; en primera línea. vt ayudar, promover; adelantar; (letters) hacer seguir; com expedir, remitir; (a parcel) despachar; (hasten) apresurar; (plants) hacer crecer. n sport delantero, m. **center-f.,** sport delantero centro, m. **from this time f.,** de hoy en adelante. **Please f.,** ¡Haga seguir! **putting f. of the clock,** el adelanto de la hora. **to carry f.,** com pasar a cuenta nueva. **to go f.,** adelantarse; estar en marcha, estar en preparación. **f. line,** sport delantera, f. **F.!** ¡Adelante!

forwarder n promotor (-ra); com remitente, m

forwarding n fomento, m, promoción, f; com expedición, f, envío, m

forwardness n progreso, adelantamiento, m; (haste) apresuramiento, m; (of persons, fruit, etc.) precocidad, f; (pertness) desenvoltura, insolencia, frescura, f, descaro, m; (eagerness) impaciencia, f

fosse n foso, m

fossil a and n fósil, m.

fossilization n fosilización, f

fossilize vt fosilizar; petrificar. vi fosilizarse

foster vt provocar, promover, suscitar; (favor) favorecer, ser propicio a. **f.-brother,** hermano de leche, m. **f.-child,** hijo (-ja) de leche. **f.-father,** padre adoptivo, m. **f.-mother,** ama de leche, f. **f.-sister,** hermana de leche, f

foul a sucio, asqueroso, puerco; (evil-smelling) hediondo, fétido; (of air) viciado; impuro; (language) ofensivo; (coarse) indecente, obsceno; (harmful) nocivo, dañino; (wicked) malvado; infame; vil; (unfair) injusto; sport sucio; (ugly) feo; (entangled) enredado; (with corrections) lleno de erratas; (choked) atascado; (of weather) borrascoso, tempestuoso; malo, desagradable; (repulsive) repugnante. n sport juego sucio, m. vt ensuciar; naut chocar, abordar; (block) atascar; (the anchor) enredar; (dishonor) deshonrar. vi atascarse; (anchor) enredarse; *naut* chocar. **to fall f. of,** *naut* abordar (un buque); *fig* habérselas con. **by fair means or f.,** a las buenas o a las malas. **f. breath,** aliento fétido, aliento corrompido, *m*. **f. brood,** peste de las abejas, *f*. **f. language,** palabras ofensivas, *f pl*; lenguaje obsceno, *m*. **f. play,** juego sucio, *m*. **f. weather,** mal tiempo, tiempo borrascoso, *m*

found *vt* fundar; (metal, glass) fundir; (create, etc.) establecer

foundation *n* fundación, *f*; establecimiento, *m*; creación, *f*; *arch* cimiento, embasamiento, *m*; (basis) base, *f*; (cause) causa, *f*, origen, principio, *m*; (endowment) dotación, *f*; *sew* refuerzo, *m*. **to lay the f.,** poner las fundaciones. **f. stone,** piedra angular, *f*; *fig* primera piedra, *f*. **to lay the f. stone,** poner la piedra angular

founder *n* fundador (-ra); (of metals) fundidor, *m*. *vt* (a ship) hacer zozobrar. *vi* zozobrar, irse a pique; *fig* fracasar

foundering *n* *naut* zozobra, *f*

founding *n* fundación, *f*; establecimiento, *m*; (of metals) fundición, *f*

foundling *n* hijo (-ja) de la cuna, expósito (-ta). **f. hospital** or **home,** casa de cuna, casa de expósitos, inclusa, *f*

foundress *n* fundadora, *f*

foundry *n* fundición, *f*

fountain *n* fuente, *f*; (spring) manantial, *m*; (jet) chorro, *m*; (artificial) fuente, *f*, surtidero, *m*; (source) origen, principio, *m*. **f.-head,** fuente, *f*. **Fountain of Youth,** Fuente de la juventud, Fuente de Juvencio, *f*. **f. pen,** pluma estilográfica, *f*

four *a* and *n* cuatro, *m*. **It is f. o'clock,** Son las cuatro. **She is f.,** Tiene cuatro años. **on all fours,** a gatas. **f.-course,** (of meals) de cuatro platos. **f.-engined,** cuadrimotor. **f.-engined plane,** cuadrimotor, *m*. **f.-footed,** cuadrúpedo. **f.-horse,** de cuatro caballos. **f. hundred,** cuatrocientos. **f.-inhand,** tiro par, *m*. **f.-part,** (of a song) a cuatro voces. **f.-wheel brakes,** freno en las cuatro ruedas, *m*

fourfold *a* cuádruple

fourposter *n* cama de matrimonio, *f*

fourscore *a* and *n* ochenta, *m*.

foursome *n* partido de cuatro personas, *m*

fourteen *a* and *n* catorce, *m*. **He is f.,** Tiene catorce años

fourteenth *a* and *n* décimocuarto *m*.; (of the month) (el) catorce, *m*; (of monarchs) catorce. **April f.,** El 14 (catorce) de abril

fourth *a* cuarto; (of the month) el cuatro; (of monarchs) cuarto. *n* (fourth part) cuarta parte, *f*; *mus* cuarta, *f*. **f. dimension,** cuarta dimensión, *f*. **f. term,** (U.S.A. *pol*) cuarto mandato, *m*

fourthly *adv* en cuarto lugar

fowl *n* gallo. *m*; gallina, *f*; (chicken) pollo, *m*; (bird) ave, *f*; (barndoor f.) ave de corral, *f*. *vi* cazar aves. **f.-house** or **run,** gallinero, *m*

fox *n* zorro, *m*; (vixen) zorra, raposa, *f*; *fig* zorro, taimado, *m*. *vi* disimular. *vt* (books) descolorar. **f.-brush,** cola de raposa, *f*. **f.-earth,** zorrera, *f*. **f.-hunting,** caza de zorras, *f*. **f. terrier,** fox-térrier, *m*

foxglove *n* digital, dedalera, *f*

foxhound *n* perro zorrero, *m*

foxiness *n* zorrería, astucia, *f*

foxtrot *n* foxtrot, *m*

foxy *a* de zorro; zorrero, astuto

foyer *n* foyer, salón de descanso, *m*

fraction *n* *math* fracción, *f*, número quebrado, *m*; pequeña parte, *f*; fragmento, *m*. **improper f.,** *math* fracción impropia, *f*. **proper f.,** *math* fracción propia, *f*

fractional *a* fraccionario

fractious *a* malhumorado, enojadizo

fractiousness *n* mal humor, *m*

fracture *n* *surg* fractura, *f*. *vt* fracturar. **compound f.,** fractura conminuta, *f*

fragile *a* frágil, quebradizo; (of persons) delicado

fragility *n* fragilidad, *f*

fragment *n* fragmento, *m*; trozo, pedazo, *m*. **to break into fragments,** hacer pedazos, hacer añicos

fragmentary *a* fragmentario

fragrance *n* fragancia, *f*, buen olor, perfume, aroma, *m*

fragrant *a* fragante, oloroso. **to make f.,** perfumar

frail *a* frágil, quebradizo; débil, endeble. *n* capacho, *m*, espuerta, *f*

frailty *n* fragilidad, *f*; debilidad, *f*

frame *n* constitución, *f*; sistema, *m*; organización, *f*; (of the body) figura, *f*, talle, *m*; (of window, picture) marco, *m*; (of machine, building) armadura, *f*; (of a bicycle) cuadro (de bicicleta), *m*; *agr* cajonera, *f*; (embroidery) bastidor (para bordar), *m*; (skeleton) esqueleto, *m*; *lit* composición, construcción, *f*; (of spectacles) armadura, *f*; (of mind) disposición (de ánimo), *f*; humor, *m*. *vt* formar; construir; arreglar; ajustar; (a picture) enmarcar; componer, hacer; (draw up) redactar; (think up) idear, inventar; (words) articular, pronunciar. **f. constitution,** elaborar una constitución

framer *n* fabricante de marcos, *m*; autor (-ra), creador (-ra), inventor (-ra)

framework *n* armadura, armazón, *f*, esqueleto, *m*; organización, *f*; (basis) base, *f*

franc *n* (coin) franco, *m*

franchise *n* (exemption) franquicia, *f*; privilegio, *m*; (vote) derecho de sufragio, *m*; (citizenship) derecho político, *m*

France Francia, *f*

Franche-Comté Franco-Condado, *m*

Franciscan *a* and *n* franciscano (-na)

Franco- (in compounds) franco- . . . *a* (Spanish *pol*— referring to General Franco) franquista

Francophile *a* and *n* afrancesado (-da)

Frank *n* franco (-ca), galo (-la)

frank *a* franco, cándido, sincero; abierto. *vt* franquear

frankincense *n* incienso, *m*

frankly *adv* francamente; sinceramente; cara a cara; sin rodeos, claramente; abiertamente. **to speak f.,** hablar claro, hablar sin rodeos

frankness *n* franqueza, *f*; sinceridad, *f*, candor, *m*

frantic *a* frenético, furioso, loco. **He drives me f.,** Me vuelve loco

fraternal *a* fraterno, fraternal

fraternity *n* fraternidad, hermandad, *f*

fraternization *n* fraternización, *f*

fraternize *vi* fraternizar

fratricidal *a* fratricida

fratricide *n* (person) fratricida, *mf*; (action) fratricidio, *m*

fraud *n* fraude, *m*; engaño, embuste, *m*; (person) farsante, *m*, embustero (-ra)

fraudulence *n* fraudulencia, fraude, *f*

fraudulent *a* fraudulento

fraught *a* (with) cargado de; lleno de, preñado de

fray *n* refriega, riña, *f*; combate, *m*, batalla, *f*; (rubbing) raedura, *f*. *vt* raer, tazar. *vi* tazarse, deshilarse

frayed *a* raído

fraying *n* raedura, deshiladura, *f*

freak *n* monstruo, *m*; fenómeno, *m*; (whim) capricho, *m*

freakish *a* monstruoso; caprichoso; extravagante; raro, singular

freakishness *n* carácter caprichoso, *m*; extravagancia, *f*; rareza, extrañeza, *f*

freckle *n* peca, *f*. *vi* tener pecas; salir pecas (a la cara, etc.)

freckled *a* pecoso, con pecas

free *a* (in most senses) libre; independiente; emancipado; desembarazado; abierto; limpio (de); franco; (voluntary) voluntario, (self-governing) autónomo, independiente; accesible; (disengaged) desocupado (vacant) vacío; (exempt) exento (de); (immune) inmune (de); ajeno; gratuito; (loose) suelto; (generous) generoso, liberal; (vicious) disoluto, licencioso; (bold) atrevido; (impudent) insolente, demasiado familiar. *adv* gratis, gratuitamente. **There are two f. seats in the train,** Hay dos asientos libres en el tren. **to get f.,**

libertarse. **to make f. with,** tomarse libertades con; usar como si fuera suyo. **to set f.,** poner en libertad. **f. agent,** libre albedrío, *m*. **f. and easy,** familiar, sin ceremonia. **f. gift,** *com* objeto de reclamo, *m*. **f.-hand drawing,** dibujo a pulso, *m*. **f. kick,** *sport* golpe franco, *m*. **f. love,** amor libre, *m*. **f. play,** rienda suelta, *f*; *mech* holgura, *f*. **f. port,** puerto franco, *m*. **f. speech,** libertad de palabra, *f*. **f. thought,** libre pensamiento, *m*. **f. ticket,** *theat* billete de favor, *m*. **f. trade,** *a* librecambista. *n* librecambio, *m*. **f. trader,** librecambista, *mf*. **f. verse,** verso libre, verso suelto, *m*. **f.-wheeling,** desenfrenado, libre. **f. will,** propia voluntad, *f*; (theology) libre albedrío, *m*

free *vt* libertar, poner en libertad (a); librar (de); (slave) salvar; emancipar; exentar; (of obstacles, difficulties) desembarazar; **to f. from,** libertar de; librar de; (clean) limpiar de

freebooter *n* pirata, filibustero, *m*

freeborn *a* nacido libre, libre por herencia

freedman *n* liberto, *m*

freedom *n* libertad, *f*; independencia, *f*; exención, *f*; inmunidad, *f*; soltura, facilidad, *f*, franqueza, *f*; (over-familiarity) insolencia, *f*; (boldness) audacia, intrepidez, *f*; (of customs) licencia, *f*. **to receive the f. of a city,** ser recibido como ciudadano de honor. **f. of speech,** libertad de palabra, *f*. **f. of the press,** libertad de la prensa, *f*. **f. of worship,** libertad de cultos, *f*

freehold *n* feudo franco, *m*

freeing *n* liberación, *f*; emancipación, *f*; salvación, *f*; (from obstruction) desembarazo, *m*; limpieza, *f*

freelance *n* *mil* soldado libre, *m*; *pol* independiente, *m*; aventurero (-ra). **f. journalist,** periodista libre, *m*

freely *adv* libremente; francamente; generosamente; sin reserva

freeman *n* hombre libre, *m*; (of a city) ciudadano de honor, *m*

freemason *n* francmasón, *m*. **freemason's lodge,** logia masónica, *f*

freemasonry *n* francmasonería, masonería, *f*

freethinker *n* librepensador (-ra)

freeze *vt* helar; (meat, etc.) congelar; *fig* helar. *vi* helarse; congelarse; (impers, of the weather) helar. **to f. to death,** morir de frío

freezing *n* hielo, *m*; congelación, *f*. *a* glacial; congelante, frigorífico. **f. mixture,** mezcla frigorífica, *f*. **f. of assets,** bloqueo de los depósitos bancarios, *m*. **f.-point,** punto de congelación, *m*. **above f.-point,** sobre cero. **below f.-point,** bajo cero

freight *n* flete, *m*; porte, *m*. *vt* fletar

freighter *n* fletador, *m*; (ship) buque de carga, *m*

French *a* francés. *n* (language) francés, *m*; (people) los franceses, *m pl*. **in F. fashion,** a la francesa. **to take F. leave,** despedirse a la inglesa. **What is the F. for "hat"?** ¿Cómo se dice «sombrero» en francés? **F. spoken,** Se habla francés. **F. bean,** judía, *f*. **F. chalk,** jabón de sastre, *m*. **F. horn,** trompa, *f*. **F. lesson,** lección de francés, *f*. **F. marigold,** flor del estudiante, *f*. **F. polish,** barniz de muebles, *m*. **F. poodle,** perro (-rra) de aguas, *f*. **F. roll,** panecillo, *m*. **F. window,** puerta ventana, *f*

Frenchify *vt* afrancesar

Frenchman *n* francés, *m*. **a young F.,** un joven francés

Frenchwoman *n* francesa, mujer francesa, *f*. **a young F.,** una joven francesa, una muchacha francesa, *f*

frenzied *a* frenético

frenzy *n* frenesí, delirio, paroxismo, *m*

frequency *n* frecuencia, *f*. **high f.,** alta frecuencia, *f*. **low f.,** baja frecuencia, *f*

frequent *a* frecuente; (usual) común, corriente. *vt* frecuentar

frequentation *n* frecuentación, *f*

frequenter *n* frecuentador (-ra)

frequently *adv* frecuentemente, con frecuencia, muchas veces; comúnmente

fresco *n* *art* fresco, *m*, pintura al fresco, *f*. *vt* pintar al fresco

fresh *a* fresco; nuevo; reciente; (newly arrived) recién llegado; (inexperienced) inexperto, bisoño; (of water, not salt) dulce; puro; (healthy) sano; (brisk) vigoroso, enérgico; (vivid) vivo, vívido; (bright) brillante; (cheeky) fresco. *adv* neuvamente, recién (with past participle). **He came to us f. from school,** Vino a nosotros recién salido de su colegio. **We are going to take the f. air,** Vamos a tomar el fresco. **The milk is not f.,** La leche no está fresca. **f.-complexioned,** de buenos colores. **f. news,** noticias nuevas, *f pl*. **f. troops,** tropas nuevas, *f pl*, (reinforcements) tropas de refuerzo, *f pl*. **f. water,** agua fresca, *f*; (not salt) agua dulce, *f*. **f. wind,** viento fresco, *m*

freshen *vt* refrescar; (remove salt) desalar. *vi* (wind) refrescar. **to f. up,** renovar; refrescar; (of dress, etc.) arreglar

freshly *adv* nuevamente; recientemente

freshness *n* frescura, *f*; (newness) novedad, *f*; (vividness, brightness) intensidad, *f*; pureza, *f*; (beauty) lozanía, hermosura, *f*; (cheek) frescura, *f*, descaro, *m*

freshwater *n* agua dulce, *f*. **f. sailor,** marinero de agua dulce, *m*

fret *n* agitación, *f*; ansiedad, preocupación, *f*; *arch* greca, *f*; (of stringed instrument) traste, *m*. *vt* roer; (of a horse) bocezar; (corrode) desgastar, corroer; (of the wind, etc.) rizar; (worry) tener preocupado (a); irritar, enojar; (lose) perder; (oneself) apurarse, consumirse; *arch* calar. *vi* torturarse, preocuparse, inquietarse; (complain) quejarse; (mourn) lamentarse, estar triste

fretful *a* mal humorado, mohíno, quejoso, irritable

fretfully *adv* irritablemente, con mal humor

fretwork *n* calado, *m*

Freudian *a* freudiano

friar *n* fraile, *m*. **Black f.,** dominicano, *m*. **Gray f.,** franciscano, *m*. **White f.,** carmelita, *m*. **f.-like,** frailesco

friction *n* frote, frotamiento, roce, *m*; *phys* rozamiento, *m*; fricción, *f*. **to give a f.,** friccionar, dar fricciones (a). **f. gearing,** engranaje de fricción, *m*. **f. glove,** guante de fricciones, *m*

Friday *n* viernes, *m*. **Good F.,** Viernes Santo, *m*

fried *a* frito. **f. egg,** huevo frito, *m*

friend *n* amigo (-ga); (acquaintance) conocido (-da); (Quaker) cuáquero (-ra); (follower) adherente, *m*; partidario (-ia); (ally) aliado (-da); *pl* **friends,** amistades, *f pl*; amigos, *m pl*. **a f. of yours,** un amigo tuyo, uno de tus amigos. **to make friends,** hacer amigos; (become friends) hacerse amigos; (after a quarrel) hacer las paces. **Friends!** (to sentinel) ¡Gente de paz!

friendless *a* sin amigos; desamparado

friendliness *n* amabilidad, afabilidad, cordialidad, amigabilidad, *f*

friendly *a* amistoso, amigable, amigo; afable, acogedor, simpático; propicio, favorable. **to be f. with,** ser amigo de. **f. society,** sociedad de socorros, *f*

friendship *n* amistad, intimidad, *f*

Friesland Frisia, *f*

frieze *n* friso, *m*; (cloth) frisa, jerga, *f*

frigate *n* *nav* fragata, *f*

fright *n* terror, susto, *m*; (guy) espantajo, *m*. *vt* asustar. **to have a f.,** tener un susto. **to take f.,** asustarse

frighten *vt* espantar, dar un susto (a), alarmar, asustar; horrorizar; (overawe) acobardar. **to be frightened out of one's wits,** estar muerto de miedo. **to f. away,** ahuyentar, espantar

frightened *a* miedoso, tímido, medroso, nervioso

frightening *a* que da miedo; alarmante, amedrentador; horrible

frightful *a* horrible, espantoso, horroroso; *inf* tremendo, enorme

frightfully *adv* horrorosamente; *inf* enormemente

frigid *a* frío; helado; *med* impotente

frigidity *n* frialdad, frigidez, *f*; *med* impotencia, *f*

frigidly *adv* fríamente

frill *n* *sew* volante, *m*; (jabot) chorrera, *f*; (round a bird's neck) collarín de plumas, *m*; (of paper) frunce, *m*. *vt* alechugar; fruncir

fringe n fleco, m, franja, f; (of hair) flequillo, m; (edge) borde, m, margen, mf. vt guarnecer con fleco, franjar; adornar; (grow by) crecer al margen (de)

Frisian a and n frisón (-ona); (language) frisón, m

frisk vi retozar, brincar

friskiness n viveza, agilidad, f

frisky a retozón, juguetón

fritter n cul fruta de sartén, f. vt (away) malgastar, desperdiciar; perder

frivolity n frivolidad, ligereza, f; futilidad, f

frivolous a frívolo, ligero, liviano; (futile) trivial, fútil

frizz vt (cloth) frisar; (hair) rizar

frizzy a (of hair) crespo, rizado

fro adv hacia atrás. **movement to and fro,** vaivén, m. **to and fro,** de un lado a otro. **to go to and fro,** ir y venir

frock n vestido, m; (of a monk) hábito, m; (of priest) sotana, f. **f.-coat,** levita, f

frog n rana, f. **to have a f. in the throat,** padecer carraspera

frolic n (play) juego, m; (mischief) travesura, f; (folly) locura, extravagancia, f; (joke) chanza, f; (amusement) diversión, f; (wild party) holgorio, m, parranda, f. vi retozar, juguetear; divertirse

frolicsome a retozón, juguetón

from prep de; desde; (according to) según; (in the name of, on behalf of) de parte de; (through, by) por; (beginning on) a contar de; (with) con; **F.** (on envelope) Remite, Remitente. **He is coming here f. the dentist's,** Vendrá aquí desde casa del dentista. **Give him this message f. me,** Dale este recado de mi parte. **Judging f. his appearance,** Juzgando por su apariencia. **prices f. five hundred pesetas upward,** precios desde quinientos pesetas en adelante. **f. what I hear,** según mi información, según lo que oigo. **f. above,** desde arriba. **f. among,** de entre. **f. afar,** de lejos, desde lejos. **f. time to time,** de cuando en cuando, de vez en cuando

frond n bot fronda, f

front n frente, f; cara, f; mil frente, m; (battle line) línea de combate, f; (of a building) fachada, f; (of shirt) pechera, f; (at the seaside) playa, f; (promenade) paseo de la playa, m; (forefront) primera línea, f; (forepart) parte delantera, f; theat auditorio, m; (organization) organización de fachada, f; (impudence) descaro, m, a delantero; anterior; de frente; primero. adv hacia delante. vi mirar a, dar a; hacer frente a. **in f.,** en frente. **in f. of,** en frente de; (in the presence of) delante de, en la presencia de. **to face f.,** hacer frente. **to put on a bold f.,** hacer de tripas corazón. **f. door,** puerta de entrada, puerta principal, f. **f. line,** mil línea del frente, f; primera línea, f. **f. seat,** (at an entertainment, etc.) delantera, f. **f. organization** organización de fachada f. **f. tooth,** diente incisivo, m. **f. view,** vista de frente, f; vista de cerca, f

frontage n (of a building) fachada, f; (site) terreno de . . . metros de fachada, m

frontal a mil de frente; anat frontal

frontier n frontera, f; fig límite, m. a fronterizo

frontispiece n (of a building) frontispicio, m, fachada, f; (of a book) portada, f

frontless a sin frente

frost n escarcha, f; helada, f. vt helar; cul escarchar; (glass) deslustrar; fig escarchar. vi helar. **f.-bitten,** helado

frostbite n efectos del frío, m pl

frosted a escarchado; helado; (of glass) deslustrado, opaco; cul escarchado

frostily adv fig glacialmente, con frialdad.

frostiness n; frío glacial, m

frosting n escarcha, f; (of glass) deslustre, m; cul cobertura, escarcha, f

frosty a helado; de hielo; (of hair) canoso; fig glacial, frío. **It was f. last night,** Anoche heló

froth n espuma, f; fig frivolidad, vanidad, f, vi espumar;

hacer espuma; echar espuma. vt hacer espumar; hacer echar espuma

frothiness n espumosidad, f; fig frivolidad, superficialidad, vaciedad, f

frothy a espumoso, espumajoso; fig frívolo, superficial

frown n ceño, m; cara de juez, expresión severa, f; desaprobación, f; (of fortune) revés, golpe, m. vi fruncir el ceño. **to f. at, on, upon,** mirar con desaprobación, ver con malos ojos; ser enemigo de; desaprobar

frowning a ceñudo; severo; amenazador

frowningly adv severamente

frowsiness n mal olor, m; (dirtiness) suciedad, f; (untidiness) desaliño, desaseo, m

frowsy a fétido, mal oliente; mal ventilado; (dirty) sucio; (untidy) desaliñado, desaseado

frozen a helado; cubierto de hielo; congelado; (geog and fig) glacial. **to be f. up,** estar helado. **f. meat,** carne congelada, f

frugal a económico; frugal; sobrio

frugality n economía, f; frugalidad, sobriedad, f

fruit n (in general sense) fruto, m; (off a tree or bush) fruta, f; fig fruto, m; resultado, m, consecuencia, f. vi frutar, dar fruto. **bottled f.,** fruta en almíbar, f. **candied f.,** fruta azucarada, f. **dried f.,** fruta seca, f. **first fruits,** primicias, f pl. **soft f.,** frutas blandas, f pl. **stone f.,** fruta de hueso, f. **f.-bearing,** frutal. **f.-cake,** pastel de fruta, m. **f.-dish,** frutero, m. **f. farming,** fruticultura, f. **f.-knife,** cuchillo de postres, m. **f. shop,** frutería, f. **f. tree,** frutal, m

fruiterer n frutero (-ra)

fruitful a fructuoso, fértil; prolífico, fecundo; provechoso

fruitfulness n fertilidad, f; fecundidad, f; provecho, m

fruition n fruición, f

fruitless a infructuoso, estéril; inútil

fruitlessness n infructuosidad, esterilidad, f; inutilidad, f

fruity a de fruta; (wines) vinoso; (of voice) melodioso

frump n estantigua, f

frumpish a estrafalario; fuera de moda

frustrate vt frustrar; defraudar; malograr; destruir; anular

frustration n frustración, f; defraudación, f; malogro, m; destrucción, f; desengaño, m

fry n cul fritada, f, vt freír. vi freírse. **small fry,** inf gente menuda, f

frying n fritura, f, el freír. **to fall out of the f.-pan into the fire,** ir de mal en peor, andar de zocos en colodros, ir de Guatemala en Guatapeor. **f.-pan,** sartén, f

fuchsia n bot fucsia, f

fuddle vt atontar, aturdir; embriagar, emborrachar

fudge n patraña, tontería, f, disparate, m. interj ¡qué disparate! ¡qué va!

fuel n combustible, m; fig cebo, pábulo, m. vt cebar, echar combustible en. vi tomar combustible. **to add f. to the flame,** echar leña al fuego. **f. consumption,** consumo de combustible, m. **f.-oil,** aceite combustible, aceite de quemar, m. **f.-tank,** depósito de combustible, m

fueling n aprovisionamiento de combustible, m

fugitive a fugitivo; pasajero, perecedero; transitorio; efímero, fugaz. n fugitivo (-va); (from justice) prófugo (-ga); mil desertor, m; (refugee) refugiado (-da)

fugue n mus fuga, f

fulcrum n mech fulcro, m

fulfil vt cumplir; (satisfy) satisfacer; (observe) observar; guardar. **to be fulfilled,** cumplirse, realizarse

fulfilment n cumplimiento, m; desempeño, ejercicio, m; (satisfaction) satisfacción, realización, f; (observance) observancia, f

full a lleno; colmado; todo; pleno; (crowded) atestado; (replete) harto; abundante; (intent on) preocupado con, pensando en; (loose) amplio; (plentiful) copioso; (occupied) ocupado; completo; (resonant) sonoro; (mature) maduro; puro; perfecto; (satiated) saciado (de); (of the moon, sails) lleno; (weighed down) agobiado, abrumado; (detailed) detallado; (with uniform, etc.) de gala; (with years, etc.) cumplido. *n* colmo, *m*; totalidad, *f*. *adv* muy; completamente, totalmente. **f. many a flower,** muchas flores. **at f. gallop,** a galope tendido. **at f. speed,** a todo correr; a toda velocidad. **His hands are f.,** Sus manos están llenas. **The moon was at the f.,** La luna estaba llena. **in f.,** por completo; sin abreviaciones; integralmente. **in f. swing,** en plena actividad. **in f. vigor,** en pleno vigor. **to the f.,** completamente; hasta la última gota; a la perfección. **to be f. to the brim,** estar lleno hasta el tope. **f.-blooded,** sanguíneo; de pura raza; *fig* viril, vigoroso; *fig* apasionado. **f.-blown,** en plena flor, abierto. **f. dress,** a de gala. *n* traje de etiqueta, traje de ceremonia, *m*. **f.-face,** de cara. **f.-flavored,** (wine) abocado. **f.-grown,** adulto; completamente desarrollado. **f.-length,** de cuerpo entero. **f. moon,** luna llena, *f*; plenilunio, *m*. **f. name,** nombre y apellidos, *m*. **f. powers,** plenos poderes, *m pl*. **f. scale,** tamaño natural, *m*. **f. scope,** carta blanca, *f*; toda clase de facilidades. **f. steam ahead,** a todo vapor. **f. stop,** *gram* punto final, *m*

full *vt* (cloth) abatanar

full-color *a* a todo color. **full-color plates,** láminas a todo color

fuller *n* batanero, *m*. **fuller's earth,** tierra de batán, galactita, *f*

fulling *n* abatanadura, *f*. **f.-mill,** batán, *m*

fullness *n* abundancia, *f*; plenitud, *f*; (repletion) hartura, *f*; (of clothes) amplitud, *f*; (stoutness) gordura, *f*; (swelling) hinchazón, *f*. **She wrote with great f. of all that she had seen,** Describía muy detalladamente todo lo que había visto. **in the f. of time,** andando el tiempo

full-page *a* a toda plana. **full-page advertisement,** anuncio a toda plana.

full-time *a* de tiempo completo

fully *adv* plenamente; enteramente. **It is f. six years since . . . ,** Hace seis años bien cumplidos que . . . **It is f. 9 o'clock,** Son las nueve bien sonadas. **f. dressed,** completamente vestido

fulminant *a med* fulminante

fulminate *n chem* fulminato, *m*. *vi* estallar; fulminar. *vt* volar; fulminar

fulminous *a* fulmíneo, fulminoso

fulsome *a* servil; insincero, hipócrita; asqueroso, repugnante

fumble *vi* (grope) ir a tientas; procurar hacer algo; chapucear (con); (for a word) titubear

fumbling *n* hesitación, *f*; tacto incierto, *m*. *a* incierto; vacilante

fumblingly *adv* de manera incierta; a tientas

fume *n* vaho, humo, gas, *m*; emanación, *f*; mal olor, *m*, fetidez, *f*; *fig* vapor, *m*; (state of mind) agitación, *f*; frenesí, *m*. *vi* humear; refunfuñar, echar pestes

fumigate *vt* fumigar; sahumar, perfumar; desinfectar

fumigation *n* fumigación, *f*; sahumerio, *m*

fumigator *n* fumigador (-ra); (apparatus) fumigador, *m*

fumigatory *a* fumigatorio

fuming *n* refunfuño, *m*. *a* refunfuñador

fumy *a* humoso

fun *n* diversión, *f*, entretenimiento, *m*; (joke) chanza, broma, *f*. **for fun,** para divertirse; en chanza. **in fun,** de burlas. **to have fun,** divertirse. **to poke fun at,** burlarse de, mofarse de, ridiculizar

funambulist *n* funámbulo (-la)

function *n* función, *f*. *vi* funcionar

functional *a* funcional

functionary *n* funcionario, *m*. *a* funcional

functioning *n* funcionamiento, *m*

fund *n* fondo, *m*; *pl* **funds,** fondos, *m pl*; *inf* dinero, *m*. **public funds,** fondos públicos, *m pl*. **sinking f.,** fondo de amortización, *m*

fundamental *a* fundamental, básico; esencial. *n* fundamento, *m*

fundamentally *adv* fundamentalmente, básicamente; esencialmente

funeral *a* funeral, fúnebre, funerario. *n* funerales, *m pl*; entierro, *m*. **to attend the f.** (of), asistir a los funerales (de). **f. feast,** banquetes fúnebres, *m pl*. **f. director, f. furnisher,** director de pompas fúnebres, *m*. **f. procession,** cortejo fúnebre, *m*. **f. pyre,** pira funeraria, *f*. **f. service,** misa de difuntos, *f*

funereal *a* fúnebre, lúgubre

fungicide *n* anticriptógamo, *m*

fungous *a* fungoso

fungus *n* hongo, *m*

funicular *a* funicular. **f. railway,** ferrocarril funicular, *m*

funk *n* pánico, *m*; miedo, *m*. *vt* temer; esquivar por miedo a

funnel *n* embudo, *m*; *naut* chimenea, *f*; (of a chimney) cañón (de chimenea), *m*. **f.-shaped,** en forma de embudo

funnily *adv* de un modo raro

funniness *n* lo divertido; rareza, extrañeza, *f*

funny *a* cómico, gracioso; divertido; (strange) extraño, raro; (mysterious) misterioso. **It struck me as f.,** (amused me) Me hizo gracia; (seemed strange) Me pareció raro. **f.-bone,** hueso de la alegría, *m*

fur *n* piel, *f*; depósito, sarro, *m*; (on tongue) saburra, *f*. *a* hecho de pieles. *vt* forrar, or adornar, or cubrir, con pieles; depositar sarro sobre; (the tongue) ensuciarse la lengua. *vi* estar forrado, or adornado, or cubierto, con pieles; formarse incrustaciones; (of the tongue) tener la lengua sucia. **fur cap,** gorra de pieles, *f*. **fur cape,** cuello de piel, *m*; capa de pieles, *f*. **fur trade,** peletería, *f*

furbish *vt* pulir; renovar; limpiar

furious *a* furioso. **to become f.,** ponerse furioso, enfurecerse

furiously *adv* furiosamente, con furia

furiousness *n* furia, *f*

furl *vt* plegar; enrollar; *naut* aferrar

furlong *n* estadio, *m*

furlough *n mil* permiso, *m*. *vt* conceder un permiso (a). **on f.,** de permiso

furnace *n* horno, *m*; (of steam boiler) fogón, *m*; (for central heating) caldera de calefacción central, *f*; (for smelting) cubilote, *m*

furnish *vt* proveer (de), equipar (de), suplir (de); amueblar; (an opportunity) proporcionar; producir

furnished *a* amueblado, con muebles. **f. house,** casa amueblada, *f*

furnisher *n* decorador, *m*; proveedor (-ra)

furnishing *n* provisión, *f*, equipo, *m*; *pl* **furnishings,** accesorios, *m pl*; mobiliario, mueblaje, *m*

furniture *n* mobiliario, mueblaje, *m*; ajuar, equipo, *m*; avíos, *m pl*; *naut* aparejo, *m*. **a piece of f.,** un mueble. **to empty of f.,** desamueblar, quitar los muebles (de). **f. dealer or maker,** mueblista, *mf*. **f. factory,** mueblería, *f*. **f. polish,** crema para muebles, *f*. **f. mover,** transportador de muebles, *m*; (packer) embalador, *m*. **f. repository,** guardamuebles, *m*. **f. van,** carro de mudanzas, *m*

furor *n* furor, *m*

furred *a* forrado or cubierto or adornado de piel; (of the tongue) sucia

furrier *n* peletero, *m*. **furrier's shop,** peletería, *f*

furrow *n* surco, *m*; *carp* muesca, *f*; *arch* estría, *f*; (wrinkle) arruga, *f*. *vt* surcar

furry *a* cubierto de piel; parecido a una piel; hecho de pieles

further *a* ulterior, más distante; (other) otro; opuesto; adicional, más. *adv* más lejos; más allá; además; también; por añadidura. *vt* promover, fomentar; ayudar. **on the f. side,** al otro lado. **till f. orders,** hasta nueva orden. **f. on,** más adelante; más allá

furtherance *n* fomento, *m*, promoción, *f*; progreso, avance, *m*

furthermore *adv* además, por añadidura

furthest *a* (el, la, lo) más lejano or más distante; extremo. *adv* más lejos

furtive *a* furtivo
furtively *adv* furtivamente, a hurtadillas. **to look at f.,** mirar de reojo
fury *n* furor, enfurecimiento, *m,* rabia, *f;* violencia, *f;* frenesí, arrebato, *m;* furia, *f.* **like a f.,** hecho una furia. **to breathe forth f.,** echar rayos
fuse *n* (of explosives) espoleta, mecha, *f; elec* fusible, *m. vt* (metals) fundir; fusionar, mezclar. *vi* (metals) fundirse; mezclarse. **safety-f.,** espoleta de seguridad, *f.* **time-f.,** espoleta de tiempo, *f.* **to blow a f.,** fundir un fusible. **f. box,** caja de fusibles, *f.* **f. wire,** fusible, *m*
fuselage *n aer* fuselaje, *m*
fusible *a* fusible
fusillade *n* descarga cerrada, *f*
fusion *n* fusión, *f;* unión, *f;* (melting) fundición, *f*
fuss *n* agitación, *f;* (bustle) conmoción, bulla, *f;* bullicio, *m. vi* agitarse, preocuparse. *vt* poner nervioso. **There's no need to make such a f.,** No es para tanto. **to make a f. of,** (a person) hacer la rueda (a), ser muy

atento (a); (spoil) mimar mucho (a). **to f. about,** andar de acá para allá
fussily *adv* nerviosamente; de un aire importante
fussy *a* meticuloso, nimio; nervioso; (of style) florido, hinchado; (of dress) demasiado adornado
fustigate *vt* fustigar
fusty *a* (moldy) mohoso; mal ventilado; mal oliente; (of views, etc.) pasado de moda
futile *a* fútil, superficial, frívolo; inútil
futility *n* futilidad, superficialidad, frivolidad, *f;* (action) tontería, estupidez, *f*
future *a* futuro, venidero. *n* futuro, porvenir, *m.* **in the f.,** en adelante, en lo venidero, en lo sucesivo. **for f. reference,** para información futura. **f. perfect tense,** *gram* futuro perfecto, *m.* **f. tense,** *gram* futuro, *m*
futurism *n* futurismo, *m*
futurist *n* futurista, *mf*
futuristic *a* futurístico
fuzz *n* tamo, *m,* pelusa, *f.* **f.-ball,** *bot* bején, *m*
fuzzy *a* crespo rizado; velloso

G

g *n* (letter) ge, *f; mus* sol, *m.* **G clef,** clave de sol, *f*
gab *n inf* labia, *f.* **to have the gift of the gab,** tener mucha labia
gabardine *n* gabardina, *f*
gabble *vi* chacharear, garlar; hablar indistintamente; (of goose and some birds) graznar. *vt* decir indistintamente; decir rápidamente; (a language) chapurrear; mascullar. *n* cháchara, *f;* vocerío, *m;* (of goose and some birds) graznido, *m*
gabbler *n* charlatán (-ana), chacharero (-ra)
gabbling *n* See **gabble**
gable *n arch* gablete, hastial, *m.* **g.-end,** alero, *m*
gad *vi* corretear, callejear. **to gad about,** correr por todos lados; divertirse
gadabout *n* azotacalles, *mf;* gandul (-la), vagabundo (-da)
gadding *a* callejero; vagabundo. *n* vagancia, *f;* vida errante, *f;* gandulería, *f*
gadfly *n ent* tábano, *m; inf* moscardón, *m*
gadget *n* accesorio, *m;* aparato, *m;* chuchería, *f*
Gadsden Purchase la Venta de la Meseta, *f*
Gael *n* escocés (-esa) del norte; celta, *mf*
Gaelic *a* gaélico. *n* gaélico, *m*
gaff *n* (hook) garfio, *m; naut* pico de cangrejo, *m; theat* teatrucho, *m*
gaffer *n* viejo, tío, abuelo, *m*
gag *n* mordaza, *f; theat* morcilla, *f. vt* amordazar; *fig* hacer callar. *vi theat* meter morcillas
gage *n* prenda, fianza, *f;* (symbol of challenge) guante, *m;* (challenge) desafío, *m.* See **gauge**
gagging *n* amordazamiento, *m*
gaggle *n* (cry) graznido, *m;* (of geese) manada (de ocas), *f. vi* graznar; cacarear
gaiety *n* alegría, *f;* animación, vivacidad, *f;* (entertainment) diversión, festividad, *f*
gaily *adv* alegremente
gain *n* ganancia, *f;* provecho, beneficio, *m;* (increase) aumento, *m; vt* ganar; adquirir; obtener; conquistar; captar; (friends) hacerse; (reach) llegar a, alcanzar. *vi* ganar; (improve) mejorar; (of a watch) adelantarse. **What have they gained by going to Canada?** ¿Qué han logrado con marcharse al Canadá? **to g. ground,** *fig* ganar terreno. **to g. momentum** adquirir velocidad **to g. time,** ganar tiempo. **to g. on, upon,** acercarse a; (overtake) alcanzar; (outstrip) dejar atrás, pasar; (of sea) invadir; (of habits) imponerse
gainful *a* ganancioso, lucrativo; ventajoso
gainfully *adv* ventajosamente; lucrativamente
gainsay *vt* contradecir; oponer; negar
gainsaying *n* contradicción, *f;* oposición, *f;* negación, *f*

gait *n* porte, andar, *m;* paso, *m,* andadura, *f*
gaiter *n* polaina, *f;* (spat) botín, *m*
gala *n* gala, fiesta, *f.* **g.-day.** día de fiesta. *m.* **g.-dress,** traje de gala, *m*
galaxy *n ast* vía láctea, *f; fig* constelación, *f;* grupo brillante, *m*
gale *n* vendaval, ventarrón, *m;* (storm) temporal, *m;* tempestad, *f*
Galician *a* and *n* gallego (-ga).
Galilean *a* and *n* galileo (-ea)
Galilee Galilea, *f*
gall *n* (on horses) matadura, *f;* (abrasion) rozadura, *f;* hiel, bilis, *f; fig* hiel, amargura, *f;* rencor, *m;* (American slang) descaro, *m,* impertinencia, *f; bot* agalla, *f. vt* rozar; *fig* mortificar, herir. **g.-apple,** agalla, *f.* **g.-bladder,** vejiga de la hiel, *f.* **g.-stone,** cálculo hepático, *m*
gallant *a* hermoso; (imposing) imponente, majestuoso; (brave) valiente, gallardo, valeroso, intrépido; (chivalrous) caballeroso; noble; (attentive to ladies, or amorous) galante. *n* galán, *m. vt* galantear, cortejar
gallantly *adv* (bravely) valientemente; caballerosamente; cortésmente; galantemente
gallantry *n* (bravery) valentía, *f,* valor, *m;* heroísmo, *m,* proeza, *f;* (chivalry) caballerosidad, *f;* (toward women, or amorousness) galantería, *f*
galleon *n* galeón, *m*
gallery *n* galería, *f;* pasillo, *m;* (of a cloister) tránsito, *m;* (cloister) claustro, *m;* (for spectators) tribuna, *f; theat* paraíso, gallinero, *m;* (theater audience) galería, *f;* (of portraits, etc.) galería, colección, *f;* (min, mil) galería, *f;* (building) museo, *m.* **art g.,** museo de pinturas, *m*
galley *n* (naut, print) galera, *f;* (kitchen) cocina, *f;* (rowboat) falúa de capitán, *f.* **to condemn to the galleys,** echar a galeras. **wooden g.,** *print* galerín. *m.* **g.-proof,** galerada, *f.* **g.-slave,** galeote, *m*
Gallic *a* gálico, galicano; francés
gallicism *n* galicismo, *m*
galling *a fig* irritante; mortificante
gallivant *vi* callejear, corretear; divertirse; ir de parranda
gallon *n* galón, *m*
galloon *n* galón, *m,* trencilla, *f*
gallop *n* galope, *m. vi* galopar; ir aprisa. *vt* hacer galopar, **at full g.,** a rienda suelta, a galope tendido. **to g. back,** volver a galope. **to g. down,** bajar a galope. **to g. off,** marcharse galopando; alejarse corriendo. **to g. past,** desfilar a galope ante. **to g. through,** cruzar a galope. **to g. up,** *vt* subir a galope. *vi* llegar a galope
gallopade *n* (dance) galop, *m*
galloping *n* galope, *m;* galopada, *f. a* que va a galope; *med* galopante. **g. consumption,** tisis galopante, *f*

gallows *n* patíbulo, *m*, horca, *f*; (framework) montante, *m*. **g.-bird,** criminal digno de la horca, *m*

galop *n* galop, *m*

galore *adv* a granel, en abundancia (e.g. **sunshine galore,** sol a granel)

galosh *n* chanclo, *m*

galvanic *a elec* galvánico; espasmódico

galvanism *n elec* galvanismo, *m*

galvanize *vt* galvanizar

gambit *n* (chess) gambito, *m*; *fig* táctica, *f*

gamble *n* juego de azar, *m*; jugada, *f*; aventura, *f*; *com* especulación, *f. vi* jugar por dinero; especular; (with) *fig* aventurar, arriesgar. **to g. on the Stock Exchange,** jugar en la bolsa. **to g. away,** perder al juego

gambler *n* jugador (-ra)

gambling *n* juego, *m. a* jugador; de juego. **g.-den,** casa de juego, *f*, garito, *m*

gambol *n* salto, brinco, retozo, *m*; cabriola, *f*; juego, *m. vi* saltar, brincar, retozar; juguetear

game *n* juego, *m*; (match) partido, *m*; (jest) chanza, *f*; (trick) trampa, *f*; (birds, hares, etc.) caza menor, *f*; (tigers, lions, etc.) caza mayor, *f*; (flesh of game) caza, *f*; *pl* **games,** deportes, *m pl. a* de caza; (courageous) valiente, animoso, brioso; resuelto. *vi* jugar por dinero. **He is g. for anything,** Se atreve a todo. **big g. hunting,** caza mayor, *f*. **head of g.,** pieza de caza, *f*. **It is a g. at which two can play,** Donde las dan las toman. **The g. is not worth the candle,** La cosa no vale la pena. **The g. is up,** *fig* El proyecto se ha frustrado. **to make g. of,** (things) burlarse de; (persons) tomar el pelo a; mofarse de. **to play the g.,** *fig* jugar limpio. **to g. away,** perder al juego. **g. of cards,** juego de naipes, *m*. **g. of chance,** juego de azar, *m*. **g.-bag,** morral, *m*. **g. drive,** batida de caza, *f*. **g.-laws,** leyes de caza, *f pl*. **g.-licence,** licencia de caza, *f*. **g.-pie,** tortada, *f*. **g. preserve,** coto de caza, *m*

gamekeeper *n* guardabosque, *m*

gamely *adv* valientemente

gameness *n* valentía, resolución, fortaleza, *f*

gamete *n* gameto, *m*

gaming *n* juego, *m, a* de juego. **g.-house,** garito, *m*. **g.-table,** mesa de juego, *f*; *fig* juego, *m*

gammon *n* (of bacon) jamón, *m. vt* curar (jamón)

gamut *n* gama, *f*

gander *n* ganso, *m*

gang *n* cuadrilla, pandilla, *f*; (squad) pelotón, *m*; (of workers) brigada, cuadrilla, *f*; group, *m*. **g.-plank,** plancha, *f*

ganglion *n* ganglio, *m*; *fig* centro, *m*

gangrene *n* gangrena, *f. vt* gangrenar. *vi* gangrenarse

gangrenous *a* gangrenoso

gangster *n* pistolero, gángster, *m*

gangway *n* pasillo, *m*; *naut* plancha, *f*, pasamano, *m*; (opening in ship's side) portalón, *m*. **midship g.,** crujía, *f*

gap *n* brecha, *f*; abertura, *f*; (hole) boquete, *m*; (pass) desfiladero, paso, *m*; (ravine) hondonada, barranca, *f*; (blank) laguna, *f*, vacío, *m*; (crack) intersticio, *m*, hendedura, *f*, resquicio, *m*. **to fill a gap,** llenar un boquete; llenar un vacío

gape *vi* estar con la boca abierta, papar moscas. **to g. at,** mirar con la boca abierta

gaping *n* huelgo, *m*; abertura, *f*, *a* que bosteza; boquiabierto; abierto

garage *n* garaje, *m*. *vt* poner (un coche, etc.) en un garaje. **g. owner,** garajista, *mf*

garb *n* traje, vestido, *m*; uniforme, *m*; *her* espiga, *f. vt* vestir, ataviar

garbage *n* basura, inmundicia, *f*

garbage can basurero, tarro de la basura, *m*

garble *vt* falsear, mutilar, pervertir

garden *n* jardín, *m*; huerto, *m*; (fertile region) huerta, *f. a* de jardín. *vi* trabajar en el jardín, cultivar un huerto. **g. city,** ciudad jardín, *f*. **g.-frame,** semillero, *m*. **g. mold,** tierra vegetal, *f*. **g.-party,** fiesta de jardín, *f*. **g.-plot,** parterre, *m*. **g. produce,** hortalizas, legum-

bres, *f pl*. **g. roller,** rodillo, *m*. **g.-seat,** banco de jardín, *m*. **g. urn,** jarrón, *m*

gardener *n* jardinero, *m*

gardenia *n* gardenia, *f*, jazmín de la India, *m*

gardening *n* jardinería, *f*; horticultura, *f. a* de jardinería

gargantuan *a* gargantuesco; tremendo, enorme

gargle *n* (liquid) gargarismo, *m*; gárgaras, *f pl. vi* hacer gárgaras, gargarizar

gargling *n* gargarismo, *m*

gargoyle *n* gárgola, *f*

garish *a* cursi, llamativo, charro, chillón

garishness *n* cursería, ostentación, *f*, lo llamativo

garland *n* guirnalda, *f*; corona, *f*; (anthology) florilegio, *m*; *arch* festón, *m*. *vt* enguirnaldar

garlic *n* ajo, *m*

garment *n* prenda de vestir, *f*; traje, vestido, *m*; *fig* vestidura, *f*; (*fig* cloak) capa, *f*

garner *n* granero, *m*; tesoro, *m*; colección, *f. vt* atesorar, guardar

garnet *n* granate, *m*

garnish *n cul* aderezo, *m*; adorno, *m*. *vt cul* aderezar; embellecer, adornar

garnishing *n*. See **garnish**

garret *n* guardilla, buhardilla, *f*, desván, *m*

garrison *n* guarnición, *f*, presidio, *m*. *vt* guarnecer, presidiar. **g. town,** plaza de armas, *f*

garrote *n* garrote, *m*. *vt* agarrotar, dar garrote (a)

garrulity *n* garrulidad, locuacidad, charlatanería, *f*

garrulous *a* gárrulo, locuaz, charlatán

garter *n* liga, *f*; (G.) Jarretera, *f*; *vt* atar con liga; investir con la Jarretera. **Order of the G.,** Orden de la Jarretera, *f*

gas *n* gas, *m*; *fig, inf* palabrería, *f*; (petrol) bencina, *f*, *a* de gas; con gas; para gases. *vt* asfixiar con gas; *mil* atacar con gas; saturar de gas. **gas attack,** ataque con gases asfixiantes, *m*. **gas-bag,** bolsa de gas, *f*; *inf* charlatán (-ana). **gas-burner,** mechero de gas, *m*. **gas-chamber,** cámara de gas, *f*. **gas detector,** detector de gases, *m*. **gas-fire,** estufa de gas, *f*. **gas-fitter,** gasista, *m*. **gas-fittings,** lámparas de gas, *f pl*. **gas-light,** luz de gas, *f*; mechero de gas, *m*. **gas-main,** cañería maestra de gas, *f*. **gas-man,** gasista, *m*. **gas-mantle,** camiseta incandescente, *f*. **gas-mask,** máscara para gases, *f*. **gas-meter,** contador de gas, *m*. **gas-pipes,** cañerías (or tuberías) de gas, *f pl*. **gas-ring,** fogón de gas, *m*. **gas-shell,** obús de gases asfixiantes, *m*. **gas-stove,** cocina de gas, *f*. **gas warfare,** guerra química, *f*. **gas-works,** fábrica de gas, *f*

Gascon *a and n* gascón (-ona)

Gascony Gascuña, *f*

gaseous *a* gaseoso

gash *n* cuchillada, *f*; herida extensa, *f. vt* acuchillar; herir extensamente

gasket *n* aro de empaquetadura, *m*

gasoline *n* gasolina, *f*

gasp *n* boqueada, *f. vi* boquear. **to be at the last g.,** estar agonizando. **to g. for breath,** luchar por respirar. **to g. out,** decir anhelante, decir con voz entrecortada

gastric *a* gástrico

gastritis *n* gastritis, *f*

gastronome *n* gastrónomo (-ma)

gastronomic *a* gastronómico

gastronomy *n* gastronomía, *f*

gate *n* puerta, *f*; cancela, verja, *f*; entrada, *f*; (of a lock, etc.) compuerta, *f*; (across a road, etc.) barrera, *f*; (money) entrada, *f*; *fig* puerta, *f*. **automatic g.,** (at level crossings, etc.) barrera de golpe, *f*. **to g.-crash,** asistir sin invitación. **g.-keeper,** portero, *m*; guardabarrera, *mf* **g.-money,** entrada, *f*. **g.-post,** soporte de la puerta, *m*

gateway *n* entrada, *f*; puerta, *f*; paso, *m*; vestíbulo, *m*; *fig* puerta, *f*

gather *vt* (assemble) reunir; (amass) acumular, amontonar; (acquire) obtener, adquirir; hacer una colección (de); cobrar; (harvest) cosechar, recolectar; (pick up) recoger; (pluck) coger; (infer) sacar en limpio, aprender; *sew* fruncir; (the brows) fruncir (el ceño). *vi* reunirse, congregarse; amontonarse; (threaten) amenazar; (sadden) amargar; (*fig* hover over) cernerse (sobre); (increase) aumentar, crecer; (be covered) cubrirse; (fester) supurar. *n sew* frunce, pliegue, *m*. **to g. breath,** tomar aliento. **to g. speed,** ganar velocidad. **to g. strength,** cobrar fuerzas. **I g. from Mary that they are going abroad,** Según lo que me ha dicho María, van al extranjero. **to g. in,** juntar; reunir; (harvest) cosechar; coger. **to g. together,** *vt* reunir. *vi* reunirse. **to g. up,** recoger; coger; tomar; (one's limbs) encoger. **to g. up the threads,** *fig* recoger los hilos.

gatherer *n* cogedor, colector, *m*; (harvester) segador, *m*; (of grapes) vendimiador (-ra); (of taxes) recaudador, *m*

gathering *n* cogedura, *f*; (fruit, etc.) recolección *f*; (of taxes) recaudación, *f*; amontonamiento, *m*; colección, *f*; *med* absceso, *m*; *sew* fruncimiento, *m*; (assembly) reunión, asamblea, *f*; (crowd) concurrencia, muchedumbre, *f*

gathers *n sew* fruncidos, pliegues, *m pl*

gauche *a* torpe, huraño

gaudily *adv* ostentosamente; brillantemente

gaudiness *n* ostentación, *f*; brillantez, *f*

gaudy *a* llamativo, vistoso, brillante, ostentoso

gauge *n* (of gun) calibre, *m*; (railway) entrevía, *f*; (for measuring) indicator, *m*; regla de medir, *f*; *naut* calado, *m*; *fig* medida, *f*; (test) indicación, *f*; (model) norma, *f*. *vt* calibrar; medir; estimar; (ship's capacity) arquear; (judge) juzgar; (size up) tomar la medida (de); *fig* interpretar; *sew* fruncir; (liquor) aforar. **broad (narrow) g. railway,** ferrocarril de vía ancha (estrecha), *m*. **pressure g.,** manómetro, *m*. **water g.,** indicador del nivel de agua, *m*

gauging *n* medida, *f*; (of ship's capacity) arqueo, *m*; (of liquor) aforamiento, *m*; *fig* apreciación, *f*; interpretación, *f*

Gaul Galia, *f*

gaunt *a* anguloso, huesudo, desvaído; (of houses, etc.) lúgubre

gauntlet *n* guante de manopla, *m*; (part of armor) manopla, *f*, guantelete, *m*. **to throw down the g.,** echar el guante, desafiar

gauntness *n* angulosidad, flaqueza, *f*

gauze *n* gasa, *f*; (mist) bruma, *f*. **wire-g.,** tela metálica, *f*

gauziness *n* diafanidad, *f*

gauzy *a* diáfano; de gasa

gavotte *n* gavota, *f*

gawkiness *n* torpeza, desmaña, *f*

gawky *a* anguloso, desgarbado, torpe

gay *a* alegre; festivo, animado; ligero de cascos, disipado; homosexual; (of colors) brillante, llamativo

Gaza Strip la franja de Gaza, *f*

gaze *n* mirada, *f*; mirada fija, *f*. *vi* mirar; mirar fijamente, contemplar

gazelle *n* gacel (-la)

gazer *n* espectador (-ra)

gazette *n* gaceta, *f*. *vt* publicar en la gaceta

gazing *n* contemplación, *f*, *a* contemplador; que presencia, que asiste a

gear *n* (apparel) atavíos, *m pl*; (harness) guarniciones, *f pl*, arneses, *m pl*; (tackle) utensilios, *m pl*, herramientas, *f pl*; *naut* aparejo, *m*; *mech* engranaje, *m*; juego, *m*, marcha, *f*. *vt* aparejar, enjaezar; *mech* poner en marcha, hacer funcionar. *vi mech* engranar, endentar. **low g.,** pimera velocidad, *f*. **neutral g.,** punto muerto, *m*. **reverse g.,** marcha atrás, *f*. **second g.,** segunda velocidad, *f*. **three-speed g.,** cambio de marchas de tres velocidades, *m*. **top g.,** tercera (or cuarta—according to gear-box) velocidad, *f*. **to change g.,** cambiar de marcha, cambiar de velocidad. **to throw out of g.,** *fig* desquiciar. **g.-box,** caja de velocidades, *f*. **g.-changing,** cambio de velocidad, *m*. **g.-changing lever,** palanca de cambio de velocidad, palanca de cambio de marchas, *f*

gearing *n* engranaje, *m*

gee up *interj* ¡arre!

gehenna *n* gehena, *m*

geisha *n* geisha, *f*

gelatine *n* gelatina, *f*. **cooking g.,** gelatina seca, *f*

gelatinous *a* gelatinoso

geld *vt* capar, castrar

gelder *n* castrador, *m*

gelding *n* castración, capadura, *f*; caballo castrado, *m*; animal castrado, *m*

gelid *a* gélido, helado; *fig* frío, frígido

gem *n* piedra preciosa, *f*; joya, alhaja, *f*; *fig* joya, *f*. *vt* adornar con piedras preciosas; enjoyar

Gemini *n* (los) Gemelos

gender *n gram* género, *m*; sexo, *m*

gene *n biol* gene, *m*

genealogical *a* genealógico. **g. tree,** árbol genealógico, *m*

genealogist *n* genealogista, *mf*

genealogy *n* genealogía, *f*

general *a* general; universal; común; corriente; (usual) acostumbrado, usual; del público, público. *n* lo general (*mil, ecc*) general, *m*; *inf* criada para todo, *f*. **in g.,** por lo general, en general, generalmente. **to become g.,** generalizarse. **to make g.,** generalizar, hacer general. **g. average,** (marine insurance) avería gruesa, *f*. **g. election,** elección general, *f*. **g. meeting,** pleno, mitin general, *m*. **g. opinion,** voz común, opinión general, *f*. **G. Post Office,** Oficina Central de Correos, *f*. **g. practitioner,** médico (-ca) general. **g. public,** público, *m*. **the general reader** el lector de tipo general *m*

generalissimo *n* generalísimo, *m*

generality *n* generalidad, *f*

generalization *n* generalización, *f*

generalize *vt* and *vi* generalizar

generally *adv* en general, por regla general, por lo general, generalmente; comúnmente, por lo común

generalship *n mil* generalato, *m*; (strategy) táctica, estrategia, *f*; dirección, jefatura, *f*

generate *vt* (beget) engendrar, procrear; (*phys, chem*) generar; *fig* producir, crear

generation *n* procreación, *f*; generación, *f*; *fig* producción, creación, *f*. **the younger g.,** los jóvenes

generative *a* generador

generator *n mech* generador, *m*; dínamo, *f*

generic *a* genérico

generosity *n* generosidad, *f*; liberalidad, *f*

generous *a* generoso; liberal, dadivoso; magnánimo; (plentiful) abundante; (of wines) generoso

generously *adv* generosamente; abundantemente

genesis *n* principio, origen, *m*; (G.) Génesis, *m*

genetic *a* genético

genetics *n* genética, *f*

Geneva Ginebra *f*

Genevan *a* and *n* ginebrés (-esa), ginebrino (-na)

genial *a* (of climate) agradable, bueno; (of persons) afable, bondadoso; de buen humor, bonachón

geniality *n* afabilidad, bondad, *f*; buen humor, *m*

genially *adv* afablemente

genie *n* genio, *m*

genital *a* genital, sexual. *n pl* **genitals,** genitales, *m pl*

genitive *a* and *n gram* genitivo *m*.

genius *n* genio, *m*; carácter, *m*, índole, *f*; ingenio, *m*; *inf* talento, *m*

Genoa Genova, *f*

Genoese *a* and *n* genovés (-esa)

genre *n* género, *m*. **g. painting,** cuadro de género, *m*

genteel *a* fino; (affected) remilgado, melindroso; de buen tono; de buena educación

gentile *a* and *n* gentil *mf*

gentility *n* aristocracia, *f*; respetabilidad, *f*

gentle *a* noble, bien nacido, de buena familia; amable; suave; ligero; dulce; (docile) manso, dócil; (affectionate) cariñoso; bondadoso; sufrido, paciente; cortés; pacífico, tolerante. **He was a man of g. birth,** Era un hombre bien nacido. **"G. reader,"** «Querido lector»

gentlefolk *n pl* gente de bien, gente fina, *f;* gente de buena familia, *f*

gentleman *n* caballero, señor, *m;* gentilhombre, *m.* **Ladies and gentlemen,** Señoras y caballeros, Señores. **young g.,** señorito, *m.* **to be a perfect g.,** ser un caballero perfecto. **g.-inwaiting,** gentilhombre de la cámara, *m*

gentlemanliness *n* caballerosidad, *f*

gentlemanly *a* caballeroso

gentleness *n* amabilidad, *f;* suavidad, *f;* dulzura, *f;* mansedumbre, docilidad, *f;* bondad, *f;* paciencia, *f;* cortesía, *f;* tolerancia, *f*

gentlewoman *n* dama, *f;* dama de servicio, *f*

gently *adv* suavemente; dulcemente; silenciosamente, sin ruido; (slowly) despacio, poco a poco. **g. born,** bien nacido

gentry *n* pequeña aristocracia, alta clase media, *f;* (disparaging) gentle, *f*

genuflect *vi* doblar la rodilla

genuflexion *n* genuflexión, *f*

genuine *a* puro; genuino; verdadero; real; sincero; auténtico

genuinely *adv* genuinamente; verdaderamente; realmente; sinceramente

genuineness *n* pureza, *f;* autenticidad, *f;* verdad, *f;* sinceridad, *f*

genus *n* género, *m*

geodesic *a* geodésico

geodesy *n* geodesia, *f*

geographer *n* geógrafo, *m*

geographical *a* geográfico

geographically *adv* geográficamente; desde el punto de vista geográfico

geography *n* geografía, *f*

geological *a* geológico

geologically *adv* geológicamente; desde el punto de vista geológico

geologist *n* geólogo, *m*

geologize *vi* estudiar la geología. *vt* estudiar desde un punto de vista geológico

geology *n* geología, *f*

geometric *a* geométrico

geometry *n* geometría, *f*

geophysics *n* geofísica, *f*

Georgian *a geog* georgiano; del principio del siglo diez y nueve

georgic *n* geórgica, *f*

geotropism *n* geotropismo, *m*

geranium *n* geranio, *m*

germ *n* embrión, germen, *m;* microbio, bacilo, *m; fig* germen, *m.* **g.-cell,** célula germinal, *f*

German *a* alemán; germánico. *n* alemán (-ana); (language) alemán, *m;* germano (-na), germánico (-ca). **Sudeten G.,** alemán (-ana) sudete. **G. measles,** rubeola, *f.* **G. silver** alpaca, *f,* melchor *m,* plata alemana *f*

germander *n bot* camedrio, *m*

germane *a* pertinente (a), a propósito (a)

Germanic *a* germánico. *n* (language) germánico, *m*

Germanization *n* germanización, *f*

Germanize *vt* germanizar. *vi* germanizarse

Germanophile *n* germanófilo (-la)

Germany Alemania, *f*

germicidal *a* bactericida

germicide *n* desinfectante, *m*

germinal *a* germinal. *n* (G.) germinal, *m*

germinate *vi* germinar, brotar. *vt* hacer germinar

germination *n* germinación, *f*

germinative *a* germinativo

gerund *n* gerundio, *m*

gerundive *n* gerundio adjetivado, *m*

Gestapo *n* Gestapo, *f*

gestation *n* gestación, *f*

gesticulate *vi* gesticular, hacer gestos; accionar. *vt* expresar por gestos

gesticulation *n* gesticulación, *f*

gesticulatory *a* gesticular

gesture *n* movimiento, *m;* gesticulación, *f;* (of the face) gesto, *m,* mueca, *f;* ademán, *m,* acción, *f. vi* gesticular. *vt* decir por gestos; acompañar con gestos

get *vt* (obtain) obtener; (acquire) adquirir; (buy) comprar; (take) tomar; (receive) recibir; (gain, win) ganar; (hit) acertar, dar; (place) poner; (achieve) alcanzar, lograr; (make) hacer; (call) llamar; (understand) comprender; (catch) coger; (procreate) procrear, engendrar; (induce) persuadir; (invite) convidar, invitar; (cause) hacer; (with have and past part.) tener; (with have and past part. followed by infin.) tener que; (followed by noun and past part.) hacer; (fetch) buscar, ir a buscar; (order) mandar, disponer; (procure) procurar; (bring) traer; (money) hacer; (a reputation, etc.) hacerse; (a prize, an advantage) llevar; (learn) aprender; (be) ser. *vi* (become) hacerse; ponerse; venir a ser; (old) envejecerse; (angry) montar (en cólera), enojarse; (arrive) llegar a; (attain) alcanzar; (accomplish) conseguir, lograr; (drunk) emborracharse; (hurt) hacerse daño; (wet) mojarse; (cool) enfriarse; (money) hacer (dinero); (of health) ponerse; (find oneself) hallarse, encontrarse; (late) hacerse (tarde); (dark) empezar a caer (la noche), empezar a caer (la noche), empezar a oscurecer; (put oneself) meterse; (grow, be) estar; (on to or on top of) montar sobre, subir a. **He has got run over,** Ha sido atropellado. **It gets on my nerves,** Se me pone los nervios en punta. **Let's get it over!** ¡Vamos a concluir de una vez! **How do you get on with her?** ¿Cómo te va con ella? **She must be getting on for twenty,** Tendrá alrededor de veinte años. **to get a suit made,** mandar hacerse un traje. **to get better,** (in health) mejorar de salud; hacer progresos adelantar. **to get dark,** obscurecer. **to get into conversation with,** trabar conversación con. **to get into bad company,** frecuentar malas compañías. **to get into the habit of,** acostumbrarse a. **to get married,** casarse. **to get near,** acercarse. **to get one's own way,** salir con la suya. **to get oneself up as,** disfrazarse de. **to get out in a hurry,** salir apresuradamente; marcharse rápidamente, *inf* salir pitando. **to get out of the way,** quitarse de en medio, apartarse. **to get rid of,** desembarazarse de, librarse de; salir de; perder. **to have got,** poseer; tener; padecer. **Get on!** ¡Adelante!; (to a horse) ¡Arre!; (continue) ¡Sigue! **Get out!** ¡Fuera! ¡Largo de aquí! ¡Sal! **Get up!** ¡Levántate!; (to a horse) ¡Arre! **to get about,** moverse mucho; andar mucho; (attend to business affairs) ir a sus negocios; (travel) viajar; (get up from sick bed) levantarse; (go out) salir; (be known) saberse, divulgarse, hacerse público. **to get above,** subir a un nivel más alto (de). **to get across,** *vi* cruzar, atravesar. *vt* hacer cruzar. **to get along,** *vi* (depart) marcharse; (continue) seguir, vivir; (manage) ir, ir tirando. *vt* llevar; traer; hacer andar por. **How are you getting along?** ¿Cómo le va? **I am getting along all right, thank you,** Voy tirando, gracias. **to get along without,** pasarse sin. **to get at,** (remove) sacar; (find) encontrar; (reach) llegar a; alcanzar; (discover) descubrir; (allude to) aludir a; (understand) comprender. **to get away,** *vi* dejar (un lugar); marcharse, irse; (escape) escaparse. *vt* ayudar a marcharse; ayudar a escaparse. **to get away with,** llevarse, marcharse con; *inf* salir con la suya. **to get back,** *vi* regresar, volver; (get home) volver a casa; (be back) estar de vuelta. *vt* (recover) recobrar; (receive) recibir; (find again) hallar de nuevo. **to get down,** *vi* bajar, descender. *vt* bajar; (take off a hook) descolgar; (swallow) tragar; (note) anotar; escribir. **to get down on all fours,** ponerse en cuatro patas. **to get down to,** ponerse a (estudiar, trabajar, etc.). **to get in,** *vi* entrar en; lograr entrar en; (slip in) colarse en; (of political party) entrar en el poder; (of a club) hacerse socio de; (return) regresar; (home) volver a casa; (find oneself) hallarse, estar; (habit) adquirir. *vt* hacer entrar en; (a club, etc.) hacer socio de; (a word) decir. **to get into.** See **to get in. to get off,** *vt* apearse de; bajar de; (send) enviar; (from punishment) librar; (bid goodbye) despedirse de; (remove) quitar, sacar. *vi* apearse; bajar; (from punishment) librarse; (leave) ponerse en camino, marcharse. **to get on,** *vi* (wear) tener puesto; (progress) hacer progresos, adelantar; (prosper) medrar, prosperar; (succeed) tener éxito; avanzar; seguir el camino; (agree) avenirse. *vt* (push) empujar; (place) poner; (cause) hacer; (clothes) ponerse; (mount) subir a. **to get open,** abrir. **to get out,** *vt* hacer salir; sacar; (publish) publicar; divulgar. *vi* salir; escapar; **to get out of a jam,** salir de un paso; (descend) bajar (de). **to get over,** (cross) atravesar, cruzar; (an illness, grief, etc.) reponerse, reponerse de; (excuse) perdonar; (surmount) superar; (ground) recorrer. **to get round,** (a person) persuadir; (surround) rodear; (avoid) evitar; (difficulties) superar, vencer. **to get through,** pasar por; (time) pasar, entretener; (money) gastar; (finish) terminar, acabar; (pierce or enter) penetrar; (communicate) comunicar (con); (difficulties) vencer; (an exam) aprobar. **to get to,** llegar a; encontrar; (begin) empezar. **to get together,** *vt* reunir, juntar. *vi* reunirse, juntarse. **to get under,** ponerse debajo de; (control) dominar. **to get up,** *vt* (raise) alzar, levantar; (carry up things) subir; hacer subir; organizar; preparar; (learn) aprender; (linen) blanquear, colar; (ascend) subir; hacer; (dress) ataviar; (steam) generar; (a play) ensayar, poner en escena. *vi* levantarse; (on a horse) montar a caballo; (of the wind) refrescarse; (of the fire) avivarse; (of the sea) embravecerse. **to get up to,** llegar a; alcanzar

get-at-able *a* accesible

getting *n* adquisición, *f*; (of money) ganancia, *f*. **g. up,** preparación, *f*; organización, *f*; (of a play) representación (de una comedia), puesta en escena, *f*

get-up *n* atavío, *m*; (of a book, etc.) aspecto, *m*

gewgaw *n* chuchería, *f*

geyser *n* géiser, *m*; (for heating water) calentador (de agua), *m*

ghastliness *n* horror, *m*; palidez mortal, *f*; aspecto miserable, *m*; (boringness) tedio, aburrimiento, *m*; lo desagradable

ghastly *a* horrible; de una palidez mortal; cadavérico; (boring) aburrido; muy desagradable

gherkin *n* cohombrillo, *m*

ghetto *n* gueto *m*

ghost *n* fantasma, espectro, aparecido, *m*; (spirit) alma, *f*, espíritu, *m*; (shadow) sombra, *f*; (writer) mercenario, *m*. Holy G., Espíritu Santo, *m*. **to give up the g.,** entregar el alma; perder la esperanza, desesperarse. **to look like a g.,** parecer un fantasma

ghostliness *n* espiritualidad, *f*; lo misterioso; palidez, *f*; tenuidad, *f*

ghostly *a* espiritual; espectral; misterioso; pálido; vaporoso, tenue; indistinto

ghost town *n* pueblo-fantasma, *m*

ghost word *n* palabra-fantasma, *f*

ghoul *n* vampiro, *m*

ghoulish *a* insano; cruel; sádico

giant *n* gigante, *m*; *fig* coloso, *m*, *a* gigantesco; de gigantes; de los gigantes. **g.-killer,** matador de gigantes, *m*. **g.-stride,** (gymnastics) paso volante, *m*

giantess *n* giganta, *f*

gibber *vi* hablar incoherentemente, hablar entre dientes; farfullar, hablar atropelladamente; decir disparates

gibberish *n* galimatías, *m*; jerigonza, *f*, griego, *m*

gibbet *n* horca, *f*, patíbulo, *m*. **to die on the g.,** morir ahorcado

gibbon *n zool* gibón, *m*

gibe *n* improperio, escarnio, *m*, burla, mofa, *f*. *vi* criticar. **to g. at,** burlarse de, ridiculizar, mofarse de

gibing *n* burlón, mofador. *n* mofas, burlas, *f pl*

gibingly *adv* burlonamente, con sorna

giblets *n* menudillos, *m pl*

giddily *adv* vertiginosamente; frívolamente, atolondradamente

giddiness *n* vértigo, *m*; atolondramiento, *m*; inconstancia, *f*; frivolidad, ligereza de cascos, *f*

giddy *a* vertiginoso; mareado; atolondrado, casquivano, frívolo; inconstante. **She felt very g.,** Se sintió muy mareada. **to make g.,** dar vértigo (a), marear

gift *n* regalo, *m*, dádiva, *f*; (quality) don, talento, *m*; prenda, *f*; poder, *m*; *law* donación, *f*; (offering) ofrenda, oblación, *f*. *vt* dotar. **deed of g.,** *law* escritura de donación, *f*. **in the g. of,** en el poder de, en las manos de. **I wouldn't have it as a g.,** No lo tomaría ni regalado. **Never look a g. horse in the mouth,** A caballo regalado no se le mira el diente. **g. of tongues,** don de las lenguas, genio de las lenguas, *m*

gifted *a* talentoso

gig *n* (carriage) carrocín, *m*; (boat) falúa, lancha, *f*; (for wool) máquina de cardar paño, *f*; (harpoon) arpón, *m*

gigantic *a* gigantesco; colosal, enorme

giggle *vi* reírse sin motivo; reírse disimuladamente. *n* risa disimulada, *f*

giggling *n* risa estúpida, *f*; risa nerviosa, *f*

gigolo *n* gigolo, mantenido, jinetero (Cuba), *m*

gild *vt* dorar; (metals) sobredorar; embellecer. **to g. the pill,** dorar la píldora

gilder *n* dorador, *m*

gilding *n* dorado, *m*, doradura, *f*; embellecimiento, *m*

Gileadite *n* and *a* galaadita, *mf*

gill *n* (of fish) agalla, branquia, *f*; (ravine) barranco, *m*; (measure) cierta medida de líquidos, *f*, ($\frac{1}{4}$ litro)

gilt *n* dorado, *m*; pan de oro, *m*; relumbrón, *m*; *fig* encanto, *m*, *a* dorado, áureo. **g.-edged,** (of books) con los bordes dorados. **g.-edged security,** papel del Estado, *m*; valores de toda confianza, *m pl*

gimcrack *n* chuchería, *f*. *a* de baratillo, cursi; mal hecho

gimlet *n* barrena, *f*, taladro, *m*

gin *n* (drink) ginebra, *f*; (snare) trampa, *f*. *vt* (snare) coger con trampa. **g. block,** *mech* garrucha, *f*

ginger *n* jengibre, *m*; *inf* energía, *f*, brío, *m*, *a* rojo. *vt* sazonar con jengibre; *inf* animar, estimular. **g.-beer,** gaseosa, *f*

gingerly *adv* con gran cuidado; delicadamente

gingham *n* guinga, *f*

gingivitis *n* gingivitis, *f*

gipsy *n*. See **gypsy**

giraffe *n* jirafa, *f*

gird *vt* ceñir; (invest) investir; (surround) cercar, rodear; (put on) revestir. **to g. oneself for the fray,** prepararse para la lucha

girder *n* viga, jácena, *f*. **main g.,** viga maestra, *f*

girdle *n* (belt) cinturón, *m*; (corset) faja, *f*; circunferencia, *f*; zona, *f*. *vt* ceñir; *fig* cercar, rodear

girl *n* niña, *f*; chica, muchacha, *f*; (maidservant) criada, muchacha, *f*; (young lady) señorita, *f*. **a young g.,** una jovencita (a little older) una joven. **old g.,** (of a school) antigua alumna, *f*; *inf* vieja, *f*; (*inf* affectionate) chica, *f*. **g. friend,** amiguita, *f*. **g. guide, girl scout,** exploradora, *f*. **girls' school,** colegio de niñas, colegio de señoritas, *m*

girlhood *n* niñez, *f*; juventud, *f*

girlish *a* de niña, de muchacha; (of boys) afeminado; joven

girth *n* (of horse, etc.) cincha, *f*; circunferencia, *f*; (of person) talle, *m*; (obesity) corpulencia, obesidad, *f*

gist *n* esencia, substancia, *f*, importe, *m*

give *vt* dar; (a present) regalar; (infect) contagiar; (impart) comunicar; (grant) otorgar; (allow, concede) conceder; (assign) asignar, señalar; (appoint) nombrar; (a toast) brindar (a la salud de); (a party, ball, etc.) dar; (a bill) presentar; (wish) desear; (punish) castigar; (pay) pagar; (hand over) entregar; (names at baptism) imponer; (produce) producir; dar; (cause) causar; (of judicial sentences) condenar a; (evoke) proporcionar; (provoke) provocar; (devote) dedicar, consagrar; (sacrifice) sacrificar; (evidence, an account, orders, a lesson, a performance, a concert) dar; (a cry, shout) lanzar, proferir; (a laugh) soltar; (describe) describir;

(paint) pintar; (write) escribir; (offer) ofrecer; (show) mostrar; (transmit) transmitir; (heed, pain) hacer; (a speech) pronunciar, hacer; (award, adjudge) adjudicar; (ear) prestar (oído (a)). *vi* dar; ser dadivoso, mostrarse generoso; (give in) ceder; (be elastic) dar de sí; ablandarse; (collapse) hundirse. **G. them my best wishes!** ¡Dales mis mejores recuerdos! **G. us a song!** ¡Cántanos algo! **I can g.** him a lift in my car, Puedo ofrecerle un asiento en mi auto. **I g. you my word,** Os doy mi palabra. **to g. a good account of oneself,** defenderse bien; hacer bien; salir bien. **to g. a person a piece of one's mind,** contarle cuatro verdades. **to g. chase,** dar caza (a). **to g. it to a person,** poner a uno como nuevo; reprender; (beat) pegar, dar de palos. **to g. of itself,** dar de sí. **to g. rise to,** dar lugar a, ocasionar, causar. **to g. way,** no poder resistir; (break) romperse; (yield) ceder; (collapse) hundirse; (retreat) retroceder. **to g. way to,** (retreat before) retirarse ante; (abandon oneself to) entregarse a, abandonarse a. **to g. away,** enajenar; dar; regalar; (sell cheaply) vender a un precio muy bajo; (get rid of) deshacerse de; (sacrifice) sacrificar; (a secret) revelar; (betray) traicionar; (expose) descubrir; (tell) contar; (a bride) conducir al altar. **He gave himself away,** Reveló su pensamiento sin querer. **to g. back,** *vt* devolver; restituir. *vi* retirarse, cejar. **to g. forth,** divulgar, publicar; (scatter) derramar; (emit) emitir, despedir; (smoke, rays) echar. **to g. in,** *vt* entregar; presentar. *vi* darse por vencido. **to g. in to,** (agree with) asentir en, consentir en; rendirse ante. **Mary always gives in to George,** María hace siempre lo que Jorge quiere. **to g. off,** (of odors, etc.) emitir, exhalar, despedir. **to g. out,** *vt* (distribute) distribuir, repartir; (allocate) asignar; (publish) publicar; (announce) anunciar; (reveal) divulgar; (allege) afirmar, hacer saber; (emit) emitir. *vi* (be exhausted) agotarse; (end) acabarse; (be lacking) faltar. **to g. over,** *vt* entregar; (transfer) traspasar; cesar de. *vi* cesar. **to g. up,** entregar; ceder; (renounce) renunciar (a); (sacrifice) sacrificar; (abandon) abandonar; (cease) dejar de; (as lost) dar por perdido; (of a patient) desahuciar; (a post) dimitir de; (return) devolver, restituir; (a problem) renunciar a resolver un problema); (lose hope) perder la esperanza; (give in) darse por vencido. **I had given you up,** (didn't expect you), Creí que no ibas a venir. **to g. oneself up to,** entregarse a; dedicarse a; *mil* rendirse a. **to g. up one's seat,** ceder su sitio (or asiento). **to g. upon,** (overlook) dar sobre

give *n* elasticidad, *f*; el dar de sí; (concession) concesión, *f*. **g. and take,** concesiones mutuas, *f pl.* **g. away,** *inf* revelación indiscreta, *f*

given *a* dado; especificado; convenido; (with to) dado a, adicto a. **in a g. time,** en un tiempo dado. **g. that,** dado que

giver *n* dador (-ra); donador (-ra)

gizzard *n* molleja, *f*. **It sticks in my g.,** *inf* No lo puedo tragar

glacial *a* glacial

glacier *n* glaciar, *m*

glad *a* feliz, alegre; contento, satisfecho; *inf* elegante. **to be g.,** alegrarse, estar contento; estar satisfecho. **to give the g. eye,** hacer ojos

gladden *vt* alegrar, regocijar

glade *n* claro, *m*; rasa, *f*

gladiator *n* gladiador, *m*

gladiatorial *a* gladiatorio

gladiolus *n bot* gladíolo, gladio, *m*; espadaña, *f*

gladly *adv* alegremente; con mucho gusto, gustoso, de buena gana

gladness *n* alegría, felicidad, *f*, contento, *m*; placer, *m*

glamorous *a* exótico; garboso

glamour *n* encanto, *m*, fascinación, *f*; garbo, *m*. **g. girl,** belleza exótica, *f*

glance *n* (of a projectile) desviación, *f*; (of light) vislumbre, *m*; relumbrón, centelleo, *m*; (look) vistazo, *m*, ojeada, *f*; mirada, *f*, *vi* desviarse; relumbrar, centellear,

brillar; (with at) ojear, echar un vistazo a, lanzar miradas a; (a book) hojear; mirar; mirar de reojo; *fig* indicar brevemente. **at a g.,** con un vistazo; en seguida. **at the first g.,** a primera vista. **to g. off,** desviarse (al chocar). **to g. over,** repasar, echar un vistazo a; (a book) hojear

glancing *a* (of a blow) que roza

gland *n* (*anat, bot*) glándula, *f*; (in the neck) ganglio, *m*. **to have swollen glands,** tener inflamación de los ganglios

glandular *a* glandular

glare *n* brillo, fulgor, *m*; luminosidad, *f*; reflejo, *m*; (look) mirada feroz, *f*. *vi* relumbrar, centellear; (stare) mirar con ferocidad, mirar fijamente

glaring *a* deslumbrante, brillante; (of colors) chillón, llamativo; (of looks) de mirada feroz; (flagrant) notorio, evidente

glaringly *adv* brillantemente; con mirada feroz; notoriamente

glass *n* vidrio, *m*; cristal, *m*; (glassware) artículos de vidrio, *m pl*; cristalería, *f*; (for drinking) vaso, *m*, copa, *f*; (pane) cristal, *m*; (mirror) espejo, *m*; (telescope) telescopio, *m*; catalejo, *m*; (barometer) barómetro, *m*; (hour-glass) reloj de arena, *m*; (of a watch) vidrio (de reloj), *m*; *pl* **glasses,** (binoculars) anteojos, *m pl*; (spectacles) gafas, lentes, *m pl*; (opera glasses) gemelos de teatro, *m pl*, *a* de vidrio; de cristal. *vt* vidriar. **John wears glasses,** Juan lleva gafas. **The g. is falling (rising),** El barómetro baja (sube). **to clink glasses,** trincar las copas. **to look in the g.,** mirarse en el espejo. **clear g.,** vidrio trasparente, *m*; cristal tallado, *m*. **frosted g.,** vidrio jaspeado, *m*. **plate-g.,** vidrio plano, *m*; **safety g.,** vidrio inastillable, *m*. **stained g.,** vidrio de color, vidrio pintado, *m*. **under g.,** bajo vidrio; en invernáculo. **g. bead,** abalorio, *m*; cuenta de vidrio, *f*. **g.-blower,** soplador de vidrio, *m*. **g.-blowing,** el soplar de vidrio. **g. case,** escaparate, *m*. **g.-cloth,** paño para vasos. *m*. **g. eye,** ojo de cristal, *m*. **g. paper,** papel de vidrio, *m*. **g. roof,** techo de cristal, *m*. **g. window,** vidriera, *f*

glasscutter *n* cortador de vidrio, *m*

glassful *n* contenido de un vaso, *m*; vaso, vaso lleno, *m*, copa, *f*

glasshouse *n* fábrica de vidrio, *f*; vidriería, *f*; invernáculo, invernadero, *m*, estufa, *f*

glassware *n* cristalería, *f*

glassy *a* vitreo; (of eyes) vidrioso; *fig* cristalino; (smooth) liso, raso

glaucous *a* de color verdemar; *bot* glauco

glaze *n* barniz, *m*; lustre, brillo, *m*. *vt* poner vidrios (a); vidriar; barnizar; (paper, leather, etc.) satinar. *vi* (of eyes) vidriarse, ponerse vidrioso

glazier *n* vidriero, *m*

glazing *n* vidriado, *m*; barnizado, *m*; satinado, *m*; (material) barniz, *m*

gleam *n* rayo, destello, *m*; (of color) viso, *m*, mancha, *f*; *fig* rayo, *m*; (in the eye) chispa, *f*. *vi* relucir, centellear, resplandecer; brillar; reflejar la luz; *fig* brillar. **g. of hope,** rayo de esperanza, *m*

gleaming *a* reluciente, centelleante; brillante. *n* see **gleam**

glean *vt* espigar, rebuscar; recoger. *vi* espigar

gleaner *n* espigador, *m*; recogedor (-ra)

gleaning *n* espigueo, *m*; rebusca, recolección, *f*; *pl* **gleanings,** fragmentos, *m pl*

glee *n* alegría, *f*, júbilo, alborozo, *m*; *mus* canción para voces solas, *f*

gleeful *a* alegre, jubiloso, gozoso

gleefully *adv* alegremente, con júbilo

glen *n* cañada, *f*, cañón, *m*, hondonada, *f*

glib *a* locuaz, voluble; (easy) fácil

glibness *n* locuacidad, volubilidad, *f*; (easiness) facilidad, *f*

glide *n* deslizamiento, *m*; *aer* planeo. *m*. *vi* deslizarse; resbalar; *aer* planear. **to g. away,** escurrirse; desaparecer silenciosamente

glider *n aer* deslizador, planeador, *m*

gliding n aer vuelo sin motor, m

glimmer n luz trémula, luz débil, f, tenue resplandor, m; vislumbre, m. vi brillar con luz trémula, rielar fig; tener vislumbres (de)

glimpse n vistazo, m; vislumbre, m; indicio, m; impresión, f; vista, f. vt entrever, divisar; tener una vista (de); ver por un instante; vislumbrar

glint n tenue resplandor, m; lustre, m; centelleo, m; reflejo, m; (in the eye) chispa, f. vi relucir, destellar, rutilar; reflejar

glisten vi brillar, relucir

glistening a coruscante; brillante, reluciente

glitter n brillo, resplandor, m, rutilación, f. vi brillar, resplandecer, relucir; rutilar. **All that glitters is not gold,** Todo lo que reluce no es oro

glittering a reluciente, resplandeciente; fig brillante

gloat (over) vi recrearse en, gozarse en, deleitarse en

globe n globo, m; esfera, f; (for fish) pecera, f; (for gas, electric light) globo, m. **geographical g.,** globo terrestre, m. **g.-trotter,** trotamundos, m

globular a globular, esférico

globule n glóbulo, m

globulous a globuloso

gloom n obscuridad, f; lobreguez, f, tinieblas, f pl; fig melancolía, tristeza, f; taciturnidad, f. vi fig ponerse melancólico; ser taciturno

gloomily adv obscuramente; fig tristemente; taciturnamente

gloomy a obscuro; sombrío, lóbrego; melancólico, triste; taciturno; (of prospects, etc.) poco halagüeño, nada atrayente

glorification n glorificación, f

glorify vt glorificar; exaltar; alabar

glorious a glorioso; espléndido, magnífico; insigne; inf estupendo

glory n gloria, f; esplendor, m, magnificencia, f; art gloria, f. vi recrearse, gozarse; glorificarse, jactarse. **to be in one's g.,** estar en la gloria. **to g. in,** hacer gala de, glorificarse en

gloss n (sheen) lustre, brillo, m; fig apariencia, f; (note) glose, m; (excuse) disculpa, f. vt pulir; glosar. **to g. over,** (faults) disculpar, excusar

glossary n glosario, m

glossiness n lustre, m, tersura, f; brillo, m

glossy a lustroso, terso; brillante; (of hair) liso

glottis n anat glotis, f

glottal stop n choque glótica, golpe de glotis, m

glove n guante. **evening gloves,** guantes largos, m pl. **to be hand in g. with,** juntar diestra con diestra. **to fit like a g.,** sentar como un guante. **to put on one's gloves,** ponerse los guantes. **g. shop,** guantería, f. **g.-stretcher,** ensanchador (or abridor) de guantes, m

glove compartment gaveta, guantera, f, guantero, portaguantes m

glove-compartment light luz de portaguantes, f

glover n guantero (-ra)

glow n incandescencia, f; claridad, f; luz difusa, f; (heat) calor, m; (of color) intensidad, f; color vivo, m; (enthusiasm) ardor, entusiasmo, m; (redness) rojez, f; (in the sky) arrebol, m; (of pleasure, etc.) sentimiento de placer, m; sensación de bienestar, f. vi estar incandescente; arder; abrasarse; sentir entusiasmo; mostrarse rojo; experimentar un sentimiento de placer o una sensación de bienestar. **to g. with health,** estar rebosando de salud. **g.-worm,** luciérnaga, f

glower n ceño, m; mirada amenazadora, f. vi poner cara de pocos amigos, mirar airadamente; tener los ojos puestos (en)

glowing a candente, incandescente; ardiente; entusiasta; satisfecho; intenso; (bright) vivo, m; (red) encendido; (with health) rebosante de salud, m see **glow**

glowingly adv encendidamente; fig con entusiasmo

glucose n glucosa, f

glue n engrudo, m, cola, f. vt encolar, engrudar; pegar; fig fijar, poner. **He kept his eyes glued on them,**

Tenía los ojos fijados (or pegados) en ellos. **g.-pot,** pote de cola, m

gluey a gomoso; pegajoso, viscoso

glueyness n viscosidad, f

gluing n encoladura, f

glum a deprimido, taciturno, sombrío

glumly adv taciturnamente

glut n superabundancia, f, exceso, m. vt (satiate) hartar; fig saciar; (the market) inundar

gluteal a glúteo

glutinous a glutinoso, pegajoso, viscoso

glutton n glotón (-ona); fig ávido (-da)

gluttonous a glotón, comilón

gluttony n glotonería, gula, f

glycerine n glicerina, f

gnarled a nudoso; (of human beings) curtido

gnash vt rechinar, crujir (los dientes)

gnashing n rechinamiento (de dientes), m

gnat n mosquito, m

gnaw vt roer; morder; (of wood by worms) carcomer; fig roer

gnawing n roedura, f; mordedura, f, a roedor; mordedor

gnome n nomo, m

gnostic a and n nóstico (-ca)

gnosticism n nosticismo, m

go vi ir; (depart) irse, marcharse; (go toward) dirigirse a, encaminarse a; (lead to, of roads, etc.) conducir a, ir a; (vanish) desaparecer; (leave) dejar, salir de; (lose) perder; (pass) pasar; (of time) transcurrir, pasar; (be removed) quitarse; (be prohibited) prohibirse; (fall) caer; (collapse) hundirse; (be torn off) desprenderse; desgajarse; mech funcionar, trabajar, andar; (sound) sonar; (of the heart) palpitar, latir; (follow) seguir; (gesture) hacer un gesto; (be stated) decirse, afirmarse; (live) vivir; (wear) llevar; (turn out) salir, resultar; (improve) mejorar; (prosper) prosperar; (turn, become) ponerse; volverse; (to sleep) dormirse; (into a faint) desmayarse; (decay) echarse a perder, estropearse; (turn sour) agriarse; (become, adopt views, etc.) hacerse; (be sold) venderse; (be decided) decidirse, ser decidido; (have) tener; (by will) pasar; (belong) pertenecer; (receive) recibir; (have its place) estar; (put) ponerse; (going plus inf.) ir a; (die) morir, irse; (do a journey, a given distance) hacer (a pace, step) dar; (take) tomar; (escape) escaparse; (contribute) contribuir (a); (harmonize) armonizar (con); (be current) ser válido; (be set; (of a document, etc., run) rezar, decir; (attend) asistir a; (be broken) estar roto; (be worn) estar raído; (be granted) darse, otorgarse. **It's gone five,** Ya dieron las cinco. **It's time to be going,** Es hora de marcharse. **Let's go!** ¡Vamos! **These two colours go well together,** Estos colores armonizan bien. **Well, how goes it?** Bueno, ¿qué tal? ¿Cómo te va? **Who goes there?** mil ¿Quién va? **to go and fetch,** ir a buscar. **to let go,** soltar; dejar ir. **to go one's way,** seguir su camino. **to go wrong,** salir mal, fracasar; (sin) descarriarse. "**Go!**" (traffic sign) «¡Siga!» **Go on!** ¡Adelante!; (continue) ¡Siga!; inf ¡Qué va! **to go about,** dar la vuelta a; rodear; recorrer; (undertake) emprender, hacer; intentar; (of news, etc.) circular; naut virar de bordo. **Go about your business!** ¡Métete en lo que te importa! ir al extranjero; salir a la calle; publicarse, divulgarse. **to go across,** cruzar, atravesar; pasar. **to go after,** andar tras; seguir; (seek) ir a buscar; (persecute) perseguir. **to go again,** ir de nuevo; (be present) asistir otra vez; volver. **to go against,** ir contra; militar contra; oponerse a; ser desfavorable a. **to go ahead,** adelantar, avanzar; progresar; (lead) ir a la cabeza (de), conducir; naut marchar hacia adelante. **to go along,** andar por; recorrer; (depart) irse, marcharse. **go apartment-hunting,** ir en busca de piso. **to go along with,** acompañar (a). **to go aside,** quitarse de en medio; apartarse, retirarse. **to go astray,** perderse; extraviarse, descarriarse. **to go at,** atacar, acometer; (undertake) emprender; empezar a. **to go at it again,** *inf* volver a la carga. **to go away,** irse, marcharse; ausentarse; alejarse; desaparecer. **to go away with,** marcharse con; (an object) llevarse. **to go back,** volver; (retreat) retroceder, volverse atrás; (in history) remontarse a. **to go back on,** (a promise, etc.) faltar a; (retract) retractarse; (betray) traicionar. **to go backwards,** retroceder, cejar; desandar lo andado; *fig* deteriorar, empeorar. **to go backwards and forwards,** ir y venir; oscilar. **to go before,** (lead) ir a la cabeza de, conducir; anteceder; proceder; (a judge, etc.) comparecer ante. **to go behind,** ir detrás de; esconderse detrás de; seguir; (evidence, etc.) mirar más allá de. **to go between,** ponerse entre; interponerse; (as a mediator) mediar; (insert) intercalarse; (travel) ir entre; llevar cartas entre, ser mensajero de. **to go beyond,** ir más allá; exceder. **to go by,** pasar por; pasar cerca de, pasar junto a; ir por; (of time) transcurrir, pasar; (follow) seguir; guiarse por, atenerse a; (judge by) juzgar por; (a name) pasar por; tomar el nombre de. **to go down,** bajar, descender; (of the sun) ponerse; (sink) hundirse; sumergirse; (fall) caer; (be remembered) ser recordado; (believe) tragar; ser creído. **to go down again,** bajar de nuevo; volver a caer. **go Dutch,** ir a escote, ir a la gringa, ir a la par, ir a limón. **to go far,** ir lejos; influir mucho (en); impresionar mucho; (contribute) contribuir (a). **to go for,** (seek) ir en busca de; procurar tener; (attack) echarse encima de, atacar. **to go for a ride (by car, bicycle, on horseback),** dar un paseo (en coche, en bicicleta, a caballo). **to go forth,** salir; publicarse. **to go forward,** adelantar, avanzar; progresar; continuar; (happen) tener lugar. **to go from,** dejar, abandonar; separarse de, apartarse de; marcharse de. **to go in,** entrar en; (a railway carriage, etc.) subir a; (compete) concurrir. **to go in again,** volver a entrar en, entrar de nuevo en. **to go in and out,** entrar y salir; ir y venir. **to go in for,** entrar a buscar; dedicarse a, entregarse a; (buy) comprarse; tomar parte en; (an examination) tomar (un examen); (for a competition) entrar en (un concurso); (try) ensayar; arriesgar. **to go into,** entrar en; examinar; investigar; ocuparse con. **to go near,** acercarse a. **to go off,** marcharse; (explode) estallar; (of fire-arms) dispararse; (of the voice, etc.) perder (la voz, etc.); (run away) huir, fugarse. **to go off badly,** salir mal, fracasar, no tener éxito. **to go off well,** salir bien, tener éxito. **to go on,** subirse a; continuar; durar; avanzar; proseguir su marcha; progresar; prosperar; *theat* entrar en escena; (of clothes) ponerse; (rely on) apoyarse en. **Don't go on like that,** No seas así, No te pongas así. **This glove will not go on me,** No puedo ponerme este guante. **to be gone on a person,** *inf* estar loco por. **I went on to say . . . ,** Después dije; Continuando mi discurso dije . . . **It was going on for six o'clock when . . .** Serían alrededor de las seis cuando . . . **He is going on for fifty,** Raya en los cincuenta años. **to go on foot,** ir a pie. **to go on with,** continuar con; empezar. **to go out,** salir; (descend) bajar; (of fires, lights) extinguirse, apagarse; (of fashion, etc.) pasar (de); (the tide) menguar; (retire) retirarse; (in society) frecuentar la alta sociedad; (die) morir; (arouse) excitar. **to go out of fashion,** pasar de moda. **to go out of one's way (to),** dejar su camino (para); (lose oneself) perder el camino, extraviarse; (take trouble) desvivirse (por), tomarse molestia (para). **to go over,** cruzar, pasar por encima; (to another party or to the other side) pasarse a; (read) repasar; examinar. **to go past,** pasar; pasar en frente de. **to go round,** dar la vuelta a; (revolve) girar; (surround) rodear; (of news, etc.) divulgarse; (be enough) ser suficiente para todos. **to go through,** ir por, pasar por; recorrer; (pierce) penetrar, atravesar; (examine) examinar; (suffer) padecer, sufrir; (experience) experimentar; (live) vivir; (of time) pasar; (of money) malgastar, derrochar. **to go through with,** llevar a cabo; terminar. **to go to,** ir a, encaminarse a; (a person) acercarse a, dirigirse a; (help, be useful) servir

para; (be meant for) destinarse a; (rise of price) subir a; (find) encontrar; (of a bid) subir una apuesta hasta. **to go to war,** declarar la guerra. **to go together,** ir juntos (juntas). **to go toward,** encaminarse hacia; ir hacia; (help) ayudar a. **to go under,** pasar por debajo de; (sink) hundirse; (fail) fracasar; (be bankrupt) arruinarse, declarar en quiebra; (the name of) hacerse pasar por. **to go up,** subir; ir arriba; (a tree) trepar; (a ladder, etc.) subir; (a river) ir río arriba; (to town) ir a; (explode) estallar. **to go up and down,** subir y bajar; oscilar; ir de una parte a otra. **to go upon,** subirse a; (rely on) apoyarse en; obrar según; emprender. **to go upstairs,** ir arriba; (to another story, as in a flat) subir al otro piso; subir la escalera. **to go up to,** acercarse a; (of a bid) subir una apuesta hasta. **to go with,** acompañar; (agree with) estar de acuerdo con; (of principles) seguir, ser fiel a; (harmonize) armonizar con; (be suitable to) ir bien con; convenir a; (*inf* get along) ir bien. **go without,** marcharse sin; (lack) pasarse sin. **It goes without saying that . . . ,** Huelga decir que **Where are you going with this?** (What do you mean?) ¿A dónde quieres llegar con esto?

go *n* (fashion) moda, boga, *f*; (happening) suceso, *m*; (fix) apuro, *m*; (energy) energía, *f*, empuje, brío, *m*; (turn) turno, *m*; (attempt) tentativa, *f*; (action) movimiento, *m*, acción, *f*; (bargain) acuerdo, *m*. **It's a go!** (agreed) ¡Trato hecho! ¡Acordado! ¡Entendidos! ¡Entendidas! **It is all the go,** Hace furor, Es la gran moda. **It is no go,** No puede ser, Es imposible. **Now it's my go,** Ahora me toca a mí, Ahora es mi turno. **on the go,** en movimiento; entre manos; ocupado. **to have a go,** probar suerte; procurar, tratar de; tener un turno

goad *n* garrocha, aguijada, *f*, aguijón, *m*; *fig* acicate, estímulo, *m*. *vt* aguijar, picar; *fig* incitar, estimular, empujar. **prick with a g.,** aguijonazo, *m*

go-ahead *a* emprendedor; progresivo

goal *n* (posts in football, etc.) meta, portería, *f*; (score) gol, *m*; (in racing) meta, *f*; (destination) destinación, *f*; *fig* ambición, *f*; (purpose, objective) fin, objeto, *m*. **to score a g.,** marcar un gol. **g.-keeper,** guardameta, *m*, portero (-ra). **g.-post,** palo de la portería, *m*

goat *n* cabra, *f*; *ast* capricornio, *m*. **he-g.,** cabrón, *m*. **young g.,** cabrito, *m*, chivo (-va). **g.-herd,** cabrero, *m*. **g. skin,** piel de cabra, *f*; (wineskin) odre, *m*

goatee *n* pera, perilla, *f*

goatish *a* cabruno; de cabra; lascivo

gobble *vt* and *vi* engullir, tragar. *vi* (of turkey) gluglutear. *n* glugluteo, *m*, voz del pavo, *f*

gobbler *n* engullidor (-ra), tragón (-ona), *inf* pavo, *m*

go-between *n* trotaconventos, *f*; alcahuete, *m*; (mediator) medianero (-ra)

goblet *n* copa, *f*

goblin *n* trasgo, duende, *m*

go-by, **to give the** evitar; pasar por alto de; omitir

go-cart *n* andaderas, *f pl*; pollera, *f*; cochecito de niño, *m*

god *n* dios, *m*; *pl* **gods,** dioses, *m pl*; (in a theater) público del paraíso, *m*; paraíso, *m*. **By God!** ¡Vive Dios! **For God's sake,** ¡Por el amor de Dios! ¡Por Dios! **Please God,** ¡Plegue a Dios! **Thank God!** ¡Gracias a Dios! **God Bless You!** (to someone who has sneezed) ¡Jesús! **God forbid!** ¡No lo quiera Dios! **God grant it!** ¡Dios lo quiera! **God keep you!** ¡Dios le guarde! ¡Vaya Vd. con Dios! **God willing,** Dios mediante. **My father, God rest his soul, was . . . ,** Mi padre, que Dios perdone, era . . .

godchild *n* ahijado (-da)

goddaughter *n* ahijada, *f*

goddess *n* diosa, *f*; *poet* dea, *f*

godfather *n* padrino, *m*. **to be a g. to,** ser padrino de, sacar de pila (a)

godfearing *a* timorato, temeroso de Dios; religioso

godforsaken *a* dejado de la mano de Dios; (of places) remoto, solitario

Godhead *n* divinidad, *f*

godkin *n* diosecillo, *m*

godless *a* impío, irreligioso; sin Dios

godlessness *n* impiedad, irreligiosidad, *f*
godlet diosecilla, *m*
godlike *a* divino
godliness *n* piedad, *f*; santidad, *f*
godling diosecillo, *m*
godly *a* devoto, piadoso, religioso
godmother *n* madrina, *f.* **fairy g.**, hada madrina, *f.* **to be a g. to**, ser madrina de
godparent *n* padrino, *m*; madrina, *f pl.* **godparents,** padrinos, *m pl*
godsend *n* bien, *m*; buena suerte, *f*; fortuna, *f*
go-getter *n* buscavidas, *mf*
goggle *n* mirada fija, *f*; *pl* **goggles,** anteojos, *m pl*, gafas, *f pl*; (of a horse) anteojeras, *f pl. vi* mirar fijamente; salirse a uno los ojos de la cabeza. **g.-eyed,** de ojos saltones. **g.-eyes,** ojos saltones, *m pl*
going *n* ida, *f*; (departure) partida, marcha, *f*; salida, *f*; (pace) paso, *m*; (speed) velocidad, *f*. **It was heavy g.,** El avance era lento; El progreso era lento; (of parties, etc.) Era aburrido. **The g. was difficult on those mountainous roads,** El conducir (or el ir or el andar) era difícil en aquellos caminos de montaña. **g. back,** vuelta, *f*, regreso, *m*. **g. down,** bajada, *f*, descenso, *m*; (of the sun, etc.) puesta, *f*. **g. forward,** avance, *m*; progreso, *m*. **g. in,** entrada, *f*. **g. in and out,** idas y venidas, *f pl.* **g. out,** salida, *f*; (of a fire, light) apagamiento, *m*
going *a* and *pres part* que va, yendo; que funciona. **G., g., gone** (at an auction) A la una, a las dos, a las tres.
goings-on, (tricks) trapujos, *m pl*; (conduct) conducta, *f.* **g. concern,** empresa próspera, *f.* **g. to,** con destino a
going-away present *n* regalo de despedida, *m*
goiter *n* bocio, *m*
gold *n* oro, *m*; color de oro, *m. a* de oro; áureo. **All that glitters is not g.,** No es oro todo lo que reluce. **cloth of g.,** tela de oro, *f.* **dull g.,** oro mate, *m.* **light g.,** oro pálido, *m.* **old g.,** oro viejo, *m.* **g.-beater,** batidor de oro, *m.* **g.-digger,** minero de oro, *m*; (woman) aventurera, *f.* **g. dust,** oro en polvo, *m.* **g.-fever,** fiebre de oro, *f.* **g. lace,** galón de oro, *m.* **g. lacquer,** sisa dorada, *f.* **g. leaf,** pan de oro, oro batido, *m.* **g.-mine,** mina de oro, *f.* **g. piece,** moneda de oro, *f.* **g. plate,** vajilla de oro, *f.* **g. standard,** patrón oro, *m.* **g.-thread,** hilo de oro, *m.* **g.-yielding,** aurífero
golden *a* de oro; dorado; áureo; amarillo; *fig* feliz; excelente. **to become g.,** dorarse. **g. age,** edad de oro, *f.* **g.-crested wren,** abadejo, *m.* **g. hair,** cabellos dorados (or de oro), *m pl.* **G. Legend,** leyenda áurea, *f.* **g. mean,** justo medio, *m.* **g. rose,** rosa de oro, *f.* **g. rule,** regla áurea, *f.* **g. syrup,** jarabe de arce, *m.* **g. voice,** voz de oro, *f.* **g. wedding,** bodas de oro, *f pl*
goldfinch *n* jilguero, *m*
goldfish *n* carpa dorada, *f.* **g. bowl,** pecera, *f*
goldrush carrera de oro, *f*
goldsmith *n* orfebre, oribe, orífice, *m*
golf *n* golf, *m.* **g.-club,** (stick) palo de golf, *m*; (organization) club de golf, *m.* **g.-course,** campo de golf, *m*
golfer *n* jugador (-ra) de golf
gonad *n* gonada, *f*
gondola *n* góndola, *f*
gondolier *n* gondolero, *m*
gone *a* and *past part* ido; (lost) perdido; (ruined) arruinado; (dead) muerto; (past) pasado; (disappeared) desaparecido; (fainted) desmayado; (suppressed) suprimido; (pregnant) encinta; (drunk) borracho; (ended) terminado; (exhausted) agotado; (ill) enfermo. **far g.,** avanzado; (in years) de edad avanzada; (of illness) cerca de la muerte, muy enfermo; (in love) loco de amor; (drunk) muy borracho. **It is all g.,** No hay más. **It is g. seven o'clock,** Son las siete y pico, Son las siete ya
gong *n* gong, *m*; (Chinese) batintín, *m*
gonorrhea *n* gonorrea, *f*
good *a* bueno (before *m sing* nouns) buen; agradable; afortunado; (appropriate) apropiado, oportuno; (beneficial) provechoso, ventajoso; (wholesome) sano,

saludable; (suitable) apto; (useful) útil; (kind) bondadoso; (much) mucho; (obliging) amable; (virtuous) virtuoso; (skilled) experto; (fresh) fresco; (genuine) genuino, legítimo; verdadero. *adv* bien. *interj* ¡bueno! ¡bien! **a g. deal,** mucho. **a g. many,** bastantes. **a g. turn,** un favor. **a g. way,** (distance) un buen trecho; mucho. **a g. while,** un buen rato. **as g. as,** tan bueno como. **Be so g. as to . . . !** Haga el favor de, Tenga Vd. la bondad de (followed by infin.). **fairly g.,** *a* bastante bueno. *adv* bastante bien. **I'm g. for another five miles,** Tengo fuerzas para cinco millas más. **It was g. of you to do it,** Vd. fue muy amable de hacerlo, Vd. tuvo mucha bondad de hacerlo. **to be no g. at this sort of thing,** no servir para tales cosas. **to have a g. time,** pasarlo bien. **to make g.,** reparar; indemnizar; (accomplish) llevar a cabo, poner en práctica; justificar; (a promise) cumplir. **very g.,** *a* muy bueno. *adv* muy bien. **g.-feeling,** buena voluntad, *f.* **g.-fellowship,** compañerismo, *m*; buena compañía, *f.* **g.-for-nothing,** *n* papanatas, badulaque, *m.* **to be g.-for-nothing,** no servir para nada. **g. luck,** buena suerte, *f.* **g. manners,** buenos modales, *m pl*; buena crianza, educación, *f.* **g. nature,** buen natural, *m*; buen humor, *m.* **g.-natured,** de buen natural; de buen humor, bonachón. **g. offices,** buenos oficios, *m pl.* **g.-tempered,** de buen humor
good *n* bien, *m*; provecho, *m*; utilidad, *f*; *pl* **goods.** See separate entry. **I am saying this for your g.,** Lo digo para tu bien. **Much g. may it do you!** ¡Buen provecho te haga! **for g. and all,** para siempre jamás. **It is no g.,** Es inútil; No vale la pena. **the g.,** el bien; (people) los buenos. **They have gone for g.,** Se han marchado para no volver. **to do one g.,** hacer bien a uno; mejorar; ser provechoso (a uno); (suit) sentar bien (a uno). **What is the g. of . . . ?** ¿Para qué sirve . . . ?; ¿Qué vale . . . ? **g. and evil,** el bien y el mal
good-bye *interj* ¡adiós! *n* adiós, *m*, despedida, *f.* **to bid g.-b.,** decir adiós. **G.-b. for the present!** ¡Hasta la vista! ¡Hasta luego! **G.-b. until tomorrow, then,** Hasta mañana pues, adiós, Hasta mañana entonces
goodness *n* bondad, *f*; (of quality) buena calidad, *f* (of persons) amabilidad, benevolencia, *f*; (essence) esencia, substancia, *f*; bien, *m*: excelencia, *f*; *interj* ¡Jesús! ¡Dios mío! **For g. sake!** ¡Por Dios! **I wish to g. that,** ¡Ojalá que . . . !
goods *n pl* bienes, efectos, *m pl*; artículos, *m pl*; *com* mercancías, *f pl*, géneros, *m pl.* **by g.-train,** en pequeña velocidad. **stolen g.,** objetos robados, *m pl.* **g. lift,** montacargas, *m pl.* **g. office,** depósito de mercancías, *m.* **g. station,** estación de carga, *f.* **g.-train,** tren de mercancías, *m.* **g. van,** furgón, *m.* **g. wagon,** vagon de mercancías, *m*
good-smelling *a* oloroso
goodwill *n* benevolencia, *f*; buena voluntad, *f*; (of a business) clientela, *f*
goose *n* oca, *f*, ganso (-sa); plancha de sastre, *f. a* de oca. **g.-flesh,** *fig* carne de gallina, *f.* **g. girl,** ansarera, *f.* **g.-step,** paso de oca, *m*
gooseberry *n* uva espina, *f*
Gordian *a* gordiano. **G. knot,** nudo gordiano, *m*
gore *n* sangre, *f*; *sew* sesga, nesga, *f. vt* acornear; desgarrar; herir (con arma blanca)
gorge *n* (valley) cañón, barranco, *m*; (heavy meal) comilona, *f*, atracón, *m. vt* engullir, tragar. *vi* hartarse, atracarse
gorgeous *a* magnífico; esplendido, suntuoso; *inf* maravilloso, estupendo
gorgeously *adv* magníficamente
gorgeousness *n* magnificencia, *f*; suntuosidad, *f*, esplendor, *m*
gorilla *n* gorila, *m*
gormandize *vi* glotonear
gormandizer *n* glotón (-ona)
gorse *n* tojo, *m*, aulaga, *f*
gory *a* ensangrentado; sangriento
gosh *interj* ¡caray! ¡caramba!

goshawk *n orn* azor, *m*

gosling *n* ansarino, *m*

gospel *n* evangelio, *m*; doctrina, *f*. **The G. according to St. Mark,** El Evangelio según San Marcos. **to believe as g. truth,** creer como si fuese el evangelio. **to preach the G.,** predicar el evangelio

gossamer *n* hilo de araña, *m*, red de araña, telaraña, *f*; (filmy material) gasa, *f*; hilo finísimo, *m*, a de gasa; sutil, delgado, fino

gossip *n* murmurador (-ra), chismoso (-sa), hablador (-ra); (scandal) chisme, *m*; habladuría, murmuración, *f*; (obsolete, of a woman) comadre, *f*; (talk) charla, *f*. *vi* charlar, conversar; (in bad sense) murmurar, chismear; criticar. **to g. about,** charlar de; poner lenguas en, cortar un sayo (a); hablar mal de. **g. column,** gacetilla, *f*

gossiping *a* charlatán, hablador; chismoso, murmurador. *n* See **gossip**

Goth *n* godo (-da); bárbaro (-ra)

Gothic *a art* gótico; (of race) godo; bárbaro. *n* (language) gótico, *m*; arquitectura gótica, *f*. **G. characters,** letra gótica, *f*

gouge *n* gubia, *f*. *vt* escoplear. **to g. out,** vaciar; sacar

gourd *n* calabaza, *f*

gourmand *n* glotón, *m*

gourmet *n* gastrónomo, *m*

gout *n med* gota, *f*

gouty *a* gotoso

govern *vt* gobernar; regir; (guide) guiar; dominar; domar, refrenar; *gram* regir; (regulate) regular

governable *a* gobernable; manejable; dócil

governess *n* institutriz, *f*; (in a school) maestra, *f*

governing *a* gubernante; director; (with principle, etc.) directivo. *n* See **government**

government *n* gobierno, *m*; dirección, *f*; autoridad, *f*. **g. bond,** bono del gobierno, *m*. **g. house,** palacio del gobernador, *m*. **g. office,** oficina del gobierno, *f*. **g. stock,** papel del Estado, *m*

governmental *a* gubernamental, gubernativo.

Government Printing Office Talleres Gráficos de la Nación, *m pl*

governor *n* gobernador (-ra); vocal de la junta de gobierno, *mf*; (of a prison) director (-ra) (de una prisión); *mech* regulador, *m*. **g.-general,** gobernador general, *m*

governorship *n* gobierno, *m*; dirección, *f*

gown *n* toga, *f*; (cassock) sotana, *f*; (dressing-g.) bata, *f*; (for sleeping) camisa de noche, *f*; (bathing-wrap) albornoz, *m*; (dress) vestido, traje, *m*

Goyesque *a* goyesco

grab *n* asimiento, *m*, presa, *f*; *mech* gancho, *m*. *vt* arrebatar, asir, agarrar; *fig* alzarse con, tomar

grabber *n* cogedor (-ra); codicioso (-sa)

grace *n* elegancia, *f*; simetría, armonía, *f*; gracia, gentileza, *f*, donaire, *m*; encanto, *m*; (goodness) bondad, *f*; gracia, *f*; merced, *f*, favor, *m*; (period of time) plazo, *m*; (privilege) privilegio, *m*; *theol* gracia divina, *f*; (at table) bendición de la mesa, *f*; (as a title) excelentísimo, (to an archbishop) ilustrísimo. *vt* adornar; favorecer; honrar. **airs and graces,** humos, *m pl*. **the Three Graces,** las Gracias. **three days' g.,** plazo de tres días, *m*. **to get into a person's good graces,** congraciarse con; caer en gracia con. **to say g.,** bendecir la mesa. **with a bad g.,** a regañadientes. **with a good g.,** de buena gana. **g.-note,** *mus* nota de adorno, *f*

graceful *a* airoso, gentil, gracioso; elegante; bonito

gracefully *adv* airosamente, gentilmente; con gracia; elegantemente

gracefulness. See **grace**

graceless *a* réprobo; dejado de la mano de Dios; sin gracia

gracious *a* (merciful) piadoso, clemente; (urbane) afable, condescendiente, agradable. **Good g.!** ¡Vamos!, ¡Dios mío!

graciously *adv* afablemente; con benevolencia. **to be g. pleased,** tener a bien

graciousness *n* amabilidad, afabilidad, condescendencia, *f*

gradate *vt* graduar; *art* degradar

gradation *n* graduación, *f*; *mus* gradación, *f*; paso gradual, *m*; serie, *f*

grade *n* grado, *m*; (quality) calidad, clase, *f*; (in a school) clase, *f*; (gradient) pendiente, *f*, declive, *m*. *vt* graduar, clasificar; (cattle breeding) cruzar. **down g.,** cuesta abajo. **up g.,** cuesta arriba. **highest g.,** *n* primera clase, *f*. *a* de primera clase; de calidad excelente

gradient *n* declive, *m*. cuesta, pendiente, *f*

gradual *a* gradual. *n ecc* gradual, *m*

gradually *adv* gradualmente; poco a poco

graduate *n* licenciado (-da). *a* graduado. *vt* graduar. *vi* graduarse; (as a doctor) doctorarse. **to g. as,** recibirse de

graduation *n* graduación, *f*

graft *n bot* injerto, *m*; *surg* injerto de piel, *m*; (swindle) estafa, *f*; (bribery) soborno, *m*. *vt bot* injertar; *surg* injertar un trozo de piel; *fig* injerir

grafting *n bot* injerto, *m*; *surg* injerto de piel, *m*; *fig* inserción, *f*

grain *n* (corn) grano, *m*; (cereal) cereal, *m*, or *f*; (seed, weight) grano, *m*; (trace) pizca, *f*; (of wood, etc.) hila, *m*, fibra, hebra, veta, *f*; (of leather) flor, *f*; (texture) textura, *f*. *vt* granear; granular; (wood, marble, etc.) vetear. **against the g.,** a contrapelo. **g. lands,** mieses, *f pl*

gram *n* gramo, *m*

grammar *n* gramática, *f*. **g. school,** instituto de segunda enseñanza, *m*

grammarian *n* gramático, *m*

grammatical *a* gramático

grammatically *adv* gramaticalmente, como la gramática lo quiere. (e.g., **She now speaks Catalan g.,** Ahora habla el catalán como la gramática lo quiere)

grammaticalness *n* corrección gramatical, *f*

gramophone *n* gramófono, *m*.

granary *n* granero, hórreo, *m*, troj, *f*. **g. keeper,** trojero, *m*

grand *a* magnífico, soberbio; imponente; (of dress) espléndido, vistoso; (of people) distinguido, importante; aristocrático; (proud) orgulloso; (of style) elevado, sublime; (morally) noble; augusto; (main) principal; (full) completo; *inf* estupendo, magnífico; (with duke, etc.) gran. gran. *n* piano de cola, *m*. **g.-aunt,** tía abuela, *f*. **g. cross,** gran cruz, *f*. **g. duchess,** gran duquesa, *f*. **g. duke,** gran duque, *m*. **g. lodge,** (of freemasons) Gran Oriente, *m*. **g. master,** gran maestre, *m*. **g.-nephew,** resobrino, *m*. **g.-niece,** resobrina, *f*. **g. opera,** ópera, *f*. **g. piano,** piano de cola, *m*. **g.-stand,** tribuna, *f*. **g.-uncle,** tío abuelo, *m*. **g. vizier,** gran visir, *m*

grandchild *n* nieto (-ta). **great-g.,** bisnieto (-ta). **great-great-g.,** tataranieto (-ta)

granddaughter *n* nieta, *f*. **great-g.,** bisnieta, *f*. **great-great-g.,** tataranieta, *f*

grandee *n* grande (de España, grande de Portugal), *m*

grandeur *n* magnificencia, *f*; grandiosidad, *f*; magnitud, grandeza, *f*; (pomp) pompa, *f*, fausto, *m*

grandfather *n* abuelo, *m*. **great-g.,** bisabuelo, *m*. **great-great-g.,** tatarabuelo, *m*

grandfather's clock reloj de péndulo, *m*

grandfatherly *a* de abuelo

grandiloquence *n* grandilocuencia, *f*

grandiloquent *a* grandílocuo

grandiose *a* grandioso, sublime; impresionante; imponente; (in a bad sense) extravagante; (of style) bombástico, hinchado

grand jury *n* jurado de acusación, jurado de juicio, *m*

grandmother *n* abuela, *f*. **great-g.,** bisabuela, *f*. **great-great-g.,** tatarabuela, *f*

grandness *n* magnificencia, *f*; aristocracia, *f*; (pride) orgullo, *m*; grandiosidad, *f*; (of style) sublimidad, *f*; (of character) nobleza, *f*

grandparent *n* abuelo, *m*; abuela, *f*; *pl* **grandparents,** abuelos, *m pl*. **great-grand-parents,** bisabuelos, *m pl*. **great-great-grandparents,** tatarabuelos, *m pl*

grandson *n* nieto, *m*. **great-g.**, bisnieto, *m*. **great-great-g.**, tataranieto, *m*

grange *n* granja, *f*; casa de campo, *f*

granite *n* granito, *m*

granny *n* abuelita, nana, *f*; abuela, *f*. **g. knot,** nudo al revés, *m*

grant *n* concesión, *f*; otorgamiento, *m*; donación, *f*; privilegio, *m*; (for study) beca, bolsa de estudio, *f*; (transfer) traspaso, *m*, cesión, *f*. *vt* conceder; (bestow) otorgar, dar; donar; (agree to) acceder a, asentir en; permitir; (transfer) traspasar; (assume) suponer. **to g. a degree,** expedir un título. **to g. a motion,** dar por entrada a una moción. **to take for granted,** descontar; dar por hecho, dar por sentado. **God g. it!** ¡Dios lo quiera! **granted that,** dado que

grantee *n* cesionario (-ia), adjudicatorio (-ia)

grantor *n* cesionista, *mf*; otorgador (-ra)

granulated *a* granulado

granule *n* gránulo, *m*

granulous *a* granuloso

grape *n* uva, *f*. **bunch of grapes,** racimo de uvas, *m*. **muscatel g.**, uva moscatel, *f*. **sour grapes,** uvas agrias, *f pl*; (phrase) ¡están verdes! **g.-fruit,** toronja, *f*. **g. gatherer,** vendimiador (-ra). **g. harvest,** vendimia, *f*. **g. juice,** mosto, *m*. **g.-shot,** metralla, *f*. **g. stone,** granuja, *f*. **g.-sugar,** glucosa, *f*. **g.-vine,** vid, parra, *f*

graph *n* gráfica, *f*; diagrama, *m*

graphic *a* gráfico

graphite *n* grafito, *m*

graphology *n* grafología, *f*

grapple *n naut* rezón, arpeo, *m*; lucha a brazo partido, *f*. *vt naut* aferrar; asir, agarrar. *vi naut* aferrarse. **to g. with,** luchar a brazo partido (con); *fig* luchar con

grappling *n naut* aferramiento, *m*; lucha cuerpo a cuerpo, *f*; (with a problem) lucha con, *f*

grasp *n* agarro, *m*; (reach) alcance, *m*; (of a hand) apretón, *m*; (power) garras, *f pl*, poder, *m*; (understanding) comprensión, *f*; inteligencia, capacidad intelectual, *f*. *vt* agarrar, asir; empuñar; abrazar; *fig* comprender, alcanzar; (a hand) estrechar. *vi* agarrarse. **within one's g.**, al alcance de uno. **to g. at,** asirse de

grasping *n* asimiento, *m*; (understanding) comprensión, *f*, a codicioso, tacaño, mezquino

graspingness *n* codicia, *f*

grass *n* hierba, *f*; (pasture) pasto, herbaje, *m*; (sward) césped, *m*. *vt* cubrir de hierba; sembrar de hierba; apacentar. **to hear the g. grow,** sentir crecer la hierba. **to let the g. grow,** dejar crecer la hierba. **to turn out to g.**, echar al pasto. **g.-blade,** brizna de hierba, *f*. **g.-green,** *a* and *n* verde como la hierba *m*.. **g.-grown,** cubierto de hierba. **g.-land,** pradera, *f*. **g.-snake,** culebra *f*. **g. widow,** mujer cuyo marido está ausente

grasshopper *n* saltamontes, *m*. **grasshopper's chirp,** chirrido (del saltamontes, *m*)

grassy *a* parecido a la hierba, como la hierba; cubierto de hierba, de hierba

grate *n* parrilla, *f*; (grating) reja, *f*. *vt* raspar, raer; *cul* rallar; (make a noise) hacer rechinar. *vi* rozar; rechinar, chirriar. **to g. on, upon,** (of sounds) irritar, molestar; chocar con. **to g. on the ear,** herir el oído

grateful *a* agradecido, reconocido; (pleasant) agradable, grato

gratefully *adv* agradecidamente; gratamente

gratefulness *n* agradecimiento, *m*, gratitud, *f*; (pleasantness) agrado, *m*

grater *n cul* rallador, *m*

gratification *n* satisfacción, *f*; (pleasure) placer, gusto, *m*

gratified *a* satisfecho, contento

gratify *vt* satisfacer; (please) gratificar, agradar

gratifying *a* satisfactorio, agradable

grating *n* reja, *f*; rejilla, *f*; *naut* jareta, *f*; (optics) retículo, *m*; (sound) rechinamiento, chirrido, *m*. *a* rechinante, chirriador; áspero

gratis *a* and *adv* gratis

gratitude *n* agradecimiento, *m*, gratitud, *f*

gratuitous *a* gratuito

gratuitousness *n* gratuidad, *f*

gratuity *n* gratificación, propina, *f*

grave *n* (hole) sepultura, fosa, *f*; (monument) tumba, *f*, sepulcro, *m*; *fig* muerte, *f*. **g.-digger,** enterrador, sepulturero, *m*

grave *a* grave; importante; serio; sobrio; (anxious) preocupado; (of accent) grave. *n* (grave accent) acento grave, *m*

gravel *n* grava, *f*; cascajo, casquijo, *m*; *med* arenillas, *f pl*, cálculo, *m*

gravely *adv* gravemente; seriamente

Graves' disease *n* bocio exoftálmico, *m*

gravestone *n* lápida mortuoria, *f*

graveyard *n* camposanto, cementerio, *m*

gravitate *vi* gravitar; tender

gravitation *n* gravitación, *f*; tendencia, *f*

gravitational *a* de gravitación, gravitacional, gravitatorio

gravitational pull *n* atracción gravitatoria, *f*

gravity *n phys* gravedad, *f*; seriedad, solemnidad, *f*; gravedad, *f*; (weight) peso, *m*; importancia, *f*; (enormity) enormidad, *f*; (danger) peligro, *m*. **center of g.**, centro de gravedad, *m*. **law of g.**, ley de la gravedad, *f*. **specific g.**, peso específico, *m*

gravy *n* salsa, *f*; jugo (de la carne), *m*. **g.-boat,** salsera, *f*

gray *a* gris; (of animals) rucio. *n* color gris, gris, *m*; caballo gris, *m*. **His hair is turning g.**, El pelo se le vuelve gris. **g.-haired,** de pelo gris. **g. matter,** materia gris, *f*; cacumen, *m*. **g. mullet,** *icht* mújol, *m*. **g. squirrel,** gris, *m*. **g. wolf,** lobo gris, *m*

grayish *a* grisáceo, agrisado; (of hair) entrecano

grayness *n* color gris, gris, *m*; *fig* monotonía, *f*

graze *n* abrasión, *f*; (brush) roce, *m*, *vi* pacer, apacentarse. *vt* pastorear, apacentar; (brush) rozar

grazing *n agr* apacentamiento, pastoreo, *m*; (brushing) rozadura, *f*. *a* que pace, herbívoro; (of land) pacedero. **g. land,** pasto, *m*

grease *n* grasa, *f*; (dirt) mugre, *f*; (of a candle) sebo, *m*, cera, *f*. *vt* engrasar; manchar con grasa; *fig inf* untar. **to g. the wheels,** *fig* untar el carro. **g.-box,** *mech* caja de sebo, *f*. **g.-gun,** engrasador de compresión, *m*. **g.-paint,** afeites de actor (o de actriz), *m pl*. **g.-proof paper,** papel impermeable, *m*. **g. spot,** lámpara, mancha de grasa, *f*, saín, *m*

greaser *n* engrasador, *m*

greasiness *n* graseza, *f*; lo aceitoso; untuosidad, *f*

greasing *n* engrasado, *m*

greasy *a* grasiento; (oily) aceitoso; (grubby) mugriento, bisunto; *fig* lisonjero. **g. pole,** cucaña, *f*

great *a* gran; grande; enorme; vasto; (much) mucho; (famous) famoso, ilustre; noble, sublime; (intimate) íntimo; importante; principal; poderoso; magnífico, impresionante; *inf* famoso, estupendo; (of time) largo; (clever) fuerte. **Alexander the G.**, Alejandro Magno. **the G. Mogul,** el Gran Mogul. **a g. deal,** mucho. **a g. man,** un grande hombre, un hombre famoso. **a g. many,** muchos (muchas). **He lived to a g. age,** Vivió hasta una edad avanzada. **so g.**, tan grande, tamaño. **the g.**, los grandes hombres. **g. on,** aficionado a. **g.-aunt,** tía abuela, *f*. **g.-grandchild,** etc. See **grandchild,** etc. **g.-hearted,** valeroso; magnánimo, generoso. **g. power,** gran poder, *m*. **G. War,** Gran Guerra, *f*. **the Great Schism,** el Gran Cisma, *m*

greater *a* comp. of **great,** mayor; más grande. **to make g.**, agrandar. **G. London,** el Gran Londres, *m*

greatest *a* sup. of **great,** más grande; mayor; máximo; más famoso; sumo

greatly *adv* mucho; con mucho; (very) muy; noblemente

greatness *n* grandeza, *f*; grandiosidad, *f*; extensión, vastedad, *f*; importancia, *f*; poder, *m*; majestad, *f*; esplendor, *m*; (intensity) intensidad, *f*; (enormity) enormidad, *f*

Grecian *a* griego

Greco- *prefix* (in compounds) greco-, greco

greed *n* (cupidity) codicia, rapacidad, avaricia, *f*; avidez, ansia, *f*; (of food) gula, glotonería, *f*

greedily *adv* codiciosamente; con avidez; (of eating) vorazmente

greedy *a* (for food) glotón; codicioso; ambicioso; ávido; deseoso

Greece Grecia, *f*

Greek *a* and *n* griego (-ga); (language) griego, *m*. **It's all G.** **to me,** Para mí es como si fuese en latín, Me es chino. **G. tunic,** peplo, *m*

green *a* verde; (inexpert) inexperto, bisoño; (recent) nuevo, reciente; (fresh) fresco; (of complexion) pálido, descolorido; (flowery) floreciente; (vigorous) lozano; (young) joven; (unripe) verde; (credulous) crédulo; (raw) crudo; (of wood, vegetables) verde. *n* verde, color verde, *m*; (vegetables) verdura, *f*; (meadow) prado, *m*; (turf) césped, *m*; (grass) hierba, *f*; (bowling) campo de juego, *m*. *vt* teñir (or pintar) de verde. **bright g.,** *n* verdegay, verde claro, *m*. **dark g.,** *n* verdinegro, *m*. **light g.,** *n* verde pálido, *m*. **to grow** or **look g.,** verdear. **g.-eyed,** de ojos verdes. **g. peas,** guisantes, *m pl*. **g. table,** tapete verde, *m*

greenery *n* follaje, *m*; verdura, *f*

greengrocer *n* verdulero (-ra)

greengrocery *n* verdulería, *f*

greenhorn *n* bisoño (-ña); papanatas, *m*

greenhouse *n* invernáculo, invernadero, *m*

greenish *a* verdoso. **g.-yellow,** cetrino

Greenland Groenlandia, *f*

Greenlander *n* groenlandés (-esa)

greenness *a* lo verde; verdor, *m*, verdura, *f*; (inexperience) falta de experiencia, *f*; (vigor) vigor, *m*, lozanía, *f*; (newness) novedad, *f*; (of wood, fruit) falta de madurez, *f*

greenroom *n theat* saloncillo, *m*

greenstuff *n* hortalizas, legumbres, *f pl*

greet *vt* saludar; recibir; (express pleasure) dar la bienvenida (a)

greeting *n* salutación, *f*, saludo, *m*; recepción, *f*; (welcome) bienvenida, *f*; *pl* **greetings,** recuerdos, *m pl*

gregarious *a* gregario

gregariousness *n* gregarismo, *m*

Gregorian *a* gregoriano

grenade *n* granada, bomba, *f*. **hand-g.,** bomba de mano, *f*

grey See **gray**

greyhound *n* galgo, lebrel, *m*. **g. bitch,** galga, *f*; **g. racing,** carreras de galgos, *f pl*

grid *n* (of electric power) red, *f*; rejilla, *f*; (for water, etc.) alcantarilla, *f*

gridiron *n cul* parrilla, *f*; (of electric power) red, *f*; *theat* telar, *m*

grief *n* angustia, pena, aflicción, *f*; dolor, suplicio, *m*. **to come to g.,** pasarlo mal, tener un desastre

grievance *n* injusticia, *f*; motivo de queja, *m*

grieve *vt* entristecer, afligir, angustiar; atormentar. *vi* entristecerse, afligirse, acongojarse. **to g. for,** lamentar: echar de menos

grievous *a* (heavy) oneroso, gravoso; opresivo; doloroso, penoso; lamentable; cruel. **g. error,** error lamentable

grievousness *n* (weight) peso, *m*; carácter opresivo, *m*; dolor, *m*, aflicción, *f*; enormidad, *f*; crueldad, *f*

griffin *n* grifo, *m*; (fig chaperon) carabina, *f*; (dog) grifón, *m*

grill *n cul* parrilla, *f*; (grating) rejilla, *f*; (before a window) reja, *f*; (food) asado a la parrilla, *m*. *vt cul* asar a la parrilla; (burn) quemar; (question) interrogar; (torture) torturar. *vi cul* asarse a la parrilla; (be burnt) quemarse. **g.-room,** parrilla, *f*

grille *n* reja, *f*; rejilla, *f*; (screen) verja, *f*

grilled *a cul* a la parrilla; con rejilla

griller *n cul* parrilla, *f*

grim *a* (fierce) feroz, salvaje; (severe) severo, ceñudo, adusto; inflexible; (frightful) horrible

grimace *n* mueca, *f*, gesto, mohín, visaje, *m*, *vi* hacer muecas

grime *n* mugre, *f*; suciedad, *f*. **to cover with g.,** enmugrecer

grimly *adv* severamente; sin sonreír; inflexiblemente; (without retreating) sin cejar; (frightfully) horriblemente; de un modo espantoso

grimness *n* (ferocity) ferocidad, *f*; (severity) severidad, *f*; inflexibilidad, *f*; (frightfulness) horror, *m*, lo espantoso

grimy *a* mugriento, sucio

grin *n* sonrisa grande, *f*; sonrisa burlona, *f*; (grimace) mueca, *f*. *vi* sonreír mostrando los dientes; sonreír bonachonamente; sonreír de un modo burlón

grind *vt* (to powder) pulverizar; moler; (break up) quebrantar; (oppress) agobiar, oprimir; (sharpen) afilar, amolar; (a barrel-organ) tocar (un manubrio); (the teeth) crujir, rechinar (los dientes); (into) reducir a; (*inf* teach) empollar. *vi* moler; *fig inf* trabajar laboriosamente. *n fig inf* trabajo pesado, *m*; *n fig inf* estudiantón, *m*

grinder *n* (of scissors, etc.) afilador, *m*; (of an organ) organillero; (mill-stone) piedra de moler, *f*; (molar) muela, *f*

grinding *a* (tedious) cansado, aburrido; opresivo; (of pain) incesante. *n* pulverización, *f*; amoladura, *f*; (of grain) molienda, *f*; (polishing) pulimento, bruñido, *m*; (oppression) opresión, *f*; (of teeth) rechinamiento, *f*

grindstone *n* amoladera, afiladera, piedra de amolar, *f*. **to have one's nose to the g.,** batir el yunque

grinning *a* sonriente; riente; (mocking) burlón

grip *n* asimiento, agarro, *m*; (claws, clutches) garras, *f pl*; (hand) mano, *f*; (of shaking hands) apretón de manos, *m*; (of a weapon, etc.) empuñadura, *f*; (reach) alcance, *m*; (understanding) comprensión, *f*; (control) dominio, *m*; (bag) portamanteo, *m*; maleta, *f*. *vt* asir, agarrar; (of wheels) agarrarse; *mech* morder; (a sword, etc.) empuñar; (pinch) pellizcar; (surround) cercar; (understand) comprender; (press; to grip the hand and *fig* the heart) apretar; (fill) llenar; (the attention) atraer, llamar; (sway, hold) dominar

gripe *n* (*inf* pain) retortijón (de tripas), *m*

grisly *a* espantoso; repugnante

grist *n* molienda, *f*. **Everything is g. to their mill,** Sacan partido de todo

gristle *n* cartílago, *m*, ternilla, *f*

gristly *a* cartilaginoso

grit *n* cascajo, *m*; polvo, *m*; *fig* firmeza (de carácter), *f*; (courage) valor, *m*; (endurance) aguante, *m*

gritty *a* arenoso, arenisco

grizzled *a* (of hair, etc.) gris; canoso; grisáceo

grizzly bear *n* oso (-sa) pardo (-da)

groan *n* gemido, *m*. *vi* gemir; (creak) crujir. **to g. out,** decir (or contar) entre gemidos. **to g. under,** sufrir bajo; gemir bajo; (of weight) crujir bajo

groaning *n* gemidos, *m pl*. *a* que gime, gemidor; (under a weight) crujiente

grocer *n* abacero (-ra) vendedor (-ra) de comestibles. **grocer's shop,** tienda de comestibles, bodega, *f*

grocery *n* tienda de comestibles, tienda de ultramarinos, abarrotería, lonja, bodega, *f*, negocio de comestibles, *m*; *pl* **groceries,** provisiones, *f pl*, comestibles, *m pl*

grog *n* grog, *m*

groin *n anat* ingle, *f*

groom *n* (in a royal household) gentilhombre, *m*; lacayo, *m*; mozo de caballos, *m*; (of a bride) novio, *m*. *vt* (a horse) cuidar; (oneself) arreglarse. **She is always well groomed,** Está siempre muy bien arreglada

groomsman *n* padrino de boda, *m*

groove *n* ranura, muesca, *f*; estría, *f*; surco, *m*; *fig* rutina, *f*. *vt* entallar; estriar

grooved *a* con ranura; estriado

grope *vi* andar a tientas; (with for) buscar a tientas; procurar, encontrar, buscar. **to g. one's way toward,** avanzar a tientas hacia; *fig* avanzar poco a poco hacia

gropingly *adv* a tientas; irresolutamente

gross *n com* gruesa, *f*; totalidad, *f*, *a* grueso; denso, espeso; (unrefined) grosero; (great) grande; (crass) craso; total; *com* bruto; (tremendous) enorme. **in g.,** en grueso. **g. amount,** total, *m; com* importe bruto, *m*. **g. weight,** peso bruto, *m*

grossly *adv* groseramente; (much) enormemente

grossness *n* gordura, *f;* (vulgarity) grosería, *f;* obscenidad, *f;* (enormity) enormidad, *f*

grotesque *a* grotesco; extravagante, estrambótico; ridiculo. *n* grotesco, *m*

grotesqueness *n* lo grotesco; ridiculez, *f*

grotto *n* gruta, *f*

ground *n* suelo, *m;* (of water and *naut*) fondo, *m;* (earth) tierra, *f; fig* terreno, *m;* (strata) capa, *f; sport* campo, *m;* (parade) plaza (de armas), *f;* (background) fondo, *m;* (basis) base, *f,* fundamento, *m;* (reason) causa, *f;* motivo, *m;* (excuse) pretexto, *m; pl* **grounds,** jardines, *m pl,* parque, *m;* (sediment) sedimento, *m,* heces, *f pl;* (reason) causa, *f. vi naut* varar, encallar. *vt* poner en tierra; *naut* hacer varar; *elec* conectar con tierra; (base) fundar (en), basar (en); (teach) enseñar los rudimentos (de). *a* molido; en polvo; (of floors, stories) bajo; (of glass) deslustrado; *bot* terrestre. **common g.,** tierra comunal, *f; fig* tierra común, *f*. **He is on his own g.,** Está en terreno propio. **It fell to the g.,** Cayó al suelo; *fig* Fracasó. **It is on the g.,** Está en el suelo. **It suits me to the g.,** Me viene de perilla. **to break fresh g.,** *fig* tratar problemas nuevos. **to be well grounded in,** conocer bien los elementos (or rudimentos) de. **to cover g.,** cubrir terreno; recorrer; (in discussion) tocar muchos puntos. **to cut the g. from beneath one's feet,** hacer perder la iniciativa (a). **to give g.,** retroceder; perder terreno. **to raze to the g.,** echar por tierra, arrasar. **to stand one's g.,** resistir el ataque; no darse por vencido; *fig* mantenerse firme, mantenerse en sus trece. **to win g.,** ganar terreno. **g. coffee,** café molido, *m*. **g.-color,** (of paint) primera capa, *f;* (color de) fondo, *m;* **g.-floor,** piso bajo, *m*. **g. glass,** vidrio deslustrado, *m*. **g.-ivy,** hiedra terrestre, *f,* **g. nut,** cacahuete, *m*. **g.-plan,** *arch* planta, *f*. **g.-rent,** censo, *m*. **g.-sheet,** tela impermeable, *f;* **g. staff,** *aer* personal del aeropuerto, *m*. **g.-swell,** mar de fondo, *m*

grounded *a* fundado. **The airplanes are g.,** Los aviones están sin volar. **His suspicions are well g.,** Tiene motivos para sus sospechas

grounding *n naut* encalladura, *f;* (teaching) instrucción en los rudimentos, *f*

groundless *a* sin fundamento, inmotivado, sin causa, sin motivo

groundwork *n* fundamento, *m;* base, *f;* principio, *m*

group *n* grupo, *m. vt* agrupar. *vi* agruparse. **g. captain,** coronel de aviación, *m*

grouping *n* agrupación, *f*

grouse *n orn* ortega, *f. vi* rezongar, refunfuñar

grove *n* soto, boscaje, *m;* arboleda, *f*

grovel *vi* arrastrarse; *fig* humillarse

groveling *a fig* servil; ruin

grow *vi* crecer; (increase) aumentar; (become) hacerse; empezar a; llegar a; (turn) volverse, ponerse; (flourish) progresar, adelantar; (develop) desarrollarse; (extend) extenderse. *vt* cultivar; dejar crecer. **I grew to fear it,** Llegué a temerlo. **to g. cold,** ponerse frío; enfriarse; (of weather) empezar a hacer frío. **to g. fat,** engordar. **to g. hard,** ponerse duro; *fig* endurecerse. **to g. hot,** ponerse caliente; calentarse; (of weather) empezar a hacer calor. **to g. like Topsy,** crecer a la buena de Dios. **to g. old,** envejecer. **to g. tall,** crecer mucho; ser alto. **to g. again,** crecer de nuevo. **to g. into,** hacerse; llegar a ser; venir a ser. **to g. out of,** brotar de; originarse en; (a habit) desacostumbrarse poco a poco. **He is growing out of his clothes,** La ropa se le hace pequeña. **to g. up,** (of persons) hacerse hombre (mujer); desarrollarse; (of a custom, etc.) imponerse. **to g. on, upon,** crecer sobre; llegar a dominar; (make think) hacer creer, empezar a pensar; (of a habit) arraigar en

grower *n* cultivador (-ra)

growing *n* crecimiento, *m;* desarrollo, *m;* (increase) aumento, *m;* (of flowers, etc.) cultivación, *f, a* creciente

growing pains *n pl* crisis de desarrollo, *f*

growl *n* gruñido, *m;* reverberación, *f;* trueno, *m. vi* gruñir; (of guns) tronar; (of thunder) reverberar. **to g. out,** decir gruñendo

grown *a* crecido; maduro; adulto. **a g. up,** una persona mayor. **to be full-g.,** estar completamente desarrollado; haber llegado a la madurez. **g. over with,** cubierto de

growth *n* crecimiento, *m;* (development) desarrollo, *m;* (progress) progreso, adelanto, *m;* (increase) aumento, *m;* (cultivation) cultivo, *m;* (vegetation) vegetación, *f; med* tumor, *m*. **He has a week's g. on his chin,** Tiene una barba de una semana

grub *n* larva, *f,* gusano, *m. vt* (with up, out) desarraigar; cavar; desmalezar; *fig inf* buscar

grubbiness *n* suciedad, *f;* (untidiness) desaliño, *m*

grubby *a* lleno de gusanos; sucio; bisunto; desaliñado

grudge *n* motivo de rencor, *m;* rencor, resentimiento, *m,* ojeriza, *f;* mala voluntad, *f;* aversión, *f. vt* envidiar. **to bear a g.,** tener ojeriza

grudging *a* (niggardly) mezquino; envidioso; poco generoso; de mala gana; nada afable

grudgingly *adv* de mala gana, contra su voluntad; con rencor; a regañadientes

gruel *n* gachas, *f pl*

gruesome *a* pavoroso, horrible; macabro

gruff *a* (of the voice) bronco, grave, áspero; (of manner) brusco, malhumorado

gruffly *adv* en una voz bronca (or áspera); bruscamente, con impaciencia, malhumoradamente

gruffness *n* aspereza, bronquedad, *f;* brusquedad, *f;* sequedad, impaciencia, *f,* mal humor, *m*

grumble *n* ruido sordo, trueno, *m;* estruendo, *m;* (complaint) refunfuño, rezongo, *m. vi* tronar; refunfuñar, rezongar; hablar entre dientes; quejarse; protestar (contra). *vt* decir refunfuñando

grumbler *n* murmurador (-ra), refunfuñador (-ra)

grumbling *a* gruñón, refunfuñador; regañón; descontento. *n* See **grumble**

grumblingly *adv* a regañadientes, refunfuñando

grumpiness *n* mal humor, *m,* irritabilidad, *f*

grumpy *a* malhumorado, irritable

grunt *n* gruñido, *m. vi* gruñir

grunting *a* gruñidor

guarantee *n law* persona de quien otra sale fiadora, *f;* garantía, *f;* abono, *m. vt* garantizar; responder de; abonar; (assure) asegurar, acreditar

guarantor *n* garante, *mf*

guard *n* (watchfulness) vigilancia, *f;* (in fencing) guardia, *f;* (of a sword) guarnición, *f;* (sentry) centinela, *m;* (soldier) guardia, *m;* (body of soldiers) guardia, *f;* (escort) escolta, *f;* (keeper) guardián, *m;* (protection) protección, defensa, *f;* (of a train) jefe de tren, *m. vt* guardar; proteger, defender; vigilar; (escort) escoltar. **to g. against,** guardarse de. **the changing of the g.,** el relevo de la guardia. **to be on g.,** *mil* estar de guardia; (in fencing) estar en guardia. **to be on one's g.,** estar prevenido, estar alerta. **to be off one's g.,** estar desprevenido. **to mount g.,** *mil* montar la guardia; vigilar. **guard's van,** furgón de equipajes, *m*. **g.-house,** cuerpo de guardia, *m;* prisión militar, *f*

guarded *a* (reticent) reservado, circunspecto, prudente, discreto

guardedly *adv* prudentemente, con circunspección, discretamente

guardian *n* protector (-ra); guardián (-ana); *law* tutor, *m. a* que guarda; tutelar. **g. angel,** ángel de la guarda, ángel custodio, *m;* deidad tutelar, *f*

guardianship *n* protección, *f;* patronato, *m; law* curaduría, tutela, *f*

guardsman *n* guardia, *m*

Guatemalan *a* and *n* guatemalteco (-ca)

guava *n bot* guayaba, *f*

Guernsey Guenesy, *m*
guerrilla *n* guerrilla, *f;* (soldier) guerrillero, *m. a de*
guerrilla. **g. warfare,** guerra de guerrillas, *f*
guess *n* adivinación, *f;* estimación, *f;* conjetura, *f;* sospecha, *f. vt* and *vi* adivinar; conjeturar; sospechar; imaginar; (suppose) suponer, creer; calcular. **to g. at,** formar una opinión sobre; imaginar. **a rough g.,** estimación aproximada, *f.* **at a g.,** a poco más o menos, a ojo de buen cubero. **g.-work,** conjeturas, suposiciones, *f pl*
guest *n* (at a meal) convidado (-da), invitado (-da); (at a hotel, etc.) cliente (-da); *biol* parásito, *m.* **g.-room,** alcoba de respeto, alcoba de honor, alcoba de huéspedes, *f,* cuarto de amigos, cuarto para invitados, *m*
guffaw *n* carcajada, *f. vi* reírse a carcajadas, soltar el trapo
Guiana Guayana, *f*
guidance *n* dirección, *f;* gobierno, *m;* (advice) consejos, *m pl;* inspiración, *f*
guide *n* (person) guía, *mf;* (girl g.) exploradora, *f;* (book and *fig*) guía, *f;* mentor, *m;* modelo, *m;* (inspiration) norte, *m; mech* guía, *f. vt* guiar; conducir; encaminar; dirigir; (govern) gobernar. **g.-book,** guía (de turistas), *f.* **g.-post,** poste indicador, *m*
guided tour *n* visita explicada, visita programada, *f*
guideline *lit* falsarregla, falsilla, *f; fig* pauta, *f*
guiding *a* que guía; directivo; decisivo. *n* See **guidance**
guild *n* gremio, *m. a* gremial. **g. member,** gremial, *m*
guilder *n* (coin) florín holandés, *m*
guile *n* astucia, superchería, maña, *f*
guileful *a* astuto
guileless *a* cándido, sin malicia, inocente
guilelessly *adv* inocentemente
guilelessness *n* inocencia, candidez, *f*
guillotine *n* guillotina, *f. vt* guillotinar
guilt *n* culpabilidad, *f;* crimen, *m;* (sin) pecado, *m*
guilt complex complejo de culpa, *m*
guiltily *adv* culpablemente; como si fuese culpable
guiltless *a* libre de culpa, inocente; puro; ignorante
guilty *a* culpable; delincuente; criminal. **to find g.,** encontrar culpable. **to plead g.,** confesarse culpable. **g. party,** culpable, *m*
Guinea Guinea, *f*
guinea *n* guinea, *f.* **g.-fowl,** gallina de Guinea, *f.* **g.-pig,** conejillo de Indias, cobayo, *m*
guise *n* manera, guisa, *f;* (garb) traje, *m;* máscara, *f; fig* pretexto, *m.* **under the g. of,** bajo el pretexto de; bajo la apariencia de
guitar *n* guitarra, *f*
guitarist *n* guitarrista, *mf*
gulf *n* golfo, *m;* abismo, *m*
Gulf Stream, the la Corriente del Golfo
gull *n orn* gaviota, *f;* (dupe) primo, *m. vt* engañar, timar, defraudar
gullet *n* esófago, *m;* garganta, *f*
gullibility *n* credulidad, *f*
gullible *a* crédulo
gully *n* hondonada, barranca, *f;* (gutter) arroyo, *m*
gulp *n* trago, sorbo, *m. vt* engullir, tragar; (repress) ahogar; (believe) tragar. **to g. up,** vomitar
gum *n* (of the mouth) encía, *f;* goma, *f. vt* engomar; pegar con goma. **gum arabic,** goma arábiga, *f.* **gum boots,** botas de goma, *f pl.* **gum-resin,** gomorresina, *f.* **gum starch,** aderezo, *m.* **gum tree,** eucalipto, *m*
gumminess *n* gomosidad, *f*
gummy *a* gomoso
gumption *n* sentido común, seso, *m*
gun *n* arma de fuego, *f;* (handgun) fusil, *m;* (sporting g.)

escopeta, *f;* (pistol) pistola, *f,* revólver, *m;* (cannon) cañón, *m;* (firing) cañonazo, *m.* **big gun,** *inf* pájaro gordo, *m.* **heavy gun,** cañón de grueso calibre, *m.* **gun-barrel,** cañón de escopeta, *m.* **gun-carriage,** cureña, *f.* **gun-cotton,** pólvora de algodón, *f.* **gun-fire,** cañonazo, *m pl,* fuego, *m.* **gun-metal,** bronce de cañón, *m;* pavón, *m.* **gun-room,** armería, *f;* (on a ship) polvorín, *m.* **gun-running,** contrabanda de armas, *f.* **gun-turret,** torre, *f.* **gun wound,** balazo, *m*
gunboat *n* cañonero, *m,* lancha bombardera, *f*
gunflint *n* piedra de escopeta, *f*
gunman *n* escopetero, armero, *m;* bandido armado, *m;* gángster, apache, *m*
gunner *n* artillero, *m;* escopetero, *m*
gun permit *n* licencia de armas, *f,* permiso de armas, *m*
gunpowder *n* pólvora, *f*
gunshot *n* escopetazo, *m;* tiro de fusil, *m*
gunsmith *n* escopetero, armero, *m*
gunwale *n naut* regala, borda, *f*
gurgle *n* murmullo, murmurio, gorgoteo, *m;* gluglú, *m;* (of a baby) gorjeo, *m. vi* murmurar; hacer gluglú; (of babies) gorjear
gurgling *a* murmurante; (of babies) gorjeador. *n* See **gurgle**
gush *n* chorro, *m;* (of words) torrente, *m;* (of emotion) efusión, *f. vi* chorrear, borbotar; surtir, surgir. **to g. out,** saltar, brotar a borbotones, salir a borbollones, salira borbotones. **to g. over,** *fig* hablar con efusión de
gushing *a* hirviente; (of people) efusivo, extremoso, empalagoso
gusset *n sew* escudete, *m*
gust *n* (of wind) ráfaga, bocanada (de aire), *f; fig* arrebato, acceso, *m*
gusto *n* brío, *m;* entusiasmo, *m*
gusty *a* borrascoso
gut *n* intestino, *m,* tripa, *f;* (catgut) cuerda de tripa, *f; naut* estrecho, *m; pl* **guts,** tripas, *f pl;* (content) meollo, *m,* substancia, *f;* (stamina) aguante, espíritu, *m. vt* (of fish, etc.) destripar; (plunder) saquear; destruir por completo; quemar completamente
gutta-percha *n* gutapercha, *f*
gutter *n* canal, *m;* (of a street) arroyo (de la calle), *m;* (ditch) zanja, *f; fig* hampa, *f. vt* surcar. *vi* gotear; (of a candle) cerotear, gotear la cera. **g. spout,** canalón, *m*
guttersnipe *n* golfillo, *m,* niño (-ña) del hampa
guttural *a* gutural. *n* letra gutural, *f*
guy *n* (rope) viento, *m; naut* guía, *f;* (effigy) mamarracho, *m;* (scarecrow) espantajo, *m, vt* sujetar con vientos o guías; burlarse de
guzzle *vt* tragar, engullir. *vi* atracarse, engullir; emborracharse. *n* comilón, *m;* borrachera, *f*
guzzler *n* tragador (-ra); borracho (-cha)
gymnasium *n* gimnasio, *m*
gymnast *n* gimnasta, *mf*
gymnastic *a* gimnástico. **g. rings,** anillas, *f pl*
gymnastics *n* gimnasia, *f*
gynecological *a* ginecológico
gynecologist *n* ginecólogo (-ga)
gynecology *n* ginecología, *f*
gypsum *n* yeso, *m*
gypsy *n* gitano (-na). *a* gitano, gitanesco; (music) flamenco
gyrate *vi* girar, rodar
gyration *n* giro, *m,* vuelta, *f*
gyratory *a* giratorio
gyro-compass *n* brújula giroscópica, *f*
gyroscope *n phys* giroscopio, *m*

H

h *n* (letter) hache, *f*
ha *interj* ¡ah!
haberdasher *n* mercero, *m*

haberdashery *n* mercería, *f*
habiliment *n* vestidura, *f; pl* **habiliments,** indumentaria, *f*

habilitate *vt* habilitar

habilitation *n* habilitación, *f*

habit *n* costumbre, *f*, hábito, *m*; (temperament) temperamento, carácter, *m*; (use) uso, *m*; (of body) complexión, constitución, *f*; *ecc* hábito, *m*. **to be in the h. of,** soler, acostumbrar, estar acostumbrado a. **to have bad habits,** estar malacostumbrado. **to have the bad h. of,** tener el vicio (or la mala costumbre) de. **to contract the h. of,** contraer la costumbre de. **h. maker,** sastre de trajes de montar, *m*

habitable *a* habitable, vividero

habitat *n* (*bot, zool*) medio, *m*, habitación, *f*

habitation *n* habitación, *f*

habit-forming *a* enviciador, que crea vicio

habitual *a* habitual, acostumbrado, usual; constante; común

habitually *adv* habitualmente; constantemente; comúnmente

habituate *vt* habituar, acostumbrar

habituation *n* habituación, *f*

habitué *n* parroquiano (-na); veterano (-na)

hack *n* caballo de alquiler, *m*; rocín, jaco, *m*; (writer) escritor mercenario, *m*. *vt* acuchillar; tajar, cortar. *vi* cortar. **to h. to pieces,** cortar en pedazos; pasar a cuchillo

hacking *a* (of coughs) seco

hackle *n* (for flax, hemp) rastrillo, *m*

hackney carriage *n* coche de plaza, coche de alquiler, *m*

hackneyed *a* gastado, trillado, muy usado, repetido, resobado

hacksaw *n* sierra de cerrajero, sierra para metal, *f*

hackwork *n* trabajo de rutina, *m*

haddock *n* merlango, *m*, pescadilla, *f*

Hades *n* Hades, *m*; *inf* el infierno, *m*

haft *n* mango, tomadero, *m*, manija, *f*; puño, *m*

hag *n* bruja, *f*

haggard *a* ojeroso, trasnochado, trasojado

haggardly *adv* ansiosamente

haggardness *n* aspecto ojeroso, *m*

haggle *vi* regatear; vacilar

haggling *n* regateo, *m*, a regatón

hagiographer *n* hagiógrafo, *m*

hagiography *n* hagiografía, *f*

Hague, The La Haya

ha, ha! *interj* ¡ja, ja!

hail *n* (salutation) saludo, *m*; (shout) grito, *m*; aclamación, *f*; (frozen rain) granizo, *m*; (of blows) lluvia, *f*. *interj* ¡salve! *vt* saludar; llamar; aclamar; *fig* lanzar, echar. *vi* (hailstones) granizar; (blows, etc.) llover. **to h. from,** proceder de, ser natural de. **within h.,** al habla. **H. Mary,** Salve Regina, Avemaría, *f*

hailstone *n* granizo, pedrisco, *m*

hailstorm *n* granizada, *f*

hair *n* (single h.) cabello, *m*; (*zool, bot*) pelo, *m*; (of horse's mane) crin, *f*; (head of h.) cabellera, mata de pelo, *f*, pelo, *m*; (superfluous) vello, *m*; (fiber) fibra, *f*, filamento, *m*; (on the pen) raspa, *f*, pelo, *m*; *fig* pelo, *m*. **lock of h.,** bucle, rizo, *m*; mecha, *f*. **to dress one's h.,** peinarse. **to have one's h. cut,** hacerse cortar el pelo. **to part the h.,** hacer(se) la raya del pelo. **to put up one's h.,** hacerse el moño; (to "come out") ponerse de largo. **to tear one's h.,** mesarse los cabellos. **h. combings,** peinaduras, *f pl*. **h.-curler,** tirabuzón, *m*. **h. dryer,** secadora de cabello, *f*. **h. dye,** tinte para el pelo, *m*. **h.-net,** redecilla, *f*. **h.-oil,** brillantina, *f*. **h.-raising,** horripilante, espeluznante. **h.-ribbon,** cinta para el pelo, *f*. **h.-shirt,** cilicio, *m*. **h. slide,** pasador, *m*. **h.-splitting,** sofistería, argucia, *f*; mez quinas argucias, quis quillas, *f pl*. **h.-spring,** muelle del volante, *m*. **h.-switch,** añadido, *m*. **h.-trigger,** pelo de una pistola, *m*

hairbreadth *n* pelo, *m*. **to have a h. escape,** escapar por un pelo.

hairbrush *n* cepillo para el cabello, *m*

hairdresser *n* peluquero (-ra), peinadora, *f*

hairdressing *n* peinado, *m*. **h. establishment** or **trade,** peluquería, *f*

haired *a* peludo, con pelo; (in compounds) de pelo . . .

hairiness *n* vellosidad, *f*

hairless *a* sin pelo; calvo

hairlike *a* filiforme

hairpin *n* horquilla, *f*. **h. bend,** viraje en horquilla, *m*

hairy *a* peludo; velloso; *bot* hirsuto

Haiti Haití, *m*

Haitian *a* and *n* haitiano (-na)

hake *n* merluza, *f*

halcyon *n* alción, martín pescador, *m*. *a fig* feliz, sereno, tranquilo

hale *a* fuerte, sano, robusto. *vt* hacer comparecer

half *n* mitad, *f*; (school term) trimestre, *m*. *a* medio; semi. *adv* a medias; mitad; (almost) casi; insuficientemente; imperfectamente. **I don't h. like it,** No me gusta nada. **It is h.-past two,** Son las dos y media. **an hour and a h.,** una hora y media. **better h.,** *inf* media naranja, cara mitad, *f*. **by halves,** a medias. **in h.,** en dos mitades. **one h.,** la mitad. **to go halves,** ir a medias. **to h. close,** entornar. **to h. open,** entreabrir. **h. a bottle,** media botella, *f*. **h. a crown,** media corona, *f*. **h.-alive,** semivivo. **h. an hour,** media hora, *f*. **h.-and-h.,** mitad y mitad; en partes iguales. **h.-asleep,** semidormido, medio dormido. **h.-awake,** medio despierto, entre duerme y vela. **h.-back,** *sport* medio, *m*. **h.-baked,** medio cocido, crudo; *fig* poco maduro. **h.-binding,** encuadernación en media pasta, *f*. **h.-breed,** *a* mestizo. *n* cruce, *m*. **h.-brother,** hermanastro, hermano de padre, hermano de madre, *m*. **h.-caste,** mestizo. **h. circle,** semicírculo, *m*. **h.-closed,** entreabierto; medio cerrado. **h.-dead,** medio muerto; más muerto que vivo. **h.-done,** hecho a medias, sin acabar. **h.-dozen,** media docena, *f*. **h.-dressed,** medio desnudo. **h. fare,** medio billete, *m*. **h.-full,** medio lleno. **h.-hearted,** débil, poco eficaz, lánguido; indiferente, sin entusiasmo. **h.-heartedness,** debilidad, *f*; indiferencia, *f*. **h.-holiday,** media fiesta, *f*. **h.-hourly,** cada media hora. **h.-length,** (portrait) de medio cuerpo. **h.-length coat,** abrigo de tres cuartos, *m*. **h.-light,** media luz, *f*. **h.-mast,** a media asta. **h.-measure,** medida poco eficaz, *f*. **h.-moon,** *n* media luna, *f*; *ast* semilunio, *m*; (of a nail) blanco (de la uña), *m*. **h.-mourning,** medio luto, *m*. **h.-pay,** media paga, *f*. **h.-price,** a mitad de precio. **h.-seas-over,** *inf* entre dos velas. **h.-sister,** hermanastra, hermana de padre, hermana de madre, *f*. **h.-time,** *sport* media parte, *f*, medio tiempo, *m*. **h.-tone,** de medio tono. **h.-tone illustration,** fotograbado a media tinta, *f*. **h.-truth,** verdad a medias, *f*. **h.-turn,** media vuelta, *f*. **h.-way,** a medio camino; medio. **h.-witted,** medio loco, tonto, imbécil. **h.-year,** medio año, *m*. **h.-yearly,** semestral

halfpenny *n* medio penique, *m*; *inf* perra gorda, *f*

half title anteportada, falsa portada, portadilla, preportada, *f*

halibut *n* halibut, *m*; (genus) hipogloso, *m*

halitosis *n* halitosis, *f*

hall *n* (mansion) mansión, casa de campo, *f*, caserón, *m*; (public building) edificio, *m*, casa (de); (town h.) casa del ayuntamiento, *f*; (room) sala, *f*; (entrance) vestíbulo, *m*; (dining room) comedor, *m*; (of residence for students) residencia, *f*. **h. door,** portón, *m*, puerta del vestíbulo, *f*. **h. porter,** conserje, *m*. **h.-stand,** perchero, *m*

hallelujah *n* aleluya, *f*

hallmark *n* marca de ley, *f*; *fig* señal, *f*; indicio, *m*. *vt* poner la marca de ley sobre; *fig* sellar

halloo *vt* (hounds) azuzar; perseguir dando voces; (call) llamar

hallow *vt* santificar; reverenciar; (consecrate) consagrar

Halloween *n* la víspera de Todos los Santos, *f*

hallucination *n* alucinación, ilusión, *f*; visión, *f*; fantasma, *m*

hallucinatory *a* alucinador

halo *n* halo, nimbo, *m*

halogen *n chem* halógeno, *m*

halt *n mil* alto, *m*; cesación, *f*; interrupción, *f*; (on a railway) apeadero, *m*; (for trams, buses) parada, *f*. *vt* parar, detener. *vi* pararse, detenerse; *mil* hacer alto; cesar; interrumpirse; (in speech) titubear; (of verse) estar cojo; (doubt) dudar; (limp) cojear. **H.!** *mil* ¡Alto!

halter *n* ronzal, cabestro, *m*; (for hanging) dogal, *m*. *vt* encabestrar, cabestrar

halting *n* parada, *f*; interrupción, *f*. *a* (of gait) cojo; incierto; vacilante; (of speech) titubeante

halve *vt* partir (or dividir) en dos mitades

ham *n* jamón, *m*; *anat* pernil, *m*; (radio-operator) radioaficionado, *m*

Hamburg Hamburgo, *m*

hamlet *n* aldea, *f*, pueblecito, *m*

hammer *n* martillo, *m*; (stone cutter's) maceta, *f*; (mason's) piqueta, *f*; (of fire-arms) percusor, *m*; (of piano) macillo, *m*. *vt* amartillar, martillar, batir. **to throw the h.,** lanzar el martillo. **under the h.,** en subasta, al remate. **h. blow,** martillazo, *m*

hammering *n* martilleo, martillazo, *m*. **by h.,** a martillo

hammock *n* hamaca, *f*; *naut* coy, *m*

hamper *n* banasta, canasta, *f*, cesto grande, *m*. *vt* estorbar, dificultar, impedir; *fig* embarazar

hamster *n zool* hámster, *m*, marmota de Alemania, rata del trigo, *f*

hand *n* mano, *f*; (of animal) pata, mano, *f*; (worker) operario (-ia); obrero (-ra); (skill) habilidad, *f*; (side) mano, *f*, lado, *m*; (measure) palmo, *m*; (of a clock) manecilla, *f*; (of instruments) aguja, *f*; (applause) aplauso, *m*; (power) poder, *m*; las manos; (at cards) mano, *f*; (card player) jugador, *m*; (signature) firma, *f*; (handwriting) letra, escritura, *f*; (influence) influencia, parte, mano, *f*. **old h.,** veterano; perro viejo. **at h.,** a mano, al lado, cerca. **have at hand,** tener a la mano. **at the hands of,** de manos de. **by h.,** a mano; (on the bottle) con biberón. **from h. to h.,** de mano a mano. **in h.,** entre manos; (of money) de contado. **in the hands of,** *fig* en el poder de. **"Hands wanted,"** «Se desean trabajadores.» **h. over h.,** mano sobre mano. **hand's breadth,** palmo, *m*. **Hands off!** ¡Fuera las manos! **Hands up!** ¡Manos arriba! **lost with all hands,** (of a ship) perdido con toda su tripulación. **off one's hands,** despachado; (of a daughter) casada. **on all hands,** por todas partes. **on h.,** entre manos; (of goods) existente; (present) presente. **on one's hands,** a cargo de uno. **on the one h.,** por un lado; a un lado. **on the other h.,** por otra parte; en cambio. **out of h.,** luego, inmediatamente; revoltoso. **to come to h.,** venir a mano; (of letters) llegar a las manos (de). **to get one's h. in,** ejercitarse. **to have a h. in,** tener parte en; intervenir en. **to have no h. in,** no tener arte ni parte en. **to have on h.,** traer entre manos. **to have the upper h.,** tener la sartén por el mango, llevar la ventaja. **to hold one's h.,** abstenerse; detenerse. **to hold hands,** cogerse de las manos. **to lay hands on,** tocar; poner mano en; echar manos a. **to set one's h. to,** emprender; (sign) firmar. **to shake hands,** estrechar la mano. **to stretch out one's hands,** tender las manos. **to take one's hands off,** no tocar. **with folded hands,** mano sobre mano. **with his hands behind his back,** con las manos en la espalda. **h.-in-h.,** cogidos (cogidas) de las manos. **h.-lever,** manija, *f*. **h.-loom,** telar de mano, *m*. **h. luggage,** equipaje de mano, *m*. **h.-made,** hecho a mano. **h.-mill,** molinillo, *m*. **h.-pump,** *n naut* sacabuche, *m*. **h. rail,** pasamano, *m*, baranda, balustrada, *f*. **h.-sewn,** cosido a mano. **h.-to-h.,** de mano en mano; (of a fight) a brazo partido, cuerpo a cuerpo. **h.-to-h. fight,** cachetina, *f*. **h.-to-mouth,** precario. **to live from h.-to-mouth,** vivir de día en día

hand *vt* dar; entregar; alargar. **to h. down,** bajar; (a person) ayudar a bajar; transmitir. **to h. in,** entregar; (a person) ayudar a entrar; (one's resignation) dimitir; (send) mandar, enviar. **to h. on,** transmitir. **to h. out,**

vt distribuir; (a person) ayudar a salir; (from a vehicle) ayudar a bajar. *vi inf* pagar. **to h. over,** *vt* entregar. *vi mil* traspasar los poderes (a). **to h. round,** pasar de mano en mano; pasar; ofrecer. **to h. up,** subir; (a person) ayudar a subir

handbag *n* bolso, saco, monedero, *m*

handbarrow *n* carretilla, *f*, angarillas, *f pl*

handbill *n* anuncio, *m*

handbook *n* manual, compendio, tratado, *m*; anuario, *m*; (guide) guía, *f*

handbreadth *n* palmo, *m*

handcart *n* carretilla de mano, *f*, carretón, *m*

handcuff *n* esposa, *f*, grillo, *m*, (gen. *pl*). *vt* poner las esposas (a), maniatar

handed *a* (in compounds) que tiene manos; de manos . . . ; con las manos . . . **four-h.,** *sport* de cuatro personas. **one-h.,** manco

handful *n* puño, puñado, manojo, *m*. **to be a h.,** *inf* tener el diablo en el cuerpo. **in handfuls,** a manojos

handgrip *n* apretón de manos, *m*

handicap *n* desventaja, *f*; obstáculo, *m*; *sport* handicap, *m*; ventaja, *f*. *vt fig* perjudicar, impedir, dificultar. **the handicapped,** los lisiados, *m pl*

handicraft *n* mano de obra, *f*; (skill) destreza manual, *f*

handiwork *n* mano de obra, *f*; trabajo manual, *m*; obra, *f*; (deed) acción, *f*, hecho, *m*

handkerchief *n* pañuelo, *m*

handle *n* mango, puño, *m*; (lever) palanca, *f*; (of baskets, dishes, jugs) asa, *f*; (of doors, windows, drawers) pomo, *m*, (of a car door) picaporte *m*; (to one's name) designación, *f*; título, *m*; (excuse) pretexto, *m*. *vt* (touch) tocar; manejar, manipular; (treat) tratar; **h. with kid gloves,** tratar con guantes de seda; (deal in) comerciar en; tomar; (paw) manosear; (direct) dirigir; (control) gobernar; (pilot) pilotar; (a theme) explicar, tratar de. **h.-bar,** manillar, *m*. **h.-bar grip,** puño de un manillar, *m*

handless *a* sin manos; manco; *fig* torpe

handling *n* manejo, *m*; manipulación, *f*; (treatment) trato, *m*, relaciones (con), *f pl*; (thumbing) manoseo, *m*; interpretación, *f*; *art* tratamiento, *m*, técnica, *f*

handmaid *n* sirvienta, criada, *f*; (thumbing) mayordomo, *m*

handsaw *n* sierra de mano, *f*, serrucho, *m*

handshake *n* apretón de manos, *m*

handsome *a* (generous) generoso; magnánimo; considerable; hermoso, bello; elegante; (of people) guapo, distinguido; excelente; (flattering) halagüeño. **He was a very h. man,** Era un hombre muy guapo

handsomely *adv* generosamente; con magnanimidad; elegantemente; bien

handsomeness *n* generosidad, *f*; magnanimidad, *f*; hermosura, *f*; elegancia, *f*; distinción, *f*

handspring *n* voltereta sobre las manos, *f*

handwork *n* obra hecha a mano, *f*, trabajo a mano, *m*; (needlework) labor de aguja, *f*

handworked *a* hecho a mano; (embroidered) bordado

handwriting *n* caligrafía, letra, escritura, *f*. **the h. on the wall,** la mano que escribía en la pared, *f*

handy *a* (of persons) diestro, mañoso, hábil; (of things) conveniente; útil; (near) cercano, a mano. *adv* cerca. **h.-man,** hombre de muchos oficios, *m*; factótum, *m*

hang *vt* colgar; suspender; (execute) ahorcar; (the head) bajar; dejar caer; (upholster) entapizar; (with wallpaper) empapelar; (drape) poner colgaduras en; (place) poner; (cover) cubrir. *vi* colgar, pender; estar suspendido; (be executed) ser ahorcado; (of garments) caer. *n* (of garments) caída, *f*; (of a machine) mecanismo, *m*; (meaning) sentido, *m*, significación, *f*. **to h. by a thread,** pender de un hilo. **to h. in the balance,** estar en la balanza. **to h. fire,** estar (una cosa) en suspenso. **to h. loose,** caer suelto; (clothes) venir ancho. **to h. about,** (surround) rodear, pegarse a; (frequent) frecuentar; (haunt) rondar; (be imminent) ser inminente, amenazar; (embrace) abrazar. **to h. back,** retroceder; quedarse atrás; *fig* vacilar, titubear. **to h. down,** colgar, pender; estar caído; caerse. **to h. on,** seguir agarrado (a); apoyarse en; *fig* persistir; (a person's words) estar pendiente de, beber; (remain) quedarse. **to h. out,** *vt* tender. *vi* (lean out) asomarse (por); (*inf* live) habitar. **to h. over,** colgar por encima; (brood) cernerse sobre; (lean over) inclinarse sobre; quedarse cerca de; (overhang) sobresalir; (overarch) abovedar; (threaten) amenazar. **to h. together,** (of persons) permanecer unidos; (of things) tener cohesión; (be consistent) ser lógico, ser consistente. **to h. up,** colgar; suspender; *fig* dejar pendiente, interrumpir. **to h. upon,** apoyarse en; (a person's words) beber las palabras de uno

hangar *n* cobertizo; *aer* hangar, *m*

hanger *n* colgadero, *m*; percha *f*. **h.-on,** parásito, *m*; dependiente, *m*

hanging *n* colgamiento, *m*; (killing) ahorcamiento, *m*; *pl* **hangings,** colgaduras, *f pl*, cortinajes, *m pl. a* pendiente colgante; péndulo; (of gardens) pensil. **It's not a h. matter,** No es una cuestión de vida y muerte. **h. bridge,** puente colgante, *m*. **h. committee,** junta (de una exposición,) *f*. **h. lamp,** lámpara de techo, *f*

hangman *n* verdugo, *m*

hangnail *n* padrastro, *m*

hangover *n* (after drinking) resaca, cruda (Mexico), *f*

hank *n* madeja, *f*

hanker *vi* (with after) ansiar, ambicionar; (with for) anhelar, suspirar por, desear con vehemencia

hankering *n* ambición, *f*; deseo vehemente, *m*

hanky-panky *n* superchería, *f*; engaño, *m*

hap *n* casualidad, suerte, *f*; suceso fortuito, *m*

haphazard *n* casualidad, *f. a* fortuito, casual

hapless *a* desgraciado, desdichado

haplessness *n* desgracia, desdicha, *f*

happen *vi* suceder, acontecer, ocurrir, pasar; (to be found, be) hallarse por casualidad; (take place) tener lugar, verificarse; (arise) sobrevenir. **Do you know what has happened to . . .?** ¿Sabes qué se ha hecho de . . .? **as if nothing had happened,** como si no hubiese pasado nada. **He turned up as if nothing had happened,** Se presentó como si tal cosa. **How did it h.?** ¿Cómo fue esto? **If they h. to see you,** Si acaso te vean. **I happened to be in London,** Me hallaba por casualidad en Londres. **It won't h. again,** No volverá a suceder. **whatever happens,** venga lo que venga

happening *n* suceso, acontecimiento, hecho, *m*, ocurrencia, *f*

happily *adv* felizmente; por suerte

happiness *n* felicidad, dicha, *f*; alegría, *f*, regocijo, *m*

happy *a* (lucky) afortunado; (felicitous) feliz, oportuno; feliz, dichoso; alegre, regocijado. **to be h.,** estar contento, ser feliz. **to be h. about,** alegrarse de. **to make h.,** hacer feliz, alegrar. **h.-go-lucky,** irresponsable, descuidado

harangue *n* arenga, *f. vt* arengar. *vi* pronunciar una arenga

harass *vt* hostigar, acosar; atormentar; preocupar; *mil* picar. **to h. the rear-guard,** picar la retaguardia

harbinger *n fig* precursor, heraldo, *m*; presagio, anuncio, *m. vt* anunciar, presagiar

harbor *n* puerto, *m*; (bay) bahía, *f*; (haven) asilo, refugio, *m. vt* dar refugio (a), albergar, acoger; (cherish) abrigar, acariciar; (conceal) esconder. **inner h.,** puerto, *m*. **outer h.,** rada del puerto, *f*. **to put into h.,** entrar en el puerto. **h. bar,** barra del puerto, *f*. **h.-dues,** derechos de puerto, *m pl*. **h.-master,** capitán de puerto, contramaestre de puerto, *m*

harborer *n* amparador (-ra), protector (-ra); (criminal) encubridor (-ra)

hard *a* duro; (firm) firme; difícil; laborioso, agotador; violento; poderoso; arduo; fuerte, recio; vigoroso, robusto; insensible, inflexible; cruel; (of weather) inclemente, severo; (unjust) injusto, opresivo; (stiff) tieso; (of water) cruda; (of wood) brava. *adv* duro; duramente; con ahínco; con fuerza; de firme; difícil-

mente; (of gazing) fijamente; severamente; (firmly) firmemente; vigorosamente; (of raining) a cántaros, mucho; (quickly) rápidamente; excesivamente; (much) mucho; (of bearing misfortune) a pechos; (attentively) atentamente; (heavily) pesadamente; (badly) mal; (closely) de cerca, inmediatamente. **It was a h. blow,** Fue un golpe recio. **to be h. put to,** encontrar difícil. **to go h.,** endurecerse. **to go h. with,** irle mal a uno. **to have a h. time,** pasar apuros, pasarlo mal. **to look h. at,** mirar atentamente, examinar fijamente; mirar fijamente. **to be a h. drinker,** ser un bebedor empedernido. **h. and fast rule,** regla inalterable, *f*. **h.-bitten,** de carácter duro. **a h.-boiled egg,** un huevo duro. **h. breathing,** resuello, *m*. **h. by,** muy cerca. **h. cash,** efectivo, *m*. **h.-earned,** difícilmente conseguido; ganado con el sudor de la frente. **h.-featured,** de facciones duras. **h.-fisted,** tacaño. **h.-fought,** arduo, reñido. **h.-headed,** práctico, perspicaz. **h.-hearted,** duro de corazón, insensible. **h.-heartedness,** insensibilidad, *f*. **h. labor,** *law* trabajos forzados, *m pl*; presidio, *m*. **h.-mouthed,** (of horses) boquiduro. **h. of hearing,** duro de oído. **h.-up,** apurado. **to be very h.-up,** ser muy pobre; *inf* estar a la cuarta pregunta. **h.-wearing,** duradero; sufrido. **h.-won,** **h.-earned.** **h.-working,** trabajador, hacendoso, diligente

harden *vt* endurecer; (metal) templar; robustecer; (to war) aguerrir; (make callous) hacer insensible. *vi* endurecerse; hacerse duro; templarse, robustecerse; (of shares) entonarse

hardening *n* endurecimiento, *m*; (of metal) temple, *m*. **h. of the arteries,** arteriosclerosis, *f*

hardiness *n* vigor, *m*, fuerza, robustez, *f*; audacia, *f*

hardly *adv* duramente; difícilmente; (badly) mal; severamente; (scarcely) apenas, casi. **h. ever,** casi nunca

hardness *n* dureza, *f*; severidad, *f*; inhumanidad, insensibilidad, *f*; (stiffness) tiesura, *f*; (difficulty) dificultad, *f*; (of water) crudeza, *f*; (of hearing) dureza de oído, *f*

hardship *n* penas, *f pl*, trabajos, *m pl*; infortunio, *m*, desdicha, *f*; (suffering) sufrimiento, *m*; (affliction) aflicción, *f*; (privation) privación, *f*. **to undergo h.,** pasar trabajos

hardware *n* ferretería, *f*

hardwood *n* madera brava, *f*

hardy *a* audaz, intrépido; (strong) fuerte, robusto; *bot* resistente

hare *n* liebre, *f*. **young h.,** lebrato, *m*. **h. and hounds,** rally paper, *m*, caza de papelitos, *f*. **h.-brained,** casquivano, atronado, con cabeza de chorlito. **hare's foot,** mano de gato, *f*. **h.-lip,** labio leporino, *m*. **h.-lipped,** labihendido

harebell *n* campanilla, campánula, *f*

harem *n* harén, serrallo, *m*

haricot *n* (green bean) judía, *f*; (dried bean) alubia, *f*

hark *vt* escuchar; oír. **to h. back,** volver al punto de partida; volver a la misma canción

harlequin *n* arlequín, *m*

harlequinade *n* arlequinada, *f*

harlot *n* ramera, prostituta, meretriz, *f*

harlotry *n* prostitución, *f*

harm *n* mal, *m*; daño, *m*; perjuicio, *m*; (danger) peligro, *m*; (detriment) menoscabo, *m*; (misfortune) desgracia, *f, vt* hacer mal (a); dañar, hacer daño (a); perjudicar. **And there's no h. in that,** Y en eso no hay mal. **to keep out of harm's way,** evitar el peligro; guardarse del mal

harmful *a* malo; dañino, perjudicial, nocivo; (dangerous) peligroso. **to be h.,** (of food, etc.) hacer mal (a); (of pests) ser dañino; (of behavior, etc.) perjudicar

harmfulness *n* lo malo; perniciosidad, *f*; daño, *m*; peligro, *m*

harmless *a* innocuo; inofensivo; inocente

harmlessness *n* innocuidad, *f*; inocencia, *f*

harmonic *n* (*phys math*) harmónica, *f*; *mus* armónico, *m*, *a mus* armónico

harmonica *n* armónica, *f*
harmonics *n* armonía, *f*; (tones) armónicos, *m pl*
harmonious *a* armonioso
harmoniously *adv* armoniosamente; *fig* en armonía
harmoniousness *n* armonía, *f*
harmonium *n* armonio, *m*
harmonization *n* armonización, *f*
harmonize *vt* armonizar. *vi* armonizarse, estar en armonía
harmony *n* armonía, *f*; *fig* paz, *f*, buenas relaciones, *f pl*; música, *f*. **to live in h.,** vivir en paz
harness *n* guarniciones, *f pl*, jaeces, *m pl*; (armor) arnés, *m*. *vt* enjaezar; (yoke) enganchar; (water) represar. **to die in h.,** *fig* morir en la brecha. **h. maker,** guarnicionero, *m*. **h. room,** guadarnés, *m*
harp *n* arpa, *f*. **to h. on,** volver a la misma canción, volver a repetir
harpist *n* arpista, *mf*
harpoon *n* arpón, *m*. *vt* arponear
harpooner *n* arponero, *m*
harpsichord *n* arpicordio, *m*
harpy *n* arpía, *f*
harridan *n* bruja, *f*
harrow *n* *agr* rastra, *f*, escarificador, *m*. *vt* *agr* escarificar; *fig* lastimar, atormentar
harrowing *a* patibulario, conmovedor, atormentador, angustioso
harry *vt* devastar, asolar; (persons) robar, perseguir; (worry) atormentar; (annoy) molestar
harsh *a* áspero; (of voice) ronco; (of sound) discordante; (of colors) áspero; duro; chillón; severo, duro; (of features) duro; (of taste) ácido, acerbo
harshly *adv* severamente
harshness *n* (roughness) aspereza, *f*; (of voice) ronquedad, aspereza, *f*; (of sound) disonancia, *f*; (of colors) aspereza, *f*; severidad, *f*; dureza, *f*; (of taste) acidez, *f*
hart *n* ciervo, *m*
harum-scarum *n* tronera, saltabarrancos, *mf* molino, *m*, *a* irresponsable
harvest *n* cosecha, siega, *f*; recolección, *f*; *fig* producto, fruto, *m*. *vt* cosechar; recoger. **h. festival,** fiesta de la cosecha, *f*
harvester *n* segador, *m*, cosechero (-ra); (machine) segadora, *f*
hash *n* *cul* picado, *m*. *vt* *cul* picar
hashish *n* hachich, hachís, quif, *m*
hasp *n* pasador, *m*; sujetador, *m*
hassock *n* cojín, *m*
haste *n* prisa, rapidez, *f*; precipitación, *f*; urgencia, *f*. *vt* dar prisa (a); acelerar; precipitar. *vi* darse prisa; acelerarse; precipitarse. **in h.,** de prisa, aprisa. **to be in h.,** estar de prisa, llevar prisa. **in great h.,** muy aprisa, aprisa y corriendo, precipitadamente; con mucha prisa. **More h. less speed,** (Spanish equivalent. Words said by Charles III of Spain to his valet) ¡Vísteme despacio que voy de prisa!
hasten *vt* acelerar, apresurar; precipitar. *vi* darse prisa, apresurarse; moverse con rapidez; correr. **to h. one's steps,** apretar el paso. **to h. away,** marcharse rápidamente. **to h. back,** regresar apresuradamente. **to h. down,** bajar rápidamente. **to h. on,** seguir el camino sin descansar; seguir rápidamente. **to h. out,** salir rápidamente. **to h. towards,** ir rápidamente hacia; correr hacia. **to h. up,** subir aprisa, correr hacia arriba; darse prisa
hastily *adv* de prisa, rápidamente; con precipitación, precipitadamente; (angrily) impacientemente, airadamente; (thoughtlessly) sin reflexión
hastiness *n* rapidez, *f*; precipitación, *f*; (anger) impaciencia, irritación, *f*
hasty *a* rápido, apresurado; precipitado; (superficial) superficial, ligero; (ill-considered) desconsiderado, imprudente; (angry) impaciente, irritable; violento, apasionado
hat *n* sombrero, *m*. **to pass round the h.,** pasar el pla-

tillo. **Andalusian h.,** sombrero calañés, *m*. **bowler h.,** sombrero hongo, *m*. **broad-brimmed h.,** sombrero chambergo, *m*. **Panama h.,** sombrero de jipijapa, *m*. **picture h.,** pamela, *f*. **shovel h.,** sombrero de teja, *m*. **soft felt h.,** sombrero flexible, *m*. **straw h.,** sombrero de paja, *m*. **three-cornered h.,** sombrero de tres picos, *m*. **top-h.,** sombrero de copa, *m*. **h. shop** or **trade,** sombrerería, *f*
hatband *n* cinta de sombrero, *f*, cintillo, *m*
hatblock *n* formillón, *f*
hatbox *n* sombrerera, *f*
hatbrush *n* cepillo para sombreros, *m*
hatch *n* (wicket) compuerta, *f*; (trap-door) puerta caediza, *f*; *naut* escotilla, *f*; compuerta de esclusa, *f*; (of chickens) pollada, *f*; (of birds) nidada, *f*. *vt* (birds) empollar; incubar, encobar; *fig* tramar, urdir. *vi* empollarse, salir del cascarón; incubarse; *fig* madurarse. **to h. a plot,** urdir un complot, conspirar. **to h. chickens,** sacar pollos
hatchet *n* hacha pequeña, *f*, machado, *m*. **to bury the h.,** hacer la paz. **h.-faced,** de cara de cuchillo
hatching *n* incubación, *f*; (of a plot) maquinación, *f*
hatchway *n* *naut* escotilla, *f*
hate *n* odio, aborrecimiento, *m*, aversión, *f*; abominación, *f*. *vt* odiar, aborrecer, detestar; repugnar; saber mal, sentir. **I h. to trouble you,** Me sabe mal molestarle, Siento mucho molestarle. **to h. the sight of,** *inf* no poder ver (a)
hateful *a* odioso, aborrecible; repugnante
hatefulness *n* odiosidad, *f*, lo odioso; maldad, *f*
hater *n* aborrecedor (-ra). **to be a good h.,** saber odiar
hatful *n* un sombrero lleno (de)
hatless *a* sin sombrero, descubierto
hatpin *n* horquilla de sombrero, *f*
hatred *n* odio, aborrecimiento, *m*, detestación, *f*; aversión, enemistad, *f*
hatstand *n* perchera, *f*
hatter *n* sombrerero, *m*. **as mad as a h.,** loco como una cabra
haughtiness *n* altanería, arrogancia, altivez, soberbia, *f*, orgullo, *m*
haughty *a* altanero, arrogante, altivo, orgulloso
haul *n* (pull) tirón, *m*; (of fish) redada, *f*; (booty) botín, *m*. *vt* arrastrar, tirar de; *naut* halar. **to h. at, upon,** (ropes, etc.) aflojar, soltar, arriar. **to h. down,** (flags, sails) arriar
haulage *n* transporte, acarreo, *m*; coste de transporte, *m*. **h. contractor,** contratista de transporte, *m*
haunch *n* anca, culata, *f*; (of meat) pierna, *f*. **h.-bone,** hueso ilíaco, *m*
haunt *n* punto de reunión, lugar frecuentado (por), *m*; (lair) cubil, nido, *m*, guarida, *f*. *vt* frecuentar; rondar; (of ideas) perseguir; (of ghosts) aparecer, visitar. **It is a h. of thieves,** Es una cueva de ladrones
haunted *a* (by spirits) encantado
haunter *n* frecuentador (-ra); (ghost) fantasma, espectro, *m*
haunting *n* frecuentación, *f*; aparición de un espectro, *f*. *a* persistente
hautboy *n* oboe, *m*
hauteur *n* altivez, *f*
Havana la Habana, *f*. *n* (cigar) habano, *m*. (native) habanero (-ra), habano (-na)
have *vt* tener; poseer; (suffer) padecer; (spend) pasar; (eat or drink) tomar; (eat) comer; (a cigarette) fumar; (a bath, etc.) tomar; (a walk, a ride) dar; (cause to be done) mandar (hacer), hacer (hacer); (deceive) engañar; (defeat) vencer; (catch) coger; (say) decir; (allow) permitir; (tolerate) tolerar, sufrir; (obtain) lograr, conseguir; (wish) querer; (know) saber; (realize) realizar; (buy) comprar; (acquire) adquirir. As an auxiliary verb, haber (e.g. **I h. done it,** Lo he hecho, etc.). **As fate would h. it,** Según quiso la suerte. **Do you h. to go?** ¿Tiene Vd. que marcharse? **H. him come here,** Hazle venir aquí. **I h. been had,** Me han engañado. **I h. a good mind to . . . ,** Tengo ganas de . . . **I had all**

my books stolen, Me robaron todos los libros. **You had better go,** Es mejor que te vayas. **I had rather,** Preferiría, Me gustaría más bien. **I h. had a suit made,** Mandé hacerme un traje, Hice hacerme un traje. **I would not h. had it otherwise,** No lo hubiese querido de otra manera. **I will not h. it,** No lo quiero; No quiero tomarlo; (object) No lo permitiré. **If we had known,** Si lo hubiésemos sabido. **It has to do with the sun,** Está relacionado con el sol, Tiene que ver con el sol. **Have a good trip!** ¡Buen viaje!, ¡Feliz viaje! **What are you going to h.?** ¿Qué quiere Vd. tomar? **Will you h. some jam?** ¿Quiere Vd. mermelada? **to h. breakfast,** desayunar. **to h. dinner, supper,** cenar. **to h. lunch,** almorzar. **to h. for tea,** invitar a tomar el té; (of food) merendar. **to h. tea,** tomar el té. **to h. it out with,** habérselas con. **to h. just,** acabar de. **I h. just done it,** Acabo de hacerlo. **to h. on hand,** traer entre manos. **to h. one's eye on,** no perder de vista (a), vigilar. **to h. one's tail between one's legs,** ir rabo entre piernas. **to h. to,** tener que; deber. **It has to be so,** Tiene que ser así. **to h. too much of,** sobrar, tener demasiado de. **He has too much time,** Le sobra tiempo. **to h. about one,** tener (or llevar) consigo. **to h. back,** aceptar; recibir. **to h. down,** hacer bajar. **She had her hair down,** El pelo le caía por las espaldas. **to h. in,** hacer entrar. **to h. on,** vestir, llevar puesto; (engagements) tener (compromisos). **to h. out,** hacer salir; llevar a paseo; llevar fuera; (have removed) hacerse sacar; quitar. **to h. up,** (persons) hacer subir; (things) subir; *law* llevar a (ante) los tribunales. **to h. with one,** tener consigo. **I h. her with me,** La tengo conmigo, Ella me acompaña

haven *n* puerto, *m*, abra, *f*; *fig* oasis, abrigo, refugio, *m*

haversack *n* mochila, *f*, morral, *m*

havoc *n* destrucción, ruina, *f*; *fig* estrago, *m*. **to wreak h. among,** destruir; *fig* hacer estragos entre (or en)

Hawaii *n* Hawai, *m*

Hawaiian *a* and *n* hawaiano; *n* (language) hawaiano, *m*

hawk *n* halcón, *m*; gavilán, milano, *m*. *vi* cazar con halcón. *vt* vender mercancías por las calles; *fig* difundir. **h.-eyed,** de ojos de lince. **h.-nosed,** de nariz aguileña

hawker *n* halconero, *m*; (vendor) buhonero, *m*, vendedor (-ra) ambulante

hawking *n* caza con halcones, cetrería, *f*; (expectorating) gargajeo, *m*; (selling) buhonería, *f*

hawser *n* maroma, *f*, calabrote, *m*

hawthorn *n* espino, *m*. **white h.,** espino blanco, *m*

hay *n* heno, *m*. **to make hay while the sun shines,** hacer su agosto. **hay fever,** fiebre del heno, *f*. **hayfork,** horca, *f*

hayloft *n* henil, *m*

haymaker *n* segador (-ra); (machine) segadora, *f*

haymaking *n* recolección del heno, *f*

haystack *n* almiar, *m*, niara, *f*

hazard *n* azar, *m*, suerte, *f*; riesgo, peligro, *m*; (game) juego de azar, *m*. *vt* arriesgar, aventurar. **at all hazards,** a todo riesgo

hazardous *a* azaroso, arriesgado, peligroso

haze *n* bruma, *f*; confusión, *f*

hazel *n* avellano, *m*. **h.-nut,** avellana, *f*

hazy *a* brumoso, calinoso; confuso

he *pers. pron* él. *n* (of humans) varón, *m*; (of animals) macho, *m*. **he who,** el que, quien. **he-goat,** macho cabrío, *m*. **he-man,** todo un hombre, hombre cabal, *m*

head *vt* golpear con la cabeza; encabezar; (lead) capitanear; (direct) dirigir, guiar; (wine) cabecear. *vi* estar a la cabeza de; dirigirse a. **headed for,** con rumbo a, en dirección a. **to h. off,** interceptar; desviar; *fig* distraer

head *n anat* cabeza, *f*; (upper portion) parte superior, *f*; (of a coin) cara, *f*; (hair) cabellera, *f*; (individual) persona, *f*; (of cattle) res, *f*; (of a mountain) cumbre, *f*; (of a ladder) último peldaño, *m*; (of toadstools) sombrero, *m*; (of trees) copa, *f*; (of a stick) puño, *m*; (of a cylinder) culata, *f*; (of a river, etc.) manantial, origen, *m*; (of a bed) cabecera, *f*; (of nails, pins) cabeza, *f*; (froth) espuma, *f*; (flower) flor, *f*; (leaves) hojas, *f pl*; (first place)

primer puesto, *m*; (of game, fish) pieza, *f*; (of a page, column) cabeza, *f*; (cape) cabo, *m*; (of an arrow, dart, lance) punta, *f*; (front) frente, *m*; (leader) jefe, cabeza, *m*; (chief) director (-ra), superior (-ra); presidente (-ta); (of a school) director (-ra); (of a cask) fondo, *m*; *mech* cabezal, *m*; (of an ax) filo, *m*; (of a bridge) cabeza, *f*; (of a jetty, pier) punta, *f*; (of a ship) proa, *f*; (of a flower) cabezuela, *f*; (of asparagus) punta, *f*; (of a table) cabeza, *f*; (of the family) jefe, cabeza, *m*; (seat of honor) cabecera, *f*; (title) título, *m*; (aspect) punto de vista, *m*; (division) capítulo, *m*; (management, direction) dirección, *f*; (talent) talento, *m*, cabeza, *f*; (intelligence) inteligencia, *f*. *a* principal; primero; en jefe. **at the h. of,** a la cabeza de. **crowned h.,** testa coronada, *f*. **from h. to foot,** de pies a cabeza; de hito en hito; de arriba abajo. **He took it into his h. to . . .,** Se le ocurrió de . . . **This story has neither h. nor tail,** Este cuento no tiene pies ni cabeza. **with h. held high,** con la frente levantada. **to come to a h.,** llegar a la crisis; llegar a punto decisivo. **to get an idea out of a person's h.,** quitar una idea a uno de la cabeza. **to keep one's h.,** *fig* conservar la sangre fría, no perder la cabeza. **to lose one's h.,** *fig* perder la cabeza. **to put into a person's h.,** *fig* meter (a uno) en la cabeza. **to run one's h. against,** golpear la cabeza contra. **h. first,** de cabeza. **h. of cattle,** res, *f*. **h. office,** central, *f*. **h. of hair,** cabellera, *f*; mata de pelo, *f*. **h.-on,** de cabeza. **h.-on collision,** choque de frente, *m*. **h. opening,** (of a garment) cabezón, *m*. **heads or tails,** cara o cruz, águila o sol (Mexico). **h. over heels,** de patas arriba. **h. over heels in love,** calado hasta los huesos. **h.-dress,** tocado, *m*; peinado, *m*; sombrero, *m*. **h. voice,** voz de cabeza, *f*. **h. waiter,** encargado de comedor, jefe de camareros, *m*

headache *n* dolor de cabeza, *m*; *fig* quebradero de cabeza, *m*

headboard *n* cabecera de una cama, *f*

headed *a* con cabeza . . .; que tiene la cabeza . . .; de cabeza . . .; (of an article) intitulado. **large h.,** cabezudo

header *n* caída de cabeza, *f*; salto de cabeza, *m*

headgear *n* tocado, *m*; sombrero, gorro, *m*

head-hunting *n* la caza de cabezas, *f*

heading *n naut* el poner la proa en dirección (a); el guiar en dirección (a); (of a book, etc.) título, encabezamiento, *m*; (soccer) golpe de cabeza, *m*. **to come under the h. of,** estar incluido entre; clasificarse bajo

headland *n* cabo, promontorio, *m*

headless *a* sin cabeza

headlight *n aut* faro, *m*; (rw, naut) farol, *m*. **to dip the headlights,** bajar los faros. **to switch on the headlights,** encender los faros (or los faroles)

headline *n* (of a newspaper) titular, *m*; (to a chapter) título de la columna, *m*

headlong *a* precipitado; despeñado. *adv* de cabeza; precipitadamente. **to fall h.,** caer de cabeza

headman *n* cacique, cabecilla, *m*; (foreman) capataz, contramaestre, *m*

headmaster *n* director de colegio, rector, *m*

headmistress *n* directora de colegio, rectora, *f*

head-on collision *n* choque frontal, *m*

head nurse enfermero-jefe, *m*

headphones *n pl* auriculares, *m pl*

headquarters *n mil* cuartel general, *m*; oficina central, *f*; jefatura, *f*; centro, *m*

headrest *n* respaldo, *m*; apoyo para la cabeza, *m*

headstone *n* piedra mortuoria, *f*

headstrong *a* impetuoso, terco, testarudo

headway *n* marcha, *f*; *fig* progreso, avance, *m*. **to make h.,** avanzar; *fig* hacer progresos; *fig* prosperar

headwind *n* viento en contra, *m*

heady *a* apasionado, violento; impetuoso, precipitado; (obstinate) terco; (of alcohol) encabezado; *fig* embriagador

heal *vt* curar, sanar; (flesh) cicatrizar. *vi* curar, sanar; cicatrizarse; (superficially) sobresanar

healable *a* curable

healer n sanador (-ra), curador (-ra); curandero, m
healing a curador, sanador; médico. n curación, f; cura, f, remedio, m
health n salud, f; higiene, sanidad, f. **Here's to your very good h.!** ¡Salud y pesetas! **He is in good h.,** Disfruta de buena salud. **to drink a person's h.,** beber a la salud de. **to enjoy good h.,** gozar de buena salud. **to look full of h.,** vender salud. **h.-giving,** saludable. **h. inspection,** visita de sanidad, f. **h. officer,** inspector de sanidad, m. **h. resort,** balneario, m
healthiness n buena salud, f; sanidad, salubridad, f
healthy a con buena salud; (healthful) saludable. **to be h.,** tener buena salud
heap n montón, m; rima, pila, f, acervo, m; (of people) muchedumbre, f, tropel, m. vt amontonar; apilar; colmar. **in heaps,** a montones. **We have heaps of time,** Nos sobra tiempo, Tenemos tiempo de sobra. **to h. together,** juntar, mezclar. **to h. up, upon,** colmar; amontonar; agr hacinar; fig acumular
hear vt oír; (listen) escuchar; (attend) asistir a; (give audience) dar audiencia (a); (a lawsuit) ver (un pleito); (speak) hablar; (be aware of, feel) sentir. vi oír; tener noticias; (learn) enterarse de; (allow) permitir. **H.! H.!** ¡Muy bien! ¡Bravo! **I have heard it said that . . .** He oído decir que . . . **Let me h. from you!** ¡Mándame noticias tuyas! **They were never heard of again,** No se volvió a saber de ellos, No se supo más de ellos. **to h. about,** oír de; (know) saber de, tener noticias de; recibir información sobre. **to h. from,** ser informado por; tener noticias de; recibir carta de. **to h. of,** enterarse de, saber; recibir información sobre; (allow) permitir
hearer n oyente, mf
hearing n (sense of) oído, m; alcance del oído, m; presencia, f; audición, f; law vista (de una causa) f. **It was said in my h.,** Fue dicho en mi presencia. **out of h.,** fuera del alcance del oído. **within h.,** al alcance del oído. **have a h. problem,** ser parcialmente sordo
hearing aid acústica, aparato auditivo, aparato acústico, audífono, m
hearsay n fama, f, rumor, m. **by h.,** de oídas
hearse n coche fúnebre, m
heart n corazón, m; (feelings) entrañas, f pl; (of the earth, etc.) seno, corazón, m; (of lettuce, etc.) cogollo, repollo, m; (suit in cards) copas, f pl; bot médula, f; (soul) alma, f; (courage) valor, m; ánimo, m. **at h.,** en el fondo, esencialmente. **by h.,** de memoria. **from the h.,** con toda sinceridad, de todo corazón. **He is a man after my own h.,** Es un hombre de los que me gustan. **I have no h. to do it,** No tengo valor de hacerlo. **in the h. of the country,** en medio del campo. **to break one's h.,** partirse el corazón. **to have one's h. in one's mouth,** tener el alma en un hilo, estar muerto de miedo. **to have no h.,** fig no tener entrañas. **to lose h.,** desanimarse, descorazonarse. **to set one's h. on,** poner el corazón en. **to take h.,** cobrar ánimo; inf hacer de tripas corazón. **to take to h.,** tomar a pechos. **to wear one's h. on one's sleeve,** tener el corazón en la mano. **with all my h.,** con toda el alma. **h.-ache,** angustia, pena, f; **h.-beat,** latido del corazón, m. **h.-breaker,** (woman) coqueta, f; (man) ladrón de corazones, m. **h. disease,** enfermedad del corazón, enfermedad cardíaca, f. **h. failure,** colapso cardíaco, m. **h.-rending,** desgarrador, angustioso. **h.-searching,** examen de conciencia, m. **h.-shaped,** acorazonado, en forma de corazón. **h.-strings,** fibras del corazón, f pl. **h.-to-h. talk,** conversación íntima, f. **h.-whole,** libre de afectos
heartbreaking a desgarrador, angustioso, doloroso, lastimoso
heartbroken a acongojado, afligido, transido de dolor
heartburn n acidez del estómago, acedia, pirosis, rescoldera, f
heartburning n rencor, m, animosidad, envidia, f
hearted a de corazón . . . que tiene el corazón . . . **kind-h.,** de buen corazón, bondadoso
hearten vt alentar, animar

heartfelt a hondo; de todo corazón, sincero; más expresivo
hearth n hogar, m; chimenea, f; fig hogar, m
heartily adv cordialmente; sinceramente; enérgicamente; con entusiasmo; (of eating) con buen apetito; (very) muy, completamente. **I am h. sick of it all,** inf Estoy harto hasta los dientes
heartiness n cordialidad, f; sinceridad, f; energía, f, vigor, m; vehemencia, f; entusiasmo, m; (of appetite) buen diente, buen apetito, m
heartless a sin corazón, sin piedad, despiadado, inhumano, cruel
heartlessness n falta de corazón, inhumanidad, crueldad, f
hearty a cordial; sincero; enérgico; vigoroso; robusto; (frank) campechano; (of appetite) voraz; bueno; (big) grande
heat n calor, m; (in animals) celo, m; (of an action) calor, m; fig vehemencia, fogosidad, f; fig fuego, m; (passion) ardor, m, pasión, f; (of a race) carrera eliminatoria, f. vt calentar; (excite) conmover, acalorar, excitar; (annoy) irritar. vi calentarse. **dead h.,** empate, m. **in h.,** en celo. **in the h. of the moment,** en el calor del momento. **to become heated,** fig acalorarse, exaltarse. **white h.,** candencia, incandescencia, f. **h. lightning,** fucilazo, m. **h. spot,** pápula, f; terminación sensible, f. **h. stroke,** insolación, f. **h. wave,** onda de calor, f
heated a calentado; caliente; excitado; apasionado
heatedly adv con vehemencia, con pasión
heater n calentador, m; calorífero, m; (stove) estufa, f; (for plates) calientaplatos, m. **water-h.,** calentador de agua, m
heath n brezal, m; yermo, páramo, m; bot brezo, m
heathen n pagano (-na); idólatra, mf; ateo (-ea), descreído (-da). a pagano; ateo; bárbaro
heathenism n paganismo, m; idolatría, f; ateísmo, m
heather n brezo, m
heating n calefacción, f, a calentador; (of drinks) fortificante. **central h.,** calefacción central, f
heave vt alzar, levantar; naut izar; (the anchor, etc.) virar; (throw) arrojar, lanzar; elevar; (extract) extraer; (emit) dar, exhalar. vi subir y bajar; palpitar; agitarse. n tirón, m; (of the sea) vaivén, m. **to h. in sight,** aparecer, surgir. **to h. out sail,** naut desenvergar. **to h. the lead,** naut escandallar. **to h. to,** naut estarse a la capa
heaven n cielo, m; firmamento, m; paraíso, m. **Heavens!** ¡Cielos! ¡Por Dios! **Thank H.!** ¡Gracias a Dios! **h.-born,** celeste. **h.-sent,** fig providencial
heavenliness n carácter celestial, m; delicia, f
heavenly a celeste, celestial; divino; fig delicioso. **h. body,** astro, m
heavily adv pesadamente; torpemente; penosamente; (slowly) lentamente; severamente; excesivamente; (of sighing) hondamente; (sadly) tristemente; (of rain, etc.) reciamente, fuertemente; (of wind) con violencia. **He fell h.,** Cayó de plomo. **to lie h. upon,** pesar mucho sobre. **to rain h.,** llover mucho, diluviar
heaviness n peso, m; (lethargy) torpor, letargo, m; sueño, m, languidez, f; (clumsiness) torpeza, f; (severity) severidad, f; importancia, responsabilidad, f; dificultad, f; (gravity) gravedad, f; tristeza, melancolía, f; (boredom) sosería, insulsez, f; (of style) monotonía, ponderosidad, f
heaving n levantamiento, m; (of the anchor, etc.) virada, f; (of the sea) vaivén, m; (of the breast) palpitación, f
heavy a pesado; torpe; sin gracia; (slow) lento; (thick) grueso; (strong) fuerte; (hard) duro; grave; difícil; oneroso; responsable, importante; (oppresive) opresivo; penoso; grande; (sad) triste, melancólico; (of the sky) anublado; (of food) indigesto; (tedious) aburrido, soso; (pompous) pomposo; (of roads) malo; (of scents) fuerte, penetrante; (of sleep, weather) pesado; (weary) rendido; (charged with) cargado de;

(of a meal) grande, abundante; (violent) violento; (of a cold, etc.) malo; (drowsy) soñoliento; (torpid) tórpido; (of rain, snow, hail) fuerte, recio; (of firing) intenso; (of sighs) profundo; (of soil) recio, de mucha miga; (*phys chem*) pesado. **to be h.,** pesar mucho. **How h. are you?** ¿Cuánto pesa Vd.? **h.-armed,** pesado; armado hasta los dientes. **h.-eyed,** con ojeras. **h. guns,** artillería pesada, *f.* **h.-handed,** de manos torpes; *fig* tiránico, opresivo. **h.-hearted,** triste, apesadumbrado. **h. industry,** la gran industria, la industria pesada, *f.* **h.-laden,** muy cargado. **h. losses,** *mil* pérdidas cuantiosas, *f pl.* **h.weight,** *sport* peso pesado, *m*

Hebraic *a* hebraico, hebreo, judaico

Hebraism *n* judaísmo, hebraísmo, *m*

Hebraist *n* hebraísta, *m*

Hebrew *n* hebreo (-ea), judío (-ía): (language) hebreo, *m*

Hebrides, the las Hébridas

hecatomb *n* hecatombe, *f*

heckle *vt fig* interrumpir, importunar con preguntas

heckler *n* perturbador (-ra)

heckling *n* interrupción, *f*

hectare *n* hectárea, *f*

hectic *a* (consumptive) hético; (feverish) febril; *fig inf* agitado

hectogram *n* hectogramo, *m*

hectoliter *n* hectolitro, *m*

hector *vt* intimidar, amenazar

hectoring *a* imperioso; amenazador

hectowatt *n elec* hectovatio, *m*

hedge *n* seto, *m*; barrera, *f.* *vt* cercar con un seto; rodear. *vi fig* titubear, vacilar. **h.-hopping,** *aer* vuelo a ras de tierra, *m*. **h.-sparrow,** acentor de bosque, *m*

hedgehog *n* erizo, *m*. **h. position,** *mil* puesto fuerte, *m*

hedonism *n* hedonismo, *m*

hedonist *n* hedonista, *mf*

heed *n* atención, *f,* cuidado, *m.* *vt* atender; observar, considerar; escuchar. *vi* hacer caso

heedful *a* atento; cuidadoso

heedless *a* desatento; descuidado, negligente; distraído

heedlessly *adv* sin hacer caso; negligentemente; distraídamente

heedlessness *n* desatención, distracción, *f,* descuido, *m*; negligencia, *f,* inconsideración, *f*

heel *n anat* talón, calcañar, *m*; (of shoe) tacón, *m*; (of a violin, etc., bow) talón, *m*; (remains) restos, *m pl.* *vt* poner tacón; poner talón a; *naut* hacer zozobrar. *vi naut* zozobrar. **rubber h.,** tacón de goma, *m.* **She let him cool his heels for half an hour,** le dio un plantón de media hora. **to follow on a person's heels,** pisarle (a uno) los talones. **to be down at h.,** (of shoes) estar gastados los tacones; estar deseaseado. **to take to one's heels,** apretar a correr, poner pies en polvorosa. **to turn on one's h.,** dar media vuelta. **h.-bone,** zancajo, *m.* **h.-piece,** talón, *m*

heeltap *n* tapa de tacón, *f*; escurridura, *f*

heft *vt* sopesar, tomar al peso

hegemony *n* hegemonía, *f*

heifer *n* ternera, vaquilla, *f*

heigh *interj* (calling attention) ¡oye! ¡ioiga! **h.-ho!** ¡ay!

height *n* altura, *f*; elevación, *f*; altitud, *f*; (stature) estatura, *f*; (high ground) cerro, *m,* colina, *f*; (sublimity) sublimidad, excelencia, *f*; colmo, *m*; (zenith) auge, *m,* cumbre, *f*

heighten *vt* hacer más alto; (enhance) realzar; (exaggerate) exagerar; (perfect) perfeccionar; (intensify) intensificar

heightening *n* elevación, *f*; (enhancement) realce, *m*; (exaggeration) exageración, *f*; (perfection) perfección, *f*; (intensification) intensificación, *f*

heinous *a* atroz, nefando, horrible.

heinousness *n* atrocidad, enormidad, *f*

heir *n* heredero, *m.* **h. apparent,** heredero aparente, *m.* **h.-at-law,** heredero forzoso, *m.* **h. presumptive,** presunto heredero, *m*

heiress *n* heredera, *f*

heirloom *n* reliquia de familia, *f*; *fig* herencia, *f*

helicopter *n* helicóptero, *m*

helium *n chem* helio, *m*

helix *n geom* hélice, *m*; (*arch geom*) espira, *f*

hell *n* infierno, *m.* **h.-fire,** fuego del infierno, *m,* llamas del infierno, *f pl*

Hellenic *a* helénico

Hellenism *n* helenismo, *m*

Hellenist *n* helenista, *mf*

Hellenistic *a* helenístico

Hellenize *vt* helenizar

hellish *a* infernal; *inf* horrible, detestable

hello *interj* ¡hola!; (on telephoning someone) ¡oiga! ¡alo!; (answering telephone) ¡diga! ¡alo!

helm *n* caña del timón, *f*; timón, gobernalle, *m.* **to obey the h.,** obedecer el timón. **to take the h.,** gobernar el timón; ponerse a pilotar

helmet *n* casco, *m*; (in olden days) yelmo, capacete, *m*; (sun) casco colonial, *m*

helminthic *a* helmíntico, vermífugo

helmsman *n* timonero, *m*

help *n* ayuda, *f*; auxilio, socorro, *m*; (protection) favor, *m,* protección, *f*; (remedy) remedio, *m*; (cooperation) cooperación, *f,* concurso, *m*; (domestic) criada, *f.* **A little h. is worth a lot of sympathy,** Más vale un toma que dos te daré. **There's no h. for it,** No hay más remedio. **to call for h.,** pedir socorro a gritos. **without h.,** a solas, sin la ayuda de nadie

help *vt* ayudar; socorrer, auxiliar; (favor) favorecer; (mitigate) aliviar; (contribute to) contribuir a, facilitar; (avoid) evitar. *vi* ayudar. **He cannot h. worrying,** No puede menos de preocuparse. **God h. you!** ¡Dios te ampare! **So h. me God!** ¡Así Dios me salve! **to h. one another,** ayudarse mutuamente, ayudarse los unos a los otros. **to h. oneself,** (to food) servirse. **to h. down, off,** ayudar a bajar; ayudar a apearse. **to h. in,** ayudar a entrar. **to h. along, forward, on,** avanzar, fomentar, promover; contribuir a. **Shall I h. you on with the dress?** ¿Quieres que te ayude a ponerte el vestido? **to h. out,** ayudar a salir; (from a vehicle) ayudar a bajar; (of a difficulty, etc.) sacar; suplir la falta de; ayudar. **to h. over,** ayudar a cruzar; (a difficulty) ayudar a salir de (un apuro); ayudar a vencer (un obstáculo, etc.); (a period) ayudar a pasar. **to h. to,** contribuir a, ayudar en; (food) servir. **to h. up,** ayudar a subir; ayudar a levantarse, levantar

helper *n* auxiliador (-ra); asistente (-ta); (protector) favorecedor (-ra); bienhechor (-ra); (colleague) colega, *m*; (co-worker) colaborador (-ra). **He thanked all his helpers,** Dio las gracias a todos los que le habían ayudado

helpful *a* útil, provechoso; (obliging) servicial, atento; (favorable) favorable; (healthy) saludable

helpfulness *n* utilidad, *f*; bondad, *f*

helping *n* ayuda, *f*; (of food) porción, ración, *f,* plato, *m.* **Won't you have a second h.?** ¿No quiere usted servirse más (or otra vez)? ¿No quiere usted repetir? **to lend a h. hand (to),** prestar ayuda (a)

helpless *a* desamparado, abandonado; (through infirmity) imposibilitado; impotente, sin fuerzas (para); (shiftless) incompetente, inútil

helplessness *n* desamparo, *m*; invalidez, debilidad, *f*; impotencia, *f*; incompetencia, *f*

helpmeet *n* compañero (-ra) perfecto (-ta); esposa, *f*

helter-skelter *adv* atropelladamente; en desorden. *n* barahunda, *f*

hem *n sew* dobladillo, filete, *m,* bastilla, *f*; (edge) orilla, *f.* *interj* ¡ejem! *vt* hacer dobladillo en, dobladillar. *vi* (cough) fingir toser. **false hem,** *sew* dobladillo falso, *m.* **running hem,** *sew* jareta, *f.* **to hem and haw,** tartamudear; vacilar. **to hem in,** cercar, sitiar

hemisphere *n* hemisferio, *m*

hemispherical *a* hemisférico, semiesférico

hemlock *n bot* cicuta, *f*

hemoglobin *n chem* hemoglobina, *f*

hemophilia *n med* hemofilia, *f*

hemorrhage *n* hemorragia, *f*, flujo de sangre, *m*

hemorrhoids *n pl med* hemorroides, *f*

hemp *n* cáñamo, *m*. **h. cloth,** lienzo, *m*. **h.-seed,** cañamón, *m*

hemstitch *n* vainica, *f*. *vt* hacer vainica en

hen *n* gallina, *f*; (female bird) hembra, *f*. **the hen pheasant,** la hembra del faisán. **hen bird,** pájara, *f*. **hen-coop** or **house,** gallinero, *m*. **hen party,** *inf* reunión de mujeres, *f*. **hen-roost,** nidal, ponedero, *m*

hence *adv* (of place) de aquí, (of time) de ahora, de aquí a, al cabo de, en; (therefore) por eso, por lo tanto, por consiguiente. *interj* ¡fuera! ¡fuera de aquí! **I shall come to see you a month h.,** Vendré a verte en un mes (or al cabo de un mes). **ten years h.,** de aquí a diez años. **h. the fact that . . . ,** de aquí que. . . . **H. it happens that . . . ,** Por eso sucede que . . .

henceforth *adv* desde aquí en adelante, de hoy en adelante

henchman *n* escudero, *m*; satélite, secuaz, *m*

henna *n* alheña, *f*

henpecked *a* gobernado por su mujer, que se deja mandar por su mujer

her *pers pron direct object* la; (with prepositions) ella. *pers. pron indirect object* le, a ella. *poss a* su, *mf*; sus, *mf pl*, de ella. **I saw her on Wednesday,** La vi el miércoles. **The message is for her,** El recado es para ella. **It is her book,** Es su libro, Es el libro de ella

herald *n* heraldo, *m*; presagio, anuncio, *m*. *vt* proclamar; anunciar, presagiar

heraldic *a* heráldico

heraldry *n* heráldica, *f*

herb *n* hierba, *f*

herbaceous *a* herbáceo

herbage *n* herbaje, *m*; pasto, *m*

herbal *a* herbario. *n* herbolaria, *f*

herbalist *n* herbario, *m*, simplista, *mf*

herbarium *n* herbario, *m*

herbivorous *a* herbívoro

herby *a* herbáceo

Herculean *a* hercúleo

herd *n* manada, *f*; (of cattle) hato, *m*; (race) raza, *f*; (*fig* contemptuous) populacho, *m*, masa, *f*. *vt* reunir en manadas; reunir en hatos; (sheep) reunir en rebaños; guiar las manadas, etc. *vi* ir en manadas, hatos o rebaños; asociarse, reunirse. **h.-instinct,** instinto gregario, *m*; instinto de las masas, *m*

herdsman *n* ganadero, pastor, manadero, *m*; (head herdsman) rabadán, *m*

here *adv* aquí; (at roll-call) ¡presente!; acá; an este punto; ahora. *n* presente, *m*. **And h. he looked at me,** Y a este punto me miró. **Come h.!** ¡Ven acá! **in h.,** aquí dentro. **h. below,** aquí abajo, en la tierra. **h. and there,** aquí y allá. **h., there and everywhere,** en todas partes. **H. I am,** Heme aquí. **h. is . . . ,** he aquí. **. . . H. they are,** Aquí los tienes, Aquí están. **Here's to you!** (on drinking) ¡Salud y pesetas! ¡A tu salud!

hereabouts *adv* por aquí cerca

hereafter *adv* en lo futuro; desde ahora; en adelante. *n* futuro, *m*. **the H.,** la otra vida

hereat *adv* en esto

hereby *adv* por esto, por los presentes

hereditarily *adv* hereditariamente, por herencia

hereditary *a* hereditario

heredity *n* herencia, *f*

herein *adv* en esto; aquí dentro; incluso

hereinafter *adv* después, más abajo, más adelante, en adelante, en lo sucesivo

hereinbefore *adv* en la anterior, en lo arriba citado, en lo antes mencianado, en lo precedente.

hereof *adv* de esto

heresy *n* herejía, *f*

heretic *n* hereje, *mf*

heretical *a* herético

hereunder *adv* abajo

hereupon *adv* en esto, en seguida

herewith *adv* junto con esto, con esto; ahora en esta ocasión

heritage *n* herencia, *f*

hermaphrodite *a* and *n* hermafrodita, *mf*

hermetic *a* hermético

hermit *n* ermitaño, *m*. **h. crab,** paguro, cangrejo ermitaño, *m*

hernia *n* hernia, *f*

hero *n* héroe, *m*. **h.-worship,** culto a los héroes, *m*

heroic *a* heroico, épico

heroin *n chem* heroína, *f*

heroine *n* heroína, *f*

heroism *n* heroísmo, *m*

heron *n* garza, *f*

herpes *n pl* herpes, *mf pl*

herring *n* arenque, *m*

hers *poss pron 3rd sing* (el) suyo, *m*; (la) suya, *f*; (los) suyos, *m pl*; (las) suyas, *f pl*; de ella. **This book is h.,** Este libro es suyo, Este libro es de ella. **This book is h., not mine,** Este libro es el suyo no el mío. **a sister of h.,** una de sus hermanas, una hermana suya

herself *pron* sí misma, sí; ella misma; (with reflexive verb) se. **She has done it by h.,** Lo ha hecho por sí misma. **She h. told me so,** Ella misma me lo dijo. **She is by h.,** Está a solas, Está sola

hesitancy. See **hesitation**

hesitant *a* indeciso, vacilante, irresoluto. **to be h.,** mostrarse irresoluto

hesitate *vi* vacilar, dudar; titubear. **I do not h. to say . . . ,** No vacilo en decir . . . **He hesitated over his reply,** Tardaba en dar su respuesta

hesitatingly *adv* irresolutamente; titubeando

hesitation *n* vacilación, hesitación, *f*; irresolución, indecisión, *f*; (reluctance) aversión, repugnancia, *f*; titubeo, *m*

heterodox *a* heterodoxo

heterodoxy *n* heterodoxia, *f*

heterogeneity *n* heterogeneidad, *f*

heterogeneous *a* heterogéneo

hew *vt* cortar, tajar; (trees) talar; (a career, etc.) hacerse

hewer *n* partidor, talador, *m*

hexagon *n* hexágono, *m*

hey *interj* ¡he! ¡oye!

heyday *n* apogeo, colmo, *m*; buenos tiempos, *m pl*; reinado, *m*; pleno vigor, *m*

hi *interj* ¡oye! ¡hola!

hiatus *n* hiato, *m*; laguna, *f*, vacío, *m*

hibernate *vi* invernar

hibernation *n* invernada, *f*

hibiscus *n bot* hibisco, *m*

hiccough *n* hipo, *m*. *vi* hipar. *vt* decir con hipo

hidden *a* escondido, secreto, oculto

hide *n* piel, *f*; pellejo, cuero, *m*

hide *vt* esconder, ocultar; (cover) cubrir, tapar; (dissemble) disimular; (meaning) obscurecer. *vi* esconderse; ocultarse; refugiarse. **to h. from each other,** esconderse el uno del otro. **h.-and-seek,** escondite, dormirlas, *m*

hidebound *a fig* muy conservador, reaccionario, de ideas muy tradicionales

hideous *a* horrible, repulsivo, horroroso; repugnante, odioso

hideously *adv* horriblemente. **to be h. ugly,** (of people) ser más feo que Picio

hideousness *n* fealdad, horribilidad, *f*; repugnancia, *f*

hiding *n* ocultación, *f*; encubrimiento, *m*; refugio, *m*; *inf* paliza, tunda, *f*. **h.-place,** escondite, escondrijo, *m*

hie *vi* apresurarse, ir a prisa

hierarch *n* jerarca, *m*

hierarchical *a* jerárquico

hierarchy *n* jerarquía, *f*

hieroglyph *n* jeroglífico, *m*

higgledy-piggledy *adv* revueltamente, en confusión; en montón, en desorden

high *a* alto; elevado; (with altar, Mass, street, festival) mayor; grande; eminente; aristocrático; (of shooting) fijante; (of quality) superior; excelente; (haughty) orgulloso; (solemn) solemne; (good) bueno; noble; supremo; sumo; (of price) subido; *mus* agudo; (of the sea) tempestuoso, borrascoso; (of wind and explosives) violento, fuerte; (of polish) brillante; (with speed) grande; (with tension, frequency) alto; (with number, etc.) importante, grande; (with colors) subido; (of food) pasado; (angry) enojado, airado; (of cheek bones) saliente, prominente; (well-seasoned) picante; (flattering) lisonjero. *adv* alto; hacia arriba; arriba; (deeply) profundamente; fuertemente; con violencia; (of price) a un precio elevado; (luxuriously) lujosamente; *mus* agudo. **a room 12 ft. h.,** un cuarto de doce pies de altura. **I knew her when she was so h.,** La conocí tamaña. **It is h. time he came,** Ya es hora de que viniese. **on h.,** en alto, arriba; en los cielos. **h. altar,** altar mayor, *m.* **h. and dry,** en la playa, varado; *fig* en seco. **h. and low,** de arriba abajo; por todas partes. **h.-born,** aristocrático, de alta alcurnia. **h.-bred,** (of people) de buena familia; (of animals) de buena raza. **h.-class,** de buena clase; de alta calidad. **h. collar,** alzacuello, *m.* **h. colored,** de colores vivos; *fig* exagerado. **h. command,** *(mil, nav)* alto mando, *m.* **h. court,** tribunal supremo, *m.* **h. day,** día festivo, *m.* **h. explosive,** explosivo violento, *m.* **h.-flown,** hinchado, retumbante, altisonante. **h. frequency,** alta frecuencia, *f.* **h.-handed,** arbitrario, dominador, despótico. **h.-heeled,** *a* de tacón alto. **h. jump,** salto de altura, *m.* **h. land,** tierras altas, *f pl*; eminencia, *f.* **h. light,** *art* realce, *m*; acontecimiento de más interés, *m*; momento culminante, *m.* **h. mass,** misa mayor, *f.* **h.-minded,** de nobles pensamientos; arrogante. **h.-necked,** con cuello alto. **h.-pitched,** de tono alto, agudo. **h.-powered,** de alta potencia. **h.-powered car,** coche de muchos caballos, *m.* **h. precision,** suma precisión, *f.* **h. pressure,** *n* alta presión, *f*; *fig* urgencia, *f*; *n* de alta presión; *fig* urgente. **h.-priced,** caro. **h. priest,** sumo pontífice, sumo sacerdote, alto sacerdote, *m.* **h. relief,** alto relieve, *m.* **h. road,** carretera mayor, *f.* **h. school,** instituto de segunda enseñanza, instituto, colegio, liceo, *m*; colegio, liceo, instituto, *m*, escuela secundaria, secundaria, *f.* **h. sea,** marejada, *f.* **h. seas,** alta mar, *f.* **h.-seasoned,** picante. **h. society,** alta sociedad, *f.* **h.-sounding,** altisonante, bombástico. **h.-speed,** de alta velocidad. **h.-spirited,** brioso; alegre. **h.-strung,** nervioso, excitable, sensitivo. **h. tension,** alta tensión, *f.* **h. tide,** marea alta, *f.* **h.-toned,** *mus* agudo; *inf* de alto copete; aristocrático. **h. treason,** alta traición, *f.* **h. water,** marea alta, pleamar, *f.* **h.-water mark,** límite de la marea, *m*; *fig* colmo, *m*; apogeo, *m*

highbrow *a* and *n* intelectual, *mf*
high-ceilinged *a* alto de techo
higher *a comp* of **high,** más alto; más elevado; superior. **on a h. plane,** en un nivel más alto. **h. education,** enseñanza superior, *f.* **h. mathematics,** la alta matemática, *f.* **h. criticism,** la alta crítica, *f.* **h. up,** más arriba. **h. up the river,** río arriba
highest *a superl* of **high,** el más alto; la más alta; los más altos; las más altas; sumo, supremo; excelente. **h. common factor,** *math* máximo común divisor, *m.* **h. references,** (of cook, gardener, etc.) informes inmejorables, *m pl*; *com* referencias excelentes, *f pl*
highland *n* altiplanicie, *f*; montañas, *f pl*, distrito montañoso, *m.* *a* montañoso
highlander *n* montañés (-esa); esocés (-esa) del norte
highlight *vtr* dar relieve a, destacar
highly *adv* altamente; mucho; muy; extremadamente; grandemente; bien; favorablemente; con lisonja, lisonjeramente. **h. seasoned,** picante. **h. strung,** nervioso, excitable
highness *n* altura, *f*; elevación, *f*; excelencia, *f*; nobleza, *f*; (title) Alteza, *f.* **His Royal H., Her Royal Highness,** Su Alteza Real
high-ranking *a* de alta jerarquía, de alto rango
highway *n* camino real, *m*, carretera, *f.* **h. code,** código

de la vía pública (or de la circulación), *m.* **h. robbery,** salteamiento de caminos, atraco, *m*
highwayman *n* salteador de caminos, *m*
highways and byways caminos y veredas
hike *vi* ir de excursión. *n* marcha con equipo, *f*
hiker *n* excursionista, *mf*
hiking *n* excursionismo, *m*; marcha con equipo, *f*
hilarious *a* alegre
hilarity *n* hilaridad, *f*
hill *n* colina, *f*, cerro, otero, *m*; monte, *m*, montaña, *f*; (pile) montón, *m.* **h.-side,** falda de montaña, ladera de una colina, *f.* **h.-top,** cumbre de una colina, *f*
hilliness *n* montuosidad, *f*, lo montañoso
hillman *n* montañés, *m*
hillock *n* altozano, montículo, collado, *m*
hilly *a* montañoso
hilt *n* puño, *m*, empuñadura, *f*
him *pron* (with prep.) él; (with a direct object) le, lo; (with prep.) él; *indirect object* le, a él; (with a direct obj. in 3rd person) se. **I gave him the magazine,** Le di la revista. **I gave it to him,** Se lo di a él. **This is for him,** Esto es para él
Himalayas, the los Himalayas, *m pl*
Himalayan *a* himalayo
himself *pron* sí, sí mismo; él mismo; (reflexive) se. **He did it by h.,** Lo hizo por sí mismo. For more examples see **herself**
hind *n* corza, cierva, *f. a* trasero, posterior. **h.-quarters,** cuarto trasero, *m*; (of a horse) ancas, *f pl*
hinder *a* trasero, posterior
hinder *vt* impedir, estorbar; embarazar, dificultar; interrumpir. *vi* ser un obstáculo; formar un obstáculo
hinderer *n* estorbador (-ra); interruptor (-ra)
hindmost *a* posterior, postrero, último
hindrance *n* obstáculo, estorbo, impedimento, *m*; perjuicio, *m*; interrupción, *f*
Hindu *n* hindú, *mf*
Hinduism *n* indoísmo, *m*
Hindustani *a* indostanés. *n* (language) indostani, *m*
hinge *n* gozne, pernio, *m*, bisagra, *f*; articulación, *f*; *fig* eje, *m. vi* moverse (or abrirse) sobre goznes; *fig* depender (de). *vt* engoznar
hinged *a* con goznes
hint *n* indirecta, insinuación, sugestión, *f*; (advice) consejo, *m. vt* dar a entender, decir con medias palabras; insinuar, sugerir. *vi* insinuar. **to take the h.,** darse por aludido
hinterland *n* interior (de un país), *m*
hip *n anat* cadera, *f*; *bot* fruto del rosal silvestre, *m.* **h.-bath,** baño de asiento, *m.* **h.-bone,** hueso ilíaco, *m.* **h.-joint,** articulación de la cadera, *f.* **h.-pocket,** faltriquera, *f*
hipped *a* de caderas
hippodrome *n* hipódromo, *m*
hippopotamus *n* hipopótamo, *m*
hire *n* alquiler, arriendo, *m*; salario, *m. vt* alquilar, arrendar; tomar en arriendo; (person) contratar; tomar a su servicio. **to h. out,** alquilar. **for** or **on h.,** de alquiler. **h.-purchase,** compra a plazos, *f*
hireling *n* mercenario, *m*
hirer *n* alquilador (-ra), arrendador (-ra)
hirsute *a* hirsuto. **non-h.** *bot* lampiño
his *poss pron 3rd sing* (el) suyo, *m*; (la) suya, *f*; (los) suyos, *m pl*; (las) suyas, *f pl*; de él. *poss a* su, *mf*; sus, *mf pl*; de él. **his handkerchiefs,** sus pañuelos. **his mother,** su madre, la madre de él. **a sister of his,** una de sus hermanas, una hermana suya. See **hers** for more examples.
Hispanism *n* hispanismo, *m*
Hispanist *n* hispanista, *mf*
hispanize *vt* españolizar
Hispano-American *a* hispano-americano
hiss *n* silbido, *m*; (sputter) chisporroteo, *m. vi* silbar
hissing *n* silbido, *m*; chisporroteo, *m. a* silbante
hist *interj* ¡chist!
histologist *n* histólogo, *m*
histology *n* histología, *f*

historian *n* historiador (-ra)
historic *a* histórico
historical *a* histórico. **h. truth,** verdad histórica, *f*
historically *adv* históricamente
historiographer *n* historiógrafo, *m*
historiography *n* historiografía, *f*
history *n* historia, *f*. **Biblical h.,** historia sagrada, *f*. **natural h.,** historia natural, *f*
histrionic *a* histriónico
hit *n* golpe, *m; aer* impacto, *m;* (success) éxito, *m;* (piece of luck) buena suerte, *f;* (satire) sátira, *f. vt* golpear; (buffet) abofetear, pegar; (find) dar con, tropezar con; (attain) acertar; (guess) adivinar; (attract) atraer; (deal) lanzar, dar; (wound) herir, hacer daño (a). **The sun hits me right in the eyes,** El sol me da en la cabeza. **direct hit,** *aer* impacto de lleno, *m.* **lucky hit,** acierto, *m.* **to hit a straight left,** (boxing) lanzar un directo con la izquierda. **to hit the mark,** dar en el blanco; *fig* dar en el clavo. **hit or miss,** acierto o error. **to hit against,** dar contra, estrellar contra. **to hit back,** defenderse; devolver golpe por golpe. **to hit off,** imitar; (a likeness) coger. **to hit out,** abofetear; *fig* atacar; golpear (la pelota) fuera. **to hit upon,** dar con; tropezar con; encontrar por casualidad; (remember) acordarse de
hitch *n* (jerk) sacudida, *f;* nudo fácil de soltar, *m; fig* obstáculo, *m; fig* dificultad, *f.* **give s.b. a hitch,** levantar a fulano. *vt* sacudir; (a chair, etc.) arrastrar, empujar; amarrar, enganchar; atar. *vi* (along a seat, etc.) correrse (en); (get entangled) enredarse, cogerse; (rub) rascarse. **without a h.,** sin dificultad alguna, viento en popa; (smoothly) a pedir de boca. **to h. up,** sacudir, dar una sacudida (a)
hitchhike *vi* ir a dedo (Argentina), pedir aventón (Mexico), pedir botella (Cuba), hacer autostop, ir por autostop (Spain)
hither *adv* acá, hacia acá; *a* citerior, más cercano. **h. and thither,** acá y aculla allá
hitherto *adv* hasta ahora, hasta el presente
Hitlerian *a* hitleriano, nacista
Hitlerism *n* hitlerismo, nacismo, *m*
Hittite *a* and *n* heteo (-ea)
hive *n* (for bees) colmena, *f;* (swarm) enjambre, *m; fig* centro, *m. vt* (bees) enjambrar. **h. of industry,** centro de industria
hoard *n* acumulación, *f;* provisión, *f;* tesoro, *m. vt* acumular, amasar, amontonar; guardar
hoarder *n* acaparador (-ra)
hoarding *n* amontonamiento, *m;* acaparamiento, *m;* (fence) empalizada, cerca, *f;* palizada de tablas, *f*
hoarfrost *n* escarcha, helada blanca, *f*
hoariness *n* (of the hair) canicie, *f;* blancura, *f;* (antiquity) vejez, vetustez, *f*
hoarse *a* ronco; discordante. **to be h.,** tener la voz ronca. **to grow h.,** enronquecerse
hoarsely *adv* roncamente
hoarseness *n* ronquera, *f; inf* carraspera, *f*
hoary *a* (of the hair) canoso; blanco; (old) vetusto, antiguo, viejo
hoax *n* estafa, *f,* engaño, *m;* broma pesada, *f;* burla, *f. vt* estafar, engañar; burlar
hoaxer *n* burlador (-ra); estafador (-ra)
hob *n* repisa interior del hogar, *f*
hobble *n* (gait) cojera, *f;* traba, maniota, *f. vi* cojear. *vt* manear. **h. skirt,** falda muy estrecha, *f*
hobby *n* pasatiempo, *m;* recreación, *f;* manía, afición, *f.* **h.-horse,** caballo de cartón, *m; fig* caballo de batalla, *m*
hobgoblin *n* trasgo, duende, *m*
hobnail *n* clavo de herradura, clavo de botas, *m*
hobnailed *a* (of boots) con clavos
hobnob *vi* codearse, tratar con familiaridad
hock *n anat* pernil, *m;* (wine) vino del Rin, *m*
hockey *n* chueca, *m.* **h. ball,** bola, pelota de chueca, *f.* **h. stick,** bastón de chueca, *m*
hocus-pocus *n* juego de pasa pasa, *m;* engaño, *m,* treta, *f*

hod *n* cuezo, *m*
hodgepodge See **hotchpotch**
hoe *n* azadón, *m. vt* azadonar; sachar
hoeing *n* cavadura con azadón, *f;* sachadura, *f*
hoer *n* azadonero, *m*
hog *n* cerdo, puerco, *m.* **to go the whole hog,** ir al extremo. **hogskin,** piel de cerdo, *f*
hoggish *a* porcuno; (greedy) comilón, tragón; (selfish) egoísta
hoist *n* levantamiento, *m;* (lift) montacargas, *m;* (winch) cabria, *f;* (crane) grúa, *f. vt* levantar, alzar; (flags) enarbolar; suspender; *naut* izar
hoity-toity *a* picajoso, quisquilloso; presuntuoso
hold *n* asimiento, agarro, *m,* presa, *f;* asidero, *m; fig* autoridad, *f,* poder, *m; fig* comprensión, *f;* (of a ship) cala, bodega, *f.* **to loose one's h.,** aflojar su presa. **to lose one's h.,** perder su presa. **to seize h. of,** asirse de, echar mano de. **h.-all,** funda, *f.* **h.-up,** (robbery) atraco, robo a mano armada, *m;* (in traffic) atasco (or obstáculo) en el tráfico, *m;* (in work) parada, cesación (de trabajo), *f*
hold *vt* tener; asir, agarrar; coger; retener; (embrace) abrazar; (a post) ocupar; (a meeting, etc.) celebrar; (bear weight of) aguantar, soportar; (own) poseer; *mil* ocupar, defender; (contain) contener; (have in store) reservar, tener capacidad para; (retain) retener; (believe) creer, sostener; (consider) opinar, tener para (mí, etc.); juzgar; (restrain) detener; contener; (of attention, etc.) mantener; (maneuvers) hacer; (observe) guardar. *vi* resistir, aguantar; (be valid) ser válido; regir; (apply) aplicarse; (last) continuar, seguir. *interj* ¡tente! ¡para! **The room won't h. more,** En este cuarto no caben más. **They h. him in great respect,** Le tienen mucho respeto. **The theory does not h. water,** La teoría es falsa, La teoría no es lógica. **to h. one's own,** defenderse, mantenerse en sus trece. **to h. one's breath,** contener la respiración. **to h. one's tongue,** callarse. **to h. sway,** mandar; reinar. **to h. tightly,** agarrar fuertemente; (clasp) estrechar. **H. the line!** (telephone) ¡Aguarde un momento! **to h. back,** *vt* detener; contener; retener; esconder; abstenerse de entregar. *vi* quedarse atrás; vacilar, dudar; tardar en. **to h. by,** seguir; basarse en, apoyarse en. **to h. down,** sujetar; (oppress) oprimir. **to h. fast,** *vt* sujetar fuertemente. *vi* mantenerse firme; *fig* estar agarrado (a). **to h. forth,** *vt* ofrecer; expresar. *vi* hacer un discurso, perorar. **to h. in,** *vt* contener; retener. *vi* contenerse. **to h. off,** *vt* apartar, alejar. *vi* apartarse, alejarse, mantenerse alejado. **to h. on,** seguir, persistir en; aguantar. **to h. out,** *vt* alargar, extender; ofrecer. *vi* aguantar; durar, resistir. **to h. over,** tener suspendido sobre; (postpone) aplazar; *fig* amenazar con. **to h. to,** agarrarse a; atenerse a. **to h. together,** *vt* unir; juntar. *vi* mantenerse juntos. **to h. up,** *vt* (display) mostrar, enseñar; levantar; sostener, soportar; (rob) atracar; saltear; (delay) atrasar; (stop) interrumpir, parar. *vi* mantenerse en pie; (of weather) seguir bueno. **The train has been held up by fog,** El tren viene con retraso a causa de la niebla
holder *n* el *m,* (*f,* la) que tiene; poseedor (-ra); *com* tenedor (-ra); inquilino (-na); propietario (-ia); (support) soporte, *m;* mango, *m;* asa, *f;* (in compounds) porta . . .
holding *n* tención, *f;* posesión, *f;* propiedad, *f;* (leasing) arrendamiento, *m;* (celebration) solemnización, *f;* (of a meeting) el celebrar, el tener; *pl* **holdings,** *com* valores habidos, *m pl*
holding company *n* compañía de cartera, *f*
hole *n* hoyo, *m;* boquete, *m;* agujero, *m;* cavidad, *f;* (hollow) depresión, *f;* hueco, *m;* orificio, *m;* (tear) roto, desgarro, *m;* (eyelet) punto, *m;* (in cheese) ojo, *m;* (in stocking) rotura, *f,* punto, *m;* (lair) madriguera, *f;* (nest) nido, *m;* (golf) hoyo, *m;* (fix) aprieto, *m. vt* agujerear; excavar; (bore) taladrar; *sport* meter la pelota (en). **to h. out,** (golf) meter la pelota en el hoyo. **h.-and-corner,** *a inf* bajo mano, secreto

hole-puncher *n* agujereadora, *f*

holiday *n* día feriado, *m*; día de fiesta, día festivo, *m*; vacación, *f*. *a* festivo, alegre; de vacación; de vacaciones; de excursión; (summer) veraniego. **day's h.,** día de asueto, *m*. **to take a h.,** tomar una vacación; hacer fiesta. **h. camp,** colonia veraniega, *f*. **h.-maker,** excursionista, turista, *mf*; (in the summer) veraneante, *mf* **holidays with pay,** vacaciones retribuidas, *f pl*

holiness *n* santidad, *f*

Holland Holanda, *f*

holland *n* lienzo crudo. *a* holandés. **H. gin,** ginebra holandesa, *f*

hollow *a* hueco; cóncavo; (empty) vacío; (of eyes, etc.) hundido; (of sound) sordo; (of a cough) cavernoso; (echoing) retumbante; (*fig* unreal) vacío, falso; insincero. *adv* vacío; *inf* completamente. *n* hueco, *m*; concavidad, *f*; (hole) hoyo, *m*; cavidad, *f*; (valley) hondanada, *f*, barranco, *m*; (groove) ranura, *f*; (depression) depresión, *f*; (in the back) curvadura, *f*. *vt* excavar, ahuecar; vaciar. **h.-cheeked,** con las mejillas hundidas. **h.-eyed,** con los ojos hundidos, de ojos hundidos

hollowness *n* concavidad, *f*; (falseness) falsedad, *f*; insinceridad, *f*

holly *n* acebo, agrifolio, *m*

holocaust *n* holocausto, *m*

holograph *n* hológrafo, *m*

holster *n* pistolera, *f*

holy *a* santo; sagrado; (blessed) bendito. **most h.,** *a* santísimo. **to make h.,** santificar. **H. Father,** Padre Santo, el Papa, *m*. **H. Ghost,** Espíritu Santo, *m*. **H. Office,** Santo Oficio, *m*, Inquisición, *f*. **H. Orders,** órdenes sagradas, *f pl*. **h. places,** santos lugares, *m pl*. **H. Scripture,** Sagrada Escritura, *f*. **H. See,** Cátedra de San Pedro, *f*. **h. water,** agua bendita, *f*. **H. Souls,** las Ánimas Benditas. **h. water stoup,** acetre, *m*. **H. Week,** Semana Santa, *f*

Holy Land, the la Tierra Santa, *f*.

homage *n* homenaje, *m*; culto, *m*; reverencia, *f*. **to pay h.,** rendir homenaje

home *n* casa, *f*; hogar, *m*; domicilio, *m*, residencia, *f*; (institution) asilo, *m*; (haven) refugio, *m*; (habitation) morada, *f*; (country of origin) país de origen, *m*; (native land) patria, *f*; (environment) ambiente natural, *m*; *sport* meta, *f*. *a* casero, doméstico; nativo; nacional, del país; indígena. *adv* a casa, hacia casa; (in one's country) en su patria; (returned) de vuelta; (of the feelings) al corazón, al alma; (to the limit) al límite. **at h.,** en casa; *fig* en su elemento; (of games) en campo propio; de recibo. **at-h. day,** día de recibo, *m*. **He shot the bolt h.,** Echó el cerrojo. **one's long h.,** su última morada. **to be at h.,** estar en casa; estar de recibo. **to be away from h.,** estar fuera de casa; estar ausente. **to bring h.,** traer (or llevar) a casa; hacer ver; convencer; llegar al alma; (a crime) probar (contra). **to go h.,** volver a casa; volver a la patria; (be effective) hacer su efecto; (move) herir en lo más vivo. **to make oneself at h.,** ponerse a sus anchas, sentirse como en casa de uno. **Please make yourself at home!** ¡Ha tomado posesión de su casa! **to strike h.,** dar en el blanco; herir; (hit) golpear; herir en lo más vivo; hacerse sentir. **h. affairs,** asuntos domésticos, *m pl*, (Ministry of) Gobernación, *f*. **h.-bred,** criado en el país; fermentado en el país; fermentado en casa. **h.-coming,** regreso al hogar, *m*. **h. counties,** condados alrededor de Londres, *m pl*. **H. Defense,** defensa nacional, *f*. **h. farm,** residencia del propietario de una finca, *f*. **h. for the aged,** asilo de ancianos, *m*. **h. front,** frente doméstico, *m*. **H. Guard,** milicia nacional, *f*. **h. life,** vida de familia, *f*. **h.-made** casero, de fabricación casera, hecho en casa. **H. Office,** Ministerio de Gobernación, *m*. **H. Rule,** autonomía, *f*. **H. Secretary,** Ministro de Gobernación, *m*. **h. stretch,** último trecho (de una carrera), *m*. **h. truth,** verdad, *inf* fresca, *f*. **to tell someone a few h. truths,** contarle cuatro verdades

homeless *a* sin casa; sin hogar. **the h.,** los sin techo

homeliness *n* comodidad, *f*; sencillez, *f*; (ugliness) fealdad, *f*

homely *a* doméstico; familiar; (unpretentious) sencillo; llano; (ugly) feo; desabrido

homeopath *n* homeópata, *mf*

homeopathic *a* homeópata

homeopathy *n* homeopatía, *f*

Homeric *a* homérico

homesick *a* nostálgico. **to be h.,** tener morriña

homesickness *n* nostalgia, añoranza, morriña, *f*

homespun *a* tejido en casa; hecho en casa; basto, grueso

homestead *n* hacienda, *f*; casa solariega, *f*; casa, *f*

homeward *adv* hacia casa, en dirección al hogar; de vuelta; hacia la patria. **h.-bound,** en dirección a casa; (of ships) con rumbo al puerto de origen; (of other traffic) de vuelta

homicidal *a* homicida

homicide *n* (act) homicidio, *m*; (person) homicida, *mf*

homily *n ecc* homilía, *f*; sermón, *m*

homing pigeon *n* palomo (-ma) mensajero (-ra)

homogeneity *n* homogeneidad, *f*

homogeneous *a* homogéneo

homologous *a* homólogo

homonym *n* homónimo, *m*

homonymous *a* homónimo

homosexual *a* and *n* homosexual, *mf*

Honduran *a* and *a* hondureño (-ña)

hone *n* piedra de afilar, *f*. *vt* afilar, vaciar

honest *a* honrado; decente, honesto; (chaste) casto; (loyal) sincero, leal; (frank) franco; imparcial. **an h. man,** un hombre de buena fe, un hombre honrado, un hombre decente

honesty *n* honradez, *f*; honestidad, *f*; (chastity) castidad, *f*; sinceridad, *f*; rectitud, imparcialidad, *f*

honey *n* miel, *f*. **h.-bee,** abeja obrera, *f*. **h.-colored,** melado. **h.-pot,** jarro de miel, *m*. **h.-tongued,** melifluo; de pico de oro

honeycomb *n* panal, *m*

honeycombed *a* apanalado

honeydew *n* mielada, *f*; *fig* ambrosia, *f*

honeyed *a* de miel; *fig* meloso, adulador

honeymoon *n* luna de miel, *f*; viaje de novios, viaje nupcial, *m*. *vi* hacer un viaje nupcial

honeysuckle *n* madreselva, *f*

honor *n* honor, *m*; honra, *f*; honradez, rectitud, integridad, *f*; *pl* **honors,** honores, *m pl*; condecoraciones, *f pl*; (at last) h.) honras, pompas fúnebres, *f pl*. *vt* honrar; (God) glorificar; (decorate) condecorar, laurear; (respect) respetar; reverenciar; *com* aceptar; (a toast) beber. **On my h.,** A fe mía. **point of h.,** punto de honor, pundonor, *m*. **word of h.,** palabra de honor, *f*. **Your H.,** (to a judge) Excelentísimo Señor Juez

honorable *a* honorable; glorioso; digno; ilustre; (sensitive of honor) pundonoroso

honorable mention *n* accésit, *m*

honorableness *n* honradez, *f*

honorably *adv* honorablemente; dignamente

honorarium *n* honorario, *m*

honorary *a* honorario, honorífico. **h. member,** socio (-ia) honorario (-ia). **h. mention,** mención honorífica, *f*

hood *n* capucha, caperuza, *f*; (folding, of vehicles) capota, cubierta, cubierta del motor *f*; (of a carriage) caparazón, fuelle, *m*; (of a car) capó, *m*, (university) muceta, *f*; (of a fireplace) campana (de hogar), *f*; (cowl of chimney) sombrerete (de chimenea), *m*. *vt* cubrir con capucha; cubrir; (the eyes) ocultar, cubrir, velar

hooded *a* con capucha

hoodwink *vt* vendar (los ojos); *fig* engañar, embaucar, burlar

hoof *n* casco, *m*; (cloven) pezuña, *f*

hoofed *a* ungulado

hoof it ir a golpe de calcetín

hook *n* gancho, garfio, *m*; (boat-) bichero, *m*; (fish-) anzuelo, *m*; (on a dress) corchete, *m*; (hanger) colgadero, *m;* (claw) garra, *f. vt* enganchar; (a dress) abrochar; (fish) pescar, coger; (nab) atrapar, pescar. **by h. or by crook,** a tuertas o a derechas. **left h.,** (boxing) izquierdo, *m.* **right h.,** (boxing) derecho, *m.* **to catch oneself on a h.,** engancharse. **h. and eye,** los corchetes. **h.-nosed,** con nariz de gancho, con nariz aguileña. **h.-up,** *rad* circuito, *m;* transmisión en circuito, *f*

hooked *a* con ganchos; corvo, ganchoso

hooking *n* enganche, *m;* (of a dress) abrochamiento, *m;* (of fish and *inf*) pesca, *f*

hookworm *n* anquilostoma, *m*

hooligan *n* rufián, *m*

hooliganism *n* rufianería, *f*

hoop *n* aro, arco, *m;* (of a skirt) miriñaque, *m;* (croquet) argolla, *f;* (toy) aro, *m;* círculo, *m. vt* poner aros a; *fig* rodear

hoot *n* (of owls) ululación, *f,* grito, *m;* (whistle) silbido, *m;* ruido, clamor, *m. vi* (of owls) ulular, gritar; silbar; *aut* avisar con la bocina. **to h. off the stage,** hacer abandonar la escena. **to h. down,** silbar

hooter *n* sirena, *f; aut* bocina, *f;* (whistle) pito, *m*

hooting *n* See **hoot**

hop *n* salto, brinco, *m; bot* lúpulo, *m; bot* flores de oblón, *f pl;* (dance) baile, *m. vi* saltar con un pie; andar dando brincos; saltar; (limp) cojear; recoger lúpulo; (of plant) dar lúpulo. *vt* saltar. **hop-garden,** huerto de lúpulo, *m.* **hop-kiln,** horno para secar lúpulo, *m.* **hop-picker,** recolector (-ra) de lúpulo. **hop-picking,** recolección de lúpulos, *f*

hope *n* esperanza, *f;* (faith) confianza, *f;* (expectation) anticipación, expectativa, *f;* (probability) probabilidad, *f;* (illusion) ilusión, *f;* sueño, *m. vi* esperar. **to live in h. that,** vivir con la esperanza de que. **to lose h.,** desesperarse. **to h. against h.,** esperar sin motivo, esperar lo imposible. **to h. for,** desear. **to h. in,** confiar en

hopeful *a* lleno de esperanzas, confiado; optimista; *(fig)* risueño. *n inf* la esperanza de la casa. **to look h.,** *fig* prometer bien

hopefully *adv* con esperanza

hopefulness *n* optimismo, *m; fig* aspecto prometedor, *m*

hopeless *a* desesperado, sin esperanza; irremediable; (of situations) imposible; (of disease) incurable. **to be h.,** (lose hope) desesperarse; (have no remedy) ser irremediable; (of disease) no tener cura. **to make h.,** hacer perder la esperanza, desesperar; dejar sin remedio; (a situation) hacer imposible; (an illness) hacer imposible de curar

hopelessly *adv* sin esperanza; sin remedio; imposiblemente; incurablemente

hopelessness *n* desesperación, *f;* (of an illness) imposibilidad de curar, *f;* lo irremediable; imposibilidad, *f* lo irremediable

hopscotch *n* infernáculo, *m,* rayuela, *f*

horal, horary *a* horario

horde *n* horda, *f*

horizon *n* horizonte, *m*

horizontal *a* horizontal. **h. suspension,** (gymnastics) plancha, *f*

horizontality *n* horizontalidad, *f*

horizontally *adv* horizontalmente

hormone *n* hormona, *f*

horn *n* (of bull, etc.) cuerno, *m;* (antler) asta, *f;* (of an insect) antena, *f;* (of a snail) tentáculo, *m; mus* cuerno, *m;* trompa, *f;* (of motor and phonograph) bocina, *f;* (of moon) cuerno (de la luna), *m.* **article made of h.,** objeto de cuerno, *m.* **on the horns of a dilemma,** entre la espada y la pared. **h. of plenty,** cuerno de abundancia, *m;* cornucopia, *f.* **h.-rimmed spectacles,** anteojos de concha, *m pl.* **h. thrust,** cornada, *f*

horned *a* cornudo; (antlered) enastado

hornet *n* avispón, abejón, *m*

horny *a* córneo; calloso; duro. **h.-handed,** con manos callosas

horoscope *n* horóscopo, *m*

horrible *a* horrible, repugnante, espantoso; (of price) enorme; *inf* horrible

horribleness *n* horribilidad, *f,* horror, *m,* lo espantoso

horribly *adv* horriblemente

horrid *a* horroroso; desagradable

horridness *n* horror, *m;* lo desagradable

horrific *a* horrífico, horrendo

horrify *vt* horrorizar; escandalizar

horrifying *a* horroroso, horripilante

horror *n* horror, *m.* **h.-stricken,** horrorizado

hors d'œuvres *n pl* entremeses, *m pl*

horse *n* caballo, *m;* (cavalry) caballería, *f;* (frame) caballete, *m;* (gymnastics and as punishment) potro, *m. a* caballar, caballuno. *vt* montar a caballo. **pack of horses,** caballada, *f.* **to ride a h.,** cabalgar, montar a caballo. **H. Artillery,** artillería montada, *f.* **h. blanket,** manta para caballos, *f;* sudadero, *m.* **h.-block,** montador, *m.* **h.-box,** vagón para caballos, *m.* **h.-breaker,** domador de caballos, *m.* **h.-cab,** simón, *m.* **h.-chestnut,** castaña pilonga, *f.* **h.-chestnut flower,** candela, *f.* **h.-collar,** collera, *f.* **h.-dealer,** chalán, *m.* **h.-doctor,** veterinario, *m.* **h.-flesh,** carne de caballo, *f.* **h.-fly,** tábano, *m.* **H. Guards,** guardias montadas, *f pl.* **h.-latitudes,** calmas de Cáncer, *f pl.* **h.-laugh,** carcajada, *f.* **h.-master,** maestro de equitación, *m.* **h. meat,** carne de caballo, *f.* **h. pistol,** pistola de arzón, *f.* **h.-play,** payasada, *f.* **h.-power,** caballo de vapor, *m;* potencia, *f.* **a twelve-h.p. car,** un coche de doce caballos. **h.-race,** carrera de caballos, *f.* **h.-radish,** rábano picante, raíz amarga, *m.* **h.-sense,** sentido común, *m,* gramática parda, *f.* **h. show,** exposición de caballos, feria equina *f;* concurso de caballos, *m.* **h.-trainer,** entrenador de caballos, *m.* **h. tram,** tranvía de sangre, *m.* **h. trappings,** monturas, *f pl*

horseback *n* lomo de caballo, *m.* **on h.,** a caballo. **to ride on h.,** ir a caballo

horseman *n* jinete, cabalgador, *m*

horsemanship *n* equitación, *f,* manejo del caballo, *m*

horseshoe *n* herradura, *f.* **h. arch,** arco de herradura, arco morisco, *m*

horsewhip *n* látigo, *m. vt* zurriagar, pegar con látigo

horsewoman *n* amazona, *f*

horsey *a* de caballo; aficionado a caballos; grosero

horticultural *a* horticultural. **h. show,** exposición de flores, *f*

horticulturalist *n* horticultor (-ra)

horticulture *n* horticultura, *f*

hosanna *n* hosanna, *m*

hose *n* (tube) manga, *f;* (breeches) calzón, *m;* (stockings) medias, *f pl;* (socks) calcetines, *m pl.* **h. man,** manguero, *m.* **h.-pipe,** manga de riego, manguera, *f*

hosier *n* calcetero (-ra)

hosiery *n* calcetería, *f.* **h. trade,** calcetería, *f*

hospice *n* hospicio, *m;* asilo, refugio, *m*

hospitable *a* hospitalario

hospitableness *n* hospitalidad, *f*

hospitably *adv* hospitalariamente

hospital *n* hospital, *m;* (school) colegio, *m.* **h. nurse,** enfermera, *f.* **h. ship,** buque hospital, *m*

hospital bed cama hospitalaria, *f*

hospitality *n* hospitalidad, *f*

host *n* huésped, convidador, *m;* (of radio or tv program) presentador, *m;* (at an inn) patrón, mesonero, *m;* (army) ejército, *m;* (crowd) multitud, muchedumbre, *f; ecc* hostia, *f; pl* **hosts,** huestes, *f pl.* **h.-plant,** planta huésped, *f*

hostage *n* rehén, *m; fig* prenda, *f*

host country *n* (of an organization) país-sede, *m*

hostel *n* hostería, *f;* club, *m;* residencia de estudiantes, *f*

hostelry *n* hospedería, *f;* parador, mesón, *m*

hostess *n* ama de la casa, *f;* la que recibe a los invitados; la que convída; (of an inn) patrona, mesonera, *f*

hostile *a* enemigo; hostil, contrario (a); (of circumstances, etc.) desfavorable

hostility *n* enemistad, *f,* antagonismo, *m,* mala voluntad, *f;* hostilidad, guerra, *f.* **suspension of hostilities,** suspensión de hostilidades, *f*

hot *a* caliente; (of a day, etc.) caluroso; (piquant) picante; ardiente; vehemente, impetuoso; violento; impaciente; colérico; entusiasta; lleno de deseo; *art* intenso; (great) grande, mucho; (vigorous) enérgico. **You are getting very hot now,** *inf* (in a game, etc.) Te estás quemando. **It is hot,** Está caliente; (of weather) Hace calor. **to grow hot,** calentarse; *fig* acalorarse; (of weather) empezar a hacer calor. **to make hot,** calentar; dar calor (a); *inf* dar vergüenza. **hot-blooded,** de sangre caliente; apasionado; colérico. **hot-foot,** aprisa, apresuradamente. **hot-headed,** impetuoso. **hot-plate,** *elec* calientaplatos, *m*. **hot springs,** termas, *f pl*. **hot-tempered,** colérico, irascible. **hot water,** agua caliente, *f*. **hot-water bottle,** bolsa de goma, *f*. **hot-water pipes,** las cañerías del agua caliente

hotbed *n* semillero, vivero, *m*; *fig* semillero, foco, *m*

hotchpotch *n* potaje, *m*; *fig* mezcolanza, *f*, fárrago, *m*

hotel *n* hotel, *m*. **h.-keeper,** hotelero (-ra)

hothead *n* exaltado (-da), fanático (-ca)

hothouse *n* invernáculo, *m*, estufa, *f*. **h. plant,** *fig* planta de estufa, *f*

hotly *adv* calurosamente; con vehemencia; coléricamente

hough *n zool* pernil, *m*; (in man) corva, *f*

hound *n* perro de caza, sabueso de artois, *m*; perro, *m*; *inf* canalla, *m*. *vt* cazar con perros; *fig* perseguir; *fig* incitar. **master of hounds,** montero, *m*. **pack of hounds,** jauría, *f*

hour *n* hora, *f*; momento, *m*; ocasión, oportunidad, *f pl*. **hours,** horas, *f pl*. **after hours,** fuera de horas. **at the eleventh h.,** en el último minuto. **by the h.,** por horas; horas enteras. **small hours,** altas horas de la noche, *inf* las tantas, *f pl*. **to keep late hours,** acostarse tarde. **to strike the h.,** dar la hora. **h.-glass,** reloj de arena, *m*. **h.-hand,** horario, *m*. **h. of death,** hora suprema, hora de la muerte, *f*

hourly *a* cada hora; por horas; continuo. *adv* a cada hora; de un momento a otro

house *n* casa, *f*; (home) hogar, *m*; (lineage) familia, *f*, abolengo, *m*; (threat.) sala, *f*, teatro, *m*; *com* casa comercial, *f*; (takings) entrada, *f*; (audience) público, *m*; (of Lords, Commons) cámara, *f*; (college) colegio, *m*; (parliament) parlamento, *m*; (building) edificio, *m*. *a* de casa; de la casa; doméstico. *vt* dar vivienda (a); alojar; recibir (or tener) en casa de uno; (store) poner, guardar. **The cottage will not h. them all,** No habrá bastante lugar para todos ellos en la cabaña, No cabrán todos en la cabaña. **country-h.,** finca, *f*; casa de campo, *f*. **full h.,** casa llena, *f*; *theat* lleno, *m*. **to bring down the h.,** *theat* hacer venirse el teatro abajo. **to keep h.,** llevar la casa; ser ama de casa. **to keep open h.,** tener mesa puesta, ser hospitalario. **to set up h.,** poner casa. **h. of cards,** castillo de naipes, *m*. **H. of Commons,** Cámara de los Comunes, *f*. **H. of Lords,** Cámara de los Lores, *f*. **h.-agent,** agente de casas, *m*. **h.-boat,** barco-habitación, *m*, casa flotante, *f*. **h.-dog,** perro de guardia, *m*; perro de casa, *m*. **h.-fly,** mosca doméstica, *f*. **h. furnisher,** mueblista, *mf*. **h. painter,** pintor de brocha gorda, *m*. **h. party,** reunión en una casa de campo, *f*. **h.-physician,** médico (-ca) interno (-na). **h. porter,** portero, *m*. **h. property,** propiedad inmueble, *f*. **h.-room,** capacidad de una casa, *f*. **h. slipper,** zapatilla, *f*, pantuflo, *m*. **h.-surgeon,** cirujano interno, *m*. **h.-to-h.,** de casa en casa. **h.-warming,** reunión para colgar la cremallera, *f*

housebreaker *n* ladrón de casas, *m*

housebreaking *n* robo de una casa, *m*

houseful *n* casa, *f*

house furnishings *n pl* artefactos para el hogar, accesorios caseros, aparatos electrodomésticos, *m pl*

household *n* casa, *f*; familia, *f*; hogar, *m*. *a* de la casa; doméstico; del hogar. **to be a h. word,** andar en lenguas. **h. accounts,** cuentas de la casa, *f pl*. **h. duties,** labores de la casa, *f pl*. **h. gods,** penates, *m pl*. **h. goods,** ajuar, mobiliario, *m*. **h. management,** gobierno de la casa, *m*

householder *n* padre de familia, *m*; dueño (-ña) (or inquilino (-na)) de una casa

house of ill repute *n* burdel, *m*, casa de citas, casa de zorras, casa pública, *f*; lupanar, *m*

housekeeper *n* ama de llaves, *f*; mujer de su casa, *f*

housekeeping *n* gobierno de la casa, *m*; economía doméstica, *f*. *a* doméstico. **to set up h.,** poner casa

housemaid *n* camarera, sirvienta, *f*. **housemaid's knee,** rodilla de fregona, *f*

housemaker *n* ama de casa, *f*

housetops *n* tejado, *m*; (flat roof) azotea, *f*. **to shout from the h.,** pregonar a los cuatro vientos

housewife *n* madre de familia, mujer de su casa, *f*; (sewing-bag) neceser de costura, *m*

housewifely *a* propio de una mujer de su casa; doméstico; (of a woman) hacendosa

housewifery *n* economía doméstica, *f*

housing *n* provisión de vivienda, *f*; (storage) almacenaje, *m*; alojamiento, *m*; *inf* casa, vivienda, *f*. **h. scheme,** urbanización, *f*. **h. shortage,** crisis de vivienda, *f*, déficit habitacional, *m*

hovel *n* casucha, *f*

hover *vi* revolotear; (of hawks, etc.) cernerse; estar suspendido; rondar; seguir de cerca, estar al lado (de); *fig* vacilar, dudar

hovering *n* revoloteo, *m*; (of birds of prey) calada, *f*; *fig* vacilación, *f*. *a* revolante, que revolotea; que se cierne (sobre); (menacing) que amenaza, inminente

how *adv* cómo; (by what means, in what manner) de qué modo; (at what price) a qué precio; qué; cuánto. *n* el cómo. **to know how,** saber. **For how long?** ¿Por cuánto tiempo? **How are you?** ¿Cómo está Vd.? *inf* ¿Qué tal? **How do you do!** ¡Mucho gusto (en conocerlo/conocerla/conocerlos/conocerlas)! **How old are you?** ¿Qué edad tiene Vd.? **How beautiful!** ¡Qué hermoso! **How big!** ¡Cuán grande! **How early?** ¿Cuán temprano?; ¿Cuándo a más tardar? **How far?** ¿A qué distancia? ¿Hasta qué punto? ¿Hasta dónde? **How fast?** ¿A qué velocidad? **How few!** ¡Qué pocos! **How little!** ¡Qué pequeño!; ¡Qué poco! **How long?** ¿Cuánto tiempo? **How many?** ¿Cuántos? *m pl*; ¿Cuántas? *f pl*. **How much is it?** ¿Cuánto vale? **How much cloth do you want?** ¿Cuánta tela quieres? **How often?** ¿Cuán a menudo? ¿Cuántas veces? **How would you like to go for a walk?** ¿Te gustaría pasearte? **How are you going to Lisbon?** ¿En qué vas a Lisboa?

however *adv* como quiera (que) (followed by subjunctive); por más que (followed by subjunctive); por . . . que (followed by subjunctive). *conjunc* (nevertheless) sin embargo, no obstante. **h. good it is,** por bueno que sea. **h. he does it,** como quiera que lo haga. **h. it may be,** sea como sea. **h. much,** por mucho que

howl *n* aullido, *m*; (groan) gemido, *m*; (cry) grito, *m*; (roar) rugido, bramido, *m*; lamento, *m*. *vi* aullar; gemir; gritar; rugir, bramar. *vt* chillar. **Each time he opened his mouth he was howled down,** Cada vez que abrió la boca se armó una bronca

howler *n* aullador (-ra); *zool* mono (-na) chillón (-ona); (blunder) coladura, plancha, *f*

howling *a* aullante; gemidor; (crying) que llora; bramante, rugiente. *n* los aullidos; (groaning) el gemir, los gemidos; (crying) los gritos; (weeping) el lloro; (roaring) los bramidos, el rugir; los lamentos

hub *n* (of a wheel) cubo (de rueda) *m*; *fig* centro, *m*. **hub cap,** tapa de cubo, *f*

hubbub *n* algarada, barahúnda, *f*

huckster *n* revendedor (-ra). *vi* revender; (haggle) regatear

huddle *n* (heap) montón, *m*; colección, *f*; (group) corrillo, grupo, *m*; (mixture) mezcla, *f*. *vt* arrebujar; amontonar; acurrucar, arrebujar; (throw on) echarse. *vi* amontonarse; apiñarse; acurrucarse, arrebujarse

hue *n* color, *m*; matiz, tono, *m*; (of opinion) matiz, *m*; (clamor) clamor, *m*, gritería, *f*. **hue and cry,** alarma, *f*

huff *n* acceso de cólera, *m*

huffily *adv* malhumoradamente; petulantemente

huffiness *n* mal humor, *m*; petulancia, *f*; arrogancia, *f*

hug *n* abrazo, *m*. *vt* abrazar, apretujar; *fig* acariciar; *naut* navegar muy cerca de. **to hug oneself,** *fig* congratularse

huge *a* enorme, inmenso; gigante; vasto

hugely *adv* inmensamente, enormemente

hugeness *n* inmensidad, enormidad, *f*; vastedad, *f*

Huguenot *a* and *n* hugonote (-ta)

hulk *n* barco viejo, *m*; pontón, *m*

hulking *a* pesado, desgarbado

hull *n naut* casco (de un buque), *m*; (shell) cáscara, *f*; (pod) vaina, *f*, *vt* mondar

hullabaloo *n* alboroto, tumulto, *m*; vocerío, *m*

hullo *interj* See **hallo**

hum *n* zumbido, *m*; ruido confuso, *m*. *vi* (sing) canturrear; zumbar; (confused sound) zurrir; (hesitate) vacilar. *vt* (a tune) tararear

human *a* humano. **the h. touch,** el don de gentes. **h. being,** ser humano, hombre, *m*

humane *a* humanitario, humano

humanely *adv* humanitariamente

humaneness *n* humanidad, *f*

humanism *n* humanismo, *m*

humanist *n* humanista, *mf*

humanistic *a* humanista

humanitarian *a* humanitario

humanitarianism *n* humanitarismo, *m*

humanity *n* humanidad, *f*; raza humana, *f*. **the humanities,** las humanidades

humanize *vt* humanizar; (milk) maternizar. *vi* humanizarse

humanly *adv* humanamente

humble *a* humilde; modesto; (cringing) servil; sumiso; pobre. *vt* humillar; mortificar. **to h. oneself,** humillarse

humbleness *n* humildad, *f*; modestia, *f*; (abjectness) servilismo, *m*; sumisión, *f*; pobreza, *f*; (of birth, etc.) obscuridad, *f*

humbling *n* humillación, *f*; mortificación, *f*

humbly *adv* humildemente; modestamente; servilmente

humbug *n* (fraud) embuste, engaño, *m*; (nonsense) disparate, *m*, tontería, *f*; mentira, *f*; (person) farsante, charlatán, *m*; (sweetmeat) caramelo de menta, *m*. *vt* engañar, embaucar; burlarse de

humdrum *a* monótono; aburrido

humeral *a* humeral. *n ecc* velo humeral, *m*

humerus *n anat* húmero, *m*

humid *a* húmedo

humidity *n* humedad, *f*

humiliate *vt* humillar, mortificar. **to h. oneself,** humillarse

humiliating *a* humillante; degradante

humiliation *n* humillación, mortificación, *f*; degradación, *f*

humility *n* humildad, *f*; modestia, *f*

humming *n* zumbido, *m*; (of a tune) tarareo, *m*. *a* zumbador. **h.-bird,** pájaro mosca, colibrí, *m*. **h.-top,** trompa, *f*

humoresque *n mus* capricho musical, *m*

humorist *n* humorista, *mf*

humorous *a* humorístico; cómico, risible

humorously *adv* humorísticamente; cómicamente

humorousness *n* humorismo, *m*; lo cómico

humor *n* humor, *m*; humorismo, *m*; (temperament) disposición, *f*, carácter, *m*; (whim) capricho, *m*. *vt* seguir el humor (a), complacer; satisfacer, consentir en; (a lock, etc.) manejar. **in a good (bad) h.,** de buen (mal) humor. **I am not in the h. to . . .** No estoy de humor para . . . **sense of h.,** sentido de humor, *m*

humored *a* (in compounds) de humor . . . **good-h.,** de buen humor. **ill-h.,** malhumorado, de mal humor

humorless *a* sin sentido humorístico, sin sentido de humor

hump *n* joroba, giba, *f*; (hillock) montecillo, *m*; *inf* depresión, *f*

humpback *n* giba, joroba, *f*; (person) jorobado (-da), giboso (-sa)

humpbacked *a* jorobado, giboso, corcovado

humph *interj* ¡qué va!; ¡patrañas!

humus *n* humus, mantillo, *m*

hunchback *n* joroba, giba, *f*; (person) jorobado (-da), corcovado (-da), giboso (-sa)

hunchbacked *a* jorobado, giboso, corcovado

hundred *n* ciento, *m*; centenar, *m*, centena, *f*. *a* ciento; (before nouns and adjectives, excluding numerals, with the exception of mil and millón) cien. **a h. thousand,** cien mil. **one h. and one,** ciento uno. **by the h.,** a centenares. **hundreds of people,** centenares de personas, *m pl*. **h.-millionth,** *a* and *n* cienmillonésimo *m*. **h.-thousandth,** *a* and *n* cienmilésimo *m*.

hundredfold *adv* cien veces. *n* céntuplo, *m*

hundredth *a* centésimo, céntimo. *n* centésimo, *m*, centésima parte, *f*

hundredweight *n* quintal, *m*

Hungary Hungría, *f*

Hungarian *a* and *n* húngaro (-ra); (language) húngaro, *m*

hunger *n* hambre, *f*; apetito, *m*; (craving) deseo, *m*, ansia, *f*. *vi* estar hambriento, tener hambre. **to h. for,** desear, ansiar. **h.-strike,** huelga de hambre, *f*

hungrily *adv* hambrientamente, con hambre; ansiosamente

hungry *a* hambriento; (of land) pobre; (anxious) deseoso. **to be h.,** tener hambre. **to make h.,** dar hambre

hunk *n* rebanada, *f*, pedazo, *m*

hunt *n* caza, cacería, montería, *f*; grupo de cazadores, *m*; (search) busca, *f*; (pursuit) persecución, *f*. *vt* cazar; cazar a caballo; (search) buscar; rebuscar, explorar; (pursue) perseguir. **to h. down,** perseguir. **to h. for,** buscar. **to h. out,** buscar; descubrir, desenterrar

hunter *n* cazador, *m*; caballo de caza, *m*; (watch) saboneta, *f*

hunting *n* caza, *f*; caza a caballo, *f*; persecución, *f*. *a* cazador, de caza. **to go h.,** ir a cazar. **h.-box,** pabellón de caza, *m*. **h.-cap,** gorra de montar, *f*. **h.-crop,** látigo para cazar, *m*. **h.-ground,** coto de caza, terreno de caza, *m*. **h.-horn,** cuerno de caza, *m*, corneta de monte, *f*. **h. party,** partido de caza, *m*, cacería, *f*

hunting lodge *n* pabellón *m*

huntress *n* cazadora, *f*

huntsman *n* cazador, montero, *m*

huntsmanship *n* montería, arte de cazar, *f*

hurdle *n* valla, *f*; zarzo, *m*. **h.-race,** carrera de obstáculos, *f*; carrera de vallas, *f*

hurdy-gurdy *n* organillo, *m*

hurl *vt* lanzar, tirar, arrojar, echar. **to h. oneself,** lanzarse. **to h. oneself against,** arrojarse a (or contra). **to h. oneself upon,** abalanzarse sobre

hurly-burly *n* alboroto, tumulto, *m*

hurrah *interj* ¡hurra! ¡viva! *n* vítor, *m*. **H. for . . . !** ¡Viva . . . !, ¡Vivan . . . ! **to shout h.,** vitorear

hurricane *n* huracán, *m*. **h.-lamp,** lámpara sorda, *f*

hurried *a* apresurado, precipitado; hecho a prisa; superficial

hurriedly *adv* apresuradamente, precipitadamente, con prisa; superficialmente; (of writing) a vuela pluma

hurry *n* prisa, *f*; precipitación, *f*; urgencia, *f*; confusión, *f*; alboroto, *m*. **in a h.,** aprisa. **in a great h.,** aprisa y corriendo. **to be in a h.,** llevar prisa, estar de prisa. **There is no h.,** No corre prisa, No hay prisa

hurry *vt* apresurar, dar prisa (a); llevar aprisa; hacer andar aprisa; enviar apresuradamente; precipitar; acelerar. *vi* darse prisa; apresurarse. **to h. after,** correr detrás de, seguir apresuradamente. **to h. away,** *vi* marcharse aprisa, marcharse corriendo; huir; salir precipitadamente. *vt* hacer marcharse aprisa; llevar con prisa. **to h. back,** *vi* volver aprisa, apresurarse a volver.

vt hacer volver aprisa. **to h. in,** *vi* entrar aprisa, entrar corriendo. *vt* hacer entrar aprisa. **to h. off.** See **to h. away. to h. on,** *vi* apresurarse. *vt* apresurar, precipitar. **to h. out,** salir rápidamente. **to h. over,** hacer rápidamente; concluir aprisa; despachar rápidamente; (travel over) atravesar aprisa; pasar rápidamente por. **to h. toward,** llevar rápidamente hacia; arrastrar hacia; impeler hacia. **to h. up,** *vi* darse prisa. *vt* apresurar, precipitar; estimular

hurt *n* herida, *f*; (harm) daño, mal, *m*; perjuicio, *m*. *vt* (wound) herir; (cause pain) doler; hacer daño (a); hacer mal (a); (damage) perjudicar, estropear; (offend) ofender; (the feelings) mortificar, lastimar, herir. *vi* doler; hacer mal; perjudicarse, estropearse. **I haven't h. myself,** No me he hecho daño. **Does it still h. you?** ¿Te duele todavía? **to h. deeply,** *fig* herir en el alma. **to h. a person's feelings,** herirle (a uno) el amor propio, lastimar, ofender

hurtful *a* nocivo, dañino; injurioso, pernicioso

hurtfulness *n* nocividad, *f*; perniciosidad, *f*

hurtle *vt* lanzar. *vi* lanzarse; volar; caer

husband *n* esposo, marido, *m*. *vt* economizar, ahorrar. **h. and wife,** los esposos, los cónyuges

husbandry *n* labor de los campos, agricultura, *f*; (thrift) frugalidad, parsimonia, *f*

hush *n* silencio, *m*, tranquilidad, *f*. *interj* ¡chitón! ¡calla! ¡silencio! *vt* silenciar, hacer callar, imponer silencio (a); (a baby) adormecer; *fig* sosegar, calmar. *vi* callarse, enmudecer. **to h. up,** mantener secreto, ocultar. **h.-h.,** secreto. **h. money,** so-borno, chantaje, *m*

hushaby *interj* ¡duerme!

husk *n* (of grain) cascabillo, *m*; zurrón, *m*; cáscara, *f*; (of chestnut) erizo, *m*

huskily *adv* roncamente

huskiness *n* ronquera, *f*; *inf* robustez, *f*

husky *a* (of voice) ronco; *bot* cascarudo; (Eskimo) esquimal; *inf* robusto, fuerte. *n* perro esquimal, *m*

hussy *n* pícara, bribona, *f*

hustle *vt* empujar, codear; *fig* precipitar; *inf* acelerar. *vi* codearse; andarse de prisa

hut *n* choza, cabaña, barraca, *f*

hutch *n* (chest) arca, *f*, cofre, *m*; (cage) jaula, *f*; (for rabbits) conejera, *f*; (for rats) ratonera, *f*; *inf* choza, *f*

hutment *n* campamento de chozas, *m*

hyacinth *n* jacinto, *m*

hybrid *a* híbrido; mestizo, mixto. *n* híbrido, *m*

hybridism *n* hibridismo, *m*

hybridization *n* hibridación, *f*

hybridize *vt* cruzar. *vi* producir (or generar) híbridos

hydrangea *n* *bot* hortensia, *f*

hydrant *n* boca de riego, *f*

hydrate *n* *chem* hidrato, *m*. *vt* hidratar

hydration *n* hidratación, *f*

hydraulic *a* hidráulico. **h. engineering,** hidrotecnia, *f*

hydraulics *n* hidráulica, *f*

hydrocarbon *n* *chem* hidrocarburo, *m*

hydrochloric *a* clorhídrico. **h. acid,** ácido clorhídrico, *m*

hydrogen *n* hidrógeno, *m*. **h. peroxide,** agua oxigenada, *f*

hydrogenation *n* hidrogenación, *f*

hydrogenize *vt* hidrogenizar

hydrolysis *n* hidrólisis, *f*

hydromel *n* aguamiel, *f*, hidromel, *m*

hydropathic *a* hidropático. **h. establishment,** balneario, *m*

hydrophobia *n* hidrofobia, rabia, *f*

hydrophobic *a* hidrofóbico, rabioso

hydroplane *n* hidroplano, *m*

hydrotherapic *a* hidroterápico

hydrotherapy *n* hidroterapia, *f*

hyena *n* hiena, *f*

hygiene *n* higiene, *f*. **personal h.,** higiene privada, *f*

hygienic *a* higiénico

hymen *n* *anat* himen, *m*; himeneo, *m*

hymeneal *a* nupcial

hymn *n* himno, *m*. **h.-book,** himnario, *m*

hyperbole *n* hipérbole, *f*

hyperbolical *a* hiperbólico

hypercorrection *n* seudocultismo, supercultismo, *m*, ultracorrección, *f*

hypercritic *n* hipercrítico, *m*

hypercritical *a* hipercrítico, criticón

hypersensitive *a* vidrioso, quisquilloso

hypertrophy *n* hipertrofia, *f*. *vi* hipertrofiarse

hyphen *n* guión, *m*

hypnosis *n* hipnosis, *f*

hypnotic *a* hipnótico. *n* (person) hipnótico (-ca); (drug) hipnótico, narcótico, *m*

hypnotism *n* hipnotismo, *m*

hypnotist *n* hipnotizador (-ra)

hypnotization *n* hipnotización, *f*

hypnotize *vt* hipnotizar

hypo *n* (sodium hyposulphite) hiposulfito sólido, *m*

hypochondria *n* hipocondría, *f*

hypochondriac *n* hipocondríaco (-ca)

hypochondriacal *a* hipocondríaco

hypocrisy *n* hipocresía, *f*; mojigatería, gazmoñería, *f*

hypocrite *n* hipócrita, *mf*; mojigato (-ta). **to be a h.,** ser hipócrita

hypocritical *a* hipócrita; mojigato, gazmoño

hypocritically *adv* hipócritamente, con hipocresía

hypodermic *a* hipodérmico. **h. syringe,** jeringa de inyecciones, *f*

hypotenuse *n* *geom* hipotenusa, *f*

hypothesis *n* hipótesis, *f*

hypothetical *a* hipotético

hysterectomy *n* *surg* histerectomía, *f*

hysteria *n* *med* histerismo, *m*; histeria, *f*, ataque de nervios, *m*

hysterical *a* histérico. **to become h.,** tener un ataque de nervios. **hysterics,** *n pl* ataque de nervios, *m*

I

i *n* (letter) i. *1st pers pron* yo. **It is I,** Soy yo. Normally omitted, the verb alone being used except when **yo** is needed for emphasis, e.g. **Hablo a María,** I speak to Mary, *but* **Yo toco el violín, pero Juan toca el piano,** I play the violin, but *John* plays the piano

Iago Yago, *m*

Iberian Peninsula, the la Peninsula Ibérica

Iberian *a* ibero, ibérico. *n* ibero (-ra)

ibex *n* *zool* íbice, *m*

ice *n* hielo, *m*; (ice cream) helado, *m*. *vt* helar; cubrir de hielo; congelar, cuajar; (a cake, etc.) garapiñar, escarchar, alcorzar. **to ice up,** (aer, aut) helarse. **to be as cold as ice,** *inf* estar hecho un hielo. **His words cut no ice,** Sus palabras ni pinchan ni cortan. **ice-age,** edad del hielo, *f*. **ice-ax,** piolet, *m*. **ice-box,** nevera, *f*.

ice-cream, helado, mantecado, *m*. **ice-cream cone,** cucurucho de helado, *m*. **ice-cream freezer,** heladora, *f*. **ice-cream vendor,** mantequero (-ra). **ice-field,** campo de hielo, *m*. **ice-floe,** témpano de hielo flotante, *m*. **ice hockey,** hockey sobre patines, *m*. **ice-pack,** bolsa para hielo, *f*. **ice-skates,** patines de cuchilla, *m pl*. **ice water,** agua helada, *f*

iceberg *n* iceberg, témpano de hielo, banco de hielo, *m*

icebound *a* aprisionado por el hielo; atascado en el hielo; (of roads, etc.) helado

iced *a* helado; congelado, cuajado; (cakes) garapiñado, escarchado; (of drinks) con hielo. **i. drink,** sorbete, *m*

Iceland Islandia, *f*

Icelander *n* islandés (-esa)

icelandic *a* islandes, islándico. *n* (language) islandés, *m*

icicle *n* carámbano, canelón, cerrión, *m*
icily *adv* fríamente; *fig* frígidamente, con indiferencia, con frialdad
iciness *n* frialdad, frigidez, *f*; *fig* indiferencia, frigidez, *f*
icing *n* helada, *f*, hielo, *m*; (on a cake, etc.) alcorza, capa de azúcar, *f*
icon *n* icono, *m*
iconoclast *n* iconoclasta, *mf*
iconoclastic *a* iconoclasta
iconography *n* iconografía, *f*
iconology *n* iconología, *f*
icy *a* helado; glacial, frío; *med* álgido; *fig* indiferente, desabrido; *poet* frígido, gélido
idea *n* idea, *f*, concepto, *m*; (opinion) juicio, *m*, opinión, *f*; (notion) impresión, noción, *f*; (plan) proyecto, plan, designio, *m*. **to form an i. of,** hacerse una idea de, formar un concepto de. **to have an i. of,** tener una idea de; tener nociones de. **An i. struck me,** Se me ocurrió una idea. **full of ideas,** preñado (or lleno) de ideas. **I had no i. that . . .** No tenía la menor idea de que . . . No sabía que . . . **What an i.!** ¡Qué idea!
ideal *a* ideal; excelente, perfecto; (utopian) utópico; (imaginary) imaginario, irreal, ficticio. *n* ideal, *m*; modelo, prototipo, *m*
idealism *n* idealismo, *m*
idealist *n* idealista, *mf*
idealistic *a* idealista
idealization *n* idealización, *f*
idealize *vt* idealizar
ideally *adv* idealmente
ideation *n* *phil* ideación, *f*
idem *adv* ídem
identical *a* idéntico, mismo, igual; muy parecido, semejante
identically *adv* idénticamente
identifiable *a* identificable
identification *n* identificación, *f*. **i. number,** placa de identidad, *f*
identify *vt* identificar. **to i. oneself with,** identificarse con
identity *n* identidad, *f*. **i. card,** cédula personal, *f*; carnet de identidad, *m*. **i. disc,** disco de identidad, *m*
ideogram, ideograph *n* ideograma, *m*
ideography *n* ideografía, *f*
ideological *a* ideológico
ideologist *n* ideólogo (-ga)
ideology *n* ideología, *f*
Ides *n* *pl* idus, *m* *pl*
idiocy *n* idiotez, imbecilidad, *f*; (foolishness) necedad, tontería, sandez, *f*
idiom *n* idiotismo, *m*; modismo, *m*, locución, *f*; (language) habla, *f*; lenguaje, *m*
idiomatic *a* idiomático
idiopathy *n* *med* idiopatía, *f*
idiosyncrasy *n* idiosincrasia, *f*
idiosyncratic *a* idiosincrásico
idiot *n* idiota, imbécil, *mf*; (fool) necio (-ia), tonto (-ta), mentecato (-ta)
idiotic *a* idiota, imbécil; (foolish) necio, tonto, sandío
idle *a* desocupado; indolente, ocioso; (unemployed) cesante, sin empleo; (lazy) perezoso, holgazán; (of machines) parado, inactivo; (useless) vano, inútil, sin efecto; (false) falso, mentiroso, infundado; (stupid) fútil, frívolo. *vi* holgar, estar ocioso; holgazanear, haraganear, gandulear. **to i. away,** malgastar, perder. **to i. away the time,** pasar el rato, matar el tiempo. **i. efforts,** vanos esfuerzos, *m* *pl*. **i. fancies,** ilusiones, fantasías, *f* *pl*, sueños, *m* *pl*. **i. hours,** horas desocupadas, *f* *pl*, ratos perdidos, *m* *pl*. **i. question,** pregunta ociosa, *f*. **i. tale,** cuento de viejas, *m*. **i. threat,** reto vacuo, *m*
idleness *n* ociosidad, indolencia, inacción, *f*; pereza, holgazanería, gandulería, *f*; (uselessness) inutilidad, futilidad, *f*
idler *n* ocioso (-sa); haragán (-ana); perezoso (-sa), holgazán (-ana), gandul (-la)

idly *adv* ociosamente, perezosamente; (uselessly) vanamente
idol *n* ídolo, *m*. **a popular i.,** el ídolo de las masas, *m*
idolater *n* idólatra, *mf*; (admirer) amante, *mf* esclavo (-va), admirador (-ra)
idolatrous *a* idólatra, idolátrico
idolatrously *adv* idolatradamente, con idolatría
idolatry *n* idolatría, *f*; (devotion) adoración, pasión, *f*
idolization *n* idolatría, *f*
idolize *vt* idolatrar, adorar
idyll *n* idilio, *m*
idyllic *a* idílico
if *conjunc* si; (even if) aunque, aun cuando; (whenever) cuando, en caso de que; (whether) si. **as if,** como si (foll. by subjunc.). **If he comes, we shall tell him,** Si viene se lo diremos. **If he had not killed the tiger, she would be dead,** Si él no hubiera matado al tigre, ella estaría muerta. **If ever there was one,** Si alguna vez lo hubiera. **if necessary,** si fuese necesario. **if not,** si no, si no es que (e.g., **Poet and philosopher are twins, if not one and the same,** Poeta y filósofo son hermanos gemelos, si no es que la misma cosa). **If only!** ¡Ojalá que! (foll. by subjunc.)
igloo *n* iglú, *m*
igneous *a* ígneo
ignite *vt* encender, pegar fuego (a), incendiar. *vi* prender fuego, incendiarse; arder
ignition *n* ignición, *f*; *aut* encendido, *m*. **i. coil,** *aut* carrete de inducción del encendido, *m*. **i. key,** *aut* llave del contacto, *f*
ignoble *a* innoble, vil, indigno
ignobly *adv* bajamente, vilmente
ignominious *a* ignominioso
ignominiously *adv* ignominiosamente
ignominy *n* ignominia, deshonra, afrenta, *f*
ignoramus *n* ignorante, *mf*
ignorance *n* ignorancia, *f*; (unawareness) desconocimiento, *m*. **to plead i.,** pretender ignorancia
ignorant *a* ignorante; inculto. **He is an i. fellow,** Es un ignorante. **to be i. of,** no saber, ignorar. **to be very i.,** ser muy ignorante, *inf* ser muy burro
ignorantly *adv* ignorantemente, por ignorancia; neciamente
ignore *vt* no hacer caso de, desatender; (omit) pasar por alto de; *law* rechazar; (pretend not to recognize) hacer semblante de no reconocer; (not recognize) no reconocer
iguana *n* *zool* iguana, *f*
ileac *a* *anat* ilíaco
ileum *n* *anat* íleon, *m*
Iliad *n* Ilíada, *f*
ilium *n* *anat* ilion, *m*
ill *n* mal, *m*. *a* (sick) enfermo, malo; (bad) malo; (unfortunate) desdichado, funesto. *adv* mal. **to be ill,** estar malo. **to be taken ill,** caer enfermo, mal aconsejado; desacertado, imprudente. **ill-advisedly,** imprudentemente. **ill at ease,** incómodo. **ill-bred,** mal criado, mal educado, mal nacido. **ill-breeding,** mala crianza, mala educación, *f*. **ill-disposed,** malintencionado. **ill fame,** mala fama, *f*. **ill-fated,** malhadado, malaventurado, aciago, fatal. **ill-favored,** mal parecido, feúcho. **ill-feeling,** hostilidad, *f*, rencor, *m*. **ill-gotten,** maladquirido. **ill-humor,** mal humor, *m*. **ill-humored,** de mal humor, malhumorado. **ill-luck,** desdicha, mala suerte, malaventura, *f*; infortunio, *m*. **ill-mannered,** mal educado. **ill-natured,** malévolo, perverso. **ill-naturedly,** malignamente. **ill-omened,** nefasto. **ill-spent,** malgastado, perdido. **ill-spoken,** mal hablado. **ill-suited,** malavenido. **ill-timed,** inoportuno, intempestivo. **ill-treat,** maltratar, malparar, tratar mal. **ill-treated,** que ha sido tratado mal; maltrecho. **ill-treatment,** maltratamiento, *m*, crueldad, *f*. **ill-turn,** mala jugada, *f*. **do an ill-turn,** hacer un flaco servicio. **ill will,** mala voluntad, *f*; rencor, *m*, ojeriza, *f*. **to bear a person ill will,** guardarle rencor

illegal *a* ilegal; indebido, ilícito
illegality *n* ilegalidad, *f*
illegally *adv* ilegalmente
illegibility *n* ilegibilidad, *f*
illegible *a* ilegible, indescifrable
illegibly *adv* de un modo ilegible
illegitimacy *n* ilegitimidad, *f;* falsedad, *f*
illegitimate *a* ilegítimo, bastardo; falso; ilícito, desautorizado
illegitimately *adv* ilegítimamente
illiberal *a* iliberal; intolerante, estrecho de miras; (mean) avaro, tacaño, ruin
illiberality *n* iliberalidad, *f;* intolerancia, *f;* (avarice) tacañería, avaricia, ruindad, *f*
illiberally *adv* avariciosamente, ruinmente
illicit *a* ilícito, indebido, ilegal
illicitly *adv* ilícitamente, ilegalmente
illicitness *n* ilicitud, ilegalidad, *f*
illimitable *a* ilimitado, sin límites, infinito
illiteracy *n* analfabetismo, *m*
illiterate *a* and *n* analfabeto (-ta), iliterato (-ta)
illness *n* enfermedad, dolencia, *f,* mal, *m*
illogical *a* ilógico; absurdo, irracional
illogicality *n* falta de lógica, *f;* absurdo, *m,* irracionalidad, *f*
illuminant *a* iluminador, alumbrador
illuminate *vt* iluminar, alumbrar; *art* iluminar; (explain) aclarar, ilustrar
illuminated *a* iluminado, encendido; *art* iluminado. **i. sign,** letrero luminoso, *m*
illuminati *n pl* secta de los alumbrados, *f*
illuminating *a* iluminador; (explanatory) aclaratorio. *n art* iluminación, *f*
illumination *n* iluminación, *f,* alumbrado, *m;* (for decoration) luminaria, *f; art* iluminación, *f; fig* inspiración, *f*
illuminator *n art* iluminador (-ra)
illumine *vt* encender, alumbrar; *fig* inspirar
illusion *n* ilusión, *f,* engaño, *m;* (dream) esperanza, ilusión, *f,* ensueño, *m.* **to harbor illusions,** tener ilusiones
illusive *a* ilusivo, engañoso, falso
illusively *adv* falsamente, aparentemente
illusoriness *n* ilusión, falsedad, *f,* engaño, *m*
illusory *a* ilusorio, deceptivo, falso, irreal
illustrate *vt* ilustrar, aclarar, explicar, elucidar; *art* ilustrar; (prove) probar, demostrar
illustration *n* ejemplo, *m;* ilustración, *f; art* grabado, *m;* estampa, *f;* (explanation) elucidación, aclaración, *f*
illustrative *a* ilustrativo, ilustrador, explicativo, aclaratorio
illustrator *n* ilustrador (-ra), grabador (-ra)
illustrious *a* ilustre, famoso, renombrado, distinguido
illustriously *adv* ilustremente, noblemente
illustriousness *n* eminencia, *f,* renombre, *m,* grandeza, *f*
image *n* (optics) imagen, *f;* efigie, imagen, *f;* (religious) imagen, estatua, *f; art* figura, *f;* (metaphor) metáfora, expresión, *f;* (of a person) retrato, *m.* **to be the i. of,** ser el retrato de. **sharp i.,** imagen nítida, *f.* **i. breaker,** iconoclasta, *mf.* **i. vendor,** vendedor (-ra) de imágenes
imagery *n art* imaginería, *f;* (style) metáforas, *f pl*
imaginable *a* imaginable
imaginary *a* imaginario; fantástico, de ensueño
imagination *n* imaginación, *f;* imaginativa, fantasía, inventiva, *f,* ingenio, *m*
imaginative *a* imaginativo; fantástico
imagine *vt* imaginar, concebir; idear, proyectar, inventar; figurarse, suponer. **Just i.!** ¡Imagínese usted!
imam *n* imán, *m*
imbecile *a* imbécil; (foolish) necio, estúpido, tonto. *n* imbécil, *mf;* (fool) necio (-ia), tonto (-ta), estúpido (-da)
imbecility *n* imbecilidad, *f;* (folly) necedad, sandez, *f*
imbibe *vt* embeber, absorber; (drink) sorber, chupar; empaparse de

imbibing *n* imbibición, absorción, *f*
imbricate *a* (zool, bot) imbricado
imbroglio *n* embrollo, lío, *m*
imbue *vt* imbuir, calar, empapar; teñir. **to i. with,** infundir de
imitable *a* imitable
imitate *vt* imitar; copiar, reproducir; (counterfeit) contrahacer
imitation *n* imitación, *f;* copia, *f;* remedo, traslado, *m. a* imitado; falso, artificial
imitative *a* imitativo; imitador
imitativeness *n* facultad imitativa (or de imitacion), *f*
imitator *n* imitador (-ra); contrahacedor (-ra), falsificador (-ra)
immaculate *a* inmaculado, puro; (of dress) elegante. **I. Conception,** la Purísima Concepción
immaculately *adv* inmaculadamente; elegantemente
immaculateness *n* pureza, *f;* (of dress) elegancia, *f*
immanence *n* inmanencia, inherencia, *f*
immanent *a* inmanente; inherente
immaterial *a* inmaterial, incorpóreo; sin importancia. **It is i. to me,** Me es indiferente, No me importa, Me da lo mismo, Me da igual
immateriality *n* inmaterialidad, *f*
immature *a* inmaturo; precoz; (of fruit) verde
immaturity *n* falta de madurez, *f;* precocidad, *f*
immeasurability *n* inmensurabilidad, inmensidad, *f*
immeasurable *a* inmensurable, inmenso, imponderable
immeasurably *adv* inmensamente, enormemente
immediate *a* (of place) inmediato, cercano, contiguo; (of time) próximo, inmediato, directo; (of action) inmediato, perentorio; (on letters) urgente. **to take i. action,** tomar acción inmediata
immediately *adv* (of place) próximamente, contiguamente; (of time) luego, seguidamente, en el acto, ahora mismo, enseguida; directamente; (as soon as) así que
immemorial *a* inmemorial, inmemorable
immemorially *adv* desde tiempo inmemorial
immense *a* inmenso, enorme; vasto, extenso; infinito
immensely *adv* inmensamente, enormemente
immensity *n* inmensidad, *f;* extensión, vastedad, *f*
immerse *vt* sumergir, hundir en, zambullir; bautizar por sumersión. *fig* **to be immersed in,** estar absorto en
immersion *n* sumersion, *f,* hundimiento, *m;* *ast* inmersión, *f*
immigrant *a* and *n* inmigrante, *mf*
immigrate *vi* inmigrar
immigration *n* inmigración, *f*
imminence *n* inminencia, *f*
imminent *a* inminente
immobile *a* inmóvil, inmoble; impasible, imperturbable
immobility *n* inmovilidad, *f;* impasibilidad, imperturbabilidad, *f*
immobilization *n* inmovilización, *f*
immobilize *vt* inmovilizar
immoderate *a* inmoderado, excesivo, indebido
immoderately *adv* inmoderadamente, excesivamente
immoderateness *n* inmoderación, *f,* exceso, *m*
immodest *a* inmodesto; indecente, deshonesto; (pert) atrevido, descarado
immodestly *adv* impúdicamente, inmodestamente
immodesty *n* inmodestia, impudicia, *f;* deshonestidad, licencia, *f;* (forwardness) descaro, atrevimiento, *m*
immolate *vt* inmolar, sacrificar
immolation *n* inmolación, *f,* sacrificio, *m*
immolator *n* inmolador (-ra)
immoral *a* inmoral; licencioso, vicioso; incontinente
immorality *n* inmoralidad, *f*
immortal *a* inmortal; perenne, eterno, imperecedero. *n* inmortal, *mf*
immortality *n* inmortalidad, *f;* fama inmortal, *f*
immortalize *vt* inmortalizar, perpetuar

immortally *adv* inmortalmente, eternamente, para siempre

immovability *n* inamovibilidad, inmovilidad, *f*; (of purpose) inflexibilidad, tenacidad, constancia, *f*

immovable *a* inmoble, fijo, inmóvil; (of purpose) inconmovible, inalterable, constante. *n pl.* **immovables** *law* bienes inmuebles, *m pl. ecc* **i. feast,** fiesta fija, *f*

immovably *adv* inmóvilmente, fijamente

immune *a* inmune, libre; *med* inmune. **i. from,** exento de; libre de

immunity *n* inmunidad, libertad, *f*; exención, *f*; *med* inmunidad, *f*

immunization *n med* inmunización, *f*

immunize *vt* inmunizar

immure *vt* emparedar, recluir, encerrar

immutability *n* inmutabilidad, inalterabilidad, *f*

immutable *a* inmutable, inalterable, constante

immutably *adv* inmutablemente

imp *n* trasgo, diablillo, duende, *m*; (child) picaruelo (-la)

impact *n* impacto, *m*, impacción, *f*; choque, *m*, colisión, *f*

impair *vt* perjudicar, echar a perder, deteriorar, empeorar, desmejorar. **to be impaired,** deteriorarse, perjudicarse

impairment *n* deterioración, perjuicio, empeoramiento, *m*

impale *vt* (punishment) empalar; (with a sword) atravesar, espetar

impalement *n* (punishment) empalamiento, *m*; atravesamiento, *m*, transfixión, *f*

impalpability *n* impalpabilidad, intangibilidad, *f*

impalpable *a* impalpable, intangible; incorpóreo

impart *vt* comunicar, dar parte (de); conferir

impartial *a* imparcial, ecuánime

impartiality *n* imparcialidad, ecuanimidad, entereza, *f*, desinterés, *m*

impartially *adv* imparcialmente, con desinterés

impassability *n* impracticabilidad, *f*

impassable *a* intransitable, impracticable; (of water) invadeable

impasse *n* callejón sin salida, *m*

impassibility *n* impasibilidad, imperturbabilidad, indiferencia, *f*

impassible *a* impasible, insensible; indiferente, imperturbable

impassion *vt* apasionar, conmover

impassioned *a* apasionado, vehemente, ardiente

impassive *a* impasible, insensible; indiferente, imperturbable; apático

impassively *adv* indiferentemente

impassivity *n* impasibilidad, *f*; indiferencia, *f*; apatía, *f*

impatience *n* impaciencia, *f*

impatient *a* impaciente; intolerante. **to make i.,** impacientar. **to grow i.,** impacientarse, perder la paciencia. **to grow i. at,** impacientarse ante. **to grow i. to,** impacientarse a or por. **to grow i. under,** impacientarse bajo

impatiently *adv* con impaciencia, impacientemente

impeach *vt law* denunciar, delatar, acusar, hacer juicio político (Argentina); censurar, criticar, tachar

impeachable *a law* delatable, denunciable, acusable; censurable

impeacher *n* acusador (-ra), denunciador (-ra), delator (-ra)

impeachment *n law* acusación, denuncia, *f*; reproche, *m*, queja, *f*

impeccability *n* (perfection) impecabilidad, perfección, *f*; elegancia, *f*

impeccable *a* impecable, intachable, perfecto; elegante

impeccably *adv* perfectamente; elegantemente

impecuniosity *n* indigencia, probreza, *f*

impecunious *a* indigente, pobre

impede *vt* impedir, obstruir, estorbar; *fig* dificultar, embarazar

impediment *n* obstáculo, estorbo, *m*; *fig* dificultad, *f*; *law* impedimento, *m*. **to have an i. in one's speech,** tener una dificultad en el hablar

impel *vt* impulsar, impeler; *fig* estimular, obligar, mover, constreñir. **I felt impelled (to),** Me sentí obligado (a)

impend *vi* ser inminente, amenazar

impending *a* inminente, pendiente

impenetrability *n* impenetrabilidad, *f*; *fig* enigma, secreto, misterio, *m*

impenetrable *a* impenetrable; intransitable; denso, espeso; *fig* enigmático, insondable, secreto

impenetrably *adv* impenetrablemente, densamente

impenitence *n* impenitencia, *f*

impenitent *a* impenitente, incorregible

impenitently *adv* sin penitencia

imperative *a* imperioso, perentorio; *gram* imperativo; (necessary) esencial, urgente. *n* mandato, *m*, orden, *f*; *gram* imperativo, *m*. **in the i.,** en el imperativo

imperatively *adv* imperativamente

imperativeness *n* perentoriedad, *f*; urgencia, importancia, *f*

imperceptible *a* imperceptible, insensible

imperceptibly *adv* imperceptiblemente

imperceptive *a* insensible

imperfect *a* imperfecto; incompleto, defectuoso. *a* and *n gram* imperfecto *m*

imperfection *n* imperfección, *f*; defecto, desperfecto, *m*; falta, tacha, *f*

imperfectly *adv* imperfectamente

imperial *a* imperial, imperatorio. *n* (beard) pera, *f.* **i. preference,** preferencia dentro del Imperio, *f*

imperialism *n* imperialismo, *m*

imperialist *n* imperialista, *mf*

imperialistic *a* imperialista

imperil *vt* arriesgar, poner en peligro, aventurar

imperious *a* imperioso, altivo, arrogante; (pressing) urgente, apremiante

imperiously *adv* imperiosamente, con arrogancia

imperiousness *n* autoridad, arrogancia, altivez, *f*; necesidad, urgencia, *f*, apremio, *m*

imperishability *n* (immortality) inmortalidad, perennidad, *f*

imperishable *a* imperecedero, inmarchitable, perenne, eterno

impermanence *n* inestabilidad, interinidad, *f*; brevedad, fugacidad, *f*

impermanent *a* interino, no permanente

impermeability *n* impermeabilidad, *f*

impermeable *a* impermeable

impersonal *a* impersonal, objetivo; *gram* impersonal

impersonality *n* objetividad, *f*

impersonally *adv* impersonalmente

impersonate *vt* personificar, simbolizar; *theat* representar

impersonation *n* personificación, simbolización, *f*; *theat* representación, *f*

impertinence *n* impertinencia, majadería, insolencia, *f*; inoportunidad, *f*; despropósito, *m*

impertinent *a* impertinente, insolente; (unseasonable) intempestivo, inoportuno; (irrelevant) fuera de propósito

impertinently *adv* con insolencia, impertinentemente

imperturbability *n* imperturbabilidad, serenidad, impasibilidad, *f*; impavidez, *f*

imperturbable *a* imperturbable, impasible, sereno; impávido

imperturbably *adv* con serenidad, imperturbablemente

impervious *a* impermeable, impenetrable; *fig* insensible. **He is i. to arguments,** No hace caso de argumentos

imperviousness *n* impermeabilidad, impenetrabilidad, *f*; *fig* insensibilidad, *f*

impetigo *n med* impétigo, *m*

impetuosity *n* impetuosidad, temeridad, irreflexión, *f*

impetuous *a* impetuoso, temerario, irreflexivo; violento, vehemente

impetuously *adv* impetuosamente; con vehemencia

impetus *n mech* ímpetu, *m*, impulsión, *f; fig* incentivo, estímulo, impulso, *m*

impiety *n* impiedad, irreligión, irreligiosidad, *f*

impinge (upon) *vi* chocar con, tropezar con

impious *a* impío, irreligioso, sacrílego; (wicked) malvado, perverso, malo

impish *a* travieso, revoltoso, enredador

implacability *n* implacabilidad, *f*

implacable *a* implacable, inexorable, inflexible, riguroso

implacably *adv* implacablemente

implant *vt fig* implantar, inculcar, instilar

implantation *n fig* implantación, instilación, inculcación, *f*

implement *n* instrumento, utensilio, *m*, herramienta, *f;* (of war) elemento, *m*. *vt* cumplir, hacer efectivo; llevar a cabo

implicate *vt* enredar, envolver; (imply) implicar, contener, llevar en sí; (in a crime) comprometer. **to be implicated in a crime,** estar implicado en un crimen.

implication *n* implicación, inferencia, repercusión, sugestión, *f;* (in a crime) complicidad, *f*

implicit *a* implícito, virtual, tácito; (absolute) ciego, absoluto, implícito. **with i. faith,** con fe ciega

implicitness *n* carácter implícito, *m*, lo implícito

implied *a* tácito, implícito

implore *vt* implorar, suplicar

imploring *a* suplicante, implorante

imploringly *adv* con encarecimiento, a súplica, de un modo suplicante

imply *vt* implicar, indicar, presuponer; (mean) querer decir, significar; (hint) insinuar, sugerir

impolicy *n* indiscreción, imprudencia, impolítica, *f*

impolite *a* descortés, mal educado

impolitely *adv* con descortesía

impoliteness *n* descortesía, falta de urbanidad, *f*

impolitic *a* impolítico

imponderability *n* imponderabilidad, *f*

imponderable *a* imponderable

import *vt com* importar; (mean) significar, querer decir. *a com* importado, de importación. *n com* importación, *f;* (meaning) significado, sentido, *m;* (value) importe, valor, *m;* (contents) contenido, tenor, *m;* importancia, *f.* **i. duty,** derechos de importación derechos de entrada, *m pl,* gravamen a la importación, *m.* **i. licence,** permiso de importación, *m.* **i. trade,** negocios de importación, *m pl*

importable *a* importable, que se puede importar

importance *n* importancia, *f;* valor, alcance, *m,* magnitud, *f;* consideración, eminencia, *f.* **to be fully conscious of one's i.,** tener plena conciencia de su importancia

important *a* importante; distinguido; presuntuoso, vanidoso. **to be i.,** importar, ser importante. **i. person,** personaje, *m,* persona importante, *f*

importantly *adv* importantemente, con importancia

importation *n* importación, *f; com* introducción (or importación) de géneros extranjeros, *f*

importer *n* importador (-ra)

importunate *a* (of a demand) insistente, importuno; (of persons) impertinente, pesado

importunately *adv* importunadamente

importune *vt* importunar, asediar, perseguir

importuning *n* persecución, importunación, *f*

importunity *n* importunidad, insistencia, impertinencia, *f*

impose *vt* (on, upon) imponer, infligir, cargar; *print* imponer. *vi* (on, upon) (deceive) engañar, embaucar

imposing *a* imponente, impresionante; (of persons) majestuoso, importante

imposition *n* imposición, *f;* (burden) impuesto, tributo, *m,* carga, *f;* (print, etc.) imposición, *f;* (trick) fraude, engaño, *m,* decepción, *f*

impossibility *n* imposibilidad, *f*

impossible *a* imposible. **Nothing is i.,** No hay nada imposible, *inf* De menos nos hizo Dios. **to do the i.,** hacer lo imposible

impost *n* impuesto, *m,* contribución, gabela, *f*

impostor *n* impostor (-ra), bribón (-ona), embustero (-ra)

imposture *n* impostura, *f,* engaño, fraude, *m*

impotence *n* impotencia, *f*

impotent *a* impotente

impound *vt* acorralar; (water) embalsar; (goods) confiscar

impoverish *vt* empobrecer, depauperar, arruinar; (health) debilitar; (land) agotar

impoverished *a* indigente, necesitado; (of land) agotado

impoverishment *n* empobrecimiento, *m,* ruina, *f;* (of land) agotamiento, *m*

impracticability *n* impracticabilidad, imposibilidad, *f*

impracticable *a* impracticable, no factible, imposible

imprecation *n* imprecación, maldición, *f*

imprecatory *a* imprecatorio, maldiciente

impregnable *a* inexpugnable, inconquistable

impregnate *vt* impregnar, empapar; *biol* fecundar. **to become impregnated,** impregnarse

impregnation *n* impregnación, *f; biol* fecundación, fertilización, *f; fig* inculcación, *f*

impresario *n* empresario, *m*

imprescriptible *a* imprescriptible, inalienable

impress *vt* imprimir; (on the mind) impresionar; inculcar, imbuir; (with respect) imponer; *mil* reclutar; (of goods) confiscar. *n* impresión, marca, señal, huella, *f*

impression *n* impresión, *f;* marca, señal, huella, *f; print* impresión, *f;* efecto, *m;* idea, noción, *f.* **He has the i. that they do not like him,** Sospecha que no les es simpático. **to be under the i.,** tener la impresión

impressionability *n* susceptibilidad, sensibilidad, *f*

impressionable *a* susceptible, impresionable, sensitivo

impressionism *n* impresionismo, *m*

impressionist *n* impresionista, *mf*

impressionistic *a* impresionista

impressive *a* impresionante; emocionante; imponente, majestuoso; enfático

impressively *adv* solemnemente, de modo impresionante; enfáticamente

impressiveness *n* efecto impresionante, *m;* grandiosidad, pompa, *f;* majestuosidad, *f;* fuerza, *f*

imprint *n* impresión, señal, marca, huella, *f; print* pie de imprenta, *m.* *vt* imprimir; (on the mind) grabar, fijar

imprison *vt* encerrar, encarcelar, aprisionar

imprisonment *n* encarcelación, prisión, *f,* encierro, *m*

improbability *n* improbabilidad, *f;* inverosimilitud, *f*

improbable *a* improbable; inverosímil

improbity *n* improbidad, *f*

improvable *a* mejorable, perfectible

improve *vt* mejorar; perfeccionar; (beautify) embellecer, hermosear; (land) bonificar; *lit* corregir, enmendar; (cultivate) cultivar; (increase) aumentar; (an opportunity) aprovechar; (strengthen) fortificar; (business) sacar provecho de, explotar. *vi* mejorar; perfeccionarse; (progress) hacer progresos, progresar, adelantarse; *com* subir; (become beautiful) hacerse hermoso, embellecerse; (increase) aumentarse. **to i. upon,** mejorar, perfeccionar; pulir

improvement *n* mejora, *f;* perfeccionamiento, *m;* aumento, *m;* adelantamiento, progreso, *m;* (in health) mejoría, *f*; embellecimiento, *m*; cultivación, *f*; (of land) abono, *m*

improver *n* aprendiz (-za)

improvidence *n* imprevisión, *f*; improvidencia, *f*

improvident *a* impróvido, desprevenido

improvidently *adv* impróvidamente

improvisation *n* improvisación, *f*

improvise *vt* improvisar

improviser *n* improvisador (-ra)

imprudence *n* imprudencia, *f*; desacierto, *m*, indiscreción, *f*

imprudent *a* imprudente; desacertado, indiscreto, mal avisado, irreflexivo

imprudently *adv* imprudentemente; sin pensar

impudence *n* impudencia, *f*, descaro, *m*, insolencia, desvergüenza, *f*, atrevimiento, *m*

impudent *a* impudente, descarado, insolente, desvergonzado, atrevido

impudently *adv* descaradamente, con insolencia

impugn *vt* impugnar, contradecir, atacar

impugnable *a* impugnable, atacable

impugnment *n* impugnación, *f*

impulse *n* ímpetu, *m*, impulsión, *f*; impulso, estímulo, *m*; incitación, instigación, *f*; motivo, *m*; (fit) arranque, arrebato, acceso, *m*

impulsion *n* ímpetu, *m*, impulsión, *f*; empuje, *m*, arranque, *m*

impulsive *a* impelente; irreflexivo, impulsivo

impulsively *adv* por impulso

impulsiveness *n* irreflexión, *f*; carácter impulsivo, *m*

impunity *n* impunidad, *f*. **with i.,** impunemente

impure *a* impuro; adulterado, mezclado; (indecent) deshonesto, indecente; (dirty) turbio, sucio

impurity *n* impureza, *f*; adulteración, mezcla, *f*; deshonestidad, liviandad, *f*; suciedad, turbiedad, *f*

imputable *a* imputable, atribuible

imputation *n* imputación, atribución, *f*; (in a bad sense) acusación, *f*, reproche, *m*

impute *vt* imputar, achacar, atribuir; acusar, reprochar

imputer *n* imputador (-ra); recriminador (-ra), acusador (-ra)

in *prep* en; a; (of duration) durante, mientras; (with) con; (through) por; dentro de; (under) bajo; (following a superlative) de; (of specified time) dentro de, de aquí a; (with afternoon, etc.) por; (out of) sobre. **course in medieval Catalan literature,** curso de literatura catalana medioeval. **dressed in black,** vestido de negro. **in London,** en Londres. **in the morning,** por la mañana; (in the course of) durante la mañana. **in time,** a tiempo; dentro de algún tiempo. **in a week,** dentro de una semana. **in the best way,** del mejor modo. **in writing,** por escrito. **in anger,** con enojo. **in one's hand,** en la mano. **in addition to,** además de, a más de. **in case,** por si acaso, en caso de que. **in order to,** a fin de, para (foll. by infin.). **in order that,** para que (foll. by subjunc.). **in so far as,** en cuanto. **in spite of,** a pesar de. **in the distance,** a lo lejos, en lontananza. **in the meantime,** entre tanto. **in the middle of,** en el medio de; a la mitad de. **in the style of,** al modo de; a la manera de, a la (francesa, etc.)

in *adv* adentro, dentro; (at home) en casa; (of sun) escondido; (of fire) alumbrado; (in power) en el poder; (of harvest) cosechado; (of boats) entrado (with haber); (of trains) llegado (with haber). **to be in,** estar dentro; haber llegado; estar en casa. **to be in for,** estar expuesto a, correr el riesgo de. **to be in with a person,** ser muy amigo de, estar muy metido con. **Come in!** ¡Adelante!; ¡Pase usted! **ins and outs,** sinuosidades, *f pl*; (of river) meandros, *m pl*; (of an affair) pormenores, detalles, *m pl*. **in less time than you can say Jack Robinson,** en menos de Jesús, en un credo, en menos que canta un gallo, en menos que se persigna un cura loco. **in the middle of nowhere,** donde Cristo dio las tres voces, (Western Hemisphere) donde el diablo perdió el poncho.

in *a* interno. **in-law** (of relations) político. **in-patient,** enfermo (-ma) de hospital

inability *n* incapacidad, inhabilidad, ineptitud, incompetencia, *f*; impotencia, *f*

inaccessibility *n* inaccesibilidad, *f*

inaccessible *a* inaccesible

inaccuracy *n* inexactitud, incorrección, *f*

inaccurate *a* inexacto, incorrecto

inaccurately *adv* inexactamente, erróneamente

inaction *n* inacción, *f*

inactive *a* inactivo, pasivo; (of things) inerte; (lazy) perezoso, indolente; (machinery) parado; (motionless) inmóvil; (at leisure) desocupado, sin empleo

inactivity *n* inactividad, pasividad, *f*; (of things) inercia, *f*; pereza, indolencia, *f*; (of machinery) paro, *m*; inmovilidad, *f*; (leisure) desocupación, *f*

inadaptable *a* inadaptable, no adaptable

inadequacy *n* insuficiencia, escasez, *f*; imperfección, *f*, defecto, *m*

inadequate *a* inadecuado, insuficiente, escaso; imperfecto, defectuoso

inadequately *adv* inadecuadamente

inadmissible *a* inadmisible, no admisible

inadvertence *n* inadvertencia, *f*; equivocación, *f*, descuido, *m*

inadvertent *a* inadvertido, accidental, casual; negligente

inadvertently *adv* inadvertidamente, sin querer

inalienability *n* inalienabilidad, *f*

inalienable *a* inajenable, inalienable

inalterability *n* inalterabilidad, *f*

inalterable *a* inalterable

inalterably *adv* inalterablemente, sin alteración

inane *a* lelo, fatuo, vacío, necio

inanimate *a* (of matter) inanimado; sin vida, exánime, muerto

inanition *n* inanición, *f*

inanity *n* vacuidad, fatuidad, necedad, *f*

inappeasable *a* implacable, riguroso

inapplicability *n* no aplicabilidad, *f*

inapplicable *a* inaplicable

inapposite *a* fuera de propósito, no pertinente, inoportuno

inappreciable *a* inapreciable, imperceptible

inappreciation *n* falta de apreciación, *f*

inappreciative *a* desagradecido, ingrato. **i. of,** insensible a, indiferente a

inapproachable *a* inaccesible, huraño, adusto

inappropriate *a* impropio, inconveniente, inadecuado, incongruente; inoportuno

inappropriately *adv* impropiamente; inoportunamente

inappropriateness *n* impropiedad, inconveniencia, incongruencia, *f*; inoportunidad, *f*

inapt *a* inepto, inhábil; impropio

inaptitude *n* ineptitud, inhabilidad, *f*; impropiedad, *f*

inarticulate *a* (of speech) inarticulado; (reticent) inexpresivo, reservado; indistinto; *anat* inarticulado

inarticulately *adv* indistintamente, de un modo inarticulado

inarticulateness *n* tartamudez, *f*; inexpresión, reserva, *f*; silencio, *m*

inartistic *a* antiartístico, antiestético

inartistically *adv* sin gusto (estético)

inasmuch (as) *adv* puesto que, visto que, dado que

inattention *n* desatención, inaplicación, abstracción, *f*; falta de solicitud, *f*

inattentive *a* desatento, distraído; poco solícito, no atento

inattentively *adv* sin atención, distraídamente

inaudibility *n* imposibilidad de oír, *f*

inaudible *a* inaudible, no audible, ininteligible

inaudibly *adv* indistintamente, de modo inaudible

inaugurate *vt* inaugurar; (open) estrenar, abrir, dedicar; (install) investir, instalar; (initiate) originar, iniciar, dar lugar (a)

inauguration *n* inauguración, *f*; (opening) estreno, *m*, apertura, *f*; (investiture) instalación, investidura, *f*

inauspicious *a* poco propicio, desfavorable; ominoso, triste, infeliz

inauspiciously *adv* en condiciones desfavorables, desfavorablemente; infelizmente, bajo malos auspicios

inauspiciousness *n* condiciones desfavorables, *f pl*; infelicidad, *f*; malos auspicios, *m pl*

inborn *a* innato, instintivo

inbred *a* innato, inherente, instintivo

Inca *a* incaico, de los incas. *n* inca, *m*

incalculability *n* imposibilidad de calcular, *f*; (of persons) volubilidad, veleidad, *f*; infinidad, immensidad, *f*

incalculable *a* incalculable, innumerable; (of persons) voluble, veleidoso, caprichoso; infinito, immenso

incalculably *adv* enormemente, infinitamente; caprichosamente

incandescence *n* incandescencia, candencia, *f*

incandescent *a* incandescente, candente. **i. light,** luz incandescente, *f*. **to make i.,** encandecer

incantation *n* hechizo, *m*, encantación, *f*, ensalmo, *m*

incapability *n* incapacidad, *f*; inhabilidad, ineptitud, incompetencia, *f*

incapable *a* incapaz; inhábil, incompetente; (physically) imposibilitado

incapacitate *vt* imposibilitar, incapacitar, inutilizar; (disqualify) inhabilitar, incapacitar

incapacitation *n* inhabilitación, *f*

incapacity *n* incapacidad, inhabilidad, *f*

incarcerate *vt* encarcelar

incarceration *n* encarcelación, prisión, *f*

incarnate *a* encarnado. *vt* encarnar

incarnation *n* encarnación, *f*

incautious *a* incauto, imprudente

incautiously *adv* incautamente

incautiousness *n* imprudencia, negligencia, falta de cautela, *f*

incendiary *a* incendiario. **i. bomb,** incendiaria, *f*

incense *n* incienso, *m*; *fig* adulación, *f*. *vt ecc* incensar; (annoy) irritar, exasperar, enojar. **i. burner,** incensario, *m*

incentive *n* incentivo, estímulo, motivo, *m*. *a* estimulador, incitativo

inception *n* comienzo, principio, *m*; inauguración, *f*

incertitude *n* incertidumbre, *f*

incessant *a* incesante, continuo, constante

incessantly *adv* incesantemente, sin cesar

incest *n* incesto, *m*

incestuous *a* incestuoso

inch *n* pulgada, *f*. **every i. a man,** hombre hecho y derecho. **Not an i.!** ¡Ni pizca! **within an i. of,** a dos dedos de. **i. by i.,** palmo a palmo, paso a paso. **i. tape,** cinta métrica, *f*

inchoate *a* rudimentario; imperfecto, incompleto

incidence *n* incidencia, *f*

incident *a* propio, característico, incidental. *n* incidente, acontecimiento, *m*, ocurrencia, *f*

incident of navigation *n* accidente de navegación, *m*

incidental *a* incidente, incidental; accidental, accesorio, no esencial. **i. expense,** gasto imprevisto, *m*

incidentally *adv* (secondarily) incidentalmente; (by the way) de propósito

incinerate *vt* incinerar

incineration *n* incineración, cremación, *f*

incinerator *n* incinerador, *m*

incipient *a* incipiente, naciente, rudimentario

incise *vt* cortar; *art* grabar, tajar

incision *n* incisión, *f*; corte, tajo, *m*; *med* abscisión, *f*

incisive *a* (of mind) agudo, penetrante; (of words) mordaz, incisivo, punzante

incisively *adv* en pocas palabras; mordazmente, incisivamente

incisiveness *n* (of mind) agudeza, penetración, *f*; (of words) mordacidad, *f*, sarcasmo, *m*

incisor *n* diente incisivo, *m*

incite *vt* incitar, estimular, animar; provocar, tentar. **to i. to,** mover a, incitar a

incitement *n* incitación, instigación, *f*; estímulo, *m*; tentación, *f*; aliciente, *m*

incivility *n* incivilidad, descortesía, *f*

inclemency *n* inclemencia, *f*, rigor, *m*

inclement *a* inclemente, riguroso, borrascoso

inclination *n* inclinación, *f*; (slope) declive, *m*, pendiente, cuesta, *f*; (tendency) propensión, tendencia, *f*; (liking) afición, *f*; amor, *m*; (bow) reverencia, *f*; *geom* inclinación, *f*

incline *vt* inclinar, torcer; doblar; (cause) inclinar (a), hacer. *vi* inclinarse, torcerse; (tend) tender, propender, inclinarse; (colors) tirar (a). *n* declive, *m*, pendiente, cuesta, inclinación, *f*. **I am inclined to believe it,** Me inclino a creerlo. **I am inclined to do it,** Estoy por hacerlo, Creo que lo haré

inclined *a* torcido, inclinado, doblado; *fig* propenso, adicto. **i. plane,** plano inclinado, *m*

include *vt* incluir, contener, encerrar; comprender, abrazar

including *present part* incluso, inclusive. **not i.,** no comprendido

inclusion *n* inclusión, *f*

inclusive *a* inclusivo. **January 2 to January 12 i.,** del 2 al 12 de enero, ambos inclusivos. **not i. of,** sin contar, exclusivo de. **i. of,** que incluye. **i. terms,** todo incluido, todos los gastos incluidos

incognito *a* and *adv* and *n* incógnito, *m*.

incoherence *n* incoherencia, inconsecuencia, *f*

incoherent *a* incoherente, inconexo, inconsecuente. **an i. piece of writing,** un escrito sin pies ni cabeza

incoherently *adv* con incoherencia

incombustibility *n* incombustibilidad, *f*

incombustible *a* incombustible

income *n* renta, *f*, ingreso, *m*; *com* rédito, *m*. **i.-tax,** impuesto de utilidades, *m*. **i.-tax commissioners,** inspectores de impuestos de utilidades, *m pl*. **i.-tax return,** declaración de utilidades, *f*

incoming *a* entrante; nuevo. *n* entrada, llegada, *f*. *n pl* **incomings,** ingresos, *m pl*

incommensurability *n* inconmensurabilidad, *f*

incommensurable *a* inconmensurable, no conmensurable

incommensurate *a* desproporcionado, desmedido

incommode *vt* incomodar, molestar, fastidiar

incommodious *a* estrecho; incómodo, inconveniente

incommodiousness *n* estrechez, *f*; incomodidad, *f*

incommunicable *a* incommunicable, indecible, inexplicable

incommunicative *a* insociable, intratable, adusto, huraño

incomparable *a* incomparable; sin par, sin igual, excelente

incomparableness *n* excelencia, perfección, *f*

incomparably *adv* incomparablemente, con mucho

incompatibility *n* incompatibilidad, *f*

incompatible *a* incompatible

incompetence *n* incompetencia, ineptitud, inhabilidad, *f*; *law* incapacidad, *f*

incompetent *a* incompetente, incapaz, inepto, inhábil; *law* incapaz

incompetently *adv* inhábilmente

incomplete *a* incompleto; imperfecto, defectuoso; (unfinished) sin terminar, inacabado, inconcluso. **incomplete sentence,** frase que queda colgando, *f*

incompletely *adv* incompletamente; imperfectamente

incompleteness *n* estado incompleto, *m*; imperfección, *f*; inconclusión, *f*

incomprehensibility *n* incomprensibilidad, *f*

incomprehensible *a* incomprensible

incomprehension *n* incomprensión, falta de comprensión, *f*

inconceivable *a* inconcebible, inimaginable

inconclusive *a* inconcluyente, cuestionable, dudoso, no convincente

inconclusiveness *n* carácter inconcluso, *m*, falta de conclusiones, *f*

incongruity *n* incongruencia, desproporción, disonancia, *f*

incongruous *a* incongruente, incongruo; chocante, desproporcionado, disonante

incongruously *adv* incongruentemente, incongruamente

inconsequence *n* inconsecuencia, *f*

inconsequent, inconsequential *a* inconsecuente, ilógico; inconsistente

inconsiderable *a* insignificante

inconsiderate *a* desconsiderado, irreflexivo, irrespetuoso

inconsiderately *adv* sin consideración, desconsideradamente

inconsiderateness *n* desconsideración, falta de respeto, *f*

inconsistency *n* inconsistencia, inconsecuencia, incompatibilidad, contradicción, anomalía, *f*

inconsistent *a* inconsistente, inconsiguiente, incompatible, contradictorio, anómalo

inconsistently *adv* contradictoriamente

inconsolable *a* inconsolable, desconsolado. **to be i.,** estar inconsolable, (*inf* of a woman) estar hecha una Magdalena

inconsolably *adv* desconsoladamente

inconspicuous *a* que no llama la atención; insignificante, humilde, modesto

inconspicuously *adv* humildemente, modestamente

inconspicuousness *n* modestia, humildad, *f*

inconstancy *n* inconstancia, movilidad, *f*; mudanza, veleidad, *f*

inconstant *a* inconstante, mudable, variable; veleidoso, volátil, voluble

incontestable *a* incontestable, evidente, indisputable

incontinence *n* incontinencia, *f*

incontinent *a* incontinente

incontrollable *a* ingobernable, indomable

incontrovertible *a* incontrovertible, incontrastable

inconvenience *n* incomodidad, inconveniencia, *f*; (of time) inoportunidad, *f*. *vt* incomodar, causar inconvenientes (a)

inconvenient *a* incómodo, inconveniente, molesto, embarazoso; (of time) inoportuno. **at an i. time,** a deshora

inconveniently *adv* incómodamente; (of time) inoportunamente

incorporate *vt* incorporar, agregar; comprender, incluir, encerrar. *vi* asociarse, incorporarse. *a* incorpóreo, inmaterial; incorporado, asociado

incorporation *n* incorporación, agregación, *f*; asociación, *f*

incorporeal *a* incorpóreo, inmaterial

incorporeity *n* incorporeidad, inmaterialidad, *f*

incorrect *a* incorrecto; inexacto, erróneo, falso

incorrectness *n* incorrección, *f*

incorrigibility *n* incorregibilidad, *f*

incorrigible *a* incorregible, empecatado

incorrigibly *adv* incorregiblemente, obstinadamente

incorrupt *a* incorrupto; recto, honrado

incorruptibility *n* incorruptibilidad, *f*; honradez, probidad, *f*

incorruptible *a* incorrupto; honrado, incorruptible

incorruption *n* incorrupción, *f*

increase *vt* aumentar, acrecentar; (in numbers) multiplicar; (extend) ampliar, extender; (of price) encarecer, aumentar. *vi* aumentar, crecer; multiplicarse; extenderse; encarecerse; aumentar. *n* aumento, crecimiento, *m*; multiplicación, *f*; (in price) encarecimiento, *m*, alza, *f*; (of water) crecida, *f*; (of moon) creciente, *f*. **It is on the i.,** Va en aumento. **to i. and multiply,** crecer y multiplicar

increasingly *adv* más y más; en creciente, en aumento

incredibility *n* incredibilidad, *f*

incredible *a* increíble; fabuloso, extraordinario. **It seems i.,** Es increíble, *inf* Parece mentira

incredibly *adv* increíblemente

incredulity *n* incredulidad, *f*, escepticismo, *m*

incredulous *a* incrédulo, escéptico

incredulously *adv* con incredulidad, escépticamente

increment *n* aumento, incremento, *m*; adición, añadidura, *f*; math incremento, *m*. **unearned i.,** plusvalía, mayor valía, *f*

incriminate *vt* incriminar

incriminating *a* incriminante, acriminador

incrust *vt* incrustar, encostrar

incrustation *n* incrustación, *f*; (scab) costra, *f*

incubate *vt* empollar; *med* incubar

incubation *n* empolladura, incubación, *f*; *med* incubación, *f*

incubator *n* incubadora, *f*

incubus *n* íncubo, *m*; (burden) carga, *f*

inculcate *vt* inculcar, implantar, instilar

inculcation *n* inculcación, implantación, instilación, *f*

incumbency *n* posesión, duración de, posesión, duración (de cualquier puesto), *f*

incumbent *a* obligatorio. *n ecc* beneficiado, *m*. **to be i. on,** incumbir a, ser de su obligación

incur *vi* incurrir (en), incidir (en). **to i. an obligation,** contraer una obligación

incurability *n* incurabilidad, *f*

incurable *a* incurable, insanable; *fig* sin solución, irremediable. *n* incurable, *mf*

incurably *adv* incurablemente, irremediablemente

incurious *a* indiferente, sin interés; incurioso, negligente, descuidado

incursion *n* incursión, invasión, irrupción, *f*, acometimiento, *m*

indebted *a* empeñado, adeudado; (obliged) reconocido

indebtedness *n* deuda, *f*; (gratitude) obligación, *f*; agradecimiento, *m*

indecency *n* indecencia, *f*

indecent *a* indecente; obsceno, deshonesto

indecently *adv* torpemente, indecentemente

indecision *n* indecisión, vacilación, irresolución, *f*

indecisive *a* indeciso, irresoluto, vacilante

indeclinable *a* indeclinable

indecorous *a* indecoroso, indecente, indigno

indecorum *n* indecoro, *m*, indecencia, *f*; incorrección, *f*

indeed *adv* en efecto, de veras, a la verdad, realmente, por cierto, claro está. *interr* ¿de veras? ¿es posible? **I shall be very glad i.,** Estaré contento de veras. **It is i. an excellent book,** Es en efecto un libro excelente. **There are differences i. between this house and the other,** Hay diferencias, claro está, entre esta casa y la otra

indefatigability *n* resistencia, *f*, aguante, *m*, tenacidad, *f*

indefatigable *a* incansable, infatigable, resistente

indefatigably *adv* infatigablemente

indefensible *a* indefendible, insostenible

indefinable *a* indefinible

indefinite *a* indefinido, incierto; (delicate) sutil, delicado; *gram* indefinido; (vague) vago. *gram* **i. article,** artículo indefinido, *m*

indefinitely *adv* indefinidamente

indefiniteness *n* lo indefinido, el carácter indefinido, *m*; vaguedad, *f*

indelibility *n* resistencia, *f*, lo indeleble; *fig* duración, tenacidad, *f*

indelible *a* indeleble, imborrable; *fig* inolvidable

indelibly *adv* indeleblemente

indelicacy *n* falta de buen gusto, grosería, *f*; (tactlessness) indiscreción, falta de tacto, *f*

indelicate *a* grosero, descortés; indecoroso, inmodesto; (tactless) inoportuno, indiscreto

indemnification *n* indemnización, compensación, *f*

indemnify *vt* indemnizar, compensar

indemnity *n* indemnización, reparación, *f*

indent *vt* endentar, mellar; *print* sangrar

indentation *n* impresión, depresión, *f;* corte, *m,* mella, *f;* línea quebrada, *f,* zigzag, *m*

indenture *n* escritura, *f,* instrumento, *m. vt* escriturar

independence *n* independencia, libertad, *f;* (autonomy) autonomía, *f.* **I. Day,** Fiesta de la Independencia, *f.* **i. movement,** movimiento en favor de la independencia, *m*

independent *a* independiente; libre; (autonomous) autónomo; **i. of,** libre de; aparte de. **a person of i. means,** una persona acomodada

independently *adv* independientemente

indescribability *n* imposibilidad de describir, *f,* lo indescriptible

indescribable *a* indescriptible; indefinible, indecible, inexplicable; incalificable

indestructibility *n* indestructibilidad, *f*

indestructible *a* indestructible

indeterminable *a* indeterminable

indeterminate *a* indeterminado, indefinido, vago; *math* indeterminado

indetermination *n* irresolución, indecisión, duda, vacilación, *f*

index *n* (forefinger) dedo índice, *m;* (of book) tabla de materias, *f,* índice, *m;* (on instruments) manecilla, aguja, *f; math* índice, *m;* (sign) señal, indicación, *f. vt* poner índice (a); poner en el índice. **i. card,** ficha, *f. I.* **expurgatorius,** Índice expurgatorio, *m*

India *n* la India, *f.* **I. paper,** papel de China, *m.* **i.-rubber,** *bot* caucho, *m;* (eraser) goma de borrar, *f.* **i.-rubber tree,** yacio, *m*

Indian *a* and *n* indio (-ia). **I. chief,** cacique, *m.* **I. club,** maza, *f.* **I. corn,** maíz, *m.* **I. ink,** tinta china, *f.* **I. summer,** veranillo, veranillo de San Martín, *m*

Indian Ocean, the el Océano Indico, *m*

indicate *vt* indicar, señalar; (show) denotar, mostrar, anunciar

indication *n* indicación, *f;* señal, *f,* indicio, síntoma, *m;* prueba, *f*

indicative *a* indicador, indicativo, demostrativo; *gram* indicativo. *n gram* indicativo, *m.* **to be i. of,** indicar, señalar

indicator *n* indicador, señalador, *m*

indict *vt* acusar; *law* demandar, enjuiciar

indictable *a* procesable, denunciable, enjuiciable

indictment *n* acusación, *f; law* procesamiento, *m*

indifference *n* indiferencia, apatía, *f,* desinterés, desapego, *m;* imparcialidad, neutralidad, *f;* (coldness) frialdad, tibieza, *f*

indifferent *a* indiferente, apático; imparcial, neutral; frío; (ordinary) regular, ordinario, ni bien ni mal

indifferently *adv* con indiferencia; imparcialmente; friamente

indigence *n* indigencia, necesidad, penuria, *f*

indigenous *a* indígena, nativo, natural

indigent *a* indigente, necesitado, menesteroso

indigestible *a* indigesto

indigestion *n* indigestión, *f; fig* empacho, ahíto, *m*

indignant *a* indignado. **to make i.,** indignar

indignantly *adv* con indignación

indignation *n* indignación, cólera, *f*

indignity *n* indignidad, *f;* ultraje, *m*

indigo *n* añil, índigo, *m*

indirect *a* indirecto; oblicuo; tortuoso; *gram* **i. case,** caso oblicuo, *m*

indirectness *n* (of route) rodeo, *m,* desviación, *f;* oblicuidad, *f;* (falsity) tortuosidad, *f*

indiscernible *a* imperceptible

indiscipline *n* indisciplina, falta de disciplina, *f*

indiscreet *a* indiscreto, imprudente, impolítico

indiscreetly *adv* indiscretamente

indiscretion *n* indiscreción, imprudencia, *f;* (slip) desliz, *m*

indiscriminate *a* general, universal; indistinto, promiscuo

indiscriminately *adv* promiscuamente

indiscrimination *n* universalidad, indistinción, *f*

indispensability *n* indispensabilidad, precisión, necesidad, *f*

indispensable *a* imprescindible, indispensable, insustituible

indispensably *adv* forzosamente, indispensablemente

indispose *vt* indisponer. **to be indisposed,** estar indispuesto, indisponerse

indisposed *a* indispuesto, enfermo, destemplado; (reluctant) maldispuesto

indisposition *n* indisposición, enfermedad, *f*

indisputability *n* verdad manifiesta, certeza, evidencia, *f*

indisputable *a* innegable, incontestable; irrefutable, evidente

indisputably *adv* indisputablemente

indissolubility *n* indisolubilidad, *f*

indissoluble *a* indisoluble

indistinct *a* indistinto; indeterminado, confuso, vago

indistinctly *adv* indistintamente; confusamente, vagamente

indistinctness *n* incertidumbre, vaguedad, indistinción, indeterminación, *f*

indistinguishable *a* indistinguible

individual *a* (single) solo, único; individual, individuo, particular, propio; personal. *n* individuo, *m,* particular, *mf*

individualism *n* individualismo, *m*

individualist *n* individualist, *mf*

individualistic *a* individualista

individuality *n* individualidad, personalidad, *f;* carácter, *m,* naturaleza, *f*

individualize *vt* particularizar, individuar

individually *adv* individualmente, particularmente

indivisibility *n* indivisibilidad, *f*

indivisible *a* incompartible, impartible, indivisible

indivisibly *adv* indivisiblemente

Indo (in compounds) indo. **I.-Chinese,** *a* and *n* indochino (-na). **I.-European,** indoeuropeo. **I.-Germanic,** indogermánico

indocile *a* indócil, desobediente, rebelde

indocility *n* indocilidad, desobediencia, falta de docilidad, *f*

indolence *n* indolencia, pereza, desidia, *f*

indolent *a* indolente, perezoso, holgazán; *med* indoloro

indolently *adv* perezosamente

indomitable *a* indomable, indómito

indoor *a* de casa; de puertas adentro, interno. **i. swimming pool,** piscina bajo techo, *f.* **i. tennis,** tenis en pistas cubiertas, tenis bajo techo, *m*

indoors *adv* en casa; adentro, bajo techo

indorsee *n* endosatario (-ia)

indubitable *a* indudable

indubitably *adv* indudablemente, sin duda

induce *vt* inducir, mover; instigar, incitar; producir, ocasionar; *elec* inducir. **Nothing would i. me to do it,** Nada me induciría a hacerlo

inducement *n* incitamento, *m;* estímulo, *m;* aliciente, atractivo, *m;* tentación, *f*

induct *vt* instalar; introducir, iniciar

induction *n* instalación, *f;* iniciación, introducción, *f; phys* inducción, *f.* **i. coil,** carrete de inducción, *m*

inductive *a* (of reasoning) inductivo; *phys* inductor

indulge *vt* (children) consentir, mimar; (a desire) satisfacer, dar rienda suelta a; (with a gift) agasajar (con), dar gusto (con). **to i. in,** *vt* consentir en. *vi* entregarse a, permitirse, gustar de

indulgence *n* (of children) mimo, cariño excesivo, *m;* (of a desire) propensión (a), afición (a), *f;* (toward others) tolerancia, transigencia, *f; ecc* indulgencia, *f*

indulgent *a* indulgente; tolerante, transigente

indult *n ecc* indulto, *m*

industrial *a* industrial. **i. alcohol,** alcohol desnaturalizado, *m.* **i. school,** escuela de artes y oficios, *f, com* **i. shares,** valores industriales, *m pl*

industrialism *n* industrialismo, *m*

industrialist *n* industrial, *m*

industrialization *n* industrialización, *f*
industrialize *vt* industrializar
industrious *a* industrioso, aplicado, diligente
industriously *adv* industriosamente, diligentemente
industriousness *n* industria, laboriosidad, *f*
industry *n* diligencia, aplicación, *f*; (work) trabajo, *m*, labor, *f*; *com* industria, *f*
inebriate *a* borracho, ebrio. *n* borracho (-cha). *vt* embriagar, emborrachar
inebriation *n* embriaguez, borrachera, *f*
inedible *a* incomible, no comestible
inedited *a* inédito
ineffable *a* indecible, inefable
ineffaceable *a* imborrable, indeleble
ineffective *a* ineficaz; vano, fútil. **to be i.**, (of persons) no pinchar ni cortar. **to prove i.**, quedar sin efecto; no tener influencia
ineffectiveness *n* ineficacia, *f*; futilidad, *f*
inefficiency *n* ineficacia, incompetencia, ineptitud, *f*
inefficient *a* ineficaz, incapaz
inefficiently *adv* ineficazmente
inelastic *a* inelástico
inelegance *n* inelegancia, fealdad, vulgaridad, *f*
inelegant *a* inelegante, ordinario, de mal gusto
inelegantly *adv* sin elegancia
ineligibility *n* ineligibilidad, *f*
ineligible *a* inelegible
inept *a* inepto, inoportuno; absurdo, ridículo; (of persons) incompetente, ineficaz
ineptitude *n* ineptitud, *f*; necedad, *f*; (of persons) incapacidad, incompetencia, *f*
ineptly *adv* ineptamente, neciamente
inequality *n* desigualdad, desemejanza, disparidad, *f*; (of surface) escabrosidad, aspereza, *f*; *fig* injusticia, *f*; (of opportunity) diferencia, *f*
inequitable *a* desigual, injusto
inequity *n* injusticia, desigualdad, *f*
ineradicable *a* indeleble, imborrable
ineradicably *adv* indeleblemente
inert *a* inerte, inactivo, pasivo; ocioso, flojo, perezoso
inertia *n* inercia, inacción, *f*; abulia, pereza, *f*; *phys* inercia, *f*
inertly *adv* indolentemente, sin mover, pasivamente
inescapable *a* ineludible, inevitable
inessential *a* no esencial
inestimable *a* inestimable
inevitability *n* fatalidad, necesidad, *f*; lo inevitable
inevitable *a* inevitable, necesario, fatal, forzoso, ineludible
inevitably *adv* inevitablemente, necesariamente, forzosamente
inexact *a* inexacto, incorrecto
inexactitude *n* inexactitud, *f*
inexcusable *a* imperdonable, inexcusable, irremisible
inexcusableness *n* enormidad, *f*; lo inexcusable
inexcusably *adv* inexcusablemente
inexhaustible *a* inagotable, inexhausto
inexorability *n* inflexibilidad, inexorabilidad, *f*
inexorable *a* inexorable, inflexible, duro
inexorably *adv* inexorablemente, implacablemente
inexpediency *n* inoportunidad, inconveniencia, imprudencia, *f*
inexpedient *a* inoportuno; inconveniente; impolítico, imprudente. **to deem i.**, creer inoportuno
inexpensive *a* poco costoso, barato
inexpensiveness *n* baratura, *f*, bajo precio, *m*
inexperience *n* inexperiencia, falta de experiencia, *f*
inexperienced *a* inexperto, novato
inexpert *a* inexperto, imperito
inexpertly *adv* sin habilidad
inexpertness *n* impericia, torpeza, *f*
inexpiable *a* inexpiable
inexplicable *a* inexplicable
inexplicit *a* no explícito
inexplosive *a* inexplosible
inexpressible *a* inexplicable, indecible, inefable

inexpressive *a* inexpresivo; (of persons) reservado, callado, poco expresivo, retraído
inexpressiveness *n* falta de expresión, *f*; (of persons) reserva, *f*, silencio, retraimiento, *m*
inexpugnable *a* inexpugnable
inextinguishable *a* inapagable, inextinguible
inextricable *a* inextricable, intrincado, enmarañado
inextricably *adv* intrincadamente
infallibility *n* infalibilidad, *f*
infallible *a* infalible
infamous *a* infame, torpe, vil, ignominioso; odioso, repugnante
infamously *adv* infamemente
infamy *n* infamia, torpeza, vileza, ignominia, *f*; deshonra, *f*
infancy *n* infancia, niñez, *f*; *law* minoridad, *f*
infant *n* criatura, *f*; crío (-ía), niño (-ña); *law* menor, *mf* **i. school,** escuela de párvulos, *f*
infanticidal *a* infanticida
infanticide *n* (act) infanticidio, *m*; (person) infanticida, *mf*
infantile *a* infantil. **i. paralysis,** parálisis infantil, *f*
infantry *n* *mil* infantería, *f*
infantryman *n* *mil* infante, peón, *m*
infatuate *vt* infatuar, embobar
infatuation *n* infatuación, *f*, encaprichamiento, *m*
infect *vt* infectar, contagiar; *fig* pegar, influir; (*fig* in a bad sense) corromper, pervertir, inficionar. **to become infected,** infectarse
infected *a* infecto
infection *n* infección, *f*, contagio, *m*; *fig* influencia, *f*; (*fig* in a bad sense) corrupción, perversión, *f*
infectious *a* infeccioso, contagioso; (*fig* in a bad sense) corruptor; *fig* contagioso
infectiousness *n* contagiosidad, *f*
infelicitous *a* poco apropiado, desacertado
infelicity *n* infelicidad, desdicha, *f*, infortunio, *m*; desacierto, *m*, inoportunidad, *f*
infer *vt* inferir, concluir, educir, deducir, implicar
inferable *a* deducible, demostrable
inference *n* inferencia, deducción, conclusión, *f*
inferential *a* ilativo, deductivo
inferior *a* inferior; (in rank) subordinado, subalterno; (of position) secundario. *n* inferior, *mf* subordinado (-da). **to be not i.,** no ser inferior, *inf* no quedarse en zaga
inferiority *n* inferioridad, *f*. **i. complex,** complejo de inferioridad, *m*
infernal *a* infernal; *poet* inferno, tartáreo
infernally *adv* infernalmente
inferno *n* infierno, *m*
infertile *a* infértil, infecundo, estéril
infertility *n* infertilidad, infecundidad, esterilidad, *f*
infest *vt* infestar. **to be infested with,** plagarse de
infestation *n* infestación, *f*
infidel *a* infiel, gentil, *mf* pagano (-na); (atheist) descreído (-da), ateo (-ea). *a* pagano; infiel, descreído, ateo
infidelity *n* infidelidad, alevosía, perfidia, *f*
infiltrate *vt* infiltrar. *vi* infiltrarse
infiltration *n* infiltración, *f*
infinite *a* infinito, ilimitado; inmenso, enorme; (of number) innumerable, infinito. *n* infinito, *m*
infinitely *adv* infinitamente
infinitesimal *a* infinitesimal. **i. calculus,** cálculo infinitesimal, *m*
infinitive *a* and *n* *gram* infinitivo, *m*.
infinitude, infinity *n* infinidad, infinitud, *f*; (extent) inmensidad, *f*; (of number) sinfín, *m*; *math* infinito, *m*
infirm *a* achacoso, enfermizo, enclenque; (shaky) inestable, inseguro; (of purpose) irresoluto, vacilante
infirmary *n* enfermería, *f*, hospital, *m*
infirmity *n* achaque, *m*, enfermedad, dolencia, *f*; (fault) flaqueza, falta, *f*
inflame *vt* encender; (excite) acalorar, irritar, provocar;

med inflamar. *vi* encenderse, arder; acalorarse, irritarse; *med* inflamarse

inflammability *n* inflamabilidad, *f*

inflammable *a* inflamable

inflammation *n* inflamación, *f*

inflammatory *a* inflamador; *med* inflamatorio

inflate *vt* inflar, hinchar; (with pride) engreír, ensoberbecer

inflation *n* inflación, hinchazón, *f*; *com* inflación, *f*

inflationism *n* inflacionismo, *m*

inflator *n mech* bomba para inflar, *f*

inflect *vt* torcer; (voice) modular; *gram* conjugar, declinar

inflection *n* dobladura, *f*; (of voice) tono, acento, *m*, modulación, *f*; *gram* conjugación, declinación, *f*

inflexibility *n* inflexibilidad, dureza, rigidez, *f*

inflexible *a* inflexible, rígido; *fig* inexorable, inalterable

inflexibly *adv* inflexiblemente

inflict *vt* infligir, imponer

infliction *n* imposición, *f*; castigo, *m*

inflorescence *n bot* inflorescencia, *f*

inflow *n* afluencia, *f*, flujo, *m*

influence *n* influencia, *f*, influjo, *m*; ascendiente, *m*; (importance) influencia, importancia, *f*. *vt* influir, afectar; persuadir, inducir. **to have i. over,** (a person) tener ascendiente sobre. *law* **undue i.,** influencia indebida, *f*

influential *a* influyente; (of person) prestigioso, importante

influenza *n med* gripe, *f*, trancazo, *m*

influx *n* influjo, *m*; (of rivers) desembocadura, afluencia, *f*

inform *vt* (fill) infundir, llenar; (tell) informar, enterar, advertir; instruir; (with about) poner al corriente de, participar. *vi* (with against) delatar (a), denunciar. **to i. oneself,** informarse, enterarse. **to be informed about,** estar al corriente de

informal *a* irregular; sin ceremonia, de confianza; (meeting) no oficial, extraoficial

informality *n* irregularidad, *f*; falta de ceremonia, sencillez, *f*; intimidad, *f*

informally *adv* sin ceremonia

informant *n* informante, *mf*; informador (-ra)

information *n* información, instrucción, *f*; noticia, *f*, aviso, *m*; *law* denuncia, delación, *f*. **piece of i.,** información, *f*. **i. bureau,** oficina de información, *f*

informative *a* informativo

informer *n* delator (-ra), denunciador (-ra)

infrared *a phys* infrarrojo, ultrarrojo

infraction *n* contravención, infracción, transgresión, *f*

infrequency *n* infrecuencia, rareza, irregularidad, *f*

infrequent *a* infrecuente, raro, irregular

infrequently *adv* rara vez, infrecuentemente

infringe *vt* infringir, violar, contravenir, quebrantar

infringement *n* contravención, violación, infracción, *f*

infringer *n* infractor (-ra), contraventor (-ra), violador (-ra), transgresor (-ra)

infuriate *vt* enfurecer, enloquecer, enojar. **to be infuriated,** estar furioso

infuse *vt* vaciar, infiltrar; *fig* infundir, inculcar, instilar

infusible *a* infundible

infusion *n* infusión, *f*; *fig* instilación, inculcación, *f*

ingathering *n* cosecha, recolección, *f*

ingenious *a* ingenioso; mañoso, hábil

ingeniously *adv* ingeniosamente, hábilmente

ingenuity *n* ingeniosidad, inventiva, listeza, habilidad, *f*

ingenuous *a* ingenuo, franco, sincero, cándido, sencillo, inocente

ingenuousness *n* ingenuidad, franqueza, sinceridad, *f*; candor, *m*

ingest *vt* ingerir

ingestion *n* ingestión, *f*

inglorious *a* vergonzoso, ignominioso, deshonroso; desconocido, obscuro

ingloriously *adv* vergonzosamente, ignominiosamente; obscuramente

ingloriousness *n* deshonra, ignominia, *f*; obscuridad, *f*

ingoing *a* entrante, que entra. *n* ingreso, *m*, entrada, *f*; **com i. and outgoing,** entradas y salidas, *f pl*

ingot *n* pepita, *f*, lingote, *m*; (of any metal) barra, *f*

ingrained *a* innato, natural

ingratiate *vt* (oneself with) congraciarse con, captarse la buena voluntad de, insinuarse en el favor de

ingratiating *a* obsequioso

ingratitude *n* ingratitud, *f*, desagradecimiento, *m*

ingredient *n* ingrediente, *m*

ingress *n* ingreso, *m*; derecho de entrada, *m*

ingrowing *a* que crece hacia adentro. **i. nail,** uñero, *m*

inhabit *vt* habitar, ocupar, vivir en, residir en

inhabitable *a* habitable, vividero

inhabitant *n* habitante, residente, *m*; vecino (-na)

inhabited *a* habitado, poblado

inhalation *n* inspiración, *f*; *med* inhalación, *f*

inhale *vt* aspirar; *med* inhalar

inharmonious *a mus* disonante, inarmónico; desavenido, discorde, desconforme. **to be i.,** disonar; (of people) llevarse mal

inhere *vi* ser inherente; pertenecer (a), residir (en)

inherence *n* inherencia, *f*

inherent *a* inherente; innato, intrínseco, natural

inherently *adv* intrínsecamente

inherit *vt* heredar

inheritance *n* herencia, *f*; patrimonio, abolengo, *m*

inheritor *n* heredero, *m*

inheritress *n* heredera, *f*

inhibit *vt* inhibir, impedir; *ecc* prohibir. **be inhibited, became inhibited,** cohibirse

inhibition *n* inhibición, *f*

inhibitory *a* inhibitorio

inhospitable *a* inhospitalario

inhospitably *adv* desabridamente

inhospitality *n* inhospitalidad, *f*

inhuman *a* inhumano; cruel, bárbaro

inhumanity *n* inhumanidad, crueldad, *f*

inhumanly *adv* inhumanamente, cruelmente

inhume *vt* inhumar, sepultar

inimical *a* enemigo, hostil, opuesto, contrario

inimically *adv* hostilmente

inimitable *a* inimitable

inimitably *adv* inimitablemente

iniquitous *a* inicuo, malvado, perverso, nefando; *inf* diabólico

iniquity *n* iniquidad, maldad, injusticia, *f*

initial *a* inicial. *n* inicial, letra inicial, *f*. *vt* firmar con las iniciales

initially *adv* al principio, en primer lugar

initiate *a* iniciado. *vt* iniciar, poner en pie, empezar, entablar; (a person) admitir

initiation *n* principio, *m*; (of a person) iniciación, admisión, *f*

initiative *n* iniciativa, *f*. **to take the i.,** tomar la iniciativa

initiator *n* iniciador (-ra)

inject *vt* inyectar

injection *n* inyección, *f*. **i. syringe,** jeringa de inyecciones, *f*

injudicious *a* imprudente, indiscreto

injudiciously *adv* imprudentemente

injudiciousness *n* imprudencia, indiscreción, *f*

injunction *n* precepto, mandato, *m*; *law* embargo, *m*

injure *vt* perjudicar, dañar; menoscabar, deteriorar; (hurt) lastimar, lisiar. **to i. oneself,** hacerse daño

injured *a* (physically) lisiado; (morally) ofendido

injurer *n* perjudicador (-ra)

injurious *a* dañoso, perjudicial, malo; ofensivo, injurioso

injuriously *adv* perjudicialmente

injury *n* perjuicio, daño, *m*; (physical) lesión, *f*; (insult) agravio, insulto, *m*

injustice *n* injusticia, desigualdad, *f*. **You do him an i.,** Le juzgas mal

ink *n* tinta, *f*. *vt* entintar. **copying-ink,** tinta de copiar, *f.* **marking-ink,** tinta indeleble, *f.* **printer's ink,** tinta de imprenta, *f.* **ink-stand** or **ink-well,** tintero, *m*

inker *n print* rodillo, *m*

inkling *n* sospecha, noción, *f*

inky *a* manchado de tinta. **i. black,** negro como el betún

inland *n* el interior de un país, *a* interior, mediterráneo; del país, regional. *adv* tierra adentro. **to go i.,** internarse en un país. **I. Revenue,** delegación de contribuciones, *f.* **i. town,** ciudad del interior, *f*

inlay *vt* taracear, ataracear, embutir; incrustar. *n* taracea, *f,* embutido, *m*

inlet *n* entrada, admisión, *f; geog* ensenada, *f.* **i. valve,** válvula de admisión, *f*

inmate *n* residente, habitante, *m*; (of hospital) paciente, *mf*; enfermo (-ma); (of prison) prisionero

inmost. See **innermost**

inn *n* posada, fonda, venta, *f,* mesón, *m.* **Inns of Court,** Colegio de Abogados, *m*

innate *a* innato, inherente, instintivo, nativo

innately *adv* naturalmente, instintivamente

innavigable *a* innavegable

inner *a* interior, interno. **i. tube** *aut* cámara de neumatico, cámara de aire, *f*

innermost *a* más adentro; *fig* más íntimo, más hondo

innings *n* (sport) turno, *m*

innkeeper *n* fondista, *mf*; tabernero (-ra), mesonero (-ra), posadero (-ra)

innocence *n* inocencia, *f*; pureza, *f*; (guilelessness) simplicidad, *f,* candor, *m*

innocent *a* inocente, puro; (guiltless) inocente, inculpable; (foolish) simple, tonto, candoroso, inocentón; (harmless) innocuo. *n* inocente, *mf* **Holy Innocents,** Santos Inocentes, *m pl*

innoculator *n* inoculador, *m*

innocuous *a* innocuo, inofensivo

innocuousness *n* inocuidad, *f*

innovate *vt* innovar

innovation *n* innovación, *f*

innovator *n* innovador (-ra)

innuendo *n* indirecta, insinuación, *f*

innumerable *a* innumerable, incalculable. **i. things,** un sinfín de cosas

inobservance *n* inobservancia, *f,* incumplimiento, *m*

inoculate *vt* inocular

inoculation *n* inoculación, *f*

inodorous *a* inodoro

inoffensive *a* inofensivo, innocuo; (of people) pacífico, apacible, manso

inoffensively *adv* inofensivamente

inoffensiveness *n* inocuidad, *f*; (of people) mansedumbre, *f*

inoperable *a* inoperable

inoperative *a* ineficaz, impracticable, inútil

inopportune *a* inoportuno, intempestivo, inconveniente

inopportunely *adv* inoportunamente, a destiempo

inopportuneness *n* inoportunidad, inconveniencia, *f*

inordinate *a* desordenado, excesivo

inordinately *adv* desmedidamente

inorganic *a* inorgánico

inoxidizable *a* inoxidable

input *n* capacidad instalada, *f,* insumo, *m*

inquest *n law* indagación, investigación, *f*

inquietude *n* inquietud, *f,* desasosiego, *m,* agitación, preocupación, *f*

inquire *vt* and *vi* preguntar, averiguar, indagar. **to i. about,** (persons) preguntar por; (things) hacer preguntas sobre. **to i. into,** investigar, examinar, averiguar. **to i. of,** preguntar a. **"I. within,"** «Se dan informaciones»

inquirer *n* indagador (-ra), inquiridor (-ra)

inquiring *a* indagador, inquiridor

inquiringly *adv* interrogativamente

inquiry *n* interrogación, pregunta, *f*; indagación, pesquisa, investigación, *f; examen, m.* **i. office,** oficina de informaciones, *f.* **on i.,** al preguntar

inquisition *n* investigación, indagación, *f*; inquisición, *f.* **Holy I.,** Santo Oficio, *m,* Inquisición, *f*

inquisitive *a* curioso, inquiridor; preguntador, impertinente, mirón

inquisitively *adv* con curiosidad, impertinentemente

inquisitiveness *n* curiosidad, *f*; impertinencia, *f*

Inquisitor *n ecc* inquisidor, *m*

inquisitorial *a* inquisitorial, inquisidor

inroad *n* incursión, *f*

insalubrious *a* malsano, insalubre

insane *a* loco, demente, insano; (senseless) insensato, ridículo. **to become i.,** enloquecer, volverse loco, perder la razón. **to drive i.,** volver a uno el juicio, enloquecer, trastornar. **i. person,** demente, *mf,* loco (-ca)

insanely *adv* locamente

insanitary *a* antihigiénico, malsano

insanity *n* demencia, locura, *f*; enloquecimiento, *m*; (folly) insensatez, ridiculez, *f*

insatiability *n* insaciabilidad, *f*

insatiable *a* insaciable

insatiably *adv* insaciablemente

inscribe *vt* inscribir

inscription *n* inscripción, *f*; letrero, *m*; (of a book) dedicatoria, *f; com* inscripción, anotación, *f,* asiento, *m*

inscrutability *n* enigma, misterio, *m*; incomprensibilidad, *f*

inscrutable *a* enigmático, insondable, incomprensible, inescrutable

inscrutably *adv* incomprensiblemente, enigmáticamente

insect *n* insecto, *m.* **i. powder,** polvos insecticidas, *m pl*

insecticide *a* and *n* insecticida *m.*

insecure *a* inseguro, precario

insecurely *adv* inseguramente

insecurity *n* inseguridad, *f*; incertidumbre, inestabilidad, *f*

inseminate *vt fig* implantar; *med* fecundar

insemination *n fig* implantación, *f; med* fecundación, *f*

insensate *a* (unfeeling) insensible, insensitivo; (stupid) insensato, sin sentido, necio

insensibility *n* insensibilidad, inconsciencia, *f*; (stupor) sopor, letargo, *m*; impasibilidad, indiferencia, *f*

insensible *a* insensible, inconsciente, indiferente, impasible, duro de corazón; (scarcely noticeable) imperceptible. **to make i.,** (to sensations) hacer indiferente (a); insensibilizar

insensibly *adv* insensiblemente, imperceptiblemente

insensitive *a* insensible, insensitivo; (person) hecho un tronco, hecho un leño

insensitiveness *n* insensibilidad, *f*

insentient *a* insensible

inseparability *n* inseparabilidad, *f*

inseparable *a* inseparable

inseparably *adv* inseparablemente

insert *vt* insertar, intercalar; (introduce) meter dentro, introducir, encajar; (in a newspaper) publicar

insertion *n* inserción, intercalación, *f*; (introduction) introducción, *f*; metimiento, encaje, *m*; *sew* entredós, *m*; (in a newspaper) publicación, *f*

inshore *a* cercano a la orilla. *adv* cerca de la orilla. **i. fishing,** pesca de arrastre, *f*

inside *a* interior, interno. *adv* adentro, dentro. *n* interior, *m*; (contents) contenido, *m*; (lining) forro, *m*; (inf stomach) entrañas, *f pl.* **to turn i. out,** volver al revés. **to walk on the i. of the pavement,** andar a la derecha de la acera. **from the i.,** desde el interior; por dentro. **on the i.,** por dentro, en el interior. **i. information,** información confidencial, *f.* **i. out,** al revés, de dentro afuera

insidious *a* insidioso, enganoso, traidor

insidiously *adv* insidiosamente

insidiousness *n* insidia, *f*; engaño, *m,* traición, *f*

insight *n* percepción, perspicacia, intuición, *f,* atisbo, *m*

insignia *n pl* insignias, *f pl*

insignificance *n* insignificancia, futilidad, pequeñez, *f*
insignificant *a* insignificante; fútil, trivial
insincere *a* insincero, hipócrita, falso
insincerely *adv* falsamente, hipócritamente
insincerity *n* insinceridad, hipocresía, falsedad, falta de sinceridad, doblez, *f*
insinuate *vt* insinuar, introducir; (hint) soltar una indirecta, sugerir; (oneself) insinuarse, introducirse con habilidad
insinuation *n* insinuación, introducción, *f*; (hint) indirecta, *f*
insipid *a* insípido, insulso; (dull) soso
insipidity *n* insipidez, insulsez, *f*, desabor, *m*; (dullness) sosería, *f*
insist *vi* insistir; persistir, obstinarse. **to i. on,** insistir en; obstinarse en, hacer hincapié en, aferrarse en (or a)
insistence *n* insistencia, *f*; obstinación, pertinacia, *f*
insistent *a* insistente; porfiado, obstinaz
insistently *adv* con insistencia; porfiadamente
insobriety *n* falta de sobriedad, *f*; embriaguez, ebriedad, *f*
insole *n* (of shoes) plantilla, *f*
insolence *n* insolencia, altanería, majadería, frescura, *f*, atrevimiento, descaro, *m*
insolent *a* insolente, arrogante, atrevido, descarado, desmesurado, fresco
insolently *adv* insolentemente, con descaro
insolubility *n* insolubilidad, *f*
insoluble *a* insoluble
insolvency *n* in olvencia, *f*
insolvent *a* insolvente
insomnia *n* insomnio, *m*
insomuch *adv* (gen. with as or that) de modo (que), así (que), de suerte (que)
inspect *vt* examinar, investigar, inspeccionar; (officially) registrar, reconocer
inspection *n* inspección, investigación, *f*; examen, *m*; (official) reconocimiento, registro, *m*
inspector *n* inspector, *m*, veedor, interventor, *m*
inspectorate *n* inspectorado, *m*; cargo de inspector, *m*
inspiration *n* (of breath) inspiración, aspiración, *f*; numen, *m*, inspiración, vena, *f*. **to find i. in,** inspirarse en.
inspire *vt* (inhale) aspirar, inspirar; (stimulate) animar, alentar, iluminar; (suggest) sugerir, inspirar; infundir. **to i. enthusiasm,** entusiasmar. **to i. hope,** dar esperanza, esperanzar
inspired *a* inspirado, intuitivo, iluminado; (of genius) genial
inspirer *n* inspirador (-ra)
inspiring *a* alentador, animador; inspirador
inspirit *vt* alentar, inspirar, estimular, animar
inspiriting *a* alentador, estimulador
instability *n* inestabilidad, mutabilidad, inconstancia, *f*
install *vt* (all meanings) instalar. **to i. oneself,** instalarse, establecerse
installation *n* (all meanings) instalación, *f*
installment *n* (of a story) entrega, *f*; *com* plazo, *m*, cuota, *f*. **by installments,** *com* a plazos. **i. plan,** pago a plazos, pago por cuotas, *m*
instance *n* ejemplo, caso, *m*; (request) solicitación, *f*, ruego, *m*; *law* instancia, *f*. *vt* citar como ejemplo, mencionar; demostrar, probar. **for i.,** por ejemplo, verbigracia. **in that i. . . .,** en el caso . . . **in the first i.,** en primer lugar, primero
instant *a* inmediato, urgente; *com* corriente, actual. *n* instante, momento, *m*; *inf* tris, santiamén, *m*. *com* **the 2nd i.,** el 2° (segundo) del corriente. **this i.,** (immediately) en seguida
instantaneous *a* instantáneo. *phot* **i. exposure,** instantánea, *f*
instantaneously *adv* instantáneamente
instantaneousness *n* instantaneidad, *f*
instantly *adv* en seguida, al instante, inmediatamente
instead *adv* en cambio; (with of) en vez de, en lugar de
instep *n* empeine, *m*

instigate *vt* instigar, incitar, aguijar, animar, provocar; fomentar
instigating *a* instigador, provocador, fomentador
instigation *n* instigación, incitación, *f*; estímulo, *m*
instigator *n* instigador (-ra), provocador (-ra), fomentador (-ra)
instil *vt* instilar; (ideas) inculcar, infundir
instilment *n* inculcación, implantación, insinuación, *f*
instinct *n* instinto, *m*. **i. with,** imbuido de, lleno de. **by i.,** por instinto, movido por instinto
instinctive *a* instintivo, espontáneo
instinctively *adv* por instinto
institute *vt* instituir, fundar, establecer; (an inquiry) iniciar, empezar. *n* instituto, *m*; *pl* **institutes,** *law* instituta, *f*
institution *n* (creation) fundación, creación, *f*; institución, *f*, instituto, *m*; (beginning) comienzo, *m*, iniciación, *f*; (charitable) asilo, *m*; (custom) uso, *m*, costumbre, tradición, *f*
institutional *a* institucional
instruct *vt* (teach) instruir, enseñar; (order) mandar, dar orden (a)
instruction *n* (teaching) instrucción, enseñanza, *f*; *pl* **instructions,** (orders) instrucciones, f *pl* orden, *f*, mandato, *m*
instructive *a* instructivo, instructor, informativo
instructively *adv* instructivamente
instructiveness *n* el carácter informativo, lo instructivo
instructor *n* instructor, preceptor, *m*
instrument *n* instrumento, *m*; (tool) herramienta, *f*, utensilio, aparato, *m*; (agent) órgano, agente, medio, *m*; *law* instrumento, *m*, escritura, *f*. *vt mus* instrumentar. **percussion i.,** instrumento de percusión, *m*. **scientific i.,** instrumento científico, *m*. **stringed i.,** instrumento de cuerda, *m*. **wind i.,** instrumento de viento, *m*
instrumental *a* instrumental; influyente. **to be i. in,** contribuir a
instrumentalist *n mus* instrumentista, *m*
instrumentality *n* mediación, intervención, agencia, *f*, buenos oficios, *m pl*
instrumentation *n mus* instrumentación, *f*; mediación, *f*
insubordinate *a* insubordinado, rebelde, desobediente, refractario
insubordination *n* insubordinación, rebeldía, desobediencia, *f*
insubstantial *a* irreal; insubstancial
insubstantiality *n* irrealidad, *f*; insubstancialidad, *f*
insufferable. See intolerable
insufficiency *n* insuficiencia, falta, carestía, *f*
insufficient *a* insuficiente, falto. **"I. Postage,"** «Falta de franqueo»
insufficiently *adv* insuficientemente
insular *a* isleño, insular; (narrow-minded) intolerante, iliberal
insularity *n* carácter isleño, *m*; (narrow-mindedness) iliberalidad, intolerancia, *f*
insulate *vt* aislar
insulating *a* aislador. **i. tape,** *elec* cinta aisladora, *f*
insulation *n* aislamiento, *m*
insulator *n elec* aislador, *m*
insulin *n med* insulina, *f*
insult *n* insulto, agravio, ultraje, *m*, afrenta, ofensa, *f*. *vt* insultar, ofender, afrentar. **He was insulted,** Fue insultado; Se mostró ofendido
insulter *n* insultador (-ra)
insulting *a* insultante, injurioso, ofensivo. **He was very i. to them,** Les insultó, Les trató con menosprecio
insultingly *adv* con insolencia, ofensivamente
insuperability *n* dificultades insuperables, *f pl*, imposibilidad, *f*, lo insuperable
insuperable *a* insuperable, invencible
insuperably *adv* invenciblemente

insupportable *a* insoportable, inaguantable, intolerable, insufrible

insupportably *adv* insufriblemente, insoportablemente

insurable *a* asegurable

insurance *n* aseguramiento, *m*; *com* seguro, *m*; aseguración, *f*. **accident i.,** seguro contra accidentes, *m*. **fire-i.,** seguro contra incendio, *m*. **life i.,** seguro sobre la vida, *m*. **maritime i.,** seguro marítimo, *m*. **National I. Act,** Ley del Seguro Nacional Obligatorio, *f*. **i. broker,** corredor de seguros, *m*. **i. company,** compañía de seguros, *f*. **i. policy,** póliza de seguros, *f*. **i. premium,** prima de seguros, *f*

insure *vt* asegurar. **to i. oneself,** asegurarse. **the insured,** (person) el asegurado

insurer *n* asegurador (-ra)

insurgent *a* insurgente, rebelde; (of sea) invasor. *n* rebelde, *mf* insurrecto (-ta)

insurmountable *a* insalvable, insuperable, invencible, intransitable

insurrection *n* insurrección, sublevación, *f*, levantamiento, *m*

insurrectionary *a* rebelde, amotinado, insurgente

insusceptible *a* no susceptible, indiferente, insensible

intact *a* intacto, íntegro, indemne

intake *n* (of a stocking) menguado, *m*; *mech* aspiración, *f*; válvula de admisión, *f*; *aer* admisión, toma, *f*; orificio de entrada, *m*

intangibility *n* intangibilidad, *f*

intangible *a* intangible; incomprensible

integer *n math* número entero, *m*

integral *a* íntegro, intrínseco, inherente; *math* integral. *n math* integral, *f*. **i. calculus,** cálculo integral, *m*

integrate *vt* integrar, completar; formar en un todo; *math* integrar

integrity *n* integridad, honradez, rectitud, entereza, *f*

intellect *n* intelecto, entendimiento, *m*

intellectual *a* intelectual, mental. *n* intelectual

intellectualism *n* intelectualismo, *m*, intelectualidad, *f*

intellectually *adv* intelectualmente, mentalmente

intelligence *n* inteligencia, comprensión, mente, *f*; (quickness of mind) agudeza, perspicacia, *f*; (news) noticia, *f*, conocimiento, informe, *m*. **the latest i.,** las últimas noticias. **i. quotient,** cociente de inteligencia, *m*. **I. Service,** Inteligencia, *f*; policía secreta, *f*. **i. test,** prueba de inteligencia, *f*

intelligent *a* inteligente

intelligentsia *n* clase intelectual, intelectualidad, *f*, *inf* masa cefálica, *f*

intelligibility *n* comprensibilidad, inteligibilidad, *f*

intelligible *a* inteligible, comprensible

intelligibly *adv* inteligiblemente

intemperance *n* intemperancia, inmoderación, *f*; exceso en la bebida, *m*

intemperate *a* intemperante, destemplado, descomedido; inmoderado; bebedor en exceso

intemperately *adv* inmoderadamente

intend *vt* intentar, proponerse, pensar; destinar, dedicar; (mean) querer decir. **to be intended,** estar destinado; tener por fin; querer decir

intendant *n* intendente, *m*

intended *a* pensado, deseado. *n inf* novio (-ia), futuro (-ra), prometido (-da)

intense *a* intenso, vivo, fuerte; (of emotions) profundo, hondo, vehemente; (of colors) subido, intenso; (great) extremado, sumo, muy grande

intensification *n* intensificación, *f*; aumento, *m*

intensify *vt* intensar, intensificar; aumentar

intensity *n* intensidad, fuerza, *f*; (of emotions) profundidad, vehemencia, violencia, *f*; (of colors) intensidad, *f*

intensive *a* intensivo

intensive-care unit *n* sala de terapia intensiva, unidad de cuidados intensivos, unidad de vigilancia intensiva, *f*

intent *n* intento, propósito, deseo, *m*. *a* atento; (ab-

sorbed) absorto, interesado; (on doing) resuelto a, decidido a. **to all intents and purposes,** en efecto, en realidad. **to be i. on,** (reading, etc.) estar absorto en, entregarse a. **with i. to defraud,** con el propósito deliberado de defraudar

intention *n* intención, voluntad, *f*, propósito, pensamiento, proyecto, *m*

intentional *a* intencional, deliberado, premeditado

intentionally *adv* a propósito, intencionalmente, de pensado

intentioned *a* intencionado

intently *adv* atentamente

inter *vt* enterrar, sepultar

inter *pref* inter, entre. **i.-allied,** interaliado, de los aliados. **i.-denominational,** intersectario. **i.-university,** interuniversitario. **i.-urban,** interurbano

interaction *n* interacción, acción recíproca, acción mutua, *f*

intercalate *vt* intercalar, interpolar

intercede *vi* interceder, mediar. **to i. for,** hablar por

intercept *vt* interceptar, detener; entrecoger, atajar

interception *n* interceptación, detención, *f*

intercession *n* mediación, intercesión, *f*

intercessor *n* intercesor (-ra), mediador (-ra)

interchange *n* intercambio, *m*; (of goods) comercio, tráfico, *m*. *vt* cambiar, trocar; alternar

interchangeable *a* intercambiable

intercom *n* teléfono interior, *m*

intercommunicate *vi* comunicarse

intercommunication *n* comunicación mutua, *f*; comercio, *m*

intercostal *a anat* intercostal

intercourse *n* (social) trato, *m*, relaciones, *f pl*; *com* comercio, tráfico, *m*; (of ideas) intercambio, *m*; (sexual) coito, trato sexual, *m*

interdependence *n* dependencia mutua, mutualidad, *f*

interdependent *a* mutuo

interdict *n* interdicto, veto, *m*, prohibición, *f*; *ecc* entredicho, *m*. *vt* interdecir, prohibir, privar; *ecc* poner entredicho

interdiction *n* interdicción, prohibición, *f*

interest *n* interés, *m*; provecho, *m*; *com* premio, rédito, interés, *m*; (in a firm) participación, *f*; (curiosity) interés, *m*; curiosidad, *f*; simpatía, *f*; (influence) influencia, *f*. *n pl* **interests,** (commercial undertakings) empresas, *f pl*, intereses, negocios, *m pl*. *vt* interesar. **to be interested in,** interesarse en, (on behalf of) por. **to be in one's own i.,** ser en provecho de uno, ser en su propio interés. **to bear eight per cent. i.,** dar interés del ocho por ciento. **to pay with i.,** pagar con creces. **to put out at i.,** dar a interés. **in the interests of,** en interés de. **compound i.,** interés compuesto, *m*. **simple i.,** interés sencillo, *m*. **vested interests,** intereses creados, *m pl*

interesting *a* interesante, curioso, atractivo

interestingly *adv* amenamente, de modo interesante

interfere *vi* intervenir, meterse, entremeterse, mezclarse; *inf* mangonear, meter las narices; (with) meterse con; (impede) estorbar, impedir

interference *n* intervención, *f*, entrometimiento, *m*; (obstacle) estorbo, obstáculo, *m*; *phys* interferencia, *f*; *rad* parásitos, *m pl*

interfering *a* entremetido, oficioso; *inf* mangoneador

interim *n* ínterin, intermedio, *m*. *a* interino, provisional. **in the i.,** entre tanto, en el ínterin. *com* **i. dividend,** dividendo interino, *m*

interior *a* interior, interno; doméstico. *n* interior, *m*

interject *vt* interponer

interjection *n* exclamación, interjección, *f*; interposición, *f*

interlace *vt* entrelazar, entretejer

interleave *vt* interfoliar, interpaginar

interline *vt* entrerrenglonar, interlinear

interlinear *a* interlineal

interlineation *n* interlineación, *f*

interlining n entretela, f
interlock vt (of wheels, etc.). endentar; trabar; cerrar. vi endentarse; entrelazarse, unirse; cerrar
interlocutor n interlocutor (-ra)
interloper n intruso (-sa); com intérlope, m
interloping a intérlope
interlude n intervalo, intermedio, m; mus interludio, m; theat entremés, m
intermarriage n casamiento entre parientes próximos, entre razas distintas, o entre grupos étnicos distintos, m
intermarry vi contraer matrimonio entre parientes próximos, entre personas de razas distintas, o entre grupos étnicos distintos
intermediary a and n intermediario (-ia)
intermediate a intermedio, medio, medianero. n sustancia intermedia, f. vi intervenir, mediar
interment n entierro, m
intermezzo n theat intermedio, m; mus intermezzo, m
interminable a interminable, inacabable
interminably adv interminablemente, sin fin, sin cesar
intermingle vt entremezclar, entreverar. vi mezclarse
intermission n intermisión, interrupción, pausa, f; theat entreacto, m. **without i.**, sin pausa, sin tregua
intermittence n intermitencia, alternación, f
intermittent a intermitente, discontinuo; (of fever) intermitente
intermittently adv a intervalos, a ratos, a pausas
intern n med practicante de hospital m, interno (-na), interno de hospital, alumno interno, m. vt confinar, encerrar
internal a interno, interior; (of affairs) doméstico, civil; intrínseco; íntimo. **i.-combustion engine,** motor de combustión interna, m
internally adv interiormente
international a internacional. n sport un partido internacional. **i. law,** derecho internacional, m
internationalism n internacionalismo, m
internationalist n internacionalista, mf
internationalization n internacionalización, f
internationalize vt hacer internacional, poner bajo un control internacional
internecine a sanguinario, feroz
internee n internado (-da)
internment n internamiento, m. **i. camp,** campo de internamiento, m
interoceanic a interoceánico
interpolate vt interpolar, intercalar, interponer
interpolation n interpolación, inserción, añadidura, f
interpolator n interpolador (-ra)
interpose vt interponer; (a remark) interpolar. vi interponerse, intervenir; (interfere) entrometerse; interrumpir
interposition n interposición, f; entrometimiento, m
interpret vt interpretar; (translate) traducir; (explain) explicar, descifrar. vi interpretar.
interpretation n interpretación, f; (translation) traducción, f; (explanation) explicación, f
interpretative a interpretativo, interpretador
interpreter n intérprete, mf
interregnum n interregno, m
interrelation n relación mutua, f
interrogate vt interrogar, examinar, preguntar
interrogation a interrogante
interrogation n interrogación, f, examen, m; pregunta, f. **mark of i.,** punto de interrogación, m
interrogative a interrogativo. n palabra interrogativa, f
interrogatively adv interrogativamente
interrogator n examinador (-ra), interrogador (-ra)
interrogatory a interrogativo. n interrogatorio, m
interrupt vt interrumpir
interruptedly adv interrumpidamente
interrupter n interruptor (-ra); elec interruptor, m
interruption n interrupción, f
intersect vt cruzar. vi cruzarse, intersecarse
intersection n intersección, f; cruce, m, (of streets) bocacalle, f

intersperse vt diseminar, esparcir; interpolar, entremezclar
interstice n intervalo, intermedio, m; (chink) intersticio, m, hendedura, f
intertwine vt entretejer, entrelazar. vi entrelazarse
interval n intervalo, intermedio, m, pausa, f; theat entreacto, m, intermisión, f; (in schools) recreo, m. **at intervals,** a trechos, de vez en cuando. **lucid i.,** intervalo claro, intervalo lúcido, m
intervene vi intervenir, tomar parte (en), mediar; (occur) sobrevenir, acaecer; law interponerse
intervening a intermedio; interventor
intervention n intervención, mediación, f
interventionist n pol partidario (-ia) de la intervención
interview n entrevista, f, interviev, m. vt entrevistarse con
interviewer n interrogador (-ra); (reporter) reportero, periodista, m
interweave vt entretejer, entrelazar
interweaving n entretejimiento, m
intestacy n ausencia de un testamento, f
intestate a and n intestado (-da)
intestinal a intestinal, intestino. **i. worm,** lombriz intestinal, f
intestine n intestino, m. **large i.,** intestino grueso, m. **small i.,** intestino delgado, m
intimacy n intimidad, f, familiaridad, f; (of nobility and others) privanza, f
intimate a íntimo; (of relations) entrañable, estrecho; intrínseco, esencial; (of knowledge) profundo, completo, detallado. n amigo (-ga) de confianza. vt intimar, dar a entender, indicar. **to become i.,** intimarse. **to be on i. terms with,** tratar de tú (a), ser amigo íntimo de
intimately adv íntimamente, al fondo
intimation n intimación, indicación, f; (hint) insinuación, indirecta, f
intimidate vt intimidar, aterrar, infundir miedo (a), espantar, acobardar, amedrentar
intimidation n intimidación, f
intimidatory a aterrador, amenazador
into prep en; a, al, a la; dentro, adentro; (of transforming, forming, etc.) en. **Throw it i. the fire,** Échalo al (or en el) fuego. **She went i. the house,** Entró en la casa. **to look i.,** mirar dentro de; mirar hacia el interior (de); investigar
intolerable a intolerable, insufrible, inaguantable, insoportable, inllevable
intolerableness n intolerabilidad, f
intolerably adv intolerablemente, insufriblemente
intolerance n intolerancia, intransigencia, f
intolerant a intolerante, intransigente; med intolerante
intonation n entonación, f
intone vt entonar; ecc salmodiar
intoxicant a embriagador. n bebida alcohólica, f
intoxicate vt emborrachar, embriagar; med intoxicar, envenenar; (excite) embriagar, embelesar
intoxicated a borracho; (excited) ebrio, embriagado; med intoxicado
intoxicating a embriagador
intoxication n borrachera, embriaguez, f; med intoxicación, f, envenenamiento, m; (excitement) entusiasmo, m, ebriedad, f
intractability n insociabilidad, hurañería, f
intractable a intratable, insociable, huraño
intramural adv intramuros
intransigence n intransigencia, intolerancia, f
intransigent a intransigente, intolerante
intransitive a intransitivo, neutro
intrauterine a med intrauterino
intravenous a med intravenoso
intrepid a intrépido, osado, audaz
intrepidity n intrepidez, osadía, audacia, f
intrepidly adv intrépidamente, audazmente
intricacy n intrincación, complejidad, f
intricate a intrincado, complejo
intricately adv intrincadamente

intrigue n intriga, maquinación, f, enredo, m; (amorous) lío, m. vi intrigar, enredar; (amorous) tener un lío. vt (interest) atraer, interesar; (with) intrigar con
intriguer n intrigante, mf, urdemalas, m, enredador (-ra)
intriguing a enredador; (attractive) atrayente, interesante, seductor
intrinsic a intrínseco, innato, inherente, esencial
intrinsically adv intrínsecamente, esencialmente
introduce vt introducir; hacer entrar; insertar, injerir; (a person) presentar; poner de moda, introducir; (a bill) presentar; (a person to a thing) llamar la atención sobre. **Permit me to i. my friend,** Permítame que le presente mi amigo
introduction n introducción, f; (of a book) prefacio, prólogo, m, advertencia, f; (of a person) presentación, f; inserción, f
introductory a introductor, preliminar, preparatorio
intromission n intromisión, f
introspection n introspección, f
introspective a introspectivo
introversion n psy introversión f
introvert a and n psy introverso (-sa)
intrude vt introducir, imponer. vi entremeterse, inmiscuirse. **Do I i.?** ¿Estorbo?
intruder n intruso (-sa)
intrusion n intrusión, f; geol intromisión, f
intrusive a intruso
intuition n intuición, f. **to know by i.,** intuir, saber por intuición
intuitive a intuitivo
inundate vt inundar, anegar; fig abrumar
inundation n inundación, anegación, f; fig diluvio, m, abundancia, f
inure vt endurecer, habituar
inurement n habituación, f
invade vt invadir, irrumpir, asaltar; med invadir
invader n invasor (-ra), acometedor (-ra), agresor (-ra)
invading a invasor, irruptor
invalid a inválido, nulo. **to become i.,** caducar
invalid n inválido (-da), enfermo (-ma). **to become an i.,** quedarse inválido. **to i. out of the army,** licenciar por invalidez. **i. carriage,** cochecillo de inválido, m
invalidate vt invalidar, anular
invalidation n invalidación, f
invalidity n invalidez, nulidad, f
invaluable n inestimable
invariability n invariabilidad, invariación, inalterabilidad, inmutabilidad, f
invariable a invariable, inmutable, inalterable
invariably adv invariablemente, inmutablemente
invariant n math invariante, m
invasion n invasión, irrupción, f; med invasión, f
invective n invectiva, diatriba, f
inveigh (against) vi desencadenarse (contra), prorrumpir en invectivas (contra)
inveigle vt seducir, engatusar, persuadir
inveiglement n seducción, persuasión, f
invent vt inventar, descubrir, originar; (a falsehood) fingir; (create) idear, componer
invention n invención, f, invento, descubrimiento, m; (imagination) ingeniosidad, inventiva, f; (falsehood) ficción, mentira, f; (finding) invención, f, hallazgo, m
inventive a inventor, inventivo; ingenioso, despejado
inventiveness n inventiva, f
inventor n inventor (-ra), autor (-ra)
inventory n inventario, m; descripción, f. vt inventariar
inverse a inverso. **i. proportion,** razón inversa, f
inversely adv inversamente, a la inversa
inversion n inversión, f, trastrocamiento, m; gram hipérbaton, m
invert vt invertir, trastornar, trastrocar. **inverted commas,** comilla, f
invertebrate a and n invertebrado m.
invest vt com invertir; mil sitiar, cercar; (foll. by with) poner, cubrir con; (of qualities) conferir, otorgar, dar.

vi (with in) poner dinero en, echar caudal en; inf comprar
investigable a averiguable
investigate vt investigar, estudiar; examinar, averiguar; explorar
investigation n investigación, f, estudio, m; examen, m, averiguación, f; encuesta, pesquisa, f
investigator n investigador (-ra); averiguador (-ra)
investigatory a investigador
investiture n investidura, instalación, f
investment n (com of money) inversión, f, empleo, m; mil cerco, m; (investiture) instalación, f; pl **investments,** com acciones, f pl, fondos, m pl
investor n inversionista, m; accionista, mf
inveteracy n antigüedad, f, lo arraigado
inveterate a inveterado, antiguo, arraigado, incurable
invidious a odioso, repugnante, injusto
invidiousness n injusticia, f, lo odioso
invigorate vt vigorizar, dar fuerza (a), avivar
invigorating a fortalecente, fortificador, vigorizador
invincibility n invencibilidad, f
invincible a invencible, indomable; fig insuperable
inviolability n inviolabilidad, f
inviolable a inviolable
inviolate a inviolado
invisibility n invisibilidad, f
invisible a invisible. **i. ink,** tinta simpática, f. **i. mending,** zurcido invisible, m
invitation n invitación, f; convite, m; (card) tarjeta de invitación, f
invite vt invitar, convidar; (request) pedir, rogar; (of things) incitar, tentar.
inviting a atrayente, incitante; (of food) apetitoso; (of looks) provocativo
invocation n invocación, f
invocatory a invocatorio, invocador
invoice n com factura, f. vt facturar. **proforma i.,** factura simulada, f. **shipping i.,** factura de expedición, f. **i. book,** libro de facturas, m
invoke vt invocar; suplicar, implorar; (laws) acogerse (a)
involuntarily adv sin querer, involuntariamente
involuntariness n involuntariedad, f
involuntary a involuntario; instintivo, inconsciente
involve vt (entangle) enredar, embrollar, enmarañar; (implicate) comprometer; (imply) implicar, ocasionar, suponer, traer consigo
involved a complejo, intrincado; (of style) confuso, obscuro
invulnerability n invulnerabilidad, f
invulnerable a invulnerable
inward a interior, interno; íntimo, espiritual. adv adentro
inwardly adv interiormente; para sí, entre sí
inwards adv hacia dentro; adentro
iodine n yodo, m. **i. poisoning,** yodismo, m
ion n chem ion, m
Ionian a and n jónico (-ca)
Ionic a jónico. **i. foot** poet jónico, m
iota n (letter) iota, f; jota, pizca, f, ápice, m. **not an i.,** ni pizca
I.O.U. n com abonaré, m
ipecacuanha n ipecacuana, f
Iranian a and n iranio (-ia)
Iraq Irak, m
irascibility n irascibilidad, iracundia, irritabilidad, f
irascible a irascible, iracundo, irritable
irate a airado, colérico, enojado
ire n ira, cólera, furia, f
Ireland Irlanda, f
iridescence n iridiscencia, f
iridescent a iridiscente. **to look i.,** irisar, tornasolarse
iridium n chem iridio, m
iris n anat iris, m; bot iridácea, f
Irish a and n irlandés (-esa). **the I.,** los irlandeses
Irish Sea Mar de Irlanda, f

irksome *a* fastidioso, tedioso, aburrido
irksomeness *n* tedio, fastidio, aburrimiento, *m*
iron *n* hierro, *m*; (for clothes) plancha, *f*; (tool) utensilio, *m*, herramienta, *f*; (golf) hierro, *m*; *pl* **irons,** grillos, *m pl*, cadenas, *f pl. a* de hierro, férreo; *fig* duro, severo. *vt* (linen) planchar; (with out) allanar. **to have too many irons in the fire,** tener demasiados asuntos entre manos. **to put in irons,** echar grillos (a). **to strike while the i. is hot,** A hierro caliente batir de repente. **cast-i.,** hierro colado, *m.* **scrap i.,** hierro viejo, *m.* **sheet i.,** hierro en planchas, *m.* **wrought i.,** hierro dulce, *m.* **i. age,** edad de hierro, *f.* **i.-foundry,** fundición de hierro, *f.* **i. lung,** *med* pulmón de hierro, pulmón de acero, *m.* **i.-mold,** mancha de orín, *f.* **i. smelting furnace,** alto horno, *m.* **i. tonic,** *med* reconstituyente ferruginoso, *m.* **i. will,** voluntad de hierro, *f*
ironclad *a* blindado, acorazado. *n* buque de guerra blindado, acorazado, *m*
ironer *n* planchador (-ra)
ironical *a* irónico
ironically *adv* con ironía, irónicamente
ironing *n* planchado, *m*; ropa por planchar, *f. a* de planchar. **i. board,** tabla de planchar, *f*
ironist *n* ironista, *mf*
ironmonger *n* ferretero (-ra). **ironmonger's shop,** ferretería, *f*
ironmongery *n* ferretería, quincallería, *f*
iron sulphide sulfuro de hierro, *m*
ironwork *n* herraje, *m*; obra de hierro, *f*
ironworks *n* herrería, *f*
irony *n* ironía, *f. a* (like iron) ferruginoso
Iroquois *a* and *n* iroqués (-esa)
irradiate *vt* irradiar; *fig* iluminar, aclarar
irradiation *n* irradiación, *f*; *fig* iluminación, *f*
irrational *a* ilógico, ridículo, irracional
irrationality *n* irracionalidad, *f*
irreclaimable *a* irrecuperable, irredimible; (of land) inservible, improductivo, *f*
irreconcilable *a* irreconciliable
irreconcilably *adv* irremediablemente
irrecoverable *a* irrecuperable, incobrable
irredeemable *a* irredimible, perdido. **i. government loan,** deuda perpetua, *f*
irredeemably *adv* perdidamente
irreducible *a* irreducible
irrefutability *n* verdad, *f*
irrefutable *a* irrefutable, indisputable, innegable, irrebatible
irregular *a* irregular; anormal; (of shape) disforme; desordenado; *gram* irregular; (of surface) desigual, escabroso
irregularity *n* irregularidad, *f*; anormalidad, *f*; (of shape) desproporción, irregularidad, *f*; (of surface) escabrosidad, desigualdad, *f*; exceso, *m*, demasía, *f*
irrelevance *n* inconexión, *f*; inoportunidad, *f*; futilidad, poca importancia, *f*; (stupidity) desatino, *m*, impertinencia, *f*
irrelevant *a* inaplicable, fuera de propósito; inoportuno; sin importancia, fútil; (stupid) impertinente
irreligion *n* irreligión, impiedad, *f*
irreligious *a* irreligioso, impío
irremediable *a* irremediable, irreparable
irremediably *adv* sin remedio, irremediablemente
irreparable *a* irreparable
irreplaceable *a* irreemplazable
irrepressible *a* incontrolable, indomable
irreproachable *a* irreprochable, intachable
irresistible *a* irresistible
irresistibleness *n* superioridad, *f*
irresolute *a* irresoluto, indeciso, vacilante
irresoluteness *n* irresolución, indecisión, *f*
irrespective *a* (with of) independiente de, aparte de, sin distinción de
irresponsibility *n* irresponsabilidad, *f*
irresponsible *a* irresponsable
irretrievable *a* irrecuperable

irretrievably *adv* irreparablemente, sin remedio
irreverence *n* irreverencia, *f*
irreverent *a* irreverente, irrespetuoso
irrevocability *n* irrevocabilidad, *f*
irrevocable *a* irrevocable; inquebrantable
irrigable *a* regadío
irrigate *vt agr* poner en regadío, regar; *med* irrigar
irrigation *n agr* riego, *m*; *med* irrigación, *f.* **i. channel,** cacera, acequia, *f*, canal de riego, *m*
irritability *n* irritabilidad, iracundia, *f*
irritable *a* irritable, irascible, iracundo
irritably *adv* con irritación, airadamente
irritant *a* irritante, irritador. *n* irritador, *m*; *med* medicamento irritante, *m*
irritate *vt* provocar, estimular; irritar, molestar, exasperar; *med* irritar
irritating *a* irritador, irritante
irritatingly *adv* de un modo irritante
irritation *n* irritación, *f*, enojo, *m*; *physiol* picazón, *f*, picor, *m*
irruption *n* irrupción, invasión, *f*
isinglass *n* cola de pescado, *f*
Islamic *a* islámico
Islamism *n* islamismo, *m*
Islamite *a* and *n* islamita *mf*
island *n* isla, *f*, a isleño
islander *n* isleño (-ña)
islet *n* isleta, *f*; isolote, *m*
isobaric *a* isobárico
isolate *vt* aislar, apartar
isolated *a* aislado, apartado, solitario; único, solo
isolation *n* aislamiento, apartamiento, *m*, soledad, *f*
isolationism *n pol* aislacionismo, aislamientismo, *m*
isolationist *a* and *n pol* aislacionista, aislamientista, *mf*
isomerism *n chem* isomería, *f*
isometric *a* isométrico
isosceles *a* isósceles
isotope *n* isotope, isotopo, *m*
Israelite *a* and *n* israelita *mf*
issue *n* salida, *f*; (result) resultado, *m*, consecuencia, *f*; (of a periodical) número, *m*; *print* edición, tirada, *f*; (offspring) prole, sucesión, *f*; (of notes, bonds) emisión, *f*; *med* flujo, *m*; cuestión, *f*, problema, *m. vi* salir, fluir, manar; nacer, originarse; resultar, terminarse. *vt* (an order) expedir, emitir, dictar; publicar, dar a luz; (of notes, bonds) poner en circulación, librar. **at i.,** en disputa, en cuestión. **to join i.,** llevar la contraria, oponer
isthmian *a* ístmico
isthmus *n* istmo, *m*
it *pron* (as subject) él, *m*; ella, *f*; (gen. omitted with all verbs in Sp.); (as object) lo, *m*; la, *f*; (as indirect object) le (se with an object in 3rd pers.); (meaning that thing, that affair) eso, ello. Sometimes omitted in other cases, e.g. **He has thought it necessary to stay at home,** Ha creído preciso de quedarse en casa. **We heard it said that . . .,** Oímos decir que . . . **to make it perfectly clear that . . .,** dejar bien claro que . . . *n* (slang) garbo, aquél, *m*; atractivos, *m pl.* **Is it not so?** ¿No es así? **That is it,** Eso es. **It's me,** Soy yo
Italy Italia, *f*
Italian *a* and *n* italiano (-na) (language) italiano, *m. art* **I. School,** escuela italiana, *f*
italic *a* (of Italy) itálico; *print* itálico, bastardillo. *n* letra bastardilla, bastardilla, letra itálica, *f.* **italics mine,** el subrayado es mío, los subrayados son míos
italicize *vt* imprimir en bastardilla; dar énfasis (a)
itch *n* sarna, *f*; *fig* picazón, *f*, prurito, capricho, *m. vi* picar; *fig* sentir picazón; (with to) rabiar por, suspirar por.
itching *n* picazón, *f*, picor, *m. a* sarnoso, picante; *med* pruriginoso. **to have an i. palm,** *fig* ser de la virgen del puño
item *n* ítem, artículo, *m*; *com* partida, *f*; punto, detalle, *m*; (of a program) número, *m*; asunto, *m. adv* ítem
iterative *a* iterativo
Ithaca Ítaca, *f*

itinerant *a* nómada, errante

itinerary *n* itinerario, *m*, ruta, *f*

its *poss a* su (with pl. obj.) sus. **a book and its pages,** un libro y sus páginas.

itself *pron* él mismo, *m*; ella misma, *f*; (with prep.) sí; (with reflex. verb) se; (with noun) el mismo, la misma; (meaning alone) solo. **in i.,** en sí

ivied *a* cubierto de hiedra

ivory *n* marfil, *m. a* ebúrneo, de marfil, marfileño. **vegetable i.,** marfil vegetal, *m.* **i. carving,** talla de marfil, *f*

ivory tower *n* torre de marfil, *f*

ivory-tower *a* de torre de marfil

ivy *n* hiedra, *f*

J

j *n* (letter) jota, *f*

jab *vt* (with a hypodermic needle, etc.) pinchar; introducir (en); clavar (con); (scrape) hurgar; (place) poner. *n* pinchazo, *m*; golpe, *m.* **He jabbed his pistol in my ribs,** Me puso la pistola en las costillas

jabber *vt* and *vi* chapurrear; (of monkeys) chillar

jabbering *n* chapurreo, *m*; (of monkeys) chillidos, *m pl*

Jack *n* Juan, *m*; (man) hombre, *m*; (sailor) marinero, *m*; (in cards) sota, *f*; (for raising weights) gato, *m*; (of a spit) torno, *m*; (of some animals) macho, *m*; (bowls) boliche, *m. vt* (with up) solevantar con gatos. **Union J.,** pabellón británico, *m.* **j.-boot,** bota de montar, *f.* **J.-in-office,** mandarín, funcionario impertinente, *m.* **J.-in-the-box,** faca, *f.* **j.-knife,** navaja, *f.* **J. of all trades,** hombre de muchos oficios, *m.* **jack of all trades, master of none,** aprendiz de todo, oficial de nada. **j.-rabbit,** liebre americana, *f.* **J.-tar,** marinero, *m*

jackal *n* chacal, adive, *m*

jackanapes *n* impertinente, *m*; mequetrefe, *m*

jackass *n* asno, *m*; (fool) tonto, asno, *m.* **laughing j.,** martín pescador, *m*

jacket *n* chaqueta, *f*; americana, *f*; (for boilers, etc.) camisa, *f*; (of a book) forro, *m*, sobrecubierta, *f.* **strait j.,** camisa de fuerza, *f*

jacks *n* (game) matatenas, *f pl*; cantillos, *m pl*

jade *n min* jade, *m*; (horse) rocín, *m*; (woman) mala pécora, *f*; (saucy wench) mozuela, picaruela, *f*

jaded *a* fatigado, agotado, rendido; (of the palate) saciado

jagged *a* dentado

jaguar *n* jaguar, *m*

jail cárcel, prisión, *f*; encierro, *m. vt* encarcelar. *a* carcelario, carcelero.

jailbird malhechor; presidiario, *m*

jailer *n* carcelero (-ra)

jalopy carcacho, *m*, (Mexico), cafetera rusa, *f*, (Spain)

jalousie *n* celosía, *f*

jam *vt* (ram) apretar; apiñar; estrujar; (a machine) atascar; (radio) causar interferencia (a); (preserve) hacer confitura de. *vi* atascarse. *n* (of people) agolpamiento, *m*; (traffic) atasco, *m*; (preserve) confitura, mermelada, compota, *f.* **He jammed his hat on,** Se encasquetó el sombrero. **She suddenly jammed down on the brakes,** Frenó de repente. **jam-dish,** compotera, *f.* **jam-jar,** pote para confitura, *m*

Jamaican *a* jamaicano, *n* jamaicano (-na)

jamboree campamento, *m*

jamming *n rad* interferencias, *f pl*

jangle *vi* cencerrear; chocar; rechinar. *n* cencerreo, *m*; choque, *m*; rechinamiento, *m*

janissary *n* jenízaro, *m*

janitor *n* portero, *m*; (in a university, etc.) bedel, *m*

Jansenist *a* and *n* jansenista, *mf*

January *n* enero, *m*

Japan el Japón, *m*

japan *n* charol, *m. vt* charolar

Japanese *a* japonés. *n* japonés (-esa); (language) japonés, *m*

jar *n* chirrido, *m*; choque, *m*; sacudida, *f*; vibración, *f*, trepidación, *f*; (quarrel) riña, *f*; (receptacle) jarra, *f*; (for tobacco, honey, cosmetics, etc.) pote, *m*; (Leyden) botella (de Leyden), *f. vi* chirriar; vibrar, trepidar; chocar; (of sounds) ser discorde; (of colors) chillar. *vt* sacu-

dir; hacer vibrar. **It jarred on my nerves,** Me atacaba los nervios. **It gave me a nasty jar,** *fig* Me hizo una impresión desagradable. **on the jar,** entreabierto

jardiniere *n* jardinera, *f*

jargon *n* jerga, jerigonza, *f*; monserga, *f*; (technical) lenguaje especial, *m*

jarring *a* discorde, disonante; en conflicto, opuesto; (to the nerves) que ataca a los nervios

jasmine *n* jazmín, *m.* **yellow j.,** jazmín amarillo, *m*

jasper *n min* jaspe, *m*

jaundice *n* ictericia, *f*

jaundiced *a* envidioso; desengañado, desilusionado

jaunt *n* excursión, *f*, *vi* ir de excursión

jauntily *adv* airosamente, con garbo

jauntiness *n* garbo, *m*, gentileza, ligereza, *f*

jaunty *a* garboso, airoso

Javanese *a* javanés, *n* javanés (-esa)

javelin *n* jabalina, *f.* **j. throwing,** lanzamiento de la jabalina, *m*

jaw *n* quijada, *f*; maxilar, *m*; *pl* **jaws,** boca, *f*; (of death, etc.) garras, *f pl*; *mech* quijada, *f*; (narrow entrance) boca, abertura, *f.* **jaw-bone,** mandíbula, *f*; *anat* hueso maxilar, *m*

jay *n* arrendajo, *m*

jazz *n* jazz, *m. vi* bailar el jazz. **j. band,** orquesta de jazz, *f*

jealous *a* celoso; envidioso. **to be j. of,** tener celos de. **to make j.,** dar celos (a)

jealously *adv* celosamente

jealousy *n* celos, *m pl*

jeans *n* vaqueros, *m pl*

jeep *n mil* yip, *m*

jeer *n* burla, mofa, *f*; insulto, *m*, *vi* burlarse; (with at) mofarse de

jeerer *n* mofador (-ra)

jeering *a* mofador. *n* burlas, *f pl*; insultos, *m pl*

jeeringly *adv* burlonamente

jellied *a* en gelatina

jelly *n* jalea, *f*; gelatina, *f*, *vi* solidificarse. **j.-bag,** manga, *f.* **j.-fish,** aguamala, aguaviva, malagna, medusa, *f*

jeopardize *vt* arriesgar, poner en juego; comprometer

jeopardy *n* peligro, *m*

jeremiad *n* jeremiada, *f*

jerk *n* sacudida, *f. vt* sacudir, dar una sacudida (a); lanzar bruscamente; (pull) tirar de; (push) empujar. *vi* moverse a sacudidas. **I jerked myself free,** Me libré de una sacudida

jerkily *adv* con sacudidas; espasmódicamente; nerviosamente

jerkin *n* justillo, *m*

jerky *a* espasmódico; nervioso (also of style)

jerry-built *a* mal construido, de pacotilla

jersey *n* jersey, *m. a* de jersey; de Jersey. **football j.,** camiseta de fútbol, *f*, jersey de fútbol, *m.* **J. cow,** vaca jerseysa, *f*

Jerusalem Jerusalén, *m*

jest *n* broma, chanza, *f*; (joke) chiste, *m*; (laughingstock) hazmerreír, *m. vi* bromear; burlarse (de). **in j.,** en broma, de guasa

jester *n* burlón (-ona); (practical joker, etc.) bromista, *mf*; (at a royal court) bufón, *m*

jesting *n* bromas, *f pl*; chistes, *m pl*; burlas, *f pl. a* de broma; burlón

jestingly *adv* en broma

Jesuit *n* Jesuita, *m*

Jesuitical *a* jesuítico

jet *n* min azabache, *m*; (stream) chorro, *m*; (pipe) surtidero, *m*; (burner) mechero, *m*, *vi* chorrear. **jet-black**, negro como el azabache, de azabache. **jet-propelled engine**, motor de retroacción, *m*. **jet-propelled plane**, aeroplano de reacción, *m*

jetsam *n* echazón, *f*; *fig* víctima, *f*

jettison *n* echazón, *f. vt* echar (mercancías) al mar; *fig* librarse de, abandonar

jetty *n* dique, malecón, *m*; (landing pier) embarcadero, muelle, *m*

Jew *n* judío, *m*. **Jew's harp,** birimbao, *m*

jewel *n* joya, alhaja, *f*; (of a watch) rubí, *m*; *fig* alhaja, *f. vt* enjoyar, adornar con piedras preciosas. **j.-box, -case,** joyero, *m*

jeweled *a* adornado con piedras preciosas, enjoyado; (of a watch) con rubíes

jeweler *n* joyero (-ra). **jeweler's shop,** joyería, *f*

jewelry *n* joyas, *f pl*; artículos de joyería, *m pl*

Jewess *n* judía, *f*

Jewish *a* judío

Jewry *n* judería, *f*

jib *n naut* foque, *m. vi* (of a horse) plantarse; (refuse) rehusar. **to jib at,** vacilar en; mostrarse desinclinado. **jib-boom,** *naut* botalón de foque, *m*

jiffy *n* instante, credo, *m*. **in a j.,** en un decir Jesús, en un credo, en un santiamén

jig *n* (dance) jiga, *f. vi* bailar una jiga; bailar, agitarse, sacudirse. *vt* agitar, sacudir; (sieve) cribar

jigger *n naut* cangreja de mesana, *f*; aparejo de mano, *m*; jigger, *m*

jigsaw puzzle *n* rompecabezas, *m*

jilt *vt* dar calabazas (a)

jingle *n* tintineo, *m*; ruido, *m*; verso, *m*; estribillo, *m. vi* tintinar; sonar; rimar

jingoism *n* jingoísmo, *m*

jitters, to have the no tenerlas todas consigo, no saber dónde meterse

job *n* tarea, *f*; trabajo, *m*; empleo, *m*; (affair) asunto, *m*; (thing) cosa, *f*; (unscrupulous transaction) intriga, *f*. **It is a good (bad) job that . . . ,** Es una buena (mala) cosa que . . . **He has done a good job,** Ha hecho un buen trabajo. **He has lost his job,** Ha perdido su empleo, Le han declarado cesante. **odd-job man,** factótum, *m*. **job-lot,** colección miscelánea, *f*; *com* saldo de mercancías, *m*

jobber *n* (workman) destajista, *m*; (in stocks) agiotista, *m*; *com* corredor, *m*

jobless *a* sin trabajo

jockey *n* jockey, *m. vt* engañar; (with into) persuadir, hacer; (with out of) quitar, robar. **j. cap,** gorra de jockey, *f*. **J. Club,** jockey-club, *m*

jocose *a* jocoso, gracioso, guasón

jocosity *n* jocosidad, *f*

jocular *a* gracioso, alegre; chistoso, zumbón

jocularity *n* alegría, jocosidad, *f*

jocularly *adv* en broma; alegremente

jocund *a* alegre, jovial; jocundo

jocundity *n* alegría, *f*; jocundidad, *f*

jog *vt* empujar; (the memory) refrescar. *vi* ir despacio; andar a trote corto. *n* empujón, *m*. **He jogged me with his elbow,** Me dio con el codo. **jog-trot,** trote corto, *m*

joie de vivre *n* goce de vivir, arregosto de vivir, *m*

join *vt* juntar; unir; añadir; (railway lines) empalmar; juntarse con; (meet) encontrarse (con); reunirse (con); (a club, etc.) hacerse miembro (de); (share) acompañar; (regiments, ships) volver (a). *vi* juntarse; unirse; asociarse. *n* unión, *f*; (railway) empalme, *m*; (roads) bifurcación, *f*. **At what time will you j. me?** ¿A qué hora me vendrás a buscar? **He has joined his ship,** Ha vuelto a su buque. **Will you j. me in a drink?** ¿Me quieres acompañar en una bebida? **to j. battle,** librar batalla. **to j. forces,** combinar; *inf* juntar meriendas. **to j. in,** tomar parte en, participar en. **to j. together,** *vt*

unir, juntar. *vi* juntarse; asociarse. **to j. up,** alistarse

joiner *n* carpintero, ensamblador, *m*,

joinery *n* ensambladuría, *f*; carpintería, *f*

joining *n* juntura, conjunción, *f*; (carp etc.) ensambladura, *f*; *fig* unión, *f*

joint *n* juntura, junta, *f*; *anat* coyuntura, articulación, *f*; (knuckle) nudillo, *m*; (of meat) cuarto, *m*; (hinge) bisagra, *f*; *bot* nudo, *m*, *a* unido; combinado; colectivo; mixto; mutuo; (in compounds) co. *vt* juntar; (meat) descuartizar. **out of j.,** dislocado; (of the times) fuera de compás. **j. account,** cuenta corriente mutua, *f*. **j.-heir,** coheredero, *m*. **j. stock company,** compañía por acciones, sociedad anónima, *f*

jointed *a* articulado; (foldable) plegadizo

jointly *adv* juntamente, en común, colectivamente

joist *n* sopanda, viga, *f*

joke *n* chiste, *m*; burla, broma, *f. vi* bromear, chancearse. *vt* burlarse (de). **Can he take a j.?** ¿Sabe aguantar una broma? **practical j.,** broma pesada, *f*. **to play a j.,** gastar una broma, hacer una burla

joker *n* bromista, *mf*; (in cards) comodín, *m*

joking *n* chistes, *m pl*, bromas, *f pl*. *a* chistoso; cómico

jokingly *adv* en broma, de guasa

jollification *n* regocijo, *m*; festividades, fiestas, *f pl*

jollity *n* alegría, *f*, regocijo, *m*

jolly *a* alegre, jovial; (tipsy) achispado; (amusing) divertido; (nice) agradable. *adv* muy. **He is a j. good fellow,** Es un hombre estupendo. **I am j. glad,** Estoy contentísimo, Me alegro mucho

jolt *n* sacudida, *f. vt* sacudir. *vi* (of a vehicle) traquetear

jolting *n* sacudidas, *f pl*, sacudimiento, *m*; (of a vehicle) traqueteo, *m*

jongleur *n* juglar, *m*

jonquil *n bot* junquillo, *m*

Jordan Jordania, *f*

joss *n* ídolo chino, *m*. **j.-stick,** pebete, *m*

jostle *vt* empujar, empellar. *vi* dar empujones, codear

jot *n* jota, pizca, *f. vt* (down) apuntar. **not a jot,** ni jota, ni pizca. **to be not worth a jot,** no valer un comino

jotter *n* taco para notas, *m*; (exercise book) cuaderno, *m*

jotting *n* apunte, *m*; observación, *f*

journal *n* (diary) diario, *m*; (ship's) diario de navegación, *m*; (newspaper) periódico, *m*; (review) revista, *f*

journalese *n* lenguaje periodístico, *m*

journalism *n* periodismo, *m*

journalist *n* periodista, *mf*

journalistic *a* periodístico

journey *n* viaje, *m*; expedición, *f*; trayecto, *m*; camino, *m. vi* viajar. **j. by sea,** viaje por mar. **Pleasant j.!** ¡Buen viaje! ¡Feliz viaje! **outward j.,** viaje de ida, *m*. **return j.,** viaje de regreso, *m*

Jove *n* Júpiter, *m*. **By J.!** ¡Pardiez! ¡Caramba!

jovial *a* jovial

joviality *n* jovialidad, *f*

jowl *n* (cheek) carrillo, *m*; (of cattle, etc.) papada, *f*; (jaw) quijada, *f*

joy *n* alegría, *f*; felicidad, *f*; deleite, placer, *m*, *vi* alegrarse. **I wish you joy,** Te deseo la felicidad. **joy-ride,** excursión en coche, *f*; vuelo en avión. *m*. **joy-stick,** (of an airplane) palanca de gobierno, *m*

joyful *a* alegre

joyfulness *n* alegría, *f*

joyless *a* sin alegría, triste

joylessness *n* falta de alegría, tristeza, *f*

joyous. See **joyful**

jubilant *a* jubiloso; triunfante

jubilantly *adv* con júbilo, alegremente; triunfalmente

jubilation *n* júbilo, *m*, alegría, *f*; ruido triunfal, *m*

jubilee *n* jubileo, *m*

jubilee volume *n* libro de homenaje, libro jubilar, *m*

Judaic *a* judaico

Judaism *n* judaísmo, *m*

Judas *n* (traitor and hole) judas, *m*

Judezmo el judesmo, *m*

judge *n* juez, *m*; (connoisseur) conocedor (-ra) (de); (umpire) árbitro, *m*. *vt* juzgar; considerar, tener por. *vi* servir como juez; juzgar. **judging by,** a juzgar por. **to be a good j. of,** ser buen juez de. **to j. for oneself,** formar su propia opinión

judgment, judgement *n law* fallo, *m*; sentencia, *f*; juicio, *m*; (understanding) entendimiento, discernimiento, *m*; (opinion) opinión, *f*, parecer, *m*. **In my j. . . . ,** Según mi parecer, . . . Según creo yo . . . **Last J.,** Juicio Final, *m*. **to pass j. on,** *law* pronunciar sentencia (en or sobre); dictaminar sobre; juzgar. **to sit in j. on,** ser juez de; juzgar. **j.-day,** Día del Juicio, *m*. **j.-seat,** tribunal, *m*

judicature *n* judicatura, *f*; (court) juzgado, *m*

judicial *a* judicial; legal; (of the mind) juicioso. **j. inquiry,** investigación judicial, *f*. **j. separation,** separación legal, *f*

judiciary *a* judicial. *n* judicatura, *f*

judicious *a* juicioso, prudente.

judiciously *adv* prudentemente, juiciosamente

judiciousness *n* juicio, *m*, prudencia, sensatez, *f*

judo *n* yudo, *m*

judoka *n* yudoca, *mf*

jug *n* jarro, *m*; cántaro, *m*; pote, *m*. *vt cul* estofar. *vi* (of nightingale) trinar, cantar. **jugged hare,** *n* liebre en estofado, *f*

juggle *vi* hacer juegos malabares. **to j. out of,** (money, etc.) quitar con engaño, estafar. **to j. with,** *fig* (facts, etc.) tergiversar, falsificar; (person) engañar

juggler *n* malabarista, *mf*; (deceiver) estafador (-ra)

jugglery *n* prestidigitación, *f*; juegos malabares, *m pl*; (imposture) engaño, *m*, estafa, *f*; trampas, *f pl*

jugular *a anat* yugular. **j. vein,** yugular, *n*

juice *n* jugo, *m*; *fig* zumo, *m*. **digestive j.,** jugo digestivo, *m*

juiciness *n* jugosidad, *f*; suculencia, *f*

juicy *a* jugoso; suculento

jujube *n* pastilla, *f*

jukebox *n* tocadiscos, vitrola, sinfonola, *f*

July *n* julio, *m*

jumble *vt* mezclar, confundir. *n* mezcla confusa, colección miscelánea, confusión, *f*. **j. sale,** tómbola, *f*

jump *n* salto, *m*; (in prices, etc.) aumento, *m*. **at one j.,** de un salto. **high j.,** salto de altura, *m*. **long j.,** salto de longitud, *m*. **to be on the j.,** *inf* estar nervioso, tener los nervios en punta

jump *vi* saltar; dar un salto; brincar; (of tea-cups, etc.) bailar; (throb) pulsar. *vt* saltar; hacer saltar; (a child) brincar; (omit) pasar por alto de, omitir. **The train jumped the rails,** El tren se descarriló. **to j. out of bed,** saltar de la cama. **to j. to the conclusion that . . . ,** darse prisa a concluir que . . . **to j. about,** dar saltos, brincar; revolverse, moverse de un lado para otro. **to j. at,** saltar sobre; precipitarse sobre, abalanzarse hacia; (an offer) apresurarse a aceptar; (seize) coger con entusiasmo. **to j. down,** bajar de un salto. **to j. over,** saltar; saltar por encima de. **to j. up,** saltar; (on to a horse, etc.) montar rápidamente; levantarse apresuradamente. **to j. with,** (agree) convenir en, estar conforme con

jumper *n* saltador (-ra); (sailor's) blusa, *f*; jersey, sweater, *m*

jumping *n* saltos, *m pl. a* saltador. **j.-off place,** base avanzada, *f*; *fig* trampolín, *m*. **j.-pole,** pértiga, *f*

jumpiness *n* nerviosidad, *f*

jumpy *a* nervioso, agitado

junction *n* unión, *f*; (of roads) bifurcación, *f*; (railway) empalme, *m*; (connection) conexión, *f*

juncture *n* coyuntura, *f*; momento, *m*; crisis, *f*, momento crítico, *m*; (joint) junta, *f*

June *n* junio, *m*

jungle *n* selva, *f*. **j.-fever,** fiebre de los grandes bosques, *f*

junior *a* joven; hijo; más joven; menos antiguo; subordinado, segundo. *n* joven, *mf* **Carmen is my j. by three years,** Carmen es tres años más joven que yo. **James Thomson, Jr.,** James Thomson, hijo. **the j. school,** los pequeños. **j. partner,** socio menor, *m*

juniper *n bot* enebro, *m*

junk *n* trastos viejos, *m pl*; (nonsense) patrañas, *f pl*; *naut* junco, *m*; (salt meat) tasajo, *m*. **j.-shop,** tienda de trastos viejos, *f*

junk bond bono-basura, *m*

junketing *n* festividades, *f pl*

juridical *a* jurídico

jurisconsult *n* jurisconsulto, *m*

jurisdiction *n* jurisdicción, *f*; competencia, *f*

jurisprudence *n* jurisprudencia, *f*

jurist *n* jurista, legista, *m*

juror *n* (miembro del) jurado, *m*

jury *n* jurado, *m*. **to be on the j.,** formar parte del jurado. **j.-box,** tribuna del jurado, *f*

juryman *n* miembro del jurado, *m*

just *a* justo; justiciero; exacto; fiel. **Peter the J.,** Pedro el justiciero

just *adv* justamente, exactamente; precisamente; (scarcely) apenas; (almost) casi; (entirely) completamente; (simply) meramente, solamente, tan sólo; (newly) recién (followed by past part.), recientemente. **He only j. missed being run over,** Por poco le atropellan. **It is j. near,** Está muy cerca. **It is j. the same to me,** Me es completamente igual. **J. as he was leaving,** Cuando estaba a punto de marcharse, En el momento de marcharse. **Just as you arrive in Spain, you must . . .** Nada más llegar a España, tienes que . . . **That's j. it!** ¡Eso es! ¡Exactamente! **to have j.,** acabar de. **They have j. dined,** Acaban de cenar. **j. as you wish,** Como Vd. quiera. **j. at that moment,** precisamente en aquel momento. **j. by,** muy cerca; al lado. **j. now,** ahora mismo; hace poco; pronto, dentro de poco. **j. yet,** todavía. **They will not come j. yet,** No vendrán todavía. **Just looking** (browser to shopkeeper) Estoy viendo, Estamos viendo

justice *n* justicia, *f*; (judge) juez, *m*; (magistrate) juez municipal, *m*. **to bring to j.,** llevar ante el juez (a). **to do j. to,** (a person) hacer justicia (a); (a meal) hacer honor (a). **to do oneself j.,** quedar bien

justifiable *a* justificable

justifiably *adv* con justicia, justificadamente

justification *n* justificación, *f*

justify *vt* justificar, vindicar; (excuse) disculpar; *print* justificar. **to be justified (in),** tener derecho a (tener motivo (para), tener razón (en)

justly *adv* justamente; con justicia; con derecho; con razón; exactamente; debidamente

justness *n* justicia, *f*; exactitud, *f*

jut (out) *vi* salir, proyectar; sobresalir

jute *n* yute, *m*

juvenile *a* juvenil; de la juventud; para la juventud; joven; de niños; para niños. *n* joven, *mf*. **j. court,** tribunal de menores, *m*. **j. lead,** *theat* galancete, galán joven, *m*. **j. offender,** delincuente infantil, *m*

juxtapose *vt* yuxtaponer

juxtaposition *n* yuxtaposición, *f*

K

k *n* (letter) ka, *f*

kaiser *n* káiser, emperador, *m*. **the K.** el emperador alemán, *m*

kaleidoscope *n* calidoscopio, *m*

kaleidoscopic *a* calidoscópico

kangaroo *n* canguro, *m*

kaolin *n* caolín, *m*

kapok *n* miraguano, *m*

keel *n* quilla, *f*. *vt* carenar. **to k. over,** volcar; caer; *naut* zozobrar

keelson *n* sobrequilla, *f*
keen *a* (of edges) afilado; agudo; penetrante; vivo; sutil; ardiente; celoso, entusiasta; mordaz; (desirous) ansioso; (of appetite) grande, bueno. **He is a k. tennis player,** Es tenista entusiasta. **Joan has a very k. ear,** Juana tiene un oído muy agudo. **I'm not very k. on apples,** No me gustan mucho las manzanas
keenly *adv* agudamente; vivamente; (of feeling) hondamente; (of looking) atentamente
keenness *n* (of a blade) afiladura, *f*; agudeza, *f*; viveza, *f*; sutileza, *f*; perspicacia, *f*; (enthusiasm) entusiasmo, *m*, afición, *f*; (desire) ansia, *f*
keep *vt* guardar; tener; que darse con; retener; conservar; mantener; (a shop, hotel, etc.) dirigir, tener; (a school) ser director de; (a promise, etc.) cumplir; (the law, etc.) observar, guardar; (celebrate) solemnizar; (a secret) guardar; (books, accounts, a house, in step) llevar; (sheep, etc., one's bed) guardar; (a city, etc.) defender; (domestic animals, cars, etc.) tener; (lodge) alojar; (detain) detener; (reserve) reservar; (cause) hacer. **They had kept this room for me,** Me habían reservado este cuarto. **Dorothy has kept the blue dress,** Dorotea se ha quedado con el vestido azul. **The government could not k. order,** El gobierno no sabía mantener el orden. **I did not know how to k. their attention,** No sabía retener su atención. **Carmen kept quiet,** Carmen guardó silencio, Carmen se calló. **Can you k. a secret?** ¿Sabes guardar un secreto? **to k. an appointment,** acudir a una cita. **to k. in repair,** conservar en buen estado. **to k. someone from doing something,** evitar que uno haga algo. **to k. someone waiting,** hacer que espere uno. **to k. something from someone,** ocultar algo de uno. **We were kept at it night and day,** Nos hacían trabajar día y noche. **I always k. it by me,** Lo tengo siempre a mi lado (or conmigo). **to k. away,** alejar; mantener a distancia; no dejar venir. **to k. back,** (a crowd, etc.) detener; cortar el paso (a); no dejar avanzar; (retain) guardar, retener; reservar; (tears, words) reprimir, contener; (evidence, etc.) callar, suprimir. **to k. down,** no dejar subir (a); sujetar; (a nation, etc.) oprimir, subyugar; (emotions) dominar; (prices, expenses) mantener bajo; (check) moderar, reprimir. **to k. in,** (feelings) contener; reprimir; (the house) hacer quedarse en casa, no dejar salir; (imprison) encerrar; (school) hacer quedar en la escuela (a). **to k. off,** alejar; tener a distancia (a); cerrar el paso (a), no dejar avanzar; no andar sobre; no tocar; (a subject) no tratar de, no discutir, no tocar. **K. your hands off!** ¡No toques! **to k. on,** guardar; retener; (eyes) fijar en, poner en. **to k. out,** no dejar entrar; excluir. **It is difficult to k. him out of trouble,** Es difícil de evitar que se meta en líos. **to k. to,** seguir; limitarse a; adherirse a; **K. to the Left,** «Tome su izquierda», **K. to the right,** «Tome su derecha»; (a path, etc.) seguir por; (one's bed) guardar; (fulfil) cumplir; (oblige) hacer, obligar. **to k. under,** subyugar, oprimir; dominar; controlar. **to k. up,** mantener; (appearances) guardar; conservar; persistir en; (prices) sostener; (in good repair) conservar en buen estado; (go on doing) continuar. **He kept me up late last night,** Anoche me entretuvo hasta muy tarde; Ayer me hizo trasnochar; Anoche me hizo velar. **to k. one's end up,** volver por sí, hacerse fuerte. **to k. up one's spirits,** no desanimarse
keep *vi* quedar; (be) estar; (continue) seguir, continuar; mantenerse; (at home, etc.) quedarse, permanecer; (be accustomed) acostumbrar, soler; (persist) perseverar; (of food) conservarse fresco. **How is he keeping?** ¿Cómo está? **to k. in with someone,** cultivar a alguien. **to k. up with the times,** mantenerse al corriente. **to k. at,** seguir; persistir; perseverar; (pester) importunar. **John keeps at it,** Juan trabaja sin descansar. **to k. away,** mantenerse apartado; mantenerse a distancia; no acudir. **to k. back,** hacerse a un lado, apartarse, alejarse. **to k. down,** quedarse tumbado; seguir acurrucado; no levantarse; esconderse. **to k.**

from, (doing something) guardarse de. **to k. off,** mantenerse a distancia. **If the storm keeps off,** Si no estalla una tempestad. **If the rain keeps off,** Si no empieza a llover, Si no hay lluvia. **to k. on,** continuar; seguir. **to k. straight on,** seguir derecho. **I'm tired, but I still k. on,** Estoy cansado, pero sigo trabajando. **to k. out,** quedarse fuera. **to k. out of,** (quarrels, trouble, etc.) no meterse en, evitar. **to k. out of sight,** no dejarse ver, no mostrarse, mantenerse oculto. **to k. together,** quedarse juntos; reunirse
keep *n* (of a castle) mazmorra, *f*; (maintenance) subsistencia, *f*; comida, *f*. **for keeps,** para siempre jamás
keeper *n* guarda, *mf*; (in a park, zoo, of a lunatic) guardián, *m*; (of a museum, etc.) director, *m*; (of animals) criador (-ra); (gamekeeper) guardabosque, *m*; (of a boardinghouse, shop, etc.) dueño (-ña); (of accounts, books) tenedor, *m*. **Am I my brother's k.?** ¿Soy yo responsable por mi hermano?
keeping *n* guarda, *f*; conservación, *f*; protección, *f*; (of a rule) observación, *f*; (of an anniversary, etc.) celebración, *f*; (of a person) mantenimiento, *m*. **in k. with,** en armonía con; de acuerdo con. **out of k. with,** en desacuerdo con. **to be in safe k.,** estar en buenas manos; estar en un lugar seguro. **k. back,** retención, *f*
keepsake *n* recuerdo, *m*
keg *n* barrilete, *m*
ken *n* alcance de la vista, *m*; vista, *f*; comprensión, *f*
Kennedy Round, the la serie Kénnedy, *f*
kennel *n* (of a dog) perrera, *f*; (of hounds) jauría, *f*; (dwelling) cuchitril, *m*; (gutter) arroyo, *m*. **k. man,** perrero, *m*
kepi *n* quepis, *m*
Kepler Keplero
kerb, kerbstone See **curb**
kerchief *n* pañuelo, *m*; pañoleta, *f*. **brightly-colored k.,** pañuelo de hierbas, *m*
kernel *n* almendra, semilla, *f*; *fig* meollo, *m*, esencia, *f*
kerosene *n* petróleo de lámpara, *m*; kerosén, *m*
ketchup *n* salsa de tomate y setas, *f*
kettle *n* caldero, *m*. **pretty k. of fish,** olla de grillos, *f*. **k.-drum,** timbal, *m*. **k.-drum player,** timbalero, *m*
key *n* llave, *f*; (*fig arch, mus*) clave, *f*; (tone) tono, *m*; (of a piano, typewriter, etc.) tecla, *f*; *mech* chaveta, *f*; (of a wind instrument) pistón, *m*; (winged fruit) sámara, *f*; *elec* conmutador, *m*. **major (minor) key,** tono mayor (menor), *m*. **latch-key,** llave de la puerta, *f*; (Yale) llavín, *m*. **master key,** llave maestra, *f*. **skeleton key,** ganzúa, *f*. **He is all keyed up,** Tiene los nervios en punta. **key industry,** industria clave, *f*. **key man,** hombre indispensable, *m*. **key point,** punto estratégico, *m*. **key-ring,** llavero, *m*. **key signature,** *mus* clave, *f*. **key word,** palabra clave, *f*
keyboard *n* teclado, *m*
keyhole *n* ojo de la cerradura, *m*. **through the k.,** por el ojo de la cerradura
keynote *n* *mus* tónica, *f*; *fig* piedra clave, idea fundamental, *f*
keystone *n* piedra clave, *f*
khaki *n* caqui, *m*
kick *vt* dar un puntapié (a); golpear; (a goal) chutar. *vi* (of horses, etc.) dar coces, cocear; (of guns) recular. **to k. one's heels,** hacer tiempo. **to kick the bucket,** palmarla. **to k. up a row,** hacer un ruido de mil diablos; (quarrel) armar camorra. **to k. about,** dar patadas (a). **to k. away,** quitar con el pie; lanzar con el pie. **to k. off,** quitar con el pie; lanzar; sacudirse. **k.-off,** *n* golpe de salida, puntapié inicial, saque, *m*. **to k. out,** echar a puntapiés
kick *n* puntapié, *m*; golpe, *m*; coz, *f*; (of guns) culatazo, *m*. **free k.,** golpe franco, *m*
kicking *n* coces, *m f pl*; acoceamiento, *m*; pataleo, *m*; golpeamiento, *m*
kid *n* cabrito, *m*, chivo (-va); carne de cabrito, *f*; (leather) cabritilla, *f*; *inf* crío, *m*. **kid gloves,** guantes de cabritilla, *m pl*
kidnap *vt* secuestrar

kidnapper *n* secuestrador (-ra); ladrón (-ona) de niños
kidnapping *n* secuestro, *m*
kidney *n* riñón, *m*; *fig* especie, índole, *f*. **k.-bean,** (plant) judía, *f*; (fruit) habichuela, judía, *f*, fréjol, *m*
Kidron Cedrón, *m*
kill *vt* matar; destruir; suprimir. **to k. off,** exterminar. **to k. time,** entretener el tiempo, pasarse las horas muertas. **to k. two birds with one stone,** matar dos pájaros de un tiro. **k.-joy,** aguafiestas, *mf*
killer *n* matador (-ra); (murderer) asesino, *mf*
killing *n* matanza, *f*; (murder) asesinato, *m*. *a* matador; destructivo; (comic) cómico; ridículo, absurdo; (ravishing) irresistible
kiln *n* horno de cerámica, horno, *m*
kilo *n* kilo, *m*
kilocycle *n elec* kilociclo, *m*
kilogram *n* kilogramo, *m*
kiloliter *n* kilolitro, *m*
kilometer *n* kilómetro, *m*
kilometric *a* kilométrico
kilowatt *n elec* kilovatio, *m*
kilt *n* enagüillas, *f pl*
kimono *n* quimono, *m*
kin *n* parientes, *m pl*; familia, *f*; clase, especie, *f*. **the next of kin,** los parientes próximos, la familia
kind *n* género, *m*, clase, *f*; especie, *f*; *inf* tipo, *m*. **He is a queer k. of person,** Es un tipo muy raro. **What k. of cloth is it?** ¿Qué clase de tela es? **Nothing of the k!** ¡Nada de eso! **payment in k.,** pago en especie, *m*
kind *a* bondadoso, bueno; cariñoso, tierno; amable; favorable, propicio. **Will you be so k. as to** . . . Tenga Vd. la bondad de . . . **With k. regards,** Con un saludo afectuoso. **You have been very k. to her,** Vd. ha sido muy bueno para ella. **k.-hearted,** bondadoso. **k.-heartedness,** bondad, benevolencia, *f*
kindergarten *n* jardín de la infancia, kindergarten, *m*
kindle *vt* encender; hacer arder; *fig* avivar. *vi* prender, empezar a arder; encenderse; *fig* inflamarse
kindliness *n* bondad, *f*
kindling *n* encendimiento (del fuego), *m*; (wood) leña menuda, *f*
kindly *a* bondadoso; bueno; benévolo; propicio, favorable; (of climate) benigno. *adv* con bondad, bondadosamente; fácilmente. **K. sit down,** Haga el favor de sentarse
kindness *n* bondad, *f*; benevolencia, *f*; amabilidad, *f*; cariño, *m*; favor, *m*, atención, *f*
kindred *n* parentesco, *m*; parientes, *m pl*; familia, *f*; afinidad, *f*, *a* emparentado; hermano
king *n* (ruler, important person, chess, cards) rey, *m*; (in draughts) dama, *f*; **king's evil,** escrófula, *f*. **k.-bolt,** perno real, *m*. **k.-craft,** arte de reinar, *m*, or *f*. **k.-cup,** *bot* botón de oro, *m*. **K.-of-Arms,** rey de armas, *m*. **k.-post,** pendolón, *m*
kingdom *n* reino, *m*. **animal k.,** reino animal, *m*
kingfisher *n* martín pescador, alción, *m*
kink *n* nudo, *m*; pliegue, *m*; (curl) rizo, *m*; *fig* peculiaridad, *f*
kinsfolk *n* parientes, *m pl*, familia, *f*
kinship *n* parentesco, *m*; afinidad, *f*
kinsman *n* pariente, deudo, *m*
kinswoman *n* parienta, *f*
kiosk *n* quiosco, *m*
kipper *n* arenque ahumado, *m*. *vt* ahumar
kiss *n* beso, *m*; (in billiards) pelo, *m*. *vt* besar; dar un beso (a); (of billiard balls) tocar. **to k. each other,** besarse. **k.-curl,** rizo de la sien, *m*, sortijilla, *f*
kit *n* (tub) cubo, *m*; (for tools, etc.) cajita, caja, *f*; (soldier's) equipo, *m*. **kit-bag,** mochila, *f*
kitchen *n* cocina, *f*. **k.-boy,** pinche (de cocina), *m*. **k.-garden,** huerta, *f*. **k.-maid,** fregona, *f*. **k.-range,** cocina económica, *f*. **k.-sink,** fregadero, *m*. **k.-stove,** horno de cocina, *m*. **k. utensils,** batería de cocina, *f*
kitchenette *n* cocinilla, *f*
kite *n orn* milano, *m*; cometa, pájara, *f*. **to fly a k.,** hacer volar una cometa. **box-k.,** cometa celular, *f*

kith and kin *n pl* parientes y amigos, *m pl*
kitten *n* gatito (-ta). *vi* (of a cat) parir
kittenish *a* de gatito; juguetón
kitty *n* michito, *m*; (in card games) platillo, *m*
kleptomania *n* cleptomanía, *f*
kleptomaniac *a* cleptómano. *n* cleptómano (-na)
knack *n* destreza, *f*; talento, *m*; (trick) truco, *m*
knapsack *n* mochila, *f*; *mil* alforja, *f*
knave *n* bellaco, truhán, tunante, *m*; (at cards) sota, *f*
knavery *n* bellaquería, truhanería, *f*
knavish *a* de bribón; taimado, truhanesco
knead *vt* amasar; (massage) sobar; *fig* formar
kneading *n* amasijo, *m*; (massaging) soba, *f*. **k.-trough,** amasadera artesa *f*
knee *n* rodilla, *f*; *fig* ángulo, codillo, *m*. **on bended k.,** de hinojos. **on one's knees,** de rodillas, arrodillado. **to go down on one's knees,** arrodillarse, ponerse de rodillas. **k.-breeches,** calzón corto, *m*; calzón ceñido, *m*; (Elizabethan) gregüescos, *m pl*. **k.-cap,** rótula, *f*. **k.-deep,** hasta las rodillas. **k.-joint,** articulación de la rodilla, *f*; *mech* junta de codillo, *f*. **k.-pad,** rodillera, *f*
kneel (down) *vi* arrodillarse, hincarse de rodillas, ponerse de rodillas
kneeling *a* arrodillado, de rodillas
knell *n* toque de difuntos, tañido fúnebre, *m*; toque de campanas, *m*; *fig* muerte, *f*. *vi* tocar a muerto. *vt fig* anunciar, presagiar
knickerbockers *n pl* bragas, *f pl*; calzón corto, *m* (women's) pantalones, *m pl*
knickknack *n* chuchería, *f*
knife *n* cuchillo, *m*. **to have one's k. in someone,** tener enemiga (a), querer mal (a). **war to the k.,** guerra a muerte, *f*. **k.-edge,** filo de cuchillo, *m*; fiel de soporte, *m*. **k. grinder,** amolador, *m*. **k.-handle,** mango de cuchillo, *m*. **k. thrust,** cuchillada, *f*
knife, fork, and spoon cuchara, tenedor, y cuchillo
knight *n* caballero, *m*; (chess) caballo, *m*. *vt* armar caballero, calzar la espuela; (in modern usage) dar el título de caballero. **untried k.,** caballero novel, *m*. **k. commander,** comendador, *m*. **k.-errant,** caballero andante, *m*. **k.-errantry,** caballería andante, *f*. **Knight of Labor,** Caballero del Trabajo *m*. **k. of the rueful countenance,** el caballero de la triste figura
knighthood *n* caballería, *f*; (in modern usage) título de caballero, *m*
knightly *a* caballeresco; de caballero; de caballería
knit *vt* and *vi* hacer calceta hacer media; juntar, ligar; unir. **Isabel is knitting me a jumper,** Isabel me hace un jersey de punto de media. **to k. one's brows,** fruncir el ceño
knitted *a* de punto. **k. goods,** géneros de punto, *m pl*
knitter *n* calcetero (-ra); (machine) máquina de hacer calceta, *f*
knitting *n* acción de hacer calceta, *f*; trabajo de punto, *m*, labor de calceta, *f*; unión, *f*. **k.-machine,** máquina de hacer calceta, *f*. **k.-needle,** aguja de media, aguja de hacer calceta, *f*
knob *n* protuberancia, *f*; (of a door, etc.) perilla, borlita, *f*; (ornamental) bellota, *f*; (of sugar) terrón, *m*; (of a stick) puño, *m*
knock *n* golpe, *m*; choque, *m*; (with a knocker) aldabada, *f*
knock *vt* golpear; chocar (contra). *vi* llamar a la puerta; (of an engine) picar. **to k. one's head against,** chocar con la cabeza contra, dar con la cabeza contra. **to k. about,** *vt* pegar; aporrear. *vi* viajar; vagar, rodar; callejear. **to k. against,** golpear contra; chocar contra. **to k. down,** derribar; (of vehicles) atropellar; (houses, etc.) demoler; (an argument, etc.) destruir; (a tender, etc.) rebajar; (of an auctioneer) rematar al mejor postor. **to k. in,** (nails, etc.) clavar. **to k. into one another,** toparse. **to k. off,** hacer caer; sacudir; quitar; (from price) descontar; (from speed, etc.) reducir; (finish) terminar pronto; (runs in cricket) hacer. **to k. out,** (remove) quitar; (boxing) dejar fuera de combate, noquear; (*fig* stun) atontar; (an idea, etc.) bosquejar. **to**

k. over, volcar. **to k. up,** hacer saltar; (call) llamar; (runs at cricket) hacer; (tire) agotar, rendir; (building) construir toscamente. **to k. up against,** chocar contra; tropezar con. **k.-kneed,** *a* patiabierto. **k.-out,** "knock-out," *m*

knocker *n* (on a door) aldaba, *f.* **k.-up,** despertador, *m*

knocking *n* golpes, *m pl,* golpeo, *m;* (with a knocker) aldabeo, *m.* **k. over,** vuelco, *m;* (by a vehicle) atropello, *m*

knoll *n* altillo, otero, *m*

knot *n* nudo, *m;* (bow) lazo, *m;* (of hair) moño, *m; naut* nudo, *m,* milla náutica, *f;* (of people) corrillo, grupo, *m;* (on timber) nudo, *m. vt* anudar. *vi* hacer nudos; enmarañarse. **to tie a k.,** hacer un nudo

knotted *a* nudoso

knotty *a* nudoso; *fig* intrincado, difícil, complicado. **a k. problem,** problema espinoso

know *vt* conocer; saber; (understand) comprender; (recognize) reconocer. **I k.** her very well by sight, La conozco muy bien de vista. **John knows Latin,** Juan sabe latín. **How can I k.?** ¿Cómo lo voy a saber yo? **I knew you at once,** Te reconocí en seguida. **They always k. best,** Siempre tienen razón. **Did you k. about Philip?** ¿Has oído lo de Felipe? **to be in the k.,** estar bien informado, saber de buena tinta. **to get to k.,** (a person) llegar a conocer, trabar amistad con. **to make known,** dar a conocer; manifestar. **Who knows?** ¿Quién sabe? **to k. by heart,** saber de coro. **to k. how,** (to do something) saber. **to k. oneself,**

conocerse a sí mismo. **k.-it-all,** sábelotodo, *mf,* marisabidilla, *f*

knowing *a* inteligente; malicioso; (of animals) sabio. **There is no k.,** No hay modo de saberlo. **worth k.,** digno de saberse

knowingly *adv* a sabiendas, de intento; conscientemente; (cleverly) hábilmente; (with look, etc.) de un aire malicioso

knowledge *n* conocimiento, *m.* **To the best of my k. the book does not exist,** El libro no existe que yo sepa. **He has a thorough k. of . . .,** Conoce a fondo **. . . lack of k.,** ignorancia, *f.* **He did it without my k.,** Lo hizo sin que lo supiera yo. **It is a matter of common k. that . . .** Es notorio que . . .

knowledgeable *a* sabedor

known *a* conocido

knuckle *n* (of a finger) nudillo, *m,* articulación del dedo, *f;* (of meat) jarrete, *m.* **He knuckled down to his work,** Se puso a trabajar con ahínco. **to k. under,** someterse. **k.-duster,** rompecabezas, *m*

kopeck *n* copec, *f*

Koran *n* Corán, Alcorán, *m*

Korea Corea, *f*

kosher *a* cosher; (slang) genuino

kowtow *vi* saludar humildemente; *fig* bajar la cerviz

Kremlin *n* Kremlín, *m*

kudos *n* prestigio, *m,* gloria, *f*

Kurdish *a* curdo

Kurd *n* curdo, *m*

kyrie eleison *n* kirieleisón, *m*

L

l *n* (letter) ele, *f*

la *n* mus la, *m*

label *n* etiqueta, (on a garment), rótula, *m,* (on a can), *f;* (on a museum specimen, etc.) letrero, *m; fig* calificación, *f. vt* poner etiqueta en; marcar, rotular; *fig* calificar, designar, clasificar

labial *a* labial. *n* letra labial, *f*

labor *n* trabajo, *m;* labor, *f;* fatiga, pena, *f;* clase obrera, *f;* (manual workers) mano de obra, *f;* (effort) esfuerzo, *m;* (of childbirth) dolores de parto, *m pl. vi* trabajar; (strive) esforzarse, afanarse; (struggle) forcejar, luchar; (try) procurar, tratar de; avanzar con dificultad; (in childbirth) estar de parto. *vt* elaborar; pulir, perfeccionar. **to l. under,** sufrir; tener que luchar contra. **hard l.,** trabajo arduo, *m; law* trabajos forzosos, *m pl,* presidio, *m.* **Ministry of L.,** Ministerio de Trabajo, *m.* **to be in l.,** estar de parto. **to l. in vain,** trabajar en balde, arar en el mar. **to l. under a delusion,** estar en el error, estar equivocado. **L. Exchange,** Bolsa de Trabajo, *f.* **l. leader,** dirigente sindical, *m.* **L. party,** partido laborista, partido obrero, *m.* **l. question,** cuestión obrera, *f;* (domestic) problema del servicio, *m.* **l.-saving,** *a* que ahorra trabajo. **l. union,** sindicato, *m*

laboratory *n* laboratorio, *m*

labored *a* (of style) premioso, artificial; forzado; (of breathing) fatigoso; (slow) torpe, lento

laborer *n* obrero, *m;* (on the land) labrador, labriego, *m;* (on the roads, etc.) peón, *m;* (by the day) jornalero, *m*

laborious *a* laborioso; arduo, difícil, penoso

laboriously *adv* laboriosamente; con dificultad, penosamente

laboriousness *n* laboriosidad, *f;* dificultad, *f*

Labrador dog *n* perro de Labrador, *m*

labyrinth *n* laberinto, *m*

labyrinthine *a* laberíntico; intrincado

lace *n* (of shoes, corsets, etc.) cordón, *m;* (tape) cinta, *f;* encaje, *m;* (narrow, for trimming) puntilla, *f;* (of gold or silver) galón, *m. vt* and *vi* (shoes, etc.) atarse los cordones; (trim) guarnecer con encajes, etc.; *fig* ornar; (a drink) echar (coñac, etc.) en. **blond l.,** blonda, *f.* **gold l.,** galón de oro, *m.* **point l.,** encaje de aguja, *m.* **l. cur-**

tain, cortina de encaje, *f;* (of net) visillo, *m.* **l. maker** or **seller,** encajera, *f.* **l. making,** obra de encaje, *f.* **l.-pillow,** almohadilla para encajes, *f.* **l. shoes,** zapatos con cordones, *m pl*

lacerate *vt* lacerar

laceration *n* laceración, *f*

lachrymal *a* lagrimal, lacrimal

lachrymose *a* lacrimoso

lack *n* falta, *f.* **l. of evidence,** falta de pruebas, *f;* carestía, escasez, *f;* (absence) ausencia, *f;* (need) necesidad, *f. vt* carecer de; no tener; necesitar. *vi* hacer falta; necesitarse. **to l. confidence in oneself,** no tener confianza en sí mismo, carecer de confianza en sí mismo. **l.-luster,** (of eyes) apagado, mortecino. **l. of evidence,** falta de pruebas, *f*

lackadaisical *a* lánguido; indiferente; (dreamy) ensimismado, distraído

lackey *n* lacayo, *m*

laconic *a* lacónico

lacquer *n* laca, *f, vt* dar laca (a), barnizar con laca. **gold l.,** sisa dorada, *f.* **l. work,** laca, *f*

lacquering *n* barnizado de laca, *m;* laca, capa de barniz de laca, *f*

lactate *n* lactato, *m, vi* lactar

lactation *n* lactancia, *f*

lacteal *a* lácteo

lactic *a* láctico

lactose *n* lactosa, *f*

lacuna *n* laguna, *f*

lacy *a* de encaje; parecido a encaje; *fig* transparente, etéreo

lad *n* muchacho, joven, mozalbete, *m;* zagal, *m;* (stable, etc.) mozo, *m.* **He's some l.!** ¡Qué tío que es! **l. of the village,** chulo, *m*

ladder *n* escalera de mano, *f; naut* escala, *f;* (in a stocking, etc.) carrera, *f.* **companion l.,** escala de toldilla, *f.* **to l. one's stocking,** escurrirse un punto de las medias

Ladies and gentlemen *n. pl* Señoras y señores, Señoras y caballeros. **ladies' man,** hombre de salón, Perico entre ellas, mujeriego, *m*

lading *n* flete, *m,* carga, *f*

ladle *n* cucharón, cazo, *m.* *vt* servir con cucharón; (a boat) achicar; *inf* distribuir, repartir

lady *n* dama, *f;* señora, *f;* (English title) milady, *f;* (woman) mujer, *f.* **to be a l.,** ser una señora. **leading l.,** *theat* dama primera, *f.* **Our L.,** Nuestra Señora. **young l.,** señorita, *f; inf* novia, *f.* **lady's maid,** doncella, *f.* **l. of the house,** señora de la casa, *f.* **l. bug,** *ent* catalina mariquita, vaca de San Antonio, *f.* **L. Chapel,** capilla de la Virgen, *f.* **L. Day,** día de la Anunciación (de Nuestra Señora), *m.* **l.-help,** asistenta, *f.* **l.-in-waiting,** dama de servicio, *f.* **l.-killer,** ladrón de corazones, castigador, tenorio, *m.* **l.-love,** querida, amada, *f.* **l. mayoress,** alcaldesa, *f*

ladylike *a* de dama; elegante; distinguido; bien educado; delicado; (of men) afeminado

ladyship *n* señoría, *f.* **Your L.,** Su Señoría

lag *vt* recubrir; aislar. *vi* retrasarse; quedarse atrás; ir (or andar) despacio; rezagarse; *naut* roncear. *n* retraso, *m; mech* retardación de movimiento, *f*

laggard *n* holgazán (-ana), haragán (-ana)

lagoon *n* laguna, *f*

laid *past part* of verb **to lay. l. up,** (ill) enfermo; *naut* inactivo; (of cars, etc.) fuera de circulación

lair *n* cubil, *m;* guarida, madriguera, *f*

laity *n* legos, *m pl*

lake *n* lago, *m;* (pigment) laca, *f.* **small l.,** laguna, *f.* **l. dwelling,** vivienda palustre, *f*

lama *n* lama, *m*

lamb *n* cordero (-ra). *vi* parir corderos. **lamb's wool,** lana de cordero. *f*

lambent *a* ondulante, vacilante; centelleante

lamblike *a* manso como un cordero; inocente

lambskin *n* corderina, piel de cordero, *f*

lame *a* estropeado, lisiado; (in the feet) cojo; (of meter) que cojea, malo; (of arguments) poco convincente; frívolo, flojo. *vt* lisiar; hacer cojo. **l. excuse,** pretexto frívolo. **to be l.,** (in the feet) (permanently) ser cojo; (temporarily) estar cojo

lamely *adv* cojeando, con cojera; *fig* sin convicción; mal

lameness *n* cojera, *f;* falta de convicción, *f*

lament *n* lamento, *m;* queja, lamentación, *f. vi* lamentarse; quejarse. *vt* lamentar, deplorar, llorar

lamentable *a* lamentable, deplorable; lastimero

lamentation *n* lamentación, *f,* lamento, *m.* **Book of Lamentations,** Libro de los lamentos, *m*

lamenting *n* lamentación, *f*

lamina *n* lámina, *f*

laminate *n* laminado, laminar. *vt* laminar

lamp *n* lámpara, *f;* (on vehicles, trains, ships and in the street) farol, *m;* luz, *f;* (oil) candil, *m,* lámpara de aceite, *f.* **safety-l.,** lámpara de seguridad, lámpara de los mineros, *f.* **street l.,** farol (de las calles), *m.* **l.-black,** negro de humo, *m.* **l.-chimney,** tubo de una lámpara, *m.* **l. factory** or **shop,** lamparería, *f.* **l.-holder,** portalámpara, *f.* **l.-lighter,** farolero, lamparero, *m.* **l.-post,** farola, *f.* **l.-shade,** pantalla (de lámpara,) *f.* **l. stand,** pie de lámpara, *m*

lamplight *n* luz de la lámpara, *f;* luz artificial, *f.* **in the l.,** a la luz de la lámpara; en luz artificial

lampoon *n* pasquinada, *f,* pasquín, *m, vt* pasquinar, satirizar

lampooner *n* escritor (-ra) de pasquinadas, libelista, *m*

lamprey *n* lamprea, *f*

lance *n* lanza, *f;* (soldier) lancero, *m. vt* alancear; *med* lancinar. **l. in rest,** lanza en ristre, *f.* **l. thrust,** lanzada, *f.* **l.-corporal,** soldado de primera clase, *m*

lancer *n mil* lancero, *m; pl* lancers, (dance and music) lanceros, *m pl*

lancet *n* apostemero, *m,* lanceta, *f.* **l. arch,** arco puntiagudo, *m*

land *n* tierra, *f;* terreno, *m;* (country) país, *m;* (region) región, *f;* territorio, *m;* (estate) bienes raíces, *m pl,* tierras, fincas, *f pl. vt* desembarcar; echar en tierra; (*fig* place) poner; *inf* dejar plantado (con); (obtain) obtener; (a fish) sacar del agua; (a blow) dar (un golpe); (leave) dejar. *vi* desembarcar; saltar en tierra; (of a

plane) aterrizar; (arrive) llegar; (fall) caer. **cultivated l.,** tierras cultivadas, *f pl.* **dry l.,** (not sea) tierra firme, *f.* **native l.,** patria, *f;* suelo natal, *m.* **on l.,** en tierra. **to see how the l. lies,** *fig* tantear el terreno. **l. of milk and honey,** jauja, *f,* paraíso, *m.* **l. of promise,** tierra de promisión, *f.* **l. agent,** procurador de fincas, *m.* **l. breeze,** brisa de tierra, *f.* **l. forces,** fuerzas terrestres, *f pl.* **l. law,** leyes agrarias, *f pl.* **l.-locked,** cercado de tierra, mediterráneo. **l.-lubber,** marinero de agua dulce, *m.* **l. mine,** mina terrestre, *f.* **l. surveying,** agrimensura, *f.* **l. surveyor,** agrimensor, *m.* **l. tax,** contribución territorial, *f*

landau *n* landó, *m*

landed *a* hacendado. **l. gentry,** hacendados, terratenientes, *m pl.* **l. property,** bienes raíces, *m pl*

landfall *n* derrumbamiento de tierras, *m*

landing *n* desembarque, desembarco, *m;* (landing place) desembarcadero, *m; aer* aterrizaje, *m;* (of steps) descanso, rellano, *m,* mesa, mesilla, *f.* **forced l.,** aterrizaje forzoso, *m.* **l. certificate,** *com* tornaguía, *f.* **l. craft,** barcaza de desembarco, *f.* **l. field,** campo de aterrizaje, *m,* pista de vuelo, *f.* **l.-net,** salabardo, *m.* **l. party,** trozo de abordaje, *m.* **l. signal,** *aer* señal de aterrizaje, *f.* **l.-stage,** desembarcadero, *m;* (jetty) atracadero, *m*

landlady *n* patrona, huéspeda, *f*

landlord *n* (of houses, land) propietario, *m;* hotelero, patrón, *m*

landmark *n* (of a hill or mountain) punto destacado, *m;* lugar conocido, *m;* característica, *f; fig* monumento, *m*

landmass *n* unidad territorial, *f*

landowner *n* hacendado, terrateniente, *m*

landscape *n* paisaje, *m;* perspectiva, *f.* **l. gardener,** arquitecto de jardines, *m.* **l. painter,** paisajista, *mf*

landslide *n* desprendimiento de tierras, *m; fig* cambio brusco de la opinión pública, *m*

landward *adv* hacia tierra

lane *n* vereda, senda, *f;* (of traffic) carril, *m,* (Argentina, Spain), línea, *f*

language *n* lenguaje, *m;* lengua, *f,* idioma, *m.* **modern l.,** lengua viva, *f.* **strong l.,** palabras mayores, *f pl*

languid *a* lánguido

languidness *n* languidez, *f*

languish *vi* languidecer

languishing *a* lánguido; amoroso, sentimental

languishingly *adv* lánguidamente; amorosamente

languor *n* languidez, *f*

languorous *a* lánguido

languorously *adv* con langor

lank *a* flaco, descarnado, alto y delgado; (of hair) lacio

lankiness *n* flacura, *f*

lanky *a* larguirucho, descarnado

lanoline *n* lanolina, *f*

lantern *n* linterna, *f;* (*naut* and of a lighthouse) farol, *m; arch* linterna, *f;* (small) farolillo, *m.* **dark l.,** linterna sorda, *f.* **magic l.,** linterna mágica, *f.* **l.-jawed,** carilargo, *m.* **l. maker,** farolero, *m.* **l. slide,** diapositiva, *f*

lap *n* regazo, *m;* falda, *f;* (knees) rodillas, *f pl;* (lick) lamedura, *f;* (of water) murmurio, susurro, *m;* (in a race) vuelta, *f;* (stage) etapa, *f. vt* (wrap) envolver; (cover) cubrir; (fold) plegar; (lick) lamer; (swallow) tragar. *vi* (overlap) traslaparse; estar replegado; (lick) lamer; (of water) murmurar, susurrar, besar. **l.-dog,** perro de faldas, perro faldero, *m*

lapel *n* solapa, *f*

lapidary *a* lapidario

lapidate *vt* lapidar

lapis lazuli *n* lapislázuli, *m*

Lapland Laponia, *f*

Laplander *n* lapón (-ona)

lapping *n* (licking) lamedura, *f;* (of water) murmurio, susurro, chapaleteo, *m*

lapse *n* lapso, *m;* (fault) desliz, *m,* falta, *f;* (of time) transcurso, intervalo, *m;* (fall) caída, *f;* (law termination) caducidad, *f.* **lapse (into),** *vi* caer (en), recaer (en), reincidir (en); volver a, caer de nuevo (en); (law cease) caducar; (*law* pass to) pasar (a); dejar de existir, desaparecer. **after the l.** of three days, después de tres días, al cabo de tres días. **with the l.** of years, en el transcurso de los años

larboard *n* babor, *m*, *a* de babor

larceny *n* latrocinio, *m*

lard *n* manteca, *f*; lardo, *m*. *vt cul* lardear, mechar; *fig* sembrar (con), adornar (con)

larder *n* despensa, *f*

large *a* grande; grueso; amplio; vasto, extenso; (wide) ancho; considerable; (in number) numeroso; (main, chief) principal; liberal; magnánimo. **at l.**, en libertad, suelto. **on the l.** side, algo grande. **l.-headed,** cabezudo. **l.-hearted,** que tiene un gran corazón, magnánimo. **l. mouth,** boca grande, boca rasgada, *f*. **l.-nosed,** narigudo. **l. scale,** en gran escala. **l.-sized,** de gran tamaño. **l.-toothed,** dentudo, que tiene dientes grandes. **l. type,** letras grandes, *f pl*

largely *adv* grandemente; en gran manera; en so mayor parte, considerablemente; muy; ampliamente; liberalmente; extensamente

largeness *n* gran tamaño, *m*; (of persons) gran talle, *m*; amplitud, *f*; vastedad, extensión, *f*; (width) anchura, *f*; liberalidad, *f*; (generosity) magnanimidad, *f*; grandeza de ánimo, *f*

larger *a comp* más grande, etc. See **large. to grow l.,** crecer, aumentarse. **to make l.,** hacer más grande; aumentar

largesse *n* liberalidad, *f*

largo *n* and *adv mus* largo, *m*

lariat *n* lazo, *m*

lark *n* alondra, *f*; (spree) juerga, *f*; (joke) risa, *f*. **to rise with the l.,** levantarse con las gallinas

larva *n* larva, *f*

laryngeal *a* laríngeo

laryngitis *n* laringitis, *f*

larynx *n* laringe, *f*

lascivious *a* lascivo, lujurioso

lasciviousness *n* lujuria, lascivia, *f*

lash *n* (thong) tralla, *f*; (whip) látigo, *m*; (blow) latigazo, *m*; azote, *m*; (of the eye) pestaña, *f*. *vt* dar latigazos (a); azotar; (of waves) romper contra; (of hail, rain) azotar; (excite) provocar; (the tail) agitar (la cola); (scold) fustigar; (fasten) sujetar, atar; *naut* trincar. **to l. out,** (of horses, etc.) dar coces; (in words) prorrumpir (en)

lashing *n* (whipping) azotamiento, *m*; (tying) ligadura, atadura, *f*; amarradura, *f*

lass *n* muchacha, chica, mozuela, *f*; zagala, *f*; niña, *f*

lassitude *n* lasitud, *f*

lasso *n* lazo, *m*, mangana, *f*, *vt* lazar, manganear

last *vi* durar; subsistir, conservarse; continuar

last *a* último; (with month, week, etc.) pasado; (supreme) extremo, (el) mayor. *adv* al fin; finalmente; por último; después de todos; por última vez; la última vez. *n* el, *m*, (*f*, la) último (-ma); los últimos, *m pl*, (*f pl*, las últimas); (end) fin, *m*; (for shoes) horma, *f*. **at l.,** en fin; por fin, a la postre. **at the l. moment,** a última hora. **I have not been there these l. five years,** Hace cinco años que no voy allá. **John spoke l.,** Juan habló el último. **She came at l.,** Por fin llegó. **to the l.,** hasta el fin. **l. but one,** penúltimo (-ma). **l. hope,** última esperanza, *f*; último recurso, *m*. **l. kick,** *inf* último suspiro, *m*. **l. night,** anoche. **l. week,** la semana pasada

lasting *a* permanente, perdurable; duradero; constante; (of colours) sólido

lastingness *n* permanencia, *f*; duración, *f*

lastly *adv* en conclusión, por fin, finalmente, por último

latch *n* pestillo, *m*, *vt* cerrar con pestillo. **l.-key,** llave de la puerta, *f*; (Yale) llavín, *m*

late *a* tarde; tardío; (advanced) avanzado; (last) último; reciente; (dead) difunto; (former) antiguo, ex . . . ; (new) nuevo. *adv* tarde. **Better l. than never,** Más vale tarde que nunca. **Helen arrived l.,** Elena llegó tarde. **The train arrived five minutes l.,** El tren llegó con cinco minutos de retraso. **He keeps l. hours,** Se acuesta muy tarde, Se acuesta a las altas horas de la

noche (*inf* las tantas). **of l.,** últimamente. **to grow l.,** hacerse tarde. **l.-eighteenth-century poetry,** la poesía de fines del siglo diez y ocho; llorado, malogrado (e.g. **the l.** Mrs. Smith, la llorada Sra. Smith, la malograda Sra. Smith);

lateen *a* latino. **l. sail,** vela latina, *f*

lately *adv* recientemente; últimamente, hace poco

latency *n* estado latente, *m*

lateness *n* lo tarde; lo avanzado; retraso, *m*. **the l.** of the hour, la hora avanzada

latent *a* latente

later *a* más tarde; posterior; más reciente. *adv* más tarde; (afterwards) luego, después; posteriormente. **sooner or l.,** tarde o temprano. **l. on,** más tarde

lateral *a* lateral, ladero

late registration *n* matrícula tardía, *f*

latest *a* and *adv sup* último; más reciente, etc. See **late. at the l.,** a lo más tarde, a más tardar. **l. fashion,** última moda, *f*. **l. news,** últimas noticias, *f pl*; novedad, *f*

latex *n* (*bot chem*) látex, *m*

lath *n* listón, *m*. **to be as thin as a l.,** no tener más que el pellejo, estar en los huesos

lathe *n* torno, *m*

lather *n* espuma de jabón, *f*, jabonaduras, *f pl*; (of sweat) espuma, *f*. *vt* enjabonar; *inf* zurrar; *vi* hacer espuma

lathering *n* jabonadura, *f*; *inf* tunda, zurra, *f*

Latin *n* latín, *m*, *a* latino. **Low L.,** bajo latín, *m*. **L.-American,** *a* latinoamericano. *n* latinoamericano (-na)

Latinism *n* latinismo, *m*

Latinist *n* latinista, *mf*

latitude *n* latitud, *f*; libertad, *f*

latitudinal *a* latitudinal

latrine *n* letrina, *f*

latter *a* más reciente; último, posterior; moderno. **the l.,** éste, *m*; ésta, *f*; esto, *neut*; éstos, *m pl*; éstas, *f pl*. **the l. half,** la segunda mitad. **toward the l. end of the year,** hacia fines del año. **L.-Day Saint,** santo de los últimos días *m*, santa de los últimos días, *f*

latterly *adv* recientemente, últimamente; en los últimos tiempos; hacia el fin

lattice *n* rejilla, *f*; celosía, reja, *f*. *vt* poner celosía (a); entrelazar. **l.-work,** enrejado, *m*

latticed *a* (of windows, etc.) con reja

Latvia Latvia, Letonia, *f*

Latvian *a* latvio. *n* latvio (-ia)

laud *n* alabanza, *f*; *pl*. **lauds,** *ecc* laudes, *f pl*. *vt* alabar, elogiar

laudability *n* mérito, *m*, lo meritorio

laudable *a* loable, meritorio

laudably *adv* laudablemente

laudatory *a* laudatorio

laugh *n* risa, *f*; carcajada, *f*. *vi* reír; (smile) sonreír; reírse. **loud l.,** risa estrepitosa, *f*. **to l. in a person's face,** reírsele a uno en las barbas. **to l. loudly,** reírse a carcajadas. **to l. to oneself,** reírse interiormente. **to l. to scorn,** poner en ridículo. **to l. at,** reírse de; burlarse de, ridiculizar

laughable *a* risible, irrisible, ridículo, absurdo

laughing *a* risueño, alegre; (absurd) risible, *n* risa, *f*. **to burst out l.,** reírse a carcajadas. **l.-gas,** gas hilarante, *m*. **l.-stock,** hazmerreír, *m*

laughingly *adv* riendo

laughter *n* risa, *f*; (in a report) risas, *f pl*. **burst of l.,** carcajada, *f*. **to burst into l.,** soltar el trapo, reírse a carcajadas, desternillarse de risa

launch *n* botadura (de un buque), *f*; (throwing) lanzamiento, *m*; (beginning) iniciación, *f*; canoa, *f*. *vt* (throw) lanzar; (a blow) asestar; (a vessel) botar, echar al agua; (begin) iniciar, dar principio a; (make) hacer. **to l. an offensive,** *mil* emprender una ofensiva. **to l. into,** arrojarse en; entregarse a. **motor l.,** canoa automóvil, *f*. **steam l.,** bote de vapor, *m*

launching *n* botadura (de un buque), *f*; (throwing) lanzamiento, *m*; (beginning) iniciación, *f*; inauguración, *f*; (of a loan, etc.) emisión, *f*. **l. site,** rampa, *f*

launder *vt* lavar y planchar (ropa)

laundress *n* lavandera, *f*

laundromat *n* lavandería automática, *f*

laundry *n* lavadero, *m*, lavandería, *f*; (washing) colada, *f*; *inf* ropa lavada or ropa para lavar, *f*. **l.-man,** lavandero, *m*

laureate *a* laureado. *n* poeta laureado, *m*

laurel *n* laurel, cerezo, *m*, a láureo. **to crown with l.,** laurear. **l. wreath,** lauréola, *f*

Lausanne Lausana, Losana, *f*

lava *n* lava, *f*

lavabo *n* lavabo, *m*; *ecc* lavatorio, *m*

lavatory *n* lavabo, *m*; retrete, excusado, *m*

lave *vt* bañar

lavender *n* espliego, *m*, lavanda, *f*. **l.-water,** agua de lavanda, *f*

lavish *a* pródigo; profuso, abundante. *vt* prodigar

lavishly *adv* pródigamente; en profusión

lavishness *n* prodigalidad, *f*; profusión, abundancia, *f*

law *n* ley, *f*; derecho, *m*; jurisprudencia, *f*; código de leyes, *m*. **according to law,** según derecho. **canon law,** derecho civil, *m*. **constitutional law,** derecho político, *m*. **criminal law,** derecho penal, *m*. **in law,** por derecho, de acuerdo con la ley; desde el punto de vista legal. **international law,** derecho internacional, *m*. **maritime law,** código marítimo, *m*. **sumptuary law,** ley suntuaria, *f*. **to be the law,** ser la ley. **to go to law,** pleitear (sobre). **to sue at law,** pedir en juicio, poner pleito. **to take the law into one's own hands,** tomar la ley por su propia mano. **law-abiding,** observante de la ley; amigo del orden. **law-breaker,** transgresor (-ra). **law court,** tribunal de justicia, *m*; palacio de justicia, *m*. **law of nature,** ley natural, *f*. **law report,** revista de tribunales, *f*. **law school,** escuela de derecho, *f*. **law student,** estudiante de derecho, *mf*

lawful *a* legítimo; legal; lícito; válido

lawfully *adv* legalmente; legítimamente, lícitamente

lawfulness *n* legalidad, *f*; legitimidad, *f*

lawgiver *n* legislador (-ra)

lawless *a* ilegal; desordenado; ingobernable, rebelde

lawlessness *n* ilegalidad, *f*; desorden, *m*; rebeldía, *f*

lawn *n* césped, prado, *m*; (cloth) estopilla, *f*. **l.-mower,** cortacésped *m*, tundidora de césped, *f*, máquina segadora del césped, *f*. **l.-tennis,** tenis (en pista de hierba), *m*

lawsuit *n* pleito, litigio, *m*, causa, acción, *f*

lawyer *n* abogado (-da). **lawyer's office** or **practice,** bufete, *m*

lax *a* laxo; indisciplinado; vago; descuidado

laxative *n* laxante, *m*, purga, *f*, *a* laxativo

laxity *n* laxitud, *f*; descuido, *m*; indiferencia, *f*

lay *a* laico, seglar, lego; profano. *n* poema, *m*, trova, *f*; romance, *m*; (song) canción, *f*. **the lay of the land,** la configuración del terreno. **lay brother,** confeso, monigote, *m*. **lay figure,** maniquí, *m*. **lay sister,** (hermana) lega, *f*

lay *vt* and *vi* poner; colocar; dejar; (strike) tumbar; (demolish) derribar; (the dust) matar; (pipes, etc.) instalar; (hands on) asentar (la mano en); (deposit) depositar; (beat down corn, etc.) encamar, abatir; (eggs, keel) poner; (the table) cubrir, poner; (stretch) extender(se); (bury) depositar en el sepulcro; (a bet) hacer; (wager) apostar; (an accusation) acusar; (the wind, etc.) sosegar, amainar; (a ghost) exorcizar; (impute) atribuir, imputar; (impose) imponer; (prepare) prepara; (make) hacer; (open) abrir; (blame, etc.) echar; (claim) reclamar; (reveal) revelar. **Don't lay the blame on me!** ¡No me eches la culpa! **We laid our plans,** Hicimos nuestros planes; Hicimos nuestros preparativos. **to lay siege to,** asediar. **to lay the colors on too thick,** *fig* recargar las tintas. **to lay the foundations,** echar los cimientos; *fig* crear, establecer; fundar. **to lay about one,** dar garrotazos de ciego. **to lay aside,** poner a un lado; arrinconar; (save) ahorrar; (cast away) desechar; abandonar; (reserve) reservar; (a person) apartar de sí; (incapacitate) incapacitar. **lay something at somebody's feet,** embutir algo en el

guante de fulano. **to lay before,** mostrar; presentar; poner a la vista; revelar. **to lay by,** See **to lay aside. to lay down,** acostar; depositar; (a burden) posar; (arms) rendir; (one's life) entregar; (give up) renunciar (a); (sketchout) trazar, dibujar; (plan) proyectar; (keep) guardar; (as a principle) establecer, sentar; (the law) dictar. **to lay oneself down,** echarse, tumbarse. **to lay in,** (a stock) proveerse de, hacer provisión de; (hoard) ahorrar; (buy) comprar. **to lay off,** *naut* virar de bordo; *inf* quitarse de encima. **to lay on,** *vt* colocar sobre; (thrash) pegar; (blows) descargar; (paint, etc.) dar; (water, etc.) instalar; (impose) imponer; (exaggerate) exagerar. *vi* atacar. **to lay open,** abrir; descubrir; revelar; manifestar; exponer. **to lay oneself open to attack,** exponerse a ser atacado. **to lay out,** poner; arreglar; (the dead) amortajar; (one's money) invertir, emplear; (at interest) poner a rédito; (plan) planear; (knock down) derribar. **to lay oneself out to,** esforzarse a; tomarse la molestia de. **to lay over,** cubrir; sobreponer; extender sobre. **to lay to,** *vi naut* estar a la capa. **to lay up,** guardar, acumular, atesorar; poner a un lado; (a ship) desarmar; (a car) poner fuera de circulación; (a person) obligar a guardar cama, incapacitar

layer *n* capa, *f*; *geol* estrato, *m*; *min* manto, *m*; (bird) gallina (pata, etc.) ponedera, *f*; (one who bets) apostador (-ra); *agr* acodo, *m*. *vt* (of plants) acodar

layette *n* canastilla, *f*

laying *n* colocación, *f*; puesta, *f*; (of an egg) postura, *f*. **l. down,** depósito, *m*; conservación, *f*; (explanation) exposición, *f*. **l. on of hands,** imposición de manos, *f*. **l. out,** tendedura, *f*; (of money) empleo, *m*; inversión, *f*; (arrangement) arreglo, *m*

layman *n* seglar, *mf*; profano (-na)

layout *n* plan, *m*; diagramación, disposición, *f*; distribución, *f*; esquema, *m*

laze *vi* holgazanear, gandulear, no hacer nada; encontrarse a sus anchas

lazily *adv* perezosamente; indolentemente; lentamente

laziness *n* pereza, holgazanería, *f*; indolencia, *f*; lentitud, *f*

lazy *a* perezoso, holgazán; indolente. **l.-bones,** gandul (-la)

lead *n* (metal) plomo, *m*; (in a pencil) mina, *f*; (plummet) sonda, *f*; *print* interlínea, *f*; *pl* **leads,** (roofs) tejados, *m pl*. *vt* emplomar; guarnecer con plomo; *print* interlinear. **black-l.,** grafito, *m*. **deep-sea l.,** *naut* escandallo, *m*. **white l.,** albayalde, *m*. **to heave the l.,** echar el escandallo, sondar. **l.-colored,** de color de plomo, plomizo. **l. mine,** mina de plomo, *f*. **l. poisoning,** saturnismo, *m*

lead *n* delantera, *f*; primer lugar, *m*; dirección, *f*, mando, *m*; (suggestion) indicación, *f*; (influence) influencia, *f*; (dog's) traílla, *f*; *theat* protagonista, *mf*; *theat* papel principal, *m*; (at cards) mano, *f*

lead *vt* and *vi* (conduct) conducir, llevar, guiar; (induce) mover, persuadir, inducir; (cause) hacer, causar; (captain) capitanear, encabezar; dirigir; (channel) encauzar; (with life) llevar; (give) dar; (head) ir a la cabeza de; *mil* mandar; (at cards) salir; (at games) jugar en primer lugar; tomar la delantera, *fig* superar a los demás; (of roads) conducir. **to take the l.,** ir delante; ir a la cabeza, tomar la delantera; tomar la iniciativa a. **to l. one to think,** hacer pensar. **to l. the way,** mostrar el camino; ir adelante. **to l. along,** llevar (por la mano, etc.), conducir; conducir por; guiar. **to l. astray,** descarriar; desviar (de), seducir (de). **to l. away,** conducir (a otra parte); llevarse (a). **to l. back,** conducir de nuevo; hacer volver. **This path leads back to the village,** Por esta senda se vuelve al pueblo. **to l. in, into,** conducir a (o ante); introducir en, hacer entrar en; invitar a entrar en; (of rooms) comunicarse con; (sin, etc.) inducir a. **to l. off,** *vi* ir adelante; (begin) empezar; (of rooms) comunicarse con. *vt* hacer marcharse, llevarse (a). **to l. on,** *vt* conducir; guiar; hacer pensar en; (make talk) dar cuerda (a). *vi* ir a la cabeza;

tomar la delantera. **to l. out,** conducir afuera; (to dance) sacar. **to l. to,** conducir a; desembocar en, salir a; (cause) dar lugar a, causar; (make) hacer; (incline) inclinar. **This street leads to the square,** Por esta calle se va a la plaza, Esta calle conduce a la plaza. **to l. up to,** conducir a; (in conversation, etc.) preparar el terreno para; preparar; tener lugar antes de, ocurrir antes de

leaden *a* hecho de plomo, plúmbeo; (of skies, etc.) plomizo, de color de plomo, aplomado. **l.-footed,** pesado; lento

leader *n* conductor (-ra); guía, *mf*; jefe (-fa); general, *m*; director (-ra); (in a journal) artículo de fondo, *m*; (of an orchestra) primer violín, *m*. **follow-the-l.,** (game) juego de seguir la fila, *m*

leadership *n* dirección, *f*; jefatura, *f*; *mil* mando, *m*

lead-in *a rad* de entrada. *n rad* conductor de entrada, *m*

leading *n* (leadwork) emplomadura, *f*

leading *n* (guidance) dirección, *f*. *a* principal; primero; importante; eminente. **l. article,** artículo de fondo, *m*; editorial, *m*. **l. card,** primer naipe, *m*. **l. counsel,** abogado (-da) principal. **l. lady,** *theat* dama primera, primera actriz, *f*; (cinema) estrella (de la pantalla), *f*. **l. man,** *theat* primer galán, *m*. **l. question,** pregunta que sugiere la respuesta, *f*; cuestión importante, *f*. **l. strings,** andadores, *m pl*; *fig* tutelaje, *m*

leaf *n* (bot and of a page, door, window, table, screen, etc.) hoja, *f*; (petal) pétalo, *m*, *vi* echar hojas. **gold l.,** pan de oro, *m*. **to turn over a new l.,** volver la hoja, hacer libro nuevo, hacer vida nueva. **to turn over the leaves of a book,** hojear (un libro). **l.-bud,** yema, *f*. **l.-mold,** abono verde, *m*. **l. tobacco,** tabaco en hoja, *m*

leafiness *n* frondosidad, *f*

leafless *a* sin hojas

leaflet *n* hojuela, *f*; (pamphlet) folleto, *m*

leafy *a* frondoso

league *n* (measure) legua, *f*; liga, federación, sociedad, *f*; (football) liga, *f*. *vt* aliar; asociar. *vi* aliarse; asociarse, confederarse. **to be in l.,** *inf* estar de manga. **L. of Nations,** Sociedad de las Naciones, *f*

leak *n* (hole) agujero, *m*, grieta, *f*; *naut* vía de agua, *f*; (of gas, liquids, etc.) escape, *m*; (in a roof, etc.) gotera, *f*; *elec* resistencia de escape, *f*. *vi naut* hacer agua; (gas, liquids, etc.) escaparse, salirse; (drip) gotear. **to l. out,** (of news, etc.) trascender, saberse. **to spring a l.,** aparecer una vía de agua, hacer agua

leakage *n* (of gas, liquids) escape, *m*, fuga, *f*; derrame, *m*; pérdida, *f*; (of information) revelación, *f*

leaky *a naut* que hace agua; agujereado; poroso; que tiene goteras

lean *a* magro, seco, enjuto, delgado; (of meat) magro; *fig* pobre, estéril. *n* carne magra, *f*, magro, *m*. **to grow l.,** enflaquecer

lean *vi* inclinarse; apoyarse (en). *vt* apoyar (en); dejar arrimado (en). **to l. out of the window,** asomarse a la ventana. **to l. against,** apoyarse en, recostarse en (or contra). **to l. back,** echarse hacia atrás; recostarse. **to l. over,** inclinarse. **to l. upon,** apoyarse en; descansar sobre

leaning *n* inclinación, tendencia, *f*; predilección, afición, *f*

leanness *n* magrura, flaqueza, *f*; (of meat) magrez, *f*; *fig* pobreza, *f*

leap *n* salto, *m*; brinco, *m*; (caper) zapateta, *f*; *fig* salto, *m*. *vi* saltar, dar un salto; brincar. *vt* saltar; hacer saltar. **at one l.,** en un salto. **by leaps and bounds,** en saltos. **My heart leaped,** Mi corazón dio un salto. **to l. to the conclusion that . . . ,** saltar a la conclusión de que . . . **to l. to the eye,** saltar a la vista. **l. frog,** salto, salto de la muerte, pídola *f*. **l. year,** año bisiesto, *m*, cabrillas, *f pl*

leaping *a* saltador. *m pl*

learn *vt* and *vi* aprender; instruirse; enterarse de. **to l. by heart,** aprender de memoria. **to l. from a reliable source,** saber de buena tinta. **to l. from experience,** aprender por experiencia

learned *a* sabio, docto; erudito; (of professions) liberal; versado (en), entendido (en). **a l. society,** una sociedad erudita

learner *n* aprendedor (-ra)

learning *n* saber, *m*; conocimientos, *m pl*; erudición, *f*; estudio, *m*; (literature) literatura, *f*

lease *n* arrendamiento, arriendo, *m*; contrato de arrendamiento, *m*. *vt* dar en arriendo, arrendar. **on l.,** en arriendo. **to take a new l. on life,** recobrar su vigor. **Lend L. Act,** ley de préstamo y arriendo, *f*

leasehold *n* censo, *m*, *a* censatario

leaseholder *n* concesionario, *m*; arrendatario (-ia)

leash *n* (of a dog) traílla, *f*

least *a sup* **little,** mínimo; el (la, etc.) menor; más pequeño. *adv* menos. **n lo menos. at l.,** siquiera; por lo menos, al menos. **at the very l.,** a lo menos. **not in the l.,** de ninguna manera, nada. **to say the l. of,** sin exagerar, para no decir más

leather *n* cuero, *m*; piel, *f*, *a* de cuero; de piel. **patent l.,** charol, *m*. **Spanish l.,** cordobán, *m*. **tanned l.,** curtido, *m*. **l. apron,** mandil, *m*. **l. bag,** saco de cuero, *m*. **l. bottle,** bota, *f*. **l. breeches,** pantalón de montar, *m*. **l. jerkin,** coleto, *m*. **l. shield,** adarga, *f*. **l. strap,** correa, *f*. **l. trade,** comercio en cueros, *m*

leatherette *n* cartón cuero, *m*

leathery *a* de cuero; (of the skin) curtido por la intemperie; (tough) correoso

leave *n* (permission) permiso, *m*; (mil etc.) licencia, *f*; (farewell) despedida, *f*. *vt* and *vi* dejar; abandonar; salir (de), quitar, marcharse (de); (as surety) empeñar; (by will) legar, mandar; (an employment) darse de baja (de), dejar; (give into the keeping of) entregar; (bid farewell) despedirse (de). **By your l.,** Con permiso de Vd. (Vds.). Con la venia de Vd. (Vds.) de permiso. **l.-taking,** despedidas, *f pl.* **to be left,** quedar. **to be left over,** quedar; sobrar. **Two from four leaves two,** De cuatro a dos van dos. **to take French l.,** despedirse a la inglesa. **to take l. of,** despedirse de. **to take one's l.,** marcharse; despedirse. **to l. a deep impression,** *fig* impresionar mucho; quedar grabado (en). **to l. undone,** dejar de hacer, no hacer; dejar sin terminar. **to l. about,** *vt* dejar por todas partes. *vi* (of time) marcharse a eso de . . . **to l. ajar,** entreabrir, entornar. **to l. alone,** dejar a solas; dejar en paz; no molestar, no meterse con. **to l. aside,** omitir; prescindir de; olvidar. **to l. behind,** dejar atrás; olvidar. **l. much to be desired,** tener mucho que desear. **to l. off,** *vt* dejar de; abandonar; (garments) no ponerse, quitarse. *vi* terminar. **to l. out,** dejar fuera; dejar a un lado, descontar; omitir; pasar por; (be silent about) callar; suprimir. **to l. to,** dejar para; dejar hacer

leaven *n* levadura, *f*, fermento, *m*, *vt* fermentar; (fig permeate) penetrar (en), infiltrar en, imbuir; (a speech) salpimentar (con)

leaving *n* salida, partida, marcha, *f*; *pl* **leavings,** sobras, *f pl*; desechos, *m pl*

Lebanon el Líbano, *m*

lecherous *a* lascivo, lujurioso

lechery *n* lascivia, lujuria, *f*

lectern *n* atril, *m*; (in a church) facistol, *m*

lecture *n* conferencia, *f*; (in a university) lección, clase, *f*; discurso, *m*; (inf scolding) sermoneo, *m*. *vi* dar una conferencia; (in a university) dar clase. *vt* (inf scold) predicar, sermonear. **l. room,** sala de conferencias, *f*; (in a university) sala de clase, aula, *f*

lecturer *n* conferenciante, *mf*; (in a university) auxiliar, *m*; (professor) catedrático (-ca), profesor (-ra)

lectureship *n* auxiliaría, *f*

ledge *n* borde, *m*; capa, *f*; (of a window) alféizar, *m*; (shelf) anaquel, *m*

ledger *n* libro mayor, *m*

lee *n naut* sotavento, *m*, *a* a sotavento

leech *n* sanguijuela, *f*

leek *n* puerro, *m*

leer *vi* mirar de soslayo; guiñar el ojo; mirar con los ojos

llenos de deseo. *n* mirada de soslayo, *f;* mirada de lascivia, *f*
lees *n pl* heces, *f pl;* sedimento, *m*
leeward *n* sotavento, *m.* **on the l.** side, a sotavento
leeway *n naut* deriva, *f; fig* amplitud, margen de holgura, márgenes de maniobra, *f pl*
left *past part* dejado, etc. See **leave.** *a* izquierdo. *adv* a la izquierda; hacia la izquierda. *n* izquierda, *f.* **on the l.,** a la izquierda. **the L.,** *pol* las izquierdas. **the Left Bank (of Paris)** la Ribera izquierda, la Orilla izquierda **L. face!** ¡Izquierda! **l.-hand,** mano izquierda, *f;* izquierda, *f.* **l.-hand drive,** conducción a la izquierda, *f.* **l.-handed,** zurdo. **l. luggage office,** consigna, *f.* **l.-overs,** sobras, *f pl,* desperdicios, *m pl*
leg *n* pierna, *f;* (of animals, birds, furniture) pata, *f;* (of a triangle) cateto, *m;* (of a pair of compasses, trousers, lamb, veal) pierna, *f;* (of boots, stockings) caña, *f;* (of pork) pernil, *m;* (support) pie, *m;* (stage) etapa, *f.* **to be on one's last legs,** estar en las últimas; estar acabándose; estar sin recursos. **to pull a person's leg,** tomar el pelo (a). **leg-pull,** tomadura de pelo, *f.* **leg-of-mutton sleeve,** manga de pernil, *f*
legacy *n* legado, *m,* manda, *f;* herencia, *f*
legal *a* legal; de derecho; jurídico; (lawful, permissible) legítimo, lícito; (of a lawyer) de abogado. **l. expenses,** litisexpensas, *f pl.* **l. inquiry,** investigación jurídica, *f*
legality *n* legalidad, *f*
legalization *n* legalización, *f*
legalize *vt* legalizar; autorizar, legitimar
legally *adv* según la ley; según derecho; legalmente
legal tender *n* moneda de curso liberatorio, *f*
legate *n* legado, *m.* **papal l.,** legado papal, *m*
legatee *n* legatario (-ia)
legation *n* legación, *f*
legend *n* leyenda, *f*
legendary *a* legendario
legerdemain *n* juegos de manos, *m pl*
legged *a* con piernas; de piernas . . . ; de patas . . . **a three-l. stool,** un taburete de tres patas. **long l.,** zancudo
leggings *n pl* polainas, *f pl*
legibility *n* legibilidad, *f*
legible *a* legible
legion *n* legión, *f.* **L. of Honor,** Legión de Honor, *f*
legionary *a* legionario. *n* legionario, *m*
legislate *vt* legislar
legislation *n* legislación, *f*
legislative *a* legislativo, legislador
legislator *n* legislador (-ra)
legislature *n* legislatura, *f*
legitimacy *n* legitimidad, *f;* justicia, *f*
legitimate *a* legítimo; justo
legitimation *n* legitimación, *f*
leguminous *a* leguminoso
leisure *n* ocio, *m,* desocupación, *f;* tiempo libre, *m.* **at one's l.,** con sosiego, despacio. **You can do it at your l.,** Puedes hacerlo cuando tengas tiempo. **to be at l.,** estar desocupado, no tener nada que hacer. **l. moments,** ratos perdidos, momentos de ocio, *m pl*
leisured *a* desocupado, libre; sin ocupación; (wealthy) acomodado
leisurely *a* pausado, lento, deliberado; tardo
lemon *n* limón, *m;* (tree) limonero, *m, a* limonado, de color de limón; hecho o sazonado con limón. **l. drop,** pastilla de limón, *f.* **l.-grove,** limonar, *m.* **l.-squash,** limonada natural, *f.* **l.-squeezer,** exprime limones, *m,* exprimidera, *f*
lemonade *n* limonada, *f.* **l. powder,** limonada seca, *f*
lemur *n* lemur, *m*
lend *vt* prestar. **to l. an ear to,** prestar atención a. **It does not l. itself to . . . ,** No se presta a . . . **to l. a hand,** echar una mano, dar una mano
lender *n* el, *m,* (*f,* la) que presta; prestador (-ra); (of money) prestamista, *mf; com* mutuante, *mf*
lending *n* prestación, *f,* préstamo, *m.* **l.-library,** biblioteca circulante, *f*

length *n* largo, *m;* longitud, *f;* (of fabric) corte, *m;* (of a ship) eslora, *f;* (in racing) largo, *m;* distancia, *f;* (in time) duración, *f;* alcance, *m.* **at l.,** por fin, finalmente; (in full) extensamente, largamente. **by a l.,** por un largo. **full-l.,** de cuerpo entero. **three feet in l.,** tres pies de largo. **to go the l. of . . . ,** llegar al extremo de . . .
lengthen *vt* alargar; prolongar; extender. *vi* alargarse; prolongarse; extenderse; (of days) crecer
lengthening *n* alargamiento, *m;* prolongación, *f;* crecimiento, *m*
lengthily *adv* largamente
lengthiness *n* largueza, *f;* prolijidad, *f*
lengthy *a* largo; demasiado largo, larguísimo; (of speech) prolijo; verboso
lenience, leniency *n* lenidad, *f;* indulgencia, *f*
lenient *a* indulgente; poco severo
leniently *adv* con indulgencia
Leningrad Leningrado, *m*
lenitive *a* lenitivo. *n* lenitivo, *m*
lens *n* lente, *m;* (of the eye) cristalino, *m*
Lent *n* Cuaresma, *f*
Lenten *a* de Cuaresma, cuaresmal
lentil *n* lenteja, *f*
lentitude *n* lentitud, *f*
Leo *n* León, *m*
leonine *a* leonino
leopard *n* leopardo, *m*
leper *n* leproso (-sa). **l. colony,** colonia de leprosos, *f*
leprosy *n* lepra, *f*
leprous *a* leproso
lesbian *a* and *n* lesbiana
lesion *n* lesión, *f*
less *a* menor; más pequeño; menos; inferior. *adv* menos; sin. **l. than,** menos de (que). **more or l.,** poco más o menos. **no l.,** nada menos. **none the l.,** sin embargo. **to grow l.,** disminuir. **l. and l.,** cada vez menos
lessee *n* arrendatario (-ia); inquilino (-na)
lessen *vi* disminuir; reducirse. *vt* disminuir; reducir; (lower) rebajar; (disparage) menospreciar
lessening *n* disminución, *f;* reducción, *f*
lesser *a comp* menor; más pequeño. See **little**
lesson *n* lección, *f.* **to give a l.,** dar lección, dar clase; *fig* dar una lección (a). **to hear a l.,** tomar la lección
lessor *n* arrendador (-ra)
lest *conjunc* para que no; por miedo de (que), no sea que. **I did not do it l. they should not like it,** No lo hice por miedo de que no les gustase
let *vt* dejar, permitir; (lease) arrendar. *vi* alquilarse, ser alquilado. **Let** as an expression of the imperative is rendered in Spanish by the subjunctive or the imperative, e.g. **Let them go!** ¡Que se vayan! ¡Déjalos marchar! **He let them go,** Les dejó marchar. **to let fall,** dejar caer. **to let go,** dejar marchar; soltar; poner en libertad (a). **to let loose,** dar suelta a; *fig* desencadenar. **to let one know,** hacer saber, comunicar. **to let the cat out of the bag,** tirar de la manta. **to let in chance slip,** perder la ocasión. **to let alone,** (a thing) no tocar; (a person) dejar en paz, dejar tranquilo; (an affair) no meterse (en or con); (omit) no mencionar, omitir toda mención de. **to let down,** bajar; (by a rope) descolgar; (hair, etc.) dejar caer; (a dress, etc.) alargar; *naut* calar; (disappoint) dejar plantado. **to let in,** dejar entrar; hacer entrar; invitar a entrar; recibir; (insert) insertar. **to let into,** (initiate) iniciar en, admitir en; (a secret) revelar. Other meanings, see **to let in. to let off,** dejar salir; dejar en libertad; exonerar; perdonar; (a gun) disparar; (fireworks, etc.) hacer estallar. **to let out,** dejar salir; poner en libertad; (from a house) acompañar a la puerta; abrir la puerta; *sew* ensanchar; (hire) alquilar; (the fire, etc.) dejar extinguirse. **to let up,** dejar subir; (decrease) disminuir; (end) terminar
let *n* estorbo, impedimento, obstáculo, *m.* **without let or hindrance,** sin estorbo ni obstáculo
lethal *a* letal. **l. weapon,** instrumento de muerte, *m*

lethargic *a* aletargado; letárgico
lethargy *n* letargo, *m*; *med* letargía, *f*
letter *n* (of the alphabet) letra, *f*; (epistle) carta, *f*; *print* carácter, *m*; (lessor) arrendador (-ra); *pl* **letters,** letras, *f pl*; (correspondence) correo, *m*; correspondencia, *f*. *vt* inscribir; imprimir. **capital l.,** letra mayúscula, *f*. **first letters,** *fig* primeras letras, *f pl*. **registered l.,** carta certificada, *f*, certificado, *m*. **small l.,** letra minúscula, *f*. **the l. of the law,** la ley escrita. **to be l.-perfect,** saber de memoria. **to the l.,** *fig* a la letra. **letters patent,** patente, *f*; título de privilegio, *m*. **l.-balance,** pesacartas, *m*. **l.-book,** *com* libro copiador, *m*. **l.-box,** buzón de correos, *m*. **l.-card,** tarjeta postal del gobierno, *f*. **l. of credit,** carta de crédito, *f*. **l. of introduction,** carta de presentación, *f*. **l.-writer,** escritor (-ra) de cartas
lettered *a* culto, instruido; (printed) impreso
lettering *n* inscripción, *f*; letrero, rótulo, *m*
letterpress *n* imprenta, *f*; (not illustrations) texto, *m*
letting *n* (hiring) arrendamiento, *m*
lettuce *n* lechuga, *f*. **l. plant,** lechuguino, *m*. **l. seller,** lechuguero (-ra)
Leuven Lovaina, *f*
Levant, the el Levante, *m*
Levantine *a* and *n* levantino (-na)
levee *n* besamanos, *m*, recepción, *f*
level *n* nivel, *m*; ras, *m*, flor, *f*; llano, *m*; (plain) llanura, *f*; (instrument) nivel, *m*, a llano; igual; al nivel (de); uniforme; imparcial. *adv* a nivel; igualmente. *vt* nivelar; igualar; allanar; (a blow) asestar; (a gun) apuntar; (raze) arrasar, derribar; adaptar; hacer uniforme. **on the l.,** a nivel; *fig* de buena fe. **spirit l.,** nivel de burbuja, *m*. **to make l. again,** rellanar. **l. country,** campaña, llanura, *f*. **l. with the ground,** a ras de la tierra. **l. with the water,** a flor de agua. **l. crossing,** paso a nivel, *m*. **l.-headed,** sensato, cuerdo. **l. stretch,** rellano, *m*; llanura, *f*
leveler *n* nivelador (-ra)
leveling *a* nivelador; de nivelación; igualador. *n* nivelación, *f*; allanamiento, *m*; (to the ground) arrasamiento, *m*; igualación, *f*
levelness *n* nivel, *m*; planicie, *f*; igualdad, *f*
lever *n* palanca, *f*; (handle) manivela, *f*; escape de reloj, *m*; (excuse) pretexto, *m*; (means) modo, *m*. *vt* sopalancar. **control l.,** *aer* palanca de mando, *f*. **hand-l.,** palanca de mano, *f*
leverage *n* sistema de palancas, *m*; acción de palanca, *f*; *fig* influencia, fuerza, *f*, poder, *m*
Leviathan *n* leviatán, *m*
levitation *n* levitación, *f*
Levite *n* levita, *m*
Levitical *a* levítico
Leviticus *n* Levítico, *m*
levity *n* levedad, frivolidad, ligereza, *f*
levy *n* exacción (de tributos), *f*; impuesto, *m*; (of a fine) imposición, *f*; *mil* leva, *f*. *vt* (taxes) exigir; (a fine) imponer; (troops) reclutar, enganchar
levying *n* (of a tax) exacción (de tributos), *f*; (of a fine) imposición, *f*; (of troops) leva, *f*
lewd *a* lascivo, lujurioso, impúdico
lewdness *n* lascivia, lujuria, impudicia, *f*
lexicographer *n* lexicógrafo, *m*
lexicography *n* lexicografía, *f*
lexicon *n* léxico, *m*
liability *n* responsabilidad, obligación, *f*; tendencia, *f*; riesgo, *m*; *pl* **liabilities,** obligaciones, *f pl*; *com* pasivo, *m*
liable *a* responsable; propenso (a); expuesto (a); sujeto (a)
liaison *n* lío, *m*; coordinación, *f*. **l. officer,** oficial de coordinación, *m*
liar *n* mentiroso (-sa)
libation *n* libación, *f*
libel *n* libelo, *m*; difamación, *f*, *vt* difamar, calumniar
libeler *n* libelista, *mf* difamador (-ra)
libelous *a* difamatorio
liberal *a* liberal; generoso; abundante. *n* liberal, *mf* **l. profession,** carrera liberal, *f*. **l.-minded,** tolerante. **l.-mindedness,** tolerancia, *f*

liberalism *n* liberalismo, *m*
liberality *n* liberalidad, *f*; generosidad, *f*
liberalize *vt* liberalizar
liberate *vt* (a prisoner) poner en libertad; librar (de); (a slave, etc.) dejar escapar
liberation *n* liberación, *f*; (of a captive) redención, *f*; (of a slave) manumisión, *f*
liberator *n* libertador (-ra)
libertinage *n* libertinaje, *m*
libertine *n* libertino, *m*
libertinism *n* libertinaje, *m*
liberty *n* libertad, *f*; (familiarity) familiaridad, *f*; (right) privilegio, *m*, prerrogativa, *f*; (leave) permiso, *m*. **at l.,** en libertad; desocupado, libre. **I have taken the l. of giving them your name,** Me he tomado la libertad de darles su nombre. **to set at l.,** poner en libertad (a). **to take liberties with,** tratar con familiaridad; (a text) tergiversar. **l. of speech,** libertad de palabra, *f*. **l. of thought,** libertad de pensamiento, *f*
libidinous *a* libidinoso
Libra *n* Libra, *f*
librarian *n* bibliotecario (-ia)
librarianship *n* carrera *f*, or empleo *m*, de bibliotecario
library *n* biblioteca, *f*; (book shop) librería, *f*. **l. catalog,** catálogo de la biblioteca, *m*
librettist *n* libretista, *mf*
libretto *n* libreto, *m*
Libya Libia, *f*
Libyan *a* and *n* libio (-ia)
license *n* licencia, *f*, permiso, *m*; autorización, *f*; (driving) carnet de chófer, permiso de conducción, *m*; (of a car) permiso de circulación, *m*; (for a wireless, etc.) licencia, *f*; (marriage) licencia de casamiento, *f*; (excess) libertinaje, desenfreno, *m*. **import l.,** permiso de importación, *m*. **poetic l.,** licencia poética, *f*. **l. number,** (of a car) número de matriculación, *m*. *vt* licenciar; autorizar; (a car) sacar la licencia del automóvil
licensee *n* concesionario (-ia)
licentiate *n* licenciado (-da)
licentious *a* licencioso, disoluto
licentiousness *n* libertinaje, *m*, disipación, *f*
lichen *n* liquen, *m*
licit *a* lícito
lick *vt* lamer; (of waves) besar; (of flames) bailar; (thrash) azotar; (defeat) vencer. **to l. one's lips,** relamerse los labios, chuparse los dedos. **to l. the dust,** morder el polvo
licking *n* lamedura, *f*; (beating) paliza, tunda, *f*; (defeat) derrota, *f*
lid *n* cobertera, *f*; tapa, *f*; (of the eye) párpado, *m*
lie *n* mentira, *f*; invención, falsedad, *f*; mentís, *m*, *vi* mentir. **to give the lie to,** desmentir, dar el mentís. **to lie barefacedly,** mentir por la mitad de la barba. **white lie,** mentira oficiosa, *f*
lie *vi* estar tumbado, estar echado; estar recostado; descansar, reposar; (in the grave) yacer; (be) estar; (be situated) hallarse, estar situado; (stretch) extenderse; (sleep) dormir; (depend) depender; (consist) consistir, estribar; (as an obligation) incumbir. **Here lies . . . ,** Aquí descansa . . . , Aquí yace . . . **It does not lie in my power,** No depende de mí. **to let lie,** dejar; dejar en paz. **to lie at anchor,** estar anclado. **to lie fallow,** estar en barbecho; *fig* descansar. **to lie about,** estar esparcido por todas partes; estar en desorden. **to lie along,** estar tendido a lo largo de; *naut* dar a la banda. **to lie back,** recostarse; apoyarse (en). **to lie by,** estar acostado al lado de; (of things, places) estar cerca (de); descansar. **to lie down,** tenderse, tumbarse, echarse, acostarse; reposar. **Lie down!** (to a dog) ¡Echate! **to lie down under,** tenderse bajo; (an insult) tragar, sufrir. **to lie in,** consistir en; depender de; (of childbirth) estar de parto. **to lie open,** estar abierto; estar expuesto (a); estar al descubierto, estar a la vista. **to lie over,** (be postponed) quedar aplazado. **to lie to,** *naut* estarse a la capa, ponerse en facha. **to lie under,** estar

bajo, hallarse bajo; estar bajo el peso de; (be exposed to) estar expuesto a. **to lie with,** dormir con; (concern) tocar (a); corresponder (a)
lie *n* configuración, *f;* disposición, *f;* posición, *f.* **the lie of the land,** la configuración del terreno
lieu *n* lugar, *m.* **in l. of,** en lugar de, en vez de
lieutenant *n* teniente, lugarteniente, *m;* (naval) alférez, *m.* **first l.,** (in the army) primer teniente, teniente, *m;* (in the navy) alférez de navío, *m.* **naval l.,** teniente de navío, *m.* **second l.,** (in the army) segundo teniente, *m;* (in the navy) alférez de fragata, *m.* **l.-colonel,** teniente coronel, *m.* **l.-commander,** capitán de fragata, *m.* **l.-general,** teniente general, *m.* **l.-governor,** subgobernador, *m*
life *n* vida, *f;* (being) ser, *m;* (society) mundo, *m,* sociedad, *f;* (vitality) vitalidad, *f;* vigor, *m, a* de vida; (of annuities, etc.) vitalicio; (life-saving) de salvamento. **for l.,** de por vida. **from l.,** del natural. **high l.,** gran mundo, *m,* alta sociedad, *f.* **low l.,** vida del hampa, vida de los barrios bajos, *f.* **to the l.,** al vivo. **to lay down one's l.,** entregar la vida. **to take one's l. in one's hands,** jugarse la vida. **l. annuity,** fondo vitalicio, *m.* **l.-belt,** (cinturón) salvavidas, *m.* **l.-blood,** sangre vital, *f; fig* nervio, *m;* vigor, *m.* **l.-boat,** (on a ship) bote salvavidas, *m;* (on the coast) lancha de salvamento, *f.* **l.-boat station,** estación de salvamento, *f.* **l.-giving,** vivificante, que da vida; tonificante. **l.-guard,** (soldier) guardia militar, *f;* Guardia de Corps, *f,* (at beach or swimming pool) guardavivas, *mf.* **l.-insurance,** seguro sobre la vida, *m.* **l.-interest,** usufructo, *m.* **l.-jacket,** chaleco salvavidas, *m.* **l.-like,** natural. **l.-line,** cable de salvamento, *m.* **l.-saving,** *a* de salvamento; curativo. **l.-saving apparatus,** aparato salvavidas, *m.* **l.-sized,** de tamaño natural
life cycle *n* ciclo vital, *m*
life imprisonment *n* reclusión perpetua, *f*
life jacket *n* chaleco salvavidas, *f*
lifeless *a* sin vida, muerto; inanimado; *fig* desanimado
lifelong *a* de toda la vida
lifetime *n* vida, *f*
lift *n* esfuerzo para levantar, *m;* acción de levantar, *f;* alza, *f;* (blow) golpe, *m;* (help) ayuda, *f;* (elevator) ascensor, *m;* (for goods) montacargas, *m; pl* **lifts,** *naut* balancines, *m pl.* **to give a l. to,** (help) ayudar; (hitchhiker etc.) dar un aventón. **l. attendant,** ascensorista, *mf*
lift *vt* levantar; alzar, elevar; (pick up) coger; (one's hat) quitarse; (steal) hurtar; exaltar. *vi* (of mist) disiparse; desaparecer. **to l. the elbow,** empinar el codo. **to l. down,** quitar (de); (a person) bajar en brazos. **to l. up,** alzar; erguir, levantar; levantar en brazos
lifting *n* acción de levantar, *f;* levantamiento, alzamiento, *m*
ligament *n* ligamento, *m*
ligature *n* (*surg mus*) ligadura, *f*
light *a* (not dark) claro, con mucha luz, bañado de luz; (of colors) claro; (not heavy, and of sleep, food, troops, movements) ligero; (of reading) de entretenimiento; (irresponsible) frívolo; (easy) fácil; (slight) leve; (of hair) rubio; (happy) alegre; (fickle) inconstante, liviano; (of complexion) blanco. *adv* ligero. **to be l.,** no pesar mucho; estar de día. **to grow l.,** (dawn) clarear; iluminarse. **to make l. of,** no tomar en serio; no preocuparse de; (suffering) sufrir sin quejarse. **l.-colored,** (de color) claro. **l.-fingeredness,** sutileza de manos, *f.* **l.-footed,** ligero de pies. **l.-haired,** de pelo rubio. **l.-headed,** casquivano, ligero de cascos; delirante. **l.-headedness,** ligereza de cascos, frivolidad, *f;* delirio, *m.* **l.-hearted,** alegre (de corazón). **l.-heartedness,** alegría, *f.* **l. horse,** *mil* caballería ligera, *f.* **l. troops,** tropas ligeras, *f pl.* **l.-weight,** *n* (*boxing*) peso ligero, *m, a* de peso ligero
light *n* luz, *f;* (day) día, *m;* (match) cerilla, *f;* (of a cigarette, etc.) fuego, *m;* (of a window) cristal, vidrio, *m;* (point of view) punto de vista, *m;* (in a picture) toque de luz, *m; pl* **lights,** (offal) bofes, *m pl.* **against the l.,**

al trasluz. **by the l. of,** a la luz de; según. **half-l.,** media luz, *f.* **high light(s),** *art* claros, *m pl; fig* momento culminante, *m;* acontecimiento de más interés, *m.* **to come to l.,** descubrirse. **to put a l. to the fire,** encender el fuego. **l.-year,** año de luz, *m*
light *vt* (a lamp, fire, etc.) encender; iluminar. *vi* encenderse; iluminarse; *fig* animarse; brillar. **to l. upon,** encontrar por casualidad; tropezar con
lighten *vt* (illuminate) iluminar; (of weight) aligerar; (cheer) alegrar; (mitigate) aliviar. *vi* (grow light) clarear; (of lightning) relampaguear; (become less heavy) disminuir de peso, aligerarse; volverse más alegre
lightening *n* aligeramiento, *m;* (easing) alivio, *m;* luz, *f*
lighter *n* (boat) lancha, barcaza, gabarra, *f;* (device) encendedor, *m.* **pocket l.,** encendedor de bolsillo, *m.* **l. man,** gabarrero, *m*
light-fingered *a* ligero de manos
lighthouse *n* faro, *m.* **l.-keeper,** guardafaro, *m*
lighting *n* iluminación, *f;* alumbrado, *m.* **flood l.,** iluminación intensiva, *f.* **l.-up time,** hora de encender los faros, *f*
lightly *adv* ligeramente; fácilmente; (slightly) levemente; ágilmente; sin seriedad. **l. wounded,** levemente herido
lightness *n* ligereza, *f;* poco peso, *m;* agilidad, *f;* (brightness) claridad, *f;* (inconstancy) liviandad, inconstancia, *f;* frivolidad, *f*
lightning *n* relámpago, rayo, *m.* **as quick as l.,** como un relámpago. **to be struck by l.,** ser herido por un relámpago. **l.-rod,** pararrayos, *m*
lightship *n* buque faro, *m*
ligneous *a* leñoso
lignite *n* lignito, *m*
likable *a* simpático
like *a* semejante; parecido; igual, mismo; (characteristic) típico, característico; (likely) probable; (equivalent) equivalente. *adv* como; igual (que); del mismo modo (que). *n* semejante, igual, *mf;* tal cosa, *f;* cosas semejantes, *f pl.* **Don't speak to me l. that,** No me hables así. **He was l. a fury,** Estaba hecho una furia. **They are very l. each other,** Se parecen mucho. **to be l.,** parecerse (a), semejar. **to look l.,** parecer ser (que); tener el aspecto de; (of persons) parecerse (a). **to return l. for l.,** pagar en la misma moneda
like *vt* gustar, agradar; estar aficionado (a), gustar de; (wish) querer. **As you l.,** Como te parezca bien, Como quieras. **If you l.,** Si quieres. **James likes painting,** Jaime está aficionado a la pintura. **Judith does not l. the north of England,** A Judit no le gusta el norte de Inglaterra. **I don't l. to do it,** No me gusta hacerlo. **I should l. him to go to Madrid,** Me gustaría que fuese a Madrid
likelihood *n* posibilidad, *f;* probabilidad, *f*
likely *a* probable; verosímil, creíble, plausible; posible; (suitable) satisfactorio, apropiado; (handsome) bien parecido. *adv* probablemente. **They are not l. to come,** No es probable que vengan
liken *vt* comparar
likeness *n* parecido, *m,* semejanza, *f;* (portrait) retrato, *m*
likewise *adv* igualmente, asimismo, también. *conjunc* además
liking *n* (for persons) simpatía, *f,* cariño, *m;* (for things) gusto, *m,* afición, *f;* (appreciation) aprecio, *m.* **I have a l. for old cities,** Me gustan (o me atraen) las viejas ciudades. **to take a l. to,** (things) aficionarse a; (persons) prendarse de, tomar cariño (a)
lilac *n* lila, *f.* **l. color,** color de lila, *m*
Lilliputian *a* liliputiense. *n* liliputiense, *mf*
lilt *n* canción, *f;* ritmo, *m;* armonía, *f*
lily *n* lirio, *m,* azucena, *f;* (of France) flor de lis, *f.* **l. of the valley,** lirio de los valles, muguete, *m.* **l.-white,** blanco como la azucena
limb *n anat* miembro, *m;* (of a tree) rama, *f*
limbless *a* mutilado
limbo *n* limbo, *m*

lime n *chem* cal, f; (for catching birds) liga, hisca, f; (linden tree) tilo, m; (tree like a lemon) limero, m; (fruit) lima, f. vt (whiten) encalar; *agr* abonar con cal. **slaked l.,** cal muerta, f. **l.-flower,** flor del tilo, tila, f; flor del limero, f. **l.-juice,** jugo de lima, m. **l.-kiln,** calera, f. **l.-pit,** pozo de cal, m

limelight n luz de calcio, f; *fig* centro de atención, m; publicidad, f. **to be in the l.,** ser el centro de atención, estar a la vista (de público)

limestone n piedra caliza, f. **l. deposit,** calar, m

limit n límite, m; confín, m; linde, m, or f; limitación, f. vt limitar; fijar; (restrict) restringir. **This is the l.!** ¡Este es el colmo! ¡No faltaba más!

limitation n limitación, f; restricción, f

limitative a restrictivo, limitativo

limited a limitado; restringido; escaso; (of persons) de cortos alcances; *com* anónimo. **l. company,** sociedad anónima, f

limited monarchy n monarquía moderada, f

limiting adjective n adjetivo determinativo, m

limitless a sin límites; ilimitado, inmenso

limousine n limousina, f, coche cerrado, m

limp a flojo; débil; fláccido; lánguido. n cojera, f. vi cojear. **to l. off,** marcharse cojeando. **to l. up,** acercarse cojeando; subir cojeando

limpid a límpido, cristalino, puro

limpidity n limpidez, f

limping a cojo

limply adv flojamente; débilmente; lánguidamente

limpness n flojedad, f; debilidad, f; languidez, f

linchpin n pezonera, f

linden n tilo, m

line vt (furrow) surcar; (troops, etc.) poner en fila; alinear; (clothes, nests, etc.) forrar; (building) revestir; (one's pocket) llenar. vi estar en línea, alinearse

line n (most meanings) línea, f; (cord) cuerda, f; *naut* cordel, m; (fishing) sedal, m; (railway) vía, f; (wrinkle) surco, m; arruga, f; (row) hilera, ringlera, fila, f; (of verse) verso, m; *print* renglón, m; (of business) ramo, m; profesión, f; (interest) especialidad, f. **bowling** or **serving l.,** línea de saque, f; **hard lines,** mala suerte, f; apuro, m, situación difícil, f. **in a l.,** en fila; en cola. **in direct l.,** (of descent) en línea recta. **It is not in my l.,** No es una especialidad mía; No es uno de mis intereses. **on the lines of,** conforme a; parecido a. **to cross the l.,** (equator) pasar la línea; (railway) cruzar la vía. **to drop a l.,** escribir unas líneas, poner unas líneas. **to read between the lines,** leer entre líneas. **l.-drawing,** dibujo de líneas, m. **l. of battle,** línea de batalla, f

lineage n linaje, m, familia, raza, f

lineal a lineal

lineament n lineamento, m; (of the face) facciones, f pl

linear a lineal. **l. equation,** ecuación de primer grado, f

lined a rayado, con líneas; (of the face) surcado, arrugado; (of gloves, etc.) forrado. **lined paper,** papel rayado, m

linen n lino, m; *inf* ropa blanca, f; a de lino. **clean l.,** ropa limpia, f. **dirty l.,** ropa sucia, f; ropa para lavar, f. **table-l.,** mantelería, f. **l. cupboard,** armario para ropa blanca, m. **l. draper,** lencero (-ra). **l.-draper's shop,** lencería, f. **l. room,** lencería, f. **l. tape,** trenzadera, f. **l. thread,** hilo de lino, m

liner n (ship) transatlántico, m; buque de vapor, m; *aer* avión de pasaje, m

linesman n soldado de línea, m; *sport* juez de línea, m

ling n *bot* brezo, m; *icht* especie de abadejo, f

linger vi (remain) quedarse; tardar en marcharse; ir lentamente; hacer algo despacio

lingerie n ropa blanca, f

lingering a lento; largo; prolongado; melancólico, triste

lingeringly adv lentamente; largamente; melancólicamente

linguist n lingüista, mf

linguistic a lingüístico

linguistics n lingüística, f

liniment n linimento, m

lining n (of a garment, etc.) forro, m; (building) revestimiento, m

link n (in a chain) eslabón, m; (of beads) sarta, f; *fig* enlace, m, cadena, f; conexión, f; *mech* corredera, f; (torch) hacha de viento, f. vt enlazar, unir; *fig* encadenar. **missing l.,** *fig* eslabón perdido, m. **to l. arms,** cogerse del brazo

linking n encadenamiento, m; *fig* conexión, f

links n pl campo de golf, m

linoleum n linóleo, m

linotype n linotipia, f

linseed n linaza, f. **l. cake,** bagazo, m. **l.-oil,** aceite de linaza, m

lint n *med* hilas, f pl; (fluff) borra, f

lintel n dintel, m; (threshold) umbral, m

lion n león, m; *fig* celebridad, f. **l. cage** or **den,** leonera, f. **l.-hunter,** cazador (-ra) de leones. **l.-keeper,** leonero (-ra). **lion's mane,** melena, f. **l.-tamer,** domador (-ra) de leones

lioness n leona, f

lionize vt dar bombo (a), hacer la rueda (a), tratar como una celebridad (a)

lion's share n parte del león, tajada del león, f

lip n labio, m; (of a vessel) pico, m; (of a crater) borde, m; *fig* boca, f. **to open one's lips,** abrir la boca. **to smack one's lips,** chuparse los dedos. **lip reading,** lectura labial, f. **lip-service,** amor fingido, m; promesas hipócritas, f pl. **lip stick,** lápiz para los labios, m

lipped a (in compounds) con labios . . . , que tiene labios; (of vessels in compounds) con . . . picos

liquefaction n licuefacción, f

liquefiable a liquidable

liquefy vt liquidar. vi liquidarse

liqueur n licor, m. **l.-glass,** copita de licor, f. **l.-set,** licorera, f

liquid n líquido, m, a líquido; límpido. **l. air,** aire líquido, m. **l. measure,** medida para líquidos, f

liquidate vt liquidar; saldar (cuentas); *mil* soldar

liquidation n liquidación, f

liquidness n liquidez, f; fluidez, f

liquor n licor, m. **l. shop,** aguardentería, f. **l. traffic,** negocio de vinos y licores, m; contrabando, m

liquorice n regaliz, m

lira n lira, f

Lisbon Lisboa, f

lisp n ceceo, m; balbuceo, m, vi cecear; balbucir

lisping a ceceoso; balbuciente. n ceceo, m; (of a child, etc.) balbuceo, m

lissom a flexible; ágil

list n lista, f; catálogo, m; matrícula, f; *naut* recalcada, f; inclinación, f; (tournament) liza, f. vt hacer una lista de; catalogar; matricular; inscribir. vi *naut* recalcar; inclinarse a un lado. **to enter the lists,** entrar en liza. **l. of wines,** lista de vinos, f

listen vi escuchar; (attend) atender. **Don't you want to l. to the music?** ¿No quieres escuchar la música? **to l. in,** (on the radio) escuchar la radio; (eavesdrop) escuchar a hurtadillas

listener n oyente, mf; (to radio) radiooyente, mf

listless a lánguido, apático, indiferente

listlessly adv lánguidamente, indiferentemente

listlessness n apatía, languidez, inercia, f

litany n letanía, f

liter n litro, m

literal a literal. **l.-minded,** sin imaginación

literalness n literalidad, f

literary a literario

literary executor n depositario de la obra literaria, m

literate a and n literato (-ta)

literature n literatura, f

lithe a flexible; sinuoso y delgado; ágil

litheness n flexibilidad, f; sinuosidad, f; delgadez, f; agilidad, f

lithograph n litografía, f, vt litografiar

lithographer n litógrafo, m

lithographic *a* litográfico
lithography *n* litografía, *f*
Lithuania Lituania, *f*
Lithuanian *a* lituano, *n* lituano (-na); (language) lituano, *m*
litigant *n* litigante, *mf*
litigate *vi* and *vt* litigar, pleitear
litigation *n* litigación, *f*
litigious *a* litigioso
litmus *n* tornasol, *m*. **l. paper,** papel de tornasol, *m*
litter *n* litera, *f*; (stretcher) camilla, *f*; (bed) lecho, *m*; cama de paja, *f*; (brood) camada, cría, *f*; (rubbish) cosas en desorden, *f pl*; (papers) papeletas, *f pl*; (untidiness) desarreglo, desorden, *m*, confusión, *f*, *vt* poner en desorden
little *a* pequeño; poco; (scanty) escaso; insignificante; bajo, mezquino. *adv* poco. **a l.,** un poco (de); un tanto. **in l.,** en pequeño. **not a l.,** no poco; bastante. **l. by l.,** poco a poco. **l. or no,** poco o nada. **however l.,** por pequeño que. **as l. as possible,** lo menos posible. **to make l. of,** no dar importancia a; sacar poco en claro de, no comprender bien; no hacer caso de; (persons) acoger mal. **l. by l.,** poco a poco. **l. finger,** dedo meñique, *m*. **l. one,** pequeñuela, *f*, pequeñito, *m*
littleness *n* pequeñez, *f*; poquedad, *f*; mezquindad, *f*; trivialidad, *f*
littoral *a* and *n* litoral, *m*
liturgical *a* litúrgico. **l. calendar,** calendario litúrgico, *m*
liturgical vestment *n* paramento litúrgico, *m*
liturgy *n* liturgia, *f*
live *a* vivo, viviente; (alight) encendido; (of a wire, etc.) cargado de electricidad. **l. cartridge,** cartucho con bala, *m*. **l. coal,** ascua, *f*. **l.-stock,** ganadería, *f*. **l. wire,** conductor eléctrico, *m*; *fig* fuerza viva, *f*
live *vi* vivir; residir, habitar; (of ships) mantenerse a flote; salvarse; subsistir. *vt* (one's life) llevar, pasar. **Long l.!** ¡Viva! **to have enough to l. on,** tener de que vivir. **to l. together,** convivir. **to l. again,** volver a vivir. **to l. at,** vivir en, habitar. **to l. down,** sobrevivir a; (a fault) lograr borrar. **to l. on,** vivir de. **to l. up to,** vivir con arreglo a, vivir en conformidad con; estar al nivel de, merecer. **to l. up to one's income,** vivir al día, gastarse toda la renta
live broadcast *n* emisión en directo, *f*
livelihood *n* vida, subsistencia, *f*. **to make a l.,** ganarse la vida
liveliness *n* vivacidad, vida, *f*; animación, *f*; alegría, *f*
livelong *a* entero, todo; eterno. **all the l. day,** todo el santo día
lively *a* vivo; vivaracho; brioso, enérgico; alegre; bullicioso; animado; (fresh) fresco; (of colours) brilliante; intenso
liver *n* vividor (-ra), el, *m*, (*f*, la) que vive; habitante, *m*; *anat* hígado, *m*. **l. cancer,** cáncer del hígado, *m*. **l. complaint,** mal de hígado, *m*. **l. extract,** extracto de hígado, *m*
livery *n* librea, *f*; uniforme, *m*; *poet* vestiduras, *f pl*. **l. stables,** pensión de caballos, *f*; cochería de alquiler, *f*
livid *a* lívido; cárdeno, amoratado
lividness *n* lividez, *f*
living *a* viviente; vivo, vital. *n* vida, *f*; modo de vivir, *m*; beneficio eclesiástico, *m*. **the l.,** los vivos. **to make one's l.,** ganarse la vida. **l. memory,** memoria de personas vivientes, memoria de los que aún viven, *f*. **l.-room,** sala de estar, *f*. **l. soul,** ser viviente; *inf* bicho viviente, *m*. **l. wage,** jornal básico, *m*
lizard *n* lagarto (-ta). **giant l.,** dragón, *m*. **wall l.,** lagartija, *f*. **l. hole,** lagartera, *f*
llama *n* llama, *f*
load *n* carga, *f*; peso, *m*; (cart) carretada, *f*; *elec* carga, *f*; (quantity) cantidad, *f*. *vt* cargar (con); (with honors) llenar (de); (*fig* weigh down) agobiar (con); (a stick with lead) emplomar; (*elec* and of dice) cargar; (wine) mezclar vino con un narcótico. **to be loaded with fruit,** estar cargado de fruta. **to l. oneself with,** car-

garse de. **to l. the dice,** cargar los dados. **to l. again,** recargar
loader *n* cargador, *m*
loading *n* carga, *f*. **l. depot,** cargadero, *m*
loaf *n* pan, *m*; (French) barra de pan, *f*. *vi* golfear, vagabundear, gandulear. **l. sugar,** azúcar de pilón, *m*
loafer *n* vago (-ga); azotacalles, *mf*; gandul (-la); golfo (-fa)
loafing *n* gandulería, *f*, vagabundeo, *m*
loam *n* marga, *f*
loamy *a* margoso
loan *n* empréstito, *m*; (lending) prestación, *f*; préstamo, *m*. *vt* prestar. **l. fund,** caja de empréstitos, *f*. **l. company office,** casa de préstamos, *f*
loath *a* desinclinado, poco dispuesto
loathe *vt* abominar, detestar, odiar, aborrecer; repugnar
loather *n* el, *m*, (*f*, la) que odia; aborrecedor (-ra)
loathing *n* aborrecimiento, odio, *m*; repugnancia, aversión, *f*
loathsome *a* odioso, aborrecible; asqueroso; repugnante
loathsomeness *n* carácter repugnante, *m*; asquerosidad, *f*
lobby *n* pasillo, *m*; antecámara, *f*; (in a hotel, house) vestíbulo, recibidor, *m*; (waiting-room) sala de espera, *f*; (in Parliament) sala de los pasos perdidos, *f*. *vt* and *vi* cabildear
lobe *n bot* lobo, *m*; (*anat arch*) lóbulo, *m*
lobster *n* langosta, *f*; bogavante, *m*. **l.-pot,** cambín, *m*, nasa, *f*
local *a* local; de la localidad. **l. anesthetic,** anestésico local, *m*. **l. color,** color local, *m*
locale *n* local, *m*
locality *n* localidad, *f*; situación, *f*
localization *n* localización, *f*
localize *vt* localizar
locate *vt* situar; colocar; localizar. **to be located,** situarse; hallarse
location *n* colocación, *f*; emplazamiento, *m*; localidad, *f*; situación, posición, *f*
loch *n* lago, *m*
lock *n* cerradura (of a door, including a vehicle) *f*; (of a gun) cerrojo, *m*; (in wrestling) llave, *f*; (on rivers, canals) presa, *f*; (at a dock) esclusa, *f*; (of hair) mechón, *m*, guedeja, *f*; (ringlet) bucle, *m*; *pl* **locks,** (hair) cabellos, *m pl*, pelo, *m*. **spring l.,** cerradura de golpe, *f*. **to put a l. on,** poner cerradura a. **under l. and key,** bajo cuatro llaves. **l.-jaw,** trismo, *m*. **l. keeper,** esclusero, *m*. **l.-out strike,** huelga patronal, *f*
lock *vt* cerrar con llave; *fig* encerrar; (embrace) abrazar estrechamente; (of wheels, etc.) trabar; (twine) entrelazar. *vi* cerrarse con llave. **to l. in,** cerrar con llave; encerrar. **to l. out,** cerrar la puerta (a); dejar en la calle (a). **to l. up,** encerrar; (imprison) encarcelar
locker *n* (drawer) cajón, *m*; (cupboard) armario, *m*; *naut* cajonada, *f*
locket *n* guardapelo, *m*; medallón, *m*
locksmith *n* cerrajero, *m*. **locksmith's trade,** cerrajería, *f*
locomotion *n* locomoción, *f*
locomotive *a* locomotor. *n* locomotora, *f*
locum tenens *n* interino (-na)
locust *n* langosta migratoria, *f*
locution *n* locución, *f*
lode *n* filón, *m*
lodestar *n* estrella polar, *f*; *fig* norte, *m*
lodge *n* casita, garita, *f*; casa de guarda, *f*; (freemason's) logia, *f*; (porter's) portería, *f*, *vi* hospedarse, alojarse, vivir, parar; penetrar; entrar (en); fijarse (en). *vt* hospedar, alojar; albergar; (a blow) asestar; (a complaint) hacer, dar; (money, etc.) depositar. **to l. an accusation against,** querellarse contra, quejarse de. **l.-keeper,** conserje, *m*
lodger *n* huésped (-eda)
lodging *n* hospedaje, alojamiento, *m*; (inn) posada, *f*; residencia, *f*; casa, *f*. **l.-house,** casa de huéspedes, *f*

loft *n* desván, sotabanco, *m*; pajar, *m*

loftily *adv* en alto; (proudly) con arrogancia, con altanería

loftiness *n* altura, *f*; sublimidad, *f*; nobleza, *f*; dignidad, *f*; (haughtiness) altanería, soberbia, *f*

lofty *a* alto; sublime; noble; eminente; (haughty) altanero, soberbio

log *n* madero, tronco, *m*; palo, *m*; leño, *m*; *naut*, diario de a bardo *m*, barquilla, *f*. **to lie like a log,** estar hecho un tronco. **log-book,** *naut* cuaderno de bitácora, *m*. **log-cabin,** cabañas de troncos, *m*. **log-wood,** palo campeche, *m*

logarithm *n* logaritmo, *m*

logarithmic *a* logarítmico

logic *n* lógica, *f*

logical *a* lógico

logician *n* lógico (-ca)

loin *n* ijar, *m*; (of meat) falda, *f*; *pl* **loins,** lomos, riñones *m pl*. **to gird up one's loins,** *fig* arremangarse los faldones. **l.-cloth,** taparrabo, *m*

loiter *vi* vagabundear, vagar, errar; haraganear; rezagarse

loiterer *n* haragán (-ana); vago (-ga); rezagado (-da)

loll *vi* recostarse (en), apoyarse (en). *vt* (the tongue) sacar

Lombardy-Venetia Lombardo-Véneto, *m*

London Londres, *m*

Londoner *n* londinense, *mf*

lone. See **lonely**

loneliness *n* soledad, *f*; aislamiento, *m*

lonely *a* solitario; solo; aislado, remoto; desierto

lonesome *a* solo, solitario

long *a* largo; prolongado; de largo; (extensive) extenso; (big) grande; (much) mucho. **a l. time,** mucho tiempo. **It is five feet l.,** Tiene cinco pies de largo. **l.-armed,** que tiene los brazos largos. **l.-boat,** falúa, *f*. **l. clothes,** (infant's) mantillas, *f pl*. **l.-distance call,** conferencia telefónica, *f*. **l.-distance race,** carrera de fondo, *f*. **l.-eared,** de orejas largas. **l.-faced,** de cara larga, carilargo. **l.-forgotten,** olvidado hace mucho tiempo. **l.-haired,** que tiene el pelo largo. **l.-headed,** dolicocéfalo; *fig* astuto, sagaz. **l.-legged,** zanquilargo, zancudo. **l.-lived,** que vive hasta una edad avanzada; longevo; duradero. **l.-lost,** perdido hace mucho tiempo. **l.-sighted,** présbita; previsor; sagaz. **l.-standing,** viejo, de muchos años. **l.-suffering,** sufrido, paciente. **l.-tailed,** de cola larga. **l.-waisted,** de talle largo. **l.-winded,** prolijo

long *adv* mucho tiempo; mucho; durante mucho tiempo. **as l. as,** mientras (que). **before l.,** dentro de poco. **the l. and the short of it,** en resumidas cuentas. **How l. has she been here?** ¿Cuánto tiempo hace que está aquí? **not l. before,** poco tiempo antes. **l. ago,** mucho tiempo ha, muchos años ha

long *vi* anhelar, suspirar (por), desear con vehemencia

longanimity *n* longanimidad, *f*

longer *a comp* más largo. *adv comp* más tiempo. **How much l. must we wait?** ¿Cuánto tiempo más hemos de esperar? **He can no l. walk as he used,** Ya no puede andar como antes

longevity *n* longevidad, *f*

longing *a* anheloso, ansioso; de envidia. *n* anhelo, *m*, ansia, *f*; deseo vehemente, *m*; envidia, *f*

longingly *adv* con ansia; impacientemente; con envidia

longish *a* algo largo

longitude *n* longitud, *f*

longitudinal *a* longitudinal

long take *n* *cinema* toma larga, *f*

loofah *n* esponja vegetal, *f*

look *n* mirada, *f*; (glance) vistazo, *m*, ojeada, *f*; (air) semblante, aire, porte, *m*; (appearance) aspecto, *m*; apariencia, *f*. **good looks,** buen parecer, *m*; guapeza, *f*. **the new l.,** la nueva línea, la nueva silueta, la nueva moda. **to be on the l.-out,** andar a la mira

look *vi* and *vt* mirar; considerar, contemplar; (appear, seem) parecer; tener aire (de); tener aspecto (de);

hacer el efecto (de); (show oneself) mostrarse; (of buildings, etc.) caer (a), dar (a); mirar (a).; (seem to be) revelar (e.g., **You don't l. thirty,** No revelas treinta años) **to l. alike,** parecerse. **to l. hopeful,** *fig* prometer bien. **to l. out of the corner of the eye,** mirar de reojo. **to l. (a person) up and down,** mirar de hito en hito. **to l. about one,** mirar a su alrededor; observar. **to l. after,** tener la mirada puesta en, mirar; (care for) cuidar; (watch) vigilar; mirar por. **to l. at,** mirar; considerar; examinar. **He looked at his watch,** Miró su reloj. **He looked at her,** La miró. **to l. away,** desviar los ojos, apartar la mirada. **to l. back,** mirar hacia atrás, volver la cabeza; (in thought) pensar en el pasado. **to l. down,** bajar los ojos; mirar el suelo; mirar hacia abajo. **to l. down upon,** dominar, mirar a; (scorn) despreciar; mirar de arriba para abajo. **to l. for,** buscar; buscar con los ojos; (await) aguardar; (expect) esperar. **to l. forward,** mirar hacia el porvenir; pensar en el futuro; esperar con ilusión. **to l. in,** entrar por un instante, hacer una visita corta. **to l. into,** mirar dentro de; mirar hacia el interior de; estudiar, investigar. **to l. on,** *vt* mirar; considerar; (of buildings, etc.) dar a. *vi* ser espectador. **to l. on to,** dar a, mirar a. **to l. out,** *vi* (be careful) tener cuidado; (look through) mirar por; asomarse a. *vt* (search) buscar; (find) hallar; (choose) escoger, elegir. **L. out!** ¡Atención! ¡Ojo! **to l. out for,** buscar; (await) aguardar, esperar; (be careful) tener cuidado con. **to l. out of,** mirar por; asomarse a. **to l. over,** mirar bien; (persons) mirar de hito en hito; examinar; visitar; (a house) inspeccionar; (a book) hojear; mirar superficialmente. **to l. round,** *vt* (a place) visitar. *vi* volver la cabeza, volverse; mirar hacia atrás. **to l. round for,** buscar con los ojos; buscar por todas partes. **to l. through,** mirar por; mirar a través de; examinar; (search) registrar; (understand) registrar. **to l. to,** (be careful of) tener cuidado de; (attend to) atender a; (care for) cuidar de; (count on) contar con; (resort to) acudir a; (await) esperar. **to l. toward,** mirar hacia, mirar en la dirección de; caer a. **to l. up,** *vi* mirar hacia arriba; (aspire) aspirar; (improve) mejorar. *vt* visitar, ir (or venir) a ver; (turn up) buscar; averiguar. **to l. upon,** mirar. Other meanings see **l. on. They l. upon her as their daughter,** La miran como una hija suya. **to l. up to,** *fig* respetar

looked-for *a* (in)esperado; deseado

looking *a* (in compounds) de . . . aspecto, de . . . apariencia. **dirty-l.,** de aspecto sucio. **l.-glass,** espejo, *m*

lookout *n* vigilancia, observación, *f*; (view) vista, *f*, panorama, *m*; (viewpoint) miradero, *m*; *mil* atalaya, *m*; *naut* gaviero, *m*; (*fig* prospect) perspectiva, *f*

loom *n* telar, *m*, *vi* asomar, aparecer

loop *n* (turn) vuelta, *f*; (in rivers, etc.) recodo, *m*, curva, *f*; (fold) pliegue, *m*; bucle, *m*; (fastening) fiador, *m*, presilla, *f*; *aer* rizo, *m*; (knot) nudo corredizo, *m*. **to l. the l.,** *aer* hacer el rizo, hacer rizos. **l.-line,** empalme de ferrocarril, *m*

loophole *n* saetera, aspillera, *f*; *fig* escapatoria, *f*; pretexto, *m*, excusa, *f*

loose *a* suelto; (free) libre; (slack) flojo; (of garments) holgado; (untied) desatado; (unfastened) desprendido; movible; (unchained) desencadenado; en libertad; (of the bowels) suelto (de vientre); (pendulous) colgante; (of a nail, tooth, etc.) inseguro; poco firme; que se mueve; (of knots, etc.) flojo; (of the mind, etc.) incoherente, ilógico; poco exacto; (of style, etc.) vago, impreciso; (of conduct) disoluto, vicioso; (careless) negligente, descuidado. *vt* (untie) desatar; desprender; soltar; aflojar; (of a priest) absolver; *fig* desencadenar. **to break l.,** desprenderse; soltarse; libertarse; escapar; *fig* desencadenarse. **to let l.,** desatar; aflojar; poner en libertad; soltar; *fig* desencadenar; (interject) lanzar. **to turn l.,** poner en libertad; dar salida (a); echar de casa, poner en la calle. **to work l.,** desprenderse; aflojarse; desvencijarse. **l.-box,** caballeriza, *f*. **f. l. change,** suelto, *m*. **l.-leaf notebook,** libreta de hojas sueltas, *f*

loosely *adv* flojamente; sueltamente; (vaguely) vagamente; incorrectamente; incoherentemente; (carelessly) negligentemente; (viciously) disolutamente

loosen *vt* (untie) desatar; aflojar; soltar; desasir; (the tongue) desatar; *fig* hacer menos riguroso, ablandar

looseness *n* flojedad, *f;* (of clothing) holgura, *f;* soltura, *f;* relajación, *f;* (of the bowels) diarrea, *f;* (viciousness) licencia, *f,* libertinaje, *m;* (vagueness) vaguedad, *f;* incoherencia, *f*

loosening *n* desprendimiento, *m;* desasimiento, *m;* aflojamiento, *m*

loot *n* botín, *m, vt* saquear

looter *n* saqueador (-ra)

looting *n* saqueo, pillaje, *m, a* saqueador

lop *vt* mochar; podar; destroncar; cortar de un golpe. *a* (of ears) gacho. **to lop off the ends,** cercenar. **to lop off the top,** desmochar. **lop-sided,** desproporcionado; desequilibrado

lopping *n* desmoche, *m;* poda, *f*

loquacious *a* locuaz, gárrulo

loquacity *n* locuacidad, garrulidad, *f*

lord *n* señor, *m;* (husband) esposo, *m;* (English title) lord, *m,* (*pl* lores); (Christ) Señor, *m.* **feudal l.,** señor de horca y cuchillo, *m.* **my l.,** milord. **my lords,** milores. **Our L.,** Nuestro Señor. **the Lord's Prayer,** el Padrenuestro. **to l. it over,** mandar como señor, mandar a la baqueta. **L. Chamberlain,** camarero mayor, *m.* **L. Chancellor,** gran canciller, *m.* **L. Chief Justice,** presidente del tribunal supremo, *m.* **L.-Lieutenant,** virrey, *m.* **L. Mayor,** alcalde, *m.* **L. Privy Seal,** guardasellos del rey, *m*

lordliness *n* suntuosidad, *f;* liberalidad, munificencia, *f;* dignidad, *f;* (haughtiness) altivez, arrogancia, *f*

lordly *a* señorial, señoril; altivo, arrogante

lordship *n* señoría, *f;* señorío, poder, *m.* **his l.,** su señoría

lore *n* saber, *m;* erudición, *f;* tradiciones, *f pl*

lorgnette *n* impertinentes, *m pl*

lorry *n* camión, *m;* carro, *m*

lose *vt* perder; hacer perder, quitar; (forget) olvidar. *vi* perder; (of clocks) atrasar. **to be lost in thought,** estar ensimismado, estar absorto. **to l. oneself (in)** perderse (en); abstraerse (en); entregarse (a). **to l. one's footing,** resbalar. **to l. one's way,** extraviarse, perder el camino. **to l. one's self-control,** perder el tino. **to l. one's head,** perder la cabeza. **to l. ground,** perder terreno. **to l. one's voice,** perder la voz. **to l. patience,** perder la paciencia, perder los estribos

loser *n* perdedor (-ra)

losing *a* perdedor. *n* pérdida, *f*

loss *n* pérdida, *f.* **at a l.,** *com* con pérdida; perplejo, dudoso. **heavy losses,** mil pérdidas cuantiosas, *f pl.* **We are at a l. for words . . . ,** No tenemos palabras para . . .

lot *n* suerte, *f;* fortuna, *f;* lote, *m;* parte, porción, cuota, *f;* (for building) solar, *m.* **a lot of people,** muchas personas. **Our lot would have been very different,** Nuestra suerte hubiera sido muy distinta, Otro gallo nos cantara. **to draw lots,** echar suertes, sortear. **to take the lot,** *inf* alzarse con el santo y la limosna

lotion *n* loción, *f*

lottery *n* lotería, *f.* **l. ticket,** billete de la lotería, *m*

lotus *n* loto, *m.* **l.-eating,** lotofagía, *f; fig* indolencia, pereza, *f*

loud *a* fuerte; (noisy) ruidoso, estrepitoso; alto; (gaudy) chillón, llamativo, cursi. *adv* ruidosamente. **l.-speaker,** *rad* altavoz, altoparlante, *m*

loudly *adv* en alta voz; fuertemente; ruidosamente, con estrépito

loudness *n* (noise) ruido, *m;* sonoridad, *f;* (force) fuerza, *f;* (of colors, etc.) mal gusto, *m,* vulgaridad, *f*

lounge *n* sala de estar, *f;* salón, *m, vi* reclinarse, ponerse a sus anchas; apoyarse (en); gandulear; vagar. **l. chair,** poltrona, *f.* **l.-lizard,** *inf* pollo pera, *m.* **l.-suit,** traje americano, *m*

lounger *n* holgazán (-ana); golfo (-fa), azotacalles, *mf*

louse *n* piojo, *m*

lousy *a* piojoso

lout *n* patán, zamacuco, *m*

loutish *a* rústico

lovable *a* amable; simpático

lovableness *n* amabilidad, *f*

love *n* amor, *m;* (friendship) amistad, *f;* (enthusiasm, liking) afición, *f;* (in tennis) cero, *m, vt* querer, amar; gustar mucho; tener afición (a). *vi* estar enamorado. **I should l. to dine with you,** Me gustaría mucho cenar con Vds. **to be in l. with,** estar enamorado de. **to fall in l. with,** enamorarse de. **They l. each other,** Se quieren. **to make l. to,** hacer el amor (a), galantear. **l. affair,** amorío, lance de amor, *m.* **l.-bird,** periquito, *m.* **l.-letter,** carta amatoria, carta de amor, *f.* **l.-making,** galanteo, *m.* **l.-philtre,** filtro, *m.* **l.-song,** canción de amor, *f.* **l.-story,** historia de amor, *f.* **l.-token,** prenda de amor, *f*

loveless *a* sin amor

loveliness *n* hermosura, belleza, *f;* encanto, *m;* amabilidad, *f*

lovely *a* hermoso, bello; delicioso; amable; *inf* estupendo

lover *n* amante, *mf;* aficionado (-da)

lovesick *a* enfermo de amor, enamorado

loving *a* amoroso; cariñoso; (friendly) amistoso; de amor

low *a* bajo; de poca altura; (of dresses, etc.) escotado; (of musical notes) grave; (soft) suave; (feeble) débil; (depressed) deprimido, triste, abatido; (plain) sencillo; (of a fever) lento; (of a bow) profundo; pequeño; inferior; humilde; (ill) enfermo; (vile) vil, ruin; obsceno, escabroso. *adv* bajo; cerca de la tierra; en voz baja; (cheaply) barato, a bajo precio. **in a low voice,** en voz baja, paso. **to lay low,** (kill) tumbar; (knock down) derribar; incapacitar. **to lie low,** descansar; estar muerto; esconderse, agacharse; callar. **to run low,** escasear. **low-born,** de humilde cuna. **low-brow,** nada intelectual. **low comedy,** farsa, *f.* **low flying,** *n* bajo vuelo, *m, a* que vuela bajo; terrero, rastrero; que vuela a ras de tierra. **low frequency,** baja frecuencia, *f.* **low Latin,** bajo latín, *m.* **Low Mass,** misa rezada, *f.* **low neck,** escote, *m.* **low-necked,** escotado. **low-pitched,** grave. **low-spirited,** deprimido. **Low Sunday,** domingo de Cuasimodo, *m.* **low tension,** baja tensión, *f.* **low trick,** mala pasada, *f.* **low water,** marea baja, bajamar, *f;* (of rivers) estiaje, *m*

low *vi* berrear, mugir. *n* berrido, mugido, *m*

low-ceiling *a* bajo de techo.

Low Countries, the Los Países Bajos, *m*

lower *vt* bajar; descolgar; disminuir; (price) rebajar; (a boat, sails) arriar. *vi* (of persons) fruncir el ceño, mostrarse malhumorado; (of the sky) encapotarse, cargarse; (menace) amenazar. **to l. a boat,** arriar un bote. **to l. oneself,** (by a rope, etc.) descolgarse. **to l. the flag,** abatir la bandera

lower *a comp* más bajo; menos alto; bajo; inferior. **l. classes,** clase obrera, *f,* clases bajas, *f pl.* **l. down,** más abajo. **L. House,** Cámara de los Comunes, *f;* cámara baja, *f.* **l. jaw,** mandíbula inferior, *f.* **l. storey,** piso bajo, *m;* piso de abajo, *m*

lowering *n* abajamiento, *m;* descenso, *m;* (of prices) baja, *f;* (of a boat) arriada, *f;* (of the flag) abatimiento, *m, a* (of persons) ceñudo; (of the sky) anublado, encapotado; (threatening) amenazador

lowest *a sup* el (la, etc.) más bajo; el (la, etc.) más profundo; ínfimo

lowing *n* berrido, mugido, *m*

lowland *n* tierra baja, *f.* **the Lowlands,** las tierras bajas de Escocia

lowliness *n* humildad, *f;* modestia, *f*

lowly *a* humilde

lowness *n* poca altura, *f;* situación poco elevada, *f;* pequeñez, *f;* (of musical notes) gravedad, *f;* (softness) suavidad, *f;* (feebleness) debilidad, *f;* (sadness) tristeza, *f,* abatimiento, *m;* (of price) baratura, *f;* inferioridad, *f;* humildad, *f;* (vileness) bajeza, *f;* obscenidad, *f*

loyal *a* leal, fiel
loyalist *n* realista, *mf*; defensor (-ra) del gobierno legítimo
loyalty *n* lealtad, fidelidad, *f*
loyalty oath *n* (approximate equivalent) certificado de adhesión, *m*
lozenge *n* pastilla, *f*
lubricant *a* and *n* lubricante *m*
lubricate *vt* lubricar, engrasar
lubricating oil *n* aceite lubricante, *m*
lubrication *n* lubricación, *f*, engrasado, *m*
lubricator *n* lubricador, *m*; engrasador, *m*
Lucerne Lucerna, *f*
lucid *a* lúcido; claro
lucidity *n* lucidez, *f*; claridad, *f*
lucidly *adv* claramente
luck *n* destino, azar, *m*; (good) buenaventura, suerte, *f*. **to bring bad l.,** traer mala suerte. **to try one's l.,** probar fortuna
luckily *adv* por fortuna, afortunadamente, felizmente
luckless *a* desdichado
lucky *a* afortunado; dichoso, venturoso; feliz. **to be l.,** tener buena suerte
lucrative *a* lucrativo
lucre *n* lucro, *m*
lucubration *n* lucubración, *f*
ludicrous *a* absurdo, risible, ridiculo
ludicrousness *n* ridiculez, *f*
lug *n* tirón, *m*; (ear and projection) oreja, *f*, *vt* tirar (de); arrastrar. **to lug about,** arrastrar (por); llevar con dificultad. **to lug in,** arrastrar adentro; introducir; hacer entrar. **to lug out,** arrastrar afuera; hacer salir
luggage *n* equipaje, *m*. **excess l.,** exceso de equipaje, *m*. **piece of l.,** bulto, *m*. **to register one's l.,** facturar el equipaje. **l. carrier,** (on buses, etc.) baca, *f*; (on a car) portaequipajes, *m*. **l. porter,** mozo de equipajes, *m*. **l. rack,** (on a car) portaequipajes, *m*; (in a train) rejilla para el equipaje, *f*. **l. receipt,** talón de equipaje, *m*. **l. room,** consigna, *f*. **l. van,** furgón de equipajes, *m*
lugubrious *a* lúgubre
lukewarm *a* tibio, templado; *fig* indiferente, frío
lukewarmness *n* tibieza, *f*; *fig* indiferencia, frialdad, *f*
lull *n* momento de calma, *m*; tregua, *f*; silencio, *m*, *vt* (a child) arrullar, adormecer; (soothe) sosegar, calmar; disminuir, mitigar
lullaby *n* canción de cuna, *f*
lumbago *n* lumbago, *m*
lumbar *a* lumbar
lumber *n* (wood) maderas de sierra, *f pl*; (rubbish) trastos viejos, *m pl*. *vt* amontonar trastos viejos; obstruir. *vi* andar pesadamente; avanzar ruidosamente, avanzar con ruido sordo. **l.-jack,** maderero, ganchero, *m*. **l.-room,** leonera, *f*. **l.-yard,** maderería, *f*, depósito de maderas, *m*
lumbering *a* pesado
luminary *n* lumbrera, *f*
luminosity *n* luminosidad, *f*
luminous *a* luminoso
lump *n* masa, *f*; bulto, *m*; pedazo, *m*; (of sugar) terrón *m*; (swelling) hinchazón, *f*; protuberancia, *f*. *vt* amontonar. **to l. together,** mezclar; incluir. **in the l.,** en la masa; en grueso. **Let him l. it!** ¡Que se rasque! l. in

one's throat, nudo en la garganta, *m*. **l. of sugar,** terrón de azúcar, *m*. **l. sum,** cantidad gruesa, *f*
lumpishness *n* hobachonería, *f*
lunacy *n* locura, *f*
lunar *a* lunar
lunatic *n* loco (-ca); demente, *mf a* de locos; loco. **l. asylum,** manicomio, *m*
lunch, luncheon *n* almuerzo, *m*; (snack) merienda, *f*. *vi* almorzar. **l. basket** or **pail,** fiambrera, *f*
lunette *n* (*arch mil*) luneta, *f*
lung *n* pulmón, *m*
lunge *n* (fencing) estocada, *f*; embestida, *f*, *vi* dar una estocada; abalanzarse sobre
lurch *n* sacudida, *f*; *naut* guiñada, *f*; tambaleo, *m*; movimiento brusco, *m*. *vi naut* guiñar; tambalearse; andar haciendo eses. **to leave in the l.,** dejar plantado
lure *n* añagaza, *f*; reclamo, *m*; aliciente, atractivo, *m*; seducción, *f*. *vt* atraer, tentar
lurid *a* misterioso, fantástico; cárdeno; ominoso; funesto, triste; (orange) anaranjado; (vicissitudinous) accidentado
lurk *vi* acechar, espiar; esconderse
lurking *a* (in ambush) en acecho; (of fear, etc.) vago
luscious *a* delicioso; suculento; meloso; atractivo, apetitoso; sensual
lusciousness *n* suculencia, *f*; melosidad, *f*; atractivo, *m*; sensualidad, *f*
lush *a* jugoso; fresco y lozano; maduro
lust *n* lujuria, lascivia, *f*; codicia, *f*; deseo, *m*. **l. for revenge,** deseo de venganza, *m*
lustful *a* lujurioso, lúbrico, lascivo
luster *n* lustre, brillo, *m*; brillantez, *f*
lusterless *a* sin brillo; mate, deslustrado; (of eyes) apagado
lustrous *a* lustroso
lusty *a* vigoroso, fuerte, lozano
lute *n* laúd, *m*, vihuela, *f*. **l.-player,** vihuelista, *mf*
Lutheran *a* luterano. *n* luterano (-na)
Lutheranism *n* luteranismo, *m*
luxation *n* luxación, *f*
Luxembourg Luxemburgo, *m*
luxuriance *n* lozanía, *f*; exuberancia, superabundancia, *f*
luxuriant *a* lozano; fértil; exuberante
luxuriate *vi* crecer con exuberancia; complacerse (en); disfrutar (de), gozar (de)
luxurious *a* lujoso
luxuriously *adv* lujosamente, con lujo
luxury *n* lujo, *m*. **l. goods,** artículos de lujo, *m pl*
lyceum *n* liceo, *m*
lye *n* lejía, *f*
lying *a* (recumbent) recostado; (untrue) mentiroso, falso. *n* mentiras, *f pl*. **l.-in,** parto, *m*
lymph *n* linfa, *f*; vacuna, *f*
lymphatic *a* linfático; flemático
lynch *vt* linchar
lynching *n* linchamiento, *m*
lynx *n* lince, *m*. **l.-eyed,** de ojos de lince
lyre *n* lira, *f*. **l.-bird,** pájaro lira, *m*
lyric *n* poesía lírica, *f*; poema lírico, *m*; letra (de una canción,) *f*
lyrical *a* lírico
lyricism *n* lirismo, *m*

M

m *n* (letter) eme, *f*
ma'am *n* señora, *f*
macabre *a* macabro
macadam *n* macadán, *m*, *a* de macadán
macadamize *vt* macadanizar
macaroni *n* macarrones, *m pl*
macaronic *a* macarrónico
macaroon *n* macarrón de almendras, *m*

Macassar oil *n* aceite de Macasar, *m*
macaw *n* macagua, *f*, guacamayo, *m*
mace *n* maza, *f*; *cul* macis, *f*. **m.-bearer,** macero, *m*
Macedonian *a* macedón, macedonio. *n* macedonio (-ia)
macerate *vt* macerar. *vi* macerarse
Machiavellian *a* maquiavélico
Machiavellism *n* maquiavelismo, *m*
machination *n* maquinación, *f*

machine n máquina, f; mecanismo, m; aparato, m; instrumento, m; organización, f, vt trabajar a máquina; sew coser a máquina. **m.-gun,** n ametralladora, f. vt ametrallar. **m.-gun carrier,** portametralladoras, m. **m.-gunner,** ametrallador, m. **m.-made,** hecho a máquina. **m.-oil,** aceite de motores, m. **m.-shop,** taller de maquinaria, m. **m.-tool,** máquina herramienta, f

machinery n maquinaria, f; mecanismo, m; organización, f; sistema, m

machinist n maquinista, mf; sew costurera a máquina, f

mackerel n caballa, f. **m. sky,** cielo aborregado, m

mackintosh n impermeable, m

macrocosm n macrocosmo, m

mad a loco; fuera de sí; (of a dog, etc.) rabioso; furioso. **as mad as a hatter,** loco como una cabra. **to drive mad,** volver loco (a). **to go mad,** volverse loco, enloquecer, perder el seso. **mad with joy (pain),** loco de alegría (dolor). **mad dog,** perro rabioso, m

madam n señora, f; (French form) madama, f. **Yes, m.,** Sí señora

madcap n loculo (-la), f, botarate, m; tarambana, mf

madden vt enloquecer; enfurecer, exasperar

maddening a exasperante, irritador

madder n bot rubia, f

made past part and a hecho; formado. **self-m. man,** un hombre hecho y derecho. **m.-to-measure,** hecho a la medida. **m.-up,** compuesto; (of clothes) confeccionado, ya hecho; (of the face) pintado; (fictitious) inventado, ficticio; artificial

Madeira n vino de Madera, m, a de Madera

madhouse n casa de locos, f, manicomio, m

madly adv locamente; furiosamente

madman n loco, m

madness n locura, f; (of a dog, etc.) rabia, f; furia, f

Madonna n Madona, f

madrigal n madrigal, m

Madrilenian a madrileño, matritense. n madrileño (-ña)

madwoman n loca, f

Maecenas n mecenas, m

maelstrom n remolino, vórtice, m

magazine n (store) almacén, m; (for explosives) polvorín, m, santabárbara, f; (periodical) revista, f. **m. rifle,** rifle de repetición, m

Magdalen n magdalena, f

magenta n color magenta, m

maggot n gusano, m, cresa, f; fig manía, f, capricho, m

maggoty a gusanoso

Magi, the n pl los reyes magos

magic n magia, f; mágica, f; fig encanto, m, a mágico. **as if by m.,** por ensalmo. **m. lantern,** linterna mágica, f

magically adv por encanto

magician n mago, mágico, brujo, m; (conjurer) jugador de manos, m

magisterial a magistral

magistracy n magistratura, f

magistrate n magistrado, m; juez municipal, m

Magna Charta n Carta Magna, f

magnanimity n magnanimidad, generosidad, f

magnanimous a magnánimo, generoso

magnanimously adv magnánimamente

magnate n magnate, m

magnesia n magnesia, f

magnesium n magnesio, m. **m. light,** luz de magnesio, f

magnet n imán, m

magnetic a magnético; fig atractivo. **m. field,** campo magnético, m. **m. needle,** brújula, f

magnetics n la ciencia del magnetismo, f

magnetism n magnetismo, m

magnetization n imanación, magnetización, f

magnetize vt magnetizar, imanar; (hypnotize) magnetizar; fig atraer

magnification n (by a lens, etc.) aumento, m; exageración, f

magnificence n magnificencia, f

magnificent a magnífico

magnify vt (by lens) aumentar; exagerar; (praise) magnificar

magnifying a de aumento, vidrio de aumento. **m. glass,** lente de aumento, m

magniloquence n grandilocuencia, f

magniloquent a grandílocuo

magnitude n magnitud, f

magnolia n magnolia, f

magnum n botella de dos litros, f

magpie n marica, picaza, f

maharaja n maharajá, m

mahogany n caoba, f, a de caoba

Mahomedan. See **Mohammedan**

maid n doncella, muchacha, f; virgen, f; soltera, f; (servant) criada, f; (daily) asistenta, f. **old m.,** solterona, f. **m.-of-all-work,** criada para todo, f. **m.-of-honor,** dama de honor, f

maiden n doncella, joven, soltera, f; virgen, f; zagala, f. a de soltera; soltera f; virginal; (of speeches, voyages, etc.) primero. **m. lady,** dama soltera, f. **m.-name,** apellido de soltera, m. **m. speech,** primer discurso, m

maidenhood n doncellez, virginidad, f

maidenly a virginal; modesto, modoso; tímido

maidservant n criada, sirvienta, f

mail n mala, f; (bag) valija, f; correo, m; correspondencia, f; (armour) cota de malla, f. vt mandar por correo; armar con cota de malla. **coat of m.,** cota de malla, f. **royal m.,** malla real, f. **m.-bag,** valija de correo, f; portacartas, m. **m.-boat,** buque correo, m. **m.-cart,** ambulancia de correos, f. **m.-clad,** vestido de cota de malla; armado. **m.-coach,** coche correo, m, diligencia, f. **m.-order,** pedido postal, m. **m.-order business,** negocio de ventas por correo, m. **m.-plane,** avión postal, m. **m. service,** servicio de correos, m. **m. steamer,** vapor correo, m. **m. train,** tren correo, m. **m. van,** (on a train) furgón postal, m

mailed a de malla; armado. **m. fist,** fig puño de hierro, m

maim vt mancar; mutilar, tullir; estropear

maimed a manco; tullido, mutilado

main a mayor; principal; más importante, esencial; maestro. n (mainland) continente, m; (sea) océano, m; (pipe) cañería maestra, f. **by m. force,** por fuerza mayor. **in the m.,** en general, generalmente; en su mayoría. **m. beam,** viga maestra, f. **m. body,** (of a building) ala principal, f; (of a church) cuerpo (de iglesia), m; (of an army) cuerpo (del ejército), m; mayor parte, mayoría, f. **m. line,** línea principal, f. **m. mast,** palo mayor, m. **m. thing,** cosa principal, f, lo más importante. **m. wall,** pared maestra, f

mainland n continente, m; tierra firme, f

mainly adv principalmente; en su mayoría; generalmente

mainsail n vela mayor, f

mainspring n (of a watch) muelle real, m; motivo principal, m; origen, m

mainstay n estay mayor, m; fig sostén principal, m

maintain vt mantener; sostener; tener; guardar; afirmar

maintainable a sostenible; defendible

maintenance n mantenimiento, m; manutención, f, sustento, m; conservación, f, subsistencia, f

maize n maíz, m. **m. field,** maizal, m

majestic a majestuoso

majesty n majestad, f; majestuosidad, f. **His** or **Her M.,** Su Majestad

majolica n mayólica, f

major a mayor; principal. n mayor de edad, m; mil comandante. **anthropology major,** alumno con la especialidad en antropología m. **m.-domo,** mayordomo, m. **m.-general,** general de división, m. **m. road,** carretera, f; ruta de prioridad, f. **m. scale,** escala mayor, f

Majorca Mallorca, f

majority *n* mayoría, *f;* mayor número, *m;* generalidad, *f.* **to have attained one's m.**, ser mayor de edad

make *vt* hacer; crear, formar; (manufacture) fabricar, confeccionar; construir; (produce) producir; causar; (prepare) preparar; (a bed, a fire, a remark, poetry, friends, enemies, war, a curtsey) hacer; (earn, win) ganar; (a speech) pronunciar; (compel) obligar (a), forzar (a); inclinar (a); (arrive at) alcanzar, llegar (a); (calculate) calcular; (arrange) arreglar; deducir; (be) ser; (equal) ser igual a; (think) creer; (appoint as) constituir (en), hacer; (behave) portarse (como). *vi* (begin) ir (a), empezar (a); (make as though) hacer (como si); (of the tide) crecer; contribuir (a); tender (a). **He made as if to go,** Hízo como si de marchara. **to m. as though . . .**, aparentar, fingir. **It made me ill,** Me hizo sentir mal. **They have made it up,** Han hecho las paces. **They m. a great deal of money,** Hacen (or ganan) mucho dinero. **You cannot m. me believe it,** No puedes hacerme creerlo. **He is making himself ridiculous,** Se está poniendo en ridículo. **to m. ready,** preparar. **to m. the tea,** hacer el té; preparar el té. **Two and two m. four,** Dos y dos son cuatro. **to m. oneself known,** darse a conocer. **to m. one of . . .**, ser uno de . . . **to m. after,** seguir; correr detrás de. **to m. again,** hacer de nuevo, rehacer. **to m. away with,** quitar; suprimir; destruir; (kill) matar; (squander) derrochar; (steal) llevarse; hurtar. **to m. away with oneself,** quitarse la vida, suicidarse. **to m. for,** encaminarse a, dirigirse a; (attack) abalanzarse sobre, atacar; (tend to) contribuir a, tender a. **to m. off,** marcharse corriendo, largarse; huir, escaparse. **to m. out,** (discern) distinguir; descifrar; (understand) comprender; (prove) probar, justificar; (draw up) redactar; (fill in a form) completar, llenar; (a check, etc.) extender; (an account) hacer; (get on, succeed or otherwise) ir (with bien o mal); (convey) dar la impresión de que; sugerir. **I cannot m. it out,** No lo puedo comprender. **How did you m. out** (get on)**?** ¿Cómo te fue? **to m. over,** hacer de nuevo, rehacer; (transfer) ceder, traspasar. **to m. up,** hacer; acabar; concluir; (clothes) confeccionar; fabricar; (the face) pintarse, maquillarse; (the fire) echar carbón, etc. a; *print* compaginar; (invent) inventar; (lies) fabricar; (compose) formar; (package) empaquetar; reparar; indemnizar; compensar; (an account) ajustar; preparar; arreglar; (conciliate) conciliar; enumerar; *theat* caracterizarse. **to m. up for,** reemplazar; compensar; (lost time, etc.) recobrar. **to m. up to,** compensar; indemnizar; (flatter) adular, halagar; procurar congraciarse con, procurar obtener el favor de; (court) galantear (con). **m. an impression (on),** dejar(le a fulano) una impresión

make *n* forma, *f;* hechura, *f;* estructura, *f;* confección, *f;* manufactura, *f;* producto, *m;* (trade name) marca, *f;* (character) carácter, temperamento, *m.* **m.-believe,** *n* artificio, pretexto, *m, a* fingido. *vi* fingir. **land of m.-believe,** reino de los sueños, *m.* **m.-up,** (for the face, etc.) maquillaje, *m; theat* caracterización, *f; print* imposición, *f;* (whole) conjunto, *m;* (character) carácter, modo de ser, *m*

maker *n* creador, *m;* autor (-ra); artífice, *mf;* (manufacturer) fabricante, *m;* constructor, *m;* (of clothes, etc.) confeccionador (-ra); (worker) obrero (-ra)

makeshift *n* expediente, *m, a* provisional

makeweight *n* añadidura (de peso), *f,* contrapeso, *m; fig* suplente, *m*

making *n* creación, *f;* hechura, *f;* (manufacture) fabricación, *f;* construcción, *f;* (of clothes, etc.) confección, *f;* formación, *f;* preparación, *f;* estructura, *f;* composición, *f; pl* **makings,** (profits) ganancias, *f pl;* (elements) elementos, *m pl;* germen, *m;* rasgos esenciales, *m pl,* características, *f pl.* **m.-up,** (of clothes) confección, *f; print* ajuste, *m;* (of the face) maquillaje, *m;* (invention) invención, *f;* fabricación, *f*

Malachite *n* malaquita, *f*

maladjustment *n* mal ajuste, *m;* inadaptación, *f*

maladministration *n* desgobierno, *m,* mala administración, *f;* (of funds) malversación, *f*

maladroit *a* torpe

maladroitness *n* torpeza, *f*

malady *n* enfermedad, *f;* mal, *m*

Malaga *n* vino de Málaga, *m*

malaria *n* paludismo, *m*

malarial *a* palúdico. **m. fever,** fiebre palúdica, *f*

Malaya Malasia, *f,* Archipiélago Malayo, *m*

Malayan *a* malayo. *n* malayo (-ya)

malcontent *n* malcontento (-ta). *a* descontento

Maldives Maldivas, *f pl*

male *a* macho; masculino. *n* macho, *m;* varón, *m.* **m. child,** niño, *m;* niño varón, *m;* (son) hijo varón, *m.* **m. flower,** flor masculina, *f.* **m. issue,** sucesión masculina, *f.* **m. nurse,** enfermero, *m.* **m. sex,** sexo masculino, *m*

malediction *n* maldición, *f*

malefactor *n* malhechor (-ra)

malefic *a* maléfico

malevolence *n* malevolencia, *f*

malevolent *a* malévolo, maligno

malformation *n* formación anormal, deformidad, deformación congénita, *f*

malice *n* malicia, *f; law* alevosía, *f.* **to bear m.,** guardar rencor

malicious *a* malicioso; maligno, rencoroso

maliciousness *n* malicia, mala intención, *f*

malign *vt* calumniar, difamar. *a* maligno; malévolo

malignancy *n* malignidad, *f;* malevolencia, *f*

malignant *a* maligno; malévolo; *med* maligno

malinger *vi* fingirse enfermo

malingerer *n* enfermo (-ma) fingido (-da)

malingering *n* enfermedad fingida, *f*

mallard *n* pato (-ta), silvestre

malleability *n* maleabilidad, *f*

malleable *a* maleable

mallet *n* mazo, *m;* (in croquet) pala, *f,* mazo, *m;* (in polo) maza (de polo), *f*

mallow *n* malva, *f*

malmsey *n* (wine) malvasía, *f*

malnutrition *n* desnutrición, alimentación deficiente, *f*

malodorous *a* de mal olor, hediondo, fétido

malpractice *n* (wrongdoing) maleficencia, *f;* (by a doctor) tratamiento equivocado, perjudicial o ilegal, *m;* (malversation) malversación, *f;* inmoralidad, *f*

malt *n* malta, *m. vt* preparar el malta. **m.-house,** fábrica de malta, *f.* **m. vinegar,** vinagre de malta, *m*

malted milk *n* leche malteada, *f*

malt shop *n* café-nevería, *f*

Maltese *a* maltés. *n* maltés (-esa). **M. cat,** gato maltés, *m.* **M. cross,** cruz de Malta, *f.* **M. dog,** perro maltés, *m*

Malthusian *a* maltusiano

Malthusianism *n* maltusianismo, *m*

maltose *n* maltosa, *f*

maltreat *vt* maltratar

maltreatment *n* maltrato, *m,*

mamma *n anat* mama, *f;* (mother) mamá, *f*

mammal *n* mamífero, *m*

mammalian *a* mamífero

mammary *a* mamario. **m. gland,** mama, teta, *f*

mammon *n* becerro de oro, *m*

mammoth *n* mamut, *m, a* gigantesco, enorme

man *n* hombre, *m;* varón, *m;* persona, *f;* (servant) criado, *m;* (workman) obrero, *m;* (soldier) soldado, *m;* (sailor) marinero, *m;* (humanity) raza humana, *f;* (husband) marido, *m;* (chess) peón, *m;* (checkers) dama, *f;* (a ship) buque, *m.* **no man,** nadie; ningún hombre. **young man,** joven, *m.* **to a man,** como un solo hombre. **to come to man's estate,** llegar a la edad viril. **Man overboard!** ¡Hombre al agua! **man and wife,** marido y mujer, *m,* cónyuges, esposos, *m pl.* **man about town,** hombre de mundo, señorito, *m.* **man-at-arms,** hombre de armas, *m.* **man-eater,** caníbal, *mf;* tigre, *m.* **man-eating,** *a* antropófago. **man hater,**

misántropo, *m;* mujer que odia a los hombres, *f.* **man-hole,** pozo, *m.* **man-hunter,** caníbal, *mf;* (woman) castigadora, *f.* **man in charge,** encargado, *m.* **man in the moon,** mujer de la luna, *f.* **man in the street,** hombre de la calle, hombre medio, *m.* **man of letters,** hombre de letras, literato, *m;* **man of straw,** bausán, *m;* (figure-head) testaferro, *m.* **man of the world,** hombre del mundo, *m.* **man of war,** buque de guerra, *m.* **man-power,** mano de obra, *f,* brazos, *m pl,* (e.g. **lack of manpower,** falta de brazos, *f*). **man servant,** criado, *m*

man *vt* armar; *mil* poner guarnición (a); ocupar; *naut* tripular; dirigir; *fig* fortificar

manacle *n* manilla, *f; pl* **manacles,** esposas, *f pl;* grillos, *m pl. vt* poner esposas (a)

manage *vt* manejar; (animals) domar; dirigir; gobernar; administrar; (arrange) agenciar, arreglar; (work) explotar; (do) hacer; (eat) comer. *vi* arreglárselas (para); (get along) ir tirando; (know how) saber hacer; (succeed in) lograr; (do) hacer

manageability *n* lo manejable; flexibilidad, *f;* (of animals, persons) docilidad, mansedumbre, *f*

manageable *a* manejable; flexible; (of persons, animals) dócil

management *n* manejo, *m;* dirección, *f;* gobierno, *m;* administración, *f;* arreglo, *m;* (working) explotación, *f; com* gerencia, *f; theat* empresa, *f;* conducta, *f;* (economy) economía, *f;* (skill) habilidad, *f;* prudencia, *f.* **the m.,** la dirección, el cuerpo de directores. **domestic m.,** economía doméstica, *f*

manager *n* director, *m;* administrador, *m;* jefe, *m; theat* empresario, *m; com* gerente, *m;* regente, *m.* **She is not much of a m.,** No es muy mujer de su casa. **manager's office,** dirección, *f*

manageress *n* directora, *f;* administradora, *f;* jefa, *f*

managerial *a* directivo; administrativo. **m. board,** junta directiva, *f*

managership *n* puesto de director, *m;* jefatura, *f*

managing *a* directivo; (officious) mandón, dominante; (niggardly) tacaño

manatee *n* manatí, *m*

Manchurian *a* manchuriano. *n* manchuriano (-na)

mandarin *n* mandarín, *m;* (language) mandarina, *f.* **m. orange,** mandarina, *f*

mandate *n* mandato, *m.* **mandated territory,** territorios bajo mandato, *m pl*

mandatory *a* obligatorio

mandible *n* mandíbula, *f*

mandolin *n* bandolín, *m,* bandurria, *f*

mandrake *n* mandrágora, *f*

mandrill *n* mandril, *m*

mane *n* melena, *f;* (of a horse) crines, *f pl*

maned *a* (in compounds) con melena . . . ; con crines . . .

maneuver *n* maniobra, *f. vi* maniobrar, hacer maniobras. *vt* hacer maniobrar; manipular

maneuvering *n* maniobras, *f pl;* maquinaciones, intrigas, *f pl*

manfully *adv* valientemente; vigorosamente

manganate *n* manganato, *m*

manganese *n* manganeso, *m*

mange *n* sarna, *f;* (in sheep) roña, *f*

manger *n* pesebre, *m*

manginess *n* estado sarnoso, *m*

mangle *n* (for clothes) exprimidor de la ropa, *m. vt* pasar por el exprimidor; (mutilate) mutilar, lacerar, magullar; (a text) mutilar

mangling *n* (mutilation) mutilación, laceración, *f*

mango *n* mango, *m*

mangy *a* sarnoso

manhandle *vt* maltratar

manhood *n:* virilidad, *f;* edad viril, *f;* masculinidad, *f;* los hombres; (manliness) hombradía, *f,* valor, *m*

mania *n* manía, *f;* obsesión, *f;* capricho, *m,* chifladura, *f*

maniac *n* maníaco (-ca). *a* maníaco, maniático

manicure *n* manicura, *f. vt* arreglar las uñas. **m.-set,** estuche de manicura, *m*

manicurist *n* manicuro (-ra)

manifest *n naut* manifiesto, *m. vt* mostrar; hacer patente, probar; manifestarse. *vi* publicar un manifiesto; (of spirits) manifestarse. *a* manifiesto, evidente, claro, patente. **to make m.,** poner de manifiesto

manifestation *n* manifestación, *f*

manifestly *adv* evidentemente, manifiestamente

manifesto *n* manifiesto, *m*

manifold *a* múltiple; numeroso; diverso, vario

manikin *n* enano, *m;* muñeco, *m; art* maniquí, *m*

Manilla *n* Manila, *f;* cigarro filipino, *m.* **M. hemp,** cáñamo de Manila, *m*

maniple *n* manípulo, *m*

manipulate *vt* manipular

manipulation *n* manipulación, *f*

manipulative *a* manipulador

mankind *n* humanidad, raza humana, *f,* género humano, *m*

manlike *a* de hombre, masculino; varonil; (of a woman) hombruno

manliness *n* masculinidad, hombradía, *f;* virilidad, *f;* valor, *m;* (of a woman) aire hombruno, *m*

manly *a* masculino, de hombre; varonil, viril; valiente; fuerte. **to be very m.,** ser muy hombre, ser todo un hombre

manna *n* maná, *m*

mannequin *n* maniquín, modelo, *f.* **m. parade,** exposición de modelos, *f*

manner *n* manera, *f,* modo, *m;* aire, porte, *m;* conducta, *f;* (style) estilo, *m;* (sort) clase, *f; gram* modo, *m; pl* **manners,** modales, *m pl,* crianza, educación, *f;* (customs) costumbres, *f pl.* **after the m. of,** en (o según) el estilo de. **in a m. of speaking,** en cierto modo, para decirlo así. **in this m.,** de este modo. **to have bad (good) manners,** tener malos (buenos) modales, ser mal (bien) criado. **the novel of manners,** la novela de costumbres

mannered *a* amanerado; (in compounds) . . . educado, de . . . modales; de costumbres . . . **well-m.,** bien educado, de buenos modales

mannerism *n* amaneramiento, *m;* afectación, *f; theat* latiguillo, *m.* **to acquire mannerisms,** amanerarse

mannerliness *n* cortesía, buena educación, urbanidad, *f*

mannerly *a* cortés, bien educado, atento

mannish *a* (of a woman) hombruno; de hombre, masculino

manor *n* feudo, *m;* finca, hacienda, *f;* casa solariega, *f;* señorío, *m*

manorial *a* señorial

mansion *n* mansión, *f;* casa solariega, *f;* hotel, *m.* **m.-house,** casa solariega, *f;* residencia del alcalde de Londres, *f*

manslaughter *n* homicidio, *m; law* homicidio sin premeditación, *m*

mantelpiece *n* repisa de chimenea, *f*

mantilla *n* mantilla, *f*

mantle *n* capa, *f,* manto, *m; fig* cobertura, *f;* (gas) camiseta, *f,* manguito, *mf; zool* manto, *m. vt* cubrir; envolver; ocultar. *vi* extenderse; (of blushes) inundar, subirse (a las mejillas)

Mantuan *a* mantuano

manual *n* manual, *m. n* manual, *m; mus* teclado de órgano, *m.* **m. work,** trabajo manual, *m*

manufactory *n* fábrica, *f,* taller, *m*

manufacture *n* fabricación, *f;* manufactura, *f. vt* manufacturar, fabricar

manufacturer *n* fabricante, industrial, *m.* **manufacturer's price,** precio de fábrica, *m*

manufacturing *a* manufacturero, fabril. *n* fabricación, *f*

manure *n* estiércol, abono, *m. vt* estercolar, abonar. **m. heap,** estercolero, *m*

manuring *n* estercoladura, *f*

manuscript *n* manuscrito, *m*, *a* manuscrito
Manx *a* manés
many *a* muchos (-as); numeroso; diversos (-as); varios (-as). *n* muchos (-as); la mayoría; las masas; muchedumbre, multitud, *f*. **a great m.,** muchísimos, *m pl*, muchísimas, *f pl*; un gran número. **as m. as . . . ,** tantos como . . . **How m. are there?** ¿Cuántos hay? ¿Cuántas hay? **m. a time,** muchas veces. **three too m.,** tres de más. **for m. long years,** por largos años. **m.-colored,** multicolor. **m.-headed,** con muchas cabezas. **m.-sided,** multilátero; polifacético; complicado
Maori *n* maorí, *m*, (*pl* maoríes)
map *n* mapa, *m*; plano, *m*; (chart) carta, *f*. *vt* hacer un mapa (or plano) de. **to map out,** *surv* señalar; trazar; (plan) proyectar. **ordnance map,** mapa del estado mayor, *m*. **map of the world,** mapamundi, mapa del mundo, *m*. **map-making,** cartografía, *f*
maple *n* (tree) arce, *m*; (wood) madera de arce, *f*. **m.-syrup,** jarabe de arce, *m*
mapping *n* cartografía, *f*
mar *vt* estropear; desfigurar; (happiness) destruir, aguar; frustrar
marabou *n* marabú, *m*
maraschino *n* marrasquino, *m*. **m. cherry,** cerezas en marrasquino, *f pl*
maraud *vi* merodear
marauder *n* merodeador, *m*
marauding *a* merodeador, *n* merodeo, *m*
marble *n* mármol, *m*; (for playing with) canica, *f*, *a* de marmol, marmóreo; *fig* insensible; (of paper, etc.) jaspeado. *vt* jaspear. **m. cutter,** marmolista, *m*. **m. works,** marmolería, *f*
marbled *a* jaspeado
March *n* marzo, *m*. **as mad as a M. hare,** loco como una cabra, loco de atar
march *n* marcha, *f*; (step) paso, *m*; *fig* marcha, *f*, progreso, *m*. **forced m.,** marcha forzada, *f*. **quick m.,** paso doble, *m*. **to steal a m. on,** tomar la delantera (a), ganar por la mano (a). **to strike up a m.,** batir la marcha. **m.-past,** desfile, *m*
march *vi* marchar; (of properties) lindar (con). *vt* hacer marchar, poner en marcha (a). **to m. back,** *vi* regresar (or volver) a pie. *vt* hacer volver a pie. **to m. in,** entrar (a pie) en. **to m. off,** marcharse. **to m. on,** seguir marchando; seguir adelante; avanzar. **to m. past,** desfilar ante
marching *n* marcha, *f*. *a* en marcha; de marcha. **to receive one's m. orders,** recibir la orden de marchar; *inf* ser despedido. **m. order,** orden de marcha, *m*. **m. song,** canción de marcha, *f*
marchioness *n* marquesa, *f*
mardi gras *n* martes de carnaval, *m*
mare *n* yegua, *f*
margarine *n* margarina, *f*
margin *n* borde, lado, *m*, orilla, *f*; (of a page) margen, *mf*; reserva, *f*; sobrante, *m*. **in the m.,** al margen
marginal *a* marginal. **m. note,** acotación, nota marginal, *f*
marigold *n* caléndula, maravilla, *f*
marine *a* marino, de mar; marítimo; naval. *n* (fleet) marina, *f*; (soldier) soldado de marina, *m*. **Tell that to the marines!** ¡Cuéntaselo a tu tía! **mercantile m.,** marina mercante, *f*. **m. forces,** infantería de marina, *f*. **m. insurance,** seguro marítimo, *m*
mariner *n* marinero, marino, *m*. **mariner's compass,** aguja de marear, brújula, *f*
marionette *n* marioneta, *f*, títere, *m*
marital *a* marital
maritime *a* marítimo
mark *n* marca, *f*; señal, *f*; mancha, *f*; impresión, *f*; (target) blanco, *m*; (standard) norma, *f*; (level) nivel, *m*; (distinction) importancia, distinción, *f*; (in examinations) nota, *f*; calificación, *f*; (signature) cruz, *f*; (coin) marco, *m*. *vt* marcar; señalar; (price) poner precio (a); (notice) observar, darse cuenta (de); (characterize) caracterizar. **trade-m.,** marca de fábrica, *f*. **to be be-**

side the m.,** no dar en el blanco; errar el tiro; *fig* no tener nada que ver con; equivocarse. **to hit the m.,** dar en el blanco; *fig* dar en el clavo. **to make one's m.,** firmar con una cruz; distinguirse. **to m. time,** marcar el paso; *fig* hacer tiempo. **to m. down,** (a person) señalar; escoger; (in price) rebajar. **to m. out,** marcar; trazar; definir; (erase) borrar; (a person) escoger; destinar **m. somebody absent,** ponerle a fulano su ausencia. **m. somebody present,** ponerle a fulano su asistencia.
Mark *n* Marcos. **the Gospel according to St. M.,** el Evangelio de San Marcos
marked *a* marcado; señalado; notable; acentuado; particular, especial. **He speaks with a m. Galician accent,** Habla con marcado acento gallego
markedly *adv* marcadamente; notablemente; especialmente, particularmente
marker *n* (billiards) marcador, *m*; (football, etc.) tanteador, *m*
market *n* mercado, *m*; tráfico, *m*; venta, *f*; (price) precio, *m*; (shop) bazar, emporio, *m*. *vt* and *vi* comprar en un mercado; vender en un mercado. **black m.,** mercado negro, estraperlo, *m*. **open m.,** mercado al aire libre, *m*; *fig* mercado libre, *m*. **m. day,** día de mercado, *m*. **m. garden,** huerto, *m*, huerta, *f*. **m. gardener,** hortelano, *m*. **m.-place,** plaza de mercado, *f*; *fig* mercado, *m*. **m. price,** precio corriente, *m*. **m. stall,** tabanco, puesto de mercado, *m*. **m.-woman,** verdulera, *f*
marketable *a* comerciable, vendible; corriente
marketing *n* venta, *f*; compra en un mercado, *f*; mercado, *m*. **to go m.,** ir al mercado
marking *n* marca, *f*; (spot on animals, etc.) pinta, *f*. **m.-ink,** tinta de marcar, *f*. **m.-iron,** ferrete, hierro de marcar, *m*
marksman *n* tirador (-ra)
marksmanship *n* puntería, *f*
marl *n* marga, *f*
marlinespike *n* pasador, *m*
marmalade *n* mermelada de naranjas amargas, *f*
marmoset *n* tití, *m*
marmot *n zool* marmota, *f*
maroon *n* (color) marrón, *m*; (slave) cimarrón (-ona); (firework) petardo, *m*. *a* de marrón. *vt* abandonar, dejar
marquee *n* marquesina, *f*
marqueterie *n* marquetería, *f*
marquis *n* marqués, *m*
marriage *n* matrimonio, *m*; unión, *f*; (wedding) boda, *f*, casamiento, *m*. **by m.,** (of relationship) político. **She is an aunt by m.,** tía política. **m. articles,** capitulaciones (matrimoniales), *f pl*. **m. contract,** contrato matrimonial, *m*. **m. license,** licencia de casamiento, *f*. **m. portion,** dote, *mf*. **m. rate,** nupcialidad, *f*. **m. register,** acta matrimonial, *f*. **m. song,** epitalamio, *m*
marriageable *a* casadero
married *past part* and *a* casado; matrimonial, conyugal. **newly-m. couple,** los recién casados. **to get m. to,** casarse con. **m. couple,** matrimonio, *m*, cónyuges, *m pl*. **m. life,** vida conyugal, *f*
married name *n* nombre de casada, *f*
marrow *n* tuétano, *m*, médula, *f*; *fig* meollo, *m*. **to the m. of one's bones,** hasta los tuétanos.
marrowbone *n* hueso medular, *m*. **on one's marrowbones,** de rodillas
marry *vt* casarse con, contraer matrimonio con; casar; (of a priest) unir en matrimonio; *fig* juntar, unir. *vi* casarse. **to m. again,** volver a casarse
Marseillaise *n* marsellesa, *f*
Marseilles Marsella, *f*
marsh *n* marjal, pantano, *m*. **m.-mallow,** *bot* malvavisco, *m*. **m. marigold,** calta, *f*
marshal *n* mariscal, *m*, *vt* poner en orden, arreglar; dirigir. **field-m.,** capitán general de ejército, *m*
marshaling *n* ordenación, *f*; dirección, *f*. **m.-yard,** (railway) apartadero ferroviario, *m*

marshy *a* pantanoso

mart *n poet* plaza de mercado, *f;* mercado, *m;* emporio, *m;* (auction rooms) martillo, *m*

marten *n* marta, *f*

martial *a* militar; marcial, belicoso. **m. array,** orden de batalla, *m.* **m. law,** derecho militar, *m;* estado de guerra, *m.* **m. spirit,** marcialidad, *f,* espíritu belicoso, *m*

martially *adv* militarmente; marcialmente

Martian *a* marciano

martinet *n mil* ordenancista, *m;* rigorista, *mf*

Martinique Martinica, *f*

Martinmas *n* día de San Martín, *m*

martyr *n* mártir, *mf vt* martirizar

martyrdom *n* martirio, *m*

martyrize *vt* martirizar

marvel *n* maravilla, *f.* **to m. at,** maravillarse de, admirarse de

marvelous *a* maravilloso

marvelousness *n* maravilla, *f,* carácter maravilloso, *m,* lo maravilloso

Marxism *n* marxismo, *m*

Marxist *a* and *n* marxista, *mf*

marzipan *n* mazapán, *m*

mascot *n* mascota, *f*

masculine *a* masculino; varonil, macho; de hombre; (of a woman) hombruno. *n* masculino, *m*

masculinity *n* masculinidad, *f*

mash *n* mezcla, *f;* amasijo, *m;* pasta, *f,* puré, *m. vt* mezclar; amasar. **mashed potatoes,** puré de patatas (de papas), *m*

mask *n* máscara, *f;* antifaz, *m;* (death) mascarilla, *f;* (person) máscara, *mf. vt* enmascarar; *fig* encubrir, disimular. *vi* ponerse una máscara; disfrazarse.

masked ball, *n* baile de máscaras, *m*

masker *n* máscara, *mf*

masochism *n* masoquismo, *m*

mason *n* albañil, *m;* (freemason) francmasón, masón, *m*

masonic *a* masónico. **m. lodge,** logia de francmasones, *f*

masonry *n* (trade) albañilería, *f;* mampostería, *f*

masque *n* mascarada, *f*

masquerade *n* mascarada, *f*

masquerader *n* máscara, *mf*

mass *n* misa, *f.* **to hear m.,** oír misa. **to say m.,** celebrar misa. **high m.,** misa mayor, *f.* **low m.,** misa rezada, *f.* **m. book,** libro de misa, *m*

mass *n* masa, *f;* (shape) bulto, *m;* (heap) montón, *m;* (great number) muchedumbre, *f;* (cloud of steam, etc.) nube, *f. vt* amasar; *mil* concentrar. *vi* congregarse en masa. **in a m.,** en masa; en conjunto. **the m. (of) . . . ,** la mayoría (de) . . . **the masses,** las masas, el vulgo, el pueblo. **m. formation,** columna cerrada, *f.* **m.-meeting,** mitin, mitin popular, *m.* **m.-production,** fabricación en serie, *f*

massacre *n* matanza, carnicería, *f, vt* hacer una carnicería (de)

massage *n* masaje, *m;* (friction) fricción, *f. vt* dar un masaje (a)

masseur, masseuse *n* masajista, *mf*

massive *a* macizo; sólido

massively *adv* macizamente; sólidamente

massiveness *n* macicez, *f;* solidez, *f*

mast *n naut* palo, árbol, *m;* (for wireless) mástil, *m;* poste, *m;* (beech) hayuco, *m;* (oak) bellota, *f. vt naut* arbolar. **at half-m.,** a media asta. **m.-head,** calcés, tope, *m*

masted *a* arbolado; (in compounds) de . . . palos

master *n* (of the house, etc.) señor, amo, *m;* maestro, *m; naut* patrón, *m;* (owner) dueño, *m;* (teacher) profesor, maestro, *m;* (young master and as address) señorito, *m;* director, *m;* jefe, *m;* (expert) perito, *m;* (of a military order) maestre, *m, a* maestro; superior. *vt* dominar; ser maestro en; dominar, conocer a fondo. **This picture is by an old m.,** Este cuadro es de un gran maestro antiguo. **to be m. of oneself,** ser dueño de sí. **to be**

one's own m., ser dueño de sí mismo; trabajar por su propia cuenta; ser independiente; estar libre. **m. builder,** maestro de obras, *m.* **m. hand,** mano maestra, *f.* **M. of Arts,** maestro (-tra) en artes. **M. of Ceremonies,** maestro de ceremonias, *m.* **M. of Foxhounds,** cazador mayor, *m.* **M. of the Horse,** caballerizo mayor del rey, *m.* **M. of the Rolls,** archivero mayor, *m.* **m.-key,** llave maestra, *f.* **m. mind,** águila, *f,* ingenio, *m.* **m. stroke,** golpe maestro, *m*

masterful *a* imperioso, dominante; autoritario, arbitrario

masterfulness *n* imperiosidad, *f;* arbitrariedad, *f*

masterless *a* sin amo

masterliness *n* maestría, *f;* excelencia, *f;* perfección, *f*

masterly *a* maestro; excelente; perfecto. **m. performance,** obra maestra, *f; theat* representación perfecta, *f;* ejecución excelente, *f*

masterpiece *n* obra maestra, *f*

master plan *n* plan regulador, *m*

masterstroke *n* golpe magistral, golpe de maestro, *m*

mastery *n* dominio, *m;* autoridad, *f;* poder, *m;* ventaja, *f;* superioridad, maestría, *f;* conocimiento profundo, *m.* **to gain the m. of,** hacerse el señor de; llegar a dominar

mastic *n* masilla, almáciga, *f*

masticate *vt* masticar, mascar

mastication *n* masticación, *f*

mastiff *n* mastín, alano, *m*

mastodon *n* mastodonte, *m*

mastoid *a* mastoides *n* apófisis mastoides, *f*

masturbate *vi* masturbarse

masturbation *n* masturbación, *f*

mat *n* esterilla, *f;* alfombrilla, *f;* (on the table) tapete individual, *m. vt* (tangle) enmarañar, desgreñar. *vi* enmarañarse

match *n sport* partido, *m;* (wrestling, boxing) lucha, *f;* (fencing) asalto, *m;* (race) carrera, *f;* (contest) concurso, *m;* (equal) igual, *mf;* (pair) pareja, *f;* compañero (-ra); (marriage) boda, *f,* casamiento, *m;* (for lighting) cerilla, *f,* fósforo, *m;* (for guns) mecha, *f. vt* competir con; (equal) igualar; ser igual (a); hacer juego con; emparejar; aparear; armonizar. *vi* ser igual; hacer juego; armonizarse. **good m.,** *inf* buen partido, *m.* **as thin as a m.,** más delgado que una cerilla. **to meet one's m.,** dar con la horma de su zapato. **to play a m.,** jugar un partido. **m.-box,** cajita de cerillas, fosforera, *f.* **m.-seller,** fosforero (-ra)

matchless *a* incomparable, sin igual, sin par

matchwood *n* madera para cerillas, *f*

mate *n* compañero, camarada, *m;* (spouse) compañero (-ra); pareja, *f;* (on merchant ships) piloto, *m;* (assistant) ayudante, *m;* (at chess) mate, *m. vt* (marry) casar; desposar; (animals, birds) aparear, acoplar; (chess) dar jaque mate (a). *vi* casarse; aparearse, acoplarse

maté *n* maté, té del Paraguay, *m*

materfamilias *n* madre de familia, *f*

material *a* material; importante, esencial; considerable; sensible, notable; grave. *n* material, *m;* materia, *f;* (fabric) tela, *f;* tejido, *m.* **raw materials,** materias primas, *f pl.* **writing materials,** utensilios de escritorio, *m pl;* papel de escribir, *m*

materialism *n* materialismo, *m*

materialist *n* materialista, *mf*

materialistic *a* materialista

materiality *n* materialidad, *f;* importancia, *f*

materialization *n* materialización, *f*

materialize *vt* materializar

maternal *a* materno, maternal. **m. grandparents,** abuelos maternos, *m pl*

maternity *n* maternidad, *f.* **m. center,** centro de maternidad, *m.* **m. hospital,** casa de maternidad, *f*

mathematical *a* matemático

mathematician *n* matemático, *m*

mathematics *n* matemáticas, *f pl.* **applied m.,** matemáticas prácticas, *f pl.* **higher m.,** matemáticas superiores, *f pl.* **pure m.,** matemáticas teóricas, *f pl*

matinee n función de tarde, f
mating n (of animals) apareamiento, acoplamiento, m; unión, f; casamiento, m
matins n pl ecc maitines, m pl
matriarch n matriarca, f
matriarchal a matriarcal
matriarchy n matriarcado, m
matricide n (crime) matricidio, m; (person) matricida, mf
matriculate vt matricular. vi matricularse
matriculation n matriculación, f
matrimonial a matrimonial, de matrimonio; marital. m. agency, agencia de matrimonios, f
matrimony n matrimonio, m
matrix n matriz, f
matron n matrona, mujer casada, madre de familia, f; (of a hospital) matrona, f; (of a school) ama de llaves, f; directora, f. m. of honor, (at a wedding) madrina, f
matronly a de matrona, matronal; respetable; serio
matt a mate
matted a enmarañado, enredado
matter n materia, f; substancia, f; caso, m; cuestión, f; asunto, m; causa, f; (distance) distancia, f; (amount) cantidad, f; (duration) espacio de tiempo, m; (importance) importancia, f; med pus, m; pl **matters,** asuntos, m pl, etc.; situación, f. **as if nothing were the m.,** como si no hubiese pasado nada. **for that m.,** en cuanto a eso. **grey m.,** substancia gris, f. **in the m. of,** en el caso de. **It is a m. of taste,** Es cuestión de gusto. **printed m.,** impresos, m pl. **What is the m.?** ¿Qué pasa? ¿Qué hay? **What is the m. with him?** ¿Qué tiene? ¿Le pasa? **m.-of-course,** cosa natural, f. **m.-of-fact,** práctico; sin imaginación; positivista. **m. of fact,** n hecho positivo, m, realidad, f. **As a m. of fact . . . ,** En realidad . . . , El caso es que . . . **m. of form,** cuestión de fórmula, f; pura formalidad, f
matter vi importar; (discharge) supurar. **What does it m.?** ¿Qué importa? **It doesn't m.,** Es igual, No importa, Da lo mismo
Matterhorn, the el Matterhorn, m
matting n estera, f
mattress n colchón, m. **spring-m.,** colchón de muelles, m. **m.-maker,** colchonero, m
mature a maduro; com vencido. vt madurar. vi madurarse; com vencer
maturity n madurez, f; edad madura, f; (com of a bill) vencimiento, m
matutinal a matutino
maudlin a sensiblero; lacrimoso; (tipsy) calamocano
maul vt maltratar; herir
maundy n lavatorio, m. **M. Thursday,** Jueves Santo, m
Mauritius Mauricio, m, Isla de Francia, f
mausoleum n mausoleo, m
mauve n color purpúreo delicado, color de malva, m, a de color de malva
maw n (of a ruminant) cuajar, m; (of a bird) buche, m; fig abismo, m
mawkish a insípido, insulso; sensiblero; asqueroso
mawkishness n insipidez, insulsez, f; sensiblería, f; asquerosidad, f
maxilla n hueso maxilar, maxilar, m
maxillary a maxilar
maxim n máxima, f
maximum a máximo. n máximo, m
may v aux poder; ser posible; (expressing wish, hope) ojalá que . . . , Dios quiera que . . . , or the present subjunctive may be used, e.g. **May you live many years!** ¡(qué) Viva Vd. muchos años! (to denote uncertainty, the future tense of the verb is often used, e.g. **You may perhaps remember the date,** Vd. quizás se acordará de la fecha. **Who may he be?** ¿Quién será?) **May God grant it!** ¡(que) Dios lo quiera! **It may be that . . . ,** Puede ser que . . . , Es posible que . . . , Quizás . . . **He may come on Saturday,** Es posible que venga el sábado; Puede venir el sábado. **May I come in?** ¿Puedo entrar? ¿Se puede entrar? **May I**

come and see you? ¿Me das permiso para hacerte una visita? ¿Me dejas venir a verte? **May I go then?** ¿Puedo irme pues? ¿Tengo permiso para marcharme entonces?
May n mayo, m; fig abril, m; bot espina blanca, f. **May Day,** primero de mayo, m. **mayflower,** flor del cuclillo, f. **mayfly,** cachipolla, f. **May queen,** maya, f
maybe adv quizás, tal vez
mayonnaise n mayonesa, f. **m. sauce,** salsa mayonesa, f
mayor n alcalde, m
mayoral a de alcalde
mayoress n alcaldesa, f
maypole n mayo, m. **m. dance,** danza de cintas, f
maze n laberinto, m; fig perplejidad, f. vt dejar perplejo, aturdir
mazurka n mazurca, f
me pron me; (after a preposition only) mí. **They sent it for me,** Lo mandaron para mí. **Dear me!** ¡Ay de mí!
meadow n prado, m, pradera, f. **m.-sweet,** reina de los prados, f
meager a magro, enjuto, flaco; (scanty) exiguo, escaso, insuficiente; pobre; fig árido
meagerly adv pobremente
meagerness n exigüidad, escasez, f; pobreza, f; fig aridez, f
meal n comida, f; (flour) harina, f. **to have a good m.,** comer bien. **test m.,** med comida de prueba, f. **m.-time,** hora de comida, f
mealy a harinoso; (of the complexion) pastoso
mean a (middle) medianero; (average) mediano; (humble) humilde; pobre; inferior; bajo, vil, ruin; (avaricious) tacaño, mezquino. **m.-spirited,** vil, de alma ruin
mean n medio, m; medianía, f; pl **means,** medio, m; expediente, m; medios, m pl; (financial) recursos, m pl; modo, m, manera, f. **by all means,** por todos los medios; (certainly) ¡ya lo creo! ¡no faltaba más! ¡naturalmente! **by means of,** mediante, por medio de; con la ayuda de. **by no means,** de ningún modo; nada. **by some means,** de algún modo, de alguna manera
mean vt destinar (para); pretender, proponerse; intentar, pensar, querer decir, significar; importar; (wish) querer; (concern, speak about) tratarse (de). vi tener el propósito, tener la intención. **I did not m. to do it,** Lo hice sin querer. **What does this word m.?** ¿Qué significa esta palabra? **What do you m. by that?** ¿Qué quieres decir con eso? **This portrait is meant to be Joan,** Este retrato quiere ser Juana. **What do they m. to do?** ¿Qué piensan (or se proponen) hacer? **Do you really m. it?** ¿Lo dices en serio? **Charles always means well,** Carlos siempre tiene buenas intenciones
meander n meandro, serpenteo, m; camino tortuoso, m, vi serpentear; errar, vagar; (in talk) divagar
meandering n meandros, m pl, serpenteo, m; (in talk) divagaciones, f pl, a serpentino, tortuoso
meaning n intención, voluntad, f; significación, f, significado, m; (of words) acepción, f; (sense) sentido, m; (thought) pensamiento, m, a significante. **double m.,** doble intención, f. **He gave me a m. look,** Me miró con intención. **What is the m. of it?** ¿Qué significa? ¿Qué quiere decir?
meaningful a significante
meaningless a sin sentido; insensato; insignificante
meaningly adv significativamente; con intención
meanness n pobreza, f; inferioridad, f; mediocridad, f; bajeza, ruindad, f; (stinginess) mezquindad, tacañería, f
meantime, meanwhile n ínterin, m, adv entre tanto, mientras tanto, a todo esto. **in the m.,** mientras tanto, en el ínterin
measles n sarampión, m. **German m.,** rubéola, f
measurable a mensurable
measure n medida, f; capacidad, f; (for measuring) regla, f; número, m; proporción, f; (limit) límite, m; (fig step) medida, f; (metre) metro, m; mus compás, m; (de-

gree) grado, *m*; manera, *f*; (parliamentary) proyecto (de ley), *m*. *vt* medir; proporcionar, distribuir; (water) aforar; (land) apear; (height of persons) tallar; (for clothes) tomar las medidas (a); (judge) juzgar; (test) probar; (*poet* traverse) recorrer. **a suit made to m.**, un traje hecho a medida. **in great m.**, en gran manera, en alto grado. **in some m.**, hasta cierto punto. **to m. one's length**, caer tendido. **to take a person's m.**, *fig* tomar las medidas (a). **to m. up to,** *fig* estar al nivel de, ser igual a
measured *a* mesurado, moderado; uniforme; limitado. **to walk with m. tread,** andar a pasos contados
measurement *n* medición, *f*; medida, *f*; dimensión, *f*
meat *n* carne, *f*; (food) alimento, *m*; (meal) comida, *f*; *fig* substancia, *f*. **to sit at m.**, estar a la mesa. **cold meats,** fiambres, *m pl*. **m.-ball,** albóndiga, *f*. **m.-chopper,** picador, *m*. **m.-dish,** fuente, *f*. **m.-eater,** comedor (-ra) de carne. **m. extract,** carne concentrada, *f*. **m.-market,** carnicería, *f*. **m.-pie,** pastel de carne, *m*. **m.-safe,** fresquera, *f*
meaty *a* carnoso; *fig* substancial
Mecca la Meca, *f*
mechanic *n* mecánico, *m*
mechanical *a* mecánico; maquinal
mechanically *adv* mecánicamente; maquinalmente
mechanical pencil *n* lapicero, *m*
mechanics *n* mecánica, *f*
mechanism *n* mecanismo, *m*; (philosophy) mecanicismo, *m*
mechanize *vt* convertir en máquina; (gen. *mil*) mecanizar; motorizar
medal *n* medalla, *f*
medallion *n* medallón, *m*
medallist *n* grabador de medallas, *m*; el, *m*, (*f*, la) que recibe una medalla
meddle *vi* tocar; meterse (con o en); entremeterse, inmiscuirse; intrigar
meddler *n* entremetido (-da); intrigante, *mf*
meddlesome *a* entremetido; oficioso; impertinente; enredador, intrigante. **to be very m.,** meterse en todo
meddlesomeness *n* entremetimiento, *m*; oficiosidad, *f*; impertinencia, *f*; intrigas, *f pl*
media, the los medios informativos, *m pl*
median *a* del medio
mediate *vi* intervenir, mediar, arbitrar; abogar (por). *a* medio; interpuesto
mediation *n* mediación, intervención, *f*; intercesión, *f*; interposición, *f*
mediator *n* mediador (-ra); arbitrador, *m*; intercesor (-ra)
mediatory *a* de mediador; intercesor
medical *a* médico; de medicina; de médico. *n inf* estudiante de medicina, *m*. **Army M. Service,** Servicio de Sanidad Militar, *m*. **m. books,** libros de medicina, *m pl*. **m. examination,** examen médico, *m*, exploración médica, *f*. **m. jurisprudence,** medicina legal, *f*. **m. knowledge,** conocimientos médicos, *m pl*. **m. practitioner,** médico (-ca). **m. school,** escuela de medicina, *f*
medicament *n* medicamento, *m*
medicate *vt* medicar; medicinar
medicated *a* medicado
medication *n* medicación, *f*
medicinal *a* medicinal
medicine *n* medicina, *f*; medicamento, *m*; (charm) ensalmo, hechizo, *m*. **patent m.,** específico farmacéutico, *m*. **m. ball,** balón medical, *m*. **m. chest,** botiquín, *m*. **m. man,** hechizador, *m*
medico- *prefix* médico-. **m.-legal,** médicolegal
medieval *a* medieval
medievalism *n* afición a la edad media, *f*; espíritu medieval, *m*
mediocre *a* mediocre
mediocrity *n* mediocridad, *f*; medianía, *f*
meditate *vt* idear, proyectar, meditar. *vi* meditar, reflexionar; pensar, intentar

meditation *n* meditación, *f*
meditative *a* meditabundo, contemplativo; de meditación
meditatively *adv* reflexivamente
Mediterranean *a* mediterráneo. *n* Mar Mediterráneo, *m*
medium *n* medio, *m*; (cooking) término medio, a medio cocer, a medio asar, *m*; (environment) medio ambiente, *m*; (agency) intermediario, *m*; (spiritualism) médium, *m*; *art* medio, *m*, *a* mediano; regular; mediocre. **through the m. of,** por medio de. **m.-sized,** de tamaño regular
medlar *n* (fruit) níspola, *f*; (tree) níspero, *m*
medley *n* mezcla, *f*; miscelánea, *f*, *a* mezclado, mixto
medulla *n* medula, *f*
meek *a* dulce, manso; humilde; modesto; pacífico
meekly *adv* mansamente; humildemente; modestamente
meekness *n* mansedumbre, *f*; humildad, *f*; modestia, *f*
meet *vt* encontrar; encontrarse con; tropezar con; (by arrangement) reunirse con; (make the acquaintance of) conocer (a); (satisfy) satisfacer; cumplir (con); (a bill) pagar, saldar; (refute) refutar; (fight) batirse (con); (confront) hacer frente (a). *vi* juntarse; encontrarse; reunirse; verse; (of rivers) confluir. *n* montería, *f*, *a* conveniente. **I shall m. you at the station,** Te esperaré en la estación. **Until we m. again!** ¡Hasta la vista! **to go to m.,** ir al encuentro de. **to m. half-way,** encontrar a la mitad del camino; partir la diferencia con; hacer concesiones (a). **to m. the eye,** saltar a la vista. **to m. with,** encontrar; experimentar; sufrir
meeting *n* encuentro, *m*; reunión, *f*; (interview) entrevista, *f*; (of rivers, etc.) confluencia, *f*; (public, etc.) mitin, *m*; (council) concilio, *m*; concurso, *m*; (race) concurso de carreras de caballos, *m*. **creditors' m.,** concurso de acreedores, *m*. **m.-house,** templo de los Cuáqueros, *m*. **m.-place,** lugar de reunión, *m*; lugar de cita, *m*; centro, *m*. **to adjourn the m.,** levantar la sesión. **to call a m.,** convocar una sesión. **to open the m.,** abrir la sesión
megalomania *n* megalomanía, monomanía de grandezas, *f*
megalomaniac *n* megalómano (-na)
megaphone *n* megáfono, portavoz, *m*
Meknès Mequínez, *f*
melancholia *n* melancolía, *f*
melancholy *a* melancólico. *n* melancolía, *f*
mellifluence *n* melifluidad, *f*
mellifluous *a* melifluo; dulce
mellow *a* maduro; dulce; (of wine) rancio; blando; suave; (of sound) melodioso; (slang) alegre; (tipsy) entre dos luces. *vt* madurar; ablandar; suavizar. *vi* madurarse
mellowing *n* maduración, *f*
mellowness *n* madurez, *f*; dulzura, *f*; (of wine) ranciedad, *f*; blandura, *f*; suavidad, *f*; melodía, *f*
melodic *a* melódico
melodious *a* melodioso
melodiously *adv* melodiosamente
melodiousness *n* melodía, *f*
melodrama *n* melodrama, *m*
melodramatic *a* melodramático
melody *n* melodía, *f*
melon *n* melón, *m*; sandía, *f*. **slice of m.,** raja de melón, *f*. **m. bed,** sandiar, *m*. **m.-shaped,** amelonado
melt *vi* derretirse; deshacerse; disolverse; evaporarse; desaparecer; (of money, etc.) hacerse sal y agua; (relent) enternecerse, ablandarse. *vt* fundir; (snow, etc.) derretir; (*fig* soften) ablandar. **He melted away,** *inf* Se escurrió. **to m. into tears,** deshacerse en lágrimas. **to m. down,** fundir
melting *a* fundente; (forgiving) indulgente; (tender) de ternura; lánguido; dulce. *n* fusión, *f*; derretimiento, *m*. **m. point,** punto de fusión. **m. m. pot,** *met* crisol, *m*; *fig* caldera de razas, *f*, *m*

member *n* miembro, *m*; (of a club, etc.) socio (-ia). **M. of Parliament,** diputado a Cortes, *m*

membership *n* calidad de miembro, socio(-ia); número de miembros (*or* socios), *m*, composición, integración, *f*

membrane *n* membrana, *f*

membranous *a* membranoso

memento *n* recuerdo, *m*

memoir *n* memoria, *f*

memorable *a* memorable

memorably *adv* memorablemente

memorandum *n* memorándum, *m*

memorial *a* conmemorativo. *n* monumento conmemorativo, *m*; memorial, *m*

memorize *vt* aprender de memoria

memory *n* memoria, *f*; recuerdo, *m*. **from m.,** de memoria. **If my m. does not deceive me,** Si mal no me acuerdo. **in m. of,** en conmemoración de; en recuerdo de

memory span *n* retentiva memorística, *f*

menace *n* amenaza, *f*, *vt* amenazar

menacing *a* amenazador

menacingly *adv* con amenazas

menagerie *n* colección de fieras, *f*; casa de fieras, *f*

mend *vt* remendar; componer; reparar; (darn) zurcir; (rectify) remediar; reformar; enmendar; (a fire) echar carbón (or leña, etc.) a; (one's pace) avivar. *vi* (in health and of the weather) mejorar. *n* remiendo, *m*; (darn) zurcido, *m*. **to be on the m.,** ir mejorando. **to m. one's ways,** reformarse, enmendarse

mendacious *a* mendaz

mendacity *n* mendacidad, *f*

Mendelism *n* mendelismo, *m*

mender *n* componedor (-ra); (darner) zurcidor (-ra); reparador (-ra); (cobbler and tailor) remendón, *m*

mendicancy *n* mendicidad, *f*

mendicant *a* mendicante. *n* mendicante, *mf*. **m. friar,** fraile mendicante, *m*

mending *n* compostura, *f*; reparación, *f*; (darning) zurcidura, *f*; ropa por zurcir, *f*

menial *a* doméstico; servil; bajo, ruin. *n* criado (-da); lacayo, *m*

meningeal *a* meningeo

meningitis *n* meningitis, *f*

menopause *n* menopausia, *f*

menses *n* menstruación, *f*

menstrual *a* menstrual

menstruate *vi* menstruar

menstruation *n* menstruación, *f*,

mental *a* mental; intelectual. **m. derangement,** enajenación mental, *f*. **m. hospital,** manicomio, *m*

mentality *n* mentalidad, *f*

mentally *adv* mentalmente. **m. deficient,** anormal

menthol *n* mentol, *m*

mention *n* mención, *f*; alusión, *f*. *vt* hacer mención (de), mencionar, mentar, hablar (de); aludir (a); (quote) citar; (in dispatches) nombrar. **Don't m. it!** (keep silent) ¡No digas nada!; (you're welcome) ¡No hay de qué!

mentor *n* mentor, *m*

menu *n* menú, *m*; lista de platos, *f*

meow *vi* maullar. *n* maullido, *m*

Mephistophelean *a* mefistofélico

mephitic *a* mefítico

mercantile *a* mercantil; mercante. **m. law,** derecho mercantil, *m*. **m. marine,** marina mercante, *f*

mercantilism *n* mercantilismo, *m*

mercenariness *n* lo mercenario

mercenary *a* mercenario. *n* (soldier) mercenario, *m*

mercer *n* mercero, *m*

mercerize *vt* mercerizar

mercery *n* mercería, *f*

merchandise *n* mercancía, *f*

merchant *n* traficante (en), *mf*, negociante (en), *m*; comerciante, *mf* mercader, *m*. *a* mercante. **The M. of Venice,** El Mercader de Venecia. **m. navy, service,** marina mercante, *f*. **m. ship,** buque mercante, *m*

merchantman *n* buque mercante, *m*

merciful *a* misericordioso, piadoso; compasivo; clemente; indulgente

mercifully *adv* misericordiosamente; compasivamente; con indulgencia

mercifulness *n* misericordia, *f*; compasión, *f*; indulgencia, *f*

merciless *a* despiadado, inhumano

mercilessly *adv* sin piedad

mercilessness *n* inhumanidad, *f*; falta de compasión, *f*

mercurial *a* mercurial; (changeable) volátil; (lively) vivo

mercury *n* mercurio, *m*; (ast and myth) Mercurio, *m*. **Mercury's wand,** caduceo, *m*

mercy *n* misericordia, *f*; compasión, *f*; clemencia, *f*; indulgencia, *f*; merced, *f*. **at the m. of the elements,** a la intemperie. **to be at the m. of,** estar a la merced de

mere *a* mero; simple; no más que, solo. *n* lago, *m*

merely *adv* meramente, solamente; simplemente, sencillamente

meretricious *a* (archaic) meretricio; (flashy) de oropel; llamativo, charro

meretriciousness *n* mal gusto, *m*

merge *vt* fundir; *com* fusionar; mezclar. *vi* fundirse; *com* fusionarse; mezclarse

merger *n* combinación, *f*; *com* fusión, *f*

meridian *n* (geog ast) meridiano, *m*; (noon) mediodía, *m*; (peak) apogeo, *m*

meringue *n* merengue, *m*

merino *a* de merino; merino. *n* (fabric and sheep) merino, *m*

merit *n* mérito, *m*, *vt* merecer, ser digno de

meritorious *a* meritorio

meritoriously *adv* merecidamente

meritoriousness *n* mérito, *m*

merlon *n* merlón, *m*, almena, *f*

mermaid *n* sirena, *f*

merrily *adv* alegremente

merriment *n* alegría, *f*; júbilo, *m*; regocijo, *m*; diversión, *f*; juego, *m*

merriness *n* alegría, *f*; regocijo, *m*; *inf* ebriedad, *f*

merry *a* alegre; jovial; feliz; regocijado, divertido; (tipsy) calamocano. **to make m.,** divertirse. **to make m. over,** reírse de. **M. Christmas!** ¡Felices Navidades! **m.-andrew,** bufón, *m*. **m.-go-round,** caballitos, *m pl*, tiovivo, *m*. **m.-making,** festividades, fiestas, *f pl*

meseta *n* meseta, *f*

mesh *n* malla, *f*; *mech* engranaje, *m*; (network) red, *f*; (snare) lazo, *m*. *vt* coger con red; *mech* endentar

mesmerism *n* mesmerismo, *m*

mesmerize *vt* hipnotizar

mess *n* (of food) plato de comida, *m*; porción, ración, *f*; rancho, *m*; (mixture) mezcla, *f*; (disorder) desorden, *m*; suciedad, *f*; (failure) fracaso, *m*. *vt* (dirty) ensuciar; desordenar; (mismanage) echar a perder. **to be in a m.,** *inf* estar aviado. **to get in a m.,** *inf* hacerse un lío. **to make a m. of,** ensuciar; desordenar; (spoil) echarlo todo a rodar

message *n* mensaje, *m*; recado, *m*; (telegraphic) parte, *m*. **I have to take a m.,** Tengo que hacer un recado

messenger *n* mensajero (-ra); (of telegrams) repartidor, *m*; heraldo, *m*; anuncio, *m*

Messiah *n* Mesías, *m*

Messianic *a* mesiánico

messrs. *n pl* (abbreviation) sres. (from señores), *m pl*

metabolism *n* metabolismo, *m*

metabolize *va* metabolizar

metal *n* metal, *m*; vidrio en fusión, *m*; (road) grava, *f*; her metal, *m*; (mettle) temple, temperamento, *m*; brío, fuego, *m*; *pl* metals, (of a railway) rieles, *m pl*. **m. engraver,** grabador en metal, *m*. **m. polish,** limpiametales, *m*. **m. shavings,** cizallas, *f pl*. **m. work,** metalistería, *f*. **m. worker,** metalario, *m*

metallic *a* metálico

metalliferous *a* metalífero

metalloid *n* metaloide, *m*

metallurgic *a* metalúrgico

metallurgist *n* metalúrgico, *m*

metallurgy *n* metalurgia, *f*

metamorphosis *n* metamorfosis, *f*

metaphor *n* metáfora, *f*

metaphorical *a* metafórico

metaphysical *a* metafísico

metaphysician *n* metafísico, *m*

metaphysics *n* metafísica, *f*

metathesis *n* metátesis, *f*

mete (out) *vt* repartir, distribuir

metempsychosis *n* metempsicosis, *f*

meteor *n* meteoro, *m*

meteoric *a* meteórico

meteorite *n* meteorito, *m*

meteorological *a* meteorológico

meteorologist *n* meteorologista, *mf*

meteorology *n* meteorología, *f*

meter *n* (for gas, etc.) contador, *m*; (verse and measure) metro, *m*

methane *n* metano, *m*

method *n* método, *m*; técnica, *f*; táctica, *f*

methodical *a* metódico; ordenado, sistemático

Methodism *n* metodismo, *m*

Methodist *n* metodista, *mf*

methyl *n* metilo, *m*. **m. alcohol,** alcohol metílico, *m*

methylated spirit *n* alcohol desnaturalizado, *m*

meticulous *a* meticuloso; minucioso

meticulously *adv* con meticulosidad

meticulousness *n* meticulosidad, *f*; minuciosidad, *f*

metric *a* métrico. **m. system,** sistema métrico, *m*

metrics *n* métrica, *f*

metronome *n* metrónomo, *m*

metropolis *n* metrópoli, *f*; capital, *f*

metropolitan *a* metropolitano; de la capital. *n ecc* metropolitano, *m*

mettle *n* temple, temperamento, *m*; fuego, brío, *m*; valor, *m*. **You have put him on his m.,** Le ha picado en el amor propio

mew *n* (gull) gaviota, *f*; (of a cat) maullido, *m*; (of seabirds) alarido, *m*. *vi* (of a cat) maullar; (of sea-birds) dar alaridos. **to mew up,** encerrar

mews *n* establos, *m pl*, caballeriza, *f*

Mexican *a* mejicano. *n* mejicano (-na)

Mexico Méjico, *m*

mezzanine *n* entresuelo, *m*

mezzosoprano *a* mezzo-soprano

mi *n mus* mi, *m*

miaow *n* miau, *m*, *vi* maullar

miasma *n* miasma, *m*

miasmatic *a* miasmático

mica *n* mica, *f*

microbe *n* microbio, *m*

microbial *a* microbiano

microbiologist *n* microbiólogo, *m*

microbiology *n* microbiología, *f*

microcosm *n* microcosmo, *m*

microphone *n* micrófono, *m*

microscope *n* microscopio, *m*

microscopic *a* microscópico

microwave *n* microonda, *f*

mid *a* medio. *prep* entre; en medio de; a mediados de. **from mid May to August,** desde mediados de mayo hasta agosto. **a mid-fourteenth century castle,** un castillo de mediados del siglo catorce. **in mid air,** en medio del aire. **in mid channel,** en medio del canal. **in mid winter,** en medio del invierno

midday *n* mediodía, *m*, *a* del mediodía, meridional. **at m.,** a mediodía

midden *n* muladar, *m*

middle *a* medio; en medio de; del centro; intermedio; (average) mediano. *n* medio, *m*; mitad, *f*; centro, *m*; (waist) cintura, *f*. **in the m. of,** en medio de. **in the m. of nowhere,** donde Cristo dio las tres voces. **toward the m. of the month,** a mediados del mes. **m. age,** edad madura, *f*. **m.-aged,** de edad madura, de cierta

edad. **M. Ages,** edad media, *f*. **m. class,** clase media, burguesía, *f*, *a* de la clase media, burgués. **m. distance,** término medio, *m*. **m. ear,** oído medio, *m*. **m. finger,** dedo de en medio (or del corazón), *m*. **m. way,** *fig* término medio, *m*. **m. weight,** peso medio, *m*

Middle East, the el Oriente Medio, el Levante, *m*

middleman *n* agente de negocios, *m*; (retailer) revendedor, *m*; intermediario, *m*

middling *a* mediano; mediocre; regular, así, así

midge *n* mosquito, *m*, mosca de agua, *f*

midget *n* enano (-na). **m. submarine,** submarino de bolsillo, *m*

midnight *n* medianoche, *f*. *a* de medianoche; nocturno. **at m.,** a medianoche. **to burn the m. oil,** quemarse las cejas. **m. mass,** misa del gallo, *f*

midriff *n* diafragma, *m*

midship *a* medio; en medio del buque, *m*. **m. beam,** bao maestro, *m*. **m. gangway,** crujía, *f*

midshipman *n* guardiamarina, *m*

midst *n* medio, *m*; seno, *m*, *prep* entre. **in the m. of,** en medio de. **There is a traitor in our m.,** Hay un traidor entre nosotros (or en nuestra compañía)

midstream, *n* **in m.** *m*. en medio de la corriente

midsummer *n* pleno verano, *m*; solsticio estival, *m*; fiesta de San Juan, *f*. **A M. Night's Dream,** El Sueño de la Noche de San Juan

midway *a* and *adv* situado a medio camino; a medio camino, a la mitad del camino; entre. *n* mitad del camino, *f*; medio, *m*. **m. between . . . ,** equidistante de . . . , entre

midwife *n* comadrona, partera, *f*

midwifery *n* obstetricia, *f*

midwinter *n* medio del invierno, *m*

mien *n* aire, *m*; porte, semblante, *m*

might *vi* poder. **It m. or m. not be true,** Podría o no podría ser verdad. **How happy Mary m. have been!** ¡Qué feliz pudo haber sido María! **I thought that you m. have seen him in the theater,** Creí que pudieras haberle visto en el teatro. **That I m. . . . !** ¡Que yo pudiese . . . ! **This m. have been avoided if . . .** Esto podía haberse evitado si . . .

might *n* fuerza, *f*; poder, *m*. **m. with m. and main,** con todas sus fuerzas

mightily *adv* fuertemente; poderosamente; *inf* muchísimo, sumamente

mightiness *n* fuerza, *f*; poder, *m*; grandeza, *f*

mighty *a* fuerte, vigoroso; poderoso; grande; *inf* enorme; (proud) arrogante. *adv inf* enormemente, muy

migraine *n* migraña, jaqueca, *f*

migrant *a* migratorio, de paso. *n* ave migratoria, ave de paso, *f*

migrate *vi* emigrar

migration *n* migración, *f*

migratory *a* migratorio, de paso; (of people) nómada, pasajero

migratory worker *n* trabajador golondrino, *m*

Milanese *a* milanés. *n* milanés (-esa)

milch *a f*, (of cows) lechera

mild *a* apacible, pacífico; manso; dulce; suave; (of the weather) blando; *med* benigno; (light) leve; (of drinks) ligero; (weak) débil

mildew *n* mildiu, añublo, *m*; moho, *m*. *vt* anublar; enmohecer. *vi* anublarse; enmohecerse

mildly *adv* suavemente; dulcemente; con indulgencia

mildness *n* apacibilidad, *f*; mansedumbre, *f*; suavidad, *f*; (of weather) blandura, *f*; dulzura, *f*; indulgencia, *f*; (weakness) debilidad, *f*

mile *n* milla, *f*

mileage *n* distancia en millas, *f*; kilometraje, *m*

milestone *n* hito, *m*, piedra miliaria, *f*; mojón kilométrico, *m*

milfoil *n* milenrama, *f*

militancy *n* carácter militante, *m*; belicosidad, *f*

militant *a* militante, combatiente; belicoso; agresivo. *n* combatiente, *mf*

militarily adv militarmente
militariness n lo militar, el carácter militar
militarism n militarismo, m
militarist n militarista, mf
militaristic a militarista
militarization n militarización, f
militarize vt militarizar
military a militar; de guerra. **the m.,** los militares. **m.
academy,** colegio militar, m. **m. camp,** campo militar,
m. **m. law,** código militar, m. **m. man,** militar, m. **m.
police,** policía militar, f. **m. service,** servicio militar, m
militate (against) vi militar contra
militia n milicia, f
militiaman n miliciano, m
milk n leche, f. a de leche; lácteo. vt ordeñar. vi dar
leche. **to have m. and water in one's veins,** tener
sangre de horchata. **condensed m.,** leche conden-
sada, leche en lata, f. **m.-can,** lechera, f. **m.-cart,** carro
de la leche, m. **m. chocolate,** chocolate con leche, m.
m. of magnesia, leche de magnesia, f. **m.-pail,** ordeñadero, m. **m.-tooth,** diente de leche, m. **m.-white,**
blanco como la leche
milkiness n lactescencia, f; carácter lechoso, m; (whiteness) blancura, f
milking n ordeño, m. **m.-machine,** máquina or-
deñadora, f. **m.-stool,** taburete, banquillo, m
milkmaid n lechera, f
milkman n lechero, m
milksop n marica, m
milky a lechero; de leche; lechoso, como leche; ast
lácteo. **the Milky Way** la Vía láctea f
mill n molino, m; (for coffee, etc.) molinillo, m; (factory)
fábrica, f; taller, m; (textile) hilandería, f; fábrica de teji-
dos, f; (fight) riña a puñetazos, f; pugilato, m. vt (grind)
moler; (coins) acordonar; (cloth) abatanar; (chocolate)
batir. **cotton m.,** hilandería de algodón, f. **hand-m.,**
molinillo, m. **paper-m.,** fábrica de papel, f. **saw-m.,**
serrería, f. **spinning m.,** hilandería, f. **water m.,**
molino de agua, m. **m.-course,** saetín, canal de
molino, m. **m.-dam,** esclusa de molino, f. **m.-hand,**
obrero (-ra). **m.-pond,** cubo, m. **m.-race,** caz, m.
m.-wheel, rueda de molino, f
millennial a milenario
millennium n milenario, m
miller n molinero, m. **miller's wife,** molinera
millet n mijo, m
milligram n miligramo, m
milliliter n mililitro, m
millimeter n milímetro, m
milliner n sombrerero (-ra), modista, mf **milliner's
shop,** sombrerería, tienda de modista, f
millinery n sombreros, m pl; modas, f pl; tienda de
modista, f
milling n molienda, f; acuñación, f; (edge of coin) cordoncillo, m. **m. machine,** fresadora, f
million n millón, m. **the m.,** las masas
millionaire a millonario. n millonario, m
millionairess n millonaria, f
millionth a millonésimo
millstone n piedra de moler, muela, f
mime n (Greek farce and actor) mimo, m; (mimicry)
mímica, f; pantomima, f. vi hacer en pantomima
mimetic a mímico, imitativo
mimic a mímico; (pretended) fingido. n imitador (-ra).
vt imitar, contrahacer; biol imitar, adaptarse a
mimicry n mímica, imitación, f; biol mimetismo, m
minaret n minarete, m; (of a mosque) alminar, m
minatory a amenazador
mince vt desmenuzar; (meat) picar; (words) medir (las
palabras). vi andar con pasos menuditos; andar o moverse con afectación; hacer remilgos. **m.-meat,** carne
picada, f; (sweet) conserva de fruta y especias, f. **m. machine,** máquina de picar carne, f
mincing a afectado. n acción de picar carne, f. **m. machine,** máquina de picar carne, f
mincingly adv con afectación; con pasos menuditos
mind n inteligencia, f; espíritu ánimo, m; imaginación,

f; alma, f; (memory) memoria, f, recuerdo, m; (understanding) entendimiento, m; (genius) ingenio, m; (cast
of mind) mentalidad, f; (opinion) opinión, f; (liking)
gusto, m; (thoughts) pensamiento, m; (intention)
propósito, m, intención, f; (tendency) propensión, inclinación, f. **I have a good m. to go away,** Por poco
me marcho; Tengo ganas de marcharme. **I have
changed my m.,** He cambiado de opinión. **I have
changed my m.,** He cambiado de opinión. olvidado. **I shall give him a piece of my m.,** Le diré
cuatro verdades. **It had quite gone out of my m.,** Lo
había olvidado completamente. **I can see it in my
mind's eye,** Está presente a mi imaginación. **I shall
bear it in m.,** Lo tendré en cuenta. **I thought in my
own m. that . . . ,** Pensé por mis adentros que . . . **We
are both of the same m.,** Ambos somos de la misma
opinión. **to be out of one's m.,** estar fuera de juicio.
to call to m., acordarse de. **to have something on
one's m.,** estar preocupado. **to make up one's m.
(to),** resolver (a), decidirse (a), determinar; animarse (a). **m.-reader,** adivinador (-ra) del pensamiento
mind vt (remember) recordar, no olvidar; (heed)
atender a; hacer caso de; tener cuidado de; (fear) tener
miedo de; (obey) obedecer; preocuparse de; (object to)
molestar; importar; (care for) cuidar. vi tener cuidado;
molestar; (feel) sentir; (fear) tener miedo; (be the same
thing) ser igual. **Do you m. being quiet a moment?**
¿Quieres hacer el favor de callarte un momento? **Do
you m. if I smoke?** ¿Le molesta si fumo? **They don't
m.,** No les importa, Les da igual. **Never m.!** ¡No se
moleste!; ¡No se preocupe!; ¡No importa! ¡Vaya! **M.
what you are doing!** ¡Cuidado con lo que haces! **M.
your own business!** ¡No te metas donde no te llaman!
minded a dispuesto, inclinado; de . . . pensamientos; de
. . . disposición
mindful a atento (a), cuidadoso (de); que se acuerda
(de)
mine a poss mío, m, (mía, f; míos, m pl; mías, f pl); el mío,
m, (la mía, f; lo mío, neut; los míos, m pl; las mías, f pl);
mi (pl mis). **a friend of m.,** un amigo mío; uno de mis
amigos
mine n mina, f. vt minar; extraer; sembrar minas en,
colocar minas en. vi minar; hacer una mina; dedicarse
a la minería. **drifting m.,** mina a la deriva, f. **land m.,**
mina terrestre, f. **magnetic m.,** mina magnética, f. **to
lay mines,** colocar (or sembrar) minas. **m.-sweeper,**
dragaminas, buque barreminas, m
minefield n campo de minas, m; barrera de minas, f
minelayer n barca plantaminas, f, barco siembraminas,
lanzaminas, m
miner n minero, m; mil zapador minador, m
mineral n mineral, m, a mineral. **m. baths,** baños, m pl.
m. water, agua mineral, f; gaseosa, f
mineralogical a mineralógico
mineralogist n mineralogista, m
mineralogy n mineralogía, f
mingle vt mezclar; confundir. vi mezclarse; confundirse
mingling n mezcla, f
miniature n miniatura, f. a en miniatura. **m. edition,**
edición diamante, f
miniature golf n minigolf, m
miniaturist n miniaturista, mf
minimize vt aminorar, reducir al mínimo; mitigar; (underrate) tener en menos, despreciar
minimum n mínimo, m, a mínimo
mining n minería, f, a minero; de mina; de minas; de
mineral. **m. engineer,** ingeniero de minas, m
minion n favorito (-ta); satélite, m; print miñona, f
minister n ministro, m. vi servir; suministrar, proveer
de; (contribute) contribuir (a). **m. of health,** ministro
de sanidad, m. **m. of war,** ministro de la guerra, m
ministerial a ministerial
ministration n ecc ministerio, m; servicio, m; agencia, f
ministry n ministerio, m. **m. of food,** Ministerio de
Abastecimientos, m

mink *n* visón, *m*

minnow *n* pez pequeño de agua dulce, *m*

minor *a* menor. *n* menor de edad, *m*; (logic) menor, *f*; *mus* tono menor, *m*; *ecc* menor, *m*. **to be a m.,** ser menor de edad. **m. key,** tono menor, *m*. **m. orders,** *ecc* órdenes menores, *f pl*. **m. scale,** escala menor, *f*

Minorca Menorca, *f*

minority *n* minoría, *f*; (of age) minoridad, *f*. **in the m.,** en la minoría

minster *n* catedral, *f*; monasterio, *m*

minstrel *n* trovador, juglar, *m*; músico, *m*; cantante, *m*

minstrelsy *n* música, *f*; canto, *m*; arte del trovador, *m*, or *f*; gaya ciencia, *f*

mint *n bot* menta, hierbabuena, *f*; casa de moneda, casa de la moneda, ceca, *f*; *fig* mina, *f*; (source) origen, *m. vt* (money) acuñar; *fig* inventar, *a* (postage stamp) en estado nuevo

minter *n* acuñador, *m*; *fig* inventor (-ra)

minting *n* (of coins) acuñación, *f*; *fig* invención, *f*

minuet *n* minué, *m*

minus *a* menos; negativo; desprovisto de; sin. *n* signo menos, *m*; cantidad negativa, *f*

minute *a* menudo, diminuto; insignificante; minucioso

minute *n* minuto, *m*; momento, *m*; instante, *m*; (note) minuta, *f*; *pl* **minutes,** actas, *f pl*. **in a m.,** en un instante. **m.-book,** libro de actas, minutario, *m*. **m.-hand,** minutero, *m*

minutely *adv* minuciosamente; en detalle; exactamente

minuteness *n* suma pequeñez, *f*; minuciosidad, *f*

minx *n* picaruela, *f*; coqueta, *f*

miracle *n* milagro, *m*. **m.-monger,** milagrero (-ra). **m. play,** milagro, *m*

miraculous *a* milagroso

miraculously *adv* milagrosamente, por milagro

miraculousness *n* carácter milagroso, *m*, lo milagroso

mirage *n* espejismo, *m*

mire *n* fango, lodo, *m*; (miry place) lodazal, *m*

mirror *n* espejo, *m. vt* reflejar. **to look in the m.,** mirarse al espejo. **full-length m.,** espejo de cuerpo entero, *m*. **small m.,** espejuelo, *m*

mirth *n* alegría, *f*, júbilo, *m*; risa, *f*; hilaridad, *f*

mirthful *a* alegre

mirthless *a* sin alegría, triste

miry *a* lodoso, fangoso, cenagoso

misadventure *n* desgracia, *f*; accidente, *m*

misanthrope *n* misántropo, *m*

misanthropic *a* misantrópico

misanthropy *n* misantropía, *f*

misapplication *n* mala aplicación, *f*; mal uso, *m*; abuso, *m*

misapply *vt* aplicar mal; hacer mal uso de; abusar de

misapprehend *vt* comprender mal; equivocarse sobre

misapprehension *n* concepto erróneo, *m*; equivocación, *f*, error, *m*

misappropriate *vt* malversar

misappropriation *n* malversación, *f*

misbehave *vi* portarse mal; (of a child) ser malo

misbehavior *n* mala conducta, *f*

miscalculate *vt* calcular mal; engañarse (sobre)

miscalculation *n* mal cálculo, error, *m*; desacierto, *m*

miscall *vt* mal nombrar; llamar equivocadamente; (abuse) insultar

miscarriage *n med* aborto, *m*; (failure) malogro, fracaso, *m*; (of goods) extravío, *m*

miscarriage of justice *n* yerro en la administración de la justicia, *m*

miscarry *vi med* abortar, malparir; (fail) malograrse, frustrarse; (of goods) extraviarse

miscellaneous *a* misceláneo; vario, diverso

miscellany *n* miscelánea, *f*

mischance *n* mala suerte, *f*; infortunio, *m*, desgracia, *f*; accidente, *m*

mischief *n* daño, *m*; mal, *m*; (wilfulness) travesura, *f*; (person) diablillo, *m*. **m.-maker,** enredador (-ra), chismoso (-sa); alborotador, *m*; malicioso (-sa).

m.-making, *a* enredador; chismoso; malicioso; alborotador

mischievous *a* dañino, perjudicial, malo; malicioso; chismoso; (wilful) travieso; juguetón; (of glances, etc.) malicioso

mischievously *adv* maliciosamente; con (or por) travesura

mischievousness *n* mal, *m*; malicia, *f*; maleficencia, *f*; travesura, *f*

misconceive *vt* formar un concepto erróneo de; concebir mal, juzgar mal

misconception *n* concepto erróneo, *m*, idea falsa, *f*; error, *m*, equivocación, *f*; engaño, *m*

misconduct *n* mala conducta, *f*. **to m. oneself,** portarse mal

misconstruction *n* mala interpretación, *f*; falsa interpretación, *f*; tergiversación, *f*; mala traducción, *f*

misconstrue *vt* interpretar mal; entender mal; tergiversar; traducir mal

miscount *vt* contar mal, equivocarse en la cuenta de; calcular mal. *n* error, *m*; yerro de cuenta, *m*

miscreant *n* malandrín, *m*; bribón, *m*, *a* vil, malandrín

misdeed *n* delito, malhecho, crimen, *m*

misdemeanor *n* mala conducta, *f*; *law* delito, *m*; ofensa, *f*, malhecho, *m*

misdirect *vt* informar mal (acerca del camino); (a letter) dirigir mal, poner unas señas incorrectas en

miser *n* avaro (-ra)

miserable *a* infeliz, desgraciado; miserable; despreciable; sin valor

miserably *adv* miserablemente

miserliness *n* avaricia, tacañería, *f*

miserly *a* avaro, tacaño

misery *n* miseria, *f*; sufrimiento, *m*; dolor, tormento, *m*

misfire *vi* no dar fuego; (of a motor-car, etc.) hacer falsas explosiones, errar el encendido

misfit *n* traje que no cae bien, *m*; zapato que no va bien, *m*; (person) inadaptado, *m*

misfortune *n* infortunio, *m*, mala suerte, adversidad, *f*; desdicha, desgracia, *f*; mal, *m*

misgive *vt* hacer temer; llenar de duda; hacer recelar; hacer presentir

misgiving *n* temor, *m*; duda, *f*; recelo, *m*; presentimiento, *m*

misgovern *vt* gobernar mal; administrar mal; dirigir mal

misgovernment *n* desgobierno, *m*; mala administración, *f*

misguided *a* mal dirigido; extraviado; engañado; (blind) ciego

misguidedly *adv* equivocadamente

mishap *n* desgracia, *f*; contratiempo, accidente, *m*. **to have a m.,** sufrir una desgracia; tener un accidente

misinform *vt* informar mal; dar informes erróneos (a)

misinformation *n* noticia falsa, *f*; información errónea, *f*

misinterpret *vt* interpretar mal; entender mal; torcer; tergiversar; traducir mal

misinterpretation *n* mala interpretación, *f*; interpretación falsa, *f*; tergiversación, *f*; mala traducción, *f*

misjudge *vt* juzgar mal; equivocarse (en or sobre); tener una idea falsa de

misjudgment *n* juicio errado, *m*; idea falsa, *f*; juicio injusto, *m*

mislay *vt* extraviar, perder

mislead *vt* extraviar; llevar a conclusiones erróneas; despistar; engañar

misleading *a* de falsas apariencias; erróneo, falso; engañoso

mismanage *vt* administrar mal; dirigir mal; echar a perder

mismanagement *n* mala administración, *f*; desgobierno, *m*

misname *vt* mal nombrar; llamar equivocadamente

misnomer *n* nombre equivocado, *m*; nombre inapropiado, *m*

misogynist *n* misógino, *m*
misogyny *n* misoginia, *f*
misplace *vt* colocar mal; poner fuera de lugar
misplaced *a* mal puesto; inoportuno; equivocado
misprint *n* error de imprenta, *m*, errata, *f*, *vt* imprimir con erratas
mispronounce *vt* pronunciar mal
mispronunciation *n* mala pronunciación, *f*
misquotation *n* cita errónea, *f*
misquote *vt* citar mal, citar erróneamente
misrepresent *vt* desfigurar; tergiversar; falsificar
misrepresentation *n* desfiguración, *f*; tergiversación, *f*; falsificación, *f*
misrule *vt* gobernar mal. *n* mal gobierno, desgobierno, *m*; confusión, *f*
miss *n* señorita, *f*
miss *vt* (one's aim) errar (el tiro, etc.); no acertar (a); (let fall) dejar caer; (lose a train, the post, etc., one's footing, an opportunity, etc.) perder; (fall short of) dejar de; no ver; no notar; pasar por alto de; omitir; echar de menos; notar la falta de; no encontrar. *vi* errar; (fail) salir mal, fracasar. **I m. you,** Te echo de menos. **to be missing,** faltar; estar ausente; haberse marchado; haber desaparecido. **to m. one's mark,** errar el blanco. **to m. out,** omitir, pasar por alto de. **She doesn't miss a beat,** (fig.) No se le escapa nada
missal *n* misal, *m*
misshapen *a* deforme
missile *n* arma arrojadiza, *f*; proyectil, *m*
missing *a* que falta; perdido; ausente; *mil* desaparecido
mission *n* misión, *f*
missionary *n* misionero, *m*
missionize *vi* misionar
missis *n* señora, *f*; *inf* mujer, *f*
Mississippi el Misisipí, *m*
missive *n* misiva, *f*
Missouri el Misuri, *m*
misspend *vt* malgastar; desperdiciar; perder
mist *n* bruma, neblina, *f*; vapor, *m*; (drizzle) llovizna, *f*; *fig* nube, *f*. *vt* anublar, empañar. *vi* lloviznar
mistakable *a* confundible
mistake *vt* comprender mal; equivocarse sobre; errar; (with for) confundir con, equivocarse con. *n* equivocación, *f*; error, *m*; inadvertencia, *f*; (in an exercise, etc.) falta, *f*. **And no m.!** *inf* Sin duda alguna. **by m.,** por equivocación; (involuntarily) sin querer. **If I am not mistaken,** Si no me engaño, Si no estoy equivocado. **to make a m.,** equivocarse
mistaken *a* (of persons and things) equivocado; (of things) erróneo; incorrecto
mistakenly *adv* equivocadamente; injustamente, falsamente
mister *n* señor, *m*
mistily *adv* a través de la neblina; obscuramente; indistintamente, vagamente
mistimed *a* intempestivo; inoportuno
mistiness *n* neblina, bruma, *f*; vaporosidad, *f*; obscuridad, *f*
mistletoe *n* muérdago, *m*
mistranslate *vt* traducir mal; interpretar mal
mistranslation *n* mala traducción, *f*; traducción inexacta, *f*
mistress *n* señora, *f*; maestra, *f*; (fiancée) prometida, *f*; (beloved) amada, dulce dueña, *f*; (concubine) amiga, querida, *f*. **M. (Mrs.) Gómez,** Sra Gómez. **m. of the robes,** camarera mayor, *f*
mistrust *vt* desconfiar de, no tener confianza en; dudar de. *n* desconfianza, *f*; recelo, *m*, suspicacia, *f*; aprensión, *f*
mistrustful *a* desconfiado; receloso, suspicaz. **to be m. of,** recelarse de
misty *a* brumoso, nebuloso; vaporoso; (of the eyes) anublado; (of windows, etc.) empañado
misunderstand *vt* comprender mal; tomar en sentido erróneo; interpretar mal

misunderstanding *n* concepto erróneo, error, *m*; equivocación, *f*; (disagreement) desavenencia, *f*
misuse *vt* emplear mal; abusar de; (funds) malversar; (ill-treat) tratar mal. *n* abuso, *m*; (of funds) malversación, *f*
mite *n* (coin) ardite, *m*; (trifle) pizca, *f*; óbolo, *m*; *ent* ácaro, *m*
miter *n* mitra, *f*; *carp* inglete, *m*, *vt carp* cortar ingletes en
mitigate *vt* (pain) aliviar; mitigar; suavizar
mitigation *n* (of pain) alivio, *m*; mitigación, *f*
mitten *n* mitón, *m*
mix *vt* mezclar; (salad) aderezar; (concrete, etc.) amasar; combinar, unir; (sociably) alternar (con); (confuse) confundir. *vi* mezclarse; frecuentar la compañía (de); frecuentar; (get on well) llevarse bien
mixed *a* mezclado; vario, surtido; mixto; (confused) confuso. **m. doubles,** parejas mixtas, *f pl.* **m. up,** (in disorder) revuelto; confuso. **m. up with,** implicado en; asociado con
mixer *n* mezclador, *m*; (person) mezclador (-ra); *inf* persona sociable, *f*. **electric m.,** mezclador eléctrico, *m*
mixture *n* mezcla, *f*; (medicine) poción, medicina, *f*
mizzen *n* mesana, *f*. **m.-mast,** palo de mesana, *m*. **m.-sail,** vela de mesana, *f*. **m.-topsail,** sobremesana, *f*
mnemonics *n* mnemotecnia, *f*
Moabite *n* moabita, *mf*
moan *vt* lamentar; llorar. *vi* gemir; quejarse, lamentarse. *n* gemido, *m*; lamento, *m*; quejido, *m*
moaning *n* gemidos, *m pl*
moat *n* foso, *m*
mob *n* (crowd) muchedumbre, multitud, *f*; (rabble) populacho, *m*, gentuza, *f*. *vt* atropellar; atacar. **mob-cap,** cofia, *f*
mobile *a* móvil; ambulante; (fickle) voluble. **m. canteen,** cantina ambulante, *f*
mobility *n* movilidad, *f*
mobilization *n* movilización, *f*
mobilize *vt* movilizar. *vi* movilizarse
moccasin *n* mocasín, *m*
mocha *n* café de Moca, *m*
mock *vt* ridiculizar; burlarse (de), mofarse (de); (cause to fail) frustrar; (mimic) imitar; (delude) engañar. *vi* mofarse, burlarse, reírse. *a* cómico, burlesco; falso; fingido; imitado. **to make a m. of,** poner en ridículo; hacer absurdo; burlarse de. **m.-heroic,** heroicocómico. **m.-orange,** *bot* jeringuilla, *f*. **m.-turtle soup,** sopa hecha con cabeza de ternera a imitación de tortuga, *f*
mocker *n* mofador (-ra); el, *m*, (*f*, la) que se burla de
mockery *n* mofa, burla, *f*; ridículo, *m*; ilusión, apariencia, *f*. **to make a m. of,** mofarse de; hacer ridículo
mocking *a* burlón. **m. bird,** pájaro burlón, *m*
mockingly *adv* burlonamente
modality *n* modalidad, *f*
mode *n* modo, *m*; manera, *f*; (fashion) moda, *f*; uso, *m*, costumbre, *f*
model *n* modelo, *m*; (artist's) modelo vivo, *m*, *a* modelo; en miniatura. *vt* modelar; moldear; formar; hacer; planear. **m. display,** (hats, etc.) exposición de modelos, *f*. **m. railway,** ferrocarril en miniatura, *m*
modeler *n* modelador (-ra); disenador, *m*
modeling *n* modelado, *m*; modelo, *m*. **m. wax,** cera para moldear, *f*
moderate *a* moderado; (of prices, etc.) módico; (fair, medium) regular, mediano; razonable; mediocre. *n* moderado, *m*. *vt* moderar; modificar; calmar. *vi* moderarse; calmarse
moderately *adv* moderadamente; módicamente; medianamente; bastante; razonablemente; mediocremente
moderation *n* moderación, *f*. **in m.,** en moderación
moderator *n* moderador, *m*; (Church of Scotland) presidente, *m*; *univ* examinador, *m*; *univ* inspector de exámenes, *m*. **m. lamp,** lámpara de regulador, *f*
modern *a* moderno. **m.** modernista, *mf*. **in the m. way,** a la moderna. **m. language,** lengua viva, *f*

modernism _n_ modernismo, _m_
modernist _n_ modernista, _mf_
modernistic _a_ modernista
modernity _n_ modernidad, _f_
modernization _n_ modernización, _f_
modernize _vt_ modernizar
modernness _n_ modernidad, _f_
modest _a_ modesto; (of a woman) púdico
modesty _n_ modestia, _f_; (of a woman) pudor, _m_
modicum _n_ porción pequeña, _f_; poco, _m_
modifiable _a_ modificable
modification _n_ modificación, _f_
modify _vt_ modificar. **It has been much modified,** Se ha modificado mucho; Se han hecho muchas modificaciones
modifying _a_ modificante, modificador
modish _a_ de moda en boga; elegante
modishness _n_ elegancia, _f_
modiste _n_ modista, _mf_
modulate _vt_ and _vi_ modular
modulation _n_ modulación, _f_
modus vivendi _n_ modo de conveniencia, _m_
Mogul _a_ mogol. _n_ mogol (-la). **the Great M.,** el Gran Mogol
Mohammedan _a_ mahometano, agareno
Mohammedanism _n_ mahometismo, _m_
Mohican _n_ mohican, _m_
moiety _n_ mitad, _f_
moiré _n_ muaré, _m_
moist _a_ húmedo
moisten _vt_ humedecer, mojar
moisture _n_ humedad, _f_
molar _n_ muela, _f_, _a_ molar
molasses _n pl_ melaza, _f_
mold _n_ (fungus) moho, _m_; (humus) mantillo, _m_; (ironmould) mancha de orín, _f_; (matrix) molde, _m_, matriz, _f_; _cul_ cubilete, _m_; _naut_ gálibo, _m_; (for jelly, etc.) molde, _m_; _arch_ moldura, _f_; (temperament) temple, _m_, disposición, _f_. _vt_ moldear; (cast) vaciar; _carp_ moldurar; _naut_ galibar; _fig_ amoldar, formar; _agr_ cubrir con mantillo. **to m. oneself on,** modelarse sobre. **m.-board,** (of a plough) orejera, _f_
Moldavian _a_ moldavo. _n_ moldavo (-va)
molder _n_ moldeador, _m_; _fig_ amolador (-ra); creador (-ra). _vi_ desmoronarse, convertirse en polvo; _fig_ decaer, desmoronarse; vegetar
moldiness _n_ moho, _m_
molding _n_ amoldamiento, _m_; vaciado, _m_; _arch_ moldura, _f_; _fig_ formación,
moldy _a_ mohoso, enmohecido; _fig_ anticuado
mole _n_ (animal) topo, _m_; (spot) lunar, _m_; (breakwater) dique, malecón, _m_; muelle, _m_
molecular _a_ molecular
molecule _n_ molécula, _f_
molehill _n_ topera, _f_
moleskin _n_ piel de topo, _f_
molest _vt_ molestar; perseguir, importunar; faltar al respeto (a)
molestation _n_ importunidad, persecución, _f_; molestia, incomodidad, _f_
mollification _n_ apaciguamiento, _m_; mitigación, _f_
mollify _vt_ apaciguar, calmar; mitigar
mollusk _n_ molusco, _m_
mollycoddle _n_ alfeñique, mírame y no me toques, _m_; niño (-ña), mimado (-da)
Moloch _n_ Moloc, _m_
molt _vi_ mudar, _n_ muda, _f_
molten _a_ fundido; derretido
Moluccas, the las Malucas, _f pl_
moment _n_ momento, _m_; instante _m_; (importance) importancia, _f_. **at this m.,** en este momento. **Do it this m.!** ¡Hazlo al instante (or en seguida)!
momentarily _adv_ momentáneamente; cada momento
momentariness _n_ momentaneidad, _f_
momentary _a_ momentáneo
momentous _a_ de suma importancia; crítico; grave

momentousness _n_ importancia, _f_; gravedad, _f_
momentum _n_ momento, _m_, velocidad adquirida _f_; _fig_ ímpetu, _m_. **to gather m.,** cobrar velocidad, acelerar
monarch _n_ monarca, _m_
monarchic _a_ monárquico
monarchism _n_ monarquismo, _m_
monarchist _n_ monárquico (-ca)
monarchy _n_ monarquía, _f_
monastery _n_ monasterio, _m_
monastic _a_ monástico. **m. life,** vida de clausura, _f_
monasticism _n_ vida monástica, _f_
Monday _n_ lunes, _m_
monetary _a_ monetario
monetization _n_ monetización, _f_
money _n_ dinero, _m_; (coin) moneda, _f_; sistema monetario, _m_. **paper m.,** papel moneda, _m_. **ready m.,** dinero contante, _m_. **to make m.,** ganar (or hacer) dinero; enriquecerse. **M. talks,** Poderoso caballero es Don Dinero. **m.-bag,** talega, _f_; (person) ricacho (-cha). **m.-bags,** riqueza, _f_. **m.-box,** alcancía, hucha, _f_. **m.-changer,** cambista, _mf_ **m.-lender,** prestamista, _mf_ **m.-making,** _n_ el hacer dinero; prosperidad, ganancia, _f_. _a_ lucrativo. **m.-order,** giro postal, _m_
moneyed _a_ adinerado; acomodado
Mongolian _a_ mogol. _n_ mogol (-la); (language) mogol, _m_
mongoose _n_ mangosta, _f_
mongrel _a_ mestizo, atravesado. _n_ perro mestizo, _m_; (in contempt) mestizo. _m_
monitor _n_ monitor, _m_
monitory _a_ monitorio. _n ecc_ monitorio, _m_
monk _n_ monje, _m_. **to become a m.,** hacerse monje, tomar el hábito. **monk's-hood,** acónito, _m_
monkey _n_ mono (-na); (imp) diablillo, _m_; (of a piledriver) pilón de martinete, _m_; (in glass-making) crisol, _m_. **to m. with,** meterse con; entremeterse. **m. nut,** cacahuete, _m_. **m.-puzzle,** (tree) araucaria, _f_. **m. tricks,** monadas, travesuras, diabluras, _f pl_. **m.-wrench,** llave inglesa, _f_
monkish _a_ monacal, de monje; monástico
monochromatic _a_ monocromo
monochrome _n_ monocromo, _m_
monocle _n_ monóculo, _m_
monogamist _n_ monógamo (-ma)
monogamous _a_ monógamo
monogamy _n_ monogamia, _f_
monogram _n_ monograma, _m_
monograph _n_ monografía, _f_, opúsculo, _m_
monolith _n_ monolito, _m_
monolithic _a_ monolítico
monologue _n_ monólogo, _m_
monomania _n_ monomanía, _f_
monomaniac _n_ monomaníaco (-ca)
monomial _n_ monomio, _m_, _a_ de un solo término
monoplane _n_ monoplano, _m_
monopolist _n_ monopolista, _mf_; acaparador (-ra)
monopolization _n_ monopolio, _m_
monopolize _vt_ monopolizar
monopoly _n_ monopolio, _m_
monotheism _n_ monoteísmo, _m_
monotheist _n_ monoteísta, _mf_
monotone _n_ monotonía, _f_
monotonous _a_ monótono
monotony _n_ monotonía, _f_
monoxide _n_ monóxido, _m_
Monroe doctrine _n_ monroísmo, _m_
monseigneur _n_ monseñor, _m_
monsoon _n_ monzón, _mf_
monster _n_ monstruo, _m_
monstrance _n_ custodia, _f_
monstrosity _n_ monstruosidad, _f_
monstrous _a_ monstruoso; horrible, atroz; enorme
montage _n_ montaje, _m_
month _n_ mes, _m_. **He arrived a m. ago,** Llegó hace un mes
monthly _a_ mensual. _adv_ mensualmente, cada mes. _n_

revista (or publicación) mensual, *f*; *pl* **monthlies,** menstruación, regla, *f*. **m. salary** or **payment,** mensualidad, *f*

monument *n* monumento, *m*

monumental *a* monumental

moo *vi* (of cattle) mugir. *n* mugido, *m*

mood *n* humor, *m*; espíritu, *m*; *gram* modo, *m*

moodily *adv* taciturnamente; tristemente, pensativamente

moodiness *n* mal humor, *m*, taciturnidad, *f*; melancolía, tristeza, *f*

moody *a* taciturno, de mal humor; triste, melancólico, pensativo

mooing *n* (of cattle) mugido, *m*

moon *n* luna, *f*; satélite, *m*; mes lunar, *m*; luz de la luna, *f*. **full m.,** plenilunio, *m*; luna llena, *f*. **new m.,** novilunio, *m*, luna nueva, *f*

moonbeam *n* rayo de luna, *m*

moonless *a* sin luna

moonlight *n* luz de la luna, *f*. **in the m.,** a la luz de la luna. **to do a m. flit,** *inf* mudarse por el aire

moonlighting *n* el pluriempleo, *m*

moonlit *a* iluminado por la luna. **moonlit night,** noche de luna, *f*

moonshine *n* claridad de la luna, *f*; *fig* música celestial, ilusión, *f*

moonstone *n* adularia, *f*

moonstruck *a* lunático

Moor *n* moro (-ra)

moor *n* páramo, brezal, *m*; (marsh) pantano, *m*; (for game) coto, *m*. *vt* amarrar, aferrar; afirmar con anclas o cables. **m.-hen,** polla de agua, *f*

mooring *n* amarre, *m*. **m.-mast,** *aer* poste de amarre, *m*

moorings *n pl* amarradero, *m*

Moorish *a* moro; árabe. **M. architecture,** arquitectura árabe, *f*. **M. girl,** mora, *f*

moorland *n* páramo, brezal, *m*

moose *n* anta, *f*

moot *n* junta, *f*; ayuntamiento, *m*. *a* discutible. *vt* (bring up) suscitar; (discuss) discutir, debatir

mop *n* (implement) trapeador, *m* (Ecuador), escoba con fleco, *f*; (of hair) mata (de pelo), *f*. *vt* trapear (Ecuador); (dry) enjugar, secar. **to mop up,** *inf* limpiar; *mil* acabar con (el enemigo)

mope *vi* replace by tristear. **to m. about,** vagar tristemente

moquette *n* moqueta, *f*

moraine *n* morena, *f*

moral *a* moral; (chaste) casto, virtuoso; honrado. *n* (maxim) moraleja, *f*; *pl* **morals,** moralidad, *f*; ética, *f*; moral, *f*; (conduct) costumbres, *f pl*. **m. philosophy,** filosofía moral, *f*. **m. support,** apoyo moral, *m*. **m. tale,** apólogo, *m*

morale *n* moral, *f*

moralist *n* moralista, *m*

morality *n* moralidad, *f*; virtud, *f*; castidad, *f*. **m. play,** moralidad, *f*, drama alegórico, *m*

moralization *n* moralización, *f*

moralize *vt* and *vi* moralizar

moralizer *n* moralizador (-ra)

moralizing *a* moralizador

morally *adv* moralmente

morals. See **moral**

morass *n* marisma, ciénaga, *f*

moratorium *n* moratoria, *f*

Moravian *a* moravo. *n* moravo (-va)

morbid *a* mórbido, morboso; (of the mind, etc.) insano

morbidezza *n* (*art* and *lit*) morbidez, *f*

morbidity *n* morbidez, *f*

mordacity *n* mordacidad, *f*

mordant *a* mordaz; (of acid) mordiente. *n* mordiente, *m*

more *a* and *adv* más. **The m. he earns, the less he saves,** Cuanto más gana, menos ahorra. **the m. the better,** cuanto más, tanto mejor. **without m. ado,** sin más ni más; sin decir nada. **Would you like some m.?** ¿Quiere Vd. más? (of food) ¿Quiere Vd. repetir?

no m., no más; (never) nunca más; (finished) se acabó. **once m.,** otra vez, una vez más. **m. and m.,** cada vez más, más y más. **m. or less,** más o menos; (about) poco más o menos

moreover *adv* además, también; por otra parte

morganatic *a* morganático

morgue *n* depósito de cadáveres, *m*

moribund *a* moribundo

Mormon *a* mormónico. *n* mormón (-ona)

Mormonism *n* mormonismo, *m*

morning *n* mañana, *f*, *a* matutino, de la mañana. **Good m.!** ¡Buenos días! **the next m.,** la mañana siguiente. **very early in the m.,** muy de mañana. **m. coat,** chaqué, *m*. **m. dew,** rocío de la mañana, *m*. **m. paper,** periódico de la mañana, *m*. **m. star,** lucero del alba, *m*. **m. suit,** chaqué, *m*

Moroccan *a* marroquí, marrueco. *n* marrueco (-ca), marroquí, *mf*

Morocco Marruecos, *m*

morocco *n* (leather) marroquí, tafilete, *m*

morose *a* sombrío, taciturno, malhumorado

morosely *adv* taciturnamente

moroseness *n* taciturnidad, *f*; mal humor, *m*

morphia, morphine *n* morfina, *f*. **m. addict,** morfinómano (-na)

morrow *n* mañana, *f*; día siguiente, *m*

Morse code *n* la clave telegráfica de Morse, *f*, el alfabeto de Morse, *m*

morsel *n* pedazo, *m*; (mouthful) bocado, *m*

mortal *a* mortal. *n* mortal, *mf*. **m. sin,** pecado mortal, pecado capital, *m*

mortality *n* mortalidad, *f*

mortally wounded *adv* herido de muerte

mortar *n* (for building) argamasa, *f*; (for mixing and mil) mortero, *m*. **m. and pestle,** mortero y majador, *m*. **m.-board,** *n* (in building) cuezo, *m*; (academic cap) birrete, *m*

mortgage *n* hipoteca, *f*. *vt* hipotecar. *a* hipotecario. **to pay off a m.,** redimir una hipoteca

mortgageable *a* hipotecable

mortgaged debt *n* deuda garantizada con una hipoteca, *f*

mortgagee *n* acreedor (-ra) hipotecario (-ia)

mortgagor *n* deudor (-ra) hipotecario (-ia)

mortification *n* mortificación, *f*; humillación, *f*; *med* gangrena, *f*

mortify *vt* mortificar; humillar. *vi med* gangrenarse

mortifying *a* humillante

mortise *n* muesca, *f*. *vt* hacer muescas (en); ensamblar

mortuary *n* mortuorio. *n* depósito de cadáveres, *m*

Mosaic *a* mosaico

mosaic *n* mosaico, *m*

Moscow Moscú, *m*

mosque *n* mezquita, *f*

mosquito *n* mosquito, *m*. **m. net,** mosquitero, *m*

moss *n* musgo, *m*; moho, *m*; (swamp) marjal, *m*

mossgrown *a* musgoso, cubierto de musgo; *fig* anticuado

mossiness *n* estado musgoso, *m*

mossy *a* musgoso

most *a* el (la, los, etc.) más; la mayor parte de; la mayoría de; (el, etc.) mayor. *adv* más; el (la, etc.) más; (extremely) sumamente; (very) muy; (before adjectives sometimes expressed by superlative, e.g. **m. reverend,** reverendísimo, **m. holy,** santísimo, etc.). *n* (highest price) el mayor precio; la mayor parte; el mayor número; lo más. **m. of all,** sobre todo. **m. people,** la mayoría de la gente. **at the m.,** a lo más, a lo sumo. **for the m. part,** en su mayor parte; casi todos; generalmente, casi siempre. **to make the m. of,** sacar el mayor partido posible de; aprovechar bien; exagerar

mostly *adv* principalmente; en su mayoría; en su mayor parte; casi siempre; en general, generalmente

mote *n* átomo, *m*; mota, *f*. **to see the m. in our neighbor's eye and not the beam in our own,** ver la paja en el ojo del vecino y no la viga en el nuestro

motet *n* motete, *m*

moth *n* mariposa nocturna, *f;* polilla, *f.* **m.ball,** bola de naftalina, *f.* **m.-eaten,** apolillado

mother *n* madre, *f;* madre de familia, *f;* (of alcoholic beverages) madre, *f. vt* cuidar como una madre (a); servir de madre (a); (animals) ahijar. **M. Church,** madre iglesia, *f;* iglesia metropolitana, *f.* **m.-in-law,** suegra, *f.* **m. land,** (madre) patria, *f.* **m.-of-pearl,** *n* madreperla, *f;* nácar, *m. a* nacarado, nacáreo. **M. Superior,** (madre) superiora, *f.* **m. tongue,** lengua materna, *f*

motherhood *n* maternidad, *f*

motherless *a* huérfano de madre, sin madre

motherlike *a* de madre, como una madre

motherliness *n* cariño maternal, *m*

motherly *a* maternal

motif *n* motivo, *m;* tema, *m; sew* adorno, *m*

motion *n* movimiento, *m; mech* marcha, operación, *f;* mecanismo, *m;* (sign) seña, señal, *f;* (gesture) ademán, gesto, *m;* (carriage) aire, porte, *m;* (of the bowels) movimiento del vientre, *m,* deyección, *f;* (will) voluntad, *f,* deseo, *m;* (proposal in an assembly or debate) proposición, moción, *f; law* pedimento, *m. vt* hacer una señal (a). *vi* hacer señas. **to set in m.,** poner en marcha. **m. picture,** fotografía cinematográfica, película, *f.* **m.-picture theater,** cine, *m*

motionless *a* inmóvil

motivate *vt* motivar

motive *n* motivo, *m. a* motor; motivo. **with no m.,** sin motivo. **m. power,** fuerza motriz, *f*

motley *a* abigarrado, multicolor; (mixed) diverso, vario. *n* traje de colores, *m,* botarga, *f*

motor *n* motor, *m;* automóvil, *m, a* motor; movido por motor; con motor; (traveling) de viaje. *vi* ir en automóvil. *vt* llevar en automóvil (a). **m.boat,** lancha automóvil, *f.* **m.bus,** autobús, ómnibus, *m.* **m.car,** automóvil, *m.* **m.-coach,** autobús, *m.* **m.cycle,** motocicleta, *f.* **m.cyclist,** motociclista, *mf* **m.-launch,** canoa automóvil, *f.* **m.oil,** aceite para motores, *m.* **m.-road,** autopista, *f.* **m.-rug,** manta de viaje, *f.* **m.-scooter,** bicicleta con motor, *f.* **m.-spirit,** bencina, *f*

motoring *n* automovilismo, *m*

motorist *n* automovilista, motorista, *mf*

mottled *a* abigarrado; (of marble, etc.) jaspeado, esquizado; manchado (con), con manchas (de); pintado (con)

motto *n her* divisa, *f;* mote, *m;* (in a book, etc.) lema, *m*

mound *n* montón, *m;* (knoll) altozano, *m;* (for defence) baluarte, *m;* (for burial) túmulo, *m*

mount *n* (hill, and in palmistry) monte, *m;* (for riding) caballería, *f;* montadura, *f;* (for a picture) borde, *m. vt* subir; (machines, etc.) montar; (jewels) engastar; (a picture) poner un borde a; (a play) poner en escena; poner a caballo; proveer de caballo. *vi* montar; subir; (increase) aumentar. **to m. a horse,** subir a caballo, montar. **to m. guard,** *mil* montar la guardia. **to m. the throne,** subir al trono

mountain *n* montaña, *f;* (mound) montón, *m. a* de montaña(s); montañés; alpino, alpestre. **to make a m. out of a molehill,** convertir un grano de arena en una montaña. hacer de una pulga un camello, hacer de una pulga un elefante. **m.-chain,** cadena de montañas, *f.* **m. dweller,** montañés (-esa). **m. railway,** ferrocarril de cremallera, *m.* **m.-side,** falda de una montaña, *f*

mountaineer *n* (inhabitant) montañés (-esa); (climber) alpinista, *mf. vi* hacer alpinismo

mountaineering *n* alpinismo, *m*

mountainous *a* montañoso; (huge) enorme

mountebank *n* saltabanco, *m;* charlatán, *m*

Mount Cenis Moncenisa

mounting *n* (ascent) subida, *f;* ascensión, *f;* (of machinery, etc.) armadura, *f;* montadura, *f;* (of a precious stone) engaste, *m.* **m.-block,** subidero, *m*

mourn *vi* afligirse, lamentarse; (wear mourning) estar de luto. *vt* llorar; lamentar; llevar luto por

mourner *n* lamentador (-ra); (paid) plañidera, *f;* el, *m,* (f, la) que acompaña al féretro

mournful *a* triste, acongojado; funesto, lúgubre; fúnebre; lamentable

mournfully *adv* tristemente

mournfulness *n* tristeza, *f;* melancolía, aflicción, *f,* pesar, *m*

mourning *n* aflicción, *f;* lamentación, *f;* luto, *m.* **deep m.,** luto riguroso, *m.* **half m.,** medio luto, *m.* **to be in m.,** estar de luto. **to be in m. for,** llevar luto por. **to come out of m.,** dejar el luto. **m.-band,** (on the hat) tira de gasa, *f;* (on the arm) brazal de luto, *m.* **m.-coach,** coche fúnebre, *m*

mouse *n* ratón (-na); *naut* barrilete, *m. vi* cazar ratones. **m.-coloured,** de color de rata. **m.-hole, m.-trap,** ratonera, *f*

mouser *n* gato ratonero, *m*

mousing *n* caza de ratones, *f*

moustache *n* bigote, mostacho, *m*

mousy *a* ratonesco, ratonil

mouth *n* (*anat* human being, of a bottle, cave) boca, *f;* entrada, *f;* (of a river) desembocadura, *f;* (of a channel) embocadero, *m;* (of a wind-instrument) boquilla, *f. vt* pronunciar con afectación; (chew) mascar. *vi* clamar a gritos, vociferar. **down in the m.,** *inf* con las orejas caídas. **It makes my m. water,** Se me hace la boca agua. **large m.,** boca rasgada, *f.* **m.-gag,** abrebocas, *m.* **m.-organ,** armónica, *f.* **m.-wash,** antiséptico bucal, *m* (Argentina), enjuague, *m*

mouthed *a* que tiene boca . . . ; de boca . . . **open-m.,** boquiabierto

mouthful *n* bocado, *m;* (of smoke, air) bocanada, *f*

mouthpiece *n* (of wind-instruments, tobacco-pipe, waterpipe) boquilla, *f;* (of a wineskin) brocal, *m;* (spokesman) portavoz, *m;* intérprete, *mf*

movable *a* movible; (of goods) mobiliario. **m. feast,** fiesta movible, *f*

movable type *n* tipos sueltos, *m pl*

movables *n pl* bienes muebles, efectos, *m pl*

move *n* movimiento, *m;* (of household effects) mudanza, *f;* (motion) marcha, *f;* (in a game) jugada, *f;* (*fig* step) paso, *m;* (device) maniobra, *f.* **Whose m. is it?** ¿A quién le toca jugar? **to be on the m.,** estar en movimiento; estar de viaje. **to be always on the m.,** *inf* parecer una lanzadera

move *vt* mover; poner en marcha; (furniture) trasladar; cambiar de lugar; (stir) remover; (shake) agitar, hacer temblar; (transport) transportar; (a piece in chess, etc.) jugar; (pull) arrancar; (impel) impulsar; (incline) inclinar, disponer; (affect emotionally) conmover, emocionar, enternecer; impresionar. *vi* moverse; ponerse en marcha; (walk) andar; ir; avanzar; (a step forward, etc.) dar; (move house) trasladarse; (act) entrar en acción; (in games) hacer una jugada; (progress) progresar; (shake) agitarse, temblar; removerse; (propose in an assembly) hacer una proposición; (in a court of law) hacer un pedimento; (grow) crecer. **to m. about,** pasearse; ir y venir; (of traffic) circular; (remove) trasladarse; (stir, tremble) agitarse. **to m. along,** caminar por; avanzar por. **to m. aside,** *vt* apartar; poner a un lado; (curtains) descorrer. *vi* ponerse a un lado; quitarse de en medio. **to m. away,** *vt* alejar. *vi* alejarse; marcharse; trasladarse; mudar de casa. **to m. back,** retroceder; volver hacia atrás. **to m. down,** bajar, descender. **to m. forward,** adelantarse; avanzar; progresar. **to m. in,** entrar (en); tomar posesión de una casa. **to m. off,** *vi* quitar. *vi* marcharse; ponerse en marcha; alejarse, apartarse. **to m. on,** avanzar; ponerse en marcha; circular; (of time) pasar, correr. **to m. out,** *vt* sacar, quitar. *vi* salir; (from a house) mudarse, abandonar (una casa, etc.). **to m. round,** dar vueltas, girar; (turn round) volverse. **to m. to,** (make) hacer, animar (a); causar. **to m. up,** *vt* montar, subir. *vi* montar; avanzar

movement *n* movimiento, *m; mech* mecanismo, *m;*

(Stock Exchange) actividad, *f.* **encircling m.**, *mil* movimiento envolvente, *m*

mover *n* motor, *m*; móvil, *m*; promotor (-ra); (of a motion, proposer) autor (-ra) de una moción

movie *n inf* cine, *m*. **m. camera,** máquina de impresionar, *f.* **m. star,** estrella de la pantalla, *f*

moving *a* móvil; motor; (affecting) emocionante, conmovedor; impresionante; patético. *n* movimiento, *m*; traslado, *m*; cambio de domicilio, *m*. **m. picture,** fotografía cinematográfica, *f.* **m. staircase,** escalera móvil, *f*

movingly *adv* con emoción; patéticamente

mow *vt* segar. *vi* (grimace) hacer muecas

mowing *n* siega, *f.* **m.-machine,** segadora, *f*

Mr. See **mister**

Mrs. See **mistress**

much *a* mucho. *adv* mucho; (by far) con mucho; (with past part.) muy; (pretty nearly) casi, más o menos. **m. of a size,** más o menos del mismo tamaño. **I was m. angered,** Estuve muy enfadado. **as m. as,** tanto como. **as m. more,** otro tanto. **How m. is it?** ¿Cuánto es? ¿Cuánto cuesta? **however m.** . . . ., por mucho que . . . **not m.,** no mucho. **not to think m. of,** tener en poco (a). **so m. so that,** tanto que. **too m.,** demasiado. **to make m. of,** dar grande importancia a; (a person) apreciar, querer; agasajar; (a child) mimar, acariciar

mucilage *n* mucílago, *m*

muck *n* (dung) estiércol, *m*; (filth) porquería, inmundicia, *f*; suciedad, *f*; (rubbish, of a literary work, etc.) porquería, *n*. **to m. up,** ensuciar; (spoil) estropear por completo

mucky *a* muy sucio; puerco; asqueroso, repugnante

mucosity *n* mucosidad, *f*

mucous *a* mucoso. **m. membrane,** mucosa, *f*

mucus *n* mucosidad, *f*; (from the nose) moco, *m*

mud *n* lodo, barro, fango, *m*. **to stick in the mud,** (of a ship, etc.) embarrancarse. **mudbath,** baño de barro, *m.* **mud wall,** tapia, *f*

muddiness *n* estado fangoso, *m*; (of liquids) turbiedad, *f*; suciedad, *f*

muddle *vt* (bewilder) dejar perplejo, aturdir; (intoxicate) emborrachar; (stupefy) entontecer; (spoil) estropear; embarullar, dejar en desorden; hacer un lío de. *n* desorden, *m*; confusión, *f*; lío, embrollo, *m*. **in a m.,** en desorden; en confusión. **to make a m.,** armar un lío. **to m. away,** derrochar sin ton ni son

muddled *a* desordenado; confuso; estúpido; torpe; (drunk) borracho

muddy *a* fangoso, lodoso, barroso; cubierto de lodo; (of liquids, etc.) turbio; (of the complexion) cetrino. *vt* enlodar, cubrir de lodo; ensuciar; (liquids) enturbiar

mudguard *n* guardabarro, *m*

muezzin *n* almuecín, almuédano, *m*

muff *n* manguito, *m*; (for a car radiator) cubierta para radiador, *f*; (*inf* at games, etc.) maleta, *m*. *vt* dejar escapar (una pelota); (an opportunity) perder

muffin *n* mollete, *m*

muffle *vt* embozar, arrebozar; envolver; encubrir, ocultar, tapar; (stifle sound of) apagar; (oars, bells) volver con tela para no hacer ruido; *fig* ahogar. **to m. oneself up,** embozarse

muffled *a* (of sound) sordo; confuso; apagado. **m. drum,** tambor enlutado, *m*

muffler *n* bufanda, tapaboca, *f*; (furnace) mufla, *f*; (of a car radiator) cubierta para radiador, *f*; (silencer) silencioso, *m*

mufti *n* mufti, *m*

mug *n* vaso, *m*; (tankard) pichel, tarro, *m*; (face) jeta, *f*; (dupe) primo, *m*; (at games, etc.) maleta, *m*

mulatto *a* mulato. *n* mulato (-ta). **m.-like,** amulatado

mulberry *n* (fruit) mora, *f*; (bush) morera, *f.* **m. plantation,** moreral, *m*

mule *n* mulo (-la); (slipper) mula, chinela, *f*; (spinning-jenny) huso mecánico, *m*

mulish *a* mular; terco como una mula

mulishness *n* terquedad de mula, *f*

mullet *n* (red) salmonete, *m*, trilla, *f*; (grey) mújol, *m*

multicolored *a* multicolor

multifarious *a* numeroso, mucho; diverso, vario

multiform *a* multiforme

multilateral *a* multilátero

multimillionaire *a* archimillonario, multimillonario, *n* multimillonario, *m*

multiple *a* múltiple, múltiplo. *n* múltiplo, *m*

multiple-choice question *n* pregunta optativa, *f*

multiplicand *n* multiplicando, *m*

multiplication *n* multiplicación, *f.* **m. table,** tabla de multiplicación, *f*

multiplicity *n* multiplicidad, *f*

multiplier *n math* multiplicador, *m*; máquina de multiplicar, *f*

multiply *vt* multiplicar. *vi* multiplicarse

multitude *n* multitud, *f.* **the m.,** las masas

multitudinous *a* muy numeroso

mumble *vi and vt* musitar, hablar entre dientes; refunfuñar; (chew) mascullar

mummer *n* momero (-ra); máscara, *mf*

mummery *n* momería, *f*; mascarada, *f*

mummification *n* momificación, *f*

mummify *vt* momificar. *vi* momificarse

mummy *n* momia, *f*; carne de momia, *f*; (*inf* mother) mama, *f.* **m. case,** sarcófago, *m*

mumps *n pl* parotiditis, papera, *f*

munch *vt* masticar, mascullar, mascar

mundane *a* mundano

municipal *a* municipal. **m. charter,** fuero municipal, *m*. **m. m. government,** gobierno municipal, *m*

municipality *n* municipio, *m*

munificence *n* munificencia, *f*

munificent *a* munífico, generoso

munition *n* munición, *f*. *vt* municionar. **m. dump,** depósito de municiones, *m*. **m. factory,** fábrica de municiones, *f.* **m. worker,** obrero (-ra) de una fábrica de municiones

mural *a* mural. *n* pintura mural, *f*

murder *n* asesinato, *m*. **m.** *vt* asesinar; dar muerte (a), matar; (a work, etc.) degollar. **He was murdered,** Fue asesinado. **willful m.,** homicidio premeditado, *m*

murderer *n* asesino, *m*

murderess *n* asesina, *f*

murderous *a* homicida; cruel, sanguinario; fatal; imposible, intolerable

murderously *adv* con intento de asesinar; (with look) con ojos asesinos; cruelmente

murkiness *n* obscuridad, lobreguez, *f*, tinieblas, *f pl*

murky *a* lóbrego, negro, obscuro; (of one's past, etc.) negro, accidentado

murmur *n* murmullo, *m*; rumor, *m*; susurro, *m*; (grumble) murmurio, *m*. *vi* murmurar, susurrar; (complain) murmurar, quejarse. *vt* murmurar, decir en voz baja

murmuring *n* murmurio, *m*, *a* que murmura, susurrante

muscatel *a* moscatel. *n* moscatel, *m*. **m. grape,** uva moscatel, *f*

muscle *n* músculo, *m*

Muscovite *a* moscovita. *n* moscovita, *mf*

muscular *a* muscular, musculoso; (brawny) membrudo, fornido. **m. pains,** (in the legs, etc.) agujetas, *f pl*

muscularity *n* fuerza muscular, *f*

musculature *n* musculatura, *f*

Muse *n* musa, *f*

muse *n* meditación, *f*. *vi* meditar, reflexionar, rumiar; mirar las musarañas, estar distraído. **to m. on,** meditar en (or sobre)

museum *n* museo, *m*

museum of arms *n* museo de armas, *m*, aploteca, *f*

mushroom *n* seta, *f*. *a* de setas; de forma de seta; (upstart) advenedizo; (ephemeral) efímero, de un día. **m.-bed,** setal, *m.* **m.-spawn,** esporas de setas, *f pl*

music *n* música, *f*; armonía, *f*; melodía, *f*. *a* de música.

to set to m., poner en música. **m.-hall,** teatro de variedades, *m*; salón de conciertos, *m*. **m. master,** profesor de música, *m*. **m. publisher,** editor de obras musicales, *m*. **m. stand,** atril, *m*; tablado para una orquesta, *m*. **m. stool,** taburete de piano, *m*
musical *a* musical; de música; armonioso, melodioso. **She is very m.,** Es muy aficionada a la música; Tiene mucho talento para la música. **m.-box,** caja de música, *f.* **m. comedy,** zarzuela, *f.* **m. instrument,** instrumento de música, *m*
musical chairs *n* escobas, *f pl,* el juego de sillas, *m sg*
musically *adv* musicalmente; melodiosamente
musician *n* músico (-ca)
musing *n* meditación, *f*; ensueños, *m pl, a* pensativo, meditabundo
musingly *adv* reflexivamente
musk *n* (substance) almizcle, *m*; perfume de almizcle, *m. a* de almizcle; almizclero; (of scents) almizcleño. **m.-deer,** almizclero, *m*. **m.-rat,** rata almizclera, *f*
musket *n* mosquete, *m*
musketeer *n* mosquetero, *m*
Muslim *a* musulmán, mahometano. *n* musulmán (-ana)
muslin *n* muselina, *f, a* de muselina
mussel *n* mejillón, *m*. **m.-bed,** criadero de mejillones, *m*
must *vi* haber de; tener que; deber; (expressing probability) deber de, ser. **This question m. be settled without delay,** Esta cuestión debe ser resuelta sin demora. **You m. do it at once,** Tienes que hacerlo en seguida. **I m. have seen him in the street sometime,** Debo haberle visto en la calle alguna vez. **One m. eat to live,** Se ha de comer para vivir. **Well, go if you m.,** Bueno, vete si no hay más remedio. **It m. be a difficult decision for him,** Debe ser una decisión difícil para él. **It m. have been about twelve o'clock when . . . ,** Serían las doce cuando . . .
must *n* mosto, zumo de la uva, *m*; (mould) moho, *m*
mustang *n* potro mesteño, *m*
mustard *n* mostaza, *f.* **m. gas,** iperita, *f.* **m. plaster,** sinapismo, *m*. **m. pot,** mostacera, *f.* **m. spoon,** cucharita para la mostaza, *f*
muster *n* lista, *f,* rol, *m*; revista, *f*; reunión, *f, vt* pasar lista (de); pasar revista (a); reunir. *vi* juntarse, reunirse. **to m. out,** (from the army) dar de baja (a). **to m. up sufficient courage,** cobrar ánimos suficientes. **to pass m.,** pasar revista; ser aceptado. **m.-roll,** mil muestra, *f; naut* rol de la tripulación, *m*
mustiness *n* moho, *m*; ranciedad, *f*; (of a room, etc.) olor de humedad, *m*
musty *a* mohoso; rancio; que huele a humedad. **to go m.,** enmohecerse
mutability *n* mutabilidad, *f*; inconstancia, inestabilidad, *f*
mutable *a* mudable; inconstante, inestable
mutation *n* mutación, *f*

mute *a* mudo; silencioso. *n* mudo (-da); *mus* sordina, *f*; (phonetics) letra muda, *f.* **deaf m.,** sordomudo (-da)
muted *a* (of sounds) sordo, apagado
mutely *adv* mudamente; en silencio
muteness *n* mudez, *f*; silencio, *m*
mutilate *vt* mutilar; estropear
mutilation *n* mutilación, *f*
mutineer *n* amotinador, rebelde, *m*
mutinous *a* amotinado; rebelde, sedicioso; turbulento
mutiny *n* motín, *m*; sublevación, insurrección, *f, vi* amotinarse, sublevarse
mutt *n* chucho, *m*
mutter *vt* and *vi* murmurar, musitar; mascullar, decir (or hablar) entre dientes; gruñir, refunfuñar; (of thunder, etc.) tronar, retumbar. *n* murmurio, *m*; rumor, *m*; retumbo, *m*
mutton *n* carnero, *m, a* de carnero. **m.-chop,** chuleta, *f*
mutual *a* mutuo, recíproco; común. **by m. consent,** de común acuerdo. **m. aid society,** sociedad de socorros mutuos, *f.* **m. insurance company,** sociedad de seguros mutuos, *f*
mutual fund *n* fondo de inversiones rentables, *m*
mutualism *n* mutualismo, *m*
mutuality *n* mutualidad, *f*
mutually *adv* mutuamente, recíprocamente
muzzle *n* (snout) hocico, *m*; (for a dog) bozal, *m*; (of a gun) boca, *f. vt* abozalar, poner un bozal (a); *(fig* gag) amordazar, imponer silencio (a)
muzzling *n* acción de abozalar, *f; (fig* gagging) amordazamiento, *m*
my *a poss* mi, *mf*; mis, *mf pl* **my relatives,** mis parientes. **My goodness!** ¡Dios mío!
myelitis *n* mielitis, *f*
myopia *n* miopía, *f*
myopic *a* miope
myriad *n* miríada, *f*
myrmidon *n* rufián, *m*; asesino, *m*; secuaz, *m*
myrrh *n* mirra, *f*
myrtle *n* mirto, arrayán, *m*
myself *pron* yo mismo; (as a reflexive with a preposition) mí; (with a reflexive verb) me. **I m. sent it,** yo mismo (-ma) lo mandé
mysterious *a* misterioso
mysteriousness *n* misterio, *m*, lo misterioso
mystery *n* misterio, *m*. **m. play,** (religious) misterio, drama litúrgico, *m*; (thriller) comedia de detectives, *f.* **m. story,** novela policíaca, *f*; novela de aventuras, *f*
mystic *a* místico
mysticism *n* misticismo, *m*
mystification *n* mistificación, *f*
mystify *vt* mistificar
myth *n* mito, *m*
mythical *a* mítico
mythologist *n* mitólogo, *m*
mythology *n* mitología, *f*

N

n *n* (letter) ene, *f*
nab *vt inf* atrapar, apresar, agazapar
nabob *n* nabab, *m*; ricacho, *m*
nacre *n* nácar, *m*, madreperla, *f*
nadir *n* nadir, *m*
nag *n* jaca, *f*; (wretched hack) rocín, jamelgo, penco, *m*. *vt* zaherir, echar en cara, regañar; (of one's conscience) remorder. *vi* criticar, regañar
nagging *n* zaherimiento, *m. a* zaheridor, criticón; (pain) continuo, incesante, constante
naiad *n myth* náyade, *f*
nail *vt* clavar, enclavar; (for ornament) clavetear, tachonar, adornar con clavos. *n* uña, *f; mech* clavo, *m*; (animal's) garra, *f.* **to n. down,** sujetar (or cerrar) con clavos. **to n. to (on to),** clavar en. **to n. together,** fijar

con clavos. *inf* **on the n.,** en el acto, en seguida. *inf* **to hit the n. on the head,** dar en el clavo. **brassheaded n.,** tachón, *m.* **French n.,** punta de París, *f.* **headless n.,** puntilla, *f.* **hob-n.,** clavo de herradura, *m.* **hook n.,** gancho, *m.* **round-headed n.,** bellota, *f.* **n.-brush,** cepillo para las (or de) uñas, *m.* **n.-file,** lima para las uñas, *f.* **n. head,** cabeza de un clavo, *f.* **n.-puller,** sacaclavos, arrancaclavos, botador, *m.* **n.-scissors,** tijeras para las uñas, *f pl.* **n. trade,** ferretería, *f.* **n. varnish,** barniz para las uñas, *m*
nailed *a* adornado con clavos, claveteado
nailer *n* fabricante de clavos, chapucero, *m*
nailing *n* enclavación, *f*
naive *a* ingenuo, candoroso, espontáneo
naively *adv* ingenuamente, espontáneamente

naiveté *n* ingenuidad, naturalidad, franqueza, *f;* candor, *m*

naked *a* desnudo, nudo; desabrigado, indefenso, desamparado; (birds) implume; calvo; (truth) simple, sencillo, puro; evidente, patente. **stark n.,** en cueros vivos, tal como le parió su madre. **with the n. sword,** con la espada desnuda. **n. eye,** simple vista, *f. n.* **light,** llama descubierta, *f*

nakedly *adv* nudamente; desabrigadamente; abiertamente, claramente

nakedness *n* desnudez, *f; fig* desabrigo, *m,* aridez, *f; fig* claridad, *f.* **the truth in all its n.,** la verdad desnuda

namby-pamby *a* soso, insípido, ñoño

name *n* nombre, *m;* título, *m;* fama, opinión, *f;* renombre, crédito, *m;* autoridad, *f;* apodo, mal nombre, *m. vt* nombrar, llamar, imponer el nombre de, apellidar; mencionar, señalar; (appoint) designar, elegir; (ships) bautizar. **by n.,** por nombre. **Christian n.,** nombre de pila, *m.* **in his n.,** en nombre de él, en nombre suyo; de parte de él. **in n. only,** nada más que en nombre. **to be named,** llamarse. **to call** (a person) **names,** poner como un trapo (a). **to go under the n. of,** vivir bajo el nombre de. **to have a good n.,** tener buena fama. **What is her n.?** ¿Cómo se llama? **n. day,** santo, *m. n.* **plate,** (machinery) placa de fábrica, *f;* (streets) rótulo, *m;* (professional) placa profesional, *f*

nameless *a* anónimo; desconocido; (inexpressible) vago, indecible

namely *adv* a saber, es decir

namesake *n* tocayo (-ya)

naming *n* bautizo, *m;* nombramiento, *m;* designación, *f*

nannygoat *n* cabra, *f*

nap *n* (cloth) pelusa, *f,* pelo, tamo, *m;* (plants) vello, *m,* pelusilla, *f;* (sleep) siesta, *f,* sueño, *m;* (cards) napolitana, *f.* **to take a nap,** *vi* dormitar, echar un sueño, echar una siesta. **to take an afternoon nap,** dormir la siesta. **to be caught napping,** estar desprevenido

nape *n* nuca, *f,* cogote, *m;* (animal's) testuz, *m,*

naphtha *n chem* nafta, *f.* **wood n.,** alcohol metílico, *m*

naphthalene *n chem* naftalina, *f*

napkin *n* (table) servilleta, *f;* (babies') pañal, *m.* **n.-ring,** servilletero, *m*

Naples Nápoles, *m*

Napoleonic *a* napoleónico

narcissism *n* narcisismo, *m*

narcissus *n* narciso, *m*

narcosis *n med* narcosis, *f*

narcotic *a med* narcótico, calmante, soporífero. *n med* narcótico, *m,* opiata, *f*

nard *n bot* nardo, *m,* tuberosa, *f*

narrate *vt* narrar, contar; referir, relatar

narration *n* narración, narrativa; relación, descripción, *f,* relato, *m*

narrative *a* narrativo. *n* narrativa, *f;* descripción, *f*

narrator *n* narrador (-ra), relator (-ra), descriptor (-ra)

narrow *vt* estrechar, angostar; reducir, limitar. *vi* reducirse, hacerse más estrecho; (eyes) entornarse; (knitting) menguar. *a* estrecho, angosto; limitado, restringido, reducido, corto; (avaricious) ruin, avaro, mezquino; (ideas) intolerante, intransigente. **"Narrow Road,"** «Camino Estrecho». *n pl* **narrows,** *naut* estrecho, *m;* desfiladero, paso estrecho, *m.* **to have a n. escape,** escapar en una tabla. **n.-brimmed** (hats), de ala estrecha. **n. circumstances,** estrechez, escasez de medios, *f.* **n.-gauge railway,** ferrocarril de vía estrecha (or de vía angosta), *m.* **n. life,** vida de horizontes estrechos, *f.* **n. majority,** escasa mayoría, *f.* **n.-minded,** cerrado al mundo, intolerante, intransigente. **n.-mindedness,** intolerancia, intransigencia, estrechez de miras, *f*

narrowing *n* estrechez, *f,* estrechamiento, *m;* reducción, limitación, *f;* (in knitting) menguado, *m*

narrowly *adv* estrechamente; por poco, con dificultad;

atentamente, cuidadosamente. **I n. escaped being run over,** Por poco me atropellan

narrowness *n* estrechez, angostura, *f;* (of means) pobreza, miseria, *f;* (of ideas) intolerancia, intransigencia, *f*

nasal *a* nasal, gangoso. *n* letra nasal, *f*

nasalize *vt* nasalizar

nasally *adv* nasalmente. **to speak n.,** hablar por las narices, ganguear

nascent *a* naciente

nastily *adv* suciamente; ofensivamente, de un modo insultante; maliciosamente, con malignidad

nastiness *n* suciedad, inmundicia, porquería, *f;* (indecency) obscenidad, indecencia, *f;* (rudeness) insolencia, impertinencia, grosería, *f;* (difficulty) dificultad, *f,* lo malo

nasturtium *n* mastuerzo, *m,* capuchina, *f*

nasty *a* nauseabundo, repugnante; asqueroso, inmundo, sucio; (obscene) indecente, obsceno; desagradable, malo; (malicious) rencoroso, malicioso; violento; malévolo, amenazador; peligroso; difícil. *fig* **to be in a n. mess,** tener el agua al cuello. **to turn n.,** *inf* ponerse desagradable

natal *a* natal, natalicio, de nacimiento, nativo

nation *n* nación, *f,* estado, país, *m;* (people) pueblo, *m*

national *a* nacional; público; patriótico. *n* nacional, *mf.* **n. anthem,** himno nacional, *m.* **n. debt,** deuda pública, *f.* **n. schools,** escuelas públicas, *f pl.* **n. socialism,** nacionalsocialismo, *m.* **n. socialist,** *a* and *n* nacionalsocialista *mf.* **n. syndicalism,** *pol* nacionalsindicalismo, *m.* **n. syndicalist,** *a* and *n pol* nacionalsindicalista, *mf*

nationalism *n* nacionalismo, patriotismo, *m*

nationalist *a* and *n* nacionalista, *mf*

nationality *n* nacionalidad, *f;* nación, *f*

nationalization *n* nacionalización, *f*

nationalize *vt* nacionalizar

National Labor Relations Board *n* Junta Nacional de Relaciones Laborales

nationally *adv* nacionalmente, como nación; del punto de vista nacional

native *a* (of a place) nativo, natal, oriundo; indígena; nacional, típico, del país; (vocabulary) patrimonial (as opposed to borrowed vocabulary); (of genius) natural, innato, instintivo; *min* nativo; (language) vernáculo. *n* nacional, *mf;* natural, *mf;* ciudadano (-na) indígena, aborigen (gen. pl.), *mf;* producto nacional, *m.* **He is a n. of Madrid,** Nació en Madrid, Es natural de Madrid, Es madrileño. **native informant,** sujeto, *m.* **n. land,** patria, tierra, *f.* **n. place,** lugar natal, *m.* **n. region,** patria chica, *f.* **n. soil,** terruño, *m.* **n. tongue,** lengua materna, *f*

nativity *n* navidad, natividad, *f;* (manger) nacimiento, *m*

natty *a inf* chulo, majo; coquetón

natural *a* natural; (wild) virgen, salvaje; nativo; (of products) crudo; normal; (usual) acostumbrado, corriente, natural; (of likeness) fiel, verdadero; (illegitimate) ilegítimo, bastardo; (of qualities) innato, instintivo; físico; característico, propio; (of people) inafectado, sencillo, genuino; *mus* natural. *n mus* becuadro, *m; mus* nota natural, *f;* imbécil, *mf* **n. features,** geografía física, *f.* **n. history,** historia natural, *f.* **n. philosophy,** filosofía natural, *f.* **n. science,** ciencias naturales, *f pl.* **n. selection,** selección natural, *f.* **n. state,** estado virgen, *m*

natural child *n* hijo ilegítimo, *m*

natural daughter *n* hija ilegítima, *f*

naturalism *n* naturalismo, *m*

naturalist *n* (*lit* and *science*) naturalista, *mf*

naturalistic *a* naturalista

naturalization *n* naturalización, *f;* aclimatación, *f.* **n. papers,** carta de naturaleza, *f*

naturalize *vt* naturalizar; aclimatar. **to become naturalized,** naturalizarse

naturally *adv* naturalmente, por naturaleza; normalmente; sin afectación; instintivamente, por instinto; (without art) al·natural

naturalness *n* naturalidad, *f;* sencillez, desenvoltura, *f;* desembarazo, *m*

nature *n* naturaleza, *f;* (of people) carácter, fondo, temperamento, genio, natural, modo de ser, *m;* (kind) género, *m,* especie, *f;* (essence) condición, esencia, cualidad, *f, art* from n., del natural. **good n.,** bondad natural, afabilidad, *f.* **ill n.,** mala índole, *f.* **nature cure,** naturismo, *m.* **n. curist,** naturista, *mf.* **n. study,** historia natural, *f.* **n. worship,** panteísmo, culto de la naturaleza, *m*

natured *a* de carácter, de índole, con un modo de ser, de condición

naught *n* nada, *f;* cero, *m. a* inútil, sin valor. **all for n.,** todo en balde. **to come to n.,** malograrse. **to set at n.,** tener en menos; despreciar

naughtily *adv* traviesamente; con picardía, con malicia

naughtiness *n* travesura, picardía, mala conducta, *f;* malicia, *f*

naughty *a* travieso, pícaro, revoltoso, malo; salado, escabroso, verde (stories, etc.). **to be n.,** (children) ser malo

nausea *n* náusea, *f,* bascas, *f pl,* mareo, *m; fig* asco, *m;* repugnancia, *f*

nauseate *vt* dar náuseas; *fig* repugnar, dar asco

nauseating *a* repugnante, horrible; asqueroso

nauseous *a* nauseabundo, asqueroso; *fig* repugnante

nauseousness *n* náusea, asquerosidad, *f; fig* repugnancia, *f,* asco, *m*

nautical *a* náutico, marítimo. **n. day, twenty-four hours,** singladura, *f*

nautilus *n zool* argonauta, nautilo, *m*

naval *a* naval; de marina, marítimo. **n. base,** base naval, *f.* **n. engagement,** batalla naval, *f.* **n. hospital,** hospital de marina, *m.* **n. law,** código naval, *m.* **n. officer,** oficial de marina, *m.* **n. power,** poder marítimo, *m.* **n. reservist,** marinero de reserva, *m.* **n. yard,** arsenal, *m*

Navarre Navarra, *f*

Navarrese *a* and *n* navarro (-rra)

nave *n arch* nave, *f;* (of wheels) cubo, *m*

navel *n* ombligo, *m.* **n. string,** cordón umbilical, *m*

navigability *n* navegación, practicabilidad de navegar, *f*

navigable *a* navegable, practicable

navigate *vt* navegar, marear, dirigir (unbuque); *fig* conducir, guiar. *vi* navegar

navigation *n* navegación, *f;* (science of) náutica, marina, *f.* **n. company,** empresa naviera, *f.* **n. laws,** derecho marítimo, *m.* **n. lights,** luces de navegación, *f pl*

navigator *n* navegador, navegante, *m;* piloto, *m*

navvy *n* peón, bracero, jornalero, *m; mech* máquina, excavadora, *f.* **road n.,** peón caminero, *m.* **to work like a n.,** estar hecho un azacán, sudar la gota gorda

navy *n* marina, *f;* armada, *f;* (color) azul marino, *m.* **n. board,** consejo de la armada, *m.* **n. department** ministerio de marina, *m.* **n. estimates,** presupuesto de marina, *m.* **n. list,** escalafón de marina, *m*

nay *adv* no; al contrario, más bien, mejor dicho. *n* negativa, *f,* voto contrario, *m*

Nazarene *a* and *n* nazareno (-na)

Nazareth Nazaret, *m*

Nazi *a* and *n* nacionalsocialista, naci, *mf*

Nazism *n* nacismo, *m*

n.d. (no date) *s.f.* (sin fecha)

Neapolitan *a* and *n* neapolitano (-na)

near *vi* acercarse, aproximarse. *a* cercano, inmediato, contiguo; (of time) inminente, próximo; (relationship) cercano, consanguíneo; (of friends) íntimo, entrañable; (mean) tacaño, avariento

near *prep* cerca de, junto a; hacia, en la dirección de; (of time) cerca de, casi. *adv* cerca; (time) cerca, próximamente. **to be n. to,** estar cerca de. **to bring n.,** acercar, aproximar. **It was a n. thing,** Escapamos por un

pelo. **n. at hand,** a la mano; (time) cerca, inminente. **n.-by,** *a* cercano, inmediato. *adv* cerca. **n. side,** (of vehicles) lado de la acera, *m.* **n.-sighted,** corto de vista, miope. **n.-sightedness,** miopía, cortedad de vista, *f*

nearest *a comp* and *sup* más cercano, más cerca; más corto. **the n. way,** el camino más corto, el camino directo

nearly *adv* casi; cerca de, aproximadamente; estrechamente; íntimamente. **It touches me n.,** Me toca de cerca, Es de sumo interés para mí. **They n. killed me,** Por poco me matan. **to be n.,** (of age) frisar en, rayar en

nearness *n* (of place) cercanía, proximidad, contigüidad, *f;* (of time) inminencia, proximidad, *f;* (relationship) consanguinidad, *f;* (avarice) avaricia, tacañería, *f;* (dearness) intimidad, amistad estrecha, *f*

neat *a zool* vacuno; elegante, sencillo, de buen gusto; (of the body) bien hecho, airoso, esbelto; (clean) limpio, aseado; (of handwriting) legible, bien proporcionado; pulido, esmerado, acabado; hábil, astuto, diestro; (of liquor, spirits) puro, solo. **to make a n. job of,** hacer (algo) bien

neatly *adv* sencillamente, con elegancia, con primor; con aseo, limpiamente; bien (proporcionado); diestramente, hábilmente

neatness *n* aseo, *m,* limpieza, *f;* elegancia, sencillez, *f;* buen gusto, *m;* destreza, habilidad, *f;* (aptness) pertinencia, *f*

nebula *n ast* nebulosa, *f*

nebulosity *n* nebulosidad, *f; ast* nebulosa, *f;* vaguedad, imprecisión, *f*

nebulous *a* nebuloso; vago, impreciso, confuso

necessarily *adv* necesariamente; inevitablemente, sin duda

necessary *a* necesario, inevitable; imprescindible, preciso, indispensable, esencial; obligatorio, debido, forzoso. *n* requisito esencial, *m.* **if n.,** en caso de necesidad; si fuera necesario. **to be n.,** hacer falta; necesitarse

necessitate *vt* necesitar, exigir, requerir, obligar

necessitous *a* pobre, indigente, miserable, necesitado

necessity *n* necesidad, *f;* menester, *m,* (e.g., **an indispensable n.,** un menester imprescindible); consecuencia, *f,* resultado, efecto, *m;* inevitabilidad, fatalidad, *f;* (poverty) indigencia, pobreza, *f.* **Fire and clothing are necessities,** El fuego y el vestir son cosas necesarias. **from n.,** por necesidad. **in case of n.,** si fuese necesario, en caso de necesidad. **of n.,** de necesidad, sin remedio. **physical necessities,** menesteres físicos, *m pl.* **prime n.,** artículo de primera necesidad, *m.* **to be under the n. of,** tener que, tener la necesidad de

Necessity is the mother of invention La necesidad es una gran inventora, La necesidad aguza el ingenio

neck *n* cuello, *m,* garganta, *f;* (of bottles) gollete, cuello, *m;* (of animals) pescuezo, *m; geog* istmo, *m,* lengua de tierra, *f;* (of musical instruments) clavijero, mástil, *m; sew* escote, *m.* **low-necked,** (of dresses) escotado. **She fell on his n.,** Se colgó de su cuello. **He won by a n.,** Ganó con un cuello; *fig* Ganó por un tris. **to break anyone's n.,** romperle el pescuezo. **to wring the n. of,** torcer el pescuezo (a). **n. and n.,** parejos. **n. or nothing,** todo o nada, perdiz o no comerla. **n. stock,** alzacuello, *m*

neckband *n* tirilla de camisa, *f*

necklace *n* collar, *m*

necklet *n* collar, *m;* (of fur) cuello, *m*

necktie *n* corbata, *f*

necrological *a* necrológico

necrology *n* necrología, *f*

necropolis *n* necrópolis, *f*

nectar *n* néctar, *m*

nectarine *n bot* variedad de melocotón, *f*

need *vt* necesitar, haber menester, requerir, exigir. *vi* ser necesario, hacer falta, carecer; haber (de). **N. I**

obey? ¿He de obedecer? **You need to write carefully,** Hay que escribir con cuidado. **The work n. not be done for tomorrow,** No es preciso hacer el trabajo para mañana

need *n* necesidad, *f;* cosa necesaria, *f;* falta; (poverty) indigencia, pobreza, *f;* urgencia, *f;* (shortage) escasez, carestía, *f.* **in case of n.,** en caso de necesidad, en caso de urgencia. **I have n.** of two more books, Me hacen falta dos libros más

needful *a* necesario, preciso; indispensable, esencial. **the n.,** lo necesario

needfulness *n* necesidad, falta, *f*

neediness *n* pobreza, penuria, miseria, estrechez, *f*

needle *n sew* aguja, *f;* (of compass) brújula, aguja imanada, *f;* (monument) obelisco, *m;* (of scales) field, *m,* lengüeta, *f;* (of phonograph) pría, *f,* (of measuring instruments) índice, *m; med* aguja de inyecciones, *f. inf* **to be as sharp as a n.,** no tener pelo de tonto. **pack n.,** aguja espartera, *f.* **n.-case,** alfiletero, agujero, *m.* **n. maker,** fabricante de agujas, *m.* **n.-shaped,** en forma de aguja, acicular

needle and thread hilo y aguja

needless *a* innecesario, supérfluo. **n. to say,** claro está que . . ., huelga decir que . . .

needlessly *adv* innecesariamente, inútilmente; en vano, de balde

needlessness *n* superfluidad, *f,* lo innecesario

needlewoman *n* (professional) cosedora, *f;* costurera, *f.* **She is a good n.,** Cose bien (or es una buena cosedora)

needlework *n* labor de aguja, labor blanca, costura, *f;* bordado, *m.* **to do n.,** hacer costura

needs *adv* necesariamente, sin remedio *n pl* necesidades, *f pl.* **if n. must,** si hace falta. **N. must when the devil drives,** A la fuerza ahorcan

needy *a* necesitado, menesteroso, corto de medios, pobre, apurado

ne'er-do-well *n* calavera, perdido, *m.* **to be a n.,** ser de mala madera

nefarious *a* nefario, vil, nefando

nefariously *adv* vilmente, nefariamente

negation *n* negación, *f*

negative *vt* negar, denegar; votar en contra (de), oponerse (a); (prevent) impedir, imposibilitar. *a* negativo. *n* negativa, negación, *f;* repulsa, denegación, *f; phot* negativo, *m,* prueba negativa, *f; elec* electricidad negativa, *f.* **to reply in the n.,** dar una respuesta negativa

negativeness *n* el carácter negativo, *m*

neglect *vt* descuidar, desatender; abandonar, dejar; (ignore) despreciar, no hacer caso (de); omitir, olvidar. *n* descuido, *m,* desatención, *f;* inobservancia, *f;* abandono, olvido, *m;* desdén, *m,* frialdad, *f.* **to fall into n.,** caer en desuso. **to n. one's obligations,** descuidar sus obligaciones

neglectful *a* negligente, descuidado, omiso

negligee *n* salto de cama, quimono, *m,* bata, *f*

negligence *n* negligencia, *f,* descuido, *m;* flojedad, pereza, *f;* (of dress) desaliño, *m*

negligent *a* negligente, descuidado; remiso, flojo, perezoso

negligently *adv* negligentemente; con indiferencia

negligible *a* insignificante, escaso, insuficiente; sin importancia, desdeñable

negotiable *a* negociable; (of a road) practicable, transitable

negotiate *vt* gestionar, agenciar, tratar; (a bend) tomar; (an obstacle) salvar, franquear; *vi* negociar. **to n. a bill of exchange,** descontar una letra de cambio. **to n. for a contract,** tratar un contrato

negotiation *n* negociación, *f; com* gestión, transacción, *f;* (of a bend) toma, *f,* (of an obstacle) salto, *m*

negotiator *n* negociador (-ra)

neigh *vi* relinchar. *n* relincho, relinchido, *m*

neighbor *n* vecino (-na); (biblical) prójimo (-ma)

neighborhood *n* vecindad, *f,* vecindario, *m;* cercanía, *f,*

afueras, *f pl,* alrededores, *m pl; a* de barrio (e.g. **neighborhood moviehouse,** cine del barrio)

neighboring *a* vecino; cercano, inmediato, adyacente

neighborliness *n* buena vecindad, *f*

neighborly *a* amistoso, sociable, bondadoso. **to be n.,** ser de buena vecindad.

neither *a* ningún; ninguno de los dos, e.g. **N. explanation is right,** Ninguna de las dos explicaciones es correcta. *conjunc* ni, tampoco, e.g. **N. Mary nor John,** Ni María ni Juan. **N. will he give it to her,** Tampoco se lo dará. *pron* ni uno ni otro, ninguno, e.g. **N. of them heard it,** Ni uno ni otro lo oyó.

nemesis *n* némesis, *f;* justicia, *f*

nenuphar *n bot* nenúfar, *m*

neo- *prefix* neo. **neo-Catholic,** *a* and *n* neo-católico (-ca). **neo-Platonic,** neoplatónico. **neo-Platonism,** neoplatonismo, *m*

neolithic *a* neolítico

neologism *n* neologismo, *m*

neon *n chem* neón, *m*

neon sign anuncio luminoso, *m*

neophyte *n* neófito (-ta); aspirante, *mf*

nephew *n* sobrino, *m*

nephritis *n med* nefritis, *f*

nepotism *n* nepotismo, *m*

nerve *n* (*anat bot*) nervio, *m;* valor, ánimo, *m;* vitalidad, *f; inf* descaro, *m,* desvergüenza, frescura, *f. vt* animar, alentar, envalentonar; esforzar; dar fuerza (a). *vi* animarse, esforzarse (a). **My nerves are all on edge,** Se me crispan los nervios. **n.-cell,** neurona, *f.* **to lose one's n.,** perder la cabeza; perder los nervios. **to strain every n.,** hacer un esfuerzo supremo. **n. center,** centro nervioso, *m.* **n.-racking,** espantoso, horripilante. **n. strain,** tensión nerviosa, *f*

nerveless *a* sin nervio; enervado

nerviness *n* nervosidad, *f*

nervous *a* nervioso, asustadizo, tímido; agitado, excitado; (of style) vigoroso. **n. breakdown,** crisis nerviosa, *f.* **n. system,** sistema nervioso, *m*

nervously *adv* nerviosamente; tímidamente

nervousness *n* nervosidad, timidez, *f;* agitación, *f;* (of style) vigor, *m;* energía, *f*

nervy *a* nervioso

nest *vi* anidar, hacerse un nido. *n* (bird's) nido, *m;* (animal's) madriguera, *f;* (of drawers) juego, *m,* serie, *f;* (of thieves) cueva, guarida, *f; inf* casita, *f,* hogar, *m.* **to feather one's n.,** hacer su agosto. **n.-egg,** *fig* nidal, *m.* **n. of eggs,** nidada de huevos, *f*

nestle *vt* apoyar. *vi* apiñarse, hacerse un ovillo. **to n. up to a person,** apretarse contra

nestling *n* pichón, pollo, *m;* pajarito, *m*

net *vt* coger con redes; obtener, coger; cubrir con redes. *vi* hacer redes. *n* red, *f;* (mesh) malla, *f;* (fabric) tul, *m.* **net making,** manufactura de redes, *f*

net *a com* líquido, neto, limpio; (of fabric) de tul. **net amount,** importe líquido, importe neto, *m.* **net balance,** saldo líquido, *m.* **net cost,** precio neto, *m.* **net profit,** beneficio neto (or líquido), *m*

nether *a* inferior, bajero, más bajo. **n. regions,** infierno, *m*

Netherland *a* neerlandés, holandés

Netherlander *n* neerlandés (-esa), holandés (-esa)

Netherlands, the *n* los Países Bajos *m pl*

nethermost *a* lo más bajo, ínfimo, más hondo

netting *n* red, (obra de) malla, *f;* *naut* jareta, *f;* manufactura de redes, *f;* pesca con redes, *f.* **wire-n.,** tela metálica, malla de alambre, *f*

nettle *vt* picar; *fig* irritar, picar, fastidiar, disgustar. *n* ortiga, *f.* **n.-rash,** urticaria, *f*

network *n* red, malla, randa, *f;* (of communications) sistema, *m,* red, *f*

neuralgia *n* neuralgia, *f*

neuralgic *a* neurálgico

neurasthenia *n* neurastenia, *f*

neurasthenic *a* and *n* neurasténico (-ca)

neuritis *n* neuritis, *f*

neurologist *n* neurólogo, *m*
neurology *n* neurología, *f*
neuropath *n* neurópata, *m*
neuropathic *a* neuropático
neurosis *n* neurosis, *f*
neurosurgeon *n* neurocirujano, *m*
neurotic *a* and *n* neurótico (-ca)
neuter *a* neutro; (of verbs) intransitivo; (*zool bot*) sin sexo
neutral *a* neutral; (*chem mech*) neutro; (of colors) indeciso, indeterminado; (of persons) imparcial, indiferente. *n* neutral, *mf mech* **to go into n.**, pasar a marcha neutra
neutrality *n* neutralidad, *f*; indiferencia, *f*; imparcialidad, *f*
neutralization *n* neutralización, *f*
neutralize *vt* neutralizar
never *adv* nunca, jamás; de ningún modo, no; ni aun, ni siquiera. **Better late than n.**, Más vale tarde que nunca. **Never look a gift horse in the mouth,** A caballo regalado no se le mira el diente. **Were the hour n.** so late, Por más tarde que fuese la hora. **n. again,** nunca jamás. **n. a one,** ni siquiera uno. **n. a whit,** ni pizca. **N. mind!** ¡No importa! ¡No te preocupes! ¡No hagas caso! **n.-ceasing,** continuo, incesante. **n.-ending,** inacabable, eterno, sin fin. **n.-failing,** infalible. **n.-to-be-forgotten,** inolvidable
nevermore *adv* nunca jamás
nevertheless *adv* sin embargo, no obstante, con todo
new *a* nuevo; novel, fresco; distinto, diferente; moderno; (inexperienced) novato, no habituado; reciente. *adv* (in compounds) recién. **as good as new,** como nuevo. **brand-new,** flamante, nuevecito. **new-born,** recién nacido. **new-comer,** recién llegado (-da). **new-fashioned,** de última moda. **new-found,** recién hallado. **new-laid egg,** huevo fresco, *m*. **new moon,** luna nueva, *f*, novilunio, *m*. **new rich,** ricacho (-cha); indio, *m*. **new student,** alumno de nuevo ingreso. **New Testament,** Nuevo Testamento, *m*. **New World,** Nuevo Mundo, *m*. **New York (er),** *a* and *n* neoyorquino (-na). **New Zealand(er),** *a* and *n* neozelandés (-esa)
newel *n* (of stair) alma, *f*, árbol, nabo, *m*. **n.-post,** pilarote (de escalera), *m*
newest *a sup* novísimo; más reciente
Newfoundland Terranova, *f*. **N. dog,** perro de Terranova, *m*
New Guinea Nueva Guinea, *f*
newish *a* bastante nuevo
newly *adv* nuevamente; hace poco, recientemente. The abb. form **recién** is used only with past part, e.g. **the n. painted door,** la puerta recién pintada. **the n.-weds,** los desposados, los recién casados
newness *n* novedad, *f*; inexperiencia, falta de práctica, *f*; innovación, *f*
New Orleans Nueva Orleans, *f*
news *n pl* noticias, *f pl*; nueva, *f*; reporte, aviso, *m*; novedad, *f*. **No n. is good n.,** Falta de noticias, buena señal. **piece of n.,** noticia, *f*. **What's the n.?** ¿Qué hay de nuevo? **n. agency,** agencia de noticias, agencia periodística, *f*. **n.-agent,** agente de la prensa, *m*; vendedor (-ra) de periódicos. **n. bulletin,** *rad* boletín de noticias, *m*. *inf* **n.-hound,** gacetillero (-ra). **n. item,** noticia de actualidad, *f*. **n.-print,** papel para periódicos, *m*. **n.-room,** gabinete de lectura, *m*. **n. reel,** película noticiera, revista cinematográfica, *f*, noticiario cinematográfico, noticiero *m*, actualidades, *f pl*. **n.-stand,** puesto de periódicos, quiosco de periódicos, *m*. **n. theater,** cine de actualidades, *m*
newscast *n* noticiario, *m*
newsletter *n* noticiera, relación de sucesos, *f*
New South Wales La Nueva Gales del Sur, *f*
newspaper *n* periódico, diario, noticiero, *m*. **n. clipping, n. cutting,** recorte de periódico, *m*. **n. paragraph,** suelto, *m*. **n. reporter,** reportero (-ra); periodista, *mf* **n. reporting,** reporterismo, *m*. **n. serial,**

folletín, *m*, novela por entregas, *f*. **n. vendor,** vendedor (-ra) de periódicos, *n*
news report *n* reportaje, *m*
newsy *a inf* lleno de noticias, noticioso
newt *n* tritón, *m*
Newtonian *a* neutoniano
New York Nueva York, *f*
New Zealand Nueva Zelandia, *f*
next *a* (of place) siguiente, vecino, contiguo; (of time) próximo, siguiente. **on the n. page,** en la página siguiente. **the n. day,** el día siguiente. **the n.-door house,** la casa vecina. **the n. life,** la otra vida. **n. month (yesar),** el mes (año) próximo (or que viene). **n. time,** otra vez, la próxima vez
next *adv* (of time) luego, en seguida; (of place) inmediatamente después. **I come n.,** Ahora me toca a mí. **It is n. to a certainty that . . . ,** Es casi seguro que . . . **the n. best,** el segundo. **the n. of kin,** los pariente más cercaro, *m*, parientes más cercanos, *m pl*. **to wear n. to the skin,** llevar sobre la piel. **n. to,** al lado de, junto a; primero después de; casi. **n. to nothing,** casi nada, muy poco. **What n.?** ¿Qué más?; ¿Y ahora qué?
nib *n* punto, tajo (de una pluma), *m*
nibble *vt* mordiscar, mordisquear, roer; (horses) rozar; (fish) picar; *fig* considerar, tantear; *vi* picar. *n* mordisco, *m*; roedura, *f*
Nicaraguan *a* and *n* nicaragüeño (-ña)
Nice Niza, *f*
nice *a* escrupuloso, minucioso, exacto; (of persons) simpático, afable, amable; fino; (of things) agradable, bonito; bueno; sutil, delicado; (*inf iron*) bonito. **a n. point,** un punto delicado. **a n. view,** una vista agradable (or bonita). **n.-looking,** guapo. **n. people,** gente fina, *f*; gente simpática, *f*
nicely *adv* muy bien; con elegancia; primorosamente; con amabilidad, gentilmente; agradablemente
Nicene *a* niceno
niceness *n* exactitud, minuciosidad, *f*; (of persons) bondad, amabilidad, *f*; amenidad, hermosura, *f*; lo bonito; sutileza, *f*; refinamiento, *m*
nicety *n* exactitud, *f*; sutileza, *f*, refinamiento, *m*. **niceties,** *n pl* detalles, *m pl*. **to a n.,** con la mayor precisión; a la perfección
niche *n* nicho, templete, *m*; (vaulted) hornacina, *f*, *fig* **to find a n. for oneself,** encontrarse una buena posición; situarse
nick *vt* cortar en muescas, mellar, tarjar. *n* mella, muesca, *f*. **n. in the n. of time,** en el momento oportuno, a tiempo
nickel *n* níquel, *m*; *com* moneda de níquel, *f*. **n.-plated,** niquelado
nickname *vt* apodar, motejar, apellidar. *n* apodo, sobrenombre, mote, mal nombre, *m*
nicotine *n* nicotina, *f*
nicotinism *n* nicotismo, *m*
nictitating membrane *n anat* membrana nictitante, *f*
niece *n* sobrina, *f*
niggardliness *n* tacañería, avaricia, parsimonia, mezquindad, *f*
niggardly *a* tacaño, avaricioso, mezquino, ruin, miserable
niggling *vt* nimio, meticuloso; escrupuloso, minucioso
nigh. See **near**
night *n* noche, *f*; *fig* oscuridad, *f*, tinieblas, *f pl*. **all n.,** toda la noche, la noche entera. **all n. service,** servicio nocturno permanente, *m*. **at** or **by n.,** de noche. **every n.,** todas las noches, cada noche. **Good n.!** ¡Buenas noches! **last n.,** ayer por la noche, anoche, la noche pasada. **restless n.,** noche mala, noche toledana, *f*. **the n. before last,** anteayer por la noche, *m*. **to-n.,** esta noche. **tomorrow n.,** mañana por la noche. **to be n.,** ser de noche. **to spend the n.,** pernoctar, pasar la noche. **n.-bird,** pájaro nocturno, *m*; *inf* trasnochador (-ra). **n.-blindness,** nictalopia, *f*. **n.-cap,** gorro de dormir, *m*. **n. clothes,** traje de dormir, *m*. **n. club,** cabaré *m*. **n. dew,** relente, sereno, *m*. **n. flying,** vuelo noc-

turno, *m*. **n.-jar,** *orn* chotacabras, *m*. **n.-light,** mariposa, lamparilla, *f*. **n. mail,** último correo, *m*; tren correo de la noche, *m*. **n. school,** escuela nocturna, *f*. **n. shift,** turno de noche, *m*. **n. watch,** ronda de noche, *f*; *naut* sonochada, *f*. **n. watchman,** (in the street) sereno, *m*; (of a building) vigilante nocturno, *m*
nightfall *n* anochecer, crepúsculo, atardecer, *m*
nightgown *n* camisa de noche, *f*
nightingale *n* ruiseñor, *m*
nightly *a* de noche; nocturno, nocturnal. *adv* todas las noches, cada noche
nightmare *n* pesadilla, *f*
nightmarish *a* de pesadilla, horrible
nightshade *n* *bot* hierba mora, *f*, solano, *m*
nihilism *n* nihilismo, *m*
nihilist *n* nihilista, *mf*
Nile, the el Nilo, *m*
nimble *a* ágil, activo; vivo, listo. **n.-fingered,** ligero de dedos. **n.-witted,** despierto, vivo
nimbleness *n* agilidad, actividad, *f*; viveza, habilidad, *f*
nimbly *adv* ágilmente, ligeramente
nimbus *n* nimbo, *m*, aureola, *f*
nincompoop *n* papirote, *m*, papanatas, *mf* tonto (-ta)
nine *a* and *n* nueve, *m*. **He is n.,** Tiene nueve años. **the N.,** las nueve Musas. **n. o'clock,** las nueve. **to be dressed up to the nines,** estar hecho un brazo de mar
ninefold *a* and *adv* nueve veces
ninepins *n* juego de bolos, *m*
nineteen *a* and *n* diez y nueve, diecinueve *m*
nineteenth *a* décimonono. *n* (of month) el diez y nueve; (of monarchs) diez y nueve. **the n. century,** el siglo diez y nueve
ninetieth *a* nonagésimo, noventa
ninety *a* and *n* noventa *m*. **n.-one,** noventa y uno. **n.-two,** noventa y dos. **the n.-first chapter,** el capítulo noventa y uno
ninny *n* parapoco, chancleta, *mf*; mentecato (-ta)
ninth *a* noveno, nono. *n* nueve, *m*; (of the month) el nueve (of sovereigns) nono. **one n.,** un noveno
ninthly *adv* en noveno (or nono) lugar
nip *vt* pellizcar, pinchar; mordiscar, morder; (wither) marchitar; (freeze) helar; (run) correr. *vi* pinchar; picar (el viento). *n* pellizco, pinchazo, *m*; mordisco, *m*; (of spirits) trago, *m*; copita, *f*; (in the air) viento frío, hielo, *m*. **to nip in,** colarse dentro, deslizarse en. **to nip off,** pirarse, mudarse. *fig* **to nip in the bud,** cortar en flor
nippers *n pl* alicates, *m pl*; tenacillas, pinzas, *f pl*
nipping *n* pinchadura, *f*; mordedura, *f*. *a* punzante; helado, glacial, mordiente. **n. off,** (of a point) despuntadura, *f*
nipple *n* pezón, *m*; pezón artificial, *m*
nit *n* *ent* liendre, *f*
nitrate *n* *chem* nitrato, *m*
nitre *n* salitre, *m*
nitric *a* nítrico
nitrite *n* *chem* nitrito, *m*
nitro- *prefix chem* nitro. **n.-cellulose,** algodón pólvora, *m*. **n.-glycerine,** nitroglicerina, *f*
nitrogen *n* *chem* nitrógeno, *m*
nitrous *a* nitroso, salitral
no *a* ningún, ninguno, ninguna, e.g. **by no means,** de ningún modo. **No** is often not translated in Sp., e.g. **I have no time,** No tengo tiempo. *adv* no. *n* voto negativo, no, *m*. **to be of no account,** no tener importancia; no significar nada. **to be no good for,** no servir para. **to be of no use,** ser inútil. **to have no connection with,** no tener nada que ver con. **for no reason,** sin motivo alguno. **"No Admittance,"** «Entrada Prohibida.» **no, indeed,** Cierto que no. **no-man's land,** tierra de nadie, *f*. **no more,** no más. **No more of this!** ¡No hablemos más de eso! **no one,** nadie, ninguno. **no sooner,** no bien, tan pronto (como). **no such thing,** no tal. **"No Thoroughfare,"** «Prohibido el Paso.» **whether or not,** sea o no sea
Noah's Ark *n* arca de Noé, *f*

nobility *n* nobleza, *f*; (of rank) aristocracia, nobleza, *f*; (of conduct) caballerosidad, hidalguía, generosidad, bondad, *f*; (grandeur) grandeza, sublimidad, *f*. **the higher n.,** los nobles de primera clase
noble *a* noble; (in rank) aristocrático, noble, linajudo; (of conduct) caballeroso, generoso; (of buildings) sublime, magnífico. *n* noble, *m*, aristócrata, *mf* **to make n.,** ennoblecer. **n.-mindedness,** generosidad, grandeza de alma, *f*. **n. title,** título de nobleza, título del reino, *m*
noblewoman *n* dama noble, mujer noble, aristócrata, *f*
nobly *adv* noblemente, generosamente. **n. born,** noble de nacimiento
nobody *n* nadie, ninguno. **There was n. there,** No había nadie allí. *inf* **a n.,** un (una) cualquiera, una persona insignificante. **n. else,** nadie más, ningún otro
nocturnal *a* nocturno, nocherniego, nocturnal
nocturne *n* *mus* nocturno, *m*
nod *vt* inclinar la cabeza; hacer una señal (or señas) con la cabeza; *vi* dar cabezadas; cabecear; (of trees) mecerse, inclinarse; inclinar la cabeza. *n* señal (or seña) con la cabeza, *f*; inclinación de la cabeza, *f*; cabeceo, *m*, cabezada, *f*. **A nod is as good as a wink,** A buen entendedor pocas palabras. **He nodded to me as he passed,** Me saludó con la cabeza al pasar. **He signed to me with a nod,** Me hizo una señal con la cabeza
nodding *a* que cabecea; *bot* colgante, inclinado; temblante. *n* cabeceo, *m*; saludo con la cabeza, *m*
noddle *n* mollera, *f*
node *n* (*bot med*) nudo, *m*
nodule *n* nódulo, *m*; nudillo, *m*
noise *n* ruido, son, *m*; tumulto, clamor, estruendo, alboroto, *m*. **to make a n.,** hacer ruido. **to n. abroad,** divulgar, publicar
noiseless *a* silencioso, callado, sin ruido
noiselessness *n* silencio, *m*, falta de ruido, *f*
noisily *adv* ruidosamente
noisiness *n* ruido, estrépito, tumulto, clamor, *m*; (of voices) gritería, *f*
noisome *a* ofensivo; fétido, apestoso
noisy *a* ruidoso; estruendoso; estrepitoso, clamoroso
nomad *a* nómada, errante; (of flocks) trashumante. *n* nómada, *mf*
nomadism *n* nomadismo, *m*
nomenclature *n* nomenclatura, *f*
nominal *a* nominal; titular; insignificante, de poca importancia. **the n. head,** el director en nombre
nominalism *n* nominalismo, *m*
nominalist *a* and *n* nominalista *mf*
nominally *adv* nominalmente, en nombre
nominate *vt* nombrar, designar, elegir; fijar, señalar
nominating *a* nominador
nomination *n* nombramiento, *m*, nominación, *f*; señalamiento, *m*
nominator *n* nominador (-ra)
nominee *n* nómino propuesto, *m*
non *adv* non; des-; in-; falta de. **non-acceptance,** rechazo, *m*. **non-acquaintance,** ignorancia, *f*. **non-admission,** no admisión, *f*; denegación, *f*, rechazo, *m*. **non-aggression,** no agresión, *f*. **non-alcoholic,** no alcohólico. **non-appearance,** ausencia, *f*; *law* no comparecencia, contumacia, *f*. **non-arrival,** ausencia, *f*; falta de recibo, *f*. **non-attendance,** falta de asistencia, ausencia, *f*. **non-carbonated,** sin gas. **non-combatant,** no combatiente, *m*. **non-commissioned officer,** oficial subalterno, *m*. **non-committal,** evasivo, equívoco, ambiguo. **non-compliance,** falta de obediencia, *f*. **non-concurrence,** falta de acuerdo, *f*. **non-conducting,** no conductivo. **non-conductor,** mal conductor, *m*; *elec* aislador, *m*. **non-contagious,** no contagioso. **non-cooperation,** *pol* resistencia pasiva, *f*; no cooperación, *f*. **non-delivery,** falta de entrega, *f*. **non-essential,** no esencial, prescindible. **non-execution,** no cumplimiento, *m*. **non-existence,** no existencia, *f*. **non-existent,** inexistente, no existente. **non-intervention,** no intervención, *f*. **non-manu-**

facturing, no industrial. **non-member,** visitante, *mf*
non-observance, incumplimiento, *m;* violación, *f.*
non-payment, falta de pago, *f.* **non-performance,**
falta de ejecución, *f.* **non-poisonous,** no venenoso,
innocuo. **non-resistance,** falta de resistencia, *f;* obediencia pasiva, *f.* **non-skid,** antideslizante, antirres-
baladizo. **non-smoking,** que no fuma; (of a railway
compartment, etc.) para no fumadores. **non-stop,**
continuo, incesante; directo, sin parar; *aer* sin escalas
nonagenarian *a* and *n* nonagenario (-ia)
non-aligned *a* no abanderado
non-alignment *n* no abanderamiento *m*
nonce word *n* palabra ocasional, *f*
nonchalance *n* aplomo, *m,* indiferencia, frialdad,
calma, *f*
nonchalant *a* indiferente, frío, impasible
nonchalantly *adv* con indiferencia
nonconformist *a* and *n* disidente *mf; a* inconforme, *n,*
inconformista, *mf*
nonconformity *n* disidencia, *f*
nondescript *a* indeterminado, indefinido, indeciso,
mediocre
none *pron* nadie, ninguno; nada. *a* and *n* ninguno (-na).
adv no; de ningún modo, de ninguna manera. **I have
n.,** No lo tengo, No tengo ninguno. **We have n. of
your things,** No tenemos ninguna de tus cosas. **I was
n. the worse,** No me hallaba peor. **N. can read his
account with pleasure,** Nadie puede leer su narración con gusto. **n. the less,** no menos; sin embargo
nonentity *n* persona sin importancia, medianía, *f,*
cero, *m*
nones *n pl ecc* nona, *f;* (Roman Calendar) nonas, *f pl,*
nonplussed *a* cortado, perplejo, confuso
non-profit *a* sin fines de lucro, sin fines lucrativos
non-self-governing *a* no autónomo
nonsense *n* disparate, despropósito, desatino, *m,* absurdidad, *f; inf* galimatías, *m;* pamplina, patraña, *f.* **to talk
n.,** hablar sin ton ni son. **N.!** ¡A otro perro con este
hueso! ¡Patrañas!
nonsensical *a* absurdo, ridículo, disparatado
noodle *n cul* tallarín, *m; inf* mentecato (-ta), bobo (-ba)
nook *n* escondrijo, lugar retirado, rincón, *m*
noon *n* mediodía, *m; fig* punto culminante, apogeo, *m,*
a de mediodía, meridional. **at n.,** a mediodía
noose *vt* coger con lazos. *n* lazo corredizo, dogal, *m*
nopal *n bot* nopal, *m*
No Parking «Se Prohibe Estacionar,» «Se Prohibe Esta-
cionarse»
nor *conjunc* ni, no, tampoco. **He removed neither his
coat nor his hat,** No se quitó ni el gabán ni el sombrero. **Nor was this the first time,** Y no fue ésta la
primera vez. **Nor I,** Ni yo tampoco
Nordic *a* and *n* nórdico (-ca)
norm *n* modelo, *m,* norma, regla, pauta, *f;* (of size)
marca, *f; (bot zool)* tipo, *m*
normal *a* normal; común, natural, corriente, regular;
math perpendicular, normal. *n* condición normal, *f,* estado normal, *m; math* normal, *f.* **to become n.,** nor-
malizarse, hacerse normal. **to make n.,** normalizar. **n.
school,** escuela normal, *f*
normality *n* normalidad, *f*
normalization *n* normalización, *f*
normalize *vt* normalizar
normally *adv* normalmente
Norman *a* and *n* normando (-da)
Normandy Normandía, *f*
Norse *n* noruego (language), *m, a* escandinavo
Norseman *n* normando, viking (*pl* -os), hombre del
norte, *m*
north *n* norte, *m. a* del norte, septentrional. **n. by west,**
norte, cuarta noroeste. **n. of the city,** al norte de la
ciudad. **N.-American,** del norte norte-americano (-na).
n.-east, *a* and *n* nordeste *m.* **n.-easter,** viento del nordeste, *m.* **n.-easterly,** del nordeste (winds). **n.-east-
ern,** del nordeste (places). **n.-eastward,** hacia el
nordeste. **n.-n.-east,** nornordeste, *m.* **n.-n.-west,**

nornorueste, *m.* **n.-polar,** ártico. **N. Star,** estrella del
norte, estrella polar, *f.* **n.-west,** noroeste, *m.*
n.-wester, viento del noroeste, *m.* **n.-westerly,** del
noroeste (winds). **n.-westerly gale,** temporal del
noroeste, *m.* **n.-western,** del noroeste; situado al
noroeste. **n.-westwards,** hacia el noroeste. **n. wind,**
el viento del norte, el cierzo
North America, Norteamérica, América del Norte, *f*
northern *a* del norte, septentrional, norteño; (of races)
nórdico. **N. Cross,** crucero, *m.* **n. lights,** aurora boreal, *f*
northerner *n* hombre del norte, *m,* habitante del
norte, *mf*
northernmost *a sup* al extremo norte, más septentrional
northwards *adv* hacia el norte
Norway Noruega, *f*
Norwegian *a* and *n* noruego (-ga); (language) noruego, *m*
nose *n* nariz, *f;* (of animals) hocico, *m;* (sense of smell)
olfato, *m;* (of ships) proa, *f;* (of jug) pico, *m,* boca, *f;*
(projecting piece) cuerno, *m,* nariz, *f;* (of airplane)
cabeza, *f, vt* acariciar con la nariz; avanzar lentamente.
vi husmear, olfatear. **to n. into,** *inf* meter las narices,
poner baza. **to n. out,** descubrir, averiguar. **to bleed
at the n.,** echar sangre por las narices. **to blow one's
n.,** sonar (o limpiarse) las narices. **to keep one's n.
to the grindstone,** estar sobre el yunque, batir el
cobre. *fig* **to lead by the n.,** tener a uno agarrado por
las narices. **to pay through the n.,** costar un ojo de la
cara. **to speak through the n.,** ganguear. **to turn up
one's n.,** *fig* hacer gestos (a), volver la cara. **flat n.,**
nariz chata, *f.* **snub n.,** nariz respingona, *f.* **well-
shaped n.,** nariz perfilada, *f.* **under one's n.,** bajo las
narices de uno. **n.-bag,** cebadera, mochila, *f;* morral,
m. **n.-bleeding,** *med* epistaxis, *f;* hemorragia de las narices, *f.* **n.-dive,** *aer* descenso de cabeza, picado, *m. vi*
picar. **n.-piece,** (of microscope) ocular, *m.* **n.-ring,** (of
a bull, etc.) narigón, *m*
-nosed *a* de nariz . . . , con la nariz . . .
nosegay *n* ramillete, *m*
nosey Parker *n inf* mequetrefe, *m;* cócora, *mf*
No Smoking «Prohibido Fumar», Se Prohibe Fumar
nostalgia *n* nostalgia, añoranza, *f*
nostalgic *a* nostálgico
nostril *n* ventana de la nariz, *f, n pl* **nostrils,** narices, *f pl*
nostrum *n* panacea, *f,* curalotodo, *m;* medicina paten-
tada, *f*
not *adv* no; sin; ni, ni siquiera. **Is it not true? We
think not,** ¿No es verdad? No lo creemos. **You have
seen Mary, have you not?** Vd. ha visto a María,
¿verdad? **not caring whether he came or not,** sin
preocuparse de que viniese o no. **not that he will
come,** no es decir que venga. **not at all,** de ningún
modo; (courtesy) ¡de nada! **not even,** ni siquiera. **not
guilty,** no culpable. **not one,** ni uno. **not so much as,**
no tanto como; ni siquiera. **It is not so much that, as
it is . . .** No es tanto eso, cuanto que . . . **not to say,** por
no decir
notability *n* notabilidad, *f;* (person) notable, *mf* persona de importancia, *f*
notable *a* notable, señalado, memorable; digno de
atención, *n* persona eminente, *f,* notable, *mf*
notably *adv* notablemente, señaladamente
notary *n* notario, escribano, *m*
notation *n* notación, *f*
notch *vt* cortar muescas (en); mellar, ranurar, entallar.
n muesca, mella, ranura, *f,* entalladura, *f*
note *vt* notar, observar; anotar, apuntar; advertir; hacerse cuenta de. *n mus* nota, *f;* son, acento, *m;* (letter)
recado, billete, *m;* anotación, glosa, *f;* apuntación, *f,*
apunte, *m,* nota, *f;* (importance) importancia, distinción, *f; com* vale, abonaré, *m;* (sign) marca, señal, *f.* **to
n. down,** anotar. **worthy of note,** digno de atención.
n.-book, libro de apuntes, cuaderno, *m,* libreta, *f.*
n.-case, cartera, *f, com* **n. of hand,** pagaré, *m.*

n.-paper, papel de escribir, *m.* **n.-taker,** apuntador (-ra)

noted *a* célebre, famoso, ilustre, eminente, insigne

noteworthy *a* digno de nota, notable, digno de atención

nothing *n* nada, *f;* la nada; cero, *m. adv* en nada. **to come to n.,** anonadarse, fracasar. **to do n.,** no hacer nada. **to do n. but,** no hacer más que. **to have n. to do with,** no tener nada que ver con; *inf* no tener arte ni parte en. **There is n. else to do,** No hay nada más que hacer; No hay más remedio. **There is n. to fear,** No hay de que tener miedo. **We could make n. of the book,** No llegamos a comprender el libro. **for n.,** de balde, en vano; gratis. **next to n.,** casi nada. **n. else or more,** nada más. **n. like,** ni con mucho. **n. much,** poca cosa. **n. new,** nada nuevo. **n. similar,** nada semejante. **n. to speak of,** poca cosa

nothingness *n* nada, *f*

notice *vt* observar, reparar en, darse cuenta (de), marcar, caer en la cuenta (de), fijarse (en). *n* observación, atención, *f;* aviso, *m,* notificación, *f;* anuncio, *m;* (term) plazo, *m;* (review) crítica, *f.* **at short n.,** a corto aviso. **until further n.,** hasta nuevo aviso (or orden). **to attract n.,** atraer la atención. **I hadn't noticed,** No me había fijado. **to be beneath one's n.,** no merecer su atención. **to be under n.,** estar dimitido. **to bring to the n. of,** dar noticia de. **to escape n.,** pasar desapercibido. **to give n.,** hacer saber, informar; (of employer) despedir (a); (of employee) dimitir, dar la dimisión. **to take n. of,** notar, darse cuenta de; hacer caso, atender (a). **n. board,** letrero, tablero de anuncios, *m.* **n. to quit,** desahúcio, *m*

noticeable *a* perceptible, evidente; digno de observación, notable

noticeably *adv* perceptiblemente; notablemente

notifiable *a* declarable, notificable

notification *n* notificación, intimación, advertencia, *f,* aviso, *m*

notify *vt* notificar, comunicar, avisar, intimar, hacer saber

notion *n* noción, idea, *f,* concepto, *m;* (view) opinión, *f,* parecer, *m;* (novelty) novedad, *f;* artículo de fantasía, *m.* **I have a n. that . . . ,** Tengo la idea de que . . . , Sospecho que . . . **I haven't a n.,** No tengo idea

No Tipping «No Se Admiten Propinas»

notoriety *n* notoriedad, publicidad, *f;* escándalo, *m;* persona notoria, *f*

notorious *a* notorio, famoso, conocido; escandaloso, sensacional

notoriously *adv* notoriamente

notwithstanding *prep* a pesar de. *adv* sin embargo, no obstante. *conjunc* aunque, bien que, por más que

nougat *n* turrón, *m*

nought *n math* cero, *m;* nada, *f*

noun *n* substantivo, nombre, *m*

nourish *vt* sustentar, alimentar, nutrir; *fig* fomentar, favorecer

nourishing *a* nutritivo, alimenticio, nutricio

nourishment *n* nutrición, *f;* sustento, *m;* alimento, *m; fig* fomento, pasto, *m*

Nova Scotia Nueva Escocia, *f*

novel *a* nuevo, original, inacostumbrado. *n* novela, *f.* **n. of roguery,** novela picaresca, *f*

novelette *n* novela corta, *f*

novelist *n* novelista, *mf*

novelty *n* novedad, *f;* innovación, *f;* cambio, *m*

November *n* noviembre, *m*

novice *n ecc* novicio (-ia); comenzante, principiante, *mf,* aspirante, *m*

novocain *n med* novocaína, *f*

now *adv* ahora, actualmente, al presente, a la fecha; en seguida, ahora, inmediatamente; poco ha, hace poco; pues bien. *interj* ¡A ver! ¡Vamos! *conjunc* pero, mas. *n* presente, *m,* actualidad, *f.* **before now,** antes, en otras ocasiones, ya, previamente. **just now,** ahora mismo,

hace poco. **now . . . now,** ya . . . ya; sucesivamente, en turno. **now and then,** de vez en cuando, de tarde en tarde. **now that,** ya que, ahora que, dado que. **until now,** hasta el presente, hasta aquí, hasta ahora

nowadays *adv* hoy en día, actualmente, en nuestros días

nowhere *adv* en ninguna parte. **in the middle of n.,** donde Cristo dio las tres voces. **n. else,** en ninguna otra parte. *inf* **n. near,** ni con mucho; muy lejos (de)

nowise *adv* de ningún modo, en modo alguno, de ninguna manera

noxious *a* dañoso, nocivo; pestífero

noxiousness *n* nocividad, *f*

nozzle *n* (of a hose-pipe) boquilla, *f; mech* gollete, *m;* tubo de salida, *m,* tobera, *f;* inyector, *m*

n.p. (no place) s.l. (sin lugar)

nuance *n* matiz, *m,* gradación, sombra, *f*

nubile *a* núbil

nuclear *a* nuclear

nucleus *n* núcleo, *m;* centro, foco, *m*

nude *a* desnudo, nudo

nudge *vt* dar un codazo (a). *n* codazo, *m*

nudism *n* nudismo, *m*

nudist *n* nudista, *mf*

nudity *n* desnudez, *f*

nugget *n min* pepita, *f*

nuisance *n* molestia, incomodidad, *f,* fastidio, *m; inf* tostón, *m,* lata, *f.* **to make a n. of oneself,** meterse donde no le llaman, ser un pelmazo. **What a n.!** ¡Qué lata! ¡Qué fastidio!

null *a* nulo, inválido, sin fuerza legal. **n. and void,** nulo, írrito

nullification *n* anulación, invalidación, *f*

nullity *n* nulidad, *f*

numb *vt* entumecer, entorpecer. *a* entumecido; torpe, dormido; paralizado; *fig* insensible, pasmado. **n. with cold,** entumecido de frío

number *vt* numerar, contar; poner número (a); (pages of a book) foliar; ascender a. *n* número, *m;* (figure) cifra, *f;* (crowd) multitud, muchedumbre, *f;* cantidad, *f;* (of a periodical) ejemplar, *m; gram* número, *m; pl* versos, *m pl.* **Numbers,** (Bible) Números, *m pl;* **to be numbered among,** figurar entre. **among the n. of,** entre la muchedumbre de. **a n. of,** varios, muchos, una cantidad de. **in great n.,** en gran número; en su mayoría. **6 Peace Street,** Calle de la Paz nº (número) 6. **one of their n.,** uno entre ellos. **n. board,** (racing) indicador, *m.* **n. plate,** *aut* chapa de identidad, placa de número, *f*

numbering *n* numeración, *f*

numberless *a* innumerable, sin número, sin fin, infinito

numbness *n* entumecimiento, entorpecimiento, *m; fig* insensibilidad, *f*

numeral *a* numeral. *n* número, *m,* cifra, *f; gram* nombre o adjetivo numeral, *m*

numerator *n* numerador

numerical *a* numérico

numerous *a* numeroso; nutrido, grande; muchos (-as)

numerousness *n* numerosidad, multitud, muchedumbre, *f*

numismatic *a* numismático. *n pl* **numismatics,** numismática, *f*

numismatist *n* numismático, *m*

numskull *n* zote, topo, *m*

nun *n* monja, religiosa, *f.* **to become a nun,** profesar, tomar el hábito, meterse monja

nuncio *n* nuncio, *m.* **acting n.,** pronuncio, *m*

nunnery *n* convento de monjas, *m*

nuptial *a* nupcial. *n pl* **nuptials,** nupcias, *f pl,* enlace, *m.* **n. mass,** *ecc* misa de velaciones, *f.* **n. song,** epitalamio, *m*

nurse *vt* criar; dar de mamar (a), amamantar; (the sick) cuidar, asistir; (fondle) acariciar, mecer; *fig* fomentar, promover. *vi* trabajar como enfermera. *n* (of the sick) enfermera, *f;* (wet) nodriza, ama de leche, *f;* (children's) niñera, *f; fig* fomentador, *m.* **male n.,** enfermero, *m*

nursery *n agr* plantel, vivero semillero, criadero, *m;* (children's room) cuarto de los niños, *m; fig* sementera, *f;* semillero, *m.* **n. governess,** aya, *f.* **n. rhyme,** canción infantil, *f*

nurseryman *n* horticultor, *m;* jardinero, *m*

nursing *n* lactancia, crianza, *f;* (of the sick) asistencia, *f,* cuido, *m.* **n. home,** clínica, *f.* **n. mother,** madre lactante, *f*

nurture *vt* alimentar; criar, educar. *n* nutrición, alimentación, *f;* crianza, educación, *f*

nut *vi* coger nueces. *n bot* nuez, *f; mech* tuerca, hembra de tornillo, *f, inf* **to be a tough nut to crack,** ser un tío de cuidado. **to crack nuts,** cascar nueces. **to go nutting,** coger nueces. **cashew nut,** anacardo, *m.*

loose nut, *mech* tuerca aflojada, *f.* **nut-brown,** castaño. **nut tree,** nogal, *m*

nutcrackers *n pl* cascanueces, quebrantanueces, *m*

nutmeg *n* nuez moscada, nuez de especia, *f*

nutria *n zool* nutria, *f*

nutriment *n* nutrimento, alimento, *m*

nutrition *n* nutrición, alimentación, *f*

nutritious, nutritive *a* nutritivo, alimenticio, alible

nutshell *n* cáscara de nuez, *f.* **to put in a n.,** decir en resumidas cuentas, decir en forma apastillada

nutty *a* de nuez

nuzzle *vt* acariciar con la nariz

nylon *n* nilón, nylon, *m.* **n. stockings,** medias de cristal (or de nilón), *f pl*

nymph *n* ninfa, *f; ent* crisálida, *f.* **n.-like,** como una ninfa; de ninfa

nymphomania *n* ninfomanía, *f,* furor uterino, *m*

O

o *n* (letter) o, *f, interj* ¡o! **O that . . . !** ¡Ojalá que!

oaf *n* zoquete, zamacuco, *m*

oafish *a* lerdo, torpe

oafishness *n* torpeza, estupidez, *f*

oak *n* (tree and wood) roble, *m, a* de roble. **carved oak,** roble tallado, *m.* **holm-oak,** encina, *f.* **oak-apple,** agalla, *f.* **oak grove,** robledo, *m*

oakum *n* estopa, *f*

oar *n* remo, *m.* **to lie on the oars,** cesar de remar. **to pull at the oars,** bogar, remar. **to put in one's oar,** *inf* meter baza. **to ship the oars,** armar los remos. **to unship the oars,** desarmar los remos. **oar-stroke,** palada, *f*

oarsman *n* remero, bogador, *m*

oarsmanship *n* arte de remar, *m,* or *f*

OAS (Organization of American States) OEA (Organización de los Estados Americanos)

oasis *n* oasis, *m*

oast *n* horno para secar el lúpulo, *m*

oat *n bot* avena, *f.* **wild oat,** avena silvestre, *f.* **to sow one's wild oats,** correrla, andarse a la flor del berro, *f.* **oat field,** avenal, *m*

oath *n* juramento, *m;* (curse) blasfemia, *f,* reniego, *m.* **on o.,** bajo juramento. **to break an o.,** violar el juramento. **to put on o.,** tomar juramento, hacer prestar juramento. **to take an o.,** prestar (or hacer) juramento. **to take the o. of allegiance,** jurar la bandera

oatmeal *n* harina de avena, *f*

obduracy *n* obduración, obstinación, terquedad, *f*

obdurate *a* obstinado, terco, porfiado. **He is o. to our requests,** Es sordo a nuestros ruegos

obedience *n* obediencia, sumisión, docilidad, *f.* **blind o.,** obediencia ciega, *f.* **in o. to,** conforme a, de acuerdo con

obedient *a* obediente, sumiso, dócil. **to be o. to,** ser obediente (a), obedecer (a)

obediently *adv* obedientemente, dócilmente. **Yours o.,** Su atento servidor (su att. s.)

obeisance *n* reverencia, cortesía, *f,* saludo, *m;* (homage) homenaje, *m*

obelisk *n* obelisco, *m*

obese *a* obeso, corpulento, grueso, gordo

obesity *n* obesidad, gordura, corpulencia, *f*

obey *vt* and *vi* obedecer. *vt* (carry out) cumplir, observar. **to be obeyed,** ser obedecido

obfuscate *vt* ofuscar, cegar

obfuscation *n* ofuscamiento, *m,* confusión, *f*

obituary *a* mortuorio, necrológico. *n* obituario, *m,* necrología, *f.* **o. column,** (in newspaper) sección necrológica, *f.* **o. notice,** esquela de defunción, *f*

object *n* objeto, artículo, *m,* cosa, *f;* (purpose) propósito, intento, *m;* (aim) fin, término, *m; gram* complemento, *m; inf* individuo, *m. vt* objetar, poner reparos (a). *vi* oponerse, poner objeciones. **I o. to that remark,** Pro-

testo contra esa observación. **If you don't o.,** Si Vd. no tiene inconveniente. **o. finder,** objetivo, *m.* **o. lesson,** lección de cosas, *f;* lección práctica, *f*

objection *n* objeción, protesta, *f,* reparo, *m;* (obstacle) dificultad, *f,* inconveniente, *m.* **to have no o.,** no tener inconveniente. **to raise an o.,** hacer constar una protesta, poner una objeción

objectionable *a* censurable, reprensible; desagradable, molesto

objective *a* objetivo; *gram* acusativo. *n* objeto, propósito, *m;* destinación, *f; mil* objetivo, *m, gram* **o. case,** caso acusativo, *m,*

objectivism *n phil* objetivismo, *m*

objectivity *n* objetividad, *f*

objector *n* objetante, *mf,* impugnador (-ra). **conscientious o.,** (dissident) el, *m,* (*f,* la) que protesta contra; (pacifist) pacifista, *mf*

oblation *n* oblación, ofrenda, *f*

obligation *n* obligación, *f;* deber, *m,* precisión, *f;* compromiso, *m.* **of o.,** de deber; de precepto. **to be under an o.,** estar bajo una obligación; deber un favor. **to place under an o.,** poner bajo una obligación

obligatory *a* obligatorio, forzoso

oblige *vt* (insist on) obligar, hacer, forzar; (gratify) hacer un favor (a), complacer. **He obliged me with a match,** Me hizo el favor de una cerilla. **They are much obliged to you,** Le están muy reconocidos. **Much obliged!** ¡Se agradece!

obliging *a* atento, condescendiente, complaciente, servicial

obligingly *adv* cortésmente

obligingness *n* cortesía, amabilidad, bondad, *f*

oblique *a* oblicuo, sesgado; (indirect) indirecto, evasivo; *gram* oblicuo

obliquely *adv* oblicuamente, al sesgo, sesgadamente; indirectamente. **to place o.,** poner al sesgo

obliquity *n* oblicuidad, *f,* sesgo, *m;* (of conduct, etc.) tortuosidad, *f*

obliterate *vt* borrar; destruir, aniquilar. **to be obliterated,** borrarse; quedar destruido

obliteration *n* testación, *f;* destrucción, *f.* **o. raid,** bombardeo de saturación, *m*

oblivion *n* olvido, *m.* **to cast into o.,** echar al olvido

oblivious *a* olvidadizo, descuidoso

oblong *a* oblongo, cuadrilongo, rectangular. *n* rectángulo, cuadrilongo, *m*

obloquy *n* infamia, maledicencia, deshonra, *f*

obnoxious *a* odioso, ofensivo, aborrecible

obnoxiously *adv* odiosamente

obnoxiousness *n* odiosidad, *f*

oboe *n mus* oboe, *m.* **o. player,** oboe, *m*

obol *n* óbolo, *m*

obscene *a* indecente, obsceno, escabroso

obscenely *adv* obscenamente, escabrosamente

obscenity *n* indecencia, obscenidad, *f*
obscurantism *n* obscurantismo, *m*
obscurantist *a* and *n* obscurantista *mf*
obscure *a* (indistinct) obscuro, indistinto; (dark) lóbrego, tenebroso; (remote) retirado, apartado; (puzzling) confuso; (unknown) desconocido; humilde; (difficult to understand) abstruso, obscuro; (vague) vago. *vt* obscurecer; (hide) esconder; (eclipse) eclipsar. **to o. the issue,** hacer perder de vista el problema
obscurely *adv* obscuramente; humildemente, retiradamente; confusamente; vagamente
obscurity *n* (darkness) obscuridad, lobreguez, *f*; (difficulty of meaning) ambigüedad, confusión, vaguedad, *f*; humildad, *f*
obsequies *n pl* exequias, *f pl*, ritos fúnebres, *m pl*
obsequious *a* servil, empalagoso, zalamero
obsequiously *adv* servilmente
obsequiousness *n* servilismo, *m*, sumisión, *f*
observable *a* observable, perceptible, visible; notable
observably *adv* notablemente
observance *n* observancia, *f*, cumplimiento, *m*; práctica, costumbre, *f*; (religious) rito, *m*
observant *a* observador; obediente, atento. **o. of,** observador de; atento a
observation *n* observación, *f*, examen, escrutinio, *m*; (experience) experiencia, *f*; (remark) advertencia, *f*, comento, *m*. **to escape o.,** no ser advertido. **o. car.,** vagón-mirador, *m*, **o. post,** puesto de observación, *m*
observatory *n* observatorio, *m*
observe *vt* (laws) cumplir; (holy days, etc.) guardar; (notice) observar, mirar, notar, ver, reparar en; (remark) decir, advertir; (examine) vigilar, atisbar, examinar; *ast* observar. *vi* ser observador. **to o. silence,** guardar silencio
observer *n* observador (-ra)
obsess *vt* obsesionar, obcecar
obsessed *a* obseso
obsession *n* obsesión, obcecación, idea fija, manía, *f*
obsidian *n min* obsidiana, *f*
obsolescent *a* que se hace antiguo, que cae en desuso
obsolete *a* obsoleto, anticuado; *biol* rudimentario, atrofiado
obstacle *n* obstáculo, impedimento, *m*; dificultad, *f*, inconveniente, *m*. **to put obstacles in the way of,** *fig* dificultar, hacer difícil. **o. race,** carrera de obstáculos, *f*
obstetric *a* obstétrico
obstetrician *n* obstétrico (-ea), médico (-ca) partero (-ra)
obstetrics *n* obstetricia, tocología, *f*
obstinacy *n* obstinación, terquedad, tenacidad, porfía, *f*, tesón, *m*; persistencia, *f*
obstinate *a* terco, porfiado, obstinado, tenaz; refractario; persistente, pertinaz. **to be o.,** ser terco; porfiar. **to be o. about,** obstinarse en.
obstinately *adv* tercamente
obstreperous *a* turbulento, ruidoso
obstruct *vt* estorbar: impedir; cerrar; (thwart) estorbar; (hinder) dificultar, embarazar; (the traffic) obstruir, atascar. *vi* estorbar. **to become obstructed,** obstruirse, cerrarse
obstruction *n* obstrucción, *f*; estorbo, obstáculo, *m*. **to cause a street o.,** obstruir el tráfico
obstructionism *n* obstruccionismo, *m*
obstructionist *n* obstruccionista, *mf*
obstructive *a* estorbador, obstructor
obtain *vt* obtener, conseguir, lograr; recibir; (by threats) arrancar. *vi* estar en boga, estar en vigor, predominar. **to o. on false pretences,** conseguir por engaño
obtainable *a* asequible, alcanzable. **easily o.,** fácil a obtener
obtainer *n* conseguidor (-ra), adquisidor (-ra)
obtainment *n* obtención, *f*, logro, *m*
obtrude *vt* imponer
obtrusion *n* imposición, *f*; importunidad, *f*
obtrusive *a* importuno; entremetido; pretencioso
obtrusiveness *n* importunidad, *f*; entremetimiento, *m*

obtuse *a* (blunt) obtuso, romo; (stupid) estúpido, torpe, lerdo. **o. angle,** obtusángulo, *m*
obtuseness *n* (bluntness) embotamiento, *m*; (stupidity) estupidez, torpeza, *f*
obverse *a* del anverso. *n* anverso, *m*
obviate *vt* obviar, evitar
obvious *a* evidente, manifiesto, patente, obvio, aparente, transparente; poco sutil
obviously *adv* evidentemente, patentemente
obviousness *n* evidencia, transparencia, *f*
occasion *n* ocasión, *f*; oportunidad, *f*, momento oportuno, tiempo propicio, *m*; (reason) motivo, origen, *m*, causa, razón, *f*; (need) necesidad, *f*. *vt* ocasionar, causar, producir. **as o. demands,** cuando las circunstancias lo exigen, en caso necesario. **for the o.,** para la ocasión. **on one o.,** una vez. **on the o. of,** en la ocasión de. **on that o.,** en tal ocasión, en aquella ocasión. **He has given me no o. to say so,** No me ha dado motivos de decirlo. **There is no o. for it,** No hay necesidad para ello. **to have o. to,** haber de, tener que, necesitar. **to lose no o.,** no perder ripio (or oportunidad). **to rise to the o.,** estar al nivel de las circunstancias. **to take this o.,** aprovechar esta oportunidad
occasional *a* (occurring at times) de vez en cuando, intermitente; poco frecuente, infrecuente; (of verse) de ocasión. **o. table,** mesilla, *f*
occasionally *adv* de vez en cuando
occiput *n anat* occipucio, *m*
occlude *vt* obstruir, cerrar; *med* ocluir; *chem* absorber
occlusion *n* cerramiento, *m*; *med* oclusión, *f*; *chem* absorción de gases, *f*
occlusive *a* oclusivo
occult *a* oculto, escondido, misterioso; mágico. **o. sciences,** creencias ocultas, *f pl*
occultation *n ast* ocultación, *f*, eclipse, *m*
occultism *n* ocultismo, *m*
occultist *n* ocultista, *mf*
occupancy *n* ocupación, posesión, *f*; (tenancy) tenencia, *f*
occupant *n* habitante, *mf*; ocupante, *mf*; (tenant) inquilino (-na)
occupation *n* ocupación *f*; (tenure) inquilinato, *m*, tenencia, *f*; (work) trabajo, quehacer, *m*, labor, *f*; (employment) empleo, oficio, *m*; profesión, *f*
occupational *a* de oficio. **o. disease,** enfermedad profesional, *f*
occupier *n* ocupante, *mf*, inquilino (-na)
occupy *vt* ocupar; (live in) vivir en, habitar; (time) emplear, pasar; (take over) apoderarse de, ocupar. **to o. oneself in** or **with,** ocuparse en, ocuparse con. **to be occupied in** or **with,** estar ocupado con, ocuparse en
occur *vi* (happen) suceder, tener lugar, acaecer; (exist) encontrarse, existir; (of ideas) ocurrirse, venirse. **to o. to one's mind,** venírsele a las mientes. **to o. again,** volver a suceder, ocurrir de nuevo. **An idea occurred to her,** Se le ocurrió una idea
occurrence *n* ocurrencia, *f*; incidente, suceso, acontecimiento, *m*. **to be of frequent o.,** ocurrir con frecuencia, acontecer a menudo
ocean *n* océano, *m*; *fig* mar, abundancia, *f*. **o.-going vessel,** buque de alta mar, *m*
Oceania el Mundo Novísmo, *m*
oceanic *a* oceánico
oceanography *n* oceanografía, *f*
ocelot *n zool* ocelote, *m*
ocher *n* ocre, *m*
octagon *n* octágono, *m*
octagonal *a* octagonal
octave *n* (*ecc* metrics, *mus*) octava, *f*
octavo *n print* libro, etc. en octavo (8°), *m*. **in o.,** en octavo. **large o.,** octavo mayor, *m*. **small o.,** octavo menor, *m*
octet *n mus* octeto, *m*
October *n* octubre, *m*, 2 October 1996, el segundo (2°) de octubre de mil novecientos noventa y seis
octogenarian *a* and *n* octogenario (-ia)

467

octopus n pulpo, m

ocular a ocular, visual. n ocular, m

oculist n oculista, mf

odd a (of numbers) impar; (of volumes, etc.) suelto; (strange) raro, curioso, extraño, extravagante; (casual) casual, accidental; (extra) y pico, y tantos, sobrante; (of gloves, etc.) sin pareja. **at odd moments,** en momentos de ocio. **at odd times,** de vez en cuando. **thirty odd,** treinta y pico. **odd number,** número impare, m. **odd or even,** pares o impares. **odd trick,** (at cards) una baza más

oddity n excentricidad, rareza, extravagancia, f; (person) ente singular, m; (curio) objeto curioso, m, antigüedad, f

oddly adv singularmente

oddment n bagatela, baratija, f

oddness n singularidad, rareza, extravagancia, f

odds n pl diferencia, desigualdad, f; (superiority) ventaja, superioridad, f; (quarrel) disputa, riña, f. **The o. are that** . . . , Lo más probable es que . . . **to fight against dreadful o.,** luchar contra fuerzas muy superiores. **o. and ends,** (remains) sobras y picos, f pl; (trifles) ñaques, m pl, chucherías, f pl

Odessa Odesa, f

odious a odioso, detestable, aborrecible, repugnante

odiousness n odiosidad, f

odium n odio, m

odor n olor, m, (fragrance) perfume, aroma, m, fragancia, f; fig sospecha, f. **in bad o.,** fig en disfavor. **o. of sanctity,** olor de santidad, m

odoriferous a odorífero; (perfumed) oloroso, perfumado

odorless a inodoro

odorous a fragante, oloroso

odyssey n odisea, f

of prep de. **of** has many idiomatic translations which are given as far as possible under the heading of the word concerned. It is also not translated. **I robbed him of his reward,** Le robé su recompensa. **I was thinking of you,** Pensaba en tí. **It was very good of you to** . . . , Vd. ha tenido mucha bondad de . . . **Your naming of the child Mary,** El que Vd. haya dado el nombre de María al niño. **29th of Sept., 1936,** el 29 de septiembre de 1936. **Of course!** ¡Claro está! ¡Ya lo creo! ¡Naturalmente! **of late,** últimamente. **of the** (before m, sing) del; (before f, sing) de la; (before m pl) de los; (before f pl) de las. **to dream of,** soñar con. **to smell of,** oler a tener olor de. **to taste of, etc.,** saber a, tener gusto de.

off prep de; fuera de; cerca de; desde; naut a la altura de. **from off,** de. **Take your gloves off the table!** ¡Quítate los guantes de la mesa! **The wheel was off the car,** La rueda se había desprendido del coche. **to be off duty,** no estar de servicio; mil no estar de guardia. **to lunch off cold meat,** almorzar de carne fría. **off one's head,** chiflado

off a (contrasted with near) de la derecha, derecho; (unlikely) improbable, remoto. adv (with intransitive verbs of motion) se (e.g. **He has gone off,** Se ha marchado); (contrasted with on) de (e.g. **He has fallen off the horse,** Ha caído del caballo); (of place at a distance) lejos, a distancia de; (of time) generally a verb is used (e.g. **The wedding is three months off,** Faltan tres meses para la boda); (completely) enteramente. **Off** is often not translated in Sp. (e.g. **to put off,** aplazar, **to cut off,** cortar). **day off,** día libre, día de asueto, m. **How far off is the house from here? The house is five miles off.** ¿Cuántas millas está la casa de aquí? La casa está a cinco millas de aquí. **His hat is off,** Está sin sombrero, Se ha quitado el sombrero. **The cover is off,** La cubierta está quitada. **The party is off,** Se ha anulado la reunión. **6% off,** un descuento de seis por ciento. interj **Off with you!** ¡Márchate! ¡Fuera! **off and on,** de vez en cuando, espasmódicamente. **off color,** (ill) malucho; (of jokes)

verde. **off season,** estación muerta, f. **off-shore,** a vista de tierra. **off-stage,** entre bastidores

offal n (butchers') menudencias, f pl, asadura, f, menudos, despojos, m pl; desperdicio, m

offend vt ofender; agraviar, insultar; herir; desagradar, disgustar; vi ofender, pecar. **to be offended,** resentirse, insultarse. **This offends my sense of justice,** Esto ofende mi sentimiento de justicia. **to o. against,** pecar contra; violar

offender n delincuente, mf; agraviador (-ra), pecador (-ra), transgresor (-ra). **old o.,** law criminal inveterado, m

offense n ofensa, transgresión, violación, f; pecado, m; law delito, crimen, m; (insult) agravio, m, afrenta, f. **the first o.,** el primer delito, m. **fresh o.,** nuevo delito, m. **political o.,** crimen político, m. **technical o.,** law cuasidelito, m. **to commit an o. against,** ofender contra. **to take o.,** resentirse, darse por ofendido

offensive a ofensivo, desagradable, repugnante; (insulting) injurioso, agraviador, agresivo. n mil ofensiva, f. **to take the o.,** tomar la ofensiva

offensiveness n lo desagradable; (insult) ofensa, f; lo injurioso

offer n oferta, f; ofrecimiento, m; (of help) promesa, f; proposición, f; com oferta, f. vt ofrecer; prometer; (opportunities, etc.) deparar, brindar; tributar. vi ofrecerse, ocurrir, surgir. **to o. up,** ofrecer; inmolar, sacrificar. **He did not offer to go,** No hizo ademán de marcharse. **to o. resistance,** oponer resistencia. **o. of marriage,** oferta de matrimonio, f

offerer n ofrecedor (-ra)

offering n ofrecimiento, m; ecc ofrenda, oblación, f, sacrificio, m; regalo, don, m, dádiva, f

offhand a sin preparación, de repente; (casual) casual, despreocupado; (discourteous) brusco, descortés

offhandedly adv sin preparación, espontáneamente; negligentemente; bruscamente

office n oficina, m; (post) cargo, puesto, destino, m; (state department) ministerio, m; (of a Cabinet minister) cartera, f; (room) oficina, f; despacho, escritorio, m; (of a newspaper) redacción, f; (lawyer's) bufete, m; departamento, m; ecc oficio, m pl. **offices,** negocio, m; oficinas, f pl; (prayers) rezos, m pl; ecc oficios, m pl. **domestic offices,** dependencias, f pl. **good offices,** fig buenos oficios, m pl. **head o.,** casa central, oficina principal, f. **private o.,** despacho particular, m. **to be in o.,** estar en el poder. **o.-bearer,** miembro de la junta, m; funcionario, m. **o.-boy,** mozo de oficina, m. **o. employee,** oficinista, mf. **o. hours,** horas de oficina, f pl; (professions) horas de consulta, f pl. **o.-seeker,** aspirante, m; pretendiente, m. **o. work,** trabajo de oficina, m

officer n oficial, funcionario, m; (police) agente de policía, m; (of the Church) dignatario, m; (mil nav aer) oficial, m. vt mandar. **commissioned o.,** oficial, m. **non-commissioned o.,** oficial subalterno, m. **to be well officered,** tener buena oficialidad, f. **Officers' Training Corps,** Escuela de Oficiales, f

office worker n oficinista, mf

official a oficial; autorizado; ceremonioso, grave. n funcionario, m; oficial público, m. **high o.,** funcionario importante, m. **o. mourning,** duelo oficial, m. **o. receiver,** fiscal de quiebras, m

officialdom n funcionarismo, m; círculos oficiales, m pl

officiant n oficiante, m

officiate vi celebrar; oficiar, funcionar

officiating a oficiante; celebrante. **o. priest,** sacerdote oficiante, celebrante, m

officious a oficioso, entremetido

officiousness n oficiosidad, f

offing n naut mar afuera, m. **in the o.,** cerca

off season fuera de temporada

offset n compensación, f, vt compensar, neutralizar

offshoot n renuevo, vástago, m

offside a (of a car) del lado derecho (or izquierda); sport fuera de juego

offspring *n* vástago, *m*; descendiente, *mf*; prole, *f*; hijos, *m pl*

often *adv* a menudo, mucho, con frecuencia, frecuentemente, muchas veces. **as o. as,** tan a menudo como, siempre que. **as o. as not,** no pocas veces. **How o.?** ¿Cuántas veces? **It is not o. that . . . ,** No ocurre con frecuencia que . . . **so o.,** tantas veces, con frecuencia. **Do you go there o.?** ¿Va Vd. allí con frecuencia (or frecuentemente)? **Not o.,** Voy rara vez allá

ogival *a arch* ojival

ogive *n arch* ojiva, *f*

ogle *vt* and *vi* comer(se) con los ojos (a), ojear, guiñar el ojo (a). *n* ojeada, *f*, guiño, *m*

ogling *n* guiño, *m*, ojeada, *f*

ogre *n* ogro, *m*

oh! *interj* ¡o! **O no!** ¡Ca! ¡Claro que no!

ohm *n elec* ohmio, *m*

oil *n* aceite, *m*; petróleo, *m*; óleo, *m*. *vt* aceitar, engrasar; olear, ungir, untar; (bribe) sobornar, untar la mano; *fig* suavizar. *a* aceitero; petrolero. **to pour oil on troubled waters,** echar aceite sobre aguas turbulentas. **to strike oil,** encontrar un pozo de petróleo; *fig* encontrar un filón. **crude oil,** petróleo bruto, *m*. **heavy oil,** aceite pesado, *m*. **thin oil,** aceite ligero, *m*. **art in oils,** al óleo. **oil-bearing,** petrolífero. **oil-box,** engrasador, *m*. **oil-burner,** quemador de petróleo, *m*. **oil-can,** aceitera, *f*. **oil-colors,** pinturas al óleo, *f pl*. **oil field,** yacimiento petrolífero, campo de petróleo, *m*. **oil-filter,** separador de aceite, *m*. **oil-gauge,** nivel de aceite, *m*. **oil lamp,** velón, candil, quinqué, *m*. **oil of turpentine,** aceite de trementina, aguarrás, *m*. esencia de trementina, *f*. **oil-painting,** pintura al óleo, *f*. **oil pipeline,** oleoducto, *m*. **oil shop,** aceitería, *f*. **oil-silk,** encerado, *m*. **oil stove,** estufa de petróleo, *f*. **oil tanker,** *naut* petrolero, *m*. **oil-well,** pozo de petróleo, *m*

oilcake *n* bagazo, *m*

oilcloth *n* hule, *m*; linóleo, *m*

oiler *n* (can) aceitera, *f*; *naut* petrolero, *m*; lubricador, *m*

oiliness *n* oleaginosidad, untuosidad, *f*

oiling *n* engrasado, *m*

oilskin *n* encerado, *m*

oil seed *n* semilla oleaginosa, *f*

oily *a* aceitoso, grasiento

ointment *n* ungüento, *m*, pomada, *f*

old *a* viejo; antiguo, anciano; (of wines, etc.) añejo; (worn out) usado, gastado; (inveterate) arraigado, inveterado. **How old are you?** ¿Cuántos años tiene usted? **to be sixteen years old,** tener dieciséis años. **He is old enough to know his own mind,** Tiene bastante edad para saber lo que quiere. **to grow old,** envejecer. **to remain an old maid,** quedar soltera; *inf* quedarse para vestir imágenes. **of old,** antiguamente. **prematurely old,** revejido averiado. **old age,** vejez, senectud, *f*. **old bachelor,** solterón, *m*. **old clothes,** ropa vieja (or usada), ropa de segunda mano, *f*. **old-clothes dealer,** ropavejero (-ra). **old-clothes shop,** ropavejería, *f*. **old-established,** viejo. **old-fashioned,** pasado de moda, viejo; (of people) chapado a la antigua. **old lady,** anciana, dama vieja, *f*. **old-looking,** de aspecto viejo, avejentado. **old maid,** solterona, *f*. **old-maidish,** remilgado. **old man,** viejo, *m*; *theat* barba, *m*. **old salt,** lobo de mar, *m*. **Old Testament,** Antiguo Testamento, *m*. **old wives' tale,** cuento de viejas, *m*. **old woman,** vieja, *f*. **Old World,** Viejo Mundo, mundo antiguo, *m*

old-age home *n* asilo de ancianos, *m*

olden *a* antiguo. **o. days,** días pasados, *m pl*

older *a comp* más viejo, mayor. **The older the madder,** A la vejez viruelas

old hat *n* viejo conocido

oldish *a* bastante viejo, de cierta edad

oldness *n* antigüedad, ancianidad, edad, *f*

oleaginous *a* oleaginoso

oleander *n bot* adelfa, *f*, baladre, *m*

olfactory *a* olfatorio, olfativo

oligarchic *a* oligárquico

oligarchy *n* oligarquía, *f*

olive *n* (tree) olivo, *m*; (fruit) aceituna, oliva, *f*, *a* aceitunado. **wild o. tree,** acebuche, *m*. **o.-complexioned,** con tez aceitunada. **o. green,** verde oliva, *m*. **o. grove,** olivar, *m*. **o. oil,** aceite de oliva, *m*

olympiad *n* olimpíada, *f*

olympian *a* olímpico

olympic *a* olímpico. **o. games,** juegos olímpicos, *m pl*

olympus *n* olimpo, *m*

omasum *n zool* librillo, libro, *m*

omber *n* tresillo, hombre, *m*

omega *n* omega, *f*

omelet *n* tortilla, *f*. **sweet o.,** tortilla dulce, *f*

omen *n* pronóstico, presagio, agüero, *m*, *vt* agorar, anunciar

ominous *a* ominoso, azaroso, siniestro, amenazante

ominously *adv* ominosamente, con amenazas

omission *n* omisión, *f*; olvido, descuido, *m*; supresión, *f*

omit *vt* omitir; olvidar, descuidar; (suppress) suprimir, excluir, callar, dejar a un lado

omitting *pres part* salvo, excepto

omnibus *n* ómnibus, autobús, *m*. **o. conductor,** cobrador de autobús, *m*. **o. driver,** conductor de autobús, *m*. **o. route,** trayecto de autobús, *m*. **o. service,** servicio de autobuses, *m*. **o. volume,** volumen de obras coleccionadas, *m*

omnipotence *n* omnipotencia, *f*

omnipotent *a* omnipotente, todopoderoso

omnipresence *n* omnipresencia, ubicuidad, *f*

omnipresent *a* ubicuo

omniscience *n* omnisciencia, *f*

omniscient *a* omniscio, omnisciente

omnivorous *a* omnívoro

on *prep* (upon) sobre, en, encima de; (concerning) de, acerca de, sobre; (against) contra; (after) después; (according to) según; (with gerund) en; (with infin.) al; (at) a; (connected with, employed in) de; (by means of) por, mediante; (near to) cerca de, sobre; (into) en. Untranslated before days of week, dates of month or time of day (e.g. **on Monday,** el lunes. **on Friday afternoons,** los viernes por la tarde). **She has a bracelet on her wrist,** Tiene una pulsera en la muñeca. **He will retire on a good income,** Se jubilará con una buena renta. **on my uncle's death,** después de la muerte de mi tío, al morir. **On seeing them, he stopped,** Al verles se paró. **on leave,** con licencia, en uso de licencia. **on the next page,** en la página siguiente. **on this occasion,** en esta ocasión. **on the other hand,** en cambio. **on second thoughts,** luego de pensarlo bien. **on the way,** en camino. **on one side,** a un lado. **on the left,** a la izquierda. **on time,** a tiempo. **on my honor,** bajo palabra de honor. **on pain of death,** so pena de muerte, bajo pena de muerte. **on an average,** por término medio. **on his part,** por su parte. **on and after,** desde, a partir de. **on credit,** de fiado. **on fire,** ardiendo, en llamas. **on foot,** a pie. **on purpose,** a propósito; con intención. **on,** *adv* puesto (e.g. **She has her gloves on,** Tiene los guantes puestos); (forward) adelante, hacia adelante; (continue, with a verb) seguir, continuar (e.g. **He went on talking,** Siguió hablando). Often on is included in Sp. verb (e.g. **The new play is on,** Se ha estrenado la nueva comedia. **The fight is on,** Ya ha empezado la lucha. **On!** *interj* ¡Adelante! **and so on,** y así sucesivamente. **to have on,** llevar puesto. **on and off,** de vez en cuando. **on and on,** sin cesar

onanism *n* onanismo, *m*

once *adv* una vez; (formerly) en otro tiempo, antiguamente; *conjunc* si (e.g. **O. you give him the opportunity,** Si le das la oportunidad). **all at o.,** todo junto, a un mismo tiempo; simultáneamente; (suddenly) súbitamente, de repente. **at o.,** en seguida, inmediatamente. **for o.,** por una vez. **more than o.,** más de una vez. **not o.,** ni siquiera una vez. **o. before,** una vez antes. **o. and for all,** una vez para siempre; por última vez. **o. in a while,** de vez en cuando. **o. more,** otra vez. **o. or twice,** una vez o dos, algunas veces. **o. too often,** una vez demasiado. **O. upon a time,** En tiempos pasados, En tiempos de Maricastaña; (as beginning of a story) Érase una vez, Había una vez, Hubo una vez

once in a blue moon a cada muerte de un obispo

one *a* un, uno, una; (first) primero; (single) único, solo; (indifferent) igual, indiferente; (some, certain) algún, cierto, un (e.g. **one day,** cierto día). *n* uno; (hour) la una; (of age) un año. Often not translated in Sp. (e.g. **I shall take the blue one,** Tomaré el azul). *pron* se; uno. **one's,** su, de uno (e.g. **one's work,** el trabajo de uno). **I for one do not think so,** Yo por uno no lo creo. **It is all one,** Es igual, No hace diferencia alguna. **only one,** un solo. **that one,** ése, *m,* ésa, *f,* eso, *neut.* **this one,** éste, *m,* ésta, *f,* esto, *neut.* **these ones,** éstos, etc. **those ones,** ésos, etc. **the one,** el (que), *m,* la (que), *f.* **with one accord,** unánimemente. **one and all,** todos. **one another,** se, uno a otro, mutuamente. **one by one,** uno a uno. **one day,** un día; un día de éstos, algún día. **one-eyed,** tuerto. **one-handed,** manco. **one-sided,** parcial. **one-way street,** calle de dirección única, *f.* **one-way traffic,** tráfico en una sola dirección, *m*

oneiric *a* onírico

oneness *n* unidad, *f*

onerous *a* oneroso, pesado, molesto, gravoso

onerousness *n* pesadez, molestia, dificultad, inconveniencia, *f*

one-seater *n* avión de una plaza, *m*

oneself *pron* se, uno mismo (una misma); (after prep.) sí mismo, sí. **It must be done by o.,** Uno mismo ha de hacerlo

onion *n* cebolla, *f.* **string of onions,** ristra de cebollas, *f.* **young o.,** babosa, *f.* **o. bed,** cebollar, *m.* **o. seed,** cebollino, *m.* **o. seller,** cebollero (-ra)

onlooker *n* espectado (-ra), observador (-ra); testigo, *mf*

only *a* único, solo. *adv* únicamente, sólo; no . . . más (que), tan sólo; con la excepción de, salvo. *conjunc* pero, salvo (que), si no fuera (que). **I shall o. give you three,** No te daré más de tres. **The o. thing one can do,** Lo único que se puede hacer. **I o. wished to see her,** Quería verla nada más. **if o.,** ¡ojalá (que)! **not o. . . . , no sólo . . . o.-begotten,** *a* unigénito. **o. child,** hijo (-ja) único (-ca)

onomatopeia *n* onomatopeya, *f*

onomatopeic *a* onomatopéyico

onrush *n* asalto, ataque, acometimiento, *m,* acometida, embestida, *f;* (of water, etc.) acceso, *m;* torrente, *m,* corriente, *f*

onset *n* ataque, *m,* acometida, *f;* (beginning) principio, *m.* **at the first o.,** al primer ímpetu

onslaught *n* asalto, ataque, *m*

ontology *n phil* ontología, *f*

onus *n* responsabilidad, *f.* **o. of proof,** obligación de probar, *f*

onward *a* progresivo. *adv* adelante, hacia adelante; (as a command) ¡Adelante!

onyx *n min* ónice, *m*

ooze *n* légamo, limo, fango, *m,* lama, *f. vi* exudar, rezumarse; manar; *vt* sudar. **to o. away,** (of money, etc.) desaparecer, volar. **to o. out,** (news) divulgarse

oozing *a* fangoso, legamoso, lamoso

opacity *n* opacidad, *f*

opal *n* ópalo, *m*

opalescence *n* opalescencia, *f*

opalescent *a* opalescente, iridiscente

opaline *a* opalino

opaque *a* opaco

opaqueness *n* opacidad, *f*

op. cit. (opere citato) obra cit. (obra citada)

open *vt* abrir; (a package) desempaquetar, desenvolver; (remove lid) destapar; (unfold) desplegar; (inaugurate) inaugurar; iniciar, empezar; establecer; (an abscess) cortar; (with arms, heart, eyes) abrir; (with mind, thought) descubrir, revelar; (make accessible) franquear, hacer accesible; (tear) romper; *vi* abrirse; empezar, comenzar; (of a view, etc.) aparecer, extenderse; inaugurarse; (of a career, etc.) prepararse. **to o. fire against,** abrir el fuego contra. **to o. into,** comunicar con, salir a. **to o. into each other,** (of rooms) comunicarse. **to o. on,** mirar a, dar a, caer a. **to o. out,** *vt* abrir; desplegar; revelar. *vi* extenderse; revelarse. **to o. the eyes of,** *fig* desengañar, desilusionar. **to o. up,** abrir; explorar, hacer accesible; revelar; *fig inf* desabrocharse. **to o. with** or **by,** empezar con

open *a* abierto; descubierto; expuesto; (unfenced) descercado; (not private) público; libre; (unfolded) desplegado, extendido; (persuasible) receptivo; no resuelto, pendiente; (frank) franco, candoroso; (with sea) alto; (liberal) generoso, hospitalario; sin prejuicios; *com* abierto, pendiente; sin defensa; (of weather) despejado; (of a letter) sin sellar; (without a lid) destapado; (well-known) manifiesto, bien conocido. *n* aire libre, *m.* **in the o.,** al descubierto. **in the o. air,** al aire libre, al raso, a cielo abierto. **to break o.,** forzar. **to cut o.,** abrir de un tajo, cortar. **to leave o.,** dejar abierto. **wide o.,** muy abierto; (of doors) de par en par. **o. boat,** barco descubierto, *m.* **o. car,** coche abierto, *m.* **o. carriage,** carruaje descubierto, *m.* **o. cast,** *min* roza abierta, *f.* **o.-eyed,** con los ojos abiertos. **o.-handed,** generoso, dadivoso. **o. letter,** carta abierta, *f.* **o.-minded,** imparcial. **o.-mouthed,** con la boca abierta, boquiabierto. **o. question,** cuestión por decidir, cuestión discutible, *f.* **o. secret,** secreto a voces, *m.* **o. sea,** alta mar, *f.* **o. town,** ciudad abierta, *f.* **o. tramcar,** jardinera, *f.* **o. truck,** vagoneta, *f.* **o.-work,** *sew* calado, enrejado, *m*

opener *n* abridor, *m*

opening *n* abertura, brecha, *f;* orificio, *m;* inauguración, apertura, *f;* principio, *m;* (chance) oportunidad, *f;* (employment) puesto, *m.* **o. price,** *com* (on Exchange) precio de apertura, *m,* primer curso *m*

openly *adv* abiertamente, francamente; públicamente

openness *n* situación expuesta, *f;* espaciosidad, *f;* franqueza, *f,* candor, *m;* imparcialidad, *f*

opera *n* ópera, *f.* **comic o.,** zarzuela, *f.* **o.-cloak,** abrigo de noche, *m.* **o.-glasses,** gemelos de teatro, *m pl.* **o.-hat,** clac, *m.* **o.-house,** teatro de la ópera, *m.* **o. singer,** cantante de ópera, operista, *mf*

operate *vi* funcionar, trabajar; obrar; (with on, upon) producir efecto sobre; influir; *surg* operar; (on Exchange) especular, jugar a la bolsa; *vt* hacer funcionar, manejar; mover, impulsar; dirigir

operatic *a* de ópera, operístico

operating *a* (of surgeons) operante; de operación. **o. table,** mesa de operaciones, *f.* **o. theater,** anfiteatro, *m;* sala de operaciones, *f*

operation *n* funcionamiento, *m,* acción, *f; surg* intervención quirúrgica, operación, *f; (mil naut)* maniobra, *f;* manipulación, *f.* **to come into o.,** ponerse en práctica; hacerse efectivo. **to continue in o.,** (laws) seguir en vigor. **to perform an o.,** *surg* operar, praticar una intervención quirúrgica; hacer una maniobra. **to put into o.,** poner en práctica

operative *a* operativo, activo. *n* operario (-ia), obrero (-ra). **to become o.,** tener efecto

operator *n* operario (-ia); (telephone) telefonista, *mf;* (machines, engines) maquinista, *mf; surg* operador, *m*

operetta *n* opereta, *f*

ophthalmologist *n* oftalmólogo, *m*

ophthalmology *n* oftalmología, *f*

opiate *n* opiata, *f,* narcótico, *m, a* opiado

opine *vi* and *vt* opinar, creer

opinion *n* opinión, *f,* parecer, juicio, *m;* concepto, *m,* idea, *f.* **in my o.,** según mi parecer. **to be of the o. that,** ser de la opinión que, opinar que. **to be of the same o.,** estar de acuerdo, concurrir. **public o.,** opinión (or voz) pública, *f*

opinionated *a* terco, obstinado
opium *n* opio, *m*. **o. addict,** opiónamo (-ma). **o. den,** fumadero de opio, *m*. **o. eater,** mascador de opio, opiófago, *m*. **o. smoker,** fumador (-ra) de opio
Oporto Oporto, Porto, *m*
opponent *n* antagonista, *mf,* enemigo (-ga); contrario (-ia), adversario (-ia), competidor (-ra)
opportune *a* oportuno, tempestivo, conveniente, a propósito. **to be o.,** venir al caso. **o. moment,** momento oportuno, *m*; hora propicia, *f*
opportunely *adv* oportunamente. **to come o.,** venir a pelo
opportuneness *n* oportunidad, tempestividad, conveniencia, *f*
opportunism *n* oportunismo, *m*
opportunist *n* oportunista, *mf*
opportunity *n* oportunidad, ocasión, posibilidad, *f.* **to give an o. for,** dar margen para. **to open new opportunities,** abrir nuevos horizontes. **to take the o.,** tomar la oportunidad
opposable *a* oponible
oppose *vt* (counterbalance) oponer, contrarrestar; combatir; hacer frente (a), contrariar, pugnar contra, oponerse (a)
opposed (to) *a* opuesto a, enemigo de, contra
opposing *a* opuesto; enemigo, contrario
opposite *a* (facing) de cara a, frente a, del otro lado de; opuesto; (antagonistic) contrario, antagónico; otro, diferente. *n* contraria, *f,* lo opuesto; antagonista, *mf;* adversario (-ia). **the o. sex,** el otro sexo. **o. leaves,** *bot* hojas opuestas, *f pl.* **o. to,** frente a; distinto de
opposition *n* oposición, *f;* (obstacle) estorbo, impedimento, *m,* dificultad, *f;* resistencia, hostilidad, *f;* (*ast pol*) oposición, *f;* (difference) contraste, *m,* diferencia, *f. a* de la oposición. **in o.,** en oposición; *pol* en la oposición. **to be in o.,** estar en oposición; *pol* ser de la oposición, estar en la oposición
oppress *vt* oprimir, tiranizar, sojuzgar, apremiar; (of moral causes) abrumar, agobiar, desanimar; (of heat, etc.) ahogar
oppression *n* opresión, tiranía, crueldad, *f;* (moral) agobio, sufrimiento, *m,* ansia, *f;* (difficulty in breathing) sofocación, *f,* ahogo, *m*
oppressive *a* opresivo, tiránico, cruel; (taxes, etc.) gravoso; (of heat) sofocante, asfixiante; agobiador, abrumador
oppressor *n* opresor (-ra), sojuzgador (-ra), tirano (-na)
opprobrious *a* oprobioso, vituperioso; infame
opprobrium *n* oprobio, *m,* ignominia, *f*
opt *vi* optar, escoger, elegir
optic, optical *a* óptico. **o. illusion,** ilusión óptica, *f;* engaño a la vista, trampantojo, *m.* **o. nerve,** nervio óptico, *m*
optician *n* óptico, *m*
optics *n* óptica, *f*
optimism *n* optimismo, *m*
optimist *n* optimista, *mf*
optimistic *a* optimista
optimum *n* lo óptimo; (used as adjective) óptimo
option *n* opción, *f,* (all meanings)
optional *a* discrecional, facultativo
opulence *n* opulencia, riqueza, magnificencia, *f;* (abundance) abundancia, copia, *f*
opulent *a* opulento, rico, acaudalado; abundante
opus *n* obra, composición, *f*
opuscule *n* opúsculo, *m*
or *conjunc* o; (before a word beginning with o or ho) u; (negative) ni. *n her* oro, *m.* **an hour or so,** una hora más o menos, alrededor de una hora. **either . . . or, o . . . o. or else,** o bien. **whether . . . or,** que . . . que, siquiera . . . siquiera, ya . . . ya. **without . . . or,** sin . . . ni
oracle *n* oráculo, *m*
oracular *a* profético, vatídico; ambiguo, misterioso, sibilino; dogmático, magistral
oral *a* verbal, hablado; *anat* oral, bucal

oral cavity *n* cavidad bucal, *f*
orange *n* (tree) naranjo, *m;* (fruit) naranja, *f;* **bitter o.,** naranja amarga, *f.* **blood o.,** naranja dulce, *f.* **tangerine o.,** naranja mandarina, *f.* **o. blossom,** azahar, *m.* **o. color,** color de naranja, *m.* **o.-colored,** de color de naranja, anaranjado. **o.-flower water,** agua de azahar, *f.* **o. grove,** naranjal, *m.* **o. grower** (or **seller**), naranjero (-ra). **o. peel,** piel de naranja, *f.* **o.-stick,** (for nails) limpiauñas, *m*
orangeade *n* naranjada, *f;* (mineral water) gaseosa, *f*
orangery *n* naranjal, *m*
orangoutan *n zool* orangután, *m*
oration *n* oración, declamación, *f,* discurso, *m*
orator *n* orador (-ra), declamador (-ra)
oratorical *a* oratorio, declamatorio, retórico
oratorio *n mus* oratorio, *m*
oratory *n* oratoria, elocuencia, *f; ecc* oratorio, *m,* capilla, *f*
orb *n* orbe, *m;* esfera, *f,* globo, *m;* astro, *m; poet* ojo, *m*
orbit *n ast* órbita, *f; anat* órbita, cuenca del ojo, *f*
orbital *a anat* orbital
orchard *n* huerto, vergel, *m;* (especially of apples) pomar, *m*
orchestra *n* orquesta, *f.* **with full o.,** con gran orquesta. *theat* **o. seat, o. stall,** butaca de piatea, *f*
orchestral *a* orquestal, instrumental
orchestrate *vt* orquestar, instrumentar
orchestration *n* orquestración, instrumentación, *f*
orchid *n* orquídea, *f*
orchitis *n med* orquitis, *f*
ordain *vt* mandar, disponer, decretar; *ecc* ordenar. **to be ordained as,** *ecc* ordenarse de
ordeal *n hist* ordalías, *f pl;* prueba severa, *f*
order *n* (most meanings) orden, *m;* (command) precepto, mandamiento, decreto, *m;* orden, *f;* (rule) regla, *f;* (for money) libranza postal, *f;* (for goods) pedido, encargo, *m;* (arrangement) método, arreglo, *m,* clasificación, *f;* (condition) estado, *m; arch* estilo, *m;* (*zool bot*) orden, *m;* (sort) clase, especie, *f;* (rank) clase social, *f; ecc* orden, *f;* (badge) condecoración, insignia, *f;* (association) sociedad, asociación, compañía, *f;* (to view a house, etc.) permiso, *m;* (series) serie, *f.* **His liver is out of o.,** No está bien del hígado. **in good o.,** en buen estado; arreglado. **in o.,** (alphabetical, etc.) en orden; arreglado; (parliamentary) en regla. **in o. that,** para que, a fin de que. **in o. to,** a fin de, para. **out of o.,** estropeado, descompuesto; (on a notice) No funciona; (parliamentary) fuera del orden del dia. **till further o.,** hasta nueva orden. **to o.,** *com* por encargo especial. **to give an o.,** dar una orden; *com* poner un pedido. **to go out of o.,** descomponerse. **to keep in o.,** mantener en orden. **to put in o.,** poner en orden, ordenar. **to take holy orders,** tomar órdenes sagradas. **O.!** ¡Orden! **O. in Council,** orden real, *f.* **o. of knighthood,** orden de caballería, *f.* **o. of the day,** orden del día, *f.* **o. paper,** orden del día, *f;* reglamento, *m*
order *vt* disponer; arreglar; (command) mandar, ordenar; (request) rogar, pedir; (direct) dirigir, gobernar; *com* encargar, cometer; (a meal, a taxi) encargar. **I ordered them to do it,** Les mandé hacerlo. **to o. about,** mandar. **to o. back,** hacer volver, mandar que vuelva. **to o. down,** hacer bajar, pedir (a uno) que baje. **to o. in,** mandar entrar. **to o. off,** despedir, decir (a uno) que se vaya. **to o. out,** mandar salir; (the troops) hacer salir la tropa; echar. **to o. up,** mandar subir, hacer subir
orderliness *n* orden, aseo, método, *m;* limpieza, *f;* buena conducta, formalidad, *f;* buena administración, *f*
orderly *a* ordenado, arreglado, metódico; aseado, en orden; (of behaviour) formal, bien disciplinado. *n mil* ordenanza, *m;* ayudante de hospital *m*
ordinal *a* and *n* ordinal *m*
ordinance *n* ordenanza, *f,* reglamento, *m; arch* ordenación, *f; ecc* rito, *m*
ordinarily *adv* de ordinario, ordinariamente, comúnmente

ordinary *a* (usual) corriente, común, usual, ordinario, normal; (average) mediano, mediocre; (somewhat vulgar) ordinario, vulgar. *n ecc* ordinario, *m*. **out of the o.**, excepcional; poco común. **o. seaman,** marinero, *m*. **o. share,** *com* acción ordinaria, *f*
ordination *n ecc* ordenación, *f*
ordnance *n* artillería, *f*, cañones, *m pl*; pertrechos de guerra, *m pl*. **o. survey map,** mapa del estado mayor, *m*. **o. survey number,** acotación, *f*
ore *n min* mena, *f*, quijo, *m*
organ *n* (all meanings) órgano, *m*. **barrel-o.,** organillo, órgano de manubrio, *m*. **o.-blower,** entonador (-ra). **o.-grinder,** organillero (-ra). **o.-loft,** tribuna del órgano, *f*. **o.-pipe,** cañón de órgano, *m*. **o.-stop,** registro de órgano, *m*
organdie *n* organdí, *m*
organic *a* orgánico. **o. chemistry,** química orgánica, *f*
organism *n* organismo, *m*
organist *n* organista, *mf*
organization *n* organización, *f*; grupo, *m*, asociación, sociedad, *f*; organismo, *m*
organize *vt* organizar; arreglar. *vi* organizarse; asociarse, constituirse
organizer *n* organizador (-ra)
organizing *a* organizador
orgasm *n med* orgasmo, *m*
orgiastic *a* orgiástico
orgy *n* orgía, *f*
oriel *n arch* mirador, *m*
orient *a poet* naciente, oriental. *n* Oriente, Este, *m*. **pearl of fine o.**, perla de hermoso oriente, *f*
oriental *a* and *n* oriental, *mf*
orientalism *n* orientalismo, *m*
orientalist *n* orientalista, *mf*
orientate *vt* orientar; dirigir, guiar. *vi* mirar (or caer) hacia el este; orientarse
orientation *n* orientación, *f*
orifice *n* orificio, *m*; abertura, boca, *f*
origin *n* origen, génesis, *m*; raíz, causa, *f*; principio, comienzo, *m*; (extraction) descendencia, procedencia, familia, *f*, nacimiento, *m*
original *a* original; primitivo, primero; ingenioso. *n* original, *m*; prototipo, modelo, *m*. **o. sin,** pecado original, *m*
originality *n* originalidad, *f*
originally *adv* originalmente; al principio; antiguamente
originate *vt* (produce) ocasionar, producir, suscitar, iniciar, engendrar; (create) inventar, crear. *vi* originarse, surgir, nacer. **to o. in,** tener su origen en, surgir de, emanar de, venir de
origination *n* origen, principio, génesis, *m*
originator *n* iniciador (-ra), fundador (-ra); autor (-ra), creador (-ra)
oriole *n orn* oropéndola, *f*
Orion *n ast* Orión, *m*
Orkneys, the las Orcadas, *f pl*
ornament *n* adorno, *m*; decoración, *f*; *fig* ornamento, *m*; (trinket) chuchería, *f*, *n pl*. **ornaments,** *ecc* ornamentos, *m pl*. *vt* ornar, adornar, decorar, embellecer
ornamental *a* ornamental, decorativo
ornamentation *n* ornamentación, decoración, *f*
ornate *a* vistoso, ornado en demasía, barroco
ornateness *n* elegancia, vistosidad, magnificencia, *f*
ornithological *a* ornitológico
ornithologist *n* ornitólogo, *m*
ornithology *n* ornitología, *f*
orphan *a* and *n* huérfano (-na)
orphanage *n* orfanato, hospicio, *m*
orphanhood *n* orfandad, *f*
Orphean *a* órfico
orthodox *a* ortodoxo
orthodoxy *n* ortodoxia, *f*
orthographic *a* ortográfico
orthography *n* ortografía, *f*
orthopedic *a* ortopédico

orthopedics *n* ortopedia, *f*
orthopedist *n* ortopedista, *mf* ortopédico (-ca)
oscillate *vi* oscilar, fluctuar; (hesitate) dudar, vacilar. *vt* hacer oscilar
oscillation *n* oscilación, fluctuación, vibración, *f*; *elec* oscilación, *f*
oscillator *n* oscilador, *m*
oscillatory *a* oscilante
osculation *n* ósculo, *m*
osier *n bot* mimbre, *m*, or *f*. **o. bed,** mimbrera, *f*
osmic *a chem* ósmico
osmosis *n* (*phys chem*) ósmosis, *f*
osprey *n orn* quebrantahuesos, *m*
osseous *a* óseo
ossification *n* osificación, *f*
ossify *vt* osificar; *vi* osificarse
ossuary *n* osario, *m*
osteitis *n med* osteítis, *f*
Ostend Ostende, *f*
ostensible *a* ostensible; aparente, engañoso, ilusorio
ostensibly *adv* en apariencia, ostensiblemente
ostentation *n* ostentación, *f*; aparato, fausto, boato, alarde, *m*, soberbia, *f*
ostentatious *a* ostentoso; aparatoso, fastuoso, rumboso
ostentatiously *adv* con ostentación
osteology *n* osteología, *f*
osteomyelitis *n med* osteomielitis, *f*
osteopath *n* osteópata, *m*
osteopathy *n* osteopatía, *f*
osteoplasty *n surg* osteoplastia, *f*
ostler *n* mozo de cuadras, establero, *m*
ostracism *n* ostracismo, *m*
ostracize *vt* desterrar; excluir del trato, echar de la sociedad
ostrich *n* avestruz, *m*. **o. farm,** criadero de avestruces, *m*
otalgia *n med* otalgia, *f*, dolor de oídos, *m*
other *a* otro. *pron* el otro, *m*; la otra, *f*; lo otro, *neut adv* (with than) de otra manera que, de otro modo que; otra cosa que. **this hand, not the o.,** esta mano, no la otra. **every o. day,** un día sí y otro no, cada dos días. **no o.,** ningún otro, *m*; otra ninguna, *f*. **someone or o.,** alguien. **the others,** los (las) demás, *m, f pl*; los otros, *m pl*; las otras, *f pl*. **o. people,** otros, *m pl*, los demás
otherwise *adv* de otra manera, de otro modo, otramente; (in other respects) por lo demás, por otra parte; (if not) si no
otitis *n med* otitis, *f*
otologist *n* otólogo, *m*
otology *n* otología, *f*
otter *n zool* nutria, *f*. **o. hound,** perro para cazar la nutria
ottoman *a* otomano, turco. *n* otomana, *f*
ouch! *interj* ¡ax!, ¡huy!
ought *v aux* deber, tener la obligación (de); ser conveniente, convenir; ser necesario (que), tener que. **I o. to have done it yesterday,** Debía haberlo hecho ayer. **She o. not to come,** No debe (debiera, debería) venir. **He o. to see them tomorrow,** (should) Conviene que les vea mañana; Tiene la obligación de verles mañana; (must) Es necesario que les vea mañana, Tiene que verles mañana.
ounce *n* (animal and weight) onza, *f*. **He hasn't an o. of common sense,** No tiene pizca de sentido común
our *a* nuestro
ours *pron* nuestro, *m*; nuestra, *f*; nuestros, *m pl*; nuestras, *f pl*; de nosotros, *m pl*; de nosotras, *f pl*; el nuestro, *m*; la nuestra, *f*; lo nuestro, *neut*; los nuestros, *m pl*; las nuestras, *f pl*. **This book is ours,** Este libro es nuestro (or el nuestro)
ourselves *pron pl* nosotros mismos, *m pl*; nosotras mismas, *f pl*
oust *vt* despedir, desahuciar, expulsar, echar
out *adv* afuera; hacia fuera; (gone out) fuera, salido, ausente; (invested) puesto; (published) publicado, salido; (discovered) conocido, descubierto; (on strike) en

huelga; (mistaken) en error, equivocado; (of journeys) de ida, (on ships) de navegación (e.g. **on the second day out,** al segundo día de navegación); (of fire, etc.) extinguido; (at sea) en el mar; (of girls in society) puesta de largo, que ha entrado en sociedad; (of fashion) fuera de moda; (of office) fuera del poder; (in holes) roto, agujereado, andrajoso; (exhausted) agotado; (expired) vencido; (of a watch) llevar . . . minutos (horas) de atraso o de adelanto; (unfriendly) reñido; (way out) salida, *f;* (sport) fuera de juego; (of flowers) abierto; (of chickens) empollado. **a scene out of one of Shakespeare's plays,** una escena de una de las comedias de Shakespeare. **I am out $6,** He perdido seis dólares. **I am out of tea,** Se me ha acabado el té. **to drink out of a glass,** beber de un vaso. **to read out of a book,** leer en un libro. **to speak out,** hablar claro. **Murder will out,** El asesinato se descubrirá. **out-and-out,** completo; (with rogue, etc.) redomado. **out of,** fuera de; (beyond) más allá de; (through, by) por; (with) con; (without) sin; (from among) entre; (in) en; (with a negative sense) no. **out of breath,** jadeante, sin aliento. **out of character,** impropio. **out of commission,** fuera de servicio. **out of danger,** fuera de peligro. **out of date,** anticuado. **out of hand,** en seguida; indisciplinado. **out of money,** sin dinero. **out of necessity,** por necesidad. **out of one's mind,** loco, demente. **out of order.** See **order. out of print,** agotado. **out of reach,** fuera de alcance, inasequible. **out of season,** fuera de temporada. **out of sight,** fuera del alcance de la vista; invisible. **Out of sight, out of mind,** Ojos que no ven, corazón que no siente. **out of sorts,** indispuesto. **out of temper,** de mal genio. **out of the question,** imposible. **out of the way,** *adv* (of work) terminado, hecho; (remote) fuera del camino; (put aside) arrinconado; donde no estorbe. **out-of-the-way,** *a* remoto, aislado; (unusual) extraordinario, singular. **out of this world,** lo máximo, lo último. **out of touch with,** alejado de; sin relaciones con; sin simpatía con. **out of work,** sin empleo, sin trabajo, en paro forzoso. **out-patient,** enfermo (-ma) de un dispensario. **Out!** *interj* ¡Fuera! ¡Fuera de aquí! ¡Márchate! **Out with it!** ¡Hable Vd.! sin rodeos! ¡Hablen claro!

outbalance *vt* exceder, sobrepujar
outbid *vt* pujar, mejorar
outbidding *n* puja, mejora, *f*
outbreak *n* (of war) declaración, *f;* comienzo, *m;* (of disease) epidemia, *f;* (of crimes, etc.) serie, *f*
outbuilding *n* dependencia, *f,* edificio accesorio, anexo, *m*
outburst *n* acceso, arranque, *m,* explosión, *f*
outcast *n* paria, *mf;* desterrado (-da), proscripto (-ta)
outclass *vt* aventajar, ser superior (a), exceder
outcome *n* consecuencia, *f,* resultado, *m*
outcry *n* clamor, grito, *m;* protesta, *f*
outdistance *vt* dejar atrás
outdo *vt* eclipsar, aventajar, sobrepujar
outdoor *a* externo; (of activities) al aire libre; fuera de casa
outdoors *adv* fuera de casa; al aire libre
outer *a* externo, exterior
outer space espacio extraatmosférico, espacio extraterreste, espacio exterior, espacio sideral, espacio sidéreo, espacio ultraterrestre, *m*
outermost *a* *sup* (el, etc.) más externo, más exterior; extremo, de más allá
outfit *n* equipo, *m;* (of clothes) traje, *m;* (of furniture or trousseau) ajuar, *m;* (gear) pertrechos, avíos, *m pl. vt* aviar equipar
outfitter *n* proveedor (-ra), abastecedor (-ra)
outflank *vt* *mil* flanquear; ser más listo (que)
outgoing *a* saliente, que sale; cesante. **outgoings,** *n pl* gastos, *m pl*
outgrow *vt* hacerse demasiado grande para; crecer más que; (ideas) perder; (illness) curarse de, curarse con la edad; pasar de la edad de, ser ya viejo para. **to o. one's**

clothes, quedársele a uno chica la ropa. **to o. one's strength,** estar demasiado crecido para su edad
outgrowth *n* excrecencia, *f;* resultado, fruto, *m,* consecuencia, *f*
outhouse *n* edificio accesorio, *m*
outing *n* excursión, vuelta, *f,* paseo, *m*
outlandish *a* extraño, singular, raro; absurdo, ridículo
outlast *vt* durar más que; (outlive) sobrevivir a
outlaw *n* bandido, proscrito, *m, vt* proscribir
outlay *n* gasto, desembolso, *m*
outlet *n* salida, *f;* orificio de salida, *m;* (of drains, etc.) desagüe, *m;* (of streets, rivers) desembocadura, *f; fig* escape, *m,* válvula de seguridad, *f*
outline *n* perfil, contorno, *m;* (drawing) esbozo, bosquejo, *m;* idea general, *f;* plan general, *m, vt* esbozar, bosquejar. **in o.,** en esbozo; en perfil. **to be outlined (against),** dibujarse (contra), destacarse (contra)
outlive *vt* sobrevivir (a); (live down) hacer olvidar
outlook *n* (view) perspectiva, vista, *f;* (opinion) actitud, *f,* punto de vista, *m;* aspecto, *m,* apariencia, *f;* (for trade, etc.) perspectiva, *f,* posibilidades, *f pl.* **o. tower,** atalaya, *f*
outlying *a* remoto, lejano, distante
outmaneuver *vt* superar en estrategia
outmatch *vt* aventajar, superar
outmoded *a* anticuado, pasado de moda
outnumber *vt* ser más numerosos que, exceder en número
out-of-court settlement *n* arreglo pacífico, *m*
out-of-town *a* de las provincias
outpost *n* *mil* avanzada, *f,* puesto avanzado, *m*
outpouring *n* derramamiento, *m;* efusión, *f*
output *n* producción, *f.* **o. capacity,** capacidad de producción, *f*
outrage *n* barbaridad infamia, atrocidad, *f;* rapto, *m,* violación, *f. vt* ultrajar; violar; violentar
outrageous *a* atroz, terrible; desaforado, monstruoso; injurioso; ridículo
outrageousness *n* lo atroz; violencia, furia, *f;* escándalo, *m;* enormidad, *f;* lo excesivo; lo horrible
outré *a* cursi, extravagante
outride *vt* cabalgar más a prisa que
outright *adv* (frankly) de plano (e.g. **to reject outright,** rechazar de plano), francamente, sin reserva; (immediately) en seguida, immediatamente. *a* categórico; completo; franco
outrival *vt* vencer, superar
outrun *vt* correr más que
outset *n* principio, comienzo, *m*
outshine *vt* brillar más que, eclipsar en brillantez; superar, eclipsar
outside *adv* afuera, fuera. *prep* fuera de, al otro lado de, al exterior de; (besides) aparte de, fuera de. *a* externo; exterior; (of labor, etc.) desde fuera; máximo; ajeno. *n* exterior, *m;* superficie, *f;* aspecto, *m,* apariencia, *f.* **at the o.,** a lo sumo, cuando más. **from the o.,** de (or desde) fuera. **on the o.,** (externally) por fuera. **o. the door,** a la puerta
outsider *n* forastero (-ra); desconocido (-da); caballo desconocido, *m;* persona poco deseable, *f*
outsize *n* artículo de talla mayor que las corrientes, *m*
outskirts *n pl* alrededores, *m pl,* afueras, *f pl,* immediaciones, cercanías, *f pl*
outspoken *a* franco. **to be o.,** decir lo que se piensa, no tener pelos en la lengua
outspokenness *n* franqueza, *f,*
outspread *a* extendido; (of wings) desplegadas
outstanding *a* excelente; sobresaliente, conspicuo; *com* pendiente, sin pagar. **to be o.,** *com* estar pendiente; *fig* sobresalir. **o. account,** *com* cuenta pendiente, *f*
outstay *vt* quedarse más tiempo que. **to o. one's welcome,** pegársele la silla
outstretched *a* extendido
outstrip *vt* dejar atrás, pasar; aventajar, superar
outvote *vt* emitir más votos que; rechazar por votación
outward *a* exterior, externo; aparente, visible. *adv* ex-

teriormente; hacia fuera; superficialmente. **o. bound,** con rumbo a . . . **o. voyage,** el viaje de ida

outwardly *adv* exteriormente; hacia fuera; en apariencia

outwear *vt* durar más que; gastar

outweigh *vt* exceder, valer más que

outwit *vt* ser más listo que; vencer

outworn *a* anticuado, ya viejo

oval *n* óvalo, *m*, *a* oval, ovalado, aovado

ovarian *a* (*bot zool*) ovárico

ovary *n* ovario, *m*

ovation *n* ovación, recepción entusiasta, *f*

oven *n* horno, *m*. **o. peel,** pala de horno, *f*. **o. rake,** hurgón, *m*

over *prep* (above, upon, over) sobre, encima de; (on the other side) al otro lado de; (across) allende, a través de; (more than) más de; (beyond) más allá de; (of rank) superior a; (during) durante; (in addition) además de; (through) por. *n* (cricket) serie de saques, *f*, *adv* encima; en; por encima; al otro lado; de un lado a otro; enfrente; al lado contrario; de un extremo a otro; (finished) terminado; (ruined) arruinado, perdido; (more) más; (excessively) demasiado, excesivamente; (covered) cubierto (de); (extra) en exceso; (completely) enteramente; (from head to foot) de pies a cabeza, de hito en hito; (of time) pasado. **over** is also used as a prefix. Indicating excess, it is generally translated by demasiado or excesivamente. In other meanings, it is either not translated or its meaning forms part of the verb, being translated as re-, super-, trans-, ultra. Very often a less literal translation is more successful than the employment of the above prefixes. **all o.,** (everywhere) en todas partes; (finished) todo acabado; (covered) cubierto (de); (up and down) de pies a cabeza. **all the world o.,** en todo el mundo. **embroidered all o.,** todo bordado. **He is o. in Germany,** Está en Alemania. **He trembled all o.,** Estaba todo tembloroso. **that which is o.,** el exceso, lo que queda. **to read o.,** leer, repasar. **o. again,** de nuevo. **o. and above,** por encima de, fuera de, en exceso de. **o. and o.,** repetidamente, muchas veces. **o. my signature,** bajo mi firma. **o. six months since . . . ,** más de seis meses desde que . . .

overabundance *n* sobreabundancia, *f*

overabundant *a* sobreabundante

overact *vt* exagerar (un papel)

overall *n* bata, *f*; guardapolvo, *m*; *a* deconjunto (e.g., **overall assessment,** evaluación de conjunto) *pl* **overalls,** mono, *m*

overanxious *a* demasiado ansioso; demasiado inquieto. **to be o.-a.,** preocuparse demasiado

overarch *vt* abovedar

overawe *vt* intimidar, acobardar

overbalance *vt* hacer perder el equilibrio. hacer caer; preponderar. *vi* perder el equilibrio, caer

overbalancing *n* pérdida del equilibrio, caída, *f*; preponderancia, *f*

overbearing *a* dominante, autoritario, imperioso

overboard *adv* al agua, al mar.

overburden *vt* sobrecargar, agobiar

overcast *a* anublado, cerrado, encapotado. *vt sew* sobrehilar. **to become o.,** anublarse

overcharge *n* recargo, *m*; (price) recargo de precio, precio excesivo, *m*. *vt* recargar, cobrar un precio excesivo; *elec* sobrecargar. *vi* cobrar demasiado

overcloud *vt* anublar; *fig* entristecer

overcoat *n* abrigo, sobretodo, gabán, *m*

overcome *vt* vencer, rendir, subyugar; (difficulties) triunfar de, allanar, dominar. *vi* saber vencer. *a* (by sleep, etc.) rendido; (at a loss) turbado, confundido; (by kindness) agradecidísimo

overconfidence *n* confianza excesiva, *f*

overcooked *a* recocido, demasiado cocido

overcrowd *vt* atestar, llenar de bote en bote; (over-populate) sobrepoblar

overcrowding *n* sobrepoblación, *f*

overdo *vt* exagerar; ir demasiado lejos, hacer demasiado; *cul* recocer; (overtire) fatigarse demasiado

overdose *n* dosis excesiva, *f*

overdraft *n com* giro en descubierto, *m*

overdraw *vt* and *vi com* girar en descubierto

over-dressed *a* que viste demasiado; cursi

overdue *a* atrasado; *com* vencido y no pagado

overeat *vi* comer demasiado, atracarse

overestimate *vt* estimar en valor excesivo; exagerar, sobreestimar, *n* presupuesto excesivo, *m*; estimación excesiva, *f*

overexcite *vt* sobreexcitar

overexposure *n phot* exceso deexposición, *m*

overfatigue *vt* fatigar demasiado. *n* cansancio excesivo, *m*

overfeeding *n* sobrealimentación, *f*

overflow *vt* inundar, derramarse por; *fig* cubrir, llenar; desbordarse. *vi* (with) rebosar de. *n* inundación, *f*, desbordamiento, derrame, *m*; *fig* residuo, resto, exceso, *m*; (plumbing) sumidero, vertedero, *m*, descarga, *f*. **The river overflowed its banks,** El río se desbordó, El río salió de cauce

overflowing *a* rebosante; superabundante. **filled to o.,** lleno hasta los bordes. **o. with health,** rebosante de salud, vendiendo salud

overgrown *a* (gawky) talludo; (plants) exuberante, vicioso; frondoso, cubierto de verdura

overhang *vt* caer a, mirar a; colgar; *fig* amenazar. *vi* colgar, sobresalir; *fig* amenazar

overhanging *a* saledizo, sobresaliente; colgante, pendiente

overhaul *vt* examinar, investigar; componer, hacer una inspección general de; (of boats overtaking) alcanzar. *n* examen, *m*, investigación, *f*; *med* exploración general, *f*

overhead *adv* arriba, en lo alto, encima de la cabeza. *a* aéreo, elevado; general, fijo. **o. cable,** cable eléctrico, *m*. **o. expenses,** gastos generales, *m pl*. **o. railway,** ferrocarril aéreo (or elevado), *m*

overhear *vt* (accidentally) oír por casualidad, oír sin querer; (on purpose) alcanzar a oír, lograr oír

overheat *vt* acalorar, hacer demasiado caliente, recalentar. *vi* (in argument) acalorarse; hacerse demasiado caliente

overheating *n* recalentamiento, *m*

overindulge *vt* mimar demasiado; dedicarse a algo con exceso; tomar algo con exceso. *vi* darse demasiada buena vida

overjoyed *a* contentísimo, lleno de alegría, encantado

overland *adv* por tierra. *a* terrestre, trascontinental

overlap *vi* traslaparse; coincidir. *n* traslapo, *m*

overlay *vt* cubrir, dar una capa; (with silver) platear; (with gold) dorar. *n* capa, *f*; cubierta, *f*

overleaf *adv* a la vuelta

overload *vt* sobrecargar, recargar. *n* sobrecarga, *f*

overlook *vt* (face) dar a, mirar a, dominar; (supervise) vigilar, examinar, inspeccionar; (not notice) no notar, pasar por alto, no hacer, caso de, no fijarse en; (neglect) desdeñar; (ignore) no darse cuenta de, ignorar; (excuse) perdonar, tolerar, hacer la vista gorda

overlord *n* señor de horca y cuchillo, señor, jefe, *m*

overmuch *adv* demasiado, en exceso

overnight *adv* la noche pasada, durante la noche; toda la noche. *a* de la víspera, nocturno. **to stay o. with,** pasar la noche con

overpaint *vt* pintar demasiado; *fig* recargar las tintas

overpass *n* pasaje elevado, viaducto, *m*

overpay *vt* pagar demasiado

overpayment *n* pago excesivo, *m*

overpopulate *vt* sobrepoblar, **become overpopulated** recargarse de habitantes (with people), recargarse de animales (with animals)

overpower *vt* vencer, subyugar; (of scents, etc.) trastornar; rendir, dominar

overpowering *a* irresistible

overpraise *vt* encarecer, alabar mucho

overproduce *vt* and *vi* sobreproducir

overproduction *n* sobreproducción, *f*

overrate *vt* exagerar el valor de; (of property) sobrevalorar

overreach *vt* sobrealcanzar. **to o. oneself,** sobrepasarse, ir demasiado lejos

override *vt* (trample) pasar por encima (de); *fig* rechazar, poner a un lado; (bully) dominar; (a horse) fatigar, reventar

overripe *a* demasiado maduro

overrule *vt law* denegar, no admitir; vencer

overrun *vt* (flood) inundar; (ravage) invadir; (infest) plagar, infestar; desbordarse, derramarse

oversea *a* ultramarino, de ultramar. *adv* en ultramar, allende los mares

oversee *vt* vigilar, inspeccionar

overseer *n* capataz, mayoral, sobrestante, contramaestre, *m*; inspector (-ra), veedor (-ra)

oversell *vt* and *vi* vender en exceso

oversensitive *a* demasiado sensitivo; vidrioso; susceptible

oversew *vt* sobrecoser

overshadow *vt* sombrear; *fig* eclipsar, obscurecer; (sadden) entristecer

overshoe *n* chanclo, *m*; (for snow) galocha, *f*

overshoot *vt* tirar más allá del blanco; *fig* exceder, rebasar el límite conveniente, **overshoot the target** (fig.) ir más allá del blanco, ir más allá de lo razonable. **to o. oneself,** exagerar; propasarse, descomedirse

oversight *n* inadvertencia, omisión, equivocación, *f*; descuido, *m*

oversimplify *vt* simplificar en exceso

oversleep *vi* dormir demasiado; *inf* pegársele a uno las sábanas, levantarse demasiado tarde

overspend *vt* and *vi* gastar demasiado

overspread *vt* desparramar, salpicar, esparcir, sembrar; cubrir

overstate *vt* exagerar, encarecer, ponderar

overstatement *n* exageración, ponderación, *f*

overstep *vt* exceder, pasar, violar; rebasar, pasar más allá (de)

overstrain *vt* fatigar demasiado, agotar. *n* fatiga, *f*. **to o. oneself,** esforzarse demasiado, cansarse demasiado

overstrung *a* nervioso, excitable; (piano) de cuerdas cruzadas

oversubscribe *vt* subscribir en exceso

overt *a* abierto, público; manifiesto, evidente

overtake *vt* alcanzar, pasar, dejar atrás; adelantarse (a); (surprise) coger, sorprender; (overwhelm) vencer, dominar

overtax *vt* oprimir de tributos; agobiar, cansar demasiado

overthrow *vt* volcar, echar por tierra, derribar; *fig* vencer, destruir, destronar. *n* vuelco, derribo, *m*; *fig* destrucción, ruina, *f*

overtime *adv* fuera de las horas estipuladas. *n* horas extraordinarias de trabajo, *f pl.* **to work o.,** trabajar horas extraordinarias

overtone *n mus* armónico, *m*

overtop *vt* dominar, sobresalir, elevarse encima de

overture *n mus* obertura, *f*

overturn *vt* volcar, derribar, echar a rodar, echar abajo; (upset) revolver, desordenar. *vi* volcar, venirse abajo, allanarse; estar revuelto

overturning *n* vuelco, salto de campana, *m*

overweening *a* arrogante, insolente, altivo

overweight *n* sobrepeso, exceso en el peso, *m.* **to be o.,** pesar más de lo debido

overwhelm *vt* (conquer) vencer, aplastar, derrotar; (of waves, etc.) sumergir, hundir, inundar, engolfar; (in argument) confundir, dejar confuso, avergonzar; (of grief, etc.) vencer, postrar, dominar; (of work) inundar

overwhelming *a* irresistible, invencible, abrumador, apabullante

overwind *vt* (a watch) dar demasiada cuerda a; romper la cuerda de

overwork *vt* hacer trabajar demasiado (or con exceso); esclavizar. *vi* trabajar demasiado. *n* exceso de trabajo, demasiado trabajo, *m*

overwrought *a* (overworked) agotado por el trabajo, rendido, muy cansado; nerviosísimo, sobreexcitado, exaltado, muy agitado

ovine *a* ovejuno

ovoid *a* ovoide

ovulation *n med* ovulación, *f*

owe *vt* deber, tener deudas (de); deber, estar agradecido (por), estar obligado (a). *vi* estar en deuda, estar endeudado, tener deudas. **He owes his tailor $30,** Le debe treinta dólares a su sastre. **I owe him thanks for his help,** Le estoy agradecido por su ayuda (*or* Le debo las gracias por . . .). **He owes his success to good fortune,** Su éxito se debe a la suerte

owing *a* sin pagar. **o. to,** debido a, a causa de, por. **We had to stay in o. to the rain,** Tuvimos que quedarnos en casa a causa de la lluvia. **What is o. to you now?** ¿Cuánto se le debe ahora?

owl *n* búho, mochuelo, *m.* **barn** or **screech owl,** lechuza, *f.* **brown owl,** autillo, *m*

owlish *a* parecido a un búho, de búho

own *a* propio. *n* (dearest) bien, *m. vt* poseer, tener, ser dueño de; (recognize) reconocer; (admit) confesar. *vi* confesar. **my (thy, his, our, your) own,** mi (tu, su, nuestro, vuestro) propio, *m,* (*f,* propia); mis (tus, sus, nuestros, vuestros) propios, *m pl,* (*f pl,* propias); (when not placed before a noun) el mío (tuyo, suyo, nuestro, vuestro), la mía (tuya, etc.), los míos (tuyos, etc.), las mías (tuyas, etc.); (relations) los suyos. **in his own house,** en su propia casa. **my (thy, his, etc.) own self,** yo (tú, él) mismo, *m,* (*f,* misma, *m pl,* mismos *f pl,* mismas). **a room of one's own,** un cuarto para sí (or para uno mismo). **to be on one's own,** ser independiente; estar a solas. **to hold one's own,** mantenerse en sus trece. **to own up,** confesar

owner *n* dueño (-ña), propietario (-ia), posesor (-ra)

ownerless *a* sin dueño, sin amo

ownership *n* posesión, *f,* dominio, *m*; propiedad, *f*

ox *n* buey (*pl* bueyes), *m.* **oxeye daisy,** margarita, *f.*

oxstall *n* boyera, *f*

oxidation *n chem* oxidación, *f*

oxide *n chem* óxido, *m*

oxidization *n* oxidación, *f*

oxidize *vt chem* oxidar; *vi* oxidarse

oxygen *n* oxígeno, *m.* **o. mask,** máscara de oxígeno, *f.* **o. tent,** tienda de oxígeno, *f*

oxygenate *vt chem* oxigenar

oxygenation *n chem* oxigenación, *f*

oyez, oyez! *interj* ¡oíd!

oyster *n* ostra, *f.* **o. bed,** pescadero (or criadero) de ostras, *m.* **o. culture,** ostricultura, *f*

ozone *n* ozono, *m*

P

p *n* (letter) pe, *f.* **to mind one's p's and q's,** poner los puntos sobre las íes; ir con pies de plomo

pabulum *n* pábulo, *m*; sustento, *m*

pace *n* paso, *m*; (gait) andar, *m,* marcha, *f*; (of a horse) andadura, *f*; (speed) velocidad, *f. vi* pasear(se); andar; (of a horse) amblar. *vt* recorrer, andar por; marcar el

paso para; (with out) medir a pasos. **at a good p.,** a un buen paso. **to keep p. with,** ajustarse al paso de, ir al mismo paso que; andar al paso de; (events) mantenerse al corriente de. **to p. up and down,** pasearse, dar vueltas. **p.-maker,** el que marca el paso

paced *a* de andar . . . ; (of a horse) de andadura . . . ; de paso . . .

pachyderm *n* paquidermo, *m*

Pacific, the el (Océano) Pacífico, *m*

pacific *a geog* pacífico; sosegado, tranquilo, pacífico. **He is of a p. disposition,** Es amigo de la paz

pacification *n* pacificación, *f*

pacificatory *a* pacificador

pacifier *n* pacificador (-ra)

pacifism *n* pacifismo, *m*

pacifist *a* pacifista. *n* pacifista, *mf*

pacify *vt* pacificar; calmar, tranquilizar; aplacar, conciliar

pack *n* (bundle) fardo, lío, *m*; paquete, *m*; (load) carga, *f*; (of hounds) jauría, *f*; (herd) hato, *m*; (of seals) manada, *f*; (of cards) baraja (de naipes), *f*; (of rogues) cuadrilla, *f*; (of lies, etc.) colección, *f*; masa, *f*; (of ice) témpanos flotantes, *m pl*; (Rugby football) delanteros, *m pl*; (for the face) compresa, *f*. **p.-horse,** caballo de carga, *m*. **p.-needle,** aguja espartera, *f*. **p.-saddle,** albarda, *f*. **p.-thread,** bramante, *m*

pack *vt* embalar; empaquetar; envasar; encajonar; (a suit-case, etc.) hacer; (cram) apretar; (crowd) atestar, llenar; (a pipe joint, etc.) empaquetar; (an animal) cargar. *vi* llenar; (one's luggage) hacer el equipaje, hacer el baúl, arreglar el equipaje. **packed like sardines,** como sardinas en banasta. **The train was packed,** El tren estababa lleno de bote en bote. **to p. off,** (a person) despachar; poner de partitas en la calle. **to p. up,** hacer el equipaje; empaquetar; embalar; *inf* liar el hato

package *n* paquete, *m*; bulto, *m*; (bundle) fardo, *m*

packer *n* embalador, *m*; envasador (-ra)

packet *n* paquete, *m*; (of cigarettes, etc.) cajetilla, *f*; (boat) paquebote, *m*. **to make one's p.,** *inf* hacer su pacotilla

packing *n* embalaje, *m*; envoltura, *f*; envase, *m*; (on a pipe, etc.) guarnición, *f*. **I must do my p.,** Tengo que hacer las maletas. **p.-case,** caja de embalaje, *f*. **p.-needle,** aguja espartera, *f*

pact *n* pacto, convenio, *m*. **to make a p.,** pactar

pad *n* almohadilla, *f*, cojinete, *m*; (on a bed, chair) colchoneta, *f*; (on a wound) cabezal, *m*; (for polishing) muñeca, *f*; (hockey) defensa, *f*; (cricket) espinillera, *f*; (writing) bloque, *m*; (of a calendar) taco, *m*; (blotting) secafirmas, *m*; (of a quadruped's foot) pulpejo, *m*; (of fox, hare) pata, *f*; (leaf) hoja grande, *f*, *vt* almohadillar; acolchar; rellenar; forrar; (out, a book, etc.) meter paja en. **inking-pad,** almohadilla de entintar, *f*. **padded cell,** celda acolchonada, *f*. **shoulder-pad,** (in a garment) hombrera, *f*

padding *n* relleno, *m*, almohadilla, *f*; (material) borra, *f*, algodón, *m*; *fig* paja, *f*, ripio, *m*,

paddle *n* (oar) canalete, zagual, *m*; paleta, *f*; (flipper) aleta, *f*, *vt* and *vi* remar con canalete; (dabble) chapotear. **double p.,** remo doble, *m*. **p.-steamer,** vapor de ruedas, vapor de paleta, *m*. **p.-wheel,** rueda de paletas, *f*

paddler *n* remero (-ra); el, *m*, (*f*, la) que chapotea

paddling *n* chapoteo, chapaleo, *m*

paddock *n* prado, *m*, dehesa, *f*; parque, *m*; (near a racecourse) en silla dero, picadero, *f*; (toad) sapo, *m*

padlock *n* candado, *m*, *vt* cerrar con candado, acerrojar

Paduan *a* and *a* paduano (-na)

paean *n* himno de alegría, *m*

pagan *a* and *n* pagano (-na)

paganism *n* paganismo, *m*

page *n* (boy) paje, *m*; (squire) escudero, *m*; (of a book, etc.) página, *f*; *fig* hoja, *f*. *vt* compaginar; (a person) vocear. **on p. nine,** en la página nueve. **to turn the p.,** *fig* volver la hoja

pageant *n* espectáculo, *m*; (procession) desfile, *m*; representación teatral, *f*; fiesta, *f*; *fig* pompa, *f*, aparato, *m*

pageantry *n* pompa, *f*, aparato, *m*, magnificencia, *f*

paginate *vt* paginar

pagination *n* paginación, *f*

pagoda *n* pagoda, *f*

paid *a* pagado; (on a parcel) porte pagado. **p. mourner,** plañidera, *f*. **p.-up share,** acción liberada, *f*

pail *n* cubo, pozal, *m*, cubeta, *f*

pailful *n* cubo (de agua, etc.), *m*

pain *n* dolor, *m*; sufrimiento, *m*; (mental) tormento, *m*, angustia, *f*; *law* pena, *f*; *pl* **pains,** (effort) trabajo, esfuerzo, *m*. *vt* doler; atormentar, afligir. **dull p.,** dolor sordo, *m*. **I have a p. in my head,** Me duele la cabeza. **on p. of death,** so pena de muerte. **to be in great p.,** sufrir mucho. **to take pains,** tomarse trabajo, esforzarse, esmerarse

pained *a* dolorido; afligido; de angustia

painful *a* doloroso; angustioso; fatigoso; (troublesome) molesto; (embarrassing) embarazoso; difícil; (laborious) arduo

painfully *adv* dolorosamente; penosamente; fatigosamente; con angustia; laboriosamente

painfulness *n* dolor, *m*; angustia, aflicción, *f*; tormento, *m*; dificultad, *f*

painless *a* sin dolor, indoloro

painlessly *adv* sin dolor; sin sufrir

painlessness *n* falta de dolor, *f*

painstaking *a* concienzudo; diligente, industrioso; cuidadoso. *n* trabajo, *m*; diligencia, industria, *f*; cuidado, *m*

paint *n* pintura, *f*; (for preserving metal) pavón, *m*; (rouge) colorete, *m*. *vt* pintar. *vi* pintar; pintarse. **The door is painted blue,** La puerta está pintada de azul. **p.-box,** caja de pinturas, *f*. **p.-brush,** pincel, *m*; (for house painting) brocha, *f*

painter *n* pintor (-ra); (house) pintor de brocha gorda, pintor de casas, *m*; (of a boat) boza, *f*. **sign-p.,** pintor de muestras, *m*

painting *n* pintura, *f*; (picture) cuadro, *m*, pintura, *f*

pair *n* par, *m*; (of people) pareja, *f*; (of oxen) yunta, *f*. *vt* parear, emparejar; (persons) unir, casar; (animals) aparear. *vi* parearse; casarse; aparearse. **a carriage and p.,** un landó con dos caballos. **a p. of steps,** una escalera de mano. **a p. of pants a p. of trousers,** unos pantalones. **in pairs,** de dos en dos; por parejas. **to p. off,** *vt* formar pareja; *inf* casarse

pal *n* camarada, compinche, *mf*; amigote, *m*

palace *n* palacio, *m*

paladin *n* paladín, *m*

paleographer *n* paleógrafo, *m*

paleography *n* paleografía, *f*

paleolithic *a* paleolítico

paleology *n* paleología, *f*

paleontology *n* paleontología, *f*

palatable *a* sabroso, apetitoso; *fig* agradable, aceptable

palatableness *n* buen sabor, gusto agradable, *m*; *fig* lo agradable

palatably *adv* agradablemente

palatal *a* paladial. *n* letra paladial, *f*

palatalize *vt* palatizar

palate *n* paladar, *m*. **hard p.,** paladar, *m*. **soft p.,** velo del paladar, *m*

palatial *a* (of a palace) palaciego; (sumptuous) magnífico, suntuoso

pale *n* (stake) estaca, *f*; límite, *m*; *her* palo, *m*, *a* pálido; (wan) descolorido; (of colours) claro, desmayado; (of light) tenue, mortecino; (lustreless) sin brillo, muerto. *vi* palidecer, perder el color; *fig* eclipsarse

palely *adv* pálidamente; vagamente, indistintamente

paleness *n* palidez, *f*; (wanness) descoloramiento, *m*, amarillez, *f*; (of light) tenuidad, *f*

Palestine Palestina, *f*

palette *n* paleta, *f*. **p.-knife,** espátula, *f*

palimpsest *n* palimpsesto, *m*

palindrome *n* capicúa *f*, (of numbers), palíndromo *m*

paling *n* palizada, estacada, valla, *f*

palisade *n* palenque, *m*, tranquera, palizada, *f*; *mil* estacada, *f*

palish *a* algo pálido; paliducho

pall *n* (on a coffin) paño mortuorio, *m*; (*fig* covering) manto, *m*, capa, *f*; *ecc* palio, *m*; (over a chalice) palia, *f*.

vi perder el sabor, hacerse insípido; saciarse (de); aburrirse (de), cansarse (de). **The music of Bach never palls on me,** No me canso nunca de la música de Bach
palladium *n min* paladio, *m*; (safeguard) paladión, *m*
pallet *n* jergón, *m*; camilla, *f*; *mech* fiador de rueda, *m*; torno de alfarero, *m*
palliate *vt* (pain) paliar, aliviar; mitigar; (excuse) disculpar, excusar
palliation *n* paliación, *f*; mitigación, *f*; disculpa, *f*
palliative *a* paliativo; (extenuating) atenuante. *n* paliativo, *m*
pallid *a* pálido
pallidness *n* palidez, *f*
pallor *n* palidez, *f*
palm *n* (of the hand, and *fig.*, victory) palma, *f*; (measurement) ancho de la mano, *m*; (tree) palmera, *f*. *vt* (a card, etc.) empalmar; (with off) defraudar (con); dar gato por liebre (a). **to bear away the p.,** llevar la palma. **p. branch,** palma, *f*. **p. grove,** palmar, *m*. **p.-oil,** aceite de palma, *m*; (bribe) soborno, *m*. **P. Sunday,** Domingo de Ramos, *m*. **p. tree,** palmera, *f*
palmate *a* palmeado
palmer *n* peregrino, *m*; (caterpillar) oruga velluda, *f*
palming *n* (in conjuring, etc.) empalme, *m*
palmist *n* quiromántico (-ca)
palmistry *n* quiromancía, *f*
palmy *a* palmar; (flourishing) floreciente; (happy) dichoso, feliz; (prosperous) próspero; triunfante
Palmyra Palmira, *f*
palp *n* palpo, *m*
palpability *n* palpabilidad, *f*
palpable *a* palpable
palpate *vt* palpar
palpation *n* palpación, *f*
palpitate *vi* palpitar
palpitating *a* palpitante
palpitation *n* palpitación, *f*
palsied *a* paralítico
palsy *n* parálisis, *f*, *vt* paralizar
paltriness *n* mezquindad, pequeñez, *f*
paltry *a* mezquino, insignificante, pobre
paludism *n med* paludismo, *m*
pampas *n* pampa, *f*
pamper *vt* mimar, consentir demasiado; criar con mimos, regalar; alimentar demasiado bien
pampered *a* mimado, consentido; demasiado bien alimentado
pamphlet *n* folleto, *m*
pamphleteer *n* folletinista, *mf*
pan *n* (vessel) cazuela, *f*; cacerola, *f*; (brain) cráneo, *m*; (of a balance) platillo, *m*; (of a firelock) cazoleta, *f*; *cinem* toma panorámica *f*, *prefix* pan-. **to pan off,** separar el oro en una gamella. **to pan out,** dar oro; *fig* suceder. **Pan-Americanism,** panamericanismo, *m*
Pan *n* Pan, *m*. **pipes of Pan,** flauta de Pan, *f*
panacea *n* panacea, *f*
panache *n* penacho, *m*
panada *n cul* panetela, *f*
Panama el Panamá, *m*
Panama *a* panameño. (-ña). **P. hat,** sombrero de jipijapa, panamá *m*
pancake *n* fruta de sartén, hojuela, *f*. **p. landing,** *aer* aterrizaje brusco, *m*. **P. Tuesday,** martes de Carnaval, *m*
panchromatic *a* pancromático
pancreas *n* páncreas, *m*
pancreatic *a* pancreático
panda *n zool* panda, *mf*
pandemic *a* pandémico
pandemonium *n* pandemonio
pander *n* alcahuete, *m*, *vi* alcahuetear. **to p. to,** prestarse a; favorecer, ayudar
pandore *n mus* bandola, *f*
pane *n* hoja de vidrio, hoja de cristal, *f*; cuadro, *m*
panegyric *a* panegírico. *n* panegírico, *m*
panegyrist *n* panegirista, *mf*

panel *n* panel, entrepaño, *m*; *art* tabla, *f*; (in a dress) paño, *m*; (list) lista, *f*, registro, *m*; (jury) jurado, *m*; lista de jurados, *f*, *vt* labrar a entrepaños; artesonar. **p. doctor,** médico (-ca) de seguros
paneled *a* entrepañado; (of ceilings) artesonado. **p. ceiling,** artesonado, *m*
paneling *n* entrepaños, *m pl*; artesonado, *m*
panful *n* cazolada, *f*
pang *n* punzada (de dolor), *f*, dolor agudo, *m*; dolor, *m*; (anguish of mind) angustia, *f*, tormento, *m*; (of conscience) remordimiento, *m*
panic *n* pánico, *m*; pavor, espanto, *m*; terror súbito, *m*, *a* pánico. *vi* espantarse. **p.-monger,** alarmista, *mf*
p.-stricken, aterrorizado, despavorido
panicky *a inf* lleno de pánico; nervioso
panicle *n bot* panoja, *f*
pannier *n* (basket) alforja, *f*; cesto, *m*; (bustle) caderillas, *f pl*
panoply *n* panoplia, *f*
panorama *n* panorama, *m*
panoramic *a* panorámico
pansy *n* pensamiento, *m*, trinitaria, *f*
pant *vi* jadear; (of dogs) hipar; resollar; (of the heart) palpitar. *n* jadeo, *m*; palpitación, *f*. **to p. after,** suspirar por
pantaloon *n* (trouser) pantalón, *m*; (Pantaloon) Pantalón, *m*
pantechnicon *n* almacén de muebles, *m*; (van) carro de mudanzas, *m*
pantheism *n* panteísmo, *m*
pantheist *n* panteísta, *mf*
pantheistic *a* panteísta
pantheon *n* panteón, *m*
panther *n* pantera, *f*
panties *n pl* pantalones, *m pl*
panting *a* jadeante, sin aliento. *n* jadeo, *m*; resuello, *m*, respiración difícil, *f*; palpitación, *f*
pantograph *n* pantógrafo, *m*
pantomime *n* pantomima, *f*; revista, *f*. **in p.,** en pantomima; por gestos
pantry *n* despensa, *f*
pants *n pl* calzoncillos, *m pl*; (trousers) pantalones, *m pl*
panzer division *n* división motorizada, *f*
pap *n* (nipple) pezón, *m*; (soft food) papilla, *f*
papa *n* papá, *m*
papacy *n* papado, pontificado, *m*
papal *a* papal, pontificio. **p. bull,** bula pontificia, *f*. **p. nuncio,** nuncio del Papa, nuncio apostólico, *m*. **p. see,** sede apostólica, *f*
paper *n* papel, *m*; hoja de papel, *f*; documento, *m*; (lecture) comunicación, *f*; (newspaper) periódico, *m*; (journal) revista, *f*; (exam.) examen escrito, trabajo, *m*; ejercicio, *m*; *pl* **papers,** (credentials) documentación, *f*, credenciales, *f pl*; *com* valores negociables, *m pl*; (packet) paquete, *m*, *a* de papel; para papeles; parecido al papel. *vt* (a room) empapelar; (a parcel) envolver. **daily p.,** diario, *m*. **in p. covers,** (of books) en rústica. **slip of p.,** papeleta. *f*. **to send in one's papers,** entregar su dimisión. **p. bag,** saco de papel, *m*. **p.-chase,** rally-paper, *m*. **p. clip,** prendedero de oficina, "sujeta papels," *m*. **p.-cutting machine,** guillotina, *f*. **p. folder,** plegadera, *f*. **p.-hanger,** empapelador, *m*. **p.-hanging,** empapelado, *m*. **p.-knife,** cortapapel, *m*. **p.-maker,** fabricante de papel, *m*. **p.-making,** manufactura de papel, *f*. **p.-mill,** fábrica de papel, *f*. **p.-money,** papel moneda, *m*. **p.-pulp,** pasta, *f*. **p.-streamer,** serpentina, *f*. **p.-weight,** pisapapeles, *m*
papering *n* (of a room) empapelado, *m*
papery *a* semejante al papel
papier-mâché *n* cartón piedra, *m*
papillary *a* papilar
papist *n* papista, *mf*; católico (-ca)
papoose *n* niño indio, *m*
paprika *n* pimienta húngara, *f*
papyrus *n* papiro, *m*
par *n* par, *f*. **at par,** *com* a la par. **above (below) par,**

com por encima (*or* debajo) de la par. **He is a little below par,** No está muy bien de salud. **to be on par with,** ser el equivalente de; ser igual a. **par excellence,** por excelencia

parable *n* parábola, *f*

parabola *n geom* parábola, *f*

parachute *n* paracaídas, *m; bot* vilano, *m*. **to p. down,** lanzarse en paracaídas. **p. troops,** cuerpo de paracaidistas, *m*

parachutist *n* paracaidista, *mf*

parade *n* alarde, *m; mil* parada, revista, *f;* (procession) desfile, *m,* procesión, *f;* (promenade) paseo, *m. vt* (display) hacer alarde de, hacer gala de, ostentar; (troops) formar en parada; pasar revista (a); (patrol) recorrer. *vi mil* tomar parte en una parada; desfilar. **to p. up and down,** pasearse. **p.-ground,** campo de instrucción, *m;* plaza de armas, *f*

paradigm *n* paradigma, *m*

paradise *n* paraíso, edén, *m; fig* jauja, *f.* **bird of p.,** ave del paraíso, *f*

paradisiac *a* paradisíaco

paradox *n* paradoja, *f*

paradoxical *a* paradójico

paradoxicality *n* lo paradójico

paraffin *n* parafina, *f. vt* parafinar. **p.-oil,** parafina líquida, *f*

paragon *n* modelo perfecto, dechado, *m*

paragraph *n* párrafo, *m;* (in a newspaper) suelto, *m, vt* dividir en párrafos; escribir un suelto sobre. **new p.,** párrafo aparte, *m*

Paraguay el Paraguay, *m*

Paraguayan *a* and *n* paraguayo (-ya)

parakeet *n orn* perico, *m*

parallel *a* paralelo; igual; semejante, análogo. *n* línea paralela, *f;* paralelo, *m; mil* paralela, *f; geog* paralelo, *m; print* pleca, *f. vt* poner en paralelo; cotejar, comparar; igualar. **to run p. to,** ser paralelo a; ser conforme a. **p. bars,** paralelas, *f pl*

parallelism *n* paralelismo, *m*

parallelogram *n* paralelogramo, *m*

paralysation *n* paralización, *f*

paralyse *vt* paralizar

paralysis *n* parálisis, *f*

paralytic *a* and *n* paralítico (-ca)

paramount *a* supremo, sumo

paramour *n* amante, querido, *m;* querida, amiga, *f*

paranoia *n* paranoia, *f*

paranoiac *n* paranoico, *m*

parapet *n* (*arch* and *mil*) parapeto, *m*

paraphernalia *n law* bienes parafernales, *m, p;* (finery) atavíos, adornos, *m pl;* equipo, *m;* arreos, *m pl;* insignias, *f pl*

paraphrase *n* paráfrasis, *f, vt* parafrasear

parasite *n* parásito, *m; inf* zángano, *m,* gorrista, *mf*

parasitic *a* parásito, parasitario; *med* parasítico

parasitology *n* parasitología, *f*

parasol *n* parasol, quitasol, *m*

parathyroid *a* paratiroides. *n* paratiroides, *f pl*

paratroops *n pl* paracaidistas, *m pl*

paratyphoid *n* paratifoidea, *f*

parboil *vt* sancochar

parcel *n* paquete, *m;* fardo, *m;* (of land) parcela, *f.* **to p. out,** repartir, distribuir; dividir. **to p. up,** envolver, empaquetar. **p. post,** servicio de paquetes, *m*

parceling *n* empaque, *m;* (out) reparto, *m,* distribución, *f;* división, *f*

parch *vt* secar; abrasar, quemar; (roast) tostar. *vi* secarse; quemarse, abrasarse

parched *a* seco, sediento. **p. with thirst,** muerto de sed

parchedness *n* sequedad, aridez, *f*

parchment *n* pergamino, *m;* (of a drum) parche, *m*. **p.-like,** apergaminado

pardon *n* perdón, *m; ecc* indulgencia, *f. vt* perdonar; indultar, amnistiar. **a general p.,** una amnistia. **I beg**

your p.! ¡Vd. dispense!; ¡Perdone Vd.! **to beg p.,** pedir perdón; disculparse. **P.?** ¿Cómo?

pardonable *a* perdonable, disculpable, excusable

pardonableness *n* disculpabilidad, *f*

pardonably *adv* disculpablemente, excusablemente

pardoner *n* vendedor de indulgencias, *m;* perdonador (-ra)

pardoning *n* perdón, *m;* remisión, *f*

pare *vt* (one's nails) cortar; (fruit) mondar; (potatoes, etc.) pelar; (remove) quitar; (reduce) reducir

parent *n* padre, *m;* madre, *f;* (ancestor) antepasado, *m;* (origin) origen, *m,* fuente, *f;* (cause) causa, *f;* (author) autor, *m;* autora, *f; pl* **parents,** padres, *m pl. a* madre, materno; principal

parentage *n* parentela, *f;* linaje, *m,* familia, alcurnia, *f;* procedencia, *f,* nacimiento, origen, *m*

parental *a* paternal; maternal, de madre

parentally *adv* como un padre; como una madre

parenthesis *n* paréntesis, *m*

parenthetical *a* entre paréntesis; de paréntesis

parenthood *n* paternidad, *f;* maternidad, *f*

pariah *n* paria, *mf*

parietal *a* parietal

paring *n* (act) raedura, *f;* peladura, mondadura, *f;* (shred) brizna, *f;* (refuse) desecho, desperdicio, *m.* **p.-knife,** trinchete, *m*

Paris París, *m*

parish *n* parroquia, *f;* feligresía, *f, a* parroquial. **p. church,** parroquia, *f.* **p. clerk,** sacristán de parroquia, *m.* **p. priest,** párroco, *m.* **p. register,** registro de la parroquia, *m*

parishioner *n* parroquiano (-na); feligrés (-esa)

Parisian *a* parisiense. *n* parisiense, *mf*

parity *n* paridad, *f*

park *n* parque, *m;* jardín, *m. vt* (vehicles) estacionar; (dump) depositar. **car p.,** parque de automóviles, *m.* **p.-keeper,** guardián del parque, *m*

parking *n* (of vehicles) estacionamiento, *m;* (dumping) depósito, *m.* **p. lights,** *aut* luces de estacionamiento, *f pl.* **p. place,** parque de estacionamiento, *m*

parking meter *n* parquímetro, *m* (Argentina)

parlance *n* lenguaje, *m.* **in common p.,** en lenguaje vulgar

parley *n* plática, conversación, *f;* discusión, *f; mil* parlamento, *m. vi mil* parlamentar; discutir; conversar. *vt* hablar

parliament *n* parlamento, *m;* cortes, *f pl;* cuerpo legislativo, *m*

parliamentarian *a* and *n* parlamentario; (of an academy) censor, *m*

parliamentarianism *n* parlamentarismo, *m,*

parliamentary *a* parlamentario. **p. immunity,** inviolabilidad parlamentaria, *f*

parlor *n* salón, gabinete, *m;* sala de recibo, *f;* (in a convent) locutorio, *m.* **p. games,** diversión de salón, *f,* juego de sociedad, *m.* **p.-maid,** camarera, *f*

parlous *a* crítico, malo. *adv* sumamente, muy

Parmesan *a* parmesano, de Parma. *n* parmesano (-na). **P. cheese,** queso de Parma, *m*

Parnassian *a* del parnaso; parnasiano. *n* parnasiano, *m*

Parnassus *n* Parnaso, *m*

parochial *a* parroquial, parroquiano; *fig* provincial

parochialism *n* provincialismo, *m*

parochially *adv* por parroquias

parodist *n* parodista, *mf*

parody *n* parodia, *f, vt* parodiar

parole *n* (of convict) libertad vigilada, *f*

paroxysm *n* paroxismo, *m;* ataque, acceso, *m*

parquet (floor) entarimado, *m;* (of theater) platea, *f*

parricide *n* (act) parricidio, *m;* (person) parricida, *mf*

parrot *n* papagayo, loro, *m*

parry *vt* (a blow, and in fencing) parar; rechazar; evitar. *n* parada, *f;* (in fencing) quite, *m,* parada, *f*

parse *vt* analizar

Parsee *n* parsi, *m*

parsimonious *a* parsimonioso

parsimoniously *adv* con parsimonia
parsimony *n* parsimonia, *f*
parsley *n* perejil, *m*
parsnip *n* chirivía, *f*
parson *n* párroco, cura, *m*; (clergyman) clérigo, *m*
parsonage *n* rectoría, *f*
part *n* parte, *f*; porción, *f*; trozo, *m*; *mech* pieza, *f*; (*gram* and of a literary work) parte, *f*; (of a living organism) miembro, *m*; (duty) deber, *m*, obligación, *f*; *theat* papel, *m*; *mus* voz, *f*; *pl* **parts,** (region) partes, *f pl*, lugar, *m*; (talents) partes, dotes, *f pl*. **foreign parts,** países extranjeros, *m pl*, el extranjero. **For my p. . . . ,** Por lo que a mí toca, Por mi parte. **for the most p.,** en su mayoría. **from all parts,** de todas partes. **in p.,** en parte; parcialmente. **spare p.,** pieza de recambio, *f*. **The funny p. of it is . . . ,** Lo cómico del asunto es . . . **the latter p. of the month,** los últimos días del mes, la segunda quincena del mes. **to form p. of,** formar parte de. **to play a p.,** hacer un papel. **to take a person's p.,** apoyar a alguien, ser partidario de alguien. **to take in good p.,** tomar bien. **to take p. in,** tomar parte en, participar en. **p. of speech,** parte de la oración, *f*. **p.-owner,** copropietario (-ia). **p.-time job,** trabajo de unas cuantas horas, *m*
part *vt* distribuir, repartir; dividir; separar (de); (open) abrir. *vi* partir, marcharse; despedirse; (of roads, etc.) bifurcarse; dividirse; (open) abrirse. **to p. one's hair,** hacerse la raya. **to p. from,** (things) separarse de; (people) despedirse de. **to p. with,** separarse de; deshacerse de; perder; (dismiss) despedir (a)
partake *vt* participar de, compartir; tomar parte en. *vi* tomar algo (de comer, de beber). **to p. of,** comer (beber) de; tener rasgos de
partaker *n* partícipe, *mf*
Parthian *a* parto. *n* parto (-ta). **P. shot,** la flecha del parto
partial *a* parcial; (fond of) aficionado (a). **p. eclipse,** eclipse parcial, *m*
partiality *n* parcialidad, *f*; preferencia, predilección, *f*
partially *adv* en parte, parcialmente; (with bias) con parcialidad
participant *a* participante. *n* partícipe, *mf*
participate *vi* participar (de), compartir; tomar parte (en)
participation *n* participación, *f*
participial *a gram* participial
participle *n gram* participio, *m*. **past p.,** participio pasado (or pretérito o pasivo), *m*. **present p.,** participio activo (or presente), *m*
particle *n* partícula, *f*; *fig* átomo, grano, *m*, pizca, *f*; *gram* partícula, *f*
parti-colored *a* bicolor
particular *a* particular; especial; individual; singular; cierto; exacto; escrupuloso; difícil, exigente. *n* detalle, pormenor, *m*; circunstancia, *f*; caso particular, *m*; *pl* **particulars,** informes, detalles, *m pl*. **further particulars,** más detalles. **in p.,** en particular; sobre todo. **He is very p. about . . . ,** Es muy exigente en cuanto a . . . ; Le es muy importante . . . , Le importa mucho . . .
particularize *vt* particularizar, detallar; especificar
particularly *adv* en particular; particularmente; sobre todo
parting *n* despedida, *f*; partida, *f*; separación, *f*; (of the hair) raya, crencha, *f*; (cross roads) bifurcación, *f*. *a* de despedida. **at p.,** al despedirse. **to reach the p. of the ways,** *fig* llegar al punto decisivo
partisan *n* partidario (-ia); (fighter) guerrillero, *m*, *a* partidario de guerrilleros
partisanship *n* partidarismo, *m*
partition *n* partición, *f*; división, *f*; (wall) pared, *f*, tabique, *m*. **the p. of Ireland,** la división de Irlanda
partly *adv* en parte
partner *n* asociado (-da); *com* socio (-ia); (dancing) pareja, *f*; (in games, and companion) compañero (-ra), *m*; (spouse) consorte, *mf*; (in crime) codelincuente, *mf*

sleeping p., socio comanditario, *m*. **working p.,** socio industrial, *m*
partnership *n* asociación, *f*; *com* sociedad, compañía, *f*. **deed of p.,** artículos de sociedad, *m pl*. **to take into p.,** tomar como socio (a). **to form a p.,** asociarse
partridge *n orn* perdiz, *f*. **young p.,** perdigón, *m*
parturient *a f*, parturienta. *n* parturienta, *f*
parturition *n* parto, *m*
party *n* partido, *m*; grupo, *m*; (of pleasure, etc.) partida, *f*; reunión, fiesta, *f*; *mil* pelotón, destacamento, *m*; *law* parte, *f*; (person) interesado (-da); (accessory) cómplice, *mf*. **rescue p.,** pelotón de salvamento, *m*. **to be a p. to,** prestarse a; ser cómplice en. **to give a p.,** dar una fiesta, dar una reunión. **p.-spirit,** espíritu del partido, *m*. **p.-wall,** pared medianera, *f*
parvenu *n* advenedizo (-za)
parvis *n arch* atrio, *m*
Paschal *a* pascual
pass *n* (in an exam.) aprobación, *f*; (crisis) crisis, situación crítica, *f*; estado, *m*; (with the hands) pase, *m*; (permit) permiso, *m*; *mil* licencia, *f*; (safe-conduct) salvoconducto, *m*; (in football, etc.) pase, *m*; (membership card) carnet, *m*; (defile) desfiladero, paso, puerto, *m*; *naut* rebasadero, *m*; (fencing) estocada, *f*. **free p.,** billete de favor, *m*. **p.-book,** libreta de banco, *f*. **p. certificate,** (in exams.) aprobado, *m*. **p.-key,** llave maestra, *f*
pass *vi* pasar; (of time) correr, pasar, transcurrir; (happen) occurrir, tomar lugar; (end) cesar, desaparecer; (die) morir. *vt* pasar; hacer pasar; (the butter, etc.) dar, alargar; (in football, hockey) pasar; (excel) aventajar, exceder; (a Bill, an examination) aprobar; (sentence) fallar, pronunciar; (a remark) hacer; (transfer) traspasar; (tolerate) sufrir, tolerar; evacuar. **He passed in psychology,** Aprobó sicología. **to allow to p.,** ceder el paso (a). **to bring to p.,** ocasionar. **to come to p.,** suceder. **to let p.,** (put up with) dejar pasar; no hacer caso de; (forgive) perdonar. **to p. a vote of confidence,** votar una proposición de confianza. **to p. the buck,** *inf* echarle a uno el muerto. **pass the hat, pass the plate,** pasar la gorra. **to p. along,** pasar por; pasar. **to p. away,** pasar; desaparecer; (die) morir, fallecer; (of time) transcurrir. **to p. by,** pasar por, pasar delante de, pasar al lado de; (omit) pasar por alto de, omitir; (ignore) pasar sin hacer caso de. **to p. for,** pasar por. **to p. in,** entrar. **to p. in and out,** entrar y salir. **to p. off,** *vi* pasar; cesar, acabarse; desaparecer; evaporarse, disiparse; (of events) tener lugar. *vt* (oneself) darse por; dar por, hacer pasar por. **to p. a cat off as hare,** dar gato por liebre. **to p. on,** *vi* pasar; seguir su camino, continuar su marcha. *vt* pasar algo de uno a otro. **to p. out,** salir. **to p. over,** pasar por encima de; cruzar, atravesar; (transfer) traspasar; (disregard) pasar por alto de, dejar a un lado; omitir. **to p. over in silence,** pasar en silencio (por). **to p. round,** circular. **to p. through,** cruzar, atravesar, pasar por; (pierce) traspasar; *fig* experimentar
passable *a* transitable, pasadero; (fairly good) regular, mediano; tolerable
passably *adv* medianamente, pasaderamente, tolerablemente
passage *n* pasaje, *m*; paso, tránsito, *m*; (voyage) viaje, *m*, travesía, *f*; (corridor) pasillo, *m*; (entrance) entrada, *f*; (way) camino, *m*; (alley) callejón, *m*; (in a mine) galería, *f*; (of time) transcurso, *m*; (of birds) pasa, *f*; (in a book, and *mus*) pasaje, *m*; (occurrence) episodio, incidente, *m*; (of a Bill) aprobación, *f*. **p. money,** pasaje, *m*. **p. of arms,** lucha, *f*, combate, *m*; disputa, *f*
passementerie *n* pasamanería, *f*
passenger *n* viajero (-ra); (on foot) peatón, *m*. **by p. train,** en gran velocidad
passerby *n* transeúnte, paseante, *mf*
passing *a* pasajero; fugitivo; momentáneo. *adv* sumamente, extremadamente. *n* pasada, *f*; paso, *m*; (death) muerte, *f*; (disappearance) desaparición, *f*; (of a law)

aprobación, *f.* **in p.,** de paso. **p.-bell,** toque de difuntos, *m*

passing grade *n* mínima calificación aprobatoria, *f*

passion *n* pasión, *f;* (Christ's) Pasión, *f;* (anger) cólera, *f.* **to fly into a p.,** montar en cólera. **p.-flower,** pasionaria, granadilla, *f.* **P. play,** drama de la Pasión, *m.* **P. Sunday,** Domingo de Pasión, *m.* **P. Week,** Semana Santa, *f*

passionate *a* apasionado; (quick-tempered) irascible, colérico; (fervid) vehemente, intenso, ardiente

passionately *adv* con pasión, apasionadamente; (irascibly) coléricamente; (fervidly) con vehemencia, ardientemente

passionless *a* sin pasión, frío; impasible; imparcial

passive *a* pasivo. *n gram* pasiva, *f.* **p. resistance,** resistencia pasiva, *f*

passiveness, passivity *n* pasividad, *f*

Passover *n* Pascua de los judíos, *f*

passport *n* pasaporte, *m*

password *n* contraseña, *f*

past *a* pasado; último; (expert) consumado; (former) antiguo, ex-. *n* pasado, *m;* historia, *f,* antecedentes, *m pl, prep* después de; (in front of) delante de; (next to) al lado de; (beyond) más allá de; (without) sin; fuera de; (of age) más de; (no longer able to) incapaz de. *adv* más allá. (The translation of **past** as an adverb is often either omitted, or included in the verb, e.g. **The years flew p.,** Los años transcurrieron. **for centuries p.,** durante siglos.) **I am p. caring,** Nada me importa ya. **It is a quarter p. ten,** Son las diez y cuarto. **It is p. four o'clock,** Son las siete pasadas, Son después de las cuatro. **what's p. is p.,** lo pasado, pasado. **p. doubt,** fuera de duda. **p. endurance,** insoportable. **p. help,** sin remedio, irremediable. **p. hope,** sin esperanza. **p.-master,** maestro, consumado, experto, *m.* **p. participle,** participio pasado, *m.* **p. president,** ex-presidente, *m.* **p. tense,** (tiempo) pasado, *m*

paste *n* pasta, *f;* (gloy) engrudo, *m. vt* (affix) pegar; (glue) engomar, engrudar

pasteboard *n* cartón, *m,* cartulina, *f, a* de cartón, de cartulina

pastel *n art* pastel, *m.* **p. drawing,** pintura al pastel, *f*

pastelist *n* pastelista, *mf*

pasteurization *n* pasteurización, *f*

pasteurize *vt* pasteurizar

pastille *n* pastilla, *f*

pastime *n* pasatiempo, entretenimiento, *m,* diversión, recreación, *f*

pastor *n* pastor, *m*

pastoral *a* pastoril; *ecc* pastoral. *n ecc* pastoral, *f; (poet mus)* pastorela, *f*

pastorate *n* pastoría, *f*

pastry *n* (dough) pasta, *f;* pastel, *m,* torta, *f;* pastelería, *f.* **p.-cook,** repostero, *m,* pastelero (-ra)

pasturage *n* (grass, etc.) pasto, *m;* pasturaje, *m;* pastoreo, *m*

pasture *n* (grass, etc.) pasto, herbaje, *m;* pasturaje, *m;* (field) prado, *m,* pradera, dehesa, *f. vi* pacer; pastar. *vt* apacentar, pastar

pasty *a* pastoso; (pale) pálido. *n* empanada, *f*

pat *n* toque, *m;* caricia, *f;* (for butter) molde (de mantequilla), *m. vt* tocar; acariciar, pasar la mano (sobre). *adv a* propósito; oportunamente; fácilmente. **pat of butter,** pedacito de mantequilla, *m.* **pat on the back,** golpe en la espalda, *m; fig* elogio, *m*

Patagonian *a* and *n* patagón (-ona)

patch *n* (mend) remiendo, *m;* (piece) pedazo, *m;* (plaster and *aut.,* etc.) parche, *m;* (beauty spot) lunar postizo, *m;* (of ground) parcela, *f;* (of flowers, etc.) masa, *f;* (stain, and *fig*) mancha, *f. vt* (mend) remendar; poner remiendo (a); pegar; (roughly) chafallar; (the face) ponerse lunares postizos. **p. of blue sky,** pedazo de cielo azul. **patch of green grass,** mancha de hierba verde. **to be not a p. on,** no ser de la misma clase que; (of persons) no llegarle a los zancajos de. **to p. up a quarrel,** hacer las paces

patchwork *n* labor de retazos, obra de retacitos, *f; fig* mezcla, mezcolanza, *f.* **p. quilt,** centón, *m*

patchy *a* desigual; manchado

patella *n anat* rótula, *f*

patency *n* evidencia, claridad, *f*

patent *a* evidente, patente; patentado. *n* patente, *f. vt* patentar. **p. of nobility,** carta de hidalguía, ejecutoria, *f.* **"P. Applied For,"** «Patente Solicitada.» **Patent Pending** marca en trámite. **p. leather,** *n* charol, *m. a* de charol. **p. medicine,** específico farmacéutico, *m*

patentee *n* el, *m,* (*f,* la) que obtiene una patente; inventor (-ra)

patently *adv* evidentemente, claramente

paterfamilias *n* padre de familia, *m*

paternal *a* paterno, paternal

paternally *adv* paternalmente

paternity *n* paternidad, *f*

path *n* senda, vereda, *f,* sendero, *m;* camino, *m;* (track) pista, *f;* (traject) trayectoria, *f.* **the beaten p.,** el camino trillado

pathetic *a* patético

pathless *a* sin senda

pathogenic *a med* patógeno

pathological *a* patológico

pathologist *n* patólogo, *m*

pathology *n* patología, *f*

pathos *n* lo patético

patience *n* paciencia, *f.* **He tries my p. very much,** Me cuesta mucho no impacientarme con él. **to lose p.,** perder la paciencia; (grow angry) perder los estribos. **to play p.,** hacer solitarios

patient *a* paciente. *n* paciente, *mf;* (ill person) enfermo (-ma); (of a physician) cliente, *mf*

patiently *adv* con paciencia, pacientemente

patina *n* pátina, *f*

patriarch *n* patriarca, *m*

patriarchal *a* patriarcal

patriarchy *n* patriarcado, *m*

patrician *a* and *n* patricio (-ia)

patrimonial *a* patrimonial

patrimony *n* patrimonio, *m*

patriot *n* patriota, *mf*

patriotic *a* patriótico

patriotism *n* patriotismo, *m*

patrol *n* patrulla, *f;* ronda, *f, vi* and *vt* patrullar; rondar; recorrer. **p. boat,** lancha escampavía, *f.* **p. flight,** vuelo de patrulla, *m*

patron *n* (of a freed slave) patrono, *m;* (of the arts, etc.) mecenas, protector, *m;* (customer) parroquiano (-na), cliente, *mf.* **p. saint,** santo (-ta) patrón (-ona)

patronage *n* (protection) patrocinio, *m;* protección, *f; ecc* patronato, *m;* (regular custom) clientela, *f;* (of manner) superioridad, *f*

patroness *n* patrona, *f;* protectora, *f;* (of a charity, etc.) patrocinadora, *f;* (of a regiment, etc.) madrina, *f*

patronize *vt* patrocinar; proteger, favorecer; (a shop) ser parroquiano de; (treat arrogantly) tratar con superioridad

patronizing *a* (with air, behavior, etc.) de superioridad, de altivez

patten *n* zueco, chanclo, *m*

patter *n* (jargon) jerga, *f;* charla, *f;* (of rain) azotes, *m pl;* (of feet) son, *m;* golpecitos, *m pl. vt* (repeat) decir mecánicamente. *vi* (chatter) charlar; (of rain) azotar, bailar; correr ligeramente

pattern *n* modelo, *m;* (*sew* and dressmaking) patrón, *m;* (in founding) molde, *m;* (templet) escantillón, *m;* (of cloth, etc.) muestra, *f;* (design) dibujo, diseño, *m;* (example) ejemplar, *m. vt* diseñar; estampar. **p. book,** libro de muestras, *m*

patty *n* empanada, *f,* pastelillo, *m*

paucity *n* poquedad, *f;* corto número, *m;* insuficiencia, escasez, *f*

paunch *n* panza, barriga, *f*

pauper *n* pobre, *mf*

pauperism *n* pauperismo, *m*

pauperization *n* empobrecimiento, *m*
pauperize *vt* empobrecer, reducir a la miseria
pause *n* pausa, *f;* intervalo, *m;* silencio, *m;* interrupción, *f; mus* pausa, *f. vi* pausar, hacer una pausa; detenerse, interrumpirse; vacilar. **to give p. to,** hacer vacilar (a)
pavan *n* (dance) pavana, *f*
pave *vt* empedrar, enlosar. **to p. the way for,** facilitar el paso de, preparar el terreno para, abrir el camino de
pavement *n* pavimento, *m;* (sidewalk) acera, *f.* **p.-artist,** pintor callejero, *m*
pavilion *n* pabellón, *m;* (for a band, etc.) quiosco, *m;* (tent) tienda de campaña, *f*
paving *n* pavimentación, *f;* empedrado, *m;* see **pavement. p.-stone,** losa, *f*
paw *n* pata, *f;* (with claws) garra, *f; inf* manaza, *f. vt* tocar con la pata; (scratch) arañar; (handle) manosear. *vi* (of a horse) piafar
pawing *n* (of a horse) el piafar; (handling) manoseo, *m*
pawn *n* (chess) peón (de ajedrez), *m;* empeño, *m; fig* prenda, *f. vt* empeñar, pignorar; dar en prenda. **p.-ticket,** papeleta de empeño, *f*
pawnbroker *n* prestamista, *mf*
pawning *n* empeño, *m,* pignoración, *f*
pawnshop *n* casa de préstamos, casa de empeño, *f,* monte de piedad, *m*
pay *n* paga, *f;* (mil nav) soldada, *f;* salario, *m;* (of a workman) jornal, *m;* (reward) recompensa, compensación, *f;* (profit) beneficio, provecho, *m.* **pay-day,** día de paga, *m.* **pay-office,** pagaduría, *f.* **pay-sheet,** nómina, *f*
pay *vt* pagar; (a debt) satisfacer; (spend) gastar; (recompense) remunerar, recompensar; (hand over) entregar; (yield) producir; (a visit) hacer; (attention) prestar; (homage) rendir; (one's respects) presentar. *vi* pagar; producir ganancia; sacar provecho; ser una ventaja, ser provechoso. **It would not pay him to do it,** No le saldría a cuenta hacerlo. **This job doesn't pay,** Este trabajo no da dinero. **to pay a compliment (to),** cumplimentar, decir alabanzas (a), echar una flor (a). **to pay attention,** prestar atención; hacer caso. **to pay cash,** pagar al contado. **to pay in advance,** pagar adelantado. **to pay in full,** saldar. **to pay off old scores,** ajustar cuentas viejas. **to pay one's addresses to,** hacer la corte (a), pretender en matrimonio (a). **to pay the penalty,** sufrir el castigo, hacer penitencia. **to pay with interest,** *fig* pagar con creces. **to pay again,** volver a pagar, pagar de nuevo. **to pay back,** devolver, restituir; (money only) reembolsar; *fig* pagar en la misma moneda, vengarse (de). **to pay down,** pagar al contado. **to pay for,** pagar, costear; satisfacer. **to pay in,** ingresar. **to pay off,** (persons) despedir; (a debt) saldar; (a mortgage) cancelar, redimir. **to pay out,** (persons) vengarse de; (money) pagar; (ropes, etc.) arriar. **to pay up,** pagar; pagar por completo; (shares, etc.) redimir
payable *a* pagadero; a pagar; que puede ser pagado
payee *n* tenedor, *m*
payer *n* pagador (-ra)
paying *n.* See **payment**
paymaster *n* pagador, *m;* tesorero, *m.* **P.-General,** ordenador general de pagos, *m*
payment *n* pago, *m,* paga, *f;* remuneración, *f; fig* recompensa, satisfacción, *f; fig* premio, *m.* **in p. of,** en pago de. **on p. of,** mediante el pago de. **p. in advance,** pago adelantado, anticipo, *m*
pea *n* guisante, *m.* **dry or split pea,** guisante seco, *m.* **sweet pea,** guisante de olor, *m.* **pea-flour,** harina de guisantes, *f.* **pea-green,** verde claro, *m.* **pea-jacket,** chaquetón de piloto, *m.* **pea-shooter,** cerbatana, *f*
peace *n* paz, *f;* tranquilidad, quietud, *f,* sosiego, *m; law* orden público, *m.* **P.!** ¡Silencio! **to hold one's p.,** callarse, guardar silencio. **to make p.,** hacer las paces. **P. be upon this house!** ¡Paz sea en esta casa! **p.-footing,** pie de paz, *m.* **p.-loving,** pacífico. **p.-offering,** sacrificio propiciatorio, *m;* satisfacción, oferta de paz, *f*
peaceable *a* pacífico; apacible; tranquilo, sosegado

peaceableness *n* paz, *f;* apacibilidad, *f;* tranquilidad, quietud, *f,* sosiego, *m*
peaceably *adv* pacíficamente; tranquilamente
peaceful *a* pacífico; tranquilo; silencioso. **to come with p. intentions,** venir de paz
peacefully *adv* en paz; pacíficamente; tranquilamente
peacefulness *n* paz, *f;* tranquilidad, calma, quietud, *f;* silencio, *m;* carácter pacífico, *m*
peacemaker *n* pacificador (-ra); conciliador (-ra)
peach *n* (fruit) melocotón, *m;* (tree) melocotonero, melocotón, *m;* (girl) breva, *f.* **p.-colour,** color de melocotón, *m*
peacock *n* pavo real, pavón, *m. vi* pavonearse; darse humos. **The p. spread its tail,** El pavo real hizo la rueda
peahen *n* pava real, *f*
peak *n* punta, *f;* (of a cap) visera, *f;* (of a mountain) peñasco, *m,* cumbre, cima, *f;* (mountain itself) pico, *m;* (naut of a hull) pico, *m; fig* auge, apogeo, *m;* punto más alto, *m. vi* consumirse, enflaquecer. **p. hours,** horas de mayor tráfico, *f pl*
peaked *a* en punta; puntiagudo; picudo; (of a cap) con visera; (wan) ojeroso; (thin) delgaducho, macilento, consumido
peal *n* toque (or repique) de campanas, *m;* campanillazo, *m;* carillón, *m;* (noise) estruendo, ruido, *m;* (of thunder) trueno, *m;* (of an organ) sonido, *m. vi* repicar; sonar. *vt* tañer, echar a vuelo (las campanas); (of a bell that one presses) hacer sonar, tocar. **a p. of laughter,** una carcajada
peanut *n* cacahuete, *m.* **p. butter,** mantequilla de cacahuete, *f*
pear *n* pera, *f.* **p.-shaped,** piriforme, de figura de pera. **p. tree,** peral, *m*
pearl *n* perla, *f;* (mother-of-pearl) nácar, *m,* a de perla; perlero. *vt* (dew) rociar, aljofarar. *vi* pescar perlas; formar perlas. **seed p.,** aljófar, *m.* **p.-ash,** carbonato potásico, *m.* **p.-barley,** cebada perlada, *f.* **p.-button,** botón de nácar, *m.* **p.-fisher,** pescador de perlas, *m.* **p.-fishery,** pescadería de perlas, *f.* **p.-grey,** gris de perla, *m*
pearly *a* perlino; de perla; nacarado; (dewy) aljofarado
peasant *n* campesino (-na), labrador (-ra). *a* campesino
peasantry *n* campesinos, *m pl,* gente del campo, *f*
peat *n* turba, *f.* **p.-bog,** turbera, *f*
pebble *n* guijarro, *m,* pedrezuela, guija, *f;* (gravel) guijo, *m;* cristal de roca, *m;* lente de cristal de roca, *m*
pebbled, pebbly *a* guijarroso, enguijarrado
peccadillo *n* pecadillo, *m*
peck *n* (of a bird) picotazo, *m,* picada, *f;* (kiss) besito, *m;* (large amount) montón, *m;* multitud, *f. vt* (of a bird) picotear; sacar (or coger) con el pico; (kiss) besar rápidamente. *vi* (with at) picotear; picar
pectoral *a* pectoral
peculiar *a* particular, peculiar, individual; propio, característico; (marked) especial; (unusual) extraño, raro, extraordinario
peculiarity *n* peculiaridad, particularidad, *f;* singularidad, *f;* (eccentricity) excentricidad, rareza, *f*
peculiarly *adv* particularmente, peculiarmente; especialmente; extrañamente
pecuniarily *adv* pecuniariamente
pecuniary *a* pecuniario
pedagogic *a* pedagógico
pedagogue *n* pedagogo, *m*
pedagogy *n* pedagogía, *f*
pedal *a zool* del pie. *n* pedal, *m. vi* pedalear
pedant *n* pedante, *mf*
pedantic *a* pedante
pedantically *adv* con pedantería, pedantescamente
pedantry *n* pedantería, *f*
peddle *vi* ser buhonero. *vt* revender
peddling *n* buhonería, *f. a* trivial, insignificante; mezquino
pedestal *n* pedestal, *m; fig* fundamento, *m,* base, *f.* **to put on a p.,** *fig* poner sobre un pedestal

pedestrian *n* peatón, peón, *m*, *a* pedestre; *fig* patoso. **p.**
  traffic, circulación de los peatones, *f*
pedestrian crosswalk, cruce peatonal (Argentina),
  cruce de peatones, *m*
pediatrician *n* pediatra, *mf*
pedigree *n* genealogía, *f;* raza, *f;* (of words) etimología,
  f. a (of animals) de raza, de casta. **p. dog,** perro de
  casta, *m*
pediment *n arch* frontón, *m*
pedlar *n* buhonero, *m*
pedometer *n* pedómetro, cuentapasos, *m*
peel *n* (baker's) pala, *f;* (of fruit, etc.) piel, *f,* hollejo, *m.*
  vt pelar, mondar; (bark) descortezar. *vi* descascararse,
  desconcharse; (of the bark of a tree) descortezarse
peeling *n* (of fruit, etc.) peladura, monda, *f;* (of bark)
  descortezadura, *f;* (of paint, etc.) desconchadura, *f*
peep *vi* (of birds) piar; (of mice) chillar; (peer) atisbar,
  mirar a hurtadillas; (appear) asomar; mostrarse; (of the
  dawn) despuntar. *n* (of birds) pío, *m;* (of mice) chillido,
  m; (glimpse) vista, *f;* (glance) ojeada, mirada furtiva, *f;*
  at the p. of day, al despuntar el día. **p.-hole,** mirilla,
  f, atisbadero, *m;* escucha, *f.* **p.-show,** óptica, *f*
peeper (eye) avizón *m*
peer *n* par, *m;* igual, *mf. vi* atisbar; escudriñar; *fig* asomar, aparecer
peerage *n* nobleza, aristocracia, *f;* dignidad de par, *f*
peeress *n* paresa, *f*
peerless *a* sin par, incomparable, sin igual
peevish *a* displicente, malhumorado; picajoso, vidrioso,
  enojadizo
peevishness *n* displicencia, *f,* mal humor, *m;* impaciencia, *f*
peg *n* clavija, *f;* (of a tent) estaca, *f;* (of a barrel) estaquilla, *f;* (of a violin, etc.) clavija, *f;* (for coats, etc.)
  colgador, *m;* (of whisky, etc.) trago, *m; fig* pretexto, *m.*
  vt clavar, enclavijar, empernar. **to take down a peg,**
  bajar los humos (a). **to peg away,** batirse el cobre. **to
  peg down,** fijar con clavijas; (a tent) sujetar con estacas; (prices) fijar
Pegasus *n* Pegaso, *m*
peignoir *n* peinador, salto de cama, *m,* bata, *f*
pekinese *n* perro (-rra) pequinés (-esa)
pelican *n* pelícano, *m*
pellagra *n med* pelagra, *f*
pellet *n* bolita, *f;* (pill) píldora, *f;* (shot) perdigón, *m*
pellmell *adv* a trochemoche; atropelladamente
pellucid *a* diáfano
Peloponesian *a* and *n* peloponense, *mf*
pelota *n* pelota vasca, *f.* **p. player,** pelotari, *m*
pelt *n* pellejo, *m;* cuero, *m;* (fur) piel, *f;* (blow) golpe, *m.*
  vt llover (piedras, etc.) sobre, arrojar . . . sobre; (questions) disparar; (throw) tirar. *vi* (of rrain) azotar,
  diluviar
pelvic *a* pélvico, pelviano
pelvis *n* pelvis, *f*
pen *n* (for sheep, etc.) aprisco, *m;* corral, *m;* (paddock)
  parque, *m;* (for hens) pollera, *f;* (for writing and *fig.,*
  author, etc.) pluma, *f. vt* (shut up) acorralar; encerrar;
  (write) escribir (con pluma). **pen-and-ink drawing,**
  dibujo a la pluma, *m.* **pen-holder,** portaplumas, *m.*
  pen-name, seudónimo, *m.* **pen-wiper,** limpia-
  plumas, *m*
penal *a* penal. **p. code,** código penal, *m.* **p. colony,** colonia penal, *f.* **p. servitude,** trabajos forzados (or forzosos), *m pl.* **p. servitude for life,** cadena perpetua, *f*
penalization *n* castigo, *m*
penalize *vt* penar, imponer pena (a); castigar
penalty *n law* penalidad, *f;* castigo, *m;* (fine) multa, *f;*
  (risk) riesgo, *m; sport* sanción, *m.* **the p. of,** la desventaja de. **under p. of,** so pena de. **p. kick,** (football)
  penalty, *m*
penance *n* penitencia, *f.* **to do p.,** hacer penitencia
penchant *n* tendencia, *f;* inclinación, *f*
pencil *n* lápiz, *m;* (automatic) lapicero, *m. vt* escribir (or
  dibujar or marcar) con lápiz. **p.-case,** estuche para lá-

pices, *m.* **p.-holder,** lapicero, *m.* **p.-sharpener,** cortalápices, afilalápices, *m*
pendant *n* (jewel) pendiente, *m; arch* culo de lámpara,
  m; (naut rope) amantillo, *m;* (flag) gallardete, *m*
pending *a* pendiente. *prep* durante. **to be p.,** pender;
  amenazar
pendulous *a* péndulo; colgante; oscilante
pendulum *n* péndola, *f,* péndulo, *m*
penetrability *n* penetrabilidad, *f*
penetrable *a* penetrable
penetrate *vt* and *vi* penetrar
penetrating *a* penetrante
penetration *n* penetración, *f*
penguin *n* pingüino, pájaro bobo, *m*
penicillin *n* penicilina, *f*
peninsula *n* península, *f*
peninsular *a* peninsular. **P. War,** Guerra de la Independencia, *f*
penis *n* pene, *m*
penitence *n* penitencia, *f*
penitent *a* penitente. *n* penitente, *mf*
penitential *a* penitencial
penitentiary *n ecc* penitenciaria, *f;* casa de corrección, *f;*
  penitenciaría, *f,* presidio, *m;* cárcel modelo, *f, a* penitenciario
penknife *n* cortaplumas, *f*
penmanship *n* caligrafía, *f*
pennant *n naut* gallardete, *m;* banderola, *f;* (ensign) insignia, bandera, *f*
penniless *a* sin un penique, sin blanca; indigente, pobre
  de solemnidad. **to leave p.,** dejar en la miseria; *inf*
  dejar sin camisa
pennilessness *n* falta de dinero, extrema pobreza, *f*
penning *n* escritura, *f;* (drawing up) redacción, *f;* (of
  bulls, etc.) acorralamiento, *m*
pennon *n* pendón, *m,* banderola, *f;* (ensign) bandera,
  insignia, *f*
Pennsylvanian *a* and *n* pensilvano (-na)
penny *n* de un centavo, penique, *m;* perra gorda, *f. a* de
  un penique. **p.-a-liner,** gacetillero, *m.* **p. dreadful,**
  folletín, *m,* novela por entregas, *f.* **p.-in-the-slot machine,** tragaperras, *m*
pennyworth *n* penique, valor de un penique, *m*
pension *n* pensión, *f; mil* retiro, *m;* (grant) beca, *f;*
  (boardinghouse) pensión de familia, *f. vt* pensionar,
  dar una pensión (a); (with off) jubilar. **old age p.,** pensión para la vejez, *f.* **retirement p.,** pensión vitalicia, *f*
pensioner *n* pensionista, *mf;* (mil and nav) inválido, *m*
pensive *a* pensativo, meditabundo; cabizbajo, triste
pensively *adv* pensativamente; tristemente
pensiveness *n* reflexión, meditación profunda, *f;* tristeza, melancolía, *f*
pentagon *n* pentágono, *m*
Pentateuch *n* pentateuco, *m*
Pentecost *n* Pentecostés, *m,* Pascua, *f*
pentecostal *a* de Pentecostés, pascual
penthouse *n* cobertizo, tinglado, *m,* tejavana, *f*
pent-up *a* encerrado; enjaulado; (of emotion) reprimido
penultimate *a* penúltimo. *n* penúltimo, *m*
penurious *a* pobre; escaso; (stingy) tacaño, avaro
penury *n* penuria, *f*
peony *n* peonía, *f,* saltaojos, *m,* rosa albardera, rosa
  montés, *f*
people *n* pueblo, *m;* nación, *f;* gente, *f;* personas, *f pl;*
  (used disparagingly, mob) populacho, vulgo, *m;* (inhabitants) habitantes, *m pl;* (subjects) súbditos, *m pl;*
  (relations) parientes, *m pl;* familia, *f. vt* poblar. **little p.,**
  (children) gente menuda, *f.* **respectable p.,** gente de
  bien, *f.* **the p. of Burgos,** los habitantes de Burgos. **P.
  say,** Se dice, La gente dice. **Very few p. think as you
  do,** Hay muy pocas personas que opinan como Vd.
  How are your p. (family)? ¿Cómo están los de tu
  casa? ¿Cómo está tu familia? **"People Working"**
  «Trabajadores»

peopling *n* población, *f*; colonización, *f*
pep *n inf* energía, *f*, ánimo, *m. p. talk,* discurso estimulante, *m. p. up,* animar
Pepin the Short Pipino el Breve
peplum *n* peplo, *m*
pepper *n* pimienta, *f*; (plant) pimentero, pimiento, *m, vt* sazonar con pimienta; (pelt) acribillar; (with questions) disparar; (a literary work with quotations, etc.) salpimentar. **black p.,** pimienta negra, *f.* **red p.,** pimiento, *m*; (cayenne) pimentón, *m. p.-castor,* pimentero, *m*
peppercorn *n* grano de pimienta, *m*
peppermint *n* menta, *f. p. drop,* pastilla de menta, *f*
peppery *a* picante; (irascible) colérico, irascible
pepsin *n chem* pepsina, *f*
peptic *a* péptico
per *prep* por. **ninety miles per hour,** noventa millas por hora. **ten pesetas per dozen,** diez pesetas la docena. **$60 per annum,** sesenta dólares al año. **per cent.,** por ciento
perambulate *vt* recorrer
perambulator *n* cochecito para niños, *m*
percale *n* percal, *m*
percaline *n* percalina, *f*
perceive *vt* percibir, comprender, darse cuenta de; percibir, discernir
percentage *n* tanto por ciento, *m*; porcentaje, *m*
perceptible *a* perceptible, visible; sensible
perceptibly *adv* visiblemente; sensiblemente
perception *n* percepción, *f*; sensibilidad, *f*
perceptive *a* perceptivo
perch *n icht* perca, *f*; (for birds) percha, *f*; (measure) pértiga, *f. vi* posarse (en or sobre). *vt* posar (en or sobre)
percolate *vi* filtrar; *fig* penetrar. *vt* filtrar, colar
percolation *n* filtración, *f*
percolator *n* filtro, *m.* **coffee p.,** colador de café, *m*
percussion *n* percusión, *f*; choque, *m.* **p. cap,** fulminante, *m. p. instrument,** instrumento de percusión, *m*
perdition *n* perdición, *f*; ruina, *f*
peregrination *n* peregrinación, *f*
peremptorily *adv* perentoriamente
peremptoriness *n* perentoriedad, *f*
peremptory *a* perentorio; (of manner, etc.) imperioso, autoritario
perennial *a bot* vivaz; perenne; eterno, perpetuo. *n* planta vivaz, *f*
perennially *adv* perennemente
perfect *a* perfecto; (of a work) acabado; completo. *n gram* (tiempo) perfecto, *m. vt* perfeccionar; (oneself) perfeccionarse. **to have a p. knowledge of . . . ,** conocer a fondo . . . **They are p. strangers to me,** Me son completamente desconocidos
perfectible *a* perfectible
perfecting *n* perfeccionamiento, *m*; terminación, *f*
perfection *n* perfección, *f*; excelencia, *f.* **to p.,** a la perfección, a las mil maravillas
perfectionist *n* perfeccionista, *mf*
perfidious *a* pérfido
perfidy *n* perfidia, *f*
perforate *vt* perforar, agujerear
perforating *a* perforador
perforation *n* perforación, *f*; agujero, *m*
perforce *adv* a la fuerza, forzosamente
perform *vt* hacer; poner por obra, llevar a cabo; desempeñar, cumplir; ejercer; (a piece of music, etc.) ejecutar; realizar; (a play) representar, dar; (a part in a play) desempeñar (el papel de . . .); (Divine Service) oficiar. *vi theat* trabajar, representar un papel; (a musical instrument) tocar; (sing) cantar; (of animals) hacer trucos
performable *a* hacedero, practicable, ejecutable; *theat* que puede representarse; *mus* tocable
performance *n* ejecución, realización, *f*; desempeño, ejercicio, *m*; cumplimiento, *m*; acción, *f*; hazaña, *f*; (work) obra, *f*; *theat* función, representación, *f*; (theat

acting of a part) interpretación, *f*; *mus* ejecución, *f*; *mech* potencia, *f.* **first p.,** *theat* estreno, *m*
performer *n mus* ejecutante, *mf*, músico, *m*; *theat* actor (-triz), representante, *mf*; artista, *mf*
performing *a* (of animals) sabio. **p. dog,** perro sabio, *m*
perfume *n* perfume, *m*; fragancia, *f*; aroma, *m. vt* perfumar; embalsamar, aromatizar, llenar con fragancia. **p. burner,** perfumador, *m*
perfumer *n* perfumista, *mf*
perfumery *n* perfumería, *f*
perfuming *n* acción de perfumar, *f*, a que perfuma
perfunctorily *adv* perfunctoriamente, sin cuidado; superficialmente
perfunctoriness *n* descuido, *m*, negligencia, *f*; superficialidad, *f*
perfunctory *a* perfunctorio, negligente; superficial; ligero, de cumplido
pergola *n* emparrado, cenador, *m*
perhaps *adv* quizá, quizás(s), tal vez
peril *n* peligro, *m*; riesgo, *m. vt* poner en peligro; arriesgar. **at one's p.,** a su riesgo. **in p.,** en peligro
perilous *a* peligroso, arriesgado
perimeter *n* perímetro, *m*
perineum *n anat* perineo, *m*
period *n* período, *m*; época, *f*; edad, *f*, tiempo, *m*; duración, *f*; término, plazo, *m*; *gram* período, *m*; (full stop) punto final, *m*; *med* menstruación, regla, *f.* **p. furniture,** muebles de época, *m pl*
periodic *a* periódico
periodical *a* periódico. *n* publicación periódica, revista, *f*
periodicity *n* periodicidad, *f*
peripatetic *a* peripatético
peripheral *a* periférico
periphery *n* periferia, *f*
periphrastic *a* perifrástico
periscope *n* periscopio, *m*
perish *vi* perecer; marchitarse; desaparecer, acabar. **to be perished with cold,** estar muerto de frío
perishable *a* perecedero, frágil
peritoneum *n* peritoneo, *m*
peritonitis *n* peritonitis, *f*
periwig *n* peluca, *f*
periwinkle *n zool* caracol marino, *m*; *bot* vincapervinca, *f*
perjure *vt* perjurar. **to p. oneself,** perjurarse
perjurer *n* perjuro (-ra); perjurador (-ra)
perjury *n* perjurio, *m.* **to commit p.,** jurar en falso, perjurar
perk (up) *vi* levantar la cabeza; recobrar sus bríos, alzar la cabeza; sacar la cabeza
perkiness *n* desenvoltura, gallardía, *f*, despejo, *m*
perky *a* desenvuelto, gallardo; coquetón; atrevido; (gay) alegre
permanence *n* permanencia, *f*; estabilidad, *f*
permanent *a* permanente; estable; (of posts, etc.) fijo. **p. wave,** ondulación permanente, *f.* **p. way,** *rw* vía, *f*
permanganate *n* permanganato, *m*
permeability *n* permeabilidad, *f*
permeable *a* permeable
permeate *vt* penetrar; impregnar; *fig* infiltrar (en)
permeation *n* penetración, *f*; impregnación, *f*; *fig* infiltración, *f*
permissible *a* permisible, admisible; lícito
permission *n* permiso, *m*, licencia, *f*
permissive *a* permisivo, tolerado; (optional) facultativo
permit *vt* permitir; dar permiso (a), dejar; tolerar, sufrir; admitir. *n* permiso, *m*, licencia, *f*; pase, *m.* **Will you p. me to smoke?** ¿Me permites fumar?
permutation *n* permutación, *f*
permute *vt* permutar
pernicious *a* pernicioso. **p. anemia,** anemia perniciosa, *f*
perniciousness *n* perniciosidad, *f*
pernickety *a* tiquismiquis
peroration *n* peroración, *f*

peroxide *n* peróxido, *m*
perpendicular *a* perpendicular. *n* perpendicular, *f*
perpendicularity *n* perpendicularidad, *f*
perpendicularly *adv* perpendicularmente
perpetrate *vt law* perpetrar; cometer
perpetration *n law* perpetración, *f*; comisión, *f*
perpetrator *n* el, *m*, (*f*, la) que comete; *law* autor (-ra); perpetrador (-ra)
perpetual *a* perpetuo, perdurable, eterno; incesante, constante; (life-long) perpetuo
perpetually *adv* perpetuamente; sin cesar; continuamente; constantemente
perpetuate *vt* perpetuar, eternizar; inmortalizar
perpetuation *n* perpetuación, *f*
perpetuity *n* perpetuidad, *f*. **in p.,** para siempre
perplex *vt* dejar perplejo, aturdir, confundir; embrollar
perplexed *a* perplejo, irresoluto; confuso; (of questions, etc.) complicado, intrincado
perplexedly *adv* perplejamente
perplexing *a* difícil; complicado; confuso
perplexity *n* perplejidad, *f*; confusión, *f*
perquisites *n pl* emolumentos, *m pl*; gajes, percances, *m pl*; (tips) propinas, *f pl*
persecute *vt* perseguir; importunar, molestar
persecution *n* persecución, *f*
persecutor *n* perseguidor (-ra)
perseverance *n* perseverancia, *f*
persevere *vi* perseverar
persevering *a* perseverante
perseveringly *adv* con perseverancia, perseverantemente
Persia (la) Persia, *f*
Persian *a* persa; de Persia; pérsico. *n* persa, *mf*; (language) persa, *m*. **P. blinds,** persianas, *f pl*. **P. cat,** gato (-ta) de Angora
persiennes *n pl* persianas, *f pl*
persist *vi* persistir; persistir (en), empeñarse (en), obstinarse (en)
persistence *n* persistencia, *f*
persistent *a* persistente
persistently *adv* con persistencia, persistentemente
person *n* persona, *f*. **first p.,** *gram* primera persona, *f*. **in p.,** en persona. **no p.,** nadie
personable *a* bien parecido
personage *n* personaje, *m*
personal *a* personal; íntimo; particular; en persona; (movable) mueble. **He is to make a p. appearance,** Va a estar presente en persona. **p. column,** (in a newspaper) columna de los suspiros, *f*. **p. equation,** ecuación personal, *f*. **p. estate,** (goods) bienes muebles, *m pl*
personality *n* personalidad, *f*; (insult) personalismo, *m*. **dual p.,** conciencia doble, *f*
personate *vt* (in a play) hacer el papel de; (impersonate) hacerse pasar por
personification *n* personificación, *f*
personify *vt* personificar
personnel *n* personal, *m*
perspective *n* perspectiva, *f*, *a* en perspectiva
perspicacious *a* perspicaz, clarividente, sagaz
perspicacity *n* perspicacia, clarividencia, sagacidad, *f*
perspicuity *n* perspicuidad, claridad, lucidez, *f*
perspicuous *a* perspicuo, claro
perspiration *n* sudor, *m*
perspire *vi* sudar, transpirar
persuadable *a* persuasible
persuade *vt* persuadir; inducir (a), instar (a), mover (a), inclinar (a)
persuasion *n* persuasión, *f*; persuasiva, *f*; opinión, *f*; creencia, *f*; religión, *f*; secta, *f*
persuasive *a* persuasivo. *n* persuasión, *f*; aliciente, atractivo, *m*
persuasively *adv* de un modo persuasivo, persuasivamente
persuasiveness *n* persuasiva, *f*
pert *a* petulante; respondón, desparpajado

pertain *vi* pertenecer (a); tocar (a), incumbir (a), convenir (a); estar relacionado (con)
pertinacious *a* pertinaz
pertinaciously *adv* con pertinacia
pertinacity *n* pertinacia, *f*
pertinence *n* pertinencia, *f*
pertinent *a* pertinente, atinado
pertinently *adv* atinadamente
pertly *adv* con petulancia; con descaro
pertness *n* petulancia, *f*; desparpajo, descaro, *m*
perturb *vt* perturbar, agitar, turbar, inquietar
perturbation *n* perturbación, agitación, inquietud, *f*; confusión, *f*; desorden, *m*
perturbed *a* perturbado, agitado, ansioso, intranquilo
perturbing *a* perturbador, inquietador
Peru el Perú
peruke *n* peluca, *f*
perusal *n* lectura, *f*; examen, *m*
peruse *vt* leer con cuidado, estudiar, examinar
Peruvian *a* and *n* peruano (-na)
pervade *vt* penetrar; llenar, saturar; difundirse por; reinar en
pervasion *n* penetración, *f*
pervasive *a* penetrante
perverse *a* (wicked) perverso, depravado; obstinado; travieso; intratable
perversion *n* perversión, *f*
perversity *n* (wickedness) perversidad, *f*; obstinacia, *f*; travesura, *f*
perversive *a* perversivo
pervert *vt* pervertir; (words, etc.) torcer, tergiversar
pervious *a* penetrable; permeable
pessary *n surg* pesario, *m*
pessimism *n* pesimismo, *m*
pessimist *n* pesimista, *mf*
pessimistic *a* pesimista
pessimistically *adv* con pesimismo
pest *n* insecto nocivo, *m*; animal dañino, *m*; parásito, *m*; (pestilence) peste, *f*; *fig* plaga, *f*; (person) mosca, *f*
pester *vt* importunar, molestar, incomodar. **to p. constantly,** *inf* no dejar a sol ni a sombra
pestering *n* importunaciones, *f pl*
pestilence *n* pestilencia, peste, *f*; plaga, *f*
pestilential *a* pestilente, pestífero; pernicioso
pestle *n* mano de mortero, *f*, *vt* pistar, machacar, majar
pet *n* animal doméstico, *m*; niño (-ña) mimado (-da); favorito (-ta); (dear) querido (-da); (peevishness) despecho, malhumor, *m*. *vt* acariciar; (spoil) mimar. **to be a great pet,** ser un gran favorito
petal *n* pétalo, *m*, hoja, *f*
Peter *n* Pedro, *m*. **blue P.,** bandera de salida, *f*. **Peter's pence,** los diezmos de San Pedro
peter (out) *vi* desaparecer; agotarse
petition *n* petición, *f*; súplica, *f*; instancia, solicitud, *f*; memorial, *m*. *vt* suplicar; pedir, demandar; dirigir un memorial (a). **to file a p.,** elevar una instancia
petitioner *n* peticionario (-ia)
Petrarchan *a* petrarquista
petrel *n* petrel, *m*
petrifaction *n* petrificación, *f*
petrify *vt* petrificar; *inf* dejar seco. **to become petrified,** petrificarse
petrol *n* bencina, gasolina, *f*. *a* de gasolina, de bencina. **to run out of p.,** tener una pana de bencina. **p. gauge,** indicador del nivel de gasolina, *m*. **p. pump,** surtidor de gasolina, *m*. **p. station,** puesto de bencina, *m*, estación de servicio, *f*. **p. tank,** depósito de bencina, *m*
petroleum *n* petróleo, *m*. *a* petrolero; de petróleo. **p. works,** refinería de petróleo, *f*
petrology *n* petrografía, *f*
petrous *a* pétreo
petticoat *n* enagua, *f*; *pl* **petticoats,** (slang) faldas, *f pl*. *a* de faldas, de mujeres; de mujer
pettifogger *n* (lawyer) picapleitos, *m*, rábula, *mf*; (quibbler) sofista, *mf*

pettifogging a charlatán, mezquino, trivial
pettiness n trivialidad, insignificancia, f; pequeñez, f; mezquindad, f; ruindad, bajeza, f
petty a trivial, sin importancia, insignificante; inferior; pequeño; mezquino; ruin; bajo. **p. cash,** gastos menores de caja, m pl. **p. expense,** gasto menudo, m. **p. officer,** suboficial, m. **p. thief,** ratero (-ra)
petulance n mal humor, m, displicencia, irritabilidad, f
petulant a malhumorado, displicente, enojadizo, irritable
petulantly adv displicentemente, con mal humor
petunia n petunia, f
pew n banco (de iglesia), m. **p.-opener,** sacristán, m
pewter n peltre, m, a de peltre
phalange n falange, f
phalanx n falange, f
phallic a fálico
phallus n falo, m
phantasmagoria n fantasmagoría, f
phantasmagoric a fantasmagórico
phantom n fantasma, espectro, m; sombra, ficción, f; visión, f
Pharisaical a farisaico
Pharisee n fariseo, m
pharmaceutical a farmacéutico; n producto farmacéutico, m
pharmacist n farmacéutico, m
pharmacological a farmacológico
pharmacologist n farmacólogo, m
pharmacology n farmacología, f
pharmacopeia n farmacopea, f
pharmacy n farmacia, f
pharyngeal a faríngeo
pharyngitis n faringitis, f
pharynx n faringe, f
phase n fase, f; aspecto, m; ast fase, f
pheasant n faisán, m. **hen p.,** faisana, f. **p. shooting,** caza de faisanes, f
phenic a fénico
phenol n fenol, m
phenomenal a fenomenal
phenomenon n fenómeno, m
phial n redoma, f
philander vi galantear
philanderer n Tenorio, galanteador, m
philandering n galanteo, m
philanthropic a filantrópico
philanthropist n filántropo, m
philanthropy n filantropía, f
philatelic a filatélico
philatelist n filatelista, mf
philately n filatelia, f
philharmonic a filarmónico
philippic n filípica, f
Philippine a and n filipino (-na)
Philippines, the las (Islas) Filipinas, f pl
Philistine a and n filisteo (-ea)
philological a filológico
philologist n filólogo, m
philology n filología, f
philosopher n filósofo, m. **philosopher's stone,** piedra filosofal, f
philosophic(al) a filosófico
philosophize vi filosofar
philosophy n filosofía, f. **moral p.,** filosofía moral, f. **natural p.,** filosofía natural, f
philter n filtro, m
phlebitis n flebitis, f
phlebotomist n sangrador, flebotomiano, m
phlebotomy n flebotomía, f
phlegm n flema, f
phlegmatic a flemático
phlox n flox, m
Phoenician a and n fenicio (-ia)
phoenix n fénix, f
phoenitic a fonético

phoneticist n fonetista, mf
phonetics n fonética, f
phonograph n fonógrafo, m
phonological a fonológico
phonology n fonología, f
phony a falso; espurio. **p. war,** guerra tonta, guerra falsa, f
phosphate n fosfato, m
phosphoresce vi fosforecer, ser fosforescente
phosphorescence n fosforescencia, f
phosphorescent a fosforescente
phosphoric a fosfórico
phosphorus n fósforo, m
photo n foto, f
photochemistry n fotoquímica, f
photogenic a fotogénico
photograph n fotografía, f. vt fotografiar, retratar. **to have one's p. taken,** hacerse retratar
photographer n fotógrafo, m
photographic a fotográfico
photography n fotografía, f
photogravure n fotograbado, m
photostat n fotostato, m
photosynthesis n fotosíntesis, f
phrase n frase, f; mus frase musical, f. vt expresar, frasear; redactar. **p.-book,** libro de frases, m
phraseology n fraseología, f
phrasing n (drawing up) redacción, f; (style) estilo, m; mus frases, f pl
phrenetic a frenético
Phrygian a and n frigio (-ia)
Phrygian cap n gorro frigio, m
phthisis n tisis, f
phylactery n filactria, f
phylloxera n filoxera, f
physical a físico. **p. fitness,** buen estado físico, m. **p. geography,** geografía física, f. **p. jerks,** ejercicios físicos, m pl. **p. sciences,** ciencias físicas, f pl. **p. training,** educación física, f
physician n médico (-ca)
physicist n físico, m
physics n física, f
physiognomist n fisonomista, mf
physiognomy n fisonomía, f
physiological a fisiológico
physiologist n fisiólogo, m
physiology n fisiología, f
physiotherapy n fisioterapia, f
physique n físico, m
pianist n pianista, mf
piano, pianoforte n piano, m. **baby grand p.,** piano de media cola, m. **grand p.,** piano de cola, m. **upright p.,** piano vertical, m. **p. maker,** fabricante de pianos, m. **p. stool,** taburete de piano, m. **p. tuner,** afinador de pianos, m
pianola n piano mecánico, m
picaresque a picaresco
piccolo n flautín, m
pick n (tool) pico, zapapico, m; (mattock) piqueta, f; (choice) selección, f; derecho de elección, m; (best) lo mejor, lo más escogido; (fig cream) flor, nata, f. **tooth-p.,** mondadientes, m. **p.-a-back,** sobre los hombros, a cuestas. **p.-ax,** zapapico, m, alcotana, f. **p.-me-up,** tónico, m; trago, m
pick vt (with a pick-ax, make a hole) picar; (pluck, pick up) coger; (remove) sacar; (clean) limpiar; (one's teeth) mondarse (los dientes); (one's nose) hurgarse (las narices); (a bone) roer; (a lock) abrir con ganzúa; (a pocket) bolsear, robar del bolsillo; (peck) picotear; (choose) escoger; (a quarrel) buscar. vi (steal) hurtar, robar; (nibble) picar. **I have a bone to p. with you,** Tengo que ajustar unas cuentas contigo. **Take your p.!** ¡Escoja! **to p. and choose,** mostrarse difícil. **to p. to pieces,** fig criticar severamente. **to p. one's way through,** abrirse camino en; andar con precaución por; andar a tientas por. **to p. off,** coger; arrancar; qui-

tar; (shoot) disparar; fusilar. **to p. out,** entresacar; escoger; (recognize) reconocer; (understand) llegar a comprender; (a tune) tocar de oídas; (a song) cantar de oídas; (of colours) contrastar, resaltar. **to p. up,** *vt* (ground, etc.) romper con pico; coger; tomar; recoger; (raise) levantar, alzar; (information, etc.) cobrar, adquirir; (a living) ganar; (make friends with) trabar amistad con; (recover) recobrar; (find) encontrar, hallar; (buy) comprar; (learn) aprender; (a wireless message) interceptar; (a radio station) oír, tener. *vi* recobrar la salud; reponerse; mejorar. *n mech* recobro, *m*

picket *n* estaca, *f;* (*mil* and during strikes) piquete, *m*. *vt* cercar con estacas; poner piquetes ante (or alrededor de); poner de guardia; estacionar

picking *n* (gathering) recolección, *f;* (choosing) selección, *f;* (pilfering) robo, *m; pl* **pickings,** desperdicios, *m pl;* (perquisites) gajes, *m pl;* ganancias, *f pl*

pickle *n* (solution) escabeche, *m;* (vegetable, etc.) encurtido, *m;* (plight) apuro, *m;* (child) diablillo, *m*. *vt* encurtir, escabechar

picklock *n* (thief and instrument) ganzúa, *f*

pickpocket *n* carterista, *mf* ratero (-ra)

picnic *n* partida de campo, jira, *f,* picnic, *m*. *vi* llevar la merienda al campo, hacer un picnic

picnicker *n* excursionista, *mf*

pictorial *a* pictórico; ilustrado. *n* revista ilustrada, *f*

pictorially *adv* pictóricamente; en grabados; por imágenes

picture *n* cuadro, *m;* (of a person) retrato, *m;* imagen, *f;* (illustration) grabado, *m,* lámina, *f;* fotografía, *f;* (outlook) perspectiva, *f;* idea, *f*. *vt* pintar; describir; imaginar. **to go to the pictures,** ir al cine. **motion p.,** película, *f*. **talking p.,** película sonora, *f*. **p. book,** libro con láminas, *m*. **p. frame,** marco, *m*. **p. gallery,** museo de pinturas, *m;* galería de pinturas, *f*. **p. hat,** pamela, *f*. **p. palace,** cine, *m*. **p. postcard,** tarjeta postal, *f*. **p. restorer,** restaurador de cuadros, *m*. **p. writing,** pictografía, *f*

picturesque *a* pintoresco

picturesqueness *n* carácter pintoresco, *m,* lo pintoresco; pintoresquismo, *m*

pie *n* (savoury) empanada, *f;* (sweet) pastel, *m,* torta, *f;* (of meat) pastelón, *m; print* pastel, *m*. **apple pie,** torta de manzanas, *f*. **to eat humble pie,** bajar las orejas. **to have a finger in the pie,** meter baza

piebald *a* pío; tordo

piece *n* pedazo, *m;* trozo, *m;* parte, porción, *f;* (literary, artistic work, coin, of fabric, at chess, etc. and slang) pieza, *f;* (of luggage) bulto, *m;* (of paper) hoja, *f;* (of ground) parcela, *f;* (of money) moneda, *f,* *vt* remendar; unir, juntar. **a p. of advice,** un consejo. **a p. of bread,** un pedazo de pan; una rebanada de pan. **a p. of folly,** un acto de locura. **a p. of furniture,** un mueble. **a p. of insolence,** una insolencia. **a p. of news,** una noticia. **a p. of paper,** un papel, una hoja de papel, una cuartilla. **a p. of poetry,** una poesía. **Peter has a five-shilling p.,** Pedro tiene una moneda de cinco chelines. **to break in pieces,** *vt* hacer pedazos, romper. *vi* hacerse pedazos, romperse. **to come or fall to pieces,** deshacerse; (of machines) desarmarse. **to cut in pieces,** cortar en pedazos; (an army) destrozar. **to give a p. of one's mind (to),** decir cuatro verdades (a), decir cuántas son cinco (a). **to go to pieces,** (of persons) hacerse pedazos. **to take to pieces,** (a machine) desmontar; deshacer. **to tear or pull to pieces,** hacer pedazos, despedazar; desgarrar. **p. goods,** géneros en piezas, *m pl*. **p.-work,** trabajo a destajo, *m*. **to do p.-work,** trabajar a destajo. **p.-worker,** destajista, *mf*

piecemeal *adv* en pedazos; a remiendos; en detalle; poco a poco

piecrust *n* pasta, *f*

pied *a* bicolor; abigarrado, de varios colores

pier *n* (jetty) dique, *m;* embarcadero, *m;* malecón, *m;* (of a bridge) pila, *f;* (pillar) columna, *f;* (between windows, etc.) entrepaño, *m*. **p.-glass,** espejo de cuerpo entero, *m*. **p. head,** punta del dique, *f*. **p. table,** consola, *f*

pierce *vt* penetrar; (of sorrow, etc.) traspasar, herir; (bore) agujerear, taladrar. *vi* penetrar

pierced ear *n* oreja perforada, *f*

piercing *a* penetrante; (of the wind, etc.) cortante; (of the voice, etc.) agudo. *n* penetración, *f*

piercingly *adv* de un modo penetrante, agudamente

pietism *n* pietismo, *m*

pietist *n* pietista, *mf*

pietistic *a* pietista

piety *n* piedad, devoción, *f*

piezometer *n phys* piezómetro, *m*

piffle *n* patrañas, tonterías, *f pl*

pig *n* puerco, cerdo, *m; inf* cochino, *m;* (metal) lingote, *m*. **to buy a p. in a poke,** cerrar un trato a ciegas. **p.-eyed,** de ojos de cerdo. **p.-iron,** arrabio; hierro colado en barras, lingote de fundición, *m*

pigeon *n* paloma, *f,* palomo, *m; inf* primo, *m*. *vt* embaucar, engañar. **carrier p.,** paloma mensajera, *f*. **clay p.,** pichón de barro, platillo de arcilla, *m*. **male p.,** pichón, *m*. **pouter p.,** paloma buchona, *f*. **young p.,** palomino, *m*. **p. fancier,** palomero, *m*. **p.-hole,** casilla, *f*. *vt* encasillar. **set of p.-holes,** encasillado, *m*. **p.-shooting,** tiro de pichón, *m*. **p.-toed,** patituerto

piggy bank *n* alcancía, *f*

pigheaded *a* terco, testarudo

pigheadedness *n* terquedad, testarudez, *f*

piglet *n* cerdito, *m*

pigment *n* pigmento, *m*

pigmentary *a* pigmentario

pigmentation *n* pigmentación, *f*

pigskin *n* piel de cerdo, *f*

pigsty *n* pocilga, *f*

pigtail *n* coleta, *f*

pike *n mil* pica, *f,* chuzo, *m;* (peak) pico, *m*

pilaster *n* pilastra, *f*

pile *n* estaca, *f;* poste, *m;* (engineering) pilote, *m;* (heap) pila, *f,* montón, *m;* (pyre) pira, *f;* (building) edificio grande, *m; elec* pila, *f;* (hair) pelo, *m;* (nap) pelusa, *f; pl* **piles,** *med* almorranas, *f pl*. *vt* clavar pilotes en; apoyar con pilotes; (heap) amontonar; (load) cargar. **to make one's p.,** *inf* hacer su pacotilla. **to p. arms,** poner los fusiles en pabellón. **to p. on,** (coal, etc.) echar; (increase) aumentar. **to p. it on,** exagerar, intensificar; (a table) cargar. **to p. up,** amontonarse; acumularse; (of a ship) encallar. **p.-driver,** machina, *f;* martinete, *m*. **p. dwelling,** vivienda palustre, sostenida por pilares, *f*

pilfer *vt* sisar, sonsacar, hurtar, ratear

pilferer *n* sisador (-ra), ratero (-ra)

pilfering *n* sisa, ratería, *f*

pilgrim *n* peregrino (-na). **pilgrim's staff,** bordón, *m*

pilgrimage *n* peregrinación, *f;* romería, *f*. **to make a p.,** hacer una peregrinación, peregrinar; ir en romería

piling *n* amontonamiento, *m;* (of buildings) pilotaje, *m*

pill *n* píldora, *f*. **to gild the p.,** *fig* dorar la píldora. **p.-box,** caja de píldoras, *f;* casamata, *f,* mil nido de ametralladoras, *m*

pillage *vt* pillar, saquear. *n* saqueo, *m*

pillager *n* saqueador (-ra)

pillaging *n* pillaje, *m,* a pillador, saqueador

pillar *n* pilar, *m,* columna, *f;* (person) sostén, soporte, *m*. **from p. to post,** de Ceca en Meca. **p. of salt,** estatua de sal, *f*. **the Pillars of Hercules,** las Columnas de Hércules. **to be a p. of strength,** *inf* ser una roca. **p.-box,** buzón, *m*

pillared *a* con columnas, sostenido por columnas; en columnas

pillion *n* (on a horse, etc.) grupera, *f;* (on a motorcycle) grupa, *f*. **to ride p.,** ir a la grupa

pillory *n* picota, argolla, *f*. *vt* empicotar; *fig* poner en ridículo; censurar duramente

pillow *n* almohada, *f;* (for lace-making) cojín, *m;* (of a machine) cojinete, *m*. *vt* apoyar; reposar; servir como almohada. **to take counsel of one's p.,** consultar con la almohada. **p.-case,** funda de almohada, *f*

pilot *n* piloto, *m*; *naut* práctico, piloto (de puerto), *m*. *vt* guiar, conducir; (*naut aer*) pilotar, pilotear. **p. boat,** vaporcito del práctico, *m*. **p. jacket,** chaquetón de piloto, *m*. **p. officer,** oficial de aviación, *m*

pilotage *n* pilotaje, *m*; *naut* practicaje, *m*

pilotless *a* sin piloto

pimento *n* pimiento, *m*

pimp *n* rufián, alcahuete, *m*, *vi* alcahuetear

pimple *n* grano, *m*

pimply *a* con granos

pin *n* alfiler, *m*; prendedor, *m*; clavija, *f*; clavo, *m*, chaveta, *f*; (bolt) perno, *m*. *vt* prender con alfileres; (with a peg) enclavijar; fijar; sujetar. **to pin up,** sujetar con alfileres; (the hair) sujetar con horquillas. **I don't care a pin,** No me importa un bledo. **to be on pins,** estar en ascuas. **to suffer from pins and needles,** tener aguijones. **pin-head,** cabeza de alfiler, *f*. **pin-money,** alfileres, *m pl*. **pin-oak,** *bot* pincarrasco, *m*, carrasca, *f*. **pin point,** punta de alfiler, *f*. **pin-prick,** alfilerazo, *m*

pinafore *n* delantal de niño, *m*

pince-nez *n* quevedos, *m pl*

pincers *n pl* pinzas, tenazas, *f pl*, alicates, *m pl*; (of crustaceans) pinzas, *f pl*. **p. movement,** movimiento de pinzas, *m*

pinch *vt* pellizcar; (crush) estrujar; aplastar; apretar; (of the cold) helar; (steal) hurtar, birlar; (arrest) coger, prender. *n* pellizco, torniscón, *m*; pulgarada, *f*; (of snuff) polvo, *m*; (distress) miseria, *f*; (pain) dolor, *m*, angustia. *f*. **at a p.,** en caso de apuro. **to know where the shoe pinches,** saber dónde le aprieta el zapato

pinched *a* (by the cold) helado; (wan) marchito, descolorido

pincushion *n* acerico, *m*

Pindaric *a* pindárico

pine *n bot* pino, *m*. *vi* languidecer, marchitarse, consumirse. **to p. for,** anhelar, suspirar por, perecer por. **pitch-p.,** pino de tea, *m*. **p.-apple,** piña de las Indias, *f*, ananás, *m*. **p. cone,** piña, *f*. **p. kernel,** piñón, *m*. **p. needle,** pinocha, *f*. **p. wood,** pinar, *m*, pineda, *f*

pineal *a* en figura de piña; *anat* pineal

ping *n* silbido de una bala, *m*; zumbido, *m*. **p. pong,** tenis de mesa, pingpong, *m*

pinion *n* (wing) ala, *f*; (small feather) piñón, *m*; (in carving) ala, *m*; (wheel) piñón, *m*. *vt* atar las alas de; cortar un piñón de; (a person) atar; (the arms of) trincar, asegurar

pink *n bot* clavel, *m*; color de rosa, *m*; (perfection) modelo, *m*; colmo, *m*; (hunting) color rojo, *m*; levitín rojo de caza, *m*. *a* de color de rosa, rosado. *vt sew* picar; (pierce) penecrar, atravesar. *vi* (of an engine) picar

pinking *n sew* picadura, *f*

pinkish *a* rosáceo

pinnacle *n naut* pinaza, *f*

pinnacle *n* pináculo, *m*

pinpoint *vt* precisar

pint *n* (measure) pinta, *f*

pintle *n* (pin) perno, *m*

piolet *n* piolet, *m*

pioneer *n* pionero, explorador, *m*; introductor, *m*. **to be a p. in . . . ,** ser el primero en (or a) . . . **pioneering role,** papel de iniciador (e.g. **She played a pioneering role,** jugó un papel de iniciadora)

pious *a* pío, devoto, piadoso

piously *adv* piadosamente, devotamente

pip *n* (of fruit) pepita, *f*; (on cards, dice) punto, *m*; (disease) moquillo, *m*; (of an army, etc., officer) insignia, *f*

pipe *n* (for tobacco) pipa de fumar, *f*; *mus* caramillo, *m*; (boatswain's) pito, *m*; (of a bird) trino, *m*; (voice) voz aguda, *f*; tubo, *m*; (for water, etc.) cañería, *f*; (of a hose) manga, *f*; (of an organ) cañón, *m*; (of wine) pipa, *f*; *pl* **pipes,** *mus* gaita, *f*. *vi* tocar el caramillo (or la gaita); empezar a cantar; silbar; (of birds) trinar. *vt* (a tune) tocar; (sing) cantar; (whistle) llamar con pito; conducir con cañerías; instalar cañerías en. **He smokes a p.,** Fuma una pipa. **I smoked a p.** (of tobacco) **before I went to bed,** Fumé una pipa antes de acostarme. **Put that in your p. and smoke it!** ¡Chúpate eso! **p. clay,** blanquizal, *m*. **p. cleaner,** limpiapipas, *m*. **p. layer,** cañero, fontanero, *m*. **p. laying,** instalación de cañerías, *f*. **p.-line,** cañería, *f*; (oil) oleoducto, *m*. **p. tobacco,** tabaco de pipa, *m*

pipeful *n* pipa, *f*

piper *n* (bagpiper) gaitero, *m*; flautista, *mf*

pipette *n chem* pipeta, *f*

piping *n* sonido del caramillo, *m*; música de la flauta, etc., *f*; (of birds) trinos, *m pl*; voz aguda, *f*; (for water, etc.) cañería, tubería, *f*; *sew* cordoncillo, *m*. **p.-hot,** hirviente

pipkin *n* ollita de barro, *f*

pippin *n* (apple) camuesa, *f*

piquancy *n* picante, *m*

piquant *a* picante

pique *n* (resentment, and score in game) pique, *m*. **to p. oneself upon,** preciarse de, jactarse de. **to be piqued,** estar enojado; *inf* amoscarse

piquet *n* juego de los cientos, *m*

piracy *n* piratería, *f*

pirate *n* pirata, *mf*. *vi* piratear. *vt* publicar una edición furtiva de. **p. edition,** edición furtiva, *f*

piratical *a* pirata, pirático; de pirata, de piratas

pirouette *n* pirueta, *f*

Pisces *n pl* peces, *m pl*

pisciculture *n* piscicultura, *f*

Pisgah Fasga, *f*

pistachio *n* pistacho, *m*

pistil *n bot* pistilo, *m*

pistol *n* pistola, *f*. **p. belt,** charpa, *f*, cinto de pistolas, *m*. **p. case,** pistolera, *f*. **p. shot,** pistoletazo, *m*

piston *n mech* émbolo, pistón, *m*; *mus* pistón, *m*, llave, *f*. **p. ring,** anillo de émbolo, segmento de émbolo, *m*. **p. rod,** biela, *f*. **p. stroke,** carrera del émbolo, *f*

pit *n* hoyo, *m*; foso, *m*; (in a garage) foso de reparación, *m*; *theat* platea, *f*; (trap) trampa, *f*; (scar) hoyo, *m*; precipicio, *m*; (hell) infierno, *m*. *vt* (with smallpox) marcar con viruelas; (against) competir con. **pithead,** boca de mina, *f*. **p. of the stomach,** boca del estómago, *f*. **pit stall,** butaca de platea, *f*

pitch *n chem* pez, brea, *f*, alquitrán, *m*; (place) puesto, *m*; (throwing) lanzamiento, *m*; (distance thrown) alcance, *m*; (for cricket) cancha, *f*; (bowling) saque, *m*; (slope) pendiente, inclinación, *f*; (height) elevación, *f*; *mus* tono, *m*; (*fig* degree) grado, extremo, *m*; (*naut aer*) cabeceo, *m*; (of threads of a screw, etc.) paso, *m*. *vt* (camp) asentar; (a tent, etc.) colocar, poner; (throw) lanzar, arrojar, tirar; (cricket, etc.) lanzar; (fix in) clavar; *mus* graduar el tono de; (tell) narrar. *vi* (fall) caer; *naut* cabecear, zozobrar; *aer* cabecear. **to paint with p.,** embrear. **to p. into,** (attack) acometer, atacar; (scold) desatarse contra; (food) engullir. **p.-black,** negro como la pez; oscuro como boca de lobo. **p.-pine,** pino de tea, *m*. **p.-pipe,** diapasón vocal, *m*

pitched battle *n* batalla campal, *f*

pitcher *n* jarro, cántaro, *m*; (in baseball) lanzador de pelota, *m*

pitcherful *n* jarro (de), *m*

pitchfork *n* horquilla, *f*, aventador, *m*. *vt* levantar con horquilla; *fig* lanzar

pitching *n* (pavement) adoquinado, *m*; (of a ship) socollada, *f*; cabeceo, *m*

piteous *a* lastimero; triste; plañidero; compasivo, tierno

piteousness *n* estado lastimero, *m*; tristeza, *f*; compasión, ternura, *f*

pitfall *n* trampa, *f*; *fig* añagaza, *f*, lazo, peligro, *m*

pith *n bot* médula, *f*; médula espinal, *f*; *fig* meollo, *m*; fuerza, *f*, vigor, *m*; substancia, *f*; quinta esencia, *f*; importancia, *f*

pithiness *n* jugosidad, *f*; fuerza, *f*, vigor, *m*

pithy *a* meduloso; *fig* jugoso; enérgico, vigoroso

pitiable *a* lastimoso, digno de compasión; (paltry) despreciable

pitiful *a* piadoso, compasivo; conmovedor, doloroso, lastimero; (contemptible) miserable

pitifully *adv* lastimosamente

pitiless *a* sin piedad, despiadado

pitilessness *n* crueldad, inhumanidad, *f*

pitman *n* minero, *m*; aserrador de foso, *m*

pittance *n* pitanza, *f*; pequeña porción, *f*; ración de hambre, *f*

pitted *a* picoso

pituitary *a* pituitario

pity *n* piedad, compasión, *f*; lástima, *f*. *vt* compadecerse de, tener lástima (a); compadecer. **It is a p. that . . . ,** Es lástima que . . . **Have p.!** ¡Ten piedad! **to take p. on,** tener lástima (de). **to move to p.,** dar lástima (a), enternecer

pityingly *adv* con lástima

pivot *n* pivote, *m*; eje, *m*; *fig* punto de partida, *m*, *vi* girar sobre un pivote o eje

pivotal *a fig* cardinal, principal, fundamental

pixy *n* duende, *m*. **p. hood,** caperuza, *f*

pizzicato *a* pichigato

placability *n* placabilidad, *f*

placable *a* aplacable, placable

placard *n* cartel, *m*. *vt* fijar carteles (en); publicar por carteles

placate *vt* aplacar, ablandar, apaciguar

placatory *a* placativo

place *n* lugar, *m*; sitio, *m*; (position) puesto, *m*; (seat) asiento, *m*; (laid at table) cubierto, *m*; (square) plaza, *f*; (house) residencia, *f*; (in the country) casa de campo, finca, *f*; (in a book) pasaje, *m*; (in an examination) calificación, *f*; (rank) posición, *f*, rango, *m*; situación, *f*; (employment) empleo, *m*, colocación, *f*. *vt* poner; colocar; (in employment) dar empleo (a); (appoint) nombrar; (an order) dar; (money) invertir; (remember) recordar, traer a la memoria; (size up) fijar; (confidence) poner. **in p.,** en su lugar; apropiado. **in p. of,** en vez de, en lugar de. **in the first p.,** en primer lugar, primero. **in the next p.,** luego, después. **out of p.,** fuera de lugar; inoportuno. **It is not my p. to . . . ,** No me toca a mí . . . **to give p. to,** ceder el paso (a); ceder (a). **to take p.,** verificarse, tener lugar, ocurrir. **p. of business,** establecimiento, local de negocios, *m*. **p. of worship,** edificio de culto, *m*

placenta *n* placenta, *f*

placid *a* plácido, apacible; calmoso; sereno, sosegado; dulce

placidity *n* placidez, *f*; serenidad, tranquilidad, *f*, sosiego, *m*

placidly *adv* plácidamente

placing *n* colocación, *f*; posición, *f*; localización, *f*

placket *n* abertura (en una falda), *f*

plagiarism *n* plagio, *m*

plagiarist *n* plagiario (-ia)

plagiarize *vt* plagiar, hurtar

plague *n* plaga, *f*; peste, pestilencia, *f*. *vt* importunar, atormentar; plagar

plaice *n* (nearest equivalent) platija, *f*

plaid *n* manta escocesa, *f*; género de cuadros, *m*, *a* a cuadros

plain *a* claro; evidente; (simple) sencillo; llano; sin adorno; (flat) liso, igual; (candid) franco; (with truth, etc.) desnudo; mero; puro, sin mezcla; (of words) redondo; (ugly) feo. *adv* claramente; llanamente; sencillamente; francamente. *n* llanura, *f*, llano, *m*. **the p. truth,** la pura verdad. **p. clothes,** traje de paisano, *m*. **p. clothes man,** detective, *m*. **p. cooking,** cocina sencilla, cocina casera, *f*. **p. dealing,** buena fe, sinceridad, *f*. **p. dweller,** llanero (-ra). **p. living,** vida sencilla, *f*. **p. people,** gente sencilla, *f*. **p. sailing,** *fig* camino fácil, *m*. **p. sewing,** costura, *f*. **p.-song,** canto llano, *m*. **p. speaking,** franqueza, *f*. **p.-spoken,** franco. **in p. English,** sin rodeos, en cristiano (e.g. **Speak in p. English!** Habla sin rodeos! Habla en cristiano!)

plainly *adv* claramente; sencillamente; llanamente; francamente; rotundamente

plainness *n* claridad, *f*; sencillez, *f*; llaneza, *f*; franqueza, *f*; (ugliness) fealdad, *f*

plainsman *n* hombre de las llanuras, *m*

plaint *n* queja, *f*, lamento, *m*; *law* demanda, querella, *f*

plaintiff *n* demandante, *mf*, actor, *m*, parte actora, actora, *f*

plaintive *a* quejumbroso, dolorido; patético

plaintively *adv* quejumbrosamente

plaintiveness *n* melancolía, tristeza, *f*; voz quejumbrosa, *f*

plait *n* trenza, *f*. *vt* trenzar; tejer. **in plaits,** (of hair) en trenzas

plan *n* plan, *m*; (map) plano, *m*; proyecto, *m*. *vt* planear; proyectar; proponerse. **the Marshall P.,** el Plan Marshall. **to make a p. of,** trazar un plano de. **to make plans,** hacer planes

planchette *n* mesa giratoria, *f*

plane *n* (tree) plátano, *m*; (tool) cepillo, *m*; *geom* plano, *m*; (level) nivel, *m*; *aer* avión, *m*, plano. *vt carp* acepillar, alisar. *vi aer* planear

planet *n* planeta, *m*

planetarium *n* planetario, *m*

planetary *a* planetario

planing *n* acepilladura, alisadura, *f*,

plank *n* tabla, *f*; *fig* fundamento, principio, *m*; *pl* **planks,** tablazón, *f*. *vt* entablar, enmaderar

planking *n* entablado, *m*, tablazón, *f*

plankton *n* plancton, *m*

planned *a* proyectado, planeado; dirigido. **p. economy,** economía dirigida, *f*

planner *n* proyectista, *mf*; autor (-ra) de un plan

planning *n* proyecto, *m*; concepción, *f*

plant *n bot* planta, *f*; instalación, *f*, material, *m*. *vt* plantar; (place) colocar; fijar; (a blow) asestar; (people) establecer; (instil) inculcar, imbuir (con); (conceal) esconder. **p. pot,** florero, *m*. **p. stand,** jardinera, *f*

plantain *n bot* llantén, *m*

plantation *n* plantación, *f*; plantío, *m*; *fig* colonia, *f*; introducción, *f*, establecimiento, *m*

planter *n* plantador, cultivador, *m*

planting *n* plantación, *f*; *fig* colonia, *f*; introducción, *f*. **p. out,** trasplante, *m*

plantlike *a* como una planta; de planta

plaque *n* placa, *f*; medalla, *f*

plash *n* (puddle) charco, *m*; (sound) chapaleteo, *m*. *vt* and *vi* chapotear, chapalear

plasma *n* plasma, *m*

plaster *n* (for walls, etc.) argamasa, *f*; yeso, *m*; *med* parche, emplasto, *m*. *vt* (walls, etc.) enlucir, enyesar; poner emplastos (a or en); (daub) embadurnar manchar; (cover) cubrir. **p. cast,** vaciado, yeso, *m*. **p. of Paris,** escayola, *f*

plasterer *n* yesero, *m*

plastering *n* revoque, enyesado, guarnecido, *m*. **p. trowel,** fratás, *m*

plastic *a* plástico. *n* plástica, *f*; *pl* **plastics,** materias plásticas, *f pl*. **p. surgery,** cirugía plástica, cirugía estética, *f*

plasticine *n* plasticina, *f*

plasticity *n* plasticidad, *f*

plate *n* plancha, chapa, *f*; (engraving and *phot.*) of a doctor, etc.) placa, *f*; (illustration) lámina, *f*; (cutlery, etc.) vajilla, *f*; (for eating) plato, *m*; (for money) platillo, *m*; electrotipo, *m*; (dental) dentadura postiza, *f*. *vt* (with armor) blindar; (with metal) planchear; (silver) platear; (electro-plate) niquelar. **silver p.,** vajilla de plata, plata, *f*. **p.-armor,** armadura, *f*; (of a ship) blindaje, *m*. **p.-draining rack,** escurreplatos, *m*. **p.-glass,** vidrio plano, *m*. **p.-rack,** escurridero para platos, *m*. **p. warmer,** calientaplatos, *m*

plateau *n* meseta, altiplanicie, *f*

plateful *n* plato (de), *m*

plater *n* plateador, *m*; platero, *m*

plateresque *a arch* plateresco

platform *n* plataforma, *f*; (railway) andén, *m*. **p. ticket,** billete de andén, *m*

plating *n* niquelado, *m*; electrogalvanización, *f*; (with armor) blindaje, *m*

platinum *n* platino, *m*. **p. blonde,** rubia platino, *f*

platitude *n* perogrullada, *f*, lugar común, *m*; trivialidad, vulgaridad, *f*

platitudinous *a* lleno de perogrulladas; trivial

platonic *a* platónico

Platonism *n* platonismo, *m*

Platonist *n* platonista, *mf*

platoon *n* *mil* pelotón, *m*

platter *n* fuente, *f*, trinchero, *m*; plato, *m*

plaudit *n* aplauso, *m*, aclamación, *f*; (praise) elogio, *m*, alabanza, *f*

plausibility *n* plausibilidad, *f*

plausible *a* plausible

plausibly *adv* plausiblemente

play *vi* jugar; (frolic) juguetear, retozar; recrearse, divertirse; *mech* moverse; (on a musical instrument) tocar; (wave) ondear, flotar; *theat* representar; (behave) conducirse. *vt* jugar; (of a searchlight, etc.) enfocar; (direct) dirigir; (a fish) agotar; (a joke, etc.) hacer; (a piece in a game) mover; (a musical instrument or music) tocar; (a string instrument) tañer; (a character in a play) hacer el papel de; (a drama, etc.) representar, poner en escena. **to p. a joke,** gastar una broma, hacer una burla. **to p. fair,** jugar limpio. **to p. false,** jugar sucio, engañar. **to p. the fool,** hacerse el tonto, hacerse el payaso. **to p. at,** jugar a; (pretend) fingir; hacer sin entusiasmo. **to p. off,** confrontar, contraponer. **to p. on.** See **to p. upon. to p. on the . . . ,** (of musical instruments) tocar. **to p. to,** (a person) tocar para. **to p. upon,** tocar; (a person's fears, etc.) explotar. **to p. up to,** (a person) adular, hacer la rueda (a). **to p. with,** jugar con; burlarse de; (an idea) acariciar play, *n* juego, *m*; diversión, *f*, recreo, *m*; (reflection) reflejo, *m*; movimiento libre, *m*; (to the imagination, etc.) rienda suelta, *f*; *mech* holgura, *f*; *lit* pieza dramática, comedia, *f*; (performance) función, representación, *f*; (theater) teatro, *m*. **fair p.,** juego limpio, *m*. **foul p.,** juego sucio, *m*; traición, perfidia, *f*. **to bring into p.,** poner en juego. **to come into p.,** entrar en juego. **to give p. to,** dar rienda a. **p. on words,** juego de palabras, *m*. **p.-pen,** cuadro enrejado, *m*

playact *vi* hacer la comedia

playbill *n* cartel, *m*; programa, *m*

played-out *a* agotado; viejo

player *n* jugador (-ra); *theat* actor (-triz), representante, *mf*; *mus* músico (-ca), tocador (-ra)

playfellow *n* camarada, *mf*; compañero (-ra) de juego, compañero de juegos

playful *a* juguetón; travieso; alegre

playfully *adv* en juego, de broma; alegremente

playfulness *n* carácter juguetón, *m*; travesuras, *f pl*; alegría, *f*

playgoer *n* persona que frecuenta los teatros, *f*; espectador de comedias, *m*

playground *n* patio de recreo, *m*

playing *n* juego, *m*. **p.-cards,** naipes, *m pl*, cartas, *f pl*. **p.-field,** campo de deportes, *m*

playlet *n* comedia corta, *f*

playmate. See **playfellow**

plaything *n* juguete, *m*

playtime *n* recreación, *f*; (in schools) hora de recreo, *f*, recreo, *m*

playwright *n* dramaturgo, *m*, autor (-ra) de comedias

plea *n* *law* informe, *m*; declaración, *f*; *law* acción, *f*, proceso, *m*; (excuse) pretexto, *m*, excusa, *f*; (entreaty) súplica, *f*. **under p. of,** bajo pretexto de, con excusa de

plead *vi law* pleitear; *law* declarar; suplicar; (of counsel, etc.) abogar (por); interceder (por). *vt* defender en juicio; aducir, alegar; pretender. **to p. guilty,** confesarse culpable. **to p. not guilty,** negar la acusación. **to p. ignorance,** pretender ignorancia

pleading *n* súplicas, *f pl*; *law* defensa, *f*; *pl* **pleadings,** alegatos, *m pl*, *a* implorante

pleasant *a* agradable; placentero; ameno; encantador;

dulce; alegre; (of persons) simpático, amable; bueno; divertido

pleasantly *adv* agradablemente; de un modo muy amable; alegremente

pleasantness *n* agrado, *m*; placer, *m*; amabilidad, *f*; alegría, *f*

pleasantry *n* jocosidad, *f*; broma, chanza, *f*

please *vi* dar placer, gustar, dar gusto, agradar; parecer bien, querer, servirse; tener a bien, placer. *vt* deleitar, agradar, gustar; halagar; contentar, satisfacer. **I will do what I p.,** Haré lo que me parezca bien. **If you p.,** Si te parece bien; Con tu permiso. **She is very easy to p.,** Es muy fácil de darle placer. **When you p.,** Cuando Vd. quiera, Cuando a Vd. le venga bien Cuando Vd. guste. **"Please Do Not Disturb,"** «No Molesten.» **P. sit down!** ¡Haga el favor de sentarse! ¡Sírvase de sentarse! **P. God!** ¡Plegue a Dios!

pleased *a* contento (de or con); encantado (de); alegre (de); satisfecho (de or con). **I am p. with my new house,** Estoy contento con mi nueva casa. **I'm p. to meet you,** Mucho gusto (en conocerle), Mucho gusto (en conocerla). **to be p.,** estar contento; complacerse en

pleasing *a* agradable, grato; placentero; halagüeño

pleasurable *a* agradable; divertido, entretenido

pleasure *n* placer, *m*; gusto, *m*; satisfacción, *f*; (will) voluntad, *f*; recreo, *m*; diversión, distracción, *f*. **to give p. (to),** dar placer (a); deleitar, agradar; complacer. **to take p. in,** gustar de, disfrutar de; complacerse en. **I shall do it with great p.,** Lo haré con mucho gusto, Lo haré con mucho placer. **p.-boat,** barco de recreo, *m*. **p.-ground,** parque de atracciones, *m*. **p.-seeking,** amigo de placeres, frívolo. **p. trip,** viaje de recreo, *m*. excursión, *f*

pleasure craft *n* barco de recreo, *m*, (one vessel); barcas de recreo (collectively); *m pl*

pleat *n* pliegue, *m*, *vt* plegar, hacer pliegues en

pleating *n* plegado, *m*

plebeian *a* plebeyo. *n* plebeyo (-ya)

plebiscite *n* plebiscito, *m*. **to take a p.,** hacer un plebiscito

plectrum *n* plectro, *m*

pledge *n* prenda, *f*; empeño, *m*; garantía, *f*; (hostage) rehén, *m*; (toast) brindis, *m*. *vt* empeñar, dar en prenda; garantizar; brindar por; prometer. **to p. oneself,** comprometerse. **to p. support for,** prometer apoyo para

Pleiades *n pl* pléyades, *f pl*

plenary *a* pleno; plenario. **p. indulgence,** indulgencia plenaria, *f*. **p. session,** sesión plenaria, *f*

plenipotentiary *a* plenipotenciario. *n* plenipotenciario, *m*

plenitude *n* plenitud, *f*

plenteous, plentiful *a* copioso, abundante. **to be p.,** abundar

plentifully *adv* en abundancia

plenty *n* abundancia, *f*; en abundancia; de sobra; mucho. *adv inf* bastante. **There is p. of food,** Hay comida en abundancia. **We have p. of time,** Tenemos tiempo de sobra

pleonasm *n* pleonasmo, *m*

plethora *n* plétora, *f*

pleurisy *n* pleuresía, *f*

plexus *n* plexo, *m*

pliability *n* flexibilidad, *f*; docilidad, *f*

pliable, pliant *a* flexible; dócil

pliers *n pl* pinzas, *f pl*, alicates, *m pl*, tenazas, *f pl*

plight *vt* (one's word) empeñar, dar; prometer en matrimonio. *n* (fix) aprieto, apuro, *m*. **to p. one's troth,** dar palabra de matrimonio

plinth *n arch* plinto, *m*

Pliny the Elder Plinio el Antiguo, Plinio el Mayor

Pliny the Younger Plinio el Menor

plod *vi* andar despacio, caminar con trabajo; *fig* trabajar con ahínco

plodder *n* trabajador lento y concienzudo, *m*; (student) empollón (-ona)

plot *n* (of land) parcela, *f;* terreno, solar, *m;* (plan) proyecto, *m;* estratagema, *m;* (literary) intriga, trama, *f;* (story) argumento, *m;* (conspiracy) conjuración, *f,* complot, *m. vt* trazar (un plano, etc.); urdir, tramar. *vi* conspirar, intrigar

plotter *n* conspirador (-ra conjurado (-da)

plotting *n* trazado (de un plano, una gráfica), *m;* (conspiracy) conspiración, *f;* maquinaciones, *f pl;* (hatching) trama, *f*

plover *n* ave fría, *f,* chorlito, *m*

plow *n* arado, *m; ast* el Carro, la Osa Mayor; (in an examination) escabechina, *f. vt and vi* arar; *fig* surcar; (in examinations) escabechar, dar calabazas (a), suspender. **plow the sands,** arar en el mar. **p. handle,** esteva, *f.* **to p. up,** roturar

plowman *n* arador, surcador, *m;* (peasant) labrador, *m*

plowshare *n* reja de arado, *f*

pluck *vt* (pick) coger; (a bird) desplumar; *mus* puntear; (in an examination) calabacear escabechar. *vi* tirar (de). *n* (tug) tirón, *m;* (of an animal) asadura, *f;* (courage) coraje, *m.* **to p. up courage,** tomar coraje, sacar ánimos. **to p. off,** quitar. **to p. out,** arrancar; quitar

pluckily *adv* valientemente

pluckiness *n* coraje, valor, *m*

plucky *a* valiente, esforzado, resuelto, animoso

plug *n* tapón, tarugo, *m;* (in building) nudillo, *m;* (of a switchboard) clave, *f; elec* enchufe, *m;* (of a w.c.) tirador, *m;* (of a bath, etc.) tapón, *m;* (of tobacco) rollo, *m. vt* atarugar, taponar, obturar; (in building) rellenar. *vi* (with away) batirse el cobre, sudar la gota gorda. **to p. in,** enchufar

plum *n* (tree) ciruelo, *m;* (fruit) ciruela, *f;* (raisin) pasa, *f; (inf* prize) breva, golosina, *f.* **p. cake,** pastel de fruta, *m*

plumage *n* plumaje, *m*

plumb *n* plomada, *f;* (sounding-lead) escandallo, *m. a* perpendiculo; recto; completo. *adv* a plomo, verticalmente; exactamente. *vt* aplomar; *naut* sondar; *(fig* pierce) penetrar; (understand) comprender. *vi* trabajar como plomero. **p.-line,** plomada, *f*

plumbago *n* plombagina, *f*

plumber *n* plomero, fontanero, *m;* instalador de cañerías, *m*

plumbic *a chem* plúmbico

plumbing *n* plomería, fontanería, *f;* instalación de cañerías, *f*

plumbless *a poet* insondable

plume *n* pluma, *f;* penacho, *m. vt* adornar con plumas; desplumar; **to p. itself,** (of a bird) limpiarse las plumas. **to p. oneself on,** echárselas de, hacer alarde de; jactarse de

plumed *a* plumado; con plumas; empenachado

plumelet *n* agujas, *f pl*

plummet *n* plomada, *f;* (weight) plomo, *m;* (sounding-lead) sonda, *f*

plump *a* gordito, llenito; rollizo; hinchado. *adv* de golpe; claramente. *vt* (swell) hinchar, rellenar; (make fall) hacer (or dejar) caer. *vi* (swell) hincharse; engordar; (fall) caer a plomo; dejarse caer. **to p. for,** escoger, dar apoyo (a); votar por. **p.-cheeked,** mofletudo

plumpness *n* gordura, *f;* lo rollizo

plumy *a* como una pluma; plumado

plunder *vt* saquear; pillar; despojar. *n* saqueo, pillaje, *m;* (booty) botín, despojo, *m*

plunderer *n* saqueador (-ra); ladrón (-ona)

plundering *n* saqueo, *m;* despojo, *m. a* saqueador

plunge *vt* chapuzar; sumergir; hundir; meter. *vi* sumergirse; (into water) zambullirse; (rush) precipitarse, lanzarse; *naut* zozobrar; (of a horse) encabritarse; (gamble) jugarse el todo. *n* sumersión, *f;* zambullida, *f;* chapuz, *m;* (rush) salto, *m; (fig* step) paso, *m*

plunger *n mech* émbolo, *m*

plunging *n* (of a ship) zozobra, *f;* (of a horse) cabriolas, *f pl;* saltos, *m pl,* For other meanings, see **plunge**

plural *a* plural. *n* plural, *m.* **in the p.,** en el plural. **to make p.,** poner en plural

plurality *n* pluralidad, *f*

pluralize *vt* pluralizar

plus *prep* and *a* más; *(math elec)* positivo. *n* signo más, *m; math* cantidad positiva, *f.* **p. fours,** pantalones de golf, *m pl*

plush *n* felpa, *f;* velludo, *m*

plushy *a* felpudo; de felpa

Pluto *n* Plutón, *m;* (pipe-line) oleoducto, *m*

plutocracy *n* plutocracia, *f*

plutocrat *n* plutócrata, *mf*

plutocratic *a* plutocrático

pluviometer *n* pluviómetro, *m*

ply *n* cabo, *m. vt* emplear, usar; manejar; ejercer; ofrecer, servir (con); importunar (con). *vi* hacer el trayecto; hacer el servicio; ir y venir; hacer viajes. **to ply for hire,** tomar viajeros; ofrecerse para ser alquilado

plywood *n* madera contrachapada, *f*

pneumatic *a* neumático. *n* (tire) neumático, *m.* **p. drill,** barreno neumático, *m*

pneumococcus *n* neumococo, *m*

pneumonia *n* pulmonía, *f.* **double p.,** pulmonía doble, *f*

poach *vi* cazar (or pescar) en vedado. *vt* robar caza de un vedado; *fig* invadir; *(fig* steal) hurtar; (eggs) escalfar. **to p. upon another's preserves,** meterse en los asuntos de otro

poacher *n* cazador furtivo, *m*

poaching *n* caza (or pesca) furtiva, *f*

pock *n* pústula, *f.* **p.-mark,** hoyo, *m.* **p.-marked,** picado de viruelas

pocket *n* bolsillo, *m;* bolsillo del reloj, *m;* faltriquera, *f; min* bolsa, *f,* depósito, *m; fig* bolsa, *f;* (in billiards) tronera, *f. vt* meter (or poner) en el bolsillo; (an insult) tragarse; (in billiards) entronerar; (a profit) ganar; apropiarse. **air-p.,** bolsa de aire, *f.* **to be out of p.,** haber perdido, tener una pérdida. **to have a person in one's p.,** calzarse a una persona. **to p. one's pride,** olvidarse de su orgullo. **p. battleship,** acorazado de bolsillo, *m.* **p.-book,** cartera, *f.* **p. dictionary,** diccionario de bolsillo, *m.* **p.-flap,** portezuela, *f.* **p.-handkerchief,** pañuelo (de bolsillo), *m.* **p.-knife,** cortaplumas, *m.* **p.-lighter,** encendedor de bolsillo, *m.* **p.-money,** alfileres, *m pl,* dinero del bolsillo, *m.* **p. picking,** ratería de carterista, *f*

pocketful *n* bolsillo lleno (de), *m;* lo que cabe en un bolsillo

pocket of resistance *n* foco de resistencia, *m*

pod *n bot* vaina, *f;* (of a silkworm) capullo, *m. vt* desvainar; mondar. *vi* hincharse, llenarse

podgy *a* gordo, grueso

poem *n* poema, *m;* *pl* **poems,** poesías, *f pl,* versos, *m pl*

poet *n* poeta, *m.* **p. laureate,** poeta laureado, *m*

poetaster *n* poetastro, *m*

poetess *n* poetisa, *f*

poetic *a* poético. **p. licence,** licencia poética, *f*

poeticize *vt* poetizar; hacer un poema (de)

poetics *n* poética, *f*

poetry *n* poesía, *f;* versos, poemas, *m pl*

pogrom *n* pogrom, *m*

poignancy *n* (of emotions) profundidad, violencia, *f,* lo patético; (of a retort, etc.) mordacidad, acerbidad, *f*

poignant *a* (moving) conmovedor, hondo, agudo; patético; (mordant) mordaz, agudo

poignantly *adv* de un modo conmovedor, patéticamente; mordazmente

poinsettia *n* flor de nochebuena, *f*

point *n* (usual meanings and *ast., math.,* in cards, in a speech, etc.) punto, *m;* característica, *f;* cualidad, *f;* (purpose) motivo, fin, *m;* (question) cuestión, *f;* asunto, *m;* (wit) agudeza, *f;* (significance) significación, *f;* (detail) detalle, *m;* (in rationing) cupón, *m;* (sharp end) punta, *f;* (of a shawl, etc.) pico, *m;* (of land) promontorio, cabo, *m;* (engraving) buril, *m;* (railway) aguja, *f;* (of horses) cabo, *m.* **Mary has many good points,** María tiene muchas cualidades buenas. **There**

is no p. in being angry, No hay para que enfadarse. **in p.,** en cuestión; a propósito. **in p. of fact,** en efecto, en verdad. **on the p. of,** a punto de. **to be to the p.,** venir al caso; ser apropiado. **to carry one's p.,** salir con la suya. **to come to the p.,** ir al grano, ir al caso, ir al mollo del asunto. **to make a p. of,** insistir en; tener por principio. **to win on points,** (boxing) ganar por puntos. **p. at issue,** cuestión bajo consideración, *f,* punto en cuestión, *m.* **p.-blank,** a boca de jarro. **p.-duty,** regulación de tráfico, *f.* **p. lace,** encaje de aguja, *m.* **p. of honor,** punto de honor, *m;* cuestión de honor, *f.* **p. or order,** cuestión de orden, *f.* **p. of view,** punto de vista, *m.* **What's your p.?** ¿A dónde quieres llegar con esto?

point *vt* sacar punta (a), afilar; (a moral, etc.) inculcar; (in building) rejuntar; *gram* puntuar; (of dogs) mostrar la caza. **He pointed his gun at them,** Les apuntó con su fusil. **The hands of the clock pointed to seven o'clock,** Las agujas del reloj marcaban las siete. **to p. with the finger,** señalar con el dedo. **to p. at,** señalar, indicar; (with a gun) apuntar; dirigir. **to p. out,** señalar, indicar; enseñar, mostrar; advertir

pointed *a* (sharpened) afilado; (in shape) puntiagudo; picudo; *arch* ojival; *fig* mordaz; satírico; (of a remark, etc.) directo; personal; aparente, evidente

pointedly *adv* explícitamente, categóricamente; mordazmente; directamente; satíricamente

pointedness *n* forma puntiaguda, *f;* (incisiveness) mordacidad, aspereza, *f;* claridad, *f*

pointer *n* (of a clock, weighing-machine, etc.) aguja, *f;* (of a balance) fiel, *m;* (wand) puntero, *m; fig* índice, *m;* (dog) perro de muestra, *m*

pointillisme *n art* puntillismo, *m*

pointing *n* (in building) rejuntado, *m;* (of a gun) puntería, *f*

pointless *a* sin motivo, innecesario; fútil; sin importancia

pointlessly *adv* sin motivo, sin necesidad; fútilmente

pointsman *n* (railway) guardagujas, *m;* (policeman) guardia del tráfico, *m*

poise *vt* balancear; pesar. *vi* balancearse; posar, estar suspendido. *n* equilibrio, *m;* (of mind) serenidad de ánimo, sangre fría, *m;* aplomo, *m;* (bearing) porte, aire, *m*

poison *n* veneno, *m; fig* ponzoña, *f,* veneno, *m. vt* envenenar; intoxicar; *fig* emponzoñar. **p. gas,** gas asfixiante, *m*

poisoner *n* envenenador (-ra); *fig* corruptor (-ra)

poisoning *n* envenenamiento, *m;* intoxicación, *f*

poisonous *a* venenoso; tóxico; *fig* ponzoñoso, pernicioso. **p. snake,** serpiente venenosa

poisonousness *n* venenosidad, *f;* toxicidad, *f; fig* veneno, *m,* ponzoña, *f*

poke *vt* (thrust) clavar; (make) hacer; (the fire) atizar; hurgar; (push) empujar; (put away) arrinconar. *vi* andar a tientas; meterse. **Don't p. your nose into other people's business!** ¡No te metas donde no te llaman! **They poked his eyes out,** Le saltaron los ojos. **to p. fun at,** burlarse de, mofarse de. **to p. the fire,** atizar la lumbre (or el fuego). **to p. about for,** buscar a tientas. **p.-bonnet,** capelina, *f*

poker *n* (game) póker, *m;* (for the fire) hurgón, atizador, *m.* **p. work,** pirograbado, *m*

poky *a* estrecho, ahogado, pequeño; miserable

Poland Polonia, *f*

polar *a* polar. **p. bear,** oso (-sa) blanco (-ca). **p. lights,** aurora boreal, *f*

polarimeter *n* polarímetro, *m*

polarity *n* polaridad, *f*

polarization *n* polarización, *f*

polarize *vt* polarizar

pole *n* palo largo, *m;* poste, *m;* (of a tent) mástil, *m;* (of a cart) pértiga, *f; sport* pértiga, garrocha, *f;* (measurement) percha, *f; (ast geog biol math elec)* polo, *m. vt* (a punt) impeler con pértiga. **from p. to p.,** de polo a polo. **greasy p.,** cucaña, *f.* **under bare poles,** *naut* a

palo seco. **p.-ax,** hachuela de mano, *f;* hacha de marinero, *f;* (butcher's) mazo, *m.* **p. jumping,** salto de pértiga, salto a la garrocha, *m.* **p.-star,** estrella polar, *f*

Pole *n* polaco (-ca)

polemic *n* polémica, *f*

polemical *a* polémico

police *n* policía, *f. vt* mantener servicio de policía en; mantener el orden público en; administrar, regular. **mounted p.,** policía montada, *f.* **p. constable,** (agente de) policía, guardia urbano, *m.* **p. court,** tribunal de la policía, *m.* **p. dog,** perro de policía, *m.* **p. force,** cuerpo de policía, *m,* policía, *f.* **p. magistrate,** juez municipal, *m.* **p. station,** comisaría de policía, *f.* **p. trap,** puesto oculto de la policía del tráfico, *m.* **p. woman,** policía, *f*

policeman *n* policía, guardia, *m*

policy *n* política, *f;* táctica, *f;* sistema, *m;* norma de conducta, *f* (ideas, *f pl,* principios, *m pl;* prudencia, *f;* (insurance) póliza, *f.* **fixed premium p.,** póliza a prima fija, *f.* **p.-holder,** asegurado (-da), tenedor (de una póliza), *m*

poliomyelitis *n* poliomielitis, *f*

polish *vt* (metals and wood) pulir; (furniture and shoes) dar brillo (a); (*lit* works) pulir, limar; (persons) descortezar, civilizar. *n* (shine) brillo, *m;* (furniture) cera para los muebles, *f;* (metal, silver) líquido para limpiar metales, *m;* (for shoes) betún para zapatos, *m;* (varnish) barniz, *m;* (of *lit.* works) pulidez, elegancia, *f;* (of persons) urbanidad, cultura, *f.* **to p. off,** terminar a prisa; (a person) acabar con; (food) engullir

Polish *a* polaco, polonés. *n* (language) polaco, *m*

polished *a* (of verses, etc.) pulido, elegante; (of person) culto, distinguido; (of manners) fino, cortés

polisher *n* (machine) pulidor, *m;* lustrador, *m.* **floor-p.,** lustrador de piso, *m.* **French p.,** barnizador, *m*

polite *a* cortés, bien educado; atento; elegante

politely *adv* cortésmente; atentamente

politeness *n* cortesía, *f.* **for p. sake,** por cortesía

politic *a* político

political *a* político. **p. agent,** agente político, *m.* **p. economist,** hacendista, *mf* **p. economy,** economía política, *f*

politically *adv* políticamente

politician *n* político (-ca)

politics *n* política, *f.* **to dabble in p.,** meterse en política

polity *n* forma de gobierno, constitución política, *f*

polka *n* polca, *f*

polka-dot *a* con puntos

poll *n* (head of person) cabeza, *f;* (voters' register) lista electoral, *f;* (voting) votación, *f;* (polling booth) colegio electoral, *m;* (counting of votes) escrutinio, *m. vt* (trees) desmochar; (vote) votar, dar su voto (a); (obtain votes) obtener, recibir; (count votes) escrutar. **p.-tax,** capitación, *f*

pollard *vt* desmochar. *n* (tree) árbol desmochado, *m*

pollen *n* polen, *m*

pollinate *vt* fecundar con polen

pollination *n* polinización, *f*

polling *n* votación, *f.* **p. booth,** colegio electoral, *m*

pollute *vt* contaminar; ensuciar; profanar; (corrupt morally) corromper

polluter *n* profanador (-ra), corruptor (-ra)

pollution *n* contaminación, *f;* profanación, *f;* corrupción, *f*

polo *n* polo, *m.* **p. mallet,** maza de polo, *f.* **p. player,** jugador de polo, *m,* polista, *mf*

polonaise *n* polonesa, *f*

poltroon *n* cobarde, *m*

polychrome *a* policromo

polygamist *n* polígamo (-ma)

polygamous *a* polígamo

polygamy *n* poligamia, *f*

polygenesis *n* poligenismo, *m*

polyglot *n* políglota (-ta). **p. Bible,** poliglota, *f*

polygon *n* polígono, *m*

Polynesia Polinesia, *f*
Polynesian *n* polinesio (-ia)
polyp *n* pólipo, *m*
polyphonic *a* polifónico
polyphony *n* polifonía, *f*
polypus *n* pólipo, *m*
polytechnic *a* politécnico
polytheism *n* politeísmo, *m*
polytheistic *a* politeísta
pomade *n* pomada, *f*
pomegranate *n* granada, *f*
Pomeranian *a* pomerano. **P. dog,** perro pomerano, *m*
pommel *n* pomo, *m*, *vt* aporrear
pomp *n* pompa, magnificencia, *f*, fausto, aparato, *m*; ostentación, *f*
Pompeian *a* pompeyano
Pompeii Pompeya, *f*
pompom *n* pompón, *m*
pomposity *n* pomposidad, presunción, *f*; (of language) ampulosidad, *f*
pompous *a* pomposo, ostentoso; (of style) ampuloso, hinchado; importante. **to be p.,** (of persons) darse tono
pompously *adv* pomposamente
pond *n* charca, *f*, estanque, *m*
ponder *vt* ponderar, estudiar, considerar. *vi* meditar (sobre), reflexionar (sobre)
ponderable *a* ponderable
ponderous *a* pesado; macizo, abultado; grave; (dull) pesado, aburrido
ponderously *adv* pesadamente; gravemente
ponderousness *n* pesadez, *f*; gravedad, importancia, *f*
poniard *n* puñal, *m*, *vt* apuñalar
pontiff *n* pontífice, *m*
pontifical *a* pontificio
pontificate *n* pontificado, *m*
pontoneer *n* pontonero, *m*
pontoon *n* pontón, *m*. **p. bridge,** puente de pontones, *m*
pony *n* jaca, *f*
poodle *n* perro (-rra) de aguas, perro de lanas, perro lanudo
pooh-pooh *vt* despreciar, desdeñar. **Pooh!** ¡Bah!
pool *n* (in a river) rebalsa, *f*; charca, *f*, estanque, *m*; (of blood, etc.) charco, *m*; (in cards) baceta, *f*; *com* asociación, *f*; *fig* fuente, *f*; *pl* **pools,** (football) apuestas benéficas de fútbol, *f pl*. *vt* (resources, etc.) combinar; juntar
poop *n* popa, *f*. **p. lantern,** fanal, *m*
poor *a* pobre; malo; (insignificant or unfortunate) infeliz, desgraciado. **the p.,** los pobres. **to be in p. health,** estar mal de salud. **to be p. stuff,** ser de pacotilla. **to be poorer than a church mouse,** ser más pobre que las ratas. **to have a p. opinion of,** tener en poco (a). **P. me!** ¡Ay de mí! ¡Pecador de mí! **p.-box,** cepillo, *m*. **p.-law,** ley de asistencia pública, *f*. **p.-spirited,** apocado
poorhouse *n* asilo, *m*
poorly *adv* pobremente; mal. *a* indispuesto, malo
poorness *n* pobreza, *f*; mala calidad, *f*; (lack) carestía, *f*; (of soil) infertilidad, *f*; (of character) mezquindad, *f*
pop *n* (of a cork) taponazo, *m*; (of a gun) detonación, *f*; (drink) gaseosa, *f*, *adv* ¡pum! *vi* (of a cork) saltar; (of guns) detonar. *vt* (corks) hacer saltar; (a gun, a question, etc.) disparar. **popgun,** escopeta de aire comprimido, *f*. **to pop down,** bajar a presuradamente. **to pop in,** (visit) dejarse caer; entrar rápidamente. **to pop off,** marcharse a prisa; (die) estirar la pata. **to pop up,** subir corriendo; aparecer de pronto
pope *n* Papa, *m*
popinjay *n* (fop) pisaverde, *m*
popish *a* papista
poplar *n* (black) chopo, álamo, *m*; (white) álamo blanco, *m*. **p. grove,** alameda, *f*
poplin *n* popelina, *f*
poppy *n* amapola, adormidera, *f*

populace *n* pueblo, *m*; (scornful) populacho, *m*
popular *a* popular; en boga, de moda; común. **He is a p. hero,** Es un héroe popular
popularity *n* popularidad, *f*
popularization *n* vulgarización, *f*
popularize *vt* popularizar, vulgarizar
popularly *adv* popularmente
populate *vt* poblar
population *n* población, *f*
populous *a* populoso; muy poblado
porcelain *n* porcelana, *f*
porch *n* pórtico, *m*; (of a house) portal, *m*
porcine *a* porcino, porcuno
porcupine *n* puerco espín, *m*
pore *n* poro, *m*. **to p. over,** estar absorto en; examinar cuidadosamente
pork *n* carne de cerdo, *f*. **salt p.,** tocino, *m*. **p. butcher,** tocinero, *m*. **p. pie,** pastel de carne de cerdo, *m*
pornographic *a* pornográfico
pornography *n* pornografía, *f*
porosity *n* porosidad, *f*
porous *a* poroso
porphyry *n* pórfido, *m*
porpoise *n* marsopa, *f*, puerco marino, *m*
porridge *n* gachas, *f pl*, *m*
port *n* puerto, *m*; (in a ship) porta, *f*; (larboard) babor, *m*; (wine) vino de Oporto, *m*; (mien) porte, *m*, presencia, *f*. *vt* (the helm) poner a babor; *mil* llevar un fusil terciado. **to put into p.,** tomar puerto. **to stop at a p.,** hacer escala en un puerto. **p. dues,** derechos de puerto, *m pl*
portable *a* portátil; móvil. **p. typewriter,** máquina de escribir portátil (or de viaje), *f*. **p. wireless,** radio portátil, *f*
portal *n* portal, *m*
portcullis *n* rastrillo, *m*
portend *vt* presagiar, anunciar
portent *n* augurio, presagio, *m*; portento, *m*
portentous *a* ominoso; portentoso; importante
porter *n* (messenger) mozo de cordel, *m*; (of a university, hotel) portero, *m*; (of a block of flats) conserje, *m*; (railway) mozo de estación, *m*; (drink) cerveza negra, *f*. **porter's lodge,** portería, *f*; conserjería, *f*
porterage *n* porte, *m*
portfolio *n* carpeta, *f*; (pol of a minister) cartera, *f*; (pol ministry) ministerio, *m*
porthole *n* tronera, *f*
portico *n* pórtico, *m*
portiere *n* antepuerta, *f*
portion *n* porción, *f*; parte, *f*; (marriage) dote, *mf*; (piece) pedazo, *m*; (in a restaurant) ración, *f*; (in life) fortuna, *f*. *vt* dividir; repartir; (dower) dotar
portliness *n* corpulencia, *f*
portly *a* corpulento, grueso
portmanteau *n* maleta, *f*
portmanteau word *n* palabra de acarreo, *f*
portrait *n* retrato, *m*. **p. painter,** pintor (-ra) de retratos, *f*
portraiture *n* retratos, *m pl*; descripción, pintura, *f*
portray *vt* retratar; pintar, representar; (in words) describir, pintar
portrayal *n* pintura, *f*; retrato, *m*; (in words) descripción, *f*
portrayer *n* retratista, *mf*, pintor (-ra)
portress *n* portera, *f*; (in a convent) tornera, *f*
Portuguese *a* portugués. *n* portugués (-esa); (language) portugués, *m*
pose *vt* colocar; (a problem, etc.) plantear; (a question) hacer; *vi* colocarse; (with as) echárselas de, dárselas de, fingir ser; hacerse pasar por. *n* actitud, postura, *f*; (affected) pose, *f*; (deception) engaño, *m*
poser *n* problema difícil, *m*; (in an examination) pega, *f*; pregunta embarazosa, *f*
position *n* posición, *f*; situación, *f*; actitud, postura, *f*; condición, *f*, estado, *m*; (post) puesto, empleo, *m*. **He is not in a p. to . . . ,** No está en condiciones de . . . , No

está para . . . **to place in p.,** poner en posición, colocar **positive** *a* positivo; absoluto; (convinced) convencido, seguro; (downright) categórico; *inf* completo. *n* realidad, *f; phot* (prueba) positiva, *f*
positively *adv* positivamente; categóricamente
positiveness *n* certitud, seguridad, *f;* terquedad, obstinacia, *f*
positivism *n* positivismo, *m*
positivist *n* positivista, *mf*
positivistic *a* positivista
posse *n* pelotón, *m;* multitud, muchedumbre, *f*
possess *vt* poseer; gozar (de); (of ideas, etc.) dominar. **to p. oneself of,** apoderarse de, apropiarse. **What possessed you to do it?** ¿Qué te hizo hacerlo?
possession *n* posesión, *f.* **to take p. of,** tomar posesión de; hacerse dueño de, apoderarse de; (a house, etc.) entrar en, ocupar
possessive *a* posesivo. *n* posesivo, *m*
possessor *n* poseedor (-ra); dueño (-ña); propietario (-ia)
possibility *n* posibilidad, *f*
possible *a* posible. **as soon as p.,** cuanto antes, lo más pronto posible. **to make p.,** hacer posible, posibilitar
possibly *adv* posiblemente; (perhaps) quizás. **I shall come as soon as I p. can,** Vendré lo más pronto posible
post *n* (pole) poste, *m;* (of a sentry, etc.) puesto, *m;* (employment) empleo, *m;* (mail) correo, *m; mil* toque, *m. vt* (a notice) fijar; anunciar; (to an appointment) destinar; (letters, etc.) echar al correo; *com* pasar al libro mayor; (inform) tener al corriente. *vi* viajar en posta. **"P. no bills!"** «Se prohibe fijar carteles.» **registered p.,** correo certificado, *m.* **p. card,** postal, *f.* **p.-chaise,** silla de posta, *f.* **p.-date,** posfecha, *f.* **p.-free,** franco de porte. **p.-haste,** con gran celeridad. **p.-horse,** caballo de posta, *m.* **p.-impressionism,** post-impresionismo, *m.* **p.-mortem,** *n* autopsia, *f.* **p.-natal,** post-natal. **p.-nuptial,** postnupcial. **p. office,** correo, *m,* correos, *m pl;* (on a train) ambulancia de correos, *f.* **p. office box,** apartado de correos, *m.* **p. office savings bank,** caja postal de ahorros, *f.* **p.-paid,** porte pagado; franco. **p.-war,** *n* postguerra, *f. a* de la postguerra
postage *n* porte de correos, franqueo, *m.* **p. stamp,** sello postal, *m*
postage meter *n* franqueadora, *f*
postal *a* postal. **p. order,** orden postal de pago, *f.* **p. packet,** paquete postal, *m*
poster *n* cartel, *m. vt* fijar carteles (a or en); anunciar por carteles. **bill-p.,** fijador de carteles, *m*
poste restante *n* lista de correos, *f*
posterior *a* posterior. *n* trasero, *m,* asentaderas, *f pl*
posteriority *n* posterioridad, *f*
posterity *n* posteridad, *f*
postern *n* postigo, *m; mil* poterna, *f*
postgraduate *n* estudiante graduado que hace estudios avanzados, *m. a* avanzado; para estudiantes graduados
posthumous *a* póstumo
posthumously *adv* después de la muerte
postman *n* cartero, *m*
postmark *n* matasellos, *m, vt* poner matasellos (a)
postmaster *n* administrador de correos, *m*
postmeridian *a* postmeridiano
postmistress *n* administradora de correos, *f*
postpone *vt* aplazar, diferir; retrasar; (subordinate) postergar
postponement *n* aplazamiento, *m;* tardanza, *f*
postscript *n* posdata, *f*
postulate *n* postulado, *m, vt* postular
posture *n* postura, actitud, *f;* (of affairs) estado, *m,* situación, *f. vi* tomar una postura
posy *n* (nosegay) ramillete de flores, *m;* flor, *f;* (motto) mote, *m*
pot *n* pote, *m;* tarro, *m;* (flower-) tiesto, *m;* (for cooking) olla marmita, *f;* jarro, *m. vt* plantar en tiestos; conservar en potes. **pot-bellied,** panzudo. **pot-boiler,** obra literaria escrita con el sólo propósito de ganar dinero, *f.*

pot-herb, hierba que se emplea para sazonar, hortaliza, *f.* **pot-hole,** bache, **pot-luck,** comida ordinaria, *f.* **pot-shot,** tiro fácil, *m;* tiro al azar, *m*
potable *a* potable
potage *n* potaje, *m*
potash *n* potasa, *f. caustic p.,* potasa cáustica, *f*
potassium *n* potasio, *m*
potato *n* patata, *f.* **sweet p.,** batata, *f.* **p. beetle,** coleóptero de la patata, *m.* **p. omelet,** tortilla a la española, *f.* **p. patch,** patatal, *m.* **p. peeler,** pelapatatas, *m*
potency *n* potencia, *f;* fuerza, eficacia, *f*
potent *a* potente, fuerte; eficaz
potentate *n* potentado, *m*
potential *a* potencial; virtual; (phys gram) potencial, *n* poder, *m; gram* modo potencial, *m; phys* energía potencial, *f; elec* tensión potencial, *f*
potentiality *n* potencialidad, *f*
pothook *n* garabato de cocina, *m;* palote, *m;* (scrawl) garabato, *m*
potion *n* poción, *f,*
potpourri *n* popurrí, *m*
potter *n* alfarero, *m. vi* gandulear. *vt* perder. **potter's clay,** barro de alfarero, *m.* **potter's wheel,** tabanque, *m.* **potter's workshop,** alfar, *m*
pottery *n* alfarería, *f;* (china) loza, porcelana, *f*
pouch *n* bolsa, *f; zool* bolsa marsupial, *f;* (for tobacco) tabaquera, *f;* (for cartridges) cartuchera, *f. vt* embolsar. *vi* bolsear
poulterer *n* pollero (-ra)
poultice *n* apósito, emplasto, *m, vt* poner emplastos (a or en)
poultry *n* volatería, *f.* **p. dealer,** gallinero (-ra) vendedor (-ra) de volatería. **p. yard,** gallinero, *m*
poultry farming *n* avicultura, *f*
pounce *n* (swoop) calada, *f. vi* (swoop) calarse; saltar (sobre); agarrar, hacer presa (en); *fig* atacar; descubrir, hacer patente
pound *n* (weight and currency) libra, *f;* (for cattle) corral de concejo, *m;* (thump) golpe, *m. vt* (break up) machacar, pistar; (beat) batir; (thump) golpear, aporrear. **p. sterling,** libra esterlina, *f.* **p. troy,** libra medicinal, *f*
pounding *n* machucamiento, *m;* batimiento, *m*
pour *vt* vaciar, verter; derramar. *vi* correr; (of rain) diluviar, llover a cántaros; (fill) llenar; (of crowds, words, etc.) derramarse. **to p. out the tea,** servir el té. **The crowd poured in,** La multitud entró en tropel
pouring *a* (of rain) torrencial
pout *vi* torcer el gesto; hacer pucheritos
poverty *n* pobreza, *f.* **p.-stricken,** menesteroso, indigente, necesitado
powder *n* polvo, *m;* (face) polvos de arroz, *m pl;* (gun) pólvora, *f. vt* polvorear; (crush) reducir a polvo, pulverizar. *vi* ponerse polvos. **p.-flash,** fogonazo, *m.* **p.-flask,** polvorín, *m.* **p.-magazine,** santabárbara, *f.* **p.-mill,** fábrica de pólvora, *f.* **p.-puff,** polvera, borla de empolvarse, *f*
powdered *a* en polvo
powdery *a* polvoriento; friable
power *n* poder, *m;* facultad, capacidad, *f;* vigor, *m,* fuerza, *f;* (pol and math) potencia, *f; mech* fuerza, *f;* influencia, *f.* **as far as lies within my p.,** en cuanto me sea posible. **It does not lie within my p.,** No está dentro de mis posibilidades, No está en mi poder. **the Great Powers,** las grandes potencias. **the powers that be,** los que mandan. **to be in p.,** estar en el poder. **p.-house, p.-station,** central eléctrica, *f.* **p. of attorney,** poderes, *m pl,* procuración, *f.* **to grant p. of attorney (to),** dar poderes (a)
powerful *a* poderoso; fuerte; eficaz; potente; (of arguments, etc.) convincente
powerfully *adv* poderosamente; fuertemente
powerless *a* impotente
power steering *n* dirección asistida *f* (Spain), servo dirección *f*
powwow *n* conferencia, *f;* conversación, *f*

pox *n* sífilis, *f*; (smallpox) viruelas, *f pl*; (chicken-pox) viruelas falsas, *f pl*

practicability *n* factibilidad, *f*

practicable *a* practicable, factible, posible; viable, transitable

practical *a* (doable) factible; práctico; virtual. **p. joke,** burla de consecuencias

practically *adv* prácticamente; en práctica; virtualmente; (in fact) en efecto. **p. nothing,** casi nada

practicalness *n* carácter práctico, *m*

practice *n* (custom) costumbre, *f*; práctica, *f*; ejercicio, *m*; (of a doctor, etc.) clientela, *f*; profesión, *f*; (religious) rito, *m*, ceremonias, *f pl*; (experience) experiencia, *f*. **It is not his p. to . . . ,** No es su costumbre de . . . **to be out of p.,** estar desentrenado. **to put into p.,** poner en práctica. **P. makes perfect,** El ejercicio hace maestro. *vt* tener la costumbre de; practicar; (a profession) ejercer; (a game) entrenarse en; (work at) estudiar; (a musical instrument) tocar; (accustom) acostumbrar. **to p. what one preaches,** predicar con el ejemplo

practiced *a* experimentado; experto

practitioner *n* médico (-ca). **general p.,** médico (-ca) general

pragmatic *a* pragmatista; (historical) pragmático; práctico

pragmatism *n* pragmatismo, *m*

pragmatist *n* pragmatista, *mf*

Prague Praga, *f*

prairie *n* pradera, sabana, pampa, *f*, *a* de la pradera, etc.

praise *vt* alabar; ensalzar, glorificar; elogiar. *n* alabanza, *f*; elogio, *m*; glorificación, *f*, ensalzamiento, *m*. **to p. to the skies,** poner en los cuernos de la luna poner por las nubes, poner sobre las estrellas hacerse lenguas de

praiseworthiness *n* mérito, *m*

praiseworthy *a* digno de alabanza, laudable

prance *vi* (of a horse) caracolear, encabritarse, cabriolar; saltar; andar airosamente. *n* corveta, cabriola, *f*; salto, *m*

prank *n* travesura, diablura, *f*. **to play pranks,** hacer diabluras

prate, prattle *vi* charlar, chacharear; (lisp) balbucir; (of brooks, etc.) murmurar, susurrar. *vt* divulgar. *n* charla, cháchara, *f*; balbuceo, *m*

prattler *n* parlanchín (-ina); (gossip) chismoso (-sa); (child) niño (-ña)

prattling *n* charla, *f*; (lisping) balbuceo, *m*; (of brooks, etc.) murmullo, susurro, ruido armonioso, *m*. *a* charlatán, gárrulo; balbuciente; (of brooks, etc.) parlero

prawn *n* camarón, *m*

pray *vt* and *vi* suplicar; implorar; rezar, orar. **P. be seated,** Haga el favor de sentarse

prayer *n* rezo, *m*, plegaria, oración, *f*; súplica, *f*; *law* petición, *f*. **p. book,** libro de devociones, devocionario, *m*. **p.-meeting,** reunión para rezar, *f*. **p.-rug,** alfombra de rezo, *f*

praying *n* rezo, *m*; suplicación, *f*

pre- *prefix* de antes de (e.g. **pre-World-War-1 publications,** publicaciones de antes de la Primera Guerra Mundial)

preach *vt* and *vi* predicar

preacher *n* predicador (-ra). **to turn p.,** meterse a predicar

preaching *n* predicación, *f*, *a* predicador

preamble *n* preámbulo, *m*

prearrange *vt* preparar de antemano, predisponer

precarious *a* precario; inseguro; incierto, arriesgado

precariousness *n* condición precaria, *f*; inseguridad, *f*; incertidumbre, *f*

precaution *n* precaución, *f*. **to take precautions,** tomar precauciones

precautionary *a* de precaución; preventivo

precede *vt* preceder (a); anteceder (a); tomar precedencia (a), exceder en importancia (a). *vi* ir delante; tener la precedencia

precedence *n* precedencia, *f*; prioridad, *f*; superioridad, *f*. **to take p. over,** tomar precedencia (a), preceder (a)

precedent *n* precedente, *m*, *a* precedente. **without p.,** sin precedente

preceding *a* anterior, precedente

precept *n* precepto, *m*

preceptor *n* preceptor, *m*

precinct *n* (police station) comisaría de sección (Argentina), delegación (Mexico), *f*

precincts *n pl* recinto, *m*; ámbito, *m*; distrito, barrio, *m*

preciosity *n* afectación, *f*

precious *a* precioso; de gran valor; hermoso; amado; muy querido; (with rogue, etc.) redomado; completo. **p. little,** muy poco. **p. nearly,** casi, por poco . . . **p. stone,** piedra preciosa, *f*

preciousness *n* preciosidad, *f*; gran valor, *m*

precipice *n* precipicio, *m*

precipitancy *n* precipitación, *f*

precipitant *a* precipitado

precipitate *vt* precipitar, despeñar, arrojar; acelerar; *chem* precipitar. *vi* precipitarse. *n* precipitado, *m*. *a* precipitado, súbito. **to p. oneself,** tirarse, lanzarse

precipitately *adv* precipitadamente

precipitation *n chem* precipitación, *f*; *chem* precipitado, *m*; (rain, etc.) precipitación pluvial, *f*

precipitous *a* precipitoso, escarpado, acantilado

precipitously *adv* en precipicio

precise *a* preciso; exacto; justo; puntual; escrupuloso; formal; claro; pedante, afectado; ceremonioso

precisely *adv* precisamente; exactamente; puntualmente; escrupulosamente; claramente; con afectación; ceremoniosamente. **at six o'clock p.,** a las seis en punto

precision *n* precisión, *f*; exactitud, *f*; puntualidad, *f*; escrupulosidad, *f*; claridad, *f*; afectación, *f*; ceremonia, *f*

preclude *vt* excluir; impedir, hacer imposible

preclusion *n* exclusión, *f*; imposibilidad, *f*

precocious *a* precoz

precocity *n* precocidad, *f*

preconceived *a* preconcebido

preconception *n* idea preconcebida, *f*; (prejudice) prejuicio, *m*

preconcerted *a* concertado de antemano

precursor *n* precursor (-ra)

precursory *a* precursor

predatory *a* rapaz; de rapiña; voraz

predecease *vt* morir antes (de or que); *law* premorir. *n law* premuerto, *m*

predecessor *n* predecesor (-ra); (ancestor) antepasado, *m*

predestination *n* predestinación, *f*

predestine *vt* predestinar

predetermination *n* predeterminación, *f*

predetermine *vt* predeterminar

predicament *n* (logic) predicamento, *m*; situación, *f*; (fix) apuro, *m*; *pl* **predicaments,** categorías, *f pl*

predicate *vt* afirmar. *n* (logic, *gram*) predicado, *m*

predict *vt* predecir, pronosticar, profetizar

prediction *n* predicción, *f*; pronóstico, vaticinio, *m*, profecía, *f*

predilection *n* predilección, *f*

predispose *vt* predisponer

predisposition *n* predisposición, *f*

predominance *n* predominio, *m*

predominant *a* predominante

predominate *vi* predominar

preeminence *n* preeminencia, *f*; primacía, superioridad, *f*

preeminent *a* preeminente; superior; extraordinario

preeminently *adv* preeminentemente; extraordinariamente; por excelencia; entre todos

preen *vt* (of birds) limpiarse; (of people) darse humos, jactarse

preexist *vi* preexistir

preexistence *n* preexistencia, *f*

prefabricated *a* prefabricado

preface *n* prólogo, *m*; *ecc* prefacio, *m*; introducción, *f*. *vt* dar principio (a), empezar. **He prefaced his remarks by . . . ,** Dijo a modo de introducción

prefatory *a* preliminar, introductorio; a manera de prólogo

prefect *n* prefecto, *m*

prefecture *n* prefectura, *f*

prefer *vt* preferir, gustar más (a); (promote) ascender, elevar; (a charge, etc.) presentar. **to p. a charge against,** pedir en juicio (a). **I p. oranges to apples,** Me gustan más las naranjas que las manzanas, Prefiero las naranjas a las manzanas

preferability *n* preferencia, ventaja, *f*

preferable *a* preferible

preferably *adv* preferiblemente, con preferencia

preference *n* preferencia, *f*; privilegio, *m*. *p.* **share,** acción privilegiada, acción preferente, *f*

preferential *a* preferente

preferment *n* promoción, *f*, ascenso, *m*; puesto eminente, *m*

preferred *a* preferente; favorito, predilecto. **p. share,** acción preferente, *f*

prefix *vt* anteponer, prefijar; (to a word) poner prefijo (a). *n* prefijo, *m*

pregnancy *n* embarazo, *m*, preñez, *f*

pregnant *a* embarazada, encinta, preñada, *f*; *fig* fértil; *fig* preñado

prehensile *a* prensil

prehistoric *a* prehistórico

prehistory *n* prehistoria, *f*

prejudge *vt* prejuzgar

prejudice *n* prejuicio, *m*; *law* perjuicio, *m*. *vt* influir, predisponer; (damage) perjudicar. **without p.,** sin perjuicio

prejudiced *a* parcial; con prejuicios

prejudicial *a* perjudicial

prelacy *n* prelacía, *f*; episcopado, *m*

prelate *n* prelado, *m*

preliminarily *adv* preliminarmente

preliminary *a* preliminar. *n* preliminar, *m*

prelude (to) *n* preludio (de) *m*; presagio (de) *m*, *vt* and *vi* preludiar

premature *a* prematuro

prematurely *adv* prematuramente

prematureness *n* lo prematuro

premeditate *vt* premeditar

premeditatedly *adv* premeditadamente, con premeditación

premeditation *n* premeditación, *f*

premier *a* primero, principal. *n* primer minístro, *m*; (in Spain) presidente del Consejo de Ministros, *m*

premiere *n* estreno, *m*

premiership *n* puesto de primer ministro, *m*; (in Spain) presidencia del Consejo de Ministros, *f*

premise *n* (logic) premisa, *f*; *pl* **premises,** local, *m*; recinto, *m*; establecimiento, *m*; propiedad, *f*; tierras, *f pl*. **on the premises,** en el local; en el establecimiento

premium *n* (prize) premio, *m*, recompensa, *f*; *com* prima, *f*; precio, *m*. **at a p.,** a premio; a una prima; (of shares) sobre la par; *fig* en boga, muy solicitado, en gran demanda

premonition *n* presentimiento, presagio, *m*

premonitory *a* premonitorio

prenatal *a* prenatal, antenatal

preoccupation *n* preocupación, *f*

preoccupied *a* preocupado; abstraído, absorto

preoccupy *vt* preocupar

prepaid *a* porte pagado, franco de porte

preparation *n* preparación, *f*; preparativo, *m*, disposición, *f*; (patent food) preparado, *m*. **I have made all my preparations,** He hecho todos mis preparativos. **The book is in p.,** El libro está en preparación

preparative *a* preparativo. *n* preparativo, *m*

preparatory *a* preparatorio, preparativo; preliminar. **p. school,** escuela preparatoria, *f*, *m*. **p. to,** como preparación para; antes de

prepare *vt* preparar; aparejar, aviar; equipar; (cloth) aprestar. *vi* prepararse; hacer preparativos

preparedness *n* estado de preparación, *m*; preparación, *f*, apercibimiento, *m*

prepay *vt* pagar adelantado; (a letter, etc.) franquear

prepayment *n* pago adelantado, *m*; (of a letter, etc.) franqueo, *m*

preponderance *n* preponderancia, *f*

preponderant *a* preponderante, predominante

preponderantly *adv* predominantemente; en su mayoría

preponderate *vi* preponderar; prevalecer (sobre), predominar (sobre)

preposition *n* preposición, *f*

prepossess *vt* predisponer; causar buena impresión (a)

prepossessing *a* atractivo

preposterous *a* ridículo, absurdo

preposterously *adv* absurdamente

preposterousness *n* ridiculez, *f*

Prep School *n* preparatoria, *f*

prepuce *n* prepucio, *m*

Pre-Raphaelite *a* and *n* prerrafaelista, *mf*

prerequisite *n* requisito necesario, esencial, *m*, *a* previamente necesario, esencial

prerogative *n* prerrogativa, *f*

presage *n* presagio, *m*; anuncio, *m*. *vt* presagiar; anunciar

Presbyterian *a* and *n* presbiteriano (-na)

prescience *n* presciencia, previsión, *f*

prescient *a* presciente

prescind *vt* prescindir (de); separar (de). *vi* separarse

prescribe *vt* and *vi* prescribir; *med* recetar; dar leyes; *law* prescribir

prescription *n* prescripción, *f*; *med* receta, *f*

presence *n* presencia, *f*; (ghost) aparición, *f*. **in the p. of,** en presencia de, delante; a vista de. **p. of mind,** presencia de ánimo, serenidad de ánimo, *f*

present *a* presente; actual; (with month) corriente; *gram* presente. **at p.,** al presente, actualmente. **at the p. day,** a la fecha, en la actualidad, hoy día. **P. company excepted!** ¡Mejorando lo presente! **the present writer,** el que suscribe, el que esto escribe, el que estas líneas traza. **to be p. at,** presenciar, ser testigo de; asistir a, acudir a; hallarse en. **p.-day,** de hoy, actual. **p. tense,** *gram* tiempo presente, *m*

present *n* (time) presente, *m*; actualidad, *f*; *gram* tiempo presente, *m*; (gift) regalo, *m*, dádiva, *f*. **By these presents . . . ,** *law* Por estas presentes . . . **to make a p. of,** regalar. **Jane made me a p. of a watch,** Juana me regaló un reloj

present *vt* presentar; ofrecer; manifestar; (a gift) regalar, dar; (*ecc mil*) presentar. **New problems presented themselves,** Nuevos problemas surgieron. **to p. arms,** presentar las armas. **He presented himself in the office,** Se presentó en la oficina. **He presented his friend Mr. Moreno to me,** Me presentó a su amigo el Sr. Moreno

presentable *a* presentable

presentation *n* presentación, *f*; homenaje, *m*; (exhibition) exposición, *f*. **on p.,** *com* a presentación

presentiment *n* presentimiento, *m*, corazonada, *f*. **I had a p. that . . . ,** Tuve el presentimiento de que . . . , Tuve una corazonada que . . . **to have a p. about,** presentir

presently *adv* pronto; en seguida; dentro de poco

preservation *n* conservación, *f*; (from harm) preservación, *f*

preservative *a* preservativo. *n* preservativo, *m*

preserve *vt* preservar (de); guardar; proteger; conservar; *cul* hacer conservas de; (in syrup) almibarar. *n cul* conserva, *f*; (of fruit) compota, confitura, *f*; (covert) coto, *m*. **preserved fruit,** dulce de almibar, *m*. **p. dish,** compotera, *f*

preserver *n* conservador (-ra); (saviour) salvador (-ra); (benefactor) bienhechor (-ra)

preserving *n* (from harm) preservación, *f*; conservación, *f*. **p. pan,** cazuela para conservas, *f*

preside *vi* (over) presidir; dirigir, gobernar. **He presided at the meeting,** Presidio la reunión
presidency *n* presidencia, *f*
president *n* presidente, *m*; (of a college) rector, *m*. **lady p.,** presidenta, *f*
presidential *a* presidencial
presidentship *n* presidencia, *f*
press *vt* prensar; (juice out of) exprimir; (clothes) planchar; (a bell, a hand, and of a shoe, etc.) apretar; (embrace) dar un abrazo (a); (a stamp, a kiss, etc.) imprimir; (an enemy) hostigar, acosar; (in a game) apretar; (crowd upon) oprimir; (emphasize) insistir en; (urge) instar, instigar; (compel) obligar; apremiar; (oppress) abrumar, agobiar; (paper) satinar; (an advantage) aprovecharse de. **Lola pressed his hand,** Lola le apretó la mano. **Time presses,** El tiempo es breve. **I did not p. the point,** No insistí. **to p. against,** pegar(se) contra. **to p. down,** comprimir; *fig* agobiar. **to p. for,** exigir, reclamar. **to p. forward, on,** avanzar; seguir el camino, continuar la marcha; (hurry) apretar el paso
press *n* (pressure) apretón, *m*; (push) golpe, *m*; (throng) muchedumbre, *f*; (of business, etc.) urgencia, *f*; (apparatus) prensa, *f*; (printing press and publishing firm) imprenta, *f*; (cupboard) armario, *m*. **Associated P.,** Prensa Asociada, *f*. **freedom of the p.,** libertad de la prensa, *f*. **in p., in the p.,** en prensa. **in the p. of battle,** en lo más reñido de la batalla. **to go to p.,** entrar en prensa. **p.-agent,** agente de publicidad, *m*. **p.-box,** tribuna de la prensa, *f*. **p. clipping, p.-cutting,** recorte de prensa, *m*. **p.-gallery,** tribuna de la prensa, *f*. **p.-gang,** ronda de enganche, *f*. **p.-mark,** número de catálogo, *m*. **p. proof,** prueba de imprenta, *f*. **p.-room,** taller de imprenta, *m*. **p.-stud,** botón automático, *m*. **p. conference,** rueda de prensa, entrevista de prensa, conferencia de pensa, *f*
pressing *a* urgente, apremiante; importuno. *n* prensado, *m*, prensadura, *f*; expresión, *f*; (of a garment) planchado, *m*
pressingly *adv* urgentemente, con urgencia; importunamente
pressman *n* tirador, *m*; (journalist) periodista, *m*
pressure *n* presión, *f*; (of the hand) apretón, *m*; apremio, *m*; opresión, *f*; (weight) peso, *m*; (force) fuerza, *f*; urgencia, *f*. **p.-cooker,** cazuela de presión, olla de presión, *f*, presto, *m*. **p.-gauge,** manómetro, *m*
prestidigitation *n* prestidigitación, *f*, juegos de manos, *m pl*
prestige *n* prestigio, *m*
prestigious *a* prestigiado
presumable *a* presumible
presume *vt* presumir; suponer, sospechar; (attempt) pretender. *vi* presumir; tomarse libertades; abusar (de)
presumption *n* presunción, *f*; suposición, *f*; (effrontery) atrevimiento, *m*; insolencia, *f*
presumptive *a* presuntivo; (with heir, etc.) presunto
presumptuous *a* presumido, insolente, presuntuoso; atrevido
presumptuously *adv* presuntuosamente
presumptuousness *n* presunción, presuntuosidad, *f*; atrevimiento, *m*
presuppose *vt* presuponer
presupposition *n* presuposición, *f*
pretence *n* (claim) pretensión, *f*; afectación, *f*; (simulation) fingimiento, *m*; pretexto, *m*. **false pretences,** apariencias fingidas, *f pl*; engaño, *m*, estafa, *f*. **to make a p. of,** fingir. **under p. of,** bajo pretexto de
pretend *vt* dar como pretexto de; aparentar, fingir; simular, hacer el papel (de). *vi* pretender (a); tener pretensiones (de); ser pretendiente (a); fingir
pretended *a* supuesto, fingido; falso
pretender *n* pretendiente, *m*; hipócrita, *mf*
pretension *n* pretensión, *f*; afectación, simulación, *f*
pretentious *a* pretencioso; (of persons) presumido
pretentiousness *n* pretensiones, *f pl*, lo pretencioso
preterite *n* (tiempo) pretérito, *m*, *a* pretérito, pasado

pretext *n* pretexto, *m*. *vt* pretextar. **under p. of,** bajo pretexto de, so color de
prettily *adv* lindamente; con gracia; agradablemente
prettiness *n* lo bonito; elegancia, *f*; gracia, *f*
pretty *a* bonito; (of women, children) guapo, mono; (of men) lindo; elegante; excelente; *iron* bueno. *adv* bastante; medianamente; (very) muy; (almost) casi. **p. good,** bastante bueno. **p.-p.,** de muñeca; mono. *n* chuchería, *f*, guapos, *m pl*. **p. ways,** monerías, *f pl*
prevail *vi* prevalecer, predominar; ser la costumbre. **to p. against or over,** triunfar de, vencer (a). **to p. on, upon,** inducir, convencer, persuadir. **to be prevailed upon to,** dejarse persuadir a
prevailing *a* prevaleciente; dominante; predominante, reinante; general; común; (fashion) en boga
prevalence *n* predominio, *m*; existencia, *f*; (habit) costumbre, *f*; (fashion) boga, *f*
prevalent *a* prevaleciente; predominante; general; común; corriente; (fashionable) en boga
prevaricate *vi* tergiversar; *law* prevaricar
prevarication *n* tergiversación, *f*, equívoco, *m*
prevaricator *n* tergiversador (-ra)
prevent *vt* evitar; (hinder) impedir (a)
preventable *a* evitable
prevention *n* prevención, *f*; (preventive) estorbo, obstáculo, *m*
preventive *a* preventivo. *n* preservativo, *m*
preview *n* vista de antemano, *f*; (of a film) avances, *m pl* (Cuba, Mexico), colas, *f pl* (Argentina), cortos *m pl* (Venezuela), sinopsis, *f* (Uruguay), tráiler, *m* (Spain)
previous *a* previo, anterior. **p. to,** antes de
previously *adv* anteriormente, antes, previamente
previousness *n* anterioridad, *f*; inoportunidad, *f*
prevision *n* previsión, *f*
prewar *a* de antes de la guerra
prey *n* presa, *f*; *fig* víctima, *f*; (booty) botín, *m*. *vi* (of animals) devorar; (plunder) robar, pillar; (of sorrow, etc.) hacer presa (de); agobiar, consumir; (sponge on) vivir a costa de. **to fall a p. to,** ser víctima de
price *n* precio, *m*; valor, *m*; costa, *f*. *vt* evaluar, tasar; poner precio a; preguntar el precio de; fijar el precio de. **at any p.,** a cualquier precio; (whatever the cost) cueste lo que cueste. **at a reduced p.,** a precio reducido. **fixed p.,** precio fijo, *m*. **p. ceiling,** precio máximo, precio tope, *m*. **p. control,** control de precios, *m*. **price list,** lista de precios, *f*; tarifa, *f*; (of shares, etc.) boletín de cotización, *m*. **Prices are subject to change without notice,** Los precios están sujetos a variación sin previo aviso.
priceless *a* sin precio; (amusing) divertidísimo. **These jewels are p.,** Estas joyas no tienen precio
prick *n* pinchazo, *m*; picadura, *f*; punzada, *f*; (prickle) espina, *f*; (with a goad) aguijonazo, *m*; (with a pin) alfilerazo, *m*; (with a spur) espolada, *f*; (of conscience) remordimiento, escrúpulo, *m*. *vt* pinchar, punzar; picar; (with remorse) atormentar, causar remordimiento (a); (urge on) incitar. **to p. the ears,** aguzar las orejas
pricking *n* picadura, *f*; punzada, *f*. **prickings of conscience,** remordimientos, *m pl*
prickle *n* espina, *f*; (irritation) escozor, *m*
prickly *a* espinoso; erizado. **p. heat,** salpullido causado por exceso de calor, *m*. **p. pear,** higo chumbo, *m*, chumbera, *f*
pride *n* orgullo, *m*; arrogancia, *f*; (splendour) pompa, *f*, fausto, aparato, *m*; belleza, *f*; vigor, *m*; (of lions) manada, *f*. **to take p. in,** estar orgulloso de. **to p. oneself,** sentirse orgulloso, ufanarse. **to p. oneself upon,** jactarse de, preciarse de
prie-dieu *n* reclinatorio, *m*
prier *n* espía, *mf*; curioso (-sa)
priest *n* sacerdote, *m*; cura, *m*. **high-p.,** sumo sacerdote, *m*. **p.-ridden,** dominado por el clero
priestess *n* sacerdotisa, *f*
priesthood *n* sacerdocio, *m*
priestly *a* sacerdotal

prig *n* fatuo (-ua), mojigato (-ta)
priggish *a* fatuo, gazmoño
priggishness *n* gazmoñería, fatuidad, *f*
prim *a* almidonado, etiquetero; peripuesto; afectado
primacy *n* primacía, *f*
prima donna *n* cantatriz, *f*
primarily *adv* en primer lugar principalmente
primary *a* primario; primitivo; principal. **p. education,** enseñanza primaria, *f*. **p. color,** color primario, *m*. **p. school,** escuela primaria, *f*. **p. election,** elección interna (dentro de un partido), *f*
primate *n* primado, *m*
prime *a* primero; principal; excelente; de primera calidad; de primera clase. *n* (spring) primavera, *f*; (of life, etc.) flor, *f*, vigor, *m*; (best) nata, crema, *f*; *ecc* prima, *f*; (number) número primo, *m*. *vt* preparar, aprestar; (fire-arms) cebar. **p. the pump,** cebar la bomba; (with paint, etc.) imprimar; (instruct) dar instrucciones (a), informar. **in his p.,** en la flor de su edad. **of p. quality,** de primera calidad. **P. Minister,** Primer Ministro, *m*. **p. necessity,** artículo de primera necesidad, *m*
primer *n* cartilla, *f*, abecedario, *m*; libro de lectura, *m*; (prayer book) devocionario, *m*
primeval *a* primevo, primitivo
priming *n* preparación, *f*; (of fire-arms) cebo, *m*; (of paint, etc.) imprimación, *f*; instrución, *f*
primitive *a* primitivo; anticuado. *n* primitivo, *m*
primitiveness *n* lo primitivo; carácter primitivo, *m*
primly *adv* afectadamente, con afectación; gravemente
primness *n* afectación, *f*; gravedad, *f*
primogeniture *n* primogenitura, *f*
primordial *a* primordial
primrose *n* primavera, *f*; color amarillo pálido, *m*
prince *n* príncipe, *m*. **P. Consort,** príncipe consorte, *m*. **P. of Wales,** (Britain) príncipe heredero, *m*; (Spanish equivalent) Príncipe de Asturias, *m*. **p. regent,** príncipe regente, *m*. **P. Charming,** el Príncipe Azul, *m*
princeliness *n* magnificencia, *f*; nobleza, *f*
princely *a* principesco; magnífico; noble
princess *n* princesa, *f*
principal *a* principal; fundamental; mayor. *n* principal, jefe, *m*; (of a university) rector, *m*; (of a school) director (-ra); *law* causante, *m*; *com* capital, *m*
principality *n* principado, *m*
principally *adv* principalmente
principle *n* principio, *m*. **in p.,** en principio
principled *a* de principios . . .
print *n* (mark) impresión, marca, *f*; (type) letra de molde, *f*, tipo, *m*; (of books) imprenta, *f*; (fabric) estampado, *m*; (picture) grabado, *m*; (photograph) positiva impresa, *f*; (mold) molde, *m*. *vt* marcar; imprimir; (on the mind) grabar; *print* tirar, hacer una tirada (de); (in photography) tirar una prueba (de); (publish) sacar a luz, publicar; (fabrics) estampar. **in p.,** impreso; publicado; **He likes to see his name in print,** Le gusta ver su nombre en letras de molde; (available) existente. **to be out of p.,** estar agotado. **p. dress,** vestido estampado, *m*
printed *a* impreso. **p. fabric,** estampado, *m*. **p. matter,** impresos, *m pl*
printer *n* impresor, *m*; tipógrafo, *m*. **printer's devil,** aprendiz de impresor, *m*. **printer's ink,** tinta de imprenta, tinta tipográfica, *f*. **printer's mark,** pie de imprenta, *f*
printing *n* imprenta, *f*; impresión, *f*; (of fabrics) estampación, *f*; (art of) tipografía, *f*. **p. house,** imprenta, *f*. **p. machine,** máquina de imprimir, *f*. **p. press,** prensa tipográfica, *f*. **p. types,** caracteres de imprenta, *m pl*
prior *n* prior, *m*, *a* anterior, previo. **p. to,** anterior a, antes de
prioress *n* priora, *f*
priority *n* prioridad, *f*
prism *n* prisma, *m*; espectro solar, *m*
prismatic *a* prismático
prison *n* prisión, cárcel, *f*. **p.-breaking,** huida de la pri-

sión, *f*. **p. camp,** campo de prisioneros, *m*. **p. van,** coche celular, *m*. **p. yard,** patio de la prisión, *m*
prisoner *n* prisionero (-ra), preso (-sa). **to take p.,** prender, hacer prisionero (a)
pristine *a* pristino, original
privacy *n* soledad, *f*, aislamiento, retiro, *m*; intimidad, *f*; secreto, *m*
private *a* particular; privado; secreto; confidencial; reservado; íntimo; personal; doméstico; (of hearings, etc.) a puertas cerradas, secreto; (own) propio. *n* (soldier) soldado raso, *m*. **in p.,** en secreto; confidencialmente, de persona a persona. **They wish to be p.,** Quieren estar a solas. **p. company,** sociedad en comandita, *f*. **p. hotel,** pensión, *f*. **p. house,** casa particular, *f*. **p. individual,** particular, *mf*. **p. interview,** entrevista privada, *f*. **p. life,** vida privada, *f*. **p. office,** despacho particular, *m*. **p. secretary,** secretario (-ia) particular. **p. viewing,** (of a film) función privada, *f*; **(of an exhibition)** día de inauguración, *m*
privateer *n* corsario, *m*
privately *adv* privadamente; en secreto; personalmente; confidencialmente; (of hearings) a puertas cerradas
privation *n* privación, *f*; carencia, escasez, *f*
privet *n* alheña, *f*
privilege *n* privilegio, *m*; derecho, *m*; inmunidad, *f*. *vt* privilegiar
privileged *a* privilegiado; confidencial
privy *a* privado; cómplice; enterado; personal, particular. *n* (latrine) retrete, *m*. **p. council,** consejo privado, *m*
prize *n* premio, *m*; recompensa, *f*, galardón, *m*; (capture) presa, *f*. *a* que ha ganado un premio; premiado; (huge) enorme; (complete) de primer orden. *vt* estimar, apreciar. **to p. open,** abrir con una palanca. **to carry off the p.,** ganar el premio. **cash p.,** premio en metálico, *m*. **first p.,** primer premio, *m*; (in a lottery) premio gordo, *m*. **p. court,** tribunal de presas, *m*. **p. fight,** partido de boxeo, *m*. **p. fighter,** boxeador, *m*. **p. giving,** distribución de premios, *f*. **p. money,** premio en metálico, *m*; (boxing) bolsa, *f*
pro *prep* pro. **pro forma invoice,** factura simulada, *f*
probability *n* probabilidad, *f*
probable *a* probable
probably *adv* probablemente
probate *n* verificación de un testamento, *f*
probation *n* probación, *f*; *law* libertad vigilada, *f*
probationary *a* de probación; de prueba
probationer *n* novicio, *m*; estudiante de enfermera, *f*; candidato, *m*; aspirante, *m*
probe *n surg* sonda, cala, tienta, *f*. *vt surg* tentar; escudriñar
probing *n* sondeo, *m*
probity *n* probidad, integridad, *f*
problem *n* problema, *m*; cuestión, *f*. **p. play,** drama de tesis, *m*
problematic *a* problemático
problem child *n* niño problemático, *m* (male), niña problemática, *f* (female)
proboscis *n* (of an elephant) trompa, *f*; (of an insect) trompetilla, *f*
Probus Probo, *m*
procedure *n* procedimiento, *m*
proceed *vi* seguir el camino, continuar la marcha; avanzar, seguir adelante; ir; proceder; ponerse (a); empezar (a); (say) proseguir; (come to) llegar a, ir a; (of a lag, etc.) desarrollarse. **Before we p. any further . . .** Antes de ir más lejos . . . **to p. to blows,** llegar a las manos. **to p. against,** proceder contra, procesar. **to p. from,** venir de. **to p. with,** proseguir; poner por obra; usar
proceeding *n* modo de obrar, *m*; conducta, *f*; procedimiento, *m*; transacción, *f*; *pl* **proceedings,** (measures) medidas, *f pl*, actos, *m pl*; (of a learned society or a conference) actas, *f pl*. **to take proceedings against,** *law* procesar

proceeds *n pl* producto, *m;* ganancias, *f pl;* beneficios, *m pl.* **net p.**, producto neto, *m*
process *n* proceso, *m;* (method) procedimiento, *m;* (course) curso, *m;* marcha, *f;* (*law zool*) proceso, *m. vt* beneficiar (ore), trasformar, elaborar. **in p. of,** en curso de. **in the p. of time,** con el tiempo marchando el tiempo
processing industry *n* industria de trasformación, industria de elaboración, *f*
procession *n* desfile, *m;* cortejo, *m;* (religious) procesión, *f.* **funeral p.**, cortejo fúnebre, *m.* **to walk in p.**, desfilar
processional *a* procesional
proclaim *vt* proclamar; publicar, pregonar; anunciar; (reveal) revelar; (outlaw) denunciar
proclamation *n* proclamación, *f;* proclama, *f,* anuncio, *m;* declaración, *f*
proclivity *n* proclividad, propensión, *f*
procrastinate *vi* tardar (en decidirse), aplazar su decisión; vacilar; perder el tiempo
procrastination *n* dilación, tardanza, *f;* vacilación, *f;* pereza, *f*
procrastinator *n* perezoso (-sa)
procreate *vt* procrear
procreation *n* procreación, *f*
procreator *n* procreador (-ra)
proctor *n* procurador, *m; univ* censor, *m*
procurable *a* procurable; asequible
procure *vt* obtener, conseguir, lograr
procurement *n* obtención, *f,* logro, *m*
procurer *n* alcahuete, *m*
procuress *n* alcahueta, celestina, trotaconventos, *f*
prod *n* (with a bayonet, etc.) punzada, *f; fig* pinchazo, *m. vt* punzar; (in the ribs, etc.) clavar; *fig* pinchar
prodigal *a* and *n* pródigo (-ga)
prodigality *n* prodigalidad, *f*
prodigally *adv* pródigamente
prodigious *a* prodigioso
prodigiousness *n* prodigiosidad, *f;* enormidad, *f*
prodigy *n* prodigio, *m;* portento, *m.* **child p.**, niño prodigio
produce *vt* producir; dar frutos; (show) mostrar, presentar; (take out) sacar; (occasion) causar, traer consigo, ocasionar; (goods) fabricar, manufacturar; (of shares, etc.) rendir; *geom* prolongar; (a play) poner en escena. *n* producto, *m;* víveres, comestibles, *m pl*
producer *n* productor (-ra); *theat* director de escena, *m*
product *n* producto, *m;* (result) fruto, resultado, *m,* consecuencia, *f; math* producto, *m*
production *n* producción, *f;* producto, *m; geom* prolongación, *f;* (of a play) dirección escénica, *f;* (performance) producción, *f.* **p. cost,** coste de producción, *m*
productive *a* productivo
productivity *n* productividad, *f*
profanation *n* profanación, *f*
profane *a* profano; sacrílego, blasfemo. *vt* profanar
profaner *n* profanador (-ra)
profanity *n* profanidad, *f;* blasfemia, *f*
profess *vt* (assert) afirmar, manifestar; declarar; (a faith, a profession, teach) profesar; (feign) fingir; (pretend) tener pretensiones de. *vi* (as a monk or nun) tomar estado, entrar en religión. **He professed himself surprised,** Se declaró sorprendido
professed *a* declarado; *ecc* profeso; ostensible, fingido
profession *n* profesión, *f;* carrera, *f;* declaración, *f.* **p. of faith,** profesión de fe, *f.* **the learned professions,** las carreras liberales
professional *a* profesional; de la profesión; de profesión; de carrera. **p. diplomat,** diplomático (-ca) de carrera. **p. etiquette,** etiqueta profesional, *f.* **p. man,** hombre profesional, *m;* hombre de carrera liberal, *m*
professor *n* catedrático (-ca), profesor (-ra)
professorate *n* profesorado, *m*
professorial *a* de catedrático; de profesor
professorship *n* cátedra, *f*
proffer *vt* proponer; ofrecer. *n* oferta, *f*

proficiency *n* pericia, habilidad, *f*
proficient *a* proficiente, experto, adepto, perito
profile *n* perfil, *m. vt* perfilar. **in p.,** de perfil
profit *n* provecho, *m;* utilidad, *f;* ventaja, *f; com* ganancia, *f, vt* aprovechar. *vi* ganar; *com* sacar ganancia. **to p. by,** aprovechar. **gross p.,** ganancia total, *f.* **p. and loss,** ganancias y pérdidas, *f pl.* **p. sharing,** participación en las ganancias, participación de utilidades, *f*
profitable *a* provechoso, útil, ventajoso; lucrativo. **p. use,** aprovechamiento, *m*
profitably *adv* con provecho, provechosamente; lucrativamente
profiteer *n* estraperlista, *mf*
profit incentive *n* acicate del lucro, *m*
profitless *a* sin provecho, infructuoso, inútil
profligacy *n* libertinaje, *m*
profligate *a* licencioso, disoluto. *n* libertino, *m*
profound *a* profundo
profundity *n* profundidad, *f*
profuse *a* profuso; pródigo; lujoso
profusely *adv* profusamente; pródigamente; lujosamente
profusion *n* profusión, abundancia, *f;* prodigalidad, *f;* exceso, *m*
progenitor *n* progenitor, *m;* (ancestor) antepasado, *m*
progeny *n* prole, *f*
prognosis *n* prognosis, *f;* presagio, *m; med* pronóstico, *m*
prognosticate *vt* pronosticar, presagiar
prognostication *n* pronosticación, *f;* pronóstico, presagio, augurio, *m*
program *n* programa, *m*
progress *n* progreso, *m;* avance, *m;* (betterment) mejora, *f;* (of events) marcha, *f. vi* avanzar, marchar; (improve) progresar, adelantar; mejorar. **to make p.,** adelantarse; hacer progresos
progression *n* progresión, *f*
progressive *a* progresivo; avanzado; *pol* progresista. *n pol* progresista, *mf*
progressiveness *n* carácter progresivo, *m*
prohibit *vt* prohibir; defender; (prevent) impedir, privar. **His health prohibited him from doing it,** Su salud le impidió hacerlo
prohibition *n* prohibición, *f;* interdicción, *f;* (of alcohol) prohibicionismo, *m*
prohibitionist *n* prohibicionista, *mf*
prohibitive *a* prohibitivo, prohibitorio
project *vt* (all meanings) proyectar. *vi* sobresalir; destacarse. *n* proyectil, plan, *m*
projectile *n* proyectil, *m, a* arrojadizo
projecting *a* saliente; (of teeth) saltón
projection *n* (hurling) lanzamiento, *m;* prominencia, protuberancia, *f;* (other meanings) proyección, *f*
projector *n* proyectista, *mf;* proyector, *m*
proletarian *a* proletario
proletariate *n* proletariado, *m*
prolific *a* prolífico; fecundo, fértil
prolix *a* prolijo
prolixity *n* prolijidad, *f*
prolog *n* prólogo, *m, vt* prologar
prolong *vt* prolongar
prolongation *n* prolongación, *f*
promenade *n* paseo, *m;* bulevar, *m;* avenida, *f. vi* pasearse. *vt* recorrer, andar por, pasearse por. **p. deck,** cubierta de paseo, *f*
Promethean *a* de Prometeo
prominence *n* prominencia, *f;* protuberancia, *f;* eminencia, *f;* importancia, *f*
prominent *a* prominente, saliente; (of eyes, teeth) saltón; (distinguished) eminente, distinguido. **They placed the vase in a p. position,** Pusieron el florero muy a la vista. **to play a p. part,** desempeñar un papel importante. **p. eyes, ojos** saltones, *m pl*
promiscuous *a* promiscuo
promiscuousness *n* promiscuidad, *f*
promise *n* promesa, *f;* (hope) esperanza, *f;* (word) pala-

bra, *f;* (future) porvenir, *m. vt* and *vi* prometer. **a young man of p.,** un joven de porvenir. **to break one's p.,** faltar a su palabra; no cumplir una promesa. **to keep one's p.,** guardar su palabra; cumplir su promesa. **to p. and do nothing,** apuntar y no dar. **under p. of,** bajo palabra de. **p. of marriage,** palabra de matrimonio, *f*

promised *a* prometido. **P. Land,** Tierra de promisión, *f*

promising *a* que promete bien, que promete mucho; prometedor; (of the future, etc.) halagüeño; (of persons) que llegará

promissory *a* promisorio. **p. note,** pagaré, abonaré, *m*

promontory *n* promontorio, *m*

promote *vt* fomentar, promover; provocar; (aid) favorecer, proteger; avanzar; estimular; (to a post) ascender; (an act bill) promover; *com* negociar

promoter *n* promotor (-ra); instigador (-ra); (*theat* etc.) empresario, *m*

promotion *n* (encouragement) fomento, *m;* (furtherance) adelanto, *m;* protección, *f,* favorecimiento, *m;* (in employment, etc.) promoción, *f,* ascenso, *m;* (of a company, etc.) creación, *f*

prompt *a* pronto; diligente; presuroso; puntual; rápido; *com* inmediato. *vt* impulsar, incitar, mover; dictar; insinuar; *theat* apuntar; (remind) recordar. **He came at five o'clock p.,** Vino a las cinco en punto. **p. book,** libro del traspunte, *m.* **p. box,** concha (del apuntador), *f*

prompter *n theat* apuntador, (in the wings) traspunte, *m*

prompting *n* sugestión, *f;* instigación, *f; pl* **promptings,** impulso, *m;* (of the heart, etc.) dictados, *m pl*

promptitude *n* prontitud, presteza, *f;* prisa, expedición, *f;* puntualidad, *f*

promptly *adv* inmediatamente, en seguida; con prontitud, con celeridad; puntualmente

promptness *n* See **promptitude**

promulgate *vt* promulgar; divulgar, diseminar

promulgation *n* promulgación, *f;* divulgación, diseminación, *f*

prone *a* postrado; inclinado, propenso

proneness *n* postración, *f;* inclinación, tendencia, propensión, *f*

prong *n* (pitchfork) horquilla, *f;* (of a fork) diente, *m,* púa, *f*

pronged *a* dentado, con púas

pronoun *n* pronombre, *m*

pronounce *vt* pronunciar; declarar; articular

pronounced *a* marcado; perceptible; bien definido

pronouncement *n* pronunciamiento, *m*

pronunciation *n* pronunciación, *f;* articulación, *f*

proof *n* prueba, *f;* demostración, *f;* ensayo, *m; law* testimonio, *m;* (*phot print*) prueba, *f; math* comprobación, *f, a* hecho a prueba (de); impenetrable (a); *fig* insensible (a). *vt* (raincoats, etc.) impermeabilizar. **in p. whereof,** en fe de lo cual. **p. against bombs,** a prueba de bombas. **p. reading,** corrección de pruebas, *f*

prop *n* apoyo, puntal, estribadero, *m;* (for a tree) horca, *f,* rodrigón, *m; naut* escora, *f; fig* báculo, *m,* columna, *f,* apoyo, *m. vt* apoyar; apuntalar; (a tree) ahorquillar; (a building) acodalar; *naut* escorar; *fig* sostener. **He propped himself against the wall,** Se apoyó en el muro, Se arrimó al muro

propaganda *n* propaganda, *f*

propagandist *n* propagandista, *mf*

propagate *vt* propagar. *vi* propagarse

propagation *n* propagación, *f*

propagator *n* propagador (-ra)

propel *vt* propulsar, empujar, mover

propeller *n* propulsor, *m; mech* hélice, *f*

propelling *n* propulsión, *f.* **p. pencil,** lapicero, *m*

propensity *n* propensión, tendencia, inclinación, *f*

proper *a* propio; apropiado; correcto; decente; (prim) afectado; serio, formal; (exact) justo, exacto; (suitable (for)) bueno (para), apto (para); (true) verdadero; (characteristic) peculiar; *her* natural; (with rascal, etc.)

redomado; (handsome) guapo. **If you think it p.,** Si te parece bien. **p. noun,** nombre propio, *m*

properly *adv* decentemente; correctamente; propiamente; bien. **to do (a thing) p.,** hacer algo bien. **p. speaking,** propiamente dicho, hablando con propiedad

propertied *a* propietario, hacendado; (rich) pudiente, adinerado

property *n* propiedad, *f;* (belongings) bienes, *m pl;* posesiones, *f pl;* (estate) hacienda, *f;* (quality) cualidad, *f; pl* **properties,** *theat* accesorios, *m pl.* **personal p.,** bienes muebles, *m pl;* cosas personales, *f pl.* **real p.,** bienes raíces, *m pl.* **p. man,** *theat* encargado de los accesorios, *m.* **p. owner,** propietario (-ia). **p. tax,** contribución sobre la propiedad, *f*

prophecy *n* profecía, *f;* predicción, *f*

prophesier *n* See **prophet**

prophesy *vt* profetizar; presagiar, predecir. *vi* hacer profecías

prophet *n* profeta, *m*

prophetess *n* profetisa, *f*

prophetic *a* profético

prophylactic *a* and *n* profiláctico, *m*

propinquity *n* propincuidad, proximidad, *f;* (relationship) parentesco, *m*

propitiate *vt* propiciar; apaciguar, conciliar

propitiation *n* propiciación, *f*

propitiator *n* propiciador (-ra)

propitiatory *a* propiciador

propitious *a* propicio, favorable

propitiousness *n* lo propicio

proportion *n* proporción, *f;* parte, *f;* porción, *f; pl* **proportions,** proporciones, *f pl;* dimensiones, *f pl. vt* proporcionar; repartir, distribuir. **in p.,** en proporción; conforme (a), según; *com* a prorrata. **in p. as,** a medida que. **out of p.,** desproporcionado. **He has lost all sense of p.,** Ha perdido su equilibrio (mental)

proportional *a* proporcional; en proporción (a); proporcionado (a). **p. representation,** representación proporcional, *f*

proportionally *adv* proporcionalmente, en proporción

proportionate *a* proporcionado; proporcional. *vt* proporcionar

proportionately *adv* See **proportionally**

proposal *n* proposición, *f;* oferta, *f;* (plan) propósito, proyecto, *m.* **p. of marriage,** oferta de matrimonio, *f*

propose *vt* proponer; ofrecer; (a toast) dar, brindar. *vi* pretender, intentar, tener la intención de; pensar; (marriage) declararse

proposer *n* proponente, *m;* (of a motion) autor (-ra) de una proposición

proposition *n* proposición, *f;* (plan) proyecto, propósito, *m*

propound *vt* proponer; plantear, presentar

proprietary *a* propietario; de propiedad

proprietor *n* propietario, *m;* dueño, *m*

proprietorship *n* propiedad, pertenencia, *f*

proprietress *n* propietaria, *f;* dueña, *f*

propriety *n* decoro, *m;* conveniencia, *f;* corrección, *f*

propulsion *n* propulsión, *f*

propulsive *a* propulsor

prorogation *n* prorrogación, *f*

prorogue *vt* prorrogar, suspender (la sesión de una asamblea legislativa)

pros and cons el pro y el contra

prosaic *a* prosaico

proscenium *n* proscenio, *m*

proscribe *vt* proscribir

proscription *n* proscripción, *f*

prose *n* prosa, *f.* **p. writer,** prosista, *mf*

prosecute *vt* proseguir, llevar adelante; (*law* a person) procesar; (*law* a claim) pedir en juicio

prosecution *n* prosecución, *f;* cumplimiento, *m; law* acusación, *f;* (*law* party) parte actora, *f.* **in the p. of his duty,** en el cumplimiento de su deber

prosecutor *n* demandante, actor, *m*. **public p.**, fiscal, *m*
proselyte *n* prosélito, *m*
proselytism *n* proselitismo, *m*
prose writer *n* prosador, *m*
prosody *n* prosodia, *f*
prospect *n* perspectiva, *f*; esperanza, *f*; probabilidad, *f*; (in mining) indicio de filón, *m*; criadero (de oro, etc.), *m*. *vi* explorar; (of a mine) prometer (bien), dar buenas esperanzas. *vt* explorar, inspeccionar; examinar. **He is a man with good prospects,** Es un hombre de porvenir
prospecting *n* la prospección, *f*
prospective *a* en expectativa, futuro; previsor
prospector *n* explorador, operador, *m*
prospectus *n* prospecto, programa, *m*
prosper *vi* prosperar. *vt* favorecer, prosperar
prosperity *n* prosperidad, *f*
prosperous *a* próspero; favorable
prostate *n* próstata, *f*
prostitute *n* prostituta, *f*, *vt* prostituir
prostitution *n* prostitución, *f*
prostrate *a* tendido; postrado; abatido. *vt* derribar; arruinar; (by grief, etc.) postrar; (oneself) postrarse
prostration *n* postración, *f*; abatimiento, *m*. **nervous p.**, neurastenia, *f*
prosy *a* aburrido, árido; pedestre, prosaico; verboso, prolijo
protagonist *n* protagonista, *mf*
protean *a* proteico
protect *vt* proteger
protection *n* protección, *f*; defensa, *f*; garantía, *f*; abrigo, *m*; refugio, *m*; (passport) salvoconducto, *m*; *pol* proteccionismo, *m*
protectionism *n* proteccionismo, *m*
protectionist *n* proteccionista, *mf*
protective *a* protector; *pol* proteccionista
protector *n* protector, *m*
protectorate *n* protectorado, *m*
protectress *n* protectriz, *f*
protein *n* proteína, *f*
protest *vt* protestar; *law* hacer el protesto de una letra de cambio. *vi* declarar; insistir (en); hacer una protesta. *n* protesta, *f*; *law* protesto, *m*. **under p.**, bajo protesta. **to p. against,** protestar contra
Protestant *a* and *n* protestante, *mf*
Protestantism *n* protestantismo, *m*
protestation *n* protestación, *f*
protester *n* el, *m*, (*f*, la) que protesta
protest literature *n* literatura de denuncia, *f*
protocol *n* protocolo, *m*, *vt* protocolizar
protoplasm *n* protoplasma, *m*
prototype *n* prototipo, *m*
protract *vt* prolongar; dilatar
protracted *a* prolongado; largo
protraction *n* prolongación, *f*
protractor *n* (*geom* and *surv*) transportador, *m*. **p. muscle,** músculo extensor, *m*
protrude *vt* sacar fuera. *vi* salir fuera; sobresalir
protuberance *n* protuberancia, *f*
protuberant *a* protuberante, prominente
proud *a* orgulloso; arrogante; noble; glorioso; magnífico; soberbio. **to be p.,** enorgullecerse. **to make p.,** enorgullecer; hacer orgulloso. **to be p. of,** ser orgulloso de, pagarse de, gloriarse en. **p. flesh,** carnosidad, *f*, bezo, *m*
proudly *adv* con orgullo, orgullosamente
provable *a* demostrable
prove *vt* probar; demostrar; (experience) experimentar, sufrir; poner a prueba; (a will) verificar; (show) mostrar; confirmar. *vi* resultar, salir (bien or mal)
provenance *n* origen, *m*
Provençal *a* provenzal. *n* provenzal, *mf*; (language) provenzal, *m*
Provence Provenza, *f*
provender *n* forraje, *m*; *inf* provisiones, *f pl*
proverb *n* refrán, *m*; proverbio, *m*. **collection of prov-**

erbs, refranero, *m*. **Book of Proverbs,** Proverbios, *m pl*
proverbial *a* proverbial
proverbially *adv* proverbialmente
provide *vt* proporcionar, dar; proveer, surtir, suplir; (stipulate) estipular; preparar (por); tomar precauciones (contra); sufragar los gastos (de); proporcionar medios de vida (a); señalar una pensión (a). **to p. oneself with,** proveerse de
provided (that) *conjunc* si; a condición de que, siempre que, con tal que
providence *n* providencia, *f*
provident *a* próvido, previsor, prudente; económico
providential *a* providencial
providentially *adv* providencialmente
provider *n* proveedor (-ra)
province *n* provincia, *f*; esfera, *f*; función, *f*; incumbencia, *f*
provincial *a* provincial, de provincia; provinciano. *n* provinciano (-na); *ecc* provincial, *m*
provincialism *n* provincialismo, *m*
provision *n* provisión, *f*; (stipulation) estipulación, *f*; *pl* **provisions,** provisiones, *f pl*; víveres, comestibles, *m pl*. *vt* abastecer, aprovisionar. **to make p. for,** hacer provisión para, proveer de. **to make p. for one's family,** asegurar el porvenir de su familia. **p. merchant,** vendedor (-ra) de comestibles
provisional *a* provisional, interino
provisioning *n* aprovisionamiento, abastecimiento, *m*
proviso *n* condición, estipulación, disposición, *f*
provisory *a* provisional; condicional
provocation *n* provocación, *f*
provocative *a* provocativo, provocador
provocatively *adv* de un modo provocativo
provoke *vt* provocar; suscitar; incitar, excitar; (irritate) sacar de madre (a), indignar
provoker *n* provocador (-ra); instigador (-ra)
provoking *a* provocativo; (irritating) enojoso, irritante
provost *n* preboste, *m*; (of a college) director, *m*; (in Scotland) alcalde, *m*. **p.-marshal,** capitán preboste, *m*
prow *n* proa, *f*
prowess *n* valor, *m*, destreza, *f*; proeza, *f*
prowl *vi* and *vt* rondar; cazar al acecho
prowler *n* rondador (-ra); ladrón (-ona)
proximity *n* proximidad, *f*
proximo *adv* en (or del) mes próximo
proxy *n* poder, *m*; delegación, *f*; apoderado, *m*; delegado (-da); substituto (-ta). **to be married by p.,** casarse por poderes
prude *n* mojigata, beata, *f*
prudence *n* prudencia, *f*
prudent *a* prudente
prudently *adv* con prudencia
prudery *n* mojigatería, beatería, damería, gazmoñería, *f*
prudish *a* mojigato, gazmoño, remilgado
prune *n* ciruela pasa, *f*; color de ciruela, *m*, *vt* podar; (cut) cortar; reducir
pruning *n* poda, *f*; reducción, *f*. **p. knife,** podadera, *f*
prurient *a* lascivo, lujurioso, salaz
Prussia Prusia, *f*
Prussian *a* and *n* prusiano (-na). **P. blue,** azul de Prusia, *m*
prussic acid *n* acido prúsico, *m*
pry *vi* escudriñar; acechar, espiar, fisgonear; (meddle) entremeterse, meterse donde no le llaman. *vt* See **prize**
prying *n* fisgoneo, *m*; curiosidad, *f*, *a* fisgón, curioso
psalm *n* salmo, *m*. **to sing psalms,** salmodiar
psalmist *n* salmista, *m*
psaltery *n* salterio, *m*
pseudo- *a* seudo. **p.-learned,** erudito a la violeta
pseudonym *n* seudónimo, *m*
psychiatrist *n* siquiatra, *m*
psychiatry *n* siquiatría, *f*

psychic *a* síquico
psychoanalysis *n* sicoanálisis, *mf*
psychoanalyst *n* sicoanalista, *mf*
psychoanalyze *vt* sicoanalizar
psychological *a* sicológico
psychologist *n* sicólogo (-ga)
psychology *n* sicología, *f*
psychopathic *a* sicopático
psychosis *n* sicosis, *f*
psychotherapy *n* sicoterapia, *f*
ptomaine poisoning *n* intoxicación por tomaínas, *f*
puberty *n* pubertad, *f*
pubescent *a* púber
pubic *a* púbico
pubis *n* pubis, *m*
public *a* and *n* público *m*. **in p.,** en público. **p. assistance,** asistencia pública, *f*. **p. funds,** hacienda pública, *f*. **p. health,** higiene pública, *f*. **p.-house,** taberna, *f*. **p. opinion,** opinión pública, *f*. *inf* el qué dirán. **p.-spirited,** patriótico. **p. thoroughfare,** vía pública, *f*. **p. works,** obras públicas, *f pl*
publican *n* tabernero, *m*
publication *n* publicación, *f*
publicist *n* publicista, *mf*
publicity *n* publicidad, *f*
publicity agent *n* publicista, *mf*
publish *vt* publicar, divulgar, difundir; (a book, etc.) dar a luz, dar a la prensa, publicar; (of a publisher) editar. **to p. abroad,** pregonar a los cuatro vientos. **to p. banns of marriage,** correr las amonestaciones
publisher *n* publicador (-ra); (of books) editor (-ra)
publishing *n* publicación, *f*. **p. house,** casa editorial, *f*. **the p. world,** el mundo de la edición, *m*
puck *n* trasgo, *m*; diablillo, picaruelo, *m*
pucker *vt* (one's brow, etc.) fruncir; (crease) arrugar. *vi* arrugarse. *n* frunce, *m*; arruga, *f*; (fold) bolsa, *f*
puckering *n* fruncido, *m*; arrugas, *f pl*
puckish *a* travieso
pudding *n* pudín, budín, *m*. **black p.,** morcilla, *f*
puddle *n* charco, *m*
puerile *a* pueril
puerility *n* puerilidad, *f*
puerperal *a* puerperal. **p. fever,** fiebre puerperal, *f*
Puerto Rican *a* and *n* puertorriqueño (-ña)
puff *vt* and *vi* (blow) soplar; (at a pipe, etc.) chupar; (smoke) lanzar bocanadas de humo; (make pant) hacer jadear; (advertise) dar bombo (a); (distend) hinchar; (make conceited) envanecerse; (of a train, etc.) bufar; resoplar. *n* soplo, *m*; (of smoke, etc.) bocanada, *f*; (of an engine, etc.) resoplido, bufido, *m*; (for powder) borla (para polvos), *f*; (pastry) bollo, *m*; (advertisement) bombo, *m*. **to be puffed up,** *fig* hincharse, inflarse. **p. of wind,** ráfaga de aire, *f*. **p.-ball,** bejín, *m*. **p.-pastry,** hojaldre, *m*, or *f*. **p.-sleeve,** manga de bullón, *f*
puffiness *n* hinchazón, *f*
puffy *a* (of the wind) a ráfagas; (panting) jadeante; (swollen) hinchado
pug *n* (dog) doguino, *m*. **p.-nosed,** de nariz respingona
pugilism *n* boxeo, pugilato, *m*
pugilist *n* pugilista, *mf*, boxeador, *m*
pugnacious *a* pugnaz, belicoso
pugnacity *n* pugnacidad, belicosidad, *f*
pull *n* tirón, *m*; sacudida, *f*; golpe, *m*; (row) paseo en barco, *m*; (with the oars) golpe (de remos), *m*; (at a bell) tirón, *m*; (bell-rope) tirador, *m*; (at a bottle) trago, *m*; (strain) fuerza, *f*; atracción, *f*; (struggle) lucha, *f*; (advantage) ventaja, *f*; (influence) influencia, *f*. **to give a p.,** tirar (de), dar un tirón (a). **to have plenty of p.,** *inf* tener buenas aldabas
pull *vt* tirar (de); (drag) arrastrar; (extract) sacar; (a boat) remar; (gather) coger; *print* imprimir. **He pulled the trigger (of his gun),** Apretó el gatillo. **He was sitting by the fire pulling at his pipe,** Estaba sentado cerca del fuego fumando su pipa. **to p. a hat well down on the head,** calarse el sombrero. **to p. a per-**

son's leg, tomar el pelo (a). **to p. oneself together,** componer el semblante, serenarse; recobrar el aplomo; (tidy oneself) arreglarse. **to p. apart,** *vt* separar; romper en dos. *vi* separarse; romperse en dos. **to p. away,** *vt* arrancar; quitar. *vi* tirar con esfuerzo. **to p. back,** tirar hacia atrás; hacer retroceder (a); retener. **to p. down,** hacer bajar, obligar a bajar; (objects) bajar; (buildings) derribar, demoler; (humble) humillar; degradar; (weaken) debilitar. **to p. in,** tirar hacia dentro; hacer entrar; (a horse) enfrenar; (expenditure) reducir. **to p. off,** arrancar; (clothes) quitarse; (a deal) cerrar (un trato), concluir con éxito; (win) ganar. **to p. on,** *vt* (gloves, etc.) meterse, ponerse. *vi* seguir remando. **to p. open,** abrir; abrir rápidamente. **to p. out,** hacer salir; obligar a salir; (teeth, daggers, etc.) sacar; (hair) arrancar. **to p. round, through,** *vt* ayudar a reponerse (a); sacar con un aprieto. *vi* restablecerse; reponerse, cobrar la salud, sanar. **to p. together,** obrar de acuerdo; (get on) llevarse (bien or mal). **He pulled himself together very quickly,** Se repuso muy pronto. **to p. up,** *vt* montar, subir; (a horse) sofrenar; (stop) parar; (by the root) desarraigar, extirpar; (interrupt) interrumpir; (scold) reñir. *vi* parar(se); (restrain oneself) reprimirse, contenerse
pullet *n* polla, *f*
pulley *n* polea, *f*; *naut* garrucha, *f*. **p. wheel,** roldana, *f*
pulling *n* tracción, *f*; tirada, *f*; arranque, *m*
pullover *n* jersey, *m*
pullulate *vi* pulular
pulmonary *a* pulmonar
pulp *n* pulpa, *f*; (of fruit) carne, *f*; (paper) pasta, *f*; (of teeth) bulbo dentario, *m*. *vt* reducir a pulpa; deshacer (el papel). **to beat to a p.,** *inf* poner como un pulpo
pulpit *n* púlpito, *m*
pulpy *a* pulposo; *bot* carnoso
pulsate *vi* pulsar, latir
pulsation *n* pulsación, *f*, latido, *m*
pulsatory *a* pulsante, pulsativo, latiente
pulse *n* pulso, *m*; pulsación, *f*, latido, *m*; vibración, *f*; (vegetable) legumbre, *f*, *vi* pulsar, latir; vibrar. **to take a person's p.,** tomar el pulso (a)
pulverization *n* pulverización, *f*
pulverize *vt* pulverizar
puma *n* puma, *f*
pumice *n* piedra pómez, *f*
pummel *vt* aporrear
pump *n* *mech* bomba, *f*; (for water, etc.) aguatocha, *f*; *naut* pompa, *f*; (slipper) escarpín, *m*, *vt* bombear, extraer por medio de una bomba; (inflate) inflar; (for information) sondear, sonsacar. **hand-p.,** bomba de mano, *f*. **to work a p.,** darle a la bomba
pumpkin *n* calabaza, *f*, (Chile) zapallo *m*; (plant) calabacera, *f*
pun *n* retruécano, *m*
punch *n* (drink) ponche, *m*; (blow) puñetazo, golpe, *m*; *mech* punzón, *m*; (for tickets, etc.) taladro, *m*; *inf* fuerza, *f*. *vt* (perforate) taladrar, punzar; estampar; (hit) dar un puñetazo (a). **p.-ball,** pelota de boxeo, *f*. **p.-bowl,** ponchera, *f*
Punchinello *n* Polichinela, *m*. **Punch and Judy show,** títeres, *m pl*
punctilious *a* formal, puntual, puntilloso
punctiliousness *n* formalidad, puntualidad, *f*
punctual *a* puntual
punctually *adv* puntualmente
punctuate *vt* puntuar
punctuation *n* puntuación, *f*
puncture *n* pinchazo, *m*; perforación, *f*; *surg* punción, *f*. *vt* pinchar; perforar; punzar. **We have a p. in the right tire,** Tenemos un pinchazo en el neumático derecho
pungency *n* picante, *m*; acerbidad, mordacidad, *f*
pungent *a* picante; acerbo, mordaz
Punic *a* púnico, cartaginés
punish *vt* castigar; maltratar
punishable *a* punible

punishment *n* castigo, *m*; pena, *f*; maltrato, *m*
punitive *a* punitivo
punt *n* batea, *f*. *vt* impeler una batea con una pértiga; ir en batea; (a ball) golpear, dar un puntapié (a)
puny *a* débil, encanijado; insignificante; pequeño
pup *n* cachorro (-rra). *vi* parir la perra
pupa *n* crisálida, *f*
pupil *n* alumno (-na), discípulo (-la); (of the eye) pupila, niña (del ojo), *f*; *law* pupilo (-la). *a* escolar. **day p.**, alumno (-na) externo (-na). **p. teacher,** maestro (-tra) alumno (-na)
puppet *n* títere, *m*, marioneta, *f*; muñeca, *f*; (person) maniquí, *m*. **p. show,** función de títeres, *f*. **p. show-man,** titiritero, titerero, *m*
puppy *n* perrito (-ta), cachorro (-rra)
purblind *a* ciego; (short-sighted and *fig*) miope
purchasable *a* comprable, que puede comprarse; *fig* sobornable
purchase *vt* comprar; adquirir; *fig* lograr, conseguir. *n* compra, *f*; adquisición, *f*; *mech* apalancamiento, *m*; fuerza, *f*; (lever) palanca, *f*, aparejo, *m*; *fig* influencia, *f*. **p. tax,** impuesto de lujo, *m*
purchaser *n* comprador (-ra)
purchasing *n* See **purchase. p. power,** poder de adquisición, *m*
pure *a* puro. **p.-bred,** de raza
pureness *n* pureza, *f*
purgation *n* purgación, *f*
purgative *a* purgativo. *n* purga, *f*
purgatorial *a* del purgatorio; (expiatory) purgatorio
purgatory *n* purgatorio, *m*
purge *n* purgación, *f*; (laxative) purga, *f*; *pol* depuración, *f*; purificación, *f*. *vt* purgar; *pol* depurar; purificar; expurgar
purging *n* purgación, *f*; *pol* depuración, *f*; *fig* purificación, *f*
purification *n* purificación, *f*
purificatory *a* purificador, purificatorio, que purifica
purifier *n* purificador (-ra)
purify *vt* purificar; (metals) acrisolar; refinar; depurar; (purge) purgar
purist *n* purista, *mf*
puritan *a* and *n* puritano (-na)
Puritanism *n* puritanismo, *m*
purity *n* pureza, *f*
purl *vi* (of a stream, etc.) murmurar, susurrar. *n* (of a stream, etc.) susurro, murmullo, *m*
purlieu *n* límite, *m*; *pl* **purlieus,** alrededores, *m pl,* inmediaciones, *f pl*; (slums) barrios bajos, *m pl*
purling *a* murmurante, que susurra, parlero. *n* murmullo, susurro, *m*
purloin *vt* hurtar, robar
purple *n* púrpura, *f*, *a* purpúreo. *vt* purpurar, teñir de púrpura. *vi* purpurear
purplish *a* purpurino, algo purpúreo
purport *vt* dar a entender, querer decir; significar; indicar; parecer; tener el objeto de; pretender. *n* importe, *m*; sentido, significado, *m*; objeto, *m*
purpose *n* objeto, *m*; propósito, fin, *m*; intención, *f*; proyecto, *m*; designio, *m*; determinación, voluntad, *f*; efecto, *m*; ventaja, utilidad, *f*, *vi* and *vt* proponerse; pensar, tener el propósito (de), intentar. **It will serve my p.,** Servirá para lo que yo quiero. **for the p. of . . . ,** con el propósito de . . . , con el fin de . . . **for purposes of . . .** para efectos de . . . **on p.,** de propósito, expresamente. **to no p.,** inútilmente; en vano
purposeful *a* resuelto; de substancia
purposeless *a* irresoluto, vacilante, vago; sin objeto; inútil
purposely *adv* expresamente, de intento
purr *vi* ronronear. *n* ronroneo, *m*
purse *n* bolsa, *f*; monedero, portamonedas, *m*. **to p. one's lips,** apretar los labios
purser *n naut* contador, sobrecargo, *m*. **purser's office,** contaduría, *f*
pursuance *n* cumplimiento, desempeño, *m*, prosecu-

ción, *f*. **in p. of,** en cumplimiento de; en consecuencia de
pursuant *a* and *adv* según; conforme (a), de acuerdo (con); en consecuencia (de)
pursue *vt* perseguir; seguir; (search) buscar; (hunt) cazar; (a submarine, etc.) dar caza (a); (continue) proseguir, continuar; (an occupation) dedicarse (a), ejercer
pursuer *n* perseguidor (-ra)
pursuit *n* perseguimiento, *m*; (search) busca, *f*; (hunt) caza, *f*; (performance) prosecución, *f*, desempeño, *m*; (employment) ocupación, *f*. **in p. of,** en busca de. **p. plane,** avión de caza, *m*
purulence *n* purulencia, *f*
purulent *a* purulento
purvey *vt* proveer, surtir, suministrar; abastecer; procurar
purveyance *n* suministro, abastecimiento, *m*; provisión, *f*
purveyor *n* suministrador (-ra), proveedor (-ra), bastecedor (-ra)
pus *n* pus, *m*
push *n* empujón, *m*; empellón, *m*; impulso, *m*; (of a person) empuje, *m*, energía, *f*; (attack) ataque, *m*; ofensiva, *f*; (effort) esfuerzo, *m*; crisis, *f*, momento crítico, *m*. **at a push,** *inf* en caso de necesidad; en un aprieto, si llegara el caso. **to give the p. to,** *inf* despedir (a). **p.-bicycle,** bicicleta, *f*. **p.-button,** botón, *m*; botón de llamada, *m*. **p.-cart,** carretilla de mano, *f*; (child's) cochecito de niño, *m*
push *vt* empujar; (jostle) empellar, dar empellones (a); (a finger in one's eye, etc.) clavar; (a button) apretar; (*fig* a person) proteger, ayudar; dar publicidad (a); (a claim, etc.) insistir en; (compel) obligar. *vi* empujar; dar empujones, empellar. **I am pushed for time,** Me falta tiempo. **He is pushed for money,** Está apurado por dinero. **I have pushed my finger in my eye,** Me he clavado el dedo en el ojo. **to p. against,** empujar contra; lanzarse contra; empellar, dar empellones (a). **to p. aside, away,** apartar con la mano; rechazar, alejar. **to p. back,** (hair, etc.) echar hacia atrás; (people) hacer retroceder; rechazar. **to p. by,** pasar. **to p. down,** hacer bajar; hacer caer; (demolish) derribar. **to p. forward,** *vt* empujar hacia delante, hacer avanzar; (a plan, etc.) llevar adelante. *vi* adelantarse a empujones; avanzar; seguir el camino. **to p. oneself forward,** *fig* abrirse camino; entremeterse; darse importancia. **to p. in,** *vt* empujar; hacer entrar; clavar, hincar. *vi* entrar a la fuerza; entremeterse. **to p. off,** *vt naut* desatracar; *inf* ponerse en camino. **to p. open,** empujar, abrir. **to p. out,** *vt* empujar hacia fuera; hacer salir; echar. *vi naut* zarpar. **to p. through,** *vt* (business, etc.) despachar rápidamente; (a crowd) abrirse camino por. *vi* aparecer, mostrarse. **to p. to,** cerrar. **to p. up,** empujar; hacer subir; (windows, etc.) levantar. **to be pushing up the daisies,** mirar los árboles de raíz
pushing *a* enérgico, emprendedor; ambicioso; agresivo. **by p. and shoving,** a empellones, a empujones
pusillanimity *n* pusilanimidad, *f*
pusillanimous *a* pusilánime
puss *n* micho (-cha). **P.! P.!** ¡Miz, Miz!
pustule *n* pústula, *f*
put *vt* poner; colocar; (pour out) echar; aplicar; emplear; (estimate) calcular; presentar; (ask) preguntar; (say) decir; (express) expresar; (a question) hacer; (a problem) plantear; (the weight) lanzar; (rank) estimar. **As the Spanish put it,** Como dicen los españoles. **If I may put it so,** Si puedo expresarlo así, Por así decirlo. **hard put to it,** en dificultades, apurado. **How will you put it to her?** ¿Cómo se lo vas a explicar a ella? **to put ashore,** echar en tierra (a). **to put a child to bed,** acostar a un niño. **to put in order,** arreglar; ordenar. **to put out of joint,** dislocar. **to put out of order,** estropear. **to put to death,** matar; (judicially)

ajusticiar. **to put about,** *vt* (a rumor) diseminar, divulgar; (worry) preocupar. *vi naut* virar, cambiar de rumbo. **to put aside,** poner a un lado; descartar; (omit) omitir, pasar por alto de; (fears, etc.) desechar. **to put away,** quitar; guardar; poner en salvo; arrinconar; (thoughts) desechar, ahuyentar; (save) ahorrar; (banish) despedir, alejar; (a wife) repudiar, divorciar; (food) tragar. **to put back,** *vt* echar hacia atrás; hacer retroceder; (replace) devolver, restituir; (the clock) retrasar; (retard) retardar, atrasar. *vi* volver; *naut* volver a puerto. **to put down,** depositar; poner en el suelo; (the blinds) bajar; (an umbrella) cerrar; (a rebellion) sofocar; (gambling, etc.) suprimir; (humble) abatir, humillar; degradar; (silence) hacer callar; (reduce) reducir, disminuir; (write) apuntar, anotar; (a name) inscribir; (to an account) poner a la cuenta de; (estimate) juzgar, creer; (impute) atribuir. **The book is so interesting that it's hard to put down,** El libro es tan interesante que es difícil dejarlo. **to put forth,** (leaves, flowers, sun's rays) echar; (a book) publicar, dar a luz; (a hand) alargar; (an arm) extender; (show) manifestar, mostrar; (strength, etc.) desplegar; (use) emplear. **to put forward,** avanzar; (a clock) adelantar; (a suggestion, etc.) hacer; (propose) proponer; (a case) presentar. **to put oneself forward,** ponerse en evidencia. **to put in,** poner dentro; (a hand, etc.) introducir; (liquids) echar en; (a government) poner en el poder; (an employment) nombrar, colocar; (insert) insertar; (a claim) presentar; (say) decir. **I shall put in two hours' work before bedtime,** Trabajaré por dos horas antes de acostarme. **He put in a good word for you,** Hablé en tu favor. **to put in writing,** poner por escrito. **to put in for,** (an employment) solicitar (un empleo); (as a candidate) presentarse como candidato para. **to put into,** meter dentro (de); (words) expresar; (port) arribar, hacer escala en (un puerto). **to put off,** desechar; (garments) quitarse, despojarse (de); (postpone) diferir, aplazar; (evade) evadir, entretener; quitarse de encima (a), desembarazarse (de); (confuse) desconcertar; (discourage) desanimar; quitar el apetito (a). **to put on,** poner sobre; (clothes) ponerse; (pretend) fingir, afectar; poner; (a play) poner en escena; (the hands of a clock) adelantar; (weight) engordar, poner carnes; (add) añadir; (*sport* score) hacer; (bet) apostar; (the light) encender; (assume) tomar; (the brake) frenar; (abuse) abusar (de). engañar. **He put the kettle on the fire,** Puso la tetera en el fuego. **to put on airs and graces,** darse humos. **to put on probation,** dar el azul a, poner a prueba a. **to put on more trains,** poner más trenes. **put one's foot down,** ponerle a fulano el alto. **to put out,** *vt* (eject) echar, expulsar; hacer salir; poner en la calle; (a tenant) desahuciar; (one's hand) alargar; (one's arm) extender; (one's tongue) sacar; (eyes) saltar; (fire, light) apagar, extinguir; (leaves, etc.) echar; (horns) sacar; (head) asomar, sacar; (use) emplear; (give) entregar, dar; (at interest) dar a interés; (finish) terminar; (dislocate) dislocar; (worry) desconcertar; turbar; poner los nervios en punta (a); (anger) enojar; (inconvenience) incomodar; (a book) publicar; (a boat) echar al mar. *vi*

(of a ship) hacerse a la vela, zarpar. **to put out to grass,** mandar a pacer. **We put out to sea,** Nos hicimos a la mar. **to put the cart before the horse,** poner la carreta por delante de los bueyes. **to put through,** (perform) desempeñar; concluir, terminar; (thrust) meter; (subject to) someter a; (exercise) ejercitar; (on the telephone) poner en comunicación (con). **to put together,** juntar; (a machine, etc.) montar, armar. **to put two and two together,** atar cabos. **to put up,** *vt* (sails, a flag) izar; (raise a window) levantar, cerrar; (open a window, or an umbrella) abrir; (one's hands, etc.) poner en alto; (one's fists) alzar; (a prayer) ofrecer, hacer; (as a candidate) nombrar; (for sale) poner (a la venta); (the price) aumentar; (a prescription) preparar; (food) conservar; (pack) empaquetar; (a sword) envainar; (lodge) alojar; (a petition) presentar; (build) construir; *mech* montar; (*inf* plan) arreglar. *vi* alojarse. **to put upon,** abusar (de); oprimir; (accuse) imputar, acusar (de). **to put up to,** incitar (a), instigar (a); dar informaciones sobre; poner al corriente (de). **to put up with,** tolerar, soportar, aguantar; resignarse a; contentarse con, conformarse con

putative *a* supuesto; (of relationship) putativo

putrefaction *n* putrefacción, *f*

putrefy *vt* pudrir. *vt* pudrirse, descomponerse

putrid *a* pútrido; *inf* apestoso

putt *vt* and *vi* patear.

putting *n* acción de poner, *f*; colocación, *f*. **p. forward of the clock,** adelanto de la hora, *m*. **p. off,** tardanza, dilación, *f*. **p. the weight,** lanzamiento del peso, *m*. **p. up,** (for office) candidatura, *f*. **p. green,** pista de golf en miniatura, *f*

putty *n* masilla, *f*, *vt* enmasillar, rellenar con masilla

puzzle *vt* dejar perplejo; desconcertar; confundir; embrollar. *n* problema, *m*; dificultad, *f*; enigma, *m*; (perplexity) perplejidad, *f*; (game) rompecabezas, *m*. **to p. out,** procurar resolver; encontrar la solución de. **to p. over,** pensar en, meditar sobre. **I am puzzled by . . . ,** Me trae (or tiene) perplejo . . .

pygmy *a* and *n* pigmeo (-ea)

pyjamas *n* pijama, *m*

pylon *n* pilón, *m*; poste, *m*; (at an airport) poste de señales, *m*

pylorus *n* píloro, *m*

pyorrhœa *n* piorrea, *f*

pyramid *n* pirámide, *f*

pyramidal *a* piramidal

pyre *n* pira, *f*

Pyrenean *a* pirineo, pirenaico

Pyrenees, the los Pirineos, *m pl*

pyrites *n* pirita, *f*

pyromancy *n* piromancia, *f*

pyrotechnic *a* pirotécnico

pyrotechnics *n* pirotecnia, *f*

pyrotechnist *n* pirotécnico, *m*

Pyrrhic *a* pírrico

Pythagorean *a* and *n* pitagórico (-ca)

Pythian *a* pitio

python *n* pitón, *m*

pythoness *n* pitonisa, *f*

Q

q *n* (letter) cu, *f*

quack *vi* (of a duck) graznar. *n* (of a duck) graznido, *m*; (charlatan) charlatán, farsante, *m*; curandero, *m*. **q. doctor,** matasanos, medicastro, curandero, *m*. **q. medicine,** curanderismo, *m*

quackery *n* charlatanería, *f*, charlatanismo, *m*

quadrangle *n* cuadrángulo, *m*; (courtyard) patio, *m*

quadrangular *a* cuadrangular

quadrant *n* (*geom ast* etc.) cuadrante, *m*

quadratic *a* cuadrático. **q. equation,** cuadrática, ecuación de segundo grado, *f*

quadrature *n* (*math ast*) cuadratura, *f*

quadrennial *a* cuadrienal

quadrilateral *a* and *n* cuadrilátero *m*

quadrille *n* cuadrilla, *f*; (card game) cuatrillo, *m*

quadruped *a* and *n* cuadrúpedo *m*

quadruple *a* cuádruple. *vt* cuadruplicar. *n* cuádruplo, *m*

quadruplet *n* serie de cuatro cosas, *f*; bicicleta de cuatro asientos, *f*; uno (una) de cuatro niños (-as) gemelos (-as)

quadruplication *n* cuadruplicación, *f*

quaff *vt* beber a grandes tragos, vaciar de un trago

quagmire *n* tremedal, pantano, *m*; *fig* cenagal, *m*
quail *n* codorniz, *f*; (U.S.A.) parpayuela, *f*. *vi* cejar, retroceder; temblar, acobardarse
quaint *a* pintoresco; curioso, raro; (eccentric) excéntrico, extravagante
quaintly *adv* de un modo pintoresco; curiosamente; con extravagancia
quaintness *n* lo pintoresco; rareza, singularidad, *f*; (eccentricity) extravagancia, *f*
quake *vi* estremecerse, vibrar; temblar. *n* estremecimiento, *m*; (of the earth) terremoto, *m*. **to q. with fear,** temblar de miedo
Quaker *n* cuáquero (-ra)
Quakerism *n* cuaquerismo, *m*
quaking *a* temblón; tembloroso. *n* temblor, *m*; estremecimiento, *m*. **q. ash,** álamo temblón, *m*
quakingly *adv* trémulamente
qualifiable *a* calificable
qualification *n* calificación, *f*; requisito, *m*; capacidad, aptitud, *f*; (reservation) reservación, salvedad, *f*
qualified *a* apto, competente; (of professions) con título universitario; habilitado; limitado
qualify *vt* habilitar; calificar; modificar; suavizar; *vi* habilitarse; prepararse; llenar los requisitos
qualifying *a gram* calificativo
qualitative *a* cualitativo
quality *n* cualidad, *f*; calidad, *f*; propiedad, *f*. **This cloth is of good q.,** Esta tela es de buena calidad. **the q.,** la alta sociedad, la aristocracia
qualm *n* náusea, *f*; mareo, desmayo, *m*; (of conscience) escrúpulo, remordimiento, *m*
quandary *n* incertidumbre, perplejidad, *f*; dilema, apuro, *m*. **to be in a q.,** estar perplejo
quantitative *a* cuantitativo
quantity *n* cantidad, *f*; gran cantidad, *f*. **unknown q.,** incógnita, *f*
quantum *n* cantidad, *f*; tanto, *m*. **q. theory,** teoría de la quanta, *f*
quarantine *n* cuarentena, *f*, *vt* someter a cuarentena
quarrel *vi* pelear, disputar; (scold) reñir; (find fault) criticar. *n* pelea, disputa, *f*; (glazier's) diamante de vidriero, *m*. **to pick a q. with,** armar pleito con, reñir con. **to q. with,** reñir con, romper con; quejarse de
quarreller *n* reñidor (-ra)
quarrelling *n* disputas, altercaciones, *f pl*
quarrelsome *a* pendenciero, peleador, belicoso
quarrelsomeness *n* belicosidad, pugnacidad, *f*
quarry *n* cantera, *f*; *fig* mina, *f*; (prey) presa, *f*; víctima, *f*. *vt* explotar una cantera; examinar
quarrying *n* explotación de canteras, *f*; cantería, *f*
quarryman *n* cantero, *m*
quart *n* cuarto de galón, *m*
quartan *a* cuartanal. *n* (fever) cuartana, *f*
quarter *n* (fourth part) cuarta parte, *f*, cuarto, *m*; (of a year) trimestre, *m*; (of an hour, the moon, a ton, an animal, etc.) cuarto, *m*; (of the compass) cuarta, *f*; *naut* cuartelada, *f*; (of a town) barrio, *m*; (mercy) cuartel, *m*; *her* cuartel, *m*; dirección, *f*; origen, *m*, fuente, *f*; *pl* **quarters,** vivienda, *f*; alojamiento, *m*; (barracks) cuartel, *m*. *vt* cuartear; (a body) descuartizar, hacer cuartos (a); (troops) alojar; (in barracks) acuartelar; *her* cuartelar. **a q. of an hour,** un cuarto de hora. **at close quarters,** de cerca. **hind quarters,** cuartos traseros, *m pl*. **It is a q. to four,** Son las cuatro menos cuarto. **It is a q. past four,** Son las cuatro y cuarto. **q.-day,** primer día de un trimestre, *m*. **q.-deck,** alcázar, *m*; cuerpo de oficiales de un buque, *m*. **q.-mile,** cuarto de milla, *m*. **q.-plate,** cuarto de placa, *m*. **q.-sessions,** sesión trimestral de los juzgados municipales, *f*. **q.-staff,** barra, *f*. **q.-tone,** cuarto de tono, *m*
quartering *n* (punishment) descuartizamiento, *m*; *her* cantón, *m*
quarterly *a* trimestral, trimestre. *n* publicación trimestral, *f*, *adv* trimestralmente
quartermaster *n mil* cabo furriel, *m*; *nav* maestre de

víveres, cabo de mar, *m*. **q.-general,** intendente de ejército, *m*
quartet *n* cuarteto, *m*
quarto *n* papel en cuarto, *m*; libro en cuarto, *m*. **in q.,** en cuarto
quartz *n* cuarzo, *m*
quash *vt law* anular, derogar; *inf* sofocar, reprimir
quasi *a* and *adv* cuasi
quasimodo *n* cuasimodo, *m*
quatrain *n* cuarteta, *f*
quaver *vi* vibrar; temblar; (trill) trinar, hacer quiebros. *vt* decir con voz temblorosa. *n* vibración, *f*; trémolo, *m*; (trill) trino, *m*; (musical note) corchea, *f*
quaveringly *adv* con voz temblorosa
quavery *a* trémulo, tembloroso
quay *n* muelle, *m*
queasiness *n* náusea, *f*; escrupulosidad, *f*
queasy *a* propenso a la náusea; nauseabundo; delicado, escrupuloso
queen *n* reina, *f*; (in a Spanish pack of cards) caballo, *m*; (in a French or English pack and in chess) reina, *f*. **to q. it,** conducirse como una reina; mandar. **q. bee,** maestra, abeja reina, *f*. **q. cell,** maestril, *m*. **q. mother,** reina madre, *f*. **q. regent,** reina regente, *f*
queenliness *n* majestad de reina, *f*
queenly *a* de reina; regio
queer *a* raro; extraño, singular; ridículo; (shady) sospechoso; (ill), malucho, algo enfermo; (mad) chiflado
queerly *adv* extrañamente; ridiculamente
queerness *n* rareza, extrañeza, singularidad, *f*; ridiculez, *f*
quell *vt* subyugar; reprimir; apaciguar, calmar
quench *vt* apagar; calmar; satisfacer. **to q. one's thirst,** apagar la sed
quenching *n* apagamiento, *m*; satisfacción, *f*
querulous *a* quejumbroso
querulousness *n* hábito de quejarse, *m*; quejumbre, *f*
query *n* pregunta, *f*; duda, *f*; punto de interrogación, *m*. *vt* preguntar; dudar (de); poner en duda. *vi* hacer una pregunta; expresar una duda
quest *n* busca, *f*; (adventure) demanda, *f*. **in q. of,** en busca de
question *n* pregunta, *f*; problema, *m*; asunto, *m*; cuestión, *f*; (discussion) debate, *m*, discusión, *f*. *vt* and *vi* interrogar; examinar; poner en duda, dudar de; preguntarse; hacer preguntas. **beyond q.,** fuera de duda. **to ask a q.,** hacer una pregunta. **without q.,** sin duda. **It is out of the q.,** Es completamente imposible. **It is a q. of whether . . . ,** Se trata de si . . . **q.-mark,** punto de interrogación, *m*
questionable *a* cuestionable, discutible, dudoso; equívoco, sospechoso
questionableness *n* lo discutible; carácter dudoso, *m*; carácter sospechoso, *m*
questioner *n* preguntador (-ra); interrogador (-ra)
questioning *n* preguntas, *f pl*; interrogatorio, *m*
questioningly *adv* interrogativamente
questionnaire *n* cuestionario, *m*
quetzal *n* (money and *orn*) quetzal, *m*
queue *n* coleta, *f*; cola, *f*; *vi* formar cola; hacer cola
quibble *n* equívoco, subterfugio, *m*; sutileza, *f*; (pun) retruécano, *m*. *vi* hacer uso de subterfugios; sutilizar
quibbler *n* sofista, *mf*
quibbling *n* sofistería, *f*, sofismas, *m pl*, sutilezas, *f pl*
quick *a* vivo; agudo; penetrante; ágil; veloz; (ready) pronto; ágil, activo; (light) ligerò. *adv* rápidamente; (soon) pronto. *n* carne viva, *f*; *fig* lo vivo. **Be q.!** ¡Date prisa! **He was very q.,** Lo hizo muy aprisa; Volvió (o Fue, according to sense) rápidamente. **the q. and the dead,** los vivos y los muertos. **to cut to the q.,** herir en lo más vivo. **q. march,** paso doble, *m*. **q.-sighted,** de vista aguda; perspicaz. **q. step,** paso rápido, *m*. **q.-tempered,** de genio vivo, colérico. **q. time,** compás rápido, *m*; *mil* paso doble, *m*. **q.-witted,** de ingenio agudo

quicken *vt* vivificar; animar; acelerar; excitar, avivar. *vi* vivificarse; despertarse; renovarse; acelerarse; (stir) moverse. **to q. one's step,** acelerar el paso

quicklime *n* cal viva, *f*

quickly *adv* rápidamente; (soon) pronto; (immediately) en seguida; (promptly) con presteza; vivamente

quickness *n* viveza, *f*; (of wit, etc.) agudeza, *f*; rapidez, velocidad, *f*; (promptness) prontitud, *f*; agilidad, *f*; (lightness) ligereza, *f*; (understanding) penetración, sagacidad, *f*

quicksand *n* arena movediza, *f*; *fig* cenagal, *m*

quicksilver *n* azogue, mercurio, *m*, *vt* azogar

quiescence *n* reposo, *m*; quietud, tranquilidad, *f*; inactividad, *f*; pasividad, *f*

quiescent *a* quieto; inactivo; pasivo

quiet *a* tranquilo; quieto; silencioso; quedo; monótono; inactivo; (informal) sin ceremonia; (simple) sencillo; (of the mind) sereno; (of colours, etc.) suave. *n* tranquilidad, quietud, *f*; silencio, *m*; paz, *f*; (of mind) serenidad, *f*. *vt* tranquilizar, sosegar; calmar. **to be q.,** callarse; no hacer ruido. **Be q.!** ¡Estate quieto! ¡A callar!

quietism *n* quietismo, *m*

quietist *n* quietista, *mf*

quietistic *a* quietista

quietly *adv* tranquilamente; en silencio; sin ruido; en calma; (simply) sencillamente; dulcemente

quietness *n* tranquilidad, quietud, *f*; calma, *f*; paz, *f*; silencio, *m*

quietus *n* (quittance) quitanza, *f*, finiquito, *m*; golpe de gracia, *m*; muerte, *f*

quill *n* pluma de ave, *f*; (of a feather) cañón, *m*; (pen) pluma, *f*; (of a porcupine) púa, *f*. **q.-driver,** cagatintas, *mf*

quilt *n* colcha, *f*, edredón, *m*. *vt* acolchar. **q. maker,** colchero, *m*

quilting *n* acolchamiento, *m*; colchadura, *f*

quince *n* (tree and fruit) membrillo, *m*. **q. cheese,** carne de membrillo, *f*. **q. jelly,** jalea de membrillo, *f*

quincentenary *n* quinto centenario, *m*

quinine *n* quinina, *f*

quinsy *n* angina, *f*

quintessence *n* quinta esencia, *f*

quintessential *a* quintaesenciado

quintet *n* quinteto, *m*

quintuple *a* quíntuplo

quintuplet *n* quintupleto, *m*; uno (una) de cinco niños (-as) gemelos (-as)

quip *n* agudeza, salida, *f*; (hint) indirecta, *f*; donaire, *m*, chanza, burla, *f*

quire *n* (of paper) mano (de papel), *f*

quirk *n* (quip) agudeza, salida, *f*; (quibble) sutileza, evasiva, *f*, (gesture) gesto, *m*

quit *vt* abandonar; dejar; renunciar (a). *vi* marcharse, *inf* tomar las de Villadiego, poner pies en polvorosa; (slang) dejar de, cesar de. **notice to q.,** aviso de desahúcio, *m*

quite *adv* completamente, enteramente; totalmente; del todo; (very) muy; (fairly) bastante. **It is not q. the thing to do,** Esto es algo que no se hace. **Q. so!** ¡Claro!; ¡Eso es! Se comprende. **It is not q. so good as we hoped,** No es tan bueno como esperábamos. **Peter is q. grown-up,** Pedro está hecho un hombre (*or* es todo un hombre)

quits *adv* quito, descargado. **be q.,** estar en paz

quittance *n* quitanza, *f*; recibo, *m*; recompensa, *f*

quitter *n* desertor (-ra); cobarde, *mf*

quiver *vi* temblar; vibrar; estremecerse; palpitar; (of light) titilar. *n* (for arrows) aljaba, *f*, carcaj, *m*. See also **quivering**

quivering *a* tremulante; vibrante; palpitante. *n* temblor, *m*; estremecimiento, *m*

quixotic *a* quijotesco

quixotism *n* quijotismo, *m*

quiz *n* examen parcial, *m*. *vt* tomar el pelo (a); burlarse (de); (stare) mirar de hito en hito (a)

quizzical *a* burlón; cómico; estrafalario

quizzically *adv* burlonamente; cómicamente

quoin *n* piedra angular, *f*; ángulo, *m*; (wedge) cuña, *f*. *vt* meter cuñas (a)

quoit *n* tejo, *m*; *pl* **quoits,** juego de tejos, *m*

quondam *a* antiguo

quorum *n* quórum, *m*. **to form a q.,** hacer un quórum

quota *n* cuota, *f*

quotable *a* citable; (Stock Exchange) cotizable

quota system *n* tablas diferenciales, *f pl*

quotation *n* citación, *f*; cita, *f*; *com* cotización, *f*. **q. mark,** comilla, *f*

quote *vt* citar; *com* cotizar. *n* *inf* comilla, *f*

quoth *vt* **q. I,** dije yo. **q. he,** dijo él

quotient *n* cociente, *m*. **intelligence q.,** cociente intelectual, *m*

R

r *n* (letter) erre, *f*

rabbet *n* ranura, *f*, rebajo, *m*. *vt* ensamblar a rebajo. **r.-joint,** junta a rebajo, *f*

rabbi *n* rabí, rabino, *m*. **grand r.,** gran rabino, *m*

rabbinical *a* rabínico

rabbinism *n* rabinismo, *m*

rabbit *n* conejo (-ja). *a* conejuno, de conejo. *vi* cazar conejos. **young r.,** gazapo, *m*. **r.-hutch,** jaula para conejos, *f*. **r.-warren,** conejera, *f*

rabble *n* populacho, vulgo, *m*, plebe, *f*

Rabelaisian *a* rabelasiano

rabid *a* rabioso; fanático; furioso, violento

rabies *n* rabia, hidrofobia, *f*

raccoon *n* mapache, *m*

race *n* carrera, *f*; (current) corriente, *f*; (prize) premio, *m*; (breed) raza, *f*; casta, estirpe, *f*; (family) linaje, *m*, familia, *f*; (scornful) ralea, *f*; (struggle) lucha, *f*. *vi* tomar parte en una carrera; correr de prisa; asistir a concursos de carreras de caballos; (of a machine) dispararse. *vt* (hacer) correr; competir en una carrera (con); desafiar a una carrera. **flat r.,** carrera llana, *f*. **mill-r.,** caz, *m*. **to run a r.,** tomar parte en una carrera; *fig* hacer una carrera. **r.-card,** programa de carreras de caballos, *m*. **r. hatred,** odio de razas, *m*. **r.-meeting,** concurso de carreras de caballos, *m*. **r. suicide,** suicidio de la raza, *m*. **r.-track,** pista, *f*

racecourse *n* hipódromo, *m*; estadio, *m*

racehorse *n* caballo de carrera, *m*

racer *n* (horse) caballo de carreras, *m*; (person) carrerista, *mf*; (car) coche de carreras, *m*; (boat) yate de carreras, *mf*; (bicycle) bicicleta de carreras, *f*

rachitic *a* raquítico

racial *a* racial, de raza

racialism *n* rivalidad de razas, *f*

raciness *n* sabor, *m*; savia, *f*, picante, *m*

racing *n* carreras, *f pl*; *mech* disparo, *m*, *a* de carreras; hípico. **r. calendar,** calendario de concursos de carreras de caballos, *m*. **r. car,** coche de carreras, *m*. **r. cycle,** bicicleta de carreras, *f*

rack *n* (for hay) percha (del pesebre), *f*; (in a railway compartment) rejilla, *f*; (for billiard cues) taquera, *f*; (for clothes) percha, *f*; (for torture) potro, *m*; *mech* cremallera, *f*. *vt* poner en el potro, torturar; atormentar. **to be on the r.,** estar en el potro **to r. one's brains,** devanarse los sesos, quebrarse la cabeza. **r. and ruin,** ruina total, *f*. **r. railway,** ferrocarril de cremallera, *m*,

racket *n sport* raqueta, *f*; (din) barahúnda, *f*; ruido, estrépito, *m*; confusión, *f*; (bustle) bullicio, *m*, agitación, *f;* (swindle) estafa, *f;* (binge) parranda, *f.* **to play rackets,** jugar a la raqueta

racking *n* tortura, *f;* (of wine) trasiego, *m, a* torturante; (of a pain or cough) persistente

racoon *n* mapache, *m*

racquet *n* See **racket**

racy *a* picante; sabroso

radar *n* radar, *m*

raddled *a* pintado de almagre; mal pintado

radial *a* radial

radiance *n* resplandor, brillo, *m,* luminosidad, *f*

radiant *a* radiante; brillante, luminoso. *n geom* línea radial, *f.* **r. heat,** calor radiante, *m*

radiantly *adv* con resplandor; brillantemente; con alegría

radiate *vi* radiar. *vt* irradiar

radiation *n* irradiación, *f; geom* radiación, *f*

radiator *n* (for central heating and of a car) radiador, *m;* (stove) calorífero, *m*

radical *a* radical. *n* (*math chem*) radical, *m; pol* radical, *mf*

radicalism *n* radicalismo, *m*

radio *n* radio, *f;* radiocomunicación, *f.* **r. amateur, r. enthusiast,** radioaficionado (-da). **r. announcer,** locutor (-ra). **r. broadcast,** radioemisión, radiodifusión, *f.* **r. listener,** radiooyente, *mf* **r. receiver,** (technical) radiorreceptor, *m;* (usual word) aparato de radio, *m.* **r. transmitter,** radiotransmisor, *m*

radioactive *a* radiactivo

radioactive fallout *n* caída radiactiva, llovizna radiactiva, precipitación radiactiva, *f*

radioactivity *n* radiactividad, *f*

radiofrequency *n* radiofrecuencia, *f*

radiolocation *n* radiolocación, *f*

radiologist *n* radiólogo, *m*

radiology *n* radiología, *f*

radiometer *n* radiómetro, *m*

radiometry *n* radiometría, *f*

radioscopy *n* radioscopia, *f*

radiotherapeutics, radiotherapy *n* radioterapia, *f*

radish *n* rábano, *m.* **horse-r.,** rábano picante, *m*

radium *n* radio, *m*

radius *n* (*geom anat*) radio, *m;* (of a wheel) rayo, *m;* (scope) alcance, *m*

raffia *n* rafia, *f*

raffish *a* disoluto, libertino

raffle *n* rifa, *f,* sorteo, *m;* lotería, *f. vt* rifar, sortear

raffling *n* sorteo, *m,* rifa, *f*

raft *n* balsa, *f;* (timber) armadía, *f. vt* transportar en balsa; cruzar en balsa

rafter *n* (of a roof) viga, traviesa, *f;* (raftsman) balsero, *m*

raftered *a* con vigas

rag *n* jirón, guiñapo, *m;* (for cleaning) paño, trapo, *m;* (for papermaking) estraza, *f;* (of smoke, etc.) penacho, *m;* (newspaper) papelucho, *m; pl* **rags,** harapos, *m pl; inf* viejos hábitos, *m pl. vt* (tease) tomar el pelo (a); burlarse de; hacer una broma pesada (a). **r.-and-boneman, ragpicker,** andrajero, trapero (Mexico), pepinador, *m.* **r. doll,** muñeca de trapo, *f*

ragamuffin *n* galopín, *m*

rage *n* (anger) cólera, rabia, ira, *f;* (of the elements) furia, violencia, *f;* (ardour) entusiasmo, ardor, *m;* (fashion) boga, moda, *f;* (craze) manía, *f;* (of the poet) furor, *m. vi* (be angry) rabiar, estar furioso; (of the sea) encresparse, alborotarse, enfurecerse; (of wind, fire, animals) bramar, rugir; (of pain) rabiar; (be prevalent) prevalecer, desencadenarse. **to r. against,** protestar furiosamente contra; culpar amargamente (de). **to be all the r.,** *inf* ser la última moda. **to fly into a r.,** montar en cólera. **to put into a r.,** hacer rabiar

ragged *a* harapiento, andrajoso; roto; (uneven) desigual; (rugged) peñascoso, áspero, escabroso; (serrated) serrado; dentellado; (of a coastline) accidentado; (unfinished) inacabado, sin terminar; (of style) descuidado, sin pulir

raggedness *n* harapos, *m pl;* estado andrajoso, *m;* as-

pereza, escabrosidad, *f;* lo serrado; lo accidentado; (of style) falta de elegancia, tosquedad, *f*

raging *a* furioso, rabioso; violento; (roaring) bramante; (of the sea) bravío; intenso. *n* furia, *f;* violencia, *f;* intensidad, *f*

raglan *n* raglán, *m.* **r. sleeve,** manga raglán, *f*

ragout *n* estofado, *m*

ragpicker *n* trapero (-ra)

ragtime *n* música sincopada, *f*

raid *n* incursión, correría, *f;* asalto, ataque, *m;* (by the police) razzia, *f;* (by aircraft) bombardeo, *m, vt* invadir; atacar, asaltar; apoderarse de; hacer una razzia en; (by aircraft) bombear, bombardear; (pillage) pillar, saquear. **obliteration r.,** hombardeo de saturación, *m*

raider *n* corsario, *m;* atacador, asaltador, *m;* (aircraft) avión enemigo, *m*

rail *n* barra, *f;* antepecho, *m;* (of a staircase) barandilla, *f,* pasamano, *m;* (track) riel, *m;* (railway) ferrocarril, *m;* (of a ship) barandilla, *f;* (of a chair) travesaño, *m pl.* **rails,** (fence) cerca, barrera, palizada, *f. vt* cercar con una palizada, poner cerca a; mandar por ferrocarril. **by r.,** por ferrocarril. **to run off the rails,** descarrilar. **to r. at,** protestar contra; prorrumpir en invectivas contra, injuriar de palabra (a)

railing *n* barandilla, *f;* antepecho, *m,* enrejado, *m;* (grille) reja, *f;* (jeers) burlas, *f pl;* insultos, *m pl,* injurias, *f pl;* quejas, *f pl*

raillery *n* jocosidad, tomadura de pelo, *f;* sátiras, *f pl*

railway *n* ferrocarril, *m;* vía férrea, *f,* camino de hierro, *m, a* de ferrocarril, ferroviario. **elevated r.,** ferrocarril aéreo, *m.* **narrow gauge r.,** ferrocarril de vía estrecha, *m.* **r. buffet,** fonda, *f,* (or restaurante, *m*) de estación. **r. carriage,** departamento de tren, *m.* **r. company,** compañía de ferrocarriles, *f.* **r. crossing,** paso a nivel, *m.* **r. engine,** locomotora, *f.* **r. guard,** jefe del tren, *m.* **r. guide,** guía de ferrocarriles, *f.* **r. line,** vía férrea, *f.* **r. marshalling yard,** apartadero ferroviario, *m.* **r. passenger,** viajero (-ra) en un tren. **r. platform,** andén, *m.* **r. porter,** mozo de estación, *m.* **r. siding,** vía muerta, *f.* **r. signal,** disco de señales, *m.* **r. station,** estación (de ferrocarril), *f.* **r. system,** sistema ferroviario, *m.* **r. ticket,** billete de tren, *m*

railwayman *n* ferroviario, empleado de los ferrocarriles, *m*

raiment *n* ropa, *f; poet* hábitos, *m pl*

rain *n* lluvia, *f. vi* and *vt* llover. **a r. of arrows,** una lluvia de flechas. **fine r.,** llovizna, *f.* **to r. cats and dogs,** llover a cántaros. **to r. hard,** diluviar. **r. cloud,** nubarrón, *m.* **r.-gauge,** pluviómetro, *m*

rainbow *n* arco iris, arco de San Martín, *m*

raincoat *n* abrigo impermeable, *m*

raindrop *n* gota de lluvia, *f*

rainfall *n* cantidad llovida, *f;* (shower) aguacero, *m*

rainless *a* sin lluvia, seco

rainstorm *n* chaparrón, *m,* tempestad de lluvia, *f*

rainwater *n* lluvia, *f;* agua lluvia, *f*

rainy *a* lluvioso. **r. day,** día de lluvia, *m; fig* tiempo de escasez, *m*

raise *vt* levantar; alzar; (the hat) quitar; solevantar; (dough) fermentar; (erect) erigir, edificar; (dust) levantar; elevar; (promote) ascender; (increase) aumentar; hacer subir; (spirits, memories) evocar; (the dead) resucitar; (cause) causar; dar lugar a; hacer concebir; (a question, a point) hacer; plantear; (breed or educate) criar; (a crop) cultivar; (an army) alistar; (gather together) juntar; (a subscription) hacer; (money, etc.) obtener, hallar; (a siege, etc.) levantar; alzar; (a laugh, a protest, etc.) suscitar, provocar; (utter) poner, dar; (a fund) abrir. **to r. oneself,** incorporarse. **He succeeded in raising himself,** Logró alzarse; Logró mejorar su posición. **He raised their hopes unduly,** Les hizo concebir esperanzas desmesuradas. **to r. an objection (to),** poner objeción (a). **to r. an outcry,** armar un alboroto. **to r. a point,** hacer una observación; plantear una cuestión. **to r. a**

siege, levantar un sitio. **to r. Cain,** armar lo de Dios es Cristo. **to r. one's voice,** alzar la voz

raised *a* (in relief) en relieve; (embossed) de realce

raiser *n* (breeder) criador (-ra); (cultivator) cultivador (-ra); (educator) educador (-ra); autor (-ra); fundador (-ra); (of objections, etc.) suscitador (-ra)

raisin *n* pasa, *f*

raising *n* levantamiento, *m*; alzamiento, *m*; (of a building, monument) erección, *f*; elevación, *f*; (increase) aumento, *m*; provocación, *f*; fundación, *f*; (breeding or education) crianza, *f*; (of spirits) evocación, *f*; (of the dead) resucitación, *f*; producción, *f*; (of crops) cultivo, *m*

rake *n agr* rastrillo, *m*, rastra, *f*; (for the fire) hurgón, *m*; (croupier's) raqueta, *f*; (of a mast, funnel) inclinación, *f*; (person) tenorio, calavera, *m. vt agr* rastrillar; (a fire, etc.) hurgar; (sweep) barrer; recoger; (ransack) buscar (en); (with fire) enfilar, tirar a lo largo de; (scan) escudriñar. *vi* trabajar con el rastrillo; (slope) inclinarse. **r. off,** tajada, *f*. **to r. together,** juntar con el rastrillo; amontonar; ahorrar. **to r. up,** (revive) resucitar, desenterrar

raking *n* rastrillaje, *m*; (the fire, etc.) hurgonada, *f*

rakish *a* (of a ship) de palos muy inclinados, (dissolute) disoluto, libertino; (dashing) elegante

rakishly *adv* disolutamente; elegantemente

rakishness *n* (licentiousness) libertinaje, *m*, disipación, disolución, *f*; (elegance) elegancia, *f*

rally *vt* reunir; *mil* rehacer; (faculties) concentrar; (tease) tomar el pelo (a). *vi* reunirse; *mil* rehacerse; (revive) mejorar, recobrar las fuerzas; (of markets, etc.) mejorar, *f*

rallying *n* reunión, *f*; (of faculties, etc.) concentración, *f*; (recovery) mejora, *f*. **r. point,** punto de reunión, *m*

ram *n zool* carnero, morueco, *m*; *ast* Aries, Carnero, *m*; (mil etc.) ariete, *m*; (tool) pisón, *m*; *nav* espolón, *m*, *vt* golpear con ariete o espolón; (of a gun) atacar; apisonar; meter a la fuerza; hacer tragar a la fuerza; (squeeze) apretar; (crowd) atestar

Ramadan *n* ramadán, *m*

ramble *vi* vagar, vagabundear; hacer una excursión. *vt* errar por

rambler *n* excursionista, *mf*; paseante, *mf*; *bot* rosa trepante, *f*

rambling *a* (of houses) encantado; laberíntico; (straggly) disperso; (of thought, etc.) incoherente, inconexo. *n* vagabundeo, *m*; excursiones, *f pl*; paseo, *m*; (digression) digresiones, *f pl*; (delirium) desvaríos, *m pl*

ramification *n* ramificación, *f*

ramify *vi* ramificarse, tener ramificaciones. *vt* ramificar; dividir en ramales

rammer *n* pisón de empedrador, *m*; baqueta (de fusil), *f*; (of a ship) espolón, *m*

ramp *n* rampa, *f*; (swindle) estafa, *f*; (storm, commotion) tormenta, *f*

rampage *vi* alborotarse; bramar

rampant *a* salvaje; *her* rampante; (of persons) impaciente, furioso; (of plants, growth) lozano, exuberante; desenfrenado; (rife) prevaleciente, predominante

rampart *n* muralla, *f*; terraplén, *m*; *fig* baluarte, *m. vt* abaluartar, abastionar

ramrod *n* baqueta, *f*

ramshackle *a* destartalado, ruinoso; desvencijado; (badly made) mal hecho

ranch *n* rancho, *m*, hacienda (de ganado), *f*

rancher *n* ranchero, *m*

rancid *a* rancio

rancidness *n* rancidez, *f*

rancorous *a* rencoroso

rancor *n* rencor, encono, *m*

random *n* azar, *m*, *a* fortuito, al azar; sin orden ni concierto. **at r.,** a la ventura, al azar; sin pensar; (of shooting) sin apuntar. **to talk at r.,** hablar a trochemoche

range *n* línea, hilera, *f*; (of mountains) cadena, *f*; serie, *f*; clase, *f*; variedad, *f*; (of goods) surtido, *m*; (of a gun,

voice, vision, etc.) alcance, *m*; (area) extensión, área, *f*; esfera de actividad, *f*; (scope) alcance, *m*; (of voice, musical instrument) compás, *m*; (of colors) gama, *f*; (for shooting) campo de tiro, *m*; (for cooking) cocina económica, *f*. **at close r.,** de cerca. **out of r.,** fuera de alcance. **within r.,** al alcance. **r.-finder,** (of guns, cameras) telémetro, *m*. **r. of mountains,** cadena de montañas, *f*; sierra, *f*

range *vt* arreglar; alinear; ordenar; clasificar; (a gun, etc.) apuntar; (place oneself) ponerse; sumarse (a); (roam) recorrer; (scan) escudriñar. *vi* extenderse (roam) vagar; (of plants) crecer (en); variar, fluctuar; oscilar, vacilar; (of guns, etc.) alcanzar; (of the mind) pasar (por); (include) incluir

ranger *n* (wanderer) vagabundo, *m*; (keeper) guardabosque, *m*; *mil* batidor, *m*

ranging *n* arreglo, *m*; alineación, *f*; ordenación, *f*; clasificación, *f*; (roving) vida errante, *f*

rank *n* línea, *f*; fila, *f*; grado, *m*; clase, *f*; rango, *m*; categoría, *f*; posición, *f*; calidad, *f*; distinción, *f. vt* ordenar; clasificar; (estimate) estimar; poner (entre). *vi* ocupar un puesto; tener un grado, rango, etc.; estar al nivel (de); ser igual (a); contarse (entre). *a* (luxuriant) lozano, exuberante; fértil; (thick) espeso; (rancid) rancio; (complete) consumado; completo; (foul-smelling) fétido; *fig* repugnante, aborrecible; (very) muy. **of the first r.,** de primera calidad; de primera clase; de distinción. **the r. and file,** los soldados, la tropa; las masas, hombres de filas, *m pl*, mujeres de fila, *f pl*, la mayoría; los socios ordinarios (de un club, etc.). **to break ranks,** *mil* romper filas. **to rise from the ranks,** ascender de las filas. **to r. high,** ocupar alta posición; ser de los mejores (de). **to r. with,** estar al nivel de; (be numbered among) contarse entre, figurar entre

rankle *vi fig* irritar, molestar; envenenarse la vida, hacerse odioso

rankly *adv* ranciamente; lozanamente; con exuberancia; abundantemente; groseramente

rankness *n* rancidez, *f*; olor rancio, *m*; fertilidad, lozanía, *f*; exuberancia, *f*, vigor, *m*; enormidad, *f*

ransack *vt* (search) registrar; (pillage) saquear; *fig* buscar en

ransacking *n* (searching) registro, *m*; (sacking) saqueo, *m*

ransom *n* rescate, *m*, redención, *f*; liberación, *f. vt* rescatar, redimir

ransomer *n* rescatador (-ra)

ransoming *n* redención, *f*; liberación, *f*

rant *vi* declamar a gritos, vociferar; despotricar (contra); desvariar; hablar por hablar, hablar sin ton ni son. *n* declamación, vociferación, *f*; desvarío, *m*

ranter *n* declamador (-ra); agitador populachero, *m*; predicador chillón, *m*

rap *n* golpecito, *m*; toque, *m*; (with the knocker) aldabada, *f*; (worthless trifle) ardite, maravedí, *m. vt* and *vi* golpear; tocar. **He doesn't care a rap,** No le importa un ardite. **to rap at the door,** tocar a la puerta. **to rap with the knuckles,** golpear con los nudillos. **to rap out an oath,** proferir una blasfemia

rapacious *a* rapaz

rapaciously *adv* con rapacidad

rapacity *n* rapacidad, *f*

rape *n* (carrying off) rapto, *m*. **the Rape of the Sabine Women,** el Rapto de las Sabinas, *m*; *law* estupro, *m*; violación, *f*; *bot* nabo silvestre, *m. vt* (carry off) raptar, robar; violar, forzar

rapid *a* rápido. *n* rápido, *m*. **r. combustion,** combustión activa, *f*

rapidity *n* rapidez, *f*

rapidly *adv* rápidamente, con rapidez

rapier *n* estoque, *m*; espadín, *m*

rapine *n* rapiña, *f*

rapping *n* golpecitos, *m pl*; golpeo, *m*; toques, *m pl*; (of the knocker) aldabeo, *m*

rapscallion *n* bribón, *m*

rapt *past part* and *a* arrebatado; absorto; extático, extasiado

rapture *n* arrebato, *m*; éxtasis, *m*; transporte, *m*; embriaguez, *f*; entusiasmo, *m*

rapturous *a* embelesado; extático; entusiasta

rapturously *adv* extáticamente; con entusiasmo

rare *a* raro; extraordinario; exótico; infrecuente

raree show *n* barracón de los fenómenos, barracón de las atracciones, *m*

rarefaction *n* rarefacción, *f*

rarefy *vt* rarefacer. *vi* rarefacerse

rareness *n* rareza, *f*; singularidad, *f*; infrecuencia, *f*

rarity *n* raridad, *f*; (uncommonness and rare object) rareza, *f*

rascal *n* sinvergüenza, *m*; truhán, bribón, pícaro, *m*; (affectionately) picaruelo, *m*

rascality *n* bellaquería, truhanería, *f*

rascally *a* redomado; vil, ruin, canallesco

rash *a* temerario, precipitado; imprudente. *n* erupción, *f*, salpullido, *m*

rasher *n* magra, *f*; (of bacon) torrezno, *m*

rashly *adv* temerariamente, precipitadamente; imprudentemente, con imprudencia

rashness *n* temeridad, precipitación, *f*; imprudencia, *f*

rasp *n* escofina, *f*, rallo, *m*; sonido áspero, *m*. *vt* raspar, escofinar; (get on one's nerves) poner los nervios en punta (a)

raspberry *n* frambuesa, *f*. **r.-cane,** frambueso, *m*. **r. jam,** mermelada de frambuesa, *f*

rasping *a* (of the voice) áspero, estridente

rat *n* rata, *f*; desertor, *m*; (black leg) esquirol, *m*. *vi* cazar ratas; ser desertor; ser esquirol. **rat-catcher,** cazador de ratas, *m*. **rat poison,** matarratas, *m*, raticida, *f*. **rat-trap,** ratonera, *f*

ratable *a* sujeto a contribución; imponible; valuable

ratafia *n* ratafía, *f*

rataplan *n* rataplán, *m*

ratchet *n mech* trinquete, *m*; (of a watch) disparador, *m*. **r.-drill,** carraca, *f*. **r.-wheel,** rueda dentada con trinquete, *f*

rate *n* velocidad, *f*; razón, proporción, *f*; (of exchange) tipo, *m*; tanto, *m*; precio, *m*; clase, *f*; modo, *m*, manera, *f*; *naut* clasificación, *f*; (tax) contribución, *f*, impuesto, *m*; *pl* **rates,** (of a house) inquilinato, *m*. *vt* tasar; estimar; fijar el precio (a); *naut* clasificar; imponer una contribución (de); (scold) reñir. **at a great r.,** rápidamente, velozmente. **at a r. of,** a razón de; a una velocidad de. **at any r.,** de todos modos; por lo menos; sea como fuere. **at this r.,** de este modo; a este paso; a esa cuenta; en esta proporción; (with seguir) así. **first-r.,** de primera clase. **rates and taxes,** contribuciones e impuestos, *f pl*. **r. of climb,** *aer* velocidad ascensional, *f*. **r. of exchange,** tipo de cambio, *m*. **r.-payer,** contribuyente, *mf*

rather *adv* más bien; antes; (more willingly) de mejor gana; (somewhat) algo, un poco; (perhaps) quizás; mejor dicho; (fairly) bastante; (very) muy; mucho; al contrario. **R.!** ¡Ya lo creo! **or r.,** o más bien. **anything r. than . . . ,** todo menos . . . **He had r.,** Preferiría. **r. than,** antes que, en vez de

ratification *n* ratificación, *f*; (of a bill) aprobación, *f*

ratifier *n* ratificador (-ra)

ratify *vt* ratificar

ratifying *n* ratificación, *f*, *a* ratificatorio

rating *n* tasación, *f*; valuación, *f*; clasificación, *f*; impuesto, *m*, contribución, *f*; repartición de impuestos, *f*; (of a ship's company) graduación, *f*; (scolding) reprensión, *f*

ratio *n* razón, *f*; proporción, *f*. **in direct r.,** en razón directa

ratiocinate *vi* raciocinar

ratiocination *n* raciocinación, *f*

ration *n* ración, *f*. *vt* racionar. **r.-book,** cartilla de racionamiento, *f*

rational *a* racional; razonable, juicioso. *n* ser racional, *m*

rationalism *n* racionalismo, *m*

rationalist *n* racionalista, *mf*

rationalistic *a* racionalista

rationality *n* racionalidad, *f*; justicia, *f*

rationalization *n* racionalización, *f*; justificación, *f*

rationalize *vt* hacer racional; concebir racionalmente; *math* quitar los radicales (a); justificar

rationing *n* racionamiento, *m*

rattan *n* rota, *f*, bejuco, *m*; junquillo, *m*

ratteen *n* ratina, *f*

ratter *n* perro ratonero, *m*; gato que caza ratas, *m*

ratting *n* caza de ratas, *f*; deserción, *f*

rattle *vi* hacer ruido; rechinar, crujir; (of loose windows, etc.) zangolotearse; (knock) golpear; tocar; (patter) bailar; sonar; (of the dying) dar un estertor. *vt* (shake) sacudir; hacer vibrar; (jolt) traquetear; (do rapidly) acabar rápidamente; (confuse) aturdir, hacer perder la cabeza (a); desconcertar. **to r. off,** (repeat) decir rápidamente; terminar apresuradamente. **to r. on about,** charlar mucho de, hablar sin cesar sobre

rattle *n* rechinamiento, crujido, *m*; zangoloteo, *m*; ruido, *m*; son (de la lluvia, etc.), *m*; (in the throat) estertor, *m*; (of a rattlesnake) cascabel, *m*; (child's) sonajero, *m*; matraca, *f*; carraca, *f*; (chatter) charla, *f*. **r.-headed,** de cabeza de chorlito, casquivano

rattlesnake *n* serpiente de cascabel, *f*, crótalo, *m*

rattling *n* See **rattle**

raucous *a* ronco, estridente

raucousness *n* ronquedad, *f*, estridor, *m*

ravage *vt* devastar; (pillage) saquear; destruir; (spoil) estropear. *n* devastación, *f*; destrucción, *f*; estrago, *m*

ravager *n* devastador (-ra); saqueador (-ra)

rave *vi* desvariar, delirar; (of the elements) bramar, rugir. **to r. about,** hablar con entusiasmo de; delirar por. **to r. against,** vociferar contra, despotricarse contra

ravel *vt* deshilar, destejer; *fig* enredar. **to r. out,** deshilarse; *fig* desenredarse, desenmarañarse

raven *n* cuervo, *m*, a negro como el azabache

ravening *a* rapaz, salvaje

Ravenna Rávena, *f*

ravenous *a* voraz

ravenously *adv* vorazmente

ravenousness *n* voracidad, *f*

ravine *n* cañada, *f*, barranco, cañón, *m*

raving *n* delirio, *m*, desvaríos, *m pl*. *a* delirante; violento; bravío

ravioli *n pl* ravioles, *m pl*

ravish *vt* (carry off) arrebatar, raptar; extasiar, encantar; (rape) violar, forzar

ravisher *n* raptador, *m*; violador, *m*

ravishing *n* violación, *f*, a encantador

ravishment *n* violación, *f*; arrobamiento, *m*; transporte, éxstasis, *m*

raw *a* (of meat, etc., silk, leather, weather) crudo; bruto; (inexpert) bisoño; (of flesh) vivo; *com* en bruto. **raw-boned,** huesudo. **raw hand,** novato (-ta). **raw material,** primera materia, *f*. **raw materials,** materias primas, *f pl*. **raw score,** puntuación bruta, *f*. **raw silk,** seda cruda, seda en rama, *f*. **raw sugar,** azúcar bruto, *m*

rawhide *a* de cuero crudo

rawness *n* crudeza, *f*; inexperiencia, *f*; (of weather) humedad, *f*

ray *n* rayo, *m*; (line) raya, *f*; (radius) radio, *m*; (fish) raya, *f*. **cathode rays,** rayos catódicos, *m pl*

rayon *n* rayón, *m*

raze *vt* arrasar, asolar; demoler; (erase) borrar, tachar

razor *n* navaja, *f*. **electric r.,** máquina de afeitar eléctrica, *f*. **safety r.,** máquina de afeitar, *f*. **slash with a r.,** navajada, *f*. **r. blade,** hoja de afeitar, *f*. **r. case,** navajero, *m*. **r. strop,** suavizador, *m*

re *n mus* re, *m*; *prep law* causa, *f*; *com* concerniente a

re *prefix* (attached to verb) re-; (after the verb) de nuevo; (followed by infin.) volver a . . . **to re-count,** volver a contar, contar de nuevo, recontar

reabsorb *vt* resorber
reabsorption *n* reabsorción, resorción, *f*
reach *vt* (stretch out) alargar; extender; alcanzar; llegar hasta; (arrive at) llegar a; (achieve) lograr, obtener. *vi* extenderse; alcanzar; penetrar. *n* alcance, *m*; extensión, *f*; poder, *m*; capacidad, *f*; (of a river) tabla, *f*. **as far as the eye could r.**, hasta donde alcanzaba la vista. **He reached home very soon**, Llegó muy pronto a casa. **out of r.**, fuera de alcance. **to r. a deadlock**, llegar a un punto muerto. **within r.**, al alcance. **within easy r.**, de fácil acceso; a corta distancia. **to r. after**, procurar alcanzar; hacer esfuerzos para obtener. **to r. back**, (of time) remontarse. **to r. down**, bajar. **r.-me-downs**, ropa hecha, *f*
react *vi* reaccionar. *vt* hacer de nuevo; *theat* volver a representar
reaction *n* reacción, *f*
reactionary *a* and *n* reaccionario (-ia)
reactive *a* reactivo
read *vt* leer; (a riddle, etc.) adivinar; descifrar; interpretar; (study) estudiar; (the Burial Service, etc.) decir; (correct) corregir; (of thermometers, etc.) marcar. *vi* leer; estudiar; (be written) estar escrito, decir. **The play acts better than it reads**, La comedia es mejor representada que leída. **to r. aloud**, leer en voz alta. **to r. between the lines**, leer entre líneas. **to r. proofs**, corregir pruebas. **to r. to oneself**, leer para sí. **to r. about**, leer; (learn) enterarse de. **to r. again**, volver a leer, leer otra vez. **to r. on**, continuar leyendo. **to r. out**, leer en alta voz. **to r. over**, leer; leerlo todo. **to r. over and over again**, leer muchas veces, leer y releer.
read *past part* leído, etc. **well-r.**, releído; instruido, culto
readability *n* legibilidad, *f*; interés, *m*, amenidad, *f*
readable *a* legible; interesante
readdress *vt* dirigir de nuevo (una carta, etc.); poner la nueva dirección en (una carta, etc.)
reader *n* lector (-ra); *ecc* lector, *m*; (proof) corrector de pruebas, *m*; (citation collector for a dictionary) cedulista, *mf*; (university) profesor (-ra) auxiliar a cátedra; (book) libro de lectura, *m*. **to be a great r.**, leer mucho. **the Spanish r.** (reader of Spanish books) el lector de español
readily *adv* fácilmente; en seguida, inmediatamente; de buena gana, con placer
readiness *n* prontitud, expedición, *f*; buena voluntad, *f*; (of speech, etc.) facilidad, *f*. **in r.**, preparado. **r. of wit**, viveza de ingenio, *f*
reading *n* lectura, *f*; (erudition) conocimientos, *m pl*; (recital) declamación, *f*; (lecture) conferencia, *f*; (study) estudio, *m*; interpretación, *f*; (of a thermometer, etc.) registro, *m*; (of a will) apertura, *f*. **r.-book**, libro de lectura, *m*. **r.-desk**, atril, *m*. **r.-glass**, lente para leer, *m*, carlita, *f*. **r.-lamp**, lámpara de sobremesa, *f*. **r.-matter**, material de lectura, *m*. **r.-room**, gabinete de lectura, *m*, sala de lectura, *f*
readjourn *vt* (a meeting) suspender (la sesión) de nuevo
readjust *vt* reajustar, reacomdar; *vi* reacomodarse
readjustment *n* reajuste, *m*, reacomodación, *f*
readmission *n* readmisión, *f*
readmit *vt* readmitir
ready *a* listo, preparado; dispuesto; pronto; (on the point of) a punto de; (easy) fácil; (near at hand) a la mano; (with money) contante; (with wit, etc.) vivo; (available) disponible; (nimble) ágil, ligero. **I am r. to do it**, Estoy dispuesto a hacerlo. **in r. cash**, en dinero contante. **to get r.**, prepararse; (dress) vestirse. **to make r.**, *vt* preparar; aprestar; *print* imponer. *vi* prepararse, disponerse. **r.-made**, hecho; confeccionado. **r.-made clothing**, ropa hecha, *f*. **r. money**, dinero contante, *m*. **r.-witted**, de ingenio vivo
reaffirm *vt* afirmar de nuevo; reiterar, volver a repetir
reaffirmation *n* reiteración, *f*
reafforestation *n* nuevas plantaciones, *f pl*
reagent *n* reactivo, *m*
real *a* real; verdadero; efectivo; (with silk, etc.) puro;

sincero. **r. estate, r. property**, bienes raíces, *m pl*
realism *n* realismo, *m*
realist *n* realista, *mf*
realistic *a* realista
reality *n* realidad, *f*; verdad, *f*
realizable *a* realizable; factible
realization *n* realización, *f*; comprensión, *f*
realize *vt* (understand) darse cuenta de, hacerse cargo de; realizar; (make real) dar vida (a); (accomplish) llevar a cabo; *com* realizar; (gain) adquirir
really *adv* realmente; en verdad; en realidad; en efecto; (frankly) francamente. **R.?** ¿De veras?
realm *n* reino, *m*, dominios, *m pl*; *fig* esfera, *f*
realty *n* bienes raíces, *m pl*
ream *n* resma, *f*
reanimate *vt* reanimar
reap *vt* segar; *fig* cosechar, recoger
reaper *n* segador (-ra); (machine) segadora mecánica, *f*
reaping *n* siega, *f*; *fig* cosecha, *f*. **r.-machine**, segadora mecánica, *f*
reappear *vi* reaparecer
reappearance *n* reaparición, *f*
reapplication *n* nueva aplicación, *f*; (of paint, etc.) otra capa, *f*; (for a post, etc.) neuva solicitud, *f*
reapply *vt* aplicar de nuevo; (paint, etc.) dar otra capa (de); (for a post, etc.) mandar una nueva solicitud
reappoint *vt* designar de nuevo
rear *vt* (lift) alzar, levantar; (breed, educate) criar; (build) erigir, construir. *vi* (of horses) encabritarse, corcovear
rear *n* cola, *f*; parte de atrás, *f*; parte posterior, *f*; última fila, *f*; (background) fondo, *m*; *inf* trasera, *f*; *mil* retaguardia, *f*. *a* de atrás; trasero; último; posterior; de última fila, *m*; de retaguardia. **in the r.**, por detrás; a la cola; a retaguardia. **to bring up the r.**, cerrar la marcha. **r.-admiral**, contra almirante, *m*. **r.-axle**, trasero, *m*. **r.-guard**, retaguardia, *f*. **r. lamp**, faro trasero, *m*. **r. rank**, última fila, *f*. **r. view**, vista por detrás, *f*; vista posterior, *f*
rearing *n* (breeding) cría, *f*; (education) crianza, *f*
rearm *vt* rearmar. *vi* rearmarse
rearmament *n* rearmamento, *m*
rearrange *vt* volver a arreglar; arreglar de otra manera; (a literary work) refundir, adaptar
rearrangement *n* nuevo arroglo, *m*; (of a literary work) refundición, adaptación, *f*
reascend *vt* and *vi* subir de nuevo, subir otra vez; montar de nuevo (sobre)
reason *n* razón, *f*. **I have plenty of r. to . . .** No me faltarían motivos para . . . *vi* and *vt* razonar. **to r. out of**, disuadir de. **by r. of**, a causa de, con motivo de; en virtud de. **for this r.**, por esto, por esta razón. **out of all r.**, fuera de razón. **to stand to r.**, ser lógico, estar puesto en razón. **with r.**, con razón. **r. of state**, razón de estado, *f*
reasonable *a* razonable; racional
reasonableness *n* lo razonable; moderación, *f*; justicia, *f*; racionalidad, *f*
reasonably *adv* razonablemente; con razón; bastante
reasoning *n* razonamiento, *m*
reassemble *vt* reunir otra vez. *vi* juntarse de nuevo
reassert *vt* afirmar de nuevo, reiterar
reassertion *n* reiteración, *f*
reassess *vt* tasar de nuevo; repartir de nuevo; (a work of art) hacer una nueva apreciación (de)
reassessment *n* nueva tasación, *f*; nuevo repartimiento, *m*; (of a work of art) nueva estimación, *f*
reassume *vt* reasumir
reassumption *n* reasunción, *f*
reassurance *n* afirmación repetida, *f*; confianza restablecida, *f*
reassure *vt* asegurar de nuevo; tranquilizar, confortar
reassuring *a* tranquilizador, consolador
rebate *n* rebaja, *f*, descuento, *m*; reducción, *f*. *vt* rebajar, descontar; reducir. **to r. pro rata**, ratear
rebec *n* *mus* rabel, *m*

rebel *n* rebelde, *mf*, insurrecto (-ta). *vi* rebelarse, sublevarse. **r. leader,** cabecilla, *m*
rebellion *n* rebelión, *f*
rebellious *a* rebelde; revoltoso; refractario
rebelliousness *n* rebeldía, *f*
rebind *vt* atar de nuevo; (a book) reencuadernar
rebirth *n* renacimiento, *m*
rebore *vt* (an engine) descarbonizar
reboring *n* (of an engine) descarburación, *f*
reborn, to be *vi* renacer; ser reincarnado
rebound *a* (of books) reencuadernado. *vi* rebotar; repercutir; (revive) reavivarse. *n* rebote, resalto, *m*; reacción, *f*, rechazo, *m*
rebuff *n* repulsa, *f*, desaire, *m*; contrariedad, *f*. *vt* rechazar; contrariar
rebuild *vt* reedificar
rebuilding *n* reedificación, *f*
rebuke *n* reconvención, reprensión, censura, *f*, reproche, *m*, *vt* reprender, censurar, reprochar
rebukingly *adv* en tono de censura; con reprensión, con reprobación
rebut *vt* refutar
rebuttal *n* refutación, *f*
recalcitrance *n* terquedad, obstinacia, *f*; rebeldía, *f*
recalcitrant *a* reacio, recalcitrante
recall *vt* llamar; hacer volver; (dismiss) destituir; (ambassador, etc.) retirar; (remind or remember) recordar; (revoke) revocar. *n* llamada, *f*; *mil* toque de llamada, *m*; (of ambassadors, etc.) retirada, *f*; (dismissal) destitución, *f*. **beyond r.,** irrevocable; (forgotten) olvidado
recant *vt* retractar, retirar. *vi* desdecirse (de), retractarse
recantation *n* recantación, *f*
recapitulate *vt* recapitular, resumir
recapitulation *n* recapitulación, *f*
recapture *vt* volver a prender, hacer prisionero nuevamente; (a place) volver a tomar; (a ship) represar
recast *vt* (metals, a literary work) refundir; (alter) cambiar; (reckon) volver a calcular
recasting *n* (metals, a literary work) refundición, *f*
recede *vi* retroceder; alejarse (de), separarse (de); desviarse (de); retirarse; desaparecer; (diminish) disminuir; (of prices) bajar
receding *a* que retrocede, etc.
receipt *n* recibo, *m*; (for money) recibí, *m*; (recipe) receta, *f*; *pl* **receipts,** ingresos, *m pl*. *vt* firmar (or extender) recibo. **on r. of,** al recibir. **to acknowledge the r. of,** acusar recibo de. **r. book,** libro talonario, *m*
receive *vt* and *vi* recibir; admitir, aceptar; acoger; (money) percibir, cobrar; (lodge) hospedar, alojar; (contain) contener. **to be well received,** tener buena acogida
receiver *n* recibidor (-ra); (of stolen goods) receptador (-ra); (in bankruptcies) síndico, *m*; (for other legal business) receptor, *m*; (of a telephone) auricular, *m*; *elec* receptor, *m*; *rad* radiorreceptor, *m*. **to hang up (the r.),** colgar (el auricular)
receivership *n* sindicatura, *f*; receptoría, *f*
receiving *n* recibimiento, *m*; (of money, etc.) cobranza, *f*, percibo, *m*; (of stolen goods) encubrimiento, *m*. *a* que recibe; recipiente; de recepción. **r. set,** aparato de radio, *m*
recency *n* lo reciente; novedad, *f*
recent *a* reciente; nuevo. **in r. years,** en estos últimos años
recently *adv* recientemente; (before past participles) recién. **until r.,** hasta hace poco. **r. painted,** recién pintado
receptacle *n* receptáculo, recipiente, *m*; *bot* receptáculo, *m*
reception *n* recepción, *f*; recibo, *m*; (welcome) acogida, *f*; (of evidence) recepción, *f*. **r. room,** pieza de recibo, *f*, gabinete, *m*
receptive *a* receptivo; susceptible
receptiveness *n* sensibilidad, susceptibilidad, *f*
recess *n* (holiday) vacaciones, *f pl*; (during school hours) hora de recreo, *f*; (fig heart) seno, *m*, entrañas,

f pl; (of the soul, heart) hondón, *m*; (in a coastline, etc.) depresión, *f*; (in a wall) nicho, *m*; (alcove) alcoba, *f*.
parliamentary r., interregno parlamentario, *m*
recessional *n* himno que se canta mientras se retiran los eclesiásticos y el coro, *m*
recharge *vt* (a gun, etc.) recargar; acusar de nuevo
recipe *n* receta, *f*
recipient *n* recibidor (-ra); el, *m*, (*f*, la) que recibe. *a* recipiente; receptivo
reciprocal *a* recíproco
reciprocate *vt* reciprocar; *mech* producir movimiento de vaivén. *vi mech* oscilar, tener movimiento alternativo; corresponder; ser recíproco
reciprocation *n* reciprocación, *f*; reciprocidad, correspondencia, *f*
reciprocity *n* reciprocidad, *f*
recital *n* narración, relación, *f*; enumeración, *f*; recitación, *f*; *mus* recital, *m*
recitation *n* recitación, *f*
recitative *n* recitado, *m*
recite *vt* recitar, repetir; narrar; declamar. *vi* decir una recitación
reciter *n* recitador (-ra); declamador (-ra)
reckless *a* temerario, audaz; precipitado; descuidado (de); indiferente (a); excesivo; imprudente
recklessly *adv* temerariamente; descuidadamente; imprudentemente
recklessness *n* temeridad, audacia, *f*; descuido, *m*; imprudencia, *f*; indiferencia, *f*
reckon *vt* calcular, computar; contar; enumerar; (believe) considerar, juzgar; (attribute) atribuir; (think) creer (que). **to r. up,** echar cuentas, calcular. **to r. with,** contar con; tomar en serio
reckoner *n* calculador (-ra). **ready r.,** tablas matemáticas, *f pl*
reckoning *n* cálculo, *m*, calculación, *f*; cuenta, *f*; *fig* retribución, *f*, castigo, *m*; *naut* estima, *f*. **the day of r.,** el día de ajuste de cuentas; el día del juicio final. **to be out in one's r.,** equivocarse en el cálculo; engañarse en el juicio
reclaim *vt* (land) entarquinar; (reform) reformar; (tame) domesticar; (claim) reclamar; (restore) restaurar
reclamation *n* (of land) entarquinamiento, *m*; cultivo, *m*; (reform) reformación, *f*; (restoration) restauración, *f*; (claiming) reclamación, *f*
recline *vt* apoyar; recostar; reclinar; descansar, reposar. *vi* recostarse, reclinarse; estar tumbado; apoyarse; descansar
reclining *n* reclinación, *f*. *a* inclinado; acostado; (of statues) yacente
recluse *a* solitario, *n* recluso (-sa); solitario (-ia); ermitaño, *m*, anacoreta, *mf*
recognition *n* reconocimiento, *m*
recognizable *a* que puede reconocerse; identificable
recognizance *n* reconocimiento, *m*; *law* obligación, *f*
recognize *vt* reconocer; confesar
recoil *n* reculada, *f*; (of a gun) culatazo, *m*; (refusal) rechazo, *m*; (result) repercusión, *f*; (repugnance) aversión, repugnancia, *f*. *vi* recular; retroceder; repercutir; sentir repugnancia
recoin *vt* acuñar de nuevo
recollect *vt* acordarse de, recordar. **to r. oneself,** reponerse, recobrarse
recollection *n* recuerdo, *m*, memoria, *f*
recommence *vt* and *vi* empezar de nuevo
recommend *vt* recomendar; aconsejar; encargar
recommendable *a* recomendable
recommendation *n* recomendación, *f*
recommendatory *a* recomendatario
recommender *n* el, *m*, (*f*, la) que recomienda
recompense *n* recompensa, *f*, *vt* recompensar
recomposition *n* recomposición, *f*
reconcilability *n* posibilidad de reconciliación, *f*; compatibilidad, *f*
reconcilable *a* reconciliable; compatible; conciliable
reconcile *vt* reconciliar; (quarrels) componer, ajustar;

(opposing theories, etc.) conciliar. **to r. oneself (to),** aceptar; acostumbrarse (a); resignarse (a)
reconciler *n* reconciliador (-ra)
reconciliation *n* reconciliación, *f*; (of theories, etc.) conciliación, *f*
reconciliatory *a* reconciliador
recondite *a* recóndito
recondition *vt* reacondicionar
reconnaissance *n* reconocimiento, *m*; exploración, *f*. **r. flight,** vuelo de reconocimiento, *m*. **r. plane,** avión de reconocimiento, *m*
reconnoiter *vt mil* reconocer; explorar. *vi mil* practicar un reconocimiento; correr la campaña
reconnoitering *n* reconocimiento, *m*, *a* de reconocimiento
reconquer *vt* reconquistar
reconquest *n* reconquista, *f*
reconsecrate *vt* consagrar de nuevo
reconsider *vt* considerar de nuevo, volver a considerar; volver a discutir
reconsideration *n* nueva consideración, *f*; nueva discusión, *f*
reconstitute *vt* reconstituir
reconstitution *n* reconstitución, *f*
reconstruct *vt* reconstruir
reconstruction *n* reconstrucción, *f*
reconversion *n* reconversión, *f*
recopy *vt* copiar de nuevo
record *vt* apuntar; inscribir; (recount) contar, escribir; recordar; registrar; (of thermometers, etc.) marcar, registrar; hacer un disco de gramófono de; (radio, cinema) impresionar. *n* relación, *f*; crónica, *f*; historia, *f*; (soldier's) hoja de servicios, *f*; (past) antecedentes, *m pl*; documento, *m*; inscripción, *f*; (entry) partida, *f*; testimonio, *m*; (memory) recuerdo, *m*; registro, *m*; (gramophone) disco de gramófono, *m*; *sport* record, *m*, plusmarca, *f*; *pl* records, *m pl*; (notes) notas, *f pl*; (facts) datos, *m pl*; anales, *m pl*. **keeper of the records,** archivero, *m*. **off the r.,** confidencialmente. **on r.,** escrito; registrado; inscrito en los anales de la historia. **to break a r.,** supremar precedentes. **r.-holder,** plusmarquista, *mf*
recorder *n* registrador, *m*; archivero, *m*; *law* juez, *m*; (historian) historiador, *m*; *mus* caramillo, *m*; *mech* contador, indicador, *m*; (scientific) aparato registrador, *m*
recording *a* registrador. **r. apparatus,** (cinema, radio, gramophone) máquina de impresionar, *f*; (scientific) aparato registrador, *m*. **r. van,** carro de sonido, *m*
recount *vt* contar de nuevo; (tell) referir, narrar, contar
recoup *vt* compensar, indemnizar; recobrar, desquitarse de
recourse *n* recurso, *m*. **to have r. to,** recurrir, *a*
recover *vt* (regain) recobrar; *fig* reconquistar; (retrieve) rescatar; *law* reivindicar. *vi* reponerse; (in health) recobrar la salud, sanar, curarse; *law* ganar un pleito. **to r. consciousness,** volver en sí
recoverable *a* recuperable
recovery *n* (regaining) recobro, *m*, recuperación, *f*; (of money) cobranza, *f*; (retrieval) rescate, *m*; *fig* reconquista, *f*; (from illness) mejoría, convalecencia, *f*; restablecimiento, *m*; *law* reivindicación, *f*
recreant *a* traidor, falso, desleal. *n* apóstata, *mf* traidor (-ra)
recreate *vt* recrear
recreation *n* recreación, *f*; (break in schools) recreo, *m*. **r. hall,** sala de recreo, *f*
recreative *a* recreativo
recriminate *vi* recriminar
recrimination *n* recriminación, reconvención, *f*
recriminator *n* recriminador (-ra)
recriminatory *a* recriminador
recross *vt* volver a cruzar, cruzar de nuevo
recrudesce *vi* recrudecer
recrudescence *n* recrudescencia, *f*
recrudescent *a* recrudescente
recruit *n* recluta, *m*. *vt* reclutar; (restore) reponer

recruiting *n* reclutamiento, *m*. **r. office,** caja de reclutamiento, *f*
recruiting flag *n* bandera de enganche, *f*
rectal *a* rectal
rectangle *n* rectángulo, *m*
rectangular *a* rectangular
rectifiable *a* rectificable
rectification *n* rectificación, *f*
rectifier *n* rectificador, *m*
rectify *vt* rectificar
rectilinear *a* rectilíneo
rectitude *n* rectitud, *f*
rector *n* (of a university or school) rector, *m*; (priest) párroco, *m*
rectorship *n* rectorado, *m*
rectory *n* rectoral, rectoría, *f*
rectum *n* recto, *m*
recumbent *a* recostado, reclinado; (of a statue) yacente
recuperable *a* recuperable
recuperate *vt* recuperar, recobrar. *vi* restablecerse, reponerse; recuperarse
recuperation *n* recuperación, *f*
recuperative *a* recuperativo
recur *vi* presentarse a la imaginación; volver (sobre); presentarse de nuevo, aparecer otra vez; repetirse; reproducirse
recurrence *n* reaparición, *f*; repetición, *f*
recurrent *a* periódico; *med* recurrente
red *a* rojo; (of wine) tinto. *n* color rojo, *m*; (in billiards) mingo, *m*, bola roja, *f*; *pol* rojo, *m*. **to catch red-handed,** coger con el hurto en las manos; coger con las manos en la masa, coger en el acto. **to grow red,** enrojecerse, ponerse rojo; volverse rojo. **red-berried,** con bayas rojas. **red cabbage,** lombarda, *f*. **red cedar,** cedro dulce, *m*. **red corpuscle,** glóbulo rojo, *m*. **Red Cross,** Cruz Roja, *f*. **red currant,** grosella, *f*. **red currant bush,** grosellero, *m*. **red-eyed,** con los ojos inyectados. **red fir,** pino silvestre, *m*. **red flush,** (in the sky) arrebol, *m*. **red-gold,** bermejo; (of hair, etc.) rojo. **red-haired,** pelirrojo, de pelo rojo. **red-handed,** con las manos ensangrentadas; *fig* en el acto. **red-head** (person) pelirrojo (-ja). **red-heat,** incandescencia, *f*. **red-hot,** candente. *m*. **red-lead,** minio, *m*. **red-letter,** de fiesta; extraordinario. **red-letter day,** día de fiesta, *m*; día extraordinario, *m*. **red mullet,** salmonete, *m*, trilla, *f*. **red ocher,** almagre, *m*. **red pepper,** pimiento, *m*; (cayenne) pimentón, *m*, **Red Sea,** mar Rojo, mar Bermejo, *m*. **red tape,** balduque, *m*; formulismo, *m*; burocracia, *f*. **red wine,** vino tinto, *m*
redbreast *n* petirrojo, *m*
redden *vt* rojear, enrojecer; pintar de rojo. *vi* enrojecerse, ponerse rojo; volverse rojo
reddish *a* rojizo
redeem *vt* (a mortgage, bonds, etc.) amortizar; (from pawn) desempeñar; (a promise, etc.) cumplir; libertar; redimir; compensar; (a fault) expiar; (reform) reformar; (rescue) rescatar
redeemable *a* redimible; amortizable
redeemer *n* rescatador (-ra); salvador (-ra); *theol* Redentor, *m*
redeeming *a* redentor; compensatorio. **r. feature,** compensación, *f*; rasgo bueno, *m*. **There is no r. feature in his work,** No hay nada bueno en su obra
redemption *n* (of a mortgage, etc.) amortización, *f*; (from pawn) desempeño, *m*; (of a promise, etc.) cumplimiento, *m*; (ransom, etc.) rescate, *m*; *theol* redención, *f*; compensación, *f*; (of a fault) expiación, *f*; reformación, *f*
redemptive *a* redentor
redescend *vi* bajar de nuevo
rediscovery *n* nuevo descubrimiento, *m*
redistribute *vt* distribuir de nuevo, volver a distribuir
redistribution *n* nueva distribución, *f*
redness *n* rojez, *f*, color rojo, *m*
redolent *a* fragante, oloroso; *fig* evocador (de)
redouble *vt* redoblar. *vi* redoblarse

redoubling *n* redoblamiento, *m*
redoubt *n* reducto, *m*
redoubtable *a* formidable, terrible; valiente
redound *vi* redundar (en)
redress *vt* rectificar; reparar; remediar; hacer justicia (a); corregir
reduce *vt* reducir; disminuir; (in price) rebajar; abreviar; (exhaust, weaken) agotar; (impoverish) empobrecer; (degrade) degradar. **to r. to the ranks,** *mil* volver a las filas; degradar. **to be in reduced circumstances,** estar en la indigencia
reducible *a* reducible
reduction *n* reducción, *f*; (in price) rebaja, *f*
redundance *n* redundancia, *f*
redundant *a* redundante; superfluo, excesivo
reduplicate *vt* reduplicar
reduplication *n* reduplicación, *f*
reecho *vt* repetir; devolver el son de, hacer reverberar. *vi* repercutirse, reverberar
reed *n bot* caña, *f*; (arrow) saeta, *f*; (pipe) caramillo, *m*; (in wind-instruments) lengüeta, *f*; *arch* junquillo, *m*; (in a loom) peine, *m*; (pastoral poetry) poesía bucólica, *f*. *vt* (thatch) bardar con cañas
reedit *vt* reeditar, volver a editar
reedy *a* juncoso, lleno de cañas; (of the voice) silbante
reef *n* arrecife, escollo, encalladero, *m*; *min* filón, *m*; *naut* rizo, *m*. *vt naut* arrizar. **to take in reefs,** *naut* hacer el rizo. **r.-knot,** nudo de marino, *m*
reek *n* humo, *m*; olor, *m*. *vi* humear; oler (de); *fig* recordar, hacer pensar (en)
reeky *a* humoso
reel *n* carrete, *m*; devanadera, *f*; (of a fishing rod) carrete, carretel, *m*; (cinema) cinta, *f*; (dance) baile escocés, *m*. *vt* devanar. *vi* tambalear, titubear; (of ships, etc.) cabecear; temblar; oscilar. **to r. about drunkenly,** (of persons) andar haciendo eses, arrimarse a las paredes. **to r. off,** recitar; enumerar; decir rápidamente
reelect *vt* reelegir
reelection *n* reelección, *f*
reeligible *a* reelegible
reeling *n* tambaleo, *m*; andar vacilante, *m*; (of a ship, etc.) cabeceo, *m*; oscilación, *f*
reembarcation *n* reembarque, *m*
reembark *vt* reembarcar. *vi* reembarcarse
reemerge *vi* reaparecer
reemergence *n* reaparición, *f*
reenact *vt* revalidar (una ley); decretar de nuevo
reenactment *n* revalidación (de una ley), *f*; nuevo decreto, *m*
reengage *vt* contratar de nuevo
reengagement *n* nuevo contrato, *m*
reenlist *vt* and *vi* alistar(se) de nuevo
reenlistment *n* reenganche, *m*
reenter *vt* volver a entrar (en); reingresar (en)
reentry *n* segunda entrada, *f*, reingreso, *m*
reequip *vt* equipar de nuevo
reestablish *vt* restablecer; restaurar
reestablishment *n* restablecimiento, *m*; restauración, *f*
reeve *vt naut* laborear, guarnir
reexamination *n* reexaminación, *f*; nuevo examen, *m*; *law* nuevo interrogatorio, *m*
reexamine *vt* reexaminar; *law* interrogar de nuevo
reexport *vt* reexportar
reexportation *n* reexportación, *f*
refashion *vt* volver a hacer; formar de nuevo
refection *n* refección, *f*
refectory *n* refectorio, *m*
refer *vt* atribuir (a); (send) enviar, remitir; (assign) referir (a), relacionar (con). *vi* referirse (a); aludir (a); hablar (de)
referee *n* árbitro, *m*; *law* juez arbitrador, *m*; (reference) garante, *mf* fiador (-ra). *vi* servir de árbitro
reference *n* referencia, *f*; consulta, *f*; mención, *f*; alusión, *f*; (relation) relación, *f*; *pl* **references,** *com* referencias, *f pl*. **for r.,** para consulta. **in r. to,** con

referencia a, respecto a, en cuanto a. **terms of r.,** puntos de consulta, *m pl.* **work of r.,** libro de consulta, *m*
reference book *n* libro de consulta, *m*
referendum *n* referéndum, *m*
refill *vt* rellenar; rehenchir; (pen) llenar de nuevo con tinta. *n* (for a pencil) mina de recambio, *f*
refine *vt* refinar; (metals) acrisolar; (fats) clarificar; *fig* perfeccionar, pulir, refinar
refined *a* refinado; fino; culto; cortés; elegante; delicado; (subtle) sutil; (affected) afectado
refinement *n* refinamiento, *m*; finura, *f*; cultura, *f*; cortesía, *f*; elegancia, *f*; delicadeza, *f*; (subtlety) sutileza, *f*; (affectation) afectación, *f*
refiner *n* refinador, *m*
refinery *n* refinería, *f*
refining *n* refinación, *f*; *fig* refinamiento, *m*
refit *vt* reparar; *naut* embonar
refitting *n* reparación, *f*; *naut* embonada, *f*
reflect *vt* reflejar; reflexionar. *vi* reflejar; reflexionar (sobre), pensar (en), meditar (sobre). **This offer reflects credit on him,** Esta oferta le hace honor. **to r. on, upon,** reflexionar sobre; (disparage) desacreditar; (affect unfavorably) perjudicar
reflecting *a* reflector
reflection *n phys* reflexión, *f*; reflejo, *m*; consideración, *f*, pensamiento, *m*; (aspersion) censura, *f*, reproche, *m*. **upon mature r.,** después de pensarlo bien
reflective *a phys* reflector; reflexivo, pensativo, meditabundo
reflectively *adv* reflexivamente
reflector *n* reflector, *m*; (shade) pantalla, *f*
reflex *a* reflejo. *n* reflejo, *m*; acción refleja, *f*. **r. action,** acción refleja, *f*
refloat *vt* (a ship) poner otra vex a flote, desvarar
reflux *n* reflujo, *m*
reform *n* reforma, *f*. *a* de reforma; reformista. *vt* reformar; formar de nuevo. *vi* reformarse
reformation *n* reformación, *f*; **Reformation,** Reforma, *f*
reformatory *a* reformatorio, reformador. *n* reformatorio, *m*, casa de corrección, *f*
reformer *n* reformador (-ra), reformista, *mf*
refract *vt* refractar
refraction *n* refracción, *f*
refractive *a* refringente
refractoriness *n* terquedad, obstinacia, *f*; rebeldía, indocilidad, *f*
refractory *a* (of substances) refractario; recalcitrante, intratable, rebelde
refrain *n* estribillo, estrambote, *m*
refrain *vi* abstenerse (de), evitar
refresh *vt* refrescar
refreshing *a* refrescante; atractivo; estimulante; interesante
refreshment *n* (solace) solaz, reposo, *m*; recreación, *f*, deleite, *m*; (food and (or) drink) refresco, *m*. **r.-room,** (at a station) fonda, *f*
refrigerate *vt* refrigerar; enfriar; refrescar
refrigeration *n* refrigeración, *f*; enfriamiento, *m*. **r. chamber,** cámara frigorífica, *f*
refrigerative *a* refrigerante, frigorífico
refrigerator *n* refrigerador, *m*, nevera, *f*
refringent *a* refringente
refuel *vt* (a furnace) cargar con carbón, etc.; (of a ship) tomar carbón; (of an airplane, motor vehicle) tomar bencina
refuge *n* refugio, *m*; asilo, *m*; (resort) recurso, *m*; subterfugio, *m*; (traffic island) refugio para peatones, *m*. **to take r.,** refugiarse; resguardarse (de)
refugee *n* refugiado, *m*. *n* refugiado (-da)
refulgence *n* refulgencia, *f*
refulgent *a* refulgente
refund *vt* reembolsar; devolver
refunding *n* reembolso, *m*; devolución, *f*
refurbish *vt* restaurar; renovar; (a literary work) refundir

refurnish *vt* amueblar de nuevo
refusal *n* negativa, *f*; (rejection) rechazo, *m*; (option) opción, *f*; preferencia, *f*
refuse *vt* negar; (reject) rechazar. *vi* negarse (a), rehusar; (of a horse) resistirse a saltar
refuse *n* desecho, *m*; desperdicios, *m pl*; residuo, *m*; basura, *f. a de* desecho. **r. dump,** muladar, *m*
refutable *a* refutable
refutation *n* refutación, *f*
refute *vt* refutar
regain *vt* recobrar, recuperar; cobrar; ganar de nuevo; *fig* reconquistar. **to r. one's breath,** cobrar aliento. **to r. consciousness,** volver en sí
regal *a* regio, real
regale *vt* regalar, agasajar; recrear, deleitar
regalia *n* regalía, *f*; insignias reales, *f pl*; distintivos, *m pl*, insignias, *f pl*
regally *adv* regiamente
regard *vt* mirar; observar; considerar; (respect) respetar; (concern) importar, concernir; relacionarse con. *n* mirada, *f*; atención, *f*; (esteem) aprecio, *m*, estimación, *f*; respeto, *m*; veneración, *f*; (relation) referencia, *f*; *pl* **regards,** recuerdos, saludos, *m pl*. **He has little r. for their feelings,** Le importan poco sus susceptibilidades. **With kindest regards,** Con mis saludos más afectuosos. **as regards, with r. to,** con referencia a, respecto a, en cuanto a
regardful *a* atento (a), cuidadoso (de); que se preocupa (de)
regarding *prep* tocante a, en cuanto a, respecto de
regardless *a* negligente (de); indiferente (a), insensible (a); que no se interesa (en); que no se inqueta (por); sin preocuparse (de)
regatta *n* regata, *f*
regency *n* regencia, *f*
regeneracy *n* regeneración, *f*
regenerate *vt* regenerar. *a* regenerado
regeneration *n* regeneración, *f*
regenerative *a* regenerador
regenerator *n* regenerador (-ra)
regent *n* regente, *mf*
régime *n* régimen, *m*
regimen *n* (*gram med*) régimen, *m*,
regiment *n* regimiento, *m*. *vt* regimentar. **r. of the line,** tropa de línea, *f*
regimental *a* de (un) regimiento, perteneciente a un regimiento
regimentation *n* regimentación, *f*
region *n* región, *f*
regional *a* regional
regionalism *n* regionalismo, *m*
regionalist *n* regionalista, *mf*
regionalistic *a* regionalista
register *n* (record and *mech mus print*) registro, *m*; (of ships, etc.) matrícula, *f*; lista, *f*. *vt* registrar; matricular; (a ship) abanderar; inscribir; (one's child in a school) anotar (Argentina), inscribir; (of thermometers, etc.) marcar; (letters) certificar; (luggage) facturar; (in one's mind) grabar; (emotion) mostrar, manifestar. *vi* (at a hotel, etc.) registrarse; *print* estar en registro. **cash r.,** caja registradora, *f*. **r. of births, marriages and deaths,** registro civil, *m*
registered letter *n* carta certificada, *f*
registrar *n* registrador, *m*; archivero, *m*; secretario, *m*; (of a school) jefe de inscripciones, secretario general (the latter has many more duties). **r. of births, marriages and deaths,** secretario del registro civil, *m*.
registrar's office, oficina del registro civil, *f*
registration *n* registro, *m*; inscripción, *f*; (of a vehicle, etc.) matrícula, *f*; *naut* abanderamiento, *m*; (of a letter, etc.) certificación, *f*. **r. number,** número de matrícula, *m*
registry *n* registro, *m*; inscripción, *f*; matrícula, *f*. **r. office,** oficina del registro civil, *f*; (for servants) agencia doméstica, *m*
regression *n* regresión, *f*, retroceso, *m*

regret *vt* sentir; lamentar, pesar; arrepentirse (de); (miss) echar de menos (a). *n* sentimiento, pesar, *m*; (remorse) remordimiento, *m*. **I r. very much that ... , Me pesa mucho que ... , Siento mucho que ... to send one's regrets,** mandar sus excusas
regretful *a* lleno de pesar; arrepentido; lamentable, deplorable. **He was most r. that ... ,** Lamentaba mucho que ...
regretfully *adv* con pesar
regrettable *a* lamentable, deplorable; doloroso; (with loss, etc.) sensible
regrettably *adv* lamentablemente; sensiblemente
regroup *vt* arreglar de nuevo; formar de nuevo; reorganizar
regular *a* regular; normal; (ordinary) corriente, común; (in order) en regla; (*gram bot ecc mil geom*) regular. *n ecc* regular, *m*; (soldier) soldado de línea, *m*; (officer) militar de carrera, *m*; (client) parroquiano habitual, *m*
regularity *n* regularidad,
regularization *n* regularización, *f*
regularize *vt* regularizar
regularly *adv* regularmente
regulate *vt* regular; ajustar, arreglar; (direct) dirigir; reglamentar
regulation *n* regulación, *f*; arreglo, *m*; (rule) reglamento, *m*, *a* de reglamento; normal
regulative *a* regulador
regulator *n mech* regulador, *m*
regurgitate *vt* and *vi* regurgitar
regurgitation *n* regurgitación, *f*
rehabilitate *vt* rehabilitar
rehabilitation *n* rehabilitación, *f*
rehash *vt* (a literary work, etc.) refundir
rehearing *n* nueva audición, *f*, (of a case) revisión, *f*
rehearsal *n theat* ensayo, *m*; recitación, *f*; relación, narración, *f*. **dress r.,** ensayo general, *m*
rehearse *vt theat* ensayar; recitar; (narrate) narrar; enumerar
reheat *vt* recalentar
reign *n* reinado, *m*. *vi* reinar; predominar
reigning *a* reinante; predominante
reimburse *vt* reembolsar
reimbursement *n* reembolso, *m*
reimport *vt* importar de nuevo, reimportar, *n* reimporte, *m*
reimportation *n* reimportación, *f*
reimpose *vt* reimponer
reimposition *n* reimposición, *f*
reimprison *vt* encarcelar de nuevo, reencarcelar
reimprisonment *n* reencarcelamiento, *m*
rein *n* rienda, *f. vt* llevar las riendas (de); (hold back) refrenar. **to give r. to,** *fig* dar rienda suelta (a)
reincarnation *n* reencarnación, *f*
reincorporate *vt* reincorporar
reincorporation *n* reincorporación, *f*
reindeer *n* reno, *m*
reinforce *vt* reforzar; (concrete) armar; fortalecer. **reinforced concrete,** *n* hormigón armado, *m*
reinforcement *n* reforzamiento, *m*; (*mil nav fig*) refuerzo, *m*
reins. *n* See **rein**
reinsert *vt* volver a insertar
reinstall *vt* reinstalar; rehabilitar
reinstalment *n* reinstalación, *f*; rehabilitación, *f*; restablecimiento, *m*
reinstate *vt* reponer, restablecer; reinstalar; rehabilitar
reinstatement *n* restablecimiento, *m*; rehabilitación, *f*
reinsurance *n* reaseguro, *m*
reinsure *vt* reasegurar
reintegrate *vt* reintegrar
reintegration *n* reintegración, *f*
reinter *vt* enterrar de nuevo
reinvest *vt* reinvertir
reinvestment *n* reinversión, *f*
reinvigorate *vt* reanimar, dar nuevo vigor (a)
reinvite *vt* invitar de nuevo (a)

reissue *n* nueva emisión, *f*; (of a book, etc.) nueva edición, reimpresión, *f. vt* hacer una nueva emisión (de); reeditar, publicar de nuevo
reiterate *vt* reiterar, repetir
reiteration *n* reiteración, *f*
reiterative *a* reiterativo
reject *vt* rechazar, rehusar; repudiar; repulsar; desechar
rejection *n* rechazamiento, *m*; repudiación, refutación, *f*; repulsa, *f*
rejoice *vt* alegrar, regocijar. *vi* alegrarse (de), regocijarse (de), gloriarse (en)
rejoicing *n* regocijo, júbilo, *m*, alegría, *f*; algazara, *f*, fiestas, *f pl*
rejoin *vt* and *vi* juntar de nuevo; volver a; reunirse con; (reply) contestar, replicar
rejoinder *n* contestación, respuesta, *f*
rejuvenate *vt* rejuvenecer
rejuvenation *n* rejuvenecimiento, *m*
rekindle *vt* encender de nuevo; despertar, reavivar. *vi* encenderse de nuevo; reavivarse
relapse *n* reincidencia, recaída, *f*; *med* recidiva, *f. vi* reincidir (en); *med* recaer
relapsed *a* relapso
relate *vt* (recount) relatar, narrar; relacionar; unir; (of kinship) emparentar. *vi* ajustarse (a); referirse (a). **The first fact is not related to the second,** El primer hecho no tiene nada que ver con el segundo
related *a* relacionado; (by kinship) emparentado. **John is well-r.,** Juan es de buena familia; Juan es de familia influyente; Juan tiene buenas relaciones
relater *n* narrador (-ra)
relation *n* (narrative) relación, narración, *f*; conexión, *f*; relación, *f*; (kinship) parentesco, *m*; (person) pariente (-ta). **in r. to,** con relación a, en cuanto a
relationship *n* parentesco, *m*; conexión, relación, *f*
relative *a* relativo. *n* pariente (-ta); *pl* **relatives,** parientes, *m pl*, parentela, *f*
relativism *n* relativismo, *m*
relativity *n* relatividad, *f*
relator *n law* relator, *f*
relax *vt* relajar; aflojar; soltar; (make less severe) ablandar; (decrease) mitigar. *vi* relajarse; aflojar; (rest) descansar
relaxation *n* relajación, *f*; aflojamiento, *m*; ablandamiento, *m*; mitigación, *f*; (rest) descanso, reposo, *m*; (pastime) pasatiempo, *m*; (amusement) diversión, *f*
relaxing *a* relajante; (of climate) enervante
relay *n* (of horses) parada, *f*; (shift) tanda, *f*; relevo, *m*; *elec* relais, *m*; *rad* redifusión, *f. vt* enviar por posta; *elec* reemitir; *rad* retransmitir; (lay again) colocar de nuevo. **r. race,** carrera de equipo, carrera de relevos, *f*
release *vt* soltar; (hurl) lanzar; (set free) poner en libertad (a); librar (de); absolver; (surrender) renunciar (a); dar al público, poner en circulación; (lease again) realquilar. *n* soltura, *f*; lanzamiento, *m*; liberación, *f*; (from pain) alivio, *m*; remisión, *f*; exoneración, *f*; publicación, *f*; (of films) representación, *f*; *law* soltura, *f*
relegate *vt* relegar
relegation *n* relegación, *f*
relent *vi* ablandarse, enternecerse; ceder
relenting *n* enternecimiento, desenojo, *m*
relentless *a* implacable, inexorable; despiadado
relentlessly *adv* inexorablemente; sin piedad
relentlessness *n* inexorabilidad, *f*; falta de piedad, *f*
relet *vt* realquilar
relevance *n* conexión, *f*; pertinencia, *f*; aplicabilidad, *f*
relevant *a* relativo; pertinente, a propósito, oportuno; aplicable
reliability *n* seguridad, *f*; formalidad, *f*; confianza, *f*; exactitud, *f*; veracidad, *f*
reliable *a* seguro; formal; digno de crédito, de confianza, solvente digno de confianza; exacto; veraz
reliably *adv* seguramente; de una manera digna de confianza; exactamente
reliance *n* confianza, *f*. **to place r. on,** tener confianza en

reliant *a* confiado
relic *n* vestigio, rastro, *m*; *ecc* reliquia, *f*
relict *n* viuda, *f*
relief *n* (alleviation) alivio, *m*; desahogo, *m*; (help) socorro, *m*, ayuda, *f*; beneficencia, *f*; *mil* relevo, *m*; (pleasure) placer, *m*, satisfacción, *f*; (consolation) consuelo, *m*; *law* remisión, *f*; *art* relieve, *m*. **high r.,** alto relieve, *m*. **low r.,** bajo relieve, *m*. **r. map,** mapa en relieve, *m*. **r. train,** tren de socorro, *m*
relieve *vt* aliviar; aligerar, suavizar; mitigar; (one's feelings, etc.) desahogar; (*mil* and to take the place of) relevar; (free) librar; (dismiss) destituir; (remove) quitar; (rob) robar; (help) socorrer, remediar; (redeem) redimir; (ornament) adornar; (from a wrong) hacer justicia (a)
relieving *n* alivio, *m*; aligeramiento, *m*; mitigación, *f*; (of the feelings) desahogo, *m*; *mil* relevo, *m*; (help) socorro, *m*. **r. arch,** sobrearco, *m*
relight *vt* volver a encender. *vi* encenderse de nuevo
religion *n* religión, *f*
religiosity *n* religiosidad, *f*
religious *a* religioso; en religión; piadoso, creyente; devoto. *n* religioso (-sa). **r. orders,** órdenes religiosas, *f pl*. **r. toleration,** libertad de cultos, *f*
religiousness *n* religiosidad, *f*
relinquish *vt* abandonar; (one's grip) soltar; renunciar; desistir (de), dejar (de); (a post) dimitir (de)
relinquishment *n* abandono, *m*; renuncia, *f*; dejamiento, *m*; (of a post) dimisión, *f*
reliquary *n* relicario, *m*
relish *n* gusto, *m*; sabor, *m*; (touch, smack) dejo, *m*; condimento, *m*; apetito, *m*, gana, *f. vt* gustar de; comer con apetito; saborear, paladear; *fig* seducir, atraer, gustar. *vi* tener gusto (de). **I do not much r. the idea,** No me seduce la idea
relishing *n* saboreo, *m*; (enjoyment) goce, *m*, fruición, *f*; consideración, *f*
relive *vt* vivir de nuevo, volver a vivir
reload *vt* recargar
reluctance *n* repugnancia, desgana, *f*. **with r.,** a regañadientes, de mala gana
reluctant *a* poco dispuesto (a), que tiene repugnancia a (hacer algo), sin gana (a); (forced) forzado; artificial; (hesitating) vacilante
reluctantly *adv* de mala gana, con repugnancia, a disgusto
rely on *vi* contar con, confiar en, depender de
remain *vi* quedar; permanecer; (be left over) sobrar; continuar. **I r. yours faithfully . . . ,** (in a letter) Queda de Vd. su att. s.s. . . . **It remains to be written,** Queda por escribir
remainder *n* resto, *m*; restos, *m pl*, sobras, *f pl*; residuo, *m*. **The r. of the people went away,** Los demás se marcharon
remaining *pres. part* and *a* que queda; sobrante
remains *n pl* restos, *m pl*; sobras, *f pl*, desperdicios, *m pl*; ruinas, *f pl*
remake *vt* rehacer; reformar
remand *vt law* reencarcelar. *n law* reencarcelamiento, *m*
remark *n* observación, *f*; nota, *f*; comentario, *m*. *vt* and *vi* observar; notar. **to r. on,** comentar, hacer una observación sobre
remarkable *a* notable, singular, extraordinario
remarkableness *n* singularidad, *f*, lo extraordinario
remarkably *adv* singularmente
remarriage *n* segundas nupcias, *f pl*, segundo casamiento, *m*
remarry *vt* volver a casar (a). *vi* casarse en segundas nupcias; volver a casarse
remediable *a* remediable
remedial *a* remediador; curativo, terapéutico
remedy *n* remedio, *m*; recurso, *m*, *vt* remediar; curar
remember *vt* recordar; tener presente; acordarse de. *vi* acordarse; no olvidarse. **R. me to your mother,** Dale recuerdos míos a tu madre. **If I r. rightly . . . ,** Si bien

me acuerdo... **And r. that I shall do no more!** ¡Y no olvides que no haré más!

remembrance *n* recuerdo, *m*; memoria, *f*; *pl* **remembrances,** recuerdos, *m pl*

remind *vt* recordar

reminder *n* recuerdo, *m*; (warning) advertencia, *f*. **a gentle r.,** una indirecta, una insinuación

reminisce *vi inf* recordar viejas historias

reminiscence *n* reminiscencia, *f*, recuerdo, *m*

reminiscent *a* evocador, que recuerda; de reminiscencia; que piensa en el pasado. **to be r. of,** recordar; *inf* oler a

reminiscently *adv* evocadoramente, como si recordara

remiss *a* negligente, descuidado

remission *n* remisión, *f*

remissly *adv* negligentemente

remissness *n* negligencia, *f*, descuido, *m*

remit *vt* remitir; *com* remesar, enviar. *vi* (pay) pagar

remittance *n* remesa, *f*, envío, *m*

remitter *n* remitente, *mf*

remnant *n* resto, *m*; (of fabric) retal, retazo, *m*; (relic) vestigio, *m*, reliquia, *f*. **r. sale,** saldo, *m*

remodel *vt* rehacer; reformar; modelar de nuevo; (a play, etc.) refundir

remodeling *n* reformación, *f*; (of a play, etc.) refundición, *f*

remonstrance *n* protesta, *f*; reconvención, *f*

remonstrate *vi* protestar, objetar. **to r. with,** reprochar, reconvenir

remorse *n* remordimiento, *m*

remorseful *a* lleno de remordimientos; penitente, arrepentido

remorsefully *adv* con remordimiento

remorseless *a* sin conciencia, sin remordimientos; despiadado, inflexible

remorselessness *n* inexorabilidad, crueldad, dureza, *f*

remote *a* distante, lejano; remoto; aislado; ajeno; (slight) leve, vago. **r. control,** mando a distancia, *m*

remotely *adv* remotamente

remoteness *n* distancia, *f*; aislamiento, *m*; alejamiento, *m*; (vagueness) vaguedad, *f*

remount *vt* subir de nuevo, montar de nuevo; *mil* remontar. *vi* (go back to) remontar (a), derivarse (de). *n* mil remonta, *f*

removable *a* que puede quitarse; (of collars, etc.) de quita y pon; transportable; (of officials, etc.) amovible

removal *n* acción de quitar o levantar, *f*; sacamiento, *m*; separación, *f*; eliminación, *f*; alejamiento, *m*; traslado, *m*; (from office, etc.) deposición, *f*; supresión, *f*; asesinato, *m*. **r. van,** carro de mudanzas, *m*

remove *vt* quitar; retirar; levantar; sacar; apartar; separar; eliminar; trasladar; (from office) destituir; suprimir; asesinar. *vi* trasladarse. *n* grado, *m*; distancia, *f*; (departure) partida, *f*. **to r. oneself,** quitarse de en medio. **to r. one's hat,** descubrirse. **first cousin once removed,** hijo de primo carnal, primo hermano del padre, primo hermano de la madre, *m*

remunerate *vt* remunerar

remuneration *n* remuneración, *f*

remunerative *a* remunerador

renaissance *n* renacimiento, *m*, *a* renacentista

Renaissance man *n* hombre del Renacimiento, *m*

Renaissance woman *n* mujer del Renacimiento, *f*

renal *a* renal

rename *vt* poner otro nombre (a)

renascent *a* renaciente, que renace

rend *vt* desgarrar, rasgar; *fig* lacerar; (split) hender; *fig* dividir. **to r. from,** arrancar (a). **to r. the air,** (with cries, etc.) llenar el aire

render *vt* (return) devolver; dar; rendir; (make) hacer; (help, service) prestar; interpretar; (translate) traducir; (fat) derretir y clarificar

rendering *n* versión, *f*; interpretación, *f*

rendezvous *n* cita, *f*; lugar de cita, *m*; reunión, *f*. *vi* reunirse

rending *n* desgarro, *m*; hendimiento, *m*

renegade *a* renegado. *n* renegado (-da)

renew *vt* renovar; (resume) reanudar; (a lease, etc.) prorrogar

renewable *a* renovable

renewal *n* renovación, *f*; (resumption) reanudación, *f*; (of a lease, etc.) prorrogación, *f*

renewed *a* renovado; nuevo

rennet *n* cuajo, *m*

renounce *vt* renunciar; (a throne) abdicar; renegar (de), repudiar; abandonar. *vi law* desistir; (cards) renunciar

renouncement *n* renuncia, *f*; (of a throne) abdicación, *f*; repudiación, *f*

renovate *vt* renovar; limpiar; restaurar

renovation *n* renovación, *f*; limpiadura, *f*; restauración, *f*

renovator *n* renovador (-ra)

renown *n* renombre, *m*, fama, *f*

renowned *a* renombrado, famoso

rent *n* (tear) rasgadura, *f*; desgarro, *m*; abertura, *f*; raja hendedura, *f*; (discord) división, *f*; (hire) alquiler, *m*; arrendamiento, *m*. *vt* arrendar, alquilar. **r.-free,** sin pagar alquiler

rentable *a* alquilable, arrendable

rental. See **rent**

renter *n* arrendador (-ra)

rentier *n* rentista, *mf*

renting *n* alquiler, arrendamiento, *m*

renumber *vt* numerar de nuevo

renunciation *n* renunciación, renuncia, *f*

reoccupy *vt* volver a ocupar, ocupar otra vez

reopen *vt* abrir de nuevo, volver a abrir. *vi* abrirse nuevamente, abrirse otra vez

reopening *n* reapertura, *f*

reorder *vt* ordenar de nuevo, *com* volver a pedir. *n com* nuevo pedido, *m*

reorganization *n* reorganización, *f*

reorganize *vt* reorganizar

reorganizing *a* reorganizador

repack *vt* reembalar; reenvasar; volver a hacer (una maleta)

repaint *vt* pintar de nuevo

repainting *n* nueva pintura, *f*

repair *vt* arreglar (e.g. a machine) componer, remendar; reparar; restaurar; rehacer. *vi* (with to) dirigirse a, ir a; acudir a. *n* arreglo *m*, reparación, *f*; compostura, *f*; restauración, *f*. **to keep in r.,** conservar en buen estado

repairable *a* que se puede componer

repairer *n* componedor (-ra); restaurador (-ra)

repairing *n* reparación

reparable *a* reparable; remediable

reparation *n* reparación, *f*

repartee *n* respuestas, agudezas, *f pl*; *inf* dimes y diretes, *m pl*

repast *n* comida, *f*; (light) colación, *f*

repatriate *vt* repatriar

repatriation *n* repatriación, *f*

repay *vt* reembolsar; recompensar, pagar; pagar en la misma moneda; *vi* pagar. **It well repays a visit,** Vale la pena de visitarse

repayable *a* reembolsable

repayment *n* reembolso, *m*; pago, retorno, *m*

repeal *n* abrogación, revocación, *f*, *vt* abrogar, rescindir, revocar

repeat *vt* repetir; reiterar; (renew) renovar; duplicar. *n* repetición, *f*

repeated *a* reiterado; redoblado

repeatedly *adv* reiteradamente, repetidamente

repeater *n* repetidor (-ra); reloj de repetición, *m*; arma de repetición, *f*

repel *vt* repeler; ahuyentar; (spurn) rechazar; *phys* resistir; repugnar

repellent *a* repulsivo

repent *vt* arrepentirse de. *vi* arrepentirse

repentance *n* arrepentimiento, *m*, penitencia, *f*

repentant *a* arrepentido, penitente, contrito
repentantly *adv* arrepentidamente, con contrición
repeople *vt* repoblar
repeopling *n* repoblación, *f*
repercuss *vt* repercutir (en)
repercussion *n* repercusión, *f*
repercussive *a* repercusivo
repertory *n* repertorio, *m*
repetition *n* repetición, *f*; recitación, *f*
repetitive *a* iterativo
repine *vi* afligirse (de); quejarse (de); padecer nostalgia
repining *n* pesares, *m pl*; quejas, *f pl*, descontento, *m*; nostalgia, *f*
replace *vt* (put back) reponer, colocar de nuevo; restituir, devolver; (renew) renovar; (in a post, etc.) reemplazar, substituir
replaceable *a* restituible; renovable; reemplazable
replacement *n* reposición, *f*; restitución, devolución, *f*; renovación, *f*; reemplazo, *m*
replant *vt* replantar
replanting *n* replantación, *f*
replenish *vt* rellenar
replenishment *n* relleno, *m*
replete *a* repleto
repletion *n* repleción, *f*
replica *n* réplica, *f*
reply *n* respuesta, contestación, *f*, *vi* responder, contestar. **Awaiting your r.**, En espera de sus noticias. **in his r.**, en su respuesta
repolish *vt* repulir
repopulate *vt* repoblar
repopulation *n* repoblación, *f*
report *n* (rumor) voz, *f*, rumor, *m*; (reputation) fama, *f*; (news) noticia, *f*; (journalistic) reportaje, *m*; (mil nav and from school) parte, *f*; (weather) boletín, *m*; (proceedings) actas, *f pl*; (statement) informe, *m*; relación, *f*; (of a gun, etc.) detonación, *f*; explosión, *f*. *vt* dar cuenta de, relatar; informar; (measure) registrar; (mil nav) dar parte de; comunicar; (journalistic) hacer un reportaje de; (transcribe) transcribir; (accuse) denunciar; quejarse de. *vi* presentar informe; ser reportero; (present oneself) presentarse, comparecer. **It is reported that . . .**, Se informa que . . .
report card *n* boletín de calificaciones, *m*
reporter *n* reportero (-ra); *law* relator, *m*
reporting *n* reporterismo, *m*
repose *n* reposo, *m*; quietud, *f*; tranquilidad, serenidad, *f*. *vt* reposar, descansar; reclinar; (place) poner. *vi* reposar; tener confianza (en); basarse (en)
repository *n* repositorio, depósito, *m*; almacén, *m*; (furniture) guardamuebles, *m*; (person) depositario (-ia)
repoussé (work) *n* repujado, *m*. **to work in r.**, repujar
reprehend *vt* reprender, reprobar
reprehensible *a* reprensible
reprehension *n* reprensión, *f*
represent *vt* representar; significar
representation *n* representación, *f*
representational *a art* realista
representative *a* que representa; representativo. *n* representante, *mf*
repress *vt* reprimir
repression *n* represión, *f*
repressive *a* represivo
reprieve *vt law* aplazar la ejecución (de); *fig* dar una tregua (a)
reprimand *n* reprimenda, *f*, *vt* reprender
reprint *n* reimpresión, tirada aparte, separata, *f*, *vt* reimprimir
reprinting *n* reimpresión, *f*
reprisal *n* represalia, *f*. **to take reprisals,** tomar represalias
reproach *n* reproche, *m*; censura, *f*; (shame) vergüenza, *f*. *vt* reprochar; censurar, echar en cara, afear
reproachful *a* severo; lleno de reproches; de censura; (shameful) vergonzoso

reproachfully *adv* con reprobación, con reprensión, severamente
reproachfulness *n* severidad, *f*. **the r. of my gaze,** mi mirada llena de reproches
reprobate *n* réprobo (-ba)
reproduce *vt* reproducir. *vi* reproducirse
reproducible *a* reproductible
reproduction *n* reproducción, *f*
reproductive *a* reproductor; de reproducción
reproof *n* reconvención, *f*
reprove *vt* censurar, culpar; reprender
reprovingly *adv*. See **rebukingly**
reptile *a* and *n* reptil, *m*
republic *n* república, *f*. **the r. of letters,** la república de las letras
republican *a* and *n* republicano (-na)
republicanism *n* republicanismo, *m*
republish *vt* publicar de nuevo; volver a editar
repudiate *vt* repudiar; negar, rechazar
repudiation *n* repudiación, *f*
repugnance *n* repugnacia, *f*
repugnant *a* repugnante; contrario; opuesto. **to be r. to,** repugnar (a)
repulse *vt* repulsar, repeler; rebatir, refutar; (refuse) rechazar, *n* repulsa, *f*; refutación, *f*; rechazo, *m*
repulsion *n phys* repulsión, *f*; repugnancia, aversión, *f*
repulsive *a* repulsivo, repugnante, repelente
repulsiveness *n* carácter repulsivo, *m*; aspecto repugnante, *m*
reputable *a* honrado, respetable, formal
reputation *n* reputación, *f*; fama, *f*, renombre, *m*. **to have the r. of,** ser reputado como, pasar por
reputed *a* supuesto; putativo
reputedly *adv* según la opinión común, según dice la gente
request *n* ruego, *m*, petición, *f*; instancia, *f*; solicitud, *f*; *com* demanda, *f*. *vt* pedir, rogar; suplicar; solicitar. **in r.,** en boga; solicitado; en demanda, **on r.,** a solicitud. **r. stop,** (for buses) parada discrecional, *f*
requiem *n* réquiem, *m*. **r. mass,** misa de difuntos, *f*
require *vt* exigir, requerir; necesitar; (wish) desear; invitar. *vi* ser necesario
required *a* necesario; obligatorio
requirement *n* deseo, *m*; requisito, *m*; formalidad, *f*; estipulación, *f*; necesidad, *f*
requisite *n* requisito, *m*. *a* necesario, requisito, preciso. **to be r.,** ser necesario, ser menester hacer falta
requisition *vt mil* requisar
requisitioning *n* requisa, *f*
requital *n* recompensa, *f*; compensación, satisfacción, *f*
requite *vt* pagar, recompensar; (affection) corresponder a
reread *vt* releer
reredos *n* retablo, *m*
resale *n* reventa, *f*
rescind *vt* rescindir
rescission *n* rescisión, *f*
rescue *vt* salvar; librar; *mil* rescatar. *n* socorro, *m*; salvamento, *m*; *mil* rescate, *m*. **to go to the r. of,** ir al socorro de. **r. party,** expedición de salvamento, *f*; *mil* expedición de rescate, *f*
rescuer *n* salvador (-ra)
reseal *vt* resellar
research *n* investigación, *f*, *vt* investigar
researcher *n* investigador (-ra)
reseda *n bot* reseda, *f*
resell *vt* revender
resemblance *n* parecido, *m*, semejanza, *f*. **The two sisters bear a strong r. to each other,** Las dos hermanas se parecen mucho
resemble *vt* parecerse (a). **Mary doesn't r. her mother,** María no se parece a su madre
resent *vt* resentirse de; ofenderse por, indignarse por; tomar a mal
resentful *a* resentido; ofendido, indignado, agraviado; vengativo

resentfully *adv* con resentimiento; con indignación

resentment *n* resentimiento, *m*

reservation *n* reservación, *f*; reserva, *f*; territorio reservado, *m*; santuario, *m*. **mental r.,** reserva mental, *f*

reserve *n* reserva, *f*. *vt* reservar. **a de reserva. without r.,** sin reserva

reserved *a* reservado; callado, taciturno. **r. compartment,** reservado, *m*. **r. list,** (*mil nav*) sección de reserva, *f*

reservedly *adv* con reserva

reservist *n* reservista, *mf*

reservoir *n* depósito, *m*; cisterna, *f*, aljibe, tanque, *m*

reset *vt* montar de nuevo

resettle *vt* repoblar; rehabilitar; (a dispute) llegar a un nuevo acuerdo sobre

resettlement *n* repoblación, *f*; rehabilitación, *f*; (of a dispute) nuevo acuerdo, *m*

reshape *vt* reformar

reship *vt* reembarcar

reshipment *n* reembarque, *m*

reshuffle *vt* volver a barajar; *fig* cambiar

reside *vi* residir, habitar; vivir

residence *n* residencia, *f*; permanencia, estada, *f*; domicilio, *m*

resident *a* residente; (of a servant) que duerme en casa; interno. *n* residente, *mf*; (diplomacy) residente, *m*

residential *a* residencial

residue *n* resto, *m*; (*law, chem*) residuo, *m*

residuum *n* residuo, *m*

resign *vt* renunciar (a); ceder; resignar. *vi* dimitir. **to r. oneself,** resignarse

resignation *n* resignación, *f*; (from a post) dimisión, *f*. **to send in one's r.,** dimitir

resigned *a* resignado

resignedly *adv* con resignación

resilience *n* elasticidad, *f*

resilient *a* elástico

resin *n* resina, *f*; (solid, for violin bows, etc.) colofonia, *f*

resinous *a* resinoso

resist *vt* and *vi* (bear) aguantar; (impede) impedir; (repel, ward off) resistir; rechazar; hacer frente (a); oponerse (a); negarse (a)

resistance *n* resistencia, *f*; aguante, *m*, tenacidad, *f*; oposición, *f*; repugnancia, *f*. **passive r.,** resistencia pasiva, *f*. **r. coil,** *elec* resistencia, *f*. **r. movement,** movimiento de resistencia, *m*

resistant *a* resistente

resister *n* el, *m*, (*f*, la) que resiste

resole *vt* remontar

resoling *n* remonta, *f*

resolute *a* resuelto, decidido

resolutely *adv* resueltamente

resolution *n* resolución, *f*; (proposal placed before a legislative body, etc.) proposición, *f*; propósito, *m*

resolve *vt* resolver; desarrollar, deshacer (an abbreviation, acronym, or initialism). *vi* resolverse. *n* propósito, *m*; (of character) resolución, firmeza, *f*

resonance *n* resonancia, *f*; sonoridad, *f*

resonant *a* resonante; reverberante, sonoro

resort *n* recurso, *m*; punto de reunión. *m*; (frequentation) frecuentación, *f*; (gathering) concurrencia, *f*; reunión, *f*. *vi* acudir (a), acogerse (a); hacer uso (de); pasar (a); (frequent) frecuentar, concurrir. **health r.,** balneario, *m*. **holiday r.,** playa de verano, *f*; pueblo de veraneo, *m*. **in the last r.,** en último recurso

resound *vi* resonar, retumbar, retronar; *fig* tener fama, ser celebrado. *vt* hacer reverberar; *fig* celebrar

resounding *a* retumbante, resonante

resource *n* recurso, *m*; (of character) inventiva, *f*; *pl* **resources;** recursos, fondos, *m pl*

resourceful *a* ingenioso

resourcefully *adv* ingeniosamente

resourcefulness *n* ingeniosidad, *f*

respect *n* respeto, *m*; consideración, *f*; (reference, regard) respecto, *m*; *pl* **respects,** (greetings) saludos, *m*

pl; homenaje, *m*. *vt* respetar; honrar; (concern, regard) concernir, tocar (a). **in other respects,** por lo demás. **in r. of,** tocante a, respecto a. **in some respects,** desde algunos puntos de vista. **out of r. for,** por consideración a

respectability *n* respetabilidad, *f*

respectable *a* respetable; pasable; considerable

respectably *adv* respetablemente

respected *a* and *part* respetado; apreciado, estimado; digno de respeto, honrado

respectful *a* respetuoso

respectfully *adv* respetuosamente

respectfulness *n* aire respetuoso, *m*; conducta respetuosa, *f*

respecting *prep* con respecto a, en cuanto a, tocante a; a propósito de

respective *a* respectivo; relativo

respectively *adv* respectivamente

respiration *n* respiración, *f*

respirator *n* respirador, *m*

respiratory *a* respiratorio

respire *vt* and *vi* respirar; exhalar; descansar

respite *n* tregua, pausa, *f*; respiro, *m*; *law* espera, *f*. *vt* dar tregua (a); (postpone) aplazar; (relieve) aliviar

resplendence *n* resplandor, *m*, refulgencia, *f*, esplendor, fulgor, *m*

resplendent *a* resplandeciente, refulgente, relumbrante. **He was r. in a new uniform,** Lucía (or Ostentaba) un nuevo uniforme. **to be r.,** ser resplandeciente; relumbrar, refulgir

resplendently *adv* esplendorosamente

respond *vi* responder; contestar; (obey) obedecer; reaccionar

respondent *n* (in a suit) demandado (-da)

response *n* respuesta, *f*; *ecc* responso, *m*

responsibility *n* responsabilidad, *f*

responsible *a* responsable

responsive *a* simpático; sensible, sensitivo

responsiveness *n* simpatía, *f*; sensibilidad, *f*

rest *n* descanso, *m*; reposo, *m*; (the grave) última morada, *f*; tranquilidad, paz, *f*; inacción, *f*; (prop) soporte, apoyo, *m*; base, *f*; (for a lance) ristre, *m*; (for a rifle) apoyo, *m*; *mus* silencio, *m*, pausa, *f*; (in verse) cesura, *f*. **in r.,** en ristre. **the r.,** el resto; los demás, los otros. **to set at r.,** calmar, tranquilizar; (remove) quitar. **r.-cure,** cura de reposo, *f*. **r.-house,** hospedería, *f*; refugio, *m*. **r.-room, lounge,** sala de descanso, *f*; (toilet) excusado, retrete, *m*; (in theaters) saloncillo, *m*

rest *vi* reposar, descansar; (lie down) acostarse, echarse; (stop) cesar, parar; estar en paz; apoyarse (en); descansar (sobre); posar; depender (de); (remain) quedar. *vt* descansar; dar un descanso (a); (lean) apoyar; basar (en). **It rests with them,** Depende de ellos. **These valuable documents now rest in the Library of Congress,** Estos valiosos documentos han parado en la Biblioteca del Congreso. **May he r. in peace!** ¡Que en paz descanse! **to r. assured,** estar seguro. **to r. on one's oars,** cesar de remar; descansar

restate *vt* repetir, afirmar de nuevo

restatement *n* repetición, *f*

restaurant *n* restaurante, restorán, *m*. **r.-car,** coche-comedor, *m*

restful *a* descansado; tranquilo, sosegado

resting *n* reposo, *m*. **last r.-place,** última morada, *f*. **r.-place,** descansadero, *m*; refugio, *m*

restitution *n* restitución, *f*

restive *a* (of a horse) repropio, ingobernable; inquieto, agitado; impaciente

restiveness *n* inquietud, agitación, *f*; impaciencia, *f*

restless *a* agitado; inquieto, intranquilo; turbulento; sin reposo; (wakeful) desvelado; (ceaseless) incesante. **r. night,** noche desvelada, noche intranquila, *inf* noche toledana, *f*

restlessly *adv* agitadamente; con inquietud; turbulentamente; incesantemente

restlessness *n* agitación, *f*; inquietud, intranquilidad, *f*;

turbulencia, *f;* falta de reposo, *f;* (wakefulness) desvelo, *m;* movimiento incesante, *m*

restock *vt* (with goods) surtir de nuevo; proveer de nuevo; restablecer; repoblar

restoration *n* restauración, *f;* renovación, *f;* restablecimiento, *m;* (returning) restitución, *f*

restorative *a* and *n* restaurativo *m*

restore *vt* restaurar; restituir; devolver; restablecer; reponer; (repair) reformar, reparar; reconstruir; (to former rank, etc.) rehabilitar. **He restored the book to its place,** Devolvió el libro a su sitio

restorer *n* restaurador (-ra)

restrain *vt* refrenar; reprimir; (restrict) limitar, restringir; (prevent) impedir; desviar; (detain) recluir. **to r. oneself,** contenerse

restrained *a* moderado, mesurado; sobrio; (of emotion) contenido

restraining *a* restrictivo; moderador, calmante

restraint *n* freno, *m;* restricción, *f;* limitación, *f;* prohibición, *f;* compulsión, *f;* (reserve) reserva, *f;* moderación, *f*

restrict *vt* restringir; limitar

restriction *n* restricción, *f;* limitación, *f*

restrictive *a* restrictivo

result *n* resultado, *m;* consecuencia, resulta, *f;* solución, *f. vi* resultar. **as the r. of,** de resultas de

resultant *a* resultante; consecuente. *n* resultado, *m; mech* resultante, *f*

resume *vt* reasumir; (continue) reanudar, continuar; (summarize) resumir

résumé *n* resumen, *m,* recapitulación, *f*

resummon *vt* convocar de nuevo (a); citar de nuevo (a)

resumption *n* (renewal) reanudación, *f;* reasunción, *f*

resurgence *n* resurgimiento, *m*

resurrect *vt inf* desenterrar; resucitar

resurrection *n* resurrección, *f*

resuscitate *vt* and *vi* resucitar

resuscitation *n* resurrección, *f;* renovación, *f;* renacimiento, *m*

retail *n* venta al por menor, reventa, *f. adv* al por menor. *vt* (goods) vender al por menor, revender; (tell) contar; repetir. **r. trade,** comercio al por menor, *m*

retailer *n* vendedor (-ra) al por menor; (of a story) narrador (-ra); el, *m,* (*f,* la) que cuenta algo

retain *vt* retener; guardar; conservar; (a barrister) ajustar; (hire) contratar

retainer *n* (dependent) criado, dependiente, *m;* partidario, adherente, *m;* (fee) honorario, *m; pl* **retainers,** séquito, *m,* adherentes, *m pl,* gente, *f*

retaining wall *n* muro de contención, *m*

retake *vt* volver a tomar; reconquistar

retaking *n* reconquista, *f*

retaliate *vt* vengarse de, desquitarse de. *vi* vengarse, tomar represalias

retaliation *n* represalias, *f pl;* desquite, *m,* satisfacción, *f.* **law of r.,** talión, *m,*

retaliatory *a* de represalias; de desquite

retard *vt* retardar

retch *vi* tener náuseas, procurar vomitar

retching *n* náusea, basca, *f*

retell *vt* repetir, volver a contar

retention *n* retención, *f;* conservación, *f*

retentive *a* retentivo

retentiveness *n* poder de retención, *m;* (memory) retentiva, *f*

reticence *n* reticencia, reserva, *f*

reticent *a* reservado, inexpresivo, taciturno

retina *n* retina, *f*

retinue *n* séquito, acompañamiento, *m,* comitiva, *f*

retire *vi* retirarse; (to bed) recogerse; acostarse; (from a post) jubilarse. *vt* retirar; jubilar. **to r. from a post,** *mil* rendir el puesto

retired *a* retirado; (remote) apartado, aislado; (hidden) escondido; (former) antiguo; (from employment, etc.) jubilado; (of an officer) retirado. **to place on the r. list,** jubilar; (*mil nav*) dar el retiro (a)

retirement *n* retirada, *f;* (solitude) apartamiento, aislamiento, *m;* retiro, *m;* (superannuation) jubilación, *f*

retiring *a* que se retira; (from a post) dimitente; (with pension, etc.) de jubilación; (reserved) reservado; modesto

retort *vi* replicar. *vt* retorcer; devolver (una acusación, etc.). *n* réplica, *f;* contestación, *f; chem* retorta, *f*

retouch *vt* retocar

retrace *vt* volver a trazar; volver a andar (un camino); (one's steps) volver sobre sus pasos, volver atrás; (in memory) rememorar, recordar; buscar el origen (de); (recount) narrar, contar

retract *vt* retractar, retirar; (draw back) retraer. *vi* retractarse

retraction *n* retracción, *f*

retranslate *vt* hacer una nueva traducción (de)

retransmission *n* retransmisión, *f*

retread *vt* pisar de nuevo; (tires) recauchetear

retreat *n* retirada, *f;* (*mil* signal) retreta, *f;* (refuge and *ecc*) retiro, *m. vi* retirarse; retroceder; refugiarse

retreat house *n* casa de ejercicios, *f*

retreating *a* que se retira; que retrocede; *mil* que se bate en retirada

retrench *vt* reducir; disminuir; *vi* economizar, hacer economías

retrenchment *n* disminución, reducción, *f;* economías, *f pl*

retrial *n* (of a person) nuevo proceso, *m;* (of a case) revisión, *f*

retribution *n* retribución, *f;* justo castigo, *m,* pena merecida, *f*

retrievable *a* recuperable, que puede recobrarse; reparable

retrieval *n* recuperación, *f;* reparación, *f;* (of game) cobra, *f;* (of one's character) rehabilitación, *f*

retrieve *vt* (game, of dogs) cobrar; (regain) recobrar, recuperar; restaurar; reparar; restablecer; (one's character) rehabilitar. *vi* cobrar la caza

retriever *n* (dog) perdiguero (-ra)

retroactive *a* retroactivo

retrocede *vi* retroceder

retrograde *a* retrógrado

retrogression *n* retrogradación, regresión, *f; med* retroceso, *m*

retrogressive *a* retrógrado

retrospect *n* mirada retrospectiva, *f,* examen del pasado, *m.* **in r.,** retrospectivamente

retrospection *n* retrospección, *f*

retrospective *a* retrospectivo

retrospectively *adv* retrospectivamente

retry *vt* (a case) rever; (a person) procesar de nuevo

return *vi* regresar; volver; reaparecer; presentarse de nuevo; *law* revertir; (answer) contestar, responder. *vt* (give back or put back) devolver; (a ball) restar; (a kindness, visit) pagar; restituir; (reciprocate) corresponder (a); recompensar; contestar (a); dar; rendir; (yield) producir; (a verdict) fallar, pronunciar; (report) dar parte de; anunciar; (exchange) cambiar; (elect) elegir. *n* regreso, *m;* vuelta, *f;* (giving or putting back) devolución, *f;* pago, *m;* restitución, *f;* correspondencia, *f;* recompensa, *f;* (reply) respuesta, *f;* (reappearance) reaparición, *f;* reinstalación, *f;* repetición, *f;* (gain) ganancia, *f,* provecho, *m;* rendimiento, *m;* (exchange) cambio, *m;* (report) parte oficial, *f;* informe, *m;* lista, *f;* (election) elección, *f; pl* **returns,** tablas estadísticas, *f pl; pl* (at an election) resultados, *m pl.* **Many happy returns!** ¡Feliz cumpleaños! **by return mail,** a vuelta de correo. **on my (his, etc.) r.,** a la vuelta, cuando vuelva. **to r. like for like,** pagar en la misma moneda. **r. journey, r. trip,** viaje de vuelta, *m.* **r. match,** partido de vuelta, *m.* **r. ticket,** billete de ida y vuelta, *m;* billete de vuelta, *m*

returnable *a* restituible; susceptible a ser devuelto; (on approval) a prueba; *law* devolutivo

returning *a* que vuelve. *n* See **return**

518

reunion *n* reunión, *f*
reunite *vt* reunir. *vi* reunirse
revaccinate *vt* revacunar
revaccination *n* revacunación, *f*
reveal *vt* revelar; descubrir
revealer *n* revelador (-ra)
revealing *a* revelador. *n* revelación, *f*; descubrimiento, *m*
reveille *n* mil diana, *f*
revel *vi* divertirse; regocijarse (en), gozarse (en); entregarse (a); (carouse) ir de parranda; emborracharse. *n* algazara, jarana, *f*; *pl* **revels,** fiestas, festividades, *f pl*
revelation *n* revelación, *f*; descubrimiento, *m*; (in the Bible) Apocalipsis, *m*
reveler *n* convidado alegre, *m*; (at night) trasnochador (-ra); (drunk) borracho (-cha); (masked) máscara, *mf*
revelry *n* festividades, *f pl*, regocijo, *m*; orgías, *f pl*
revenge *n* venganza, *f*. *vt* vengarse de; desquitarse de
revengeful *a* vengativo
revengefully *adv* vengativamente
revengefulness *n* deseo de venganza, *m*; carácter vengativo, *m*
revenger *n* vengador (-ra)
revenue *n* rentas públicas, *f pl*; (treasury) fisco, *m*; *com* rédito, *m*, ingresos, *m pl*; beneficio, *m*. **Inland R.,** delegación de contribuciones, *f*. **r. officer,** agente fiscal, *m*
reverberate *vt* and *vi* (of sound) retumbar, resonar; (of light, etc.) reverberar
reverberation *n* (reflection) reverberación, *f*; (of sound) retumbo, eco, *m*
revere *vt* reverenciar, venerar, honrar
reverence *n* reverencia, *f*, *vt* reverenciar
reverend *a* reverendo
reverent *a* reverente
reverently *adv* reverentemente, con reverencia
reverie *n* ensueño, *m*
reversal *n* inversión, *f*; (of a verdict) revocación, *f*
reverse *vt* invertir; (a steam engine) dar contra vapor (a); (a vehicle) poner en marcha atrás; (arms) llevar a la funerala; (a judgment, etc.) revocar, derogar. *vi* (dancing) dar vueltas al revés. *n* lo contrario, lo opuesto; (back) dorso, revés, *m*; (change) cambio, *m*; (check) revés, *m*, vicisitud, *f*; (loss) pérdida, *f*; (defeat) derrota, *f*; *mech* marcha atrás, *f*, a inverso; contrario, opuesto. **quite the r.,** todo el contrario. **r. turn,** (of an engine) cambio de dirección, *m*; (in dancing) vuelta al revés, *f*
reversible *a* reversible
reversion *n* reversión, *f*; *biol* atavismo, *m*; (of offices) futura, *f*; (of property) reversión, *f*
revert *vi* *law* revertir; volver (a)
review *n* examen, análisis, *m*; juicio crítico, *m*; (journal and *mil*) revista, *f*; (criticism) revista, reseña, *f*; *law* revisión, *f*. *vt* examinar, analizar; (*mil* etc.) pasar revista (a); revisar; repasar; (a book, etc.) reseñar; *law* revisar. *vi* escribir revistas
review article *n* artículo de reseña, *m*
reviewer *n* revistero (-ra), crítico, *m*
revile *vt* injuriar, maldecir, difamar
reviler *n* maldiciente, *m*, insultador (-ra)
reviling *n* insultos, *m pl*, injurias, *f pl*
revisal *n* revisión, *f*
revise *vt* revisar; repasar; corregir; (change) cambiar
reviser *n* revisor, *m*; corrector de pruebas, *m*
revision *n* revisión, *f*; repaso, *m*; corrección de pruebas, *f*
revisit *vt* volver a visitar, visitar de nuevo
revival *n* resurgimiento, *m*; renovación, *f*; (awakening) despertamiento, *m*; restablecimiento, *m*; resurrección, *f*; (of learning) renacimiento, *m*; *theat* reposición, *f*; (religious) despertar religioso, *m*
revive *vi* reponerse; restablecerse; resucitar; renovarse; renacer; cobrar fuerzas; (recover consciousness) volver en sí. *vt* hacer revivir; resucitar; restablecer; renovar; restaurar; despertar; (fire, colours) avivar

reviver *n* resucitador (-ra)
revivification *n* revivificación, *f*
revivify *vt* revivificar
revocable *a* revocable
revocation *n* revocación, *f*
revoke *vt* revocar, anular, derogar; (wills) quebrantar. *vi* revocar, anular; (at cards) renunciar. *n* (cards) renuncio, *m*
revolt *n* rebelión, *f*, *vi* rebelarse, sublevarse. *vt* repugnar, indignar, dar asco (a)
revolting *a* repugnante, asqueroso; (rebellious) rebelde
revolution *n* revolución, *f*; (turn) vuelta, *f*, giro, *m*
revolutionary *a* and *n* revolucionario (-ia)
revolutionize *vt* revolucionar
revolve *vi* dar vueltas, girar; suceder periódicamente. *vt* hacer girar; (ponder) revolver, discurrir
revolver *n* revólver, *m*
revolving *a* giratorio; que vuelve; periódico. **r. chair,** silla giratoria, *f*. **r. door,** puerta giratoria, *f*. **r. stage,** escenario giratorio, *m*
revue *n* *theat* revista, *f*
revulsion *n* revulsión, *f*
revulsive *a* *med* revulsivo
rev up *vt* (an engine) calentar
reward *n* recompensa, *f*; retribución, *f*. *vt* recompensar; satisfacer, premiar
rewarding *a* premiador; que recompensa. *n* recompensación, *f*. **a rewarding experience,** una experiencia compensadora, *f*
rewrite *vt* escribir de nuevo; volver a escribir; redactar otra vez
rhapsody *n* rapsodia, *f*
rheostat *n* reóstato, *m*
rhetoric *n* retórica, *f*
rhetorical *a* retórico; declamatorio
rhetorician *n* retórico (-ca)
rheumatic *a* reumático. **r. fever,** reumatismo poliarticular agudo, *m*
rheumatism *n* reumatismo, reuma, *m*
rheumy *a* catarroso; (of the eyes) legañoso
Rhine, the el Rin, *m*
rhinestone *n* circón, *m*
rhinoceros *n* rinoceronte, *m*
Rhodes Rodas, *m*
rhododendron *n* rododendro, *m*
rhubarb *n* ruibarbo, *m*
rhyme *n* rima, *f*; verso, *m*. *vi* and *vt* rimar. **without r. or reason,** sin ton ni son; a tontas y a locas
rhymer *n* rimador (-ra)
rhyming *a* rimador
rhythm *n* ritmo, *m*
rhythmic *a* rítmico
rib *n* (anat, bot, aer, naut, arch) costilla, *f*; (of an umbrella or fan) varilla, *f*; (in cloth) cordoncillo, *m*, lista, *f*
ribald *a* escabroso, ribaldo, indecente
ribaldry *n* ribaldería, escabrosidad, indecencia, *f*
ribbed *a* con costillas; (of cloth) listado, con listas
ribbon *n* cinta, *f*; tira, *f*; (tatter) jirón, *m*. **to tear to ribbons,** hacer jirones
rice *n* arroz, *m*. *a* de arroz; con arroz. **r. field,** arrozal, *m*. **r.-paper,** papel de paja de arroz, *m*. **r.-pudding,** arroz con leche, *m*
rich *a* rico; opulento; (happy) dichoso; (of land, etc.) fértil; abundante; (of objects) magnífico, suntuoso, hermoso; precioso; (of food) exquisito; suculento; (highly seasoned) muy sazonado; (creamy) con mucha nata; (of colours) brillante, vivo. **new r.,** ricacho (-cha). **newly-r.,** advenedizo. **to grow r.,** enriquecerse
riches *n* riqueza, *f*
richly *adv* ricamente, abundantemente; magníficamente; bien
richness *n* riqueza, *f*; opulencia, *f*; (of land, etc.) fertilidad, *f*; abundancia, *f*; (of objects) magnificencia, suntuosidad, hermosura, *f*; preciosidad, *f*; (of food)

gusto exquisito, *m*; suculencia, *f*; (piquancy) gusto picante, *m*; (of colours) viveza, *f*
rickets *n* raquitismo, *m*
rickety *a med* raquítico; destartalado, desvencijado; (unsteady) tambaleante; cojo
rickshaw *n* riksha, *m*
ricochet *n* rebote, *m*, *vi* rebotar
rid *vt* librar (de). **to get rid of,** librarse de; quitarse de encima (a); perder, quitarse; (dismiss) despedir. **to rid oneself of,** librarse de, deshacerse de
riddance *n* libramiento, *m*
riddle *n* acertijo, *m*; enigma, problema, *m*; misterio, *m*; (sieve) tamiz de alambre, *m*; *vt* (guess) adivinar; (sift) cribar; (with holes) acribillar
ride *vi* (a horse) montar a caballo, cabalgar; pasear a caballo; (a mule, a bicycle) montar en, pasear en; (a vehicle, train) ir en; (a carriage, car) andar en, pasear en; (float) flotar; (on the wind) dejarse llevar por el viento; ser llevado por el viento; (go) ir; (come) venir; (a distance) hacer . . . a caballo, en coche, etc.; *naut* estar al ancla; *mech* tener juego. *vt* (a horse, mule, bicycle) montar; ir montado sobre; manejar; (a race) hacer; (float) flotar en; (cleave, the sea, etc.) surcar. *n* paseo (a caballo, en bicicleta, en coche, etc.), *m*; viaje (en un autobús, de tren, etc.), *m*; (bridle path) camino de herradura, *m*; cabalgata, *f*, desfile a caballo, *m*. **a r. on horseback,** un paseo a caballo. **They gave me a r. in their car,** (e.g. to see the sights) Me llevaron a paseo en su auto, (a lift to a certain place) Me dieron un aventón. **ride at anchor,** estar fondeado. **to r. a bicycle,** montar en bicicleta. **to r. rough-shod over,** mandar a la baqueta (a), mandar a puntapiés (a). **to r. sidesaddle,** cabalgar a mujeriegas. **to r. at,** embestir con. **to r. away,** marcharse, alejarse; marcharse a caballo, etc. **to r. back,** volver; volver a caballo, en bicicleta, etc. **to r. behind,** seguir a caballo; ir inmediatamente detrás (de); (on the back seat) ocupar el asiento de atrás; (on the same animal) cabalgar en la grupa. **to r. down,** atropellar; (trample) pisotear, pasar por encima de. **to r. on,** seguir su camino. **to r. out,** salir a paseo en caballo, etc.; irse a paseo en coche, etc.; (a storm) hacer frente a, luchar con. **to r. over,** pasar por encima de; recorrer. **to r. up,** *vi* llegar, acercarse; (of a tie, etc.) subir. *vt* montar
rider *n* cabalgador (-ra); jinete, *m*; persona que va en coche, etc., *f*; (on a bicycle) ciclista, *mf*; (on a motorcycle) motociclista, *mf*; (horsebreaker) domador de caballos, *m*; (clause) añadidura, *f*; corolario, *m*
ridge *n* cumbre, cima, *f*; (of mountains) cordillera, sierra, *f*; (of a roof, of a nose) caballete, *m*; *agr* lomo, caballón, *m*; (wrinkle) arruga, *f*; (on coins) cordoncillo, *m*. *vt* surcar; formar lomos (en); (wrinkle) arrugar
ridicule *n* ridículo, *m*, *vt* poner en ridículo, ridiculizar, burlarse (de), mofarse (de)
ridiculous *a* ridículo, absurdo
ridiculously *adv* absurdamente
ridiculousness *n* ridiculez, *f*
riding *a* cabalgante; que va a caballo; montado (a, en, sobre); *naut* al ancla; (in compounds) de equitación; de montar. *n* equitación, *f*; paseo a caballo, *f*; bicicleta, etc., *m*; acción de ir a caballo, etc., *f*; (district) comarca, *f*. **r.-boots,** botas de montar, *f pl*. **r.-habit,** traje de montar, *m*; (woman's) amazona, *f*. **r.-master,** profesor de equitación, *m*. **r.-saddle,** silla de montar, *f*. **r.-school,** escuela de equitación, *f*
rife *a* común; frecuente; prevalente; abundante; general. **r. with,** abundante en; lleno de
riffraff *n* desperdicios, *m pl*; (rabble) gentuza, canalla, *f*
rifle *n* rifle, fusil rayado, *m*. *vt* robar; (a suitcase, etc.) desvalijar; (a gun) rayar. **r.-range,** campo de tiro, *m*. **r.-sling,** portafusil, *m*. **r.-shot,** fusilazo, *m*
rifleman *n* fusilero, *m*
rifler *n* saqueador (-ra)
rifling *n* (robbing) saqueo, robo, *m*; (of a suitcase, etc.) desvalijamiento, *m*
rift *n* hendedura, abertura, *f*; grieta, *f*

rig *n naut* aparejo, *m*; *inf* atavío, *m*. *vt* (a ship) aparejar; equipar; (elections) falsificar. **to rig out,** proveer de; equipar con; ataviar. **to rig up,** arreglar; armar, construir
rigging *n* (of a ship) aparejo, *m*
right *a* recto; correcto; conveniente, debido; apropiado; exacto; (opposite of left hand) derecho; (straight) directo; en línea recta; razonable; (true) verdadero, genuino, legítimo; (just) justo; (prudent) prudente; (in health) sano. **All r.!** ¡Está bien! **I feel all r.,** Me siento perfectamente bien, Estoy bien. **He is the r. man for the job,** Él es el hombre que hace falta para el puesto. **It is the r. word,** Es la palabra apropiada. **on the r.,** a la derecha. **to be r.,** (of persons) tener razón. **to make r.,** poner en orden; arreglar. **r.-angle,** ángulo recto, *m*. **r.-angled,** rectangular. **r.-angled triangle,** triángulo rectángulo, *m*. **the R. Bank (of Paris),** la Orilla derecha, la Ribera derecha, *f*. **r. hand,** *n* (mano) derecha, diestra, *f*; derecha, *f*; (person) brazo derecho, *m*. *a* de la mano derecha; de la derecha; a la derecha. **r.-handed,** derecho; diestro, hábil. **r. mind,** entero juicio, *m*. **r.-minded,** juicioso, prudente; honrado. **r.-of-way,** derecho a la vía, *m*
right *adv* directamente; inmediatamente; derechamente; correctamente; debidamente; exactamente; bien; (quite, thoroughly) completamente; honradamente; (very) muy. **r. on,** adelante; en frente. **R. about face!** ¡Media vuelta a la derecha! **r. at the bottom,** al fondo; al final; el último (de la clase, etc.). **r. at the end of his speech,** al fin de su discurso. **r. away,** en seguida, inmediatamente
right *n* razón, *f*; verdad, *f*; justicia, *f*; (good) bien, *m*; derecho, *m*; (not left side) derecha, *f*; (of political parties) derechas, *f pl*. **r. and wrong,** el bien y el mal. **"All rights reserved,"** «Derechos reservados.» **by rights,** por derecho. **It is on the r.,** Está a la derecha. **to exercise one's r.,** usar de su derecho. **r. of association,** derecho de asociación, *m*. **r. of way,** derecho de paso, *m*. **to be in the r.,** tener razón; estar en su derecho
right *vt* enderezar; rectificar; corregir; poner en orden; *naut* enderezar; hacer justicia (a). **to r. wrongs,** deshacer agravios
righteous *a* recto, virtuoso, justo; justificado
righteously *adv* virtuosamente; justamente
righteousness *n* rectitud, integridad, virtud, *f*; justicia, *f*
rightful *a* justo; legítimo; verdadero
rightfully *adv* justamente; legítimamente; verdaderamente
rightfulness *n* justicia, *f*; legitimidad, *f*; verdad, *f*
rightly *adv* justamente; debidamente; correctamente; bien. **r. or wrongly,** mal que bien
rightness *n* rectitud, *f*; derechura, *f*; justicia, *f*; exactitud, *f*
rigid *a* rígido; inflexible; severo, riguroso
rigidity *n* rigidez, *f*; inflexibilidad, *f*; severidad, *f*
rigmarole *n* monserga, *f*, galimatías, *m*, jerigonza, *f*
rigor *n* rigor, *m*
rigorous *a* riguroso
rigorously *adv* rigurosamente
rigor *n* rigor, *m*
rile *vt inf* irritar, sacar de tino (a)
rim *n* borde, *m*; orilla, *f*; (of a wheel) llanta, *f*, aro, *m*
rime *n* escarcha, *f*, *vt* cubrir còn escarcha. See also **rhyme**
rind *n* (of fruit) cáscara, corteza, *f*; (of cheese) costra, *f*; (of bacon) piel, *f*
ring *n* círculo, *m*; (round the eyes) ojera, *f*; (for curtains, etc.) anilla, *f*; (for the finger) anillo, *m*, sortija, *f*; (for children's games) corro, *m*; (for the ears) arete, *m*; (of smoke and for the nose) anillo, *m*; (for hitching, etc.) argolla, *f*; (for boxing) cuadrilátero, *m*; (on a racecourse) picadero, *m*; (at a circus, bull-fight) ruedo, redondel, *m*; *fig* arena, *f*; (group) camarilla, *f*, grupo, *m*; (metallic sound) sonido metálico, *m*; resonancia, *f*;

(tinkle) tintín, *m*; (of a bell) repique, tañido, son (de la campana), *m*; (of bells) juego de campanas, *m*; (of laughter, etc.) ruido, *m*; (of truth, etc.) apariencia, *f.* **r.-bolt,** *naut* cáncamo, *m.* **r. finger,** dedo anular, *m.* **r.-master,** director de circo, *m*

ring *vt* (surround) cercar, rodear; (a bull, etc.) poner un anillo (a); (sound) hacer sonar; sonar; (a door bell, etc.) tocar, apretar; (bells) echar a vuelo; (announce by pealing the bells) anunciar, proclamar; sonar, tañer. *vi* (of bells) sonar; (re-echo) resonar; (of the ears) zumbar; (tinkle) tintinar. **to r. the bell,** tocar la campana; tocar el timbre. **to r. off,** colgar el teléfono. **to r. up,** llamar por teléfono, telefonear

ringing *n* acción de tocar las campanas o el timbre, *f*; toque, *m*; repique, *m*; campanilleo, *m*; (in the ears) zumbido, *m. a* resonante, sonoro. **r. signal,** señal de llamada, *f.* **the r. of the bells,** el son de las campanas

ringleader *n* cabecilla, *m*

ringlet *n* rizo, bucle, *m*

ringworm *n* tiña, *f*

rink *n* pista, *f.* **skating-r.,** sala de patinar, *f*; pista de patinar, *f*

rinse *n* enjuague, *m*; enjuagadura, *f*; (of clothes) aclarado, *m. vt* enjuagar; (clothes) aclarar; lavar

rinsing *n* See **rinse;** *pl* **rinsings,** lavazas, *f pl, a* de aclarar

riot *n* motín, *m*; tumulto, *m*; desorden, *m*; exceso, *m*; orgía, *f*; disipación, *f. vi* amotinarse; alborotarse; entregarse a la disipación (or al placer); (enjoy) gozar, disfrutar. **to run r.,** hacer excesos; perder el freno; desmandarse; *fig* extenderse por todas partes; crecer en abundancia, cubrir todo

rioter *n* amotinador (-ra); alborotador (-ra)

riotous *a* sedicioso; bullicioso; disoluto; desordenado; desenfrenado

riotously *adv* sediciosamente; bulliciosamente; disolutamente; con exceso

riotousness *n* sedición, *f*; disolución, *f*; excesos, *m pl*, desenfreno, *m*; desorden, *m*

rip *vt* rasgar; (unsew) descoser; (wood, etc.) partir; (make) hacer. *vi* rasgarse. *n* rasgón, *m*; rasgadura, *f*; desgarro, *m*; (libertine) calavera, *m.* **to rip off,** arrancar; quitar. **to rip open,** abrir; (an animal) abrir en canal

riparian *a* and *n* ribereño (-ña)

ripe *a* maduro; preparado; perfecto, acabado

ripen *vt* and *vi* madurar

ripeness *n* madurez, *f*

ripening *n* maduración, *f*

ripping *n* rasgadura, *f*; (unstitching) deshiladura, *f. a inf* estupendo

ripple *n* rizo, *m*; onda, *f*; (of sound) murmullo, *m. vt* rizar. *vi* rizarse; murmurar

rippling *n* rizado, *m*; murmullo, *m*

rise *vi* ascender; subir; levantarse; ponerse de pie; (of a meeting) suspenderse; (from the dead) resucitar; (grow) crecer; (swell) hincharse; (of sun, moon) salir; (of sound, gradient, price, stock exchange quotations) subir; (of river source) nacer; (in revolt) sublevarse, rebelarse; (to the mind) presentarse, surgir; (appear) aparecer; (of buildings, etc.) elevarse, alzarse; (in the world) mejorar de posición; (originate) originarse (en), proceder (de); (of mercury) alzarse; (of fish) picar. **He has risen in my estimation,** Ha ganado en mi estimación. **She rose early,** Se levantó temprano. **The color rose in her cheeks,** Se le subieron los colores a la cara. **to r. to the occasion,** estar al nivel de las circunstancias. **to r. to one's feet,** ponerse de pie. **to r. to the bait,** morder el anzuelo. **to r. again,** levantarse de nuevo; resucitar; renovarse; suscitarse otra vez. **to r. above,** alzarse por encima de; mostrarse superior a

rise *n* ascensión, *f*; subida, *f*; levantamiento, *m*; (in price, temperature) alza, *f*; (increase) aumento, *m*; (of the sun, moon) salida, *f*; (of a river) nacimiento, *m*; (origin) origen, *m*; (growth, development) desarrollo, *m*; crecimiento, *m*; (promotion) ascenso, *m*; (slope)

cuesta, *f*; pendiente, *f*; (high ground) eminencia, altura, *f.* **to give r. to,** dar lugar a, causar. **r. and fall,** subida y baja, *f*; (of the voice) ritmo, *m*; (of music) cadencia, *f*; (of institutions) grandeza y decadencia, *f.* **r. to power,** subida al poder, *f*

riser *n* el, *m,* (*f,* la) que se levanta; (of a step) contrahuella, *f.* **early r.,** madrugador (-ra). **late r.,** el, *m,* (*f,* la) que se levanta tarde

risibility *n* risibilidad, *f*

risible *a* risible

rising *n* subida, *f*; (of the source of rivers) nacimiento, *m*; (overflowing of rivers) crecimiento, *m*; (of sun, moon) salida, *f*; (from the dead) resurrección, *f*; (rebellion) sublevación, insurrección, *f*; (of the tide) crecida, *f*; (of bread) levadura, *f*; (of an assembly) suspensión, *f*; (of a theater curtain) subida, *f*; (literary) renacimiento, *m, a* creciente; naciente; saliente; (promising) de porvenir; (young) joven. **the r. generation,** los jóvenes, la generación joven. **He is r. forty,** Raya en los cuarenta. **He likes early r.,** Le gusta madrugar. **On the r. of the curtain . . . ,** Al levantarse el telón . . . **the r. of the moon,** la salida de la luna, *f.* **the r. tide,** la marea creciente

risk *n* riesgo, *m*; peligro, *m. vt* arriesgar; atreverse (a), osar. **at the r. of,** al riesgo de. **to take a r.,** tomar un riesgo; correr peligro. **to r. everything on the outcome,** jugar el todo por el todo

risk capital *n* capital-riesgo, *m*

riskiness *n* peligro, *m*

risky *a* arriesgado, peligroso

rissole *n* risol, *m,* (*pl* risoles)

rite *n* rito, *m*

rite of passage *n* rito de tránsito, *m*

ritual *a* ritual. *n* rito, *m,* ceremonia, *f*

ritualist *n* ritualista, *mf*

ritualistic *a* ritualista

rival *n* rival, *mf a* competidor; rival. *vt* rivalizar con, competir con

rivalry *n* rivalidad, *f*

river *n* río, *m,* a del río; fluvial. **r.-basin,** cuenca de un río, *f.* **r.-bed,** lecho, cauce de un (río), *m.* **r. civilization,** civilización fluvial, *f.* **r.-god,** dios de los ríos, *m.* **r.-mouth,** ría, *f.* **r. port,** puerto fluvial, *m*

riverside *n* ribera, orilla de un río, *f. a* de la(s) orilla(s) de un río; situado a la orilla de un río; ribereño

rivet *n* remache, roblón, *m. vt* remachar; clavar; *fig* fijar, concentrar; *fig* cautivar, absorber

Riviera, the la Riviera, *f*

riveter *n* remachador, *m*

riveting *n* remachado, remache, *m; fig* fijación, concentración, *f; fig* absorción, *f.* **r. machine,** remachadora, *f*

rivulet *n* riachuelo, arroyo, *m*

road *n* camino, *m*; carretera, *f*; ruta, *f*; *pl* **roads,** *naut* rada, *f.* **high r.,** camino real, *m.* **main r.,** carretera, *f.* **secondary r.,** carretera de segunda clase, *f.* **on the r. to . . . ,** en el camino de . . . **to get out of the r.,** *inf* quitarse de en medio. **to go by r.,** ir por carretera. **"R. up!"** «Carretera en reparaciones.» **r.-book,** guía de carreteras, *f.* **r. house,** albergue de carretera, *m.* **r. maker,** constructor de caminos, *m*; (navvy) peón caminero, *m.* **r. making,** construcción de caminos, *f.* **r. map,** mapa de carreteras, *m.* **r. sign,** señal de carretera, señal de tránsito, señal vial, *f*, poste indicador, *m.* **The r. to hell is paved with good intentions,** El camino del infierno está empedrado de buenas intenciones. **"R. Repairs,"** «Camino en Reparación»

roadmender *n* peón caminero, *m*

roadside *n* borde del camino, *m, a* al lado del camino

roadstead *n* rada, *f*

roadster *n* automóvil de turismo, *m*; bicicleta de carreras, *f*; caballo de aguante, *m*; buque fondeado en rada, *m*

roadway *n* calzada, carretera, *f*

roam *vi* vagar, vagabundear, andar errante. *vt* errar por

roamer *n* vagabundo (-da), hombre errante, *m*

roaming *n* vagabundeo, *m*; excursiones, *f pl*, paseos, *m pl*; *a* errante, vagabundo; nómada
roan *a* roano, sabino. *n* caballo roano, *m*
roar *vi* rugir; (of a bull, of the wind, of a person in anger) bramar; dar voces; (of the fire) crepitar; (of cannon) retumbar; (of thunder) estallar. *vt* gritar. *n* rugido, bramido, *m*; (shout) grito, *m*; (of the fire) crepitación, *f*; (of cannon, thunder) estallido, *m*; (noise) ruido, *m*. **to r. with laughter,** reírse a carcajadas
roaring *n* (of horses) asma de los caballos, *f*, For other meanings, see under **roar.** *a* rugiente, bramante; *inf* magnífico. **to do a r. trade,** hacer un buen negocio
roast *n* asado, *m*, carne asada, *f*. *a* asado; tostado. *vt* asar; (coffee and to warm one's feet, etc.) tostar; (metals) calcinar; (scold) desollar vivo (a). *vi* asarse; tostarse. **r. beef,** rosbif, *m*
roaster *n* asador, *m*; (for coffee or peanuts) tostador, *m*; (for chestnuts, etc.) tambor, *m*
roasting *n* asación, *f*; (of coffee) tostado, *m*; (of metals) calcinación, *f*. **r. spit,** asador, *m*
rob *vt* robar; quitar, privar (de). **They have robbed her of her pocketbook,** Le han robado la cartera
robber *n* ladrón (-ona); (footpad) salteador de caminos, *m*; (brigand) bandido, *m*
robbery *n* robo, *m*. **It's daylight r.!** ¡Es un desuello! **to commit a r.,** cometer un robo. **r. with violence,** robo armado, *m*
robe *n* traje talar, *m*, toga, *f*; (of a monk, nun) hábito, *m*; (of a priest, etc.) sotana, *f*; *poet* manto, *m*; (infant's) mantillas, *f pl*; *pl* **robes,** traje de ceremonia, *m*. *vt* vestir; cubrir, revestir (de). *vi* vestirse. **bath r.,** albornoz, *m*
robin *n* petirrojo, *m*
roble *n* rublo, *m*
robot *n* hombre mecánico, *m*; *aer* piloto mecánico, *m*. **traffic r.,** torre del tráfico, *f*, aparato automático, *m*. **r. plane,** avión sin piloto, *m*
robust *a* robusto; fuerte, vigoroso. **to make r.,** robustecer
robustness *n* robustez, *f*; vigor, *m*, fuerza, *f*
rock *n* roca, *f*; (in the sea) abrojo, escollo, *m*; peña, *f*, peñasco, *m*. **as firm as a r.,** como una roca. **to be on the rocks,** estar a la cuarta pregunta. **r. bottom,** *m* fondo, *m*. *a* mínimo, más bajo. **r. crystal,** cuarzo, *m*. **r.-garden,** jardincito rocoso, jardin alpestre, *m*. **r.-plant,** planta alpestre, *f*. **r.-rose,** heliantemo, *m*. **r.-salt,** sal gema, *f*
rock *vt* mecer; (shake) hacer temblar, sacudir; (to sleep) arrullar. *vi* mecerse, balancearse; tambalearse; agitarse; temblar
rocker *n* (of a chair, cradle) balancín, *m*; (chair) mecedora, *f*
rockery *n* jardincito rocoso, *m*
rocket *n* cohete, volador, *m*. *vi* lanzarse. **r.-launching aircraft,** caza lanzacohetes, *f*
rockiness *n* abundancia de rocas, *f*; fragosidad, escabrosidad, *f*
rocking *n* balanceo, *m*; (staggering) tambaleo, *m*; oscilación, *f*; (of an infant) arrullo, *m*. **r.-chair,** mecedora, *f*. **r.-horse,** caballo balancín, caballo mecedor, *m*
rocky *a* rocoso; de roca; roqueño; (rough) fragoso, escabroso; (rugged) peñascoso, escarpado. **the R. Mountains,** las Montañas Rocosas, *f pl*
rococo *n* rococó, *m*
rod *n* vara, *f*; bastón de mando, *m*; (for fishing) caña, *f*; (measure) pértiga, *f*; (surveying) jalón, *m*; palo, *m*; (for punishment) vergajo, *m*; *mech* vástago, *m*. **connecting rod,** biela, *f*. **to fish with rod and line,** pescar con caña
rodent *a* and *n* roedor, *m*
roe *n* (deer) corzo (-za); (of fish) hueva, *f*. **soft roes,** lechas, *f pl*
rogue *n* bribón, pícaro, pillo, *m*; *law* vago, *m*; (affectionate) picaruelo (-la)
roguery *n* truhanería, picardía, *f*; (knaves) pícaros, *m pl*; (mischief) travesuras, *f pl*. **novel of r.,** novela picaresca, *f*

roguish *a* picaresco, bellaco; (mischievous) travieso, juguetón; malicioso
roguishly *adv* como un pícaro; con malicia
roguishness *n* picardía, bribonería, bellaquería, *f*; (mischievousness) travesuras, *f pl*; malicia, *f*
role *n* papel, *m*
roll *n* rollo, *m*; (list) rol, *m*, lista, *f*; (of bread) panecillo, *m*; (of a drum) redoble, *m*; (of thunder) tronido, *m*; (of cloth) pieza, *f*; (of tobacco) rollo, *m*; (of meat, etc.) pastel, *m*; (of a ship) balanceo, *m*; *pl* **rolls,** (records) archivos, *m pl*. **He has a nautical r.,** Tiene un andar de marinero. **to call the r.,** pasar lista. **r. film,** película fotográfica, *f*. **r. of honour,** lista de honor, *f*. **r.-on corset,** faja elástica, *f*, corsé de goma, *m*. **r.-top desk,** buró de cierre enrollable, *m*
roll *vi* rodar; dar vueltas; (wallow) revolcarse; (of a ship) balancearse, bambolearse; (in money, etc.) nadar; (flow) correr, fluir; (*fig* of time) pasar tranquilamente; (of vehicle) rodar; pasar rodando; (of country) ondular; (of the sea) ondear; (of drums) redoblar; (of thunder) retumbar. *vt* hacer rodar; arrollar; (a cigarette) liar; (metals) laminar; (move) mover; (the eyes) guiñar (los ojos); (the ground) apisonar; (pastry) aplanar; (of an organ) sonar; (a drum) redoblar. **Mary rolled her eyes heavenwards,** María puso los ojos en blanco. **to r. away,** alejarse; desaparecer; (of time) pasar. **to r. back,** volver, retirarse; desaparecer. **to r. by,** pasar rodando; desaparecer. **to r. down,** bajar rodando, rodar por. **to r. in,** llegar en gran cantidad (or en gran número). **to r. off,** caer de. **to r. on,** seguir su marcha; fluir sin cesar; seguir su curso; (of time) avanzar. **to r. out,** (metal) laminar; (pastry) aplanar; (bring out) sacar; desenrollar. **to r. over,** *vt* volcar; tumbar; dar la vuelta (a). *vi* dar la vuelta; volverse al otro lado. **to r. up,** arrollar; envolver; (of hedgehogs, etc.) enroscarse, hacerse un ovillo
roll-call vote *n* votación nominal, *f*
roller *n* rodillo, *m*; cilindro, *m*; (wheel, castor) rueda, *f*; (for flattening the ground) apisonadora, *f*; *print* rodillo, *m*; (wave) ola grande, *f*. **r.-bandage,** venda, *f*. **r. canary,** canario de raza flauta, *m*. **r.-skate,** patín de ruedas, *m*. **r.-skating,** patinaje de ruedas, *m*. **r.-towel,** toalla continua, *f*
rollicking *a* alegre, jovial; juguetón
rolling *a* rodante; (of landscape) ondulante, quebrado. *n* rodadura, *f*; (wallowing) revuelco, *m*; (of metals) laminación, *f*; (of a ship) balanceo, *m*; (rolling up) enrollamiento, *m*. **r.-pin,** rollo, rodillo de pastelero, *m*. **r.-stock,** material móvil ferroviario, *m*
Roman *a* romano, de los romanos; (of noses and *print*) romano. *n* romano (-na). **in R. fashion,** a la romana. **R. Catholic,** *a* católico; católico apostólico romano. *n* el católico (-ca). **R. Catholicism,** catolicismo, *m*. **R. figures,** números romanos, *m pl*. **R. nose,** nariz romana, *f*. **R. road,** vía romana, *f*. **R. type,** *print* tipo romano, *m*
Romance *a* (of languages) romance *n* (language) romance, *m*
romance *n* novela de caballería, *f*; romance, *m*; aventura, *f*; cuento, *m*, novela, *f*; romanticismo, *m*; *mus* romanza, *f*. *vi* inventar ficciones; exagerar
romancer *n* romancerista, *mf*; mentiroso (-sa), embustero (-ra)
Romanesque *a* románico; romanesco
romantic *a* and *n* romántico (-ca)
romantically *adv* románticamente; de un modo romántico
romanticism *n* romanticismo, *m*
romanticist *n* romántico (-ca)
Rome Roma, *f*
romp *vi* juguetear, brincar, retozar, loquear; correr rápidamente. *n* locuelo (-la), saltaparedes, *mf*; (game) retozo, *m*. **The horse romped home easily,** El caballo ganó la carrera fácilmente
rompers *n* mono, *m*
romping *n* juegos, *m pl*, travesuras, *f pl*

rondo *n* rondó, *m*

rood *n* cruz, *f*; crucifijo, *m*; cuarto de acre, *m*. **By the r.!** ¡Por mi santiguada!

roof *n* tejado, techado, *m*; (of a motor-car, bus) tejadillo, *m*; (of coaches, etc.) imperial, *f*; cubierta, *f*; (of the mouth) paladar, *m*; (bower) enramada, *f*; (of heaven) bóveda (del cielo), *f*. *vt* techar, tejar; (shelter) abrigar. **r.-garden,** azotea, *f*. **r.-gutter,** canalera, *f*

roofer *n* techador, *m*; constructor de tejados, *m*

rook *n* chova, *f*, grajo, *m*; (chess) torre, *f*. *vt* engañar, estafar; (overcharge) desollar vivo (a)

rookery *n* manada de grajos, *f*; colonia de grajos, aves marinas or focas, *f*

room *n* (in a house) habitación, *f*, cuarto, *m*; sala, *f*; cámara, *f*; (behind a shop) trastienda, *f*; (space) sitio, espacio, *m*; lugar, *m*; (opportunity) oportunidad, *f*; (cause) motivo, *m*, causa, *f*. *vi* alojarse. **bath-r.,** cuarto de baño, *m*. **dining-r.,** comedor, *m*. **drawing-r.,** salón, *m*. **There is no r. for us in this car,** No cabemos en este coche. **There is still r. for improvement,** Se puede mejorar todavía. **There isn't r. for anything else,** No cabe más. **to be r.,** caber, haber sitio. **to make r.,** hacer sitio

roomed *a* (in compounds) de . . . habitaciones; de . . . salas

roominess *n* espaciosidad, amplitud, amplitud de habitación, *f*; (of garments) holgura, *f*

rooming house *n* casa de huéspedes, *f*

roommate *n* compañero de cuarto, compañero de pieza, *m*

roomy *a* espacioso, amplio; (of garments) holgado

roost *n* percha de gallinero, *f*. *vi* dormir en una percha; recogerse. **to rule the r.,** ser el amo del cotarro

rooster *n* gallo, *m*,

root *n* raíz, *f*; *gram* radical, *m*; *mus* base, *f*; origen, *m*; explicación, *f*. *vt* arraigar; *fig* fijar, clavar. *vi* echar raíces; *fig* arraigarse; (of pigs, etc.) hozar, escarbar; revolver. **to r. out,** arrancar de raíz; *fig* desarraigar; (destroy) extirpar. **cubed r.,** raíz cúbica, *f*. **from the r.,** (entirely) de raíz. **square r.,** raíz cuadrada, *f*. **to cut close to the r.,** cortar a raíz

rooted *a* (in compounds) de raíces . . . ; arraigado

rope *n* soga, cuerda, *f*; (hawser) maroma, *f*; *naut* cabo, *m*; (tight-rope) cable, *m*, cuerda de volatinero, *f*; (string) ristra, sarta, *f*; hilo, *m*; *pl* **ropes,** (boxing) cuerdas del cuadrilátero, *f pl*. *vt* encordelar, atar con cuerdas. **to r. in,** encerrar; (a person) enganchar, coger. **a r. of pearls,** una sarta de perlas. **to give a person plenty of r.,** dar mucha latitud (a). **to know the ropes,** conocer todos los trucos. **r.-ladder,** escala de cuerda, *f*. **r.-maker,** cordelero (-ra), soguero, *m*. **r.-making,** cordelería, soguería, *f*. **r.-trick,** truco de la cuerda, *m*. **r.-walk,** cordelería, *f*. **r.-yarn,** *naut* filástica, *f*

rosary *n* rosario, *m*. **to say the r.,** rezar el rosario

rose *n* rosa, *f*; color de rosa, *m*; (rosette) roseta, *f*; *arch* rosetón, *m*; (of watering-can) pomo, *m*, roseta, *f*. *a* de rosa, rosado. **to see the world through r.-colored spectacles,** ver las cosas en color de rosa. **to turn to r.,** volverse color de rosa, rosear. **r.-bay,** *bot* rododafne, adelfa, *f*. **r.-bush,** rosal, *m*. **r.-color,** color de rosa, rosa, *m*. **r.-colored,** de color de rosa, rosado. **r.-garden,** rosalera, rosaleda, *f*. **r. grower,** cultivador (-ra) de rosas. **r. hip,** escaramujo, *m*. **r. leaf,** hoja de rosa, *f*; pétalo de rosa, *m*. **r.-like,** como una rosa, de rosa. **r.-red,** de color de rosa; como una rosa. **climbing r.-tree,** rosal trepador, *m*. **dwarf r.-tree,** rosal bajo, *m*. **standard r.-tree,** rosal de tallo, *m*. **r.-water,** agua de rosas, *f*. **r.-window,** rosetón, *m*, rosa, *f*. **r.-wood,** palo de rosa, *m*

rosé *a* (of wines) rosado

rosebud *n* capullo de rosa, *m*

rosemary *n* romero, *m*

rosin *n* (solid, for violin-bows, etc.) colofonia, *f*; resina, *f*. *vt* dar con colofonia; dar con resina

rosiness *n* color de rosa, *m*

roster *n* lista, *f*; registro, *m*, matrícula, *f*

rostrum *n* tribuna, *f*; *zool* pico, *m*; (of a ship) espolón, *m*

rosy *a* róseo, rosado; sonrosado; *fig* de color de rosa, halagüeño; optimista. **r.-cheeked,** con (de) mejillas sonrosadas

rot *n* putrefacción, podredumbre, *f*; (in trees) caries, *f*; (in sheep) comalía, *f*; (slang) patrañas, *f pl*, disparates, *m pl*, *vi* pudrirse; descomponerse; *fig* echarse a perder; (slang) decir disparates. *vt* pudrir; *fig* corromper; (slang) tomar el pelo (a)

rota *n* lista, *f*; orden del día, *m*

rotary *a* rotativo. **r. printing press,** rotativa, *f*

rotary telephone *n* teléfono de discado, *m*

rotate *vi* girar, dar vueltas; alternarse. *vt* hacer girar

rotating *a* rotativo; giratorio

rotation *n* rotación, *f*; turno, *m*. **in r.,** por turnos. **r. of crops,** rotación de cultivos, *f*

rotatory *a* rotatorio

rote, to learn by *vt* aprender de memoria, aprender por repetición, aprender de cotorra

rotogravure *n* rotograbado, *m*

rotten *a* putrefacto; podrido; (of bones, teeth) cariado; dañado, echado a perder; *fig* corrompido; (slang) pésimo. **to smell r.,** oler a podredumbre; apestar

rottenness *n* putrefacción, podredumbre, *f*; *fig* corrupción, *f*

rotter *n* (slang) perdido, *m*

rotting *n* pudrición, *f*, *a* que se pudre

rotund *a* rotundo

rotunda *n* rotonda, *f*

rotundity *n* redondez, *f*; rotundidad, *f*

roué *n* calavera, libertino, *m*

rouge *n* colorete, *m*, *vt* and *vi* pintar de rojo, poner(se) colorete

rough *a* áspero; duro; (of country) fragoso, escabroso; (uneven) desigual; (stormy) borrascoso, tempestuoso; (of the sea) encrespado, bravo; (of movement) violento; (bristling) erizado; (of the hair) despeinado; (unpolished) tosco; basto; (unskilled, clumsy) torpe; (of sounds, tastes) áspero; (of persons) rudo, inculto; (severe) severo; (of behavior) brutal; (of manners) brusco; (rude) grosero; (approximate) aproximado. *adv* duramente, mal. *n* estado tosco, *m*; (person) matón, *m*. **in the r.,** en bruto; (roughed out) bosquejado. **to grow r.,** (of the sea) encresparse, embravecerse. **to take the r. with the smooth,** *fig* aceptar la realidad; tomar lo bueno con lo malo. **to r. it,** luchar contra las dificultades, pasar apuros; llevar una vida sencilla; vivir mal. **to r. out,** bosquejar. **r. and ready,** improvisado; provisional. **r. and tumble,** *n* camorra, pendencia, *f*. **r.-cast,** *vt* dar una primera capa de mezcla gruesa (a); bosquejar. **r. diamond,** diamante bruto (en or en bruto), *m*. **r.-draft,** borrador, *m*; bosquejo, *m*. **r.-haired,** (of a dog) de pelo crespo. **r.-hewn,** modelado toscamente; desbastado; *fig* cerril, tosco. **r.-house,** jarana, *f*. **r.-rider,** domador (de caballos), *m*. **r. sketch,** bosquejo, esbozo, *m*. **r.-spoken,** malhablado

roughen *vt* poner áspero. *vi* ponerse áspero

roughly *adv* rudamente, toscamente; duramente; brutalmente; bruscamente; (of tastes, sounds) ásperamente; (approximately) aproximadamente, más o menos

roughness *n* aspereza, *f*; dureza, *f*; tosquedad, *f*; rudeza, *f*; (of the sea, wind) braveza, *f*; violencia, *f*; (of manner) brusquedad, *f*; brutalidad, *f*; (vulgarity) grosería, *f*. **the r. of the way,** la aspereza del camino

roulette *n* ruleta, *f*

round *a* redondo; (plump) rollizo; rotundo, categórico; sonoro. **a r. sum,** una cantidad redonda; un número redondo. **to walk at a r. pace,** andar a un buen paso. **r. dance,** baile en ruedo, *m*. **r.-faced,** carrilleno, de cara redonda. **r.-house,** cuerpo de guardia, *m*; *naut* tumbadillo, *m*. **r.-shouldered,** cargado de espaldas. **r. table,** mesa redonda, *f*; (of King Arthur) Tabla

Redonda, *f*. **r. trip,** viaje redondo, viaje de ida y vuelta, *m*. **r.-up,** rodeo de ganado, *m*; arresto, *m*

round *n* círculo, *m*; esfera, *f*; redondez, *f*; (slice) rodaja, *f*; (of a ladder) peldaño, *m*; (patrol and *mil*) ronda, *f*; circuito, *m*; vuelta, *f*, giro, *m*; serie, *f*; rutina, *f*; (of ammunition) andanada, descarga, *f*; (of cartridge) cartucho con bala, *m*; (of applause, etc.) salva, *f*; (of golf) partido, *m*; (in a fight) asalto, *m*; *sport* vuelta, *f*; (of drinks) ronda, *f*; (doctor's) visitas, *f pl*

round *vt* redondear; (*fig* complete) acabar, perfeccionar; (go round, e.g. a corner) dar vuleta (a), doblar, trasponer; rodear, cercar; (of a ship) doblar. *vi* redondearse. **to r. off,** redondear; terminar; coronar. **to r. up,** (cattle) rodear. **to r. upon,** volverse contra

round *adv* alrededor, en derredor; por todos lados; a la redonda, en torno; en circunferencia; en conjunto (**r.** is not translated in Spanish, e.g. **I shall come r. to your house,** Vendré a tu casa). *prep* alrededor de. **all the year r.,** todo el año, el año entero. **r. about,** a la redonda de, al derredor de; (nearly) cerca de; (of time by the clock) a eso de. **The road is closed and we shall have to go r.,** El camino está cerrado y tendremos que dar una vuelta. **to come r.,** volver; dejarse persuadir; recobrar su buen humor. **to go r.,** (spin) dar vueltas; (of the wind) cambiar. **There is enough to go r.,** Hay bastante para todos

roundabout *a* indirecto; desviado; vago. *n* tiovivo, *m*; (traffic) redondel, *m*. **He spoke in a r. way,** Hablaba con circunloquios. **We went there by a r. way,** Fuimos dando un rodeo

roundly *adv* en redondo; rotundamente, claramente

roundness *n* redondez, *f*; rotundidad, *f*

rouse *vt* despertar; animar; excitar; suscitar, provocar. **to r. oneself,** despertarse; animarse (a hacer algo)

rousing *a* que despierta; (moving) emocionante; (enthusiastic) entusiasta; grande, bueno

rout *n* (rabble) chusma, *f*; (party) sarao, *m*; (defeat) derrota, *f*; (meeting) reunión, *f*. *vt* derrotar, poner en fuga; vencer

route *n* ruta, *f*; camino, *m*; itinerario, *m*. **r. march,** marcha de maniobras, *f*

routine *n* rutina, *f*, *a* rutinario, de rutina

rove *vi* vagar, errar

rover *n* vagabundo (-da); pirata, *m*

roving *a* vagabundo, errante; ambulante

row *n* (line) hilera, fila, hila, *f*; (in a theater, etc.) fila, *f*; (string) ristra, *f*; (in a boat) paseo en bote, *m*; (commotion) alboroto, *m*; (noise) ruido, *m*; (shindy) gresca, camorra, *f*; (scolding) regaño, *m*, *vi* (a boat) remar, bogar. *vt* conducir remando; (scold) regañar. **to be a row,** (shindy) haber la de San Quintín. **to start a row,** (shindy) armar camorra.

rowboat *n* bote de remos, *m*

rowdiness *n* alboroto, *m*

rowdy *a* alborotador. *n* trafalmejas, *mf* rufián, *m*

rower *n* remero (-ra); bogador (-ra)

rowing *a* que rema; de remos. *n* deporte del remo, *m*; paseo en bote, *m*. **r.-boat,** bote de remos, *m*. **r.-club,** club náutico, *m*. **r.-seat,** bancada, *f*. **r.-stroke,** bogada, *f*

royal *a* real; regio. *n naut* sobrejuanete, *m*. **r. academy,** real academia, *f*. **r. eagle,** águila real, *f*. **R. Highness,** Alteza Real, *f*. **r. letters patent,** cédula real, *f*. **R. Mail,** mala real, *f*. **R. Standard,** estandarte real, *m*

royalism *n* realismo, *m*

royalist *a* and *n* realista, *mf*

royally *adv* realmente; regiamente

royalty *n* realeza, *f*; miembro de la familia real, *m*; tanto por ciento de los ingresos, *m*; derechos de autor, *m pl*

R.R. (abbrev. of *railroad*) F.R. (abbrev. of *ferrocarril*)

rub *vt* frotar, estregar; fregar; rozar; friccionar; (make sore) raspar. **to rub one's hands together,** frotarse las manos. **to rub the wrong way,** frotar a contrapelo. **to rub against,** rozar. **to rub along,** *inf* ir tirando. **to rub down,** (a horse) bruzar; limpiar; (dry) secar; (wear down) desgastar. **to rub in,** dar fricciones

con; frotar con; (an idea, etc.) machacar. **to rub off,** *vt* quitar (frotando); borrar. *vi* borrarse; separarse (de). **to rub out,** *vt* borrar. *vi* borrarse. **to rub up,** (polish) limpiar; *fig* refrescar

rub *n* frotación, *f*; roce, *m*; fricción, *f*; *fig* obstáculo, *m*; dificultad, *f*. **to give a rub,** frotar, etc. **rub-a-dub,** rataplán, *m*

rubber *a* de caucho, de goma. *n* caucho, *m*, goma, *f*; (for erasing) goma de borrar, *f*; (masseur) masajista, *mf*; (at whist, etc.) partida, *f*; *pl* **rubbers,** zapatos de goma, chanclos, *m pl*. **synthetic r.,** caucho artificial, *m*. **r. band,** goma, banda de goma, *f*. **r. belt,** *mech* correa de transmisión de caucho, *f*. **r.-plant, tree,** cauchera, *f*. **r. plantation,** cauchal, *m*. **r. planter,** cauchero, *m*. **r. stamp,** estampilla, *f*

rubbing *n* frotación, *f*; fricción, *f*; roce, *m*; (of floors, dishes, etc.) fregado, *m*

rubbish *n* basura, *f*; desperdicios, *m pl*, desecho, *m*; (of goods) pacotilla, *f*; (nonsense) pamplinas, patrañas, *f pl*, disparates, *m pl*. **r. cart,** carro del basurero, *m*

rubbishy *a* sin valor, malo; (of goods) de pacotilla, de calidad inferior

rubble *n* escombros, *m pl*; cascote, *m*; piedra bruta, *f*

rubicund *a* rubicundo

rubric *n* rúbrica, *f*

ruby *n* rubí, *m*. *a* de rubíes; de rubí. **r. lips,** labios de rubí, *m pl*

rucksack *n* mochila, *f*

rudder *n* timón, *m*, gobernalle, *m*

ruddiness *n* rubicundez, *f*; rojez, *f*; frescura, *f*

ruddy *a* rubicundo; rojo; frescote; (of animals) barcino

rude *a* rudo; tosco; vigoroso; grosero, descortés

rudely *adv* toscamente; groseramente

rudeness *n* rudeza, *f*; tosquedad, *f*; grosería, incivilidad, descortesía, *f*

rudiment *n* rudimento, *m*

rudimentary *a* rudimentario

rue *vt* lamentar, llorar. *n bot* ruda, *f*

rueful *a* triste, melancólico; lamentable

ruefully *adv* tristemente

ruefulness *n* tristeza, *f*

ruff *n* golilla, lechuguilla, *f*; (of a bird) collarín de plumas, *m*; (of an animal) collarín de pelo, *m*

ruffian *n* rufián, *m*

ruffle *n sew* volante fruncido, *m*; (of a bird) collarín de plumas, *m*; (of an animal) collarín de pelo, *m*; (ripple) rizo, *m*; (annoyance) irritación, *f*. *vt* (ripple) rizar; (pleat) fruncir; (feathers) erizar; (hair) despeinar; agitar; (annoy) irritar, incomodar

ruffling *n* (rippling) rizado, *m*; (pleating) fruncido, *m*; (of the temper) irritación, *f*

rug *n* (floor) alfombra, *f*; manta de viaje, *f*. **rug strap,** portamantas, *m*

rugged *a* áspero, escabroso; escarpado, abrupto; (wrinkled) arrugado; tosco; (harsh) duro, severo; inculto; rudo; mal acabado; vigoroso

ruggedness *n* aspereza, escabrosidad, *f*; lo escarpado; dureza, severidad, *f*; rudeza, *f*; vigor, *m*

ruin *n* ruina, *f*. *vt* arruinar; echar a perder, estropear por completo; (a woman) perder

ruination *n* ruina, perdición, *f*

ruined *a* arruinado; en ruinas

ruinous *a* ruinoso; en ruinas

ruinously *adv* ruinosamente

rule *n* regla, *f*; gobierno, *m*; autoridad, *f*, mando, *m*; administración, *f*; (reign) reinado, *m*; (of a court, etc.) orden, *f*; (for measuring) regla, *f*; *print* regleta, *f*; *pl* **rules,** reglas, *f pl*; reglamento, *m*. *vt* gobernar; regentar; regir; (control) dominar; (of a chairman, etc.) disponer, decidir; (guide) guiar; (lines) reglar. *vi* gobernar; (of a monarch) reinar; (of prices) mantenerse; estar en boga, prevalecer. **as a r.,** por regla general, en general. **slide-r.,** regla de cálculo, *f*. **to make it a r.,** tener por regla; tener por costumbre; tener por máxima. **to r. out,** excluir; *law* no admitir. **to r. over,** (of a king, etc.) reinar sobre. **r. of the road,** reglamento del

tráfico, *m*. **r. of thumb,** regla empírica, *f*; rutina, *f*
ruler *n* gobernador (-ra); soberano (-na); (master) amo (ama); (for ruling lines) regla, *f*
ruling *a* regente; dominante; (current) vigente. *n* gobierno, *m*; *law* decisión, *f*, fallo, *m*; (with lines) rayado, *m*. **r. pen,** tiralíneas, *m*
rum *n* ron, *m*
Rumanian *a* rumano. *n* rumano (-na); (language) rumano, *m*
rumble *vi* retumbar, tronar; (of vehicles) rugir; crujir. *n* retumbo, trueno, *m*; rugido, *m*; ruido sordo, *m*; rumor, *m*; crujido, *m*
rumbling *a* que retumba, etc. *n* ruido sordo, *m*; retumbo, *m*; crujido, *m*; (in the bowels) rugido, *m*
ruminant *a* and *n* rumiante, *mf*
ruminate *vi* and *vt* rumiar
rumination *n* rumia, *f*; meditación, reflexión, *f*
rummage *vt* revolver, desordenar, trastornar; explorar. **to r. out,** desenterrar
rumor *n* rumor, *m*, fama, *f*. **It is rumored that . . . ,** Hay rumores de que . . . , La voz corre que . . . , Se dice que . . .
rump *n* (of an animal) nalgas, ancas, *f pl*; cuarto trasero, *m*; (of a bird) rabadilla, *f*; (scornful) culo, *m*, posaderas, *f pl*. **r.-steak,** solomillo, *m*
rumple *vt* arrugar; desordenar
run *vi* correr; acudir; (flee) huir; (rush) precipitarse, lanzarse; (in a race) tomar parte en una carrera; competir; (pass over) deslizarse (por); (of machines) andar, marchar; (of traffic) circular; (leave, of trains, ships, etc.) salir; (ply between) hacer el trayecto entre . . . y . . . ; (flow) fluir, correr; (into the sea, of rivers) desembocar (en); (spurt) chorrear, manar; (drip) gotear; (leak) dejar fugar (el agua, etc.); (of colors) correrse; caer; (of tears) correr; derramarse; (of eyes) llorar; (melt) derretirse; (of a sore) supurar; (travel or go) ir; moverse; (work) trabajar; funcionar; (of editions of a book) agotarse; (of a play) representarse; (cross) cruzar; (elapse) correr; transcurrir, pasar; (become) hacerse; (of wording) decir; (be current) correr; (for parliament, etc.) hacerse candidato; (navigate) navegar; (spread) extenderse; (be) estar; ser; (of thoughts) pasar; (last) durar; (tend) tender (a). *vt* (a race, a horse) correr; (drive) conducir; (a business, etc.) administrar; dirigir; (govern) gobernar, regir; (hunt) cazar; perseguir; (water, etc.) hacer correr; (pierce) clavar; introducir; (push) empujar; (one's hand, eye, etc.) pasar; (risks, etc.) correr; (possess) tener; establecer un servicio de (autobuses, etc.); (smuggle) hacer contrabando de. **The ship ran aground,** El barco encalló. **to run dry,** secarse; agotarse. **to run in the family,** estar en la familia. **to run into debt,** endeudarse, contraer deudas. **to run to seed,** granar; agotarse. **Steamers run daily between Barcelona and Mallorca,** Hay servicio diario de vapores entre Barcelona y Mallorca. **A stab of pain ran up his leg,** Sintió un dolor agudo en la pierna. **Feeling was running high,** Los ánimos estaban excitados. **My arrangements ran smoothly,** Mis planes marchaban bien. **Funds are running low,** El dinero escasea. **The tune runs in my head,** Tengo la canción metida en la cabeza. **The message runs like this,** El mensaje reza así, El mensaje dice así. **He ran his fingers through his hair,** Se mesaba los cabellos. **to run about,** andar de un lado a otro, correr por todas partes; (gad) corretear. **to run across,** cruzar corriendo; (meet) topar con, tropezar con. **to run after,** correr detrás (de); perseguir; buscar. **to run against,** (collide with) dar contra; (meet) tropezar con. **to run at,** abalanzarse hacia, precipitarse sobre; atacar. **to run away,** huir, escaparse; (slip away) escurrirse; (of a horse) dispararse, desbocarse. **to run away with,** huir con, fugarse con; (carry off) arrebatar; (steal) llevarse; (imagine) imaginarse, figurarse; (of temper, etc.) dominar, poseer. **to run back,** volver corriendo; llegar corriendo; retroceder rápidamente, correr hacia atrás. **to run backwards,** correr hacia

atrás; **to run backwards and forwards,** ir y venir. **to run behind,** correr detrás (de); quedarse atrás; (be late) estar atrasado. **to run down,** *vi* bajar corriendo; descender, bajar; (of a clock) parar; (of a battery) gastarse; (of liquids) correr; fluir; (drop by drop) destilar. *vt* (capture) coger; alcanzar; (a person by a vehicle) atropellar; (a ship) echar a pique; (disparage) hablar mal de. **run-down,** (in health) agotado; (of a clock) parado. **to run for,** buscar corriendo; correr para coger (el autobús, etc.); (president, etc.) ser candidato para. **to run in,** *vi* entrar corriendo. *vt* arrestar; hacer prisionero; *print* encerrar. **to run into,** tropezar con; chocar con; (plunge into) meterse de cabeza en; (of sums of money, etc.) ascender a; (of streets, rivers, etc.) desembocar en. **to run off,** *vi* escaparse corriendo; marcharse corriendo. *vt* deslizarse por; (drain) vaciar; *print* imprimir; (compose) componer. **to run off with,** huir con. **to run on,** correr delante; continuar; (of the mind) pensar en, entregarse a; hablar sin cesar; *print* recorrer. **to run out,** *vi* salir corriendo; (of liquids) derramarse; salir; (end) acabarse; agotarse; (project) sobresalir. *vt* (cricket) coger al lanzador fuera de la línea de saque. **to run out of,** no tener más de, haber terminado. **to run over,** *vi* rebosar; derramarse. *vt* (of a vehicle) atropellar, pasar por encima de; (peruse) repasar; revisar. **run pell-mell,** salir pitando, salir volando, salvarse por pies. **to run through,** correr por; pasar por; recorrer; (go directly) ir directamente a; (pierce) traspasar, pasar de parte a parte; (squander) derrochar, malbaratar; (read) hojear, leer por encima. **to run up,** *vt* (hoist) izar; hacer de prisa; construir rápidamente; (incur) incurrir. *vi* subir corriendo; (of plants) trepar (por); (shrink) encogerse; (of expenses) aumentar. **to run up to time,** llegar a su hora. **to run up against,** tropezar con; (opposition, etc.) encontrar.

run *n* carrera, corrida, *f*; (excursion) visita, excursión, *f*; (cricket) carrera, *f*; (walk) paseo, *m*; (by train or sea) viaje, *m*; (by bus, tram) trayecto, *m*; (sea crossing) travesía, *f*; (distance run) recorrido, *m*; (of events, etc.) curso, *m*; marcha, *f*; (of markets, etc.) tendencia, *f*; (rhythm) ritmo, *m*; dirección, *f*; distancia, *f*; *mus* serie de notas, *f*; serie, *f*; duración, *f*; *theat* serie de representaciones, *f*; (freedom to use) libre uso, *m*; (majority) mayoría, *f*; (on a bank) asedio, *m*; (on a book, etc.) demanda, *f*; (for sheep, etc.) terreno de pasto, *m*; (for fowls) gallinero, *m*. **a run of bad luck,** una temporada de mala suerte. **at a run,** corriendo. **in the long run,** a la larga, al fin y al cabo. **on the run,** en fuga; ocupado. **Prices came down with a run,** Los precios bajaron de golpe. **take-off run,** *aer* recorrido de despegue, *m*
runaway *a* fugitivo; (of a horse) desbocado
rune *n* runa, *f*
rung *n* (of a ladder) peldaño, *m*; (of a chair) travesaño, *m*; (lath) listón, *m*
runic *a* rúnico
runner *n* corredor (-ra); (carrier of sedan chair, etc.) silletero, *mf*; (smuggler) contrabandista, *m*; (courier) estafeta, *f*; (messenger) mensajero, *m*; (ring) anillo movible, pasador corredizo, *m*; rueda móvil, *f*; (of a sledge) patín, *m*; *bot* tallo rastrero, *m*. **r.-up,** el segundo
running *a* corredor; (of water, bank accounts) corriente; (of a knot) corredizo; (of a sore) supurante; (continuous) continuo; (consecutive) consecutivo. *n* carrera, *f*; marcha, *f*; funcionamiento, *m*; administración, *f*; gobierno, *m*; dirección, *f*; (flowing) derrame, *m*; (of trains, buses, etc.) servicio, *m*; (smuggling) contrabando, *m*; (of a sore) supuración, *f*. **six times r.,** seis veces consecutivas. **The car is in r. order,** El auto está en buen estado. **r. away,** fuga, *f*. **r.-board,** (of a car, etc.) estribo, *m*; (of a locomotive) plataforma, *f*. **r. costs,** gastos de mantenimiento, *m pl*; (railway) gastos de tracción, *m pl*. **r. fight,** acción de retirada, *f*. **r.-knot,** lazo corredizo, *m*. **r. title,** *print* título de la columna, *m*

run-off match *n* desempate, *m*
runway *n* (for launching a ship) grada, *f*; (of an airfield) pista de aterrizaje, *f*
rupee *n* rupia, *f*
rupestrian *a* rupestre
rupture *n* rompimiento, *m*, rotura, *f*; ruptura, *f*; *med* hernia, *f*
ruptured *a med* herniado, quebrado
rupturing *n* ruptura, *f*
rural *a* rural, campestre, del campo; agrario
ruse *n* artimaña, treta, ardid, *f*
rush *n bot* junco, *m*; acometida, *f*; ataque, *m*; (of water) torrente, *m*; (bustle) bullicio, *m*; (speed) prisa, *f*; precipitación, *f*; acceso, *m*; (crowd) tropel, *m*, masa, *f*; (struggle) lucha, *f*; furia, *f*. *vi* precipitarse, lanzarse; agolparse. *vt* llevar rápidamente (a); despachar rápidamente; precipitar; (attack) asaltar, atacar; (capture) tomar, capturar; hacer de prisa; (a bill) hacer aprobar de prisa. **to r. upon,** abalanzarse hacia; embestir. **in a r.,** en tropel, en masa; de prisa. **to r. to a conclusion,** precipitarse a una conclusión. **r.-bottomed,** con asiento de enea. **r. hour,** hora de mayor circulación, *f*, hora de aglomeración, hora-pico (Argentina), hora brava (Argentina, informal). **r. order,** pedido urgente, *m*
rushy *a* juncoso
russet *a* rojizo; rojo. **r. apple,** manzana asperiega, *f*
Russia Rusia, *f*
Russian *a* ruso. *n* ruso (-sa); (language) ruso, *m*. **R. leather,** piel de Rusia, *f*
rust *n* herrumbre, *f*, orín, *m*; moho, *m*; (disease) añublo,

tizón, *m*. *vt* aherrumbrar; enmohecer. *vi* aherrumbrarse; enmohecerse
rustic *a* rústico; campesino, aldeano; (scornful) palurdo, grosero. *n* aldeano, *m*; (scornful) patán, *m*
rusticate *vi* rusticar, vivir en el campo. *vt* enviar al campo
rustication *n* rusticación, *f*
rusticity *n* rusticidad, *f*
rustiness *n* herrumbre, *f*; enmohecimiento, *m*; color rojizo, *m*; *fig* falta de práctica, *f*
rustle *n* susurro, *m*; murmurio, *m*; (of silk, a dress, etc.) frufru, *m*; (of paper, etc.) crujido, *m*. *vi* susurrar; murmurar; crujir. *vt* (a paper) hacer crujir
rustless *a* inoxidable
rustling *n see* **rustle**
rusty *a* herrumbroso; enmohecido, mohoso; (red) rojizo, (worn out) usado, viejo; (out of practice) desacostumbrado; (forgotten) empolvorado, oxidado (e.g. **My Portuguese is rusty,** Mi portugués está empolvorado)
rut *n* rodera, *f*, bache, surco, *m*; *fig* sendero trillado, *m*; *fig* rutina, *f*; (sexual appetite) celo, *m*, *vi* estar en celo
ruthless *a* inhumano, insensible, despiadado; inexorable, inflexible
ruthlessly *adv* inhumanamente; inflexiblemente, inexorablemente
ruthlessness *n* inhumanidad, *f*; inflexibilidad, inexorabilidad, *f*
Rwanda Ruanda, *f*
rye *n* centeno, *m*. **rye field,** centenar, *m*

S

s *n* (letter) ese, *f*
sabbatarian *a* sabatario
Sabbath *n* (Jewish) sábado, *m*; (Christian) domingo, *m*
sabbatical *a* sabático
sable *n* (animal and fur) marta, *f*; her sable, *m*. *a* her sable; *poet* negro
sabotage *n* sabotaje, *m*, *vt* cometer un acto de sabotaje en
saboteur *n* saboteador, *m*
sabre *n* sable, *m*; (soldier) jinete, *m*. *vt* dar sablazos (a), acuchillar. **s. cut, thrust,** sablazo, *m*
sac *n biol* saco, *m*
saccharin *n* sacarina, *f*
sachet *n* sachet, *m*; bolsa, *f*. **handkerchief s.,** bolsa para pañuelos, *f*
sack *n* (bag) saco, *m*; *mil* saqueo, saqueamiento, saco, *m*. *vt* meter en sacos; (dismiss) dar pasaporte (a), despedir; *mil* saquear. **to get the s.,** recibir el pasaporte. **to give the s.,** dar el pasaporte (a), poner de patitas en la calle (a). **s. coat,** saco, *m*
sackcloth *n* harpillera, *f*. **to repent in s. and ashes,** ponerse cenizas en la cabeza
sacking *n* harpillera, *f*; *mil* saqueo, *m*
sacrament *n* sacramento, *m*; Eucaristía, *f*. **the Blessed S.,** el Santísimo Sacramento. **to receive the Holy S.,** comulgar. **to receive the last sacraments,** recibir los sacramentos, recibir la Extremaunción
sacramental *a* sacramental
sacramentalist *n* sacramentario (-ia)
sacred *a* sagrado; sacro, santo; consagrado. **Nothing is s. to them,** No hay nada sagrado para ellos, No respetan nada. **the S. Heart of Jesus,** el Sagrado Corazón (de Jesús). **S. to the memory of . . .** Consagrado a la memoria de . . . **s. music,** música sagrada, *f*
sacredness *n* carácter sagrado, *m*; santidad, *f*; inviolabilidad, *f*
sacrifice *n* sacrificio, *m*. *vt* and *vi* sacrificar. **s. of the mass,** sacrificio del altar, *m*
sacrificial *a* sacrificador; del sacrificio
sacrilege *n* sacrilegio, *m*

sacrilegious *a* sacrílego
sacristan *n* sacristán, *m*
sacristy *n* sacristía, *f*
sacrosanct *a* sacrosanto
sacrum *n anat* sacro, *m*
sad *a* triste; melancólico; (of a mistake) deplorable, funesto; *inf* redomado; (pensive) pensativo. **How s.!** ¡Qué lástima! ¡Qué triste! **It made me s.,** Me entristeció
sadden *vt* entristecer, acongojar, afligir
saddle *n* (riding) silla de montar, *f*; (of a bicycle, etc.) sillín, *m*; *mech* silla, *f*; *anat* espalda, *f*. *vt* ensillar. **to s. with the responsibility of,** echar la responsabilidad de (a). **s. of mutton,** lomo de carnero, *m*. **s.-bag,** alforja, *f*. **s.-cloth,** mantilla de silla, *f*. **s.-tree,** arzón, *m*
saddler *n* sillero, guarnicionero, *m*
Sadducee *n* saduceo (-ea)
sadism *n* sadismo, *m*
sadist *n* sadista, *mf*
sadistic *a* sadístico
sadly *adv* tristemente; (very) muy
sadness *n* tristeza, melancolía, *f*
safe *a* al abrigo (de); seguro; salvo; (certain) cierto; prudente; digno de confianza. *n* caja de caudales, *f*; (for food) alacena, *f*. **I stood beneath a tree s. from the rain,** Estaba de pie bajo un árbol, al abrigo de la lluvia. **to put something in a s. place,** poner algo en salvo; poner algo en un lugar seguro. **s. and sound,** sano y salvo. **s.-conduct,** salvoconducto, *m*. **s.-keeping,** lugar seguro, *m*; (of a person) buenas manos, *f pl*
safeguard *n* protección, garantía, *f*; precaución, *f*. *vt* proteger, guardar; tomar precauciones (contra)
safely *adv* seguramente; sin accidente, sin novedad, sano y salvo; sin peligro. **You may s. tell him,** Puedes decírselo con toda seguridad. **to put** (something) **away s.,** poner (algo) en un lugar seguro
safety *n* seguridad, *f*. *a* de seguridad; (of locks) de golpe. **a place of s.,** un lugar seguro. **in s.,** en salvo, en seguro; con seguridad. **to believe in s. first,** poner la seguridad en primer lugar. **to play for s.,** jugar seguro.

with complete s., con toda seguridad. **s.-belt,** (cinto) salvavidas, *m.* **s.-catch,** fiador, *m.* **s.-curtain,** telón de seguridad, telón contra incendios, *m.* **s.-fuse,** espoleta de seguridad, *f.* **s.-glass,** vidrio inastillable, *m.* **s.-island,** refugio para peatones, *m.* **s.-lamp,** lámpara de seguridad, *f.* **s.-latch,** pestillo de golpe, *m.* **s.-lock,** (of fire-arms) seguro, *m;* (of doors, etc.) cerradura de seguridad, *f.* **s.-pin,** imperdible, *m.* **s.-razor,** máquina de afeitar, *f.* **s.-valve,** válvula de seguridad, *f*

saffron *n* azafrán, *m,* a azafranado, de color de azafrán.

sag *vi* doblegarse, ceder; inclinarse; *naut* caer a sotavento; (of prices) bajar; (of spirits, etc.) flaquear

saga *n* saga, *f;* epopeya, *f*

sagacious *a* sagaz, perspicaz; (of animals) sabio

sagacity *n* sagacidad, perspicacia, *f;* (of animals) sagacidad, *f*

sage *n* sabio, *m; bot* salvia, *f. a* sabio; sagaz; cuerdo

Sagittarius *n* Sagitario, *m*

Sahara, the el Sáhara, *m*

said *a* antedicho; tal dicho. **No sooner s. than done,** Dicho y hecho. **the s. Mr. Martínez,** el tal Sr. Martínez

sail *n* (of a ship) vela, *f;* (sailing-ship) velero, *m;* (of a windmill) aspa, *f; mech* ala, *f;* (trip) paseo en barco, *m. vi* navegar; ir en barco; dar un paseo en barco; (leave) salir en barco; zarpar; (of swans, etc.) deslizarse; (of clouds, etc.) flotar. *vt* (a ship) gobernar; (the sea) navegar por. **She sailed into the room,** Entró majestuosamente en la sala. **The ship sailed at eight knots,** El buque navegaba a ocho nudos. **to go for a s.,** dar un paseo en barco. **to s. round the world,** dar la vuelta al mundo. **to s. the seas,** navegar por los mares. **to set s.,** darse a la vela, zarpar. **to take in the sails,** amainar. **s.-maker,** velero, *m.* **to s. into,** entrar en. **to s. round,** (the Cape, etc.) doblar. **to s. up,** subir en barco; (of a boat) ir río arriba

sailcloth *n* lona, *f*

sailing *n* navegación, *f;* (departure) salida, *f.* **It's all plain s.,** Todo va viento en popa. **s.-boat,** bote de vela, *m.* **s.-ship,** buque de vela, velero, *m*

sailor *n* marinero, *m.* **John is a bad s.,** Juan se marea fácilmente. **to be a good s.,** no marearse. **s.-blouse, s.-suit,** traje de marinero, *m*

saint *n* santo (-ta); (before masculine names of Sts., excluding Sts. Dominic and Thomas) San; *inf* ángel, *m.* **All Saints' Day,** el día de Todos los Santos. **saint's day,** fiesta de un santo (or de una santa), *f;* (of a person) santo, *m.* **St. Bernard dog,** perro de San Bernardo, *m.* **St. John the Baptist,** San Juan Bautista. **St. Martin's summer,** el veranillo de San Martín. **St. Vitus's dance,** el baile de San Vito

sainthood *n* santidad, *f*

saintliness *n* santidad, *f*

saintly *a* de santo; de santa; santo; *inf* angelical

Saint Petersburg San Petersburgo, *m*

sake *n* amor, *m;* causa, *f.* **for God's s.,** por el amor de Dios. **for the s. of,** para; por amor de. **to talk for talking's s.,** hablar por hablar

salable *a* vendible

salaciousness *n* salacidad, *f*

salad *n* ensalada, *f;* (lettuce) lechuga, *f.* **fruit s.,** macedonia de frutas, *f.* **s.-bowl,** ensaladera, *f.* **s.-dressing,** aderezo, aliño, *m,* salsa para ensalada, *f.* **s.-oil,** aceite para ensaladas, *m*

salamander *n* salamandra, *f*

salaried *a* a sueldo; (of posts) retribuido

salary *n* sueldo, salario, *m*

sale *n* venta, *f;* (auction) almoneda, subasta pública, *f.* **clearance s.,** liquidación, *f,* saldo, *m.* **to be on s.,** estar de venta. **"Piano for s.,"** «Se vende un piano.» **s. price,** precio de venta, *m;* precio de saldo, *m*

sales contract *n* contrato de compraventa, *m*

salesman *n* dependiente de tienda, *m;* (traveller) viajante, *m*

salesmanship *n* arte de vender, *mf*

salesroom *n* salón de ventas, *m*

saleswoman *n* dependiente de tienda, vendedera, *f*

salient *a* saliente; *fig* prominente, conspicuo, notable, *n* saliente, *m.* **s. angle,** ángulo saliente, *m*

saline *a* salino. *n* (marsh) saladar, *m; med* salino, *m*

saliva *n* saliva, *f*

salivary *a* salival

salivate *vi* salivar

salivation *n* salivación, *f*

sallow *a* cetrino, oliváceo, lívido

sallowness *n* amarillez, lividez, *f;* palidez, *f*

sally *n* (mil etc.) salida, *f;* (quip) ocurrencia, salida, *f. vi* hacer una salida, salir. **to s. forth,** ponerse en camino

salmon *n* salmón, *m;* color de salmón, *m.* **s.-net,** salmonera, *f.* **s. trout,** trucha asalmonada, *f*

salon *n* salón, *m*

Salonika Salónica, *f*

saloon *n* sala, *f;* (of a steamer) cámara, *f,* salón, *m;* (on train, for sleeping) departamento de coche cama, *m;* (on train, for dining) coche comedor, *m; aut* coche cerrado, *m.* **billiard s.,** salón de billares, *m.* **dancing s.,** salón de baile, *m.* **hair-dresser's s.,** salón de peluquero, *m.* **s. bar,** bar, *m*

salsify *n bot* salsifí, *m*

salt *n* sal, *f;* (spice) sabor, *m;* (wit) sal, agudeza, *f. a* salobre, salino; salado; (of land) salitroso. *vt* (season) poner sal en; (cure) salar. **kitchen s.,** sal de cocina, *f.* **old s.,** *inf* lobo de mar, *m.* **rock s.,** sal gema, *f.* **sea s.,** sal marina, *f.* **to be not worth one's s.,** no merecer el pan que se come. **to take with a pinch of s.,** tomar con su grano de sal. **s.-cellar,** salero, *m.* **s. lagoon,** albufera, *f.* **s. lake,** lago salado, *m.* **s. marsh,** saladar, *m.* **s. meat,** carne salada, cecina, *f.* **s. merchant,** salinero, *m.* **s.-mine,** mina de sal, *f.* **s.-spoon,** cucharita de sal, *f.* **s. water,** agua salada, *f;* agua de mar, *f.* **s.-water fish,** pez de mar, *m.* **s.-works,** salinas, *f pl*

saltiness *n* sabor de sal, *m;* salobridad, *f*

salting *n* saladura, *f;* (salt marsh) salado, *m*

saltless *a* sin sal, soso, insípido; *fig* soso

saltpeter *n* salitre, *m.* **s. bed,** salitral, *m.* **s. works,** salitrería, *f*

salty *a* salado; salobre

salubrious *a* salubre, saludable, sano

salubriousness *n* salubridad, *f*

salutary *a* saludable, beneficioso

salutation *n* salutación, *f,* saludo, *m*

salute *vt* and *vi* saludar. *n* saludo, *m;* (of guns) salva, *f.* **to fire a s.,** hacer salvas, saludar con . . . salvas. **The soldier saluted them,** El soldado les saludó. **to take the s.,** tomar el saludo. **saluting base,** puesto de mando, *m*

Salvadoran, Salvadorian *a* and *n* salvadoreño (-ña)

salvage *n* salvamento, *m, vt* salvar

salvation *n* salvación, *f.* **to work out one's own s.,** salvar el alma. **the S. Army,** el Ejército de la Salvación, *m*

salve *n* pomada, *f; fig* bálsamo, *m. vt* curar; (overcome) vencer; (soothe) tranquilizar; *naut* salvar. **to s. one's conscience,** tranquilizar la conciencia

salver *n* salva, bandeja, *f*

salvo *n* (of guns or applause) salva, *f;* (reservation) salvedad, reservación, *f.* **s. of applause,** salva de aplausos, *f*

Samaritan *a* and *n* samaritano (-na)

same *a* mismo; igual; parecido; idéntico. *adv* lo mismo; del mismo modo. **all the s.,** sin embargo; con todo, a pesar de eso. **at the s. time,** al mismo tiempo; a la vez. **just the s.,** igual; (nevertheless) sin embargo. **He bowed deeply and I did the s.,** Él hizo una profunda reverencia y yo hice lo mismo. **They do not look at things the s. as we do,** No ven las cosas del mismo modo que nosotros. **If it is the s. to her,** Si le da igual. **It's all the s.,** Es igual, Lo mismo da, Es todo uno. **Ávila, capital of the province of the s. name,** Ávila, capital de la provincia de su nombre

"Same-Day Service" «En el día» (Argentina)

sameness *n* identidad, *f;* semejanza, *f,* parecido, *m;* monotonía, *f*
samovar *n* samovar, *m*
sampan *n* (boat) champán, *m*
sample *n* muestra, *f;* prueba, *f;* ejemplo, *m. vt* sacar una muestra de; (try) probar. **s. book,** muestrario, *m*
sampler *n* probador, *m;* (of wines) catador, *m; sew* dechado, *m*
sanatorium *n* sanatorio, *m*
sanctification *n* santificación, *f;* consagración, *f*
sanctify *vt* santificar; consagrar
sanctimonious *a* santurrón, mojigato, beato
sanctimoniousness *n* beatería, mojigatería, santurronería, *f*
sanction *n* sanción, *f. vt* sancionar; autorizar. **to apply sanctions,** *pol* aplicar sanciones
sanctity *n* santidad, *f;* lo sagrado; inviolabilidad, *f.* **odor of s.,** olor de santidad, *f*
sanctuary *n* santuario, *m;* (historical) sagrado, sagrado asilo, *m;* refugio, asilo, *m.* **to take s.,** acogerse a sagrado; refugiarse
sand *n* arena, *f;* (for drying writing) arenilla, *f;* granos de arena, *m pl; pl* **sands,** playa, *f;* (of life) horas de la vida, *f pl. vt* arenar. **to plough the s.,** arar en el mar. **s.-bag,** *n* saco de arena, *m. vt* (a building) proteger con sacos de arena; (a person) golpear con un saco de arena. **s.-bank,** banco de arena, *m,* barra, *f.* **to run on a s.-bank,** encallar. **s.-colored,** de color de arena. **s.-dune,** médano, *m.* **s.-paper,** *n* papel de lija, *m. vt* pulir con papel de lija, lijar. **s.-pit,** arenal, *m.* **s. shoes,** alpargatas, *f pl*
sandal *n* sandalia, *f;* (rope-soled) alpargata, *f.* **s.-wood,** sándalo, *m*
sandiness *n* naturaleza arenosa, *f;* (of hair) color bermejo, *m*
sandstone *n* arenisca, *f*
sandstorm *n* tempestad de arena, *f;* simún, *m*
sandwich *n* emparedado, bocadillo, *m. vt* insertar. **I found myself sandwiched between two fat men,** Me encontré aplastado entre dos hombres gordos. **s.-man,** hombre sándwich, *m*
sandy *a* arenoso; sabuloso; (of hair) rojo, rufo, bermejo. **a s. beach,** una playa arenosa
sane *a* de juicio sano; razonable, prudente; sesudo. **He is a very s. person,** Es un hombre con mucho sentido común. **to be s.,** estar en su juicio; (of a policy, etc.) ser prudente, ser razonable
sangfroid *n* sangre fría, *f;* aplomo, *m*
sanguinary *a* sanguinario
sanguine *a* (of complexion) rubicundo; sanguíneo; optimista, confiado. *n* (drawing) sanguina, *f.* **to be s. about the future,** ser optimista acerca del porvenir, tener confianza en el porvenir
sanhedrin *n* sanedrín, *m*
sanitary *a* sanitario; higiénico, **s. inspector,** inspector de sanidad, *m.* **s. napkin, s. towel,** servilleta higiénica, toalla sanitaria, *mf,* paño higiénico, *m*
sanitation *n* higiene, *f;* sanidad pública, *f;* (apparatus) instalación sanitaria, *f*
sanity *n* juicio sano, *m;* prudencia, *f;* (common sense) sentido común, *m,* sensatez, *f*
Sanskrit *a* and *n* sánscrito, *m*
Santa Claus *n* (Spanish equivalent) los Reyes Magos, *m pl*
São Paulo San Pablo, *m*
sap *n* (*bot* and *fig*) savia, *f; mil* zapa, *f. vt* (undermine) debilitar, agotar; *mil* zapar
sapidity *n* sapidez, *f*
sapling *n* arbolillo, *m*
sapper *n mil* zapador, *m*
Sapphic *a* sáfico. **S. verse,** verso sáfico, *m*
sapphire *n* zafiro, *m. a* de zafiros; cerúleo, de zafiro
Saracen *a* and *n* sarraceno (-na)
Saragossa Zaragoza, *f*
sarcasm *n* sarcasmo, *m*
sarcastic *a* sarcástico

sarcastically *adv* con sarcasmo, sarcásticamente
sarcophagus *n* sarcófago, *m*
sardine *n* sardina, *f.* **packed like sardines,** como sardinas en banasta. **s.-net,** sardinal, *m*
Sardinia Cerdeña, *f*
Sardinian *a* and *n* sardo (-da)
sardonic *a* sardónico
sarsaparilla *n* zarzaparrilla, *f*
sash *n* (with uniform) faja, *f;* (belt) cinto, cinturón, *m;* (of a window) cerco, *m.* **s. window,** ventana de guillotina, *f*
Satan *n* Satanás, *m*
satanic *a* satánico
satchel *n* saquito de mano, *m,* bolsa, *f;* (school) vademécum, *m;* cartapacio, *m,* cartera, *f*
sate *vt* saciar, hartar; satisfacer
sateen *n* satén, *m*
satellite *n* satélite, *m*
satiable *a* saciable
satiate *vt* saciar, hartar; satisfacer. *a* harto; repleto
satiety *n* saciedad, *f*
satin *n* raso, *m. a* de raso; (glossy) lustroso, terso. *vt* (paper) satinar
satiny *a* arrasado; lustroso, brillante
satire *n* sátira, *f*
satiric *a* satírico
satirist *n* escritor (-ra) satírico (-ca)
satirize *vt* satirizar
satisfaction *n* satisfacción, *f;* (contentment) contento, *m,* satisfacción, *f;* (for sin) expiación, *f;* (of a debt) pago, *m;* desquite, *m;* recompensa, *f.* **to demand s.,** pedir satisfacción. **to give** (someone) **s.,** dar contento (a), alegrar
satisfactorily *adv* satisfactoriamente
satisfactoriness *n* carácter satisfactorio, *m,* lo satisfactorio
satisfactory *a* satisfactorio; (for sin) expiatorio
satisfy *vt* satisfacer; (convince) convencer; (allay) tranquilizar, apaciguar. **I am satisfied with him,** Estoy satisfecho (Estoy contento) con él. **The explanation did not s. me,** La explicación no me convenció. **to s. oneself that . . . ,** asegurarse de que . . . **to s. one's thirst,** apagar la sed
satisfying *a* que satisface; satisfactorio; (of food) nutritivo
satrap *n* sátrapa, *m*
saturate *vt* saturar (de), empapar (de); *chem* saturar; *fig* imbuir; *fig* empapar. **to s. oneself in,** (a subject) emparse en
saturation *n* saturación, *f.* **s. point,** (*chem* etc.) punto de saturación, *m*
Saturday *n* sábado, *m*
Saturn *n* Saturno, *m*
saturnine *a* saturnino, taciturno
satyr *n* sátiro, *m*
sauce *n* salsa, *f;* (thick fruit) compota, *f; inf* insolencia, *f.* **s.-boat,** salsera, *f*
saucepan *n* cazuela, cacerola, *f.* **double s.,** baño de María, *m*
saucer *n* platillo, *m.* **flying s.,** platillo volante, *m.* **s.-eyed,** con ojos redondos
sauciness *n* impertinencia, insolencia, *f*
saucy *a* respondón, descarado; (cheerful) alegre; (of hats, etc.) coquetón, majo
sauerkraut *n* chucruta, *f*
saunter *vi* pasearse, vagar, *n* paseo, *m,* vuelta, *f*
sausage *n* chorizo, *m;* salchicha, *f.* **s.-balloon,** globo cautivo, *m.* **s.-curl,** bucle, *m.* **s.-machine,** choricera, *f.* **s.-maker,** choricero (-ra)
savage *a* salvaje; feroz; (cruel) inhumano, cruel; (furious) furioso. *n* salvaje, *mf*
savagely *adv* bárbaramente; ferozmente; furiosamente
savagery *n* salvajismo, *m;* ferocidad, *f;* brutalidad, crueldad, *f*
savannah *n* sabana, *f.* **s. dweller,** sabanero (-ra)
save *vt* salvar; (keep) guardar; conservar; reservar;

(money, one's clothes, etc.) ahorrar; (time) ganar; (avoid) evitar. *vi* salvar; hacer economías; ahorrar. **He saved my life,** Me salvó la vida. **They have saved a room for me,** Me han reservado una habitación. **to s. appearances,** guardar las apariencias. **to s. oneself trouble,** ahorrarse molestias. **to s. the situation,** estar al nivel de las circunstancias

save *prep* salvo, excepto, menos. *conjunc* sino, a menos que; con la excepción de. **all s. one,** todos menos uno. **all the conspirators s. he,** todos los conspiradores con la excepción de él

saving *a* frugal, económico; (stingy) tacaño, avaricioso; (clause) condicional. *n* salvación, *f;* (of money, time, etc.) ahorro, *m,* economía, *f; pl* **savings,** ahorros, *m pl.* *prep* salvo, excepto, fuera de. *conjunc* con excepción de que, fuera de que. **s. grace,** único mérito, *m.* **savings bank,** caja de ahorros, *f.* **savings fund,** montepío, *m*

savior *n* salvador (-ra). **the S.,** el Salvador, el Redentor

savor *n* sabor, gusto, *m;* (aftertaste) dejo, *m;* (zest) salsa, *f.* *vi* saber (a), tener sabor (de); *fig* oler (a). *vt* saborear, paladear; (flavor) sazonar

savoriness *n* buen sabor, *m;* (of a district) respetabilidad, *f*

savory *a* sabroso, apetitoso; (not sweet) no dulce; (of places) respetable; (of reputation, etc.) bueno. *n* entremés salado, *m.* **s. omelette,** tortilla, *f*

Savoy Saboya, *f*

saw *n* (maxim) sentencia, *f;* (proverb) refrán, decir, *m;* (tool) sierra, *f.* *vt* aserrar; (the air) cortar. *vi* usar una sierra. **two-handled saw,** tronzador, *m.* **saw-fish,** pez sierra, *m.* **saw-mill,** molino de aserrar, *m.* **sawpit,** aserradero, *m*

sawdust *n* aserrín, *m*

sawinghorse *n* caballete de aserrar, *m*

sawyer *n* aserrador, *m*

Saxon *a* and *n* sajón (-ona)

Saxony Sajonia, *f*

saxophone *n* saxófono, saxofón *m*

say *vt* decir; recitar. *vi* decir. **Let us say that the house is worth $100,000,** Pongamos por ejemplo que la casa vale cien mil dólares. **He has no say in the matter,** No entra ni sale en el asunto. **I have said my say,** He dicho lo que quería. **They say,** Se dice, Dicen, La gente dice. **You don't say!** ¡Calle! ¿De veras? ¡Imposible! **that is to say . . . ,** es decir . . . ; esto es . . . , a saber . . . **to say one's prayers,** rezar, decir sus oraciones. **to say again,** volver a decir; decir otra vez, repetir. **to say over and over again,** repetir muchas veces, decir repetidamente. **What do you say to that?** ¿Qué dices a esto?

saying *n* decir, *m;* (proverb) refrán, *m;* (maxim) sentencia, *f.* **As the s. is,** Como suele decirse; Según el refrán. **It goes without s.,** Huelga decir. **It's only a s.,** Es un decir, nada más

scab *n* (of a wound) costra, *f;* (disease) escabro, *m;* (blackleg) esquirol, *m*

scabbard *n* vaina (de espada), *f*

scabby *a* costroso; (diseased) roñoso, sarnoso

scabies *n* sarna, *f.* **s. mite,** arador de la sarna, *m*

scaffold *n* (in building) andamio, *m;* (for execution) cadalso, patíbulo, *m.* **to go to the s.,** ir al patíbulo; acabar en el patíbulo

scaffolding *n* andamiada, *f;* (building, scaffold) andamio, *m*

scald *vt* escaldar; quemar; (instruments) esterilizar. *n* quemadura, escaldadura, *f.* **to s. oneself,** escaldarse. **scalding hot,** hirviendo

scale *n* (of a balance) platillo, *m;* *zool* escama, *f;* *bot* bráctea, *f; bot* hojuela, *f;* (flake) laminita, *f;* (mus, math) escala, *f;* (of charges, etc.) tarifa, *f;* (of salaries) escalafón, *m;* (of a thermometer) escala, *f.* *vt* escalar; (fish) escamar. **major s.,** escala mayor, *f.* **minor s.,** escala menor, *f.* **on a grand s.,** en gran escala. **on a small s.,** en pequeña escala. **pair of scales,** balanza, *f;* (for heavy weights) báscula, *f.* **social s.,** escala social, *f.* **The Scales,** *ast* Libra, *f.* **to draw to s.,** dibujar a escala. **to s.**

turn the scales, pesar; *fig* inclinar la balanza. **to s. down,** (art and of charges) reducir

scaling *n* (of fish) escamadura, *f;* (of buildings) desconchadura, *f;* (ascent) escalamiento, *m*

scallop *n* (*icht* and badge) venera, *f;* concha, *f; sew* onda, *f,* festón, *m.* *vt cul* guisar en conchas; *sew* ondear, festonear

scalp *n* *anat* pericráneo, *m;* cuero cabelludo, *m; fig* trofeo, *m.* *vt* escalpar. **s.-hunter,** cazador de cabelleras, *m*

scalpel *n* escalpelo, *m*

scaly *a* escamoso, conchado; (of boilers) incrustado

scamp *n* bribón, granuja, *m,* *vt* (work) frangollar

scamper *vi* retozar, brincar; correr. *n* carrerita, *f.* **to s. off,** salvarse por los pies, huir; marcharse corriendo

scan *vt* (verse) medir, escandir; (examine) escudriñar, examinar; (glance at) dar una vistazo (a)

scandal *n* escándalo, *m;* maledicencia, *f;* (slander) calumnia, *f.* **to talk s.,** murmurar

scandalize *vt* escandalizar

scandalous *a* escandaloso; infame; calumnioso

scandalously *adv* escandalosamente

scandalousness *n* carácter escandaloso, *m*

Scandinavia Escandinavia, *f*

Scandinavian *a* escandinavo. *n* escandinavo (-va);

scant *a* escaso; insuficiente

scantily *adv* insuficientemente

scantiness *n* escasez, *f;* insuficiencia, *f*

scanty *a* insuficiente; escaso; (of hair) ralo; (of crops, etc.) pobre

scapegoat *n* víctima propiciatoria, *f;* cabeza de turco, *f.* **to be a s. for,** pagar el pato por

scapegrace *n* bribón, *m*

scapula *n* *anat* escápula, *f*

scapulary *n* *ecc* escapulario, *m*

scar *n* cicatriz, *f; fig* señal, *f.* *vt* marcar con una cicatriz. **to s. over,** cicatrizarse

scarab *n* escarabajo, *m;* escarabajo sagrado, *m*

scarce *a* escaso; insuficiente; raro. *adv poet* apenas. **to make oneself s.,** largarse, pirarse, escabullirse; ausentarse, esconderse

scarcely *adv* apenas; no bien; casi; (with difficulty) a duras penas, con dificultad. **It is s. likely he said that,** No es muy probable que lo hubiese dicho. **There were s. twenty people in the building,** Había apenas veinte personas en el edificio. **S. anyone likes his pictures,** Sus cuadros no le gustan a casi nadie

scarcity *n* escasez, insuficiencia, *f;* (famine) carestía, *f;* (rarity) rareza, *f*

scare *vt* asustar, espantar, llenar de miedo (a); intimidar. *n* susto, pánico, *m;* alarma, *f.* **What a s. I got!** ¡Qué susto me ha llevado! **to s. away,** ahuyentar

scarecrow *n* espantapájaros, *m; inf* estantigua, *f,* mamarracho, espantajo, *m*

scaremonger *n* alarmista, *mf*

scarf *n* bufanda, *f;* (tie) corbata, *f; mil* faja, *f*

scarlatina *n* *med* escarlatina, *f*

scarlet *n* escarlata, *f.* *a* de color escarlata. **to turn s.,** (of persons) enrojecerse. **s. fever,** escarlatina, *f.* **s. hat,** *ecc* capelo (cardenalicio), *m.* **s. runner,** *bot* judía verde, *f*

scatheless *a* ileso, sano y salvo

scathing *a* mordaz, cáustico

scathingly *adv* mordazmente, cáusticamente

scatter *vt* esparcir, sembrar con; (benefits, etc.) derramar; (put to flight) derrotar; dispersar; disipar; *fig* frustrar; (squander) derrochar, desparramar. *vi* dispersarse. **The crowd scattered,** La muchedumbre se dispersó. **s.-brained,** de cabeza de chorlito, atolondrado

scattered *a* disperso; esparcido

scattered showers *n* lluvias aisladas, *f pl*

scattering *n* dispersión, *f;* (defeat) derrota, *f;* esparcimiento, *m;* (small number) número pequeño, *m*

scavenge *vt* (streets) recoger la basura de, barrer

scavenger *n* (of the streets) barrendero, *m;* (dustman) basurero, *m; zool* animal que se alimenta de carne

muerta, *m*; insecto que se alimenta de estiércol, *m. vt*
See **scavenge**
scenario *n* escenario, *m*
scene *n* escena, *f*; teatro, lugar, *m*; espectáculo, *m*; (*theat* décor) decoración, *f*; (of a play) escena, *f*; (view) vista, perspectiva, *f*. **behind the scenes,** entre bastidores. **The s. is laid . . . ,** La acción pasa . . . **to come on the s.,** entrar en escena. **to make a s.,** hacer una escena. **s.-painter,** *n* escenógrafo (-fa). **s.-shifter,** tramoyista, *mf*
scenery *n theat* decorado, *m*; (landscape) paisaje, *m*
scenic *a* dramático; escénico; pintoresco. **s. railway,** montaña rusa, *f*
scenography *n* escenografía, *f*
scent *vt* perfumar; (smell) oler; (out) husmear, olfatear; (suspect) sospechar. *n* perfume, *m*; fragancia, *f*, aroma, *m*; (smell) olor, *m*; (of hounds) viento, *m*; (of game, etc.) rastro, viento, *m*; (*fig* of person) nariz, *f*; (trail) pista, *f*. **to lose the s.,** perder la pista. **to s. danger,** oler el peligro. **to throw off the s.,** despistar. **s.-bottle,** frasco de perfume, *m*. **s.-spray,** pulverizador, *m*
scented *a* perfumado; (of roses, etc.) de olor, oloroso; (in compounds) de . . . olfato. **s. sweet pea,** guisante de olor, *m*
scentless *a* sin olor; inodoro
scepter *n* cetro, *m*
sceptic *n* escéptico (-ca)
sceptical *a* escéptico
scepticism *n* escepticismo, *m*
schedule *n* lista, *m*; programa, *m*; (of taxes) clase, *f*; (of trains, etc.) horario, *m. vt* poner en una lista; inventariar
scheme *n* plan, *m*; proyecto, *m*; diagrama, esquema, *m*; (summary) resumen, *m*; (of colors, etc.) combinación, *f*; (plot) intriga, maquinación, *f. vt* proyectar. *vi* planear, formar planes; (intrigue) intrigar, conspirar. **color s.,** combinación de colores, *f*
schemer *n* (plotter) intrigante, *mf*
scheming *a* intrigante; astuto. *n* planes, proyectos, *m pl*; intrigas, maquinaciones, *f pl*
schism *n* cisma, *mf*
schismatic *a* cismático. *n* cismático (-ca)
scholar *n* (at school) colegial (-la); (disciple) alumno (-na); (student) estudiante, *mf*; (learned person) erudito (-ta), hombre de letras, *m*; (scholarship holder) becario, *m*. **to be a poor s.,** *fig* ser analfabeto
scholarly *a* de sabio, de hombre de letras; erudito
scholarship *n* erudición, *f*; saber, *m*; (exhibition) beca, *f*. **s. holder,** becario, *m*
scholastic *a* escolar, escolástico; pedante; (medieval) escolástico. *n* escolástico, *m*. **the s. profession,** el magisterio
school *n* escuela, *f*; colegio, *m*; academia, *f*; *univ* departamento, *m*; (faculty) facultad, *f*; (of fish) banco, *m. vt* enseñar, instruir; formar; disciplinar. **in s.,** en clase.
day s., escuela, *f*, colegio, *m*. **the Florentine s.,** (of painting) la escuela florentina. **the Lower s.,** los alumnos del preparatorio. **private s.,** colegio particular, *m*.
s.-bag, vademécum, *m*. **s.-book,** libro escolar, *m*.
s.-days, los días de escuela; los años de colegio. **in his s.-days,** cuando él iba a la escuela. **s.-fees,** gastos de la enseñanza, *m pl*, cuota escolar, *f*,
schoolboy *n* muchacho de escuela, colegial, *m*
school district *n* sector escolar, *m*
schoolfellow *n* compañero de colegio, condiscípulo, *m*
schoolgirl *n* colegiala, *f*
schooling *n* educación, enseñanza, *f*
schoolmaster *n* maestro de escuela, professor, *m*
schoolmistress *n* maestra de escuela, profesora, *f*
school of hard knocks *n* universidad sin tejados, *f*
schoolroom *n* aula, sala de clase, salón de clase, *m*
schooner *n naut* escuna, goleta, *f*
sciatic *a* ciático
sciatica *n* ciática, *f*
science *n* ciencia, *f*
scientific *a* científico; exacto, sistemático

scientifically *adv* científicamente
scientist *n* hombre de ciencia, *m*, científico (-ca)
scimitar *n* cimitarra, *f*
scintilla *n fig* átomo, vestigio, *m*
scintillate *vi* centellear, lucir, chispear; (of persons) brillar
scion *n* (sucker) acodo, *m*; (shoot) vástago, renuevo, *m*; (human) descendiente, *mf*. **s. of a noble race,** vástago de una raza noble, *m*
scissors *n pl* tijeras, *f pl*. **s.-sharpener,** amolador, *m*
sclerosis *n med* esclerosis, *f*
sclerotic *n anat* esclerótica, *f*
scoff *n* burla, mofa, *f. vi* burlarse. **to s. at,** burlarse de, mofarse de
scoffer *n* mofador (-ra); (at religion, etc.) incrédulo (-la)
scoffing *a* burlón. *n* mofas, burlas, *f pl*
scold *n* virago, *f*, *vt* reñir, reprender
scolding *n* reprensión, increpación, *f*
sconce *n* cubo de candelero, *m*; candelabro de pared, *m*; cornucopia, *f*
scone *n* bollo, *m*
scoop *n* pala de mano, *f*; cuchara de draga, *f*; (boat) achicador, *m*; (financial) golpe, *m*; (journalistic) éxito periodístico, *m. vt* sacar con pala (de); sacar con cuchara (de); (shares, etc.) comprar, obtener. **to s. out,** vaciar; excavar; (bail) achicar
scooter *n* (child's) patinete, patín del diablo, *m*; monopatín, *m*
scope *n* alcance, *m*; esfera de acción, *f*; lugar, *m*. **to give full s. to,** dar rienda suelta a. **to have full s.,** tener plena oportunidad; tener todas las facilidades. **within the s. of,** dentro del alcance de
scorbutic *a med* escorbútico
scorch *vt* chamuscar; (the skin) tostar; (of the sun) abrasar, quemar; (wither) agostar. **to s. along,** ir como un relámpago. **scorching,** *a* abrasador, ardiente; *fig* mordaz
score *n* (scratch) rasguño, *m*; señal, *f*; (crossing out) raya, *f*; (reckoning) cuenta, *f*, escote, *m*; (notch) muesca, *f*; *sport* tanteo, *m*, puntuación, *f*; (point) punto, tanto, *m*; (twenty) veintena, *f*; (reason) motivo, *m*, causa, *f*; respecto, *m*; *mus* partitura, *f. vt* marcar; rayar; (erase) tachar, borrar; (cricket runs, etc.) hacer; (goals) marcar; (points) ganar; (reckon) apuntar. **s. a triumph,** apuntarse un triunfo; *mus* instrumentar; (for orchestra) orquestar. *vi* (be fortunate) llevar la ventaja. **to pay off old scores,** ajustar cuentas viejas. **to s. off someone,** ganar un punto (a); triunfar de. **upon that s.,** a ese respecto; por esa causa. **Upon what s.?** ¿Con qué motivo? **s.-board,** marcador, *m*
scorer *n* (of a goal, etc.) tanteador, *m*; (keeper of score) marcador, *m*
scoria *n* escoria, *f*
scorn *n* desprecio, desdén, *m. vt* despreciar, desdeñar; reírse de. **to s. to do,** no dignarse hacer
scornful *a* desdeñoso, despreciativo
scornfully *adv* desdeñosamente, con desprecio
Scorpion *n* Escorpión, *m*
scorpion *n* escorpión, alacrán, *m*; *ast* Escorpión, *m*
Scot *n* escocés, *m*
scotch *vt* (kill) matar; (thwart) frustrar; (a wheel) calzar
Scotland Escocia, *f*
Scotswoman *n* escocesa, *f*
Scottish *a* escocés
scoundrel *n* canalla, sinvergüenza, *mf*
scour *vt* (traverse) recorrer, batir; (pans, etc.) fregar, estregar; (free from) limpiar (de); (of water) arrastrar
scourge *vt* azotar, flagelar; castigar, mortificar. *n* disciplinas, *f pl*; *fig* verdugo, *m*, plaga, *f*
scout *n mil* batidor, explorador, *m*. *vi mil* explorar, reconocer; (of flout) rechazar a mano airada, rechazar con desdén. **boy s.,** muchacho explorador, *m*
scowl *vi* fruncir el ceño. *n* ceño, *m. to s. at,** mirar con ceño
scowling *a* amenazador
scragginess *n* magrez, flaqueza, *f*

scraggy *a* flaco, magro, descarnado

scramble *vi* trepar. *vt* (throw) arrojar; (eggs) revolver.

scrambled eggs, huevos revueltos, *m pl.* **to s. for,** andar a la rebatiña por; (for coins, etc.) luchar para. **to s. up,** escalar; subir a gatas

scrap *n* pedazo, *m*; fragmento, *m*; pizca, brizna, *f*; (shindy) suiza, camorra, *f*; (boxing) combate de boxeo, *m*; *pl* **scraps,** desperdicios, *m pl*; (food) restos de la comida, *m pl. vt* desechar; (expunge) borrar; *vi* (fight) armar camorra. **a few scraps of news,** algunas noticias. **Do you mind not coming? Not a s.,** ¿Te importa no venir? Ni pizca. **s.-book,** álbum de recortes, *m*; **s.-heap,** depósito de basura, *m*; *fig* olvido, *m*. **s. iron,** chatarra, *f*, hierro viejo, *m*

scrape *vt* raspar, rascar, raer; (one's shoes) restregar; (a musical instrument) rascar. *n* rasguño, *m*; ruido de raspar, *m*; (predicament) lío, apuro, *m*; dificultad, *f*. **to s. acquaintance with,** trabar amistad con. **to s. along,** *inf ir* tirando. **to s. away,** rascar; quitar. **to s. through,** (an examination) aprobar justo. **to s. together,** amontonar poco a poco

scrappy *a* escaso; fragmentario; (incoherent) descosido. **a s. meal,** una comida escasa

scratch *vt* arañar; (the earth) escarbar; (rub) rascar; (a hole) hacer; (sketch) dibujar, trazar; (a horse) retirar de una carrera. *vi* arañar; rascar; escarbar; (of a pen) rasguear; (back out) retirarse. *n* arañazo, *m*; (of a pen) rasgueo, *m*; (in a race) línea de salida, *f*; (in games) cero, *m. a* improvisado. **The dog scratched at the door,** El perro arañó la puerta. **to come up to s.,** estar al nivel de las circunstancias. **to s. one's head,** rascarse la cabeza. **to s. a person's eyes out,** sacar los ojos con las uñas (a). **to s. the surface of,** (a subject) tratar superficialmente. **to s. out,** tachar

scrawl *vi* hacer garabatos. *vt* garabatear, garrapatear. *n* garabato, *m*

scream *vt* and *vi* chillar. *n* chillido, *m*. **It was a perfect s.** Era para morirse de risa. **to s. with laughter,** reírse a carcajadas, morirse de risa

screaming *n* chillidos, *m pl. a* chillador; (piercing) penetrante, agudo; (funny) divertidísimo

screech *vi* chillar; (of owls, etc.) ulular; graznar. *n* chillido, *m*, ululación, *f*; graznido, *m*. **s.-owl,** úlula, *f*

screed *n* arenga, *f*; cita larga, *f*

screen *n* biombo, *m*; (wire) tela metálica, *f*; (nonfolding) mampara, *f*; (eco) cancel, *m*; (cinema, television) pantalla, *f*; (of trees, etc., and *mil*) cortina, *f*; (*fig* protection) abrigo, *m. vt* proteger; (shelter) abrigar; (hide) esconder, ocultar; (a light) proteger con pantalla; (a film) proyectar; (sieve) cribar, cerner; (examine) investigar. **to s. from view,** ocultar la vista (de), esconder. **s. star,** estrella de la pantalla, *f*

screw *n* tornillo, *m*; (propeller) hélice, *f*; vuelta de tornillo, *f*; presión, *f*; (miser) tacaño, *m*; (salary) salario, *m. vt* atornillar; torcer; apretar, oprimir. **He has a s. loose,** Le falta un tornillo. **to s. down,** sujetar con tornillos. **to s. up,** cerrar con tornillos. **to s. up one's courage,** tomar coraje. **to s. up one's eyes,** desojarse, entornar los ojos. **s.-driver,** destornillador, *m*

scribble *vt* escribir de prisa, *vi* garabatear, garrapatear; escribir, ser autor. *n* garabato, garrapato, *m*; mala letra, letra ilegible, *f*; (note) billete, *m*

scribbler *n* el, *m*, (f, la) que tiene mala letra; (author) autor (-ra) malo (-la)

scribbling *n* garabateo, *m*. **s.-block,** bloque de papel, *m*

scribe *n* escribiente, copista, *mf*; (Jewish history) escriba, *m*

scrimmage *n* reyerta, pelea, camorra, *f*; (Rugby) mêlée, *f*

script *n* letra cursiva, *f*; *print* plumilla, *f*; manuscrito, *m*; *law* escritura, *f*; examen escrito, *m*; (film) escenario, *m*

scriptural *a* bíblico

Scripture *n* Sagrada Escritura, *f*. **Scriptures,** Escrituras, *f pl*; (of non-Christian religions) los libros sagrados

scrivener *n* chupatintas, *mf*

scrofula *n* escrófula, *f*

scrofulous *a* escrofuloso

scroll *n* (of paper, etc.) rollo, *m*; pergamino, *m*; (flourish) rúbrica, *f*; (of an Ionic capital) voluta, *f*. **s. of fame,** lista de la fama, *f*

scrotum *n* *anat* escroto, *m*

scrounge *vi* sablear. *vt* dar un sablazo (a); hurtar

scrounger *n* sablista, *mf*

scrub *vt* fregar; limpiar; restregar. *n* fregado, *m*; limpieza, *f*; fricción, *f*; (brushwood) matorral, breñal, *m*, maleza, *f*

scrubbing *n* fregado, *m*. **s.-brush,** cepillo para el suelo, *m*

scrubby *a* (of plants) anémico; (of persons) insignificante, pobre; (of land) cubierto de maleza

scruff *n* nuca, *f*, pescuezo, *m*

scruple *n* escrúpulo, *m*. *vi* tener escrúpulos. **to have no scruples,** no tener escrúpulos

scrupulous *a* escrupuloso; exacto, meticuloso

scrupulously *adv* escrupulosamente; meticulosamente

scrupulousness *n* escrupulosidad, *f*; meticulosidad, *f*

scrutinize *vt* escudriñar, examinar; (votes) escrutar

scrutinizer *n* escudriñador (-ra); (of votes) escrutador (-ra)

scrutinizing *a* escrutador

scrutiny *n* escrutinio, *m*

scud *vi* correr; deslizarse; flotar. **to s. before the wind,** ir viento en popa

scuffle *vi* pelear, forcejear, andar a la rebatiña. *n* refriega, pelea, sarracina, arrebatiña, *f*

scull *n* remo, *m*, *vi* remar

scullery *n* fregadero, *m*. **s. maid,** fregona, *f*

sculptor *n* escultor, *m*, escultora, *f*

sculptural *a* escultural, escultórico

sculpture *n* escultura, *f*, *vt* esculpir

scum *n* espuma, *f*; (dregs) heces, *f pl. vt* espumar. **s. of the earth,** las heces de la sociedad

scupper *n* *naut* clava, *f*. *vt* abrir las clavas (de); (frustrate) frustrar, destruir

scurrility *n* grosería, indecencia, *f*

scurrilous *a* grosero, indecente

scurry *vi* echar a correr. *n* fuga precipitada, *f*; (of rain) chaparrón, *m*; (of snow) remolino, *m*. **to s. off,** escabullirse. **to s. through,** hacer de prisa, terminar rápidamente

S-curve *n* curva doble, *f*

scurvy *a* tiñoso, vil, ruin. *n* escorbuto, *m*. **a s. trick,** una mala pasada

scuttle *n* (trap-door) escotillón, *m*; *naut* escotilla, *f*; (for coal) carbonera, *f*; (flight) huida precipitada, *f*. *vt* (a boat) echar a pique, *vi* (run away) escabullirse, apretar a correr

scythe *n* dalle, *m*, guadaña, *f*, *vt* dallar, segar

sea *n* mar, *m*, or *f*; ola, *f*; multitud, *f*. **Black Sea,** Mar Negro. **Mediteranean Sea,** (Mar) Mediterráneo, *m*. **at sea,** en el mar; perplejo. **beyond the seas,** allende los mares. **by sea,** por mar. **by the sea,** a la orilla del mar. **high seas,** alta mar, *f*. **the seven seas,** todos los mares del mundo. **to go to sea,** hacerse marinero. **to put to sea,** hacerse a la mar, hacerse a la vela. **sea-anemone,** anémone de mar. *f*. **sea-bathing,** baños de mar, *m pl.* **sea-breeze,** brisa de mar, *f*. **sea captain,** capitán de mar, *f*. **sea chart,** carta de marear, *f*. **sea-coast,** litoral, *m*, costa marítima, *f*. **sea-cow,** manatí, *m*. **sea dog,** lobo de mar, *m*. **sea-fight,** combate naval, *m*. **sea-foam,** espuma de mar, *f*. **sea-girt,** rodeado por el mar. **sea-going** *a* de altura; navegante. **sea-going craft,** embarcación de alta mar, *f*. **sea-green,** verdemar, *m*. **sea-gull,** gaviota, *f*. **sea-horse,** caballo marino, *m*. **sea-legs,** piernas de marino, *f pl*. **sea-level,** nivel del mar, *m*. **sea-lion,** león marino, *m*. **sea-mist,** bruma, *f*. **sea-nymph,** nereida, *f*. **sea-power,** potencia naval, *f*. **sea-serpent,** serpiente de mar, *f*. **sea-sick,** mareado. **to be sea-sick,** marearse. **sea-sickness,** mal de mar, *m*. **sea-trip,** viaje por mar, *m*. **sea-urchin,** erizo de mar, *m*. **sea-wall,** dique de mar, *m*

seafarer *n* (traveller) viajero (-ra) por mar; (sailor) marinero, *m*

seafaring *a* marinero, marino. *n* viajes por mar, *m pl*; vida del marinero, *f*

seal *n zool* foca, *f*, lobo marino, *m*; piel de foca, *f*; sello, *m*; (stamp) estampillo, timbre, *m*; *vt* sellar; (stamp) estampar; (letters, etc.) cerrar; *vi* cazar focas. **His fate is sealed,** Su suerte está determinada. **His lips were sealed,** Sus labios estaban cerrados. **under my hand and s.,** firmado y sellado por mí. **s.-ring,** sortija de sello, *f*

sealing wax *n* lacre, *m*

sealskin *n* piel de foca, *f*

seam *n sew* costura, *f*; *naut* costura de los tablones, *f*; *anat* sutura, *f*; *surg* cicatriz, *f*; (wrinkle) arruga, *f*, surco, *m*; *geol* capa, *f*, yacimiento, *m*; *min* vena, *f*, filón, *m*. *vt* coser; juntar; (a face) surcar, arrugar

seaman *n* marinero, *m*; hombre de mar, *m*; navegante, *m*. **able-bodied s.,** marinero práctico, *m*

seamanlike *a* de marinero, marino; de buen marinero

seamanship *n* marinería, *f*; náutica, *f*

seamstress *n* costurera, *f*

seamy *a* con costuras. **the s. side of life,** el lado peor de la vida

seance *n* sesión, junta, *f*; sesión de espiritistas, *f*

seaplane *n* hidroavión, hidroplano, *m*

seaport *n* puerto de mar, *m*

sear *a* marchito. *vt* agostar, secar; (a wound) cauterizar; marchitar, ajar; (a conscience) endurecer

search *vt* registrar; (a wound) explorar; examinar; escudriñar; investigar. *vi* buscar. *n* busca, *f*; (of luggage, etc.) reconocimiento, *m*. **in s. of,** en busca de. **to s. after, for,** buscar; ir al encuentro de. **to s. out,** ir en busca de; preguntar por. **right of s.,** (international law) derecho de visita, *m*. **s.-party,** pelotón de salvamento, *m*. **s.-warrant,** auto de reconocimiento, auto de registro domiciliario, orden de allanamiento, orden de cateo, *m*

searching *a* escrutador; penetrante; minucioso. **a s. look,** una mirada penetrante. **a s. wind,** un viento penetrante. **a s. question,** una pregunta perspicaz

searchlight *n* reflector, proyector, *m*

seashore *n* playa, *f*; orilla del mar, *f*

seaside *n* orilla del mar, *f*; playa, *f*. **to go to the s.,** ir al mar, ir a la playa

season *n* estación, *f*; sazón, *f*; temporada, *f*; tiempo, *m*. *vt* (food) sazonar; (wood, wine) madurar; (accustom) acostumbrar, aclimatar; (with wit, etc.) salpimentar; (temper) templar, moderar. *vi* madurarse. **at that s.,** a la sazón. **close s.,** veda, *f*. **in s.,** en sazón; a su tiempo. **out of s.,** fuera de sazón; fuera de tiempo, inoportuno. **the dead s.,** la estación muerta. **the autumn s.,** el otoño; (for social functions, etc.) la temporada de otoño. **s.-ticket,** billete de abono, *m*

seasonable *a* de estación; tempestivo, oportuno

seasonably *adv* en sazón; oportunamente

seasonal *a* estacional; de temporada

seasonal worker *n* trabajador por temporada, *m*

seasoned *a* (of food) sazonado; (of wood, etc.) maduro. **highly-s.,** (of a dish) picante, con muchas especies

seasoning *n cul* condimento, *m*; madurez, *f*; aclimatación, *f*; *fig* salsa, sal, *f*

seat *n* asiento, *m*; (bench) banco, *m*; (chair) silla, *f*; (in a cinema, etc.) localidad, *f*; (theat etc., ticket) entrada, *f*; (of a person) trasero, *m*, asentaderas, *f pl*; (of trousers) fondillos, *m pl*; (of government, etc.) sede, capital, *f*; (of war, etc.) teatro, *m*; (place) sitio, lugar, *m*; (house) casa solar, *f*. *vt* sentar; poner en una silla (a); encontrar sitio; (of buildings) tener . . . asientos; (a chair) poner asiento (a). **The hall seats a thousand,** La sala tiene mil asientos, Hay mil asientos en la sala. **Please be seated!** ¡Haga el favor de sentarse! **to be seated,** estar sentado; sentarse. **to have a good s.,** (on a horse) caer bien a caballo. **to hold a s. in parliament,** ser diputado a Cortes. **to keep one's s.,** permanecer sen-

tado. **to take a s.,** tomar asiento, sentarse. **s.-back,** respaldo, *m*; **s. belt,** cinturón de seguridad, *m*

seater *n* de . . . asientos. **four-s.,** automóvil de cuatro asientos, *m*

seaweed *n* alga marina, *f*

seaworthy *a* (of a ship) en buen estado; marinero

sebaceous *a* sebáceo

secede *vi* retirarse (de); separarse (de)

secession *n* secesión, *f*

secessionist *n* secesionista, *mf*; *pol* separatista, *mf*. *a* secesionista; *pol* separatista

secluded *a* apartado, retirado; solitario

seclusion *n* reclusión, *f*; apartamiento, retiro, *m*; soledad, *f*

second *a* segundo; otro; igual. *adv* en segundo lugar; después. *n* segundo, *m*; (in a duel) padrino, *m*; (helper) ayudante, *m*; (boxing) segundo, *m*; (railway compartment) departamento de segunda (clase), *m*; *mus* segunda, *f*; (of time) segundo, *m*; (moment) instante, momento, *m*. *vt* secundar; (a motion) apoyar; *mil* ayudar. **the s. of May,** el dos de mayo. **James the S.,** Jaime el segundo. **on s. thoughts,** después de pensarlo bien. **every s. day,** cada dos días. **They live on the s. floor,** Viven en el primer piso (since the ground floor is not counted separately in Spanish speaking areas, the American second floor = the Spanish **primer piso**). **the s. largest,** el más grande menos uno. **to be s. to none,** no ser inferior a ninguno; (of persons) no ser inferior a nadie; no ceder a nadie. **to come off s.,** llegar el segundo; ser vencido. **seconds hand,** (of watch) segundero, *m*. **s.-in-command,** segundo, *m*; subjefe, *m*. **My s.-best hat,** Mi sombrero número dos. **to come off s.-best,** salir mal parado, ser vencido. **s. class,** segunda clase, *f*. **s.-class,** de segunda clase; de calidad inferior; mediocre. **s. cousin,** primo (-ma) segundo (-a). **s. gear,** segunda velocidad, *f*. **s.-hand,** *a* usado; de ocasión; no nuevo. *adv* de segunda mano. **s.-hand car,** un coche de segunda mano. **s.-hand clothing,** ropa usada, *f*. **s. lieutenant,** *mil* subteniente, segundo teniente, *m*; *nav* alférez de fragata, *m*. **s.-rate,** *a* inferior, mediocre. **s. sight,** doble vista, *f*

secondary *a* secundario; subordinado; accesorio; poco importante. **s. education,** enseñanza secundaria, *f*

seconder *n* ayudante, *m*; el, *m*, (*f*, la) que apoya una proposición

secondly *adv* en segundo lugar

secrecy *n* secreto, *m*; reserva, *f*, silencio, *m*. **in the s. of one's own heart,** en lo más íntimo de su corazón

secret *a* secreto; clandestino; (of persons) reservado; taciturno; (secluded) remoto, apartado; oculto; misterioso. *n* secreto, *m*; (key) clave, *f*. **a s. code,** un código secreto. **in s.,** en secreto, secretamente. **open s.,** secreto a voces. **to keep a s.,** guardar un secreto. **to keep s.,** tener secreto, ocultar. **s. drawer,** secreto, *m*. **S. Service,** servicio de espionaje, *m*

secretaire *n* secreter, escritorio, *m*

secretarial *a* de secretario. **s. college,** academia comercial, *f*

secretariat *n* secretaría, *f*

secretary *n* secretario (-ia). **private s.,** secretario (-ia) particular. **S. of State,** ministro, *m*; Ministro de Estado, *m*

secrete *vt* esconder, ocultar; *med* secretar

secretion *n* escondimiento, *m*; *med* secreción, *f*

secretive *a* reservado, callado

secretly *adv* en secreto, secretamente; ocultamente, a escondidas

sect *n* secta, *f*

sectarian *a* and *n* sectario (-ia)

sectarianism *n* sectarismo, *m*

section *n* sección, *f*; porción, *f*; subdivisión, *f*; (of a law) artículo, *m*. *vt* seccionar. **conic s.,** sección cónica, *f*

sectional *a* en secciones. **s. bookcase,** biblioteca desmontable, *f*

sector *n* sector, *m*

secular *a* (very old) secular; (lay) seglar; laico; profano. **s. music,** música profana, *f.* **s. school,** escuela laica, *f*
secularization *n* secularización, *f*
secularize *vt* secularizar
secure *a* seguro; (certain) asegurado; (safe) en seguridad; sano y salvo; (firm) firme; fijo; (confident (in)) confiado (en). *vt* asegurar; (insure) garantizar; (lock) cerrar; (confine) prender; (acquire) adquirir, obtener; lograr, conseguir
securely *adv* seguramente; en seguridad, sin peligro; con confianza; (firmly) firmemente
security *n* seguridad, *f*; protección, defensa, *f*; garantía, *f*; (faith) confianza, *f*; com fianza, *f*; (person) fiador, *m*; *pl* **securities,** valores, títulos, *m pl.* **government securities,** papel del Estado, *m.* **to give s.,** com dar fianza. **to stand s. for,** com salir fiador por
sedan-chair *n* silla de manos, *f*
sedate *a* tranquilo, sosegado; formal, serio, grave
sedately *adv* sosegadamente; seriamente
sedateness *n* sosiego, *m,* tranquilidad, *f*; formalidad, compostura, *f*
sedative *a* and *n* sedativo, calmante *m*
sedentary *a* sedentario
sediment *n* sedimento, *m*
sedimentation *n* sedimentación, *f*
sedition *n* sedición, *f*
seditious *a* sedicioso
seduce *vt* seducir
seducer *n* seductor, *m*
seduction *n* seducción, *f*
seductive *a* seductivo, atractivo; persuasivo
sedulous *a* asiduo, diligente
see *n* sede, *f.* **The Holy S.,** la Santa Sede, *f*
see *vt* and *vi* ver; mirar; (understand) comprender; (visit) visitar; (attend to) atender a; ocuparse de. **He sees the matter quite differently,** Él mira el asunto de un modo completamente distinto, Su punto de vista sobre el asunto es completamente distinto. **You are not fit to be seen,** No eres nada presentable. **See you next Tuesday!** ¡Hasta el miércoles que viene! **I see!** ¡Ya! ¡Ahora comprendo! **Let's see!** ¡Vamos a ver! **Shall I see you home?** ¿Quieres que te acompañe a casa? **to go and see,** ir a ver. **to see red,** echar chispas. **to see the sights,** visitar los monumentos. **to see life,** ver mundo. **to see service,** servir (en el ejército, etc.). **to see about,** atender a; pensar en; ocuparse de. **to see after,** cuidar de; atender (a); ocuparse de. **to see again,** volver a ver. **to see into,** investigar, examinar. **to see off,** (at the station, etc.) ir a despedir; acompañar. **to see out,** (a person) acompañar a la puerta; (a play, etc.) quedarse hasta el fin (de); no dejar el puesto. **to see over,** inspeccionar. **to see through,** (a house, etc.) inspeccionar; (a person) calarle las intenciones; (a mystery) penetrar; (a person through trouble) ayudar. **to see it through,** llevarlo al cabo; quedarse hasta el fin. **to see to,** atender a; ocuparse de; encargarse de. **to see to everything,** encargarse de todo
seed *n* semilla, *f*; simiente, *f*; (of fruit) pepita, *f,* grano, *m*; *fig* germen, *m*; (offspring) prole, descendencia, *f. vi* granar. *vt* sembrar. **s.-bed,** almáciga, *f,* semillero, *m.* **s.-pearl,** aljófar, *m.* **s.-plot,** sementera, *f*; *fig* semillero, *m.* **s.-time,** tiempo de sembrar, *m*
seedling *n* planta de semilla, *f*
seedsman *n* tratante en semillas, *m*
seedy *a* granado; (of clothes) raído, roto; (of persons) andrajoso, desharrapado; infeliz, desgraciado; (ill) indispuesto, malucho
seeing *n* vista, *f*; visión, *f.* **It is worth s.,** Vale la pena de verse. **s. that ...,** visto que, dado que, como que. **S. is believing,** Ver es creer
seek *vt* buscar; solicitar, pretender; (demand) pedir; (investigate) investigar; (to do something) procurar, tratar de. **They are much sought after,** Son muy populares, Están en demanda. **to s. after,** buscar; perseguir. **to s. for,** buscar
seeker *n* el, *m,* (*f,* la) que busca; investigador (-ra)

seem *vi* parecer. **He seemed honest,** Parecía honrado. **It seemed to me,** Me pareció a mí. **It seems that they were both at home last night,** Parece ser que ambos estaban en casa anoche
seeming *a* aparente; supuesto
seemingly *adv* aparentemente; en apariencia
seemliness *n* decoro, *m*
seemly *a* decoroso, decente
seep *vi* filtrar; rezumarse
seer *n* profeta, *m*
seesaw *n* columpio, *m*; vaivén, *m. vi* columpiarse; balancearse, oscilar. *a* de vaivén, oscilante
seethe *vi* hervir; *fig* bullir
segment *n* segmento, *m*
segregate *vt* segregar. *vi* segregarse. *a* segregado
segregation *n* segregación, *f*
Seine, the el Sena, *m*
seismic *a* sísmico
seismograph *n* sismógrafo, *m*
seismological *a* sismológico
seismology *n* sismología, *f*
seize *vt* law embargar; apoderarse de; asir; (a person) prender; coger; (a meaning) comprender; (an occasion, etc.) aprovecharse de; (of emotions) dominar; (of illnesses) atacar. *vi mech* atascarse. **He was seized by fear,** Le dominó el miedo. **to s. the opportunity,** aprovecharse de la oportunidad. **to s. upon a pretext,** valerse de un pretexto
seizure *n* asimiento, *m*; (of property) embargo, secuestro, *m*; (of a person) captura, *f*; arresto, *m*; *med* ataque, *m*
seldom *adv* rara vez, raramente; pocas veces
select *a* escogido, selecto; exclusivista. *vt* escoger
selection *n* selección, *f.* **selections from Cervantes,** trozos escogidos de Cervantes, *m pl.* **to make a s. from,** escoger entre. **s. committee,** comité de selección, *m*
selective *a* selectivo
self *n* mismo (-a), propio (-a); sí mismo (-a), se; personalidad, *f*; ser, *m.* **all by one's s.,** sin ayuda de nadie; solo; *inf* solito. **my other s.,** mi otro yo. **my better s.,** mi mejor parte. **the s. and yo. s.-abasement,** humillación de sí mismo, *f.* **s.-acting,** automático. **s.-apparent,** evidente, patente. **s.-appointed,** nombrado por uno mismo. **s.-assertion,** presunción, *f.* **s.-assertive,** presumido. **s.-assurance,** confianza en sí mismo, *f*; aplomo, *m*; (impertinence) cara dura, frescura, *f.* **s.-centered,** egocéntrico. **s.-colored,** del mismo color; de su color natural. **s.-command,** dominio de sí mismo, *m*; sangre fría, ecuanimidad, *f.* **s.-complacent,** satisfecho de sí mismo. **s.-conceit,** vanidad, arrogancia, petulancia, *f.* **s.-confidence,** confianza en sí mismo, *f*; aplomo, *m.* **s.-confident,** seguro de sí mismo, lleno de confianza en sí mismo. **s.-conscious,** turbado, confuso, apocado. **s.-consciousness,** turbación, confusión, *f,* apocamiento, azoramiento, *m.* **s.-contained,** (of a person) reservado, poco comunicativo; dueño de sí mismo; (of things) completo; (of flats, etc.) independiente; con entrada independiente. **s.-contradictory,** contradictorio. **s.-control,** dominio de sí mismo, *m*; ecuanimidad, serenidad, sangre fría, *f.* **s.-controlled,** dueño de sí mismo; ecuánime, sereno. **s.-deception,** engaño de sí mismo, *m*; ilusiones, *f pl.* **s.-defense,** defensa propia, *f.* **s.-denial,** abnegación, *f*; renunciación, *f*; frugalidad, *f.* **s.-destruction,** suicidio, *m.* **s.-determination,** libre albedrío, *m*; (of peoples) autonomía, *f,* independencia, *f.* **s.-educating,** autodidacto. **s.-esteem,** respeto para uno mismo, *m*; amor propio, *m.* **s.-evident,** aparente, que salta a la vista. **s.-explanatory,** que se explica a sí mismo; evidente. **s.-generating,** autógeno. **s.-government,** (of a person) dominio de sí mismo, *m*; (of a state) autonomía, *f.* **s.-importance,** presunción, petulancia, *f.* **s.-important,** pagado de sí mismo. **to be s.-important,** darse importancia, darse tono. **s.-indulgence,** indulgencia con sí mismo, *f*; (of food, drink,

etc.) excesos, *m pl,* falta de moderación, *f.* **s.-indulgent,** indulgente con sí mismo; dado a los placeres, sibarita. **s.-interest,** propio interés, *m.* **s.-knowledge,** conocimiento de sí mismo, *m.* **s.-love,** egolatría, *f.* **s.-made man,** hombre que ha llegado a su posición actual por sus propios esfuerzos, *m.* **self-medication,** automedicación, *f.* **s.-opinionated,** terco, obstinaz. **s.-portrait,** autorretrato, *m.* **s.-possessed,** dueño de sí mismo; reservado; de sangre fría. **s.-possession,** aplomo, *m,* sangre fría, serenidad, *f.* **s.-preservation,** protección de sí mismo, *f.* **s.-reliance,** independencia, *f;* confianza en sí mismo, *f.* **s.-reliant,** independiente; confiado en sí mismo. **s.-reproach,** remordimiento, *m.* **s.-respect,** respeto de sí mismo, *m;* amor propio, *m,* dignidad, *f.* **s.-respecting,** que se respeta; que tiene amor propio **s.-restraint,** dominio de sí mismo, *m;* moderación, *f.* **s.-righteous,** farisaico. **s.-sacrifice,** abnegación, *f.* **s.-sacrificing,** abnegado. **s.-same,** mismo, idéntico. **s.-satisfaction,** satisfacción de sí mismo, *f;* vanidad, *f;* (of desires, etc.) satisfacción, indulgencia, *f.* **s.-satisfied,** satisfecho de sí mismo, pagado de sí mismo. **s.-seeking,** *a* egoísta, interesado. *n* egoísmo, *m.* **s.-starter,** *mech* arranque automático, *m.* **s.-styled,** autodenominado, autotitulado, llamado por sí mismo. **s.-sufficiency,** suficiencia, *f;* presunción, *f.* **s.-sufficient,** que basta a sí mismo; contento de sí mismo. **s.-supporting,** que vive de su propio trabajo; (of an institution, business) independiente. **s.-taught,** autodidacto. **s.-willed,** voluntarioso
selfish *a* egoísta, interesado
selfishly *adv* interesadamente; por egoísmo
selfishness *n* egoísmo, *m*
sell *vt* vender. *vi* vender; venderse. **They sold him to his enemies,** Le vendieron a sus enemigos. **House to s.,** «Se vende una casa.» **to s. at a loss,** malvender, vender con pérdida. **to s. for cash,** vender al contado. **to s. retail,** vender al por menor. **to s. wholesale,** vender al por mayor. **to s. one's life dearly,** vender cara la vida. **They sold the chair for $10,** Vendieron la silla por diez dólares. **to s. off,** (goods) liquidar, saldar. **to s. out,** vender; agotar. **The best edition is sold out,** La mejor edición está agotada. **All the nylons have been sold out,** Se han vendido todas las medias de nilón (de cristal). **to s. up,** vender
seller *n* vendedor (-ra); comerciante (en), *m*
selling *n* venta, *f.* **s. off,** liquidación, *f.* **s. price,** precio de venta, *m*
selvage *n* (in cloth) orillo, *m*
semantics *n* semántica, *f*
semaphore *n* semáforo, *m, vt* and *vi* hacer señales semafóricas (a)
semaphoric *a* semafórico
semblance *n* apariencia, *f.* **to put on a s. of woe,** aparentar ser triste
semen *n* semen, *m,* esperma, *f*
semester *n* semestre, *m*
semi *prefix* semi; medio. **s.-conscious,** medio consciente. **s.-detached house,** casa doble, *f*
semicircle *n* semicírculo, *m*
semicircular *a* semicircular
semicolon *n* punto y coma, *m*
semidetached *a* (house) apartado
semiformal *a* de media ceremonia
seminarist *n* seminarista, *mf*
seminary *n* seminario, *m;* (for girls) colegio interno, *m*
Semite *n* semita, *mf*
Semitic *a* semítico, semita
Semitism *n* semitismo, *m*
semolina *n* sémola, *f*
senate *n* senado, *m*
senator *n* senador, *m*
senatorial *a* senatorio
send *vt* enviar, mandar; *com* remitir; (a ball) lanzar; (grant) conceder; permitir; (inflict) afligir (con). **I sent Jane for it,** Envié a Juana a buscarlo. **He sent us word that he could not come,** Nos mandó que

recado diciéndonos que no podía venir. **to s. mad,** hacer enloquecer. **to s. packing,** mandar a paseo. **to s. again,** volver a mandar. **to s. away,** *vt* enviar; (dismiss) destituir; despedir; (scare off) ahuyentar, *vi* enviar a otra parte. **to s. back,** (goods) devolver; (persons) volver. **to s. down,** hacer bajar; (rain, etc.) mandar, derramar; (a student) suspender, expulsar. **to s. in,** mandar; (persons) hacer entrar, introducir; (food) servir; (a bill) presentar; (one's name) dar. **Please s. him in!** ¡Sírvase de invitarle a entrar! **to s. in one's resignation,** mandar su dimisión. **to s. off,** enviar, mandar; (goods) despachar; (persons) destituir; (scare) ahuyentar. **s.-off,** *n* despedida, *f.* **a good s.-off,** una despedida afectuosa. **to s. on,** (a letter) hacer seguir; (instructions) trasmitir. **to s. out,** hacer salir; mandar; (emit) despedir, dar; (new shoots, etc.) echar. **to s. round,** (the hat, etc.) hacer circular. **to s. up,** enviar arriba; mandar subir, hacer subir; mandar, enviar; (a ball) lanzar
sender *n* remitente, *mf; elec* transmisor, *m*
sending *n* envío, *m*
Senegal Senegal, *m*
Senegalese *a* and *n* senegalés (-esa)
senile *a* senil
senility *n* senilidad, *f*
senior *a* mayor, de mayor edad; más antiguo. **Martinez s.,** Martínez padre. **Charles is Mary's s. by five years,** Carlos es cinco años mayor que María. **s. member,** decano, *m*
seniority *n* ancianidad, *f;* antigüedad, *f*
senna *n bot* sena, *f*
sensation *n* sensación, *f;* sentimiento, *m;* impresión, *f.* **to create a s.,** causar una sensación
sensational *a* sensacional
sensationalism *n phil* sensualismo, *m;* efectismo, *m*
sensationalist *n phil* sensualista, *mf;* efectista, *mf*
sense *n* sentido, *m. vt* sentir. **in a s.,** hasta cierto punto; desde un punto de vista. **in the full s. of the word,** en toda la extensión de la palabra. **common s.,** sentido común, *m.* **He has no s. of smell,** No tiene olfato. **the five senses,** los cinco sentidos. **to be out of one's senses,** estar fuera de sí, estar trastornado. **You must be out of your senses!** ¡Debes de haber perdido el juicio! ¡Estás loco! **to come to one's senses,** (after unconsciousness) volver en sí; (after folly) recobrar el sentido común. **to talk s.,** hablar con sentido común, hablar razonablemente. **s. organ,** órgano de los sentidos, *m.* **have a good s. of direction,** saber orientarse, tener buena orientación. **have no s. of smell,** ser incapaz de percibir olores. **have no s. of taste,** ser incapaz de distinguir gustos
senseless *a* (unconscious) sin sentido, insensible; desmayado; (silly) necio, estúpido. **to knock s.,** derribar, tumbar
senselessness *n* falta de sentido común, *f;* locura, absurdidad, *f*
sensibility *n* sensibilidad, *f*
sensible *a* sensible; (conscious) consciente (de); sesudo. **to be s. of,** estar consciente de; estar persuadido de
sensibly *adv* sensiblemente; sesudamente, cuerdamente
sensitive *a* sensitivo; susceptible (a); impresionable. **s. plant,** sensitiva, *f*
sensitivity *n* sensibilidad, *f;* susceptibilidad, *f;* delicadeza, *f*
sensitize *vt phot* sensibilizar
sensory *a* sensorio
sensual *a* sensual; voluptuoso
sensualism *n* sensualismo, *m*
sensualist *n* sensualista, *mf*
sensuality *n* sensualidad, *f*
sensually *adv* sensualmente
sensuous *a* sensorio
sensuousness *n* sensualidad, *f*
sentence *n law* sentencia, *f;* (penalty) pena, *f; gram* frase, *f;* (maxim) máxima, sentencia, *f. vt* sentenciar,

condenar. **to pass s.,** pronunciar sentencia, fallar. **under s. of,** bajo pena de
sententious *a* sentencioso
sentient *a* sensible
sentiment *n* sentimiento, *m;* (sentimentality) sentimentalismo, *m;* opinión, *f*
sentimental *a* sentimental; (mawkish) sensiblero
sentimentalist *n* romántico (-ca), persona sentimental, *f*
sentimentality *n* sentimentalismo, *m,* sensiblería, *f*
sentimentalize *vt* idealizar
sentimentally *adv* sentimentalmente
sentinel *n* centinela, *mf*
sentry *n* centinela, *m.* **to be on s. duty,** estar de guardia. **s.-box,** garita de centinela, *f*
separable *a* separable
separate *a* separado; distinto; independiente. *vt* separar; dividir. *vi* separarse; (of husband and wife) separarse de bienes y de cuerpos
separately *adv* separadamente; aparte
separation *n* separación, *f; law* separación de bienes y de cuerpos, *f*
separatism *n* separatismo, *m*
separatist *a* and *n* separatista *mf*
Sephardic *a* Sefaradí
sepia *n* (color and fish) sepia, *f*
September *n* setiembre, septiembre, *m*
septic *a* séptico
septicemia *n* septicemia, *f*
septuagenarian *n* setentón (-ona); septuagenario (-ia)
septum *n* septo, tabique, *m*
sepulcher *n* sepulcro, *m*
sepulchral *a* sepulcral
sequel *n* (of a story, etc.) continuación, *f;* consecuencia, *f;* resultado, *m*
sequence *n* sucesión, *f;* serie, *f;* orden, *mf;* (at cards) serie, *f; gram* correspondencia, *f; (ecc* and cinema) secuencia, *f.* **s. of tenses,** correspondencia de los tiempos, *f*
sequestered *a* aislado, remoto
sequestrate *vt* secuestrar
sequestration *n* secuestro, *m,*
sequin *n* lentejuela, *f*
seraglio *n* serrallo, *m*
seraph *n* serafín, *m*
seraphic *a* seráfico
seraphim *n* serafín, *m*
Serbia Servia, *f*
Serbian *a* servio. *n* servio (-ia); (language) servio, *m*
serenade *n* serenata, *f, vt* dar una serenata (a)
serene *a* sereno. **His S. Highness,** Su Alteza Serenísima
serenity *n* serenidad, *f;* tranquilidad, *f*
serf *n* siervo (-va)
serfdom *n* servidumbre, *f*
serge *n* estameña, *f;* (silk) sarga, *f*
sergeant *n mil* sargento, *m;* (police) sargento de policía, *m.* **s.-at-arms,** macero, *m.* **s.-major,** sargento instructor, *m*
serial *a* en serie; (of a story) por entregas. *n* novela por entregas, *f.* **s. number,** número de serie, *m*
sericulture *n* sericultura, *f*
series *n* serie, *f;* cadena, *f; math* serie, progresión, *f.* **in s.,** en serie
serious *a* serio; sincero; verdadero; (of illness, etc.) grave; importante. **He was s.** (not laughing) **when he said it,** Lo dijo en serio. **He is very s. about it,** Lo toma muy en serio. **to grow s.,** (of persons) ponerse serio; (of events) hacerse grave
seriously *adv* seriamente; en serio; gravemente. **to take** (something) **s.,** tomar (algo) en serio. **to take oneself s.,** tomarse muy en serio
seriousness *n* seriedad, *f;* gravedad, *f.* **in all s.,** en serio, seriamente
sermon *n* sermón, *m*
sermonize *vt* and *vi* sermonear

serpent *n* serpiente, *f; mus* serpentón, *m*
serpentine *a* serpentino; (of character) tortuoso. *n min* serpentina, *f*
serrated *a* serrado; dentellado
serried *a* apretado, apiñado
serum *n* suero, *m*
servant *n* servidor (-ra); (domestic) criado (-da); (employee) empleado (-da); (slave and *fig*) siervo (-va); *pl* **servants,** (domestic) servidumbre, *f,* servicio, *m.* **I remain your obedient s.,** Quedo de Vd. atento y seguro servidor (att. y s.s.). **civil s.,** empleado del estado, *m.* **general s.,** criada para todo, *f.* **man s.,** criado, *m.* **the s. problem,** el problema del servicio. **Your s., sir,** Servidor de Vd., señor. **s.-girl,** criada, *f*
serve *vt* servir (a); ser útil (a); satisfacer; (in a shop) despachar; (an apprenticeship, etc.) hacer; (a prison sentence) cumplir; (treat) tratar; (of stallion) cubrir; (a warrant, etc.) ejecutar; (a notice) entregar; (a ball) servir; (on a jury, etc.) formar parte de; *naut* aforrar. *vi* servir; (mil, nav) hacer el servicio. *n sport* saque, *m.* **It serves you right!** ¡Lo tienes merecido! **to s. at table,** servir a la mesa. **to s. as,** servir de. **to s. out,** distribuir; servir. **Serves 8,** (recipe) Da 8 porciones
server *n ecc* acólito, *m; sport* saque, *m;* (tray) bandeja, *f;* (for fish, etc.) pala, *f*
service *n* servicio, *m; ecc* oficio, *m;* servicio de mesa, *m;* (of a writ) entrega, *f; sport* saque, *m.* **cup of coffee s.,** juego de café, *m.* **diplomatic s.,** cuerpo diplomático, *m.* **At your s.,** Para servir a Vd., A su disposición. **on active s.,** en acto de servicio; en el campo de batalla. **to go into s.,** (of servants) ir a servir. **to render s.,** prestar servicios. **s. tree,** serbal, *m*
serviceable *a* (of persons) servicial; (of things) servible, utilizable; útil; (lasting) duradero
service road *n* vía de servicio, *f*
serviette *n* servilleta, *f.* **s. ring,** servilletero, *m*
servile *a* servil
servility *n* servilismo, *m*
serving *a* sirviente; al servicio (de). **s. maid,** criada, *f.* **s. table,** trinchero, *m*
servitude *n* servidumbre, esclavitud, *f.* **penal s.,** cadena perpetua, *f*
session *n* sesión, *f;* junta, *f.* **petty sessions,** tribunal de primera instancia, *m*
set *vt* poner; colocar; fijar; (seeds, etc.) plantar; (bones) reducir, componer; (gems) engastar, montar; (a clock) regular; (sails) desplegar; (the teeth of a saw) trabar; triscar; (congeal) hacer coagular; (a trap) armar; (a snare) tender; (a razor) afilar; (make ready) preparar; (type) componer; (cause) hacer; *mus* poner en música; *mus* adaptar; (order) mandar; (prescribe) dar, asignar; (estimate) estimar, evaluar; (an example, etc.) dar; (establish) establecer, crear. *vi* (of the sun, etc.) ponerse; (solidify) coagularse; solidificarse; (of tides) fluir; (of the wind) soplar; (of dogs) hacer punta. **The joke set him laughing,** El chiste le hizo reír. **set an example,** dar ejemplo, dar el ejemplo. **set a precedent,** sentar precedente. **to set a person's mind at rest,** tranquilizar, sosegar. **to set a trap,** armar lazo. **to set at ease,** poner a sus anchas (a), hacer cómodo (a). **to set at naught,** despreciar. **to set eyes on,** poner los ojos en. **to set fire to,** pegar fuego a, incendiar. **to set free,** poner en libertad, librar (de). **to set in motion,** poner en marcha. **to set one's teeth,** apretar los dientes. **to set people talking,** dar que hablar a la gente. **to set the fashion,** fijar la moda; poner de moda. **to set the alarm at seven o'clock,** poner el despertador a las siete. **to set the table,** poner la mesa. **to set to work,** ponerse a trabajar. **to set about,** *vi* (begin) comenzar (a); empezar; (undertake) emprender. *vt* (a rumour, etc.) divulgar. **They set about each other,** Empezaron a golpearse. Vinieron a las manos. **to set against,** indisponer (con), enemistar (con); hacer el enemigo (de), ser hostil (a); (balance) oponer, balancear. **to set oneself against,** oponerse a; atacar, luchar contra. **to set aside,** poner a un lado; apartar;

(discard) desechar; (omit) omitir, pasar por alto de; dejar aparte, excluir; (keep) reservar; (money, etc.) ahorrar; (reject) rechazar; (quash) anular. **to set back,** retrasar; hacer retroceder. **set-back,** *n* revés, *m*; contrariedad, *f.* **to set before,** poner ante; (facts) exponer; (introduce) presentar. **to set down,** poner en tierra; depositar; (of a bus, etc.) dejar; (in writing) poner por escrito; anotar, apuntar; narrar, contar; (attribute) atribuir; (fix) fijar, formular; (believe to be) creer. **Passengers are set down at . . . ,** Los viajeros pueden apearse en . . . **to set forth,** *vt* (one's opinions, etc.) exponer; publicar; (display) exhibir, mostrar; (make) hacer. *vi* ponerse en camino. **to set going,** poner en marcha; echar a andar. **to set in,** empezar; (of the tide) fluir. **A reaction has set in,** Se ha hecho sentir una reacción. **to set off,** *vt* (explode) hacer estallar; (cause) hacer; (heighten) realzar; hacer resaltar; (counterbalance) contraponer. *vi* ponerse en camino. **set-off,** *n* contraste, *m*, contraposición, *f.* **to set off against,** contraponer. **to set on,** *vt* (a dog) azuzar; (incite) instigar, incitar. *vi* atacar. **to set out,** *vt* (state) exponer, manifestar; (embellish) realzar; (display) arreglar, disponer. *vi* ponerse en camino, partir. **to set over,** (rule) tener autoridad sobre, gobernar. **to set to,** (begin to) ponerse a, empezar a; (work) ponerse a trabajar. **set-to,** *n* lucha, *f*; (boxing) asalto, *m*; (quarrel) pelea, riña, *f.* **to set up,** *vt* (a monument, etc.) erigir, levantar; (fix) fijar; (apparatus, machinery) montar; (exalt) exaltar; (found) establecer; crear; (propound) exponer; (a howl, etc.) dar; (equip with) proveer de; instalar; (make strong) robustecer; fortificar; (type) componer; (raise) alzar. *vi* establecerse; dárselas de. **He sets himself up as a painter,** Se las da de pintor. **to set up** (a person) **up as a model,** poner como modelo (a). **to set up house,** poner casa. **to set up a business,** establecer un comercio. **set-up,** *n* establecimiento, *m*; arreglo, *m.* **to set upon,** atacar

set *n* (of sun, etc.) puesta, *f*, ocaso, *m*; (of the head, etc.) porte, *m*; (of a garment) corte, *m*; (of the tide, etc.) dirección, *f*; (slant) inclinación, *f*; (*fig* drift) tendencia, *f*, movimiento, *m*; (of the teeth of a saw) triscamiento, *m*; (of men, houses, etc.) grupo, *m*; (of tools, golf clubs, china, etc.) juego, *m*; (gang) pandilla, camarilla, *f*; clase, *f*; (dance) tanda, *f*; (tennis) partido, *f*; *theat* decoración, *f*; *rad* aparato de radio, *m*, radio, *f.* **coffee set,** juego de café, *m.* **all-mains set,** radio de corriente eléctrica, *f.* **battery set,** radio de batería, *f.* **portable set,** radio portátil, *f.* **the smart set,** el mundo elegante. **to have a shampoo and set,** hacerse lavar y marcar (el pelo). **to make a set,** hacer juego. **to make a dead set at,** hacer un ataque vigoroso (a), atacar resueltamente; procurar insinuarse en el favor de. **set of teeth,** dentadura, *f*

set *a* fijo; inmóvil; (of a smile) forzado; (of a task) asignado; (of times) señalado, fijo; (prescribed) prescrito, establecido; (firm) firme; (resolved) resuelto; (well-known) consabido; (obstinate) terco, nada adaptable. **well set-up,** apuesto, bien plantado. **He is set on doing it,** Se empeña en hacerlo. **to be dead set against,** estar completamente opuesto a. **set phrase,** frase hecha, *f.* **set-square,** cartabón, *m*

settee *n* canapé, *m.* **s.-bed,** cama turca, *f*

setter *n* (perro) séter, perdiguero, *m.* **s.-on,** instigador (-ra)

setting *n* (of the sun, etc.) puesta, *f*; (of mortar, etc.) fraguado, *m*; (of a jelly) solidificación, *f*; (of jewels) engaste, *m*, montadura, *f*; (of bones) aliño, *m*; (of teeth of saw) traba, *f*; (of razor) afiladura, *f*; (of a trap) armadura, *f*; (of a machine, etc.) ajuste, *m*; (frame) marco, *m*; *mus* arreglo, *m*; *theat* decorado, *m*; (emplacement) lecho, *m.* **the s. sun,** el sol poniente. **s. free,** liberación, *f.* **s. off,** partida, salida, *f.* **s. out,** ida, marcha, *f*; principio, *m.* **s.-up,** creación, institución, *f*, establecimiento, *m*; (of a machine) montaje, *m*; *print* composición, *f*

settle *vt* colocar; asegurar; afirmar; (a country) coloni-

zar; (live in) establecer (en); (populate) poblar; (in a profession, etc.) dar; (install) instalar; (the imagination, etc.) sosegar, calmar; (resolve) resolver; (arrange) disponer, arreglar; (differences) componer, concertar; (an opponent, etc.) confundir; (a bill) saldar, pagar; (a claim) satisfacer; (clarify) depositar, clarificar; (end) poner fin (a). *vi* establecerse; (of weather) serenarse; (to work, etc.) empezar a, ponerse a; aplicarse a; (decide) decidirse; (alight) posarse; (of foundations, etc.) asentarse; (of a ship) zozobrar; (of sediment) depositarse; (of liquid) clarificarse. **to s. accounts with,** *fig* ajustar cuentas con. **to s. down,** establecerse, arraigarse; adaptarse (a); (become calm) sosegarse, calmarse; sentar el juicio; (of foundations) asentarse; (of a ship) zozobrar; (of sediment) depositarse. **to s. in,** *vi* instalar. *vi* instalarse. **to s. on,** (choose) escoger; (decide on) decidirse (a). **to s. a pension on,** señalar pensión (a). **to s. up,** *vt* (one's affairs) poner en orden; (bill) pagar, saldar. *vi* llegar a un acuerdo; pagar cuentas

settled *a* fijo; permanente; invariable; (of countries) colonizado; (of weather) sereno

settlement *n* (of a country) colonización, *f*; (of a dispute) arreglo, ajuste, *m*; (of a question) solución, *f*; decisión, *f*; (of a bill) saldo, pago, *m*, liquidación, *f*; (of an obligation) satisfacción, *f*; (colony) colonia, *f*; (creation) creación, institución, *f*; establecimiento, arraigo, *m.* **deed of s.,** escritura de donación, *f.* **marriage s.,** contrato matrimonial, *m*; **s. out of court,** arreglo pacífico, *m*

settler *n* colono, *m*; colonizador (-ra)

seven *a* and *n* siete *m.* **It is s. o'clock,** Son las siete. **the s. deadly sins,** los siete pecados capitales

seventeen *a* diecisiete, diez y siete. *n* diecisiete, *m.* **She is just s.,** Acaba de cumplir los diez y siete años

seventeenth *a* décimoséptimo; (of monarchs and of the month) diez y siete. *n* décimoséptimo, *m.* **Louis the S.,** Luis diez y siete. **the s. of June,** el diez y siete de junio

seventh *a* séptimo; (of the month) siete. *n* séptimo, *m*; séptima parte, *f*; *mus* séptima, *f.* **Edward the S.,** Eduardo séptimo. **the s. of August,** el siete de agosto

seventieth *a* septuagésimo, setentavo. *n* setentavo, *m*

seventy *a* and *n* setenta, *m*

sever *vt* separar; romper; dividir

several *a* distinto, diferente; respectivo; varios, *m pl*, (*f pl*, varias); algunos, *m pl*, (*f pl*, algunas)

severally *adv* separadamente; individualmente; independientemente

severance *n* separación, *f*; (of friendship, etc.) ruptura, *f*

severe *a* severo; riguroso; fuerte; duro; (of style) austero; (of pain) agudo; (of illness) grave

severely *adv* severamente; intensamente; gravemente

severity *n* severidad, *f*; intensidad, *f*; (of weather) inclemencia, *f*; (of illness) gravedad, *f*

sew *vt* and *vi* coser. **to sew on,** coser, pegar

sewage *n* aguas residuales, *f pl.* **s. system,** alcantarillado, *m*

sewer *n* alcantarilla, cloaca, *f*, albañal, *m*

sewing *n* costura, *f.* **s. bag,** costurero, *m.* **s. cotton,** hilo de coser, *m.* **s.-machine,** máquina de coser, *f.* **s. silk,** torzal, *m*

sex *n* sexo, *m.* **the fair sex,** el bello sexo. **the weaker sex,** el sexo débil. **sex appeal,** atractivo, *m*

sexagenarian *n* sexagenario (-ia)

sexless *a* neutro; frígido

sexologist *n* sexólogo (-ga)

sexology *n* sexología, *f*

sextant *n* sextante, *m*

sexton *n* sacristán, *m*; sepulturero, *m*; (bell-ringer) campanero, *m*

sexual *a* sexual

sexuality *n* sexualidad, *f*

Sforza Esforcia, *f*

sh! *interj* ¡Chitón! ¡Chis!

shabbily *adv* (of dressing) pobremente; (of treatment) mezquinamente

shabbiness *n* pobreza, *f*; estado andrajoso, *m*; (of behavior) mezquindad, ruindad, *f*

shabby *a* (of persons) desharrapado, andrajoso; (of garments) raído, roto; (of a neighborhood, etc.) pobre; (mean) ruin, mezquino

shack *n* choza, *f*

shackle *n* traba, *f*; *pl* **shackles**, grillos, *m pl*, esposas, *f pl*; *fig* cadenas, *f pl*. *vt* poner esposas (a), encadenar; (a horse) apear; *fig* atar; (impede) estorbar

shad *n* sábalo, *m*

shade *n* sombra, *f*; (in a picture) toque de obscuro, *m*; (for the eyes) visera, *f*; (of a lamp) pantalla, *f*; (ghost) espectro, fantasma, *m*; (of color) matiz, *m*; (tinge) dejo, *m*. *vt* sombrear, dar sombra (a); (the face, etc.) proteger, resguardar; (a drawing) esfumar. **in the s.,** a la sombra. **80° in the s.,** ochenta grados a la sombra. **to put** (a person) **in the s.,** eclipsar

shadiness *n* sombra, *f*

shading *n* sombra, *f*; *art* degradación, *f*

shadow *n* sombra, *f*; obscuridad, *f*; (in a picture) toque de obscuro, *m*. *vt* sombrear; obscurecer; (a person) seguir **to cast a s.,** proyectar una sombra. **to s. forth,** indicar; simbolizar. **s. show,** sombras chinescas, *f pl*

shadowy *a* umbroso; vago, indistinto, indefinido

shady *a* sombreado, umbrío; sombrío; (of persons, etc.) sospechoso. **It was s. in the wood,** Hacía sombra en el bosque

shaft *n* fuste, *m*; (arrow) flecha, saeta, *f*, dardo, *m*; (of a golf club, etc.) mango, *m*; (of a cart) vara, *f*; *mech* árbol, eje, *m*; (of a column and a feather) cañón, *m*; (of light) rayo, *m*; (of a mine) pozo, tiro, *m*; (air-shaft) conducto de aire, ventilador, *m*. **cam-s., árbol de levas, *m*. driving s.,** árbol motor, *m*

shaggy *a* peludo; lanudo

shagreen *n* chagrén, *m*

shah *n* cha, *m*

shake *vt* sacudir; agitar; hacer temblar; (weaken) debilitar, hacer flaquear. *vi* estremecerse; temblar; (trill) trinar. **He managed to s. himself free,** Consiguió librarse por una sacudida. **to s. hands,** darse la mano, estrecharse la mano. **to s. one's finger at,** señalar con el dedo (a). **to s. one's fist at,** amenazar con el puño (a). **to s. one's head,** mover la cabeza; negar con la cabeza. **to s. one's sides,** (with laughter) reírse a carcajadas. **to s. with fear,** temblar de miedo. **to s. down,** sacudir, hacer caer. **s.-down,** *n* cama improvisada, *f*. **to s. off,** sacudirse; librarse (de), perder; quitar de encima (a). **to s. out,** (unfurl) desplegar; sacudir. **to s. up,** agitar; sacudir, remover

shake *n* sacudida, *f*; (of the head) movimiento (de la cabeza), *m*; (of the hand) apretón (de manos), *m*; temblor, *m*; *mus* trino, gorjeo, *m*. **in two shakes,** *inf* en un periquete. **to give a person a good s.,** sacudir violentamente (a)

Shakespearean *a* shakespeariano

shakiness *n* inestabilidad, *f*; poca firmeza, *f*; temblor, *m*; lo dudoso. **the s. of his voice,** su voz trémula

shaking *n* sacudimiento, *m*; temblor, *m*; (of windows, etc.) zangoloteo, *m*

shaky *a* inestable; poco firme; (of hands, etc.) tembloroso; (of the voice) trémulo; (of gait) vacilante; dudoso

shale *n* esquisto, *m*

shall *v aux* (expressing simple future) **I s. arrive tomorrow,** Llegaré mañana. **S. we go to the sea next week?** ¿Iremos al mar la semana próxima?; (expressing obligation, compulsion) **You s. not go out,** No has de salir, No quiero que salgas. **He s. see her immediately,** Tiene que verla en seguida; (as a polite formula) **S. I go?** ¿Quiero Vd. que vaya? **S. we buy the soap?** ¿Quiere Vd. que compremos el jabón? ¿Compraremos el jabón?

shallot *n bot* chalote, *m*, ascalonia, *f*

shallow *a* poco profundo; (of a receptacle) llano; (of

persons) superficial, frívolo; (of knowledge, etc.) superficial, ligero, somero. *n* bajío, *m*

shallowness *n* poca profundidad, *f*; superficialidad, *f*

sham *vt* fingir, simular. *n* farsa, *f*; imitación, *f*; engaño, *m*; (person) farsante, *m*. *a* fingido; falso; espurio. **to s. illness,** fingirse enfermo. **to s. dead,** hacer la mortecina. **You're just a s.,** Eres un farsante

sham battle *n mil* simulacro de combate, simulacro guerrero, *m*

shamble *vi* andar arrastrándose. *n* andar pesado, *m*; *pl* **shambles,** matadero, *m*; *fig* carnicería, *f*

shambling *a* pesado, lento

shame *n* vergüenza, *f*; ignominia, *f*; deshonra, *f*. *vt* avergonzar; deshonrar. **For s.!** ¡Qué vergüenza! **What a s.!** ¡Qué lástima! **to put to s.,** avergonzar

shamefaced *a* (bashful) vergonzoso, tímido; (ashamed) avergonzado

shamefacedly *adv* vergonzosamente, tímidamente; con vergüenza

shameful *a* vergonzoso, escandaloso; indecente

shamefully *adv* escandalosamente

shamefulness *n* vergüenza, infamia, *f*; indecencia, *f*

shameless *a* desvergonzado; impúdico, indecente

shamelessly *adv* desvergonzadamente

shamelessness *n* desvergüenza, poca vergüenza, *f*; impudicia, deshonestidad, *f*

shampoo *n* champú, *m*. *vt* dar un champú (a); dar un masaje (a). **dry s.,** champú seco, *m*

shamrock *n* trébol blanco, *m*

shank *n* zanca, *f*; *mech* pierna, *f*; (handle) mango, *m*; (of a button) rabo, *m*, cola, *f*. **go on Shank's mare, ride on Shank's mare,** caminar en coche de San Francisco, ir en la boridad de Villadiego

shanty *n* choza, *f*

shanty town *n* barriada (Peru), callampa, población, población callampa (Chile), *f*, Rancho (Venezuela), *m*, villa-miseria (Argentina), *f*

shape *n* forma, *f*; bulto, *m*; fantasma, *m*; (of a garment) corte, *m*; (of a person) talle, *m*; *cul* molde, *m*; (of a hat) forma, *f*. *vt* formar; (a garment) cortar; (ideas) dar forma (a); adaptar; (stone, etc.) labrar; (one's life) dominar. *vi* (of events) desarrollarse. **to go out of s.,** perder la forma. **to take s.,** tomar forma. **to s. one's course,** dirigirse (hacia, a); *naut* dar el rumbo. **to s. well,** prometer bien

shaped *a* de forma de . . . , que tiene figura de . . . **pear-s.,** piriforme

shapeless *a* informe; disforme

shapelessness *n* informidad, *f*; deformidad, *f*

shapeliness *n* belleza de forma, *f*; simetría, *f*

shapely *a* bien formado; simétrico

share *n* porción, *f*; parte, *f*; cuota, *f*; contribución, *f*; (part ownership) interés, *m*; (in a company) acción, *f*. *vt* distribuir; compartir; dividir; tomar parte en. *vi* participar (de); tomar parte (en). **to fall to one's s.,** tocar, corresponder. **to go shares with,** dividir con, compartir con. **to take a s. in the conversation,** tomar parte en la conversación. **paid-up s.,** *com* acción liberada, *f*. **to s. out,** repartir, distribuir

shareholder *n* accionista, *mf*

sharer *n* partícipe, *mf*

shark *n icht* tiburón, *m*; *inf* caimán, *m*

sharp *a* (of edges) afilado, cortante; (of points) punzante, puntiagudo; (of features, etc.) anguloso; (of bends, etc.) brusco; (of outlines, etc.) definido, distinto; (of pain, sound) agudo; (marked) marcado; (intense) intenso; (of winds, glance, etc.) penetrante; (of hearing) fino; (of appetite) bueno; (of showers) fuerte; (quick) rápido; (clever, etc.) vivo, listo; perspicaz; (of children) despierto, precoz; (unscrupulous) astuto, sin escrúpulos; (of criticism, remarks) mordaz; (of rebukes, sentences, etc.) severo; (of winters, etc.) riguroso; (of fighting) encarnizado; (of taste) picante; (sour) ácido; *mus* sostenido. *adv* en punto; puntualmente. **s.** *n mus* sostenido, *m*. **at five o'clock s.,** a las

cinco en punto. **Look s.!** ¡Date prisa! **s.-edged,** afilado. **s.-eyed,** con ojos de lince; de mirada penetrante. **s.-featured,** de facciones angulosas. **s.-nosed,** de nariz puntiaguda. **s.-pointed,** puntiagudo. **s. practice,** procedimientos poco honrados, *m pl.* **s.-tongued,** de lengua áspera. **s. turn,** curva brusca, curva cerrada, *f.* **s.-witted,** de inteligencia viva, listo **sharpen** *vt* (knives) afilar, amolar; (pencils, etc.) sacar punta (a); (wits, etc.) despabilar; (appetite) abrir. **This walk has sharpened my appetite,** Este paseo me ha abierto el apetito. **to s. one's claws,** afilarse las uñas **sharper** *n inf* caballero de industria, timador, *m;* (at cards) fullero, *m*
sharply *adv* claramente; bruscamente; severamente; ásperamente
sharpness *n* (of cold, etc.) intensidad, *f;* severidad, *f;* (cleverness) agudeza, perspicacia, *f;* (of a child) precocidad, *f;* (sarcasm, etc.) mordacidad, *f;* aspereza, *f;* brusquedad, *f*
sharpshooter *n* franco tirador, *m*
sharpsighted *a* de vista penetrante, listo, perspicaz
shatter *vt* romper, quebrantar; hacer añicos; *fig* destrozar. **You have shattered my illusions,** Has destrozado todas mis ilusiones
shave *vt* afeitar, rasurar; (wood, etc.) acepillar. *vi* afeitarse; (of razors) afeitar. *n* afeitada, *f.* **to have a s.,** hacerse afeitar. **to have a close s.,** *inf* escapar por un pelo
shaving *n* afeitada, *f;* (of wood, etc.) viruta, acepilladura, *f.* **s.-bowl,** bacía, *f.* **s.-brush,** brocha de afeitar, *f.* **s.-glass,** espejo de afeitar, *m.* **s.-soap,** jabón de afeitar, *m.* **s.-stick,** barra de jabón de afeitar, *f*
shawl *n* chal, mantón, rebozo, *m*
she *pers pron* ella; la; (female) hembra, *f;* (translated by fem. ending in the case of animals, etc., e.g. **she bear,** osa, **she cat,** gata). **It is her,** Es ella. **she who is dancing,** la que baila
sheaf *n* (of corn, etc.) gavilla, garba, *f;* (of arrows) haz, *m;* (of papers, etc.) paquete, atado, *m.* **to bind in sheaves,** agavillar
shear *vt* (sheep) esquilar, trasquilar; tonsurar; cortar; (cloth) tundir
shearer *n* (of sheep) esquilador, *m*
shearing *n* (of sheep) esquileo, *m,* tonsura, *f;* (of cloth) tunda, *f.* **s. machine,** esquiladora, *f.* **s. season,** esquileo, *m*
shears *n pl* tijeras grandes, *f pl,* cizalla, *f*
sheath *n* vaina, *f.* **s.-knife,** cuchillo de monte, *m*
sheathe *vt* envainar; *naut* aforrar
shed *vt* derramar; (skin, etc.) mudar; perder; (remove) quitarse, desprenderse de; (get rid of) deshacerse de. *n* cobertizo, sotechado, *m;* cabaña, *f.* **to s. light on,** echar luz sobre, iluminar
sheen *n* lustre, *m;* brillo, *m*
sheep *n* oveja, *f;* carnero, *m;* ganado lanar, *m.* **He is the black s. of the family,** Es el garbanzo negro de la familia. **to cast sheep's eyes at,** lanzar miradas de carnero degollado. **s. breeder,** ganadero, *m.* **s.-dip,** desinfectante para ganado, *m.* **s.-dog,** perro de pastor, *m.* **s.-like,** ovejuno, de oveja. **s.-shearing,** esquileo, *m*
sheepfold *n* aprisco, redil, *m*
sheepish *a* tímido, vergonzoso; estúpido
sheepishly *adv* tímidamente
sheepishness *n* timidez, cortedad, *f;* estupidez, *f*
sheepskin *n* piel de carnero, *f.* **s. jacket,** zamarra, *f*
sheer *a* puro; completo, absoluto; (steep) escarpado, acantilado; a pico; (of fabrics) transparente; ligero, fino. *adv* completamente; de un golpe; (perpendicularly) a pico. **to s. off,** desviarse; largarse, marcharse
sheet *n* (bed) sábana, *f;* (shroud) mortaja, *f;* (of paper) hoja, *f;* cuartilla, *f;* (pamphlet) folleto, *m;* (news) periódico, *m,* hoja, *f;* (of metal, etc.) lámina, plancha, *f;* (of water, etc.) extensión, *f;* *naut* escota, *f. vt* poner sábanas en; envolver en sábanas; (a corpse) amortajar. **to be as white as a s.,** estar pálido como un muerto. **s. bend,** (knot) nudo de tejedor, *m.* **s. glass,** vidrio en lámina, *m.* **s. iron,** hierro en planchas, *m*

sheik *n* jeque, *m*
shekel *n* (coin) siclo, *m; pl* **shekels,** dinero, *m*
shelf *n* estante, anaquel, *m;* (reef) banco de arena, bajío, *m;* (of rock) escalón, *m.* **to be on the s.,** *inf* quedarse para tía, quedarse para vestir imágenes
shell *n* (of small shellfish) concha, *f;* (of tortoise) coraza, *f;* (of insects, lobsters, etc.) caparazón, *m;* (of a nut) cáscara, *f;* (of an egg) cascarón, *m;* (of peas, beans) vaina, *f;* (corn and mus) concha, *f;* (of a building) casco, *m;* (outside) exterior, *m;* (empty form) apariencia, *f;* mil granada, *f. vt* pelar; (nuts) descascarar; (beans, etc.) desvainar; *mil* bombardear. **to be under s.-fire,** sufrir un bombardeo. **s. shock,** neurosis de guerra, *f*
shellfish *n* crustáceo, *m;* (as food) marisco, *m*
shelling *n mil* bombardeo, *m*
shelter *n* abrigo, amparo, *m;* refugio, *m;* asilo, *m. vt* dar asilo (a); abrigar; (defend) amparar, proteger; (hide) esconder. *vi* refugiarse; resguardarse; esconderse
sheltered *a* abrigado
sheltering *a* protector
shelve *vt* (books) poner en un estante; (persons) destituir; (questions, etc.) aplazar, arrinconar; proveer de estantes, *vi* (slope) inclinarse, formar declive; (of sea bed) formar escalones
shelving *a* inclinado; (of ocean bed) acantilado
shepherd *n* pastor, *m. vt* guardar; guiar, conducir. **s. boy,** zagal, *m.* **shepherd's pouch,** zurrón, *m*
shepherdess *n* pastora, *f*
sherbet *n* sorbete, *m*
sheriff *n* (in U.K.) sheriff, *m;* (U.S.A.) jefe de la policía, *m*
sherry *n* (vino de) jerez, *m.* **dry s.,** jerez seco, *m*
Shetlands, the las Islas de Shetland, *f pl*
shield *n* escudo, *m;* (round) rodela, *f; her* escudo de armas, *m; fig* defensa, *f,* amparo, *m. vt* proteger, amparar. **to s. a person,** proteger a una persona. **to s. one's eyes from the sun,** proteger los ojos del sol. **s.-bearer,** escudero, *m*
shift *vt* mover; trasladar; quitar, librarse de; cambiar. *vi* moverse; (of the wind) girar; cambiar. *n* cambio, *m;* (expedient) recurso, expediente, *m;* (dodge) artificio, *m,* trampa, *f;* (of workmen) tanda, *f,* turno, *m.* **to make s.,** arreglárselas (para hacer algo); procurar (hacer algo); (manage) ir tirando. **to s. for oneself,** componérselas, arreglárselas. **to s. the scenes,** *theat* cambiar de decoración. **to s. the helm,** *naut* cambiar el timón. **to work in shifts,** trabajar por turnos
shiftiness *n* falta de honradez, informalidad, *f;* astucia, *f*
shifting *a* (of light, etc.) cambiante; (of sand, etc.) movedizo; (of wind) mudable; (of moods) voluble. **s. sand,** arena movediza, *f*
shiftless *a* perezoso; sin energía, ineficaz
shiftlessness *n* pereza, *f;* falta de energía, *f*
shifty *a* (tricky) tramposo, astuto; (dishonest) informal, falso; (of gaze) furtivo. **s.-eyed,** *a* de mirada furtiva
Shiite *a* and *n* chiíta
shilling *n* chelín, *m.* **nine shillings in the £,** nueve chelines por libra. **to cut off with a s.,** desheredar
shilly shally *n* irresolución, vacilación, *f, vi* estar irresoluto, titubear, no saber qué hacer
shimmer *vi* rielar; relucir. *n* luz trémula, *f;* resplandor, *m;* viso, *m*
shin *n* espinilla, *f;* (of beef) corvejón, *m.* **to s. up,** trepar
shindy *n* suiza, reyerta, tasquera, *f.* **to kick up a s.,** armar camorra
shine *vi* brillar; resplandecer, relucir, relumbrar. *vt* (hacer dar lustre (a). *n* brillo, *m;* lustre, *m.* **in rain or s.,** en buen o mal tiempo. **to s. with happiness,** radiar felicidad. **to take the s. out of,** eclipsar
shingle *n* (pebbles) guijarros, *m pl;* cascajo, *m; carp* barda, *f;* (hair) pelo a la garçonne, *m; pl* **shingles,** *med* zona, *f,* herpe zóster, *m. vt* (the hair) cortar a la garçonne
shining *a* resplandeciente, brillante, reluciente; ra-

diante. **s. with happiness,** radiante de felicidad. **s. example,** ejemplo notable, *m*

shintoism *n* sintoísmo, *m*

shiny *a* brillante; lustroso, terso; (of trousers, etc.) reluciente; (of paper) glaseado

ship *n* buque, barco, *m*; (sailing) velero, *m. vt* embarcar; (oars) armar. *vi* embarcar; (as a member of crew) embarcarse. **on board s.,** a bordo. **to s. a sea,** embarcar agua. **to take s.,** embarcar. **to s. off,** mandar. **ship's boat,** lancha, *f.* **ship's boy,** grumete, *m.* **ship's carpenter,** carpintero de ribera, *m.* **ship's company,** tripulación, *f.* **s.-breaker,** desguazador, *m.* **s.-canal,** canal de navegación, *m.* **s.-load,** cargamento, *m*

shipbuilder *n* constructor de buques, arquitecto naval, *m*

shipbuilding *n* construcción naval, *f*

shipment *n* embarque, *m*; despacho por mar, *m*; (consignment) remesa, *f*

shipowner *n* naviero, *m*

shipper *n* naviero, *m*; importador, *m*; exportador, *m*

shipping *n* embarque, *m*; buques, barcos, *m pl*; (of a country) marina, *f.* **s. agent,** consignatario de buques, *m.* **s. company,** compañía de navegación, *f.* **s. offices,** oficinas de una compañía de navegación, *f pl*

shipshape *a* en buen orden; bien arreglado

shipwreck *n* naufragio, *m, vt* hacer naufragar, echar a pique

shipwrecked person *n* náufrago (-ga). **to be shipwrecked,** naufragar

shipyard *n* astillero, varadero, *m*

shire *n* condado, *m*

shirk *vt* eludir, esquivar; desentenderse de. *vi* faltar al deber

shirker *n* gandul (-la); persona que no cumple con su deber, *f*

shirr *vt* fruncir

shirt *n* camisa, *f.* **dress s.,** camisa de pechera dura, *f.* **hair-s.,** cilicio, *m..* **in one's s.-sleeves,** en mangas de camisa. **s.-blouse,** blusa sencilla, *f.* **s.-collar,** cuello de camisa, *m.* **s. factory** or **shop,** camisería, *f.* **shirtfront,** pechera, *f.* **s.-maker,** camisero (-ra)

shirting *n* tela para camisas, *f*

shiver *vi* temblar, tiritar; dar diente con diente; (of a boat) zozobrar. *vt* (break) hacer añicos, romper; (sails) sacudir. *n* temblor, estremecimiento, *m*; escalofrío, *m*; (of glass, etc.) fragmento, *m,* astilla, *f.* **You give me the shivers,** Me das escalofríos

shivery *a* tembloroso; friolero. **I feel s.,** Tengo escalofríos

shoal *n* (of fish) banco, *m*; gran cantidad, *f*; (of people) multitud, muchedumbre, *f*; (water) bajo fondo, *m*; (sand-bank) banco, bajío, *m,* a poco profundo. **I know shoals of people in Valencia,** Conozco a muchísima gente de Valencia

shock *n* choque, *m*; *elec* conmoción, *f*; *med* shock, *m*; (*med* stroke) conmoción cerebral, *f*; (fright) sobresalto, susto, *m. vt* sacudir, dar una sacudida (a); chocar; escandalizar, horrorizar. *vi* chocar. **electric s.,** conmoción eléctrica, *f.* **She is easily shocked,** Ella se escandaliza fácilmente. **s. of hair,** mata de pelo, *f.* **s. absorber,** *mech* amortiguador, *m*; *aut* amortiguador (de los muelles), *m.* **s. troops,** tropas de asalto, *f pl,* elementos de choque, *m pl*

shocking *a* escandaloso; repugnante, horrible; espantoso. **How s.!** ¡Qué horror! **s. bad,** malísimo

shockingly *adv* horriblemente

shod *a* calzado; (of horses) herrado

shoddy *n* pacotilla, *f.* a de pacotilla; espurio, falso

shoe *n* zapato, *m*; (horse) herradura, *f*; (*naut mech*) zapata, *f. vt* (horses) herrar. **I should not like to be in his shoes,** No me gustaría estar en su pellejo. **That is quite another pair of shoes,** Eso es harina de otro costal. **to cast a s.,** (of horses) desherrarse, perder una herradura. **to put on one's shoes,** ponerse los zapatos, calzarse. **to remove one's shoes,** quitarse los zapatos, descalzarse. **wooden shoes,** zuecos, *m pl.*

s.-buckle, hebilla de zapato, *f.* **s.-lace,** cordón de zapato, *m.* **s.-leather,** cuero para zapatos, *m*; calzado, *m.* **s.-scraper,** limpiabarros, *m*, estregadera, *f.* **s.-shop,** zapatería, *f*

shoeblack *n* betún, *m*; (person) limpiabotas, *m*

shoehorn *n* calzador, *m*

shoemaker *n* zapatero (-ra)

shoemaking *n* fabricación de calzado, zapatería, *f*

shoo! *interj* ¡fuera!; ¡zape! *vt* ahuyentar

shoot *vt* (throw) lanzar; precipitar; (empty) vaciar; (a rapid) salvar; (rays, etc.) echar; (an arrow, a gun, etc.) disparar; (a person, etc.) pegar un tiro (a); *sport* tirar; *mil* fusilar, pasar por las armas; (a film) hacer, impresionar. *vi* lanzarse, precipitarse; (of pain) latir; (sprout) brotar; disparar; tirar; (at football) tirar a gol, chutar. **to s. a glance at,** lanzar una mirada (a). **I was shot in the foot,** Una bala me hirió en el pie. **to s. the sun,** *naut* tomar el sol. **to s. ahead,** tomar la delantera. **to s. at,** tirar a. **to s by,** pasar como una bala. **to s. down,** *aer* derribar; matar de un tiro. **to s. up,** (of children) espigarse; (of prices) subir mucho; (of cliffs, etc.) elevarse

shoot *n* partida de caza, *f*; tiro, *m*; *bot* renuevo, retoño, *m*

shooting *n* tiro, *m*; caza con escopeta, *f*; (of guns) tiroteo, *m*; (of an arrow) disparo, *m*; (of a film) rodaje, *m.* **to go s.,** ir a cazar con escopeta. **s.-box,** pabellón de caza, *m.* **s. butts,** tiradero, *m.* **s. dog,** perro de caza, *m.* **s.-gallery,** tiro al blanco, *m.* **s. match,** concurso de tiro, *m.* **s. pain,** punzada de dolor, *f.* **s. party,** partida de caza, *f.* **s. practice,** ejercicios de tiro, *m pl.* **s.-range,** campo de tiro, *m.* **s. star,** estrella fugaz, *f*

shop *n* tienda, *f*; (workshop) taller, *m. vi* ir de compras, ir de tiendas; comprar. **to talk s.,** hablar de negocios. **s.-assistant,** dependiente (-ta). **s.-soiled,** deslucido. **s.-steward,** representante de los obreros de una fábrica o taller, *m.* **s. window,** escaparate, *m*

shopkeeper *n* tendero (-ra)

shoplifter *n* ladrón (-ona) de tiendas, ratero (-ra) de tiendas

shoplifting *n* ratería en las tiendas, *f*

shopper *n* comprador (-ra)

shopping *n* compra, *f*; compras, *f pl.* **to go s.,** ir de compras. **s. basket,** cesta para compras, *f.* **s. center,** centro comercial, *m*

shopwalker *n* jefe de recepción, *m*

shore *n* orilla, ribera, *f*; costa, *f*; (sands) playa, *f.* **off s.,** en alta mar. **on s.,** en tierra. **to come on s.,** desembarcar. **to s. up,** apuntalar, acodalar; *fig* apoyar

short *a* corto; (of persons) bajo; breve; (of temper) vivo; insuficiente; distante (de); (brusque) seco; (of money) alcanzado. *adv* súbitamente; brevemente. *n* (vowel) vocal breve, *m*; *pl* **shorts,** calzones cortos, *m pl.* **for s.,** para mayor brevedad. **for a s. time,** por poco tiempo. **in a s. time,** dentro de poco. **in s.,** en breve, en resumen, en pocas palabras. **on s. notice,** con poco tiempo de aviso. **s. of,** con la excepción de, menos. **to be s.,** faltar, ser escaso. **to be s. with someone,** tratar con sequedad (a). **to fall s. of expectations,** no cumplir las esperanzas. **to go s. of,** pasarse sin. **to grow s.,** escasear. **s.-circuit,** corto circuito, *m.* **s. cut,** atajo, *m.* **s.-haired,** pelicorto. **s.-handed,** falto de mano de obra. **s.-lived,** de vida corta; efímero, fugaz. **to be short-lived,** tener vida corta. **s.-sighted,** corto de vista. **s.-sightedness,** miopía, cortedad de vista, *f.* **s. story,** cuento, *m.* **s.-tempered,** irascible, irritable, de genio vivo. **s.-waisted,** corto de talle, *m.* **s.-winded,** corto de resuello; asmático

shortage *n* falta, escasez, *f*; carestía, *f.* **water s.,** carestía de agua, *f*

shortcoming *n* defecto, *m*; imperfección, *f*

shorten *vt* acortar; reducir, disminuir; abreviar. *vi* acortarse

shorthand *n* taquigrafía, estenografía, *f. a* taquigráfico, estenográfico. **to take down in s.,** taquigrafiar. **s. writer,** estenógrafo (-fa); taquígrafo (-fa)

shortly *adv* dentro de poco, pronto; brevemente, en resumen, en pocas palabras; (curtly) bruscamente, secamente

shortness *n* cortedad, *f;* brevedad, *f;* (of a person) pequeñez, *f;* (lack) falta, *f;* (of memory, sight) cortedad, *f;* brusqueness) sequedad, brusquedad, *f.* **s. of breath,** falta de aliento, respiración difícil, *f*

shot *n* perdigón, *m; inf* perdigones, *m pl;* bala, *f;* (firing) tiro, *m;* (person) tirador (-ra); (stroke, etc.) golpe, *m,* tirada, *f;* (cinema) fotograma, *m. a* (of silk) tornasolado. **at one s.,** de un tiro. **like a s.,** *fig* como una bala. **to exchange shots,** tirotearse. **to fire a s.,** disparar un tiro. **to have a s. at,** probar suerte. **s.-gun,** escopeta, *f.* **s. silk,** seda tornasolada, *f*

should *v aux* (expressing future) **I s. like to go to the sea,** Me gustaría ir al mar; (expressing conditional) **I s. like to see them if I could,** Me gustaría verlos si pudiera; (expressing obligation) **You s. go at once,** Debes ir en seguida; (expressing probability) **They s. arrive tomorrow,** Seguramente llegarán mañana; (expressing doubt) **If the moment s. be opportune,** Si el momento fuera oportuno. **I s. just think so!** ¡Ya lo creo! ¡No lo dudo!

shoulder *n* hombro, *m;* (of mutton) espalda, *f;* (of a hill) falda, *f. vt* echar al hombro, echar sobre sí; (a responsibility) cargar con, hacerse responsable para; (jostle) dar codazos (a). **s. to s.,** hombro a hombro. **S. arms!** ¡Armas al hombro! **s.-blade,** omoplato,. *m.* **s.-knot,** charretera, *f.* **s.-pad,** hombrera, *f.* **s.-strap,** *mil* dragona, *f;* (of a dress, etc.) tirante, *m;* (of a water carrier, etc.) correón, *m*

shouldered *a* de hombros . . . , de espaldas . . . **round-s.,** cargado de espaldas

shout *vi* gritar, hablar a gritos. *vt* gritar. *n* grito, *m.* **shouts of applause,** aclamaciones, *f pl,* aplausos, *m pl.* **to s. from the housetops,** pregonar a los cuatro vientos. **to s. with laughter,** reírse a carcajadas. **to s. down,** silbar. **to s. out,** gritar

shouting *n* gritos, *m pl,* vocerío, clamor, *m;* (applause) aclamaciones, *f pl*

shove *vt* empujar; poner. *n* empujón, *m.* **to s. along,** empujar. **to s. aside,** empujar a un lado; apartar a codazos. **to s. away,** rechazar. **to s. back,** hacer retroceder. **to s. forward,** hacer avanzar, empujar hacia adelante. **to s. off,** (a boat) echar afuera. **to s. out,** empujar hacia fuera

shovel *n* pala, *f. vt* traspalar. **s. hat,** sombrero de teja, *m*

show *vt* mostrar; hacer ver; (disclose) descubrir; revelar; (exhibit) exhibir; (indicate) indicar; (prove) demostrar, probar; (conduct) conducir, llevar, guiar; (explain) explicar; (oneself) presentarse. *vi* mostrarse; verse; parecer. **to s. cause,** mostrar causa. **to s. fight,** ofrecer resistencia. **s. signs of,** dar señales de. **to s. itself,** declararse, asomarse, surgir. **to s. to the door,** acompañar a la puerta. **to s. in,** (a person) hacer entrar, introducir (en). **to s. off,** *vt* exhibir; realzar; (new clothes, etc.) lucir. *vi* darse importancia; pavonearse. **to s. out,** (a person) acompañar a la puerta; (in anger) poner de patitas en la calle. **to s. through,** *vi* trasparentarse. *vt* conducir por. **to s. up,** *vt* insinuar a subir; (a fraud, etc.) descubrir; (a swindler) desenmascarar; (defects) revelar. *vi* (stand out) destacarse; (be present) asomarse, asistir

show *n* (exhibition) exposición, *f;* espectáculo, *m;* (sign) indicio, *m,* señal, *f;* (ostentation) pompa, *f,* aparato, *m,* ostentación, *f;* (appearance) apariencia, *f;* (affair) negocio, *m.* **to give the s. away,** echar los títeres a rodar. **to make a s. of,** hacer gala de. **s.-case,** escaparate, *m,* vitrina, *f.* **s. of hands,** votación por manos levantadas, *f.* **s.-room,** salón de muestras, *m*

showdown *n* cartas boca arriba, *m*

shower *n* chaparrón, chubasco, *m;* (of spray, etc.) chorro, *m;* (of stones, arrows, etc.) lluvia, *f;* (of honors) cosecha, *f,* (bridal) despedida de soltera, despedida de soltería, *f. vt* derramar; rociar; mojar; llover. *vi* chaparrear, llover. **s.-bath,** ducha, *f*

shower cap *n* gorro de ducha, *m*

showery *a* lluvioso

showily *adv* aparatosamente, con ostentación

showiness *n* ostentación, *f;* esplendor, *m,* magnificencia, *f*

showman *n* director de un espectáculo de feria, *m;* titiritero, *m;* pregonero, *m*

showy *a* vistoso; ostentoso

shrapnel *n* granada, *m,* granada de metralla, *f*

shred *n* fragmento, *m;* (of cloth) jirón, *m;* brizna, *f; fig* pizca, *f. vt* desmenuzar. **to tear in shreds,** hacer pedazos

shrew *n zool* musaraña, *f;* (woman) fiera, *f*

shrewd *a* sagaz, perspicaz; prudente; (of the wind) penetrante; (pain) punzante. **to have a s. idea of,** tener una buena idea de. **a s. diplomat,** un fino diplomático

shrewdly *adv* sagazmente, con perspicacia; prudentemente

shrewdness *n* sagacidad, perspicacia, *f;* prudencia, *f*

shrewish *a* regañón

shrewishness *n* mal genio, *m*

shriek *vi* chillar, gritar. *vt* decir a voces, gritar. *n* chillido, *m;* grito agudo, *m.* **shrieks of laughter,** carcajadas, *f pl*

shrieking *n* gritos, chillidos, *m pl*

shrift to give short, enviar normala (a), enviar a paseo (a)

shrill *a* estridente, agudo

shrillness *n* estridencia, *f*

shrimp *n* camarón, *m,* gamba, *f, vi* pescar camarones

shrine *n* relicario, *m;* sepulcro de santo, *m;* templete, *m,* capilla, *f;* santuario, *f*

shrink *vi* encogerse; contraerse; disminuir, reducirse. *vt* encoger; reducir, disminuir; desaparecer; disiparse. **I shrank from doing it,** Me repugnaba hacerlo. **to s. away from,** retroceder ante; recular ante; huir de. **to s. back,** recular (ante)

shrinkage *n* encogimiento, *m;* contracción, *f;* reducción, disminución, *f*

shrinking *a* tímido

shrive *vt* confesar

shrivel *vi* avellanarse; (of persons, through old age) acartonarse, apergaminarse; (wither) marchitarse; arrugarse. *vt* arrugar; secar, marchitar

shroud *n* sudario, *m,* mortaja, *f; naut* obenque, *m.* **to wrap in a s.,** amortajar

Shrove Tuesday *n* martes de carnaval, *m*

shrub *n* arbusto, *m;* matajo, *m*

shrubbery *n* arbustos, *m pl,* maleza, *f;* bosquecillo, *m*

shrug *vi* encogerse de hombros. *n* encogimiento de hombros, *m*

shrunken *a* contraído; acartonado, apergaminado; seco, marchito. **shrunken head,** cabeza reducida, *f*

shudder *vi* estremecerse; vibrar. *n* estremecimiento, *m;* escalofrío, *m;* (of an engine, etc.) vibración, *f*

shuffle *vt* (the feet) arrastrar; (scrape) restregar; (cards) barajar; (papers) mezclar. *vi* arrastrar los pies, arrastrarse; (cards) barajar; *fig* tergiversar. *n* (of the cards) barajadura, *f; fig* evasiva, *f;* embuste, *m.* **to s. along,** andar arrastrando los pies

shuffling *n* el arrastrar, *m,* (e.g. **the shuffling of chairs,** el arrastrar de sillas)

shun *vt* evitar, rehuir, esquivar

shunt *vt rw* apartar; *elec* shuntar. *vi rw* hacer maniobras

shunting *n* (of trains) maniobras, *f pl*

shut *vt* and *vi* cerrar. **to s. again,** volver a cerrar. **to s. down,** *vt* cerrar; (a machine) parar. *vi* (of factories, etc.) cerrar. **to s. in,** encerrar; (surround) cercar, rodear. **to s. off,** (water, etc.) cortar; (isolate) aislar (de). **to s. out,** excluir; obstruir, impedir; negar la entrada (a). **to s. up,** *vt* cerrar; encerrar; *inf* hacer callar (a); *vi inf* callarse; cerrar la boca. **to s. oneself up,** encerrarse

shutter *n* (window) contraventana, *f,* postigo, *m;* (of a camera) obturador, *m;* (of a fireplace) campana (de hogar), *f. vt* poner contraventanas (a); cerrar los postigos de

shuttle *n* (weaver's, and sewing-machine) lanzadera, *f*, (airplane service) puente aéreo, *m*. **s.-cock,** volante, gallito, *m*

shy *a* (of animals) tímido, salvaje; (of persons) huraño, tímido; vergonzoso. *vi* (of a horse) respingar; (of persons) asustarse (de). *vt* (a ball, etc.) lanzar. *n* (of a horse) respingo, *m*; (of a ball) lanzamiento, *m*; (try) prueba, tentativa, *f*. **to fight shy of,** procurar evitar. **to have a shy at,** probar

shyly *adv* tímidamente; con vergüenza, vergonzosamente

shyness *n* timidez, *f*; huraña, *f*; vergüenza, *f*

Siamese *a* siamés. *n* siamés (-esa); (language) siamés, *m*. **S. cat,** gato siamés, *m*

Siberia Siberia, *f*

Siberian *a* and *n* siberiano (-na)

sic *vt* atacar; abijar, azuzar (a dog); *adv* así (in academic prose)

Sicilian *a* and *n* siciliano (-na)

Sicily Sicilia, *f*

sick *a* enfermo; mareado. **the s.,** los enfermos. **to be s.,** vomitar; estar enfermo. **to be s. of,** estar harto de. **to feel s.,** sentirse mareado. **to be on the s.-list,** estar enfermo. **s.-bed,** lecho de dolor, *m*. **s.-headache,** jaqueca, con náuseas, *f*. **s.-leave,** *mil* permiso por enfermedad, *m*. **s.-nurse,** enfermera, *f*

sicken *vi* caer enfermo, enfermar; (feel sick) marearse; (recoil from) repugnar; (weary of) cansarse (de), aburrirse (de). *vt* marear; dar asco (a), repugnar; cansar, aburrir. **It sickens me,** Me da asco. **He is sickening for measles,** Muestra síntomas de sarampión

sickening *a* nauseabundo; repugnante; (tedious) fastidioso

sickle *n* hoz, segadera, *f*

sickliness *n* falta de salud, *f*; náusea, *f*; (paleness) palidez, *f*

sickly *a* enfermizo, achacoso, malucho; (of places, etc.) malsano; (pale) pálido; débil; (of a smell) nauseabundo; (mawkish) empalagoso

sickness *n* enfermedad, *f*; mal, *m*; náusea, *f*, mareo, *m*

side *n* lado, *m*; (hand) mano, *f*; (of a river, etc.) orilla, *f*, margen, *m*; (of a person) costado, *m*; (of an animal) ijada, *f*; (of a hill) falda, pendiente, ladera, *f*; (of a ship) banda, *f*, costado, *m*; (aspect) aspecto, *m*; punto de vista, *m*; (party) partido, grupo, *m*; (team) equipo, *m*; (of descent) lado, *m*. *a* lateral, de lado; oblicuo. **on all sides,** por todas partes. **on both sides,** por ambos lados. **s. by s.,** lado a lado. **the other s. of the picture,** el revés de la medalla. **to change sides,** cambiar de partido. **to pick sides,** escoger el equipo. **to put on s.,** darse tono, alzar el gallo. **to split one's sides,** desternillarse de risa, reírse a carcajadas. **to s. with,** declararse por, ponerse al lado de, tomar el partido de. **wrong s. out,** al revés. **s.-car,** sidecar, asiento lateral, *m*. **s.-chain,** *chem* cadena lateral, *f*. **s.-dish,** entremés, *m*. **s. door,** puerta lateral, *f*. **s.-face,** *a* de perfil. *n* perfil, *m*. **s.-glance,** mirada de soslayo, *f*. **s.-issue,** cuestión secundaria, *f*. **s.-line,** negocio accesorio, *m*; ocupación secundaria, *f*; *rw* vía secundaria, *f*. **s.-saddle,** silla de señora, silla de montar de lado, *f*. **s.-show,** (at a fair) barraca, *f*, puesto de feria, *m*; exhibición secundaria, *f*; función secundaria, *f*. **s.-table,** trinchero, *m*. **s.-track,** *n* *rw* apartadero, *m*. *vt* desviar (de), apartar (de). **s.-view,** perfil, *m*. **s.-walk,** acera, *f*. **s.-whiskers,** patillas, *f pl*

sidelight *n* luz lateral, *f*; (on a ship) ojo de buey, *m*; *fig* información incidental, *f*

sidelong *adv* de lado, lateralmente; (of glances) de soslayo. *a* oblicuo

side road *n* camino lateral, *m*

sideways *adv* oblicuamente, de lado; (edgewise) de soslayo. *a* de soslayo

siding *n* *rw* apartadero, *m*

sidle *vi* andar (or ir) de lado. **to s. up to,** acercarse servilmente a; arrimarse (a)

siege *n* asedio, sitio, cerco, *m*. **to lay s. to,** poner cerco

(a), sitiar, asediar cercar. **to raise a s.,** levantar un sitio

sienna *n* tierra de siena natural, *f*. **burnt s.,** tierra de siena tostada, *f*

sieve *n* cedazo, tamiz, *m*, criba, *f*, *vt* tamizar, cerner, cribar

sift *vt* (sieve) cerner, cribar; (sugar, etc.) salpicar (con) (a question) escudriñar, examinar minuciosamente

sifting *n* cribado, *m*; (of a question) investigación minuciosa, *f*; *pl* **siftings,** cerniduras, *f pl*

sigh *vi* suspirar; (of the wind) susurrar. *n* suspiro, *m*; (of the wind) susurro, *m*. **to s. for,** suspirar por; lamentar

sighing *n* suspiros, *m pl*; (of the wind) susurro, *m*

sight *n* vista, *f*; visión, *f*; espectáculo, *m*; (fright) estantigua, *f*. *vt* ver, divisar; (aim) apuntar. **front s.,** (of guns) alza, *f*. **short s.,** (of eyes) vista corta, *f*. **at first s.,** a primera vista. **in s.,** a la vista. **in s. of,** a vista de. **out of s.,** que no está a la vista; perdido de vista. **Out of s., out of mind,** Ojos que no ven, corazón que no siente. **to be lost to s.,** perderse de vista. **to lose s. of,** perder de vista (a). **to catch a s. of,** vislumbrar. **to come in s.,** aparecer, asomarse. **to know by s.,** conocer de vista (a). **s.-reading,** lectura a primera vista, *f*

sightly *a* hermoso; deleitable

sightseeing *n* turismo, *m*. **to go s.,** visitar los monumentos, ver los puntos de interés

sightseer *n* curioso (-sa); turista, *mf*

sign *n* señal, *f*; seña, *f*; indicio, *m*; (of the zodiac and *mus*) signo, *m*; marca, *f*; *ecc* símbolo, *m*; (of a shop, etc.) muestra, *f*, rótulo, *m*; (symptom) síntoma, *m*. *vt* firmar; indicar; *ecc* persignar. **as a s. of,** en señal de. **to converse by signs,** hablar por señas. **to make the s. of the cross over,** santiguar. **to show signs (of),** dar señas (de); indicar. **s.-painter,** pintor de muestras, *m*

signal *n* señal, *f*. *vt* señalar; hacer señas (a). *vi* hacer señales. *a* insigne, notable. **fog-s.,** señal de niebla, *f*. **landing s.,** *aer* señal de aterrizaje, *f*. **to give the s. for,** dar la señal para. **s.-box,** garita de señales, *f*. **s. code,** *naut* código de señales, *m*

signalize *vt* señalar, distinguir

signaler *n* señalador, *m*

signalman *n* *rw* guardavía, *m*

signatory *a* and *n* signatario (-ia)

signature *n* firma, *f*; (mus and print) signatura, *f*

signboard *n* letrero, *m*, muestra, *f*

signet *n* sello, *m*. **s.-ring,** anillo de sello, *m*

significance *n* significación, *f*, significado, *m*; importancia, *f*

significant *a* significativo, significante; expresivo; importante

significantly *adv* significativamente; expresivamente

signify *vt* significar; querer decir; importar. *vi* significar, tener importancia; importar

signpost *n* indicador de dirección, *m*

Sikh *n* sik, *mf* (*pl* siks)

silage *n* forraje conservado en silo, *m*

silence *n* silencio, *m*, interj ¡silencio! *vt* hacer callar, imponer silencio (a); silenciar. **to keep s.,** guardar silencio, callarse. **to pass over in s.,** pasar en silencio (por), pasar por alto de. **S. gives consent,** Quien calla otorga

silencer *n* (of fire-arms) silencioso, *m*; *aut* silenciador, silencioso, *m*

silent *a* silencioso. **to become s.,** enmudecer; callar. **to remain s.,** callarse, guardar silencio; permanecer silencioso. **s. partner,** *n* socio (-ia) comanditario (-ia)

silent film, silent movie *n* película muda, *f*

silently *adv* silenciosamente, en silencio

silhouette *n* silueta, *f*. *vt* representar en silueta; destacar. **in s.,** en silueta. **to be silhouetted against the sky,** destacarse contra el sielo

silica *n* sílice, *f*

silk *n* seda, *f*, *a* de seda. **artificial s.,** seda artificial, *f*. **floss s.,** seda ocal, *f*. **sewing s.,** seda de coser, *f*. **twist s.,** seda cordelada, *f*. **as smooth as s.,** como una seda. **s. growing,** sericultura, *f*. **s. hat,** sombrero de copa, *m*.

s. merchandise, sedería, *f.* **s. stocking,** media de seda, *f*
silken *a* de seda; sedoso
silkiness *n* carácter sedoso, *m*; suavidad, *f*
silk-screen process *n* imprenta por tamiz, imprenta serigráfica, imprenta tamigráfica, impresión con estarcido de seda, *f*, proceso tamigráfico, *m*, serigrafía, tamigrafía, *f*
silkworm *n* gusano de seda, *m*
silky *a* sedoso; (of wine) suave
sill *n* (of a window) alféizar, antepecho, *m*; (of a door) umbral, *m*
silliness *n* tontería, estupidez, *f*
silly *a* tonto, estúpido; imbécil. *n* tonto (-ta). **You are a s. ass,** Eres un imbécil
silo *n* silo, *m*
silt *n* aluvión, *m*, sedimentación, *f.* **to s. up,** *vt* cegar (or obstruir) con aluvión. *vi* cegarse con aluvión
silver *n* plata, *f. a* de plata; argénteo; (of the voice, etc.) argentino. *vt* platear; (mirrors) azogar; (hair) blanquear. **s. birch,** abedul, *m*. **s. fox,** zorro plateado, *m*. **s.-gry,** gris perla, *m*. **s.-haired,** de pelo entrecano. **s.-paper,** papel de estaño, *m*. **s.-plate,** *n* vajilla de plata, *f. vt* platear. **s.-tongued,** de pico de oro; de voz argentina. **s. wedding,** bodas de plata, *f pl*
silversmith *n* platero, *m*. **silversmith's shop,** platería, *f*
silvery *a* plateado, argentado; (of sounds) argentino
simian *a* símico
similar *a* parecido (a), semejante (a); similar; *geom* semejante. **to be s. to,** asemejarse (a), parecerse (a)
similarity *n* parecido, *m*, semejanza, similitud, *f*
similarly *adv* de un modo parecido, asimismo
simile *n* símil, *m*
simmer *vi* hervir a fuego lento; *fig* estar a punto de estallar. **to s. down,** *fig* moderarse poco a poco. **to s. over,** *fig* estallar
simper *vi* sonreírse bobamente
simpering *n* sonrisilla tonta, *f*
simperingly *adv* con sonrisa necia
simple *a* sencillo; simple; ingenuo, inocente; crédulo; (humble) humilde; (mere) mero. **s.-hearted,** inocente, cándido, sin malicia. **s.-minded,** ingenuo; crédulo. **s.-mindedness,** ingenuidad, *f*; credulidad, *f*
simpleton *n* primo (-ma); papanatas, *m*, tonto (-ta)
simplicity *n* sencillez, *f*; simplicidad, candidez, *f*
simplifiable *a* simplificable
simplification *n* simplificación, *f*
simplify *vt* simplificar
simply *adv* sencillamente; simplemente, meramente; absolutamente
simulacrum *n* simulacro, *m*
simulate *vt* fingir, aparentar, simular
simulation *n* simulación, *f*, fingimiento, *m*
simultaneous *a* simultáneo
simultaneously *adv* simultáneamente; al mismo tiempo (que)
simultaneousness *n* simultaneidad, *f*
sin *n* pecado, *m*, *vi* pecar; faltar (a)
since *adv* desde entonces, desde (que). *prep* desde. *conjunc* desde que; ya que, puesto que. **a long time s.,** hace mucho. **not long s.,** hace poco. **How long is it s. . . . ?** ¿Cuánto tiempo hace que . . . ? **s. then,** desde entonces
sincere *a* sincero
sincerely *adv* sinceramente. **Yours s.,** Su afectísimo . . .
sincerity *n* sinceridad, *f*
sine *n* *math* seno, *m*
sinecure *n* canonjía, sinecura, *f*, empleo de aviador (Mexican slang), *m*
sinew *n* tendón, *m*; *pl* **sinews,** nervio, *m*, fuerza, *f*
sinewy *a* (stringy) fibroso; musculoso, nervudo
sinful *a* (of persons) pecador; (of thoughts, acts) pecaminoso

sinfulness *n* pecado, *m*; culpabilidad, perversidad, maldad, *f*
sing *vi* cantar; (of the ears) zumbar; (of wind, water) murmurar, susurrar; (of a cat) ronronear. *vt* cantar. **to s. a child to sleep,** dormir a un niño cantando. **to s. another song,** *inf* bajar el tono. **to s. small,** hacerse el chiquito. **to s. the praises of,** hacer las alabanzas de. **to s. out,** vocear, gritar. **s.-song,** *n* canturía, *f*; concierto improvisado, *m. a* monótono
Singapore Singapur, *m*
singe *vt* chamuscar; (a fowl) aperdigar; (hair) quemar las puntas de los cabellos
singer *n* cantor (-ra); (professional) cantante, *mf*; (bird) ave cantora, *f*
singing *n* canto, *m*; (of the ears) zumbido, *m. a* cantante. **s.-bird,** ave cantora, *f.* **s.-master,** maestro de cantar, *m*
single *a* único; sencillo; solo; simple; (individual) particular; individual; (unmarried) soltero. *n* (tennis) juego sencillo, individual, *m*. **in s. file,** de reata. **to s. out,** escoger; singularizar. **s. bed,** cama de monja, *f.* **s. bedroom,** habitación individual, habitación con una sola cama, *f.* **s.-breasted,** (of coats) recto. **s. combat,** combate singular, *m*. **s. entry,** *com* partida simple, *f.* **s.-handed,** de una mano; para una sola persona; sin ayuda, solo, en solitario. **s.-minded,** sin doblez, sincero de una sola idea. **s. ticket,** billete sencillo, *m*
singleness *n* celibato, *m*, soltería, *f.* **with s. of purpose,** con un solo objeto
singlet *n* camiseta, *f*
singly *adv* separadamente, uno a uno; a solas, solo; sin ayuda
singular *a* and *n* singular, *m*
singularity *n* singularidad, *f*
singularly *adv* singularmente
sinister *a* siniestro
sink *vi* ir al fondo; bajar; hundirse; (of ships) irse a pique, naufragar; sumergirse; disminuir; caer (en); penetrar; (of persons, fires) morir; (of the sun, etc.) ponerse. *vt* (a ship) echar a pique; sumergir; hundir; dejar caer; bajar; (wells) cavar; reducir, disminuir; (invest) invertir; (one's identity, etc.) tener secreto; (differences) olvidar; (engrave) grabar. **My heart sank,** Se me cayeron las alas del corazón. **He sank to his knees,** Cayó de rodillas. **He is sinking fast,** Está en las últimas. **Their words began to s. in,** Sus palabras empezaban a tener efecto (or hacer mella). **I found her sunk in thought,** La encontré ensimismada. **to s. one's voice,** bajar la voz. **to s. down on a chair,** dejarse caer en una silla. **to s. into misery,** caer en la miseria. **to s. under,** (a responsibility, etc.) estar agobiado bajo
sink *n* (kitchen) fregadero, *m*; sumidero, *m*, sentina, *f.* **s. of iniquity,** sentina, *f*
sinker *n* (engraver) grabador (-ra); (of a fishing line) plomada, *f*
sinking *n* hundimiento, *m*; (of the sun) puesta, *f*; (of wells) cavadura, *f*; sumergimiento, *m*. **the s. of a boat,** el hundimiento de un buque. **with s. heart,** con la muerte en el alma. **s. fund,** fondo de amortización, *m*
sinless *a* sin pecado, inocente, puro
sinner *n* pecador (-ra)
sinuosity *n* sinuosidad, *f*; flexibilidad, agilidad, *f*
sinuous *a* sinuoso, tortuoso; flexible, ágil
sinus *n* (anat etc.) seno, *m*
sip *vt* sorber; (wine) saborear, paladear. *n* sorbo, *m*
siphon *n* sifón, *f*, *m*, *vt* sacar con sifón
sir *n* señor, *m*; (British title) sir. **Dear s.,** Muy Señor mío
sire *n* (to a monarch) Señor, *m*; (father) padre, *m*; (stallion) semental, *m*. *vt* procrear, engendrar
siren *n* sirena, *f.* **s. suit,** mono, *m*
sirloin *n* solomillo, *m*
sirocco *n* siroco, *m*
sister *n* hermana, *f*; (before nun's christian name) Sor; (hospital) hermana del hospital, *f*; enfermera, *f.* **s. language,** lengua hermana, *f.* **s. ship,** buque gemelo, *m*.

s.-in-law, cuñada, hermana política, *f.* **S. of Mercy,** Hermana de la Caridad, *f*

sisterhood *n* hermandad, *f*; comunidad de monjas, *f*

sisterly *a* de hermana

sit *vi* sentarse; estar sentado; (of birds) posarse; (of hens) empollar; (in Parliament, etc.) ser diputado; (of a committee, etc.) celebrar sesión; (on a committee, etc.) formar parte de; (function) funcionar; (of garments, food, and *fig*) sentar. **to sit a horse,** mantenerse a caballo; montar a caballo. **to sit oneself,** sentarse, tomar asiento. **to sit by,** (a person) sentarse (or estar sentado) al lado de. **to sit for** (a portrait) servir de modelo para; hacerse retratar. **to sit tight,** no moverse. **to sit down,** sentarse; (besiege) sitiar. **to sit on,** sentarse (en or sobre); (eggs) empollar; (a committee, etc.) formar parte de; (investigate) investigar; (snub) dejar aplastado (a). **to sit out,** quedarse hasta el fin (de). **to sit out a dance,** conversar un baile. **to sit up,** incorporarse en la cama; tenerse derecho; (at night) velar; (of dogs, etc.) pedir. **to sit up and take notice,** abrir los ojos. **to sit up in bed,** incorporarse en la cama. **to sit up late,** estar de pie hasta muy tarde

sit-down strike *n* huelga de brazos caídos, huelga de sentados, *f*

site *n* sitio, local, *m*; (for building) solar, *m*

sitting *n* asentada, *f*; (of Parliament, etc.) sesión, *f*; (for a portrait) estadia, *f*; (of eggs) nidada, *f*. **at a s.,** de una asentada. **s.-room,** sala de estar, *f*

situated *a* situado. **How is he s.?** ¿Cómo está situado? ¿Cuál es su situación?

situation *n* situación, *f*; (job) empleo, *m*

six *a* and *n* seis, *m*. **It is six o'clock,** Son las seis. **Everything is at sixes and sevens,** Todo está en desorden.

six-foot, de seis pies. **six hundred,** seiscientos (-as)

sixfold *a* séxtuplo

sixteen *a* and *n* diez y seis, dieciséis, *m.* **John is s.,** Juan tiene dieciséis años

sixteenth *a* décimosexto; (of the month) (el) diez y seis; (of monarch) diez y seis. *n* dieciseisavo, *m*

sixth *a* sexto; (of the month) (el) seis; (of monarchs) sexto. *n* seisavo, *m*; sexta parte, *f*; *mus* sexta, *f.* **Henry the S.,** Enrique sexto. **May the s.,** el seis de mayo

sixtieth *a* sexagésimo. *n* sesentavo, *m*; sexagésima parte, *f*

sixty *a* and *n* sesenta *m.* **John has turned s.,** Juan ha pasado los sesenta

sizable *a* bastante grande

size *n* tamaño, *m*; dimensión, *f*; (height) altura, *f*; (measurement) medida, *f*; talle, *m*; (in gloves, etc.) número, *m*; (glue) cola, *f. vt* clasificar por tamaños; (glaze, etc.) encolar. **to s. up,** tomar las medidas (a).

sizzle *vi* chisporrotear, chirriar. *n* chisporroteo, chirrido, *m*

skate *n* patín, *m*; *icht* raya, *f, vi* patinar

skater *n* patinador (-ra)

skating *n* patinaje, *m.* **s. rink,** sala de patinar, *f*; pista de hielo, pista de patinar, *f*, patinadero, *m*

skein *n* madeja, *f*

skeleton *n* esqueleto, *m*; (of a building) armadura, *f*; (of a literary work) esquema, *m.* **s. key,** ganzúa, *f*

sketch *n* croquis, apunte, *m*; (for a literary work) esbozo, esquema, *m*; (article) cuadro, artículo, *m*; descripción, *f*; *theat* entremés, sainete, *m. vt* dibujar; esbozar, bosquejar; trazar; describir. **s.-book,** álbum de croquis, *m*

sketchily *adv* incompletamente

sketching *n* arte de dibujar, *mf.* **He likes s.,** Le gusta dibujar

sketchy *a* bosquejado; incompleto; escaso

skewer *n* broqueta, *f, vt* espetar

ski *n* esquí, *m, vi* esquiar

skid *n* (of a vehicle) patinazo, *m, vi* patinar

skidding *n* patinaje, *m*

skier *n* esquiador, *m*

skiff *n* esquife, *m*

skiing *n* patinaje sobre la nieve, *m*, el esquiar. **to go s.,** ir a esquiar

skill *n* habilidad, *f*

skilled *a* hábil; experto

skilled worker *n* obrero calificado, *m*

skillful *a* hábil

skim *vt* espumar; (milk) desnatar; (touch lightly) deslizarse sobre, rozar; (a book) hojear

skimp *vt* escatimar; escasear; (work) frangollar. *vi* ser parsimonioso

skimpy *a* escaso

skin *n* tez, *f*, cutis, *m*; piel, *f*; (of fruit) pellejo, *m*, piel, *f*; (for wine) odre, pellejo, *m*; (on milk) espuma, *f. vt* despellejar; pelar, mondar; (graze) hacerse daño (a); *inf* desollar. **next to one's s.,** sobre la piel. **to s. over,** cicatrizarse. **to have a thin s.,** *fig* ser muy susceptible. **to save one's s.,** salvar el pellejo. **s.-deep,** superficial. **s.-tight,** escurrido, muy ajustado

skinflint *n* avaro (-ra)

skinned *a* de . . . piel

skinny *a* flaco, descarnado, magro

skip *vi* retozar, brincar, saltar; saltar a la comba; (bolt) largarse, escaparse. *vt* saltar; (a book) hojear; (omit) omitir; pasar por alto de. *n* brinco, pequeño salto, *m*

skipper *n* *naut* patrón, *m*; (*inf* and *sport*) capitán, *m*

skirmish *vi* escaramuzar. *n* escaramuza, *f*

skirt *n* falda, *f*; (edge) margen, borde, *m*, orilla, *f*; (of a jacket, etc.) faldón, *m. vt* ladear; (hug) rodear, ceñir

skit *n* sátira, *f*; parodia, *f*

skittish *a* (of a horse) retozón; (of persons) frívolo; caprichoso

skittle *n* bolo, *m*; *pl* **skittles,** juego de bolos, *m.* **s. alley,** pista de bolos, bolera, *f*

skulk *vi* estar en acecho; esconderse; rondar

skull *n* cráneo, *m*; calavera, *f.* **s.-cap,** gorro, casquete, *m*; (for ecclesiastics) solideo, *m*

skunk *n* *zool* mofeta, *f*, chingue, mapurite, yaguré, zorrillo, zorrino, zorro hediondo, *m*

sky *n* cielo, *m.* **to praise to the skies,** poner en los cuernos de la luna. **s.-blue,** *n* azul celeste, *m. a* de color azul celeste, cerúleo. **s.-high,** hasta las nubes, hasta el cielo. **s.-line,** horizonte, *m.* **s.-scraper,** rascacielos, *m.* **s.-sign,** anuncio luminoso, *m*

skylight *n* claraboya, *f*, tragaluz, *m*

slab *n* bloque, *m*; losa, *f*; plancha, *f*

slack *a* lento; flojo; (lazy) perezoso; negligente, descuidado; *com* encalmado; débil. *vi* ser perezoso. **the s. season,** la estación muerta. **to be s. in one's work,** ser negligente en el trabajo. **to s. off,** disminuir sus esfuerzos; dejar de trabajar

slacken *vt* and *vi* aflojar; disminuir, reducir. **The wind slackened,** El viento amainaba, El viento aflojaba. **to s. one's efforts,** disminuir sus esfuerzos. **to s. speed,** disminuir la velocidad

slackening *n* aflojamiento, *m*; disminución, *f*

slacker *n* gandul (-la)

slackness *n* flojedad, *f*; pereza, falta de energía, *f*; negligencia, *f*; *com* desanimación, *f*

slacks *n pl* pantalones, *m pl*

slag *n* escoria, *f.* **s. heap,** escorial, *m*

slake *vt* (one's thirst and lime) apagar; satisfacer

slam *vt* cerrar de golpe; golpear. *n* (of a door) portazo, *m*; golpe, *m*; (cards) capote, *m.* **He went out and slammed the door,** Salió dando un portazo

slander *n* calumnia, *f*; *vt* calumniar

slanderer *n* calumniador (-ra)

slanderous *a* calumnioso

slang *n* argot, *m*, jerga, *f*, *vt* poner como un trapo (a), llenar de insultos

slant *vi* estar al sesgo; inclinarse; ser oblicuo. *vt* inclinar. *n* inclinación, *f*; oblicuidad, *f.* **on the s.,** inclinado; oblicuo

slanting *a* al sesgo, inclinado; oblicuo

slap *vt* pegar con la mano. *n* bofetada, *f*; palmada, *f.* **to s. on the back,** golpear en la espalda. **s.-dash,** (of persons) irresponsable, descuidado; (of work) chapucero, sin cuidado.

slash vt (gash, also sleeves, etc.) acuchillar; cortar; (with a whip) dar latigazos (a). n cuchillada, f; corte, m; latigazo, m

slashing a mordaz, severo

slat n tablilla, f, vi (of sails) dar zapatazos, zapatear

slate n pizarra, f, esquisto, m; (for roofs and for writing) pizarra, f, vt (a roof) empizarrar; (censure) criticar severamente, censurar. **s.-colored,** apizarrado. **s. pencil,** pizarrín, m. **s. quarry,** pizarrería, f, pizarral, m

slater n pizarrero, m

slating n empizarrado, m; (criticism) crítica severa, censura, f; (scolding) peluca, f

slattern n pazpuerca, f

slatternly a desgarbado, desaliñado

slaughter n matanza, f; carnicería, f. vt (animals) sacrificar, matar; matar, hacer una carnicería de. **s.-house,** matadero, m

slaughterer n jifero, carnicero, m

Slav a and n eslavo (-va)

slave n esclavo (-va). vi trabajar como un negro. **white s. traffic,** trata de blancas, f. **s.-bangle,** esclava, f. **s.-driver,** capataz de esclavos, negrero, m; fig negrero, sayón de esclavos, m. **s.-trade,** trata de esclavos, f

slaver n negrero, m

slaver vi babear. n baba, f

slavering a baboso

slavery n esclavitud, f; trabajo muy arduo, m

slavish a de esclavo; servil

slavishly adv como esclava; servilmente

Slavonic a eslavo. n (language) eslavo, m, lengua eslava, f

slay vt matar; asesinar

slayer n matador (-ra); asesino, mf

slaying n matanza, f; asesinato, m

sledge n trineo, m. vi ir en trineo. vt transportar por trineo. **s.-hammer,** acotillo, m

sleek a liso, lustroso; (of general appearance) pulcro, bien aseado, elegante; (of manner) obsequioso

sleekness n lustre, m, lisura, f; (of an animal) gordura, f; elegancia, f

sleep n sueño, m. vi dormir; reposar, descansar. vt dormir. **a deep s.,** un sueño pesado. **He walks in his s.,** Es un sonámbulo. **to court s.,** conciliar el sueño. **to go to s.,** dormirse; entumecerse. **My foot has gone to s.,** Se me ha dormido (or Se me ha entumecido) el pie. **to send a person to s.,** adormecer. **to s. like a top,** dormir como un lirón. **to s. oneself sober,** dormir la mona. **to s. in,** dormir tarde; dormir en casa. **to s. off,** (a cold, etc.) curarse . . . durmiendo; (drunkenness) dormirla. **to s. on,** vt (consider) dormir sobre, consultar con la almohada. vi seguir durmiendo. **to s. out,** dormir fuera de casa; dormir al aire libre

sleeper n durmiente, mf; rw traviesa, f; (on a train) coche cama, m. **to be a bad s.,** dormir mal. **to be a good s.,** dormir bien.

sleepily adv soñolientamente

sleepiness n somnolencia, f; letargo, m

sleeping a durmiente. n el dormir. **between s. and waking,** entre duerme y vela. **s.-bag,** saco-cama, m. **s.-car,** coche camas, m. **s.-draught,** narcótico, m. **s. partner,** n socio (-ia) comanditario (-ia). **s. sickness,** enfermedad del sueño, f

sleepless a (of persons) insomne, desvelado; (unremitting) incansable; (of the sea, etc.) en perpetuo movimiento. **to spend a s. night,** pasar una noche en vela, pasar una noche toledana, pasar una noche sin dormir

sleeplessness n insomnio, m

sleepwalker n sonámbulo (-la)

sleepwalking n sonambulismo, m

sleepy a soñoliento; letárgico. **to be s.,** tener sueño. **s.-head,** lirón, m, marmota, f

sleet n aguanieve, cellisca, nevisca, f, vi caer aguanieve, cellisquear, neviscar

sleeve n manga, f; (of a hose pipe, etc.) manguera, f;

mech manguito, m. **to have something up one's s.,** traer algo en la manga

sleeved a con mangas . . . ; de . . . manga(s)

sleeveless a sin manga

sleigh n trineo, m, vi ir en trineo

sleight of hand n prestidigitación, f; juego de manos, m

slender a delgado; esbelto; tenue; escaso; pequeño; ligero. **Their means are very s.,** Sus recursos son muy escasos. **It is a very s. hope,** Es una esperanza muy remota

slenderness n delgadez, f; esbeltez, f; tenuidad, f; escasez, f

sleuth n (dog) sabueso, m; inf detective, m

slice n lonja, tajada, f; (of fruit) raja, f; (of bread, etc.) rebanada, f; (share) parte, porción, f; (for fish, etc.) pala, f. vt cortar en tajadas, etc.; rajar; cortar

slick a hábil, diestro

slide vi deslizarse, resbalar; (over a question) pasar por alto de; (into a habit, etc.) caer (en). n resbalón, m; pista de hielo, f; (chute) tobogán, m; (of a microscope) portaobjetos, m; (lantern) diapositiva, f; (for the hair) pasador, m; (of rock, etc.) desprendimiento, m; mech guía, f. **to let things s.,** dejar rodar la bola. **s.-rule,** regla de cálculo, f

sliding a resbaladizo; corredizo; movible. **s.-door,** puerta corrediza, puerta de corradera, f. **s.-roof,** techo corredizo, m. **s.-scale,** escala graduada, f. **s.-seat,** asiento movible, m; (in a rowing-boat) bancada corrediza, f

slight a delgado; débil, frágil; ligero; (small) pequeño; escaso; (trivial) insignificante, poco importante. vt desairar, despreciar. n desaire, desprecio, m; falta de respeto, f

slighting a despreciativo, de desprecio

slightingly adv con desprecio

slightly adv ligeramente; poco. **I only know her s.,** La conozco muy poco. **s. built,** de talle delgado

slightness n (slimness) delgadez, f; ligereza, f; (triviality) poca importancia, insignificancia, f

slim a delgado; escaso. vi adelgazarse. **He has very s. chances of success,** Tiene muy pocas posibilidades de conseguir el éxito

slime n légamo, limo, lodo, cieno, m; (of a snail) limazo, m; fig cieno, m

sliminess n limosidad, f; viscosidad, f

slimness n delgadez, f; escasez, f

slimy a limoso, legamoso; pecinoso, viscoso; (of persons) rastrero, servil

sling vt arrojar, lanzar; tirar con honda (a sword, etc.) suspender; (lift) embragar; (a limb) poner en cabestrillo. n (for missiles) honda, f; naut balso, m; (for a limb) cabestrillo, m, charpa, f

slink vi (away, off) escurrirse, escabullirse

slip vi resbalar, deslizar; (stumble) resbalar, tropezar; (fall) caer; (out of place) salirse; (become untied) desatarse; (steal away) escabullirse; (glide) deslizarse; (of years) correr, pasar; (skid) patinar. vt deslizar; (garments, shoes) ponerse; (dogs, cables) soltar; (an arm round, etc.) pasar; rw desacoplar; (escape) escaparse de; (free oneself of) librarse de. n resbalón, m; (skid) patinazo, m; (stumble) tropezón, traspié, m; (oversight) inadvertencia, f; (mistake) falta, equivocación, f; (moral lapse) desliz, m; (petticoat) combinación, f; (cover) funda, f; bot vástago, m; print galerada, f; (of paper) papeleta, f; pl **slips,** naut anguilas, f pl. **It slipped my memory,** Se me fué de la memoria. **There's many a s. 'twixt the cup and the lip,** Del dicho al hecho hay muy gran trecho, De la mano a la boca desaparece la sopa. **to give** (someone) **the slip,** escaparse de. **You ought not to let the opportunity s.,** No debes perder la oportunidad. **to let s. a secret,** revelar un secreto. **to let s. an exclamation,** soltar (dar) una exclamación. **to s. into,** colarse en, deslizarse en. **to s. into,** colarse en, deslizarse en. **to s. into one's clothes,** vestirse rápidamente. **to s. on,** (a garment) ponerse. **to s. out,** salir a hurtadillas; escaparse; (of information) divulgarse. **s. of a boy,** mozalbete, joven imberbe, *m*. **s. of the tongue,** error de lengua, *m*. **s.-knot,** nudo corredizo, *m*

slipcover *n* cubierta, cubierta para muebles, funda, funda para muebles, *f*

slipper *n* babucha, chinela, *f*, pantuflo, *m*; (heelless) chancleta, *f*; (dancing) zapatilla de baile, *f*. **s.-shaped,** achinelado

slippered *a* en zapatillas

slipperiness *n* lo resbaladizo; (of persons) informalidad, *f*

slippery *a* resbaladizo; poco firme, inestable; (of persons) informal, sin escrúpulos

slipshod *a* descuidado, negligente; poco correcto

slipway *n* surtida, *f*, anguilas, *f pl*

slit *vt* cortar; hender, rajar; (the throat) degollar. *n* cortadura, *f*; resquicio, *m*. **to s. open,** abrir de un tajo

slither *vi* resbalar; deslizarse

sliver *n* raja, *f*; (of wood) astilla, *f*; (of cloth) tira, *f*

slobber *vi* babear; (blubber) gimotear, *n* baba, *f*

sloe *n* (fruit) endrina, *f*; (tree) endrino, *m*. **s.-colored,** endrino. **s.-eyed,** con ojos de mora

slog *vt* golpear duramente. **to s. away,** batirse el cobre, trabajar como un negro

slogan *n* grito de batalla, *m*; reclamo, *m*; frase hecha, *f*; mote, *m*

slop *n* charco, *m*; *pl* **slops,** agua sucia, *f*; alimentos líquidos, *m pl*. *vi* derramarse, verterse. *vt* verter, derramar

slope *n* inclinación, *f*; pendiente, *f*; (of a mountain, etc.) falda, ladera, cuesta, *f*; vertiente, *mf*. *vi* inclinarse; estar en declive; bajar (hacia). **to s. down,** declinar

sloping *a* inclinado; en declive; (of shoulders) caídos, *m pl*

sloppy *a* casi líquido; (muddy) lodoso, lleno de barro; (of work) chapucero; (of persons) baboso, sobón. **s. sentiment,** sensiblería, *f*

slot *n* ranura, muesca, *f*. **s.-machine,** máquina expendedora, *f*, expendedor, *m*; (in amusement arcades, etc.) tragaperras, *m*

sloth *n* pereza, indolencia, *f*; *zool* perezoso, *m*

slothful *a* perezoso, indolente

slouch *n* inclinación del cuerpo, *f*. *vi* andar cabizbajo, andar arrastrando los pies. **to s. about,** vagar, golfear. **s.-hat,** sombrero gacho, *m*

slough *n* (bog) cenagal, pantano, *m*, marisma, *f*; (of a snake) camisa, *f*. *vt* (a skin) mudar; (prejudices, etc.) desechar

Slovak *n* eslovaco (-ca)

Slovakian *a* eslovaco

sloven *n* puerco, *m*; (at work) chapucero, *m*

Slovene *a* and *n* esloveno (-na)

slovenliness *n* desaseo, desaliño, *m*; (carelessness) descuido, *m*, negligencia, *f*; (of work) chapucería, *f*

slovenly *a* desgarbado, desaseado; (careless) descuidado, negligente; (of work) chapucero

slow *a* despacio; lento; (stupid) torpe; tardo; (of clocks) atrasado; (boring) aburrido; (inactive) flojo. *adv* despacio, lentamente. **I was not s. to . . . ,** No tardé en . . . **The clock is ten minutes s.,** El reloj lleva diez minutos de atraso. **to s. down,** aflojar el paso; ir más despacio. **s.-motion,** velocidad reducida, *f*. **s. train,** tren ómnibus, *m*. **s.-witted,** lerdo tardo

slowcoach *n* perezoso (-sa)

"Slow Down" «Moderar Su Velocidad»

slow learner *n* alumno de lento aprendizaje, *m*

slowly *adv* despacio, lentamente; poco a poco

slowness *n* lentitud, *f*; (delay) tardanza, *f*; (stupidity) torpeza, estupidez, *f*

slug *n* babosa, *f*

sluggard *n* gandul (-la), perezoso (-a)

sluggish *a* perezoso; (of the market) flojo; (of temperament, etc.) calmoso, flemático; (slow) lento

sluggishness *n* pereza, *f*; (of the market) flojedad, *f*; (slowness) lentitud, *f*

sluice *n* esclusa, *f*; canal, *m*, acequia, *f*. **to s. down,** lavar; echar agua sobre; (a person) dar una ducha (a),

dar un baño (a). **s.-gate,** compuerta de esclusa, *f*; tajaderas, *f pl*, tablacho, *m*

slum *n* barrio pobre, *m*, banda de miseria (Argentina), barriada (Peru), población (Chile), villa-miseria (Argentina), *f*, tugurio (Colombia), *m*; *pl* **slums,** barrios bajos, *m pl*

slumber *vi* dormir; (go to sleep) dormirse, caer dormido; (be latent) estar latente. *n* sueño, *m*

slump *n com* baja repentina, *f*; *fig* baja, racha mala, *f*. *vi com* bajar repentinamente. **the s.,** la crisis económica. **to s. into an armchair,** dejarse caer en un sillón

slur *vt* (words) comerse sílabas o letras (de); (in writing) unir (las palabras); (*mus* of notes) ligar. **to cast a s. on,** difamar, manchar. **to s. over,** pasar por alto de, omitir, suprimir

slush *n* lodo, *m*; agua nieve, *f*; (sentimentality) ñoñería, *f*

slushy *a* lodoso, fangoso

slut *n* pazpuerca, marrana, *f*

sly *a* astuto, taimado, socarrón; disimulado; (arch) malicioso. **on the sly,** a hurtadillas

slyly *adv* astutamente; disimuladamente; (archly) maliciosamente

slyness *n* astucia, socarronería, *f*; disimulo, *m*; malicia, *f*

smack *n* (taste) sabor, gusto, *m*; (tinge) dejo, *m*; (blow) golpe, *m*; (with the hand) bofetada, palmada, *f*; (with a whip) latigazo, *m*; (crack of whip) restallido, chasquido, *m*; (kiss) beso sonado, *m*; (boat) lancha de pescar, *f*. *vi* (taste of) tener gusto de, saber a; (be tinged with) oler a. *vt* (a whip) hacer restallar; (slap) pegar con la mano. **to s. one's lips over,** chuparse los dedos

small *a* pequeño; menudo; menor; poco; (petty) mezquino, vulgar. *n* parte estrecha, *f*. **a s. number,** un pequeño número. **to make a person look s.,** humillar. **to make oneself s.,** hacerse chiquito. **s.-arms,** armas portátiles, *f pl*. **s. change,** suelto, *m*. **s. craft,** embarcaciones menores, *f pl*. **s. fry,** pececillos, *m pl*; (children) gente menuda, *f*; gente sin importancia, *f*. **s. hours,** altas horas de la noche, *f pl*. **s.-minded,** adocenado, de cortos alcances. **s.-talk,** trivialidades, *f pl*, charla frívola, *f*

smallish *a* bastante pequeño; más bien pequeño que grande

smallness *n* pequeñez, *f*; escasez, exigüidad, *f*

smallpox *n* viruelas, *f pl*

smart *vi* picar; dolerse (de). *n* escozor, *m*; dolor, *m*. *a* severo; vivo; rápido; pronto; (competent) hábil; (clever) listo; (unscrupulous) cuco, astuto; (of personal appearance) majo; elegante, distinguido; (neat) aseado; (fashionable, etc.) de moda; de buen tono. **to s. for,** ser castigado por. **to s. under,** sufrir

smarten *vt* embellecer. *vi* (up) ponerse elegante, mejorar. **I must go and s. myself up a little,** Tengo que arreglarme un poco

smartly *adv* severamente; vivamente; rápidamente; hábilmente; elegantemente

smartness *n* viveza, *f*; prontitud, rapidez, *f*; (cleverness) despejo, *m*, habilidad, *f*; (wittiness) agudeza, *f*; (astuteness) cuquería, astucia, *f*; (of dress, etc.) elegancia, *f*; buen tono, *m*

smash *vt* romper, quebrar; (a ball, etc.) golpear; (annihilate) destruir; (an opponent) aplastar. *vi* romperse, quebrarse; hacerse pedazos; (collide) chocar (con, contra); estallarse (contra); (financially) hacer bancarrota. *n* rotura, *f*; quebrantamiento, *m*; estruendo, *m*; (financial) quiebra, ruina, *f*; (car, etc.) accidente, *m*; desastre, *m*, catástrofe, *f*. **to s. to atoms,** hacer trizas. **to s. up,** hacer pedazos. **s. and grab raid,** atraco a mano armada, *m*

smash hit *n* éxito arrollador, éxito rotundo, *m*

smattering *n* conocimiento superficial, *m*, tintura, *f*, barniz, *m*

smear *n* mancha, *f*; *biol* frotis, *m*. *vt* embadurnar (de); manchar (con), ensuciar (con); (oneself) untarse; (blur) borrar

smell *n* (sense of) olfato, *m*; (odor) olor, *m*. *vt* oler. *vi*

oler; tener olor; (disagreeably) oler mal, tener mal olor; (stink) apestar. **How good it smells!** ¡Qué bien huele! **to s. of,** oler a. **to s. out,** husmear
smelling n olfateo, m. **s.-bottle,** frasco de sales, m. **s.-salts,** sales (inglesas), f pl
smelt vt fundir. n icht eperlano, m
smelter n fundidor, m
smelting n fundición, f. **s. furnace,** horno de fundición, m
smile vi sonreír; reírse. vt expresar con una sonrisa. n sonrisa, f. **Mary smiled her thanks,** María dio las gracias con una sonrisa. **smile at adversity,** ponerse buena cara a mal tiempo. **to s. at threats,** reírse de las amenazas
smiling a sonriente, risueño
smilingly adv sonriendo, con una sonrisa, con cara risueña
smirch vt manchar. n mancha, f
smirk vi sonreír con afectación; hacer visajes. n sonrisa afectada, f
smirking a afectado; sonriente
smite vt golpear; (kill) matar; (punish) castigar; (pain) doler; (of bright light, sounds, etc.) herir; (cause remorse) remorder. **My conscience smites me,** Tengo remordimientos de conciencia. **to be smitten by,** inf estar prendado de. **I was smitten by a desire to smoke,** Me entraron deseos de fumar
smith n herrero, m. **smith's hammer,** destajador, m
smithereens n pl añicos, m pl
smithy n herrería, f
smock n blusa, f; (child's) delantal, m
smoke n humo, m. vi humear, echar humo; (tobacco) fumar. vt ahumar; ennegrecer; (tobacco) fumar. **smoked glasses,** gafas ahumadas, f pl. **s. helmet,** casco respiratorio, m. **s.-screen,** cortina de humo, f. **s. signal,** ahumada, f. **s.-stack,** chimenea, f
smokeless a sin humo
smoker n fumador (-ra)
smoking a humeante. n el fumar. **"S. Prohibited,"** «Se prohíbe fumar.» **non-s. compartment,** rw departamento de no fumadores, m. **s.-carriage,** rw departamento para fumadores, m. **s.-room,** fumadero, m
smoky a humeante; lleno de humo; (black) ahumado
smooth a liso; igual; (of the skin, etc.) suave; (of water) calmo, tranquilo; (flattering, etc.) lisonjero; obsequioso; afable. vt allanar; (hair, etc.) alisar; (paths, etc.) igualar. **to s. down,** (a person) tranquilizar, calmar. **to s. over,** (faults) exculpar. **to s. the way for,** allanar el camino para. **s.-faced,** barbilampiño, lampiño, bien afeitado, todo afeitado; fig obsequioso, untuoso. **s.-haired,** de pelo liso. **s.-spoken,** de palabras lisonjeras; obsequioso
smoothly adv lisamente; (of speech) afablemente; con lisonjeras. **Everything was going s.,** Todo iba viento en popa
smoothness n igualdad, f; lisura, f; (of skin, etc.) suavidad, f; (of water) calma, tranquilidad, f; (of manner, etc.) afabilidad, f
smother vt ahogar, sofocar; (a fire) apagar; (cover) envolver, cubrir
smoulder vi arder sin llama, arder lentamente; (of passions, etc.) arder; estar latente
smouldering a que arde lentamente; fig latente
smudge vt manchar, ensuciar; (blur) borrar. n mancha, f
smug a satisfecho de sí mismo, pagado de sí mismo; farisaico
smuggle vt pasar de contrabando. vi hacer contrabando
smuggler n contrabandista, mf
smuggling n contrabando, m
smugly adv con presunción, de un aire satisfecho
smugness n satisfacción de sí mismo, f; fariseísmo, m
smut n copo de hollín, m; mancha, f; (disease) tizón, m
smutty a tiznado; ahumado; inf verde
snack n tentempié, piscolabis, bocado, m. **to take a s.,** tomar un piscolabis

snack bar n merendero, m
snaffle n filete, m. vt (a horse) refrenar. **s.-bridle,** bridón, m
snag n (of a tree) tocón, m; (of a tooth) raigón, m; (problem) busilis, m; obstáculo inesperado, m
snail n caracol, m. **at a snail's pace,** a paso de tortuga
snake n serpiente, f. **s.-charmer,** encantador de serpientes, m
snakelike a de serpiente; serpentino
snap vt morder; (break) romper; (one's fingers) castañetear; (a whip) chasquear; (down a lid, etc.) cerrar de golpe; (beaks, etc.) cerrar ruidosamente; phot sacar una instantánea de. vi partirse; quebrarse; hablar bruscamente. n (bite) mordedura, f; golpe seco, m; chasquido, m; rotura, f; (clasp) cierre, m; (of weather) temporada, f; (spirit) vigor, brío, m; phot instantánea, f. **to s. at,** procurar morder; (an invitation, etc.) aceptar gustoso. **to s. one's fingers at,** fig burlarse de. **to s. up,** coger, agarrar; (a person) cortar la palabra (a), interrumpir. **s.-fastener,** botón de presión, m
snapdragon n dragón, m, becerra, boca de dragón, f
snappily adv irritablemente
snappishness n irritabilidad, f
snappy a irritable; vigoroso
snapshot n instantánea, foto, f
snare n cepo, lazo, m, trampa, f; fig red, f. vt coger en lazo; fig enredar
snarl vi (of dogs) regañar; (cats, etc.) gruñir. n regañamiento, m; gruñido, m
snarling n regañamiento, m; gruñidos, m pl, a gruñidor
snatch vt asir; agarrar; (enjoy) disfrutar; (an opportunity) tomar, aprovecharse de. n asimiento, agarro, m; (of time) rato, m; instante, m; (of song) fragmento, m. **to make a s. at,** procurar agarrar; alargar la mano hacia. **to s. a hurried meal,** comer aprisa. **to s. away,** arrebatar, quitar; (carry off) robar. **to s. up,** coger rápidamente; coger en brazos
sneak vi deslizarse (en), colarse (en); (lurk) rondar; (inform) acusar. n mandilón, m; (accuser) acusón (-ona). **to s. off,** escabullirse, irse a hurtadillas. **s.-thief,** n garduño (-ña)
sneaker n (shoe) zapatilla de tenis, f
sneaking a furtivo, ruin, mezquino; secreto
sneer vi sonreír irónicamente; burlarse, mofarse. n sonrisa sardónica, sonrisa de desprecio, f; burla, mofa, f. **to s. at,** mofarse de, burlarse de; hablar con desprecio de
sneering a mofador, burlón
sneeringly adv con una sonrisa sardónica; burlonamente
sneeze vi estornudar. n estornudo, m. **It's not to be sneezed at,** No es moco de pavo
sniff vi respirar fuertemente; resollar. vt oler, olfatear; aspirar. **to s. at,** oler. **to s. out,** inf husmear
snigger vi reírse por lo bajo, reírse disimuladamente. n risa disimulada, f
snip vt (with cut on tijeras; cortar, quitar. n tijeretada, f; (of cloth, etc.) recorte, pedacito, m
snipe n orn agachadiza, f. **to s. at,** mil pacar
sniper n mil paco, m
snippet n pedacito, fragmento, m; (of prose, etc.) trocito, m; (of news) noticia, f
snivel vi lloriquear, gimotear
sniveling n lloriqueo, gimoteo, m. a llorón; mocoso
snob n esnob, mf
snobbery n snobismo, m
snobbish a esnob
snood n (for the hair) redecilla, f; (turkey's) moco (de pavo), m; (fishing) cendal, m
snoop vi espiar; entremeterse
snooze vi dormitar, echar un sueño. n sueñecito, m; (afternoon) siesta, f
snore vi roncar. n ronquido, m
snoring n ronquidos, m pl
snort vi bufar; resoplar. n bufido, m; resoplido, m
snout n hocico, m; (of a pig) jeta, f
snow n nieve, f. vi nevar. vt nevar; fig inundar. **to s.**

under (with), inundar con. **to be snowed up,** estar aprisionado por la nieve. **s.-blindness,** deslumbramiento causado por la nieve, *m*. **s.-boot,** bota para la nieve, *f*. **s.-bound,** aprisionado por la nieve; bloqueado por la nieve. **s.-capped,** coronado de nieve. **s.-clad,** cubierto de nieve. **s.-drift,** acumulación de nieve, *f*. **s.-field,** ventisquero, *m*. **s.-goggles,** gafas ahumadas, *f pl*. **s.-line,** límite de las nieves perpetuas, *m*. **s.-man,** figura de nieve, *f*. **s.-plough,** quitanieve, *m*. **s.-shoe,** raqueta de nieve, *f*. **s.-white,** blanco como la nieve

snowball *n* bola de nieves, *f*; *bot* bola de nieve, *f*

snowdrop *n* campanilla de invierno, violeta de febrero, *f*

snowfall *n* nevada, *f*

snowflake *n* copo de nieve, *m*

snowstorm *n* ventisca, *f*

snowy *a* nevoso; de nieve

snub *vt* repulsar; desairar, tratar con desdén. *n* repulsa, *f*, desaire, *m*; (nose) nariz respingona, *f*. **s.-nosed,** de nariz respingona

snuff *vt* (breathe) oler, olfatear; inhalar; (a candle) atizar, despabilar. *n* (of a candle) moco, *m*, despabiladura, *f*; (tobacco) rapé, *m*. **to take s.,** tomar rapé. **to s. out,** extinguir. **s.-box,** caja de rapé, tabaquera, *f*

snuffers *n pl* tenacillas, despabiladeras, *f pl*

snuffle *vi* hacer ruido con la nariz; respirar fuerte; (in speaking) ganguear

snuffling *a* mocoso; (of the voice) gangoso

snug *a* caliente; cómodo; (hidden) escondido, **to have a s. income,** tener el riñón bien cubierto, ser acomodado

snuggle *vi* hacerse un ovillo; acomodarse; ponerse cómodo. **to s. up to,** arrimarse a, apretarse contra

snugly *adv* cómodamente

snugness *n* comodidad, *f*

so *adv* así; de este modo, de esta manera; por lo tanto; tanto; (before adjs. and advs. but not before **más, mejor, menos, peor,** where **tanto** is used) tan; (in the same way) del mismo modo, de igual modo; (therefore) de modo que, de manera que; (also) también; (approximately) más o menos, aproximadamente. **Is that so?** ¿De veras? **if so . . . ,** si así es **. . . He has not yet done so,** no lo ha hecho todavía. **I told you so!** ¡Ya te lo dije yo! **So be it!** ¡Así sea! **so far,** hasta aquí; hasta ahora. **so forth,** etcétera. **So long!** ¡Nos vemos! **so much,** tanto. **So much the worse for them,** Tanto peor para ellos. **so to speak . . . ,** por decirlo así. **so as to,** a fin de, para. **So long as,** con tal que, a condición de que. **so on,** etcétera. **so soon as,** tan pronto como. **so that,** de suerte que, de modo que, para que; con que. **so-and-so,** *n* fulano (-na); mengano (-na). **so-called.** así llamado, supuesto. **so-so,** así-así, regular

soak *vt* remojar; empapar; (skins) abrevar. *vi* estar en remojo. *n* remojo, *m*; (rain) diluvio, *m*; (booze) borrachera, *f*. **to s. into,** filtrar en; penetrar. **to s. through,** penetrar; filtrar **so-called,** así llamado, supuesto. **so-so,** así, regular

soaked *a* remojado. **He is s. to the skin,** Está calado hasta los huesos

soaking *n* remojo, *m*; empapamiento, *m*,

soap *n* jabón, *m*. *vt* jabonar; (flatter) enjabonar. **a tablet of s.,** una pastilla de jabón. **soft s.,** jabón blando, *m*. **toilet s.,** jabón de tocador, jaboncillo, *m*. **s.-bubble,** burbuja de jabón, *f*. **s. dish,** jabonera, *f*. **s. factory,** jabonería, *f*. **s.-flakes,** copos de jabón, *m pl*

soapbark tree *n* quillay, palo de jabón, *m*

soap box *n lit* caja de jabón, *f*; *fig* tribuna callejera, *f*

soap opera *n* radionovela (on radio), telenovela (on television), *f*; serial lacrimógeno (derogatory), *m*

soapsuds *n pl* jabonaduras, *f pl*

soapy *a* cubierto de jabón; jabonoso

soar *vi* remontarse; *fig* elevarse; (of prices, etc.) subir de golpe

soaring *n* remonte, vuelo, *m*; *fig* aspiración, *f*; (of prices, etc.) subida repentina, *f*

sob *vi* sollozar. *n* sollozo, *m*. **to sob one's heart out,** llorar a lágrima viva. **to sob out,** decir sollozando, decir entre sollozos

s.o.b. *n* (son of a bitch) hache de pe (hijo de puta)

sobbing *n* sollozos, *m pl*, *a* sollozante

sober *a* sobrio; moderado; (of colors) obscuro. **s.-minded,** serio; reflexivo

sobriety *n* sobriedad, *f*; moderación, *f*; seriedad, *f*; calma, tranquilidad, *f*

sobriquet *n* apodo, *m*

soccer *n* fútbol (Asociación), *m*

sociability *n* sociabilidad, *f*

sociable *a* sociable; amistoso

sociably *adv* sociablemente; amistosamente

social *a* social; sociable. *n* reunión, velada, *f*. **s.-democrat,** *a* and *n* socialdemócrata, *mf*. **s. event,** acontecimiento social, *m*. **s. insurance,** previsión social, *f*. **s. services,** servicios sociales, *m pl*. **s. work,** asistencia social, *f*

socialism *n* socialismo, *m*

socialist *a* socialista, laborista. *n* socialista, *mf*

socialization *n* socialización, *f*

socialize *vt* socializar

socially *adv* socialmente

society *n* sociedad, *f*; (fashionable) mundo elegante, *m*, alta sociedad, *f*; compañía, *f*. **to go into s.,** (of girls) ponerse de largo; entrar en el mundo elegante. **s. hostess,** dama de sociedad, *f*. **society for the prevention of cruelty to animals,** sociedad protectora de animales, *f*. **s. news,** noticias de sociedad, *f pl*

sociological *a* sociológico

sociologist *n* sociólogo (-ga)

sociology *n* sociología, *f*

sock *n* calcetín, *m*; (for a shoe) plantilla, *f*

socket *n mech* encaje, cubo, ojo, *m*; (of a lamp, and *elec*) enchufe, *m*; (of the eye) órbita, cuenca, *f*; (of a tooth) alvéolo, *m*; (of a joint) fosa, *f*. **His eyes started out of their sockets,** Sus ojos estaban fuera de su órbita

Socratic *a* socrático

sod *n* césped, *m*; (cut) tepe, *m*

soda *n* sosa, *f*. **caustic s.,** sosa cáustica, *f*. **s.-ash,** carbonato sódico, *m*. **s.-fountain,** aparato de aguas gaseosas, *m*. **s.-water,** sifón, *m*

sodden *a* saturado, empapado

sodium *n* sodio, *m*

Sodomite *n* sodomita, *mf*

sodomy *n* sodomía, *f*

sofa *n* sofá, *m*

soft *a* blando; suave; muelle; (flabby) flojo; (of disposition, etc.) dulce; (effeminate) muelle, afeminado; (lenient) indulgente; (easy) fácil; (silly) tonto. **to have a s. spot for,** (a person) tener una debilidad para. **s. coal,** carbón bituminoso, *m*. **s. drink,** bebida no alcohólica, *f*. **s. felt hat,** sombrero flexible, *m*. **s. fruit,** fruta blanda, *f*. **s.-boiled,** (of eggs) pasado por agua; (of persons) inocente, ingenuo. **s.-hearted,** de buen corazón; compasivo; bondadoso. **s.-heartedness,** buen corazón, *m*, bondad, *f*. **s.-spoken,** de voz suave; que habla con dulzura, meloso. **s. water,** agua blanda, *f*

soften *vt* ablandar, reblandecer; (weaken) debilitar; (mitigate) mitigar, suavizar; (the heart, etc.) enternecer. *vi* reblandecerse; enternecerse

softening *n* reblandecimiento, *m*; (relenting) enternecimiento, *m*

softly *adv* suavemente; dulcemente, tiernamente; sin ruido, silenciosamente

softness *n* blandura, *f*; suavidad, *f*; (sweetness, etc.) dulzura, *f*; (of character) debilidad de carácter, *f*; (silliness) necedad, estupidez, *f*

soggy *a* empapado de agua; saturado

soil *n* tierra, *f*; (country) país, *m*, tierra, *f*. *vt* ensuciar; *fig* manchar. **my native s.,** mi tierra, mi patria

soiled *a* sucio. **s. linen,** ropa sucia, *f*

soiree *n* velada, *f*
sojourn *vi* morar, residir, permanecer. *n* residencia, permanencia, *f*
sojourner *n* morador (-ra), residente, *mf*
sol *n mus* sol, *m*. **sol-fa,** *n* solfa, *f*, solfeo, *m*. *vt* solfear
solace *n* consuelo, solaz, *m*. *vt* consolar; solazar
solar *a* solar. **s. plexus,** *anat* plexo solar, *m*. **s. system,** sistema solar, *m*
solder *n* soldadura, *f*, *vt* soldar
soldering *n* soldadura, *f*
soldier *n* soldado, *m*; militar, *m*. **He wants to be a s.,** Quiere ser militar
soldierly *a* militar; marcial
soldiery *n* soldadesca, *f*
sole *n* (of a foot) planta, *f*; (of a shoe) suela, *f*; (of a plough) cepa, *f*; *icht* lenguado, *m*, suela, *f*. *vt* (shoes) solar, poner suela (a). *a* solo, único; exclusivo. **s. right,** exclusiva, *f*, derecho exclusivo, *m*
solecism *n* solecismo, *m*
solely *adv* sólo; únicamente, puramente; meramente
solemn *a* solemne; grave; serio; (sacred) sagrado. **Why do you look so s.?** ¿Por qué estás tan serio?
solemnity *n* solemnidad, *f*
solemnization *n* solemnización, celebración, *f*
solemnize *vt* solemnizar
solemnly *adv* solemnemente; gravemente
solicit *vt* solicitar; implorar, rogar encarecidamente
solicitation *n* solicitación, *f*
solicitor *n* abogado (-da)
solicitous *a* ansioso (de), deseoso (de); solícito, atento; (worried) preocupado
solicitude *n* solicitud, *f*, cuidado, *m*; (anxiety) preocupación, *f*
solid *a* sólido; macizo; (of persons) serio, formal; (unanimous) unánime. *n* sólido, *m*. **a s. meal,** una comida fuerte. **He slept for ten s. hours,** Durmió por diez horas seguidas. **solid-colored material,** tela lisa, *f*. **s. food,** alimentos sólidos, *m pl*. **s. geometry,** geometría del espacio, *f*. **solid gold,** oro de ley, *m*. **s. tire,** llanta de goma maciza, *f*
solidarity *n* solidaridad, *f*
solidification *n* solidificación, *f*
solidify *vt* solidificar. *vi* solidificarse; congelarse
solidity *n* solidez, *f*; unanimidad, *f*
solidly *adv* sólidamente
soliloquize *vi* soliloquiar, hablar a solas
soliloquy *n* soliloquio, *m*
solitaire *n* (diamond and game) solitario, *m*
solitary *a* solitario; solo, aislado, único. **He was in s. confinement for three months,** Estuvo incomunicado durante tres meses. **There is not a s. one,** No hay ni uno
solitude *n* soledad, *f*
solo *n* (performance and cards) solo, *m*. **to sing a s.,** cantar un solo. **It was his first s. flight,** Era su primer vuelo a solas
soloist *n* solista, *mf*
solstice *n* solsticio, *m*. **summer s.,** solsticio vernal, *m*. **winter s.,** solsticio hiemal, *m*
solubility *n* solubilidad, *f*
soluble *a* soluble
solution *n* solución, *f*
solvable *a* que se puede resolver, soluble
solve *vt* resolver, hallar la solución de
solvency *n* solvencia, *f*
solvent *a com* solvente; (*chem* and *fig*) disolvente. *n* disolvente, *m*
somatic *a* somático
somber *a* sombrío
somberly *adv* sombríamente
somberness *n* lo sombrío; sobriedad, *f*; melancolía, *f*
some *a* alguno (-a), algunos (-as); (before a masculine sing. noun) algún; unos (-as); un poco de, algo de; (a partitive, often not translated, e.g. **Give me s. wine,** Dame vino); (approximately) aproximadamente, unos (-as). *pron* algunos (-as), unos (-as); algo, un poco. **I**

should like s. strawberries, Me gustaría comer unas fresas. **s. day,** algún día. **S. say yes, others no,** Algunos dicen que sí, otros que no. **There are s. sixty people in the garden,** Hay unas sesenta personas en el jardín
somebody, someone *n* alguien, *mf*. **s. else,** otro (-a), otra persona, *f*. **S. or other said that the book is worth reading,** No sé quién dijo que el libro vale la pena de leerse. **to be s.,** *inf* ser un personaje
somehow *adv* de un modo u otro, de alguna manera. **S. I don't like them,** No sé por qué, pero no me gustan
somersault *n* salto mortal, *m*, *vi* dar un salto mortal
something *n* algo, *m*, alguna cosa, *f*. *adv* algún tanto. **Would you like s. else?** ¿Quiere Vd. otra cosa? **He left s. like fifty thousand pounds,** Dejó algo así como cincuenta mil libras. **He has s. to live for,** Tiene para que vivir
sometime *adv* algún día, alguna vez; en algún tiempo. *a ex-*. **Come and see me s. soon,** Ven a verme algún día de estos. **He will have to go abroad s. or another,** Tarde o temprano, tiene que ir al extranjero. **s. last month,** durante el mes pasado
sometimes *adv* algunas veces, a veces. **s. happy, s. sad,** algunas veces feliz y otras triste, ora feliz ora triste
somewhat *adv* algo; algún tanto, un tanto; un poco. **I am s. busy,** Estoy algo ocupado. **He is s. of a lady-killer,** Tiene sus puntos de castigador, Tiene algo de castigador
somewhere *adv* en alguna parte. **s. about,** por ahí. **s. else,** en otra parte
somnambulism *n* somnambulismo, *f*
somnambulist *n* somnámbulo (-la)
somnolence *n* somnolencia, *f*
somnolent *a* soñoliento; soporifero
son *n* hijo, *m*. **son-in-law,** yerno, hijo político, *m*
sonata *n* sonata, *f*
song *n* canto, *m*; canción, *f*; (poem) poema, verso, *m*. **It's nothing to make a s. about,** No es para tanto. **to break into s.,** ponerse a cantar. **to be not worth an old s.,** no valer un pito. **the S. of Songs,** Cantar de los Cantares, *m*. **s.-bird,** ave canora, *f*. **s.-book,** libro de canciones, *m*. **s.-writer,** compositor (-ra) de canciones
sonic *adj* sónico. **sonic boom,** estampido sónico, *m*
sonnet *n* soneto, *m*
sonorous *a* sonoro
sonorousness *n* sonoridad, *f*
soon *adv* pronto; dentro de poco, luego. **as s. as,** así que, en cuanto, luego que, no bien . . . **as s. as possible,** lo antes posible, lo más pronto posible, con la mayor antelación posible, cuanto antes. **s. after,** poco después (de). **See you s.!** ¡Hasta pronto! **sooner or later,** tarde o temprano. **the sooner the better,** cuanto antes mejor. **No sooner had he left the house, when . . .** Apenas hubo dejado la casa, cuando . . . **Emily would sooner go to London,** Emilia preferiría ir a Londres (A Emilia le gustaría más ir a Londres)
soot *n* hollín, *m*, *vt* cubrir de hollín
soothe *vt* tranquilizar, calmar, (pain) aliviar, mitigar
soothing *a* calmante, tranquilizador, sosegador; (of powders, etc.) calmante
soothingly *adv* con dulzura; suavemente; como un consuelo
soothsayer *n* adivino (-na), adivinador (-ra)
soothsaying *n* adivinanza, *f*
sooty *a* cubierto de hollín; negro como el hollín
sop *n* sopa, *f*; (bribe) soborno, *m*
sophism *n* sofisma, *m*
sophist *n hist* sofista, *m*; (quibbler) sofista, *mf*
sophistic *a phil* sofista; (of persons, arguments) sofístico
sophisticated *a* nada ingenuo; mundano; (cultured) culto
sophistication *n* falta de simplicidad, *f*; mundanería, *f*; cultura, *f*
sophistry *n* sofistería, *f*
Sophoclean *a* sofocleo
soporific *a* soporífico

sopping *a* muy mojado. **s. wet,** hecho una sopa

soprano *n* (voice and part) soprano, *m*; (singer) soprano, tiple, *mf*

sorcerer *n* encantador, mago, brujo, *m*

sorceress *n* hechicera, bruja, *f*

sorcery *n* sortilegio, *m*, hechicería, brujería, *f*; encanto, *m*

sordid *a* sórdido; (of motives, etc.) ruin, vil

sordidness *n* sordidez, *f*; (of motives, etc.) vileza, bajeza, *f*

sordine *n mus* sordina, *f*

sore *a* doloroso, malo; (sad) triste; (annoyed) enojado; (with need, etc.) extremo. *n* llaga, *f*; (on horses, etc., caused by girths) matadura, *f*; *fig* herida, *f*; recuerdo doloroso, *m*. **to open an old s.,** *fig* renovar la herida. **running s.,** úlcera, *f*. **s. throat,** dolor de garganta, *m*

sorely *adv* grandemente; muy; urgentemente. **He was s. tempted,** Tuvo grandes tentaciones

soreness *n* dolor, *m*; (resentment) amargura, *f*, resentimiento, *m*; (ill-feeling) rencor, *m*

sorrel *a* alazán. *n* (horse) alazán, *m*; *bot* acedera, *f*

sorrow *n* pesar, *m*, aflicción, pesadumbre, *f*; tristeza, *f*. *vi* afligirse; entristecerse. **To my great s.,** Con gran pesar mío. **s.-stricken,** afligido, agobiado de pena

sorrowful *a* afligido, angustiado; triste

sorrowfully *adv* con pena, tristemente

sorrowing *a* afligido. *n* aflicción, *f*; lamentación, *f*

sort *n* especie, *f*; clase, *f*; tipo, *m*. *vt* separar (de); clasificar. **a s. of hat,** una especie de sombrero. **all sorts of,** toda clase de. **He is a good s.,** Es buen chico. **He is a queer s.,** Es un tipo raro. **in some s.,** hasta cierto punto. **I am out of sorts,** Estoy destemplado. **Nothing of the s.!** ¡Nada de eso!

sorter *n* oficial de correos, *m*; clasificador (-ra)

sorting *n* clasificación, *f*

sot *n* zaque, pellejo, *m*

sotto voce *adv* a sovoz, en voz baja

soul *n* alma, *f*; espíritu, *m*; (departed) ánima, *f*; (being) ser, *m*; (life) vida, *f*; (heart) corazón, *m*. **All Souls' Day,** Día de los Difuntos, *m*. **He is a good s.!** ¡Es un bendito! **She is a simple s.,** Ella es una alma de Dios. **without seeing a living s.,** sin ver un bicho viviente. **Upon my s.!** ¡Por mi vida! **s. in purgatory,** alma en pena, *f*. **s.-stirring,** emocionante

soulful *a* sentimental, emocional; espiritual; romántico

soulless *a* sin alma; mecánico

sound *n* sonido, *m*; son, *m*; ruido, *m*; (strait) estrecho, *m*. *vi* sonar; hacer ruido; resonar; (seem) parecer. *vt* sonar; (the horn, the alarm, musical instrument) tocar; (express) expresar; proclamar; (praise) celebrar; *naut* hondear; *med* tentar; (the chest) auscultar; (try to discover) tentar, sondar; (experience) experimentar. **to the s. of,** al son de. **s.-box,** (of a gramophone) diafragma, *m*. **s.-detector,** fonolocalización de aviones, *f*. **s.-film,** película sonora, *f*. **s.-proof,** (of radio studios, etc.) aislado de todo sonido. **s.-track,** guía sonora, banda sonora, *f*. **s.-wave,** onda sonora, *f*

sound *a* sano; (of a person) perspicaz; (reasonable) lógico, razonable; (of a policy, etc.) prudente; (of an argument, etc.) válido; (of an investment) seguro; (solvent) solvente, *f*; (good) bueno; (deep) profundo. *adv* profundamente, bien

sounding *n naut* sondeo, *m*; *pl* **soundings,** sondas, *f pl*. *a* sonoro. **to take soundings,** sondar, echar la plomada. **s.-board,** tabla de armonía, *f*

soundless *a* sin ruido, silencioso

soundly *adv* sanamente; juiciosamente, prudentemente; bien; (deeply) profundamente

soundness *n* (of a person) perspicacia, *f*; (of a policy, etc.) prudencia, *f*; (of an argument, etc.) validez, fuerza, *f*; (financial) solvencia, *f*

soup *n* sopa, *f*. **clear s.,** consommé, *m*. **thick s.,** puré, *m*. **to be in the s.,** *inf* estar aviado. **s.-ladle,** cucharón, *m*. **s.-plate,** plato sopero, *m*. **s.-tureen,** sopera, *f*

sour *a* ácido, agrio; (of milk) agrio; (of persons, etc.) agrio, desabrido. *vt* agriar. **to go s.,** volverse agrio. **S. grapes!** ¡Están verdes!

source *n* (of a river, etc.) nacimiento, *m*; fuente, *f*; (of infection) foco, *m*. **to know from a good s.,** saber de buena tinta

sourly *adv* agriamente

sourness *n* acidez, agrura, *f*; acrimonia, *f*

south *n* sur, *m*; mediodía, *m*. *a* del sur. *adv* hacia el sur. **S. African,** *a* and *n* sudafricano (-na). **S. American,** *a* and *n* sudamericano (-na). **s.-east,** *n* sudeste, *m*. *a* del sudeste. *adv* hacia el sudeste. **s.-easter,** viento del sudeste, *m*. **s.-easterly,** *a* del sudeste; al sudeste. *adv* hacia el sudeste. **s.-eastern,** del sudeste. **s.-s.-east,** *n* sudsudeste, *m*. **s.-s.-west,** sudsudoeste, *m*. **s.-west,** *n* sudoeste, *m*. *a* del sudoeste. *adv* hacia el sudoeste. **s.-west wind,** viento sudoeste, ábrego, *m*. **s.-westerly,** *a* del sudoeste. *adv* hacia el sudoeste. **s.-western,** *a* del sudoeste

South Africa República Sudafricana, *f*

South America América del Sur, *f*

southerly *a* del sur; hacia el sur. **The house has a s. aspect,** La casa está orientada al sur

southern *a* del sur; del mediodía; meridional. **S. Cross,** Cruz, *f*, Crucero, *m*. **s. express,** sudexpreso, *m*

southerner *n* habitante del sur, *m*

South Sea Mar del Sur, Mar del Pacífico, *m*

southward *a* del sur; al sur. *adv* hacia el sur

souvenir *n* recuerdo, *m*

sovereign *a* soberano. *n* soberano (-na); (coin) soberano, *m*

sovereignty *n* soberanía, *f*

soviet *n* soviet, *m*, a soviético

Soviet Union, the la Unión Soviética, *f*

sow *n* cerda, puerca, marrana, *f*; (of a wild boar) jabalina, *f*; (of iron) galápago, *m*

sow *vt* sembrar; esparcir; diseminar

sower *n* sembrador (-ra)

sowing *n* sembradura, siembra, *f*. **s. machine,** sembradora, *f*. **s. time,** tiempo de la siembra, *m*

soya bean *n* soja, *f*

spa *n* balneario, *m*; (spring) manantial mineral, *m*, caldas, *f pl*

space *n* espacio, *m*; (of time) temporada, *f*; intervalo, *m*; (print, mus) espacio, *m*. *vt* espaciar. **blank s.,** blanco, *m*. **s.-bar,** tecla de espacios, *f*, espaciador, *m*

spacious *a* espacioso; amplio

spaciousness *n* espaciosidad, *f*; amplitud, *f*

spade *n* pala, azada, *f*; (cards) espada, *f*. **to call a s. a s.,** llamar al pan pan y al vino vino, llamar a las cosas por su nombre. **s.-work,** trabajo preparatorio, *m*, labor de pala, *f*

spaghetti *n* fideos, macarrones, *m pl*

Spain España, *f*

span *vt* medir a palmos; rodear; medir; (cross) atravesar, cruzar. *n* palmo, *m*; espacio, *m*, duración, *f*; (of a bridge) vano, *m*; (of wing, *aer*, *zool*) envergadura, *f*; (distance) distancia, *f*. **single-s. bridge,** puente de vano único. **the brief s. of human life,** la corta duración de la vida humana

spangle *n* lentejuela, *f*; (tinsel) oropel, *m*. *vt* adornar con lentejuelas; sembrar (de), esparcir (de). **spangled with stars,** sembrado de estrellas

Spaniard *n* español (-la). **a young S.,** un joven español

spaniel *n* perro de aguas, perro sabueso español *m*; (cocker) sabueso, *m*

Spanish *a* español. *n* (language) español, castellano, *m*. **a S. girl,** una muchacha española. **in S. fashion,** a la española. **S. American,** *a* and *n* hispanoamericano (-na). **S. broom,** retama de olor, *f*. **S. fly,** cantárida, *f*

Spanish America Hispanoamérica, *f*

spank *vt* pegar con la mano, azotar. *n* azotazo, *m*. **to s. along,** correr rápidamente; (of a horse) galopar

spanking *n* azotamiento, vapuleo, *m*

spanner *n* llave inglesa, llave de tuercas, *f*

spar *n naut* mastel, *m*; *min* espato, *m*; (boxing) boxeo, *m*; (quarrel) disputa, *f*. *vi* boxear; (argue) disputar

spare *a* (meager) frugal, escaso; (of persons) enjuto, flaco; (available) disponible; (extra) de repuesto. *n* re-

cambio, *m*. **s. part,** pieza de recambio, pieza de repuesto, *f*. **s. room,** cuarto de amigos, *m*. **s. time,** ratos de ocio, *m pl*, tiempo disponible, *m*. **s. wheel,** rueda de repuesto, *f*
spare *vt* (expense, etc.) escatimar; ahorrar; (do without) pasarse sin; (give) dar; (a life, etc.) perdonar; (avoid) evitar; dispensar de; (grant) hacer gracia de; (time) dedicar. **I cannot s. her,** No puedo estar sin ella. **They have no money to s.,** No tienen dinero de sobra. **to be sparing of,** ser avaro de
sparingly *adv* frugalmente; escasamente. **to eat s.,** comer con frugalidad
spark *n* chispa, *f*; (gallant) pisaverde, *m*. *vi* chispear, echar chispas
sparking *a* chispeante. *n* emisión de chispas, *f*. **s.-plug,** bujía de encendido, *f*
sparkle *vi* centellear, rutilar, destellar; *fig* brillar; (of wines) ser espumoso. *n* centelleo, destello, *m*; *fig* brillo, *m*
sparkling *a* rutilante, centelleante, reluciente; *fig* brillante, chispeante; (of wines) espumante
sparring match *n* combate de boxeo amistoso, *m*
sparrow *n* gorrión, *m*. **s.-hawk,** gavilán, esparaván, *m*
sparse *a* claro, ralo; esparcido
sparsely *adv* escasamente
Sparta Esparta, *f*
Spartan *a* and *n* espartano (-na)
spasm *n* espasmo, *m*; ataque, *m*; acceso, *m*
spasmodic *a* espasmódico; intermitente
spasmodically *adv* espasmódicamente
spat *n* (gaiter) polaina de tela, *f*
spate *n* crecida, *f*; *fig* torrente, *m*. **in s.,** crecido
spatter *vt* salpicar; (*fig* smirch) manchar. *vi* rociar. *n* salpicadura, *f*; rociada, *f*
spatula *n* espátula, *f*
spawn *vt* and *vi* desovar; engendrar. *n* huevas, *f pl*, freza, *f*; (offspring) producto, *m*
spawning *n* desove, *m*
speak *vi* hablar; pronunciar un discurso; (sound) sonar. *vt* decir; (French, etc.) hablar. **She never spoke to him again,** Nunca volvió a dirigirle la palabra. **roughly speaking,** aproximadamente, más o menos. **Speaking for myself,** En cuanto a mí, Por mi parte. **without speaking,** sin decir nada, sin hablar. **to s. for,** (a person) hablar por. **to s. for itself,** hablar por sí mismo, ser evidente. **to s. one's mind,** decir lo que se piensa. **to s. of,** hablar de. **to s. out,** hablar claro; hablar alto. **to s. up for,** (a person) hablar en favor de (alguien)
speaker *n* el, *m*, (*f*, la) que habla; (public) orador (-ra). **the S.,** el Presidente de la Cámara de los Comunes
speaking *a* hablante; para hablar; elocuente, expresivo. *n* habla, *f*, discurso, *m*. **They are not on s. terms,** No se hablan. **within s. distance,** al habla. **s.-trumpet,** portavoz, *m*. **s.-tube,** tubo acústico, *m*
spear *n* lanza, *f*; (javelin) venablo, *m*; (harpoon) arpón, *m*. *vt* herir con lanza, alancear; (fish) arponear. **s.-head,** punta de la lanza, *f*. **s.-thrust,** lanzada, *f*
special *a* especial; particular; extraordinario. *n* (train) tren extraordinario, *m*. **s. correspondent,** corresponsal extraordinario, *m*. **s. friend,** amigo (-ga) del alma, amigo íntimo
specialist *n* especialista, *mf*
speciality *n* particularidad, *f*; especialidad, *f*
specialization *n* especialización, *f*
specialize *vt* especializar. *vi* especializarse
specially *adv* especialmente; particularmente; sobre todo
species *n* especie, *f*; raza, *f*
specific *a* específico; explícito. *n* específico, *m*. **s. gravity,** peso específico, *m*, densidad, *f*
specifically *adv* específicamente; explícitamente
specification *n* especificación, *f*
specify *vt* especificar
specimen *n* espécimen, *m*; ejemplo, *m*; *inf* tipo, *m*
specious *a* especioso

speciousness *n* plausibilidad, *f*; apariencia engañosa, *f*
speck *n* pequeña mancha, *f*; punto, *m*; átomo, *m*; (on fruit) maca, *f*
speckle *vt* motear, manchar
speckled *a* abigarrado; con manchas . . .
spectacle *n* espectáculo, *m*; escena, *f*; *pl* **spectacles,** gafas, *f pl*, anteojos, *m pl*. **s.-case,** cajita para las gafas, *f*
spectacled *a* con gafas, que lleva gafas
spectacular *a* espectacular
spectator *n* espectador (-ra)
spectral *a* espectral
specter *n* espectro, fantasma, *m*
spectroscope *n* espectroscopio, *m*
spectrum *n phys* espectro, *m*
speculate *vi* especular (sobre, acerca de); *com* especular (en)
speculation *n* especulación, *f*
speculative *a* especulativo
speculator *n* especulador (-ra)
speech *n* habla, *f*; palabra, *f*; (idiom) lenguaje, *m*; (language) idioma, *m*; *gram* oración, *f*; (address) discurso, *m*; disertación, *f*. **part of s.,** parte de la oración, *f*. **to make a s.,** pronunciar un discurso. **s.maker,** orador (-ra)
speechless *a* mudo; sin habla; desconcertado, turbado
speed *n* prisa, rapidez, *f*; velocidad, *f*. *vt* dar la bienvenida (a); conceder éxito (a); (accelerate) acelerar. *vi* darse prisa; correr a toda prisa; (of arrows) volar. **at full s.,** a toda prisa; a toda velocidad; a todo correr. **maximum s.,** velocidad máxima, *f*. **with all s.,** a toda prisa. **s. of impact,** velocidad del choque, *f*. **s.-boat,** lancha de carrera, *f*. **s.-limit,** velocidad máxima, *f*, límite de velocidad, *m*
speedily *adv* aprisa, rápidamente; prontamente
speediness *n* rapidez, prisa, celeridad, *f*; prontitud, *f*
speeding *n* exceso de velocidad, *m*. **s. up,** aceleración, *f*
speedometer *n* cuentakilómetros, *m*
speedway *n* autódromo, *m*, pista de ceniza, *f*
speedy *a* rápido; pronto
spell *n* ensalmo, hechizo, *m*; encanto, *m*; (bout) turno, *m*; (interval) rato, *m*; temporada, *f*. *vt* (a word) deletrear; (a word in writing) escribir; (mean) significar; (be) ser. **a s. of good weather,** una temporada de buen tiempo. **by spells,** a ratos. **to learn to s.,** aprender la ortografía. **s.-bound,** encantado, fascinado; asombrado
spelling *n* deletreo, *m*; ortografía, *f*. **s.-book,** silabario, *m*; **s. mistake,** falta de ortografía, *f*
spelling bee *n* certamen de deletreo, *m*
spend *vt* gastar; (time, etc.) pasar; perder; consumir, agotar. *vi* gastar, hacer gastos. **to s. oneself,** agotarse
spendthrift *n* derrochador (-ra), manirroto (-ta). *a* despilfarrado, pródigo
spent *a* agotado, rendido. **The night is far s.,** La noche está avanzada. **s. bullet,** bala fría, *f*
sperm *n biol* esperma, *f*; (whale) cachalote, *m*
spermaceti *n* esperma de ballena, *f*
sphere *n* esfera, *f*. **s. of influence,** zona de influencia, *f*
spherical *a* esférico
sphinx *n* esfinge, *f*. **s.-like,** de esfinge
spice *n* especia, *f*; *fig* sabor, *m*; (trace) pizca, *f*. *vt* especiar. **s. cupboard,** especiero, *m*
spick and span *a* limpio como una patena; (brand-new) flamante; (of persons) muy compuesto
spicy *a* especiado; aromático; *fig* picante
spider *n* araña, *f*. **spider's web,** telaraña, *f*
spidery *a* de araña; lleno de arañas. **s. writing,** letra de patas de araña, *f*
spigot *n* espiche, *m*
spike *n* punta (de hierro, etc.), *f*; escarpia, *f*; (for boots) clavo, *m*; *bot* espiga, *f*. *vt* clavetear; (a cannon) clavar
spill *vt* derramar. *n* (fall) caída, *f*
spilling *n* derramamiento, derrame, *m*
spin *vt* hilar; (a cocoon) tejer; (a top) bailar; (a ball) tor-

near; (a coin) lanzar. *vi* hilar; girar, bailar. *n* vuelta, *f*; paseo, *m*. **to send spinning downstairs,** hacer rodar por la escalera (a). **to s. a yarn,** contar un cuento. **to s. out,** prolongar

spinach *n* espinaca, *f*

spinal *a* espinal. **s. anaesthesia,** raquianestesia, *f*. **s. column,** columna vertebral, *f*

spindle *n* huso, *m*; *mech* eje, *m*. **s.-shaped,** ahusado

spine *n anat* espinazo, *m*, columna vertebral, *f*; *bot* espina, *f*; (of a porcupine, etc.) púa, *f*

spineless *a zool* invertebrado; *fig* débil

spinet *n* espineta, *f*

spinner *n* hilandero (-ra); máquina de hilar, *f*

spinney *n* arboleda, *f*; bosquecillo, *m*

spinning *n* hilado, *m*; hilandería, *f*. **s.-machine,** máquina de hilar, *f*. **s.-top,** trompo, *m*, peonza, *f*. **s.-wheel,** rueca, *f*

spinster *n* soltera, *f*. **confirmed s.,** solterona, *f*

spiny *a* con púas; espinoso

spiral *a* espiral; en espiral. *n* espiral, *f*

spirally *adv* en espiral

spire *n* (of a church) aguja, *f*; espira, *f*

spirit *n* espíritu, *m*; alma, *f*; (ghost) aparecido, fantasma, *m*; (outstanding person) ingenio, *m*, inteligencia, *f*; (disposition) ánimo, *m*; (courage) valor, espíritu, *m*; (for a lamp, etc.) alcohol, *m*. **the Holy S.,** El Espíritu Santo. **to be in high spirits,** no caber de contento, saltar de alegría. **to be in low spirits,** estar desalentado, estar deprimido. **to be full of spirits,** ser bullicioso, tener mucha energía. **to keep up one's spirits,** sostener el valor. **to s. away,** quitar secretamente, hacer desaparecer; (kidnap) secuestrar. **s.-level,** nivel de burbuja, *m*. **s.-stove,** cocinilla, *f*

spirited *a* animado, vigoroso; fogoso, animoso, brioso

spiritless *a* sin espíritu, apático; flojo, débil; (depressed) abatido, desalentado; (cowardly) sin valor, cobarde

spiritual *a* espiritual

spiritualism *n* espiritismo, *m*; *phil* espiritualismo, *m*

spiritualist *n* espiritista, *mf*; *phil* espiritualista, *mf*

spiritualistic *a* espiritista; *phil* espiritualista. **s. séance,** sesión espiritista, *f*

spirituality *n* espiritualidad, *f*

spiritually *adv* espiritualmente

spirituous *a* espiritoso

spirt *vi, vt, n*. See **spurt**

spit *n* (for roasting) espetón, asador, *m*; (sand-bank) banco de arena, *m*; (of land) lengua de tierra, *f*; (spittle) saliva, *f*. **the spit of, the spit and image of, the spitting image of,** la imagen viva de, la segunda edición de, *f*. *vt* (skewer) espetar; (saliva, etc.) escupir; (curses, etc.) vomitar. *vi* escupir, expectorar; (of a cat) fufear, decir fu; (sputter) chisporrotear; (rain) lloviznar

spite *n* malevolencia, mala voluntad, hostilidad, *f*; rencor, *m*, ojeriza, *f*. *vt* contrariar; hacer daño (a). **He has a s. against them,** Les tiene rencor. **in s. of,** a pesar de; a despecho de

spiteful *a* rencoroso, malévolo

spitefully *adv* malévolamente; con rencor; por maldad; por despecho

spitefulness *n* malevolencia, *f*; rencor, *m*

spitfire *n* cascarrabias, *mf*, furia, *f*

spittle *n* saliva, *f*

splash *vt* salpicar (de); manchar (con). *vi* derramarse, esparcirse; chapotear, chapalear. *n* chapoteo, *m*; (of rain, etc.) chapaleteo, *m*; (stain or patch) mancha, *f*. **John was splashing about in the sea,** Juan chapoteaba en el mar. **to make a s.,** *fig* causar una sensación. **s.-board,** alero, *m*

spleen *n anat* bazo, *m*; esplín, *m*

splendid *a* espléndido; magnífico; glorioso; excelente

splendidly *adv* espléndidamente; magníficamente; excelentemente

splendor *n* resplandor, *m*; magnificencia, *f*; (of exploits, etc.) esplendor, brillo, *m*

splice *vt* (ropes, timbers) empalmar; (marry) unir, casar. *n* empalme, *m*

splint *n surg* férula, *f*. **to put in a s.,** entablar

splinter *vt* astillar, hacer astillas. *vi* hacerse astillas

splintery *a* astilloso

split *vi* henderse; resquebrajarse; (of seams) nacerse; abrirse; dividirse. *vt* hender; partir; dividir; abrir; (the atom) escindir. *n* hendedura, *f*; grieta, *f*; división, *f*; (in fabric) rasgón, *m*; (quarrel) ruptura, *f*. **to s. hairs,** andar en quisquillas, pararse en pelillos, sutilizar. **I have a splitting headache,** Tengo un dolor de cabeza que me trae loco. **to s. one's sides,** reírse a carcajadas, desternillarse de risa. **to s. on a rock,** estrellarse contra una roca. **to s. the difference,** partir la diferencia. **The blow s. his head open,** El golpe le abrió la cabeza. **to s. on,** *inf* delatar, denunciar

splodge *n* mancha, *f*, borrón, *m*

splutter *vi* chisporrotear; (of a person) balbucir. *n* chisporroteo, *m*. **to s. out,** decir tartamudeando

spoil *n* botín, despojo, *m*; (of war) trofeo, *m*. *vt* estropear; echar a perder; (diminish) mitigar; (a child) mimar; (injure) dañar; (destroy) arruinar, destruir. *vi* estropearse; echarse a perder. **to be spoiling for a fight,** tener ganas de pelearse. **You have spoilt my fun,** Me has aguado la fiesta. **s.-sport,** aguafiestas, *mf*

spoilt *a* (of a child, etc.) mimado, consentido, malacostumbrado

spoke *n* (of a wheel) rayo, *m*; (of a ladder) travesaño, peldaño, *m*; *naut* cabilla (de la rueda del timón), *f*

spoken *a* hablado. **well-s.,** bien hablado; cortés

spokesman *n* portavoz, *m*. **to be s.,** llevar la palabra

spoliation *n* expoliación, *f*; despojo, *m*

sponge *n* esponja, *f*; (cadger) gorrón (-ona); (cake) bizcocho, *m*. *vt* limpiar con esponja. **to s.,** *inf* vivir de gorra. **s.-holder,** esponjera, *f*

sponger *n* gorrón (-ona), vividor, *m*, sablista, *mf*

sponginess *n* esponjosidad, *f*

sponging *n* esponjadura, *f*; *inf* sablazo, *m*

spongy *a* esponjoso

sponsor *n* garante, *mf*; valedor (-ra), patron (-na); (godfather) padrino, *m*; (godmother) madrina, *f*, (radio and TV) auspiciador, patrocinador, *m*

spontaneity *n* espontaneidad, *f*

spontaneous *a* espontáneo. **s. combustion,** combustión espontánea, *f*

spontaneously *adv* espontáneamente

spook *n* fantasma, espectro, *m*

spool *n* (for thread) bobina, *f*, carrete, *m*; (in a sewing machine) canilla, *f*; (of a fishing rod) carrete, *m*

spoon *n* cuchara, *f*. *vt* sacar con cuchara. *vi* (slang) besuquearse. **to s.-feed,** dar de comer con cuchara (a); tratar como a un niño (a)

spoonful *n* cucharada, *f*

spoor *n* pista, huella de animal, *f*; rastro, *m*

sporadic *a* esporádico

spore *n bot* espora, *f*; *zool* germen, *m*

sport *n* deporte, sport, *m*; deportismo, *m*; (jest) broma, *f*; (game) juego, *m*; (plaything) juguete, *m*; (pastime) pasatiempo, *m*. *vi* jugar; recrearse, divertirse. *vt* llevar; ostentar, lucir. **He is a s.,** Es un buen chico. **to make s. of,** burlarse de. **sports car,** coche de deporte, *m*. **sports ground,** campo de recreo, *m*. **sports jacket,** chaqueta de deporte, americana, *f*. **sports shirt,** camisa corta, *f*

sporting *a* deportista; caballeroso. **I think there is a s. chance,** Me parece que hay una posibilidad de éxito

sporting goods *n* artículos de deporte, efectos de deportes, *m pl*

sportive *a* juguetón; bromista

sportsman *n* deportista, *m*; aficionado al sport, *m*; *fig* caballero, sportman, *m*; buen chico, *m*

sportsmanlike *a* de deportista; caballeroso

sportsmanship *n* deportividad, *f*

spot *n* mancha, *f*; pinta, *f*; (on the face, etc.) peca, *f*; grano, *m*; (place) sitio, *m*; lugar, *m*; (of liquor) trago, *m*; (of food) bocado, *m*; (of rain) gota, *f*. *vt* manchar; motear; (recognize) reconocer; (understand) darse cuenta de, comprender. **a tender s.,** *fig* debilidad, *f*. **on the s.,**

en el acto. **s. ball,** (billiards) pinta, *f.* **s. cash,** dinero contante, *m*

spotless *a* saltando de limpio; sin mancha; inmaculado; puro; virgen

spotlight *n* luz del proyector, *f;* proyector, *m*

spotted *a* (stained) manchado; (of animals, etc.) con manchas; (of garments, etc.) con pintas

spotty *a* lleno de manchas; moteado; (pimply) con granos

spouse *n* esposo, *m;* esposa, *f*

spout *vi* chorrear; *inf* hablar incesantemente. *vt* arrojar; vomitar; *inf* declamar, recitar. *n* (of a jug, etc.) pico, *m;* (for water, etc.) tubo, *m,* cañería, *f;* canalón, *m;* (gust) ráfaga, nube, *f.* **down s.,** tubo de bajada, *m*

spouting *n* chorreo, *m; inf* declamación, *f*

sprachgefühl *n* sentido del idioma, *m*

sprain *vt* dislocar, torcer. *n* dislocación, *f,* esguince, *m.* **Victoria has sprained her foot,** Victoria se ha torcido el pie

sprat *n* sardineta, *f*

sprawl *vi* recostarse (en); extenderse; (of plants) trepar. **He went sprawling,** Cayó cuan largo era

spray *n* (branch) ramo, *m;* (of water, etc.) rocío, *m;* (of the sea) espuma, *f;* (mechanical device) pulverizador, *m. vt* pulverizar; rociar; regar; (the throat) jeringar

spread *vt* tender; cubrir (de); poner; (stretch out) extender; (open out) desplegar; (of disease, etc.) propagar; diseminar; divulgar, difundir. *vi* extenderse; propagarse; difundirse; divulgarse; (become general) generalizarse. *n* extensión, *f;* expansión, *f;* propagación, *f;* divulgación, *f;* (aer and of birds) envergadura, *f.* **Carmen s. her hands to the fire,** Carmen extendió las manos al fuego. **The peacock s. its tail,** El pavo real hizo la rueda. **The dove s. its wings,** La paloma desplegó sus alas. **to s. out,** *vt* extender; desplegar; (scatter) esparcir, *vi* extenderse. **spread like wildfire,** correr como pólvora en reguero, propagarse como un reguero de pólvora, ser un reguero de pólvora

spreading *n* (of a disease) propagación, *f;* (of knowledge, etc.) divulgación, *f;* expansión, *f;* extensión, *f*

spree *n* juerga, parranda, *f;* excursión, *f.* **to go on the s.,** ir de juerga, ir de picos pardos

sprig *n* ramita, *f;* (of heather, etc.) espiga, *f;* (scion) vástago, *m*

sprightliness *n* vivacidad, *f,* despejo, *m;* energía, *f*

sprightly *a* vivaracho, despierto; enérgico

spring *vi* saltar, brincar; (become) hacerse; (seek) buscar; (of plants, water) brotar; (of tears) arrasar, llenar; (from) originarse (en), ser causado (por); inspirarse (en). *vt* (a mine) volar; (a trap) soltar. **to s. a surprise,** dar una sorpresa. **to s. a surprise on a person,** coger a la imprevista (a). **to s. at a person,** precipitarse sobre. **to s. to one's feet,** ponerse de pie de un salto. **to s. back,** saltar hacia atrás; recular; volver a su sitio. **to s. open,** abrirse súbitamente. **to s. up,** (of plants) brotar, crecer; (of difficulties, etc.) surgir, asomarse

spring *n* (jump) salto, brinco, *m;* (of water) fuente, *f,* manantial, *m;* (season) primavera, *f;* (of a watch, etc.) resorte, *m;* (of a mattress, etc.) muelle, *m. a* primaveral. *vi* saltar, brincar. **at one s.,** en un salto. **to give a s.,** dar un salto. **s.-board,** trampolín, *m.* **s.-mattress,** colchón de muelles, *m.* **s.-tide,** marea viva, *f*

springiness *n* elasticidad, *f*

springlike *a* primaveral

springtime *n* primavera, *f*

sprinkle *vt* esparcir; salpicar; rociar

sprinkling *n* salpicadura, *f;* rociadura, *f;* pequeño número, *m.* **a s. of snow,** una nevada ligera

sprint *vi* sprintar. *n* sprint, *m*

sprite *n* trasgo, *m;* hada, *f*

sprout *vi* brotar, despuntar, retoñar, tallecer; germinar. *vt* salir. *n* brote, retoño, pimpollo, *m;* germen, *m.* **Brussels sprouts,** coles de Bruselas, *f pl*

spruce *a* peripuesto, muy aseado, pulido; elegante, *n bot* pícea, *f.* **to s. oneself up,** arreglarse, ponerse elegante

spruceness *n* aseo, buen parecer, *m,* elegancia, *f*

spry *a* activo, ágil

spur *n* espuela, *f;* aguijada, *f;* (of a bird) espólon, *m; bot* espuela, *f;* (of a mountain range) espolón, estribo, *m; fig* estímulo, *m. vt* espolear, picar con la espuela; calzarse las espuelas; *fig* estimular, incitar. **on the s. of the moment,** bajo el impulso del momento

spurious *a* espurio; falso

spurn *vt* rechazar; tratar con desprecio; menospreciar

spurt *vi* (gush) chorrear, borbotar; brotar, surgir; (in racing, etc.) hacer un esfuerzo supremo. *vt* hacer chorrear; lanzar. *n* (jet) chorro, *m;* esfuerzo supremo, *m*

sputter *vi* chisporrotear; crepitar; (of a pen) escupir; (of a person) balbucir

sputtering *n* chisporroteo, *m;* crepitación, *f;* (of a person) balbuceo, *m*

sputum *n* esputo, *m*

spy *vt* observar, discernir. *vi* espiar, ser espía. *n* espía, *mf.* **to spy out the land,** explorar el terreno. **to spy upon, espiar,** seguir los pasos (a). **spy-glass,** catalejo, *m*

spying *n* espionaje, *m*

squabble *n* disputa, *f;* riña, *f. vi* pelearse; disputar

squabbling *n* riñas, querellas, *f pl;* disputas, *f pl*

squad *n* escuadra, *f;* pelotón, *m*

squadron *n mil* escuadrón, *m; nav* escuadra, *f; aer* escuadrilla, *f;* (of persons) pelotón, *m.* **s.-leader,** comandante, *m*

squalid *a* escuálido; (of quarrels, etc.) sórdido, mezquino

squall *vi* berrear; chillar. *n* berrido, *m;* chillido, *m;* (storm) chubasco, turbión, *m;* (storm) chubasco, turbión, *m; fig* tormenta, tempestad, *f*

squalor *n* escualidez, *f;* sordidez, mezquindad, *f*

squander *vt* derrochar, tirar, desperdiciar; (time, etc.) malgastar

squanderer *n* derrochador (-ra)

squandering *n* derroche, desperdicio, dispendio, *m;* (of time, etc.) pérdida, *f,* desperdicio, *m*

square *n math* cuadrado, *m;* rectángulo, *m;* (of a chessboard) escaque, *m;* (of a draughtboard and of graph paper) casilla, *f;* (in a town) plaza, *f;* (of troops) cuadro, *m, a* cuadrado; justo; igual; (honest) honrado, formal; (unambiguous) redondo, categórico; *math* cuadrado. **She wore a silk s. on her head,** Llevaba un pañuelo de seda en la cabeza. **five s. feet,** cinco pies cuadrados. **nine feet s.,** nueve pies en cuadro. **on the s.,** honradamente. **a s. dance,** contradanza, *f.* **a s. meal,** una buena comida. **s. dealing,** trato limpio, *m.* **The account is s.,** La cuenta está justa. **to get s. with,** desquitarse (de), vengarse de. **s. measure,** medida de superficie, *f.* **s. root,** raíz cuadrada, *f.* **s.-shouldered,** de hombros cuadrados

square *vt* cuadrar; *carp* escuadrar; (arrange) arreglar; (bribe) sobornar; (reconcile) acomodar; *math* cuadrar. *vi* conformarse (con), cuadrar (con). **to s. the circle,** cuadrar el círculo. **to s. one's shoulders,** enderezarse. **to s. accounts with,** saldar cuentas con. **to s. up to,** (a person) avanzar belicosamente hacia

squarely *adv* en cuadro; directamente; sin ambigüedades, rotundamente; (honestly) de buena fe, honradamente

squareness *n* cuadratura, *f;* (honesty) honradez, buena fe, *f*

squash *vt* aplastar. *vi* aplastarse; apretarse. *n* aplastamiento, *m;* (of fruit, etc.) pulpa, *f;* (of people) agolpamiento, *m;* muchedumbre, *f;* (drink) refresco (de limón, etc.), *m,* (sport) frontón con raqueta, *m*

squashy *a* blando y húmedo

squat *vi* acuclillarse, agacharse, agazaparse ponerse en cuclillas; estar en cuclillas; (on land, etc.) apropiarse sin derecho. *a* rechoncho

squatter *n* intruso (-sa); colono usurpador, *m*

squatter town *n.* See **shanty town**

squawk *vi* graznar; lanzar gritos agudos. *n* graznido, *m;* grito agudo, *m*

squeak *vi* (of carts, etc.) chirriar, rechinar; (of shoes)

crujir; (of persons, mice, etc.) chillar; (slang) cantar. *n* chirrido, crujido, *m*; chillido, *m*. **to have a narrow s.**, escapar por un pelo
squeaking *n* chirrido, rechinamiento, *m*; crujido, *m*; (of humans, mice, etc.) chillidos, *m pl*
squeal *vi* lanzar gritos agudos, chillar; (complain) quejarse; (slang) cantar. *n* grito agudo, chillido, *m*
squealing *n* gritos agudos, chillidos, *m pl*
squeamish *a* que se marea fácilmente; mareado; (nauseated) asqueado; delicado; remilgado
squeamishness *n* tendencia a marearse, *f*; delicadeza, *f*; remilgos, *m pl*
squeeze *vt* apretar; estrujar; (fruit) exprimir; (extort) arrancar; (money from) sangrar. *n* (of the hand, etc.) apretón, *m*; estrujón, *m*; (of fruit juice) algunas gotas (de). **It was a tight s. in the car,** Íbamos muy apretados en el coche. **He was in a tight s.**, Se encontraba en un aprieto. **to s. one's way through the crowd,** abrirse camino a codazos por la muchedumbre. **to s. in,** *vt* hacer sitio para. *vi* introducirse con dificultad (en)
squelch *vi* gorgotear, chapotear. *vt* aplastar
squib *n* (firework) rapapiés, buscapiés, *m*; (lampoon) pasquinada, *f*
squid *n* calamar, *m*
squint *n* estrabismo, *m*; mirada furtiva, *f*; *inf* vistazo, *m*, mirada, *f*. *vi* ser bizco; bizcar. **to s. at,** mirar de soslayo. **s.-eyed,** bizco. **to be s.-eyed,** mirar contra el gobierno
squire *n* escudero, *m*; hacendado, *m*. *vt* escoltar, acompañar
squirm *vi* retorcerse; (with embarrassment) no saber dónde meterse. *n* retorcimiento, *m*. **to s. along the ground,** arrastrarse por el suelo
squirrel *n* ardilla, *f*
squirt *vt* (liquids) lanzar. *vi* chorrear, salir a chorros. *n* chorro, *m*; (syringe) jeringa, *f*
stab *vt* apuñalar, dar de puñaladas (a); herir. *n* puñalada, *f*; herida, *f*; (of pain, and *fig*) pinchzo, *m*. **a s. in the back,** una puñalada por la espalda
stability *n* estabilidad, *f*; solidez, firmeza, *f*
stabilize *vt* estabilizar
stable *a* estable; fijo, firme. *n* cuadra, caballeriza, *f*; (for cows, etc.) establo, *m*. *vt* poner en la cuadra; alojar. **s.-boy,** mozo de cuadra, *m*
stack *n* (of hay) niara, *f*, almiar, *m*; (heap) montón, *m*; (of rifles) pabellón, *m*; (of a chimney) cañón, *m*. *vt agr* hacinar; amontonar; *mil* poner (las armas) en pabellón
stacked *a* (woman) abultada de pechera
stadium *n* estadio, *m*
staff *n* vara, *f*; (bishop's, and *fig*) báculo, *m*; (pilgrim's) bordón, *m*; (pole) palo, *m*; (flagstaff) asta, *f*; (of an office, etc.) personal, *m*; (editorial) redacción, *f*; (corps) cuerpo, *m*; *mil* plana mayor, *f*, estado mayor, *m*; *mus* pentagrama, *m*. *vt* proveer de personal. **general s.**, estado mayor general, *m*. **s. officer,** *mil* oficial de estado mayor, *m*
stag *n* ciervo, *m*. **s.-beetle,** ciervo volante, *m*. **s.-hunting,** caza del ciervo, *f*
stage *n* (for workmen) andamio, *m*; (of a microscope) portaobjetos, *m*; *theat* escena, *f*, tablas, *f pl*; teatro, *m*; (of development, etc.) etapa, *f*; fase, *f*. *vt theat* escenificar, poner en escena; *theat* representar; (a demonstration, etc.) arreglar. **by easy stages,** poco a poco; (of a journey) a pequeñas etapas. **to come on the s.**, salir a la escena. **to go on the s.**, hacerse actor (actriz), dedicarse al teatro. **s. carpenter,** tramoyista, *m*. **s.-coach,** diligencia, *f*. **s.-craft,** arte de escribir para el teatro, *f*; arte escénica, *f*. **s.-direction,** acotación, *f*. **s.-door,** entrada de los artistas, *f*. **s.-effect,** efecto escénico, *m*. **s.-fright,** miedo al público, *m*. **s.-hand,** tramoyista, sacasillas, metesillas y sacamuertos, *m*. **s. manager,** director de escena, *m*. **s.-whisper,** aparte, *m*
stager, old *n* veterano, *m*
stagger *vi* tambalear; andar haciendo eses; (hesitate) titubear, vacilar. *vt* desconcertar. *n* titubeo, tambaleo,

m; *aer* decalaje, *m*. **staggered working hours,** horas de trabajo escalonadas, *f pl*
staggering *a* tambaleante; (surprising) asombroso, sorprendente; (dreadful) espantoso. **a s. blow,** un golpe que derriba
staging *n* (scaffolding) andamio, *m*; *theat* producción, *f*; representación, *f*; decorado, *m*
stagnancy *n* (of water) estancación, *f*; (inactivity) estagnación, *f*; paralización, *f*
stagnant *a* estancado; paralizado. **to be s.**, estar estancado. **s. water,** agua estancada, *f*
stagnate *vi* estancarse; estar estancado; (of persons) vegetar
stagnation *n* (of water) estancación, *f*; estagnación, *f*; parálisis, *f*
staid *a* serio, formal, juicioso
staidness *n* seriedad, formalidad, *f*
stain *vt* manchar; (dye) teñir. *n* mancha, *f*; colorante, *m*. **without a s.**, *fig* sin mancha. **stained glass,** vidrio de color, *m*. **s.-remover,** quitamanchas, *m*
stainless *a* sin mancha; inmaculado, puro
stair *n* escalón, peldaño, *m*; escalera, *f*; *pl* **stairs,** escalera, *f*. **a flight of stairs,** una escalera; un tramo de escaleras. **below stairs,** escalera abajo. **s.-carpet,** alfombra de escalera, *f*. **s.-rod,** varilla para alfombra de escalera, *f*
staircase *n* escalera, *f*. **spiral s.,** escalera de caracol, *f*
stake *n* estaca, *f*; (for plants) rodrigón, *m*; (gaming) envite, *m*, apuesta, *f*; (in an undertaking) interés, *m*; *pl* **stakes,** (prize) premio, *m*; (race) carrera, *f*. *vt* estacar; (plants) rodrigar; (bet) jugar. **at s.,** en juego; en peligro. **to be burnt at the s.,** morir en la hoguera. **to s. one's all,** jugarse el todo por el todo. **to s. a claim,** hacer una reclamación. **to s. out,** jalonar
stalactite *n* estalactita, *f*
stalagmite *n* estalagmita, *f*
stale *a* no fresco; (of bread, etc.) duro, seco; (of air) viciado; viejo; pasado de moda; (tired) cansado
stalemate *n* (chess, checkers) tablas, *f pl*; *fig* punto muerto, *m*. **to reach a s.,** llegar a un punto muerto
staleness *n* rancidez, *f*; (of bread, etc.) dureza, *f*; (of news, etc.) vejez, *f*
stalk *n bot* tallo, *m*; *bot* pedúnculo, *m*; (of a glass) pie, *m*. *vi* andar majestuosamente; *fig* rondar. *vt* (game) cazar al acecho; (a person) seguir los pasos (a)
stalking horse *n* boezuelo, *m*; *fig* pretexto, disfraz, *m*
stall *n* (in a stable) puesto (individual), *m*; (stable) establo, *m*; (choir) silla de coro, *f*; (in a fair, etc.) barraca, *f*, puesto, *m*; *theat* butaca, *f*; (finger-stall) dedal, *m*. *vt* (an engine) cortar accidentalmente. *vi aut* pararse de pronto; *aer* perder velocidad; (of a cart, etc.) atascarse. **pit s.,** *theat* butaca de platea, *f*
stalling *n aut* parada accidental, *f*; *aer* pérdida de velocidad, *f*. **Stop s.!** ¡Déjate de rodeos!
stallion *n* semental, *m*
stalwart *a* robusto, fornido; leal; valiente
stalwartness *n* robustez, *f*; lealtad, *f*; valor, *m*
stamen *n bot* estambre, *m*
stamina *n* resistencia, *f*
stammer *vi* tartamudear; (hesitate in speaking) titubear, balbucir. *n* tartamudez, *f*; titubeo, balbuceo, *m*
stammerer *n* tartamudo (-da)
stammering *a* tartamudo; balbuciente. *n* tartamudeo, *m*; balbuceo, *m*
stamp *vt* estampar; imprimir; (documents) timbrar; pegar el sello de correo (a); (characterize) sellar; (*fig* engrave) grabar; (coins) acuñar; (press) apisonar; (with the foot) golpear con los pies, patear; (in dancing) zapatear. *n* (with the foot) patada, *f*, golpe con los pies, *m*; (mark, etc.) marca, *f*; (rubber, etc.) estampilla, *f*; matasellos, *m*; cuño, *m*; (for documents) póliza, *f*; timbre, *m*; (for letters) sello, *m*; (machine) punzón, *m*; mano de mortero, *f*; (*fig* sign) sello, *m*; (kind) temple, *m*, clase, *f*. **The events of that day are stamped on my memory,** Los acontecimientos de aquel día están grabados en mi memoria. **to s. out,** (a fire, etc.) extin-

guir, apagar; (resistance, etc.) vencer; destruir. **post-age-s.**, sello de correos, *m.* **s.-album,** álbum de sellos, *m.* **s.-duty,** impuesto del timbre, *m.* **s.-machine,** expendedor automático de sellos de correo, *m*
stampede *n* fuga precipitada, *f*; pánico, *m. vi* huir precipitadamente; (of animals) salir de estampía; huir en desorden. *vt* hacer perder la cabeza (a), sembrar el pánico entre
stamping *n* selladura, *f*; (of documents) timbrado, *m*; (of fabrics, etc.) estampado, *m*; (with the feet) pataleo, *m*; (in dancing) zapateo, *m*
stance *n* posición de los pies, *f*; postura, *f*
stanch *vt* restañar
stand *vi* estar de pie; ponerse de pie, incorporarse; estar; hallarse; sostenerse; ser; ponerse; (halt) parar; (remain) permanecer, quedar. *vt* poner; (endure) resistir; tolerar; sufrir; (entertain) convidar. **S.!** ¡Alto! **as things s.,** tal como están las cosas. **I cannot s. any more,** No puedo más. **I cannot s. him,** No le puedo ver. **Nothing stands between them and ruin,** No hay nada entre ellos y la ruina. **I stood him a drink,** Le convidé a un trago. **How do we s.?** ¿Cómo estamos? **It stands to reason that . . . ,** Es lógico que . . . **Edward stands six feet,** Eduardo tiene seis pies de altura. **to s. accused of,** ser acusado de. **to s. godfather** (or **godmother) to,** sacar de pila (a). **to s. in need (of),** necesitar, tener necesidad (de). **to s. on end,** (of hair) ponerse de punta, despeluzarse, **to s. one in good stead,** ser útil, ser ventajoso. **to s. to attention,** cuadrarse, permanecer en posición de firmes. **to s. well with,** tener buenas relaciones con, ser estimado de. **to s. aside,** tenerse a un lado; apartarse; (in favor of someone) retirarse. **to s. back,** quedarse atrás; recular, retroceder. **to s. by,** estar de pie cerca de; estar al lado de; estar presente (sin intervenir); ser espectador; estar preparado; (one's friends) ayudar, proteger; (a promise, etc.) atenerse (a); ser fiel (a); (of a ship) mantenerse listo. **s.-by,** *n* recurso, *m.* **to s. for,** representar; simbolizar; (mean) significar; (Parliament, etc.) presentarse como candidato; (put up with) tolerar, sufrir. **to s. in,** colaborar. **to s. in with,** estar de acuerdo con, ser partidario de; compartir. **to s. off,** mantenerse a distancia. **to s. out,** (in relief, and *fig.* of persons) destacarse; (be firm) resistir, mantenerse firme; *naut* gobernar más afuera. **S. out of the way!** ¡Quítate del medio! **to s. over,** (be postponed) quedar aplazado. **to s. up,** estar de pie; ponerse de pie, incorporarse; tenerse derecho. **to s. up against,** resistir; oponerse a. **to s. up for,** defender; volverpor. **to s. up to,** hacer cara a
stand *n* puesto, *m*; posición, actitud, *f*; (for taxis, etc.) punto, *m*; (in a market, etc.) puesto, *m*; *sport* tribuna, *f*; (for a band) quiosco, *m*; (of a dish, etc.) pie, *m*; *mech* sostén, *m*; (opposition) resistencia, oposición, *f.* **to make a s. against,** oponerse resueltamente (a); ofrecer resistencia (a). **to take one's s.,** fundarse (en), apoyarse (en). **to take up one's s. by the fire,** ponerse cerca del fuego
standard *n* (flag) estandarte, *m*, bandera, *f*; (for gold, weights, etc.) marco, *m*; norma, *f*; convención, regla, *f*; (of a lamp) pie, *m*; (pole) poste, *m*; columna, *f*; (level) nivel, *m. a* corriente; normal; típico; clásico. **It is a s. type,** Es un tipo corriente. **gold s.,** patrón de oro, *m.* **s. author,** autor clásico, *m.* **s. formula,** fórmula clásica, *f.* **s. of living,** nivel de vida, *m.* **s.-bearer,** abanderado, *m.* **s.-lamp,** lámpara vertical, *f*
standardization *n* (of armaments, etc.) unificación de tipos, *f*; (of dyestuffs, medicinals, etc.) control, *m*, estandardización, *f*
standardize *vt* hacer uniforme; controlar
standing *a* de pie, derecho; permanente, fijo; constante. *n* posición, *f*; reputación, *f*; importancia, *f*; antigüedad, *f.* **It is a quarrel of long s.,** Es una riña antigua. **s. committee,** comisión permanente, *f.* **s. room,** sitio para estar de pie, *m.* **s. water,** agua estan-

cada, *f.* **standoffish,** frío, etiquetero; altanero. **standoffishness,** frialdad, *f*; altanería, *f.* **standpoint,** punto de vista, *m*
standstill *n* parada, *f*; pausa, *f.* **at a s.,** parado; (of industry) paralizado
stanza *n* estrofa, estancia, *f*
staple *n* (fastener) grapa, *f*; (of wool, etc.) hebra, fibra, *f*; producto principal (de un pais), *m*; (raw material) materia prima, *f*; *a* principal; más importante; corriente
stapler, (device) cosepapeles, engrapador, *m*, atrochadora (Argentina), *f*
star *n* (all meanings) estrella, *f*; (asterisk) asterisco, *m. vt* estrellar, sembrar de estrellas; marcar con asterisco. *vi* (theat cinema) presentarse como estrella, ser estrella. **stars and stripes,** las barras y las estrellas. **to be born under a lucky s.,** tener estrella. **to see stars,** ver estrellas. **s.-gazing,** observación de las estrellas, *f*; ensimismamiento, *m.* **s.-spangled,** estrellado, tachonado de estrellas, sembrado de estrellas. **s.-turn,** gran atracción, *f*
starboard *n naut* estribor, *m*
starch *n* almidón, *m*, las harinas, *f pl*, *vt* almidonar
starchy *a* almidonado; (of food) feculento; *fig* tieso, entonado, estirado
stare *vi* mirar fijamente; abrir mucho los ojos. *n* mirada fija, *f.* **stony s.,** mirada dura, *f.* **to s. at,** (a person) clavar la mirada en; mirar de hito en hito (a). **The explanation stares one in the face,** La explicación salta a la vista (o está evidente). **to s. into space,** mirar las telarañas. **to s. out of countenance,** avergonzar con la mirada
starfish *n* estrella de mar, *f*
staring *a* (of colors) chillón, llamativo, encendido. **s. eyes,** ojos saltones, *m pl*; ojos espantados, *m pl*
stark *a* rígido; *poet* poderoso; absoluto. **s. staring mad,** loco de atar. **s.-naked,** en cueros vivos, en pelota
starless *a* sin estrellas
starlight *n* luz de las estrellas, *f*, *a* estrellado
starry *a* estrellado, sembrado de estrellas
start *vi* estremecerse, asustarse; saltar; (set out) salir; ponerse en camino; (of a train, a race) arrancar; ponerse en marcha; *aer* despegar; (begin) empezar; (of timbers) combarse. *vt* empezar (a car, etc.) poner en marcha; (a race) dar la señal de partida; (a hare, etc.) levantar; (cause) provocar, causar; (a discussion, etc.) abrir; iniciar. *n* (fright) susto, *m*; (setting out) partida, salida, *f*; (beginning) principio, comienzo, *m*; (starting-point of a race) arrancadero, *m*; *aer* despegue, *m*; (advantage) ventaja, *f.* **at the s.,** al principio. **for a s.,** para empezar. **from s. to finish,** desde el principio hasta el fin. **She started to cry,** Se puso a llorar. **He has started his journey to Canada,** Ha empezado su viaje al Canadá. **I started up the engine,** Puse el motor en marcha. **to get a s.,** asustarse; tomar la delantera. **to give** (a person) **a s.,** asustar, dar un susto (a); dar la ventaja (a). **to give** (a person) **a s. in life,** ayudar a alguien a situarse en la vida. **to make a fresh s.** (in life), hacer vida nueva, empezar la vida de nuevo. **to s. after,** lanzarse en busca de; salir tras. **to s. back,** retroceder; emprender el viaje de regreso; marcharse. **to s. off,** salir, partir; ponerse en camino. **to s. up,** *vi* incorporarse bruscamente, ponerse de pie de un salto; (appear) surgir, aparecer. *vt* (an engine) poner en marcha
starter *n* iniciador (-ra); (for a race) starter, juez de salida, *m*; (competitor in a race) corredor, *m*; (of a car, etc.) arranque, *m*
starting *n* (setting out) salida, partida, *f*; (beginning) principio, *m*; (fear) estremecimiento, *m*; susto, *m.* **s.-gear,** palanca de arranque, *f.* **s.-handle,** manivela de arranque, *f.* **s.-point,** punto de partida, *m*; *fig* arrancadero, punto de arranque, *m.* **s.-post,** puesto de salida, *m*
startle *vt* asustar, sobresaltar, alarmar. **The news startled him out of his indifference,** Las noticias le hicieron salir de su indiferencia

startling *a* alarmante; (of dress, etc.) exagerado; (of colors) chillón

starvation *n* hambre, *f;* *med* inanición, *f.* **s. diet,** régimen de hambre, *m.* **s. wage,** ración de hambre, *f*

starve *vi* morir de hambre; pasar hambre, no tener bastante que comer; no comer. *vt* matar de hambre; privar de alimentos (a). **I am simply starving,** Tengo una hambre canina, Me muero de hambre. **to s. with cold,** *vi* morir de frío. *vt* matar de frío

starved *a* muerto de hambre, hambriento. **s. of affection,** hambriento de cariño

starving *a* que muere de hambre, hambriento

state *n* estado, *m;* condición, *f;* (anxiety) agitación, ansiedad, *f;* (social) rango, *m;* (pomp) magnificencia, pompa, *f;* (government, etc.) Estado, *m;* nación, *f. a* de Estado; de gala, de ceremonia. **the married s.,** el estado matrimonial. **s. of war,** estado de guerra. **in s.,** con gran pompa. **to lie in s.,** (of a body) estar expuesto. **s. apartments,** habitaciones de gala, *f pl.* **s. banquet,** comida de gala, *f.* **s. coach,** coche de gala, *m.* **s. control,** control por el Estado, *m.* **S. Department,** Ministerio de Estado, *m.* **s. education,** instrucción pública, *f.* **State of the Union message,** Mensaje al Congreso, *m.* **s. papers,** documentos de Estado, *m pl*

state *vt* decir (que), afirmar (que); (one's case, etc.) exponer; explicar; *math* proponer

statecraft *n* arte de gobernar, *m*

stated *a* arreglado, indicado; fijo. **the s. date,** la fecha indicada. **at s. intervals,** a intervalos fijos

statehood *n* estadidad, *f*

stateliness *n* dignidad, *f;* majestad, *f*

stately *a* majestuoso; imponente; noble; digno

statement *n* afirmación, declaración, *f;* resumen, *m;* exposición, *f; law* deposición, *f; com* estado de cuenta, *m.* **to make a s.,** hacer una declaración

stateroom *n* sala de recepción, *f;* (on a ship) camarote, *m*

statesman *n* hombre de estado, *m*

statesmanlike *a* de hombre de estado

statesmanship *n* arte de gobernar, *m*

static *a* estático

statics *n* estática, *f*

station *n* (place) puesto, sitio, *m;* (rw and ecc) estación, *f;* (social) posición social, *f; naut* apostadero, *m; surv* punto de marca, *m. vt* estacionar, colocar, poner. **to s. oneself,** colocarse. **Stations of the Cross,** Estaciones, *f pl.* **s.-master,** jefe de la estación, *m*

stationary *a* estacionario; inmóvil; *ast* estacional

stationer *n* papelero (-ra). **stationer's shop,** papelería, *f*

stationery *n* papelería, *f,* efectos de escritorio, *m pl;* papel de escribir, *m*

station wagon *n* pisicorre, coche camioneta, coche rural, *m*

statistical *a* estadístico

statistician *n* estadista, *m*

statistics *n* estadística, *f*

statuary *a* estatuario. *n* estatuaria, *f;* estatuas, *f pl;* (sculptor) estatuario, *m*

statue *n* estatua, *f;* imagen, *f*

statuesque *a* escultural

statuette *n* figurilla, *f*

stature *n* estatura, *f;* (moral, etc.) valor, *m*

status *n* (law etc.) estado, *m;* posición, *f;* rango, *m.* **What is his s. as a physicist?** ¿Cómo se le considera entre los físicos? **social s.,** posición social, *f;* rango social, *m*

statute *n* ley, *f;* acto legislativo, *m;* estatuto, *m;* regla, *f.* **s. book,** código legal, *m*

statutory *a* establecido; reglamentario; estatutario

staunch *a* leal, fiel; firme, constante. *vt* restañar

staunchness *n* lealtad, fidelidad, *f;* firmeza, *f*

stave *n* (of a barrel, etc.) duela, *f;* (of a ladder) peldaño, *m;* (stanza) estrofa, *f; mus* pentagrama, *m.* **to s. in,** abrir boquete en; romper a golpes; quebrar. **to s. off,** apartar, alejar; (delay) aplazar, diferir; (avoid) evitar; (thirst, etc.) dominar

stay *vt* detener; (a judgment, etc.) suspender. *vi* permanecer; quedarse; detenerse; (of weather, etc.) durar; (lodge) hospedarse, vivir. **to come to s.,** venir a ser permanente. **to s. a person's hand,** detenerle a fulano el brazo. **to s. at home,** quedarse en casa. **s.-at-home,** *a* casero. *n* persona casera, *f.* **to s. the course,** terminar la carrera. **S.! Say no more!** ¡Calle! ¡No diga más! **to s. away,** ausentarse. **to s. up,** no acostarse; velar. **to s. with,** quedarse con; alojarse con; quedarse en casa de, vivir con

stay *n* estancia, permanencia, *f;* residencia, *f;* (restraint) freno, *m; law* suspensión, *f;* (endurance) aguante, *m;* resistencia, *f; naut* estay, *m;* (prop) puntal, *m; fig* apoyo, soporte, *m; pl* **stays,** corsé, *m*

stead *n* lugar, *m.* **in the s. of,** en el lugar de, como substituto de. **It has stood me in good s.,** Me ha sido muy útil

steadfast *a* fijo; constante; firme; tenaz. **s. gaze,** mirada fija, *f*

steadfastly *adv* fijamente; con constancia; firmemente; tenazmente

steadfastness *n* fijeza, *f;* constancia, *f;* firmeza, *f;* tenacidad, *f*

steadily *adv* firmemente; (without stopping) sin parar; continuamente; (assiduously) diligentemente; (uniformly) uniformemente. **Prices have gone up s.,** Los precios no han dejado de subir. **He looked at it s.,** Lo miraba sin pestañear (or fijamente)

steadiness *n* estabilidad, *f;* firmeza, *f;* constancia, *f;* (of persons) seriedad, formalidad, *f;* (of workers) diligencia, asiduidad, *f*

steady *a* firme; seguro; fijo; constante; uniforme; continuo; estacionario; (of persons) serio, formal, juicioso; (of workers) diligente, asiduo. *vt* afirmar; (persons) hacer más serio (a); (nerves, etc.) calmar, fortificar. **a s. job,** un empleo seguro. **S.!** ¡Calma! *naut* ¡Seguro! **He steadied himself against the table,** Se apoyó en la mesa

steak *n* tajada, *f;* biftec, *m*

steal *vt* robar, hurtar; tomar. *vi* robar, ser ladrón; (glide) deslizarse; (overwhelm) dominar, ganar insensiblemente (a). **to s. a kiss,** robar un beso. **to s. a look at,** mirar de soslayo (or de lado). **to s. away,** escurrirse, escabullirse; marcharse a hurtadillas. **to s. in,** deslizarse en, colarse en

stealthily *adv* a hurtadillas; a escondidas, furtivamente

stealthiness *n* carácter furtivo, *m*

stealthy *a* furtivo; cauteloso

steam *n* vapor, *m. a* de vapor. *vi* echar vapor. *vt cul* cocer al vapor; (clothes) mojar; (windows, etc.) empañar. **to have the s. up,** estar bajo presión. **The windows are steamed,** Los cristales están empañados. **s.-boiler,** caldera de vapor, *f.* **s.-engine,** máquina de vapor, *f.* **s.-hammer,** maza de fragua, *f.* **s.-heat,** calefacción por vapor, *f.* **s.-roller,** *lit* apisonadora, *fig* fuerza arrolladora, *f*

steamboat *n* vapor, *m*

steamer *n cul* marmita al vacío, *f; naut* buque de vapor, *m*

steamship *n* buque de vapor, piróscafo, *m*

steamy *a* lleno de vapor

steed *n* corcel, *m*

steel *n* (metal, and *poet* sword) acero, *m;* (for sharpening) afilón, *m. a* de acero; acerado. *vt* acerar; *fig* endurecer. **to be made of s.,** *fig* ser de bronce. **He cannot s. himself to do it,** No puede persuadirse a hacerlo. **to s. one's heart,** hacerse duro de corazón. **cold s.,** arma blanca, *f.* **stainless s.,** acero inoxidable, *m.* **s.-engraving,** grabado en acero, *m*

steel mill *n* fábrica de acero, *f*

steep *a* acantilado, escarpado; precipitoso; (of stairs, etc.) empinado; (of price) exorbitante. *vt* (soak) remojar, empapar; *fig* absorber; (in a subject) empaparse (en). *n* remojo, *m.* **It's a bit s.!** *inf* ¡Es un poco demasiado!

steeping *n* remojo, *m,* maceración, *f*

steeple *n* campanario, *m*, torre, *f*; aguja, *f*
steeplechase *n* steeplechase, *m*, carrera de obstáculos, *f*
steepness *n* carácter escarpado, *m*, lo precipitoso
steer *vt naut* gobernar; (a car, etc.) conducir; *fig* guiar,
conducir. *vi naut* timonear; *naut* navegar; *aut* conducir.
n zool novillo, *m*. **to s. clear of,** evitar. **to s. one's way
through the crowd,** abrirse paso entre la mu-
chedumbre
steerage *n* gobierno, *m*; (stern) popa, *f*; (quarters) entrepuente, *m*. **to go s.,** viajar en tercera clase
steering *n naut* gobierno, *m*; (tiller, etc.) gobernalle,
timón, *m*; (of a vehicle) conducción, *f*. **s.-column,**
barra de dirección, *f*. **s.-wheel,** *aut* volante de dirección, *m*; *naut* rueda del timón, *f*
stellar *a* estelar
stem *n* (of a tree) tronco, *m*; (of a plant) tallo, *m*; (of a
glass, etc.) pie, *m*; (mus of a note) rabo, *m*; (of a pipe)
tubo, *m*; (of a word) radical, *m*. *vt* (check) contener;
(the tide) ir contra; (the current) vencer; (dam) estancar. **from s. to stern,** de proa a popa
stench *n* tufo, hedor, *m*, hediondez, *f*
stencil *n* patrón para estarcir, *m*; estarcido, *m*. *vt* estarcir
stenographer *n* estenógrafo (-fa), taquígrafo (-fa)
stenography *n* estenografía, taquigrafía, *f*
stentorian *a* estentóreo
step *n* paso, *m*; (footprint) huella, *f*; (measure) medida,
f; (of a stair, etc.) escalón, peldaño, *m*, grada, *f*; (of a
ladder) peldaño, *m*; (of vehicles) estribo, *m*; (grade) escalón, *m*; *mus* intervalo, *m*. **at every s.,** a cada paso.
flight of steps, escalera, *f*; (before a building, etc.) escalinata, *f*. **in steps,** en escalones. **to bend one's
steps towards,** dirigirse hacia. **to keep in s.,** llevar el
paso. **to take a s.,** dar un paso. **to take steps,** tomar
medidas. **s. by s.,** paso a paso; poco a poco. **s.-dance,**
baile típico, *m*. **s.-ladder,** escalera de tijera, *f*
step *vi* dar un paso; pisar; andar. **Please s. in!** Sírvase
de entrar. **Will you s. this way, please?** ¡Haga el
favor de venir por aquí! **to s. aside,** ponerse a un lado;
desviarse; *fig* retirarse (en favor de). **to s. in,** entrar;
intervenir (en); (meddle) entrometerse. **He stepped
into the train,** Subió al tren. **to s. on,** pisar. **to s. on
board,** *naut* ir a bordo. **to s. out,** salir; (from a vehicle)
bajar; (a dance) bailar. **He stepped out a moment
ago,** Salió hace un instante
stepbrother *n* hermanastro, medio hermano, *m*
stepchild *n* hijastro (-ra)
stepdaughter *n* hijastra, *f*
stepfather *n* padrastro, *m*
stepmother *n* madrastra, *f*
steppe *n* estepa, *f*
steppingstone *n* pasadera, *f*; *fig* escabel, escalón, *m*
stepsister *n* hermanastra, media hermana, *f*
stepson *n* hijastro, *m*
stereotype *n* estereotipia, *f*, clisé, *m*, *vt* (*print* and *fig*)
estereotipar
sterile *a* estéril; árido
sterility *n* esterilidad, *f*; aridez, *f*
sterilization *n* esterilización, *f*
sterilize *vt* esterilizar
sterilizer *n* esterilizador, *m*
sterling *a* esterlina *f*; *fig* genuino. **pound s.,** libra esterlina, *f*
stern *a* severo, austero; duro. *n naut* popa, *f*
sternly *adv* con severidad, severamente, duramente
sternness *n* severidad, *f*; dureza, *f*
sternum *n anat* esternón, *m*
stethoscope *n* estetoscopio, *m*
stevedore *n* estibador, *m*
stew *vt* guisar a la cazuela, estofar; (mutton, etc.) hervir;
(fruit) cocer. *n* estofado, *m*; *inf* agitación, *f*. **to be in a
s.,** *inf* sudar la gota gorda. **stewed fruit,** compota de
frutas, *f*. **s.-pot,** cazuela, olla, *f*, puchero, *m*
steward *n* administrador, *m*; mayordomo, *m*; (provision) despensero, *m*; *naut* camarero, *m*
stewardess *n naut* camarera, *f*

stick *vt* clavar (en); hundir (en); (put) poner; sacar;
(stamps, etc.) pegar; fijar; (endure) resistir; tolerar. *vi*
clavarse, hundirse; estar clavado; pegarse; (remain)
quedar; (in the mud, etc.) atascarse, embarrancarse,
(on a reef) encallarse; (in the throat, etc.) atravesarse;
(stop) detenerse. **It sticks in my throat,** *inf* No lo
puedo tragar. **Friends always s. together,** Los
amigos no se abandonan. **The nickname stuck to
him,** El apodo se le quedó. **to s. at,** persistir en; desistir
(ante); pararse (ante); tener escrúpulos sobre. **to s. at
nothing,** no tener escrúpulos. **He stuck at his work,**
Siguió trabajando. **to s. down,** pegar. **to s. out,** *vi*
proyectar; sobresalir. *vt* (one's chest) inflar; (one's
tongue) sacar. **His ears, s. out,** Tiene las orejas sa-
lientes. **to s. to,** (one's job) no dejar; (one's plans)
adherirse (a); (one's principles) ser fiel (a); (one's
friends) no abandonar; (one's word, etc.) cumplir; atenerse a. **to s. up,** *vi* (of hair) erizarse, ponerse de
punta; salirse. *vt* clavar; (a notice) fijar. **to s. up for,** (a
person) defender
stick *n* estaca, *f*; (for the fire) leña, *f*; (walking-s.) bastón, *m*; (of office) vara, *f*; (of sealing-wax, etc.) barra, *f*;
palo, *m*; (baton) batuta, *f*; (of celery) tallo, *m*. **in a cleft
s.,** entre la espada y la pared. **to give** (a person) **the s.,**
dar palo (a)
stickiness *n* viscosidad, *f*
stickingplaster *n* esparadrapo, *m*
stick-in-the-mud *n* chapado a la antigua, *m*
stickler *n* rigorista, *mf*. **to be a s. for etiquette,** ser
etiquetero
sticky *a* pegajoso, viscoso; *fig* difícil
stiff *a* rígido; inflexible; tieso; (of paste) espeso; (of
manner) distante; (of a bow, etc.) frío; (of a person)
almidonado, etiquetero; severo; (of examinations,
etc.) difícil; (strong) fuerte; (of price, etc.) alto, exorbitante; (of a shirt front, etc.) duro. **s. with cold,**
aterido de frío. **s. neck,** torticolis, *m*. **s.-necked,** terco,
obstinaz
stiffen *vt* reforzar; atiesar; (paste, etc.) hacer más espeso; (*fig* strengthen) robustecer; (make more obstinate) hacer más tenaz. *vi* atiesarse; endurecerse;
(straighten oneself) enderezarse; (of manner) volverse
menos cordial; (become firmer) robustecerse; (become
more obstinate) hacerse más tenaz. **The breeze stiffened,** Refrescó el viento
stiffly *adv* tiesamente; rígidamente; obstinadamente
stiffness *n* rigidez, *f*; tiesura, *f*; dureza, *f*; (of manner)
frialdad, *f*; (obstinacy) terquedad, obstinación, *f*; (of an
examination, etc.) dificultad, *f*
stifle *vt* ahogar, sofocar; apagar; suprimir
stifling *a* sofocante, bochornoso
stigma *n* estigma, *m*
stigmatize *vt* estigmatizar
stile *n* (nearest equivalent) portilla con escalones, *f*
stiletto *n* estilete, *m*
still *a* tranquilo; inmóvil; quedo; silencioso; (of wine)
no espumoso. *n* silencio, *m*. **in the s. of the night,** en
el silencio de la noche. **Keep s.!** ¡Estate quieto! **to
keep s.,** quedarse inmóvil, no moverse. **s.-birth,** nacimiento de un niño muerto, *m*. **s.-born,** nacido muerto.
s. life, *art* bodegón, *m*, naturaleza muerta, *f*
still *vt* hacer callar, acallar; calmar, tranquilizar; apaciguar; (pain) aliviar
still *adv* todavía, aún; (nevertheless) sin embargo, no
obstante; (always) siempre. **I think she s. visits them
every week,** Me parece que sigue visitándolos cada
semana. **s. and all,** con todo y eso. **s. more,**
aún más
still *n* alambique, *m*. **salt water s.,** adrazo, *m*
stillness *n* quietud, calma, tranquilidad, *f*; silencio, *m*. **in the s.
of the night,** en el silencio de la noche
stilt *n* zanco, *m*
stilted *a* ampuloso, campanudo, hinchado
stimulant *a* and *n* estimulante, *m*
stimulate *vt* estimular; incitar (a), excitar (a)

stimulating *a* estimulante; (encouraging) alentador; (inspiring) sugestivo, inspirador

stimulation *n* excitación, *f*; (stimulus) estímulo, *m*

stimulus *n* estímulo, *m*; *med* estimulante, *m*; (incentive) impulso, incentivo, *m*; acicate, aguijón, *m*

sting *vt* picar, pinchar; (of snakes, etc.) morder; (of hot dishes) resquemar; (of hail, etc.) azotar; (pain) atormentar; (provoke) provocar (a), incitar (a). *n* (*zool* organ) aguijón, *m*; *bot* púa, *f*; (of a scorpion) uña, *f*; (of a serpent) colmillo, *m*; (pain and wound) pinchazo, *m*; (serpent's) mordedura, *f*; (stimulus) acicate, estímulo, *m*; (torment) tormento, dolor, *m*

stingily *adv* avaramente, tacañamente

stinginess *n* tacañería, avaricia, *f*

stinging *a* picante; *fig* mordaz; (of blows) que duele

stingy *a* tacaño, avaro, mezquino

stink *vi* apestar, heder, oler mal. *n* tufo, *m*, hediondez, *f*

stinking *a* apestoso, hediondo, fétido, mal oliente

stint *vt* escatimar; limitar. *n* límite, *m*, restricción, *f*. **without s.,** sin límite; sin restricción.

stipend *n* estipendio, salario, *m*

stipple *vt art* puntear. *n* punteado, *m*

stipulate *vi* estipular, poner como condición. *vt* estipular, especificar. **They stipulated for a five-day week,** Pusieron como condición (*or* Estipularon) que trabajasen cinco días por semana

stipulation *n* estipulación, *f*; condición, *f*

stir *vt* agitar; revolver; (the fire) atizar; (move) mover; (emotionally) conmover, impresionar; (the imagination) estimular. *vi* moverse. *n* movimiento, *m*; conmoción, *f*; (bustle) bullicio, *m*; sensación, *f*. **to make a s.,** causar una sensación. **to s. one's coffee,** revolver el café. **to s. up discontent,** fomentar el descontento

stirring *a* conmovedor, emocionante, impresionante; (of times, etc.) turbulento, agitado

stirrup *n* estribo, *m*. **s.-cup,** última copa, *f*. **s.-pump,** bomba de mano (para líquidos), *f*

stitch *n* (action) puntada, *f*; (result) punto, *m*; *surg* punto de sutura, *m*; (pain) punzada, *f*, pinchazo, *m*. *vt* coser; *surg* suturar

stoat *n* armiño, *m*; (weasel) comadreja, *f*

stock *n* (of a tree) tronco, *m*; (of a rifle) culata, *f*; (handle) mango, *m*; (of a horse's tail) nabo, *m*; (stem for grafting etc.) injerto, *m*; (race) raza, *f*; (lineage) linaje, *m*, estirpe, *f*; (supply) provisión, *f*; reserva, *f*; (of merchandise) surtido, *m*; *cul* caldo, *m*; (collar) alzacuello, *m*; *bot* alhelí, *m*; (government) papel del estado, *m*, valores públicos, *m pl*; (financial) valores, *m pl*, (of a company) capital, *m*; *pl* **stocks,** *hist* cepo, *m*; (of goods) existencias, *f pl*, stock, *m*, a corriente; del repertorio. **in s. en existencia. lives.,** ganado *m*. **rolling-s.,** *rw* materia móvil ferroviaria, *m*. **s. phrase** frase hecha, *f*. **s. size,** talla corriente, *f*. **to lay in a s. of,** hacer provisión de, almacenar, **to stand s.-still,** quedarse completamente inmóvil. **to take s.,** *com* hacer inventario. **to take s. of,** inventariar; examinar, considerar. **s.-breeder,** ganadero, *m*. **s.-broker,** corredor de bolsa, bolsista, *m*. **s. exchange,** bolsa, *f*. **s.-in-hand,** *com* existencias, *f pl*. **s.-in-trade** (*com* etc.) capital, *m*. **s.-raising,** cría de ganados, ganadería, *f*. **s.-taking,** *com* inventario, *m*

stock *vt* proveer (de), abastecer (de); (of shops) tener existencia de

stockade *n* estacada, empalizada, *f*, *vt* empalizar

stocking *n* media, *f*. **nylon stockings,** medias de cristal (or de nilón), *f pl*

stocky *a* rechoncho, doblado, achaparrado

stodgy *a* (of food) indigesto; (of style, etc.) pesado, amazacotado

stoic *a* and *n* estoico (-ca)

stoical *a* estoico

stoicism *n* estoicismo, *m*

stoke *vt* (a furnace, etc.) cargar, alimentar; (a fire) echar carbón, etc., en. **s.-hole,** cuarto de fogoneros, *m*; *naut* cámara de calderas, *f*

stoker *n* fogonero, *m*; (mechanical) cargador, *m*

stole *n* (*ecc* and of fur, etc.) estola, *f*

stolid *a* impasible, imperturbable

stolidity *n* imperturbabilidad, impasibilidad, *f*

stolidly *adv* imperturbablemente

stomach *n* estómago, vientre, *m*; apetito, estómago, *m*; (courage) corazón, valor, *m*. *vt* digerir; (tolerate) tragar, sufrir. **s.ache,** dolor de estómago, *m*

stone *n* piedra, *f*; (gem) piedra preciosa, *f*; (of cherries, etc.) hueso, *m*; (of grapes, etc.) pepita, *f*; *med* cálculo, *m. a* de piedra. *vt* apedrear; (a wall, etc.) revestir de piedra; (fruit) deshuesar. **to pave with stones,** empedrar. **to leave no s. unturned,** no dejar piedra sin remover. **within a stone's throw,** a corta distancia, a un paso. **S. Age,** edad de piedra, *f*. **s.-breaker,** cantero, picapedrero, *m*. **s.-cold,** muy frío, completamente frío **s.-deaf,** *a* completamente sordo. **s.-fruit,** fruta de hueso, *f*. **s.-mason,** mazonero, albañil, *m*; picapedrero, *m*. **s.-quarry,** pedrera, cantera, *f*

stonily *adv* fríamente; fijamente, sin pestañear

stoniness *n* lo pedregoso; (of hearts, etc.) dureza, *f*; (of stares, etc.) fijeza, inmovilidad, *f*

stoning *n* apedreamiento, *m*, lapidación, *f*

stony *a* pedregoso; (of hearts, etc.) duro, insensible, empedernido; (of a stare, etc.) fijo, duro

stool *n* banquillo, taburete, *m*; (feces) excremento, *m*

stoop *vi* inclinarse, doblarse; encorvarse; ser cargado de espaldas; andar encorvado; (demean oneself) rebajarse (a). *vt* inclinar, doblar. *n* inclinación, *f*; cargazón de espaldas, *f*

stooping *a* inclinado, doblado; (of shoulders) cargado

stop *vt* (a hole) obstruir, atascar; (a leak) cegar, tapar; (a tooth) empastar; (stanch) restañar; (the traffic, etc.) parar; detener; (prevent) evitar; (discontinue) cesar (de), dejarse de; (cut off) cortar; (end) poner fin (a), acabar con; (payment) suspender. *vi* parar; detenerse; cesar; terminar; (stay) quedarse, permanecer. **I stopped myself from saying what I thought,** Me abstuve de decir lo que pensaba, Me mordí la lengua. **They stopped the food-supply,** Cortaron las provisiones. **to s. beating about the bush,** dejarse de historias. **to s. one's ears,** *fig* taparse los oídos. **to s. payments,** suspender pagos

stop *n* parada, *f*; pausa, *f*; interrupción, *f*; cesación, *f*; (of an organ) registro, *m*. **"Stop,"** (road sign) «Alto.» **full s.,** *gram* punto, *m*. **tram s.,** parada de tranvía, *f*. **to come to a full s.,** pararse de golpe; cesar súbitamente. **to put a s. to,** poner fin a, poner coto a, acabar con. *f pl.* **s.-watch,** cronógrafo, *m*

stopgap *n* (person) tapagujeros, *m*; substituto, *m*

stoppage *n* parada, *f*; cesación, *f*; suspensión, *f*; interrupción, *f*; pausa, *f*; (obstruction) impedimento, *m*; obstrucción, *f*. **s. of work,** suspensión de trabajo, *f*

stopper *n* tapón, *m*; obturador, *m*, *vt* cerrar con tapón, taponar

stopping *n* parada, *f*; cesación, *f*; suspensión, *f*; (of a tooth) empaste, *m*. **without s.,** sin parar. **without s. to draw breath,** de un aliento. **s.-place,** paradero, *m*; (of buses, etc.) parada, *f*. **s. train,** tren ómnibus, *m*. **s. up,** obturación, *f*

storage *n* almacenamiento, *m*; (charge) almacenaje, *m*; (place) depósito, *m*. **cold s.,** cámara frigorífica, *f*. **s. battery,** acumulador, *m*

store *n* provisión, *f*; abundancia, *f*; reserva, *f*; (of knowledge, etc.) tesoro, *m*; (for furniture, etc.) depósito, almacén, *m*; *pl* **stores,** (shop) almacenes, *m pl*; (food) provisiones, *f pl*; (mil etc.) pertrechos, *m pl. vt* proveer; guardar, acumular; tener en reserva; (furniture, etc.) almacenar; (hold) caber en, tomar. **in s.,** en reserva; en depósito, en almacén. **to set s. by,** estimar en mucho; dar importancia a. **to set little s. by,** estimar en poco; conceder poca importancia a. **s.-room,** despensa, *f*

storehouse *n* almacén, *m*; *fig* mina, *f*, tesoro, *m*

storied *a* de . . . pisos. **two-s.,** de dos pisos

stork *n* cigüeña, *f*

storm *n* tempestad, tormenta, *f*, temporal, *m*; *fig* tempestad, *f; mil* asalto, *m. vt mil* tomar por asalto, asaltar. *vi* (of persons) bramar de cólera. **to take by s.,** tomar por asalto; *fig* cautivar, conquistar. **s. cloud,** nubarrón, *m.* **s.-signal,** señal de temporal, *f.* **s.-tossed,** *a* sacudido por la tempestad. **s. troops,** tropas de asalto, *f pl.* **s. window,** contravidriera, *f*

stormily *adv* tempestuosamente; con tormenta

storming *n* (*mil* etc.) asalto, *m;* violencia, *f.* **s.-party,** pelotón de asalto, *m*

stormy *a* tempestuoso; de tormenta; (of life, etc.) borrascoso; (of meetings, etc.) tempestuoso

story *n* historia, *f;* cuento, *m;* anécdota, *f;* (funny) chiste, *m;* (plot) argumento, enredo, *m;* (fib) mentira, *f;* (floor) piso *m.* **It's always the same old s.,** Es siempre la misma canción (or historia). **That is quite another s.,** Eso es harina de otro costal. **short s.,** cuento, *m.* **s. book,** libro de cuentos, *m.* **s. teller,** cuentista, *mf;* (fibber) mentiroso (-sa)

stoup *n* copa, *f;* pila de agua bendita, *f*

stout *a* fuerte; (brave) intrépido, indómito; (fat) gordo, grueso; (firm) sólido, firme; (decided) resuelto; vigoroso. *n* (drink) cerveza negra, *f.* **s.-hearted,** valiente, intrépido

stove *n* estufa, *f;* (open, for cooking) cocina económica, *f;* (gas, etc., for cooking) cocina, *f,* fogón, *m.* **s. pipe,** tubo de la chimenea, *m*

stow *vt* meter, poner; colocar; (hide) esconder; (cargo) estibar, arrimar

stowaway *n* polizón, llovido, *m, vi* embarcarse secretamente

straddle *vi* (*nav* etc.) graduar el tiro. *vt* montar a horcajadas en. **s.-legged,** patiabierto

strafe *vt* bombardear concentradamente; castigar; reñir

straggle *vi* rezagarse; vagar en desorden; dispersarse; estar esparcido; extenderse.

straggler *n* rezagado (-da)

straggling *a* disperso; esparcido

straight *a* derecho; recto; (of hair) lacio; directo; (tidy) en orden; (frank) franco; (honest) honrado. *adv* derecho; en línea recta; directamente. **Keep s. on!** ¡Siga Vd. derecho! **to go s. to the point,** dejarse de rodeos, ir al grano. **to look s. in the eyes,** mirar derecho en los ojos. **s. away,** inmediatamente, en seguida. **s. out,** sin rodeos

straighten *vt* enderezar; poner derecho; poner en orden; arreglar. *vi* ponerse derecho; enderezarse. **to s. one's face,** componer el semblante. **to s. the line,** *mil* rectificar el frente. **to s. out,** poner en orden; *fig* desenredar. **to s. oneself up,** erguirse

straightforward *a* honrado, sincero; franco; (simple) sencillo. **s. answer,** respuesta directa, *f*

straightforwardly *adv* honradamente; francamente

straightforwardness *n* honradez, integridad, *f;* franqueza, *f;* (simplicity) sencillez, *f*

straightness *n* derechura, rectitud, *f;* (of persons) honradez, probidad, *f*

straightway *adv* al instante, inmediatamente

strain *vt* estirar; forzar; esforzar; (one's eyes) quebrarse; (one's ears) aguzar (el oído); (a muscle, etc.) torcer; (a friendship) pedir demasiado (a), exigir demasiado (de); (a person's patience, etc.) abusar (de); (words) tergiversar; (embrace) abrazar estrechamente (a); (filter) filtrar; *cul* colar. *vi* hacer un gran esfuerzo, esforzarse (para). *n* tirantez, *f;* tensión, *f;* (effort) esfuerzo, *m;* (sprain) torcedura, *f;* (nervous) tensión nerviosa, *f; mech* esfuerzo, *m;* (breed) raza, *f; biol* cepa, *f;* (tendency) tendencia, *f;* (heredity) herencia, *f;* rasgo, *m,* vena, *f;* (style) estilo, *m; mus* melodía, *f;* (of mirth, etc.) son, ruido, *m;* (poetry) poesía, *f.* **to s. a point,** hacer una excepción. **to s. after effect,** buscar demasiado el efecto

strained *a* tenso; (of muscles, etc.) torcido; (of smiles, etc.) forzado. **s. relations,** *pol* estado de tirantez, *m*

strainer *n* filtro, *m;* coladero, *m*

strait *n geog* estrecho, *m.* **to be in great straits,** estar en un apuro. **s. laced,** *fig* de manga estrecha.

straiten *vt* estrechar; limitar, **in straitened circumstances,** en la necesidad

Strait of Magellan Estrecho de Magallanes, *m*

Straits Settlements Establecimientos del Estrecho, *m pl*

strand *n* (shore) playa, *f;* (of a river) ribera, orilla, *f;* (of rope) cabo, ramal, *m;* (of thread, etc.) hebra, *f;* (of hair) trenza, *f. vt and vi* (a ship) encallar, varar. **to be stranded,** hallarse abandonado; (by missing a train, etc.) quedarse colgado. **to leave stranded,** abandonar, dejar plantado (a)

strange *a* (unknown) desconocido; nuevo; (exotic, etc.) extraño, singular; extraordinario; raro; exótico. **I felt very s. in a s. country,** Me sentía muy solo en un país desconocido. **He is a very s. person,** Es una persona muy rara

strangely *adv* extrañamente, singularmente; de un modo raro

strangeness *n* novedad, *f;* singularidad, *f;* rareza, *f*

stranger *n* desconocido (-da); (from a foreign country) extranjero (-ra); (from another region, etc.) forastero (-ra).

strangle *vt* estrangular; (a sob, etc.) ahogar

stranglehold *n* collar de fuerza, *m.* **to have a s. (on),** tener asido por la garganta; paralizar

strap *n* correa, *f;* tirante de botas, *m, vt* atar con correas

strapping *a* rozagante, robusto

Strasburg Estrasburgo, *m*

stratagem *n* estratagema, *f,* ardid, *m*

strategic *a* estratégico

strategist *n* estratego, *m*

strategy *n* estrategia, *f*

stratification *n* estratificación, *f*

stratosphere *n* estratosfera, *f*

stratum *n geol* estrato, *m,* capa, *f;* (social, etc.) estrato, *m*

straw *n* paja, *f.* **I don't care a s.,** No se me da un bledo. **to be not worth a s.,** no valer un ardite. **to be the last s.,** ser el colmo. **to drink through a s.,** sorber con una paja. **s. hat,** sombrero de paja, *m.* **s.-coloured,** pajizo

strawberry *n* (plant and fruit, especially small or wild) fresa, *f;* (large cultivated) fresón, *m.* **s. bed,** fresal, *m.* **s. ice,** helado de fresa, *m*

stray *vi* errar, vagar; perderse; (from a path, etc., also *fig*) descarriarse. *n* animal perdido, *m;* niño (-ña) sin hogar. *a* descarriado, perdido; errante; (sporadic) esporádico

stray bullet *n* bala perdida, *f*

streak *n* raya, *f;* (in wood and stone) vena, *f;* (of light) rayo, *m;* (of humor, etc.) rasgo, *m. vt* rayar. **like a s. of lightning,** como un relámpago

streaky *a* rayado (-a); (of bacon) entreverado

stream *n* arroyo, riachuelo, *m;* río, *m;* (current) corriente, *f;* (of words, etc.) torrente, *m. vi* correr, fluir; manar, brotar; (float) flotar, ondear. *vt* (blood, etc.) manar, echar. **The tears streamed down Jean's cheeks,** Las lágrimas corrían por las mejillas de Juana. **s.-lined,** fuselado

stream-of-consciousness *n* escritura automática, *f,* fluir de la conciencia, *m,* flujo de la subconciencia, monólogo interior, *m*

streamer *n* gallardete, *m,* serpentina, *f;* (on a hat, etc.) cinta colgante, *f,* siguemepollo, *m*

street *n* calle, *f.* **the man in the s.,** el hombre medio. **at s. level,** a ras de suelo. **s. arab,** golfo, *m.* **s. cries,** gritos de vendedores ambulantes, *m pl.* **s. entertainer,** saltabanco, *m.* **s. brawl, s. fight,** algarada callejera, *f.* **s. fighting,** luchas en las calles, *f pl.* **s. musician,** músico ambulante, *m.* **s.-sweeper,** barrendero, *m.* **s.-walker,** buscona, prostituta, *f*

strength *n* fuerza, *f;* (of colors, etc.) intensidad, *f;* (of character) firmeza (de carácter), *f;* (of will) resolución, decisión, *f; mil* complemento, *m.* **The enemy is in s.,** El enemigo está presente en gran número. **by sheer s.,** a viva fuerza. **on the s. of,** confiando en, en razón de

strengthen *vt* fortificar; consolidar; reforzar. *vi* fortificarse; consolidarse; reforzarse

strengthening *a* fortificante; tonificante. *n* refuerzo, *m*; fortificación, *f*; consolidación, *f*

strenuous *a* activo, enérgico; vigoroso; (arduous) arduo

strenuously *adv* enérgicamente, vigorosamente

strenuousness *n* energía, *f*; vigor, *m*; (arduousness) arduidad, *f*

streptococcus *n med* estreptococo, *m*

streptomycine *n med* estreptomicina, *f*

stress *n* tensión, *f*; impulso, *m*; importancia, *f*, énfasis, *m*; *gram* acento (tónico), *m*; acentuación, *f*; *mech* esfuerzo, *m*. *vt* acentuar; poner énfasis en, insistir en. **under s. of circumstance,** impulsado por las circunstancias. **times of s.,** tiempos turbulentos, *m pl*. **to lay great s. on,** insistir mucho en; dar gran importancia a

stretch *vt* (make bigger) ensanchar; (pull) estirar; (one's hand, etc.) alargar, extender; (knock down) tumbar. *vi* ensancharse; dar de sí; ceder; extenderse. **to s. oneself,** estirarse, desperezarse. **to s. as far as,** llegar hasta, extenderse hasta. **to s. a point,** hacer una concesión. **to s. one's legs,** estirar las piernas

stretch *n* estirón, *m*; tensión, *f*; (of country, etc.) extensión, *f*; (scope) alcance, *m*. **by a s. of the imagination,** con un esfuerzo de imaginación. **He can sleep for hours at a s.,** Puede dormir durante horas enteras

stretcher *n* (for gloves) ensanchador, *m*; dilatador, *m*; (for canvas) bastidor, *m*; (for wounded, etc.) camilla, *f*.

s.-bearer, camillero, *m*

strew *vt* esparcir; derramar

stricken *a* (wounded) herido; (ill) enfermo; (with grief) afligido, agobiado de dolor. **s. in years,** entrado en años

strict *a* exacto; estricto; escrupuloso; severo

strictly *adv* exactamente; estrictamente; severamente, con severidad. **s. speaking,** en rigor, en realidad

strictness *n* exactitud, *f*; escrupulosidad, *f*; rigor, *m*; severidad, *f*

stricture *n fig* crítica severa, censura, *f*. **to pass strictures on,** criticar severamente

stride *vi* andar a pasos largos, dar zancadas; cruzar a grandes trancos. *vt* cruzar de un tranco; poner una pierna en cada lado de. *n* zancada, *f*, paso largo, tranco, *m*. **to s. up and down,** dar zancadas

strident *a* estridente; (of colors) chillón

strife *n* lucha, *f*, conflicto, *m*

strike *vt* golpear; pegar, dar una bofetada (a); (wound) herir; (a coin) acuñar; (a light) encender; (of a snake) morder; (a blow) asestar, dar; (of ships, a rock, etc.) chocar contra; estrellarse contra; (flags) bajar, arriar; (a tent) desmontar; (camp) levantar; (come upon) llegar a; (discover) encontrar por casualidad, tropezar con; hallar, descubrir; (seem) parecer; (impress) impresionar; (of ideas) ocurrirse; (an attitude) tomar, adoptar; llegar a; (level) nivelar; (cuttings) enraizar. *vi* golpear; (of a clock) dar la hora; (of a ship) encallar; (go) ir; (penetrate) penetrar; (of a cutting) arraigar; (sound) sonar. **He struck the table with his fist,** Golpeó la mesa con el puño. **I was very much struck by the city's beauty,** La belleza de la ciudad me impresionó mucho. **The news struck fear into their hearts,** La noticia les llenó el corazón de miedo. **The clock struck three,** El reloj dio las tres. **The hour has struck,** *fig* Ha llegado la hora. **How did the house s. you?** ¿Qué te pareció la casa? **to s. a bargain,** cerrar un trato. **to s. a blow,** asestar un golpe. **to s. across country,** ir a campo traviesa. **to s. an attitude,** tomar una actitud. **to s. home,** dar en el blanco; herir; herir en lo más vivo; hacerse sentir. **to s. at,** asestar un golpe (a); acometer, embestir; atacar. **to s. down,** derribar; (of illness) acometer. **to s. off,** (a head, etc.) cortar; (a name) borrar, tachar; (print) imprimir. **to s. out,** *vi* asestar un golpe (a); (of a swimmer) nadar; echarse, lanzarse. *vt* (a word, etc.) borrar, rayar; (begin) iniciar.

to s. through, (cross out) rayar, tachar; (of the sun's rays, etc.) penetrar. **to s. up,** *vt* tocar; empezar a cantar; (a friendship) trabar. *vi* empezar a tocar. **to s. up a march,** *mil* batir la marcha

strike *n* huelga, *f*. *vi* declararse en huelga. **go-slow s.,** tortuguismo, *m*. **lock-out s.,** huelga patronal, *f*. **sit-down s.,** huelga de brazos caídos, *f*. **to go on s.,** declararse en huelga. **s.-breaker,** esquirol, *m*. **s.-pay,** subsidio de huelga, *m*

striker *n* huelguista, *mf*

striking *a* notable, sorprendente; (impressive) impresionante; que llama la atención; llamativo

string *n* bramante, *m*; cuerda, *f*; (ribbon) cinta, *f*; (of beads, etc.) sarta, *f*; (of onions) ristra, *f*; (of horses, etc.) reata, *f*; hilera, *f*; (of a bridge) cable, *m*; (of oaths, lies) sarta, serie, *f*; (of beans) fibra, *f*. *vt* encordar; (beads, etc.) ensartar; (beans) quitar las fibras (de). **He is all strung up,** Se le crispan los nervios. **the strings,** los instrumentos de cuerda. **a s. of pearls,** un collar de perlas. **for strings,** *mus* para arco. **to pull strings,** *fig* manejar los hilos. **to s. up,** (an instrument) templar; (a person) pender, ahorcar. **s. bean,** judía verde, *f*

stringed *a* (of musical instruments) de cuerda. **s. instrument,** instrumento de cuerda, *m*

stringency *n* severidad, *f*; estrechez, *f*

stringent *a* estricto, severo

stringy *a* fibroso; filamentoso; correoso; arrugado

strip *vt* desnudar; despojar (de), quitar; robar; (a cow) ordeñar hasta agotar la leche. *vi* desnudarse. *n* (tatter) jirón, *m*; tira, lista, *f*; (of wood) listón, *m*; (of earth) pedazo, *m*; (*geog* of land) zona, *f*. **to s. off,** *vt* quitar; (bark from a tree) descortezar; (one's clothes) despojarse de. *vi* desprenderse, separarse

stripe *n* raya, lista, *f*; (*mil* etc.) galón, *m*; (lash) azote, *m*. *vt* rayar. **the stripes of the tiger,** las rayas del tigre

striped *a* listado, a rayas; con rayas. **s. trousers,** pantalón de corte, *m*

stripling *n* joven imberbe, pollo, mancebo, *m*

strive *vi* esforzarse (a); pugnar (por, para); trabajar (por); (fight against) luchar contra; pelear con. **He was striving to understand,** Pugnaba por (or Se esforzaba a) comprender

stroke *n* (blow) golpe, *m*; (of the oars) golpe del remo, *m*, remada, *f*; (at billards) tacada, *f*; (in golf) tirada, *f*; (in swimming) braza, *f*; (of a clock) campanada, *f*; (of a pen) rasgo de la pluma, *m*; (of a brush) pincelada, *f*; *mech* golpe de émbolo, *m*; (caress) caricia con la mano, *f*. *vt* acariciar con la mano. **on the s. of six,** al acabar de dar las seis. **to have a s.,** tener un ataque de apoplejía. **s. of genius,** rasgo de ingenio, *m*. **s. of good luck,** racha de buena suerte, *f*

stroll *vi* pasearse, vagar. *n* vuelta, *f*, paseo, *m*. **to go for a s.,** dar una vuelta

stroller *n* paseante, *mf*

strolling *a* errante; ambulante. **s. player,** *n* cómico (-ca) ambulante

strong *a* fuerte; vigoroso; robusto; enérgico; firme; poderoso; (of colours) intenso, vivo; (of tea, coffee) cargado; *gram* fuerte. **The government took s. measures,** El gobierno tomó medidas enérgicas. **They gave very s. reasons,** Alegaron unas razones muy poderosas. **Grammar is not his s. point,** La gramática no es su punto fuerte. **The enemy is s. in numbers,** El enemigo es numéricamente fuerte. **The society is four thousand s.,** La sociedad tiene cuatro mil miembros. **s. box,** caja de caudales, *f*. **s. man,** hombre fuerte, *m*; (in a circus) hércules, *m*. **s.-minded,** de espíritu fuerte; independiente. **s. room,** cámara acorazada, *f*

stronghold *n* fortaleza, *f*; refugio, *m*

strongly *adv* vigorosamente; fuertemente; firmemente

strop *n* (razor) suavizador, *m*, *vt* suavizar

strophe *n* estrofa, *f*

structural *a* estructural

structurally *adv* estructuralmente, desde el punto de vista de la estructura

structure *n* estructura, *f*; edificio, *m*; construcción, *f*
struggle *vi* luchar; pelear; disputarse. *n* lucha, *f*; combate, *m*; conflicto, *m*. **to s. to one's feet,** luchar por levantarse. **without a s.,** sin luchar
struggling *a* pobre, indigente, que lucha para vivir
strum *vt* (a stringed instrument) rascar; tocar mal
strumpet *n* ramera, *f*
strut *vi* pavonearse. *vt* (prop) apuntalar. *n* pavonada, *f*; (prop) puntal, *m*. **to s. out,** salir de un paso majestuoso
strychnine *n* estricnina, *f*
stub *n* (of a tree) tocón, *m*; (of a pencil, candle, etc.) cabo, *m*; pedazo, fragmento, *m*; (of a cigarette or cigar) colilla, *f*. **s.-book,** talonario, *m*
stubble *n* rastrojo, *m*; (beard) barba de tres días, *f*
stubborn *a* inquebrantable, tenaz; persistente; (pigheaded) terco, testarudo
stubbornness *n* tenacidad, *f*; terquedad, testarudez, *f*
stucco *n* estuco, *m*, *vt* estucar
stud *n* (of horses) caballeriza, *f*; (nail) tachón, *m*; (for collars) pasador para camisas, *m*. *vt* tachonar; sembrar. **dress s.,** botón de la pechera, *m*. **s.-farm,** potrero, *m*
student *n* estudiante, *mf*. *a* estudiantil
studied *a* estudiado; calculado; (of style) cerebral, reflexivo; (intentional) deliberado
studio *n* estudio, *m*. **broadcasting s.,** estudio de emisión, *m*
studious *a* estudioso, aplicado; (deliberate) intencional, deliberate; (eager) solícito, ansioso
studiously *adv* estudiosamente; con intención, deliberadamente; solícitamente
study *n* estudio, *m*; solicitud, *f*, cuidado, *m*; investigación, *f*; (room) gabinete, cuarto de trabajo, *m*. *vt* ocuparse de, cuidar de, atender a; considerar; estudiar; examinar; (the stars) observar; (try) procurar. *vi* estudiar. **in a brown s.,** en Babia. **to make a s. of,** hacer un estudio de, estudiar. **to s. for an examination,** prepararse para un examen
stuff *n* substancia, materia, *f*; (fabric) tela, *f*, paño, *m*; (rubbish) cachivaches, *m pl*, cosas, *f pl*. *a* de estofa. *vt* henchir; llenar; *cul* rellenar; (with food) ahitar (de); (cram) atestar, apretar; (furniture) rehenchir; (an animal, bird) disecar; (put) meter, poner. **S. and nonsense!** ¡Patrañas! **to be poor s.,** ser de pacotilla; no valer para nada
stuffed animal *n* animal disecado, *m*
stuffiness *n* mala ventilación, *f*; falta de aire, *f*; calor, *m*
stuffing *n* (of furniture) rehenchimiento, *m*; *cul* relleno, *m*
stuffy *a* mal ventilado, poco aireado, ahogado
stultify *vt* hacer inútil; invalidar; hacer ridiculo
stumble *vi* tropezar; dar un traspié; (in speaking) tartamudear. *n* tropezón, *m*; traspié, *m*. **to s. through a speech,** pronunciar un discurso a tropezones. **to s. against,** tropezar contra. **to s. upon, across,** tropezar con; encontrar por casualidad
stumblingblock *n* tropiezo, impedimento, *m*
stump *n* (of a tree) tocón, *m*; (of an arm, leg) muñón, *m*; (of a pencil, candle) cabo, *m*; (of a tooth) raigón, *m*; (of a cigar) colilla, *f*; (cricket) poste, montante, *m*; *art* esfumino, *m*; (leg) pata, *f*. *vt* (disconcert) desconcertar; *art* esfumar; recorrer. **to s. up,** *inf* pagar
stun *vt* dejar sin sentido (a); aturdir de un golpe (a); (astound) pasmar
stunning *a* aturdidor; que pasma; *inf* estupendo
stunt *vt* impedir el crecimiento de; encanijar. *n* (advertising) anuncio de reclamo, *m*; recurso (para conseguir algo), *m*; proeza, *f*
stunted *a* (of trees, etc.) enano; (of children) encanijado; (of intelligence) inmaduro
stupefaction *n* estupefacción, *f*; estupor, *m*
stupefy *vt* atontar, embrutecer; causar estupor (a), asombrar
stupendous *a* asombroso; enorme
stupid *a* (with sleep, etc.) atontado; (silly) estúpido, tonto. *n* tonto (-ta)
stupidity *n* estupidez, *f*; tontería, *f*

stupor *n* estupor, *m*
sturdiness *n* robustez, *f*, vigor, *m*; firmeza, tenacidad, *f*
sturdy *a* robusto, vigoroso, fuerte; firme, tenaz
sturgeon *n* *icht* esturión, *m*
stutter *vi* tartamudear. *vt* balbucir. *n* tartamudeo, *m*
stutterer *n* tartamudo (-da)
stuttering *a* tartamudo; balbuciente. *n* tartamudeo, *m*
sty *n* (pig) pocilga, *f*; *med* orzuelo, *m*
Stygian *a* estigio
style *n* (for etching) buril, *m*; (lit, art, arch, etc.) estilo, *m*; (fashion) moda, *f*; (model) modelo, *m*; (behavior, etc.) tono, *m*; elegancia, *f*; (kind) especie, clase, *f*; (designation) tratamiento, *m*; *vt* llamar, nombrar. **the latest styles from Madrid,** los últimos modelos de Madrid. **He has a very individual s.,** Su estilo es muy personal. **They live in great s.,** Viven en gran lujo
stylet *n* estilete, *m*
stylish *a* elegante
stylishness *n* elegancia, *f*
stylist *n* estilista, *mf*
stylize *vt* estilizar
suasion *n* persuasión, *f*
suasive *a* suasorio, persuasivo
suave *a* afable, cortés, urbano; (of wine) suave
suavity *n* afabilidad, urbanidad, *f*
subaltern *n* *mil* subalterno, *m*, *a* subalterno, subordinado
subcommittee *n* subcomisión, *f*
subconscious *a* subconsciente. **the s.,** la subconsciencia
subconsciously *adv* subconscientemente
subcutaneous *a* subcutáneo
subdivide *vt* subdividir. *vi* subdividirse
subdivision *n* subdivisión, *f*
subdominant *n* *mus* subdominante, *f*
subdue *vt* subyugar, sojuzgar, vencer; (one's passions) dominar; (colors, voices) suavizar; (lessen) mitigar; apagar
subdued *a* (of colors) apagado; (of persons) sumiso; (depressed) deprimido, melancólico. **in a s. voice,** en voz baja
subheading *n* subtítulo, *m*
subhuman *a* subhumano
subject *a* sujeto; sometido (a); expuesto (a). *n* (of a country) súbdito (-ta); sujeto, *m*; (of study) asignatura, materia, *f*; (theme) tema, *m*; (gram, phil) sujeto, *m*. *vt* subyugar; someter. **It can only be done s. to his consent,** Podrá hacerse únicamente si él lo consiente. **He is a British s.,** Es súbdito británico. **to change the s.,** cambiar de conversación. **to s. to criticism,** criticar (a). **s.-matter,** materia, *f*; (of a letter) contenido, *m*
subjection *n* sujeción, *f*; sometimiento, *m*. **He was in a state of complete s.,** Estaba completamente sumiso. **to bring into s.,** subyugar
subjective *a* subjetivo
subjectiveness *n* subjetividad, *f*
subjectivism *n* subjetivismo, *m*
subjoin *vt* añadir, adjuntar
subjugate *vt* subyugar, someter
subjugation *n* subyugación, *f*
subjunctive *a* and *n* subjuntivo, *m*
sublet *vt* subarrendar. *n* subarriendo, *m*
sublimate *vt* sublimar. *n* sublimado, *m*
sublimation *n* sublimación, *f*
sublime *a* sublime; absoluto, completo; extremo. **the s.,** lo sublime
sublimely *adv* sublimemente; completamente
submachine gun *n* pistola ametralladora, metralleta, *f*, subfusil ametrallador, *m*
submarine *a* submarino. *n* submarino, *m*. **midget s.,** submarino enano, submarino de bolsillo, *m*. **s. chaser,** cazasubmarino, *m*
submerge *vt* sumergir; inundar. *vi* sumergirse. **The submarine submerged,** El submarino se sumergió
submergence *n* sumergimiento, *m*, sumersión, *f*; hundimiento, *m*

submersible *a* sumergible
submersion *n* sumersión, *f;* hundimiento, *m*
submission *n* sometimiento, *m;* sumisión, resignación, *f;* docilidad, *f*
submissive *a* sumiso, dócil, manso
submissively *adv* sumisamente, con docilidad
submissiveness *n* sumisión, docilidad, *f*
submit *vt* someterse (a); doblarse ante; (a scheme, etc.) someter; presentar; (urge) proponer. *vi* someterse; resignarse; (surrender) rendirse, entregarse. **to s. to arbitration,** someter a arbitraje
subnormal *a* anormal
subordinate *a* subordinado; subalterno, inferior; secundario. *n* subordinado (-da). *vt* subordinar
subordination *n* subordinación, *f*
suborn *vt* sobornar, cohechar
subpena *n* citación, *f, vt* citar
subplot *n* intriga secundaria, trama secundaria, *f*
subscribe *vt* and *vi* subscribir; (to a periodical, etc.) abonarse (a)
subscriber *n* subscriptor (-ra); abonado (-da)
subscription *n* subscripción, *f;* (to a periodical, series of concerts, etc.) abono, *m;* (to a club) cuota, *f*
subsection *n* subsección, *f*
subsequent *a* subsiguiente, subsecuente; posterior. **s. to,** después de, posterior a. **s. upon,** de resultas de
subsequently *adv* más tarde; subsiguientemente; posteriormente
subservience *n* servilidad, *f;* utilidad, *f*
subservient *a* servil; subordinado; útil
subside *vi* (of water) bajar; (of ground) hundirse; (of foundations) asentarse; disminuir; calmarse; (be quiet) callarse. **to s. into a chair,** dejarse caer en un sillón
subsidence *n* hundimiento, *m;* desplome, derrumbamiento, *m;* (of floods) bajada, *f;* (of anger, etc.) apaciguamiento, *m*
subsidiary *a* subsidiario
subsidize *vt* subvencionar
subsidy *n* subvención, *f,* subsidio, *m;* prima, *f*
subsist *vi* subsistir
subsistence *n* subsistencia, *f*
subsoil *n* subsuelo, *m*
substance *n* substancia, *f*
substantial *a* substancial; sólido; importante
substantially *adv* substancialmente; sólidamente
substantiate *vt* establecer, verificar; justificar
substantiation *n* comprobación, verificación, *f;* justificación, *f*
substantive *a* real, independiente; *gram* substantivo. *n gram* substantivo, *m*
substitute *n* substituto (-ta); (material) substituto, *m. vt* substituir, reemplazar. **to be a s. for,** hacer las veces de
substitution *n* substitución, *f,* reemplazo, *m*
substratum *n* substrato, *m*
subterfuge *n* subterfugio, *m;* evasiva, *f*
subterranean *a* subterráneo
subtitle *n* subtítulo, *m;* (on films) guión, *m*
subtle *a* sutil; delicado; penetrante; (crafty) astuto
subtlety *n* sutileza, *f;* delicadeza, *f;* (craftiness) astucia, *f*
subtly *adv* sutilmente; con delicadeza
subtract *vt* restar, substraer
subtraction *n* resta, substracción, *f*
suburb *n* suburbio, *m;* pl **suburbs,** las afueras, *f pl* los arrabales, *m pl*
suburban *a* suburbano
subvention *n* subvención, *f*
subversion *n* subversión, *f*
subversive *a* subversivo
subvert *vt* subvertir
subway *n* (passageway) pasaje subterráneo, *m;* (underground railway) metro (Spain, Puerto Rico), subte (Argentina), *m*
succeed *vt* seguir (a); suceder (a); heredar. *vi* seguir (a); suceder (a); (be successful) tener éxito. **I did not s. in**

doing it, No logré hacerlo. **to s. to the throne,** subir al trono
succeeding *a* subsiguiente; futuro; consecutivo; sucesivo
success *n* éxito, *m;* triunfo, *m.* **to be a s.,** tener éxito. **The film was a great s.,** La película tuvo mucho éxito
successful *a* que tiene éxito; afortunado, venturoso; próspero.
successfully *adv* con éxito; prósperamente
succession *n* sucesión, *f;* (series) serie, *f;* (inheritance) herencia, *f;* (descendants) descendencia, *f.* **in s.,** sucesivamente
successive *a* sucesivo
successor *n* sucesor (-ra)
succinct *a* sucinto, conciso
succinctly *adv* sucintamente, brevemente, en pocas palabras
succor *vt* socorrer, auxiliar. *n* socorro, *m,* ayuda, *f*
succulence *n* suculencia, *f*
succulent *a* suculento
succumb *vi* sucumbir; someterse, ceder
such *a* tal; parecido, semejante; así; tanto; (before an adjective, adverb) tan. *n* el, *m,* (*f,* la) que, los, *m pl,* (*f pl,* las) que; tal. **s. men,** tales hombres. **I have never seen s. magnificence,** Nunca no he visto tanta magnificencia. **s. an important man,** un hombre tan importante. **s. pictures as these,** cuadros como estos. **S. is life!** ¡Así es la vida! **science as s.,** la ciencia como tal. **s.-and-s.,** tal y tal
suchlike *a* parecido, semejante; de esta clase
suck *vt* chupar; (the breast) mamar; sorber; (of a vacuum cleaner, etc.) aspirar. *n* chupada, *f;* succión, *f.* **to s. down,** tragar. **to s. up,** aspirar; absorber
sucker *n zool* ventosa, *f; bot* acodo, mugrón, *m;* (greenhorn) primo, *m;* (pig) lechón, *m*
suckingpig *n* lechón, cochinillo, *m*
suckle *vt* amamantar, dar el pecho (a)
suction *n* succión, *f;* aspiración, *f.* **s.-pump,** bomba aspirante, *f*
Sudan, the el Sudán, *m*
Sudanese *a* and *n* sudanés (-esa)
sudden *a* súbito; (unexpected) inesperado, impensado; (of bends) brusco. **all of a s.,** de repente; súbitamente
suddenly *adv* súbitamente; de pronto, de repente
suddenness *n* carácter repentino, *m;* (of a bend, etc.) brusquedad, *f*
suds *n pl* jabonaduras, *f pl;* espuma, *f*
sue *vt law* proceder contra, pedir en juicio; *law* demandar; (beg) suplicar. **to sue for peace,** pedir la paz
suede *n* ante, *m.* **s. glove,** guante de ante, *f*
suet *n* sebo, *m*
Suez Canal, the el Istmo de Suez, *m*
suffer *vt* sufrir, padecer; pasar, experimentar; (tolerate) tolerar, sufrir; (allow) permitir. *vi* sufrir. **She suffers from her environment,** es la víctima de su medio ambiente
sufferance *n* tolerancia, *f.* **on s.,** por tolerancia
sufferer *n* enfermo (-ma); víctima, *f*
suffering *n* sufrimiento, padecimiento, *m;* dolor, *m. a* sufriente
suffice *vi* ser suficiente, bastar. *vt* satisfacer
sufficiency *n* suficiencia, *f;* (of money) subsistencia, *f*
sufficient *a* suficiente, bastante. **to be s.,** bastar, ser suficiente
sufficiently *adv* suficientemente, bastante
suffix *n gram* sufijo, *m*
suffocate *vt* ahogar, sofocar, asfixiar. *vi* sofocarse, asfixiarse
suffocating *a* sofocante, asfixiante
suffocation *n* sofocación, asfixia, *f;* ahogo, *m*
suffrage *n* sufragio, *m;* voto, *m.* **universal s.,** sufragio universal, *m*
suffragette *n* sufragista, *f*
suffuse *vt* bañar, inundar, cubrir
sugar *n* azúcar, *m. vt* azucarar. **brown s.,** azúcar moreno, *m.* **loaf s.,** azúcar de pilón, *m.* **white s.,** azú-

car blanco, *m*. **to s. the pill,** dorar la píldora. **s.-almond,** peladilla, *f*. **s.-basin,** azucarera, *f*. **s.-beet,** remolacha, *f*. **s.-candy,** azúcar candi, *m*. **s.-cane,** caña de azúcar, *f*. **s.-cane syrup,** miel de caña, *f*. **s.-paste,** alfeñique, *m*, alcorza, *f*. **s.-refinery,** fábrica de azúcar, *f*. **s.-tongs,** tenacillas para azúcar, *f pl*
sugary *a* azucarado; *fig* meloso, almibarado
suggest *vt* implicar; indicar, dar a entender; sugerir; (advise) aconsejar; (hint) insinuar; (evoke) evocar. **I suggested they should go to London,** Les aconsejé que fueran a Londres. **An idea suggested itself to him,** Se le ocurrió una idea
suggestion *n* sugestión, *f*; insinuación, *f*
suggestive *a* sugestivo; estimulante
suicidal *a* suicida. **s. tendency,** tendencia suicida, tendencia al suicidio, *f*
suicide *n* (act) suicidio, *m*; (person) suicida, *mf*. **to commit s.,** darse la muerte, quitarse la vida suicidarse
suit *n* (request) petición, súplica, *f*; oferta de matrimonio, *f*; *law* pleito, *m*; (of clothes) traje, *m*; (cards) palo, *m*; (of cards held) serie, *f*, *vt* convenir; sentar; ir bien (a); venir bien (a); (adapt) adaptar. **S. yourself!** ¡Haz lo que quieras! **The arrangement suits me very well,** El arreglo me viene muy bien. **The climate doesn't s. me,** El clima no me sienta bien. **The color does not s. you,** El color no te va bien. **to follow s.,** seguir el ejemplo (de); (cards) jugar el mismo palo. **s.-case,** maleta, *f*
suitability *n* conveniencia, *f*; aptitud, *f*
suitable *a* conveniente; apropiado; apto; a propósito. **Not s. for children,** No apto para menores. **to make s. for,** adaptar a las necesidades de
suitably *adv* convenientemente; apropiadamente
suite *n* (of retainers, etc.) séquito, acompañamiento, *m*; (of furniture, etc.) juego, *m*; *mus* suite, *f*. **private s.,** habitaciones particulares, *f pl*. **s. of rooms,** apartamiento, *m*
suitor *n law* demandante, *m*; pretendiente, *m*
sulk *vi* ponerse malhumorado, ser mohíno
sulkiness *n* mohína, *f*, mal humor, *m*
sulky *a* mohíno, malhumorado
sullen *a* taciturno, hosco; malhumorado, sombrío; (of a landscape, etc.) triste, sombrío
sullenly *adv* taciturnamente, hoscamente
sullenness *n* taciturnidad, hosquedad, *f*, mal humor, *m*
sully *vt* desdorar, empañar; manchar
sulphur *n* azufre, *m*
sulphuric *a* sulfúrico
sulphurous *a* sulfuroso
sultan *n* sultán, *m*
sultriness *n* bochorno, calor sofocante, *m*
sultry *a* bochornoso, sofocante
sum *n* suma, *f*; total, *m*; cantidad, *f*; (in arithmetic) problema (de aritmética), *m*. *vt* sumar, calcular. **in sum,** en suma; en resumen. **to sum up,** recapitular; resumir; (a person) tomar las medidas (a)
summarily *adv* someramente; *law* sumariamente
summarize *vt* resumir brevemente; compendiar
summary *a* somero; *law* sumario. *n* resumen, sumario, compendio, *m*. **summary records,** actas resumidas, *f pl*
summer *n* verano, estío, *m*. **to spend the s.,** veranear. **s.-house,** cenador, *m*. **s.-time,** verano, *m*; hora de verano, *f*. **s. wheat,** trigo tremesino, *m*
summing-up *n* recapitulación, *f*
summit *n* cima, cumbre, *f*; *fig* apogeo, *m*
summitry *n* diplomacia en la cumbre, *f*
summon *vt* llamar, hacer venir; mandar, requerir; *law* citar. **to s. up one's courage,** cobrar ánimos
summons *n* llamamiento, *m*; *mil* intimación, *f*; *law* citación, *f*. *vt law* citar
sump *n* (of a motor-car) pozo colector, *m*; *min* sumidero, *m*
sumptuous *a* suntuoso, lujoso, magnífico
sumptuousness *n* suntuosidad, magnificencia, *f*
sun *n* sol, *m*. **The sun was shining,** Hacía sol, El sol

brillaba. **to bask in the sun,** tomar el sol. **sun-bathing,** baños de sol, *m pl*. **sun-blind,** toldo para el sol, *m*. **sun-bonnet,** capelina, *f*. **sun-glasses,** gafas ahumadas, *f pl*. **sun-helmet,** casco colonial, *m*. **sun-spot,** *ast* mancha del sol, *f*; (freckle) peca, *f*. **sun-worship,** adoración del sol, *f*
sunbeam *n* rayo de sol, *m*
sunburn *n* quemadura del sol, *f*; bronceado, *m*
sunburnt *a* quemado por el sol; bronceado, tostado por el sol
sundae *n* helado de frutas, *m*
Sunday *n* domingo, *m*. **in his S. best,** en su traje dominguero, endomingado. **S. school,** escuela dominical, *f*
Sunday's child *n* niño nacido de pies, niño nacido un domingo, niño mimado de la fortuna
sunder *vt* dividir en dos, hender; separar
sundial *n* reloj de sol, reloj solar, *m*
sundown *n* puesta del sol, *f*
sundry *a* varios (-as). *n pl* **sundries,** artículos diversos, *m pl*; *com* varios, *m pl*. **all and s.,** todo el mundo, todos y cada uno
sunflower *n* girasol, tornasol, *m*, trompeta de amor, *f*
sunken *a* (of eyes, etc.) hundido
sun letter *n* letra solar, *f*
sunless *a* sin sol
sunlight *n* luz del sol, *f*, rayos del sol, *m pl*. **artificial s.,** sol artificial, *m*. **in the s.,** al sol
sunny *a* de sol; bañado de sol; asoleado; expuesto al sol; (face) risueño; (of disposition, etc.) alegre. **to be s.,** hacer sol
sunrise *n* salida del sol, *f*. **from s. to sunset,** de sol a sol
sunset *n* puesta del sol, *f*. **at s.,** a la caída (or puesta) del sol
sunshade *n* parasol, quitasol, *m*, sombrilla, *f*
sunshine *n* luz del sol, *f*. **in the s.,** al sol
sunstroke *n* insolación, *f*
sup *vt* sorber. *vi* cenar. *n* sorbo, *m*
super *n* (actor) comparsa, *mf*; (film) superproducción, *f*; (of a beehive) alza, *f*
superabundance *n* superabundancia, sobreabundancia, *f*
superabundant *a* superabundante, sobreabundante. **to be s.,** sobreabundar
superannuate *vt* (retire) jubilar
superannuated *a* (retired) jubilado; (out-of-date) anticuado
superannuation *n* (retirement and pension) jubilación, *f*
superb *a* magnífico, espléndido
superbly *adv* magníficamente
supercargo *n naut* sobrecargo, *m*
supercharger *n* (aut, aer) compresor, *m*
supercilious *a* altanero, altivo, orgulloso; desdeñoso
superciliousness *n* altanería, altivez, *f*, orgullo, *m*; desdén, *m*
superficial *a* superficial
superficiality *n* superficialidad, *f*
superficially *adv* superficialmente
superfine *a* superfino
superfluity *n* superfluidad, *f*
superfluous *a* superfluo. **to be s.,** sobrar
superfortress *n aer* superfortaleza volante, *f*
superhuman *a* sobrehumano
superimpose *vt* sobreponer
superintend *vt* superintender, dirigir
superintendent *n* superintendente, *mf*; director (-ra); (school) inspector; (police) subjefe de la policía, *m*
superior *a* superior; (in number) mayor; (smug) desdeñoso. *n* superior (-ra). **Mother S.,** (madre) superiora, *f*. **s. to,** superior a; encima de
superiority *n* superioridad, *f*
superlative *a* extremo, supremo; *gram* superlativo. *n gram* superlativo, *m*
superlatively *adv* en sumo grado, superlativamente
superman *n* superhombre, *m*

supernatural *a* sobrenatural
supernumerary *a* and *n* supernumerario (-ia)
superposition *n* superposición, *f*
superscribe *vt* sobrescribir; poner el sobrescrito (a)
superscription *n* (on letters, documents) sobrescrito, *m*; leyenda, *f*
supersede *vt* reemplazar; suplantar
supersensible *a* suprasensible
superstition *n* superstición, *f*
superstitious *a* supersticioso
supertax *n* impuesto suplementario, *m*
supervene *vi* sobrevenir
supervise *vt* superentender, vigilar; dirigir
supervision *n* superintendencia, *f*; dirección, *f*
supervisor *n* superintendente, *mf*; inspector (-ra); director (-ra)
supine *a* supino; indolente, negligente. *n gram* supino, *m*
supper *n* cena, *f*. **the Last S.**, la Última Cena. **to have s.**, cenar. **s.-time**, hora de cenar, *f*
supplant *vt* suplantar; usurpar; reemplazar
supplanter *n* suplantador (-ra)
supple *a* flexible; dócil, manso; (fawning) adulador, servil, lisonjero
supplement *n* suplemento, *m*; (of a book) apéndice, *m*
supplementary *a* suplementario; adicional
suppleness *n* flexibilidad, *f*; docilidad, *f*; servilidad, *f*
suppliant *a* and *n* suplicante, *mf*
supplicate *vt* and *vi* suplicar
supplication *n* suplicación, *f*; súplica, *f*
supply *vt* proveer (de); suministrar; proporcionar, dar; (a deficiency) suplir; (a post) llenar; (a post temporarily) reemplazar. *n* suministro, surtimiento, *m*; provisión, *f*; (of electricity, etc.) suministro, *m*; *com* oferta, *f*; (person) substituto (-ta); *pl* **supplies,** *com* existencias, *f pl*; *mil* pertrechos, *m pl*; víveres, *m pl*, provisiones, *f pl*. **s. and demand,** oferta y demanda, *f*
support *vt* apoyar, sostener; mantener; (endure) soportar; (a cause) apoyar, defender; (corroborate) confirmar, vindicar. *n* apoyo, *m*; sostén, *m*; soporte, *m*. **to speak in s. of,** defender, abogar por. **to s. oneself,** ganarse la vida, mantenerse
supporter *n* apoyo, *m*; defensor (-ra); partidario (-ia)
suppose *vt* suponer; imaginar(se); creer. **always supposing,** dado que, en el caso de que. **Supposing he had gone out?** ¿Y si hubiera salido? **I don't s. they will go to Spain,** No creo que vayan a España. **He is supposed to be clever,** Tiene fama de listo
supposed *a* supuesto; que se llama a sí mismo
supposition *n* suposición, hipótesis, *f*
suppress *vt* reprimir; (yawns, etc.) ahogar; (heresies, rebellions, books, etc.) suprimir; (dissemble) disimular, esconder; (a heckler, etc.) hacer callar
suppressed *a* reprimido; contenido; disimulado
suppression *n* represión, *f*; supresión, *f*; disimulación, *f*
suppurate *vi* supurar
suppuration *n* supuración, *f*
supremacy *n* supremacía, *f*
supreme *a* supremo; sumo. **with s. indifference,** con suma indiferencia, *f*. **s. court,** tribunal supremo, *m*
surcharge *n* sobrecarga, *f*
sure *a* seguro; cierto. *adv* seguramente. **Be s. to . . . !** ¡Ten cuidado de . . . ! ¡No dejes de . . . ! **to be s.,** seguramente, sin duda; ¡claro!; (fancy!) ¡no me digas!; ¡qué sorpresa! **I am not so s. of that,** No diría yo tanto. **Come on Thursday for s.,** Venga el jueves sin falta. **It is s. to rain tomorrow,** Seguramente va a llover mañana. **to make s. of,** asegurarse de. **to be (or feel) s.,** estar seguro. **s.-footed,** de pie firme, seguro
surely *adv* seguramente; sin duda, ciertamente; por supuesto
sureness *n* seguridad, *f*; certeza, *f*
surety *n* garantía, fianza, *f*; (person) garante, *mf*. **to go s. for,** ser fiador (de), salir garante (por)
surf *n* resaca, *f*; rompiente, *m*; oleaje, *m*. **s.-board,** aquaplano, *m*. **s.-riding,** patinaje sobre las olas, *m*

surface *n* superficie, *f*; exterior, *m*. *a* superficial. *vi* (of a submarine) salir a la superficie. **on the s.,** en apariencia
surface mail *n* correo por vía ordinaria, servicio ordinario, servicio per vía de superficie, *m*
surfeit *n* exceso, *m*, superabundancia, *f*; saciedad, *f*. *vt* hartar; saciar
surge *vi* (of waves) embravecerse, hincharse; (of crowds) agitarse, bullir; (of emotions) despertarse. *n* (of sea, crowd, blood) oleada, *f*; (of anger) ola, *f*. **The blood surged into his face,** La sangre se le subió a las mejillas
surgeon *n* cirujano, *m*; (nav, mil) médico, *m*
surgery *n* cirugía, *f*; (doctor's) consultorio, *m*; (dispensary) dispensario, *m*
surgical *a* quirúrgico
surliness *n* mal genio, *m*, taciturnidad, *f*; brusquedad, *f*
surly *a* taciturno, huraño, malhumorado; brusco
surmise *n* conjetura, suposición, *f*. *vt* conjeturar, adivinar; imaginar, suponer. *vi* hacer conjeturas
surmount *vt* superar, vencer; coronar
surname *n* apellido, *m*, *vt* denominar, nombrar
surpass *vt* superar, exceder; aventajarse (a); eclipsar
surpassing *a* sin par, incomparable
surplus *n* exceso, sobrante, *m*; (com of accounts) superávit, *m*. **sale of s. stock,** liquidación de saldos, *f*
surplusage *n* material de desecho, *m*
surprise *n* sorpresa, *f*; asombro, *m*. *vt* sorprender; asombrar. **to s. (someone) in the act,** coger en el acto. **to take (a person) by s.,** sorprender (a). **He was surprised into admitting it,** Cogido a la imprevista, lo confesó
surprising *a* sorprendente
surrealism *n* surrealismo, *m*
surrealist *a* and *n* surrealista, *mf*
surrender *vt* rendir, entregar; (goods) ceder, renunciar (a). *vi* rendirse, entregarse; abandonarse. *n* rendición, capitulación, *f*; entrega, *f*; (of goods) cesión, *f*; (of an insurance policy) rescate, *m*. **to s. oneself to remorse,** abandonar (or entregarse) al remordimiento. **to s. unconditionally,** entregarse a discreción
surreptitious *a* subrepticio
surreptitiously *adv* subrepticiamente, a hurtadillas
surround *vt* rodear; cercar; *mil* asediar, sitiar. *n* borde, *m*. **Peter was surrounded by his friends,** Pedro estaba rodeado por sus amigos
surrounding *a* (que está) alrededor de; vecino. **the s. country,** los alrededores
surroundings *n pl* cercanías, *f pl*, alrededores, *m pl*; (environment) medio, *m*; (medio) ambiente, *m*
surtax *n* impuesto suplementario, *m*
surveillance *n* vigilancia, *f*
survey *vt* contemplar, mirar; (events, etc.) pasar en revista; estudiar; (land, etc.) apear; (a house, etc.) inspeccionar. *n* vista general, *f*; inspección, *f*; (of facts, etc.) examen, *m*; estudio, *m*; (of land, etc.) apeo, *m*; (of literature, etc.) bosquejo, breve panorama, *m*
surveying *n* agrimensura, *f*
surveyor *n* agrimensor, *m*; (superintendent) inspector, *m*; superintendente, *m*
survival *n* supervivencia, *f*. **s. of the fittest,** supervivencia de los más aptos, *f*
survive *vt* sobrevivir a. *vi* sobrevivir; (of customs) subsistir, durar
survivor *n* sobreviviente, *mf*
susceptibility *n* susceptibilidad, *f*; tendencia, *f*; *pl* **susceptibilities,** susceptibilidad, *f*
susceptible *a* susceptible; impresionable; sensible; (to love) enamoradizo. **He is s. to bronchitis,** Es susceptible a la bronquitis
suspect *a* and *n* sospechoso (-sa). *vt* sospechar; dudar; imaginar, suponer. *vi* tener sospechas
suspend *vt* suspender. **suspended animation,** muerte aparente, *f*

suspender / swell

suspender *n* liga, *f*; *pl* **suspenders**, (braces) tirantes del pantalón, *m pl*. **s.-belt,** faja, *f*
suspense *n* incertidumbre, *f*. **to keep** (a person) **in s.**, dejar en la incertidumbre (a)
suspension *n* suspensión, *f*. **s.-bridge,** puente colgante, *m*. **s. of payments,** suspensión de pagos, *f*,
suspicion *n* sospecha, *f*; (touch) dejo, *m*; cantidad muy pequeña, *f*. **to be above s.,** estar por encima de toda sospecha. **to be under s.,** estar bajo sospecha. **I had no suspicions . . . ,** No sospechaba . . .
suspicious *a* (by nature) suspicaz; sospechoso. **to make s.,** hacer sospechar
suspiciously *adv* suspicazmente, desconfiadamente; de un modo sospechoso. **It seems s. like . . . ,** Tiene toda la apariencia de . . .
suspiciousness *n* carácter sospechoso, *m*, lo sospechoso; suspicacia, *f*
sustain *vt* sostener; mantener; sustentar; apoyar; corroborar, confirmar; (a note) prolongar. **to s. injuries,** recibir heridas
sustenance *n* mantenimiento, *m*; sustento, *m*, alimentos, *m pl*
suture *n* sutura, *f*
svarabhakti *adj* esvarabático
svelte *a* esbelto, gentil
swab *vt naut* lampacear; limpiar con lampazo; *surg* tamponar. *n* lampazo, *m*; *surg* torunda, *f*, tampón, *m*
swaddle *vt* envolver; (infants) fajar
swaddling clothes *n pl* pañales, *m pl*. **to be still in s. clothes,** *fig* estar en mantillas, estar en pañales
swag *n* botín, *m*
swagger *vi* fanfarronear, pavonearse; darse importancia. *n* pavoneo, *m*; aire importante, *m*; (coat) tonto, *m*. *a* majo; de última moda
swaggering *a* fanfarrón, jactancioso; importante
Swahili suaili; *n* suaili, *m*
swain *n* zagal, *m*; enamorado, *m*; pretendiente, amante, *m*
swallow *vt* tragar, engullir. *n* trago, *m*; sorbo, *m*; *orn* golondrina, *f*. **to s. an insult (a story),** tragar un insulto (una historia). **to s. one's words,** retractarse. **to s. one's pride,** bajar la cerviz, humillarse. **to s. up,** tragar; absorber. **s.-tailed coat,** frac, *m*
swamp *n* pantano, *m*, marisma, *f*. *vt* sumergir; (a boat) echar a pique, hundir; (inundate) inundar
swampy *a* pantanoso
swan *n* cisne, *m*. **swan's down,** plumón de cisne, *m*. **s.-song,** canto del cisne, *m*
swank *n* pretensiones, *f pl*, *vi* darse humos
sward *n* césped, *m*, hierba, *f*
swarm *n* enjambre, *m*; (of people) muchedumbre, multitud, *f*; tropel, *m*. *vi* (of bees) enjambrar; (of other insects) pulular; (of people) hormiguear, bullir, pulular. *vt* (climb) trepar. **to s. with,** estar infestado de
swarthiness *n* tez morena, *f*; color moreno, *m*
swarthy *a* moreno
swashbuckler *n* perdonavidas, matasiete, *m*
swashbuckling *a* matamoros, valentón, fanfarrón
swastika *n* esvástica, cruz gamada, *f*
swathe *vt* envolver; fajar; (with bandages) vendar
swathing *n* envoltura, *f*; (bandages) vendas, *f pl*
sway *vi* balancearse; oscilar; (stagger, of persons) bambolearse; (totter, of things) tambalearse; (of carriages) cabecear; (gracefully, in walking) cimbrarse. *vt* balancear, mecer; oscilar; hacer tambalear; (influence) influir, inclinar; (govern) regir, gobernar. *n* balanceo, *m*; oscilación, *f*; vaivén, *m*; tambaleo, *m*; (influence) ascendiente, dominio, *m*, influencia, *f*; (rule) imperio, poder, *m*. **to hold s.** over, dominar, regir
swear *vt* jurar; (*law* etc.) declarar bajo juramento. *vi* jurar; (curse) echar pestes, blasfemar. **to s. at,** maldecir. **to s. by,** jurar por; poner fe implícita en. **to be sworn in,** prestar juramento. **to s. in,** tomar juramento (a). **to s. to,** atestiguar
sweat *n* sudor, *m*; *inf* trabajo arduo, *m*. *vi* sudar. *vt* sudar; hacer sudar; (workers) explotar. **by the s. of**

one's brow, con el sudor de la frente, con el sudor del rostro. **s.-gland,** glándula sudorípara, *f*
sweated *a* (of persons) explotado; (of labor) mal retribuido
sweater *n* suéter, jersey, *m*
sweating *n* transpiración, *f*; (of workers) explotación, *f*
sweaty *a* sudoroso
Swede *n* sueco (-ca); (vegetable) naba, *f*
Sweden Suecia, *f*
Swedish *a* sueco. *n* (language) sueco, *m*
sweep *vi* extenderse (por); (cleave) surcar; pasar rápidamente (por); invadir; dominar; andar majestuosamente; (with a' brush) barrer. *vt* barrer; pasar (por); (the strings of a musical instrument) rasguear; (the sea) navegar por; (mines) barrer; (the horizon, etc.) examinar; (a chimney) deshollinar; (with a brush) barrer; (remove) arrebatar; quitar; llevarse; (abolish) suprimir. **to s. along,** *vt* (of the current, crowds, etc.) arrastrar. *vi* pasar majestuosamente; correr rápidamente (por). **to s. aside,** apartar con la mano; abandonar; (a protest) desoír, no hacer caso de. **to s. away,** barrer; (remove) llevarse; destruir; suprimir. **to s. down,** *vt* barrer; (carry) arrastrar. *vi* (of cliffs, etc.) bajar; (of an enemy) abalanzarse (sobre); lanzarse (por). **to s. off,** barrer; (a person) llevarse sin perder tiempo; arrebatar con violencia (a). **to be swept off one's feet,** ser arrastrado (por); perder el balance; (of emotion) ser dominado por. **to s. on,** seguir su avance inexorable; seguir su marcha. **to s. up,** recoger, barrer
sweep *n* barredura, *f*; (of a chimney) deshollinador, *m*; (of the tide) curso, *m*; (of a scythe, etc.) golpe, *m*; (range) alcance, *m*; (fold) pliegue, *m*; (curve) curva, *f*; (of water, etc.) extensión, *f*; (of wings) envergadura, *f*. **with a s. of the arm,** con un gesto del brazo. **to make a clean s. of,** hacer tabla rasa de
sweeping *a* completo; comprensivo; demasiado general; radical. **a s. judgment,** un juicio demasiado general. **s. change,** cambio radicale, *m pl*. **s. brush,** escoba, *f*
sweepings *n pl* barreduras, *f pl*; residuos, *m pl*; (of society) heces, *f pl*
sweepstake *n* lotería, *f*
sweet *a* dulce; (of scents) oloroso, fragante; (of sounds) melodioso, dulce; (charming) encantador; amable; (pretty) bonito. *n* bombón, *m*; golosina, *f*; (at a meal) (plato) dulce, *m*; dulzura, *f*; (beloved) amor, *m*, querido (-da). **How s. it smells!** ¡Qué buen olor tiene! **the sweets of life,** las dulzuras de la vida. **s.-pea,** guisante de olor, *m*, haba de las Indias, *f*. **s.-potato,** batata, *f*. **s.-scented,** perfumado, fragante. **s.-tempered,** amable, de carácter dulce. **s.-toothed,** goloso. **s.-william,** *bot* clavel de la China, clavel de ramillete, clavel de San Isidro, ramillete de Constantinopla, *m*, minutisa, *f*
sweetbread *n* lechecillas, *f pl*
sweeten *vt* azucarar; endulzar. **Cervantes sweetens one's bitter moments,** Cervantes endulza los momentos ásperos
sweetheart *n* amante, *mf*, amado (-da); (as address) querido (-da)
sweetish *a* algo dulce
sweetly *adv* dulcemente; (of scents) olorosamente; (of sounds) melodiosamente; (of behaviour, etc.) amablemente
sweetmeat *n* bombón, dulce, *m*
sweetness *n* dulzura, *f*; (of scents) buen olor, *m*, fragancia, *f*; (of sounds) melodía, dulzura, *f*; (of character) bondad, amabilidad, *f*
sweet potato *n* batata, *f*, boniato, buniato, camote, *m*
sweet sixteen *n* (age) los dieciséis abriles, *m pl*; (party) quinceañera (at age fifteen) *f*
swell *vi* hincharse; (of the sea) entumecerse; crecer; aumentarse. *vt* hinchar; aumentar. *n* (of the sea) oleada, *f*, oleaje, *m*; (of the ground) ondulación, *f*; (of sound) crescendo, *m*; (increase) aumento, *m*; (dandy) pisaverde, elegante, *m*; (important person) pájaro

gordo, *m*; (at games, etc.) espada, *m*. *a* estupendo; elegantísimo; de primera, excelente. **to suffer from swelled head,** tener humos, darse importancia. **This foot is swollen,** Este pie está hinchado (or tumefacto). **The refugees have swelled the population,** Los refugiados han aumentado la población. **eyes swollen with tears,** ojos arrasados de lágrimas. **to s. with pride,** hincharse de orgullo

swelling *n* hinchazón, *f*; *med* tumefacción, *f*; (bruise, etc.) chichón, *m*

swelter *vi* abrasarse; arder. *n* bochorno, calor sofocante, *m*

swerve *vi* desviarse; apartarse (de); torcerse. *n* desvío, *m*

swift *a* rápido, veloz; pronto. *adv* velozmente, rápidamente. *n orn* vencejo, *m*. **s.-flowing,** (of rivers, etc.) de corriente rápida. **s.-footed,** de pies ligeros

swiftly *adv* rápidamente, velozmente

swiftness *n* rapidez, velocidad, *f*; prontitud, *f*

swim *vi* nadar; flotar; (glide) deslizarse; (fill) inundarse. *vt* (a horse) hacer nadar; pasar a nado; nadar. *n* natación, *f*. **eyes swimming with tears,** ojos inundados de lágrimas. **He enjoys a s.,** Le gusta nadar. **My head swims,** Se me va la cabeza. **Everything swam before my eyes,** Todo parecía bailar ante mis ojos. **to be in the s.,** formar parte (de), ser (de); (be up to date) estar al corriente. **to s. the Channel,** atravesar el canal de la Mancha a nado. **to s. with the tide,** ir con la corriente

swimmer *n* nadador (-ra). **He is a bad s.,** Nada mal

swimming *n* natación, *f*; (of the head) vértigo, *m*. **s.-bath,** piscina, *f*. **s.-costume,** traje de baño, *m*. **s.-pool,** piscina al aire libre, *f*

swindle *vt* engañar, estafar; defraudar (de). *n* estafa, *f*, timo, *m*; engaño, *m*; impostura, *f*

swindler *n* estafador (-ra), trampeador (-ra); engañador (-ra)

swine *n* cerdo, puerco, *m*; (person) cochino (-na). **a herd of s.,** una manada de cerdos

swineherd *n* porquero, *m*

swing *vi* balancearse; oscilar; (hang) colgar, pender; columpiarse; girar; dar la vuelta; (of a boat) bornear. *vt* balancear; (hang) colgar; (rock) mecer; (in a swing, etc.) columpiar; hacer oscilar; (raise) subir. *n* oscilación, *f*; vaivén, *m*; balanceo, *m*; (rhythm) ritmo, *m*; (seat, etc.) columpio, *m*; (reach) alcance, *m*. **The door swung open,** La puerta se abrió silenciosamente. **He swung the car round,** Dio la vuelta al auto. **He swung himself into the saddle,** Montó de un salto. **to be in full s.,** estar a toda marcha. **to go with a s.,** tener mucho éxito. **s.-boat,** columpio, *m*. **s.-bridge,** puente giratorio, *m*. **s.-door,** puerta giratoria, *f*

swinging *a* oscilante; pendiente; rítmico. *n* balanceo, *m*; oscilación, *f*; vaivén, *m*; ritmo, *m*. **s. stride,** andar rítmico, *m*

swinish *a* porcuno, de cerdo; cochino, sucio

swipe *vt* golpear duro; aplastar. *n* golpe fuerte, *m*

swirl *vi* arremolinarse. *n* remolino, *m*

swish *vt* (of an animal's tail) agitar, mover, menear; (of a cane) blandir; (thrash) azotar. *vi* silbar; (of water) susurrar; (of a dress, etc.) crujir. *n* silbo, *m*; (of water) susurro, murmullo, *m*; (of a dress, etc.) crujido, *m*

Swiss *a* and *n* suizo (-za)

switch *n* vara, *f*; (riding) látigo, *m*; (of hair) trenza, *f*; *elec* interruptor, *m*; *rw* aguja, *f*; (*rw* siding) desviadero, *m*. *vt* azotar; (a train) desviar; *elec* interrumpir; (transfer) trasladar; (of an animal, its tail) remover, mover rápidamente. **to s. off,** (*elec* and telephone) cortar; (*rad* and *aut*) desconectar. **to s. on,** conectar; (a light) poner (la luz); (a radio) encender

switchback *n* subida en zigzag, *f*; (amusement) montañas rusas, *f pl*

switchboard *n* cuadro de distribución, *m*

Switzerland Suiza, *f*

swivel *n* torniquete, *m*; anillo móvil, *m*; pivote, *m*. *vi* girar sobre un eje; dar una vuelta. **s.-chair,** silla giratoria, *f*. **s.-door,** puerta giratoria, *f*

swoon *vi* desvanecerse, desmayarse. *n* desmayo, desvanecimiento, *m*

swoop *vi* calarse, abatirse; (of robbers, etc.) abalanzarse (sobre). *n* calada, *f*. **at one fell s.,** de un solo golpe

sword *n* espada, *f*; sable, *m*. **to measure swords with,** cruzar espadas con. **to put to the s.,** pasar a cuchillo (a). **s.-arm,** brazo derecho, *m*. **s.-belt,** talabarte, *m*. **s.-cut,** sablazo, *m*. **s.-dance,** danza de espadas, *f*. **s.-fish,** pez espada, pez sierra, espadarte, *m*, jifia, *f*. **s.-play,** esgrima, *f*; manejo de la espada, *m*. **s.-stick,** bastón de estoque, *m*. **s.-thrust,** golpe de espada, *m*; estocada, *f*

swordsman *n* espadachín, *m*; esgrimidor, *m*

swordsmanship *n* manejo de la espada, *m*; esgrima, *f*

sybarite *a* and *n* sibarita, *mf*

sybaritic *a* sibarítico, sibarita

sycamore *n* sicomoro, *m*; falso plátano, *m*

sycophancy *n* servilismo, *m*

sycophant *n* sicofanta, *m*

syllabic *a* silábico

syllable *n* sílaba, *f*

syllabus *n* programa, *m*; compendio, *m*

syllogism *n* silogismo, *m*

sylph *n* sílfide, *f*, silfo, *m*; (woman) sílfide, *f*; (hummingbird) colibrí, *m*. **s.-like,** de sílfide; como una sílfide

sylvan *a* selvático, silvestre; rústico

symbiosis *n* simbiosis, *f*

symbol *n* símbolo, emblema, *m*; *math* símbolo, *m*; (of rank, etc.) insignia, *f*

symbolical *a* simbólico

symbolism *n* simbolismo, *m*

symbolist *n* simbolista, *mf*

symbolize *vt* simbolizar

symmetrical *a* simétrico

symmetry *n* simetría, *f*

sympathetic *a* simpático; compasivo; (of the public, etc.) bien dispuesto. *n anat* gran simpático, *m*. **s. words,** palabras de simpatía, *f pl*. **s. ink,** tinta simpática, *f*

sympathetically *adv* simpáticamente; con compasión

sympathize *vi* simpatizar (con); (understand) comprender; (condole) compadecerse (de), condolerse (de); dar el pésame

sympathizer *n* partidario (-ia)

sympathy *n* simpatía, *f*; compasión, *f*. **Paul is in s. with their aims,** Pablo está de acuerdo con sus objetos. **Please accept my s.,** (on a bereavement) Le acompaño a Vd. en su sentimiento

symphonic *a* sinfónico

symphony *n* sinfonía, *f*

symposium *n* colección de artículos, *f*

symptom *n* síntoma, *m*; señal, *f*, indicio, *m*. **to show symptoms of,** dar indicios de

symptomatic *a* sintomático

synagogue *n* sinagoga, *f*

synchronization *n* sincronización, *f*

synchronize *vi* coincidir, tener lugar simultáneamente; sincronizar. *vt* sincronizar

synchronous *a* sincrónico

syncopate *vt* (*gram mus*) sincopar

syncopation *n mus* síncopa, *f*

syncope *n* (*med gram*) síncope, *m*

syndical *a* sindical

syndicalism *n* sindicalismo, *m*

syndicalist *n* sindicalista, *mf*

syndicate *n* sindicato, *m*, *vt* sindicar

syndication *n* sindicación, *f*

synod *n ecc* sínodo, *m*

synonym *n* sinónimo, *m*

synonymous *a* sinónimo

synopsis *n* sinopsis, *f*

synoptic *a* sinóptico

syntax *n* sintaxis, *f*

synthesis *n* síntesis, *f*

synthetic *a* sintético

synthetize *vt* sintetizar

syphilis *n* sífilis, *f*
syphilitic *a* and *n* sifilítico (-ca)
Syracuse Siracusa, *f*
syren *n*. See **siren**
Syria Siria, *f*
Syrian *a* and *n* siríaco (-ca), sirio (-ia)
syringe *n* jeringa, *f*, *vt* jeringar
syrup *n* jarabe, *m*; (for bottling fruit, etc.) almíbar, *m*
syrupy *a* siroposo

system *n* sistema, *m*; régimen, *m*; método, *m*; (body) organismo, *m*. **He has no s. in his work,** No tiene método en su trabajo. **the nervous s.,** el sistema nervioso. **the feudal s.,** el feudalismo, el sistema feudal
systematic *a* sistemático, metódico
systematically *adv* sistemáticamente, metódicamente
systematization *n* sistematización, *f*
systematize *vt* sistematizar
systole *n med* sístole, *f*

T

t *n* (letter) te, *f*. *a* en T, en forma de T. **T bandage,** vendaje en T, *m*. **T square,** regla T, *f*
tab *n* oreja, *f*
tabby *n* gato romano, *m*; (female) gata, *f*; *inf* vieja chismosa, *f*
tabernacle *n* tabernáculo, *m*; templo, *m*; *arch* templete, *m*; *ecc* custodia, *f*
tabes *n med* tabes, *f*
table *n* mesa, *f*; (food) comida, mesa, *f*; (of the law, weights, measures, contents, etc.) tabla, *f*; (of land) meseta, *f*; (of prices) lista, tarifa, *f*. *vt* (parliament) poner sobre la mesa; enumerar, apuntar, hacer una lista de. **to clear the t.,** alzar (or levantar) la mesa. **to lay the t.,** cubrir (or poner) la mesa. **to have at.-d'hôte meal,** tomar el menú. **to rise from t.,** levantarse de la mesa. **to sit down to t.,** ponerse a la mesa. **The tables are turned,** Se volvió la tortilla. **side t.,** aparador, trinchero, *m*. **small t.,** mesilla, *f*. **t. of contents,** tabla de materias, *f*, índice, índice de materias, índice general, *m*. **t.-centrepiece,** centro de mesa, *m*. **t.-cloth,** mantel, *m*. **t.-companion,** comensal, *mf* **t.-knife,** cuchillo de mesa, *m*. **t.-lamp,** quinqué, *m*; lampara de mesa, *f*. **t.-land,** meseta, *f*. **t.-leg,** pata de una mesa, *f*. **t.-linen,** mantelería, *f*. **t.-napkin,** servilleta, *f*. **t.-runner,** camino de mesa, *m*. **t.-spoon,** cuchara para los legumbres, *f*. **t.-talk,** conversación de sobremesa, *f*. **t.-turning,** mesas que dan vueltas, *f pl*. **t.-ware,** artículos para la mesa, *m pl*
tableau *n* cuadro, *m*. **tableaux vivants,** cuadros vivos, *m pl*
tablespoonful *n* cucharada, *f*
tablet *n* tabla, *f*; (with inscription) tarjeta, losa, lápida, *f*; *med* comprimido, *m*, tableta, *f*; (of soap, chocolate) pastilla, *f*. **writing t.,** taco de papel, *m*
tabloid *n* comprimido, *m*, pastilla, *f*
taboo *n* tabú, *m*. *a* prohibido, tabú. *vt* declarar tabú, prohibir
tabor *n mus* tamboril, tamborín, *m*. **t. player,** tamborilero, *m*
tabouret (stool) taburete, *m*; (for embroidery) tambor de bordar, *m*; *mus* tamborilete, *m*
tabulate *vt* resumir en tablas; hacer una lista de, catalogar
tabulation *n* distribución en tablas, *f*
tacit *a* tácito
taciturn *a* taciturno, sombrío, reservado, de pocas palabras
taciturnity *n* taciturnidad, *f*; reserva, *f*
tack *n* (nail) tachuela, puntilla, *f*; *sew* hilván, embaste, *m*; *naut* amura, *f*; *naut* puño de amura, *m*; *naut* bordada, *f*; *fig* cambio de política, *m*. *vt* clavar con tachuelas; *sew* hilvanar, embastar; *fig* añadir. *vi naut* virar; *fig* cambiar de política, adoptar un nuevo plan de acción. **t. puller,** sacabrocas, *m*
tackle *n* aparejo, *m*; maniobra, *f*; *naut* cuadernal, *m*, jarcia, *f*; (gear) aparejos, avíos, *m pl*; (football) carga, *f*. *vt* agarrar, asir; *fig* atacar, abordar; (football) cargar; (undertake) emprender; (a problem) luchar con. **t.-block,** polea, *f*
tackling *n* aparejo, *m*, maniobra, *f*; *naut* cordaje, *m*
tacky *a* pegajoso, viscoso
tact *n* tacto, *m*, discreción, diplomacia, delicadeza, *f*

tactful *a* lleno de tacto, diplomático, discreto
tactfully *adv* discretamente, diplomáticamente
tactical *a* táctico
tactically *adv* según la táctica; del punto de vista táctico
tactician *n* táctico, *m*
tactics *n pl* táctica, *f*
tactile *a* táctil; tangible
tactless *a* que no tiene tacto, sin tacto alguno, indiscreto
tactlessly *adv* impolíticamente, indiscretamente
tactlessness *n* falta de tacto, *f*
tadpole *n* renacuajo, *m*
taffeta *n* tafetán, *m*
tag *n* herrete, *m*; (label) marbete, *m*, etiqueta, *f*; (of tail) punta del rabo, *f*; (of boot) tirador de bota, *m*; (game) marro, *m*; (rag) arrapiezo, *m*; (quotation) cita bien conocida, *f*; (of song, poem) refrán, *m*. **to play t.,** jugar al marro
Tagus el Tajo, *m*
Tahiti Taiti, Tahiti, *m*
tail *n* cola, *f*, rabo, *m*; (plait) trenza, *f*; (wisp of hair) mechón, *m*; (of a comet) cola, cabellera, *f*; (of a note in music) rabito, *m*; (of a coat) faldon, *m*; (of a kite) cola, *f*; (of the eye), rabo, *m*; (retinue) séquito, *m*, banda, *f*; (of an aeroplane) cola, *f*; (end) fin, *m*; (of coin) cruz, *f*; (line) fila, cola, *f*. *vt* seguir de cerca, pisarle (a uno) los talones. **to t. after,** seguir de cerca. **to t. away,** disminuir; desaparecer, perderse de vista. **to t. on,** unir, juntar. **to turn t.,** volver la espalda, poner los pies en polvorosa. **with the t. between the legs,** con el rabo entre piernas. **t.-board,** (of a cart) escalera, *f*. **t.-coat,** frac, *m*. **t.-end,** extremo, *m*; fin, *m*; lo último. **t.-feather,** pena, *f*. **t.-fin,** aleta caudal, *f*; *aer* timón de dirección, *m*. **t.-light,** farol trasero, *m*. **t.-piece,** (of a violin, etc.) cola, *f*; *print* marmosete, culo de lámpara, *m*. **t. spin** *aer* barrena de cola, *f*. **t. wind,** viento de cola, *m*
tailed *a* de rabo. **big-t.,** rabudo, de cola grande. **long-t.,** rabilargo. **short-t.,** rabicorto
tailless *a* rabón, sin rabo
tailor *n* sastre, *m*. **t.-made,** *n* traje sastre, *m*, *a* de hechura de sastre. **tailor's shop,** sastrería, *f*
tailoress *n* sastra, *f*
tailoring *n* sastrería, *f*; (work) corte, *m*
taint *n* corrupción, *f*; infección, *f*; (blemish) mancha, *f*; (tinge) dejo, *m*. *vt* corromper, pervertir; inficionar; (meat) corromper. *vi* corromperse, inficionarse; (meat) corromperse
take *vt* tomar; (receive) aceptar; (remove) quitar; (pick up) coger; (grab) asir, agarrar; *math* restar; (carry) llevar; (a person) traer, llevar; (guide) conducir, guiar; (win) ganar; (earn) cobrar, percibir; obtener; (make prisoner) hacer prisionero, prender; (a town, etc.) tomar, rendir, conquistar; (appropriate) apoderarse de, apropiarse; (steal) robar, hurtar; (ensnare) coger, cazar con trampas; (fish) pescar, coger; (a trick, in cards) hacer (una baza); (an illness) contraer, coger; (by surprise) sorprender, coger desprevenido (a); (attract) atraer; (drink) beber; (a meal) tomar; (select) escoger; (hire) alquilar; (suppose) suponer; (a journal) estar abonado a; (use) emplear, usar; (impers., require) necesitarse, hacer falta; (purchase) comprar; (assume)

adoptar, asumir; (a leap) dar (un salto); (a walk) dar (un paseo); (a look) echar (un vistazo); (measures) tomar (medidas); (the chair) presidir; (understand) comprender; (a photograph) sacar (una fotografía); (believe) creer; (consider) considerar; (a note) apuntar; (jump over) saltar; (time) tomar, emplear. **I t. size three in shoes,** Calzo el número tres. **to t. to be,** (believe) suponer; (mistake) creer quivocadamente. **to t. (a thing) badly,** tomarlo (or llevarlo) a mal. **The book took me two hours to read,** Necesité dos horas para leer el libro, Leí el libro en dos horas. **And this, I t. it, is Mary?** ¿Y supongo que ésta será María? **to be taken with,** ser entusiasta de; (of persons) estar prendado de. **to t. aback,** desconcertar, coger desprevenido (a). **to t. again,** volver a tomar; llevar otra vez; (a photograph) retratar otra vez. **to t. along,** llevar; traer. **to t. away,** quitar; llevarse. **to t. back,** devolver; (retract) retractar; (receive) recibir (algo) devuelto. **to t. down,** bajar; (a building) derribar; (machinery) desmontar; (hair) deshacerse (el cabello); (swallow) tragar; (in writing) apuntar; (humble) quitar los humos (a), humillar. **to t. for,** creer, imaginar; (a walk, etc.) llevar a; (mistake) creer erróneamente; tomar por. **Whom do you t. me for?** ¿Por quién me tomas? **to. t. for granted (assume),** dar por descontado, dar por lecho, dar por sentado, dar por supuesto; (underestimate) no hacer caso de, tratar con indiferencia. **t. the lion's share (of),** llevarse la parte del león (de), llevarse la tajada del león (de). **t. shape,** cobrar perfiles más nítidos, estructurarse con más nitidez, ir adquiriendo consistencia, tomar forma. **t. the law into one's own hands,** tomar la justicia por la mano. **to t. from,** privar, quitar de; (subtract) restar; substraer de. **to t. in,** (believe) tragar, creer; (sail) acortar las velas; (deceive) engañar; (lead in) hacer entrar; (accept) recibir, aceptar. **to t. off,** quitar; (surgically) amputar; (one's hat, etc.) quitarse (el sombrero); (eyes) sacar; (take away) llevarse; (mimic) imitar; (ridicule) ridiculizar; (unstick) despegar; (discount) descontar. **to t. on,** emprender; aceptar; (at sports) jugar. **to t. on oneself,** encargarse de, tomar por su cuenta, asumir. **to t. out,** sacar; extraer; (remove) quitar; (outside) llevar fuera; (for a walk) llevar a paseo; (obtain) obtener, sacar; (tire) agotar, rendir. **to t. over,** tomar posesión de; asumir; (show) mostrar, conducir por. **t. the bull by the horns,** ir al toro por los cuernos. **take seriously,** tomar en serio. **to t. up,** subir; (pick up) recoger; tomar; (a challenge, etc.) aceptar; (a dress, etc.) acortar; (absorb) absorber; (of space) ocupar; (of time) ocupar, hacer perder; (buy) comprar; (adopt) dedicarse a; (arrest) arrestar, prender; (criticize) censurar, criticar; (begin) empezar; (resume) continuar

take vi tomar; (be successful) tener éxito; (of vaccination, etc.) prender; (a good (bad) photograph) salir bien (mal). **to t. after,** salir a, parecerse a; (of conduct) seguir el ejemplo de; **to t. off,** salir; aer despegar. **to t. on,** inf lamentarse. **to t. to,** dedicarse a; darse a; (of persons) tomar cariño a; (grow accustomed) acostumbrarse a. **to t. up with,** hacerse amigo de

take n toma, f; cogida, f; print tomada, f; theat taquilla, f. **t.-in,** engaño, m. **t.-off,** aer (recorrido de) despegue, m; caricatura, f; sátira, f

taker n tomador (-ra)

taking n toma, f; secuestro, m, an pl **takings,** ingresos, m pl; theat taquilla, entrada, f. a atractivo, encantador; simpático; (of disease) contagioso

talc n min talco, m

talcum powder n talco, polvo de talco, m

tale n (recital) narración, historia, f; relato, m; cuento, m; leyenda, historia, fábula, f; (number) cuenta, f, número, m; (gossip) chisme, m. **old wives' t.,** cuento de viejas, m. **to tell a t.,** contar una historia. **to tell tales,** contar cuentos; revelar secretos, chismear

talebearer n correveidile, mf; chismoso (-sa), soplón (-ona)

talebearing n el chismear, m

talent n (coin) talento, m; (ability) ingenio, m; habilidad, f. **the best t. in Spain,** la flor de la cultura española

talented a talentoso, ingenioso

talisman n talismán, m

talit taled, m

talk vi and vt hablar, decir. **to t. business,** hablar de negocios. **to t. for talking's sake,** hablar por hablar. **to t. French,** hablar francés. **to t. nonsense,** decir disparates. **to t. too much,** hablar demasiado; inf hablar por los codos, irse (a uno) la lengua. **to t. about,** hablar de; conversar sobre. **to t. at,** decir algo a alguien para que lo entienda otro. **Are you talking at me?** ¿Lo dices por mí? **to t. away,** seguir hablando; disipar. **to t. into,** persuadir, inducir (a). **to t. of,** hablar de; charlar sobre. **to t. on,** hablar acerca de (or sobre); (continue) seguir hablando. **to t. out of,** disuadir de. **to t. out of turn,** meterse donde no le llaman, meter la pata. **to t. over,** hablar de; discutir, considerar. **to t. round,** persuadir. **to t. to,** (address) hablar a; (consult) hablar con; (scold) reprender. **to t. to each other,** hablarse. **to t. up,** hablar claro

talk n conversación, f; (informal lecture) charla, f; (empty words) palabras, f pl; (notoriety) escándalo, m; rumor, m. **There is t. of . . . ,** Se dice que . . . ; Se habla de que. **to give a t.,** dar una charla. **to indulge in small t.,** hablar de cosas sin importancia, hablar de naderías

talkative a locuaz, gárrulo, hablador, decidor. **to be very t.,** ser muy locuaz; inf tener mucha lengua

talkativeness n locuacidad, garrulidad, f

talker n hablador (-ra), conversador (-ra); (lecturer) orador (-ra); (in a derogatory sense) fanfarrón (-ona), charlatán (-ana). **to be a good t.,** hablar bien, ser buen conversacionista

talking a que habla, hablante; (of birds, dolls, etc.) parlero. **to give a good t. to,** dar una peluca (a). **t.-film,** película sonora, f. **t.-machine,** fonógrafo, m

tall a alto; (of stories) exagerado. **five feet tall,** de cinco pies de altura

tallboy n cómoda alta, f

tallness n altura, f; estatura, talla, f; (of stories) lo exagerado

tallow n sebo, m. **t. candle,** vela de sebo, f. **t. chandler,** velero (-ra). **t.-faced,** con cara de color de cera

tallowy a seboso

tally n tarja, tara, f; cuenta, f. vt llevar la cuenta (de). vi estar conforme, cuadrar

Talmud n Talmud, m

Talmudic a talmúdico

tamable a domable, domesticable

tambour n mus tambor, m; (for embroidery) tambor (or bastidor) para bordar, m

tambourine n pandereta, f

tame a domesticado, manso; (spiritless) sumiso; (dull) aburrido, soso. vt domar, domesticar; (curb) reprimir, gobernar, domar, suavizar. **to grow t.,** domesticarse

tameness n mansedumbre, f; sumisión, timidez, f

tamer n domador (-ra)

taming n domadura, f. **The T. of the Shrew,** La Fierecilla Domada

tamp vt apisonar; (in blasting) atacar (un barreno)

tamper vi (with) descomponer, estropear; (meddle with) meterse con; (witnesses) sobornar; (documents) falsificar

tampon n surg tampón, tapón, m, vt taponar

tan vt curtir, adobar; (of sun) tostar, quemar; (slang) zurrar. vi tostarse por el sol. n color café claro, m; bronceado, cutis tostado, m. a de color café claro

tandem n tándem, m

tang n (of sword, etc.) espiga, f; (flavor) fuerte sabor, m; (sound) retintín, m

tangent a and n tangente f. **to fly off at a t.,** fig salir por la tangente

tangerine a and n tangerino (-na). **t. orange,** naranja mandarina, f

tangible *a* tangible; *fig* real
Tangier Tánger, *m*
tangle *n* embrollo, enredo, nudo, *m*; (of streets) laberinto, *m*; *fig* confusión, *f*. *vt* embrollar, enmarañar; (entangle) enredar; *fig* poner en confusión, complicar. *vi* enmarañarse
tank *n* tanque, depósito (de agua, etc.), *m*; cisterna, *f*; (as a reservoir) aljibe, estanque, *m*; *mil* tanque, carro de asalto, *m*
tankard *n* pichel, bock, *m*
tanker *n* petrolero, *m*
tanned *a* bronceado, quemado por el sol, dorado por el sol
tanner *n* curtidor, *m*; (slang) medio chelín, *m*. **tanner's scraper,** descarnador, *m*. **tanner's vat, noque,** *m*
tannery *n* curtiduría, *f*
tannic *a chem* tánico. **t. acid,** ácido tánico, *m*
tannin *n chem* tanino, *m*
tanning *n* curtido, adobamiento, *m*
tantalize *vt* tentar, atormentar, provocar
tantalizing *a* tentador, atormentador; provocativo
tantamount *a* equivalente, igual. **to be t. to,** ser equivalente a
tantrum *n* paleta, rabieta, *f*, berrinche, *m*
taoism *n* taoísmo, *m*
taoist *n* taoísta, *mf*
tap *n* (blow) pequeño golpe, toque ligero, *m*; palmadita, *f*; (for drawing water, etc.) grifo, *m*, llave, *f*; (of a barrel) canilla, *f*; (brew of liquor) clase de vino, *f*; (tap-room) bar con mostrador, *m*; (tool) macho de terraja, *m*; (piece of leather on shoe) tapa, *f*; *pl* **taps,** *mil* toque de apagar las luces, *m*. *vt* (strike) golpear ligeramente, dar una palmadita a; (pierce) horadar; (a barrel) decentar; *surg* hacer una puntura en; (trees) sangrar; *elec* derivar (una corriente); (of water, current) tomar; (information) descubrir; (telephone) escuchar las conversaciones telefónicas. *vi* golpear ligeramente. **to tap at the door,** llamar suavemente a la puerta. **on tap,** en tonel. **screw-tap,** terraja, *f*. **tap-dance,** claqué, *m*.
tap-root, raíz pivotante, *f*
tape *n* (linen) cinta de hilo, *f*; (cotton) cinta de algodón, *f*; (telegraph) cinta de papel, *f*; (surveying) cinta para medir, *f*. **adhesive t.,** cinta adhesiva, *f*. **red t.,** balduque, *m*; *fig* burocracia, *f*; formulismo, *m*. **t.-machine,** telégrafo de cotizaciones, bancarias, *m*. **t.-measure,** cinta métrica, *f*
taper *n* bujía, cerilla, *f*; *ecc* cirio, *m*. *vi* ahusarse, rematar en punta. *vt* afilar
tapering *a* cónico, piramidal; (of fingers) afilado
tapestried *a* cubierto de tapices, tapizado
tapestry *n* tapiz, *m*. **t. weaver,** tapicero, *m*
tapeworm *n* tenia, lombriz solitaria, *f*
tapioca *n* tapioca, *f*
tapir *n zool* danta, *f*
tapis, to be on the estar sobre el tapete
tar *n* alquitrán, *m*, brea, *f*. *vt* embrear, alquitranar. **to tar and feather,** emplumar. **coal t.,** alquitrán mineral, *m*
tarantella *n* tarantela, *f*
tarantula *n* tarántula, *f*
tardily *adv* tardíamente; lentamente
tardiness *n* tardanza, lentitud, *f*
tardy *a* (late) tardío; (slow) lento; (reluctant) desinclinado
tare *n bot* yero, *m*; (in the Bible) cizaña, *f*; *com* tara, *f*; (of a vehicle) peso en vacío, *m*
target *n* blanco (de tiro), *m*; (shield) rodela, tarja, *f*. **t. practice,** tiro al blanco, *m*
tariff *n* tarifa, *f*. **to put a t. on,** tarifar
tarlatan *n* tarlatana, *f*
tarmac *n* alquitranado, *m*
tarn *n* lago de montaña, *m*
tarnish *n* deslustre, *m*. *vt* deslustrar, empañar; *fig* obscurecer, manchar. *vi* deslustrarse
tarpaulin *n* alquitranado, encerado, *m*
tarred *a* alquitranado, embreado

tarring *n* embreadura, *f*
tarry *vi* tardar, detenerse
tart *a* ácido, acerbo, agridulce; *fig* áspero. *n* tarta, *f*; pastelillo de fruta, *m*
tartan *n naut* tartana, *f*; (plaid) tartán, *m*
tartar *n chem* tártaro, *m*; (in teeth) sarro, tártaro, *m*; **cream of t.,** (cremor) tártaro, *m*. **t. emetic,** tártaro emético, *m*. **Tartar,** *a* and *n* tártaro (-ra)
Tartary Tartaria, *f*
tartly *adv* ásperamente, agriamente
tartness *n* acidez, *f*; *fig* aspereza, *f*
task *n* tarea, labor, *f*; empresa, *f*; misión, *f*. **to take to t.,** regañar, censurar. **t.-force,** (naval or military) contingente, *m*
taskmaster *n* el que señala una tarea; amo, *m*
tassel *n* borla, *f*; (of corn) panoja, espiga, *f*
taste *n* gusto, *m*; (flavor) sabor, *m*; (specimen) ejemplo, *m*, idea, *f*; (small quantity) un poco, muy poco; (liking) afición, inclinación, *f*; (of drink) sorbo, trago, *m*; (tinge) dejo, *m*. *vt* (appraise) probar; gustar, percibir el gusto de; (experience) experimentar, conocer. *vi* tener gusto, tener sabor. **a matter of t.,** cuestión de gusto. **Each to his own t.,** Entre gustos no hay disputa. **He had not tasted a bite,** No había probado bocado. **in bad (good) t.,** de mal (buen) gusto; de mal (buen) tono. **to have a t. for,** ser aficionado a, gustar de. **to t.,** *cul* a gusto, a sabor. **to t. of,** tener gusto de, saber a
tasted *a* (in compounds) de sabor . . .
tasteful *a* de buen gusto
tastefully *adv* con buen gusto
tastefulness *n* buen gusto, *m*
tasteless *a* insípido, soso, insulso; de mal gusto
tastelessness *n* insipidez, insulsez, *f*; mal gusto, *m*
taster *n* catador, *m*; (vessel) catavino, *m*
tasting *n* saboreo, *m*, gustación, *f*, *a* (in compounds) de sabor . . .
tasty *a* apetitoso, sabroso
tatter *n* andrajo, harapo, *m*; jirón, *m*. **to tear in tatters,** hacer jirones
tattered *a* andrajoso, haraposo
tatting *n* frivolité, *m*
tattoo *n* tatuaje, *m*; *mil* retreta, *f*; (display) parada militar, *f*. *vt* tatuar
tattooing *n* tatuaje, *m*; tamboreo, *m*
taunt *n* mofa, *f*, insulto, escarnio, *m*. *vt* insultar, atormentar. **to t. with,** echar en cara
taunting *a* insultante, burlón, insolente
tauntingly *adv* burlonamente, insolentemente
Taurus *n* tauro, toro, *m*
taut *a* tieso, tirante, tenso; en regla; *naut* **to make t.,** tesar
tauten *vt* tesar; poner tieso
tautness *n* tensión, *f*
tautological *a* tautológico
tautology *n* tautología, *f*
tavern *n* taberna, *f*; (inn) mesón, *m*, posada, *f*. **t.-keeper,** tabernero, *m*
tawdrily *adv* llamativamente, de un modo cursi
tawdriness *n* charrería, *f*
tawdry *a* chillón, charro, cursi
tawny *a* leonado
tax *n* contribución, gabela, imposición, *f*; *fig* carga, *f*; *vt* imponer contribuciones (a); *law* tasar; *fig* cargar, abrumar. **to tax with,** tachar (de), acusar (de). **direct (indirect) tax,** contribución directa (indirecta), *f*. **tax-collector,** recaudador de contribuciones, *m*. **tax-free,** libre de impuestos. **tax-rate,** tarifa de impuestos, *f*, cupo, *m*. **tax-register,** lista de contribuyentes, *f*
taxable *a* imponible, sujeto a impuestos
taxation *n* imposición de contribuciones (or impuestos), *f*
tax evasion *n* evasión tributaria, *f*
taxi *n* taxi, *m*. *vi* ir en un taxi; *aer* correr por tierra. **t. driver,** chófer de un taxi, taxista, *m*. **t. rank, taxi stand,** parada de taxis, *f*
taxidermist *n* taxidermista, *mf*

taxidermy *n* taxidermia, *f*
taximeter *n* taxímetro, *m*
taxpayer *n* contribuyente, *mf*
taxpaying *a* tributario, que paga contribuciones
tax reform *n* reforma impositiva, reforma tributaria, *f*
tea *n* (liquid) té, *m*; (meal) merienda, *f*. **to have tea,** tomar el té, merendar. **tea-caddy,** bote para té, *m*. **tea-chest,** caja para té, *f*. **tea-cosy,** cubretetera, *m*. **tea-cup,** taza para té, *f*. **tea-dance,** té baile, *m*. **tea-kettle** or **tea-pot,** tetera, *f*. **tea-leaf,** hoja de té, *f*. **tea-party,** reunión para tomar el té, *f*. **tea-room,** salón de té, *m*. **tea-rose,** rosa de té, *f*. **tea-set,** juego de té, *m*. **tea-strainer,** colador de té, *m*. **tea-time,** hora de té, *f*. **tea-urn,** samowar, *m*, tetera para hacer té, *f*. **tea-waggon,** carrito para el té, *m*
teach *vt* (a person) enseñar, instruir; (a subject) enseñar; (to lecture on) ser profesor de; (a lesson) dar una lección (de). *vi* (be a teacher) dedicarse a la enseñanza. **to teach at . . . ,** desempeñar una cátedra en . . . **to t. a person Spanish,** enseñar el castellano a alguien. **to t. how to,** enseñar a (followed by infin.)
teachability *n* docilidad, *f*
teachable *a* educable; dócil
teacher *n* preceptor, *m*; profesor, maestro, *m*. **woman t.,** profesora, maestra, *f*
teaching *n* enseñanza, *f*; (belief) doctrina, *f*, *a* docente. **t. profession,** magisterio, *m*
teaching method *n* método didáctico, *f*
teak *n* *bot* teca, *f*; (wood) madera de teca, *f*
team *n* (of horses) tiro, *m*; (of oxen, mules) par, *m*, pareja, yunta, *f*; *sport* partido, equipo, *m*; compañía, *f*, grupo, *m*. *vt* enganchar, uncir. **t.-work,** cooperación, *f*
teamster *n* gañán, *m*
tear *vt* rasgar; romper; lacerar; (in pieces) hacer pedazos, despedazar; (scratch) arañar; *fig* atormentar. **to t. asunder,** romper; desmembrar. **to t. away,** arrancar, quitar violentamente. **to t. down,** derribar, echar abajo. **to t. off,** arrancar; desgajar. **to t. oneself away,** arrancarse, desgarrarse. **to t. one's hair,** arrancarse los pelos, mesarse. **to t. open,** abrir apresuradamente. **to t. up,** hacer pedazos; (uproot) arrancar, desarraigar.
tear *vi* rasgarse; romperse; correr precipitadamente. **to t. along,** correr rápidamente (por). **to t. away,** marcharse corriendo. **to t. down,** bajar corriendo. **to t. into,** entrar corriendo en. **to t. off,** irse precipitadamente, marcharse corriendo. **to t. up,** subir corriendo; llegar corriendo; atravesar rápidamente
tear *n* lágrima, *f*; (drop) gota, *f*. **with tears in one's eyes,** con lágrimas en los ojos. **to shed tears,** llorar, lagrimear. **to wipe away one's tears,** secarse las lágrimas. **t.-drop,** lágrima, *f*. **t.-duct,** conductor lacrimal, *m*. **t.-gas,** gas lacrimante, *m*. **t.-stained,** mojado de lágrimas
tear *n* (rent) rasgón, *m*
tearful *a* lloroso, lacrimoso
tearfully *adv* con lágrimas en los ojos
tearing *n* rasgadura, *f*, desgarro, *m*
tearjerker *n* drama lacrimón, *m*
tease *vt* (card) cardar; (annoy) fastidiar, irritar, molestar; (chaff) tomar el pelo (a), embromar; (pester) importunar. *n* bromista, *mf*
teasel *n* *bot* cardencha, *f*, *vt* cardar
teaser *n* (problem) rompecabezas, *m*; (person) bromista, *mf*
teaspoon *n* cucharita, *f*
teaspoonful *n* cucharadita, *f*
teat *n* pezón, *m*; (of animals) teta, *f*
technical *a* técnico. **t. offence,** *law* cuasidelito, *m*. **t. school,** escuela industrial, *f*
technicality *n* carácter técnico, *m*; tecnicismo, *m*; detalle técnico, *m*
technician *n* técnico, *m*
technicolor *n* tecnicolor, *m*
technique *n* técnica, *f*; ejecución, *f*; mecanismo, *m*
technological *a* tecnológico
technologist *n* tecnólogo, *m*

technology *n* tecnología, *f*
teddy bear *n* osito de trapo, *m*
tedious *a* aburrido, tedioso, pesado
tediously *adv* aburridamente
tediousness *n* aburrimiento, *m*, pesadez, *f*
tedium *n* tedio, *m*, monotonía, *f*
tee *n* *sport* teca, *f*; (golf) tee, *m*; (letter) te, *f*; cosa en forma de te, *f*. *vt* (golf) colocar la pelota en el tee
teem *vi* rebosar (de), abundar (en); pulular, hormiguear, estar lleno (de); (with rain) diluviar
teeming *a* prolífico, fecundo. **t. with,** abundante en, lleno de
teens *n pl* números y años desde trece hasta diez y nueve; edad de trece a diez y nueve años de edad. **to be still in one's t.,** no haber cumplido aún los veinte
teeter *vi* balancearse, columpiarse
teethe *vi* endentecer, echar los dientes
teething *n* dentición, *f*. **t.-ring,** chupador, *m*
teetotal *a* abstemio
teetotalism *n* abstinencia completa de bebidas alcohólicas, *f*
teetotaller *n* abstemio (-ia)
teetotum *n* perinola, *f*
telecast *vt* telefundir
telecommunication *n* telecomunicación, *f*
telegram *n* telegrama, *m*
telegraph *n* telégrafo, *m*. *vi* telegrafiar; *fig* hacer señas. *vt* telegrafiar, enviar por telégrafo. **t. line,** línea telegráfica, *f*. **t. office,** central de telégrafos, *f*. **t. pole,** poste telegráfico, *m*. **t. wire,** hilo telegráfico, *m*
telegraphic *a* telegráfico
telegraphist *n* telegrafista, *mf*
telegraphy *n* telegrafía, *f*. **wireless t.,** telegrafía sin hilos, *f*
telemetry *n* telemetría, *f*
teleology *n* teleología, *f*
telepathic *a* telepático
telepathy *n* telepatía, *f*
telephone *n* teléfono, *m*. *vi* telefonear. *vt* telefonear, llamar por teléfono. **to be on the t.,** (speaking) estar comunicando; (of subscribers) tener teléfono. **dial t.,** teléfono automático, *m*. **t. call,** comunicación telefónica, *f*; conversación telefónica, *f*. **t. call box,** teléfono público, *m*. **t. directory,** guía de teléfonos, *f*. **t. exchange,** central telefónica, *f*. **t. number,** número de teléfono, *m*. **t. operator,** telefonista, *mf* **t. receiver,** receptor telefónico, *m*. **t. wire,** hilo telefónico, *m*
telephonic *a* telefónico
telephonist *n* telefonista, *mf*
telephony *n* telefonía, *f*. **wireless t.,** telefonía sin hilos, *f*
teleprinter *n* teletipo, *m*
telescope *n* telescopio, catalejo, *m*. *vt* enchufar. *vi* enchufarse, meterse una cosa dentro de otra
telescopic *a* telescópico; de enchufe
televise *vt* trasmitir por televisión
television *n* televisión, *f*. **on television,** por televisión. **I saw her on television,** La vi por televisión
television series *n* serie televisiva, *f*
tell *vt* contar, narrar; decir; revelar; expresar; (the time, of clocks) marcar; (inform) comunicar, informar; (show) indicar, manifestar; (explain) explicar; (distinguir; (order) mandar; (compute) contar. *vi* decir; (have effect) producir efecto. **We cannot t.,** No sabemos. **Who can t.?** ¿Quién sabe? **T. that to the marines!,** Cuéntaselo a tu tía! **to t. again,** volver a decir; contar otra vez. **to t. off,** regañar, reñir; (on a mission) despachar, mandar. **to t. on,** delatar. **to t. upon,** afectar
teller *n* narrador (-ra) de (votes) escrutador (-ra) de votos; (payer) pagador; (bank) cajero (-ra), *m*
telling *a* notable, significante. *n* narración, *f*
telltale *n* chismoso (-sa), soplón (-ona); (informer) acusón (-ona); *fig* indicio, *m*, señal, *f*, *a* revelador
temerity *n* temeridad, *f*
temper *n* (of metals) temple, *m*; (nature) naturaleza, *f*,

carácter, *m*; espíritu, *m*; (mood) humor, *m*; (anger) mal genio, *m*. *vt* (of metals) templar; moderar, mitigar; mezclar. *vi* templarse. **bad (good) t.,** mal (buen) humor. **to keep one's t.,** no enojarse, no impacientarse. **to lose one's t.,** enojarse, perder la paciencia
tempera *n art* templa, *f.* **in t.,** al temple, *m*
temperament *n* temperamento, *m*; modo de ser, natural, *m*, naturaleza, índole, *f*; *mus* temple, *m*
temperamental *a* natural, innato; caprichoso
temperamentally *adv* por naturaleza
temperance *n* moderación, templanza, *f*; sobriedad, abstinencia, *f*
temperate *a* moderado; sobrio; (of regions) templado. **t. zone,** zona templada, *f*
temperately *adv* sobriamente
temperateness *n* moderación, sobriedad, mesura, *f*; (of regions) templanza, *f*
temperature *n* temperatura, *f.* **to have a t.,** tener fiebre
tempered *a* de humor . . . , de genio . . . **to be good (bad) t.,** ser de buen (mal) humor
tempering *n* temperación, *f*
tempest *n* tempestad, borrasca, *f*, temporal, *m*; *fig* tormenta, *f*
tempest in a teapot borrasca en un vaso de agua, *m*
tempestuous *a* tempestuoso, borrascoso; *fig* impetuoso, violento
tempestuousness *n* lo tempestuoso; *fig* impetuosidad, violencia, *f*
temple *n* templo, *m*; *anat* sien, *f*
tempo *n mus* tiempo, *m*
temporal *a* temporal; (transient) transitorio, fugaz; *anat* temporal. *n anat* hueso temporal, *m*
temporality *n* temporalidad, *f*
temporarily *adv* provisionalmente
temporariness *n* interinidad, *f*
temporary *a* provisional, interino
temporize *vi* ganar tiempo; contemporizar
temporizing *n* contemporización, *f*, *a* contemporizador
tempt *vt* tentar; atraer, seducir
temptation *n* tentación, *f*; aliciente, atractivo, *m*
tempter *n* tentador (-ra)
tempting *a* tentador, atrayente; seductor
ten *a* diez; (of the clock) las diez, *f pl*; (of age) diez años, *m pl*, *n* diez, *m*; (a round number) decena, *f*. **ten-millionth,** *a* and *n* diezmillonésimo *m*. **ten months old,** diezmesino. **ten syllable,** decasílabo. **ten thousand,** *a* and *n* diez mil *m*. **There are ten thousand soldiers,** Hay diez mil soldados. **ten-thousandth,** *a* and *n* diezmilésimo *m*
tenable *a* sostenible, defendible
tenacious *a* tenaz; (stubborn) porfiado, obstinaz, terco; (sticky) adhesivo. **to be t. of life,** estar muy apegado a la vida
tenaciously *adv* tenazmente; porfiadamente
tenacity *n* tenacidad, *f*; porfía, *f*; tesón, *m*
tenancy *n* inquilinato, *m*; tenencia, *f*
tenant *n* arrendatario (-ia), inquilino (-na); habitante, *m*; morador (-ra)
tench *n icht* tenca, *f*
tend *vt* cuidar, atender; guardar; vigilar. *vi* tender; inclinarse (a), propender (a)
tendency *n* tendencia, inclinación; propensión, *f*; proclividad, *f*
tendentious *a* tendencioso
tender *n* guardián, *m*; *com* oferta, propuesta, *f*; *naut* falúa, *f*; (of a railway engine) ténder, *m*. **legal t.,** moneda corriente, *f*
tender *a* tierno; delicado; (of conscience) escrupuloso; (of a subject) espinoso; compasivo, afectuoso, sensible; muelle, blando. **t.-hearted,** compasivo, tierno de corazón
tender *vt* ofrecer; dar; presentar. *vi* hacer una oferta. **to t. condolences,** dar el pésame. **to t. one's resignation,** presentar la dimisión. **to t. thanks,** dar las gracias

tenderly *adv* tiernamente
tenderness *n* ternura, *f*; sensibilidad, *f*; delicadeza, *f*; dulzura, *f*; indulgencia, *f*; compasividad, benevolencia, *f*; escrupulosidad, *f*; mimo, cariño, *m*
tendon *n anat* tendón, *m*. **t. of Achilles,** tendón de Aquiles, *m*
tenement *n* casa de vecindad, *f*; vivienda, *f*; *poet* morada, *f*
Teneriffe Tenerife, *f*
tenet *n* principio, dogma, *m*, doctrina, *f*
tenfold *a* décuplo. *adv* diez veces
tennis *n* tenis, *m*. **to play t.,** jugar al tenis. **t. ball,** pelota de tenis, *f*. **t. court,** campo de tenis, *m*, cancha de tenis, pista de tenis, *f*. **tennis club,** club de tenis, *m*. **t. racket,** raqueta de tenis, *f*; **tennis shoe,** zapatilla de tenis, *f*
tenon *n carp* espiga, *f*, *vt* espigar
tenor *n* curso, tenor, contenido, *m*; *mus* tenor, *m*; *mus* alto, *m*; (mus. instrument) viola, *f*. *a mus* de tenor
tense *n gram* tiempo, *m*. *a* tirante, estirado, tieso; tenso
tenseness *n* tirantez, *f*; tensión, *f*
tensile *a* tensor; extensible
tension *n* tensión, *f*; *elec* voltaje, *m*, tensión, *f*; (of sewing-machine) tensahílo, *m*. **state of t.,** (diplomatic) estado de tirantez, *m*
tent *n* tienda (de campaña), *f*; (bell) pabellón, *m*; *surg* tienda, *f*. **oxygen t.,** tienda oxígena, *f*. **to pitch tents,** armar las tiendas de campaña; acamparse. **to strike tents,** plegar tiendas. **t. fly,** toldo de tienda, *m*. **t. maker,** tendero, *m*. **t. peg,** clave que sujeta las cuerdas de una tienda, *f*. **t. pole,** mástil (or montante) de tienda, *m*
tentacle *n* tentáculo, *m*
tentative *a* tentativo, interino, provisional, de prueba, *n* tentativa, *f*, ensayo, *m*
tentatively *adv* por vía de ensayo, experimentalmente
tenth *a* décimo; (of monarchs) diez; (of the month) (el) diez. *n* décimo, *m*; (part) décima parte, *f*; *mus* decena, *f*
tenthly *adv* en décimo lugar
tenuity *n* tenuidad, *f*; sutilidad, *f*; delgadez, *f*
tenuous *a* tenue; sutil; delgado; fino
tenure *n* tenencia, posesión, *f*; (duration) duración, *f*; (of office) administración, *f*
tepid *a* tibio
tepidity *n* tibieza, *f*
tercentenary *n* tercer centenario, *m*
tercet *n* terceto, *m*
term *n* (limit) límite, fin, *m*; (period) plazo, tiempo, período, *m*; (schools, universities) trimestre, *m*; (math, law, logic) término, *m*; (word) expresión, palabra, *f pl*. **terms,** (conditions) condiciones, *f pl*; (charges) precios, *m pl*, tarifa, *f*; (words) términos, *m pl*, palabras, *f pl*. *vt* llamar, calificar. **for a t. of years,** por un plazo de años. **in plain terms,** en palabras claras. **on equal terms,** en condiciones iguales. **to be on bad (good) terms with,** estar en (or tener) malas (buenas) relaciones con. **to come to terms,** llegar a un acuerdo; hacer las paces. **What are your terms?** ¿Cuáles son sus condiciones? (price) ¿Cuáles son sus precios? **terms of sale,** condiciones de venta, *f pl*
termagant *n* arpía, fiera, *f*
terminable *a* terminable
terminal *a* terminal, final; (of schools, universities) trimestre. *n* término, *m*; *elec* borne, *m*; (schools, universities) examen de fin de trimestre, *m*; (railway) estación terminal, *f*; (arch and figure) término, *m*; *arch* remate, *m*
terminate *vt* limitar; terminar; concluir; poner fin (a). *vi* terminarse, concluirse (por); cesar
termination *n* terminación, conclusión, *f*; fin, *m*; *gram* terminación, *f*; cabo, remate, *m*
terminology *n* nomenclatura, terminología, *f*
terminus *n* (railway) estación terminal, *f*; (arch and figure) término, *m*; *arch* remate, *m*; *myth* Término
termite *n ent* termita, *m*
term paper *n* trabajo de examen, *m*

terms of trade *n* relación de los precios de intercambio, *f*

terrace *n* terraza, *f*, *vt* terraplenar

terraced *a* en terrazas; con terrazas

terracotta *n* terracota, *f*

terrain *n* terreno, campo, *m*, región, *f*

terrapin *n* tortuga de agua dulce, *f*

terrestrial *a* terrestre, terrenal

terrible *a* terrible, pavoroso, espantoso; *inf* tremendo

terribleness *n* terribilidad, *f*, lo horrible

terrier *n* terrier, *m*; *inf* soldado del ejército territorial, *m*

terrific *a* espantoso, terrible; *inf* atroz, tremendo

terrify *vt* aterrorizar, espantar, horrorizar

terrifying *a* aterrador, espantoso

territorial *a* territorial. *n* soldado del ejército territorial, *m*

territoriality *n* territorialidad, *f*

territory *n* región, comarca, *f*; (state) territorio, *m*; jurisdicción, *f*. **mandated territory,** territorio bajo mandato, *m pl*

terror *n* terror, pavor, espanto, *m*. **the Reign of T.,** el Reinado del Terror, *m*. **t.-stricken,** espantado, muerto de miedo

terrorism *n* terrorismo, *m*

terrorist *n* terrorista, *m*

terrorization *n* aterramiento, *m*

terrorize *vt* aterrorizar

terse *a* conciso, sucinto; seco, brusco

tersely *adv* concisamente; secamente

terseness *n* concisión, *f*; brusquedad, *f*

tertiary *a* tercero; *geol* terciario. *n ecc* terciario, *m*

tessera *n* tesela, *f*

test *n* (proof) prueba, *f*; examen, *m*; investigación, *f*; (standard) criterio, *m*, piedra de toque, *f*; *chem* análisis, *m*; (trial) ensayo, *m*; *zool* concha, *f*. *vt chem* ensayar; probar, poner a prueba; examinar; (eyes) graduar (la vista). **to put to the t.,** poner a prueba. **to stand the t.,** soportar la prueba. **t. match,** partido internacional de cricket, *m*. **t. meal,** *med* comida de prueba, *f*. **t. pilot,** *aer* piloto de pruebas, *m*. **t. tube,** tubo de ensayo, *m*

testament *n* testamento, *m*. **the New T.,** el Nuevo Testamento, *m*. **the Old T.,** el Antiguo Testamento, *m*

testamentary *a* testamentario

testate *a* testado

testator *n* testador, *m*, (**testatrix,** testadora, *f*)

testicle *n* testículo, *m*

testification *n* testificación, *f*

testify *vt* and *vi* declarar, atestar; *law* atestiguar, testificar, dar fe

testily *adv* malhumoradamente

testimonial *n* recomendación, *f*; certificado, *m*; (tribute) homenaje, *m*

testimony *n* testimonio, *m*, declaración, *f*; (proof) prueba, *f*. **in t. whereof,** en fe de lo cual. **to bear t.,** atestar

testiness *n* mal humor, *m*, irritación, *f*

testing grounds *n* campo de experimentación, campo de pruebas, *m*

testy *a* enojadizo, irritable, irascible, quisquilloso

tetanus *n* tétano, *m*

tether *n* traba, atadura, maniota, *f*. *vt* atar con una correa. **to be at the end of one's t.,** acabarse la resistencia; acabarse la paciencia

Teuton *n* teutón (-ona)

Teutonic *a* teutónico

text *n* texto, *m*; (subject) tema, *m*; (motto) lema, *m*; (of a musical composition) letra, *f*. **t.-book,** libro de texto, *m*

textile *a* textil, de tejer. *n* textil, *m*, materia textil, *f*; tejido, *m*

textual *a* textual

texture *n* (material and *biol*) tejido, *m*; textura, *f*

Thailand Tailandia, *f*

thalamus *n* (*anat, bot*) tálamo, *m*

Thames, the *n* el Támesis, *m*. **to set the T. on fire,** descubrir la pólvora

than *conjunc* que; (between **more, less,** or **fewer** and a number) de; (in comparisons of inequality) que, but que becomes *a* del (de la, de los, de las) que if the point of comparison is a noun in the principal clause, which has to be supplied mentally to fill up the ellipsis; (*b*) de lo que if there is no noun to act as a point of comparison, e.g. **He was older than I thought,** Era más viejo de lo que yo pensaba. **They have less than they deserve,** Tienen menos de lo que merecen. **They lose more money than (the money) they earn,** Pierden más dinero del que ganan. **He will meet with more opposition than he thought,** Va a encontrar más oposición de la que pensaba. **I have more books than you,** Tengo más libros que tú. **She has fewer than nine and more than five,** Ella tiene menos de nueve y más de cinco

thank *vt* agradecer, dar las gracias (a). **to t. for,** agradecer. **I will t. you to be more polite,** Le agradecería que fuese más cortés. **He has himself to t. for it,** Él mismo tiene la culpa de ello. **No, t. you,** No, muchas gracias. **T. goodness!** ¡Gracias a Dios!

thank *n* (now in pl. only, **thanks**) gracias, *f pl*. **a vote of thanks,** un voto de gracias. **Many thanks!** ¡Muchas gracias! **to return thanks,** dar las gracias. **thanks to,** merced a, debido a. **thanks to you,** gracias a tí. **t.-offering,** ofrecimiento en acción de gracias, *m*

thankful *a* agradecido. **I am t. to see,** Me alegro de ver, Me es grato ver

thankfully *adv* con gratitud, agradecido

thankfulness *n* agradecimiento, *m*; gratitud, *f*

thankless *a* ingrato; desagradecido; desagradable

thanksgiving *n* acción de gracias, *f*. **t. service,** servicio de acción de gracias, *m*. **Thanksgiving (Day),** *n* día de acción de dar gracias, día de gracias, *m*

that *dem a* ese, *m*; esa, *f*; aquel, *m*; aquella, *f*, *dem. pron* ése, *m*; ésa, *f*; eso, *neut*; aquél, *m*; aquélla, *f*; aquello, *neut*; (standing for a noun) el, *m*; la, *f*; lo, *neut* **All t. there is,** Todo lo que hay. **His temperament is t. of his mother,** Su temperamento es de su madre. **We have not come to t. yet,** Todavía no hemos llegado a ese punto. **T. is what I want to know,** Eso es lo que quiero saber. **with t.,** con eso; (thereupon) en eso. **Go t. way,** Vaya Vd. por allí; Tome Vd. aquel camino. **T. is to say . . . ,** Es decir . . . **What do you mean by t.?** ¿Qué quieres decir con eso? **The novel is not as bad as all t.,** La novela no es tan mala como tú piensas (*or* como dicen, etc.)

that *pron. rel* que; el cual, *m*; la cual, *f*; lo cual, *neut*; (of persons) a quien, *mf*; a quienes, *mf pl*; (with from) de quien, *mf*; de quienes, *mf pl*; (of place) donde. **the letter t. I sent you,** la carta que te mandé. **The box t. John put them in,** la caja en la cual los puso Juan. **The last time t. I saw her,** La última vez que la vi

that *conjunc* que; (of purpose) para que; afin de que; (before infin.) para; (because) porque. **O t. he would come!** ¡Ojalá que viniese! **so t.,** para que; (before infin.) para; (as a result) de manera que; de modo que. **It is better t. he should not come,** Es mejor que no venga. **now t.,** ahora que

thatch *n* barda, *f*, *vt* bardar

thaw *n* deshielo, *m*. *vt* deshelar; derretir. *vi* deshelarse; derretirse

the *def art.* el, *m*; la, *f*; lo, *neut*; los, *m pl*; las, *f pl*; (before feminine sing. noun beginning with stressed a or ha) el; (untranslated between the name and number of a monarch, pope, ruler, e.g. **Charles the Tenth,** Carlos diez). *adv* (before a comparative) cuanto, tanto más. **at the** or **to the,** al, *m*, (also before feminine sing. noun beginning with a or ha); a la, *f*; a lo, *neut*; a los, *m pl*; a las, *f pl*. **from the** or **of the,** del, *m*, (also before feminine sing. noun beginning with stressed a or ha); de la, *f*; de lo, *neut*; de los, *m pl*; de las, *f pl*. **the one,** see **one.** **The sooner the better,** Cuanto antes mejor. **The room will be all the warmer,** El cuarto estará tanto más caliente

theater *n* teatro, *m*; (lecture) anfiteatro, *m*; (drama) tea-

tro, *m*, obra dramática, *f;* (scene) teatro, *m*, escena, *f.* **t. attendant,** acomodador (-ra)
theater-in-the-round *n* teatro circular, teatro en círculo, *m*
theatin *a* and *n ecc* teatino *m*
theatrical *a* teatral. *n pl* **theatricals,** funciones teatrales, *f pl.* **amateur theatricals,** función de aficionados, *f.* **t. company,** compañía de teatro, *f.* **t. costumier,** mascarero (-ra), alquilador (-ra) de disfraces. **t. manager,** empresario de teatro, *m*
theatricality *n* teatralidad, *f*
theban *a* and *n* tebeo (-ea), tebano (-na)
Thebes Tebas, *f*
thee *pers pron* te; (after prep.) tí. **with t.,** contigo
theft *n* robo, hurto, *m*
their *poss a* su, *mf sing;* sus, *pl;* de ellos, *m pl;* de ellas, *f pl.* **They have t. books,** Tienen sus libros. **I have t. books,** Tengo los libros de ellos
theirs *poss pron* (el) suyo, *m;* (la) suya, *f;* (los) suyos, *m pl;* (las) suyas, *f pl;* de ellos, *m pl;* de ellas, *f pl.* **These hats are t.,** Estos sombreros son los suyos
them *pers pron* ellos, *m pl;* ellas, *f pl;* (as object of a verb) los, *m pl;* las, *f pl;* (to them) les
thematic *a* temático
theme *n* tema, asunto, *m;* tesis, *f; mus* tema, motivo, *m*
themselves *pers pron pl* ellos mismos, *m pl;* ellas mismas, *f pl, reflexive pron* sí; sí mismos; (with a reflexive verb) se. **They t. told me about it,** Ellos mismos me lo dijeron. **They left it for t.,** Lo dejaron para sí (mismos)
then *adv* (of future time) entonces; (of past time) a la sazón, en aquella época, entonces; (next, afterwards) luego, después, en seguida; (in that case) en este caso, entonces; (therefore) por consiguiente. *a* de entonces. *n* entonces, *m. conjunc* (moreover) además; pues. **And what t.?** ¿Y qué pasó después?; ¿Y qué pasará ahora?; ¿Y qué más? **by t.,** por entonces. **now and t.,** de vez en cuando. **now . . . t.,** ya . . . ya, ora . . . ora. **since t.,** desde aquel tiempo; desde entonces; desde aquella ocasión. **until t.,** hasta entonces; hasta aquella época. **well t.,** bien, pues. **t. and there,** en el acto, en seguida; allí mismo
thence *adv* desde allí, de allí; (therefore) por eso, por esa razón, por consiguiente
thenceforth *adv* de allí en adelante, desde entonces
theocracy *n* teocracia, *f*
theocratic *a* teocrático
theologian *n* teólogo, *m*
theological *a* teológico, teologal
theologize *vi* teologizar
theology *n* teología, *f*
theorem *n* teorema, *m*
theoretical *a* teórico
theoretically *adv* teóricamente, en teoría
theorist *n* teórico, *m*
theorize *vi* teorizar
theory *n* teoría, *f*
theosophical *a* teosófico
theosophist *n* teósofo, *m*
theosophy *n* teosofía, *f*
therapeutic *a* terapéutico. *n* **therapeutics,** terapéutica, *f*
therapeutist *n* terapeuta, *mf*
therapy *suffix* terapia, *f*
there *adv* allí; ahí, allá; (at that point) en eso; (used pronominally as subject of verb) haber, e.g. **T. was once a king,** Hubo una vez un rey; **What is t. to do here?** ¿Qué hay que hacer aquí? *interj* ¡vaya!; (I told you so!) ¡ya ves! ¡ya te lo dije yo!; (in surprise) ¡toma! **about t.,** cerca de allí. **down t.,** allí abajo. **in t.,** allí dentro. **out t.,** allí fuera. **over t.,** ahí; allá a lo lejos. **up t.,** allí arriba. **T. came a time when . . . ,** Llegó la hora cuando . . . **T. it is!** ¡Allí está! **t. is** or **t. are,** hay. **t. was** or **t. were,** había, hubo. **t. may be,** puede haber, quizás habrá. **t. must be,** tiene que haber. **t. will be,** habrá. **T., t.!** (to a child, etc.) ¡Vamos!

thereabouts *adv* (near to a place) cerca de allí, por ahí, allí cerca; (approximately) approximadamente, cerca de
thereafter *adv* después, después de eso
thereby *adv* (near to that place) por allí cerca; (by that means) con lo cual, de este modo
therefore *adv* por lo tanto, por eso, así, por consiguiente; por esta razón
therein *adv* (inside) allí dentro; (in this, that particular) en estre, en eso, en ese particular
thereinafter *adv* posteriormente, más adelante
thereupon *adv* (in consequence) por consiguiente, por lo tanto; (at that point) luego, en eso; (immediately afterwards) inmediatamente después, en seguida
thermal *a* termal. **t. springs,** aguas termales, termas, *f pl*
thermodynamics *n* termodinámica, *f*
thermoelectric *a* termoeléctrico
thermometer *n* termómetro, *m*
Thermopylae Termópilas, *f*
thermos flask *n* termos, *m*
thermostat *n* termostato, *m*
thermostatic *a* termostático
thesaurus *n* tesoro, tesauro, *m*
these *dem pron pl* of **this,** éstos, *m pl;* éstas, *f pl, dem a* estos, *m pl;* estas, *f pl.* **Are not t. your flowers?** ¿No son éstas tus flores? **T. pictures have been sold,** Estos cuadros han se han vendito
thesis *n* tesis, *f*
Thespian *a* dramático
Thessaly Tesalia, *f*
they *pers pron pl* ellos, *m pl;* ellas, *f pl;* (people) se (followed by sing. verb). **T. say,** Dicen, Se dice
thick *a* espeso; (big) grueso, (wall) grueso, (string, cord) gordo; (vapors) denso; (muddy) turbio; (dense, close) tupido apretado; (numerous) numeroso, repetido, continuo; (full of) lleno (de); (of voice) velado, indistinto; (obtuse) estúpido, lerdo; (friendly) íntimo. *adv* densamente; continuamente, sin cesar. **three feet t.,** de tres pies de espesor. **That's a bit t.!** ¡Eso es un poco demasiado! **to be as t. as thieves,** estar unidos como los dedos de la mano. **t.-lipped,** con labios gruesos, bezudo. **t.-headed,** estúpido, lerdo. **t.-skinned,** de piel gruesa; *zool* paquidermo; *fig* sin vergüenza, insensible. **t. stroke,** (of letters) grueso, *m*
thick *n* espesor, *m;* parte gruesa, *f;* lo más denso; (of a fight) lo más reñido; centro, *m.* **in the t. of,** en el centro (de), en medio de
thicken *vt* espesar; (increase) aumentar, multiplicar; *cul* espesar. *vi* espesarse; condensar; aumentar, multiplicarse; (of a mystery, etc.) complicarse; hacerse más denso; *cul* espesarse
thickening *n* hinchamiento, *m;* gordura, *f;* (cul and of paints) espesante, *m*
thicket *n* matorral, soto, *m*, maleza, *f;* (grove) boscaje, *m*
thickly *adv* densamente; espesamente; continuamente, sin cesar; (of speech) indistintamente
thickness *n* espesor, *m;* grueso, *m;* densidad, *f;* (of liquids) consistencia, *f;* (layer) capa, *f;* (of speech) dificultad (en el hablar), *f*
thickset *a* doblado
thief *n* ladrón (-ona); (in a candle) moco de vela, *m.* **Stop t.!** ¡Ladrones! **thieves' den,** *fig* cueva de ladrones, *f*
thieve *vi* hurtar, robar. *vt* robar
thievish *a* ladrón
thigh *n* muslo, *m.* **t.-bone,** fémur, *m*
thimble *n* dedal, *m*
thimbleful *n* lo que cabe en un dedal; *fig* dedada, *f*
thin *a* delgado; (lean) flaco; (small) pequeño; delicado; fino; (of air, light) tenue, sutil; (clothes) ligero; (sparse) escaso; transparente; (watery) aguado; (of wine) bautizado; (not close) claro; (of arguments) flojo. *vt* adelgazar; aclarar; *agr* limpiar; reducir. *vi* adelgazarse; afilarse; reducirse. **somewhat t.,** (of persons) del-

gaducho, algo flaco. **to grow t.,** enflaquecer; afilarse. **to make t.,** hacer adelgazar volver flaco. **t.-clad,** ligero de ropa; mal vestido. **t.-faced,** de cara delgada. **t.-lipped,** de labios apretados. **t.-skinned,** de piel fina; *fig* sensitivo, sensible

thine. See **theirs.** *poss pron* (el) tuyo, *m*; (la) tuya, *f*; (los) tuyos, *m pl*; (las) tuyas, *f pl*; tu, *mf*; tus, *mf pl*; de tí. **The fault is t.,** La culpa es tuya, La culpa es de tí

thing *n* cosa, *f*; objeto, artículo, *m*; (affair) asunto, *m*; (contemptuous) sujeto, tipo, *m*; (creature) ser, *m*, criatura, *f*; *pl* **things,** (belongings) efectos, trastos, *m pl*; (luggage) equipaje, *m*; (clothes) trapitos, *m pl*; (circumstances) circunstancias, condiciones, *f pl*. **above all things,** ante todo, sobre todo. **a very pretty little t.,** (child) una pequeña muy mona. **as things are,** tal como están las cosas. **for one t.,** en primer lugar. **Her behavior is not quite the t.,** La conducta de ella no está bien vista. **It is a bad t. that . . . ,** Lo malo es que . . . **It is a good t. that . . . ,** Menos mal que . . . ; Lo bueno es que . . . **No such t.!** ¡No hay tal!; ¡Nada de eso! **Poor t.!** ¡Pobrecito!; (woman) ¡Pobre mujer!; (man) ¡Pobre hombre! **to be just the t.,** venir al pelo. **with one t. and another,** entre unas cosas y otras. **I like things Spanish,** Me gusta lo español

think *vt* and *vi* pensar; (believe) creer; (deem) considerar, juzgar; imaginar; (suspect) sospechar; (opine) ser de opinión (que). **And to t. that . . . !** ¡Y pensar que . . . ! **As you t. fit,** Como usted quiera, Como a usted le parezca bien. **He thought as much,** Se lo figuraba. **He little thought that . . . !** ¡Cuán lejos estaba de pensar que . . . ! **He thinks nothing of . . . ,** No le importa . . . ; Desprecia, Tiene una opinión bastante mala de. **I don't t. so,** No lo creo. **I should just t. not!** ¡Claro que no! ¡Eso sí que no! **I should just t. so!** ¡Claro! ¡Ya lo creo! **It makes me t. of . . . ,** Me hace pensar en . . . **One might t.,** Podría creerse . . . **to t. better of something,** cambiar de opinión, considerar mejor. **to t. highly (badly) of,** tener buen (mal) concepto sobre. **to t. over carefully,** pensarlo bien, considerar detenidamente; *inf* consultar con la almohada. **to t. proper,** creer conveniente. **to t. to oneself,** pensar para sí (or entre sí). **to t. too much of oneself,** pensar demasiado en sí; tener demasiada buena opinión de sí mismo; tener humos. **What do you t. about it?** ¿Qué te parece? **to t. about,** (of persons) pensar en; (of things) pensar de (or sobre); meditar, considerar, reflexionar sobre. **to t. for,** pensar por. **to t. of,** pensar en; pensar de (or sobre). **What do you t. of this?** ¿Qué te parece esto? **to t. out,** idear, proyectar, hacer planes para; (a problem) resolver. **to t. over,** pensar; reflexionar sobre, meditar sobre. **I shall t. it over,** Lo pensaré.

thinker *n* pensador, *m*

thinking *n* pensamiento, *m*, reflexión, meditación, *f*; juicio, *m*; opinión, *f*, parecer, *m*. *a* pensador; inteligente; racional; serio. **To my way of t.,** Según pienso yo, A mi parecer. **way of t.,** modo de pensar, *m*

thinly *adv* delgadamente; esparcidamente; (lightly) ligeramente; poco numeroso

thinness *n* delgadez, *f*; (leanness) flaqueza, *f*; sutileza, tenuidad, *f*; (lack) escasez, *f*; pequeño número, *m*; poca consistencia, *f*

third *a* tercero (tercer before *m*, *sing* noun); (of monarchs) tercero; (of the month) (el) tres. *n* tercio, *m*, tercera parte, *f*; *mus* tercera, *f*. **T. time lucky!** ¡A la tercera va la vencida! **t. class,** *n* tercera clase, *f*. *a* de tercera clase. **t. party,** tercera persona, *f*. **t.-party insurance,** seguro contra tercera persona, *m*. **t. person,** tercero (-ra); *gram* tercera persona, *f*. **t.-rate,** de tercera clase

thirdly *adv* en tercer lugar

thirst *n* sed, *f*; *fig* deseo, *m*, ansia, *f*; entusiasmo, *m*. **to satisfy one's t.,** apagar (or matar) la sed

thirsty *a* sediento. **to be t.,** tener sed. **to make t.,** dar sed.

thirteen *a* and *n* trece *m*. **t. hundred,** *a* and *n* mil trescientos *m*

thirteenth *a* décimotercio; (of monarchs) trece; (of month) (el) trece, *m*, *n* décimotercio, trezavo, *m*

thirtieth *a* trigésimo; (of month) (el) treinta, *m*. *n* treintavo, *m*

thirty *a* and *n* treinta, *m*. **t.-first,** treinta y uno

this *dem a* este, *m*; esta, *f*, *dem pron* éste, *m*; ésta, *f*; esto, *neut* by t., de este modo, así. **T. is Wednesday,** Hoy es miércoles. **What is all t.?** ¿Qué es todo esto?

thistle *n* cardo, *m*. **t.-down,** papo de cardo, vilano de cardo, *m*

thither *adv* allá, hacia allá; a ese fin. *a* más remoto

thong *n* correa, tira, *f*

thoracic *a* torácico

thorax *n* tórax, *m*

thorn *n* espina, *f*; (tree) espino, *m*; *fig* abrojo, *m*, espina, *f*. **to be a t. in the flesh of,** ser una espina en el costado de. **t. brake,** espinar, *m*

thornless *a* sin espinas

thorny *a* espinoso; *fig* difícil, arduo

thorough *a* completo; perfecto; (conscientious) concienzudo; (careful) cuidadoso. **t.-bred,** (of animals) de pura raza, de casta; (of persons) bien nacido. **t.-paced,** cabal, consumado

thoroughfare *n* vía pública, *f*. **"No t.,"** «Prohibido el paso», Calle cerrada

thoroughly *adv* completamente; (of knowing a subject) a fondo; concienzudamente

thoroughness *n* perfección, *f*; minuciosidad, *f*

those *dem a pl* of **that,** esos, *m pl*; esas, *f pl*; aquellos, *m pl*; aquellas, *f pl*, *dem pron* ésos, *m pl*; ésas, *f pl*; aquéllos, *m pl*; aquéllas, *f pl*; (standing for a noun) los, *m pl*; las, *f pl*. **t. who,** quienes, *mf pl*; los que, *m pl*; las que, *f pl*. **t. that or which,** los que, *m pl*; las que, *f pl*. **Your eyes are t. of your mother,** Tus ojos son los de tu madre

thou *pers pron* tú

though *conjunc* (followed by subjunc. when doubt is implied or uncertain future time) aunque, bien que; (nevertheless) sin embargo, no obstante; (in spite of) a pesar de que; (but) pero. **as t.,** como si (followed by subjunc.). **even t.,** aunque (followed by subjunc.)

thought *n* pensamiento, *m*; meditación, reflexión, *f*. **some thoughts on . . .** algunas reflexiones sobre . . . ; opinión, *f*; consideración, *f*; idea, *f*, propósito, *m*; (care) cuidado, *m*, solicitud, *f*; *inf* pizca, *f*. **on second thought,** después de pensarlo bien. **The t. struck him,** Se le ocurrió la idea. **to collect one's thoughts,** orientarse; informarse (de). **t.-reading,** adivinación del pensamiento, *f*. **t.-transference,** telepatía, transmisión del pensamiento, *f*

thoughtful *a* pensativo, meditabundo; serio; especulativo; (provident) previsor; (kind) atento, solícito; cuidadoso; (anxious) inquieto, intranquilo

thoughtfully *adv* pensativamente; seriamente; (providently) con previsión; (kindly) atentamente, solícitamente

thoughtfulness *n* natural reflexivo, *m*, seriedad, *f*; (kindness) solicitud, atención, *f*; (forethought) previsión, *f*

thoughtless *a* irreflexivo; (careless) descuidado, negligente; (unkind) inconsiderado; (silly) necio, estúpido

thoughtlessly *adv* sin pensar, irreflexivamente; negligentemente

thoughtlessness *n* irreflexión, *f*; descuido, *m*, negligencia, *f*; (unkindness) inconsideración, *f*; (silliness) neciedad, *f*

thousand *a* mil. *n* mil, *m*; millar, *m*. **one t.,** mil, *m*. **one t. three hundred,** *a* mil trescientos, *m pl*; mil trescientas, *f pl*. *n* mil trescientos, *m pl*. **two (three) t.,** dos (tres) mil. **by thousands,** por millares, por miles. **t.-fold,** mil veces más

thousandth *a* and *n* milésimo *m*

Thrace Tracia, *f*

thrall *n* esclavo (-va); esclavitud, *f*

thrash *vt* azotar, apalear; *agr* trillar, desgranar; *inf* triunfar sobre, derrotar. *vi agr* trillar el grano; arrojarse, agitarse. *fig* **to t. out,** ventilar

thrashing *n* apaleamiento, *m*, paliza, *f*; *agr* See **threshing**

thread *n* hilo, *m*; (fibre) hebra, fibra, *f*, filamento, *m*; (of a screw) filete, *m*; *fig* hilo, *m*, *a* de hilo. *vt* (a needle) enhebrar; (beads) ensartar; (make one's way) colarse a través de, atravesar; pasar por. **to hang by a t.,** pender de un hilo. **to lose the t. of,** *fig* perder el hilo de

threadbare *a* raído; muy usado; *fig* trivial, viejo

threadlike *a* como un hilo, filiforme

threadworm *n m,* lombriz intestinal, *f*

threat *n* amenaza, *f*

threaten *vt* and *vi* amenazar. **to t. with,** amenazar con

threatening *a* amenazador. *n* amenazas, *f pl*

threateningly *adv* con amenazas

three *a* and *n* tres *m*; (of the clock) las tres, *f pl*; (of one's age) tres años, *m pl*. **t.-color process,** tricromía, *f.* **t.-colored,** tricolor. **t.-cornered,** triangular; (of hats) de tres picos, tricornio. **t.-cornered hat,** sombrero de tres picos, tricornio, *m*. **t. decker,** *naut* navío de tres puentes, *m*; novela larga, *f.* **t. deep,** en tres hileras. **t. hundred,** *a* and *n* trescientos *m*. **t.-hundredth,** *a* and *n* tricentésimo *m*. **t.-legged,** de tres patas. **t.-legged stool,** banqueta, *f.* **t.-per-cents,** accion al tres por ciento (3%), *f.* **t.-phase,** *elec* trifásico. **t.-ply,** (of yarn) triple; (of wood) de tres capas. **t.-quarter,** de tres cuartos. **t. quarters of an hour,** tres cuartos de hora, *m pl.* **t.-sided,** trilátero. **t. speed gear box,** cambio de marcha de tres velocidades, *m*. **t.-stringed,** *mus* de tres cuerdos. **t. thousand,** a tres mil, *mf pl; n* tres mil, *m*

threefold *a* triple

Three Musketeers, the los Tres Mosqueteros

threescore *a* and *n* sesenta, *m pl*

threesome *n* partido de tres, *m*

threnody *n* treno, *m*

thresh *vt* trillar, desgranar. *vi* trillar el grano. **to t. out,** ventilar

threshing *n* trilla, *f.* **t. floor,** era, *f.* **t. machine,** trilladora, *f*

threshold *n* umbral, *m*; *psy* limen, *m*; *fig* comienzo, principio, *m*; (entrance) entrada, *f.* **to cross the t.,** atravesar (or pisar) los umbrales

thrice *adv* tres veces

thrift *n* frugalidad, parsimonia, *f*

thriftless *a* malgastador, manirroto

thrifty *a* frugal, económico

thrill *n* estremecimiento, *m*; emoción, *f. vt* conmover, emocionar; penetrar. *vi* estremecerse, emocionarse

thriller *n* libro, *m*, (or comedia, *f*) sensacional; (detective novel) novela policíaca, *f*

thrilling *a* sensacional, espeluznante; (moving) emocionante, conmovedor

thrive *vi* prosperar, medrar; enriquecerse, tener éxito; (grow) desarrollarse, robustecerse; florecer; (of plants) acertar

thriving *a* próspero; floreciente; robusto, vigoroso

throat *n* garganta, *f*; orificio, *m*; (narrow entry) paso, *m*. **sore t.,** dolor de garganta, *m*. **to cut one's t.,** cortarse la garganta. **to take by the t.,** asir (or agarrar) por la garganta

throat cancer *n* cáncer de la garganta, *m*

throaty *a* indistinto, ronco

throb *n* latido, *m*; pulsación, *f*; vibración, *f*; *fig* estremecimiento, *m*. *vi* palpitar, latir; vibrar

throbbing *n* pulsación, *f*; vibración, *f. a* palpitante; vibrante. **t. pain,** dolor pungente, *m*

throe *n* dolor, *m*, agonía, *f.* angustia, *f.* **in the throes of,** en medio de; luchando con; en las garras de. **throes of childbirth,** dolores de parto, *m pl.* **throes of death,** agonía de la muerte, *f*

thrombosis *n med* trombosis, *f*

throne *n* trono, *m*; (royal power) corona, *f*, poder real,

m. vt elevar al trono. **speech from the t.,** el discurso de la corona, *m*

throng *n* muchedumbre, multitud, *f. vi* apiñarse remolinarse, acudir. *vt* atestar, llenar de bote en bote

throstle *n orn* tordo, malvís, *m*

throttle *n mech* regulador, *m*; *aut* estrangulador, *m*; *inf* garganta, *f. vt* estrangular; *fig* ahogar, suprimir. **to open (close) the t.,** abrir (cerrar) el estrangulador

throttling *n* estrangulación, *f*

through *prep* por; al través de; de un lado a otro de; por medio de; (between) entre; por causa de; gracias a. *adv* al través; de un lado a otro; (whole) entero, todo; (from beginning to end) desde el principio hasta el fin; (to the end) hasta el fin. *a* (of passages, etc.) que va desde . . . hasta . . . ; (of trains) directo. **to look t. the window,** mirar por la ventana, asomarse a la ventana. **to be wet t.,** estar calado hasta los huesos; estar muy mojado. **to carry t.,** llevar a cabo. **to fall t.,** caer por; (fail) fracasar. **to sleep the whole night t.,** dormir durante toda la noche, dormir la noche entera. **t. and t.,** completamente. **through the length and breadth of,** a lo largo y a lo ancho de, hasta los últimos rincones de. **t. traffic,** tráfico directo, *m.* **t. train,** tren directo, *m*

throughout *prep* por todo; durante todo. *adv* completamente; (from beginning to end) desde el principio hasta el fin; (everywhere) en todas partes

throw *vt* arrojar, lanzar, echar; (fire) disparar; (pottery) plasmar; (knock down) derribar; (slough) mudar (la piel); (cast off) despojarse de; (a rider) desmontar; (a glance) echar, dirigir (una mirada, etc.); (silk) torcer; (dice) echar; (light) dirigir, enfocar. **to t. oneself at the head of,** echarse a la cabeza de. **to t. open,** abrir de par en par; abrir. **to t. overboard,** *naut* echar al mar; desechar; (desert) abandonar. **to t. about,** esparcir, desparramar; derrochar. **to t. aside,** echar a un lado, desechar; abandonar, dejar. **to t. away,** tirar, desechar; (spend) malgastar, derrochar; (waste) sacrificar; (of opportunities) malograr, perder. **to t. back,** devolver; echar hacia atrás. **to t. down,** derribar, dar en el suelo con; echar abajo; (arms) rendir. **to t. down the glove,** arrojar el guante. **to t. oneself down,** tumbarse, echarse; (descend) echarse abajo. **to t. oneself down from,** arrojarse de. **to t. in,** echar dentro; (give extra) añadir; (the clutch) embragar; insertar; (a remark) hacer (una observación). **to t. off,** despojarse de; quitarse; (refuse) rechazar; sacudirse; (get rid of) despedir; (renounce) renunciar; (exhale) emitir, despedir; (verses) improvisar. **to t. on,** echar sobre; (garments) ponerse. **to t. oneself upon,** lanzarse sobre. **to t. out,** expeler; hacer salir; plantar en la calle; (utter) proferir, soltar; (one's chest) inflar. **to t. over,** (desert) abandonar, dejar. **to t. up,** (build) levantar; lanzar en el aire; (a remark) renunciar (a), abandonar; vomitar

throw *n* echada, *f*; tiro, *m*; (at dice) lance, *m*; jugada, *f*; (wrestling) derribo, *m*. **within a stone's t.,** a tiro de piedra. **t.-back,** retroceso, *m*; *biol* atavismo, *m*

thrower *n* tirador (-ra), lanzador (-ra)

throwing *n* lanzamiento, *m*, lanzada, *f.* **t. the hammer,** lanzamiento del martillo, *m*

thrum *vt* and *vi* tocar mal; (of keyed instruments) teclear; (of stringed instruments) rascar las cuerdas (de)

thrush *n orn* tordo, *m*

thrust *n* empujón, *m*; (with a sword) estocada, *f*; (fencing) golpe, *m*; (with a lance) bote, *m*; ataque, *m*; asalto, *m*. *vt* empujar; (put) meter; (insert) introducir; (pierce) atravesar; (out, through, of the head, etc.) asomar. *vi* acometer, atacar, embestir; meterse, introducirse; (intrude) entrometerse; (fencing) dar un golpe. **to t. aside,** empujar a un lado; (proposals) rechazar. **to t. back,** hacer retroceder, empujar hacia atrás; (words) tragarse; (thoughts) apartar, rechazar. **to t. down,** empujar hacia abajo; hacer bajar; *fig* reprimir. **to t. forward,** empujar hacia delante; hacer seguir. **to t. oneself forward,** adelantarse; *fig* ponerse delante de los otros, darse importancia. **to t. in,** introducir; (stick) hincar; (insert) intercalar. **to t. on,** hacer seguir; empujar sobre; (garments) ponerse rápidamente. **to t. oneself in,** introducirse; entrometerse. **to t. out,** echar fuera; hacer salir, echar; expulsar; (the tongue) sacar (la lengua); (the head, etc.) asomar. **to t. through,** atravesar; (pierce) traspasar. **to t. one's way through,** abrirse paso por. **to t. upon,** imponer, hacer aceptar

thud *n* sonido sordo, *m;* golpe sordo, *m*

thug *n* asesino, criminal, *m*

thumb *n* pulgar, *m. vt* hojear; ensuciar con los dedos. **under the t. of,** *fig* en el poder de. **t. index,** índice pulgar, *m*. **t.-mark,** huella del dedo, *f*. **t.-screw,** tornillo de orejas, *m*, **t.-stall,** dedil, *m*. **t.-tack,** chinche, *m*

thump *n* golpe, porrazo, *m. vt and vi* golpear, aporrear; (the ground, of rabbits) zapatear

thunder *n* trueno, *m;* (of hooves, etc.) estampido, *m;* estruendo, *m. vi* tronar; retumbar; *fig* fulminar. *vt* gritar en una voz de trueno, rugir. **to t. along,** avanzar como el trueno; galopar ruidosamente. **t.-clap,** trueno, *m*. **t.-cloud,** nube de tormenta, *f,* nubarrón, *m*. **t.-storm,** tronada, *f*. **t. struck,** muerto, estupefacto. **to be thunderstruck,** quedarse frío

thunderbolt *n* rayo, *m*

thunderer *n* fulminador, *m*. **the Thunderer,** Júpiter tonante, Júpiter tronante, *m;* el «Times» londinense, *m*

Thuringia Turingia, *f*

Thursday *n* jueves, *m*. **Holy T.,** Jueves Santo, *m*

thus *adv* así; de este modo; en estos términos; hasta este punto. **t. far,** hasta ahora; hasta este punto; hasta aquí. **Thus it is that . . . ,** Así es que . . .

thwack *n* golpe, *m; vt* golpear

thwart *vt* frustrar, impedir

thy *poss* a tu, *mf;* tus, *m pl,* and *f pl*

thyme *n bot* tomillo, *m*

thymus *n anat* timo, *m*

thyroid *a* tiroideo. **t. gland,** tiroides, *f*

thyself *poss pron* tu mismo, *m;* tu misma, *f;* (with prep.) tí mismo, *m;* tí misma, *f;* (in a reflexive verb) te

tiara *n* tiara, *f*

Tiberias Tiberíades, *f*

Tibetan *a* and *n* tibetano (-na); (language) tibetano, *m*

tibia *n anat* tibia, *f*

tic *n* (twitch) tic nervioso, *m*

tick *n ent* ácaro, *m;* (sound) tictac, *m;* (cover) funda de colchón, *f; inf* fiado, crédito, *m;* (mark) marca, *f vi* hacer tictac. *vt* poner una marca contra. **on t.,** *inf* al fiado. **to t. off,** poner una marca contra; *inf* reñir. **to t. over,** *aut* andar, marchar

ticket *n* billete, *m;* (for an entertainment) entrada, localidad, *f;* (label) etiqueta, *f;* (pawn) papeleta de empeño, *f;* (for luggage) talón, *m;* (*pol* U.S.A.) candidatura, *f, vt* marcar. **to take one's t.,** sacar el billete (or for entertainment) la entrada, *f*). **excursion t.,** billete de excursión, *m*. **return t.,** billete de ida y vuelta, *m*. **season t.,** billete de abono, *m*. **single t.,** billete sencillo, *m*. **t. agency,** (for travel) agencia de viajes, *f;* (for entertainments) agencia de teatros, *f*. **t. collector or inspector,** revisor, *m*. **t. holder,** tenedor de billete, *m;* abonado (-da). **t. office,** (railway) despacho de billetes, *m;* taquilla, *f*. **t.-of-leave,** libertad condicional, *f*. **t. punch,** sacabocados, *m;* (on tramcars) clasificador de billetes, *m*

ticking *n* (sound) tictac, *m;* (cloth) cotí, *m*

tickle *vt* hacer cosquillas (a), cosquillear; irritar; (gratify) halagar; (amuse) divertir. *vi* tener cosquillas; hacer cosquillas; ser irritante

ticklish *a* cosquilloso; (of persons) difícil, vidrioso; (of affairs) espinoso, delicado

tidal *a* de marea. **t. wave,** marejada, *f; fig* ola popular, *f*

tidbit *n* See **titbit**

tiddlywinks *n* juego de la pulga, *m*

tide *n* marea, *f;* (season) tiempo, *m,* estación, *f;* (trend) corriente, *f;* (progress) curso, *m;* marcha, *f. vi* (with over) vencer, superar; aguardar la ocasión. **to go**

against the t., ir contra la corriente. **to go with the t.,** seguir la corriente. **high t.,** marea alta, *f*. **low t.,** marea baja, *f,* bajamar, *m*. **neap t.,** marea muerta, *f*. **t. mark,** lengua del agua, *f*

tideless *a* sin mareas

tidily *adv* aseadamente; en orden, metódicamente

tidiness *n* aseo, *m;* buen orden, *m*

tidings *n pl* noticias, nuevas, *f pl*

tidy *a* aseado; metódico, en orden; pulcro; *inf* considerable. *vt* poner en orden, asear; limpiar; (oneself) arreglarse

tie *n* lazo, *m,* atadura, *f;* (knot) nudo, *m;* (for the neck) corbata, *f; sport* empate, *m; mus* ligado, *m; arch* tirante, *m;* (spiritual bond) lazo, *m;* (burden) carga, responsabilidad, *f*. **tie-pin,** alfiler de corbata, *m*. **tie clasp,** pisa corbata, *mf*. **tie seller,** corbatero (-ra)

tie *vt* atar; (bind) ligar; (lace) lacear; (a knot) hacer; (with a knot) anudar; (unite) unir; (*fig* bind) constreñir, obligar; (limit) limitar, restringir; (occupy) ocupar, entretener; (hamper) estorbar, impedir. *vi* atarse; *sport* empatar. **to tie one's tie,** hacer la corbata. **to tie down,** atar a; limitar; obligar. **They tied him down to a chair,** Le ataron a una silla. **to tie together,** enlazar, ligar; unir. **to tie up,** liar, atar; (wrap) envolver; recoger; *naut* amarrar, atracar; (restrict) limitar, restringir; (invest) invertir

tie-breaker *n* desempate, *m*

tier *n* fila, hilera, *f*. **in tiers,** en gradas; (of a dress) en volantes

tiff *n* disgusto, *m*

tiger *n* tigre, *m*. **t.-cat,** gato (-ta) atigrado (-da). **t.-lily,** tigridia, *f*

tigerish *a* atigrado, de tigre; salvaje, feroz

tight *a* apretado; (not leaky) hermético, impermeable; (taut) tieso, tirante; (narrow) estrecho; (trim) compacto; (of clothes) muy ajustado; (shut) bien cerrado; *naut* estanco; (risky) peligroso, difícil; (miserly) tacaño; (of money, goods) escaso; (tipsy) borracho. **to be t.-fisted,** ser como un puño. **to hold t.,** agarrar fuerte. **t. corner,** *fig* aprieto, lance apretado, *m*. **t.-rope,** cuerda de volatinero, *f*. **t.-rope walker,** alambrista, equilibrista, *mf;* volatinero (-ra), bailarín de la cuerda floja, *m*. **t.-rope walker's pole,** balancín, *m*

tighten *vt* estrechar, apretar; (stretch) estirar; (of saddle girths) cinchar. *vi* estrecharse; estirarse

tightly *adv* estrechamente

tightness *n* estrechez, *f;* tirantez, tensión, *f;* (feeling of constriction) opresión, *f;* (drunkenness) emborrachamiento, *m*

tights *n pl* mallas, *f pl*

tigress *n* tigresa, *f*

tile *n* teja, *f;* (for flooring) baldosa, losa, *f;* (ornamental) azulejo, *m;* (hat) chistera, *f. vt* tejar; embaldosar. **t. floor,** enlosado, embaldosado, *m*. **t. manufacturer,** tejero, *m*. **t. works** or **yard,** tejar, *m,* (Colombia) galpón *m*

tiler *n* solador, *m;* tejero, *m*

till *n* (for money) cajón, *m. vt agr* cultivar, labrar. *prep* hasta. *conjunc* hasta que

tillable *a* laborable

tillage *n* labranza, *f,* cultivo, *m;* tierra de labrantío, *f*

tiller *n agr* labrador, *m; bot* mugrón, renuevo, vástago, *m; naut* caña del timón, *f*

tilling *n agr* cultivo, laboreo, *m*

tilt *n* inclinación, *f;* ladeo, *m;* (fight) torneo, *m,* justa, *f. vt* inclinar; ladear; (a drinking vessel) empinar. *vi* inclinarse; ladearse; (fight) justar. **to t. against,** *fig* arremeter contra, atacar. **at full t.,** a toda correr. **t. hammer,** martinete de báscula, *m*. **t.-yard,** palestra, *f*

tilting *n* inclinación, *f;* (fighting) justas, *f pl. a* inclinado

timber *n* madera de construcción, *f;* (trees) árboles de monte, *m pl;* bosque, *m;* (beam) viga, *f; naut* cuaderna, *f. vt* enmaderar. **t. line,** límite del bosque maderable, *m*. **t. merchant,** maderero, *m*. **t. wolf,** lobo gris, *m*. **t. work,** maderaje, *m*. **t. yard,** maderería, *f,* corral de madera, *m*

timbered *a* enmaderado; (with trees) arbolado

timbre *n mus* timbre, *m*

timbrel *n mus* tamborete, tamboril, *m*

time *n* (in general) tiempo, *m*; (epoch) época, edad, *f*; tiempos, *m pl*; (of the year) estación, *f*; (by the clock) hora, *f*; (lifetime) vida, *f*; (particular moment of time) momento, *m*; (occasion) sazón, ocasión, *f*; (day) día, *m*; (time allowed) plazo, *m*; (in repetition) vez, *f*; *mus* compás, *m*; mil paso, *m*. *vt* ajustar al tiempo; hacer con oportunidad; (regulate) regular; calcular el tiempo que se emplea en hacer una cosa; (a blow) calcular. **all the t.**, todo el tiempo; continuamente, sin cesar. **a long t.**, mucho tiempo. **a long t. ago**, mucho tiempo ha, hace mucho tiempo. **at a t.**, a la vez, al mismo tiempo; (of period) en una época. **at any t.**, a cualquier hora; en cualquier momento; (when you like) cuando gustes. **at no t.**, jamás, nunca. **at some t.**, alguna vez; en alguna época. **at some t. or another**, un día u otro; en una u otra ocasión; en alguna época. **at that t.**, en aquella época; en la sazón; en aquel instante. **at the one t.**, de una vez. **at the present t.**, en la actualidad, al presente. **at the proper t.**, a su debido tiempo; a la hora señalada; a la hora conveniente. **at the same t.**, al mismo tiempo. **at the same t. as**, mientras, a medida que; al mismo instante que, **at times**, a veces, en ocasiones. **behind the times**, *fig* atrasado de noticias; pasado de moda. **behind t.**, atrasado. **by that t.**, para entonces. **every t.**, cada vez; siempre. **for some t.**, durante algún tiempo. **for some t. past**, de algún tiempo a esta parte. **for the t. being**, de momento, por ahora, por lo pronto. **from this t.**, desde hoy; desde esta fecha. **from this t. forward**, de hoy en adelante. **from t. to t.**, de vez en cuando, de cuando en cuando, de tarde en tarde. **in a month's t.**, en un mes. **in a short t.**, en breve, dentro de poco. **in good t.**, puntualmente; temprano. **in my t.**, en mis días, en mis tiempos. **in olden times**, antiguamente, en otros tiempos. **in the course of t.**, andando el tiempo, en el transcurso de los años. **in the t. of**, en la época de. **in t.**, (promptly) a tiempo; con el tiempo. **in t. to come**, en el porvenir. **It is t. to . . .**, Es hora de . . . **many times**, frecuentemente, muchas veces. **Once upon a t.**, Érase una vez, Una vez había, Érase que érase. Érase que se era. **Since t. out of mind**, Desde tiempo inmemorial. **the last (next) t.**, la última (próxima) vez. **this t. of year**, esta estación del año. **T. hangs heavy on his hands**, El tiempo se le hace interminable. **T. flies**, El tiempo vuela. **T. will tell!** ¡El tiempo lo dirá! ¡Veremos lo que veremos! **What t. is it?** ¿Qué hora es? **The t. is . . .**, La hora es . . . **within a given t.**, dentro de un plazo dado. **to be out of t.**, estar fuera de compás. **to gain t.**, ganar tiempo. **to have a good t.**, pasarlo bien, divertirse. **to have a bad t.**, pasarlo mal; *inf* tener un mal cuarto de hora. **to have no t. to**, no tener tiempo para + noun or pronoun, no tener tiempo de + infinitive. **to keep t.**, guardar el compás. **to kill t.**, engañar (or entretener) el tiempo. **to mark t.**, marcar el paso; *fig* hacer tiempo. **to pass the t.**, pasar el rato; pasar el tiempo. **to pass the t. of day**, saludar. **to serve one's t.**, (to a trade) servir el aprendizaje; (in prison) cumplir su condena; mil hacer el servicio militar. **to take t. to**, tomar tiempo para. **to take t. by the forelock**, asir la ocasión por la melena. **to waste t.**, perder el tiempo. **t. exposure**, pose, *f*. **t. fuse**, espoleta de tiempo, espoleta graduada, *f*. **t.-honored**, tradicional, consagrado por el tiempo. **t.-keeper**, capataz, *m*; reloj, *m*. **t.-saving**, que ahorra el tiempo. **t.-server**, lameculos, *mf* **t.-signal**, señales horarias, *f pl*. **t.-table**, horario, *m*; itinerario, programa, *m*; (railway) guía de ferrocarriles, *f*. **t. to come**, porvenir, *m*, lo venidero

timed *a* calculado; (ill-) intempestivo; (well-) oportuno

timeless *a* eterno

timeliness *n* tempestividad, oportunidad, *f*

timely *a* oportuno

timepiece *n* reloj, *m*

time zone *n* huso esférico, huso horario, *m*

timid *a* tímido, asustadizo, medroso; (shy) vergonzoso

timidity *n* timidez, *f*; vergüenza, *f*

timing *n* medida del tiempo, *f*; *mech* regulación, *f*; (timetable) horario, *m*

timorous *a* timorato, apocado, asustadizo

timorousness *n* encogimiento, *m*, timidez, *f*

tin *n* (metal) estaño, *m*; (container) lata, *f*; (sheet) hojalata, *f*; (money) plata, *f*. *vt* estañar; (place in tins) envasar en lata; cubrir con hojalata, hoja de aluminio, *f*. **tin-foil**, papel de estaño, *m*. **tin hat**, casco de acero, *m*. **tin opener**, abrelatas, abridor de latas, *m*. **tinplate**, hojalata, *f*. **tin soldier**, soldado de plomo, *m*. **tin ware**, hojalatería, *f*

tincture *n* tintura, *f*, tinte, *m*; *med* tintura, *f*; (trace) dejo, *m*; (veneer) capa, *f*. *vt* teñir, tinturar

tinder *n* yesca, *f*. **t. box**, yescas, lumbres, *f pl*

tinge *n* tinte, matiz, *m*; *fig* dejo, toque, *m*. *vt* matizar, tinturar; *fig* tocar

tingle *n* picazón, comezón, *f*; (thrill) estremecimiento, *m*. *vi* picar; (of ears) zumbar; (thrill) estremecerse (de); vibrar

tingling *n* picazón, *f*; (of the ears) zumbido, *m*; (thrill) estremecimiento, *m*

tinker *n* calderero remendón, *m*. *vt* remendar. *vi* chafallar. **to t. with**, jugar con

tinkle *n* tilín, retintín, *m*; campanilleo, *m*; cencerreo, *m*. *vi* tintinar. *vt* hacer tintinar

tinkling *n* retintín, tintineo, *m*; campanilleo, *m*

tinned *a* (of food) en lata, en conserva

tinsel *n* oropel, *m*; (cloth) lama de oro o plata, *f*, brocadillo, *m*; *fig* oropel, *m*. *a* de oropel; de brocadillo; *fig* charro. *vt* adornar con oropel

tinsmith *n* hojalatero, estañador, *m*

tint *n* tinta, *f*, color, *m*; matiz, *m*; tinte, *m*. *vt* colorar, teñir; matizar

tinting *n* tintura, *f*, teñido, *m*

tiny *a* diminuto, minúsculo, menudo, chiquito

tip *n* punta, *f*; cabo, *m*, extremidad, *f*; (of an umbrella, etc.) regatón, *m*; (of a lance) borne, *m*; (of a cigarette) boquilla, *f*; (of a shoe) puntera, *f*; (of a finger) yema, *f*; (for rubbish) depósito de basura, *m*; (gratuity) propina, *f*; (information) informe oportuno, *m*; (tap) golpecito, *m*. **to have on the tip of one's tongue**, tener en la punta de la lengua. **tip-cart**, volquete, *m*. **tip-up seat**, asiento plegable, *m*

tip *vt* inclinar; volcar, voltear; (drinking vessel) empinar; poner regatón, etc. (a); *poet* tocar, golpear ligeramente; (reward) dar propina (a). *vi* inclinarse; (topple) tambalearse; (reward) dar propina. **to tip the wink**, guiñar el ojo (a). **to tip off**, (liquids) echar; hacer caer; (inform) decir en secreto; informar oportunamente. **to tip over**, *vt* volcar; hacer caer. *vi* volcarse; caer; (of a boat) zozobrar. **to tip up**, *vt* (a seat) levantar; (money) proporcionar (el dinero); (upset) volcar; hacer perder el equilibrio. *vi* volcarse; (of a seat) levantarse; (lose the balance) perder el equilibrio

tipple *n* bebida, *f*. *vi* beber, sorber. *vi* empinar el codo

tippler *n* borracho (-cha)

tipsily *adv* como borracho

tipsiness *n* borrachera, *f*

tipsy *a* achispado, algo borracho. **to be t.**, estar entre dos luces, estar entre dos velas

tiptoe (on) *adv* de puntillas; *fig* excitado, ansioso. **to stand on t.**, ponerse de puntillas, empinarse

tirade *n* diatriba, *f*

tire *n* (of a cart, etc.) llanta, *f*; *aut* neumático, *m*; (of a perambulator, etc.) rueda de goma, *f*. **balloon t.**, neumático balón, *m*. **pneumatic t.**, neumático, *m*. **slack t.**, neumático desinflado, *m*. **solid t.**, neumático macizo, *m*. **spare t.**, neumático de recambio (or de repuesto), *m*. **t. burst**, estallido de un neumático, *m*. **t. valve**, válvula de cámara (del neumático), *f*

tire *vt* cansar, fatigar; (bore) aburrir. *vi* cansarse, fatigarse; aburrirse. **to be tired of**, estar cansado de. **to**

grow tired, empezar a cansarse. **to t. out,** rendir de cansancio

tired *a* cansado, fatigado. **to be sick and t. of,** estar hasta la coronilla (de), (of persons) con. **t. of,** cansado de; disgustado de

tiredness *n* cansancio, *m*, fatiga, *f*; aburrimiento, *m*

tireless *a* infatigable, incansable

tirelessly *adv* sin tregua, sin cesar

tiresome *a* fastidioso, molesto, pesado; (dull) aburrido

tiresomeness *n* pesadez, *f*, fastidio, *m*; tedio, aburrimiento, *m*

tiring *a* fatigoso

tissue *n* (cloth) tisú, *m*, lama, *f*; (paper) pañuelito *m*; *biol* tejido, *m*; (series) serie, sarta, *f*. **t. paper,** papel de seda, *m*

tit *n* *orn* paro, *m*. **tit for tat,** tal para cual

Titan *n* titán, *m*

titanic *a* titánico

titbit *n* golosina, *f*

tithe *n* décima, *f*; fracción, pequeña parte, *f*, *vt* diezmar. **t. gatherer,** diezmero (-ra)

titillate *vt* titilar, estimular

titivate *vi* arreglarse

title *n* título, *m*; (right) derecho, *m*; documento, *m*. **to give a t. to,** intitular; ennoblecer. **t. deed,** títulos de propiedad, *m*. **t. page,** portada, *f*. **t. role,** papel principal, *m*

titter *vi* reírse disimuladamente. *n* risa disimulada, *f*

tittle *n* adarme, tilde, ápice, *m*

titular *a* titular; nominal

to *prep* a; (as far as) hasta; (in the direction of) en dirección a, hacia; (with indirect object) a; (until) hasta; (compared with) en comparación con, comparado con; (against) contra; (according to) según; (as) como; (in) en; (so that, in order to, for the purpose of) para; (indicating possession) a, de; (of time by the clock) menos; (by) por; (before verbs of motion or which imply motion) a (sometimes para); (before some other verbs) de; en; (before verbs of beginning, inviting, exhorting, obliging) a; (indicating indirect object) a; (before a subjunctive or infinitive indicating future action or obligation) que. **To** is often not translated. With most Spanish infinitives no separate translation is necessary, e.g. leer, decir, to read, to speak. Some verbs are always followed by a preposition (e.g. **to begin to speak,** empezar a hablar, etc.). *adv* (shut) cerrado. **to come to,** volver en sí. **to lie to,** *naut* ponerse a la capa. **to and from,** de un lado a otro. **face to face,** cara a cara. **He has been a good friend to them,** Ha sido un buen amigo para ellos. **That is new to me,** Eso es nuevo para mí. **He went to London,** Se fue a Londres. **to go to France (Canada),** ir a Francia (al Canadá). **the road to Madrid,** la carretera de Madrid. **She kept the secret to herself,** Guardó el secreto para sí. **to go to the dentist,** ir al dentista. **We give it to them,** Se lo damos a ellos. **It belongs to me,** Pertenece a mí. **What does it matter to you?** ¿Qué te importa a tí? **I wish to see him,** Quiero verle. **They did it to help us,** Lo hicieron para ayudarnos. **I have to go to see her,** Tengo que ir a verla. **to this day,** hasta hoy, hasta el presente. **It is a quarter to six,** Son las seis menos cuarto. **to the last shilling,** hasta el último chelín. **the next to me,** el que me sigue. **closed to the public,** cerrado para el público

toad *n* sapo, *m*

toadstool *n* hongo, *m*. **poisonous t.,** seta venenosa, *f*

toady *n* lameculos, *mf* adulador (-ra). *vt* lamer el culo (a), adular

toast *n* *cul* tostada, *f*; (drink) brindis, *m*. *vt* tostar; brindar, beber a la salud de. *vi* brindar. **buttered t.,** mantecada, *f*. **t.-rack,** portatostadas, *m*

toaster *n* (device) tostador, *m*; (person) brindador, *m*

toasting *n* tostadura, *f*, tueste, *m*, *a* de tostar. **t.-fork,** tostadera, *f*

tobacco *n* tabaco, *m*. *a* tabacalero. **black** or **cut t.,** picadura, *f*. **leaf t.,** tabaco de hoja, *m*. **mild t.,** tobaco

flojo, *m*. **pipe t.,** tabaco de pipa, *m*. **plug t.,** tabaco para mascar, *m*. **strong t.,** tabaco fuerte, *m*. **Turkish t.,** tabaco turco, *m*. **Virginian t.,** tabaco rubio, *m*. **t.-pipe,** pipa (de tabaco), *f*. **t.-pipe cleaner,** escobillón para limpiar pipas, *m*. **t. plantation,** tabacal, *m*. **t. planter,** tabacalero (-ra). **t. poisoning,** tabaquismo, *m*. **t.-pouch** or **jar,** tabaquera, *f*

tobacconist *n* tabaquero (-ra). **tobacconist's shop,** tabaquería, *f*

toboggan *n* tobogán, *m*. *vi* ir en tobogán. **t. run,** pista de tobogán, *f*

tocsin *n* rebato, *m*

today *adv* hoy; ahora, actualmente, al presente, hoy día. *n* el día de hoy. **from t.,** desde hoy. **from t. forward,** de hoy en adelante

toddle *vi* hacer pinos, empezar a andar; (stroll) dar una vuelta; (leave) marcharse

toddy *n* ponche, *m*

toe *n* dedo del pie, *m*; (cloven) pezuña, *f*; uña, *f*; (of furniture) base, *f*, pie, *m*; (of stockings, shoes) punta, *f*. **He stepped on my toe,** Me pisó el dedo del pie. **big toe,** dedo pulgar del pie, dedo gordo del pie, *m*. **little toe,** dedo pequeño del pie, *m*. **to toe the line,** ponerse en la raya; *fig* cumplir con su deber. **toe-cap,** puntera, *f*. **toe-dancing,** baile de puntillas, *m*. **toe-nail,** uña del dedo del pie, *f*

toffee *n* caramelo, *m*

toga *n* toga, *f*

together *adv* junto; (uninterruptedly) sin interrupción; (in concert) simultáneamente, a la vez, al mismo tiempo; (consecutively) seguido. **t. with,** con; junto con; en compañía de; (simultaneously) a la vez que

toil *n* labor, *f*, trabajo, *m* *pl*. **toils,** lazos, *m pl*; *fig* redes, *f pl*. *vi* trabajar, afanarse. **to t. along,** caminar penosamente (por); adelantar con dificultad. **to t. up,** subir penosamente

toiler *n* trabajador (-ra)

toilet *n* tocado, *m*; atavío, *m*; vestido, *m*; (w.c.) retrete, excusado, *m*; (for ladies) tocador, *m*. **to make one's t.,** arreglarse. **t. case,** neceser, *m*. **t.-paper,** papel higiénico, *m*. **t.-powder,** polvos de arroz, *m pl*. **t. roll,** rollo de papel higiénico, *m*. **t.-set,** juego de tocador, *m*. **t. soap,** jabón de olor, jabón de tocador, *m*

toiling *n* trabajo duro, *m*, *a* laborioso, trabajador

token *n* señal, muestra, *f*; prueba, *f*; (presage) síntoma, indicio, *m*; (remembrance) recuerdo, *m*. **as a t. of,** en señal de; como recuerdo de

Tokyo Tokio, *m*

tolerable *a* tolerable, soportable, llevadero; (fairly good) mediano, mediocre, regular

tolerably *adv* bastante

tolerance *n* tolerancia, *f*; paciencia, indulgencia, *f*

tolerant *a* tolerante; indulgente

tolerate *vt* tolerar, sufrir, soportar; permitir

toleration *n* tolerancia, *f*; indulgencia, paciencia, *f*. **religious t.,** libertad de cultos, *f*

toll *n* (of a bell) tañido, doble, *m*; (for passage) peaje, portazgo, *m*; (for grinding) derecho de molienda, *m*. *vt* and *vi* doblar, tañer. **to t. the hour,** dar la hora. **t. call,** conferencia telefónica interurbana, llamada a larga distancia, *f*. **t. gate,** barrera de peaje, *f*. **t. house,** oficina de portazgos, *f*

toll booth *n* caseta de pago, *f*

tolling *n* tañido, clamor (de las campanas), *m*

Tom *n* Tomás, *m*; (cat) gato, *m*. **Tom, Dick and Harry,** Fulano, Zutano y Mengano

tomahawk *n* hacha de guerra de los indios, *f*

tomato *n* tomate, jitomate, (Mexico) *m*. **t. plant,** tomatera, *f*. **t. sauce,** salsa de tomate, *f*

tomb *n* tumba, *f*, sepulcro, *m*

tombac *n* tombac, *m*, tumbaga, *f*

tomboy *n* muchachote, torbellino, *m*

tombstone *n* piedra mortuoria, *f*, monumento funerario, *m*

tome *n* tomo, volumen, *m*

tomfoolery *n* necedad, tontería, *f*; payasada, *f*

tommy gun *n* pistola automática

tomorrow *adv* and *n* mañana, *f.* **a fortnight t.,** mañana en quince. **the day after t.,** pasado mañana. **t. afternoon (morning),** mañana por la tarde (mañana). **T. is Friday,** Mañana es viernes

ton *n* tonelada, *f*

tonality *n* tonalidad, *f*

tone *n* tono, *m;* (*mus, med, art*) tono, *m;* (of the voice) acento, *m,* entonación, *f;* (of musical instruments) sonido, *m;* (shade) matiz, *m. vt* entonar; *phot* virar. **to t. down,** *vt* (*art, mus*) amortiguar; *fig* suavizar, modificar. *vi* (*art, mus*) amortiguarse; *fig* suavizarse, modificarse. **to t. in with,** (of colors) *vt* armonizar con. *vi* armonizarse, corresponder en tono o matiz. **to t. up,** *vt* subir de color, intensificar el color de; *med* entonar, robustecer. **t. poem,** poema sinfónico, *m*

tonelessly *adv* sin tono; apáticamente

tongs *n pl* tenazas, *f pl;* tenacillas, *f pl.* **curling t.,** tenacillas para el pelo, *f pl.* **sugar t.,** tenacillas para azúcar, *f pl*

tongue *n anat* lengua, *f;* (language) idioma, *m,* lengua, *f;* (speech) modo de hablar, *m,* habla, *f; mus* lengüeta, *f;* (of buckle) diente, *m;* (of shoe) oreja, *f;* (of land) lengua, *f;* (of a bell) badajo, *m;* (flame) lengua, *f.* **My t. ran away with me,** *inf* Se me fue la mula. **to give t.,** ladrar. **to hold one's t.,** cerrar el pico, tener la boca. **t. of fire,** lengua de fuego, *f.* **t. tied,** con impedimento en el habla; turbado, confuso; mudo. **t.-twister,** trabalenguas, *m*

-tongued *a* de voz . . .

tonic *a* tónico. *n med* tónico, reconstituyente, *m; mus* tónica, *f*

tonight *adv* and *n* esta noche

tonnage *n* tonelaje, porte, *m;* (duty) derecho de tonelaje, *m*

tonner *n naut* de . . . toneladas

tonsil *n* amígdala, *f*

tonsillitis *n* amigdalitis, *f*

tonsure *n ecc* tonsura, *f, vt* tonsurar

tonsured *a* tonsurado

too *adv* demasiado; (very) muy; también; además. **too hard,** demasiado difícil, demasiado rígido; (of persons) demasiado duro. **too much,** demasiado. **too often,** con demasiada frecuencia

tool *n* herramienta, *f;* utensilio, *m;* instrumento, *m;* (person) criatura, *f. vt* labrar con herramienta; (a book) estampar en seco. **t.-bag,** capacho, *m.* **t. box,** caja de herramientas, *f*

tooling *n* (of books) estampación en seco, *f*

toot *n* sonido de bocina, *m, vi* sonar una bocina

tooth *n* diente, *m;* muela, *f;* (of comb) púa, *f;* (taste) gusto, paladar, *m;* (cog) diente de rueda, *m;* (of saw) diente, *m. vt* dentar; mellar. *vi mech* engranar. **armed to the teeth,** armado hasta los dientes. **double t.,** muela, *f.* **false teeth,** dentadura postiza, *f.* **set of teeth,** dentadura, *f.* **to cut one's teeth,** echar los dientes. **to have a sweet t.,** ser muy goloso. **to show one's teeth,** enseñar los dientes. **t.-brush,** cepillo para los dientes, *m.* **t. drawing,** extracción de un diente, *f.* **t.-paste,** pasta dentífrica, *f*

toothache *n* dolor de muelas, *m*

toothed *a* con dientes; dentado

toothless *a* desdentado, sin dientes; (of combs) sin púas

toothpick *n* mondadientes, *m*

top *n* (summit) cima, cumbre, *f;* (of a tree) copa, *f;* (of the head) coronilla, *f;* (of a page) cabeza, *f;* (crest) copete, *m,* cresta, *f;* (surface) superficie, *f;* (of a wall) coronamiento, *m;* (tip) punta, *f;* (point) ápice, *m;* (of a tram, bus) imperial, baca, *f;* (of a wave) cresta, *f;* (acme) auge, *m;* (of a class) primero (de la clase), *m;* (highest rank) último grado, *m;* (of a plant) hojas, *f pl;* (of a piano) cima, *f; naut* cofa, *f;* (head of a bed, etc.) cabeza, *f;* (lid) tapadera, *f;* (toy) trompo, peón, *m;* (humming) trompa, *f. a* más alto; máximo; (chief) principal, primero. *vt* (cover) cubrir de; (cut off) desmochar; (come level with) llegar a la cima de; (rise above) elevarse por encima (de), coronar, dominar; (be superior to) exceder, aventajar; (golf) topear. **at the top,** a la cabeza; a la cumbre. **from top to bottom,** de arriba abajo. **on top of,** encima de; (besides) en adición a, además de. **to be top-dog,** ser un gallito. **to sleep like a top,** dormir como un lirón. **top boots,** botas de campaña, *f pl.* **top-dog,** vencedor, *m;* poderoso, *m.* **top-hat,** sombrero de copa, *m.* **top-heavy,** más pesado por arriba que por abajo

topaz *n* topacio, jacinto occidental, *m*

topcoat *n* sobretodo, gabán, *m*

top floor *n* piso alto, *m*

topic *n* asunto, tema, *m*

topical *a* tópico; actual

topknot *n* cresta, *f,* penacho, *m;* (of birds) moño, *m;* copete, *m*

topmast *n* mastelero, *m*

topmost *a* más alto; más importante

topographer *n* topógrafo, *m*

topographical *a* topográfico

topography *n* topografía, *f*

topple *vi* tambalearse, estar al punto de caer. **to t. down,** volcarse; derribarse; caer. **to t. over,** *vi* venirse abajo; perder el equilibrio. *vt* derribar, hacer caer

topsail *n* gavia, *f*

topsyturvy *a* desordenado. *adv* en desorden, patas arriba, de arriba abajo

toque *n* toca, *f*

torch *n* antorcha, hacha, tea, *f.* **electric t.,** lamparilla eléctrica, *f.* **t.-bearer,** hachero, *m*

torchlight *n* luz de antorcha, *f.* **by t.,** a la luz de las antorchas

torment *n* tormento, *m,* angustia, *f;* (torture) tortura, *f;* suplicio, *m;* mortificación, *f;* disgusto, *m. vt* atormentar; martirizar; (torture) torturar; molestar

tormentor *n* atormentador (-ra)

tornado *n* tornado, *m; icht* pez torpedo, *m. vt* torpedear

torpedo *n* torpedo, *m; fig* tormenta, *f.* **self-propelling t.,** torpedo automóvil, *m.* **t.-boat,** torpedero, *m.* **t.-boat destroyer,** cazatorpedero, contratorpedero, *m.* **t. netting,** red contra torpedos, *f.* **t. station,** base de torpedos, *f.* **t. tube,** tubo lanzatorpedos, *m*

torpedoing *n* torpedeamiento, torpedeo, *m*

torpid *a* aletargado, entorpecido; (of the mind) torpe, tardo, apático

torpidity, torpor *n* letargo, *m;* apatía, *f*

torrent *n* torrente, *m*

torrential *a* torrencial

torrid *a* tórrido. **t. zone,** zona tórrida, *f*

torsion *n* torsión, *f*

torso *n* torso, *m*

tort *n law* tuerto, *m*

tortoise *n* tortuga, *f.* **t.-shell,** carey, *m. a* de carey

tortuous *a* tortuoso

tortuousness *n* tortuosidad, *f*

torture *n* tortura, *f,* tormento, *m;* angustia, *f. vt* torturar, dar tormento (a); martirizar

torturer *n* atormentador (-ra)

torturing *a* torturador, atormentador; angustioso

toss *n* sacudimiento, *m,* sacudida, *f;* (of the head) movimiento (de cabeza), *m;* (bull fighting) cogida, *f;* (from a horse) caída de caballo, *f. vt* echar, lanzar; agitar, sacudir; (of bulls) acornear. *vi* agitarse; (of plumes, etc.) ondear; (in a boat) balancearse a la merced de las olas; jugar a cara o cruz. **to t. in a blanket,** mantear, dar una manta (a). **to t. aside,** echar a un lado; abandonar. **to t. off,** beber de un trago. **to t. up,** jugar a cara o cruz

tot *n* (child) nene (-na), crío (-ía); (of drink) vaso pequeño, *m.* **to tot up,** sumar

total *a* total; absoluto, completo, entero. *n* total, *m,* suma, *f. vt* sumar. *vi* ascender (a). **t. employment,** ocupación total, *f.* **t. war,** guerra total, *f*

totalitarian *a* totalitario

totality *n* totalidad, *f*

totally *adv* totalmente, completamente

totem *n* tótem, *m*

totemism *n* totemismo, *m*

totter *vi* (of persons) bambolearse; tambalear, estar al punto de caer; *fig* aproximarse a su fin

tottering *a* vacilante; tambaleante. *n* bamboleo, *m*; tambaleo, *m*

toucan *n orn* tucán, *m*

touch *vt* tocar; (brush against) rozar; (reach) alcanzar; (musical instruments) tocar; (move) emocionar, enternecer; (spur on) aguijar; (food) tomar; (affect) influir, afectar; (arouse) despertar, estimular; (equal) compararse con, igualar; (consider) tratar ligeramente (de); (money) dar un sablazo (a). *vi* tocarse; imponer las manos para curar. **I have not touched a bite,** No he probado un bocado. **This touches me nearly,** Esto me toca de cerca. **to t. at,** hacer escala en, tocar en (un puerto). **to t. off,** descargar. **to t. up,** retocar; corregir. **to t. upon,** (a subject) tratar superficialmente de, tratar ligeramente de; hablar de; considerar

touch *n* (sense of) tacto, *m*; (contact) toque, contacto, *m*; (brushing) roce, *m*; (tap) golpe ligero, *m*; palmadita, *f*; (of an illness) ataque ligero, *m*; *mus* dedeo, *m*; (little) dejo, *m*; (test) prueba, *f*, toque, *m*; *art* toque, *m*, pincelada, *f*. **by the t.,** a tiento. **in t. with,** en relaciones con; en comunicación con; al corriente de. **to give the finishing t.,** dar la última pincelada; dar el último toque. **t.-line,** (football) línea de toque, línea lateral, *f*. **t.-me-not,** *inf* erizo, *m*. **t.-stone,** piedra de toque, *f*

touched *a* emocionado, conmovido

touchiness *n* susceptibilidad, *f*

touching *a* patético, conmovedor. *prep* tocante a, acerca de. *n* tocamiento, *m*

touchy *a* susceptible, quisquilloso, vidrioso

tough *a* (hard) duro; vigoroso, fuerte, robusto; resistente; (of character) tenaz, firme; (of a job) difícil; espinoso. *n* chulo, *m*

toughen *vt* endurecer. *vi* endurecerse

toughness *n* dureza, *f*; vigor, *m*, fuerza, *f*; resistencia, *f*; tenacidad, firmeza, *f*; dificultad, *f*

Toulouse Tolosa, *f*

toupee *n* tupé, *m*

tour *n* viaje, *m*, excursión, *f*. *vi* viajar. *vt* viajar por. **circular t.,** viaje redondo, *m*. **on t.,** *theat* en tour, de gira

touring *a* de turismo. *n* turismo, *m*; viaje, *m*. **t. car,** coche de turismo, *m*

tourist *n* turista, *mf*; viajero (-ra). **t. agency,** agencia de turismo, *f*, patronato de turismo, *m*. **t. ticket,** billete kilométrico, *m*

tournament *n* torneo, *m*, justa, *f*; (of games) concurso, *m*

tourniquet *n* torniquete, *m*

tousle *vt* despeinar; desordenar el pelo

tout *n* buhonero, *m*. **to t. for,** pescar, solicitar

tow *n* remolque, *m*; (rope) estopa, *f*. *vt* (*naut, aut*) remolcar. **on tow,** a remolque. **tow-path,** camino de sirga, *m*. **tow rope,** cable de remolque, *m*

towage *n* remolque, *m*; (fee) derechos de remolque, *m pl*

towards *prep* hacia, en dirección a; (of time) sobre, cerca de; (concerning) tocante a; (with persons) para, con

towel *n* toalla, *f*. **roller t.,** toalla continua, *f*. **t. rail,** toallero, *m*

toweling *n* tela para toallas, *f*

tower *n* torre, *f*; (fortress) fortaleza, *f*; (belfry) campanario, *m*; (large) torreón, *m*. *vi* elevarse. **to t. above,** destacarse sobre, sobresalir; *fig* sobrepujar, superar

towered *a* torreado; de las . . . torres. **high t.,** de las altas torres

towering *a* elevado; dominante; orgulloso; *fig* violento, terrible

town *n* población, *f*, pueblo, *m*; ciudad, *f*. **t. clerk,** secretario de ayuntamiento, *m*. **t. council,** concejo municipal, *m*. **t. councilor,** concejal municipal, *m*. **t. crier,** pregonero, *m*. **t. hall,** (casa de) ayuntamiento, *m*

casa consistorial, *f*. **t. house,** casa de ciudad, *f*. **t. planning,** urbanismo, *m*; reforma urbana, *f*. **t. wall,** muralla, *f*

"Town Ahead" «Poblado Próximo»

townsman *n* ciudadano, *m*

town worthy *n* persona principal de la ciudad, *f*

toxic *a* tóxico

toxicological *a* toxicológico

toxicologist *n* toxicólogo, *m*

toxicology *n* toxicología, *f*

toxin *n* toxina, *f*

toy *n* juguete, *m*. *vi* (with) jugar con; acariciar. **toy maker,** fabricante de juguetes, *m*

toyshop *n* juguetería, tienda de juguetes, *f*

trace huella, pista, *f*; rastro, *m*; vestigio, *m*; indicio, *m*, evidencia, *f*; (of a harness) tirante, *m*; (touch) dejo, *m*; (of fear, etc.) sombra, *f*. *vt* trazar; (through transparent paper) calcar; seguir la pista (de); (write) escribir; (discern) distinguir; investigar; descubrir; determinar; (walk) atravesar, recorrer. **to t. back,** (of ancestry, etc.) hacer remontar (a)

traceable *a* que se puede trazar; atribuible

tracer *n* trazador (-ra). **t. bullet,** bala luminosa, *f*

tracery *n* tracería, *f*

trachea *n anat* tráquea, *f*

trachoma *n med* tracoma, *f*

tracing *n* calco, *m*; trazo, *m*; seguimiento, *m*. **t.-paper,** papel de calcar, *m*

track *n* huella, *f*, rastro, *m*; (for racing, etc.) pista, *f*; (of wheels) rodada, *f*; (railway) vía, *f*; (of a boat) estela, *f*; (path) senda, vereda, *f*; (sign) señal, evidencia, *f*; (course) ruta, *f*. *vt* rastrear, seguir la pista (de); *naut* sirgar. **to t. down,** seguir y capturar. **double t.,** vía doble, *f*. **off the t.,** extraviado; (of a train) descarrilado; *fig* por los cerros de Úbeda. **side t.,** desviadero, *m*. **to keep t. of,** *inf* no perder de vista (a); seguir las fortunas de

trackless *a* sin camino; sin huella; (of trams, etc.) sin rieles; (untrodden) no pisado

tract *n* tracto, *m*; región, *f*; *anat* vía, *f*; (written) tratado, *m*

tractability *n* docilidad, *f*

tractable *a* dócil

traction *n* tracción, *f*. **t.-engine,** máquina de arrastre (or de tracción), *f*

tractor *n* máquina de arrastre, *f*; tractor, *m*

trade *n* comercio, *m*; tráfico, *m*; negocio, *m*; industria, *f*; (calling) oficio, *m*, profesión, *f*; (dealers) comerciantes, *mf pl*. *vi* comerciar, traficar. *vt* cambiar. **to t. on,** explotar, aprovecharse de. **by t.,** de oficio, por profesión. **t.-mark,** marca de fábrica, *f*. **t.-name,** razón social, *f*. **t. price,** precio para el comerciante, *m*. **t. union,** sindicato, *m*. **T. Union Congress,** Congreso de Sindicatos, *m*. **t. unionism,** sistema de sindicatos obreros, *m*. **t.-winds,** vientos alisios, *m pl*

trader *n* comerciante, traficante, *mf*; mercader, *m*; (boat) buque mercante, *m*

tradesman *n* tendero, *m*. **tradesmen's entrance,** puerta de servicio, *f*

trading *n* comercio, tráfico, *m*. *a* mercantil, comerciante, mercante, *m*. **t. ship,** buque mercante, *m*. **t. station,** factoría, *f*

tradition *n* tradición, *f*

traditional *a* tradicional; del lugar

traditionalism *n* tradicionalismo, *m*

traditionalist *n* tradicionalista, *mf*

traditionally *adv* según la tradición, tradicionalmente

traduce *vt* calumniar, denigrar, vituperar

traducer *n* calumniador (-ra)

traffic *n* comercio, negocio, tráfico, *m*; (in transit) transporte, *m*; (in movement) circulación, *f*. *vi* comerciar, traficar, negociar. **to cause a block in the t.,** interrumpir la circulación. **t. block,** obstrucción del tráfico, *f*, atasco en la circulación, *m*. **t. indicator,** (on a car) indicador de dirección, *m*. **t. island,** refugio para peatones, salvavidas, *m*. **t. light,** disco, *m*, luz (de tráfico), *f*, semáforo, *m*. **t. roundabout,** redondel, *m*

trafficker *n* traficante, *mf*

tragedian *n* trágico, *m*

tragedy *n* tragedia, *f*

tragic *a* trágico

tragicomedy *n* tragicomedia, *f*

tragicomic *a* tragicómico

trail *n* rastro, *m*, pista, huella, *f*; (path) sendero, *m*; (of a comet) cola, cabellera, *f*. *vt* rastrear, seguir el rastro de; (drag) arrastrar; (the anchor) garrar. *vi* arrastrar; (of plants) trepar. **on the t. of,** en busca de; siguiendo el rastro de; **put somebody on the t. of . . .** darle a fulano la pista de . . .

trailer *n* cazador (-a); perseguidor (-ra); *aut* remolque, *m*; (cinema) anuncio de próximas atracciones, *m*; *bot* talle rastrero, *m*

train *n* (railway) tren, *m*; (of a dress) cola, *f*; (retinue) séquito, *m*; (procession) desfile, *m*, comitiva, *f*; (series) serie, sucesión, *f*; (of gunpowder) reguero de pólvora, *m*. **down t.,** tren descendente, *m*. **excursion t.,** tren de excursionistas, *m*. **express t.,** exprés, tren expreso, *m*. **fast t.,** rápido, *m*. **goods t.,** tren de mercancías, *m*. **mail t.,** tren correo, *m*. **next t.,** próximo tren, *m*. **passenger t.,** tren de pasajeros, *m*. **stopping t.,** tren ómnibus, *m*. **through t.,** tren directo, *m*. **up t.,** tren ascendente, *m*. **t.-bearer,** paje que lleva la cola, *m*; dama de honor, *f*; (of a cardinal, etc.) caudatario, *m*. **t.-ferry,** buque transbordador, *m*. **t.-oil,** aceite de ballena, *m*. **t. service,** servicio de trenes, *m*

train *vt* educar; adiestrar; enseñar; *sport* entrenar; (firearms) apuntar; (plants) guiar; (accustom) habituar, acostumbrar; (a horse for racing) entrenar; (circus) amaestrar. *vi* educarse; adiestrarse; *sport* entrenarse

trainer *n* (of men and racehorses) entrenador, *m*; (of performing animals) domador, *m*

training *n* educación, *f*; enseñanza, instrucción, *f*; *sport* entrenamiento, *m*. **t.-college,** escuela normal, *f*. **t.-ship,** buque escuela, *m*

trait *n* rasgo, *m*, característica, *f*

traitor *n* traidor, *m*

traitress *n* traidora, *f*

trajectory *n* trayectoria, *f*

tram *n* tranvía, *m*. *a* tranviario. **t. conductor,** cobrador de tranvía, *m*. **t. depot,** cochera de tranvías, *f*. **t. stop,** parada de tranvía, *f*

trammel *n* (of a horse) traba, *f*; *fig* obstáculo, estorbo, *m*. *vt* travar; *fig* estorbar, impedir

tramp *n* (person) vagabundo (-da); vago (-ga); (walk) caminata, *f*, paseo largo, *m*; ruido de pasos, *m*; *naut* vapor volandero, *m*. *vi* ir a pie; patear; vagabundear. *vt* vagar por

trample *n* pisoteo, *m*; (of feet) ruido de pasos, *m*. *vt* pisotear, pisar, hollar. *vi* pisar fuerte. **to t. on,** *fig* atropellar humillar

trance *n* rapto, arrobamiento, *m*; *med* catalepsia, *f*

tranquil *a* tranquilo, apacible; sereno, sosegado

tranquilizer *n* calmante, *m*

tranquility *n* tranquilidad, paz, quietud, *f*; serenidad, *f*, sosiego, *m*; calma, *f*

tranquilize *vt* tranquilizar, sosegar, calmar

tranquilizing *a* sosegador, tranquilizante

trans *prefix* trans-. **t.-Pyrenean,** *a* traspirenaico. **to t.-ship,** trasbordar. **t.-shipment,** trasbordo, *m*. **t.-Siberian,** trasiberiano

transact *vt* despachar, hacer. *vi* despachar un negocio

transaction *n* desempeño, *m*; negocio, *m*; transacción, operación, *f*; *pl* **transactions** (of a society) actas, *f pl*

transatlantic *a* transatlántico. **t. liner,** transatlántico, *m*

transcend *vt* exceder, superar, rebasar. *vi* trascender

transcendence *n* superioridad, *f*; trascendencia, *f*

transcendental *a* trascendental

transcontinental *a* transcontinental

transcribe *vt* trascribir, copiar; *mus* trascribir, adaptar

transcriber *n* copiador (-ra); *mus* adaptador (-ra)

transcript *n* traslado, trasunto, *m*; (student's) certificado de estudios, certificado de materias aprobadas, *m*, constancia de estudios, copia del expediente académico, hoja de estudios, *f*

transcription *n* trascripción, copia, *f*, trasunto, *m*; *mus* trascripción, adaptación, *f*, arreglo, *m*

transept *n* *arch* transepto, crucero, *m*

transfer *n* traslado, *m*; trasferencia, *f*, traspaso, *m*; *law* cesión, enajenación, *f*; (picture) calcomanía, *f*. *vt* trasladar; trasferir; pasar; *law* enajenar, ceder; estampar; calcografiar. *vi* trasbordarse. **deed of t.,** escritura de cesión, *f*. **t.-paper,** papel de calcar, *m*

transferable *a* trasferible

transferee *n* cesionario (-ia)

transference *n* traslado, *m*; transferencia, *f*; *law* cesión, enajenación, *f*

transferor *n* cesionista, *mf*

transfiguration *n* trasfiguración, *f*

transfigure *vt* trasfigurar, trasformar

transfix *vt* traspasar; *fig* paralizar

transfixion *n* trasfixión, *f*

transform *vt* trasformar; convertir, cambiar. **It is completely transformed,** Está completamente trasformado

transformation *n* trasformación, *f*; conversión, *f*, cambio, *m*

transformative *a* trasformador

transformer *n* *elec* trasformador, *m*

transfuse *vt* trasfundir

transfusion *n* trasfusión, *f*. **blood t.,** trasfusión de sangre, *f*

transgress *vt* exceder, sobrepasar; (violate) contravenir, violar, pecar contra. *vi* pecar

transgression *n* contravención, trasgresión, *f*; pecado, *m*

transgressor *n* trasgresor (-ra), pecador (-ra)

transient *a* transitorio, fugaz, pasajero; perecedero

transiently *adv* pasajeramente

transit *n* tránsito, paso, *m*; trasporte, *m*; *ast* tránsito, *m*. **in t.,** de tránsito

transition *n* transición, *f*; cambio, *m*; tránsito, paso, *m*

transitional *a* de transición, transitorio

transitive *a* *gram* transitivo, activo. **t. verb,** verbo transitivo, verbo activo, *m*

transitively *adv* transitivamente

transitorily *adv* transitoriamente; provisionalmente

transitoriness *n* brevedad, *f*, lo fugaz

transitory *a* transitorio, fugaz, pasajero, breve

translatable *a* traducible

translate *vt* traducir; interpretar; (transfer) trasladar

translation *n* traducción, *f*; versión, *f*; traslado, *m*

translator *n* traductor (-ra)

translucence *n* traslucidez, *f*

translucent *a* traslúcido, transparente

transmigrate *vi* trasmigrar

transmigration *n* trasmigración, *f*

transmissibility *n* trasmisibilidad, *f*

transmissible *a* trasmisible

transmission *n* trasmisión, *f*

transmit *vt* trasmitir; remitir, dar

transmitter *n* trasmisor (-ra); *rad* radiotrasmisor, *m*; *elec* trasmisor, *m*

transmutable *a* trasmutable

transmutation *n* trasmutación, *f*

transmute *vt* trasmutar

transoceanic *a* transoceánico

transom *n* *carp* travesaño, *m*; *naut* yugo de popa, *m*

transpacific *a* traspacífico

transparency *n* trasparencia; diafanidad, *f*; (picture) trasparente, *m*

transparent *a* trasparente; diáfano; (of style) claro, limpio

transpiration *n* traspiración, *f*

transpire *vi* traspirar; rezumarse; hacerse público; *inf* acontecer. *vt* exhalar

transplant *vt* trasplantar

transplantation n trasplante, m, trasplantación, f,

transport n trasporte, m; naut navío de trasporte, m; aer avión de trasporte, m; (fit) acceso, paroxismo, m. vt trasportar; (convicts) deportar; fig (joy) colmar; (rage) llenar

transportable a trasportable

transportation n trasporte, m; (convicts) deportación, f

transporter n trasportador (-ra)

transpose vt trasponer; mus trasportar

transposition n trasposición, f

transversal a and n trasversal, m

transverse a trasverso, trasversal

transversely adv trasversalmente

trap n trampa, f; cepo, m; (net) lazo, m, red, f; (for mice, rats) ratonera, f; mech sifón de depósito, m; pequeño carruaje de dos ruedas, m; (door) puerta caediza, f; theat escotillón, m; pl **traps**, trastos, m pl; equipaje, m. vt coger con trampa; hacer caer en el lazo; fig tender el lazo. vi armar una trampa; armar lazo. **to fall into a t.,** fig caer en la trampa. **to pack one's traps,** liar el hato

trapeze n trapecio (de gimnasia), m

trapper n cazador de animales de piel, m

trappings n pl arneses, jaeces, m pl; arreos, aderezos, m pl, galas, f pl

trash n paja, hojarasca, f; (of sugar, etc.) bagazo, m; trastos viejos, m pl; cachivaches, m pl; (literary) paja, f

trashy a de ningún valor, inútil, despreciable

traumatic a med traumático

traumatism n med traumatismo, m

travail n dolores de parto, m pl. vi estar de parto; trabajar

travel n el viajar, viajes, m pl. vi viajar; ver mundo; (of traffic) circular, pasar, ir. vt viajar por; recorrer; (with number of miles) hacer. **to t. over,** viajar por; recorrer. **t. worn,** fatigado por el viaje

travel agent n agente de viajes, mf

traveled a que ha viajado, que ha visto muchas partes

traveler n viajero (-ra); pasajero (-ra). **commercial t.,** viajante, mf **traveler's check,** cheque de viajeros, m. **traveler's joy,** bot clemátide, f

traveling n viajes, m pl. a viajero; para (or de) viajar; (itinerant) ambulante. **t. crane,** grúa móvil, f. **t. expenses,** gastos de viaje, m pl. **t. requisites,** objetos de viaje, m pl. **t. rug,** manta, f. **t. show,** circo ambulante, m

traversable a atravesable, transitable, practicable

traverse n carp travesaño, m; law navegación, f; (mil arch) través, m; (crossing) travesía, f, a transversal. adv transversalmente. vt atravesar, cruzar; law negar

travesty n parodia, f, vt parodiar

trawl vt rastrear. vi pescar a la rastra. **t.-net,** red de arrastre, f

trawler n barco barredero, m; pescador a la rastra, m

trawling n pesca a la rastra, f

tray n bandeja, f; (of a balance) platillo, m; (in a wardrobe, etc.) cajón, m; (trough) artesa, f

treacherous a traidor, falso, pérfido, fementido; (of memory) infiel; engañoso; (of ice, etc.) peligroso

treacherously adv traidoramente, a traición

treachery n perfidia, traición, falsedad, f

treacle n melado, m

tread n pisada, f; paso, m; (of a stair) peldaño, m; (of tire) pastilla, f; (walk) andar, porte, m, vi pisar; (trample) pisotear; hollar; (oppress) oprimir. vt hollar; (a path) abrir; recorrer; caminar por; bailar. **to t. the grapes,** pisar las uvas. **to t. the stage,** pisar las tablas. **to t. under foot,** hollar; pisotear. **to t. on,** pisar. **to t. on one's heels,** pisarle los talones a uno; seguir de cerca. **to t. out,** (a measure) bailar

treading n pisoteo, m

treadle n pedal, m; (of a loom) cárcola, f

treadmill n molino de rueda de escalones, m; fig rueda, f

treason n traición, f. **high t.,** alta traición, lesa majestad, f

treasonable a desleal, traidor

treasonably adv traidoramente

treasure n tesoro, m; riqueza, f, caudal, m; fig perla, f. vt atesorar; acumular (or guardar) riquezas; (a memory) guardar. **t. trove,** tesoro hallado, m

treasurer n tesorero (-ra)

treasury n tesorería, f; (government department) Ministerio de Hacienda, m; (anthology) tesoro, m. **t. bench,** banco del Gobierno, m

treat n (pleasure) gusto, placer, m; (present) obsequio, m; (entertainment) fiesta, f. vt tratar; med tratar, curar; (regale) obsequiar. vi (stand host) convidar; (of) tratar de, versar sobre; (with) negociar con

treatise n tesis, monografía, disertación, f, tratado, m

treatment n tratamiento, m; (of persons) conducta hacia, f, modo de obrar con, m; med tratamiento, m; (lit, art) procedimiento, m, técnica, f

treaty n tratado, pacto, m; (bargain) contrato, m

treble n mus tiple, m; voz de tiple, f. a triple; mus sobreagudo. vt triplicar; vi triplicarse. **t. clef,** clave de sol, f

trebling n triplicación, f

tree n árbol, m; (for shoes) horma, f; (of a saddle) arzón, m. **breadfruit t.,** árbol del pan, m. **Judas t.,** árbol de amor, m. **t. of knowledge,** árbol de la ciencia, m. **t.-covered,** arbolado. **t.-frog,** rana de San Antonio, f

treeless a sin árboles

trefoil n trébol, trifolio, m

trek vi caminar, andar

trellis n enrejado, m; (for plants) espaldera, f. vt cercar con un enrejado; construir espalderas

tremble vi temblar; estremecerse; trepidar; vibrar; (sway) oscilar; (of flags) ondear; agitarse; ser tembloroso. **His fate trembled in the balance,** Su suerte estaba en la balanza. **to t. all over,** temblar de pies a cabeza

trembling n temblor, m; estremecimiento, m; trepidación, f; vibración, f; (fear) agitación, ansiedad, f; temor, m. a tembloroso; trémulo

tremendous a terrible, espantoso; formidable; grande; importante; inf tremendo; enorme

tremendously adv terriblemente; inf enormemente

tremor n temblor, movimiento sísmico, m; (thrill) estremecimiento, m; vibración, f

tremulous a trémulo, tembloroso; vacilante; tímido

tremulously adv trémulamente; tímidamente

tremulousness n lo tembloroso; vacilación, f; timidez, f

trench n zanja, f, foso, m; (for irrigation) acequia, f; mil trinchera, f. vt hacer zanjas (en); acequiar; mil atrincherar. **t.-fever,** tifus exantemático, m. **t.-foot,** pie de trinchera, m. **t.-mortar,** mortero de trinchera, m

trenchant a mordaz

trencher n trinchero, m

trend n curso, rumbo, m; fig tendencia, f; dirección, f. vi fig tender

trepan vt surg trepanar

trepanning n surg trepanación, f

trepidation n trepidación, f

trespass n violación de propiedad, f; ofensa, f; pecado, m; (in the Lord's Prayer) deuda, f. vi (on land) entrar sin derecho, violar la propiedad; (upon) entrar sin permiso en; (with patience, etc.) abusar de; (against) pecar contra, infringir

trespasser n violador (-ra) de la ley de propiedad. **"Trespassers will be prosecuted,"** «Entrada prohibida,» «Prohibido el paso»

tress n (plait) trenza, f; rizo, bucle, m; pl **tresses,** cabellera, f

trestle n caballete, m; armazón, m. **trestle-table,** mesa de caballete, f

triad n terna, f; mus acorde, m

trial n prueba, f, ensayo, m; examen, m; (experiment) tentativa, f, experimento, m; (misfortune) desgracia, pena, f; (nuisance) molestia, f; law vista de una causa, f. **on t.,** a prueba; law en proceso. **to bring to t.,** procesar. **to stand one's t.,** ser procesado. **t. run,** marcha de ensayo, *f.* **t. trip,** *naut* viaje de ensayo, *m*

trial and error *n* tanteos, *m.* **by trial and error,** por tanteos.

triangle *n* triángulo, *m.* **acute-angled t.,** triángulo acutángulo, *m.* **obtuse-angled t.,** triángulo obtusángulo, *m.* **right-angled t.,** triángulo rectángulo, *m.* **the eternal t.,** el eterno triángulo

triangular *a* triangular, triángulo

triangulation *n* (in surveying) triangulación, *f*

tribal *a* tribal

tribe *n* tribu, *f*

tribesman *n* miembro de una tribu, *m*

tribulation *n* tribulación, *f*; pena, aflicción, desgracia, *f*

tribunal *n* (seat) tribunal, *m*; (court) juzgado, *m*; (confessional) confesionario, *m*

tribunary *a* tribúnico

tribunate *n* tribunado, *m*

tribune *n* (person) tribuno, *m*; tribuna, *f*

tributary *a* and *n* tributario *m*

tribute *n* tributo, *m*; contribución, imposición, *f*

trice *n* tris, soplo, *m.* **in a t.,** en un periquete, en un avemaría, en dos trancos

tricentennial *a* de trescientos años; *n* tercer centenario, tricentenario, *m*

trick *n* (swindle) estafa, *f*, engaño, *m*; (ruse) truco, *m*, estratagema, ardid, *f*; (mischief) travesura, *f*; burla, *f*; (illusion) ilusión, *f*; (habit) costumbre, *f*; (affectation) afectación, *f*; (jugglery) juego de manos, *m*; (knack) talento, *m*; (at cards) baza, *f*. *vt* engañar, estafar; (with out) adornar, ataviar; (with into) inducir fraudulentamente. *vi* trampear. **dirty t.,** *inf* mala pasada, perrada, *f*. **His memory plays him tricks,** La memoria le engaña. **to play a t. on,** gastar una broma (a). **to play tricks,** hacer travesuras. **t. riding,** acrobacia ecuestre, *f*

trickery *n* maullería, superchería, *f*; fraude, engaño, *m*

trickle *n* chorrito, hilo (de agua, etc.) *m. vi* gotear. **to t. down,** deslizar por, correr por, escurrir por

trickling *n* goteo, *m*; (sound) murmullo, *m*

trickster *n* embustero (-ra), trampeador (-ra). **to be a t.,** ser buena maula

tricky *a* informal, maullero; (of things) difícil; complicado; (clever) ingenioso

tricolor *a* tricolor

tricycle *n* triciclo, *m*

tried *a* probado

triennial *a* trienal

trifle *n* (object) baratija, fruslería, *f*; pequeñez, tontería, bagatela, *f*; *cul, f*; (small amount) pequeña cantidad, *f*, muy poco (de); (adverbially) algo. *vi* entretenerse, jugar. *vt* (away) malgastar. **to t. with,** jugar con

trifler *n* persona frívola, *f*; (with affections) seductor (-ra)

trifling *a* insignificante, sin importancia, trivial

trigger *n* (of a fire-arm) gatillo, *m*; *mech* tirador, *m*

trigonometric *a* trigonométrico

trigonometry *n* trigonometría, *f*

trilingual *a* trilingüe

trill *n* trino, *m*, *vi* trinar

trillion *n* trillón, *m*

trilogy *n* trilogía, *f*

trim *a* aseado; bien arreglado; bien ajustado; elegante; bonito; (of sail) orientado. **She has a t. waist,** *inf* Tiene un talle juncal. *n* orden, *m*; buen estado, *m*; buena condición, *f*; (toilet) atavío, *m*. *vt* arreglar; (tidy) asear; pulir; (ornament) ornar, adornar; (adapt) ajustar, adaptar; *sew* guarnecer; (lamps) despabilar; (a fire) atizar; (hair, moustache) atusar, recortar; (trees) mondar, atusar; *carp* alisar; (sails) templar, orientar; distribute weight in a boat) equilibrar; (of quill pens) tajar. *vi* (waver) nadar entre dos aguas. **to t. oneself up,** arreglarse

trimly *adv* aseadamente; lindamente

trimmer *n* guarnecedor (-ra); contemporizador (-ra)

trimming *n* arreglo, *m*; guarnición, *f*; (on a dress) pasamanería, *f*; adorno, *m*; *agr* poda, *f*; adaptación, *f*, ajuste, *m*; *pl* **trimmings,** accesorios, *m pl*

trimness *n* aseo, buen orden, *m*; buen estado, *m*; elegancia, lindeza, *f*; (slimness) esbeltez, *f*

Trinidad and Tobago Trinidad, *f*, y Tobago, *m*

Trinidadian *n* and *a* trinitario

Trinity *n* Trinidad, *f*

trinket *n* joya, alhaja, *f*; dije, *m*, chuchería, baratija, *f*

trinomial *a math* de tres términos. *n math* trinomio, *m*

trio *n* trío, *m*

trip *n* excursión, *f*; viaje, *m*; (slip) traspié, tropiezo, *m*; (in wrestling) zancadilla, *f*; (mistake) desliz, *m. vi* (stumble) tropezar, caer; (move nimbly) andar airosamente, ir (or correr) ligeramente; (frolic) bailar, saltar; (wrestling, games) echar la zancadilla; (err) equivocarse; cometer un desliz. *vt* (up) hacer caer; echar la zancadilla (a); coger en una falta; hacer desdecirse; coger en un desliz; *naut* levantar (el ancla)

tripartite *a* tripartito

tripartition *n* tripartición, *f*

tripe *n* callos, *m pl*

triple *a* triple. *vt* triplicar. *vi* triplicarse

triplet *n poet* terceto, *m*; *mus* tresillo, *m*; cada uno (una) de tres hermanos (hermanas) gemelos (-as)

triplicate *a* triplicado. *vt* triplicar

triplication *n* triplicación, *f*

tripod *n* trípode, *m*

Tripoli Trípoli, *m*

tripper *n* turista, excursionista, *mf*

tripping *a* ligero, ágil

trippingly *adv* ligeramente

triptych *n* tríptico, *m*

trite *a* vulgar, trivial

triteness *n* trivialidad, vulgaridad, *f*

triumph *n* triunfo, *m. vi* triunfar; (over) triunfar de, vencer

triumphal *a* triunfal. **t. arch,** arco de triunfo, *m*

triumphant *a* triunfante, victorioso

triumvirate *n* triunvirato, *m*

trivet *n* trébedes, *f pl*, trípode, *m*

trivial *a* trivial, frívolo; insignificante, sin importancia

triviality *n* trivialidad, frivolidad, *f*; insignificancia, *f*

trochlea *n anat* tróclea, *f*

trodden *a* trillado, batido

troglodyte *a* and *n* troglodita, *mf*

Trojan *a* and *n* troyano (-na). **the T. War,** la guerra de Troya, *f*

trolley *n elec* trole, *m*; (for children) carretón, *m.* **t.-bus,** trolebús, *m. n* **trolley car** tranvía, *m.* **t.-pole,** trole, *m*

trollop *n* tarasca, ramera, *f*

trombone *n* trombón, *m.* **t. player,** trombón, *m*

troop *n* banda, muchedumbre, *f; theat* compañía, *f*; (of cavalry) escuadrón, *m; pl* **troops,** mil tropas, *f pl*; ejército, *m. vi* ir en tropel, congregarse; (with away) marcharse en tropel, retirarse; (with out) salir en masa. **fresh troops,** tropas frescas, *f pl.* **storm troops,** tropas de asalto, *f pl.* **t.-ship,** transporte de guerra, *m*

trooper *n* soldado de caballería, *m*

trope *n* tropo, *m*

trophy *n* trofeo, *m*

tropic *a* and *n* trópico, *m*

tropical *a* tropical; (figurative) figurativo

tropism *n* tropismo, *m*

trot *n* trote, *m. vi* trotar. *vt* hacer trotar. **to t. out,** *inf* sacar a relucir

troth *n* fe, *f*; palabra, *f*. **to plight one's t.,** dar palabra de matrimonio, desposarse

trotting *a* trotón. *n* trote, *m*

troubadour *n* trovador, *m*, *a* trovadoresco

trouble *n* (grief) aflicción, angustia, *f*; (difficulty) dificultad, *f*; (effort) esfuerzo, *m*; pena, desgracia, *f*; (annoyance) disgusto, sinsabor, *m*; (unrest) confusión, *f*, disturbio, *m*; (illness) enfermedad, *f*; mal, *m*; (disagreement) desavenencia, *f*. **The t. is . . . ,** Lo malo es; La dificultad está en que . . . **to be in t.,** estar afligido; estar en un apuro, estar entre la espada y la pared. **to**

be not worth the t., no valer la pena. to stir up t., revolver el ajo; armar un lío. to take the t. to, tomarse la molestia de.

trouble *vt* turbar; agitar; afligir, inquietar; (badger) importunar; (annoy) molestar; (cost an effort) costar trabajo (e.g., **Learning Spanish did not t. him much,** No le costó mucho trabajo aprender el castellano). *vi* preocuparse; darse la molestia; inquietarse

troubled *a* agitado; inquieto; preocupado; (of life) accidentado, borrascoso. **to fish in t. waters,** pescar en agua turbia, pescar en río revuelto

troublesome *a* dificultoso; molesto; inconveniente; importuno; fastidioso

trough *n* gamella, *f*; (for kneading bread) artesa, *f*; (of the waves) seno, *m*; (meteorological) mínimo, *m*. **drinking t.,** abrevadero, *m*. **stone t.,** pila, *f*

trounce *vt* zurrar, apalear; *fig* fustigar

troupe *n* compañía, *f*

trousers *n pl* pantalones, *m pl*. **plus four t.,** pantalones de golf, *m pl*. **striped t.,** pantalón de corte, *m*. **t. pocket,** bolsillo del pantalón, *m*. **t. press,** prensa para pantalones, *f*

trousseau *n* ajuar de novia, *m*

trout *n* trucha, *f*

trowel *n agr* almocafre, *m*; (mason's) paleta, *f*, palustre, *m*

Troy Troya, *f*

troy weight *n* peso de joyería, *m*

truant *n* novillero, *m*; haragán (-ana). *a* haragán, perezoso. **to play t.,** (from school) hacer novillos; ausentarse

truce *n* tregua, *f*; suspensión, cesación, *f*

truck *n* (lorry) camión, *m*; carretilla de mano, *f*; (railway) vagón de carga, *m*; (intercourse) relaciones, *f pl*; (trash) cachivaches, *m pl*, cosas sin valor, *f pl*

truckage *n* camionaje, *m*; acarreo, *m*

truckle *vi* humillarse, no levantar los ojos. **t. bed,** carriola, *f*

truculence *n* truculencia, agresividad, *f*

truculent *a* truculento, agresivo

trudge *vi* caminar a pie; andar con dificultad, caminar lentamente, andar trabajosamente, *n* caminata, *f*

true *a* verdadero; real; leal, sincero; fiel; exacto; honesto; genuino; auténtico; alineado, a plomo. That is t. of . . . Es propio de . . . *adv* realmente; exactamente. **t.-bred,** de casta legítima. **t.-hearted,** leal, fiel, sincero

truffle *n* trufa, *f*. **to stuff with truffles,** trufar

truism *n* perogrullada, *f*

truly *adv* lealmente; realmente, verdaderamente; en efecto, por cierto; sinceramente, de buena fe. **Yours t.,** su seguro servidor (su s.s.)

trump *n* (cards) triunfo, *m*; son de la trompeta, *m*; *inf* gran persona, joya, *f*. *vt* ganar con el triunfo. **to t. up,** inventar. **t.-card,** naipe de triunfo, *m*

trumpery *a* de pacotilla; ineficaz. *n* oropel, *m*

trumpet *n* trompeta, *f*. *vt* trompetear; *fig* pregonar. *vi* (of elephant) barritar. **ear.-t.,** trompetilla (acústica), *f*. **speaking t.,** portavoz, *m*. **t. blast,** trompetazo, *m*. **t. shaped,** en trompeta

trumpeter *n* trompetero, trompeta, *m*

trumpeting *n* trompeteo, *m*; (of elephant) barrito, *m*

truncate *a* truncado. *vt* truncar

truncheon *n* porra (de goma), *f*; bastón de mando, *m*. **blow with a t.,** porrazo, *m*

trundle *vt* and *vi* rodar

trunk *n* (*anat bot*) tronco, *m*; (elephant's) trompa, *f*; (railway) línea principal, *f*; baúl, *m*; cofre, *m*; *pl* **trunks,** (Elizabethan, etc.) trusas, *f pl*; calzoncillos cortos, *m pl*. **wardrobe t.,** baúl mundo, *m*. **t.-call,** conferencia telefónica, *f*. **t.-line,** tronco, *m*. **t.-road,** carretera de primera clase, carretera mayor, *f*

truss *n med* braguero, *m*; (of straw, etc.) haz, *m*; (of blossom) racimo, *m*; (framework) armazón, *f*. *vt* atar; *cul* espetar; (a building) apuntalar

trust *n* fe, confianza, *f*; deber, *m*; *law* fideicomiso, *m*;

(credit) crédito, *m*; esperanza, expectación, *f*; *com* trust, *m*. *vt* tener confianza en; confiar en; esperar; creer; *com* dar crédito (a). *vi* confiar; *com* dar crédito. **in t.,** en confianza; en administración, en depósito. **on t.,** al fiado

trustee *n* guardián, *m*; *law* fideicomisario, depositario, consignatario, *m*

trustful *a* confiado

trustingly *adv* confiadamente

trust release *n* extinción de fideicomiso, *f*

trustworthiness *n* honradez, probidad, integridad, *f*; (of statements) exactitud, *f*

trustworthy *a* digno de confianza, honrado; fidedigno, seguro; exacto

trusty *a* leal, fiel; firme, seguro

truth *n* verdad, *f*; realidad, *f*; exactitud, *f*. **the plain t.,** la pura verdad. **to tell the t.,** decir la verdad

truthful *a* veraz; exacto, verdadero

truthfulness *n* veracidad, *f*; exactitud, *f*

try *vt* and *vi* procurar, tratar de; (test) probar, ensayar; (a case, *law*) ver (el pleito); (strain) poner a prueba; (tire) cansar, fatigar; (annoy) molestar, exasperar; (afflict) hacer sufrir, afligir; (attempt) intentar; (judge) juzgar; (the weight of) tomar a pulso; (assay) refinar. *n* tentativa, *f*; (football) tiro, *m*. **Try as he would . . . ,** Por más que hizo . . . **to try hard to,** hacer un gran esfuerzo para. **to try one's luck,** probar fortuna. **to try on,** (clothes) probarse (un vestido, etc.). **to try out,** poner a prueba, probar. **to try to,** tratar de, procurar

trying *a* molesto; fatigoso; irritante; (painful) angustioso, penoso

tryst *n* cita, *f*; lugar de cita, *m*. *vt* citar. *vi* citarse

tsar *n* zar, *m*

tsarina *n* zarina, *f*

tsetse fly *n* mosca tsetsé, *f*

tub *n* cuba, *f*; artesón, *m*; cubeta, *f*. *vi* bañarse. **tub thumper,** *inf* gerundio, *m*

tuba *n mus* tuba, *f*

tube *n* tubo, *m*; (railway) metro, ferrocarril subterráneo, *m*; tubo, *m*; *anat* trompa, *f*. **Eustachian t.,** *anat* trompa de Eustaquio, *f*. **Fallopian t.,** trompa de Falopio, *f*. **inner t.,** *aut* cámara de aire, *f*. **speaking t.,** tubo acústico, *m*. **test t.,** tubo de ensayo, *m*

tuber *n* tubérculo, *m*

tubercular *a* tuberculoso

tuberculosis *n* tuberculosis, *f*

tuberose *n* nardo, *m*, tuberosa, *f*

tubing *n* tubería, *f*

tubular *a* tubular

tuck *n sew* alforzar, *f*; pliegue, *m*. *vt* recoger; *sew* alforzar. *vi* hacer alforzas. **to t. in,** (in bed) arropar; *inf* tragar. **to t. under,** poner debajo; doblar. **to t. up,** (in bed) arropar; (skirt) sofaldar; (sleeves) arremangar

tucker *n* camisolín, *m*

Tuesday *n* martes, *m*. **Shrove T.,** martes de carnaval, *m*

tuft *n* (bunch) manojo, *m*; (on the head) copete, moño, *m*, cresta, *f*; (tassel) borla, *f*; mechón, *m*

tug *n* tirón, *m*; sacudida, *f*; (boat) remolcador, *m*. *vt* tirar de; halar; sacudir. *vi* tirar con fuerza. **to give a tug,** dar una sacudida. **tug of war,** *lit* lucha de la cuerda, *f*; *fig* estira y afloja, *msg*

tuition *n* (teaching) instrucción, enseñanza, *f*; lecciones, *f pl*; (fee) cuota, *f*

tulip *n* tulipán, *m*. **t. wood,** palo de rosa, *m*

tulle *n* tul, *m*

tumble *n* caída, *f*; (somersault) tumbo, *m*; voltereta, *f*. *vi* caer; (acrobats) voltear, dar saltos. *vt* hacer caer; desarreglar. **to t. down,** venirse abajo; caer por. **t. down,** ruinoso, destartalado. **to t. off,** caer de. **to t. out,** *vt* hacer salir; arrojar. *vi* salir apresuradamente. **to t. over,** *vt* tropezar con. *vi* volcarse. **to t. to,** *inf* caer en la cuenta

tumbler *n* (acrobat) volteador (-ra); vaso para beber, *m*

tumbrel *n* carreta, *f*

tumefaction *n* tumefacción, *f*

tumid *a* túmido, hinchado

tumor *n* tumor, *m*

tumult *n* alboroto, tumulto, *m*; conmoción, agitación, *f*; confusión, *f*

tumultuous *a* tumultuoso, alborotado; ruidoso; confuso; turbulento, violento

tumulus *n* túmulo, *m*

tun *n* tonel, *m*, cuba, *f*. *vt* entonelar, embarrilar

tune *n* melodía, *f*; son, *m*; armonía, *f*; *fig* tono, *m*; *inf* suma, *f*. *vt mus* afinar, templar; *rad* sintonizar; (up, an engine) ajustar (un motor). *vi* (in) sintonizar el receptor; (up, *mus*) templar (afinar) los instrumentos. **in t.,** *mus* afinado, templado; *fig* armonioso; (agreement) de acuerdo, conforme. **out of t.,** *mus* desafinado, destemplado. **to be out of t.,** desentonar, discordar; *fig* no armonizar, no estar en armonía. **to go out of t.,** desafinar. **to put out of t.,** destemplar. **to change one's t.,** *inf* bajar el tono

tuneful *a* melodioso

tunefully *adv* melodiosamente, armoniosamente

tunefulness *n* melodía, *f*

tuneless *a* disonante, discordante

tuner *n* afinador, templador, *m*; *rad* sintonizador, *m*

tungsten *n* tungsteno, *m*

tunic *n* túnica, *f*

tuning *n* afinación, *f*; *rad* sintonización, *f*. **t. fork,** diapasón normal, *m*. **t. key,** templador, *m*

Tunis Túnez, *m*

Tunisian *a* and *n* tunecino (-na)

tunnel *n* túnel, *m*. *vt* hacer (or construir) un túnel por. *vi* hacer un túnel

tunneling *n* construcción de túneles, *f*; horadación, *f*

tunny *n* atún, *m*. **striped t.,** bonito, *m*. **t. fishery,** almadraba, *f*

turban *n* turbante, *m*

turbid *a* turbio; *fig* confuso, **to make t.,** enturbiar

turbine *n* turbina, *f*

turbulence *n* turbulencia, *f*; desorden, *m*; agitación, *f*

turbulent *a* turbulento; alborotado; (stormy) borrascoso; agitado

tureen *n* sopera, *f*

turf *n* césped, *m*; (fuel) turba, *f*; (racing) carreras de caballos, *f pl*

turgid *a* turgente, hinchado; (of style) pomposo

turgidity *n* turgencia, *f*; pomposidad, *f*

Turk *n* turco (-ca). **Turk's head,** (duster) deshollinador, *m*; *naut* cabeza de turco, *f*

Turkey Turquía, *f*

turkey *n* (cock) pavo, *m*; (hen) pava, *f*; **t. red,** rojo turco, *m*

Turkish *a* turco. *n* (language) turco, idioma turco, *m*. **T. bath,** baño turco, *m*. **T. slipper,** babucha, *f*. **T. towel,** toalla rusa, *f*

turmeric *n* cúrcuma, *f*. **t. paper,** papel de cúrcuma, *m*

turmoil *n* alboroto, tumulto, desorden, *m*

turn *n* turno, *m*; (twist) torcimiento, *m*; (bend) recodo, *m*, vuelta, *f*; (in a river) meandro, *m*; (in a road) viraje, *m*; (revolution) vuelta, revolución, *f*; (direction) dirección, *f*; (in spiral stair) espira, *f*; *theat* número, *m*; (change) cambio, *m*; vicisitud, *f*; (appearance) aspecto, *m*; (service) servicio, *m*; (nature) índole, naturaleza, *f*; (of phrase) giro, *m*, expresión, *f*; (walk) vuelta, *f*, paseo, *m*; (talent) talento, *m*. **a sharp t.,** (in a road) un viraje rápido. **at every t.,** a cada instante; en todas partes. **bad t.,** flaco servicio, *m*. **by turns,** por turnos. **good t.,** servicio, favor, *m*. **in its t.,** a su vez. **in t.,** sucesivamente. **Now it's my t.,** Ahora me toca a mí. **The affair has taken a new t.,** El asunto ha cambiado de aspecto. **turn of the century,** vuelta del siglo, *f*; **turn of the millenium,** vuelta del milenio, *f*. **t. to a t.,** *cul* a la perfección. **to have a t. for,** tener talento para. **to take turns at,** alternar en. **t.-table,** (railway) plataforma, *f*; (of a gramophone) disco giratorio, *m*. **t. up,** barahúnda, conmoción, *f*; (of trousers) dobladillo (del pantalón), *m*

turn *vt* (on a lathe) tornear; (revolve) dar vueltas a, girar; (a key, door handle, etc.) torcer; (the leaves of a book) hojear; (the brain) trastornar; (a screw) enros-

car; (the stomach) revolver (el estómago), marear; (go round) doblar, dar la vuelta a; (change) cambiar, mudar; (translate) traducir, verter; (dissuade) disuadir; (deflect) desviar; (apply) adaptar; (direct, move) volver; (concentrate) dirigir; concentrar; (turn over) volver del revés al derecho; (upside-down) volver lo de arriba abajo; (make) hacer, volver; (make sour) volver agrio; (transform) transformar convertir; *mil* envolver. **He has turned thirty,** Ha cumplido los treinta. **He said it without turning a hair,** Lo dijo sin pestañear. **He turned his head,** Volvió la cabeza. **They have turned the corner,** Han doblado la esquina; *fig* Han pasado la crisis. **"Please t. over,"** «A la vuelta (de la página).» **to t. a deaf ear to,** no dar oídos a, no hacer caso de. **to t. one's hand to,** aplicarse a. **to t. to account,** sacar ventaja (de). **to t. adrift,** dejar a la merced de las olas; echar de casa, poner en la calle; abandonar. **to t. against,** causar aversión, hacer hostil. **to t. aside,** desviar. **to t. away;** despedir; rechazar; (the head, etc.) volver; desviar. **to t. back,** hacer volver; enviar de nuevo; (raise) alzar; (fold) doblar; (the clock) retrasar. **to t. down,** doblar; (gas) bajar; (a glass, etc.) poner boca abajo; (reject) rechazar; (a suitor) dar calabazas (a). **to t. from,** alejar de, desviar de. **to t. in,** doblar hacia dentro; entregar. **to t. in one's toes,** ser patizambo. **to t. inside out,** volver al revés. **to t. into,** (enter) entrar en; (change) cambiar en, transformar en; convertir en; (translate) traducir a. **to t. off,** (dismiss) despedir; (from) desviarse de, dejar; (light) apagar; (water) cortar; *mech* cerrar; (disconnect) desconectar; (avoid) evitar; (refuse) rechazar. **to t. off the tap,** (water, gas) cerrar la llave (del agua, del gas). **to t. on,** (light) encender; (water, gas, etc.) abrir la llave (del agua, del gas); (steam) dar (vapor); (electric current) establecer (la corriente eléctrica); (eyes) fijar. **to t. out,** (expel) expeler, echar; (dismiss) despedir; (animals) echar al campo; (produce) producir; (dress) vestir; (equip) equipar, guarnecer; (a light) apagar. **to t. over,** (the page) volver (la hoja); (transfer) ceder, traspasar; revolver; (upset) volcar; considerar, pensar. **to t. round,** dar vuelta a; girar; (empty) descargar. **to t. up,** levantar; apuntar; hacia arriba; (the earth) labrar, cavar; (a glass) poner boca arriba; (one's sleeves, skirt) arremangar; (fold) doblar. **to t. up one's nose at,** mirar con desprecio. **to t. upon,** atacar, volverse contra, acometer; depender de, estribar en. **to t. upside down,** volver lo de arriba abajo; revolver; revolcar

turn *vi* (in a lathe) tornear; (revolve) girar, dar vueltas a; (depend) depender (de); torcer; volverse; dar la vuelta; girar sobre los talones; dirigirse (a, hacia); (move) mudar de posición; (deviate) desviarse (de); (be changed) convertirse (en); (become) hacerse, venir a ser; (begin) meterse (a); (take to) dedicarse a; (seek help) acudir; (change behavior) enmendarse, corregirse; (the stomach) revolver (el estómago); (go sour) agriarse, avinagrarse; (rebel) sublevarse. **He turned to the left,** Dio la vuelta a la izquierda; Torció hacia la izquierda. **My head turns,** (with giddiness) Se me va la cabeza. **to t. about,** voltearse, dar la vuelta. **to t. against,** coger aversión (a), disgustarse con; volverse hostil (a). **to t. aside,** desviarse; dejar el camino. **to t. away,** volver la cabeza; apartarse; alejarse. **to t. back,** volver atrás; volver de nuevo; retroceder; volver sobre sus pasos. **to t. down,** doblarse; reducirse. **to t. from,** alejarse de; apartarse de, huir de. **to t. in,** doblarse hacia dentro; (retire) acostarse. **to t. into,** transformarse en; convertirse en. **to t. off,** (depart from) desviarse (de); (fork) torcer, bifurcarse. **to t. out,** estar vuelto hacia fuera; (leave home) salir de casa; (rise) levantarse (de la cama); (arrive) llegar, presentarse; (attend) asistir, acudir; (result) resultar. **to t. over,** mudar (or cambiar) de posición, revolverse; (upset) voltearse, volcarse. **to t. round,** girar; volverse; cambiar de frente; cambiar de dirección, dar la vuelta; (*aut, aer*) virar; (change views) cambiar de opinión; (change sides) cambiar de partido. **to t. round and round,** dar vueltas, girar. **to t. to,** (apply to) acudir a; (begin) ponerse a; (become) convertirse en; (face) dirigirse hacia; (address) dirigirse a. **to t. up,** (crop up), surgir, aparecer; (arrive) llegar; (happen) acontecer; (be found again) volver a hallarse, reaparecer; (cards) venir; (of hats) levantar el ala; (of hair, etc.) doblarse. **His nose turns up,** Tiene la nariz respingona

turncoat *n* desertor (-ra), renegado (-da). **to become a t.,** volver la casaca

turned-up *a* (of hats) con el ala levantada; (of noses) respingona

turner *n* (craftsman) tornero, torneador, *m*

turnery *n* tornería, *f*

turning *n* (bend) vuelta, *f*; (turnery) tornería, *f*; (of milk, etc.) agrura, *f*; *pl* **turnings,** *sew* ensanche, *m*. **t.-point,** punto decisivo, *m*, crisis, *f*

turnip *n* nabo, *m*. **t. field,** nabar, *m*

turnover *n com* ventas, *f pl*; *cul* pastelillo, *m*

turnpike *n* barrera de portazgo, *f*

turnstile *n* torniquete, *m*

turpentine *n* aguarrás, *m*, trementina, *f*

turpitude *n* infamia, maldad, *f*

turquoise *n* turquesa, *f*

turret *n* torrecilla, almenilla, *f*; *naut* torre blindada, *f*

turreted *a* con torres, guarnecido de torres; en forma de torre

turtle *n* (dove) tórtolo (-la); (sea) tortuga de mar, *f*. **to turn t.,** voltearse patas arriba; *naut* zozobrar. **t. soup,** sopa de tortuga, *f*

Tuscan *a* and *n* toscano (-na)

Tuscany Toscana, *f*

tusk *n* colmillo, *m*

tussle *n* lucha, *f*; agarrada, *f*. *vi* luchar, pelear; tener una agarrada

tutelage *n* tutela, *f*

tutelar *a* tutelar

tutor *n* (private) ayo, *m*; profesor (-ra); (Roman law) tutor, *m*; (supervisor of studies) preceptor. *vt* enseñar, instruir. *vi* ser profesor, dar clases

tutorial *n* (university) seminario, *m*; (private) clase particular, *f*

tutoring *n* enseñanza, instrucción, *f*

TWA la TWA, *f*, (pronounced as if written *túa*)

twaddle *n* disparates, *m pl*, tonterías, patrañas, *f pl*

twain *a* and *n* dos, *m*

twang *n* punteado de una cuerda, *m*; (of a guitar) zumbido, *m*; (in speech) gangueo, *m*. *vt* puntear; (las cuerdas de un instrumento) rasguear. *vi* zumbar. **to speak with a t.,** hablar con una voz gangosa

tweak *n* pellizco, *m*; sacudida, *f*, tirón, *m*. *vt* pellizcar; sacudir, tirar

tweed *n* mezcla, *f*, cheviot, *m*

tweezers *n pl* pinzas, tenacillas, *f pl*

twelfth *a* duodécimo; (of the month) (el) doce; (of monarchs) doce. *n* duodécimo, *m*; (part) dozavo, *m*, duodécima parte, *f*. **T.-night,** Día de Reyes, *m*, Epifanía, *f*

twelve *a* and *n* doce *m*; (of age) doce años, *m pl*. **t. o'-clock,** las doce; (mid-day) mediodía, *m*; (midnight) media noche, *f*, las doce de la noche. **t.-syllabled,** dodecasílabo

twentieth *a* vigésimo; (of the month) (el) veinte; (of monarchs) veinte, *n* vigésimo, *m*; (part) vientavo, *m*, vigésima parte, *f*

twenty *a* veinte; (of age) veinte años, *m pl*, *n* veinte, *m*; (score) veintena, *f*. **t.-first,** vigésimo primero; (of date) (el) veintiuno, *m*, (In modern Spanish the ordinals above *décimo* "tenth" are generally replaced by the cardinals, e.g. **the twenty-ninth chapter,** el capítulo veintinueve.)

twice *adv* dos veces. **t. as many** or **as much,** el doble

twiddle *vt* jugar con; hacer girar. *vi* girar; vibrar. *n* vuelta, *f*. **to t. one's thumbs,** dar vuelta a los pulgares, estar mano sobre mano

twig *n* ramita, pequeña rama, *f*

twilight *n* crepúsculo, *m*; media luz, *f. a* crepuscular. **in the t.,** en el crepúsculo; en la media luz. **t. sleep,** parto sin dolor, *m*

twin *a* gemelo, mellizo; doble. *n* gemelo (-la), mellizo (-za); (of objects) pareja, *f*, par, *m*. **t.-engined,** bimotor. **t. screw,** (*naut aer*) de dos hélices

twine *n* bramante, cordel, *m*; guita, *f*. *vt* enroscar; (weave) tejer; (encircle) ceñir; (round, about) abrazar. *vi* (of plants) trepar; entrelazarse; (wind) serpentear

twinge *n* punzada, *f*, dolor agudo, *m*; *fig* remordimiento, tormento, *m*. *vi* causar un dolor agudo

twining *a bot* trepante, voluble. **t. plant,** planta enredadera (or trepante), *f*

twinkle *vi* centellear, chispear, titilar; (of eyes) brillar; (of feet) moverse rápidamente, bailar. *n* (in the eye) chispa, *f*

twinkling *n* centelleo, *m*; titilación, *f*; (of the eye) brillo, *m*; (glimpse) vislumbre, *m*; *fig* instante, momento, *m. a* titilante, centelleador. **in a t.,** en un dos por tres. **in the t. of an eye,** en un abrir y cerrar de ojos

twin-tailed comet *n* ceratias, *m*

twirl *n* rotación, vuelta, *f*; pirueta, *f*. *vi* hacer girar; voltear; torcer; (a stick, etc.) dar vueltas (a). *vi* girar, dar vueltas; dar piruetas

twirp *n inf* renacuajo, *m*

twist *n* (skein) mecha, *f*; trenza, *f*; (yarn) torzal, *m*; (of tobacco) rollo, *m*; (of bread) rosca de pan, *f*; (act of twisting) torcimiento, *m*, torsión, *f*; (in a road, etc.) recodo, *m*, curva, vuelta, *f*; (pull) sacudida, *f*; (contortion) regate, esguince, *m*; (in a winding stair) espira, *f*; (in ball games) efecto, *m*; (in a person's nature) peculiaridad, *f*; falta de franqueza, *f*; (to words) interpretación, *f*. *vt* torcer; enroscar; (plait) trenzar; (wring) estrujar; (weave) tejer; (encircle) ceñir; (a stick, etc.) dar vueltas a; (of hands) crispar; (distort) interpretar mal, torcer. *vi* torcerse; enroscarse; (wind) serpentear; dar vueltas; (coil) ensortijarse; (writhe) undular, retorcerse; (of a stair) dar vueltas

twisted *a* torcido; (of persons) contrahecho

twisting *n* torcimiento, *m*; torcedura, *f*; serpenteo, *m*; (interlacing) entrelazamiento, *m. a* sinuoso, serpenteado

twit (with) *vt* echar en cara

twitch *n* sacudida, *f*; tirón, *m*; (nervous) contracción nerviosa, *f. vt* tirar bruscamente, quitar rápidamente; agarrar; (ears, etc.) mover; (hands) crispar, retorcer. *vi* crisparse; (of ears, nose) moverse

twitching *n* sacudida, *f*; (contraction) crispamiento, *m*, contracción nerviosa, *f*; (pain) punzada, *f*; (of conscience) remordimiento, *m*

twitter *n* piada, *f*, gorjeo, *m*. *vi* piar, gorjear

two *a* and *n* dos, *m*; (of the clock) (las) dos, *f pl*; (of age) dos años, *m pl. a* de a dos. **in two,** en dos partes. **in two's,** de dos en dos. **one or two,** uno o dos; algunos, *m pl*; algunas, *f pl*. **two against two,** dos a dos. **two by two,** de dos en dos, a pares. **Two can live as cheaply as one,** Donde come uno comen dos. **to put two and two together,** atar cabos. **two-edged,** de dos filos. **two-faced,** de dos caras; *fig* de dos haces. **to be two-faced,** hacer a dos caras. **two-headed,** de dos cabezas; bicéfalo. **two hundred,** *a* and *n* doscientos, *m*. **two hundredth,** *a* ducentésimo. *n* ducentésima parte, *f*; doscientos, *m*. **two-legged,** bípedo. **two-ply,** de dos hilos. **two-seater,** *a* de dos asientos. **two-speed gear box,** cambio de marcha de dos velocidades, *m*. **two-step,** paso doble, *m*. **two of a kind,** (well-matched) tal para cual. **two-way switch,** *elec* interruptor de dos direcciones, *m*

twofold *a* doble. *adv* doblemente, dos veces

twosome *n* partido de dos, *m*

two's words theory *n* teoría de los dos gladios, *f*

tying *n* ligadura, *f*; atadura, *f*

tympanum *n* (*anat, arch*) tímpano, *m*

type *n* tipo, *m*; *print* carácter, *m*, letra de imprenta, *f*, tipo, *m*. *vt* and *vi* escribir a máquina. **t. case,** caja de

imprenta, *f*. **t. founder,** fundidor de letras de imprenta, *m*. **t. foundry,** fundición de tipos, *f*. **t.-setter,** cajista, *mf* **t.-setting,** composición tipográfica, *f*
typewrite *vt* and *vi* escribir a máquina
typewriter *n* máquina de escribir, *f*
typewriting *n* mecanografía, *f*, a mecanográfico
typewritten *a* escrito a máquina
typhoid *n* tifoidea, fiebre tifoidea, *f*
typhoon *n* tifón, *m*
typhus *n* tifus, tabardillo pintado, *m*
typical *a* típico, característico; simbólico
typify *vt* simbolizar, representar; ser ejemplo de
typing pool central *n* mecanográfico, grupo mecanográfico, *m*, sala mecanográfica, *f*

typist *n* mecanografista, *mf*; mecanógrafo (-fa)
typographic *a* tipográfico
typography *n* tipografía, *f*
typographer *n* tipógrafo, *m*
tyrannical *a* tiránico, despótico
tyrannization *n* tiranización, *f*
tyrannize *vi* tiranizar
tyranny *n* tiranía, *f*, despotismo, *m*
tyrant *n* déspota, *m*, tirano (-na)
Tyre Tiro, *m*
Tyrol, the el Tirol
Tyrolese *a* and *n* tirolés (-esa)
Tyrrhenian *a* tirreno
Tyrrhenian Sea, the el Mar Tirreno, *m*

U

U *n* (letter) u, *f*. **U-boat,** submarino, *m*. **u-shaped,** en forma de U
ubiquitous *a* ubicuo, omnipresente
ubiquity *n* ubicuidad, omnipresencia, *f*
udder *n* ubre, teta, mama, *f*
ugh *interj* ¡uf!
ugliness *n* fealdad, *f*; (moral) perversidad, *f*; (of a situation) peligro, me, lo difícil
ugly *a* feo; (morally) repugnante, asqueroso, perverso; (of a situation) peligroso, difícil; (of a wound) grave, profundo; (of a look) amenazador; *inf* desagradable; (of weather) borrascoso. **to make u.,** afear, hacer feo
Ukraine Ucrania, *f*
Ukrainian *a* and *n* ucranio (-ia)
ukulele *n mus* ucelele, *m*
ulcer *n* úlcera, *f*
ulcerate *vt* ulcerar. *vi* ulcerarse
ulceration *n* ulceración, *f*
ulcerous *a* ulceroso
ulterior *a* (of place) ulterior; (of time) posterior, ulterior; (of motives) interesado, oculto; **ulterior motive,** segunda intención, *f*
ultimate *a* último; fundamental, esencial
ultimately *adv* por fin, al final; esencialmente
ultimatum *n* ultimátum, *m*
ultimo *adv* del mes anterior
ultra *a* exagerado, extremo. *prefix* ultra-. **u-red,** ultrarrojo. **u.-violet,** ultravioleta
ultramarine *a* ultramarino. *n* azul de ultramar, *m*
ultramontane *a* ultramontano
ululation *n* ululación, *f*, ululato, *m*
umbilical *a* umbilical
umbilicus *n* ombligo, *m*
umbra *n ast* cono de sombra, *m*
umbrage *n poet* sombra, *f*; resentimiento, enfado, *m*. **to take u.,** ofenderse, resentirse
umbrella *n* paraguas, *m*. **u. maker,** paragüero (-ra). **u. shop,** paragüería, *f*. **u. stand,** paragüero, *m*
umpire *n sport* árbitro, *m*; *law* juez arbitrador, tercero en discordia, *m*. *vt* arbitrar
un- *prefix* Used before adjectives, adverbs, abstract nouns, verbs and translated in Spanish by **in-, des-, nada, no, poco, sin,** as well as in other ways
unabashed *a* desvergonzado, descarado, insolente; (calm) sereno, sosegado
unabashedly *adv* sin rubor
unabated *a* no disminuido; cabal, entero
unabbreviated *a* íntegro, sin abreviar
unable *a* incapaz, impotente; (physical defect) imposibilitado. **to be u. to,** no poder, serle a uno imposible. **to be u. to control,** no poder controlar
unabridged *a*. See **unabbreviated**
unaccented *a* sin acento
unacceptability *n* lo inaceptable
unacceptable *a* inaceptable
unaccepted *a* rechazado, no aceptado

unaccommodating *a* poco complaciente, nada servicial
unaccompanied *a* solo, sin compañía; *mus* sin acompañamiento
unaccomplished *a* incompleto, sin terminar, inacabado; (not clever) sin talento
unaccountability *n* lo inexplicable; falta de responsabilidad, irresponsabilidad, *f*
unaccountable *a* inexplicable; irresponsable
unaccountably *adv* inexplicablemente, extrañamente
unaccredited *a* no acreditado, extraoficial
unaccustomed *a* no habituado; (unusual) desacostumbrado, insólito, inusitado
unacknowledged *a* no reconocido; (of letter) sin contestación, por contestar; no correspondido, sin devolver; (of crimes, etc.) inconfeso, no declarado
unacquainted *a* que no conoce; que desconoce, que ignora; no habituado. **to be u. with,** no conocer; ignorar; no estar acostumbrado a
unadaptable *a* inadaptable (also of persons)
unadorned *a* sin adorno sencillo, que no tiene adornos
unadulterated *a* sin mezcla, no adulterado, natural; genuino, verdadero; puro
unadventurous *a* nada aventurero, que no busca aventuras, tímido; tranquilo, sin incidente
unadvisability *n* imprudencia, *f*; inoportunidad, *f*
unadvisable *a* imprudente; inoportuno, no conveniente
unadvisedly *adv* imprudentemente
unesthetic *a* antiestético
unaffected *a* natural, llano, sin melindres; impasible; genuino, sincero. **u. by,** no afectado por
unaffectedly *adv* sin afectación
unaffectedness *n* naturalidad, sencillez, *f*; sinceridad, franqueza, *f*
unaffiliated *a* no afiliado
unafraid *a* sin temor
unaided *a* sin ayuda, solo a solas
unaired *a* sin ventilar, no ventilado; húmedo, sin airear
unalloyed *a* sin mezcla, puro
unalterability *n* lo inalterable; constancia, *f*
unalterable *a* inalterable; invariable, constante
unambiguous *a* no ambiguo, nada dudoso, claro
unambitious *a* sin ambición; modesto
unamusing *a* nada divertido
unanimity *n* unanimidad, *f*
unanimous *a* unánime
unanimously *adv* unánimemente, por unanimidad. **carried u.,** adoptado por unanimidad
unanswerability *n* imposibilidad de negar, *f*; lo irrefutable
unanswerable *a* incontestable, incontrovertible, incontrastable, irrefutable
unanswered *a* no contestado, sin contestar; (unrequited) no correspondido
unapparent *a* no aparente
unappealable *a* inapelable

unappeasable *a* implacable

unappeased *a* no satisfecho; implacable

unappetizing *a* no apetitoso; (unattractive) repugnante, feo

unappreciated *a* desestimado, no apreciado, tenido en poco; (misunderstood) mal comprendido

unapproachable *a* inaccesible

unapproachableness *n* inaccesibilidad, *f*

unappropriated *a* no concedido; libre

unapproved *a* sin aprobar, no aprobado

unarm *vt* desarmar. *vi* desarmarse, quitarse las armas

unarmed *a* desarmado; indefenso; (*zool, bot*) inerme

unarranged *a* no arreglado, sin clasificar; (accidental) fortuito, casual

unartistic *a* no artístico

unascertainable *a* no verificable

unashamed *a* sin vergüenza; tranquilo, sereno; insolente, descarado

unasked *a* sin pedir; no solicitado; espontáneo; (uninvited) no convidado

unassailable *a* inexpugnable; irrefutable; incontestable

unassisted *a*. See **unaided**

unassuming *a* modesto, sin pretensiones

unattached *a* suelto; *law* no embargado; *mil* de reemplazo; independiente

unattainable *a* inasequible, irrealizable

unattainableness *n* imposibilidad de alcanzar (or realizar), *f*; inaccesibilidad

unattended *a* solo, sin acompañamiento; (of ill person) sin tratamiento; (of entertainment, etc.) no concurrido

unattested *a* sin atestación

unattractive *a* poco atrayente, desagradable, antipático, feo

unattractiveness *n* fealdad, falta de hermosura, *f*; lo desagradable

unauthentic *a* no auténtico, sin autenticidad; apócrifo

unauthorized *a* no autorizado

unavailable *a* inaprovechable

unavailing *a* inútil, vano

unavenged *a* no vengado, sin castigo

unavoidable *a* inevitable, preciso, necesario. **to be u.,** no poder evitarse, no tener remedio

unavoidableness *n* inevitabilidad, necesidad, *f*

unavoidably *adv* irremediablemente

unaware *a* ignorante; inconsciente. **to be u. of,** ignorar, desconocer; no darse cuenta de

unawareness *n* ignorancia, *f*, desconocimiento, *m*; inconsciencia, *f*

unawares *adv* (by mistake) sin querer, inadvertidamente; (unprepared) de sobresalto, de improviso, inopinadamente. **He caught me u.,** Me cogió desprevenido

unbalance *vt* desequilibrar, hacer perder el equilibrio; *fig* trastornar

unbalanced *a* desequilibrado; *fig* trastornado; *com* no balanceado

unbaptized *a* no bautizado, sin bautizar

unbar *vt* desatrancar; *fig* abrir

unbearable *a* intolerable, insufrible, inaguantable, inllevable, insoportable

unbearably *adv* insoportablemente

unbeatable *a* inmejorable

unbeaten *a* (of paths) no frecuentado, no pisado; (of armies) no derrotado, no batido; invicto

unbecoming *a* impropio, inapropiado, inconveniente; indecoroso, indigno; indecente; (of clothes) que no va bien, que sienta mal

unbelief *n* incredulidad, *f*

unbelievable *a* increíble

unbelievably *adv* increíblemente

unbeliever *n* incrédulo (-la), descreído (-da)

unbeloved *a* no amado

unbend *vt* desencorvar, enderezar; entretenerse, descansar; (*naut* of sails) desenvergar; (*naut* of cables) desamarrar. *vi* enderezarse; mostrarse afable

unbending *a* inflexible, rígido, tieso; *fig* inexorable, inflexible, duro, terco; (amiable) afable, jovial

unbiased *a* imparcial, ecuánime

unbidden *a* espontáneo; (uninvited) no convidado, no invitado

unbind *vt* desligar, desatar; (bandages) desvendar; (books) desencuadernar

unbleached *a* crudo, sin blanquear

unblemished *a* no manchado; (pure) sin mancha, inmaculado, puro

unblessed *a* no bendecido, no consagrado; (accursed) maldito; (unhappy) desdichado

unblushing *a* desvergonzado, insolente

unbolt *vt* descerrojar, desempernar

unborn *a* sin nacer, no nacido todavía; venidero

unbosom *vt* confesar, declarar. **to u. oneself,** abrir su pecho (a) or (con)

unbought *a* no comprado; gratuito, libre; (not bribed) no sobornado

unbound *a* suelto, libre; (of books) en rama, no encuadernado

unbounded *a* ilimitado, infinito; inmenso

unbowed *a* erguido; no encorvado; (undefeated) invicto

unbreakable *a* irrompible, inquebrantable

unbridled *a* desenfrenado, violento; licencioso

unbroken *a* no quebrantado, intacto, entero; continuo, incesante; no interrumpido; (of soil) virgen; (of a horse) indomado; inviolado; (of the spirit) indómito; (of a record) no batido

unbrotherly *a* poco fraternal, indigno de hermanos

unbuckle *vt* deshebillar

unburden *vt* descargar; aliviar. **to u. oneself,** (express one's feelings) desahogarse

unburied *a* insepulto

unburnt *a* no quemado; incombusto

unbusinesslike *a* informal; poco comercial, descuidado

unbutton *vt* desabrochar, desabotonar

uncalled *a* no llamado, no invitado. **u.-for,** impertinente; innecesario

uncannily *adv* misteriosamente

uncanniness *n* lo misterioso

uncanny *a* misterioso, horroroso, pavoroso

uncared-for *a* abandonado, desatendido, desamparado

uncarpeted *a* sin alfombra

uncaught *a* no prendido, libre

unceasing *a* continuo, incesante, sin cesar, constante

unceasingly *adv* incesantemente, sin cesar

uncensored *a* no censurado

unceremonious *a* sin ceremonia, familiar; descortés, brusco

unceremoniousness *n* falta de ceremonia, familiaridad, *f*; incivilidad, descortesía, *f*

uncertain *a* incierto, dudoso; inseguro; precario; (hesitant) indeciso, vacilante, irresoluto

uncertainly *adv* inciertamente

uncertainty *n* incertidumbre, duda, *f*; inseguridad, *f*; irresolución, *f*

uncertificated *a* sin certificado (of teachers, etc.) sin título

uncertified *a* sin garantía; no garantizado; (of lunatics) sin certificar

unchain *vt* desencadenar

unchallenged *a* incontestable

unchangeable *a* invariable, inalterable, inmutable

unchangeableness *n* invariabilidad, inalterabilidad, *f*

unchanging *a* inmutable, invariable

uncharitable *a* nada caritativo, duro; intolerante, intransigente

uncharitableness *n* falta de caridad, *f*; intolerancia, intransigencia *f*

uncharitably *adv* sin caridad; con intolerancia

unchaste *a* incasto, incontinente; deshonesto, impuro, lascivo

unchecked *a* desenfrenado; (unproved) no comprobado; *com* no confrontado

unchivalrous *a* nada galante, nada caballeroso

unchristened *a* no bautizado, sin bautizar

unchristian *a* (heathen) pagano; poco cristiano, indigno de un cristiano, nada caritativo

uncircumcised *a* incircunciso

uncircumscribed *a* incircunscripto

uncivil *a* descortés, incivil

uncivilizable *a* reacio a la civilización

uncivilized *a* no civilizado, bárbaro, salvaje, inculto

uncivilly *adv* descortésmente

unclad *a* sin vestir; desnudo

unclasp *vt* (jewelery) desengarzar; desabrochar; (of hands) soltar, separar

unclassifiable *a* inclasificable

unclassified *a* sin clasificar

uncle *n* tío, *m*; (pawnbroker) prestamista, *m*

unclean *a* sucio, puerco, inmundo; desaseado; impuro, obsceno; (ritually) poluto

uncleanliness *n* suciedad, porquería, *f*; desaseo, *m*; falta de limpieza, *f*

uncleanly *a* sucio, puerco; desaseado

uncleanness *n* suciedad, *f*; impureza, obscenidad, inmoralidad, *f*

unclench *vt* (of hands) abrir

Uncle Tom's Cabin La Cabaña del Tío Tom

unclouded *a* sin nubes, despejado, claro

uncoil *vt* desarrollar. *vi* desovillarse; (of snakes) desanillarse

uncollected *a* disperso; no cobrado; (in confusion) confuso, desordenado

uncolored *a* incoloro; *fig* imparcial, objetivo, sencillo

uncombed *a* despeinado, sin peinar

uncomfortable *a* incómodo; (anxious) intranquilo, inquieto, desasosegado, preocupado; (awkward) molesto, difícil, desagradable. **to be u.,** (people) estar incómodo; (anxious) estar preocupado; (of things) ser incómodo

uncomfortableness *n* incomodidad, *f*; malestar, *m*; intranquilidad, preocupación, *f*; dificultad, *f*; lo desagradable

uncomfortably *adv* incómodamente; intranquilamente; desagradablemente

uncomforted *a* desconsolado, sin consuelo

uncommercial *a* no comercial

uncommon *a* poco común, extraordinario, singular, raro, extraño; infrecuente; insólito

uncommonly *adv* extraordinariamente, muy; infrecuentemente, raramente

uncommonness *n* infrecuencia, rareza, *f*; singularidad, *f*

uncommunicative *a* reservado, poco expresivo

uncommunicativeness *n* reserva, *f*

uncomplaining *a* resignado, que no se queja

uncomplainingly *adv* con resignación

uncompliant *a* sordo, inflexible

uncomplicated *a* sencillo, sin complicaciones

uncomplimentary *a* descortés, poco halagüeño, ofensivo

uncompromising *a* inflexible, estricto, intolerante; irreconciliable

unconcealed *a* no oculto; abierto

unconcern *n* indiferencia, frialdad, *f*, desapego, *m*; (lack of interest) apatía, despreocupación, *f*; (nonchalance) desenfado, *m*, frescura, *f*

unconcerned *a* indiferente, frío, despegado; apático, despreocupado; desenfadado, fresco

unconcernedly *adv* con indiferencia; sin preocuparse; con desenfado

unconditional *a* incondicional, absoluto. **u. surrender,** rendición incondicional, *f*

unconditionally *adv* incondicionalmente; *mil* a discreción

unconfessed *a* inconfeso

unconfined *a* suelto, libre; ilimitado; sin estorbo

unconfirmed *a* no confirmado; (report) sin confirmar

uncongenial *a* incompatible, antipático; desagradable, repugnante

uncongeniality *n* incompatibilidad, antipatía, *f*; repugnancia, *f*; lo desagradable

unconnected *a* inconexo; *mech* desconectado; (relationship) sin parentesco; (confused) incoherente

unconquerable *a* invencible, indomable, inconquistable

unconquered *a* no vencido

unconscientious *a* poco concienzudo

unconscionable *a* excesivo, desmedido; sin conciencia

unconscious *a* inconsciente; (senseless) insensible, sin sentido; espontáneo; (unaware) ignorante. **to be u. of,** ignorar; perder la consciencia de. **to become u.,** perder el sentido

unconsciously *adv* inconscientemente, involuntariamente

unconsciousness *n* inconsciencia, *f*; (hypnosis, swoon) insensibilidad, *f*; (unawareness) ignorancia, falta de conocimiento, *f*

unconsecrated *a* no consagrado

unconsidered *a* indeliberado; sin importancia, trivial

unconstitutional *a* anticonstitucional, inconstitucional

unconstitutionally *adv* inconstitucionalmente

unconstrained *a* libre; voluntario; sin freno

uncontaminated *a* incontaminado; puro, sin mancha, impoluto

uncontested *a* sin oposición

uncontradicted *a* sin contradicción; incontestable

uncontrollable *a* irrefrenable, incontrolable, inmanejable; (temper) ingobernable; indomable

uncontrolled *a* libre, no controlado; desenfrenado, desgobernado

unconventional *n* poco convencional; bohemio, excéntrico, extravagante; original

unconventionality *a* excentricidad, extravagancia, independencia de ideas, *f*; (of a design) originalidad, *f*

unconversant *a* poco familiar, poco versado (en)

unconverted *a* no convertido; sin transformar

unconvinced *a* no convencido

unconvincing *a* no convincente, poco convincente, que no me (nos, etc.) convence; frívolo

uncooked *a* crudo, no cocido, sin cocer

uncork *vt* destapar, descorchar, quitar el corcho

uncorrected *a* sin corregir, no corregido

uncorroborated *a* no confirmado, sin confirmar

uncorrupted *a* incorrupto; puro, no pervertido; (unbribed) no sobornado, honrado

uncorruptible *a* incorruptible

uncountable *a* innumerable

uncounted *a* no contado, sin cuenta

uncouple *vt* soltar; desenganchar, desconectar

uncouth *a* grosero, chabacano, tosco, patán

uncouthness *n* grosería, tosquedad, patanería, *f*

uncover *vt* descubrir; (remove lid of) destapar; (remove coverings of) desabrigar, desarropar; (leave unprotected) desamparar; (disclose) revelar, dejar al descubierto. *vi* descubrirse, quitar el sombrero

uncovered *a* descubierto; desnudo; sin cubierta

uncreated *a* increado

uncritical *a* sin sentido crítico, poco juicioso

uncross *vt* (of legs) descruzar

uncrossed *a* (of check) sin cruzar

uncrowned *a* antes de ser coronado; sin corona

unction *n* unción, *f*; untadura, *f*; untamiento, *m*; (unguent) ungüento, *m*; (zeal) fervor, *m*; (flattery) insinceridad, hipocresía, *f*; (relish) gusto, entusiasmo, *m*. **extreme u.,** extremaunción, *f*

unctuous *a* untuoso, craso; insincero, zalamero

uncultivable *a* incultivable

uncultivated *a* inculto, yermo; (barbarous) salvaje, bárbaro; (uncultured) inculto, tosco; no cultivado

uncultured *a* inculto, iletrado

uncurbed *a* sin freno; *fig* desenfrenado

uncurl *vt* desrizar *vi* desrizarse; desovillarse

uncurtained *a* sin cortinas; con las cortinas recogidas

uncut *a* sin cortar, no cortado; (of gems) sin labrar

undamaged *a* indemne, sin daño

undated *a* sin fecha

undaunted *a* intrépido, atrevido

undeceive *vt* desengañar, desilusionar

undecided *a* (of question) pendiente, indeciso; dudoso; vacilante, irresoluto

undecipherable *a* indescifrable; ilegible

undeclared *a* no declarado

undefended *a* indefenso

undeferable *a* inaplazable

undefiled *a* impoluto, incontaminado; puro

undefinable *a* indefinible; inefable, vago

undefined *a* indefinido; indeterminado

undelivered *a* no recibido; (speech) no pronunciado; (not sent) no enviado

undemonstrative *a* poco expresivo, reservado

undeniable *a* incontestable, innegable, indudable; excelente; inequívoco, evidente

undeniably *adv* indudablemente

undenominational *a* sin denominación

undependable *a* indigno de confianza

under *prep* debajo de; bajo; (in) en; (less than) menos de, menos que; (at the orders of) a las órdenes de, al mando de; (in less time than) en menos de; (under the weight of) bajo el peso de; (at the foot of) al abrigo de; (for less than) por menos de; (at the time of) en la época de, en tiempos de; (according to) según, conforme a, en virtud de (e.g. **under the law,** en virtud de la ley); (of monarchs) bajo (or durante) el reinado de; (of rank) inferior a; (in virtue of) en virtud de; (of age) menor de; (with penalty, pretext, etc.) so; en; a (see below for examples); (*agr* of fields) plantado de, sembrado de. **u. arms,** bajo las armas. **u. contract,** bajo contrato. **u. cover,** al abrigo, bajo cubierto. **u. cover of,** bajo pretexto de, so color de. **u. fire,** bajo fuego. **u. oath,** bajo juramento. **u. pain of,** so pena de. **u. sail,** a la vela. **u. separate cover,** bajo cubierta separada, en sobre apartado, por separado. **u. steam,** al vapor. **u. way,** en camino; en marcha; en preparación. **to be u. an obligation,** deber favores; (to) tener obligación de; estar obligado a

under *a* inferior; (of rank) subalterno, subordinado; bajo, bajero. *adv* debajo; abajo; más abajo; menos; (for less) para menos; (ill) mal; (insufficient) insuficiente. **to bring u.,** someter. **to keep u.,** dominar, subyugar

underact *vt* hacer un papel sin fogosidad

underarm *n* sobaco, *m*. *a* sobacal; (of bowling) de debajo del brazo. **to serve u.,** sacar por debajo

underbid *vt* ofrecer menos que

underbred *a* mal criado, mal educado

undercharge *vt* cobrar menos de lo debido

underclothes *n* ropa interior, *f*, paños menores, *m pl*

undercurrent *n* corriente submarina, *f*; *fig* tendencia oculta, *f*

undercut *n* (of meat) filete, *m*

underdeveloped *a* de desarrollo atrasado; *phot* no revelado lo suficiente

underdog *n* víctima, *f*; débil, paciente, *m*. **underdogs,** los de abajo, *m pl*

underdone *a* (of meat) crudo, medio asado

underdress *vt* and *vi* vestir(se) sin bastante elegancia

underestimate *vt* tasar en menos; desestimar, menospreciar

underfeed *vt* alimentar insuficientemente

underfoot *adv* debajo de los pies, en el suelo

undergo *vt* sufrir, padecer, pasar por. **undergo surgery,** someterse a la cirugía

undergraduate *n* estudiante no graduado, *m*

underground *a* subterráneo; *fig* oculto, secreto. *adv* bajo tierra, debajo de la tierra; fig en secreto, ocultamente. *n* sótano, *m*; metro, ferrocarril subterráneo, *m*

undergrown *a* enclenque

undergrowth *n* maleza, *f*

underhand *adv* *fig* bajo mano, ocultamente, a escondidas. *a* *fig* secreto, oculto

underlie *vt* estar debajo de; servir de base a, caracterizar

underline *vt* subrayar

underling *n* subordinado (-da)

underlying *a* fundamental, básico, esencial

undermentioned *a* abajo citado

undermine *vt* socavar, excavar; minar, destruir poco a poco

undermining *n* socava, excavación, *f*; destrucción, *f*, a minador

underneath *adv* debajo. *prep* bajo, debajo de

undernourished *a* mal alimentado

undernourishment *n* desnutrición, *f*

underpaid *a* insuficiente retribuido, mal pagado

underpass *n* pasaje por debajo, *m*

underpay *vt* pagar mal, remunerar (or retribuir) deficientemente

underpayment *n* retribución mezquina, *f*, pago insuficiente, *m*

underpin *vt* apuntalar, socalzar

underpopulated *a* con baja densidad de población

underprivileged *a* menesteroso, pobre, necesitado

underrate *vt* tasar en menos; tener en poco, desestimar, menospreciar

underripe *a* verde

undersecretary *n* subsecretario (-ia)

undersell *vt* vender a un precio más bajo que

underside *n* revés, envés, *m*

undersigned *a* infrascrito, suscrito. **the u.,** el abajo firmado, el infrascrito

undersized *a* muy pequeño, enclenque, enano

underskirt *n* enagua, *f*; refajo, *m*

underslung *a aut* con bajo centro de gravedad

understand *vt* comprender, entender; (know) saber; (be acquainted with) conocer; (hear) oír, tener entendido; (mean) sobrentender. *vi* comprender, entender; oír, tener entendido. **to u. each other,** comprenderse. **It being understood that . . .,** Bien entendido que . . .

understandable *a* comprensible; inteligible. **It is very u. why he does not wish to come,** Se comprende muy bien por qué no quiere venir

understanding *n* (intelligence) entendimiento, *m*, inteligencia, *f*; (agreement) acuerdo, *m*; (knowledge) conocimiento, *m*; (wisdom) comprensión, sabiduría, *f*. *a* inteligente; sabio; (sympathetic) comprensivo, simpático. **to come to an u.,** ponerse de acuerdo

understandingly *adv* con inteligencia; con conocimiento (de); con simpatía

understate *vt* decir menos que, rebajar, describir sin énfasis

understatement *n* moderación, *f*

understudy *n* sobresaliente, *mf*. *vt* sustituir

undertake *vt* comprometerse a, encargarse de; emprender, abarcar, acometer

undertaker *n* empresario, director de pompas fúnebres, *m*

undertaking *n* empresa, tarea, *f*; garantía, promesa, *f*; (funerals) funeraria, *f*

undertone *n* voz baja, *f*; *art* color tenue (or apagado), *m*. **in an u.,** en voz baja

undervalue *vt* tasar en menos; tener en poco, despreciar

underwater *a* subacuático, submarino. **underwater flipper,** aleta de bucear

underweight *a* de bajo peso, que pesa menos de lo debido, flaco

underworld *n* (hell) infierno, averno, *m*; (slums) hampa, *f*, fondos bajos de la sociedad, *m pl*; heces de la sociedad, *f pl*

underwrite *vt com* asegurar contra riesgos; reasegurar; obligarse a comprar todas las acciones de una compañía no subscritas por el público, mediante un pago convenido

underwriter *n* asegurador, *m*; reasegurador, *m*

underwriting *n* aseguro, *m*; reaseguro, *m*
undeserved *a* inmerecido, no merecido
undeserving *a* indigno, desmerecedor; que no merece
undesirable *a* no deseable; nocivo, pernicioso; (unsuitable) inconveniente
undesired *a* no deseado; no solicitado, no buscado
undesirous *a* no deseoso
undestroyed *a* sin destruir, no destruido, intacto
undetected *a* no descubierto
undeveloped *a* no desarrollado; rudimentario; inmaturo; (of a country) no explotado, virgen; *phot* no revelado; (of land) sin cultivar
undeviating *a* directo; constante, persistente
undigested *a* no digerido, indigesto
undignified *a* sin dignidad; poco serio; indecoroso
undiluted *a* sin diluir, puro
undiminished *a* no disminuido, sin disminuir, cabal, íntegro
undimmed *a* no obscurecido, brillante
undiplomatic *a* impolítico, indiscreto
undirected *a* sin dirección; (of letters) sin señas
undiscernible *a* imperceptible, invisible
undiscerning *a* sin percepción, obtuso, sin discernimiento
undisciplined *a* indisciplinado
undisclosed *a* no revelado, secreto
undiscouraged *a* animoso, sin flaquear, sin desaliento
undiscovered *a* no descubierto, ignoto
undiscriminating *a* sin distinción; sin sentido crítico
undisguised *a* sin disfraz; abierto, claro
undismayed *a* intrépido, impávido; sin desaliento
undisposed *a* desinclinado; (of property) no enajenado, no invertido
undisputed *a* incontestable, indisputable
undistinguishable *a* indistinguible
undistinguished *a* (of writers) poco conocido; indistinto; sin distinción
undisturbed *a* sin tocar; tranquilo, sereno, impasible
undivided *a* indiviso, íntegro; junto; completo, entero
undo *vt* anular; reparar; desatar, deshacer; desasir; abrir
undoing *n* anulación, *f*; (reparation) reparación, *f*; (opening) abrir, *m*; ruina, *f*
undomesticated *a* salvaje, no domesticado; poco casero
undone *a* and *part* sin hacer; deshecho; arruinado, perdido. **I am undone!** ¡Estoy perdido! **to come u.,** desatarse. **to leave u.,** dejar sin hacer
undoubted *a* indudable, evidente, incontestable
undoubtedly *adv* sin duda
undrained *a* sin drenaje
undramatic *a* no dramático
undreamed *a* no soñado. **u. of,** inopinado, no imaginado
undress *vt* desnudar, desvestir. *vi* desnudarse. *n* traje de casa, *m*; paños menores, *m pl*; *mil* traje de cuartel, *m*
undressed *a* desnudo; en paños menores; (of wounds) sin curar; *com* en rama, en bruto
undrinkable *a* impotable
undue *a* excesivo, indebido; injusto; impropio; (of a bill of exchange) por vencer
undulant *a* ondulante. **u. fever,** fiebre mediterránea, fiebre de Malta, *f*
undulate *vi* ondular, ondear
undulating *a* ondulante
undulation *n* ondulación, undulación, *f*; ondeo, *m*; fluctuación, *f*
undulatory *a* ondulatorio, undoso
unduly *adv* excesivamente, demasiado, indebidamente; injustamente
undutiful *a* desobediente, irrespetuoso
undutifulness *n* desobediencia, falta de respeto, *f*
undying *a* inmortal, imperecedero; eterno
unearned *a* no ganado; inmerecido
unearth *vt* desenterrar; *fig* descubrir, sacar a luz
unearthing *n* desenterramiento, *m*; *fig* descubrimiento, *m*, revelación, *f*

unearthly *a* sobrenatural; misterioso, aterrador, espantoso
uneasily *adv* con dificultad; incómodamente; inquietamente
uneasiness *n* malestar, *m*; (discomfort) incomodidad, *f*; (anxiety) inquietud, intranquilidad, *f*, desasosiego, *m*
uneasy *a* incómodo; inseguro; inquieto, intranquilo, desasosegado; aturdido, turbado. **to become u.,** inquietarse
uneatable *a* incomible
uneaten *a* no comido
uneconomical *a* poco económico, costoso, caro
unedifying *a* poco edificante
unedited *a* inédito
uneducated *a* ignorante; ineducado, inculto, indocto
unembarrassed *a* sereno, tranquilo, imperturbable; (financially) sin deudas, acomodado
unemotional *a* frío, impasible
unemployable *a* sin uso, inservible; (of persons) inútil para el trabajo
unemployed *a* sin empleo; (out of work) sin trabajo, parado; desocupado, ocioso; inactivo. *n* paro obrero, *m*. **the u.,** los sin trabajo, los cesantes, los desocupados
unemployment *n* paro forzoso, *m*. **u. benefit,** subvención contra el paro obrero, *f*. **u. insurance,** seguro contra el paro obrero, *m*,
unencumbered *a* libre, independiente; (of estates) libre de gravamen; (untaxable) saneado
unending *a* perpetuo, eterno, sin fin; incacabable, constante, continuo, incesante
unendurable *a* insoportable, insufrible, intolerable
unenlightened *a* ignorante
unenterprising *a* poco emprendedor, tímido
unenthusiastic *a* sin entusiasmo, tibio
unenviable *a* no envidiable
unequal *a* desigual; inferior; (out of proportion) desproporcionado; injusto; insuficiente; incapaz; (of ground) escabroso. **to be u. to the task,** ser incapaz de la tarea; no tener fuerzas para la tarea
unequalled *a* sin igual, incomparable, sin par, único
unequally *adv* desigualmente
unequivocal *a* inequívoco; redondo, claro, franco
unerring *a* infalible; seguro
unerringly *adv* infaliblemente; sin equivocarse
unessential *a* no esencial
uneven *a* desigual; (of roads) escabroso, quebrado; (of numbers) impar; irregular
unevenly *adv* desigualmente
unevenness *n* desigualdad, *f*; desnivel, *m*, irregularidad, *f*. **the unevenness of the terrain,** lo desigual del terreno, lo accidentado del terreno, *m*
uneventful *a* sin incidentes, sin acontecimientos notables; tranquilo
unexaggerated *a* nada exagerado
unexamined *a* no examinado, sin examinar
unexampled *a* sin igual, sin par
unexceptionable *a* intachable, irreprensible; correcto; impecable, perfecto
unexhausted *a* no agotado; inexhausto
unexpected *a* inesperado, imprevisto, inopinado, impensado; repentino, súbito
unexpectedly *adv* inesperadamente; de repente
unexpectedness *n* lo inesperado
unexpired *a* (of bill of exchange) no vencido; (of lease) no caducado
unexplored *a* inexplorado
unexpressed *a* no expresado; tácito, sobrentendido
unexpurgated *a* sin expurgar, completo
unfading *a* inmarcesible, inmarchitable; eterno, inmortal
unfailing *a* inagotable; inexhausto; seguro; indefectible
unfailingly *adv* siempre, constantemente; sin faltar
unfair *a* injusto; vil, bajo, soez; de mala fe, engañoso; (of play) sucio
unfairly *adv* injustamente; de mala fe
unfairness *n* injusticia, *f*; mala fe, *f*

unfaithful *a* infiel; desleal; inexacto, incorrecto. **to be u. to,** ser infiel a; faltar a

unfaithfulness *n* infidelidad, *f*; deslealtad, *f*; inexactitud, *f*

unfaltering *a* sin vacilar; resuelto, firme

unfamiliar *a* poco familiar; desconocido. **to be u. with,** ser ignorante de

unfashionable *a* pasado de moda, fuera de moda; poco elegante

unfashionableness *n* falta de elegancia, *f*

unfashionably *adv* contra la tendencia de la moda; sin elegancia

unfasten *vt* desatar; desabrochar; desenganchar; abrir; aflojar; soltar

unfathomable *a* insondable; impenetrable, inescrutable

unfavorable *a* desfavorable, adverso, contrario

unfavorably *adv* desfavorablemente

unfeathered *a* implume, sin plumas

unfeeling *a* insensible, impasible, frío; duro, cruel

unfeigned *a* sincero, natural, verdadero

unfenced *a* descercado, sin tapia; abierto

unfermented *a* no fermentado;

unfetter *vt* desencadenar, destrabar; poner en libertad, librar

unfilial *a* poco filial, desobediente

unfinished *a* incompleto, inacabado; sin acabar; imperfecto

unfit *a* incapaz; incompetente, inepto; (unsuitable) impropio; (useless) inservible, inadecuado; (unworthy) indigno; (ill) enfermo, malo. *vt* inhabilitar, incapacitar. **u. for human consumption,** impropio para el consumo humano

unfitness *n* incapacidad, *f*; incompetencia, ineptitud, *f*; impropiedad, *f*; falta de mérito, *f*; falta de salud, *f*

unfix *vt* desprender, despegar, descomponer; soltar. **to come unfixed,** desprenderse

unflagging *a* incansable, infatigable; persistente, constante

unflattering *a* poco halagüeño

unflinching *a* inconmovible, resuelto, firme

unfold *vt* desplegar, desdoblar; tender; abrir; (plans) revelar, descubrir; contar, manifestar. *vi* abrirse

unfolding *a* que se abre. *n* despliegue, *m*; revelación, *f*; narración, *f*

unforced *a* libre; espontáneo; fácil; natural

unforeseen *a* imprevisto, inesperado

unforgettable *a* involvidable

unforgivable *a* inexcusable, imperdonable

unforgiving *a* implacable, que no perdona, inexorable

unforgotten *a* no olvidado

unformed *a* informe; rudimentario; inmaturo; (inexperienced) inexperto, sin experiencia

unfortunate *a* desdichado, infortunado, desgraciado, desventurado. *n* desdichado (-da); pobre, *mf*; (prostitute) perdida, *f*

unfortunately *adv* por desdicha, desgraciadamente

unfounded *a* infundado, inmotivado, sin fundamento, injustificado

unframed *a* sin marco

unfrequented *a* poco frecuentado, solitario, retirado, aislado

unfriendliness *n* hostilidad, falta de amistad, frialdad, *f*; huraña, insociabilidad, *f*

unfriendly *a* hostil, enemigo; (of things, events) perjudicial; huraño, insociable

unfrock *vt* degradar, exclaustrar

unfruitful *a* estéril, infecundo; infructuoso, improductivo, vano

unfulfilled *a* incumplido, sin cumplir; malogrado

unfurl *vt* desplegar; *naut* izar (las velas)

unfurnished *a* desamueblado, sin muebles; desprovisto (de), sin

ungainliness *n* falta de gracia, torpeza, *f*, desgarbo, *m*

ungainly *a* desgarbado

ungallant *a* poco caballeroso, nada galante

ungenerous *a* poco generoso; avaro, tacaño, mezquino; injusto

ungentlemanly *a* poco caballeroso, indigno de un caballero

unglazed *a* sin vidriar; (paper) sin satinar; deslustrado

ungloved *a* sin guante(s)

unglue *vt* desencolar, despegar

ungodliness *n* impiedad, *f*

ungodly *a* impío, irreligioso

ungovernable *a* ingobernable, indomable; irrefrenable

ungraceful *a* desagraciado, desgarbado, sin gracia

ungracious *a* desagradable, poco cortés, desdeñoso

ungraciousness *n* descortesía, aspereza, inurbanidad, *f*

ungrammatical *a* antigramatical, incorrecto

ungrateful *a* ingrato, desagradecido; desagradable, odioso

ungratefulness *n* ingratitud, *f*; lo desagradable

ungrounded *a* infundado; sin motivo

ungrudging *a* no avaro, liberal; generoso, magnánimo

ungrudgingly *adv* de buena gana

unguarded *a* indefenso, sin protección; descuidado; indiscreto, imprudente; sin reflexión

unguided *a* sin guía

unhallowed *a* impío, profano

unhampered *a* desembarazado, libre

unhappily *adv* desafortunadamente, por desgracia

unhappiness *n* infelicidad, desgracia, desdicha, tristeza, *f*

unhappy *a* infeliz, desgraciado, desdichado, triste; (ill-fated) aciago, funesto, malhadado; (remark) inoportuno, inapropiado

unharmed *a* ileso, sano y salvo; (of things) indemne, sin daño

unharness *vt* desaparejar; desenganchar; desarmar

unhealthiness *n* falta de salud, *f*; (of place) insalubridad, *f*

unhealthy *a* enfermizo; malsano, insalubre

unheard *a* no oído; sin ser escuchado; desconocido. **u.-of,** inaudito, no imaginado

unheeding *a* distraído; desatento, sin prestar atención (a); descuidado

unhelpful *a* poco servicial; inútil

unhesitating *a* resuelto, decidido; pronto, inmediato

unhesitatingly *adv* sin vacilar

unhinge *vt* desgoznar, desquiciar; (of the mind) trastornar

unhitch *vt* desenganchar; descolgar

unholy *a* impío, sacrílego

unhonored *a* sin que se reconociese sus méritos; despreciado; (check) protestado

unhook *vt* desenganchar; desabrochar; descolgar

unhoped-for *a* inesperado

unhurt *a* ileso, incólume, sano y salvo; (of things) sin daño

unicellular *a* unicelular

unicolored *a* unicolor

unicorn *n* unicornio, *m*

unidentified *a* no reconocido, no identificado

unification *n* unificación, *f*

uniform *a* uniforme; igual, constante, invariable; homogéneo. *n* uniforme, *m*. **in full u.,** de gran uniforme. **to make u.,** uniformar, igualar, hacer uniforme

uniformity *n* uniformidad, igualdad, *f*

uniformly *adv* uniformemente

unify *vt* unificar; unir

unilateral *a* unilateral

unimaginable *a* inimaginable, no imaginable

unimaginative *a* sin imaginación

unimpaired *a* no disminuido; sin alteración; intacto, entero; sin menoscabo

unimpeachable *a* irreprochable, intachable

unimportance *n* no importancia, insignificancia, trivialidad, *f*

unimportant *a* sin importancia, nada importante, insignificante, trivial

unimpressive *a* poco impresionante; nada conmovedor; (of persons) insignificante

uninflammable *a* no inflamable, incombustible

uninfluenced *a* no afectado (por), libre (de)

uninformed *a* ignorante

uninhabitable *a* inhabitable

uninhabited *a* deshabitado, inhabitado, vacío, desierto

uninjured *a* ileso; sin daño

uninspired *a* sin inspiración; pedestre, mediocre

uninstructive *a* nada instructivo

uninsured *a* no asegurado

unintelligent *a* nada inteligente, corto de alcances, tonto

unintelligibility *n* incomprensibilidad, *f*, lo ininteligible

unintelligible *a* ininteligible, incomprensible

unintentional *a* involuntario, inadvertido

unintentionally *adv* sin querer, involuntariamente

uninterested *a* no interesado, despreocupado

uninteresting *a* sin interés, poco interesante, soso

uninterrupted *a* ininterrum pido, sin interrupción; continuo, incesante

uninvited *a* no invitado, no convidado, sin invitación; (unlooked-for) no buscado

uninviting *a* poco atrayente; inhospitalario

union *n* unión, *f*; *mech* manguito de unión, *m*; conexión, *f*; (poverty) asociación, *f*; (of trade) gremio de oficios, *m*; sindicato (obrero), *m*; (workhouse) asilo, *m*; (U.S.A.) Estados Unidos de América, *m pl*

unionism *n* unionismo, *m*

unionist *n pol* unionista, *mf*

unique *a* único, sin igual, sin par

uniqueness *n* unicidad, *f*; lo singular

unisexual *a* unisexual

unison *n* unisonancia, *f*. **in u.,** al unísono

unit *n* unidad, *f*. **u. bookcase,** librería en secciones, *f*

Unitarian *a* and *n* unitario (-ia)

Unitarianism *n* unitarismo, *m*

unite *vt* unir, juntar; combinar, incorporar; (of countries) unificar; (of energies, etc.) reunir. *vi* unirse, juntarse; reunirse, concertarse; convenirse

united *a* unido; junto. **the U. Nations,** las Naciones Unidas, *f pl*

unitedly *adv* unidamente; armoniosamente, de acuerdo

United States of America los Estados Unidos, *m pl*

unity *n* unidad, *f*; *math* la unidad; unión, *f*; conformidad, armonía, *f*. **the three unities,** las tres unidades

universal *a* universal; general; común. **to make u.,** universalizar, generalizar. **u. joint,** junta universal, *f*; *aut* cardán, *m*

universality *n* universalidad, *f*

universalize *vt* universalizar

universe *n* universo, *m*; creación, *f*, mundo, *m*

university *n* universidad, *f*. *a* universitario. **u. degree,** grado universitario, *m*

unjust *a* injusto

unjustifiable *a* injustificable, indisculpable, inexcusable

unjustifiably *adv* injustificadamente, inexcusablemente

unjustly *adv* injustamente, sin razón

unkempt *a* despeinado; desaseado, sucio

unkind *a* nada bondadoso, nada amable; poco complaciente; duro, cruel; desfavorable, nada propicio

unkindly *adv* sin bondad; con dureza, cruelmente

unkindness *n* falta de bondad, *f*; severidad, crueldad, dureza, *f*, rigor, *m*; acto de crueldad, *m*

unknowable *a* impenetrable, incomprensible, insondable

unknowingly *adv* sin querer, involuntariamente; sin saberlo; insensiblemente

unknown *a* ignoto, desconocido; *math* incógnito. *n* lo desconocido, misterio, *m*; *math* incógnita, *f*; (person)

desconocido (-da), forastero (-ra). *math* **u. quantity,** incógnita, *f*

unlabeled *a* sin etiqueta

unlace *vt* desenlazar; desatar

unladylike *a* indigno (or impropio) de una dama; vulgar, ordinario, cursi

unlamented *a* no llorado, no lamentado

unlatch *vt* alzar el pestillo de, abrir

unlawful *a* ilegal, ilícito

unlawfulness *n* ilegalidad, *f*

unlearn *vt* olvidar, desaprender

unleash *vt* soltar

unleavened *a* ázimo, sin levadura

unless *conjunc* a no ser que, a menos que, como no, si no (all followed by subjunc.); salvo, excepto, con excepción de

unlicensed *a* no autorizado, sin licencia

unlike *a* disímil, desemejante; distinto, diferente. *prep* a distinción de, a diferencia de, al contrario de. **They are quite u.,** No se parecen nada

unlikeliness *n* improbabilidad, *f*

unlikely *a* improbable, inverosímil; arriesgado

unlikeness *n* desemejanza, diferencia, *f*

unlimited *a* ilimitado, infinito, inmenso; sin restricción; excesivo, exagerado. **unlimited telephone,** teléfono no medido (Argentina)

unlined *a* no forrado, sin forro; sin rayas; (of face) sin arrugas

unlit *a* no iluminado, oscuro, sin luz

unload *vt* descargar; aligerar; *naut* hondear; (of shares) deshacerse de. *vi* descargar

unloading *n* descarga, *f*, descargue, *m*

unlock *vt* desencerrar, abrir; *fig* revelar, descubrir

unlooked-for *a* inopinado, inesperado

unloose *vt* desatar; soltar; poner en libertad

unlovable *a* indigno del querer; antipático, poco amable; repugnante

unloveliness *n* falta de hermosura, fealdad, *f*

unlovely *a* nada hermoso, feo; desagradable

unluckily *adv* desafortunadamente, por desgracia

unluckiness *n* mala suerte, *f*; (unsuitability) inoportunidad, *f*; lo nefasto, lo malo

unlucky *a* de mala suerte; desdichado, desgraciado, infeliz; (ill-omened) funesto, nefasto, fatal; inoportuno, inconveniente

unmanageable *a* indomable, indócil; ingobernable, inmanejable; (unwieldy) difícil de manejar, pesado

unmannerliness *n* mala crianza, descortesía, *f*

unmannerly *a* mal educado, descortés

unmarketable *a* invendible

unmarriageable *a* incasable

unmarried *a* soltero, célibe

unmask *vt* desenmascarar; *fig* quitar la careta (a). *vi* quitarse la máscara; *fig* quitarse la careta, descubrirse

unmeaning *a* sin sentido, vacío, sin significación

unmelodious *a* sin melodía, discorde

unmendable *a* incomponible

unmentionable *a* que no se puede mencionar; indigno de mencionarse

unmerciful *a* sin piedad, sin compasión; cruel, despiadado, duro

unmerited *a* inmerecido, desmerecido

unmethodical *a* poco metódico

unmindful *a* olvidadizo; desatento; negligente. **u. of,** sin pensar en, olvidando

unmistakable *a* inequívoco; manifiesto, evidente, indudable

unmistakably *adv* indudablemente

unmitigated *a* no mitigado; completo, absoluto; (of rogue) redomado

unmixed *a* sin mezcla; puro, sencillo; (free) limpio

unmoor *vt* desamarrar

unmoral *a* amoral, no moral; sin fin didáctico

unmounted *a* desmontado

unmoved *a* fijo; (unemotional) impasible, frío; (determined) firme, inflexible, inexorable

unmuffle *vt* desembozar, descubrir

unmusical *a* sin afición a la música; sin oído (para la música); inarmónico

unnamable *a* que no se puede nombrar, innominable

unnatural *a* desnaturalizado; (of vices, etc.) contra natural; innatural; (of style) rebuscado; artificial; inhumano, cruel

unnaturalness *n* lo monstruoso; lo innatural; artificialidad, *f*; inhumanidad, *f*

unnavigable *a* innavegable, no navegable

unnecessarily *adv* inútilmente, innecesariamente, sin necesidad

unnecessariness *n* inutilidad, *f*; superfluidad, *f*; lo innecesario

unnecessary *a* innecesario, superfluo, inútil

unneighborly *a* de mala vecindad, impropio de vecinos, poco servicial

unnerve *vt* acobardar quitar el valor, desanimar

unnoticed *a* inadvertido, no observado

unobliging *a* nada servicial

unobservable *a* inobservable

unobservant *a* inobservante

unobserved *a* sin ser notado, desapercibido

unobtainable *a* inalcanzable, inasequible

unobstructed *a* no obstruido; sin obstáculos; libre

unobtrusive *a* discreto, modesto

unobtrusiveness *n* discreción, modestia, *f*

unoccupied *a* (at leisure) desocupado, ocioso, sin ocupación; vacío, vacante, libre; (untenanted) deshabitado

unofficial *a* no oficial

unopened *a* sin abrir, cerrado; (of exhibitions, etc.) no inaugurado

unopposed *a* sin oposición

unorganized *a* inorganizado; *biol* inorgánico

unoriginal *a* poco original

unorthodox *a* heterodoxo

unostentatious *a* sencillo, modesto, sin ostentación

unostentatiousness *n* sencillez, modestia, falta de ostentación, *f*

unpack *vt* desempaquetar; (trunks) vaciar; (bales) desembalar. *vi* desempaquetar; deshacer las maletas

unpacking *n* desembalaje, *m*

unpaid *a* sin pagar, no pagado

unpalatable *a* de mal sabor; desagradable

unparalleled *a* sin paralelo, sin par, sin igual

unpardonable *a* imperdonable, inexcusable, irremisible

unparliamentary *a* poco parliamentario

unpatriotic *a* antipatriótico

unpaved *a* sin empedrar

unperceived *a* inadvertido, sin ser notado

unperturbed *a* impasible, sin alterarse, sereno

unpleasant *a* desagradable, desapacible; ofensivo; (troublesome) enfadoso, molesto

unpleasantly *adv* desagradablemente

unpleasantness *n* lo desagradable; disgusto, sinsabor, *m*; (disagreement) disputa, riña, *f*

unpleasing *a* nada placentero; desagradable, sin atractivos

unplug *vt* desenchufar

unpoetic, unpoetical, *a* poco poético

unpolished *a* sin pulir, tosco, mate; *fig* inculto, cerril. **u. diamond,** diamante en bruto, *m*

unpolluted *a* impoluto, incontaminado; puro, sin pervertir

unpopular *a* impopular

unpopularity *n* impopularidad, *f*

unpractical *a* impracticable, imposible; (of persons) sin sentido práctico

unpracticed *a* no practicado; inexperto, inhábil

unpraiseworthy *a* inmeritorio

unprecedented *a* sin precedente, inaudito

unprejudiced *a* sin prejuicios, imparcial

unpremeditated *a* sin premeditación, indeliberado, impremeditado

unprepared *a* sin preparación, no preparado; desprevenido; desapercibido (unready)

unpreparedness *n* falta de preparación, imprevisión, *f*, desapercibimiento, *m*

unprepossessing *a* poco atrayente, antipático

unpresentable *a* impresentable

unpretentious *a* sin pretensiones, modesto

unpriced *a* sin precio

unprincipled *a* sin consciencia, sin escrúpulos

unprinted *a* sin imprimir, no impreso

unprocurable *a* inalcanzable, inasequible

unproductive *a* improductivo; infructuoso, estéril

unproductiveness *n* infructuosidad, *f*; esterilidad, *f*

unprofessional *a* sin profesión; contrario a la ética profesional

unprofitable *a* improductivo, infructuoso; sin provecho; inútil; nada lucrativo

unprogressive *a* reaccionario

unpromising *a* poco halagüeño

unpronounceable *a* impronunciable

unpropitious *a* desfavorable, nada propicio, nada halagüeño

unprosperous *a* impróspero

unprotected *a* sin protección; (of persons) indefenso, desválido

unproved *a* no probado, sin demostrar

unprovided *a* desapercibido, desprovisto. **u. for,** sin provisión (para); sin medios de vida, desamparado

unprovoked *a* no provocado, sin provocación; sin motivo

unpublished *a* inédito, no publicado, sin publicar

unpunctual *a* no puntual, retrasado

unpunctuality *n* falta de puntualidad, *f*, retraso, *m*

unpunctually *adv* sin puntualidad, tarde, con retraso

unpunishable *a* no punible

unpunished *a* impune, sin castigo

unpurchasable *a* que no puede comprarse

unqualified *a* incapaz, incompetente; (with professions) sin título; (downright) incondicional, absoluto

unquenchable *a* inextinguible, inapagable; insaciable

unquestionable *a* indiscutible, indudable, indubitable

unquestionably *adv* indudablemente

unquiet *a* inquieto, intranquilo; agitado

unravel *vt* deshilar; destejer; (a mystery, etc.) desentrañar, desembrollar, descifrar

unraveling *n* deshiladura, *f*; aclaración, *f*

unreadable *a* ilegible

unreadiness *n* falta de preparación, *f*, desapercibimiento, *m*; lentitud, *f*

unready *a* desapercibido, desprevenido; lento

unreal *a* irreal; falso, imaginario, ilusorio; ficticio; artificial; insincero, hipócrita; ideal; incorpóreo

unreality *n* irrealidad, *f*; falsedad, *f*; artificialidad, *f*; lo quimérico

unreasonable *a* irrazonable, irracional; disparatado, extravagante; (with price, etc.) exorbitante, excesivo

unreasonableness *n* irracionalidad, *f*; exorbitancia, *f*

unreasonably *adv* irracionalmente

unreasoning *a* irracional; sin motivo, sin causa

unreceipted *a* sin recibo

unrecognizable *a* que no puede reconocerse; imposible de reconocer

unrecognized *a* no reconocido

unreconciled *a* no resignado, no reconciliado

unrectified *a* no corregido, sin rectificar

unredeemed *a* no redimido; no mitigado; (of pledges) sin desempeñar

unrefined *a* no refinado, impuro; inculto, grosero

unreformed *a* no reformado

unrefuted *a* no refutado

unregenerate *a* no regenerado

unregretted *a* no llorado, sin lamentar

unrehearsed *a* sin preparación; *theat* sin ensayar; (extempore) improvisado

unrelated *a* inconexo; (of persons) sin parentesco

unrelenting *a* implacable, inflexible, inexorable

unreliability n incertidumbre, f; el no poder confiar en, informalidad, inestabilidad, f

unreliable a incierto, dudoso, indigno de confianza; (of persons) informal

unrelieved a no aliviado; absoluto, complete, total

unremitting a incansable

unremunerative a sin remuneración, no remunerado

unrepealed a vigente

unrepentant a impenitente

unrepresentative a poco representativo

unrepresented a sin representación

unrequited a no correspondido

unreserved a no reservado; expresivo, comunicativo, expansivo, franco

unreservedly adv sin reserva; con toda franqueza

unresisting a sin oponer resistencia

unresolved a sin resolverse, vacilante; incierto, dudoso, inseguro; sin solución

unresponsive a flemático; insensible, sordo

unresponsiveness n flema, f; insensibilidad, f

unrest n desasosiego, m, agitación, inquietud, f

unrestful a agitado, inquieto, intranquilo

unrestrained a desenfrenado; ilimitado, sin límites; sin reserva

unrestricted a sin restricción; ilimitado

unrevealed a no revelado, por descubrir, no descubierto

unrewarded a sin premio, no recompensado

unrighteous a injusto, malo, perverso

unrighteousness n injusticia, f; maldad, perversidad, f

unripe a verde, inmaturo

unripeness n falta de madurez, f

unrivaled a sin igual, sin par

unroll vt desarrollar. vi desarrollarse; (unfold) desplegarse (a la vista)

unromantic a poco (or nada) romántico

unruffled a sereno, plácido, ecuánime; no arrugado; (of hair) liso

unruliness n turbulencia, indisciplina, f; insubordinación, rebeldía, f

unruly a ingobernable, revoltoso; refractario, rebelde; (of hair) indomable

unsaddle vt desensillar; derribar (del caballo, etc.)

unsafe a inseguro; peligroso; arriesgado; (to eat) nocivo

unsafeness n inseguridad, f; peligro, riesgo, m

unsaid a sin decir, no dicho

unsalable a invendible

unsalaried a no asalariado

unsalted a soso, sin sal

unsanctioned a no permitido, sin sancionar

unsanitary a antihigiénico

unsatisfactoriness n lo insatisfactorio

unsatisfactory a poco (or nada) satisfactorio; no aceptable

unsatisfied a no satisfecho; descontento; no convencido; (hungry) no harto; com no saldado

unsatisfying a que no satisface

unsavoriness n insipidez, f, mal sabor, m; lo desagradable; sordidez, suciedad, f

unsavory a insípido, de mal sabor; desagradable; sórdido, sucio

unscalable a inascendible, virgen

unscathed a sin daño, ileso

unscented a sin perfume, sin olor, no fragante

unscholarly a nada erudito; fuera de un erudito; indigno de un erudito

unscientific a no científico

unscrew vt destornillar. vi destornillarse

unscrewing n destornillamiento, m

unscrupulous a sin escrúpulos, poco escrupuloso, desaprensivo

unscrupulousness n falta de escrúpulos, desaprensión, f

unseal vt desellar, romper (or quitar) el sello (de)

unseasonable a intempestivo, fuera de sazón; inoportuno, inconveniente. **at an u. hour,** a una hora inconveniente, a deshora

unseasonableness n lo intempestivo, inoportunidad, f

unseasonably adv intempestivamente; a deshora; inoportunamente

unseasoned a cul sin sazonar, soso; (wood) verde; no maduro, sin madurar

unseat vt (from horse) tirar, echar al suelo; pol desituir

unseaworthy a innavegable

unseemliness n falta de decoro, f; indecencia, f

unseemly a indecoroso, indigno; indecente; impropio

unseen a no visto, invisible; inadvertido; secreto, oculto. n versión al libro abierto, f. **the u.,** lo invisible

unselfish a desinteresado, abnegado, nada egoísta; generoso

unselfishness n abnegación, f; desinterés, m; generosidad, f

unsentimental a no sentimental

unserviceable a inservible, inútil, que no sirve para nada, sin utilidad

unsettle vt desarreglar; desorganizar; hacer inseguro; agitar, perturbar

unsettled a inconstante, variable; com pendiente, sin pagar; incierto; sin resolver; (of estates) sin solucionar

unshackle vt desencadenar

unshakable a inconmovible, firme

unshapely a desproporcionado

unshaven a sin afeitar

unsheathe vt desenvainar, sacar

unsheltered a desabrigado, desamparado; no protegido, sin protección; (of places) sin abrigo, expuesto; (from) sin defensa contra

unship vt desembarcar; (the oars) desarmar

unshod a descalzo; (of a horse) sin herraduras

unshorn a sin esquilar; intonso

unshrinkable a que no se encoge

unshrinking a intrépido; resoluto, sin vacilar

unsightly a feo, horrible, repugnante, antiestético

unsinkable a insumergible

unskilled a inexperto, inhábil, imperito, torpe

unsmokable a (of tobacco) infumable

unsociability n insociabilidad, huraña, esquivez, f

unsociable a insociable, huraño, esquivo, arisco

unsocial a insocial, antisocial

unsold a no vendido, sin vender

unsolder vt desoldar, desestañar

unsoldierly a indigno de un soldado; poco marcial

unsophisticated a ingenuo, inocente, cándido

unsought a no solicitado; no buscado

unsound a enfermo; defectuoso; (rotten) podrido; (fallacious) erróneo, poco convincente; (of persons) informal, indigno de confianza; (of religious views) heterodoxo. **of u. mind,** insano

unsoundness n lo defectuoso; mal estado, m; falsedad, f; informalidad, f; heterodoxia, f

unsparing a severo, implacable; generoso, pródigo

unspeakable a indecible, inefable; que no puede mencionarse, horrible

unspecified a no especificado

unspoilt a intacto; ileso, indemne; no corrompido; no estropeado; (of children) no mimado

unspoken a no pronunciado

unsportsmanlike a indigno de un cazador; indigno de un deportista; nada caballeroso. **to play in an u. way,** jugar sucio

unstable a inestable; variable; inconstante; vacilante, irresoluto

unstained a no manchado; no teñido; inmaculado, sin mancha

unstamped a sin sello; no sellado

unstatesmanlike a impropio (or indigno) de un hombre de estado

unsteadiness n inestabilidad, falta de firmeza, f; inconstancia, f

unsteady a inestable, inseguro; inconstante

unstick vt despegar

unstitch vt desapuntar

unstressed a sin énfasis; (of syllables) sin acento

unstudied *a* no estudiado; natural, espontáneo

unsubstantial *a* insubstancial; ligero; irreal, imaginario; incorpóreo; aparente

unsuccessful *a* sin éxito; infructuoso. **to be u.**, no tener éxito

unsuccessfully *adv* en vano, sin éxito

unsuitability *n* impropiedad, *f*; inconveniencia, incongruencia, *f*; incapacidad, *f*; inoportunidad, *f*

unsuitable *a* inapropiado; inconveniente; impropio; inservible; incapaz; inoportuno

unsung *a* no cantado; no celebrado en verso

unsupported *a* sin apoyo; sin defensa; no favorecido

unsurmountable *a* insuperable, infranqueable

unsurpassable *a* inmejorable, insuperable

unsurpassed *a* sin par

unsuspecting *a* no suspicaz, confiado, no receloso

unswerving *a* directo; sin vacilar, constante

unsymmetrical *a* asimétrico

unsympathetic *a* indiferente, incompasivo; antipático

unsystematic *a* sin sistema, asistemático, no metódico

untalented *a* sin talento

untamed *a* indomado, cerril, bravío, no domesticado; desenfrenado, violento

unteach *vt* desenseñar

untenable *a* insostenible

untenanted *a* desalquilado, deshabitado; vacío, desierto

unthankful *a* ingrato, desagradecido

unthinkable *a* inconcebible; imposible

unthinking *a* sin reflexión; desatento; indiscreto

unthinkingly *adv* sin pensar

unthread *vt* deshebrar

untidily *adv* en desorden, sin aseo

untidiness *n* desorden, *m*; desaseo, desaliño, *m*; falta de pulcritud, *f*

untidy *a* desarreglado; desaseado; abandonado; en desorden, sin concierto

untie *vt* desatar, desanudar; (knots) deshacer

until *prep* hasta. *conjunc* hasta que. (The subjunc. is required in clauses referring to future time, e.g. **No venga usted hasta que le avise yo,** Don't come until I tell you. In clauses referring to past or present time the indicative is generally used, e.g. **No la reconocí hasta que se volvió,** I didn't recognize her until she turned round)

untilled *a* sin cultivar

untimeliness *n* inoportunidad, *f*; lo prematuro

untimely *a* inoportuno, intempestivo; prematuro

untiring *a* incansable, infatigable

unto *prep* hacia

untold *a* no revelado; no narrado; sin decir, no dicho; incalculable

untouchable *a* que no puede tocarse, intangible; (of castes) intocable

untouched *a* sin tocar; intacto, incólume

untrained *a* indisciplinado; inexperto; no adiestrado

untranslatable *a* intraducible

untraveled *a* no frecuentado; (of persons) provinciano

untried *a* no experimentado. **u. knight,** caballero novel, *m*

untrodden *a* no hollado, no frecuentado; inexplorado, virgen

untroubled *a* tranquilo, sosegado

untrue *a* mentiroso, falso, engañoso; ficticio, imaginario; traidor, desleal; infiel

untrustworthiness *n* incertidumbre, inseguridad, *f*; (of persons) informalidad, *f*

untrustworthy *a* indigno de confianza; incierto, dudoso; desleal

untruth *n* mentira, falsedad, *f*; ficción, *f*

untruthful *a* mentiroso; falso

untruthfulness *n* falsedad, *f*

untwist *vt* destorcer

unused *a* no empleado; desacostumbrado; inusitado; (postage stamp) sin sellar

unusual *a* fuera de lo común, desacostumbrado; extraño, raro, peregrino, extraordinario

unusually *adv* excepcionalmente; infrecuentemente

unusualness *n* lo insólito; rareza, *f*

unutterable *a* indecible, inexpresable

unvarnished *a* sin barnizar; *fig* sencillo

unvarying *a* invariable, constante, uniforme

unveil *vt* quitar el velo; (memorial) descubrir; *fig* revelar. *vi* quitarse el velo; revelarse, quitarse la careta

unventilated *a* sin ventilación; sin aire, ahogado; (of topics) no discutido

unverifiable *a* que no puede verificarse

unverified *a* sin verificar

unvisited *a* no visitado; no frecuentado

unvoiced *a* no expresado

unwanted *a* no deseado; superfluo, de más

unwarlike *a* nada marcial, pacífico

unwarranted *a* sin garantía; inexcusable, injustificable

unwary *a* incauto, imprudente

unwashed *a* sin lavar; sucio

unwatched *a* no vigilado

unwavering *a* resuelto, firme; inexorable; (gaze) fijo

unwaveringly *adv* sin vacilar; inexorablemente

unwearied *a* incansable; infatigable

unwelcome *a* mal acogido; inoportuno; desagradable

unwell *a* indispuesto

unwholesome *a* malsano, nocivo, insalubre

unwholesomeness *n* insalubridad, *f*

unwieldiness *n* pesadez, dificultad de manejarse, *f*

unwieldy *a* pesado, abultado, difícil de manejar

unwilling *a* desinclinado, reluctante

unwillingly *adv* de mala gana

unwillingness *n* falta de inclinación, repugnancia, *f*

unwind *vt* desenvolver; (thread) desdevanar, desovillar. *vi* desarrollarse; desdevanarse

unwise *a* imprudente, indiscreto, incauto; (lacking wisdom) tonto

unwisely *adv* imprudentemente, indiscretamente

unwitting *a* inconsciente

unwittingly *adv* sin darse cuenta

unwomanly *a* poco femenino

unwonted *a* insólito, inusitado

unworkable *a* impráctico

unworkmanlike *a* chapucero, charanguero

unworldly *a* poco, mundano, espiritual

unworn *a* sin llevar, nuevo

unworthiness *n* indignidad, *f*

unworthy *a* indigno

unwounded *a* no herido, sin herida, ileso

unwrap *vt* desenvolver, desempapelar

unwritten *a* no escrito. **u. law,** ley consuetudinaria, *f*

unyielding *a* duro, firme; (of persons) inflexible, terco, resuelto, obstinado

unyoke *vt* desuncir, quitar el yugo

up *adv* (high) arriba, en alto; (higher) hacia arriba; (out of bed) levantado; (standing) de pie; (finished) concluido, terminado; (of time) llegado; (excited) agitado; (rebellious) sublevado; (of sun, etc.) salido; (come or gone up) subido; (of universities) en residencia; (for discussion) bajo consideración; (abreast of) al lado, al nivel; (incapable) incapaz, incompetente; (ill) enfermo, indispuesto. **"Up,"** (on elevators) «Para subir.» (For various idiomatic uses of **up** after verbs, see verbs themselves.) *a* (in a few expressions only) ascendente. *prep* en lo alto de; hacia arriba de; a lo largo de; (with country) en el interior de; (with current) contra. **to be up in arms,** sublevarse, rebelarse. **to be very hard up,** ser muy pobre, estar a la cuarta pregunta. **to drink up,** beberlo todo. **to go or come up,** subir. **to lay up,** acumular. **to speak up,** hablar en voz alta. **He has something up his sleeve,** Tiene algo en la manga. **It is all up,** Todo se acabó, Mi gozo en el pozo. **It is not up to much,** Vale muy poco; No es muy fuerte. **It is up to you,** Tú dirás, Tú harás lo que te parezca. **What is he up to?** ¿Qué está tramando? **What's up?** ¿Qué pasa? ¿Qué hay? **up and down,**

adv bajando y subiendo, de arriba abajo; de un lado a otro; por todas partes. **up-and-down,** *a* fluctuante; (of roads) undulante; (of life) accidentado, borrascoso. **ups and downs,** vicisitudes, *f pl,* altibajos, *m pl.* **upgrade,** subida, *f.* **up in,** versado en, perito en. **well up in,** fuerte en. **up North,** al norte; en el norte; hacia el norte. **up there,** allí arriba, allí en lo alto. **up to,** hasta; (aware) al corriente de, informado de. **up to date,** *adv* hasta la fecha. **up-to-date,** *a* de última moda; al día. **up to now,** hasta ahora. **up train,** tren ascendente. **Up with . . . !** ¡Arriba! **Up you go!** (to children) ¡Upa!

upbraid *vt* reprender, echar en cara

upbringing *n* crianza, educación, *f*

upcountry *n* tierra adentro, *f;* lo interior (de un país). *a* de tierra adentro, del interior. *adv* tierra adentro, hacia el interior

update *vt* actualizar, poner al día

upheaval *n* solevantamiento, *m;* trastorno, *m*

uphill *a* ascendente; penoso, fatigoso, difícil. *adv* cuesta arriba, pendiente arriba

uphold *vt* sostener, apoyar; (help) ayudar, consolar; (protect) defender; (countenance) aprobar; *law* confirmar

upholder *n* sostenedor (-ra), defensor (-ra)

upholster *vt* entapizar, tapizar

upholsterer *n* tapicero, *m*

upholstery *n* tapicería, *f;* (of car) almohadillado, *m*

upkeep *n* mantenimiento, *m,* conservación, *f*

upland *n* tierra alta, *f,* a alto, elevado

uplift *vt* elevar. *n* elevación, *f; inf* fervor, *m*

upon *prep.* See **on**

upper *a comp* superior; alto; de arriba. *n* (of shoe) pala, *f, sport* **u.-cut,** golpe de abajo arriba, upper-cut, *m.* **U. Egypt,** Alto Egipto, *m.* **u. hand,** dominio, *m;* superioridad, ventaja, *f.* **u. house,** cámara alta, *f;* senado, *m.* **u. ten,** los diez primeros

upper classes *a* clases altas, capas altas, *f pl*

uppermost *a* más alto, más elevado; predominante, principal; más fuerte. *adv* en primer lugar; en lo más alto. **to be u.,** predominar

upright *a* recto, derecho; vertical; (honorable) honrado, digno, recto. *n* (stanchion) mástil, soporte, palo derecho, montante, *m. adv* en pie; derecho

uprightly *adv* rectamente, honradamente

uprightness *n* rectitud, honradez, probidad, *f*

uprising *n* insurrección, sublevación, *f*

uproar *n* alboroto, tumulto, estrépito, *m,* conmoción, *f*

uproarious *a* tumultuoso, estrepitoso

uproot *vt* desarraigar; *fig* arrancar; (destroy) extirpar

uprooting *n* desarraigo, *m;* arranque, *m;* extirpación, *f*

upset *vt* volcar; (overthrow) derribar, echar abajo; (frustrate) contrariar; desarreglar; (distress) trastornar, turbar; (of food) hacer mal. *vi* volcarse. *n* vuelco, *m;* trastorno, *m.* **u. price,** tipo de subasta, *m*

upsetting *a* turbante, inquietante

upshot *n* resultado, *m;* consecuencia, *f*

upside *n* lado superior, *m;* parte superior, *f;* (of trains) andén ascendente, *m.* **u. down,** al revés, de arriba abajo; en desorden

upstairs *adv* arriba, en el piso de arriba; (with go or come) al piso de arriba

upstanding *a* gallardo, guapo. **an u. young man (woman),** un buen mozo (una buena moza)

upstart *n* arribista, *mf;* advenedizo (-za), insolente, *mf;* presuntuoso (-sa)

upstream *a* and *adv* contra la corriente, agua arriba, río arriba

upturned *a* (of noses) respingada

upward *a* ascendente, hacia arriba

upwards *adv* hacia arriba; en adelante. **u. of,** más de

Urals, the los Urales, *m pl*

uranium *n min* uranio, *m*

Uranus *n ast* Urano, *m*

urban *a* urbano, ciudadano

urban renewal *n* renovación urbana, renovación urbanística, *f*

urbane *a* cortés, urbano, fino

urbanity *n* urbanidad, cortesía, finura, *f*

urbanization *n* urbanización, *f*

urbanize *vt* urbanizar

urchin *n* galopín, granuja, pilluelo, *m*

ureter *n anat* uréter, *m*

urethra *n anat* uretra, *f*

urge *vt* empujar, impeler; incitar, estimular, azuzar, animar; pedir con urgencia, recomendar con ahínco, instar, insistir (en). *n* instinto, impulso, *m;* deseo, *m;* ambición, *f*

urgency *n* urgencia, *Y;* importancia, perentoriedad, *f*

urgent *a* urgente; importante, apremiante, perentorio. **to be u.,** urgir

urgently *adv* urgentemente

uric *a* úrico

urinal *n* orinal, urinario, *m*

urinalysis *n* análisis de orina, urinálisis, *m*

urinary *a* urinario

urinary tract *n* conducto urinario, *m,* vías urinarias, *f pl*

urinate *vi* orinar

urine *n* orín, *m*

urn *n* urna, *f;* (for coffee) cafetera, *f;* (for tea) tetera, *f*

Ursa *n ast* osa, *f.* **U. Major,** osa mayor, *f.* **U. Minor,** osa menor, *f*

urticaria *n med* urticaria, *f*

Uruguayan *a* and *n* uruguayo (-ya)

us *pron* nos; (with prep.) nosotros. **He came toward us,** Vino hacia nosotros

usable *a* aprovechable, servible

usage *n* (handling) tratamiento, *m;* uso, *m,* costumbre, *f*

use *n* uso, *m;* manejo, empleo, *m;* (custom) costumbre práctica, *f;* (need) necesidad, *f;* (usefulness) aprovechamiento, *m; law* usufructo, *m.* **directions for use,** direcciones para el uso, *f pl,* **for the use of . . .,** para uso de . . . **in use,** en uso. **out of use,** anticuado; fuera de moda. **to be of no use,** no servir; ser inútil. **to have no use for,** no tener necesidad de; *inf* tener en poco. **to make use of,** servirse de, aprovechar; *law* ejercer. **to put to use,** poner en uso, poner en servicio

use *vt* usar; (employ) emplear; (utilize) servirse de, utilizar; (handle) manejar; hacer uso de; (consume) gastar, consumir; (treat) tratar; practicar. **to use up,** agotar; acabar con; consumir. *vi impers* acostumbrar, soler (e.g. **It used to happen that . . . ,** Solía ocurrir que . . .). (**Used to** and the verb which follows are often translated simply by the imperfect tense of the following verb, e.g. **I used to see her every day,** La veía todos los días. Use of the verbs **acostumbrar** or **soler** to translate used to adds emphasis to the statement)

used *a* and *past part* acostumbrado, habituado; empleado; (clothes) usado; (postage stamp) sellado. **to become u. to,** acostumbrarse a

useful *a* útil; provechoso; servicial

usefully *adv* útilmente; con provecho

usefulness *n* utilidad, *f;* valor, *m*

useless *a* inútil; vano, infructuoso. **to render u.,** inutilizar

uselessness *n* inutilidad, *f*

user *n* el, *m,* (*f,* la) que usa, comprador (-ra)

usher *n* ujier, *m;* (in a theater) acomodador (-ra). *vt* introducir, anunciar; acomodar

usual *a* usual, acostumbrado, habitual; normal, común. **as u.,** como siempre. **in the u. form,** *com* al usado; como de costumbre. **with their usual courtesy,** con la cortesía que les es característica

usually *adv* por lo general, ordinariamente. **We u. go out on Sundays,** Acostumbramos salir los domingos

usurer *n* usurero (-ra)

usurious *a* usurario

usurp *vt* usurpar; asumir, arrogarse

usurpation *n* usurpación, *f;* arrogación, *f*

usurper *n* usurpador (-ra)

usurping *a* usurpador

usury *n* usura, *f.* **to practice u.,** usurear, dar (or tomar) a usura

utensil *n* utensilio, instrumento, *m;* herramienta, *f.* **kitchen utensils,** batería de cocina, *f*

uterine *a med* uterino

uterus *n* útero, *m*

utilitarian *a* utilitario

utilitarianism *n* utilitarismo, *m*

utility *n* utilidad, *f;* ventaja, *f,* beneficio, provecho, *m.* **u. goods,** artículos fabricados bajo la autorizacion del gobierno, *m pl*

utilizable *a* utilizable, aprovechable

utilization *n* empleo, aprovechamiento, *m*

utilize *vt* utilizar, servirse de; aprovechar

utmost *a* (outermost) extremo; (farthest) más remoto, más distante; (greatest) mayor, más grande. *n* lo más; todo lo posible. **to do one's u.,** hacer todo lo posible, hacer todo lo que uno pueda

utopian *a* utópico

utter *a* completo, total; terminate, absoluto; sumo, extremo. **He is an u. fool,** Es un tonto de capirote

utter *vt* pronunciar, proferir, decir, hablar; (a sigh, cry, etc.) dar; (express) manifestar, expresar, explicar; (coin) poner en circulación; (a libel) publicar; (disclose) revelar, descubrir

utterance *n* expresión, manifestación, *f;* pronunciación, *f;* (style) lenguaje, *m*

utterly *adv* enteramente, completamente

uttermost *a.* See **utmost**

uvula *n anat* úvula, *f*

uxorious *a* uxorio

V

v *n* (letter) ve, *f;* pieza en forma de V, *f*

vacancy *n* vacío, *m;* vacancia, *f;* (mental) vacuidad, *f;* (of offices, posts) vacante, *f;* (leisure) desocupación, ociosidad, *f;* (gap, blank) vacío, *m,* laguna, *f*

vacant *a* vacío; despoblado, deshabitado; (free) libre; (of offices, etc.) vacante; (leisured) ocioso; (absentminded) distraído; (vague) vago; (foolish) estúpido, estólido

vacantly *adv* distraídamente; estúpidamente

vacate *vt* dejar vacío; (a post) dejar; (a throne) renunciar a; dejar vacante; *mil* evacuar; *law* anular, rescindir

vacation *n* (of offices) vacante, *f;* (holiday) vacaciones, *f pl, f.* **the long v.,** las vacaciones de verano. **to be on a v.,** estar de vacaciones

vaccinate *vt* vacunar

vaccination *n* vacunación, *f*

vaccine *n* vacuna, *f*

vacillate *vi* (sway) oscilar; (hesitate) vacilar, titubear, dudar

vacillating *a* vacilante

vacillation *n* vacilación, *f*

vacuity *n* vacuidad, *f*

vacuous *a* desocupado, ocioso; estúpido, vacío

vacuum *n* vacío, *m.* **v. brake,** freno al vacío, *m.* **v. cleaner,** aspirador de polvo, *m.* **v. flask,** termos, *m.* **v. pump,** bomba neumática, *f.* **vacuum-shelf dryer,** secador al vacío, *m*

vade mecum *n* vademécum, *m*

vagabond *n* vagabundo (-da); vago, *m;* (beggar) mendigo (-ga). *a* vagabundo, errante

vagabondage *n* vagabundeo, *m,* vagancia, *f*

vagary *n* (whim) capricho, antojo, *m,* extravagancia, *f;* (of the mind) divagación, *f*

vagina *n* vagina, *f*

vaginal *a* vaginal

vagrancy *n* vagancia, *f*

vagrant *n* vago, *m, a* vagabundo, errante

vague *a* vago; indistinto; equívoco, ambiguo; (uncertain) incierto

vaguely *adv* vagamente

vagueness *n* vaguedad, *f*

vain *a* vano; (fruitless) infructuoso; (useless) inútil; (unsubstantial) fútil, insubstancial; fantástico; (empty) vacío; (worthless) despreciable; (conceited) vanidoso, presumido. **in v.,** en vano, en balde, inútilmente. **v. about,** orgulloso de

vainglorious *a* vanaglorioso

vaingloriousness *n* vanagloria, *f*

vainly *adv* vanamente; inútilmente; (conceitedly) vanidosamente, con vanidad

valance *n* cenefa, *f*

vale *n* (valley) valle, *m. interj* ¡adiós! *n* (good-bye) vale, *m*

valediction *n* despedida, *f;* vale, *m*

valedictory *a* de despedida

Valencian *a* and *n* valenciano (-na)

valency *n chem* valencia, *f*

valet *n* criado, *m.* **v. de chambre,** ayuda de cámara, *m*

valetudinarian *a* valetudinario

Valhalla *n* el Valhala, *m*

valiant *a* valiente, esforzado, animoso, bravo

valiantly *adv* valientemente

valid *a* válido, valedero; (of laws in force) vigente

validate *vt* validar

validation *n* validación, *f*

validity *n* validez, *f*

validly *adv* válidamente

valise *n* valija, *f,* saco de viaje, *m*

Valkyrie *n* Valquiria, *f*

valley *n* valle, *m*

valor *n* valor, *m,* valentía, *f*

valorous *a* valoroso, esforzado, intrépido

valse *n* vals, *m*

valuable *a* valioso; costoso; precioso; estimable; excelente. *n pl* **valuables,** objetos de valor, *m pl*

valuableness *n* valor, *m*

valuation *n* valuación, tasación, *f;* estimación, *f*

valuator *n* tasador, *m*

value *n* valor, *m;* precio, *m;* estimación, *f;* importancia, *f;* (gram mus) valor, *m; pl* **values,** valores morales, principios, *m pl. vt* tasar, valorar; estimar; apreciar; tener en mucho; hacer caso de; considerar. **to be of v.,** ser de valor

valued *a* apreciado, estimado; precioso

valueless *a* sin valor; insignificante

valuer *n* tasador, *m*

valve *n* (elec, mech, anat) válvula, *f;* (bot, zool) valva, *f*

valved *a* con válvulas; (in compounds) de . . . válvulas

valvular *a* valvular

vamp *n* (of a shoe) pala (de zapato), *f;* (patch) remiendo, *m;* mus acompañamiento improvisado, *m; inf* aventurera, *f. vt* (of shoes) poner palas (a); (patch) remendar; *mus* improvisar un acompañamiento; (of a woman) fascinar, engatusar

vampire *n* vampiro, *m*

van *n* (mil, nav, fig) vanguardia, *f;* camión, *m;* (for delivery) camión de reparto, *m;* (for furniture) conductora de muebles, *f;* (removal) carro de mudanzas, *m;* (mail) camión postal, *m;* (for bathing) caseta de baño, *f;* (for guard on trains) furgón de equipajes, *m;* (railroad car) vagón, *m*

vandal *a* and *n* vándalo (-la); bárbaro (-ra)

vandalism *n* vandalismo, *m*

Vandyke *n* cuadro de Vandyke, *m.* **V. beard,** perilla, *f.* **V. collar,** cuello de encaje, *m*

vane *n* (weathercock) veleta, *f;* (of a windmill) aspa, *f;* (of a propeller) paleta, *f;* (of a feather) barba, *f;* (of a surveying instrument) pínula, *f*

vanguard *n* vanguardia, *f.* **in the v.,** a vanguardia; *fig* en la vanguardia

vanilla *n* vainilla, *f*

vanish *vi* desaparecer; desvanecerse; disiparse
vanishing *n* desaparición, *f*; disipación, *f*. **v. cream,** crema desvanecedora, *f*. **v. point,** punto de la vista, *m*
vanity *n* vanidad, *f*. **v. case,** polvera de bolsillo, *f*
vanquish *vt* vencer, derrotar
vanquisher *n* vencedor (-ra)
vantage *n* ventaja (also in tennis), *f*. **v.-ground,** posición ventajosa, *f*, sitial de privilegio, *m*
vapid *a* insípido, insulso; (of speeches, etc.) soso, aburrido, insípido
vapidity *n* insipidez, sosería, *f*
vapor *n* vapor, *m*; *pl* **vapors,** (hysteria) vapores, *m pl*. *vi* (boast) jactarse, baladronear; decir disparates. **v. bath,** baño de vapor, *m*
vaporizable *a* vaporizable
vaporization *n* vaporización, *f*
vaporize *vt* vaporizar. *vi* vaporizarse
vaporizer *n* vaporizador, *m*
vaporous *a* vaporoso
variability *n* variabilidad, *f*
variable *a* variable. *n math* variable, *f*
variably *adv* variablemente
variance *n* variación, *f*, cambio, *m*; desacuerdo, *m*, disensión, *f*; diferencia, contradicción, *f*. **at v.,** en desacuerdo, reñidos; hostil (a), opuesto (a); (of things) distinto (de), en contradicción (con)
variant *n* variante, *f*
variation *n* variación, *f*; cambio, *m*; variedad, *f*; diferencia, *f*; (*mus* magnetism) variación, *f*
varicose *a* varicoso
varied success éxito vario, *m*
variegate *vt* abigarrar, matizar, salpicar
variegated *a* abigarrado; variado; mezclado
variegation *n* abigarramiento, *m*; diversidad de colores, *f*
variety *n* variedad, *f*; diversidad, *f*; (choice) surtido, *m*. **v. show,** función de variedades, *f*
various *a* vario, diverso; diferente
variously *adv* diversamente
varix *n* várice, *f*
varnish *n* barniz, *m*. *vt* barnizar; (pottery) vidriar; (conceal) disimular. **copal v.,** barniz copal, *m*. **japan v.,** charol japonés, *m*. **lacquer v.,** laca, *f*. **v. remover,** (for nails) quitaesmalte, *m*
varnishing *n* barnizado, *m*; (of pottery) vidriado, *m*
vary *vt* variar; cambiar; diversificar; modificar. *vi* variar; cambiar; (be different) ser distinto (de); (deviate) desviarse (de); (disagree) estar en desacuerdo, distar, estar en contradicción. **to v. directly (indirectly),** *math* variar en razón directa (inversa)
varying *a* variante, cambiante, diverso
vascular *a* vascular
vase *n* vaso, jarrón, *m*; urna, *f*
vaseline *n* vaselina, *f*
vassal *n* vasallo (-lla); esclavo (-va), siervo (-va). *a* tributario
vast *a* vasto, extenso; enorme; grande. *n* vastedad, inmensidad, *f*
vastly *adv* enormemente; muy; con mucho
vastness *n* vastedad, extensión, *f*; inmensidad, *f*; enormidad, *f*, gran tamaño, *m*; grandeza, *f*
vat *n* cuba, tina, *f*; alberca, *f*, estanque, *m*. **dyeing vat,** cuba de tintorero, *f*. **tanning vat,** noque, *m*. **wine vat,** lagar, *m*
Vatican *a* and *n* Vaticano, *m*
vaticinate *vt* and *vi* vaticinar, profetizar
vaticination *n* vaticinio, *m*, predicción, *f*
vaudeville *n* vodevil, *m*, zarzuela cómica, *f*
vault *n arch* bóveda, *f*; caverna, *f*; (for wine) bodega, cueva, *f*; (in a bank) cámara acorazada, *f*; (in a church) cripta, *f*; sepultura, *f*; (of the sky) bóveda celeste, *f*; (leap) salto, *m*; voltereta, *f*. *vi* (jump) saltar; (with a pole) saltar con pértiga; saltar por encima de; voltear. *vt arch* abovedar; saltar
vaulted *a* abovedado
vaulter *n* saltador (-ra)

vaulting *n* construcción de bóvedas, *f*; bóvedas, *f pl*; edificio abovedado, *m*; (jumping) salto, *m*. **v.-horse,** potro de madera, *m*
vaunt *vi* jactarse (de), hacer gala (de); triunfar (sobre). *vt* ostentar, sacar a relucir; (praise) alabar. *n* jactancia, *f*
veal *n* ternera, *f*. **v.-cutlet,** chuleta de ternera, *f*
vector *n* vector, *m*
Veda *n* Veda, *m*
veer *vi* (of the wind) girar; (of a ship) virar; *fig* cambiar (de opinión, etc.). *vt* virar
vegetable *n* vegetal, *m*; legumbre, *f*; *pl* **vegetables,** (green and generally cooked) verduras, *f pl*; (raw green) hortalizas, *f pl*. **v. dish,** fuente de legumbres, *f*. **v. garden,** huerto de legumbres, *m*; **v. ivory,** marfil vegetal, *m*. **v. kingdom,** reino vegetal, *m*. **v. soup,** sopa de hortelano, *f*
vegetal *a* vegetal
vegetarian *a* and *n* vegetariano (-na)
vegetarianism *n* vegetarianismo, *m*
vegetate *vi* vegetar
vegetation *n* vegetación, *f*
vehemence *n* vehemencia, *f*; violencia, *f*; impetuosidad, *f*; pasión, *f*, ardor, *m*
vehement *a* vehemente; violento; impetuoso; apasionado
vehemently *adv* con vehemencia; violentamente; con impetuosidad; apasionadamente
vehicle *n* vehículo, *m*; (means) medio, *m*; instrumento, *m*
vehicular *a* vehicular, de los vehículos; de los coches. **v. traffic,** circulación de los coches, *f*; los vehículos
veil *n* velo, *m*; (curtain) cortina, *f*; (disguise) disfraz, *m*; (excuse) pretexto, *m*; (appearance) apariencia, *f*. *vt* velar; cubrir con un velo; (hide) tapar, encubrir; (dissemble) disimular; (disguise) disfrazar. **to take the v.,** tomar el velo, profesar
vein *n* (anat, bot) vena, *f*; (geol, min) veta, *f*, filón, *m*; (in wood) fibra, hebra, *f*; (fig streak) rasgo, *m*; (inspiration) vena, *f*; (mood) humor, *m*
veined, veiny *a* venoso; de venas; veteado
velar *a* velar
vellum *n* vitela, *f*
velocity *n* velocidad, *f*; rapidez, *f*
velodrome *n* velódromo, *f*
velours *n* terciopelo, *m*
velvet *n* terciopelo, *m*, *a* hecho de terciopelo; aterciopelado
velveteen *n* pana, *f*, velludillo, *m*
velvety *a* aterciopelado
venal *a* venal
venality *n* venalidad, *f*
vend *vt* vender
vendor *n* vendedor (-ra)
veneer *vt* chapear, taracear; (conceal) disimular, disfrazar. *n* taraceado, chapeado, *m*; (plate) chapa, hoja para chapear, *f*; (fig gloss) barniz, *m*, apariencia, *f*
venerability *n* venerabilidad, respetabilidad, *f*
venerable *a* venerable
venerate *vt* venerar, reverenciar
veneration *n* veneración, *f*
venerator *n* venerador (-ra)
venereal *a* venéreo. **v. disease,** enfermedad venérea, *f*
Venetian *a* and *n* veneciano (-na). **v. blinds,** persianas, celosías, *f pl*
Venezuelan *a* and *n* venezolano (-na)
vengeance *n* venganza, *f*
vengeful *a* vengativo
venial *a* venial
veniality *n* venialidad, *f*
Venice Venecia, *f*
venison *n* venado, *m*
venom *n* veneno, *m*
venomous *a* venenoso; maligno, malicioso
venomously *adv* con malignidad, maliciosamente
venomousness *n* venenosidad, *f*; malignidad, *f*

venous *a* venoso

vent *n* abertura, *f*; salida, *f*; (air-hole) respiradero, *m*; (in pipes) ventosa, *f*; (in fire-arms) oído, *m*; *anat* ano, *m*; (*fig* outlet) desahogo, *m*; expresión, *f*. *vt* dejar escapar; (pierce) agujerear; (discharge) emitir, vomitar; (relieve) desahogar; expresar, dar expresión (a), dar rienda suelta (a)

venter *n law* vientre, *m*

ventilate *vt* ventilar; discutir

ventilation *n* ventilación, *f*

ventilator *n* ventilador, *m*

ventricle *n* ventrículo, *m*

ventriloquism *n* ventriloquia, *f*

ventriloquist *n* ventrílocuo (-ua)

venture *n* ventura, *f*; riesgo, *m*; aventura, *f*; especulación, *f*. *vt* arriesgar, aventurar; (stake) jugar; (state) expresar. *vi* aventurarse; (dare) atreverse, osar; permitirse. **at a v.,** a la ventura. **to v. on,** arriesgarse a; probar ventura con; lanzarse a; (a remark) permitirse. **to v. out,** atreverse a salir

venturesome *a* atrevido, audaz; (dangerous) arriesgado, peligroso

venturesomeness *n* atrevimiento, *m*, temeridad, *f*; (risk) riesgo, peligro, *m*

Venus *n* (planet) Venus, *m*; (woman) venus, *f*

veracious *a* veraz, verídico; verdadero

veracity *n* veracidad, *f*; verdad, *f*

veranda *n* veranda, *f*

verb *n* verbo, *m*. **auxiliary v.,** verbo auxiliar, *m*. **intransitive v.,** verbo intransitivo (neutro), *m*. **reflexive v.,** verbo reflexivo, *m*. **transitive v.,** verbo transitivo, *m*

verbal *a* verbal

verbally *adv* de palabra, verbalmente

verbatim *a* textual. *adv* textualmente, palabra por palabra

verbiage *n* verbosidad, palabrería, *f*

verbose *a* verboso, prolijo

verbosity *n* verbosidad, *f*

verdancy *n* verdura, *f*, verdor, *m*

verdant *a* verde

verdict *n law* veredicto, fallo, *m*, sentencia, *f*; opinión, *f*, juicio, *m*. **to bring in a v.,** fallar sentencia.

verdigris *n* cardenillo, verdín, *m*

verdure *n* verdura, *f*, verdor, *m*; *fig* lozanía, *f*

verge *n* (wand) vara, *f*; (edge) margen, borde, *m*; (of a lake, etc.) orilla, *f*; (horizon) horizonte, *m*; *fig* víspera, *f*, punto, *m*. **on the v. of,** al margen de, a la orilla de. **to be on the v. of,** *fig* estar a punto de; estar en vísperas de

verger *n* macero, *m*; (in a church) pertiguero, *m*

verifiable *a* verificable

verification *n* verificación, *f*

verifier *n* verificador (-ra)

verify *vt* verificar, confirmar; probar

verily *adv* de veras, en verdad

verisimilitude *n* verosimilitud, *f*

veritable *a* verdadero

veritably *adv* verdaderamente

verity *n* verdad, *f*

vermicelli *n* fideos, *m pl*

vermilion *n* bermellón, *m*

vermin *n* bichos dañinos, *m pl*; (insects) parásitos, *m pl*

vermouth *n* vermut, *m*

vernacular *a* vernáculo; nativo; vulgar. *n* lengua popular, *f*; lenguaje vulgar, *m*

versatile *a zool* versátil; inconstante, voluble; (clever) de muchos talentos; de muchos intereses; adaptable; completo, cabal

versatility *n* (cleverness) muchos talentos, *m pl*; adaptabilidad, *f*

verse *n* verso, *m*; (stanza) estrofa, *f*; (in the Bible) versículo, *m*; (poetry) poesía, *f*, versos, *m pl*. **to make verses,** escribir versos

versed *a* versado, experimentado

versicle *n* versículo, *m*

versification *n* versificación, *f*

versifier *n* versificador (-ra)

versify *vt* and *vi* versificar

version *n* versión, *f*; traducción, *f*; interpretación, *f*

versus *prep* contra

vertebra *n* vértebra, *f*

vertebral *a* vertebral

vertebrate *n* vertebrado, *m*

vertex *n* (geom, anat) vértice, *m*; *ast* cenit, *m*; cumbre, *f*

vertical *a* vertical

verticality *n* verticalidad, *f*

vertiginous *a* vertiginoso

vertigo *n* vértigo, *m*

verve *n* brío, *m*, fogosidad, *f*

very *a* mismo; (mere) mero; (true) verdadero; (with adjective and comparative) más grande; *inf* mismísimo; (complete) perfecto, completo. **The v. thought of it made him laugh,** Sólo con pensarlo se rió (*or* La mera idea le hizo reír). **this v. minute,** este mismísimo instante. **the v. day,** el mismo día

very *adv* muy; mucho; demasiado; (exactly) exactamente; completamente; absolutamente. **He is v. worried,** Está muy preocupado. **He is not v. well,** (i.e. rather ill) Está bastante bien. **This cloth is the v. best,** Esta tela es la mejor que hay. **I like it v. much,** Me gusta muchísimo. **He is v. much pleased,** Está muy contento. **so v. little,** tan poco; tan pequeño. **v. well,** muy bien

vesicle *n* vesícula, *f*

vesper *n* estrella vespertina, *f*, héspero, *m*; *pl* **vespers,** *ecc* vísperas, *f pl*

vessel *n* vasija, *f*, recipiente, *m*; (boat) barco, buque, *m*; (anat, bot) vaso, *m*

vest *n* camiseta, *f*; (waistcoat) chaleco, *m*. *vt* vestir; (with authority, etc.) revestir de; (property, etc.) hacer entrega de, ceder. *vi* tener validez; (dress) vestirse. **vested interests,** intereses creados, *m pl*. **v.-pocket,** bolsillo del chaleco, *m*. **v.-pocket camera,** cámara de bolsillo, *f*

vestal *a* vestal; virgen, casto. *n* vestal, *f*; virgen, *f*

vestibule *n* vestíbulo, *m*; (anteroom) antecámara, *f*; (of a theatre box) antepalco, *m*; *anat* vestíbulo, *m*

vestige *n* vestigio, rastro, *m*; sombra, *f*; *biol* rudimento, *m*

vestment *n* hábito, *m*; *ecc* vestidura, *f*

vestry *n* vestuario, *m*, sacristía, *f*

vesture *n* traje, hábito, *m*, vestidura, *f*

Vesuvius Vesubio, *m*

veteran *a* veterano; de los veteranos; aguerrido; anciano; experimentado. *n* veterano (-na)

veterinary *a* veterinario. **v. science,** veterinaria, *f*. **v. surgeon,** veterinario, *m*

veto *n* veto, *m*; prohibición, *f*. *vt* poner el veto; prohibir

vex *vt* contrariar, irritar; enojar; (make impatient) impacientar; fastidiar; (afflict) afligir, acongojar; (worry) inquietar

vexation *n* contrariedad, irritación, *f*; enojo, enfado, *m*; (impatience) impaciencia, *f*; fastidio, *m*; aflicción, *f*; inquietud, *f*; disgusto, *m*

vexatious *a* irritante; enojoso, enfadoso; fastidioso, molesto

vexatiousness *n* fastidio, *m*, molestia, *f*; incomodidad, *f*; contrariedad, *f*

vexed *a* discutido; contencioso; (thorny) espinoso, difícil

vexing *a* irritante; molesto; enfadoso

via *n* vía, *f*, *prep* por, por la vía de

viability *n* viabilidad, *f*

viable *a* viable

viaduct *n* viaducto, *m*

vial *n* frasco, *m*, ampolleta, *f*

vibrant *a* vibrante

vibrate *vi* vibrar; (of machines) trepidar; oscilar. *vt* hacer vibrar, vibrar

vibration *n* vibración, *f*; trepidación, *f*; oscilación, *f*

vibrator *n elec* vibrador, *m*; *rad* oscilador, *m*

vicar *n* vicario, *m*; (of a parish) cura, *m*. **v.-general,** vicario general, *m*

vicarious *a* vicario; sufrido por otro; experimentado por otro

vicariously *adv* por delegación; por substitución. **I know it only vicariously,** Lo conozco sólo por referencia

vice *n* vicio, *m*; defecto, *m*; (in a horse) vicio, resabio, *m*; (tool) tornillo de banco, *m*, *prefix* vice. **v.-admiral,** vicealmirante, *m*. **v.-chairman,** vice-presidente (-ta). **v.-chancellor,** vicecanciller, *m*. **v.-consul,** vice-cónsul, *m*. **v.-consulate,** vice-consulado, *m*. **v.-president,** vicepresidente (-ta)

viceroy *n* virrey, *m*

viceversa *adv* viceversa

vicinity *n* vecindad, *f*; (nearness) cercanía, proximidad, *f*. **to be in the v. of,** estar en la vecindad de

vicious *a* vicioso. **v. circle,** círculo vicioso, *m*

viciousness *n* viciosidad, *f*; (in a horse) resabios, *m pl*

vicissitude *n* vicisitud, *f*

vicissitudinous *a* accidentado, vicisitudinario

victim *n* víctima, *f*

victimization *n* sacrificio, *m*; tormento, *m*

victimize *vt* hacer víctima (de); sacrificar; ser víctima (de), sufrir; (cheat) estafar, engañar

victor *n* víctor, vencedor, *m*

victoria *n* victoria, *f*

Victorian *a* victoriano

victorious *a* victorioso, triunfante. **to be v.,** triunfar, salir victorioso

victoriously *adv* victoriosamente, triunfalmente

victory *n* victoria, *f*

victress *n* vencedora, *f*

victual *n* vitualla, vianda, *f*; *pl* **victuals,** víveres, *m pl*, provisiones, *f pl*. *vt* avituallar; abastecer. *vi* tomar provisiones

victualler *n* abastecedor (-ra), proveedor (-ra)

victualling *n* abastecimiento, *m*

vide *Latin imperative* véase, véanse

videlicet *adv* a saber

video, *n* vídeo, *m*

videotape *n* videograbación, videocinta, *f*

vie *vi* (with) competir con; rivalizar con; (with a person for) disputar; luchar con

Vienna Viena, *f*

Viennese *a* and *n* vienés (-esa)

view *n* vista, *f*; perspectiva, *f*; panorama, *m*; (landscape) paisaje, *m*; escena, *f*; inspección, *f*; (judgment) opinión, *f*, parecer, *m*; consideración, *f*; (appearance) apariencia, *f*; aspecto, *m*; (purpose) propósito, *m*, intención, *f*; (sight) alcance de la vista, *m*; (show) exposición, *f*. *vt* examinar; inspeccionar; (look at) mirar; (see) ver, contemplar; considerar. **in v. of,** en vista de. **in my v.,** en mi opinión, segun creo yo. **on v.,** a la vista. **to keep in v.,** no perder de vista; *fig* no olvidar, tener presente. **to take a different v.,** pensar de un modo distinto. **to v. a house,** inspeccionar una casa. **with a v. to,** con el propósito de. **v.-finder,** enfocador, *m*. **v.-point,** punto de vista, *m*

viewer *n* espectador (-ra); examinador (-ra)

viewing *n* inspección, *f*, examen, *m*

vigil *n* vela, vigilia, *f*; *ecc* vigilia, *f*

vigilance *n* vigilancia, *f*, desvelo, *m*

vigilant *a* vigilante, desvelado

vigilantly *adv* vigilantemente

vignette *n* viñeta, *f*

vigorous *a* vigoroso, enérgico, fuerte

vigorously *adv* con vigor

vigor *n* vigor, *m*, fuerza, *f*

Viking *n* vikingo, *m*

vile *a* vil; bajo; despreciable; infame; *inf* horrible

vilely *adv* vilmente; *inf* mal, horriblemente

vileness *n* vileza, *f*; bajeza, *f*; infamia, *f*

vilification *n* vilipendio, *m*, difamación, *f*

vilifier *n* difamador (-ra)

vilify *vt* vilipendiar, difamar

villa *n* villa, torre, casa de campo, *f*; hotel, *m*

village *n* aldea, *f*, pueblo, *m*

villager *n* aldeano (-na)

villain *n* *hist* villano, *m*; malvado, *m*

villainous *a* malvado; infame; vil

villainously *adv* vilmente

villainy *n* vileza, infamia, maldad, *f*

vindicate *vt* vindicar, justificar; defender

vindication *n* vindicación, justificación, *f*; defensa, *f*

vindicative *a* vindicativo, vindicador, justificativo

vindicator *n* vindicador (-ra)

vindictive *a* vengativo; rencoroso

vindictively *adv* vengativamente; rencorosamente

vindictiveness *n* deseo de venganza, *m*; rencor, *m*

vine *n* vid, parra, *f*; (twining plant) enredadera, *f*. **v.-arbor,** emparrado, *m*. **v.-branch,** sarmiento, *m*. **v.-clad,** cubierto de parras. **v.-grower,** vinicultor, *m*. **v.-growing,** vinicultura, *f*. **v.-leaf,** hoja de parra, *f*. **v.-pest,** filoxera, *f*. **v.-stock,** cepa, *f*

vinegar *n* vinagre, *m*. **v.-cruet,** vinagrera, *f*. **v.-sauce,** vinagreta, *f*

vinegary *a* vinagroso

vineyard *n* viña, *f*, viñedo, *m*. **v.-keeper,** viñador, *m*

vinification *n* vinificación, *f*

vinosity *n* vinosidad, *f*

vinous *a* vinoso

vintage *n* vendimia, *f*; (of wine) cosecha (de vino), *f*

vintner *n* vinatero, *m*

viola *n* (*mus, bot*) viola, *f*. **v. player,** viola, *mf*

violate *vt* (desecrate) profanar; (infringe) contravenir, infringir; (break) romper; (ravish) violar

violation *n* profanación, *f*; (infringement) contravención, *f*; (rape) violación, *f*

violator *n* violador (-ra); (ravisher) violador, *m*

violence *n* violencia, *f*

violent *a* violento

violently *adv* con violencia

violet *n* violeta, *f*. *a* violado, **v. color,** violeta, color violado, *m*

violin *n* violín, *m*

violinist *n* violinista, *mf*

violoncellist *n* violoncelista, *mf*

violoncello *n* violoncelo, *m*

viper *n* víbora, *f*

viperish *a* viperino

virago *n* virago, *f*,

Virgilian *a* virgiliano

virgin *n* virgen, *f*; (sign of the zodiac) Virgo, *m*. *a* virginal; (untouched) virgen. **the V.,** la Virgen. **v. soil,** tierra virgen, *f*

virginal *a* virginal

virginity *n* virginidad, *f*

Virgo *n* Virgo, *m*

virile *a* viril

virility *n* virilidad, *f*

virtual *a* virtual

virtue *n* virtud, *f*

virtuosity *n* virtuosidad, *f*

virtuoso *n* virtuoso (-sa)

virtuous *a* virtuoso

virulence *n* virulencia, *f*

virulent *a* virulento

virulently *adv* con virulencia

virus *n* virus, *m*

visa *n* visa, *f*

visage *n* cara, *f*, rostro, *m*; semblante, aspecto, *m*

viscera *n* víscera, *f*

visceral *a* visceral

viscid *a* viscoso

viscosity *n* viscosidad, *f*

viscount *n* vizconde, *m*

viscountess *n* vizcondesa, *f*

viscous *a* viscoso

visé *n* visado, *m*, *vt* visar

visibility *n* visibilidad, *f*. **poor v.,** mala visibilidad, *f*

visible *a* visible; aparente, evidente

visibly *adv* visiblemente; a ojos vistas
Visigoth *n* visigodo (-da)
Visigothic *a* visigodo, visigótico
vision *n* visión, *f*; (eyesight) vista, *f*. **field of v.,** campo visual, *m*
visionary *a* and *n* visionario (-ia)
visit *n* visita, *f*; (inspection) inspección, *f*; (doctor's) visita de médico, *f*. *vt* visitar; hacer una visita (a); ir a ver; inspeccionar; (frequent) frecuentar; (Biblical) visitar. **to be visited by an epidemic,** sufrir una epidemia. **to go visiting,** ir de visita. **to pay a v.,** hacer una visita
visitation *n* visita, *f*; *ecc* visitación, *f*; (inspection) inspección, *f*; (punishment) castigo, *m*
visiting *a* de visita. **v. card,** tarjeta de visita, *f*. **v. card case,** tarjetero, *m*. **visiting hours,** horas de visita, *f pl*
visitor *n* visita, *f*; (official) visitador, *m*
visor *n* visera, *f*
vista *n* vista, perspectiva, *f*
visual *a* visual. **the v. arts,** las artes visuales
visualize *vt* and *vi* imaginarse, ver mentalmente
vital *a* vital; esencial; trascendental
vitalism *n* vitalismo, *m*
vitality *n* vitalidad, *f*
vitalize *vt* vitalizar, vivificar; reanimar
vitals *n pl* partes vitales, *f pl*; *fig* entrañas, *f pl*
vitamin *n* vitamina, *f*
vitiate *vt* viciar; corromper, contaminar
viticultural *a* vitícola
viticulture *n* viticultura, *f*
vitreous *a* vítreo, vidrioso
vitrification *n* vitrificación, *f*
vitrify *vt* vitrificar. *vi* vitrificarse
vitriol *n* vitriolo, ácido sulfúrico, *m*
vitriolic *a* vitriólico
Vitruvius Vitrubio, *m*
vituperable *a* vituperable
vituperate *vt* vituperar
vituperation *n* vituperio, *m*
vituperative *a* vituperador
vivacious *a* animado, vivaracho
vivaciously *adv* animadamente
vivacity *n* vivacidad, animación, *f*
viva voce *a* oral. *n* examen oral, *m*
vivid *a* vivo; brillante; intenso; (of descriptions, etc.) gráfico
vividly *adv* vivamente; brillantemente
vividness *n* vivacidad, *f*; intensidad, *f*; (strength) fuerza, *f*
vivification *n* vivificación, *f*
vivify *vt* vivificar, avivar
vivifying *a* vivificante
vivisection *n* vivisección, *f*
vixen *n* raposa, zorra, *f*; (woman) arpía, *f*
viz *adv* a saber
vizier *n* visir, *m*. **grand v.,** gran visir, *m*
vocabulary *n* vocabulario, *m*
vocal *a* vocal. **v. cords,** cuerdas vocales, *f pl*
vocalist *n* cantante, *mf*, voz, *f*
vocalization *n* vocalización, *f*
vocalize *vt* vocalizar
vocation *n* vocación, *f*; oficio, *m*; empleo, *m*; profesión, *f*
vocational *a* profesional; práctico. **vocational guidance,** guía vocacional, orientación profesional, *f*. **v. training,** instrucción práctica, *f*; enseñanza de oficio, *f*
vociferate *vt* gritar. *vi* vociferar, vocear
vociferation *n* vociferación, *f*
vociferous *a* (noisy) ruidoso; vocinglero, clamoroso
vociferously *adv* ruidosamente; a gritos
vodka *n* vodca, *m*
vogue *n* moda, *f*. **in v.,** en boga, de moda
voice *n* voz, *f*. *vt* expresar, interpretar, hacerse eco de; hablar. **in a loud v.,** en voz alta. **in a low v.,** en voz baja

voiced *a* (in compounds) de voz . . . ; hablado
void *a* (empty) vacío; (vacant) vacante; deshabitado; (lacking in) privado (de), desprovisto (de); (without) sin; *law* inválido, nulo; sin valor. *n* vacío, *m*. *vt* evacuar; *law* anular; invalidar
voile *n* espumilla, *f*
volatile *a* volátil; (light) ligero; (changeable) voluble, inconstante
volatility *n* volatilidad, *f*; ligereza, *f*; volubilidad, *f*
volatilization *n* volatilización, *f*
volatilize *vt* volatilizar. *vi* volatilizarse
volcanic *a* volcánico
volcano *n* volcán, *m*. **extinct v.,** volcán extinto, *m*
volition *n* volición, *f*; voluntad, *f*
volley *n* (of stones, etc.) lluvia, *f*; (of fire-arms) descarga, *f*; (of cannon, naval guns) andanada, *f*; *sport* voleo, *m*; (of words, etc.) torrente, *m*; (of applause and as a salute) salva, *f*. *vt sport* volear; (abuse, etc.) dirigir. *vi* lanzar una descarga, hacer una descarga
volt *n elec* voltío, *m*; (of a horse and in fencing) vuelta, *f*. **v.-ampere,** voltamperio, *m*
voltage *n* voltaje, *m*. **v. control,** mando del voltaje, *m*
voltaic *a* voltaico
Voltairian *a* volteriano
voltmeter *n* voltímetro, *m*
volubility *n* garrulidad, locuacidad, *f*
voluble *a* gárrulo, locuaz
volume *n* (book) tomo, *m*; (amount, size, space) volumen, *m*; (of water) caudal (de río), *m*; (mass) masa, *f*; (of smoke) humareda, *f*, nubes de humo, *f pl*
volumed *a* (in compounds) en . . . volúmenes, de . . . tomos
volumetric *a* volumétrico
voluminous *a* voluminoso
voluminousness *n* lo voluminoso
voluntarily *adv* voluntariamente
voluntariness *n* carácter voluntario, *m*
voluntary *a* voluntario; espontáneo; libre; (charitable) benéfico; (intentional) intencional, deliberado. *n* solo de órgano, *m*
volunteer *n mil* voluntario (-ia). *a* de voluntarios. *vt* ofrecer; contribuir; expresar. *vi* ofrecerse para hacer algo; *mil* alistarse, ofrecerse a servir como voluntario
volunteering *n* voluntariado, *m*
voluptuary *n* voluptuoso (-sa); sibarita, *mf*
voluptuous *a* voluptuoso
voluptuously *adv* voluptuosamente
voluptuousness *n* voluptuosidad, *f*; sensualidad, *f*
volute *n arch* voluta, *f*
vomit *vt* and *vi* vomitar; arrojar, devolver. *n* vómito, *m*
vomiting *n* vómito, *m*
voodoo *n* vudú, *m*
voracious *a* voraz
voracity *n* voracidad, *f*
vortex *n* torbellino, *m*, vorágine, *f*; *fig* vórtice, *m*
vortical *a* vortiginoso
votaress, votary *n* devoto (-ta), adorante, *mf*; partidario (-ia)
vote *n* voto, *m*; (voting) votación, *f*; (suffrage) sufragio, *m*; (election) elección, *f*. *vt* votar; asignar; nombrar; elegir; (consider) tener por. *vi* votar, dar el voto. **casting v.,** voto de calidad, *m*. **to put to the v.,** poner a votación. **to v. down,** desechar, rechazar. **v. of confidence,** voto de confianza, *m*. **v. of thanks,** voto de gracias, *m*
voter *n* votante, *mf*, votador (-ra); elector (-ra)
voting *n* votación, *f*; elección, *f*. *a* de votar; electoral. **v. paper,** papeleta de votación, *f*
votive *a* votivo. **v. offering,** exvoto, *m*
vouch *vi* atestiguar, afirmar; garantizar; responder (de)
voucher *n* (guarantor) fiador (-ra); (guarantee) garantía, *f*; (receipt) recibo, *m*; (proof) prueba, *f*; documento justificativo, *m*; vale, bono, *m*
vouchsafe *vt* conceder, otorgar
vouchsafement *n* concesión, *f*, otorgamiento, *m*

vow *n* voto, *m*; promesa solemne, *f*. *vt* hacer voto (de), hacer promesa solemne (de); jurar. **to take a vow,** hacer un voto

vowel *n* vocal, *f*

voyage *n* viaje (por mar), *m*; travesía, *f*. *vi* viajar por mar. **Good v.!** ¡Buen viaje!, Feliz viaje!

voyager *n* viajero (-ra)

vulcanite *n* ebonita, *f*

vulcanization *n* vulcanización, *f*

vulcanize *vt* vulcanizar

vulgar *a* vulgar; (ill-bred) ordinario, cursi; (in bad taste) de mal gusto; trivial; adocenado; (coarse) grosero. *n*

vulgo, populacho, *m*. **v. fraction,** fracción común, *f*

vulgarism *n* vulgarismo, *m*; vulgaridad, *f*

vulgarity *n* vulgaridad, *f*; grosería, *f*; mal tono, *m*, cursilería, *f*

vulgarize *vt* vulgarizar; popularizar

vulgarly *adv* vulgarmente; comúnmente; groseramente

Vulgate *n* Vulgata, *f*

vulnerability *n* vulnerabilidad, *f*

vulnerable *a* vulnerable

vulpine *a* vulpino; astuto

vulture *n* buitre, *m*

vulva *n* vulva, *f*

W

w *n* ve doble, *f*

wabble *vi*. See **wobble**

wad *n* (of straw, etc.) atado, *m*; (of notes, etc.) rollo, *m*; (in a gun) taco, *m*. *vt sew* acolchar; (furniture) emborrar; (guns) atacar; (stuff) rellenar

wadding *n* borra, *f*; (lining) entretela, *f*; (for guns) taco, *m*; (stuffing) relleno, *m*

waddle *n* anadeo, *m*, *vi* anadear

waddling *a* patojo, que anadea

wade *vi* and *vt* andar (en el agua, etc.); vadear; (paddle) chapotear. **to w. in,** entrar en (el agua, etc.); *fig* meterse en. **to w. through,** (a book) leer con dificultad; estudiar detenidamente; ir por

wader *n* el, *m*, (*f*, la) que vadea; (bird) ave zancuda, *f*; *pl* **waders,** botas de vadear, *f pl*

wafer *n* (host) hostia, *f*; (for sealing) oblea, *f*; (for ices) barquillo, *m*

waffle *n cul* fruta de sartén, *f*

waft *vt* llevar por el aire o encima del agua; hacer flotar; (stir) mecer; (of the wind) traer. *n* (fragrance) ráfaga de olor, *f*

wag *n* (of the tail) coleada, *f*; movimiento, *m*; meneo, *m*; (jester) bromista, *mf*. *vt* mover ligeramente; agitar; (of the tail) menear (la cola), colear. *vi* menearse; moverse; oscilar; (of the world) ir. **And thus the world wags,** Y así va el mundo

wage, wages *n* salario, *m*; *fig* premio, galardón, *m*. **minimum wage,** salario mínimo, *m*. **wages clerk,** pagador (-ra). **wage-earner,** asalariado (-da); (worker) trabajador (-ra)

wage *vt* emprender; sostener; hacer. **to w. war,** hacer guerra

wager *n* (bet) apuesta, *f*; (test) prueba, *f*, *vt* (bet) apostar; (pledge) empeñar. **to lay a w.,** hacer una apuesta

wages *n pl*. See **wage**

waggish *a* zumbón, jocoso; cómico

waggishness *n* jocosidad, *f*

waggle *vt* menear; mover; agitar; oscilar. *vi* menearse; moverse; agitarse; oscilar. *n* meneo, movimiento, *m*; oscilación, *f*

wagon *n* carro, *m*; carreta, *f*; (railway) vagón, *m*. **w.-lit,** coche cama, *m*. **w.-load,** carretada, *f*; vagón, *m*

wagoner *n* carretero, *m*

Wagnerian *a* wagneriano

waif *n* niño (-ña) sin hogar; animal perdido o abandonado, *m*; objeto extraviado, *m*; objeto sin dueño, *m*. **waifs and strays,** niños abandonados, *m pl*

wail *n* lamento, gemido, *m*; (complaint) queja, *f*. *vi* lamentarse, gemir; quejarse (de). *vt* lamentar, deplorar

wailer *n* lamentador (-ra)

wailing *n* lamentaciones, *f pl*, gemidos, *m pl*, *a* lamentador, gemidor

wainscot *n* entablado de madera, *m*. *vt* enmaderar; poner friso de madera (a)

waist *n* cintura, *f*; (blouse) blusa, *f*; (belt) cinturón, *m*; (bodice) corpiño, *m*; (narrowest portion) cuello, *m*, garganta, *f*; *naut* combés, *m*. **w.-band,** pretina, *f*. **w.-deep,** hasta la cintura. **w.-line,** cintura, *f*. **w. mea-**

surement, medida de la cintura, *f*. **w.-coat,** chaleco, *m*. **w. strap,** trincha, *f*

wait *vi* and *vt* esperar, aguardar; (serve) servir. **to keep waiting,** hacer esperar. **to w. at table,** servir a la mesa. **to w. on oneself,** servirse a sí mismo; cuidarse a sí mismo; hacer las cosas por sí solo. **to w. one's time,** aguardar la ocasión. **to w. for,** (until) esperar hasta que; (of persons) esperar (a), aguardar (a); (in ambush) acechar. **to w. upon,** (serve) servir (a); (visit) visitar; presentar sus respetos (a); (*fig* accompany) acompañar; (follow) seguir a

wait *n* espera, *f*; (pause) pausa, *f*, intervalo, *m*; (ambush) asechanza, *f*; *pl* **waits,** coro de nochebuena, *m*. **to lie in w. for,** estar en acecho para

waiter *n* camarero, mozo, *m*; (tray) bandeja, *f*

waiting *n* espera, *f*. *a* que espera; de espera; de servicio. **lady-in-w.,** dama de servicio, *f*. **w.-maid,** camarera, doncella, *f*. **w.-room,** (of a bus station, etc.) sala de espera, *f*; (of an office) antesala, *f*

waitress *n* camarera, *f*

waive *vt* renunciar (a); desistir (de)

wake *vi* estar despierto; despertarse; (watch) velar. *vt* despertar; (a corpse) velar (a). *n* vela, *f*; vigilia, *f*; (of a corpse) velatorio, *m*; (holiday) fiesta, *f*; (of a ship) estela, *f*. **in the w. of,** *naut* en la estela de; después de; seguido por

wakeful *a* vigilante; (awake) despierto. **to be w.,** pasar la noche en vela

wakefulness *n* vigilancia, *f*; (sleeplessness) insomnia, *f*

waken *vi* despertarse. *vt* despertar; (call) llamar

waking *a* despierto; de vela. *n* despertar, *m*; (watching) vela, *f*

wale *n* (weal) verdugo, *m*, huella de azote, *f*, *vt* azotar

Wales (País de) Gales, *m*

walk *n* (pace) paso, *m*; (modo de) andar, *m*; (journey on foot) paseo, *m*, vuelta, *f*; (long) caminata, *f*; (promenade) paseo, *m*, avenida, *f*; (path) senda, *f*; (rank) clase social, *f*; esfera, *f*; profesión, *f*; ocupación, *f*. **quick w.,** paseo rápido, *m*; (pace) andar rápido, *m*. **to go for a w.,** ir de paseo. **to take a w.,** dar un paseo (or una vuelta), pasear. **to take for a w.,** llevar a paseo, sacar a paseo. **w.-out,** (strike) huelga, *f*. **w.-over,** triunfo, *m*, (or victoria, *f*) fácil. **w. past,** desfile, *m*

walk *vi* andar; caminar; ir a pie; (take a walk) pasear, dar un paseo; (of ghosts) aparecer; (behave) conducirse. *vt* hacer andar; (take for a walk) sacar a paseo; andar de una parte a otra (de), recorrer; (a specified distance) hacer a pie, andar; (a horse) llevar al paso. **to w. abroad,** dar un paseo; salir. **to w. arm in arm,** ir de bracero. **to w. past,** pasar; (in procession) desfilar. **to w. quickly,** andar de prisa. **to w. slowly,** andar despacio, andar lentamente. **to w. the hospitals,** estudiar en los hospitales. **to w. the streets,** recorrer las calles; vagar por las calles. **to w. about,** pasearse; ir y venir. **to w. after,** seguir (a), ir detrás de. **to w. along,** andar por; recorrer. **to w. away,** marcharse, irse. **to w. away with,** (win) ganar, llevarse; (steal) quitar, tomar, alzarse con. **to w. back,** volver; volver a pie, regresar a pie. **to w. down,** bajar; bajar a pie; andar por. **to w. in,** entrar en; entrar a pie en; (walk about) pasearse en. **to w. on,** seguir andando; (step on) pisar. **to w. out,** salir. **to w. over,** andar por; llevar la victoria (a); triunfar fácilmente sobre. **to w. round,** dar la vuelta a. **to w. round and round,** dar vueltas. **to w. up,** subir andando; subir. **to w. up and down,** dar vueltas, ir y venir

walker *n* (pedestrian) peatón, *m*; andador (-ra); (promenader) paseante, *mf*

walking *n* el andar; (excursion on foot) paseo, *m*. *a* andante; de andar; a pie; ambulante. **at a w. pace,** a un paso de andadura. **w. encyclopedia,** enciclopedia ambulante, *f*. **w. match,** marcha atlética, *f*. **w.-stick,** bastón, *m*. **w. tour,** excursión a pie, *f*

Walkyrie *n* valquiria, *f*

wall *n* muro, *m*; (rampart) muralla, *f*; (*fig* and of an organ, cavity, etc.) pared, *f*. **partition w.,** tabique, *m*. **Walls have ears,** Las paredes oyen. **w. lizard,** lagartija, *f*. **w. map,** mapa mural, *m*. **w.-painting,** pintura mural, *f*. **w.-paper,** papel pintado, *m*. **w. socket,** *elec* enchufe, *m*

wall *vt* cercar con un muro; amurallar. **to w. in,** murar. **to w. up,** tapiar, tabicar

wallet *n* cartera, *f*; bolsa de cuero, *f*

wallflower *n* alhelí, *m*

Walloon *a* and *n* valón (-ona)

wallop *n* golpe, *m*, *vt* tundir, zurrar

wallow *vi* revolcarse; encenagarse; (in riches, etc.) nadar (en). *n* revuelco, *m*

walnut *n* (tree and wood) nogal, *m*; (nut) nuez de nogal, *f*

walrus *n* morsa, *f*

waltz *n* vals, *m*, *vi* valsar

wan *a* ojeroso, descolorido; (of the sky, etc.) pálido, sin color

wand *n* vara, *f*; (conductor's) batuta, *f*. **magic w.,** varita mágica, *f*

wander *vi* errar, vagar; (deviate) extraviarse; (from the subject) desviarse del asunto; divagar; (be delirious) delirar. *vt* vagar por, errar por, recorrer

wanderer *n* vagabundo (-da); hombre, *m*, (*f*, mujer) errante; (traveler) viajero (-ra)

wandering *a* errante; vagabundo; nómada; (traveling) viajero; (delirious) delirante; (of thoughts, the mind) distraído; (of cells, kidneys, etc.) flotante. *n* vagancia, *f*; viaje, *m*; (delirium) delirio, *m*; (digression) divagación, *f*; (of a river, etc.) meandro, *m*. **the w. Jew,** el judío errante

wane *vi* (of the moon, etc.) menguar; (decrease) disminuir; (*fig* decay) decaer. *n* (of the moon) menguante de la luna, *f*; mengua, *f*; disminución, *f*; decadencia, *f*

waning *a* menguante

wanly *adv* pálidamente; *fig* tristemente

wanness *n* palidez, *f*; *fig* tristeza, *f*

want *vt* (lack) carecer de, faltar; (need) necesitar, haber menester de; (require or wish) desear, querer; (demand) exigir; (ought) deber; (do without) pasarse sin. *vi* hacer falta; carecer (de); (be poor) estar necesitado. **I don't w. to,** No quiero, No me da la gana. **to be wanted,** hacer falta; (called) ser llamado. **You are wanted on the telephone,** Te llaman por teléfono **wanted** se necesita; (advertisement) demanda, *f*. **Estelle wants me to write a letter,** Estrella quiere que escriba una carta. **What do you w. me to do?** ¿Qué quiere Vd. que haga?; ¿En qué puedo servirle? **What does Paul w.?** ¿Qué quiere Pablo?; (require) ¿Qué necesita Pablo? **He wants (needs) a holiday,** Le hacen falta unas vacaciones, Necesita unas vacaciones **want** *n* (lack) falta, *f*; escasez, carestía, *f*; (need) necesidad, *f*; (poverty) pobreza, indigencia, *f*; (absence) ausencia, *f*; (wish) deseo, *m*; exigencia, *f*. **in w. of,** por falta de; en la ausencia de. **to be in w.,** estar en la necesidad, ser indigente

wanting *a* deficiente (en); falto (de); (scarce) escaso; ausente; (in intelligence) menguado. *prep* (less)

menos; (without) sin. **to be w.,** faltar. **to be w. in,** carecer de

wanton *a* (playful) juguetón; (wilful) travieso; (loose) suelto, libre; (unrestrained) desenfrenado; extravagante; excesivo; caprichoso; (dishevelled) en desorden; (reckless) indiscreto; (of vegetation) lozano; (purposeless) inútil; imperdonable; frívolo; (unchaste) disoluto; lascivo. *n* mujer disoluta, *f*; ramera, *f*; (child) niño (-ña) juguetón (-ona)

wantonly *adv* innecesariamente; sin motivo; excesivamente; lascivamente

war *n* guerra, *f*. *a* de guerra; guerrero. *vi* guerrear. **at war with,** en guerra con. **cold war,** guerra tonta, *f*. **on a war footing,** en pie de guerra. **We are at war,** Estamos en guerra. **to be on the war-path,** *fig inf* buscar pendencia, tratar de armarla. **to declare war on,** declarar la guerra (a). **to make war on,** hacer la guerra (a). **war to the death,** guerra a muerte, *f*. **war correspondent,** corresponsal en el teatro de guerra, *m*. **war-cry,** alarido de guerra, grito de combate, grito de guerra *m*. **war-dance,** danza guerrera, *f*. **war horse,** caballo de batalla, *m*. **war loan,** empréstito de guerra, *m*. **war-lord,** adalid, caudillo, jefe militar, *m*. **war material,** pertrechos de guerra, *m pl*; municiones, *f pl*. **war memorial,** monumento a los caídos, *m*. **war minister,** Ministro de la Guerra, *m*. **war neurosis,** neurosis de guerra, *f*. **War Office,** Ministerio de la Guerra, *m*. **war plane,** avión de guerra, *m*. **war-ship,** barco (o buque) de guerra, *m*. **war-wearied,** agotado por la guerra

warble *vt* and *vi* trinar; gorjear; murmurar. *n* trino, *m*; gorjeo, *m*; murmurio, *m*

ward *n* protección, *f*; (of a minor) pupilo (-la); (of locks, keys) guarda, *f*; (of a city) barrio, distrito, *m*; (of a hospital, etc.) sala, *f*; (of a prison) celda, *f*; (fencing) guardia, *f*. **w.-room,** cuarto de los oficiales, *m*. **w. sister,** hermana de una sala de hospital, *f*

ward *vt* proteger, defender. **to w. off,** desviar; evitar

warden *n* guardián, *m*; director (-ra); (of a prison) alcaide, *m*; (of a church) mayordomo de la iglesia, *m*; (of a port) capitán, *m*

warder *n* (gaoler) guardián, *m*; alabardero, guardia, *m*

Wardour-Street English *n* inglés arcaizante de magüerista, *m*

wardress *n* guardiana, *f*

wardrobe *n* guardarropa, ropero, *m*; (clothes) ropa, *f*; *theat* vestuario, *m*. **w. trunk,** baúl mundo, *m*

ware *n* mercadería, *f*; (pottery) loza, *f*; *pl* **wares,** mercancías, *f pl*

war effort *n* esfuerzo bélico, esfuerzo de guerra, esfuerzo guerrero, *m*

warehouse *n* almacén, *m*, *vt* almacenar

warehouseman *n* almacenero, *m*

warfare *n* guerra, *f*; lucha, *f*; arte militar, *m*, or *f*. **chemical w.,** guerra química, *f*

war head *n* (of torpedo) cabeza de combate, punto de combate, *f*; (of missile) detonante, *m*

war heroe *n* héroe de guerra, *m*

war heroine *n* heroína de guerra, *f*

warily *adv* con cautela, cautelosamente; prudentemente

wariness *n* cautela *f*; prudencia, *f*

warlike *a* belicoso, guerrero; militar, de guerra; marcial. **war-spirit,** espíritu belicoso, *m*, marcialidad, *f*

warm *a* caliente; (lukewarm) tibio; (hot) caluroso; (affectionate) cordial, cariñoso, afectuoso; (angry) acalorado; (enthusiastic) entusiasta, ardiente; (art) cálido; (of coats, etc.) de abrigo; (fresh) fresco, reciente; *inf* animado. *vt* calentar; *fig* encender; entusiasmar. *vi* calentarse; *fig* entusiasmarse (con). **to have a w. at the fire,** calentarse al lado del fuego. **to be w.,** (of things) estar caliente; (of coats, etc.) ser de abrigo; (of the weather) hacer calor; (of people) tener calor. **to grow w.,** calentarse; (grow angry) excitarse, agitarse; (of a discussion) hacerse acalorado. **to keep w.,** conservar caliente; calentar. **to keep oneself w.,** estar caliente, no enfriarse. **to w. up,** calentar. **w.-blooded,** de sangre caliente; ardiente. **w.-hearted,** de buen corazón; generoso; afectuoso, cordial. **w.-hearted-ness,** buen corazón, *m*; generosidad, *f*; cordialidad, *f*

warming *n* calentamiento, *m*; calefacción, *f. a* calentador; para calentar. **w.-pan,** calentador, *m*

warmly *adv* (affectionately) cordialmente, afectuosamente; con entusiasmo; (angrily) acaloradamente. **to be w.** wrapped up, estar bien abrigado

warmonger *n* atizador de guerra, belicista, fautor de guerra, fomentador de guerra, propagador (-ra) de guerra

warmth *n* calor, *m*

warn *vt* advertir; prevenir; amonestar; (inform) avisar

warning *n* advertencia, *f*; aviso, *m*; amonestación, *f*; (lesson) lección, *f*, escarmiento, *m*; alarma, *f. a* amonestador; de alarma. **to give w.,** prevenir, advertir; (dismiss) despedir. **to take w.,** escarmentar

warningly *adv* indicando el peligro; con alarma; con amenaza

warp *vt* torcer; combar; *naut* espiar; (the mind) pervertir. *vi* torcerse; combarse, bornearse; *naut* espiarse. *n* (in a fabric) urdimbre, *f*; (in wood) comba, *f*, torcimiento, *m*; *naut* espía, *f.* **w. and woof,** trama y urdimbre, *f*

warping *n* (of wood) combadura, *f*; (weaving) urdidura, *f*; *naut* espía, *f*; (of the mind) perversión, *f.* **w. frame,** urdidera, *f*

warrant *n* autoridad, *f*; justificación, *f*; autorización, *f*; garantía, *f*; decreto de prisión, *m*; orden, *f*; *com* orden de pago, *f*; *mil* nombramiento, *m*; motivo, *m*, razón, *f. vt* justificar; autorizar; garantizar, responder por; asegurar. **pay w.,** boletín de pago, *m*

warrantable *a* justificable

warrantor *n* garante, *mf*

warranty *n* autorización, *f*; justificación, *f*; *law* garantía, *f*

warren *n* (for hunting) vedado, *m*; (rabbit) conejera, *f*; vivar, *m*, madriguera, *f*

warrior *n* guerrero, *m*; soldado, *m*

Warsaw Varsovia, *f*

wart *n* verruga, *f*

wary *a* cauto, cauteloso; prudente

wash *vt* lavar; (dishes) fregar; (lave) bañar; (clean) limpiar; (furrow) surcar; (wet) regar, humedecer; (with paint) dar una capa de color o de metal. *vi* lavarse; lavar ropa. **Two of the crew were washed overboard,** El mar arrastró a dos de los tripulantes. **Will this material w.?** ¿Se puede lavar esta tela? ¿Es lavable esta tela? **to w. ashore,** echar a la playa. **w. away,** (remove by washing) quitar lavando; derrubiar; (water or waves) arrastrar, llevarse. **to w. one's hands,** lavarse las manos. **to look washed out,** estar ojeroso. **to w. down,** lavar; limpiar; (remove) llevarse; (accompany with drink) regar. **to w. off,** *vt* quitar lavando; hacer desaparecer; borrar; (of waves, etc.) llevarse; (of color) desteñir. *vi* borrarse; desteñirse. **to w. up,** lavar los platos, fregar la vajilla; (cast up) desechar. **w. one's dirty laundry in public,** sacar los más sucios trapillos a la colada

wash *n* lavadura, *f*, lavado, *m*; baño, *m*; (clothes) ropa para lavar, ropa sucia, *f*; colada, *f*; (of the waves) chapoteo, *m*; (lotion) loción, *f*; (coating) capa, *f*; (silt) aluvión, *m*. **w.-basin,** palangana, *f*; lavabo, *m*. **w.-board,** tabla de lavar, *f.* **w.-house,** lavadero, *m*. **w.-leather,** gamuza, badana, *f.* **w.-stand,** lavabo, *m*. **w.-tub,** cuba de lavar, *f*

washable *a* lavable

washer *n* lavador (-ra); (washerwoman) lavandera, *f*; (machine) lavadora, *f*; *mech* arandela, *f*

washerwoman *n* lavandera, *f*

washing *n* lavamiento, *m*; ropa sucia, ropa para lavar, *f*; ropa limpia, *f*; ropa, *f*; (bleaching) blanqueadura, *f*; (toilet) abluciones, *f pl*; *ecc* lavatorio, *m*; *pl* **washings,** lavazas, *f pl.* **There is a lot of w. to be done,** Hay mucha ropa que lavar. **w.-board,** tabla de lavar, *f*

w.-day, día de colada, *m*. **w.-machine,** lavadora, máquina de lavar, *f.* **w.-soda,** carbonato sódico, *m*. **w.-up,** lavado de los platos, *m*. **w.-up machine,** fregador mecánico de platos, *m*

wasp *n* avispa, *f.* **wasp's nest,** avispero, *m*.

w.-waisted, (of clothes) ceñido, muy ajustado

waspish *a* enojadizo, irascible; malicioso; mordaz

wastage *n* desgaste, desperdicio, *m*

waste *vt* desperdiciar, derrochar, malgastar; (time) perder; consumir; corroer; (devastate) asolar, devastar; echar a perder; malograr; disipar; agotar. *vi* gastarse; consumirse; perderse. **to w. time,** perder el tiempo. **to w. away,** (of persons) demacrarse, consumirse

waste *n* (wilderness) yermo, desierto, *m*; (vastness) inmensidad, vastedad, *f*; (loss) pérdida, *f*; (squandering) despilfarro, derroche, *m*; disminución, *f*; (refuse) desechos, *m pl*; (of cotton, etc.) borra, *f*; disipación, *f. a* (of land) sin cultivar; yermo; inútil; desechado, de desecho; superfluo. **to lay w.,** devastar. **w. land,** yermo, *m*; tierras sin cultivar, *f pl.* **w. paper,** papel usado, papel de desecho, *m*. **w.-paper basket,** cesto para papeles, *m*. **w.-pipe,** desaguadero, tubo de desagüe, *m*

wasteful *a* pródigo, derrochador, manirroto; antieconómico; ruinoso; inútil

wastefully *adv* pródigamente; antieconómicamente; inútilmente

wastefulness *n* prodigalidad, *f*, despilfarro, *m*; pérdida, *f*; gasto inútil, *m*; falta de economía, *f*

waster *n* gastador (-ra); disipador (-ra); (loafer) golfo, *m*

watch *vi* velar; mirar. *vt* mirar; observar; guardar; (await) esperar; (spy upon) espiar, acechar. **to w. for,** buscar aguardar. **to w. over,** vigilar, guardar; (care for) cuidar; proteger

watch *n* (at night) vela, *f*; (wakefulness) desvelo, *m*; observación, vigilancia, *f*; (mil naut) guardia, *f*; (sentinel) centinela, *m*; (watchman) sereno, vigilante, *m*; (guard) ronda, *f*; (timepiece) reloj de bolsillo, *m*. **to be on the w.,** estar al acecho, estar al alerta, estar a la mira. **to keep w.,** vigilar. **dog w.,** media guardia, *f.* **pocket w.,** reloj de bolsillo, *m*. **wrist w.,** reloj de pulsera, *f*. **w.-case,** caja de reloj, relojera, *f.* **w.-chain,** cadena de reloj, leontina, *f.* **w.-dog,** perro guardián, *m*. **w.-glass,** cristal de reloj, *m*. **w.-making,** relojería, *f.* **w.-night,** noche vieja, *f.* **w.-spring,** muelle de reloj, *m*, espiral, *f.* **w.-tower,** vigía, atalaya, *f*

watcher *n* observador (-ra); espectador (-ra); (at a sick bed) el, *m*, (*f*, la) que vela a un enfermo

watchful *a* vigilante, alerto; observador; atento, cuidadoso

watchfully *adv* vigilantemente; atentamente

watchfulness *n* vigilancia, *f*; cuidado, *m*; desvelo, *m*

watching *n* observación, *f*; (vigil) vela, *f*

watchmaker *n* relojero (-ra). **watchmaker's shop,** relojería, *f*

watchman *n* vigilante, sereno, *m*; guardián, *m*

watchword *n* (password) consigna, contraseña, *f*; (motto) lema, *m*

water *n* agua, *f*; (tide) marea, *f*; (of precious stones) aguas, *f pl*; (urine) orina, *f*; (quality) calidad, clase, *f. a* de agua; por agua; acuático; hidráulico. **fresh w.,** (not salt) agua dulce, *f*; agua fresca, *f.* **hard w.,** agua cruda, *f.* **high w.,** marea alta, *f.* **low w.,** marea baja, *f.* **of the first w.,** de primera clase. **running w.,** agua corriente, *f.* **soft w.,** agua blanda, *f.* **to make w.,** *naut* hacer agua; orinar. **to take the waters,** tomar las aguas. **under w.,** *adv* debajo del agua. *a* acuático. **w.-bird,** ave acuática, *f.* **w. blister,** ampolla, *f.* **w.-boatman,** chinche de agua, *f.* **w.-borne,** flotante. **w.-bottle,** cantimplora, *f.* **w.-brash,** acedia, *f.* **w.-butt,** barril, *m*, pipa, *f.* **w.-carrier,** aguador (-ra). **w.-cart,** carro de regar, *m*. **w.-closet,** retrete, excusado, *m*. **w.-color,** acuarela, *f.* **w.-color painting,** pintura a la acuarela, *f.* **w.-colorist,** acuarelista, *mf* **w.-cooled,** enfriado por agua. **w.-cooler,** cantimplora, *f.* **w.-finder,** zahorí, *m*. **w. front,** (wharf) muelle, *m*; puerto, *m*; litoral, *m*. **w.-gauge,** indicador de nivel de agua, *m*, vara de aforar, *f.* **w.-glass,** vidrio soluble, silicato de sosa, *m.* **w. heater,** calentador de agua, *m.* **w.-ice,** helado, *m.* **w.-level,** nivel de las aguas, *m.* **w.-lily,** nenúfar, *m,* azucena de agua, *f.* **w.-line,** lengua de agua, *f;* (of a ship) línea de flotación, *f.* **w.-logged,** anegado en agua. **w.-main,** cañería maestra de agua, *f.* **w. man,** barquero, *m.* **w.-melon,** sandía, *f.* **w. mill,** aceña, *f.* **w.-nymph,** náyade, *f.* **w.-pipe,** cañería del agua, *f.* **w. pitcher,** jarro, *m.* **w. plant,** planta acuática, *f.* **w.-polo,** polo acuático, *m.* **w.-power,** fuerza hidráulica, *f.* **w.-rate,** cupo del consumo de agua, *m.* **w. snake,** culebra de agua, *f.* **w. softener,** generador de agua dulce, *m;* purificador de agua, *m.* **w. spaniel,** perro (-rra) de aguas. **w. sprite,** ondina, *f.* **w.-supply,** abastecimiento de agua, *m;* traída de aguas, *f.* **w. tank,** depósito para agua, *m.* **w. tower,** arca de agua, *f.* **w. wave,** ondulado al agua, *m.* **w.-way,** canal, río *m,* o vía *f,* navegable. **w.-wheel,** rueda hidráulica, *f,* azud, *m;* (for irrigation) aceña, *f.* **w. wings,** nadaderas, *f pl*

water *vt* (irrigate, sprinkle) regar; (moisten) mojar; (cattle, etc.) abrevar; (wine, etc.) aguar; diluir con agua; (bathe) bañar. *vi* (of animals) beber agua; (of engines, etc.) tomar agua; (of the eyes, mouth) hacerse agua. **My mouth waters,** Se me hace agua la boca

watercourse *n* corriente de agua, *f;* cauce, *m;* lecho de un río, *m*

watercress *n* berro, mastuerzo, *m*

watered *a* regado, abundante en agua; (of silk) tornasolado

watered-down *fig* pasado por agua

waterfall *n* salto de agua, *m,* cascada, catarata, *f*

wateriness *n* humedad, *f;* acuosidad, *f*

watering *n* riego, *m;* irrigación, *f;* (of eyes) lagrimeo, *m;* (of cattle, etc.) el abrevar (a); *naut* aguada, *f.* **w.-can,** regadera, *f.* **w.-cart,** carro de regar, *m.* **w.-place,** (for animals) aguadero, *m;* (for cattle) abrevadero, *m;* (spa) balneario, *m;* (by the sea) playa de veraneo, *f*

watermark *n* (in paper) filigrana, *f;* nivel del agua, *m. vt* filigranar

waterproof *a* impermeable; a prueba de agua. *n* impermeable, *m. vt* hacer impermeable, impermeabilizar

water-repellent *a* repelente al agua

watershed *n* vertiente, *f;* línea divisoria de las aguas, *f;* (river-basin) cuenca, *f*

waterspout *n* bomba marina, manga, trompa, *f*

watertight *a* impermeable, estanco; a prueba de agua; (of arguments, etc.) irrefutable

watertightness *n* impermeabilidad, *f*

waterworks *n* establecimiento para la distribución de las aguas, *m;* obras hidráulicas, *f pl*

watery *a* (wet) húmedo; acuoso; (of the sky) de lluvia; (of eyes) lagrimoso, lloroso; (sodden) mojado; (of soup, etc.) claro; insípido

watt *n* vatio, *m.* **w. hour,** vatio hora, *m.* **w.-meter,** vatímetro, *m*

wattage *n* vatiaje, *m*

wattle *n* zarzo, *m;* (of turkey) barba, *f;* (of fish) barbilla, *f*

wave *vi* ondear; ondular; flotar; hacer señales. *vt* (brandish) blandir; agitar; (the hair) ondular; ondear; hacer señales (de). **They waved goodby to him,** Le hicieron adiós con la mano; Le hicieron señas de despedida; Se despidieron de él agitando el pañuelo

wave *n* (of the sea) ola, *f; phys* onda, *f;* (in hair or a surface) ondulación, *f;* (movement) movimiento, *m;* (of anger, etc.) ráfaga, *f.* **long w.,** onda larga, *f.* **medium w.,** onda media, *f.* **short w.,** onda corta, *f.* **sound w.,** onda sonora, *f.* **to have one's hair waved,** hacerse ondular el pelo. **w. band,** franja undosa, escala de longitudes de onda, *f.* **w. crest,** cresta de la ola, cabrilla, *f.* **w.-length,** longitud de onda, *f*

wavelet *n* pequeña ola, olita, *f;* (ripple) rizo (del agua), *m*

wave of immigration una imigración, *f*

waver *vi* ondear; oscilar; (hesitate) vacilar, titubear; (totter) tambalearse; (weaken) flaquear

waverer *n* irresoluto (-ta), vacilante, *m*

wavering *n* vacilación, irresolución, *f. a* oscilante; vacilante, irresoluto; flotante

waving *n* ondulación, *f;* oscilación, *f;* agitación, *f;* movimiento, *m. a* ondulante; oscilante; que se balancea

wavy *a* ondulado; flotante

wax *n* cera, *f;* (cobblers') cerote, *m;* (in the ear) cerilla, *f. a* de cera. *vt* encerar. *vi* crecer; hacerse; ponerse. **to wax enthusiastic,** entusiasmarse. **waxed paper,** papel encerado, *m.* **wax chandler,** cerero, *m.* **wax doll,** muñeca de cera, *f.* **wax modeling,** modelado en cera, *m,* ceroplástica, *f.* **wax taper,** blandón, *m*

waxen *a* de cera; como la cera; de color de cera

waxing *n* enceramiento, *m;* (of the moon) crecimiento, *m;* aumento, *m*

wax museum *n* museo de cera, *m*

waxwork *n* figura de cera, *f*

waxy *a.* See **waxen**

way *n* camino, *m;* senda, *f;* paso, *m;* ruta, *f;* (railway, etc.) vía, *f;* dirección, *f;* rumbo, *m;* distancia, *f;* (journey) viaje, *m;* (sea crossing) travesía, *f;* avance, progreso, *m;* (*naut* etc.) marcha, *f;* método, *m;* modo, *m;* (means) medio, *m;* manera, *f;* (habit) costumbre, *f;* (behavior) conducta, *f,* modo de obrar, *m;* (line of business, etc.) ramo, *m;* (state) estado, *m,* condición, *f;* (course) curso, *m;* (respect) punto de vista, *m;* (particular kind) género, *m;* (scale) escala, *f.* **a long way off,** a gran distancia, a lo lejos. **a short way off,** a poca distancia, no muy lejos. **by way of,** pasando por; por vía de; como; por medio de; a modo de. **by the way,** de paso; durante el viaje; durante la travesía; a propósito, entre paréntesis. **in a small way,** en pequeña escala. **in a way,** hasta cierto punto; desde cierto punto de vista. **in many ways,** de muchos modos; por muchas cosas. **in no way,** de ningún modo; nada. **in the way,** en el medio. **in the way of,** en cuanto a, tocante a; en materia de. **I went out of my way to,** Dejé el camino para; Me di la molestia de. **Is this the way to . . . ?** ¿Es este el camino a . . . ? **Make way!** ¡Calle! **Milky Way,** vía láctea, *f.* **on the way,** en camino; al paso; durante el viaje. **out of the way,** puesto a un lado; arrinconado; apartado, alejado; (imprisoned) en prisión; fuera del camino; remoto; (unusual) original. **over the way,** en frente; al otro lado (de la calle, etc.). **right of w.,** derecho de paso, *m.* **The ship left on its way to . . . ,** El barco zarpó con rumbo a . . . **the Way of the Cross,** vía crucis, *f.* **This way!** ¡Por aquí!; De este modo, Así. **this way and that,** en todas direcciones, por todos lados. **"This way to . . . ,"** «Dirección a . . .» A . . . **under way,** en camino; en marcha; en preparación. **to bar the way,** cerrar el paso. **to be in the way,** estorbar. **to be out of the way of doing,** haber perdido la costumbre de hacer (algo). **to clear the way,** abrir paso, abrir calle; *fig* preparar el terreno. **to force one's way through,** abrirse paso por. **to find a way,** encontrar un camino; *fig* encontrar medios. **to find one's way,** hallar el camino; orientarse. **to get into the way of,** contraer la costumbre de. **to get under way,** *naut* zarpar, hacerse a la vela; ponerse en marcha. **to give way,** ceder; (break) romper. **to go a long way,** ir lejos; contribuir mucho (a). **to have one's own way,** salir con la suya. **to keep out of the way,** *vt* and *vi* esconder(se); mantener(se) alejado; mantener(se) apartado. **to lose one's way,** perder el camino; desorientarse; *fig* extraviarse. **to make one's way,** abrirse paso. **to make one's way down,** bajar. **to make one's way round,** dar la vuelta a. **to make one's way up,** subir. **to make way,** hacer lugar; hacer sitio; dar paso (a). **to pay one's way,** ganarse la vida; pagar lo que se debe. **to prepare the way for,** preparar el terreno para. **to put out of the way,** poner a un lado; apartar; (kill) matar; (imprison) poner en la cárcel; hacer cautivo (a). **to see one's way,** poder ver el camino; poder orientarse; ver el modo de hacer algo; ver cómo se puede hacer algo. **ways and means,** medios y arbitrios, *m pl.* **way back,** camino de regreso, *m*; vuelta, *f.* **way down,** bajada, *f.* **way in,** entrada, *f.* **way out,** salida, *f.* **way round,** camino alrededor, *m*; solución, *f*; modo de evitar . . . , *m.* **way through,** paso, *m.* **way up,** subida, *f*

wayfarer *n* transeúnte, *mf*; viajero (-ra)

wayfaring *a* que va de viaje; errante, ambulante

waylay *vt* asechar, salir al paso (de)

wayside *n* borde del camino, *m. a* (of flowers) silvestre; (by the side of the road) en la carretera

wayward *a* caprichoso; desobediente; voluntarioso; travieso; rebelde

waywardness *n* desobediencia, indocilidad, *f*; voluntariedad, *f*; travesura, *f*; rebeldía, *f*

we *pron* nosotros, *m pl*; nosotras, *f pl*, (Usually omitted except for emphasis or for clarity.) **We are in the garden,** Estamos en el jardín. **We have come, but they are not here,** Nosotros hemos venido pero ellos no están aquí

weak *a* débil; flojo; frágil; delicado; (insecure) inseguro; (of arguments) poco convincente; (of prices, markets, etc.) flojo, en baja. **w.-eyed,** de vista floja. **w.-kneed,** débil de rodillas; *fig* sin voluntad. **w.-minded,** sin carácter; pusilánime; **w. spot,** debilidad, *f*; flaco, *m*; lado débil, *m*; desventaja, *f*

weaken *vt* debilitar; (diminish) disminuir. *vi* debilitarse; flaquear, desfallecer; (give way) ceder

weakening *n* debilitación, *f. a* debilitante; enervante

weaker *a comp* más débil. **the w. sex,** el sexo débil

weakling *n* ser delicado, *m*, persona débil, *f*; cobarde, *m*; *inf* alfeñique, *m*

weakly *a* enfermizo, delicado, enclenque. *adv* débilmente

weakness *n* debilidad, *f*; imperfección, *f*

weal *n* bienestar, *m*; prosperidad, *f*; (blow) verdugo, *m*

wealth *n* riqueza, *f*; abundancia, *f*; bienes, *m pl*

wealthy *a* rico, adinerado, acaudalado; abundante (en)

wean *vt* destetar, ablactar; separar (de); privar (de); enajenar el afecto de; (of ideas) desaferrar (de)

weaning *n* ablactación, *f*, destete, *m*

weapon *n* arma, *f*; *pl* **weapons,** (zool, bot) medios de defensa, *m pl.* **steel w.,** arma blanca, *f*

wear *n* uso, *m*; gasto, *m*; deterioro, *m*; (fashion) moda, boga, *f.* **for hard w.,** para todo uso. **for one's own w.,** para su propio uso. **for evening w.,** para llevar de noche. **for summer w.,** para llevar en verano. **w. and tear,** uso y desgaste, *m*; deterioro natural, *m*

wear *vt* llevar; llevar puesto; traer; usar; (have) tener; (exhibit) mostrar; (be clad in) vestir; (waste) gastar; deteriorar; (make) hacer; (exhaust) agotar, cansar, consumir. *vi* (last) durar; (of persons) conservar(se); (of time) correr; avanzar. **She wears well,** Está bien conservada. **to w. one's heart on one's sleeve,** tener el corazón en la mano. **to w. the trousers,** *fig inf* llevar los pantalones. **to w. well,** durar mucho. **to w. away,** *vt* gastar, roer; (rub out) borrar; consumir. *vi* (of time) pasar lentamente, transcurrir despacio. **to w. down,** gastar; consumir; reducir; agotar las fuerzas de; destruir; (tire) fatigar. **to w. off,** *vt* destruir; borrar. *vi* quitarse; fatigar; *fig* desaparecer, pasar. **to w. on,** (of time) transcurrir, correr, pasar. **to w. out,** *vt* (use) romper con el uso; consumir, acabar con; (exhaust) agotar; (tire) rendir. *vi* usarse; romperse con el uso; consumirse

wearable *a* que se puede llevar

wearer *n* el, *m*, (*f*, la) que lleva alguna cosa

weariness *n* cansancio, *m*, fatiga, lasitud, *f*; aburrimiento, *m*; aversión, repugnancia, *f*

wearing *n* uso, *m*; desgaste, *m. a* (tiring) agotador; cansado. **w. apparel,** ropa, *f*

wearisome *a* cansado; laborioso; aburrido, tedioso, pesado

wearisomely *adv* tediosamente

wearisomeness *n* cansancio, *m*; aburrimiento, tedio, hastío, *m*

weary *a* cansado, fatigado; aburrido; hastiado; impaciente; tedioso, enfadoso. *vt* cansar, fatigar; aburrir;

hastiar; molestar. *vi* cansarse, fatigarse; aburrirse. **to w. for,** anhelar, suspirar por; (miss) echar de menos (a). **to w. of,** aburrirse de; (things) impacientarse de; (people) impacientarse con

weasel *n* comadreja, *f*

weather *n* tiempo, *m*; intemperie, *f*; (storm) tempestad, *f. a naut* del lado del viento; de barlovento. *vt* (of rain, etc.) desgastar; curtir; secar al aire; *naut* pasar a barlovento; (bear) aguantar, capear; (survive) sobrevivir a; luchar con. *vi* curtirse a la intemperie. **Andrew is a little under the w.,** Andrés está algo destemplado; (with drink) Andrés tiene una mona; (depressed) Andrés está melancólico. **to be bad (good) w.,** hacer mal (buen) tiempo. **What is the w. like?** ¿Qué tiempo hace? ¿Cómo está el tiempo? **w.-beaten,** curtido por la intemperie. **w. chart,** carta meteorológica, *f.* **w. conditions,** condiciones meteorológicas, *f pl.* **w. forecast,** pronóstico del tiempo, *m.* **w.-hardened,** endurecido a la intemperie. **w. prophet,** meteorologista, *mf* **w. report,** boletín meteorológico, *m.* **w.-worn,** gastado por la intemperie; curtido por la intemperie

weathercock *n* veleta, *f*

weathering *n* desintegración por la acción atmosférica, *f*

weather-resistant *a* resistente a la intemperie

weave *vt* tejer; trenzar; entrelazar; *fig* tejer. *vi* tejer. *n* tejido, *m*; textura, *f*

weaver *n* tejedor (-ra)

weaving *n* tejido, *m*; tejeduría, *f.* **w. machine,** telar, *m*

web *n* tejido, *m*; tela, *f*; (network) red, *f*; (spider's) telaraña, *f*; (of a feather) barba, *f*; (of birds, etc.) membrana interdigital, *f*; (of intrigue) red, *f*; (snarl) lazo, *m*, trampa, *f.* **web-foot,** pie palmado, *m.* **web-footed,** palmípedo.

webbed *a* (of feet) unido por una membrana

wed *vt* casarse con; (join in marriage, cause to marry) casar; *fig* unir. *vi* estar casado; casarse

wedded *a* casado; matrimonial, conyugal; *fig* unido (a); aficionado (a), entusiasta (de), devoto (de); aferrado (a). **to be w. to one's own opinion,** estar aferrado a su propia opinión

wedding *n* boda, *f*, casamiento, *m*; (with golden, etc.) bodas, *f pl*; (union) enlace, *m*, *a* de boda, nupcial, matrimonial, conyugal; de novios, de la novia. **golden w.,** bodas de oro, *f pl.* **silver w.,** bodas de plata, *f pl.* **w. bouquet,** ramo de la novia, *m.* **w.-breakfast,** banquete de bodas, *m.* **w.-cake,** torta de la boda, *f*, pan de la boda, *m.* **w.-day,** día de la boda, *m.* **w.-march,** marcha nupcial, *f.* **w.-present,** regalo de boda, regalo de la boda, *m.* **w.-ring,** anillo de la boda, *m.* **w. trip,** viaje de novios, *m*

wedge *n* cuña, *f*; (under a wheel) calza, alzaprima, *f*; *mil* cuña, mella, *f*; (of cheese) pedazo, *m. vt* acuñar, meter cuñas; (a wheel) calzar; (fix) sujetar. **to be the thin end of the w.,** ser el principio, ser el primer paso. **to drive a w.,** *mil* hacer mella, practicar una cuña. **to w. oneself in,** introducirse con dificultad (en). **w.-shaped,** cuneiforme

wedlock *n* matrimonio, *m*

Wednesday *n* miércoles, *m*

wee *a* pequeñito, chiquito. **a wee bit,** un poquito

weed *n* mala hierba, *f*; tabaco, *m*; (cigar) cigarro, *m*; (person) madeja, *f*; (*fig* evil) cizaña, *f. vt* carpir, desherbar, sachar, sallar, escardar; *fig* extirpar, arrancar. **w.-grown,** cubierto de malas hierbas. **to w. out,** extirpar; quitar

weeder *n* (person) escardador (-ra); (implement) sacho, *m*

weeding *n* (also *fig*) escarda, *f*

weedy *a* lleno de malas hierbas; *fig* raquítico

week *n* semana, *f.* **in a w.,** de hoy en ocho (días); en una semana; después de una semana. **once a w.,** una vez por semana. **a w. ago,** hace una semana. **Michael will come a w. from today,** Miguel llegará hoy en ocho. **w. in, w. out,** semana tras semana. **w.-day,** día de trabajo, día laborable, día de la semana que no sea el domingo. **on weekdays,** entre semana, *m.* **w.-end,** fin de semana, *m.* **w.-end case,** saco de noche, *m*

weekly *a* semanal, semanario; de cada semana. *adv* semanalmente, cada semana. *n* semanario, *m,* revista semanal, *f*

weep *vt* and *vi* llorar. **to w. for,** (a person) llorar (a); (on account of) llorar por; (with happiness, etc.) llorar de. **They wept for joy,** Lloraron de alegría

weeping *n* lloro, llanto, *m,* lágrimas, *f pl. a* lloroso, que llora; (of trees) llorón. **w.-willow,** sauce llorón, *m*

weevil *n* gorgojo, *m*

weigh *vt* pesar; (consider) considerar, ponderar, tomar en cuenta; comparar; (the anchor) levar. *vi* pesar; ser de importancia. **to w. anchor,** zarpar, levar el ancla, hacerse a la vela. **to w. down,** pesar sobre; sobrecargar; hacer inclinarse bajo; *fig* agobiar. **to be weighed down,** hundirse por su propio peso; *fig* estar agobiado. **to w. out,** pesar. **to w. with,** influir (en). **w.-bridge,** báscula, *f*

weighing *n* pesada, *f;* (weight) peso, *m;* (of the anchor) leva, *f;* (consideration) ponderación, consideración, *f.* **w.-machine,** báscula, *f*

weight *n* peso, *m;* (heaviness) pesantez, *f;* cargo, *m;* (of a clock and as part of a system) pesa, *f; fig* peso, *m,* importancia, *f. vt* cargar; (a stick) emplomar; aumentar el peso (de); poner un peso (a). **gross w.,** peso bruto, *m.* **heavy w.,** peso pesado, *m.* **light w.,** peso ligero, *m.* **middle w.,** peso medio, *m.* **net w.,** peso neto, *m.* **to lose w.,** adelgazar. **loss of w.,** (of a person) adelgazamiento, *m.* **to put on w.,** cobrar carnes, hacerse más gordo. **to put the w.,** *sport* lanzar el peso. **to throw one's w. about,** *inf* darse importancia. **to try the w. of,** sopesar. **weights and measures,** pesas y medidas, *f pl.* **weightlifting,** halterofilia, *f*

weighty *a* pesado; (influential) influyente; importante, de peso; grave

weir *n* presa, esclusa, *f;* (for fish) cañal, *m*

weird *a* misterioso, sobrenatural; fantástico; mágico; (queer) raro, extraño. **the W. Sisters,** las Parcas

weirdly *adv* misteriosamente; fantásticamente; (queerly) de un modo raro, extrañamente

weirdness *n* misterio, *m;* cualidad fantástica, *f;* lo sobrenatural; (queerness) rareza, *f*

welcome *a* bienvenido; (pleasant) grato, agradable. *n* bienvenida, *f;* buena acogida, *f;* (reception) acogida, *f. vt* dar la bienvenida (a); acoger con alegría, acoger con entusiasmo; agasajar, festejar; (receive) acoger, recibir; recibir con gusto. **W.!** ¡Bienvenido! **to bid w.,** dar la bienvenida (a). **You are w.,** Estás bienvenido. **You are w. to it,** Está a su disposición

welcoming *a* acogedor, cordial, amistoso

weld *vt* soldar; combinar; unificar

welder *n* soldador, *m*

welding *n* soldadura, *f;* unión, fusión, *f*

welfare *n* bienestar, bien, *m;* (health) salud, *f;* prosperidad, *f;* intereses, *m pl.* **w. state,** estado benefactor, estado de beneficencia, estado socializante, *m.* **w. work,** trabajo social, *m*

well *a* bien; bien de salud; bueno; conveniente; (advantageous) provechoso; favorable; (happy) feliz; (healed) curado; (recovered) repuesto. **I am very w.,** Estoy muy bien. **to get w.,** ponerse bien. **to make w.,** curar. **w. enough,** bastante bien

well *adv* bien; (very) muy; favorablemente; convenientemente; (easily) sin dificultad. **as w.,** también. **as w. as,** tan bien como; además de. **That is all very w. but . . . ,** Todo eso está muy bien pero . . . **to be w. up in,** estar versado en. **to get on w. with,** llevarse bien con. **Very w.!** ¡Está bien! Muy bien. **w. and good,** bien está. **w. now,** ahora bien. **w. then,** conque; pues bien. **w.-advised,** bien aconsejado; prudente. **w.-aimed,** certero. **w.-appointed,** bien provisto; (furnished) bien amueblado. **w.-attended,** concurrido. **w.-balanced,** bien equilibrado. **w.-behaved,** bien educado; (of animals) manso. **w.-being,** bienestar, *m;* felicidad, *f.* **w.-born,** bien nacido, de buena familia. **w.-bred,**

bien criado, bien educado; (of animals) de pura raza. **w.-chosen,** bien escogido. **w.-defined,** bien definido. **w.-deserved,** bien merecido. **w.-disposed,** bien dispuesto; favorable; bien intencionado. **w.-doing,** *n* el obrar bien; obras de caridad, *f pl,* a bondadoso, caritativo. **w.-done,** *a* bien hecho. *interj* ¡bravo! **w.-educated,** instruido, culto. **w.-favored,** guapo, de buen parecer. **w.-founded,** bien fundado. **w.-groomed,** elegante. **w.-grounded,** bien fundado; bien instruido. **w.-informed,** instruido; culto, ilustrado. **w.-intentioned,** bien intencionado. **w.-known,** bien conocido, notorio. **w.-meaning,** bien intencionado. **w.-modulated,** armonioso. **w.-off,** acomodado, adinerado; feliz. **w.-read,** culto, instruido. **w.-shaped,** bien hecho; bien formado. **w.-shaped nose,** nariz perfilada, *f.* **w.-spent,** bien empleado. **w.-spoken,** bien hablado; bien dicho. **w.-stocked,** bien provisto. **w.-suited,** apropiado. **w.-timed,** oportuno. **w.-to-do,** acomodado, rico. **w.-wisher,** amigo (-ga). **w.-worn,** raído; (of paths) trillado

well *n* pozo, *m;* (of a stair) caja, *f;* cañón de escalera, *m;* (fountain) fuente, *f,* manantial, *m;* (of a fishing boat) vivar, *m;* (of a ship) sentina, *f.* **w.-sinker,** pocero, *m*

well *vi* chorrear, manar, brotar, fluir

Welsh *a* galés, de Gales. *n* (language) galés, *m.* **the W.,** los galeses

Welshman *n* galés, *m*

Welshwoman *n* galesa, *f*

welt *n* (of shoe) vira, *f,* cerquillo, *m;* (in knitting) ribete, *m;* (weal) verdugo, *m*

Weltanschauung *n* cosmovisión, postura de vida, *f*

welter *vi* revolcarse; bañarse (en), nadar (en). *n* confusión, *f,* tumulto, *m;* mezcla, *f.* **w.-weight,** peso welter, *m*

wench *n* mozuela, muchacha, *f*

wend *vt* dirigir, encaminar. *vi* ir. **to w. one's way,** dirigir sus pasos, seguir su camino

Wesleyan *a* wesleyano, metodista. *n* metodista, *mf*

west *n* oeste, *m;* poniente, *m;* occidente, *m. a* del oeste; occidental. *adv* hacia el oeste, a poniente; al oeste. **W. Indian,** de las Antillas, de las Indias Occidentales. **w.-north-w.,** oesnoroeste, *m.* **w.-south-w.,** oessudeste, *m.* **w. wind,** viento del oeste, poniente, *m*

westerly *a* del oeste; hacia el oeste; occidental

western *a* occidental; del oeste. *n* (novel) novela caballista, *f;* (film) película del oeste, *f*

westernized *a* influido por el occidente

westernmost *a* más al oeste

West Indies Indias Occidentales, *f pl*

westward *a* que está al oeste. *adv* hacia el oeste; hacia el occidente

wet *a* mojado; húmedo; (rainy) lluvioso. *vt* mojar; humedecer. *n* (rain) lluvia, *f.* **"Mind the wet paint!"** «¡Cuidado, recién pintado!» **to be wet,** estar mojado; (of the weather) llover. **to get wet,** mojarse. **wet blanket,** *fig* aguafiestas, *mf* **w. through,** (of persons) calado, hecho una sopa. **wet-nurse,** nodriza, *f*

wetness *n* humedad, *f;* (rain) lluvia, *f*

wetting *n* mojada, *f;* humectación, *f;* (soaking) remojo, *m*

whack *n* golpe, *m;* (try) tentativa, *f;* (portion) porción, parte, *f. vt* golpear, aporrear, pegar

whale *n* ballena, *f.* **sperm w.,** cachalote, *m.* **w.-oil,** aceite de ballena, *m*

whalebone *n* barbas de ballena, *f pl,* ballena, *f*

whaler *n* (man) ballenero, pescador de ballenas, *m;* (boat) buque ballenero, *m*

whaling *a* ballenero. *n* pesca de ballenas, *f.* **w.-gun,** cañón arponero, *m*

wharf *n* muelle, embarcadero, descargadero, *m, vt* amarrar al muelle

what *a* *pron* (interrogative and exclamatory) qué; cómo; (relative) que; el que, *m;* la que, *f;* lo que, *neut;* los que, *m pl;* las que, *f pl;* (which, interrogative) cuál, *mf;* cuáles, *mf pl;* (how many) cuantos, *m pl;* cuantas, *f* *pl;* (interrogative and exclamatory) cuántos, *m pl;* cuántas, *f pl;* (how much, interrogative and exclamatory) cuánto, *m;* cuánta, *f.* **And w. not,** Y qué sé yo qué más. **Make w. changes you will,** Haz los cambios que quieras. **W. confidence he had . . . ,** La confianza que tenía . . . **W. is this called?** ¿Cómo se llama esto? **W. did they go there for?** ¿Por qué fueron? **W. do you take me for?** ¿Por quién me tomas? **That was not w.** he said, No fue eso lo que dijo. **to know what's w.,** saber cuántas son cinco. **You have heard the latest news, w.?** Has oído las últimas noticias, ¿verdad? **W. a pity!** ¡Qué lástima! **W., do you really believe it?** ¿Lo crees de veras? **W. else?** ¿Qué más? **W. for?** ¿Para qué? **what's-his-name,** fulano (-na) de tal, *m.* **W. ho!** ¡Hola! **W. if . . . ?** ¿Qué será si . . . ? **W. is the matter?** ¿Qué pasa? ¿Qué hay? **w. though . . . ,** aun cuando . . . ; ¿Qué importa qué? **w. with one thing, w. with another,** entre una cosa y otra. **What's more, . . .** Es más, . . .

whatever *a pron* cuanto; todo lo que; cualquier cosa que; cualquier. **W. sacrifice is necessary,** Cualquier sacrificio que sea necesario. **W. I have is yours,** Todo lo que tenga es vuestro. **W. happens,** Venga lo que venga. **It is of no use w.,** No sirve absolutamente para nada

wheal *n.* See **weal**

wheat *n* trigo, *m.* a de trigo. **summer w.,** trigo tremesino, *m.* **whole w.,** a de trigo entero. **w.-ear,** espiga de trigo, *f.* **w.-field,** trigal, *m.* **w.-sheaf,** gavilla de trigo, *f*

wheaten *a* de trigo; del color del trigo

wheedle *vt* lagotear, engatusar; (flatter) halagar; (with out) sacar con mimos

wheedling *a* zalamero, mimoso; marrullero. *n* lagotería, *f,* mimos, *m pl;* (flattery) halagos, *m pl;* marrullería, *f*

wheel *n* rueda, *f;* (bicycle) bicicleta, *f;* (for steering a ship) timón, *m;* rueda del timón, *f;* (for steering a car) volante, *m;* (for spinning) rueca, *f;* (potter's) rueda de alfarero, *f;* (of birds) vuelo, *m;* (turn) vuelta, *f; mil* conversión, *f.* **Catherine w.,** (firework) rueda de Santa Catalina, *f.* **back w.,** rueda trasera, *f.* **front w.,** rueda delantera, *f.* **to break on the w.,** enrodar. **to go on wheels,** ir en ruedas; *fig* ir viento en popa. **to take the w.,** (in a ship) tomar el timón; tomar el volante. **w. of fortune,** rueda de la fortuna, *f.* **w.-chair,** silla de ruedas, *f.* **w.-house,** timonera, *f.* **w.-mark,** rodada, *f*

wheel *vt* hacer rodar; (push) empujar; (drive) conducir; transportar; llevar; pasear; (turn) hacer girar. *vi* girar; dar vueltas; ir en bicicleta. **to w. about,** cambiar de frente; volverse; cambiar de rumbo

wheelbarrow *n* carretilla, *f*

wheeled *a* de . . . ruedas; con ruedas. **w. chair,** silla de ruedas, *f*

wheeling *n* rodaje, *m; mil* conversión, *f;* (of birds) vuelos, *m pl,* vueltas, *f pl.* **free-w.,** rueda libre, *f*

wheelwright *n* carpintero de carretas, ruedero, *m*

wheeze *vi* ser asmático, jadear, respirar fatigosamente, resollar

wheezing *n* resuello, jadeo, *m;* respiración fatigada, *f*

whelp *n* cachorro (-rra). *vi and vt* parir

when *adv* cuando (interrogative, cuándo); (as soon as) tan pronto como, en cuanto; (meaning 'and then') y luego, y entonces; (although) aunque. **I will see you w. I return,** Te veré cuando vuelva. **W. he came to see me he was already ill,** Cuando vino a verme estaba enfermo ya. **We returned a week ago, since w. I have not been out,** Volvimos hace ocho días y desde entonces no he salido. **Since w.?** ¿Desde cuándo?

whence *adv* de donde (interrogative, ¿de dónde?); a donde (interrogative a dónde); por donde, de que; por lo que. **W. does he come?** ¿De dónde viene? **W. comes it that?** ¿Cómo es que . . . ?

whenever *adv* cuando quiera que, siempre que; cada vez que, todas las veces que; cuando

en que (interrogative, en qué); (to where with verbs of motion) a donde (interrogative, a dónde); (from where with verbs of motion) de donde (interrogative, de dónde). **W. are you going to?** ¿A dónde va Vd.? **This is w. we get out,** (of a bus, etc.) Nos apeamos aquí

whereabouts *adv* (interrogative) dónde; (relative) donde. *n* paradero, *m*

whereas *conjunc* (inasmuch as) visto que, ya que; (although) mientras (que)

whereat *adv* por lo cual; a lo cual

whereby *adv* cómo; por qué; por el cual, con el cual

wherefore *adv* (why) por qué; por lo cual. *n* porqué, *m*

wherein *adv* en donde (interrogative, en dónde); en que (interrogative, en qué)

whereinto *adv* en donde; dentro del cual; en lo cual

whereof *adv* de que; (whose) cuyo

whereon *adv* sobre que; en qué

whereto *adv* adonde; a lo que

whereupon *adv* dónde; sobre lo cual, con lo cual; en consecuencia de lo cual

wherever *adv* dondequiera (que), en cualquier sitio; adondequiera (que). **Sit w. you like,** Siéntate donde te parezca bien

wherewith *adv* con que (interrogative, con qué)

wherewithal *n* lo necesario; dinero necesario, *m*

whet *vt* (knives, etc.) afilar, amolar, aguzar; (curiosity, etc.) excitar, estimular

whether *conjunc* si; que; sea que, ya que. **W. he will or no,** Que quiera, que no quiera. **w. or not,** si o no

whetstone *n* afiladera, amoladera, piedra de amolar, *f*

whetting *n* aguzadura, amoladura, *f;* (of curiosity, etc.) estimulación, excitación, *f*

whey *n* suero (de la leche), *m*

which *a and pron* cuál, *mf;* cuáles, *mf pl;* que (interrogative, qué); el cual, *m;* la cual, *f;* lo cual, *neut;* los cuales, *m pl;* las cuales, *f pl;* el que, *m;* la que, *f;* lo que, *neut;* los que, *m pl;* las que, *f pl;* (who) quien. **all of w.,** todo lo cual, etc. **in w.,** en donde, en el que; donde. **the w.,** el cual, la cual, etc. **W. would you like?** ¿Cuál quieres? **The documents w. I have seen,** Los documentos que he visto. **W. way have we to go?** ¿Por dónde hemos de ir?

whichever *a and pron* cualquiera (que), *mf;* cualesquiera, *mf pl;* el que, *m;* la que, *f;* (of persons only) quienquiera (que), *mf;* quienesquiera (que), *mf pl* **Give me w. you like,** Dame el que quieras. **I shall take w. you would like to come,** Me llevaré a cualquiera de Vds. que guste de venir

whiff *n* (of air) soplo, *m;* vaho, *m;* fragancia, *f*

while *n* rato, *m;* momento, *m;* tiempo, *m.* **after a w.,** al cabo de algún tiempo, después de algún tiempo. **a little w. ago,** hace poco. **all this w.,** todo este tiempo. **at whiles,** a ratos, de vez en cuando. **between whiles,** de cuando en cuando, entre tanto. **It is worth your w. to do it,** Vale la pena de hacerse. **Mary smiled the w.,** María mientras tanto se sonreía. **once in a w.,** de vez en cuando; en ocasiones

while *conjunc* mientras (que); al (followed by an infinitive); al mismo tiempo que; a medida que; (although) aunque; si bien. **w. I was walking down the street,** mientras andaba por la calle, al andar yo por la calle. *vt* **to w. (away),** pasar, entretener. **to w. away the time,** pasar el rato

whim *n* capricho, antojo, *m;* manía, *f;* extravagancia, *f;* fantasía, *f*

whimper *n* quejido, sollozo, gemido, *m, vi* lloriquear, quejarse, sollozar, gemir

whimpering *n* lloriqueo, llanto, *m, a* que lloriquea

whimsical *a* antojadizo, caprichoso; fantástico

whimsicality *n* capricho, *m,* extravagancia, *f;* fantasía, *f*

whimsically *adv* caprichosamente; fantásticamente

whine *vi* gimotear, lloriquear; quejarse

whining *n* gimoteo, lloriqueo, *m;* quejumbres, *f pl. a* que lloriquea; quejumbroso

whinny *n* relincho, hin, *m, vi* relinchar

whip *vt* azotar; pegar; *cul* batir; *sew* sobrecoser; (ropes, etc.) ligar; (defeat) vencer. *vi* moverse rápidamente. **to w. down,** *vi* bajar volando, bajar corriendo. *vt* arrebatar (de). **to w. in,** entrar apresuradamente (en), penetrar apresuradamente (en). **to w. off,** cazar a latigazos, despachar a golpes; (remove) quitar rápidamente; (persons) llevar corriendo, llevar aprisa. **to w. open,** abrir rápidamente. **to w. out,** *vt* (draw) sacar rápidamente; (utter) saltar diciendo (que); proferir. *vi* escabullirse, escaparse, salir apresuradamente. **to w. round,** volverse de repente. **to w. up,** *vt* (horses, etc.) avivar con el látigo; (snatch) coger de repente agarrar; (gather) reunir. *vi* (mount) subir corriendo

whip *n* azote, zurriago, *m*; (riding) látigo, *m*. **blow with a w.,** latigazo, *m*. **to have the w.-hand,** mandar, tener la sartén por el mango; tener la ventaja. **w.-cord,** tralla del látigo, *f*

whippet *n* especie de perro (-rra) lebrero (-ra)

whipping *n* paliza, *f*, vapuleo, azotamiento, *m*. **w. post,** picota, *f*. **w. top,** trompo, *m*, peonza, *f*

whirl *n* vuelta, *f*, giro, *m*; rotación, *f*; *fig* torbellino, *m*. *vi* girar; dar vueltas; (dance) bailar, danzar. *vt* hacer girar; dar vueltas (a); (carry) llevar rápidamente. **to w. along,** volar (por), pasar aprisa (por); dejar atrás los vientos, correr velozmente. **to w. past,** pasar volando (por); pasar como una exhalación. **to w. through,** atravesar rápidamente, cruzar volando

whirligig *n* perinola, *f*; (merry-go-round) tiovivo, *m*

whirlpool *n* vórtice, remolino, *m*; *fig* vorágine, *f*

whirlwind *n* torbellino, *m*, manga de viento, *f*

whirr *n* zumbido, *m*; (of wings) ruido (de las alas), *m*. *vi* girar; zumbar

whirring *n* zumbido, *m*; ruido, *m*. *a* que gira; que zumba

whisk *n* cepillo, *m*; *cul* batidor, *m*; (movement) movimiento rápido, *m*. *vt cul* batir; (wag) menear, mover rápidamente; (with off, away) quitar rápidamente; sacudirse; arrebatar; (take away a person) llevarse (a). *vi* moverse rápidamente; andar rápidamente

whiskers *n pl* mostacho, *m*, patillas, barbas, *f pl*; (of a feline) bigotes, *m pl*

whiskered *a* bigotudo

whisky *n* güisqui, *m*

whisper *n* cuchicheo, *m*; (rumour) voz, *f*; (of leaves, etc.) susurro, murmullo, *m*. *vi* and *vt* cuchichear, hablar al oído; (of leaves, etc.) susurrar; (of rumors) murmurar. **in a w.,** al oído, en un susurro

whisperer *n* cuchicheador (-ra); (gossip) murmurador (-ra)

whispering *n* cuchicheo, *m*; susurro, *m*; (gossip) murmurio, *m*. **w. gallery,** galería de los murmullos, *f. inf* sala de los secretos, *f*

whistle *n* (sound) silbido, silbo, *m*; (instrument) pito, silbato, *m*; *inf* gaznate, *m*. *vi* and *vt* silbar. **blast on the w.,** pitido, *m*. **to w. for,** llamar silbando; *inf* esperar sentado, buscar en vano

whistler *n* silbador (-ra)

whistling *n* silbido, *m*, *a* silbador

whit *n* pizca, *f*, bledo, *m*. **not a w.,** ni pizca

Whit, Whitsun *a* de Pentecostés. **W. Monday,** lunes de Pentecostés, *m*

white *a* blanco; pálido; puro. *n* color blanco, blanco, *m*; (pigment) pintura blanca, *f*; (whiteness) blancura, *f*; (of egg) clara (del huevo), *f*; (person) blanco, *m*. **Elizabeth went w.,** Isabel se puso pálida. **the w.,** (billiards) la blanca. **the w. of the eye,** lo blanco del ojo. **w. ant,** hormiga blanca, termita, *f*. **w. cabbage,** repollo, *m*. **w. caps,** (of waves) cabrillas, *f pl*; (of mountains) picos blancos, *m pl*. **w. clover,** trébol blanco, *m*. **w. corpuscle,** glóbulo blanco, *m*. **w. currant,** grosella blanca, *f*. **w. elephant,** elefante (-ta) blanco (-ca). **w. ensign,** pabellón blanco, *m*. **w.-faced,** de cara pálida. **w. fish,** pescado blanco, *m*. **w. flag,** bandera blanca, *f*. **w.-haired,** de pelo blanco. **w. heat,** calor blanco, *m*, candencia, *f*; ardor, *m*. **w. horses,** cabrillas, palomas, *f pl*. **w.-hot,** incandescente.

W. House, the, la Casa Blanca, *f*. **w. lead,** albayalde, *m*. **w. lie,** mentira inocente, mentira oficiosa, mentira piadosa, la mentirilla, *f*. **w. man,** blanco, hombre de raza blanca, *m*. **the white man's burden,** la misión sagrada de la civilización blanca, *f*. **w. meat,** carne blanca, pechuga, *f*. **w. paper,** libro blanco, *m*. **w. sauce,** salsa blanca, *f*. **w. slave,** víctima de la trata de blancas, *f*. **w. slavery,** trata de blancas, *f*. **w. sugar,** azúcar blanco, azúcar de flor, *m*. **w. woman,** mujer de raza blanca, *f*

whiten *vt* blanquear. *vi* blanquearse

whiteness *n* blancura, *f*; palidez, *f*; pureza, *f*; *poet* nieve, *f*

whitening *n* blanqueo, *m*; blanco de España, *m*; blanco para los zapatos, *m*

whitewash *vt* blanquear, jalbegar, encalar; (*fig* of faults) disculpar, justificar

whitewashing *n* blanqueo, *m*, encaladura, *f*

whither *adv* (interrogative) adónde; (with a clause) adonde

whithersoever *adv* adondequiera

whiting *n* blanco de España, *m*; blanco para los zapatos, *m*; (fish) pescadilla, *f*, merlango, *m*

whitish *a* blanquecino

whitlow *n* panadizo, *m*

Whitsunday *n* domingo de Pentecostés, *m*

Whitsuntide *n* pascua de Pentecostés, *f*

whittle *n* navaja, *f*. *vt* cercenar, cortar; (sharpen) afilar, sacar punta (a); tallar; *fig* reducir. **to w. away, down,** *fig* reducir a nada

whizz *n* silbido, zumbido, *m*, *vi* silbar, zumbar

whizzing *n* silbido, *m*, *a* que zumba

who *pron* (interrogative) quién, *mf*; quiénes, *mf pl*; (relative) quien, *mf*; quienes, *mf pl*; que; (in elliptical constructions the person that, etc.) el que, *m*; la que, *f*; los que, *m pl*; las que, *f pl*

whoa *interj* ¡so!

whoever *pron* quienquiera (que); cualquiera (que); quien. **Give it to w. you like,** Dáselo a quien te parezca bien

whole *a* (healthy) sano; (uninjured) ileso, entero; todo. *n* todo, *m*; total, *m*; totalidad, *f*; conjunto, *m*. **on the w.,** por regla general, en general; en conjunto. **the w. week,** la semana entera, toda la semana. **w.-hearted,** sincero, genuino; entusiasta. **w.-heartedly,** de todo corazón. **w.-heartedness,** sinceridad, *f*; entusiasmo, *m*. **w. length,** *a* de cuerpo entero. **w. number,** número entero, *m*

wholemeal *n* harina de trigo entero, *f*, *a* de trigo entero

wholeness *n* totalidad, *f*; integridad, *f*; todo, *m*

wholesale *a com* al por mayor; en grueso; *fig* general; en masa. *n* venta al por mayor, *f*. **w. price,** precio al por mayor, *m*. **w. trade,** comercio al por mayor, *m*

wholesaler *n* comerciante al por mayor, *mf* mercader de grueso, *m*

wholesome *a* sano; saludable; (edifying) edificante

wholesomeness *n* sanidad, *f*; lo sano; lo saludable

wholly *adv* completamente, enteramente, totalmente; integralmente; del todo

whom *pron* quien, a quien, *mf*; a quienes, *mf pl*; (interrogative) a quién, *mf*; a quiénes, *mf pl*; al que, *m*; a la que, *f*; a los que, *m pl*; a las que, *f pl*. **from w.,** de quien, (interrogative) de quién. **the man w. you saw,** el hombre a quien viste

whoop *n* alarido, grito, *m*; estertor de la tos ferina, *m*. *vi* dar gritos, chillar; (whooping-cough) toser

whooping cough *n* tos ferina, coqueluche, *f*

whore *n* puta, ramera, *f*

whorl *n* (of a shell) espira, *f*; *bot* verticilo, *m*; (of a spindle) tortera, *f*

whorled *a bot* verticilado; (of shells) en espira

whose *pron* cuyo, *m*; cuya, *f*; cuyos, *m pl*; cuyas, *f pl*; de quien, *mf*; de quienes, *mf pl*; (interrogative) de quién, de quiénes; **W. daughter is she?** ¿De quién es ella la hija? **This is the writer w. name I always forget,** Este es el autor cuyo nombre siempre olvido

whosoever *pron.* See **whoever**

why *adv* (*interrogative*) por qué; (on account of which) por el cual, *m*; por la cual, *f*; por lo cual, *neut*; por los cuales, *m pl*; por las cuales, *f pl*; (how) cómo. *n* ni porqué, *m*, *interj* ¡qué!; ¡cómo!; ¡toma!; si. **not to know the why or wherefore,** no saber ni el porqué ni el cómo, no saber ni el qué ni el por qué. **Why! I have just come,** ¡Si no hago más de llegar! **Why not?** ¿Por qué no? ¡Cómo no!

wick *n* mecha, torcida, *f*

wicked *a* malo; malvado, perverso; pecaminoso; malicioso; (mischievous) travieso

wickedly *adv* mal; perversamente; maliciosamente

wickedness *n* maldad, *f*; perversidad, *f*; pecado, *m*; (mischievousness) travesura, *f*

wicker *n* mimbre, *m*, *a* de mimbre

wicket *n* postigo, portillo, *m*; (half-door) media puerta, *f*; (at cricket) meta, *f*. **w.-keeper,** guardameta, *m*

wide *a* ancho; (in measurements) de ancho; vasto; extenso; grande; amplio; (loose) holgado; (distant) lejos; liberal; general, comprensivo. *adv* lejos; completamente. **far and w.,** por todas partes. **to be too w.,** ser muy ancho; estar muy ancho; (of garments) venir muy ancho. **two feet w.,** dos pies de ancho. **w.-awake,** muy despierto; despabilado; vigilante. **w.-eyed,** con los ojos muy abiertos; asombrado. **w.-open,** abierto de par en par

widely *adv* extensamente; generalmente; (very) muy

widen *vt* ensanchar; extender. *vi* ensancharse; extenderse

widening *n* ensanche, *m*; extensión, *f*

widespread *a* universal, generalizado; extenso; esparcido. **to become w.,** generalizarse

widow *n* viuda, *f*. *vt* dejar viuda; dejar viudo; *fig* privar. **to be a grass w.,** estar viuda. **to become a w.,** enviudar, perder al esposo. **widow's pension,** viudedad, *f*. **widow's weeds,** luto de viuda, *m*

widowed *a* viudo

widower *n* viudo, *m*. **to become a w.,** perder a la esposa, enviudar

widowhood, widowerhood *n* viudez, *f*

width *n* anchura, *f*; (of cloth) ancho, *m*; (of mind) liberalismo, *m*. **double w.,** (cloth) doble ancho, *m*

wield *vt* (a scepter) empuñar; (power, etc.) ejercer; (a pen, sword) manejar

wife *n* esposa, mujer, *f*; mujer, *f*; comadre, *f*. **husband and w.,** los cónyuges, los esposos. **old wives' tale,** cuento de viejas, *m*. **The Merry Wives of Windsor,** Las alegres comadres de Windsor. **to take to w.,** contraer matrimonio con, tomar como esposa (a)

wifely *a* de esposa, de mujer casada; de mujer de su casa; conyugal

wig *n* peluca, *f*; (hair) cabellera, *f*. **top wig,** peluquín, *m*. **wigmaker,** peluquero, *m*

wigged *a* con peluca, de peluca

wigging *n* (scolding) peluca, *f*

wigwam *n* tienda de indios, *f*

wild *a* (of animals, men, land) salvaje; (barren) desierto, yermo; (mountainous) riscoso, montañoso; (of plants, birds) silvestre; montés; (disarranged) en desorden, desarreglado; (complete) absoluto, completo; (dissipated) disipado; vicioso; (foolish) alocado; (of the sea) bravío; (of weather, etc.) borrascoso; (mad with delight, etc.) loco; (frantic, mad) frenético, loco; (with 'talk,' etc.) extravagante; insensato, desatinado; (shy) arisco; (incoherent) inconexo, incoherente; (frightened) alarmado, espantado; (wilful) travieso, indomable. *n* tierra virgen, *f*; desierto, *m*; soledad, *f*. **It made me w.,** (angry) Me hizo rabiar. **to run w.,** volver a un estado silvestre; (of persons) llevar una vida de salvajes; volverse loco. **to shoot w.,** errar el tiro. **to spread like w. fire,** propagarse como el fuego. **w. beast,** fiera, *f*. **w. boar,** jabalí, *m*. **w. cat,** gato montés, *m*. **w. duck,** pato silvestre, *m*. **w. goat,** cabra montesa, *f*. **w.-goose chase,** caza infructuosa, *f*; empresa quimérica, *f*. **w. oats,** avenas locas, *f pl*; *fig* indiscre-

ciones de la juventud, *f pl*. **to sow one's w. oats,** andarse a la flor del berro

wilderness *n* desierto, *m*; yermo, páramo, despoblado, *m*; soledad, *f*; (jungle) selva, *f*; (maze) laberinto, *m*; infinidad, *f*

wildly *adv* en un estado salvaje; sin cultivo; (rashly) desatinadamente; sin reflexión, sin pensar; (incoherently) incoherentemente; (stupidly, of looking, etc.) tontamente; (in panic) con ojos espantados, con terror en los ojos, alarmado

wildness *n* salvajez, *f*; estado silvestre, *m*; naturaleza silvestre, *f*; (ferocity) ferocidad, *f*; (of the wind, sea) braveza, *f*; (of the wind) violencia, *f*; (wilfulness) impetuosidad, *f*; (of statements, etc.) extravagancia, *f*; (incoherence) incoherencia, *f*; (disorder) desorden, *m*; (wilfulness, of children) travesuras, *f pl*; (of the expression) gesto espantado, *m*

wile *n* estratagema, *f*, engaño, *m*, ardid, *f*

wilily *adv* astutamente

wiliness *n* astucia, *f*

will *n* voluntad, *f*; albedrío, *m*; (wish) deseo, *m*; (pleasure) discreción, *f*, placer, *m*; (legal document) testamento, *m*. **against my w.,** contra mi voluntad. **at w.,** a voluntad; a gusto; a discreción. **free w.,** libre albedrío, *m*. **of one's own free w.,** por su propia voluntad. **iron w.,** voluntad de hierro, *f*. **last w. and testament,** última disposición, última voluntad, *f*. **to do with a w.,** hacer con toda el alma, hacer con entusiasmo. **to make one's w.,** otorgar (hacer) su testamento. **w.-power,** fuerza de voluntad, *f*

will *vt* querer; disponer, ordenar; (bequeath) legar, dejar en testamento, mandar; (oblige) sugestionar (a una persona) para que haga algo; hipnotizar. *vi aux.* querer; (As a sign of the future it is not translated separately in Spanish) **I w. come tomorrow,** Vendré mañana. **John does not approve, but I w. go,** Juan no lo aprueba pero yo quiero ir. **Do what you w.,** Haga lo que a Vd. le parezca bien, Haga lo que Vd. quiera; Haga lo que haga. **Boys w. be boys,** Los niños son siempre niños. **He w. not (won't) do it,** No lo hará; No quiere hacerlo

wilful *a* rebelde, voluntarioso; (of children) travieso; (of crimes, etc.) premeditado

wilfully *adv* voluntariosamente; intencionadamente; (of committing crimes) con premeditación

wilfulness *n* rebeldía, *f*; (obstinacy) terquedad, obstinación, *f*

William the Silent Guillermo el Taciturno

willing *a* dispuesto, inclinado; (serviceable) servicial; deseoso; espontáneo; complaciente; gustoso; (willingly) de buena gana. **to be w.,** estar dispuesto (a), querer; consentir (en)

willingly *adv* de buena gana, con gusto

willingness *n* buena voluntad, *f*; deseo de servir, *m*; complacencia, *f*; (consent) consentimiento, *m*

will-o'-the-wisp *n* fuego fatuo, *m*

willow *n* sauce, *m*. **weeping w.,** sauce llorón, *m*. **w.-pattern china,** porcelana de estilo chino, *f*. **w. tree,** sauce, *m*

willowy *a* lleno de sauces; (slim) cimbreño, esbelto, alto y delgado

willy nilly *adv* de buen o mal grado, mal que bien

wilt *vi* (of plants) marchitarse, secarse; *fig* languidecer; ajarse. *vt* marchitar; *fig* ajar; hacer languidecer

wily *a* astuto, chuzón

wimple *n* toca, *f*

win *vt* ganar; (reach) alcanzar, lograr; (a victory, etc.) llevarse; conquistar. *vi* ganar; triunfar. *n* triunfo, *m*. **to win back,** volver a ganar; recobrar

wince *vi* retroceder, recular; (flinch) quejarse; (of a horse) respingar. *n* respingo, *m*. **without wincing,** sin quejarse; estoicamente

winch *n* cabria, *f*; (handle) manubrio, *m*

wind *n* viento, *m*; aire, *m*; (flatulence) flatulencia, *f*; (breath) respiración, *f*, aliento, *m*; (idle talk) paja, *f*. **breath of w.,** soplo de viento, *m*. **following w.,**

viento en popa, *m.* **high w.,** viento alto, viento fuerte, *m.* **land w.,** viento terrenal, *m.* **It's an ill w. that blows nobody good,** No hay mal que por bien no venga. **There is something in the w.,** Hay algo en el aire, Se trama algo. **to get w. of,** husmear. **to sail before the w.,** navegar de viento en popa. **The w.** **stiffened,** Refrescó el viento. **You took the w. out of his sails,** Le deshinchaste las velas. **w.-instrument,** instrumento de viento, *m.* **w.-proof,** a prueba del viento. **w.-swept,** expuesto a todos los vientos. **w. storm,** ventarrón, *m*

wind *vi* serpentear; desfilar lentamente; torcerse. *vt* (turn) dar vueltas (a); (a handle) manejar, mover; (a watch) dar cuerda (a); (wool, etc.) devanar, ovillar; (wrap) envolver; (of arms, embrace) rodear (con); (a horn) tocar. **to w. off,** devanar; desenrollar. **to w. round,** (wrap) envolver; (skirt) rodear; (embrace) ceñir con (los brazos); (pass by) pasar por; (of snakes) enroscarse. **to w. up,** (a watch) dar cuerda (a); (thread) devanar; (conclude) concluir; *com* liquidar; (excite) agitar, emocionar

windbag *n* pandero, *m,* sacamuelas, *mf*

winder *n* (person) devanador (-ra); (machine) devanadera, *f;* (of a clock) llave, *f*

windfall *n* fruta caída del árbol, *f;* (good luck) breva, *f;* ganancia inesperada, lotería, *f*

windiness *n* tiempo ventoso, *m;* situación expuesta a todos los vientos, *f;* (of speech) pomposidad, verbosidad, *f*

winding *a* tortuoso; (e.g., road) sinuoso; serpentino; en espiral. *n* tortuosidad, *f;* meandro, recoveco, *m,* vuelta, curva, *f.* **w. sheet,** mortaja, *f,* sudario, *m.* **w. stair,** escalera de caracol, *f.* **w.-up,** conclusión, *f; com* liquidación, *f*

windlass *n* torno, *m*

windless *a* sin viento

windmill *n* molino de viento, *m*

window *n* ventana, *f;* (of a shop) escaparate, *m;* (in a train, car, bank, etc.) ventanilla, *f;* (booking office) taquilla, *f;* (of a church) vidriera, *f.* **casement w.,** ventana, *f.* **sash w.,** ventana de guillotina, *f.* **small w.,** ventanilla, *f.* **stained glass w.,** vidriera, *f.* **to lean out of the w.,** asomarse a la ventana. **to look out of the w.,** mirar por la ventana. **w. blind,** (Venetian) persiana, *f;* transparente, *m;* (against the sun) toldo, *m.* **w.-dresser,** decorador (-ra) de escaparates. **w. frame,** marco de ventana, *m.* **w.-pane,** cristal (de ventana), *m.* **w.-shutter,** contraventana, *f.* **w.-sill,** repisa de la ventana, *f,* alféizar, *m*

windpipe *n* tráquea, *f*

windscreen *n* parabrisas, guardabrisa, *m.* **w.-wiper,** limpiaparabrisas, limpiavidrios, *m*

windward *n* barlovento, *m. a* de barlovento. *adv a* barlovento

windy *a* ventoso; expuesto al viento; (of style) hinchado, pomposo. **It is w.,** Hace viento

wine *n* vino, *m;* zumo fermentado (de algunas frutas), *m. a* de vino; de vinos; para vino. **in w.,** *cul* en vino; (drunk) ebrio, borracho. **heavy w.,** vino fuerte, *m.* **light w.,** vino ligero, *m.* **local w.,** vino del país, *m.* **matured w.,** vino generoso, *m.* **red w.,** vino tinto, *m.* **thin w.,** vinillo, *m.* **white w.,** vino blanco, *m.* **w.-cellar,** bodega, cueva, *f.* **w.-colored,** de color de vino. **w.-cooler,** cubo para enfriar vinos, *m.* **w. country,** tierra de vino, *f.* **w. decanter,** garrafa para vino, *f.* **w.-grower,** vinicultor (-ra). **w.-growing,** *n* vinicultura, *f. a* vinícola. **w. lees,** zupia, *f.* **w. merchant,** comerciante en vinos, *mf.* vinatero, *m.* **w.-press,** lagar, *m.* **w.-taster,** catavinos, *m.* **w. waiter,** bodeguero, *m*

wineskin *n* bota, *f,* odre, pellejo, *m*

wing *n* (of a bird and *zool, arch, aer, mil, bot*) ala, *f;* (flight) vuelo, *m; theat* bastidor, *m; fig* protección, *f. vt* dar alas (a); llevar sobre las alas; (wound) herir en el ala; herir en el brazo; volar por. *vi* volar. **beating of wings,** batir de alas, aleteo, *m.* **in the wings,** *theat* entre bastidores. **on the w.,** al vuelo. **to clip a (per-**

son's) **wings,** cortar (*or* quebrar) las alas (a). **under his w.,** bajo su protección. **w.-case,** élitro (de un insecto), *m.* **w. chair,** sillón con orejas, *m.* **w.-commander,** teniente coronel de aviación, *m.* **w.-span,** (*zool* and *aer*) envergadura, *f.* **w.-spread,** extensión del ala, *f.* **w.-tip,** punta del ala, *f*

winged *a* alado, con alas; (in compounds) de alas . . .; (swift) alado; (of style) elevado, alado

wink *vi* (blink) pestañear; (as a signal, etc.) guiñar; (of stars, etc.) titilar, parpadear, centellear. *vt* guiñar (el ojo). *n* pestañeo, *m;* guiño, *m.* **not to sleep a w.,** no pegar los ojos. **to w. at,** guiñar el ojo (a); (ignore) hacer la vista gorda

winking *n* (blinking) parpadeo, *m;* (as a signal) guiños, *m pl;* (of stars, etc.) titilación, *f,* pestañeo, *m. a* (of stars, etc.) titilante. **like w.,** en un abrir y cerrar de ojos.

winner *n* ganador (-ra); vencedor (-ra)

winning *a* ganador; vencedor; (attractive) encantador. *n* ganancia, *f.* **w. number,** número galardonado, número premiado, número vencedor, *m.* **w.-post,** meta, *f.* **w. side,** *sport* equipo vencedor, *m;* (politics, etc.) partido vencedor, *m*

winnings *n* ganancias, *f pl*

winnow *vt* aventar, abalear; *fig* separar

winnower *n* aventador (-ra)

winnowing *n* abaleo, aventamiento, *m; fig* separación, *f.* **w. fork,** bieldo, *m.* **w. machine,** aventador mecánico, *m*

winsome *a* sandunguero; dulce, encantador

winsomeness *n* sandunga, *f;* encanto, *m,* dulzura, *f*

winter *n* invierno, *m. a* de invierno; hiemal. *vi* pasar el invierno, invernar. *vt* (of cattle, etc.) guardar en invierno. **in w.,** en invierno, durante el invierno. **w. clothes,** ropa de invierno, *f.* **w. palace,** palacio de invierno, *m.* **w. quarters,** invernadero, *m.* **w. season,** invierno, *m;* temporada de invierno, *f.* **w. sleep,** invernada, *f.* **w. solstice,** solsticio hiemal, *m.* **w. sports,** deportes de nieve, *m pl.* **w. wheat,** trigo de invierno, *m*

wintry *a* de invierno; invernal; (of a smile, etc.) glacial

wipe *vt* limpiar; (rub) frotar; (dry) secar; (remove) quitar. *n* limpión, *m;* (blow) golpe de lado, *m.* **to w. one's eyes,** enjugarse las lágrimas. **to w. off,** limpiar; (remove) quitar; (erase) borrar; (kill) destruir completamente, exterminar; (a military force) destrozar; (a debt) cancelar

wire *n* alambre, *m;* hilo metálico, *m;* telégrafo (eléctrico), *m; inf* telegrama, *m. vt* atar con alambre; (fence) alambrar; (snare) coger con lazo de alambre; (of electrical equipment, etc.) instalar; (telegraph) telegrafiar. *vi* (telegraph) telegrafiar. **barbed w.,** alambre espinoso, *m.* **live w.,** alambre cargado (de electricidad), *m;* (person) fuerza viva, *f.* **w.-cutters,** cortaalambres, *m pl.* **w.-entanglement,** *mil* alambrada, *f.* **w. fence,** alambrera, *f,* cercado de alambre, *m.* **w. gauze,** tela metálica, *f.* **w. nail,** punta de París, *f.* **w.-netting,** malla de alambre, *f;* alambrado, *m.* **w.-pulling,** influencias secretas, *f pl;* intrigas políticas, *f pl*

wiredraw *vt* estirar (alambre), tirar (el hilo de hierro, plata, etc.); (arguments, etc.) sutilizar

wiredrawer *n* estirador, *m*

wiredrawing *n* tirado, *m; fig* sutileza, *f*

wireless *a* sin hilos; (of a message) radiotelegráfico; por radio. *n* telegrafía sin hilos, *f;* radiotelefonía, *f;* (telegram) radiocomunicación, *f;* (broadcasting) radio, *f. vt* radiotelegrafiar. **Let's listen to the w.,** Vamos a escuchar la radio. **portable w.,** radio portátil, *f.* **w. engineer,** ingeniero radio-telegrafista, *m.* **w. enthusiast,** radioaficionado (-da). **w. licence,** permiso de radio-receptor, *m.* **w. operator,** radiotelegrafista, *mf. w.* **room,** cuarto de telegrafía sin hilos, *m.* **w. set,** aparato de radio, *m.* **w. station,** estación de radiotelegrafía, *f;* (broadcasting) radioemisora, *f.* **w. telegraph,** telégrafo sin hilos, *m.* **w. telegraphy,** telegrafía sin hilos, radiotelegrafía, *f.* **w. telephony,** telefonía sin hilos, *f.* **w. transmission,** radioemisión, *f*

wiretap *vi* poner escucha. *vt* poner escucha a

wiring *n* instalación de alambres eléctricos, *f*

wiry *a* semejante a un alambre; (of persons) nervudo

wisdom *n* sabiduría, *f;* (learning) saber, *m;* (judgment) juicio, *m.* **Book of W.,** Libro de la Sabiduría, *m.* **w.-tooth,** muela del juicio, *f*

wise *a* sabio; juicioso, prudente; (informed) enterado, informado. **a w. man,** un sabio. **in no w.,** de ningún modo. **the W. Men of the East,** los magos. **w. guy,** *inf* toro corrido, *m*

wisely *adv* sabiamente; prudentemente, con prudencia

wish *n* deseo, *m.* **Best wishes for the New Year,** Los mejores deseos para el Año Nuevo. **w.-bone,** espoleta, *f*

wish *vt* querer; desear; ansiar; (with 'good morning', etc.) dar. **I w. he were here!** ¡Ojalá que estuviera aquí! **Theresa wishes us to go,** Teresa quiere que vayamos. **I w. it had happened otherwise,** Quisiera que las cosas hubiesen pasado de otra manera. **I w. you would make less noise,** Me gustaría que hicieses menos ruido. **I only w. one thing,** Solamente deseo una cosa. **I w. you good luck,** Te deseo mucha suerte. **I wished him a merry Christmas,** Le deseé unas Pascuas muy felices, Le felicité las Pascuas. **to w. a prosperous New Year,** desear un próspero Año Nuevo. **to w. good-by,** despedirse (de). **to w. good day,** dar los buenos días. **to w. for,** desear

wisher *n* el que, *m,* (*f,* la que) desea, deseador (-ra)

wishful *a* deseoso; ansioso; ávido. **w. thinking,** ilusiones, *f pl;* optimismo injustificado, optimismo exagerado, *m*

wisp *n* mechón, *m;* jirón, *m;* trozo, pedazo, *m*

wistaria *n* vistaria, *f*

wistful *a* ansioso; triste; patético; (envious) envidioso; (regretful) de pesar; (remorseful) de remordimiento; (thoughtful) pensativo

wistfully *adv* con ansia; tristemente; patéticamente; con envidia; con pesar; con remordimiento; pensativo

wistfulness *n* ansia, *f;* tristeza, *f;* (envy) envidia, *f;* (regret) pesar, *m;* (remorse) remordimiento, *m;* (thoughtfulness) lo pensativo, lo distraído

wit, to *adv* a saber

wit *n* (reason) juicio, *m;* agudeza, gracia, *f,* rasgo de ingenio, *m;* ingenio, *m;* inteligencia, *f,* talento, *m;* (person) hombre de ingenio, *m;* mujer de ingenio, *f.* **my five wits,** mis cinco sentidos. **to be at one's wits' end,** no saber qué hacer. **to live by one's wits,** ser caballero de industria. **to lose one's wits,** perder el juicio

witch *n* bruja, *f.* **witches' sabbath,** aquelarre, *m.* **w.-doctor,** hechizador, mago, *m.* **witch-hazel,** carpe, *m;* loción de carpe, *f*

witchcraft *n* brujería, *f;* sortilegio, encantamiento, *m*

witchery *n* brujería, *f; fig* encanto, *m,* magia, *f*

with *prep* con; en compañia de; de; (against) contra; (among) entre; en; (by) por; (towards) hacia; para con; (according to) según; (notwithstanding) a pesar de; a; (concerning) con respecto a; en el caso de. **Rose is w. Antony,** Rosa está con Antonio. **He was w. his dog,** Estaba acompañado por su perro. **He pulled at it w. both hands,** Lo tiró con las dos manos. **filled w. fear,** lleno de miedo. **to shiver w. cold,** temblarse de frío. **the girl w. golden hair,** la muchacha del pelo dorado. **They killed it w. one blow,** Lo mataron de un solo golpe. **It rests w. you to decide,** Tú tienes que decidirlo; Te toca a tí decidirlo. **to begin w.,** para empezar; *v* empezar por. **w. all speed,** a toda prisa. **to part w.,** desprenderse de; (of people) despedirse de; separarse de. **w. that . . .,** (at once) en esto . . . (disease and poverty, etc.) **are still with us,** están todavía en el mundo

withal *adv* además; al mismo tiempo. *prep* con

withdraw *vt* retirar; (words) retractar; (remove) quitar; privar (de); (a legal action) apartar. *vi* retirarse; retroceder; apartarse; irse

withdrawal *n* retirada, *f;* (retirement) retiro, *m;* apartamiento, *m*

withdrawn *a* (abstracted) ensimismado, meditabundo

wither *vi* marchitarse, secarse, ajarse. *vt* marchitar, secar, ajar; *fig* hacer languidecer, matar; (snub) avergonzar

withered *a* marchito, mustio; muerto; (of persons) acartonado, seco

witheredness *n* marchitez, *f;* sequedad, *f*

withering *a* que marchita; (scorching) abrasador, ardiente; (scornful) despreciativo, desdeñoso; (biting) mordaz, cáustico

withers *n* cruz, *f*

withhold *vt* retener; detener; (restrain) refrenar; apartar; (refuse) negar; abstenerse de; (refuse to reveal) ocultar

withholding *n* detención, *f;* (refusal) negación, *f*

within *adv* dentro, adentro; en el interior; en casa; *fig* en su interior. **He stayed w.,** Se quedó dentro. **Is Mrs. González w.?** ¿Está en casa la Sra. González?

within *prep* dentro de; el interior de; en; entre; (within range of) al alcance de; a la distancia de; (near) cerca de; a poco de; (of time) en el espacio de, en; dentro de; (almost) por poco, casi. **He was w. an ace of being killed,** Por poco le matan. **to be w. hearing,** estar al alcance de la voz. **seen from w.,** visto desde dentro. **twice w. a fortnight,** dos veces en quince días. **w. himself,** por sus adentros, entre sí. **w. an inch of,** *fig* a dos dedos de. **w. a few miles of Edinburgh,** a unas millas de Edimburgo. **w. a short distance,** en una corta distancia; a poca distancia

without *prep* sin; falto de; (outside) fuera de; (beyond) más allá de. *adv* exteriormente; por fuera; hacia afuera; fuera. **It goes w. saying,** No hay que decir. **w. more ado,** sin más ni más. **w. my knowledge,** sin que yo lo supiese. **w. regard for,** sin miramientos por. **w. saying more,** sin decir más. **without batting an eyelash,** sin sobresaltos

withstand *vt* resistir, oponerse (a); soportar

withstanding *n* resistencia, oposición (a), *f*

witless *a* sin seso, tonto, necio

witness *n* (evidence) testimonio, *m;* (person) testigo, *mf;* espectador (-ra). **in w. whereof,** en fe de lo cual. **to bear w.,** atestiguar, dar testimonio. **to bring forward witnesses,** hacer testigos. **w. my hand,** en fe de lo cual, firmo. **w.-box,** puesto de los testigos, *m.* **w. for the defence,** testigo de descargo, *mf.* **w. for the prosecution,** testigo de cargo, *mf*

witness *vt* (show) mostrar, señalar; (see) ser testigo de, ver, presenciar; *law* atestiguar. *vi* dar testimonio; servir de testigo

witticism *n* rasgo de ingenio, donaire, *m,* agudeza, *f*

wittily *adv* ingeniosamente, donairosamente, agudamente

wittiness *n* viveza de ingenio, donosura, *f*

witty *a* salado, gracioso. **w. sally,** agudeza, *f*

wizard *n* mago, hechicero, *m*

wizardry *n* magia, *f*

wizened *a* seco, arrugado; (of persons) acartonado

wobble *vi* tambalearse, balancearse; (quiver) temblar; oscilar; *mech* galopar; (stagger) titubear; *fig* vacilar

wobbly *a* que se bambolea; inestable; *fig* vacilante

woe *n* dolor, *m;* congoja, aflicción, *f;* mal, desastre, infortunio, *m.* **Woe is me!** ¡Ay de mí! ¡Desdichado de mí!

woebegone *a* angustiado

woeful *a* triste; doloroso; funesto

woefully *adv* tristemente; dolorosamente

wolf *n* lobo (-ba). **a w. in sheep's clothing,** un lobo en piel de cordero. **to cry w.,** gritar «el lobo!» **to keep the w. from the door,** ponerse a cubierto del hambre. **w.-cub,** lobezno, *m.* **w.-hound,** perro lobo, *m.* **w. pack,** manada de lobos, *f*

wolfish *a* lobuno, de lobo

wolfram *n* volframio, *m*

woman *n* mujer, *f;* hembra, *f;* (lady-in-waiting) dama de servicio, *f.* **a fine figure of a w.,** una real hembra. **w. doctor,** médica, *f.* **w.-hater,** misógino, *m.* **w. of**

the town, mujer de la vida airada, f. w. of the world, mujer de mundo, f

womanhood n feminidad, f; sexo feminino, m

womanish a afeminado

womankind n el sexo femenino, las mujeres

womanliness n feminidad, f; carácter femenino, m

womanly a femenino, de mujer

womb n útero, m, matriz, f; fig seno, m

women's dormitory n residencia para señoritas, f

wonder n maravilla, f; prodigio, m; portento, milagro, m; (surprise) sorpresa, f; admiración, f; asombro, m; (problem) enigma, m; misterio, m. vi admirarse, asombrarse, maravillarse; sorprenderse. vt (ask oneself) preguntarse; desear saber. **I wondered what the answer would be,** Me preguntaba qué sería la respuesta. **It is no w. that . . . ,** No es mucho que . . . , No es sorprendente que . . . **It is one of the wonders of the world,** Es una de las maravillas del mundo. **to work wonders,** hacer milagros. **to w. at,** asombrarse de, maravillarse de; sorprenderse de. **w.-working,** milagroso

wonderful a maravilloso; magnífico; asombroso; inf estupendo

wonderfully adv maravillosamente; admirablemente

wondering a de asombro, sorprendido; perplejo

wonderingly adv con asombro

wonderland n mundo fantástico, m; reino de las hadas, m; país de las maravillas, m. **"Alice in W.,"** Alicia en el país de las maravillas

wonderment n. See **wonder**

wondrous a maravilloso. adv extraordinariamente

wont n costumbre, f. vi soler. **as he was w.,** Como solía

won't. See **will not**

wonted a sólito, acostumbrado

woo vt galantear; hacer la corte (a), solicitar amores a; cortejar; fig solicitar; perseguir

wood n bosque, m; madera, f; (for the fire, etc.) leña, f; (cask) barril, m. a de (the woods) selvático. **dead w.,** ramas muertas, f pl; fig paja, f. **w. alcohol,** alcohol metílico, m. **w.-anemone,** anémona de los bosques, f. **w.-block floor,** entarimado, m. **w.-borer,** xiló-fago, m. **w.-carver,** tallista, mf **w.-carving,** talla en madera, f. **w.-craft,** conocimiento del campo, m. **w.-cut,** grabado en madera, m. **w.-cutter,** leñador, m. **w.-engraver,** grabador (-ra) en madera. **w.-engraving,** grabado al boj, m. **w.-fibre,** fibra de madera, f. **w.-louse,** cochinilla, f. **w.-nymph,** ninfa de los bosques, f. **w.-pigeon,** paloma torcaz, f. **w.-pile,** pila de leña, leñera, f. **w.-pulp,** pulpa de madera, f. **w.-shaving,** acepilladura, f. **w.-splinter,** tasquil, m, astilla, f. **w.-wind,** mus madera, f. **w.-worm,** carcoma, f

wooded a provisto de árboles, plantado de árboles, arbolado

wooden a de madera; de palo; (of smiles) mecánico; (stiff) indiferente, sin emoción; (clumsy) torpe; (of character) inflexible. **He has a w. leg,** Tiene una pata de palo. **w. beam,** madero, m; viga de madera, f. **w. bridge,** pontón, m. **w. galley,** print galerín, m

woodland n bosques, m pl. a de bosque; silvestre

woodpecker n pájaro carpintero, picamaderos, m

woodshed n leñera, f

woodwork n maderaje, m; molduras, f pl; carpintería, f

woody a leñoso; arbolado, con árboles. **w. tissue,** tejido leñoso, m

wooer n pretendiente, galanteador, m

woof n trama, f

wooing n galanteo, m

wool n lana, f. a de lana; lanar. **to go w.-gathering,** estar distraído. **to pull the w. over a person's eyes,** engañar como a un chino. **w.-bearing,** lanar. **w.-carding,** cardadura de lana, f. **w.-growing,** cría de ganado lanar, f. **w. merchant,** comerciante en lanas, mf, lanero, m. **w.-pack,** fardo de lana, m. **w. trade,** comercio de lana, m

woollen a de lana; lanar. n paño de lana, m; género de punta de lana, m

woolliness n lanosidad, f

woolly a lanudo, lanoso; de lana; bot velloso; (of hair) lanoso, crespo. n género de punta de lana, m; (sweater) jersey, m

word n palabra, f; gram vocablo, m; theol verbo, m; (maxim) sentencia, f, dicho, m; (message) recado, m; (news) aviso, m, noticias, f pl; (mil command) voz de mando, f; (order) orden, f; (password) contraseña, f; (term) término, m. vt expresar; formular; (draw up) redactar; escribir. **He was as good as his w.,** Fue hombre de palabra. **I do not know how to w. this letter,** No sé cómo redactar esta carta. **in a w.,** en una palabra; en resumidas cuentas. **in other words,** en otros términos; en efecto. **the W. (of God),** el Verbo (de Dios). **to have a w. with,** hablar con; conversar con; entablar conversación con. **to leave w.,** dejar recado. **to have words with,** tener palabras con. **to keep one's w.,** cumplir su palabra

word index n índice de vocablos, m

wordiness n palabrería, verbosidad, f

wording n fraseología, f; expresión, f; estilo, m; (terms) términos, m pl; (drawing up) redacción, f

wordy a verboso, prolijo

work n trabajo, m; (sewing) labor, f; (literary, artistic production and theological) obra, f; (behavior) acción, f, acto, m; (employment) empleo, m; (business affairs) negocios, m pl; pl **works,** obras, fortificaciones, f, pl; obras públicas, f pl; construcciones, f pl; (of a machine) mecanismo, m; motor, m; (factory) fábrica, f, taller, m. **w. of art,** obra de arte. **w. accident,** accidente del trabajo, m. **w.-bag,** bolsa de costura, f, saco de labor, m. **w.-box,** (on legs) costurero, m; (small) neceser de costura, m. **w.-people,** obreros (-as). **w.-room,** taller, m; (study) estudio, m; (for sewing) cuarto de costura, m. **w.-table,** banco de taller, m; (for writing) mesa de escribir, f

work vi trabajar; sew hacer labor de aguja, coser; (embroider) bordar; mech funcionar, marchar; (succeed) tener éxito; ser eficaz; (be busy) estar ocupado; (be employed) tener empleo; (of the face) demudarse, torcerse; (ferment) fermentar; (operate) obrar vt trabajar; operar, hacer funcionar; mover; (control) manejar; (a mine) explotar; (embroider) bordar; (wood) tallar; (a problem) resolver; calcular; (iron, etc.) labrar; (the soil) cultivar; (a ship) maniobrar; (do) hacer; (bring about) efectuar; traer consigo; producir; (agitate oneself) agitarse, emocionarse, excitarse. **to w. in repoussé,** repujar. **to w. loose,** desprenderse. **to w. one's passage,** trabajar por el pasaje. **to w. overtime,** trabajar horas extraordinarias. **to w. two ways,** ser espada de dos filos. **to w. at,** trabajar en; ocuparse en; dedicarse a; elaborar. **to w. in,** vt introducir; insinuar. vi combinarse. **to w. into,** penetrar en. **to w. off,** usar, emplear; (get rid of) deshacerse de, librarse de. **to w. on, upon,** influir en; obrar sobre; estar ocupado en. **to w. out,** vt calcular; resolver; (a mine, topic, etc.) agotar; (develop) elaborar, desarrollar; trazar, planear; (find) encontrar. vi llegar (a); resultar; venir a ser. **to w. up,** crear; (promote) fomentar; producir; (excite) agitar, excitar; (fashion) dar forma (a), labrar; (finish) terminar

workable a laborable; factible, practicable; (of a mine) explotable

workableness n practicabilidad, f

workaday a de todos los días; prosaico

workbench banco de mecánico, f, banco de taller, banco de trabajo, m, mesa de trabajo, f

workday n día de trabajo, día laborable, m

worker n trabajador (-ra); (manual) obrero (-ra); (of a machine) operario (-ia). **w.-ant,** hormiga obrera, f. **w.-bee,** abeja obrera, f

workhouse n asilo, m

working *a* de trabajo; (of capital) de explotación; trabajador, que trabaja; obrero. *n* trabajo, *m*; (of a machine, organism, institution) funcionamiento, *m*; explotación, *f*; (of a mine) laboreo, *m*; (of a ship) maniobra, *f*; (of metal, stone, wood) labra, *f*; operación, *f*; (result) efecto, resultado, *m*; (calculation) cálculo, *m*. "Not w.," «No funciona.» **to be in w. order,** funcionar bien. **w.-class,** clase obrera, *f*; pueblo, *m*. **w.-clothes,** ropa de trabajo, *f*. **w.-day,** día de trabajo, *m*. **w.-hours,** horas de trabajo, horas hábiles, *f pl*. **w. hypothesis,** postulado, *m*. **w.-man,** obrero, *m*; trabajador, *m*. **w.-out,** elaboración, *f*; ensayo, *m*. **w.-plan,** plan de trabajo, *m*. **w.-woman,** obrera, *f*; trabajadora, *f*

workless *a* sin trabajo

workman *n* obrero, *m*; (agricultural) labrador, *m*

workmanlike *a* bien hecho, bien acabado; (clever) hábil

workmanship *n* trabajo, *m*; manufactura, *f*; hechura, *f*; (cleverness) habilidad, *f*

works *n* fábrica, *f*

workshop *n* taller, *m*

world *n* mundo, *m*. **For all the w. as if . . . ,** Exactamente como si . . . **to see the w.,** ver mundo. **to treat the w. as one's oyster,** ponerse el mundo por montera. **w. without end,** por los siglos de los siglos. **w.-power,** potencia mundial, gran potencia, *f*. **w.-wide,** mundial, universal

world almanac *n* compendio mundial, *m*

worldliness *n* mundanería, *f*, conocimiento del mundo, *m*; frivolidad, vanidad mundana, *f*; egoísmo, *m*; prudencia, *f*

worldly *a* de este mundo; mundano; humano; profano; frívolo. **to be w.-wise,** tener mucho mundo

worm *n* gusano, *m*; lombriz, *f*; *chem* serpentín, *m*; (of a screw) tornillo sinfin, *m*; (person) gusano, *m*; *fig* gusano roedor, remordimiento, *m*. **intestinal w.,** lombriz intestinal, *f*, gusano de la conciencia. **w.-eaten,** carcomido. **w.-hole,** picadura de gusano, lombriguera, *f*. **w.-powder,** polvos antihelmínticos, *m pl*. **w.-shaped,** vermiforme

worm *vt* (a dog) dar un vermífugo (a). *vi* arrastrarse como un gusano. **to w. one's way into,** deslizarse en; *fig* insinuarse en, introducirse en. **to w. out,** (secrets, information) sonsacar

wormwood *n* ajenjo, *m*

wormy *a* gusanoso, lleno de gusanos

worn *a* (of garments) raído; estropeado; gastado; (of paths) trillado; (of the face) arrugado, cansado. **w. out,** acabado; muy usado; (tired) rendido; (exhausted) agotado

worrier *n* inquietador (-ra); receloso (-sa); aprensivo (-va)

worry *n* preocupación, inquietud, ansiedad, *f*; problema, cuidado, *m*. *vt* (prey) zamarrear; preocupar, inquietar; molestar; importunar. *vi* estar preocupado, estar intranquilo, inquietarse. **Don't worry,** Pierda cuidado, No pase cuidado

worrying *a* inquietante, perturbador; molesto

worse *a comp* peor; inferior. *adv* peor; menos. *n* lo peor. **so much the w.,** tanto peor. **to be w. off,** estar peor; estar en peores circunstancias; ser menos feliz. **to be the w. for wear,** ser muy usado; estar ajado; ser ya viejo. **to grow w.,** empeorarse; (of an ill person) ponerse peor. **w. and w.,** de mal en peor, peor que peor. **w. than ever,** peor que nunca

worsen *vt* agravar, hacer peor; exasperar. *vi* agravarse, empeorarse; exasperarse

worsening *n* agravación, *f*, empeoramiento, *m*; exasperación, *f*

worship *n* culto, *m*; adoración, *f*; veneración, *f*. *vt* adorar; reverenciar. *vi* adorar; rezar; dar culto (a). **place of w.,** edificio de culto, *m*. **Your W.,** vuestra merced

worshipful *a* venerable, respetable

worshipper *n* adorador (-ra); *pl* **worshippers,** (in a church, etc.) fieles, *m pl*, congregación, *f*

worshipping *n* adoración, *f*, culto, *m*

worst *a* el (la, etc.) peor; más malo. *adv* el (la, etc.) peor. *n* el (la, etc.) peor; lo peor. *vt* vencer, derrotar; triunfar sobre **If the w. comes to the w.,** En el peor de los casos. **The w. of it is that . . . ,** Lo peor es que . . . **to have the w. of it,** salir perdiendo, llevar la peor parte

worsted *n* estambre, *m, a* de estambre

worth *n* valor, *m*; precio, *m*; mérito, *m, a* (que) vale; de precio de; cuyo valor es de; equivalente a; (que) merece; digno de. **He bought six hundred pesetas w. of sweets,** Compró seiscientas pesetas de dulces. **He sang for all he was w.,** Cantó con toda su alma. **It is w. seeing,** Es digno de verse, Vale la pena de verse. **to be w.,** valer. **to be w. while,** valer la pena, merecer la pena

worthily *adv* dignamente

worthiness *n* mérito, valor, *m*

worthless *a* sin valor; sin mérito; inútil; malo; (of persons) vil, despreciable, indigno

worthlessness *n* falta de valor, *f*; falta de mérito, *f*; inutilidad, *f*; (of persons) bajeza, vileza, *f*

worthy *a* digno de respeto, benemérito, respetable; digno, merecedor; meritorio. *n* varón ilustre, hombre célebre, *m*; héroe, *m*; (*inf iron*) tío, *m*. **to be w. of,** ser digno de, merecer

would *preterite* and *subjunctive* of **will.** (indicating a conditional tense) **They w. come if . . . ,** Vendrían si . . . ; (indicating an imperfect tense) **Often he w. sing,** Muchas veces cantaba, **Now and then a blackbird w. whistle,** De vez en cuando silbó un mirlo; (expressing wish, desire) **What w. they?** ¿Qué quieren? **The place where I w. be,** El lugar donde quisiera estar. **W. I were at home!** ¡Ojalá que estuviese en casa! **I thought that I w. tell you,** Se me ocurrió la idea de decírselo. **It w. seem that . . . ,** Parece ser que . . . , Según parece . . . ; Se diría que . . . **He said that he w. never have done it,** Dijo que no lo hubiera hecho nunca. **They w. have been killed if he had not rescued them,** Habrían sido matados si él no los hubiese salvado. **He w. go,** Se empeñó en ir. **He w. not do it,** Rehusó hacerlo, Se resistió a hacerlo; No quiso hacerlo. **This w. probably be the house,** Sin duda esta sería la casa. **W. you be good enough to . . . ,** Tenga Vd. la bondad de . . . , Haga el favor de . . .

would-be *a* supuesto; llamado; aspirante (a); en esperanza de (followed by infin.); (frustrated) frustrado, malogrado

wound *n* herida, *f*. *vt* herir; (the feelings) lastimar, lacerar. **deep w.,** herida penetrante, *f*. **the wounded,** los heridos.

wounding *n* herida, *f, a* digno lastimador

wraith *n* fantasma, espectro, *m*, sombra, *f*

wrangle *vi* discutir; altercar, disputar acaloradamente; reñir; (bargain) regatear. *n* argumento, *m*; disputa, *f*, altercado, *m*; riña, *f*

wrangler *n* disputador (-ra); (Cambridge University) laureado en matemáticas, *m*

wrangling *n* disputas, *f pl*, altercación, *f*; (bargaining) regateo, *m*

wrap *vt* envolver; arrollar; cubrir; abrigar; (conceal) ocultar. *n* envoltorio, *m*; abrigo, *m*; *pl* **wraps,** abrigos y mantas de viaje, *m pl*. **W. yourself up well!** ¡Abrígate bien! **to be wrapped up in,** estar envuelto en; *fig* estar entregado a, estar absorto en; (a person) estar embelesado con

wrapper *n* envoltura, *f*; embalaje, *m*; (of a newspaper) faja, *f*; (of a book) sobrecubierta, *f*; (dressing-gown) bata, *f*, salto de cama, *m*

wrapping *n* envoltura, cubierta, *f*. **w.-paper,** papel de envolver, *m*

wrath *n* ira, *f*

wrathful *a* airado

wreak *vt* ejecutar; (anger, etc.) descargar. **to w. one's vengeance,** vengarse

wreath *n* guirnalda, *f*; corona, *f*; trenza, *f*. **funeral w.,** corona funeraria, *f*

wreathe *vt* trenzar; (entwine) entrelazar (de); (garland) coronar (de), enguirnaldar (con); (encircle) ceñir, rodear; (a face in smiles) iluminar

wreck *n* naufragio, *m*; buque naufragado, *m*; destrucción, *f*; *fig* ruina, *f*; (remains) restos, *m pl*; (person) sombra, *f*. *vt* hacer naufragar; destruir; *fig* arruinar; hacer fracasar. **I am a complete w.,** *inf* Estoy hecho una ruina. **to be wrecked,** irse a pique, naufragar; *fig* arruinarse; frustrarse

wreckage *n* naufragio, *m*; restos de naufragio, *m pl*; ruinas, *f pl*; (of a car, plane, etc.) restos, *m pl*; accidente, *m*

wrecked *a* naufragado

wrecker *n* destructor (-ra); (of ships) raquero, *m*

wren *n* reyezuelo, *m*

wrench *n* (jerk) arranque, *m*; (pull) tirón, *m*; (sprain) torcedura, *f*; (tool) llave, *f*; (pain) dolor, *m*. *vt* arrancar; forzar; torcer, dislocar. **He has wrenched his arm,** Se ha torcido el brazo

wrest *vt* arrebatar, arrancar

wrestle *vi* luchar. *n* lucha grecorromana, *f*; *fig* lucha, *f*. **to w. with,** *fig* luchar con; luchar contra

wrestler *n* luchador, *m*

wrestling *n* lucha grecorromana, *f*. **all-in-w.,** lucha libre, *f*. **w.-match,** lucha, *f*

wretch *n* infeliz, *mf*; (ruffian) infame, *m*; (playful) picaruelo (-la). **a poor w.,** un pobre diablo

wretched *a* (unhappy) infeliz, desdichado; miserable; pobre; (ill) enfermo; horrible; malo; mezquino; despreciable; lamentable

wretchedly *adv* tristemente; pobremente; muy mal; ruinmente

wretchedness *n* infelicidad, desdicha, *f*; miseria, pobreza, *f*; escualidez, *f*; ruindad, *f*

wriggle *vi* agitarse, moverse; menearse; serpear, culebrear; retorcerse. *n* See under **wriggling. to w. into,** insinuarse en, deslizarse dentro (de). **to w. out,** escaparse. **to w. out of a difficulty,** extricarse de una dificultad

wriggling *n* meneo, *m*; retorcimiento, *m*; serpenteo, culebreo, *m*

wring *vt* torcer; estrujar; exprimir; arrancar; (force) forzar. **to w. one's hands,** restregarse las manos. **to w. the neck of,** torcer el pescuezo (a). **to w. out,** exprimir; estrujar

wringer *n* torcedor (-ra); (for clothes) exprimidor de ropa, *m*

wringing *n* torsión, *f*. **w.-machine,** exprimidor de ropa, *m*

wrinkle *n* arruga, *f*; pliegue, *m*; *inf* noción, *f*. *vt* arrugar. *vi* arrugarse. **to w. one's brow,** (frown) fruncir el ceño; (in perplexity) arrugar la frente

wrinkling *n* arrugamiento, *m*

wrinkly *a* arrugado

wrist *n* muñeca, *f*. **w.-band,** tira del puño de la camisa, *f*. **w. bandage,** pulsera, *f*

wristlet *n* pulsera, *f*; manguito elástico, *m*. **w. watch,** reloj de pulsera, *m*

writ *n* escritura, *f*; *law* decreto judicial, mandamiento, *m*; orden, *f*; título ejecutorio, *m*; hábeas corpus, *m*. **Holy W.,** la Sagrada Escritura. **to issue a w.,** dar orden. **to serve a w.,** notificar una orden. **w. of privilege,** auto de excarcelación, *m*

write *vt* and *vi* escribir; *fig* mostrar. **He writes a good hand,** Tiene buena letra. **I shall w. to them for a list,** Les escribiré pidiendo una lista. **to w. back,** contestar por escrito; contestar a una carta. **to w. down,** poner por escrito; anotar, apuntar; describir. **to w. for,** escribir para; escribir para pedir algo; escribir algo en vez de otra persona. **to w. off,** escribir; escribir rápidamente; cancelar. **to w. on,** seguir escribiendo; escribir sobre. **to w. out,** copiar; redactar. **to w. over again,** escribir de nuevo, escribir otra vez, volver a escribir. **to w. up,** redactar; *com* poner al día; (praise) escribir alabando

writer *n* escritor (-ra); autor (-ra). **the present w.,** el que, *m*, (*f*, la que) esto escribe. **writer's cramp,** calambre del escribiente, *m*

writhe *vi* retorcerse

writhing *n* retorsión, *f*

writing *n* escritura, *f*; (work) escrito, *m*; inscripción, *f*; documento, *m*; (style) estilo, *m*; (hand) letra, *f*; el arte de escribir; trabajo literario, *m*. **in one's own w.,** de su propia letra. **in w.,** por escrito. **w.-case,** escribanía, *f*. **w.-desk,** escritorio, *m*. **w.-pad,** taco de papel, *m*. **w.-paper,** papel de escribir, *m*. **w.-table,** mesa de escribir, *f*

written *a* escrito

wrong *a* injusto; mal; equivocado, erróneo; inexacto; falso; incorrecto; desacertado; inoportuno. **It is the w. one,** No es el que hacía falta; No es el que quería. **to be in the w. place,** estar mal situado; estar mal colocado. **to be w.,** estar mal; no tener razón; (mistaken) estar equivocado; (of deeds or things) estar mal hecho; (be unjust) ser injusto; (of clocks) andar mal. **to do w.,** hacer mal; obrar mal. **to get out of bed on the w. side,** levantarse del izquierdo. **to go w.,** (of persons) descarriarse; (of affairs) ir mal; salir mal; frustrarse; (of apparatus) estropearse, no funcionar. **We have taken the w. road,** Nos hemos equivocado de camino. **You were very w. to . . . ,** Has hecho muy mal en . . . **w.-headed,** terco, obstinado; disparatado. **w.-headedness,** terquedad, obstinación, *f*. **w. number,** (telephone) número errado, *m*. **w. side,** revés, *m*; lado malo, *m*. **w. side out,** al envés; al revés

wrong *adv* mal; injustamente; sin razón; incorrectamente; equivocadamente; (inside out) al revés. **to get it w.,** (a sum) calcular mal; (misunderstand) comprender mal

wrong *n* mal, *m*; injusticia, *f*; perjuicio, *m*; ofensa, *f*, agravio, *m*; culpa, *f*; error, *m*. **to be in the w.,** no tener razon; haber hecho mal. **to put one in the w.,** echar la culpa (a), hacer responsable (de)

wrong *vt* hacer mal (a); perjudicar; ser injusto con; ofender

wrongdoer *n* malhechor (-ra); pecador (-ra); perverso (-sa)

wrongdoing *n* maldad, maleficencia, *f*; pecado, *m*; injusticia, *f*

wrongful *a* injusto; perjudicial; falso

wrongfully *adv* injustamente; falsamente

wrongly *adv* injustamente; erróneamente, equivocadamente; perversamente; mal

wrongness *n* mal, *m*; injusticia, *f*; falsedad, *f*; inexactitud, *f*, error, *m*

wrought *a* forjado; labrado; (hammered) batido; trabajado. **w. iron,** hierro dulce, hierro forjado, *m*. **w. up,** muy excitado, muy agitado, muy nervioso

wry *a* torcido; tuerto; triste; pesimista; desilusionado; irónico. **wry face,** mueca *f*, de desengaño, de ironía, de disgusto, etc. **to make a wry face,** torcer el gesto. **wry neck,** *orn* torcecuello, *m*

wryly *adv* tristemente; irónicamente

Wuthering Heights Cumbres borrascosas

wye *n* (letter) ye, i griega, *f*; horquilla, cosa en forma de Y, *f*

X

x *n* equis, *f*

x-ray *vt* tomar una radiografía (de). **x-ray,** rayo x, *m pl*. **x-ray examination,** examen con rayos x, *m*. **x-ray photograph,** radiografía, *f*

xylophone *n* xilófono, *m*

Y

y *n* (letter) i griega, ye, *f*
yacht *n* yate, *m*. **y. club,** club marítimo, *m*. **y. race,** regata de yates, *f*
yachting *n* navegación en yate, *f*, paseo en yate, *m*
yachtsman *n* deportista náutico, balandrista, balandrismo, *m*
yank *n* tirón, *m*, sacudida, *f*. *vt* dar un tirón (a); sacar de un tirón
Yankee *a* and *n* yanqui, *mf*
yap *vi* ladrar. *n* ladrido, *m*
yapper *n* (yapping dog) gozque, gozquejo, *m*
yapping *n* ladridos, *m pl*, *a* que ladra
yard *n* (measure) yarda, *f*; *naut* verga, *f*; corral, *m*; (courtyard) patio, *m*. *vt* acorralar. **goods y.,** estación de mercancías, *f*. **y.-arm,** penol (de la verga), *m*. **y.-stick,** vara de medir de una yarda, *f*
yarn *n* hilaza, *f*; hilo, *m*; (story) historia, *f*, cuento, *m*. **to spin a y.,** contar una historia
yaw *vi naut* guiñar; *aer* serpentear. *n naut* guiñada, *f*; *aer* serpenteo, *m*
yawl *n* yola, *f*; bote, *m*
yawn *vi* bostezar; quedarse con la boca abierta; (of chasms, etc.) abrirse. *n* bostezo, *m*. **to stifle a y.,** ahogar un bostezo
yawning *a* abierto. *n* bostezos, *m pl*
ye *pers pron* vos, vosotros
yea *adv* en verdad, ciertamente; y aun . . . no sólo . . . sino. *n* si, *m*
year *n* año, *m*; *pl* **years,** años, *m pl*, edad, *f*. **We are getting on in years,** Nos vamos haciendo viejos. **He is five years old,** Tiene cinco años. **all the y. round,** todo el año, el año entero. **by the y.,** al año. **every other y.,** cada dos años, un año sí y otro no. **in after years,** en años posteriores. **last y.,** el año pasado. **next y.,** el año próximo. el año que viene. **y. after y.,** año tras año. **New Y.,** Año Nuevo, *m*. **to see the New Y. in,** ver empezar el Año Nuevo. **New Year's Day,** día de Año Nuevo, *m*. **(A) Happy New Y.!** ¡Feliz Año Nuevo! **y.-book,** anuario, *m*
yearling calf *n* becerra *f*
yearly *a* anual. *adv* anualmente, cada año; una vez al año
yearn *vi* anhelar, suspirar (por); desear vivamente
yearning *n* sed, ansia, *f*; anhelo, deseo vehemente, *m*. *a* ansioso; anhelante; (tender) tierno
yeast *n* levadura, *f*
yell *vi* and *vt* chillar; gritar. *n* chillido, *m*; grito, *m*
yelling *n* chillidos, *m pl*; gritos, *m pl*, gritería, *f*
yellow *a* amarillo; (of hair) rubio; (cowardly) cobarde; (newspaper) amarillista, sensacionalista. **to turn y.,** *vi* ponerse amarillo; amarillear. *vt* volver amarillo. **y. fever,** fiebre amarilla, *f*. **y.-hammer,** *orn* emberizo, *m*
yellowing *n* amarilleo, *m*
yellowish *a* amarillento
yellowness *n* amarillez, *f*
yellow pages *n* páginas amarillas, páginas doradas, *f pl*
yelp *vi* gañir. *n* gañido, *m*
yelping *n* gañidos, *m pl*
yen *n* (currency) yen, *m*; (desire) deseovivo, *m*
yeoman *n* pequeño propietario rural, *m*; soldado de caballería, *m*. **Y. of the Guard,** alabardero de la Casa Real, *m*
yes *adv* sí. **Yes?** ¿De verdad? ¿Y qué pasó después? ¿Y entonces? **to say yes,** decir que sí; dar el sí. **yes-man,** amenista, sacristán de amén, *m*
yesterday *adv* ayer. *n* ayer, *m*. **the day before y.,** anteayer
yet *adv* aún, todavía. **as yet,** hasta ahora; todavía. **He has not come yet,** No ha venido todavía. **yet again,** otra vez
yet *conjunc* sin embargo, no obstante, con todo; pero.

The book is well written and yet I do not like it, El libro está bien escrito, y sin embargo no me gusta
yew *n* tejo, *m*; madera de tejo, *f*
Yiddish *n* yídis, yídish, yídico, *m*; *a* yídico
yield *vt* producir; dar; (grant) otorgar; (afford) ofrecer; (surrender) ceder. *vi* producir; (submit) rendirse, someterse; (of disease) responder; (give way) flaquear, doblegarse; dar de sí; (consent) consentir (en); (to circumstances, etc.) ceder (a), sucumbir (a). *n* producción, *f*, producto, *m*; *com* rédito, *m*; (crop) cosecha, *f*. **to y. to temptation,** ceder a la tentación. **to y. up,** entregar; devolver
yielding *a* flexible; (soft) blando; dócil, sumiso; fácil; condescendiente
yogurt *n* yogur, *m*
yoke *n* yugo, *m*; (of oxen) yunta, *f*; (for pails) balancín, *m*; (of a garment) canesú, *m*; *fig* férula, *f*, yugo, *m*. *vt* uncir, acoplar. **to throw off the y.,** sacudir el yugo
yokel *n* patán, rústico, *m*
yolk *n* (of an egg) yema, *f*
yonder *a* aquel, *m*; aquella, *f*; aquellos, *m pl*; aquellas, *f pl*. *adv* allí; allí a lo lejos
yore *n* in days of y., antaño; en otro tiempo
you *pers pron nominative* (polite form) usted (Vd.), *mf*; ustedes (Vds.), *mf pl*; (familiar form) *sing* tu, *mf*; (plural) vosotros, *m pl*; vosotras, *f pl*; (one) uno, *m*; una, *f*; se (followed by 3rd pers. sing. of verb). *pers pron accusative* (polite form) le, *m*; la, *f*; les, *m pl*; las, *f pl*; a usted, a ustedes; (informal form) te, *mf*, os, *mf pl*; (after most prepositions) ti, *mf*; vosotros, *m pl*; vosotras, *f pl*. **Are you there?** (telephone) ¡Oiga! **I gave the parcel to you,** Te (os) di el paquete; Di el paquete a usted (a ustedes). **I shall wait for you in the garden,** Te (os) esperaré en el jardín; Esperaré a Vds. (a Vd.) en el jardín. **This present is for you,** Este regalo es para ti (para vosotros, para Vd. (Vds.)). **Away with you!** ¡Vete! ¡Marchaos! **Between you and me,** Entre tú y yo. **you can't eat your cake and have it too,** no hay rosa sin espinas. **You never can tell,** No se sabe nunca, Uno no sabe nunca
young *a* joven; nuevo; reciente; inexperto; poco avanzado. *n* cría, *f*, hijuelos, *m pl*. **y. blood,** *inf* pollo pera, *m*. **y. girl,** jovencita, *f*. **y. man** joven, *m*. **y. people,** jóvenes, *mf pl*. **in his y. days,** en su juventud. **The night is y.,** La noche está poca avanzada. **to grow y. again,** rejuvenecer. **with y.,** (of animals) preñada
younger *a* más joven; menor. **Peter is his y. brother,** Pedro es su hermano menor. **to look y.,** parecer más joven
youngish *a* bastante joven
youngster *n* jovencito, chico, muchacho, *m*; niño, *m*
your *a poss* (polite form) su (*pl* sus), de usted (Vd.), (*pl* de ustedes (Vds.)); (familiar form) tu (*pl* vuestro). **I have y. papers,** Tengo tus (vuestros) papeles; Tengo los papeles de Vd. (or de Vds.). **How is y. mother?** ¿Cómo está su (tu) madre? **It is y. turn,** Te toca a ti, Le toca a Vd.
yours *pron poss* (polite form) (el) suyo, *m*; (la) suya, *f*; (los) suyos, *m pl*; (las) suyas, *f pl*; el, *m*; la, *f*; lo, *neut*; los, *m pl*; las, *f pl*; de usted (Vd.), *mf sing* or de ustedes (Vds.), *mf pl*; (familiar form) (el) tuyo, *m*; (la) tuya, *f*; (los) tuyos, *m pl*; (las) tuyas, *f pl*; (el) vuestro, *m*; (la) vuestra, *f*; (los) vuestros, *m pl*; (las) vuestras, *f pl*. **This is a picture of y.,** (addressing one person), Este es uno de los cuadros de usted (Vd.), Este es uno de tus cuadros. **This hat is mine, it is not y.,** Este sombrero es el mío, no es tuyo. **The horse is y.,** El caballo es tuyo (de Vd.). **Y. affectionately,** Un abrazo de tu amigo . . . **Y. faithfully,** Queda de Vd. su att. (atentísimo) s.s. (seguro servidor). **Y. sincerely,** Queda de Vd. su aff. (afectuoso)

yourself *pron pers* (familiar form *sing*) tú mismo, *m*; tú misma, *f*; (after a preposition) tí, *mf*; (polite form) usted (Vd.) mismo, *m*; usetd misma, *f*; *pl* **yourselves,** (familiar form) vosotros mismos, *m pl*; vosotras mismas, *f pl*; (polite form) ustedes (Vds.) mismos, *m pl*; ustedes mismas, *f pl*. **This is for y.,** Esto es para ti; Esto es para Vd.

youth *n* juventud, *f*; (man) joven, chico, mozalbete, *m*; (collectively) jóvenes, *m pl*, juventud, *f*

youthful *a* joven, juvenil; de la juventud
yowl *n* gañido, aullido, *m*. *vi* gañir, aullar
Yucatan *a* yucateco
yucca *n bot* yuca, *f*
Yugoslav *n* yugoeslavo (-va). *a* yugoeslavo
Yugaslavia Yugoeslavia, *f*
Yukon, the el Yukón, *m*
Yule *n* Navidad, *f*. **y.-log,** leño de Navidad, *m*. **y-tide,** Navidades, *f pl*

Z

z *n* (letter) zeda, zeta, *f*
zeal *n* celo, entusiasmo, *m*; ardor, fervor, *m*
zealot *n* fanático (-ca)
zealous *a* celoso, entusiasta
zealously *adv* con entusiasmo
zebra *n* cebra, *f*
zenith *n* cenit, *m*; *fig* apogeo, punto culminante, *m*
zephyr *n* céfiro, *m*, brisa, *f*
zero *n* cero, *m*. **below z.,** bajo cero. **z. hour,** hora cero, *f*
zest *n* sabor, gusto, *m*; entusiasmo, *m*. **to eat with z.,** comer con buen apetito. **to enter on with z.,** emprender con entusiasmo
zigzag *n* zigzag, *m*. *a* and *adv* en zigzag. *vi* zigzaguear, hacer zigzags, serpentear; (of persons) andar haciendo eses
Zimbabwe Zimbabue
zinc *n* cinc, *m*. **z. oxide,** óxido de cinc, *m*
Zion *n* Sión, *m*

Zionism *n* sionismo, *m*
Zionist *n* and *a* sionista
zip *n* (of a bullet) silbido, *m*; *inf* energía, *f*. **zip fastener,** cierre de cremallera, *m*
zip code *n* código postal, *m*
zipper *n* cremallera, *f*, cierre relámpago, cierre, cerrador, *m*
zircon *n* circón, *m*
zither *n* cítara, *f*
zodiac *n* zodiaco, *m*
zone *n* zona, *f*; faja, *f*
zoo *n* jardín zoológico, *m*
zoological *a* zoológico. **Z. garden,** jardín zoológico, *m*
zoologist *n* zoólogo, *m*
zoology *n* zoología, *f*
zoom *n* zumbido, *m*. *vi* zumbar; *aer* empinarse
Zulu *a* and *n* zulú *mf*
Zuyder Zee, the el Zuyderzée, *m*

Numbers/Números

Cardinal/Cardinales

one	1	uno, una	one hundred	100	cien
			one hundred one	101	ciento uno
one	1	uno, una	one hundred two	102	ciento dos
two	2	dos	two hundred	200	doscientos, -as
three	3	tres	three hundred	300	trescientos, -as
four	4	cuatro	four hundred	400	cuatrocientos, -as
five	5	cinco	five hundred	500	quinientos, -as
six	6	seis	six hundred	600	seiscientos, -as
seven	7	siete	seven hundred	700	setecientos, -as
eight	8	ocho	eight hundred	800	ochocientos, -as
nine	9	nueve	nine hundred	900	novecientos, -as
ten	10	diez	one thousand	1,000	mil
eleven	11	once	two thousand	2,000	dos mil
twelve	12	doce	one hundred thousand	100,000	cien mil
thirteen	13	trece			
fourteen	14	catorce	one million	1,000,000	un millón
fifteen	15	quince	two million	2,000,000	dos millones
sixteen	16	dieciséis			
seventeen	17	diecisiete			
eighteen	18	dieciocho			
nineteen	19	diecinueve			
twenty	20	veinte			
twenty-one	21	veinte y uno (or veintiuno)			
twenty-two	22	veinte y dos (or veintidós)			
thirty	30	treinta			
thirty-one	31	treinta y uno			
thirty-two	32	treinta y dos			
forty	40	cuarenta			
fifty	50	cincuenta			
sixty	60	sesenta			
seventy	70	setenta			
eighty	80	ochenta			
ninety	90	noventa			

Ordinal/Ordinales

first	1st /	1°	primero
second	2nd /	2°	segundo
third	3rd /	3°	tercero
fourth	4th /	4°	cuarto
fifth	5th /	5°	quinto
sixth	6th /	6°	sexto
seventh	7th /	7°	séptimo
eighth	8th /	8°	octavo
ninth	9th /	9°	noveno
tenth	10th /	10°	décimo

Weights and Measures/Pesos y Medidas

1 centímetro	=	.3937 inches		1 kilolitro	=	264.18 gallons
1 metro	=	39.37 inches		1 inch	=	2.54 centímetros
1 kilómetro	=	.621 mile		1 foot	=	.305 metros
1 centigramo	=	.1543 grain		1 mile	=	1.61 kilómetros
1 gramo	=	15.432 grains		1 grain	=	.065 gramos
1 kilogramo	=	2.2046 pounds		1 pound	=	.455 kilogramos
1 tonelada	=	2.204 pounds		1 ton	=	.907 toneladas
1 centilitro	=	.338 ounces		1 ounce	=	2.96 centilitros
1 litro	=	1.0567 quart (liquid);		1 quart	=	1.13 litros
		.908 quart (dry)		1 gallon	=	4.52 litros

Signs/Señales

Caution	Precaución	**No smoking**	Prohibido fumar
Danger	Peligro	**No admittance**	Entrada prohibida
Exit	Salida	**One way**	Dirección única
Entrance	Entrada	**No entry**	Dirección prohibida
Stop	Alto	**Women**	Señoras, Mujeres, Damas
Closed	Cerrado	**Men**	Señores, Hombres, Caballeros
Open	Abierto	**Ladies' Room**	El cuarto de damas
Slow	Despacio	**Men's Room**	El servicio

Days of the Week/Días de la Semana

Sunday	domingo	Thursday	jueves
Monday	lunes	Friday	viernes
Tuesday	martes	Saturday	sábado
Wednesday	miércoles		

Months/Meses

January	enero	October	octubre
February	febrero	November	noviembre
March	marzo	December	diciembre
April	abril		
May	mayo		
June	junio		
July	julio		
August	agosto		
September	septiembre		

Useful Phrases/Locuciones Útiles

Good day, Good morning. Buenos días.
Good afternoon. Buenas tardes.
Good night, Good evening. Buenas noches.
Hello. ¡Hola!
Welcome! ¡Bienvenido!
See you later. Hasta luego.
Goodbye. ¡Adiós!
How are you? ¿Cómo está usted?
I am fine, thank you. Estoy bien, gracias.
I am pleased to meet you. Mucho gusto en conocerle.
May I introduce . . . Quisiera presentar . . .
Thank you very much. Muchas gracias.
You're welcome. De nada *or* No hay de qué.
Please. Por favor.
Excuse me. Con permiso.
Good luck. ¡Buena suerte!
To your health. ¡Salud!

Please help me. Ayúdeme, por favor.
I don't know. No sé.
I don't understand. No entiendo.
Do you understand? ¿Entiende usted?
I don't speak Spanish. No hablo español.
Do you speak English? ¿Habla usted inglés?
How do you say . . . in Spanish? ¿Cómo se dice . . . en español?
What do you call this? ¿Cómo se llama esto?
Speak slowly, please. Hable despacio, por favor.
Please repeat. Repita, por favor.
I don't like it. No me gusta.
I am lost. Ando perdido; Me he extraviado.

What is your name? ¿Cómo se llama usted?
My name is . . . Me llamo . . .
I am an American. Soy norteamericano.
Where are you from? ¿De dónde es usted?
I'm from . . . Soy de . . .

How is the weather? ¿Qué tiempo hace?
It's cold (hot) today. Hace frío (calor) hoy.
What time is it? ¿Qué hora es?

How much is it? ¿Cuánto es?
It is too much. Es demasiado.
What do you wish? ¿Qué desea usted?
I want to buy . . . Quiero comprar . . .
May I see something better? ¿Podría ver algo mejor?
May I see something cheaper? ¿Podría ver algo menos caro?
It is not exactly what I want. No es exactamente lo que quiero.

I am hungry. Tengo hambre.
I am thirsty. Tengo sed.
Where is there a restaurant? ¿Dónde hay un restaurante?
I have a reservation. Tengo una reservación.
I would like . . . Quisiera . . . ; Me gustaría . . .
Please give me . . . Por favor, déme usted . . .
Please bring me . . . Por favor, tráigame usted . . .
May I see the menu? ¿Podría ver el menú?
The bill, please. La cuenta, por favor.
Is service included in the bill? ¿El servicio está incluido en la cuenta?
Where is there a hotel? ¿Dónde hay un hotel?
Where is the post office? ¿Dónde está el correo?
Is there any mail for me? ¿Hay correo para mí?
Where can I mail this letter? ¿Dónde puedo echar esta carta al correo?

Take me to . . . Lléveme a . . .
I believe I am ill. Creo que estoy enfermo.
Please call a doctor. Por favor, llame al médico.

Please call the police. Por favor, llame a la policía.

I want to send a telegram. Quiero poner un telegrama.

As soon as possible. Cuanto antes.

Round trip. Ida y vuelta.

Please help me with my luggage. Por favor, ayúdeme con mi equipaje.

Where can I get a taxi? ¿Dónde puedo coger un taxi?

What is the fare to . . . ¿Cuánto es el pasaje hasta . . . ?

Please take me to this address. Por favor, lléveme a esta dirección.

Where can I change my money? ¿Dónde puedo cambiar mi dinero?

Where is the nearest bank? ¿Dónde está el banco más cercano?

Can you accept my check? ¿Puede aceptar usted mi cheque?

Do you accept traveler's checks? ¿Aceptan cheques de viaje?

What is the postage? ¿Cuánto es el franqueo?

Where is the nearest drugstore? ¿Dónde está la farmacia más cercana?

Where is the men's (women's) room? ¿Dónde está el servicio de caballeros (de señoras)?

Please let me off at . . . Por favor, déjeme bajar en . . .

Right away. ¡Pronto!

Help. ¡Socorro!

Who is it? ¿Quién es?

Just a minute! ¡Un momento no más!

Come in. ¡Pase usted!

Pardon me. Dispense usted.

Stop. ¡Pare!

Look out. ¡Cuidado!

Hurry. ¡De prisa! *or* ¡Dése prisa!

Go on. ¡Siga!

To (on, at) the right. A la derecha.

To (on, at) the left. A la izquierda.

Straight ahead. Adelante.